PAGE 52 ON THE ROAD

YOUR COMPLETE DESTINATION GUIDE
In-depth reviews, detailed listings and insider tips

TOP EXPERIENCES MAP NEXT PAGE

PAGE 1053 SURVIVAL GUIDE

YOUR AT-A-GLANCE REFERENCE
How to get around, get a room, stay safe, say hello

Directory A-Z 1054
Transport 1064
Glossary 1071
Index 1077
Map Legend 1101

Transport

GETTING THERE & AWAY

Air

Airports

THIS EDITION WRITTEN AND RESEARCHED BY

David Else,
David Atkinson, Oliver Berry, Joe Bindloss, Fionn Davenport, Marc Di Duca, Belinda Dixon, Peter Dragicevich, Catherine Le Nevez, Etain O'Carroll, Andy Symington, Neil Wilson

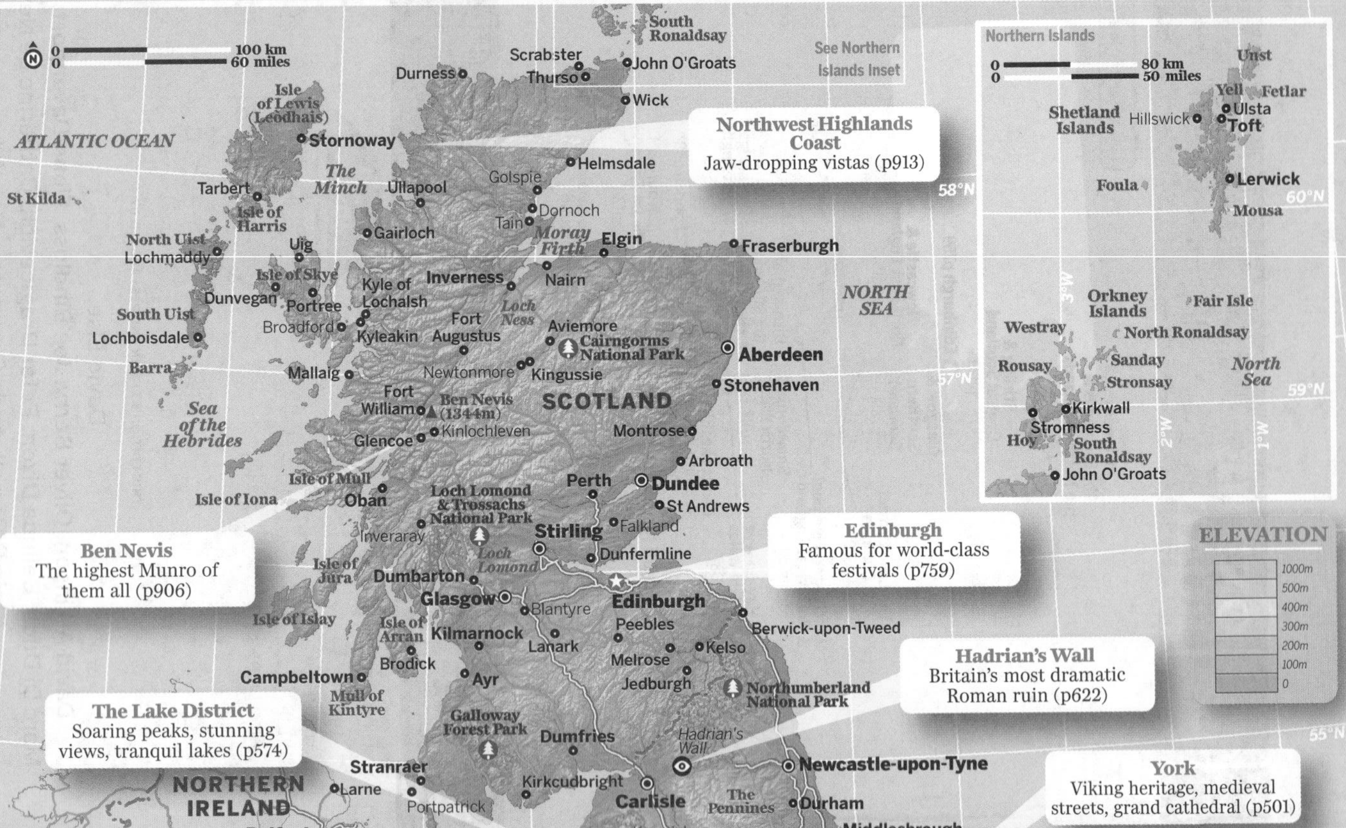

Northwest Highlands Coast
Jaw-dropping vistas (p913)
Ben Nevis
The highest Munro of them all (p906)
Edinburgh
Famous for world-class festivals (p759)
Hadrian's Wall
Britain's most dramatic Roman ruin (p622)
The Lake District
Soaring peaks, stunning views, tranquil lakes (p574)
York
Viking heritage, medieval streets, grand cathedral (p501)
ATLANTIC OCEAN
NORTH SEA
SCOTLAND
NORTHERN IRELAND
Sea of the Hebrides
The Minch
Moray Firth
See Northern Islands Inset
100 km
60 miles
St Kilda
Isle of Lewis (Leodhais)
Stornoway
Tarbert
Isle of Harris
North Uist
Lochmaddy
South Uist
Lochboisdale
Barra
Uig
Isle of Skye
Dunvegan
Portree
Broadford
Kyleakin
Kyle of Lochalsh
Mallaig
Durness
Ullapool
Gairloch
Scrabster
Thurso
John O'Groats
South Ronaldsay
Wick
Helmsdale
Golspie
Dornoch
Tain
Inverness
Loch Ness
Fort Augustus
Nairn
Elgin
Fraserburgh
Aviemore
Cairngorms National Park
Newtonmore
Kingussie
Aberdeen
Stonehaven
Fort William
Ben Nevis (1344m)
Kinlochleven
Glencoe
Montrose
Arbroath
Dundee
St Andrews
Perth
Isle of Mull
Oban
Isle of Iona
Loch Lomond & Trossachs National Park
Inveraray
Loch Lomond
Stirling
Falkland
Dunfermline
Isle of Jura
Dumbarton
Glasgow
Edinburgh
Blantyre
Isle of Islay
Isle of Arran
Kilmarnock
Lanark
Peebles
Berwick-upon-Tweed
Melrose
Kelso
Brodick
Campbeltown
Ayr
Jedburgh
Northumberland National Park
Mull of Kintyre
Galloway Forest Park
Dumfries
Hadrian's Wall
Stranraer
Newcastle-upon-Tyne
Larne
Portpatrick
Kirkcudbright
Carlisle
The Pennines
Durham
Northern Islands
80 km
50 miles
Shetland Islands
Hillswick
Unst
Yell
Fetlar
Ulsta
Toft
Foula
Lerwick
Mousa
Orkney Islands
Fair Isle
Westray
North Ronaldsay
Rousay
Sanday
Stronsay
North Sea
Kirkwall
Stromness
Hoy
South Ronaldsay
John O'Groats
ELEVATION
1000m
500m
400m
300m
200m
100m
0
58°N
57°N
55°N
60°N
59°N
3°W
2°W
1°W

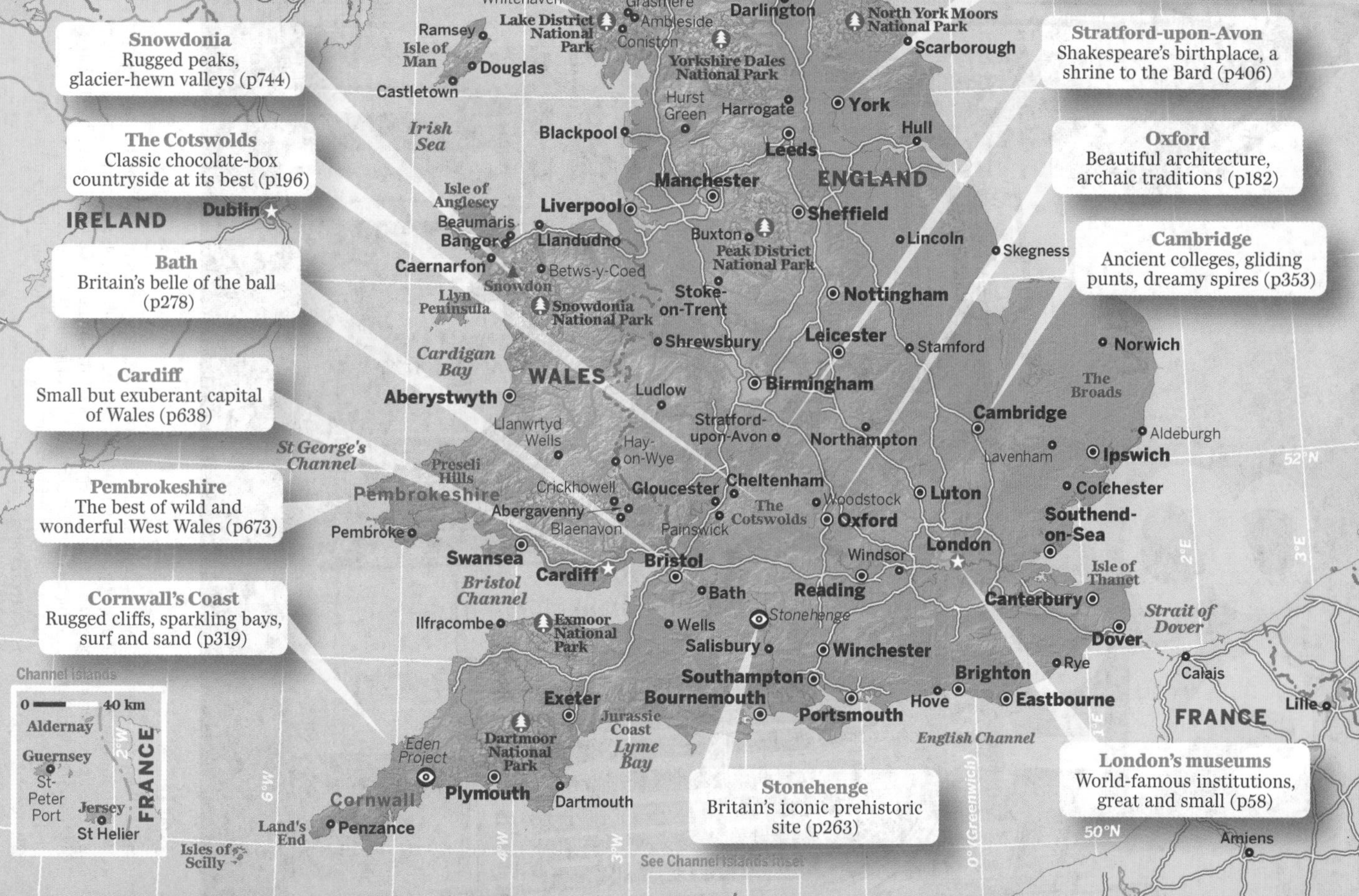
Snowdonia
Rugged peaks, glacier-hewn valleys (p744)
The Cotswolds
Classic chocolate-box countryside at its best (p196)
Bath
Britain's belle of the ball (p278)
Cardiff
Small but exuberant capital of Wales (p638)
Pembrokeshire
The best of wild and wonderful West Wales (p673)
Cornwall's Coast
Rugged cliffs, sparkling bays, surf and sand (p319)
Stratford-upon-Avon
Shakespeare's birthplace, a shrine to the Bard (p406)
Oxford
Beautiful architecture, archaic traditions (p182)
Cambridge
Ancient colleges, gliding punts, dreamy spires (p353)
Stonehenge
Britain's iconic prehistoric site (p263)
London's museums
World-famous institutions, great and small (p58)
IRELAND
Dublin
WALES
ENGLAND
FRANCE
Irish Sea
Cardigan Bay
St George's Channel
Bristol Channel
English Channel
Strait of Dover
Lyme Bay
Isle of Man
Ramsey
Douglas
Castletown
Lake District National Park
Yorkshire Dales National Park
North York Moors National Park
Peak District National Park
Snowdonia National Park
Exmoor National Park
Dartmoor National Park
Grasmere
Ambleside
Coniston
Darlington
Scarborough
York
Harrogate
Hurst Green
Blackpool
Leeds
Hull
Manchester
Liverpool
Sheffield
Lincoln
Skegness
Isle of Anglesey
Beaumaris
Bangor
Llandudno
Caernarfon
Betws-y-Coed
Snowdon
Llyn Peninsula
Buxton
Stoke-on-Trent
Nottingham
Shrewsbury
Leicester
Stamford
Norwich
The Broads
Aberystwyth
Ludlow
Birmingham
Llanwrtyd Wells
Hay-on-Wye
Stratford-upon-Avon
Northampton
Cambridge
Aldeburgh
Lavenham
Ipswich
Preseli Hills
Pembrokeshire
Crickhowell
Abergavenny
Blaenavon
Gloucester
Cheltenham
Painswick
The Cotswolds
Woodstock
Oxford
Luton
Colchester
Southend-on-Sea
Pembroke
Swansea
Cardiff
Bristol
Bath
Windsor
Reading
London
Isle of Thanet
Canterbury
Dover
Ilfracombe
Wells
Stonehenge
Salisbury
Winchester
Rye
Southampton
Brighton
Hove
Eastbourne
Exeter
Bournemouth
Portsmouth
Jurassic Coast
Eden Project
Plymouth
Dartmouth
Cornwall
Penzance
Land's End
Isles of Scilly
Calais
Lille
Amiens
52°N
50°N
2°E
3°E
1°E
0°(Greenwich)
3°W
4°W
6°W
See Channel Islands Inset
Channel Islands
0 40 km
Alderney
Guernsey
St-Peter Port
Jersey
St Helier
FRANCE
2°W

28 TOP EXPERIENCES

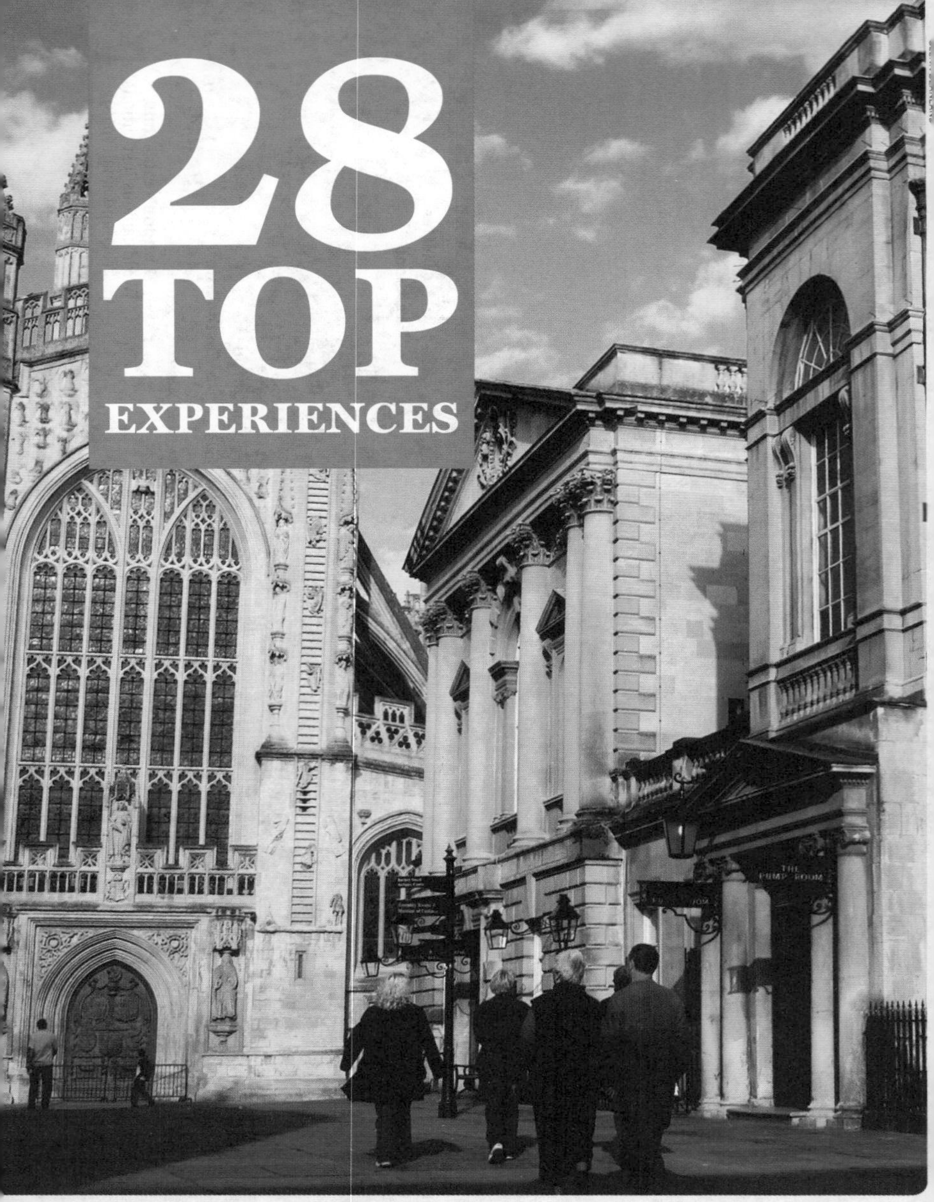

Bath

1 Britain can boast many great cities, but Bath (p278) stands out as the belle of the ball. Thanks to natural hot water bubbling to the surface, the Romans built a health resort here. The waters were rediscovered in the 18th century, and Bath became the place to see and be seen by British high society. Today, the stunning Georgian architecture of grand town houses, sweeping crescents and Palladian mansions (not to mention Roman remains, a beautiful cathedral, and a cutting-edge 21st-century spa), means Bath demands your undivided attention.

Edinburgh

2 Edinburgh (p759) is a city of many moods. It's famous for its festivals and is especially lively in the summer. It's also worth visiting out of season for sights such as the castle silhouetted against a blue spring sky with a yellow haze of daffodils misting the slopes below the esplanade. Or a chill December morning with the fog snagging the spires of the Old Town, the dark mouths of the wynds more mysterious than ever, rain on the cobblestones and a warm glow beckoning from the window of a pub.

Lake District

3 William Wordsworth and his Romantic chums were the first to champion the charms of the Lake District (p574), and it's not hard to see what stirred them. Pocked by whale-backed fells, razor-edge valleys and misty mountain tarns (as well as England's highest peak), this craggy corner of northwest England is still considered by many to be the spiritual home of British hiking. Strap on the boots, stock up on mintcake and drink in the views – inspiration is sure to follow.

ANDREW MARSHALL & LEANNE WALKER

Stonehenge

5 Mysterious and compelling, Stonehenge (p263) is Britain's most iconic ancient site. People have been drawn to this myth-rich ring of bluestones for more than 5000 years. And we still don't know quite why it was built. Most visitors get to gaze at the 50-ton megaliths from behind the perimeter fence, but with enough planning you can book an early-morning or evening tour and walk around the inner ring itself. In the slanting sunlight, away from the crowds, it's an ethereal place – an experience that certainly stays with you.

DAVID RYAN

Hadrian's Wall

4 Hadrian's Wall (p622) is one of Britain's most revealing and dramatic Roman ruins, its procession of abandoned forts, garrisons, towers and milecastles disclosing much about the everyday life of the international crew posted along its length. But walls are always about more than the stones from which they are built – this edge-of-empire barrier symbolised the boundary of civilised order. To the south was the bridled Roman world of underfloor heating, bathhouses and orderly taxpaying, to the north the unruly land of the marauding Celts.

NEIL SETCHFIELD

London's Live Entertainment

6 Can you hear that, music lovers? That's London calling – from the numerous theatres, concert halls, nightclubs, pubs and even tube stations, where on any given night hundreds if not thousands of performers are taking to the stage. Search out your own iconic London experience (p122), whether it's the Proms at the Royal Albert Hall, an East End singalong, a performance of *Oliver!* on the West End, a superstar DJ set at Fabric or a floppy-fringed guitar band at a Hoxton boozer.

Eating in Britain

7 Britain is packed with high-quality eateries – from Michelin-starred restaurants and welcoming gastropubs, to classic city cafes and quaint country teashops – with a choice of food to match. Tuck into national favourites such as fish and chips or toad in the hole, followed of course by rhubarb and custard or spotted dick. Then move on to regional specialities such as Scottish haggis, Cumberland sausage, Stilton cheese, Welsh cakes or the quintessential multicultural dish of northern England: a big fresh Yorkshire pudding filled with curry. See p1008.

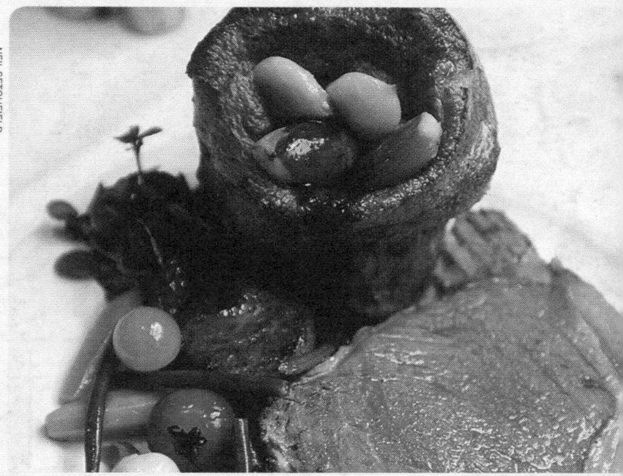

NEIL SETCHFIELD

GLENN VAN DER KNIJFF

Yorkshire Dales

8 From well-known Wensleydale and Swaledale, to obscure and evocative Langstrothdale and Arkengarthdale, this national park (p490) is characterised by a distinctive landscape of high moorland, stepped skylines and flat-topped hills rising above green valley floors. The park is patchworked with walls and ancient stone barns, and remote settlements where sheep and cattle still graze on village greens. Pull on your hiking boots or hire a mountain bike and explore the 500 miles of footpaths, bridleways and green lanes that criss-cross the landscape.

Snowdonia

9 The rugged northwest corner of Wales has rocky mountain peaks, glacier-hewn valleys, sinuous ridges, sparkling lakes and rivers, and charm-infused villages. The busiest part is around Snowdon itself, where many people hike to the summit, and many more take the jolly cog railway, while to the south and west are rarely trod areas perfect for off-the-beaten-track exploration (p744). And just nearby sit the lovely Llŷn Peninsula and Isle of Anglesey, where the sun often shines, even if it's raining on the mountains.

GARETH MCCORMACK

LAWRENCE WORCESTER

Oxford's Glorious Architecture

10 For most of us a visit to Oxford (p182) is as close as we're going to get to the brilliant minds and august institutions that have made this city famous across the globe. But you'll get a glimpse of this other world in the hushed quads and cobbled lanes where student cyclists and dusty academics roam. The beautiful college buildings, archaic traditions and stunning architecture have changed little over the centuries leaving the city centre much as Einstein or Tolkien would have found it.

Historic Buildings

11 Britain's history is rich and turbulent, and nowhere is this more apparent than in the mighty castles and stately homes that dot the landscape, from romantic clifftop ruins like Corfe (p248) or sturdy fortresses such as Caernarfon (p736), to formidable Stirling (p833) and still-inhabited Windsor (p216). And when the aristocracy no longer needed castles, they built 'stately homes' at the heart of their country estates. Classics of the genre include Blenheim Palace (p194) – see picture, right – and Chatsworth House (p473) in England, Powis Castle (p721) in Wales and Hopetoun House (p787) in Scotland.

GLENN BEANLAND

Glasgow

12 Scotland's biggest city (p789) lacks Edinburgh's classical beauty but more than makes up for it with a barrelful of things to do, and a warmth and energy that leave every visitor impressed. It's edgy and contemporary, a great spot to browse art galleries and – despite the awful fried-Mars-bar reputation – the country's best place to eat. Add to that what's perhaps Britain's best pub culture, and one of the world's best live music scenes, and the only thing to do is live it.

HOLGER LEUE

Newquay & Cornwall's Coast

13 Cornwall (p319) boasts more miles of unbroken coastline than anywhere else in Britain, but if it's rugged cliffs and sparkling bays you're looking for, there's only one place that fits the bill. The cluster of white sandy beaches around Newquay (p323) are some of the loveliest of England, favoured by everyone from bucket-and-spaders to beach-bronzed surfers. Visit in early spring or late autumn and you might even have the sands to yourself.

Gower Peninsula

14 Just along the coast from the cities of Cardiff and Swansea, but a different world entirely, the Gower Peninsula (p668) has been a favourite with local holidaymakers for years and now tempts visitors from further afield. Not surprisingly, this 15-mile-long thumb of land is an Area of Outstanding Natural Beauty (AONB), with broad butterscotch beaches, pounding surf, dreamy sand dunes, precipitous clifftop walks and rugged, untamed uplands. It's a perfect place for cycling and walking, with excellent surfing, and some wonderful low-key beaches for families.

CHERYL FORBES

Punting the Cambridge 'Backs'

15 No trip to Cambridge (p353) would be complete without an attempt to punt by the picturesque 'Backs', the leafy, green lawns behind the city's finest colleges. Hop off to marvel at the intricate vaulting of King's College Chapel, a show-stopping Gothic concoction, glide under the curious-looking Mathematical Bridge, or down a pint in one of the city's many historic pubs. You'll soon wonder how you could have studied anywhere else.

DENNIS JOHNSON

Canterbury Cathedral

17 Few other English cathedrals come close to Canterbury (p135), top temple of the Anglican Church and a place of worship for over 15 centuries. Its intricate tower dominates the Canterbury skyline, its grandeur unsurpassed by later structures. At its heart lies a 12th-century crime scene, the very spot where Archbishop Thomas Becket was put to the sword – an epoch-making event that launched a million pilgrimages and still pulls in the crowds today. A lone candle mourns the gruesome deed, the pink sandstone before it smoothed by 800 years of devout kneeling.

ORIEN HARVEY

Stratford-upon-Avon

16 What could be more English than taking in a Shakespeare play in the birthplace of the Bard? The pretty town of Stratford-upon-Avon (p406) is also where the world's most famous playwright shuffled off this mortal coil, and its tight knot of Tudor streets form a living map of Shakespeare's life and times. Huge crowds of theatre lovers and would-be thespians congregate here to visit the five historic houses owned by Shakespeare and his relatives, with a respectful detour to the old stone church where the Bard was laid to rest.

Northumberland Coast

18 For a complete contrast to Britain's busy tourist destinations head for the peace and quiet of Northumberland (p630). It wasn't always so tranquil, though, as the legacy of castles in the area shows. Places like Dunstanburgh, Bamburgh and Alnwick were built to control the borderlands with Scotland but today attract less aggressive visitors who are also drawn here by the wonderful opportunities for walking along windswept beaches, boat trips out to the puffin- and seal-covered Farne Islands, and cracking pubs and restaurants to relax in at the end of the day.

DAVID ELSE

Cardiff

19 The exuberant capital of Wales, Cardiff (p638) has recently emerged as one of Britain's leading urban centres. If its mid-20th-century decline seemed terminal, the city has entered the new millennium with vigour and confidence, flexing new-found architectural muscles. From the historic castle to the ultramodern waterfront, from the Victorian shopping arcades to the gigantic rugby stadium that is the pulsating heart of the city on match days, Cardiff has a buzz that reverberates through the streets, and a nightlife that's as famous as it's infectious.

ORIEN HARVEY

A Pint Down the Pub

20 Whether it's a long congenial evening with friends, or a swift half after work, the pub is still the centre of British social life, and the best traditional drink has to be beer. Not your fizzy lager, but honest to goodness ale. To outsiders it may be 'warm and flat', but give it a chance and you'll soon learn to savour the complex flavours and explore the country's many regional varieties, from Tinners Ale in Cornwall and Double Dragon in Wales to Cumbria's Sneck Lifter and Orkney's Dark Island.

Ben Nevis

21 The allure of Scotland's best-known natural features is strong. Around 100,000 people a year set off to reach the highest point in Britain (p906), though not all make it to the top. The reward for those that do is a truly magnificent view (weather permitting) and a great sense of achievement. Real enthusiasts can warm up by trekking the 95-mile West Highland Way first, while a hike in nearby Glen Coe (p902), Scotland's most famous glen, combines those two essential qualities of the Highland landscape – dramatic scenery and deep history.

GARETH MCCORMACK

York

22 With its Roman and Viking heritage, ancient city walls, spectacular Gothic cathedral and maze of medieval streets, York (p501) is a living showcase for the highlights of English history. Join one of the city's many walking tours and plunge into the network of snickleways (narrow alleys), each one the focus of a ghost story or historical character, then explore the intricacies of York Minster, the biggest medieval cathedral in all of Northern Europe. And don't miss the Flying Scotsman at the National Railway Museum, the world's largest collection of historic locomotives.

CHRIS MELLOR

Cotswolds

23 The most wonderful thing about the Cotswolds (p196) is that no matter where you go or how lost you get, you'll still end up in an impossibly picturesque village of rose-clad cottages and honey-coloured stone. And when you do, there'll be a quaint village green, a pub with sloping floors and fine ales, and a view of the lush green hills. It's easy to leave the crowds behind and find your very own slice of medieval England – and some of the best boutique hotels in the country.

BARBARA VAN ZANTEN

BRITAIN ON VIEW

Northwest Highland Coast

24 In the Highlands of Scotland (p887) you're never far from a breathtaking view, but the far northwest (p913) is awe-inspiring even by these high standards. The coast between Durness and Kyle of Lochalsh offers a jaw-dropping moment at every turn of the narrow road; the rugged mountainscapes of Assynt, the desolate beauty of Loch Torridon, the piercing incisions of sea lochs and the remote cliffs of Cape Wrath. Add to this some warm Highland hospitality – romantic hotels, gourmet restaurants, classic rural pubs – and you've got an unforgettable corner of the country.

DAVID TOMLINSON

Perthshire

25 In the heart of Scotland, this is a landscape where blue-grey lochs shimmer and reflect the changing moods of the weather, swaths of noble woodland clothe the hills, majestic glens scythe their way into remote wilderness, and salmon leap upriver to the place of their birth. Picturesque towns bloom with flowers, distilleries emit tempting malty odours, and sheep graze in impossibly green meadows. Here in Perthshire (p864), there's a feeling of the bounty of nature that few other places can match.

ROCCO FASANO

London's Museums

26 Institutions bright and beautiful, great and small, wise and wonderful – London's (p58) got them all. The range of museums is vast: from generalist collections (British Museum, V&A) to specific themes (Imperial War Museum, London Transport Museum, Natural History Museum). From intriguing private collections (Sir John Soane's Museum, Wallace Collection) to those celebrating people associated with the city (Handel, Dickens, Freud). Seriously, you could spend weeks without even scratching the surface. And most of it's free!

Football

27 The rest of the world may call it 'soccer', but here in Britain it's definitely 'football' (p1049). Despite what the fans may say in Italy or Brazil, the English Premier League has some of the world's finest teams. Big names include the globally renowned Arsenal, Liverpool and Chelsea – plus of course THE most famous club on the planet: Manchester United. North of the border, Scotland's best-known teams are Glasgow Rangers and Glasgow Celtic – and their 'old firm' rivalry is legend – while in Wales the national sport is most definitely rugby.

DAVID TOMLINSON

DAVID TIPLING

Pembrokeshire

28 Perched at the tip of wild and wonderful West Wales, Pembrokeshire (p673) boasts one of Britain's most beautiful and dramatic stretches of coast, with sheer cliffs, natural arches, blowholes, sea stacks, and a wonderful hinterland of tranquil villages and secret waterways. It's a landscape of Norman castles, Iron Age hill forts, holy wells and Celtic saints – including the nation's patron, St David – and the remnants of an even older people that left behind intriguing stone circles.

welcome to Great Britain

Edinburgh Castle, Buckingham Palace, Stonehenge, Snowdon, Manchester United, The Beatles – Britain does icons like no other place on earth, and travel here is a fascinating mix of famous names and hidden gems.

Variety Packed

From the graceful architecture of Canterbury Cathedral in the south to the soaring ramparts of Edinburgh Castle in the north, via the mountains of Wales or the Roman ruins of Hadrian's Wall, Britain's astounding variety is a major reason to travel here. City streets buzz day and night, with tempting shops and restaurants, and some of the world's finest museums. After dark, cutting-edge clubs, top-class theatre and formidable live music provide nights to remember. Next day, you're deep in the countryside, high in the hills or enjoying a classic seaside resort. In Britain, there really is something for everyone, whether you're eight or 80, going solo or travelling with your friends, your kids or your grandma.

Time Travel

A journey through Britain is a journey through history – but not history that's dull and dusty; history you can feel and relive. You can lay your hands on the megaliths of a 5000-year-old stone circle, or walk the battlements of a medieval fortress – just as they were patrolled by knights seven centuries ago. Fast forward to the future and you're admiring 21st-century architecture in Glasgow, or exploring the space-age domes of Cornwall's Eden Project.

English Spoken Here

While Britain boasts complex traditions and culture, on the surface at least it's familiar to many visitors thanks to a vast catalogue of British film and TV exports. The same applies when it comes to communication: this is home turf for the English language, so many visitors don't need to carry a phrasebook. Of course Wales and Scotland have their own languages, but everyone speaks English too – and all outsiders get a little confused by local accents in places such as Devon, Snowdonia and Aberdeen.

Easy Does It

A final thing to remember while you're planning a trip to Britain: travel here is a breeze. Although the locals may grumble (in fact, it's a national pastime), the public transport is pretty good, and a train ride through the British landscape can be a highlight in itself. But however you get around, in this compact country you're never far from the next town, the next pub, the next restaurant, the next national park or the next impressive castle on your hit-list of highlights. The choice is endless, and we've hand-picked the best places to create this book. Use it to steer you from place to place, and mix it with making your own discoveries. You won't be disappointed.

need to know

CURRENCY

» Pound – also called 'pound sterling' (£)

LANGUAGE

» English (also Scottish Gaelic and Welsh)

When to Go

High season

(Jun–Aug)

» Weather at its best. Accommodation rates at their highest – especially for August school holidays.

» Roads are busy, especially in seaside areas, national parks and popular cities such as Oxford, Edinburgh, Bath and York.

Shoulder

(Easter–end May; mid-Sep–end Oct)

» Crowds reduce. Prices drop.

» Weather often good; sunny spells mix with sudden showers March to May, while balmy 'Indian summers' feature September to October.

Low season

(Dec–Feb)

» Wet and cold; snow in mountain areas, especially in the north.

» Opening hours reduced October to Easter; some places shut down. Big-city sights (especially London's) operate all year.

Your Daily Budget

Budget less than £50

» Dorm beds: £10-£25

» Cheap meals in cafes and pubs: £5-£9

» Long-distance coach fare: £10-£30 (200 miles)

Midrange £50-£100

» Midrange hotel or B&B: £50-£130 (London £80-£180) per double room

» Main course in midrange restaurant: £9-£18

» Long-distance train: £15-£50 (200 miles)

» Car rental: from £30 per day

Top end over £100

» Four-star hotel room: from £200

» Three-course meal in a good restaurant: around £40 per person

MONEY

» Change bureaux and ATMs widely available, especially in cities and major towns.

VISAS

» Not required for most citizens of Europe, Australia, NZ, USA and Canada.

MOBILE PHONES

» Phones from most other countries operate in Britain but attract roaming charges. For local calls, local SIM cards cost from £10; SIM and basic handset around £30.

DRIVING

» Traffic drives on the left. Steering wheels are on the right side of the car. Most rental cars have manual gears (stick shift).

Websites

» **BBC** (www.bbc.co.uk) News and entertainment from the nation's broadcaster.

» **Visit Britain** (www.visitbritain.com) Official tourism website.

» **Lonely Planet** (http://lonelyplanet.com/great-britain) Destination information, hotel bookings, traveller forum and more.

» **Seize the Days** (http://lonelyplanet.com/132days) Weekly updates on UK activities and events.

» **National Traveline** (www.traveline.org.uk) Great portal site for all UK public transport.

Exchange Rates

Australia	A$1	61p
Canada	C$1	61p
euro zone	€1	87p
Japan	¥100	78p
New Zealand	NZ$1	47p
USA	US$1	68p

For current exchange rates see www.xe.com.

Important Numbers

Omit the area code if you're inside that area. Drop the initial 0 if you're calling from abroad.

Country code	☎+44
International access code	☎00
Emergency (police, fire, ambulance, mountain rescue or coastguard)	☎999

Arriving in Britain

» **Heathrow airport**
Train to Paddington station every 15 minutes (from £16)

» **Gatwick airport**
Train to Victoria station every 15 minutes (from £15)

» **Eurostar trains from Paris or Brussels**
Arrive at St Pancras International station in central London

» **London Victoria Coach Station**
Arrival point for buses/coaches from Europe

» **Taxis from airports**
Trips to central London run from £40 (Heathrow) to £90 (Luton); more at peak hours p131 and p133

Great Britain on a Shoestring

If you're on a tight budget, there's no getting away from it – Britain ain't cheap. Public transport, admission fees, restaurants and hotel rooms all tend to be expensive compared with their equivalents in many other European countries. But with some careful planning, a trip here doesn't have to break the bank. You can save money by staying in B&Bs instead of hotels, or hostels instead of B&Bs. You can also save by prebooking long-distance coach or train travel – and by avoiding times when everyone else is on the move (like Friday afternoon). Many attractions are free (or offer discounts on quiet days, such as Monday). And don't forget that you won't have to stump up a penny to enjoy Britain's best asset: the wonderful countryside and coastline.

what's new

For this new edition of Great Britain, our authors hunted down the fresh, the transformed, the hot and the happening. Here are a few of our favourites. For up-to-the-minute recommendations, see lonelyplanet.com/great-britain.

Darwin Centre, Natural History Museum, London

1 The Natural History Museum has attracted visitors for a hundred years with the constant addition of features. Latest is the striking new home for the Darwin Centre, where you catch a lift to the top of the 'Cocoon' – a seven-storey egg-shaped structure encased within a glass pavilion – and snoop through the windows at boffins studying 20 million animal and plant specimens (p85).

Ashmolean Museum, Oxford

2 Britain's oldest public museum re-opened in late 2009 after a massive £61 million redevelopment; it's now lauded as one of the finest in the world (p189).

Hotel Missoni, Edinburgh

3 The Italian fashion house turns to luxury hotels, comes to Scotland and instantly establishes a style icon in the heart of the city (p778).

Fallen Angel, Durham

4 Kip in a sleeper train compartment or in your own personal cinema at the one of the northeast's newest – and most bizarre – digs (p619).

English Whisky Company, Norfolk

5 Usually associated with Scotland, the first whisky distillery in England for 120 years bottled its landmark spirits in November 2009. Take a tour and savour the historic moment (p381).

Agatha Christie's Greenway, Devon

6 The famous crime writer's riverside holiday home opened to visitors in 2009; you can wander between rooms much as she left them, admire the books in her library and even piles of hats in the lobby (p305).

Hafod Eryri, Mount Snowdon

7 Just below Snowdon's summit, this striking piece of architecture opened in 2009 to replace the dilapidated visitor centre once famously labelled 'the highest slum in Europe' (p747).

Turner Contemporary, Margate

8 Launching in 2011, Margate's brand new state-of-the-art gallery stands right on the seafront, bathed in the sea-refracted light that the artist JMW Turner loved so much. The first exhibition, naturally, focuses on Turner himself (p144)

if you like...

Castles

Britain's turbulent history bequeaths a landscape dotted with defensive masterpieces of the medieval era, complete with moats, keeps, battlements, dungeons and all the classic features we know from history books or legends of knights and maidens in distress.

Windsor Castle The largest and oldest occupied fortress in the world, a majestic vision of battlements and towers, and the Queen's weekend retreat (p216)

Warwick Castle Among the finest castles in Britain; preserved enough to be impressive, ruined enough to be romantic (p403)

Edinburgh Castle The focal point of the Scottish capital, and its very reason for being (p764)

Stirling Castle Perched on a volcanic crag, with stunning views from the battlements; a classic historic royal fortress (p833)

Carreg Cennen Castle The most dramatically positioned fortress in Wales, standing guard over a lonely stretch of Brecon Beacons National Park (p670)

Cathedrals

Along with castles, the cathedrals of Britain are the country's most impressive and inspiring historic structures. Many were works in progress for centuries, so display an eclectic mix of styles with solid Norman naves later enjoying the addition of graceful Gothic arches or soaring spires, and – most beautiful of all – vast extents of stained-glass windows.

St Paul's Cathedral A symbol of the city for centuries, and still an essential part of the London skyline (p74)

York Minster One of the largest medieval cathedrals in all of Europe, especially renowned for its windows (p501)

Canterbury Cathedral The mother ship of the Anglican Church, still attracting pilgrims and visitors in their thousands (p138)

St David's Cathedral An ancient place of worship in Britain's smallest city (p680)

Glasgow Cathedral A shining example of Gothic architecture, and the only mainland Scottish cathedral to have survived the Reformation (p793)

Ruined Abbeys

Thanks to the work of industrious monks from the 12th to the 14th centuries, great abbeys are a feature of the British landscape. Thanks to Henry VIII's spat with the Catholic Church around 1540, many are now in ruins – but they're no less impressive for today's visitor.

Fountains Abbey Extensive ruins set in more recently landscaped water-gardens – one of the most beautiful sites in Britain (p517)

Rievaulx Abbey Tranquil remains of columns and arches hidden away in a secluded valley (p523)

Melrose Abbey The finest of all the great Border abbeys; the heart of Robert the Bruce is buried here (p812)

Whitby Abbey Stunning clifftop ruin with an eerie atmosphere that inspired the author of *Dracula* (p526)

Glastonbury Abbey The legendary burial place of King Arthur and Queen Guinevere (p289)

Tintern Abbey Riverside ruins that inspired generations of poets and artists (p660)

» Lavenham (p368) is home to a wonderful collection of half-timbered and pargeted houses

Stately Homes

Where France has endless chateaux, and Germany a schloss on every corner, Britain boasts a raft of stately homes – vast mansions where the landed gentry have lived for generations, recently opening their doors so the rest of us can admire the fabulous interiors.

Blenheim Palace A monumental baroque fantasy and one of Britain's greatest stately homes (p194)

Castle Howard Another stunning baroque edifice, best known as the setting for *Brideshead Revisited* (p512)

Hopetoun House One of Scotland's finest stately homes, with a superb location in lovely grounds beside the Firth of Forth (p787)

Powis Castle Rising above a fantastical cloud of manicured yew trees, this one-time fortress was enriched by generations of aristocratic families (p721)

Chatsworth House The quintessential stately home, a treasure trove of heirlooms and works of art (p473)

Village idylls

If you want to see the Britain you've always imagined, or the Britain you know so well from period movies and TV costume dramas, you'll absolutely love the country's villages, all very different in character, but all a reminder of a simpler age.

Lavenham A wonderful collection of exquisitely preserved medieval buildings virtually untouched since the 15th century (p368)

Hutton-le-Hole One of Yorkshire's most attractive villages, with sheep grazing on a wide green amid a scattering of cottages (p524)

Mousehole Southwest England overflows with picturesque pint-sized ports, but this is one of the best (p331)

Beddgelert A conservation village of rough grey stone buildings in the heart of Snowdonia National Park (p744)

Cromarty At the northeastern tip of the Black Isle, with a fine collection of 18th-century sandstone houses (p895)

Moors & Mountains

For a crowded country, Britain has a surprising proportion of countryside, some of it even more surprisingly high and wild – a playground for hikers, bikers, birdwatchers and other lovers of the great outdoors.

Torridon A stunning collection of imposing mountains: is there a place in Scotland more forbiddingly beautiful? (p918)

Assynt These weirdly shaped mountains epitomise the epic geological essence of Scotland's northwest (p916)

Lake District A feast of mountains, valleys, views and – of course – lakes; the landscape that inspired William Wordsworth (p574)

Northumberland National Park The vast and dramatically empty landscapes of England's far north (p628)

Snowdonia National Park The best-known slice of nature in Wales, with grand but surprisingly accessible Snowdon at its heart (p744)

Brecon Beacons A dramatic collection of high mountains, glacier-scoured hollows and waterfall-splashed valleys (p693)

If you like... clifftop drama

The Minack is a unique theatre, carved into vertiginous cliffs overlooking the Atlantic in Cornwall. The classic play to catch is *The Tempest*, but any performance is spell-binding (p333)

Industrial Heritage

Britain's history is not all about big castles or twee cottages; the nation also drove the world's industrialisation in the 18th and 19th centuries, and this golden (though rather grimy) era is celebrated at several sites around the country.

Ironbridge The place where it all started, the crucible of the Industrial Revolution, where 10 museums for the price of one give fascinating insights (p427)

Blaenavon A World Heritage Site of well-preserved ironworks and the fascinating Big Pit coal mine (p661)

New Lanark Once the largest cotton-spinning complex in Britain and a testament to enlightened capitalism (p809)

National Railway Museum A cathedral to Britain's great days of steam; for railway fans of all ages it's the perfect place to go loco (p503)

Roman Remains

For 400 years the province of Britannia was part of the Roman Empire, a legacy still visible at various sites around the country – from sturdy defences for soldiers to fancy houses for wealthy citizens.

Roman Baths at Bath Perhaps the most famous Roman remains in England – a complex of bathhouses around natural thermal waters – plus additions from the 17th century when restorative waters again became fashionable (p279)

Hadrian's Wall Snaking coast-to-coast across lonely hills, this 2000-year-old fortified line once marked the northern limit of imperial Roman jurisdiction (p622)

Caerleon One of three legionary forts in Britain, with impressive remains of barracks, baths and amphitheatre (p662)

Outdoor Art

Many of the great stone sculptures by well-known British artists are from, and of, the earth, so it's fitting that we can now admire many of them in a natural setting. Works in steel and other materials complete the picture.

Yorkshire Sculpture Park England's biggest outdoor sculpture collection, dominated by the works of Henry Moore and Barbara Hepworth (p487)

Scottish National Gallery of Modern Art The park surrounding the gallery features sculptures by Henry Moore, Rachel Whiteread and Barbara Hepworth among others (p773)

Tout Quarry An unsung artistic gem: around 50 rock-carved sculptures still in situ, including works by Antony Gormley and Dhruva Mistry (p253)

Angel of the North England's best-known public work of art spreads its rusty wings and stands sentinel near Newcastle (p616)

Grizedale Forest A maze of walking and biking routes, passing around 90 outdoor sculptures created by local and international artists (p587)

If you like... kooky collections
Portmeirion is a private village built in a mix of styles – from Moorish to Ancient Greek; it's most famous as the set for cult TV show *The Prisoner* (p743)

Shopping

For every identikit megastore in Britain there's an independent shop with soul and character – whether you're in the market for books, clothes, jewellery, arts and crafts, retro handbags or 1960s vinyl.

Hay-on-Wye The self-proclaimed secondhand book capital of the world boasts over 30 bookshops and millions of volumes, attracting browsers, collectors and academics from around the world (p704)

Arcades, Cardiff Half a dozen arcades branch off the main streets in Cardiff city centre, lined with speciality shops and cafes (p651)

Victoria Quarter, Leeds Lovely arcades of wrought ironwork and stained glass, home to several top fashion boutiques (p485)

North Laine, Brighton The perfect place to pick up essential items such as vegetarian shoes, Elvis outfits and circus monocycles (p173)

Royal Arcade, Norwich Art-nouveau classic with ornate tiling, stained glass and a host of speciality shops (p377)

Galleries

Fans of the visual arts are spoilt for choice in Britain. Galleries abound, from long-standing classics and famous works in the larger cities, to quirky and off-beat locations featuring experimental and up-and-coming artists.

Tate Britain One of the best-known galleries in London, full to the brim with the finest local works (p84)

Tate Modern London's other Tate focuses on modern art in all its wonderful permutations (p77)

BALTIC Newcastle's 'Tate of the North' features work by some of contemporary art's biggest show-stoppers (p612)

National Museum Cardiff An excellent collection of Welsh artists, plus works by Monet, Renoir, Matisse, Van Gogh, Francis Bacon and David Hockney (p641)

Kelvingrove Art Gallery & Museum A national landmark in Glasgow – great collection, and a cracking spot to learn about Scottish art (p797)

Barber Institute of Fine Arts With works by Rubens, Turner and Picasso, this Birmingham gallery is no lightweight (p395)

Arts & Music Festivals

Whatever your taste in music or the arts, there's a festival for you somewhere in Britain.

Edinburgh International Festival & Fringe The world's biggest festival of art and culture. 'Nuff said (p777)

Glastonbury Britain's biggest and best-loved music festival (p289)

Hay Festival A world-class celebration of all things literary at the country's bookshop capital (p704)

Notting Hill Carnival London's Caribbean community shows the city how to party (p99)

Pride Gay and lesbian street parade through London culminating in a concert in Trafalgar Sq (p99)

Birmingham Artsfest A cultural extravaganza featuring everything from ballet and bhangra to rhythm and blues (p397)

Latitude An eclectic mix of music, literature, dance, drama and comedy, with stunning location in Southwold and manageable size (p373)

» The bustling seaside city of Brighton (p166) has a bohemian, cosmopolitan and hedonistic vibe

CHRISTER FREDRIKSSON

Coastal Beauty

It won't have escaped your notice that Britain is an island. Surrounded by the sea, the country boasts a nautical heritage and a long coastline with many beautiful spots.

Ardnamurchan The most westerly point on the British mainland is also one of the most scenic, with superb views across to the islands of Skye and Mull (p853)

Pembrokeshire coast Towering cliffs, rock arches, clean waters and perfect sandy beaches at the tip of West Wales (p673)

Tongue Sea lochs penetrate the rocky coast in this wild stretch of Scotland's north (p913)

Holkham Bay This pristine expanse of sand gives a real sense of isolation with giant skies stretching overhead (p386)

Jurassic Coast An exhilarating 3D geology lesson, with towering rock stacks, sea-carved arches and fossils aplenty (p248)

Beachy Head & Seven Sisters Where the South Downs plunge into the sea, these mammoth chalk cliffs provide a dramatic finale (p166)

Beach Action

Maybe you want to do more than just look at Britain's wonderful coastal scenery. Down on the beach, or out in the swell, you can be a bit more active.

Newquay Beautifully positioned above a cluster of golden beaches; the undisputed capital of British surfing (p323)

Burnham Deepdale Eastern England's unexpected centre for wind-powered beach activities, thanks to strong breezes and big stretches of flat sand (p386)

Gower Peninsula Sand dunes, lovely family-friendly beaches and some key surfer hang-outs (p668).

Thurso At the top of Scotland, this is an unlikely surf spot, but once you've got the dry-suit on the breaks are worth it (p912)

Classic Seaside Resorts

Quiet coves or surfy beaches are one thing, but for a different view of Britain's coast you have to sample a traditional seaside resort. This is the place for Victorian piers, buckets and spades, fairy floss and a stroll along the prom-prom-prom...

Scarborough The original British seaside resort, where it all began back in the 17th century (p517)

Southwold A genteel seaside resort with lovely sandy beach, charming pier and rows of colourful beach huts (p373)

Bournemouth Seven miles of sandy beach, 3000 deckchairs and a pair of Edwardian cliff-lifts (p243)

Brighton Away from the ubercool scene there are still plenty of naughty postcards and kiss-me-quick hats in 'London-by-the-Sea' (p166)

Llandudno Beach-side Punch and Judy shows, a step-back-in-time pier and a classic esplanade (p726)

month by month

Top Events

1 **Edinburgh International Festival & Fringe,** August

2 **Glyndebourne,** late May–August

3 **Trooping the Colour,** mid-June

4 **Glastonbury**, late June

5 **Abergavenny Food Festival,** September

January

January is mid-winter in Britain. Festivals and events to brighten the mood are thin on the ground, but luckily some include fire – lots of it.

London Parade

A ray of light in the gloom, the New Year's Day Parade in London (to use its official title) is one of the biggest events of its kind in the world, featuring marching bands, street performers, classic cars, floats and displays winding their way through the streets, watched by over half a million people. www.londonparade.co.uk

Up-Helly-Aa

Half of Shetland dresses up with horned helmets and battleaxes in this spectacular re-enactment of a Viking fire festival, with a torchlit procession leading the burning of a full-size Viking longship. www.uphellyaa.org

Celtic Connections

Glasgow plays host to a celebration of Celtic music, dance and culture, with participants from all over the globe. www.celticconnections.com

February

The country may be scenic under snow and sunshine, or more likely grey and gloomy. Hang in there...

Jorvik Viking Festival

The ancient Viking capital of York becomes home once again to invaders and horned helmets galore, with the intriguing addition of longship races. p507

Fort William Mountain Festival

Britain's capital of the outdoors celebrates the peak of the winter season with ski workshops, mountaineering films and talks by famous climbers. www.mountainfilmfestival.co.uk

March

Spring finally arrives. There's a hint of better weather and a few classic sporting fixtures grace the calendar. Most people stay hunkered down, though, so hotels offer special rates to tempt them out from under the duvet.

Six Nations Rugby Championship

The highlight of the rugby calendar, with the home nations playing at London's Twickenham, Edinburgh's Murrayfield and Cardiff's Millennium Stadium. www.rbs6nations.com

University Boat Race

Annual race down the River Thames in London between the rowing teams from Cambridge and Oxford Universities, an institution since 1856 that still captures the imagination of the country (p99).

April

The weather slowly improves – getting imperceptibly warmer and drier – and attractions that closed for the low season open around the middle of the month.

Grand National

Half the country has a flutter on the highlight of the three-day horse race meeting at Aintree on the first Saturday of the month – a steeplechase with a testing course and notoriously high jumps (p561).

London Marathon

Super-fit athletes cover 26 miles 385 yards in just over two hours, while others dress up in daft costumes and take considerably longer (p99).

Camden Crawl

Your chance to spot the next big thing in the music scene or witness a secret gig by an established act, with 40 of Camden's venues given over to live music for two full days (p99).

Beltane

Thousands of revellers climb Edinburgh's Calton Hill for this modern revival of a pagan fire festival marking the end of winter. www.beltane.org

Spirit of Speyside

Based in Dufftown, a Scottish festival of whisky, food and music, with five days of art, cooking, distillery tours and outdoor activities. www.spiritofspeyside.com

May

The weather is usually good, with more events to enjoy. There are two public holidays this month (first and last Mondays) so traffic is very busy over the corresponding long weekends.

FA Cup Final

The highlight of the football season for over a century. All winter teams from all England's football divisions have been battling it out in a knock-out tournament, culminating in this heady spectacle at Wembley Stadium – the home of English football (p1049).

Brighton Festival

The lively three-week arts fest takes over the streets of buzzy south-coast resort Brighton – and alongside the mainstream performances there's a festival fringe as well (p167).

Chelsea Flower Show

The Royal Horticultural Society flower show at Chelsea is the highlight of the gardener's year (p99).

Hay Festival

The ever-expanding 'festival of the mind' brings an intellectual influx to book-town Hay-on-Wye (p704).

Glyndebourne

Open-air festival of world-class opera in the pastoral surroundings of Glyndebourne House in East Sussex. www.glyndebourne.com

June

Now it's almost summer. You can tell because this month sees the music-festival season kick off properly, while sporting events – from rowing to racing – fill the calendar.

Derby Week

Horse-racing, people-watching and clothes-spotting are on the agenda at this week-long meeting in Epsom, Surrey. www.epsomderby.co.uk

Download Festival

Expect ear-splitting feedback and fists thrust aloft at this heavy-metal fest in Donington Park, Derbyshire. www.downloadfestival.co.uk

Cotswolds Olimpicks

Welly-wanging, pole-climbing and shin-kicking are the key disciplines at this traditional Gloucestershire sports day, held every year since 1612. www.olimpickgames.co.uk

Trooping the Colour

Military bands and bearskinned grenadiers march down London's Whitehall in this martial pageant to mark the monarch's birthday (p99).

Royal Ascot

It's hard to tell which matters more, the fashion or the fillies, at this highlight of the horse-racing year in Berkshire. www.ascot.co.uk

Wimbledon Tennis

The world's best-known grass-court tennis tournament, Wimbledon attracts all the big names, while crowds cheer or eat tons of strawberries and cream (p99).

Glastonbury Festival

One of the country's favourite pop and rock gatherings, invariably muddy and still a rite of passage for every self-respecting British teenager (p288).

Meltdown Festival

London's Southbank Centre hands over the curatorial reins to a legend of contemporary music (such as David Bowie, Morrissey or Patti Smith) to create a program of concerts, talks and films. http://meltdown.southbankcentre.co.uk

Royal Regatta

Boats of every description take to the water for Henley's upper-crust river regatta (p196).

Pride

Highlight of the gay and lesbian calendar, a technicolour street parade heads through London's West End (p99).

Glasgow Festivals

Scotland's second city hosts a major celebration of music and arts **West End Festival**. www.westendfestival.co.uk, www.jazzfest.co.uk)

July

Proper summer. Festivals every week. Schools break up at the end of the month, so there's a holidays tingle in the air, dulled only by busy roads on Friday because everyone's going somewhere for the weekend.

Great Yorkshire Show

Harrogate plays host to one of Britain's largest county shows. Expect Yorkshire grit, Yorkshire tykes, Yorkshire puddings, Yorkshire beef... www.greatyorkshireshow.co.uk

T in the Park

World-class acts since 1994 ensure this major music festival is Scotland's answer to Glastonbury. www.tinthepark.com

Latitude Festival

A small but fast-growing gathering in the seaside town of Southwold, with theatre, cabaret, art and literature, plus top names from the alternative music scene (p373).

International Musical Eisteddfod

A week-long festival of international folk music at Llangollen, with an eclectic fringe and big-name evening concerts (p726).

Royal Welsh Show

Prize bullocks and local produce at this national farm and livestock event in Builth Wells. www.rwas.co.uk

Cowes Week

The country's biggest yachting spectacular on the choppy seas around the Isle of Wight (p240).

Womad

Roots and world music take centre stage at this festival in a country park in the south Cotswolds. www.womad.org

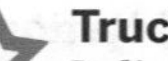

Truck

Indie music festival in Oxfordshire, known for its eclectic acts. www.thisistruck.com

August

Schools and colleges are closed, parliament is in recess, the sun is shining (hopefully), most people go away for a week or two, and the nation is in holiday mood.

International Festival & Fringe

Edinburgh's most famous August happening is its International Festival and Fringe, but this month the city also has an event for anything you care to name – books, art, theatre, music, comedy, marching bands... www.edinburghfestivals.co.uk

Notting Hill Carnival

A multicultural Caribbean-style street carnival in the London district of Notting Hill. Steel drums, dancers, outrageous costumes (p99).

Reading Festival

Venerable rock and pop festival, always still a good bet for big-name bands. www.readingfestival.com

Leeds Festival

Reading's northern sister. Same weekend, same line-up, with bands shuttling between the two (p481).

National Eisteddfod of Wales

The largest celebration of native Welsh culture, steeped in

history, pageantry and pomp; held at various venues around the country (p726).

Brecon Jazz Festival

Smoky sounds at one of Europe's leading jazz festivals, in the charming mid-Wales town of Brecon. p698

September

The first week of September is still holiday time, but then schools reopen, traffic returns to normal, and the summer party's over for another year. Ironically, the weather's often better than August's, now everyone's back at work.

Bestival

Quirky music festival with a different fancy dress theme every year, at Robin Hill Country Park on the Isle of Wight. www.bestival.net

Great North Run

Tyneside plays host to the biggest half marathon in the world with the greatest number of runners in any race at this distance. www.greatrun.org

Abergavenny Food Festival

The mother of all epicurean festivals and the champion of Wales' burgeoning food scene. www.abergavennyfoodfestival.com

Braemar Gathering

The biggest and most famous Highland Games in the Scottish calendar, traditionally attended by members of the royal family. Highland dancing, caber-tossing and bagpipe-playing. www.braemargathering.org

October

October means autumn. The leaves are falling from the trees. Sights and attractions start to shut down for the low season, and accommodation rates drop as hoteliers try to entice a final few guests before winter.

Horse of the Year Show

The country's major indoor horse event, with dressage, show-jumping and other equine activities, at the NEC arena near Birmingham (p397).

Dylan Thomas Festival

A celebration of the Welsh laureate's work with readings, events and talks in Swansea (p665).

November

Winter's here, and November is a dull month. The weather is often cold and damp, summer is a distant memory and Christmas is still too far away.

Guy Fawkes Night

Also called Bonfire Night, 5 November sees fireworks fill the country's skies in commemoration of a failed attempt to blow up parliament way back in 1605. www.bonfirenight.net

Remembrance Day

Red poppies are worn and wreaths are laid in towns and cities around the country on 11 November in commemoration of fallen military personnel. www.poppy.org.uk

December

Schools break up earlier, but shops and businesses keep going until Christmas Eve; the last weekend before Christmas Day is busy on the roads as people visit friends and family, or head for the airport.

Stonehaven Fireball Festival

The Scottish fishing town of Stonehaven celebrates Hogmanay with a spectacular procession of fireball-swinging locals. www.stonehavenfireballs.co.uk

New Year Celebrations

The last night of December sees fireworks and street parties in town squares across the country. London's Trafalgar Sq is where the city's largest crowds gather to herald in the New Year.

itineraries

Whether you've got six days or 60, these itineraries provide a starting point for the trip of a lifetime. Want more inspiration? Head online to lonelyplanet .com/thorntree to chat with other travellers.

Two weeks

Best of Britain

Start with a full day in the nation's capital, **London**, simply walking the streets to admire the world-famous sights: Buckingham Palace, Tower Bridge, Trafalgar Sq and more. Then head southwest to the grand cathedral cities of **Winchester** and **Salisbury**, across to the iconic menhirs of **Stonehenge**, and their less well-known counterpart **Avebury Stone Circle**, then onwards to the beautiful historic city of **Bath**.

Loop over to **Chepstow** and **Cardiff** for a taste of Wales, then cruise across the classic English countryside of the **Cotswolds** to reach **Oxford**. Not far away is **Stratford-upon-Avon**, for everything Shakespeare.

Strike out north to **Edinburgh** for another great castle, before crossing down to **York** for its glorious cathedral and first-class train museum. Keep going south to reach **Cambridge**, another ancient university city, and enjoy the last few days back in **London**, immersed in galleries, museums, luxury shops, street markets, West End shows or East End cafes – or whatever takes your fancy.

One month

The Full Monty

This is a trip for those with time, or an urge to see everything. So brace yourself, and let's be off.

After a day or two in **London**, head southeast to **Canterbury**, then along the coast to hip and happening **Brighton**. For a change of pace, divert to the **New Forest**, then up to historic **Winchester** and **Salisbury** with their awe-inspiring cathedrals. Next, religion of a different kind: the ancient stone circles at **Stonehenge** and **Avebury**.

Go westwards to **Bath**, with its grand Georgian architecture, Roman remains and famous spas, and then over the border to reach Wales. Stop off at the energetic little city of **Cardiff**, then head north through to the whaleback hills of **Brecon Beacons National Park** to reach the quirky book-mad town of **Hay-on-Wye**.

Then it's back to England, and east into the **Cotswolds**, with its rolling hills, quintessential rural scenery and chocolate-box towns like **Chipping Norton**. Not far away is the famous university town of **Oxford**, as well as the ancient town of **Warwick** with its spectacular castle, and Shakespeare's birthplace **Stratford-upon-Avon**.

Continue north to **Chester**, for its famous city walls, diverting into North Wales for the grand castles at **Conwy** and **Caernarfon**, and the equally stunning mountains of **Snowdonia**. If time allows and the weather's good, you can take a train to the top of the highest peak!

Then ferry across the Mersey to **Liverpool**, with a famous musical heritage and revitalised waterfront, or to **Manchester** for a taste of big-city life, followed by a total change of scenery in the tranquil mountains of the **Lake District**.

Just to the north is the sturdy border town of **Carlisle**, and one of Britain's most impressive Roman remains, **Hadrian's Wall**.

Hop across the border to Scotland, via the tranquil **Southern Uplands**, to reach good-time **Glasgow**. Then trek to **Fort William**, maybe diverting up **Ben Nevis**, from where it's easy to reach the beautiful **Isle of Skye**. Then it's time to head south again, via **Stirling Castle** to **Edinburgh**, and on through the abbey towns of **Melrose** and **Jedburgh**.

Back in England, you can marvel at the castle and cathedral of **Durham** and the ancient Viking capital of **York**, before taking in the ancient university city of **Cambridge**, and enjoying the last few days back in **London**.

One month

Walk on the Wild Side

Some itineraries focus on cities, but this is a tour through the best of Britain's natural landscape. So put on your hiking boots, or have a camera at the ready, as we take a south–north meander through some of the country's finest stretches of countryside.

Start in the **New Forest**, for a spot of walking, cycling or horse-riding, then keep heading west, via Dorset's fossil-ridden **Jurassic Coast**, to reach the lonely hills and granite tors of **Dartmoor**. Detour to **Land's End**, where the English mainland plunges into the Atlantic, then travel the stunning cliffs and bays of **Cornwall's North Coast** and the rich farmland of **Devon** to reach the gorse-clad hills of **Exmoor**.

Cross the River Severn into Wales; hike through the rolling hills of the **Brecon Beacons** or go down to the sea in **Pembrokeshire**. Then aim north through remote and little-visited **Mid-Wales** to reach **Snowdonia** – with mountains for walkers and steam trains for all the family. Nearby is the beautiful **Isle of Anglesey**.

Then it's back to England, through the moors and valleys of the **Peak District** and **Yorkshire Dales** – two of England's best-known and best-loved national parks. Westwards from Yorkshire and across the **Pennines** – the chain of hills known as 'England's backbone' – takes you into Cumbria, and the high peaks of the **Lake District**, once the spiritual home for Wordsworth and the Romantic poets, now providing inspiration for walkers and hikers – including England's highest summit **Scafell Pike**.

Head northwards again, over (or along) the spectacular Roman remains of **Hadrian's Wall** to reach **Northumberland National Park**, England's final frontier. The landscape is wild and often unforgiving – but for outdoor fans that's its very attraction.

Next, it's across the border into Scotland, and the delightful hills and forests of the **Southern Uplands**. Further north two new national parks await: the glorious combination of **Loch Lomond & the Trossachs**, and the mountain wilderness of the **Cairngorms**.

That may be wonder enough, but Britain's pastoral pleasures are crowned by **Northwest Scotland**, the famous Highlands and islands, where jewels include peaks like **Ben Nevis** (Britain's highest summit) and remote ranges such as **Torridon** and **Assynt**, while out to sea the lovely islands – **Arran, Skye, Mull, Islay, Jura, North Uist, South Uist, Lewis, Harris** – bask in the afternoon sun...

Two to Three Weeks

Urban Odyssey

To get away from the main track and dig under Britain's skin a little, take this ride through some of the country's less well-known and revitalised cities.

Kick off in **Bristol**, former poor cousin to neighbouring Bath, but today a city with fierce pride, a rich historic legacy and a music scene that rivals cool northern outposts. Divert to **Cardiff**, once a provincial backwater, but now the seat of the devolved Welsh government – and another musical hotbed.

Next stop is **Birmingham**, a city that oozes transformation, with a renovated waterside, energised museums and a space-age shopping centre. Nearby is **Nottingham**, forever associated with Robin Hood, but renowned today for very merry nightlife. If hitting the dance floor isn't your thing, relax in the city's great pubs.

But don't dawdle. Sup up your pint. We're off again, this time to **Leeds**, where rundown factories and abandoned warehouses have been turned into loft apartments, ritzy boutiques and stylish department stores, hence the nickname 'Knightsbridge of the North'.

Shopping not your thing? No problem. On we go to **Newcastle-upon-Tyne**, the one-time king of coal and steel, now given up on heavy industries in favour of art and architecture – and also famous for to-the-hilt partying. Cross the Millennium Bridge to twin-city **Gateshead** to visit Baltic, a former grain mill turned cutting-edge art gallery, before catching a show at the fabulous Sage concert hall. And don't miss Britain's best-known work of public art, the iconic (and gigantic) Angel of the North.

Still want more? It's got to be **Glasgow**. No longer completely overshadowed by Edinburgh, Scotland's other great city boasts fabulous galleries, welcoming pubs and clubs, some truly electric venues, and – only in Scotland – slick but unpretentious bars.

Pausing only for coffee and toast, it's back to England again and the city of **Liverpool**. The Beatles are done to death, but there's a lively *current* music scene, and this one-time port is reinventing itself as a cultural hot spot, epitomised by the new museums and galleries along the historic waterfront.

To finish your tour, it's just a few miles east to **Manchester**, the self-styled 'Barcelona of Britain' and a long-time stage for musical endeavour, with thriving arts and club scenes, galleries a go-go, dramatic new architecture and – oh yes – a rather well-known football team.

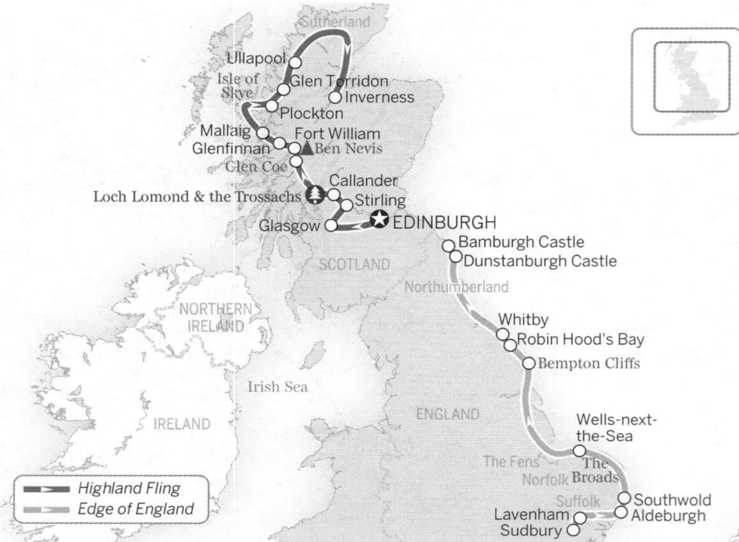

Two weeks

Highland Fling

This itinerary is a circuit of Scotland's finest and most famous sights, and naturally starts in **Edinburgh**, where highlights include the famous castle, as well as the Royal Mile, the new parliament and the haunts of the Old Town. For a change of pace, hop over to **Glasgow** for a day or two as well.

Then head northwest to see Scotland's other great castle at **Stirling**. Next stop is **Callander**, a good base for exploring the **Trossach mountains** – part of Loch Lomond & the Trossachs National Park – for a first taste of Highland scenery.

Continue north, and the landscape becomes ever more impressive, culminating in the grandeur of **Glen Coe**. Keen hillwalkers will pause for a day at **Fort William** to trek to the top of **Ben Nevis** (plus another day to recover!) before taking the **'Road to the Isles'** past glorious **Glenfinnan** to the lovely little port of **Mallaig**.

Take the ferry to the **Isle of Skye**, then head back to the mainland to reach pretty **Plockton** and magnificent **Glen Torridon**. Onwards, via the lively outpost of **Ullapool**, takes you into the British mainland's furthest reaches, the big-sky wilderness of **Sutherland**, before looping south to finish your tour at **Inverness**.

Two weeks

Edge of England

If you like the outdoors, and prefer flocks of birds to crowds of people, try this backwater route along England's eastern fringe.

Start in sleepy **Suffolk**, a favourite spot for boaters, bikers, painters and birdwatchers. Quaint villages and stout market towns such as **Sudbury** and **Lavenham** dot the landscape, while along the coast are wildlife reserves, shingly beaches, fishing ports such as **Aldeburgh** and the delightfully retro seaside resort of **Southwold**.

Things get even quieter as you head into **Norfolk**, especially around the misty lakes and windmill-lined rivers of **the Broads**. For big-sky strolls or historic country pubs, head for the villages along the coast near **Wells-next-the-Sea**.

Across the border in Lincolnshire lies the eerie, pan-flat landscape of **The Fens**, now a haven for otters and all kinds of birdlife. Then it's north again into Yorkshire, where the massive breeding seabird colonies at **Bempton Cliffs** are one of England's finest wildlife spectacles.

Enjoy quirky **Robin Hood's Bay** and bustling **Whitby**, to finally round things off with a blustery stroll between the landmark castles of **Bamburgh** and **Dunstanburgh** on the wild **Northumberland coast**.

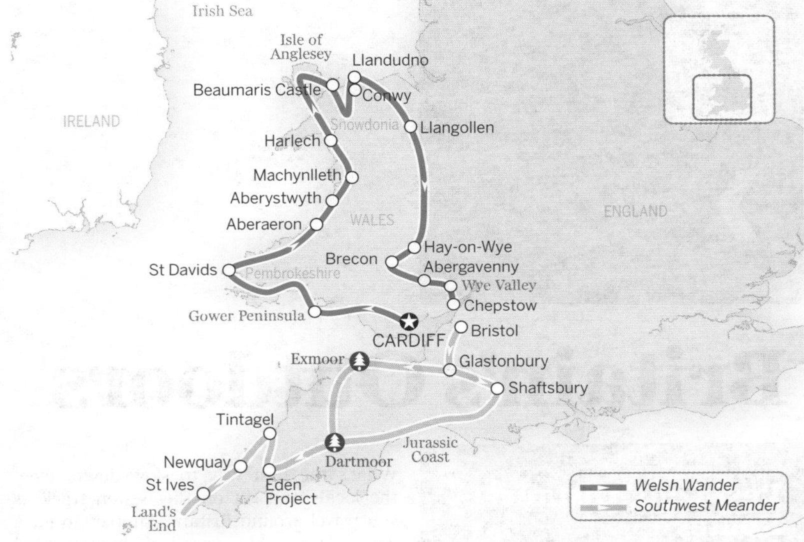

Two weeks

Welsh Wander

The coast and countryside of Wales has long been a favourite with visitors, and this tour includes most of the hot spots. Combine it with the Southwest Meander for a longer jaunt along part of Britain's Celtic fringe. Start in **Cardiff**, with its fantastical castle, gigantic rugby stadium, revitalised waterfront and stunning Millennium Centre concert hall. Head west via the beautiful beaches of the **Gower** to reach the clear waters and sandy beaches of **Pembrokeshire**. Don't miss the charming market town of **St Davids** and its beautiful cathedral. Continue up the coast via pretty **Aberaeron** to **Aberystwyth**, through 'alternative' **Machynlleth** to reach **Harlech** and its ancient castle. Divert to tranquil **Isle of Anglesey** and historic **Beaumaris Castle**, then strike through the mountains of **Snowdonia** to reach **Conwy** (another stunning castle) and the seaside resort **Llandudno**. Southwards takes you through **Llangollen**, with its jolly steam trains and vertiginous aqueduct, then along the England–Wales borderlands to book-mad **Hay-on-Wye**. Loop inland to peaceful **Brecon** and foodie **Abergavenny**, then saunter down the **Wye Valley** to finish at the frontier town of **Chepstow** – and yet another amazing castle.

Two weeks

Southwest Meander

The southwest of England takes a bit of effort to reach but repays in full with a rich green landscape dotted with hills and moors, surrounded by glistening seas.

Start in **Bristol**, the capital of the West-country, then saunter down through the flatlands of Somerset to reach **Glastonbury** – famous for its annual music festival and the best place to stock up on candles or crystals at any time of year. West leads to heathery **Exmoor**. South leads into **Dorset**, where highlights include picturesque **Shaftsbury** and the fossil-strewn **Jurassic Coast**.

Onwards into Devon, and there's a choice of coasts, as well as **Dartmoor**, the highest and wildest hills in southern Britain.

Cross into Cornwall to explore the **Eden Project**, where giant space-age greenhouse domes are home to a range of habitats from jungle to desert. In another era entirely is **Tintagel Castle**, the legendary birthplace of King Arthur. Nearby, you can wax your board in **Newquay**, epicentre of England's surf scene, or browse the galleries at **St Ives**.

The natural finish to this wild west tour is **Land's End**, where the mainland comes to a final full stop. Sink a drink in the First and Last pub, and promise yourself a return trip some day...

Britain's Outdoors

Best Long-Distance Routes

Coast to Coast Walk, Cotswold Way, West Highland Way, Southwest Coast Path, Pembrokeshire Coast Path, Offa's Dyke Path

Best for Short Walks

Yorkshire Dales, Cotswolds, South Downs, Brecon Beacons, Southern Uplands

Best for Coast Walks

Dorset, Devon, Cornwall, Northumberland, Norfolk and Suffolk, Pembrokeshire, Isle of Skye

Best for Leisurely Cycling

Norfolk and Suffolk, Somerset, Wiltshire, Dorset, Cotswolds, Gower Peninsula, Isle of Anglesey, Central Scotland

Best Mountain Biking

Yorkshire, Peak District, Southern Uplands, Mid-Wales, Snowdonia

Best Time to Go

Summer (June–August) Best time for walking and cycling in England and Wales; weather is usually hot and dry

Late spring (May) and early autumn (September) The seasons either side of summer can also be good in England and Wales, and are often the best time for outdoor activities in Scotland

What's the best way to slow down, meet the locals and get off the beaten track as you travel around Britain? Simple: go for a walk, get on a bike or enjoy any other kind of outdoor activity. With a bit of hiking or cycling you'll appreciate and understand Britain more than you ever can on a coach tour, and becoming *actively* involved in the country's way of life is much more rewarding than staring at it through a camera lens or car window.

Walking and cycling are the most popular of all outdoor activities – for locals and visitors alike – because they open up some beautiful corners of the country and can be done virtually on a whim. For walkers, there's no need to apply for trekking permits, arrange sherpas or carry tents. Cyclists can be equally spontaneous; if you don't have a bike, you can easily hire one.

How much you do is your choice. On foot or two wheels you can enjoy relaxed saunters or work up a sweat on long tours, amble across plains or conquer lofty mountains. There's something for young and old, and these activities are often perfect for families, too.

But if walking or cycling is too gentle for your tastes, Britain supplies the goods for thrill seekers, too. The coast has excellent spots for surfing and sailing, while rock-climbers can test their skills on mountains, cliffs and crags – and that's before we get onto cutting-edge activities like coasteering and kite-surfing.

So pack your bags and your sense of adventure. Whatever your budget, a walk or ride through the British countryside – and possibly something involving a bit more adrenalin – could be a highlight of your trip.

Walking

Britain can sometimes seem a crowded place, so open areas are highly valued by the British, and every weekend millions of people go walking in the countryside. It might be a short riverside stroll or a major hike over mountain ranges – or anything in between. You could do a lot worse than join them.

You can walk from place to place in true backpacking style, maybe following one of Britain's famous long-distance national trails. Or you can base yourself in one spot for a week or so, and go out on walks each day to explore the surrounding countryside. The options really are limitless.

Where to Walk

Although you can walk pretty much anywhere in Britain, some areas are better than others. Here's a rundown of our favourites:

Southern England

» The chalky hills of the South Downs stride across the counties of West Sussex (p174) and East Sussex (p160), but the highest and wildest area in southern England is Dartmoor (p312), dotted with Bronze Age remains and granite outcrops called 'tors' – looking for all the world like abstract sculptures. Nearby Exmoor (p291) has heather-covered hills cut by deep valleys and a lovely stretch of coastline, while the entire coast of the southwest peninsula from Dorset to Somerset offers dramatic walking conditions – especially along the beautiful cliff-lined shore of Cornwall.

Central England

» The gem of central England is the Cotswold hills (p196), classic English countryside with gentle paths through neat fields, mature woodland and pretty villages of honey-coloured stone. The Marches (p392), where England borders Wales, are similarly bucolic with more good walking options. For something higher, aim for the Peak District (p462), divided into two distinct areas: the White Peak, characterised by limestone, farmland and verdant dales, ideal for gentle strolls; and the Dark Peak, with high peaty moorlands, heather and gritstone outcrops, for more serious hikes.

SAMPLING THE LONG ROUTES

Although Britain's long-distance trails have official start and finish points, you don't have to do the whole thing end-to-end in one go. Many people walk just a section for a day or two, or use the main route as a basis for loops exploring the surrounding area.

Northern England

» The Lake District (p574) is the heart and soul of walking in England, a wonderful area of soaring peaks, endless views, deep valleys and, of course, beautiful lakes. On the other side of the country, the rolling hills of the Yorkshire Dales (p490) make it another very popular walking area. Further north, keen walkers love the starkly beautiful hills of Northumberland National Park (p628), while the nearby coast is less daunting but just as dramatic – perfect for wild seaside strolls.

South & Mid-Wales

» The Brecon Beacons (p693) is a large range of gigantic rolling whaleback hills with broad ridges and table-top summits, while out in the west is Pembrokeshire (p673), a wonderful array of beaches, cliffs, islands, coves and harbours, with a hinterland of tranquil farmland and secret waterways, and a relatively mild climate year-round.

North Wales

» For walkers, North Wales *is* Snowdonia (p744), where the remains of ancient volcanoes bequeath a striking landscape of jagged peaks, sharp ridges and steep cliffs. There are challenging walks on Snowdon itself – at 1085m, the highest peak in Wales – and many more on the surrounding Glyders or Carneddau ranges, or further south around Cadir Idris.

Southern & Central Scotland

» This extensive region embraces several areas just perfect for keen walkers, including Ben Lomond, the best-known peak in the area, and the nearby Trossachs range (p837), now within the new Loch Lomond & the Trossachs National Park. Also here is the splendid Isle of Arran (p817), with a great choice of coastal rambles and high-mountain hikes.

THE ANCIENT ART OF MUNRO BAGGING

At the end of the 19th century an eager hill walker named Sir Hugh Munro published a list of 545 Scottish mountains measuring over 3000ft (914m) – a height at which he believed they gained special significance. Of these summits he classified 277 as mountains in their own right (new surveys have since revised this to 283), the rest being satellite peaks of lesser consequence (known as 'tops'). Today any Scottish mountain over the magical 3000ft mark is called a Munro, and many keen hill walkers now set themselves the target of summiting (or 'bagging') all 283.

Munro bagging started soon after the list was published. By 1901 the Reverend AE Robertson had become the first person to bag the lot, and between 1901 and 1981 another 250 people managed to climb all the Munros, but the huge increase in hill walking from the 1980s saw the number of 'Munroists' soar; by 2010 the total was to 4500.

To the uninitiated it may seem odd that Munro baggers see plodding around in the mist as time well spent, but the quest is, of course, more than merely ticking names on a list – it takes walkers to some of the wildest, most beautiful parts of Scotland.

Once you've bagged all the Munros you can move on to the Corbetts – hills over 2500ft (700m) with a drop of at least 500ft (150m) on all sides – and the Donalds, lowland hills over 2000ft (610m).

Northern & Western Scotland

» For serious walkers, this is heaven, where the forces of nature have created a mountainous landscape of utter grandeur, including two of Scotland's most famous place names, Glen Coe (p902) and Ben Nevis (p906), Britain's highest mountain at 1343m. Off the west coast lie the dramatic mountains of the Isle of Skye (p920). Keep going north and west, and things just keep getting better: a remote and beautiful area, sparsely populated, with scenic glens and lochs, and some of the largest, wildest and finest mountains in Britain.

HILL WALKING IN SCOTLAND – A MATTER OF TIMING

Consider the following when planning your trip. Get up-to-date information at www.outdooraccess-scotland.com.

October–March May need ice axe and crampons for higher hills; for experienced mountaineers only.

Mid-June–August Midges; see www.midgeforecast.co.uk and p911.

Mid-April–end May Avoid lambing areas.

12 August–third week in October Grouse shooting.

1 July–15 February Deer stalking; peaks August to October.

Long-Distance Walks

Many walkers savour the chance of completing one of Britain's famous long-distance routes, and there are so many to choose from you'd easily wear out your boots trying to do them all. Some long-distance walking routes are obscure and exist only in dedicated guidebooks, while others are high profile with signposts and route markers as well as being highlighted on Ordnance Survey maps. The most high-profile routes are the national trails – clearly marked on the ground and on the map, so ideal for beginners or visitors from overseas – although this doesn't mean they're all easy; some are long and pass through tough terrain. Most routes take between one and two weeks to complete, although some are longer. As with the short walks, there are many options, and it's easy to pick a route that suits your experience and the time you have available.

Because Britain doesn't have the endless tracts of wilderness found in some other countries, when you're on the route you're rarely more than a few miles from a village, meaning overnight stops can be at inns or B&Bs – you don't *have* to camp. And you don't even have to carry your pack if you don't want to; baggage services operate on most popular routes, carrying your kit between each night's accommodation. It may be the soft option, but it certainly makes the walking far more enjoyable.

FRESH-AIR FREEDOM

The absolute pleasure of walking in Britain is mostly thanks to the 'right of way' network – public paths and tracks across private property, especially in England and Wales. In Britain nearly all land (including in national parks) is privately owned, but if there's a right of way you can follow it through fields, pastures, woods, even farmhouse yards, as long as you keep to the route and do no damage. In some mountain and moorland areas, walkers can move freely beyond the rights of way, and explore at will. Known as 'freedom to roam', where permitted it's clearly advertised with markers on gates and signposts. For more see www.countrysideaccess.gov.uk.

Scotland has a different legal system, so there aren't so many actual rights of way, but the Scottish Outdoor Access Code allows walkers to cross most land providing they act responsibly. There are restrictions during lambing time, birth-nesting periods and the grouse- and deer-hunting seasons. For details see www.outdooraccess-scotland.com.

Coast to Coast Walk (190 miles) A top-quality trail across northern England, through three national parks and a spectacular mix of valleys, plains, mountains, dales and moors.

Cotswold Way (102 miles) A delightful walk through classic picture-postcard countryside with fascinating smatterings of English history along the way.

Cumbria Way (68 miles) A wonderful Lake District hike, keeping mainly to the valleys, with breathtaking views of the mountains on either side.

Hadrian's Wall (84 miles) A new national trail following the famous Roman structure all the way across northern England, and giving the Coast to Coast a run for its money in the popularity stakes.

Pennine Way (256 miles) The granddaddy of them all, Britain's oldest national trail; an epic hike along the mountainous spine of northern England.

South West Coast Path (610 miles) A roller-coaster romp round England's southwest peninsula, past beaches, bays, shipwrecks, seaside resorts, fishing villages and clifftop castles.

Thames Path (173 miles) A journey of contrasts beside England's best-known river, from rural Gloucestershire to the heart of London.

Pembrokeshire Coast Path (186 miles) Marking the line where West Wales drops suddenly into the sea, passing popular beaches and isolated clifftop stretches.

Offa's Dyke Path (178 miles) Following Britain's longest archaeological monument, the 8th-century ditch that still largely marks the boundary between Wales and England

Great Glen Way (73 miles) A largely level walk on paths and forest tracks beside Loch Ness and the Caledonian Canal.

St Cuthbert's Way (62 miles) Following the footsteps of the 6th-century missionary through southern Scotland and northern England.

Southern Upland Way (212 miles) Scotland's coast to coast, a tough and committing trek through remote hills and moorlands.

West Highland Way (95 miles) One of Britain's top favourites, through glens and beside lochs with spectacular scenery all the way.

Cycling

A bike is the perfect mode of transport for exploring back-road Britain. Once you escape the busy main highways, a vast network of quiet country lanes winds through fields and peaceful villages, ideal for cycle touring.

Mountain bikers can go further into the wilds on the tracks and bridleways that cross Britain's hills and high moors, or head for the dedicated mountain-bike centres where specially built single-track trails wind through the forests, with options of

ROUTE OF ALL KNOWLEDGE

For comprehensive coverage of a selection of long and short walking routes, we (naturally) recommend Lonely Planet's very own *Walking in Britain*, which also covers places to stay and eat along the way. If you're on two wheels, we have *Cycling Britain*, a selection of touring routes around the country. For more ideas, *Cycling in the UK* is an excellent route book published by bike campaign group Sustrans, while *100 Greatest Cycling Climbs* by Simon Warren is essential reading for those who delight in an uphill challenge.

THE NATIONAL CYCLE NETWORK

Anyone riding a bike through Britain will almost certainly come across the National Cycle Network (NCN), a UK-wide, 10,000-mile web of roads and traffic-free tracks.

The whole scheme is the brainchild of Sustrans (derived from 'sustainable transport'), a campaign group barely taken seriously way back in 1978 when the network idea was first announced. But the growth of cycling, coupled with car congestion, has earned the scheme lots of attention – not to mention serious millions from government and regional authorities.

Strands of the network in cities are aimed at commuters or school kids (where the network follows streets and cyclists normally have their own lane, separate from motor traffic), while other sections follow the most remote roads in the country.

Several long-distance touring routes use the most scenic sections of the NCN – plus a few less-than-scenic urban sections, it has to be said. Other features include a great selection of artworks to admire along the way. In fact, the network is billed as the country's largest outdoor-sculpture gallery. The whole scheme is a resounding success and a credit to the visionaries who persevered against inertia all those years ago. For more details see www.sustrans.org.uk.

varying difficulty, all indicated green to black in ski-resort style.

Whether on-road or off-road is your thing, the options are truly enticing. You can cruise through gently rolling landscapes, taking it easy and stopping for cream teas, or you can thrash all day through hilly areas, revelling in steep ascents and swooping downhill sections.

You can cycle from place to place, staying in B&Bs (many of which are cyclist friendly), or you can base yourself in one area for a few days. All you need is a map and a sense of adventure, and the highways and byways of Britain are yours for the taking.

Where to Cycle

While you can cycle anywhere in Britain, some areas are better than others. Here's an overview of some favourite areas.

Southern England

» Down in Southwest England, Cornwall and Devon are beautiful and enjoy a good climate, but the rugged landscape can mean tough days in the saddle if you overdo the mileage. The neighbouring counties of Somerset, Dorset and Wiltshire have more gentle hills (plus a few steep valleys to keep you on your toes) and a beautiful network of quiet lanes, making them perfect for leisurely cycle touring. In Hampshire, the ancient woodland and open heath of the New Forest (p234) is especially good for on-road and off-road rides, while in Sussex the South Downs have numerous mountain-bike options.

Eastern England

» Norfolk and Suffolk are generally low-lying counties, with quiet lanes winding through picturesque villages, past rivers, lakes and welcoming country pubs – easy-pedalling country.

Central England

» The Cotswold hills (p196) offer good cycling options, with lanes through farmland and quaint villages. From the western side of the hills you get fantastic views over the Severn Valley, but you wouldn't want to go up this escarpment too often! Further west, the Marches (p392) are another rural delight, with good quiet lanes and some off-road options in the hills. The Peak District (p462) is a very popular area for mountain biking and road cycling, although the hills are steep in places. More leisurely options are excellent cycle routes cutting through the landscape along disused railways – dramatic and effortless at the same time.

Northern England

» It's no accident that many of Britain's top racing cyclists come from northern England – the mountain roads make an excellent training ground. The North York Moors (p521) and Yorkshire Dales (p490) both offer exhilarating off-road rides and great cycle touring; the hills mean some routes can be strenuous, but the scenery is superb and well worth the effort.

Wales

» The varied Welsh landscape, crossed by a wonderful network of lanes and tracks, makes an excellent place to cycle, although much of it is hilly, so low gears will often be the order of the day. The lovely lanes of Pembrokeshire (p673) are excellent on a bike – although the bits near the coast can be hilly. The Brecon Beacons National Park (p693) is popular for cycle tourists and off-roaders, while north of the park much of Mid-Wales offers excellent on- and off-road cycling in a scenic and surprisingly little-visited region. In the north, the rugged peaks of Snowdonia (p744) provide a dramatic backdrop to any cycling trip. The nearby Isle of Anglesey (p733) is not so hilly and the quiet lanes are perfect for touring. For mountain biking there are several dedicated areas, Coed-y-Brenin being one of the favourites.

Scotland

» The Scottish Borders (p810) is an excellent area for cycle touring, with a combination of rolling farmland, lochs, glens, hills and a peaceful, intimate charm. For off-road fans, the 7Stanes (p826) is a fantastic range of specially constructed routes in Galloway Forest Park and several other sites across the region. Cyclists in search of the wild and remote will love the Highlands (p887); there aren't many roads, but traffic is usually light. As you pass majestic mountains, beautiful lochs and coasts with views of mystical islands, it won't just be the pedalling that takes your breath away.

Other Outdoor Activities

While walking and cycling can be done at the drop of a hat, many other outdoor activities need a bit more organisation – and often specialist kit, as well as guides or instructors. Below are a few ideas to inform and inspire. If you need more details while you're travelling in Britain, tourist offices can advise about specialist local operators and adventure centres.

Coasteering

If sometimes a simple clifftop walk doesn't cut the mustard, then the wacky activity of coasteering might appeal. It's like mountaineering, but instead of going up a mountain, you go sideways along a coast – a steep and rocky coast – with waves breaking around your feet. And if the rock gets too steep, no problem – you jump in and start swimming. The mix of steep cliffs, sandy beaches and warm water makes Pembrokeshire the UK's prime coasteering spot, and it's also offered in Anglesea, Cornwall and Devon. Outdoor centres provide wetsuits, helmets and buoyancy aids. You provide an old pair of training shoes and a sense of adventure. For more information see www.coasteering.org.

Kitebuggying

Bring together a wing-shaped parachute, three wheels, a good breeze and – whoosh – you're picking up serious speed across the beach. Welcome to kitebuggying. Often available wherever you find big stretches of flat sand, good places to start include various beaches in Cornwall and Devon, as well as Pembrey in Carmarthenshire and Burnham Deepdale in Norfolk, a great backpacker-friendly base for other activities, too.

Horse Riding & Pony Trekking

If you want to explore the hills and moors, but walking or cycling is too much of a

RULES OF THE ROAD

Bicycles aren't allowed on motorways, but you can ride on all other public roads, although main roads (A roads) tend to be busy with cars and trucks so should be avoided. Many B roads suffer heavy motor traffic too, so the best places for cycling are the small C roads and unclassified roads ('lanes') that cover rural Britain, especially in lowland areas, meandering through quiet countryside and linking small, picturesque villages.

For off-roaders, cycling is *not* allowed on footpaths in England and Wales, but it is allowed on unmade roads or bridleways (originally for horses but now for bikes, too) that are a public right of way. Scotland's separate laws allow mountain-bikers the same access to open country enjoyed by walkers, which means you can legally ride on footpaths, though in reality you're often better off sticking to established tracks and trails. More details are available at local tourist offices or www.outdooraccess-scotland.com.

BOOTS & BIKES – HANDY RESOURCES

www.ctc.org.uk Cyclists' Touring Club (the UK's recreational cycling and campaigning body); includes cycle-hire directory and mail-order service for maps and books.

www.mtbbritain.co.uk For off-road rides.

www.nationaltrail.co.uk Specifics on some longer walking routes.

www.ramblers.org.uk Ramblers' Association (Britain's leading organisation for walkers); a mine of background information and it produces *Walk Britain*, an invaluable annually updated handbook listing walker-friendly accommodation.

sweat, seeing the wilder parts of Britain from horseback is highly recommended. In rural areas and national parks like Dartmoor, the Brecon Beacons, Northumberland and southern Scotland, riding centres cater to all levels of proficiency – with ponies for kids and beginners, and horses for the more experienced. The British Horse Society (www.bhs.org.uk) lists approved riding centres offering day rides or longer holidays on horseback.

Mountain Boarding & Kite-Boarding

Imagine hurtling down a grassy hillside on a gigantic skateboard with four oversize wheels, and you've pretty much got mountain boarding. If that's not enough, add a wing-shaped parachute, and it's a kiteboard – so you can get the wind to pull you around whenever gravity gives up. There are mountain- and kite-boarding centres in Yorkshire, Derbyshire, Shropshire, Cornwall, the Brecon Beacons and near Helensburgh in Scotland (among other places). For more information see www.atbauk.org.

Rock Climbing & Mountaineering

Britain is the birthplace of modern rock climbing, and few places in the world offer such a wide range of mountains, cliffs and crags in such a compact area – not to mention an ever-growing number of indoor climbing walls.

Areas for mountaineering include the high mountains of Scotland (especially the northwest), with favourite spots including Glen Coe, the area around Ben Nevis and the Cuillin Ridge on the Isle of Skye. In Wales the crags, cliffs and quarries of Snowdonia offer long and short routes, while England's main centre for long routes is the Lake District, and there are some fine short routes here as well.

Popular areas for short or single-pitch climbing are the Peak District and Yorkshire Dales. In southern England, good climbing areas include Cheddar Gorge and Dartmoor. Britain also offers the exhilaration of sea-cliff climbing, most notably in Pembrokeshire and Cornwall; nothing makes you concentrate more on finding the next hold than waves crashing 30m below!

The website of the British Mountaineering Council (www.thebmc.co.uk) covers access rules (don't forget: all mountains and outcrops are privately owned), indoor climbing walls, competitions and so on. In Scotland the main bodies are the Scottish Mountaineering Club (www.smc.org.uk) and the Mountaineering Council of Scotland (www.mountaineering-scotland.org.uk).

Skiing & Snowboarding

Scotland is far enough north to offer Britain's only serious ski conditions, and even then the snow is thin on the ground some years. The main season is from January to April, but it's sometimes possible to ski from as early as November to as late as May. Just turn up at the slopes, hire some kit, buy a day pass and off you go. Ski and snowboarding centres include Cairngorm (p897) near Aviemore, with almost 30 runs spread over an extensive area; Glenshee between Perth and Braemar, with the largest network of lifts and the widest range of runs; Lecht between Ballater and Grantown-on-Spey, the smallest and most remote centre; and the Nevis Range (p906) near Fort William, offering the highest runs, the grandest setting and some of the best off-piste potential. For more information see www.snowsportscotland.org and www.ski-scotland.com.

Sailing & Windsurfing

Britain's nautical heritage means sailing is a very popular pastime, in everything from tiny dinghies to ocean-going yachts. More recently there's been a massive surge in windsurfing, too. Favourite spots include the

WEATHER WATCH

It's always worth remembering the fickle nature of Britain's weather. At any time of year, if you're walking on the hills or open moors:

- ☐ carry warm and waterproof clothing (even in summer)
- ☐ take a map and compass (and know how to use them)
- ☐ bring some drink, food and high-energy stuff such as chocolate
- ☐ leave details of your route with someone if going off the beaten track

coasts of Norfolk and Suffolk, southeast England, Devon, Cornwall, the Isle of Wight, the Gower Peninsula, Pembrokeshire, the Menai Strait and Llŷn Peninsula. In Scotland head for the Firth of Forth near Edinburgh, the area north of Largs (west of Glasgow) or Inverness. Britain also has many inland lakes and reservoirs, ideal for training, racing or just pottering. The Royal Yachting Association (www.rya.org.uk) can provide details on training centres where you can improve your skills or simply charter a boat for pleasure.

Surfing

Britain may not seem an obvious place for surfing, but conditions are surprisingly good, and the huge tidal range means a completely different set of breaks at low and high tides. If you've come from the other side of the world, you'll be delighted to learn that summer water temperatures in Britain are roughly equivalent to winter temperatures in southern Australia. But wetsuit-protected, there are many excellent surf opportunities. Top of the list is the Atlantic-facing west coast of Cornwall and Devon – Newquay (p323) is surf central, with all the trappings from Kombi vans to bleached hair – and there are smaller surf scenes on the west coast, notably Norfolk and Yorkshire. In Wales, the main surf areas include the Gower, Pembrokeshire, Anglesey and the Llŷn Peninsula, while Scotland has some of the best breaks in Europe – though water temperatures can be, er, bracing – notably around Thurso and in the Outer Hebrides, where conditions are outstanding. At the main spots, it's easy enough to hire boards and wetsuits. The British Surfing Association (www.britsurf.co.uk) can provide details on instruction centres, courses, competitions and so on.

Kitesurfing

If regular surfing doesn't offer enough airtime, strap on a wing-shaped parachute and let the wind do the work. Brisk breezes, decent waves and great beaches make Cornwall a favourite spot for kitesurfing, but it's possible all round the British coastline, and there are several training centres to show you the ropes. The British Kite Surfing Association (www.kitesurfing.org) has more information.

Scrambling

Scrambling is a specific activity in Britain, covering the twilight zone between serious hiking and relatively easy rock climbing, and basically means moving up a steep rocky section of cliff or hillside, using your hands as well as your feet – and often involves a little rush of adrenalin too. While experienced climbers may cruise effortlessly up a scramble route, someone new to the game may need a rope and a lot of encouragement. Classic scrambles in Britain include Bristly Ridge and Crib Coch in Snowdonia, Jack's Rake and Striding Edge in the Lake District, and the Aonach Eagach Ridge in Glen Coe. Local guidebooks can suggest many more. It's great fun, as long as you know what you're doing.

MAPS

The UK's national mapping agency, Ordnance Survey, produces some of the finest mapping in the world. Use the 1:50,000 Landranger series for cycling and 1:25,000-scale Explorer maps for walking. In the mountains, Harvey maps are excellent.

Travel with Children

Best Regions for Kids

London
The capital has children's attractions galore; many are free

Devon, Cornwall & Wessex
Lovely beaches and reliable weather, though crowded in summer

The Midlands
Caverns and 'show caves', plus former railways now traffic-free cycle routes

Oxford & the Cotswolds
Oxford has Harry Potter connections; the Cotswolds is ideal for little-leg strolls

Lake District & Cumbria
Longer walks, zip-wires and kayaks for teenagers; boat-rides and Beatrix Potter for the youngsters

Wales
Long coast of beaches and pony-trekking in the hill-country. And loads of castles...

Southern Scotland
Edinburgh and Glasgow have kid-friendly museums; the Southern Uplands offer mountain-biking for a range of levels

Scottish Highlands & Islands
Hardy teenagers can plunge into various outdoor activities, while dolphin-spotting boat trips are fun for all the family

Britain is great for travel with children because it's compact, with a lot of attractions in a small area. So when the kids in the back of the car say 'are we nearly there yet?' your answer can often be 'yes'. Throughout this book, we've highlighted many family-friendly attractions. With a bit of planning, and some online research to get the best bargains, having the kids on board can make your trip even more enjoyable.

Britain for Kids

Many places of interest cater for kids as much as adults. At the country's historic castles, for example, mum and dad can admire the medieval architecture, while the kids will have great fun striding around the battlements. In the same way, many national parks and holiday resorts organise specific activities for children. It goes without saying that everything ramps up in the school holidays.

Bargain Hunting

Most visitor attractions offer family tickets – usually two adults plus two children, for less than the sum of the individual entrance charges. Most offer cheaper rates for solo parents and kids, too. Be sure to ask, as these are not always clearly displayed.

On the Road

If you're going by public transport, trains are great for families: intercity services have plenty of room for luggage and extra stuff like buggies, and the kids can move about a bit when bored. In contrast, they need to stay in their seats on long-distance coaches.

If you're hiring a car, most (but not all) rental firms can provide child seats – but you'll need to check this in advance. Most will not actually fit the child seats; you need to do that yourself, for insurance reasons.

Dining, not Whining

When it comes to refuelling, most cafes and teashops are child friendly. Restaurants are mixed: some offer high chairs and kiddy portions; others firmly say 'no children after 6pm'.

Children under 18 are usually not allowed in pubs serving just alcohol. Pubs also serving meals usually allow children of any age (with their parents) in England and Wales, but in Scotland they must be over 14 and must leave by 8pm. If in doubt, simply ask the bar staff.

And finally, a word on another kind of refuelling: Britain is still slightly buttoned up about breastfeeding; older folks may tut-tut a bit if you give junior a top-up in public, but if done modestly it's usually considered OK.

Children's Highlights

Best Hands-on Action

Please do not touch? No chance. Here are some places where grubby fingers and enquiring minds are positively welcomed.

» **Science Museum, London** Seven floors of educational exhibits, at the mother of all science museums.

» **Magna, Yorkshire** Formerly one of the world's largest steel works, and now a science adventure centre.

» **Enginuity, Ironbridge** Endless hands-on displays at the birthplace of the Industrial Revolution.

» **National Waterfront Museum, Swansea** Great interactive family fun.

» **Glasgow Science Centre** Bringing science and technology alive through hundreds of engaging exhibits.

» **Discovery Museum, Newcastle** Tyneside's rich history on display; highlights include a buzzers-and-bells science maze.

Best Fresh Air Fun

If the kids tire of castles and museums, you're never far from a place for outdoor activities to blow away the cobwebs.

» **Wildlife Cruises, Scotland's west coast** What child could resist a boat trip to see seals, porpoises and dolphins, maybe even a whale?

» **Puzzle Wood, Forest of Dean** Wonderful woodland playground with mazy paths, weird rock formations and eerie passageways.

» **Whinlatter Forest, Cumbria** Highlights include a Go Ape adventure park and excellent mountain-bike trails, plus live video feeds from red squirrel cams.

» **Bewilderwood, Norfolk** Zip wires, jungle bridges, tree-houses, marsh walks, boat trips, mazes and all sorts of old-fashioned outdoor adventure.

» **Lyme Regis & the Jurassic Coast, Dorset** Guided tours to find your very own prehistoric fossil.

» **Tissington Trail, Derbyshire** Cycling this former railway is fun and almost effortless. You can hire kids' bikes, tandems and trailers. Don't forget to hoot in the tunnels!

HANDY WEBSITES

Baby Goes 2 (www.babygoes2.com) Advice, tips and encouragement (and a stack of adverts) for families on holiday.

Mums Net (www.mumsnet.com) No-nonsense advice on travel and more from a gang of UK mothers.

Planning

When to Go

The best time for families to visit Britain is pretty much the best time for everyone else – from April/May to the end of September. It's worth avoiding August – the heart of school summer holidays – when prices go up and roads are busy, especially near the coast. Other school holidays are two weeks around Easter Sunday, and mid-December to early January, plus three week-long 'half-term' breaks – usually late February (or early March), late May and late October.

Places to Stay

Some hotels welcome kids (with their parents) and provide cots, toys and babysitting services, while others maintain an adult atmosphere. Many B&Bs offer 'family suites' of two adjoining bedrooms with one bathroom, and an increasing number of hostels (YHA/SYHA and

ALL CHANGE

On the sticky topic of dealing with nappies, most museums and other attractions in Britain usually have good baby-changing facilities (cue old joke: I swapped mine for a nice souvenir). Elsewhere, some city-centre public toilets have baby-changing areas, although these can be a bit grimy; your best bet for clean facilities is an upmarket department store. On the road, baby-changing facilities are usually bearable at motorway service stations and OK at out-of-town supermarkets.

independent) have family rooms with four or six beds – some even with private bathroom attached. If you want to stay in one place for a while, renting a holiday cottage is ideal (see p1054). Camping is very popular with British families, and there are lots of fantastic campsites, but you'll usually need all your own kit.

Best Rainy-Day Distractions

For those inevitable gloomy days, head for the indoor attractions. Don't forget the nation's great collection of museums. Alternatively, try outdoor stuff like coasteering in Cornwall or canyoning in the Lake District. It's always fun – wet or dry.

» **Cadbury World, Birmingham** Dentists may cry, but kids love the story of chocolate. And yes, there are free samples.

» **Underground Edinburgh** Take a guided tour of the haunted vaults beneath the medieval Old Town.

» **Eden Project, Cornwall** It may be raining outside, but inside these giant domes it's forever tropical forest or Mediterranean climate.

» **Cheddar Gorge Caves, Wessex** Finally nail the difference between stalactites and stalagmites in the Westcountry's deep caverns.

» **Underground Passages, Exeter** Explore medieval catacombs – the only system of its kind open to the public in England.

Best Stealth Learning

Secretly exercise their minds while the kids think they are 'just' having fun.

» **At-Bristol** One of Britain's best interactive science museums, covering space, technology and the human brain.

» **Jorvik Centre, York** Excellent smells-and-all Viking settlement reconstruction.

» **Natural History Museum, London** Highlights include the life-size blue whale and animatronic dinosaurs.

» **Thinktank, Birmingham** Every display comes with a button or a lever at this edu-taining science museum.

» **National Space Centre, Leicester** Spacesuits, zero-gravity toilets and mini-astronaut training – guaranteed to boost little minds.

» **Centre for Alternative Technology, Machynlleth** Educational, fun and truly green – great for curious kids.

» **Our Dynamic Earth, Edinburgh** A slick extravaganza of whiz-bang special effects and 3D movies about all things geological and environmental.

regions at a glance

London

History ✓✓✓
Entertainment ✓✓✓
Museums ✓✓✓

Historic Streetscapes

London's ancient streets contain many of Britain's best-known and history-steeped landmarks. The echoes of the footfalls of monarchs, poets, whores and saints can still be detected in places like the Tower of London, Westminster Abbey, St Paul's Cathedral and the capital's many palaces, while pubs and coaching inns that once served the likes of Dickens, Shelley, Keats and Byron are still pouring pints today.

Entertainment

From West End theatres to East End clubs, from Camden's rock venues to Covent Garden's opera house, from tennis at Wimbledon to cricket at Lord's or football at Wembley, London's world-famous venues and arenas offer a perpetual clamour of entertainment.

Museums & Galleries

London has museums and galleries of every shape and size – and most of the very best are free.

p58

Canterbury & Southeast England

Churches ✓✓✓
History ✓✓
Food & Drink ✓✓

Canterbury Cathedral

One of the finest cathedrals in Europe, one of the most holy places in Christendom and a highlight of any visit to Britain – today's tourists do little to diminish its ancient venerable status.

Invasion Heritage

The southeast has always been a gateway for Continental arrivals. Castles and fortresses, the 1066 battlefield and secret wartime tunnels tell the region's story of invasion and defence.

Food & Drink

Kent is deseredly known as the Garden of England, long celebrated for hops, fruit, fish and vineyards. Sussex isn't far behind, with England's finest sparkling wine giving the French stuff a run for its euro.

p134

Oxford, Cotswolds & Around

Houses ✓✓✓
Villages ✓✓
Food & Drink ✓

Stately Homes

Favoured by the rich and powerful for centuries, this region is scattered with some of the finest stately homes and country houses in Britain. Top of the pile is the baroque masterpiece of Blenheim Palace.

Villages

Littered with implausibly picturesque 'chocolate-box' scenes of stone cottages with thatched roofs, the Cotswolds villages provide a charming snapshot of rural England, little changed since medieval times.

Cream Teas

If you're craving a proper cream tea with all the trimmings in historic surroundings, nearly every scenic village in this region has at least one tearoom – and you couldn't find a better place to indulge.

p179

Southwest England

Coastline ✓✓✓
History ✓✓✓
Activities ✓✓✓

Beaches
Britain's southwest peninsula juts determinedly into the Atlantic and an almost endless chain of sandy beaches – some big, some small, some brash, some tranquil – offering something for everyone.

Stone Circles
This ancient landscape is nowhere more epitomised than the mysterious stone circle of Stonehenge. Nearby is Avebury, even bigger than Stonehenge, surrounded by many other reminders of the past.

Outdoor Activities
If you like to take it nice and easy, come to walk the moors or tootle along cycle trails. If you prefer life fast and furious, come to surf the best waves in England, or learn to dive or kitesurf.

p221

Cambridge & East Anglia

Churches ✓✓✓
Coastline ✓✓
Lakes ✓✓

Cathedrals
The magnificent cathedrals of East Anglia soar above the flat landscape, testament to the region's past wealth and prosperity. Highlights are Ely and Norwich, while lesser-known gems include Peterborough and St Albans.

Coastline
With historic villages still proud of their nautical heritage, seaside resorts like Southwold or Great Yarmouth, wide sandy beaches, delightful old pubs and globally important bird reserves, this coast is rich and varied.

The Broads
This tranquil haven of lakes and meandering waterways in Norfolk and Suffolk is protected as a national park – an ideal spot for pleasure boating, birding, canoeing, cycling or walking.

p349

Birmingham, the Midlands & the Marches

Activities ✓✓✓
Houses ✓✓✓
Food & Drink ✓✓

Outdoor Activities
The Peak District National Park, along with Cannock Chase, the Shropshire Hills, the Roaches, the Malvern Hills, Offa's Dyke Path, the Tissington Trail and the Pennine Cycleway, makes this region great for hiking and biking.

Stately Homes
Grand houses like Haddon Hall, Burghley House and Chatsworth promise walls dripping with oil paintings, sprawling, deer-filled grounds and priceless heirlooms.

Food & Drink
Foodies take note: Birmingham is the curry capital of the country (and, increasingly, a magnet for Michelin-starred chefs), while the tiny town of Ludlow is an epicentre of gastronomic exploration.

p389

Yorkshire

Activities ✓✓✓
Food & Drink ✓✓✓
History ✓✓✓

Outdoor Activities
With rolling hills, scenic valleys and high moors and a cliff-lined coast all protected by national parks, Yorkshire is a natural adventure playground for hiking, biking, surfing and rock climbing.

Food & Drink
Lush pasture means Yorkshire beef and lamb is sought after, while the famous breweries of Masham turn out excellent real ales, always best sampled in one of Yorkshire's excellent traditional pubs.

History
From York's Viking heritage and the ancient abbeys of Rievaulx, Fountains and Whitby, to the industrial archaeology of Leeds, Bradford and Sheffield, you can follow several of Britain's most important historical narratives in Yorkshire.

p474

Manchester, Liverpool & Northwest England

Museums ✓✓✓
Sport ✓✓✓
Towns ✓✓

Museums

The northwest's collection of heritage sites – from the wonderful People's History Museum in Manchester to the International Slavery Museum in Liverpool – is testament to the region's rich history and its ability to keep it alive.

Football

Two cities – Liverpool and Manchester – give the world four famous clubs, including the two most successful in English history. The National Football Museum in Manchester is just another reason for fans to visit this region.

Blackpool

The queen of England's classic seaside resorts keeps going, thanks to the rides of the Pleasure Beach amusement park, where adrenalin junkies can always find a fix.

p530

Lake District & Cumbria

Mountains ✓✓✓
Lakes ✓✓✓
Activities ✓✓✓

Mountains

Cumbria is the most mountainous part of England, a stunningly beautiful region that famously moved William Wordsworth to write his ode to 'a host of golden daffodils'.

Lakes

Dotted between the mountains sit numerous lakes. Some are big and famous – Windermere, Coniston, Ullswater – while others are small, hidden and little known. The Lake District National Park protects this striking and valuable landscape.

Walking

If anywhere is the heart and soul of walking in England, it's the Lake District. Casual strollers find gentle routes through the foothills and valleys, while serious hikers tackle the high peaks and fells.

p570

Newcastle & Northeast England

History ✓✓✓
Landscapes ✓✓✓
Castles ✓✓✓

Hadrian's Wall

One of the world's premier Roman Empire sites, this potent symbol of power and defence strides its way for over 70 miles across the neck of England, from Tyneside to the Solway Firth. You can travel its length, stopping off at forts along the way.

Big Landscapes

If it's widescreen vistas you're after, the northeast never fails to please. From the golden beaches of Northumberland to the high moors of the Pennine uplands, great views are guaranteed.

Castles

Northumberland's vast expanse is dotted with some of Britain's finest castles, all acting as reminders of the centuries-long scrap between Scots and English over these remote borderlands.

p605

Cardiff

Architecture ✓✓
Sport ✓✓
Nightlife ✓✓

Architecture

From the medieval battlements of Caerphilly Castle and the fantastical structures of Cardiff Castle to Victorian shopping arcades and Cardiff Bay's ultramodern waterfront, the Welsh capital has plenty to keep building buffs interested.

Sport

Cardiff is the home of Welsh sport, with Millennium Stadium dominating the centre. The city is never more alive than during a rugby international, when the singing from the stands resonates through the streets.

Nightlife

A lively alternative music scene, some swish bars and a swath of old- fashioned pubs attract hordes of generally good-humoured lads and ladettes every weekend.

p638

Pembrokeshire & South Wales

Coastline ✓✓✓
Castles ✓✓✓
Countryside ✓✓

Coastal Scenery
South Wales boasts two of Britain's most beautiful stretches of coast – the Gower Peninsula and Pembrokeshire. Between them offering clifftop walks, family-friendly beaches, surfing hot spots and watery adventures such as sea-kayaking and coasteering.

Castles
South Wales has some of the best castles, including Chepstow and Pembroke, while remote Carreg Cennen in the heart of the Brecon Beacons is the most spectacularly positioned of them all.

Countryside
Inland from the coast, and away from the towns and cities, South Wales is spoilt with bucolic green pastures, most notably in Monmouthshire and Carmarthenshire.

p657

Hay-on-Wye & Mid-Wales

Wildlife ✓✓✓
Towns ✓✓
Food ✓✓

Wildlife
In the mountains and moors of Brecon Beacons and many other parts of the region you can spot birds of prey, most famously the once-rare red kites – and most easily at feeding stations such as Gigrin Farm in Rhyader – while coastal Ceredigion shelters important wetland habitats.

Market Towns
From book-obsessed Hay-on-Wye and food-obsessed Abergavenny to quirky Llanwrtyd Wells and quaint Llandrindod Wells, the market towns of Mid-Wales are full of charm.

Food
Restaurants, inns and country gastropubs throughout the region are at the forefront of a new Welsh gastronomy, focussing on the finest fresh, locally grown, organic ingredients.

p687

Snowdonia & North Wales

Mountains ✓✓✓
History ✓✓✓
Coastline ✓✓

Mountains
Home to some of Britain's finest mountain scenery south of the Scottish Highlands – and for most visitors much more accessible – Snowdonia's imposing peaks provide a scenic backdrop for innumerable outdoor pursuits.

Industrial Heritage
Welsh slate once roofed much of the world and the region's quarries and caverns bear witness to the lives of generations of workers, while rejuvenated railways now shunt tourists through spectacular terrain.

Beaches
From the North Coast's popular resort towns to the surf spots on Anglesey and the quiet bays of the Llŷn Peninsula, North Wales has plenty of beach to go round.

p722

Edinburgh

History ✓✓✓
Culture ✓✓✓
Food ✓✓✓

History
Perched on a brooding black crag overlooking the city centre, Edinburgh Castle has played a pivotal role in Scottish history. And on the edge of the city lies medieval Rosslyn Chapel, Scotland's most beautiful and enigmatic church.

Culture
Dubbed the Athens of the North, the Scottish capital is a city of high culture and lofty ideals, of art and literature, philosophy and science.

Food
The last decade has seen a boom in the number of restaurants in Edinburgh – while Scottish cuisine has been given a makeover with inventive chefs using top-quality local produce.

p759

Glasgow & Southern Scotland

Museums ✓✓✓
Churches ✓✓✓
Houses ✓✓

Museums & Galleries

Glasgow's mercantile, industrial and academic history has left the city with a wonderful legacy of museums and art galleries, dominated by the grand Victorian cathedral of culture that is the Kelvingrove.

Historic Abbeys

Rolling countryside and ruined abbeys are the big draws along the country's southern border, where you'll find the Gothic ruins of Melrose, Jedburgh and Dryburgh abbeys.

Stately Homes

The peace that followed the Act of Union saw landowners build luxurious homes for their families. Highlights of this region include Culzean Castle, Paxton House, Floors Castle and Mellerstain House.

p789

Stirling & Central Scotland

Castles ✓✓✓
Islands ✓✓✓
Drinks ✓✓

Castles

Central Scotland is home to the greatest concentration of castles in the country, from regal Stirling and the turreted splendour of Craigievar to the more restrained elegance of Crathie and Balmoral.

Islands

Island hopping is a great way to explore Scotland's western seaboard, and the islands of this region – wild Jura, scenic Mull and the jewel of Iona – provide a brilliant introduction.

Whisky

No trip to Scotland is complete without a visit to a whisky distillery – the Speyside region and the isle of Islay are epicentres of the industry.

p829

Inverness, the Highlands & Northern Islands

Activities ✓✓✓
Landscapes ✓✓✓
History ✓✓

Outdoor Activities

Between them, the Cairngorm resort of Aviemore, gateway to snow sports in winter and wild hill walking in summer, and Fort William, self-styled Outdoor Capital of the UK, offer enough adventure to keep you busy for a year.

Scenery

Landscape photographers are spoilt for choice, with classic views ranging from the mountain beauty of Glen Coe and the snow-patched summits of the Cairngorms to the rock pinnacles of the Cuillin Hills.

History

The region is rich in prehistoric remains, including the standing stones of Callanish and the neolithic settlement of Skara Brae, while abandoned rural communities are a sombre reminder of the 18th-century Clearances.

p887

Channel Islands

Coastline ✓✓✓
Wildlife ✓✓✓
Museums ✓✓✓

Coastline

The Channel Islands take in spectacular sea cliffs, coves and beaches – from Jersey and Guernsey's surf beaches to idylic swimming spots like Herm's Shell Beach and Sark's tidal Venus Pool.

Wildlife

The islands are a haven for wildlife, including birdlife. Alderney is a particular hot spot: see thousands of gannets and the world's only breeding colony of blonde hedgehogs onshore, and puffins and grey Atlantic seals offshore.

Museums

Medieval castles, fortresses and old war tunnels are some of the atmospheric settings for museums spanning subjects from shipwrecks to the islands' occupation during WWII, as well as island life over the centuries.

p967

Look out for these icons:

Our author's recommendation

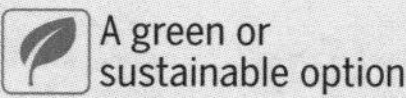
A green or sustainable option

No payment required

ENGLAND.......... 55

London.............58

Canterbury & Southeast England..134
Kent 135
East Sussex.............160
West Sussex 174
Surrey...................177

Oxford, Cotswolds & Around............179
Oxfordshire 182
The Cotswolds 196
Gloucestershire 205
Hertfordshire 214
Bedfordshire & Buckinghamshire.........215
Berkshire................216

Southwest England..221
Hampshire............. 225
New Forest............. 234
Isle Of Wight........... 238
Dorset.................. 242
Wiltshire............... 258
Bristol.................. 270
Bath 278
Somerset............... 285
Exmoor National Park....291
Devon 296
Cornwall................319
Isles Of Scilly 344

Cambridge & East Anglia............. 349
Cambridgeshire 352
Essex 365
Suffolk 367
Norfolk..................374

Birmingham, The Midlands & The Marches.......389
Birmingham 392
Warwickshire........... 402
Staffordshire............411
Worcestershire 414
Herefordshire 418
Shropshire............. 423
Nottinghamshire 436
Lincolnshire............ 442
Northamptonshire...... 449
Leicestershire.......... 450
Derbyshire............. 456
Peak District 462

Yorkshire 474
South Yorkshire 478
West Yorkshire 480
Yorkshire Dales National Park 490
East Riding Of Yorkshire . 497
North Yorkshire......... 500
North York Moors National Park 521

Manchester, Liverpool & Northwest England..530
Manchester 531
Cheshire.................547
Liverpool 552
Around Liverpool 562
Lancashire............. 562
Isle Of Man 566

The Lake District & Cumbria...........570
The Lake District 574
Cumbrian Coast........ 598
Northern & Eastern Cumbria............... 600

Newcastle & Northeast England..605
Newcastle-Upon-Tyne ... 609
Around Newcastle 616
County Durham 617
Hadrian's Wall.......... 622
Northumberland National Park 628
Northumberland........ 630

See the Index for a full list of destinations covered in this book.

On the Road

WALES 636

Cardiff (Caerdydd). .638
Around Cardiff 653

Pembrokeshire & South Wales 657
Southeast Wales. 659
Swansea & The Gower. . . 663
Carmarthenshire (Sir Gaerfyrddin) 670
Pembrokeshire (Sir Benfro). 673

Hay-On-Wye & Mid-Wales 687
Ceredigion. 689
Brecon Beacons National Park 693
Powys. 713

Snowdonia & North Wales 722
North Coast & Borders. . .724
Isle Of Anglesey 733
West Of Snowdonia 736
Snowdonia National Park. . 744

SCOTLAND 757

Edinburgh 759
Around Edinburgh 787

Glasgow & Southern Scotland. .789
Glasgow 792
Around Glasgow 809
Borders Region. 810
Ayrshire & Arran. 816
Dumfries & Galloway. . . . 822

Stirling & Central Scotland 829
Stirling Region 832
Argyll 840
Fife 855
Perthshire 864
Dundee & Angus. 871
Aberdeenshire & Moray . . .876

Inverness, The Highlands & The Northern Islands 887
Inverness & The Great Glen 890
The Cairngorms 897
Central Western Highlands. 902
Northeast Coast. 908
Caithness. 910
North & Northwest Coast . .913
Isle Of Skye 920
Outer Hebrides. 927
Orkney Islands 942
Shetland Islands. 956

THE CHANNEL ISLANDS 966

England

DOUG MCKINLAY

England Highlights

1. Spend more time (and money) than you'd planned in England's (and Britain's) endlessly entertaining capital, **London** (p58)
2. Be a Jane Austen character for the day in elegant **Bath** (p278)
3. Wander lonely as a cloud in the idyllic **Lake District** (p574)
4. Explore medieval walls, Viking sights and smells, soaring Gothic minister – **York** (p501) is a history buff's delight
5. Fall in love with the impossibly quaint villages of the **Cotswolds** (p196)
6. Get some higher education among the dreamy spires of **Oxford** (p182)
7. Punt along the river in **Cambridge** (p353)
8. See how wild scenery and ancient engineering combine at **Hadrian's Wall** (p622)
9. Catch a play or visit the Bard's grave in **Stratford-upon-Avon** (p406)

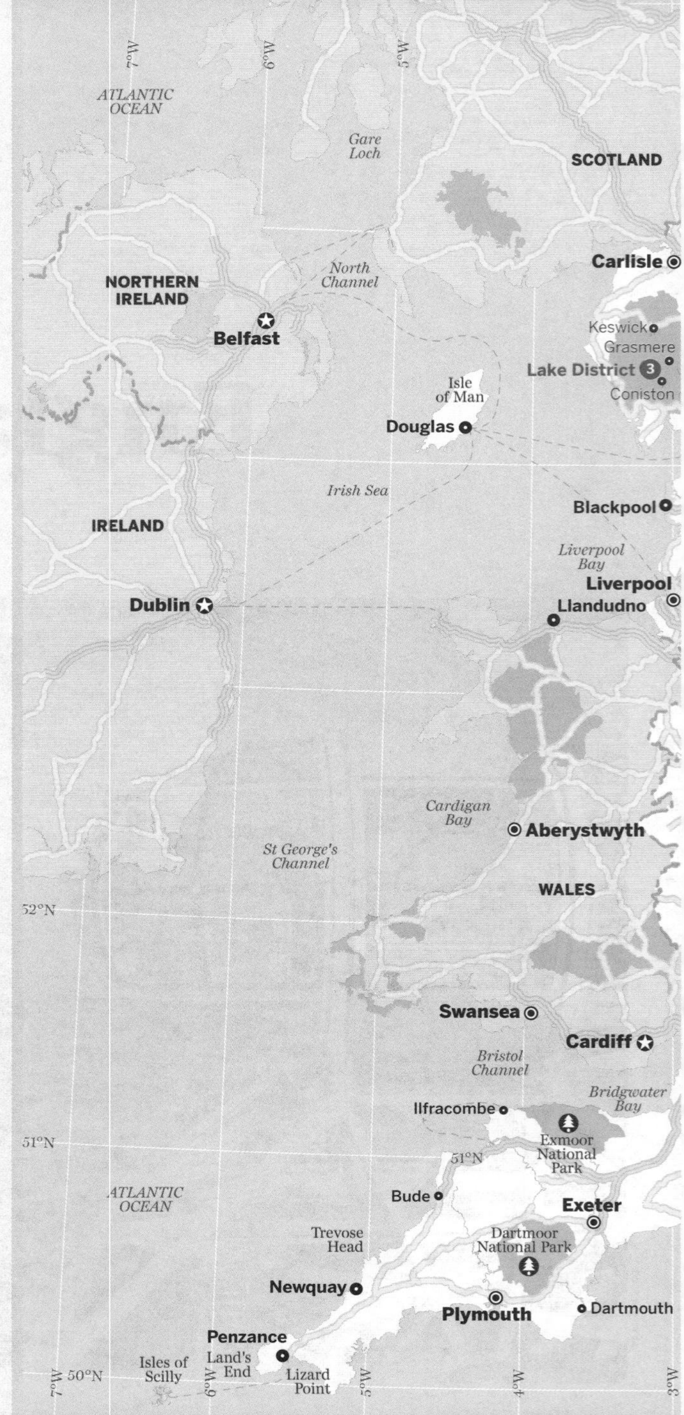

Berwick-upon-Tweed
Northumberland National Park
Alnwick
Hadrian's Wall
8
Newcastle-upon-Tyne
Tynemouth
Durham
Penrith
Darlington
Whitby
North York Moors National Park
Scarborough
Yorkshire Dales National Park
Lancaster
Forest of Bowland
4 York
Hurst Green
Leeds
Spurn Head
Grimsby
Manchester
Peak District National Park
Sheffield
Chester
Buxton
Chesterfield
Lincoln
Skegness
Derby
Nottingham
Boston
The Wash
Holkam
Stoke-on-Trent
The Fens
King's Lynn
Norwich
Shrewsbury
Leicester
Stamford
The Broads
Birmingham
Ludlow
Cambridge
7
Worcester
9 Stratford-upon-Avon
5 Cotswolds
Lavenham
Hereford
ENGLAND
Cheltenham
Woodstock
Colchester
Gloucester
Forest of Dean
Painswick
6 Oxford
St Albans
Southend-on-Sea
River Thames
Bristol
1 London
Windsor
Isle of Thanet
2 Bath
Newbury
Canterbury
Wells
Dover
Salisbury
Winchester
Calais
Rye
Strait of Dover
New Forest National Park
Hove
Brighton
Bournemouth
Portsmouth
Eastbourne
Lyme Bay
Weymouth
FRANCE
English Channel
North Sea
To Bergen, Gothenburg & Ijmuiden
To Hamburg
0 150 km
0 100 miles
55°N
54°N
53°N
52°N
3°E
2°E
1°E
0°
1°W
2°W

London

TELEPHONE CODE: 020 / POP: 7.51 MILLION / AREA: 609 SQ MILES

Includes »

Sights 62
Tours 98
Festivals & Events 99
Sleeping 99
Eating 107
Drinking 117
Entertainment 122
Shopping 127

Why Go?

Everyone comes to London with a preconception shaped by a multitude of books, movies, TV shows and songs. Whatever yours is, prepare to have it shattered by this endlessly fascinating, amorphous city. You could spend a lifetime exploring it and find that the slippery thing's gone and changed on you. One thing is constant: that great serpent of a river enfolding the city in its sinuous loops, linking London both to the green heart of England and the world. From Roman times the world has come to London, put down roots and whinged about the weather. There is no place on earth that is more multicultural; any given street yields a rich harvest of languages. Those narrow streets are steeped in history, art, architecture and popular culture. With endless reserves of cool, London is one of the world's great cities, if not the greatest.

Best Places to Eat

» Bistrot Bruno Loubet (p115)

» Ottolenghi (p113)

» Tamarind (p107)

» Hakkasan (p113)

» St John (p115)

When to Go?

April in the city sees daffodils in bloom, costumed marathon runners and London's edgiest music event, the Camden Crawl. In June you'll find the parks filled with people, Trooping the Colour, summer arts festivals, gay pride and Wimbledon. London in December is all about Christmas lights on Oxford and Regent Sts, and perhaps a whisper of snow.

Best Places to Stay

» Haymarket Hotel (p100)

» Hazlitt's (p100)

» Hoxton (p106)

» Zetter Hotel (p106)

» Palmers Lodge (p106)

History

London first came into being as a Celtic village near a ford across the River Thames, but it wasn't until after the Roman invasion, in the year 43, that the city really began to take off. The Romans enclosed their Londinium in walls that are still echoed in the shape of the City of London (the big 'C' City) today.

By the end of the 3rd century AD, Londinium was almost as multicultural as it is now, with 30,000 people of various ethnic groups and temples dedicated to a variety of cults. Internal strife and relentless barbarian attacks took their toll on the Romans, who abandoned Britain in the 5th century, reducing the conurbation to a sparsely populated backwater.

The Saxons then moved in to the area, establishing farmsteads and villages. Their 'Lundenwic' prospered, becoming a large, well-organised town divided into 20 different wards. As the city grew in importance, it caught the eye of Danish Vikings, who launched many invasions and razed the city in the 9th century. The Saxons held on until, finally beaten down in 1016, they were forced to accept the Danish leader Knut (Canute) as King of England, after which London replaced Winchester as its capital. In 1042 the throne reverted to the Saxon Edward the Confessor, whose main contribution to the city was the building of Westminster Abbey.

The Norman Conquest saw William the Conqueror marching into London, where he was crowned king. He built the White Tower (the core of the Tower of London), negotiated taxes with the merchants, and affirmed the city's independence and right to self-government. From then until the late 15th century, London politics was largely taken up by a three-way power struggle between the monarchy, the church and city guilds.

The greatest threat to the burgeoning city was that of disease caused by unsanitary living conditions and impure drinking water. In 1348 rats on ships from Europe brought the bubonic plague, which wiped out a third of London's population of 100,000 over the following year.

London was consolidated as the seat of law and government in the kingdom during the 14th century. An uneasy political compromise was reached between the factions, and the city expanded rapidly in the 16th century under the House of Tudor.

The Great Plague struck in 1665 and by the time the winter cold arrested the epidemic, 100,000 Londoners had perished. Just as the population considered a sigh of relief, another disaster struck. The mother of all blazes, the Great Fire of 1666, virtually razed the place. One consequence was that it created a blank canvas upon which master architect Sir Christopher Wren could build his magnificent churches.

London's growth continued unabated, and by 1700 it was Europe's largest city, with 600,000 people. An influx of foreign workers brought expansion to the east and south, while those who could afford it headed to the more salubrious environs of the north and west, divisions that still largely shape London today.

Georgian London saw a surge in artistic creativity, with the likes of Dr Johnson, Handel, Gainsborough and Reynolds enriching the city's culture while its architects fashioned an elegant new metropolis. At the same time the gap between rich and poor grew ever wider, and lawlessness was rife.

In 1837, 18-year-old Victoria ascended the throne. During her long reign (1837–1901), London became the fulcrum of the expanding British Empire, which covered a quarter of the earth's surface. The Industrial Revolution saw the building of new docks and railways (including the first underground line in 1863), while the Great Exhibition of 1851 showcased London to the world. The city's population mushroomed from just over two million to 6.6 million during Victoria's reign.

Although London suffered relatively minor damage during WWI, it was devastated by the Luftwaffe in WWII, when huge

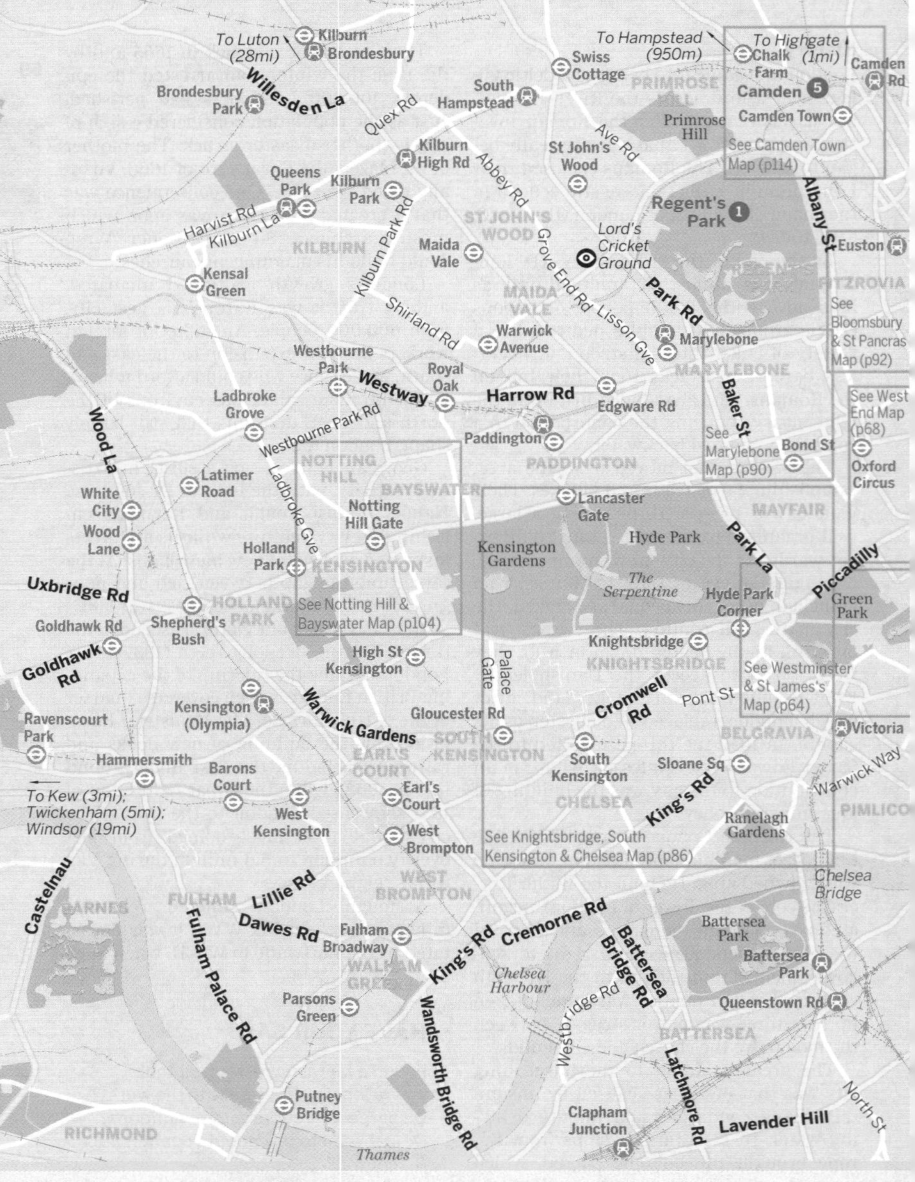

London Highlights

1 Watching the world pass by on a sunny day in **Regent's Park** (p89) or any of London's other green oases

2 Admiring the booty of an empire at the **British Museum** (p90)

3 Losing your head in history at the **Tower of London** (p73)

4 Meeting the dead famous in **Westminster Abbey** (p62)

5 Discovering the next cool thing in skinny jeans in one of Camden's **live music venues** (p124)

6 Seeing the locals through beer goggles on a **Hoxton** (p121) bar hop

7 Getting closer to God at the top of the dome of **St Paul's Cathedral** (p74)

8 Enjoying some proper Cockney barrow boy banter at **Columbia Road Flower Market** (p128)

9 Ending the day on the Thames near **Tower Bridge** (p74) – a Waterloo sunset's fine but one by the bridge is even better

swaths of the centre and East End were flattened and 32,000 people were killed. Ugly housing and low-cost developments were hastily erected in postwar London, and immigrants from around the world flocked to the city and once again changed its character. On 6 December 1952 the Great Smog descended, a lethal combination of fog, smoke and pollution caused by residential coal fires, vehicle exhausts and industry, killing some 4000 people.

Prosperity gradually returned, and the creative energy that had been bottled up in the postwar years was suddenly unleashed. London became the capital of cool in fashion and music in the 'Swinging Sixties'. The party didn't last long, however, and London returned to the doldrums in the harsh economic climate of the 1970s. Since then the city has surfed up and down the waves of global economics, hanging on to its position as the world's leading financial centre even during the recent international banking crisis.

In 2000 the modern metropolis got its first Mayor of London (as opposed to the Lord Mayor of the City of London), an elected role covering the City and all 32 urban boroughs, a position held (at the time of research) by bicycle-riding Boris Johnson, a Conservative known for his unruly shock of blond hair and appearances on TV game shows.

July 2005 was a roller-coaster month for London. Snatching victory from the jaws of Paris (the favourites), the city won its bid to host the 2012 Olympics and celebrated with a frenzy of flag waving. The following day, the celebrations abruptly ended as suicide bombers struck on three tube trains and a bus, killing 52 people. Only two weeks later a second terrorist attack was foiled. But Londoners are not easily beaten and they immediately returned to the tube, out of both defiance and pragmatism.

WANT MORE?

For in-depth information, reviews and recommendations at your fingertips, head to the Apple App Store to purchase Lonely Planet's London City Guide iPhone app.

Alternatively, head to Lonely Planet (www.lonelyplanet.com/england/london) for planning advice, author recommendations, traveller reviews and insider tips.

At the time of writing, preparations for the Olympics were in full swing. A new East London overground line opened in 2010, while new sporting venues were sprouting all over the East End.

Sights

The city's main geographical feature is the murky Thames, which snakes around but roughly divides the city into north and south. The old City of London (note the big 'C') is the capital's financial district, covering roughly a square mile bordered by the river and the many gates of the ancient (long-gone) city walls: Newgate, Moorgate etc. The areas to the east of the City are collectively known as the East End. The West End, on the City's other flank, is effectively the centre of London nowadays. It actually falls within the City of Westminster, which is one of London's 32 boroughs and has long been the centre of government and royalty.

Surrounding these central areas are dozens of former villages (Camden Town, Islington, Clapham etc), each with their own High St, which were long ago swallowed by London's sprawl.

With so much to see and do, it can be hard to know where to start. Weather will be a determining factor: the museums and galleries are great for a rainy day, but when the sun shines make like a Londoner and head to the parks – you never know whether this fine day will be your last. Otherwise, attack the sights by area using the ordering of this section as your guide.

WESTMINSTER & ST JAMES'S

Purposefully positioned outside the old City (London's fiercely independent burghers preferred to keep the monarch and parliament at arm's length), Westminster has been the centre of the nation's political power for nearly a millennium. The area's many landmarks combine to form an awesome display of authority and gravitas.

Put on your best rah-rah voice to wander around St James's, an aristocratic enclave of palaces, famous hotels, historic shops and elegant buildings. There are some 150 historically noteworthy buildings within its 36 hectares.

Westminster Abbey CHURCH

(Map p64; ☎020-7654 4834; www.westminster-abbey.org; 20 Dean's Yard SW1; adult/child £15/6, tours £3; ⏲9.30am-4.30pm Mon, Tue, Thu & Fri, to 7pm Wed, to 2.30pm Sat; ⊖Westminster) If

LONDON IN...

Two Days

Only two days? Start in **Trafalgar Sq** and see at least the outside of all the big-ticket sights – **London Eye**, **Houses of Parliament**, **Westminster Abbey**, **St James's Park and Palace**, **Buckingham Palace**, **Green Park**, **Hyde Park**and **Kensington Gardens and Palace** – and then motor around **Tate Modern** until you get booted out. In the evening, explore **Soho**. On day two, race around the **British Museum**, then head to the City. Start with our **walking tour** and finish in the **Tower of London**. Head to the East End for an evening of **ethnic food** and **hip bars**.

Four Days

Take the two-day itinerary but stretch it to a comfortable pace. Stop at the **National Gallery** while you're in Trafalgar Sq, explore inside Westminster Abbey and **St Paul's Cathedral** and allow half a day for each of Tate Modern, British Museum and Tower of London. On your extra evenings, check out **Camden** and **Islington** or splurge on a slap-up dinner in **Chelsea**.

One Week

As above, but add in a day each for **Greenwich**, **Kew Gardens** and **Hampton Court Palace**.

you're one of those boring sods who boast about spending months in Europe without ever setting foot in a church, get over yourself and make this the exception. Not merely a beautiful place of worship, Westminster Abbey serves up the country's history cold on slabs of stone. For centuries the country's greatest have been interred here, including most of the monarchs from Henry III (died 1272) to George II (1760).

Westminster Abbey has never been a cathedral (the seat of a bishop). It's what is called a 'royal peculiar' and is administered directly by the Crown. Every monarch since William the Conqueror has been crowned here, with the exception of a couple of unlucky Eds who were murdered (Edward V) or abdicated (Edward VIII) before the magic moment. Look out for the strangely ordinary-looking **Coronation Chair**.

The building itself is an arresting sight. Though a mixture of architectural styles, it is considered the finest example of Early English Gothic in existence. The original church was built in the 11th century by King (later Saint) Edward the Confessor, who is buried in the chapel behind the main altar. Henry III began work on the new building in 1245 but didn't complete it; the French Gothic nave was finished in 1388. Henry VII's magnificent Late Perpendicular–style **Lady Chapel** was consecrated in 1519 after 16 years of construction.

Apart from the royal graves, keep an eye out for the many famous commoners interred here, especially in **Poets' Corner**, where you'll find the resting places of Chaucer, Dickens, Hardy, Tennyson, Dr Johnson and Kipling, as well as memorials to the other greats (Shakespeare, Austen, Brontë etc). Elsewhere you'll find the graves of Handel and Sir Isaac Newton.

The octagonal **Chapter House** (⌚10.30am-4pm) dates from the 1250s and was where the monks would meet for daily prayer before Henry VIII's suppression of the monasteries. Used as a treasury and 'Royal Wardrobe', the cryptlike **Pyx Chamber** (⌚10.30am-3.30pm) dates from about 1070. The neighbouring **Abbey Museum** (⌚10.30am-4pm) has as its centrepiece the death masks of generations of royalty.

Parts of the Abbey complex are free to visitors. This includes the **Cloister** (⌚8am-6pm) and the 900-year-old **College Garden** (⌚10am-6pm Tue-Thu Apr-Sep, to 4pm Oct-Mar). Free concerts are held here from 12.30pm to 2pm on Wednesdays from mid-July to mid-August. Adjacent to the abbey is **St Margaret's Church** (⌚9.30am-3.30pm Mon-Sat, 2-4.45pm Sun), the House of Commons' place of worship since 1614. There are windows commemorating churchgoers Caxton and Milton, and Sir Walter Raleigh is buried by the altar.

Verger-led tours are held several times a day (except Sundays) and are limited to 25

Westminister & St James's

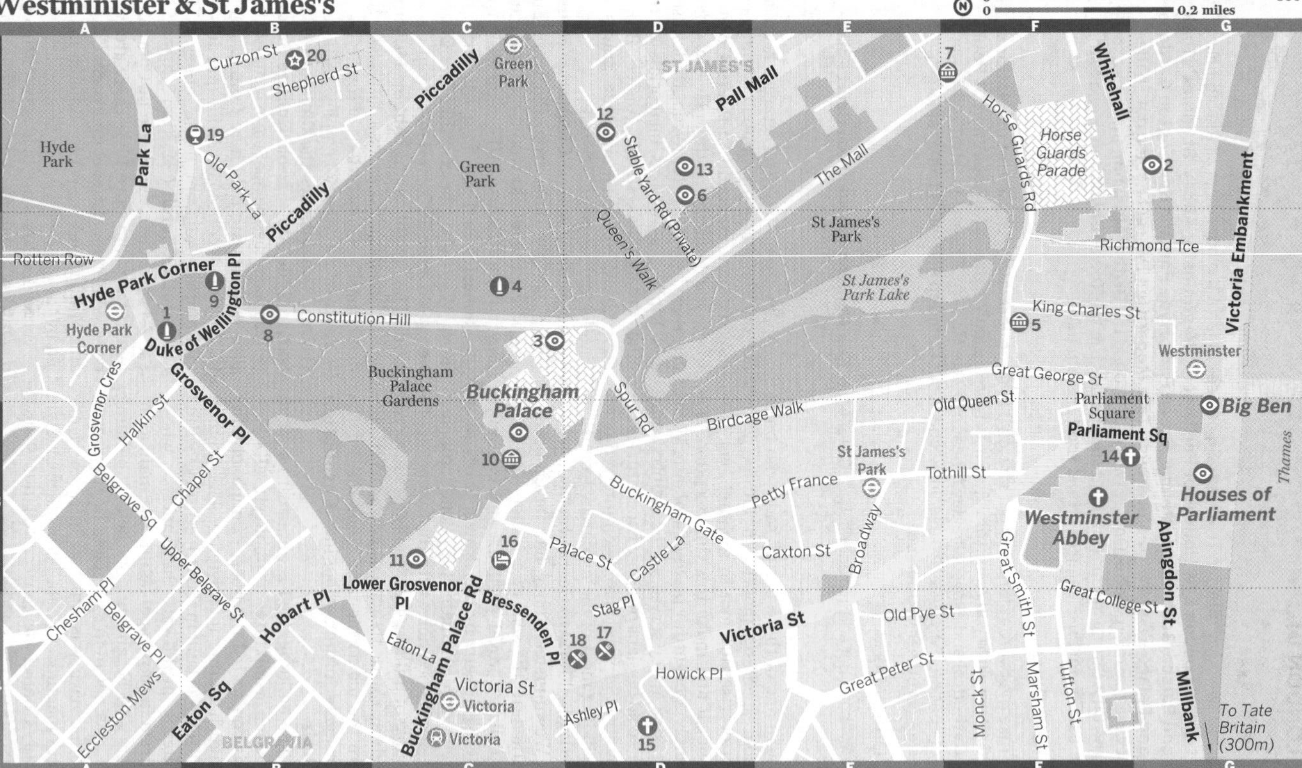
500 m
0.2 miles
Hyde Park
Park La
Curzon St
Shepherd St
Old Park La
Piccadilly
Green Park
St James's
Pall Mall
Stable Yard Rd (Private)
Queen's Walk
The Mall
Horse Guards Rd
Horse Guards Parade
Whitehall
Victoria Embankment
Richmond Tce
St James's Park
St James's Park Lake
King Charles St
Westminster
Big Ben
Rotten Row
Hyde Park Corner
Duke of Wellington Pl
Constitution Hill
Buckingham Palace Gardens
Buckingham Palace
Spur Rd
Birdcage Walk
Great George St
Old Queen St
Parliament Square
Parliament Sq
Houses of Parliament
Thames
Grosvenor Cres
Halkin St
Grosvenor Pl
Chapel St
Belgrave Sq
Upper Belgrave St
Chesham Pl
Belgrave Pl
Eccleston Mews
Eaton Sq
Belgravia
Hobart Pl
Lower Grosvenor Pl
Buckingham Palace Rd
Bressenden Pl
Eaton La
Victoria St
Victoria
Palace St
Castle La
Stag Pl
Buckingham Gate
Petty France
Tothill St
Caxton St
Broadway
Howick Pl
Ashley Pl
Great Peter St
Old Pye St
Great Smith St
Westminster Abbey
Great College St
Abingdon St
Monck St
Marsham St
Tufton St
Millbank
To Tate Britain (300m)

Westminster & St James's

Top Sights

Big Ben G3
Buckingham Palace C3
Houses of Parliament G3
Westminster Abbey F3

Sights

1 Australian War Memorial A2
2 Banqueting House G1
3 Canada Gate C2
4 Canada Memorial C2
5 Churchill Museum & Cabinet War Rooms F2
6 Clarence House D1
7 Institute of Contemporary Arts F1
8 Memorial Gates B2
9 New Zealand War Memorial B2
10 Queen's Gallery C3
11 Royal Mews C3
12 Spencer House D1
13 St James's Palace D1
14 St Margaret's Church F3
15 Westminster Cathedral D4

Sleeping

16 Rubens at the Palace C3

Eating

17 Wagamama D4
18 Zizzi D4

Drinking

19 Galvin at Windows B1

Entertainment

20 Curzon Mayfair B1

people per tour; call ahead to secure your place. Of course, admission to the Abbey is free if you wish to attend a service. On weekdays, Matins is at 7.30am, Holy Communion at 8am and 12.30pm, and Choral Evensong at 5pm. There are services throughout the day on Sundays. You can sit and soak in the atmosphere, even if you're not religious.

Houses of Parliament HISTORIC BUILDING
(Map p64; www.parliament.uk; Parliament Sq SW1; ⊖Westminster) Coming face to face with one of the world's most recognisable landmarks is always a surreal moment, but in the case of the Houses of Parliament it's a revelation. The BBC's standard title shot just doesn't do justice to the ornate stonework and golden filigree of Charles Barry and Augustus Pugin's neo-Gothic masterpiece (1840).

Officially called the Palace of Westminster, the oldest part is **Westminster Hall** (1097), which is one of only a few sections that survived a catastrophic fire in 1834. Its roof, added between 1394 and 1401, is the earliest known example of a hammerbeam roof and has been described as the greatest surviving achievement of medieval English carpentry.

The palace's most famous feature is its clock tower, aka **Big Ben** (Map p64). Ben is actually the 13-ton bell, named after Benjamin Hall, who was commissioner of works when the tower was completed in 1858.

At the business end, parliament is split into two houses. The green-hued **House of Commons** is the lower house, where the 650 elected Members of Parliament sit. Traditionally the home of hereditary bluebloods, the scarlet-decorated **House of Lords** now has peers appointed through various means. Both houses debate and vote on legislation, which is then presented to the Queen for her Royal Assent (in practice, this is a formality; the last time Royal Assent was denied was 1708). At the annual State Opening of Parliament (usually in November), the Queen takes her throne in the House of Lords, having processed in the gold-trimmed Irish State Coach from Buckingham Palace. It's well worth lining the route for a gawk at the crown jewels sparkling in the sun.

When parliament is in session, visitors are admitted to the **House of Commons Visitors' Gallery** (admission free; ⌚2.30-10.30pm Mon & Tue, 11.30am-7.30pm Wed, 10.30am-6.30pm Thu, 9.30am-3pm some Fridays). Expect to queue for at least an hour and possibly longer during Question Time (at the beginning of each day). The **House of Lords Visitors' Gallery** (admission free; ⌚2.30-10pm Mon & Tue, 3-10pm Wed, 11am-7.30pm Thu, from 10am some Fridays) can also be visited.

Parliamentary recesses (ie holidays) last for three months over summer and a couple of weeks over Easter and Christmas. When parliament is in recess there are guided **tours** (☎0844 847 1672; www.ticketmaster.co.uk/housesofparliament; 75min tours adult/child £14/6) of both chambers and other historic areas. UK residents can approach their MPs to arrange a free tour and to climb the clock tower.

Buckingham Palace PALACE
(Map p64; ☎020-7766 7300; www.royalcollection.org.uk; Buckingham Palace Rd SW1; tours adult/child £17/9.75; ⊙late Jul-Sep; ⊖Victoria) With so many imposing buildings in the capital, the Queen's well-proportioned but relatively plain city pad is an anticlimax for some. Built in 1803 for the Duke of Buckingham, Buckingham Palace replaced St James's Palace as the monarch's London home in 1837. When she's not off giving her one-handed wave in far-flung parts of the Commonwealth, Queen Elizabeth II divides her time between here, Windsor and Balmoral. If you've got the urge to drop in for a cup of tea, a handy way of telling whether she's home is to check whether the yellow, red and blue royal standard is flying.

Nineteen lavishly furnished State Rooms – hung with artworks by the likes of Rembrandt, van Dyck, Canaletto, Poussin and Vermeer – are open to visitors when HRH (Her Royal Highness) takes her holidays. The two-hour tour includes the **Throne Room**, with his-and-hers pink chairs initialled 'ER' and 'P'.

'A Royal Day Out' is a combined ticket including the State Rooms, Queen's Gallery and Royal Mews (adult/child £31/18).

Changing of the Guard
If you're a fan of bright uniforms, bearskin hats, straight lines, marching and shouting, join the throngs outside the palace at 11.30am (daily from May to July and on alternate days for the rest of the year, weather permitting), when the regiment of guards outside the palace changes over in one of the world's most famous displays of pageantry. It does have a certain freak show value, but gets dull very quickly. If you're here in November, the procession leaving the palace for the State Opening of Parliament is much more impressive.

Queen's Gallery
(Map p64; adult/child £8.75/4.50; ⊙10am-5.30pm) Originally designed by John Nash as a conservatory, it was smashed up by the Luftwaffe in 1940 before being converted to a gallery in 1962, housing works from the extensive Royal Collection.

Royal Mews
(Map p64; adult/child £7.50/4.80; ⊙11am-4pm) Indulge your Cinderella fantasies while inspecting the exquisite state coaches and immaculately groomed royal horses housed in the Royal Mews. Highlights include the 1910 royal wedding's Glass Coach and the 1762 Gold Coach, which has been used for every coronation since that of George IV. We're pretty sure that these aren't about to change back into pumpkins any time soon.

St James's Park & Palace PARK
(Map p64; ⊖St James's Park) With its manicured flowerbeds and ornamental lake, St James's Park is a wonderful place to stroll and take in the surrounding palaces. The striking Tudor gatehouse of **St James's Palace** (Map p64; Cleveland Row SW1; ⊖Green Park), initiated by the palace-mad Henry VIII in 1530, is best approached from St James's St, to the north of the park. This was the residence of Prince Charles and his sons before they shifted next door to **Clarence House** (1828), following the death of its previous occupant, the Queen Mother, in 2002. It's a great place to pose for a photograph beside one of the resolutely unsmiling royal guards.

Green Park PARK
(Map p64; ⊖Green Park) Green Park's 47-acre expanse of meadows and mature trees links St James's Park to Hyde Park and Kensington Gardens, creating a green corridor from Westminster all the way to Kensington. It was once a duelling ground and served as a vegetable garden during WWII. Although it doesn't have lakes, fountains or formal gardens, it's blanketed with daffodils in spring and seminaked bodies whenever the sun shines.

The only concessions to formality are the war memorials of various Commonwealth countries: the **Canada Memorial** near **Canada Gate**, which links the park to Buckingham Palace; the **Memorial Gates** at its western end, which recognise the contribution of various African, Caribbean and Indian subcontinent countries; and the nearby **Australian** and **New Zealand War Memorials** in Hyde Park Corner.

Westminster Cathedral CATHEDRAL
(Map p64; www.westminstercathedral.org.uk; Victoria St SW1; ⊙7am-7pm; ⊖Victoria) Begun in 1895, this neo-Byzantine cathedral is the headquarters of Britain's once-suppressed Roman Catholic Church. It's still a work in progress, the vast interior part dazzling marble and mosaic and part bare brick; new sections are completed as funds allow. Look out for Eric Gill's highly regarded stone **Stations of the Cross** (1918).

The **Chapel of St George and the English Martyrs** displays the body of St John Southwark, a priest who was hanged, drawn and quartered in 1654 for refusing to reject the supremacy of the Pope.

The distinctive 83m red-brick and white-stone **tower** (adult/child £5/2.50) offers splendid views of London and, unlike St Paul's dome, you can take the lift.

Banqueting House PALACE
(Map p64; www.hrp.org.uk/BanquetingHouse; Whitehall SW1; adult/child £4.80/free; ⏲10am-5pm Mon-Sat; ⊖Westminster) The beautiful, classical design of the Banqueting House was conceived by Inigo Jones for James I in 1622. It's the only surviving part of Whitehall Palace after the Tudor bit burnt down in 1698. The key attraction is the ceiling, painted by Rubens in 1635 at the behest of Charles I. The king didn't get to enjoy it for long, as in 1649 he was frogmarched out of the 1st-floor balcony to lose his head for treason. A bust outside commemorates him. An audio guide is included in the price.

Churchill Museum & Cabinet War Rooms MUSEUM
(Map p64; www.iwm.org.uk/cabinet; Clive Steps, King Charles St SW1; adult/child £15/free; ⏲9.30am-6pm; ⊖Westminster) The Cabinet War Rooms were Prime Minister Winston Churchill's underground military HQ during WWII. Now a wonderfully evocative and atmospheric museum, the restored and preserved rooms (including Churchill's bedroom) capture the drama of the time. The interactive displays offer an intriguing exposé of the public and private faces of the man.

FREE **Institute Of Contemporary Arts** GALLERY
(Map p64; www.ica.org.uk; The Mall SW1; ⏲noon-7pm Wed & Fri-Sun, to 9pm Thu; ⊖Charing Cross) A one-stop contemporary-art bonanza, the exciting program at the ICA includes film, photography, theatre, installations, talks, performance art, DJs, digital art and book readings. Stroll around the galleries, watch a film, browse the bookshop, then head to the bar for a beer.

Spencer House HISTORIC HOME
(Map p64; ☎020-7499 8620; www.spencerhouse.co.uk; 27 St James's Pl SW1; adult/child £9/7; ⏲10.30am-5.45pm Sun Feb-Jul & Sep-Dec; ⊖Green Park) The ancestral home of Princess Diana's family, Spencer House was built in the Palladian style between 1756 and 1766. It was converted into offices after the Spencers moved out in 1927, but 60 years later an £18 million restoration returned it to its former glory. Visits are by guided tour.

ESCALATOR ETIQUETTE

The fastest way to get abused in London (apart from jumping a queue – you'd need to have a death wish to attempt that) is to block an escalator, especially at a busy tube station. Always, always, always stand in single file to the right. Don't expect any mercy if you forget. And while you're at it, make sure you have your ticket/Oyster card ready when you get to the tube exit. Fumbling in your wallet or purse is guaranteed to elicit a sharply passive-aggressive 'Excuse me!' from the person behind you.

WEST END

Synonymous with big-budget musicals and frenzied flocks of shoppers, the West End is a strident mix of culture and consumerism. More a concept than a fixed geographical area, it nonetheless takes in Piccadilly Circus and Trafalgar Sq to the south, Regent St to the west, Oxford St to the north and Covent Garden and the Strand to the east.

Named after the elaborate collars (picadils) that were the sartorial staple of a 17th-century tailor who lived nearby, **Piccadilly** became the fashionable haunt of the well-heeled (and collared), and still boasts establishment icons such as the Ritz hotel and Fortnum & Mason department store. It meets Regent St, Shaftesbury Ave and Haymarket at neon-lit, turbo-charged **Piccadilly Circus**, home to the popular but unremarkable Eros statue. Ironically, the love god looks over an area that's long been linked to prostitution, both male and female, although it's less conspicuous these days.

Mayfair hogs all of the most expensive streets on the Monopoly board, including Park Lane and Bond St, which should give you an idea of what to expect: lots of pricey shops, Michelin-starred restaurants, society hotels and gentlemen's clubs. Elegant **Regent St** and frantic **Oxford St** are the

West End

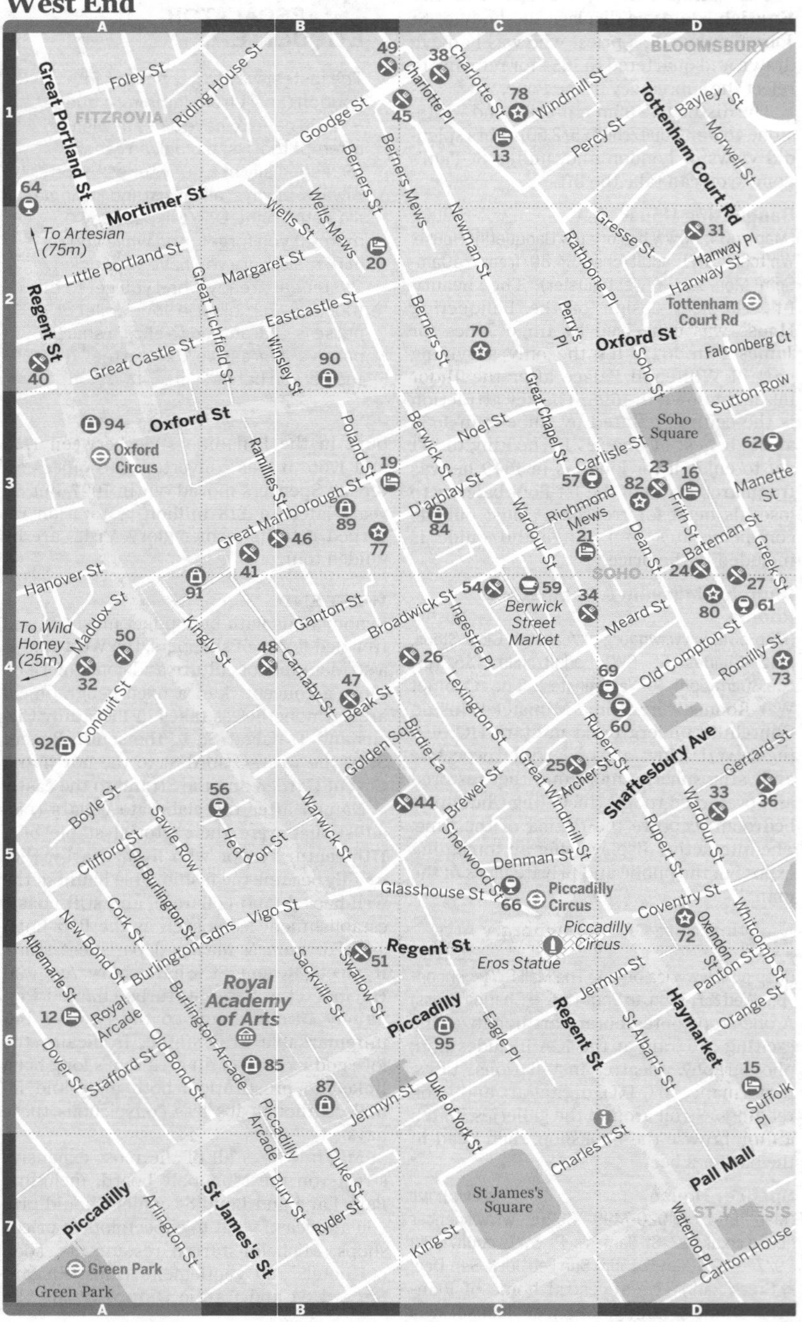

FITZROVIA
BLOOMSBURY
SOHO
ST JAMES'S
Great Portland St
Foley St
Riding House St
Goodge St
Charlotte St
Charlotte Pl
Windmill St
Tottenham Court Rd
Bayley St
Morwell St
Percy St
Mortimer St
Berners St
Berners Mews
Wells St
Wells Mews
Newman St
Rathbone Pl
Gresse St
Hanway Pl
Hanway St
Tottenham Court Rd
Little Portland St
Margaret St
Regent St
Great Tichfield St
Eastcastle St
Perry's Pl
Oxford St
Soho St
Falconberg Ct
Great Castle St
Winsley St
Great Chapel St
Sutton Row
Oxford St
Oxford Circus
Poland St
Berwick St
Noel St
Soho Square
Ramillies St
Carlisle St
Manette St
D'arblay St
Great Marlborough St
Richmond Mews
Wardour St
Frith St
Dean St
Bateman St
Greek St
Hanover St
Maddox St
Ganton St
Broadwick St
Ingestre Pl
Berwick Street Market
Meard St
Old Compton St
Romilly St
To Wild Honey (25m)
To Artesian (75m)
Kingly St
Carnaby St
Lexington St
Beak St
Conduit St
Golden Sq
Birdie La
Rupert St
Archer St
Great Windmill St
Shaftesbury Ave
Gerrard St
Boyle St
Savile Row
Heddon St
Warwick St
Brewer St
Sherwood St
Wardour St
Rupert St
Clifford St
Old Burlington St
Denman St
Glasshouse St
Piccadilly Circus
Whitcomb St
Coventry St
New Bond St
Cork St
Vigo St
Burlington Gdns
Piccadilly Circus
Eros Statue
Oxendon St
Panton St
Albemarle St
Sackville St
Swallow St
Regent St
Jermyn St
Royal Arcade
Burlington Arcade
Royal Academy of Arts
Piccadilly
Eagle Pl
Regent St
St Alban's St
Haymarket
Orange St
Dover St
Stafford St
Old Bond St
Jermyn St
Duke of York St
Suffolk Pl
Piccadilly Arcade
Charles II St
Pall Mall
Piccadilly
Arlington St
St James's St
Bury St
Duke St
Ryder St
St James's Square
King St
Waterloo Pl
Carlton House
Green Park
A
B
C
D
1
2
3
4
5
6
7
49
38
78
45
13
64
31
20
70
90
40
94
62
57
23
16
19
82
89
84
46
77
21
41
91
54
59
34
24
27
80
61
50
48
26
32
47
69
73
60
92
25
56
33
36
44
66
72
51
12
95
85
15
87

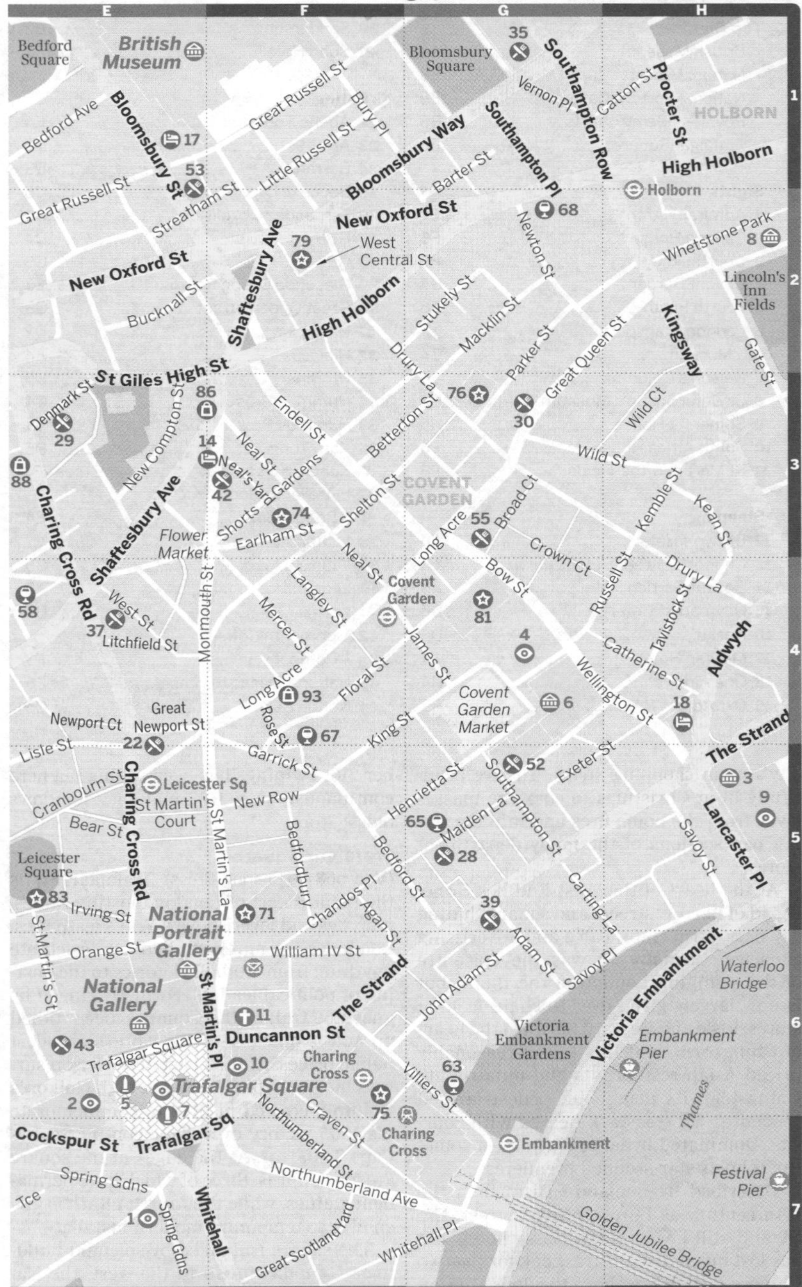
0 250 m
0 0.2 miles
E
F
G
H
1
2
3
4
5
6
7
Bedford Square
British Museum
Bloomsbury Square
Southampton Row
Procter St
Vernon Pl
Catton St
HOLBORN
Great Russell St
Bury Pl
Bedford Ave
Bloomsbury St
Little Russell St
Bloomsbury Way
Southampton Pl
Barter St
High Holborn
Holborn
Great Russell St
Streatham St
New Oxford St
Newton St
Whetstone Park
West Central St
Shaftesbury Ave
New Oxford St
Stukely St
Lincoln's Inn Fields
Bucknall St
High Holborn
Macklin St
Kingsway
Parker St
Great Queen St
Gate St
Drury La
St Giles High St
Denmark St
New Compton St
Endell St
Betterton St
Wild Ct
Neal St
Wild St
Neal's Yard
Gardens
Shelton St
COVENT GARDEN
Broad Ct
Kemble St
Kean St
Charing Cross Rd
Shaftesbury Ave
Shorts
Earlham St
Long Acre
Crown Ct
Flower Market
Neal St
Bow St
Russell St
Drury La
Monmouth St
Langley St
Covent Garden
Tavistock St
West St
Mercer St
James St
Catherine St
Aldwych
Litchfield St
Floral St
Wellington St
Long Acre
Covent Garden Market
Great Newport St
Newport Ct
Rose St
King St
The Strand
Lisle St
Garrick St
Exeter St
Charing Cross Rd
Leicester Sq
Henrietta St
Southampton St
Cranbourn St
St Martin's Court
New Row
Bear St
Bedfordbury
Maiden La
Lancaster Pl
Savoy St
Leicester Square
Bedford St
Carting La
Chandos Pl
Agar St
Irving St
National Portrait Gallery
St Martin's La
St Martin's St
Orange St
William IV St
Adam St
Savoy Pl
Victoria Embankment
Waterloo Bridge
National Gallery
The Strand
John Adam St
St Martin's Pl
Duncannon St
Victoria Embankment Gardens
Embankment Pier
Trafalgar Square
Charing Cross
Villiers St
Trafalgar Square
Thames
Craven St
Charing Cross
Cockspur St
Trafalgar Sq
Northumberland St
Embankment
Spring Gdns
Northumberland Ave
Festival Pier
Tce
Whitehall
Spring Gdns
Golden Jubilee Bridge
Whitehall Pl
Great Scotland Yard
35
17
53
68
8
79
76
30
86
29
14
88
42
74
55
58
81
37
4
93
6
18
22
67
52
3
9
65
28
83
71
39
11
43
10
63
2
5
7
75
1

West End

Top Sights		
	British Museum	E1
	National Gallery	E6
	National Portrait Gallery	E6
	Royal Academy of Arts	B6
	Trafalgar Square	E6
Sights		
1	Admiralty Arch	E7
2	Canada House	E6
3	Courtauld Gallery	H5
4	Covent Garden	G4
5	Fourth Plinth	E6
6	London Transport Museum	G4
7	Nelson's Column	E6
8	Sir John Soane's Museum	H2
9	Somerset House	H5
10	South Africa House	F6
11	St Martin-in-the-Fields	F6
Sleeping		
12	Brown's Hotel	A6
13	Charlotte Street Hotel	C1
14	Covent Garden Hotel	F3
15	Haymarket Hotel	D6
16	Hazlitt's	D3
17	Morgan Hotel	E1
18	One Aldwych	H4
19	Oxford St YHA	B3
20	Sanderson	B2
21	Soho Hotel	C3
Eating		
22	Abeno Too	E4
23	Arbutus	D3
24	Barrafina	D3
25	Bocca di Lupo	C5
26	Fernandez & Wells	C4
27	GBK	D4
28	GBK	G5
29	Giaconda Dining Room	E3
30	Great Queen Street	G3
31	Hakkasan	D2
32	Hibiscus	A4
33	HK Diner	D5
34	Hummus Bros	C4
35	Hummus Bros	G1
36	Kam Tong	D5
	Konditor & Cook	(see 73)
37	L'Atelier de Joël Robuchon	E4
38	Lantana	C1
39	Leon	G5
40	Leon	A2
41	Leon	B3
42	Monmouth Coffee Company	F3
43	National Dining Rooms	E6
44	Nordic Bakery	C5

city's main shopping strips. They're beautifully lit at Christmas to coax the masses away from the home fires and into the frying pan sections of the many department stores.

At the heart of the West End lies **Soho**, a grid of narrow streets and squares hiding gay bars, strip clubs, cafes and advertising agencies. **Carnaby St** was the epicentre of the swinging London of the 1960s, but is now largely given over to chain fashion stores. Lisle and Gerrard Sts form the heart of **Chinatown**, which is full of reasonably priced Asian restaurants and unfairly hip youngsters. Its neighbour, pedestrianised **Leicester Sq (les-ter)**, heaves with tourists. Dominated by large cinemas, it sometimes hosts star-studded premieres.

Described by Benjamin Disraeli in the 19th century as Europe's finest street, **the Strand** still boasts a few classy hotels but has lost much of its lustre. Look for the two Chinese merchants above the door at number 216; Twinings has been selling tea here continuously since 1787, making it London's oldest store.

Trafalgar Square SQUARE

(Map p68; Charing Cross) Trafalgar Sq is the public heart of London, hosting rallies, marches and feverish New Year's festivities. Londoners congregate here to celebrate anything from football victories to the ousting of political leaders. Formerly ringed by gnarling traffic, the square's been tidied up and is now one of the world's grandest public places. At the heart of it, Nelson surveys his fleet from the 43.5m-high **Nelson's Column**, erected in 1843 to commemorate his 1805 victory over Napoleon off Spain's Cape Trafalgar. At the edges of the square are four plinths, three of which have permanent statues, while the **fourth plinth** is given over to temporary modern installations.

The square is flanked by splendid buildings: **Canada House** to the west, the National Gallery and National Portrait Gallery

45 Ping Pong	C1	**Entertainment**	
46 Ping Pong	B3	**70** 100 Club	C2
47 Polpo	B4	**71** Coliseum	F5
Sacred	(see 93)	**72** Comedy Store	D5
48 Sacred	B4	**73** Curzon Soho	D4
49 Salt Yard	B1	**74** Donmar Warehouse	F3
50 Sketch	A4	**75** G-A-Y Club @ Heaven	F6
51 Veeraswamy	B6	**76** Guanabara	G3
52 Wagamama	G5	**77** Lucky Voice	B3
53 Wagamama	E1	**78** Pear Shaped	C1
54 Yauatcha	C4	**79** Popstarz	F2
55 Zizzi	G3	**80** Ronnie Scott's	D4
		81 Royal Opera House	G4
Drinking		**82** Soho Theatre	D3
56 Absolut Ice Bar	B5	**83** tkts	E5
57 Candy Bar	C3		
58 Coach & Horses	E4	**Shopping**	
59 Flat White	C4	**84** BM Soho	C3
60 Friendly Society	D4	**85** Burlington Arcade	B6
61 G-A-Y Bar	D4	**86** Forbidden Planet	E3
62 G-A-Y Late	D3	**87** Fortnum & Mason	B6
63 Gordon's Wine Bar	G6	**88** Foyle's	E3
64 Heights	A1	**89** Grant & Cutler	B3
65 Jewel Covent Garden	G5	**90** HMV	B2
66 Jewel Piccadilly Circus	C5	**91** Liberty	A4
67 Lamb & Flag	F4	Ray's Jazz	(see 88)
68 Princess Louise	G2	**92** Rigby & Peller	A4
69 Village	D4	**93** Stanford's	F4
		94 Topshop Oxford Circus	A3
		95 Waterstone's	C6

to the north, **South Africa House** and the church of **St Martin-in-the-Fields** to the east. Further south stands **Admiralty Arch**, built in honour of Queen Victoria in 1910, and beyond that The Mall (rhymes with 'shall', not 'shawl') is the ceremonial route leading to Buckingham Palace.

FREE **National Gallery** GALLERY
(Map p68; www.nationalgallery.org.uk; Trafalgar Sq WC2; 10am-6pm Sat-Thu, to 9pm Fri; Charing Cross) Gazing grandly over Trafalgar Sq through its Corinthian columns, the National Gallery is the nation's most important repository of art. Four million visitors come annually to admire its 2300-plus Western European paintings, spanning the years 1250 to 1900.

Highlights include Turner's *The Fighting Temeraire* (voted Britain's greatest painting), Botticelli's *Venus and Mars* and van Gogh's *Sunflowers*. The medieval religious paintings in the Sainsbury Wing are fascinating, but for a short, sharp blast of brilliance, you can't beat the truckloads of Monets, Manets, Cézannes and Renoirs in rooms 43 to 46.

It's all a bit overwhelming for one visit, but as admission's free it's possible to dip into it again and again. Themed audio guides are available (£3.50). If you prefer, you can devise and print off your own tour from the flashy computer screens of ArtStart, the gallery's interactive multimedia system. Visit on Friday evenings for live music and free talks.

FREE **National Portrait Gallery** GALLERY
(Map p68; www.npg.org.uk; St Martin's Pl WC2; 10am-6pm Sat-Wed, to 9pm Thu & Fri; Charing Cross) The fascinating National Portrait Gallery is like stepping into a picture book of English history or, if you're feeling trashy, an *OK* magazine spread on history's celebrities ('what's *she* wearing?').

Founded in 1856, the permanent collection (around 11,000 works) starts with the Tudors on the 2nd floor and descends to contemporary figures (from pop stars to scientists). An audiovisual guide (£3) will lead you through the gallery's most famous pictures. Look out for the temporary exhibitions, especially the prestigious BP Portrait Award (June to September). There's also an interesting view over the rooftops to Trafalgar Sq and Nelson's backside from the top-floor restaurant.

Royal Academy of Arts GALLERY

(Map p68; ☎020-7300 8000; www.royalacademy.org.uk; Burlington House, Piccadilly W1; admission depending on exhibition £6-20; ⊙10am-6pm Sat-Thu, to 10pm Fri; ⊖Green Park) Set back from Piccadilly, the grandiose Royal Academy of Arts hosts high-profile exhibitions and a small display from its permanent collection. The crafty Academy has made it a condition of joining its exclusive club of 80 artists that new members donate one of their artworks. Past luminaries have included Constable, Gainsborough and Turner, while Norman Foster, David Hockney and Tracey Emin are among the current crop.

Covent Garden SQUARE

(Map p68; ⊖Covent Garden) A hallowed name for opera fans due to the presence of the esteemed Royal Opera House (p125), Covent Garden is one of London's biggest tourist traps, where chain restaurants, souvenir shops, balconied bars and street entertainers vie for the passer-by's pound. Better, marginally less-frenetic shopping can be had in the atmospheric narrow streets surrounding it, such as Floral St and Neal St.

In the 7th century the Saxons built Lundenwic here, a satellite town to the City of London. It reverted back to fields until the 1630s, when the Duke of Bedford commissioned Inigo Jones to build London's first planned square. Covent Garden's famous fruit, vegetable and flower market, immortalised in the film *My Fair Lady,* eventually took over the whole piazza, before being shifted to Nine Elms in South London in 1974.

In the 18th and 19th centuries, the area immediately north of Covent Garden was the site of one of London's most notorious slums, the 'rookery' of St Giles. Much of it was knocked down in the 1840s to create New Oxford St, but the narrow lanes and yards around Monmouth St still carry an echo of the crammed conditions of the past.

TOP CHOICE **Sir John Soane's Museum** MUSEUM

(Map p68; www.soane.org; 13 Lincoln's Inn Fields WC2; ⊙10am-5pm Tue-Sat, 6-9pm 1st Tue of month ⊖Holborn) Not all of this area's inhabitants were poor, as is aptly demonstrated by the remarkable home of celebrated architect and collector extraordinaire Sir John Soane (1753–1837). Now a fascinating museum, the house has been left largely as it was when Sir John was taken out in a box. Among his eclectic acquisitions are an Egyptian sarcophagus, dozens of Greek and Roman antiquities and the original *Rake's Progress,* William Hogarth's set of caricatures telling the story of a late-18th-century London cad. Soane was clearly a very clever chap – check out the ingenious folding walls in the picture gallery. Tours (£5) are given at 11am Saturdays.

London Transport Museum MUSEUM

(Map p68; www.ltmuseum.co.uk; Covent Garden Piazza WC2; adult/child £10/free; ⊙10am-6pm; ⊖Covent Garden) Newly refurbished, this museum houses vintage vehicles, ranging from sedan chairs to train carriages, along with fascinating posters, videos and photos. You can buy your tube-map boxer shorts at the museum shop.

Somerset House GALLERIES

(Map p68; www.somersethouse.org.uk; Strand WC2; ⊙7.30am-11pm; ⊖Temple) The first Somerset House was built for the Duke of Somerset, brother of Jane Seymour, in 1551. For two centuries it played host to royals (Elizabeth I once lived here), foreign diplomats, wild masked balls, peace treaties, the parliamentary army (during the Civil War) and Oliver Cromwell's wake. Having fallen into disrepair, it was pulled down in 1775 and rebuilt in 1801 to designs by William Chambers. Among other weighty organisations, it went on to house the Royal Academy of the Arts, the Society of Antiquaries, the Navy Board and that most popular of institutions, the Inland Revenue.

The tax collectors are still here, but that doesn't dissuade Londoners from attending open-air events in the grand central courtyard, such as live performances in summer and ice skating in winter. The riverside terrace is a popular spot to get caffeinated with views of the Thames.

Near the Strand entrance, the **Courtauld Gallery** (Map p68; www.courtauld.ac.uk; adult/child £5/free, admission free 10am-2pm Mon; ⊙10am-6pm) displays a wealth of 14th- to 20th-century art, including a room of Rubens and works by van Gogh, Renoir and Cézanne. Downstairs, the **Embankment Galleries** are devoted to temporary exhibitions; prices and hours vary.

Handel House Museum MUSEUM

(Map p90; www.handelhouse.org; 25 Brook St W1; adult/child £5/2; ⏲10am-6pm Tue, Wed, Fri & Sat, 10am-8pm Thu, noon-6pm Sun; ⊖Bond St) George Frideric Handel's pad from 1723 until his death in 1759 is now a moderately interesting museum dedicated to his life. He wrote some of his greatest works here, including the *Messiah,* and music still fills the house during live recitals (see the website for details).

From songs of praise to *Purple Haze,* Jimi Hendrix lived next door at number 23 many years (and genres) later.

Burlington Arcade SHOPPING ARCADE

(Map p68; 51 Piccadilly W1; ⊖Green Park) The well-to-do Burlington Arcade, built in 1819, is most famous for the Burlington Berties, uniformed guards who patrol the area keeping an eye out for offences such as running, chewing gum or whatever else might lower the arcade's rarefied tone.

THE CITY

For most of its history, the City of London *was* London. Its boundaries have changed little since the Romans first founded their gated community here two millennia ago. You can always tell when you're within it as the Corporation of London's coat of arms appears on the street signs.

It's only in the last 250 years that the City has gone from being the very essence of London and it's main population centre to just its central business district. But what a business district it is – despite the hammering its bankers have taken in recent years, the 'square mile' remains at the very heart of world capitalism.

Currently fewer than 10,000 people actually live here, although some 300,000 descend on it each weekday, when they generate almost three-quarters of Britain's entire GDP before squeezing back onto the tube. On Sundays it becomes a virtual ghost town; it's a good time to poke around but come with a full stomach – most shops and eateries are closed.

Apart from the big-ticket sights, visitors tend to avoid the City, which is a shame as it's got enough interesting churches, intriguing architecture, hidden gardens and atmospheric lanes to spend weeks exploring.

Tower of London CASTLE

(Map p74; ☎0844-482 7777; www.hrp.org.uk; Tower Hill EC3; adult/child £17/9.50, audio guides £4/3; ⏲9am-5.30pm Tue-Sat, from 10am Sun & Mon Mar-Oct, until 4.30pm Nov-Feb; ⊖Tower Hill). If you pay only one admission fee while you're in London, make it the Tower. One of the city's three World Heritage Sites (joining Westminster Abbey and Maritime Greenwich), it offers a window on to a gruesome and fascinating history.

In the 1070s, William the Conqueror started work on the White Tower to replace the castle he'd previously had built here. By 1285, two walls with towers and a moat were built around it and the defences have barely been altered since. A former royal residence, treasury, mint and arsenal, it became most famous as a prison when Henry VIII moved to Whitehall Palace in 1529 and started dishing out his preferred brand of punishment.

The most striking building is the central **White Tower**, with its solid Romanesque architecture and four turrets. Today it houses a collection from the Royal Armouries. On the 2nd floor is **St John's Chapel**, dating from 1080 and therefore the oldest church in London. To the north is **Waterloo Barracks**, which now contains the spectacular **Crown Jewels**. On the far side of the White Tower is the **Bloody Tower**, where the 12-year-old Edward V and his little brother were held 'for their own safety' and later murdered, probably by their uncle, the future Richard III. Sir Walter Raleigh did a 13-year stretch here, when he wrote his *History of the World*.

On the small green in front of the **Chapel Royal of St Peter ad Vincula** stood Henry VIII's **scaffold**, where seven people, including Anne Boleyn and her cousin Catherine Howard (Henry's second and fifth wives) were beheaded.

Look out for the latest in the Tower's long line of famous ravens, which legend says could cause the White Tower to collapse should they leave. Their wings are clipped in case they get any ideas.

MAPS

No Londoner would be without a pocket-size *London Mini A-Z,* which lists nearly 30,000 streets and still doesn't cover the capital in its entirety. If you're going to be in London for more than a few weeks, it's worth getting one.

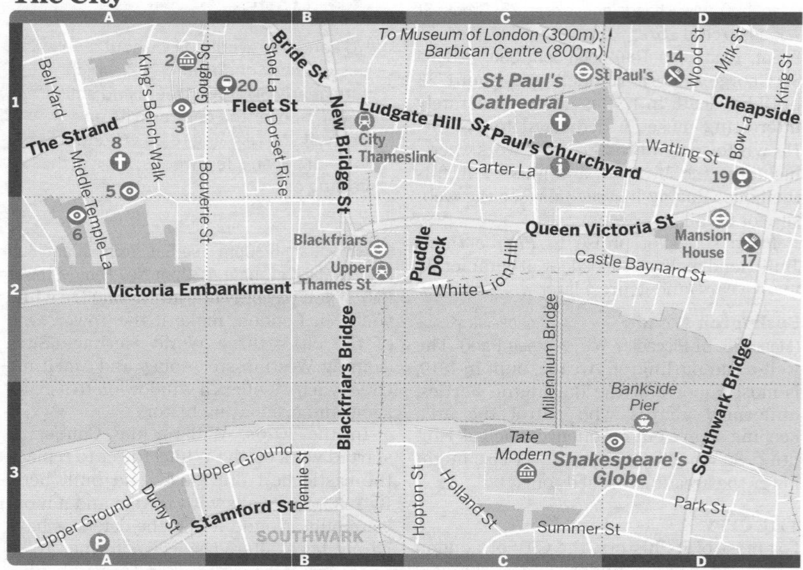

To get your bearings, take the hugely entertaining free guided tour with any of the Tudor-garbed Beefeaters. Hour-long tours leave every 30 minutes from the bridge near the main entrance; the last tour's an hour before closing.

St Paul's Cathedral CATHEDRAL
(Map p74; www.stpauls.co.uk; adult/child £12.50/4.50; ⌚8.30am-4pm Mon-Sat; ⊖St Paul's) Dominating the City with a dome second in size only to St Peter's in Rome, St Paul's Cathedral was designed by Wren after the Great Fire and built between 1675 and 1710. Four other cathedrals preceded it on this site, the first dating from 604.

The dome is renowned for somehow dodging the bombs during the Blitz and became an icon of the resilience shown in the capital during WWII. Outside the cathedral, to the north, is a **monument to the people of London**, a simple and elegant memorial to the 32,000 Londoners who weren't so lucky.

Inside, some 30m above the main paved area, is the first of three domes (actually a dome inside a cone inside a dome) supported by eight huge columns. The walkway round its base is called the **Whispering Gallery**, because if you talk close to the wall, your words will carry to the opposite side 32m away. It can be reached by a staircase on the western side of the southern transept (9.30am to 3.30pm only). There are 528 lung-busting steps to the **Golden Gallery** at the very top, and an unforgettable view of London.

The **Crypt** has memorials to up to 300 military demigods, including Wellington, Kitchener and Nelson, whose body lies below the dome. But the most poignant memorial is to Wren himself. On a simple slab bearing his name, a Latin inscription translates as: 'If you seek his memorial, look about you'.

Audio tours lasting 45 minutes are available for £4. Guided tours (adult/child £3/1) leave the tour desk at 10.45am, 11.15am, 1.30pm and 2pm (90 minutes). Evensong takes place at 5pm (3.15pm on Sunday).

Tower Bridge LANDMARK
London was still a thriving port in 1894 when elegant Tower Bridge was built. Designed to be raised to allow ships to pass, electricity has now taken over from the original steam engines. A lift leads up from the northern tower to the overpriced **Tower Bridge Exhibition** (Map p74; www.towerbridge.org.uk; adult/child £7/3; ⌚10am-5.30pm Apr-Sep, 9.30am-5pm Oct-Mar; ⊖Tower Hill), where the story of its building is recounted within the upper walkway. The same ticket gets you into the engine

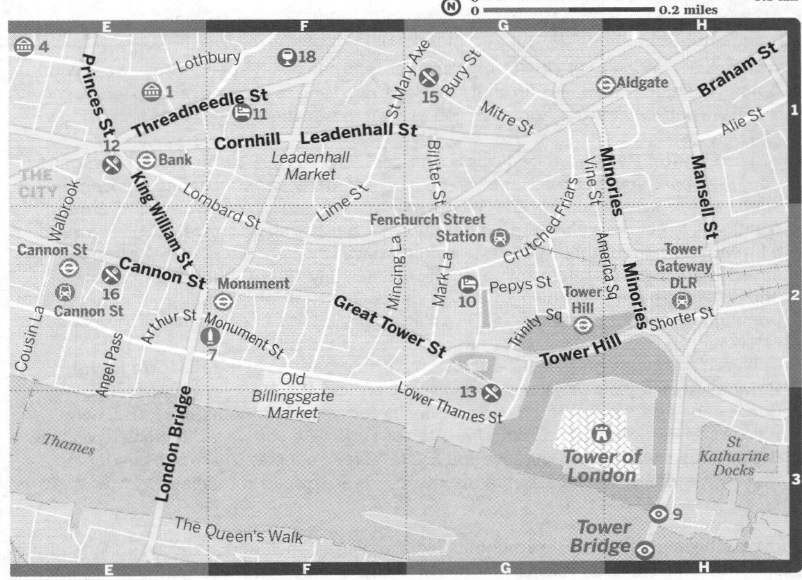

The City

Top Sights
Shakespeare's Globe D3
St Paul's Cathedral C1
Tower Bridge H3
Tower of London G3

Sights
1 Bank of England Museum E1
2 Dr Johnson's House A1
3 Fleet St A1
4 Guildhall E1
5 Inner Temple A1
6 Middle Temple A2
7 Monument F2
8 Temple Church A1
9 Tower Bridge Exhibition H3

Sleeping
10 Apex City of London G2
11 Threadneedles F1

Eating
12 1 Lombard Street E1
13 GBK G3
14 Hummus Brothers D1
15 Konditor & Cook G1
16 Leon E2
17 Wagamama D2
Wagamama ..... (see 13)

Drinking
18 Vertigo 42 ..... F1
19 Ye Old Watling D1
20 Ye Olde Cheshire Cheese B1

rooms below the southern tower. Below the bridge on the City side is Dead Man's Hole, where corpses that had made their way into the Thames (through suicide, murder or accident) were regularly retrieved.

FREE **Museum of London** MUSEUM (www.museumoflondon.org.uk; 150 London Wall EC2; ⏲10am-6pm; ⊖Barbican) Visiting the fascinating Museum of London early in your stay helps to make sense of the layers of history that make up this place. The Roman section, in particular, illustrates how the modern is grafted onto the ancient; several of the city's main thoroughfares were once Roman roads, for instance.

The museum's £20 million Galleries of Modern London opened in 2010, encompassing everything from 1666 (the Great Fire) to the present day. While the Lord Mayor's ceremonial coach is the centrepiece, an

POUND SAVERS

As many of London's very best sights are free, you can easily spend a busy week without paying much on admission charges. However, if you're hanging around for longer and have particular attractions that you're keen to see, there are options for saving a few pounds.

The **London Pass** (www.londonpass.com; per 1/2/3/6 days £40/55/68/90) is a smart card that gains you fast-track entry to 55 different attractions, including pricier ones such as the Tower of London and St Paul's Cathedral. You'd have to be racing around frantically to get real value from a one-day pass, but you could conceivably save quite a bit with the two- or three-day version. You'll have to weigh up whether the money saved justifies the cramming of so much into each day. Passes can be booked online and collected from the Britain & London Visitor Centre. They also sell a version with a preloaded Transport For London (TFL) travel pass, but it's cheaper to buy this separately.

If you're a royalty buff, taking out an annual membership to the **Historic Royal Palaces** (www.hrp.org.uk; individual/joint membership £41/63) allows you to jump the queues and visit the Tower of London, Kensington Palace, Banqueting House, Kew Palace and Hampton Court Palace as often as you like. If you were intending to visit all five anyway, membership will save you £12 (£43 for a couple). There can be a lengthy wait for membership cards, but temporary cards are issued immediately.

effort has been made to create an immersive experience: you can enter reconstructions of an 18th-century debtors' prison, a Georgian pleasure garden and a Victorian street.

FREE **Guildhall** HISTORIC BUILDING

(Map p74; ☎020-7606 3030; www.guildhall.cityoflondon.gov.uk; Gresham St EC2; ⊙10am-4pm unless in use; ⊖Bank) Plum in the middle of the 'square mile', the Guildhall has been the seat of the City's local government for eight centuries. The present building dates from the early 15th century.

Visitors can see the **Great Hall**, where the city's mayor is sworn in and where important fellows like the Tsar of Russia and the Prince Regent celebrated beating Napoleon. It's an impressive space decorated with the shields and banners of London's 12 principal livery companies, carved galleries (the west of which is protected by disturbing statues of giants Gog and Magog) and a beautiful oak-panelled roof. There's also a lovely bronze statue of Churchill sitting in a comfy chair. Beneath it is London's largest **medieval crypt** (visit by free guided tour only, bookings essential), with 19 stained-glass windows showing the livery companies' coats of arms.

The **Clockmakers' Museum** (admission free; ⊙9.30am-4.45pm Mon-Sat) charts 500 years of timekeeping with more than 600 ticking exhibits, and the **Guildhall Art Gallery** (adult/child £2.50/1; ⊙10am-5pm Mon-Sat, noon-4pm Sun) displays around 250 artworks. Included in the art gallery admission is entry to the remains of an ancient **Roman amphitheatre**, which lay forgotten beneath this site until 1988.

FREE **Bank of England Museum** MUSEUM

(Map p74; www.bankofengland.co.uk/museum; Bartholomew Lane EC2; ⊙10am-5pm Mon-Fri; ⊖Bank) Guardian of the country's financial system, the Bank of England was established in 1694 when the government needed to raise cash to support a war with France. It was moved here in 1734 and largely renovated by Sir John Soane. The surprisingly interesting museum traces the history of the bank and banking system. Audio guides are free and you even get to pick up a £230,000 gold bar.

Monument MEMORIAL

(Map p74; www.themonument.info; Monument St; adult/child £3/1; ⊙9.30am-5.30pm; ⊖Monument) Designed by Wren to commemorate the Great Fire, the Monument is 60.6m high, the exact distance from its base to the bakery on Pudding Lane where the blaze began. Climb the 311 tight spiral steps (not advised for claustrophobes) for an eye-watering view from beneath the symbolic vase of gold-leaf flames.

Dr Johnson's House MUSEUM

(Map p74; www.drjohnsonshouse.org; 17 Gough Sq EC4; adult/child £4.50/1.50; ⊙11am-5pm Mon-Sat; ⊖Chancery Lane) The Georgian house where Samuel Johnson and his assistants compiled the first English dictionary (between 1748 and 1759) is full of prints and portraits of friends and intimates, including the good doctor's Jamaican servant to whom he bequeathed this grand residence.

Inns of Court HISTORIC BUILDINGS
All London barristers work from within one of the four atmospheric Inns of Court, positioned between the walls of the old City and Westminster. It would take a lifetime working here to grasp all the intricacies of their arcane protocols, originating in the 13th-century. It's best just to soak up the dreamy ambience of the alleys and open spaces and thank your lucky stars you're not one of the bewigged barristers scurrying about. A roll call of former members would include the likes of Oliver Cromwell, Charles Dickens, Mahatma Gandhi and Margaret Thatcher.

Lincoln's Inn (Map p108; www.lincolnsinn.org.uk; Lincoln's Inn Fields WC2; ⏲grounds 9am-6pm Mon-Fri, chapel & gardens noon-2.30pm Mon-Fri; ⊖Holborn) still has some original 15th-century buildings. It's the oldest and most attractive of the bunch, with a 17th-century chapel and pretty landscaped gardens.

Gray's Inn (Map p108; www.graysinn.org.uk; Gray's Inn Rd WC1; ⏲grounds 10am-4pm Mon-Fri; ⊖Chancery Lane) was largely rebuilt after the Luftwaffe levelled it.

Middle Temple (Map p74; www.middletemple.org.uk; Middle Temple Lane EC4; ⏲10-11.30am & 3-4pm Mon-Fri; ⊖Temple) and **Inner Temple** (Map p74; www.innertemple.org.uk; King's Bench Walk EC4; ⏲10am-4pm Mon-Fri; ⊖Temple) both sit between Fleet St and Victoria Embankment. The former is the better preserved, while the latter is home to the intriguing 12th-century **Temple Church** (Map p74; ☎020-7353 8559; www.templechurch.com; ⏲hours vary), built by the Knights Templar and featuring nine stone effigies of knights in its round chapel. Check the church's website or call ahead for opening hours.

Fleet St FAMOUS THOROUGHFARE
(Map p74; ⊖Temple) As 20th-century London's 'Street of Shame', Fleet St was synonymous with the UK's scurrilous tabloids until the mid-1980s, when the press barons embraced computer technology, ditched a load of staff and largely relocated to the Docklands. It's named after the River Fleet, which it once crossed. This substantial river was a major feature of the London landscape until the 18th century, when it was relegated to the sewers. It now flows subterraneously from Hampstead Heath and joins the Thames near Blackfriars Bridge.

St Katharine Docks HARBOUR
(Map p74; ⊖Tower Hill) A centre of trade and commerce for 1000 years, St Katharine Docks is now a buzzing waterside area of pleasure boats, shops and eateries. It was badly damaged during the war, but survivors include the popular **Dickens Inn**, with its original 18th-century timber framework, and **Ivory House** (built 1854) which used to store ivory, perfume and other precious goods.

SOUTH BANK

Londoners once crossed the river to the area controlled by the licentious Bishops of Southwark for all kinds of raunchy diversions frowned upon in the City. It's a much more seemly area now, but the theatre and entertainment tradition remains. While South Bank only technically refers to the area of river bank between Westminster and Blackfriars Bridges (parts of which are actually on the east bank due to the way the river bends), we've used it as a convenient catch-all for those parts of Southwark and Lambeth that sit closest to the river. In reality you'll find that many Londoners refer to sections of this largish stretch by the nearest tube station, especially Waterloo, Borough and London Bridge.

Tate Modern GALLERY
(Map p82; www.tate.org.uk; Queen's Walk SE1; ⏲10am-6pm Sun-Thu, to 10pm Fri & Sat; ⊖Southwark) It's hard to miss this surprisingly elegant former power station on the side of the river, which is fortunate as the tremendous Tate Modern really shouldn't be missed. Focusing on modern art in all its wacky and wonderful permutations, it's been extraordinarily successful in bringing

TATE-A-TATE

To get between London's Tate galleries in style, the **Tate Boat** (www.thamesclippers.com) will whisk you from one to the other, stopping en route at the London Eye. Services run from 10.10am to 5.28pm daily at 40-minute intervals. A River Roamer hop-on/hop-off ticket (purchased on board) costs £12; single tickets are £5.

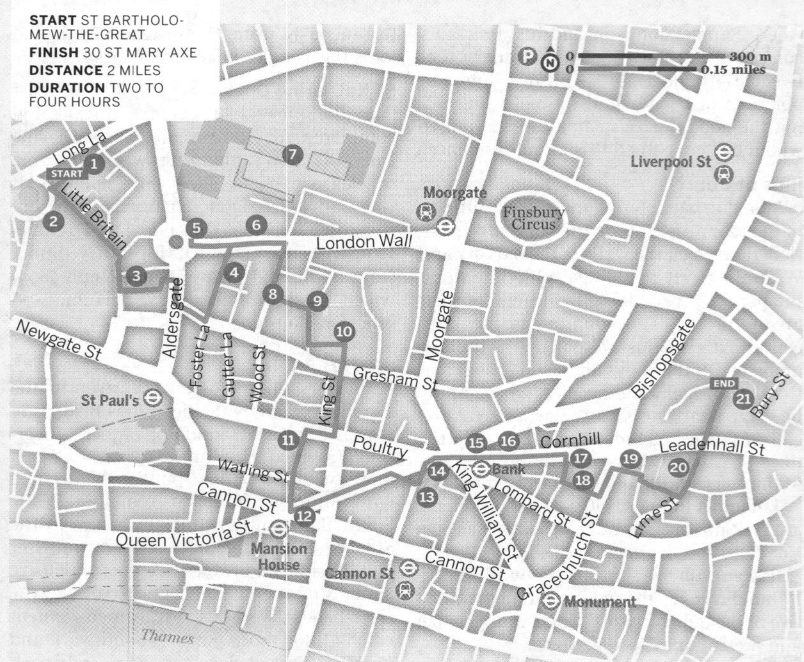

Walking Tour

City of London

The City of London has as much history and interesting architecture in its square mile as the rest of London put together. This tour focuses on the City's hidden delights (secluded parks, charming churches) in a journey from the ancient to the ultramodern.

It's fitting to start at 1 **St Bartholomew-the-Great**, as this fascinating 12th-century church was once a pilgrimage stop for travellers to London. In more recent times, it's been used for scenes in *Four Weddings & A Funeral, Shakespeare In Love* and *Sherlock Holmes*.

Head out through the Tudor gatehouse. In the distance you'll see the Victorian arches of Smithfield's meat market, which has occupied this site just north of the old city walls for 800 years. Executions were held here, most famously the burning of Protestants under Mary I and the grisly killing of Scottish hero William Wallace (Braveheart) in 1305; a plaque on the front of 2 **St Bartholomew's Hospital** commemorates him. Also note the shrapnel damage to the wall – the legacy of an attack in 1916 by a German Zeppelin.

Head back towards the gate and turn right into Little Britain. Follow it as it curves to the right and look out for the large oak marking the entrance to 3 **Postman's Park**. This lovely space includes a touching legacy of Victorian socialism: a tiled wall celebrating everyday heroes.

Turn right at the end of the park, then left and left again into Noble St. You're now inside what was once the old City's 4 **walls**, remnants of which you'll pass on your left. Commenced in Roman times, the fortifications were demolished in the 18th and 19th centuries, but the shape of them can be traced in street names such as Newgate, Moorgate, Bishopsgate and Aldgate. This section was only uncovered after WWII bombs destroyed the buildings covering it. Take the stairs up to the footbridge crossing the street called London Wall towards the 5 **Museum of London** (p75). The museum's Roman section will give you a feel for the layout of the City.

Turn left when leaving the museum and follow the Highwalk. On your left you'll see 6 **ruins** of the barbicans (defensive towers) that once guarded the northwestern corner of the walls, with the 7 **Barbican Centre** behind them. Like Marmite, you either love or hate the concrete Barbican. Parts of it are extraordinarily ugly, particularly the forbidding high-rise tower blocks (romantically named Shakespeare, Cromwell and Lauderdale). However, in 2001 the complex became heritage-listed and more people are admitting to finding beauty in its curved roofs, brightly planted window boxes and large central 'lake'. At the time of its construction, this vast complex of offices and residences was revolutionary. At its heart is an arts centre consisting of concert halls, cinemas, galleries, eateries, a library and a school. It was designed by Chamberlain, Powell and Bon, disciples of Le Corbusier, to fill a WWII bomb–pummelled space with democratic modern housing. Sadly this dream never really materialised, and today around 80% of the flats are privately owned.

Follow the painted lines on the Highwalk for a closer look, or turn right at Pizza Express, take the escalator down to Wood St and head towards the remaining tower of 8 **St Alban's**, a Wren-designed church destroyed in WWII. Turn left and you'll find a sweet garden on the site of 9 **St Mary Aldermansbury**, capped by a bust of Shakespeare. The 12th-century church was ruined in the war then shipped to Missouri where it was re-erected.

Turn right on to Aldermansbury and head to the 10 **Guildhall** (p76). Take King St down to Cheapside, cross the road and head right to elegant 11 **St Mary-le-Bow**. The church was rebuilt by Wren after the Great Fire, and then rebuilt again after WWII. The term 'Cockney' traditionally refers to someone born within the sound of this church's bell.

Backtrack to Bow Lane and follow this narrow path to beautiful 12 **St Mary Aldermary**, rebuilt in the Perpendicular Gothic style in 1682 following the fire. Turn left on to Queen Victoria St and then right into Bucklersbury, where you'll see 13 **St Stephen's Walbrook** directly in front of you. In the 3rd century, a Roman temple stood here, and in the 7th century a Saxon church. Rebuilt after the Great Fire, the current St Stephen's is one of Wren's greatest masterpieces, with elegant Corinthian columns supporting a beautifully proportioned dome. Henry Moore sculpted the round central altar from travertine marble in 1972.

Leaving the church, you'll pass 14 **Mansion House**, built in 1752 as the official residence of the Lord Mayor. As you approach the busy Bank intersection, lined with neoclassical temples to commerce, you might think you've stumbled into the ancient Roman forum (the actual forum was a couple of blocks east). Head for the 15 **equestrian statue of the Iron Duke**, behind which a metal pyramid details the many significant buildings here. Directly behind you is the 16 **Royal Exchange**; walk through it and exit through the door on the right, then turn left onto Cornhill.

If you're not churched out, cross the road to 17 **St Michael's**, a 1672 Wren design that still has its box pews. Hidden in the warren of tiny passages behind the church is its 18 **churchyard**. Head through to Gracechurch St, turn left and cross the road to wonderful 19 **Leadenhall Market**. This is roughly where the ancient forum once stood. As you wander out the far end, the famous 20 **Lloyd's building** displays its innards for all to see.

Once you turn left onto Lime St, you'll see ahead of you Norman Foster's 180m 21 **30 St Mary Axe building**. Its dramatic curved shape has given birth to many nicknames (the Crystal Phallus, the Towering Innuendo), but it's the Gherkin by which it's fondly referred. Built nearly 900 years after St Bartholomew-the-Great, it's testimony to the City's ability to constantly reinvent itself for the times.

South Bank – Around Waterloo Station

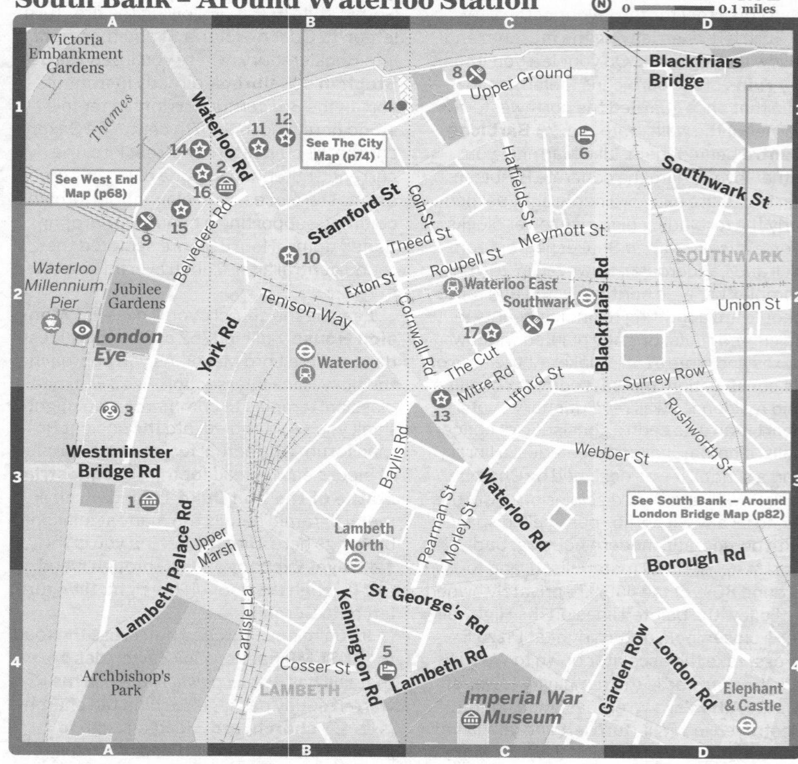

challenging work to the masses, becoming one of London's most popular attractions.

Outstanding temporary exhibitions (on the 4th floor; prices vary) continue to spark excitement, as does the periodically changing large-scale installation in the vast Turbine Hall. The permanent collection is organised into four themed sections, which change periodically but include works by the likes of Mark Rothko, Pablo Picasso, Francis Bacon, Roy Lichtenstein, Andy Warhol and Tracey Emin.

The multimedia guides (£3.50) are worthwhile for their descriptions of selected works, and there are free guided tours of the collection's highlights (Level 3 at 11am and midday; Level 5 at 2pm and 3pm). Make sure you cop the view from the top floor's restaurant and bar.

Shakespeare's Globe HISTORIC THEATRE
(Map p82; ☎020-7401 9919; www.shakespeares-globe.org; 21 New Globe Walk SE1; adult/child £11/7; ⏰10am-5pm; ⊖London Bridge) Today's Londoners might grab a budget flight to Amsterdam to behave badly. Back in Shakespeare's time they'd cross London Bridge to Southwark. Free from the city's constraints, they could hook up with a prostitute, watch a bear being tortured for their amusement and then head to a theatre. The most famous of them was the Globe, where a clever fellow was producing box-office smashes like *Macbeth* and *Hamlet*.

Originally built in 1599, the Globe burnt down in 1613 and was immediately rebuilt. The Puritans, who regarded theatres as dreadful dens of iniquity, eventually closed it in 1642. Its present incarnation was the vision of American actor and director Sam Wanamaker, who sadly died before the opening night in 1997.

Admission includes a guided tour of the open-roofed theatre, faithfully reconstructed from oak beams, handmade bricks, lime

South Bank – Around Waterloo Station

Top Sights
Imperial War Museum C4
London Eye A2

Sights
1 Florence Nightingale Museum A3
2 Hayward Gallery B1
3 Sea Life A3

Activities, Courses & Tours
4 London Bicycle Tour Company B1
London Duck Tours Departure Point .... (see 3)

Sleeping
5 Captain Bligh House B4
6 Mad Hatter Hotel C1

Eating
7 Anchor & Hope C2
8 Oxo Tower Brasserie C1
Ping Pong .... (see 15)
9 Wagamama A2

Entertainment
10 BFI IMAX B2
11 BFI Southbank B1
12 National Theatre B1
13 Old Vic C3
Purcell Room .... (see 14)
14 Queen Elizabeth Hall A1
15 Royal Festival Hall A2
16 Southbank Centre A1
17 Young Vic C2

plaster and thatch. There's also an extensive exhibition about Shakespeare and his times.

From April to October plays are performed, and while Shakespeare and his contemporaries dominate, modern plays are also staged (see the website for upcoming performances). As in Elizabethan times, 'groundlings' can watch proceedings for a modest price (£5; seats are £15 to £35). There's no protection from the elements and you'll have to stand, but it's a memorable experience.

London Eye RIDE, VIEWPOINT
(Map p80; ☎0871 781 3000; www.londoneye.com; adult/child £18/9.50; ⏲10am-8pm; ⊖Waterloo) It may seem a bit Mordor-ish to have a giant eye overlooking the city, but the London Eye doesn't actually resemble an eye at all, and, in a city where there's a CCTV camera on every other corner, it's probably only fitting. Originally designed as a temporary structure to celebrate the millennium, the Eye is now a permanent addition to the cityscape, joining Big Ben as one of London's most distinctive landmarks.

This 135m-tall, slow-moving Ferris-wheel-like attraction is the largest of its kind in the world. Passengers ride in an enclosed egg-shaped pod; the wheel takes 30 minutes to rotate completely and offers 25-mile views on a clear day. Visits are preceded by a short '4D' film offering a seagull's view of London, enhanced with bubbles, rain and snow.

Book your ticket online to speed up your wait (you also get a 20% discount), or you can pay an additional £10 to jump the queue. Joint tickets for the London Eye and Madame Tussauds (adult/child £43/31) are available, as is a 40-minute, sightseeing **River Cruise** (adult/child £12/6) with a multilingual commentary.

FREE **Imperial War Museum** MUSEUM
(Map p80; www.iwm.org.uk; Lambeth Rd SE1; ⏲10am-6pm; ⊖Lambeth North) You don't have to be a lad to appreciate the Imperial War Museum and its spectacular atrium with *Spitfires* hanging from the ceiling, rockets (including the massive German V2), field guns, missiles, submarines, tanks, torpedoes and other military hardware. Providing a telling lesson in modern history, highlights include a recreated WWI trench and WWII bomb shelter as well as a Holocaust exhibition.

Old Operating Theatre Museum & Herb Garret MUSEUM
(Map p82; www.thegarret.org.uk; 9A St Thomas St SE1; adult/child £5.80/3.25; ⏲10.30am-4.45pm; ⊖London Bridge) One of London's most genuinely gruesome attractions, the Old Operating Theatre Museum is Britain's only surviving 19th-century operating theatre, rediscovered in 1956 within the garret of a church. The display of primitive surgical tools is suitably terrifying, while the pickled bits of humans are just unpleasant.

It's a hands-on kind of place, with signs saying 'please touch', although obviously the pointy things are locked away. For a more intense experience, check the website for the regular 20-minute 'special events'.

South Bank – Around London Bridge

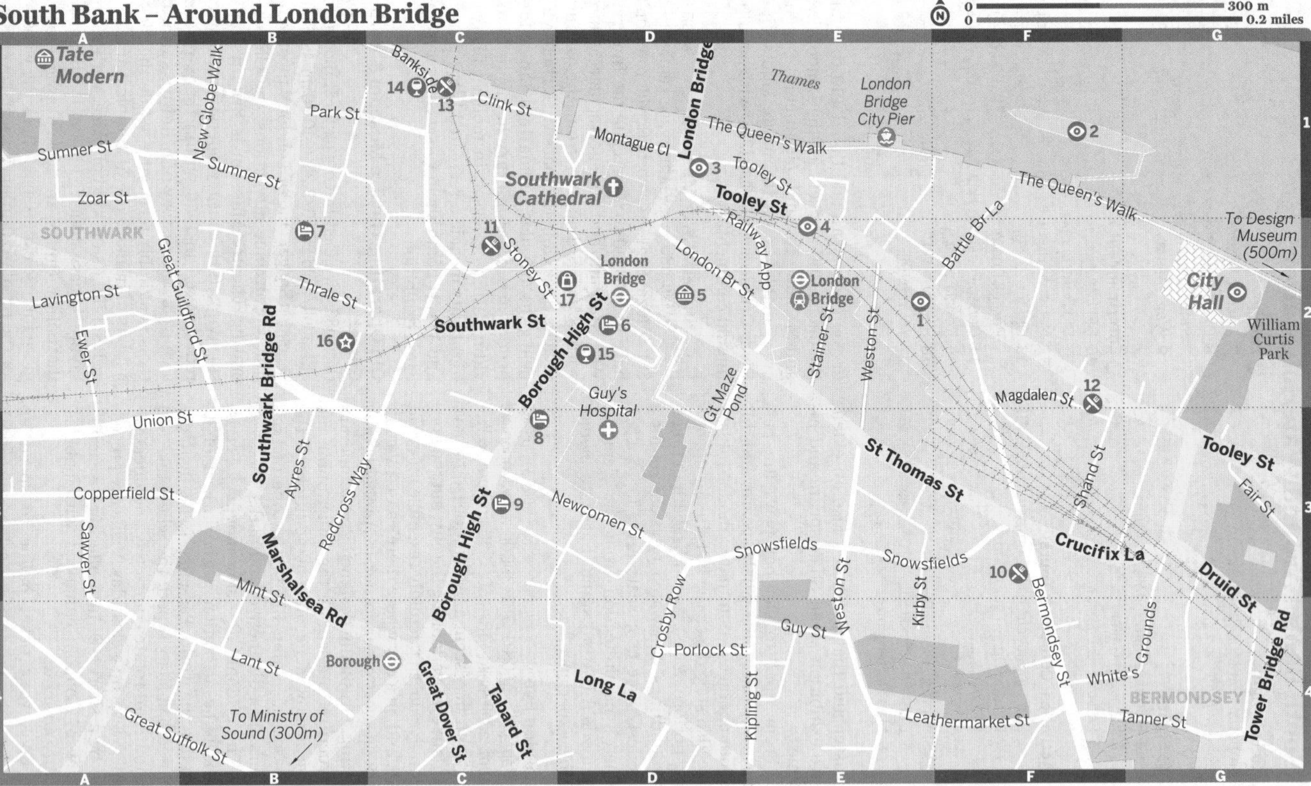

South Bank – Around London Bridge

Top Sights
City Hall G2
Southwark Cathedral D1
Tate Modern A1

Sights
1 Britain at War Experience E2
2 HMS Belfast F1
3 London Bridge Experience & London Tombs D1
4 London Dungeon E2
5 Old Operating Theatre Museum & Herb Garret D2

Sleeping
6 Orient Express D2
7 Southwark Rose Hotel B2
8 St Christopher's Inn C3
9 St Christopher's Village C3

Eating
10 Delfina F3
GBK .... (see 13)
11 Konditor & Cook C2
12 Magdalen F2
13 Wagamama C1

Drinking
14 Anchor C1
15 George Inn D2
Monmouth Coffee Company .... (see 11)

Entertainment
16 Menier Chocolate Factory B2

Shopping
17 Borough Market D2

Southwark Cathedral CATHEDRAL
(Map p82; www.southwark.anglican.org/cathedral; Montague Close SE1; suggested donation £4-6.50; 8am-6pm; London Bridge) Although the central tower dates from 1520 and the choir from the 13th century, Southwark Cathedral is largely Victorian. Inside are monuments galore, including a Shakespeare Memorial. Catch evensong at 5.30pm on Tuesdays, Thursdays and Fridays, 4pm on Saturdays and 3pm on Sundays.

City Hall LANDMARK
(Map p82; www.london.gov.uk; Queen's Walk SE1; 8.30am-6pm Mon-Fri; London Bridge) The Norman Foster–designed, wonky-egg-shaped City Hall is an architectural feast and home to the mayor's office, the London Assembly and the Greater London Assembly (GLA). Visitors can see the mayor's meeting chamber and attend debates.

Design Museum MUSEUM
(www.designmuseum.org; 28 Shad Thames SE1; adult/child £8.50/5; 10am-5.45pm; Tower Hill) The whiter-than-white Design Museum is a must for anyone interested in beautiful, practical things. The permanent collection has displays of modern British design and there are also regular temporary exhibitions including the annual Designs of the Year competition. To get here from Tower Bridge, head east along Shad Thames, an evocative lane between old warehouses.

HMS Belfast SHIP
(Map p82; http://hmsbelfast.iwm.org.uk; Queen's Walk SE1; adult/child £13/free; 10am-5pm; London Bridge) Launched in 1938, HMS *Belfast* took part in the D-Day landings and saw action in Korea. Explore the nine decks and see the engine room, gun decks, galley, chapel, punishment cells, canteen and dental surgery.

Britain at War Experience MUSEUM
(Map p82; www.britainatwar.co.uk; 64-66 Tooley St SE1; adult/child £13/5.50; 10am-5pm Apr-Oct, to 4.30pm Nov-Mar) You can pop down to the London Underground air-raid shelter, look at gas masks and ration books, stroll around Southwark during the Blitz and learn about the battle on the home front. It's crammed with fascinating WWII memorabilia.

London Dungeon FRIGHT EXPERIENCE
(Map p82; 020-7403 7221; www.thedungeons.com; 28-34 Tooley St SE1; adult/child £20/15; 10.30am-5pm, extended during holidays; London Bridge) Older kids tend to love the London Dungeon, as the terrifying queues during school holidays and weekends testify. It's all spooky music, ghostly boat rides, macabre hangman's drop-rides, fake blood and actors dressed up as torturers and gory criminals (including Jack the Ripper and Sweeney Todd). Beware the interactive bits.

London Bridge Experience & London Tombs FRIGHT EXPERIENCE

(Map p82; www.thelondonbridgeexperience.com; 2-4 Tooley St SE1; adult/child £22/17; ⏲10am-5pm; ⊖London Bridge) Another coronary-inducing attraction, similar to but not related to nearby London Dungeon, this one starts with the relatively tame London Bridge Experience, where actors bring to life the bridge's history with the assistance of plenty of severed heads. Once the entertaining educational bit is out the way, the London Tombs turns up the terror. Adding to the general creepiness is the knowledge that these were once plague pits and therefore actual tombs. The experience takes about 45 minutes, with the tombs an optional additional 25 minutes. Tickets are much cheaper if bought in advance online.

Florence Nightingale Museum MUSEUM

(Map p80; www.florence-nightingale.co.uk; 2 Lambeth Palace Rd SE1; adult/child £5.80/4.80; ⏲10am-5pm; ⊖Waterloo) The thought-provoking Florence Nightingale Museum recounts the story of 'the lady with the lamp' who led a team of nurses during the Crimean War. She established a training school for nurses here at St Thomas' Hospital in 1859.

Sea Life AQUARIUM

(Map p80; ☎0871 663 1678; www.sealife.co.uk/london; County Hall SE1; adult/child £18/13; ⏲10am-6pm; ⊖Waterloo) One of the largest aquariums in Europe, Sea Life has all sorts of aquatic creatures organised into different zones (coral cave, rainforest, River Thames), culminating with the shark walkway. Check the website for shark-feeding times and book online for a 10% discount.

Hayward Gallery GALLERY

(Map p80; www.southbankcentre.co.uk; Belvedere Rd SE1; admission prices vary; ⏲10am-6pm Sat-Thu, to 10pm Fri; ⊖Waterloo) Part of the Southbank Centre, the Hayward hosts a changing roster of contemporary art (video, installations, photography, collage, painting etc) in a 1960s Brutalist building.

PIMLICO

Handy to the big sights but lacking a strong sense of neighbourhood, the streets get prettier the further you stray from Victoria station.

FREE **Tate Britain** GALLERY

(www.tate.org.uk; Millbank SW1; ⏲10am-5.40pm; ⊖Pimlico) Unlike the National Gallery, Britannia rules the walls of Tate Britain. Reaching from 1500 to the present, it's crammed with local heavyweights like Blake, Hogarth, Gainsborough, Whistler, Spencer and, especially, Turner, whose work dominates the **Clore Gallery**. His 'interrupted visions' – unfinished canvasses of moody skies – wouldn't look out of place in the contemporary section alongside the work of David Hockney, Francis Bacon, Tracey Emin, Angela Bulloch and Damien Hirst. The always-controversial annual Turner Prize is exhibited in the gallery from October to January.

There are free hour-long guided tours, taking in different sections of the gallery, held daily at midday and 3pm (as well as 11am and 2pm on weekdays). The popular **Rex Whistler Restaurant** (☎020-7887 8825; mains £14-21), featuring an impressive mural from the artist, is open for breakfast, lunch and snacks.

CHELSEA & KENSINGTON

Known as the royal borough, residents of Chelsea and Kensington are certainly paid royally, earning the highest incomes in the UK (shops and restaurants will presume you do, too). Kensington High St has a lively mix of chains and boutiques. Thanks to the surplus generated by the 1851 Great Exhibition, which allowed the purchase of a great chunk of land, South Kensington boasts some of London's most beautiful and interesting museums all on one road.

FREE **Victoria & Albert Museum** MUSEUM

(V&A; Map p86; www.vam.ac.uk; Cromwell Rd SW7; ⏲10am-5.45pm Sat-Thu, to 10pm Fri; ⊖South Kensington) A vast, rambling and wonderful museum of decorative art and design, the V&A is part of Prince Albert's legacy to Londoners in the wake of the Great Exhibition. It's a bit like the nation's attic, comprising four million objects collected from Britain and around the globe. Spread over nearly 150 galleries, it houses the world's greatest collection of decorative arts, including ancient Chinese ceramics, modernist architectural drawings, Korean bronzes, Japanese swords, cartoons by Raphael, spellbinding Asian statues and Islamic carpets, Rodin sculptures, actual-size reproductions of famous European architecture and sculpture (including Michelangelo's *David*), Elizabethan gowns, ancient jewellery, an all-wooden Frank Lloyd Wright study and a pair of Doc Martens. Yes, you'll need to plan. To top it all off, it's a fabulous building, with an attractive garden cafe as well as the original, lavishly decorated V&A cafe.

Natural History Museum MUSEUM
(Map p86; www.nhm.ac.uk; Cromwell Rd SW7; admission free; ⏲10am-5.50pm; ⊖South Kensington) Let's start with the building itself: stripes of pale blue and honey-coloured stone are broken by Venetian arches decorated with all manner of carved critters. Quite simply, it's one of London's finest.

A sure-fire hit with kids of all ages, the Natural History Museum is crammed full of interesting stuff, starting with the giant dinosaur skeleton that greets you in the main hall. In the dinosaur section, the fleshless fossils are brought to robotic life with a very realistic 4m-high animatronic Tyrannosaurus Rex and his smaller, but no less sinister-looking, cousins.

The other galleries are equally impressive. An escalator slithers up and into a hollowed-out globe where two exhibits – The Power Within and Restless Surface – explain how wind, water, ice, gravity and life itself impact on the earth. For parents unsure of how to broach the facts of life, a quick whiz around the Human Biology section should do the trick.

The **Darwin Centre** houses a team of biologists and a staggering 20-million-plus species of animal and plant specimens. Take a lift to the top of the Cocoon, a seven-storey egg-shaped structure encased within a glass pavilion, and make your way down through the floors of interactive displays. Glass windows allow you to watch the scientists at work.

FREE **Science Museum** MUSEUM
(Map p86; www.sciencemuseum.org.uk; Exhibition Rd SW7; ⏲10am-6pm; ⊖South Kensington) With seven floors of interactive and educational exhibits, the Science Museum covers everything from the Industrial Revolution to the exploration of space. There is something for all ages, from vintage cars, trains and aeroplanes to labour-saving devices for the home, a wind tunnel and flight simulator. Kids love the interactive sections. There's also a 450-seat **Imax cinema**.

Kensington Palace PALACE
(Map p104; www.hrp.org.uk/Kensingtonpalace; Kensington Gardens W8; adult/child £13/6.25; ⏲10am-6pm; ⊖High St Kensington) Kensington Palace (1605) became the favourite royal residence under the joint reign of William and Mary and remained so until George III became king and moved across the park to Buckingham Palace. It still has private apartments where various members of the royal extended family live. In popular imagination it's most associated with three intriguing princesses: Victoria (who was born here in 1819 and lived here with her domineering mother until her accession to the throne), Margaret (sister of the current queen, who lived here until her 2002 death) and, of course, Diana. More than a million bouquets were left outside the gates following her death in 1997.

The building is undergoing major restoration work until January 2012. Rather than closing completely, sections of the palace have been transformed into a giant art installation. Leading artists and fashion designers have been given free rein to create their own enchanted spaces within the ornately painted and gilded rooms, which are changed every six months. All museum-like elements have been removed – there are no information panels, display cases, audio guides or tours. If you're hungry for historical information, ask the warders, who have been rebranded 'explainers' for this very purpose.

Kensington Gardens PARK
(Map p104; ⏲dawn-dusk; ⊖Queensway) Blending in with Hyde Park, these royal gardens are part of Kensington Palace and hence popularly associated with Princess Diana. Diana devotees can visit the **Diana, Princess of Wales Memorial Playground** in its northwest corner, a much more restrained royal remembrance than the over-the-top **Albert Memorial** (Map p86). The latter is a lavish marble, mosaic and gold affair opposite the Royal Albert Hall, built to honour Queen Victoria's husband, Albert (1819–61).

The gardens also house the **Serpentine Gallery** (Map p86; www.serpentinegallery.org; admission free; ⏲10am-6pm), one of London's edgiest contemporary art spaces. The **Sunken Garden** (Map p104), near the palace, is at its prettiest in summer, while tea in the **Orangery** (Map p104) is a treat any time of the year.

Hyde Park PARK
(Map p86; ⏲5.30am-midnight; ⊖Marble Arch, Hyde Park Corner or Queensway) At 145 hectares, Hyde Park is central London's largest open space. Henry VIII expropriated it from the Church in 1536, when it became a hunting ground and later a venue for duels, executions and horse racing. The 1851 Great Exhibition was held here, and during WWII the park became an enormous potato field. These days, it serves as an occasional concert venue and a

Knightsbridge, South Kensington & Chelsea

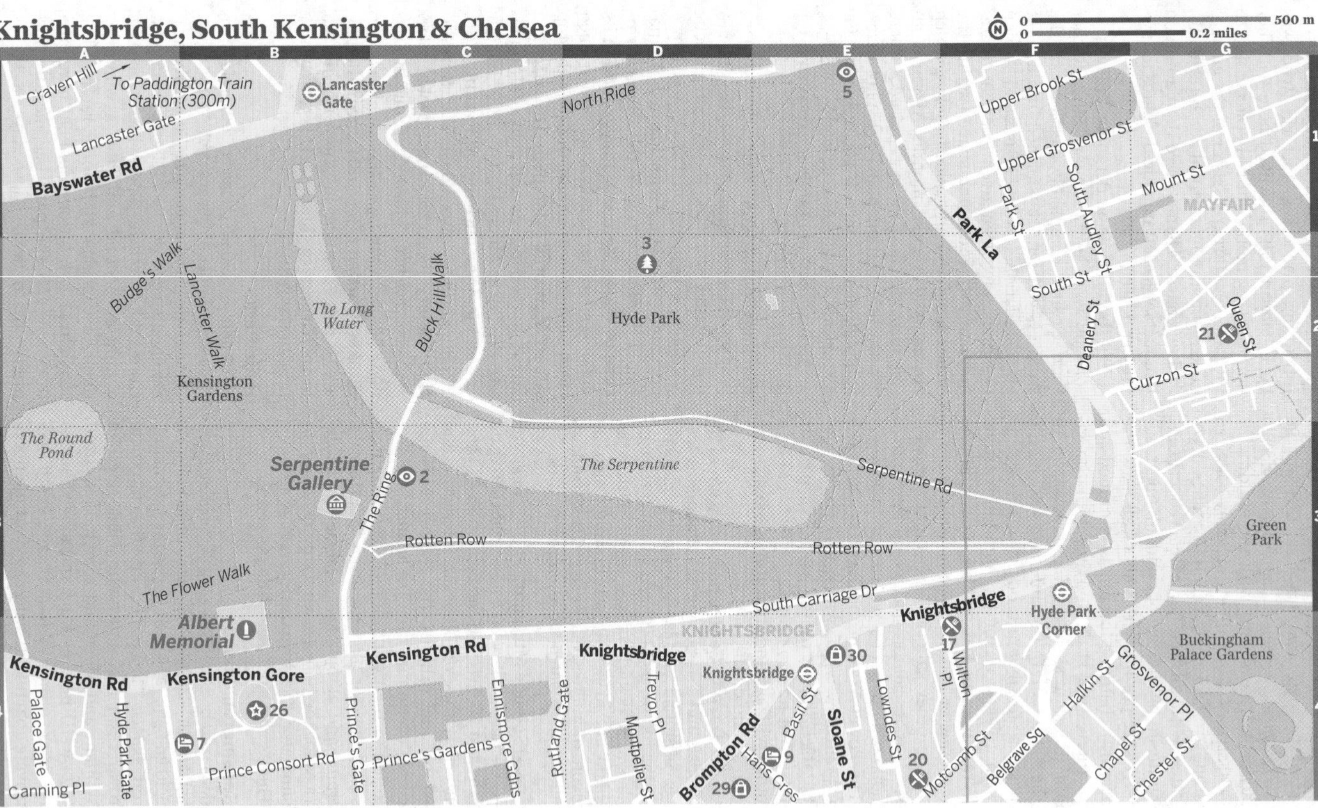

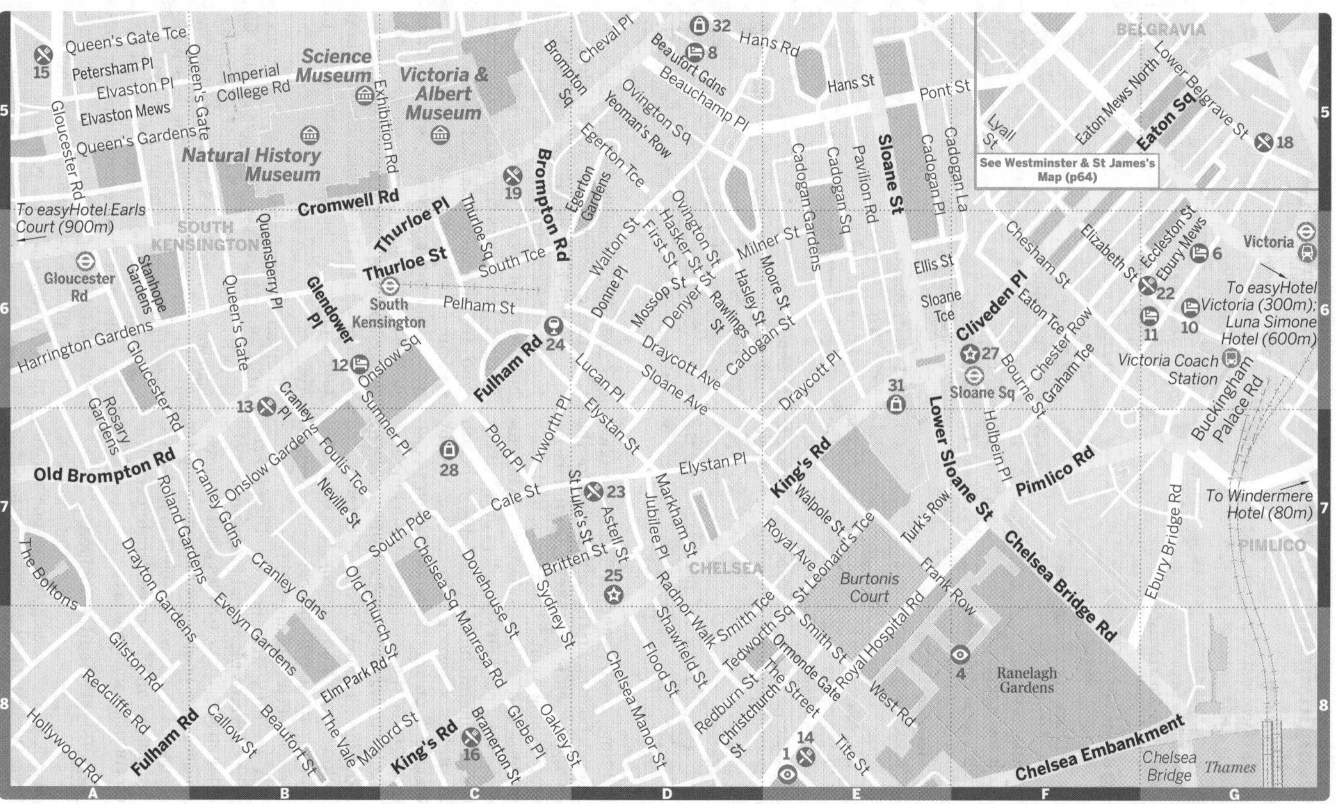
Queen's Gate Tce
Petersham Pl
Elvaston Pl
Elvaston Mews
Queen's Gardens
Gloucester Rd
Queen's Gate
Imperial College Rd
Science Museum
Exhibition Rd
Victoria & Albert Museum
Natural History Museum
Cromwell Rd
To easyHotel Earls Court (900m)
SOUTH KENSINGTON
Gloucester Rd
Stanhope Gardens
Queensberry Pl
Glendower Pl
Thurloe Pl
Thurloe St
Thurloe Sq
South Tce
South Kensington
Pelham St
Brompton Rd
Brompton Sq
Cheval Pl
Beaufort Gdns
Hans Rd
Beauchamp Pl
Ovington Sq
Yeoman's Row
Egerton Tce
Egerton Gardens
Hans St
Pont St
Sloane St
Cadogan Pl
Cadogan La
Cadogan Gardens
Cadogan Sq
Pavilion Rd
BELGRAVIA
Lyall St
Eaton Mews North
Eaton Sq
Lower Belgrave St
See Westminster & St James's Map (p64)
Harrington Gardens
Gloucester Rd
Rosary Gardens
Onslow Sq
Sumner Pl
Cranley Pl
Fulham Rd
Walton St
Donne Pl
First St
Hasker St
Ovington St
Mossop St
Denyer St
Rawlings St
Hasley St
Moore St
Milner St
Cadogan St
Draycott Ave
Sloane Ave
Lucan Pl
Ixworth Pl
Elystan St
Draycott Pl
Ellis St
Sloane Tce
Cliveden Pl
Chesham St
Elizabeth St
Eccleston St
Ebury Mews
Victoria
To easyHotel Victoria (300m); Luna Simone Hotel (600m)
Eaton Tce
Chester Row
Graham Tce
Bourne St
Sloane Sq
Victoria Coach Station
Buckingham Palace Rd
Old Brompton Rd
Cranley Gdns
Onslow Gardens
Foulis Tce
Neville St
Pond Pl
Cale St
Elystan Pl
St Luke's St
Astell St
Jubilee Pl
Markham St
King's Rd
Walpole St
Lower Sloane St
Holbein Pl
Pimlico Rd
Turk's Row
To Windermere Hotel (80m)
Ebury Bridge Rd
PIMLICO
The Boltons
Roland Gardens
Drayton Gardens
Cranley Gdns
South Pde
Chelsea Sq
Dovehouse St
Manresa Rd
Old Church St
Britten St
Sydney St
CHELSEA
Radnor Walk
Royal Ave
St Leonard's Tce
Burtonis Court
Frank Row
Chelsea Bridge Rd
Gilston Rd
Evelyn Gardens
Elm Park Rd
Chelsea Manor St
Flood St
Shawfield St
Smith Tce
Tedworth Sq
Smith St
Royal Hospital Rd
Ranelagh Gardens
Redcliffe Rd
Hollywood Rd
Fulham Rd
Callow St
Beaufort St
The Vale
Mallord St
King's Rd
Bramerton St
Glebe Pl
Oakley St
Redburn St
Christchurch St
The Street
Ormonde Gate
Tite St
West Rd
Chelsea Embankment
Chelsea Bridge
Thames

Knightsbridge, South Kensington & Chelsea

Top Sights
Albert Memorial B4
Natural History Museum B5
Science Museum B5
Serpentine Gallery B3
Victoria & Albert Museum C5

Sights
1 Chelsea Physic Garden E8
2 Diana, Princess of Wales Memorial Fountain C3
3 Hyde Park D2
4 Royal Hospital Chelsea F8
5 Speaker's Corner E1

Sleeping
6 B&B Belgravia G6
7 Gore B4
8 Knightsbridge Hotel D5
9 Levin E4
10 Lime Tree Hotel G6
11 Morgan House G6
12 Number Sixteen B6

Eating
Boxwood Cafe .... (see 17)
13 GBK B6
14 Gordon Ramsay E8
15 L'Etranger A5
16 Made in Italy C8
17 Marcus Wareing at the Berkeley F4
18 Olivomare G5
19 Orsini C5
20 Ottolenghi Belgravia E4
21 Tamarind G2
22 Thomas Cubitt G6
23 Tom's Kitchen D7
Wagamama .... (see 30)

Drinking
24 Bibendum Oyster Bar C6

Entertainment
25 Curzon Chelsea D7
26 Royal Albert Hall B4
27 Royal Court Theatre F6

Shopping
28 Butler & Wilson C7
29 Harrods D4
30 Harvey Nichols E4
31 Rigby & Peller E6
32 Rigby & Peller D5

full-time green space for fun and frolics. There's boating on the **Serpentine** for the energetic, while **Speaker's Corner** is for oratorical acrobats. These days, it's largely nutters and religious fanatics who address the bemused stragglers at Speaker's Corner, maintaining the tradition begun in 1872 as a response to rioting. Nearby **Marble Arch** was designed by John Nash in 1828 as the entrance to Buckingham Palace. It was moved here in 1851. The infamous Tyburn Tree, a three-legged gallows, once stood nearby. It is estimated that up to 50,000 people were executed here between 1196 and 1783.

A soothing structure, the **Diana, Princess of Wales Memorial Fountain** is a circular stream that cascades gently and reassembles in a pool at the bottom; paddling is encouraged. It was unveiled in mid-2004, instigating an inevitable debate over matters of taste and gravitas.

FREE Royal Hospital Chelsea
HISTORIC BUILDINGS

(Map p86; www.chelsea-pensioners.co.uk; Royal Hospital Rd SW3; 10am-noon Mon-Sat & 2-4pm daily; Sloane Sq) Designed by Christopher Wren, the Royal Hospital Chelsea was built in 1692 to provide shelter for ex-servicemen. Today it houses hundreds of war veterans known as Chelsea Pensioners, charming old chaps who are generally regarded as national treasures. As you wander around the grounds or inspect the elegant chapel and interesting museum, you'll see them pottering about in their winter blue coats or summer reds. The Chelsea Flower Show takes place in the hospital grounds in May.

Chelsea Physic Garden
GARDEN

(Map p86; www.chelseaphysicgarden.co.uk; 66 Royal Hospital Rd SW3; adult/child £8/5; noon-5pm Wed-Fri, noon-6pm Sun; Sloane Sq) One for the garden obsessives (the less hardcore should head to the many free parks or Kew), this historic botanical garden is one of the oldest in Europe, established in 1673 for apprentice apothecaries to study medicinal plants. An audio guide is included in the price, and tours commence at 3pm on Sundays.

WORTH A TRIP

ABBEY ROAD

Beatles aficionados can't possibly visit London without making a pilgrimage to **Abbey Road Studios** (3 Abbey Rd) in posh St John's Wood. The fence outside is covered with decades of fans' graffiti. Local traffic is by now accustomed to groups of tourists lining up on the zebra crossing to re-create the cover of the fab four's 1969 album *Abbey Road*. To get here, take the tube to St John's Wood, cross the road, follow Grove End Rd to its end and turn right.

MARYLEBONE

Hip Marylebone isn't as exclusive as Mayfair, its southern neighbour, but it does have one of London's nicest high streets and the very famous, if somewhat disappointing, Baker St. Apart from being immortalised in a hit song by Gerry Rafferty, Baker St is strongly associated with Sherlock Holmes (there's a museum and gift shop at his fictional address, 221B).

FREE **Wallace Collection** MUSEUM
(Map p90; www.wallacecollection.org; Manchester Sq W1; 10am-5pm; Bond St) Housed in a beautiful, opulent, Italianate mansion, the Wallace Collection is a treasure trove of exquisite 18th-century French furniture, Sèvres porcelain, arms, armour and art by masters such as Rubens, Titian, Rembrandt and Gainsborough. Audio guides are £4. Oliver Peyton's Wallace Restaurant occupies a glassed-in courtyard at its centre.

Regent's Park PARK
(Map p90; Regent's Park) A former royal hunting ground, Regent's Park was designed by John Nash early in the 19th century, although what was actually laid out is only a fraction of the celebrated architect's grand plan. Nevertheless, it's one of London's most lovely open spaces – at once serene and lively, cosmopolitan and local – with football pitches, tennis courts and a boating lake. **Queen Mary's Gardens**, towards the south of the park, are particularly pretty, with spectacular roses in summer. **Open Air Theatre** (0844 826 4242; www.openairtheatre.org) hosts performances of Shakespeare and other classics here on summer evenings, along with comedy and concerts.

London Zoo ZOO
(Map p114; www.londonzoo.co.uk; Outer Circle, Regent's Park NW1; adult/child £18/14; 10am-5.30pm Mar-Oct, to 4pm Nov-Feb; Camden Town) A huge amount of money has been spent to bring London Zoo, established in 1828, into the modern world. It now has a swanky £5.3 million gorilla enclosure and is involved in gorilla conservation in Gabon. Feeding times, reptile handling and the petting zoo are guaranteed winners with the kids.

Madame Tussauds WAXWORKS
(Map p90; 0870 400 3000; www.madame-tussauds.co.uk; Marylebone Rd NW1; adult/child £26/22; 9.30am-5.30pm; Baker St) With so much fabulous free stuff to do in London, it's a wonder that people still join lengthy queues to visit pricey Madame Tussauds, but in a celebrity-obsessed, camera-happy world, the opportunity to pose beside Posh and Becks is not short on appeal. The full-size wax figures are remarkably lifelike and are as close to the real thing as most of us will get. It's interesting to see which are the most popular; nobody wants to be photographed with Richard Branson, but Prince Charles and Camilla do a brisk trade.

Honing her craft making effigies of victims of the French revolution, Tussaud brought her wares to England in 1802. Her Chamber of Horrors still survives (complete with the actual blade that took Marie Antoinette's head), but it's now joined by Chamber Live, where actors lunge at terrified visitors in the dark. The Spirit of London ride is wonderfully cheesy.

Tickets are cheaper when ordered online; combined tickets with London Eye and London Dungeon are also available (adult/child £65/48).

BLOOMSBURY & ST PANCRAS

With the University of London and British Museum within its genteel environs, it's little wonder that Bloomsbury has attracted a lot of very clever, bookish people over the years. Between the world wars, these pleasant streets were colonised by a group of artists and intellectuals known collectively as the Bloomsbury Group, which included novelists Virginia Woolf and EM Forster and the economist John Maynard Keynes. Russell Square, its very heart, was laid out in 1800 and is one of London's largest and loveliest.

Marylebone

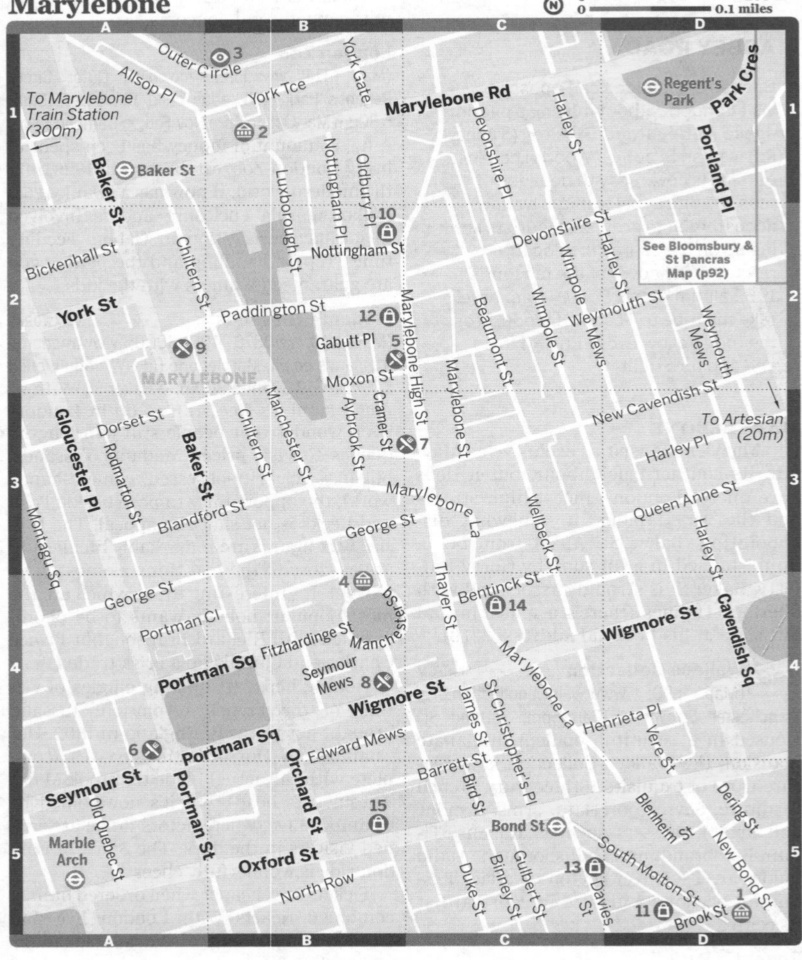

Most people are content to experience Kings Cross St Pancras subterraneously, as it's a major interchange on the tube network, but the conversion of spectacular St Pancras station into the new Eurostar terminal and a ritzy apartment complex seems to be reviving the area's fortunes. The streets are still grey and car-choked, but some decent accommodation options and interesting bars have sprung up.

FREE **British Museum** MUSEUM
(Map p68; ☎020-7323 8000; www.britishmuseum.org; Great Russell St WC1; ⊙10am-5.30pm Sat-Wed, to 8.30pm Thu & Fri; ⊖Russell Sq) The country's largest museum and one of the oldest and finest in the world, this famous museum boasts vast Egyptian, Etruscan, Greek, Roman, European and Middle Eastern galleries, among many others.

Begun in 1753 with a 'cabinet of curiosities' bequeathed by Sir Hans Sloane to the nation on his death, the collection mushroomed over the ensuing years partly through the plundering of the empire. The grand **Enlightenment Gallery** was the first section of the redesigned museum to be built (in 1823).

Marylebone

Sights

1 Handel House Museum....D5
2 Madame Tussauds....B1
3 Regent's Park....B1
4 Wallace Collection....B4

Eating

5 La Fromagerie....B2
6 Locanda Locatelli....A4
7 Providores & Tapa Room....C3
8 Zizzi....B4
9 Zizzi....A2

Shopping

10 Apartment C....B2
11 Butler & Wilson....D5
12 Daunt Books....B2
13 Grays....C5
14 KJ's Laundry....C4
15 Selfridges....B5

Among the must-sees are the **Rosetta Stone**, the key to deciphering Egyptian hieroglyphics, discovered in 1799; the controversial **Parthenon Sculptures** (aka Elgin Marbles) stripped from the walls of the Parthenon in Athens by Lord Elgin (the British ambassador to the Ottoman Empire), and which Greece wants returned; the stunning **Oxus Treasure** of 7th- to 4th-century-BC Persian gold; and the Anglo-Saxon **Sutton Hoo** burial relics.

The **Great Court** was restored and augmented by Norman Foster in 2000 and now has a spectacular glass-and-steel roof, making it one of the most impressive architectural spaces in the capital. In the centre is the **Reading Room**, with its stunning blue-and-gold domed ceiling, where Karl Marx wrote the *Manifesto of the Communist Party*.

You'll need multiple visits to savour even the highlights here; happily there are 15 half-hour free 'eye opener' tours between 11am and 3.45pm daily, focusing on different parts of the collection. Other tours include the 90-minute highlights tour at 10.30am, 1pm and 3pm daily (adult/child £8/5), and audio guides are available (£4.50).

FREE **British Library** LIBRARY

(Map p92; www.bl.uk; 96 Euston Rd NW1; ⏲9.30am-6pm Mon & Wed-Fri, 9.30am-8pm Tue, 9.30am-5pm Sat, 11am-5pm Sun; ⊖King's Cross St Pancras) You need to be a 'reader' (ie member) to use the vast collection of the library, but the Treasures gallery is open to everyone. Here you'll find Shakespeare's first folio, Leonardo da Vinci's notebooks, the lyrics to 'A Hard Day's Night' scribbled on the back of Julian Lennon's birthday card, Oscar Wilde's handwritten 'Ballad Of Reading Gaol', religious texts from around the world and, most importantly, the 4th-century *Codex Sinaiticus* (one of the earliest Bibles) and 1215 *Magna Carta*.

FREE **Wellcome Collection** MUSEUM

(Map p92; www.wellcomecollection.org; 183 Euston Rd NW1; ⏲10am-6pm Tue, Wed, Fri & Sat, 10am-10pm Thu, 11am-6pm Sun; ⊖Euston Sq) Focusing on the interface of art, science and medicine, this clever museum is surprisingly fascinating. There are interactive displays where you can scan your face and watch it stretched into the statistical average; wacky modern sculptures inspired by various medical conditions; and downright creepy things, like an actual cross-section of a body and enlargements of parasites (fleas, body lice, scabies) at terrifying proportions.

Foundling Museum MUSEUM

(Map p92; www.foundlingmuseum.org.uk; 40 Brunswick Sq WC1; adult/child £7.50/free; ⏲10am-5pm Tue-Sat, 11am-5pm Sun; ⊖Russell Sq), The Foundling Hospital opened in 1741 at a time of such extreme poverty that a thousand babies were abandoned annually. Hogarth was a founding governor, and in order to raise funds he hung his own artwork in the hospital's picture gallery and encouraged other artists to do the same – creating the first permanent exhibition space in Britain. The hospital closed and was demolished in 1928, but this neighbouring building recalls its social and artistic legacy.

Leading-edge artists still exhibit their work here, along with art from throughout the hospital's history. Most affecting is the display of the trinkets and tokens that mothers left as a parting gift to their children; they were never passed on.

The top floor is devoted to a collection of Handel memorabilia – including concert programs, tickets and the composer's handwritten will. Handel staged an annual performance of his greatest work, *Messiah,* as a fundraiser for the hospital.

Charles Dickens Museum MUSEUM

(Map p92; www.dickensmuseum.com; 48 Doughty St WC1; adult/child £6/3; ⏲10am-5pm Mon-Sat,

Bloomsbury & St Pancras

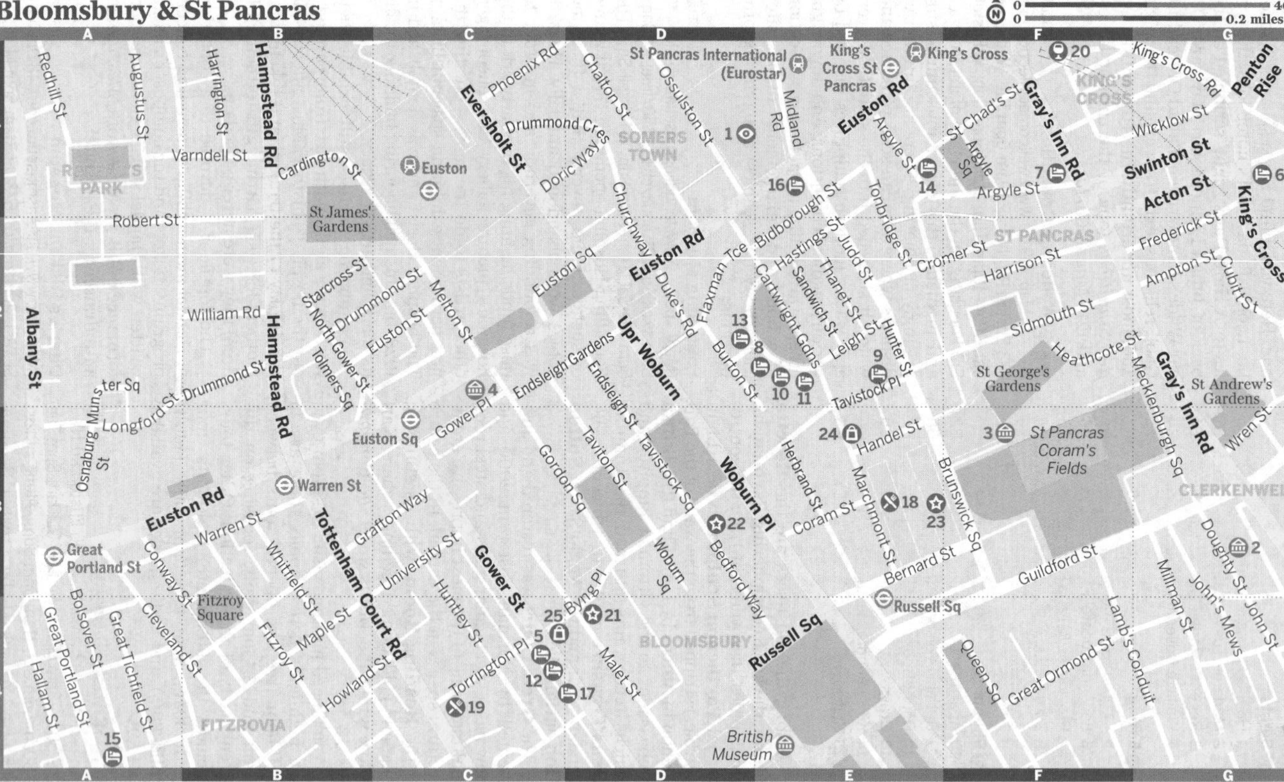

Bloomsbury & St Pancras

Sights
1 British Library ... D1
2 Charles Dickens Museum ... G3
3 Foundling Museum ... F3
4 Wellcome Collection ... C2

Sleeping
5 Arosfa Hotel ... C4
Arran House Hotel ... (see 5)
6 Clink78 ... G1
7 Clink261 ... F1
8 Crescent Hotel ... E2
9 Generator ... E2
10 George ... E2
11 Harlingford Hotel ... E2
12 Hotel Cavendish ... C4
13 Jenkins Hotel ... D2
14 Jesmond Dene Hotel ... E1
15 London Central YHA ... A4
16 London St Pancras YHA ... E1
17 Ridgemount Hotel ... D4

Eating
18 GBK ... E3
19 Planet Organic ... C4

Drinking
20 Big Chill House ... F1

Entertainment
21 Barfly ... D4
22 Bloomsbury Bowling Lanes ... D3
23 Curzon Renoir ... E3

Shopping
24 Gay's the Word ... E3
25 Waterstone's ... C4

11am-5pm Sun; ⊖Russell Sq) Dickens' sole surviving London residence is where his work really flourished – *The Pickwick Papers, Nicholas Nickleby* and *Oliver Twist* were all written here. The handsome four-storey house opened as a museum in 1925, and visitors can stroll through rooms chock-a-block with fascinating memorabilia.

CAMDEN TOWN

Once well outside the city limits, the former hamlets of North London have long since been gobbled up by the metropolis, and yet they still maintain a semblance of a village atmosphere and distinct local identity. Not as resolutely wealthy as the west or as gritty as the east, the 'Norf' is a strange mix of genteel terrace houses and council estates, and contains some of London's hippest neighbourhoods.

Technicolor hairstyles, facial furniture, intricate tattoos and ambitious platform shoes are the look of bohemian Camden Town, a lively neighbourhood of pubs, live-music venues, interesting boutiques and, most famously, Camden Market. There are often some cartoon punks hanging around earning a few bucks for being photographed by tourists, as well as none-too-discreet dope dealers.

HOXTON, SHOREDITCH & SPITALFIELDS

Fans of the long-running TV soap *Eastenders* may find it hard to recognise its setting in traditionally working-class but increasingly trendy enclaves like these. The fact is you're more likely to hear a proper Cockney accent in Essex these days than you are in much of the East End. Over the centuries waves of immigrants have left their mark here, and it's a great place to come for diverse ethnic cuisine and vibrant nightlife.

TOP CHOICE **Dennis Severs' House** MUSEUM
(Map p94; ☎020-7247 4013; www.dennisseversshouse.co.uk; 18 Folgate St E1; ⊖Liverpool St) This extraordinary Georgian House is set up as if its occupants had just walked out the door. There are half-drunk cups of tea, lit candles and, in a perhaps unnecessary attention to detail, a full chamber pot by the bed. More than a museum, it's an opportunity to meditate on the minutiae of everyday Georgian life through silent exploration.

Bookings are required for the Monday evening candlelit sessions (£12; 6pm to 9pm), but you can just show up on the first and third Sundays of the month (£8; noon to 4pm) or the following Mondays (£5; noon to 2pm).

FREE **Geffrye Museum** MUSEUM
(www.geffrye-museum.org.uk; 136 Kingsland Rd E2; ⊙10am-5pm Tue-Sat, noon-5pm Sun; ⊖Old St) If you like nosing around other people's homes, the Geffrye Museum will be a positively orgasmic experience. Devoted to middle-class domestic interiors, these former almshouses (1714) have been

Hoxton, Shoreditch & Spitalfields

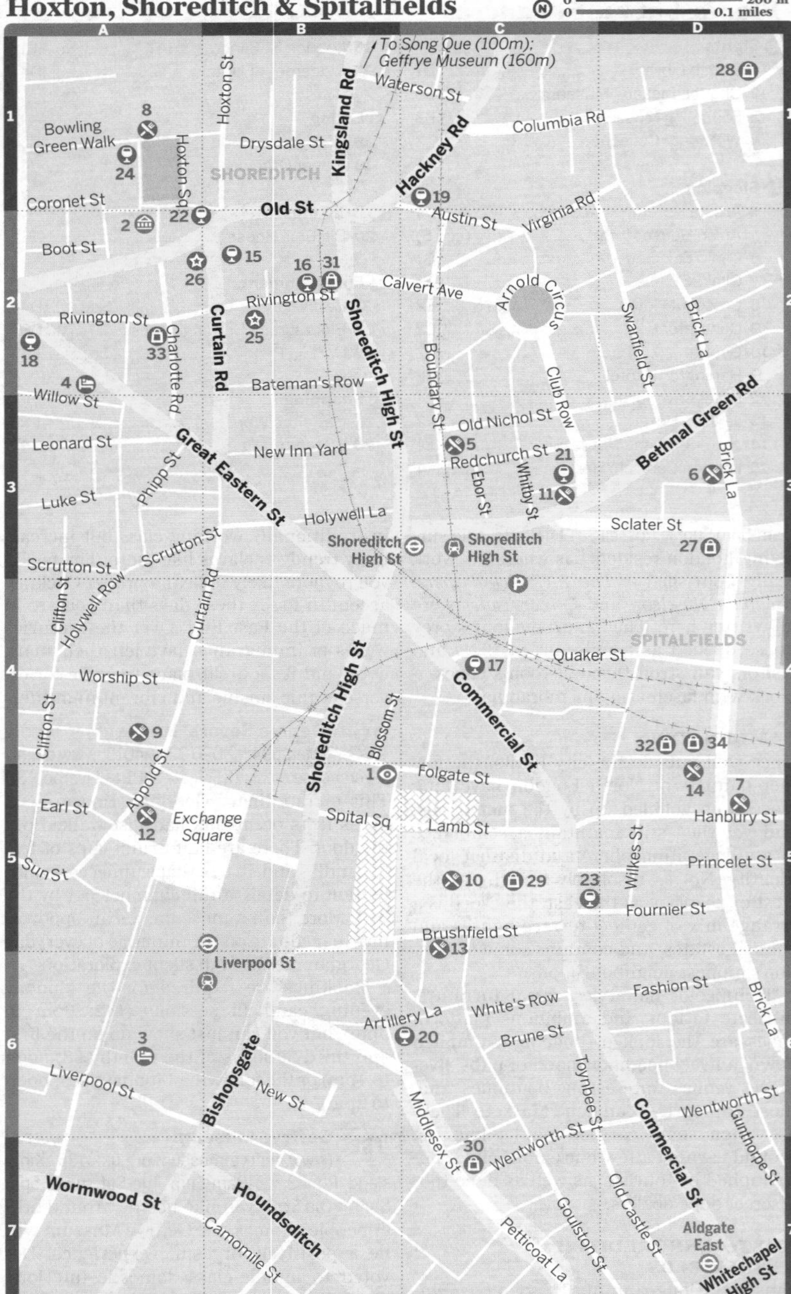

Hoxton, Shoreditch & Spitalfields

Sights
1 Dennis Severs' House B5
2 White Cube A2

Sleeping
3 Andaz A6
4 Hoxton A2

Eating
5 Albion C3
6 Brick Lane Beigel Bake D3
7 Cafe Bangla D5
GBK .... (see 10)
8 Hoxton Apprentice A1
9 L'Anima A4
10 Leon C5
11 Les Trois Garçons C3
12 Ping Pong A5
13 S&M Cafe C5
14 Story Deli D5
Wagamama .... (see 10)

Drinking
15 Bar Music Hall B2
16 Cargo B2
17 Commercial Tavern C4
18 Favela Chic A2
19 George & Dragon C1
20 Grapeshots C6
21 Loungelover C3
22 Mother A2
23 Ten Bells C5
24 Zigfrid Von Underbelly A1

Entertainment
25 Comedy Cafe B2
26 Plastic People A2

Shopping
27 Brick Lane Market D3
28 Columbia Road Flower Market D1
29 Old Spitalfields Market C5
30 Petticoat Lane Market C7
31 Present B2
32 Rough Trade D4
33 Start A2
34 Sunday (Up)Market D4

converted into a series of living rooms dating from 1630 to the current Ikea generation. On top of the interiors porn, the back garden has been transformed into period garden 'rooms' and a lovely walled herb garden (April to October only).

The museum is three blocks along Kingsland Rd, the continuation of Shoreditch High St.

FREE **White Cube** GALLERY
(Map p94; www.whitecube.com; 48 Hoxton Sq N1; ⏲10am-6pm Tue-Sat; ⊖Old St) Set in an industrial building with an impressive glazed-roof extension, White Cube has an interesting program of contemporary-art exhibitions, from sculptures to video, installations and painting.

DOCKLANDS

Docklands' Canary Wharf and Isle of Dogs, to the east of the City, are now an island of tower blocks, rivalling those of the City itself. London's port was once the world's greatest, the hub of the enormous global trade of the British Empire. Since being pummelled by the Luftwaffe in WWII, its fortunes have been topsy-turvy, but the massive development of Canary Wharf has replaced its crusty seadogs with battalions of dark-suited office workers. It's an interesting if slightly sterile environment, best viewed while hurtling around on the DLR (Docklands Light Railway).

FREE **Museum of London Docklands** MUSEUM
(www.museumoflondon.org.uk/docklands; Hertsmere Rd, West India Quay E17; ⏲10am-6pm; DLR West India Quay) Housed in a heritage-listed warehouse, this outpost of the Museum of London uses a combination of artefacts and multimedia to chart the history of the city through its river and docks. There's a lot to see here, including an affecting section on the slave trade. The museum faces West India Quay; head west (towards the city) from the DLR station.

GREENWICH

Simultaneously the first and last place on earth, Greenwich (*gren*-itch) straddles the hemispheres as well as the ages. More than any of the villages swamped by London, Greenwich has retained its own sense of identity based on splendid architecture and strong connections with the sea and science. All the great architects of the Enlightenment made their mark here, leaving an extraordinary cluster of buildings that have earned 'Maritime Greenwich' its place on Unesco's World Heritage list.

Greenwich is easily reached on the DLR or via train from London Bridge. **Thames River Services** (020-7930 4097; www.thamesriverservices.co.uk) has boats departing from Westminster Pier (single/return £9.50/12.50, one hour, every 40 minutes), or alternatively take the cheaper Thames Clippers ferry. The *Cutty Sark,* a famous Greenwich landmark, remains closed while repairs continue on the boat, which was damaged by fire in 2007.

FREE Old Royal Naval College HISTORIC BUILDINGS

(www.oldroyalnavalcollege.org; 2 Cutty Sark Gardens SE10; 10am-5pm; DLR Cutty Sark) Designed by Wren, the Old Royal Naval College is a magnificent example of monumental classical architecture. Parts are now used by the University of Greenwich and Trinity College of Music, but you can visit the **chapel** and the extraordinary **Painted Hall**, which took artist Sir James Thornhill 19 years of hard graft to complete.

The complex was built on the site of the 15th-century Palace of Placentia, the birthplace of Henry VIII and Elizabeth I. This Tudor connection, along with Greenwich's industrial and maritime history, is explored in the **Discover Greenwich** centre. The tourist office is based here, along with a cafe and microbrewery. Tours of the complex leave at 2pm daily, taking in areas not otherwise open to the public (£5, 90 minutes). You can also buy 'walkcards' (50p) for themed self-guided tours of Greenwich: *Highlights* (40 minutes), *Royal* (80 minutes), *Viewpoints* and *Architecture* (both 90 minutes).

Greenwich Guided Walks (0757-577 2298; www.greenwichtours.co.uk; adult/child £6/5; 12.15pm & 2.15pm) leave from the tourist office.

FREE National Maritime Museum MUSEUM

(020-8858 4422; www.nmm.ac.uk; Romney Rd SE10; 10am-5pm; DLR Cutty Sark) Directly behind the old college, the National Maritime Museum completes Greenwich's trump hand of historic buildings. The museum itself houses a large collection of paraphernalia recounting Britain's seafaring history. Exhibits range from interactive displays to humdingers like Cook's journals and Nelson's uniform, complete with a hole from the bullet that killed him. The mood changes abruptly between galleries (one is devoted to toy ships while another examines the slave trade).

At the centre of the site, the elegant Palladian **Queen's House** has been restored to something like Inigo Jones' intention when he designed it in 1616 for the wife of Charles I. It's a refined setting for a gallery focusing on illustrious seafarers and historic Greenwich.

Behind Queen's House, idyllic **Greenwich Park** climbs up the hill, affording great views of London. It's capped by the **Royal Observatory** (same hours as rest of museum, until 7pm May-Aug), which Charles II had built in 1675 to help solve the riddle of longitude. Success was confirmed in 1884 when Greenwich was designated as the prime meridian of the world, and Greenwich Mean Time (GMT) became the universal measurement of standard time. Here you can stand with your feet straddling the western and eastern hemispheres.

If you arrive just before lunchtime, you will see a bright-red ball climb the observatory's northeast turret at 12.58pm and drop at 1pm – as it has every day since 1833 when it was introduced for ships on the Thames to set their clocks by.

The observatory's galleries are split into those devoted to astronomy and those devoted to time. There's also a 120-seat **planetarium** (adult/child £6.50/4.50) screening a roster of digital presentations; the website is updated daily with details.

O2 PERFORMANCE VENUE

(www.theo2.co.uk; Peninsula Sq SE10; North Greenwich) The world's largest dome (365m in diameter) opened on 1 January 2000, at a cost of £789 million, as the Millennium Dome, but closed on 31 December, only hours before the third millennium began. Renamed the O2, it's now a 20,000-seat sports and entertainment arena surrounded by shops and restaurants. It has hosted some massive concerts, including the one-off Led Zeppelin reunion and a 21-night purple reign by Prince; but alas not Michael Jackson's sold-out 50-show run that was imminent at the time of his death. There are ferry services from central London on concert nights.

HAMPSTEAD & HIGHGATE

These quaint and well-heeled villages, perched on hills north of London, are home to an inordinate number of celebrities.

Hampstead Heath PARK

(Gospel Oak or Hampstead Heath) With its 320 hectares of rolling meadows and wild woodlands, Hampstead Heath is a million miles away – well, approximately four – from central London. A walk up **Parliament Hill** affords one of the most spectacular views of the city, and on summer days it's popular with picnickers. Also bewilderingly popular are the murky brown waters of the single-sex and mixed bathing ponds (basically duck ponds with people splashing about in them), although most folk are content just to sun themselves around London's 'beach'.

Kenwood House (www.english-heritage.org.uk; Hampstead Lane NW3; admission free; 11.30am-4pm) is a magnificent neoclassical mansion (1764) on the northern side of the heath that houses a collection of paintings by English and European masters including Rembrandt, Vermeer, Turner and Gainsborough.

Highgate Cemetery CEMETERY

(020-8340 1834; www.highgate-cemetery.org; Swain's Lane N6; Archway) The cemetery weaves a creepy kind of magic with its Victorian symbols – shrouded urns, obelisks, upturned torches (life extinguished) and broken columns (life cut short) – eerily overgrown graves and the twisting paths of the **West Cemetery** (adult/child £7/3; tours 2pm Mon-Fri Mar-Nov, hourly 11am-3pm Sat & Sun year-long), where admission is by tour only; bookings are essential for weekday tours. In the less atmospheric **East Cemetery** (adult/child £3/2; 10am-5pm Mon-Fri, 11am-5pm Sat & Sun Mar-Oct, to 4pm Nov-Feb), you can pay your respects to Karl Marx and George Eliot.

From Archway station, walk up Highgate Hill until you reach Waterlow Park on the left. Go through the park; the cemetery gates are opposite the exit.

Freud Museum MUSEUM

(www.freud.org.uk; 20 Maresfield Gardens NW3; adult/child £6/3; noon-5pm Wed-Sun) After fleeing Nazi-occupied Vienna in 1938, Sigmund Freud lived the last year of his life here. The fascinating Freud Museum maintains his study and library much as he left it, with his couch, books and collection of small Egyptian figures and other antiquities. Excerpts of dream analyses are scattered around the house, and there's a video presentation upstairs.

OUTSIDE CENTRAL LONDON

Kew Gardens PARK

(020-8332 5655; www.kew.org.uk; Kew Rd; adult/child £14/free; 9.30am-6.30pm, earlier closing in winter; Kew Gardens) In 1759 botanists began rummaging around the world for specimens they could plant in the 3-hectare plot known as the Royal Botanic Gardens. They never stopped collecting, and the gardens, which have bloomed to 120 hectares, provide the most comprehensive botanical collection on earth (including the world's largest collection of orchids). It's now recognised as a Unesco World Heritage Site.

You can easily spend a whole day wandering around, but if you're pressed for time, the **Kew Explorer** (adult/child £4/1) is a hop-on/hop-off road train that leaves from Victoria Gate and takes in the gardens' main sights.

Highlights include the enormous **Palm House**, a hothouse of metal and curved sheets of glass; the impressive **Princess of Wales Conservatory**; the red-brick, 1631 **Kew Palace** (www.hrp.org.uk/kewpalace; adult/child £5/free; 10am-5pm Easter-Sep), formerly King George III's country retreat; the celebrated **Great Pagoda** designed by William Chambers in 1762; and the **Temperate House**, which is the world's largest ornamental glasshouse and home to its biggest indoor plant, the 18m Chilean wine palm.

The gardens are easily reached by tube, but you might prefer to take a cruise on a riverboat from the **Westminster Passenger Services Association** (020-7930 2062; www.wpsa.co.uk), which runs several daily boats from April to October, departing from Westminster Pier (return adult/child £18/9, 90 minutes).

Hampton Court Palace PALACE

(www.hrp.org.uk/HamptonCourtPalace; adult/child £14/7; 10am-6pm Apr-Oct, to 4.30pm Nov-Mar; Hampton Court) Built by Cardinal Thomas Wolsey in 1514 but coaxed out of him by Henry VIII just before the chancellor fell from favour, Hampton Court Palace is England's largest and grandest Tudor structure. It was already one of the most sophisticated palaces in Europe when, in the 17th century, Wren was commissioned to build an extension. The result is a beautiful blend of Tudor and 'restrained baroque' architecture.

Take a themed tour led by costumed historians or, if you're in a rush, visit the highlights: **Henry VIII's State Apartments**, including the Great Hall with its spectacular hammer-beamed roof; the **Tudor Kitchens**, staffed by 'servants'; and the **Wolsey Rooms**. You could easily spend a day exploring the palace and its 60 acres of riverside gardens, especially if you get lost in the 300-year-old **maze**.

Hampton Court is 13 miles southwest of central London and is easily reached by train from Waterloo. Alternatively, the riverboats that head from Westminster to Kew continue here (return adult/child £23/12, three hours).

Richmond Park PARK
(⊖Richmond) London's wildest park spans more than 1000 hectares and is home to all sorts of wildlife, most notably herds of red and fallow deer. It's a terrific place for bird-watching, rambling and cycling.

To get there from Richmond tube station, turn left along George St then left at the fork that leads up Richmond Hill.

☞ Tours

One of the best ways to orient yourself when you first arrive in London is with a 24-hour hop-on/hop-off pass for the double-decker bus tours. The buses loop around interconnecting routes throughout the day, providing a commentary as they go, and the price includes a river cruise and three walking tours. You'll save a couple of pounds by booking online.

Original London Sightseeing Tour BUS TOURS
(☎020-8877 1722; www.theoriginaltour.com; adult/child £25/12)

Big Bus Company BUS TOURS
(☎020-7233 9533; www.bigbustours.com; adult/child £26/10)

Citisights WALKING TOURS
(☎020-8806 3742; www.chr.org.uk/cswalks.htm) Focuses on the academic and the literary.

London Beatles Walks WALKING TOURS
(☎07958 706329; www.beatlesinlondon.com) Following the footsteps of the Fab Four.

London Walks WALKING TOURS
(☎020-7624 3978; www.walks.com) Harry Potter tours, ghost walks and the ever-popular Jack the Ripper tours.

London Mystery Walks WALKING TOURS
(☎07957 388280; www.tourguides.org.uk)

City Cruises FERRY TOURS
(☎020-7740 0400; www.citycruises.com; single/return trips from £8/11, day pass £13) Ferry service between Westminster, Waterloo, Tower and Greenwich piers.

Black Taxi Tours of London TAXI TOURS
(☎020-7935 9363; www.blacktaxitours.co.uk; 8am-6pm £100, 6pm-midnight £110, plus £5 on weekends) Takes up to five people on a two-hour spin past the major sights with a chatty cabbie as your guide.

London Bicycle Tour Company CYCLING TOURS
(Map p80; ☎020-7928 6838; www.londonbicycle.com; 1A Gabriel's Wharf, 56 Upper Ground SE1; tour incl bike £16-19; ⊖Waterloo) Themed 2½- to 3½-hour tours of the 'East', 'Central' or 'Royal West'.

City Jogging Tours JOGGING TOURS
(☎0845 544 0433; www.cityjoggingstories.co.uk; tours £26) Combine sightseeing with keeping fit on a 6km route, graded for 'gentle joggers' or 'recreational runners'.

London Duck Tours AMPHIBIOUS-VEHICLE TOURS
(Map p80; ☎020-7928 3132; www.londonducktours.co.uk; County Hall SE1; adult/child from £20/16; ⊖Waterloo) Cruise the streets in the same sort of amphibious landing craft used on D-Day before making a dramatic plunge into the Thames.

LONDON FOR CHILDREN

London has plenty of sights that parents and kids can enjoy together, and many of them are free, including the Natural History Museum, Science Museum and all of the city's parks, many of which have excellent playgrounds. Pricier but popular attractions include London Dungeon (for older children), London Zoo, Madame Tussauds, Tower of London, Sea Life and the London Eye. On top of that, there are city farms (see www.londonfootprints.co.uk/visitfarms.htm) and the big galleries have activities for children. However, don't expect a warm welcome in swanky restaurants or pubs.

All top-range hotels offer in-house babysitting services. Prices vary enormously from hotel to hotel, so ask the concierge about hourly rates. Alternatively try www.sitters.co.uk: membership costs £12.75 for three months, then sitters cost around £8 per hour plus a £4 booking fee.

Festivals & Events

Chinese New Year ETHNIC CELEBRATION
Late January or early February sees Chinatown snap, crackle and pop with fireworks, a colourful street parade and eating aplenty.

University Boat Race BOAT RACE
(www.theboatrace.org) A posh-boy grudge match held annually since 1829 between the rowing crews of Oxford and Cambridge Universities (late March).

London Marathon MARATHON
(www.london-marathon.co.uk) Up to half a million spectators watch the whippet-thin champions and bizarrely clad amateurs take to the streets in late April.

Camden Crawl MUSIC FESTIVAL
(www.thecamdencrawl.com; 1-/2-day pass £39/62) Your chance to spot the next big thing on the music scene or witness a secret gig by an established act, with 40 of Camden's venues given over to live music for two full days (late April/early May).

Chelsea Flower Show HORTICULTURAL SHOW
(www.rhs.org.uk/chelsea; Royal Hospital Chelsea; admission £19-42) Held in May, arguably the world's most renowned horticultural show attracts green fingers from near and far.

Trooping the Colour ROYAL PAGEANT
Celebrating the Queen's official birthday (in June), this ceremonial procession of troops, marching along the Mall for their monarch's inspection, is a pageantry overload.

Royal Academy Summer Exhibition ART EXHIBITION
(www.royalacademy.org.uk; adult/child £9.50/5) Running from mid-June to mid-August, this is an annual showcase of works submitted by artists from all over Britain, mercifully distilled to 1200 or so pieces.

Meltdown Festival MUSIC FESTIVAL
(www.southbankcentre.co.uk) The Southbank Centre hands over the curatorial reins to a legend of contemporary music (such as David Bowie, Morrissey or Patti Smith) to pull together a full program of concerts, talks and films in late June.

Wimbledon Lawn Tennis Championships TENNIS TOURNAMENT
(www.wimbledon.org) Held at the end of June, the world's most prestigious tennis event is as much about strawberries, cream and tradition as smashing balls.

Pride GAY & LESBIAN PARADE
(www.pridelondon.org) The big event on the gay and lesbian calendar, a Technicolor street parade heads through the West End in late June or early July, culminating in a concert in Trafalgar Sq.

Lovebox MUSIC FESTIVAL
(www.lovebox.net) London's contribution to the summer music festival circuit is held in Victoria Park in mid-July.

Notting Hill Carnival ETHNIC CARNIVAL
(www.nottinghillcarnival.biz) Held over two days in August, this is Europe's largest and London's most vibrant outdoor carnival, where London's Caribbean community shows the city how to party. Unmissable and truly crazy.

Sleeping

Take a deep breath and sit down before reading this section because no matter what your budget, London is a horribly pricey city to sleep in – one of the most expensive in the world, in fact. Anything below £80 per night for a double is pretty much 'budget', and at the top end, how does a £3500 penthouse sound? For this book we've defined the price categories for London differently from the other chapters. Double rooms ranging between £80 and £180 per night are considered midrange; cheaper or more expensive options fall into the budget or the top-end categories, respectively.

Ignoring the scary money stuff for a minute, London has a wonderful selection of interesting hotels, whether brimming with history or zany modern decor. Most of the ritzier places offer substantial discounts on the weekends, for advance bookings and at quiet times (if there is such a thing in London).

Public transport is good, so you don't need to be sleeping at Buckingham Palace to be at the heart of things. However, if you're planning some late nights and don't fancy enduring the night buses (a consummate London experience, but one you'll want only once) it'll make sense not to wander too far from the action.

London's a noisy city, so expect a bit of the din to seep into your room. If you're a light sleeper, earplugs are a sensible precaution, as is requesting a room back from the street and higher up.

It's now becoming the norm for budget and midrange places to offer free wireless internet. The expensive places will offer it, too, but often charge. Hostels tend to serve free breakfast (of the toast-and-cereal variety). If your hotel charges for breakfast, check the prices; anything over £8 just isn't worth it when there are so many eateries to explore.

Budget accommodation is scattered about, with some good options in Southwark and St Pancras. For something a little nicer, check out Bloomsbury, Fitzrovia, Bayswater and Earl's Court. If you've the cash to splash, consider the West End, Clerkenwell and Kensington.

WESTMINSTER & ST JAMES'S

A bed in the Queen's own hood can be as ritzy as the Ritz, but there are some surprisingly affordable options.

Rubens at the Palace HOTEL ££
(Map p64; ☎020-7834 6600; www.rubenshotel.com; 39 Buckingham Palace Rd SW1; r from £149; @ 📶; ⊖Victoria) Opposite Buckingham Palace, it's perhaps not surprising to find that Rubens is a firm favourite with Americans looking for that quintessential British experience. The rooms are monarchist chic: heavy patterned fabrics, dark wood, thick drapes and crowns above the beds.

WEST END

Like on the Monopoly board, if you land on a Mayfair hotel you may have to sell a house, or at least remortgage. This is the heart of the action, so naturally accommodation comes at a price, and a hefty one at that. A couple of hostels cater for would-be Soho hipsters of more modest means.

THE KIT KEMP CLUB

Kit Kemp's interiors purr loudly rather than whisper. She's waved her magically deranged wand over all the hotels of London's boutique **Firmdale chain** (www.firmdalehotels.com), creating bold, playful spaces full of zany fabrics, crazy sculpture and sheer luxury. Yet somehow she manages to create an old-fashioned feel from a thoroughly modern sensibility. While nonconformity is the norm, key values are shared throughout the chain: welcoming staff, inviting guest lounges with honesty bars, a dressmaker's dummy in each bedroom (some in miniature) and beautiful grey-flecked granite bathrooms.

TOP CHOICE **Haymarket Hotel** HOTEL £££
(Map p68; ☎020-7470 4000; www.haymarkethotel.com; 1 Suffolk Pl SW1; r/ste from £250/1750; @ 📶 🏊; ⊖Piccadilly Circus) The building was designed by John Nash (Buckingham Palace's main man), but the rest is Kit Kemp all the way. We love the gold lounges around the sunset-lit indoor swimming pool.

Hazlitt's HOTEL £££
(Map p68; ☎020-7434 1771; www.hazlittshotel.com; 6 Frith St W1; s £206, d/ste from £259/646; @ 📶; ⊖Tottenham Court Rd) Staying in this charming Georgian house (1718) is a trip back into a time when four-poster beds and claw-foot baths were the norm for gentlefolk. Each of the individually decorated 30 rooms is packed with antiques and named after a personage connected with the house.

One Aldwych HOTEL £££
(Map p68; ☎020-7300 1000; www.onealdwych.com; 1 Aldwych WC2; d/ste from £195/440; @ 📶 🏊; ⊖Covent Garden) Granite bathrooms, long swimming pool with underwater music, majestic bar and restaurant, modern art, and a lift that changes colour to literally lift your mood.

Brown's Hotel HOTEL £££
(Map p68; ☎020-7493 6020; www.brownshotel.com; 30 Albemarle St W1; d £340-645, ste £885-3200; @ 📶; ⊖Green Park) Rudyard Kipling penned many of his works here, Kate Moss has frequented the spa and both Queen Victoria and Winston Churchill dropped in for tea. There's a lovely old-world feel to Browns, but without the snootiness of other Mayfair hotels. The rooms have every modern comfort.

Soho Hotel HOTEL £££
(Map p68; ☎020-7559 3000; www.sohohotel.com; 4 Richmond Mews W1; d £290-360, ste £400-2750; @ 📶; ⊖Oxford Circus) Hello Kitty! This Kit Kemp–designed hotel has a giant cat sculpture in a reception that looks like a psychedelic candy store; try to refrain from licking the walls.

Covent Garden Hotel HOTEL £££
(☎020-7806 1000; www.coventgardenhotel.co.uk; 10 Monmouth St WC2; d/ste from £240/395; @ 📶; ⊖Covent Garden) This well-positioned Firmdale hotel (see p100) has a gym and private cinema.

Oxford St YHA HOSTEL £
(☎0845 371 9133; www.yha.org.uk; 14 Noel St W1; dm/tw from £18/44; @ 📶; ⊖Oxford Circus) In most respects, this is a bog-standard YHA

hostel, with tidy rooms and all the usual facilities (kitchen, TV room, laundry). What it's got going for it are a terrific (albeit noisy) location and decent views over London's rooftops from some of the rooms.

THE CITY

Bristling with bankers during the week, you can often pick up a considerable bargain in the City on weekends.

Threadneedles HOTEL ££
(Map p74; ☎020-7657 8080; www.theetoncollection.com; 5 Threadneedle St EC2; r weekend/weekday from £175/345; @; Bank) The incredible stained-glass dome in the lobby points to Threedneedles' former status as a bank HQ. Today it's still popular with suits, but the atmosphere is chic rather than stuffy. Request one of the two deluxe rooms with balconies.

Apex City of London HOTEL ££
(Map p74; ☎020-7702 2020; www.apexhotels.co.uk; 1 Seething Lane EC3; r from £100; ; Tower Hill) Business-focused but close enough to the Tower to hear the heads roll, the Apex offers particularly enticing weekend rates, a gym, huge TVs, free wi-fi and a rubber ducky in every room.

SOUTH BANK

Immediately south of the river is a good spot if you want to immerse yourself in workaday London and still be central.

Captain Bligh House B&B ££
(Map p80; ☎020-7928 2735; www.captainblighhouse.co.uk; 100 Lambeth Rd SE1; s/d £58/80; ; Lambeth North) The blue disc by the door confirms that this 1780 house, opposite the Imperial War Museum, belonged to the unfortunate Bligh, of Mutiny on the Bounty and Rum Rebellion infamy. No such bad luck awaits guests who manage to snag one of the two comfortable, reasonably priced rooms nowadays.

Mad Hatter Hotel HOTEL ££
(Map p80; ☎020-7401 9222; www.fullershotels.com; 3-7 Stamford St SE1; r £155; Southwark) There's nothing particularly mad (or even unusual) about it, but this is a good hotel with decent-sized rooms and unassuming decor hiding behind a lovely Victorian frontage. Prices fall considerably on weekends.

Southwark Rose Hotel HOTEL ££
(Map p82; ☎020-7015 1480; www.southwarkrosehotel.co.uk; 47 Southwark Bridge Rd SE1; r/ste from £85/115; @; Borough) Though it's somewhat pricey during the week, this generic but comfortable business hotel drops its rates considerably to attract the weekender visitors.

St Christopher's Village HOSTEL £
(Map p82; ☎020-7939 9710; www.st-christophers.co.uk; 163 Borough High St SE1; dm/r from £14/62; @; London Bridge) The Village – a huge, up-for-it party hostel, with a club that opens until 4am on the weekends and a roof terrace bar – is the main hub of three locations on the same street. It's either heaven or hell, depending on what side of 30 you're on. The others are much smaller, quieter and, frankly, more pleasant. **St Christopher's Inn** (121 Borough High St) is above a very nice pub, while **Orient Express** (59 Borough High St) is a dude-free zone.

PIMLICO

Luna Simone Hotel B&B ££
(☎020-7834 5897; www.lunasimonehotel.com; 47-49 Belgrave Rd SW1; s £70-75, d £95-120; @; Pimlico) The blue-and-yellow rooms aren't huge, but they're clean and calming; the ones at the back are quieter. Belgrave Rd follows on from Eccleston Bridge, directly behind Victoria Station.

Windermere Hotel B&B ££
(Map p86; ☎020-7834 5163; www.windermere-hotel.co.uk; 142-144 Warwick Way SW1; s £105-155, d £129-165; @; Victoria) Chintzy but comfortable early-Victorian town house. The cheapest rooms share bathrooms.

BELGRAVIA

Lime Tree Hotel B&B ££
(Map p86; ☎020-7730 8191; www.limetreehotel.co.uk; 135-137 Ebury St SW1; s £95, d £135-160; @; Victoria) A smartly renovated Georgian town house hotel with a beautiful back garden to catch the late-afternoon rays. Contemporary renovations have left it the best of the Belgravia crop.

Also recommended:

B&B Belgravia B&B ££
(Map p86; ☎020-7259 8570; www.bb-belgravia.com; 64-66 Ebury St SW1; s/d £99/120; @; Victoria) This small hotel's unassuming facade belies a contemporary interior, although a new coat of paint wouldn't go astray.

Morgan House B&B £
(Map p86; ☎020-7730 2384; www.morganhouse.co.uk; 120 Ebury St SW1; s £58, d £78-98; ; Victoria) Pleasant Georgian town house with homely rooms, some en suite.

BOOKING SERVICES

At Home in London (☎020-8748 1943; www.athomeinlondon.co.uk) B&Bs.

British Hotel Reservation Centre (☎020-7592 3055; www.bhrconline.com)

GKLets (☎020-7613 2805; www.gklets.co.uk) Apartments.

London Homestead Services (☎020-7286 5115; www.lhslondon.com) B&Bs.

LondonTown (☎020-7437 4370; www.londontown.com) Hotel and B&Bs.

Uptown Reservations (☎020-7937 2001; www.uptownres.co.uk) Upmarket B&Bs.

Visit London (☎0871 222 3118, per min 10p; www.visitlondonoffers.com) Hotels.

KNIGHTSBRIDGE

Knightsbridge is where you'll find some of London's best-known department stores, including Harrods and Harvey Nicks.

Levin HOTEL £££
(Map p86; ☎020-7589 6286; www.thelevinhotel.co.uk; 28 Basil St SW3; r £285-485; ⊖Knightsbridge) As close as you can get to sleeping in Harrods, the Levin knows its market. Despite the baby-blue colour scheme, there's a subtle femininity to the decor, although it's far too elegant to be flouncy.

Knightsbridge Hotel HOTEL £££
(Map p86; ☎020-7584 6300; www.knightsbridgehotel.com; 10 Beaufort Gardens SW3; s/d from £170/220; @📶; ⊖Knightsbridge) Another Firmdale property (see p100), the Knightsbridge is on a quiet, tree-lined cul-de-sac very close to Harrods.

CHELSEA & KENSINGTON

Classy Chelsea and Kensington offer easy access to the museums and fashion retailers. It's all a bit sweetie-darling, along with the prices.

Number Sixteen HOTEL £££
(Map p86; ☎020-7589 5232; www.numbersixteenhotel.co.uk; 16 Sumner Pl SW7; s/d from £120/205; @📶; ⊖South Kensington) The least pricey of the Firmdale hotels (see p100), with a lovely garden tucked away.

Gore HOTEL ££
(Map p86; ☎020-7584 6601; www.gorehotel.com; 190 Queen's Gate SW7; r from £135; @📶; ⊖Gloucester Rd) A short stroll from the Royal Albert Hall, the Gore serves up British grandiosity (antiques, carved four-posters, a secret bathroom in the Tudor room) with a large slice of camp. How else could you describe the Judy Garland, Dame Nellie and Miss Fanny rooms, named after famous former occupants?

Vicarage Private Hotel B&B ££
(Map p104; ☎020-7229 4030; www.londonvicaragehotel.com; 10 Vicarage Gate W8; s/d £95/125, without bathroom £56/95; @📶; ⊖High St Kensington) You can see Kensington Palace from the doorstep of this grand Victorian town house, which opens on to a cul-de-sac. The cheaper rooms (without bathrooms) are on floors three and four, so you may get a view as well as a workout.

EARL'S COURT & FULHAM

West London's Earl's Court is lively, cosmopolitan and so popular with travelling Antipodeans it's been nicknamed Kangaroo Valley. There are no real sights, but it does have inexpensive digs and an infectious holiday atmosphere.

Barclay House B&B ££
(☎020-7384 3390; www.barclayhouselondon.com; 21 Barclay Rd SW6; s/d £69/89; @📶; ⊖Fulham Broadway) A proper homestay B&B, the two comfy bedrooms in this charming Victorian town house share a bathroom and an exceptionally welcoming hostess. You'll be well set up to conquer London with helpful tips, maps, umbrellas and a full stomach. From the tube station head west on Fulham Broadway and then look out for Barclay Rd on your left.

Twenty Nevern Square HOTEL ££
(☎020-7565 9555; www.20neversquare.com; 20 Nevern Sq SW5; r from £95; @📶; ⊖Earl's Court) An Ottoman theme runs through this Victorian town-house hotel, where a mix of wooden furniture, luxurious fabrics and natural light helps maximise space – even in the cheaper bedrooms, which are not particularly large. Exit the tube station from the rear and turn right into Warwick St and then take the second right.

Base APARTMENT HOTEL ££
(☎020-7244 2255; www.base2stay.com; 25 Courtfield Gardens SW5; s/d from £93/99; @📶; ⊖Earl's Court) With smart decor, power showers, flatscreen TVs with internet access and artfully concealed kitchenettes, this boutique establishment feels like a four-star hotel without the hefty price tag.

Enter the tube station from the front entrance, cross Earl's Court Rd and take Earl's Court Gardens, turning right at the end.

easyHotel CAPSULE HOTEL £
(www.easyhotel.com; r from £25; @📶) Earls Court (44 West Cromwell Rd SW5; ⊖Earl's Court); Paddington (10 Norfolk Pl W2; ⊖Paddington); South Kensington (14 Lexham Gardens W8; ⊖Gloucester Rd); Victoria (36 Belgrave Rd SW1; ⊖Victoria) Run along the same principles as its sibling business easyJet, this no-frills chain has tiny rooms with even tinier bathrooms, all bedecked in their trademark garish orange.

NOTTING HILL, BAYSWATER & PADDINGTON

Don't be fooled by Julia Roberts and Hugh Grant's shenanigans, Notting Hill and the areas immediately north of Hyde Park are as shabby as they are chic. There are some nice gated squares surrounded by Georgian town houses, but the area is better exemplified by the Notting Hill Carnival, where the West Indian community who made the area their home from the 1950s party up big time.

Scruffy Paddington has lots of cheap hotels, with a major strip of unremarkable ones along Sussex Gardens, which are worth checking if you're short on options.

Vancouver Studios APARTMENT HOTEL ££
(Map p104; ☎020-7243 1270; www.vancouverstudios.co.uk; 30 Prince's Sq W2; apt £89-170; @📶; ⊖Bayswater) It's the addition of kitchenettes and a self-service laundry that differentiates these smart, reasonably priced studios (sleeping from one to three people) from a regular Victorian town-house hotel. In spring, the garden is filled with colour and fragrance.

New Linden Hotel HOTEL ££
(Map p104; ☎020-7221 4321; www.newlinden.co.uk; 58-60 Leinster Sq W2; s/d from £79/105; @📶; ⊖Bayswater) Cramming in a fair amount of style for the price, this terrace-house hotel has interesting modern art in the rooms and carved wooden fixtures in the guest lounge. The quiet location, helpful staff and monsoon shower heads in the deluxe rooms make this an excellent proposition.

FITZROVIA

Sanderson HOTEL £££
(Map p68; ☎020-7300 1400; www.sandersonlondon.com; 50 Berners St W1; r from £253; @📶; ⊖Goodge St) Liberace meets Philippe Starck in an 18th-century French bordello – and that's just the reception. A 3D space scene in the lift shuttles you into darkened corridors leading to blindingly white rooms complete with sleigh beds, oil paintings hung on the ceiling, en suites behind glass walls and pink silk curtains.

Charlotte Street Hotel HOTEL £££
(Map p68; ☎020-7806 2000; www.charlottestreethotel.com; 15 Charlotte St W1; d/tw/ste from £270/340/447; @📶; ⊖Goodge St) Another of the Firmdale clan (see p100), this one's a favourite with media types, with a small gym and a screening room.

London Central YHA HOSTEL £
(Map p92; ☎0845 371 9154; www.yha.org.uk; 104-108 Bolsover St W1; dm £21-32, q from £70; @📶; ⊖Great Portland St) One of London's new breed of YHA hostels, most of the four- to six-bed rooms have en suites. There's a flash cafe-bar attached to reception and a wheelchair-accessible kitchen downstairs.

BLOOMSBURY & ST PANCRAS

Only one step removed from the West End and crammed with Georgian town-house conversions, these neighbourhoods are much more affordable. You'll find a stretch of lower-priced hotels along Gower St and on the pretty Cartwright Gardens crescent. While hardly a salubrious location, St Pancras is handy to absolutely everything and has some excellent budget options.

Arran House Hotel B&B ££
(Map p92; ☎020-7636 2186; www.arranhotel-london.com; 77-79 Gower St WC1; s/d/tr/q £70/110/128/132, without bathroom £60/80/105/111; @📶; ⊖Goodge St) Period features such as cornicing and fireplaces, a pretty pergola-decked back garden and a comfy lounge with PCs and TV lift this hotel from the average to the attractive. Squashed en suites or shared bathrooms are the trade-off for these reasonable rates.

Arosfa Hotel B&B ££
(Map p92; ☎020-7636 2115; www.arosfalondon.com; 83 Gower St WC1; s £60-65, d/tr/q £90/102/110; @📶; ⊖Goodge St) While the decor of the immaculately presented rooms is unremarkable, Arosfa's guest lounge has been blinged up with chandeliers, clear plastic chairs and a free internet terminal. Recent refurbishments have added en suites to all 15 bedrooms, but

Notting Hill & Bayswater

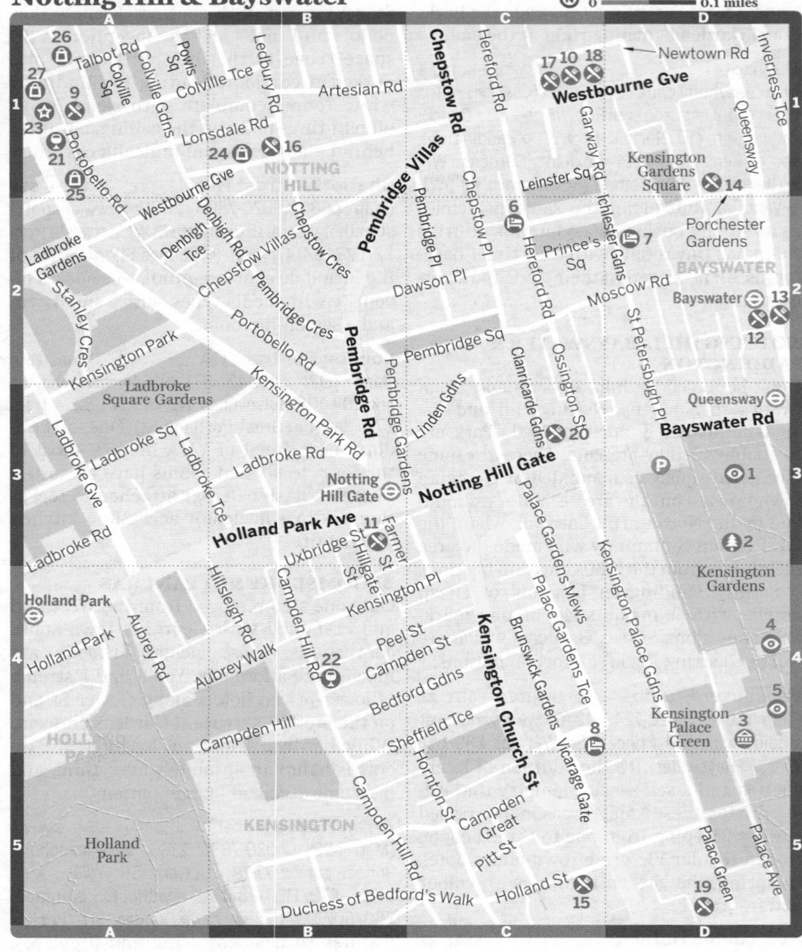

they're tiny (putting the 'closet' back into water closet).

Jesmond Dene B&B £

(Map p92; ☎020-7837 4654; www.jesmonddenehotel.co.uk; 27 Argyle St, WC1; s/d incl breakfast from £60/65; P@; ⊖Kings Cross) A surprisingly pleasant option for a place so close to busy Kings Cross station, this modest hotel has clean but small rooms, some of which share bathrooms.

London St Pancras YHA HOSTEL £

(Map p92; ☎020-7388 9998; www.yha.org.uk; 79 Euston Rd NW1; dm/r from £20/61; @; ⊖Kings Cross) A renovation in 2009 has made this 185-bed hostel one of the best in central London – even if it is on a busy road. Rooms range from private doubles to six-bed dorms; most have bathrooms. There's a good bar and cafe but no kitchen.

Ridgemount Hotel B&B £

(Map p92; ☎020-7636 1141; www.ridgemounthotel.co.uk; 65-67 Gower St WC1; s/d/tr/q £55/78/96/108, without bathroom £43/60/81/96; @; ⊖Goodge St) There's a comfortable, welcoming feel at this old-fashioned, slightly chintzy place that's been in the same family for 40 years.

Notting Hill & Bayswater

Sights

1 Diana, Princess of Wales Memorial Playground D3
2 Kensington Gardens D3
3 Kensington Palace D4
4 Orangery D4
5 Sunken Garden D4

Sleeping

6 New Linden Hotel C2
7 Vancouver Studios D2
8 Vicarage Private Hotel C4

Eating

Electric Brasserie .... (see 23)
9 GBK A1
10 GBK C1
11 Geales B3
12 Kam Tong D2
13 Kiasu D2
14 Le Café Anglais D1
15 Ottolenghi C5
16 Ottolenghi B1
17 Ping Pong C1
18 Planet Organic C1
19 Wagamama D5
20 Zizzi C3

Drinking

21 Trailer Happiness A1
22 Windsor Castle B4

Entertainment

23 Electric A1

Shopping

24 EC One B1
25 Portobello Road Market A1
26 Rough Trade A1
27 Travel Bookshop A1

Harlingford Hotel B&B ££
(Map p92; ☎020-7387 1551; www.harlingfordhotel.com; 61-63 Cartwright Gardens WC1; s/d £86/112; @; ⊖Russel Sq) This family-run hotel sports refreshing, upbeat decor: bright-green mosaic-tiled bathrooms (with trendy sinks), fuchsia bedspreads and colourful paintings. There's lots of stairs and no lift; request a 1st-floor room.

Jenkins Hotel B&B ££
(Map p92; ☎020-7387 2067; www.jenkinshotel.demon.co.uk; 45 Cartwright Gardens WC1; s/d from £52/95; ⊖Russell Sq) This modest hotel has featured in the TV series of Agatha Christie's *Poirot*. Rooms are small but the hotel has charm.

Morgan Hotel B&B ££
(Map p68; ☎020-7636 3735; www.morganhotel.co.uk; 24 Bloomsbury St WC1; s/d £95/115; ⊖Tottenham Court Rd) In a row of Georgian town houses alongside the British Museum, the Morgan has 20 guest rooms at its disposal. Don't fret about the busy location, though – the windows are double-glazed. The warmth and hospitality more than make up for the slightly cramped quarters.

Crescent Hotel B&B ££
(Map p92; ☎020-7387 1515; www.crescenthoteloflondon.com; 49-50 Cartwright Gardens WC1; s/d from £52/105; @; ⊖Russell Sq) There's a homely feel to this humble hotel, despite the odd saggy bed. It's one of the cheaper options on the crescent overlooking Cartwright Gardens.

Clink78 HOSTEL £
(Map p92; ☎020-7183 9400; www.clinkhostel.com; 78 Kings Cross Rd WC1; dm/r from £12/60; @; ⊖Kings Cross) If anyone can think of a more right-on London place to stay than the courthouse where The Clash went on trial, please let us know. You can watch TV from the witness box or sleep in the cells, but the majority of the rooms are custom-built and quite comfortable.

Clink261 HOSTEL £
(Map p92; ☎020-7833 9400; www.ashleehouse.co.uk; 261 Grays Inn Rd WC1; dm/r £12/50; @; ⊖Kings Cross) This hostel is a cheery surprise in a gritty but central location. It's not as massive as its sister, the 740-bed Clink around the corner, but neither does it have its historic import.

Generator HOSTEL £
(Map p92; ☎020-7388 7666; www.generatorhostels.com/london; 37 Tavistock Pl WC1; dm/r from £18/55; @; ⊖Russell Sq) Lashings of primary colours and shiny metal are the hallmarks of this futuristic hostel. This former police barracks has 820 beds; a bar that stays open until 2am and hosts quizzes, pool competitions, karaoke and DJs; safe-deposit boxes; and a large eating area (but no kitchen). Come to party.

George B&B £

(Map p92; ☎020-7387 8777; www.georgehotel.com; 58-60 Cartwright Gardens WC1; s/d from £55/69; @📶; ⊖Russell Sq) A friendly chap, this George, if a little old-fashioned. Cheaper rooms share bathrooms.

Hotel Cavendish B&B ££

(Map p92; ☎020-7636 9079; www.hotelcavendish.com; 75 Gower St WC1; s/d/tr/q £75/90/120/140; @📶; ⊖Goodge St) Bedrooms have flatscreen TVs and compact en suite shower rooms (some have pretty tiles and bumper mirrors). The two gardens at the back are a good place to catch some rays.

CLERKENWELL & FARRINGDON

In these now fashionable streets, it's hard to find an echo of the notorious 'rookeries' of the 19th century, where families were squeezed into damp, fetid basements, living in possibly the worst conditions in the city's history. This is the London documented so vividly by Dickens. It was also the traditional place for a last drink on the way to the gallows at Tyburn Hill – fitting, as many of the condemned hailed from here, as did many of those who were transported to Australia.

The availability of accommodation hasn't kept pace with Clerkenwell's revival, but it's still a great area to stay in. The best pickings aren't exactly cheap.

TOP CHOICE **Zetter Hotel** HOTEL £££

(Map p108; ☎020-7324 4444; www.thezetter.com; 86-88 Clerkenwell Rd EC1; d £180-423; @📶; ⊖Farringdon) A slick 21st-century conversion of a Victorian warehouse. The furnishings and facilities are cutting edge. You can even choose the colour of your room's lighting.

Rookery HOTEL £££

(Map p108; ☎020-7336 0931; www.rookeryhotel.com; Peter's Lane, Cowcross St EC1; s £205, d £258-582; @📶; ⊖Farringdon) Taking its name from London's notorious slums (Fagin's house in *Oliver Twist* was nearby), this antique-strewn luxury hotel recreates an 18th-century ambience with none of the attendant grime or crime. For a bird's-eye view of St Paul's, book the Rook's Nest, but be warned: Fagin never had a lift.

HOXTON, SHOREDITCH & SPITALFIELDS

It's always had a rough-edged reputation, but London's East End is being gentrified faster than you can say 'awrigh' guv'. Staying here, you'll be handy to some of London's best bars.

TOP CHOICE **Hoxton** HOTEL £

(Map p94; ☎020-7550 1000; www.hoxtonhotels.com; 81 Great Eastern St; d & tw £59-199; @📶; ⊖Old St) A novel approach to pricing means that while all the rooms are identical, the first ones on any given day are offered at £59: an absolute steal for a hotel of this calibre. The reasonably sized rooms all have comfy beds, quality linen and TVs that double as computers.

Andaz HOTEL ££

(Map p94; ☎020-7961 1234; www.london.liverpoolstreet.andaz.com; 40 Liverpool St EC2; r from £145; @📶; ⊖Liverpool St) The former Great Eastern Hotel is now the London flagship for Hyatt's youth-focused Andaz chain. There's no reception here, just black-clad staff who check you in on laptops. Rooms are a little generic but have free juice, snacks and wi-fi.

GREENWICH

If you'd rather keep the bustle of central London at arm's length and nightclubbing is your idea of hell, Greenwich offers a villagey ambience and some great old pubs to explore.

Number 16 B&B ££

(☎020-8853 4337; www.st-alfeges.co.uk; 16 St Alfege Passage SE10; s/d £75/90; @📶; DLR Cutty Sark) Both the house and the host have personality plus, so much so that they were featured on TV's *Hotel Inspector* series. The two double rooms are elegant and comfortable, but the single would only suit the vertically challenged and going to the toilet in the wardrobe might take some getting used to. From the DLR station head up Greenwich High St and look for St Alfege Passage on your left – it's the lane that skirts the church.

HAMPSTEAD & HIGHGATE

A little further out but still in transport Zone 2, the following are excellent options within walking distance of Hampstead Heath.

Palmers Lodge HOSTEL £

(☎020-7483 8470; www.palmerslodge.co.uk; 40 College Cres NW3; dm £18-38; P@📶; ⊖Swiss Cottage) Reminiscent of a period murder mystery (in a good way), this former children's hospital has bags of character. Listed by English Heritage, it's stuffed with cornicing, moulded ceilings, original fireplaces and imposing wooden panelling. Ceilings are high, rooms are spacious, there's a chapel bar with pews, a grand stairway and a roomy lounge. Privacy curtains make the 28-bed men's dorm bearable (imagine you're in the hold of a pirate ship), but they don't shut out the amorous noises in the couples' dorm. From Swiss Cottage tube station, cross Finchley Rd, turn left and take College Cres, which heads straight up the hill.

Hampstead Village Guesthouse B&B ££
(020-7435 8679; www.hampsteadguesthouse.com; 2 Kemplay Rd NW3; s £55-75, d £80-95, apt £100-175; ; Hampstead) Eclectic and thoroughly charming, this grand Victorian house has an easygoing hostess, comfy beds and a delightful back garden. There's also a studio flat, which can accommodate up to five people. From the tube station, turn left down Hampstead High St. After a few streets and lanes turn left into Willoughby Rd and then first right into Kemplay Rd.

AIRPORTS

Yotel CAPSULE HOTEL ££
(020-7100 1100; www.yotel.com; s/d £69/85, or per 4hr £29/45 then per additional hr £8;) Gatwick (South Terminal); Heathrow (Terminal 4) The best news for early-morning flyers since coffee-vending machines, Yotel's smart 'cabins' offer pint-sized luxury: comfy beds, soft lights, internet-connected TVs, monsoon showers and fluffy towels. Swinging cats isn't recommended, but when is it ever?

Eating

Dining out in London has become so fashionable that you can hardly open a menu without banging into some celebrity chef or other: at the time of writing, London's eateries had 59 Michelin stars between them. The range and quality of eating options has increased exponentially over the last few decades, with waves of immigrants bringing with them the flavours of their respective homelands. You'll still find relics of the London food scene's stodgy, surly past, but these days Londoners expect better.

In this section, we steer you towards restaurants and cafes distinguished by their location, value for money, unique features, original settings and, of course, good food. Vegetarians needn't worry; London has a host of dedicated meat-free joints, while most others offer at least a token dish.

There are supermarkets absolutely everywhere in central London. Look out for the big names: Waitrose, Tesco, Sainsbury's, Marks & Spencer, Morrisons and Asda.

WEST END

Mayfair, Soho and Covent Garden are the gastronomic heart of London, with stacks of restaurants and cuisines to choose from at budgets to suit both booze hounds and theatre-goers. If you're craving a decent coffee, this is the place to come.

TOP CHOICE **Hibiscus** FRENCH, BRITISH £££
(Map p68; 020-7629 2999; www.hibiscusrestaurant.co.uk; 29 Maddox St W1; 3-course lunch/dinner £30/70; Oxford Circus) Claude and Claire Bosi have generated an avalanche of praise and two Michelin stars since moving their restaurant from Shropshire to Mayfair. Expect adventurous, intricate dishes and perfect service.

Tamarind INDIAN ££
(Map p86; 020-7629 3561; www.tamarindrestaurant.com; 20 Queen St W1; mains £14-26; Green Park) A mix of spicy Moghul classics and new creations have earned this northwest Indian restaurant a Michelin star. The set lunches are a good deal (two/three courses £17/19).

Polpo ITALIAN ££
(Map p68; www.polpo.co.uk; 41 Beak St W1; dishes £1-7; closed dinner Sun; Piccadilly Circus) Come early or late, or expect to queue: this hip Venetian place doesn't take bookings and it's often as packed as a rush-hour tube. The friendly young staff maintain the waiting list efficiently and help you negotiate the delicious tapas-style menu. Serendipitously, Venetian painter Canaletto once resided here.

Great Queen Street BRITISH ££
(Map p68; 020-7242 0622; 32 Great Queen St WC2; mains £9-19; lunch daily, dinner Mon-Sat; Holborn) There's no tiara on this Great Queen, her claret-coloured walls and mismatched wooden chairs suggesting cosiness and informality. But the food's still the best of British, including lamb that melts in the mouth and Arbroath smokie (a whole smoked fish with creamy sauce).

Clerkenwell & Farringdon

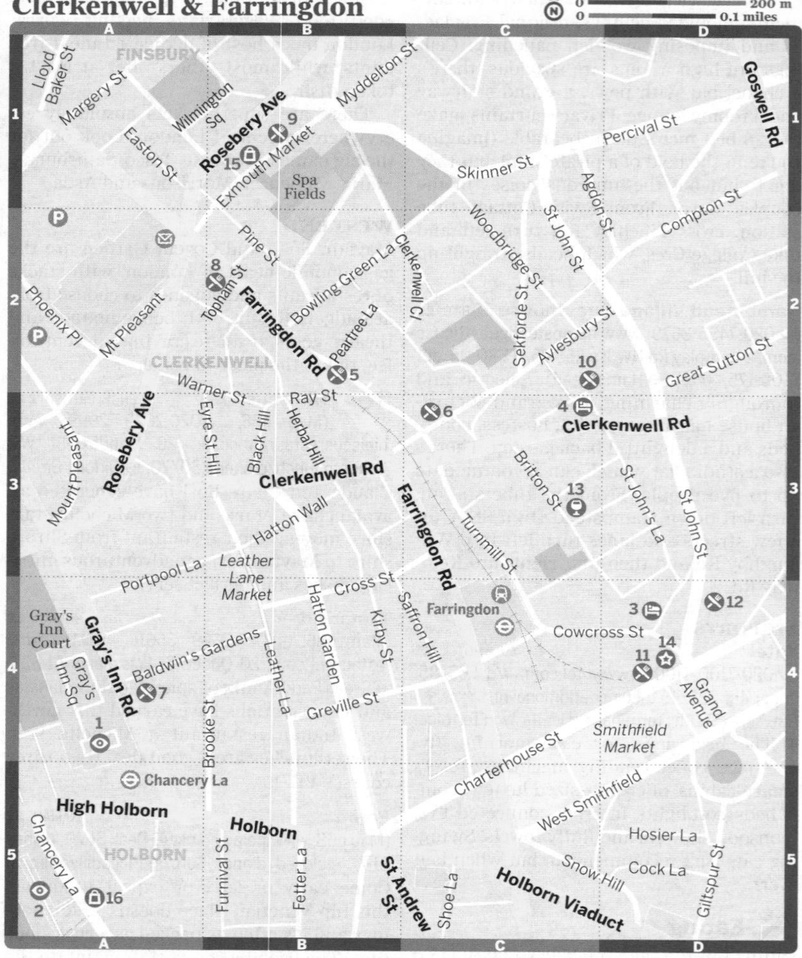

Veeraswamy INDIAN ££
(Map p68; ☎020-7734 1401; www.veeraswamy.com; 99 Regent St W1; mains £15-30, pre- & post-theatre 2-/3-course £18/21; ⊖Piccadilly Circus) Since 1926 Veeraswamy has occupied this prime 1st-floor location, with windows looking over Regent St – making it Britain's longest-running Indian restaurant. The excellent food, engaging service and exotic, elegant decor make for a memorable eating experience. The entrance is on Swallow St.

Wild Honey MODERN EUROPEAN ££
(☎020-7758 9160; www.wildhoneyrestaurant.co.uk; 12 St George St W1; mains £15-24; ⊖Oxford Circus) If you fancy a relatively affordable meal within the oak-panelled ambience of a top Mayfair restaurant, Wild Honey offers excellent lunch and pre-theatre set menus (respectively, £19 and £22 for three courses).

Sketch FRENCH £££
(Map p68; ☎020-7659 4500; www.sketch.uk.com; 9 Conduit St W1; Parlour mains £5-16, Gallery mains £11-32, Lecture Room 2-course lunch/8-course dinner £30/95; ⊖Oxford Circus) A design enthusiast's dream, with shimmering white rooms, video projections,

Clerkenwell & Farringdon

Sights

1 Gray's Inn A4
2 Lincoln's Inn A5

Sleeping

3 Rookery D4
4 Zetter Hotel C3

Eating

5 5ifty 4our B2
Bistrot Bruno Loubet .... (see 4)
6 Dans le Noir C3
7 Konditor & Cook A4
8 Little Bay B2
9 Medcalf B1
10 Modern Pantry C2
11 Smiths of Smithfield D4
12 St John D4

Drinking

13 Jerusalem Tavern C3

Entertainment

14 Fabric D4

Shopping

15 EC One B1
16 London Silver Vaults A5

designer Louis XIV chairs and toilet cubicles shaped like eggs. And that's just the Gallery, which becomes a buzzy restaurant and bar at night. The ground-floor Parlour has decadent cakes and decor, but is surprisingly affordable: perfect for breakfast, or afternoon tea served on fine bone china. The swanky Lecture Room upstairs is the realm of Pierre Gagnaire, whose book *Reinventing French Cuisine* gives a hint of what to expect.

Giaconda Dining Room MODERN EUROPEAN ££
(Map p68; ☎020-7240 3334; www.giacondadining.com; 9 Denmark St WC2; mains £12-15; ⏰Mon-Fri; ⊖Tottenham Court Rd) Blink and you'll miss this 10-table restaurant (we did at first). It's well worth hunting down for quality British, French and Italian dishes and attentive service. Pig trotters are a speciality, but for those less au fait with offal, there's always a choice of fish dishes.

Abeno Too JAPANESE £
(Map p68; www.abeno.co.uk; 17-18 Great Newport St WC2; mains £8-13; ⊖Leicester Sq) This restaurant specialises in soba (noodles) and *okonomi-yaki* (Japanese-style pancakes), which are cooked in front of you on a hotplate. Sit at the bar or by the window and feast.

Yauatcha CHINESE ££
(Map p68; ☎020-7494 8888; www.yauatcha.com; 15 Broadwick St W1; dishes £3-17; ⊖Piccadilly Circus) Dim sum restaurants don't come much cooler than this, and the menu is fantastic and Michelin-starred. It's housed in an architecturally interesting building, with a choice of light-filled ground floor tables or a hip basement area.

Arbutus MODERN EUROPEAN ££
(Map p68; ☎020-7734 4545; www.arbutusrestaurant.co.uk; 63-64 Frith St W1; mains £14-20; ⊖Tottenham Court Rd) Focusing on seasonal produce, inventive dishes and value for money, Anthony Demetre's Michelin-starred restaurant just keeps getting better.

L'Atelier de Joël Robuchon FRENCH ££
(Map p68; ☎020-7010 8600; www.joel-robuchon.com; 13 West St WC2; mains £16-34; ⊖Leicester Sq) Superchef Robuchon has 25 Michelin stars to his name – and two of them are derived from this, his London flagship. A wall of living foliage adds lushness to the dimly lit dining room, with a sparkling open kitchen as its showcase. Degustation (£125) and set lunch and pre-theatre menus (two-/three-courses £22/27) are available.

Sacred CAFE £
(Map p68; www.sacredcafe.co.uk; mains £4-6) Ganton St (13 Ganton St W1; ⏰7.30am-8pm Mon-Fri, 10am-7pm Sat & Sun; ⊖Oxford Circus); Covent Garden (Stanfords, 12-14 Long Acre ⏰9am-7.30pm Mon-Fri, 10am-8pm Sat, noon-6pm Sun; ⊖Covent Garden) The spiritual paraphernalia and blatant Kiwiana don't seem to deter the smart Carnaby St set from lounging around this eclectic cafe. That's down to the excellent coffee and appealing counter food.

National Dining Rooms BRITISH £££
(Map p68; ☎020-7747 2525; www.thenationaldiningrooms.co.uk; Sainsbury Wing, National Gallery WC2; 2-/3-course meals £23/26; ⏰10am-5pm Sat-Thu, 10am-8.30pm Fri; ⊖Charing Cross) It's fitting that this acclaimed restaurant should celebrate British food, being in the National Gallery and overlooking Trafalgar Sq. For a much cheaper option with the same views, ambience, quality produce and excellent service, try a salad, pie or tart at the adjoining bakery.

Fernandez & Wells DELICATESSEN CAFE £
(Map p68; www.fernandezandwells.com; 73 Beak St W1; mains £4-5; Piccadilly Circus) With its sister deli around the corner, there's no shortage of delicious charcuterie and cheese to fill the fresh baguettes on the counter of this teensy cafe. The coffee's superb.

HK Diner CHINESE £
(Map p68; 22 Wardour St W1; mains £6-13; 11am-4am; Piccadilly Circus) If you've a hankering for soft-shelled crab or barbecued pork in the wee hours of the morning, this Hong Kong–style cafe (delicious food, no-nonsense decor) is the place to come.

Nordic Bakery SCANDINAVIAN £
(Map p68; www.nordicbakery.com; 14a Golden Sq W1; snacks £3-5; 8am-8pm Mon-Fri, 9am-7pm Sat, 11am-6pm Sun; Piccadilly Circus) As simple and stylish as you'd expect from the Scandinavians, this small cafe has bare wooden walls and uncomplicated Danish snacks, such as sticky cinnamon buns and salmon served on dark rye bread.

Bocca di Lupo ITALIAN ££
(Map p68; 020-7734 2223; www.boccadilupo.com; 12 Archer St W1; mains £11-25; Piccadilly Circus) A new Italian restaurant that has sent ecstatic tremors down Londoners' taste buds, Bocca di Lupo hides down a dark Soho backstreet and radiates elegant sophistication.

Barrafina SPANISH ££
(Map p68; 020-7813 8016; www.barrafina.co.uk; 54 Frith St W1; tapas £4-13; Tottenham Court Rd) They may not be as reasonably priced as you'd get in Spain, but the quality of the tapas served here is excellent.

Hummus Bros BUDGET £
(Map p68; www.hbros.co.uk; mains £4-8;); Soho (88 Wardour St W1; Piccadilly Circus); Holborn (Map p68; 37-63 Southampton Row W1; Holborn); Cheapside (Map p74; 128 Cheapside EC2; St Pauls) Don't come here if you're chickpea-challenged, because this informal place is hummus heaven. It comes in small or regular bowls with a choice of meat or veggie toppings and a side of pita bread.

THE CITY

You'll be sorely dismayed if you've got an empty belly on a Sunday morning in the City. Even during the busy weekdays, the chain eateries are often your best option.

1 Lombard St FRENCH ££
(020-7929 6611; www.1lombardstreet.com; 1 Lombard St EC3; mains £15-30; Bank) Cassoulet goes head-to-head with bangers and mash in the brasserie, under the domes of a heritage-listed bank building, and both the French and the Brits come out winners.

SOUTH BANK

You'll find plenty of touristy eateries on the riverside, making the most of the constant foot traffic and iconic London views. For a feed with a local feel, head to Borough Market or Bermondsey St.

Oxo Tower Brasserie FUSION £££
(Map p80; 020-7803 3888; www.harveynichols.com; Barge House St SE1; mains £18-26; Waterloo) The spectacular views are the big drawcard, so skip the restaurant and head for the slightly less extravagantly priced brasserie, or if you're not hungry, the bar. The food is excellent, combining European and East Asian flavours. Set-price menus (two/three courses £23/27) are offered at lunchtime, before 6.15pm and after 10pm.

Magdalen BRITISH ££
(Map p82; 020-7403 1342; www.magdalenrestaurant.co.uk; 152 Tooley St SE1; mains £14-18, lunch 2-/3-course £16/19; lunch Mon-Fri, dinner Mon-Sat; London Bridge) Roasting up the best of the critters that walk, hop, flap and splash around these fair isles, Magdalen isn't the place to bring a vegetarian or a weight-conscious waif on a date. Carnivorous couples, however, will appreciate the elegant room and traditional treats presented in interesting ways.

Delfina MODERN EUROPEAN ££
(Map p82; 020-7357 0244; www.thedelfina.co.uk; 50 Bermondsey St SE1; mains £10-15; lunch Sun-Fri, dinner Fri; London Bridge) This white-walled restaurant in a converted Victorian chocolate factory serves delicious modern cuisine to a backdrop of contemporary canvases. Sunday roasts are popular.

Anchor & Hope GASTROPUB ££
(Map p80; 36 The Cut SE1; mains £12-17; lunch Tue-Sun, dinner Mon-Sat; Southwark) The hope is that you'll get a table without waiting hours because you can't book at this quintessential gastropub. The Anchor serves gutsy, unashamedly meaty British food.

CHAIN-CHAIN-CHAIN, CHAIN OF FOODS

It's an unnerving, but not uncommon, experience to discover the idiosyncratic cafe or pub you were so proud of finding on your first day in London popping up on every other high street. But among the endless Caffe Neros, Pizza Expresses and All-Bar-Ones are some gems – or, at least, great fallback options. Some of the best:

GBK GOURMET BURGERS

(Map p104, p92, p86, p74, p94, p82, p68; www.gbk.co.uk) Gourmet Burger Kitchens dish up creative burger constructions, including lots of vegetarian options.

Konditor & Cook BAKERY

(Map p108, p74, p82, p68; www.konditorandcook.com) London's best bakery chain serves excellent cakes, pastries, bread and coffee.

Leon BISTRO

(p74, p94, p68; www.leonrestaurants.co.uk) Focuses on fresh, seasonal food (salads, wraps and the like).

Ping Pong CHINESE

(Map p104, Map p80, p94, p68; www.pingpongdimsum.com) Stylish Chinese dumpling joints.

S&M Cafe BRITISH

(Map p116, Map p94; www.sandmcafe.co.uk) The sausages and mash served in these retro diners won't give your wallet a spanking.

Wagamama JAPANESE

(Map p116, p74, p64, p104, p114, p94, p86, p68,p80, p82; www.wagamama.com) Japanese noodles that ar taking over the world from their London base.

Zizzi ITALIAN

(Map p104, p64, p68,p90; www.zizzi.co.uk) Wood-fired pizza.

BELGRAVIA

Olivomare ITALIAN ££

(Map p86; ☎020-7730 9022; www.olivorestaurants.com; 10 Lower Belgrave St SW1; mains £14-21; ⊖Victoria) The Sardinian seaside comes to Belgravia in a dazzling white dining room with flavoursome seafood dishes, regional wines and impeccable service.

Thomas Cubitt BRITISH ££

(Map p86; ☎020-7730 6060; www.thethomascubitt.co.uk; 44 Elizabeth St SW1; mains £17-23; ⊖Victoria) The bar below gets jammed to the impressively high rafters with the swanky Belgravia set, but don't let that put you off this excellent, elegant dining room. The culinary focus is thoroughly British and deftly executed. The downstairs menu is cheaper (£10 to £17).

KNIGHTSBRIDGE

Marcus Wareing at the Berkeley FRENCH £££

(Map p86; ☎020-7235 1200; www.marcus-wareing.com; Berkeley Hotel, Wilton Pl SW1; 3-course lunch/dinner £38/75; ⊖Knightsbridge) A very public spat between Marcus Wareing and his former boss Gordon Ramsay has added an entertaining frisson of drama to the London scene. Wareing now runs this one-time Ramsay restaurant under his own name, and its reputation for exquisite food and exemplary service has only been enhanced.

Boxwood Cafe BRITISH, FRENCH £££

(Map p86; ☎020-7235 1010; www.gordonramsay.com/boxwoodcafe; Berkeley Hotel, Wilton Pl SW1; mains £18-25; ⊖Knightsbridge) An accessible entry point into Gordon Ramsay's eating empire, Boxwood offers set-price lunch and pre-7pm menus (two/three courses £21/25). It's intended as an informal option – although you wouldn't guess it from the attentive staff, faultless food and staid decor.

CHELSEA & KENSINGTON

These highbrow neighbourhoods harbour some of London's very best (and priciest) restaurants. Perhaps the Chelsea toffs are secretly titillated by the foul-mouthed tele-chefs in their midst.

Tom's Kitchen FRENCH ££
(Map p86; ☎020-7349 0202; www.tomskitchen.co.uk; 27 Cale St SW3; breakfast £4-15, mains £15-30; ⊙breakfast Mon-Fri, lunch & dinner daily; ⊖South Kensington) A much more informal and considerably cheaper option than Tom Aikens' eponymous restaurant, just around the corner, the firebrand chef's kitchen maintains the magic throughout the day. The breakfasts are excellent.

L'Etranger FRENCH, JAPANESE ££
(Map p86; ☎020-7584 1118; www.etranger.co.uk; 36 Gloucester Rd SW7; mains £15-29; ⊖Gloucester Rd) A refined grey and burgundy interior (echoed in waitress uniforms that are part kimono, part Parisian runway) sets the tone for a romantic formal dining experience. While most of the menu is mainly French, it's also possible to blow the budget on sashimi and five types of caviar. The two-/three-course set weekday lunches and pre-6.45pm dinners are £17/20.

Made in Italy ITALIAN £
(Map p86; ☎020-7352 1880; www.madeinitalygroup.co.uk; 249 King's Rd SW3; pizzas £5-11, mains £8-17; ⊙lunch Sat & Sun, dinner daily; ⊖Sloane Sq) Pizza is served by the tasty quarter-metre at this traditional trattoria. Sit on the Chelsea roof terrace and dream of Napoli.

Orsini ITALIAN ££
(Map p86; www.orsiniristorante.com; 8a Thurloe Pl SW3; snacks £2-6, mains £9-16; ⊙8am-10pm; ⊖South Kensington) Marinated in authentic Italian charm, this tiny family-run eatery serves excellent espresso and deliciously fresh baguettes stuffed with Parma ham and mozzarella. More substantial fare is offered in the evenings.

Gordon Ramsay FRENCH £££
(Map p86; ☎020-7352 4441; www.gordonramsay.com; 68 Royal Hospital Rd SW3; 3-course lunch/dinner £45/90; ⊖Sloane Sq) Like or loathe the ubiquitous Scot, his eponymous restaurant is one of Britain's finest – one of only four in the country with three Michelin stars. Book ahead and dress up: jeans and T-shirts are forbidden – if you've seen the chef on the telly, you know not to argue.

NOTTING HILL, BAYSWATER & PADDINGTON

Notting Hill teems with good places to eat, from cheap takeaways to atmospheric pubs and restaurants worthy of the fine-dining tag. Queensway has the best strip of Asian restaurants this side of Soho.

Kiasu SOUTHEAST ASIAN £
(Map p104; www.kiasu.co.uk; 48 Queensway W2; mains £6-9; ⊖Bayswater) Local Malaysians and Singaporeans rate this place highly, as do those who know a tasty cheap thing when they see it. Kiasu serves 'Food from the Straits of Malacca'. You'll also find Thai and Vietnamese food on the menu, but it's hard to go past the delicious and filling laksa.

Geales SEAFOOD ££
(Map p104; ☎020-7727 7528; www.geales.com; 2 Farmer St W8; 2-course lunch £10, mains £10-18; ⊙closed lunch Mon; ⊖Notting Hill Gate) It may have opened in 1939 as a humble chippy, but now it's so much more. Fresh fish stars in a variety of guises – either battered and British or with an Italian sensibility. Tables spill out onto the pleasant side street.

Electric Brasserie FRENCH ££
(Map p104; ☎020-7908 9696; www.electricbrasserie.com; 191 Portobello Rd W11; breakfasts £5-13, mains £11-20; ⊖Ladbroke Grove) The leather-and-cream look is suitably cool for the brasserie that's attached to the Electric Cinema. And the food's very good, too; head to the back area for a darker, more moody dinner. The two-/three-course pre-7pm dinner (£14/17) is served Monday to Friday.

Kam Tong CHINESE £
(www.kam-tong.co.uk; mains £8-17) Bayswater (Map p104; 59-63 Queensway W2; ⊖Bayswater); Chinatown (Map p68; 14 Lisle St WC2; ⊖Leicester Sq) When most of the clientele are actually Chinese, you know you're on to a good thing. Kam Tong serves genuine Cantonese and Szechuan dishes and wonderful yum cha (£3 to £4).

Satay House MALAYSIAN £
(☎020-7723 6763; www.satay-house.co.uk; 13 Sale Pl W2; mains £5-19; ⊖Edgware Rd) Authentic Malaysian cuisine, including some dishes that will blow your head off, have been served here for nearly 40 years. Book ahead for an upstairs table, although the communal tables in the basement can be fun. Sale Pl is one block along Sussex Gardens from Edgware Rd.

Le Café Anglais MODERN EUROPEAN ££
(Map p104; ☎020-7221 1415; www.lecafeanglais.co.uk; 8 Porchester Gardens W2; mains £13-25, 3-course menu £30; ⊖Bayswater) This bustling restaurant has a very eclectic menu (from gigantic roasts to Thai curries) that means to please everybody and usually does.

MARYLEBONE

You won't go too far wrong planting yourself on a table anywhere along Marylebone's charming High Street.

Providores & Tapa Room FUSION £££
(Map p90; ☎020-7935 6175; www.theprovidores.co.uk; 109 Marylebone High St W1; 2-/3-/4-/5-course meals £30/43/53/60; ⊖Baker St) New Zealand's greatest culinary export since kiwi fruit, chef Peter Gordon works his fusion magic here, matching his creations with NZ wines. Downstairs, in a cute play on words, the Tapa Room (as in the Polynesian barkcloth) serves sophisticated tapas, along with excellent breakfasts.

La Fromagerie CAFE, DELI £
(Map p90; www.lafromagerie.co.uk; 2-6 Moxon St W1; mains £6-13; ⊖Baker St) This deli-cafe has bowls of delectable salads, antipasto, peppers and beans scattered about the long communal table. Huge slabs of bread invite you to tuck in, and all the while the heavenly waft from the cheese room beckons.

Locanda Locatelli ITALIAN ££
(Map p90; ☎020-7935 9088; www.locandalocatelli.com; 8 Seymour St W1; mains £11-30; ⊖Marble Arch) Known for its sublime pasta dishes, this dark but quietly glamorous restaurant in an otherwise unremarkable hotel is one of London's hottest tables.

FITZROVIA

Tucked away behind busy Tottenham Court Rd, Fitzrovia's Charlotte and Goodge Sts form one of central London's most vibrant eating precincts.

Hakkasan CHINESE ££
(Map p68; ☎020-7927 7000; www.hakkasan.com; 8 Hanway Pl W1; mains £11-58; ⊖Tottenham Court Rd) Hidden down a lane like all fashionable haunts need to be, the first Chinese restaurant to get a Michelin star combines celebrity status, a dimly lit basement dining room, persuasive cocktails and sophisticated food.

Salt Yard SPANISH, ITALIAN ££
(Map p68; ☎020-7637 0657; www.saltyard.co.uk; 54 Goodge St W1; tapas £4-8; ⊖Goodge St) Named after the place where cold meats are cured, this softly lit joint serves delicious Spanish and Italian tapas. Try the roasted chicken leg with gnocchi, wild garlic and sorrel, or flex your palate with courgette flowers stuffed with cheese and drizzled with honey.

Lantana CAFE £
(Map p68; www.lantanacafe.co.uk; 13 Charlotte Pl W1; mains £4-10; ⏲breakfast & lunch Mon-Sat; ⊖Goodge St) Excellent coffee and substantial, inventive brunches induce queues on Saturday mornings outside this Australian-style cafe.

CAMDEN TOWN

Camden's great for cheap eats, while neighbouring Chalk Farm and Primrose Hill are salted with gastropubs and upmarket restaurants.

Engineer GASTROPUB ££
(Map p114; ☎020-7722 0950; 65 Gloucester Ave NW1; mains £13-21; ⊖Chalk Farm) One of London's original gastropubs, the Engineer has been serving up consistently good international cuisine to hip north Londoners for a fair while now. The courtyard garden is a real treat on balmy summer nights.

Mango Room CARIBBEAN ££
(Map p114; ☎020-7482 5065; www.mangoroom.co.uk; 10-12 Kentish Town Rd NW1; mains £11-14; ⊖Camden Town) With exposed-brick walls hung with bright cartoonish paintings, Mango Room is an upmarket Caribbean experience serving a mix of modern and traditional dishes: Creole fish, goat curry, jerk chicken etc. The rum-based happy hour cocktails (£4, 6pm to 8pm) will get you in the tropical mood.

ISLINGTON

Allow at least an evening to explore Islington's Upper St, along with the lanes leading off it.

TOP CHOICE **Le Mercury** FRENCH £
(Map p116; ☎020-7354 4088; www.lemercury.co.uk; 140A Upper St N1; mains £7-10; ⊖Highbury & Islington) A cosy Gallic haunt ideal for cash-strapped Casanovas, given that it appears much more expensive than it is. Sunday lunch by the open fire upstairs is a treat, although you'll have to book.

Ottolenghi BAKERY, MEDITERRANEAN ££
(www.ottolenghi.co.uk; mains £10-15; ⏲8am-8pm Mon-Sat, 9am-6pm Sat) Islington (Map p116; ☎020-7288 1454; 287 Upper St N1; ⏲8am-11pm Mon-Sat, 9am-7pm Sun; ⊖Angel); Belgravia (Map p86; 13 Motcomb St SW1; ⊖Knightsbridge); Kensington (Map p104; 1 Holland St W8; ⊖High St Kensington); Notting Hill (Map p104; 63 Ledbury Rd W11; ⊖Notting Hill Gate) Mountains of meringues tempt you through the door, where

Camden Town

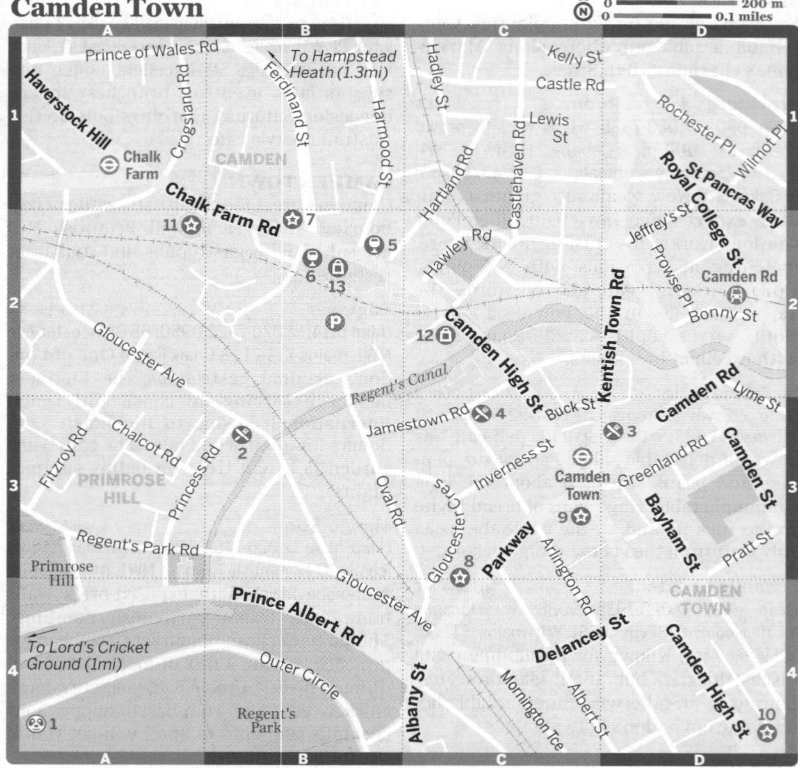

Camden Town

Sights

1 London Zoo A4

Eating

2 Engineer B3
3 Mango Room D3
4 Wagamama C3

Drinking

5 Lock Tavern B2
6 Proud B2

Entertainment

7 Barfly B2
8 Dublin Castle C3
9 Jazz Cafe C3
10 Koko D4
11 Roundhouse A2

Shopping

12 Camden Lock Market C2
13 Camden Stables Market B2

a sumptuous array of bakery treats and salads greets you. Meals are as light and tasty as the oh-so-white interior design. Vegetarians are well catered for. The Islington branch is open till later – until 11pm, and 7pm on Sundays.

Regent PIZZA £

(Map p116; 201 Liverpool Rd N1; mains £7-11; Angel) Delicious crispy-based pizza with deli toppings is what the regular crowd of youngish Islingtonians come here for. The ambience is more pub than gastropub, and the jukebox is loaded with indie pop gems.

Duke of Cambridge GASTROPUB ££

(Map p116; 020-7359 3066; www.dukeorganic.co.uk; 30 St Peter's St N1; mains £14-18; Angel) Pioneers in bringing sustainability to the table, this tucked-away gastropub serves only organic food, wine and beer, fish from sustainable sources and locally sourced fruit, vegetables and meat.

Planet Organic GROCERIES
(www.planetorganic.co.uk) Islington (Map p116; 64 Essex Rd, N1; ⊖Angel); Bayswater (Map p104; 42 Westbourne Grove W2; ⊖Bayswater); Fitzrovia (Map p92; 22 Torrington Pl WC1; ⊖Goodge St) As the name suggests, everything in this cafe/supermarket is organic. Fresh veggies are sourced (where possible) directly from British farms.

CLERKENWELL & FARRINGDON

Clerkenwell's hidden gems are well worth digging for. Pedestrianised Exmouth Market is a good place to start.

TOP CHOICE **Bistrot Bruno Loubet** FRENCH ££
(Map p108; 020-7324 4455; www.bistrotbrunoloubet.com; 86-88 Clerkenwell Rd EC1; mains £12-17; breakfast, lunch & dinner; ⊖Farringdon) There are London restaurants that charge twice as much for food half as good as what's on offer at this informal but stylish bistro below the Zetter Hotel. Top-quality ingredients, surprising taste combinations and faultless execution all come together – in the food, the cocktails and the home-infused aperitifs.

St John BRITISH ££
(Map p108; 020-7251 0848; www.stjohnrestaurant.com; 26 St John St EC1; mains £14-22; ⊖Farringdon) Bright whitewashed brick walls, high ceilings and simple wooden furniture keep diners free to concentrate on the world-famous nose-to-tail offerings. Expect offal, ox tongue and bone marrow.

5ifty 4our MALAYSIAN ££
(Map p108; 020-7336 0603; www.54farringdon.com; 54 Farringdon Rd; mains £11-16; ⊖Farringdon) Britain and Malaysia go back a long way and this smart-looking restaurant celebrates that fact with tasty fusion dishes such as lamb shanks with a spicy *redang* sauce.

Smiths of Smithfield BRITISH ££
(Map p108; 020-7251 7950; www.smithsofsmithfield.co.uk; 67-77 Charterhouse St EC1; mains 1st fl £13-15, top floor £19-30; ⊖Farringdon) This converted meat-packing warehouse endeavours to be all things to all people and succeeds. Hit the ground-floor bar for a beer, follow the silver-clad ducts and wooden beams upstairs to a relaxed dining space, or continue up for two more floors of feasting, each slightly smarter and pricier than the last.

Little Bay EUROPEAN £
(Map p108; 020-7278 1234; www.little-bay.co.uk; 171 Farringdon Rd EC1; mains before/after 7pm £6.45/8.45; ⊖Farringdon) The crushed-velvet ceiling, handmade twisted lamps that improve around the room (as the artist got better) and elaborately painted bar and tables showing nymphs frolicking are bonkers but fun. The hearty food is very good value.

Modern Pantry FUSION ££
(Map p108; 020-7553 9210; www.themodernpantry.co.uk; 47-48 St John's Sq EC1; mains £15-22; breakfast, lunch & dinner; ⊖Farringdon) Currently one of London's most talked-about eateries, this three-floor Georgian town house in the heart of Clerkenwell has a cracking, innovative, all-day menu.

Medcalf BRITISH ££
(Map p108; 020-7833 3533; www.medcalfbar.co.uk; 40 Exmouth Market EC1; mains £10-16; closed dinner Sun; ⊖Angel) Medcalf is one of the best value hang outs on Exmouth Market. Housed in a beautifully converted 1912 butcher's shop, it serves up interesting and well-realised British fare.

Dans le Noir THEME RESTAURANT £££
(Map p108; 020-7253 1100; 30-31 Clerkenwell Green EC1; 2-/3-course meals £39/44; dinner Mon-Sat; ⊖Farringdon) If you've ever felt in the dark about food, eating in the pitch black might suit you. A visually impaired waiter guides you to your table, plate and cutlery. Then it's up to you to guess what you're eating and enjoy the anonymous conviviality of the dark.

HOXTON, SHOREDITCH & SPITALFIELDS

From the hit-and-miss Bangladeshi restaurants of Brick Lane to the Vietnamese strip on Kingsland Rd, plus the Jewish, Spanish, French, Italian and Greek eateries in between, the East End's cuisine is as multicultural as its residents.

Fifteen ITALIAN ££
(0871 330 1515; www.fifteen.net; 15 Westland Pl N1; breakfast £2-8.50, trattoria mains £6-11, restaurant mains £11-25; breakfast, lunch & dinner; ⊖Old St) Jamie Oliver's culinary philanthropy started at Fifteen, set up to give unemployed young people a shot at a career. The Italian food is beyond excellent, and, surprisingly, even those on limited budgets can afford a visit. In the trattoria, a croissant and coffee will only set you

Islington

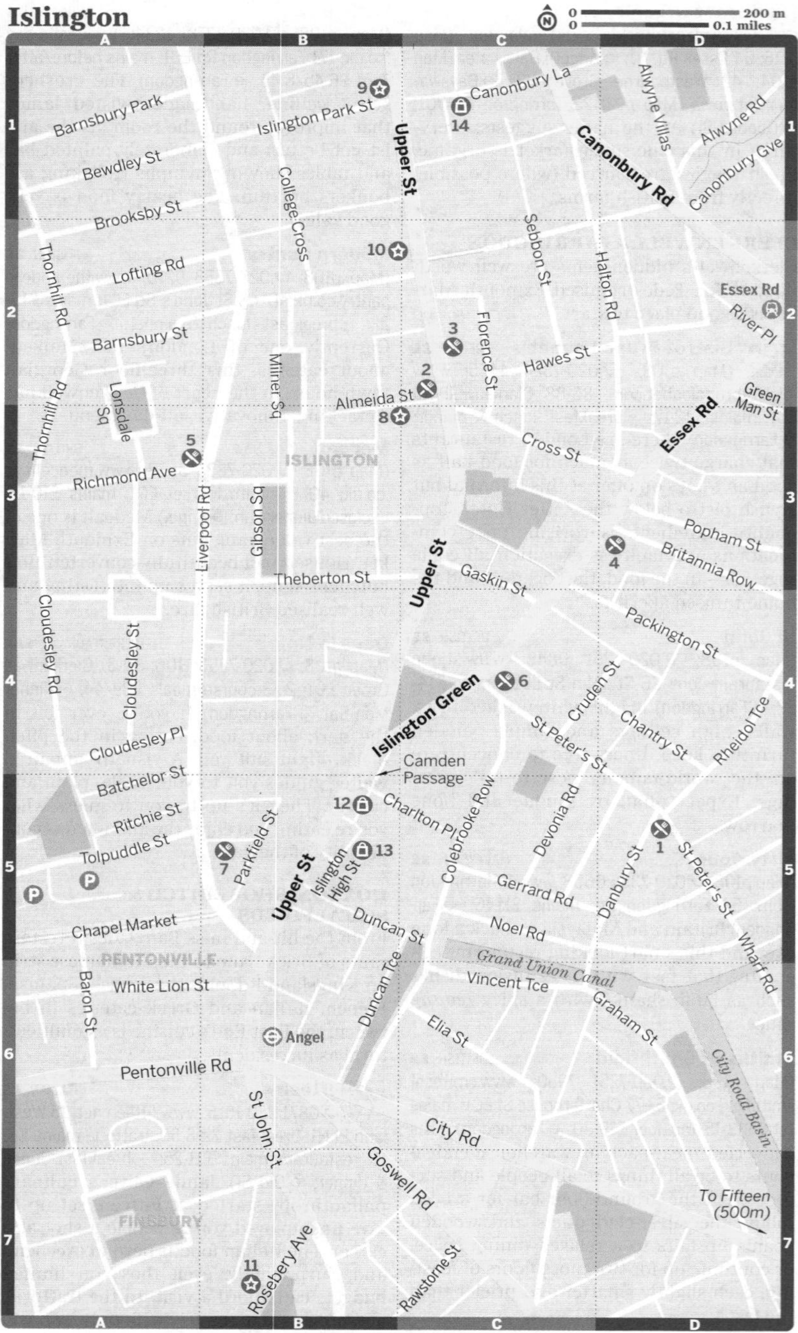

0 200 m
0 0.1 miles
A
B
C
D
1
2
3
4
5
6
7
Barnsbury Park
Islington Park St
Canonbury La
Alwyne Villas
Alwyne Rd
Canonbury Gve
Canonbury Rd
Upper St
College Cross
Bewdley St
Brooksby St
Lofting Rd
Thornhill Rd
Sebbon St
Halton Rd
Essex Rd
River Pl
Barnsbury St
Florence St
Hawes St
Milner Sq
Almeida St
Lonsdale Sq
Green Man St
Essex Rd
Cross St
ISLINGTON
Richmond Ave
Liverpool Rd
Gibson Sq
Popham St
Britannia Row
Theberton St
Gaskin St
Packington St
Cloudesley Rd
Cloudesley St
Islington Green
Cruden St
Chantry St
Rheidol Tce
St Peter's St
Cloudesley Pl
Camden Passage
Batchelor St
Charlton Pl
Colebrooke Row
Devonia Rd
Ritchie St
Tolpuddle St
Parkfield St
Islington High St
Danbury St
Gerrard Rd
Chapel Market
Duncan St
Noel Rd
PENTONVILLE
Grand Union Canal
Wharf Rd
White Lion St
Duncan Tce
Vincent Tce
Graham St
Baron St
Elia St
Angel
City Road Basin
Pentonville Rd
St John St
City Rd
Goswell Rd
To Fifteen (500m)
FINSBURY
Rosebery Ave
Rawstorne St

Islington

Eating

1	Duke of Cambridge	D5
2	Le Mercury	C2
3	Ottolenghi	C2
4	Planet Organic	D3
5	Regent	A3
6	S&M Cafe	C4
7	Wagamama	B5

Entertainment

8	Almeida	B3
9	Hope & Anchor	B1
10	Lucky Voice	B2
11	Sadler's Wells	B7

Shopping

12	Camden Passage Market	B5
13	Laura J London	B5
14	Palette London	C1

back £3.50, while a £10 pasta makes for a delicious lunch. From Old St tube station, take City Rd and after 300m turn right into Westland Place.

Song Que VIETNAMESE £
(134 Kingsland Rd E2; mains £5-8; Old St) If you arrive after 7.30pm, expect to queue: this humble eatery has already had its cover blown as one of the best Vietnamese restaurants in London. There's never much time to admire the institutional-green walls, fake lobsters and bizarre horse portrait, as you'll be shunted out shortly after your last bite. Song Que is 300m along Kingsland Rd, the continuation of Shoreditch High St.

L'Anima ITALIAN ££
(Map p94; 020-7422 7000; www.lanima.co.uk; 1 Snowden St EC2; mains £11-32; lunch Mon-Fri, dinner Mon-Sat; Liverpool St) Sleek design meets accomplished cooking – what could be more Italian? The capacious space is divided into a formal dining room and a bar/lounge where you can drop in for a quick pasta fix.

Story Deli PIZZA ££
(Map p94; www.storydeli.com; 3 Dray Walk; pizzas £13; Liverpool St) This organic cafe, with mismatched cutlery poking out of jam jars, vintage mirrors leaning haphazardly against walls, high ceilings and solid wooden furniture (mismatched of course) is justifiably popular. The pizzas are thin and crispy, and you can rest assured that anything fishy has been sustainably caught.

Albion BRITISH ££
(Map p94; www.albioncaff.co.uk; 2-4 Boundary St E2; mains £9-13; Old St) For those wanting to be taken back to Dear Old Blighty's cuisine but with rather less grease and stodge, this self-consciously retro 'caff' serves up top-quality bangers and mash, steak-and-kidney pies, devilled kidneys and, of course, fish and chips.

Les Trois Garçons FRENCH £££
(Map p94; 020-7613 1924; www.lestroisgarcons.com; 1 Club Row E1; Mon-Thu 2-/3-courses £27/31, Fri & Sat £40/46; closed Sun; Liverpool St) The name may prepare you for the French menu, but nothing on earth could prepare you for the camp decor. A virtual menagerie of stuffed or bronze animals fills every surface, while chandeliers dangle between a set of suspended handbags. The food is great, if overpriced, and the small army of bow-tie-wearing waiters unobtrusively delivers complimentary bread and tasty gifts from the kitchen.

Hoxton Apprentice EUROPEAN ££
(Map p94; 020-7749 2828; www.hoxtonapprentice.com; 16 Hoxton Sq N1; mains £11-15; 11am-11pm Tue-Sat, to 6pm Sun; Old St) Both professionals and apprentices work the kitchen in this restaurant, under the auspices of the Training For Life charity. Appropriately enough, it's housed in a Victorian school building.

Cafe Bangla BANGLADESHI £
(Map p94; 128 Brick Lane E1; mains £5-15; Liverpoool St) Dining in the famous curry houses of Brick Lane is inevitably more about the experience than the food. Among the hordes of practically interchangeable restaurants, this one stands out for its murals of scantily clad women riding dragons, alongside a tribute to Princess Di.

Brick Lane Beigel Bake BAGELS £
(Map p94; 159 Brick Lane E2; most bagels less than £2; 24hr; Liverpool St) A relic of London's Jewish East End, it's more a takeaway than a cafe and sells dirt-cheap bagels. They're a top snack on a bellyful of booze.

Drinking

As long as there's been a city, Londoners have loved to drink – and, as history shows, often immoderately. The pub is the focus of social life and there's always one near at hand. When the sun shines, drinkers spill out into the streets, parks and squares as well. It was only in 2008 that drinking was banned on the tube!

Soho is undoubtedly the heart of bar culture, with enough variety to cater to all tastes. Camden's great for grungy boozers and rock kids, although it has lost ground on the bohemian-cool front to the venues around Hoxton and Shoreditch.

Now that Princes William and Harry have hit their stride, the Sloane Ranger (cashed-up young aristocrat in the heady pre-crash 1980s) scene has been reborn in exclusive venues in South Ken(sington), although the 'Turbo Sloanes' now count megarich commoners among their numbers.

Us mere mortals will find plenty of pub-crawl potential in places like Clerkenwell, Islington, Southwark, Notting Hill, Earl's Court...hell, it's just not that difficult. The reviews below are simply to make sure you don't miss out on some of the most historic, unusual, best-positioned or excellent examples of the genre.

WEST END

Flat White CAFE

(Map p68; www.flat-white.co.uk 17 Berwick St W1; ⌚8am-7pm Mon-Fri, 9am-6pm Sat & Sun; ⊖Piccadilly Circus) Trailblazers of the unexpected but thoroughly welcome Kiwi invasion of Soho cafes, Flat White is both named after and delivers the holy grail of Antipodean coffee. The beach scenes on the walls are a comfort on a cold day.

Gordon's Wine Bar BAR

(Map p68; www.gordonswinebar.com; 47 Villiers St WC2; ⊖Embankment) What's not to love about this cavernous wine cellar that's lit by candles and practically unchanged over the last 120 years? In summer, the crowd spills out into Embankment Gardens.

Princess Louise PUB

(Map p68; 208 High Holborn WC1; ⊖Holborn) This late-19th-century Victorian boozer is arguably London's most beautiful pub. Spectacularly decorated with fine tiles, etched mirrors, plasterwork and a gorgeous central horseshoe bar, it gets packed with the after-work crowd.

Coach & Horses PUB

(Map p68; www.coachandhorsessoho.co.uk; 29 Greek St W1; ⊖Leicester Sq) Regulars at this no-nonsense Soho institution have included Francis Bacon, Peter O'Toole and Lucien Freud. The Wednesday and Saturday night singalongs are tops.

Lamb & Flag PUB

(Map p68; 33 Rose St WC2; ⊖Covent Garden) Everyone's Covent Garden 'find', this historic pub is often jammed. Built in 1623, it was formerly called the 'Bucket of Blood'.

Galvin at Windows HOTEL BAR

(Map p64; www.galvinatwindows.com; The Hilton, 22 Park Lane W1; ⊖Hyde Park Corner) Drinks are pricey, but the view's magnificent from this 28th-floor eyrie.

Jewel COCKTAIL BAR

(Map p68; www.jewelbar.com) Piccadilly Circus (4-6 Glasshouse Street W1; ⊖Piccadilly Circus); Covent Garden (29-30 Maiden Lane WC2; ⊖Covent Garden) Chandeliers, banquettes, cocktails and, in Piccadilly, sunset views.

Monmouth Coffee Company CAFE

(⌚Mon-Sat) Covent Garden (Map p68; 27 Monmouth St WC2; ⊖Covent Garden); Borough (Map p82; 2 Park St SE1; ⊖London Bridge) While the array of treats displayed on the counter is alluring, it's the coffee that's the star, nay god, here. Chat to a caffeinated stranger on one of the tight tables at the back, or grab a takeaway and slink off to a nearby lane for your fix.

Absolut Ice Bar NOVELTY BAR

(Map p68; ☎020-7478 8910; www.belowzerolondon.com; 31-33 Heddon St W1; admission Thu-Sat £16, Sun-Wed £13; ⊖Piccadilly Circus) At -6°C, this bar made entirely of ice is literally the coolest in London. Entry is limited to 40 minutes, and your ticket includes a vodka cocktail served in an ice glass. It's a gimmick, sure, but a good one, and there are plenty of places nearby that charge the same for a cocktail alone. Book ahead.

THE CITY

Ye Olde Watling PUB

(Map p74; 29 Watling St; ⊖Mansion House) An atmospheric 1668 pub with a good selection of wine and tap beer.

Ye Olde Cheshire Cheese PUB

(Map p74; Wine Office Ct, 145 Fleet St EC4; ⊖Holborn) Rebuilt six years after the Great Fire, it was popular with Dr Johnson, Thackeray, Dickens and the visiting Mark Twain. Touristy but always atmospheric and enjoyable for a pub meal.

LOCAL KNOWLEDGE

SUE OSTLER: FLIRT DIVA

JOB Running practical 'flirtshops' in London's bars, helping women hone their man-meeting skills.

Where's the best place in London to get your flirt on?

Piccadilly Circus, because it's the gateway to London and you get all kinds of people there. If the girls say 'Hey Sue, we want a fun night out', I take them to Jewel bar (p118). It's a meat market without the trash – a m-e-e-t market, if you like.

And once you m-e-e-t, any ideas for a first date that doesn't waste any valuable sightseeing time?

Meet at the Wallace (p89) for afternoon tea among the art, then grab a bottle of bubbly at Tesco and find an enchanted corner of Regent's Park (p89) to quaff it in.

And for a meal to impress?

You'd have to be seriously loaded, but I can guarantee that if you took a date to Marcus Wareing's restaurant at The Berkeley (p111) it would certainly make an impression.

Vertigo 42 CHAMPAGNE BAR

(Map p74; ☎020-7877 7842; www.vertigo42.co.uk; Tower 42, Old Broad St, EC2; ⊖Liverpool St) Book a two-hour slot in this 42nd-floor bar with vertiginous views across London.

SOUTH BANK

George Inn PUB

(Map p82; www.nationaltrust.org.uk/main/w-georgeinn; 77 Borough High St SE1; ⊖London Bridge) Tucked away in a cobbled courtyard is London's last surviving galleried coaching inn, dating in its current form from 1677 and now belonging to the National Trust. Dickens and Shakespeare used to prop up the bar here (not together, obviously). There are outdoor tables for sunny days.

Anchor PUB

(Map p82; 34 Park St SE1; ⊖London Bridge) An 18th-century boozer replacing the 1615 one where Samuel Pepys witnessed the Great Fire, it has a terrace offering superb views over the Thames. Dr Johnson was once a regular.

CHELSEA & KENSINGTON

Bibendum Oyster Bar CHAMPAGNE BAR

(Map p86; www.bibendum.co.uk; 81 Fulham Rd SW3; ⊖South Kensington) If rubber-clad men happen to be your thing, slurp up a bivalve and knock back a champers in the foyer of the wonderful art nouveau Michelin House (1911). The Michelin Man is everywhere: in mosaics, stained glass, crockery and echoed in the architecture itself.

NOTTING HILL, BAYSWATER & PADDINGTON

Trailer Happiness COCKTAIL BAR

(Map p104; www.trailerhappiness.com; 177 Portobello Rd W11; ⊖Ladbroke Grove) Think shag carpets, 1960s California kitsch and trashy trailer-park glamour. Try the tiki cocktails and share a flaming volcano bowl of Zombie with a friend to ensure your evening goes off with a bang.

Windsor Castle PUB

(Map p104; www.thewindsorcastlekensington.co.uk; 114 Campden Hill Rd W11; ⊖Notting Hill Gate) A memorable pub with oak partitions separating the original bars, the panels have tiny doors so big drinkers will have trouble getting past the front bar. It also has one of the loveliest walled gardens of any pub in London. Thomas Paine (*Rights of Man* writer) is rumoured to be buried in the cellar.

MARYLEBONE

Artesian HOTEL BAR

(www.artesian-bar.co.uk; Langham Hotel, 1C Portland Pl W1; ⊖Oxford Circus) For a dose of colonial glamour with a touch of the Orient, the sumptuous bar at the Langham hits the mark. Rum is the speciality here – award-winning cocktails (£15) are concocted from the 60 varieties on offer.

GAY & LESBIAN LONDON

London's had a thriving scene since at least the 18th century, when the West End's 'Mollie houses' were the forerunners of today's gay bars. The West End, particularly Soho, remains the visible centre of gay and lesbian London, with numerous venues clustered around Old Compton St and its surrounds. However, Soho doesn't hold a monopoly on gay life. One of the nice things about the city is that there are local gay bars in many neighbourhoods.

Despite, or perhaps because of, its grimness and griminess, Vauxhall's taken off as a hub for the hirsute, hefty and generally harder-edged sections of the community. The railway arches are now filled with dance clubs, leather bars and a sauna. Clapham (South London), Earl's Court (West London), Islington (North London) and Limehouse (East End) have their own miniscenes.

Generally, London's a safe place for lesbians and gays. It's rare to encounter any problem with sharing rooms or holding hands in the inner city, although it would pay to keep your wits about you at night and be conscious of your surroundings.

The easiest way to find out what's going on is to pick up the free press from a venue *(Pink Paper, Boyz, QX)*. The gay section of *Time Out* is useful, as are www.gaydarnation.com (for men) and www.gingerbeer.co.uk (for women). The hard-core circuit club nights run on a semiregular basis at a variety of venues: check out **DTPM**, **Fiction** (both at www.dtpmevents.co.uk), **Matinee**, **SuperMartXé** (both at www.loganpresents.com) and **Megawoof!** (www.megawoof.com).

Some venues to get you started:

Candy Bar (Map p68; www.candybarsoho.co.uk; 4 Carlisle St W1; ⊖Tottenham Court Rd) Long-running lesbian hang-out.

Friendly Society (Map p68; 79 Wardour St W1; ⊖Piccadilly Circus) Soho's quirkiest gay bar, this Bohemian basement is bedecked in kid's-room wallpaper and Barbie dolls.

G-A-Y (Map p68; www.g-a-y.co.uk) Bar (30 Old Compton St W1; ⊖Leicester Sq); Late (5 Goslett Yard WC2; 11pm-3am; ⊖Tottenham Court Rd); Club @ Heaven (The Arches, Villiers St WC2; 11pm-4am Thu-Sat; ⊖Charing Cross) Too camp to be restricted to one venue, G-A-Y now operates a pink-lit bar on the strip, a late-night bar a few streets away and club nights at one of gaydom's most internationally famous venues, Heaven. Cover charges vary; entry is usually cheaper with a flyer from G-A-Y Bar.

Gay's the Word (Map p92; 66 Marchmont St WC1; ⊖Russell Sq) Books and mags of all descriptions.

George & Dragon (Map p94; 2 Hackney Rd E2; ⊖Old St) Appealing corner pub where the crowd is often as eclectically furnished as the venue.

Popstarz (Map p68; www.popstarz.org; The Den, 18 West Central St WC1; 10pm-4am Fri; ⊖Tottenham Court Rd) London's legendary indie pop club night. The online flyer gets you in free.

Royal Vauxhall Tavern (RVT; www.rvt.org.uk; 372 Kennington Lane SE11; admission free-£9; ⊖Vauxhall) Much-loved pub with crazy cabaret and drag acts. Head under the arches from Vauxhall tube station onto Kennington Lane, where you'll see the tavern immediately to your left.

Two Brewers (www.thetwobrewers.com; 114 Clapham High St SW4; admission free-£5; ⊖Clapham Common) Popular bar with regular acts and a nightclub out the back. From the tube station, head north along Clapham High St (away from the common).

Village (Map p68; www.village-soho.co.uk; 81 Wardour St W1; ⊖Piccadilly Circus) Glitzy gay bar with excellent, lengthy happy hours.

Heights HOTEL BAR
(Map p68; St George's Hotel, 14 Langham Pl W1; ⊖Oxford Circus) Take the lift up to this understated bar with huge windows showcasing the panorama. It is an unusual view, managing to miss most of the big sights, but it is impressive, nonetheless.

KING'S CROSS

Big Chill House BAR, DJS

(Map p92; www.bigchill.net; 257-259 Pentonville Rd N1; entry £5 after 10pm Fri & Sat; ⊖King's Cross) Come the weekend, the only remotely chilled-out space in this busy bar, split over two levels, is its first-rate and generously proportioned rooftop terrace.

CAMDEN TOWN

Lock Tavern PUB, BANDS

(Map p114; www.lock-tavern.co.uk; 35 Chalk Farm Rd NW1; ⊖Camden Town) The archetypal Camden pub, the Lock has both a rooftop terrace and a beer garden and attracts an interesting crowd with its mix of ready conviviality and regular live music.

Proud BAR, BANDS

(Map p114; www.proudcamden.com; Stables Market NW1; admission free-£10; ⊖Camden Town) No, despite the name it's not a gay bar. Proud occupies a former horse hospital within Stables Market, with booths in the stalls, ice-cool rock photography on the walls and deck chairs printed with images of Pete Doherty and Blondie. Spin around the gallery during the day or enjoy bands at night.

CLERKENWELL & FARRINGDON

Jerusalem Tavern PUB

(Map p108; www.stpetersbrewery.co.uk; 55 Britton St; ⊖Farringdon) Pick a wood-panelled cubbyhole to park yourself in at this 1720 coffee shop-turned-inn, and choose from a selection of St Peter's beers and ales, brewed in Suffolk.

HOXTON, SHOREDITCH & SPITALFIELDS

TOP CHOICE **Commercial Tavern** PUB

(Map p94; 142 Commercial St E1; ⊖Liverpool St) The zany decor's a thing of wonder in this reformed East End boozer. Check out the walls coated in buttons and jigsaw puzzle pieces. The little boy's room has been wallpapered like, well, a little boy's room: Popeye, astronauts and cyclists all make an appearance.

TOP CHOICE **Loungelover** COCKTAIL BAR

(Map p94; ☎020-7012 1234; www.lestriosgarcons.com; 1 Whitby St E1; ⏱6pm-midnight Sun-Thu, 6pm-1am Fri & Sat; ⊖Liverpool St) Book a table, sip a cocktail and admire the Louis XIV chairs, the huge hippo head, the cage turned living room, the jewel-encrusted stag's head and the loopy chandeliers. Utterly fabulous.

Bar Music Hall BAR, BANDS

(Map p94; www.barmusichall.com; 134 Curtain Rd EC2; ⊖Old St) Keeping the East End music-hall tradition alive but with a modern twist, this roomy space with a central bar hosts DJs and live bands. Music runs the gamut from punk to jazz to rock and disco.

Grapeshots WINE BAR

(Map p94; www.davywine.co.uk/grapeshots; 2/3 Artillery Passage E1; ⊖Liverpool St) Half the fun of this place is walking down the Dickensian passage, complete with old street lamps, that leads to it. The old-world ambience continues inside.

Ten Bells PUB

(Map p94; cnr Commercial & Fournier Sts E1; ⊖Liverpool St) The most famous Jack the Ripper pub, Ten Bells was patronised by his last victim before her grisly end, and possibly by the slayer himself. Admire the wonderful 18th-century tiles and ponder the past over a pint.

Other good stops on a Hoxton hop:

Favela Chic BAR, DJS

(Map p94; www.favelachic.com; 91-93 Great Eastern St EC2; entry £5-10 after 8pm; ⊖Old St) Ticks the following boxes: hip young things, crazy theme nights, lumberyard meets jungle decor, fun and funky music.

Mother BAR, NIGHTCLUB

(Map p94; www.333mother.com; 333 Old St EC1; entry free-£5; ⊖Old St) Red-and-gold flocked wallpaper, chequerboard floors and live alternative music and DJs on weekends. Downstairs, 333 is part nightclub, part live venue.

Zigfrid Von Underbelly BAR, DJS

(Map p94; www.zigfrid.com; 11 Hoxton Sq N1; ⊖Old St) Furnished like an oversized lounge room (check out the disturbing family portrait over the fireplace), it's the kookiest of the Hoxton Sq venues.

HAMPSTEAD & HIGHGATE

Spaniard's Inn PUB

(www.thespaniardshampstead.co.uk; Spaniard's Rd NW3; ⊖Hampstead, then bus 21) An enigmatic tavern that dates from 1585, complete with dubious claims that Dick Turpin, the dandy highwayman, was born here and used it as a hideout. More savoury sorts like Dickens, Shelley, Keats and Byron certainly availed themselves of its charms. There's a big, blissful garden and good food. From the tube station take Heath St and then veer left onto Spaniard's Rd.

Flask PUB
(77 Highgate West Hill N6; ⊖Highgate) Charming nooks and crannies, an old circular bar and an enticing beer garden make this 1663 pub the perfect place for a pint en route between Hampstead Heath and Highgate Cemetery. It's like a village pub in the city. From Highgate tube station, cross Archway, turn right and then left onto Southwood Lane. At the lane's end, the Flask is a block to the right.

Holly Bush PUB
(22 Holly Mount NW3; ⊖Hampstead) Dating from the early 19th century, this beautiful pub has a secluded hilltop location, open fires in winter and a knack for making you stay a bit longer than you had intended. It's above Heath St, reached via the Holly Bush Steps, which you'll find across the road and slightly up the hill from the tube station.

☆ Entertainment

From West End luvvies to End End geezers, Londoners have always loved a spectacle. With bear-baiting and public executions no longer an option, they've learnt to make do with having the one of the world's best theatre, nightclub and live-music scenes to divert them. Yet the gladiatorial contests that the Romans brought to these shores still survive on the football fields, especially when Chelsea goes head-to-head with Arsenal.

For a comprehensive list of what to do on any given night, check out *Time Out*. The listings in the free tube papers are also handy.

Theatre

London is a world capital for theatre and there's a lot more than mammoth musicals to tempt you into the West End. As far as the blockbuster musicals go, you can be fairly confident that *Les Miserables* and *Phantom of the Opera* will still be chugging along, as well as Phantom's sequel *Love Never Dies*, *Legally Blonde*, *Sister Act* and *The Wizard of Oz*.

On performance days, you can buy half-price tickets for West End productions (cash only) from the official agency **tkts** (Map p68; www.tkts.co.uk; ⏲10am-7pm Mon-Sat, noon-4pm Sun; ⊖Leicester Sq), on the south side of Leicester Sq. The booth is the one with the clock tower; beware of touts selling dodgy tickets. For a comprehensive look at what's being staged and where, visit www.officiallondontheatre.co.uk, www.theatremonkey.com or http://london.broadway.com.

The term 'West End' – as with Broadway – generally refers to the big-money productions like musicals, but also includes other heavyweights.

Some recommended options:

Royal Court Theatre THEATRE
(Map p86; ☎020-7565 5000; www.royalcourttheatre.com; Sloane Sq SW1; ⊖Sloane Sq) The patron of new British writing.

National Theatre THEATRE
(Map p80; ☎020-7452 3000; www.nationaltheatre.org.uk; South Bank SE1; ⊖Waterloo) Cheaper tickets for both classics and new plays from some of the world's best companies.

Royal Shakespeare Company THEATRE COMPANY
(RSC; ☎0844 800 1110; www.rsc.org.uk) Productions of the Bard's classics and other quality stuff.

Old Vic THEATRE
(Map p80; ☎0844 871 7628; www.oldvictheatre.com; The Cut SE1; ⊖Waterloo) Kevin Spacey continues his run as artistic director (and occasional performer).

Donmar Warehouse THEATRE
(Map p68; ☎0844 871 7624; www.donmarwarehouse.com; 41 Earlham St WC2; ⊖Covent Garden) A not-for-profit company that has forged itself a West End reputation.

Off West End is where you'll generally find the most original works. Some venues to check out:

Almeida THEATRE
(Map p116; ☎020-7359 4404; www.almeida.co.uk; Almeida St N1; ⊖Highbury & Islington)

Young Vic THEATRE
(Map p80; ☎020-7922 2922; www.youngvic.org; 66 The Cut SE1; ⊖Waterloo)

Menier Chocolate Factory THEATRE
(Map p82; ☎020-7907 7060; www.menierchocolatefactory.com; 55 Southwark St SE1; ⊖London Bridge)

Nightclubs

London's had a lot of practice perfecting the art of clubbing – Samuel Pepys used the term in 1660! – and the volume and

NOVEL NIGHTS OUT

It seems that the cool kids are bored with simply going clubbing, listening to a band or propping up a bar with a pint. To plant your finger on the party pulse, check out some of these activity-based haunts.

Bloomsbury Bowling Lanes TENPIN BOWLING

(Map p92; ☎020-7183 1979; www.bloomsburybowling.com; Bedford Way WC1; ⏲1pm-late; ⊖Russell Sq) With eight 10-pin bowling lanes, a diner and authentic 1950s decor shipped in from America (even the carpet), this place is the real deal. And the fun doesn't stop with dubious footwear and a burger; there are also private karaoke rooms, a cinema screening independent movies, DJs and up-and-coming live bands.

Lucky Voice KARAOKE

(www.luckyvoice.com; 4-person booth per 2hr £20-50) Soho (Map p68; ☎020-7439 3660; 52 Poland St W1; ⏲5.30pm-1am Mon-Thu, 3pm-1am Fri & Sat, 3-10.30pm Sun; ⊖Oxford Circus); Islington (Map p116; ☎020-7354 6280; 173-174 Upper St N1; ⏲5pm-midnight Mon-Thu, 3pm-2am Fri & Sat, 3pm-midnight Sun; ⊖Highbury & Islington) Moulded on the private karaoke bars of Tokyo, Lucky Voice is a low-lit maze of dark walls with hidden doors revealing snug leather-clad soundproofed booths for your secret singalong. Select one of 50,000 songs from a touch screen, pick up a microphone and you're away. In the Super Lucky rooms there are wigs and blow-up guitars to enhance your performance. Drinks and bento boxes are ordered by the touch of a button; expect to spend a fortune in Dutch courage.

SRO Audiences LIVE TV

(www.sroaudiences.com) British telly is saturated with chat shows and quiz shows hosted by famous comedians with even more famous guests. It's surprisingly easy to be part of a **live TV studio audience** – for free. Follow the instructions on the website and be prepared to queue, whoop and cheer on demand.

variety of venues in today's city is staggering. Clubland's no longer confined to the West End, with megaclubs scattered throughout the city wherever there's a venue big enough, cheap enough or quirky enough to hold them. Some run their own regular weekly schedule, while others host promoters on an ad hoc basis. The big nights are Friday and Saturday, although you'll find some of the most cutting-edge sessions midweek. Admission prices vary widely; it's often cheaper to arrive early or prebook tickets.

Fabric SUPERCLUB

(Map p108; www.fabriclondon.com; 77A Charterhouse St EC1; admission £8-18; ⏲10pm-6am Fri, 11pm-8am Sat; 11pm-6am Sun; ⊖Farringdon) Consistently rated by DJs as one of the world's greatest, Fabric's three dance floors occupy a converted meat cold-store opposite the Smithfield meat market. Friday's FabricLive offers drum and bass, breakbeat and hip hop, Saturdays see house, techno and electronica, while hedonistic Sundays are delivered by the Wetyourself crew.

Plastic People NIGHTCLUB

(Map p94; www.plasticpeople.co.uk; 147-149 Curtain Rd EC2; admission £5-10; ⏲10pm-3.30am Fri & Sat, 10pm-2am Sun; ⊖Old St) Taking the directive 'underground club' literally, Plastic People provides a low-ceilinged subterranean den of dubsteppy, wonky, funky, no-frills fun times.

Guanabara BRAZILIAN

(Map p68; www.guanabara.co.uk; cnr Parker St & Drury Lane WC2; admission free-£10; ⏲5pm-2.30am Mon-Sat, 5pm-midnight Sun; ⊖Covent Garden) Brazil comes to London with live music and DJs nightly.

Ministry of Sound SUPERCLUB

(www.ministryofsound.com; 103 Gaunt St SE1; admission £13-22; ⏲11pm-6.30am Fri & Sat; ⊖Elephant & Castle) Where the global brand started, it's London's most famous club and still packs in a diverse crew with big local and international names.

Cargo NIGHTCLUB

(Map p94; www.cargo-london.com; 83 Rivington St EC2; admission free-£16; ⊖Old St) A popular club with a courtyard where you can simultaneously enjoy big sounds and the great outdoors. Hosts live bands and gay bingo, too.

Mass NIGHTCLUB
(www.mass-club.com; St Matthew's Church, Brixton Hill SW2; cover charges vary; ⊖Brixton) The congregation's swollen at this Brixton church under its new high priests, with regular services of live music and club nights. Turn left when leaving Brixton tube station and you'll see the church on your left, immediately after the first major intersection.

Matter SUPERCLUB
(www.matterlondon.com; The O2 Arena SE10; admission £10-20; ⊖North Greenwich) London's newest superclub, courtesy of the Fabric crew, Matter is the latest word in high-tech club design. No regular nights, just a busy roster of visiting promoters.

Rock, Pop & Jazz

While London may have stopped swinging in the 1960s, every subsequent generation has given birth to a new set of bands in the city's thriving live venues: punk in the 1970s, New Romantics in the 1980s, Brit Pop in the 1990s and the current crop of skinny-jeaned rockers and electro acts thrilling the scenesters today. You'll find interesting young bands gigging around venues all over the city. Big-name gigs sell out quickly, so check www.seetickets.com before you travel. See also the Drinking reviews, especially Bar Music Hall and Mother in Hoxton, and Proud and the Lock Tavern in Camden.

Koko CLUB
(Map p114; www.koko.uk.com; 1A Camden High St NW1; ⊖Mornington Cres) Occupying the grand Camden Palace theatre, Koko hosts live bands most nights and the regular Club NME (£5) on Friday.

O2 Academy Brixton CONCERT HALL
(☎0844 477 2000; www.o2academybrixton.co.uk; 211 Stockwell Rd SW9; ⊖Brixton) This Grade II–listed art deco venue is always winning awards for 'best live venue' (something to do with the artfully sloped floor, perhaps) and hosts big-name acts in a relatively intimate setting (5000 capacity).

Dublin Castle PUB
(Map p114; ☎020-7485 1773; www.thedublincastle.com; 94 Parkway NW1; ⊖Camden Town) There's live punk or alternative music most nights in this pub's back room (cover usually £6).

Jazz Cafe CLUB
(Map p114; www.jazzcafe.co.uk; 5 Parkway NW1; ⊖Camden Town) Jazz is just one part of the picture at this intimate club that stages a full roster of rock, pop, hip hop and dance, including famous names.

Barfly PUB
(www.barflyclub.com; ☎0844 847 2424) Camden (Map p114; 49 Chalk Farm Rd NW1; ⊖Chalk Farm); ULU (Map p92; Byng Pl NW1; ⊖Goodge St) Pleasantly grungy, and a good place to see the best new bands. The same crew runs a couple of other joints around town.

Ronnie Scott's CLUB
(Map p68; ☎020-7439 0747; www.ronniescotts.co.uk; 47 Frith St W1; ⊖Leicester Sq) London's legendary jazz club has been pulling in the hep cats since 1959.

100 Club CLUB
(Map p68; ☎020-7636 0933; www.the100club.co.uk; 100 Oxford St W1; ⊖Oxford Circus) This legendary London venue once showcased the Stones and was at the centre of the punk revolution. It now divides its time between jazz, rock and even a little swing.

Hope & Anchor PUB
(Map p116; ☎020-7700 0550; 207 Upper St; admission free-£6; ⊖Angel) Live music's still the focus of the pub that hosted the first London gigs of Joy Division and U2 (only nine people showed up).

Roundhouse CONCERT HALL
(Map p114; ☎0844 482 8008; www.roundhouse.org.uk; Chalk Farm Rd NW1; ⊖Chalk Farm) Built in 1847 as a railway shed, Camden's Roundhouse has been an iconic concert venue since the 1960s (capacity 3300), hosting the likes of the Rolling Stones, Led Zeppelin and The Clash. It's also used for theatre and comedy.

Classical Music

With four world-class symphony orchestras, two opera companies, various smaller ensembles, brilliant venues, reasonable prices and high standards of performance, London is a classical capital. Keep an eye out for the free (or nearly so) lunchtime concerts held in many of the city's churches.

Royal Albert Hall CONCERT HALL
(Map p86; ☎020-7589 8212; www.royalalberthall.com; Kensington Gore SW7; ⊖South Kensington) A beautiful circular Victorian arena that hosts classical concerts and contemporary artists, but is best known as the venue for the annual classical music festival, the Proms.

LONDON CALLING

Download these to your MP3 player before tackling the tube.

» **London in general:** Blur – 'London Loves'; Chemical Brothers – 'Hold Tight London'; The Clash – 'London Calling'; The Jam – 'Down In The Tube Station At Midnight'; Pet Shop Boys – 'London'

» **West End:** David Bowie – 'London Boys'; The Kinks – 'Lola'; Pet Shop Boys – 'West End Girls'; Roll Deep – 'Good Times'; The Who – 'Who Are You'

» **The City:** The Beatles – 'Being for the Benefit of Mr Kite'; Roxy Music – 'Do The Strand'; T-Rex – 'London Boys'

» **South London:** The Clash – 'Guns of Brixton'; Dire Straits – 'Sultans of Swing'; Eddie Grant – 'Electric Avenue'; The Kinks – 'Waterloo Sunset'; Morrissey – 'You're the One for Me, Fatty'

» **West London:** Blur – 'Fool's Day'; The Clash – 'London's Burning'; Elvis Costello – 'Chelsea'; Hard-Fi – 'Tied Up Too Tight'; Rolling Stones – 'You Can't Always Get What You Want'

» **North London:** Dizzee Rascal – 'Dream'; Morrissey – 'Come Back to Camden'; Pet Shop Boys – 'Kings Cross'; The Pogues – 'London Girl'; The Smiths – 'London'

» **East End:** Billy Bragg – 'Dreadbelly'; Morrissey – 'Dagenham Dave'; Pulp – 'Mile End'; Rolling Stones – 'Play With Fire'

Barbican Centre ARTS CENTRE
(☎0845 121 6823; www.barbican.org.uk; Silk St EC2; ⊖Barbican) This hulking complex has a full program of film, music, theatre, art and dance, including loads of concerts from the **London Symphony Orchestra** (www.lso.co.uk), which is based here. The centre is in the City and is well signposted from both the Barbican and Moorgate tube stations.

Southbank Centre CONCERT HALLS
(Map p80; ☎0844 875 0073; www.southbankcentre.co.uk; Belvedere Rd; ⊖Waterloo) Home to the London Philharmonic Orchestra (www.lpo.co.uk), Sinfonietta (www.londonsinfonietta.org.uk) and the Philharmonia Orchestra (www.philharmonia.co.uk), among others, this centre hosts classical, opera, jazz and choral music in three premier venues: the **Royal Festival Hall**, the smaller **Queen Elizabeth Hall** and the **Purcell Room**. The precinct is a riverside people-watching mecca of shops and restaurants. Look out for free recitals in the foyer.

Opera & Dance

Royal Opera House OPERA, BALLET
(Map p68; ☎020-7304 4000; www.roh.org.uk; Bow St WC2; tickets £5-195; ⊖Covent Garden) Covent Garden is synonymous with opera thanks to this world-famous venue, which is also the home of the Royal Ballet, Britain's premier classical ballet company. Backstage tours take place on weekdays (£10, book ahead).

Sadler's Wells DANCE
(Map p116; ☎0844 412 4300; www.sadlers-wells.com; Rosebery Ave EC1; tickets £10-49; ⊖Angel) A glittering modern venue that was, in fact, first established in the 17th century, Sadler's Wells has been given much credit for bringing modern dance to the mainstream.

Coliseum OPERA
(Map p68; ☎0871 911 0200; www.eno.org; St Martin's Lane WC2; tickets £10-87; ⊖Leicester Sq) Home of the progressive English National Opera; all performances are in English.

Comedy

When London's comics aren't being terribly clever on TV, you might find them doing stand-up somewhere in your neighbourhood. There are numerous venues to choose from, and many pubs getting in on the act.

Comedy Store CLUB
(Map p68; ☎0844 847 1728; www.thecomedystore.co.uk; 1A Oxendon St SW1; admission £14-20; ⊖Piccadilly Circus) One of London's first comedy clubs, featuring the capital's most famous improvisers, the Comedy Store Players, on Wednesdays and Sundays.

Comedy Cafe CLUB
(Map p94; ☎020-7739 5706; www.comedycafe.co.uk; 68 Rivington St EC2; admission free-

£15; ⏲Wed-Sat; ⊖Old St) Have dinner and watch comedy; Wednesday is free New Act Night.

99 Club MULTIVENUE CLUB
(☎0776 048 8119; www.the99club.co.uk; admission £10-30) Not quite the famous 100 Club, this virtual venue takes over various bars around town nightly, with three rival clones on Saturdays.

Soho Theatre THEATRE
(Map p68; ☎020-7478 0100; www.sohotheatre.com; 21 Dean St W1; ⊖Tottenham Court Rd) Where grown-up comedians graduate to once they start pulling the crowds.

Pear Shaped COMEDY NIGHT
(Map p68; www.pearshapedcomedy.com; Fitzroy Tavern, 16a Charlotte Street W1; admission £5; ⏲8.30pm Wed; ⊖Goodge St) Advertising themselves as 'London's second-worst comedy club', Pear Shaped is the place to destroy the hopes of enthusiastic amateurs.

Cinemas

Glitzy premieres usually take place in one of the mega multiplexes in Leicester Sq.

Electric CINEMA
(Map p104; ☎020-7908 9696; www.electriccinema.co.uk; 191 Portobello Rd W11; tickets £8-15; ⊖Ladbroke Grove) Grab a glass of wine from the bar, head to your leather sofa (£30) and snuggle down to watch a flick. All cinemas should be like this. Tickets are cheapest on Mondays.

BFI Southbank CINEMA, MEDIATHEQUE
(Map p80; ☎020-7928 3232; www.bfi.org.uk; Belvedere Rd SE1; tickets £9; ⏲11am-11pm; ⊖Waterloo) A film-lover's fantasy, it screens some 2000 flicks a year, ranging from classics to foreign art-house. There's also the Mediatheque viewing stations, where you can explore the British Film Institute's extensive archive of movies and watch whatever you like free.

BFI IMAX IMAX CINEMA
(Map p80; ☎020-7199 6000; www.bfi.org.uk/imax; Waterloo Rd SE1; tickets £9-16; ⊖Waterloo) Watch 3D movies and cinema releases on the UK's biggest screen: 20m high (nearly five double-decker buses) and 26m wide.

Curzon Cinemas CINEMA
(www.curzoncinemas.com; tickets £8-12) Chelsea (Map p86; 206 Kings Rd SW3; ⊖Sloane Sq); Mayfair (Map p64; 38 Curzon St W1; ⊖Green Park); Renoir (Map p92; Brunswick Sq WC1; ⊖Russell Sq); Soho (Map p68; 99 Shaftesbury Ave W1; ⊖Leicester Sq) Part of a clutch of independent cinemas spread throughout the capital showing less-mainstream fare.

Sport

As the capital of a football-mad nation, you can expect London to be brimming over with sporting spectacles during the cooler months. The Wimbledon Lawn Tennis Championships (p99) is one of the biggest events on the city's summer calendar.

FOOTBALL

Tickets for Premier League football matches are ridiculously hard to come by for casual fans these days, but you could try your luck. Contacts for London's Premier League clubs:

Arsenal (www.arsenal.com)

Chelsea (www.chelseafc.com)

Fulham (www.fulhamfc.com)

Tottenham Hotspur (www.tottenhamhotspur.com)

West Ham United (www.whufc.com)

RUGBY

Twickenham (www.rfu.com; Rugby Rd, Twickenham; 🚉Twickenham) is the home of English rugby union, but as with football, tickets for tests are difficult to get unless you have contacts. The ground also has the **World Rugby Museum** (☎020-8892 8877; adult/child £6/4; ⏲10am-5pm Tue-Sat, 11am-5pm Sun), which can be combined with a tour of the stadium (adult/child £14/8, bookings recommended).

CRICKET

Cricket is as popular as ever in the land of its origin. Test matches take place at two venerable grounds: Lord's Cricket Ground (which also hosts tours) and the **Brit Oval** (☎0871 246 1100; www.britoval.com; Kennington SE11; ⊖Oval). Tickets cost from £20 to £80, but if you're a fan it's worth it. If not, it's an expensive and protracted form of torture.

Lord's Cricket Ground CRICKET GROUND
(☎020-7616 8595; www.lords.org; St John's Wood Rd NW8; tours adult/child £14/8; ⏲tours 10am, noon & 2pm; ⊖St John's Wood) The next best thing to watching a test at Lord's is the absorbingly anecdotal 100-minute tour of the ground and facilities, held when there's no play. It takes in the famous (members only) Long Room and the **MCC Museum**, featuring evocative memorabilia, including the tiny Ashes trophy.

Shopping

Napoleon famously described Britain as a nation of shopkeepers, which doesn't sound at all bad to us! From world-famous department stores to quirky backstreet retail revelations, London is a mecca for shoppers with an eye for style and a card to exercise. If you're looking for something distinctly British, eschew the Union Jack–emblazoned kitsch of the tourist thoroughfares and fill your bags with London fashion, music, books and antiques.

London's famous department stores are a tourist attraction in themselves, even if you don't intend to make a personal contribution to the orgy of consumption. If there's a label worth having, you'll find it in central London. The capital's most famous designers (Paul Smith, Vivienne Westwood, Stella McCartney, the late Alexander McQueen) have their own stores scattered about and are stocked in major department stores. Look out for dress agencies that sell secondhand designer clothes, bags and shoes – there are particularly rich pickings in the wealthier parts of town.

Nick Hornby's book *High Fidelity* may have done for London music workers what *Sweeney Todd* did for barbers, but those obsessive types still lurk in wonderful independent stores all over the city.

WEST END

Oxford St is the place for High St fashion, while Regent St cranks it up a notch. Carnaby St is no longer the hip hub that it was in the 1960s, but the lanes around it still have some interesting boutiques. Bond St has designers galore, Savile Row is famous for bespoke tailoring and Jermyn St is the place for Sir to buy his smart clobber (particularly shirts). For musical instruments, visit Denmark St (off Charing Cross Rd).

Selfridges DEPARTMENT STORE
(Map p90; www.selfridges.com; 400 Oxford St W1; ⊖Bond St) The funkiest and most vital of London's one-stop shops, where fashion runs the gamut from street to formal. The food hall is unparalleled, and the cosmetics hall the largest in Europe.

Fortnum & Mason DEPARTMENT STORE
(Map p68; www.fortnumandmason.com; 181 Piccadilly W1; ⊖Piccadilly Circus) The byword for quality and service from a bygone era, steeped in 300 years of tradition. It is particularly noted for its old-world basement food hall, where Britain's elite come for their Marmite and bananas.

Liberty DEPARTMENT STORE
(Map p68; www.liberty.co.uk; Great Marlborough St W1; ⊖Oxford Circus) An irresistible blend of contemporary styles and indulgent pampering in a mock-Tudor fantasyland of carved dark wood.

Topshop Oxford Circus CLOTHES
(Map p68; www.topshop.com; 216 Oxford St W1; ⊖Oxford Circus) Billed as the 'world's largest fashion store', the Topshop branch on Oxford Circus is a constant frenzy of shoppers searching for the latest look at reasonable prices. It's been given a shot of cool by being home to a range by London's favourite local supermodel rock chick, Kate Moss. Topman is upstairs.

Grays ANTIQUES
(Map p90; www.graysantiques.com; 58 Davies St W1; ⊖Bond St) Top-hatted doormen welcome you to this wonderful building full of specialist stallholders. Make sure you head to the basement where the Tyburn River still runs through a channel in the floor.

Also check out:

HMV MUSIC
(Map p68; www.hmv.com; 150 Oxford St W1; ⊖Oxford Circus) Giant store selling music, DVDs and magazines.

Foyle's BOOKS
(Map p68; www.foyles.co.uk; 113-119 Charing Cross Rd WC2; ⊖Tottenham Court Rd) Venerable independent store with an excellent collection of poetry and women's literature.

Ray's Jazz JAZZ
(Map p68; www.foyles.co.uk; Foyles, 113-119 Charing Cross Rd WC2; ⊖Tottenham Court Rd) Where aficionados find those elusive back catalogues from their favourite jazz and blues artists.

Stanfords TRAVEL BOOKS
(Map p68; www.stanfords.co.uk; 12-14 Long Acre WC2; ⊖Covent Garden) The granddaddy of travel booksshops.

Waterstone's BOOKS
(www.waterstones.com) Piccadilly (Map p68; 203-206 Piccadilly W1; ⊖Piccadilly Circus); Bloomsbury (Map p92; 82 Gower St WC1; ⊖Goodge St) Beautiful branches of the chain. Check out the 5th View bar in the Piccadilly store.

ROLL OUT THE BARROW

London has more than 350 markets selling everything from antiques and curios to flowers and fish. Some, such as Camden and Portobello Rd, are full of tourists, while others exist just for the locals.

Columbia Road Flower Market FLOWERS
(Map p94; Columbia Rd; ⏲8am-2pm Sun; ⊖Old St) The best place for East End barrow boy banter ('We got flowers cheap enough for ya muvver-in-law's grave'). This market is unmissable.

Borough Market FOOD
(Map p82; www.boroughmarket.org.uk; 8 Southwark St SE1; ⏲11am-5pm Thu, noon-6pm Fri, 8am-5pm Sat; ⊖London Bridge) A farmers' market sometimes called London's Larder, it has been here in some form since the 13th century. It's wonderfully atmospheric; you'll find everything from organic falafel to boars' heads.

Camden Market ALTERNATIVE
(Map p114; ⏲10am-5.30pm; www.camdenmarkets.org; ⊖Camden Town) London's most famous market is actually a series of markets spread along Camden High St and Chalk Farm Rd. Despite a major fire in 2008, the **Camden Lock Market** and **Camden Stables Market** are still the places for punk fashion, cheap food, hippy shit and a whole lotta craziness.

Portobello Road Market CLOTHES, ANTIQUES
(Map p104; www.portobellomarket.org; Portobello Rd W10; ⏲8am-6.30pm Mon-Sat, closes 1pm Thu; ⊖Ladbroke Grove) One of London's most famous (and crowded) street markets. New and vintage clothes are its main attraction, with antiques at its south end and food at the north.

Old Spitalfields Market ASSORTED
(Map p94; www.oldspitalfieldsmarket.com; 105a Commercial St E1; ⏲10am-4pm Mon-Fri, 9am-5pm Sun; ⊖Liverpool St) It's housed in a Victorian warehouse, but the market's been here since 1638. Thursdays are devoted to antiques and vintage clothes, Fridays to fashion and art, but Sunday's the big day, with a bit of everything.

Rigby & Peller LINGERIE
(www.rigbyandpeller.com) Mayfair (Map p68; 22A Conduit St W1; ⊖Oxford Circus); Knightsbridge (Map p86; 2 Hans Rd SW3; ⊖Knightsbridge); Chelsea (Map p86; 13 Kings Rd SW3; ⊖Sloane Sq); Westfield mall (see p130) Get into some right royal knickers with a trip to the Queen's corsetière.

Butler & Wilson JEWELLERY
(www.butlerandwilson.co.uk) Mayfair (Map p90; 20 South Moulton St W1; ⊖Bond St); Chelsea (Map p86; 189 Fulham Rd SW3; ⊖South Kensington) Camp jewellery, antique baubles and vintage clothing.

BM Soho DANCE MUSIC
(Map p68; www.bm-soho.com; 25 D'Arblay St W1; ⊖Oxford Circus) Your best bet for dance – if they haven't got what you're after, they'll know who has.

Forbidden Planet COMICS
(Map p68; 179 Shaftesbury Ave WC2; ⊖Tottenham Court Rd) On a different planet from our lonely one, populated by comic-book heroes, sci-fi figurines, horror and fantasy literature.

Grant & Cutler BOOKS
(Map p68; www.grantandcutler.com; 55-57 Great Marlborough St W1; ⊖Oxford Circus) Specialises in foreign languages.

KNIGHTSBRIDGE

Knightsbridge draws the hordes with quintessentially English department stores.

Harrods DEPARTMENT STORE
(Map p86; www.harrods.com; 87 Brompton Rd SW1; ⊖Knightsbridge) A pricy but fascinating theme park for fans of Britannia, Harrods is always crowded with slow tourists.

Harvey Nichols DEPARTMENT STORE
(Map p86; www.harveynichols.com; 109-125 Knightsbridge SW1; ⊖Knightsbridge) London's temple of high fashion, jewellery and perfume.

Broadway Market FOOD

(www.broadwaymarket.co.uk; Broadway Mkt E8; 9am-5pm Sat; Bethnall Green) Graze from the organic food stalls, choose a cooked meal and then sample one of the 200 beers on offer at the neighbouring Dove Freehouse. It's a bit of a schlep from the tube. Head up Cambridge Heath Rd until you cross the canal. Turn left, following the canal and you'll see the market to the right after a few short blocks.

Brixton Market ASSORTED

(www.brixtonmarket.net; Electric Ave & Granville Arcade; 8am-6pm Mon-Sat, to 3pm Wed; Brixton) Immortalised in the Eddie Grant song, Electric Ave is a cosmopolitan treat that mixes everything from reggae music to exotic foods and spices.

Sunday (Up)market CLOTHES

(Map p94; www.sundayupmarket.co.uk; The Old Truman Brewery, Brick Lane E1; 10am-5pm Sun; Liverpool St) Handmade handbags, jewellery, new and vintage clothes and shoes, plus food if you need refuelling.

Brick Lane Market ASSORTED

(Map p94; www.visitbricklane.org; Brick Lane E1; 8am-2pm Sun; Liverpool St) An East End pearler, this sprawling bazaar features everything from fruit and veggies to paintings and bric-a-brac.

Camden Passage Market ANTIQUES

(Map p116; www.camdenpassageislington.co.uk; Camden Passage N1; 10am-2pm Wed, to 5pm Sat; Angel) Get your fill of antiques and trinkets galore. Not in Camden (despite the name).

Greenwich Market ASSORTED

(www.greenwichmarket.net; College Approach SE10; 10am-5.30pm Wed-Sun; DLR Cutty Sark) Rummage through antiques, vintage clothing and collectibles (Thursday and Friday), arts and crafts (Wednesday and weekends), or just chow down in the food section.

Petticoat Lane Market ASSORTED

(Map p94; Wentworth St & Middlesex St E1; 9am-2pm Sun-Fri; Aldgate) A cherished East End institution overflowing with cheap consumer durables and jumble-sale ware.

NOTTING HILL, BAYSWATER & PADDINGTON

Portobello Rd and the lanes surrounding it are the main focus, both for the famous market and the quirky boutiques and gift shops.

Travel Bookshop TRAVEL BOOKS

(Map p104; www.thetravelbookshop.com 13 Blenheim Cres W11; Ladbroke Grove) Hugh Grant's haunt in *Notting Hill* is a wealth of guidebooks and travel literature.

MARYLEBONE

Daunt Books TRAVEL BOOKS

(Map p90; 83 Marylebone High St W1; Baker St) An exquisitely beautiful shop, with guidebooks, travel literature, fiction and reference books, all sorted by country.

KJ's Laundry WOMEN'S CLOTHES

(Map p90; www.kjslaundry.com; 74 Marylebone Lane W1; Bond St) Break out of the High St uniform in this women's boutique, which sources collections from up-and-coming designers.

Apartment C LINGERIE

(Map p90; www.apartment-c.com; 70 Marylebone High St W1; Baker St) 'Apartment C is about hanging out in your knickers, drinking gin out of a teacup, and reading *Last Tango in Paris* out loud.' Quite.

ISLINGTON

Curios, baubles and period pieces abound along Camden Passage. Upper and Cross Sts have an interesting mix of shops.

Palette London WOMEN'S CLOTHES

(Map p116; www.palette-london.com; 21 Canonbury Lane N1; Highbury & Islington) Fancy an original 1970s Halston dress or 1980s Chanel? Vintage meets modern and fashion meets collectables in this interesting shop.

Laura J London WOMEN'S SHOES

(Map p116; www.laurajlondon.com; 114 Islington High St N1; Angel) A girlie boutique stocking shoes and accessories from a local designer.

CLERKENWELL & FARRINGDON

London Silver Vaults SILVER

(Map p108; www.thesilvervaults.com; 53-63 Chancery Lane WC2; ⊖Chancery Lane) Thirty subterranean shops form the world's largest retail collection of silver under one roof.

EC One JEWELLERY

(www.econe.co.uk) Clerkenwell (Map p108; 41 Exmouth Market EC1; ⊖Farringdon); Notting Hill (Map p104; 56 Ledbury St W11; ⊖Notting Hill Gate) Husband-and-wife team Jos and Alison Skeates sell contemporary collections by British and international jewellery designers.

HOXTON, SHOREDITCH & SPITALFIELDS

Rough Trade ALTERNATIVE MUSIC

(www.roughtrade.com) East (Map p94; Dray Walk, 91 Brick Lane E1; ⊖Liverpool St); West (Map p104; 130 Talbot Rd W11; ⊖Ladbroke Grove) At the forefront of the punk explosion of the 1970s, it's the best place to come for anything of an indie or alternative bent.

Present MEN'S CLOTHES

(Map p94; www.present-london.com; 140 Shoreditch High St E1; ⊖Old St) Hip men's designer duds.

Start CLOTHES

(Map p94; www.start-london.com; 42-44 Rivington St EC2; ⊖Old St) Spilling over three shops on the same lane (womenswear, menswear and men's formal), your quest for designer jeans starts here.

SHEPHERD'S BUSH

Westfield MALL

(http://uk.westfield.com/london; Ariel Way W12; ⊖Wood Lane) A new concept for London, this giant mall has 265 shops, restaurants and cinemas.

Information

Dangers & Annoyances

Considering its size and disparities in wealth, London is generally safe. That said, keep your wits about you and don't flash your cash unnecessarily. A contagion of youth-on-youth knife crime is cause for concern, so walk away if you sense trouble brewing and take care at night. When travelling by tube, choose a carriage with other people in it and avoid deserted suburban stations. Following reports of robberies and sexual attacks, shun unlicensed or unbooked minicabs.

Nearly every Londoner has a story about a wallet/phone/bag being nicked from under their noses – or arses, in the case of bags on floors in bars. Watch out for pickpockets on crowded tubes, night buses and streets. That friendly drunk who bumped into you may now be wandering off with your wallet.

When using ATMs, guard your PIN details carefully. Don't use one that looks like it's been tampered with as there have been incidents of card cloning.

Emergency

Police/fire/ambulance (☎999)

Rape & Sexual Abuse Support Centre (☎0808 802 9999)

Samaritans (☎08457 90 90 90)

Internet Access

You'll find free wireless access at many bars, cafes and hotels. Large tracts of London, notably Canary Wharf and the City, are covered by pay-as-you-go wireless services that you can sign up to in situ – and London's mayor is promising blanket wireless coverage of this sort for all of London by 2012. You'll usually pay less at the numerous internet cafes (about £2 per hour).

Internet Resources

BBC London (www.bbc.co.uk/london)

Evening Standard (www.thisislondon.co.uk)

Londonist (www.londonist.com)

Time Out (www.timeout.com/london)

Urban Path (www.urbanpath.com)

View London (www.viewlondon.co.uk)

Walk It (www.walkit.com) Enter your destination and get a walking map, time estimate and information on calories burnt and carbon dioxide saved.

Media

Two free newspapers bookend the working day – *Metro* in the morning and the *Evening Standard* in the evening – both available from tube stations. All of the national dailies have plenty of London coverage. Published every Wednesday, *Time Out* (£2.99) is the local listing guide par excellence.

Medical Services

To find a local doctor, pharmacy or hospital, consult the local telephone directory or call ☎0845 46 47. Hospitals with 24-hour accident and emergency units:

St Thomas' Hospital (Map p80; ☎020-7188 7188; Lambeth Palace Rd SE1; ⊖Waterloo)

University College Hospital (Map p92; ☎0845 155 5000; 235 Euston Rd WC1; ⊖Euston Sq)

Toilets

If you're caught short around London, public toilets can be hard to find. Only a handful of tube stations have them, but the bigger National Rail stations usually do (although they're often coin operated). If you can face five floors on an escalator, department stores are a good bet. In a busy pub, no one's going to notice you sneaking in to use the loo, but if you're spotted it would be polite to order a drink afterwards.

Tourist Information

For a list of all tourist offices in London and around Britain, see www.visitmap.info/tic.

Britain & London Visitor Centre (Map p68; www.visitbritain.com; 1 Regent St SW1; 9am-6.30pm Mon-Fri, 10am-4pm Sat & Sun; Piccadilly Circus) Books accommodation, theatre and transport tickets; *bureau de change;* international telephones; and internet terminals. Longer hours in summer.

City of London Information Centre (Map p74; 020-7332 1456; www.visitthecity.co.uk; 9.30am-5.30pm Mon-Sat, 10am-4pm Sun; St Paul's Churchyard EC4; St Paul's) Tourist information, fast-track tickets to City attractions and guided walks (adult/child £6/4).

Greenwich tourist office (0870 608 2000; www.visitgreenwich.org.uk; Discover Greenwich, 2 Cutty Sark Gardens SE10; 10am-5pm) Information plus guided tours.

Getting There & Away

London is the major gateway to England, so further transport information can be found in the main Transport chapter.

AIR For a list of London's airports see p1064.

BUS Most long-distance coaches leave London from **Victoria Coach Station** (Map p86; 020-7824 0000; 164 Buckingham Palace Rd SW1; Victoria).

CAR See p1067 for reservation numbers of the main car-hire firms, all of which have airport and various city locations.

TRAIN London's main-line terminals are all linked by the tube and each serve different destinations. Most stations have left-luggage facilities (around £4) and lockers, toilets (a 20p coin) with showers (around £3), newsstands and bookshops, and a range of eating and drinking outlets. St Pancras, Victoria and Liverpool St stations have shopping centres attached.

If you can't find your destination below, see the journey planner at www.nationalrail.co.uk.

Charing Cross (Map p68) Canterbury.

Euston (Map p92) Manchester, Liverpool, Carlisle, Glasgow.

King's Cross (Map p92) Cambridge, Hull, York, Newcastle, Scotland.

Liverpool St (Map p94) Stansted airport, Cambridge.

London Bridge (Map p82) Gatwick airport, Brighton.

Marylebone (Map p60) Birmingham.

Paddington (Map p60) Heathrow airport, Oxford, Bath, Bristol, Exeter, Plymouth, Cardiff.

St Pancras (Map p92) Gatwick and Luton airports, Brighton, Nottingham, Sheffield, Leicester, Leeds, Paris.

Victoria (Map p86) Gatwick airport, Brighton, Canterbury.

Waterloo (Map p80) Windsor, Winchester, Exeter, Plymouth.

Getting Around

To/From the Airports

GATWICK There are **National Rail** (www.nationalrail.co.uk) services from Gatwick's South Terminal to Victoria (from £12, 37 minutes), running every 15 minutes during the day and hourly through the night. Other trains head to St Pancras (from £12, 66 minutes), stopping at London Bridge, City Thameslink, Blackfriars and Farringdon. Fares are cheaper the earlier you book. If you're racing to make a flight, the **Gatwick Express** (0845 850 1530; www.gatwickexpress.com) departs Victoria every 15 minutes from 5am to 11.45pm (one way/return £16/26, 30 minutes, first/last train 3.30am/12.32am).

Prices start from £2, depending on when you book, for the **EasyBus** (www.easybus.co.uk) minibus service between Gatwick and Earls Court (£10, allow 1¼ hours, every 30 minutes from 4.25am to 1am). You'll be charged extra if you have more than one carry-on and one check-in bag.

Gatwick's taxi partner, **Checker Cars** (www.checkercars.com), has a counter in each terminal. Fares are quoted in advance (about £95 for the 65-minute ride to Central London).

HEATHROW The transport connections to Heathrow are excellent, and the journey to and from the city is painless. The cheapest option is the Underground. The Piccadilly line is accessible from every terminal (£4.50, one hour to central London, departing from Heathrow every five minutes from around 5am to 11.30pm). If it's your first time in London, it's a good chance to practise using the tube as it's at the beginning of the line and therefore not too crowded when you get on. If there are vast queues at the ticket office, use the automatic machines instead; some accept credit cards as well as cash. Keep your bags near you and expect a scramble to get off if you're hitting the city at rush hour (7am to 9am and 5pm to 7pm weekdays).

You might save some time on the considerably more expensive **Heathrow Express** (0845 600 1515; www.heathrowexpress.co.uk), an ultramodern train to Paddington station (one way/return £16.50/32, 15 minutes, every 15 minutes 5.12am to 11.42pm). You can purchase tickets on board (£5 extra), from self-service machines (cash and credit cards accepted) at both stations, or online.

There are taxi ranks for black cabs outside every terminal; a fare to the centre of London will cost between £50 and £70.

LONDON CITY The Docklands Light Railway connects London City Airport to the tube network, taking 22 minutes to reach Bank station (£4). A black taxi costs around £25 to/from central London.

LUTON There are regular **National Rail** (www.nationalrail.co.uk) services from St Pancras (£9.50, 29 to 39 minutes) to Luton Airport Parkway station, where a shuttle bus (£1) will get you to the airport within 10 minutes. EasyBus (p131) minibuses head from Victoria and Baker St to Luton (from £2, walk-on £10, allow 1½ hours, every 30 minutes). A taxi costs around £65.

STANSTED The **Stansted Express** (☎0845 850 0150; www.stanstedexpress.com) connects with Liverpool St station (one way/return £18/27, 46 minutes, every 15 minutes 6am to 12.30am).

EasyBus (p131) also has services between Stansted and Baker St (from £2, £10 walk-on, 1¼ hours, every 20 minutes). The **Airbus A6** (☎0870 580 8080; www.nationalexpress.com) links with Victoria Coach Station (£11, allow 1¾ hours, at least every 30 minutes).

A black cab to/from central London costs about £100.

Bike

The central city is flat and relatively compact and the traffic moves slowly – all of which make it surprisingly good for cyclists. It can get terribly congested though, so you'll need to keep your wits about you – and lock your bike (including both wheels) securely. At the time of writing, **TFL** (www.tfl.gov.uk) was about to launch a Cycle Hire Scheme, with 6000 cycles available to hire from self-service docking stations within Zone 1 (£1/6/15/35/50 for up to one/two/three/six/24 hours).

Car

The M25 ring road encompasses the 609 sq miles that is broadly regarded as Greater London. For motorists it's the first circle of hell; London was recently rated western Europe's second-most congested city (congratulations Brussels). Don't even think about driving within it: traffic is heavy, roadwork continuous, parking is either impossible or expensive, and wheel-clampers keep busy.

If you drive into central London from 7am to 6pm on a weekday, you'll need to pay an £8 per day congestion charge (visit www.tfl.gov.uk for payment options) or face a hefty fine. If you're hiring a car to continue your trip, take the tube to Heathrow and pick it up from there.

Public Transport

Although locals love to complain about it, London's public transport is excellent, with tubes, trains, buses and boats conspiring to get you anywhere you need to go. **TFL** (www.tfl.gov.uk) is the glue that binds the network together. Its website has a handy journey planner and information on all services, including cabs. As a creature of leisure, you'll be able to avoid those bits that Londoners hate (especially the sardine

LONDON'S OYSTER DIET

To get the most out of London, you need to be able to jump on and off public transport like a local, not scramble to buy a ticket at hefty rates each time. The best and cheapest way to do this is with an Oyster card, a reusable smartcard on which you can load either a season ticket (weekly/monthly £26/100) or prepaid credit. The card itself is £3, which is fully refundable when you leave.

London is divided into concentric transport zones, although almost all of the places covered in this book are in Zones 1 and 2. The season tickets quoted above will give you unlimited transport on tubes, buses and rail services within these zones. All you need to do is touch your card to the yellow sensors on the station turnstiles or at the front of the bus.

If you opt for pay as you go, the fare will be deducted from the credit on your card at a much lower rate than if you were buying a one-off paper ticket. An oyster bus trip costs £1.20 as opposed to £2, while a Zone 1 tube journey is £1.80 as opposed to £4. Even better, in any single day your fares will be capped at the equivalent of the Oyster day-pass rate for the zones you've travelled in (Zones 1–2 peak/off-peak £7.20/5.60).

Assuming you avoid peak hours (6.30am to 9.30am and 4pm to 7pm), this ready reckoner gives the cheapest options for your length of stay:

- » 1–4 days: prepay
- » 5–24 days: weeklies topped up with prepay for any remaining days
- » 25–31 days: monthly

squash of rush-hour tubes), so get yourself an Oyster card and make the most of it.

LONDON UNDERGROUND, DLR & OVERGROUND 'The tube', as it's universally known, extends its subterranean tentacles throughout London and into the surrounding counties, with services running every few minutes from roughly 5.30am to 12.30am (from 7am to 11.30pm Sunday).

It's easy to use. Tickets (or Oyster card top-ups) can be purchased from counters or machines at the entrance to each station using either cash or credit card. They're then inserted into the slot on the turnstiles (or you touch your Oyster card on the yellow reader), and the barrier opens. Once you're through you can jump on and off different lines as often as you need to get to your destination.

Also included within the network are the driverless Docklands Light Railway (DLR), and the train lines shown on tube maps as 'Overground'. The DLR links the City to Docklands, Greenwich and London City Airport. It's very Jetsons-like, especially when it hurtles between the skyscrapers of Canary Wharf; try to get the front row seat.

The tube map itself is an acclaimed graphic design work, using coloured lines to show how the 14 different routes intersect. However, it's not remotely to scale. The distances between stations become greater the further from central London you travel, while Leicester Sq and Covent Garden stations are only 250m apart.

BUS Travelling round London by double-decker bus is an enjoyable way to get a feel for the city, but it's usually slower than the tube. Heritage 'Routemaster' buses with conductors operate on route 9 (from Aldwych to Royal Albert Hall) and 15 (between Trafalgar Sq and Tower Hill); these are the only buses without wheelchair access.

Buses run regularly during the day, while less frequent night buses (prefixed with the letter 'N') wheel into action when the tube stops. Single-journey bus tickets (valid for two hours) cost £2 (£1.20 on Oyster, capped at £3.90 per day); a weekly pass is £17. Children ride free. At stops with yellow signs, you have to buy your ticket from the automatic machine (or use an Oyster) *before* boarding. Buses stop on request, so clearly signal the driver with an outstretched arm.

TRAIN Particularly south of the river, where tube lines are in short supply, the various rail companies are an important part of the public transport picture. Most stations are now fitted with Oyster readers and accept TFL travelcards. If you travel outside your zone you'll need to have enough prepaid credit on your Oyster card to cover the additional charge. As not all stations have turnstiles, it's important to remember to tap-in and tap-out at the Oyster reader at the station or your card will register an unfinished journey and you're likely to be charged extra. You can still buy a paper ticket from machines or counters at train stations.

BOAT The myriad boats that ply the Thames are a great way to travel, avoiding traffic jams while affording great views. Passengers with daily, weekly or monthly travelcards (including on Oyster) get a third off all fares.

Thames Clippers (www.thamesclippers.com) runs regular commuter services between Embankment, Waterloo, Blackfriars, Bankside, London Bridge, Tower, Canary Wharf, Greenwich, North Greenwich and Woolwich piers (adult/child £5.30/2.65) from 7am to midnight (from 9.30am weekends).

Leisure services include the Tate-to-Tate boat (see p77) and Westminster–Greenwich services (p96). For boats to Kew Gardens and Hampton Court Palace, see p97.

London Waterbus Company (☎020-7482 2660; www.londonwaterbus.com, single/return £6.70/9.70) and **Jason's Trip** (www.jasons.co.uk; opposite 42 Blomfield Rd W9; single/return £7.50/8.50) both run canal boat journeys between Camden Lock and Little Venice; see websites for times. London has some 40 miles of inner-city canals, mostly built in the 19th century.

Taxi

London's famous black cabs are available for hire when the yellow light above the windscreen is lit. To get an all-London licence, cabbies must do 'The Knowledge', which tests them on up to 25,000 streets within a 6-mile radius of Charing Cross and all points of interest from hotels to churches. Fares are metered, with flag fall of £2.20 and the additional rate dependent on time of day, distance travelled and taxi speed. A one-mile trip will cost between £4.60 and £8.60. To order a black cab by phone, try **Dial-a-Cab** (☎020-7253 5000; www.dialacab.co.uk); you must pay by credit card and will be charged a premium.

Licensed minicabs operate via agencies (most busy areas have a walk-in office with drivers waiting). They're a cheaper alternative to black cabs and quote trip fares in advance. The cars are recognisable by the ⊖ symbol displayed in the window. To find a local minicab firm, visit www.tfl.gov.uk.

There have been many reports of sexual assault and theft by unlicensed minicab drivers. Only use drivers from proper agencies; licensed minicabs aren't allowed to tout for business or pick you up off the street without a booking, so avoid the shady characters who hang around outside nightclubs or bars.

Canterbury & Southeast England

Includes »

KENT 135
Canterbury 135
Whitstable. 143
Margate 144
Dover 156
Leeds Castle. 159
EAST SUSSEX 160
Rye 160
Battle. 162
Bodiam Castle 163
Hastings 163
Brighton & Hove 166
WEST SUSSEX. 174
SURREY. 177

Best Places to Eat

- » Deeson's (p142)
- » Allotment (p158)
- » Eddie Gilbert's (p154)
- » Terre á Terre (p170)
- » Town House (p174)

Best Places to Stay

- » Abode Canterbury (p141)
- » Jeake's House (p161)
- » Wallett's Court (p158)
- » Neo Hotel (p167)
- » Bell Hotel (p156)

Why Go?

Rolling chalk downs, venerable Victorian resorts, fields of hops and grapes sweetening in the sun – welcome to England's affluent southeast. Four soothing counties' worth of country houses, fairytale castles and Cinque Ports, and with the country's finest food and drink to boot.

That fruit-ripening sun shines brightest and longest on the southeast, gently warming a string of seaside towns wedged between formidable chalk cliffs. There's something for everyone here, from the understated charm of Whitstable, to the Bohemian spirit of hedonistic Brighton, to more genteel Eastbourne.

But the southeast is also pockmarked with less idyllic reminders of darker days. From the 1066 battlefield to Dover Castle's secret war tunnels to the scattered Roman ruins, the region's position as the front line against Continental invaders has left a wealth of turbulent history.

England's spiritual heart is Canterbury, its cathedral and ancient Unesco-listed attractions are essential viewing for any camera-toting, 21st-century pilgrim.

When to Go?

May is a good time to get creative at Great Britain's second-largest arts festival, held in Brighton. During June don your top hat and britches to revel in frilly Victoriana at the Dickens festivals in Broadstairs. Any time between May and October is ideal for a hike along the South Downs Way, running the length of England's newest national park. And between September and October enjoy an Indian summer on Eastbourne's 'sunshine coast', officially the sunniest place in Britain.

Activities

The southeast of England may be Britain's most densely populated corner, but there are still plenty of off-the-beaten-track walking and cycling routes to enjoy. Below are some of the highlights, but you'll find more information throughout the chapter.

CYCLING

Finding quiet roads for cycle touring takes a little extra perseverance in the southeast of England, but the effort is richly rewarded. Long-distance routes that form part of the **National Cycle Network** (NCN; www.sustrans.org.uk):

Downs & Weald Cycle Route (110 miles; NCN Routes 2, 20 & 21) London to Brighton and on to Hastings.

Garden of England Cycle Route (165 miles; NCN Routes 1, 2) London to Dover and then Hastings.

You'll also find less-demanding routes on the NCN website. Meanwhile there are plenty of uppers and downers to challenge mountain bikers on walking trails, such as the South Downs Way National Trail (100 miles), which takes hard nuts two days but mere mortals around four.

WALKING

Two long-distance trails meander steadily westward through the region, but there are plenty of shorter ambles to fit your schedule, stamina and scenery wish list.

South Downs Way National Trail (100 miles) This trail through England's newest national park is a beautiful rollercoaster walk along prehistoric drove ways between the ancient capital, Winchester, and the seaside resort of Eastbourne.

North Downs Way (153 miles) This popular walk begins near Farnham in Surrey but one of its most beautiful sections runs from near Ashford to Dover in Kent; there's also a loop that takes in Canterbury near its end.

Both long-distance routes have sections ideal for shorter walks. History buffs will revel in the 1066 Country Walk which connects with the South Downs Way. The Devil's Punchbowl (p178) offers breathtaking views, sloping grasslands and romantic wooded areas.

Information

Kent Attractions (www.kentattractions.co.uk)

Tourism South East (www.visitsoutheastengland.com) The official website for south and southeast England.

Visit Kent (www.visitkent.co.uk)

Visit Surrey (www.visitsurrey.com)

Visit Sussex (www.visitsussex.org)

Getting There & Around

The southeast is easily explored by train or bus and many attractions can be visited in a day trip from London. Contact the **National Traveline** (☎0871 200 2233; www.travelinesoutheast.org.uk) for comprehensive information on public transport in the region.

Bus

Explorer tickets (adult/child £6.50/4.50) provide day-long unlimited travel on most buses throughout the region; you can buy them at bus stations or on your first bus.

Train

You can secure 33% discounts on most rail fares in the southeast by purchasing a **Network Railcard** (www.railcard.co.uk/network; per yr £25). Children under 15 can save 60%, but a minimum fare of £1 applies.

KENT

Kent isn't described as the garden of England for nothing. Inside its sea-lined borders you'll find a clipped landscape of gentle hills, fertile farmland, cultivated country estates and fruitful orchards. It also serves as the booze garden of England, producing the world-renowned Kent hops, some of the country's finest ales and award-winning wines from its numerous vineyards. At its heart is spellbinding Canterbury crowned by its enthralling cathedral.

Here, too, are beautiful coastal stretches dotted with beach towns and villages, from old-fashioned Broadstairs to gentrified Whitstable, to the aesthetically challenged port town of Dover, close enough to France to smell the garlic or hop over on a day trip to taste it.

Canterbury

POP 43,432

Canterbury tops the charts when it comes to English cathedral cities and is one of southern England's top attractions. The World Heritage–listed cathedral that dominates its centre is considered by many to be one of Europe's finest, and the town's narrow medieval alleyways, riverside gardens and ancient city walls are a joy to explore. But Canterbury isn't just a showpiece to times

Canterbury & Southeast England Highlights

1 Shopping, tanning and partying in **Brighton & Hove** (p166), bustling hedonist capital of the southeast

2 Making a pilgrimage to **Canterbury Cathedral** (p138), one of England's most important religious sites

3 Wandering the cobbled lanes of **Rye** (p160), one of England's prettiest towns

4 Being transported back to the age of chivalry at the moated marvel that is **Leeds Castle** (p159)

5 Scrambling up **Beachy Head** (p166), a spectacular headland in snow-white chalk

6 Exploring the atmospheric WWII tunnels beneath sprawling **Dover Castle** (p157)

7 Packing your thirst for a **vineyard or brewery tour** (p161)

8 Shaking out your beach towel for some seaside fun on the **Isle of Thanet** (p153)

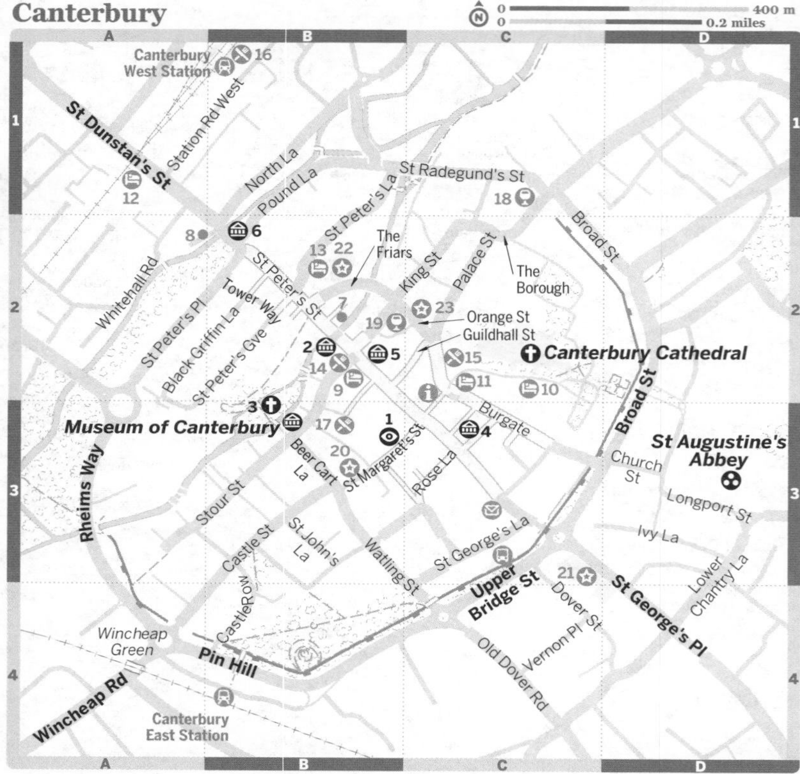

past; it's a spirited place with an energetic student population and a wide choice of contemporary bars, restaurants and arts. But book ahead for the best hotels and eateries: pilgrims may no longer flock here in their thousands but tourists certainly do.

History

Canterbury's past is as rich as it comes. From AD 200 there was a Roman town here, which later became the capital of the Saxon kingdom of Kent. When St Augustine arrived in England in 597 to carry the Christian message to the pagan hordes, he chose Canterbury as his *cathedra* (primary seat) and set about building an abbey on the outskirts of town. Following the martyrdom of Thomas Becket, Canterbury became northern Europe's most important centre of pilgrimage, which in turn led to Geoffrey Chaucer's *The Canterbury Tales,* one of the most outstanding poetic works in English literature.

Blasphemous murders and rampant tourism thrown aside, the city of Canterbury still remains the primary seat for the Church of England.

Sights

Canterbury Cathedral CATHEDRAL

(www.canterbury-cathedral.org; adult/concession £8/7; 9am-5pm Mon-Sat, 12.30pm-2.30pm Sun) The Church of England could not have a more imposing mother church than this extraordinary early Gothic cathedral, the centrepiece of the city's World Heritage Site and repository of more than 1400 years of Christian history.

It's an overwhelming edifice filled with enthralling stories, striking architecture and a very real and enduring sense of spirituality, although visitors can't help but pick up on the ominous undertones of violence and bloodshed that whisper from its walls.

Canterbury

Top Sights
Canterbury Cathedral C2
Museum of Canterbury B3
St Augustine's Abbey D3

Sights
1 Canterbury Tales B3
2 Eastbridge Hospital B2
3 Greyfriars Chapel B3
Main Library .... (see 5)
4 Roman Museum C3
5 Royal Museum & Art Gallery B2
6 West Gate Towers B2

Activities, Courses & Tours
7 Canterbury Historic River Tours B2
8 Canterbury River Navigation Company A2
Ghost Tours .... (see 20)

Sleeping
9 Abode Canterbury B2
10 Canterbury Cathedral Lodge C2
11 Cathedral Gate Hotel C2
12 House of Agnes A1
13 White House B2

Eating
14 Boho B2
15 Deeson's C2
16 Goods Shed B1
17 Veg Box Cafe B3

Drinking
18 Parrot C1
19 Thomas Beckett B2

Entertainment
20 Alberry's Wine Bar B3
21 Chill Nightclub C3
22 New Marlowe Theatre B2
23 Orange St Music Club C2

This ancient structure is packed with monuments commemorating the nation's battles. Also here is the grave and heraldic tunic of one of the nation's most famous warmongers, Edward the Black Prince (1330–76). The spot in the northwest transept where Archbishop Thomas Becket met his grisly end has been drawing pilgrims for more than 800 years and is marked by a flickering candle and striking modern altar.

The doorway to the crypt is beside the altar. This cavernous space is the cathedral's highlight, an entrancing 11th-century survivor from the cathedral's last devastating fire in 1174, which destroyed the rest of the building. Look for original carvings among the forest of pillars.

The wealth of detail in the cathedral is immense and unrelenting, so it's well worth joining a one-hour **tour** (adult/child £5/3; 10.30am, noon & 2.30pm Mon-Fri, 10.30am, noon & 1.30pm Sat Easter-Oct), or you can take a 40-minute self-guided **audiotour** (adult/concessions £3.50/2.50).

Museum of Canterbury MUSEUM
(www.canterbury-museums.co.uk; Stour St; adult/child £3.60/2.30; 11am-4pm Mon-Sat year-round, also 1.30-4pm Sun Jun-Sep) A fine 14th-century building, once the Poor Priests' Hospital, now houses the city's absorbing museum which has a jumble of exhibits from pre-Roman times to the assassination of Becket, Joseph Conrad to locally born celebs. The kids' room is excellent, with a memorable glimpse of real medieval poo among other fun activities. There's also a fun **Rupert Bear Museum** (Rupert's creator, Mary Tourtel, was born in Canterbury) and a gallery celebrating that other children's favourite of old, Bagpuss. The museum will also house the Royal Museum & Art Gallery's collections until restoration work is completed there.

St Augustine's Abbey ABBEY RUINS
(EH; adult/child £4.50/2.30; 10am-6pm Jul & Aug, to 5pm Apr-Jun) An integral but often overlooked part of the Canterbury World

CANTERBURY ATTRACTIONS PASSPORT

The **Canterbury Attractions Passport** (adult/child £19/15.25) gives entry to the cathedral, St Augustine's Abbey, the Canterbury Tales and any one of the city's museums. It's available from the tourist office.

KEEP YOUR ENEMIES CLOSE...

Not one to shy away from nepotism, in 1162 King Henry II appointed his good mate Thomas Becket to the highest clerical office in the land, figuring it would be easier to force the increasingly vocal religious lobby to toe the line if he was pally with the archbishop. Unfortunately for Henry, he had underestimated how seriously Thomas would take the job, and the archbishop soon began disagreeing with almost everything the king said or did. By 1170 Henry had become exasperated with his former favourite and, after a few months of sulking, 'suggested' to four of his knights that Thomas was too much to bear. The dirty deed was done on 29 December. Becket's martyrdom – and canonisation in double-quick time (1173) – catapulted Canterbury Cathedral to the top of the premier league of northern European pilgrimage sites. Mindful of the growing criticism at his role in Becket's murder, Henry arrived here in 1174 for a dramatic *mea culpa*, and after allowing himself to be whipped and scolded was granted absolution.

Heritage Site, St Augustine's Abbey was founded in AD 597, marking the rebirth of Christianity in southern England. Later requisitioned as a royal palace, it was to fall into disrepair and now only stumpy foundations remain. A small museum and a worthwhile audiotour (free) do their best to underline the site's importance and put flesh back on its now humble bones.

FREE St Martin's Church CHURCH

(North Holmes Rd; ⌚11am-4pm Tue, Thu & Sat Apr-Sep) This stumpy little building is thought to be England's oldest parish church in continuous use, and where Queen Bertha (the wife of the Saxon King Ethelbert) welcomed Augustine upon his arrival in the 6th century. The original Saxon church has been swallowed by a medieval refurbishment, but it's still worth the 900m walk east of the abbey.

Eastbridge Hospital HISTORICAL ALMSHOUSE

(www.eastbridgehospital.org.uk; 25 High St; adult/child £1/50p; ⌚10am-5pm Mon-Sat) A 'place of hospitality' for pilgrims, soldiers and the elderly since 1180, the Hospital of St Thomas the Martyr, Eastbridge is worth a visit for the Romanesque undercroft and historic chapel. The 16th-century almshouses, still in use today, sit astride Britain's oldest road bridge dating back over 800 years.

Roman Museum MUSEUM

(Butchery Lane; adult/child £3.10/2.10; ⌚10am-4pm Mon-Sat year-round, also 1.30-4pm Sun Jun-Sep) A fascinating subterranean archaeological site forms the basis of this museum where you can walk around reconstructed rooms, including a kitchen and a market place and view Roman mosaic floors. At the time of writing there were plans afoot to close this piece of the city's heritage for good in 2011.

West Gate Towers MUSEUM

(St Peter's St; adult/concession £1.30/80p; ⌚11am-12.30pm & 1.30-3.30pm Sat) The city's only remaining medieval gateway – a brawny 14th-century bulk through which traffic still passes – is home to a small museum with superb rooftop views. As with the Roman Museum, this too was to become a victim of cuts in 2011.

FREE Greyfriars Chapel CHAPEL

(⌚2-4pm Mon-Sat Easter-Sep) In serene riverside gardens behind the Eastbridge Hospital you'll find Greyfriars Chapel, the first English monastery built by Franciscan monks in 1267. The grounds are a tranquil spot to shake out the picnic blanket.

Canterbury Tales CHAUCER ATTRACTION

(www.canterburytales.org.uk; St Margaret's St; adult/child £7.75/5.75; ⌚10am-5pm Mar-Oct) A three dimensional interpretation of Chaucer's classic tales through jerky animatronics and audio guides, the ambitious Canterbury Tales is certainly entertaining but could never do full justice to Chaucer's tales. It's a lively and fun introduction for the young or uninitiated, however.

FREE Royal Museum & Art Gallery MUSEUM

(High St; ⌚10am-5pm Mon-Sat) The building's mock-Tudor facade is a splendid display of Victorian foppery, with intricate carving and big wooden gables. The interior houses mostly ho-hum art and military memorabilia as well as the city's **main library**, but the whole caboodle was closed for lengthy renovation at the time of research.

Tours

Canterbury Historic River Tours RIVER TOURS

(07790-534744; www.canterburyrivertours.co.uk; adult/child £7.50/5; 10am-5pm Mar-Oct) Knowledgeable guides double up as energetic oarsmen on these fascinating minicruises that leave from behind The Old Weaver's House on St Peter's St.

Canterbury River Navigation Company RIVER TOURS

(07816-760869; www.crnc.co.uk; Westgate Gardens; adult/child £8/4; Apr-Oct) Relaxing punt trips on the River Stour.

Canterbury Walks WALKING TOURS

(01227-459779; www.canterbury-walks.co.uk; adult/under 12yr/senior & student £6/5.50/4.25; 11am daily Feb-Oct, also 2pm Jul-Sep) Chaperoned walking tours leave from the tourist office.

Ghost Tours WALKING TOURS

(0845 5190267; www.canterburyghosttour.com; adult/child £8/6; 8pm Fri & Sat) Award-winning ghost hunts departing from outside Alberry's Wine Bar (p142) on St Margaret's St. Only groups need book.

Festivals & Events

Myriad musicians, comedians, theatre groups and other artists from around the world come to the party for two weeks in mid-October, during the **Canterbury Festival** (01227-787787; www.canterburyfestival.co.uk).

Sleeping

TOP CHOICE **Abode Canterbury** HOTEL ££

(01227-766266; www.abodehotels.co.uk; 30-33 High St; s/d from £89/109;) The only boutique hotel in town, the 72 rooms here are graded from 'comfortable' to 'fabulous' and for the most part they live up to their names. They come with little features such as handcrafted beds, cashmere throws, velour bathrobes, beautiful modern bathrooms and little tuck boxes of locally produced snacks. There's a splendid champagne bar, restaurant and tavern here, too.

House of Agnes HOTEL ££

(01227-472185; www.houseofagnes.co.uk; 71 St Dunstan's St; r from £83; @) Situated near the West Gate, this 13th-century beamed inn, mentioned in Dickens' *David Copperfield*, has eight themed rooms bearing names such as 'Marrakesh' (Moorish), 'Venice' (inevitable carnival masks), 'Boston' (light and airy) and 'Canterbury'. The last in the list arguably the pick of the bunch, packed with antiques and heavy fabrics.

Cathedral Gate Hotel HOTEL ££

(01227-464381; www.cathgate.co.uk; 36 Burgate; s/d £70/105, without bathroom £44/75) This often-photographed 15th-century hotel adjoins the spectacular cathedral gate, which it predates – a fact that becomes evident upon exploring its labyrinthine passageways, where few rooms lack an angled floor, low door or wonky wall. Rooms are simple but worth it for the fantastic position.

White House B&B ££

(01227-761836; www.whitehousecanterbury.co.uk; 6 St Peter's Lane; s/d from £60/80;) This elegant white Regency town house, supposedly once home to Queen Victoria's head coachman, has a friendly welcome, seven period rooms with modern touches and a grand guest lounge. Some of the rooms would have cathedral views were it not for the New Marlowe Theatre under construction in-between.

THE CANTERBURY TALES

If English literature has a father figure, then it is Geoffrey Chaucer (1342–1400). Chaucer was the first English writer to introduce characters – rather than 'types' – into fiction, and he did so to greatest effect in his most popular work, *The Canterbury Tales.*

Written in the now hard-to-decipher Middle English of the day between 1387 and his death, Chaucer's *Tales* is an unfinished series of 24 vivid stories as told by a party of pilgrims on their journey from London to Canterbury and back. Chaucer successfully created the illusion that the pilgrims, not Chaucer (though he appears in the tales as himself), are telling the stories, which allowed him unprecedented freedom as an author. *The Canterbury Tales* remains one of the pillars of the literary canon, but more than that it's a collection of rollicking good yarns of adultery, debauchery, crime and edgy romance, and filled with Chaucer's witty observances of human nature.

Kipp's Independent Hostel HOSTEL £
(☎01227-786121; www.kipps-hostel.com; 40 Nunnery Fields; dm/s/d £16/22/36; @) This red-brick town house is popular for its laid-back, homely atmosphere with friendly hosts and long-term residents, lots of communal areas, clean though cramped dorms, bike hire and garden. It's just south of the centre.

Canterbury Cathedral Lodge HOTEL ££
(☎01227-865350; www.canterburycathedrallodge.org; Canterbury Cathedral precincts; r from £65; @ ☎) Located opposite the cathedral within the precinct itself, the position of this modern, circular lodge is pretty special. Modern, recently refurbished rooms – done out in white and blond wood – have excellent facilities but what really makes this place are the views and the unlimited access to the cathedral for guests. Often full, so book ahead.

Yew Tree Park CAMPSITE £
(☎01227-700306; www.yewtreepark.com; Stone St, Petham; tent & 2 adults £12.20-17.20; ⏰Mar-Sep; P @ ☎ ≋) Set in gentle rolling countryside 5 miles southeast of the city, this lovely family-run campsite has plenty of soft grass to pitch a tent on and a heated swimming pool. Call for directions and transport information.

Eating

TOP CHOICE **Deeson's** BRITISH ££
(☎01227-767854; 25-27 Sun St; mains £4.50-16; ⏰lunch & dinner) Put the words 'local', 'seasonal' and 'tasty' into a make-believe restaurant search engine and this superb new British eatery would magically pop up first under Canterbury. Kentish fruit and veg, local award-winning wines, beers and ciders, fish from Kent's coastal waters and the odd ingredient from the proprietor's very own allotment, all served in a straightforward, contemporary setting a Kentish apple's throw from the Cathedral gates. What more do you want? Bookings recommended.

Boho INTERNATIONAL £
(43 St Peter's St; snacks £3-7; ⏰9am-6pm Mon-Sat) In a prime spot on the main drag, next to the Eastbridge Hospital, this hip eatery is extraordinarily popular and you'd be lucky to get a table on busy shopping days. The coolest sounds on CD lilt through the chic retro dining space as chilled diners chow down on humungous burgers, full-Monte breakfasts and imaginative, owner-cooked international mains. Boho doesn't do bookings so be prepared to queue.

Veg Box Cafe VEGETARIAN CAFE £
(1 Jewry Lane; soups £4.95, specials £6.95; ⏰9am-5pm Mon-Sat) Perched above Canterbury's top veggie food store, this welcoming, laid-back spot uses only the freshest, locally sourced organic ingredients in its dishes; served at stocky timber tables under red paper lanterns.

Goods Shed MARKET RESTAURANT ££
(☎01227-459153; Station Rd West; mains £11-19; ⏰market 9am-7pm Tue-Sat, to 4pm Sun, restaurant breakfast, lunch & dinner Tue-Sat, lunch Sun) Farmers market, food hall and fabulous restaurant all rolled into one, this converted station warehouse by the railway is a hit with everyone from self-caterers to sit-down gourmets. The chunky wooden tables sit slightly above the market hubbub but in full view of its appetite-whetting stalls, and country-style daily specials exploit the freshest farm goodies the Garden of England has to offer.

Drinking

Parrot PUB
(1-9 Church Lane) Built in 1370 on Roman foundations, Canterbury's oldest boozer has a snug, beam-rich pub downstairs and a much-lauded dining room upstairs under yet more aging oak. Needless to say many a local microbrewed ale is pulled in both.

Thomas Beckett PUB
(21 Best Lane) A classic English pub with a garden's worth of hops hanging from its timber frame, several quality ales to sample and a traditional decor of copper pots, comfy seating and a fireplace to cosy up to on winter nights. It also serves decent pub grub.

Entertainment

Alberry's Wine Bar NIGHTCLUB
(St Margaret's St) Every night is different at this after-hours music bar, which puts on everything from smooth live jazz to DJ-led drum and bass to commercial pop. It's a two-level place where you can relax over a French Kiss (cocktail or otherwise) above, before partying in the basement bar below.

Chill Nightclub NIGHTCLUB
(www.chill-nightclub.com; St George's Pl, New Dover Rd) Canterbury's most visible nightclub

is a large, fun, cheesy place with a popular student night on Mondays and house anthems and old skool at the weekends.

Orange St Music Club MUSIC VENUE
(www.orangestreetmusic.com; 15 Orange St) This Bohemian music and cultural venue in a 19th-century hall puts on a medley of jazz, salsa, folk, DJ competitions, comedy and even poetry and film screenings.

New Marlowe Theatre THEATRE
(☎01227-787787; www.newmarlowetheatre.org.uk; The Friars) The old Marlowe Theatre was bulldozed in 2009 and a spanking new, state-of-the-art building was being bolted together at the time of writing. When it reopens in 2011, the New Marlowe is set to become the southeast's premier venue for performing arts, attracting top companies and productions.

Information

Canterbury Health Centre (☎01227-597 000; 26 Old Dover Rd) For general medical consultations.

Dotcafe (19-21 St Dunstan's St; per hr £3; ⏲9am-9pm Mon-Sat, 10am-6pm Sun) Large cyber cafe near the Canterbury West train station.

Kent & Canterbury Hospital (☎01227-766877; Etherbert Rd) Has a minor injuries emergency unit and is a mile from the centre.

Post office (19 St George's St, 1st fl, WH Smiths; ⏲9am-5.30pm Mon-Sat)

Tourist office (☎01227-378100; www.canterbury.co.uk; 12 Sun St; ⏲9.30am-5pm Mon-Sat, 9.30am-4.30pm Sun) Situated opposite the Cathedral gate; staff can help book accommodation, excursions and theatre tickets.

Getting There & Away

The city's bus station is just within the city walls on St George's Lane. There are two train stations: Canterbury East for London Victoria; and Canterbury West for London's Charing Cross and St Pancras stations.

Bus

Canterbury connections:

London Victoria National Express, £13.40, two hours, hourly

Dover National Express, 40 minutes, hourly

Margate 48 minutes, three per hour

Ramsgate 46 minutes, twice hourly

Sandwich 37 minutes, three hourly

Whitstable 35 minutes, every 15 minutes)

Train

Canterbury connections:

London St Pancras High-speed service; £27.80, one hour, hourly

London Victoria/Charing Cross £23.40, one hour 40 minutes, two to three hourly

Dover Priory £6.50, 25 minutes, every 30 minutes

Getting Around

Canterbury's centre is mostly pedestrianised. Car parks are dotted along and just within the walls, but due to Canterbury's traffic issues day trippers may prefer to use one of the three Park & Ride sites, which cost £2.50 per day and are connected to the centre by bus every eight minutes (7am to 7.30pm Monday to Saturday, 10am to 6pm Sunday). Further sites are planned.

Downland Cycles (☎01227-479643; www.downlandcycles.co.uk) rents bikes from the Malthouse on St Stephen's Rd. Bikes cost £15 per day with helmet.

Taxi companies:

Cabwise (☎01227-712929)

Canterbury Cars (☎01227-453333)

Whitstable

POP 30,195

Best known for its succulent oysters, which have been harvested here since Roman times, charming Whitstable has morphed into a popular destination for weekending metropolitans, attracted by the weatherboard houses, shingle beach and candy-coloured beach huts lining the shore. The town has nevertheless managed to retain the character of a working fishing town, its thriving harbour and fish market co-existing with boutiques, organic delis and swanky restaurants. In recent years assorted campaigns by steadfast locals have kept some of the biggest names of the retail world out of the town, thus preserving its eccentric, artisanal air.

Sights

Whitstable Museum & Gallery MUSEUM
(www.whitstable-museum.co.uk; 8 Oxford St; ⏲10am-4pm Mon-Sat year-round, 1-4pm Sun Jul & Aug) This modest museum has glass cases examining Whitstable's oyster industry, the Crab & Winkle Railway which once ran from Canterbury, and the local fishing fleet, as well as a corner dedicated to the actor Peter Cushing, star of several Hammer

Horror films and the town's most famous resident, who died in 1994.

Sleeping & Eating

Hotel Continental HOTEL ££
(01227-280280; www.hotelcontinental.co.uk; Beach Walk; s/d/huts from £62.50/85/130; P) The rooms in this elegant seaside art-deco building are nothing special – come for the quirky converted fishermen's huts right on the beach. These should be booked well in advance.

Wheeler's Oyster Bar OYSTER BAR £££
(01227-273311; 8 High St; mains £17-22; lunch & dinner Thu-Tue) Squeeze onto a stool by the bar or into the Victorian four-table dining room of this baby blue and pink restaurant, choose from a seasonal menu and enjoy the best seafood in Whitstable. It knows its-stuff – it's been serving oysters since 1856. Bookings highly recommended unless you're travelling solo.

Crab & Winkle SEAFOOD ££
(South Quay, The Harbour; mains £9.50-22.95; lunch & dinner Mon-Sat, lunch Sun) Sitting above the Whitstable Fish Market in a black clapboard house, this bright restaurant has large windows overlooking the harbour, a buzzing vibe and excellent seafood with a few options for meat lovers thrown in.

Information

Whitstable has no tourist office, but you can pick up maps and other information at the **library** (31-33 Oxford St; 9am-6pm Mon-Fri, to 5pm Sat, 10am to 4pm Sun) which also lays on free internet access (bring ID).

Getting There & Away

Buses 4, 5 and 6 go to Canterbury (35 minutes) several times an hour.

Margate

POP 57,000

A popular seaside resort for more than 250 years thanks to its fine-sand beaches, Margate's tatty seafront and amusement arcades seem somewhat removed from the candy-striped beach huts and crowd-pleasing Punch and Judy puppet shows of its Victorian heyday. Major cultural regeneration projects – including the spectacular new Turner Contemporary art gallery – are slowly reversing the town's fortunes.

Sights

Shell Grotto GROTTO
(www.shellgrotto.co.uk; Grotto Hill; adult/child £3/1.50; 10am-5pm Apr-Oct). Margate's unique attraction is this mysterious, subterranean grotto discovered in 1835. It's a claustrophobic collection of rooms and passageways embedded with millions of shells arranged in symbol-rich mosaics. It has inspired feverish speculation over the years but presents few answers; some think it a 2000-year-old pagan temple, others an elaborate 19th-century hoax. Either way, it's an exquisite place worth seeing.

Turner Contemporary ART GALLERY
(www.turnercontemporary.org) Due to open in spring of 2011 this long-awaited and much-delayed gallery will highlight the town's links with the artist JMW Turner. At the time of writing the state-of-the-art building was under construction on the site of the seafront guest house where Turner used to stay. The gallery is set to become East Kent's top attraction and the first exhibition is expected to focus on Turner and his relationship with Margate.

Sleeping & Eating

Walpole Bay Hotel HOTEL ££
(01843-221703; www.walpolebayhotel.co.uk; 5th Ave, Cliftonville; s/d from £60/80) For Margate's most eccentric night's sleep, look no further than this peculiar part-hotel, part-shrine to interwar trinkets. The pink, flouncy rooms are furnished with antiques, while public spaces are lined with glass-cased displays of memorabilia from the early 20th century. The hotel is a mile from central Margate, in Cliftonville.

Mad Hatter CAFE £
(9 Lombard St; mains £4-8; lunch & dinner) Insanely unmissable, this completely cuckoo eatery run by a top-hatted proprietor packs two rooms of a 1690s house with bonkers regalia and miscellaneous knick-knackery from down the ages. Christmas decorations stay up all year and the toilets are original Victorian porcelain. The yummy cakes and snacks are all homemade.

Information

Tourist office (01843-577577; www.visitthanet.co.uk; 12-13 The Parade; 10am-5pm Apr-Sep) Following the closure of Broadstairs and Ramsgate tourist offices, the Margate office now serves all of Thanet. Surf the net for £1.50 per 30 minutes and pick up a copy of *The Isle* (£1.50), a glossy magazine crammed with listings and Thanet essentials.

(Continued on page 153)

Iconic England

Tower of London »
The River Thames »
Hadrian's Wall »

DAVID TOMLINSON

» The clock tower of Big Ben (p65) is actually the moniker of its 13-ton bell, named after Benjamin Hall

Tower of London

TACKLING THE TOWER

Although it's usually less busy in the late afternoon, don't leave your assault on the Tower until too late in the day. You could easily spend hours here and not see it all. Start by getting your bearings with the hour-long Yeoman Warder (Beefeater) tours; they're included in the cost of admission, entertaining and the only way to access the Chapel Royal of St Peter ad Vincula 1 which is where they finish up.

When you leave the chapel, the Tower Green scaffold site 2 is directly in front. The building immediately to your left is Waterloo Barracks , where the Crown Jewels 3 are housed. These are the absolute highlight of a Tower visit, so keep an eye on the entrance and pick a time to visit when it looks relatively quiet. Once inside, take things at your own pace. Slow-moving travelators shunt you past the dozen or so crowns that are the treasury's centrepiece, but feel free to double-back for a second or even third pass – particularly if you ended up on the rear travelator the first time around. Allow plenty of time for the White Tower 4, the core of the whole complex, starting with the exhibition of royal armour. As you continue onto the 2nd floor, keep an eye out for St John's Chapel 5. The famous ravens 6 can be seen in the courtyard around the White Tower. Head next through the towers that formed the Medieval Palace 7, then take the East Wall Walk 8 to get a feel for the castle's mighty battlements. Spend the rest of your time poking around the many, many other fascinating nooks and crannies of the Tower complex.

BEAT THE QUEUES

» **Buy** your fast-track ticket in advance online or at the City of London Information Centre in St Paul's Churchyard.

» **Palacepalooza** An annual Historic Royal Palaces membership allows you to jump the queues and visit the Tower (and four other London palaces) as often as you like.

MIKE BOOTH/ALAMY

Chapel Royal of St Peter ad Vincula
The chapel serves as the resting place for the royals and other members of the aristocracy who were executed on the small green out front. Several notable identities are buried under the chapel's altar.

Tower Green scaffold site
Seven people, including three queens (Anne Boleyn, Catherine Howard and Jane Grey), lost their heads here during Tudor times, saving the monarch the embarrassment of the usual public execution on Tower Hill.

Main Entrance

White Tower
Much of the White Tower is taken up with this exhibition of 500 years of royal armour. Look for the virtually cuboid suit made to match Henry VIII's bloated body, complete with an oversized armoured pouch to protect his, ahem, crown jewels.

PAWEL LIBERA IMAGES/ALAMY

St John's Chapel

Kept as plain and unadorned as it would have been in Norman times, the White Tower's 2nd-floor chapel is the oldest surviving church in London, dating from 1080.

TOM HANLEY/ALAMY

Crown Jewels

When they're not being worn for affairs of state, Her Majesty's bling is kept here. Among the 23,578 gems, look out for the 530-carat Cullinan diamond at the top of the Royal Sceptre, the largest part of what was (until 1985) the largest diamond ever found.

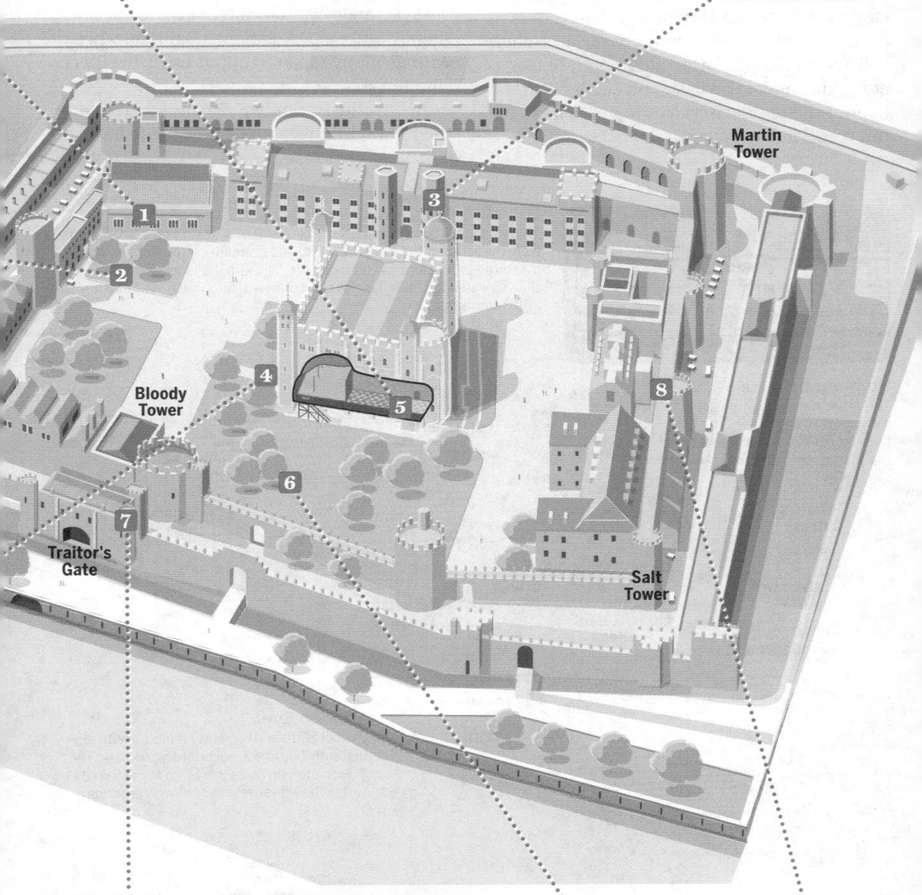

Martin Tower

Bloody Tower

Traitor's Gate

Salt Tower

1 2 3 4 5 6 7 8

Medieval Palace

This part of the Tower complex was commenced around 1220 and was home to England's medieval monarchs. Look for the recreations of the bedchamber of Edward I (1272–1307) in St Thomas's Tower and the throne room on the upper floor of the Wakefield Tower.

ENIGMA/ALAMY

Ravens

This stretch of green is where the Tower's famous ravens are kept, fed on raw meat and blood-soaked bird biscuits. According to legend, if the birds were to leave the Tower, the kingdom would fall.

East Wall Walk

Follow the inner ramparts, starting from the 13th-century Salt Tower, passing through the Broad Arrow and Constable Towers, and ending at the Martin Tower, where the Crown Jewels were once stored.

The River Thames

A FLOATING TOUR

London's history has always been determined by the Thames. The city was founded as a Roman port nearly 2000 years ago and over the centuries since then many of the capital's landmarks have lined the river's banks. A boat trip is a great way to experience the attractions.

There are piers dotted along both banks at regular intervals where you can hop-on/hop-off the regular services to visit places of interest. The best place to board is Westminster Pier, from where boats head downstream, taking you from the City of Westminster, the seat of government, to the original City of London, now the financial district and dominated by a growing band of skyscrapers. Across the river, the once shabby and neglected South Bank now bristles with as many top attractions as its northern counterpart.

In our illustration we've concentrated on the top highlights you'll enjoy at a fish's-eye

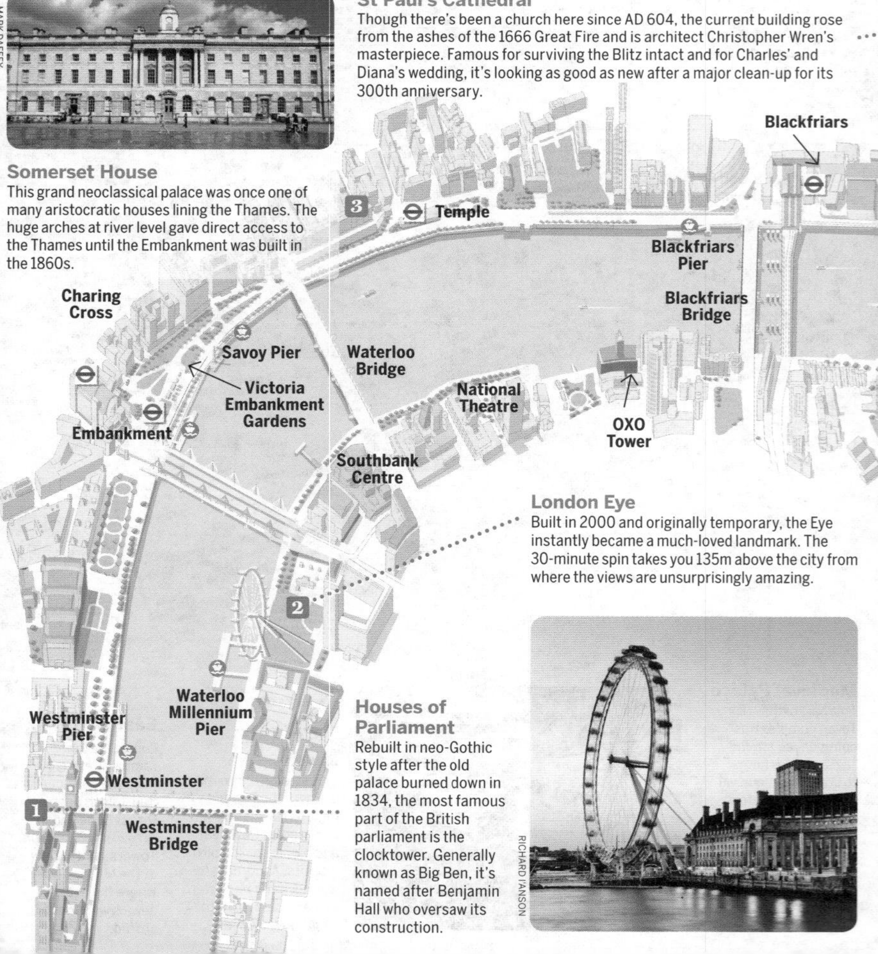

MARK DAFFEY
St Paul's Cathedral
Though there's been a church here since AD 604, the current building rose from the ashes of the 1666 Great Fire and is architect Christopher Wren's masterpiece. Famous for surviving the Blitz intact and for Charles' and Diana's wedding, it's looking as good as new after a major clean-up for its 300th anniversary.
Somerset House
This grand neoclassical palace was once one of many aristocratic houses lining the Thames. The huge arches at river level gave direct access to the Thames until the Embankment was built in the 1860s.
Blackfriars
3
Temple
Blackfriars Pier
Blackfriars Bridge
Charing Cross
Savoy Pier
Waterloo Bridge
Victoria Embankment Gardens
National Theatre
OXO Tower
Embankment
Southbank Centre
London Eye
Built in 2000 and originally temporary, the Eye instantly became a much-loved landmark. The 30-minute spin takes you 135m above the city from where the views are unsurprisingly amazing.
2
Waterloo Millennium Pier
Westminster Pier
Westminster
1
Westminster Bridge
Houses of Parliament
Rebuilt in neo-Gothic style after the old palace burned down in 1834, the most famous part of the British parliament is the clocktower. Generally known as Big Ben, it's named after Benjamin Hall who oversaw its construction.
RICHARD I'ANSON

view as you sail along. These are, from west to east, the Houses of Parliament 1, the London Eye 2, Somerset House 3, St Paul's Cathedral 4, Tate Modern 5, Shakespeare's Globe 6, the Tower of London 7 and Tower Bridge 8.

Apart from covering this central section of the river, boats can also be taken upstream as far as Kew Gardens and Hampton Court Palace, and downstream to Greenwich and the Thames Barrier.

BOAT HOPPING

Thames Clippers hop-on/hop-off services are aimed at commuters but are equally useful for visitors, operating every 15 minutes on a loop from piers at Embankment, Waterloo, Blackfriars, Bankside, London Bridge and the Tower. Other services also go from Westminster. Oyster cardholders get a discount off the boat ticket price.

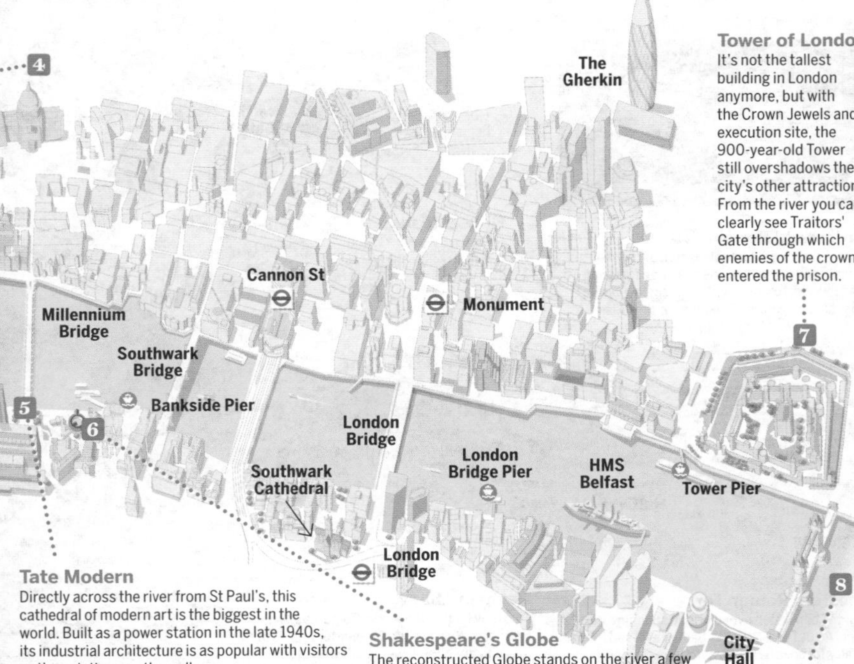

Tower of London

It's not the tallest building in London anymore, but with the Crown Jewels and execution site, the 900-year-old Tower still overshadows the city's other attractions. From the river you can clearly see Traitors' Gate through which enemies of the crown entered the prison.

Tate Modern

Directly across the river from St Paul's, this cathedral of modern art is the biggest in the world. Built as a power station in the late 1940s, its industrial architecture is as popular with visitors as the paintings on the walls.

DOUG MCKINLAY

Shakespeare's Globe

The reconstructed Globe stands on the river a few hundred metres from where the original stood (and burnt down in 1613 during a performance). The life's work of American actor Sam Wanamaker, the theatre runs a hugely popular season from April to October each year.

DOUG MCKINLAY

Tower Bridge

It might look as old as its namesake neighbour but one of the world's most iconic bridges was only completed in 1894. Not to be confused with London Bridge upstream, this one's famous raising bascules allowed tall ships to dock at the old wharves to the west and are still lifted up to 1000 times a year.

Hadrian's Wall

ROME'S FINAL FRONTIER

Of all Britain's Roman ruins, Emperor Hadrian's 2nd-century wall, cutting across northern England from the Irish Sea to the North Sea, is by far the most spectacular; Unesco awarded it world cultural heritage status in 1987.

We've picked out the highlights, one of which is the prime remaining Roman fort on the wall, Housesteads, which we've reconstructed here.

GEOGPHOTOS/ALAMY

Housesteads' granaries

Nothing like the clever underground ventilation system, which kept vital supplies of grain dry in Northumberland's damp and drizzly climate, would be seen again in these parts for 1500 years.

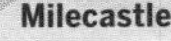

North Gate

JASON SMALLEY/ALAMY

Birdoswald Roman Fort

Explore the longest intact stretch of the wall, scramble over the remains of a large fort then head indoors to wonder at a full-scale model of the wall at its zenith. Great fun for the kids.

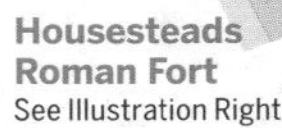

Housesteads Roman Fort

See Illustration Right

Chesters Roman Fort

Built to keep watch over a bridge spanning the River North Tyne, Britain's best-preserved Roman cavalry fort has a terrific bathhouse, essential if you have months of nippy northern winter ahead.

Hexham Abbey

This may be the finest non-Roman sight near Hadrian's Wall, but the 7th-century parts of this magnificent church were built with stone quarried by the Romans for use in their forts.

Housesteads' hospital

Operations performed at the hospital would have been surprisingly effective, even without anaesthetics; religious rituals and prayers to Aesculapius, the Roman god of healing, were possibly less helpful for a hernia or appendicitis.

NEIL HOLMES/ALAMY

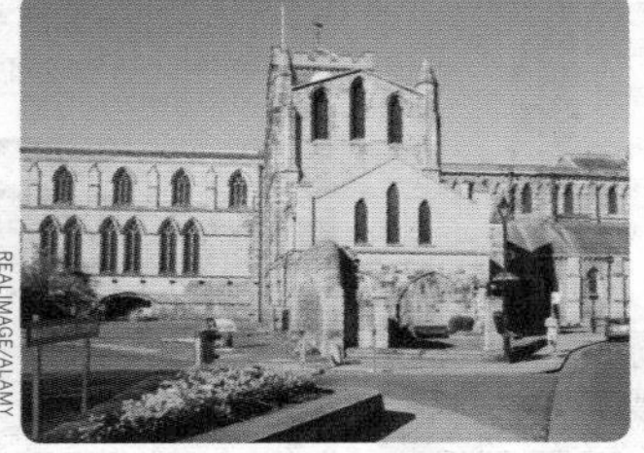

REALIMAGE/ALAMY

GLYN THOMAS/ALAMY

Housesteads' latrines
Communal toilets were the norm in Roman times and Housesteads' are remarkably well preserved – fortunately no traces remain of the vinegar-soaked sponges that were used instead of toilet paper.

QUICK WALL FACTS & FIGURES

» **Latin name** Vallum Aelium

» **Length** 73.5 miles (80 Roman miles)

» **Construction date** AD 122–128

» **Manpower for construction**
Three legions (around 16,000 men)

» **Features** at least 16 forts, 80 milecastles, 160 turrets.

» **Did you know** Hadrian's wasn't the only wall in Britain – the Antonine Wall was built across what is now central Scotland in the AD 140s, but it was abandoned soon after

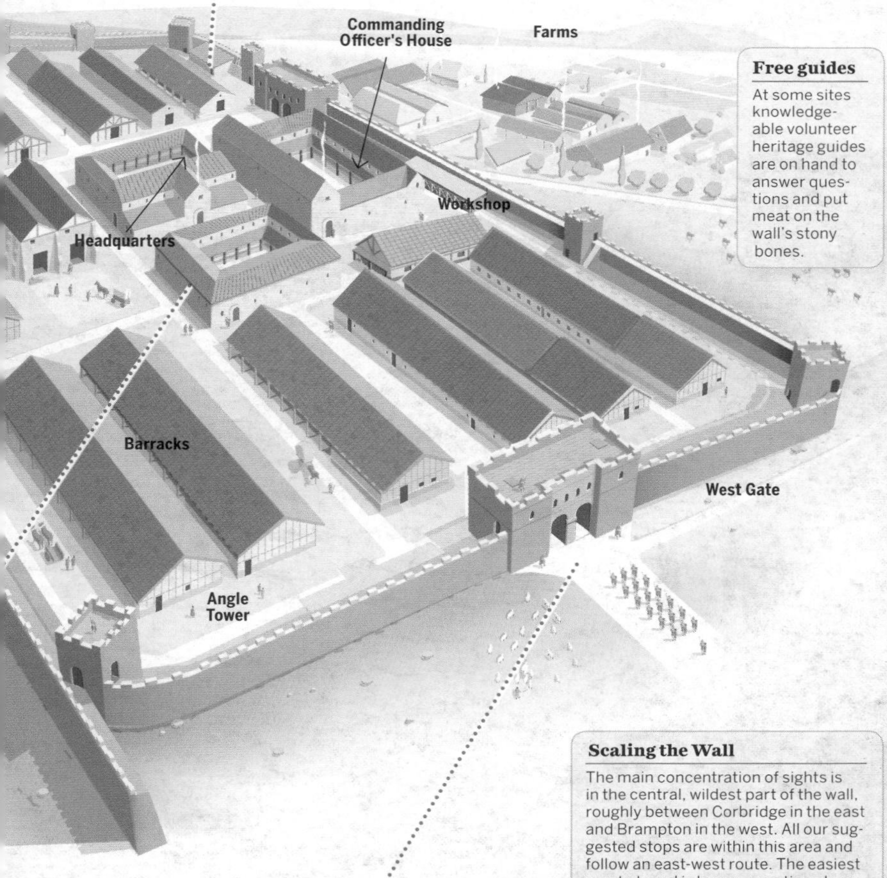

Commanding Officer's House
Farms
Workshop
Headquarters
Barracks
West Gate
Angle Tower

Free guides

At some sites knowledgeable volunteer heritage guides are on hand to answer questions and put meat on the wall's stony bones.

Housesteads' gatehouses
Unusually at Housesteads neither of the gates faces the enemy, as was the norm at a Roman fort – builders aligned them east-west. Ruts worn by cart wheels are still visible in the stone.

Scaling the Wall

The main concentration of sights is in the central, wildest part of the wall, roughly between Corbridge in the east and Brampton in the west. All our suggested stops are within this area and follow an east-west route. The easiest way to travel is by car, scooting along the B6318, but special bus AD122 will also get you there. Hiking along the designated Hadrian's Wall Path (84 miles) allows you to appreciate the achievement up close.

» Hiking along Hadrian's Wall (p622)

(Continued from page 144)

Getting There & Away

Margate has good connections with London and East Kent.

Bus

Canterbury Bus 8, 48 minutes, three hourly

London Victoria National Express, £12, 2½ hours, four daily

Train

London St Pancras High-speed service; £31.40, 1½ hours, hourly

London Victoria £27, one hour 50 minutes, twice hourly

Broadstairs

POP 24,370

Unlike its bigger, brasher neighbours, the charming resort village of Broadstairs revels in its quaintness, plays the Victorian nostalgia card at every opportunity, and names every second business after the works of its most famous holidaymaker, Charles Dickens. The town's elegant clifftop buildings, neatly manicured gardens, scythe of saffron sand and colourful beach huts hide a far grittier history of smuggling and shipbuilding.

Sights

Dickens House Museum MUSEUM

(2 Victoria Pde; adult/child £3.25/1.80; ⏲10am-5pm Jun-Sep) Broadstairs' top attraction is this quaint museum which was actually the home of Mary Pearson Strong, inspiration for the character of Betsey Trotwood in *David Copperfield*. Diverse Dickensiana on display includes letters from the author.

Dickens wrote parts of *Bleak House* and *David Copperfield* in the handsome, if slightly worse for wear, **clifftop house** above the harbour wall between 1837 and 1859. It's now a private property.

Festivals & Events

Broadstairs' biggest bash is the annual, nine-day-long **Dickens Festival** (www.broadstairsdickensfestival.co.uk) held in late June and culminating in a banquet and ball in Victorian fancy dress.

Sleeping & Eating

East Horndon Guesthouse B&B ££

(☎01843-868306; www.easthorndonhotel.com; 4 Eastern Esplanade; s £44, d £80-90; wi-fi) This elegant guest house sits on manicured lawns a few yards from the cliff edge. The eight comfortable rooms are decorated in warm colours, the front four enjoying views of the sea and the world's largest off-shore wind farm.

Tartar Frigate PUB ££

(42 Harbour St; mains £14-16.50) Dating back to the 18th century, this seafront pub is a great place to be in summer when tourists and locals alike spill out onto the beach. The seafood restaurant upstairs serves excellent fare and there are great views of the bay. The pub also puts on regular live folk music.

Getting There & Away

The handy Thanet Loop bus runs every 10 minutes through the day to Ramsgate (20 minutes) and Margate (20 minutes).

Bus

Canterbury Bus 8/9, 1½ hours

London Victoria National Express, £12, three hours, four daily

Train

London St Pancras High-speed service; £31.40, one hour 20 minutes, hourly

London Victoria £27, two hours, twice hourly

ISLE OF THANET

Margate, Ramsgate and Broadstairs are all towns on the Isle of Thanet, but you won't need a wetsuit or a ferry to reach them – the 2-mile-wide Wantsum Channel, which divided the island from the mainland, silted up in the 16th century, transforming the East Kent landscape forever. In its island days Thanet was the springboard to several epoch-making episodes in English history. It was here that the Romans kicked off their invasion in the first century AD and where Augustine landed in AD 597 to launch his conversion of the pagans.

Ramsgate

POP 39,639

The most diverse of Kent's coastal towns, Ramsgate has a friendlier feel than rival Margate and is more vibrant than quaint little neighbour Broadstairs. A forest of sails whistle serenely in the breeze below the town's handsome curved harbour walls, surrounded by seafront bars and cosmopolitan street cafes that give things a laid-back feel. One celebrity chef away from being described as 'up-and-coming', Ramsgate retains a shabbily undiscovered charm, with its superb Blue Flag beaches, some spectacular Victorian architecture and a few welcoming places to stay and eat making it worth the trip.

Sights & Activities

Ramsgate Maritime Museum MUSEUM
(www.ekmt.fogonline.co.uk; The Clock House, Royal Harbour; adult/child £1.50/75p; ⏲10am-5pm Tue-Sun Easter-Sep) More than 600 ships have been wrecked on the notorious Goodwin Sands off this stretch of coast, and an intriguing assortment of loot from their barnacled carcasses fills the town's 19th-century clock tower near the harbour. Here, too, is a line marking Ramsgate's meridian (the town once had its own Ramsgate Mean Time almost 6 minutes ahead of GMT).

Sleeping & Eating

Glendevon Guesthouse B&B ££
(☎01843-570909; www.glendevonguesthouse.co.uk; 8 Truro Rd; s/d from £45/65; P) Run by energetic and outgoing young hosts, this comfy guest house takes the whole ecofriendly thing very seriously, with guest recycling facilities, ecoshowers and even energy-saving hairdryers. The hallways of this grand Victorian house, a block back from the seafront road, are decorated with watercolours by local artists, and there are bookshelves full of games, books and DVDs to borrow. All the rooms have kitchenettes and breakfast is a convivial affair taken around a communal table.

Eddie Gilbert's SEAFOOD ££
(32 King St; mains £6-17; ⏲lunch & dinner Mon-Sat, extended lunch Sun) Indulge in England's favourite aroma (battered fish and chips) at Thanet's best seafood and gourmet fish and chips restaurant above a traditional fishmonger's. The beamed dining space decorated with lobster cages, fish nets and sea charts is the ideal setting for platters of locally caught fish prepared in some very inventive ways by a Michelin-trained chef.

Getting There & Away

Ramsgate is linked to Margate, Broadstairs and Sandwich by frequent local bus services.

Air

The only scheduled service out of nearby **Kent International Airport** (☎08707 605 755; www.kia-m.com) is the daily flight to Edinburgh operated by **Flybe** (www.flybe.com). More may be added in coming years.

Boat

Euroferries (☎0844-4145355; www.euroferries.co.uk) Runs high-speed ferries to Boulogne (from £49 per car, 1¼ hours, four daily).

Transeuropa Ferries (☎01843-595522; www.transeuropaferries.com) Operates ferries from Ramsgate New Port to Ostend in Belgium (from £49 per car, five hours, four daily).

Bus

London Victoria National Express, £12, three hours, four daily

Train

London Charing Cross £27.30, two hours, hourly

London St Pancras High-speed service; £31.40, one hour 20 minutes, hourly

Sandwich

POP 4398

With a top slice of ancient churches, Dutch gables and peg-tiled roofs, a juicy filling of medieval lanes and timber-framed houses, and a wholesome base of riverside strolls and great pubs, Sandwich makes a very tasty morsel for passing travellers. Today it's a sleepy little inland settlement, but the town retains a certain salty tang from its days as one of the original Cinque Ports when it ran a close second to the Port of London. Decline set in when the entrance to the harbour silted up in the 16th century, leaving this once vital gateway to and from the Continent to spend the last 400 years retreating into very quaint rural obscurity.

Of course, though the town makes precious little of it, Sandwich indirectly gave the world its favourite snack when the 4th Earl of Sandwich called for his meat to be served between two slices of bread, thus freeing him to gamble all night long without leaving the table or smudging his cards. It hence became de rigueur to ask for meat 'like Sandwich' and the rest is fast-food history.

Sights & Activities

Sandwich's spider web of medieval and Elizabethan streets is perfect for ambling and getting pleasantly lost. **Strand Street** in particular has one of the highest concentrations of half-timbered buildings in the country. Stepped gables betray the strong influence of 350 Protestant Flemish refugees (the 'Strangers') who settled in the town in the 16th century on the invitation of Elizabeth I.

Guildhall Museum MUSEUM
(adult/child £1/50p; 10.30am-12.30pm & 2-4pm Tue, Wed, Fri & Sat, 2-4pm Thu & Sun Apr-Nov) A good place to start is the small but thorough guildhall with its exhibitions on Sandwich's rich past as a Cinque Port, the town at war and gruesome punishments meted out to felons, fornicators and phoney fishermen.

Sandwich Quay QUAY
Several attractions line the River Stour; first up is a cute little flint-chequered **Barbican** tollgate, built by Henry VIII, which controls traffic flow over the only road bridge across the river. Nearby rises the **Fishergate**, built in 1384 and once the main entrance to the town through which goods from the Continent and beyond, unloaded on the quay, once passed. On fair-weather days, hop aboard the **Sandwich River Bus** (07958-376183; www.sandwichriverbus.co.uk; adult/child 30min trip £6/4, 1hr £10/7; every 30-60min 11am-6pm Thu-Sun Apr-Sep) beside the toll bridge for seal spotting trips along the River Stour and in Pegwell Bay or an interesting way to reach Richborough (p156).

Salutation Gardens GARDENS
(www.the-secretgardens.co.uk; adult/child £6/3; 10am-5pm) Just along from Fishergate is Sandwich's top attraction, a set of exquisite gardens laid out by leading early-20th-century garden designers Jekyll and Lutyens behind a 1912 mansion. There's a superb new tea room in the grounds.

Churches CHURCHES
Architecture buffs should head for **St Clement's Church** (Church St St Clement's), topped with a handsome Norman tower. The oldest church in Sandwich is **St Peter's** (King St), now no longer used for worship. It's a real mixture of styles and years: its tower collapsed in dramatic fashion in 1661 and it was rebuilt with a bulbous cupola by the Strangers. It houses the town's old horse-drawn fire engine and sparse displays on the often scandalous earls of Sandwich. **St Mary's** (Cnr Church St St Mary's and Strand St), the town's third church, is now a multipurpose venue, but open during the day for perusal.

CINQUE PORTS

Due to their proximity to Europe, southeast England's coastal towns were the front line against raids and invasion during Anglo-Saxon times. In the absence of a professional army and navy, these ports were frequently called upon to defend themselves, and the kingdom, on land and at sea.

In 1278, King Edward I formalised this already ancient arrangement by legally defining the Confederation of Cinque Ports. The five original ports – Sandwich, Dover, Hythe, Romney and Hastings – were granted numerous perks and privileges in exchange for providing the king with ships and men. At their peak, the ports were deemed England's most powerful institution after Crown and Church.

The ports' real importance evaporated eventually, when the shifting coastlines silted up several Cinque Port harbours and a professional navy was based at Portsmouth. Yet, the pomp and ceremony remains. The Lord Warden of the Cinque Ports is a prestigious post now given to faithful servants of the Crown. The Queen Mother was warden until she passed away, succeeded by Admiral Lord Boyce. Previous incumbents include the Duke of Wellington and Sir Winston Churchill.

'Who names us sank and not sink is a foreigner and foe' once went the saying on the south coast, describing a faux pas committed today by just about every unknowing tourist, both foreign and British (cinque, as in Cinque Port, is pronounced 'sink' and not 'sank' as the French would say).

Sleeping & Eating

TOP CHOICE **Bell Hotel** HOTEL ££
(01304-613388; www.bellhotelsandwich.co.uk; The Quay; s/d from £95/110; P) Today the haunt of celebrity golfers, the Bell Hotel has been sitting on the town's quay since Tudor times, though much of the remaining building is from the 19th century. A splendid, sweeping staircase leads up to luxurious rooms, some with great quay views. The service here could not be better.

King's Arms INN ££
(01304-617330; cnr Church St St Mary's & Strand St; light meals £3-8, mains £10.50-18; lunch & dinner) This 15th-century inn opposite St Mary's church serving quality English food and very popular Sunday lunches has a beamed dining room heated by large fireplaces. For sunny days there's a walled, vine-covered beer garden. There are six B&B rooms upstairs.

Information

Tourist office (01304-613565; www.open-sandwich.co.uk; New St; 10am-4pm Mon-Sat Apr-Oct plus noon-3pm Sun Jun-Aug) Hands out maps and audio guides (£2).

Getting There & Away

Trains run from Dover Priory train station (21 minutes, hourly), Ramsgate (12 minutes, hourly) and London Charing Cross (£26.90, two hours 18 minutes, hourly).

Buses also go to Ramsgate (22 minutes, hourly), Dover (47 minutes, hourly) and Canterbury (40 minutes, three hourly).

Richborough

Roman Britain began here amid the windswept ruins of **Richborough Roman Fort** (EH; adult/child £4.50/2.30; 10am-6pm Mar-Sep), just 2 miles north of Sandwich. This is the spot from which the successful AD 43 invasion of Britain was launched. To celebrate their victory, a colossal triumphal arch was planted here, the base of which remains. The fort's clearest features today – high walls and scores of deep defensive ditches that give it the appearance of a vast jelly mould – came later as the Romans were forced to stave off increasingly vicious seaborne attacks.

There's a small onsite museum and an audiotour to steer you through the rise and fall of Roman Richborough. To arrive as the Romans did – by boat – take the Sandwich River Bus from Sandwich quay.

Dover

POP 39,078

Down-in-the-dumps Dover has certainly seen better days and its derelict, postwar architecture and shabby town centre of va-

LOCAL KNOWLEDGE

COLIN CARR: SANDWICH HARBOURMASTER & BOATMAN

You could say I've had the sea and the southeast in my blood since birth, having arrived in Sandwich via the net shops of Hastings and my own boatyard on the Medway. For the last decade I've been continuing ancient boating traditions as harbourmaster of this Cinque Port, but when I'm not overseeing the navigation way on the River Stour, you'll find me restoring my 1903 barge, which I hope to use for river tours from 2011. You can't live in Sandwich without developing a passion for local history and wildlife, so here are my tips.

Hidden gems

Sandwich is one big hidden gem! Wander aimlessly through its medieval web of streets to unearth a wealth of history and architecture or take a tour. Most atmospheric is around 8pm when the 'curfew bell' is still rung from the tower of St Peter's, as it has been for 800 years.

Must-sees

The exquisite Salutation Gardens, Sandwich's redundant Norman churches and Richborough Roman Fort, where the Romans gained their first foothold in Britain in AD 43, should be on every visitor's checklist.

Top tip

Head down the meandering River Stour towards Pegwell Bay and the Channel at low tide for the best bird- and wildlife-spotting; high tide is more picturesque.

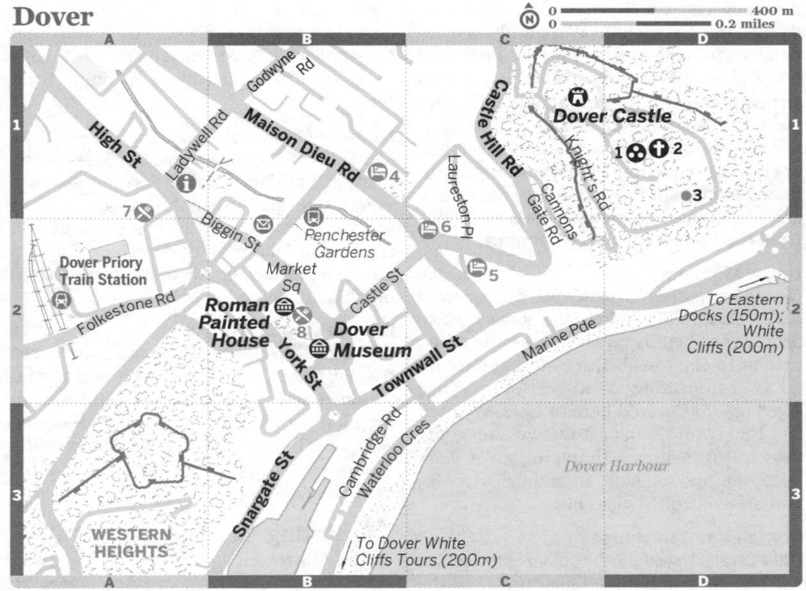

cant shops is a sad introduction to Blighty for travellers arriving from the Continent, most of whom pass through quickly. Lucky, then, that the town has a couple of stellar attractions to redeem it. The port's vital strategic position so close to mainland Europe gave rise to a sprawling hilltop castle, with some 2000 years of history to its credit. The spectacular white cliffs, as much a symbol of English wartime resilience as Winston Churchill or the Battle of Britain, rise in chalky magnificence to the east and west.

Dover

Top Sights

- Dover Castle ... C1
- Dover Museum ... B2
- Roman Painted House ... B2

Sights

1. Roman Lighthouse ... D1
2. Saxon Church ... D1

Activities, Courses & Tours

3. Secret Wartime Tunnels ... D1

Sleeping

4. East Lee Guest House ... B1
5. Hubert House ... C2
6. Number One Guest House ... C2

Eating

7. Allotment ... A1
8. La Salle Verte ... B2

Sights & Activities

Dover Castle CASTLE

(EH; adult/child £13.90/7; 10am-6pm Apr-Sep; P) The almost impenetrable Dover Castle, one of the most impressive in England, was built to bolster the country's weakest point at this, the shortest sea-crossing to mainland Europe. It sprawls across the city's hilltop, commanding a tremendous view of the English Channel as far as the French coastline.

The site has been in use for as many as 2000 years. On the vast grounds are the remains of a **Roman lighthouse**, which date from AD 50 and may be the oldest standing building in Britain. Beside it lies a restored **Saxon church**.

The robust 12th-century **Great Tower**, with walls up to 7m thick, is filled with interactive exhibits and light-and-sound shows which take visitors back to the times of Henry II. But it's the warren of claustrophobic **secret wartime tunnels** under the castle that are the biggest draw. Excellent 50-minute tours delve into the hillside passageways, which were first excavated during the Napoleonic Wars and then expanded to house a command post and hospital in WWII. They now house reconstructed scenes of their wartime use, complete with sounds, smells and erratic lighting. One of Britain's most famous wartime operations, code-named Dynamo, was directed from here in 1940. It saw the evacuation of hundreds of thousands of troops from the French beaches of Dunkirk.

Dover Museum MUSEUM
(www.dovermuseum.co.uk; Market Sq; adult/child £3/2; ⌚10am-5.30pm Mon-Sat year-round, noon-5pm Sun Apr-Aug) By far the most enthralling exhibit in the town's three-storey museum is an astonishing 3600-year-old Bronze Age boat, discovered here in 1992. Vaunted as the world's oldest-known seagoing vessel, it measures a thumping great 9.5m by 2.4m and is kept in a huge, low-lit, climate-controlled glass box.

Roman Painted House ROMAN ART
(New St; adult/child £3/2; ⌚10am-5pm Tue-Sun Apr-Sep) A crumbling 1960s bunker is the unlikely setting for some of the most extensive, if stunted, Roman wall paintings north of the Alps. Several scenes depict Bacchus (the god of wine and revelry), which makes perfect sense as this large villa was built around AD 200 as a *mansio* (hotel) for travellers in need of a little lubrication to unwind.

Sleeping

B&Bs cluster along Castle St, Maison Dieu Rd and Folkestone Rd.

TOP CHOICE **Wallett's Court** HOTEL £££
(☎01304-852424; www.wallettscourt.com; Westcliffe, St Margaret's-at-Cliffe; d from £150; P 📶 ✲) Weekend haunt of de-stressing London highfliers, romantic couples and the odd moneyed cliff walker, this place is just a bit special. Digs at this country house in rolling open country range from spacious Jacobean guestrooms to beamed converted barns to a canvass wigwam in the grounds. Add to that a soothing spa, a first-rate restaurant and perky service, and you have yourself one very relaxing country retreat. Heading towards Deal, turn right off the A258 for Westcliffe after almost 2 miles.

Hubert House B&B ££
(☎01304-202253; www.huberthouse.co.uk; 9 Castle Hill Rd; s/d from £40/55; P @ 📶) The comfortable bedrooms in this Georgian house may be overly flowery but the welcome is warm, and it uses ecofriendly and fair-trade products. It has its own little bistro downstairs which opens out onto a front terrace.

Number One Guest House B&B ££
(☎01304-202007; www.number1guesthouse.co.uk; 1 Castle Street; d from £50; P) Set in a grand Georgian town house at the foot of Dover Castle, with rooms decorated in traditional Victorian style. There's also a quaint walled garden with lovely views and breakfast is served in bed.

East Lee Guest House B&B ££
(☎01304-210176; www.eastlee.co.uk; 108 Maison Dieu Rd; d £60; P 📶) This lovely terracotta-shingled town house makes quite an impression with its grand, elegantly decorated communal areas, energetic hosts, recently renovated rooms and excellent, varied breakfasts.

Eating

TOP CHOICE **Allotment** BRITISH ££
(www.theallotmentdover.com; 9 High St; mains £7.50-16; ⌚8.30am-11pm Tue-Sat) Dover's best dining spot plates up local fish and meat from around Canterbury, seasoned with herbs from the tranquil garden out back, in a relaxed, understated setting. Swab the decks with a Kentish wine as you admire the view of the Maison Dieu directly opposite through the exquisite stained glass frontage.

La Salle Verte CAFE £
(14-15 Cannon St; snacks £2-5.50; ⌚9am-5pm Mon-Sat) The funkiest little coffee shop in Dover serves great cakes, coffee and snacks both inside and in a little suntrap patio garden.

Information

Post office (68-72 Pencester Rd)

Tourist office (☎01304-205108; www.whitecliffscountry.org.uk; Biggin St; ⌚9am-5.30pm daily Jun-Aug, 9am-5.30pm Mon-Fri & 10am-4pm Sat & Sun Apr, May & Sep, closed Sun Oct-Mar) Located in the Old Town Gaol on Biggin St; can book accommodation and ferries for a small fee.

White Cliffs Medical Centre (☎01304-201705; 143 Folkestone Rd)

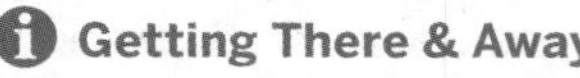

Getting There & Away

For information on the Channel Tunnel services, see p1065.

Boat

Ferries depart for France from the Eastern Docks below the castle. Fares vary according to season and advance purchase. See the websites for specials.

LD Lines (☎0800 917 1201; www.ldlines.co.uk) Services to Boulogne (50 minutes, up to seven daily).

Norfolk Line (☎0844 847 5042; www.norfolkline.com) Services to Dunkirk (two hours, every two hours).

P&O Ferries (☎08716 642020; www.poferries.com) Runs to Calais (1½ hours, every 40 minutes to an hour).

Seafrance (☎0871 423 7119; www.seafrance.com) Ferries to Calais roughly every 90 minutes.

Bus

Dover connections:

Canterbury Bus 15, 45 minutes, twice hourly

London Victoria Coach 007, £13.50, 2¾ hours, 19 daily

Sandwich Bus 87, 45 minutes, hourly

Train

Dover connections:

London Charing Cross £18.50, two hours, twice hourly

London St Pancras High-speed service; £31.70, one hour, hourly

Ramsgate £7.50, 35 minutes, hourly, via Sandwich

 Getting Around

The ferry companies run regular shuttle buses between the docks and the train station (five minutes) as they're a long walk apart.

Heritage (☎01304-204420) Provides a 24-hour service.

Star Taxis (☎01304-228822) Also has a 24-hour service.

Around Dover

THE WHITE CLIFFS

Immortalised in song, film and literature, these iconic cliffs are embedded in the national consciousness, acting as a big, white 'Welcome Home' sign to generations of travellers and soldiers.

The cliffs rise 100m high and extend for 10 miles on either side of Dover, but it is the 6-mile stretch east of town – properly known as the Langdon Cliffs – that particularly captivates visitors' imaginations. The chalk here is about 250m deep, and the cliffs themselves are about half a million years old, formed when the melting icecaps of northern Europe were gouging a channel between France and England.

The Langdon Cliffs are managed by the National Trust, which has a **tourist office** (☎01304-202756; ⏲10am-5pm Mar-Oct, 11am-4pm Nov-Feb) and **car park** (£3 for nonmembers) 2 miles east of Dover along Castle Hill Rd and the A258 road to Deal or off the A2 past the Eastern Docks.

From the tourist office, follow the stony path east along the clifftops for a bracing 2-mile walk to the stout Victorian **South Foreland Lighthouse** (NT; adult/child £4/2; ⏲guided tours 11am-5.30pm Fri-Mon mid-Mar-Oct). This was the first lighthouse to be powered by electricity, and is the site of the first international radio transmissions in 1898.

A mile further on the same trail brings you to delightful **St Margaret's Bay**, a gap in the chalk with a sun-trapping shingle beach and the welcoming **Coastguard Pub** (www.thecoastguard.co.uk; mains £10-15; ⏲lunch & dinner). As this is the closest point to France many a cross-Channel swimmer has stepped into the briny here. From the top of the hill the hourly bus 15 shuttles back to Dover or onwards to Deal.

To see the cliffs in all their full-frontal glory, **Dover White Cliffs Tours** (☎01303-271388; www.doverwhiteclifftours.com; adult/child £8/4; ⏲daily Jul & Aug, Sat & Sun Apr-Jun & Sep-Oct) runs 40-minute sightseeing trips at least three times a day from the Western Docks.

Leeds Castle

This immense moated pile is for many the world's most romantic **castle** (www.leeds-castle.com; adult/child £17.50/10; ⏲10am-6pm Apr-Sep), and it's certainly one of the most visited in Britain. While it looks formidable enough from the outside – a hefty structure balancing on two islands amid a large lake and sprawling estate – it's actually known as something of a 'ladies castle'. This stems from the fact that in its more than 1000 years of history, it has been home to a who's who of medieval queens, most famously Henry VIII's first wife, Catherine of Aragon.

The castle was transformed from fortress to lavish palace over the centuries, and its last owner, the high-society hostess Lady Baillie, used it as a princely family

WORTH A TRIP

DOWN HOUSE

Charles Darwin's home from 1842 until his death in 1882, **Down House** (EH; Luxted Rd, Downe; adult/child £9.30/4.70; ⌚11am-5pm Jul & Aug, Wed-Sun Mar, Jun, Sep & Oct) witnessed the development of Darwin's theory of evolution by natural selection. The house and gardens have been restored to look much as they would have in Darwin's time, including Darwin's study, where he undertook much of his reading and writing; the drawing room, where he tried out some of his indoor experiments; and the gardens and greenhouse, where some of his outdoor experiments are re-created. There are three self-guided trails in the area, where you can follow in the great man's footsteps.

Down House is in Downe, off the A21. Take bus 146 from Bromley North or Bromley South railway station, or service R8 from Orpington.

home and party pad to entertain the likes of Errol Flynn, Douglas Fairbanks and JFK.

The castle's vast estate offers enough attractions of its own to justify a day trip: peaceful walks, a duckery, aviary and falconry demonstrations. You'll also find possibly the world's sole **dog collar museum**, plenty of kids' attractions and a **hedge maze**, overseen by a grassy bank where fellow travellers can shout encouragement or misdirections.

Since Lady Baillie's death in 1974, a private trust has managed the property. This means that some parts of the castle are periodically closed for private events.

Leeds Castle is just east of Maidstone. Trains run from London Victoria to Bearsted (£17.10, one hour) where you catch a special shuttle coach to the castle (£5 return).

EAST SUSSEX

Home to rolling countryside, medieval villages and gorgeous coastline, this inspiring corner of England is besieged by weekending Londoners whenever the sun pops out. And it's not hard to see why as you explore the cobbled medieval streets of Rye, wander historic Battle, where William the Conqueror first engaged the Saxons in 1066, and peer over the edge of the breathtaking Seven Sisters chalk cliffs and Beachy Head near the genteel seaside town of Eastbourne. Brighton, a highlight of any visit, offers some kicking nightlife, offbeat shopping and British seaside fun. But you needn't follow the crowds to enjoy East Sussex. It's just as rewarding to get off the beaten track, linger along its winding country lanes and stretch your legs on the South Downs Way, which traverses England's newest national park, the South Downs National Park.

Rye

POP 4195

If you're searching for a perfect example of a medieval settlement, look no further than Rye, described by many as the most attractive little town in England. Once a Cinque Port this exquisite place looks as if it's been pickled, put on a shelf and promptly forgotten about by old Father Time. Even the most hardened cynic can't fail to be bewitched by Rye's cobbled lanes, mysterious passageways and crooked half-timbered Tudor buildings. Romantics can lap up the townsfolk's tales of resident smugglers, ghosts, writers and artists, and hole up in one of a slew of gorgeous accommodation options in its heart.

Sights

A short walk from the Rye Heritage Centre, most start their exploration of Rye in the famous **Mermaid St**, bristling with 15th-century timber-framed houses with quirky house names such as 'The House with Two Front Doors' and 'The House Opposite'.

Ypres Tower MUSEUM

(Tower & museum adult/child £3/free; ⌚10.30am-5pm Apr-Oct) Just off Church Sq stands the sandcastle-esque Ypres Tower (pronounced 'wipers'). This 13th-century building looks out over Romney Marsh and Rye Bay, and houses one part of Rye Museum. It's overseen by a friendly warden, who's full of colourful tales from the tower's long history as fort, prison, mortuary and museum (the last two at overlapping times). New exhibitions dedicated to women and children in Rye and a medieval garden are planned. The other branch of the **museum** (www.ryemuseum.co.uk; 3 East St; adult/child £2.50/free; ⌚2-5pm Thu, Fri & Mon, 10.30am-1pm & 2-5pm Sat & Sun Apr-Oct), a short stroll away on East St, is home to an 18th-century leather fire engine and other intriguing loot.

Lamb House HOUSE MUSEUM
(NT; West St; adult/child £4/2.10; ⌚2-6pm Thu & Sat late Mar-Oct) This Georgian town house is a favourite stomping ground for local apparitions, but not that of its most famous resident, American writer Henry James, who lived here from 1898 to 1916, during which he wrote *The Wings of the Dove*.

Church of St Mary the Virgin CHURCH
(Church Sq; ⌚9.15am-5.30pm Apr-Sep) Rye's church is a hotchpotch of medieval and later styles and its turret clock is the oldest in England (1561) still working with its original pendulum, which swings above your head as you enter. Climb the **tower** (adult/child £2.50/1) for panoramic views of the town and surroundings.

Landgate TOWN GATE
At the northeastern edge of the village, this thickset pale-stone gate dating from 1329 is the only remaining gate out of four and is still in use. The name comes from the fact that when first built, it was the only gate linking the town to the mainland at high tide.

Sleeping

TOP CHOICE **Jeake's House** HOTEL ££
(☎01797-222828; www.jeakeshouse.com; Mermaid St; s/d from £70/114; P 📶) Superbly situated on cobbled Mermaid St, this labyrinthine 17th-century town house once belonged to US poet Conrad Aitken. The '11 Rooms' are named after writers who actually stayed here, though the decor was probably slightly less bold back then, minus the beeswaxed antiques and lavish drapery. You can literally take a pew in the snug book-lined bar and, continuing the theme, breakfast is served in an 18th-century former chapel.

Mermaid Inn HOTEL £££
(☎01797-223065; www.mermaidinn.com; Mermaid St; d £160-250; P) Few inns can claim to be as atmospheric as this ancient hostelry, dating from 1420. Every room is different – but each is thick with dark beams and lit by leaded windows, and some are graced by secret passageways that now act as fire escapes. Small wonder it's such a popular spot – these days you're as likely to spot a celeb or a royal as the resident ghost.

George in Rye HOTEL £££
(☎01797-222114; www.thegeorgeinrye.com; 98 High St; d from £135; @📶) This old coaching inn has managed to reinvent itself as a contemporary boutique hotel while

A SWIG OF KENT & SUSSEX

With booze cruises over to Calais now almost a thing of the past, many Kent and Sussex drinkers are rediscovering their counties' superb home-grown beverages. Both counties produce some of the most delicious ales in the country and the southeast's wines are even outgunning some traditional Continental vintners.

Kent's **Shepherd Neame Brewery** (☎01795-532206; www.shepherd-neame.co.uk; 10 Court St, Faversham; admission £10; ⌚on request) is Britain's oldest and cooks up aromatic ales brewed from Kent-grown premium hops. Sussex's reply is **Harveys Brewery** (☎01273-480209; www.harveys.org.uk; Bridge Wharf, Lewes; ⌚tours evenings only) which perfumes Lewes town centre with a hop-laden scent. Book in advance for tours of either brewery.

Mention 'English wine' not too long ago and you'd likely hear a snort of derision. Not any more. Thanks to warmer temperatures and determined winemakers, English wine, particularly of the sparkling variety, is developing a fan base all of its own.

Award-winning vineyards can be found in both Sussex and Kent, whose chalky soils are likened to France's Champagne region. Many vineyards now offer tours and wine tastings. Some of the most popular are **Biddenden Vineyards** (☎01580-291726; biddendenvineyards.co.uk; 1.2 miles from Wealden; admission free; ⌚tours 10am daily) and **Chapel Down Vinery** (☎01580-766111; www.englishwinesgroup.com; Tenterden; admission £9; ⌚tours Jun-Sep).

staying true to its roots. Downstairs, an old-fashioned wood-panelled lounge is warmed by roaring log fires, while the 24 guest-rooms, created by the set designer from the film *Pride & Prejudice*, are chic and understated. The George's contemporary restaurant can contend with Rye's best and if you stay here, ask to see the incredible, and unexpectedly large, 18th-century ballroom.

Eating

Haydens CAFE £
(108 High St; snacks/meals from £3/9; ⏲10am-5pm daily, dinner Fri & Sat) Staunch believers in organic and fair-trade produce, these guys dish up delicious omelettes, ploughman's lunches, salads and pancakes in their light, breezy cafe. There's a wonderful elevated terrace at the back with great views over the town and surrounding countryside.

Ypres Castle Inn PUB ££
(Gun Gardens; meals £5.50-17; ⏲lunch & dinner) You can have a match on a boules pitch, enjoy some live bands or chow down on scrumptious seasonal food like Rye bay scallops at this warm, country-style pub. The beer's not bad either.

Information

Post office (Unit 2, Station Approach)

Rye Heritage Centre (☎01797-226696; www.ryeheritage.co.uk; Strand Quay; ⏲10am-5pm Apr-Oct) Runs a town-model audiovisual history for £3.50 and upstairs is a freaky collection of penny-in-the-slot novelty machines. It also sells a *Rye Town Walk* map (£1) and rents out multilingual audiotours (adult/child £4/2).

Rye Internet Cafe (46 Ferry Rd; per hr £2; ⏲10am-9pm Tue-Thu, 10am-7pm Fri, 11am-6pm Sat & Sun)

Tourist office (☎01797-229049; www.visit1066country.com; 4/5 Lion St; ⏲10am-5pm Apr-Sep) New but rather spartan office. Can help with accommodation bookings.

Getting There & Away

Bus

Dover Bus 100, two hours, hourly

Hastings Bus 344 or 100, 40 minutes, two per hour

Train

London Charing Cross £25.80, two hours, hourly; change either in Hastings or Ashford

Battle

POP 5190

This unassuming village grew up around the spot where invading French duke William of Normandy, aka William the Conqueror, scored a decisive victory over local King Harold in 1066, so beginning Norman rule and changing the face of the country forever. If there'd been no battle, there'd be no Battle, as locals sometimes say.

Sights

Battle Abbey BATTLEFIELD
(EH; adult/child £7/3.50; ⏲10am-6pm Apr-Sep) Another day, another photogenic ruin? Hardly. On this spot raged *the* pivotal battle in the last successful invasion of England in 1066: an event with unparalleled impact on the country's subsequent social structure, architecture and well...pretty much every-

THE LAST INVASION OF ENGLAND

The most famous battle in the history of England took place in 1066: a date seared into every English schoolchild's brain. The Battle of Hastings began when Harold's army arrived on the scene on 14 October and created a three-ring defence consisting of archers, then cavalry, with massed infantry at the rear. William marched north from Hastings and took up a position about 400m south of Harold and his troops. He tried repeatedly to break the English cordon, but Harold's men held fast. William's knights then feigned retreat, drawing some of Harold's troops after them. It was a fatal mistake. Seeing the gap in the English wall, William ordered his remaining troops to charge through, and the battle was as good as won. Among the English casualties was King Harold who, as tradition has it, was hit in the eye by an arrow, and struck down by Norman knights as he tried to pull it out. At news of his death the last English resistance collapsed.

In their wonderfully irreverent *1066 And All That* (1930), WC Sellar and RJ Yeatman suggest that 'the Norman conquest was a Good Thing, as from this time onward England stopped being conquered and thus was able to become top nation...' When you consider that England hasn't been successfully invaded since, it's hard to disagree.

thing. Only four years later, the conquering Normans began constructing an abbey right in the middle of the battlefield: a penance ordered by the Pope for the loss of life incurred here.

Only the foundations of the original church remain, the altar's position marked by a **plaque** – also supposedly the spot England's King Harold famously took an arrow in his eye. Other impressive monastic buildings survive and make for atmospheric explorations.

The battlefield's innocently rolling lush hillsides do little to evoke the ferocity of the event, but high-tech interactive presentations and a film at the new visitors centre, as well as blow-by-blow audiotours, do their utmost to bring the battle to life.

Yesterday's World MUSEUM
(www.yesterdaysworld.co.uk; 89-90 High St; adult/child £7/5; ⏲10am-6pm Apr-Sep) Overshadowed literally and figuratively by the abbey, this growing museum is an incredible repository of England's retail past. The first building houses entire streets of quaint old shops where costumed dummies proffer long discontinued brands, every space in between stuffed with yesteryear products, enamel advertising signs, battered toys, wartime memorabilia and general nostalgia-inducing knick-knackery. The second building is much the same except for the Royalty Room where a cardboard cut-out illustrates just how tiny Queen Victoria was (1.40m).

Information

The **tourist office** (☎01424-776789; Gatehouse; ⏲10am-6pm Apr-Sep, to 4pm Oct-Mar) is in the entrance to Battle Abbey. The post office, banks and ATMs are also on High St.

Getting There & Away

Bus

London Victoria National Express bus 023, £13.40, 2¼ hours, daily

Hastings Bus 304/305, 26 minutes, hourly

Train

London Charing Cross £18.30, one hour 20 minutes, twice hourly

Bodiam Castle

Surrounded by a square moat teeming with oversized goldfish, four-towered archetypal **Bodiam Castle** (NT; adult/child £6.40/3.20; ⏲10am-6pm mid-Feb–Oct) makes you half expect to see a fire-breathing dragon appear or a golden-haired princess lean over its walls. It is the legacy of 14th-century soldier of fortune (the polite term for knights who slaughtered and pillaged their way around France) Sir Edward Dalyngrigge, who married the local heiress and set about building a castle to make sure everybody knew who was boss.

Parliamentarian forces left the castle in ruins during the English Civil War, but in 1917 Lord Curzon, former viceroy of India, bought it and restored the exterior. Much of the interior remains unrestored, but it's possible to climb to the battlements for some sweeping views.

While here you'll most likely hear the tooting of the nearby **Kent & East Sussex steam railway** (www.kesr.org.uk; day ticket adult/child £12.80/7.80), which runs from Tenterden in Kent through 11 miles of gentle hills and woods to Bodiam village, from where a bus takes you to the castle. It operates three to five services on most days from May to September and at the weekend and school holidays in October, December and February.

The castle is 9 miles northeast of Battle off the B2244. Stagecoach bus 349 stops at Bodiam from Hastings (40 minutes) once every two hours during the day Monday to Saturday.

Hastings

POP 85,000

Forever associated with the Norman invasion of 1066 even though the crucial events took place 6 miles away, Hastings thrived as a Cinque Port, and in its Victorian heyday was one of the country's most fashionable seaside resorts. After a period of steady decline, the town is enjoying a mini-renaissance, and these days it's an intriguing mix of tacky resort, fishing port and arty New-Age hang-out.

Hastings last hit the news in October 2010 when its Victorian pier burnt down following an alleged arson attack. The ballroom at the end of the pier, where groups like The Clash, The Sex Pistols and The Rolling Stones once performed, was completely destroyed. It's very unlikely the money will be found to rebuild this reminder of the town's seaside holiday heyday.

Sights

The best place for aimless wandering is the **Old Town**, a hotchpotch of narrow streets and half-timbered buildings filled with junk shops, quirky boutiques, street cafes, quaint local pubs and galleries.

Down by the seafront, the **Stade** – the stretch of shingle in front of Rock-a-Nore Rd – is home to distinctive, tall black clapboard huts known as **Net Shops**, built as storage for fishing gear back in the 17th century. Some now house fishmongers where the catch brought home by Europe's largest beach-launched fishing fleet is sold.

Three nautical attractions line up one after the other on Rock-a-Nore Rd itself: the **Fishermen's Museum** (www.hastingsfish.co.uk; Rock-a-Nore Rd; admission free; 10am-5pm Apr-Oct), the **Shipwreck and Coastal Heritage Centre** (www.shipwreck-heritage.org.uk; Rock-a-Nore Rd; admission free; 10am-5pm) and the **Blue Reef Aquarium** (www.bluereefaquarium.co.uk/hastings; Rock-a-Nore Rd; adult/child £7.95/5.95; 10am-5pm).

Two Victorian funicular railways scale the high cliffs that shelter the town, the most useful of which is the **West Hill Cliff Railway** (George St; adult/child £2.20/1.30; 10am-5.30pm Apr-Sep), which takes visitors up to West Hill and the ruins of a Norman fortress built by William the Conqueror in 1069, now known as **Hastings Castle** (www.discoverhastings.co.uk; Castle Hill Rd; adult/child £4.25/3.50; 10am-5pm Easter-Sep). The **Smugglers Adventure** (www.smugglersadventure.co.uk; St Clement Caves; adult/child £7.20/5.20; 10am-5pm Easter-Sep) is also on West Hill. Meander through underground caverns to hear yarns of smuggling along the Sussex coast, told through interactive exhibits and a ghostly narrator. The **East Hill Cliff Railway** (Rock-a-Nore Rd; adult/child £2.20/1.30; 10am-5.30pm Apr-Sep) reopened in March 2010, and once again elevates walkers and nature-lovers up to the 267-hectare **Hastings Country Park**.

Sleeping & Eating

The Laindons B&B ££

(01424-437710; www.thelaindons.com; 23 High St; s/d from £80/110;) This newcomer occupying a Georgian Grade II–listed former coaching inn is five minutes' amble from the seafront at the quieter end of High St. The three beautifully appointed rooms flood with sea-refracted light from the huge Georgian windows, illuminating the blend of breezy contemporary design and antique furnishings. Owner-cooked breakfasts are taken around a communal table.

Dragon Bar BAR, RESTAURANT ££

(71 George St; mains £10-16; lunch & dinner Mon-Sat, lunch Sun) Atmospheric, laid-back bar full of dark walls, mismatched furniture and beaten leather sofas, attracting the younger end of the alternative old-town crowds. The eclectic menu features everything from Thai curry to Winchelsea lamb to pizzas.

Information

Tourist office (01424-451111; Queen's Sq; 8.30am-6.15pm Mon-Fri, 9am-5pm Sat, 10.30am-4pm Sun) This large office sells all kinds of bus, ferry and train tickets as well as locally themed publications.

Getting There & Away

Bus

Eastbourne Bus 99, one hour 20 minutes, three per hour

London Victoria National Express, £13.40, 2½ to four hours, twice daily

Rye Buses 100 & 344, 40 minutes, twice hourly

Train

Brighton £11.20, one hour to one hour 20 minutes, three per hour; via Eastbourne

London Charing Cross £25.90, 1½ hours, twice hourly

London Victoria £25.90, two hours, hourly

Eastbourne

POP 89,667

This classic, old-fashioned seaside resort has long brought to mind images of octogenarians dozing in deck chairs. While many of Eastbourne's seafront hotels still have that retirement-home feel, in recent years an influx of students and one of the largest new Polish communities in the southeast have given the town a sprightlier feel. The creation of the new South Downs National Park to the west also means Eastbourne's pebbly beaches, scrupulously snipped seaside gardens and picturesque arcade-free promenade are likely to see increasing numbers of walkers and cyclists, finishing or embarking on a trip along the South Downs Way.

Sights & Activities

FREE **Towner Art Gallery** ART GALLERY

(01323-434670; www.townereastbourne.org.uk; Devonshire Park, College Rd; 10am-6pm Tue-Sun, bldg tours 11.30am) Until Turner Margate is up and running, Eastbourne's Towner Gallery will be far and away the most exciting new exhibition space on the south coast. The purpose-built, state-of-the-art gallery building has temporary shows of contemporary work on the ground and second floors, while the first floor is given over to rotating themed shows created from the 4000-piece-strong Towner collection. Building tours include a peek inside the climate-controlled art store.

Pier PIER
(seafront) Eastbourne's striking filigree-trimmed pier is a lovely place to watch the sunset, and also has a curious Victorian **Camera Obscura** that projects images of the outside world into a dish within a darkened room (when it's working).

Other sights:

Museum of Shops MUSEUM
(20 Cornfield Tce; adult/child £4.50/3.50; 10am-5pm) This small museum is swamped by an obsessive collection of how-we-used-to-live memorabilia.

Eastbourne Heritage Centre MUSEUM
(www.eastbournesociety.co.uk; 2 Carlisle Rd; adult/child £2.50/1; 2-5pm Apr-Oct) Livens up exhibits on the town's history with eccentric asides, such as on Donald McGill, the pioneer of the 'naughty postcard'.

Tours

City Sightseeing BUS TOURS
(0170-886 6000; www.city-sightseeing.co.uk; adult/child £5/3; tours every 30min 10am-4.30pm) Open-top bus tours around local sights and up to Beachy Head.

Allchorn Pleasure Boats BOAT TRIPS
(01323-410606; www.allchornpleasureboats.co.uk; adult/child £9/5.50; hourly 10.30am-3.30pm Jun-Oct) The dramatic white cliffs to the west are best viewed from the sea; tours leave from just west of the pier, weather permitting.

Sleeping

The Big Sleep DESIGN HOTEL ££
(01323-722676; www.thebigsleephotel.com; King Edward's Pde; s/d from £45/59;) Hip, fresh and friendly, this seafront design hotel has 50 gobsmacking rooms with big-print wallpaper, retro furnishings and curtains that look as though they might have been grazing on Beachy Head just a few hours prior. Home to Eastbourne's trendiest bar, a big basement games room and Channel views make this BN21's coolest kip.

Albert & Victoria B&B ££
(01323-730948; www.albertandvictoria.com; 19 St Aubyns Rd; s/d £45/70) Book ahead to stay at this delightful Victorian terraced house with opulent rooms, canopied beds, crystal chandeliers and wall frescoes in the breakfast room, mere paces from the seafront promenade.

Eating & Drinking

Lamb Inn PUB ££
(36 High St; mains £9.50-12; lunch & dinner) This Eastbourne institution located less than a mile northwest of the train station in the undervisited Old Town has been plonking Sussex wet ones on the bar for eight centuries. A holidaying Dickens also left a few beer rings and smudged napkins here (he stayed across the road). Take bus 1, 1A or 10.

Dal Maestro ITALIAN ££
(01323-417733; www.dalmaestro.co.uk; 17 Carlisle Rd; mains £4-18; 10am-5pm Mon-Sat) This chic new Italian job near the Towner Gallery has old curved-glass vitrines, an elegantly contemporary dining room and perfectly crafted meat dishes, pastas, salads and desserts.

Shopping

Camilla's Bookshop SECONDHAND BOOKSHOP
(www.camillasbookshop.com; 57 Grove Rd) Literally packed to the rafters with musty volumes, this incredible book repository, a short amble from the train station, fills three floors of a crumbling Victorian town house. The owner claims to have over a million books for sale, making it the best stocked, if not the biggest, secondhand bookstore in England.

Information

Tourist office (0871-663 0031; www.visiteastbourne.com; Cornfield Rd; 9.15am-5.30pm Mon-Fri, to 4pm Sat Apr-Oct) Can book accommodation for a £3 fee.

Getting There & Away

Bus

Brighton Bus 12, one hour 15 minutes, three per hour

Hastings Bus 99, one hour 20 minutes, three per hour

Train

Brighton £8.50, 30 to 40 minutes, twice hourly

London Victoria £23.90, 1½ hours, twice hourly

Around Eastbourne

After decades of campaigning, planning and deliberation, the **South Downs National Park**, stretching west from Eastbourne for around 100 miles, finally came into being in March 2010.

BEACHY HEAD

The famous cliffs of Beachy Head are the highest point in a string of chalky rock faces that slice across this rugged stretch of coast at the southern end of the South Downs. It's a spot of thrilling beauty, at least until you remember that this is also officially one of the top suicide spots in the world!

From Beachy Head, the stunning **Seven Sisters Cliffs** undulate their way west, a clifftop path (a branch of the South Downs Way) rides the waves of chalk as far as the picturesque Cuckmere Haven. Along the way, you'll stumble upon the tiny seaside hamlet of **Birling Gap**, where you can stop for a drink, snack or ice cream at the **Birling Gap Hotel** (Seven Sisters Cliffs, Birling Gap, East Dene). The secluded sun-trap beach here is popular with locals and walkers taking a breather.

Beachy Head is off the B2103, from the A259 between Eastbourne and Newhaven. Eastbourne's City Sightseeing tour bus stops at the clifftop.

PEVENSEY CASTLE

The ruins of William the Conqueror's first stronghold, **Pevensey Castle** (EH; adult/child £4.50/2.30; ⏲10am-6pm Apr-Sep), sit 5 miles east of Eastbourne, off the A259. Picturesquely dissolving into its own moat, the castle marks the point where William the Conqueror landed in 1066, just two weeks before the Battle of Hastings. And shortly afterwards, Old Bill wasted no time in building upon sturdy Roman walls to create a castle, which was used time and again through the centuries, right up to WWII. You can roam about its decaying husk with an enlightening audio guide, free with entry.

The 14th-century **Mint House** (High St; admission £1), just across the road from the castle, is worth visiting for its nutty collection of antiques and curios.

Regular train services between London Victoria and Hastings via Eastbourne (10 minutes) stop at Westham, half a mile from Pevensey.

ALFRISTON

Eight miles west of Eastbourne lies the excruciatingly quaint village of Alfriston, an essential stop for South Downs Way hikers and south coast explorers.

Most of the action takes place on boutique- and tavern-lined **High St**, a crooked hodgepodge of medieval half-timbered houses, some (such as the Star Inn) still supporting their original flagstone roofs. Just off High St, in a bend in the River Cuckmere, stands musty **St Andrew's Church**, a 14th-century creation in flint known as the 'Cathedral of the Downs' due to its size. Notice the rare bell ropes that descend into the chancel crossing (where the nave meets the transepts). The **Clergy House** (NT; adult/child £4.05/2.05; ⏲10.30am-5pm Wed, Thu, Sat-Mon) is the church's old vicarage and the first property to be acquired by the National Trust in 1896.

Guided tours (⏲3pm Sat Jul & Aug) leave from the Market Cross.

Where the A27 meets the access road to the village is **Drusillas** (www.drusillas.co.uk; admission £14.30; ⏲10am-5pm), perhaps the best small zoo in England. There's heaps of turtle-stroking, cow-milking, dino-hunting fun to be had, including playgrounds and rides.

Brighton & Hove

POP 247, 817

Raves on the beach, Graham Greene novels, Mods and Rockers in bank holiday fisticuffs, hens and stags on naughty weekends, classic car runs from London, the UK's biggest gay scene and the Channel's best clubbing – this city by the sea evokes many images among the British, but one thing is for certain: with its Bohemian, cosmopolitan, hedonistic vibe, Brighton is where England's seaside experience goes from cold to cool.

Brighton rocks all year round, but really comes to life during the summer months, when tourists, language students and revellers from London, keen to explore the city's legendary nightlife, summer festivals and multitude of trendy restaurants, slick boutique hotels and shops, pour into the city. The city has embraced the outlandish ever since the Prince Regent built his party palace here in the 19th century. Celebrities rub shoulders with dreadlocked hippies, drag queens party next to designer-clad urbanites, and kids toddle around the tables of mocha-quaffing media types.

Brighton last hit the news in 2010 in the wake of the British General Election when the city centre constituency found itself with the UK's very first Green Party MP, Caroline Lucas. Perhaps more surprising to many in this supposed hip nest of alternativism is that the city's other two constituencies (Kemptown and Hove) plumped for the Tories.

Sights

Royal Pavilion ROYAL RESIDENCE
(www.royalpavilion.org.uk; adult/child £9.50/5.40; ⏲9.30am-5.45pm Apr-Sep, 10am-5.15pm Oct-Mar) The city's must-see attraction is the Royal Pavilion, the glittering party-pad and palace of Prince George, later Prince Regent then King George IV. It's one of the most decadent buildings in England and an apt symbol of Brighton's reputation for hedonism. The Indian-style domes and Moorish minarets outside are only a prelude to the palace's lavish oriental-themed interior, where no colour is deemed too strong, dragons swoop and snarl from gilt-smothered ceilings, gem-encrusted snakes slither down pillars, and crystal chandeliers seem ordered by the tonne. While gawping is the main activity, you can pick up an audiotour (included in the admission price) to learn more about the palace.

FREE **Brighton Museum & Art Gallery** MUSEUM, GALLERY
(Royal Pavilion Gardens; ⏲10am-7pm Tue, to 5pm Wed-Sat, 2-5pm Sun) Set in the Royal Pavilion's renovated stable block, this museum and art gallery has a glittering collection of 20th-century art and design, including a crimson Salvador Dalí sofa modelled on Mae West's lips. There's also an enthralling gallery of world art, an impressive collection of Egyptian artefacts and an 'images of Brighton' multimedia exhibit containing a series of oral histories and a model of the now defunct West Pier.

Brighton Pier PIER
(www.brightonpier.co.uk) This grand old centenarian pier, full of glorious gaudiness, is the place to come to experience the tackier side of Brighton. There are plenty of stomach-churning fairground rides and dingy amusement arcades to keep you amused, and candy floss and Brighton rock to chomp on while you're doing so.

Look west and you'll see the sad remains of the **West Pier** (www.westpier.co.uk), a skeletal iron hulk that attracts flocks of birds at sunset. It's a sad end for a Victorian marvel upon which the likes of Charlie Chaplin and Stan Laurel once performed.

So far there's no sign of the i360 observation tower ('hurray!', some may cry), a spectacularly space-age piece of architecture from the creators of the London Eye that may one day loom 150m above the seafront. This would include a West Pier Heritage Centre – a pavilion where AV exhibits will relate the pier's history.

WANT MORE?

Head to **Lonely Planet** (http://www.lonelyplanet.com/england/southeast-england/brighton-and-hove) for planning advice, author recommendations, traveller reviews and insider tips.

Tours

City Sightseeing BUS TOURS
(www.city-sightseeing.co.uk; adult/child £8/3; ⏲tours every 30min May-late Sep) Open-top hop-on/hop-off bus tours leaving from Grand Junction Rd near Brighton Pier.

Tourist Tracks MP3 TOURS
(www.tourist-tracks.com) MP3 audio guides downloadable from the website (£5) or available on a preloaded MP3 player at the tourist office (£6 per half-day).

Festivals & Events

There's always something fun going on in Brighton, from **Gay Pride** (www.brightonpride.org; ⏲early Aug) to food and drink festivals, but the showpiece is May's three-week-long **Brighton Festival** (☎01273-709 709; www.brightonfestival.org), the biggest arts festival in Britain after Edinburgh, drawing theatre, dance, music and comedy performers from around the globe.

Sleeping

Despite a glut of hotels in Brighton, prices are relatively high and you'd be wise to book well ahead for summer weekends and for the Brighton Festival in May. Expect to pay up to a third more at weekends across the board.

TOP CHOICE **Neo Hotel** BOUTIQUE HOTEL ££
(☎01273-711104; www.neohotel.com; 19 Oriental Pl; d from £100; 📶) You won't be surprised to learn that the owner of this

Brighton & Hove

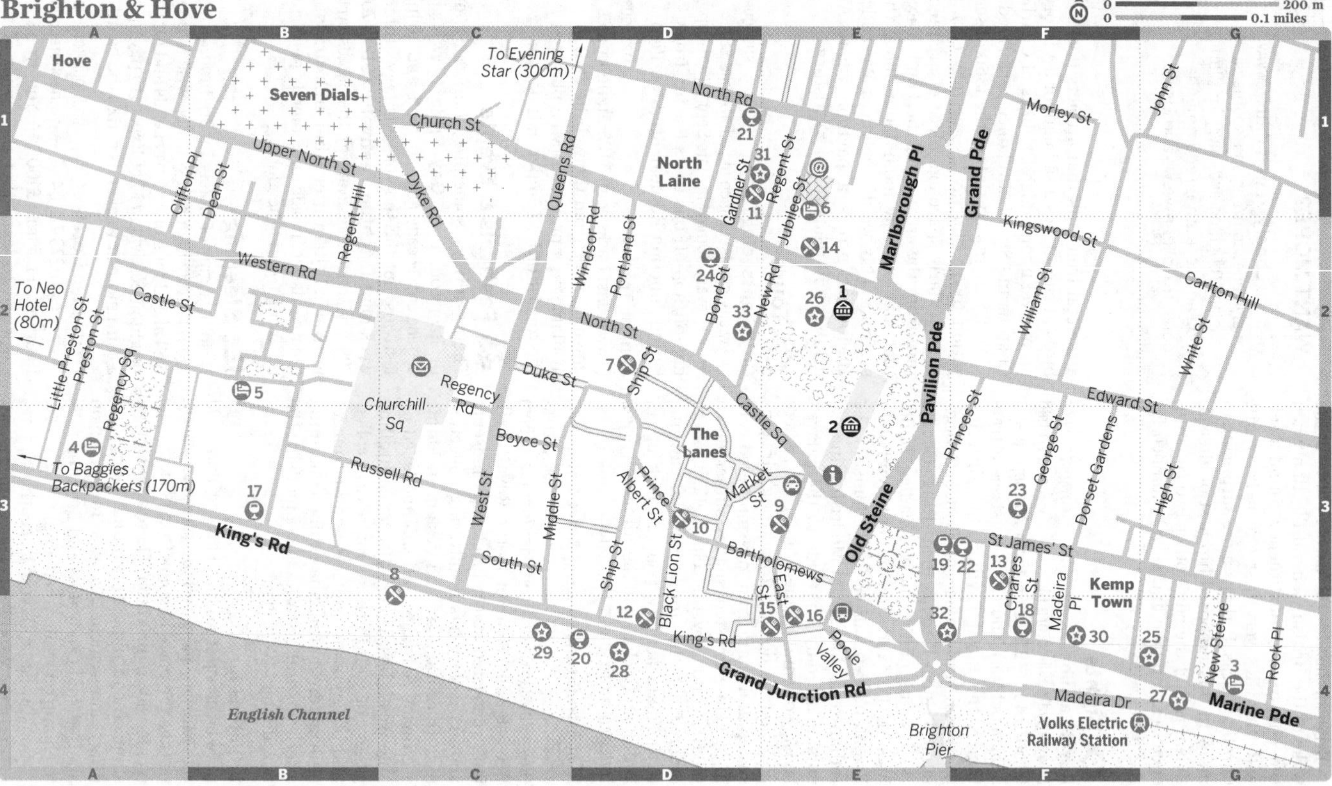

Brighton

Sights

1 Brighton Museum & Art Gallery ... E2
2 Royal Pavilion ... E3

Sleeping

3 Drakes ... G4
4 Hotel Pelirocco ... A3
5 Motel Schmotel ... B2
6 myhotel ... E1

Eating

7 Bombay Aloo ... D2
8 Due South ... C3
9 English's Oyster Bar ... E3
10 Food for Friends ... D3
11 Infinity Foods Cafe ... D1
12 JB's American Diner ... D4
13 Pomegranate ... F3
14 Pompoko ... E2
15 Scoop & Crumb ... E4
16 Terre à Terre ... E4

Drinking

17 106 Bar & Brasserie ... B3
18 Amsterdam ... F4
19 Candy Bar ... E3
20 Coalition ... D4
21 Dorset ... D1
22 Hub ... F3
23 Queen's Arms ... F3
24 Riki Tik ... D2

Entertainment

Audio ... (see 18)
25 Basement Club ... G4
26 Brighton Dome ... E2
27 Concorde 2 ... G4
28 Digital ... D4
29 Funky Buddha ... C4
30 Funky Fish Club ... F4
31 Komedia Theatre ... D1
32 Revenge ... E4
33 Theatre Royal ... D2

gorgeous hotel is an interior stylist. The nine rooms could have dropped straight out of the pages of a design magazine, each finished in rich colours and tactile fabrics, with bold floral and Asian motifs and black-tiled bathrooms. Kick back in satin kimono robes and watch a DVD on your wafer-thin-screen TV, or indulge in massage and beauty treatments. Wonderful breakfasts include homemade smoothies and fruit pancakes.

Baggies Backpackers HOSTEL £
(01273-733740; www.baggiesbackpackers.com; 33 Oriental Pl; dm/d £13/35; wi-fi) A warm familial atmosphere, worn-in charm, motherly onsite owners and clean, snug dorms have made this long-established hostel something of an institution. It's also blessed with a homely kitchen, an inexpensive laundry, a cosy basement music and chill-out room and a TV lounge piled high with video cassettes. The hostel only takes phone bookings and is a stag- and hen-free zone.

Snooze HOTEL ££
(01273-605797; www.snoozebrighton.com; 25 St George's Tce; s/d from £60/85; @ wi-fi) This eccentric Kemptown pad is very fond of retro styling. Rooms feature vintage posters, bright '60s and '70s patterned wallpaper, flying wooden ducks, floral sinks and mad clashes of colour. It's more than just a gimmick though – rooms are comfortable and spotless, and there are great veggie breakfasts. You'll find it just off St James' St about 500m east of New Steine.

Hotel Pelirocco THEME HOTEL ££
(01273-327055; www.hotelpelirocco.co.uk; 10 Regency Sq; s £50-65, d £95-130, ste from £230; @ wi-fi) One of Brighton's first theme hotels, this is the sexiest and nuttiest place to stay in town and the ultimate venue for a flirty weekend in style. There's a range of flamboyantly designed rooms, some by artists, some by big-name sponsors, from a basic single done up like a boxing ring, to Betty's Boudoir with leopard skin throws and a big-enough-for-two bath, to the Play Room suite with a 3m circular bed, mirrored ceiling and pole-dancing area.

myhotel DESIGN HOTEL ££
(01273-900300; www.myhotels.com; 17 Jubilee St; r from £94; P @ wi-fi) With trend-setting rooms looking like space-age pods, full of curved white walls, floor-to-ceiling observation windows and suspended flatscreen TVs, with the odd splash of neon orange or pink, there's nothing square about

this place, daddio. You can even hook up your iPod and play music through speakers in the ceiling. There's a cocoon-like cocktail bar downstairs, and if you've money to burn, a suite with a steam room and harpooned vintage carousel horse.

Motel Schmotel B&B ££

(☎01273-326129; www.motelschmotel.co.uk; 37 Russell Sq; s/d from £50/60;) If you can overlook the petite rooms and miniscule bathrooms, this 11-room B&B in a Regency town house, a short stroll from virtually anywhere, is a sound and very central place to hit the sack. Rooms are accented with colourful oversize prints and an uncluttered design, and guests heap praise on the breakfast cooked by the always-around-to-help couple who run the place.

Paskins Town House B&B ££

(☎01273-601203; www.paskins.co.uk; 18/19 Charlotte St; d from £60; @) An environmentally friendly B&B spread between two elegant town houses. It prides itself on using ecofriendly products such as recycled toilet paper, low-energy bulbs and biodegradable cleaning materials. The individually designed rooms are beautifully maintained, and excellent organic and vegetarian breakfasts are served in the art deco–inspired breakfast room.

Drakes BOUTIQUE HOTEL £££

(☎01273-696934; www.drakesofbrighton.com; 43-44 Marine Pde; r £105-275; P@) Drakes oozes understated class: a stylish, minimalist boutique hotel that eschews the need to shout its existence from the rooftops (you could easily miss it). Feature rooms have giant free-standing tubs set in front of full-length bay windows with stunning views out to sea.

Blanch House BOUTIQUE HOTEL £££

(☎01273-603504; www.blanchhouse.co.uk; 17 Atlingworth St; r £100-230; @) Themed rooms are the name of the game in this boutique hotel, but there's nothing tacky about them – plush fabrics and a Victorian roll-top bath rule in the 'Decadence' suite and the 'Snowstorm' room is a frosty vision in white and tinkling ice. There's a magnificently stylish fine dining restaurant here – all white leather banquettes and space-age swivel chairs – and a fine cocktail bar. No wonder it's the hotel of choice for celebs in transit. To reach it from New Steine, walk for 150m east along St James' St then turn right into Atlingworth St.

Seadragon Backpackers HOSTEL £

(☎01273-711854; www.seadragonbackpackers.co.uk; 36 Waterloo St; dm/tw incl breakfast £20/50;) Perched on the edge of Hove, but just a short bus ride from Churchill Sq, this simple, uncluttered and well-equipped hostel lacks vibe but is ideal for budget nomads, who like to snooze in peace and party outside the hostel. The 20 beds are divided into four-bed dorms and twins with one set of facilities per six beds. The best hostel kitchen you're likely to see, memory foam mattresses and a free breakfast make these very respectable no-frills lodgings.

Eating

Brighton easily has the best choice of eateries on the south coast, with cafes, diners and restaurants to fulfil every whim. It's also one of the UK's best destinations for vegetarians, and its innovative meat-free menus are terrific value for anyone on a tight budget.

TOP CHOICE **Terre á Terre** VEGETARIAN ££

(71 East St; mains £10-15; noon-10.30pm Tue-Fri, to 11pm Sat, to 10pm Sun) Even staunch meat eaters will come out raving about this legendary vegetarian restaurant. Terre á Terre offers a sublime dining experience, from the vibrant, modern space, to the entertaining menus, to the delicious, inventive dishes full of rich robust flavours.

Infinity Foods Cafe VEGETARIAN £

(50 Gardner St; mains £3-7; 10.30am-5pm Mon-Sat, noon-4pm Sun) The sister establishment of Infinity Foods wholefoods shop, a health-food cooperative and Brighton institution, this place serves a wide variety of vegetarian and organic food, with many vegan and wheat- or gluten-free options including tofu burgers, mezze plates and falafel.

JB's American Diner AMERICAN DINER £

(31 King's Rd; burgers £7, other mains £6.50-12; lunch & dinner) The waft of hotdog aroma as you push open the door, the shiny red-leather booths, the stars and stripes draped across the wall, the '50s soundtrack twanging in the background and the colossal portions of burgers, fries and milkshakes – in short, a hefty slab of authentic Americana teleported to Brighton seafront.

Food for Friends RESTAURANT ££

(www.foodforfriends.com; 17-18 Prince Albert St; mains £9-13; lunch & dinner) This airy, glass-sided restaurant attracts the attention of passers-by as much as it does the loyalty of its customers with an ever-inventive choice of vegetarian and vegan food. Children are also catered for.

English's Oyster Bar SEAFOOD ££
(www.englishs.co.uk; 29-31 East St; mains £11-25; ⏲lunch & dinner) A 60-year institution, this Brightonian seafood paradise dishes up everything from oysters to lobster to Dover sole. It's converted from fishermen's cottages, with echoes of the elegant Edwardian era inside and buzzing alfresco dining on the pedestrian square outside.

Pomegranate KURDISH ££
(www.eatpomegranates.com; 10 Manchester St; mains £11-15; ⏲lunch & dinner) Take your taste buds on a trip to the Middle East at this fascinating Kemptown nosh spot where mains such as Kurdish-style roast lamb, stuffed aubergine and baked swordfish are dished up in a cosy setting. There are plenty of veggie choices as well as lip-smacking desserts such as revani (semolina cake) and stuffed figs with pomegranate paste.

Due South LOCAL CUISINE ££
(www.duesouth.co.uk; 139 Kings Rd Arches; mains £12-18; ⏲lunch & dinner Mon-Sat, lunch Sun) Sheltered under a cavernous Victorian arch on the seafront, with a curvaceous front window and small bamboo-screened terrace on the promenade, this refined yet relaxed and convivial restaurant specialises in dishes cooked with the best environmentally sustainable and seasonal Sussex produce.

Pompoko JAPANESE £
(110 Church St; mains £4-5; ⏲lunch & dinner) Simple Japanese food in a small but perfectly formed little cafe. It's quick, cheap and delicious, with an emphasis on home-style curries, soups and noodle dishes.

Also try:

Bombay Aloo INDIAN BUFFET £
(39 Ship St; buffet £4.95; ⏲noon-midnight) Cheap and cheerful all-you-can-eat Indian buffet with big pots of vegetarian curry, acres of salad and mountains of rice.

Scoop & Crumb ICE-CREAM PARLOUR £
(5-6 East St; snacks £3-5, sundaes £2.50-6; ⏲10am-6pm Sun-Fri, to 7pm Sat) The sundaes (over 50 types) stacked at this ice-cream parlour, belonging to the city's artisan ice-cream producer, are second to none. Freshly cut sandwiches and monster toasties also available.

Drinking

Outside London, Brighton's nightlife is the best in the south, with its unique mix of seafront clubs and bars. Drunken stag and hen parties and charmless, tacky nightclubs rule on West St, which is best avoided. For more ideas, visit www.drinkinbrighton.co.uk.

Evening Star PUB
(www.eveningstarbrighton.co.uk; 55/56 Surrey St) This cosy, unpretentious pub is a beer-drinker's nirvana, with a wonderful selection of award-winning real ales, Belgian beers, organic lagers and real ciders. It's a short stagger away from the station.

Coalition BAR, CLUB
(171-181 Kings Rd Arches) On a summer's day, there's nowhere better to sit and watch the world go by than at this popular beach bar, diner and club. It's a cavernous place with a funky brick-vaulted interior and a wide terrace spilling onto the promenade. All sorts happen here, from comedy, to live music, to club nights.

106 Bar & Brasserie BAR
(www.106brasseries.com; Kings Rd; ⏲3-11pm Fri, noon-11pm Sat, 11am-5pm Sun) Huge sea-view windows deluge this weekend venue in light as you sip a pre-club 'pretty Pink' or 'Flirtini' champagne cocktail and watch the sun go down. There's a limited choice of light meals available between noon and 5pm.

Dorset GASTRO PUB
(www.thedorset.co.uk; 28 North Rd; wi-fi) This laid-back Brighton institution throws open its doors and windows in fine weather and spills tables onto the pavement. You'll be just as welcome for a morning coffee as for an evening pint here, and if you decide not to leave between the two, there's always the decent gastropub menu.

Riki Tik BAR
(18a Bond St; ⏲10am-late) Coffee bar by day, popular preclub venue by night, this place has been pumping out cool cocktails and funky breaks for years. It's stylish, dark and sexy and much bigger than it looks from the outside. DJs play here most nights.

Entertainment

Brighton offers the best entertainment line-up on the south coast, with clubs to rival London and Manchester for cool. Keep tabs on what's hot and what's not by searching

GAY & LESBIAN BRIGHTON

Perhaps it's Brighton's long-time association with the theatre, but for more than 100 years the city has been a gay haven. With more than 25,000 gay men and around 15,000 lesbians living here, it is the most vibrant queer community in the country outside London.

Kemptown (aka Camptown), on and off St James' St, is where it's all at. For up-to-date information on gay Brighton, check out www.gay.brighton.co.uk and www.real-brighton.com, or pick up the free monthly magazine **Gscene** (www.gscene.com) from various venues or the tourist office.

For drinking...

Hub CAFE
(129 St James' St; ⌚8am-6pm Mon-Fri, 10am-6pm Sat & Sun) This cool coffeeshop hang-out and internet cafe is *the* place to get word on everything going on in town.

Amsterdam RESTAURANT, BAR
(www.amsterdam.uk.com; 11-12 Marine Pde; ⌚noon-2am) Hotel, sauna, restaurant and extremely hip bar above the pier; its sun terrace is a particular hit.

Candy Bar CAFE
(www.thecandybar.co.uk; 129 St James' St; ⌚9pm-2am) Slick cafe-bar-club for the girls, with pink-lit arches, curvaceous bar, pool table and dance floor.

Queen's Arms PUB
(www.queensarmsbrighton.com; 7 George St; ⌚3pm-late) And they don't mean Victoria or Elizabeth! Plenty of camp cabaret and karaoke at this pub.

For dancing...

Bars and pubs may be fun, but the real action takes place on and off the dance floor.

Revenge NIGHTCLUB
(www.revenge.co.uk; 32-34 Old Steine; ⌚10.30pm-3am) Nightly disco with occasional cabaret.

Basement Club NIGHTCLUB
(31-34 Marine Pde; ⌚9am-2am) Located beneath the Legends Hotel, arguably the best gay hotel in town and winner of the Golden Handbag award 2009.

out publications such as the *List*, the *Source* and *What's On*.

Nightclubs

When Britain's top DJs aren't plying their trade in London, Ibiza or Aya Napia, chances are you'll spy them here. All Brighton's clubs open until 2am, and many as late as 5am.

Funky Buddha NIGHTCLUB
(Kings Rd Arches) Twin giant, brick, subterranean tunnels, with bars at the front and back, playing funky house, 70s, R&B and disco to a stylish and attitude-free crowd.

Audio NIGHTCLUB
(www.audiobrighton.com; 10 Marine Pde) Some of the city's top club nights can be found at this ear-numbing venue, where the music's top priority is attracting a young, up-for-it crowd. Every night is different, with music ranging from breakbeat to electro to indie. Next to the Amsterdam Hotel.

Funky Fish Club NIGHTCLUB
(www.funkyfishclub.co.uk; 19-23 Marine Pde) Fun, friendly and unpretentious little club playing soul, funk, jazz, Motown and old-skool breaks. No big-name DJs or stringent door policies, just cheap drinks and a rocking party atmosphere.

Digital NIGHTCLUB
(www.yourfutureisdigital.com/brighton; 187-193 Kings Rd Arches) This inconspicuous place on the Brighton seafront hosts indie, house and cheesy student nights.

Concorde 2 NIGHTCLUB
(www.concorde2.co.uk; Madeira Dr, Kemptown) Brighton's best-known and best-loved club is a disarmingly unpretentious den, where DJ Fatboy Slim pioneered the Big Beat Boutique and still occasionally graces the

decks. There's a huge variety of club nights and live bands each month, from world music to rock.

Theatre

Brighton Dome THEATRE
(☎01273-709709; www.brightondome.org; 29 New Rd) Once the stables and exercise yard of King George IV, this art-deco complex houses three theatre venues within the Royal Pavilion estate. ABBA famously won the 1974 Eurovision Song Contest here.

Theatre Royal THEATRE
(☎01273-328488; New Rd) Built by decree of the Prince of Wales in 1806, this grand venue hosts plays, musicals and operas.

Komedia Theatre COMEDY
(☎0845 293 8480; www.komedia.co.uk; 44-47 Gardner St) This former billiards hall and supermarket is now a stylish comedy, theatre and cabaret venue attracting some of the brightest stars on the stand-up circuit.

Shopping

A busy maze of narrow lanes and tiny alleyways that was once a fishing village, the **Lanes** is Brighton's most popular shopping district. Its every twist and turn is jam-packed with jewellers and gift shops, coffee shops and boutiques selling everything from antique firearms to hard-to-find vinyls. There's another, less-claustrophobic shopping district in **North Laine**, a series of streets north of the Lanes, including Bond, Gardner, Kensington and Sydney Sts, that are full of retro-cool boutiques and Bohemian cafes. Head west from the Lanes and you'll hit Churchill Square Shopping Centre and Western Rd, where all the mainstream high street stores gather.

Information

Brighton City Guide (www.brighton.co.uk)

Brighton Internet Centre (109 Western Rd; per hr £1)

City Council (www.brighton-hove.gov.uk) A mine of information on every aspect of the city.

Jubilee Library (Jubilee St; ⏲10am-7pm Mon & Tue, to 5pm Wed, Fri & Sat, to 8pm Thu, 11am-4pm Sun) Bring ID and sign up to use machines for free.

Post office (2-3 Churchill Square Shopping Centre)

Royal Sussex County Hospital (☎01273-696955; Eastern Rd) Has an accident and emergency department 2 miles east of the centre.

Tourist office (☎0300-300 0088; www.visitbrighton.com; Royal Pavilion Shop, Royal Pavilion; ⏲10am-5.30pm) The guys to turn to for anything Brighton-related, from tide times to train times.

visitbrighton.com (www.visitbrighton.com)

Wistons Clinic (☎01273-506263; 138 Dyke Rd) For general medical consultations, under a mile from the centre.

Getting There & Away

Brighton is 53 miles from London and transport is fast and frequent. If arriving by car, parking is plentiful but pricey, city-centre traffic, bus-clogged lanes and road layouts confusing.

Bus

Standard connections:

Arundel Bus 700, two hours, hourly

Chichester Bus 700, 2¾ hours, twice hourly

Eastbourne Bus 12, one hour 10 minutes, up to every 10 minutes

London Victoria National Express, £11.80, two hours, hourly

Train

All London-bound services pass through Gatwick Airport.

Chichester £11.40, 50 minutes, half hourly

Eastbourne £8.50, 30 to 40 minutes, half hourly

Hastings £11.80, one hour, half hourly

London St Pancras £16.90, 1¼ hours, half hourly

London Victoria £13.90, 50-70 minutes, half hourly

Portsmouth £13.90, 1½ hours, hourly

Getting Around

Most of Brighton can be covered on foot. Alternatively, buy a day ticket (£3.60) from the driver to scoot back and forth on Brighton & Hove buses.

Parking can be expensive. The city operates a pay-and-display parking scheme. In the town centre, it's usually £1.50 per half hour with a maximum stay of two hours. Alternatively, there's a Park & Ride 2.5 miles northwest of the centre at Withdean, from where bus 27 zips into town.

Cab companies include **Brighton Streamline Taxis** (☎01273-747474) and **City Cabs** (☎01273- 205205), and there's a taxi rank on the junction of East St with Market St. All Brighton taxis have a distinctive white and turquoise livery.

Planet Cycle Hire (West Pier Promenade; bikes per half day/day £8/12; ⏲10am-6pm Thu-Tue), next to West Pier, rents bikes. Deposit and ID required.

WEST SUSSEX

After the fast-paced adventures of Brighton and East Sussex, West Sussex is welcome respite. The serene hills and valleys of the South Downs ripple across the county, fringed by sheltered coastline. Beautiful Arundel and cultured Chichester make good bases from which to explore the county's winding country lanes and remarkable Roman ruins.

Arundel

POP 3408

Arguably West Sussex's prettiest town, Arundel is clustered around a vast fairy-tale castle, its hillside streets overflowing with antique emporiums, teashops, a host of eateries and the odd boutique hotel. While much of the town appears medieval – the whimsical castle has been home to the dukes of Norfolk for centuries – most of it dates back to Victorian times.

Sights & Activities

Arundel Castle CASTLE

(www.arundelcastle.org; adult/child £16/7.50; 10am-5pm Tue-Sun Apr-Oct) Originally built in the 11th century, all that's left of the first structure are the modest remains of the keep at its core. Thoroughly ruined during the English Civil War, most of what you see today is the result of passionate reconstruction by the eighth, 11th and 15th dukes of Norfolk between 1718 and 1900. The current duke still lives in part of the castle. Highlights include the atmospheric keep, the massive Great Hall and the library, which has paintings by Gainsborough and Holbein. The castle does a good impression of Windsor Castle and St James' Palace in the popular 2009 film *The Young Victoria*.

Cathedral CATHEDRAL

(www.arundelcathedral.org; 9am-6pm Apr-Oct) Arundel's ostentatious 19th-century Catholic cathedral is the other dominating feature of the town's impressive skyline. Commissioned by the 15th duke in 1868, this impressive structure was designed by Joseph Aloysius Hansom (inventor of the Hansom cab) in the French Gothic style, but marked with much Victorian economy and restraint. Although small for a cathedral – it only holds 500 worshippers – Hansom's clever layout makes the building seem a lot bigger.

A 1970s shrine in the north transept holds the remains of St Philip Howard, a canonised Catholic martyr who was banged up in the Tower of London by Elizabeth I until his death in 1595 for reverting to Catholicism.

Other attractions:

Arundel Ghost Experience GHOST EXPERIENCE

(www.arundeljailhouse.co.uk; High St; adult/child £5/3; noon-6pm) Hear hair-raising ghost stories and explore supposedly haunted prison cells by candlelight at this kids' attraction.

Wildfowl & Wetlands Centre WILDLIFE RESERVE

(www.wwt.org.uk; Mill Rd; adult/child £9.70/4.85; 9.30am-5.30pm Easter-Oct) Bird fanciers will be rewarded by an electric boat safari through this 26-hectare reserve, a mile east of the centre as the duck flies.

FREE **Arundel Museum** MUSEUM

(www.arundelmuseum.org.uk; 11am-3pm) Temporarily located in a small metal container at the Mill Rd car park, poor old Arundel Museum has been waiting for a new home to be erected on an adjacent plot for years. The modern, Lottery-funded structure should appear by 2013.

Sleeping & Eating

Arundel House HOTEL ££

(01903-882136; www.arundelhouseonline.com; 11 High St; d from £80;) The modern rooms in this lovely 'restaurant-with-rooms' may be slightly low-ceilinged but they're clean-cut and very comfortable, with showers big enough for two. The restaurant downstairs serves some of the best food in Arundel (three-course dinner £28), which happily extends to breakfast.

Norfolk Arms HOTEL ££

(0808-144 9494; www.norfolkarmshotel.com; High St; s/d from £60/70; P) You'll be warmly welcomed at this rambling old Georgian coaching inn built by the 10th duke. Although the rooms are spacious, they are looking dated and a little scruffy.

TOP CHOICE **Town House** BRITISH £££

(01903-883847; 65 High St; set lunch £14-18, set dinner £22-27.50; Tue-Sat) The only thing that rivals the stunning 16th-century Florentine gilded-walnut ceiling at this compact and very elegant eatery is the acclaimed British cuisine with a

European twist and sparkling atmosphere. Book ahead.

Bay Tree INTERNATIONAL ££
(☎01903-883679; www.thebaytreearundel.com; 21 Tarrant St; mains lunch £7-13, dinner £12-17; ⊙lunch & dinner Tue-Sat, lunch Sun) Frequented by famished antique hunters, this uncluttered eatery keeps things surprisingly free of yesteryear knickknacks. Everything from basic panini to sophisticated dishes blending local produce with Mediterranean flavours populates the menu.

Information

Tourist office (☎01903-882268; www.sussexbythesea.com; 1-3 Crown Yard Mews; ⊙10am-5pm Mon-Sat, 10am-4pm Sun Apr-Oct) Supplies maps and provides an accommodation-booking service but may close in 2011.

Getting There & Away

Trains run to London Victoria (£22.80, 1½ hours, twice hourly), and to Chichester (20 minutes, twice hourly); change at Barnham. There are also links to Brighton (£8.40, one hour 20 minutes, twice hourly); again change at Barnham. Bus 700 (two hours, twice hourly) is a slower option to Brighton.

Chichester

POP 27,477

A lively Georgian market town still almost encircled by its medieval town walls, the administrative capital of West Sussex keeps watch over the plains between the South Downs and the sea. Visitors flock to its splendid cathedral, streets of handsome 18th-century town houses, famous theatre and an annual arts festival, as well as a superb modern-art gallery, and nearby Petworth House, a must-visit for culture vultures. A Roman port garrison in its early days, the town is also a launch pad to other fascinating Roman remains as well as Arundel and the coast.

Sights

Chichester Cathedral CATHEDRAL
(www.chichestercathedral.org.uk; West St; donation requested; ⊙7.15am-6pm) This understated cathedral was begun in 1075 and largely rebuilt in the 13th century. The freestanding church tower, now in fairly bad shape, was built in the 15th century and the spire dates from the 19th century when its predecessor famously toppled over. Inside, three storeys of beautiful arches sweep upwards, and Romanesque carvings are dotted around. Interesting features to track down include a smudgy stained-glass window added by Marc Chagall in 1978 and a glassed-over section of Roman mosaic flooring about a metre below ground level.

Guided tours operate at 11.15am and 2.30pm Monday to Saturday, Easter to October, and the excellent cathedral choir is guaranteed to give you goosebumps during the daily **Evensong** (⊙5.30pm Mon-Sat, 3.30pm Sun).

Pallant House Gallery ART GALLERY
(www.pallant.org.uk; 9 North Pallant; adult/child £8.25/2.30; ⊙10am-5pm Tue-Sat, 12.30-5pm Sun) A Queen Anne mansion built by a local wine merchant, handsome Pallant House, along with a recently opened modern wing, hosts this superb gallery focusing on 20th-century, mostly British, art. Showstoppers such as Caulfield, Freud, Sutherland, Auerbach and Moore are interspersed with international names such as Filla, Le Corbusier and Kitaj. Most of these older works are in the mansion while the new wing is packed with pop art and temporary shows of modern and contemporary work.

Other Sights:

FREE **Guildhall** CHURCH BUILDING
(Priory Park; ⊙noon-4pm Sat Jun-Sep) This church building is all that remains of a Franciscan Monastery, which didn't survive Henry VIII's 1536 Dissolution. The church later served as a court of law, where William Blake was tried for sedition in 1804, and Chichester's first museum.

FREE **District Museum** MUSEUM
(29 Little London; ⊙10am-5.30pm Wed-Sat) The eclectic collections once housed at the Guildhall can now be viewed at this somewhat ramshackle museum where the ground-floor Roman finds and mosaic fragments are the clear-cut winners.

Market Cross COVERED MARKET
(crossroads of North, South, East & West Sts) Chichester's epicentre is marked by a dinky market building constructed in 1501 by the bishop of the time to enable impoverished locals to sell their wares without paying hefty market fees.

Festivals & Events

For three weeks in June and July, the annual **Chichester Festivities** (☎01243-528356; www.chifest.org.uk) puts on an abundance of terrific theatre, art, guest lectures, fireworks and performances of every musical genre.

Sleeping

Chichester is about to get a spanking new Travelodge! 'So what?', you may say, but this one will be located right opposite the cathedral, meaning the views out may be worth bearing the blandness within.

Ship Hotel HOTEL ££
(☎01243-778000; www.theshiphotel.net; North St; s/d £75/99; wifi) The grand central staircase in this former Georgian town house climbs to 36 fairly spacious rooms of commandingly clean-cut period chic. It's the most enticing option in the city centre and also boasts an excellent all-day brasserie.

Trents B&B ££
(☎01243-773714; www.trentschichester.co.uk; 50 South St; s/d from £65/85; wifi) Right in the thick of the city centre, the five snazzy rooms above this trendy bar-restaurant are understandably popular.

Eating

St Martin's Tea Rooms TEAROOMS £
(www.organictearooms.co.uk; 3 St Martins St; mains £4-10; ⏰10am-6pm Mon-Sat) A little cocoon of nooks and crannies tucked away in a part-18th-century, part-medieval town house, this passionately organic cafe serves freshly ground coffee, wholesome, mostly vegetarian, food and a sinful selection of desserts. There's also a guest piano with which to shatter the tranquil scene if you so wish.

Comme Ça FRENCH ££
(☎01243-788724; 67 Broyle Rd; mains £8-14; ⏰lunch Wed-Sun, dinner Tue-Sat) Run by a Franco-English couple, this friendly French place does traditional Normandy cuisine in a converted Georgian inn, with a lovely vine-covered alfresco area. It's a short walk north of the centre.

Cloisters Cafe CAFE £
(Cathedral Cloisters; snacks £2.50-7; ⏰9am-5pm Mon-Sat, 10am-4pm Sun) Sparkling marble-floored cafe in the cathedral grounds with sunny walled garden and airy atmosphere. It's a good spot for simple sandwiches, cakes and fair-trade drinks.

Entertainment

Chichester Festival Theatre THEATRE
(☎01243-781312; www.cft.org.uk; Oakland's Park) This somewhat Soviet-looking playhouse was built in 1962 and has a long and distinguished history. Sir Laurence Olivier was the theatre's first director and Ingrid Bergman, Sir John Gielgud and Sir Anthony Hopkins are a few of the other famous names to have played here.

Information

Click Computers (2 Southdown Bldg, Southgate; per hr £1; ⏰9am-7pm Mon-Fri, 11am-7pm Sat, 11am-5pm Sun) Mega-fast net access opposite the train station.

Post office (10 West St)

Tourist office (☎01243-775888; www.visitchichester.org; 29a South St; ⏰10.15am-5.15pm Mon, 9.15am-5.15pm Tue-Sat year-round, also 10.30am-3pm Sun Apr-Sep) Organises guided walks (£4) on Tuesdays at 11am and Saturdays at 2.30pm.

Getting There & Away

Bus

Brighton Bus 700, 2¾ hours, twice hourly

London Victoria National Express, £13.30, four hours, daily

Portsmouth Bus 700, one hour, twice hourly

Train

Chichester has connections to:

Arundel £4, 20 to 30 minutes, twice hourly, change at Barnham

Brighton £10.10, 50 minutes, twice hourly

London Victoria £22.80, 1½ hours, half hourly

Portsmouth £6.70, 30 to 40 minutes, twice hourly

Around Chichester

FISHBOURNE ROMAN PALACE & MUSEUM

Mad about mosaics? Then head for **Fishbourne Palace** (www.sussexpast.co.uk; Salthill Rd; adult/child £7.60/4; ⏰10am-4pm Feb-Nov, to 5pm Mar-Oct), the largest known Roman residence in Britain. Happened upon by labourers in the 1960s, it's thought that this once-luxurious mansion was built around AD 75 for a Romanised local king. Housed in a modern pavilion are its foundations, hypocaust and painstakingly relaid mosaics. The centrepiece is a spectacular floor depicting cupid riding a dolphin flanked by sea horses and panthers. There's also a fascinating little museum and replanted Roman gardens.

Fishbourne Palace is 1½ miles west of Chichester, just off the A259. Bus 700 leaves from outside Chichester Cathedral and stops at the bottom of Salthill Rd (five minutes' walk away; four hourly). The museum is a 10-minute amble from Fishbourne train station.

PETWORTH

On the outskirts of its namesake village, the imposing 17th-century stately home, **Petworth House** (NT; adult/child £9.90/5; ⏲11am-5pm Sat-Wed Mar-Nov), has an extraordinary art collection, the National Trust's finest. JMW Turner was a regular visitor and the house is still home to the largest collection of his paintings outside London's Tate Gallery. There are also many paintings by Van Dyck, Reynolds, Gainsborough, Titian, Bosch and William Blake. Other highlights are the fabulously theatrical grand staircase and the exquisite Carved Room, which ripples with wooden reliefs by master chiseller Grinling Gibbons.

The surrounding **Petworth Park** (⏲11am-6pm Wed-Sun Mar-Nov) is the highlight – the fulfilment of Lancelot 'Capability' Brown's romantic natural landscape theory. It's home to herds of deer and becomes an open-air concert venue in summer.

Petworth is 5 miles from the train station at Pulborough, from where bus 1 runs to Petworth Sq (15 minutes, hourly Monday to Saturday). If driving, it's 12 miles northeast of Chichester off the A285.

SURREY

Surrey is the heart of commuterville, chosen by well-off Londoners when they spawn, move out of the city and buy a country pad. For the most part, though, it's made up of uninspiring towns and dull, sprawling suburbs. Further away from the roaring motorways and packed rush-hour trains, the county reveals some inspiring landscapes made famous by authors Sir Arthur Conan Doyle, Sir Walter Scott and Jane Austen.

Farnham

POP 37,055

Nudging the border with Hampshire and joined at the hip with the garrison settlement of Aldershot, affluent Farnham is Surrey's prettiest town and its most worthwhile destination. Blessed with lively shopping streets of Georgian symmetry, a 12th-century castle and some soothing river walks, this easy-going market town makes for an undemanding day trip from the capital just an hour away.

Farnham has no tourist office but maps and leaflets are available from the library (28 West St), the museum (38 West St) and the town hall (South St).

Sights

Farnham Castle CASTLE

(EH; adult/child £3.20/1.60; ⏲noon-5pm Fri-Sun Mar-Sep) Constructed in 1138 by Henry de Blois, the grandson of William the Conqueror, there's not much left of the castle keep today except the beautiful old ramparts. Even if the keep is closed, it's worth walking around the outside for the picturesque views.

A residential palace house, Farnham Castle was built in the 13th century for the bishops of Winchester as a stopover on London journeys. From 1926 to the 1950s, it was taken over by the bishops of Guildford. It's now owned by the Farnham Castle International Briefing & Conference Centre, but you can visit it on a **guided tour** (☎01252-721194; adult/child £2.50/1.50; ⏲2-4pm Wed & 2.30pm Fri Apr-Aug). Farnham Castle is located up the old steps at the top of Castle St.

FREE **Museum of Farnham** MUSEUM

(38 West St; ⏲10am-5pm Tue-Sat) This engaging little museum is located in the splendid Willmer House, a Georgian mansion built for wealthy hop merchant and maltster John Thorne in 1718.

Themed rooms trace Farnham's history from flint tool days to Bakelite nostalgia, with a corner dedicated to William Cobbett, the town's most famous son and 19th-century reformer, radical MP, writer and journalist who established *Hansard* (the official record of what is said in Parliament). Cobbett's bust takes pride of place in the peaceful garden out back where you'll also find a spanking new timber gallery housing temporary exhibitions by local artists.

Sleeping & Eating

Bush Hotel HOTEL £££

(☎01252-715237; www.mercure-uk.com; The Borough; r from £140; P ❄ ☎) This 17th-century inn is right in the heart of the action and benefits from recently renovated rooms, a cosy beamed bar and a superb restaurant that spills out into the pretty courtyard.

Mulberry GOURMET BURGERS ££
(Station Hill; burgers £7-11; ⏲lunch & dinner) Right by the station, all this bar-restaurant does is humungous gourmet burgers, and boy does it do 'em well. There are snazzy rooms upstairs where you can sleep off any excesses and a bi-monthly local DJ open-deck night (Sundays) you may wish to avoid.

Getting There & Away

Bus

London Victoria National Express, £9.30, one hour 40 minutes, daily

Train

London Waterloo £19.30, one hour, twice hourly, change at Woking

Winchester £16.10, one hour, twice hourly, change at Woking

Hindhead

The tiny hamlet of Hindhead, 8 miles south of Farnham off the A287, lies in the middle of the largest area of open heath in Surrey. During the 19th century, a number of prominent Victorians bought up property in the area, including Sir Arthur Conan Doyle (1859–1930). One of the three founders of the National Trust, Sir Robert Hunter, lived in nearby Haslemere, and today much of the area is administered by the foundation.

The most beautiful part of the area is to the northeast, where you'll find a natural depression known as the **Devil's Punchbowl**. There are a number of excellent trails and bridleways here. To get the best view, head for **Gibbet Hill** (280m), which was once an execution ground.

The **Hindhead YHA Hostel** (☎0845 371 9022; www.yha.org.uk; Punchbowl La, Thursley; dm £15.95) is a completely secluded cottage run by the National Trust on the northern edge of the Punchbowl – perfect digs for walkers.

Bus 19 runs hourly to Hindhead from Farnham.

Oxford, Cotswolds & Around

Includes »

OXFORDSHIRE...... 182
Oxford 182
Henley-on-Thames... 195
THE COTSWOLDS ... 196
Cirencester 203
Bibury............. 204
Tetbury............ 204
Painswick.......... 205
GLOUCESTERSHIRE. 205
Cheltenham........ 206
Gloucester.......... 211
HERTFORDSHIRE ... 214
BERKSHIRE 216
Windsor & Eton...... 216

Best Places to Eat

» Le Champignon Sauvage (p209)

» Daffodil (p209)

» Chef's Table (p205)

» Trout (p192)

Best Places to Stay

» St Briavels Castle YHA (p213)

» Malmaison (p191)

» Old Parsonage Hotel (p191)

» Lamb Inn (p198)

Why Go?

Dripping with charm and riddled with implausibly pretty villages, this part of the country is as close to the old-world English idyll as you'll get. It's a haven of lush rolling hills, rose-clad cottages, graceful stone churches, thatched roofs, cream teas and antique shops. Add to the mix the legendary city of Oxford, and it's easy to see why the region is a magnet for tourists.

Although the roads and the most popular villages are busy in summer, it's easy to get off the tourist trail. The Cotswolds are at their best when you find your own romantic refuge and discover the fire-lit inns and grandiose manors that persuade A-list celebrities and the merely moneyed to buy property here.

Most of the area is an easy day trip from London, but Oxford and the Cotswolds deserve at least an overnight stay.

When to Go

On 1 May you can welcome the dawn with Oxford's Magdalen College Choir, which sings hymns from the college tower. In July you can swill champagne and watch the rowing at Henley's Royal Regatta and Festival. September is the best time to sample England's finest ales at the four-day St Alban's Beer Festival.

Oxford, Cotswolds & Around Highlights

1. Following in the footsteps of Lyra, Tolkien, CS Lewis and Inspector Morse as you tour the **Oxford colleges** (p183)
2. Meandering around **Painswick** (p205), one of the most beautiful and unspoilt towns in the Cotswolds
3. Getting a glimpse of the high life at the Queen's very own hideaway, **Windsor Castle** (p216)
4. Touring the elegant cloisters and taking in a concert at the magnificent **Gloucester Cathedral** (p211)
5. Stepping back in time as you down a pint by the fire in the **Falkland Arms** (p199)
6. Strolling the tree-lined streets, soaking up the architecture and browsing the chichi shops of Regency **Cheltenham** (p206)
7. Touring the monumental **Blenheim Palace** (p194), one of the country's greatest stately homes
8. Exploring the vast collection and swanky new makeover at the **Ashmolean Museum** in Oxford (p189)

History

A Bronze Age chalk horse at Uffington is the earliest evidence of settlement in this part of England, but in Roman times, the region was traversed by a network of roads, some of which still exist today, and as word of the good hunting and fertile valleys spread, the area became heavily populated.

By the 11th century, the wool and grain trade had made the locals rich, William the Conqueror had built his first motte and bailey in Windsor, and the Augustinian abbey in Oxford had begun training clerics. In the 12th century, Henry II fortified the royal residence at Windsor by adding a stone tower and protective walls, and in the 13th century, Oxford's first colleges were established, along with its reputation as England's foremost centre of learning.

Meanwhile, local farmers continued to supply London with corn, wool and clothing. The Cotswolds in particular flourished and amassed great wealth. By the 14th century, the wool merchants were rolling in money and happy to show off their good fortune by building the beautiful villages and graceful wool churches that still litter the area today.

The region's proximity to London also meant that it became a popular retreat for wealthy city dwellers. The nobility and aristocracy flocked to Hertfordshire and Buckinghamshire, building country piles as retreats from the city. Today, the area remains affluent and is home to busy commuters and is a popular choice for wealthy Londoners looking for second homes.

Activities

Walking or cycling through the Cotswolds is an ideal way to get away from the crowds and discover some of the lesser-known vistas and villages of the region. You'll also find great walking and cycling opportunities in Buckinghamshire's leafy Chiltern Hills and along the meandering River Thames. There are specific suggestions for walks and rides throughout this chapter.

CYCLING

Gentle gradients and scenic vistas make the Cotswolds ideal for cycling, with only the steep western escarpment offering a challenge to the legs. Plenty of quiet country lanes and gated roads crisscross the region, or you can follow the signposted **Thames Valley Cycle Way** (NCN Routes 4, 5).

Mountain bikers can use a variety of bridleways in the **Cotswolds** and **Chilterns**, and in the west of the region the **Forest of Dean** has many dirt-track options, and some dedicated mountain-bike trails.

WALKING

The **Cotswold Hills** offer endless opportunities for day hikes, but if you're looking for something more ambitious, the **Cotswold Way** (www.nationaltrail.co.uk/Cotswold) is an absolute classic. The route covers 102 miles from Bath to Chipping Campden and takes about a week to walk.

Alternatively, the **Thames Path** (www.national trail.co.uk/thamespath) follows the river downstream from its source near Cirencester to London. It takes about two weeks to complete the 184-mile route, but there's a very enjoyable five-day section from near Cirencester to Oxford.

Finally, the 87-mile **Ridgeway National Trail** (www.nationaltrail.co.uk/ridgeway) meanders along the chalky grassland of the Wiltshire downs near Avebury, down into the Thames Valley and then along the spine of the Chilterns to Ivinghoe Beacon near Aylesbury in Buckinghamshire, offering wonderful views of the surrounding area.

Getting There & Around

Thanks to its proximity to London and the rash of commuters who live in the area, there are frequent trains and buses here from the capital. Getting across the region by public transport can be frustrating and time-consuming, though. Renting a car gives you the most freedom, but be prepared for busy roads in the Cotswolds during the summer months and daily rush-hour traffic closer to London.

Traveline (☎0871-200 22 33; www.traveline eastanglia.org.uk) provides timetables for all public transport across the country. For specific information on travelling across the Cotswolds, try www.cotswoldsaonb.org.uk, which has downloadable guides on all bus and rail options in the region.

BUS Major bus routes are run by **Stagecoach** (www.stagecoachbus.com) and **Arriva** (www.arrivabus.co.uk), with a host of smaller companies offering services to local towns and villages. Pick up a copy of Oxfordshire County Council's *Public Transport Map & Guide*, or the *Explore the Cotswolds by Public Transport* brochures in any tourist office.

TRAIN Services in the region are limited, with the exception of the area immediately outside London. For general rail information, call **National Rail** (☎08457-48 49 50; www.nationalrail.co.uk).

WANT MORE?

Head to **Lonely Planet** (www.lonelyplanet.com/england/oxfordshire/oxford) for planning advice, author recommendations, traveller reviews and insider tips.

OXFORDSHIRE

The whiff of old money, academic achievement and genteel living wafts from Oxfordshire's well-bred, well-preened pores. Rustic charm, good manners and grand attractions are in abundant supply here, with a host of charming villages surrounding the world-renowned university town.

Oxford is a highlight on any itinerary, with over 1500 listed buildings, a choice of excellent museums and an air of refined sophistication. Between the gorgeous colleges and hushed quads students in full academic dress cycle along cobbled lanes little changed by time.

Yet there is a lot more to the county. Just to the north is Blenheim Palace, an extravagant baroque pile that's the birthplace of Sir Winston Churchill, while to the south is the elegant riverside town of Henley, famous for its ever-so-posh Royal Regatta.

Activities

As well as the long-distance national trails, walkers may be interested in the **Oxfordshire Way**, a scenic, 65-mile signposted trail running from Bourton-on-the-Water to Henley-on-Thames, and the **Wychwood Way**, a historic, 37-mile route from Woodstock, which runs through an ancient royal forest. The routes are divided up into manageable sections, described in leaflets available at most local tourist offices and libraries.

The quiet roads and gentle gradients also make Oxfordshire good cycling territory. The main signposted route through the county is the **Oxfordshire Cycleway**, which takes in Woodstock, Burford and Henley. If you don't have your own wheels, you can hire bikes in Oxford.

You'll find more information at www.oxfordshire.gov.uk/countryside.

Getting Around

You can pick up bus and train timetables for most routes at local tourist offices. The main train stations are in Oxford and Banbury and have frequent connections to London Paddington and Euston, Hereford, Birmingham, Bristol and Scotland.

The main bus operators are the **Oxford Bus Company** (☎01865-785400; www.oxfordbus.co.uk) and **Stagecoach** (☎01865-772250; www.stagecoachbus.com/oxfordshire).

Oxford

POP 134,248

The genteel city of Oxford is a privileged place, one of the world's most famous university towns – it's soaked in history, dripping with august buildings and yet incredibly insular. The 39 colleges that make up the University jealously guard their elegant honey-coloured buildings, and inside their grounds, a reverent hush and studious calm descends.

Oxford is highly aware of its international standing and yet is remarkably restrained for a city driven by its student population. It's a conservative, bookish kind of place where academic achievement and intellectual ideals are the common currency. The University buildings wrap around narrow cobbled lanes, cyclists in academic gowns blaze along the streets and the vast library collections run along shelves deep below the city streets.

Oxford is a wonderful place to ramble: the oldest colleges date back almost 750 years, and little has changed inside the hallowed walls since then. But along with the rich history and tradition, there is a whole other world beyond the college walls. Oxford has a long industrial past and was the birthplace of the Morris motor car as well as of Mensa. Today, the new Mini runs off the production lines, and the real-world majority still outnumber the academic elite.

The university buildings are scattered throughout the city, with the most important and architecturally significant in the centre. Jericho, in the northwest, is the trendy, artsy end of town, with slick bars and restaurants and an art-house cinema, while Cowley Rd, southeast of Carfax, is the gritty student and immigrant area packed with cheap places to eat and drink. Further out, in the salubrious northern suburb of Summertown, you'll find more upmarket restaurants and bars.

History

Strategically placed at the confluence of the Rivers Cherwell and Thames (called the Isis here, from the Latin *Tamesis*), Oxford was a key Saxon town heavily fortified by Alfred the Great during the war against the Danes.

By the 11th century, the Augustinian abbey in Oxford had begun training clerics, and when Henry II banned Anglo-Norman students from attending the Sorbonne in 1167, the abbey began to attract students in droves. Whether bored by the lack of distractions or revolted by the ignorance of the country folk we'll never know, but the new students managed to create a lasting enmity with the local townspeople, culminating in the St Scholastica's Day Massacre in 1355. Thereafter, the king ordered that the university be broken up into colleges, each of which then developed its own traditions.

The first colleges, Balliol, Merton and University, were built in the 13th century, with at least three more being added in each of the following three centuries. Newer colleges, such as Keble, were added in the 19th and 20th centuries to cater for an ever-expanding student population. However, old habits die hard at Oxford, and it was 1877 before lecturers were allowed to marry, and another year before female students were admitted. Even then, it still took another 42 years before women would be granted a degree for their four years of hard work. Today, there are 39 colleges that cater for about 20,000 students, and in 2008 the last all-female college, St Hilda's, eventually opened its door to male students.

Meanwhile, the arrival of the canal system in 1790 had a profound effect on the rest of Oxford. By creating a link with the Midlands' industrial centres, work and trade suddenly expanded beyond the academic core. However, the city's real industrial boom came when William Morris began producing cars here in 1913. With the success of his Bullnose Morris and Morris Minor, his Cowley factory went on to become one of the largest motor plants in the world. Although the works have been scaled down since their heyday, new Minis still run off BMW's Cowley production line today.

Sights

University Buildings & Colleges

Much of the centre of Oxford is taken up by graceful university buildings and elegant colleges, each one individual in its appearance and academic specialities. However, not all are open to the public. For those that are, visiting hours change with the term and exam schedule. Check www.ox.ac.uk/colleges for full details of visiting hours and admission.

ST SCHOLASTICA'S DAY MASSACRE

The first real wave of students arrived in Oxford in the 12th century, and right from the start an uneasy relationship grew between the townspeople and the bookish blow-ins. Name-calling and drunken brawls escalated into full-scale riots in 1209 and 1330, when browbeaten scholars abandoned Oxford to establish new universities in Cambridge and Stamford, respectively. The riots of 10 and 11 February 1355 changed everything, however, and left a bitter scar on relations for hundreds of years.

It all began when celebrations for St Scholastica's Day grew out of hand and a drunken scuffle spilled into the street. Years of simmering discontent and frustrations were let loose, and soon students and townspeople took to one another's throats. The chancellor ordered the pealing of the university bells, and every student who heard it rushed to join the brawl. By the end of the day, the students had claimed victory and an uneasy truce was called.

The next morning, however, the furious townspeople returned with the help of local villagers armed with pickaxes, shovels and pikes. By sundown, 63 students and 30 townspeople were dead. King Edward III sent troops in to quell the rioting and eventually decided to bring the town under the control of the university.

To prove its authority, the university ordered the mayor and burgesses (citizens) to attend a service and pay a penny for every student killed on the anniversary of the riot each year. For 470 years, the vengeful practice continued, until one mayor flatly refused to pay the fine. His successors all followed suit, but it took another 130 years for the university to extend the olive branch and award a Doctorate of Civil Law to Mayor William Richard Gowers, MA, Oriel in 1955.

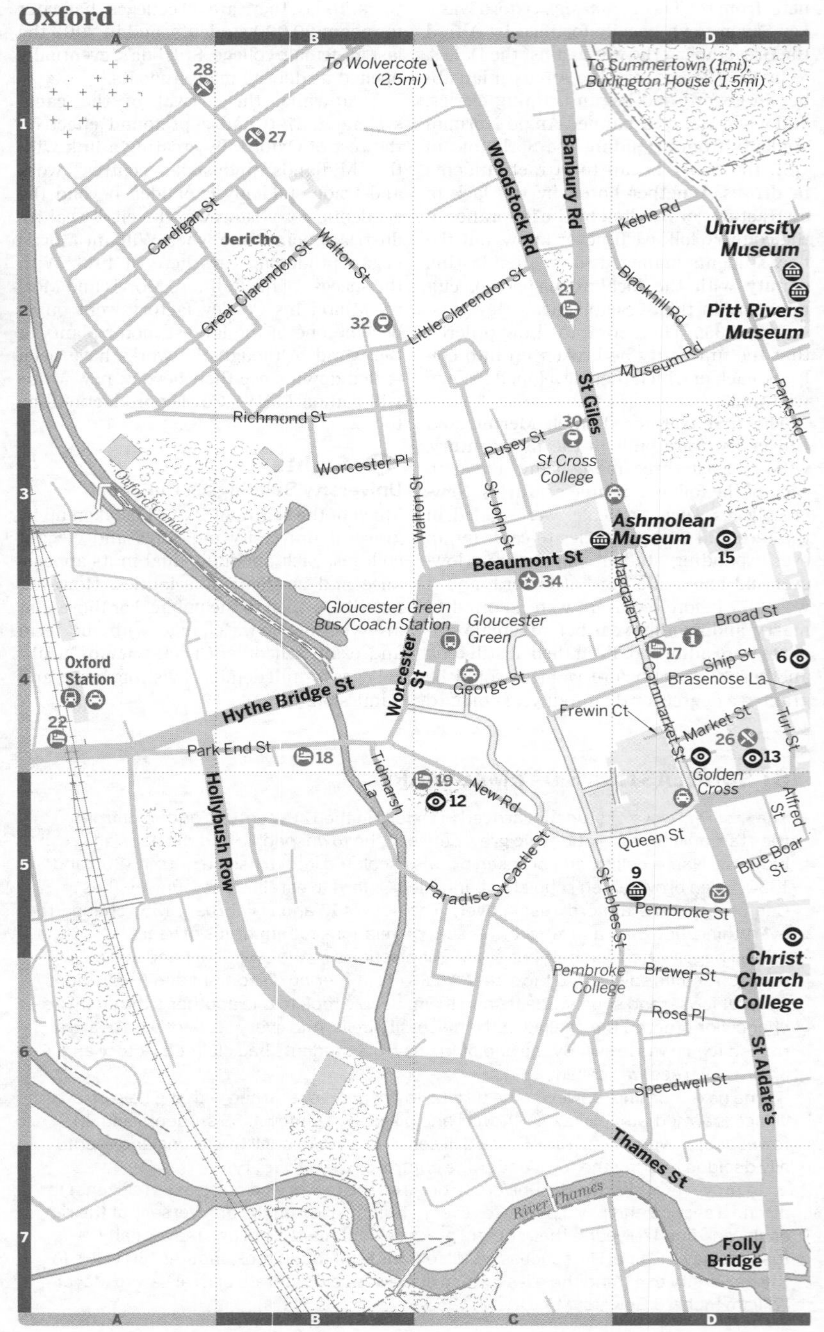
A
B
C
D
1
2
3
4
5
6
7
To Wolvercote (2.5mi)
To Summertown (1mi); Burlington House (1.5mi)
28
27
Jericho
Cardigan St
Walton St
Great Clarendon St
Little Clarendon St
Woodstock Rd
Banbury Rd
Keble Rd
Blackhall Rd
University Museum
Pitt Rivers Museum
Museum Rd
Parks Rd
21
32
Richmond St
St Giles
30
Pusey St
St Cross College
Worcester Pl
Walton St
St John St
Oxford Canal
Ashmolean Museum
15
Beaumont St
34
Magdalen St
Gloucester Green Bus/Coach Station
Gloucester Green
Broad St
17
6
Ship St
Brasenose La
Oxford Station
Hythe Bridge St
Worcester St
George St
Frewin Ct
Cornmarket St
Market St
Turl St
22
Park End St
18
26
13
Golden Cross
Hollybush Row
Tidmarsh La
19
12
New Rd
Alfred St
Queen St
Blue Boar St
Castle St
Paradise St
9
St Ebbes St
Pembroke St
Christ Church College
Pembroke College
Brewer St
Rose Pl
St Aldate's
Speedwell St
Thames St
River Thames
Folly Bridge

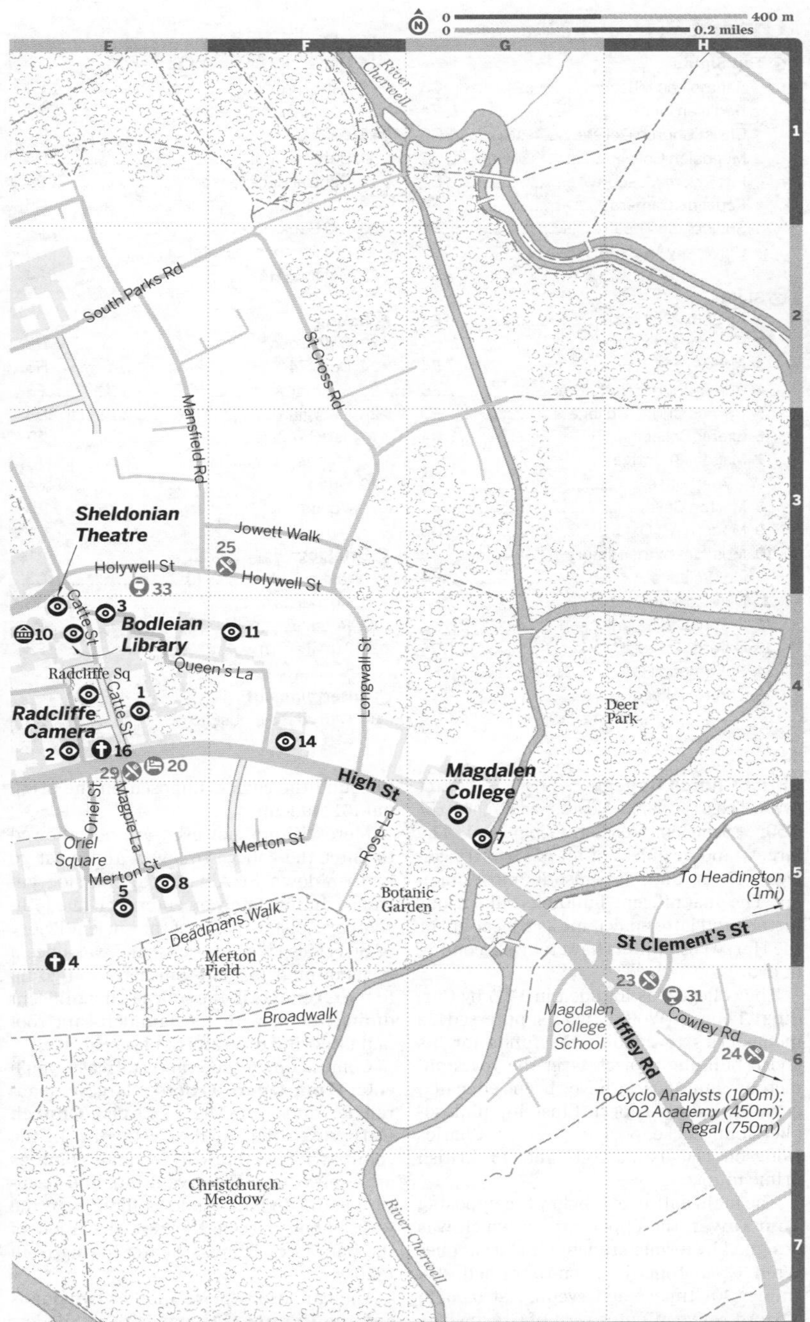

0 400 m
0 0.2 miles
E
F
G
H
1
2
3
4
5
6
7
River Cherwell
South Parks Rd
St Cross Rd
Mansfield Rd
Sheldonian Theatre
Jowett Walk
25
Holywell St
33
Holywell St
3
10
Bodleian Library
11
Catte St
Queen's La
Radcliffe Sq
Catte St
1
Longwall St
Radcliffe Camera
14
2
16
29
20
High St
Magdalen College
Deer Park
Oriel St
Magpie La
7
Oriel Square
Merton St
Rose La
Merton St
8
5
Botanic Garden
To Headington (1mi)
Deadmans Walk
St Clement's St
4
Merton Field
23
31
Broadwalk
Magdalen College School
Iffley Rd
Cowley Rd
24
To Cyclo Analysts (100m); O2 Academy (450m); Regal (750m)
Christchurch Meadow
River Cherwell

Oxford

Top Sights

	Ashmolean Museum	C3
	Bodleian Library	E4
	Christ Church College	D5
	Magdalen College	G5
	Pitt Rivers Museum	D2
	Radcliffe Camera	E4
	Sheldonian Theatre	E4
	University Museum	D2

Sights

1	All Souls College	E4
2	Brasenose College	E4
3	Bridge of Sighs	E4
4	Christ Church Cathedral	E5
5	Corpus Christi College	E5
6	Exeter College	D4
7	Magdalen Bridge Boathouse	G5
8	Merton College	E5
9	Modern Art Oxford	D5
10	Museum of the History of Science	E4
11	New College	F4
12	Oxford Castle Unlocked	C5
13	Oxford Covered Market	D4
14	St Edmund Hall	F4
15	Trinity College	D3
16	University Church of St Mary the Virgin	E4

Sleeping

17	Buttery Hotel	D4
18	Central Backpackers	B4
19	Malmaison	C5
20	Old Bank Hotel	E4
21	Old Parsonage Hotel	C2
22	Oxford YHA	A4

Eating

23	Café Coco	H6
24	Door 74	H6
25	Edamame	F3
26	Georgina's	D4
27	Jericho Café	B1
28	Manos	A1
29	Quod	E4
	Vaults	(see 16)

Drinking

30	Eagle & Child	C3
31	Kazbar	H6
32	Raoul's	B2
33	Turf Tavern	E3

Entertainment

34	Oxford Playhouse	C3

Christ Church College COLLEGE
(www.chch.ox.ac.uk; St Aldate's; adult/child £6/4.50; ⌚9am-5pm Mon-Sat, 2-5pm Sun) The largest and grandest of all of Oxford's colleges, Christ Church is also its most popular. The magnificent buildings, illustrious history and latter-day fame as a location for the Harry Potter films have tourists coming in droves.

The college was founded in 1525 by Cardinal Thomas Wolsey, who suppressed 22 monasteries to acquire the funds for his lavish building project. Over the years numerous luminaries have been educated here, including Albert Einstein, philosopher John Locke, poet WH Auden, Charles Dodgson (Lewis Carroll) and 13 British prime ministers.

The main entrance is below the imposing **Tom Tower**, the upper part of which was designed by former student Sir Christopher Wren. Great Tom, the 7-ton tower bell, still chimes 101 times each evening at 9.05pm (Oxford is five minutes west of Greenwich), to sound the curfew imposed on the original 101 students.

Mere visitors, however, are not allowed to enter the college this way and must go further down St Aldate's to the side entrance. Immediately on entering is the 15th-century cloister, a relic of the ancient Priory of St Frideswide, whose shrine was once a focus of pilgrimage. From here, you go up to the **Great Hall**, the college's magnificent dining room, with its hammerbeam roof and imposing portraits of past scholars.

Coming down the grand staircase, you'll enter **Tom Quad**, Oxford's largest quadrangle, and from here, **Christ Church Cathedral**, the smallest cathedral in the country. Inside, brawny Norman columns are topped by elegant vaulting, and beautiful stained-glass windows illuminate the walls. Look out for the rare depiction of the murder of Thomas Becket dating from 1320.

You can also explore another two quads and the **Picture Gallery**, with its modest collection of Renaissance art. To the south of the college is **Christ Church Meadow**, a leafy expanse bordered by the Rivers Isis and Cherwell and ideal for leisurely walking.

Christ Church is a working college, and the hall often closes between noon and 2pm and the cathedral in late afternoon.

Magdalen College COLLEGE

(www.magd.ox.ac.uk; High St; adult/child £4.50/3.50; ⌚1-6pm) Set amid 40 hectares of lawns, woodlands, river walks and deer park, Magdalen (*mawd*-len) is one of the wealthiest and most beautiful of Oxford's colleges.

An elegant Victorian gateway leads into a medieval chapel, with its glorious 15th-century tower, and on to the remarkable cloisters, some of the finest in Oxford. The strange gargoyles and carved figures here are said to have inspired CS Lewis' stone statues in *The Chronicles of Narnia*. Behind the cloisters, the lovely **Addison's Walk** leads through the grounds and along the banks of the River Cherwell for just under a mile.

Magdalen has a reputation as an artistic college, and some of its most famous students and fellows have included Oscar Wilde, Poet Laureate Sir John Betjeman and Nobel Laureate Seamus Heaney.

The college also has a fine choir that sings *Hymnus Eucharisticus* at 6am on May Day (1 May) from the top of the 42m bell tower. The event now marks the culmination of a solid night of drinking for most students as they gather in their glad rags on Magdalen Bridge to listen to the dawn chorus.

Opposite the college and sweeping along the banks of the River Cherwell is the beautiful **Botanic Garden** (www.botanic-garden.ox.ac.uk; adult/child £3.50/free; ⌚9am-5pm). The gardens are the oldest in Britain and were founded in 1621 for the study of medicinal plants.

Sheldonian Theatre CEREMONIAL HALL

(www.sheldon.ox.ac.uk; Broad St; adult/child £2.50/1.50; ⌚10am-12.30pm & 2-4.30pm Mon-Sat) The monumental Sheldonian Theatre was the first major work of Christopher Wren, at that time a university professor of astronomy. Inspired by the classical Theatre of Marcellus in Rome, it has a rectangular front end and a semicircular back, while inside, the ceiling of the main hall is blanketed by a fine 17th-century painting of the triumph of truth over ignorance. The Sheldonian is now used for college ceremonies and public concerts, but you can climb to the cupola for good views of the surrounding buildings.

Bodleian Library LIBRARY

(www.bodley.ox.ac.uk; Broad St; ⌚9am-5pm Mon-Fri, 9am-4.30pm Sat, 11am-5pm Sun) Oxford's Bodleian Library is one of the oldest public libraries in the world, and one of England's three copyright libraries. It holds more than 7 million items on 118 miles of shelving and has seating space for up to 2500 readers.

The oldest part of the library surrounds the stunning Jacobean-Gothic **Old Schools Quadrangle**, which dates from the early 17th century. On the eastern side of the quad is the **Tower of Five Orders**, an ornate building depicting the five classical orders of architecture. On the west side is the **Divinity School** (adult/child £1/free), the university's first teaching room. It is renowned as a masterpiece of 15th-century English Gothic architecture and has a superb fan-vaulted ceiling. A self-guided **audio tour** (£2.50, 40 minutes) to these areas is available.

Most of the rest of the library is closed to visitors, but **library tours** (admission £6.50; ⌚10.30am, 11.30am, 2pm & 3pm) allow access to the medieval Duke Humfrey's library, where, the library proudly boasts, no less than five kings, 40 Nobel Prize winners, 25 British prime ministers and writers such as Oscar Wilde, CS Lewis and JRR Tolkien studied. You'll also get to see 17th-century **Convocation House and Court**, where parliament was held during the Civil War. The tour takes about an hour and is not suitable for children under 11 years old.

Radcliffe Camera LIBRARY

(Radcliffe Sq) Just south of the library is the Radcliffe Camera, the quintessential Oxford landmark and one of the city's most photographed buildings. The spectacular circular library was built between 1737 and 1749 in grand Palladian style, and has Britain's third-largest dome. The only way to see the library is to join an **extended tour** (£13). Tours take place on some Saturdays at 10am and most Sundays at 11.15am and last about an hour and a half. Check the website for up-to-date details.

For excellent views of the Radcliffe Camera and surrounding buildings, climb the 14th-century tower in the beautiful **University Church of Saint Mary the Virgin** (www.university-church.ox.ac.uk; High St; tower admission adult/child £3/2.50). On Sunday the tower does not open until about noon, after the morning service.

New College COLLEGE

(www.new.ox.ac.uk; Holywell St; admission £2; ⏲11am-5pm) From the Bodleian, stroll under the **Bridge of Sighs**, a 1914 copy of the famous bridge in Venice, to New College. This 14th-century college was the first in Oxford for undergraduates and is a fine example of the glorious Perpendicular style. The chapel here is full of treasures, including superb stained glass, much of it original, and Sir Jacob Epstein's disturbing statue of Lazarus.

During term time, visitors may attend the beautiful **Evensong**, a choral church service held nightly at 6pm. Access for visitors is through the New College Lane gate from Easter to early October, and through the Holywell St entrance the rest of the year.

William Spooner was once a college warden here, and his habit of transposing the first consonants of words gave rise to the term 'spoonerism'. Local lore suggests that he once reprimanded a student by saying, 'You have deliberately tasted two worms and can leave Oxford by the town drain'.

Merton College COLLEGE

(www.merton.ox.ac.uk; Merton St; admission £2; ⏲2-5pm Mon-Fri, 10am-5pm Sat & Sun) From the High St, follow the wonderfully named Logic Lane to Merton College, one of Oxford's original three colleges. Founded in 1264, Merton was the first to adopt collegiate planning, bringing scholars and tutors together into a formal community and providing a planned residence for them. The charming 14th-century **Mob Quad** was the first of the college quads.

Just off the quad is a 13th-century **chapel** and the **Old Library** (admission on guided tour only), the oldest medieval library in use. It is said that Tolkien spent many hours here writing *The Lord of the Rings*. Other literary giants associated with the college include TS Eliot and Louis MacNeice.

During the summer months it may be possible to join a **guided tour** (£2, 45 minutes) of the college grounds. These usually take place in the afternoon, but are dependent on the availability of the graduate students who run them. If you're visiting in summer, look out for posters advertising candlelit concerts in the chapel.

FREE **All Souls College** COLLEGE

(www.all-souls.ox.ac.uk; High St; ⏲2-4pm Mon-Fri) One of the wealthiest of Oxford's colleges and unique in not accepting undergraduate students, All Souls is primarily an academic research institution. It was founded in 1438 as a centre of prayer and learning, and today fellowship of the college is one of the highest academic honours in the country. Each year, the university's top finalists are invited to sit a fellowship exam, with an average of only two making the grade annually.

Much of the college facade dates from the 1440s, and, unlike other older colleges, the front quad is largely unchanged in five centuries. It also contains a beautiful 17th-century sundial designed by Christopher Wren. Most obvious, though, are the twin mock-Gothic towers on the north quad. Designed by Nicholas Hawksmoor in 1710, they were lambasted for ruining the Oxford skyline when first erected.

Brasenose College COLLEGE

(www.bnc.ox.ac.uk; Radcliffe Sq; admission £1; ⏲noon-4pm) Small and select, this elegant 16th-century place is truly charming. Look out for the door-knocker above the high table in the dining hall – and ask about its fascinating history.

FREE **Exeter College** COLLEGE

(www.exeter.ox.ac.uk; Turl St; ⏲2-5pm) Exeter is known for its elaborate 17th-century dining hall and ornate Victorian Gothic chapel housing *The Adoration of the Magi,* a William Morris tapestry.

Trinity College COLLEGE

(www.trinity.ox.ac.uk; Broad St; adult/child £1.50/75p; ⏲10am-noon & 2-4pm Sun-Fri, 2-4pm Sat) This small 16th-century college is worth a visit to see its exquisitely carved chapel, one of the most beautiful in the city, and the lovely garden quad designed by Sir Christopher Wren.

FREE **St Edmund Hall** COLLEGE

(www.seh.ox.ac.uk; Queen's Lane; ⏲noon-4pm Mon-Fri term time only) St Edmund Hall is the sole survivor of the original medieval halls, the teaching institutions that preceded colleges in Oxford. The Mohawk chief Oronhyatekha studied here in 1862 (and eloped with the principal's daughter) but it is best known for its small chapel decorated by William Morris and Edward Burne-Jones.

LOCAL KNOWLEDGE

PETER BERRY, BLACKWELL TOUR GUIDE

Although it's a small city, Oxford is such a big world, with a wealth of famous people who have studied here. There's no shortage of material for a tour guide.

Must see:

» **Christ Church Cathedral** (p186)

» **Bridge of Sighs** (p188)

» **Radcliffe Camera** (p187)

» **Turf Tavern** (p193)

Must do:

» Climb the tower of **University Church** (p187) – it's the highest point in the city and offers great views of the dreamy spires.

Favourite chapel:

» **Exeter College** (p188) Don't miss it.

Oxford inspires:

» CS Lewis' office at **Magdalen** (p187) looked out over the deer park, and this was probably the inspiration for the fawn in the *Narnia* series.

» Tolkien lived at 99 Holywell St and neighbours can recall him coming out to the street to test his stories on the local children.

» The *Jabberwocky* tree still stands at the back of **Christ Church Cathedral** (p186); you can see it through a gate in the high wall. It's almost 400 years old.

Hidden gem:

The Elizabethan murals in the **Golden Cross Inn** (now Pizza Express). The Prince's Chamber was Shakespeare's overnight Oxford stop between London and Stratford.

Things the university would rather you didn't know:

Percy Bysshe Shelley was infamous for playing schoolboy pranks, in particular, swapping babies left in prams outside the shops on the High St.

FREE **Corpus Christi College** COLLEGE (www.ccc.ox.ac.uk; Merton St; ⌚1.30-4.30pm) Reputedly the friendliest and most liberal of Oxford's colleges, Corpus Christi is small but strikingly beautiful. The pelican sundial in the front quad calculates the time by the sun and the moon, although it is always five minutes fast.

Other Sights

FREE **Ashmolean Museum** MUSEUM (www.ashmolean.org; Beaumont St; ⌚10am-6pm Tue-Sun) Britain's oldest public museum, the Ashmolean reopened in 2009 after a massive £61 million redevelopment and is now being lauded as the finest university museum in the world. The makeover has made the once intimidating building and stuffy collection a real joy to browse, with a giant atrium, glass walls revealing galleries on different levels, and a beautiful rooftop restaurant.

The museum was established in 1683 when Elias Ashmole presented the University with the collection of artefacts amassed by John Tradescant, gardener to Charles I. It contains everything from Egyptian, Islamic and Chinese art to rare porcelain, tapestries and silverware, priceless musical instruments and extensive displays of European art (including works by Raphael and Michelangelo). Set in one of Britain's best examples of neo-Grecian architecture, it is one of the region's top attractions.

FREE **University & Pitt Rivers Museums** MUSEUM
Housed in a glorious Victorian Gothic building with slender, cast-iron columns, ornate capitals and a soaring glass roof, the **University Museum** (www.oum.ox.ac.uk; Parks Rd; ⌚10am-5pm; 👪) is worth a visit for its architecture alone. However, the real draw is the mammoth natural-history collection of more than 5 million exhibits,

ranging from exotic insects and fossils to a towering *T. rex* skeleton.

Hidden away through a door at the back of the main exhibition hall, the **Pitt Rivers Museum** (www.prm.ox.ac.uk; ⏲10am-4.30pm Tue-Sun, noon-4.30pm Mon; 👪) is a treasure trove of weird and wonderful displays to satisfy every armchair adventurer's wildest dreams. In the half light inside are glass cases and mysterious drawers stuffed with Victorian explorers' prized booty. Feathered cloaks, necklaces of teeth, blowpipes, magic charms, Noh masks, totem poles, fur parkas, musical instruments and shrunken heads lurk here, making it a fascinating place for adults and children.

Both museums run workshops for children almost every weekend and are known for their child-friendly attitude.

Oxford Castle Unlocked PRISON
(www.oxfordcastleunlocked.co.uk; 44-46 Oxford Castle; adult/child £7.75/5.50; ⏲10am-4.20pm) Oxford Castle Unlocked explores the 1000-year history of Oxford's castle and prison. Tours begin in the 11th-century Crypt of St George's Chapel, possibly the first formal teaching venue in Oxford, and continue on into the Victorian prison cells and the 18th-century Debtors' Tower, where you can learn about the inmates' grisly lives, daring escapes and cruel punishments. You can also climb the Saxon St George's Tower, which has excellent views of the city, and clamber up the original medieval motte.

FREE **Modern Art Oxford** ART GALLERY
(www.modernartoxford.org.uk; 30 Pembroke St; ⏲10am-5pm Tue-Sat, noon-5pm Sun; 👪) Far removed from Oxford's musty hallways of history, this is one of the best contemporary-art museums outside London, with heavyweight exhibitions, a wonderful gallery space and plenty of activities for children.

FREE **Museum of the History of Science** MUSEUM
(www.mhs.ox.ac.uk; Broad St; ⏲noon-5pm Tue-Fri, 10am-5pm Sat, 2-5pm Sun) Science, art, celebrity and nostalgia come together at this fascinating museum where the exhibits include everything from a blackboard used by Einstein to the world's finest collection of historic scientific instruments, all housed in a beautiful 17th-century building.

Oxford Covered Market INDOOR MARKET
(www.oxford-covered-market.co.uk; ⏲9am-5.30pm) A haven of traditional butchers, fishmongers, cobblers and barbers, this is the place to go for Sicilian sausage, handmade chocolates, traditional pies, funky T-shirts and expensive brogues. It's a fascinating place to explore and, if you're in Oxford at Christmas, a must for its traditional displays of freshly hung deer, wild boar, ostrich and turkey.

Activities

A typical Oxford experience, **punting** is all about sitting back and quaffing Pimms (the quintessential English summer drink) as you watch the city's glorious architecture float by. Which, of course, requires someone else to do the hard work – punting is far more difficult than it appears. Be prepared to spend much of your time struggling to get out of a tangle of low branches or avoiding the path of an oncoming rowing team. For tips on how to punt, see p359.

Punts are available from mid-March to mid-October, 10am to dusk, and hold five people including the punter (£13/15 per hour weekdays/weekends, £65 deposit).

The most central location to rent punts is **Magdalen Bridge Boathouse** (www.oxfordpunting.co.uk; High St). From here, you can punt downstream around the Botanic Garden and Christ Church Meadow or upstream around Magdalen Deer Park. Alternatively, head for the **Cherwell Boat House** (www.cherwellboathouse.co.uk; Bardwell Rd) for a countryside amble, where the destination of choice is the busy boozer, the **Victoria Arms** (Mill Lane). To get to the boathouse, take bus 2 or 7 from Magdalen St to Bardwell Rd and follow the signposts.

Tours

The tourist office can also advise on a number of self-guided (brochure or audio) tours of the city.

Tourist Office WALKING TOURS
(☎01865-252200; www.visitoxford.org; 15-16 Broad St; ⏲9.30am-5pm Mon-Sat, 10am-4pm Sun) Runs two-hour tours of Oxford city and colleges (adult/child £7/3.75) at 10.45am and 2pm year-round, and at 11am and 1pm in July and August. The Inspector Morse tours (adult/child £7.50/4) start at 1.30pm on Saturdays, family walking tours (adult/child £5.75/3.50) at 1.30pm on school holidays, and a bewildering array of themed tours (adult/child £7.50/4) – including an Alice [in Wonderland] tour,

a Literary Tour, and a Harry Potter tour – run on various dates throughout the year.

Blackwell WALKING TOURS
(☎01865-333606; oxford@blackwell.co.uk; 48-51 Broad St; adult/child £7/6.50; ⌚mid-Apr–Oct) Oxford's most famous bookshop runs 1½-hour guided walking tours, including a literary tour at 2pm Tuesday and 11am Thursday, a tour devoted to 'Inklings' – an informal literary group whose membership included CS Lewis and JRR Tolkien – at 11.45am on Wednesday, and a Chapels, Churches and Cathedral tour (adult/child £9/8) at 2pm on Friday. Book ahead.

Bill Spectre's Ghost Trail WALKING TOURS
(☎07941 041811; www.ghosttrail.org; adult/child £6/3; ⌚6.30pm Fri & Sat) For a highly entertaining and informative look at Oxford's dark underbelly, join Victorian undertaker Bill Spectre on a tour of Oxford's most haunted sites. The tour lasts one hour 45 minutes and departs from Oxford Castle Unlocked.

City Sightseeing BUS TOURS
(www.citysightseeingoxford.com; adult/child £12.50/6; ⌚9.30am-6pm Apr-Oct) Hop-on/hop-off bus tours depart every 10 to 15 minutes from the bus and train stations or any of the 20 dedicated stops around town.

Sleeping

Oxford accommodation is generally overpriced and underwhelming, with suffocating floral patterns as the B&B norm. The following places stand out for their value for money and good taste. Book ahead between May and September. If you're stuck, you'll find a string of B&Bs along Iffley, Abingdon, Banbury and Headington roads.

TOP CHOICE **Malmaison** HOTEL £££
(☎01865-268400; www.malmaison-oxford.com; Oxford Castle; d/ste from £160/245; P@) Lock yourself up for the night in one of Oxford's most spectacular settings. This former Victorian prison has been converted into a sleek and slinky hotel, with plush interiors, sultry lighting, dark woods and giant beds. If you're planning a real treat, go for the Governor's Suite, complete with four-poster bed and mini-cinema. Look out for online promotions: you might bag a room for as little as £115.

Oxford Rooms STUDENT ROOMS ££
(www.oxfordrooms.co.uk; r from £40) Didn't quite make the cut for a place at Oxford? Well at least you can experience life inside the hallowed college grounds and breakfast in a grand college hall by staying overnight in one of their student rooms. Most rooms are singles and pretty functional, with basic furnishings, shared bathrooms and internet access, though there are some en suite, twin and family rooms available. Some rooms have old-world character and views over the college quad, while others are more modern but in a nearby annexe. There's limited availability during term time, but a good choice of rooms during university holidays.

Old Parsonage Hotel HOTEL £££
(☎01865-310210; www.oldparsonage-hotel.co.uk; 1 Banbury Rd; r from £138; P@) Wonderfully quirky and instantly memorable, the Old Parsonage is a small boutique hotel with just the right blend of old-world character, period charm and modern luxury. The 17th-century building oozes style, with a contemporary-art collection, artfully mismatched furniture and chic bedrooms with handmade beds and marble bathrooms. Oscar Wilde once made it his home. Ask for a room in the old building to see just how he might have lived.

Ethos Hotel HOTEL ££
(☎01865-245800; www.ethoshotels.co.uk; 59 Western Rd; d from £80; @) Hidden away off Abingdon Rd, this funky new hotel has bright, spacious rooms with bold, patterned wallpaper, enormous beds and marble bathrooms. You'll also get a minikitchen with a microwave, a breakfast basket and free wi-fi – all just 10 minutes' walk from the city centre. Some rooms open directly to the street, but with online deals for as little as £68, it's incredible value. To get here, cross Folly Bridge to Abingdon Rd and take the first right onto Western Rd.

Buttery Hotel HOTEL ££
(☎01865-811950; www.thebutteryhotel.co.uk; 11-12 Broad St; s/d from £55/95; @) Right in the heart of the city with views over the college grounds, the Buttery is Oxford's most central hotel. It's a modest enough place, but considering its location, it's a great deal, with spacious if innocuous modern rooms, decent bathrooms and the pick of the city's attractions on your doorstep.

Oxford YHA HOSTEL £
(☎01865-727275; www.yha.org.uk; 2a Botley Rd; dm/d from £18/46; @) Bright, well-kept, clean, and tidy, this is Oxford's best budget option, with simple but comfortable dorm accommodation, private rooms and loads of facilities, including a restaurant, library, garden, laundry

and a choice of lounges. All rooms are en suite and are bright and cheery, a far better option than some of the city's cheapest B&Bs.

Old Bank Hotel HOTEL £££
(☎01865-799599; www.oldbank-hotel.co.uk; 92 High St; r from £150; P @) Slap bang in the centre of Oxford, rooms here look over the college walls and spires into the very heart of the university. The rooms are sleek and spacious, all neutral colours and silky throws, but they lack a little soul. Downstairs there's a buzzing restaurant with brash modern art and a tumult of eager diners.

Burlington House B&B ££
(☎01865-513513; www.burlington-house.co.uk; 374 Banbury Rd, Summertown; s/d from £65/85; P @ wi-fi) Simple, elegant rooms decked out in restrained, classical style are available at this Victorian merchant house. The rooms are big, bright and uncluttered, with plenty of period character and immaculately kept bathrooms. The Burlington isn't central, but it has good public transport to town and is well worth the trip.

Central Backpackers HOSTEL £
(☎01865-242288; www.centralbackpackers.co.uk; 13 Park End St; dm £17-20; @) A good budget option right in the centre of town, this small hostel has basic, bright and simple rooms that sleep four to 12 people. There's a small but decent lounge with satellite TV, a rooftop terrace and free internet and luggage storage.

Eating

Oxford has plenty of choice when it comes to eating out, but unfortunately, the ubiquitous chain restaurants dominate the scene, especially along George St and around the pedestrianised square at the castle. Head to Walton St in Jericho, to Summertown, St Clements or up Cowley Rd for a quirkier selection of restaurants. Look out for local chain G&D's for excellent ice cream and cakes.

TOP CHOICE **Edamame** JAPANESE £
(www.edamame.co.uk; 15 Holywell St; mains £6-8; ⏲lunch Wed-Sun, dinner Thu-Sat) It may not be the place for a leisurely dinner thanks to its cramped quarters, but the queue out the door speaks volumes about the quality of the food here. This tiny Japanese joint is the best place in town for rice and noodle dishes, and the sushi (Thursday night only, £2.50 to £4) is divine. Arrive early and be prepared to wait – it's well worth it. Last orders at 8.30pm.

Trout MODERN BRITISH ££
(☎01865-510930; www.thetroutoxford.co.uk; 195 Godstow Rd, Wolvercote; mains £8-16) Possibly the prettiest location in Oxford, 2½ miles north of the city centre, this charming old-world pub has been a favourite haunt of town and gown for many years. Immortalised by Inspector Morse, it's generally crammed with happy diners enjoying the riverside garden and the extensive menu, though you can also just come for a quiet pint outside meal times. Book ahead.

Vaults CAFE £
(www.vaultsandgarden.com; Church of St Mary the Virgin; mains £3.50-5; ⏲10am-5pm) Set in a vaulted 14th-century Congregation House, this place serves a wholesome line of soups, salads, pastas and paellas with plenty of choice for vegetarians. It's one of the most beautiful lunch venues in Oxford, with a lovely garden overlooking Radcliffe Sq. Come early for lunch as it's a local favourite.

Manos GREEK £
(www.manosfoodbar.com; 105 Walton St; mains £6-8) For delicious home-cooked tastes of the Med, head for this Greek deli and restaurant where you'll find a great selection of dishes bursting with flavour. The ground floor has a cafe and deli, while downstairs has more style and comfort, with giant cushions surrounding low tables.

Door 74 MODERN BRITISH ££
(☎01865-203374; www.door74.co.uk; 74 Cowley Rd; mains £8-13; ⏲closed Mon & Sun dinner) This cosy little place woos its fans with a rich mix of British and Mediterranean flavours and friendly service. The menu is limited and the tables tightly packed, but the food is consistently good and combines classic ingredients with a modern twist. Book ahead as seating is limited.

Café Coco MEDITERRANEAN £
(www.cafe-coco.co.uk; 23 Cowley Rd; mains £6-10.50) Chilled out but always buzzing, this Cowley Rd institution is a hip hang-out, with classic posters on the walls and a bald plaster-cast clown in an ice bath. The food is vaguely Mediterranean and can be a bit hit-and-miss, but most come for the atmosphere.

Jericho Café MEDITERRANEAN ££
(www.thejerichocafe.co.uk; 112 Walton St; mains £7-12) Chill out and relax with the paper over a coffee and a slab of cake, or go for some

of the wholesome lunch and dinner specials, which encompass everything from sausages and mash to Lebanese lamb *kibbeh*. Plenty of hearty salads and veggie options.

Quod MODERN BRITISH ££
(www.quod.co.uk; 92 High St; mains £12-15) Bright, buzzing and decked out with modern art and beautiful people, Quid dishes up modern brasserie-style food to the masses. It's always bustling and at worst, will tempt you to chill by the bar with a cocktail while you wait. The two-course set lunch (£9.95) is great value.

Georgina's CAFE £
(Ave 3, Oxford Covered Market; mains £3-6; ⌚8.30am-5pm Mon-Sat, 10am-4pm Sun) Hidden up a scruffy staircase in the covered market and plastered with old cinema posters, this funky little cafe serves bulging salads, hearty soups and goodies such as goat-cheese quesadillas and scrumptious cakes.

Drinking

Oxford is blessed with some wonderful traditional pubs as well as a good selection of funky bars. Stroll along the towpaths to find a few riverside gems, or check out Cowley Rd for student haunts or George St for rowdy weekend revellers.

Turf Tavern TRADITIONAL PUB
(4 Bath Pl) Hidden away down a narrow alleyway, this tiny medieval pub is one of the town's best-loved and bills itself as 'an education in intoxication'. Home to real ales and student antics, it's always packed with a mix of students, professionals and the lucky tourists who manage to find it. One of of few pubs with plenty of outdoor seating.

Eagle & Child TRADITIONAL PUB
(49 St Giles) Affectionately known as the 'Bird & Baby', this atmospheric place dates from 1650 and is a hotchpotch of nooks and crannies. It was once the favourite haunt of Tolkien, CS Lewis and their literary friends and still attracts a mellow crowd.

Raoul's COCKTAIL BAR
(www.raoulsbar.co.uk; 32 Walton St; ⌚4pm-midnight) This trendy retro-look bar is one of Jericho's finest and is always busy. Famous for its perfectly mixed cocktails and funky music, it's populated by effortlessly cool customers trying hard not to spill their drinks as people squeeze by.

Kazbar BAR
(www.kazbar.co.uk; 25-27 Cowley Rd; ⌚4pm-midnight) This funky Moroccan-themed bar has giant windows, low lighting, warm colours and a cool vibe. It's buzzing most nights with hip young things sipping cocktails and filling up on the Spanish and North African tapas (£3 to £5).

Entertainment

Despite its large student population, Oxford's club scene is fairly limited, with several cattle-mart clubs in the centre of town and a lot of crowd-pleasing music. If you're a fan of classical music, however, you'll be spoilt for choice, with a host of excellent venues and regular concerts throughout the year. See www.dailyinfo.co.uk or www.musicatoxford.com for listings.

Creation Theatre THEATRE COMPANY
(www.creationtheatre.co.uk) Performing in a variety of nontraditional venues including city parks, the BMW plant and Oxford Castle, this theatre company produces highly original, mostly Shakespearean shows featuring plenty of magic and special effects. If you're in town when a performance is running, don't miss it.

O2 Academy LIVE VENUE
(www.o2academy.co.uk; 190 Cowley Rd) Oxford's best club and live-music venue had a recent makeover and now hosts everything from big-name DJs and international touring artists to indie bands, hard rock and funk nights across three performance spaces. Expect a mixed crowd of students, professionals and dusty academics.

Oxford Playhouse THEATRE
(www.oxfordplayhouse.com; Beaumont St) The city's main stage for quality drama also hosts an impressive selection of touring theatre, music and dance, while the Burton Taylor Studio has quirky student productions.

Regal PERFORMANCE SPACE
(www.the-regal.com; 300 Cowley Rd; ⌚Thu-Sat) Set in a restored art deco building, the regal hosts an eclectic mix of dance classes, live music, headline DJs, club nights and theatre performances.

Information

Emergency

Police (☎0845 8 505 505; St Aldate's)

Internet Access

C-Works (1st fl, New Bailey House, New Inn Hall St; per 50min £1; ⌚9am-9pm Mon-Sat, to 7pm Sun)

Central Library (Westgate; ⏲9am-7pm Mon-Thu, to 5.30pm Fri & Sat) Free internet access.

Links (33 High St; per 45min £1; ⏲10am-7pm Mon-Sat, 11am-6pm Sun)

Internet Resources

Daily Info (www.dailyinfo.co.uk) Daily listings for events, gigs, performances, accommodation and jobs.

Oxford City (www.oxfordcity.co.uk) Accommodation and restaurant listings as well as entertainment, activities and shopping.

Oxford Online (www.visitoxford.org) Oxford's official tourism website.

Medical Services

John Radcliffe Hospital (☎01865-741166; Headley Way, Headington) Three miles east of the city centre in Headington.

Money

You'll find that every major bank and ATM is handily represented on or close to Cornmarket St.

Post

Post office (102 St Aldate's; ⏲9am-5.30pm Mon-Sat)

Tourist Information

Tourist office (☎01865-252200; www.visitoxford.org; 15-16 Broad St; ⏲9.30am-5pm Mon-Sat, 10am-4pm Sun)

Getting There & Away

Bus

Oxford's main bus/coach station is at Gloucester Green. Services to London (£16 return) run up to every 15 minutes, day and night, and take about 90 minutes.

Airline (www.oxfordbus.co.uk) Runs to Heathrow (£20, 90 minutes) half-hourly from 4am to 10pm and at midnight and 2am, and Gatwick (£26, two hours) hourly 5.15am to 8.15pm and every two hours from 10pm to 4am.

National Express (www.nationalexpress.com) Runs buses to Birmingham, Bath and Bristol, but all are easier to reach by train.

Stagecoach (www.stagecoachbus.com) Serves most of the small towns in Oxfordshire and runs the X5 service to Cambridge (£10.90, 3½ hours) roughly every half-hour.

Car

Driving and parking in Oxford is a nightmare. Use the five Park & Ride car parks on major routes leading into town. Parking is free and buses (10 to 15 minutes, every 10 minutes) cost £2.50.

Train

Oxford's train station is conveniently placed at the western end of Park End St. There are half-hourly services to London Paddington (£19.90, one hour) and roughly hourly trains to Birmingham (£27, 1¼ hours). Hourly services also run to Bath (£22.50, 1¼ hours) and Bristol (£24.50, 1½ hours), but require a change at Didcot Parkway.

Getting Around

Bicycle

Cyclo Analysts (☎01865-424444; 150 Cowley Rd; per day/week £17/54) Rents hybrid bikes.

Bus

Buses 1 and 5 go to Cowley Rd from St Aldate's, 2 and 7 go along Banbury Rd from Magdalen St, and 16 and 35 run along Abingdon Rd from St Aldate's.

A multi-operator Plus Pass (per day/week £6/19) allows unlimited travel on Oxford's bus system.

Taxi

There are taxi ranks at the train station and bus station, as well as on St Giles and at Carfax. Be prepared to join a long queue after closing time. For a green alternative, call **Oxon Carts** (☎07747 024600; info@oxoncarts.com), a pedicab service.

Woodstock

POP 2924

The charming village of Woodstock is full of picturesque creeper-clad cottages, elegant town houses, buckled roofs, art galleries and antique shops. It's an understandably popular spot, conveniently close to Oxford, yet a quintessential rural retreat. The big draw here is Blenheim Palace, the opulent country pile of the Churchill family, but the village itself is a gracious and tranquil spot even on busy summer days.

Sights

The hub of the village is the imposing **town hall**, built at the Duke of Marlborough's expense in 1766. Nearby, the **Church of St Mary Magdalene** had a 19th-century makeover but retains its Norman doorway, early English windows and a musical clock.

Opposite the church, the **Oxfordshire Museum** (www.tomocc.org.uk; Park St; admission free; ⏲10am-5pm Tue-Sat, 2-5pm Sun) has displays on local history, art, archaeology and wildlife. It also houses the **tourist office** (☎01993-813276).

Blenheim Palace PALACE
(www.blenheimpalace.com; adult/child £18/10, park & garden only £10.30/5; ⏲10.30am-5.30pm

daily mid-Feb–Oct, Wed-Sun Nov–mid-Dec) One of the country's greatest stately homes, Blenheim Palace is a monumental baroque fantasy designed by Sir John Vanbrugh and Nicholas Hawksmoor between 1705 and 1722. The land and funds to build the house were granted to John Churchill, Duke of Marlborough, by a grateful Queen Anne after his decisive victory at the 1704 Battle of Blenheim. Now a Unesco World Heritage Site, Blenheim (pronounced *blen*-num) is home to the 11th duke and duchess.

Inside, the house is stuffed with statues, tapestries, ostentatious furniture and giant oil paintings in elaborate gilt frames. Highlights include the **Great Hall**, a vast space topped by 20m-high ceilings adorned with images of the first duke in battle; the opulent **Saloon**, the grandest and most important public room; the three **state rooms**, with their plush decor and priceless china cabinets; and the magnificent **Long Library**, which is 55m in length.

From the library, you can access the **Churchill Exhibition**, which is dedicated to the life, work and writings of Sir Winston, who was born at Blenheim in 1874. For an insight into life below stairs, the **Untold Story** exhibition explores the family's history through the eyes of the household staff.

If the crowds in the house become too oppressive, retire to the lavish gardens and vast parklands, parts of which were landscaped by Lancelot 'Capability' Brown. To the front, an artificial lake sports a beautiful bridge by Vanbrugh, and a minitrain is needed to take visitors to a maze, adventure playground and butterfly house. For a quieter and longer stroll, glorious walks lead to an arboretum, cascade and temple.

Sleeping & Eating

Woodstock has a good choice of accommodation, but it's not cheap. Luxurious, old-world hotels are the thing here, so plan a day trip from Oxford if you're travelling on a budget.

Kings Arms Hotel HOTEL £££
(01993-813636; www.kings-hotel-woodstock.co.uk; 19 Market St; s/d from £75/140; @) Set in a lovely Georgian town house, the rooms here are sleek and stylish, with warm woods, soft, neutral tones and black-and-white images on the walls. Downstairs, there's a bright bistro serving modern British fare (mains £11 to £15) and a good bar with leather sofas and cheaper snacks.

Hampers DELI & CAFE £
(31-33 Oxford St; snacks £1.50-5; lunch) On a fine day you couldn't do better than a picnic in the grounds of the palace, and this deli provides all the essential ingredients: fine cheeses, olives, cold meats, Cotswold smoked salmon and delicious cakes. If it's raining, pop in to the cafe and feast on the delicious soups, sandwiches and cakes instead.

Getting There & Around

Stagecoach bus S3 runs every half-hour (hourly on Sunday) from George St in Oxford. **Cotswold Roaming** (01865-308300; www.cotswold-roaming.co.uk) offers a Cotswolds/Blenheim combination tour (adult £47.50), with a morning at Blenheim and a half-day Cotswolds tour in the afternoon. The price includes admission to the palace.

Henley-on-Thames

POP 10,646

A conservative but well-heeled kind of place, Henley is an attractive town set on the banks of the river, studded with elegant stone houses, a few Tudor relics and a host of chichi shops. The town bursts into action in July when it becomes the location for the Henley Royal Regatta, a world-famous boat race and weeklong posh picnic.

The **tourist office** (01491-578034; www.visithenley-on-thames.com; 10am-5pm Mon-Sat) is in the town hall.

Sights

Walking around Henley, you'll come across a wealth of historic buildings, with many Georgian gems lining Hart St, the main drag. You'll also find the imposing **town hall** here, and the 13th-century **St Mary's Church**, with its 16th-century tower topped by four octagonal turrets.

River & Rowing Museum MUSEUM
(www.rrm.co.uk; Mill Meadows; adult/child £7.50/5.50; 10am-5.30pm;) Life in Henley has always focused on the river, and this impressive museum takes a look at the town's relationship with the Thames, the history of rowing, and the wildlife and commerce supported by the river. Hands-on activities and interactive displays make it a good spot for children, and the *Wind in the Willows* exhibition brings Kenneth Grahame's stories of Ratty, Mole, Badger and Toad to life.

Festivals & Events

Henley Royal Regatta ROWING FESTIVAL

(www.hrr.co.uk) The first ever Oxford and Cambridge boat race was held in Henley in 1839, and ever since, the cream of English society has descended on this small town each year for a celebration of boating, backslapping and the beau monde.

The five-day Henley Royal Regatta has grown into a major fixture in the social calendar of the upwardly mobile and is a massive corporate entertainment opportunity. These days, hanging out on the lawn swilling champagne and looking rich and beautiful is the main event, and although rowers of the highest calibre compete, most spectators appear to take little interest in what's happening on the water.

The regatta is held in the first week of July, but you'll need contacts in the rowing or corporate worlds to get tickets in the stewards' enclosure. Mere mortals should head for the public enclosure (tickets £12 to £15), where you can lay out your gourmet picnic and hobnob with the best of them.

Henley Festival ARTS FESTIVAL

(www.henley-festival.co.uk) In the week following the regatta, the town continues its celebrations with the Henley Festival, a vibrant black-tie affair that features everything from big-name international stars to quirky, alternative acts – anything from opera to rock, jazz, comedy and swing. The main events take place on a floating stage on the Thames, and tickets vary in price from £80 for a seat in the grandstand to £35 for a space in the enclosure.

Sleeping & Eating

Henley has a good choice of accommodation, especially at the top end, but if you're planning to visit during either festival, book well in advance.

TOP CHOICE **Hotel du Vin** HOTEL £££

(☎01491-848400; www.hotelduvin.com; New St; d from £145; P @ ☎) Set in the former Brakspears Brewery, this upmarket hotel chain scores high for its blend of industrial chic and top-of-the-line designer sophistication. The spacious rooms and opulent suites are slick and stylish and are matched by a walk-in humidor, incredible billiards rooms, huge wine cellar and a popular bistro (mains £13 to £21).

Old School House B&B ££

(☎01491-573929; www.oldschoolhousehenley.co.uk; 42 Hart St; d £85; P) This small, quiet guest house in the town centre is a 19th-century schoolhouse in a walled garden, with a choice of two pretty guest rooms decked out in simple but comfortable style. Exposed timber beams and rustic furniture give it plenty of character, and the central location can't be beat at this price.

Green Olive GREEK £

(www.green-olive.co.uk; 28 Market Pl; mezedhes £4-10) A popular Henley haunt, Green Olive dishes up piled plates of traditional *mezedhes* (appetisers) in a bright and airy building with a lovely garden to the rear. Choose from over 50 dishes, including *spanakopita* (spinach pie), souvlaki, mussels with feta, *stifadho* (meat cooked with onions in a tomato puree) and *mousakas* (baked layers of eggplant or zucchini, minced meat and potatoes topped with cheese sauce).

Chez Gerard Brasserie FRENCH ££

(www.brasseriegerard.co.uk; 40 Hart St; mains £11-17) This stalwart chain of French brasseries has a chilled atmosphere, wooden floors, modern art on the walls and a selection of mismatched furniture. The menu features French classics as well as Moroccan tagines, fish and grills.

Getting There & Around

There are no direct train or bus services between Henley and Oxford. Trains to London Paddington take about one hour (£12.80, hourly).

If you fancy seeing the local area from the river, **Hobbs & Son** (☎01491-572035; www.hobbs-of-henley.com) runs hour-long afternoon river trips from April to September (adult/child £7.75/5) and hires five-seater rowing boats (£20 per hour) and four-seater motorboats (£25 per hour).

THE COTSWOLDS

Glorious honey-coloured villages riddled with beautiful, old mansions, thatched cottages, atmospheric churches and rickety almshouses draw crowds of tourists to the Cotswolds. The booming medieval wool trade brought the area its wealth and left it with such a glut of beautiful buildings that its place in history is secured for evermore. If you've ever craved exposed beams, dreamed of falling asleep under English-rose wallpaper or lusted after a cream tea in the mid afternoon, there's no finer place to fulfil your fantasies.

This is prime tourist territory, however, and the most popular villages can be besieged by tourists and traffic in summer. Plan to visit the main centres early in the morning or late in the evening, focus your attention on the south or take to the hills on foot or by bike to avoid the worst of the crowds. Better still, just leave the crowds behind and meander down deserted country lanes and bridleways until you discover your very own bucolic village seemingly undisturbed since medieval times.

Activities

The gentle hills of the Cotswolds are perfect for walking, cycling and riding. The 102-mile **Cotswold Way** (www.nationaltrail.co.uk/cotswold) gives walkers a wonderful overview of the area. The route meanders from Chipping Campden to Bath, with no major climbs or difficult stretches, and is easily accessible from many points en route if you fancy tackling a shorter section. Ask at local tourist offices for details of day hikes, or pick up a copy of one of the many walking guides to the region.

Away from the main roads, the winding lanes of the Cotswolds make fantastic cycling territory, with little traffic, glorious views and gentle gradients. Again, the local tourist offices are invaluable in helping to plot a route.

Information

For information on attractions, accommodation and events:

Cotswolds (www.the-cotswolds.org)

Cotswolds Tourism (www.cotswolds.com)

Oxfordshire Cotswolds (www.oxfordshirecotswolds.org)

Getting Around

Public transport through the Cotswolds is fairly limited, with bus services running to and from major hubs only, and train services just skimming the northern and southern borders. However, with a little careful planning and patience, you can see all the highlights. Tourist offices stock useful *Explore the Cotswolds* brochures with bus and rail summaries.

For the most flexibility, and the option of getting off the beaten track, your own car is unbeatable; car hire can be arranged in most major centres.

Alternatively, **Cotswold Roaming** (☎01865-308300; www.cotswold-roaming.co.uk) runs guided bus tours from Oxford between April and October. Half-day tours of the Cotswolds (£25) include Minster Lovell, Burford and Bibury, while full-day tours of the North Cotswolds (£40) feature Chipping Campden and Stow-on-the-Wold.

The Cotswolds

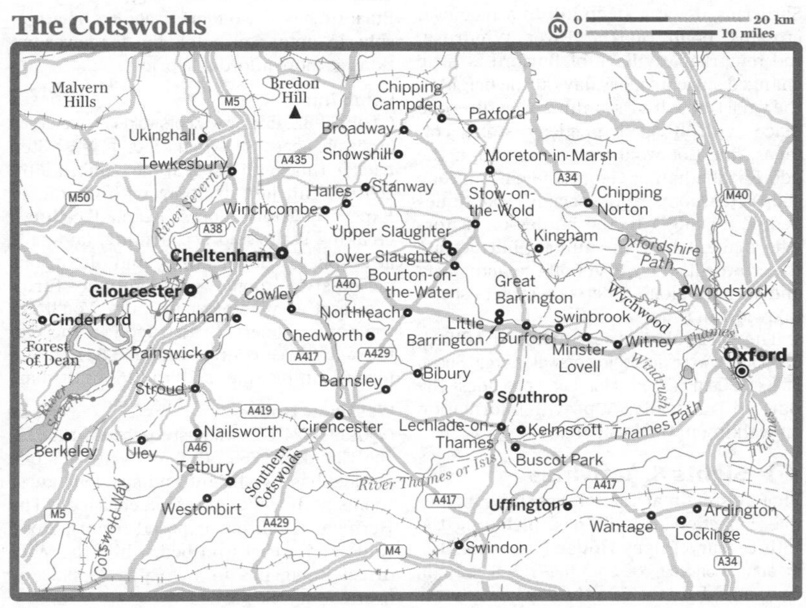

Minster Lovell

POP 1348

Set on a gentle slope leading down to the meandering River Windrush, Minster Lovell is a gorgeous village with a cluster of stone cottages nestled beside an ancient pub and riverside mill. One of William Morris' favourite spots, the village has changed little since medieval times and is a glorious place for an afternoon pit stop, quiet overnight retreat or start to a valley walk.

The main sight here is the ruins of **Minster Lovell Hall**, the 15th-century manor-house that was home to Viscount Francis Lovell. Lovell fought with Richard III at the Battle of Bosworth in 1485 and joined Lambert Simnel's failed rebellion after the king's defeat and death. Lovell's mysterious disappearance was never explained, and when a skeleton was discovered inside a secret vault in the house in 1708, it was assumed he had died while in hiding.

Swanbrook coaches stop here on the Oxford to Cheltenham run. Stagecoach bus 233 en route to Burford stops here Monday to Saturday (10 minutes each way, 10 daily).

Burford

POP 1340

Slithering down a steep hill to a medieval crossing point on the River Windrush, the remarkable village of Burford is little changed since its glory days at the height of the wool trade. It's a stunningly picturesque place with higgledy-piggledy stone cottages, fine Cotswold town houses and the odd Elizabethan or Georgian gem. Antique shops, tearooms and specialist boutiques peddle nostalgia to the hordes of visitors who make it here in summer, but despite the crowds it's easy to get off the main drag and wander along quiet side streets seemingly lost in time.

The helpful **tourist office** (☎01993-823558; www.oxfordshirecotswolds.org; Sheep St; ⏲9.30am-5.30pm Mon-Sat) provides the Burford Trail leaflet (50p), with information on walking in the local area.

Sights & Activities

Burford's main attraction lies in its incredible collection of buildings, including the 16th-century **Tolsey House** (Toll House; High St; admission free; ⏲2-5pm Tue-Fri & Sun, 11am-5pm Sat), where the wealthy wool merchants held their meetings. This quaint building perches on sturdy pillars and now houses a small museum on Burford's history.

Just off the High St, you'll find the town's 14th-century **almshouses** and the gorgeous **Church of St John the Baptist**. The Norman tower here is topped by a 15th-century steeple, and inside you'll find a fine fan-vaulted ceiling and medieval screens dividing the chapels.

If you fancy getting away from the crowds, it's worth the effort to walk east along the picturesque river path to the untouched and rarely visited village of **Swinbrook** (3 miles), where the beautiful church has some remarkable tombs.

Sleeping & Eating

Burford has a wonderful choice of atmospheric, upmarket hotels but far fewer options at more affordable prices.

Lamb Inn HOTEL **£££**
(☎01993-823155; www.cotswold-inns-hotels.co.uk/lamb; Sheep St; r from £150; P@) Step back in time with a stay at the Lamb, a 15th-century inn just dripping with character. Expect flagstone floors, beamed ceilings, creaking stairs and a charming, laid-back atmosphere downstairs, and luxurious period-style rooms with antique furniture and cosy comfort upstairs. You'll get top-notch modern British food in the restaurant (three-course dinner, £35) or less formal dining (mains £9 to £16) in the bar.

Westview House B&B **££**
(☎01993-824723;www.westview-house.co.uk;151 The Hill; s/d from £60/80) This lovely old stone cottage has two bright and spacious guest rooms with plenty of period character. The Heritage Room has exposed beams, stone walls and a cast-iron bed, while the Windrush Room has its own private balcony overlooking the garden.

A COTTAGE OF YOUR OWN

If you'd like to rent your own Cotswold cottage, try these websites:

Campden Cottages (www.campdencottages.co.uk)

Cotswold Retreats (www.cotswoldretreats.co.uk)

Manor Cottages (www.manorcottages.co.uk)

Angel MODERN BRITISH ££
(☎01993-822714; www.theangelatburford.co.uk; 14 Witney St; mains £14.50-18) Set in a lovely 16th-century coaching inn, this atmospheric brasserie serves up an innovative menu of modern British and European food. Dine in by roaring fires in winter, or eat alfresco in the lovely walled garden in warmer weather.

Getting There & Away

From Oxford, Swanbrook runs three buses a day (one on Sunday) to Burford (45 minutes) and on to Cheltenham.

Chipping Norton

POP 5972

The sleepy but attractive town of Chipping Norton – or 'Chippy' as it is locally known – is somewhat spoiled by the traffic running along the main street, but it has plenty of quiet side streets to wander and none of the Cotswold crowds. Handsome Georgian buildings, stone cottages and old coaching inns cluster around the market square, and on Church St you'll find a row of beautiful honey-coloured **almshouses** built in the 17th century. Further on is the secluded **Church of St Mary**, a classic example of the Cotswold wool churches, with a magnificent 15th-century Perpendicular nave and clerestory.

Chippy's most enduring landmark, however, is the arresting **Bliss Mill** (now converted to apartments) on the outskirts of town. This monument to the industrial architecture of the 19th century is more like a stately home than a factory, topped by a domed tower and chimney stack of the Tuscan order.

For lunch or dinner your best bet is **Wild Thyme** (☎01608-645060; www.wildthymerestaurant.co.uk; 10 New St; mains £9-19, s/d from £40/60; ⏲Tue-Sat), a simple but stylish restaurant-with-rooms. The menu is modern British and the food is top-notch, and the three upstairs rooms are pretty and excellent value.

Alternatively, make your way 4 miles southwest of town to the pretty village of Kingham, where two fine gastropubs offer stylish rooms and sublime food.

Stagecoach bus S3 runs between Chippy and Oxford (55 minutes) roughly every half-hour.

Moreton-in-Marsh

POP 3198

Home to some beautiful buildings but utterly ruined by through traffic, Moreton-in-Marsh is a major road hub and useful for its transport links.

Pulham's Coaches (www.pulhamscoaches.com) runs seven services between Moreton and Cheltenham (one hour, Monday to Saturday) via Stow-on-the-Wold (15 minutes). Two Sunday services run from May to September only.

There are trains roughly every two hours to Moreton from London Paddington (£26.90, one hour 40 minutes) via Oxford (£7.90, 40 minutes) and on to Worcester (£9.90, one hour) and Hereford (£15.20, one hour 45 minutes).

DON'T MISS

A STEP BACK IN TIME

Squirreled away in the gorgeous village of Great Tew is a real gem of a 16th-century pub. Original flagstone floors, open fireplaces and low beams give the **Falkland Arms** (☎01608-683653; www.falklandarms.org.uk; Great Tew; r £85-115) oodles of medieval charm. The pub sits on the village green and serves a fine collection of real ales from ancient hand pumps, as well as ciders, perries and malt whiskies. There are boxes of snuff and clay pipes behind the bar, beams hung with a dusty collection of beer mugs and jugs, benches out front and a small garden at the rear. You can also grab a decent meal (mains £9 to £17) or stay in one of the five guest rooms that come complete with four-poster or cast-iron beds and period style. On Sunday nights the pub is packed for its regular folk music sessions.

If you get the chance take a walk around the village, the stone cottages, thatched roofs and winding lanes remain virtually untouched and rival anything the rest of the Cotswolds has to offer. It simply doesn't get much more authentic than this.

Great Tew is about 4 miles east of Chipping Norton.

Chipping Campden

POP 2206

An unspoiled gem in an area full of achingly pretty villages, Chipping Campden is a glorious reminder of life in the Cotswolds in medieval times. The graceful curving main street is flanked by a wonderful array of wayward stone cottages, fine terraced houses, ancient inns and historic homes, liberally sprinkled with chichi boutiques and upmarket shops. Despite its obvious allure, the town remains relatively unspoiled by tourist crowds and is a wonderful place to visit.

Pop into the helpful **tourist office** (01386-841206; www.chippingcampdenonline.org; High St; 9.30am-5pm) to pick up a town trail guide (£1) for information on the most historic buildings and to get you off the main drag and down some of the gorgeous back streets. If you are visiting on a Tuesday between July and September, it is well worth joining a **guided tour** at 2.30pm (suggested donation £3) run by the Cotswold Wardens.

Sights & Activities

The most obvious sight is the wonderful 17th-century **Market Hall**, with multiple gables and an elaborate timber roof. Further on, at the western end of the High St, is the 15th-century **St James'**, one of the Cotswolds' great wool churches. Built in the Perpendicular style, it has a magnificent tower and some graceful 17th-century monuments. Nearby on Church St is a remarkable row of **almshouses** dating from the 17th century, and the Jacobean lodges and gateways of the now-ruined Campden House.

The surviving **Court Barn** (01386-841951; www.courtbarn.org.uk; Church St; adult/child £3.75/free; 10.30am-5.30pm Tue-Sat, 11.30am-5.30pm Sun) is now a craft and design museum featuring work from the Arts and Crafts Movement. CR Ashbee and the Guild of Handicrafts moved to Chipping Campden in 1902, and a collection of their work is showcased here.

About 4 miles northeast of Chipping Campden, **Hidcote Manor Garden** (NT; www.nationaltrust.org.uk; Hidcote Bartrim; adult/child £8.60/4.30; 10am-6pm) is one of the finest examples of Arts and Crafts landscaping in Britain.

Sleeping & Eating

Cotswold House Hotel HOTEL £££
(01386-840330; www.cotswoldhouse.com; The Square; r £140-650; P @) If you're after a spot of luxury, look no further than this chic Regency town house turned boutique hotel. Bespoke furniture, massive beds, Frette linens, cashmere throws, private gardens and hot tubs are the norm here. You can indulge in some treatments at the hotel spa, dine in luxuriant style at Juliana's (three-course set dinner, £49.50) or take a more informal approach at Hick's Brasserie (mains £10 to £19), a slick operation with an ambitious menu.

Chance B&B ££
(01386-849079; www.the-chance.co.uk; 1 Aston Rd; d £75; P) Two pretty rooms with floral bedspreads, fresh flowers and a cast-iron fireplace make this B&B a good choice. The owners are particularly helpful, and little extras such as bathrobes and hot-water bottles are waiting in the rooms.

Eight Bells PUB ££
(01386-840371; www.eightbellsinn.co.uk; Church St; mains £13-17) Dripping with old-world character and charm, but also decidedly modern, this 14th-century inn serves real ales and a fine selection of modern British and Continental dishes in rustic settings.

Getting There & Around

Between them, buses 21 and 22 run almost hourly to Stratford-upon-Avon or Moreton-in-Marsh. Bus 21 also stops in Broadway. There are no Sunday services.

To catch a real glimpse of the countryside, try hiring a bike from **Cotswold Country Cycles** (01386-438706; www.cotswoldcountrycycles.com; Longlands Farm Cottage; per day £15) and discover the quiet lanes and gorgeous villages around town.

Broadway

POP 2496

This absurdly pretty village has inspired writers, artists and composers in times past with its graceful, golden-hued cottages set at the foot of a steep escarpment. It's a quintessentially English place pitted with antique shops, tearooms and art galleries and is justifiably popular in the summer months. But take the time to wander away from the main street and you'll be rewarded with quiet back roads lined with stunning cottages, flower-filled gardens and picturesque churches.

Next door to the tourist office is the **Gordon Russell Museum** (www.gordonrussellmuseum.org; adult/child £3.50/1; ⏲11am-5pm Tue-Sun), celebrating the work of the renowned furniture designer. Set in his restored workshop, it features samples of his furniture, metalwork and glassware. Beyond the charm of the village itself, there are few other specific attractions.

If you're feeling energetic, the lovely, 12th-century **Church of St Eadburgha** is a signposted 1-mile walk from town. Near here, a more challenging path leads uphill for 2 miles to **Broadway Tower** (www.broadwaytower.co.uk; adult/child £4/2.50; ⏲10.30am-5pm), a crenulated, 18th-century Gothic folly on the crest of the escarpment. It has a small William Morris exhibition on one floor and stunning views from the top.

Broadway is littered with chintzy B&Bs, but for something more modern, try **Windrush** (☎01386-853577; www.broadway-windrush.co.uk; Station Rd; d from £90; P 📶), a stunning little B&B with newly refurbished rooms done in great style. Neutral colour schemes, bold patterned wallpapers and plush fabrics give it a real edge over the competition. Alternatively, try sleek and stylish **Russells** (☎01386-853555; www.russellsofbroadway.co.uk; 20 High St; d £95-225), where you'll find a range of slick, modern rooms with simple design and lots of little luxuries. This is also the town's best bet for food, and the award-winning modern British fare (mains £12 to £18) here is well worth a detour if you're in the area. Almost next door is the less formal **Swan** (www.theswanbroadway.co.uk; 2 The Green; mains £9-16), another swish joint with contemporary decor, wooden floors, leather seats and a tempting, modern menu.

Information

Tourist office (☎01386-852937; www.beautifulbroadway.com; Russell Sq; ⏲10am-5pm Mon-Sat, 2-5pm Sun) Just off the High St.

Getting There & Away

Bus 21 goes to Moreton-in-Marsh, Chipping Campden and Stratford (50 minutes, four daily Monday to Saturday). Bus 606 goes to Cheltenham (50 minutes, four daily Monday to Saturday).

Winchcombe

POP 4379

Winchcombe is a sleepy Cotswold town, very much a working, living place, with butchers, bakers and small independent shops giving it a lived-in, authentic feel. It was capital of the Saxon kingdom of Mercia and one of the most important towns in the Cotswolds until the Middle Ages, and today the remnants of its illustrious past can still be seen. Winchcombe is also blessed with good accommodation and fine-dining choices, making it a great base for exploring the area.

The helpful **tourist office** (☎01242-602925; www.visitcotswoldsandsevernvale.gov.uk; High St; ⏲10am-5pm Mon-Sat, 10am-4pm Sun) can help plan an itinerary.

Sights & Activities

Just wander around the town to take in its charms, but don't miss the picturesque cottages on **Vineyard St** and **Dents Tce** and look out for the fine gargoyles that adorn the lovely **St Peter's Church**.

THROW AWAY YOUR GUIDEBOOK!

As wonderful as the Cotswolds villages may be, in the summer months they can be a nightmare of camera-wielding crowds, slow-moving pensioners and chaotic coach parking. However, most tourists stick to a well-trodden path, so it's easy to get away from the crowds and discover the rarely visited villages lurking in the hills. Stick to the B-roads and visit places like the **Slaughters** and **Guiting Power** near Bourton-on-the-Water; **Broadwell**, **Maugersbury**, **Adlestrop** and the **Swells** near Stow; **Sheepscombe** and **Slad** near Painswick; **Blockley** near Chipping Campden; **Great Tew** near Chipping Norton; **Taynton**, **Sherborne** and the **Barringtons** near Burford; **Ampney St Mary** and **Ampney Crucis** near Cirencester; or **Coln St Aldwyns** and **Hatherop** near Bibury. Better still, see the region on foot or by bike and just meander at your own pace, or join a walking tour with **Cotswold Walking Holidays** (www.cotswoldwalks.com) or a bike tour with **Cotswold Country Cycles** (www.cotswoldcountrycycles.com).

Sudeley Castle CASTLE
(www.sudeleycastle.co.uk; adult/child £7.20/4.20; ⌚10.30am-5pm) The town's main attraction, this magnificent castle was once a favoured retreat of Tudor and Stuart monarchs. The house is still used as a family home, and much of the interior is off limits to visitors, but you can get a glimpse of its grand proportions while visiting the exhibitions of costumes, memorabilia and paintings and the surrounding gardens. If you want an insight into real life in the castle, join one of the 'Connoisseur Tours' (£12, Tuesday, Wednesday and Thursday at 11am, 1pm and 3pm).

Belas Knap BURIAL CHAMBER
If you're feeling energetic, there's easy access to the Cotswold Way from Winchcombe, and the 2½-mile hike to Belas Knap is one of the most scenic short walks in the region. Five-thousand-year-old Belas Knap is the best-preserved Neolithic burial chamber in the country. Visitors are not allowed inside, but the views down to Sudeley Castle and across the surrounding countryside are breathtaking.

Hailes Abbey RUINS
(EH; www.english-heritage.org.uk; adult/child £4/2; ⌚10am-5pm) Just outside the town are the evocative ruins of this Cistercian Abbey, once one of the country's main pilgrimage centres.

Sleeping & Eating

White Hart Inn HOTEL ££
(☎01242-602359; www.wineandsausage.co.uk; r £40-115) An excellent option in the centre of town. Choose the cheaper 'rambler' rooms, with shared bathrooms, or go for more luxury in a superior room. You'll also get pub staples in the bar (mains £7 to £9) and modern British fare in the 'wine and sausage' restaurant (mains £9 to £17).

5 North St MODERN EUROPEAN £££
(☎01242-604566; 5 North St; 2-/3-course lunch £21.50/25.50, 3-course dinner £31-46; ⌚lunch Wed-Sun, dinner Tue-Sat) The top spot to eat for miles around, this Michelin-starred restaurant has no airs and graces, just beautifully prepared food in down-to-earth surroundings. Deep-red walls, wooden tables and friendly service make it a very unpretentious place, but the food is thoroughly ambitious with a keen mix of British ingredients and French flair.

Getting There & Away

Bus 606 runs from Broadway (65 minutes, four daily Monday to Saturday) to Cheltenham via Winchcombe.

Stow-on-the-Wold

POP 2794

A popular stop on a tour of the Cotswolds, Stow is anchored by a large market square surrounded by handsome buildings and steep-walled alleyways, originally used to funnel the sheep into the fair. The town has long held a strategic place in Cotswold history, standing as it does on the Roman Fosse Way and at the junction of six roads. Today, it's littered with antique shops, boutiques, tearooms and delis, and thronging with people from passing coach tours. On a quiet day, it's a wonderful place, but all a little artificial if you're looking for true Cotswold charm.

Sleeping & Eating

Mole End B&B ££
(☎01451-870348; www.moleendstow.co.uk; Moreton Rd; s/d from £55/80; P@) This charming and immaculately kept B&B on the outskirts of town is a real gem. There are three stunning rooms with acres of space, huge beds and a whiff of refined French styling. There's a large garden with bucolic views, as well as great breakfasts and amiable hosts.

Number 9 B&B ££
(☎01451-870333; www.number-nine.info; 9 Park St; s/d from £45/65; wifi) Centrally located and wonderfully atmospheric, this beautiful B&B is all sloping floors and exposed beams. The three rooms are cosy but spacious and have brand-new bathrooms and subtle decor.

Stow-on-the-Wold YHA HOSTEL £
(☎0845 371 9540; www.yha.org.uk; The Square; dm £18; P@family) Slap bang on the market square, this hostel is in a wonderful 16th-century town house and has small dorms, a children's play area and a warm welcome for families.

Old Butchers MODERN EUROPEAN ££
(☎01451-831700; www.theoldbutchers.com; 7 Park St; mains £13-18) Simple, smart and sophisticated, this is Stow's top spot for dining, serving robust, local ingredients whipped up into sublime dishes. For all its fanfare, there's little pretension here, just fine modern British cuisine with more than a hint of Continental European influence thrown in.

Getting There & Away

Bus 855 links Stow with Moreton, Bourton, Northleach and Cirencester (eight daily Monday to Saturday). Bus 801 runs to Cheltenham, Moreton and Bourton (four daily Monday to Friday, nine on Saturday).

The nearest train stations are 4 miles away at Kingham and Moreton-in-Marsh.

Cirencester

POP 18,324

Refreshingly unpretentious, with narrow, winding streets and graceful town houses, charming Cirencester is an affluent, elegant kind of place. The lovely market square is surrounded by wonderful 18th-century and Victorian architecture, and the nearby streets showcase a harmonious medley of buildings from various eras.

Under the Romans, Cirencester was second only to London in terms of size and importance and, although little of this period remains, you can still see the grassed-over ruins of one of the largest amphitheatres in the country. The medieval wool trade was also good to the town, with wealthy merchants funding the building of a superb church.

The **tourist office** (☎01285-654180; www.cotswold.gov.uk; Park St; ⏲10am-5pm Mon-Sat, 2-5pm Sun) is in the museum and has a leaflet detailing a guided walk around the town and its historic buildings.

Sights & Activities

Church of St John the Baptist CHURCH
(suggested donation £3; ⏲10am-5pm) Standing elegantly on the Market Sq, the cathedral-like St John's is one of England's largest parish churches. An outstanding Perpendicular-style tower with wild flying buttresses dominates the exterior, but it is the majestic three-storey south porch that is the real highlight. Built as an office by late 15th-century abbots, it subsequently became the medieval town hall.

Soaring arches, magnificent fan vaulting and a Tudor nave adorn the light-filled interior, where you'll also find a 15th-century painted stone pulpit and memorial brasses recording the matrimonial histories of important wool merchants. The east window contains fine medieval stained glass, and a wall safe displays the **Boleyn Cup**, made for Anne Boleyn, second wife of Henry VIII, in 1535.

Corinium Museum MUSEUM
(www.cotswold.gov.uk/go/museum; Park St; adult/child £4.50/2.25; ⏲10am-5pm Mon-Sat, 2-5pm Sun) Modern design, innovative displays and computer reconstructions bring one of Britain's largest collections of Roman artefacts to life at the Corinium Museum. You can dress as a Roman soldier, meet an Anglo-Saxon princess and discover what Cirencester was like during its heyday as a wealthy medieval wool town. Highlights of the Roman collection include the beautiful Hunting Dogs and Four Seasons floor mosaics, and a reconstructed Roman kitchen and butcher's shop.

Roman Amphitheatre AMPHITHEATRE
(Cotswold Ave) The grassed-over remains of one of Britain's largest amphitheatres are worth a visit for their sheer scale.

Sleeping & Eating

No 12 B&B ££
(☎01285-640232; www.no12cirencester.co.uk; 12 Park St; d £95) This Georgian town house right in the centre of Cirencester has gloriously unfussy rooms kitted out with a tasteful mix of antiques and modern furnishings. Think feather pillows, merino blankets, extra-long beds, slick modern bathrooms and a host of little extras to make you smile.

Old Brewhouse B&B ££
(☎01285-656099; www.theoldbrewhouse.com; 7 London Rd; s/d from £56/68; P 📶) Set in a charming 17th-century town house, this lovely B&B has bright, pretty rooms with cast-iron beds and subtle, country-style florals or patchwork quilts. The courtyard rooms are newer and larger, and the beautiful garden room even has its own patio.

Jesse's Bistro MODERN BRITISH ££
(☎01285-641497; www.jessesbistro.co.uk; Blackjack St; mains £12-20; ⏲lunch Tue-Sun & dinner Wed-Sat) Hidden away in a cobbled stable yard with its own fishmonger and cheese shop, Jesse's is a great little place, with flagstone floors, wrought-iron chairs and mosaic tables. The modern menu features a selection of great dishes, but the real treat is the fresh fish and meat cooked in the wood-burning oven.

Getting There & Away

National Express buses run roughly hourly from Cirencester to London (£12, 2½ hours) and to Cheltenham Spa (30 minutes) and Gloucester (one hour). Stagecoach bus 51 also runs to Cheltenham Monday to Saturday (40 minutes, hourly). Bus 852 goes to Gloucester (four daily Monday to Saturday).

Bibury

POP 1235

Once described by William Morris as 'the most beautiful village in England', Bibury is another Cotswold gem with a cluster of gorgeous riverside cottages and tangle of narrow streets flanked by wayward stone buildings. It's an impossibly quaint place whose main attraction is **Arlington Row**, a stunning sweep of cottages now thought to be the most photographed street in Britain. The street was originally home to one long, 14th-century sheep house, but in the 17th century this was divided up and converted into weavers' cottages. Also worth a look is the 17th-century **Arlington Mill**, just a short stroll away across Rack Isle, a wildlife refuge once used as a cloth-drying area.

Few visitors make it past these two sights, but for a glimpse of the real Bibury, venture into the village proper behind Arlington Row, where you'll find a cluster of stunning cottages and the Saxon **Church of St Mary**. Although much altered since its original construction, many 8th-century features are still visible among the 12th- and 13th-century additions.

Despite its popularity, Bibury is seriously lacking in decent accommodation. The best place to stay is in the nearby village of Coln, where the jasmine-clad **New Inn** (☎0844-815 3434; www.new-inn.co.uk; Coln-St-Aldwyns; s/d from £120/130) offers quirky luxury in 16th-century surroundings. Look out for online deals offering rooms from £70. It's also the best bet in the area for food, with its modern British menu (mains £11 to £18.50) served in the main restaurant, bar and gorgeous garden.

Buses 860, 865, and 866 pass through Bibury en route to Cirencester (15 minutes) at least once daily from Monday to Saturday (15 minutes).

Tetbury

POP 5250

Once a prosperous wool-trading centre, Tetbury has managed to preserve most of its architectural heritage – its busy streets are lined with medieval cottages, sturdy old town houses and Georgian Gothic gems. It's an unspoilt place with a rather regal character: even HRH Prince Charles has a shop here – Highgrove – though it's unlikely you'll find him serving behind the counter.

Along with goodies from the Highgrove Estate, Tetbury is a great place for antique fans, with a shop of old curios on almost every corner. You'll also find plenty of chichi boutiques and interior-design shops, but they're tempered by the bakers, butchers and delis that ground the town and give it a sense of real identity.

The friendly **tourist office** (☎01666-503552; www.visittetbury.co.uk; 33 Church St; ⏲10am-4pm Mon-Sat) has plenty of information on the town and its history.

Sights & Activities

Just wander around the town to soak up the atmosphere, but look out for the row of gorgeous medieval weavers' cottages that line the steep hill at **Chipping Steps**, leading up to the **Chipping** (market), which is surrounded by graceful 17th- and 18th-century town houses. From here, it's a short stroll to Market Sq, where the 17th-century **Market House** stands as if on stilts. Close by, the Georgian Gothic **Church of St Mary the Virgin** has a towering spire and wonderful interior.

Just south of Tetbury is the **National Arboretum** (www.forestry.gov.uk/westonbirt; adult £6-9, child £2-4; ⏲9am-dusk) at Westonbirt. The park boasts a magnificent selection of temperate trees, with some wonderful walks and great colour throughout the year, especially in autumn.

Sleeping & Eating

Oak House No 1 B&B £££

(☎01666-505741; www.oakhouseno1.com; The Chipping; d £135-255; wi-fi) Indulge in the over-the-top interior design at this luxury pad in the centre of town. Set in a Georgian town house, it's all eclectic art, antique furniture and trinkets from far-off places. The rooms are suitably luxurious, with a mix of contemporary and old-school styling, all the usual high-tech gadgets and a plate of homemade cakes and scones ready for you on arrival. It's a heady mix which you may love or loathe.

Ormond HOTEL ££

(☎01666-505690; www.theormond.co.uk; 23 Long St; s/d from £59/79; P wi-fi family) This modern hotel has a range of individually styled rooms with subtle but striking fabrics and funky wallpapers. It's an unassuming place that offers excellent value for money. Expect duck-down duvets, flatscreen TVs, a DVD library and warm welcome for families. The modern bar and grill downstairs serve surprisingly good food (mains £10 to £14).

Chef's Table MODERN BRITISH ££
(☎01666-504466; www.thechefstable.co.uk; 49 Long St; mains £9-13; ⊙closed dinner Sun-Tue) This fantastic deli and bistro is the place to go to stock up for a picnic in the Arboretum or to sit down for a mouth-watering lunch of local organic ingredients rustled up into stunning rustic dishes. If you're feeling inspired, you can learn how to cook the dishes under the guidance of Michelin-starred chef Michael Bedford: his cookery school runs on selected days during the summer months (day course £130).

Getting There & Away

Bus 29 runs between Tetbury and Stroud (30 minutes, six daily Monday to Saturday). Bus 620 goes to Bath (1¼ hours, six daily Monday to Friday, four on Saturday), stopping at Westonbirt Arboretum en route.

Painswick

POP 1666

One of the most beautiful and unspoilt towns in the Cotswolds, hilltop Painswick is an absolute gem. Largely untouched since medieval times, totally unassuming and gloriously uncommercial, it's like gaining access to an outdoor museum that is strangely lost in time. Despite its obvious charms, Painswick sees few visitors, so you can wander the narrow winding streets and admire the picture cottages, handsome stone town houses and medieval inns in your own good time.

Sights & Activities

Running downhill beside and behind the church is a series of gorgeous streetscapes. Look out for **Bisley St**, the original main drag, which was superseded by the now ancient-looking **New St** in medieval times. Just south of the church, stand rare **iron stocks**.

St Mary's Church CHURCH
The village centres on a fine, Perpendicular wool church surrounded by tabletop tombs and 99 clipped yew trees. Legend has it that if the hundredth yew tree were allowed to grow, the devil would appear and shrivel it. They planted it anyway – to celebrate the millennium – but there's been no sign of the Wicked One.

Painswick Rococo Garden ORNAMENTAL GARDEN
(www.rococogarden.co.uk; adult/child £6/3; ⊙11am-5pm Jan-Oct; 🚸) Just a mile north of town, the ostentatious Painswick Rococo Garden is the area's biggest attraction. These flamboyant pleasure gardens were designed by Benjamin Hyett in the 1740s and have now been restored to their former glory. Winding paths soften the otherwise strict geometrical precision, bringing visitors around the central vegetable garden to the many Gothic follies dotted in the grounds. There's also a children's nature trail and maze.

Sleeping & Eating

St Michaels HOTEL ££
(☎01452-814555; www.stmichaelsrestaurant.co.uk; Victoria St; s/d £65/80; @) The three rooms at St Michaels are a handsome mix of luxurious fabrics, exposed stonework, rustic furniture and carved woods. Each is individual in style and has flatscreen TVs, fresh-cut flowers and a sense of tranquil calm. The restaurant downstairs serves modern British and European cuisine with a touch of Asian and Czech influence (two-/three-course dinner £28/31, open lunch and dinner Wednesday to Sunday, dinner Sunday).

Cardynham House HOTEL ££
(☎01452-814006; www.cardynham.co.uk; Tibbiwell St; s/d from £55/75; 📶) The rooms at 15th-century Cardynham House have four-poster beds, heavy patterned fabrics and buckets of character. Choose the Shaker-style New England room, the opulent Arabian Nights room, the chintzy Old Tuscany room or for a private pool and garden, the Pool Room. Downstairs, the bistro (mains £9 to £18, open lunch Tuesday to Sunday, dinner Tuesday to Saturday) serves modern British cuisine.

Getting There & Away

Bus 46 connects Cheltenham (30 minutes) and Stroud (10 minutes) with Painswick hourly Monday to Saturday.

GLOUCESTERSHIRE

After the crowds and coaches of the Cotswolds, Gloucestershire's languid charms are hard to beat, with its host of mellow stone villages and rustic allure. The county's greatest asset, however, is the elegant Regency town of Cheltenham, with its graceful, tree-lined terraces, upmarket boutiques and a tempting collection of accommodation and dining options.

The county capital, Gloucester, seems a dowdy cousin by comparison, but is well worth a visit for its magnificent Gothic cathedral. To the north, Tudor Tewkesbury follows the ecclesiastical splendour with a gracious Norman abbey surrounded by a town full of crooked, half-timbered houses. To the west, the picturesque Forest of Dean is a leafy backwater perfect for cycling and walking.

Activities

Gloucestershire's quiet roads, gentle gradients and numerous footpaths are ideal for walking and cycling. Tourist offices can help with route planning and stock numerous guides to the trails.

Compass Holidays (www.compass-holidays.com) offers guided cycling and walking tours of the area.

Cheltenham

POP 110,013

The shining star of the region, Cheltenham is a historic but cosmopolitan hub at the western edge of the rustic Cotswolds. The city oozes an air of gracious refinement, its streetscapes largely left intact since its heyday as a spa resort in the 18th

Cheltenham

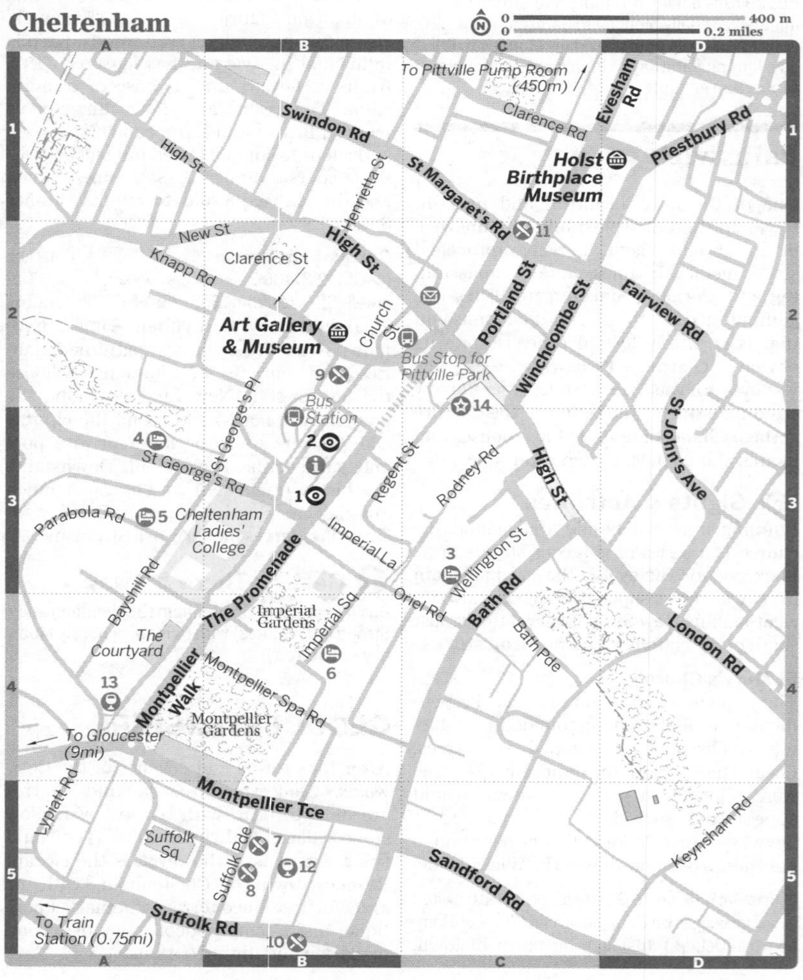

century. At the time, it rivalled Bath as *the* place for the sick, hypochondriac and merely moneyed to go, and today it is still riddled with historic buildings, beautifully proportioned terraces and manicured squares.

Cheltenham is an affluent kind of place, its well-heeled residents attracted by the genteel architecture, leafy crescents, wrought-iron balconies and expansive parks – all of which are kept in pristine condition. Add on a slew of festivals of all persuasions and a host of fine hotels, restaurants and shops, and it's easy to come to the conclusion that it's the perfect base from which to explore the region.

History

Cheltenham languished in relative obscurity until pigeons were seen eating and thriving on salt crystals from a local spring in the early 18th century. It wasn't long before a pump was bored and Cheltenham began to establish itself as a spa town. Along with the sick, property speculators arrived in droves, and the town started to grow dramatically. Graceful terraced housing was thrown up, parks were laid out and the rich and famous followed.

Cheltenham

Top Sights

	Art Gallery & Museum	B2
	Holst Birthplace Museum	D1

Sights

1	Edward Wilson Statue	B3
2	Municipal Offices	B3

Sleeping

3	Big Sleep	C3
4	Hanover House	A3
5	Hotel du Vin	A3
6	Thirty Two	B4

Eating

7	Brosh	B5
8	Daffodil	B5
9	Dfly	B2
10	Le Champignon Sauvage	B5
11	Storyteller	C2

Drinking

12	Beehive	B5
13	Montpellier Wine Bar	A4

Entertainment

14	Everyman Theatre	C2

By the time George III visited in 1788, the town's fate had been sealed and Cheltenham became the most fashionable holiday destination for England's upper crust. Today, Cheltenham is the most complete Regency town in England, with millions being spent propping up the quick-buck buildings that the Regency entrepreneurs rushed to erect.

Sights

The Promenade & Montpellier BOULEVARD

Famed as one of England's most beautiful streets, the **Promenade** is a wide, tree-lined boulevard flanked by imposing period buildings. The **Municipal Offices**, built as private residences in 1825, are among the most striking on this street and they face a **statue of Edward Wilson** (1872–1912), a local man who joined Captain Scott's ill-fated second expedition to the South Pole.

Continuing on from here, you'll pass the grandiose **Imperial Gardens**, built to service the Imperial Spa (now the Queens Hotel), en route to **Montpellier**, Cheltenham's most fashionable district. Along with the handsome architecture of the area, there's a buzzing collection of bars, restaurants and boutiques. Along Montpellier Walk, **caryatids** (draped female figures based on those on the Acropolis in Athens) act as structural supports between the shops, each balancing an elaborately carved cornice on its head.

FREE **Pittville Pump Room** CONCERT HALL

(01242-523852; www.pittvillepumproom.org.uk; Pittville Park; 9am-noon) Built in 1830 as a centrepiece to a vast estate, the Pittville Pump Room is Cheltenham's finest Regency building. Originally used as a spa and social centre, it is now used as a concert hall and wedding venue. You can wander into the main auditorium and sample the pungent spa waters when the building is not in use for a private event, or just explore the vast parklands and the lake it overlooks. It's best to phone in advance to check the opening hours as the building is about 2 miles from the city centre.

FREE **Art Gallery & Museum** MUSEUM

(www.cheltenham.artgallery.museum; Clarence St; 10am-5pm Mon-Sat) Cheltenham's excellent Art Gallery & Museum is well worth a visit for its depiction of Cheltenham life through the ages. It also has wonderful displays on William Morris and the Arts and Crafts Movement, as well as

Dutch and British art, rare Chinese and English ceramics and a section on Edward Wilson's expedition to Antarctica. The museum is closed for redevelopment in 2011. Check the website for details on reopening.

Holst Birthplace Museum MUSEUM
(www.holstmuseum.org.uk; 4 Clarence Rd; adult/child £4.50/4; ⏲10am-4pm Tue-Sat) The composer Gustav Holst was born in Cheltenham in 1874, and his childhood home has been turned into a museum celebrating his life and work. The rooms are laid out in typical period fashion and feature much Holst memorabilia, including the piano on which most of *The Planets* was composed. You can also visit the Victorian kitchen, which explains what life was like 'below stairs'.

Tours

Guided 1½-hour **walking tours** (£4; ⏲11.30am Sat Apr-Oct, plus Sun Jul & Aug) of Regency Cheltenham depart from the tourist office. You can also book tickets for a rolling program of daylong **coach tours** (adult/child £29/15; ⏲10.15am Thu) to various locations in the Cotswolds here.

Festivals & Events

Cheltenham is renowned as a city of festivals, and throughout the year you'll find major events going on in the city. For more information or to book tickets, visit www.cheltenhamfestivals.com.

Folk Festival A showcase of traditional and new-age folk talent in February.

Jazz Festival An imaginative program hailed as the UK's finest jazz fest, held in late April.

Science Festival Exploring the delights and intrigues of the world of science in June.

Music Festival A celebration of traditional and contemporary sounds with a geographical theme, in July.

Literature Festival A 10-day celebration of writers and the written word in October.

Sleeping

Cheltenham has an excellent choice of hotels and B&Bs, but few options in the budget range. Book as far in advance as possible during the festivals – especially for race week.

Beaumont House B&B ££
(☎01242-223311; www.bhhotel.co.uk; 56 Shurdington Rd; s/d from £68/78; P @) Set in a large garden just a short way from the centre of town, this boutique guest house is a memorable place with a range of carefully designed rooms with opulent decor. The cheaper standard rooms are elegant but simple, while the pricier suites are sumptuous. Go for the full-on safari look in Out of Africa, sultry boudoir in Out of Asia or more subtle design in the Prestbury Suite. To get here follow Bath Rd south from the city for about 1 mile.

Thirty Two B&B £££
(☎01242-771110; www.thirtytwoltd.com; 32 Imperial Square; s/d from £155/170; P @ wifi) In a league of its own, this slick boutique B&B is a rare find. It may charge hotel prices, but it's well worth it. You get the personal service of a B&B but the luxury, style and comfort of a top-notch hotel. Expect views over the Imperial Gardens, muted colours, contemporary artwork, luxurious fabrics and rooms that could easily feature in a glossy style magazine.

Big Sleep HOTEL ££
(☎01242-696999; www.thebigsleephotel.com; Wellington St; r £55-300; P @ wifi family) A luxury budget hotel, this place is all designer looks and no-frills minimalism. The thoroughly modern rooms have playful wallpapers and simple furniture, the family rooms have their own kitchenette, and breakfast is included in the price. If you can grab one of the cheaper deals, it's an absolute steal, and a brilliant option if you're travelling with family or friends.

Hotel du Vin HOTEL £££
(☎01242-588450; www.hotelduvin.com; Parabola Rd; r from £145; P @) Sleek, stylish and very hip, this is another winning offer from the Hotel du Vin luxury hotel chain. A spiral staircase anchors the spacious public areas, which are decked out with a subtle horsey theme, while the bedrooms ooze minimalist sophistication. Some of the standard rooms are quite small so it's worth paying the extra for the superior option.

Hanover House B&B ££
(☎01242-541297; www.hanoverhouse.org; 65 St George's Rd; s/d from £70/90; P wifi) A real gem, this Victorian town house has three lovely rooms with high ceilings, big sash windows and quirky, vibrant decor. Blending period details and modern style, the rooms feel lived in, with well-stocked bookcases, colourful throws and a decanter of sherry

'to ease any stress'. Breakfast is organic and seriously good.

Eating

Cheltenham has a great choice of top-end places to eat, but apart from the usual chains there's little choice for those on a more meagre budget. For the best range of options, head to Montpellier or the area around Suffolk Square.

Daffodil MODERN BRITISH ££
(01242-700055; www.thedaffodil.com; 18-20 Suffolk Pde; mains £13.50-17.50; closed Sun) A perennial favourite, the Daffodil is as loved for its top-notch modern British brasserie-style food as for its flamboyant surroundings. Set in a converted art deco cinema, it harks back to the Roaring Twenties and features live jazz and blues every Monday night. The atmosphere is suitably bubbly and the food consistently good.

Le Champignon Sauvage FRENCH £££
(01242-573449; www.lechampignonsauvage.co.uk; 24-26 Suffolk Rd; set menu 2-/3-course £45/55; Tue-Sat) This unpretentious but oh-so-delectable restaurant has earned two Michelin stars for its inspired cuisine. The atmosphere is refined but relaxed, the tables big and the decor simple. It's the kind of place where you can just wallow in the food, which is worth every penny. Perfect for a special occasion. Book ahead.

Brosh MEDITERRANEAN ££
(www.broshrestaurant.co.uk; 8 Suffolk Pde; mains £14-18; dinner Wed-Sat) This lovely little place serves excellent eastern Mediterranean food with everything from the *merguez* to the sourdough bread prepared on site from scratch. The menu is limited but the flavours are superb. For something lighter (£2 to £4), come for the *mezedhes* bar, which opens on Wednesday to Friday nights.

Dfly FUSION £
(1a Crescent Pl; dishes £3.50-8; Tue-Sat) Bar, restaurant and hip hang-out rolled into one, Dfly is a style-conscious place serving great sushi and tapas in sultry surroundings. Think deep red, oversize cushions, dark woods, liberally scattered church candles and Asian carvings. By night it's a buzzing watering hole with soulful music and monthly live gigs.

Storyteller INTERNATIONAL ££
(www.storyteller.co.uk; 11 North Pl; mains £8-16) Feel-good comfort food draws the crowds to this enduringly popular restaurant. It dishes up generous portions of barbecue ribs, seafood platters and vegetarian burritos on a menu fusing tastes from as far afield as Mexico and Asia. The place is always buzzing and is a popular spot for parties.

Drinking & Entertainment

Beehive PUB
(www.thebeehivemontpellier.com; 1-3 Montpellier Villas) A local favourite with a mixed following, this traditional pub is always busy but still manages to feel like a great place to chill out. There's an open fire in winter, a pleasant garden in summer and a great choice of local ales and ciders on tap.

Montpellier Wine Bar WINE BAR
(www.montpellierwinebar.com; Bayshill Lodge, Montpellier St) Slick, sophisticated and self-consciously cool, this is where Cheltenham's beautiful people come to hang out, sip wine and dine on modern British food (mains £9 to £14). There's an extensive wine list, cask ales and plenty of people-watching.

Everyman Theatre THEATRE
(www.everymantheatre.org.uk; Regent St) Cheltenham's main stage hosts everything from Elvis impersonators to comedy and panto.

Pittville Pump Room CONCERT HALL
(01242-523852; www.pittvillepumproom.org.uk; Pittville Park) Cheltenham's best bet for classical music.

Information

You'll find all the major banks and the main **post office** on High St.

Cheltenham Library (Clarence St; 9am-7pm Mon, Wed & Fri, to 5.30pm Tue & Thu, to 4pm Sat) Free web browsing.

Loft (8-9 Henrietta St; per hr £4; 10am-7pm Mon-Thu, to 6pm Fri & Sat) Internet access.

Tourist Office (01242-522878; www.visitcheltenham.info; 77 The Promenade; 9.30am-5.15pm Mon-Sat) The tourist office will move into the Cheltenham Museum & Art Gallery once it reopens.

Getting There & Away

For information on public transport to and from Cheltenham, pick up a free copy of the handy *Getting There by Public Transport* guide from the tourist office. The bus station is behind the Promenade in the town centre, but the train station is to the west of town.

Bus

National Express runs buses to London (£7, 2½ hours, hourly). Other bus routes:

Broadway Bus 606 (45 minutes) via **Winchcombe** (20 minutes); four times daily Monday to Friday.

Cirencester Bus 51 (40 minutes, hourly).

Gloucester Bus 94 (30 minutes, every 10 minutes Monday to Saturday, every 20 minutes on Sunday).

Moreton Bus 801 (one hour) via **Bourton** (35 minutes) and **Stow** (50 minutes); seven times daily Monday to Saturday.

Oxford Bus 853 (£7.50, 1½ hours, three daily Monday to Saturday, one Sunday).

Train

Trains run to **London** (£31, 2¼ hours), **Bristol** (£7.30, 50 minutes), **Gloucester** (£3.60, 11 minutes) and **Bath** (£11.60, 1¼ hours) roughly every half-hour.

Getting Around

Bus D runs to Pittville Park and the train station from Clarence St every 10 minutes.

Tewkesbury

POP 10,016

Sitting at the confluence of the Rivers Avon and Severn, Tudor-heavy Tewkesbury is all crooked little half-timbered houses, buckled roof lines and narrow alleyways stuck in a medieval time warp. Throw in a few Georgian gems and the town's higgledy-piggledy charm is hard to resist. Take time to wander the ancient passageways that lead up to the main streets from the rivers, and then wander along Church St to the town's most glorious building, the magnificent medieval abbey church.

The **tourist office** (☎01684-855040; www.visitcotswoldsandsevernvale.gov.uk; 100 Church St; ⌚10am-5pm Mon-Sat, to 4pm Sun) is housed in a 17th-century hat shop that's also home to the **Out of the Hat** (www.outofthehat.org.uk; adult/child £3.50/2.50; ⌚10am-5pm Mon-Sat, to 4pm Sun) heritage centre.

Sights

Tewkesbury Abbey CHURCH

(www.tewkesburyabbey.org.uk; ⌚7.30am-6pm) This magnificent abbey is one of Britain's largest churches, far bigger than many of the country's cathedrals. The Norman abbey, built for the Benedictine monks, was consecrated in 1121 and was one of the last monasteries to be dissolved by Henry VIII. Although many of the monastery buildings were destroyed, the abbey church survived after being bought by the townspeople for the princely sum of £453 in 1542.

The church has a massive 40m-high tower and some spectacular Norman piers and arches in the nave. The Decorated-style chancel dates from the 14th century, however, and still retains much of its original stained glass. The church also features an organ dating from 1631, originally made for Magdalen College, Oxford, and an extensive collection of medieval tombs. The most interesting is that of John Wakeman, the last abbot, who is shown as a vermin-ridden skeleton.

You can take a **guided tour** (£4) of the abbey on weekdays in summer or visit an exhibition on the abbey's history at the **visitor centre** (⌚10am-5.30pm Mon-Sat Apr-Sep) by the main gate. The church also makes a wonderfully atmospheric venue for a range of summer concerts.

John Moore Countryside Museum MUSEUM

(www.johnmooremuseum.org; adult/child £1.50/1; ⌚10am-1pm & 2-5pm Tue-Sat) This small museum, set in a wonderfully atmospheric 15th-century dwelling, gives an insight into life in Tudor times and features a fully restored late-medieval home and shop.

Tewkesbury Museum MUSEUM

(www.tewkesburymuseum.org; 64 Barton St; admission £2; ⌚1-4pm Tue-Fri, 11am-4pm Sat) Displays finds from Roman and medieval times as well as a diorama on the Battle of Tewkesbury.

Sleeping & Eating

Jessop Townhouse HOTEL ££

(☎01684-292017; www.jessophousehotel.com; 65 Church St; s/d from £59/79; P) A lovely little hotel set in a Georgian town house, this place has large rooms with high ceilings, big windows, old fireplaces and elegant style. The rooms are all different – some in period style, others more contemporary – but all are warm and cosy, with large TVs and new bathrooms. It's a great deal at these rates.

Owens MODERN BRITISH ££

(www.eatatowens.co.uk; 73 Church St; mains £10-15; ⌚11am-10pm Tue-Sat, 2-4pm Sun) Set in a 15th-century building that's decidedly modern inside, this place is a welcome change from Tewkesbury's tearooms. The menu features big, honest flavours and a modern take on classic British and French cuisine. Try the excellent two-course set lunch for £10.

Getting There & Away

Bus 41 runs to Cheltenham (25 minutes) every 15 minutes, hourly on Sunday, and bus 71 (30 minutes) goes to Gloucester hourly. The nearest train station is 1½ miles away at Ashchurch, from where there are trains every two hours to Cheltenham (10 minutes) and Worcester (£6.60; 26 minutes).

Gloucester

POP 136,203

Gloucester (*glos*-ter) began life as a settlement for retired Roman soldiers but really came into its own in medieval times, when the pious public brought wealth and prosperity to what was then a prime pilgrimage city. The faithful flocked to see the grave of Edward II and soon financed the building of what remains one of England's most beautiful cathedrals.

In more recent years, Gloucester bore the brunt of hard times and the city fell into serious decline. The centre remains a rather dowdy, workaday place but scratch the surface and you'll find a glimmer of medieval character.

Sights

Gloucester Cathedral CATHEDRAL

(www.gloucestercathedral.org.uk; College Green; suggested donation £3; ⏲8am-6pm) The main reason to visit Gloucester is to see its magnificent Gothic cathedral, a stunning example of English Perpendicular style. Originally the site of a Saxon abbey, a Norman church was built here by a group of Benedictine monks in the 12th century, and when Edward II was murdered in 1327, the church was chosen as his burial place. Edward's tomb proved so popular, however, that Gloucester became a centre of pilgrimage and the income generated from the pious pilgrims financed the church's conversion into the magnificent building seen today.

Inside, the cathedral skilfully combines the best of Norman and Gothic design with sturdy columns creating a sense of gracious solidity, and wonderful Norman arcading draped with beautiful mouldings. From the elaborate 14th-century wooden choir stalls, you'll get a good view of the imposing **Great East Window**, one of the largest in England.

To see the window in more detail, head for the **Tribune Gallery**, where you can also see an **exhibition** (admission £2; ⏲10.30am-4pm Mon-Fri, to 3.30pm Sat) on its creation. As you walk around the **Whispering Gallery,** you'll notice that even the quietest of murmurs reverberates across the wonderfully elaborate lierne vaulting. Beneath the window in the northern ambulatory is Edward II's magnificent tomb, and nearby is the late 15th-century **Lady Chapel**, a glorious patchwork of stained glass.

One of the cathedral's greatest treasures, however, is the exquisite **Great Cloister**. Completed in 1367, it is the first example of fan vaulting in England and is only matched in beauty by Henry VIII's Chapel at Westminster Abbey. You (or your children) might recognise the cloister from the first two Harry Potter films: it was used in the corridor scenes at Hogwart's School.

A wonderful way to take in the glory of the cathedral is to attend one of the many musical recitals and concerts held here. The stunning acoustics and breathtaking surroundings are pretty much guaranteed to make your hair stand on end.

Civic Trust volunteers provide **guided tours** (⏲10.30am-4pm Mon-Sat, noon-2.30pm Sun) of the cathedral. For more insights and a fantastic view of the town, join an hour-long guided **tower tour** (adult/child £3/1; ⏲2.30pm Mon-Fri, 1.30pm & 2.30pm Sat). Because of the steep steps it's not recommended for children under 10.

National Waterways Museum MUSEUM

(www.nwm.org.uk/gloucester; adult/child £4.25/3.25; ⏲10.30am-5pm; 👪) A major part of the city's regeneration is taking place at **Gloucester Docks**, once Britain's largest inland port. Fifteen beautiful Victorian warehouses, many now restored, surround the canal basins and house a series of museums, shops and cafes. The largest warehouse at the docks, Llanthony, is home to the National Waterways Museum, a hands-on kind of place where you can discover the history of Britain's inland waterways. Exhibitions explain what it was like living, working and moving on the water, featuring plenty of historic boats and interactive exhibits that are great for children.

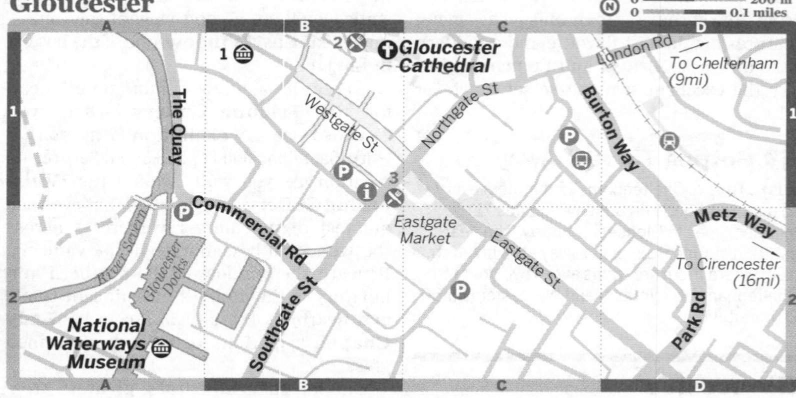

FREE **Gloucester Folk Museum** MUSEUM (www.gloucester.gov.uk/folkmuseum; 99-103 Westgate St; ⏲10am-5pm Tue-Sat) This folk museum examines domestic life, crafts and industries from 1500 to the present and is housed in a wonderful series of Tudor and Jacobean timber-framed buildings dating from the 16th and 17th centuries.

Sleeping & Eating

Gloucester's accommodation options are pretty grim. You'd be far better off staying in Cheltenham (10 minutes by train) instead.

Tigers Eye ASIAN ££
(www.theoldbell-tigerseye.co.uk; 9a Southgate St; mains £6-14; ⏲closed Sun & Mon) This place attempts to please everyone with a menu that veers from baguettes and wraps to sushi, noodles and Black Rock grills (where you cook your own meat or fish on a sizzling volcanic plate). It's a strange mix, but somehow it manages to work and the food is some of the best in town.

Cathedral Coffee Shop CAFE £
(College Green; snacks £2-4; ⏲10am-5pm Mon-Fri, 10am-4.30pm Sat, 11am-3pm Sun) For hearty soups, diet-busting cakes and sticky buns, the cathedral coffee shop provides a wonderful setting for a quick cuppa.

Information

Tourist Office (☎01452-396572; www.visitgloucester.info; 28 Southgate St; ⏲10am-5pm Mon-Sat, 11am-3pm Sun) Pick up a free *Via Sacra* brochure to guide you around the city's most historic buildings.

Getting There & Away

National Express has buses roughly every two hours to London (£6, 3¼ hours). Bus 94 goes to Cheltenham (30 minutes) every 10 minutes Monday to Saturday, and every 20 minutes on Sunday. However, the train (11 minutes, every 20 minutes) is faster.

Forest of Dean

POP 79,982

An ancient woodland with a unique, almost magical character, the Forest of Dean is the oldest oak forest in England and a wonderfully scenic place to walk, cycle or paddle. Its steep, wooded hills, winding, tree-lined roads and glimmering lakes make it a remarkably tranquil place to visit and an excellent spot for outdoor pursuits.

The forest was formerly a royal hunting ground and a centre of iron and coal mining, and its mysterious depths were supposedly the inspiration for Tolkien's setting in *The Lord of the Rings* and for JK Rowling's Harry Potter adventures. Numerous other writers, poets, artists and craftspeople have been inspired by the stunning scenery, designated England's first National Forest Park in 1938.

Covering 42 sq miles between Gloucester, Ross-on-Wye and Chepstow, the forest is in an isolated position, but Coleford, the main population centre, has good transport connections. You'll find more information on the area if you check out www.visitforestofdean.co.uk.

Gloucester

Top Sights

Gloucester Cathedral B1
National Waterways Museum A2

Sights

1 Gloucester Folk Museum.................. B1

Eating

2 Cathedral Coffee Shop...................... B1
3 Tigers Eye.. B1

Sights & Activities

Dean Heritage Centre MUSEUM
(www.deanheritagemuseum.com; Camp Mill, Soudley; adult/child £5.40/2.75; 10am-5pm) For an insight into the history of the forest since the Ice Age, this entertaining museum looks at everything from the forest's geology to Roman occupation, medieval hunting laws, free mining, cottage crafts and industrial coal mining. There's also a reconstructed forest home, adventure playground and art gallery on site.

Puzzle Wood ADVENTURE PARK
(www.puzzlewood.net; adult/child £5/3.50; 10am-5pm;) If you're travelling with children, this wonderful forest playground is a must. An overgrown pre-Roman, opencast ore mine, it has a maze of paths, weird rock formations, tangled vines and eerie passageways and offers a real sense of discovery. Puzzle Wood is 1 mile south of Coleford on the B4228.

Clearwell Caves CAVES
(www.clearwellcaves.com; adult/child £5.80/3.80; 10am-5pm) Mined for iron ore for more than 4000 years, these caves are a warren of passageways, caverns and pools that help explain the forest's history of mining. There is also a blacksmith's workshop and the possibility of deep-level caving for small groups. The caves are signposted off the B4228 a mile south of Coleford.

Sleeping & Eating

TOP CHOICE **St Briavels Castle YHA** HOSTEL £
(01594-530272; www.yha.org.uk; Lydney; dm from £18; P) Live like a king for a night at this unique hostel set in an imposing moated castle once used as King John's hunting lodge. Loaded with character and a snip at this price, this 13th-century castle comes complete with round towers, drawbridge and gruesome history. The dorms sleep four to six, and you can even join in the ancient spirit with full-blown medieval banquets on Wednesdays and Saturdays in August.

Three Choirs Vineyard B&B ££
(01531-890223; www.threechoirs.com; Newent; d from £115; P) This working vineyard has a range of extremely comfortable, classically styled rooms overlooking the sweeping fields of vines. You can also take a guided tour of the vineyard (£7.50), try the award-winning wines and then relax over lunch (mains £12.50 to £16.50) or dinner (mains £19 to £20) in the bright and airy restaurant. There's also a gift shop and microbrewery on site.

Dome Garden BOUTIQUE CAMPING ££
(01730-261458; www.domegarden.co.uk; Mile End, Coleford; 4-bed dome from £375, B&B d £96) For something completely different why not get back to nature in luxurious style in a cool geodesic dome? Linked by paths of recycled glass and set in glorious gardens, the domes sleep between two and eight people and have giant bean bags, wood burners and their own kitchen and showers. Yes, it's camping, just not like you know it.

Garden Cafe MODERN BRITISH ££
(01594-860075; www.gardencafe.co.uk; Lwr Lydbrook; mains £8-13; lunch Fri-Sun, dinner Fri, Sat & Mon) An award-winning organic cafe on the banks of the River Wye, this place is set in a converted malt house and surrounded by a beautiful walled garden. The food is all seasonal and locally sourced, with vegetables from the cafe's garden. Monday night is tapas night (set menu £10).

Getting There & Around

From Gloucester, bus 31 (one hour, hourly) runs to Coleford, and there are trains to Lydney (20 minutes, hourly). The **Dean Forest Railway** (www.deanforestrailway.co.uk) runs steam trains from Lydney to Parkend (day tickets adult/child £10/5) on selected days from March to December.

You can hire bikes (£15 per day), buy maps and get advice on cycling routes at **Pedalabikeaway** (01594 860065; www.pedalabikeaway.co.uk; Cannop Valley; Tue-Sun) near Coleford.

HERTFORDSHIRE

Firmly on the commuter belt and within easy reach of the capital, Hertfordshire is a small, sleepy county liberally scattered with satellite towns that threaten to overtake the fast-disappearing countryside. However, it is also home to the historic town of St Albans, with its elegant Georgian streetscapes and Roman remains.

St Albans

POP 129,005

A bustling market town with a host of crooked Tudor buildings and elegant Georgian town houses, St Albans makes a pleasant day trip from London. The town was founded as Verulamium after the Roman invasion of AD 43 but was renamed St Albans in the 3rd century after a Roman soldier, Alban, lost his head in punishment for sheltering a Christian priest. He became England's first Christian martyr, and the small city soon became a site of pilgrimage.

The pilgrims brought business and, subsequently, wealth to the town, and eventually the object of their affection was enshrined in what is now a magnificent cathedral. The town is also home to an excellent Roman museum, an array of chichi shops and upmarket restaurants and some wonderful pubs.

Sights

St Albans Cathedral CATHEDRAL

(www.stalbanscathedral.org.uk; admission by donation; ⌚8am-5.45pm) Set in tranquil grounds away from the din of the main streets, St Albans' magnificent cathedral is a lesson in architectural history. The church began life as a Benedictine monastery in 793, built by King Offa of Mercia around the tomb of St Alban. In Norman times it was completely rebuilt using material from the old Roman town of Verulamium, and then, in the 12th and 13th centuries, Gothic extensions and decorations were added.

The deceptively simple nave gives way to stunningly ornate ceilings, semi-lost wall paintings, an elaborate nave screen and, of course, the shrine of St Alban. There's also a luminescent rose window from the 20th century. The best way to appreciate the wealth of history contained in the building is to join a free **guided tour** (⌚11.30am & 2.30pm Mon-Fri, 11.30am & 2pm Sat, 2.30pm Sun). If you miss the tour you can pick up a very helpful free plan and guide at the entrance.

Verulamium Museum & Roman Ruins MUSEUM

(www.stalbansmuseums.org.uk; St Michael's St; adult/child £3.50/2; ⌚10am-5.30pm Mon-Sat, 2-5.30pm Sun) A fantastic exposé of everyday life under the Romans, the Verulamium Museum is home to a large collection of arrowheads, glassware and grave goods. Its centrepiece, however, is the **Mosaic Room**, where five superb mosaic floors, uncovered between 1930 and 1955, are laid out. You can also see re-creations of Roman rooms, and learn about life in the settlement through interactive and audiovisual displays. Every second weekend, the museum is 'invaded' by Roman soldiers who demonstrate the tactics and tools of the Roman army.

Adjacent **Verulamium Park** has remains of a basilica, bathhouse and parts of the city wall. You can pick up a map of the area with information on the site from the museum or tourist office.

Across the busy A4147 are the grassy foundations of a **Roman theatre** (☎01727-835035; www.romantheatre.co.uk; adult/child £2.50/1.50; ⌚10am-5pm), which once seated 2000 spectators.

Sleeping & Eating

You'll find plenty of chain restaurants around the centre of town.

Fleuchary House B&B ££

(☎01727-766764; www.29stalbans.com; 29 Upper Lattimore Rd; s/d £45/60; P 📶) A beautiful Victorian house with many original features, this boutiquey B&B has elegantly stylish rooms with freshly plumped cushions, crisp, white linens, subtly patterned wallpapers and bejewelled lamps. It's about 600m from the train station: walk west down Victoria St and take the second right onto Upper Lattimore Rd.

Lussmanns Eatery MEDITERRANEAN ££

(☎01727-851941; www.lussmans.com; Waxhouse Gate; mains £11-18; ⌚11.30am-10pm Mon-Thu, to 10.30pm Fri & Sat, to 9pm Sun) This bright, modern restaurant just off the High St is enduringly popular with locals despite ample competition around town. It serves a menu of mainly Mediterranean dishes, all in a bright, modern space with oak, leather and metal decor. Ingredients are ethically sourced with plenty of information on the menu about where your food has come from. Book ahead.

ST ALBANS BEER FESTIVAL

Beer is big business in England, and to pint-swilling connoisseurs, real ale is the only brew that matters. To celebrate its key role in national culture, Camra (the Campaign for Real Ale) hosts a four-day beer festival in St Albans at the end of September. Over 9000 people converge on the Alban Arena off St Peter's St to sample and talk about the 350-odd real ales on tap and the 500 or so cask and bottled beers, ciders and perries. With food, music and good booze on offer, and tickets a mere £2 to £4, it's a great excuse for a party. For more information, see www.hertsale.org.uk/beerfest.

Drinking

TOP CHOICE **Ye Olde Fighting Cocks** TRADITIONAL PUB

(16 Abbey Mill Lane) Reputedly the oldest pub in England, this unusual, octagon-shaped inn has oodles of charm. Oliver Cromwell spent a night here, stabling his horses in what's now the bar, and underground tunnels lead to the cathedral. Drink in this historic atmosphere while you nurse your pint.

Information

Tourist office (01727-864511; www.stalbans.gov.uk; Market Pl; 10am-4.30pm Mon-Sat) In the grand town hall in the marketplace. Can book themed guided walks (adult/child £3/1.50) of the city.

Getting There & Away

Trains run between London St Pancras and St Albans (£9, 20 minutes) every 10 minutes. The station is on Victoria St, 800m east of St Peter's St.

BEDFORDSHIRE & BUCKINGHAMSHIRE

The sweeping valleys and chalky, forested hills of Bedfordshire and Buckinghamshire once attracted the rich and famous, who used them as a rural hideaway for their majestic stately homes. Today, commuters populate the pretty villages surrounding these vast and magnificent estates and enjoy the quiet woodland walks and mountain-bike trails that criss-cross the undulating Chiltern Hills.

Woburn Abbey & Safari Park

The pretty Georgian village of Woburn is home to Bedfordshire's biggest attractions: a palatial stately home and Europe's largest conservation park.

Once a Cistercian abbey but dissolved by Henry VIII and awarded to the earl of Bedford, **Woburn Abbey** (www.woburn.co.uk; adult/child £12.50/6; 11am-4pm) is a wonderful country pile set within a 1200-hectare deer park. The house is stuffed with 18th-century furniture, porcelain and silver, and displays paintings by Gainsborough, van Dyck and Canaletto. Highlights include the bedroom of Queen Victoria and Prince Albert; the beautiful wall hangings and cabinets of the Chinese Room; the mysterious story of the Flying Duchess; and the gilt-adorned dining room.

On an equally grand scale is **Woburn Safari Park** (www.woburn.co.uk/safari; adult/child £18.50/13.50; 10am-5pm), the country's largest drive-through animal reserve. Rhinos, tigers, lions, zebras, bison, monkeys, elephants and giraffes roam the grounds, while in the 'foot safari' area, you can see sea lions, penguins and lemurs.

For both attractions, buy a **passport ticket** (adult/child £22.50/15.50), which can be used on two separate days within any 12-month period.

The abbey and safari park are easily accessible by car off the M1 motorway. First Capital Connect runs trains from King's Cross to Flitwick, the nearest station. From here it's a 15-minute taxi journey (£15 to £20) to Woburn.

Waddesdon Manor

Dripping with gilt, crystal chandeliers, tapestries, fine porcelain and elaborate furniture, **Waddesdon Manor** (01296-653226; www.waddesdon.org.uk; house & gardens adult/child £15/11; noon-4pm Wed-Fri, 11am-4pm Sat & Sun) is a stunning Renaissance-style chateau built by Baron Ferdinand de Rothschild to showcase his collection of French decorative arts. The baron liked to do things on a grand scale, and the ostentatious magnificence of the house, designed by French architect Destailleur and completed in 1889, is almost overwhelming.

Very little space is left unadorned – only the Bachelor's Wing stands out as being noticeably more restrained. The baron used the house for his glamorous parties, and it's not hard to imagine the great and good of the 19th century living it up in the palatial rooms. Visitors can view his outstanding collection of art, Sèvres porcelain, expensive furniture and the extensive wine cellar. The house hosts a variety of events throughout the year, from Christmas fairs to wine-tasting days, Valentine's dinners and opera and theatre events. Weekends get busy, so book tickets in advance.

The beautiful **gardens** (gardens only adult/child £7/3.50; ⏲10am-5pm Wed-Sun) boast rare flowers, divine views and a Rococo-revival aviary filled with exotic birds.

Waddesdon is 6 miles northwest of Aylesbury off the A41. Trains to Aylesbury (£13, one hour, half-hourly) depart from London Marylebone. From Aylesbury bus station take bus 16 (25 minutes), which runs roughly half-hourly Monday to Friday and every two hours on Saturday.

BERKSHIRE

Long known as the 'Royal County of Berkshire', this rather posh and prosperous part of the world acts as a country getaway for some of England's most influential figures. Within easy reach of London and yet entirely different in character, the pastoral landscape is littered with handsome villages and historic houses as well as some of the top attractions in the country. Few visitors make it past the historic towns of Windsor and Eton, home to the Queen's favourite castle and the world-renowned public school, but wander further afield and you'll be rewarded with tranquil rural countryside and exquisitely maintained villages.

Windsor & Eton

POP 30,568

Dominated by the massive bulk and heavy influence of Windsor Castle, these twin towns have a rather surreal atmosphere, with the morning pomp and ceremony of the changing of the guards in Windsor and the sight of school boys dressed in formal tailcoats wandering the streets of Eton.

Windsor Castle, with its romantic architecture and superb state rooms, is an absolute must-see, while across the bridge over the Thames, England's most famous public school has an altogether different flavour. To cater for the droves of tourists that visit these star attractions, Windsor town centre is full of expensive boutiques, grand cafes and trendy restaurants. Eton, by comparison, is far quieter, its pedestrianised centre lined with antique shops and art galleries. Both towns exude an air of affluence, and if you're travelling on a tight budget, a day trip from London is probably your best bet.

Sights

Windsor Castle CASTLE

(www.royalcollection.org.uk; adult/child £16/9.50; ⏲9.45am-5.15pm) The largest and oldest occupied fortress in the world, Windsor Castle is a majestic vision of battlements and towers used for state occasions and as the Queen's weekend retreat.

William the Conqueror first established a royal residence in Windsor in 1070 when he built a motte and bailey here, the only naturally defendable spot in the Thames valley. Since then successive monarchs have rebuilt, remodelled and refurbished the castle complex to create the massive and sumptuous palace that stands here today. Henry II replaced the wooden stockade in 1165 with a stone round tower and built the outer walls to the north, east and south; Charles II gave the state apartments a baroque makeover; George IV swept in with his preference for Gothic style; and Queen Victoria refurbished a beautiful chapel in memory of her beloved Albert.

The castle largely escaped the bombings of WWII, but in 1992 a devastating fire tore through the building, destroying or damaging more than 100 rooms. By chance, the most important treasures were in storage at the time, and with skilled craftsmanship and painstaking restoration, the rooms were returned to their former glory.

Join a free guided tour (every half hour) or take a multilingual audio tour of the lavish state rooms and beautiful chapels. The State Apartments and St George's Chapel are closed at times during the year; check the website for details. If the Queen is in residence, you'll see the Royal Standard flying from the Round Tower.

Windsor Castle is one of England's most popular attractions. Come early and be prepared to queue.

Queen Mary's Dolls' House

Your first sight will be an incredible dolls' house, designed by Sir Edwin Lutyens for Queen Mary in 1924. The attention to detail is spellbinding – there's running water, electricity and lighting and vintage wine in the cellar! The house was intended to accurately depict households of the day, albeit on a scale of 1:12.

State Apartments

After the dolls' house, a **gallery** with drawings by Leonardo da Vinci and a **China Museum**, you'll enter the stunning State Apartments, which are home to some exquisite paintings and architecture and are still used by the Queen.

The **Grand Staircase** sets the tone for the rooms, all of which are elaborate, opulent and suitably regal. Highlights include **St George's Hall,** which incurred the most damage during the fire of 1992. The dining chairs here, dwarfed by the scale of the room, are standard size. On the ceiling, the shields of the Knights of the Garter (originally from George IV's time here) were re-created after the fire.

For intimate gatherings (just 60 people), the Queen entertains in the **Waterloo Chamber** – the super shiny table is French-polished and then dusted by someone walking over it with dusters on their feet.

The **King's Dressing Room** has some of the most important Renaissance paintings in the royal collection. Alongside Sir Anthony van Dyck's magnificent *Triple Portrait* of Charles I, you will see works by Hans Holbein, Rembrandt, Peter Paul Rubens and Albrecht Dürer. Charles II kipped in here instead of in the **King's Bedchamber** – maybe George IV's magnificent bed (now on display) would have tempted him.

St George's Chapel

This elegant chapel, commissioned for the Order of the Garter by Edward IV in 1475, is one of Britain's finest examples of Perpendicular Gothic architecture.

The chapel – along with Westminster Abbey – serves as a **royal mausoleum**, and its tombs read like a history of the British monarchy.

St George's Chapel closes on Sunday, but time your visit well and you can attend **Evensong** at 5.15pm daily except Wednesday.

Albert Memorial Chapel

Originally built in 1240 and dedicated to Edward the Confessor, this small chapel was the place of worship for the Order of the Garter until St George's Chapel snatched that honour. After the death of Prince Albert at Windsor Castle in 1861, Queen Victoria ordered its elaborate redecoration as a tribute to her husband. A major feature of the restoration is the magnificent vaulted roof, whose gold mosaic pieces were crafted in Venice.

Windsor Great Park

Stretching behind Windsor Castle almost all the way to Ascot, Windsor Great Park covers about 40 sq miles and features a lake, walking tracks, a bridleway and gardens. The **Savill Garden** (www.theroyallandscape.co.uk; adult/child £8/3.75; ⌚10am-6pm) is particularly lovely and has a stunning visitor centre. The Savill Garden is about 4 miles south of Windsor Castle. Take the A308 out of town and follow the brown signs.

The **Long Walk** is a 3-mile jaunt along a tree-lined path from King George IV Gate to the Copper Horse statue (of George III) on Snow Hill, the highest point of the park. The walk is signposted from the town centre.

Changing of the guard

A fabulous spectacle of pomp, with loud commands, whispered conversations, triumphant tunes from a military band and plenty of shuffling and stamping of feet, the **changing of the guard** (11am Mon-Sat Apr-Jul, alternate days Aug-Mar) draws the crowds to the castle gates each day.

Eton College BOYS' SCHOOL

Cross the bridge over the Thames to Eton and you'll enter another world, one where old-school values and traditions seem to ooze from the very walls. The streets here are surprisingly hushed as you make your way down to the most enduring and illustrious symbol of England's class system, **Eton College** (www.etoncollege.com; adult/child £6.20/5.20; ⌚guided tours 2pm & 3.15pm daily during school holidays, Wed, Fri, Sat & Sun during term time).

Those who have studied here include 18 prime ministers, countless princes, kings and maharajahs, famous explorers, authors, and economists – among them the Duke of Wellington, Princes William and Harry, George Orwell, Ian Fleming, Aldous Huxley, Sir Ranulph Fiennes and John Maynard Keynes.

Windsor & Eton

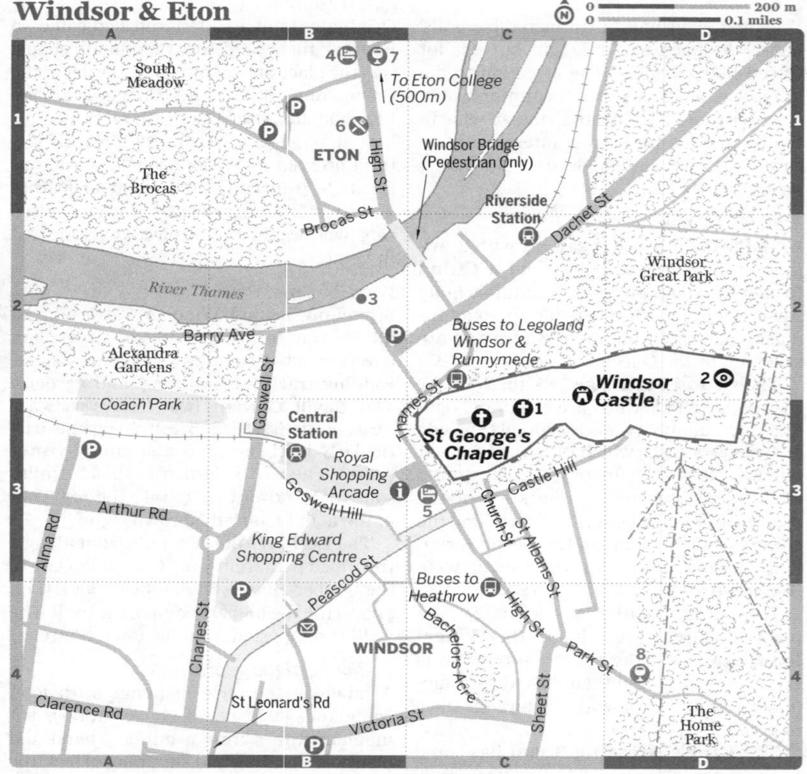

Eton is the largest and most famous public (meaning very private) school in England. It was founded by Henry VI in 1440 with a view towards educating 70 highly qualified boys awarded a scholarship from a fund endowed by the king. Every year since then, 70 King's Scholars (aged 12 to 14) have been chosen based on the results of a highly competitive exam; these pupils are housed in separate quarters from the rest of the 1300 or so other students who are known as Oppidans.

While the King's Scholars are chosen exclusively on the basis of exam results, Oppidans must be able to foot the bill for £28,800 per-annum fees as well as passing entrance exams. All the boys are boarders and must comply with the strong traditions at Eton. The boys still wear formal tailcoats, waistcoats and white collars to lessons, the school language is full of in-house jargon, and fencing, shooting, polo and beagling are on the list of school sporting activities.

Luckily for the rest of us, the college is open to visitors taking the guided tour, which gives a fascinating insight into how this most elite of schools functions. Tours take in the **chapel** (which you can see from Windsor Castle), the **cloisters**, the **Museum of Eton Life**, the **lower school** and the **school yard**. As you wander round, you may recognise some of the buildings, as the college is often used as a film set. *Chariots of Fire, The Madness of King George, Mrs Brown* and *Shakespeare in Love* are just some of the movies that have been filmed here. To get here cross the bridge to Eton and follow the High St to its end.

Legoland Windsor THEME PARK
(www.legoland.co.uk; adult/3-15yr £38/28; hours vary) A fun-filled theme park of white-knuckle rides, Legoland is more about the thrills of scaring yourself silly

Windsor & Eton

Top Sights

St George's Chapel........C3
Windsor Castle........C2

Sights

1 Albert Memorial Chapel........C3
2 State Apartments........D2

Activities, Courses & Tours

3 French Brothers........B2

Sleeping

4 Christopher Hotel........B1
5 Harte & Garter........C3

Eating

6 Gilbey's........B1
Tower........(see 5)

Drinking

7 Henry VI........B1
8 Two Brewers........D4

than the joys of building your own make-believe castle from the eponymous bricks.

The Legoland shuttle bus departs opposite the Theatre Royal from 10am, with the last bus returning 30 minutes after the park has closed.

Tours

French Brothers BOAT TOURS
(www.frenchbrothers.co.uk; Clewer Court Rd; 11am-5pm Easter-Oct) Run a variety of boat trips to Runnymede (adult/child £5.20/2.60, 45 minutes) and around Windsor and Eton (adult/child £8.40/4.20, two hours). Boats leave from just next to Windsor Bridge. If you fancy doing the hop-on/hop-off bus plus a 35-minute boat trip, a combined boat and bus ticket costs £12.50/6 per adult/child.

Tourist Office WALKING TOURS
(01753-743900; www.windsor.gov.uk; adult/child £6/3; 11.30am Sat & Sun) Themed guided walks of the city.

Sleeping

Windsor has a good selection of quality hotels and B&Bs, but few budget options.

Harte & Garter HOTEL £££
(01753-863426; www.foliohotels.com/harteandgarter; High St; d from £135;) Right opposite the castle, this Victorian hotel blends period style with modern furnishings. High ceilings, giant fireplaces, decorative cornices and dark woods seamlessly combine with contemporary fabrics, plasma-screen TVs and traditional, cast-iron baths. Some rooms enjoy wonderful views over the castle, and all guests can enjoy the luxurious spa in the converted stable block.

Frances Lodge B&B ££
(01753-832019; www.franceslodge.co.uk; 53 Frances Rd; s/d £70/90; P) Set in a traditional Victorian villa, this contemporary B&B blends original period features with simple, uncluttered minimalism. Cool neutral colour schemes, stylish bathrooms, an extremely warm welcome and the relaxed atmosphere make it a great bet. Frances Lodge is 700m from High St along Sheet St.

Christopher Hotel HOTEL £££
(01753-852359; www.thechristopher.co.uk; High St, Eton; d from £120; P) Set in a former coaching inn, this modern hotel offers clean-cut, uncluttered rooms with contemporary, if a little corporate, styling. The grill downstairs has big windows overlooking the street, and serves up a modern European menu (mains £9 to £15) in slick surroundings.

Eating

You'll find plenty of choice when it comes to restaurants; try Peascod St and the Windsor Royal Shopping Arcade for the old reliables.

Gilbey's MODERN BRITISH ££
(01753-854921; www.gilbeygroup.com; 82-83 High St, Eton; mains £14.50-20) Small but perfectly formed, this little restaurant with a big heart is one of the area's finest. Terracotta tiling and a sunny courtyard garden and conservatory give it a Continental cafe feel. But the bold artwork and understated decor are reflected in a superb modern British menu, which is almost surpassed by the wide and interesting choice of wines.

Tower CLASSIC BRITISH ££
(01753-863426; High St; mains £9-16) Giant windows with views over the castle give this place an immediate allure, as do the grand chandeliers and high ceilings. The menu is brasserie style with a choice of classic British cuisine, featuring grills, fish and steaks simply and perfectly done. It's also a good spot to sample the finest of English institutions: afternoon tea.

A WORLD FIRST

In June 1215, King John met his barons and bishops in a large field 3 miles southeast of Windsor, and over the next few days they hammered out an agreement on a basic charter of rights guaranteeing the liberties of the king's subjects and restricting the monarch's absolute power. The document they signed was the Magna Carta, the world's first constitution. It formed the basis for statutes and charters throughout the world's democracies. (Both the national and state constitutions of the United States, drawn up more than 500 years later, paraphrase this document.)

Today, the field remains pretty much as it was, except that now it features two **lodges** (1930) designed by Sir Edward Lutyens. In the woods behind the field are two **memorials**.

Runnymede is on the A308, 3 miles southeast of Windsor. Bus 71 stops near here on the Windsor–Egham route.

Drinking

Windsor and Eton are packed with pubs, with a cluster late night venues under the railway arches of the central station.

TOP CHOICE **Two Brewers** TRADITIONAL PUB
(34 Park St) This 17th-century inn perched on the edge of Windsor Great Park is close to the castle's tradesmen's entrance and supposedly frequented by staff from the castle. It's a quaint and cosy place, with dim lighting, obituaries to castle footmen and royal photographs with irreverent captions on the wall.

Henry VI PUB
(37 High St, Eton) Another old pub, but this time the low ceilings and subtle lighting are mixed with leather sofas and modern design. It's the kind of place where you can sit back with an afternoon pint and read the paper. There's a nice garden for alfresco dining and live music at weekends.

Information

Royal Windsor Information Centre (www.windsor.gov.uk; Old Booking Hall, Windsor Royal Shopping Arcade; ⏲9.30am-5pm Mon-Sat, 10am-4pm Sun) Has information on a self-guided heritage walk around town.

Getting There & Away

Bus 702 connects Windsor with London Victoria coach station (£8.50, one hour, hourly), and bus 77 connects Windsor with Heathrow airport (one hour, hourly).

Trains from Windsor Central station on Thames St go to London Paddington (30 to 45 minutes). Trains from Windsor Riverside station go to London Waterloo (one hour). Services run half-hourly from both stations and tickets cost £8.

Southwest England

Includes »

HAMPSHIRE........225
NEW FOREST.......234
ISLE OF WIGHT.....238
DORSET...........242
WILTSHIRE.........258
BRISTOL...........270
BATH...............278
SOMERSET.........285
EXMOOR NATIONAL PARK..............291
DEVON.............296
CORNWALL........319
ISLES OF SCILLY....344

Best Places to Eat

- Porthminster Beach Café (p328)
- Riverford Field Kitchen (p307)
- Boathouse (p242)
- Bordeaux Quay (p275)

Best Places to Stay

- Urban Beach (p244)
- Queensberry Hotel (p283)
- Really Green (p242)
- Scarlet (p325)
- Cary Arms (p303)

Why Go?

England's southwest is simply spectacular. Here the past is ever present - prepare for close encounters with iconic stone circles, Iron Age hillforts and Roman baths. Blockbuster stately homes border romantic castles and serene cathedrals frame sumptuous Georgian cityscapes. The landscape immerses you in the myths of Kings Arthur and Alfred the Great – and the writings of Thomas Hardy, Jane Austen and Daphne du Maurier.

But the southwest also has an eye to the future. Here you can tour counter-culture eco-towns, pioneering restaurants and cool surfer hang-outs, and sleep in campsites peppered with chic yurts and retro campervans. Then there are three wildlife-rich national parks, fossil-studded shores, England's best surf spots and a coastline flecked with exquisite bays, towering rock formations and tranquil sweeps of sandy beach. It all gives you a bit of a dilemma. With the southwest it's not so much why go, as what to do first.

When to Go?

This region appeals at any time of year, but spring, summer and early autumn enjoy better weather; they're also when most sights are open. In April and May, cliffs, hillsides and formal gardens burst into a profusion of fragrance and blooms. June offers the chance to catch music festival fever at ultra-cool Glastonbury and on the funky Isle of Wight, and the Port Eliot Festival in mid-July brings music, theatre, dance and literary events to Cornwall. In July and August, coastal areas and blockbuster city sights can get overwhelmed by visitor numbers. But early September brings the end of school summer holidays, cheaper sleeps-spots, quieter beaches and warmer seas.

St George's Channel
To Rosslare (Ireland)
WALES
Carmarthen Bay
Swansea
To Cork (Ireland)
Bristol Channel
Bridgwater Bay
Isles of Scilly
St Martin's
Tresco
St Mary's
Hugh Town
To Penzance (38mi)
0 4 km
0 1.8 miles
Lundy Island
Ilfracombe
Lynton
Porlock
Minehead
Dunster
Combe Martin
Exmoor National Park
Dunkery Beacon
Brendon Hills
Croyde
Braunton
Barnstaple
Barnstaple Bay
Bideford
Dulverton
Clovelly
ATLANTIC OCEAN
A39
Torridge
Taw
Exe
A361
Tiverton
A377
South West Coast Path
Bude
M5
Okehampton
Exeter
Tamar
A30
Chagford
Tintagel
Boscastle
Dartmoor
8
Exmouth
A38
Rough Tor
Brown Willy
Jamaica Inn
Widecombe-in-the-Moor
Padstow
Bodmin Moor
Princetown
Dart
Newton Abbot
Bodmin
Cotehele
Buckfastleigh
Torquay
Newquay
Lanhydrock House
St Just-in-Penwith
Eden Project
7
A38
Totnes
Paignton
Perranporth
A30
Fowey
Looe
Plymouth
Greenway
9
Brixham
St Agnes Head
St Agnes
St Austell
Polperro
Whitsand Bay
Yealm
A379
Dartmouth
Porthtowan
St Austell Bay
Truro
Kingsbridge
Zennor
St Ives
Veryan
Portloe
South West Coast Path
Falmouth
Penzance
10
St Mawes
Roseland Peninsula
Sennen
Helston
St Michael's Mount
Land's End
Mousehole
To Isles of Scilly (see inset) (28mi)
Lizard Point
The Lizard

Southwest England Highlights

1. Bagging a place on an early-morning walk inside the massive sarsen ring at **Stonehenge** (p263)
2. Cooling off amid Georgian splendour in a super-slick spa in **Bath** (p282)
3. Foraging for 200-million-year-old fossils in Dorset's constantly crumbling **Jurassic Coast** (p248)
4. Clambering aboard the pride of Nelson's navy in the historic dockyard at **Portsmouth** (p230)
5. Falling in love with the utterly romantic ruin of **Corfe Castle** (p248)

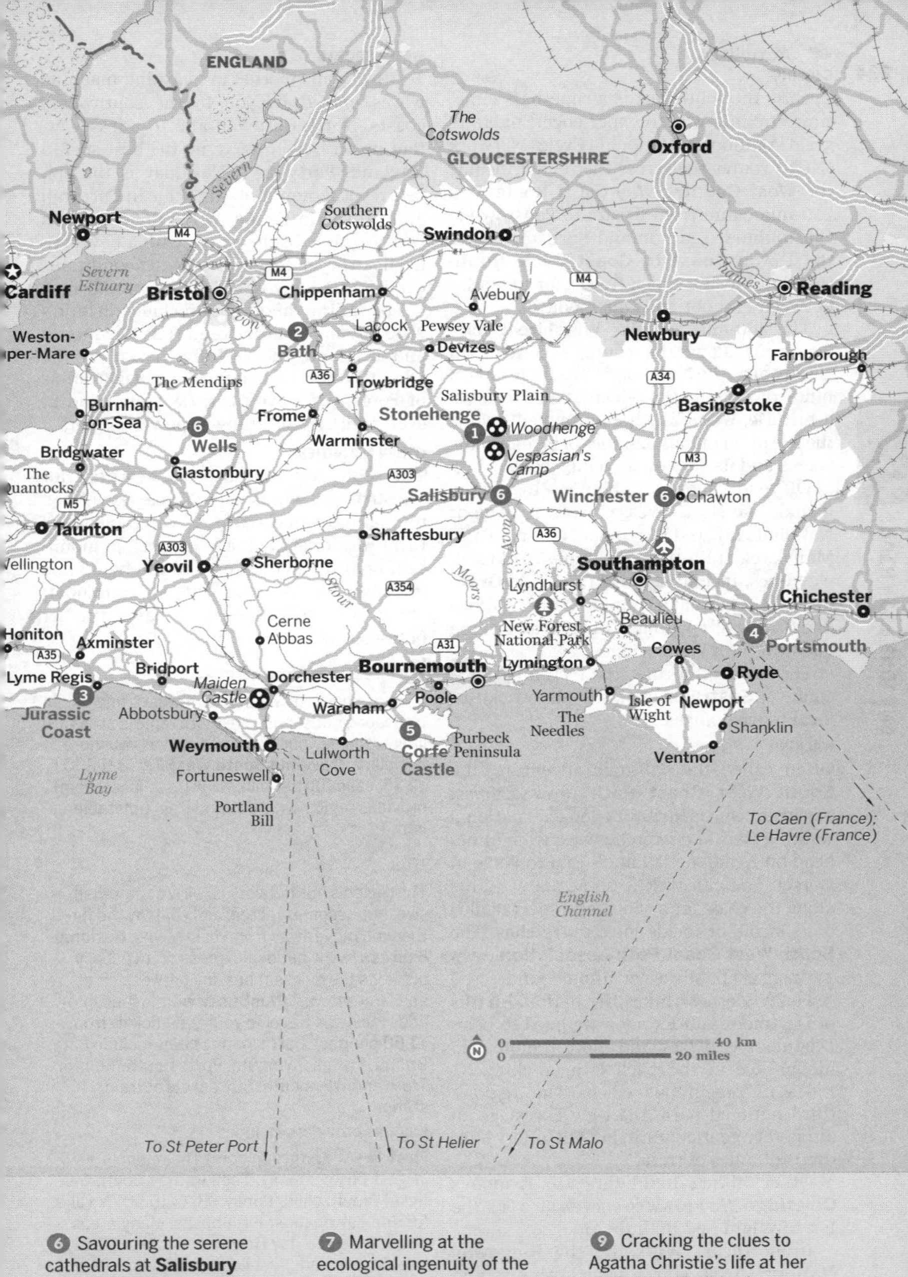

6 Savouring the serene cathedrals at **Salisbury** (p259), **Winchester** (p225) and **Wells** (p286)

7 Marvelling at the ecological ingenuity of the **Eden Project** (p341)

8 Discovering your very own slice of wilderness in natural breakout-zone **Dartmoor** (p312)

9 Cracking the clues to Agatha Christie's life at her enchanting holiday home, **Greenway** (p305)

10 Crossing the causeway to **St Michael's Mount** (p333)

Activities

CYCLING

Cycling the southwest is a superb, if sometimes taxing, way to experience England's great outdoors. National Cycle Network (NCN) routes that cross the region include the **West Country Way** (NCN Route 3), a 250-mile jaunt from Bristol to Padstow via Glastonbury, Taunton and Barnstaple, and the Devon **Coast to Coast Cycle Route** (NCN Route 27), which travels for 102 miles between Exmoor and Dartmoor.

The 160-mile circular **Wiltshire Cycleway** runs along the county's borders. In Hampshire, the New Forest has hundreds of miles of cycle paths which snake through a historic, wildlife-rich environment, while the Isle of Wight has 62-miles of bike-friendly routes and its very own cycling festival.

Off-road mountain-biking highlights include the North Wessex Downs, Exmoor National Park and Dartmoor National Park. Many cycle trails trace the routes of old railway lines, including Devon's 11-mile **Granite Way** between Okehampton and Lydford and Cornwall's popular **Camel Trail** linking Padstow with Wadebridge.

For further information on cycling trails, contact **Sustrans** (www.sustrans.org.uk) or local tourist offices.

WALKING

Often called the 630-mile adventure, the **South West Coast Path** (www.southwestcoastpath.com) is Britain's longest national walking trail, and stretches west from Minehead on Exmoor, via Land's End to Poole in Dorset. You can pick it up at many points along the coast for a short (and spectacular) day's stroll, or tackle longer stretches. The **South West Coast Path Association** (www.swcp.org.uk) publishes an annual guide.

For wilderness hikes the national parks of Dartmoor and Exmoor are hard to beat. Dartmoor is bigger and more remote; Exmoor's ace in the pack is a cracking 34 miles of precipitous coast. The region's third national park, the New Forest, is an altogether gentler affair, but still offers hundreds of miles of trails.

Other hiking highlights are Exmoor's **Coleridge Way** (www.coleridgeway.co.uk), the Isle of Wight and Bodmin Moor.

In northeast Wiltshire, the **Ridgeway National Trail** starts near Avebury and winds 44 miles through chalk hills to meet the River Thames at Goring. The trail then continues another 41 miles (another three days) through the Chiltern Hills.

WATER SPORTS

Testing your mettle in washing-machine waves may draw you to the southwest's coasts. North Cornwall and to a lesser extent north Devon, serve up the best surf in England. Party-town Newquay is the epicentre; other top spots are Bude in Cornwall and Croyde in Devon; while Bournemouth is trying to boost its waves with a new artificial surf reef. Region-wide surf conditions can be found at www.magicseaweed.com.

For sailing, highlights includes Britain's 2012 Olympic sailing venues at Weymouth and Portland, the yachting havens of the Isle of Wight, and the watery playgrounds of Poole, where you can try your hand at everything from sailing to powerboating.

OTHER ACTIVITIES

The southwest is also prime territory for kitesurfing, windsurfing, sea kayaking, diving and wakeboarding; while plenty of firms also offer caving, coasteering, mountain boarding, climbing and kitebuggying. We give details of providers throughout; www.visitsouthwest.co.uk has further options.

Getting Around

It is possible to travel the southwest using public transport, but services to more remote areas are limited; using your own wheels gives you more flexibility. **Traveline South West** (0871 200 22 33, calls 10p per min; www.travelinesw.com) provides region-wide bus and train timetable info.

Bus

The region's bus network is fairly comprehensive, but becomes increasingly patchy the further you move away from main towns. **National Express** (www.nationalexpress.com) usually provides the quickest bus link between cities and larger towns. **PlusBus** (www.plusbus.info) adds local bus travel to your train ticket (from £1.60 per day). Participating cities include Bath, Bristol, Exeter, Plymouth, Portsmouth, Taunton, Truro and Weymouth. Buy tickets at train stations.

Key bus providers include:

First (www.firstgroup.com) The region's largest bus company. The FirstDay Southwest ticket (adult/child/family £8/5/16.50) is valid for one day on most First buses. Many areas also have three-day (from adult/child £12/9) or weekly (from adult/child £21/15) variations.

Stagecoach (www.stagecoachbus.com) A key provider in Hampshire and Devon. Does a one-day Explorer Ticket (adult/child/family £6.50/4/16).

Wilts & Dorset (www.wdbus.co.uk) Useful service across Wiltshire and Dorset. Seven-day network tickets (£20) can be used on all its buses.

Western Greyhound (www.westerngreyhound.com) Key operator in Cornwall.

Car

The main car-hire firms have offices at the region's airports and main-line train stations; rates are similar to elsewhere in the UK.

Train

Bristol is a main train hub; its links include those to London Paddington, Scotland and Birmingham, plus services to Bath, Swindon, Chippenham, Weymouth, Southampton and Portsmouth. Trains from London Waterloo travel to Bournemouth, Salisbury, Southampton, Portsmouth and Weymouth.

Stops on the London Paddington–Penzance service include Exeter, Plymouth, Liskeard, St Austell and Truro. Spur lines run to Barnstaple, Paignton, Gunnislake, Looe, Falmouth, St Ives and Newquay.

The Freedom of the SouthWest Rover pass (adult/child £95/45) allows eight days' unlimited travel over 15 days in an area west of, and including, Salisbury, Bath, Bristol and Weymouth.

HAMPSHIRE

Hampshire's history is regal and rich. Kings Alfred the Great, Knut and William the Conqueror all based their reigns in its ancient cathedral city of Winchester, whose jumble of historic buildings sits in the centre of undulating chalk downs. The county's coast is awash with heritage too – in rejuvenated Portsmouth you can clamber aboard the pride of Nelson's navy, HMS *Victory,* wonder at artefacts from the *Mary Rose* (Henry VIII's flagship), and wander wharfs buzzing with restaurants, shops and bars. Hampshire's southwestern corner claims the open heath and woods of the New Forest and, just off shore, the hip holiday hot-spot that is the Isle of Wight – both areas are covered in separate sections in this chapter.

Winchester

POP 41,420

Calm, collegiate Winchester is a mellow must-see for all visitors. The past still echoes strongly around the flint-flecked walls of this ancient cathedral city. It was the capital of Saxon kings and a power base of bishops, and its statues and sights evoke two of England's mightiest myth-makers: Alfred the Great and King Arthur (he of the round table). Winchester's architecture is exquisite, from the handsome Elizabethan and Regency buildings in the narrow winding streets to the wondrous cathedral at its core. Thanks to its location, nestled in a valley of the River Itchen, there are also charming waterside trails to explore, and the city marks the beginning of the beautiful South Downs Way (see p135).

History

The Romans first put their feet under the table here, but Winchester really took off when the powerful West Saxon bishops moved their episcopal see here in AD 670. Thereafter, Winchester was the most important town in the powerful kingdom of Wessex. King Alfred the Great (r 871–99) made it his capital, and it remained so under Knut (r 1016–35) and the Danish kings. After the Norman invasion of 1066, William the Conqueror arrived here to claim the English throne. In 1086 he commissioned local monks to write the ground-breaking Domesday Book, an administrative survey of the entire country and the most significant clerical accomplishment of the Middle Ages. Winchester thrived until the 12th century, when a fire gutted most of the city – after this, London took its crown. A long slump lasted until the 18th century, when the town was revived as a trading centre.

Sights

Winchester Cathedral CATHEDRAL
(www.winchester-cathedral.org.uk; adult/child £6/free, combined admission & tower tour £9; 9am-5pm Mon-Sat, 12.30-3pm Sun) Almost 1000 years of history are crammed into Winchester's cathedral, which is not only the city's star attraction but one of southern England's most awe-inspiring buildings. The exterior, with a squat tower and a slightly sunken rear, isn't at first glance appealing, despite a fine Gothic facade. But the interior contains one of the longest **medieval naves** (164m) in Europe, and a fascinating jumble of features from all eras.

The cathedral sits beside foundations that mark the town's original 7th-century minster church. The cathedral was begun in 1070 and completed in 1093, and was subsequently entrusted with the bones of its patron saint, St Swithin (bishop of Winchester from 852 to 862). He is best known

Winchester

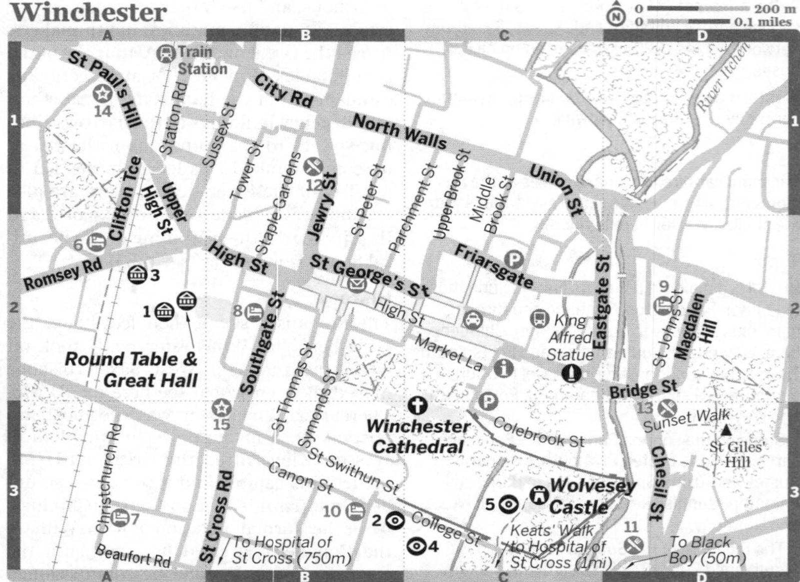

for the proverb that states that if it rains on St Swithin's Day (15 July) it will rain for a further 40 days and 40 nights.

Soggy ground and poor workmanship spelled disaster for the early church; the original tower collapsed in 1107 and major restructuring continued until the mid-15th century. Look out for the monument at the rear to diver William Walker, who saved the cathedral from collapse by delving repeatedly into its waterlogged underbelly from 1906 to 1912 to bolster rotting wooden foundations with vast quantities of concrete and brick.

The transepts are the most original parts of the cathedral, and the intricately carved **medieval choir stalls** are another must-see, sporting everything from mythical beasts to a mischievous green man.

Evensong is held at 5.30pm Monday to Saturday, on Sunday services take place at 8am and 10am, with Evensong at 3.30pm.

Winchester

Top Sights
- Round Table & Great Hall A2
- Winchester Cathedral C3
- Wolvesey Castle C3

Sights
- Gurkha Museum .... (see 1)
- 1 Horsepower A2
- 2 Jane Austen's House B3
- 3 Royal Green Jackets Museum A2
- 4 Winchester College C3
- 5 Wolvesey Palace C3

Sleeping
- 6 5 Clifton Terrace A2
- 7 Dolphin House A3
- 8 Hotel du Vin B2
- 9 No 21 .... D2
- 10 Wykeham Arms B3

Eating
- 11 Black Rat D3
- 12 Brasserie Blanc B1
- 13 Chesil Rectory D3
- Wykeham Arms .... (see 10)

Drinking
- Wykeham Arms .... (see 10)

Entertainment
- 14 Railway Inn A1
- 15 Screen B3

The cathedral's tree-fringed lawns are a tranquil spot to take time out, especially on the quieter south side beyond the cloisters; the permanent secondhand book stall in the Deanery porch provides great bargain hunting.

Cathedral Library & Triforium Gallery

(10.30am-3.30pm Tue-Sat, 2-4pm Mon Apr-Oct) Tucked away on the south side of the nave, this section provides a fine elevated view of the cathedral body and contains the dazzlingly illuminated pages of the 12th-century **Winchester Bible** – its colours as bright as if it was painted yesterday.

Jane Austen's Grave

Jane Austen, one of England's best-loved authors, is buried near the entrance in the cathedral's northern aisle. Austen died a stone's throw from the cathedral in 1817 at **Jane Austen's House** (8 College St), where she spent her last six weeks. It's now a private residence and is marked by a slate plaque. Her former home is 18 miles away (see also boxed text, p228).

Tours

Cathedral body tours (free; hourly 10am-3pm Mon-Sat) last one hour. **Tower and roof tours** (£6; tours at 2.15pm Wed & Sat, plus 11.30am Sat) see you clambering up narrow stairwells, and being rewarded with fine views as far as the Isle of Wight. There's an extra tour at 2.15pm Monday to Friday in July and August; tours are only open to those aged between 12 and 70, for safety reasons. **Crypt Tours** (free; 10.30am, 12.30pm & 2.30pm Mon-Sat Apr-Oct) aren't always available because of flooding. If the crypt is open, look for the poignant solitary sculpture by Anthony Gormley called *Sound 2*.

The Round Table & Great Hall HISTORIC ARTEFACT

(Castle Ave; suggested donation adult/child £1/50p; 10am-5pm) Winchester's other showpiece sight is the cavernous Great Hall, the only part of 11th-century Winchester Castle that Oliver Cromwell spared from destruction. Crowning the wall like a giant-sized dartboard of green and cream spokes is what centuries of mythology have dubbed King Arthur's Round Table. It's actually a 700-year-old copy, but is fascinating nonetheless. It's thought to have been constructed in the late 13th century and then painted in the reign of Henry VIII (King Arthur's image is unsurprisingly reminiscent of Henry's youthful face).

This hall was also the stage for several dramatic English courtroom dramas, including the trial of adventurer Sir Walter Raleigh in 1603, who was sentenced to death but received a reprieve at the last minute.

FREE **Wolvesey Castle** CASTLE

(EH; www.english-heritage.org.uk; 10am-5pm Apr-Sep) The fantastic, crumbling remains of early-12th-century Wolvesey Castle huddle in the protective embrace of the city's walls, despite the building having been largely demolished in the 1680s. It was completed by Henry de Blois, and it served as the Bishop of Winchester's residence throughout the medieval era. Queen Mary I and Philip II of Spain celebrated their wedding feast here in 1554. According to legend, its odd name comes from a Saxon king's demand for an annual payment of 300 wolves' heads. Access is via College St. Today the bishop lives in the (private) **Wolvesey Palace** next door.

Winchester College SCHOOL

(www.winchestercollege.org; College St; tours £4; tours at 10.45am & noon Mon-Sat, plus 2.15pm & 3.30pm Fri, Sat & Sun) Winchester College gives you a rare chance to nosey around a prestigious English private school. It was set up by William Wykeham, Bishop of Winchester in 1393, 14 years after he founded Oxford's New College. Hour-long guided tours trail through the school's medieval core, taking in the 14th-century Gothic Chapel, complete with wooden vaulted roof, the dining room (called College Hall), and a vast 17th century open-class room (called School), where exams are still held. It's all deeply atmospheric and unshakably affluent; a revealing insight into how the other half learns. Tours start from the Porter's Lodge.

Hospital of St Cross HISTORIC HOSPITAL

(www.stcrosshospital.co.uk; St Cross Rd; adult/child £3/1; 9.30am-5pm Mon-Sat, 1-5pm Sun Apr-Oct, 10.30am-3.30pm Mon-Sat Nov-Mar) Monk, bishop, knight, politician and grandson of William the Conqueror, Henry de Blois was a busy man. But he found time to establish this still-impressive hospital in 1132. As well as healing the sick and housing the needy, the hospital was built to feed and house pilgrims and crusaders en route to the Holy Land. It's the oldest charitable institution in the country, and is still roamed

WORTH A TRIP

JANE AUSTEN'S HOUSE MUSEUM

There's more than a touch of the period dramas she inspired about the former home of Jane Austen (1775–1817) in Chawton village. This appealing red-brick house, where the celebrated English novelist lived with her mother and sister from 1809 to 1817, is now a **museum** (www.jane-austens-house-museum.org.uk; Chawton; adult/child £7/2; ⏲10.30am-4.30pm mid-Feb–Dec). While here she wrote *Mansfield Park, Emma* and *Persuasion*, and revised *Sense and Sensibility, Pride and Prejudice* and *Northanger Abbey.*

The interior depicts a typical well-to-do Georgian family home, complete with elegant furniture and copper pans in the kitchen. Highlights include the occasional table Austen used as a desk, first editions of her novels and the delicate handkerchief she embroidered for her sister.

The museum is 18 miles east of Winchester; take bus 64 from Winchester to Chawton roundabout (50 minutes, hourly Monday to Saturday, six on Sunday) then walk 500m to Chawton village.

by 25 elderly black- or red-gowned brothers in pie-shaped trencher hats, who continue to hand out alms. Take a peek into the stumpy church, the brethren hall, the kitchen and the peaceful gardens. The best way to arrive is via the one-mile Keats' Walk. Upon entering, claim the centuries-old Wayfarer's Dole – a crust of bread and horn of ale (now a small swig of beer) from the Porter's Gate.

Military Museums

Of Winchester's clutch of army museums, the pick is the **Royal Green Jackets Museum** (The Rifles; www.winchestermilitarymuseums.co.uk; Peninsula Barracks, Romsey Rd; adult/child £3/1; ⏲10am-5pm Mon-Sat, noon-4pm Sun), which has a mini rifle-shooting range, a room of 6000 medals and an impressive blow-by-blow diorama of Napoleon's downfall, the Battle of Waterloo. The **Gurkha Museum** (www.thegurkhamuseum.co.uk; Peninsula Barracks, Romsey Rd; adult/child £2/free; ⏲10am-5pm Mon-Sat, noon-4pm Sun) features the regiment's history, combining a jungle tableau with a history of Gurkha service to the British crown. **Horsepower** (www.horsepowermuseum.co.uk; Peninsula Barracks, Romsey Rd; admission free; ⏲10am-4pm Tue-Fri, noon-4pm Sat & Sun) gallops through the combat history of the Royal Hussars, from the Charge of the Light Brigade to armour-clad vehicles.

Activities

Winchester has a tempting range of walks. The one-mile **Keats' Walk** meanders through the water meadows to the Hospital of St Cross. Its beauty is said to have prompted the poet to pen the ode To Autumn – pick up the trail near Winchester College. Alternatively, head down Wharf Hill, through the water meadows to St Catherine's Hill (1 mile). The tranquil **Riverside Walk** trails a short distance from the castle along the bank of the River Itchen to High St.

Tours

Guided Walks HISTORY

(adult/child £4/free; ⏲11am & 2.30pm Mon-Sat Apr-Oct, 11am Sat Nov-Mar) Tourist office–run, 1½ hour, heritage-themed walks that include Jane Austen's Winchester, Ghost Walks and Canons and Courtesans.

Sleeping

Wykeham Arms HISTORIC INN ££

(☎01962-853834; www.fullershotels.com; 75 Kingsgate St; s/d/ste £70/119/150; P 📶) At 250-odd years old, the Wykeham is bursting with history – it used to be a brothel and also put up Nelson for a night (some say the two events coincided). Creaking, winding stairs lead to the cosy, traditionally styled bedrooms above the pub, while sleeker rooms (over the converted post office, opposite), look out onto a pocked-sized courtyard garden.

5 Clifton Terrace BOUTIQUE B&B ££

(☎01962-890053; cliftonterrace@hotmail.co.uk; 5 Clifton Tce; s/d/f £60/70/110; P 📶) Blending old and new, this tall Georgian town house sees plush furnishings rub shoulders with antiques, and modern comforts coexist alongside claw-foot baths. The owners are utterly charming.

Dolphin House B&B ££

(☎01962-853284; www.dolphinhousestudios.co.uk; 3 Compton Rd; s/d £55/70; P 📶) At this kind of B&B-plus, your continental breakfast is delivered to a compact kitchen – perfect for lazy lie-ins. The terrace, complete with cast-iron tables and chairs, overlooks a gently sloping lawn.

No 21 B&B ££
(☎01962-852989; St Johns St; s/d £45/90) Gorgeous cathedral views, a flower-filled cottage garden and rustic-chic rooms (think painted wicker and woven bedspreads) make this art-packed house a tranquil city bolt hole.

Hotel du Vin HISTORIC HOTEL £££
(☎01962-841414; www.hotelduvin.com; Southgate St; r £140-225; P @) An oh-so-stylish oasis, boasting ultracool minimalist furniture, ornate chaises longues and opulent stand-alone baths.

Eating

TOP CHOICE **Chesil Rectory** ENGLISH ££
(☎01962-851555; www.chesilrectory.co.uk; 1 Chesil St; mains £16; ⊙lunch & dinner Mon-Sat, lunch Sun) Duck through the hobbit-sized door, settle down amid the 15th-century beams and savour perfectly prepared modern British cuisine, cooked up by the former head chef at Fortnum and Masons. New Forest rabbit, seared scallops, truffles and local watercress all feature on an assured menu. The two-course evening menu (served 6pm to 7pm) is a snip at £15.

Black Rat ENGLISH ££
(☎01962-844465; www.theblackrat.co.uk; 88 Chesil St; mains £17-20; ⊙dinner daily, lunch Sat & Sun) Worn wooden floorboards and warm red-brick walls give this relaxed restaurant a cosy feel. Locally sourced treats such as roast venison with asparagus, and Weymouth crab with marsh samphire find their way onto the sanded-down tables.

Wykeham Arms ENGLISH ££
(☎01962-853834; www.fullershotels.com; 75 Kingsgate St; mains £10-17; ⊙lunch & dinner Mon-Sat, lunch Sun;) The food at this super-quirky pub is legendary – try the pan-fried salmon, or sausages flavoured with local bitter, then finish off with some seriously addictive sticky toffee pudding.

Brasserie Blanc FRENCH ££
(☎01962-810870; www.brasserieblanc.com; 19 Jewry St; mains £13; ⊙lunch & dinner) Get a taste of French home cooking, Raymond (Blanc) style, at this super-sleek chain. The celebrity chef may not necessarily sauté your starter, but the chicken stuffed with morel mushrooms and the Toulouse sausage with onion gravy are full of Gallic charm.

Drinking

TOP CHOICE **Wykeham Arms** PUB
(www.fullershotels.com; 75 Kingsgate St;) Somehow reminiscent of an endearingly eccentric old uncle, this is just the sort of pub you'd love to have as a local: 1400 tankards, school canes and a riot of flags hang from the ceiling, while seating comes in the form of worn school desks, lending pint-supping an illicit air.

Black Boy PUB
(www.theblackboypub.com; 1 Wharf Hill; ⊙noon-11pm, to midnight Fri & Sat) This adorable old boozer is filled with obsessive and sometimes freaky collections, from pocket watches to wax facial features; bear traps to sawn-in-half paperbacks. The pumps produce five locally-brewed real ales. It'ss located just south of Black Rat.

Entertainment

For listings, pick up the free *What's On in Winchester* from the tourist office.

Railway Inn LIVE MUSIC
(☎01962-867795; www.liveattherailway.co.uk; 3 St Paul's Hill; ⊙5pm-midnight Sun-Thu, to 2am Fri, to 1am Sat) Bands ranging from acoustic to punk play at this grungy venue.

Screen MAINSTREAM CINEMA
(☎0870-0664777; www.screencinemas.co.uk; Southgate St) Shows the standard features.

Information

Discovery Centre (Jewry St; ⊙9am-7pm Mon-Fri, 9am-5pm Sat, 10am-4pm Sun) A library with free internet access.

Tourist office (☎01962-840500; www.visitwinchester.co.uk; High St; ⊙10am-5pm Mon-Sat plus 11am-4pm Sun May-Sep)

Getting There & Away

Winchester is 65 miles west of London.

Bus

Regular, direct National Express buses shuttle to **London Victoria** (£14.40, 1¾ hours). Stagecoach Explorer Tickets (adult/child £8/6) cover Winchester and Salisbury.

Train

Trains leave every 30 minutes for London Waterloo (£26, 1¼ hours) and hourly for Portsmouth (£9.10, one hour). There are also fast links to the Midlands.

Getting Around

Bicycle

Bikeabout (www.winchester.gov.uk/bikeabout; membership £20) Members can borrow bikes (free) for 24 hours; pick them up from the tourist office.

Car

The **Park & Ride** (£2 to £3 per day) is signed off junctions 10 and 11 of the M3.

Taxi

Ranks for taxis are on Middle Brook St, or you can phone **Wintax Taxis** (01962-878727).

Portsmouth

POP 187,056

Prepare to splice the main brace, hoist the halyard and potter around the poop deck. Portsmouth is the principal port of Britain's Royal Navy, and its historic dockyard ranks alongside Greenwich as one of England's most fascinating centres of maritime history. Here you can jump aboard Lord Nelson's glorious warship HMS *Victory,* which led the charge at Trafalgar, and see atmospheric artefacts from Henry VIII's 16th-century flagship, the *Mary Rose.*

Regeneration at the nearby Gunwharf Quays has added fresh glitz to the city's waterfront, where a spectacular millennium-inspired structure, the Spinnaker Tower, provides jaw-dropping views. But Portsmouth is by no means noted for its beauty; it was bombed heavily during WWII and chunks of the city feature soulless postwar architecture. However, the city's fine array of naval museums, a clutch of superb French restaurants and some chic places to sleep, justify a longer visit. The suburb of Southsea, which begins a mile southeast of Gunwharf Quays, is rich in good hotels and eateries.

Sights & Activities

TOP CHOICE Portsmouth Historic Dockyard

HISTORIC SHIPS

(www.historicdockyard.co.uk; adult/child/family £20/14/55; 10am-6pm Apr-Oct, 10am-5.30pm Nov-Mar) This is Portsmouth's blockbuster attraction. Set in the heart of one of the country's most important naval ports, it comprises two stunning ships and a cluster of museums that pay homage to the historical might of the Royal Navy. The ticket price also includes a boat trip round the harbour. Together it makes for a full day's outing, the last admission is 1½ hours before closing.

The Ships

As resplendent as she is venerable, the dockyard's star sight is **HMS Victory** (www.hms-victory.com), Lord Nelson's flagship at the Battle of Trafalgar (1805) and the site of his infamous dying words 'Kiss me, Hardy...' when victory over the French had been secured. This remarkable ship is topped by a forest of ropes and masts, and weighted by a swollen belly filled with cannon and paraphernalia for an 850-strong crew. Clambering through the low-beamed decks and crew's quarters is an evocative experience.

Anywhere else, the magnificent warship **HMS Warrior**, built in 1860, would grab centre stage. This stately dame was at the cutting edge of technology in her day, riding the transition from wood to iron and sail to steam. The gleaming upper deck, vast gun deck and the dimly-lit cable lockers conjure up a vivid picture of life in the Victorian navy.

Mary Rose Museum

The raising of the 16th-century warship the *Mary Rose* was an extraordinary feat of marine archaeology. This 700-tonne floating fortress and favourite of Henry VIII, sank suddenly off Portsmouth while fighting the French in 1545 and was only raised from her watery grave in 1982. Of a crew of 400, its thought 360 men died. The vessel herself currently can't be seen – a £35 million museum is being built around her, it's due to open in mid-2012.

You can still see the wealth of artefacts from the warship that fills the **Mary Rose Museum** (www.maryrose.org). Artefacts range from the military, including scores of cannons and hundreds of longbows, to the touchingly prosaic: water jugs, hair combs and even leather shoes. The museum also features a 15-minute film chronicling the extraction of the still-preserved hulk from Portsmouth Harbour.

Royal Naval Museum

Expect model ships, battle dioramas, medals and paintings in this huge museum. Audiovisual displays recreate the Battle of Trafalgar and one even lets you take command of a warship – see if you can cure the scurvy and avoid mutiny. One gallery is entirely devoted to Lord Nelson.

Trafalgar Sail Exhibition

This small exhibition showcases the only HMS *Victory* sail to survive the Battle of Trafalgar. Clearly bearing the scars of conflict, it's riddled with the holes made by Napoleonic cannon – a telling illustration of the battle's ferocity.

Action Stations!

Stroll into this warehouse-based **interactive experience** (www.actionstations.org) and you'll soon be piloting a replica Merlin helicopter, controlling an aircraft carrier, upping periscope or jumping aboard a ship simulator. The whole set-up is a thinly disguised recruitment drive for the modern navy, but it's fun nonetheless.

The Point SIGNIFICANT AREA

Some 500m south of Gunwharf Quays, the Point (also known locally as Spice Island), is home to characterful cobbled streets dotted with salty sea-dog pubs; their water-side terraces are top spots to gaze at the Spinnaker Tower and the passing parade of ferries and navy ships. You can clatter up the steps of the **Round Tower** (originally built by Henry V) and stroll along the old fort walls to the **Square Tower**, which was built in 1494. Underneath, cavernous vaults frame **Sally Ports**; historic openings in the defences that give access to the sea and a strip of shingle beach. To walk to the Point follow the chain link design set into the pavement from Gunwharf Quays.

Spinnaker Tower LANDMARK TOWER

(www.spinnakertower.co.uk; Gunwharf Quays; adult/child £7.25/5.75; ⏲10am-10pm) Soaring to 170m above Gunwharf Quays, the Spinnaker Tower is an unmistakable symbol of Portsmouth's new-found razzle-dazzle. Its two sweeping white arcs resemble a billowing sail from some angles, and a sharp skeletal ribcage from others.

As the UK's tallest publicly accessible structure, it offers truly extraordinary views over Portsmouth, the Isle of Wight, the South Downs and even Chichester, 23 miles to the east. **Observation Deck 1** has a hair-raising view through the glass floor, while the roofless **Crow's Nest** on Deck 3 allows you to feel the wind on your face.

D-Day Museum MILITARY MUSEUM

(www.ddaymuseum.co.uk; Clarence Esplanade; adult/child £6/4.20; ⏲10am-5pm) Two miles southeast of Gunwharf Quays, exhibits here recount Portsmouth's crucial role as a departure point for Allied D-Day forces in 1944.

Blue Reef AQUARIUM

(www.bluereefaquarium.co.uk; Towan Promenade; adult/child £9.20/7.20; ⏲10am-5pm Mar-Oct, to 4pm Nov-Feb) Open-topped tanks, huge underwater walkways and a captivating 'seahorse ranch'.

HMS VICTORY

In the summer, tours of Nelson's flagship are self-guided. But between autumn and spring, hugely-popular 40-minute **guided tours** are held. Arrive early to bag a place – you can't book in advance.

Tours

Boat Trips BOAT TRIP

(☎023-9272 8060; Historic Dockyard; ⏲11am-3pm Easter-Oct) Weather permitting, 45-minute harbour tours leave on the hour. They're free with the Dockyard ticket or can be bought separately (adult/child £5/3).

Walking Tours HERITAGE

(adult/child £3/free; ⏲2.30pm Sun Apr-Oct) Guided walk themes include Nelson, Henry VIII and Old Fortifications. Check with the tourist office for departure points.

Sleeping

Florence House BOUTIQUE HOTEL **££**

(☎023-9275 1666; www.florencehousehotel.co.uk; 2 Malvern Rd, Southsea; d £75-145; P @ 🛜) Edwardian elegance combines beautifully with modern flourishes at this superstylish oasis of boutique bliss. It's a winning combination of plush furnishings, sleek bathrooms, open fireplaces and the odd chaise longue – the suite, complete with spa bath, is top-notch.

Fortitude Cottage B&B **££**

(☎023-9282 3748; www.fortitudecottage.co.uk; 51 Broad St, The Point; s £45, d £60-120; P) The ferry-port views from this fresh and airy guest house are interesting, while the top-floor penthouse boasts a private balcony, roof terrace and 360-degree vistas; binoculars are provided. The bay-windowed breakfast room is ideal for tucking into smoked salmon and scrambled eggs.

Somerset House BOUTIQUE HOTEL **£££**

(☎023-9275 3555; www.somersethousehotel.co.uk; 10 Florence Rd, Southsea; d £95-190) At this late-Victorian sister to Florence House opposite, the same team has created another achingly tasteful haven of designer

Portsmouth

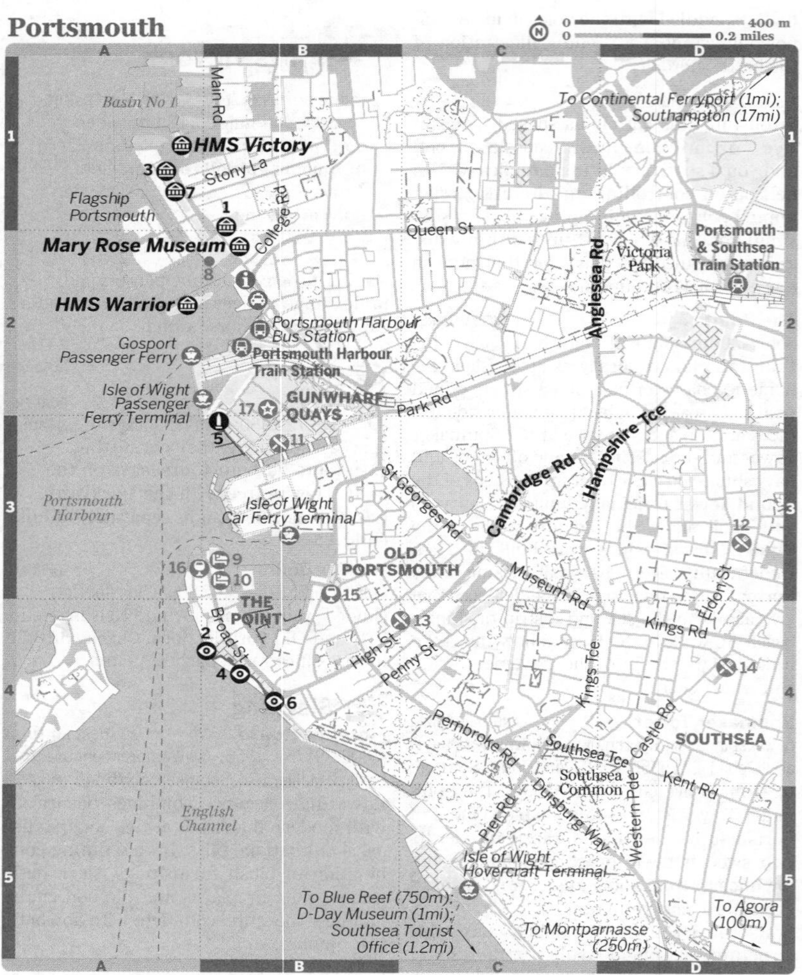

calm. Here, stained glass, dark woods and polished floors cosy up to Balinese figurines and the last word in luxury bathrooms.

Cecil Cottage B&B ££
(☎078 9407 2253; www.cecilcottage.co.uk; 45 Broad St, The Point; s/d £50/70; P) Luxury smellies in the bathroom, use of a ferry-view lounge and a pot of tea and plate of biscuits on arrival make this Spice Island B&B another great option. The crisp white and soft grey colour scheme completes the soothing effect.

Southsea Backpackers HOSTEL £
(☎023-9283 2495; www.portsmouthbackpackers.co.uk; 4 Florence Rd, Southsea; dm £15, d £33-38; P @) A well-run, old-fashioned backpackers with four- to eight-bed dorms. A pool table, patio and BBQ compensates for a low shower-to-people ratio. In Southsea.

Eating

TOP CHOICE **Truffles** FRENCH ££
(☎023-9273 0796; www.trufflesfrancais.co.uk; 67 Castle Rd, Southsea; 2-course lunch/dinner £7.50/22; ⊙lunch & dinner Tue-Sat, lunch Sun) The perfect marriage of Hampshire ingredients and continental gastronomy, this chic little bistro rustles up super-stylish

Portsmouth

Top Sights
- HMS Victory ... A1
- HMS Warrior ... A2
- Mary Rose Museum ... B2

Sights
1. Action Stations! ... B1
2. Round Tower ... B4
3. Royal Naval Museum ... A1
4. Sally Ports ... B4
5. Spinnaker Tower ... B3
6. Square Tower ... B4
7. Trafalgar Sail Exhibition ... A1

Activities, Courses & Tours
8. Boat Trips ... B2

Sleeping
9. Cecil Cottage ... B3
10. Fortitude Cottage ... B3

Eating
11. Custom House ... B3
12. Kitsch'n d'or ... D3
13. Lemon Sole ... C4
14. Truffles ... D4

Drinking
15. A Bar ... B3
16. Still & West ... A3

Entertainment
17. Vue ... B2

food at bargain prices. British rump steak combines with truffle sauce, while sea bass comes laced with vermouth. The painters' palettes, Eiffel Tower silhouettes and gendarme's uniform reinforce the Parisienne air.

Kitsch'n d'or FRENCH ££
(023-9286 1519; www.kitschndor.com; 37 Eldon St, Southsea; mains £13, 4-courses £18-23; lunch & dinner Mon-Sat, lunch Sun) Prepare to be transported to rural Provence. Dishes are rich with hearty rustic flavours, from venison with blackberry sauce, to mountain chorizo with baked duck eggs and Madeira. Seafood is a speciality too: mounds of lobster, steaming clams and scallops are topped off with a zingy spiced butter.

Lemon Sole ENGLISH ££
(023-928 11303; www.lemonsole.co.uk; 123 High St, Old Portsmouth; mains £9.50-18; lunch & dinner) At Lemon Sole you get to pick-your-own piece of fish at a counter then choose how you want it cooked. Try the seafood chowder, devilled mackerel or stunning shellfish platters (£45 for two). It's all tucked away in a lemon-yellow interior with a whole wall full of wine bottles at the end.

Custom House PUB £
(Gunwharf Quays; mains £9; lunch & dinner) The best of Gunwharf Quays' numerous eateries, this smart pub occupies an 18th-century former Royal Marine hospital. Now better-than-average bar food (think glazed ham, steak and ale pie and gourmet burgers) is served up amid its raspberry-red walls and gilt-framed mirrors.

Drinking

Rows of bars and trendy balconied eateries line Gunwharf Quays.

A Bar PUB
(www.abarbistro.co.uk; 58 White Hart Rd, Old Portsmouth; 11am-midnight) There's actually been a pub on this site since 1784 – these days it's home to worn floorboards, squishy leather sofas, a soundtrack of groovy tunes and a chilled, gently trendy vibe.

Still & West PUB
(2 Bath Sq, The Point) This relaxed, salty sea-dog boozer has served many a sailor and smuggler in the last 300 years. The waterside terrace is the place to down a beer to a backdrop of passing yachts and ferries.

Entertainment

Southsea is thick with nightclubs and live-music venues.

Wedgewood Rooms NIGHTCLUB
(www.wedgewood-rooms.co.uk; Albert Rd, Southsea) One of Portsmouth's best live-music venues; also hosts DJs and comedians.

Vue CINEMA
(www.myvue.com; Gunwharf Quays)

Information

Online Café (163 Elm Grove, Southsea; per 10min/1hr 50p/£2.50; 10am-10pm) Internet access.

Main tourist office (023-9282 6722; www.visitportsmouth.co.uk; The Hard; 9.30am-5.45pm Jul & Aug, to 5.15pm Sep-Jun)

Southsea tourist office (023-9282 6722; Clarence Esplanade, Southsea; 9.30am-5.15pm daily Mar-Aug, to 4pm Fri-Tue Sep-Feb)

SOUTHAMPTON

Southhampton is a useful transport hub. **Southampton International Airport** (www.southamptonairport.com) sits between Winchester, Portsmouth and Bournemouth. It connects with 40 UK and European destinations, including Amsterdam, Paris and Dublin.

Trains run direct from the airport to Bournemouth (£10, 30 minutes, three per hour) via Brockenhurst in the New Forest (£7.40, 22 minutes). Five trains an hour link the airport to Southampton's main train station (seven minutes).

From there, three trains an hour run to **Portsmouth** (£8.30, 1¼ hours) and **Winchester** (£5.20, 20 minutes).

Ferries shuttle from Southampton to the Isle of Wight (see p240).

Getting There & Away

Portsmouth is 100 miles southwest of London.

Boat

For details on how to reach the Isle of Wight from Portsmouth, see p239.

Several routes run from Portsmouth to France. Prices vary wildly depending on times and dates of travel – an example fare is £300 return for a car and two adults on the Portsmouth–Cherbourg route. Book in advance, be prepared to travel off-peak and look out for special deals.

Brittany Ferries (www.brittanyferries.co.uk) Services run regularly to St Malo (10¾ hours), Caen (four hours) and Cherbourg (three hours) in France, and twice-weekly to Santander (13 hours) in Spain.

Condor Ferries (www.condorferries.co.uk) Runs a weekly car-and-passenger service to Cherbourg (6½ hours).

LD Lines (www.ldlines.co.uk) Shuttles to Le Havre (three to eight hours) in France.

Bus

There are 13 National Express buses from London (£18, 2¼ hours) daily; some go via Heathrow Airport (£17.60, 3½ hours). Bus 700 runs to Chichester (one hour) and Brighton (four hours) half-hourly Monday to Saturday, and hourly on Sunday.

Train

Trains run every 30 minutes from London Victoria (£27, two hours) and Waterloo (£27, 1¾ hours) stations. For the Historic Dockyard get off at the final stop, Portsmouth Harbour.

Departures include:

Brighton (£14, 1½ hours, hourly)
Chichester (£6, 40 minutes, twice an hour)
Southampton (£8.30, 1¼ hours, three hourly)
Winchester (£9, one hour, hourly)

Getting Around

Bus

Bus 6 runs every 15 minutes between Portsmouth Harbour bus station and South Parade Pier in Southsea.

Taxi

Ranks for taxis are near the bus station. Or call **Aquacars** (☎023-9266 6666) in Southsea.

NEW FOREST

With typical, accidental English irony, the New Forest is anything but new – it was first proclaimed a royal hunting preserve in 1079. It's also not much of a forest, being mostly heathland ('forest' is from the Old French for 'hunting ground'). Today the forest's combined charms make it a joy to explore. Wild ponies mooch around pretty scrubland, deer flicker in the distance and rare birds flit among the foliage. Genteel villages dot the landscape, connected by a web of walking and cycling routes.

Activities

CYCLING

With all that picturesque scenery, the New Forest makes for superb cycling country, and hundreds of miles of trails link the main villages and the key railway station at Brockenhurst.

The *New Forest Cycle Map* (£2) shows the approved off-road and quieter 'on-road' routes. The *New Forest Cycle Experience RoutePack* (£4) features seven trips, including a 4-mile jaunt. The *Forest Leisure Cycling Route Pack* (£4) has six circular cycle routes for all abilities – all start from the village of Burley.

Maps and guides can be bought from Lyndhurst tourist office (p236) or via its website.

To rent bikes you'll need to pay a deposit (usually £20) and provide identification.

AA Bike Hire BIKE HIRE
(☎023-8028 3349; www.aabikehirenewforest.co.uk; Fern Glen, Gosport Lane, Lyndhurst; adult/child per day £10/5)

Country Lanes BIKE HIRE
(☎01590-622627; www.countrylanes.co.uk; Railway Station, Brockenhurst; bike/tandem per day £15/28; ⏲Easter-Oct)

Cyclexperience BIKE HIRE
(☎01590-624204; www.newforestcyclehire.co.uk; Brookley Rd, Brockenhurst; adult/child per day £14/7)

Forest Leisure Cycling BIKE HIRE
(☎01425-403584; www.forestleisurecycling.co.uk; The Cross, Village Centre, Burley; adult/child per day from £14/6)

HORSE RIDING

No, we're not talking about saddling up one of the wild ponies. But riding is a wonderful way to roam the New Forest. Stables welcoming beginners:

Arniss Equestrian Centre STABLE
(☎01425-654114; www.arnissequestrian.co.uk; Godshill, Fordingbridge; per hr £20)

Burley-Villa STABLE
(Western Riding; ☎01425-610278; www.burleyvilla.co.uk; New Milton; per 1/2 hr £29/49)

Forest Park STABLE
(01590-623429; www.forestparkridingstables.co.uk; Rhienfield Rd, Brockenhurst; per 1/2 hr £30/50)

OTHER ACTIVITIES

The forest is prime **hiking** territory. Ordnance Survey (OS) produces a detailed, 1:25 000 Explorer map (New Forest; No 22, £8); Crimson Publishing's *New Forrest Short Walks* (£7) features 20 day-hikes.

Rambles with a Ranger TOUR
(☎023-8028 6840; www.forestry.gov.uk; adult £6-8, child £4-5) Memorable dusk deer-watching safaris and wild food foraging trips.

New Forest Activities WATER SPORTS
(☎01590-612377;www.newforestactivities.co.uk) Near Beaulieu. Offers canoeing (adult/child per two hours £28/22), kayaking (per two hours £28), sea kayaking (per three hours/day £40/70) and archery (adult/child per 1½ hours £20/15).

ℹ Getting There & Around

BUS

Regular services run to Bournemouth and Southampton.

New Forest Tour (www.thenewforesttour.info; adult/child £9/4.50; ⏲hourly 10am-5pm mid-Jun–mid-Sep) The hop-on/hop-off bus

New Forest

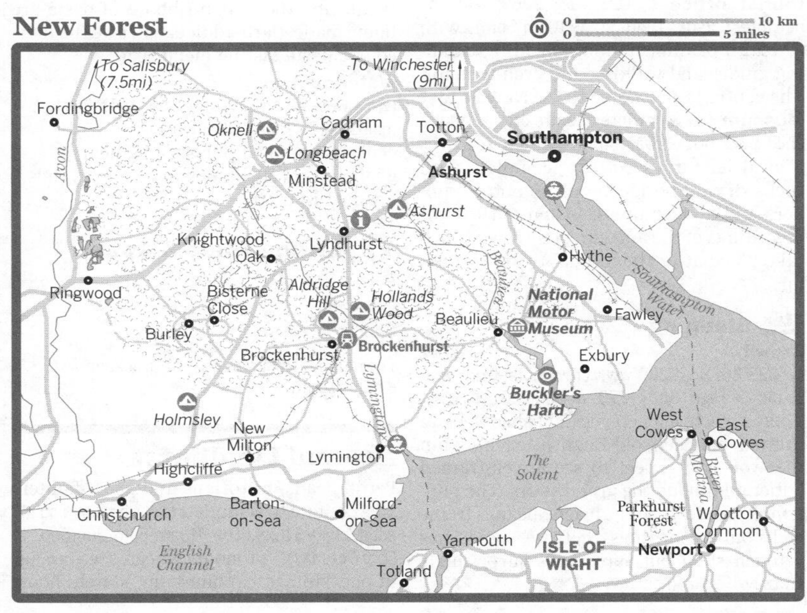

CAMPING IN THE NEW FOREST

The New Forest is hugely popular with campers; Lyndhurst's tourist office has a free brochure detailing designated areas. For more information, go to www.thenewforest.co.uk.

passes through Lyndhurst's main car park, Brockenhurst station, Lymington, Beaulieu and Exbury.

TRAIN

Trains run every hour to Brockenhurst from London Waterloo (£34, two hours) via Winchester (£10, 30 minutes) and on to Bournemouth (£5.80, 25 minutes). Local trains also link Brockenhurst with Lymington.

Lyndhurst

POP 2281

A good base from which to explore the national park or simply stop off for a pint, a cuppa or a map, the quaint country village of Lyndhurst is one of the New Forest's larger settlements. It boasts an evocative museum, a quintessentially English pub and an authentically Italian restaurant.

The **New Forest Centre** contains a **tourist office** (☎023-8028 2269; www.thenewforest.co.uk; High St; ⏲10am-5pm) with a wealth of information, including camping guides and walking and cycling maps. The centre is also home to the **New Forest Museum** (www.newforestcentre.org.uk; adult/child £3/2.50; ⏲10am-4pm), which features a local labourer's cottage (complete with socks drying beside the fire), potato dibbers and a cider press. Listen out too for recordings of the autumn pony sales which take place after the annual drifts (round-ups).

Sleeping

Crown HOTEL ££

(☎023-8028 2922; www.crownhotel-lyndhurst.co.uk; 9 High St; s £70 d £80-130; P@) There's such a deeply established feel to this oak-panelled, old-English coaching inn that you half expect to see a well-trained butler gliding up the grand stairs. The mullioned windows and ancient beams frame bedroom furnishings that are sometimes a touch staid but sometimes surprisingly snazzy.

Whitley Ridge HOTEL £££

(☎01590-622354; www.whitleyridge.com; Beaulieu Rd; r £95-155; P) If you hanker after pure country-house atmosphere, head here. Set in 6 hectares of dappled grounds, this ivy-clad Georgian pile pampers guests amid elegant rooms finished with contemporary twists (think sleigh beds meets gilt mirrors). The classy restaurant conjures up organic, seasonal, locally sourced creations finished with Anglo-French flair. It's all tucked away 4 miles south of Lyndhurst at Brockenhurst.

Little Hayes B&B ££

(☎023-8028 3816; www.littlehayes.co.uk; 43 Romsey Rd; d £70-80; P) Moulded ceilings, old oak banisters and the odd chandelier speak of this Edwardian guest house's age. Bursts of scatter-cushion-smartness liven up the good-sized rooms, while the breakfasts are full of New Forest produce.

Eating & Drinking

Fra Noi ITALIAN ££

(☎023-8028 3745; www.franoi.co.uk; 74 High St; mains £11-19; ⏲dinner Tue-Sat, lunch Sun) The techniques may be pure Tuscany, but the chefs at this swish trattoria have definitely raided the New Forest larder. The beef and venison is free-range, local and organic; the richly-flavoured lasagne comes with black truffle and the golden ribbons of pasta are home made. Carb-addicts will love the four-course pasta tasting menu (£30).

Waterloo Arms PUB £

(www.waterlooarmsnewforest.co.uk; Pikes Hill; mains £6-9; ⏲lunch & dinner) Cosy 17th-century thatched pub serving hearty grub and excellent ales in a snug, wood-beamed interior.

Getting There & Away

Bus

See p235.

Train

The nearest train station is at Brockenhurst, 8 miles south

Around Lyndhurst

Petrol-heads, historians and ghost-hunters all gravitate to **Beaulieu** (www.beaulieu.co.uk; adult/child £16/8.60; ⏲10am-6pm Jun-Sep, to 5pm Oct-May) – pronounced *bew*-lee – an all-in-one vintage car museum, stately home and tourist complex based on the site of what was once England's most important 13th-century Cistercian monastery. Following Henry VIII's monastic land-grab of 1536, the abbey fell to the ancestors of current proprietors, the Montague family.

Motor-maniacs will be in raptures at Lord Montague's **National Motor Museum**, a splendid collection of vehicles that will sometimes leave you wondering if they really are cars, or strange hybrid planes, boats or metal bubbles with wheels. It's hard to resist the romance of the early classics, or the oomph of winning F1 cars. Here, too, are several jet-powered land-speed record-breakers including *Bluebird,* which famously broke the record (403mph, or 649km/h) in 1964. There are even celebrity wheels – look out for Mr Bean's Austin Mini and James Bond's whizz-bang speed machines.

Beaulieu's grand but indefinably homely **palace** began life as a 14th-century Gothic abbey gatehouse, but received a 19th-century Scottish Baronial makeover from Baron Montague in the 1860s. Don't be surprised if you hear eerie Gregorian chanting or feel the hairs on the back of your neck quiver – the abbey is supposedly one of England's most haunted buildings.

The New Forest Tour Bus stops directly outside the complex on its circular route via Lyndhurst, Brockenhurst and Lymington. You can also get here from Lymington (35 minutes) by catching bus 112.

Buckler's Hard

For such a tiny place, this picturesque huddle of 18th-century cottages, near the mouth of the River Beaulieu, has a big history. It started life in 1722, when one of the dukes of Montague decided to build a port to finance an expedition to the Caribbean. His dream was never realised, but when the war with France came, this embryonic village with a sheltered gravel waterfront became a secret boatyard where several of Nelson's triumphant Battle of Trafalgar warships were built. In the 20th century it played its part in more clandestine wartime manoeuvrings – the preparations for the D-Day landings.

The hamlet is now a fascinating heritage centre – **Buckler's Hard Story** (www.bucklershard.co.uk; adult/child £6/4.30; ⏲10am-5pm Mar-Oct, to 4.30pm Nov-Feb) – which features immaculately preserved 18th-century labourers' cottages. The **maritime museum** charts the inlet's shipbuilding history and its role in WWII – for a little light relief, seek out Nelson's dinky baby clothes.

The luxurious **Master Builder's House Hotel** (☎01590-616253; www.themasterbuilders.co.uk; d £105-160; P) is also part of the complex. This beautifully restored 18th-century hotel has 25 grandly chic rooms, featuring soft lighting, burnished trunks and plush fabrics. The gorgeous **restaurant** (mains £12 to £20) overlooks the river, while the wood-panelled **Yachtsman's Bar** serves classy pub grub from £5.

Buckler's Hard is 2 miles downstream from Beaulieu; a picturesque riverside walking trail links the two.

Lymington

POP 14,227

Yachting haven, New Forest base and jumping-off point to the Isle of Wight – the appealing Georgian harbour town of Lymington has several strings to its tourism bow. This former smuggler's port offers great places to eat and sleep, plenty of nautical shops and, in Quay St, an utterly quaint cobbled lane.

Sights & Activities

Puffin Cruises BOAT TRIP

(☎07850 947618; www.puffincruiseslymington.com; Town Quay) Your chance to ride the waves without owning your own yacht. The best trip (adult/child £15/6, daily May to October) is an exhilarating blast down the river and across the Solent to the Isle of Wight, where the Needles lighthouse (p242) and towering chalk stacks loom from the water. It also does a two-hour sunset cruise in high summer.

St Barbe Museum MUSEUM

(www.stbarbe-museum.org.uk; New St; adult/child £4/2; ⏲10am-4pm Mon-Sat) Explores tales of boat-builders, sailing ships, contraband and farming through a mix of models and artefacts.

Sleeping

TOP CHOICE **Stanwell House** BOUTIQUE HOTEL £££

(☎01590-677123; www.stanwellhouse.com; 14 High St; s £99, d £138-175, ste £215; @ wi-fi) The epitome of discreet luxury, this is the place to wait for your ship to come in. Cane chairs dot the elegant conservatory, while bedrooms are an eclectic mix of stand-alone baths, rococo mirrors, gently distressed furniture and plush throws. The **seafood restaurant** (tapas £6, mains £17-22; ⏲noon-10pm) rustles up bouillabaisse and seafood platters, while the chic bistro tempts you with fine dining (two-/three-courses from £22/27). There's even a vaguely decadent satin cushion-strewn bar.

Gorse Meadow B&B ££
(☎01590-673354; www.gorsemeadowguesthouse.co.uk; Sway Rd; d £80-120; P) With views from the bedrooms of fields, woods and ponies in paddocks, this rambling farmhouse eases you into the New Forest's rural vibe. Reassuringly old-fashioned rooms are packed with gilt plant stands, antique maps and velvet arm chairs, and it's all run by the indomitable Mrs Tee, a professional mushroom picker – so expect mounds of perfectly cooked King Oysters for breakfast.

Bluebird B&B ££
(☎01590-676908; www.bluebirdrestaurant.co.uk; 4 Quay St; d/f £80/120) An ancient cottage of dark beams, white walls and gleaming new bathrooms in the midst of quaintly cobbled Quay St.

Eating

Egan's EUROPEAN ££
(☎01590-676165; Gosport St; 2-/3-course lunch £14/16, mains £16; ⏲lunch & dinner Tue-Sat) The wooden tables here are highly polished and so is the food. Rich local ingredients are transformed by well-travelled flavours: marinated salmon combines with vodka; lobster with shellfish bisque; and beef with basil.

Vanilla Pod CAFE £
(Gosport St; snacks £5; ⏲breakfast & lunch Tue-Sun) Munch through Belgian muffins, English breakfasts and mounds of American pancakes at this top brunch spot.

Information

Library (North Close; ⏲9.30am-7pm Mon, Tue, Thu & Fri, 9.30am-1pm Wed, 9.30am-5pm Sat) Free internet access.

Tourist office (☎01590-689000; www.thenewforest.co.uk; New St; ⏲10am-5pm Mon-Sat Jul-Sep, to 4pm Mon-Sat Oct-Jun)

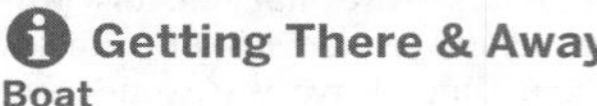

Getting There & Away

Boat

Wightlink Ferries (☎0871 376 1000; www.wightlink.co.uk) Carries cars and passengers to Yarmouth on the Isle of Wight. Puffin Cruises (p237) take foot passengers.

Bus

See p235.

Train

Lymington has two train stations: Lymington Town and Lymington Pier. Isle of Wight ferries connect with Lymington Pier. Trains run to Southampton (£9, 45 minutes), via Brockenhurst, every half-hour.

ISLE OF WIGHT

On the Isle of Wight these days there's something groovy in the air. For decades this slab of rock anchored off Portsmouth has been a magnet for family holidays, and it still has sea-side kitsch by the bucket and spade. But now the proms and amusement arcades are framed by pockets of pure funkiness. A brace of music festivals draws the party crowd, you can feast on just-caught seafood in cool fishermen's cafes, and 'glamping' (camping's more glamorous cousin) rules – here campsites are dotted with eco-yurts and vintage camper vans. Yet still the isle's principal appeal remains: a mild climate, myriad outdoorsy activities and a 25-mile shore lined with beaches, dramatic white cliffs and tranquil sand dunes.

ISLE OF WIGHT FESTIVALS

The isle's festival tradition stretches back to the early-1970s when an incredible 600,000 hippies gathered to see the Doors, the Who, Joni Mitchell and the last performance of rock icon Jimi Hendrix. Decades later the gatherings are still some of England's top musical events. The **Isle of Wight Festival** (www.isleofwightfestival.org), held in mid-June, has been headlined by the likes of REM, Coldplay, The Feeling, the Kaiser Chiefs and Keane, while **Bestival** (www.bestival.net), in early to mid-September, revels in an eclectic, counter-culture feel, drawing the Pet Shop Boys, Scissor Sisters, Dizzee Rascal and more.

Isle of Wight

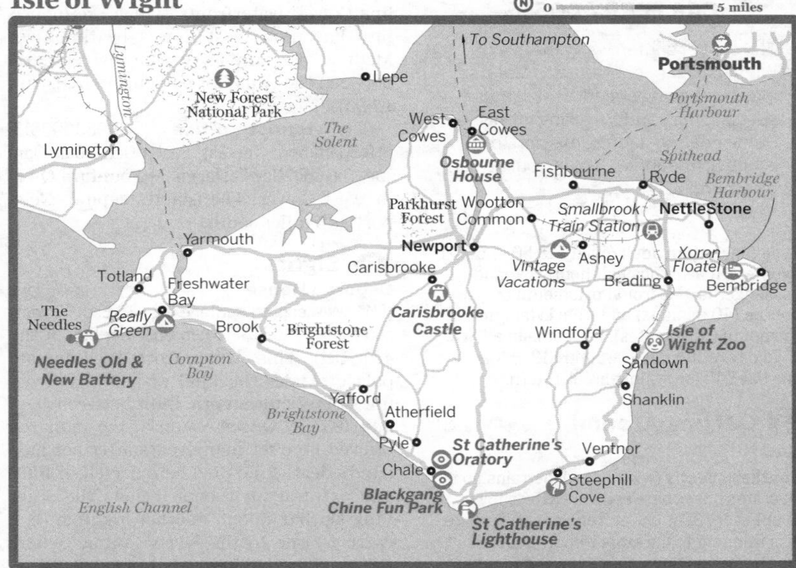

Activities

CYCLING

The Isle of Wight will make pedal-pushers smile with its 62-mile cycleway and **Cycling Festival** (☎01983-203891; www.sunseaandcycling.com) every September. The tourist office can advise and sell trail guides (£2).

Bike rentals cost around £12 to £14 per day, or £45 per week.

Tavcycles (☎01983-812989; www.tavcycles.co.uk; 140 High St, Ryde)

Wight Cycle (☎0800 112 3751; www.thewightcycle.com; Zigzag Rd, Ventnor)

Wight Cycle Hire (☎01983-761800; www.wightcyclehire.co.uk) Brading (Station Rd, Brading); Yarmouth (Station Rd, Yarmouth) Delivers and collects across the island.

WALKING

This is one of the best spots in southern England for rambling, with 500 miles of well-marked walking paths, including 67 miles of coastal routes. The island's **Walking Festival** (www.isleofwightwalkingfestival.co.uk), held over two weeks in May, is billed as the UK's largest. Tourist offices sell trail pamphlets (from £4).

OTHER ACTIVITIES

Water sports are a serious business on Wight's northern shores – especially sailing but also windsurfing, sea-kayaking and surfing. Powerboat trips also run out to the Needles. Wight also offers gliding lessons, paragliding, and even llama-trekking.

Information

Main tourist office (☎01983-813813; The Guildhall, High St, Newport; ⏰9.30am-5pm Mon-Sat 10am-3pm Sun Apr-Oct, 10am-3pm Nov-Mar) The main office is in Newport; there are also branches at Cowes (p240) and Ryde (p241).

Useful websites include www.islandbreaks.co.uk and www.isleofwight.com.

Getting There & Away

Hovertravel (☎01983-811000; www.hovertravel.co.uk) Shuttles foot passengers between **Southsea** (near Portsmouth) and Ryde (day-return adult/child £13/6, 10 minutes, every half-hour).

Red Funnel (☎0844 844 9988; www.redfunnel.co.uk) Operates car ferries between Southampton and East Cowes (day-return adult/child £13/7, from £45 with car, 55 minutes) and high-speed passenger ferries between Southampton and West Cowes (day-return adult/child £19/10, 25 minutes).

Wightlink Ferries (☎0871 376 1000; www.wightlink.co.uk) Operates passenger ferries every half hour from Portsmouth to

CAR FERRY COSTS

The cost of car ferries to the Isle of Wight can vary enormously. Make savings by booking ahead, asking about special offers and travelling off-peak. Some deals include admission to island attractions. Booking online can be around £20 cheaper.

Ryde (day-return adult/child £13.50/6.50, 20 minutes). It also runs half-hourly car-and-passenger ferries from Portsmouth to Fishbourne (40 minutes) and from Lymington to Yarmouth (30 minutes). For both, an adult/child day return costs around £12/5. Car fares start at £45 for a short-break return.

Getting Around

Bus

Southern Vectis (www.islandlinetrains.co.uk) Operates buses between the eastern towns about every 30 minutes; regular services are less frequent to the more remote southwest side between Blackgang Chine and Brook. Twice daily between Easter and September, the **Island Coaster** also shuttles between Ryde, around the southern shore to Alum Bay in the far southwest. Rover Tickets are available for a day (adult/child £10/5) or a week (adult/child £20/10).

Car

1st Call (☎01983-400055; 15 College Close, Sandown; from £30 per day) Collects and delivers island wide.

Train

Island Line (www.island-line.com) Runs trains twice-hourly from **Ryde to Shanklin**, via Sandown and Brading (25 minutes). Day rover tickets are available (adult/child £12/6).

Isle of Wight Steam Railway (☎01983-885923; www.iwsteamrailway.co.uk; ⏲May-Sep) Branches off at Smallbrook Junction and chugs to **Wootton Common** (adult/child £9.50/5, 1st class £14.50/10).

Cowes & Around

Pack your yachting cap – the hilly Georgian harbour town of Cowes is famous for **Cowes Week** (www.skandiacowesweek.co.uk), one of the longest-running and biggest annual sailing regattas in the world. Started in 1826, the regatta still sails with as much gusto as ever in late July or early August. Fibreglass playthings and vintage sailboats line Cowes' waterfronts, which are lopped into East and West Cowes by the River Medina; a chain ferry shuttles regularly between the two (foot passengers free, cars £1.80).

The **tourist office** (☎01983-813813; ⏲9.30am-5pm Tue-Sat Easter-Oct, 10am-3pm Tue, Thu & Fri Nov-Easter) is at Fountain Quay in West Cowes. The island's capital, Newport, is 5 miles south.

Sights

Osborne House ROYAL HOME

(EH; www.english-heritage.org.uk; East Cowes; adult/child £10/5; ⏲10am-6pm Apr-Sep, 10am-4pm Oct) This lemon-frosted, Italianate palace exudes the kind of pomp that defines the Victorian era. Built between 1845 and 1851 by Queen Victoria, the monarch grieved here for many years after her husband's death, and died here herself in 1901. The extravagant rooms include the stunning Durbar Room; another highlight is a carriage ride to the Swiss Cottage where the royal ankle-biters would play. Between November and March, visits are by pre-booked tours only.

Carisbrooke Castle CASTLE

(EH; www.english-heritage.org.uk; Newport; adult/child £7/3.50; ⏲10am-5pm Apr-Sep, to 4pm Oct-Mar) Charles I was imprisoned here before his execution in 1649. Today you can clamber the sturdy ramparts and play bowls on the very green the doomed monarch used.

Sleeping & Eating

Fountain HOTEL ££

(☎01983-292397; www.fountaininn-cowes.com; High St, West Cowes; s £90, d £100-120) They may be in a classic old pub, but the bedrooms are all sleigh beds, leather headboards and red and gold velvet – the best have views across the Solent. Enjoy espressos and pastries in the cool **cafe,** hearty pub grub (mains £10) in the cosy **bar**; and watching the boats drifting from the seafront patio.

Anchorage B&B ££

(☎01983-247975; www.anchoragecowes.co.uk; 23 Mill Hill Rd, West Cowes; s £40, d £60-80; P ᯤ) Unfussy cream and blue rooms combine with ecofriendly water and heating systems. Breakfasts are full of fair-trade and island foods.

Ryde to Shanklin

The nippiest foot-passenger ferries between Wight and Portsmouth alight in **Ryde**, a work-a-day Victorian town rich in seaside kitsch and lined with amusement arcades. Next comes the cutesy village of **Brading**, with its fine Roman villa; photogenic **Bembridge Harbour**, fringed by tranquil sand dunes; and the twin resort towns of **Sandown** and **Shanklin**, boasting beaches, a zoo full of tigers, and hordes of families wielding buckets and spades. The area also features unique sleep spots including a decommissioned warship and vintage airstream trailers.

Sights

Brading Roman Villa ROMAN VILLA
(www.bradingromanvilla.co.uk; Morton Old Rd, Brading; adult/child £6.50/3; 10am-4pm) The exquisitely preserved mosaics here (including a famous cockerel-headed man) make this one of the finest Romano-British sites in the UK. Wooden walkways lead over the rubble walls and brightly painted tiles, allowing you to gaze right down onto the ruins below.

Isle of Wight Zoo ZOO
(www.isleofwightzoo.com; Yaverland Rd, Sandown; adult/child £7.50/6.50; 10am-6pm Apr-Sep, to 4pm Oct & Feb-Mar) One of Europe's largest collections of tigers, plus scores of cute lemurs.

Sleeping & Eating

TOP CHOICE **Xoron Floatel** FLOATING B&B ££
(01983-874596; www.xoronfloatel.co.uk; Bembridge Harbour; s/d £45/60) Your chance to go to sleep on a gunboat – this former WWII warship is now a cheery, bunting-draped houseboat. Comfy cabins come complete with snug bathrooms, while the views from the flower-framed sun deck are simply superb.

Vintage Vacations CAMPSITE £
(07802-758113; www.vintagevacations.co.uk; Ashey, near Ryde; 4-person caravans per week £390-600; Apr-Oct; P) The 10 airstream trailers from the 1960s on this farm are retro-chic personified. Their gleaming aluminium shells shelter lovingly selected furnishings ranging from cheerful patchwork blankets to vivid tea cosies.

Kasbah B&B, BISTRO ££
(01983-810088; www.kas-bah.co.uk; 76 Union St, Ryde; s £60, d £65-85; @) More North Africa than East Wight, Kasbah brings a funky blast of the Mediterranean to Ryde. Intricate lanterns, stripy throws and furniture fresh from Marrakesh dot the chic rooms; falafel, tapas and paella (£4) are on offer in the chilled-out **bar** (lunch & dinner).

Information

Ryde tourist office (01983-813813; 81 Union St, Ryde; 9.30am-5pm Mon-Sat, 10am-3.30pm Sun Apr-Oct, 10am-3pm Nov-Mar).

Ventnor & Around

The Victorian town of **Ventnor** slaloms so steeply down the island's southern coast that you'd be forgiven for mistaking it for the south of France. The winding streets are home to a scattering of quirky boutiques, while local hotels, eateries and the atmospheric Steephill Cove are well worth a detour.

To the west, the island's southernmost point is marked by the stocky 19th-century **St Catherine's Lighthouse** and its 14th-century counterpart: **St Catherine's Oratory**. Nearby, kid-friendly **Blackgang Chine**

WORTH A TRIP

STEEPHILL COVE

You can't drive to Steephill Cove, which makes it all the more special. Its tiny, sandy beach is fringed by an eclectic mix of buildings, ranging from stone cottages to rickety-looking shacks. A dinky clapper-board lighthouse presides over the scene, while the beach finds festoon porches dotted with driftwood furniture and draped with fishing nets. Two great places to eat: the Boathouse restaurant (p242) and the Crab Shed cafe (p242), add to the appeal.

Steephill Cove is 1 mile west of Ventnor; either walk down from the Botanical Gardens, or hike from the hill-side car park 200m west of Ventnor Esplanade, then follow the (steep) coast path until you arrive.

Fun Park (www.blackgangchine.com; admission £10), features water gardens, animated shows and a hedge maze. Times are varied; check the website.

Sleeping

Hambrough BOUTIQUE HOTEL £££
(☎01983-856333; www.thehambrough.com; Hambrough Rd, Ventnor; d £150-187, ste £210; P) It's hard to say which views are better: the 180-degree vistas out to sea, or those of rooms full of subtle colours, clean lines and satiny furnishings. Espresso machines, dressing gowns and heated floors keep the luxury gauge set to high.

Harbour View HOTEL ££
(☎01983-852285; www.harbourviewhotel.co.uk; Esplanade, Ventnor; d £92-108; P 📶) Expansive sea views and crisp white linen fill this Victorian villa with bursts of period charm. The window-seated Tower Room sees light and views pour in from three sides.

Eating

TOP CHOICE **Boathouse** SEAFOOD ££
(☎01983-852747; Steephill Cove; mains £15-30; ⊙lunch Thu-Tue Jun-Sep) Arrive early enough, and you'll see the cove's fishermen (Jimmy and Mark) landing your lunch – the sanded wooden tables here are just steps from the sea. It's an idyllic spot to sip some chilled wine, sample succulent lobster and revel in Wight's new-found driftwood-chic.

Crab Shed CAFE £
(Steephill Cove; snacks £4; ⊙11am-3.30pm Apr-Oct) Lobster pots and fishing boats line the slipway right outside a fisherman's shack, that's a riot of sea-smoothed spas, cork floats and faded buoys. Irresistible treats include meaty crab salads, mackerel ciabatta and freshly baked crab pasties.

West Wight

Rural and remote, Wight's westerly corner is where the island really comes into its own. Sheer white cliffs rear from a surging sea and the stunning coastline peels west to Alum Bay and the most famous chunks of chalk in the region: the Needles. These jagged rocks rise shardlike out of the sea, forming a line like the backbone of a prehistoric sea monster.

Sights & Activities

Needles Old Battery FORT
(NT; www.nationaltrust.org.uk; adult/child £4.80/2.50; ⊙10.30am-5pm mid-Mar–Oct) Established in 1862, this remote gun emplacement was used as an observation post during WWII – today you can explore the Victorian cartridge store, trek down a 60m cliff tunnel to a searchlight look out and drink in extraordinary views.

Also on the same site is **New Battery** (⊙11am-4pm Tue, Sat & Sun mid-Mar–Oct). Displays in its vaults outline the clandestine space-rocket testing carried out here in the 1950s.

You can hike to the battery along the cliffs from Alum Bay (1 mile) or hop on the tourist bus that runs between the bay and battery hourly (twice hourly in July and August).

Boat Trips BOAT TRIPS
(☎01983-761587; www.needlespleasurecruises.co.uk; adult/child £5/3; ⊙10.30am-4.30pm Apr-Oct) Twenty minute voyages from Alum Bay to the Needles, providing close-up views of those towering white cliffs.

Sleeping

TOP CHOICE **Really Green** CAMPSITE £
(☎07802 678591; www.thereallygreenholidaycompany.com; Blackbridge Rd, Freshwater Bay; yurt per week £395-490; P) The epitome of 'glamping' (glamorous camping), the five-person, fully-furnished yurts on this tree-shaded site feature four-poster beds, futons, wood-burning stoves and shabby-chic antiques. You can even have continental breakfast delivered to your tent flap – roughing it has never been so smooth.

Totland Bay YHA HOSTEL £
(☎0845 371 9348; www.yha.org.uk; Hirst Hill, Totland; dm £16; P) Family-friendly Victorian house overlooking the water, with a maximum of eight beds per room.

DORSET

For many, Dorset conjures up the kind of halcyon holiday memories you find in flickering 1970s home movies. But this county's image deserves a dramatic revamp. In party-town Bournemouth the snapshots are as likely to be of stag- and hen-party frenzies as buckets and spades on the sand; Poole provides images of the super-rich, while Dorset's Jurassic Coast would catch the eye of even the most jaded cinematographer. This stunning shoreline is studded with exquisite sea-carved bays and creamy-white rock arches around Lulworth Cove, while beaches at Lyme Regis are littered with fossils ripe for the picking. Dorchester provides a biopic of Thomas Hardy; the massive Iron Age hill fort at Maiden Castle is a battle-ground epic; and the really rather rude chalk figure at Cerne Abbas delivers a comic interlude. Then comes the regenerated resort of Weymouth, preparing to be catapulted onto TV screens worldwide as the sailing venue for England's 2012 Olympics.

Information

Jurassic Coast (www.jurassiccoast.com) Official World Heritage Site guide.

Visit Dorset (www.visit-dorset.com) The county's official tourism website.

Getting Around

Bus

A key provider is **First** (www.firstgroup.com). **Wilts & Dorset** (www.wdbus.co.uk) connects Dorset's rural and urban areas.

Train

One mainline runs from Bristol and Bath through Dorchester West to Weymouth, the other connects London and Southampton with Bournemouth and Poole.

Bournemouth

POP 163,600

In Bournemouth, four worlds collide: old folks, families and corporate delegates meet club-loads of determined drinkers. Sometimes the edges rub and on weekend evenings parts of town transform into a frenzy of massive party zones, full of angels with L plates and blokes in frocks, blond wigs and slingbacks. But there's also a much sunnier side to the town. A recent survey revealed Bournemouth had the happiest residents in the UK – thanks partly to its glorious 7-mile sandy beach. The town sprang up as a Victorian resort, but these days it's busy adding a much more modern attraction: it's hoped Europe's first artificial surf reef will bring even bigger barrels and more amped-up board riders to town.

Sights & Activities

Bournemouth Beach BEACH

Backed by 3000 deckchairs, Bournemouth's expansive, sandy shoreline regularly clocks up seaside awards. It stretches from Southborne in the far east to Alum Chine in the west – an immense promenade backed by ornamental gardens, cafes and toilets. The resort also prides itself on two piers (Bournemouth and Boscombe). Around **Bournemouth Pier** you can hire beach **chalets** (☎0845 0550968; per day/week from £17/55), deckchairs (£2 per day), windbreaks (£2.50) and parasols (£4).

At the **East Cliff Lift Railway** (☎01202-451781; Undercliff Dr; adult/child £1.20/80p; ⏰Easter-Oct), cable-cars-on-rails wiz up bracken-covered slopes, cutting out the short, steep hike up the zig zag paths.

Alum Chine GARDEN

(Mountbatten Rd; ⏰24hr) This award winning sub-tropical enclave dates from the 1920s, providing a taste of Bournemouth's golden age. Set 1.5 miles west from Bournemouth Pier, its plants include those from the Canary Islands, New Zealand, Mexico and the Himalayas; their bright-red bracts, silver thistles and purple flowers frame views of a glittering sea.

FREE **Russell-Cotes** MUSEUM

(www.russell-cotes.bournemouth.gov.uk; Russell-Cotes Rd; ⏰10am-5pm Tue-Sun) This ostentatious mix of Italianate villa and Scottish baronial pile was built at the end of the 1800s for Merton and Annie Russell-Cotes as somewhere to showcase the remarkable range of souvenirs gathered on their world travels. Look out for a plaster version of the Parthenon frieze by the stairs, Maori woodcarvings and Persian tiles. The house also boasts fine art, including paintings by Rossetti, Edwin Landseer and William Frith.

Dorset Cruises BOAT TRIP

(☎0845 4684640; www.dorsetcruises.co.uk; Bournemouth Pier; adult/child £12.50/5; ⏰daily Apr-Sep) Dorset's extraordinary World Heritage Jurassic Coast (p248) starts some 5 miles west of Bournemouth at the chalk Old Harry Rocks. These 2½ hour cruises cross the mouth of Poole Harbour, providing up-close views of the chalky columns. The stacks used to be massive arches before erosion brought the tops tumbling down – huge scooped-out sections of cliff clearly show how the sea begins the erosion process.

SURF REEF

Bournemouth is now home to Europe's first ever artificial surf reef. Made up of 55 immense sandbags (some 70m-long), it sits submerged beneath the sea 220m off-shore at **Boscombe Pier**. Despite delays and initial teething problems, the aim remains to harness and increase existing waves, push them up and form them into better breaks for surfers. The result would be a faster, more challenging ride.

The reef isn't for beginners, but you can learn nearby. The **Sorted Surf School** (☎01202-300668; www.bournemouth-surfschool.co.uk; Undercliff Drive, Boscombe Beach), 300m west of Boscombe Pier, does lessons (£30 for two hours) and hires out wetsuits (four/eight hours £10/15), surfboards (four/eight hours £10/15), bodyboards (four/eight hours £5/10) and kayaks (one/two/four hours £10/15/25).

Sleeping

Bournemouth has huge concentrations of budget B&Bs, especially around the central St Michael's Rd and to the east of the train station.

TOP CHOICE **Urban Beach** BOUTIQUE HOTEL £££
(☎01202-301509; www.urbanbeachhotel.co.uk; 23 Argyll Rd; d £95-170; P @) Bournemouth's finest hipster hotel is packed with chic flourishes: oatmeal, brown leather and rippling velvet define the rooms; the hall sports brightly-coloured Wellingtons for guests to borrow. There's a cool **bistro** downstairs and a heated deck for pre-dinner cocktails. It's all just a 10 minute walk from Boscombe Pier.

Balincourt B&B ££
(☎01202-552962; www.balincourt.co.uk; 58 Christchurch Rd; s £40-70, d £75-120; P) This Victorian guest house is a labour of love – even the china on the tea tray is hand painted to match each room's colour scheme. The decor is bright and deeply tasteful, respecting both the house's heritage and modern anti-frill sensibilities.

Langtry Manor HOTEL ££
(☎01202-553887; www.langtrymanor.com; Derby Rd; s from £100, d £105-200; P) Prepare for a delicious whiff of royal indiscretion – this minimansion was built by Edward VII for his mistress Lillie Langtry. Opulent grandeur is everywhere, from the red-carpeted entrance to immense chandeliers. Bedrooms include modern touches such as recessed lights and Jacuzzis, while the King's Suite is a real jaw-dropper: a monumental, climb-up-to-get-in four-poster bed, and a fireplace big enough to sit in.

Amarillo B&B ££
(☎01202-553884; www.amarillohotel.co.uk; 52 Frances Rd; s £25-45, d £50-90, f £80; P) Minimalist decor, beige throws and clumps of twisted willow – an inexpensive Bournemouth sleep spot with style.

Bournemouth Backpackers HOSTEL £
(☎01202-299491; www.bournemouthbackpackers.co.uk; 3 Frances Rd; dm £14) Plain dorms in small (19-bed), friendly suburban house. Reservations by email, or by phone between 5.30pm and 6.30pm, Sunday to Friday in summer (5pm to 7pm Sundays only in winter).

Eating

West Beach ENGLISH ££
(☎01202-587785; www.west-beach.co.uk; Pier Approach; mains £11-18; breakfast, lunch & dinner) A firm favourite with Bournemouth's foodie crowd, this buzzy eatery delivers both top-notch dishes and the best views in town. Try monkfish medallions with Parma ham or a seafood platter crammed with crab claws, lobster, razor clams and crevettes – best enjoyed on a decked dining terrace that juts out over the sand.

Print Room FRENCH ££
(☎01202-789669; Richmond Hill; mains £10-25; breakfast, lunch & dinner) This charismatic brasserie exudes Parisian chic, from the black and white tiled floors to the burnished wooden booths. Dishes are well travelled too, try the beetroot gnocchi, grilled calves livers, or steak with black truffle potato. Or that most excellent French tradition: the *plat du jour* (plate of the day), including wine, for only £10.

Basilica EUROPEAN £
(73 Seamoor Rd; tapas from £3, mains £6-10; Mon-Sat) The menu tours more Mediterranean countries than your average InterRailer – expect mezze, Parma ham parcels, grilled haloumi and pasta with chorizo.

Drinking & Entertainment

Most of the main entertainment venues are clustered around Firvale Rd, St Peter's Rd and Old Christchurch Rd. The gay scene kicks off around the Triangle.

Sixty Million Postcards PUB
(www.sixtymillionpostcards.com; 19 Exeter Rd; ⏲noon-midnight Sun-Wed, to 1am Thu, to 2am Fri & Sat) A hip crowd inhabits this quirky drinking den. The worn wooden floors, battered sofas and fringed lampshades are home to everything from DJ sets (including indie, synth-pop and space disco), to board games and impromptu Sunday jumble sales.

Lava Ignite NIGHTCLUB
(www.lavaignite.com; Firvale Rd) Four room megaclub playing R&B, pop, house, hip hop and dubstep.

Information

Cyber Place (25 St Peter's Rd; per hr £2; ⏲10am-10pm)

Tourist office (☎0845 0511700; www.bournemouth.co.uk; Westover Rd; ⏲10am-5pm Mon-Sat, plus 11am-4pm Sun Jun & Aug).

Getting There & Away

Bus

Standard routes:

Bristol (£19, four hours, daily) National Express.

London (£20, 2½ hours, hourly) National Express.

Oxford (£21, three hours, three daily) National Express.

Poole (15 minutes, every 10 minutes) Buses M1 and M2.

Salisbury (1¼ hours, half-hourly Monday to Saturday, nine on Sunday) Bus X3.

Southampton (£5.50, 50 minutes, 10 daily) National Express.

Train

Trains run every half-hour from **London Waterloo** (£35, two hours). Regular connections:

Dorchester South (£9.50, 45 minutes, hourly)

Poole (10 minutes, half-hourly)

Weymouth (£12, one hour, hourly)

Poole

POP 144,800

Just a few miles west of Bournemouth, Poole was once the preserve of hard-drinking sailors and sunburned day trippers. But these days you're as likely to encounter super-yachts and Porsches because the town borders Sandbanks, one of the most expensive chunks of real estate in the world. But you don't have to be knee-deep in cash to enjoy Poole's quaint old harbour, excellent eateries and nautical pubs. The town is also the springboard for some irresistible boat trips and a tempting array of water sports.

Sights & Activities

Brownsea Island ISLAND
(NT; adult/child £5.50/2.70; ⏲10am-5pm late-Mar–Nov) This small, wooded island in the middle of Poole harbour played a key role in a global movement famous for three-fingered salutes, shorts and toggles – Lord Baden-Powell staged the first ever scout camp here in 1907. Today trails weave through heath and woods, past peacocks, red squirrels, red deer and a wealth of birdlife.

Guided walks (free; ⏲11am & 2pm Jul & Aug) include ones on the war-time island, smugglers and pirates.

Boats run by **Brownsea Island Ferries** (www.brownseaislandferries.com; Poole Quay) leave from **Poole Quay** (adult/child return £8.50/5.50) and **Sandbanks** (adult/child return £5/4). Services operate when the island is open only and the last boat is normally at about 4.30pm.

Poole Old Town SIGNIFICANT AREA
The attractive old buildings on Poole Quay range from the 15th to the 19th century, and include the Tudor **King Charles pub** on Thames St; the cream **Old Harbour Office** (1820s) next door; and the impressive red-brick **Custom House** (1813) opposite, complete with Union Jack and gilded coat of arms. The tourist office stocks a free heritage walking trail leaflet.

FREE **Waterfront Museum** MUSEUM
(☎01202-262600; 4 High St; ⏲10am-4pm Tue-Sat, noon-4pm Sun Apr-Oct) This beautifully restored 15th-century warehouse is home to a 2300-year old **Iron Age logboat** dredged up from Poole Harbour. At 10m-long and 14 tonnes, it's the largest to be found in southern Britain and probably carried 18 people. It was hand-chiselled from a single tree; centuries later you can still see the blade marks in the wood.

Sandbanks BEACH

A 2-mile, wafer-thin peninsula of land that curls around the expanse of Poole Harbour, Sandbanks is studded with some of the most expensive houses in the world. But the golden beaches that border them are free, and have some of the best water-quality standards in the country. They're also home to a host of water-sport operators.

Brownsea Island Ferries (www.brownseaislandferries.com; adult/child return £8/5; ⏲10am-5pm Apr-Oct) shuttle between Poole Quay and Sandbanks every half hour.

Sleeping

TOP CHOICE **Saltings** BOUTIQUE B&B ££

(☎01202-707349; www.the-saltings.com; 5 Salterns Way; d £80-90; P) You can almost hear the languid drawl of Noël Coward in this utterly delightful 1930s guest house. Charming art-deco flourishes include curved windows, arched doorways and decorative up-lighters. Immaculate rooms feature dazzling white, spearmint and pastel blue as well as minifridges, digital radios and Lush toiletries. One room is more like a little suite, with its own seating area and pocket-sized balcony. Saltings is halfway between Poole and Sandbanks.

Milsoms B&B ££

(☎01202-609000; www.milsomshotel.co.uk; 47 Haven Rd; d £60-75; P 📶) Supersleek and semi-boutique, this minihotel sits above Poole's branch of the Loch Fyne seafood restaurant chain. Bedrooms are decked out in achingly tasteful tones of chrome and cream, and finished with thoughtful extras such as cafetières and Molton Brown bath products.

Quayside B&B ££

(☎01202-683733; www.poolequayside.co.uk; 9 High St; s £35-50, d £55-75, f £60-80; P) Snug rooms, pine, and jazzy prints in the heart of the old harbour.

Eating & Drinking

Guildhall Tavern FRENCH ££

(☎01202-671717; 15 Market St; mains £15-20, 2-course lunch £15; ⏲lunch & dinner Tue-Sat) More Provence than Poole, the grub at this brasserie is Gallic gourmet charm at its best: unpretentious and top-notch. Expect double-baked cheese soufflé, chargrilled sea bass flambéed with pernod, or Charolais beef with peppercorns. Exquisite aromas fill the dining room, along with the quiet murmur of people enjoying very good food.

Storm SEAFOOD ££

(☎01202-674970; www.stormfish.co.uk; 16 High St; mains £17; ⏲lunch & dinner Mon-Sat) The superbly cooked fish on the robust, eclectic menu here depends on what the owner's caught.

Custom House BAR, BISTRO ££

(www.customhouse.co.uk; Poole Quay; snacks £6, mains from £11; ⏲lunch & dinner) Harbourside terrace, funky eatery and fine-dining venue all rolled into one.

Information

Tourist office (☎01202-253253; www.pooletourism.com; Poole Quay; ⏲10am-5pm Apr-Oct, 10am-4pm Mon-Sat Nov-Mar) Opens longer (9.15am to 6pm) in July and August.

Getting There & Around

Bus

National Express runs hourly to London (£19, three hours). Buses M1 and M2 go to Bournemouth every 10 minutes (15 minutes). Bus 52 shuttles between Poole and Sandbanks (15 minutes, hourly).

Boat

Brittany Ferries (www.brittany-ferries. com) Sails between Poole and Cherbourg in France (2½-6½ hours, one to three daily). Expect to

WATER SPORTS – POOLE HARBOUR

Poole Harbour's sheltered coasts may inspire you to get on the water. Operators cluster near the start of the Sandbanks peninsula. **Pool Harbour Watersports** (☎01202-700503; www.pooleharbour.co.uk; 284 Sandbanks Rd, Lilliput) does lessons in windsurfing (£50 for three hours) and kitesurfing (one/two/three days £99/175/240), as well as kayak tours (one/two day £35).

The nearby **FC Watersports** (☎01202-708283; www.fcwatersports.co.uk; 19 Banks Rd) provides similarly priced kite- and windsurfing lessons, as does **Watersports Academy** (☎01202-708283; www.thewatersportsacademy.com; Banks Rd), which also runs sailing courses (two hours/two days £55/165) and wakeboarding and waterskiing (per 15 minutes £20).

WORTH A TRIP

KINGSTON LACY

Dorset's must-see stately home, **Kingston Lacy** (NT; www.nationaltrust.org.uk; house adult/child £10.50/5, grounds only £6/3; ⊙house 11am-5pm Wed-Sun mid-Mar–Oct;) looks every inch the setting for a period drama; it overflows with rich decor, most famously in the Spanish Room which is smothered with gold and gilt. Other highlights include the hieroglyphics in the Egyptian Room, and the elegant marble staircase and loggia.

The house became the home of the aristocratic Bankes family when it was evicted from Corfe Castle (p249) by the Roundheads; look out for the bronze statue of Dame Mary Bankes in the loggia – she's shown still holding the keys to her much-loved castle in her hand. Art works include the overwhelming ceiling fresco *The Separation of Night and Day*, by Guido Reni in the library, and paintings by Rubens, Titian and Van Dyck. In the extensive landscaped grounds, hunt out the restored Japanese Tea Garden, and the **Iron Age hillfort** of Badbury Rings.

Kingston Lacy is 12.5 miles west of Bournemouth, off the B3082.

pay around £90 for foot passengers; £400 for a car and two adults.

Sandbanks Ferry (www.sandbanksferry.co.uk; per pedestrian/car one-way £1/3.20; ⊙7am-11pm) Takes cars from Sandbanks to Studland every 20 minutes. It's a short-cut from Poole to Swanage, Wareham and the Isle of Purbeck, but the summer queues can be horrendous.

Taxi

Dial-a-Cab (☎01202-666822).

Train

Rail connections are as for Bournemouth; just add 13 minutes to times to London Waterloo (£30).

Southeast Dorset

With its string of glittering bays and towering rock formations, the southeast Dorset shoreline is the most beautiful in the county. Also known as the 'Isle' of Purbeck (although it's actually a peninsula), it's also the start of the Jurassic Coast and the scenery and geology, especially around Lulworth Cove, make swimming irresistible and hiking memorable. The hinterland harbours the immense, fairy-tale ruins of Corfe Castle, while Wareham sheds light on the mysterious figure of Lawrence of Arabia.

WAREHAM & AROUND

POP 2568

Saxons established the sturdy settlement of Wareham on the banks of the River Frome in the 10th century, and their legacy lingers in the remains of their defensive walls and one of Dorset's last remaining Saxon churches. Wareham is also famous for its links to the enigmatic TE Lawrence, the British soldier immortalised in the 1962 David Lean epic *Lawrence of Arabia*.

Sights

Clouds Hill HISTORIC HOME

(NT; www.nationaltrust.org.uk; near Bovington; adult/child £4.50/2; ⊙noon-5pm Thu-Sun mid-Mar–Oct) This tiny cottage was home to **TE Lawrence** (1888–1935), the British scholar, military strategist and writer made legendary for his role in helping unite Arab tribes against Turkish forces in WWI. The house's four rooms provide a compelling insight into a complex man, they're also much as he left them – he died at the age of 46 after a motorbike accident on a nearby road.

Highlights include the deeply evocative photos Lawrence took during his desert campaign and his sketches of French crusader castles. There's also a surprisingly comfortable cork-lined bathroom, an aluminium foil-lined bunk room and a heavily beamed music room, which features the desk where Lawrence abridged *Seven Pillars of Wisdom*.

Clouds Hill is 7 miles northeast of Wareham on an unclassified road.

St Martin's on the Walls CHURCH

(North St; ⊙10am-4pm Mon-Sat Easter-Oct) Dating from 1020, it features a 12th-century fresco on the northern wall, and a marble effigy of Lawrence of Arabia.

Monkey World ZOO

(www.monkeyworld.co.uk; Long-thorns; adult/child £10.75/7.50; ⊙10am-5pm Sep–Jun, to 6pm Jul & Aug) A sanctuary for rescued chimpanzees, orang-utans, gibbons, marmosets and some ridiculously cute ring-tailed lemurs.

JURASSIC COAST

The kind of massive, hands-on geology lesson you wish you had at school, the Jurassic Coast is England's first natural World Heritage Site, putting it on a par with the Great Barrier Reef and the Grand Canyon. This striking shoreline stretches from Exmouth in East Devon to Swanage in Dorset, encompassing 185 million years of the earth's history in just 95 miles. It means you can walk, in just a few hours, many millions of years in geological time.

It began when layers of rocks formed; their varying compositions determined by different climates: desert-like conditions gave way to higher then lower sea levels. Massive earth movements then tilted all the rock layers to the east. Next, erosion exposed the different strata, leaving most of the oldest formations in the west and the youngest in the east.

The differences are very tangible. Devon's rusty-red Triassic rocks are 200 to 250 million years old. Lyme Regis (see boxed text, p255) has fossil-rich, dark-clay Jurassic cliffs 190 million-year old. Pockets of much younger, creamy-coloured Cretaceous rocks (a mere 140 to 65 million years old) also pop up, notably around Lulworth Cove, where erosion has sculpted a stunning display of bays, stacks and rock arches.

The coast's **website** (www.jurassiccoast.com) is a great information source; also look out locally for the highly readable *Official Guide to the Jurassic Coast* (£4.95).

Sleeping & Eating

Trinity B&B ££
(01929-556689; www.trinitybnb.co.uk; 32 South St; s/d/f £40/60/80) This 15th-century cottage oozes so much character, you half expect to bump into a chap in doublet and hose. The staircase is a swirl of ancient timber, floors creak under plush rugs, and bathrooms gleam with yellow and green tiles and smart new fittings.

Anglebury PUB, B&B ££
(01929-552988; www.angleburyhouse.co.uk; 15 North St; mains £10; lunch daily, dinner Tue-Sat) Lawrence of Arabia and Thomas Hardy have, apparently, had cuppas in the coffee shop attached to this 16th-century inn. The restaurant rustles up hearty dishes such as chilli and garlic sea bass, while simple bedrooms (single/double £40/70) are done out in creams, floral fabrics and pine.

Information

Purbeck tourist office (01929-552740; www.purbeck.gov.uk; Holy Trinity Church, South St, Wareham; 9.30am-4pm Mon-Sat, plus 10am-4pm Sun Jul & Aug)

Getting There & Away

Bus

Bus 40 runs hourly between Poole (35 minutes) and Swanage (30 minutes) via Wareham and Corfe Castle.

Train

Wareham is on the main railway line from London Waterloo (£17, 2½ hours, hourly) to Weymouth (£8, 30 minutes, hourly).

CORFE CASTLE

The massive, shattered ruins of Corfe Castle loom so dramatically from the landscape it's like blundering into a film set. The defensive fragments tower over an equally photogenic village, which bears the castle's name, and makes for a romantic spot for a meal or an overnight stay.

Sights & Activities

TOP CHOICE **Corfe Castle** CASTLE
(NT; www.nationaltrust.org.uk; adult/child £5.60/2.80; 10am-6pm Apr-Sep, 10am-4pm Oct-Mar) One of Dorset's most iconic landmarks, these towering battlements were once home to Sir John Bankes, right-hand man and attorney general to Charles I. The castle was besieged by Cromwellian forces during the Civil War – for six weeks the plucky Lady Bankes directed the defence and the castle fell only after being betrayed from within. The Bankes decamped to Kingston Lacy (p247) and the Roundheads immediately gunpowdered Corfe Castle apart, an action that's still startlingly apparent today: turrets and soaring walls sheer off at precarious angles; the gatehouse splays out as if it's just been blown up. Today you can roam over most of the site, peeping through slit windows and prowling the fractured defences.

Swanage Steam Railway RAILWAY
(www.swanagerailway.co.uk; adult/child return £9/7; Apr-Oct & many weekends in Nov, Dec, Feb & Mar) Vintage steam trains run (hourly) between Swanage and Norden (20 minutes), stopping at Corfe Castle.

Sleeping & Eating

Mortons House HOTEL ££££

(☎01929-480988; www.mortonshouse.co.uk; East St; d £130-225; P ☎) This is a place to break open the Bollinger: a romantic, luxurious 16th-century, mini-baronial pile. The rooms are festooned with red brocade and gold tassels; an occasional chaise longue adds to the effect.

Olivers B&B, BISTRO ££

(☎01929-477111; www.oliverscorfecastle.co.uk; 5 West St; s/d £35/70) The spacious, simple, light-blue rooms here are finished with willow displays – for intricate beams and village views bag an upstairs one. The **bistro** (mains £8-12; ⊙lunch & dinner daily, closed Mon & Sun Oct-Easter) rustles up gourmet burgers for lunch, and some surprises for dinner: expect venison and chocolate sauce or pork terrine with onion marmalade.

Getting There & Away

Bus 40 shuttles hourly between Poole, Wareham, Corfe Castle and Swanage.

LULWORTH COVE & AROUND

South of Corfe Castle the coast steals the show. For millions of years the elements have been creating an intricate shoreline of curved bays, caves, stacks and weirdly wonderful rock formations – most notably the massive natural arch at Durdle Door.

At Lulworth Cove, a pleasing jumble of thatched cottages and fishing gear leads down to a perfect circle of white cliffs. It's a charismatic place to stay; inevitably, it draws coach party crowds in the height of summer.

Sights & Activities

TOP CHOICE **Durdle Door** ROCK ARCH

This immense, 150-million-year-old Portland stone arch plunges into the sea near Lulworth Cove. Part of the Jurassic Coast (p248), it was created by a combination of massive earth movements and then erosion. Today it's framed by shimmering bays – bring a swimsuit and head down the hundreds of steps for an unforgettable dip.

There's a car park at the top of the cliffs, but it's best to hike along the coast from Lulworth Cove (1 mile), passing the delightfully named **Lulworth Crumple**, where layers of rock have been forced into dramatically zigzagging folds.

Secondwind Watersports KAYAK TOUR

(☎01305-834951; www.jurassic-kayaking.com; Lulworth Cove; per person £50; ⊙up to two tours daily) This three-hour paddle offers a jaw-dropping view of Dorset's heavily eroded coast. Starting at Lulworth Cove, you glide through Stair Hole's intricate caves and stacks, across Man O'War Bay then under the massive stone arch at Durdle Door, stopping for swims and picnics along the way.

Lulworth Castle STATELY HOME

(EH; www.lulworth.com; East Lulworth; adult/child £8.50/4; ⊙10.30am-6pm Sun-Fri Apr-Sep, to 4pm Oct-Mar) A creamy, dreamy, white, this baronial pile looks more like a French chateau than a traditional English castle. Built in 1608 as a hunting lodge, it's survived extravagant owners, extensive remodelling and a disastrous fire in 1929; it has now been sumptuously restored. Check out the massive four-poster bed, and the suits of armour in the basement.

Sleeping & Eating

Beach House HOTEL ££

(☎01929-400404; www.lulworthbeachhotel.com; Main St; d £90-120; P ☎) At this oh-so-stylish sleep spot 200m from the beach, rooms feature blonde woods, coconut matting and flashes of leather and lime – the best has its own private sea-view deck

Bishops Cottage B&B ££

(☎01929-400880; www.bishopscottage.co.uk; Main St; d £100; P ☎) As cool as the coolest kid in the year, this shabby-chic bolt hole throws together antique furniture and sleek modern fabrics – and makes it work. Chill out on your own window seat or in the funky bar-bistro downstairs.

Fish Shack FISH SHOP £

(Lulworth Cove; ⊙Fri-Wed Easter-Oct, Sat & Sun Nov-Easter) Set right beside the path to the beach, this shed is piled with plaice, sole and brill. Settle at the tiny table outside, and tuck into crab landed at Lulworth Cove – a meal that's travelled food yards, not miles.

Durdle Door Holiday Park CAMPSITE

(☎01929-400200; www.lulworth.com; sites from £15; ⊙Mar-Oct; P) Clifftop site, just metres from the famous rock arch.

Information

Lulworth Cove Heritage Centre (☎01929-400587; admission free; ⊙10am-5pm April-Oct, till 4pm Nov-March) Has excellent displays outlining how geology and erosion have combined to shape the area's remarkable shoreline.

Dorchester

POP 16,171

With Dorchester, you get two towns in one: a real-life, bustling county town, and Thomas Hardy's fictional Casterbridge. The Victorian writer was born just outside Dorchester and clearly used it to add authenticity to his writing – so much so that his literary locations can still be found amid the town's white Georgian terraces and red-brick buildings. You can also visit his former homes here, and see his original manuscripts. Add incredibly varied museums and some attractive places to eat and sleep, and you get an appealing base for a night or two.

Sights

Dorset County Museum MUSEUM
(www.dorsetcountymuseum.org; High West St; admission £6; ⏲10am-5pm Jul-Sep, closed Sun Oct-Jun) The Thomas Hardy collection here is the biggest in the world. It offers extraordinary insights into his creative process – reading his cramped handwriting, it's often possible to spot where he's crossed out one word and substituted another. There's also a wonderful reconstruction of his study at Max Gate and a letter from Siegfried Sassoon, asking Hardy if Sassoon can dedicate his first book of poems to him.

As well as the superb Hardy exhibits, look out for Jurassic Coast fossils, especially the huge ichthyosaur and the 6ft fore paddle of a plesiosaur. Bronze and Iron Age finds from Maiden Castle (p251) include a treasure trove of coins and neck rings, while Roman artefacts include 70 gold coins, nail cleaners and ear picks.

Max Gate HISTORIC HOME
(NT; www.nationaltrust.org.uk; Alington Ave; adult/child £3/1.50; ⏲2-5pm Mon, Wed & Sun Apr-Sep) Hardy was a trained architect and designed this house, where he lived from 1885 until his death in 1928. *Tess of the D'Urbervilles* and *Jude the Obscure* were both written here, and the house contains several pieces of original furniture, but otherwise it's a little slim on sights. The house is a mile east of Dorchester on the A352.

Hardy's Cottage HISTORIC HOME
(NT; www.nationaltrust.org.uk; admission £4; ⏲11am-5pm Sun-Thu Apr-Oct) The author was born at this picturesque cob-and-thatch house. Again it's a little short on attractions, but makes an evocative stop for Hardy completists. It's in Higher Bockhampton, 3 miles northeast of Dorchester.

FREE **Roman Town House** ROMAN VILLA
(www.romantownhouse.org; High West St; ⏲24hr) The knee-high flint walls and beautifully preserved mosaics here conjure up the Roman occupation of Dorchester (then Durnovaria). You can also peek into the summer dining room and study the underfloor heating system (hypocaust), where charcoal-warmed air circulated around pillars to produce a toasty 18°C.

Tutankhamen MUSEUM
(www.tutankhamun-exhibition.co.uk; High West St; adult/child £7/5.50; ⏲9.30am-5.30pm) Experience the sights, sounds and smells of ancient Egypt, including a fake-gold mock-up of a pharaoh's tomb.

Other Thomas Hardy Sites
Hardy's **statue** is at the top of High West St. **Lucetta's House**, a grand Georgian affair with ornate door posts, is near the tourist office, while in parallel South St, a red-brick mid-18th century building (now a bank) has a plaque identifying it as the inspiration for the **Mayor of Casterbridge's house**. The tourist office sells 'location' guides to the Dorset places in Hardy's novels.

Sleeping

TOP CHOICE **Beggar's Knap** BOUTIQUE B&B ££
(☎01305-268191; www.beggarsknap.co.uk; 2 Weymouth Ave; s £45, d £70-90; P) Despite the name, this utterly fabulous, vaguely decadent guest house is far from impoverished. Opulent raspberry-red rooms drip with chandeliers and gold brocades; beds draped in fine cottons range from French sleigh to four-poster. The breakfast room, with its towering plants and a huge harp, is gorgeous. You could pay much, much more and get something half as nice.

Slades Farm B&B ££
(☎01305-264032; www.bandbdorset.org.uk; Charminster; s/d/f £50/70/110; P) Barn conversions don't come much more subtle and airy than this: done out in oatmeal and cream, tiny skylights dot ceilings that meet walls in gentle curves. The riverside paddock (complete with grazing alpacas) is perfect to laze in. It's 2 miles north of Dorchester.

Westwood B&B ££

(☎01305-268018; www.westwoodhouse.co.uk; 29 High West St; s £60-65, d £70-90, f £85-120;) Elegant Georgian town house with painted wicker chairs, cast iron bedsteads and dinky cushions.

Eating

Billy the Fish SEAFOOD £

(Trinity St; mains from £8; ⊙lunch Mon-Sat, dinner Thu-Sat) Former fisherman Billy doesn't catch his own anymore; he's too busy cooking up a storm at this kooky bistro. The walls are hung with fabric, lobster pots and buoys; the tables are lined by locals enjoying skilfully cooked food. Try the super-fresh turbot, brill and scallops, or the intensely flavoured fish soup.

Sienna EUROPEAN £££

(☎01305-250022; 36 High West St; 2-course set lunch/dinner £24/35; ⊙lunch & dinner Tue-Sat) Dorchester's Michelin-starred eatery is rich in seasonal produce; look out for wild garlic and pungent white truffles; partridge might be teamed with spiced pear. The cheeseboard bears the best of the west, served with fig chutney and Bath Oliver biscuits. Booking is required.

Information

Tourist office (☎01305-267992; www.westdorset.com; Antelope Walk; ⊙9am-5pm Mon-Sat Apr-Oct, to 4pm Nov-Mar)

Getting There & Around

Bicycle

Dorchester Cycles (☎01305-268787; 31 Great Western Rd; adult/child per day £8/12)

Bus

London (£22, four hours, one direct service daily) National Express.

Lyme Regis (1¾ hours, hourly) Bus 31; runs via Weymouth (30 minutes).

Poole (1¼ hours, three daily Monday to Saturday) Bus 347/387.

Sherborne (one hour, two to three daily Monday to Friday) Bus D12; via Cerne Abbas.

Weymouth (35 minutes, three per hour Monday to Saturday, six on Sunday) Bus 10/110.

Train

Trains run twice-hourly from Weymouth (11 minutes) to London Waterloo (£30, 2¾ hours) via Dorchester South, Bournemouth (£9.50, 45 minutes) and Southampton (£20, 1¼ hours). Dorchester West has connections with Bath (£14, two hours) and Bristol (£15, 2½ hours); trains run every two hours.

Around Dorchester

CERNE ABBAS & THE CERNE GIANT

If you had to describe an archetypal sleepy Dorset village, you'd come up with something a lot like Cerne Abbas: its houses run the gamut of England's architectural styles, roses climb countless doorways, and half-timbered houses frame a honey-coloured, 12th-century church.

But this village also packs one heck of a surprise – a real nudge-nudge, wink-wink tourist attraction in the form of the **Cerne Giant**. Nude, full frontal and notoriously well endowed, this chalk figure is revealed in all his glory on a hill on the edge of town. And he's in a stage of excitement that wouldn't be allowed in most magazines. The giant is around 60m high and 51m wide and his age remains a mystery; some claim he's Roman but the first

WORTH A TRIP

MAIDEN CASTLE

Occupying a massive slab of horizon on the southern fringes of Dorchester, **Maiden Castle** (EH; www.english-heritage.org.uk; ⊙24hr) is the largest and most complex Iron Age hill fort in Britain. The huge, steep-sided chalk ramparts flow along the contour lines of the hill and surround 48 hectares – the equivalent of 50 football pitches. The first hill fort was built on the site around 500 BC and in its heyday was densely populated with clusters of roundhouses and a network of roads. The Romans besieged and captured it in AD 43 – an ancient Briton skeleton with a Roman crossbow bolt in the spine was found at the site. The sheer scale of the ramparts is awe-inspiring, especially from the ditches immediately below, and the winding complexity of the west entrance reveals just how hard it would be to storm. Finds from the site are displayed at Dorset County Museum (p250). Maiden Castle is 1½ miles southwest of Dorchester.

historical reference comes in 1694, when three shillings were set aside for his repair. The Victorians found it all deeply embarrassing and allowed grass to grow over his most outstanding feature. Today the hill is grazed on by sheep and cattle – though only the sheep are allowed to do their nibbling over the giant, the cows would do too much damage to his lines.

The village has the not-so-new **New Inn** (☎01300-341274; www.newinncerneabbas.co.uk; 14 Long St; mains £9-22; ⏲lunch daily, dinner Fri & Sat), a 13th-century pub with rustic, comfy rooms (doubles £100), sophisticated bar meals, such as local venison casserole, and a restaurant menu including gurnard and spiced pork belly.

Dorchester is 8 miles to the south. Bus D12 (two to three daily Monday to Friday) connects Cerne Abbas with Dorchester (20 minutes) and Sherborne.

Weymouth & Around

As the venues for the sailing events in Britain's 2012 Olympics, Weymouth and neighbouring Portland are preparing to welcome some of the world's best seafarers to their shores. But despite the waterfront spruce-up, evidence of their core characters remains. Weymouth's billowing deckchairs, candy-striped beach kiosks and Punch and Judy stands are the epitome of a faded Georgian resort, while Portland's pock-marked central plateau still proudly proclaims a rugged, quarrying past. Portland also offers jaw-dropping views down onto 17-mile Chesil Beach, which is backed by the Fleet; Britain's biggest tidal lagoon – a home to 600 nesting swans.

WEYMOUTH

POP 48,279

Weymouth has been a popular seaside spot since King George III (the one with a 'nervous disorder') took an impromptu dip here in 1789. Some 200-plus years later, the town is still popular with holidaymakers, drawn by a 3-mile sandy beach, a revitalised historic harbour and oodles of seaside kitsch.

Sights & Activities

Weymouth Beach BEACH

Weymouth's fine sandy shore is perfect for a stroll down seaside memory lane. Here you can rent a **deckchair**, **sun-lounger** or **pedalo** (each £6 per hr), watch donkey rides, and see professional sandsculptors turn the golden grains into works of art. Alternatively, go all Californian and join a volleyball game. For watersports, see boxed text.

White Motor Boats BOAT TRIP

(www.whitemotorboat.freeuk.com; adult/child return £7.50/6; ⏲Apr-Oct) This wind-blown 40-minute jaunt crosses Portland Harbour's vast Olympic sailing waters, before dropping you off at Portland Castle (p254). Boats leave from Cove Row on Weymouth Harbour (three to four daily).

Nothe Fort HISTORIC FORT

(www.nothefort.org.uk; Barrack Rd; adult/child £6/1; ⏲10.30am-5.30pm May-Oct) Crowning the headland beside Weymouth Harbour, these photogenic 19th-century defences are studded with cannons, rifles, searchlights and 12-inch coastal guns. Exhibits detail the Roman invasion of Dorset, a Victorian soldier's drill, and Weymouth in WWII. Commanding an armoured car and clambering around the magazine prove popular with regiments of children.

WATER SPORTS – PORTLAND HARBOUR

Just south of Weymouth, the 890-hectare Portland Harbour is the sailing venue for the 2012 Olympics. The brand new **Weymouth & Portland National Sailing Academy** (☎0845 3373214; www.wpnsa.org.uk; Portland Harbour) runs sailing lessons (two/four days £170/325) and hires lasers (two hours/day £40/85). **Windtek** (☎01305-787900; www.windtek.co.uk; 109 Portland Rd, Wyke Regis) runs lessons in windsurfing (one/two days £90/150) and kitesurfing (per day £95).

Local waters offer super diving, with a huge variety of depths, seascapes, and wrecks. Operators include **Underwater Explorers** (☎01305-824555; www.underwaterexplorers.co.uk; 15 Castletown, Portland) and **Fathom & Blues** (☎01305-766220; www.fathomandblues.co.uk; 262 Portland Rd, Wyke Regis). Lessons start at around £95 a day; some operators shuttle qualified divers to a site (around £20) and rent equipment (from £50).

Sea Life AQUARIUM
(www.sealife.co.uk; Lodmoor Country Park; adult/child £17.50/15; ⏲10am-5pm) Sharks, penguins and seahorses entertain you at this 3-hectare aquatic park.

Sleeping

Harbourside APARTMENT ££
(☎01305-776757; www.mallamsrestaurant.co.uk; 5 Trinity Rd; 2-/4-person apt £100/150; P 📶) Antique chairs, brass bedsteads and fine Egyptian cotton fill two bedrooms and a lounge that looks out directly onto the bustling harbour. This bundle of elegance is often rented out as a weekly let (from £500), but the nightly rates are a bargain.

Old Harbour View B&B ££
(☎01305-774633; www.oldharbourviewweymouth.co.uk; 12 Trinity Rd; d £80-88) In this Georgian terrace you get boating themes in the fresh, white bedrooms and boats right outside the front door – one room overlooks the bustling harbour, the other faces the back.

Chatsworth B&B ££
(☎01305-785012; www.thechatsworth.co.uk; 14 The Esplanade; s £45, d £78-108) A sunny waterside terrace lets you watch yachts cast off just metres away while you eat breakfast. Inside you'll find leather armchairs, vanilla candles, worn wood and bursts of sea-side chintz.

Eating & Drinking

Clusters of bars line the old harbour; ice cream kiosks dot the prom.

Perry's EUROPEAN ££
(☎01305-785799; www.perrysrestaurant.co.uk; 4 Trinity Rd; mains £12-20; ⏲lunch Tue-Fri & Sun, dinner Tue-Sat) Effortlessly stylish, but also relaxed, this Georgian town house is a study of snowy white tablecloths and flashes of pink. The local seafood is irresistible: sea bass with crushed saffron potatoes, and spiced tian of Portland crab. The cognoscenti book the 1st floor window table (complete with fabulous harbour view) for a two-course lunch – a bargain at £15.

King Edward's CHIP SHOP £
(100 The Esplanade; mains £6; ⏲lunch & dinner) It has to be done: sit on Weymouth seafront scoffing fish 'n' chips. This classic Victorian chippy is lined with burgundy tiles and wrought iron; its menu is a feast of battered fish, chipped potatoes, mushy peas and pickled eggs.

Information

Tourist office (☎01305-785747; www.visitweymouth.co.uk; Pavilion Theatre, The Esplanade; ⏲9.30am-5pm Apr-Oct, 9.30am-4pm Nov-Mar)

Getting There & Away

Bus

National Express operates one direct coach to London (£21, 4¼ hours) daily. Bus 10/110 shuttles to Dorchester (35 minutes, three per hour Monday to Saturday, six on Sunday). Bus 31 goes hourly to Lyme Regis (1¾ hours) and Axminster (two hours). Bus X53 (two to six daily) travels from Weymouth to Wareham (50 minutes) and Poole (1½ hours), and to Abbotsbury (35 minutes), Lyme Regis (1¾ hours) and Exeter (2¾ hours) in the opposite direction. Bus 1 runs from Weymouth to Fortuneswell on the Isle of Portland every half-hour, between June and September it also goes on to Portland Bill.

Boat

Condor Ferries (www.condorferries.co.uk) Shuttle daily between Weymouth and the Channel Islands.

Train

Trains run twice-hourly between Weymouth and London (£50, three hours) via Dorchester South (11 minutes) and Bournemouth, (£10.90, one hour), and hourly to Bath (£15.60, two hours) and Bristol (£20.60, 2½ hours).

ISLE OF PORTLAND

The 'Isle' of Portland is really a hard, high comma of rock fused to the rest of Dorset by the ridge of Chesil Beach. Portland is where the pre-Olympic building boom is most apparent; chunks of waterside waste ground have been transformed into a shiny new sailing centre, a glitzy apartment block and a hotel. But inland on Portland's 500ft central plateau, a quarrying past still holds sway, evidenced by huge craters and large slabs of limestone. Proud, and at times bleak and rough around the edges, it's decidedly different from the rest of Dorset, and is all the more compelling because of it. The watersports on offer, rich birdlife and starkly beautiful cliffs make it worthy of at least a day trip.

Sights

TOP CHOICE **Tout Quarry** INDUSTRIAL ART
(⏲24hr) Portland's unique white limestone has been quarried for centuries, and has been used in some of the world's finest buildings – including the British Museum and St Paul's Cathedral. Tout Quarry

WORTH A TRIP

ABBOTSBURY SWANNERY

Every May some 600 free-flying swans choose to nest at the **Abbotsbury Swannery** (www.abbotsbury-tourism.co.uk; New Barn Rd; adult/child £9.50/6.50; 10am-5pm or 6pm late-Mar–Oct), which shelters in the Fleet lagoon, protected by the ridge of Chesil Beach. The swannery was founded by local monks about 600 years ago, and feathers from the Abbotsbury swans are still used in the helmets of the Gentlemen at Arms (the Queen's official bodyguard). Wandering the network of trails that wind between the swans' nests is an awe-inspiring experience that is often punctuated by occasional territorial displays (think snuffling cough and stand-up flapping), ensuring that even the liveliest children are stilled.

The swannery is at the picturesque village of Abbotsbury, 10 miles from Weymouth off the B3157.

is a disused working quarry where 53 sculptures have been carved into the rock in situ. The result is a fascinating combination of the raw material, the detritus of the quarrying process and the beauty of chiselled works. Labyrinthine paths snake through hacked-out gullies and around jumbled piles of rock, revealing the half-formed bears, bison and lizards that emerge out of stone cliffs. Highlights include *Still Falling* by Antony Gormley, *Woman on Rock* by Dhruva Mistry and the well-hidden *Green Man*. Tout Quarry is signed off the main road, just south of Fortuneswell.

Portland Lighthouse LIGHTHOUSE
(adult/child £2.50/1.50; 11am-5pm Sun-Fri Apr-Sep) For a real sense of the isle's remote nature, head to its southern tip, **Portland Bill**. Then climb the 13m-high, candy-striped lighthouse for breathtaking views of rugged cliffs and The Race, a surging vortex of conflicting tides.

Portland Castle CASTLE
(EH; www.english-heritage.org.uk; Castletown; adult/child £4.20/2.10; 10am-5pm Apr-Sep, to pm Jul & Aug, to 4pm Oct) A particularly fine product of Henry VIII's castle-building spree, with expansive views over Portland harbour.

Eating & Drinking

Crab House Café RESTAURANT ££
(01305-788867; www.crabhousecafe.co.uk; Portland Rd, Wyke Regis; mains £16; lunch & dinner Wed-Sat, lunch Sun) At this funky cabin beside the Fleet lagoon, the oyster beds are right alongside, meaning the molluscs (£8.50 per half dozen) are in your mouth minutes after leaving the water. Gutsy dishes include skate with chorizo and paprika, or get cracking on crab still in its shell (half/whole £11/19). The cafe is near the start of the road onto Portland.

Cove House PUB £
(Chiswell, Portland; mains £8; lunch & dinner) Extraordinary Chesil Beach views, memorable sunsets and great grub in a history-rich fishermen's inn.

Information

Tourist office (01305-861233; www.visitweymouth.co.uk; Portland Bill; 11am-5pm Easter-Sep)

Getting There & Away

Bus

Bus 1 runs to Portland from Weymouth every half-hour, going onto Portland Bill between June and September.

Boat

See White Motor Boats (p252) for links to Weymouth.

CHESIL BEACH

One of the most breathtaking beaches in Britain, Chesil is 17 miles long, 15m high and moving inland at the rate of 5m a century. This mind-boggling, 100-million-tonne pebble ridge is the baby of the Jurassic Coast (see boxed text, p248); a mere 6000 years old, its stones range from pea-sized in the west to hand-sized in the east. More recently it became famous as the setting for Ian McEwan's acclaimed novel about sexual awakening, *On Chesil Beach*.

Chesil Beach Centre (www.chesilbeach.org; Ferrybridge; admission free; 10am-5pm Apr-Sep, 11am-4pm Oct-Mar), just over the bridge to Portland, is a good place to get onto the beach. The pebble ridge is at its highest around this point - 15m compared to 7m at **Abbotsbury**. From the car park an energy-sapping hike up sliding pebbles leads to the constant surge and rattle of sea on stones and dazzling views of the sea, the thin pebble line and the expanse of the Fleet behind. The centre details geology, bird and plant life that includes ringed plover, redshank and oyster catchers, as well as drifts of thrift and sea campion. It also provides information, and organises talks and guided walks.

Lyme Regis

POP 4406

Fantastically fossiliferous, Lyme Regis packs a heavyweight historical punch. Rock-hard relics of the past pop out repeatedly from the surrounding cliffs – exposed by the landslides of a retreating shoreline. Now a pivot point of the Unesco-listed Jurassic Coast (see p248), fossil fever is definitely in the air and everyone, from proper palaeontologists to those out for a bit of fun, can engage in a spot of coastal rummaging.

Lyme was also famously the setting for *The French Lieutenant's Woman*, the film version – starring Meryl Streep – immortalised the iconic Cobb harbour defences in movie history. Add sandy beaches and some delightful places to sleep and eat, and you get a charming base for explorations.

Sights & Activities

Lyme Regis Museum MUSEUM

(www.lymeregismuseum.co.uk; Bridge St; adult/child £3/free; ⏲10am-5pm Mon-Sat, 11am-5pm Sun Apr-Oct, 11am-4pm Wed-Sun Nov-Mar) In 1814 a local teenager called Mary Anning found the first full ichthyosaurus skeleton near Lyme, propelling the town onto the word stage. An incredibly famous fossilist in her day, Miss Anning did much to pioneer the science of modern-day palaeontology. The museum, on the site of her former home, exhibits her story along with spectacular fossils and other prehistoric finds.

Dinosaurland FOSSIL MUSEUM

(www.dinosaurland.co.uk; Coombe St; adult/child £5/4; ⏲10am-5pm mid-Feb–Nov) This mini, indoor Jurassic Park is packed with the remains of belemnites and the graceful plesiosaurus. Lifelike dinosaur models will thrill youngsters – the fossilised tyrannosaurus eggs and 73kg dinosaur dung will have them in raptures.

Cobb HARBOUR WALL

(⏲24hr) First built in the 13th century, this curling, protective barrier has been strengthened and extended over the years, so it doesn't present the elegant line it once did, but it's still hard to resist wandering its length for a wistful, sea-gazing Meryl moment at the tip.

Sleeping

Coombe House B&B ££

(☎01297-443849; www.coombe-house.co.uk; 41 Coombe St; s/d £36/72; P) Easygoing and stylish, this fabulous value guest house is full of airy rooms, bay windows, wicker and white wood. Breakfast is delivered to your door on a trolley, complete with toaster – perfect for a lazy lie-in in Lyme.

Alexandra HOTEL ££

(☎01297-442010; www.hotelalexandra.co.uk; Pound St; s £75, d £120-190; P) This grand 18th-century villa was once home to a countess; today, it's all dignified calm and murmured chatter. Rooms are scattered with antique chairs and fine drapes and most have captivating views of the Cobb and the sea. The glorious terrace prompts patrons to peruse the *Telegraph* in a panama hat.

FOSSIL HUNTING

Lyme Regis sits in one of the most unstable sections of Britain's coast and regular landslips mean nuggets of prehistory constantly tumble from the cliffs. If you are bitten by the hunting bug, the best cure is one of the regular fossil walks staged locally.

In the village of **Charmouth**, 3 miles east of Lyme, they're run two to four times a week by the **Charmouth Heritage Coast Centre** (☎01297-560772; www.charmouth.org; adult/child £7/5). Or in Lyme itself, **Lyme Regis Museum** (☎01297-443370; 2-hr walks adult/child £9/5) offers four to six walks a week, and local expert **Brandon Lennon** (☎07944 664757; www.lymeregisfossilwalks.com; adult/child £7/5; ⏲Sat-Tue) also leads expeditions.

For the best chances of a find, time your trip to Lyme to within two hours of low tide; to be sure of a place on the walks, book ahead. If you choose to hunt by yourself, official advice is to check tide times, always collect on a falling tide, observe warning signs, keep away from the cliffs, stay on public paths, only pick up from the beach (never dig out from cliffs) and always leave some behind for others. Oh, and tell the experts if you find a stunner.

Old Lyme B&B ££
(☎01297-442929; www.oldlymeguesthouse.co.uk; 29 Coombe St; d £75; P) A 17th-century cottage featuring pastel-painted rooms, patterned curtains and china trinkets.

Eating & Drinking

TOP CHOICE **Hix Oyster & Fish House** SEAFOOD ££
(☎01297-446910; Cobb Rd; mains £8-20; ⊙lunch & dinner Wed-Sun) Expect grandstand views of the Cobb and dazzling food at this super-stylish open-plan cabin. Cuttlefish comes with ink stew; ray with hazelnuts; and steak with baked bone marrow. Or plump for potted Morecambe Bay shrimps on toast, or oysters – choose from Brownsea Island or Falmouth – at £2 to £3 a pop.

Jurassic Seafood FUSION ££
(47 Silver St; mains £10-15; ⊙dinner) Bright and buzzy in blue and orange, this eatery revels in its prehistoric theme: fossil maps, hunting tips and replica dinosaur remains abound. A tasty, eclectic menu includes crab sushi, mussels and chips, and local mackerel, as well as salads and steaks.

Alexandra AFTERNOON TEA
(www.hotelalexandra.co.uk; Pound St, afternoon tea from £5.20; ⊙2.30-5.30pm) Head to this grand hotel's sea-view lawns for the ultimate English experience: afternoon tea, complete with scones, clotted cream and cucumber sandwiches.

Harbour Inn PUB £
(Marine Pde; mains £5-10; ⊙lunch & dinner) Stone walls, wooden settles and a harbour-side beer garden

Information

Tourist Office (☎01297-442138; www.westdorset.com; Church St; ⊙10am-5pm Mon-Sat & 10am-4pm Sun Apr-Oct, 10am-3pm Mon-Sat Nov-Mar)

Getting There & Away

Bus 31 runs to Dorchester (1¼ hours) and Weymouth (1¾ hours) hourly (every two hours on Sunday). Bus X53 (six to nine daily, three on Sunday) goes west to Exeter (1¾ hours) and east to Weymouth (1½ hours).

Sherborne

POP 9350

Sherborne gleams with a mellow, orangey-yellow stone – it's been used to build a central cluster of 15th-century buildings and the impressive abbey church at their core. This serene town exudes wealth. The five local fee-paying schools include the famous Sherborne School, and its pupils are a frequent sight as they head off to lessons from boarding houses scattered around the town. The number of boutique shops and convertibles in the car parks reinforces the well-heeled feel. Evidence of splashing the cash 16th- and 18th-century style lies on the edge of town with two castles: one a crumbling ruin, the other a marvellous manor house, complete with a Capability Brown lake.

Sights & Activities

FREE **Sherborne Abbey** CATHEDRAL
(www.sherborneabbey.com; suggested donation £3.50; ⊙8am-6pm late Mar–late Oct, to 4pm Nov–mid-Mar) At the height of its influence, the magnificent Abbey Church of St Mary the Virgin was the central cathedral of the 26 Saxon bishops of Wessex. Established early in the 8th century, it became a Benedictine abbey in 998 and functioned as a cathedral until 1075. The church has mesmerising fan vaulting that's the oldest in the country; a central tower supported by Saxon-Norman piers; and an 1180 Norman porch. Its tombs include the elaborate marble effigy belonging to John Lord Digby, Earl of Bristol, and those of the elder brothers of Alfred the Great, Ethelred and Ethelbert.

On the edge of the abbey lie the beautiful 15th-century **St Johns' Almshouses** (admission £2; ⊙2-4pm Tue & Thu-Sat May-Sep); look out, too, for the six-sided **conduit** now at the foot of Cheap St. This arched structure used to be the monks' lavatorium (washhouse), but was moved to provide the townsfolk with water when the abbey was disbanded.

Old Castle CASTLE
(EH; www.english-heritage.org.uk; adult/child £3/1.50; ⊙10am-5pm Apr-Sep, to 4pm Oct) These days the epitome of a picturesque ruin, Sherborne's Old Castle was built by Roger, Bishop of Salisbury in around 1120. Elizabeth I gave it to her one-time favourite Sir Walter Raleigh in the late 16th century. He spent large sums of money modernising it before opting for a new-build instead – moving across the River Yeo to start work on the next Sherborne Castle. The old one became a Royalist

WORTH A TRIP

FORDE ABBEY

A former Cistercian monastery, **Forde Abbey** (www.fordeabbey.co.uk; abbey adult/child £10.50/free, gardens £8.50/free; ⏲abbey noon-4pm Tue-Fri & Sun Apr-Oct, gardens 10am-4.30pm) was built in the 12th century, updated in the 17th century, and has been a private home since 1649. The building boasts magnificent plasterwork ceilings and fine tapestries but it's the gardens that are the main attraction: 12 hectares of lawns, ponds, shrubberies and flower beds with many rare and beautiful species.

It's 10 miles north of Lyme Regis; public transport is a nonstarter.

stronghold during the English Civil War, but Cromwell reduced the 'malicious and mischievous castle' to rubble after a 16-day siege in 1645, leaving the crumbling southwest gatehouse, great tower and north range. It stays open until 6pm in July and August.

Sherborne Castle STATELY HOME
(www.sherbornecastle.com; house adult/child £9.50/free, gardens only £5/free; ⏲11am-4.30pm Tue-Thu & weekends Apr-Oct) Having had enough of the then 400-year-old Old Castle, Sir Walter Raleigh began building New Castle, really a splendid manor house, in 1594. Raleigh got as far as the central block before falling out of favour with the royals and ending up back in prison – this time at the hands of James I. In 1617 James sold the castle to Sir John Digby, Earl of Bristol, who added the wings we see today. In 1753, the grounds received a mega-makeover at the hands of landscape-gardener extraordinaire Capability Brown – visit today and marvel at the massive lake he added, along with a remarkable 12 hectares of waterside gardens.

Walking Tours HERITAGE TOURS
(tour £3; ⏲11am Fri Jun-Sep) One and a half hour trips exploring the photogenic old town, leaving from the tourist office.

Sleeping

Cumberland House B&B ££
(☎01935-817554; www.bandbdorset.co.uk; Green Hill; s £50-55, d £65-75; P) There are few straight lines in this 17th-century cottage; instead, walls undulate towards each other in charming rooms finished in white, beige and bursts of vivid pink. Breakfast is either continental (complete with chocolate croissants) or full English – either way, there's freshly squeezed orange juice.

Stoneleigh Barn B&B ££
(☎01935-815964; www.stoneleighbarn.com; North Wootton; s £55, d £80-90, f £80-100; P ⊠) Outside, this gorgeous 18th-century barn delights the senses – it's smothered in bright, fragrant flowers. Inside, exposed trusses frame rooms calmly decorated in cream and gold and crammed with books and jigsaws. Stoneleigh is 3 miles southeast of Sherborne.

Eastbury HOTEL £££
(☎01935-813131; www.theeastburyhotel.co.uk; Long St; s £70, d £135-175; P) The best rooms here have real 'wow' factor – black and gold lacquer screens frame minimalist freestanding baths, and shimmering fabrics swathe French sleigh beds. The standard rooms are much more standard, but are still elegant with stripy furnishings and pared-down wicker chairs.

Eating

Green ENGLISH ££
(☎01935-813821; 3 The Green; mains £9-17; ⏲lunch & dinner Tue-Sat) As mellow as the honey-coloured building it's set in, this intimate restaurant's menu is full of local ingredients; try the mushroom and thyme risotto with roasted butternut squash, or the guinea fowl with apples and redcurrants.

Pear Tree DELI £
(Half Moon St; snacks £4-8; ⏲9am-5pm Mon-Sat, 10am-4pm Sun) Full of mouth-watering aromas, this delectable deli is packed with gourmet picnic supplies. Spinach and feta pie, homemade soups and a wealth of local cheeses are coupled with irresistible cakes and puddings.

Information

Tourist office (☎01935-815341; www.westdorset.com; Digby Rd; ⏲9am-5pm Mon-Sat Apr-Oct, 10am-3pm Nov-Mar) Stocks the free *All About Sherborne* leaflet, which has a map and town trail.

Getting There & Away

Bus

Buses 57 and 58 shuttle hourly between Sherborne and Yeovil (30 minutes). National Express runs one coach a day from Sherborne to Shaftesbury (30 minutes). Bus D12 runs from Sherborne to Dorchester (two to three daily Monday to Friday), via Cerne Abbas.

Train

Hourly trains go to Exeter (£16, 1¼ hours), London Waterloo (£28, 2½ hours) and Salisbury (£11, 40 minutes).

Shaftesbury & Around

POP 6665

Perched on a hilltop overlooking a panorama of pastoral meadows and hogbacked hills, the village of Shaftesbury was home to the largest community of nuns in England until 1539, when Henry VIII came knocking during the Dissolution. Now its attractions are rather more prosaic; the town's best-known landmark is Gold Hill. This cobbled slope, lined by chocolate-box cottages, graces many a local postcard and also starred in a famous TV advert for Hovis bread.

Sights

Shaftesbury Abbey ECCLESIASTICAL RUINS
(www.shaftesburyabbey.org.uk; Park Walk; adult/child £4/1; 10am-5pm Apr-Oct) These hill-top ruins mark the site of what was England's largest and richest nunnery. It was founded in 888 by King Alfred the Great, and was the first religious house in Britain built solely for women; Alfred's daughter, Aethelgifu, was its first abbess. St Edward is thought to have been buried here, and King Knut died at the abbey in 1035. Most buildings were dismantled by Henry VIII, but you can still wander around its foundations with a well-devised audio guide, and visit the intriguing museum.

Old Wardour Castle CASTLE
(EH; adult/child £3.50/1.80; 10am-5pm Apr-Sep, to 4pm Oct, 10am-4pm Sat & Sun Nov-Mar) The six-sided Old Wardour Castle was built around 1393 and suffered severe damage during the English Civil War, leaving the magnificent remains you see today. It's an ideal spot for a picnic and there are fantastic views from the upper levels. It's open until 6pm in July and August. Bus 26 runs from Shaftesbury (four daily Monday to Friday), 4 miles west.

Sleeping & Eating

Fleur de Lys HOTEL-RESTAURANT £££
(01747 853717; Bleke St; s £80-90, d £110-135; P @ wi-fi) For a lovely dollop of luxury, immerse yourself in the world of Fleur de Lys. Fluffy bathrobes, minifridges and laptops ensure you click into pamper mode. The elegant **restaurant** (2/3 courses £25/30, mains £23; lunch pre-booked Wed-Sun, dinner Mon-Sat) rustles up lobster ravioli, venison in Armagnac, and lemon sole with a dash of vermouth. Lunch has to be pre-booked, reserving a space for dinner is advisable too.

Up Down SELF CATERING ££
(www.updowncottage.co.uk; Gold Hill; per week from £500; P wi-fi) This whitewashed, 4-bedroom cottage clinging to Gold Hill is a supremely picturesque place to sleep. Snug, beam-lined rooms, open fires and a hillside garden make it one to remember, the boutique bathrooms make it hard to leave.

Mitre PUB ££
(23 High St; mains £6-10; lunch & dinner Mon-Sat, lunch Sun) An atmospheric old inn with drink-them-in views over Blackmore Vale from its decked terrace.

Information

Tourist office (01747-853514; www.shaftesburydorset.com; 8 Bell St; 10am-5pm Mon-Sat Apr-Sep, to 3pm Oct-Mar)

Getting There & Away

National Express runs one bus a day to London Victoria (£19, four hours), via Heathrow, and one daily service to Sherborne (30 minutes). Buses 26 and 27 go to Salisbury (1¼ hours, four to five Monday to Saturday).

WILTSHIRE

Wiltshire is rich in the reminders of ritual. Its verdant landscape is littered with more ancient barrows, processional avenues and mysterious stone circles than anywhere else in Britain. It's a place that teases and tantalises the imagination – here you'll find the prehistoric majesty of Stonehenge, atmospheric Avebury and, in soaring Silbury Hill, the largest constructed earth mound in Europe. Then there's the serene 800-year-old cathedral at Salisbury – a relatively modern religious monument. Add the supremely stately homes at Stourhead and Longleat and the impossibly pretty village of Lacock, and you have a county crammed full of English charm waiting to be explored.

Information

Visit Wiltshire (www.visitwiltshire.co.uk)

Getting Around

Bus

The bus coverage in Wiltshire can be patchy, especially in the northwest of the county. The two main operators:

First (www.firstgroup.com) Serves west Wiltshire.

Wilts & Dorset Buses (www.wdbus.co.uk) Covers many rural areas. It sells 1-day Explorer tickets (adult/child £7.50/4.50) and 7-day Network passes (£20).

Train

Rail lines run from London to Salisbury and beyond to Exeter and Plymouth, branching off north to Bradford-on-Avon, Bath and Bristol, but most of the smaller towns and villages aren't served by trains.

WORTH A TRIP

CANAL TRIPS

The 87-mile-long **Kennet & Avon Canal** (www.katrust.org) runs all the way from Bristol to Reading. **Sally Boats** (☎01225-864923; www.sallyboats.ltd.uk; Bradford-on-Avon) and **Foxhangers** (☎01380-828795; www.foxhangers.co.uk; Devizes) both hire out narrowboats. Weekly rates for a four-berth boat range from around £680 in the winter to £950 in high-summer.

Salisbury

POP 43,335

Centred on a majestic cathedral that's topped by the tallest spire in England, the gracious city of Salisbury makes a charming base from which to discover the rest of Wiltshire. It's been an important provincial city for more than a thousand years, and its streets form an architectural timeline ranging from medieval walls and half-timbered Tudor town houses to Georgian mansions and Victorian villas. Salisbury is also a lively, modern town, boasting plenty of bars, restaurants and terraced cafes, as well as a concentrated cluster of excellent museums.

Sights

Salisbury Cathedral CATHEDRAL

(www.salisburycathedral.org.uk; requested donation adult/child £5/3; ⏲7.15am-6.15pm) England is endowed with countless stunning churches, but few can hold a candle to the grandeur and sheer spectacle of Salisbury Cathedral. Built between 1220 and 1258, the cathedral bears all the hallmarks of the early English Gothic style, with an elaborate exterior decorated with pointed arches and flying buttresses, and a sombre, austere interior designed to keep its congregation suitably pious.

Beyond the highly decorative **West Front**, a small passageway leads into the 70m-long nave, lined with handsome pillars of Purbeck stone. In the north aisle look out for a fascinating **medieval clock** dating from 1386, probably the oldest working timepiece in the world. At the eastern end of the ambulatory the glorious **Prisoners of Conscience** stained-glass window (1980) hovers above the ornate tomb of Edward Seymour (1539–1621) and Lady Catherine Grey. Other monuments and tombs line the sides of the nave, including that of William Longespée, son of Henry II and half-brother of King John. When the tomb was excavated a well-preserved rat was found inside Longespée's skull.

The intensely atmospheric Evensong takes place at 5.30pm Monday to Saturday and 3pm on Sunday, during term time only.

Spire

Salisbury's 123m crowning glory was added in the mid-14th century, and is the tallest spire in Britain. It represented an enormous technical challenge for its medieval builders; it weighs around 6500 tons and required an elaborate system of cross-bracing, scissor arches and supporting buttresses to keep it upright. Look closely and you'll see that the additional weight has buckled the four central piers of the nave.

Sir Christopher Wren surveyed the cathedral in 1668 and calculated that the spire was leaning by 75cm. A brass plate in the floor of the nave is used to measure any shift, but no further lean was recorded in 1951 or 1970. Despite this, reinforcement of the notoriously 'wonky spire' continues to this day.

Chapter House

(⏲10am-4.30pm Mon-Sat, 12.45-4.30pm Sun) Salisbury Cathedral is home to one of only four surviving original copies of the **Magna Carta**, the historic agreement made between King John and his barons in 1215 that acknowledged the fundamental principle that the monarch was not above the law. It's an evocative document; beautifully written and remarkably well-preserved.

Salisbury

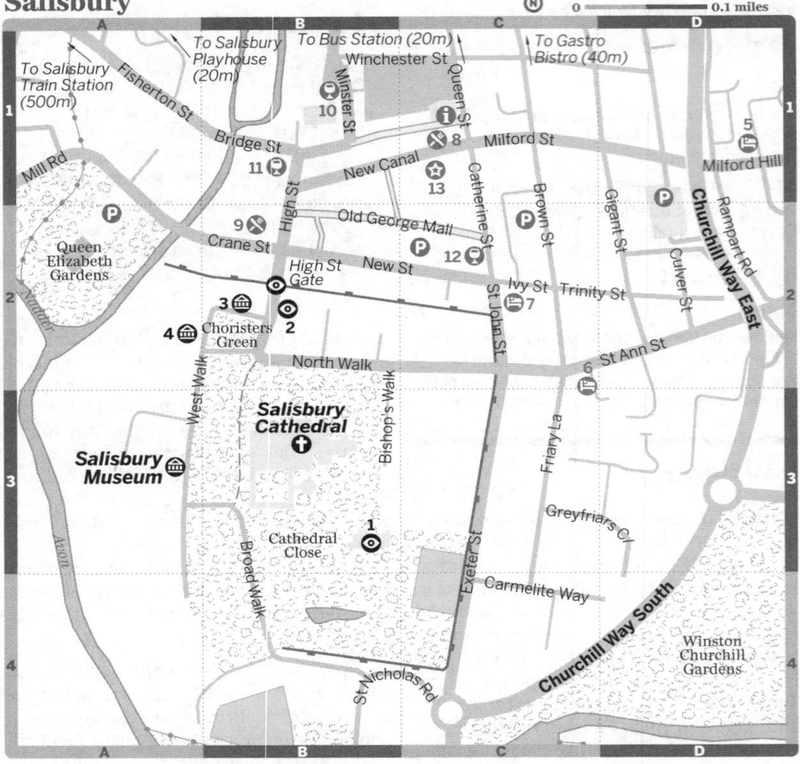

Tower Tours

These 1½ hour **trips** (☎01722-555156; adult/child £8.50/6.50; ⏱1-4pm) climb up 332 vertigo-inducing steps to the base of the spire, revealing jaw-dropping views across the city and the surrounding countryside. Bookings are required.

Cathedral Close SIGNIFICANT AREA

Salisbury's medieval cathedral close, a tranquil enclave surrounded by beautiful houses, has an other-worldly feel. Many of the buildings date from the same period as the cathedral, although the area was heavily restored during an 18th-century clean-up by James Wyatt.

The close is encircled by a sturdy outer wall, constructed in 1333; the stout gates leading into the complex are still locked every night. Just inside narrow High St Gate is the **College of Matrons**, founded in 1682 for widows and unmarried daughters of clergymen. South of the cathedral is the **Bishop's Palace**, now the private Cathedral School, parts of which date back to 1220. The close is also home to three museums and historic buildings – Mompesson House, Salisbury Museum and the Rifles.

Salisbury Museum MUSEUM

(www.salisburymuseum.org.uk; 65 Cathedral Close; adult/child £6/2; ⏱10am-5pm Mon-Sat, plus 2-5pm Sun Jul & Aug) The hugely important archaeological finds here include the Stonehenge Archer (the bones of a man found in the ditch surrounding the stone circle – one of the arrows found alongside probably killed him). Add gold coins dating from 100 BC and a Bronze Age gold necklace, and it's a great introduction to Wiltshire's prehistory.

Mompesson House HISTORIC BUILDING

(NT; www.nationaltrust.org.uk; Cathedral Close; adult/child £5/2.50; ⏱11am-5pm Sat-Wed Mar-Oct) Built in 1701, this fine Queen Anne

Salisbury

Top Sights
- Salisbury Cathedral B3
- Salisbury Museum A3

Sights
- 1 Bishop's Palace B3
- 2 College of Matrons B2
- 3 Mompesson House B2
- 4 Rifles A2

Sleeping
- 5 Salisbury YHA D1
- 6 St Anns House C2
- 7 White Hart C2

Eating
- 8 Bird & Carter C1
- 9 Lemon Tree B2
- One .... (see 10)

Drinking
- 10 Haunch of Venison B1
- 11 Moloko B1
- 12 Spirit C2

Entertainment
- Goldfingers .... (see 12)
- 13 Odeon Cinema C1

building boasts magnificent plasterwork ceilings, exceptional period furnishings and a wonderful carved staircase. All that made it the perfect location for the 1995 film *Sense and Sensibility*.

Rifles MILITARY MUSEUM
(The Wardrobe; www.thewardrobe.org.uk; 58 Cathedral Close; adult/child £3.50/1; ⏲10am-5pm Mar-Sep, 10am-5pm Tue-Sat Oct-Nov & Feb) Collections include ranks of medals, Victorian redcoat uniforms and displays on 19th and 21st century conflicts in Afghanistan.

Tours

Salisbury Guides HERITAGE TOURS
(www.salisburycityguides.co.uk; adult/child £4/2; ⏲11am Apr-Oct, 11am Sat & Sun Nov-Mar) One and a half hour trips leave from the tourist office. There's an 8pm ghost walk on Fridays from May to September.

Festivals

Salisbury Festival MUSIC & ARTS
(www.salisburyfestival.co.uk) A prestigious, eclectic event running from late May to early June, encompassing classical, world and pop music, plus theatre, literature and art.

Sleeping

TOP CHOICE **St Anns House** BOUTIQUE B&B ££
(☎01722-335657; www.stannshouse.co.uk; 32 St Ann St; s/d £60/110) For some perfectly priced indulgence head to this sumptuous town house which overflows with antiques, fine silk and linen direct from Istanbul. Gourmet breakfasts include beef and chilli sausages, smoked salmon and Parma ham. The chef-proprietor has spent decades working for the great and the good, ask after some past jobs and prepare for some great stories.

Rokeby Guesthouse B&B ££
(☎01722-329800; www.rokebyguesthouse.co.uk; 3 Wain-a-long Rd; s/d from £50/60; P@) Fancy furnishings, free-standing baths and lovely bay windows make this cheerful B&B stand out from the crowd. The decking overlooking the lawn and the minigym help, too. Rokeby is a mile northeast of the cathedral.

White Hart HOTEL ££
(☎01722-327476; www.mercure-uk.com; St John St; s from £90, d £122-142; P@) This 17th-century coaching inn is the place for a bit of pomp and pampering. Its white porticos face Cathedral Close, the service is appropriately attentive and rooms are suitably swish – the wood-rich four-poster bedrooms are positively opulent.

Websters B&B ££
(☎01722-339779; www.websters-bed-breakfast.com; 11 Hartington Rd; s £45-53, d £60-70; P@) Websters' exterior charms include quaint blue shutters and arched windows. Inside it's all flowery wallpaper, patterned duvets, extra tea-tray treats and a genuinely warm welcome. Websters is a mile northwest of the cathedral.

Salisbury YHA HOSTEL £
(☎0845 371 9537; www.yha.org.uk; Milford Hill; dm £18; P@) A real gem: neat rooms in a rambling, listed Victorian building. Choose from doubles or dorms – a cafe-bar, laundry and dappled gardens add to the appeal.

Eating

Gastro Bistro FRENCH ££
(☎01722-414926; www.restaurant-salisbury.com; 19 Salt La; mains £7-16; ⏲lunch & dinner)

Prepare for a Gallic, gastronomic assault on the senses. The aroma of robust French cooking fills the air, while tastebuds delight in dishes such as escargots, terrines, Toulouse sausages and confit of duck with redcurrant sauce. The three-course menu, including wine, is a bargain at £18.

Lemon Tree ENGLISH ££
(☎01722-333471; www.thelemontree.co.uk; 92 Crane St; mains £10; ⊙lunch & dinner Mon-Sat) The menu at this tiny eatery is packed with character – how about chicken laced with white wine, butternut squash with Provençal sauce, or crab claw and avocado salad? The patio-garden makes warm weather dining a delight.

Bird & Carter DELI £
(3 Fish Row, Market Sq; snacks from £4.50; ⊙8.30am-6pm Mon-Sat, 10am-4pm Sun) Nestling amid 15th-century beams, this deli-cafe blends old-world charm with a tempting array of antipasti, charcuterie and local goodies. Grab a goats' cheese and aubergine panini to go, or duck upstairs to eat alongside weathered wood, stained glass and old church pews.

One ENGLISH ££
(☎01722-411313; www.haunchofvenison.uk.com; 1 Minster St; mains £9-13; ⊙lunch & dinner) Sloping floors, slanting beams and fake ponyhide chairs surround you in this chic eatery, located above the Haunch of Venison pub. The menu is equally eclectic, featuring mustard-rubbed pork chops, duck mousse with red onion marmalade and, yes: a haunch of venison (with garlic mash).

Drinking

Haunch of Venison HERITAGE PUB
(www.haunchofvenison.uk.com; 1 Minster St) Featuring wood-panelled snugs, spiral staircases and wonky ceilings, this 14th-century drinking den is packed with atmosphere – and ghosts. One is a cheating whist player whose hand was severed in a game – look out for his mummified bones on display inside.

Spirit BAR
(46 Catherine St; ⊙4pm-midnight Tue-Sat) Hip hang-out with a multi-coloured light-up floor, crowd-pleasing tunes on the decks and a choice of vivid cocktails.

Moloko BAR
(5 Bridge St) Red radiators, Soviet stars and flavoured vodkas create a Cold War theme.

Entertainment

Salisbury Arts Centre ARTS CENTRE
(www.salisburyartscentre.co.uk; Bedwin St) Housed in the converted St Edmund's church some 800m northeast of the cathedral, this innovative arts centre showcases cutting-edge theatre, dance and live gigs; photography and arts exhibitions are held in the foyer.

Salisbury Playhouse THEATRE
(www.salisburyplayhouse.com; Malthouse Lane) Hosts top touring shows, musicals and new plays.

Goldfingers NIGHTCLUB
(www.goldfingersnightclub.com; 48 Catherine St; ⊙11pm-3am Thu-Sat) Live music on Fridays, dance-floor fillers on Saturdays, plus monthly comedy nights.

Odeon Cinema CINEMA
(www.odeon.co.uk; New Canal)

Information

Library (Market Pl; ⊙10am-7pm Mon-Wed & Fri, to 5pm Sat & Thu) Internet access; first 30 minutes free.

Tourist office (☎01722-334956; www.visitwiltshire.co.uk/salisbury; Fish Row, Market Sq; ⊙9.30am-6pm Mon-Sat, 10am-4pm Sun Jun-Sep, 9.30am-5pm Mon-Sat Oct-Apr)

Getting There & Away

Bus

National Express operates coaches to London via Heathrow (£16, three hours, three daily), and Bath (£10, 1¼ hours, one daily) and Bristol (£10, 2¼ hours, daily). Regular buses run to Shaftesbury, Devizes and Avebury. Tour buses leave Salisbury for Stonehenge regularly; see p265.

Train

Trains run half-hourly from London Waterloo (£32, 1½ hours) and hourly to Exeter (£27, two hours) and further west. Another line provides hourly connections between Salisbury, Portsmouth (£15.30, 1½ hours) and Southampton (£7.60, 30 minutes), with hourly connections to Bath (£8, one hour) and Bristol (£9, 1¼ hours).

Around Salisbury

OLD SARUM

The huge ramparts of **Old Sarum** (EH; www.english-heritage.org.uk; adult/child £3.50/1.80; ⊙10am-5pm Apr-Sep, 11am-3pm Oct-Mar) sit on a grassy rise about 2 miles from Salisbury. It began life as a hill fort during the Iron Age, and was later occupied by both the Romans and the Saxons. By the mid-11th century it was a town – one of the most important in the west of England; William the Conqueror convened one of his earliest councils here, with the first cathedral being built in 1092, snatching the bishopric from nearby Sherborne Abbey. But Old Sarum always had problems: it was short on water and exposed to the elements, and in 1219 the bishop was given permission to move the cathedral to a new location beside the River Avon, founding the modern-day city of Salisbury. By 1331 Old Sarum's cathedral had been demolished for building materials and the settlement was practically abandoned.

Today you can wander the grassy ramparts, see the stone foundations of the original cathedral, and look across the Wiltshire countryside to the spire of Salisbury's new cathedral. Medieval tournaments, open-air plays and mock battles are held on selected days. There are free guided tours at 3pm in June, July and August. Old Sarum stays open longer in July and August (9am to 6pm).

Between them, buses 5, 6 and 8 run twice an hour from Salisbury to Old Sarum (hourly on Sundays).

WILTON HOUSE

Stately **Wilton House** (www.wiltonhouse.com; house & gardens adult/child £12/6.50; ⌚11.30am-4.30pm Sun-Thu May-Aug) provides an insight into the exquisite, rarefied world of the British aristocracy. One of the finest stately homes in England, the Earls of Pembroke have lived here since 1542, and it's been expanded, improved and embellished by successive generations since a devastating fire in 1647. The result is quite staggering and delivers a whistle-stop tour of the history of European art and architecture: magnificent period furniture, frescoed ceilings and elaborate plasterwork frame paintings by Van Dyck, Rembrandt and Joshua Reynolds. Highlights are the **Single** and **Double Cube Rooms**, designed by the pioneering 17th-century architect Inigo Jones. The fine landscaped **grounds** (adult/child £5/3.50; ⌚11am-5pm daily May-Aug) were largely laid out by Capability Brown.

All that architectural eye candy makes the house a favoured film location: *The Madness of King George, Sense and Sensibility* and *Pride and Prejudice* were all shot here. But Wilton was serving as an artistic haven long before the movies – famous guests include Ben Jonson, Edmund Spenser, Christopher Marlowe and John Donne. Shakespeare's *As You Like It* was performed here in 1603, shortly after the bard had written it.

Wilton House is 2½ miles west of Salisbury; buses 3 and 13 run from Salisbury (10 minutes, three hourly Monday to Saturday, hourly on Sunday).

Stonehenge

This compelling ring of monolithic **stones** (EH; ☎01980-624715; www.english-heritage.org.uk; adult/child £6.90/3.50; ⌚9am-7pm Jun-Aug, 9.30am-6pm Mar-May & Sep-Oct, 9.30-4pm Oct-Feb) has been attracting a steady stream of pilgrims, poets and philosophers for the last 5000 years and is Britain's most iconic archaeological site. Despite the constant flow of traffic from the main road beside the monument, and the huge numbers of visitors who traipse around the perimeter on a daily basis, Stonehenge still manages to be a mystical, ethereal place – a haunting echo from Britain's forgotten past, and a reminder of the people who once walked the many ceremonial avenues across Salisbury Plain. Even more intriguingly, it's still one of Britain's great archaeological mysteries: despite countless theories about what the site was used for, ranging from a sacrificial centre to a celestial timepiece, in truth, no one really knows what drove prehistoric Britons to expend so much time and effort on its construction.

Stone Circle Access Visits (☎01722-343830; www.english-heritage.org.uk; adult/child £14.50/7.50) are unforgettable. Visitors normally have to stay outside the stone circle itself. But on these trips, you get to wander round the core of the site, getting up-close views of the iconic bluestones and trilithons. The walks take place in the evening or early morning so the quieter atmosphere and slanting sunlight add to the effect. Each visit only takes 26 people; to secure a place book at least two months in advance.

THE SITE

The first phase of construction at Stonehenge started around 3000 BC, when the outer circular bank and ditch were erected. A thousand years later, an inner circle of granite stones, known as bluestones, was added. It's thought that these mammoth 4-ton blocks were hauled from the Preseli Mountains in South Wales, some 250 miles away – an almost inexplicable feat for Stone Age builders equipped with only the simplest of

Stonehenge

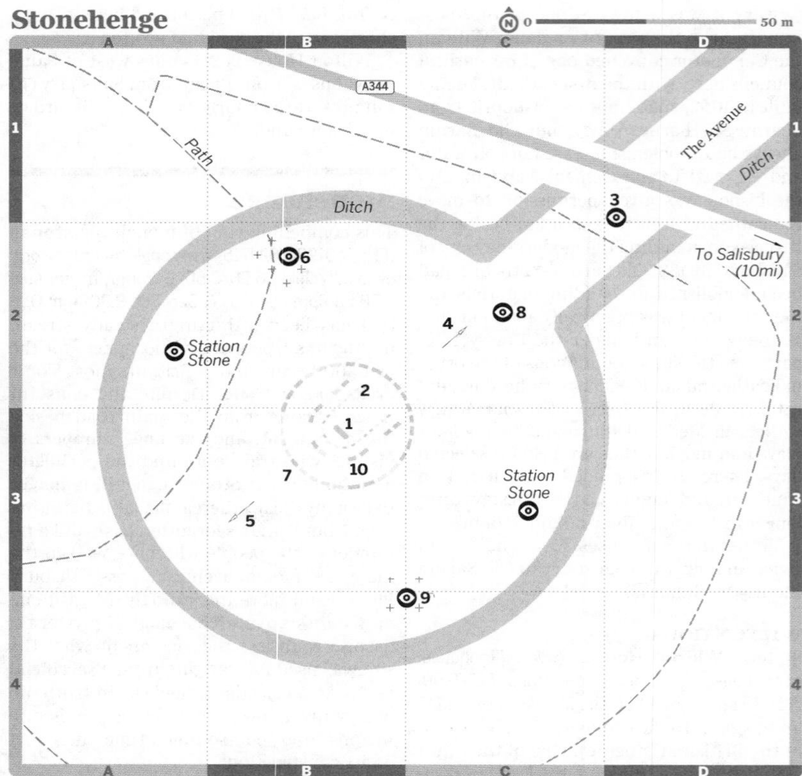

tools. Although no one is entirely sure how the builders transported the stones so far, it's thought they probably used a system of ropes, sledges and rollers fashioned from tree trunks – Salisbury Plain was still covered by forest during Stonehenge's construction.

Around 1500 BC, Stonehenge's main stones were dragged to the site, erected in a circle and crowned by massive lintels to make the trilithons (two vertical stones topped by a horizontal one). The sarsen (sandstone) stones were cut from an extremely hard rock found on the Marlborough Downs, 20 miles from the site. It's estimated that dragging one of these 50-ton stones across the countryside would require about 600 people.

Also around this time, the bluestones from 500 years earlier were rearranged as an inner **bluestone horseshoe** with an **altar stone** at the centre. Outside this the **trilithon horseshoe** of five massive sets of stones was erected. Three of these are intact; the other two have just a single upright. Then came the major **sarsen circle** of 30 massive vertical stones, of which 17 uprights and six lintels remain.

Much further out, another circle was delineated by the 58 **Aubrey Holes**, named after John Aubrey, who discovered them

Stonehenge

Sights

1 Altar Stone B3
2 Bluestone Horseshoe B2
3 Heel Stone D1
4 Midsummer Sunrise C2
5 Midwinter Sunset B3
6 North Barrow B2
7 Sarsen Circle B3
8 Slaughter Stone C2
9 South Barrow C4
10 Trilithon Horseshoe B3

in the 1600s. Just inside this circle are the **South and North Barrows**, each originally topped by a stone. Like many stone circles in Britain (including Avebury, p267), the inner horseshoes are aligned to coincide with sunrise at the midsummer solstice, which some claim supports the theory that the site was some kind of astronomical calendar.

Prehistoric pilgrims would have entered the site via the **Avenue**, whose entrance to the circle is marked by the **Slaughter Stone** and the **Heel Stone**, located slightly further out on one side.

A marked pathway leads around the site, and although you can't walk freely in the circle itself, it's possible to see the stones fairly close up. An audio guide is included in the admission price, and can be obtained from the tourist office, which is 50m north of the main circle.

 Tours

The **Stonehenge Tour** (☎01722-336855; www.thestonehengetour.info; return adult/child £11/5) leaves Salisbury's railway and bus stations half-hourly in June and August, and hourly between September and May. Tickets last all day, so you can hop off at Old Sarum on the way back. For guided tours, try **Salisbury Guided Tours** (☎0777 567 48 16; www.salisburyguidedtours.com; from £65 per group).

Getting There & Around

Bus

No regular buses go to the site. See also Tours.

Taxi

Taxis charge £35 to go to the site from Salisbury, wait for an hour and come back.

Around Stonehenge

Stonehenge actually forms part of a huge complex of ancient monuments. Leaflets available from the Stonehenge visitor centre detail walking routes around the main sites; most are accessible to the public although a few are on private land.

North of Stonehenge and running roughly east–west is the **Cursus**, an elongated embanked oval; the slightly smaller **Lesser Cursus** is nearby. Theories abound as to what these sites were used for, ranging from ancient sporting arenas to processional avenues for the dead.

Other prehistoric sites around Stonehenge include a number of burial mounds, such as the **New King Barrows**, and **Vespasian's Camp**, an Iron Age hill fort.

Just north of Amesbury and 1½ miles east of Stonehenge is **Woodhenge**, a series of concentric rings that would once have been marked by wooden posts. It's thought there might be some correlation between the use of wood and stone in both structures, but it's unclear what the materials would have meant to ancient Britons. Excavations in the 1970s at Woodhenge revealed the skeleton of a child with a cloven skull, buried near the centre.

Stourhead

Overflowing with vistas, temples and follies, **Stourhead** (NT; www.nationaltrust.org.uk; Stourton; house or garden adult/child £7/3.80, house & garden £11.60/5.80; ⌚house 11am-5pm Fri-Tue mid-Mar–Oct) is landscape gardening

STONEHENGE'S FUTURE

For such a celebrated site, Stonehenge has seen a surprising amount of upheaval. While the reasons behind its creation have provoked debate, how the site is used today has proved equally controversial. The tense stand-offs between solstice-goers and police that marked the 1980s and '90s have been replaced by fresh controversy about the impact the modern world has on the jewel in Britain's archaeological crown. This World Heritage Site is framed by busy roads and wire fences; crowded with visitors throughout the summer; and underscored by the hum of traffic. For some, it's a long way from the haven of peace and spiritual tranquillity they expected to find.

Ambitious plans to tunnel the A303 under the monument and to turn the surrounding arable fields back into chalk downland came to nothing. Smaller-scale changes, involving a new visitor centre and closing part of the quieter A344, have been beset by planning and funding problems – meaning the future of this supremely mystical site is as mysterious as its past.

at its finest. The Palladian house has some fine Chippendale furniture and paintings by Claude and Gaspard Poussin, but it's a sideshow to the magnificent 18th-century gardens, which spread out across the valley. A lovely 2-mile circuit takes you past the most ornate follies, around the lake and to the **Temple of Apollo**; a 3½-mile side trip can be made from near the Pantheon to **King Alfred's Tower** (adult/child £2.20/1.20; ⏲11.30am-4.30pm mid-Mar–Oct), a 50m-high folly with wonderful views. The garden is open, year round, from 9am to 7pm or dusk.

Stourhead is off the B3092, 8 miles south of Frome (in Somerset).

Longleat

Half ancestral mansion and half safari park, **Longleat** (www.longleat.co.uk; house & grounds adult/child £12/6, safari park £12/8, all-inclusive passport £24/17; ⏲house 10am-5pm Apr-Oct, safari park 10am-4pm Apr-Oct, other attractions 11am-5pm Apr-Oct) became the first stately home in England to open its doors to the public, in 1946. It was prompted by finance: heavy taxes and mounting bills after WWII meant the house had to earn its keep. Britain's first safari park opened on the estate in 1966, and soon Capability Brown's landscaped grounds had been transformed into an amazing drive-through zoo, populated by a menagerie of animals more at home in an African wilderness than the fields of Wiltshire. These days the zoo is backed up by a throng of touristy attractions, including a narrow-gauge railway, a Dr Who exhibit, a Postman Pat village, pets' corner and a butterfly garden.

Under all these tourist trimmings it's easy to forget the house itself, which contains fine tapestries, furniture and decorated ceilings, as well as seven libraries containing around 40,000 tomes. The highlight, though, is an extraordinary series of paintings and psychedelic murals by the present-day marquess, who trained as an art student in the '60s and upholds the long-standing tradition of eccentricity among the English aristocracy – check out his website at www.lordbath.co.uk.

Longleat House is just off the A362, 3 miles from both Frome and Warminster.

Malmesbury Abbey

The mellow hilltop town of Malmesbury is peppered with ancient buildings constructed out of honey-coloured Cotswold stone. It's the oldest borough in England, having been awarded that civic status in AD 880, and boasts one of the county's finest market crosses – a 15th century crown-like structure built to shelter the poor from the rain.

The town's big draw is **Malmesbury Abbey** (www.malmesburyabbey.com; suggested donation £2; ⏲10am-5pm mid-Mar–Oct, 10am-4pm Nov–mid-Mar), a wonderful blend of ruin and living church, with a somewhat turbulent history. It began life as a 7th-century monastery, which was later replaced by a Norman church. By the mid-15th century the abbey had been embellished with a spire and twin towers, but in 1479 a storm toppled the east tower and spire, destroying the eastern end of the church. The west tower followed suit in 1662, destroying much of the nave. The present-day church is about a third of its original size, and is flanked by ruins at either end. Notable features include the **Norman doorway** decorated with biblical figures, the Romanesque **Apostle carvings** and a four-volume **illuminated bible** dating from 1407. A window at the western end of the church depicts Elmer the Flying Monk, who in 1010 strapped on wings and jumped from the tower. Although he broke both legs during this leap of faith, he survived and became a local hero.

Just below the abbey are the **Abbey House Gardens** (www.abbeyhousegardens.co.uk; adult/child £6.50/2.50; ⏲11am-5pm mid-Mar–Oct), which include a herb garden, river, waterfall and 2 hectares of colourful blooms.

Bus 31 runs to Swindon (45 minutes, hourly Monday to Saturday), while bus 91 heads to Chippenham (35 minutes, hourly Monday to Saturday).

Lacock

With its geranium-covered cottages, higgledy-piggledy rooftops and idyllic location next to a rushing brook, pockets of the medieval village of Lacock seem to have been preserved in aspic since the mid-19th century. The village has been in the hands of the National Trust since 1944, and in many places is remarkably free of modern development – there are no telephone poles or electric street lights, and although villagers drive around the streets, the main car park on the outskirts keeps it largely traffic-free. Unsurprisingly, it's also a popular location for costume dramas and feature films – the village and its abbey pop up in the Harry Potter films, *The Other Boleyn Girl* and BBC adaptations of *Moll Flanders* and *Pride and Prejudice*.

Sights

Lacock Abbey ABBEY
(NT; www.nationaltrust.org.uk; adult/child £10/5; 11am-5pm Mar-Oct, 11am-4pm Nov-Feb) Lacock Abbey was founded as an Augustinian nunnery in 1232 by Ela, Countess of Salisbury. After the Dissolution the abbey was sold to Sir William Sharington in 1539, who converted the nunnery into a home, demolished the church, tacked a tower onto the corner of the abbey and added a brewery. Highlights are the wonderfully atmospheric medieval rooms, while the stunning Gothic entrance hall is lined with bizarre terracotta figures; spot the scapegoat with a lump of sugar on its nose. Some of the original 13th-century structure is evident in the cloisters and there are traces of medieval wall paintings. The recently restored botanic garden is also worth a visit.

On Tuesdays year-round and on winter weekends, access to the Abbey is limited to the cloisters. It's possible to buy a **cheaper ticket** (adult/child £7.20/3.60) which gets you into the grounds, museum and Abbey cloisters, but not the Abbey building itself.

Fox Talbot Museum of Photography
The ticket into the Abbey also includes admission into this exhibition about the man who pioneered the photographic negative – William Henry Fox Talbot (1800–77). A prolific inventor, he began developing the system in 1834 while working at the abbey. The museum details his ground-breaking work and displays a superb collection of his images.

Sleeping & Eating

Sign of the Angel B&B-RESTAURANT ££
(01249-730230; www.lacock.co.uk; 6 Church St; s £82, d £120-145; P) If you want to slumber amid a slice of history, check into this 15th-century beamed bolt-hole. Filled with antique beds, tapestries and burnished chests, comfort levels are brought up to date with free-standing sinks and slipper baths. The **restaurant** (mains from £14) revels in English classics – try the pigeon, Stilton and walnut pâté, then squeeze in treacle tart with clotted cream.

King John's Hunting Lodge B&B, CAFE ££
(01249-730313; www.kingjohnslodge.2day.ws; 21 Church St; s/d/f £65/95/115; tearooms 11am-5.30pm) Lacock's oldest building is a picturesque venue for a quintessentially English **afternoon tea** (£7 to £15): smoked salmon, cucumber sandwiches, scones, clotted cream and home-made jam. Upstairs, snug, resolutely old-fashioned rooms are crammed with creaky furniture and Tudor touches.

Lacock Pottery B&B ££
(01249-730266; www.lacockbedandbreakfast.com; d from £80; P) A serene, airy former workhouse graced by an oatmeal colour scheme and antiques.

George Inn PUB £
(4 West St; mains from £8; lunch & dinner) An ancient, horse brass–hung pub dispensing good grub and local ales.

Getting There & Away

Bus 234 runs hourly, Monday to Saturday, from Chippenham (15 minutes).

Avebury

While the tour buses usually head straight for Stonehenge, prehistoric purists make for the massive stone circle at Avebury. Though it lacks the dramatic trilithons of its sister site across the plain, Avebury is arguably a much more rewarding place to visit. A large section of the village is actually inside the ring of stones; you get much closer to the action than you do at Stonehenge; and it's bigger, older and a great deal quieter. It may also have been a more important ceremonial site, judging by its massive scale and its location at the centre of a complex of barrows, burial chambers and processional avenues.

Sights

Avebury Stone Circle STONE CIRCLE
With a diameter of about 348m, Avebury is the largest stone circle in the world. It's also one of the oldest, dating from around 2500 to 2200 BC, between the first and second phase of construction at Stonehenge. The site originally consisted of an outer circle of 98 standing stones from 3m to 6m in length, many weighing up to 20 tons, carefully selected for their size and shape. The stones were surrounded by another circle delineated by a 5.5m-high earth bank and a 6m- to 9m-deep

Avebury

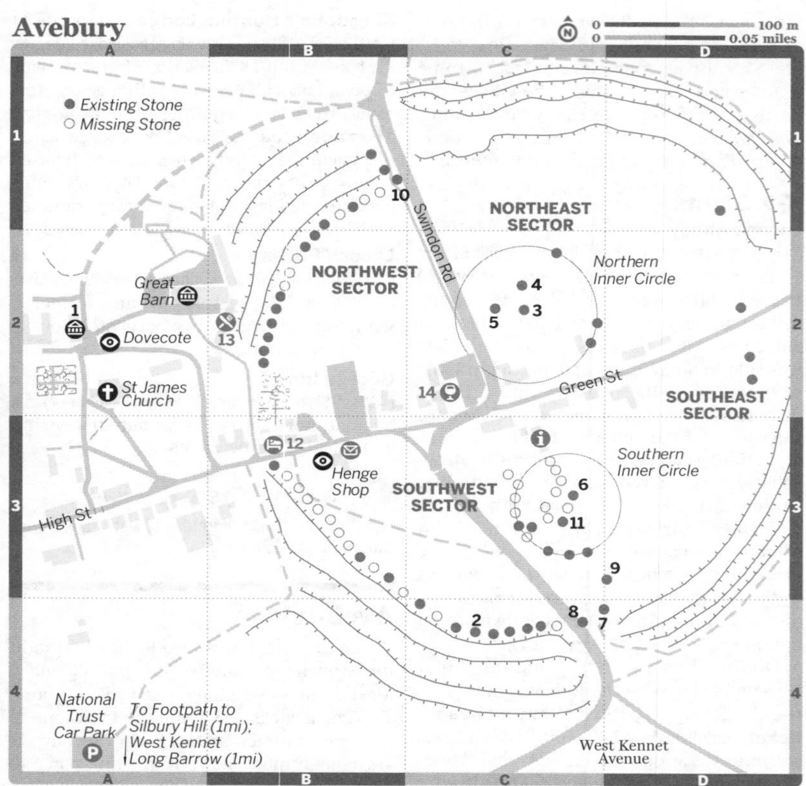

ditch. Inside were smaller stone circles to the north (27 stones) and south (29 stones).

The present-day site represents just a fraction of the circle's original size; many of the stones were buried, removed or broken up during the Middle Ages, when Britain's pagan past became something of an embarrassment to the church. In 1934, wealthy businessman and archaeologist Alexander Keiller supervised the re-erection of the buried stones, and planted markers to indicate those that had disappeared; he later bought the site for posterity using funds from his family's marmalade fortune.

Self Guided Tour

Modern roads into Avebury neatly dissect the circle into four sectors. Starting at High St, near the Henge Shop, and walking round the circle in an anticlockwise direction, you'll encounter 11 standing stones in the southwest sector. They include the **Barber Surgeon Stone**, named after the skeleton of a man found under it. The equipment buried with him suggested he was a medieval travelling barber-surgeon, possibly killed when a stone accidentally fell on him.

The southeast sector starts with the huge portal stones marking the entry to the circle from the West Kennet Avenue. The **southern inner circle** stood in this sector and within this circle was the **obelisk** and a group of stones known as the **Z Feature**. Just outside this smaller circle, only the base of the **Ring Stone** remains.

In the **northern inner circle** in the northeast sector, three sarsens remain of what would have been a rectangular **cove**. The northwest sector has the most complete collection of standing stones, including the massive 65-ton **Swindon Stone**, one of the few never to have been toppled.

Avebury

Sights

1 Alexander Keiller Museum.................A2
2 Barber Surgeon Stone.......................C4
3 Cove Stones.......................................C2
4 Cove Stones.......................................C2
5 Cove Stones.......................................C2
6 Obelisk...C3
7 Portal Stones.....................................C4
8 Portal Stones.....................................C4
9 Ring Stone..D3
10 Swindon Stone..................................B1
11 Z Feature...C3

Sleeping

12 Manor Farm......................................B3

Eating

13 Circle Restaurant..............................B2

Drinking

14 Red Lion..C2

Silbury Hill PREHISTORIC SITE

This huge mound rises abruptly from the surrounding fields just west of Avebury. At more than 40m high, it's the largest artificial mound in Europe, and was built in stages from around 2500 BC. No significant artefacts have been found at the site, and the reason for its construction remains unclear. A massive project to stabilise the hill took place in 2008 after a combination of erosion and damage caused by earlier excavations caused part of the top to collapse. Direct access to the hill isn't allowed, but you can view it from a car park on the A4. Hiking across the fields from Avebury (1½ miles each way) is a more atmospheric way to arrive; the tourist office sells guides (50p).

West Kennet Long Barrow BURIAL MOUND

Set in the fields south of Silbury Hill, this is England's finest burial mound and dates from around 3500 BC. Its entrance is guarded by huge sarsens and its roof is made out of gigantic overlapping capstones. About 50 skeletons were found when it was excavated, and finds are on display at the Wiltshire Heritage Museum in Devizes. A footpath just to the east of Silbury Hill leads to West Kennet (half-mile).

Alexander Keiller Museum MUSEUM

(NT; www.nationaltrust.org.uk; Avebury Village; adult/child £4.90/2.45; 10am-6pm Apr-Oct, to 4pm Nov-Mar) Explores the archaeological history of the circle and traces the story of the man who dedicated his life to unlocking the secret of the stones.

Sleeping & Eating

TOP CHOICE **Manor Farm** B&B ££

(01672-539294; www.manorfarmavebury.com; High St; d £80-90) A rare chance to sleep in style inside a stone circle – this red-brick farmhouse snuggles just inside the henge. The elegant, comfy rooms blend old woods with bright furnishings, there's a splendid free-standing claw-foot bath, and the views out onto the 4000-year-old standing stones provide spine-tingling views.

Circle CAFE ££

(mains from £7; lunch) Veggie and wholefood cafe serving homemade quiches and cakes, chunky sandwiches and afternoon teas.

Drinking

Red Lion PUB £

(Swindon Rd; mains from £10; lunch & dinner) Having a pint here means downing a drink at the only pub in the world inside a stone circle. It's also haunted by Flori, who was killed during the Civil War when her husband threw her down a well – it now forms the centrepiece of the dining room.

RITUAL LANDSCAPE

Avebury is surrounded by a network of ancient monuments, including Silbury Hill and West Kennet Long Barrow. To the south of the village, the **West Kennet Avenue** stretched out for 1½ miles, lined by 100 pairs of stones. It linked the Avebury circle with a site called the **Sanctuary**. Post holes indicate that a wooden building surrounded by a stone circle once stood at the Sanctuary, although no one knows quite what the site was for.

The **Ridgeway National Trail** starts near Avebury and runs eastwards across Fyfield Down, where many of the sarsen stones at Avebury (and Stonehenge) were collected.

Information

Tourist office (☎01672-539179; www.visitwiltshire.co.uk; Chapel Centre, Green St; ⏲9.30am-5pm Tue-Sun Apr-Oct, 9.30am-4.30pm Tue-Sun Nov-Mar)

Getting There & Away

Bus 5/6/96 runs to Avebury from Salisbury (1¾ hours, hourly Monday to Saturday, five on Sunday). Bus 49 serves Swindon (30 minutes) and Devizes (25 minutes, hourly Monday to Saturday, five on Sunday).

BRISTOL

POP 393,300

Bristol's buzzing. After decades of neglect, there's change happening everywhere you look in the southwest's biggest city: the historic docks have been redeveloped, the harbourside is crammed with cutting-edge galleries, designer flats and urban pieds-à-terre, and the tired old city centre is now almost unrecognisable thanks to the addition of one of Britain's largest new shopping centres at Cabot Circus and über-exclusive Quakers Friars. Long known for its industrial connections, more recently Bristol has garnered a reputation as one of the region's most creative corners, thanks to its thriving media industry and its lively music, theatre and art scenes. Bristol might not be as elegant as Exeter or as beautiful as Bath, but the city has plenty of life in it yet.

History

The city began as a small Saxon village and the medieval river-port of Brigstow. Bristol developed as a trading centre for cloth and wine, before 'local hero' John Cabot (actually a Genoese sailor called Giovanni Caboto) really put the city on the map, when he set sail from Bristol to discover Newfoundland in 1497. Over the following centuries, Bristol became one of Britain's major ports, and grew rich on the proceeds of the transatlantic slave trade, and from dealing in cocoa, sugar and tobacco.

By the 18th century Bristol was suffering from competition from other UK ports, especially London and Liverpool. The city repositioned itself as an industrial centre, becoming an important hub for shipbuilding and the terminus for the pioneering Great Western Railway line from London. During the 20th century Bristol also played a key role in Britain's burgeoning aeronautics industry: many key components of Concorde were developed in the nearby suburb of Filton.

During WWII the city's heavy industry became a key target for German bombing, and much of the city centre was reduced to rubble. The postwar rush for reconstruction left Bristol with plenty of concrete eyesores, but over the last decade the city has undergone extensive redevelopment, especially around the dockside.

In 2006, the city celebrated the bicentenary of the birth of Isambard Kingdom Brunel, the pioneering Victorian engineer responsible (among many other things) for developing the Great Western Railway, the Clifton Suspension Bridge and SS *Great Britain*.

A £25-million scheme to turn the city's old Industrial Museum on the harbour into a flagship Museum of Bristol is due for completion in 2011.

Sights

TOP CHOICE **SS Great Britain** MUSEUM

(www.ssgreatbritain.org; Great Western Dock, Gas Ferry Rd; adult/child £11.95/9.50; ⏲10am-5.30pm Apr-Oct, 10am-4.30pm Nov-Mar; [wi-fi]) In 1843 Brunel designed the

BRISTOL IN...

Two Days

Start off your Bristol trip with a morning exploring **Clifton**. Factor in a walk across the **Suspension Bridge**, a stroll across the **Downs**, and lunch at one of the many cafés and restaurants round Clifton – we particularly like the **Primrose Café** and the **Thali Café**. Spend the afternoon at **Bristol Zoo** or lounging around the **Bristol Lido**, then overnight at the gorgeous **Hotel du Vin**.

On day two, set out for the city's historic docks. Stop off for some avant-garde art at the **Arnolfini** en route to Brunel's stately steamer, **SS Great Britain**. Enjoy lunch at the thoroughly brilliant **Bordeaux Quay**, and then in the afternoon take a cruise with the **Bristol Ferry Boat**, mosey round the shops in **Cabot Circus** or **St Nicholas Market**, or visit the city's historic **Georgian House**. Finish up with dinner at **riverstation**.

THE TRIANGLE TRADE

It's a sobering thought that much of Bristol's 18th-century wealth and splendour was founded on human exploitation. In the late 1600s, the first slave ship set sail from Bristol harbour, kick-starting the city's connections with the so-called 'triangular trade', in which Africans had been kidnapped from their homes (or traded, usually for munitions) before being shipped across the Atlantic and sold into a life of slavery in the New World. Conditions on the boats were horrific; it was expected that one in 10 of those captured would die en route – in reality, many more did. Their human cargo unloaded, the merchants stocked their vessels with luxury goods such as sugar, rum, indigo, tobacco and cotton, and sailed back to Britain.

Bristol, London and Liverpool were the three main British ports engaged in the practice. By the time the slave trade (not slavery itself) was finally abolished in the British Empire in 1807, it's thought that 500,000 Africans were enslaved by Bristol merchants – a-fifth of all people sold into slavery by British vessels.

The financial profits for Bristol's traders were immense, and that legacy lingers. Many of the grand houses in Clifton were built on the proceeds of the 'trade', and several of the city's most elegant edifices – such as the Bristol Old Vic theatre – were partly financed by slave-trading investors.

There are many more connections – for further insights, download the MP3 audio tour from the **Visit Bristol** (www.visitbristol.co.uk) website, or pick up the *Slave Trade Trail* leaflet (£3) from the tourist office.

mighty *SS Great Britain*, the first transatlantic steamship to be driven by a screw propeller. For 43 years the ship served as a luxury ocean-going liner and cargo vessel, but huge running costs and mounting debts meant she was eventually sold off to serve as a troop ship and coal hulk, a sorry fate for such an important vessel. By 1937 she was no longer watertight and was abandoned near Port Stanley in the Falklands, before finally being towed back to Bristol in 1970.

Since then a massive 30-year restoration program has brought SS *Great Britain* back to stunning life. The ship's rooms have been refurbished in impeccable detail, including the galley, surgeon's quarters, mess hall, and the great engine room; but the highlight is the amazing 'glass sea' on which the ship sits, enclosing an airtight dry dock that preserves the delicate hull and allows visitors to see the ground-breaking screw propeller up close. Moored nearby is a replica of John Cabot's ship **Matthew**, which sailed from Bristol to Newfoundland in 1497.

Tickets to SS *Great Britain* also allow access to the neighbouring **Maritime Heritage Centre** (☎0117-927 9856; Great Western Dockyard, Gas Ferry Rd; ⊙10am-5.30pm Apr-Oct, to 4.30pm Nov-Mar), which has exhibits relating to the ship's illustrious past and the city's boat-building heritage.

Clifton
HISTORIC AREA

During the 18th and 19th centuries, wealthy Bristol merchants transformed the former spa resort of Clifton into an elegant hilltop suburb packed with porticoed mansions – especially around **Cornwallis Cres** and **Royal York Cres**. These days, Clifton is still the poshest postcode in Bristol, with a wealth of streetside cafes and designer shops, and a villagey atmosphere that's far removed from the rest of the city.

Clifton Suspension Bridge
BRIDGE

(www.clifton-suspension-bridge.org.uk) Clifton's most famous (and photographed) landmark is another Brunel masterpiece, the 76m-high Clifton Suspension Bridge, which spans the Avon Gorge from Clifton over to Leigh Woods in northern Somerset. Construction began in 1836, but sadly Brunel died before the bridge's completion in 1864. It was mainly designed to carry light horse-drawn traffic and foot passengers, but these days around 12,000 cars cross it every day – testament to the quality of the construction and the vision of Brunel's design.

It's free to walk or cycle across the bridge; car drivers pay a 50p toll. There's a **visitor information point** (visitinfo@clifton-suspension-bridge.org; ⊙10am-5pm) near the tower on the Leigh Woods side. Free guided tours of the bridge take place at 3pm on Saturdays and Sundays from May to October.

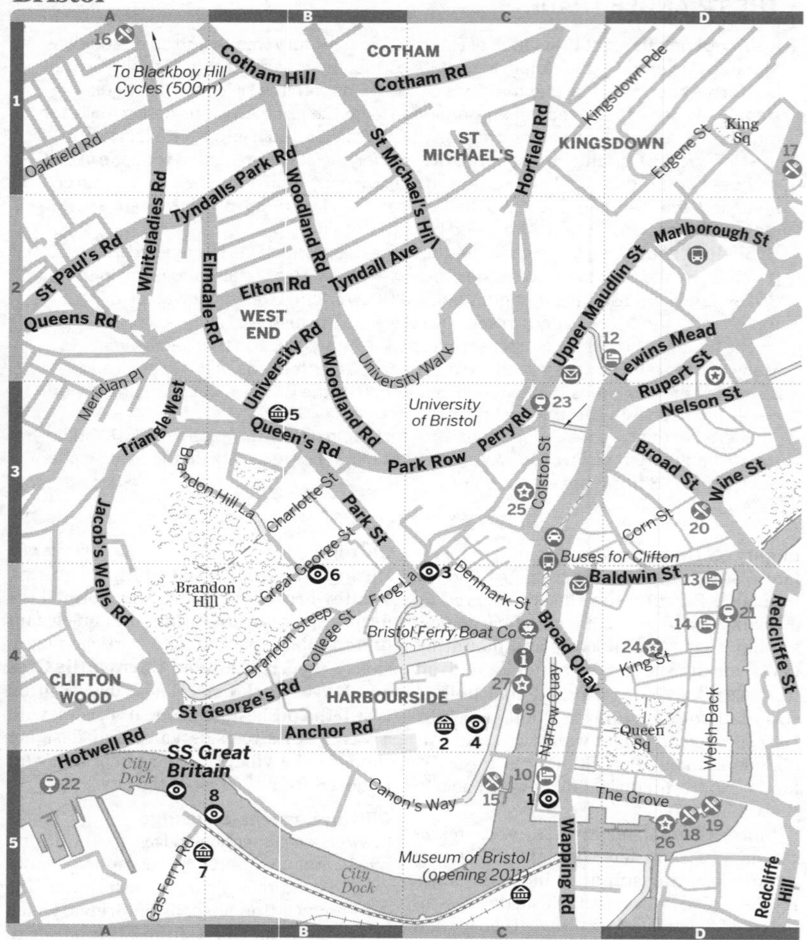

The Downs PARKS

Near the bridge, the grassy parks of Clifton Down and Durdham Down (often referred to as just the Downs) make a fine spot for a picnic. Nearby, a well-worn observatory houses Britain's only **camera obscura** (adult/child £2/1; ⏲10.30am-5.30pm) and a tunnel leading down to the **Giant's Cave** (adult/child £1.50/0.50), a natural cavern that emerges halfway down the cliff with dizzying views across the Avon Gorge.

Bristol Lido BATHS

(☎0117-933-9530; www.lidobristol.com; Oakfield Place; pool adult/child £15/7.50; ⏲7am-10pm) Bristol's public hot tub dates back to 1849, but it's been through its fair share of trials and tribulations over the last century. Having closed in 1990, it's now been completely renovated, and the original outdoor heated pool is back to its sparkling best. Elsewhere you'll find a sauna, bar and a rather good restaurant, and needless to say there are plenty of spa treatments on offer to help you unwind after a long day's sightseeing.

Bristol Zoo ZOO

(www.bristolzoo.org.uk; Clifton; adult/child £11.81/7.27; ⏲9am-5.30pm mid-Mar–mid-Oct, 9am-5pm mid-Oct–mid-Mar) The city's award-

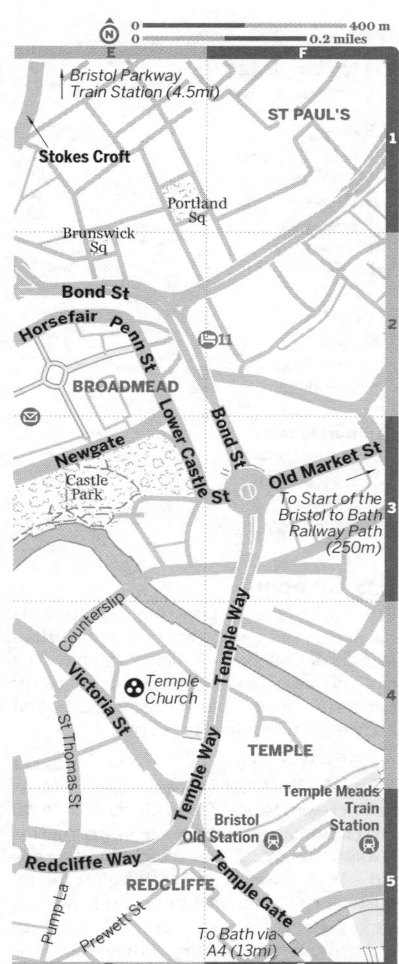

winning zoo occupies a huge site on the north side of Clifton. Highlights include gorilla and gibbon islands, a reptile and bug house, a butterfly forest, a lion enclosure, a monkey jungle and the new **Zooropia** (adult/child £7.50/6), a treetop adventure park strung with net ramps, rope bridges, hanging logs and a zip-line.

At-Bristol SCIENCE MUSEUM
(www.at-bristol.org.uk; Anchor Rd; adult/child £10.80/7; ⏲10am-5pm Mon-Fri, to 6pm Sat & Sun) Bristol's interactive science museum has several zones spanning space, technology and the human brain. In the Curiosity Zone you get to walk through a tornado, spin on a human gyroscope and strum the strings of a virtual harp. It's fun, imaginative and highly interactive, and should keep kids enthralled for a few hours.

Blue Reef Aquarium AQUARIUM
(www.bluereefaquarium.co.uk; Harbourside; adult/child £13.50/9.20; ⏲10am-5pm Mon-Fri, to 6pm Sat & Sun) Across the square is Bristol's brand-new aquarium, with tanks re-creating 40 underwater environments from tropical seas to mangrove forests and coral reefs, complete with underwater viewing tunnel. The 3D IMAX cinema shows marine-themed films.

FREE **Arnolfini** GALLERY
(www.arnolfini.org.uk; 16 Narrow Quay; ⏲10am-6pm Tue-Sun) The city's avant-garde art gallery occupies a hulking redbrick warehouse by the river, and remains the top venue in town for modern art, as well as occasional exhibitions of dance, film and photography.

FREE **City Museum & Art Gallery** MUSEUM
(Queen's Rd; ⏲10am-5pm) Housed in a stunning Edwardian baroque building, the City Museum & Art Gallery has an excellent collection of British and French art; galleries dedicated to ceramics and decorative arts; and archaeological, geological and natural-history wings.

FREE **Georgian House** ARCHITECTURE
(7 Great George St; ⏲10am-5pm Wed-Sat) This 18th-century house provides an atmospheric illustration of aristocratic life in Bristol during the Georgian era – and the city's links to the slave trade. The six-storeyed house was home to West India merchant John Pinney, along with his slave Pero (after whom Pero's Bridge across the harbour is named). It's decorated throughout in period style, typified by the huge kitchen (complete with cast-iron roasting spit) and the grand drawing rooms.

☞ Tours

Bristol Highlights Walk WALKING TOUR
(adult/under 12yr £3.50/free; ⏲11am Sat Apr-Sep) Tours the old town, city centre and Harbourside. It's run every Saturday; just turn up outside the tourist office. Themed tours exploring Clifton, Brunel and the history of Bristol traders are run on request.

Bristol

Top Sights

SS Great Britain A5

Sights

1 Arnolfini C5
2 At-Bristol C4
3 Banksy's Love Triangle Stencil C4
4 Blue Reef Aquarium C4
5 City Museum & Art Gallery B3
6 Georgian House B4
7 Maritime Heritage Centre A5
8 Matthew B5

Activities, Courses & Tours

9 Bristol Packet Boat Trips C4

Sleeping

10 Bristol YHA C5
11 Future Inns Cabot Circus F2
12 Hotel du Vin D2
13 Mercure Brigstow Hotel D4
14 Premier Inn, King St D4

Eating

15 Bordeaux Quay C5
16 Cowshed A1
17 Pieminister D1
18 riverstation D5
19 Severnshed D5
20 St Nicholas Market D3

Drinking

21 Apple D4
22 Grain Barge A5
23 Zerodegrees C3

Entertainment

24 Bristol Old Vic D4
25 Colston Hall C3
26 Thekla D5
27 Watershed C4

FREE **MP3 Tours** WALKING TOUR
(http://visitbristol.co.uk/site/visitor-information/multimedia/mp3-audio-tours) Free MP3 guides covering Brunel, the slave trade, the harbour area and the city's heritage.

Bristol Packet Boat Trips BOAT TOUR
(www.bristolpacket.co.uk; adult/child £5.25/4.75; 11am-4.15pm Sat & Sun) Cruises around the harbour area (departures every 45 minutes, operates daily during school holidays). There are also weekly cruises along the Avon from May to October (adult/child £14/12), and less frequent trips to Bath and local pubs.

Festivals & Events

Bristol Shakespeare Festival THEATRE
(www.bristolshakespeare.org.uk) Britain's biggest outdoor festival devoted to the Bard, held between May and September.

Bristol Harbour Festival FESTIVAL
(www.bristolharbourfestival.co.uk) Bands, events and historic ships take over the city's docks in early August.

International Balloon Fiesta FESTIVAL
(www.bristolballoonfiesta.co.uk) Hot-air balloonfest at Ashton Court in August.

Encounters FILM FESTIVAL
(www.encounters-festival.org.uk) Bristol's largest film-fest is in November.

Sleeping

Bristol's hotels are largely aimed towards the business crowd; function rather than form is definitely the order of the day. The city also has a real shortage of quality B&Bs, but there are a couple of decent chains and a great hostel in the city centre.

TOP CHOICE **Hotel du Vin** HOTEL £££
(0117-925 5577; www.hotelduvin.com; Narrow Lewins Mead; d £150-205, ste £225; P) For elegance and indulgence in Bristol this is the only choice. Sensitively built inside old sugar warehouses, with plenty of industrial character still in situ, this hotel is simply a treat from start to finish: giant futon beds, clawfoot baths, frying-pan showerheads and a sexy minimalist sheen. The double-height loft-suites wouldn't look out of place in a Manhattan loft apartment.

Bristol YHA HOSTEL £
(bristol@yha.org.uk; 14 Narrow Quay; dm £20, s £25-35, d £40-45; @) It's at the opposite end of the price scale, but this warehouse hostel actually has an even better location, in a renovated redbrick dockhouse overlooking the harbour. Facilities are superb: modern four-bed dorms and doubles, a cycle store, games room and the excellent Grainshed coffee lounge.

Premier Inn, King St HOTEL ££
(0117-910 0619; www.premiertravelinn.com; The Haymarket; r £59-79;) Swallow those

preconceptions – in the absence of any decent B&Bs near the city centre, this budget chain is a real find. It's literally steps from the harbour and the Old Vic, the rooms have big beds, workdesk and wi-fi, and some even have harbour glimpses. Worth considering – although the pub next door can get rowdy on weekends. The hotel offers 15% discounted parking at the NCP on Queen Charlotte Street (although it's still pretty expensive).

Future Inns Cabot Circus HOTEL ££
(☎0845-094 5588; reservations.bristol@futureinns.co.uk; d £59-89; P 📶) This hotel mini-chain has outlets in Plymouth, Cardiff and Bristol. It's modern, functional and businessy, and the concrete skin is charmless, but the rooms are clean in beige, white and pine, and the rates are pretty fantastic this close to the centre. Rates include free parking at the Cabot Circus car-park.

Mercure Brigstow Hotel HOTEL £££
(☎0117-929 1030; H6548@accor.com; Welsh Back; d £99-250; 📶) Despite the concrete-and-glass facade, this Mercure hotel's surprisingly cool inside. Bedrooms boast trendy floating beds, curved wood-panel walls and tiny TVs set into bathroom tiles (gimmicky, yes, but rather fun).

Eating

Eating out in Bristol is a real highlight – the city is jammed with restaurants of every description, ranging from classic British 'caffs' to designer dining emporiums.

TOP CHOICE **riverstation** RESTAURANT ££
(☎0117-914 4434; www.riverstation.co.uk; 2-/3-course lunch £12/14.75, dinner mains £13-19; ⊙lunch & dinner) The city's original, award-winning riverside restaurant, still renowned for its super-sophisticated modern British cooking. The downstairs cafe rustles up light lunches, coffee and feather-light pastries, while up on the 1st floor it's all effortless elegance and European cuisine.

Bordeaux Quay RESTAURANT ££
(☎0117-943 1200; www.bordeaux-quay.co.uk; Canons Way; brasserie mains £10, restaurant mains £17-21; ⊙lunch & dinner) Top-class dining with sustainable credentials, in a fabulous converted dock warehouse overlooking the harbour. It has multiple guises: there's a restaurant, brasserie, bar, deli, bakery and even a cookery school if you feel like brushing up your kitchen skills. The same industrial-chic decor and continental-style food runs throughout, but it's a hot ticket: reservations recommended.

Cowshed RESTAURANT ££
(☎0117-973 3550; www.thecowshedbristol.com; 46 Whiteladies Rd; 3-course lunch £10, dinner mains £13.95-21.95; ⊙lunch & dinner) Country dining in a city setting. Hearty roast chicken, perfect pork chop and the house special 'Hot Stone' steak (which you cook yourself at your table) are the order of the day, served in sophisticated surroundings blending big glass windows, wooden furniture and rough stone walls. It's a bit of a walk up the old Whiteladies Rd, but you'll be extremely glad you made the trip.

Thali Café INDIAN £
(☎0117-974 3793; www.thethalicafe.co.uk; 1 Regent St; set meal £6.95; ⊙lunch Tue-Sun, dinner daily) The bustle and buzz of an Indian street market comes to this much-loved ethnic café, which now has four outlets round the city, including this one in Clifton. It specialises in fresh, spicy and authentic thalis (multicourse Indian meals), and the six-course £6.95 menu is just ridiculously cheap. For big, bold flavours and dining-on-a-budget, there's nowhere better in Bristol.

Primrose Café BISTRO ££
(☎0117-946 6577; www.primrosecafe.co.uk; 1-2 Boyce's Ave; dinner mains £12.50-16.50; ⊙cafe 9am-5pm Mon-Sat, 9am-3pm Sun) The classic Clifton cafe, is as popular for coffee with the Sunday papers as for an evening meal with chums. Pavement tables are dotted around

TYNTESFIELD

Formerly the aristocratic home of the Gibbs family, **Tyntesfield** (NT; ☎01275-461900; Wraxall; adult/child £10/5; ⊙11am-5pm Sat-Wed Mar-Oct) is an ornate Victorian pile that prickles with spiky turrets and towers. The house was built in grand Gothic Revival style by the architect John Norton, and is crammed with Victorian decorative arts, a working kitchen garden and a magnificent private chapel. The house is undergoing extensive renovation (due to finish in 2012, allowing a fascinating insight into the conservation process). Tyntesfield is 7 miles southwest of Bristol, off the B3128.

BANKSY

Bristol brings you closer to a man who specialises in stencils, subverted art and stunts: the guerrilla graffiti artist **Banksy**. Banksy's true identity is a closely guarded secret, but it's rumoured he was born in 1974 in Yate (near Chipping Sodbury), 12 miles from Bristol, and cut his teeth in a city graffiti outfit. Headline-grabbing works include issuing spoof British £10 notes (with Princess Diana's head on them instead of the Queen's); replacing 500 copies of Paris Hilton's debut album in record shops with remixes (featuring tracks titled *Why Am I Famous*? and *What Have I Done*?); painting an image of a ladder going up and over the Israeli West Bank Barrier; and covertly inserting his own version of a primitive cave painting (with a human hunter-gatherer pushing a shopping trolley) into the British Museum in London. He also recently had Bristolians queuing round the block for his first official exhibition in the city at the City Museum and Art Gallery – although needless to say no-one managed to catch a glimpse of the artist himself.

Banksy's art has proved to be a divisive issue in Bristol. Most people love him, but the city authorities were initially less keen: many of his public works have long since been washed away, although the powers-that-be finally seem to have come round to Banksy's potential as a tourist magnet.

A few of his works around the city centre have survived. Look out for his notorious **love triangle** stencil (featuring an angry husband, a two-timing wife, and a naked man dangling from a window) at the bottom of Park St. Banksy's ghostly take on Charion, the River Styx boatman, graces the side of the Thekla, and there's a large mural called **Mild Mild West** featuring a Molotov cocktail-wielding teddy bear on Cheltenham Rd, opposite the junction with Jamaica St.

For more, check out www.banksy.co.uk; the tourist office has produced a free mini-guide.

Parisian-style, while the dining room is a cosy grotto of fairy-lights, white linen and church candles. British food with a French accent. A 2-/3-course menu (£15.95/18.95) is available.

Pieminister PIES £

(24 Stokes Croft; pies £3; ⏲10am-7pm Sat, 11am-4pm Sun) Forget boring old steak-and-kidney – the creations at Bristol's beloved pie shop range from Thai Chook (chicken with green curry sauce) to Chicken of Aragon (chicken, bacon, garlic and vermouth) and Mr Porky (pork, bacon, leeks and Somerset cider). Veggies are well cared for, too: you can even ask for meat-free mash and gravy. The main shop's on Stokes Croft, but there's another outlet in St Nick's market.

Severnshed RESTAURANT ££

(☎0117-925 1212; www.shedrestaurants.co.uk; The Grove; mains from £12, menus £18.95-22.95; ⏲lunch & dinner) Typifying 'new-Bristol', this former boathouse was built by Brunel – now it's home to a designer bar, bistro and waterside cafe. The renovation is a beautiful blend of industrial trappings and contemporary chrome, while the food offers Euro-fusion flavours. Check out the cool floating bar.

St Nicholas Market MARKET

(Corn St; ⏲9.30am-5pm Mon-Sat) The city's lively street market has a bevy of food stalls selling everything from artisan bread to cheese toasties. Look out for local **farmers markets** on Wednesdays, and a **slow-food market** on the first Sunday of each month

Drinking

Apple PUB

(Welsh Back) Bristol's legendary cider boat stocks an impressive 40 varieties of the golden elixir and specialises in organic and craft-produced varieties (try a tipple of the raspberry and strawberry varieties).

Grain Barge PUB

(www.grainbarge.com; Mardyke Wharf, Hotwell Rd) Built in 1936, overhauled in 2007, this tow-barge near SS *Great Britain* is owned by the city's microbrewery, the Bristol Beer Factory. Boutique beers include traditional No. 7 Bitter, creamy Milk Stout, pale Sunrise Ale and dark Exhibition ale.

Albion PUB

(Boyce's Ave) Lovely old-fashioned pub packed with evening drinkers from Clifton's well-heeled streets.

Zerodegrees PUB
(www.zerodegrees.co.uk; 53 Colston St) Plentiful glass, chrome and steel in Bristol's boutique brewery. Options range from fruit beers and pale wheat ale to Czech-style Black and Pilsner lagers.

☆ Entertainment

The Bristol club scene moves fast; so check the latest listings at *Venue* (www.venue.co.uk; £1.50). The freebie mag *Folio* is published monthly.

Watershed CINEMA, MEDIA CENTRE
(www.watershed.co.uk; 1 Canon's Rd) Bristol's digital media centre also hosts regular art-house programs and film-related events, including the Encounters Festival in November.

Bristol Old Vic THEATRE
(www.bristololdvic.org.uk; 103 The Cut) Bristol's stately theatre (one of England's oldest) has been through troubled times, but it's recently reopened its doors and puts on big touring productions in its famously ornate auditorium, plus more experimental work in its smaller studio.

Thekla LIVE MUSIC, CLUB
(www.thekla.co.uk; The Grove) Bristol's venerable club-boat has something to suit all moods: nights devoted to electro-punk, indie, disco and new wave, plus regular live gigs. Look out for the stencil of the River Styx boatman on the side, courtesy of the city's maverick street artist, Banksy.

Colston Hall LIVE MUSIC
(www.colstonhall.org; Colston St) Bristol's historic concert hall hosts everything from big-name comedy to touring bands, and a recent £20-million refit has added a shiny glass-and-copper foyer to the old building.

ⓘ Information

Bristol Central Library (College Green; ⌚9.30am-7.30pm Mon, Tue & Thu, 10am-5pm Wed, 9am-5pm Fri & Sat, 1-5pm Sun) Free internet access.

Bristol Royal Infirmary (Marlborough Street; ⌚24hr)

Bristol tourist office (☎0333-321 0101; www.visitbristol.co.uk; E-Shed, 1 Canons Rd; ⌚10am-6pm) In a new purpose-built location on the harbour.

Police station Nelson St (☎0845 456 7000; Nelson St); New Bridewell (☎0845-456 7000; Rupert St; ⌚9.30am-5pm Mon-Fri); Trinity Rd (☎0845-456-7000; Trinity Rd; ⌚24hr)

Getting There & Away

Air

Bristol International Airport (BRS; ☎0871-334-4344; www.bristolairport.co.uk) Eight miles southwest of the city.

Budget carriers:

Air Southwest (www.airsouthwest.com) Several UK destinations including Jersey, Leeds, Manchester, Newquay and Plymouth.

easyJet (www.easyjet.com) Budget flights to UK destinations including Belfast, Edinburgh, Glasgow, Newcastle and Inverness, plus European cities.

Ryanair (www.ryanair.com) Flights to Irish airports including Derry, Dublin and Shannon, as well as European destinations.

Bus

Bristol has excellent bus and coach connections. The main bus station on Marlborough St has an **enquiry office** (⌚7.30am-6pm Mon-Fri, 10am-6pm Sat).

COACHES National Express coaches go to Birmingham (£17, two hours, nine daily), London (£18, 2½ hours, at least hourly), Cardiff (£7, 1¼ hours, nine daily) and Exeter (£12.40, two hours, four daily).

BUSES There are regular buses from Bristol to destinations across Somerset.

Bath (one hour, several per hour) Express bus X39/339.

Wells (one hour, hourly Monday to Friday) Bus 376, with onward connections to Glastonbury (1¼ hours).

Weston-super-Mare (one hour, several per hour) Bus X1/352/353.

Train

Bristol is an important rail hub, with regular services to London provided by **First Great Western** (www.firstgreatwestern.co.uk) and services to northern England and Scotland mainly covered by **Cross Country** (www.crosscountrytrains.co.uk).

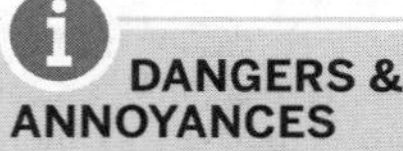

DANGERS & ANNOYANCES

As in any big city, it pays to keep your wits about you after dark, especially around the suburb of St Paul's, just northeast of the centre.

DESTINATION	FARE (ONE WAY)	DURATION (HR)	FREQ
Birmingham	£40	1½	hourly
Edinburgh	£82.50	6½	hourly
Exeter	£22.50	1	hourly
Glasgow	£82.50	6½	hourly
London	£34	1¾	hourly
Penzance	£37	5½	hourly
Truro	£37	5	hourly

Getting Around

To/From the Airport

Bristol International Flyer (http://flyer.bristolairport.co.uk) Runs shuttle buses (one way/return £6/9, 30 minutes, every 10 minutes at peak times) from the bus station and Temple Meads.

Bicycle

Bristol to Bath Railway Path (www.bristolbathrailwaypath.org.uk) The 13-mile off-road path follows the course of an old train track between the two cities. In Bristol pick it up around half a mile northeast of Temple Meads Train Station.

Blackboy Hill Cycles (☎0117-9731420; 180 Whiteladies Rd; ⊙9am-5.30pm Mon-Sat) For bike hire.

Boat

Bristol Ferry Boat Co (☎0117-9273416; www.bristolferry.com; adult/child return £3.30/2.70, day-pass £7/5) Runs two hourly commuter routes from the city centre dock, near the tourist office. The blue route goes east to Temple Meads via Millennium Sq, Welsh Back and Castle Park (for Broadmead and Cabot Circus); the red route goes west to Hotwells via Millennium Sq and SS *Great Britain*.

Bus

Useful city buses:

Bus 8/9 to Clifton (10 minutes), Whiteladies Rd and Bristol Zoo Gardens every 15 minutes from St Augustine's Pde. Add another 10 minutes from Temple Meads.

Bus 73 Runs from Parkway Station to the centre (30 minutes).

Taxi

The taxi rank on St Augustine's Pde is a central but rowdy place on weekend nights. There are plenty of companies; try **Streamline Taxis** (☎0117-926 4001).

BATH

POP 90,144

Ask any visitor for their ideal image of an English city, and chances are they'll come up with something pretty close to Bath – an architectural icon, cultural trendsetter and fashionable haunt for the last 300 years.

This honey-stoned city is especially renowned for its architecture: along its stately streets you'll find a celebrated set of Roman bathhouses, a grand medieval abbey and some of the finest Georgian terraces anywhere in England (in fact, Bath has so many listed buildings the entire place has been named a World Heritage Site by Unesco). Throw in some fabulous restaurants, gorgeous hotels and top-class shopping (especially since the arrival of the new SouthGate shopping centre), and you have a city that demands your undivided attention. Just don't expect to dodge the crowds.

History

Prehistoric peoples probably knew about the hot springs; legend has it King Bladud, a Trojan refugee and father of King Lear, founded Bath some 2800 years ago when his pigs were cured of leprosy by a dip in the muddy swamps. The Romans established the town of Aquae Sulis in AD 44 and built the extensive baths complex and a temple to the goddess Sulis-Minerva.

Long after the Romans decamped, the Anglo-Saxons arrived, and in 944 a monastery was founded on the site of the present abbey. Throughout the Middle Ages, Bath was an ecclesiastical centre and a wool-trading town, but it wasn't until the early 18th century that Ralph Allen and the

DRIVING IN BRISTOL

Heavy traffic and pricey parking make driving in Bristol a bit of a nightmare. If you can, it's best to ditch the car altogether: the train station's within walking distance of the centre, and pretty much everywhere can be reached on foot or by bus. If you do drive, make sure your hotel has parking, or use the **Park & Ride buses** (☎0117-922 2910; return before 10am Mon-Fri £3.50, after 10am Mon-Fri £2.50, Sat £2.50; ⊙every 10mins Mon-Sat) from Portway, Bath Rd and Long Ashton. Note that overnight parking is not permitted at the Park & Ride car parks.

celebrated dandy Richard 'Beau' Nash made Bath the centre of fashionable society. Allen developed the quarries at Coombe Down, constructed Prior Park and employed the two John Woods (father and son) to create some of Bath's most glorious buildings.

During WWII, Bath was hit by the Luftwaffe during the so-called Baedeker raids, which deliberately targeted historic cities in an effort to sap British morale. Several houses on the Royal Crescent and the Circus were badly damaged, and the city's Assembly Rooms were gutted by fire, although all have since been carefully restored.

More recently, the city's futuristic (and controversial) Thermae Bath Spa has been joined by a huge new shopping centre at SouthGate, seamlessly blending in with the rest of Bath's amber-coloured buildings.

Sights & Activities

Roman Baths ARCHITECTURE, MUSEUM

(www.romanbaths.co.uk; Abbey Churchyard; adult/child £11.50/7.50, Jul & Aug £12.25/7.50; ⌚9am-8pm Jul & Aug, 9am-6pm Mar, Jun, Sep & Oct, 9.30am-5.30pm Jan, Feb, Nov & Dec, last admission one hr before closing) Ever since the Romans arrived in Bath, life in the city has revolved around the three natural springs that bubble up near the abbey. In typically ostentatious style, the Romans constructed a glorious complex of bathhouses above these thermal waters to take advantage of their natural temperature – a constant 46°C. The buildings were left to decay after the Romans departed and, apart from a few leprous souls who came looking for a cure in the Middle Ages, it wasn't until the end of the 17th century that Bath's restorative waters again became fashionable.

The 2000-year-old baths now form one of the best-preserved ancient Roman spas in the world. The site gets very, very busy in summer; you can usually dodge the worst crowds by visiting early on a midweek morning, or by avoiding July and August. Multilingual audioguides (including an optional one read by the bestselling author Bill Bryson) are included in the price.

The heart of the complex is the **Great Bath**. Head down to water level and along the raised walkway to see the Roman paving and lead base. A series of excavated passages and chambers beneath street level leads off in several directions and lets you inspect the remains of other smaller baths and hypocaust (heating) systems.

One of the most picturesque corners of the complex is the 12th-century **King's Bath**, built around the original sacred spring; 1.5 million litres of hot water still pour into the pool every day. You can see the ruins of the vast **Temple of Sulis-Minerva** under the **Pump Room**, and recent excavations of the **East Baths** give an insight into its 4th-century form.

Bath Abbey CHURCH

(www.bathabbey.org; requested donation £2.50; ⌚9am-6pm Mon-Sat Easter-Oct, to 4.30pm Nov-Easter, 1-2.30pm & 4.30-5.30pm Sun year-round) King Edgar was crowned in a church in Abbey Courtyard in 973 – though he had ruled since 959 – but the present Bath Abbey was built between 1499 and 1616, making it the last great medieval church raised in England. The nave's wonderful fan vaulting was erected in the 19th century.

Outside, the most striking feature is the west facade, where angels climb up and down stone ladders, commemorating a dream of the founder, Bishop Oliver King. Among those buried here are Sir Isaac Pitman, who devised the Pitman method of shorthand, and Beau Nash.

On the abbey's southern side, the steps lead down to the small **Heritage Vaults Museum** (admission free; ⌚10am-3.30pm Mon-Sat), which explores the abbey's history and its links with the nearby baths. It also contains fine stone bosses, archaeological artefacts and a weird model of the 10th-century monk Aelfric, dressed in his traditional black Benedictine habit.

Royal Crescent & The Circus HISTORIC AREA

Bath has so many listed buildings that the entire city has been named a World Heritage Site by Unesco. The city's crowning glory is the Royal Crescent, a semicircular terrace of majestic houses overlooking a private lawn and the green sweep of Royal Victoria Park. Designed by John Wood the Younger (1728–82) and built between 1767 and 1775, the houses would have originally been rented for the season by wealthy socialites. These days flats on the crescent are still keenly sought after, and entire houses almost never come up for sale.

For a glimpse into the splendour and razzle-dazzle of Georgian life, head for **No 1 Royal Crescent** (www.bath-preservation-trust.org.uk; adult/child £6/2.50; ⌚10.30am-5pm Tue-Sun mid-Feb–mid-Oct, 10.30am-4pm mid-Oct–Dec), given to the city by the shipping magnate Major Bernard

Bath

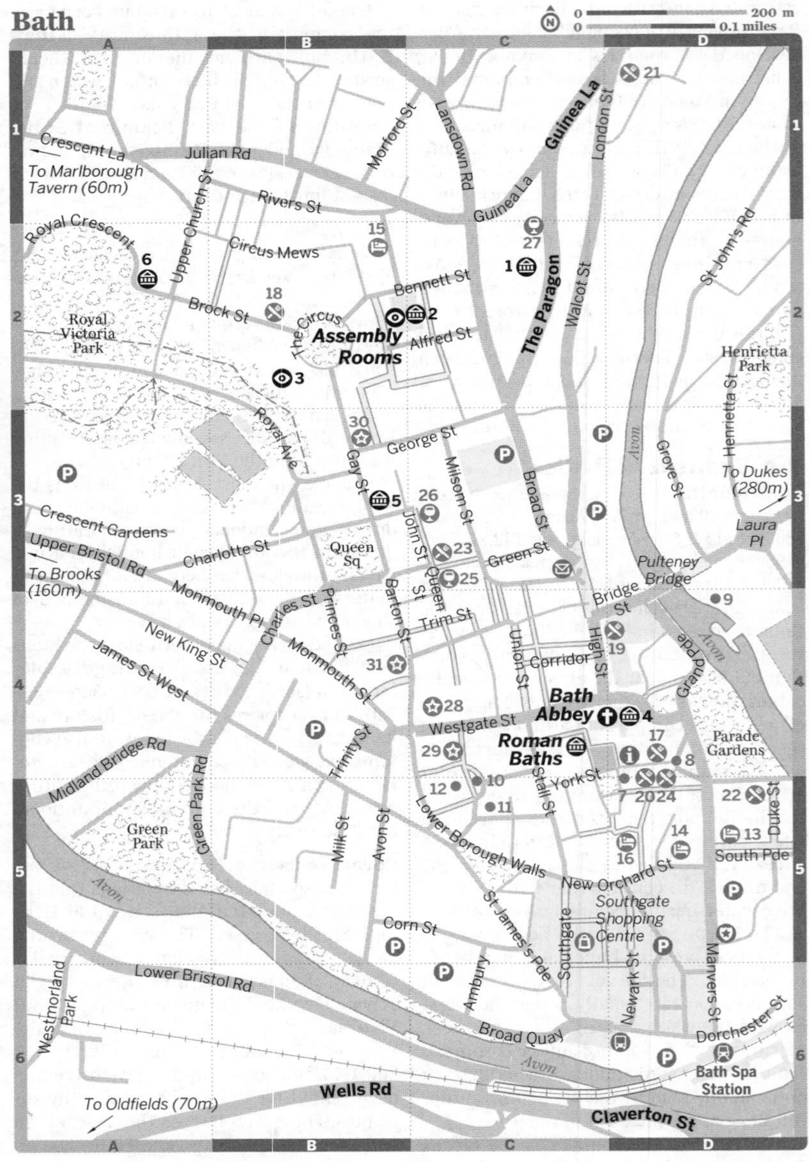

Cayzer, and since restored using only 18th-century materials. Among the rooms on display are the drawing room, several bedrooms and the huge kitchen, complete with massive hearth, roasting spit and mousetraps.

A walk east along Brock St from the Royal Crescent leads to the **Circus**, a ring of 30 symmetrical houses divided into three terraces. Plaques on the houses commemorate famous residents such as Thomas Gainsborough, Clive of India and David

Bath

Top Sights

Assembly Rooms ... B2
Bath Abbey ... C4
Roman Baths ... C4

Sights

1 Building of Bath Museum ... C2
2 Fashion Museum ... C2
3 Georgian Garden ... B2
4 Heritage Vaults Museum ... D4
5 Jane Austen Centre ... B3
6 No 1 Royal Crescent ... A2

Activities, Courses & Tours

7 Bath Festivals ... D5
8 Bizarre Bath Comedy Walk ... D4
9 Boat Trips ... D4
10 Cross Bath ... C5
11 Hot Bath ... C5
12 Thermae Bath Spa ... C5

Sleeping

13 Halcyon ... D5
14 Henry ... D5
15 Queensberry Hotel ... B2
16 Three Abbey Green ... D5

Eating

17 Café Retro ... D4
18 Circus ... B2
19 Deli Shush ... D4
20 Demuth's ... D5
21 Hudson Steakhouse ... D1
22 Onefishtwofish ... D5
23 Paxton & Whitfield ... C3
24 Sally Lunn's ... D5

Drinking

25 Raven ... C3
26 Salamander ... C3
27 Star Inn ... C2

Entertainment

28 Komedia ... C4
29 Little Theatre Cinema ... C4
30 Moles ... B3
31 Theatre Royal ... B4

Livingstone. To the south along Gravel Walk is the **Georgian Garden**, restored to resemble a typical 18th-century town house garden.

FREE **Assembly Rooms** ARCHITECTURE
(Bennett St; 10.30am-5pm Mar-Oct, 10.30am-4pm Nov-Feb) Opened in 1771, the city's glorious Assembly Rooms were where fashionable Bath socialites once gathered to waltz, play cards and listen to the latest chamber music. You're free to wander around the rooms, as long as they haven't been reserved for a special function. Highlights include the card room, tearoom and the truly splendid ballroom, all of which are lit by their original 18th-century chandeliers. The Assembly Rooms were all but gutted by incendiary bombs during WWII but have since been carefully restored.

Fashion Museum MUSEUM
(www.fashionmuseum.co.uk; adult/child £7/5, joint ticket with Roman Baths £15/9; 10.30am-5pm Mar-Oct, 10.30am-4pm Nov-Feb) In the basement of the Assembly Rooms, this museum displays costumes worn from the 16th to late-20th centuries, including some alarming crinolines that would have forced women to approach doorways side on.

Boat Trips CRUISES
Various cruise operators offer boat trips up and down the River Avon from the landing station underneath Pulteney Bridge. Try **Pulteney Cruisers** (01225-312900; www.bathboating.com; adult/child £8/4), the **Pulteney Princess** (07791-910650; www.pulteneypriness.co.uk; adult/child £7/3) or **Bath City Boat Trips** 07974-560197; www.bathcityboattrips.com; adult/child £6.95/4.95).

You can also pilot your own vessel down the Avon from the **Bathwick Boating Station** (01225-312900; www.bathboating.co.uk; Forrester Rd, Bathwick; first hr per adult/child £7/3.50, subsequent hr £3/1.50; 10am-6pm Easter-Oct), which rents out traditional skiffs and Canadian canoes.

Prior Park LANDSCAPED GARDEN
(NT; 01225-833422; priorpark@nationaltrust.org.uk; Ralph Allen Dr; adult/child £5/2.80; 11am-5.30pm Wed-Mon mid-Feb–Nov, 11am-5.30pm Sat & Sun Nov-Jan) Celebrated landscape gardener Capability Brown and satirical poet Alexander Pope both had a hand in the creation of Prior Park, an 18th-century ornamental garden dreamt up by local entrepreneur Ralph Allen, who founded Britain's postal service, owned many local quarries and funded the construction

DON'T MISS

THERMAE BATH SPA

Taking a dip in the Roman Baths might be off the agenda, but you can still sample the city's curative waters at **Thermae Bath Spa** (☎0844-888-0844; www.thermaebathspa.com; Hot Bath St; New Royal Bath spa session per 2hr/4hr/day £24/34/54, spa packages from £65; ⏱New Royal Bath 9am-10pm). Here the old **Cross Bath**, incorporated into an ultramodern shell of local stone and plate glass, is now the setting for a variety of spa packages. The New Royal Bath ticket includes steam rooms, waterfall shower and a choice of bathing venues – including the jaw-dropping open-air rooftop pool, where you can swim in the thermal waters in front of a backdrop of Bath's stunning cityscape.

Across the street are treatment rooms above the old **Hot Bath**, while the Hetling Pump Room, opposite, houses a **visitor centre** (⏱10am-5pm Mon-Sat, to 4pm Sun) that explores the history of bathing in Bath.

of many of Bath's most notable buildings. Cascading lakes and a famous Palladian bridge can be found around the garden's winding walks, and the sweeping views of the Bath skyline are something to behold.

Prior Park is 1 mile south of Bath's centre; it can be reached on foot or by Bus 2 (every 10 minutes), as well as by the City Skyline tour.

Jane Austen Centre MUSEUM
(www.janeausten.co.uk; 40 Gay St; adult/child £6.50/3.50; ⏱9.45am-5.30pm Apr-Sep, 11am-4.30pm Oct-Mar) Bath is known to many as a location in Jane Austen's novels. *Persuasion* and *Northanger Abbey* were both largely set in the city; the writer visited it many times and lived here from 1801 to 1806. The author's connections with the city are explored at the Jane Austen Centre, where displays also include period costume and contemporary prints of Bath.

Building of Bath Museum MUSEUM
(www.bath-preservation-trust.org.uk; The Vineyards, The Paragon; adult/child £4/2; ⏱10.30am-5pm Tue-Sun mid-Feb–Nov) This architectural museum details how Bath's Georgian splendour came into being, tracing the city's evolution from a sleepy spa town to one of the centres of Georgian society. There are some displays on contemporary construction methods, and the museum also explores the way in which social class and interior decor were intimately linked during the Georgian era; heaven forbid should you use a wallpaper that outstripped your station...

Tours

Bath City Sightseeing BUS TOUR
(☎01225-330444; www.city-sightseeing.com; adult/child £10/6; ⏱9.30am-5pm Mar-May, Oct & Nov, to 6.30pm Jun-Sep) Hop-on/hop-off city tour on an open-topped bus. Commentary is in seven languages. Buses stop every 20 minutes or so at various points around town. There's also a second route, the **Skyline tour** that runs year-round and travels out to Prior Park (p281); the same tickets are valid on both routes.

Bizarre Bath Comedy Walk WALKING TOUR
(☎01225-335124; www.bizarrebath.co.uk; adult/student £8/5; ⏱8pm Mar-Oct) Daft city tour mixing street theatre and live performance. Leaves from outside the Huntsman Inn on North Parade Passage.

Jane Austen's Bath WALKING TOUR
(☎01225-443000; adult/child £5/4; ⏱11am Sat & Sun) Focuses on the Georgian city and Jane Austen sites. Tours leave from the Abbey Churchyard.

FREE **Mayor's Guide Tours** WALKING TOUR
(☎01225-477411; www.thecityofbath.co.uk; ⏱10.30am & 2pm Sun-Fri, 10.30am Sat) Excellent historical tours provided free by The Mayors Corp of Honorary guides. Leave from outside the Pump Rooms. Extra tours at 7pm on Tuesday, Friday and Saturday May to September.

Festivals & Events

Bath has lots of festivals. All bookings are handled by **Bath Festivals** (☎01225-463362; www.bathfestivals.org.uk; 2 Church St; ⏱9.30am-5.30pm Mon-Sat).

Bath Literature Festival BOOKS
(www.bathlitfest.org.uk) Annual book festival in late February or early March.

Bath International Music Festival MUSIC
(www.bathmusicfest.org.uk) Mainly classical

and opera, plus smaller gigs of jazz, folk and world. Mid-May to early June.

Bath Fringe Festival THEATRE
(www.bathfringe.co.uk) Major theatre festival around mid-May to early June.

Sleeping

Bath gets incredibly busy, especially in the height of summer and at weekends, when prices have a tendency to skyrocket. The tourist office books last-minute rooms for a £3 fee, but you're better off booking online as early as you can.

TOP CHOICE **Queensberry Hotel** HOTEL £££
(01225-447928; www.thequeensberry.co.uk; 4 Russell St; s £95-300, d £105-425;) There's no getting away from it – the quirky Queensberry is eye-poppingly expensive – but for a right royal spoil, it's worth a splash. Four classic Georgian town houses have been combined into one seamless boutique whole, and all the rooms are different: some are sleek and zen, others indulgent and elegant, but the whole package is effortlessly chic. No parking, but give 'em your keys and they'll whisk your wheels to a private garage.

Halcyon HOTEL ££
(01225-444100; www.thehalcyon.com; 2/3 South Parade; d £99-125;) A shabby terrace of old hotels has been knocked through, polished up and totally reinvented, and the Halcyon is now by far and away the best place in the city centre. It's style on a budget: the lobby is cool and monochrome; off-white rooms have splashes of colour, Philippe Starck bath fittings and White Company smellies; studio rooms even have kitchens. We like it a lot.

Brooks B&B ££
(01225-425543; www.brooksguesthouse.com; 1 & 1a Crescent Gardens; d £69-175;) On the west side of Bath, this is another plush option, with heritage fixtures blending attractively with snazzy finishes. The owners have tried hard on the details: goosedown duvets, pocket-sprung mattresses, DAB radios and several breakfast spoils, including smoked salmon brioche and homemade muesli. Parking can be problematic.

Three Abbey Green B&B ££
(01225-428558; www.threeabbeygreen.com; 3 Abbey Green; d £85-135;) Considering the location, this place is a steal – tumble out of the front door and you'll find yourself practically on the abbey's doorstep. It's on a leafy square, and though the rooms lack sparkle, the suites have adjoining singles – ideal for travellers en famille.

Appletree Guest House B&B ££
(01225-337642; www.appletreeguesthouse.co.uk; 7 Pulteney Gardens; s £55-66, d £85-110, f £120-132;) It's absolutely tiny, but this welcoming B&B is worth recommending mainly for the sunny disposition of its husband-and-wife owners (Lynsay mainly sticks to the kitchen, while Les is a non-stop fizz of energy). Rooms are small and simple, but very cosy. Street parking is available free if you can find a space.

Henry B&B ££
(01225-424052; www.thehenry.com; 6 Henry St; s £50-55, d £90-130, f £90-110) Thorough renovations have removed the clutter and brought a palette of crisp whites and smooth beiges to the old Henry – unfortunately the prices have taken an upwards hike too. Still, the city-centre position is a winner.

Bath YHA HOSTEL ££
(bath@yha.org.uk; dm £14, d from £35; P @) Hostels don't come much grander than this Italianate mansion, a steep climb (or a short hop on bus 18) from the city centre. The refurbished rooms are surprisingly modern and many look out across the private tree-lined gardens; book early if you're after a double.

Eating

TOP CHOICE **Circus** RESTAURANT ££
(01225-318918; www.thecircuscafeandrestaurant.co.uk; 34 Brock St; lunch mains £5.50-9.70, dinner mains £11-13.90; lunch & dinner) Quite simply, our favourite place to eat in Bath. In a city that's often known for its snootiness, the Circus manages to be posh but not in the slightest pretentious. The attractive town house is steps from the Royal Crescent, and you can choose to eat on the ground floor or the intimate cellar dining room: either way, expect classic modern British, beautifully presented, at bargain prices. Book now while you still can.

Marlborough Tavern GASTROPUB ££
(01225-423731; www.marlborough-tavern.com; 35 Marlborough Buildings; mains £10.95-15.95; lunch & dinner) Bath's best address for gastrogrub, especially if you like your flavours rich and rustic. Chef Richard Whiting's food is defined by big country dishes, and it's earned him a big following – it's not often you have to book at a pub, but we recommend you do at the Marlborough.

Demuth's RESTAURANT ££
(☎01225-446059; 2 North Parade Passage; mains £9.75-14.25; ⏰lunch & dinner) Yes, it's vegetarian – but this place is a world away from stodgy quiches and nut roasts. For the last 20-something years this brilliant meat-free bistro has been turning out some of Bath's most creative and imaginative food – from a chive tart made with Devon Blue cheese to a simply divine apricot and fennel tagine.

Hudson Steakhouse RESTAURANT £££
(☎01225-332323; www.hudsonbars.com; 14 London St; mains £15-30; ⏰dinner Mon-Sat) Steak, steak and more steak is this much-garlanded restaurant's raison d'être. Top-quality cuts take in everything from delicate *filet mignon* to cowboy rib steak, all sourced from a Staffordshire farmers' co-op.

Onefishtwofish RESTAURANT ££
(☎01225-330236; 10a North Pde; mains £13-18; ⏰dinner Tue-Sun) Piscatarians would do well to plump for this super seafooderie, with cute little tables crammed in under a barrel-brick roof dotted with twinkly lights. Seafood is shipped in daily: there's always a *poisson du jour*, but you'll have to order bouillabaisse ahead.

Café Retro CAFÉ £
(18 York St; mains £5-11; ⏰breakfast, lunch & dinner Tue-Sat, breakfast & lunch Mon) This place is a poke in the eye for the corporate coffee chains. The paint-job's scruffy, the crockery's ancient and none of the furniture matches, but that's all part of the charm: this is a cafe from the old-school, and there's nowhere better for a hearty burger, a crumbly cake or a good old mug of tea. Takeaway's on offer from Retro to Go next door.

Sally Lunn's TEAROOM £
(4 North Parade Passage; lunch mains £5-6, dinner mains from £8; ⏰lunch & dinner) Classic chintzy tearoom serving the trademark Sally Lunn's bun.

Deli Shush DELI £
(8a Guildhall Market; ⏰8am-5.30pm Mon-Sat) Serrano ham, antipasti, samosas and 20 types of olives fill the shelves of this designer deli.

Paxton & Whitfield CHEESE SHOP £
(1 John St; ⏰Mon-Sat) Cheese connoisseurs beware – this fantastic fromagerie has enough stinky Stiltons and award-winning cheddars to send your olfactory senses into overdrive.

Drinking

Raven PUB
(Queen St) Highly respected by real ale aficionados, this fine city drinking den commands a devoted following for its well-kept beer and trad atmosphere.

Salamander PUB
(3 John St) The city's bespoke brewery, Bath Ales, owns this place, and you can sample all of their ales here. At the lighter end are amber-coloured Gem and Golden Hare, while the strongest of all is dark Rare Hare at a punchy 5.2%.

Star Inn PUB
(www.star-inn-bath.co.uk; 23 The Vineyards off the Paragon; 📶) Not many pubs are registered relics, but the Star is – it still boasts many of its 19th-century bar fittings. It's the brewery tap for Bath-based Abbey Ales; some ales are served in traditional jugs, and you can ask for a pinch of snuff in the 'smaller bar'.

Entertainment

Venue magazine (www.venue.co.uk, £1.50) has comprehensive listings of Bath's theatre, music and gig scenes. Pick up a copy at any newsagency.

Moles LIVE MUSIC
(www.moles.co.uk; 14 George St; ⏰9pm-2am Mon-Thu, to 4am Fri & Sat, 8pm-12.30am Sun) Bath's historic music club has hosted some big names down the years, and it's still the place to catch the hottest breaking acts.

Theatre Royal THEATRE
(www.theatreroyal.org.uk; Sawclose) Exclusive theatre featuring major drama, opera and ballet in the main auditorium, experimental productions in the Ustinov Studio, and young people's theatre at 'the egg'.

Komedia CABARET, COMEDY
(www.komedia.co.uk; 22-23 Westgate St) The Brighton-based comedy and cabaret venue has recently extended its reach west to Bath.

Little Theatre Cinema CINEMA
(St Michael's Pl) Bath's arthouse cinema, screening fringe and foreign-language flicks.

Information

Main post office (27 Northgate St)

Police station (Manvers St; ⏰7am-midnight)

Royal United Hospital (☎01225-428331; Combe Park)

Tourist office (enquiries ☎0906-711-2000, accommodation 0844-847-5256; www.visitbath.co.uk; Abbey Churchyard; ⏰9.30am-6pm Mon-Sat & 10am-4pm Sun Jun-Sep, 9.30am-5pm Mon-Sat & 10am-4pm Sun Oct-May) Phone enquiries to the main office are charged at premium rate (50p per minute).

Getting There & Away

Bus

Bath's bus and coach station (henquiries office 9am-5pm Mon-Sat) is on Dorchester St near the train station. National Express coaches run to London (£21.25, 3½ hours, 10 daily) via Heathrow (£17.50, 2¾ hours), and to Bristol (45 minutes, every 30 minutes). Services to most other cities require a change at Bristol or Heathrow.

Other services:

Bristol (55 minutes, four per hour Monday to Saturday, half-hourly Sunday) Bus X39/339.

Devizes (one hour, 15 daily Monday to Saturday, six on Sunday) Bus 271/272/273.

Frome (hourly Monday to Saturday) Bus 184.

Wells (1 hour 10 minutes, hourly Monday to Saturday, seven on Sunday) Bus 173.

Train

There are several trains per hour from Bath Spa to Bristol (£5.80, 11 minutes), which has connections to most major British cities. There are also direct trains to London Paddington and London Waterloo (£22 to £39, 1½ hours, at least hourly), as well as Cardiff Central (£15.90, one hour, six to 10 daily).

Getting Around

Bicycle

Bath's hills make getting around by bike challenging, but the canal paths along the Kennet & Avon Canal and the 13-mile **Bristol & Bath Railway Path** (www.bristolbathrailwaypath.org.uk) offer great cycling.

Bus

Bus 18 runs from the bus station, High St and Great Pulteney St up Bathwick Hill past the YHA to the university every 10 minutes. Bus 4 runs every 20 minutes to Bathampton from the same places.

Car & Motorcycle

Bath has serious traffic problems (especially at rush hour). **Park & Ride services** (☎01225-464446; return £2.50; ⏰6.15am-7.30pm) operate from Lansdown to the north, Newbridge to the west and Odd Down to the south. It takes about 10 minutes to the centre; buses leave every 10 to 15 minutes. If you brave the city, the best value car-park is underneath the new SouthGate shopping centre (two/eight hours £3/9.50, after 6.30pm £2).

SOMERSET

Sleepy Somerset provides the type of pleasing pastoral wanderings that are reminiscent of a simpler, calmer, kinder world. Its landscape of hedgerows, hummocks and russet-coloured fields is steeped in ancient rites and scattered with ancient sites. The cloistered calm of the cathedral city of Wells acts as a springboard for the limestone caves and gorges around Cheddar; while the hippie haven of Glastonbury

BABINGTON HOUSE

You'll definitely need to save your pennies, but for out-and-out luxury this much-lauded design **hotel** (☎01373-812266; www.babingtonhouse.co.uk; near Frome; r £380-450; P📶🏊) in rolling countryside near Frome is quite simply one of the top spots in Britain. It's part of a small chain of ultra-boutique hotels which also includes the Electric House in Notting Hill, Shoreditch House in East London and various Soho Houses (in London, New York, Berlin and Hollywood).

Combining Georgian architecture with urban invention, it comes across somewhere between *Homes & Gardens* and *Wallpaper*. Heritage beds, antique dressers and period fireplaces sit side-by-side with über-minimalist furniture, sanded wood floors and retro anglepoise lamps. There's a choice of rooms in the manor house, a stable block, a twin-storeyed lodge or the mezzanine-floored coach house, but top spot goes to the lavish Playroom, with a huge canopied bed, complimentary bar and views of green grounds from every angle.

And as if all that wasn't enough, there's the Cowshed Spa for relaxing, the Log Room restaurant (dinner mains £12 to £19) for eating, the Library for reading and a 45-seat cinema for – well, watching your latest directorial magnum opus, of course.

Very expensive, very exclusive and very lovely indeed.

provides an ancient abbey, mud-drenched festival and masses of Arthurian myth.

Somerset hugs the coast of the Bristol Channel and includes much of Exmoor National Park, which we cover separately. Glastonbury and Wells make good bases.

Information

Somerset Visitor Centre (01934-750833; www.visitsomerset.co.uk; Sedgemoor Services M5 South, Axbridge; 9.15am-5pm daily Easter-Oct, 9.15am-5pm Mon-Fri Nov-Easter) Provides general information.

Visit South Somerset (www.visitsouthsomerset.co.uk)

Getting Around

Most buses in Somerset are operated by **First** (0845-606-4446; www.firstgroup.com), supplemented by smaller operators. For timetables and general information contact **Traveline South West** (0871-200 2233; www.travelinesw.com).

Key train services link Bath, Bristol, Bridgwater, Taunton and Weston-Super-Mare. The M5 heads south past Bristol, to Bridgwater and Taunton, with the A39 leading west across the Quantocks to Exmoor.

Wells

POP 10,406

With Wells, small is beautiful. This tiny, picturesque metropolis is England's smallest city, and only qualifies for the 'city' title thanks to a magnificent medieval cathedral, which sits in the centre beside the grand Bishop's Palace. Wells has been the main seat of ecclesiastical power in this part of Britain since the 12th century, and is still the official residence of the Bishop of Bath and Wells. Medieval buildings and cobbled streets radiate out from the cathedral green to a marketplace that has been the bustling heart of Wells for some nine centuries (Wednesday and Saturday are market days). A quiet provincial city, Wells' excellent restaurants and busy shops help make it a good launching pad for exploring the Mendips and northern Somerset.

Sights

Wells Cathedral CHURCH

(www.wellscathedral.org.uk; Chain Gate, Cathedral Green; requested donation adult/child £5.50/2.50; 7am-7pm Apr-Sep, 7am-dusk Oct-Mar) Set in a marvellous medieval close, the Cathedral Church of St Andrew was built in stages between 1180 and 1508. The building incorporates several Gothic styles, but its most famous asset is the wonderful **west front**, an immense sculpture gallery decorated with more than 300 figures, built in the 13th century and restored to its original splendour in 1986. The facade would once have been painted in vivid colours, but has long since reverted to its original sandy hue. Apart from the figure of Christ, installed in 1985 in the uppermost niche, all the figures are original.

Inside, the most striking feature is the pair of **scissor arches** that separate the nave from the choir, designed to counter the subsidence of the central tower. High up in the north transept you'll come across a wonderful **mechanical clock** dating from 1392 – the second-oldest surviving in England after the one at Salisbury Cathedral (p259). The clock shows the position of the planets and the phases of the moon.

Other highlights are the elegant **Lady Chapel** (1326) at the eastern end and the seven effigies of Anglo-Saxon bishops ringing the choir. The 15th-century **chained library** houses books and manuscripts dating back to 1472. It's only open at certain times during the year or by prior arrangement.

From the north transept follow the worn steps to the glorious **Chapter House** (1306), with its delicate ceiling ribs sprouting like a palm from a central column. Externally, look out for the **Chain Bridge** built from the northern side of the cathedral to Vicars' Close to enable clerics to reach the cathedral without getting their robes wet. The cloisters on the southern side surround a pretty courtyard.

Guided tours (Mon-Sat) of the cathedral are free, and usually take place every hour. Regular concerts and cathedral choir recitals are held here throughout the year. You need to buy a permit (£3) from the cathedral shop to take pictures.

Cathedral Close SIGNIFICANT AREA

Wells Cathedral forms the centrepiece of a cluster of ecclesiastical buildings dating back to (and even earlier than) the Middle Ages. Facing the west front, on the left are the 15th-century **Old Deanery** and the **Wells & Mendip Museum** (www.wellsmuseum.org.uk; 8 Cathedral Green; adult/child £3/1; 10am-5.30pm Easter-Oct, 11am-4pm Wed-Mon Nov-Easter), with exhibits on local life, cathedral architecture and the infamous Witch of Wookey Hole (see p287).

Further along, **Vicars' Close** is a stunning cobbled street of uniform houses dating back to the 14th century, with a chapel at the end; members of the cathedral choir still live here. It is thought to be the oldest complete medieval street in Europe.

Penniless Porch, a corner gate leading onto Market Sq and built by Bishop Bekynton around 1450, is so-called because beggars asked for alms here.

Bishop's Palace HISTORIC BUILDING
(www.bishopspalacewells.co.uk; adult/child £5/2; ⌚10.30am-6pm summer, 10.30-4pm winter) Beyond the cathedral, the moated 13th-century Bishop's Palace is a real delight. Purportedly the oldest inhabited building in England, ringed by water and surrounded by a huge fortified wall, the palace complex contains several fine Italian Gothic state rooms, an imposing Great Hall and beautiful tree-shaded gardens. The natural wells that gave the city its name bubble up in the palace's grounds, feeding the moat and the fountain in the market square. The swans in the moat have been trained to ring a bell outside one of the windows when they want to be fed.

Sleeping

Beryl B&B ££
(☎01749-678738; www.beryl-wells.co.uk; Hawkers Lane; d £75-130; P) A mile from the city centre, this tree-shaded, gabled Victorian mansion is run by an eccentric local family and is stuffed to the rafters with antique atmosphere: grandfather clocks, chaises longues and stately four-posters aplenty. The rooms have a heritage feel, and outside there are acres of private gardens and a heated pool to enjoy.

Stoberry House B&B ££
(☎01749-672906; www.stoberry-park.co.uk; Stoberry Park; d £70-95; P) Another extravagant Wells house has thrown open its doors to provide supremely posh B&B. Four rooms are richly furnished in silky fabrics: top of the heap are sultry Black Orchid and regal Lady Hamilton. The truly gorgeous art-filled garden is the icing on the cake. There's a £10 to £15 supplement for one-night stays.

Number Twelve B&B ££
(☎01749-679406; www.numbertwelve.info; 12 North Rd; d £80-95; P) Two rooms in an Arts and Crafts house on the outskirts of Wells, both finished with taste and class. The best room is number 1, which has a glass-bricked bathroom with freestanding bath and a small balcony with cathedral views. Tea and cake is served on arrival, and there's kedgeree and smoked salmon and scrambled eggs for brekkie.

Eating

TOP CHOICE **Old Spot** BRITISH ££
(☎01749-689099; 12 Sadler St; 2-/3-course lunch £15/17.50, dinner £21.50/26.50; ⌚lunch Wed-Sun, dinner Tue-Sat) Little Wells conceals a culinary star in the shape of the Old Spot, run by renowned chef Ian Bates. It's a favourite with the foodie guides and the Sunday supplements, and the menu specialises in giving a modern twist to old country favourites – saddle of pork, smoked eel, rabbit stew.

Goodfellows BISTRO, BAKERY ££
(☎01749-673866; 5 Sadler St) Two eateries rolled into one. Downstairs is a super **café-bakery** (mains £7-10; ⌚8.30am-5pm Mon-Sat & 6-10pm Wed-Sat), which rustles up treats like goats' cheese bruschetta and hand-made pastries, while upstairs is a more formal seafood **bistro** (mains £11.50-25, 3-course dinner menu £35; ⌚lunch Tue-Sat, dinner Wed-Sat). The quality of the food in both is top-drawer, and it's a favourite with Wells' ladies-who-lunch.

Information

Tourist office (☎01749-672552; www.wellstourism.com; Market Pl; ⌚9.30am-5.30pm Apr-Oct, 10am-4pm Nov-Mar) Stocks the *Wells City Trail* leaflet (30p) and sells discount tickets to Wookey Hole and Cheddar Gorge.

Getting There & Away

The bus station is south of Cuthbert St, on Princes Rd. Useful services:

Bath (1 hour 10 minutes, hourly Monday to Saturday, seven on Sunday) Bus 173.

Bristol (one hour, hourly Monday to Saturday, seven on Sunday) Bus 376/377 stops in Wells en route to Glastonbury (15 minutes) and Street (25 minutes). The 377 continues to Yeovil (1¼ hours).

Cheddar (25 minutes, 10 daily Monday to Saturday, seven on Sunday) Bus 126; continues on to Weston-super-Mare (1½ hours).

Taunton (1¼ hours, nine daily Monday to Saturday, six on Sunday) Bus 29; runs via Glastonbury.

Wookey Hole

(www.wookey.co.uk; adult/child £16/11; ⌚10am-5pm Apr-Oct, 10.30am-4pm Nov-Mar) On the southern edge of the Mendips, the River Axe has carved out a series of deep limestone

CHEDDAR CHEESE

As well as its caves, Cheddar is also famous as the spiritual home of the nation's favourite cheese. Cheddar's strong, crumbly, tangy cheese is the essential ingredient in any self-respecting ploughman's, and has been produced in the area since at least the 12th century; Henry II boldly proclaimed cheddar to be 'the best cheese in Britain', and the king's accounts from 1170 record that he purchased 10,240lbs (around 4644kg) of the stuff. In the days before refrigeration, the Cheddar caves made the ideal cool store for the cheese, with a constant temperature of around 7°C. However, the powerful smell attracted rats and the practice was eventually abandoned.

These days most cheddar cheese is made far from the village, but if you're interested in seeing how the genuine article is made, head for the **Cheddar Gorge Cheese Company** (☎01934-742810; www.cheddargorgecheeseco.co.uk; ⏰10am-4pm). You can take a guided tour of the factory from Easter to October, and pick up some tangy, whiffy souvenirs at the on-site shop.

caverns collectively known as Wookey Hole. The caves are littered with dramatic natural features, including a subterranean lake and some fascinating stalagmites and stalactites: one of which is supposedly the legendary Witch of Wookey Hole, who was turned to stone by a local priest.

The caves were inhabited by prehistoric people for some 50,000 years, but these days the deep pools and underground rivers are more often frequented by cave divers – the deepest subterranean dive ever recorded in Britain was made here in September 2004, when divers reached a depth of more than 45m.

Admission to the caves is by guided tour. Despite its natural attractions, it's very touristy: the rest of the complex is taken up by kid-friendly attractions including mirror mazes, an Edwardian penny arcade, a paper-mill and a valley stuffed with 20 giant plastic dinosaurs. Look out for Wookey's newly appointed witch, Carla Calamity (aka Carole Bonahan, an ex-estate agent who beat 300 other applicants to the job after a series of gruelling auditions in mid-2009).

Cheddar Gorge

(www.cheddarcaves.co.uk; Explorer Ticket adult/child/family £17/11/44; ⏰10am-5.30pm Jul & Aug, 10.30am-5pm Sep-Jun) If Wookey Hole is a little too touristy for your tastes, then you'd better brace yourself for Cheddar Gorge, a spectacular series of limestone caverns that's always jam-packed with coach-parties and day trippers.

Despite the tourist throng, the natural wonders on display are genuinely impressive. The gorge itself is England's deepest, in places towering 138m above the twisting, turning road, and a network of caves extends deep into the surrounding rock on every side. Only a few are open to the public, including **Cox's Cave** and **Gough's Cave**, both decorated by an amazing gallery of stalactites and stalagmites, and subtly lit to bring out the spectrum of colours in the limestone rock. After the end of the last ice age, the caves were inhabited by prehistoric people; a 9000-year-old skeleton (imaginatively named Cheddar Man) was discovered here in 1903, and genetic tests have revealed that some of his descendants are still living in the surrounding area.

When the throngs become too much, you can clamber up the 274 steps of **Jacob's Ladder**; on a clear day you can see all the way to Glastonbury Tor and Exmoor.

Nearby, a signposted 3-mile-round walk follows the cliffs along the most spectacular parts of the gorge. Most visitors only explore the first section of the path, and you can usually escape the crowds by venturing further up the valley.

If a visit to the caves piques your interest, **Rocksport** (☎01934-742343; caves@visitcheddar.co.uk; adult/child £31/25) offers full-day subterranean trips into many of the more remote caverns which are normally closed to the public. Needless to say, you'll get cold, wet and muddy, and if you're even vaguely claustrophobic, don't even think about it.

Glastonbury

POP 8429

If you suddenly feel the need to get your third eye cleansed or your chakras realigned, then there's really only one place in England which fits the bill: good old Glastonbury, a bohemian haven and centre for New Age culture since the days of the Summer of Love, and still a favourite hangout for hippies, mystics and counter-cultural types of all descriptions. The main street is more Haight Ashbury than Somerset hamlet, thronged with a bewildering assortment of crystal sellers, veggie cafes, mystical bookshops and bong emporiums, but Glastonbury has been a spiritual centre since long before the weekend Buddhists and white witches arrived. It's supposedly the birthplace of Christianity in England, and several of Britain's most important ley lines are said to converge on nearby Glastonbury Tor.

The town is also famous for the June **Glastonbury Festival** (www.glastonburyfestivals.co.uk). This massive, often mud-soaked extravaganza of music, dance, spirituality and general all-round weirdness has been held on and off on farmland near Glastonbury (near Pilton) for the last 40 years.

Sights

Glastonbury Abbey ABBEY
(www.glastonburyabbey.com; Magdalene St; adult/child £5.50/3.50; 9.30am-6pm or dusk Sep-May, from 9am Jun-Aug) Legend has it that Joseph of Arimathea, great-uncle of Jesus, owned mines in this area and returned here with the Holy Grail (the chalice from the Last Supper) after the death of Christ. Joseph supposedly founded England's first church on the site, now occupied by the ruined abbey, but the earliest proven Christian connection dates from the 7th century, when King Ine gave a charter to a monastery in Glastonbury. In 1184 the church was destroyed by fire and reconstruction began in the reign of Henry II.

In 1191, monks claimed to have had visions confirming hints in old manuscripts that the 6th-century warrior-king Arthur and his wife Guinevere were buried in the abbey grounds. Excavations uncovered a tomb containing a skeletal couple, who were reinterred in front of the high altar of the new church in 1278. The tomb survived until 1539, when Henry VIII dissolved the monasteries and had the last abbot hung, drawn and quartered on the tor.

Glastonbury

Top Sights
- Chalice Well & Gardens ... D2
- Glastonbury Abbey ... B1
- Glastonbury Tor ... D2
- Rural Life Museum ... C2

Sights
- 1 Lake Village Museum ... A1
- 2 White Spring ... D2

Sleeping
- 3 Chalice Hill ... C1
- 4 Glastonbury Backpackers ... A1
- 5 Parsnips ... B2

Eating
- 6 Hundred Monkeys Cafe ... B1
- 7 Mocha Berry ... A1
- 8 Rainbow's End ... B1

Drinking
- 9 Who'd A Thought It Inn ... A1

Glastonbury

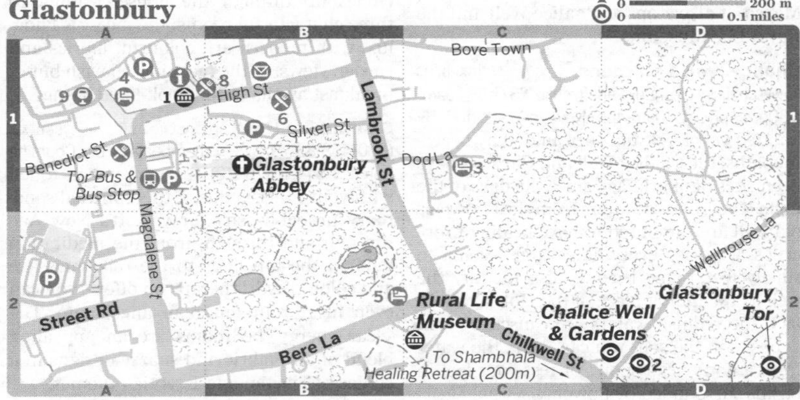

The remaining ruins at Glastonbury mainly date from the church that was built after the 1184 fire. It's still possible to make out some of the nave walls, the ruins of St Mary's chapel, and the remains of the crossing arches, which may have been scissor-shaped, like those in Wells Cathedral. The grounds also contain a small **museum**, cider **orchard** and **herb garden**, as well as the **Holy Thorn tree**, which supposedly sprung from Joseph's staff and mysteriously blooms twice a year, at Christmas and Easter.

FREE **Glastonbury Tor** LANDMARK

The iconic hump of Glastonbury Tor looms up from flat fields to the northwest of town. This 160m-high grassy mound provides glorious views over the surrounding countryside, and a focal point for a bewildering array of myths. According to some it's the home of a faery king, while an old Celtic legend identifies it as the stronghold of Gwyn ap Nudd (ruler of Annwyn, the Underworld) – but the most famous legend identifies the tor as the mythic Isle of Avalon, where King Arthur was taken after being mortally wounded in battle by his nephew Mordred, and where Britain's 'once and future king' sleeps until his country calls again.

Whatever the truth of the legends, the tor has been a site of pilgrimage for many years, and was once topped by the medieval church of **St Michael**, although today only the tower remains.

It takes 45 minutes to walk up and down the tor. Parking is not permitted nearby, but the **Tor Bus** (adult/child £2.50/1.50) leaves from Dunstan's car park near the abbey. The bus runs every 30 minutes from 10am to 7.30pm from April to September, and from 10am to 3.30pm from October to March. It also stops at Chalice Well and the Rural Life Museum.

Chalice Well & Gardens GARDENS

(www.chalicewell.org.uk; adult/child £3/1; ⏲10am-5.30pm Apr-Oct, 10am-4pm Nov-Mar) Shaded by knotted yew trees and surrounded by peaceful paths, the Chalice Well and Gardens have been sites of pilgrimage since the days of the Celts. The iron-red waters from the 800-year-old well are rumoured to have healing properties, good for everything from eczema to smelly feet; some legends also identify the well as the hiding place of the Holy Grail. In fact, the reddish waters are caused by iron deposits in the soil. You can drink the water from a lion's-head spout, or rest your feet in basins surrounded by flowers.

The Chalice Well is also known as the 'Red Spring' or 'Blood Spring'; its sister, **White Spring**, surfaces across Wellhouse Lane.

FREE **Rural Life Museum** MUSEUM

(Abbey Farm, Chilkwell St; ⏲10am-5pm Tue-Fri, 2-6pm Sat & Sun Apr-Oct, 10am-5pm Tue-Sat Nov-Mar) Somerset's agricultural heritage is explored at the Rural Life Museum, which contains a varied collection of artefacts relating to traditional trades such as willow growing, peat digging, cider making and cheese making. There are often live displays of local skills, so if you fancy trying your hand at beekeeping, lace making and spinning, this is the place to do it. The late-14th-century tithe barn has fine carvings on the gables and porch, and an impressive timber roof; it now houses a collection of vintage agricultural machinery.

Lake Village Museum MUSEUM

(The Tribunal, 9 High St; adult/child £2/1.50; ⏲10am-5pm Apr-Sep, to 4pm Oct-Mar) Upstairs from Glastonbury's tourist office, in the medieval courthouse, the Lake Village Museum displays finds from a prehistoric bog village discovered in nearby Godney. The houses in the village were clustered in about six groups and were built from reeds, hazel and willow. It's thought they were occupied by summer traders who lived the rest of the year at Glastonbury Tor.

Sleeping

Chalice Hill B&B ££

(☎01458-838828; www.chalicehill.co.uk; Dod Lane; d £100; P) This grand Georgian B&B has been renovated with flair by its artistic owner Fay Hutchcroft. A sweeping staircase circles up through the house, leading to three characterful rooms: the nicest is Phoenix, with modern art, colourful fabrics and garden views. In the morning, a lavish buffet breakfast awaits in the book-lined lounge.

Shambhala Healing Retreat B&B ££

(☎01458-831797; www.shambhala.co.uk; Coursing Batch; s £44, d £76-112) If you're not in touch with your inner goddess, this spiritual sanctuary probably isn't for you. It's New Age through and through, from the meditation tent on the top floor to the reiki massage and colonic hydrotherapy on offer – you can even meet your guardian angel here. The 'clear energy' bedrooms are an appealing blend of airy fabric and snazzy designs in a choice of Tibetan and Egyptian themes.

Parsnips B&B ££
(☎01458-835599; www.parsnips-glastonbury.co.uk; 99 Bere La; s/d £50/65; P @) The house is modern, but if you're looking for an escape from tie-dye and crystals, this solid B&B's a decent bet. Rooms are in gingham and cream; there's a bright conservatory and massages available.

Glastonbury Backpackers HOSTEL £
(☎01458-833353; www.glastonburybackpackers.com; 4 Market Pl; dm £14-16, tw £35-45, d £45-50; P @) A fresh lick of paint has made this basic hostel more presentable, but it's still pretty basic. Still, it's very friendly, and there's a TV lounge, kitchen and cafe-bar downstairs.

Eating & Drinking

Rainbow's End CAFÉ £
(17a High St; mains £4-7; ⌚10am-4pm) A Glasto classic, this charming wholefood cafe cooks up generous portions of veggie chilli, fresh quiches and hearty soups, served up in a cheery dining room dotted with potted plants and mix-and-match furniture, plus a little patio out back. The homemade cakes are particularly yummy.

Hundred Monkeys Cafe BISTRO ££
(52 High St; mains £8-15; ⌚10am-6pm Mon-Wed, to 9pm Thu-Sat, to 3.30pm Sun) Surprisingly sleek bistro, decked out with leather sofas, pine tables and a big blackboard listing fresh pastas, salads and mains. If you've a spare half-hour ask about the origin of the name – the original 100th monkey.

Who'd A Thought It Inn PUB ££
(17 Northload St; mains £8.25-16.95; ⌚lunch & dinner) In keeping with Glastonbury's outsider spirit, this town pub is brimming with wacky character, from the vintage signs and upside-down bike on the ceiling to the reclaimed red telephone box tucked in one corner.

Mocha Berry CAFE £
(14 Market Pl; mains £5-8; ⌚Sun-Wed) This ever-popular cafe is the top spot in Glastonbury for a frothy latte, a fresh milkshake or a stack of breakfast pancakes.

Information

Glastonbury Tourist Office (☎01458-832954; www.glastonburytic.co.uk; The Tribunal, 9 High St; ⌚10am-5pm Apr-Sep, to 4pm Oct-Mar) Stocks maps and accommodation lists, and sells leaflets describing local walks and the *Glastonbury Millennium Trail* (60p).

Getting There & Away

There is no train station in Glastonbury, so buses are the only public transport option.

Bus 29 runs to Taunton (50 minutes, nine daily Monday to Saturday, six on Sunday). Bus 376/377 travels northwest to Wells (30 minutes, hourly Monday to Saturday, seven on Sundays) and Bristol (1¼ hours), and south to Street (15 minutes). The 377 runs on to Yeovil (one hour).

EXMOOR NATIONAL PARK

Barely 21 miles across and 12 miles north to south, Exmoor might be the little sister of England's national parks, but what she lacks in scale she more than makes up in scenery. Part wilderness expanse, part rolling fields, dotted with bottle-green meadows, wooded combes and crumbling cliffs, Exmoor seems to sum up everything that's

Exmoor National Park

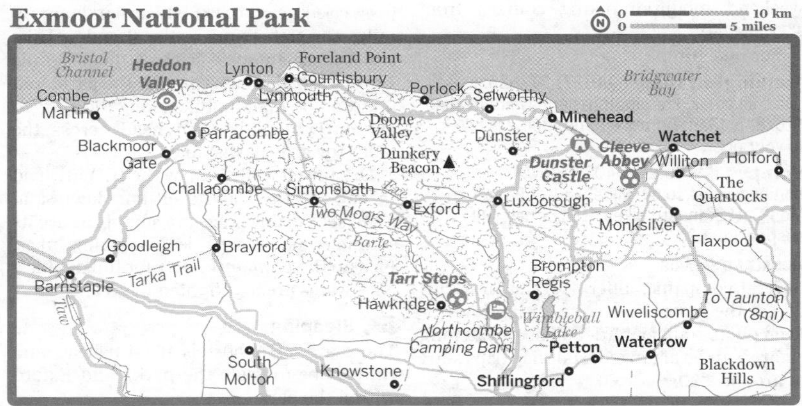

green and pleasant about the English landscape. Waymarked paths criss-cross the moor, and a dramatic section of the **South West Coast Path** runs from Minehead (a family-fun resort just outside the park) all the way to Padstow in Cornwall.

It's a haven for ramblers, mountain-bikers and horse-riders, and it's also home to lots of rare wildlife, including some of England's largest herds of wild red deer. These skittish creatures are notoriously elusive, however, so if you want to spot them your best bet is to get up early for a dawn safari.

Activities

Active Exmoor (01398-324599; www.activeexmoor.com) A central contact point for all the park's outdoor activity providers, ranging from riding to rowing and sailing to surfing.

CYCLING

A network of bridleways and quiet lanes makes Exmoor great cycling country, but you're not going to get away without tackling a few hills. Popular trails travel through the Brendon Hills, the Crown Estate woodland and along the old Barnstaple railway line. National Park Authority (NPA) centres sell the map *Exmoor for Off-Road Cyclists* (£10), and the *Bike It Dunster* and *Bike It Wimbleball* leaflets (75p) – both of which feature a family, beginner and explorer route. All are also available at the NPA's online shop.

Several sections of the **National Cycle Network** (NCN; www.sustrans.org.uk) cross the park, including the **West Country Way** (NCN route 3) from Bristol to Padstow, and the **Devon Coast to Coast Cycle Route** (NCN route 27) between Exmoor and Dartmoor.

Exmoor & Quantocks MTB Experiences (01643-705079; www.exqumtb.co.uk) runs weekend mountain-biking courses from £75 to £150.

For bike hire:

Fremington Quay (01271-372586; www.biketrail.co.uk; Fremington; per day adult/child £16/8; 10am-5pm Wed-Sun) Delivers bikes to your door.

Pompys (01643-704077; www.pompyscycles.co.uk; Minehead; 9am-5pm Mon-Sat) Standard bikes £15 per day, full-suspension £25.

MOORLAND SAFARIS

Several companies offer 4WD 'safari' trips across the moor. If you're a nature-lover or keen photographer, bird- and deer-watching safaris can be arranged. Half-day trips start at around £30.

Barle Valley Safaris SAFARI
(01643-851386; www.exmoorwildlifesafaris.co.uk; Dulverton & Dunster)

Discovery Safaris SAFARI
(01643-863080; www.discoverysafaris.com; Porlock)

Exmoor Safari SAFARI
(01643-831229; www.exmoorsafari.co.uk; Exford)

Red Stag Safari SAFARI
(01643-841831; www.redstagsafari.co.uk)

PONY TREKKING & HORSE RIDING

Exmoor is popular riding country and lots of stables offer pony and horse treks from around £40 for a two-hour hack – see the *Exmoor Visitor* for full details.

Brendan Manor Stables HORSE RIDING
(01598-741246) Near Lynton.

Burrowhayes Farm HORSE RIDING
(01643-862463; www.burrowhayes.co.uk; Porlock)

Knowle Riding Centre HORSE RIDING
(01643-841342; www.knowleridingcentre.co.uk; Dunster)

Outovercott Stables HORSE RIDING
(01598-753341; www.outovercott.co.uk; Lynton)

WALKING

The open moors and profusion of marked bridleways make Exmoor an excellent area for hiking. The best-known routes are the **Somerset & North Devon Coast Path**, which is part of the **South West Coast Path** (www.southwestcoastpath.com), and the Exmoor section of the **Two Moors Way**, which starts in Lynmouth and travels south to Dartmoor and beyond.

Other routes include the **Coleridge Way** (www.coleridgeway.co.uk) which winds for 36 miles through Exmoor, the Brendon Hills and the Quantocks. Part of the 180-mile **Tarka Trail** also cuts through the park; join it at Combe Martin, hike along the cliffs to Lynton/Lynmouth, then head across the moor towards Barnstaple.

Organised walks run by the NPA are held throughout the year. Its autumn dawn safaris to see rutting stags are superb, as are its summertime evening deer-watching hikes. Pick up the *Exmoor Visitor* for full details – NPA walks are highlighted in green.

Sleeping

There are YHA hostels in Minehead and Ilfracombe (outside the park), and Exford within the park.

ADVENTUROUS EXMOOR

For budding backcountry adventurers, **Mountains+Moor** (☎01643-841610; www.mountainsandmoor.co.uk) offers navigation lessons (from £80 per two days) and summer mountain-craft courses (two/five days £110/270), which include camp-craft, rope work and river crossings, and take the form of mini-expeditions. Eat your heart out, Ray Mears...

There's also YHA hostel-style accommodation at the **Pinkery Bunkhouse** (☎0164-831437; pinkery@exmoor-nationalpark.gov.uk) near Simonsbath.

The YHA also runs camping barns (often known as 'stone tents') at **Mullacott Farm** (☎01629-592700) near Ilfracombe and **Northcombe Farm** (☎01629-592700) near Dulverton. Prices start at around £8 per night, and you'll need all the usual camping supplies.

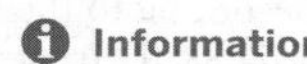

Information

TOURIST OFFICES

There are three NPA Centres around the park – the main one is in Dulverton.

Dulverton (☎01398-323841; NPCDulverton@exmoor-nationalpark.gov.uk; 7-9 Fore St)

Dunster (☎01643-821835; NPCDunster@exmoor-nationalpark.gov.uk)

Lynmouth (☎01598-752509; NPCLynmouth@exmoor-nationalpark.gov.uk)

INTERNET RESOURCES

Exmoor National Park (www.exmoor-nationalpark.gov.uk) The official NPA site.

Exmoor Tourist Association (www.exmoor.com) Accommodation and activities.

Visit Exmoor (www.visit-exmoor.info) Excellent information site with advice on activities, events, accommodation and eating out.

What's On Exmoor (www.whatsonexmoor.com) Local listings and information.

Getting Around

Once outside the key towns, getting around Exmoor by bus can be very tricky.

Coastal bus Bus 28 (hourly, nine on Sunday). Departs from Taunton with stops at Crowcombe, Bicknoller, Williton, Watchet, Dunster and Minehead.

Cross-moor bus Bus 399 (three daily Monday to Saturday). Crosses the moor from Minehead to Tiverton via Dunster, Wheddon Cross, Exford and Dulverton.

'Coastal Link' Bus 39/300. Seasonal open-top bus from Minehead to Lynmouth via Selworthy and Porlock.

'Exmoor Explorer' Bus 401. Summer-only service which follows the coast from Porlock to Dunster and then circles inland via Wheddon Cross and Exford.

Dulverton

Dulverton is the southern gateway to Exmoor National Park, and sits at the base of the Barle Valley near the confluence of two key rivers, the Exe and Barle. It's a no-nonsense sort of country town, home to a collection of gun-sellers, fishing-tackle stores and gift shops.

There's a lovely 12-mile circular walk along the river from Dulverton to **Tarr Steps** – an ancient stone clapper bridge haphazardly placed across the River Barle and shaded by gnarled old trees. The bridge was supposedly built by the devil for sunbathing. It's a four- to five-hour trek for the average walker. You can add another three or four hours to the walk by continuing from Tarr Steps up Winsford Hill for distant views over Devon.

Sleeping

TOP CHOICE **Tarr Farm** HOTEL **£**

(☎01643-851507; www.tarrfarm.co.uk; s/d £90/150; P) This valley getaway is snuggled near the Tarr Steps, 5 miles from Dulverton. Despite the farmhouse appearance, it's a top-class retreat: nine rooms in rich creams and yellows, with organic bath goodies and old-fashioned bath taps, plus spoils such as home-baked cookies, in-room fridges, DVD players and a fab country **restaurant** (mains £13-18; lunch & dinner).

Town Mills B&B **££**

(☎01398-323124; www.townmillsdulverton.co.uk; High St; s/d £60/85; P) The nicest B&B near Dulverton's town centre, with creamy-and-beam rooms squeezed into a converted mill, livened up by bits of art and crisp fabrics. The attic rooms are a bit small, but you can hear the rush of the river from your window.

Three Acres B&B ££
(☎01398-323730; www.threeacrescountryhouse.co.uk; Brushford; s £60-75, d £90-120; P) A sweet retreat reached by narrow, twisty lanes from Dulverton. It's scooped lots of B&B awards, and with good reason: there are six prim rooms overlook rolling Exmoor hills, and there's a different daily special for breakfast, from Exe trout to homemade bangers. Lovely.

Eating

Woods RESTAURANT ££
(☎01398-324007; 4 Bank Sq; lunch £9.95-15, dinner £11-16.50; ⏲lunch & dinner) This deservedly popular restaurant has built up a devoted following for its rustic dishes, quaint atmosphere and excellent service. Tummy treats include local lobster, pork belly with samphire, and Ruby Red sirloin steak.

Lewis' Tea Rooms CAFE ££
(☎01398-323850; 13 High St; mains £5-18; ⏲breakfast & lunch Mon-Sat, dinner Thu-Sat Jul & Aug) Top-class afternoon teas (including many rare estate varieties) are the main draw at this delightful town tearoom, but it's worth leaving room for the Welsh rarebits and crumbly cakes too. It's frilly and floral, but hugely friendly – and it opens late for country suppers in summer, too.

Getting There & Away

For buses, see p293.

Lynton & Lynmouth

The attractive harbour of Lynmouth is rooted at the base of a steep, tree-lined valley, where the West Lyn River empties into the sea along Exmoor's northern coastline. Its similarity to the harbour at Boscastle (p321) is striking, and, in fact, the two harbours share more than just a common geography: like Boscastle, Lynmouth is famous for a devastating flash flood. A huge wave of water swept through Lynmouth in 1952 and the town paid a much heavier price than its Cornish cousin; 34 people lost their lives, and memory of the disaster remains strong in the village today.

Lynmouth is a busy tourist harbour town lined with pubs, souvenir sellers and fudge shops. At the top of the rocky cliffs is the more genteel Victorian resort of Lynton, which can be reached via an amazing water-operated railway, or a stiff climb up the cliff path.

Sights

Lyn & Exmoor Museum MUSEUM
(St Vincent's Cottage, Market St, Lynton; adult/child £1/20p; ⏲10am-12.30pm & 2-5pm Mon-Fri, 2-5pm Sun Apr-Oct) The history of Lynmouth's flood is explored at this museum which also houses some interesting archaeological finds and a collection of tools, paintings and period photos.

Cliff Railway RAILWAY
(www.cliffrailwaylynton.co.uk; single/return adult £2/3, child £1.20/1.85; ⏲10am-6pm Easter-Oct, later at peak times) This extraordinary piece of Victorian engineering was designed by George Marks, believed to be a pupil of Brunel. Two cars linked by a steel cable descend or ascend the slope according to the amount of water in the cars' tanks. It's been running like clockwork since 1890, and it's still the best way to commute between the two villages.

Activities

There are some beautiful short walks in and around the two villages, as well as access to some longer routes: the **South West Coast Path**, the **Coleridge Way** and the **Tarka Trail** all pass through Lynmouth, and it is the official starting point of the **Two Moors Way**.

The most popular hike is to the stunning **Valley of the Rocks**, described by poet laureate Robert Southey as 'rock reeling upon rock, stone piled upon stone, a huge terrifying reeling mass'. It's just over a mile west of Lynton, and is believed to mark the original course of the River Lyn. Many of the tortuous rock formations have been named over the years – look out for the **Devil's Cheesewring** and **Ragged Jack** – the valley is also home to a population of feral goats.

Other popular trails wind to the lighthouse at **Foreland Point**, east of Lynmouth, and **Watersmeet**, 2 miles upriver from Lynmouth, where a handily placed National Trust teashop is housed in a Victorian fishing lodge.

Sleeping

There are plenty of mid-price B&Bs dotted along Lee Rd in Lynton.

St Vincent House

B&B ££

(☎01598-752244; www.st-vincent-hotel.co.uk; Castle Hill, Lynton; d £75-80; P) No sea view, but this classy lodge is still our favourite Lynton base. The house has history – it was built by a sea captain who sailed with Nelson. The decor is full of cosy heritage and there's a rather grand central staircase.

Sea View Villa

B&B ££

(☎01598-753460; www.seaviewvilla.co.uk; 6 Summer House Path, Lynmouth; d £100-150) Georgian grandeur in seaside Lynmouth. In this 1721 villa Egyptian cotton, Indian silk and suede fabrics grace rooms done out in 'Champagne', 'ginger' and 'vanilla'. Eggs Benedict, smoked salmon and cafetière coffee ensure the breakfast is classy, and they'll even pack you a picnic.

Chough's Nest

B&B £

(☎01598-753315; www.choughsnesthotel.co.uk; North Walk, Lynton; d £94-110; P) For clifftop position, this Lynton B&B is unbeatable. It goes a bit overboard with the frips and floral fabrics, but if you can get a room with a sea-view, you'll be a happy bunny.

Eating

St Vincent Restaurant

RESTAURANT ££

(☎01598-752244; Castle Hill, Lynton; 2/3 courses £24/27; ⊙dinner Wed-Sun Easter-Oct) With the local dining scene largely limited to tearooms and seaside pubs, the St Vincent's accomplished eatery looks all the more appealing. Exmoor produce is given a Mediterranean zing by the proprietor-chef, Belgian-born Jean-Paul Salpetier: think Exmoor boar with honey, thyme and sage, or noisettes of lamb with tomatoes, capers and olives.

Rising Sun

PUB ££

(☎01598-753223; Lynmouth; mains £11.25-17.70; ⊙lunch & dinner) A historic thatched pub a little walk uphill from the Lynmouth harbour. Chef Oliver Wood's food is a world way from the usual boring bar fare, and makes maximum use of the ingredients on his doorstep – especially lamb, game and riverfish. The Sunday roast is a real cracker, too.

Information

Lynton Tourist Office (☎01598-752225; info@lyntourism.co.uk; Lynton Town Hall, Lee Rd; ⊙10am-4pm Mon-Sat, to 2pm Sun) Publishes the free newspaper *Lynton & Lynmouth Scene* (www.lyntonandlynmouthscene.co.uk), which has accommodation, eating and activities listings.

Getting There & Away

For buses see p293.

Porlock & Around

The small village of Porlock is one of the prettiest on the north Exmoor coast; the huddle of thatched cottages lining its main street is framed on one side by the sea, and on the other by a jumble of houses that cling to the steeply sloping hills behind. Winding lanes lead to the picturesque breakwater of **Porlock Weir**, a compact collection of pubs, shops and hotels, 2 miles to the west.

Coleridge's famous poem *Kubla Khan* was written during a brief sojourn in Porlock (helped along by a healthy slug of laudanum and a vicious head cold), and the villages are popular with summertime tourists, as well as walkers on the Coleridge Way and the South West Coast Path.

The village of **Selworthy**, 2½ miles southeast of Porlock, forms part of the 5060-hectare **Holnicote Estate**, the largest NT-owned area of land on Exmoor. Though its cob-and-thatch cottages look ancient, the village was almost entirely rebuilt in the 19th century by local philanthropist and landowner Thomas Acland, to provide accommodation for elderly workers on his estate.

Sleeping & Eating

TOP CHOICE Andrews on the Weir

RESTAURANT £££

(☎01643-863300; www.andrewsontheweir.co.uk; Porlock Weir; 2-/3-course menu £31.50/38.50) Exmoor's starriest and starchiest restaurant is nestled behind the Porlock breakwater. Chef Andrew Dixon makes a point of sourcing all his produce from local farmers and fishing boats, so the menu is a riot of local flavours – Withycombe pork, Exmoor lamb and Devon scallops. Dinner can be pricey, but the £10 lunch menu is fab value. He also runs regular cooking courses if you fancy finding out how the magic happens.

Ship Inn

PUB £

(www.shipinnporlock.co.uk; High St; mains £7.75-11.95) Coleridge and pal Robert Southey both downed pints in this venerable thatched Porlock pub – you can even sit in 'Southey's Corner'. Substantial pub food – mainly steaks, roasts and stews – are served in the wood-filled bar, and there are 10 surprisingly light **rooms** (single/double £40/60) in pine and cream.

Information

Porlock Tourist Office (☎01643-863150; www.porlock.co.uk; West End, High St; ⏲10am-5pm Mon-Sat, 10am-1pm Sun Mar-Oct, 10.30am-1pm Tue-Fri, 10am-2pm Sat Nov-Feb) Main point of contact for info on the Coleridge Way.

Getting There & Away

For buses see p293.

If you're driving, the most scenic route to Porlock is the steep, twisting **toll-road** (cars/motorbikes/bicycles £2.50/1.50/1) that hugs the coast all the way from Lynmouth. Better still, you get to avoid the 1:4 gradient on Porlock Hill.

Dunster

Centred around a scarlet-walled castle and an original medieval yarn market, Dunster is one of Exmoor's oldest villages, sprinkled with bubbling brooks, packhorse bridges and a 16th-century dovecote.

Sights

Dunster Castle CASTLE

(NT; dunster@nationaltrust.co.uk; castle adult/child £8.10/4, garden & park only £4.50/2; ⏲11am-5pm Sat-Wed Mar-Oct, 11am-4pm Nov) The castle was originally owned by the aristocratic Luttrell family whose manor encompassed much of northern Exmoor. Although it served as a fortress for around a thousand years, present-day Dunster Castle bears little resemblance to the original Norman stronghold. The 13th-century gateway is probably the only original part of the castle; the turrets, battlements and towers were all added later during a romantic remodelling at the hands of Victorian architects. Despite its 19th-century makeover, the castle is still an impressive sight, and is decorated with Tudor furnishings, gorgeous 17th-century plasterwork and ancestral portraits of the Luttrell family. The terraced gardens are also worth exploring, with fine views across Exmoor and the coastline, and an important national collection of strawberry trees.

St George's Church CHURCH

The beautiful church dates mostly from the 15th century and boasts a wonderfully carved fan-vaulted rood screen.

Watermill MILL

(Mill Lane; adult/child £3.50/2; ⏲11am-4.45pm Jun-Sep, 11am-4.45pm Sat-Thu Apr, May & Oct) Further down the road is this working 18th-century mill.

Sleeping & Eating

Dunster Castle Hotel HOTEL ££

(☎01643 82 30 30; www.thedunstercastlehotel.co.uk; 5 High St; d £90-150; 📶) Fresh from an expensive refurb, this old Dunster hostelry is now all uncluttered simplicity. The rooms are light and soothing – it's worth bumping up to one of the Superior Kingsize Rooms (£125) for more space, and we particularly liked the Grabbist and Aville Rooms. Downstairs the restaurant has the same stripped-down feel – grey wicker chairs, crimson key-notes and modern Brit-bistro food.

Spears Cross B&B ££

(☎01643-821439; www.spearscross.co.uk; 1 West St; s £55, d £82-92) This Dunster house mostly dates back to the mid 15th-century, but if you're a sucker for low ceilings, inglenook grates and quirky crannies, you couldn't ask for a quainter sleep. The rooms are obviously small, but luxuries including Bose hi-fis and Penhaligons toiletries are a really welcome surprise, and the breakfast is simply fab: Quantock Mueslis, locally made jams and sausages from rare-breed pigs.

Reeve's RESTAURANT ££

(☎01643-821414; www.reevesrestaurantdunster.co.uk; lunch £4.95-14.25, dinner £12.95-24.95; ⏲lunch Thu-Sun, dinner Tue-Sat) Oak girders, worn-wood tables and twinkling candles create a bewitchingly cosy atmosphere at Reeve's, a reliable stalwart for dining in Dunster. Rich, indulgent dishes are the watchword – guineafowl, lamb's liver, venison, slow-roasted partridge – but it's refreshingly unstuffy.

Luttrell Arms PUB, HOTEL ££

(☎01643-821555; www.luttrellarms.co.uk; High St; Ⓟ) In medieval times this glorious old coaching inn was the guest house of the Abbots of Cleeve. Huge flagstones, heavy armchairs and faded tapestries dot the lounge – a perfect fit for the hearty bar food. The beamed **rooms** (B&B d £116-150) might be too olde-worlde for some.

Getting There & Away

The **West Somerset Railway** (☎01643-704996; www.west-somerset-railway.co.uk) stops at Dunster during the summer. For buses, see p293.

DEVON

If counties were capable of emotions, those in the rest of England would envy Devon.

It's all to do with a rippling landscape studded with prehistoric sites, historic homes, vibrant cities, ancient villages, intimate coves and wild, wild moors. If exhilaration is your thing, you'll be right at home: here you can get churned around by crashing surf, ride white-water rapids or hike hundreds of miles along precipitous cliffs. Landscape and lifestyle ensure food is fresh from furrow or sea – eat a Michelin-starred meal at a swanky restaurant or a fresh crab sandwich sitting on the beach – it's up to you. In Devon a day's drive can take you from Exeter's serene cathedral, via Torbay's touristy coast to the yachting haven of Dartmouth, where Agatha Christie's mysterious house waits in the wings. Totnes provides the eco-awareness, Plymouth provides the party and wilderness, Dartmoor provides the great escape, while the North Coast – rugged, remote and surf-dashed – draws you into the waves. The delights of Devon are tempting indeed.

Information

Visit Devon (www.visitdevon.co.uk)

Getting Around

Tourist offices stock timetables, the *Devon Bus Map* and the *Discovery Guide to Dartmoor*.

Traveline South West (www.travelinesw.com) Details all bus and train timetables.

Bus

First (www.firstgroup.com) The key bus operator in Dartmoor, north, south and east Devon.

Stagecoach Devon (www.stagecoachbus.com) Operates mostly local buses, especially in Exeter and Torbay.

Bus passes:

First Seven day (adult/family £32.50/49) Week-long equivalent.

Firstday Southwest (adult/child/family £7/5.70/17.20) A day's unlimited bus travel on First buses in Devon and Cornwall.

Stagecoach Explorer (adult/child/family £6.50/4/16) One day's travel on its southwest network.

Train

Devon's main line skirts southern Dartmoor, running from Exeter to Plymouth and on to Cornwall. Branch lines include the 39-mile Exeter–Barnstaple Tarka Line; the 15-mile Plymouth–Gunnislake Tamar Valley Line and the scenic Exeter–Torquay Paignton line.

The Devon and Cornwall Rover allows unlimited, off-peak train trips across Devon and Cornwall. Eight day's travel in 15 costs an adult £60; and three day's travel in one week is £40.

REGIONAL RESOURCES

www.visitsouthwest.com Covers the region from Bath and Dorset west to Cornwall.

www.visithampshire.co.uk Hampshire-specific site.

Exeter

POP 116,393

Well-heeled and comfortable, Exeter exudes evidence of its centuries-old role as the spiritual and administrative heart of Devon. The city's gloriously Gothic cathedral presides over stretches of cobbled streets, fragments of the terracotta Roman city wall and a tumbling of medieval and Georgian buildings. A snazzy new shopping centre brings bursts of the modern, thousands of university students ensure a buzzing nightlife and the vibrant quayside acts as a launch pad for cycling or kayaking trips. Throw in some stylish places to stay and eat and you have a relaxed but lively base for further explorations.

History

Exeter's past can be read in its buildings. The Romans marched in around AD 55 – their 17-hectare fortress included a 2-mile defensive wall, crumbling sections of which remain, especially in Rougemont and Northernhay Gardens. Saxon and Norman times saw growth: a castle went up in 1068, the cathedral 40 years later. The Tudor wool boom brought Exeter an export trade, riches and half-timbered houses; prosperity continued into the Georgian era when hundreds of merchants built genteel homes. The Blitz of WWII brought devastation. In just one night in 1942, 156 people died and 12 hectares of the city were flattened. In the 21st century the £220 million Princesshay shopping centre added himmering glass and steel lines to the architectural mix.

Sights

Exeter Cathedral CATHEDRAL

(www.exeter-cathedral.org.uk; The Close; adult/child £5/free; ⌚9.30am-4.45pm Mon-Sat) Magnificent in warm, honey-coloured stone, Exeter's Cathedral Church of St Peter is framed by lawns and wonky half-timbered buildings – a quintessentially English scene often peopled by picnickers snacking to the sound of the bells.

The site has been a religious one since at least the 5th-century but the Normans started the current building in 1114; the towers of today's cathedral date from that period. In 1270 Bishop Bronescombe remodelled the whole building, a process that took 90 years and introduced a mix of Early English and Decorated Gothic styles.

Above the **Great West Front** scores of weather-worn figures line a screen that was once brightly painted. It now forms the largest collection of 14th-century sculpture in England. Inside, the ceiling is mesmerising – the longest unbroken Gothic vaulting in the world, it sweeps up to meet ornate ceiling bosses in gilt and vibrant colours. Look out for the 15th-century **Exeter Clock** in the north transept: in keeping with medieval astronomy it shows the earth as a golden ball at the centre of the universe with the sun, a fleur-de-lys, travelling round. Still ticking and whirring, it chimes on the hour.

The huge oak canopy over the **Bishop's Throne** was carved in 1312, while the 1350 **minstrels' gallery** is decorated with 12 angels playing musical instruments. Cathedral staff will point out the famous sculpture of the lady with two left feet and the tiny **St James Chapel**, built to repair the one destroyed in the Blitz in 1942. Look out for its unusual carvings: a cat, a mouse and, oddly, a rugby player.

In the **Refectory** (⌚10am-4.45pm Mon-Sat) you can tuck into cakes, quiches and soups at trestle tables surrounded by vaulted ceilings, stained glass and busts of the great, the good and the dead.

Guided tours (free; ⌚11am & 2.30pm Mon-Fri & 11am Sat) are excellent and last

Exeter

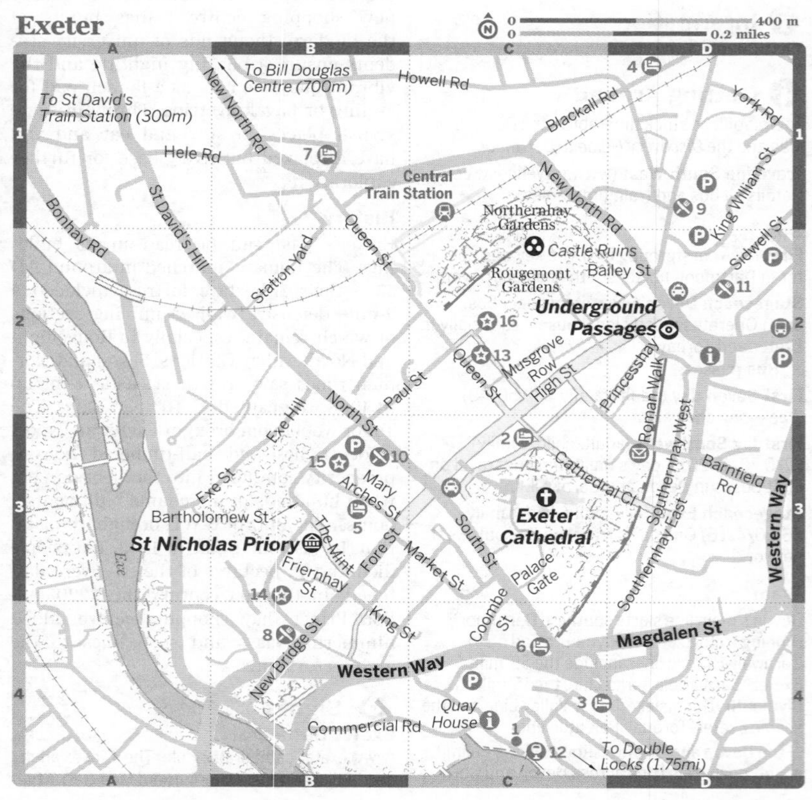

45 minutes. Intensely atmospheric Evensong services are held at 5.30pm Monday to Friday and 3pm on Saturday and Sunday.

FREE **Bill Douglas Centre** MUSEUM
(www.billdouglas.org; Old Library, Prince of Wales Rd; ⏲10am-5pm Mon-Fri) A delightful homage to film and fun, the Bill Douglas Centre is a compact collection of all things celluloid, from magic lanterns to Mickey Mouse. Inside discover just what the butler did see and why the flicks are called the flicks. In a mass of movie memorabilia Charlie Chaplin bottle stoppers mingle with Ginger Rogers playing cards, James Bond board games and Star Wars toys.

St Nicholas Priory MEDIEVAL BUILDING
(www.exeter.gov.uk/priory; Mint La; adult/child £2/free; ⏲10am-5pm Mon-Sat school holidays) This 900 year-old former Benedictine monastery is built out of beautiful russet stone and vividly evokes life inside a late-Elizabethan town house. Expect brightly coloured furnishings, elaborate plaster ceilings and intricate oak panelling.

Exeter

Top Sights

Exeter Cathedral....C3
St Nicholas Priory....B3
Underground Passages....D2

Activities, Courses & Tours

1 Saddles & Paddles....C4

Sleeping

2 ABode at the Royal Clarence....C3
3 Globe Backpackers....C4
4 Raffles....D1
5 St Olaves....B3
6 White Hart....C4
7 Woodbine....B1

Eating

8 @Angela's....B4
9 Harry's....D1
10 Herbies....B3
Michael Caines....(see 2)
11 tyepyedong....D2

Drinking

12 On The Waterfront....C4

Entertainment

13 Cavern Club....C2
14 Exeter Picturehouse....B3
15 Mamma Stone's....B3
16 Phoenix....C2

Activities

The River Exe and the Exeter Canal are framed by foot and cycle paths which wind south from **the Quay**, past pubs (see p300), beside an ever broadening estuary towards the sea, 10 miles away. **Saddles & Paddles** (☎01392-424241; www.sadpad.com; 4 Kings Wharf, the Quay; ⏲9.30am-5.30pm) rents out bikes (adult per hour/day £6/15), kayaks (per hour/day £7/25) and Canadian canoes (per hour/day £15/35); the tourist office stocks maps.

Tours

FREE **Redcoat Tours** HERITAGE TOUR
(www.exeter.gov.uk/visiting; ⏲2-5pm daily Apr-Oct, 2-3pm daily Nov-Mar) For an informed and entertaining introduction to Exeter's history, it's hard to beat these 1½ hour tours. Themes range from murder and trade to Romans and religion – there are even torch-lit prowls through the catacombs and night-time ghost walks. Tours leave from Cathedral Yard or the Quay, pick up a program from the tourist office.

Underground Passages SUBTERRANEAN TOUR
(☎01392-665887; www.exeter.gov.uk/passages; Paris St; adult/child £5/3.50; ⏲9.30am-5.30pm Mon-Sat Jun-Sep, 11.30am-4pm Tue-Sun Oct-May) Prepare to crouch down, don a hard hat and possibly get spooked in what is the only system of its kind open to the public in England. These medieval, vaulted passages were built to house pipes bringing fresh water to the city. Unlike modern utility companies, the authorities opted to have permanent access for repairs, rather than dig up the streets each time – genius. Guides lead you on a scramble through the network regaling you with tales of ghosts, escape routes and cholera. The last tour is an hour before closing; it can get busy so it's best to book.

Sleeping

ABode at the Royal Clarence HOTEL ££
(☎01392-319955; www.abodehotels.co.uk/exeter; Cathedral Yard; r £115-135, ste £175-260; 📶) Georgian grandeur meets minimalist chic in these, the poshest rooms in town, where wonky floors and stained glass blend with pared-down furniture and neutral tones. The top-end suite is bigger

than most people's apartments; its slanted ceilings and beams frame a grandstand Cathedral view.

Raffles B&B ££
(☎01392-270200; www.raffles-exeter.co.uk; 11 Blackall Rd; s/d £42/72; P) Creaking with antiques and oozing atmosphere, this late-Victorian town house is an appealing blend of old woods and tasteful modern fabrics. Plant stands and dado rails add to the turn-of-the-century feel, while the largely organic breakfasts, walled garden and much coveted parking make it a great value choice.

Woodbine B&B ££
(☎01392-203302; www.woodbineguesthouse.co.uk; 1 Woodbine Tce; s/d £38/66; wifi) A bit of a surprise sits behind this archetypal flower-framed terrace: fresh, contemporary rooms with low beds and flashes of burgundy – there's even underfloor heating in the showers.

White Hart HOTEL ££
(☎01392-279897; www.english-inns.co.uk; 66 South St; s £60, d £60-70; P) They've been putting people up here since the Plantagenets were on the throne in the 14th century. The courtyard is a wisteria-fringed bobble of cobbles and the bar is book-lined and beamed. Rooms are either traditional (dark woods and rich drapes) or contemporary (laminate floors and light fabrics).

St Olaves HOTEL ££
(☎01392-217736; www.olaves.co.uk; Mary Arches St; d/ste/f £125/155/165; P) This hotel's swirling spiral staircase is so gorgeous it's tempting to sleep beside it. But if you did, you'd miss out on the 18th century-with-contemporary-twist bedrooms: expect rococo mirrors, brass bedsteads and plush furnishings.

Globe Backpackers HOSTEL £
(☎01392-215521; www.exeterbackpackers.co.uk; 71 Holloway St; dm £16.50, d £42; @wifi) A spotlessly clean, relaxed, rambling house near the Quay. There's only one double room, so book ahead.

Eating

Michael Caines FINE DINING ££
(☎01392-223638; www.michaelcaines.com; Cathedral Yard; mains £25; ⏱breakfast, lunch & dinner) Housed in the Royal Clarence and run by a double Michelin-starred chef, the food here is a complex blend of Westcountry ingredients and full-bodied French flavours. Try the cauliflower and truffle soup with roasted scallops, or the slow-roast beef with celeriac purée and Madeira sauce. The set lunches are a bargain (per two/three courses £15/20), while the seven-course tasting menu (£65) really is one to linger over.

@Angela's BRITISH ££
(☎01392 499038; www.angelasrestaurant.co.uk; 38 New Bridge St; dinner mains £17; ⏱dinner Tue-Sat, lunch Wed-Sat) Dedication to sourcing local ingredients sometimes sees the chef at this smart bistro rising before dawn to bag the best fish at Brixham Market; his sea bass with caramelised ginger is worth the trip alone. The lamb and beef has grazed Devon fields, while local venison is made memorable by a rich redcurrant and chocolate sauce. Wise foodies opt for the pre-booked, three-course lunch (£18).

Herbies VEGETARIAN £
(15 North St; mains £5-9; ⏱lunch Mon-Sat, dinner Tue-Sat) Cosy and gently groovy, Herbies has been cheerfully feeding Exeter's vegetarians for more than 20 years. It's *the* place in town to tuck into delicious butterbean and vegetable pie, Moroccan *tagine* or cashew nut loaf. They're strong on vegan dishes too.

Harry's EUROPEAN ££
(www.harrys-exeter.co.uk; 86 Longbrook St; mains £8-12; ⏱lunch & dinner Mon-Sat) Harry's is the kind of welcoming neighbourhood bistro you wish was on your own doorstep, but rarely is. The decor is all wooden chairs, blackboards and gilt mirrors; the food includes seared tuna, Spanish ham with marinated figs, and a hearty three bean chilli.

tyepyedong NOODLE BAR £
(www.tyepyedong.com; 175 Sidwell St; mains £7-9; ⏱lunch & dinner Mon-Sat) Tucked away in an unlikely terrace of postwar shops, this minimalist eatery rustles up great value *ramen* and *udon* noodles – at lunchtime a dish-and-a-drink will only cost you £5.40.

Drinking

Double Locks PUB
(www.doublelocks.com; Canal Banks) A bit of a local legend, this atmospheric former lock-house sits 2 miles south of the quay, beside the Exeter Ship Canal. Scarred floorboards, battered board games and excellent ale lend it a chilled vibe – helped by the real fires, waterside terrace and better-than-average bar food (mains £9).

WORTH A TRIP

COMBE HOUSE

The sumptuous **Combe House** (☎01404-540400; www.thishotel.com; Gittisham; s £159-364, d £179-344, ste £384) is more like a National Trust property than a hotel. The great hall of this Elizabethan country manor is floor-to-ceiling wood panels, while ancient oak furniture and original Tudor paintings pop up everywhere. The historic splendour is matched by modern luxuries – guests are pampered with crisp cottons, monogrammed towels, rain showers and sumptuous throws. One room even has a vast copper washtub for a bath. It's all set on a massive estate near Gittisham, 14 miles east of Exeter.

On The Waterfront BAR
(www.waterfrontexeter.co.uk; The Quay) In 1835 this was a warehouse, now its red-brick, barrel-vaulted ceilings stretch back from a thoroughly modern bar. The tables outside are a popular spot for a riverside pint.

☆ Entertainment

Phoenix ARTS CENTRE
(www.exeterphoenix.org.uk; Gandy St) The city's art and soul; Phoenix is a vibrant hub of exhibitions, performance, music, dance, film, classes and workshops. There's a buzzing cafe-bar too.

Exeter Picturehouse CINEMA
(www.picture houses.co.uk; 51 Bartholomew St West) An intimate, independent cinema, screening mainstream and art-house movies.

Mamma Stone's LIVE MUSIC
(www.mamastones.com; 1 Mary Arches St; ⌚8pm-midnight, 9pm-2am when bands play) Über-cool venue showcasing everything from acoustic sets to pop, folk and jam nights. Mamma Stone's daughter, Joss (yes, *the* Joss Stone), plays sometimes too.

Cavern Club LIVE MUSIC
(www.cavernclub.co.uk; 83-84 Queen St; ⌚11am-5pm Mon-Sat, 8pm-1am Sun-Thu, 11am-2am Fri & Sat) A long-standing club-performance space, staging big-name DJs and breaking acts from the indie scene.

Information

Exeter Library (Castle St; per 30 min £2; ⌚9.30am-7pm Mon, Tue, Thu & Fri, 10am-5pm Wed, 9.30am-4pm Sat, 11am-2.30pm Sun).

Police station (☎08452 777444; Heavitree Rd; ⌚24hr)

Royal Devon & Exeter Hospital (Barrack Rd)

Tourist office Main (☎01392-665700; www.exeterandessentialdevon.com; Paris St; ⌚9am-5pm Mon-Sat, 10am-4pm Sun Jul & Aug); Quay House (☎01392-271611; The Quay; ⌚10am-5pm Easter-Oct, 11am-4pm Sat & Sun only Nov-Easter)

ⓘ Getting There & Away

Air

Exeter International Airport (www.exeter-airport.co.uk) Scheduled services link with cities in Europe and the UK, including Glasgow, Manchester and Newcastle, as well as the Channel Islands and the Isles of Scilly.

FlyBe (ww.flybe.com) Key operator.

Bus

On Sundays between June and mid-September Bus 82, the Transmoor Link, makes five trips from Exeter to Plymouth via Moretonhampstead, Postbridge, Princetown and Yelverton. Standard routes:

Bude (£5.90, three hours, five Monday to Saturday) Bus X9; runs via Okehampton.

Moretonhampstead (45 minutes, seven daily Monday to Saturday) Bus 359.

Plymouth (£6, 1¼ hours, hourly Monday to Saturday, three on Sunday) Bus X38.

Sidmouth (50 minutes, one to three hourly) Bus 52.

Totnes (one hour, six daily Monday to Saturday, two on Sunday) Bus X64.

Weymouth (six to nine daily, three on Sunday) The Jurassic Coastlinx (Bus X53) runs via Beer and Lyme Regis.

Train

Main-line and branch-line trains run from Exeter St David's and Exeter Central stations:

Barnstaple (£8, 1¼ hours, hourly Monday to Saturday, four to six on Sunday) The picturesque Tarka Line.

Bristol (£18, 1¼ hours, half-hourly)

Exmouth (£4, hourly, 40 minutes)

London Paddington (£45, 2½ hours, hourly)

Paignton (£6.30, 50 minutes, half-hourly)

Penzance (£17, three hours, hourly)

Plymouth (£7.40, one hour, two or three per hour)

Torquay (£6, 45 minutes, hourly)

Totnes (£6, 35 minutes, two or three per hour)

Getting Around

To/From the Airport

Buses 56 and 379 run from the bus station and Exeter St David's train station to Exeter Airport (20 to 30 minutes, hourly 7am-6pm).

Bicycle

See Saddle & Paddles (p299).

Bus

Bus H1/2 links St David's train station and the High St, passing near the bus station.

Car

Hire options include **Europcar** (www.europcar.co.uk). Park & Ride buses (adult/child £2/1.30) run from Sowton (near M5, junction 30), Matford and Honiton Rd (near M5, junction 29) every 10 minutes, Monday to Saturday.

Taxi

Ranks are at St David's train station and on High St. Other options:

Capital Taxis (☎01392-758472)

Club Cars (☎01392-341615)

Gemini (☎01392-342152)

Around Exeter

POWDERHAM CASTLE

The historic home of the Earl of Devon is **Powderham** (www.powderham.co.uk; adult/child £9.50/7.50; ⏰11am-4.30pm Sun-Fri Apr-Oct). A stately but still friendly place, it was built in 1391, damaged in the Civil War and remodelled in the Victorian era. A visit takes in a fine wood-panelled Great Hall, parkland with 650 deer and a glimpse of life 'below stairs' in the kitchen. The earl and family are still resident and, despite its grandeur, for charming, fleeting moments it feels like you're actually wandering through someone's sitting room.

Powderham is on the River Exe near Kenton, 8 miles south of Exeter. Bus 2 runs from Exeter (30 minutes, every 20 minutes Monday to Friday.

A LA RONDE

The delightfully quirky 16-sided **cottage** (NT; www.nationaltrust.org.uk; Summer Lane, Exmouth; adult/child £6.70/3.40; ⏰11am-5pm Sat-Wed mid-Mar–Jun & Sep-Oct, 11am-5pm Fri-Wed Jul-Aug) was built in 1796 for two spinster cousins to display a mass of curiosities acquired on a 10-year European grand tour. Its glass alcoves, low lintels and tiny doorways mean it's like clambering through a doll's house – highlights are a delicate feather frieze in the drawing room and a gallery smothered with a thousand seashells. In a fabulous collision of old and new, this can only be seen via remote control CCTV from the butler's pantry. The house is 10 miles south of Exeter, near Exmouth; bus 57 runs close by.

Torquay & Paignton

POP 110,370

For decades the bright 'n' breezy seaside resort of Torquay pitched itself as an exotic 'English Riviera' – playing on a mild microclimate, palm trees and promenades. But these days Torquay's nightclubs and bars attract a much younger crowd and the result is a sometimes bizarre clash of cultures: coach parties meet stag parties on streets lined by fudge shops and slightly saucy postcards. Chuck in some truly top-notch restaurants, a batch of good beaches and an Agatha Christie connection, and it all makes for some grand days out beside the sea. Just to the south of Torquay is Paignton with its seafront prom, multi-coloured beach huts and faded 19th-century pier.

Sights & Activities

Beaches — BEACHES

Torquay boasts no fewer than 20 beaches and a surprising 22 miles of coast. Holidaymakers flock to the central **Torre Abbey Sands** (covered by water at very high tides); the locals opt for the sand-and-shingle beaches beside the 240ft red-clay cliffs at **Babbacombe**. These can be accessed by a glorious 1920s **funicular railway** (Torquay; adult/child return £1.75/1.20; ⏰9.30am-5.25pm Easter-Sep); a memorable trip in a tiny wooden carriage that shuttles up and down rails set into the cliff.

Paignton Zoo — ZOO

(www.paigntonzoo.org.uk; Totnes Rd, Paignton; adult/child £11.90/8.40; ⏰10am-5pm) This 80-acre site is dotted with spacious enclosures re-creating habitats as varied as savannah, wetlands, tropical forest and

WORTH A TRIP

RIVER COTTAGE CANTEEN

TV chef Hugh Fearnley-Whittingstall campaigns on sustainable food, so it makes sense that his **bistro** (www.rivercottage.net; Trinity Sq, Axminster; mains £8; ⏲breakfast & lunch daily, dinner Thu-Sat) champions local, seasonal and organic ingredients. Hearty flavours include pike and parsley soup, Portland crab with fennel, and garlic mushrooms on toast with sorrel and goat's cheese shavings – a kind of deeply satisfying English crostini. Drinks include Stinger Beer, brewed from (carefully) handpicked Dorset nettles; it's spicy with just a hint of tingle. Alternatively, book a four-course gastronomic delight at the nearby **River Cottage HQ** (☎01297-630313; www.rivercottage.net; 4-course meal £60; ⏲dates vary) for a truly memorable evening.

Axminster is 30 miles east of Exeter. Trains (£8.40, 40 minutes, hourly) leave from Exeter's St David's station.

desert. Highlights are the crocodile swamp, orang-utan island, vast glass-walled lion enclosure, and a lemur wood, where you walk over a plank suspension bridge as the primates leap around in the surrounding trees.

Living Coasts ZOO
(www.livingcoasts.org.uk; Beacon Quay, Torquay; adult/child £9.50/7.25; ⏲10am-5pm) A vast open-plan aviary bringing you up-close to free-roaming penguins, punk-rocker style tufted puffins and disarmingly cute bank cormorants.

Ferry to Brixham BOAT TRIP
(www.greenwayferry.co.uk; Princess Pier; adult/child return £7/4; ⏲10 sailings daily April-Oct) Among other operators, Greenway Ferry offers grandstand views of beaches, crumbling cliffs and grand Victorian hotels.

Sleeping

Cary Arms BOUTIQUE HOTEL £££
(☎01803-327110; www.caryarms.co.uk; Babbacombe Beach, Torquay; d £150-250, ste £200-350) The great British seaside has just gone seriously stylish. At this oh-so-chic bolthole, neutral tones are jazzed up by candy-striped cushions; balconies directly overlook the beach and there's even a stick of rock with the hotel's name running through it on your pillow.

Headland View B&B ££
(☎01803-312612; www.headlandview.com; Babbacombe Downs, Torquay; s/d £45/70; P) Set high on the cliffs at Babbacombe, this cheery terrace is awash with nauticalia: from boat motifs on the curtains to 'welcome' lifebelts on the walls. Four rooms have tiny flower-filled balconies overlooking a cracking stretch of sea.

Torquay International Backpackers HOSTEL £
(☎01803-299924; www.torquaybackpackers.co.uk; 119 Abbey Rd, Torquay; dm/d £15/32; @☜) Relics of happy travels (world maps, board games and homemade wind chimes) are everywhere in this funky, friendly, laid-back hostel. The owner, Jane, hands out guitars and organise barbecues, beach trips and local pub tours.

Hillcroft BOUTIQUE B&B ££
(☎01803-297247; www.thehillcroft.co.uk; 9 St Lukes Rd, Torquay; s £65-110, d £75-85, ste £100-130; @☜) Classy rooms veer from French antique to Asian chic; the top-floor suite is gorgeous.

Eating & Drinking

Room in the Elephant FINE DINING £££
(☎01803-200044; www.elephantrestaurant.co.uk; 3 Beacon Tce, Torquay; 6 courses £45; ⏲dinner Tue-Sat) A restaurant to remember. Torbay's Michelin-starred eatery is defined by seriously good food and imaginative flavour fusions: squid and cauliflower risotto or chicken with liver and fig salad. The sumptuous cheeseboard groans under the very best Westcountry offerings.

Number 7 SEAFOOD ££
(☎01803-295055; www.no7-fish.com; Beacon Tce, Torquay; mains £15; ⏲lunch Wed-Sat, dinner daily) Fabulous smells fill the air at this buzzing harbourside bistro, where the menu is packed with super-fresh crab, lobster and monkfish, often with unexpected twists. Try the king scallops with vermouth or fish and prawn tempura.

Elephant Brasserie EUROPEAN ££
(☎01803-200044; www.elephantrestaurant.co.uk; 3 Beacon Tce, Torquay; 2/3 courses £23/27;

AGATHA CHRISTIE

Torquay is the birthplace of the 'Queen of Crime', Agatha Christie (1890–1976), author of 75 novels and 33 plays, anbrid creator of Hercule Poirot, the moustachioed, immodest Belgian detective, and Miss Marple, the surprisingly perceptive busy-body spinster. Born Agatha Miller, she grew up, courted and honeymooned in the resort town of Torquay and also worked as a hospital dispenser here during WWI, thus acquiring her famous knowledge of poisons.

The tourist office stocks the Agatha Christie Mile leaflet (free), which guides you round significant local sites, while **Torquay Museum** (529 Babbacombe Rd, Torquay; adult/child £4/2.50; ⊙10am-5pm Mon-Sat & 1.30-5pm Sun Jul-Sep) has a huge collection of photos, handwritten notes and display cases devoted to her famous detectives. The highlight though is **Greenway** (p306), her summer home near Dartmouth. The **Greenway Ferry** (☎01803-844010; www.greenwayferry.co.uk) sails there from Princess Pier in Torquay, and from Dartmouth and Totnes. Boats sail only when the property is open; times vary and it's best to book.

⊙lunch & dinner Tue-Sat) The setting may be less formal, but the bistro below Torquay's Michelin-starred Room in the Elephant (p303) is still super-stylish. Treatments include lemon sole with shellfish ragout and Noilly Prat cream, and Devon duckling with spiced honey jus.

Orange Tree EUROPEAN ££
(☎01803-213936; www.orangetreerestaurant.co.uk; 14 Park Hill Rd, Torquay; mains £17; ⊙dinner Mon-Sat) This award-winning brasserie adds a dash of Continental flair to local fish, meat and game. Try to resist the Brixham crab lasagne with crab bisque or the south Devon steak with a rich blue cheese sauce. Then succumb to Chocolate Temptation, a brownie-mousse and parfait combo.

Hole in the Wall PUB
(6 Park Lane, Torquay) Heavily beamed, Tardis-like boozer with a tiny terrace; an atmospheric spot for a pint.

ℹ Information

Tourist office (☎01803-211211; www.theenglishriviera.co.uk; Vaughan Pde, Torquay; ⊙9.30am-5pm Mon-Sat, daily Jun-Sep)

ℹ Getting There & Away

Bus

Bus 12 runs to Paignton from Torquay (20 minutes, every 15 minutes) and onto Brixham (40 minutes). Bus 111 goes from Torquay to Totnes (one hour, hourly Monday to Saturday, four on Sunday) and on to Dartmouth.

Ferry

Regular ferries shuttle between Torquay and Brixham.

Train

A branch train line runs from Exeter via Torquay (£5.20, 45 minutes, hourly) to Paignton (£5.40, 50 minutes).

Paignton & Dartmouth Steam Railway (www.dartmouthrailriver.co.uk; Paignton Station, Paignton; adult/child return £10/7.50; ⊙May-Sep) Puffs from Paignton to Kingswear (30 minutes, four to nine trains a day), which is linked by ferry to Dartmouth (car/pedestrian £3.50/1, six minutes).

Brixham

POP 17,460

An appealing, pastel-painted tumbling of fishermen's cottages leads down to Brixham's horseshoe harbour, signalling a very different place from Torquay. Here gently tacky arcades coexist with winding streets, brightly coloured boats and one of England's busiest fishing ports. Although picturesque, Brixham is far from a neatly packaged resort, and its brand of gritty charm offers a more accurate glimpse of life along Devon's coast.

Sights

Golden Hind SAILING SHIP
(The Quay; adult/child £4/3; ⊙10am-4pm Mar-Sep) Devon sailor and explorer Sir Francis Drake carried out a treasure-seeking circumnavigation of the globe aboard the *Golden Hind*, in the late 1500s. On this remarkably small, but full-sized, replica you get to cross the gangplank, peer in the captain's cabin and prowl around the poop deck.

Brixham Heritage Museum MUSEUM
(www.brixhamheritage.org.uk; Bolton Cross; adult/child £2/free; ⊙10am-4pm Tue-Sat

Apr-Oct, 10am-1pm Tue-Fri Mar) Explores the town's salty history with exhibits on smuggling and the curious items dragged up by local trawlers.

Eating & Drinking

David Walker FISHMONGER £
(Unit B, Fish Market; 9am-4pm Mon-Fri, to 1pm Sat) The place to connect with Brixham's fishing heritage, the counters here are piled high with the day's catch, plus picnic goodies such as huge, cooked shell-on prawns (per 500g £7) and dressed crab (£4.50 each).

Maritime PUB
(79 King St) Gloriously eccentric old boozer smothered in thousands of key rings, stone jugs and chamber pots and presided over by a chatty parrot called Mr Tibbs.

Information

Tourist office (01803-211211; www.theenglishriviera.co.uk; The Quay; 9.30am-4.30pm Mon-Sat, plus 10am-4pm Sun Jun-Sep)

Getting There & Away

Bus

Bus 22 shuttles to Kingswear (20 minutes, one to two hourly); where you can catch the ferry to Dartmouth. Bus 12 connects Torquay and Brixham via Paignton (see p304).

Ferry

Regular ferries shuttle between Brixham and Torquay.

Dartmouth & Around

POP 5693

A bewitching blend of primary-coloured boats and delicately shaded houses, Dartmouth is hard to resist. Buildings cascade down steep, wooded slopes towards the River Dart while 17th-century shops with splendidly carved and gilded fronts line narrow lanes. Its popularity with a trendy sailing set risks imposing too many boutiques and upmarket restaurants, but Dartmouth is also a busy port and the constant traffic of working boats ensures an authentic tang of the sea. Agatha Christie's summer home and a captivating art-deco house are both nearby, adding to the town's appeal.

Dartmouth hugs the quay on the west side of the Dart estuary, it's linked to the village of **Kingswear** on the east bank by a string of car and foot ferries, providing a key transport link to Torbay.

Sights

TOP CHOICE **Greenway** HISTORIC HOME
(NT; 01803-842382; www.nationaltrust.org.uk; Greenway Rd, Galmpton; adult/child £8/4; 10.30am-5pm Wed-Sun Mar-Oct, Tue-Sun mid-Jul–Aug) The enchanting summer home of crime writer Agatha Christie sits beside the River Dart near Dartmouth. Part-guided tours allow you to wander between rooms where the furnishings and knick-knacks are much as she left them. So you can check out the piles of hats in the lobby, the books in her library and the clothes in her wardrobe, and listen to her speak (via a replica radio) in the drawing room.

Woods speckled with splashes of magnolias, daffodils and hydrangeas, frame the water, while the planting creates intimate, secret spaces – the boathouse and views over the river are delightful. In Christie's book *Dead Man's Folly,* Greenway doubles as Nasse House, with the boathouse making an appearance in a murder scene.

Driving to Greenway is discouraged and you have to pre-book parking spaces. The **Greenway Ferry** (0845 489418; www.greenwayferry.co.uk) runs regularly from Dartmouth (adult/child return £7.50/5.50), Totnes (adult/child return £11/7.50) and Torquay (adult/child return £19/12). Times vary and it's best to book. Alternatively, hike along the **Dart Valley Trail** from Kingswear (4 miles).

Coleton Fishacre HISTORIC HOME
(NT; www.nationaltrust.org.uk; Brownstone Rd, Kingswear; adult/child £7.40/3.70; 10.30am-5pm Sat-Wed Mar-Oct) For an enchanting glimpse of Jazz Age glamour, drop by this former home of the D'Oyly Carte family of theatre impresarios. Built in the 1920s, its gorgeous art deco embellishments include original Lalique tulip uplighters, comic bathroom tiles and a stunning saloon – complete with tinkling piano. The croquet terrace leads to deeply shelved subtropical gardens and suddenly revealed vistas of the sea. Hike the 4 miles along the cliffs from Kingswear, or drive.

Dartmouth Castle CASTLE
(EH; www.english-heritage.org.uk; adult/child £4.50./2.30; 10am-5pm Apr-Sep, to 4pm Oct, 10am-4pm Sat & Sun Nov-Mar) Mazy passages, atmospheric guardrooms and great views

from the battlements. Get there via the tiny, open-top **Castle Ferry** (return £1.40; ⌚10am-4.45pm Easter-Oct).

Sleeping

Brown's BOUTIQUE HOTEL ££
(☎01803-832572; www.brownshoteldartmouth.co.uk; 29 Victoria Rd; s £70, d £90-180; P) How do you combine leather curtains, pheasant feather-covered lampshades, animal-print chairs and still make it look classy? The owners of this smoothly sumptuous sleep spot have worked it out. Look out for the lobster and frites evenings in their tapas bar too.

Just B ROOMS £
(☎01803-834311; www.justbdartmouth.com; reception Fosse St; r £64, apt £65) The 11 stylish options here range from bedrooms with bathrooms to mini-apartments. All feature snazzy furnishings, crisp cottons and comfy beds. They're scattered over three central properties, and the 'just B' policy (no '&B' means no breakfast) keeps the price down.

Hill View House B&B ££
(☎01803-839372; www.hillviewdartmouth.co.uk; 76 Victoria Rd; s/d £47/70) This eco-conscious house features environmentally-friendly toiletries, natural cotton linen, long-life light bulbs and organic breakfasts. Rooms are tastefully decked out in cream and brown and there's a 5% discount for travellers not using cars.

Eating

TOP CHOICE **Seahorse** SEAFOOD £££
(☎01803-835147; 5 South Embankment; mains £17-23, 2-course lunch £15; ⌚lunch Wed-Sat, dinner Tue-Sat) The fish here is so fresh they change the menu twice a day. So depending on what's been landed at Brixham (7 miles away) or Dartmouth (a few yards away) you might get cuttlefish in Chianti, sea bream with roasted garlic, or fried local squid with garlic mayonnaise. The river views are charming, the atmosphere relaxed; definitely one not to miss.

New Angel FINE DINING £££
(☎01803-839425; 2 South Embankment; mains £19-27, 2 courses £19-28; ⌚breakfast, lunch & dinner Tue-Sat) Dartmouth's Michelin-starred eatery is run by celebrity chef John Burton Race (of *French Leave* fame), so it serves up pheasant, Devon duck and local fish with more than a dash of Continental flair.

Alf Resco CAFE £
(Lower St; mains from £6; ⌚breakfast, lunch & dinner Wed-Sun) Tucked under a huge canvas awning, this cool hang-out brings a dash of cosmopolitan charm to town. Rickety wooden chairs and old street signs are scattered around a front terrace, making a great place for brunch alongside the riverboat crews.

Information

Tourist office (www.discoverdartmouth.com; Mayor's Ave; ⌚9.30am-5.30pm Mon-Sat, 10am-2pm Sun Apr-Oct, 9.30am-4.30pm Mon-Sat Nov-Mar)

Getting There & Away

Boat

River Link (www.dartmouthrailriver.co.uk) Cruises along the River Dart to Totnes (1¼ hours, two to four daily April to September).

Bus

Plymouth (£5.50, two hours, three to four daily) Bus 93; runs via Kingsbridge (one hour).

Torquay (1¾ hours, hourly Monday to Saturday, four on Sunday) Bus 111; goes via Totnes.

Ferry

Dartmouth's Higher and Lower Ferries both take cars and foot passengers; they shuttle across the river to Kingswear (car/pedestrian £3.50/1) every six minutes between 6.30am and 10.45pm.

Train

For the Paignton & Dartmouth Steam Railway, see p304.

Totnes & Around

POP 8194

Totnes has such a reputation for being alternative that local jokers wrote 'twinned with Narnia' under the town sign. For decades famous as Devon's hippie haven, eco-conscious Totnes also became Britain's first 'transition town' in 2005, when it began trying to wean itself off a dependence on oil. Sustainability aside, Totnes boasts a number of attractions.

Sights & Activities

Sharpham Vineyard VINEYARD
(☎01803-732203; www.sharpham.com; Ashprington; ⌚10am-5pm Mon-Sat Mar-Dec, daily Jun-Sep) The riverside terraces here give you the chance to wander among the vines, while a variety of **tours and tastings** (£5 to £50) allow you to learn about vinifica-

tion and indulge in tutored slurpings; it also makes cheese on the estate, so you can nibble that too. The vineyard is 3 miles south of Totnes, signed off the A381 – or walk from town along the Dart Valley Trail.

Totnes Castle CASTLE
(EH; www.english-heritage.org.uk; Castle St; adult/child £3.20/1.60; ⏲10am-5pm Apr-Sep, to 4pm Oct) The outer keep of Totnes' Norman motte-and-bailey fortress crowns a hill at the top of town, providing captivating views. Look out for the medieval loo too. The castle stays open until 6pm in July and August.

Devonshire Collection of Period Costume MUSEUM
(43 High St; adult/child £2/80p; ⏲11am-5pm Tue-Fri May-Sep) Beautifully displayed garments.

Canoe Adventures CANOE TRIPS
(☎01803-865301; www.canoe adventures.co.uk; adult/child £20/17) Voyages in 12-seater Canadian canoes – the monthly moonlit paddles are a treat.

Sleeping

Maltsters Arms B&B ££
(☎01803-732350; www.tuckenhay.com; Tuckenhay; d £75-115; P) The rooms in this old creekside pub are anything but ordinary, ranging from silky and eastern to authentically nautical – one even sports painted oil drums and real anchors. It's hidden away in the hamlet of Tuckenhay, 4 miles south of Totnes.

Steam Packet INN ££
(☎01803-863880; www.steampacketinn.co.uk; St Peters Quay; s/d/f £60/80/95; P) It's almost as if the minimalist bedrooms of this wharfside former warehouse have been plucked from the pages of a design magazine; expect painted wood panels, willow arrangements and neutral tones. Ask for a riverview room then watch the world float by.

Old Forge B&B ££
(☎01803-862174; www.oldforgetotnes.com; Seymour Pl; s £60, d £70-85, f £105; P wi-fi) This 600-year-old B&B used to be a smithy and the town jail – thankfully comfort has now replaced incarceration: deep red and sky blue furnishings cosy up to bright throws and spa baths. The delightful family room even has its own decked sun terrace.

Eating & Drinking

TOP CHOICE **Riverford Field Kitchen** EUROPEAN ££
(☎01803-762074; www.riverford.co.uk; Wash Barn; 2/3 courses £18/23; ⏲lunch daily, dinner Tue-Sat) At this futuristic farm bistro vegetables are plucked to order from the fields in front of you and the meats are organic and locally sourced. Eating is a convivial affair – diners sit at trestle tables and platters laden with food are passed around. Rich flavours and imaginative treatments might include marinated, grilled Moroccan lamb and British veg transformed by cumin or saffron. Planning laws require you to book, and take a free tour of the fields. The farm is 3 miles west of Totnes.

Rumour PUB RESTAURANT ££
(☎01803-864682; www.rumourtotnes.com; 30 High St; mains £9-15; ⏲lunch & dinner) It's so friendly here it's almost like dining in a friend's front room. The menu is packed with pizzas, pan-fried sea trout and Salcombe ice cream; their pioneering eco-policy includes using heat from the kitchen to warm the water.

Willow VEGETARIAN £
(87 High St; mains £7; ⏲lunch Mon-Sat, dinner Wed, Fri & Sat) A favourite hang-out for Totnes' New Agers. Tuck into couscous, quiches, hotpots and homemade cakes – look out for their curry nights too.

Information

Tourist office (☎01803-863168; www.totnesinformation.co.uk; Coronation Rd; ⏲9.30-5pm Mon-Fri & 10am-4pm Sat Apr-Oct, 10am-4pm Mon-Fri & 10am-1pm Sat Nov-Mar)

Getting There & Away

Boat

For river trips to Dartmouth, see p306.

Bus

Bus 111 goes to Torquay (30 minutes, hourly Monday to Saturday, four on Sunday) via Dartmouth.

Train

Trains shuttle at least hourly to Exeter (£5.40, 35 minutes) and Plymouth (£5, 30 minutes). The privately run South Devon Steam Railway (www.southdevonrailway.org) chuffs to Buckfastleigh (adult/child return £10/6, four or five a day, Easter to October) on the edge of Dartmoor.

Plymouth

POP 256,633

If parts of Devon are costume dramas or nature programs, Plymouth is a healthy dose of reality TV. Gritty, and certainly not always pretty, its centre has been subjected to buildings even the architects' mothers might question. But despite often being dismissed for its partying, poverty and urban problems, this is a city that's huge in spirit – and it comes with great assets. Its setting on the fringes of an impressive natural harbour and just a few miles from the wilderness expanse of Dartmoor makes it an ideal base for activities. Add a rich maritime history, a Barbican area creaking with half-timbered houses, some unusual attractions and a decidedly lively nightlife, and you have a place to reconnect with the real before another foray into the delights of Devon's chocolate-box-pretty moors and shores.

History

Plymouth's history is dominated by the sea. The first recorded cargo left the city in 1211 and by the late 16th century it was the port of choice for explorers and adventurers. It's waved off Sir Francis Drake, Sir Walter Raleigh, the fleet that defeated the Spanish Armada, the pilgrims who founded America, Charles Darwin, Captain Cook and countless boats carrying emigrants to Australia and New Zealand.

During WWII Plymouth suffered horrendously at the hands of the Luftwaffe – more than 1000 civilians died in the Blitz, which reduced the city centre to rubble. The 21st-century has brought large-scale regeneration of the city's waterfront areas and the architectural mishmash of the £200-million Drake Circus shopping centre.

Sights & Activities

Plymouth Hoe HISTORIC HEADLAND

Francis Drake supposedly spied the Spanish fleet from this grassy strip overlooking Plymouth Sound; the fabled bowling green on which he finished his game was probably where his **statue** now stands. Later the Hoe became a favoured holiday spot for the Victorian aristocracy, and the wide promenade is backed by an impressive array of multistoreyed villas and once-grand hotels.

Dominating the scene is the red-and-white-striped former lighthouse, **Smeaton's Tower** (The Hoe; adult/child £2/1; 10am-noon & 1-4pm Tue-Sat Apr-Oct, 10am-noon & 1-3pm Tue-Sat Nov-Mar), which was built 14 miles off shore on the Eddystone Rocks in 1759, then moved to the Hoe in 1882. Climbing its 93 steps provides an illuminating insight into lighthouse keepers' lives and stunning views of the city, Dartmoor and the sea.

Barbican HISTORIC DISTRICT

(www.plymouthbarbican.com) To get an idea of what old Plymouth was like before the Blitz, head for the Barbican, a district of cobbled streets and Tudor and Jacobean buildings, many now converted into galleries, craft shops and restaurants.

The Pilgrim Fathers' *Mayflower* set sail for America from the Barbican on 16 September 1620. The **Mayflower Steps** mark the point of departure – track down the passenger list displayed on the side of **Island House** nearby. Scores of other famous voyages are also marked by plaques at the steps, including one led by Captain James Cook, who set out from the Barbican in 1768 in search of a southern continent.

Plymouth Gin Distillery DISTILLERY

(01752-665292; www.plymouthgin.com; 60 Southside St; tours £6; tours at 11.30am, 12.30pm, 2.30pm & 3.30pm) This is the oldest producer of this kind of spirit in the world – it has been making gin here since 1793. The Royal Navy ferried it round the world in countless officers' messes and the brand was specified in the first recorded recipe for a dry martini in the 1930s. Tours wind past the stills and take in a tutored tasting before depositing you in the heavily beamed medieval bar for a free tipple. Between Easter and October, there are extra tours at 10.30am and 4.30pm.

National Marine Aquarium AQUARIUM

(www.national-aquarium.co.uk; Rope Walk; adult/child £11/6.50; 10am-6pm Apr-Oct, 10am-5pm Nov-Mar). The sharks here swim in coral seas that teem with moray eels and vividly coloured fish – there's even a loggerhead turtle called Snorkel who was rescued from a Cornish beach. Walk-through glass arches ensure huge rays glide over your head, while the immense Atlantic Reef tank, reveals just what's lurking a few miles offshore.

Boat Trips BOAT TRIPS

Sound Cruising (www.soundcruising.com; The Barbican) offers regular cruises from the Barbican Pontoon to the huge warships at Plymouth's naval base (adult/child £6.25/3, 1½ hours) and up the River Tamar to the Cornish village of Calstock (adult/child £10/7, 4½ hours).

The little yellow **Mount Batten Ferry** (adult/child return £3/2, 10 minutes, half hourly) shuttles from beside the Mayflower Steps across to the Mount Batten Peninsula.

Plymouth Mayflower MUSEUM
(3 The Barbican; adult/child £2/1; ⏲10am-4pm daily May-Oct, 10am-4pm Mon-Sat Nov-Apr) Runs through Plymouth's nautical heritage, providing the background to the Pilgrim Fathers' trip via interactive gizmos and multisensory displays.

Mount Batten Centre WATERSPORTS
(☎01752-404567; www.mount-batten-centre.com; 70 Lawrence Rd, Mount Batten) Courses include kayaking (£85 for two days), sailing (£158, two days) and windsurfing (£135, two days).

Sleeping

Fertile B&B hunting grounds are just back from Hoe, especially around Citadel Rd.

St Elizabeth's House HOTEL £££
(☎01752-344840; www.stelizabeths.co.uk; Longbrook St; d £140-160 ste £180-250; P) A manor house in the 17th century, this minihotel now oozes boutique-chic. Free-standing slipper baths, oak furniture and Egyptian cotton grace the rooms; the suites feature palatial bathrooms and private terraces. It's set in the suburb-village of Plympton St Maurice, 5 miles east of Plymouth city centre.

Bowling Green HOTEL ££
(☎01752-209090; www.bowlinggreenhotel.co.uk; 10 Osborne Pl; s/d/f £47/68/78; P) Some of the airy cream-and-white rooms in this family-run hotel look out onto the modern incarnation of Drake's famous bowling green. If you tire of watching people throw woods after jacks you can play chess in the conservatory.

Four Seasons B&B £
(☎01752-223591; www.fourseasons guesthouse.co.uk; 207 Citadel Rd East; s £32-42, d £48-58, f £60) This place is crammed full of treats, from the big bowls of free sweets to the mounds of Devon bacon for breakfast. They've got the basics right too: tasteful rooms decorated in gold and cream.

Jewell's B&B £
(☎01752-254760; www.jewellsguesthouse.com; 220 Citadel Rd; s/d/f £28/50/65) Traces of the Victorian era linger in the high ceilings and ornate plasterwork of this friendly town house. Rooms are bright and modern with deep armchairs and filmy curtains; top-quality bathrooms add another layer of class.

Berkeleys of St James B&B ££
(☎01752-221654; www.onthehoe.co.uk; 4 St James Pl East; s/d/f £40/60/75) A cosy terrace, dishing up breakfasts full of local, organic goodies.

Eating

TOP CHOICE **Barbican Kitchen** BRITISH ££
(☎01752-604448; 60 Southside St; mains £11; ⏲lunch & dinner, closed Sun evening) In this bistro-style baby sister of Tanners Restaurant, the stone interior fizzes with bursts of shocking pink and lime. The food is attention grabbing too – try the calves' liver with horseradish mash or the honey, goat's cheese and apple crostini. Its Devon beefburger, with a slab of stilton, is divine.

Tanners Restaurant FINE DINING £££
(☎01752-252001; www.tannersrestaurant.com; Finewell St; 2-/3-course dinner £32/39; ⏲lunch & dinner Tue-Sat) At Plymouth's top table reinvented British and French classics are the mainstay; expect lamb with gnocchi, char-grilled asparagus with soft poached egg, and roasted quail with pancetta.

TINSIDE LIDO

Tucked between the Hoe and the shore, **Tinside Lido** (Hoe Rd; adult/child £3.65/2.40; ⏲noon-6pm Mon-Fri, 10am-6pm Sat & Sun late-May–Jul, 10am-6pm daily Aug) is an outdoor, saltwater art-deco pool which was first opened in 1935. During its heyday in the '40s and '50s, thousands of Plymouthians flocked to the pool on summer days, to swim to the soothing strains of a string orchestra. In the '70s and '80s the pool fell into disrepair before closing in 1992. It's since been restored to its former glory thanks to a hefty £3.4 million refurbishment and now it's packed throughout summer with school kids and sun worshippers; sadly, though, there's no sign of the string orchestra returning just yet.

Plymouth

0 200 m
0 0.1 miles

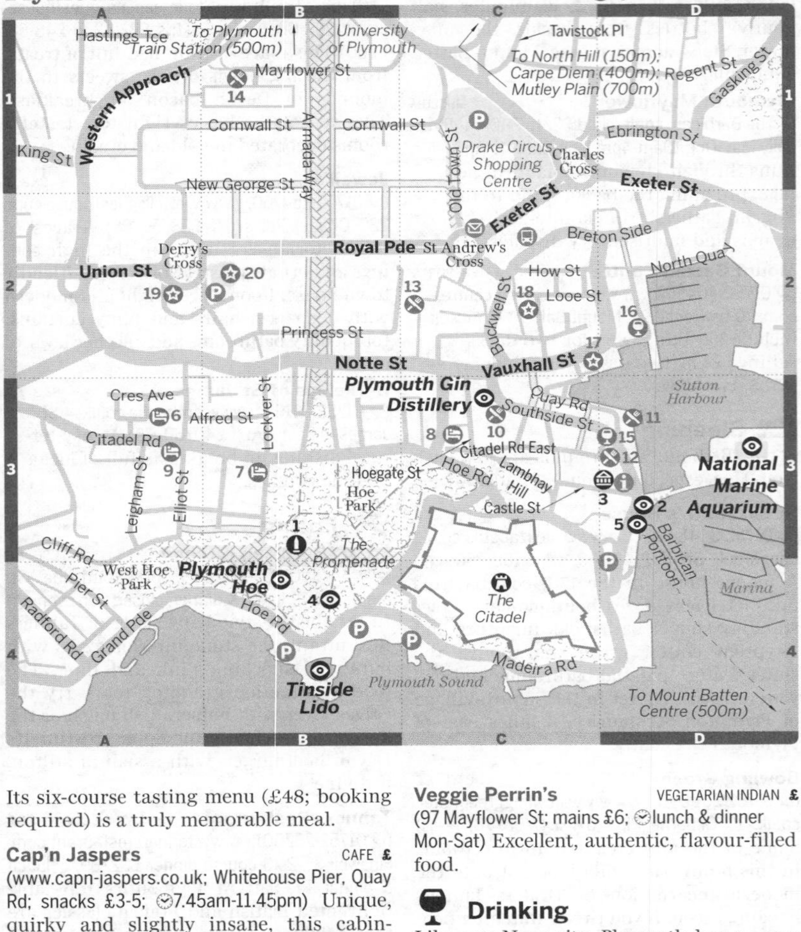

Hastings Tce
To Plymouth Train Station (500m)
University of Plymouth
Tavistock Pl
To North Hill (150m); Carpe Diem (400m); Mutley Plain (700m)
Regent St
Gasking St
Mayflower St
14
Western Approach
Cornwall St
Armada Way
Cornwall St
Ebrington St
King St
Old Town St
Drake Circus Shopping Centre
Charles Cross
Exeter St
New George St
Exeter St
Breton Side
Derry's Cross
Royal Pde
St Andrew's Cross
North Quay
Union St
20
19
How St
13
18
Looe St
Buckwell St
16
Princess St
17
Notte St
Vauxhall St
Sutton Harbour
Plymouth Gin Distillery
Quay Rd
Cres Ave
6
Alfred St
Southside St
11
Lockyer St
10
8
15
Citadel Rd
Citadel Rd East
12
National Marine Aquarium
9
7
Hoegate St
Hoe Rd
Lambhay Hill
3
Leigham St
Elliot St
Hoe Park
Castle St
2
5
Barbican Pontoon
1
The Promenade
Cliff Rd
Pier St
West Hoe Park
Plymouth Hoe
4
The Citadel
Marina
Radford Rd
Grand Pde
Hoe Rd
Madeira Rd
Plymouth Sound
Tinside Lido
To Mount Batten Centre (500m)

Its six-course tasting menu (£48; booking required) is a truly memorable meal.

Cap'n Jaspers CAFE £

(www.capn-jaspers.co.uk; Whitehouse Pier, Quay Rd; snacks £3-5; ⏲7.45am-11.45pm) Unique, quirky and slightly insane, this cabin-kiosk has been delighting bikers, tourists, locals and fishermen for decades with its motorised gadgets and teaspoons attached by chains. The menu is of the burger and bacon butty school – trying to eat a 'half a yard of hot dog' is a Plymouth rite of passage. Try the local crab rolls – the filling could have been caught by the bloke sitting next to you.

Platters SEAFOOD ££

(12 The Barbican; mains £16; ⏲lunch & dinner) A down-to-earth eatery with fish so fresh it's just stopped flapping – try the skate in butter or the locally caught sea bass.

Veggie Perrin's VEGETARIAN INDIAN £

(97 Mayflower St; mains £6; ⏲lunch & dinner Mon-Sat) Excellent, authentic, flavour-filled food.

Drinking

Like any Navy city, Plymouth has a more than lively nightlife. Union St is clubland; Mutley Plain and North Hill have a studenty vibe, while the Barbican has more restaurants amid the bars. All three areas get rowdy, especially at weekends.

View 2 BAR

(www.barbicanleisurebars.com; Vauxhall Quay; ⏲10am-midnight Sun-Thu, 10am-3am Fri, 10am-2am Sat) Just round from the heart of the Barbican, this cool venue's flagstone terrace is perfect for a waterside drink. Enjoy comedy, easy listening, soul, funk and R&B.

Plymouth

Top Sights
- National Marine Aquarium ... D3
- Plymouth Gin Distillery ... C3
- Plymouth Hoe ... B4
- Tinside Lido ... B4

Sights
- 1 Drake Statue ... B3
- Island House ... (see 12)
- 2 Mayflower Steps ... D3
- 3 Plymouth Mayflower ... D3
- 4 Smeaton's Tower ... B4

Activities, Courses & Tours
- 5 Mount Batten Ferry ... D3
- Sound Cruising ... (see 5)

Sleeping
- 6 Berkeleys of St James ... A3
- 7 Bowling Green ... B3
- 8 Four Seasons ... C3
- 9 Jewell's ... A3

Eating
- 10 Barbican Kitchen ... C3
- 11 Cap'n Jaspers ... D3
- 12 Platters ... D3
- 13 Tanners Restaurant ... C2
- 14 Veggie Perrin's ... B1

Drinking
- 15 Dolphin ... D3
- 16 View 2 ... D2

Entertainment
- 17 Annabel's ... C2
- 18 Plymouth Arts Centre ... C2
- 19 Revolution ... A2
- 20 Theatre Royal ... B2

Dolphin PUB
(14 The Barbican) This wonderfully unreconstructed Barbican boozer is all scuffed tables, padded bench seats and an authentic, no-nonsense atmosphere.

Carpe Diem BAR
(www.carpediemnh.co.uk; 50 North Hill; ⌚noon-1am Tue-Sun) A beautifully lit, funky hang-out done out in a kaleidoscope of colours – there's a heated, open-air chill-out room too.

Entertainment

Annabel's CABARET CLUB
(www.annabelscabaret.co.uk; 88 Vauxhall St; ⌚8.30am-2am Thu-Sat) The stage spots in this quirky venue are filled by an eclectic collection of acts (expect anything from burlesque to comedy). Crowd-pleasing tunes fill the dance floor while classy cocktails fill your glass.

Revolution CLUB-BAR
(www.revolution-bars.co.uk; Derry's Cross; ⌚11.30am-2.30am Mon-Fri, 11.30am-3am Sat) A cavernous chrome-lined drinking den with a two-bar club room (open Thursday to Sunday). If you don't like the scene here the mega clubs of Union St are just a totter away.

Plymouth Arts Centre ARTS CENTRE
(www.plymouthac.org.uk; 38 Looe Street; ⌚10am-8.30pm Tue-Sat, 4-8.30pm Sun) This cultural hot-spot combines an independent cinema, modern-art exhibitions, and a licensed veggie-friendly **cafe** (⌚11am to 8.30pm Tue-Sat).

Theatre Royal THEATRE
(www.theatreroyal.com; Royal Pde) Plymouth's main theatre stages large-scale touring and home-grown productions; its studio space, the Drum, is renowned for featuring new writing.

Information

Plymouth Library (Drake Circus; ⌚9am-7pm Mon-Fri, 9am-5pm Sat) Internet access.

Police station (Charles Cross; ⌚24hr)

Tourist office (☎01752-306330; www.visitplymouth.co.uk; Plymouth Mayflower, 3 The Barbican; ⌚9am-5pm Mon-Sat, 10am-4pm Sun Apr-Oct, 9am-5pm Mon-Fri, 10am-4pm Sat Nov-Mar)

Getting There & Away

Bus

On Sundays between June and mid-September Bus 82, the Transmoor Link, makes five trips from Plymouth to Exeter, via Yelverton, Princetown, Postbridge and Moretonhampstead.

Other services:

Birmingham (£48, 5½ hours, five daily)

Bristol (£29, three hours, five daily)

Exeter (£6, 1¼ hours, one to three daily) Bus X38.

London (£33, five to six hours, eight daily)

Penzance (£8, three hours, six daily)

Train

Bristol (£32, two hours, two or three per hour)

Exeter (£7.40, one hour, two or three per hour)

London (£40, 3¼ hours, half-hourly)

Penzance (£8, two hours, half-hourly)

Totnes (£5, 30 minutes, at least hourly)

Around Plymouth

Stately **Buckland Abbey** (NT; www.nationaltrust.org.uk; near Yelverton; adult/child £7.80/3.90; ⏲10.30am-5.30pm daily Apr-Oct, 11am-4.30pm Fri-Sun Nov-Dec & Feb-Mar) was originally a Cistercian monastery and 13th-century abbey church, but was transformed into a family residence by Sir Richard Grenville before being purchased in 1581 by his cousin and nautical rival Sir Francis Drake. Its displays include Drake's Drum, said to beat by itself when Britain is in danger of being invaded. There's also a very fine Elizabethan garden.

Buckland Abbey is 11 miles north of Plymouth. You'll need your own transport to get here.

Dartmoor National Park

Dartmoor is an ancient, compelling landscape, so different from the rest of Devon that a visit can feel like falling straight into Tolkien's *Return of the King*. Exposed granite hills (called tors) crest on the horizon, linked by swaths of honey-tinged moors. On the fringes, streams tumble over moss-smothered boulders in woods of twisted trees. The centre of this 368-sq-mile wilderness is the higher moor; a vast, treeless expanse. Moody and utterly empty

Dartmoor National Park

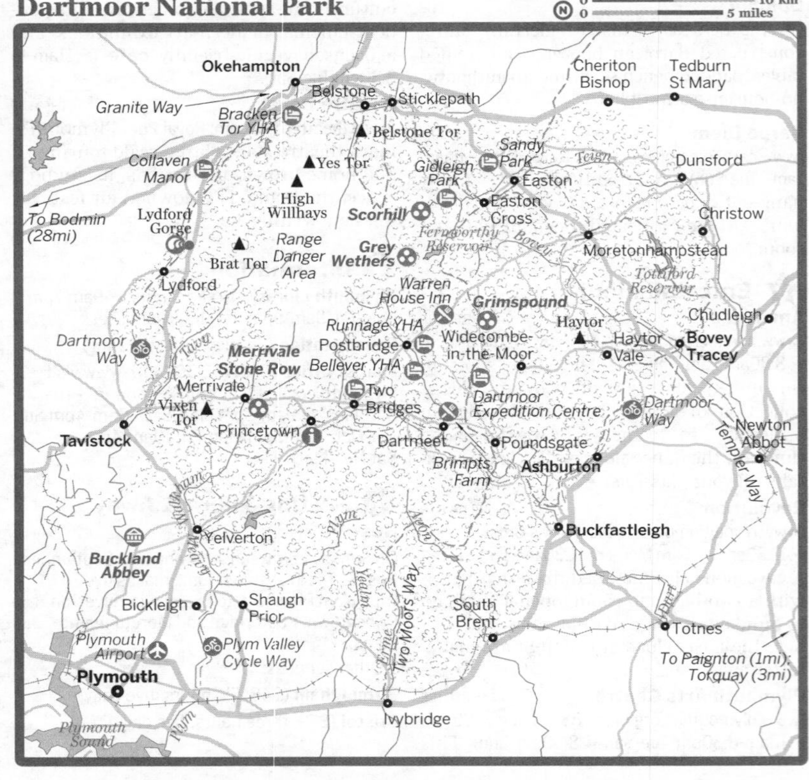

you'll find its desolate beauty exhilarating or chilling, or quite possibly a bit of both.

Dartmoor can be picture-postcard pretty; ponies wander at will here and sheep graze beside the road, but peel back the picturesque and there's a core of hard reality – stock prices mean many farming this harsh environment struggle to make a profit. It's also a mercurial place where the urban illusion of control over our surroundings is stripped away and the elements are in charge. Dartmoor inspired Sir Arthur Conan Doyle to write *The Hound of the Baskervilles* and in sleeting rain and swirling mists you suddenly see why; the moor morphs into a bleak, wilderness where tales of a phantom hound can seem very real indeed.

But Dartmoor is also a natural breakout zone with a checklist of charms: superb walking, cycling, riding, climbing and white-water kayaking; rustic pubs and fancy restaurants; wild camping nooks and country-house hotels – the perfect boltholes when the fog rolls in.

Activities

Walking

Some 730 miles of public footpaths snake across Dartmoor's open heaths and rocky tors. Crimson's *Dartmoor, Short Walks* (£5.99) is a good introduction for family day strolls, while the local tourist office can advise on all types of self-guided trails or **guided walks** (2-/6-hr £3/8). Themes include Sherlock Holmes, myths, geology, industry and archaeology. Look out for the memorable moonlit rambles amid stone rows.

Cycling

Marked cycling routes include the 11-mile Granite Way which runs along a former railway line between Okehampton and Lydford. The Dartmoor Way is a 90-mile circular cycling and walking route that goes through Okehampton, Chagford, Buckfastleigh, Princetown and Tavistock.

Devon Cycle Hire BIKE HIRE
(☎01837-861141; www.devoncycle hire.co.uk; Sourton Down, near Okehampton; per full/half day £10/14; ⏲9am-5pm Apr-Sep) On the Granite Way.

Horse Riding

A half-day ride costs around £36.

Babeny Farm RIDING STABLE
(☎01364-631296; Poundsgate)

> **THE DARTMOOR GUIDE**
>
> The free *Dartmoor Guide* newspaper is packed with useful info, including details of activities, attractions, campsites and the full diary of guided walks. Pick it up at visitor centres and venues across the moor.

Skaigh RIDING STABLES
(☎01837-840917; www.skaighstables.co.uk; Belstone; ⏲Apr-Oct)

Shilstone Rocks RIDING STABLES
(☎01364-621281; Widecombe-in-the-Moor)

White Water

The raging River Dart makes Dartmoor a top spot for thrill seekers. Experienced kayakers can get permits from www.dartaccess.co.uk or the **British Canoe Union** (BCU; ☎0845 370 9500; www.bcu.org.uk). **CRS Adventures** (☎01364-653444; www.crsadventures.co.uk) near Ashburton runs a range of white-water activities (from £35 for a half day). Rivers are only open in the winter.

Climbing

Rock Centre ROCK CLIMBING
(☎01626-852717; www.rockcentre.co.uk; Rock House, Chudleigh; 1-/2-hr lessons £40/80)

Information

The main tourist office is in Princetown (see p314); it stocks walking guides, maps and clothes. See also the official website at www.dartmoor.co.uk. Other offices:

Haytor Vale (DNPA; ☎01364-661520; ⏲10am-5pm Easter-Oct, 10am-4pm Sat & Sun Nov & Dec)

Postbridge (DNPA; ☎01822-880272; ⏲10am-5pm Easter-Oct, 10am-4pm Sat & Sun Nov & Dec)

Getting There & Around

For environmental reasons, the local national parks authority advocates using public transport and, with a bit of planning, it is a real option. The *Discovery Guide to Dartmoor,* free from most tourist offices, details bus and train services in the park.

Bus

Key routes onto the moor:

Bus 83/84/86 (hourly) From Plymouth to Tavistock, via Yelverton.

DARTMOOR HIKES

The **West Devon Way** (part of the Dartmoor Way) is a 14-mile trek between Tavistock and Okehampton, while the 18-mile **Templer Way** is a two- to three-day leg stretch from Haytor to Teignmouth. The 90-mile **Dartmoor Way** circles from Buckfastleigh in the south, through Moretonhampstead, northwest to Okehampton and south through Lydford to Tavistock. But the blockbuster route is the 103-mile **Two Moors Way**, which runs from Ivybridge, across Dartmoor and Exmoor to Lynmouth on the north Devon coast.

Be prepared for Dartmoor's notoriously fickle weather and carry a map and compass as many trails are not way-marked. The Ordnance Survey (OS) Explorer 1:25,000 map No 28, *Dartmoor* (£7.99), is the most comprehensive and shows park boundaries and MOD firing-range areas, see Warning, p315.

Bus 359 (two hourly Monday to Saturday) From Exeter to Moretonhampstead.

Bus 118 (one to four daily) From Barnstaple to Tavistock (2¼ hours), via Lydford and Okehampton.

Key routes around the Moor:

Haytor Hoppa (four on Saturdays April to October, plus three on Thursdays June to mid-September) A circular route taking in Haytor, Widdecombe-in-the-Moor and Bovey Tracey.

Transmoor Link/Bus 82 On Sundays between June and mid-September it makes five trips between Exeter and Plymouth (2½ hours) via Moretonhampstead, Warren House Inn, Postbridge, Two Bridges, Princetown and Yelverton. It also runs between Moretonhampstead and Yelverton (45 minutes) five times on Saturdays between April and October, and three times on Thursdays between June and mid-September.

Travel passes:

Dartmoor Sunday Rover (adult/child £6.50/4.30, Sundays June to September) Buys unlimited travel on most bus routes, and train travel on the Tamar Valley line from Plymouth to Gunnislake. Buy tickets from bus drivers or at Plymouth train station.

PRINCETOWN

Set in the heart of the remote, higher moor, Princetown is dominated by the grey, foreboding bulk of Dartmoor Prison. The jail has dictated the town's fortunes for hundreds of years. When it stopped housing French and American prisoners of war in the early 1800s, Princetown fell into decline and on bad weather days the town can still have a bleak feel. But it's also a useful insight into the harsh realities of moorland life and makes an atmospheric base for some excellent walks.

The prison reopened as a convict jail in 1850 and just up from its looming gates the **Dartmoor Prison Heritage Centre** (www.dartmoor-prison.co.uk; Princetown; adult/child £2.50/1.50; 9.30am-12.30pm & 1.30-4.30pm Mon-Thu & Sat, to 4pm Fri & Sun) provides a chilling glimpse of life (past and present) inside – look out for the straight jackets, manacles and mock-up cells, and the escape tale of Frankie 'the mad axeman' Mitchell, supposedly sprung by 1960s gangster twins, the Krays. The centre also sells the bizarrely cheery garden ornaments made by the inmates.

The Moor's main **tourist office** (DNPA; 01822-890414; www.dartmoor-npa.gov.uk; 10am-5pm Apr-Oct, 10am-4pm Nov-Mar) stocks maps, guides and books. The building started life as Princetown's main hotel, where Arthur Conan Doyle began his classic Dartmoor tale *The Hound of the Baskervilles*. Ask staff to point you towards Foxtor Mires (2 to 3 miles away), the inspiration for the book's Grimpen Mire, then detect the story's other locations.

The **Plume of Feathers** (01822-890240; www.theplumeoffeathers.co.uk; Plymouth Hill; dm £14.50-17, d £34, sites £13) in the heart of town serves up typical bar food. It also offers no-nonsense rooms with shared bathrooms, as well as basic bunk-bed dorms and camping.

Getting There & Away

For the Transmoor Link bus east across the moor, see p313. Bus 98 shuttles between Tavistock and Princetown (four daily). Bus 98 runs from Princetown to Postbridge (one per day Monday to Friday).

POSTBRIDGE

There's not much to the quaint village of Postbridge apart from a couple of shops, pubs and whitewashed houses. It's best known for its 13th-century **clapper bridge** across the East Dart, made of large granite slabs supported by stone pillars.

There's an **information centre** (☎01822-880272; ⏰10am-5pm Easter-Oct, 10am-4pm Sat & Sun Nov & Dec) in the car park, and a post office and shop in the village.

Sleeping

Two Bridges HOTEL £££
(☎01822-890581; www.twobridges.co.uk; Two Bridges; s £95-125, d £140-190; P) There's a real feel of a classy country house to this classic moorland hotel. That's no doubt down to the gently elegant rooms, huge inglenook fireplaces and squishy leather sofas; former guests Wallis Simpson, Winston Churchill and Vivien Leigh probably liked it too. It's 3 miles southwest of Postbridge.

Runnage YHA CAMPING BARN £
(☎01629-592700; ww.yha.org.uk; sites per adult/child £4.50/3.50, dm £8.50; P) Set in a working farm, this converted hayloft allows you to bed down to the soundtrack of bleating sheep. It's 1½ miles from Postbridge: take the 'Widecombe' turning off the Moretonhampstead road.

Bellever YHA HOSTEL £
(☎0845 371 9622; www.yha.org.uk; dm £14; ⏰Mar-Oct; P) A characterful former farm on the edge of a conifer plantation, with a huge kitchen, lots of rustic stone walls and cosy dorms. It's a mile south of Postbridge.

Eating & Drinking

Warren House Inn PUB £
(www.warrenhouseinn.co.uk; mains from £7; ⏰11am-11pm) Plonked amid miles of open moor, this former tin miners' haunt exudes the kind of hospitality you only get in a pub in the middle of nowhere. A Dartmoor institution, its stone floors, trestle tables and hearty food (served noon-8.30pm) are warmed by a fire that's reputedly been crackling since 1845. Between November and March the pub closes at 5pm on Monday and Tuesday. It's on the B3212, 2 miles northeast of Postbridge.

Brimpts Farm CAFE £
(www.brimptsfarm.co.uk; cream teas £3; ⏰11.30am-5.30pm weekends & school holidays, 2-5.30pm weekdays) It has been serving cream teas here since 1913, and is still one of the best places to tuck in on the moor. Expect freshly baked scones, homemade jams and utterly gooey clotted cream. It's signed off the B3357, Two Bridges–Dartmeet road.

Getting There & Away

As well as being on the Transmoor Link bus 82 route (see p313), Postbridge has connections to **Princetown** via bus 98 (one per day Monday to Friday).

WIDECOMBE-IN-THE-MOOR

POP 652

This is archetypal Dartmoor, down to the ponies grazing on the village green. Widecombe's honey-grey, 15th-century buildings circle a church whose 40m tower has seen it dubbed the Cathedral of the Moor. Inside search out the boards telling the fire-and-brimstone tale of the violent storm of 1638 – it knocked a pinnacle from the roof, killing several parishioners. As ever on Dartmoor, the devil was blamed; said to be in search of souls.

PREHISTORIC DARTMOOR

Dartmoor is ripe for archaeological explorations. The moor has an estimated 11,000 monuments, including the largest concentration of Bronze Age (c 2300-700 BC) remains in the country. It also has around 75 stone rows (half the national total), 18 stone circles and 5000 huts.

The **Merrivale Stone Rows**, near Princetown, are a handy one-stop-shop for most monument types – the site has a parallel stone row, a stone circle, a menhir, burial chambers and dozens of hut circles. To the northeast, near Chagford, the **Grey Wethers** stone circles stand side by side on a stretch of open moor; they're about a third of a mile from another stone circle near Fernworthy. Also nearby, at Gidleigh, **Scorhill** stone circle is sometimes called the Stonehenge of Dartmoor, although only half of the original stones remain. The biggest site is the Bronze Age village of **Grimspound**, just off the B3212, where you can wander inside the circular stone wall that once surrounded an entire village, and the ruins of several granite round houses.

There are a series of archaeology-themed walks (£3 to £8) all over the moor, as well as mini guides to some sites (£4). Enquire at the tourist office.

WARNING

The military uses three adjoining areas of Dartmoor as training ranges where live ammunition is used. The local tourist office can explain their locations; they're also marked on OS maps. In general you're advised to check if the route you're planning falls within a range; if it does, find out if firing is taking place when you want to walk via the **Firing Information Service** (☎0800 458 4868; www.dartmoor-ranges.co.uk). During the day red flags fly at the edges of in-use ranges, and red flares burn at night. Even when there's no firing, beware of unidentified metal objects lying in the grass. Don't touch anything you find: note its position and report it to the **Commandant** (☎01837-650010).

The village is commemorated in the traditional English folksong of 'Widecombe Fair'; the event of the same name takes place on the second Tuesday of September.

Sleeping & Eating

Dartmoor Expedition Centre BUNK HOUSE £
(☎01364-621249; www.dartmoorbase.co.uk; dm £13, loft room £15; P) The real fires, hot showers and dorm beds at this 300-year-old converted barn are all best enjoyed after the climbing, orienteering and caving the centre organises. It's 2 miles west of Widecombe.

Higher Venton Farm B&B ££
(☎01364-621235; www.ventonfarm.com; Widecombe; d £50-60; P) This 16th-century farmhouse could be used to define the architectural style 'picture-postcard thatch'. With low lintels and winding stone stairs, there's not a straight line in the place.

Rugglestone Inn PUB £
(www.rugglestoneinn.co.uk; mains £4-9; ⏲lunch & dinner) You'll find plenty of locals in front of this intimate old pub's wood-burning stove. Its stone floor and low beams set the scene for hearty helpings of handmade sausages and mash, or fisherman's pie.

Getting There & Away

Bus 272 goes to Tavistock (1¼ hours, three buses, late May to early September) via Two Bridges (50 minutes) and Princetown (55 minutes), but only on Sundays in the summer.

Bus 274 runs to Okehampton (1¾ hours, three on summer Sundays only) via Moretonhampstead. In the summer Widdecombe is also served by the Haytor Hoppa, see p313.

CHAGFORD & AROUND

POP 1470

With its wonky thatches and cream-and-white-fronted buildings, Chagford gathers round a busy square – at first glance every inch a timeless moorland town. But the purveyors of waxed jackets and hip flasks have also been joined by health-food shops and contemporary pottery galleries. A former Stannary town (where local tin was weighed and checked), Chagford was also the first town west of London to get electric street lights.

Sleeping & Eating

Gidleigh Park HOTEL/RESTAURANT £££
(☎01647-432367; www.gidleigh.com; near Gidleigh; s £340, d £310-1155; P 📶) This sumptuous oasis of supreme luxury teams crests, crenellations and roaring fires with shimmering sanctuaries of blue marble, waterproof TVs and private saunas. Rates include dinner at the double-Michelin-starred **restaurant** (⏲lunch & dinner), where three courses would normally set you back a hefty £95 – crafty local foodies opt for the £35 two-course lunch instead. This dollop of utter extravagance is 2 miles west of Chagford.

22 Mill Street B&B/RESTAURANT ££
(☎01647-432 244; www.22millst.com; 22 Mill St; d £110-130; P) The elegant rooms of this sleek retreat feature exposed stone walls, wooden floorboards, satin cushions and bursts of modern art. Its intimate **restaurant** (2-courses £15-36; ⏲lunch & dinner) delivers imaginative dishes packed with produce from the moors and the shores – look out for seared Exmoor venison, and rabbit with parmesan risotto.

Sparrowhawk HOSTEL £
(☎01647-440318; www.sparrowhawkbackpackers.co.uk; 45 Ford St; dm/d/f £16/36/45) The bright, light dorms in this ecofriendly hostel are set in converted stables. Set in the village of Moretonhampstead, 5 miles south of Chagford, the central courtyard, ringed by rickety outbuildings, is a great spot to swap traveller's tales.

Sandy Park INN ££
(☎01647-433267; www.sandyparkinn.co.uk; Sandy Park; s/d £55/85; P) Part pub (mains £8 to £12), part chic place to stay. At this 17th-century thatch you can sip a pint of real ale in a cosy, exposed-beam bar, sample classy Dartmoor fare in the restaurant, then totter upstairs to sleep amid plump pillows and classic furnishings.

Getting There & Away

Bus 179 runs to Okehampton (one hour, two daily Monday to Saturday). Bus 173 travels from Moretonhampstead to Exeter via Chagford twice daily, Monday to Saturday.

OKEHAMPTON & AROUND

POP 7029

Okehampton has a staging post feel, huddling as it does on the edge of the mind-expanding sweep of the higher moor; an uninhabited tract of bracken-covered slopes and granite tors. With its clusters of traditional shops and pubs, it's an agreeable place to stock up before a foray into the wilderness.

Sights & Activities

Lydford Gorge WATERFALL
(NT; www.nationaltrust.org.uk; adult/child £5.50/2.80; ⌚10am-4pm or 5pm mid-Mar–Oct) The 1½-mile rugged riverside hikes here snake past a series of bubbling whirlpools (including the fearsome 'Devil's Cauldron') to the thundering, 30m-high White Lady waterfall. Lydford is 9 miles southwest of Okehampton.

Okehampton Castle CASTLE
(EH; www.english-heritage.org.uk; adult/child £3.50/1.80; ⌚10am-5pm Apr-Jun & Sep, to 6pm Jul & Aug) Clinging to a wooded spur, the crumbling Norman motte and ruined keep of what was once Devon's largest castle allow for some picturesque rampart clambering.

Finch Foundry FORGE
(NT; www.nationaltrust.org.uk; Sticklepath; adult/child £4.40/2.20; ⌚11am-5pm Wed-Mon Apr-Oct) The last working water-powered forge in England sits at the end of a 3½-hour walk along the Tarka Trail from Okehampton.

Sleeping & Eating

Collaven Manor B&B ££
(☎01837-861522; www.collavenmanor.co.uk; Sourton; s £65, d £106-146; P) At this delightful, clematis-clad mini-manor house a wooden chandelier crowns a 16th-century hall. Restful bedrooms are lined with tapestries and window seats that provide tor-top views. Collaven Manor is 5 miles west of Okehampton.

Bracken Tor YHA HOSTEL £
(☎01837-53916; www.yha.org.uk; Saxon Gate; dm £16; P @) This 100-year old country house sits in four acres of grounds on the fringe of the higher moor, making a perfect base for memorable hikes. It's a mile south of Okehampton and a YHA activity centre, so you can do some climbing and canoeing too.

Tors PUB ££
(☎01837-840689; www.thetors.co.uk; Belstone; mains £7-17; ⌚lunch & dinner) Tucked away in the picturesque moorland village of Belstone, this welcoming country pub offers simple, traditional **rooms** (singles/doubles £33/66), hearty food and views onto the moor. It's 2 miles east of Okehampton.

Information

Tourist office (☎01837-53020; www.okehamptondevon.co.uk; Museum Courtyard, 3 West St; ⌚10am-5pm Mon-Sat Easter-Oct, 10am-4.30pm Mon-Tue & Fri & Sat Nov-Easter)

Getting There & Away

Bus X9 runs from Exeter (50 minutes, hourly Monday to Saturday) via Okehampton to Bude (one hour). Bus 179 (two daily Monday to Saturday) goes to Chagford (30 minutes) and Moretonhampstead (50 minutes). Bus 118 (one to four daily) runs from Tavistock to Barnstaple (2¼ hours), via Lydford and Okehampton.

> **DRIVING ON DARTMOOR**
>
> Much of Dartmoor is unfenced grazing so you're very likely to come across Dartmoor ponies, sheep and even cows in the middle of the road. Many sections have a 40mph speed limit. Car parks on the moor can be little more than lay-bys for half a dozen cars; their surface can be rough to very rough.

Braunton & Croyde

POP 8319

The cheerful, chilled village of Croyde is Devon's surf central. Here olde-worlde meets new wave: thatched roofs peep out over racks of wetsuits; and crowds of cool guys in board shorts sip beer outside 17th-century inns. Inland, Braunton also has surf shops, board hire and a **tourist office** (☎1271-816400; www.brauntontic.co.uk; Caen St; ⏲10am-3pm Mon-Fri, 10am-2pm Sat).

The water's hard to resist. **Le Sport** (☎01271-890147; Hobbs Hill, Croyde; ⏲9am-5.30pm daily Mar-Oct, to 9pm Jul & Aug, 9.30am-5.30pm Sat & Sun Nov-Feb) is among those hiring wetsuits and boards (half-/full day £13/20). The British Surfing Association (BSA) -approved **Surf South West** (☎01271-890400; www.surfsouthwest.com; Croyde; per half-day £30; ⏲Mar-Nov) and **Surfing Croyde Bay** (☎01271-891200; www.surfingcroydebay.co.uk; 8 Hobbs Hill, Croyde; per half day £35) provide lessons.

Sleeping & Eating

Croyde gets very busy in the summer – book ahead, even for campsites.

Thatch B&B ££
(☎01271-890349; www.thethatchcroyde.com; 14 Hobbs Hill, Croyde; d £60-80) Set above a legendary surfer's hang out, the bedrooms in this thatched drinking-den are smart and modern, featuring delicate creams, browns and subtle checks. Some share bathrooms. It also offers a range of swish **rooms** (d £50-110, f £100-130) at neighbouring cottages and above Billy Budd's (a few doors away).

Chapel Farm B&B ££
(☎01271-890429; www.chapelfarmcroyde.co.uk; Hobbs Hill, Croyde; s/d £30/70; P) Walls and ceilings shoot off at atmospherically random angles in this cosy, thatched cob farmhouse, formerly a home to monks. Some of the light, pretty rooms share bathrooms. Self catering is available too.

Bay View Farm CAMPSITE £
(☎01271-890501; www.bayviewfarm.co.uk; Croyde; sites per adult £11) One of the area's best campsites, with laundry, showers and surf-view pitches. Often requires a week's minimum booking in summer.

Mitchum's CAMPSITE £
(☎07875 406473; www.croydebay.co.uk; Croyde; sites per adult £17-27; ⏲mid-Jun–Aug) There are two locations, one in Croyde village and one by the beach. There's often a two night minimum booking in July and August.

Getting There & Away

Bus 308 (hourly Monday to Saturday, five on Sunday) goes from Barnstaple to Braunton and Croyde (40 minutes).

Bus 3 (every 30 minutes Monday to Saturday, hourly Sunday) runs between Ilfracombe and Barnstaple, via Braunton.

Ilfracombe & Around

POP 12,430

Like a matinée idol past his prime, for years Ilfracombe had a sagging, crumpled feel. The steeply sloping streets of this Victorian watering hole are lined by town houses with cast-iron balconies; formal gardens, crazy golf and ropes of twinkling lights line the promenade. But these days there's more to Ilfracombe, as evidenced by a string of smart eateries and places to sleep, a Damien Hirst connection and the chance to go surfing or take a 'dip' in the past.

Sights & Activities

TOP CHOICE **Tunnelsbeaches** HISTORIC POOL
(www.tunnelsbeaches.co.uk; Granville Rd; adult/child £2/1.50; ⏲10am-5pm or 6pm Easter-Oct, to 7pm Jul & Aug) These Victorian tidal swimming pools beautifully evoke Ilfracombe's hey-day. Passageways hacked out of solid rock lead to a pocket-sized beach where you can still plunge into the sea. Sepia photos depict the same spot in the 19th-century, conveying a world of woollen bathing suits, segregated swimming and boating etiquette ('Gentlemen who cannot swim should never take ladies upon the water').

Nick Thorn Hunter SURFING LESSONS
(☎01271-871337 www.nickthornhuntersurfacademy.com; ⏲9am-5pm Apr-Sep) Stationed at the best local surf beach, Woolacombe, 5 miles west of Ilfracombe. Lessons cost from £30 for 2½ hours.

Sleeping & Eating

Westwood BOUTIQUE B&B £
(☎01271-867443; www.west-wood.co.uk; Torrs Park Rd; d £80-110; P 📶) Modern, minimal and marvellous, this ultra-chic guest house is a study of neutral tones and dashes of vivid colour. It's graced by pony-skin chaises longues and stand-alone baths; some rooms have sea glimpses.

Norbury House Hotel B&B ££
(☎01271-863888; www.norburyhouse.co.uk; Torrs Park; d £80-100, f £100-135; P) This exquisite former gentleman's residence is now dotted with low-level beds, cool lamps and artfully placed cushions. Set on the hill

overlooking Ilfracombe, there are impressive views from its terraced gardens.

11 The Quay EUROPEAN ££
(☎01271-868090; www.11thequay.com; 11 The Quay; snacks £2-9, mains £13-22; ⊙lunch & dinner Wed-Sat, dinner Sun) Full of Chelsea-chic, this distinctive eatery is owned by the artist Damien Hirst, a man famous for exhibiting preserved dead cows and sharks. The menu's less controversial; sample cured ham with pickled garlic or lobster risotto with chives while admiring Hirst's artwork. It includes his *Pharmacy* installation and, with delicious irony, fish in formaldehyde. The **bistro** is open for lunch and dinner with snacks served all day.

Ocean Backpackers HOSTEL £
(☎01271-867835; www.oceanbackpackers.co.uk; 29 St James Pl; dm £10-14, d £35; P@) A well-run indie hostel stalwart with snug dorms and a convivial lounge. There's surfing, kayaking and archery on offer too.

Information

Tourist office (☎01271-863001; www.visitilfracombe.co.uk; Landmark Theatre, the Seafront; ⊙10am-5pm daily Easter-Sep, 10am-4pm Mon-Sat Oct-Mar)

Getting There & Away

Bus 3 (40 minutes, every half-hour Monday to Saturday, hourly Sunday) runs to Barnstaple, via Braunton. Bus 300 heads to Lynton (one hour, three daily), with connections on to Minehead (40 minutes).

Clovelly

POP 452

Clovelly is the quintessential picture-postcard pretty Devon village. Its white cottages cascade down cliffs to meet a curving crab claw of a harbour, which is lined with lobster pots and set against a deep blue sea. Clovelly's cobbled streets are so steep cars can't negotiate them so supplies are still brought in by sledge – you'll see these big bread baskets on runners leaning outside homes. Clovelly's tenants enjoy enviably low rents (around £400 a year) and although the village is often branded artificial, 98% of the houses are occupied – in some Westcountry villages half the properties are second homes.

Entry to the privately owned village is via the **visitor centre** (www.clovelly.co.uk; adult/child £6/4; ⊙8.45am-6.30pm Jun-Sep, 9am-5pm Apr & May, 10am-4pm Nov-Mar).

Charles Kingsley, author of the children's classic *The Water Babies,* spent much of his early life in Clovelly. You can visit his former house, as well as an old fisherman's cottage and the village's twin chapels. By the harbour, the **Red Lion** (☎01237-431237; www.clovelly.co.uk) has stylish rooms with superb views (d £120 to £136), a classy restaurant (three-courses £30), and a welcoming bar (mains £6 to £10).

Bus 319 (four to six Monday to Saturday, two on Sunday between May and September only) runs between Clovelly, Hartland Village, Bideford (40 minutes) and Barnstaple (one hour).

Hartland Abbey

This 12th-century **former monastery** (www.hartlandabbey.com; adult/child £9.50/2.50; ⊙2-4.30pm Sun-Thu Jun-Sep, Wed-Thu & Sun Apr-May) was another post-Dissolution hand-out, given to the sergeant of Henry VIII's wine cellar in 1539. Now a stately home, it boasts fascinating murals, ancient documents, paintings by English masters, Victorian photos, as well as bewitching **gardens** (⊙noon-5pm Sun-Fri Apr-Sep). Hartland Abbey is 15 miles west of Bideford, off the A39 between Hartland and Hartland Quay.

CORNWALL

You can't get any further west than the ancient Celtic kingdom of Cornwall (or Kernow, as it's often referred to around these parts). Blessed with the craggiest cliffs, wildest coastline and most breathtakingly beautiful coves anywhere in England, this proud, independent corner of the Westcountry has always marched to its own tune. While the staple industries of old – mining, fishing and farming – have all but disappeared, Cornwall has picked itself up, dusted itself down and reinvented itself as one of the nation's creative and cultural corners. Whether it's exploring the space-age domes of the Eden Project, sampling the creations of a celebrity chef or chilling out on the faraway beaches of the Isles of Scilly, you're guaranteed to get inspired out west. Time to let a little Kernow into your soul.

Getting Around

Most of Cornwall's main bus, train and ferry timetables are collected into a handy brochure, available free from bus stations and tourist

PUBLIC TRANSPORT PASSES

Several passes are available covering public transport in Cornwall.

Bus

» **FirstDay Southwest** (adult/child/family £7.10/5.80/16.50) Buys a day's unlimited bus travel on most First buses. There's also a seven-day equivalent (adult/family £32.50/49). Cheaper day and weekly passes are available for smaller zones.

» **Western Greyhound Day Explorer** (adult/child £7/4.50) Covers all Western Greyhound buses in Cornwall.

Train

» **Devon & Cornwall Rover** Allows unlimited off-peak train travel across Devon and Cornwall. Eight days' travel in 15 costs an adult £60; three days' travel in one week is £40.

Bus & Train

» **Ride Cornwall** (adult/child £10/7.50/20) Unlimited travel on all rail and bus services within Cornwall after 9am Monday to Friday and weekends.

offices). **Traveline South West** (☎0871-200-2233; www.travelinesw.com) can also answer timetable queries.

Bus

Cornwall has two main bus operators.

First (☎timetables 0871-200-2233, customer services 0845-600-1420; www.firstgroup.com) Operates buses and trains across Cornwall.

Western Greyhound (☎01637-871871; www.westerngreyhound.com)

Train

Cornwall's main railway line follows the coast as far as Penzance, with spurs to Gunnislake, Looe, Falmouth, St Ives and Newquay.

CrossCountry (☎0844-811-0124; www.crosscountrytrains.co.uk) Shuttles between the southwest and Scotland, the north and the Midlands.

First Great Western (☎08457-000-125; www.firstgreatwestern.co.uk) Links London Paddington with Exeter, Penzance, Plymouth and Truro; plus branch lines to Falmouth, Newquay and St Ives.

Bude

POP 9242

Travelling west from Devon, the first Cornish town across the border is Bude, a popular family getaway and surfing hangout thanks to its fantastic nearby beaches.

Sights & Activities

Beaches

Closest to town is **Summerleaze**, a classic bucket-and-spade affair with bags of space at low tide, as well as a saltwater **sea pool** (⏲10am-6pm May-Sep), built in the 1930s and fed straight from the bracing waters of the Atlantic. Just to the north is **Crooklets**, which often has decent surf, as does **Widemouth Bay** (pronounced *widmouth*) 3 miles south of town. Further along the coast, the most spectacular beach scenery is saved for the dramatic beaches of **Crackington Haven** and the **Strangles**.

Several steps removed from the high-octane hustle of Newquay, Bude is ideal for some low-key surf lessons. Try **Big Blue Surf School** (☎01288-331764; www.bigbluesurfschool.co.uk), **BSX Surf Centre** (☎0870-777-5511; www.budesurfingexperience.co.uk) or **Raven Surf School** (☎01288-353693; www.ravensurf.co.uk). Which beach is used depends on the tide and weather conditions, but Summerleaze and Crooklets are the favourites.

Bude Castle — MUSEUM

(The Castle; adult/child £3.50/2.50; ⏲10am-6pm Easter-Oct, 10am-4pm Nov-Easter) Other than the beaches, there's not a huge amount to keep you occupied in Bude, although it's worth taking a peek around the **Castle Heritage Centre,** which rummages through Bude's maritime, geological and social history. Look out for exhibits on local inventor Sir Goldsworthy Gurney, whose pioneering creations included theatrical limelight and steam carriages – he also built the peculiar pint-sized castle in which the museum is now housed.

Sleeping

Dylan's Guesthouse B&B £
(☎01288-354705; www.dylansguesthouseinbude.co.uk; Downs View; s £45-50, d £50-65) This friendly, fizzy little B&B has nine rooms decked out in white linen, chocolate throws and pleasant pine, and a friendly owner full of info on the local area.

Elements Hotel HOTEL ££
(☎01288-275066; www.elements-life.co.uk; Marine Drive; s/d/f £70/105/160; P) Smart clifftop hotel with 11 soothing rooms in whites and creams, big views from the outdoor deck, a gym and Finholme sauna, and surf lessons courtesy of nearby Raven Surf School.

Eating

Life's a Beach CAFE ££
(www.lifesabeach.info; Summerleaze; lunch £4-6, dinner mains £16-21.50; Mon-Sat) By day it's a breezy beach caff serving the Summerleaze punters with coffees, paninis and ice-creams: by night it's a snazzy candlelit restaurant specialising in seafood.

Scrummies CAFE £
(Lansdown Rd; mains from £8; 8am-10pm) Fab fish cafe where the skate and monkfish are caught by the owner – try their crab pasta or lobster (half/whole £12/24) and chips.

Information

Bude tourist office (☎01288-354240; www.visitbude.info; The Crescent; 10am-5pm Mon-Sat, plus 10am-4pm Sun summer) In a car park at the end of town.

Getting There & Away

Boscastle (30 minutes, six daily Monday to Saturday, four on summer Sundays) Bus 594/595; runs via Widemouth and Crackington Haven. From Boscastle there are connections to Tintagel, Wadebridge, Newquay and Truro.

Boscastle

With its sturdy harbour, quaint cottages and steep valley setting, Boscastle is the perfect picture of a Cornish port, but in August 2004 the village hit the headlines for all the wrong reasons: devastating flash floods swept through the village, carrying away cars, bridges and even a couple of buildings, and forcing the emergency evacuation of many residents by naval helicopter (somewhat miraculously, not a single person lost their life).

Residents have spent the last few years piecing Boscastle back together, and most of its properties have now been completely refurbished, almost as though the floods never were. Look closely, though, and you might still be able to spot flood-marks halfway up some of the buildings, and a much-reinforced stone bridge at the centre of the village.

Elsewhere, there's plenty of fine coastal walking around Boscastle, plus a couple of woodland trails leading to local churches: ask at the tourist office for leaflets.

Sights

Museum of Witchcraft MUSEUM
(☎01840-250111; The Harbour; adult/child £3/2.50; 10.30am-6pm Mon-Sat, 11.30am-6pm Sun) Among Boscastle's renovated buildings, this quirky museum rather improbably houses the world's largest collection of witchy memorabilia, from haunted skulls to hags' bridles and voodoo dolls.

Sleeping & Eating

Boscastle House B&B ££
(☎01840-250654; www.boscastlehouse.com; Tintagel Rd; d £120; P) The fanciest of Boscastle B&Bs, in a Victorian house overlooking the valley, with six rooms named after Cornish legends. Charlotte has bay window-views, Nine Windows has his-and-hers sinks and a freestanding bath, Trelawney has space and its own sofa.

Orchard Lodge B&B £
(☎01840-250418; www.orchardlodgeboscastle.co.uk; Gunpool Ln; d £74-84; P) A short walk uphill from the village, this is a fine example of a thoroughly modern B&B, crisply finished in slinky fabrics and cool colours and run with efficiency by B&B newbies Geoff and Shirley Barratt. Rates get cheaper the longer you stay.

Boscastle YHA HOSTEL £
(boscastle@yha.org.uk; dm £14) Having been all but swept away by the floods, Boscastle's shoebox hostel has been polished up and now looks spanking fresh. It's in one of the village's oldest buildings by the harbour.

Boscastle's dining scene is limited almost entirely to the village pubs: try the cosy **Cobweb** (☎01840-250278; www.cobwebinn.co.uk; The Bridge; mains £5-14) and the old-time **Napoleon** (☎01840-250204; High Street; mains £6-12).

Information

Boscastle tourist office (☎01840-250010; www.visitboscastleandtintagel.com; ⊙10am-5pm Mar-Oct) In a new building by the harbour.

Getting There & Away

For buses see Tintagel.

Tintagel

POP 1822

The spectre of King Arthur looms large over the village of Tintagel and its spectacular clifftop **castle** (EH; ☎01840-770328; adult/child £5.20/2.60; ⊙10am-6pm Apr-Sep, 10am-5pm Oct, 10am-4pm Nov-Mar). Though the present-day ruins mostly date from the 13th century, archaeological digs have revealed the foundations of a much earlier fortress, fuelling speculation that the legendary king may indeed have been born at the castle as local fable claims. Part of the crumbling stronghold stands on a rock tower cut off from the mainland, accessed via a bridge and steep steps, and it's still possible to make out several sturdy walls and much of the castle's interior layout.

The village is awash with touristy shops and tearooms making the most of the King Arthur connection, but there's not that much to see. The **Old Post Office** (NT; ☎01840-770024; Fore St; adult/child £3.20/1.60; ⊙11am-5.30pm mid-Mar–Sep, 11am-4pm Oct) is a beautiful example of a traditional Cornish longhouse and mostly dates from the 1500s; it was still used as the village's post office during the 19th-century.

Information

Tintagel Tourist Office (☎01840-779084; www.visitboscastleandtintagel.com; Bossiney Rd; ⊙10am-5pm Mar-Oct, 10.30am-4pm Nov-Feb) Has exhibits exploring local history and the Arthur legend.

Getting There & Away

Bus 597 runs from Truro to St Columb Major where the connecting 594 goes via Wadebridge to Tintagel (two hours, seven daily Monday to Saturday) and onto Boscastle (10 minutes).

Padstow

POP 3162

If anywhere symbolises Cornwall's culinary renaissance, it's Padstow. Decades ago this was an industrious fishing village where the day's catch was battered and served up in newspaper. Today it's seared, braised or chargrilled, garnished with wasabi and dished up in some of the poshest restaurants this side of the Tamar.

The transformation is largely due to celebrity chef Rick Stein, whose property portfolio has now mushroomed to include restaurants, shops, hotels, a seafood school and even a fish and chip outlet. Inevitably, the town's much-bandied nickname of 'Padstein' raises the hackles of the locals, but there's no doubt the town has changed beyond recognition since its days as a quiet fishing harbour; while the cash has certainly swelled Padstow's coffers, it hasn't always been good for its soul.

Sights & Activities

National Lobster Hatchery MARINE CENTRE

(www.nationallobsterhatchery.co.uk; adult/child £3/1.50; ⊙10am-7.30pm Jul & Aug, 10am-5pm Apr-Jun & Sep-Oct, earlier closing Nov-Mar) In order to ensure sustainable stocks for future generations, baby lobsters are reared in special tanks at this harbourside hatchery before being returned to the wild. It's a fascinating place to learn about the life-cycle of this tasty crustacean.

Camel Trail CYCLE PATH

The disused Padstow–Bodmin railway now forms the Camel Trail, one of Cornwall's most popular cycling tracks. Starting in Padstow, it runs east through Wadebridge (5¾ miles), Bodmin (11 miles) and beyond. Bikes can be hired from **Padstow Cycle Hire** (☎01841-533533; www.padstowcyclehire.com; ⊙9am-5pm) or **Bridge Bike Hire** (☎01208-813050; www.bridgebikehire.co.uk), at the Wadebridge end.

Boat Trips CRUISES

Several operators leave from the harbour for scenic spins around the bay. **Padstow Boat Trips** (www.padstowboattrips.com) collects together schedules and details. Operators include **Jubilee Queen** (☎07836-798457) and **Padstow Sealife Safaris** (☎01841-521613; www.padstowsealifesafaris.co.uk).

Beaches

Padstow is surrounded by excellent beaches, including the so-called Seven Bays: Trevone, Harlyn, Mother Ivey's, Booby's, Constantine, Treyarnon and Porthcothan. Bus 556 runs fairly close by most of the beaches, and also stops at the surfy community of Polzeath, where you'll find plenty of outfits who can help you learn the basics of catching a break. **Animal Surf Academy** (☎01208-880617; www.animalsurfacademy.co.uk) offers options including female-only coaching and sessions with pro surfers; and **Surf's Up Surf School** (☎01208-862003; www.surfsupsurfschool.com) is a family-run outfit.

Sleeping

Treverbyn House B&B £
(☎01841-532855; www.treverbynhouse.com; Station Rd; d £80-115; P) This smart Padstow townhouse is topped by little turrets and has five rooms subtly themed around different colours. It's elegant and understated, and the choice of brekkies is about the best in Padstow.

Ballaminers House B&B ££
(☎01841-540933; www.ballaminershouse.co.uk; Little Petherick; d £90; P) Two miles south of Padstow, this smart stone farmhouse blends old-world atmosphere with modern elegance. Rooms feature Balinese furniture and antique chests, and boast sweeping views of the surrounding fields.

Treyarnon Bay YHA HOSTEL £
(treyarnon@yha.org.uk; Tregonnan; dm £14; P@) Settings don't get much better than this 1930s beach house on the bluffs above Treyarnon Bay. Bus 556 from Padstow stops at nearby Constantine several times a day.

Eating

TOP CHOICE **Paul Ainsworth at No 6** RESTAURANT ££
(☎01840-532093; www.number6inpadstow.co.uk; 6 Middle St; mains £13.50-15.50; ⏲lunch & dinner) You might not have heard of him yet, but take our word for it – Paul Ainsworth is the chef to watch in Padstow. He's trained under some of the country's top names, and his elegant townhouse eatery is a treat. Black-and-white chequerboard tiles, besuited waiters and simple, classic decor provide the perfect setting for Ainsworth's quietly stunning food.

Rick Stein's Cafe BISTRO ££
(☎01841-532700; Middle St; mains £9-18; ⏲closed Sun) Rick Stein's original Padstow establishment, The Seafood Restaurant, is a real budget blower, but this backstreet bistro offers stripped-down samples of his trademark Med-influenced cuisine at much more reasonable prices.

Basement BISTRO ££
(☎01841-532846; 11 Broad Street; lunch mains £7.50-9, dinner mains £12.50-19.50; ⏲lunch & dinner) Newly arrived on Padstow's harbourside, this Continental cafe is a welcome addition for its breezy brasserie-style food. Plump for the smart interior or bag one of the sought-after pavement tables, sheltered under big black umbrellas.

Margot's Bistro BISTRO ££
(☎01840-533441; 11 Duke St; mains £12-15; ⏲lunch Wed-Sat, dinner Tue-Sat) Padstow's not all about big-name chefs – in fact, Margot's owner isn't even called Margot (it's now run by local boy, Adrian Oliver). It's strong on seasonal food, and the decor's cosily chaotic – but there are only a few tables, so booking's a good idea.

Rojano's RESTAURANT ££
(9 Mill Sq; pizzas & pastas from £9; ⏲lunch & dinner Tue-Sun) This bright, buzzy Italian joint turns out excellent pizza and pasta, served either in the snug, sunlit dining room or on the tiny front terrace.

Information

Padstow Tourist Office (☎01841-533449; www.padstowlive.com; North Quay; ⏲10am-5pm Mon-Sat) On the quay.

Getting There & Away

From Padstow, bus 557 (six daily Monday to Saturday) travels to St Columb Major (30 minutes) with connecting buses to Newquay (30 minutes) and Truro (1¼ hours) via the 597.

Newquay

POP 19,423

Bright, breezy and unashamedly brash: that's Newquay, Cornwall's premier party town and the undisputed capital of British surfing. Beautifully positioned above a cluster of golden beaches, a decade ago Newquay was one of Cornwall's top family resorts. But it's recently become infamous for its after-dark antics: throughout the summer, a non-stop parade of beach-blond surfers, boozed-up clubbers and cackling hen parties descends on the town in search of some high jinks beside the seashore, creating a drink-till-dawn atmosphere that's closer to the Costa-del-Sol than Cornwall.

Change might well be afoot in Newquay, however. The recent deaths of two teenagers after nights of heavy drinking have

Newquay

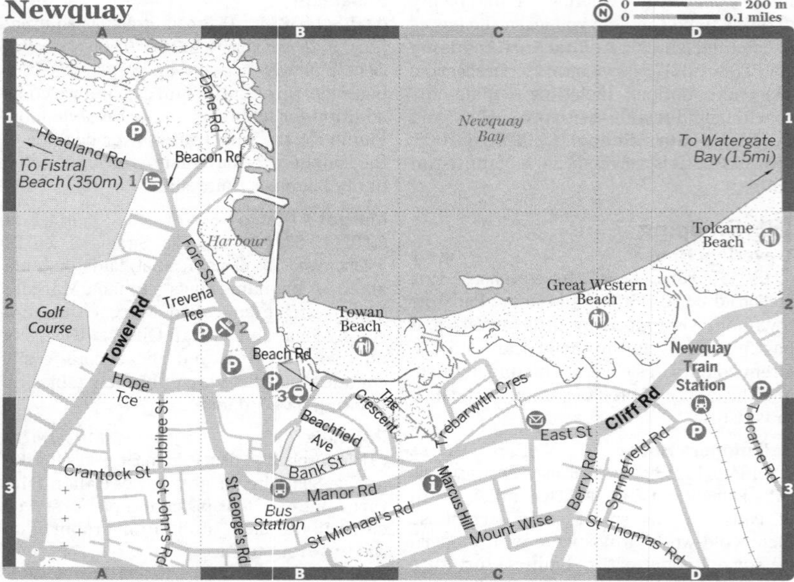

Newquay

Sleeping

1 Goofys A1

Eating

2 Café Irie B2

Drinking

3 Chy B2

Koola ..... (see 3)

prompted many local residents to think again about the direction their town's taken, and perhaps contemplate a return to the family-friendly days of old. But for now the party shows no sign of slowing down, and if you're looking to learn how to brave the waves, Newquay's definitely the place.

Sights & Activities

Beaches

Newquay is set amid some of the finest beaches on the North Coast. **Fistral**, west of Towan Head, is England's best-known surfing beach and the venue for the annual Boardmasters surfing festival. Below town are **Great Western** and **Towan**; a little further up the coast you'll find **Tolcarne**, **Lusty Glaze**, **Porth** and **Watergate Bay**. All these beaches are good for swimming and supervised by lifeguards in summer.

The stately rock towers of **Bedruthan Steps** are a few miles further east towards Padstow; **Crantock** lies 3 miles to the southwest. Further west again is family-friendly **Holywell Bay**.

Surfing

SURF LESSONS

Newquay's awash with places to learn to surf, offering everything from half-day taster lessons (£25 to £30) to full-blown multi-day 'surfaris' (from £130). When choosing your school, make sure it's approved by the BSA (British Surfing Association. Reputable operators include **National Surfing Centre** (☎Fistral Beach 01637-850737, Lusty Glaze 01637-851487; www.nationalsurfingcentre.com) and **Extreme Academy** (☎01637-860840; Watergate Bay; www.extreme academy.co.uk).

Adventure Sports

For those after even more thrills and spills, there are several multi-activity providers in and around Newquay specialising in outdoor sports, from paddle surfing and kitebuggying to the latest Cornish craze, coasteering (pitched somewhere between rock-climbing, scrambling and wild swimming). On Lusty Glaze try **Adventure Centre** (☎01637-872444; www.adventure-centre.org), while on Holywell Bay see **EboAdventure** (☎0800-781-6861; www.penhaleadventure.com).

Sleeping

Although Newquay has stacks of sleeping options, in high season prices rocket, the best get booked up, and some require a week's booking. Surf lodges seem to be on the wane in Newquay – several of the big ones have recently been sold off and redeveloped as holiday flats.

TOP CHOICE **Scarlet** HOTEL £££
(☎01637-861600; www.scarlethotel.co.uk; d £180-395; P 📶 🏊) For out-and-out luxury, there's no topping Cornwall's newest eco-chic hotel. In a regal location above Mawgan Porth, it simply screams designer style: a fabulous infinity pool, a boutique bar straight out of Soho and huge seaview rooms full of funky fabrics, stripped-back surfaces and ridiculously oversized TVs. Stunning really doesn't do it justice.

The Hotel HOTEL ££
(☎01637-860543; www.watergatebay.co.uk; Watergate Bay; d £95-295, ste £205-400; P) Fresh from a multi-million pound refit, the old Watergate has been reinvented as a beachside beauty. The rooms dazzle in slinky pinks, candy-stripes and sea-blues, partnered with wicker chairs, stripped wood and mini sea-view balconies. It's pricey, but for this kind of location it's hardly surprising.

Goofys HOSTEL £
(☎01637-872684; www.goofys.co.uk; 5 Headland Rd; r per person £32.50-40; P @) The town's top surf lodge bills itself as a 'boutique hostel', and it is certainly head and shoulders above the rest. There are only six rooms, so it never feels overcrowded even when it's full, and all the rooms are nicely furnished with posh cotton sheets and 'zip-a-link' beds. There are even several doubles for those who prefer their privacy. Prices fall outside the high season.

Eating

TOP CHOICE **Fifteen Cornwall** RESTAURANT £££
(☎01637-861000; www.fifteencornwall.com; Watergate Bay; lunch/dinner menu £26/55; ⊙lunch & dinner) Jamie Oliver's social enterprise restaurant opened on Watergate Bay back in 2006, and it's proved enormously popular. Underprivileged youngsters learn their trade in the kitchen preparing Oliver's trademark zesty, Italian-influenced food, while diners soak up the beach views and the buzzy, beachy vibe. It's a red-hot ticket: bookings essential.

Beach Hut BISTRO ££
(☎01637-860877; Watergate Bay; mains £9.75-19.95; ⊙breakfast, lunch & dinner) If you can't get a table at Fifteen, head downstairs to the by-the-sand bistro at the Watergate Bay Hotel. It's similarly beachy in feel, and the menu's classic surf 'n' turf: fish curries, 'extreme' burgers and a different fresh fish dish every day.

Café Irie CAFE £
(☎01637-859200; www.cafeirie.co.uk; 38 Fore St; lunch £3-8; ⊙9am-5.30pm Mon-Sat) Run by surfers for surfers, this cafe's famous for its coffee and hot chocolate (just the ticket after a morning in the ocean swell) plus veggie wraps, piping-hot jacket spuds and gooey cakes. The decor's cool, too: vintage vinyl on the walls, multi-coloured plates and coffee mugs, and chalkboards scrawled with specials.

Drinking & Entertainment

Chy BAR
(www.thekoola.com/the-chy-bar; 12 Beach Rd) Chrome, wood and leather dominate this stylish cafe-bar overlooking Towan Beach. The patio is perfect for a gourmet breakfast

WORTH A TRIP

TRERICE

Built in 1751, the charming Elizabethan manor of **Trerice** (NT; ☎01637-875404; adult/child £6.70/3.30; ⊙house 11am-5pm Sat-Thu Mar-Oct, gardens from 10.30am) is famous for the elaborate barrel-roofed ceiling of the Great Chamber, but has plenty of other intriguing features, including ornate fireplaces, original plasterwork and a fine collection of period furniture. There's also an amusing lawnmower museum in the barn, with over 100 grass-cutters going back over a century.

Trerice is 3 miles southeast of Newquay. Bus 527 runs from Newquay to Kestle Mill, about a mile from the manor house.

or lunchtime salad, or pitch up late when the DJs take to the decks and the beers start to flow.

Koola CLUB
(www.thekoola.com; 12 Beach Rd) Underneath Chy, Koola is a world away from most of Newquay's cheese-heavy clubs. The music's eclectic – house, Latin, drum and bass, plus occasional big-name gigs.

Information

Newquay tourist office (☎01637-854020; www.newquay.co.uk; Marcus Hill; ⏰9.30am-5.30pm Mon-Sat, 9.30am-12.30pm Sun)

Tad & Nick's Talk'n'Surf (72 Fore St; per hr £3; ⏰10am-6pm) Net access.

Getting There & Away

Air

Bus 556 (£2.80, 22 minutes, hourly) shuttles to the airport from Newquay's bus station on Manor Rd.

Newquay Airport (☎01637-860600; www.newquaycornwallairport.com) Regular flights to UK airports, including London, Belfast, Birmingham, Cardiff, Edinburgh and the Isles of Scilly.

Bus

The 585/586 is the fastest service to Truro (50 minutes, twice hourly Monday to Saturday), while the hourly 587 follows the coast via Crantock (14 minutes), Holywell Bay (25 minutes) and Perranporth (50 minutes).

Train

There are trains every couple of hours between Newquay and Par (£3.80, 45 minutes) on the main London–Penzance line.

St Agnes & Around

Once a centre for Cornish tin-mining, the coastline around St Agnes is littered with the remains of old minestacks and engine houses, most notably at Wheal Coates, a famously photogenic mine perched on the cliff's edge above the National Trust cove of Chapel Porth. The coast path winds through stunning scenery between the surfers' beaches of Perranporth to the north and Porthtowan to the south.

Sights

Blue Hills Tin Streams
(☎01872-553341; www.bluehillstin.com; adult/child £5.50/3; ⏰10am-4pm Mon-Sat Jul-Aug, 10am-2pm Mon-Sat late-Mar–late-Oct) A mile or so east of St Agnes in the rocky valley of Trevellas Coombe (locally known as Blue Hills, thanks to the copious heather that cloaks the hillsides hereabouts) is one of Cornwall's last (and tiniest) tin manufacturers. Guided tours of this family-run operation take in the whole tinning process, from mining and smelting through to casting and finishing.

The site is reached via a turn-off from the St Agnes–Perranporth road, signed to Wheal Kitty. It's very steep and parking is limited, so take care when driving down. Better still, walk down.

Sleeping & Eating

Aramay B&B ££
(☎01872-553546; www.aramay.com; Quay Rd; d £95-105; P 📶) Not long on the scene, but with five fine rooms and a sweet St Agnes location, it won't stay secret for long. Try No 1, with contemporary four-poster and crimson-and-cream decor, or swanky No 3, with silky throws and views of the Stippy Stappy.

Driftwood Spars HOTEL ££
(☎01872-552428; www.driftwoodspars.com; d £86-110; P) This old warhorse by Trevaunance Cove near St Agnes has something to suit all-comers: local beers and brassy trinkets in the low-ceilinged pub, good bistro **food** (mains £10.95-16.95) in the conservatory restaurant, and nautically-themed upstairs rooms, many of which overlook the cove.

Blue Bar BAR, BISTRO ££
(www.blue-bar.co.uk; Porthtowan; ⏰lunch & dinner) Porthtowan's popular surfers' hang-out has a decent pub-grub menu and plenty of beachside tables, tailor-made for sinking a cold one as the sun goes down.

Getting There & Away

Western Greyhound's bus 583 (12 daily Monday to Saturday) runs between Truro, St Agnes and Perranporth, while bus 304 (10 to 12 Monday to Friday, six on Saturday) goes from Truro to Porthtowan. First's bus 85 (hourly Monday to Saturday) is the most regular from Truro to St Agnes.

St Ives

POP 9870

Sitting on the fringes of a glittering arc-shaped bay, St Ives was once one of Cornwall's busiest pilchard-fishing harbours, but it's better known now as the centre of the county's arts scene. From the old harbour, cobbled alleyways and switchback lanes lead up into the jumble of buzzy galleries, cafes and brasseries that cater for thousands of summer visitors. It makes for an intriguing mix of boutique chic and traditional seaside, and while the high-season traffic can take the shine off things, St Ives is still an essential stop on any Cornish grand tour.

Sights & Activities

Tate St Ives GALLERY

(☎01736-796226; www.tate.org.uk/stives; Porthmeor Beach; adult/child £5.75/3.25; ⊙10am-5pm Mar-Oct, 10am-4pm Tue-Sun Nov-Feb) The artwork almost takes second place to the surroundings at the stunning Tate St Ives, which hovers above Porthmeor Beach. Built in 1993, the gallery contains work by celebrated local artists, including Terry Frost, Patrick Heron and Barbara Hepworth, and hosts regular special exhibitions. On the top floor there's a stylish cafe-bar with imaginative bistro food and some of the best sea views in St Ives. A joint ticket with the **Barbara Hepworth museum** can be purchased for £8.75/4.50 per adult/child.

There are plenty more galleries around town; at the **Sloop Craft Market** you'll find a treasure trove of tiny artists' studios selling everything from handmade jewellery to driftwood furniture.

Barbara Hepworth Museum & Sculpture Garden MUSEUM

(☎01736-796226; www.tate.org.uk/stives; Barnoon Hill; adult/child £5.75/3.25; ⊙10am-5pm Mar-Oct, 10am-4pm Tue-Sun Nov-Feb) Barbara Hepworth (1903–75) was one of the leading abstract sculptors of the 20th century, and a key figure in the St Ives art scene; fittingly her former studio has been transformed into a moving archive and museum. The studio itself has remained almost untouched since her death in a fire, and the adjoining garden contains some of her most famous sculptures. A joint ticket for **Tate St Ives** can be purchased for £8.75/4.50 per adult/child. Hepworth's work is scattered throughout St Ives; look for her sculptures outside the Guildhall and inside the 15th-century parish church of St Ia.

Beaches

The largest town beaches are **Porthmeor** and **Porthminster**, but the tiny cove of **Porthgwidden** is also popular. Nearby, on a tiny peninsula of land known locally as The Island, sits the pre-14th-century Chapel of St Nicholas. **Carbis Bay**, to the southeast, is popular with families and sun seekers.

On the opposite side of the bay from St Ives, the receding tide reveals over 3 miles of golden beach at **Gwithian** and **Godrevy Towans**, both popular spots for kiteboarders and surfers. The lighthouse just offshore at Godrevy was the inspiration for Virginia Woolf's classic stream-of-consciousness novel *To The Lighthouse*.

Gwithian boasts some of the best beach breaks in Cornwall. The **Gwithian Surf Academy** (☎01736-757579; www.surfacademy.co.uk) is one of only four BSA Schools of Excellence, so lessons get booked up fast.

Boat Trips

Boats heading out on sea-fishing trips and cruises to the grey seal colony on Seal Island (adult/child £9/7) include those of the **St Ives Pleasure Boat Association** (☎07821-774178).

Sleeping

Primrose Valley HOTEL £££

(☎01736-794939; www.primroseonline.co.uk; Porthminster Beach; d £105-155, ste £175-225; P 📶) A swash of style on the St Ives seafront. The rooms of the Edwardian house are all deliberately different: some chase a faintly maritime theme, with pale pine and soothing blues, while others plump for rich fabrics, cappuccino throws and exposed brick. It's full of spoils – therapy room, metro-modern bar, locally sourced breakfasts – and needless to say, the sea-views are sensational.

Boskerris HOTEL ££

(☎01736-795295; www.boskerrishotel.co.uk; Boskerris Rd; d £130-195; P 📶) This Carbis Bay beauty is a favourite with the weekend supplements: a 1930s guest house which has had a metro-minimalist makeover. Cool monotones contrast with bespoke wallpaper, artful scatter cushions, shell-shaped chandeliers or curvy lamps; bay views extend in grandstand style from the floaty patio.

Treliska B&B ££

(☎01736-797678; www.treliska.com; 3 Bedford Rd; d £60-80; 📶) The smooth decor at this B&B is attractive – chrome taps, wooden furniture, cool sinks – but what really sells it is the fantastic position, literally steps from St Ives' centre.

Organic Panda B&B ££

(☎01736-793890; www.organicpanda.co.uk; 1 Pednolver Tce; d £80-120; 📶) Sleep

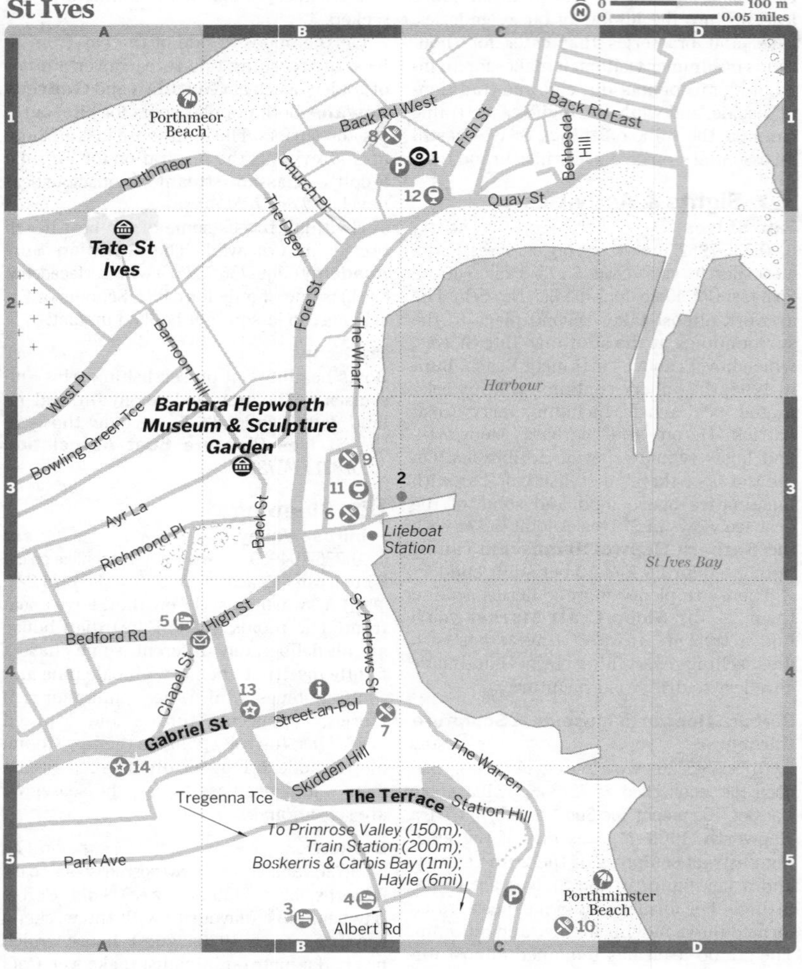

with a clear conscience at this elegant B&B, run along all-organic lines. Spotty cushions, technicolour artwork and timber-salvage beds keep the funk factor high, and local artists showcase their works on the walls. The lack of parking's a pain though.

11 Sea View Terrace B&B ££

(☎01736-798440; www.11stives.co.uk; 11 Sea View Tce; d £100-120; P) Creams, checks and cappuccino carpets distinguish this chic St Ives B&B. The two front rooms have lovely town and sea views, while the rear one overlooks a garden patio; for more space there's a smart holiday flat (£500 to £925 per week).

Eating

St Ives' harbourside is awash with brasseries, but the backlanes conceal plenty of tempting options too.

TOP CHOICE **Porthminster Beach Café** BISTRO ££

(☎01736-795352; www.porthminstercafe.co.uk; Porthminster Beach; lunch £10.50-16.50, dinner £10-22; ⊙9am-10pm) Fresh from scooping

St Ives

Top Sights

Barbara Hepworth Museum & Sculpture Garden B3
Tate St Ives A2

Sights

1 Sloop Craft Market C1

Activities, Courses & Tours

2 Boat Trips C3

Sleeping

3 11 Sea View Terrace B5
4 Organic Panda B5
5 Treliska A4

Eating

6 Alba B3
7 Blas Burgerworks B4
8 Loft B1
9 Onshore B3
10 Porthminster Beach Café C5

Drinking

11 Hub B3
12 Sloop Inn C1

Entertainment

13 Crow Rooms B4
14 Royal Cinema A5

top prize in a recent survey to find Britain's top coastal cafe, the Porthminster boasts a sexy Riviera vibe, a suntrap patio and a seasonal menu ranging from Provençal fish soup to pan-fried scallops. The result? Cornwall's top beach cafe, bar none.

Alba RESTAURANT ££
(01736-797222; Old Lifeboat House; mains £11-18; lunch & dinner) Split-level sophistication next to the lifeboat house, serving some of the best seafood this side of Padstow. In-the-know locals bag tables 5, 6 or 7 for their gorgeous harbour views.

Loft RESTAURANT ££
(01736-794204; www.theloftrestaurantandterrace.co.uk; Norway Ln; dinner £10.95-19.95; lunch & dinner) Great new tip hidden away in a fisherman's net loft just behind the Sloop Craft Centre. The dining room's set out attic-style under A-frame beams, and window tables peep out over St Ives slate rooftops. Solid seafood, locally-sourced meat, Cornish game, delivered with a minimum of fuss or frills: lovely.

Blas Burgerworks CAFE £
(The Warren; burgers £5-10; dinner Tue-Sun) This pocket-sized burger joint has a big reputation: sustainable sourcing, ecofriendly packaging and lots of wacky burger variations have earned it a loyal following. Traditionalists go for the 6oz, 100%-beef Blasburger, while veggies might plump for a halloumi stack or a ginger, coriander and chilli tofu burger.

Onshore PIZZA ££
(01736-796000; The Wharf; pizzas £8-16; lunch & dinner) Pizza, pizza and more pizza – woodfired and award-winning, with super harbour views from the front deck.

Drinking

Hub CAFE
(www.hub-stives.co.uk; The Wharf) As its name suggests, the open-plan Hub is the heart of St Ives' (admittedly limited) nightlife. Think frothy lattes by day, cocktails and boutique beers after-dark, plus sliding doors that open onto the harbour when the sun shines.

Sloop Inn PUB
(The Wharf) A classic fishermen's boozer, complete with low ceilings, tankards behind the bar and a comprehensive selection of Cornish ales.

Entertainment

Crow Rooms VENUE
(www.thecrowrooms.co.uk; Tregenna Hill) The old Isobar has gone under and come up again as this grungy rehearsal space-gig venue – check the website for forthcoming events.

Royal Cinema CINEMA
(www.merlincinemas.co.uk; Royal Sq) Shows new films and often has cheap matinees.

Information

Library (01736-795377; 1 Gabriel St; per hr £3; 9.30am-9.30pm Tue, to 6pm Wed-Fri, to 12.30pm Sat) Internet access.

St Ives Info (www.stives-cornwall.co.uk) Official town website with accommodation and activity guides.

Tourist office (01736-796297; ivtic@penwith.gov.uk; Street-an-Pol; 9am-5.30pm Mon-Fri, 9am-5pm Sat, 10am-4pm Sun) Inside Guildhall.

Getting There & Away

Bus

Quickest bus to Penzance is bus 17 (30 minutes, twice hourly Monday to Saturday, hourly on Sunday). In summer the open-top 300 takes the scenic route via Zennor, Land's End and St Just.

Train

The gorgeous branch line from St Ives is worth taking just for the coastal views: trains terminate at St Erth (£3, 14 minutes, half-hourly), where you can catch connections along the Penzance–Paddington main line.

Zennor

POP 217

For one of Cornwall's most stunning drives, follow the twisting B3306 coast road all the way from St Ives to the windswept village of **Zennor**. The village itself is little more than a collection of cottages collected around the medieval church of **St Senara**. Inside, a famous carved chair depicts the legendary Mermaid of Zennor, who is said to have fallen in love with the singing voice of local lad Matthew Trewhella; it's said you can still sometimes hear them singing down at nearby Pendour Cove.

The **Wayside Folk Museum** (admission £3; 10.30am-5pm Sun-Fri May-Sep, 11am-5pm Sun-Fri Apr & Oct) houses a treasure trove of artefacts gathered by inveterate collector Colonel 'Freddie' Hirst in the 1930s. The displays range from blacksmiths' hammers and cobblers' tools to an 18th-century kitchen and two reclaimed watermills.

Even if you normally don't 'do' dorms, the **Old Chapel Backpackers Hostel** (01736-98307; dm/f £15/50; P) is a top sleeping spot. Set in a sensitively renovated former church, the smart rooms sleep four to six – ask for one with a sea view. There's a comfy, high-ceilinged cafe-lounge too.

DH Lawrence's local while he lived at Zennor was the **Tinner's Arms** (01736-792697; lunch £7-10), a classic Cornish inn with a rambling main bar sheltering under a slate roof.

St Just-in-Penwith

Beyond Zennor, the Penwith landscape really starts to feel big, wild and empty. Blustery cliffs, lonely fields and heather-clad hills unfurl along the horizon en route to the stern granite mining town of **St Just** and the rocky promontory of **Cape Cornwall**, a notorious shipwreck spot in centuries past, now guarded by the blinking lighthouse at **Pendeen Watch**.

Sights

It's hard to imagine today, the St Just area was once at the heart of Cornwall's booming tin and copper mining industry.

Geevor Tin Mine MINE

(01736-788662; www.geevor.com; adult/child £9.50/4.50; 9am-5pm Sun-Fri Mar-Oct, 9am-4pm Sun-Fri Nov-Feb) Just north of St Just near Pendeen, this historic mine closed in 1990 and now provides an amazing insight into the dark and dangerous conditions in which Cornwall's miners worked. You can view the dressing floors and much of the original machinery used to sort the minerals and ores, before taking a tour deep into some of the underground shafts. Claustrophobes need not apply.

WORTH A TRIP

GURNARD'S HEAD

Pubs don't get much more remote than the gorgeous **Gurnard's Head** (01736-796928; www.gurnardshead.co.uk; lunch £5.50-12, dinner £12.50-16.50; 12.30-2.30pm & 6.30-9.30pm). It's flung 6 miles out along the Zennor coast road, but don't worry about missing it – it's the only building for miles around, and has its name spelled out in huge white letters on the roof. Having been taken over by renowned pub-hoteliers the Inkin Brothers (who previously developed the equally swish Felin Fach Griffin near Hay-on-Wye) it's become one of Cornwall's top gastropubs. Book-lined shelves, sepia prints, scruffy wood and rough stone walls create a reassuringly lived-in feel, and the menu's crammed with cockle-warming fare – haddock and mash, spring lamb and belly pork, followed by lashings of Eton Mess or sticky marmalade pudding. If you feel like overnighting, there are country-cosy rooms (doubles without dinner £90 to £160, with dinner for two £135 to £205) upstairs with views of nothing but farms and fields.

Levant Mine & Beam Engine MINE
(www.nationaltrust.org.uk/main/w-levantmineandbeamengine; adult/child £5.80/2.90; ⌚11am-5pm Tue-Fri & Sun Jul-Sep, Wed-Fri & Sun Jun, Wed & Fri Apr-May & Oct) More mining heritage comes to life at this National Trust–owned mine, one of the world's only working Cornish beam engines.

Botallack Mine MINE
Clinging to the cliffs near Levant Mine, one of Cornwall's most dramatic engine houses, which has abandoned mine shafts extending right out beneath the raging Atlantic waves.

 Getting There & Away

St Just is 6 miles north of Land's End. Buses 17/17A/17B travel from St Ives (1¼ hours) via Penzance (half-hourly Monday to Saturday, five on Sunday).

Sennen & Land's End

Further west, the coastline peaks and plunges all the way into the sandy scoop of **Sennen**, which overlooks one of Penwith's most stunning stretches of sand on **Whitesand Bay** (pronounced Whitsand).

From here, there's a wonderful stretch of coast path that leads for about a mile-and-a-half along the clifftops all the way to **Land's End**, the westernmost point of mainland England, where the coal-black cliffs plunge dramatically down into the pounding surf, and the views stretch all the way to the Isles of Scilly on a clear day.

Unfortunately, the decision to build the **Legendary Land's End** (☎0870 458 0099; www.landsend-landmark.co.uk; adult/child £11/7; ⌚10am-4pm or 5pm Easter-Oct, 10.30am-3.30pm Nov-Easter) theme park just behind the headland in the 1980s hasn't done much to enhance the view. Take our advice: skip the tacky multimedia shows and opt for an exhilarating clifftop stroll instead.

Land's End is 9 miles from Penzance. Bus 1/1A travels from Penzance (one hour, eight daily, five on Saturday) to Land's End; half the buses go via Sennen, the other half via Treen and Porthcurno. In summer, the number 300 double-decker runs three or five times daily taking in Penzance, St Ives, and all the main Penwith spots.

Mousehole

The compact harbour town Mousehole (pronounced *mowzle*) was once at the heart of Cornwall's thriving pilchard industry, but these days it's better known for its colourful Christmas lights.

With a tightly-packed knot of slate-roofed cottages gathered around the picturesque harbour, Mousehole is one of Cornwall's most appealing villages, but the picture-perfect location has its drawbacks: huge numbers of second homes means the village is practically a ghost town out of season. It's also the traditional home of 'stargazey pie', a pilchard pie in which the fish-heads are left poking up through the pie's crust. It's traditionally eaten on Tom Bawcock's Eve (23rd December), named after a local lad who reputedly rescued the town from a famine by braving stormy seas to land a bumper haul of pilchards.

To stay the night, set yourself up at the **Old Coastguard Hotel** (☎01736-731222; www.oldcoastguardhotel.co.uk; d £140-210), a swish seaside hotel with jaw-dropping sea views on the edge of Mousehole. The sunlit restaurant (mains £10.50 to £16) also looks out over the glittering bay and specialises, unsurprisingly, in fantastic seafood.

Bus 6 makes the 20-minute journey to Penzance half-hourly.

Penzance & Newlyn

POP 21,168

Stretching along the glittering sweep of Mount's Bay, Penzance has been the last stop on the main railway line from London since the days of the Great Western Railway. With its hotchpotch of winding streets, old shopping arcades and its grand seafront promenade, Penzance is much more authentic than the polished-up, prettified towns of Padstow and St Ives, and makes an excellent base for exploring the rest of west Cornwall and Land's End.

The salty old harbour of Newlyn, on the western edge of Penzance, is one of the UK's busiest fishing ports and offers the chance to buy fresh-cooked lobster, crab and seafood straight off the boats. During the 19th century the port was home to the Newlyn School of artists, a group of figurative painters headed by Stanhope Forbes and his wife Elizabeth.

Penzance

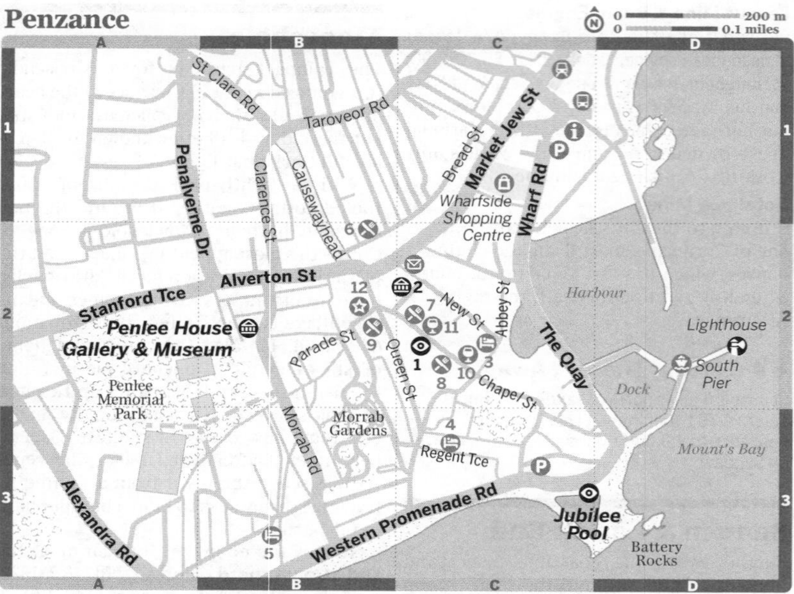

Penzance

Top Sights

Jubilee Pool....C3
Penlee House Gallery & Museum....B2

Sights

1 Egyptian House....C2
2 Exchange....C2

Sleeping

3 Abbey Hotel....C2
4 Camilla House....C3
5 Summer House....B3

Eating

6 Archie Brown's....B2
7 Bakehouse....C2
8 Chapel Street Brasserie....C2
9 Honey Pot....B2

Drinking

10 Turk's Head....C2
11 Zero Lounge....C2

Entertainment

12 Acorn Arts Centre....B2

Sights

Penzance's old town is littered with elegant Georgian and Regency houses, especially around Chapel St; hunt down the 19th-century **Egyptian House**, which looks like a bizarre cross between a Georgian town house and an Egyptian sarcophagus.

Penlee House Gallery & Museum GALLERY
(www.penleehouse.org.uk; Morrab Rd; adult/child £3/2; ⏲10am-5pm Mon-Sat May-Sep, 10.30am-4.30pm Mon-Sat Oct-Apr) Penzance's historic art gallery displays a fine range of paintings by artists of the Newlyn School (including Stanhope Forbes) and hosts regular exhibitions on Cornwall's art history. Admission is free on Saturday.

Jubilee Pool SWIMMING POOL
(www.jubileepool.co.uk; adult/child/family £4/2.90/12.20; ⏲10.30am-6pm May-Sep) At the eastern end of Penzance's 19th-century promenade, the glorious 1930s lido is a fantastic place for a summer dip. Since falling into disrepair in the 1980s, it's been thoroughly spruced-up and is now open to alfresco bathers throughout the summer – just don't expect the water to be warm. Entry is half-price after 3.30pm.

FREE **Newlyn Art Gallery** GALLERY
(www.newlynartgallery.co.uk; ⏲10am-5pm Mon-Sat Easter-Sep, Wed-Sat Oct-Easter) Newlyn's artistic connections live on at this contemporary art gallery.

FREE **Exchange** GALLERY
(www.theexchangegallery.co.uk; Princes Street, Penzance; 10am-5pm Mon-Sat Easter-Sep, Wed-Sat Oct-Easter) Housed in Penzance's old telecoms building, this is the sister gallery to the Newlyn Art Gallery. The pulsating light installation outside is by the artist Peter Freeman, and is best seen after dark.

St Michael's Mount MONUMENT
(NT; 01736-710507; castle & gardens adult/child £8.75/4.25; 10.30am-5.30pm Sun-Fri late-Mar–Oct) Looming up from the waters of Mount's Bay is the unmistakeable silhouette of St Michael's Mount, one of Cornwall's most iconic landmarks. Set on a craggy island connected to the mainland by a cobbled causeway, there's been a monastery here since at least the 5th century, but the present abbey largely dates from the 12th century. After the Norman conquest, the Benedictine monks of Mont St Michel in Normandy raised a new chapel on the island in 1135, and the abbey later became the family seat of the aristocratic St Aubyns (who still reside here).

It's now under the stewardship of the National Trust. Highlights include the rococo drawing room, the original armoury, the 14th-century priory church and the abbey's subtropical gardens, which teeter dramatically above the sea. You can walk across the causeway at low tide, or catch a ferry at high tide in the summer from the little town of Marazion, 3 miles from Penzance.

Sleeping

Penzance has lots of low-price B&Bs, especially along Alexandra Rd and Morrab Rd.

Summer House B&B ££
(01736-363744; www.summerhouse-cornwall.com; Cornwall Tce; d £120-150; closed Nov-Mar; P) For a touch of Chelsea-on-Sea, check into this elegant Regency house. Checks, pinstripes and cheery colours characterise the five bedrooms, and downstairs there's a Mediterranean restaurant with alfresco terrace.

Abbey Hotel HOTEL £££
(01736-366906; www.theabbeyonline.co.uk; Abbey St; d £130-200) This superbly creaky sea-captain's house just off Chapel Street offers a tempting taste of Penzance in its 18th-century heyday. It's brimming with heritage touches – antique dressers, wonky corridors, canopied beds – and a couple of rooms even have their bathrooms tucked away in the cupboard. There's a divine garden out back that's perfect for an early-evening tipple.

Camilla House B&B ££
(01736-363771; www.camillahouse.co.uk; 12 Regent Tce; s £37.50, d £75-95; P) One of several quality B&Bs on Regent's Terrace, this old-fashioned five-starrer stands out for its classy rooms, period features and eco-conscious stance. Fluffy bathrobes, pillow treats and views over the prom will tempt you too.

Penzance YHA HOSTEL £
(penzance@yha.org.uk; Castle Horneck, Alverton; dm £14; P @) Housed inside an 18th-century Georgian manor on the outskirts of town, this official hostel has an on-site cafe, laundry and four- to 10-bed dorms. Buses 5 and 6 run from the bus station to Alverton; it's a 500m walk from the bus stop.

DON'T MISS

MINACK THEATRE

In terms of theatrical settings, the **Minack** (01736-810181; www.minack.com) really has to take top billing. Carved directly into the crags overlooking Porthcurno Bay and the azure-blue Atlantic, this amazing clifftop amphitheatre was the lifelong passion of local lady Rowena Cade, who dreamt up the idea in the 1930s and oversaw the theatre until her death in 1983. It's now a hugely popular place for alfresco theatre, with a 17-week season running from mid-May to mid-September: regulars bring wine, picnic supplies, wet-weather gear and – most importantly of all, considering the seats are carved out of granite – a very comfy cushion.

Above the theatre, the **visitor centre** (adult/child £3.50/1.40; 9.30am-5.30pm Apr-Sep, 10am-4pm Oct-Mar) recounts the theatre's history; it's closed when there's a matinée.

The Minack is three miles from Land's End and 9 miles from Penzance. Bus 1/1A from Penzance stops several times daily.

Eating

Chapel Street Brasserie BISTRO ££

(☎01736-350222; 13 Chapel St; mains £10-15; ⏰10am-11pm) Formerly Bar Coco's, this well-groomed Gallic bistro makes the perfect place for a hearty plate of French food, from steaming bowls of mussels to rich cassoulet. The two-course *prix fixe* menu is super value at £12.50, and it's served at lunch and supper.

Bakehouse BISTRO ££

(☎01736-331331; www.bakehouserestaurant.co.uk; Chapel St; mains £8.95-19.50; ⏰lunch Wed-Sat, dinner daily) This funky double-floored diner caters for seafood-lovers and veggies, but it's the carnivores who do best: copious steak choices are partnered with your choice of sauce or spicy rub.

Archie Brown's CAFE £

(☎01736-362828; Bread St; mains £3-10; ⏰9.30am-5pm Mon-Sat) A cosier whole-food caff you couldn't hope to find. Archie Brown's has been serving Penzance's earth-mothers and artsy crowd for years and shows no signs of flagging, with stocked-up counters full of crispy salads, veggie quiches and carrot cake.

Honey Pot CAFE £

(☎01736-368686; 5 Parade St; mains £4-10; ⏰9am-5pm Mon-Sat) Another wonderfully friendly Penzance cafe, opposite the Acorn Arts Centre. It's a popular spot for afternoon tea and cake, but also turns out tempting fare such as jacket potatoes and homemade homity pies. Naturally, nearly everything's made on site and locally sourced, and the big glass windows keep it sunny and light-filled.

Drinking & Entertainment

Turk's Head PUB

(Chapel St) They pull a fine pint of real ale at this, the oldest boozer in Penzance. It's said a smugglers' tunnel used to link the pub with the harbour – handy for sneaking in that liquid contraband – and the bar's covered in maritime memorabilia.

Zero Lounge BAR

(Chapel St) More urban chic than olde-worlde, this open-plan bar also boasts the town's best beer patio.

Acorn Arts Centre THEATRE

(www.acornartscentre.co.uk; Parade St) An excellent independent arts centre, with regular programs of film, theatre and live music.

Information

Library (Morrab Rd; per hr £3; ⏰9.30am-6pm Mon-Fri, to 4pm Sat) Internet access.

Penzance Online (www.penzance.co.uk) Useful local guide.

Tourist office (☎01736-362207; penzance-tic@cornwall.gov.uk; Station Approach; ⏰9am-5pm Mon-Sat, 10am-1pm Sun) Next to the bus station.

Getting There & Away

For travel to the Isles of Scilly, see p345.

Bus

Penzance is the main local bus hub for the Penwith area.

Helston (45 minutes, six to eight daily) Buses 2/2A/2B; via Marazion and Praa Sands.

St Ives (30 minutes, twice hourly Monday to Saturday, hourly on Sunday) Buses 17/17A/17B.

Truro (one hour, four daily Monday to Saturday) Bus X18; express service.

Train

Penzance is the last stop on the main rail route from Paddington. Sample fares:

Bodmin (£8.40, 1¼ hours)

Bristol (£37, four hours)

Exeter (£11.50, three hours)

London Paddington (5½ hours, £57.50, hourly)

St Ives (£3.30, 30 minutes)

Truro (£5.40, 30 minutes)

The Lizard

For a taste of Cornwall's stormier side, head for the ink-black cliffs, rugged coves and open heaths of the Lizard Peninsula. Wind-lashed in winter, in summer it bristles with wildflowers, butterflies and coves that are perfect for a secluded swim.

The Lizard used to be at the centre of Cornwall's smuggling industry and is still alive with tales of Cornish 'free-traders', contraband liquor and the government's preventive boats. The most notorious excise dodger was John Carter, the so-called King of Prussia – Prussia Cove near Marazion is named after him. It was also an ill-famed graveyard for ships – more vessels have come to grief on the Lizard's treacherous reefs than almost anywhere else in Britain.

The Lizard's main town is **Helston**, which is famous for its annual street party, Flora Day, held on 8 May.

Sights & Activities

Lizard Lighthouse Heritage Centre LANDMARK, MUSEUM

(www.lizardlighthouse.co.uk; adult/child £4/2; ⏲Sun-Thu most of year, plus extra days in summer) Right at the tip of the peninsula is **Lizard Point**, the southernmost point in England. The vista from the surrounding cliffs is breathtaking, but it's especially worth a visit for this maritime museum, housed in a historic lighthouse built in 1751. The museum explore's the Lizard's connections with smuggling, shipwrecks and nautical navigation: you even get the chance to climb up into the tower and, if you're lucky, let off a deafening blast from the foghorn.

National Seal Sanctuary WILDLIFE

(☎0871-423-2110; www.sealsanctuary.co.uk; adult/child £10.95/6.95; ⏲10am-5pm May-Sep, 9am-4pm Oct-Apr) This sanctuary cares for sick and orphaned seals washed up along the Cornish coastline before returning them to the wild. It's six miles from Helston at the western end of the Helford River.

Sleeping

Chydane B&B ££

(☎01326-241232; www.chydane.co.uk; Gunwalloe; s/d £50/100; P 📶) This much-touted Lizard B&B teeters on the cliff edge right above Gunwalloe Cove, and both rooms peep over the beach and bay beyond (although the window in the Porthole Room is, as it's name suggests, tiny). Elsewhere, there are plenty of local books to browse in the lounge, and a panoramic patio where the coastal vistas truly dazzle; and the excellent Halzephron Inn is only a short walk away.

Beacon Crag B&B ££

(☎01326-573690; www.beaconcrag.com; d £85-95; P @) Built for a local artist, this Victorian villa above Porthleven is now one of the Lizard's loveliest B&Bs. Rooms are

West Cornwall

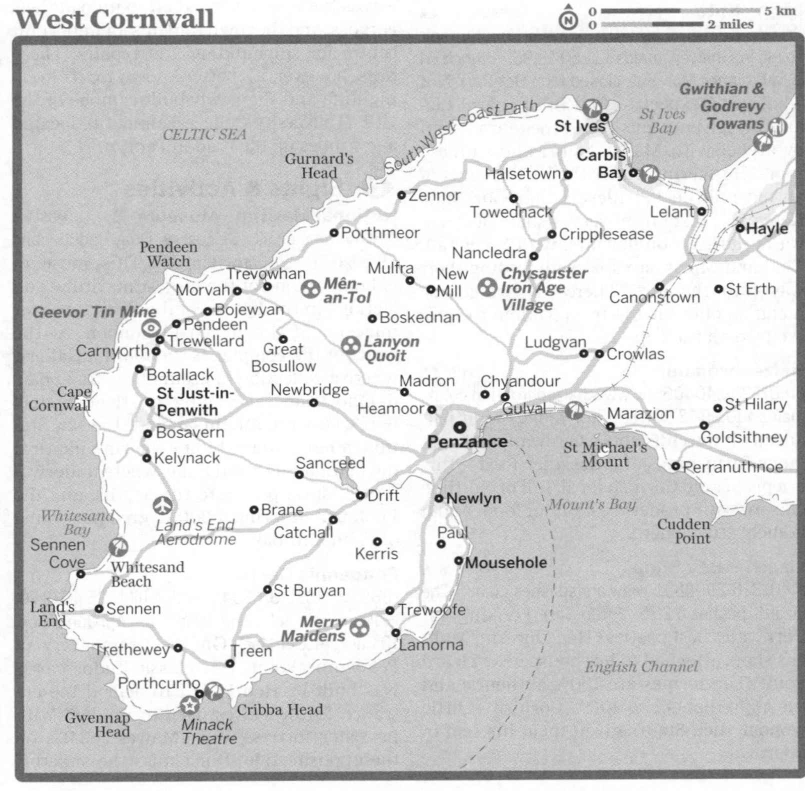

plainly furnished to make the most of the house's grandstand position: craggy coastline unfurls in abundance around the house.

Lizard YHA HOSTEL £
(lizard@yha.org.uk; dm £14; ⏲Apr-Oct) Wow – this absolutely marvellous hostel commands the kind of sea view you'd normally have to pay through the nose for. Housed in former lighthouse-keeper's cottages, it's quite simply one of the most spectacularly situated hostels anywhere in England.

Coverack YHA HOSTEL £
(coverack@yha.org.uk; Coverack; dm from £14; ⏲Mar-Oct) Set above the pretty harbour of Coverack, this was a decent hostel even before its recent refit. Five of the nine bedrooms are now ensuite (making them a great B&B alternative) and the setting in a Victorian clifftop villa surrounded by private grounds is simply out of this world.

Eating

TOP CHOICE **Kota** RESTAURANT ££
(☎01326-562407; www.kotarestaurant.co.uk; Porthleven; mains £11.50-19.95; ⏲lunch Fri & Sat, dinner Mon-Sat, closed Mon Oct-Apr) Not what you'd expect to find in the rural Lizard: an adventurous fusion restaurant run by a chef with Malay, Maori and Chinese roots. Hunkering under the hefty beams of an old mill on Porthleven's harbour, Jude Kereama's restaurant serves some of Cornwall's most exotic flavours, with Szechuan, Thai and Malaysian spices all finding their way into the mix. There's a two-course menu on offer for £14 from 5.30pm to 7pm. Well worth the trip.

Halzephron Inn PUB ££
(☎01326-240406; www.halzephron-inn.co.uk; mains £10.95-18.50) Hugger-mugger inn balanced on the cliffs above Gunwalloe. Forget fancy furnishings and designer food – this is a proper old Cornish local, full of old-time charm, with proper ales, filling food, and a homely atmosphere.

Lizard Pasty Shop PASTIES £
(☎01326-290889; www.annspasties.co.uk; The Lizard; pasties £2.75; ⏲Tue-Sat) Looking for Cornwall's best pasties? Head for Ann Muller's shop, attached to her house near Lizard Point. The recipes are 100% authentic and the ingredients are 100% Cornish – little wonder Rick Stein's given them his seal of approval.

Getting There & Away

Buses are the only public transport option on the Lizard.

Bus 2 Penzance to Falmouth, with stops at Porthleven and Helston (eight to ten Monday to Saturday, six on Sunday).

Bus 32 Helston to Gunwalloe, Gweek, Coverack and St Keverne (two on Sundays only).

Bus 33 Helston to Poldhu, Mullion and the Lizard (three daily Monday to Friday).

Bus 82 Helston to Truro (hourly Monday to Saturday, five on Sunday).

Falmouth

POP 20,775

The maritime port of Falmouth sits on the county's south coast at the end of the Carrick Roads, a huge river estuary that empties out into the third deepest natural harbour in the world. Falmouth's fortunes were made during the 18th and 19th centuries, when clippers, trading vessels and mail packets from across the world stopped off to unload their cargoes, and the town remains an important centre for shipbuilding and repairs. These days, however, it's better known for its lively nightlife and the newly-built campus of the UCF (University College Falmouth), located a few miles up the road in Penryn.

Sights & Activities

National Maritime Museum MUSEUM
(www.nmmc.co.uk; Discovery Quay; adult/child £9.50/6.50; ⏲10am-5pm; 📶) This museum is home to one of the largest maritime collections in the UK, second only to its sister museum in Greenwich in London. At the heart of the complex is the Flotilla Gallery, where a collection of groundbreaking boats dangle from the ceiling on slender steel wires. Other highlights include the Nav Station, a hands-on exhibit exploring nautical navigation, the Tidal Zone, where underwater windows peer into the depths, and the Look Out, offering a 360-degree panorama of Falmouth Bay.

Pendennis Castle CASTLE
(EH; ☎01326-316594; adult/child £5.40/2.70; ⏲10am-6pm Jul & Aug, 10am-5pm Apr-Jun & Sep, 10am-4pm Oct-Mar) On the promontory of Pendennis Point, this classic Tudor castle was built by Henry VIII to defend the entrance to the Fal estuary in tandem with its sister fortress at St Mawes (p340), on the opposite side. Don't miss the superbly

atmospheric Tudor gun deck (complete with cannon flashes, smoke and shouted commands), the WWI guard house and the WWII observation post.

Boat Trips

Passenger ferries make the harbour-mouth dash across to St Mawes and Flushing every hour in summer. For a longer trip, several operators run from the Prince of Wales Pier or Customs House Quay along the Fal River, making stops at National Trust–owned Trelissick Gardens, the 500-year-old Smuggler's Cottage pub and Truro. Try **Enterprise Boats** (☎01326-374241; www.enterprise-boats.co.uk) or **Newman's Cruises** (☎01872-580309; www.newmanscruises.co.uk).

Beaches

Falmouth has three main beaches. The nearest beach to town is busy **Gyllyngvase**, a short walk from the town centre, where you'll find plenty of flat sand and a decent beach cafe. Further around the headland, **Swanpool** and **Maenporth** are usually quieter. The regular Bus 500 from Falmouth stops at all three.

Trebah GARDENS
(☎01326-252200; www.trebahgarden.co.uk; adult/child £7.50/2.50 Mar-Oct, £3/1 Nov-Feb; ⏲10.30am-6.30pm, last entry 4.30pm) Two of Cornwall's great gardens sit side by side along the northern bank of the Helford River, both of which can be visited on a day trip from Falmouth. Trebah, first planted in 1840, is one of Cornwall's finest subtropical gardens, dramatically situated in a steep ravine filled with giant rhododendrons, huge Brazilian rhubarb plants and jungle ferns.

Glendurgan GARDENS
(NT; ☎01326-250906; adult/child £6/3; ⏲10.30am-5.30pm Tue-Sat Feb-Oct) Next-door to Trebah, this garden was established in the 18th century by the wealthy Fox family, who imported exotic plants from the New World. Look out for the stunning views of the River Helford, the 19th-century maze and the secluded beach near Durgan village. The garden is also open on Mondays in July and August.

Sleeping

Falmouth has plenty of B&Bs and hotels, especially around Melvill Rd and Avenue Rd.

Falmouth Townhouse HOTEL ££
(☎01326-312009; www.thefalmouthtownhouse.co.uk; Grove Place; d £85-120; 📶) The choice for the design-conscious, in an elegant mansion halfway between the high street and Discovery Quay. Despite the heritage building, the feel is studiously modernist: slate greys, retro bits-and-bobs and funky scatter cushions throughout, plus walk-in showers and king-size tellies in the top-of-the-line rooms.

St Michael's Hotel HOTEL £££
(☎01326-312707; www.stmichaelshotel.co.uk; r £129-333; P 🏊) One of a string of places along the Falmouth seafront, but St Michael's stands head and shoulders above the rest. Comprehensive renovations have reinvented the bedrooms in gingham checks, stripes and slatted wood, giving them a feel akin to a New England beach retreat, and the whole place is sprinkled with maritime touches, from portholes in the doors to a soothing palette of sea-greens and bottle-blues.

Hawthorne Dene Hotel B&B ££
(☎01326-311427; www.hawthornedenehotel.co.uk; 12 Pennance Rd; d £80-90; P) Edwardian elegance rules the roost at this family-run hotel, with its ranks of old photos and booklined gentleman's lounge. The antique-themed bedrooms feature springy beds, polished woods and teddy bears – most also have a sea view.

Chelsea House B&B ££
(☎01326-212230; www.chelseahousehotel.com; 2 Emslie Rd; d £63-73) On a terrace of tucked-away B&Bs just off the seafront, the Chelsea's attractive rooms include a 'Ships and Castle' family suite, spacious 'Pendennis' with a sea-view bay window and a miniscule 'Captain's Cabin' in the attic.

Falmouth Backpacker's HOSTEL £
(⏲01326-319996; www.falmouthbackpackers.co.uk; 9 Gyllyngvase Terrace; dm/s £19/25, d £50-60) New owners have given this old Falmouth hostel a new lease of life, and its rooms are now much enlivened with bright colours, cosy beds and the odd funky print. There's an Aga in the kitchen and a DVD lounge, but the real asset is owner Judy, who's full of fizzy fun and often lays on BBQs and paella nights.

Eating

TOP CHOICE **Cove** RESTAURANT £££
(☎01326-251136; www.thecovemaenporth.co.uk; Maenporth; mains £14.25-22.50; ⏲lunch & dinner) It's a trek down to Maenporth, but you'll be more than happy you made the effort. This gorgeous and much garlanded

WORTH A TRIP

PANDORA INN

One of Cornwall's oldest and loveliest creekside pubs, the **Pandora Inn** (☎01326-372678; www.pandorainn.com; Restronguet Creek; mains £10-16) is nestled in a beautiful river setting. Inside, blazing hearths, snug alcoves and ships-in-cabinets; outside, thatched roof, cob walls and a pontoon snaking out onto Restronguet Creek. The location really has the wow-factor, but the food's lost some star quality since a recent change of ownership. It's a bit tricky to find if you've never been – you'll need a decent map.

modern fine diner has earned a big reputation thanks to the creative talents of head man Arty Williams, who imparts his own individual spin on contemporary Brit cuisine. The pièce de la resistance is the glorious beach-view deck: reserve well ahead.

Oliver's RESTAURANT ££
(☎01326-218138; 33 High St; mains £12.95-19.95; ⏲lunch & dinner Tue-Sun) There's nothing remotely fancy about the decor at this new French-style bistro – it's plain pine meets plain white walls – but here simplicity is definitely a virtue. The food is classic, unfussy and impeccably presented, with the emphasis placed on essential flavours rather than cheffy flourishes. It's particularly strong on seafood.

Indaba on the Beach RESTAURANT £££
(☎01326-311886; www.indabafish.co.uk; Swanpool; mains £10.50-37.95; ⏲lunch daily, dinner Mon-Sat) The former Three Mackerel has recently been snapped up by the folk behind Indaba Fish in Truro. It offers the same upmarket seafood menu from mussels to full-blown lobster platters, with the added benefit of a top-drawer position on the rocks above Swanpool.

Stein's Fish & Chips CAFE ££
(☎01841-532700; Discovery Quay; dishes £6.65-10.95; ⏲12-2.30pm & 5-9pm) It had to happen – the Stein empire is spreading. Offering the same menu as his Padstow original (top-quality battered fish fried in beef dripping, or fish grilled in sunflower oil, both accompanied with hand-cut chips), Stein's Falmouth fish-and-chip shop has the addition of a snazzy **oyster bar** (mains £3.50-15.50; ⏲5-9pm) on the top floor. Pricey, mind.

Gylly Beach Café CAFE ££
(☎01326-312884; www.gyllybeach.com; Gyllyngvase Beach; mains £10.95-15.95; ⏲breakfast, lunch & dinner) The decked patio over Gyllyngvase is the main draw at this lively beach restaurant. It covers all bases: fry-ups and pancakes for brekkie, platters of antipasti for lunch, quality steak, seafood and pasta after dark. It's open late for drinks, too, but gets very busy.

Drinking

Top spots for a pint include the **Quayside** (Arwenack St), with outside seating on the harbour, and the **Chain Locker** (Quay St), crammed with maritime atmosphere.

Information

Falmouth Tourist Office (☎01326-312300; falmouthtic@yahoo.co.uk; 11 Market Strand, Prince of Wales Pier; ⏲9.30am-5.15pm Mon-Sat) On the pier.

Getting There & Away

Bus

Falmouth is well served by buses.

Glendurgan, the Helford Passage and Gweek (nine or ten daily Monday to Saturday, two on Sunday) Bus 35. Some services continue to Helston.

Helford Passage (four to six daily in summer) Western Greyhound bus 500; to the outer beaches.

Truro (hourly) Bus 88; fastest option.

Truro & Newquay (eight daily Monday to Saturday) Bus 89/90.

Train

Falmouth is at the end of the branch line from Truro (£3.20, 20 minutes), which also stops at Penryn.

Truro

POP 17,431

Cornwall's capital city has been at the centre of the county's fortunes for over eight centuries. Truro first grew up around a now vanished hilltop castle, and throughout the Middle Ages it was one of Cornwall's five stannary towns, where tin and copper was assayed and stamped. The 18th and 19th centuries saw it become a key industrial centre, and its wealthy merchants built swathes of elegant town houses, best seen along Lemon St and Falmouth Rd. Truro was granted its own bishop in 1877, with the city's three-spired cathedral following soon after. Today the city makes an appealing base, with a good selection of shops, galleries and restaurants and Cornwall's main museum.

Sights

FREE **Royal Cornwall Museum** MUSEUM
(☎01872-272205; www.royalcornwallmuseum.org.uk; River St; ⏰10am-5pm Mon-Sat) The county's main repository for all things industrial and archaeological, with an eclectic collection taking in everything from geological specimens to Celtic torques and a ceremonial carriage. Upstairs there's a small Egyptian section and a little gallery with some surprising finds: a Turner here, a van Dyck there, and several works by Stanhope Forbes.

Truro Cathedral CHURCH
(☎01872-276782; www.trurocathedral.org.uk; High Cross; suggested donation £4; ⏰7.30am-6pm Mon-Sat, 9am-7pm Sun) Built on the site of a 16th-century parish church in soaring Gothic Revival style, Truro Cathedral was finally completed in 1910, making it the first new cathedral in England since London's St Paul's. It contains a soaring high-vaulted nave, some fine Victorian stained glass and the impressive Father Willis Organ.

Trelissick Gardens COUNTRY ESTATE
(NT; ☎01872-862090; Feock; adult/child £7.40/3.70; ⏰10.30am-5.30pm Feb-Oct, 11am-4pm Nov-Jan) At the head of the Fal estuary, 4 miles south of Truro, Trelissick is one of Cornwall's most beautiful estates, with a formal garden filled with magnolias and hydrangeas, and a huge expanse of fields and parkland criss-crossed by walking trails.

Sleeping

Mannings Hotel HOTEL ££
(☎01872-270345; www.manningshotels.co.uk; Lemon St; s £79, d £99-109; P 📶) Truro's best option (formerly known as the Royal Hotel) is this efficient city-centre hotel, geared mainly towards the business crowd. Bold, bright colours, wall-mounted TVs and up-to-date furniture keep things uncluttered, and there are 'aparthotels' with all the mod-cons for longer stays (£129 a night). The restaurant's none too shabby either.

Carlton Hotel HOTEL ££
(☎01872-223938; www.carltonhotel.co.uk; 49 Falmouth Rd; s £50-59, d £68-79; P) This double-fronted Victorian house is a coach-tour favourite, so it's often booked out in summer. The furnishings are pretty much bog-standard B&B (pastel colours, easy-clean carpets), but on the up side, it's only a five minute walk down the hill into town.

Eating

Saffron RESTAURANT ££
(☎01872-263771; www.saffronrestauranttruro.co.uk; 5 Quay St; mains £10-16.50; ⏰lunch Mon-Fri, dinner Tue-Sat) It's been around for ages, but this titchy restaurant tucked down a Truro side-street still packs an impressive culinary punch. It's strong on seasonal Cornish produce served with a Mediterranean twist: spider-crab served bisque-style, pollock dished up with saffron mash, mutton with turnip dauphinoise.

French Bistro RESTAURANT ££
(☎01872-223068; www.thefrenchbistro.co.uk; 19 New Bridge St; plat du jour £5.95-7.50, mains £10-12; ⏰lunch & dinner Thu-Sat) Ooh la la – Karen Cairns' opulent eatery has brought a flash of French sophistication to Truro, and it's a lovely place to tuck into classic casseroles, *coq au vin* and *oeuf cocottes*. The jumble shop decor just adds to the charm. Wine is bring-your-own; corkage is £3.

Indaba Fish RESTAURANT ££
(☎01872-274700; Tabernacle St; mains £14-18; ⏰dinner) The chef here used to work for Rick Stein, and this swish fish emporium has a similar emphasis on classic, straightforward seafood, ranging from Falmouth oysters and Newlyn lobster to sea bream with garlic mash. Vegetarians and fish-phobes are catered for too.

Drinking

Old Ale House PUB
(Quay St) What a relief – a city-centre pub that eschews chrome 'n' cocktails and sticks with burnished wood 'n' beer mats. The daily ales are chalked up behind the bar and there's often live jazz at weekends.

Heron PUB
(Malpas; ⏰11am-3pm & 6-10.30pm Mon-Fri, 11am-11pm Fri & Sat, noon-10.30pm Sun) Two miles along the river estuary from Truro, this Malpas pub is an idyllic place for a riverside pint.

Old Grammar School PUB
(19 St Mary St; ⏰10am-late) Open-plan drinking den with big tables and soft sofas to sink into. Lunch is served from noon to 3pm; later it's cocktails, candles and imported Belgian and Japanese beers.

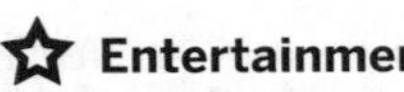

Hall for Cornwall THEATRE
(☎01872-262466; www.hallforcornwall.co.uk; Lemon Quay) The county's main venue for touring theatre and music.

Plaza Cinema CINEMA
(☎01872-272894; www.wtwcinemas.co.uk; Lemon St) A four-screen cinema showing mainstream releases.

Information

Library (☎01872-279205; Union Pl; per hr £3; ⏲9am-6pm Mon-Fri, 9am-4pm Sat) Net access.

Tourist office (☎01872-274555; tic@truro.gov.uk; Boscawen St; ⏲9am-5.30pm Mon-Fri, 9am-5pm Sat)

Bus

Truro is the county's main bus terminus, with regular services all over the county and frequent National Express coaches to Exeter, Bristol, Heathrow, and London Victoria. The bus station is beside Lemon Quay. Useful local lines:

Falmouth (hourly) Bus 88.

Helston (one hour, hourly, five on Sunday) Bus 82.

St Ives (1½ hours, hourly Monday to Saturday) Bus 14/14A/14B.

Newquay (hourly Monday to Saturday, six on Sun) Bus 85/85A. Runs to St Agnes then along the coast via Perranporth.

Newquay (ten daily Monday to Saturday) Bus 89/90.

Penzance (one hour, hourly Monday to Saturday, six on Sunday) Bus X18. Express service via Redruth and Camborne.

Train

Truro is on the main Paddington-Penzance line and the branch line to Falmouth. Destinations:

Bodmin (£7.40, 30 minutes)

Bristol (£37, 3½ hours)

Exeter (£15.40, 2¼ hours)

Falmouth (£3.60, 30 minutes)

London Paddington (£57.50, five hours)

Penzance (£5.40, 30 minutes)

Around Truro

THE ROSELAND

Stretching into the sea south of Truro, this beautiful rural peninsula gets its name not from flowers but from the Cornish word *ros,* meaning promontory. Highlights include the coastal villages of **Portloe**, a wreckers' hang out on the South West Coast Path, and **Veryan**, awash with daffodils in spring and framed by two thatched roundhouses. Nearby are the beaches of **Carne** and **Pendower**, which join at low tide to form one of the best stretches of sand on Cornwall's south coast.

St Mawes has a beautifully preserved clover-leaf **castle** (EH; ☎01326-270526; adult/child £4.20/2.10; ⏲10am-6pm Jul & Aug, 10am-5pm Apr-Jun & Sep, 10am-4pm Oct, 10am-4pm Fri-Mon Nov-Mar), commissioned by Henry VIII and designed as the sister fortress to Pendennis across the estuary.

St Just-in-Roseland boasts one of the most beautiful churchyards in the country, tumbling down to a creek filled with boats and wading birds.

CORNISH MINING SITES

Since 2006, Cornwall and West Devon's historic mining areas have formed part of the UK's newest Unesco World Heritage Site, the **Cornwall & West Devon Mining Landscape** (www.cornish-mining.org.uk).

The **Cornish Mines & Engines** (☎01209-315027; cornishmines@nationaltrust.org.uk) centre in Pool, near Redruth, makes an ideal place to get acquainted with this once great industry. At the heart of the complex are two working beam engines, both once powered by steam boilers designed by local lad Richard Trevithick (who was born in Redruth in 1771, and whose cottage at Penponds is now open to the public). Films, photos and artefacts trace the area's rich mining history, while you can see more mining gear in action at **King Edward Mine** (☎01209-614681; www.kingedwardmine.co.uk; adult/child £5/1; ⏲10am-5pm May-Sep).

It's also well worth making a visit to the historic beam engine at Levant (p331) and the mine at Geevor (p330), where you can take an underground tour into the old mineshafts.

THE EDEN PROJECT

If any one thing is emblematic of Cornwall's regeneration, it's the **Eden Project** (01726-811911; www.edenproject.com; Bodelva; adult/child/family £16/6/39; 10am-6pm Apr-Oct, 10am-4.30pm Nov-Mar). Ten years ago the site was a dusty, exhausted clay pit, a symbol of the county's industrial decline. Now, thanks to the vision of ex-record producer turned environmental pioneer Tim Smit, it's home to three giant biomes, the largest greenhouses anywhere in the world.

Inside, a huge variety of plants recreate tropical, temperate and desert habitats, from dry savannah to tropical rainforest and wild jungle, elegantly illustrating the diversity of life on earth and our own dependence on its continued survival. It's informative, educational and enormous fun, but it does get very busy: booking in advance online will allow you to dodge the worst queues, and also bag a £1 discount.

In summer the biomes also become a spectacular backdrop to a series of outdoor gigs during the **Eden Sessions** (www.edensessions.com), and in winter Eden is transformed for the seasonal **Time of Gifts** festival, complete with a full-size ice rink.

It's three miles by road from St Austell; you can catch buses from St Austell, Newquay, Helston, Falmouth and Truro, but arriving on foot or by bike snags you £3 off the admission price. Last entry is 90 minutes before the site closes.

LOST GARDENS OF HELIGAN

Cornwall's own real-life secret **garden** (01726-845100; www.heligan.com; Pentewan; adult/child £8.50/5; 10am-6pm Mar-Oct, 10am-5pm Nov-Feb). Formerly the family estate of the Tremaynes, the gardens fell into disrepair following WWI (when many staff were killed) and have since been restored to their former splendour by Tim Smit (the man behind the Eden Project and a huge army of gardeners, horticultural specialists and volunteers. Among the treats in store at Heligan are a working kitchen garden, formal terraces, a secret grotto and a wild jungle valley – as well as the world's largest rhododendron, measuring an impressive 82 feet from root to tip.

Heligan is 7 miles from St Austell. Bus 526 (30 minutes, hourly, ten on Sunday) links Heligan with Mevagissey and St Austell train station.

Fowey

POP 2273

Nestled on the steep tree-covered hillside overlooking the River Fowey, opposite the old fishing harbour of Polruan, Fowey (pronounced Foy) is a pretty tangle of pale-shaded houses and snaking lanes. Its long maritime history includes being the base for 14th-century raids on France and Spain; to guard against reprisals Henry VIII constructed **St Catherine's Castle** above Readymoney Cove, south of town. The town later prospered by shipping china clay extracted from pits at St Austell, but the industrial trade has long declined and Fowey has now reinvented itself for summer-time tourists and second-home owners.

The **tourist office** (01726-833616; www.fowey.co.uk; 5 South St; 9am-5.30pm Mon-Sat, 10am-5pm Sun) is also home to the compact **Daphne du Maurier Literary Centre** (01726-833616; www.fowey.co.uk; 5 South St; 9am-5.30pm Mon-Sat, 10am-5pm Sun), which is devoted to the author of *Rebecca*, *Frenchman's Creek* and the short story that inspired Hitchcock's film *The Birds*, who spent much of her life in Fowey. Every May the town hosts the **Daphne du Maurier Literary Festival** (www.dumaurier.org) in her honour.

Sleeping

Old Quay House HOTEL £££

01726-833302; 28 Fore St; www.theoldquayhouse.com; d £180-250;) The epitome of Fowey's upmarket trend, this extremely exclusive quayside hotel is all natural fabrics, rattan chairs and tasteful tones, and the rooms are a mix of estuary-view suites and attic penthouses. Very Kensington; not at all Cornish.

Coriander Cottages B&B ££

(01726-834998; www.foweyaccommodation.co.uk; Penventinue Ln; r £90-130, cottages £130-220; P) A delightful cottage complex on the outskirts of Fowey, with ecofriendly accommodation in a choice of B&B garden rooms or deluxe open-plan barns, all of which

TREVALSA COURT

Perched on the clifftops above the old fishing village of Mevagissey, this Edwardian **pile** (☎01726-842468; www.trevalsa-hotel.co.uk; School Hill, Mevagissey; d £125-225; P) is one of the best places to stay on the south coast, but the word's out so you'll need to reserve well ahead. Its restoration-meets-retro approach is enormously persuasive: some rooms have sleigh beds and leather sofas, others funky fabrics and modernist lamps, while a lounge with mullioned windows opens onto coast views.

offer a gloriously quiet rural atmosphere far removed from Fowey's tourist fizz.

Fowey Marine Guest House B&B ££
(☎01726-833920; www.foweymarine.com; 21-27 Station Rd; s/d £50/70; wi-fi) Snug room in a teeny harbour guest house, run by a friendly husband-and-wife team. It's especially handy for the harbour car park.

Golant YHA HOSTEL £
(golant@yha.org.uk; Penquite House; dm from £12; P @) Sheltering amid 16 hectares of tree-shaded grounds, this whitewashed Georgian manor house makes a fantastic base. There's a super kitchen and a lounge filled with leather sofas, and some rooms have estuary views. It's at the end of a long private drive – take a torch if you're venturing out at night.

Eating & Drinking

Sam's BISTRO ££
(www.samsfowey.co.uk; 20 Fore St; mains £5.95-13.95; ⏲lunch & dinner) This much-loved local's diner has long been a favourite for Fowey punters, but a recent refit has added extra space upstairs and new premises down by Polkerris Beach. Both offer a similar '60s-retro vibe, with booth seats and big specials blackboards: the Samburgers are particularly worth a mention. No bookings.

Pinky Murphy's Café CAFE £
(www.pinkymurphys.com; 19 North St; ⏲9am-5pm Mon-Sat, 9.30am-4pm Sun) Cafes don't come much quirkier than this oddbod establishment, where mismatching crockery is a virtue and seating ranges from tie-dyed beanbags to patched-up sofas. Ciabattas, paninis and generous platters are washed down with Pinky's Cream Tease, mugs of Horlicks and fresh-brewed smoothies.

King of Prussia PUB £
(www.kingofprussia.co.uk; Town Quay) The king of Fowey's many pubs takes its name from the local 'free trader' John Carter, and makes a superior spot for a quayside pint or a quick crab sandwich.

Getting There & Away

Bus

Buses to Fowey all stop at Par Station, with onward connections on the Penzance–Paddington mainline.

25 First bus to St Austell (45 minutes, hourly Monday to Saturday).

525 Western Greyhound bus to St Austell (45 minutes, 10 or 11 daily in summer).

Ferry

Bodinnick Ferry (car/pedestrian £2.20/1; ⏲last ferry 8.45pm Apr-Oct, 7pm Nov-Mar) Car ferry crossing the river to Bodinnick.

Polruan Ferry (foot passengers & bikes only; £1) Foot passenger ferry across the estuary to the village of Polruan.

Polperro

The ancient fishing village of Polperro is a picturesque muddle of narrow lanes and cottages set around a tiny harbour, best approached along the coastal path from Looe or Talland Bay. It's always jammed with day trippers and coach tours in summer, so arrive in the evening or out of season if possible.

Polperro was once heavily involved in pilchard fishing by day and smuggling by night; the displays at the small **Heritage Museum** (☎01503-272423; The Warren; adult/child £1.75/50p; ⏲10am-6pm Mar-Oct) include sepia photos, pilchard barrels and fascinating smuggling memorabilia.

For buses, see Looe, p343.

Looe

POP 5280

Looe is a pleasing mixture of breezy bucket-and-spade destination and historic fishing port. Although the industry has declined, Looe has the second-biggest fish market in Cornwall (after Newlyn), and high tide still brings the bustle of landing and ice-packing the catch. The port has been a holiday hotspot since Victorian times when bathing machines rolled up to the water's edge off Banjo Pier. Split into East and West Looe and divided by a broad estuary, inter-village rivalry is intense, with locals referring to living on the 'sunny' or the 'money' side of town.

Sights & Activities

Boat Trips
Various boat-trips set out from Buller Quay for destinations including Polperro (£19) and Fowey (£12). Check the signs on the quay for sailings, then leave your contact details in one of the books alongside.

Looe Island
Half a mile off-shore is tiny St George's Island (known locally as Looe Island), a 22-acre nature reserve run by the Cornwall Wildlife Trust. The boat **Islander** (☎07814-139223; adult/child return £6/4, plus £2.50/1 landing fee) runs regular summer trips depending on the weather and tides: check the board on the quay for forthcoming sailings.

Wild Futures Monkey Sanctuary WILDLIFE
(☎01503-262532; www.monkeysanctuary.org; St Martins; adult/child £7.50/3.50; ⏲11am-4.30pm Sun-Thu Easter-Sep) Half a mile west of town, this monkey centre is guaranteed to raise a few 'aaahhhhs' over its unfeasibly cute woolly and capuchin monkeys, many of which were rescued from illegal captivity.

Sleeping & Eating

Looe's B&Bs tend towards the chintzy, so choose carefully. There are plenty of cheap-and-cheerful restaurants in West Looe, but nothing that'll set your world on fire, so it's probably sensible to follow the crowd and plump for fish-and-chips.

Barclay House B&B ££
(☎01503-262929; www.barclayhouse.co.uk; St Martins Rd, East Looe; d £115-145; [pool][P][wifi]) This gorgeous detached Victorian villa in six acres of private gardens has the best bedrooms in Looe, decorated in graceful shades of peach, pistachio and aquamarine, and some of the most glorious river views you could possibly wish for.

Beach House B&B ££
(☎01503-262598; www.thebeachhouselooe.co.uk; Hannafore Point; d £100-130; [P]) Smart B&B in a striking modern house overlooking Hannafore Point. The compact rooms are named after Cornish beaches: top of the pile is Kynance, with a massive bed and private balcony.

Information

Looe Tourist Office (☎01503-262072; www.visit-southeastcornwall.co.uk; Fore St; ⏲10am-5pm Easter-Oct, plus occasional days Nov-Easter) In the Guildhall.

Getting There & Away

The scenic Looe Valley Line (day ranger adult/child £3.40/1.70; every two hours Monday to Saturday, eight on Sunday) trundles along the gorgeous stretch to Liskeard on the London–Penzance line.

Bus 572 travels to Plymouth (1¼ hours, seven daily Monday to Saturday); bus 573 goes to Polperro (30 minutes, hourly in summer).

Around Looe

Lanhydrock STATELY HOME
(NT; ☎01208-265950; house & gardens adult/child £9.90/4.90, ⏲11am-5.30pm Tue-Sun Mar-Sep, 11am-5pm Tue-Sun Oct) Reminiscent of the classic 'upstairs-downstairs' film, *Gosford Park*. Set in 365 hectares of sweeping grounds above the River Fowey, parts date from the 17th century but the property was

PORT ELIOT

Stretching across the far eastern end of Cornwall is the 6000-acre estate of **Port Eliot** (☎01503-230211; www.porteliot.co.uk; house & grounds adult/child £7/free, grounds only £4/2; ⏲2-6pm Sat-Thu Mar-Jun), the family seat of the Earl of St Germans. Since March 2008 the house and grounds have been opened to the public for a hundred days every year, and the estate has also become renowned for its annual outdoor bash, the **Port Eliot Festival** (www.porteliotfestival.com), which began life as a literary festival but has now branched out into live music, theatre and outdoor art.

Occasional trains from Plymouth stop at the tiny station of St Germans, otherwise you'll need your own transport to get to the estate.

extensively rebuilt after a fire in 1881, creating the Victorian county house. Highlights include the gentlemen's smoking room (complete with old Etonian photos, moose heads and tiger-skin rugs), the children's toy-strewn nursery, and the huge original kitchens. The **gardens** (adult/child £5.80/3.10; ⏲10am-6pm) are open year-round.

Lanhydrock is 2½ miles southeast of Bodmin; you'll need your own transport to get here.

Cotehele STATELY HOME
(NT; ☎01579-351346; St Dominick; adult/child £8.70/4.35; ⏲11am-4.30pm Sat-Thu Apr-Oct) Seven miles from Tavistock, this Tudor manor served as the family seat of the aristocratic Edgcumbe dynasty for some 400 years. It's stocked with some of Britain's finest Tudor interiors, best seen in the great hall, and dotted throughout with impressive tapestries and suits of armour. It's also notoriously haunted – several ghostly figures are said to wander through the house, accompanied by music and a peculiar herbal smell.

Outside, the lovely terraced **gardens** (adult/child £5.20/2.60) include both a medieval dovecote, a working mill and a restored quay with a restored river barge moored alongside.

ISLES OF SCILLY

Twenty-eight miles southwest of mainland Cornwall lie the tiny Isles of Scilly, a miniature archipelago of over 140 islands, five of which are inhabited. Nurtured by the Gulf Stream and blessed with a balmy sub-tropical climate, the Scillys have long survived on the traditional industries of farming, fishing and flower-growing, but these days tourism is by far the biggest moneyspinner. St Mary's is the largest and busiest island, closely followed by Tresco,

Isles of Scilly

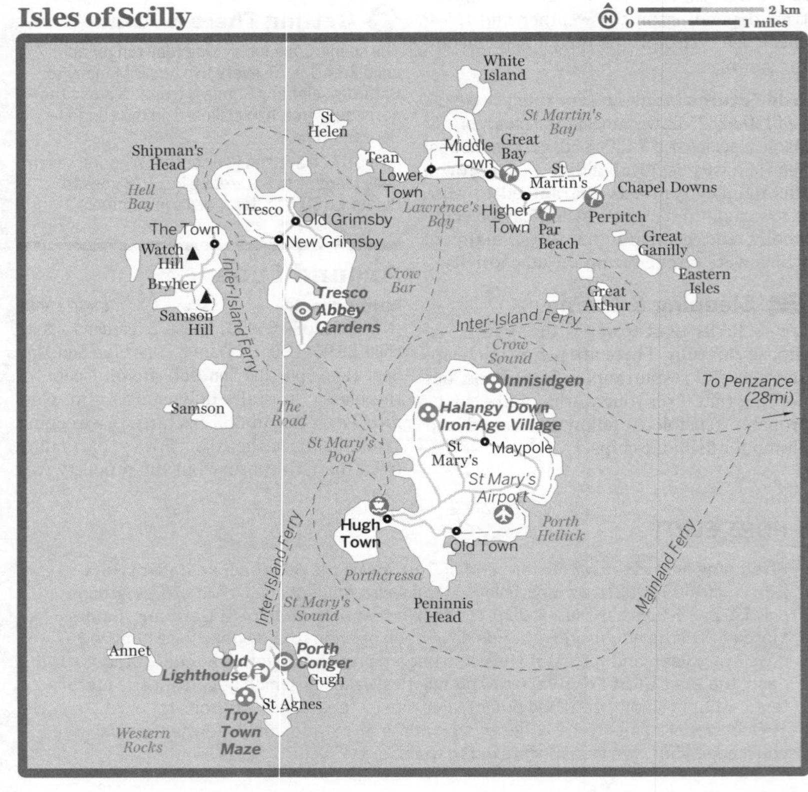

BODMIN MOOR

Cornwall's 'roof' is a high heath pock-marked with bogs, ancient remains and lonely granite hills, including **Rough Tor** (pronounced *row-tor*, 400m) and **Brown Willy** (419m), Cornwall's highest points. It's a desolate place that works on the imagination; for years there have been reported sightings of the Beast of Bodmin, a large, black cat-like creature, although no one's ever managed to snap a decent picture.

The wild landscape offers some superb walking, and there are some great trails suitable for hikers and mountain-bikers around **Cardinham Woods** (www.forestry.gov.uk/cardinham) on the moor's eastern edge. Other landmarks to look out for are **Dozmary Pool**, at the centre of the moor and said to have been where Arthur's sword, Excalibur, was thrown after his death. Nearby is **Jamaica Inn** (☎01566-86250; www.jamaicainn.co.uk; s £65, d £80-110; P), made famous by Daphne du Maurier's novel of the same name (although it's sadly been modernised since du Maurier's day). It also has a small smuggling museum and a room devoted to du Maurier.

The **Bodmin & Wenford Railway** (www.bodminandwenfordrailway.co.uk; rover pass adult/child £11.50/6; ⏲Mar-Oct) is the last standard-gauge railway in Cornwall plied by steam locomotives. Trains are still decked out in original 1950s livery and chug from Bodmin Parkway and Bodmin General station to Boscarne Junction, where you can join up with the Camel Trail cycle route (p322). There are two to four return trips daily depending on the season.

For general information on the moor, contact **Bodmin tourist office** (☎01208-76616; www.bodminlive.com; Mount Folly; ⏲10am-5pm Mon-Sat).

while only a few hardy souls remain on Bryher, St Martin's and St Agnes.

With a laid-back island lifestyle, a strong community spirit and some of the most glorious beaches anywhere in England, it's hardly surprising that many visitors find themselves drawn back to the Scillys year after year. While life moves on at breakneck speed in the outside world, time in the Scillys seems happy to stand still.

Information

Isles of Scilly Tourist Board (☎01720-422536; tic@scilly.gov.uk; Hugh Town, St Mary's; ⏲8.30am-6pm Mon-Fri, 9am-5pm Sat, 9am-2pm Sun May-Sep, shorter hours in winter) On St Mary's.

Scilly Online (www.scillyonline.co.uk) Locally run site with lots of info on the islands.

Simply Scilly (www.simplyscilly.co.uk) Official tourist site with comprehensive listings.

Getting There & Away

Air

There are two ways to get to Scilly by air – chopper and plane – but neither's cheap.

British International (☎01736-363871; www.islesofscillyhelicopter.com) Helicopters run to St Mary's and Tresco from Penzance heliport. Full return fares are £175/105 per adult/child. Saver fares (for travel Monday to Friday) and Daytrip fares are much cheaper.

Isles of Scilly Skybus (☎0845-710-5555; www.ios-travel.co.uk) Several daily flights from Land's End (adult/child return £140/89.25) and Newquay (£165/100.25), plus at least one from Exeter, Bristol and Southampton daily in summer.

Boat

Scillonian (☎0845-710-5555; www.ios-travel.co.uk; ⏲Mar-Oct) Scilly's ferry plies the choppy waters between Penzance and St Mary's (adult/child return £95/47.50). There's at least one daily crossing in summer (except on Sundays), dropping to four a week in the shoulder months.

Getting Around

Boat

Inter-island launches sail regularly from St Mary's harbour in summer to the other main islands. Trips to all islands cost adult/child £7.80/3.90; you don't need to book, but label your luggage clearly so it can be deposited at the right harbour.

Bus

The only bus services are on St Mary's. The airport bus (£3) departs from Hugh Town 40 minutes before each flight, while the **Island Rover** (☎01720-422131; www.islandrover.co.uk; £7), offers a twice-daily sightseeing trip in a vintage bus in summer.

Taxi

For taxis, try **Island Taxis** (☎01720-22126), **Scilly Cabs** (☎01720-422901) or **St Mary's Taxis** (☎01720-422555).

St Mary's

The largest and busiest island in the Scillys is St Mary's, which contains most of the islands' big hotels, B&Bs, restaurants and shops. The Scillonian ferry and most flights from the mainland arrive on St Mary's, but the other main islands (known as the 'off-islands') are easily reached via regular inter-island launches.

The traditional sport of gig racing is still hugely popular in the Scillys. These six-oared wooden boats were originally used to race out to secure valuable pilotage of sailing ships. You can often see gig racing around the shores of St Mary's between May and September, and every May the island hosts the World Pilot Gig Championships, which attracts teams from as far away as Holland and the USA.

Sights

Hugh Town & Old Town

About a mile west of the airport is the main settlement of **Hugh Town**, where you'll find the bulk of the island's hotels and guest houses. The islands have an absorbing, unique history, which is explored to the full in the **Isles of Scilly Museum** (Church St; adult/child £3.50/1; 10am-4.30pm Mon-Fri, 10am-noon Sat Easter-Sep, 10am-noon Mon-Sat Oct-Easter or by arrangement) where exhibits include artefacts recovered from shipwrecks (including muskets, a cannon and a ship's bell), Romano-British finds and a fully rigged 1877 pilot gig.

A little way east of Hugh Town is **Old Town**, once the island's main harbour but now home to a few small cafes, a village pub and a curve of beach. Look out for the minuscule Old Town Church where evocative services are still conducted by candlelight – the graveyard contains a memorial to Augustus Smith, founder of the Abbey Garden, as well as the grave of former British prime minister Harold Wilson, who often holidayed here.

Beaches

The small inlets scattered around the island's coastline are best reached on foot or by bike. Porth Hellick, Watermill Cove and the remote Pelistry Bay are worth seeking out.

Ancient Ruins

St Mary's prehistoric sites include the Iron Age village at **Halangy Down**, a mile north of Hugh Town, and the barrows at **Bant's Carn** and **Innisidgen**.

VISITING SCILLY

Scilly gets extremely busy in summer, while many businesses shut down completely in winter. All of the islands, except Tresco, have a simple campsite, but many visitors choose to stay in self-catering accommodation as a way of keeping costs down – the two big companies are **Island Properties** (01720-422082; www.scillyhols.com) or **Sibley's Island Homes** (01720-422431; www.sibleysonscilly.co.uk).

Travelling to the islands is the major expense, although there are usually discounted fares on flights leaving Land's End after 2pm or St Mary's before 11am. Look in the local papers for discount coupons on helicopter trips and the *Scillonian* ferry, too.

Activities

Scilly Walks HISTORICAL TOURS

(01720-423326; www.scillywalks.co.uk) Excellent three-hour archaeological and historical tours, costing £5/2.50 per adult/child, as well as visits to the off-islands.

Island Wildlife Tours WILDLIFE TOURS

(01720-422212; www.islandwildlifetours.co.uk) Regular birdwatching and wildlife walks with local boy Will Wagstaff.

Island Sea Safaris WATER TOURS

(01720-422732; www.scillyonline.co.uk/seasafaris.html) Speedboat rides (adult/child £30/20) and snorkelling trips (£35) to local seabird and seal colonies.

Sleeping

Belmont B&B £

(01720-423154; www.the-belmont.co.uk; Church Rd; s £28-65, d £56-80, f £90-120) Solid St Mary's guest house, in a double-fronted detached house 15 minutes' walk from the quay. The six rooms are clean and bright and the price is definitely right.

Blue Carn Cottage B&B £

(01720-422214; Old Town; 3-night stay d £276-284; Mar-Oct) Removed from the relative bustle of Hugh Town, this whitewashed B&B near Old Town is a welcoming affair.

DVD players and cosy surroundings distinguish the rooms, while there's a game-stocked guest lounge and hearty brekkies with home-reared eggs.

Star Castle Hotel HOTEL £££
(☎01720-422317; www.star-castle.co.uk; The Garrison; r incl dinner £188-312, ste incl dinner £242-362;) Shaped like an eight-pointed star, this former fort on Garrison Point is one of Scilly's star hotels, with a choice of heritage-style castle rooms or more modern garden suites. It's a bit stuffy, but prices include dinner at a choice of restaurants.

St Mary's Hall Hotel HOTEL £££
(☎01720-422316; www.stmaryshallhotel.co.uk; Church St, Hugh Town; r £180-240) Say *ciao* to this Italianate mansion which is full of grand wooden staircases, bits of art and panelled walls. Rooms are either flowery and chintzy or candy-striped, while the superplush designer suites have LCD TVs and a galley kitchen.

Garrison Campsite CAMPSITE
(☎01720-422670; tedmoulson@aol.com; Tower Cottage, Garrison; sites per person £6-10) This 4-hectare site sits on the garrison above Hugh Town. Fairly basic facilities, but a cut above many other sites on Scilly.

Eating

Juliet's Garden Restaurant RESTAURANT, CAFE ££
(☎01720-422228; www.julietsgardenrestaurant.co.uk; lunch £4-10, dinner £12-16; 10am-5pm daily, 6pm-late Wed-Sun) Apart from a couple of pubs, cafes and a deli around Hugh Town, eating choices are pretty limited on St Mary's, which makes this converted barn 15 minutes' walk from town extra-special. Light lunches by day, candlelit fare by night, all treated with loving care and attention.

Tresco

Once owned by Tavistock Abbey, Tresco is the second-largest island, and the second most visited after St Mary's. The main attraction is the magical **Tresco Abbey Garden** (☎01720-424105; www.tresco.co.uk/stay/abbey-garden; adult/child £10/5; 10am-4pm), first laid out in 1834 on the site of a 10th-century Benedictine abbey. The terraced gardens feature more than 5000 subtropical plants, including species from Brazil, New Zealand and South Africa, and the intriguing Valhalla collection made up of figureheads and nameplates salvaged from the many ships that have foundered off Tresco's shores.

Sleeping & Eating

Apart from self-catering cottages, there are now three places to stay on the island, but the two big hotels are eye-poppingly expensive. By far the most affordable choice is the **New Inn** (☎01720-422844; newinn@tresco.co.uk; d £140-230), the island's popular pub, which also has pleasant pastel rooms, some of which have views over the channel to Bryher.

Other options:

Island Hotel HOTEL £££
(☎01720-422883; www.tresco.co.uk; d incl dinner £370-720;) The island's original luxury hotel, with regal rooms and a price-tag to match.

Flying Boat Club APARTMENTS £££
(☎01720-422849; flyingboatclub@tresco.co.uk; apts £4500-5000;) Fabulously lavish sea-view apartments; prices drop to a mere £1375 to £1950 in winter.

Bryher & Samson

Only around 70 people live on Bryher, Scilly's smallest and wildest inhabited island. Covered by rough bracken and heather, this chunk of rock takes the full force of Atlantic storms; **Hell Bay** in a winter gale is a truly powerful sight.

Watch Hill provides cracking view over the islands, and **Rushy Bay** is one of the finest beaches in the Scillys. From the quay, occasional boats visit local seal and bird colonies and deserted **Samson Island**, where abandoned settlers' cottages tell a story of hard subsistence living.

Sleeping & Eating

Hell Bay HOTEL £££
(☎01720-422947; www.tresco.co.uk; d incl dinner £260-600) The island's only hotel is a real pamper pad, run by the owners of Tresco's pricey pamper-pads, and offering similarly upmarket accommodation. All the rooms are huge suites, most with their own sitting rooms and private balconies. Dinner at one of the hotel's two restaurants is included in the price.

Fraggle Rock CAFE, PUB £
(☎01720-422222; 10.30am-4.30pm & 7-11pm;) Pretty much the only place to eat on

Bryher is this relaxed cafe which also doubles as the island pub. The menu's mainly pizzas, salads and burgers, and there are a few local ales on tap and fairtrade coffees which help support the Cornwall Wildlife Trust.

Bryher Campsite CAMPSITE £
(☎01720-422886; www.bryhercampsite.co.uk; sites from £9.50) Bare-bones camping near the quay. Hot showers and transport from the boat is included in the rates.

St Martin's

The northernmost of the main islands, St Martin's is renowned for its beaches. Worth hunting out are **Lawrence's Bay** on the south coast, which becomes a broad sweep of sand at low tide; **Great Bay** on the north, arguably Scilly's finest beach; **White Island** in the northwest, which you can cross to (with care) at low tide; and the secluded cove of **Perpitch** in the southeast.

The largest settlement is **Higher Town** where you'll find a small village shop and **Scilly Diving** (☎01720-422848; www.scillydiving.com; Higher Town), which offers snorkelling trips and diving courses.

Sleeping

Accommodation options on the island are almost non-existent, apart from one super-expensive hotel, **St Martin's on the Isle** (☎01720-422090; www.stmartinshotel.co.uk; d £300-560), a campsite and a handful of B&Bs.

Polreath B&B £
(☎01720-422046; Higher Town; d £90-110, open all year, but weekly stays only May-Sep) This robust granite cottage is one of the few B&Bs on the island. Squeeze yourself into one of the titchy traditional rooms or sip a cool lemonade in the sunny conservatory; cream teas, baguettes and light bites are also on offer several days a week, and sometimes you'll even get a hot evening meal too.

Campsite CAMPSITE £
(☎01720-422888; www.stmartinscampsite.co.uk; sites £8-10) Towards the western end of Lawrence's Bay; has a laundry, showers and fresh-water well. Eggs and vegetables are usually available in season.

Eating

Apart from the hotel's super-expensive restaurant, St Martin has few eating options:

Little Arthur Farm FARM £
(☎01720-422457; www.littlearthur.co.uk; ⌚10.30am-4pm daily, 6.30-8.30pm Mon-Fri) Wonderful little organic farm where you can buy fresh eggs, milk, homemade cakes and other goodies.

St Martin's Bakery BAKERY £
(☎01720-423444; www.stmartinsbakery.co.uk; ⌚9am-6pm Mon-Sat, 9am-2pm Sun) Fresh bread, pastries and patisseries.

St Agnes

England's most southerly community somehow transcends even the tranquillity of the other islands in the Isles of Scilly; with its cloistered coves, coastal walks and a scattering of prehistoric sites, it's an ideal spot to stroll, unwind and reflect.

Visitors disembark at Porth Conger, near the decommissioned **Old Lighthouse** – one of the oldest lighthouses in the country. Other points of interest include the 200-year-old stone **Troy Town Maze**, and the inlets of Periglis Cove and St Warna's Cove (dedicated to the patron saint of shipwrecks). At low tide you can cross over to the island of **Gugh**, where you'll find intriguing standing stones and Bronze Age remains.

Sleeping & Eating

Covean Cottage B&B £
(☎01720-422620; http://st-agnes-scilly.org/covean.htm; d £60-80) A little stone-walled cottage B&B, which makes the perfect location for getting away from the crowds. It offers four pleasant, good-value rooms and serves excellent cream teas, light meals and sticky treats during the day.

Troytown Farm Campsite CAMPSITE £
(☎01720-422360; www.troytown.co.uk; Troy Town Farm; sites £7-8, tents £1-7 depending on size) At the southwestern corner of the island. Originally a flower-farm, it's now home to Scillys' only dairy herd.

Turk's Head PUB £
(☎01720-422434; mains £7-12) The most southwesterly pub in all of England is a real treat, with fine views, excellent beers, good pub grub and a hearty island atmosphere.

Cambridge & East Anglia

Includes »

CAMBRIDGESHIRE . . 352
Cambridge 353
ESSEX 365
Colchester 365
SUFFOLK 367
Sutton Hoo 367
Lavenham 368
Bury St Edmunds . . . 369
Aldeburgh 372
Southwold 373
NORFOLK 374
Norwich 375
Around Norwich 380
Norfolk Broads 381
King's Lynn 387

Best Places to Eat

- Midsummer House (p360)
- Great House (p369)
- Butley Orford Oysterage (p373)
- Alimentum (p361)
- Roger Hickman's (p379)

Best Places to Stay

- Lavenham Priory (p369)
- Cley Windmill (p385)
- Hotel du Vin (p359)
- Hotel Felix (p360)
- Swan Hotel (p369)

Why Go?

Unfurling gently eastwards to the sea, the vast flatlands of East Anglia are a rich web of lush farmland, melancholy fens and sparkling rivers. The area is justly famous for its sweeping sandy beaches, big skies and the bucolic landscape that once inspired Constable and Gainsborough.

It's not all rural idyll, though: rising out of the fens is the world-famous university town of Cambridge, with its stunning classical architecture and earnest attitude, and to the east is the cosmopolitan city of Norwich. Around them magnificent cathedral cities, pretty market towns and implausibly picturesque villages are testament to the enormous wealth amassed here during medieval times, when the wool and weaving industries flourished.

Meanwhile, the meandering coastline is peppered with pretty fishing villages and traditional bucket-and-spade resorts, while inland is the languid, hypnotic charm of the Norfolk Broads, an ideal location for serious relaxation.

When to Go

Aldeburgh swings into action with its classical music festival in June. You can chill out and tune in at the Latitude Festival in Southwold in July. On 24 December the King's College Chapel is at its best at the Festival of Nine Lessons and Carols.

Cambridge & East Anglia Highlights

1. Dreaming of your student days as you **punt** past Cambridge's historic colleges (p359)
2. Soaking up the medieval atmosphere in topsy-turvy **Lavenham** (p368)
3. Marvelling at the exquisite rib vaulting at **Norwich Cathedral** (p375)
4. Walking the prom, dining on sublime food and just chilling out in understated **Aldeburgh** (p372)
5. Wallowing in the heavenly sounds of Evensong at **King's College Chapel** (p353)
6. Canoeing your way through the tranquil waterways of the **Norfolk Broads** (p381)
7. Wandering aimlessly along the pristine sands of **Holkham beach** (p386)

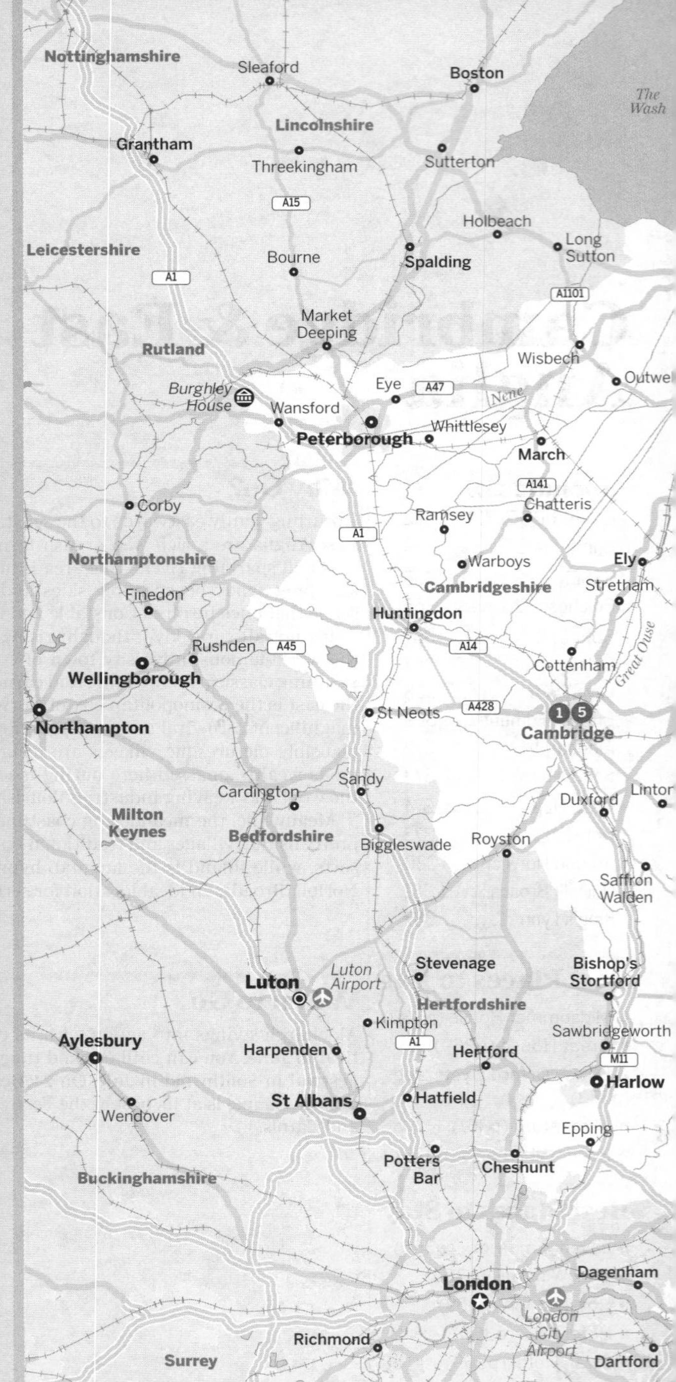

0
40 km
0
20 miles
Holkham Beach
Wells-next-the-Sea
Burnham Market
Holkham Hall
Sheringham
Blakeney
Cromer
Sustead
Ringstead
Little Walsingham
Baconsthorpe
Mundesley
Castle Rising Castle
Sandringham House
Houghton Hall
Fakenham
Blickling Hall
A149
Palling
Aylsham
Castle Rising
Harpley
A1067
Potter Heigham
Winterton
King's Lynn
Wroxham
How Hill
Norfolk
Dereham
Norwich
Acle
Great Yarmouth
Swaffham
Norfolk Broads National Park
Stradsett
Wymondham
Reedham
A1065
Swainsthorpe
A134
A11
Loddon
Mundford
Attleborough
Lowestoft
Norfolk Broads
Thetford Forest
Military Camp
Bungay
Kessingland
Thetford
Scole
A143
Southwold
Suffolk Coast National Nature Reserve
A143
Ferry Route
Ixworth
Dunwich
RSPB Minsmere
Bury St Edmunds
Newmarket
A1120
Saxmundham
Thorpeness
Stowmarket
A12
Suffolk
Aldeburgh
A143
North Sea
Lavenham
Woodbridge
Suffolk Coast Path
Orford
Ipswich
Sutton Hoo
Long Melford
Kersey
Hadleigh
Alderton
Sudbury
Dedham Vale
Felixstowe
Finchingfield
Halstead
Wormingford
Harwich
To Hamburg
Colchester
Baintree
Frinton-on-Sea
Walton-on-the-Naze
Layer de la Haye
Blackwater
Tiptree
Brightlingsea
Clacton-on-Sea
Witham
A12
Chelmsford
Essex
Brentwood
Southend-on-Sea
Canvey Island
Kent
Leysdown-on-Sea
Rochester
Chatham
Margate

History

East Anglia was a major Saxon kingdom, and the treasures unearthed in the Sutton Hoo burial ship proved that they enjoyed something of the good life here.

The region's heyday, however, was in the Middle Ages, during the wool and weaving boom, when Flemish weavers settled in the area and the grand churches and the world-famous university began to be established.

By the 17th century much of the region's marshland and bog had been drained and converted into arable land, and the good times rolled.

East Anglia's fortunes waned in the 18th century, however, when the Industrial Revolution got under way up north. The cottage industries dwindled, and today crops have replaced sheep as the rural mainstay. During WWII East Anglia became central to the fight against Nazi Germany. With plenty of flat open land and its proximity to mainland Europe, it was an ideal base for the RAF and the United States Air Force.

Activities

East Anglia is a great destination for walking and cycling enthusiasts, with miles of coastline to discover, vast expanses of flat land for leisurely touring and plenty of inland waterways for quiet boating. Try www.visiteastofengland.com for information, or visit local tourist offices for maps and guides.

CYCLING

East Anglia is famously flat and riddled with quiet roads; even the unfit can find vast swaths for a gentle meander on two wheels. All four counties boast networks of quiet country lanes, where the biggest natural hazard is the wind sweeping in unimpeded from the coast. When it's behind you though, you can free-wheel for miles. There's gorgeous riding to be had along the Suffolk and Norfolk coastlines and in the Fens. Finding quiet roads in Essex is a little more of a challenge. Mountain bikers should head for Thetford Forest, near Thetford, while much of the popular on- and off-road Peddars Way walking route is also open to cyclists.

WALKING

East Anglia is not everybody's idea of classic walking country; you won't find any challenging peaks here, but gentle rambles through farmland, beside rivers and lakes and along the wildlife-rich coastline are in ample supply.

The **Peddars Way and Norfolk Coast Path** (www.nationaltrail.co.uk/peddarsway) is a six-day, 93-mile national trail from Knettishall Heath near Thetford to Cromer on the coast. The first half trails along an ancient Roman road, then finishes by meandering along the beaches, sea walls, salt marshes and fishing villages of the coast. Day trippers and weekend walkers tend to dip into its coastal stretches, which also cover some of the best birdwatching country in England.

Curving round further south, the 50-mile **Suffolk Coast Path** (www.suffolkcoastandheaths.org) wanders between Felixstowe and Lowestoft, via Snape Maltings, Aldeburgh, Dunwich and Southwold, but is also good for shorter rambles.

OTHER ACTIVITIES

With wind and water so abundant here, it's a popular destination for **sailing**, both along the coast and in the Norfolk Broads, where you can easily hire boats and arrange lessons. It's also possible to just put-put your way around the Broads in **motorboats** or gently **canoe** along the slow-moving rivers. Alternatively, the wide and frequently empty beaches of the Norfolk coast make great spots for **land yachting** and **kitesurfing**.

Getting There & Around

Getting about East Anglia on public transport, both rail and coach, is straightforward. Consult **Traveline** (☎0871 200 2233; www.travelineeastanglia.org.uk) for all public transport information.

BUS **Stagecoach** (www.stagecoachbus.com) and **First Group** (www.firstgroup.com), along with a host of smaller companies, offer bus services across the region.

TRAIN **National Express East Anglia** (www.nationalexpresseastanglia.com) offers the handy Anglia Plus Pass (one day/three days out of seven £13.50/27), which allows you to explore Norfolk, Suffolk and parts of Cambridgeshire. The pass is valid for unlimited regional travel after 8.45am on weekdays and anytime at weekends. Up to four accompanying children can travel for £2 each.

CAMBRIDGESHIRE

Many visitors to Cambridgeshire never make it past the beautiful university town of Cambridge, where august old buildings, student cyclists in academic gowns and glorious chapels await. But beyond the breathtaking city lies a county of vast open landscapes, epic sunsets and unsullied horizons. The flat reclaimed fen, lush farmland and myriad waterways make perfect walking and cycling territory, while the extraordinary cathedrals at Peterborough and Ely, and the rip-roaring Imperial War Museum at Duxford, would be headline attractions anywhere else.

Getting Around

The region's public transport radiates from Cambridge, which is a mere 55-minute train ride from London. This line continues north through Ely to King's Lynn in Norfolk. From Ely, branch lines run east through Norwich, southeast into Suffolk and northwest to Peterborough. Local tourist offices stock bus and train timetables.

Cambridge

POP 108,863

Drowning in exquisite architecture, steeped in history and tradition and renowned for its quirky rituals, Cambridge is a university town extraordinaire. The tightly packed core of ancient colleges, the picturesque 'Backs' (college gardens) leading on to the river, and the leafy green meadows that seem to surround the city give it a far more tranquil appeal than its historic rival Oxford.

Like 'the other place', as Oxford is known, the buildings here seem unchanged for centuries, and it's possible to wander the college buildings and experience them as countless prime ministers, poets, writers and scientists have done. The sheer weight of academic achievement seems to seep from the very walls, with cyclists who are loaded down with books negotiating narrow cobbled passageways, earnest students relaxing on manicured lawns and great minds debating life-changing research in historic pubs. Meanwhile, distracted punters drift into the river banks as they soak up the breathtaking views, tills whir with brisk trade in the city's designer boutiques, and those long past their student days wonder what it would have been like to study in such auspicious surroundings.

History

First a Roman fort and then a Saxon settlement, Cambridge was little more than a rural backwater until 1209, when the university town of Oxford exploded in a riot between town and gown (see boxed text, p191). Fed up with the constant brawling between locals and students, a group of scholars upped and left to found a new university in Cambridge.

Initially students lived in halls and religious houses, but gradually a collegiate system, where tutors and students lived together in a formal community, developed. The first Cambridge college, Peterhouse, was founded in 1284.

By the 14th century, the royalty, nobility, church, trade guilds and anyone rich enough to court the prestige that their own institution offered began to found their own colleges. It was 500 years before female students were allowed into the hallowed grounds, though, and even then in women-only colleges Girton and Newnham, founded in 1869 and 1871 respectively. By 1948 Cambridge minds had broadened sufficiently to allow the women to actually graduate.

The honour roll of famous Cambridge graduates reads like an international who's who of high achievers: 87 Nobel Prize winners (more than any other institution in the world), 13 British prime ministers, nine archbishops of Canterbury, an immense number of scientists, and a healthy host of poets and authors.

WANT MORE?

Head to **Lonely Planet** (www.lonelyplanet.com/england/eastern-england/cambridge) for planning advice, author recommendations, traveller reviews and insider tips.

Sights

CAMBRIDGE UNIVERSITY

Cambridge University comprises 31 colleges, though not all are open to the public. Most colleges close to visitors for the Easter term and all are closed for exams from mid-May to mid-June. Opening hours vary from day to day, so contact the colleges or the tourist office for information as hours given below are only a rough guide.

King's College Chapel CHAPEL

(www.kings.cam.ac.uk/chapel; King's Pde; adult/child under 12 £5/free; ⌚9.30am-4.30pm Mon-Sat, 10am-5pm Sun) In a city crammed with show-stopping architecture, this is the show-stealer. Chances are you will already

Cambridge

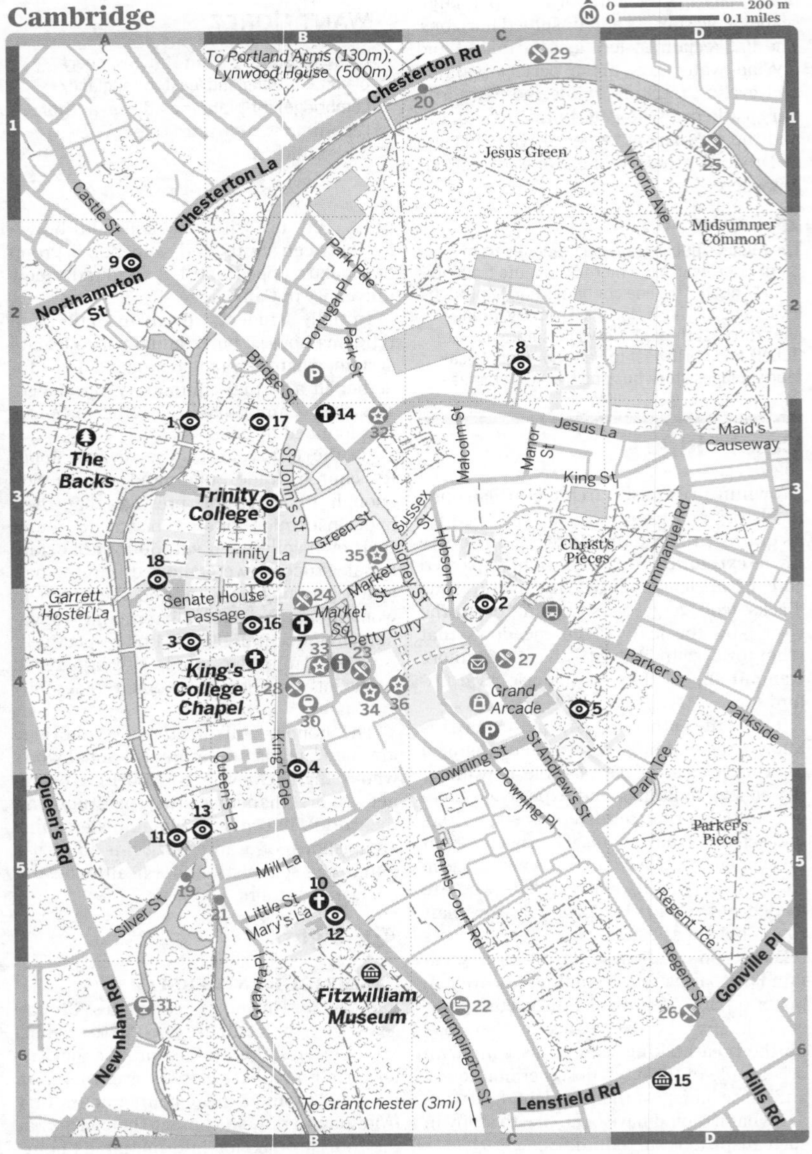

have seen it on a thousand postcards, tea towels and choral CDs before you catch your first glimpse of the grandiose King's College Chapel, but still it inspires awe. It's one of the most extraordinary examples of Gothic architecture in England, and was begun in 1446 as an act of piety by Henry VI and finished by Henry VIII around 1516.

While you can enjoy stunning front and back views of the chapel from King's Pde and the river, the real drama is within. Mouths drop open upon first glimpse of

Cambridge

Top Sights

Fitzwilliam Museum ... B6
King's College Chapel ... B4
The Backs ... A3
Trinity College ... B3

Sights

1 Bridge of Sighs ... A3
2 Christ's College ... C4
3 Clare College ... A4
4 Corpus Christi College ... B4
5 Emmanuel College ... C4
Folk Museum ... (see 9)
6 Gonville & Caius College ... B3
7 Great St Mary's Church ... B4
8 Jesus College ... C2
9 Kettle's Yard ... A2
10 Little St Mary's Church ... B5
11 Mathematical Bridge ... A5
12 Peterhouse ... B5
13 Queens' College ... A5
14 Round Church ... B3
15 Scott Polar Research Institute ... D6
16 Senate House ... B4
17 St John's College ... B3
18 Trinity Hall College ... A3

Activities, Courses & Tours

19 Cambridge Chauffer Punts ... A5
Granta ... (see 31)
20 Riverboat Georgina ... C1
21 Scudamore's ... B5

Sleeping

22 Hotel du Vin ... C6

Eating

23 Jamie's Italian ... B4
24 Michaelhouse ... B4
25 Midsummer House ... D1
26 Oak Bistro ... D6
27 Origin8 ... C4
28 Rainbow Vegetarian Bistro ... B4
29 Twenty-Two ... C1

Drinking

30 Eagle ... B4
31 Granta ... A6

Entertainment

32 ADC ... B3
33 Arts Theatre ... B4
34 Corn Exchange ... B4
35 Fez ... B3
36 Soul Tree ... B4

the inspirational **fan-vaulted ceiling**, its intricate tracery soaring upwards before exploding into a series of stone fireworks. This vast 80m-long canopy is the work of John Wastell and is the largest expanse of fan vaulting in the world.

The chapel is also remarkably light, its sides flanked by lofty **stained-glass windows** that retain their original glass – rare survivors of the excesses of the Civil War in this region. It's said that these windows were ordered to be spared by Cromwell himself, who knew of their beauty from his own studies in Cambridge.

The antechapel and the choir are divided by a superbly carved **wooden screen**, designed and executed by Peter Stockton for Henry VIII. The screen bears his master's initials entwined with those of Anne Boleyn. Look closely and you may find an angry human face – possibly Stockton's – amid the elaborate jungle of mythical beasts and symbolic flowers. Above is the magnificent bat-wing organ, originally constructed in 1686 though much altered since.

The thickly carved wooden stalls just beyond the screen are a stage for the chapel's world-famous **choir**. You can hear them in full voice during the magnificent **Evensong** (5.30pm Mon-Sat, 10.30am & 3.30pm Sun term time only; admission free). If you happen to be visiting at Christmas, it is also worth queuing for admission to the incredibly popular **Festival of Nine Lessons and Carols** on Christmas Eve.

Beyond the dark-wood choir, light suffuses the **high altar**, which is framed by Rubens' masterpiece *Adoration of the Magi* (1634) and the magnificent east window. To the left of the altar in the side chapels, an **exhibition** charts the stages and methods of building the chapel.

The chapel is open for reduced hours during term time.

Trinity College COLLEGE
(www.trin.cam.ac.uk; Trinity St; adult/child £1/50p; 9am-4pm) The largest of Cambridge's colleges, Trinity is entered through an impressive Tudor gateway first created in 1546. As you walk through, have a look at

the statue of the college's founder, Henry VIII, that adorns it. His left hand holds a golden orb, while his right grips not the original sceptre but a table leg, put there by student pranksters and never replaced. It's a wonderful introduction to one of Cambridge's most venerable colleges, and a reminder of who really rules the roost.

As you enter the **Great Court**, scholastic humour gives way to wonderment, for it is the largest of its kind in the world. To the right of the entrance is a small tree, planted in the 1950s and reputed to be a descendant of the apple tree made famous by Trinity alumnus Sir Isaac Newton. Other alumni include Tennyson, Francis Bacon, Lord Byron, HRH Prince Charles and at least nine prime ministers, British and international, and a jaw-dropping 32 Nobel Prize winners.

The square is also the scene of the run made famous by the film *Chariots of Fire* – 350m in 43 seconds (the time it takes the clock to strike 12). Although many students attempt it, Harold Abrahams (the hero of the film) never actually did, and the run wasn't even filmed here. If you fancy your chances remember that you'll need Olympian speed to even come close.

The college's vast hall has a dramatic hammerbeam roof and lantern, and beyond this are the dignified cloisters of Nevile's Court and the renowned **Wren Library** (⌚noon-2pm Mon-Fri). It contains 55,000 books dated before 1820 and more than 2500 manuscripts, including AA Milne's original *Winnie the Pooh*. Both Milne and his son, Christopher Robin, were graduates.

Henry VIII would have been proud to note, too, that his college would eventually come to throw the best party in town, the lavish May Ball in June.

Corpus Christi College COLLEGE

(www.corpus.cam.ac.uk; King's Pde; admission £2) Entry to this illustrious college is via the so-called New Court, which dates back a mere 200 years. To your right is the door to the Parker Library, which holds the finest collection of Anglo-Saxon manuscripts in the world. As you enter take a look at the statue on the right, that of the eponymous Matthew Parker, who was college master in 1544 and Archbishop of Canterbury to Elizabeth I. Mr Parker was known for his curiosity, and his endless questioning gave rise to the term 'nosy parker'. Meanwhile, a monastic atmosphere still oozes from the inner Old Court, which retains its medieval form. Look out for the fascinating sundial and plaque to playwright and past student Christopher Marlowe (1564–93), author of *Dr Faustus* and *Tamburlaine*.

On the corner of Bene't St you'll find the college's new **Corpus Clock**. Made from 24-carat gold, it displays the time through a series of concentric LED lights. A hideous-looking insect 'time-eater' crawls across the top. The clock is only accurate once every five minutes. At other times it slows or stops and then speeds up, which according to its creator, JC Taylor, reflects life's irregularity.

Trinity Hall College COLLEGE

(www.trinhall.cam.ac.uk; Trinity Lane; admission by donation) Henry James once wrote of the delightfully diminutive Trinity Hall, 'If I were called upon to mention the prettiest corner of the world, I should draw a thoughtful sigh and point the way to the gardens of Trinity Hall.' Wedged cosily among the great and the famous, but unconnected to better-known Trinity, it was founded in 1350 as a refuge for lawyers and clerics escaping the ravages of the Black Death, thus earning it the nickname, the 'Lawyers' College'. The college's 16th-century library has original Jacobean reading desks and chained books (an early antitheft device) on the shelves, while the chapel is one of the most beautiful of the colleges. You can attend Evensong here on Thursdays (6.30pm) and Sundays (6pm) during term time. Writer JB Priestley, astrophysicist Stephen Hawking and actor Rachel Weisz are among Trinity Hall's graduates.

Gonville & Caius College COLLEGE

(www.cai.cam.ac.uk; Trinity St; admission free) Known locally as Caius (pronounced keys), Gonville and Caius was founded twice, first by a priest called Gonville, in 1348, and then again in 1557 by Dr Caius (his given name was Keys – it was common for academics to use the Latin form of their names), a brilliant physician who supposedly spoilt his legacy by insisting the college admit no 'deaf, dumb, deformed, lame, chronic invalids, or Welshmen'! Fortunately for the college, his policy didn't last long, and the wheelchair-using megastar of astrophysics, Stephen Hawking, is now a fellow here.

The college is of particular interest thanks to its three fascinating gates: Virtue, Humility and Honour. They symbolise the progress of the good student, since the third gate (the *Porta Honoris,* a fabulous domed and sundial-sided confection) leads to the Senate House and thus graduation.

Christ's College COLLEGE
(www.christs.cam.ac.uk; St Andrew's St; admission free 9.30am-noon, Darwin room £2.50; ⌚9.30am-noon, Darwin room 10am-noon & 2-4pm) Over 500 years old and a grand old institution, Christ's is worth visiting if only for its gleaming Great Gate emblazoned with heraldic carving of spotted Beaufort yale (antelope-like creatures), Tudor roses and portcullis. Its founder, Lady Margaret Beaufort, hovers above like a guiding spirit. A stout oak door leads into First Court, which has an unusual circular lawn, magnolias and wisteria creepers. Pressing on through the Second Court there is a gate to the Fellows' Garden, which contains a mulberry tree under which 17th-century poet John Milton reputedly wrote *Lycidas*. Charles Darwin also studied here, and his **room** (admission £2; ⌚10am-noon & 2-4pm) has been restored as it would have been when he lived in it. You can buy a guided walk brochure (£1) to Darwin-related sites in the college from the porter's lodge.

FREE **Peterhouse** COLLEGE
(www.pet.cam.ac.uk; Trumpington St) The oldest and smallest college, Peterhouse is a charming place founded in 1284. Much of the college was rebuilt or added over the years, including the exceptional little chapel built in 1632, but the main hall is bona fide 13th century and beautifully restored. Just to the north is **Little St Mary's Church**, which has a memorial to Peterhouse student Godfrey Washington, great-uncle of George. His family coat of arms was the stars and stripes, the inspiration for the US flag.

Queens' College COLLEGE
(www.queens.cam.ac.uk; Silver St; adult/child £2.50/free; ⌚10am-4.30pm) The gorgeous 15th-century Queens' College sits elegantly astride the river and has two enchanting medieval courtyards: Old Court and Cloister Court. Here, too, is the beautiful half-timbered President's Lodge and the tower in which famous Dutch scholar and reformer Desiderius Erasmus lodged from 1510 to 1514. He had plenty to say about Cambridge: the wine tasted like vinegar, the beer was slop and the place was too expensive, but he did note that the local women were good kissers.

St John's College COLLEGE
(www.joh.cam.ac.uk; St John's St; adult/child £3.20/free; ⌚10am-5.30pm) After King's College, St John's is one of the city's most photogenic colleges, and is also the second-biggest after Trinity. Founded in 1511, it sprawls along both banks of the river, joined by the Bridge of Sighs, a masterpiece of stone tracery. Over the bridge is the 19th-century New Court, an extravagant neo-Gothic creation, and out to the left stunning views of the Backs.

Emmanuel College COLLEGE
(www.emma.cam.ac.uk; St Andrew's St) The 16th-century Emmanuel College is famous for its exquisite chapel designed by Sir Christopher Wren. Here, too, is a plaque commemorating John Harvard (BA 1632), a scholar here who later settled in New England and left his money to found his namesake university in the Massachusetts town of Cambridge.

Jesus College COLLEGE
(www.jesus.cam.ac.uk; Jesus Lane) This tranquil 15th-century college was once a nunnery before its founder, Bishop Alcock, expelled the nuns for misbehaving. Highlights include a Norman arched gallery, a 13th-century chancel and art nouveau features by Pugin, William Morris (ceilings), Burne-Jones (stained glass) and Madox Brown.

OTHER SIGHTS

The Backs PARKLANDS
Behind the grandiose facades, stately courts and manicured lawns of the city's central colleges lies a series of gardens and parklands butting up against the river. Collectively known as the Backs, these tranquil green spaces and shimmering waters offer unparalleled views of the colleges and are often the most enduring image of Cambridge for visitors. The picture-postcard snapshots of college life, graceful bridges and weeping willows can be seen from the pathways that cross the Backs, from the comfort of a chauffeur-driven punt or from the lovely pedestrian bridges that criss-cross the river.

The fanciful **Bridge of Sighs** (built in 1831) at St John's is best observed from the stylish bridge designed by Wren just to the south. The oldest crossing is at **Clare College**, built in 1639 and ornamented with decorative balls. Its architect was paid a grand total of 15p for his design and, feeling aggrieved at such a measly fee, it's said he cut a chunk out of one of the balls adorning the balustrade so the bridge would never be complete. Most curious of all is the flimsy-looking wooden construction joining the two halves of Queen's College known as the **Mathematical Bridge**, first built in 1749. Despite what unscrupulous guides may tell you, it wasn't the handiwork of Sir Isaac Newton (he died in 1727), originally built without nails, or taken apart by students who then couldn't figure how to put it back together.

FREE **Fitzwilliam Museum** MUSEUM
(www.fitzmuseum.cam.ac.uk; Trumpington St; ⏲10am-5pm Tue-Sat, noon-5pm Sun) Fondly dubbed 'the Fitz' by locals, this colossal neoclassical pile was one of the first public art museums in Britain, built to house the fabulous treasures that the seventh Viscount Fitzwilliam had bequeathed to his old university. An unabashedly over-the-top building, it sets out to mirror its contents in an ostentatious jumble of styles that mixes mosaic with marble, Greek with Egyptian and more. It was begun by George Basevi in 1837, but he did not live to see its completion: while working on Ely Cathedral he stepped back to admire his handiwork, slipped and fell to his death.

The lower galleries are filled with priceless treasures from ancient Egyptian sarcophagi to Greek and Roman art, Chinese ceramics to English glass, and some dazzling illuminated manuscripts. The upper galleries showcase works by Leonardo da Vinci, Titian, Rubens, the Impressionists, Gainsborough and Constable, right through to Rembrandt and Picasso. You can join a one-hour **guided tour** (£3.50) of the museum on Saturdays at 2.30pm.

FREE **Kettle's Yard** ART COLLECTION
(www.kettlesyard.co.uk; cnr Northampton & Castle Sts; ⏲house 2-4pm Tue-Sun, gallery 11.30am-5pm Tue-Sun) Neither gallery nor museum, this house nonetheless oozes artistic excellence, with a collection of 20th-century art, furniture, ceramics and glass that would be the envy of many an institution. It is the former home of HS 'Jim' Ede, a former assistant keeper at the Tate Gallery in London, who opened his home to young artists, resulting in a beautiful collection by the likes of Miró, Henry Moore and others. There are also exhibitions of contemporary art in the modern **gallery** next door.

While here, take a peek in the neighbouring **Folk Museum** (www.folkmuseum.org.uk; 2/3 Castle St; adult/child £3.50/1; ⏲10.30am-5pm Tue-Sat, 2-5pm Sun), a 300-year-old former inn now cluttered with a wonderfully diverse collection of domestic tools and equipment from 1700 onwards.

FREE **Scott Polar Research Institute** MUSEUM
(www.spri.cam.ac.uk/museum; Lensfield Rd; ⏲10am-4pm Tue-Sat) For anyone interested in polar exploration or history the Scott Polar Research Institute has a fantastic collection of artefacts, journals, paintings, photographs, clothing, equipment and maps in its museum. Reopened in 2010 after a thorough redesign, the museum is a fascinating place to learn about the great polar explorers and their harrowing expeditions, and to read the last messages left to wives, mothers and friends by Scott and his polar crew. You can also examine Inuit carvings and scrimshaw (etched bones), sledges and snow scooters and see the scientific and domestic equipment used by various expeditions.

Great St Mary's Church CHURCH
(www.gsm.cam.ac.uk; Senate House Hill; tower adult/child £2.50/1.25; ⏲9am-5pm Mon-Sat, 12.30-5pm Sun) Cambridge's staunch university church was built between 1478 and 1519 in the late-Gothic Perpendicular style. If you're fit and fond of a view, climb the 123 steps of the tower for superb vistas of the dreamy spires, albeit marred by wire fencing.

The beautiful classical building directly across King's Pde is the **Senate House**, designed in 1730 by James Gibbs; graduations are held here in summer, when gowned and mortar-boarded students parade the streets to pick up those all-important scraps of paper.

Round Church CHURCH
(www.christianheritageuk.org.uk; Bridge St; adult/child £2/free; ⏲10am-5pm Tue-Sat, 1-5pm Sun) The beautiful Round Church is another of Cambridge's gems and one of only four such structures in England. It was built by the mysterious Knights Templar in 1130 and shelters an unusual circular nave ringed by chunky Norman pillars. It now houses an exhibition on Cambridge's Christian heritage and the city's contribution to the world.

Cambridge University Botanic Garden BOTANIC GARDEN
(www.botanic.cam.ac.uk; entrance on Bateman St; adult/child £4/free; ⌚10am-6pm) Founded by Charles Darwin's mentor, Professor John Henslow, the beautiful Botanic Garden is home to 8000 plant species, a wonderful arboretum, tropical houses, a winter garden and flamboyant herbaceous borders. You can take an hour-long **guided tour** (£7, includes garden admission) of the garden on the first Saturday of the month at 11am. The gardens are 1200m south of the city centre via Trumpington St.

Activities

Punting

Gliding a self-propelled punt along the Backs is a blissful experience once you've got the knack, though it can also be a manic challenge to begin. If you wimp out you can always opt for a relaxing chauffeured punt.

Punt hire costs £14 to £16 per hour, chauffeured trips of the Backs cost £10 to £12, and a return trip to Grantchester will set you back £20 to £30. All companies offer discounts if you pre-book tickets online. Some recommended outlets:

Cambridge Chauffer Punts (www.punting-in-cambridge.co.uk; Silver St Bridge)

Granta (www.puntingincambridge.com; Newnham Rd)

Scudamore's (www.scudamores.com; Silver St) Also hires rowboats, kayaks and canoes.

Walking & Cycling

For an easy stroll into the countryside, you won't find a prettier route than the 3-mile walk to **Grantchester** following the meandering River Cam and its punters southwest through flower-flecked meadows.

Scooting around town on a bike is easy thanks to the pancake-flat landscape, although the surrounding countryside can get a bit monotonous. The Cambridge tourist office stocks several useful guides.

Tours

Visit www.visitcambridge.org for information on self-guided walking and audio tours of the city.

City Sightseeing BUS TOUR
(www.city-sightseeing.com; adult/child £13/7; ⌚every 20min 10am-4.40pm) Hop-on/hop-off bus tours.

Riverboat Georgina BOATING
(☎01223-307694; www.georgina.co.uk) One-/two-hour cruises £6/12 with the option of including lunch or a cream tea.

Tourist Office WALKING TOUR
(☎01223-457574; www.visitcambridge.org) Conducts two-hour city tours (adult/child £12.50/6, 11am and 1pm Monday to Saturday, 1pm Sunday); 1½-hour city tours (adult/child £11/6, noon Monday to Friday, noon and 2pm Saturday); and ghost tours (adult/child £6/4; 6pm Friday). Book in advance.

Sleeping

Some of Cambridge's most central B&Bs use their convenient location as an excuse not to upgrade. Some of the better places are a bit of a hike from town but well worth the effort.

Hotel du Vin HOTEL **£££**
(☎01223-227330; www.hotelduvin.com; Trumpington St; d from £140; @📶) This boutique hotel chain really knows how to do things

HOW TO PUNT

Punting looks pretty straightforward but, believe us, it's not. As soon as we dried off and hung our clothes on the line, we thought it was a good idea to offer a couple of tips on how to move the boat and stay dry.

» Standing at the end of the punt, lift the pole out of the water at the side of the punt.

» Let the pole slide through your hands to touch the bottom of the river.

» Tilt the pole forward (that is, in the direction of travel of the punt) and push down to propel the punt forward.

» Twist the pole to free the end from the mud at the bottom of the river, and let it float up and trail behind the punt. You can then use it as a rudder to steer with.

» If you haven't fallen in yet, raise the pole out of the water and into the vertical position to begin the cycle again.

right. Its Cambridge offering has all the usual trademarks, from quirky but incredibly stylish rooms with monsoon showers and luxurious Egyptian cotton sheets to the atmospheric vaulted cellar bar and the French-style bistro (mains £14.50 to £20). The central location, character-laden building and top-notch service make it a great deal at this price.

Cambridge Rooms COLLEGE ROOMS **££**
(www.cambridgerooms.co.uk; r £35-120) If you fancy experiencing life inside the hallowed college grounds, you can stay in a student room, wander the grounds, see the chapel and have breakfast in the ancient college hall. Accommodation varies from functional singles (with shared bathroom) overlooking college quads to more modern, en suite rooms in nearby annexes. There's limited availability during term time but a good choice of rooms during university holidays.

Hotel Felix HOTEL **£££**
(☎01223-277977; www.hotelfelix.co.uk; Whitehouse Lane, Huntingdon Rd; d £180-305; P @ wi-fi) This luxurious boutique hotel occupies a lovely grey-brick Victorian villa in landscaped grounds a mile from the city centre. Its 52 rooms embody designer chic with minimalist style but lots of comfort. The slick restaurant serves Mediterranean cuisine with a modern twist (mains £12.50 to £20). To get here follow Castle St and then Huntingdon Rd out of the city for about 1.5 miles.

Alexander B&B **££**
(☎01223-525725; www.beesley-schuster.co.uk; 56 St Barnabas Rd; s/d from £40/65) Set in a Victorian house in a quiet residential area, the Alexander has two homey rooms with period fireplaces, big windows and lots of light. There's a two-night minimum stay, but with a convenient location and friendly atmosphere it's worth booking in advance. Continental breakfast only. The B&B is off Mill Rd, about 1 mile from the corner of Parker's Piece.

Tenison Towers Guest House B&B **££**
(☎01223-363924; www.cambridgecitytenisontowers.com; 148 Tenison Rd; s/d from £40/60) This exceptionally friendly and homey B&B is really handy if you're arriving by train, but well worth seeking out whatever way you arrive in town. The rooms are bright and simple, with pale colours and fresh flowers, and the aroma of freshly baked muffins greets you in the morning. The B&B is about a mile from the city centre. Follow Regent St south from the city, veer left onto Station Rd and then left onto Tension Rd just before you reach the train station.

Lynwood House B&B **££**
(☎01223-500776; www.lynwood-house.co.uk; 217 Chesterton Rd; s/d from £40/75; P wi-fi) Newly redecorated rooms with white linens, silky throws, trendy wallpapers and brocade curtains give contemporary style to this Victorian semi-close to Midsummer Common. Breakfasts are hearty and made with organic, free-range ingredients. No children under 12 allowed.

Benson House B&B **££**
(☎01223-311594; www.bensonhouse.co.uk; 24 Huntingdon Rd; d £85-110; P wi-fi) Just a 1200m-walk from the city centre, this lovely B&B has some beautifully renovated rooms offering hotel-standard accommodation. The tasteful decor ranges from monochrome minimalism to muted classical elegance. No children. To get here follow Castle St north of the city centre into Huntingdon Rd.

Cambridge YHA HOSTEL **£**
(☎0845 371 9728; www.yha.org.uk; 97 Tenison Rd; dm/tw £16/40; @) Within walking distance of the city centre and cheap and cheerful; this well-worn hostel close to the train station fills up fast. The dorms are small and pretty basic and with lots of groups using the hostel it can be noisy. Book well ahead. To get to the hostel follow Regent St south out of the city, following signs for the train station. Veer left onto Station Rd and then left onto Tenison Rd.

Eating

Cambridge is packed with chain restaurants, particularly around the city centre. You'll find upmarket chains such as Browns and Loch Fyne on Trumpington St and plenty of Asian eateries on Regent St. If you're looking for something more independent you'll have to search a little harder.

Midsummer House MODERN BRITISH **£££**
(☎01223-369299; www.midsummerhouse.co.uk; Midsummer Common; 2-/3-course lunch £30/35, 2/3-course dinner £55/72; ⏲lunch Wed-Sat, dinner Tue-Sat) Set in a wonderful Victorian villa backing onto the river, but simple and modern inside, this sophisticated place is sheer gastronomic delight. It serves what is probably the best food in East Anglia, has

a host of rave reviews from famous foodies and two Michelin stars, but none of the pretension you'd expect of a restaurant of its calibre. Book ahead.

Alimentum MODERN EUROPEAN £££
(01223-413001; www.restaurantalimentum.co.uk; 152-154 Hills Rd; mains £17.50-21; closed Sun dinner) Slick and stylish and eager to impress, this place aims to wow you with its ambitious menu and effortlessly casual service. The food is divine, with slow cooking and ethically sourced local produce a priority. On the down side it's way out of town (off Hills Rd) in a far-from-pretty location, and the piped music is a tad too loud.

Michaelhouse MODERN BRITISH £
(www.michaelhousecafe.co.uk; Trinity St; mains £7-9; 8am-5pm Mon-Sat) Sip fair-trade coffee and nibble focaccias among soaring medieval arches or else take a pew within reach of the altar at this stylishly converted church, which still has a working chancel. The simple lunch menu features quiche, soup and salads, as well as more substantial hot dishes, and has a good range of vegetarian options.

Origin8 DELI CAFE £
(www.origin8delicafes.com; 62 St Andrew's St; mains £4-6.50; 8am-6pm Mon-Sat, 11am-5.30pm Sun) Bright and airy, this cafe, deli and butchers shop prides itself on its local organic ingredients. It's a great place to stop for hearty soups, hog roast baps, home-cooked sausage rolls, fresh salads or luscious cakes. The shop showcases foodstuffs from East Anglia's finest producers, making it a perfect bet for picnic supplies.

Oak Bistro MODERN BRITISH ££
(01223-323361; www.theoakbistro.co.uk; 6 Lensfield Rd; mains £11-17, set 2-/3-course lunch £12/15; closed Sun) This little place on a busy corner is a great local favourite and serves up simple, classic dishes with modern flair. The atmosphere is relaxed and welcoming, the decor minimalist and the food perfectly cooked. There's even a hidden walled garden for alfresco dining. It's a popular spot so book ahead.

CB2 MODERN BRITISH ££
(www.cb2bistro.com; 5-7 Norfolk St; mains £6-13) Internet cafe, bistro, music venue and cinema all rolled into one, this lively place dishes up a great range of rustic cuisine in a relaxed and friendly atmosphere. The menu features everything from salads, pastas and wraps to heartier bistro specials. There's live music on the top floor on Wednesday nights and every other Thursday. To get here take a left off Parkside onto East Rd. Norfolk St is about 300m along on the right.

Jamie's Italian ITALIAN ££
(www.jamieoliver.com/italian; Old Library, Wheeler St; mains £8-18) Set in the city's Guildhall, the celebrity chef's 'neighbourhood Italian' is a great place to eat. The building itself has loads of character, and the funky modern design has the city's young trendsters flocking in droves. The food's great, too: simple, unpretentious dishes that leave you wanting more. Be prepared to queue.

Twenty-Two MODERN EUROPEAN £££
(01223-351880; www.restaurant22.co.uk; 22 Chesterton Rd; set dinner £28.50; 7-9.45pm Tue-Sat) Hidden away amid a row of Victorian terraced housing is this slightly odd, yet outstanding restaurant. It's an intimate kind of place, with a hushed atmosphere and old-school decor where diners chose from a delicate set menu. Dishes are of the highest standard and the wine list is impressive. Book ahead.

Rainbow Vegetarian Bistro VEGETARIAN ££
(www.rainbowcafe.co.uk; 9a King's Pde; mains £8-10; 10am-10pm Tue-Sat, to 4pm Sun & Mon) First-rate vegetarian food and a pious glow emanate from this snug subterranean gem, accessed down a narrow passageway off King's Pde. It's decorated in funky colours and serves up organic dishes with a hint of the exotic, such as scrumptious Indonesian gado gado and Cuban peccadillo pie.

Drinking

Cambridge is awash with historic pubs that have the same equal mix of intellectual banter and rowdy merrymaking that they have had for centuries past.

Eagle TRADITIONAL PUB
(Bene't St) Cambridge's most famous pub has loosened the tongues and pickled the grey cells of many an illustrious academic in its day; among them Nobel Prize-winning scientists Crick and Watson, who discussed their research into DNA here. It's a traditional 17th-century pub with five cluttered, cosy rooms, the back one once popular with WWII airmen, who left their signatures on the ceiling.

Kingston Arms PUB
(33 Kingston St) Down to earth and full of character, this bright blue pub is tucked away off Mill Rd. Real ales, decent pub grub (mains £8.50 to £13.50, served 6pm to 10pm Monday to Thursday and all day Friday to Sunday), a walled garden, free wi-fi and a friendly attitude make it well worth the effort to get here. You can even challenge the regulars to a game of tiddlywinks. To get here follow Parker St past Parker's Piece onto Mill Rd, turning left onto Kingston St after about 600m.

Granta PUB
(☎01223-505016; Newnham Rd) If the exterior of this picturesque waterside pub, overhanging a pretty mill pond, looks strangely familiar, it could be because it's the darling of many a TV director. Its terrace sits directly beside the water, and when your Dutch courage has been sufficiently fuelled, there are punts for hire alongside.

Portland Arms PUB
(www.theportlandarms.co.uk; 129 Chesterton Rd) The best spot in town to catch a gig and see the pick of up-and-coming bands, the Portland is a popular student haunt and music venue. Its wood-panelled interior, honest attitude and spacious terrace make it a good bet any day of the week.

☆ Entertainment

Thanks to a steady stream of students and tourists there's always something on in Cambridge. You'll find all the railings in the city centre laden down with posters advertising classical concerts, theatre shows, academic lectures and live music. It's also worth picking up a *What's On* events guide from the tourist office or logging on to www.admin.cam.ac.uk/whatson for details of university events. Despite the huge student population, Cambridge isn't blessed with the best nightclubs in the country. Many students stick to the college bars late at night and swear that they are the best venues in town. Pity they're not open to the rest of us.

Fez NIGHTCLUB
(www.cambridgefez.com; 15 Market Passage) Hip-hop, dance, R&B, techno, funk, top-name DJs and club nights – you'll find it at Cambridge's most popular club, the Moroccan-themed Fez.

Soul Tree NIGHTCLUB
(www.soultree.co.uk; 1-6 Guildhall Chambers, Corn Exchange St; ⌚Mon, Fri & Sat) Funk, disco, '80s classics, and not-so-big-name DJs at this popular club.

Corn Exchange THEATRE
(www.cornex.co.uk; Wheeler St) The city's main centre for arts and entertainment, attracting the top names in pop and rock to ballet.

Arts Theatre THEATRE
(www.cambridgeartstheatre.com; 6 St Edward's Passage) Cambridge's biggest bona fide theatre puts on everything from pantomime to drama fresh from London's West End.

ADC STUDENT THEATRE
(www.adctheatre.com; Park St) Students' theatre and home to the university's Footlights comedy troupe, which jump-started the careers of scores of England's comedy legends.

ℹ Information

You'll find all the major banks and a host of ATMs around St Andrew's St and Sidney St. The going rate for internet access is about £1 per hour.

Addenbrooke's Hospital (☎01223-245151; Hills Rd) Southeast of the centre.

Budget Internet Cafe (30 Hills Rd; ⌚10am-9pm Mon-Sat, 11am-7pm Sun)

CB2 (5-7 Norfolk St; ⌚noon-midnight) Internet access.

Jaffa Internet Cafe (22 Mill Rd; ⌚10am-10pm)

Police station (☎01223-358966; Parkside)

Post office (9-11 St Andrew's St)

Tourist office (☎0871 266 8006; www.visitcambridge.org; Old Library, Wheeler St; ⌚10am-5.30pm Mon-Fri, to 5pm Sat, 11am-3pm Sun) Pick up a guide to the Cambridge colleges (£4.99) in the gift shop or a leaflet (£1) outlining two city walks. You can also download audio tours from the website.

ℹ Getting There & Away

BUS From Parkside there are regular buses to Stansted (£12.40, 50 minutes), Heathrow (£30, 2½ to three hours) and Gatwick (£31, four hours) airports, while a Luton (£15, 1½ hours) service runs roughly every two hours. Buses to Oxford (£11, 3½ hours) are regular but take a very convoluted route.

TRAIN Trains run at least every 30 minutes to London's King's Cross and Liverpool St stations (£19, 45 minutes to 1¼ hours). There are also three trains per hour to Ely (£4, 20 minutes) and hourly connections to Bury St Edmunds (£8, 45 minutes) and King's Lynn (£8, 50 minutes).

CAR Cambridge's centre is largely pedestrianised. Use one of the five free Park & Ride car parks on major routes into town. Buses (£2.50) serve the city centre every 10 minutes between 7am and 7pm daily, then every 20 minutes until 10pm.

Getting Around

BICYCLE Cambridge is very bike-friendly, and two wheels provide a great way of getting about town.

Cambridge Station Cycles (www.stationcycles.co.uk; Station Bldg, Station Rd; per half-day/day/week £8/12/20) Near the train station.

City Cycle Hire (www.citycyclehire.com; 61 Newnham Rd; per half-day/day/week from £6/10/20)

BUS A free gas-powered City Circle bus runs around the centre, stopping every 15 minutes from 9am to 5pm, on Downing St, King's Pde and Jesus Lane. City bus lines run around town from Drummer St bus station; C1, C3 and C7 stop at the train station. Dayrider passes (£3.30) offer unlimited travel on all buses within Cambridge for one day.

Around Cambridge

GRANTCHESTER

Old thatched cottages with gardens covered in flowers, breezy meadows and some classic cream teas aren't the only reason to make the pilgrimage along the river to the picture-postcard village of Grantchester. You'll also be following in the footsteps of some of the world's greatest minds on a 3-mile walk, cycle or punt that has changed little since Edwardian times.

The journey here is idyllic on a sunny day, and once you arrive you can flop into a deck chair under a leafy apple tree and wolf down calorific cakes or light lunches at the quintessentially English **Orchard Tea Garden** (www.orchard-grantchester.com; Mill Way; lunch mains £6-8; ⌚9.30am-7pm). This was the favourite haunt of the Bloomsbury Group and other cultural icons who came to camp, picnic, swim and discuss their work.

IMPERIAL WAR MUSEUM

The romance of the winged war machine is alive and well at Europe's biggest **aviation museum** (http://duxford.iwm.org.uk; Duxford; adult/child £16.50/free; ⌚10am-6pm) where almost 200 lovingly waxed aircraft are housed. The vast airfield, once a frontline fighter station in WWII, showcases everything from dive bombers to biplanes, Spitfire and Concorde.

Also included is the stunning **American Air Museum** hangar, designed by Norman Foster, which has the largest collection of American civil and military aircraft outside the USA, and the slick **AirSpace hangar** which houses an exhibition on British and Commonwealth aviation. WWII tanks and artillery can be seen in the **land-warfare hall**, and the regular **airshows** of modern and vintage planes are legendary.

Duxford is 9 miles south of Cambridge at Junction 10 of the M11. Bus C7 runs from Emmanuel St in Cambridge to Duxford (45 minutes, every half-hour, Monday to Saturday). The last bus back from the museum is at 5.30pm. The service is hourly on Sundays.

Ely

POP 15,102

A small but charming city steeped in history and dominated by a jaw-dropping cathedral, Ely (*ee*-lee) makes an excellent day trip from Cambridge. Beyond the dizzying heights of the cathedral towers lie medieval streets, pretty Georgian houses and riverside walks reaching out into the eerie fens that surround the town. The abundance of eels that once inhabited the undrained fens gave the town its unusual name, and you can still sample eel stew or eel pie in local restaurants. Ely is a sleepy kind of place where traditional tearooms and antiques shops vie for attention, but it also ranks as one of the fastest-growing cities in Europe, so change is surely on the way.

Sights

Ely Cathedral CATHEDRAL
(www.elycathedral.org; adult/child £6/free; ⌚9am-5pm) Dominating the town and visible across the flat fenland for vast distances, the stunning silhouette of Ely Cathedral is locally dubbed the 'Ship of the Fens'.

Walking into the early 12th-century Romanesque nave, you're immediately struck by its clean, uncluttered lines and lofty sense of space. The cathedral is renowned for its entrancing ceilings and the masterly 14th-century octagon and lantern towers, which soar upwards in shimmering colours.

The vast 14th-century Lady Chapel is the biggest in England; it's filled with eerily empty niches that once held statues of saints and martyrs. They were hacked out unceremoniously by iconoclasts during the English Civil War. However, the astonishingly delicate tracery and carving remain.

The cathedral is a breathtaking place, its incredible architecture and light making it a popular film location. You may recognise some of its fine details from scenes in *Elizabeth: The Golden Age* or *The Other Boleyn Girl*, but wandering back to the streets it can be difficult to imagine how such a small and tranquil city ended up with such a fine monument.

Although a sleepy place today, Ely has been a place of worship and pilgrimage since at least 673, when Etheldreda, daughter of the king of East Anglia, founded a nunnery here. A colourful character, Ethel shrugged off the fact that she had been twice married in her determination to become a nun and was canonised shortly after her death. The nunnery was later sacked by the Danes, rebuilt as a monastery, demolished and then resurrected as a church after the Norman Conquest. In 1109 Ely became a cathedral, built to impress mere mortals and leave them in no doubt about the power of the church.

For more insight into the fascinating history of the cathedral join a free **guided tour**, or a **tower tour** (£4 Mon-Sat, £6 Sun, Apr-Oct) of the Octagon Tower or the West Tower. Tour times change daily and by season so check in advance. It's also worth timing a visit to attend the spine-tingling **Evensong** (⏲5.30pm Mon-Sat, 4pm Sun) or **choral service** (⏲10.30am Sun).

Near the entrance a **stained-glass museum** (www.stainedglassmuseum.com; adult/child £3.50/2.50; ⏲10.30am-5pm Mon-Fri, to 5.30pm Sat, noon-6pm Sun) tells the history of decorated glasswork from the 14th century onwards.

Historic sites cluster about the cathedral's toes. Look out for the **Bishop's Palace**, now used as a nursing home, and **King's School**, which keeps the cathedral supplied with fresh-faced choristers.

Cromwell's House MUSEUM
(☎01353-662062; adult/child £4.50/4; ⏲10am-5pm Apr-Oct, 11am-4pm Nov-Mar) A short hop from the cathedral across St Mary's Green is the attractive half-timbered house where England's warty warmonger lived with his family from 1636 to 1646, when he was the local tithe collector. The house now has Civil War exhibits, portraits, waxworks and echoes with canned commentaries of – among other things – the great man's grisly death, exhumation and posthumous decapitation.

Ely Museum MUSEUM
(www.elymuseum.org.uk; Market St; adult/child £3.50/2.50; ⏲10.30am-5pm Mon-Sat, 1-5pm Sun, closed Tue Nov-Apr) Housed in the Old Gaol House complete with prisoners' cells and their scrawled graffiti, this place has everything from Roman remains to archive footage of eel-catching. It's the place to catch up on local history, from the formation of the fens to the local role in the World Wars.

Sleeping & Eating

You'll find a good choice of pubs serving decent food along the waterfront and the lanes off it.

Cathedral House B&B **££**
(☎01353-662124; www.cathedralhouse.co.uk; 17 St Mary's St; s/d £50/80; P) Set in a lovely Georgian house bursting with antiques and curios, this elegant B&B offers three individually decorated rooms, all with period features and cast-iron baths. Outside there's a beautiful walled garden and views of the cathedral.

Riverside Inn B&B **££**
(☎01353-439396; www.riversideinn-ely.co.uk; 8 Annesdale; s/d £65/90; P) You'll get great views of the river from this elegant house right on the waterfront. It has four spacious rooms with king-size beds, silky, brocade bedspreads, dark furniture and sparkling new bathrooms.

Old Fire Engine House TRADITIONAL BRITISH **££**
(☎01353-662582; www.theoldfireenginehouse.co.uk; 25 St Mary's St; two-/three-course set lunch £15/20, mains £14-17; ⏲closed dinner Sun) Backed by beautiful gardens and showcasing a variety of artwork, this delightfully homely place serves classic English food and excellent afternoon teas. Expect the likes of steak-and-kidney pie or rabbit with prunes and bacon washed down with a carefully chosen wine. Book in advance.

Boathouse MODERN BRITISH **££**
(☎01353-664388; www.cambscuisine.com; 5 Annesdale; two-/three-course set lunch £12/16, dinner mains £10.50-17) This sleek riverside restaurant dishes up excellent modern English food at very reasonable prices. It has wonderful patio dining overlooking the water, while the stylish interior is lined with oars. Book ahead.

Information

Tourist office (☎01353-662062; www.visitely.org.uk; 29 St Mary's St; ⏲10am-5pm) Stocks a leaflet on the 'Eel Trail' town walk and organises guided walking tours of the city at 2.30pm on some Sundays (£3.70).

Getting There & Away

The easiest way to get to Ely from Cambridge is by train (15 minutes, every 20 minutes); don't even consider the bus – it takes a roundabout route and five times as long. There are also trains to Norwich (£13, one hour, every 20 minutes), and hourly services to King's Lynn (£5.50, 30 minutes).

Following the Fen Rivers Way (map available from tourist offices), it's a lovely 17-mile towpath walk from Cambridge to Ely.

ESSEX

Ah, Essex; home to chavs (bling, bling youfs), bottle blonds, boy racers and brash seaside resorts – or so the stereotype goes. The county's inhabitants have been the butt of some of England's cruellest jokes and greatest snobbery for years, but beyond the fake Burberry bags and slots 'n' bumper car resorts, there's a rural idyll of sleepy medieval villages and rolling countryside. One of England's best-loved painters, Constable, found inspiration here, and the rural Essex of his time remains hidden down winding lanes little changed for centuries. Here, too, is the historic town of Colchester, Britain's oldest, with a sturdy castle and vibrant arts scene, and even Southend-on-Sea, the area's most popular resort, has a softer side in the traditional cockle-sellers and cobbled lanes of sleepy suburb Leigh.

Colchester

POP 104,390

Dominated by its sturdy castle and ancient walls, Colchester claims the title as Britain's oldest recorded city, with settlement noted here as early as the 5th century BC. Centuries later in AD 43, the Romans came, saw, conquered and constructed their northern capital Camulodunum here. So, too, the invading Normans, who saw Colchester's potential and built the monstrous war machine that is the castle.

Today the city has a rather dowdy atmosphere, but amid the maze of narrow streets in the city centre you'll find a few half-timbered gems, the fine castle and a host of new regeneration projects under way.

Sights

Colchester Castle CASTLE
(www.colchestermuseums.org.uk; adult/child £5.70/3.60; ⏲10am-5pm Mon-Sat, from 11am Sun) England's largest surviving Norman keep (bigger even than that of the Tower of London), once a hair-raising symbol of foreign invasion, now slumbers innocently amid a lush park. Built upon the foundations of a Roman fort, the castle was first established in 1076 and now houses an exceptional interactive museum, with plenty of try-on togas and sound effects to keep young curiosity alive. There are also illuminating guided tours (adult/child £2/1, hourly noon to 3pm) of the Roman vaults, Norman rooftop chapel and castle walls.

FREE **Hollytrees Museum** MUSEUM
(www.colchestermuseums.org.uk; High St; ⏲10am-5pm Mon-Sat, from 11am Sun) Housed in a graceful Georgian town house beside the castle, this museum trawls through 300 years of domestic life with quirky surprises that include a shipwright's baby carriage in the shape of a boat and a make-your-own Victorian silhouette feature. There are also temporary exhibitions and events throughout the year.

Dutch Quarter HISTORIC DISTRICT
The best of the city's half-timbered houses and rickety roof lines are clustered together in this Tudor enclave just a short stroll north of High St. The area remains as a testament to the 16th-century Protestant weavers who fled here from Holland.

FREE **firstsite** ARTS CENTRE
(www.firstsite.uk.net; St Botolph's) Already being promoted as a star attraction, this sparkly new arts centre was just taking shape at the time of writing. A stunning curved-glass and copper building, it will contain gallery space, a library, auditorium and conference facilities and will play host to exhibitions, workshops, lectures and performances. Check the website or tourist office for the latest information.

Sleeping & Eating

Colchester has some excellent, lovingly cared for and reasonably priced B&Bs that give the town's ancient hotels a real run for their money. Independent restaurants are in short supply, but you'll find all the usual chains along North Hill.

Charlie Browns B&B ££
(☎01206-517541; www.charliebrownsbedandbreakfast.co.uk; 60 East St; s/d £45/65; P@) A former hardware shop turned boutique B&B, this place offers incredible value, with a couple of stunning rooms blending

14th-century character with 21st-century style. Antique and modern furniture mix seamlessly with the half-timbered walls, limestone bathrooms and rich fabrics to create an intimate, luxurious feel. It's an absolute steal at these rates and should be your first port of call.

Trinity Townhouse B&B ££
(01206-575955; www.trinitytownhouse.co.uk; 6 Trinity St; s/d from £70/85;) This central Tudor town house has five lovely rooms, each with its own character. Go for four-poster Wilbye, cottage-style Darcy or the more modern Furley. Each has period features, king-size beds, flatscreen TV and a designer bathroom. No children under five.

Lemon Tree MODERN EUROPEAN ££
(01206-767337; www.the-lemon-tree.com; 48 St John's St; mains £11-16; closed Sun) This zesty little eatery serves a refreshing menu of European classics with a modern twist. The decor strikes a nice chic-to-rustic balance, with a section of knobbly Roman wall flanking the main dining area. There are tasty blackboard specials, frequent gourmet nights, a pianist on Monday nights and regular special events.

Information

Compuccino (www.compuccino.co.uk; 17-19 Priory Walk; per hr £2.50; 9am-6.30pm Mon-Sat, 11am-5pm Sun) Internet access.

Post office (North Hill & Longe Wyre St)

Tourist office (01206-282920; www.visitcolchester.com; 1 Queen St; 9.30am-5pm Mon-Sat) Opposite the castle.

Getting There & Away

The bus station is on Queen St. There are three daily National Express buses to London Victoria (£13, 2½ hours).

There are two train stations, but mainline services stop at Colchester Station, about half a mile north of the centre. Trains run to London Liverpool St (£21, one hour, every 15 minutes).

Southend-on-Sea

POP 160,257

Crass, commercialised and full of flashing lights, Southend is London's lurid weekend playground, full of gaudy amusements and seedy nightclubs. But beyond the tourist tat, roller coasters and slot machines there's a glorious stretch of sandy beach, an absurdly long pier and in the suburb of Old Leigh, a traditional fishing village of cobbled streets, cockle sheds and thriving art galleries.

Sights & Activities

Other than miles upon miles of tawny imported-sand and shingle **beaches**, Southend's main attraction is its **pier** (01702-215620; pier train adult/child £3/1.50, pier walk & ride £2.50/1.50; 8.15am-8pm Easter-Oct, to 4pm Mon-Fri, to 6pm Sat & Sun Nov-Easter), built in 1830. At a staggering 1.33 miles long – the world's longest – it's an impressive edifice and a magnet for boat crashes, storms and fires, the last of which ravaged its tip in 2005. It's a surprisingly peaceful stroll to the lifeboat station at its head, and you can hop on the Pier Railway to save the long slog back.

Afterwards, dip beneath the pier's entrance to see the antique slot machines at the **museum** (www.southendpiermuseum.co.uk; adult/child £1/free; 11am-5pm Sun-Wed).

If the seaside tat is not your thing, swap the candy floss for steaming cockles wrapped in newspaper in the traditional fishing village of **Old Leigh**, just west along the seafront. Wander the cobbled streets, cockle sheds, art galleries and craft shops for a taste of life before the amusement arcades took over. The **Leigh Heritage Centre** (01702-470834; High St, Old Leigh) offers an insight into the history and heritage of the village and its buildings. The centre is run by volunteers so call in advance to check opening times.

Sleeping & Eating

Hamiltons HOTEL ££
(01702-332350; www.hamiltonsboutiquehotel.co.uk; 6 Royal Tce; d from £60; @) Set in a classic Georgian terrace house, this gorgeous boutique hotel offers plenty of period character yet has all your 21st-century comforts. Subtle floral wallpapers, weighty traditional fabrics, tasteful reproduction furniture and crystal chandeliers give the rooms a warm, luxurious charm without overloading the senses.

Pipe of Port BRITISH ££
(01702-614606; www.pipeofport.com; 84 High St; mains £10-21) A Southend institution, this subterranean wine bar and bistro is an atmospheric place, with old-world character, candlelit tables, sawdust-covered floor and its own unique charm. It's famous for its pies, casseroles and fish dishes as well as the lengthy wine list. Book ahead.

Information

Tourist Office (01702-618747; www.visitsouthend.co.uk; Southend Pier, Western Esplanade; 8.15am-8pm high season, to 6pm low season) At the entrance to the pier.

Getting There & Around

The easiest way to arrive is by train. There are trains roughly every 15 minutes from London Liverpool St to Southend Victoria and from London Fenchurch St to Southend Central (£9.40, 55 minutes). The seafront is a 10- to 15-minute walk from either train station. Trains leave Southend Central for Leigh-on-Sea (10 minutes, every 10 to 15 minutes).

SUFFOLK

Littered with picturesque villages seemingly lost in time, and quaint seaside resorts that have doggedly refused to sell their souls to tourism, this charming county makes a delightfully tranquil destination. Suffolk built its wealth and reputation on the back of the medieval wool trade, and although the once-busy coastal ports little resemble their former selves, the inland villages remain largely untouched, with magnificent wool churches and lavish medieval homes attesting to the once-great might of the area. To the west are the picture-postcard villages of Lavenham and Long Melford; further north the languid charm and historic buildings attract visitors to Bury St Edmunds; and along the coast the genteel seaside resorts of Aldeburgh and Southwold seem miles away from their more brash neighbours to the north and south.

Information

You can whet your appetite for the region further by visiting www.visit-suffolk.org.uk.

Getting Around

Consult **Suffolk County Tourism** (www.suffolkonboard.com) or **Traveline** (www.travelineeastanglia.co.uk) for local transport information. The two main bus operators in rural areas are **Constable** (www.constablecoachesltd.co.uk) and **Chambers** (www.chamberscoaches.co.uk).

Ipswich is the main transport hub of the region but not really worth a visit in itself. Trains from Ipswich:

Bury St Edmunds £7, 40 minutes, twice hourly

London Liverpool St £37.40, 1¼ hours, every 20 minutes

Norwich £12, 40 minutes, twice hourly

Sutton Hoo

Somehow missed by plundering grave robbers and left undisturbed for 1300 years, the hull of an enormous Anglo-Saxon ship was discovered here in 1939, buried under a mound of earth. The ship was the final resting place of Raedwald, King of East Anglia until AD 625, and was stuffed with a fabulous wealth of Saxon riches. The massive effort that went into his burial gives some idea of just how important an individual he must have been.

Many of the original finds and a full-scale reconstruction of his ship and burial chamber can be seen in the **visitors centre** (NT; www.nationaltrust.org.uk/suttonhoo; Woodbridge; adult/child £7/3.50; 10.30am-5pm). The finest treasures, including the king's exquisitely crafted helmet, shields, gold ornaments and Byzantine silver, are displayed in London's British Museum, but replicas are on show here.

Access to the original burial mounds is restricted, but you can join a one-hour **guided tour** (adult/child £2.50/1.25; 11.30am & 12.30pm), which explores the area and does much to bring this fascinating site back to life. The site is open year-round but has restricted opening hours in low season. Check the website.

Sutton Hoo is 2 miles east of Woodbridge and 6 miles northeast of Ipswich off the B1083. Buses 71 and 73 go to Sutton Hoo 10 times per day Monday to Saturday, passing through Woodbridge (10 minutes) en route to Ipswich (40 minutes).

Stour Valley

The soft, pastoral landscape and impossibly pretty villages of the Stour Valley have provided inspiration for some of England's best-loved painters. Constable and Gainsborough grew up or worked here, and the topsy-turvy timber-framed houses and elegant churches that date to the region's 15th-century weaving boom are still very much as they were. This now-quiet backwater once produced more cloth than anywhere else in England, but in the 16th century, production gradually shifted elsewhere and the valley reverted to a rustic idyll. Wander through the region and you'll happen on any number of picturesque villages far from the crowds.

Long Melford

POP 3675

Strung out along a winding road, the village of Long Melford is home to a clutch of historic buildings and two impressive country piles. The 2-mile High St is supposedly the longest in England; it's flanked by some stunning timber-framed houses, Georgian gems and Victorian terraces, and at one end has a sprawling village green lorded over by the magnificently pompous **Holy Trinity Church** (9am-6pm Apr-Sep, to 5pm Nov-Mar). A spectacular example of a 15th-century wool church, it has wonderful stained-glass windows and a tower dating from 1903.

From outside, the romantic Elizabethan mansion of **Melford Hall** (NT; www.nationaltrust.org.uk/melfordhall; adult/child £6.30/3.15; 1.30-5pm Wed-Sun May-Oct, 1.30-5pm Sat & Sun Apr & Oct) seems little changed since it entertained the queen in 1578. Inside, there's a panelled banqueting hall, much Regency and Victorian finery and a display on Beatrix Potter, who was related to the Parker family, which owned the house from 1786 to 1960.

There's a noticeably different atmosphere at Long Melford's other red-brick Elizabethan mansion, **Kentwell Hall** (www.kentwell.co.uk; adult/child £9.40/6.10; noon-4pm Apr-Sep;). Despite being full of Tudor pomp and centuries-old ghost stories, it is still used as a private home and has a wonderfully lived-in feel. It's surrounded by a rectangular moat, and there's a Tudor-rose maze and a rare-breeds farm that'll keep the kids happy. Kentwell hosts special events throughout the year, including several full **Tudor re-creations**, when the whole estate bristles with bodices and hose. Check the website for details.

Long Melford is also famed for its **antique shops**. Viewing appointments are required in some.

Sleeping & Eating

Black Lion Hotel & Restaurant HOTEL ££
(01787-312356; www.blacklionhotel.net; the Green; s/d from £102/157; P) Flamboyant rooms with serious swag curtains, four-poster and half-tester beds, rich fabrics and a creative combination of contemporary style and traditional elegance are on offer at this small hotel on the village green. Go for the deep red Yquem for pure, sultry passion, or try the Sancerre for something a little more restful. The hotel has two restaurants (mains £12 to £19) and a lovely walled Victorian garden.

High Street Farmhouse B&B ££
(01787-375765; www.highstreetfarmhouse.co.uk; High St; r from £60; P) This 16th-century farmhouse offers a choice of cosy but bright rooms full of rustic charm. Expect patchwork quilts, pretty florals, knotty pine and cast-iron or four-poster beds. There's a lovely mature garden outside and hearty breakfasts on offer.

Scutcher's Bistro BRITISH ££
(01787-310200; www.scutchers.com; Westgate St; mains £14-22; closed Sun & Mon) Despite the rather mismatched decor, this unpretentious place is renowned throughout the Stour Valley for its exquisite food. The menu features classic and modern English dishes that leave locals coming back regularly for more. It's just off the Green.

Getting There & Away

Buses leave from the High St outside the post office. A service goes to Bury St Edmunds (50 minutes, hourly Monday to Saturday).

Lavenham

POP 1738

One of East Anglia's most beautiful and rewarding towns, topsy-turvy Lavenham is home to a wonderful collection of exquisitely preserved medieval buildings that lean and lurch to dramatic effect. Lavenham's 300 half-timbered and pargeted houses and thatched cottages have been left virtually untouched since its heyday in the 15th century when it made its fortunes on the wool trade. Curiosity shops, art galleries, quaint tearooms and ancient inns line the streets, where the predominant colour is 'Suffolk pink', a traditional finish of whitewash mixed with red ochre. On top of the medieval atmosphere and beautiful street scenery, Lavenham has an excellent choice of accommodation, making it one of the most popular spots in the area with visitors.

Sights

Many of Lavenham's most enchanting buildings cluster along High St, Water St and around Market Pl, which is dominated by the early 16th-century **guildhall** (NT; www.nationaltrust.org.uk/lavenham; adult/child £3.90/1.60; 11am-5pm Apr-Oct, 11am-4pm Sat & Sun Nov, 11am-4pm Wed-Sun Mar), a superb example of a close-studded, timber-framed building. It is now a local-history museum with displays on the wool trade, and in its tranquil garden you can see dye plants that produced the typical medieval colours.

Also on Market Pl, the atmospheric 14th-century **Little Hall** (www.littlehall.org.uk; adult/child £3/free; 2-5.30pm Wed, Thu, Sat & Sun Apr-Oct) was once home to a successful wool merchant. It's another medieval gem, with soft ochre plastering, timber frame and crown-post roof. Inside, the rooms are restored to period splendour.

At the village's southern end rises the stunning **Church of St Peter & St Paul** (8.30am-5.30pm Apr-Sep, to 3.30pm Oct-Mar), a late Perpendicular church that seems to lift into the sky, with its beautifully proportioned windows and soaring steeple. Built between 1485 and 1530, it was one of Suffolk's last great wool churches, completed on the eve of the Reformation, and now a lofty testament to Lavenham's past prosperity.

If you're visiting at a weekend it's well worth joining a guided village walk (£3, 2.30pm Saturday, 11am Sunday) run by the **tourist office** (01787-248207; lavenhamtic@babergh.gov.uk; Lady St; 10am-4.45pm mid-Mar–Oct, 11am-3pm Sat & Sun Nov–mid-Mar).

Sleeping & Eating

TOP CHOICE Lavenham Priory B&B ££
(01787-247404; www.lavenhampriory.co.uk; Water St; s/d from £79/105; P) A rare treat, this sumptuously restored 15th-century B&B steals your heart as soon as you walk in the door. Every room oozes Elizabethan charm, with cavernous fireplaces, leaded windows, oak floors, original wall paintings and exquisite period features throughout. Now an upmarket six-room B&B, it must be booked well in advance.

Swan Hotel HOTEL £££
(01787-247477; www.theswanatlavenham.co.uk; High St; s/d from £85/170; P) A warren of stunning timber-framed 15th-century buildings now shelters one of the region's best-known hotels. Rooms are suitably spectacular, some with immense fireplaces, colossal beams and magnificent four-posters. Elsewhere the hotel cultivates a gentlefolk's country-club feel. The stunning beamed Great Hall is an atmospheric place to try the modern English cuisine (three-course set dinner £36).

Great House HOTEL ££
(01787-247431; www.greathouse.co.uk; Market Pl; d from£90; lunch Wed-Sat, dinner Tue-Fri;) Chic design blends effortlessly with 15th-century character at this much-loved restaurant in the centre of town. The guest accommodation is decidedly contemporary, with funky wallpaper, sleek furniture and plasma-screen TVs, but there are plenty of period features and a decanter of sherry on the side. The acclaimed **restaurant** (3-course lunch/dinner £20/32) serves classic French dishes with a modern flourish.

Angel Hotel HOTEL ££
(01787-247388; www.maypolehotels.com/angelhotel; Market Pl; s/d from £80/95; P) Dating back to 1420, this old coaching inn has been much altered and now offers eight comfortable rooms with exposed beams or brickwork, crisp white linens and minimalist furniture. There's a busy bar and a decent restaurant serving a modern British menu (mains £10 to £16).

Getting There & Away

Regular buses connect Lavenham with Bury St Edmunds (30 minutes) and Sudbury (20 minutes) hourly until 6pm Monday to Saturday (no service on Sunday). The nearest train station is Sudbury.

Bury St Edmunds

POP 36,218

Once home to one of the most powerful monasteries of medieval Europe, Bury has long attracted travellers for its powerful history, atmospheric ruins, handsome Georgian architecture and bustling agricultural markets. It's a genteel kind of place with tranquil gardens, a newly completed

A COTTAGE OF YOUR OWN

For self-catering country cottages in the area, have a browse through these sites:

Heritage Hideaways (www.heritage-hideaways.com)

Farm Stay Anglia (www.farmstayanglia.co.uk)

Just Suffolk (www.justsuffolk.com)

Norfolk Cottages (www.norfolkcottages.co.uk)

Suffolk Secrets (www.suffolk-secrets.co.uk)

Bury St Edmunds

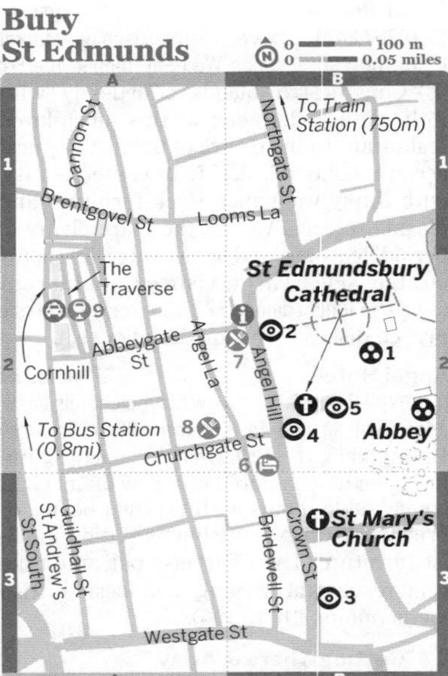

Bury St Edmunds

Top Sights

Abbey B2
St Edmundsbury Cathedral B2
St Mary's Church B3

Sights

1 Abbot's Palace B2
Great Court .... (see 2)
2 Great Gate B2
3 Greene King Brewery B3
4 Norman Tower B2
5 Western Front B2

Sleeping

6 Angel Hotel B2

Eating

7 Grid B2
8 Maison Bleue A2

Drinking

9 Nutshell A2

cathedral and a lively buzz. Bury is also home to Greene King, the famous Suffolk brewer.

History

St Edmund, last Saxon king of East Anglia, was decapitated by the Danes in 869, and in 903 the martyr's body was reburied here. Soon a series of ghostly miracles emanated from his grave, and the shrine became a centre of pilgrimage and the core of a new Benedictine monastery. In the 11th century, King Canute built a new abbey that soon became one of the wealthiest and most famous in the country.

Such was its standing that in 1214 the English barons chose the abbey to draw up a petition that would form the basis of the Magna Carta. The town prospered and in medieval times the town grew rich on the wool trade, that is until Henry VIII got his grubby hands on the abbey in 1539 and closed it down as part of the Dissolution.

Sights

Abbey & Park ABBEY RUINS

(dawn-dusk) Now a picturesque ruin residing in beautiful gardens behind the cathedral, the once all-powerful abbey still impresses despite the townspeople having made off with much of the stone after the Dissolution. The Reformation also meant an end to the veneration of relics, and St Edmund's grave and bones have long since disappeared.

You enter the park via one of two well-preserved old gates: opposite the tourist office, the staunch mid-14th-century **Great Gate** is intricately decorated and ominously defensive, complete with battlements, portcullis and arrow slits. The other entrance sits further up Angel Hill, where a gargoyle-studded early 12th-century **Norman Tower** looms.

Just beyond the Great Gate is a peaceful garden where the **Great Court** was once a hive of activity, and further on a dovecote marks the only remains of the **Abbot's Palace**. Most impressive, however, are the remains of the **western front**, where the original abbey walls were burrowed into in the 18th century to make way for houses. The houses are still in use and look as if they have been carved out of the stone like caves. The rest of the abbey spreads eastward like a ragged skeleton, with various lumps and pillars hinting at its immense size.

St Edmundsbury Cathedral CATHEDRAL

(St James; www.stedscathedral.co.uk; Angel Hill; requested donation £3; 8.30am-6pm) Completed in 2005, the 45m-high Millennium Tower of St Edmundsbury Cathedral is a vision in Lincolnshire limestone, and its traditional Gothic-style construction gives a good idea of how the towers of many other English cathedrals must have looked fresh from the stonemason's chisel.

Most of the rest of the building dates from the early 16th century, though the eastern end is postwar 20th-century, and the northern side was completed in 1990. The overall effect is light and lofty, with a gorgeous hammerbeam roof and a striking sculpture of the crucified Christ by Dame Elisabeth Frink in the north transept. The impressive entrance porch has a tangible Spanish influence, a tribute to Abbot Anselm (1121–48), who opted against pilgrimage to Santiago de Compostela in favour of building a church dedicated to St James (Santiago in Spanish) right here.

For an insight into the church's history and heritage join one of the **guided tours** (⌚11.30am Mon-Sat Apr-Sep) of the cathedral.

St Mary's Church CHURCH
(www.stmarystpeter.net/stmaryschurch; Honey Hill; ⌚10am-4pm Mar-Oct, to 3pm Nov-Feb) One of the biggest parish churches in England, St Mary's contains the tomb of Mary Tudor (Henry VIII's sister and a one-time queen of France). Built around 1430, it also has a host of somewhat vampirelike angels swooping from its roof, and a bell is still rung to mark curfew, as it was in the Middle Ages.

Greene King Brewery BREWERY
(www.greeneking.co.uk; Crown St; tours day/evening £8/10; ⌚museum 10.30am-4.30pm Mon-Sat, tours 11am Wed-Mon, 2pm Tue-Sat, 7pm Mon-Fri) Churning out some of England's favourite booze since Victorian times, this famous brewery has a museum (admission free) and runs tours, after which you can appreciate what all the fuss is about in its brewery bar. Tours are popular so book ahead.

Sleeping & Eating

Angel Hotel HOTEL ££
(☎01284-714000; www.theangel.co.uk; 3 Angel Hill; r from £100; P 📶) Peeking out from behind a shaggy mane of vines, this famous old coaching inn has hosted many a dignitary in its long history, including fictional celebrity Mr Pickwick, who, Dickens wrote, enjoyed an 'excellent roast dinner' here. Rooms are split between a slick contemporary wing and a traditional Georgian building. The modern restaurant has bright artwork, high ceilings and a stylish menu (mains £13 to £17).

Fox Inn HOTEL ££
(☎01284-705562; www.thefoxinnbury.co.uk; 1 Eastgate St; s/d from £84/90) Set in an old courtyard barn attached to an even older inn, the rooms here blend the warmth of exposed brick and beams with minimalist contemporary styling. You'll find trendy but subtle wallpapers, tasteful furniture and a relaxed, calming vibe. The restaurant serves a good selection of modern British food (mains £10 to £18). The Fox is about 600m from the cathedral. Head up Angel Hill, bearing right at the end into Mustow St and on to Eastgate St.

Maison Bleue SEAFOOD £££
(☎01284-760623; www.maisonbleue.co.uk; 31 Churchgate St; mains £15-27; ⌚Tue-Sat) Muted colours, pale leather banquettes, white linens and contemporary style merge with a menu of imaginative dishes in this excellent seafood restaurant. The food is superb but not fussy, the service impeccable and the setting very stylish yet relaxed. The three-course set lunch/dinner menu (£19/29) is a great way to sample everything.

Grid BRITISH ££
(www.thegridgrill.co.uk; 34 Abbeygate St; mains £10-14) Set in a 16th-century building but all slick, modern style, this restaurant has a menu revolving around locally reared meats. Don't worry, it's not all steaks: there are fish and vegetarian choices, too, and a good range of pasta and risotto dishes. It's bright and cheery, has a relaxed atmosphere and is enduringly popular with the locals.

Drinking

Nutshell PUB
(The Traverse) Recognised by the *Guinness Book of Records* as Britain's smallest, this tiny timber-framed pub is an absolute gem. Mind how you knock back a pint here: in the crush you never know who you're going to elbow.

Information

Tourist Office (☎01284-764667; tic@stedsbc.gov.uk; 6 Angel Hill; ⌚9.30am-5pm Mon-Sat Easter-Oct, 10am-3pm Sun May-Sep, 10am-4pm Mon-Fri, 10am-1pm Sat Nov-Easter) Has internet access and is the starting point for guided walking tours (£4, 2pm May to September).

Getting There & Around

The central bus station is on St Andrew's St North. The train station is 900m north of the tourist office, with frequent buses to the centre.

BUS The central bus station is on St Andrew's St North.

London National Express (£14, 2½ hours, daily)

Cambridge Stagecoach (bus 11, 65 minutes, hourly Monday to Saturday)

TRAIN The train station is 900m north of the tourist offi ce, with frequent buses to the centre.

Cambridge (£8, 45 minutes, hourly)

Ely (£8, 30 minutes, every two hours)

Aldeburgh

POP 2790

One of the region's most charming coastal towns, the small fishing and boat-building village of Aldeburgh has an understated charm that attracts visitors back year after year. Handsome pastel-colour houses, independent shops, art galleries and ramshackle fishing huts selling fresh-from-the-nets catch line the High St, while a sweeping shingle beach stretches along the shore offering tranquil big-sky views. Although it's a popular place, the town remains defiantly unchanged, with a low-key atmosphere and a great choice of food and accommodation.

Aldeburgh also has a lively cultural scene. Composer Benjamin Britten and lesser-known poet George Crabbe both lived and worked here; Britten founded East Anglia's primary arts and music festival, the **Aldeburgh Festival** (www.aldeburgh.co.uk), which takes place in June and has been going for over 60 years. Britten's legacy is commemorated by Maggi Hambling's wonderful *Scallop* sculpture, a short stroll north along the seashore.

Aldeburgh's other photogenic gem is the intricately carved and timber-framed **Moot Hall** (www.aldeburghmuseum.org.uk; adult/child £1/free; ⌚2.30-5pm), which now houses a local history museum.

Information can be found at the **tourist office** (☎01728-453637; atic@suffolkcoastal.gov.uk; 152 High St; ⌚9am-5.30pm Mon-Sat, 10am-4pm Sun).

Sleeping & Eating

Most places in Aldeburgh ask for a two-night minimum stay at weekends.

TOP CHOICE **Ocean House** B&B ££

(☎01728-452094; www.oceanhousealdeburgh.co.uk; 25 Crag Path; s/d £70/90) Right on the seafront and with only the sound of the waves to lull you to sleep at night, this beautiful Victorian guesthouse has wonderfully cosy, period-style rooms. Expect pale pastels, subtle florals and tasteful furniture, and the sound of classical music wafting from the rooms occupied by visiting music students. There's a baby grand piano on the top floor, a gaily painted rocking horse and bikes to borrow.

Number Six B&B ££

(☎01728-454226; www.numbersixaldeburgh.co.uk; 6 St Peters Rd; d £95; P) Guests can stay on the self-contained second floor of this New England–style home, where you'll find a spacious bedroom, kitchenette, and a private lounge with balcony and sea views. There's also an option of a second 'secret' adjoining room for children or friends. The decor is cosy contemporary with lots of attention to detail and loads of space.

Regatta Restaurant SEAFOOD ££

(☎01728-452011; www.regattaaldeburgh.com; 171 High St; mains £11-18.50; ⌚noon-2pm & 6-10pm) Good ol' English seaside food is given star treatment at this sleek, contemporary restaurant where local fish is the main attraction. The celebrated owner-chef supplements his wonderful seafood with meat and vegetarian options and regular gourmet nights. Book ahead.

Lighthouse MODERN EUROPEAN ££

(☎01728-453377; www.lighthouserestaurant.co.uk; 77 High St; mains £10-15; 👪) This unassuming bistro-style restaurant is a fantastic place to dine, with wooden tables and floors, a menu of simple but sensational international dishes, and a relaxed and friendly atmosphere. Despite the excellent food and accolades piled upon it, children are very welcome.

Getting There & Away

Aldeburgh is not well connected in terms of transport. There are frequent bus services to Ipswich (1¼ hours), where you can make connections to the rest of the country.

Around Aldeburgh

Strung along the coastline north of Aldeburgh is a poignant trail of serene and little-visited coastal heritage towns that are gradually succumbing to the sea. Most dramatically, the once-thriving port town of **Dunwich** is now a quiet village, with 12 churches and chapels and hundreds of houses washed away by the water.

The region is a favourite haunt of the binocular-wielding birdwatcher brigade, and **RSPB Minsmere** (www.rspb.org.uk; Westleton; adult/child £5/1.50; ⏲9am-dusk) flickers with airborne activity year-round. Another step south towards Aldeburgh is the odd early 20th-century 'Tudorbethan' holiday village of **Thorpeness**, which sports idiosyncratic follies, a windmill and a boating lake.

With public transport lacking you'll need your own wheels, or the will to walk or bike this stretch of peaceful and varied coastline.

ORFORD

Secluded and seductive, the gorgeous village of Orford, 6 miles south of Snape Maltings, is well worth a detour. It's a laid-back place littered with pretty houses and dominated by the odd polygonal keep of **Orford Castle** (EH: www.english-heritage.org.uk; adult/child £5.30/2.70; ⏲10am-5pm). The 12th-century castle is remarkably intact and has an innovative, 18-sided drum design with three square turrets. You can explore right from the basement to the roof, where there are glorious views of **Orford Ness** (NT; www.nationaltrust.org.uk/orfordness; admission incl ferry crossing adult/child £7.20/3.60; ⏲10am-2pm Tue-Sat), the largest vegetated shingle spit in Europe. Once used as a secret military testing ground, it is now home to a nature reserve and many rare wading birds, animals and plants. Ferries run from Orford Quay: the last ferry departs at 2pm and returns from the reserve at 5pm.

On your return make a beeline for the **Butley Orford Oysterage** (www.butleyorfordoysterage.co.uk; mains £7-13), where you'll find fresh seafood, smoked fish and local oysters just waiting to be gobbled up..

Southwold

POP 3858

Southwold is the kind of genteel seaside resort where beach huts cost an arm and a leg (upwards of £100,000 in some cases if local estate agents are to be believed) and the visitors are ever so posh. Its reputation as a well-heeled holiday getaway has earned it the nickname 'Kensington-on-Sea' after the upmarket London borough, and its lovely sandy beach, pebble-walled cottages, cannon-dotted clifftop and rows of beachfront bathing huts are all undeniably picturesque. Over the years the town has attracted many artists, including Turner, Charles Rennie Mackintosh, Lucian Freud and Damien Hirst.

However, this down-to-earth town also has a traditional pier, boat rides, fish and chips and its very own brewery.

Starting inland, the **Church of St Edmund** (Church St; admission free; ⏲9am-6pm Jun-Aug, to 4pm rest of year) is worth a quick peek for its fabulous medieval screen and 15th-century bloodshot-eyed Jack-o-the-clock, which grumpily overlooks the church's rear. A mere stone's throw away is an old weavers' cottage that now houses the **Southwold Museum** (www.southwold-museum.org; 9-11 Victoria St; admission free; ⏲10.30am-noon & 2-4pm Aug, 2-4pm Apr-Oct), where you can learn about the explosive 132-ship and 50,000-men Battle of Solebay (1672), fought just off the coast. You can also take a tour (£10) of the town's brewery, **Adnams** (www.adnams.co.uk; Adnams Pl). The one-hour tours are followed by a 30-minute tutored beer tasting. They take place daily in high season but at unpredictable times, so check the website for details.

For most visitors Southwold's shorefront is the main attraction. Take time to amble along its promenade and admire the squat 19th-century **lighthouse** before ending up at the cute little **pier** (www.southwoldpier.co.uk), first built in 1899 but recently reconstructed. In the 'under the pier' show you'll find a quirky collection of hand-made slot machines, a mobility masterclass for zimmerframe (walker) users, and a dog's-eye view of Southwold.

If you fancy a bit of a water jaunt, the **Coastal Voyager** (www.coastalvoyager.co.uk) offers a range of boat trips, including a 30-minute high-speed fun trip (adult/child £20/10), a leisurely river cruise (£25/12.50) to nearby Blythburgh, and a three-hour trip to Scroby Sands (£29/14.50) to see a seal colony and wind farm.

Southwold's hippest event is the **Latitude Festival** (www.latitudefestival.co.uk) held in Henham Park in mid-July. An eclectic mix of music, literature, dance, drama and comedy, its stunning location and manageable size make it popular with festival-goers fed up with fields of mud and never-ending queues.

The **tourist office** (☎01502-724729; www.visit-sunrisecoast.co.uk; 69 High St; ⏲10am-5pm Mon-Sat, 11am-4pm Sun) can help with accommodation and information.

Sleeping & Eating

Despite Southwold's charm and popularity, decent accommodation is thin on the ground.

Sutherland House HOTEL £££
(☎01502-724544; www.sutherlandhouse.co.uk; 56 High St; d £140-220; P 📶) Set in a beautiful 15th-century house dripping with character and period features, this small hotel has just three rooms featuring pargeted ceilings, exposed beams and elm floorboards but decked out in sleek, modern style. The top-notch restaurant (mains £10 to £17) specialises in local food, with the menu showing how many miles the principal ingredient in each dish has travelled.

Swan HOTEL ££
(☎01502-722186; www.adnams.co.uk; Market Sq; s/d from £95/135) There's a timeless elegance to the public rooms at the Swan, where large fireplaces, grandfather clocks and old-fashioned lamps induce a kind of soporific calm. You can choose between similarly period-style rooms or the newly refurbished lighthouse rooms with their garden views. The atmospheric restaurant serves a mainly fishy menu (mains £14 to £20).

Gorse House B&B ££
(☎01502-725468; www.gorsehouse.com; 19B Halesworth Rd, Reydon; d from £65; P) A 10-minute walk from the seafront but well worth the effort, this lovely B&B is one of the best in the area. The two rooms here are newly decorated in simple, contemporary style with subtle-patterned wallpapers, silky throws and flatscreen TVs.

Coasters MODERN BRITISH ££
(☎01502-724734; www.coastersofsouthwold.co.uk; 12 Queen St; mains £8-15; ⊙closed Mon) Right on the main drag, this unassuming restaurant has a great reputation and a loyal local following. The menu is short but sweet, and every dish is memorable. On top of the main meals there are a range of tapas for quick snacks, and sandwiches and cakes for a light lunch. Book ahead for evening meals.

Getting There & Away

Bus connections are surprisingly limited: your best bet is to catch one of the hourly services to Lowestoft (45 minutes) or Halesworth train station (30 minutes) and continue from there.

NORFOLK

Big skies, sweeping beaches, windswept marshes, meandering inland waterways and pretty flint houses make up the county of Norfolk, a handsome rural getaway with a thriving regional capital. You're never far from water here, whether it's the tranquil setting of rivers and windmills in the Norfolk Broads or the wide sandy beaches, fishing boats and nature reserves along the coast. They say the locals have 'one foot on the land, and one in the sea', and beach and boating holidays are certainly a highlight of the area. But twitchers flock here, too, for some of the country's best birdwatching. Meanwhile, in Norwich, the county's bustling capital, you'll find a stunning cathedral and castle, medieval churches, a lively market and an excellent choice of pubs, clubs and restaurants.

Activities

Signposted walking trails include the well-known Peddars Way and Norfolk Coast Path. Other long-distance paths include the **Weavers Way**, a 57-mile trail from Cromer to Great Yarmouth, and the **Angles Way** (www.eastsuffolklinewalks.co.uk/anglesway), which negotiates the valleys of the Rivers Waveney and Little Ouse for 70 miles. Meanwhile the **Wherryman's Way** (www.wherrymansway.net) is a 35-mile walking and cycling route through the Broads, following the River Yare from Norwich to Great Yarmouth.

For a real challenge, the **Around Norfolk Walk** is a 220-mile circuit that combines most of the above.

If you're planning to do the Norfolk Coast Path and don't fancy carrying your bags, **Walk Free** (www.walk-free.co.uk; per bag £10) provides a bag courier service.

Information

Some handy websites:

Independent Traveller's Norfolk (www.itnorfolk.co.uk)

Norfolk Tourist Attractions (www.norfolktouristattractions.co.uk)

Tour Norfolk (www.tournorfolk.co.uk)

Visit Norfolk (www.visitnorfolk.co.uk)

Getting Around

For comprehensive travel advice and timetables, contact **Traveline East Anglia** (☎0871-200 22 33; www.travelineeastanglia.co.uk).

Norwich

POP 121,550

The affluent and easygoing city of Norwich (pronounced norritch) is a rich tapestry of meandering laneways liberally sprinkled with architectural gems – spoils of the city's heyday at the height of the medieval wool boom. A magnificent cathedral lords over it all from one end of the city centre and a sturdy Norman castle from the other. Around these two landmarks a series of leafy greens, grand squares, quiet lanes, crooked half-timbered buildings and a host of medieval churches pan out across this compact and artsy city. Meanwhile thriving markets, modern shopping centres, contemporary-art galleries and a young student population give the city a genial, debonair attitude that makes it one of the most appealing cities in East Anglia. Add easy access to the Broads and sweeping beaches along the coast and you have an excellent base to use for touring the area.

History

Though Norwich's history stretches back well over a thousand years, the city's golden age was during the Middle Ages, when it was England's most important city after London. Its relative isolation meant that it traditionally had stronger ties to the Low Countries than to London, and when Edward III encouraged Flemish weavers to settle here in the 14th century this connection was sealed. The arrival of the immigrants helped establish the wool industry that fattened the city and sustained it right through to the 18th century.

Mass immigration from the Low Countries peaked in the troubled 16th century. In 1579 more than a third of the town's citizens were foreigners of a staunch Protestant stock, which proved beneficial during the Civil War when the Protestant parliamentarians caused Norwich little strife.

Sights

Norwich is a fantastic city to see on foot, with winding laneways and narrow passageways criss-crossing the centre of town. Most radiate from the candy-stripe canopied **Market Square** (⌚8am-4.30pm), one of the biggest and oldest markets in England, running since 1025. As you walk it's impossible to miss the huge number of **medieval churches** (www.norwich-churches.org) in the city. There are 36, to be precise – a testament to the city's wealth during the Middle Ages.

Norwich Cathedral CATHEDRAL

(www.cathedral.org.uk; admission by donation; ⌚7.30am-6pm) Norwich's most stunning landmark is the magnificent Anglican cathedral, its barbed spire soaring higher than any in England except Salisbury, while the size of its cloisters is second to none.

Begun in 1096, the cathedral is one of the finest Anglo-Norman abbey churches in the country, rivalled only perhaps by Durham. The sheer size of its nave is impressive, but its most renowned feature is the superb **Gothic rib vaulting** added in 1463. Among the spidery stonework are 1200 sculpted roof bosses depicting Bible stories. Together they represent one of the finest achievements of medieval English masonry.

Similar bosses can be seen in closer detail in the cathedral's remarkable cloisters. Built between 1297 and 1430, the **two-storey cloisters** are unique in England today and were originally built to house a community of about 100 monks.

Outside the cathedral's eastern end is the grave of the WWI heroine Edith Cavell, a Norfolk-born nurse who was executed for helping hundreds of Allied soldiers escape from German-occupied Belgium. The **cathedral close** also contains handsome houses and the old chapel of King Edward VI School (where English hero Admiral Nelson was educated). Its current students make up the choir, which performs in at least one of the three services held daily.

The visitor entrance to the cathedral is through the stunning new **Hostry** (9.30am-4.30pm Mon-Sat) building, which rises within the walls of its original equivalent. Inside you can learn about the history and role of the Cathedral. For a deeper insight join one of the fascinating **guided tours** (10.45am, 12.30pm & 2.15pm); the tours are free but a donation is expected.

Tombland & Elm Hill MEDIEVAL STREETS

Leave the cathedral complex by Erpingham gate and turn left onto leafy Tombland, where the market was originally located. Despite its ominous overtones, 'tomb' is an old Norse word for empty, hence space for a market. Cross over and follow Princes St to reach Elm Hill, an utterly charming medieval cobbled street of crooked timber beams and doors, intriguing shops and snug cafes. It's one of the oldest intact streets in the city and now centre of the local antiques business.

Norwich

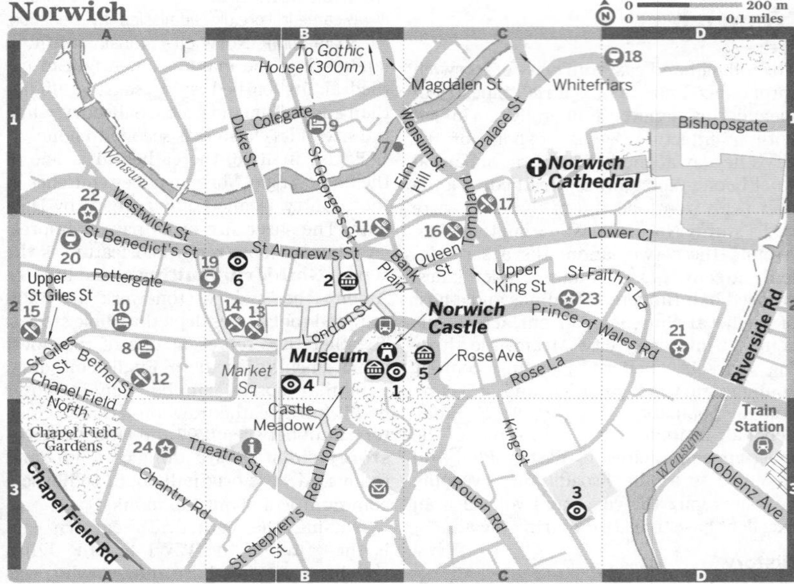

Norwich Castle, Museum & Art Gallery

CASTLE

(www.museums.norfolk.gov.uk; castle & exhibitions adult/child £6.20/4.40, exhibitions £3.30/2.40; 10am-5pm Mon-Sat, 1-5pm Sun;) Perched on a hilltop overlooking central Norwich, this massive Norman castle keep is a sturdy example of 12th-century aristocratic living. The castle is one of the best-preserved examples of Anglo-Norman military architecture in the country, despite a 19th-century facelift and a gigantic shopping centre grafted to one side.

It's now home to an art gallery and superb interactive museum. The **museum** crams in a wealth of history, including lively exhibits on Boudica and the Iceni, the Anglo-Saxons and Vikings, natural-history displays and even an Egyptian gallery complete with mummies. Every room is enlivened with plenty of fun for kids, but best of all is the atmospheric keep itself, which sends shivers down the spine, with graphic displays on grisly punishments meted out in its days as a medieval prison. **Guided tours** (£2.20) also wander around the battlements (minimum age eight) and dungeons (minimum age five).

Meanwhile the **art gallery** houses paintings of the acclaimed 19th-century Norwich School of landscape painting founded by John Crome and – trust the English – the world's largest collection of ceramic teapots.

A claustrophobic tunnel from the castle also emerges into a reconstructed WWI trench at the **Royal Norfolk Regimental Museum** (www.rnrm.org.uk; Shirehall, Market Ave; adult/child £3/1.60; 10am-4.30pm Tue-Fri, to 5pm Sat), which details the history of the local regiment since 1830. It has another, less dramatic entrance from the road.

FREE Sainsbury Centre for Visual Arts

GALLERY

(www.scva.org.uk; 10am-5pm Tue-Sun) Housed in the first major building by Norman Foster, now the darling of Britain's architectural set, the Sainsbury Centre is the most important centre for the arts in East Anglia. Filled with an eclectic collection of works by Picasso, Moore, Degas and Bacon, displayed beside art from Africa, the Pacific and the Americas, it also houses changing exhibitions that cover everything from local heritage to international art movements. Even if you're not an art buff you're almost guaranteed to find something of interest going on here.

Norwich

Top Sights

Museum ... B2
Norwich Castle ... B2
Norwich Cathedral ... C1

Sights

1 Art Gallery ... B2
2 Bridewell Museum ... B2
3 Dragon Hall ... C3
4 Mustard Shop ... B2
5 Royal Norfolk Regimental Museum ... C2
6 Strangers' Hall ... B2

Activities, Courses & Tours

7 Broads Boatrains ... B1

Sleeping

8 38 St Giles ... A2
9 By Appointment ... B1
10 St Giles House Hotel ... A2

Eating

11 Elm Hill Brasserie ... B2
12 Greenhouse ... A2
13 Library ... B2
14 Pulse Cafe ... B2
15 Roger Hickman's ... A2
16 Shiki ... C2
17 Tatlers ... C1

Drinking

18 Adam & Eve's ... D1
19 Birdcage ... B2
20 Ten Bells ... A2

Entertainment

21 Mercy ... D2
22 Norwich Arts Centre ... A1
23 Optic ... C2
24 Theatre Royal ... A3

The gallery is about 2 miles west of the city centre. To get here take bus 25, 26 or 35 from Castle Meadow (20 minutes).

Strangers' Hall MEDIEVAL HOUSE
(www.museums.norfolk.gov.uk; Charing Cross; adult/child £3.50/2; ⏲10.30am-4pm Wed & Sat) A maze of atmospheric rooms furnished in different medieval styles is on view in this early 14th-century town house. You can see the Great Hall set for a banquet, examine historic toys or try your hand making a bed Tudor style. Outside is a pretty 17th-century knot garden.

Bridewell Museum MUSEUM
(www.museums.norfolk.gov.uk; Bridewell Alley) Closed for major redevelopment at the time of writing, the 14th-century bridewell or 'prison for women, beggars and tramps', is housed in a former merchant's house and is filled with fascinating paraphernalia and reconstructions of Norwich's principal shops and industries. Check the website to find out about new opening hours.

Dragon Hall MEDIEVAL HALL
(www.dragonhall.org; 115-123 King St; adult/child £4.50/3.50; ⏲10am-4pm Mon-Fri, noon-4pm Sun) Another remarkable medieval building, this magnificent trading hall dates from 1430. The first floor great hall has a stunning crown-post roof with a carved dragon figure which gave the building its name. Guided tours are available on Tuesdays at 2pm.

Mustard Shop HISTORIC SHOP
(www.colmansmustardshop.com; 15 Royal Arcade; ⏲9.30am-5pm Mon-Sat, 11am-4pm Sun) Though it's more shop than museum, this replica Victorian shop tells the 200-year story of Colman's Mustard, a famous local product. It's in the lavish art-nouveau **Royal Arcade**.

Tours

Tourist Office WALKING TOUR
(☎01603-213999; www.visitnorwich.co.uk; adult/child £4/1.50; ⏲11.30am or 2pm Thu-Sat Easter-Oct) The tourist office organises a dizzying array of guided tours and has free downloadable pdf and audio city tours on its website.

City Sightseeing BUS TOUR
(www.city-sightseeing.com; adult/child £8/4; ⏲hourly 10am-4pm Apr-Oct) Hop-on/hop-off bus service stopping at nine destinations around the city centre.

Broads Boatrains BOAT TOUR
(www.cityboats.co.uk; 1hr city cruise adult/child £8.50/6.50) Runs a variety of cruises from Griffin Lane, Station Quay, and Elm Hill Quay.

Tombland Tours WALKING TOUR
(www.tomblandtours.com; adult/child £4/1.50; ⏲1pm Tue-Sun) Walking tours of Norwich's medieval heart around Tombland, the cathedral and Elm Hill. Departs from the Great West Doors of the cathedral.

Sleeping

Norwich has a dearth of budget-range accommodation, and battle-worn floral-patterned B&Bs are currently the only choice in this price category. You'll find most of them around the train station or outside the ring road. A new youth hostel is planned by the river in the near future; ask at the tourist office for details.

Gothic House B&B ££
(01603-631879; www.gothic-house-norwich.com; King's Head Yard, Magdalen St; s/d £65/95; P wi-fi) Step back in time at this faithfully restored Grade II Regency house hidden away in a quiet courtyard in the heart of the city. There are just two rooms here, but if period style is your thing, they are *the* place to be. From the fabrics and furnishings to the ornaments and mirrors, it just oozes great character and charm. The rooms are bright and spacious, immaculately kept and each has a private bathroom. To get here follow Wensum St north across the river into Magdalen St for 300m.

38 St Giles B&B ££
(01603-662944; www.38stgiles.co.uk; 38 St Giles St; s/d from £90/130; P family) Ideally located, beautifully styled and reassuringly friendly, this boutique B&B is a real gem. There are no airs and graces here – just handsome, homely rooms with wooden floors, hand-made rugs, original fireplaces and the odd chaise longue. The decor is restrained, with calming colour schemes and a contemporary feel, yet the whole place seems to have oodles of character. It's a wonderful find right in the centre of town.

St Giles House Hotel HOTEL £££
(01603-275180; www.stgileshousehotel.com; 41-45 St Giles St; d incl breakfast £120-210; wi-fi) Right in the heart of the city in a stunning 19th-century building, you'll find this large hotel with individually styled rooms. There's a grandiose air to the whole place, but the rooms range from fashionably art deco in style to less personal modern decor so check the website before booking. There's a good restaurant serving a modern British menu (mains £13.50 to £22), a spa and a lovely terrace for sipping cocktails.

By Appointment HOTEL ££
(01603-630730; www.byappointmentnorwich.co.uk; 25-29 St George's St; s/d incl breakfast from £90/120; @) This fabulously theatrical and delightfully eccentric B&B occupies three heavy-beamed 15th-century merchants' houses, and is also home to a labyrinthine restaurant well known for its classic English fare. Its antique furniture, creaky charm and superb breakfasts make this well worth booking in advance.

Eaton Bower B&B ££
(01603-462204; www.eatonbower.co.uk; 20 Mile End Rd; s/d from £50/60; P wi-fi) A little out of town but worth the effort, this small B&B has a choice of cosy rooms with subtle patterns and traditional styling. En suite bathrooms, free wi-fi, private parking and a touch of period character make it one of the best bets in this price range. The B&B is about 2 miles west of the city centre just off the A11. Or take bus 25 from the railway station.

No 15 B&B ££
(01603-250283; www.number15bedandbreakfast.co.uk; 15 Grange Rd; s/d £45/65; wi-fi) There are just two cosy but uncluttered bedrooms at this serene B&B in a leafy residential street. The rooms have period satinwood furniture, white linens and good bathrooms; breakfasts are vegetarian; holistic massage is on offer; and the whole experience is like a home away from home. No 15 is about a mile west of the city centre. Bus 25 passes nearby.

Beaufort Lodge B&B ££
(01603-667402; www.beaufortlodge.com; 60-62 Earlham Rd; s/d £55/70; P @) Giant windows wash the rooms in this Victorian house with light, and the spacious bedrooms have pretty fabrics and wallpapers in period style. The effect is bright and airy, with tasteful traditional touches. It's a great deal and only about a mile west of Market Sq (following Theatre St into Chapel Field North and across the roundabout to Earlham Rd).

Georgian House HOTEL ££
(01603-615655; www.georgian-hotel.co.uk; 32-34 Unthank Rd; s/d from £80/95; P wi-fi) A rambling, elegant Victorian house turned hotel, this place has a choice of spacious, modern rooms decked out in contemporary style. There's a large tree-filled garden and a popular restaurant (mains £12 to £22). The hotel is about 700m west of Market Sq. Follow theatre St into Chapel Field North and turn left at the roundabout to reach Unthank Rd.

Eating

Norwich has a great choice of places to eat with plenty of options for vegetarians. You'll find a cluster of good restaurants around Tombland.

Roger Hickman's MODERN BRITISH £££
(☎01603-633522; www.rogerhickmansrestaurant.com; 79 Upper St Giles St; 2-/3-course set menu lunch £16/19, dinner £30/35; ⊙closed Sun) Understated, classic elegance is what this place is all about: pale floorboards, white linen, bare walls and professional, unobtrusive service. In fact, there's nothing to distract you from the glorious food. Expect top-quality dishes made with flair and imagination and a simple dedication to quality. The set lunch menu is well worth the expense. Book ahead.

Tatlers MODERN BRITISH ££
(☎01603-766670; www.butlersrestaurants.co.uk; 21 Tombland; mains £10-17; ⊙closed Sun) This converted Victorian town house is home to one of the city's best eateries, where local suppliers and ingredients are as important as the final menu. The truly divine dishes are served in a series of unpretentious dining rooms. Come for the set lunch, an excellent-value choice, but be sure to book in advance.

Elm Hill Brasserie FRENCH ££
(☎01603-624847; www.elmhillbrasserie.co.uk; 2 Elm Hill; mains £12-16; ⊙12.30-2.30pm & 5.45-10.30pm Mon-Sat, noon-6pm Sun) On the corner of the city's most famous street, this simple and elegant restaurant is bathed with light from its giant windows. Scrubbed wooden floors, contemporary style, a relaxed atmosphere and a menu of unfussy, classic French dishes made from seasonal, local ingredients make it always busy. Book in advance.

Library MODERN EUROPEAN ££
(www.thelibraryrestaurant.co.uk; 1a Guildhall Hill; mains £10-13; ⊙closed dinner Sun) Set in a 19th-century library complete with original shelving, this chilled-out brasserie is a great spot for a good-value lunch. The menu is heavy on meats and fish, with dishes cooked in a nifty wood-fired grill, while the interior is sleek and stylish, with exhibitions of work by contemporary local artists.

Shiki JAPANESE ££
(6 Tombland; sushi £1.50-2.80, mains £9-11; ⊙closed Sun) This minimalist Japanese restaurant has a stylish, contemporary interior and a reputation for some of the best Asian food in town. From delicate sushi to superb *teppanyaki*, it's a firm local favourite with a particularly friendly vibe.

Greenhouse VEGETARIAN £
(www.greenhousetrust.co.uk; 42-48 Bethel St; snacks & mains £3.50-7; ⊙10am-5pm Tue-Sat) This organic, free-trade, vegetarian/vegan cafe is bound to leave you feeling wholesome, with a menu of simple dishes, noticeboards crammed with posters for community events, and a lovely vine-covered, herb-planted terrace.

Pulse Cafe VEGETARIAN £
(www.pulsecafebar.co.uk; Labour in Vain Yard, Guildhall Hill; mains £5-7.50;) This funky lounge-bar in the old fire station stables serves a bumper crop of hearty vegetarian dishes. There's also a great choice of sandwiches, organic ciders and beers and scrummy desserts.

Drinking

It was once said that Norwich had a pub for every day of the year, and although that may not be completely true, there's certainly plenty of choice. You'll find hip and trendy or quaint and traditional pubs all across the city centre, but start your quest in Tombland or St Benedict's St for a taste of what's on offer.

Adam & Eve's TRADITIONAL PUB
(www.adamandevenorwich.co.uk; Bishopsgate) A 13th-century brew-house built to quench the thirst of cathedral builders, this is now Norwich's oldest-surviving pub and an adorable little sunken-floored gem. It's a tiny place just loaded with character and popular with discerning locals, old timers and those in search of a quiet pint. There's a pleasant outdoor courtyard for sunny days.

Ten Bells PUB
(76 St Benedict's St) This is this kind of faded 18th-century pub where people feel instantly at ease, calmed by the real ales, mellow red velvet, battered armchairs and quirky memorabilia, including an ancient red phone booth in the corner. It also fancies itself as an intellectuals' hang-out, with poetry readings and arts-school regulars.

Birdcage BAR
(www.thebirdcagenorwich.co.uk; 22 Pottergate;) A bohemian hang out, this is one of Norwich's quirkiest bars, with slightly kitsch decor that includes strips of

bunting, mismatched furniture and a much-loved juke box. There's eclectic music in the back room, plenty of board games, free wi-fi, cabaret nights and a lovely outside deck area.

 Entertainment

Norwich has a flourishing arts scene and pulsating weekend nightlife. For what's on information from ballet to boozing try www.norwichtonight.com or, for live music, www.norfolkgigs.co.uk.

Optic NIGHTCLUB

(www.optic-club.co.uk; 50 Prince of Wales Rd; ⌚Mon, Wed, Fri & Sat) Supposedly Norwich's upmarket club, this place features everything from '70s funk to chart-topping anthems.

Mercy NIGHTCLUB

(www.mercynightclub.com; 86 Prince of Wales Rd; ⌚Thu-Sat) A massive club set in a former cinema, with DJs that favour R&B and club classics.

Theatre Royal THEATRE

(www.theatreroyalnorwich.co.uk; Theatre St) Features programs by touring drama, opera and ballet companies.

Norwich Arts Centre ARTS CENTRE

(www.norwichartscentre.co.uk; St Benedict's St) A wide-ranging program of alternative drama, concerts, dance and jazz set in a medieval church.

 Information

Library (The Forum; ⌚9am-8pm Mon-Fri, 9am-5pm Sat, 10.30am-4.30pm Sun) Free internet for those with ID and the patience to fill out a few forms.

Norfolk & Norwich University Hospital (☎01603-286286; Colney Lane) Four miles west of the centre.

Post office (84-85 Castle Mall)

Tourist office (☎01603-213999; www.visitnorwich.co.uk; The Forum; ⌚9.30am-6pm Mon-Sat, to 2.30pm Sun) Just inside the Forum on Millennium Plain.

 Getting There & Around

Norwich has free parking at six Park & Ride locations. Buses (£2) run to the city centre up to every 15 minutes from 6.40am to 7.50pm.

AIR **Norwich International Airport** (www.norwichinternational.com) Four miles north of town; has cheap flights to Europe and several British destinations.

BUS The bus station is on Queen's Rd 400m south of the castle. Follow Red Lion St into Stephen's St and then turn left onto Surrey St. The bus station is on the right. **National Express** (www.nationalexpress.com) and **First Eastern Counties** (www.firstgroup.com) run several services out of Norwich.

London £16.60, three hours, seven daily

Cromer one hour, hourly

King's Lynn 1½ hours, hourly

Great Yarmouth 45 minutes, twice hourly

TRAIN The train station is off Thorpe Rd 600m east of the castle.

London Liverpool St £40.40, two hours, twice hourly

Cambridge £13.40, 1¼ hours, twice hourly

Ely £12.90, one hour, twice hourly

Around Norwich

Largely remodelled in the 17th century for Sir Henry Hobart, James I's chief justice, **Blickling Hall** (NT; www.nationaltrust.org.uk/blickling; Blickling; adult/child £9.30/4.60, garden only £6.30/3.15; ⌚house Wed-Mon late-Jul–early-Sep, Wed-Sun late-Sep, Oct & Feb-Jul, gardens 10.15am-5.15pm Mar-Oct, 11am-4pm Thu-Sun Nov-Feb) began life in the 11th century as a manor house and bishop's palace. Today it is a grand Jacobean mansion set in vast parklands and as famous for its ghostly sightings as its spectacular Long Gallery.

In 1437 the isolated house was claimed by the Boleyn family and passed through the generations to Thomas, father of Anne Boleyn. Poor old Anne was executed by her husband Henry VIII in 1533, and it's said that on the anniversary of her death a coach drives up to the house, drawn by headless horses, driven by headless coachmen and containing the queen with her head on her lap.

If you're not around to witness the spectacle that day, there's still quite a lot to see. The grand state rooms are stuffed with fine Georgian furniture, pictures and tapestries, and the Long Gallery has an impressive Jacobean plaster ceiling. There's also an exhibition describing life below stairs, with stories from those who lived and worked at Blickling over the centuries.

Blickling Hall is 15 miles north of Norwich off the A140. Buses run twice hourly from Castle Meadow and Tombland in Norwich. Aylsham is the nearest train station, 1.5 miles away.

Norfolk Broads

A mesh of navigable slow-moving rivers, freshwater lakes, wild water meadows, fens, bogs and saltwater marshes make up the Norfolk Broads, a 125-mile stretch of lock-free waterways and the county's most beautiful attraction. The official name of the area is the 'Norfolk and Suffolk Broads', but as most of the lakes and waterways are in Norfolk, it's generally called the Norfolk Broads.

The Broads are home to some of the UK's rarest plants and animals and are protected as a national park, with flourishing nature reserves and bird sanctuaries attracting gangs of birdwatchers. But the area's appeal reaches far further, with boaters, families and those in search of scenic tranquillity all wanting a slice of the action.

Despite the Broads' popularity, it's easy to lose yourself in the hypnotic peace of the waterways. A boat is by far the best vantage point from which to spy on its myriad wildlife, and anyone fond of splashing about will undoubtedly want to linger here. Apart from the waterways and the wildlife there are restored windmills, medieval churches and glorious gardens to explore. Walkers and cyclists will also find a web of trails crossing the region, and with the Broads' highest point, How Hill, just 12m above sea level, they're accessible for all.

History

The low-lying nature of the land here was the key to its modern appearance. In the 12th century the land was dug for peat, the only local source of fuel. But dig gaping holes in low-lying land and they're bound to spring a leak. Water gradually seeped through, causing marshes and eventually lakes to develop. As water levels rose, the peat-cutting industry died out and the broads became a landscape of interconnected lakes and rivers. In no other area of England has human effort changed the natural landscape so dramatically. Around How Hill you'll find many of the picturesque wind pumps first built to drain the marshland and to return water to the rivers.

Sights & Activities

The Broads cover a meandering area that roughly follows the Rivers Wensum, Yare, Waveney, Bure, Thurne and Ant. There are more than 150 medieval churches across the area, many of which are made from flint with distinctive round towers. In addition you'll find plenty of waterside pubs, villages and market towns and stretches of river where you can feel you are the only person around.

Cruising is extremely popular in high season and some stretches of the most popular rivers are clogged with boats on sunny weekends. Getting away from the crowds by canoe, on foot or by bike is a far more memorable experience.

Bike and canoe hire are available at numerous points across the Broads from Easter to October. Bikes cost about £14 per day (you can also hire child seats and tandems), while canoe hire costs about £35 per day.

Bewilderwood ACTIVITY CENTRE
(www.bewilderwood.co.uk; Hornig Rd, Hoveton; adult/child £11.50/7; 10am-5.30pm Mar-Oct;) A forest playground for children and

ENGLAND'S FINEST SPIRITS

For 600 years the Nelstrop family have been growing and processing grain, but it was a brave decision to branch out into the ancient art of whisky-making. It's apparently such a daunting task that there has not been a whisky distillery in England for 120 years.

You can visit the **English Whisky Company** (www.englishwhisky.co.uk; Harling Rd, Roudham; tours hourly 10am-4pm) and take a guided tour (adult/child £5/2) around the distillery, which bottled its first whisky in November 2009. The tour explains the whole process, takes you through the distilling and casking room and ends with a tasting of company whiskies, liqueurs and creams. The company shop stocks a vast array of unusual and rare whiskies, and once a month there's a 'World Whisky' tour (£20), which includes a tour of the distillery with the chief whisky-maker as well as an hour-long tutored tasting of whiskies from around the world. Bring a driver to get you home.

St George's Distillery is just off the A11 between East Harling and Roudham on the B1111.

adults alike, this place is littered with zip wires, jungle bridges, tree houses and all sorts of old-fashioned outdoor adventure. It's a magical kind of place where children can run, jump, swing and climb to their hearts' content. There are marsh walks, boat trips, mazes, den-building activities, plenty of mud and peals of laughter all over the site. You and your young ones will wish you'd found it sooner.

Bus No 12a from Norwich (hourly) drops you right at the door.

Museum of the Broads MUSEUM
(www.northnorfolk.org/museumofthebroads; Staithe, Stalham; adult/child £4/3.50; ⏲10.30am-5pm Easter-Oct) Learn about the traditional Broads' boats, the wherries, the marshmen who gathered reeds and sedge for thatching and litter, and the history and lifestyles of the area at this modest museum. There are displays on everything from early settlements to peat extraction and modern conservation. Visitors can also take a trip on a steam launch (adult/child £3.50/2.50) hourly from 11am to 3pm.

The museum is about 5 miles north of Potter Heigham off the A149.

St Helen's Church CHURCH
(Ranworth; ⏲8am-7pm) Known locally as the 'Cathedral of the Broads', this 14th-century church dominates the pretty village of Ranworth. Inside there's a magnificent painted medieval rood screen, some wonderful stained glass and in a bulletproof cabinet by the main door, a 15th-century antiphoner, a rare illustrated book of prayers. The second antiphoner from the church is in the British Library in London.

For wonderful views of the surrounding broads, climb the series of ladders to the top of the tower. There's also a small visitors centre in a converted coach house next door with displays on East Anglia's churches.

The church is next to a large nature reserve. Follow the leafy woodland path to get to the **Norfolk Wildlife Conservation Centre** (admission free; ⏲10am-5pm Apr-Oct), which is set in an unusual thatched floating building right on the edge of the broad. It has information about the area and its history.

Horsey Windpump WINDMILL
(NT; www.nationaltrust.org.uk; Horsey; adult/child £2.50/1; ⏲10am-5pm) A Grade II–listed building, this five-storey drainage windpump is typical of the area, but unlike many of its counterparts it has been faithfully restored. Built in 1912, it lies just a mile from the sea and it offers great views of the coast and Broads.

The windpump is about 15 miles north of Great Yarmouth on B115.

FREE **Toad Hole Cottage** MUSEUM
(How Hill; ⏲9.30am-6pm Jun-Sep, 10.30am-5pm Apr, May & Oct) This tiny cottage was home to a marshman and his family and is restored in period style, showing how the family lived and the tools they used to work the marshes around them. Nearby is a beautiful thatched Edwardian mansion and a picturesque nature trail.

Bure Valley Steam Railway STEAM TRAIN
(www.bvrw.co.uk; adult/child £7.50/5; ⏲Feb-Oct) This narrow-gauge steam train runs between Aylsham and Wroxham and is an ideal way to see some hidden parts of the Broads. Trains operate on different schedules depending on the month so check the website for details. For an even better experience, take the train in one direction and canoe or cruise your way back. The Canoe Man and Broads Tours both operate a connecting service.

Canoe Man CANOE TRIP
(www.thecanoeman.com; half-day trip £22.50) To see the broads at a slower pace, take to the water by canoe. Day and overnight guided trips to areas the cruisers can't reach are available, as well as canoe and kayak hire, weekend camping canoe trails (two nights £85), bushcraft courses (two/three days £125/175), geo-caching challenges, and paddle-steamer trips, which combine a canoe and steam train trip.

Canoe & Bike Hire

Broadland Cycle Hire (www.norfolkbroadscycling.co.uk; Bewilderwood, Hoveton) Bike hire.

Clippesby (www.clippesby.com; Clippesby) Bike hire.

Otney Meadow (www.outneymeadow.co.uk; Bungay) Bike and canoe hire.

Rowan Craft (www.rowancraft.com; Geldeston) Canoe hire.

Waveney River Centre (www.waveneyrivercentre.co.uk; Burgh St Peter) Bike and canoe hire.

Boat Hire

You can hire a variety of launches, from large cabin cruisers to little craft with outboards for anything from a couple of hours' gentle messing about on the water to a week-long trip. Depending on boat size, facilities and season, a boat costs from around £60 for four hours, £100 for one day, up to £600 to £1200 for a week, including fuel and insurance.

Barnes Brinkcraft (www.barnesbrinkcraft.co.uk; per half-day/day £58/102) Short-term rental from Wroxham.

Blakes (www.blakes.co.uk) Boating holidays from Wroxham and Potter Heigham.

Boats for the Broads (www.dayboathire.com) Short-term rental from Wroxham.

Hoseasons (www.hoseasons.co.uk) Boating holidays from a variety of points across the Broads.

Luxury Day Cruisers (www.daycruisers.co.uk; per half-day/day £75/110) Short-term rental from Horning and Burgh St Peter.

Boat Trips

Broads Tours (www.broads.co.uk; adult/child £7.50/6; ⏲Apr-Oct) Frequent 1½-hour pleasure trips from Potter Heigham and Wroxham.

Broads Authority (www.broads-authority.gov.uk; adult/child £7/6; ⏲Apr-Oct) Short boat trips from Beccles, Neatishead, Ranworth and How Hill.

Sleeping & Eating

Broad House HOTEL £££
(☎01603-783567; www.broadhousehotel.co.uk; The Avenue, Wroxham; d from £118-231; P @) An intimate boutique hotel with just nine rooms, this place really knows how to look after you. Set in beautiful gardens surrounding an 18th-century country house, it's a character-laden place with plenty of charm. The rooms range from full period style, with four-poster beds, swag curtains and cast-iron baths, to more modern attic rooms with contemporary design.

Recruiting Sergeant MODERN BRITISH ££
(☎01603-737077; www.recruitingsergeant.co.uk; Norwich Rd, Horstead; mains £13-22) Close to the lovely village of Coltishall is this award-winning gastropub serving a fine selection of locally sourced meat and fish dishes. There's no contrived design style here: just honest food deftly cooked and served in hearty portions.

Information

Broads Authority (www.broads-authority.gov.uk) Has the low-down on all you could want to know about the Broads.

Enjoy the Broads (www.enjoythebroads.com) Information for visitors with accommodation, activity and event listings.

RSPB (www.rspb.org.uk) Information on birdwatching and habitats.

Getting There & Away

Wroxham, on the A1151 from Norwich, and Potter Heigham, on the A1062 from Wroxham, are the main centres. Buses leave Norwich twice hourly for Wroxham (40 minutes). You can get to Potter Heigham by bus from Great Yarmouth (40 minutes) roughly hourly.

Great Yarmouth

POP 90,810

On first glance Great Yarmouth is little more than a tatty traditional seaside resort complete with neon-lit esplanade, jingling amusement arcades, grim greasy spoons, crazy golf and cheek-by-jowl hotels. But scratch the surface, and you'll find the old town rich in history and heritage.

Sights

Yarmouth's 'heritage quarter' looks on to the river rather than the sea and boasts a fine collection of stately period buildings.

Row Houses HISTORIC HOUSES
(EH; www.english-heritage.org.uk; South Quay; adult/child £4.20/2.10; ⏲noon-5pm Apr-Sep) You can see how life once was in Great Yarmouth in these preserved houses. One is reconstructed as it would have been in 1870, the other in 1940s style. Displays show how the 'herring girls' lived and how life was for tenants – from wealthy merchants to tenement families – over the centuries.

Time & Tide MUSEUM
(www.museums.norfolk.gov.uk; Blackfriars Rd; adult/child £4.50/3.30; ⏲10am-5pm) This is the most absorbing of Yarmouth's museums, set in a Victorian herring-curing works. It tackles everything from prehistory to penny arcades and naughty postcards, but dwells on maritime heritage with evocative reconstructions of typical fishermen's row houses.

LOCAL KNOWLEDGE

MARK WILKINSON: THE CANOE MAN, NORFOLK BROADS

Best paddle

The **Buxton to Coltishall** stretch of the River Bure. It's really beautiful and you'll see kingfishers, otters, marsh harriers and a very tame barn owl here. You start in the wide open fields with their big skies and great views, then there's a tree-lined section that is like a different world – totally calm even when there's a gale howling elsewhere – the water's crystal clear and you can just meander along at a slow pace. There are no other people here – sometimes another canoeist but even this is quite unusual. At **Horstead Mill** there's a lovely open lock and weir: a great place for picnics and for families. Then you paddle on to **Coltishall Green**, where there are some lovely pubs.

Secret Spot

It's very difficult to access the **River Wensum**, but the stretches you can paddle are simply stunning.

Favourite time of year

Late September. The holidaymakers are gone, the colours are gorgeous and there's lots of wildlife scurrying about preparing for winter.

A spot of history

At **Bargate** you can see the remains of 14 wherries (sailing barges traditionally used on the Broads). It's known as the 'wherry graveyard' and you can see the ribs sticking up out of the water.

Elizabethan House HISTORIC HOUSE
(NT; www.museums.norfolk.gov.uk; 4 South Quay; adult/child £3.50/1.90; ⏲10am-5pm Mon-Fri, noon-4pm Sat & Sun Apr-Oct) This fine 16th-century merchant's house is faithfully reconstructed to showcase Tudor and Victorian domestic life, and is home to the 'Conspiracy Room' where Cromwell and his cronies decided Charles I must be executed.

Nelson Museum MUSEUM
(www.nelson-museum.co.uk; 26 South Quay; adult/child £3.20/1.90; ⏲10am-5pm Mon-Fri, 1-4pm Sat & Sun) Celebrates the life, times, romances and death of the one-eyed hero of Trafalgar.

Sleeping & Eating

B&Bs are everywhere, especially on chock-a-block Trafalgar St.

No 78 B&B ££
(☎01493-850001; www.no78.co.uk; 78 Marine Pde; d £50-85; @) A chic, modern place that bucks the chintzy local trends and offers really beautiful, bright, contemporary rooms with an eco-conscience. The toilets have water-saving devices, tea and coffee come in resealable containers and the house uses 'green' electricity.

Olive Garden MEDITERRANEAN ££
(☎01493-844641; www.olivegardenrestaurant.co.uk; 42 Regent Rd; mains £10-18; ⏲closed Mon lunch) Away from the kiss-me-quick diners and bang up to date, this vibrant, modern place serves a long and interesting menu of dishes that take the best Mediterranean ingredients and shape them into something irresistible. Lunch is a great deal, with mains costing just £5.95. Book ahead for dinner.

Information

Tourist office (☎01493-846345; www.great-yarmouth.co.uk; 25 Marine Pde; ⏲10am-5pm) On the seafront. Staff can point you towards the lovely Weavers Way walking trail, which cuts into the Broads from here.

Getting There & Away

There are hourly buses (40 minutes) and trains (£5.60, 33 minutes) to Norwich.

North Coast Norfolk

The north coast of Norfolk has something of a split personality, with a string of busy seaside towns with brash attractions and hordes of people clustering along the eastern end and a collection of small villages with trendy gastropubs and boutique hotels littering the western end. In between sit stunning beaches and the marshy coast that attracts crowds of visiting seabirds.

The Coast Hoppper bus runs from Cromer to Hunstanton, serving Cley, Blakeney, Wells, Holkham, Burnham Deepdale and (with a connection) King's Lynn.

CROMER

POP 3800

Once a fashionable Victorian coastal resort, Cromer is now firmly part of the bucket-and-spade brigade, with a wonderful stretch of safe, sandy beachfront, family entertainment on the pier, a glut of fish-and-chip shops and plenty of trashy amusement arcades. The town has recently seen some major investment and may yet return to its former glory.

Stay long enough to wander off the beach and you'll find the quaint **Cromer Museum** (www.museums.norfolk.gov.uk; East Cottages, Tucker St; adult/child £3.20/1.80; ⏲10am-5pm Mon-Sat, 1-4pm Sun), set in a Victorian fisherman's cottage. The museum depicts life in the town in the 19th century and displays a series of historic photos of the area.

Just 2 miles southwest of town off the B1436 is **Felbrigg Hall** (NT; www.nationaltrust.org.uk; adult/child £7.80/3.65; ⏲11am-5pm Sat-Wed Mar-Oct), an elegant stately home with a fine Georgian interior. The walled gardens and orangery are particularly lovely, with access to the **Weavers Way** running through the estate.

Cromer has direct trains to Norwich (£5.60, 45 minutes) hourly Monday to Saturday and services every two hours on Sunday. The Coasthopper bus runs from Cromer west along the coast roughly half-hourly in summer.

CLEY MARSHES

One of England's premier birdwatching sites, Cley (pronounced cly) Marshes, is a mecca for twitchers, with over 300 species recorded here. There's a **visitors centre** (www.norfolkwildlifetrust.org.uk; adult/child £4/free; ⏲10am-5pm) built on high ground and a series of hides hidden amid the golden reed beds.

For food head to the lovely **Wiveton Hall Cafe** (☎01263-740515; www.wivetonhall.co.uk; mains £7-9; ⏲9.30am-5pm daily, 6.30-8.30pm Fri & Sat Mar-Oct), set in the grounds of a dreamy Jacobean manor house. For an extra-special experience, you can stay in the gorgeous manor house on a self-catering basis (sleeps eight, per week £850 to £2000).

Alternatively, the stunning 17th-century **Cley Windmill** (☎01263-740209; www.cleymill.co.uk; d £80-165) has nine bedrooms with the one at the top reached by ladder alone. It's a wonderfully quirky place to stay, with a circular living room, great views across the marshes and rooms with four-poster, half-tester or cast-iron beds.

BLAKENEY POINT

The pretty village of **Blakeney** was once a busy fishing and trading port before its harbour silted up. These days it's a good place to jump aboard boat trips out to a 500-strong colony of common and grey seals that live, bask and breed on nearby Blakeney Point. The hour-long trips (adult/child £8/4) run daily April to October, but the best time to come is between June and August when the common seals pup. Trips run either from Blakeney Harbour or nearby Morston.

Beans Boat Trips (www.beansboat trips.co.uk; Morston)

Bishop's Boats (www.norfolkseal trips.co.uk; Blakeney Harbour)

Temples Seal Trips (www.sealtrips.co.uk; Morston)

WELLS-NEXT-THE-SEA

POP 2451

Thronged with crowds on holiday weekends, this harbour town has plenty of seaside tat on the waterfront but a surprisingly tranquil old town set back from the sea. Attractive Georgian houses and flint cottages surround a large green, while kids bounce between toy shops and ice-cream parlours, and pensioners check out the curios.

The **narrow-gauge steam train** (www.wellswalsinghamrailway.co.uk; adult/child return £6.50/5; ⏲Apr-Oct) chuffs 5 miles to **Little Walsingham**, where there are shrines and a ruined abbey that have drawn pilgrims since medieval times. The trip takes 30 minutes.

If you fancy staying overnight, the **Wells YHA** (☎0845-371 9544; www.yha.org.uk; Church Plains; dm £16; P) has simple rooms in an ornately gabled early 20th-century church hall. Alternatively try **Admiral House** (☎01328-711669; www.admiralhouse-wells.co.uk; 6 Southgate Close; d £95; P Wi-Fi) for its smart, modern rooms and clean-cut decor.

The small **tourist office** (☎01328-710885; www.visitnorthnorfolk.com; Staithe St; ⏲10am-5pm Mon-Sat, to 4pm Mar-Oct) can help with all enquiries.

The Coasthopper bus goes through Wells roughly half-hourly in summer on its way between Cromer (one hour) and Kings Lynn (1½ hours).

HOLKHAM

The pretty village of **Holkham** is well worth a stop for its imposing stately home, incredible stretch of beach and for the pleasure of walking its picturesque streets lined with elegant buildings.

The main draw here is **Holkham Hall** (www.holkham.co.uk; adult/child £11/5.50, parking £2.50; ⏲noon-4pm Sun, Mon & Thu Apr-Oct), a grand Palladian mansion set in a vast deer park designed by Capability Brown. The slightly industrial-looking brick mansion is the ancestral seat of the Earls of Leicester and has a sumptuous interior, dripping with gilt, tapestries, fine furniture and family history. The Marble Hall (it's actually alabaster), magnificent state rooms and giant kitchen shouldn't be missed. You can also visit the **Bygones Museum** (museum only adult/child £4/2; ⏲10am-5pm Apr-Oct) in the stable block. It showcases everything from mechanical toys to agricultural equipment and vintage cars.

For many, Holkham's true delight is not the stately home but the pristine 3-mile **beach** that meanders along the shore. Regularly voted one of England's best, it's a popular spot with walkers. The vast expanse of sand swallows people up and gives a real sense of isolation with giant skies stretching overhead. The only place to park for access to the beach is Lady Anne's Drive (parking up to £5).

Recover after a jaunt on the beach with tea or a snack at the **Marsh Larder** (Main Rd; ⏲10am-5pm) in the stunning Ancient House or a more substantial meal at the much-lauded **Victoria Arms** (☎01328-711008; www.victoriaatholkham.co.uk; Park Rd; mains £12-18; r £125-560). The menu here is modern English with an emphasis on local ingredients. The Victoria also has a choice of quirky, but extremely plush rooms, with exotic fabrics, eclectic bric-a-brac and a relaxed, colonial feel. You'd be well advised to book ahead.

The Coasthopper bus goes through Holkham roughly half-hourly in summer.

BURNHAM DEEPDALE

In-the-know backpackers and walkers flock to this lovely coastal spot, with its tiny twin villages of **Burnham Deepdale** and **Brancaster Staithe** strung along a rural road. Stroked by the beautiful Norfolk Coastal Path, surrounded by beaches and reedy marshes, alive with birdlife, criss-crossed by cycling routes and a base for a whole host of water sports, Burnham Deepdale is also home to one of the country's best backpacker hostels.

Ecofriendly **Deepdale Farm** (☎01485-210256; www.deepdalefarm.co.uk; sites per adult/child £9/5, dm/tw £13.50/56, 2-/6-person tepees £80/114; P @ 📶) is a backpackers' haven. It has spotless en suite rooms set in converted 17th-century stables as well as camping space and a collection of Native American–style tepees and Mongolian yurts for extra comfort. There's a large kitchen and lounge area, picnic tables, a barbecue and a laundry and cafe next door. It's an enduring popular spot so be sure to book ahead.

The hostel also operates a **tourist office** (☎01485-210256; ⏲10am-4pm), the best place to go to organise kitesurfing or windsurfing on nearby beaches. Bike hire is also available.

Just west of the hostel is the award-winning **White Horse** (☎01485-210262; www.whitehorsebrancaster.co.uk; mains £10-14, s/d from £95/130; P @), a gastropub with a menu strong on fish and seafood. It also has some light and fresh, New England–style guest rooms, but it lacks a little soul and some rooms have terraces overlooking the car park.

The Coasthopper bus stops outside Deepdale Farm roughly half-hourly in summer.

AROUND BURNHAM DEEPDALE

Littered with pretty little villages and a host of ancient watering holes, trendy gastropubs and boutique hotels, this part of the Norfolk coast is one of the most appealing.

At the oh-so-fashionable Georgian town of **Burnham Market**, you'll find plenty of elegant old buildings, flint cottages, delis and independent retailers. It's another excellent base, with a trio of accommodation options to suit any taste. The **Hoste Arms** (☎01328-738777; www.hostearms.co.uk; The Green; d £118-234; P) and its sister properties the **Vine House** (d £145-207) and the **Railway Inn** (s/d £78/94) offer everything from over-the-top classical rooms with swags and florals to trendy, contemporary suites with bold wallpaper, luscious fabrics and mountains of towels.

Just past Burnham Deepdale you come to Titchwell, home to **Titchwell Manor** (☎01485-210221; www.titchwellmanor.com; Titchwell; d £130-250, mains £10-18; P @), a slick contemporary hotel set in a grand Victorian house. The conservatory restaurant serves modern English cuisine, and there's a large garden loved by visiting children.

Continue west along the coast road to the village of Thornham for a choice of three more great places to eat. Right by the road is the **Orange Tree** (☎01485-512213; www.theorangetreethornham.co.uk; High St; mains £10-19;) an old-world pub with a modern interior. The food here is excellent and the seafood in particular is worth a detour. There's a garden with a playground for children and a selection of newly refurbished rooms (doubles from £99).

Hidden from passing traffic on the village back road is the **Lifeboat Inn** (☎01485-512236; www.lifeboatinn.co.uk; Ship Lane; 3-course dinner £29), a 16th-century pub laden with character and famous for its traditional food, while just west of the village is the **Yurt** (☎01485-525108; www.theyurt.co.uk; Drove Orchards; mains £8.50-12.50; closed dinner Sun & Mon;), a restaurant in, er, a yurt. The food is all local, with doorstop sandwiches and wholesome salads at lunch and hearty fish, meat and game dishes for dinner.

King's Lynn

POP 34,565

Once one of England's most important ports, King's Lynn was long known as 'the Warehouse on the Wash'. It was said you could cross from one side of the River Great Ouse to the other by simply stepping from boat to boat in its heyday. Something of the salty port-town tang can still be felt in old King's Lynn, with its cobbled lanes and narrow streets flanked by old merchants' houses. Unfortunately, the rest of the town is not so pretty, with modern architectural blunders and high-street chain stores blighting the landscape.

Sights

Old Lynn huddles along the eastern bank of the river. Walk between the two market places to take in the most handsome buildings in town, or pick up a heritage trail leaflet from the tourist office.

St Margaret's Church CHURCH

(www.stmargaretskingslynn.org.uk; Margaret Plain) A patchwork of architectural styles, this church is worth a look for its two extraordinarily elaborate Flemish brasses. You can also see a remarkable 17th-century moon dial, which tells the tide, not the time. You'll find historic flood-level markings by the west door.

Old Gaol House MUSEUM

(Saturday Market Pl; adult/child £3/2.15; 10am-5pm Tue-Sat Easter-Oct;) Explore the old cells and hear grisly tales of smugglers, witches and highwaymen in the town's old jail. Also here is the **Regalia Room**, which houses the town civic treasures, including the 650-year-old King John Cup, exquisitely decorated with scenes of hunting and hawking.

Lynn Museum MUSEUM

(www.museums.norfolk.gov.uk; Market St; adult/child £3.30/1.80) The town's main museum features displays on maritime life in Lynn and Norfolk history, but its highlight is the new Seahenge gallery, which showcases a 4000-year-old timber circle and explores the lives of the people who created it.

True's Yard MUSEUM

(www.truesyard.co.uk; North St; adult/child £3/1.50; 10am-4pm Tue-Sat) Housed in two restored fishermen's cottages, this museum looks at the difficult life fishermen endured and the traditions and lifestyle of the close-knit community that once lived in this part of the city.

Town House Museum MUSEUM

(www.museums.norfolk.gov.uk; 46 Queen St; adult/child £3.30/1.80; 10am-5pm Mon-Sat May-Sep;) Petite museum dealing with the history of the town from the Middle Ages up to the 1950s. Next door is the magnificent flint-and-brick **town hall**, which dates from 1421.

FREE **Green Quay** MUSEUM

(www.thegreenquay.co.uk; South Quay; 9am-5pm) This museum charts life in the Wash (the estuary) with exhibitions on the wildlife, flora and fauna of the area and the effects of climate change.

Sleeping & Eating

Bank House B&B ££

(☎01553-660492; www.thebankhouse.co.uk; Kings Staithe Sq; s/d from £80/100; P) This outstanding B&B has ticks in all the right boxes: history, location, atmosphere, comfort and welcome. Overlooking the water, the 18th-century former bank is now an elegantly furnished town house with five luxurious rooms, mixing original features and modern furnishings. There's also a lovely, modern brasserie (mains £8 to £16) serving seriously good food made from locally sourced ingredients.

Bradley's MODERN BRITISH **££**
(☎01553-819888; www.bradleysbytheriver.co.uk; 10 South Quay; mains £13-19; ⊙no dinner Sun) Eat in the elegant Georgian dining room at this riverside restaurant, or relax in the popular wine bar with some lighter meals (£8 to £10); either way you're bound to be pleased as this is probably the finest food the city has to offer.

ℹ Information

Tourist office (☎01553-763044; www.visitwestnorfolk.com; Purfleet Quay; ⊙10am-5pm Mon-Sat, noon-5pm Sun) Housed in the lovely 17th-century Custom House, the tourist office arranges guided walks (adult/child £4/1) at 2pm on Tuesdays, Fridays and Saturdays in high season.

ℹ Getting There & Away

There are hourly trains from Cambridge (£8.40, 50 minutes) and London Kings Cross (£27.40, 1¾ hours). Bus 35 runs to Hunstanton (30 minutes, half hourly) and connects with the Coasthopper (www.coasthopper.co.uk) service, which runs along the north Norfolk coast.

Around King's Lynn

CASTLE RISING CASTLE

There's something bordering on ecclesiastical about the beautifully embellished keep of this **castle** (EH; www.castlerising.co.uk; adult/child £4/2.50; ⊙10am-6pm Apr-Nov), built in 1138 and set in the middle of a massive earthwork upon which pheasants scurry about like guards. So extravagant is the stonework that it's no surprise to learn that it shares stonemasons with some of East Anglia's finest cathedrals. It was once the home of Queen Isabella, who (allegedly) arranged the gruesome murder of her husband, Edward II.

It's well worth the trip 4 miles northeast of King's Lynn off the A149. Bus 41 runs here (15 minutes) hourly from the King's Lynn bus station.

SANDRINGHAM HOUSE

Royalists and those bemused by the English sovereigns will have plenty to mull over at this, the Queen's **country estate** (www.sandringhamestate.co.uk; adult/child £10/5, gardens & museum only £7/3.50; ⊙11am-4.30pm Apr-Oct), set in 25 hectares of landscaped gardens and lakes, and open to the hoi polloi when the court is not at home. (If they are in residence, the estate is closed.)

Queen Victoria bought the estate in 1862 for her son, the Prince of Wales (later Edward VII), but he promptly had it overhauled in the style later named Edwardian. Half of the surrounding 8000 hectares is leased to farm tenants, while the rest is managed by the Crown Estate as forestry.

Visitors can shuffle around the ground-floor rooms, regularly used by the royal family, then head out to the old stables, which house a flag-waving **museum** filled with diverse royal memorabilia. The superb royal **vintage-car collection** includes the very first royal motor from 1900, darling electrical toy cars driven by various princes, and the buggy in which the recently deceased Queen Mother would bounce around race tracks. For another oddity, look for the pet cemetery just outside the museum.

There are **guided tours** of the gardens on Wednesdays and Saturdays at 11am and 2pm. The **shop** is also worthy of a visit if only to browse the organic goodies produced on the sprawling estate.

Sandringham is 6 miles northeast of King's Lynn off the B1440. Bus 41 runs here from the station (30 minutes, hourly).

Birmingham, the Midlands & the Marches

Includes »

BIRMINGHAM......392
WARWICKSHIRE ...402
STAFFORDSHIRE... 411
WORCESTERSHIRE . 414
HEREFORDSHIRE .. 418
SHROPSHIRE......423
NOTTINGHAMSHIRE............436
LINCOLNSHIRE 442
NORTHAMPTONSHIRE............449
LEICESTERSHIRE ..450
DERBYSHIRE 456
PEAK DISTRICT 462

Best Places to Eat

- » Balti Triangle (p398)
- » Simpsons (p398)
- » La Bécasse (p435)
- » Golden Mile (p454)

Best Places to Stay

- » Hotel du Vin (p397)
- » Feathers Hotel (p435)
- » Hotel Maiyango (p453)
- » George Hotel (p447)

Why Go?

Because few other places in the country come so close to the dream of England. If you are searching for green and pleasant valleys and chocolate-box villages of wonky timbered houses, or the chance to walk in the footsteps of William Shakespeare, or stately homes that look like the last lord of the manor just clip-clopped out of the stables, then you'll find it here. You'll also find the dust and grime of centuries of industrial history – best exemplified by the World Heritage–listed mills of Ironbridge and the Derwent Valley – as well as tumbling hills where the air is so clean you can taste it. Walkers and cyclists flock to the Peak District National Park and the Shropshire Hills, only to vanish into the vastness of the landscape. Then there's Birmingham, England's second city, an industrial crucible reinvented as cultural melting pot, with the best food and nightlife in the Midlands.

When to Go?

February and March see the wonderful chaos of Shrovetide football in Ashbourne. Literary buffs take note: Shakespeare takes a back seat to contemporary wordsmiths at Stratford's Literary Festival in April/May. If you're up for a belt-loosening, belly-stretching good time, head to Ludlow's famous Food & Drink Festival in September.

On weekends from April to September, Shropshire Hills Shuttles provides access to wonderful walking trails on the Long Mynd and the Shropshire Hills, and June to September is the peak season for walking and cycling in the Peak District.

Birmingham, the Midlands & the Marches Highlights

1. Enjoying England's great contribution to the world of curry in the balti restaurants of **Birmingham** (p392)
2. Walking in the footsteps of the Bard in Shakespeare-obsessed **Stratford-upon-Avon** (p406)
3. Eating up a storm at the foodie mecca that is **Ludlow** (p434)
4. Aiming pedals or walking boots at the rugged trails of the **Peak District National Park** (p462)
5. Admiring the abundance of flamboyant architecture and leafy parks in the former spa town of **Buxton** (p464)
6. Stepping back into Jane Austen's England in the stone-lined streets of **Stamford** (p446)
7. Getting lost in the grandeur of **Chatsworth House** (p473), one of the nation's finest country houses

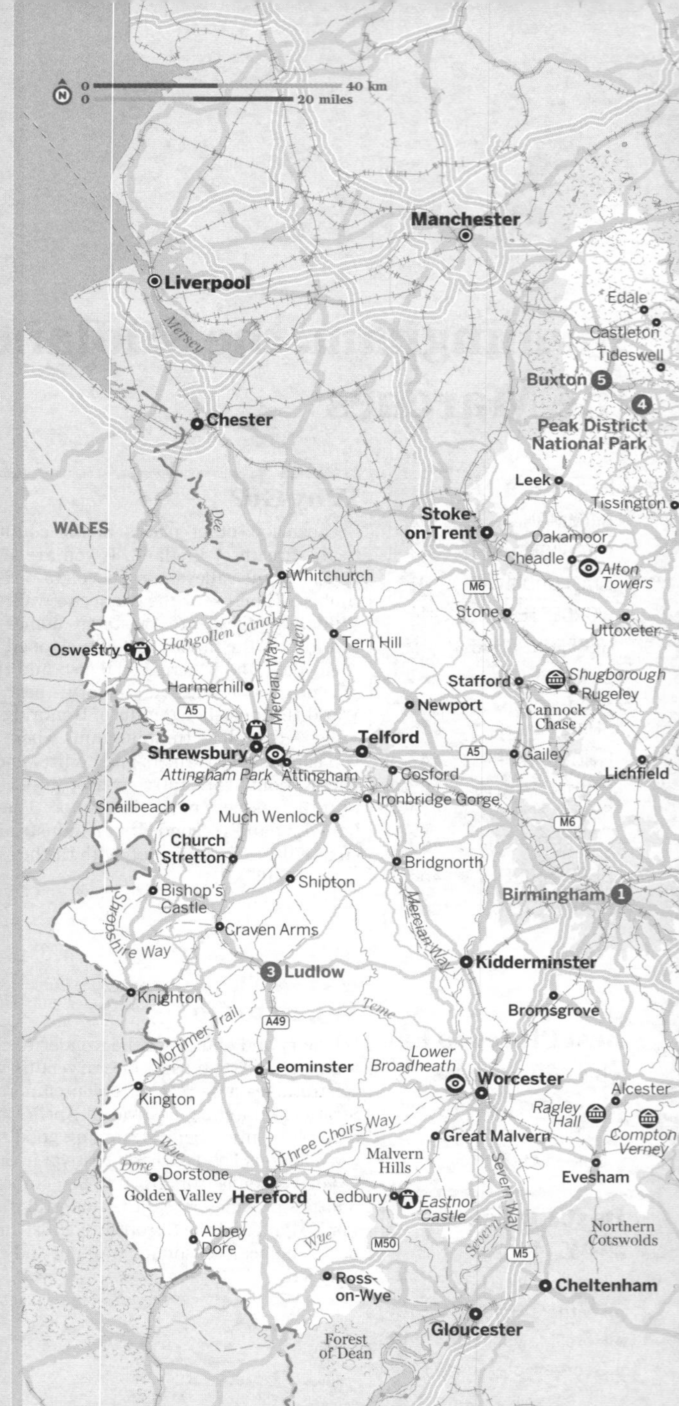

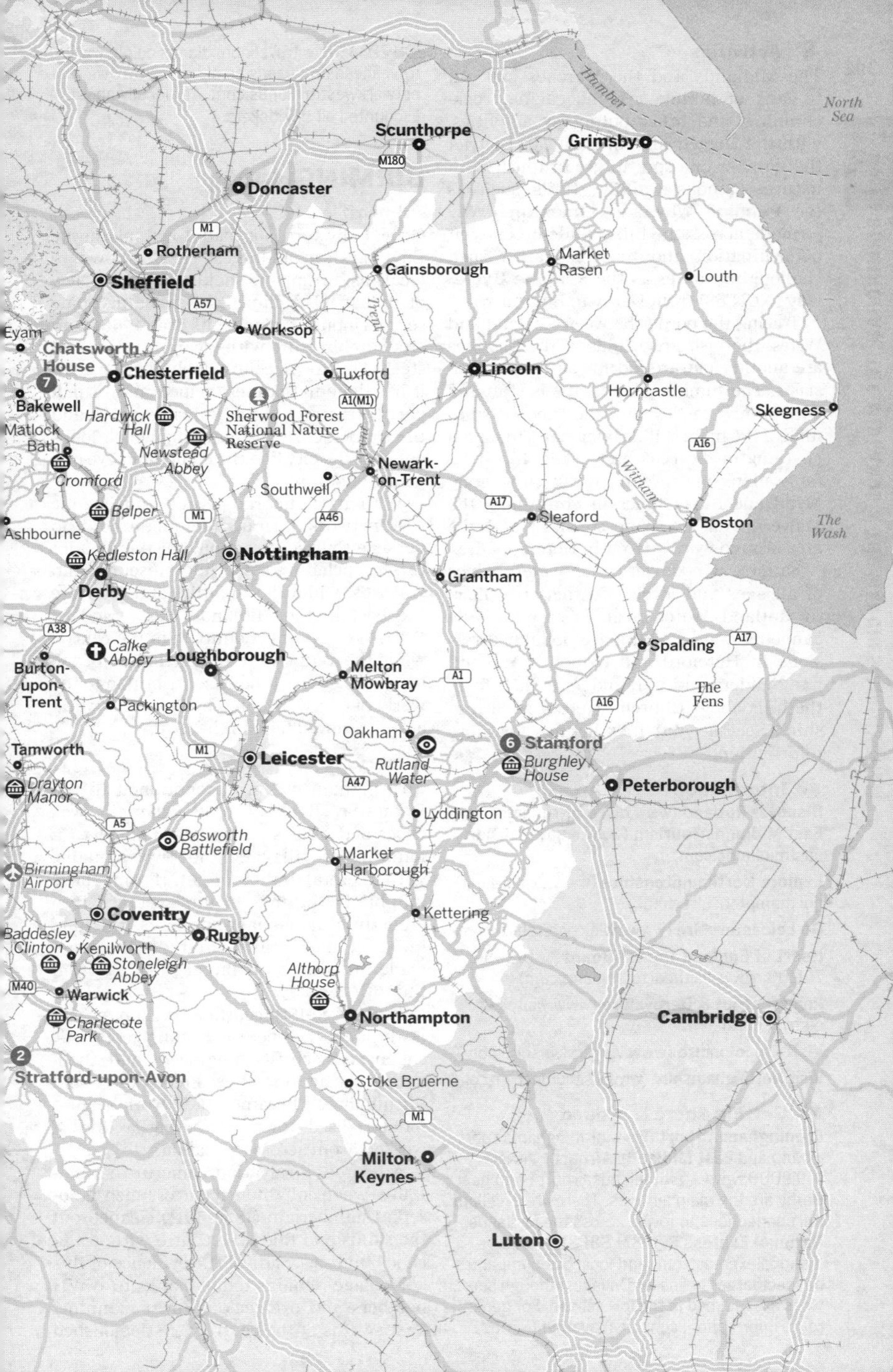

North Sea
Humber
Scunthorpe
Grimsby
M180
Doncaster
M1
Rotherham
Market Rasen
Gainsborough
Louth
Sheffield
A57
Trent
Worksop
Eyam
Chatsworth House
7
Chesterfield
Tuxford
Lincoln
Horncastle
Bakewell
A1(M1)
Skegness
Hardwick Hall
Sherwood Forest National Nature Reserve
Matlock Bath
Newstead Abbey
A16
Witham
Cromford
Newark-on-Trent
Southwell
A17
Belper
M1
A46
Sleaford
Boston
The Wash
Ashbourne
Kedleston Hall
Nottingham
Grantham
Derby
A38
Calke Abbey
Spalding
A17
Loughborough
Burton-upon-Trent
Melton Mowbray
A1
The Fens
Packington
A16
Oakham
6
Stamford
Tamworth
M1
Leicester
Rutland Water
Burghley House
Peterborough
Drayton Manor
A47
Lyddington
A5
Bosworth Battlefield
Market Harborough
Birmingham Airport
Kettering
Coventry
Rugby
Baddesley Clinton
Kenilworth
Stoneleigh Abbey
Althorp House
M40
Warwick
Northampton
Cambridge
Charlecote Park
2
Stratford-upon-Avon
Stoke Bruerne
M1
Milton Keynes
Luton

Activities

The Midlands and the Marches call out to fans of hiking, cycling, caving, rock-climbing, and other outdoorsy activities, with the rugged hills of the Peak District the number-one spot to get in touch with nature. Famous walking trails such as the **Pennine Way** and **Limestone Way** struggle across the hills, while cyclists pit determination and muscle against such challenging routes as the **Pennine Cycleway** (NCN 68) from Derby to Buxton.

Tracing the border between England and Wales, the lush green hills of the Marches are another playground for outdoor enthusiasts. The tumbling landscape is scattered with ruined castles, and the exposed summits of the highest hills offer views to match anything in the Peak and Lakes. Top spots for walking and cycling include the Long Mynd and Stiperstones in Shropshire, the Malvern Hills in Worcestershire and the area around Symonds Yat in Herefordshire.

Sailors, windsurfers and water babies of all ages and levels of experience flock to Rutland Water near Leicester, while canoeing and kayaking are popular diversions in Hereford and Symonds Yat and hang-gliders and paragliders launch from the hills above Church Stretton in Shropshire. See the Activities listings for more information.

Information

Discover Rutland (www.discover-rutland.co.uk)
East Midlands Tourism (www.enjoyenglands eastmidlands.com)

Explore Northamptonshire (www.explore northamptonshire.co.uk)

Go Leicestershire (www.goleicestershire.com)

Heart of England Tourist Board (☎01905-761100; www.visitheartofengland.com)

Peak District & Derbyshire (www.visitpeak district.com)

Visit Lincolnshire (www.visitlincolnshire.com)

Visit Nottinghamshire (www.visitnottingham.com)

Getting There & Around

Birmingham Airport (www.birminghamairport .co.uk) and **East Midlands Airport** (☎0871 919 9000; www.eastmidlandsairport.com) near Derby are the main air hubs. There are excellent rail connections to towns across the Midlands. **National Express** (☎0871 881 8181; www .nationalexpress.com) and local bus companies connect larger towns and villages, though services are reduced in the low season. For general route information, consult **Traveline** (☎0871 200 2233; www.travelinemidlands.co.uk, www .travelineeastmidlands.co.uk) or visit www .networkwestmidlands.com. Ask locally about discounted all-day tickets.

BIRMINGHAM

POP 977,087

Once a byword for bad town planning, England's second-largest city – known to locals as 'Brum' – is shaking off the legacy of industrial decline, and spending some serious money replacing its drab 1960s concrete architecture with gleaming glass and steel. The town centre looks better than it has done in decades, helped in no small part by the revitalised Bullring centre and the iconic Selfridges building, which looks out over the city like the compound eye of a giant robot insect.

With its industrial legacy and chaotic road network, Birmingham might not leap out as a tourist attraction, but there's a lot to see, including some fine museums and galleries, while the nightlife and food are the best in the Midlands. Sleek Modern British restaurants dominate in the centre, while the 'burbs were the birthplace of the balti – England's unique contribution to the world of curry, invented by Pakistani workers who moved here in the 1970s.

History

Birmingham was first mentioned in the Domesday Book of 1086, where it was described as a small village, home to a handful of villagers and two ploughs, with a total value of £1. From these humble beginnings, Brum exploded into a bustling industrial and mercantile hub, building its fortunes first on the wool trade, and then on metal-working from the 16th century.

In the mid-18th century, the Lunar Society brought together the leading geologists, chemists, scientists, engineers and theorists of the age – see boxed text, p397 – and Birmingham became the world's first industrialised town, attracting a tide of workers from across the nation.

A degree of salvation came in the mid-1800s, when enlightened mayors such as Joseph Chamberlain (1836–1914) cleaned out the slums and filled the centre with grand civic buildings. Sadly, little evidence of this golden age remains today thanks to WWII bombers and overzealous town planning. Vast swaths of the centre were demolished

BIRMINGHAM IN...

Two Days

Start off in the centre, dropping into Victoria Sq and the eclectic **Birmingham Museum & Art Gallery**. Go west through Centenary Sq to reach the Birmingham Canals, where you can while away an afternoon at the **National Sea Life Centre** or **Ikon gallery**, before an evening of rock and cocktails at the **Island Bar** or **Sunflower Lounge**. On day two, indulge your inner shopaholic at the gleaming malls of the **Bullring** and **Mailbox**, which both have good options for lunch. In the afternoon, catch up on some social history at the **Birmingham Back to Backs**. After dark, roam south to the **Balti Triangle** to sample Birmingham's unique contribution to the world of curry.

Four Days

Follow the two-day itinerary, but add a **canal cruise**. On day three, head north from the centre to **Aston Hall** and **Soho House**, or south to the famous **Barber Institute**, then take in a show at the **Repertory Theatre** or a concert at **Symphony Hall**. Use day four to explore the fascinating **Jewellery Quarter**, with an upmarket Indian lunch at **Itihaas** or **Lasan**, and spend the afternoon reliving *Charlie and the Chocolate Factory* fantasies at **Cadbury World**.

in a bid to transform Birmingham into 'Britain's Motor City'.

Whatever the mistakes of the past, recent years have seen a series of successful regeneration projects as part of the 'Big City Plan', with 21st-century landmarks appearing all over the city.

Sights & Activities

For information on all of Birmingham's museums, visit www.bmag.org.uk.

CITY CENTRE

Birmingham's grandest civic buildings are clustered around pedestrianised **Victoria Sq**, at the western end of New St, dominated by the stately facade of **Council House**, erected in 1874–79. The square was given a facelift in 1993, with modernist sphinxes and a **fountain** topped by a naked female figure, nicknamed 'the floozy in the jacuzzi' by locals, overlooked by a disapproving **statue of Queen Victoria**.

Housed in the annexe at the back of Council House, the delightful **Birmingham Museum & Art Gallery** (☎0121-303 2834; www.bmag.org.uk; Chamberlain Sq; admission free; ⏲10am-5pm Mon-Thu & Sat, 10.30am-5pm Fri, 12.30-5pm Sun) houses an impressive collection of ancient treasures and Victorian art, including an important collection of major Pre-Raphaelite works by Rossetti, Edward Burne-Jones and others. The museum's latest arrival is part of the Staffordshire Hoard, a treasure trove of 7th-century Anglo-Saxon gold, unearthed in a field near Lichfield in 2009.

The west side of the square is marked out by the neoclassical **Town Hall** (☎0121-780 3333; www.thsh.co.uk), constructed in 1834 and styled after the Temple of Castor and Pollux in Rome, and now used as a venue for classical concerts and stage performances.

North of the New St shopping precinct, the small but perfectly formed **Cathedral Church of St Philip** (☎0121-262 1840; Colmore Row; donations requested; ⏲7.30am-6.30pm Mon-Fri, 8.30am-5pm Sat & Sun) was constructed in a neoclassical style between 1709 and 1715. The Pre-Raphaelite artist Edward Burne-Jones was responsible for the magnificent stained-glass windows.

On the other side of the Bullring, **Birmingham Back to Backs** (NT; ☎0121-666 7671; 55-63 Hurst St; adult/child £5.45/2.70; ⏲10am-5pm Tue-Sun, guided tour only) is a cluster of restored back-to-back terraced houses – a quirky tour

BIRMINGHAM'S HISTORY BUS

Every Sunday from May to October, a free bus runs around Birmingham's museums, stopping at the Birmingham Museum & Art Gallery, Soho House, Aston Hall and Sarehole Mill, as well as several smaller museums. Contact any of the museums for details.

takes you through four working-class homes, telling the stories of the people who lived here from the 1840s to the 1970s.

BIRMINGHAM CANALS

During the industrial age, Birmingham was a major hub on the English canal network (the city technically has more miles of canals than Venice), and visiting narrowboats still float into Gas St Basin in the heart of the city, passing a string of swanky wharfside developments.

Across the canal from the International Convention Centre and Symphony Hall, the glitzy Brindley Pl development contains banking offices, designer restaurants and the sleek **Ikon Gallery** (☎0121-248 0708; www.ikon-gallery.co.uk; 1 Oozells Sq; admission free; ⏲11am-6pm Tue-Sun). This cutting-edge art gallery is housed in a stylishly converted Gothic schoolhouse. Prepare to be thrilled, bemused or outraged, depending on your take on conceptual art.

Nearby, the Norman Foster–designed **National Sea Life Centre** (☎0121-643 6777; www.sealifeeurope.com; 3a Brindley Pl; adult/child £17.50/14; ⏲10am-4pm Mon-Fri, to 5pm Sat & Sun) is the largest inland aquarium in England, and the tanks teem with exotic marine life including razor-jawed hammerhead sharks, turtles and otters. During the school holidays, the queues can stretch around several blocks – buy tickets online ahead of time for fast-track entry.

Jewellery Quarter NEIGHBOURHOOD

Birmingham has been a major player on the British jewellery scene ever since Charles II brought back a taste for fancy buckles and sparkly brocade from France in the 17th century. Stretching north from the last Georgian square in Birmingham, the Jewellery Quarter still produces 40% of the jewellery manufactured in the UK, and dozens of workshops are open to the public. The tourist office provides a free booklet, *Jewel-*

Birmingham

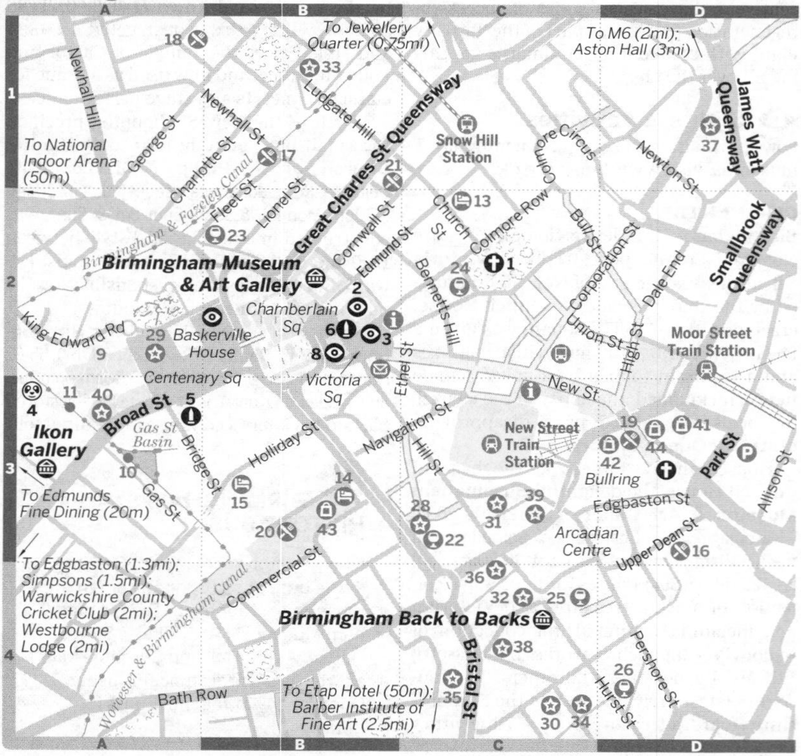

lery Quarter: The Essential Guide, describing the main workshops and showrooms, or you can take a virtual tour at www.jewelleryquarter.net.

In the **Museum of the Jewellery Quarter** (☎0121-554 3598; 75-79 Vyse St; admission free; ⊙10.30am-4pm Tue-Sun), the Smith & Pepper jewellery factory is preserved as it was on its closing day in 1981, after 80 years of operation. You can explore the long history of the trade in Birmingham and watch master jewellers at work.

About 1.5 miles northwest of the Jewellery Quarter is **Soho House** (☎0121-554 9122; Soho Ave, Handsworth; admission free; ⊙11.30am-4pm Tue-Sun Apr-Oct), where industrialist Matthew Boulton lived from 1766 to 1809. Among the restored 18th-century chambers is the dining room where Boulton and members of the Lunar Society met to discuss their world-changing ideas (see boxed text, p397).

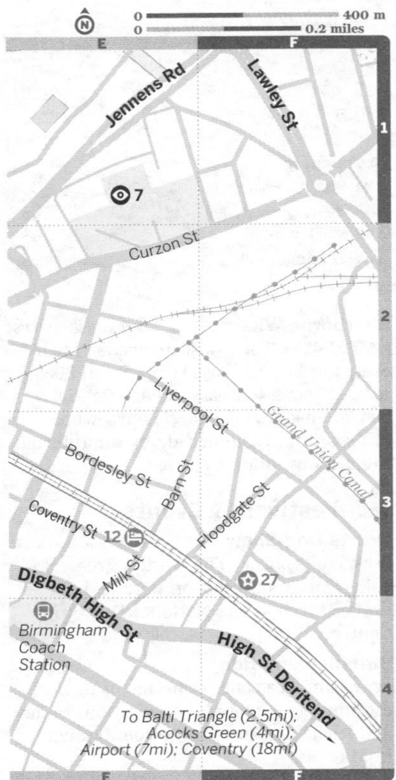

The Jewellery Quarter is three-quarters of a mile northwest of the centre; take bus 101 or ride the metro from Snow Hill or the train from Moor St to Jewellery Quarter station. Buses 74 and 79 pass close to Soho House.

OUTLYING AREAS

A 10-minute walk northeast of the centre, surrounded by the footprints of vanished factories, the Millennium Point development contains the entertaining **Thinktank** (☎0121-202 2222; www.thinktank.ac; Curzon St; adult/child £11.75/7.95; ⊙10am-5pm, last admission 4pm), an ambitious attempt to make science accessible to children (and anyone else with an interest in levers, pulleys and bubbling test tubes). There's also a **Planetarium**, covered by the same ticket, and an **IMAX cinema**.

Around 2.5 miles south of the centre at the University of Birmingham, the **Barber Institute of Fine Art** (☎0121-414 7333; www.barber.org.uk; admission free; ⊙10am-5pm Mon-Sat, noon-5pm Sun) takes in Renaissance masterpieces, European masters such as Rubens and Van Dyck, British greats including Gainsborough, Reynolds and Turner, and modern classics by the likes of Picasso and Schiele. To get here, take the train from New St to University station, or catch bus 61, 62 or 63 from Corporation St.

The next best thing to Willy Wonka's Chocolate Factory, **Cadbury World** (☎0844 880 7667; www.cadburyworld.co.uk; Linden Rd; adult/child £13.90/10.10, under 3yr free; ⊙hours vary, see website) is about 4 miles south of Birmingham in the village of Bournville. This sweet-toothed attraction aims to educate visitors about the history of cocoa and the Cadbury family, but sweetens the deal with free samples, displays of chocolate-making machines, and chocolate-themed rides. Surrounding the chocolate works, pretty **Bournville Village** was built by the philanthropic Cadbury family to accommodate early-20th-century factory workers. Opening hours vary through the year and bookings are essential in July and August. The easiest way to get to Bournville is by train from Birmingham New St (11 minutes).

About 3 miles north of the centre in Aston (of Aston Villa fame), well-preserved **Aston Hall** (☎0121-675 4722; Trinity Rd, Aston; ⊙noon-4pm Tue-Sun Apr-Oct) was built in extravagant Jacobean style between 1618 and 1635. The lush grounds are a wonderful

Birmingham

Top Sights
- Birmingham Back to Backs ... C4
- Birmingham Museum & Art Gallery ... B2
- Ikon Gallery ... A3

Sights
- 1 Cathedral Church of St Philip ... C2
- 2 Council House ... B2
- 3 Fountain ... B2
- 4 National Sea Life Centre ... A3
- Planetarium ... (see 7)
- 5 Statue of Boulton, Watt & Murdoch ... A3
- 6 Statue of Queen Victoria ... B2
- 7 Thinktank ... E1
- 8 Town Hall ... B2

Activities, Courses & Tours
- 9 International Convention Centre ... A2
- 10 Second City Canal Cruises ... A3
- 11 Sherborne Wharf ... A3

Sleeping
- 12 Birmingham Central Backpackers ... E3
- 13 Hotel du Vin ... C2
- 14 Malmaison ... B3
- 15 Nitenite ... B3

Eating
- 16 Cafe Soya ... D3
- 17 Itihaas ... B1
- 18 Lasan ... A1
- 19 Mount Fuji ... D3
- 20 Oriental ... B3
- 21 Purnells ... B1

Drinking
- 22 Island Bar ... C3
- 23 Mechu ... B2
- 24 Old Joint Stock ... C2
- 25 Sobar ... C4
- 26 Village Inn ... D4

Entertainment
- 27 Air ... F3
- 28 Alexandra Theatre ... C3
- 29 Birmingham Repertory Theatre ... A2
- 30 Club DV8 ... C4
- 31 Electric Cinema ... C3
- 32 Hippodrome ... C4
- IMAX ... (see 7)
- 33 Jam House ... B1
- 34 Nightingale Club ... C4
- 35 O2 Academy ... C4
- 36 Oceana ... C4
- 37 Q Club ... D1
- 38 Queens Tavern ... C4
- 39 Sunflower Lounge ... C3
- 40 Symphony Hall ... A3

Shopping
- 41 Bullring East Mall ... D3
- 42 Bullring West Mall ... D3
- 43 Mailbox ... B3
- 44 Selfridges ... D3

retreat from the city streets, and the sumptuous interiors are full of friezes, moulded ceilings and tapestries. To get here, take a train to Aston station from New St station, or jump on bus 65 from Corporation St, north of the Old Sq junction.

Tours

Birmingham Tours WALKING/BUS TOUR
(☎0121-427 2555; www.birmingham-tours.co.uk; prices vary) Runs popular walking tours and the hop-on/hop-off Big Brum Buz (all day ticket adult/child £10/5, Saturdays from May to September).

Second City Canal Cruises CANAL CRUISE
(☎0121-236 9811; www.secondcityboats.co.uk; fares vary) Narrowboat tours of Birmingham's canals lasting anything from one hour to two days, leaving from the Gas St Basin.

Sherborne Wharf NARROWBOAT CRUISE
(☎0121-455 6163; www.sherbornewharf.co.uk; Sherborne St; adult/child £6.50/5; ⌚11.30am, 1pm, 2.30pm & 4pm daily mid-Apr–Oct, Sat & Sun Nov–mid-Apr) Nostalgic narrowboat cruises from the quayside by the International Convention Centre.

Festivals & Events

Crufts Dog Show DOG SHOW
(www.crufts.org.uk) The world's greatest collection of pooches on parade, held every March at the National Exhibition Centre.

Birmingham Pride GAY FESTIVAL
(www.birminghampride.com) One of the largest and most colourful celebrations of gay and lesbian culture in the country, held in May.

Artsfest ARTS FESTIVAL
(www.artsfest.org.uk) The UK's largest free arts festival features visual arts, dance and musical performances in venues across the city in September.

Horse of the Year Show HORSE SHOW
(www.hoys.co.uk) Held in October, the UK's biggest annual equestrian event, with jumping, mounted sports and dressage.

Sleeping

Most Birmingham hotels are aimed at business travellers, ensuring high prices during the week. Look out for cheap deals at weekends or for longer stays. B&Bs are concentrated outside the centre in Acocks Green (to the southeast) or Edgbaston and Selly Oak (to the southwest). The tourist office has a long accommodation list.

TOP CHOICE **Hotel du Vin** HOTEL £££
(0121-200 0600; www.hotelduvin.com; Church St; d from £160; P @) Housed in the handsome Victorian precincts of the former Birmingham Eye Hospital, this upmarket hotel has real class. Polished communal areas give way to art deco–inspired rooms with spectacular bathrooms, and the hotel boasts a pampering spa and a bistro with a stellar wine list.

Malmaison HOTEL £££
(0121-246 5000; www.malmaison-birmingham.com; 1 Wharfside St; d from £160; P @) Within tickling distance of Harvey Nichols and the posh eateries of the Mailbox, there is nothing 'mal' about this sleek hotel. Mood lighting and Regency tones set the scene in the stylish rooms, which offer floor-to-ceiling views. Indulgences include a brasserie, champagne bar and miniature spa. Wheelchair accessible.

Birmingham Central Backpackers HOSTEL £
(0121-643 0033; www.birminghamcentralbackpackers.com; 58 Coventry St; dm from £13; @) Despite the setting in down-at-heel Digbeth, Birmingham's backpacker hostel is handy for the bus station, and guests have a choice of standard dorms or funky Japanese-style pods. The excellent facilities include a lounge with DVD movies, a guest kitchen and a bar.

Nitenite HOTEL ££
(0121-631 5550; www.nitenite.com; 18 Holliday St; r from £56; P @) Taking the chain hotel concept to another level, Nitenite offers catwalk style on a shoestring budget. The compact rooms feel a little like yacht cabins, with panelled walls, floating double beds and giant plasma TV screens with webcam images of the city streets. Wheelchair accessible.

Etap Hotel HOTEL £
(0121-622 7575; www.etaphotel.com; 1 Great Colmore St; r from £38; P @) The Birmingham branch of this cost-effective European chain has a breakfast room and net-cafe and a handy location for the O2 Academy and the clubs around Bristol St. Rooms are simple but good value and the hotel attracts plenty of party-minded young folk.

Westbourne Lodge B&B ££
(0121-429 1003; www.westbournelodge.co.uk; Fountain Rd; s/d from £49.50/69; P @) Removed from the bustle of the city centre, this B&B is still conveniently located, about 2 miles out in the suburb of Edgbaston (follow the A456). Rooms are a little chintzy but spacious, and there's a pleasant terrace to enjoy in summer.

BIRMINGHAM BRAINS

The Industrial Revolution was a great time for entrepreneurs, and nowhere more so than in Birmingham, where the industrialists, philosophers and intellectuals of the Lunar Society came together to swap ideas for the greatest technological leap forward since the invention of wheel. As well as engineers like Matthew Boulton, James Watt and gaslight mogul William Murdoch, the society drew in such great thinkers as philosopher and naturalist Erasmus Darwin, oxygen discoverer Joseph Priestley, pottery boss Josiah Wedgwood, botanist Joseph Banks (who sailed to Australia with Captain Cook) and US founding father Benjamin Franklin. Between 1765 and 1813, this esteemed company held regular meetings at Soho House (now an engaging museum) to thrash out their groundbreaking ideas. If you don't feel like dragging yourself out to the 'burbs, there's a gleaming golden statue of Boulton, Watt and Murdoch near Centenary Sq.

Eating

Birmingham is best known for its brilliant baltis but the city has a growing reputation for fine dining and gastronomy. For cheap eats, look to the myriad Asian eateries in Chinatown, just south of the centre.

Lasan INDIAN ££
(www.lasangroup.com; 3-4 Dakota Bldgs, James St; mains £12-18; ⌚lunch Sun-Fri, dinner daily) Expletive-loving chef Gordon Ramsay gave his endorsement to this elegant and upmarket Indian as Britain's best local restaurant. From our experience, the service and style are spot on and the North and South Indian dishes are masterpieces.

Simpsons MODERN BRITISH £££
(☎0121-454 3434; www.simpsonsrestaurant.co.uk; 20 Highfield Rd, Edgbaston; 3-course set lunch/dinner £30/32.50; ⌚closed dinner Sun) Simpsons is far from the centre in a gorgeous Victorian house, but it's worth making the journey for the imaginative creations sliced and diced by Michelin-starred chef Andreas Antona. Reservations recommended.

Purnells MODERN BRITISH £££
(☎0121-212 9799; www.purnellsrestaurant.com; 55 Cornwall St; 2/3 courses £36/42; ⌚lunch Tue-Fri, dinner Tue-Sat) Exquisite, inventive dishes (such as ox cheek with lentils cooked in toffee) are served in an airy Victorian red-brick building with a striking modern interior. Run by celebrated chef Glynn Purnell.

Itihaas INDIAN ££
(☎0121-212 3383; www.itihaas.co.uk; 18 Fleet St; mains £11-17; ⌚lunch Mon-Fri, dinner daily) Voted best Indian restaurant in the UK by drinkers of Cobra beer, Itihaas does everything right – presentation, decor, service, flavours. It's a big hit with Birmingham's wealthy Indian expats.

Edmunds Fine Dining MODERN BRITISH £££
(☎0121-633 4944; www.edmundsbirmingham.com; 6 Central Sq, Brindley Pl; 2/3 courses from £19/21; ⌚lunch Mon-Fri, dinner Mon-Sat) The latest venture for Michelin-starred chef Andy Waters, this sleek place is where traders from the surrounding banking houses come to spend their bonuses. Expect lots of locally sourced meats, fish and farm-fresh produce. The restaurant is just back from the river in the Brindley Place precinct.

Oriental PAN-ASIAN ££
(☎0121-633 9988; www.theoriental.uk.com; 4 The Mailbox, 128–130 Wharfside St; mains £8-13) The most glamorous of the eateries around the Mailbox wharf, wok-tastic dishes from China, Thailand and Malaysia are served in a funky dining room full of designer wallpaper and prints of Asian celebs.

THE BEAUTIFUL BALTI

If curry is the unofficial national dish of England, then the balti is its finest interpretation. First cooked up in the curry houses of Sparkbrook in southern Birmingham, this one-pot curry is prepared in a cast-iron wok with plenty of onion and chilli. Tracing its origins back to Baltistan in northern Pakistan, the balti is traditionally served with a giant *karack* naan bread that's big enough to feed the whole table.

The best place to sample this Brummie delicacy is in the so-called Balti Triangle about 2.5 miles southeast of the centre, formed by Ladypool Rd, Stoney Lane and Stratford Rd. Reflecting the religious sensibilities of local residents, restaurants serve soft drinks, fruit juices and *lassis* (yoghurt shakes) instead of alcohol, but diners are welcome to bring their own beer and wine. Expect to pay £7 to £9 for a balti and rice or naan bread. To get here, take bus 2, 5, 5A or 6 from Corporation St and ask the driver for Ladypool Rd.

Here are our picks of the Birmingham baltis:

Grameen Khana (☎0121-449 9994; www.grameenkhana.com; 310-12 Ladypool Rd) Multicoloured lights and Bollywood movies provide a backdrop to Birmingham's best balti – according to a city-wide poll in 2009.

Saleem's Restaurant & Sweet House (☎0121-449 1861; 256-8 Ladypool Rd) Long established and understandably popular for its tasty milk-based Indian sweets and generous portions of balti.

Al Faisal's (☎0121-449 5695; www.alfaisal.co.uk; 136-140 Stoney Lane) Come here for delicious dishes from the mountains of Kashmir, as well for as classic Birmingham baltis.

Mount Fuji JAPANESE ££
(☎0121-633 9853; www.mountfuji.co.uk/Bullring.htm; Bullring; mains £7-14) When you tire of retail therapy, sashay to this minimalist Japanese sushi cafe under the West Mall for raw fish, bento boxes and sake.

Cafe Soya ASIAN £
(☎0121-622 3888; Upper Dean St; mains £5-9) The Soya is an excellent cafe that dishes up tasty dim sum and filling bowls of *pho* (Vietnamese noodle soup). There's also a branch in the Arcadian Centre (closed Wednesday).

Drinking

The pub scene in the centre is dominated by bland commercial chains, but there are a few gems if you know where to look.

Island Bar BAR
(☎0121-632 5296; www.bar-island.co.uk; 14-16 Suffolk St; ⌚5pm-late Mon-Sat) Locals rave about the cocktails at this funky nightspot, where you can sit in perspex chairs in front of giant blow-ups of Hawaiian beaches and groove to rock and roll.

Old Joint Stock PUB
(☎0121-200 1892; www.oldjointstocktheatre.co.uk; 4 Temple Row West; ⌚noon-5pm Sun) A vast, high-ceilinged temple of a pub, housed in a former bank and appealing to a high-spirited after-work crowd. There's an 80-seat theatre upstairs that puts on plays and comedy shows.

Sobar BAR
(☎0121-693 5084; Arcadian Centre, Hurst St; ⌚5pm-late Tue & Wed, noon-2am Thu, noon-3am Fri & Sat) A glammed-up, shirted and booted crowd packs out this black-and-red bar to the strains of mainstream dance and house.

Mechu BAR
(☎0121-710 4233; www.summerrow.com/mechu; 47-59 Summer Row; ⌚noon-1am Mon-Wed, noon-3am Fri, 5pm-3am Sat) Work-eat-drink-play is the motto at this slick bistro and club northwest of the centre. Accordingly, most patrons come straight from the office to sup, sip and sway.

Entertainment

Tickets for most Birmingham events can be purchased through the entertainment megacorp **TicketWeb** (☎0870 060 0100; www.ticketweb.co.uk).

Nightclubs

The main party district is south of New St station, where a series of defunct warehouses and pubs have found new life as bars and clubs. Chinatown's **Arcadian Centre** (www.thearcadian.co.uk; Hurst St) is the gateway to this hedonistic quarter, with numerous party bars and dancing spots.

Air CLUB
(www.airbirmingham.com; Heath Mill Lane) Don't be put off by the grungy Digbeth location; this superclub is home to the renowned Godskitchen night (www.godskitchen.com), where some of the country's top DJs whip the crowd into a frenzy.

Q Club CLUB
(www.qclub.co.uk; 212 Corporation St; ⌚from 8.30pm or 10pm) The old brick Central Hall that houses this legendary club is on its last legs, but the 'Q' is still going strong. DJs pump out boisterous electro, house, jungle and old-school club classics.

Oceana CLUB
(www.oceanaclubs.com; Hurst St; ⌚to 3.30am Thu-Sat) Huge and unashamedly commercial, Oceana offers multiple rooms, multiple dance floors and more drinks promotions than you can shake a shot glass at.

Glee Club COMEDY
(www.glee.co.uk; Arcadian Centre; tickets £9.50-17.50; ⌚from 7.30pm Thu-Sat) No connection to the hit TV show, this rib-tickler is Birmingham's favourite comedy club, attracting local talent and big names on tour.

Live Music

As well as the following venues, the **National Indoor Arena** (☎0121-767 2937; www.thenia.co.uk; King Edwards Rd), north of Brindley Pl, and the giant **National Exhibition Centre Arena** (☎0121-780 4141; www.thenec.co.uk; off the M42), near Birmingham International Airport, host stadium-fillers from the world of rock and pop.

Sunflower Lounge LIVE MUSIC
(☎0121-632 6756; www.thesunflowerlounge.co.uk; 76 Smallbrook Queensway; ⌚to 2am Fri & Sat) A quirky little mod bar tucked away on the dual carriageway near New St train station, with a great alternative soundtrack and a regular program of live gigs and DJ nights.

Jam House BAR
(www.thejamhouse.com; 1 St Paul's Sq; ⌚noon-midnight Tue & Wed, noon-1am Thu, noon-2am

GAY & LESBIAN BIRMINGHAM

Birmingham's loud and lively gay scene is centred on the streets south of the Bullring, which throng with the bold, bright and beautiful on weekend nights. For up-to-the-minute information on the Brummie scene visit www.gaybrum.com and www.visitgaybrum.com, or ask the crowds during the bustling Pride march (www.birminghampride.com) in May.

Top gay nightspots:

Nightingale Club (0121-622 1718; www.nightingaleclub.co.uk; Kent St) Birmingham's most established gay nightclub, the Nightingale rocks on three levels, with mainstream pop on the bottom floor and hardcore techno upstairs.

Village Inn (0121-622 4742; www.villagebirmingham.co.uk; 152 Hurst St; noon-2am Sun-Thu, to 4am Fri & Sat) A lively late bar with a side line in drag nights and camp cabaret.

Queens Tavern (0121-622 7091; www.queenstavern.co.uk; 23 Essex St) This bustling, unpretentious corner pub switches to risqué stage shows at weekends.

Club DV8 (0121-666 6366; www.clubdv8.co.uk; 16 Lower Essex St) Dance tunes dominate at this animated dance spot, where the focus is on frolics and flirting.

Fri & Sat) Nasal-toned piano-meister Jools Holland was the brains behind this moody music venue in posh St Paul's Sq. Acts range from jazz big bands to famous soul crooners. Over 21s only.

O2 Academy LIVE MUSIC
(www.birmingham-academy.co.uk; 16-18 Horsefair, Bristol St) Replacing the defunct Carling Academy at Dale End, this is Birmingham's leading venue for big-name rockers and tribute bands.

Symphony Hall MUSIC HALL
(www.symphonyhall.co.uk; Broad St) To hear top talent from the world of classical music, head to the ultramodern Symphony Hall, the official home of the City of Birmingham Symphony Orchestra. Shows also take place in the handsome auditorium at the Town Hall (p393).

Theatre & Cinema

Birmingham Repertory Theatre THEATRE
(www.birmingham-rep.co.uk; Centenary Sq, Broad St) With two performances spaces – the Main House and the more experimental Door – 'the Rep' presents edgy drama and musicals, with an emphasis on contemporary work.

Electric Cinema CINEMA
(www.theelectric.co.uk; 47-49 Station St; deluxe seats £12) At the oldest working cinema in the UK (the projectors have been rolling since 1909), you can enjoy a mix of mainstream and art-house cinema, while sitting in plush two-seater sofas.

IMAX CINEMA
(www.imax.ac; Curzon St; adult/child £9.60/7.75) Coming into its own in the age of the 3D blockbuster, Birmingham's five-storey IMAX cinema is housed in the same building as the Thinktank.

Other venues:

Hippodrome THEATRE
(www.birminghamhippodrome.com; Hurst St) The place to come to see stars off the telly, plus highbrow entertainment from the Birmingham Royal Ballet.

Alexandra Theatre THEATRE
(www.alexandratheatre.org.uk; Suffolk St Queensway) This Brummie institution has been around even longer than the veteran comedians and touring stage shows that grace its stage.

Sport

Villa Park FOOTBALL
(www.avfc.co.uk; Aston) The fourth most successful British football club of all time, Aston Villa Football Club packs out its ground with loyal fans on match days. General sale tickets for Premiership matches can be purchased from the Premier League website (www.premierleague.com). The ground is northwest of the centre, a five-minute walk from Witton train station.

Warwickshire County Cricket Club CRICKET
(www.edgbaston.com; County Ground, Edgbaston) Tickets for tests and one-day internationals sell out early, but seats are often available for county matches and fast-paced Twenty20 games.

Shopping

The workshops of the Jewellery Quarter are well worth a browse – see p394 – and there are several bustling markets selling cheap imported clothes in the pedestrian precincts surrounding the Bullring.

Bullring MALL

(www.bullring.co.uk; St Martin's Circus; 9.30am-8pm Mon-Fri, 9am-8pm Sat, 11am-5pm Sun) Split into two vast retail spaces – the East Mall and West Mall – the Bullring has all the international brands and chain cafes you could ask for, plus the architectural wonder that is the **Selfridges** department store.

Mailbox MALL

(www.mailboxlife.com; Wharfside St; 10am-6pm Mon-Wed, to 7pm Thu-Sat, 11am-5pm Sun) Birmingham's newest 'shopping experience' could hold its own on Madison Ave, with a designer hotel, a fleet of upmarket restaurants, a branch of posh department store Harvey Nichols, and a new extension in a metallic cube that resembles a prop from the *Transformers* movie.

Information

Dangers & Annoyances

As in most large cities, it's wise to avoid walking alone late at night in unlit areas. The area around Digbeth bus station can be quite rough after dark – stick to the High St if you are walking to central Birmingham.

Emergency

Police station (0845 113 5000; Steelhouse Lane)

Internet Access

Internet Lounge (loft level, Pavilions Shopping Centre; per 30min £2; 9.30am-6pm Mon-Wed, Fri & Sat, to 7pm Thu, 11am-5pm Sun) Internet lounge and coffee bar.

Left Luggage

New St train station has left luggage facilities, but there are cheaper bag lockers in the East and West Malls at the Bullring (£2 to £4 per 24 hours).

Media

Numerous free listings magazines are available in hotel lobbies, bars and restaurants, including the fortnightly *What's On* and the monthly *Birmingham 24seven* magazine, which cover everything from exhibitions to club nights.

Medical Services

Birmingham Children's Hospital (0121-333 9999; www.bch.nhs.uk; Steelhouse Lane)

Heartlands Hospital (0121-424 2000; www.heartofengland.nhs.uk; Bordesley) Catch bus 15, 17, 97 or 97A.

Money

You can't walk more than a block in the town centre without coming across a bank or an ATM, particularly around Brindley Pl and New St.

Thomas Cook (0121-643 5057; Middle Mall, Bullring; 10am-8pm Mon-Fri, 9am-8pm Sat, 11am-5pm Sun) Bureau de change.

Post

Central post office (1 Pinfold St, Victoria Sq; 9am-5.30pm Mon-Sat) With bureau de change.

Tourist Information

Tourist office Main Office (0121-202 5115; www.visitbirmingham.com; The Rotunda, 150 New St; 9.30am-5.30pm Mon & Wed-Sat, 10am-5.30pm Tue, 10.30am-4.30pm Sun); Welcome Centre (cnr New & Stephenson Sts; 9am-5pm Mon-Sat, 10am-6pm Sun) With racks of brochures, maps and info on activities, transport and sights.

Getting There & Away

Air

Birmingham's **international airport** (0844 576 6000; www.birminghamairport.co.uk) is about 8 miles east of the centre, with flights to destinations around the UK and Europe, plus a few long-haul connections to America and Dubai.

Bus

Most intercity buses run from the Birmingham Coach Station on Digbeth High St, but the X20 to Stratford-upon-Avon (1¼ hours, hourly, every two hours at weekends) leaves from a stop on Moor St, just north of the Pavilions mall. **National Express** (08717 81 81 81; www.nationalexpress.com) runs coaches between Birmingham and major cities across the country, including:

Oxford £11.60, 1½ to two hours, five daily

London £15.70, 2¾ hours, every 30 minutes

Manchester £12.60, 2½ hours, 12 daily

THE SHAKESPEARE EXPRESS

In July and August, this nostalgic **steam train** (0121-708 4960; www.shakespeareexpress.com; adult/child £10/5) chugs its way southwest from Birmingham Snow Hill to Stratford-upon-Avon, blowing out clouds of vapour as it goes. The train runs twice each Sunday and the journey takes one hour.

Train

Most long-distance trains leave from New St station, beneath the Pallasades shopping centre, but Chiltern Railways runs to London Marylebone (£31.90, 2½ hours, two per hourly) from Birmingham Snow Hill, and London Midland runs to Stratford-upon-Avon (£6.30, one hour, hourly) from Snow Hill and Moor St station.

Useful services from New St:

Derby £13.80, 45 minutes, four per hour

Leicester £13.10, one hour, two per hour

London Euston £40.90, 1½ hours, every 30 minutes

Manchester £30.50, 1¾ hours, every 15 minutes

Shrewsbury £11.70, one hour, two per hour

Getting Around

To/From the Airport

Fast and convenient trains run regularly between New St and Birmingham International station (20 minutes, every 10 minutes), or take bus 58 or 900 (45 minutes, every 20 minutes) from Moor St Queensway. A taxi from the airport to the centre costs about £20.

Car

All the big car-hire companies have town offices:

Avis (☎0844 544 6038; www.avis.co.uk; 17 Horse Fair)

Enterprise Rent-a-Car (☎0121-782 5158; www.enterprise.co.uk; 9-10 Suffolk St Queensway)

Public Transport

Local buses run from a convenient hub on Corporation St, just north of the New St junction. For routes, pick up a free copy of the *Network Birmingham Map & Guide* from the tourist office. Commuter trains to destinations in the north of Birmingham (including Aston) operate from Moor St station, close to Selfridges. Birmingham's single tram line, the **Metro** (www.travelmetro.co.uk), runs from Snow Hill to Wolverhampton via the Jewellery Quarter, West Bromwich and Dudley.

Special saver tickets covering all the buses and trains are available from **Network West Midlands** (☎0121-214 7214; www.networkwestmidlands.com; 9am-5.30pm Mon-Fri, to 5pm Sat) on the lower ground floor of the Pavilions mall.

TOA Taxis (☎0121-427 8888; www.toataxis.net) are a reliable black-cab taxi firm.

NAVIGATING BRUM

The endless ringroads, roundabouts and underpasses make driving in Birmingham a descent into madness. Do as the locals do and ditch your wheels in one of the car parks around the Bullring, then explore the city on foot. For a downloadable map of car park locations, search for 'car park' at www.birmingham.gov.uk.

WARWICKSHIRE

Warwickshire could have been just another picturesque English county of rolling hills and market towns were it not for the birth of a rather well-known wordsmith. William Shakespeare was born, and died, in Stratford-upon-Avon, and the sights linked to his life are a magnet for tourists from around the globe. Famous Warwick Castle attracts similar crowds. Visitor numbers dwindle away from these tourist hubs, but Kenilworth boasts atmospheric castle ruins and Coventry has two fine cathedrals and an excellent motoring museum.

Information

Shakespeare Country (www.shakespeare-country.co.uk)

Getting There & Around

The Warwickshire transport site (www.warwickshire.gov.uk/transport) covers all aspects of travel in the county, including bus and train timetables. Coventry is the main transport hub, with frequent rail connections to London Euston and Birmingham New St.

Coventry

POP 300,848

Over the centuries, Coventry has been a bustling hub for the production of cloth, clocks, bicycles, automobiles and munitions. It was this last industry that attracted the attention of the German Luftwaffe in WWII. The city was blitzed so badly that the Nazis coined a new verb, 'Coventrieren', meaning 'to flatten'.

However, it's not all doom and gloom – a handful of medieval streets escaped the bombers, offering a taste of what the city must have been like in its heyday.

Sights

Coventry Cathedrals CATHEDRAL

The evocative ruins of **St Michael's Cathedral** (Priory Row), built around 1300 but destroyed by Nazi incendiary bombs in the blitz of 14 November 1940, still stand as a permanent memorial to Coventry's darkest hour. You can climb the 180 steps of its **Gothic spire** for panoramic views (adult/child £2.50/1).

Symbolically adjoining the old cathedral's sandstone walls, the Basil Spence–designed **Coventry Cathedral** (024-7652 1200; www.coventrycathedral.org.uk; Priory Row; adult/child under 7 £4.50/3.50; 9.30am-4.30pm) is a modernist architectural masterpiece, with a futuristic organ, stained glass, a Jacob Epstein statue of the devil and St Michael, and ghostlike angels etched into its glass facade.

FREE **Coventry Transport Museum** MUSEUM

(024-7623 4270; www.transport-museum.com; Hales St; 10am-5pm) Down by the bus station, this stupendous museum is every schoolboy's dream. Inside you can view hundreds of motor cars from across the ages, from the earliest 'horseless carriages' produced by Daimler in the 1890s to the jet-powered car that broke the land speed record (and the sound barrier) in 1997.

FREE **Herbert Art Gallery & Museum** GALLERY

(024-7683 2386; www.theherbert.org.uk; 10am-4pm Mon-Sat, noon-4pm Sun) Behind the twin cathedrals, the Herbert has an eclectic collection of paintings and sculptures (including work by TS Lowry and Stanley Spencer), a delightful cafe, and lots of exhibitions and activities aimed at kids.

FREE **St Mary's Guildhall** HISTORIC BUILDING

(024-7683 3328; Bayley Lane; admission free; 10am-4pm) On the other side of the cathedral ruins is one of the country's finest medieval guildhalls. Inside rooms that once imprisoned Mary Queen of Scots, you can view arms and armour, ancient oil paintings and 15th-century tapestries.

Sleeping & Eating

Spire View Guest House B&B £

(024-7625 1602; www.spireviewguesthouse.co.uk; 36 Park Rd; s/d from £25/51; P) Crisp, clean rooms in a quiet residential street a few minutes' walk from the train station. The hosts are eager to please and there's a guest lounge with plenty of books for browsing.

Playwrights CAFE ££

(024-7623 1441; www.playwrightsrestaurant.co.uk; 4-6 Hay Lane; mains £10-14; closed Sun) On the cobbled lane leading from Earl St to the cathedral, this bright, inviting cafe, bar and bistro is as good for breakfast as it is for a working lunch or an intimate dinner.

Tin Angel BAR/LIVE MUSIC

(www.thetinangel.co.uk; Medieval Spon St) Looking like something you'd find in an arty part of Berlin or Barcelona, Tin Angel is where local hipsters come to sip, chat and groove. There are regular live gigs, film screenings and comedy nights.

Information

Tourist office (024-7622 5616; www.visitcoventry.co.uk; 9.30am-4.30pm Mon-Fri, 10am-4.30pm Sat, 10am-noon & 1-4.30pm Sun) Housed in the restored tower of St Michael's.

Getting There & Away

Trains go south to London Euston (£37.80, 1¼ hours, every 20 minutes) and you will rarely have to wait for a train to Birmingham (30 minutes, every 10 minutes).

From the main bus station, National Express buses serve most parts of the country. Bus X17 (every 20 minutes) goes to Kenilworth (25 minutes), Leamington Spa (40 minutes) and Warwick (1¼ hours).

Warwick

POP 25,434

Regularly name-checked by Shakespeare, Warwick was the ancestral seat of the Earls of Warwick, who played a pivotal role in the Wars of the Roses, ousting Henry VI and installing the young Edward IV on the English throne. Despite a devastating fire in 1694, Warwick remains a treasure-house of medieval architecture, dominated by the soaring turrets of Warwick Castle, which has been transformed into a major tourist attraction by the team behind Madame Tussauds. Unfortunately, the summer queues at the castle can resemble a medieval siege – you can escape the melee in the surrounding streets, which are jammed with interesting buildings and museums.

Sights & Activities

Warwick Castle CASTLE

(0870 442 2000; www.warwick-castle.co.uk; castle adult/child £19.95/11.95, castle & dungeon £27.45/19.45; 10am-6pm Apr-Sep, to 5pm

Warwick

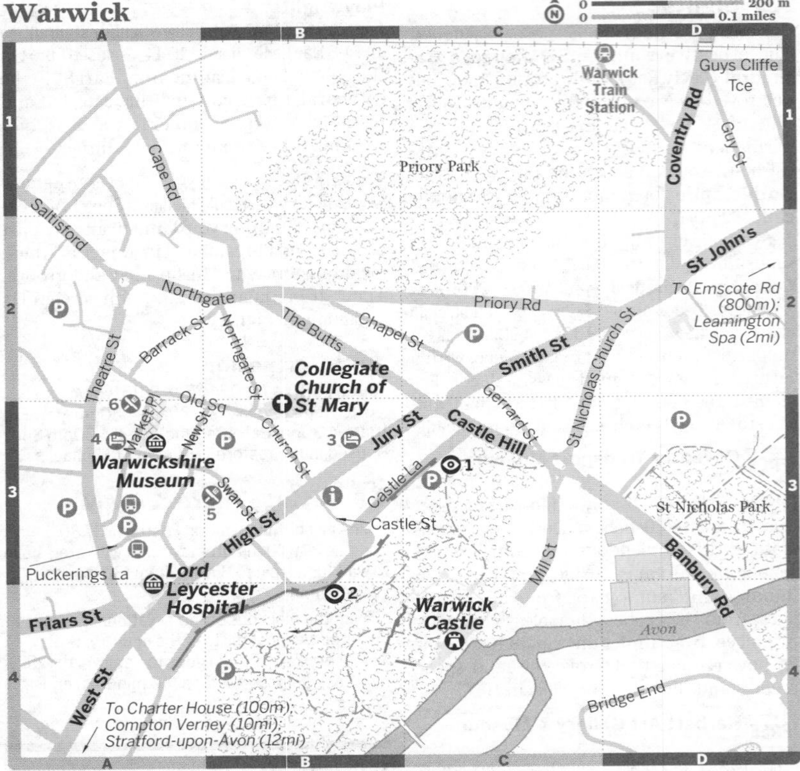

Oct-Mar; P) Founded in 1068 by William the Conqueror, the stunningly preserved Warwick Castle is the biggest show in town.

With waxwork-populated private apartments, sumptuous interiors, landscaped gardens, towering ramparts, displays of arms and armour, medieval jousting and a theme-park dungeon (complete with torture chamber and ham actors in grisly make-up), there's plenty to keep the family busy for a whole day. Tickets are discounted if you buy online.

FREE Collegiate Church of St Mary CHURCH

(01926-492909; Old Sq; suggested donation £2; 10am-6pm Apr-Oct, to 4.30pm Nov-Mar) Drag yourself away from the castle ramparts to explore this magnificent Norman church, founded in 1123 and packed with 16th- and 17th-century tombs. Highlights include the Norman crypt, the Beauchamp Chapel (built between 1442 and 1464 to enshrine the mortal remains of the Earls of Warwick) and the clock tower (admission adult/child £2.50/1), which offers supreme views over town.

Lord Leycester Hospital HISTORIC BUILDING

(01926-491422; www.lordleycester.com; High St; adult/child £4.90/3.90; 10am-5pm Tue-Sun Apr-Sep, to 4.30pm Oct-Mar) Leaning against the Westgate like a rest home for Hobbits, the wonderfully wonky Lord Leycester Hospital has been used as a retirement home for soldiers (but not as a hospital) since 1571. Visitors can wander around the courtyard, chapel, guildhall and regimental museum.

Warwickshire Museum MUSEUM

(01926-412501; Market Pl; admission free; 10am-5pm Tue-Sat year-round, plus 11.30am-5pm Sun Apr-Sep) Housed in Warwick's striking 17th-century market hall, this museum has some entertaining displays on local history and the Warwick Sea Dragons (ancient dinosaurs that once roamed the Jurassic seas).

Warwick

Top Sights
Collegiate Church of St Mary.............B3
Lord Leycester Hospital.....................A3
Warwick Castle.................................C4
Warwickshire Museum.......................A3

Sights
1 Warwick Castle Pedestrian Entrance...C3
2 Warwick Castle Ticket Office.............B4

Sleeping
3 Lord Leycester Hotel..........................B3
4 Rose & Crown.....................................A3

Eating
5 Art Kitchen & Gallery..........................B3
6 Tailors..A3

Sleeping

The nearest YHA (Youth Hostels Association) hostel is in Stratford-upon-Avon (see p407), but reasonably priced B&Bs line Emscote Rd, which runs northeast towards Leamington Spa.

Rose & Crown PUB/HOTEL ££
(☎01926-411117; www.roseandcrownwarwick.co.uk; 30 Market Pl; mains from £8; r incl breakfast from £70; P @) Warwick's finest, this convivial gastropub has five appealing rooms with tasteful modern trim (some with views of the town square), as well as good beer and superior food.

Charter House B&B ££
(☎01926-496965; sheila@penon.gotadsl.co.uk; 87-91 West St; s/d from £65/85; P @) Found southwest of the centre, this cute little timbered cottage has three rooms convincingly decorated in medieval period styles, and a long list of options for breakfast. Book well ahead.

Lord Leycester Hotel HOTEL ££
(☎01926-491481; www.lord-leycester.co.uk; 17 Jury St; r from £79.50; P) This rambling stone town house–turned-hotel, built in 1726, has helpful staff but dated rooms.

Eating

Tailors MODERN BRITISH £££
(☎01926-410590; www.tailorsrestaurant.co.uk; 22 Market Pl; 2-/3-course dinner £28/32.50; Tue-Sat) Set in a former gentlemen's tailor shop, this elegant eatery serves prime ingredients – guinea fowl, pork belly and lamb from named farms – presented oh-so-delicately in neat little towers.

Art Kitchen & Gallery THAI £
(☎01926-494303; www.theartkitchen.com; 7 Swan St; mains £7-13) Come for zingy Thai dishes prepared with lots of local produce, served up in a snug dining room that doubles as a gallery. All of the art on display is for sale.

Information

Tourist office (☎01926-492212; www.warwick-uk.co.uk; Court House, Jury St; 9.30am-4.30pm Mon-Fri, from 10am Sat, 10am-3.30pm Sun) Found near the junction with Castle St, the tourist office sells the informative *Warwick Town Trail* leaflet (45p).

Getting There & Away

National Express coaches operate from Puckerings Lane. Stagecoach X17 runs to Coventry (1¼ hours, every 15 minutes Monday to Saturday), via Kenilworth (30 minutes). Stagecoach bus 16 goes to Stratford-upon-Avon (40 minutes, hourly) in one direction, and Coventry in the other. The main bus stops are on Market St.

Trains run to Birmingham (£7.40, 45 minutes, half-hourly), Stratford-upon-Avon (£5.20, 30 minutes, hourly) and London (£30, 1¾ hours, every 20 minutes), from the station northeast of the centre.

Kenilworth

POP 23,219

It's well worth deviating from the A46 between Warwick and Coventry to visit the spine-tinglingly atmospheric ruins of Kenilworth Castle. A refreshing counterpoint to the commercialism of Warwick's royal ruin, the castle was the inspiration for Walter Scott's *Kenilworth,* and it still feels pretty inspiring today.

Sights & Activities

Kenilworth Castle CASTLE
(EH; ☎01926-852078; adult/child £7.60/3.80; 10am-5pm Mar-Oct, to 4pm Nov-Feb) This wonderful ruin sprawls among fields and hedges on the outskirts of Kenilworth. Built in the 1120s, the castle survived the longest siege in English history in 1266, when the forces of Lord Edward (later Edward I) threw themselves at the moat and battlements for six solid months.

The excellent audio-tour will tell you all about the relationship between former owner Robert Dudley and the 'Virgin

Queen', who was wined and dined here at tremendous expense, almost bankrupting the castle.

Sleeping & Eating

As well as the following choices, there are numerous pubs and eateries along the High St (just north of the castle) and Warwick Rd (just south).

Castle Laurels Hotel B&B ££
(01926-856179; www.castlelaurels.co.uk; 22 Castle Rd; s/d £45/60; P @) A stately guest house opposite the castle, where the owners pride themselves on the spotless rooms and the warmth of the welcome. The home-cooked breakfasts (with free-range eggs) are lovely.

Clarendon Arms PUB £
(01926-852017; www.clarendonarmspub.co.uk; 44 Castle Hill; mains £8-13) Almost opposite the castle, this bright and homey alehouse has home-cooked food, a warm ambience and a cosy little beer garden.

Information

For tourist information, browse the brochures at the town **library** (01926-852595; 11 Smalley Pl; 9am-7pm Mon & Thu, to 5.30pm Tue & Fri, 10.30am-5.30pm Wed, 9.30am-4pm Sat).

Getting There & Away

From Monday to Saturday, bus X17 runs every 15 minutes from Coventry to Kenilworth (25 minutes) and on to Leamington Spa (from Kenilworth, 15 minutes) and Warwick (20 minutes). On Sunday, take bus U17 (half-hourly) for Coventry or bus 18A (hourly) for Warwick.

Stratford-upon-Avon

POP 22,187

The author of some of the most quoted lines ever written in the English language, William Shakespeare was born in Stratford in 1564 and died here in 1616, and the five houses linked to his life form the centrepiece of a tourist attraction that verges on a cult of personality.

Experiences in this unmistakably Tudor town range from the touristy (medieval recreations and bard-themed tearooms) to the humbling (Shakespeare's modest grave in Holy Trinity Church) and the sublime (taking in a play by the world-famous Royal Shakespeare Company). Nevertheless, if can leave without buying at least a Shakespeare novelty pencil, you'll have resisted one of the most keenly honed marketing machines in the nation.

Sights & Activities

The Shakespeare Houses MUSEUMS
Five of the most important buildings associated with Shakespeare contain museums that form the core of the visitor experience at Stratford, run by the **Shakespeare Birthplace Trust** (01789-204016; www.shakespeare.org.uk; adult/child all five properties £19/12, three in-town houses £12.50/8; 9am-5pm Apr-Oct, see website for low-season hours). You can buy individual tickets, but it's more cost-effective to buy a combination ticket covering the three houses in town, or all five properties.

Shakespeare's Birthplace
(Henley St) Start your Shakespeare tour at the house where the world's most famous playwright supposedly spent his childhood days. In fact, the jury is still out on whether this really was Shakespeare's birthplace, but devotees of the bard have been dropping in since at least the 19th century, leaving their signatures scratched onto the windows. Set behind a modern facade, the house contains restored Tudor rooms, live presentations from famous Shakespearean characters and an engaging exhibition on Stratford's favourite son.

Nash's House & New Place
(01789-292325; cnr Chapel St & Chapel Lane) When Shakespeare retired, he swapped the bright lights of London for a comfortable town house at New Pl, where he died of unknown causes in April 1616. The house was demolished in 1759, but an attractive Elizabethan **knot garden** occupies part of the grounds.

Displays in the adjacent **Nash's House**, where Shakespeare's granddaughter Elizabeth lived, describe the town's history, and there's a collection of 17th-century furniture and tapestries.

Hall's Croft
(01789-292107; Old Town) Shakespeare's daughter Susanna married respected doctor John Hall, and their fine Elizabethan town house is south of the centre on the way to Holy Trinity Church. Deviating from the main Shakespearean theme, the exhibition offers fascinating insights into medicine in the 16th century.

Anne Hathaway's Cottage
(☎01789-292100, Cottage Lane, Shottery) Before marrying Shakespeare, Anne Hathaway lived in Shottery, a mile west of the centre, in this pretty thatched farmhouse. As well as period furniture, there's an orchard and arboretum, with examples of all the trees mentioned in Shakespeare's plays. A footpath (no bikes allowed) leads to Shottery from Evesham Pl.

Mary Arden's Farm
(☎01789-293455; Station Rd, Wilmcote) If you fancy going back even further, you can visit the childhood home of Shakespeare's mum at Wilmcote, 3 miles west of Stratford. Aimed firmly at families, the farm has exhibits tracing country life over the centuries, with nature trails, falconry displays and a collection of rare-breed farm animals. You can get here on the City Sightseeing bus, or cycle via Anne Hathaway's Cottage, following the Stratford-upon-Avon Canal towpath.

FREE **Holy Trinity Church** CHURCH
(☎01789-266316; www.stratford-upon-avon.org; Old Town; admission to church free, Shakespeare's grave adult/child £1.50/50p; ⏲8.30am-6pm Mon-Sat, 12.30-5pm Sun Apr-Sep, reduced low season hours) The final resting place of the bard is said to be the most visited parish church in England. Inside are handsome 16th- and 17th-century tombs (particularly in the Clopton Chapel), some fabulous carvings on the choir stalls and, of course, the grave of William Shakespeare, with its ominous epitaph: 'cvrst be he yt moves my bones'.

Other Sights

Set in an old timbered building, **Falstaff's Experience** (☎01789-298070; www.falstaffsexperience.co.uk; 40 Sheep St; adult/child £4.80/1.30; ⏲10.30am-5.30pm) offers a ghost-train take on Shakespeare's tales, with olde-worldey walk-throughs, mannequins of Tudor celebs and live actors hamming it up like Olivier. Night-time ghost tours (adults only) are led by famous mediums.

Also at this end of town is the **Guild Chapel** (cnr Chapel Lane & Church St), founded in 1269 and painted with motivational frescoes showing the fate of the damned in the 15th century. It's only open to the public for services (10am Wednesday and noon on the first Saturday of the month, April to September).

Tours

Popular and informative two-hour **guided town walks** (☎01789-292478; adult/child £5/2; ⏲11am Mon-Wed, 2pm Thu-Sun) depart from Waterside, opposite Sheep St, which is also the starting point for the spooky **Stratford Town Ghost Walk** (adult/child £6/3; ⏲7.30pm Mon, Thu, Fri & Sat).

Other options:

City Sightseeing BUS TOURS
(☎01789-412680; www.citysightseeing-stratford.com; adult/child £11.50/6; ⏲every 20min Apr-Sep, less frequently in low season) Open-top, hop-on/hop-off bus tours leave from the tourist office and go to each of the Shakespeare properties. Tickets are valid for 24 hours.

Avon Boating RIVER CRUISES
(☎01789-267073; www.avon-boating.co.uk; The Boathouse, Swan's Nest Lane; 30min river cruises adult/child £4.50/3) Runs river cruises that depart every 20 minutes from either side of the main bridge.

Bancroft Cruisers RIVER CRUISES
(☎01789-269669; www.bancroftcruisers.co.uk; 45min river cruises adult/child £5/3.50; ⏲daily departures Apr-Oct) These fun trips leave from the riverbank by the Holiday Inn, off Bridgeway.

Sleeping

B&Bs are plentiful, particularly along Grove Rd and Evesham Pl, but vacancies can be hard to find during the high season – the tourist office can help with bookings, for a fee.

Stratford-upon-Avon YHA HOSTEL £
(☎0845 371 9661; www.yha.org.uk; Hemmingford House, Alveston; dm from £16; P @) Set in a large, 200-year-old mansion 1.5 miles east of the town centre along Tiddington Rd, this superior hostel attracts travellers of all ages. There's a canteen, bar and kitchen, and buses 18 and 18a run here from Bridge St.

Shakespeare Hotel HOTEL £££
(☎01789-294997; www.mercure.com; Chapel St; s/d £135/150; P @) For the full Tudor inn experience, head to this atmospheric Mercure property in a timbered medieval charmer on the main street. As well as a perfect location, you get tasteful rooms – some with four-poster beds and wood panels – and a sense of history that's missing from the competition.

Stratford-upon-Avon

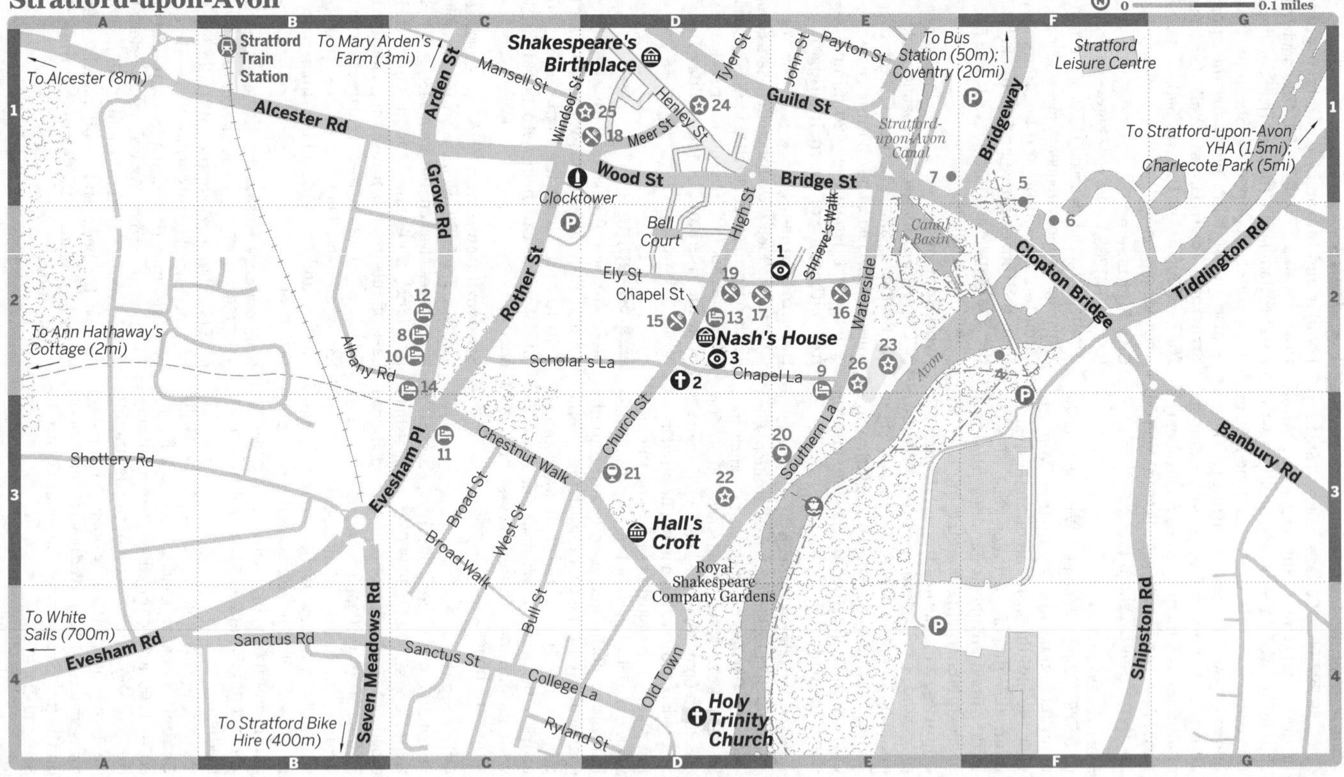

Stratford-upon-Avon

Top Sights
- Hall's Croft ... D3
- Holy Trinity Church ... D4
- Nash's House ... D2
- Shakespeare's Birthplace ... D1

Sights
- 1 Falstaff's Experience ... E2
- 2 Guild Chapel ... D2
- 3 Knot Garden ... D2

Activities, Courses & Tours
- 4 Avon Boating River Cruises ... F2
- 5 Avon Boating River Cruises ... F1
- 6 Bancroft Cruisers ... F2
- 7 City Sightseeing Bus Tours ... E1

Sleeping
- 8 Ambleside Guest House ... C2
- 9 Arden Hotel ... E2
- 10 Ashgrove Guest House ... C2
- 11 Broadlands Guest House ... C3
- 12 Salamander Guest House ... C2
- 13 Shakespeare Hotel ... D2
- 14 Woodstock Guest House ... C2

Eating
- 15 Edward Moon's ... D2
- 16 Georgetown ... E2
- 17 Lambs ... D2
- 18 Oscar's ... D1
- 19 Vintner Wine Bar ... D2

Drinking
- 20 Dirty Duck (Black Swan) ... E3
- 21 Windmill Inn ... D3

Entertainment
- 22 Courtyard Theatre ... D3
- 23 Royal Shakespeare Theatre ... E2
- 24 Saint Club ... D1
- 25 Stratford Picture House ... D1
- 26 Swan Theatre ... E2

Arden Hotel HOTEL £££
(☎01789-298682; www.theardenhotelstratford.com; Waterside; r incl breakfast from £125; P@) Formerly the Thistle, this elegant property facing the Swan Theatre has been stylishly revamped, with a sleek brasserie and champagne bar, and rooms featuring designer fabrics and bathrooms full of polished stone.

White Sails B&B ££
☎01789-264326; www.white-sails.co.uk; 85 Evesham Rd; r from £95; P@) Plush fabrics, framed prints, brass bedsteads and shabby-chic tables and lamps set the scene at this gorgeous, intimate guest house. The four individually furnished rooms come with flatscreen TVs, climate control and glamorous bathrooms.

Eating

Sheep St is clustered with upmarket eating options, mostly aimed at theatregoers (look out for good-value pre-theatre menus).

Lambs MODERN EUROPEAN ££
(☎01789-292554; www.lambsrestaurant.co.uk; 12 Sheep St; mains £12-16; ⊙lunch Tue-Sun, dinner daily) The classiest joint in town – Lambs skips the Shakespeare chintz in favour of Venetian blinds and modern elegance. The menu includes slow cooked lamb, Gressingham duck and the like, and the wine list is excellent.

Edward Moon's MODERN BRITISH ££
(☎01789-267069; www.edwardmoon.com/moonsrestaurant; 9 Chapel St; mains £10-15) Named after a famous travelling chef, who cooked up the flavours of home for the British colonial service, this snug eatery serves delicious, hearty English dishes, many livened up with herbs and spices from the East.

Vintner Wine Bar MODERN BRITISH ££
(☎01789-297259; www.the-vintner.co.uk; 5 Sheep St; mains £10-20; ⊙breakfast, lunch & dinner) Set in a town house from 1600, this quirky place is full of beams, exposed brickwork and low ceilings on which to bang your head. Locals as well as out-of-towners come here for good food (mostly steaks, salads and roasts) and lively conversation.

Other recommendations:

Oscar's CAFE £
(13/14 Meer St; sandwiches & lunches £4-7; ⊙11.30am-late) A casual cafe serving appetising breakfasts, lunches and afternoon teas; it turns into a bar after hours.

Georgetown MALAYSIAN ££
(☎01789-204445; www.georgetownrestaurants.co.uk; 23 Sheep St; mains £12-26) This classy Malaysian restaurant serves Straits cuisine at tables with starched white linen and wicker chairs.

STRATFORD BED & BREAKFASTS

Stratford is well stocked with old-fashioned B&Bs, to the level that some streets are a continuous line of almost identical guest houses, offering almost identical facilities at almost identical prices.

With so much choice, it pays to be selective – here are our top five beds (and breakfasts):

Ambleside Guest House (☎01789-297239; www.amblesideguesthouse.co.uk; 41 Grove Rd; s/d from £25/50; P @) Lovely, nonfrilly B&B, with spotless rooms, amiable, well-informed hosts and big organic breakfasts.

Ashgrove Guest House (☎01789-297278; www.ashgrovehousestratford.co.uk; 37 Grove Rd; s/d from £25/50; P) Tidy, airy rooms decked out in varying degrees of burgundy. Look for the wooden bear sculpture outside.

Broadlands Guest House (☎01789-299181; www.broadlandsguesthouse.co.uk; 23 Evesham Pl; s/d from £48/80; P) Prim and blue, with classic English B&B rooms and filling breakfasts served in a pretty breakfast room.

Salamander Guest House (☎01789-205728; www.salamanderguesthouse.co.uk; 40 Grove Rd; s/d incl breakfast from £20/40; P @ wi-fi) Comfortable and homey, with the added appeal of wi-fi.

Woodstock Guest House (☎01789-299881; www.woodstock-house.co.uk; 30 Grove Rd; s/d from £30/55; P) Agreeable flowery rooms, soft carpets and a warm welcome, in a house with a tidy garden and gravel drive.

Drinking

Dirty Duck PUB

(Waterside) Officially called the 'Black Swan', this enchanting riverside alehouse is a favourite thespian watering hole, and has a roll-call of former regulars (Olivier, Attenborough etc) that reads like an actors' *Who's Who*. Just be sure not to mention Macbeth...

Windmill Inn PUB

(Church St) Ale was flowing here at the same time as rhyming couplets flowed from Shakespeare's quill – this pub has been around a while. Despite its age it's still one of the liveliest places in town, and slightly removed from the tourist hubbub.

Entertainment

Royal Shakespeare Company THEATRE

(RSC; ☎0844 800 1110; www.rsc.org.uk; tickets £8-38) Coming to Stratford without seeing a production of Shakespeare would be like going to Rome and not visiting the Vatican.

There are three grand stages in Stratford: **Royal Shakespeare Theatre** and **Swan Theatre** on Waterside and the **Courtyard Theatre** on Southern Lane. The first two properties were extensively redeveloped between 2007 and 2010 – contact the RSC for the latest news on performance times at the three venues. There are often special deals for under 25-year-olds, students and seniors, and a few tickets are held back for sale on the day of the performance, but eager backpackers tend to snap these up fast. Wise theatregoers book well ahead.

Stratford Picture House CINEMA

(www.picturehouses.co.uk; Windsor St) This cinema, tucked away just off the main drag, shows Hollywood blockbusters as well as art-house films.

Saint Club CLUB

(www.worshipsaint.com; 4-5 Henley St; ⏲events Mon, Fri & Sat) Another night of Shakespeare is pretty low on the list of must-dos for young folk in Stratford – instead, they bop to '80s classics and mainstream dance at this nightclub on the main street.

Information

Cyber Junction (www.thecyberjunction.co.uk; 28 Greenhill St; per 30min £2; ⏲10.30am-8pm Mon-Fri, to 5.30pm Sat)

Tourist office (☎0870 160 7930; www.shakespeare-country.co.uk; Bridgefoot; ⏲call for opening times) Under refurbishment at the time of writing, but due to reopen on same site.

Getting There & Away

If you drive to Stratford, be warned that town car parks charge high fees, 24 hours a day. From Stratford train station, London Midland runs to Birmingham (£6.30, one hour, hourly) and Chiltern Railways runs to London Marylebone

(£49.50, 2¼ hours, four daily). **Shakespeare Express steam train** (0121-708 4960; www.shakespeareexpress.com; one way adult/child £10/5) runs twice every Sunday in July and August between Stratford and Birmingham Snow Hill.

National Express coaches and other bus companies run from Stratford's Riverside bus station (behind the Stratford Leisure Centre on Bridgeway). Destinations served:

Birmingham National Express, £7.70, one hour, twice daily

London Victoria National Express, £17.10, three to four hours, five daily

Moreton-in-Marsh Bus 21/22, one hour, hourly

Oxford National Express, £9.90, one hour, twice daily

Warwick Bus 16, 40 minutes, hourly

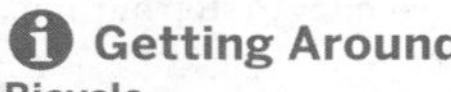

Getting Around

Bicycle

A bicycle is handy for getting out to the outlying Shakespeare properties, and **Stratford Bike Hire** (07711-776340; www.stratfordbikehire.com; 7 Seven Meadows Rd; per half/full day from £7/13) will deliver to your accommodation.

Around Stratford-upon-Avon

CHARLECOTE PARK

A youthful Shakespeare is said to have poached deer in the grounds of **Charlecote Park** (NT; 01789-470277; Wellesbourne; adult/child £8.15/4.05; noon-5pm Fri-Tue Mar-Oct, noon-4pm Sat & Sun Dec), a lavish Elizabethan pile that backs onto the River Avon. Fallow deer still roam the grounds today, and the interiors were restored from Georgian chintz to Tudor splendour in 1823. Charlecote is around 5 miles east of Stratford-upon-Avon. Bus 18 (18A on Sunday) runs to Charlecote hourly from Stratford (30 minutes), continuing to Leamington Spa (30 minutes).

RAGLEY HALL

In a region crammed with stately homes, **Ragley Hall** (01789-762090; www.ragleyhall.com; adult/child £8.50/5; house noon-4pm, grounds 10am-6pm Sat & Sun Feb-Oct) stands out as a testament to the extravagance of inherited wealth. The family home of the Marquess and Marchioness of Hertford, this grand Palladian mansion was built between 1679 and 1683, and it features some truly opulent interior design, from the scarlet damask walls of the Red Saloon to the astonishing *trompe l'oeil* murals in the South Staircase, showing the temptation of Christ in a garden full of toucans and marmosets. Youngsters can run wild in the attached adventure playground.

The house and grounds are open most weekends plus additional weekdays in summer – see the website for details. The mansion is about 10 miles west of Stratford-upon-Avon, easily accessible by taxi. With your own vehicle, follow the A46 and look for the signs.

COMPTON VERNEY

The once-decrepit 18th-century mansion of **Compton Verney** (01926-645500; www.comptonverney.org.uk, adult/child £8/2; 11am-5pm Tue-Sun mid-Mar–mid-Dec) opened to the public in 2004 after a multimillion-pound overhaul. It now houses a grand art gallery, with an impressive collection of British folk art Neapolitan masterpieces, Germanic medieval art and Chinese bronzes, as well as visiting exhibitions. If it gets too packed, retreat to the lovely grounds, landscaped by Lancelot 'Capability' Brown. Bus 269 runs directly here from Stratford-upon-Avon (not on Sunday). You can also reach Compton Verney on the City Sight-Seeing 'Heart of Warwickshire' bus from Stratford (adult/child £9.50/5, half-hourly May to October).

STAFFORDSHIRE

Despite being wedged between the ever-expanding conurbations of Birmingham and Manchester, Staffordshire is surprisingly green and pleasant, and the northern half of the county rises to meet the rugged hills of the Peak District. Highlights of this under-explored neck of the woods include cathedral-crowned Lichfield, and the famous theme parks at Drayton Manor and Alton Towers.

Information

Staffordshire Tourism (www.enjoystaffordshire.co.uk)

Getting There & Around

Regular trains and National Express buses serve Stafford and other major towns. The main local bus operator is **First Group** (0870 850 0868; www.firstgroup.com). For details of services, browse the public transport pages at www.staffordshire.gov.uk/transport.

Stafford

POP 63,681

The capital of Staffordshire is a quiet little place that seems somewhat overshadowed by Lichfield and other towns around the county. The main shopping street has some handsome Georgian and medieval buildings, but little evidence remains that this was once the capital of the Anglo-Saxon kingdom of Mercia. For local info, drop into the **tourist office** (01785-619619; www.visitstafford.org; Eastgate St; 9.30am-5pm Mon-Fri, 10am-4pm Sat) at the Stafford Gatehouse Theatre.

Surrounded by high-street shops, the **Ancient High House** (01785-619131; Greengate St; admission free; 10am-4pm Tue-Sat) is the largest timber-framed town house in the country, artistically assembled in 1595. Creaking stairways lead to carefully restored rooms, and to displays on the history of the town and medieval construction techniques.

The hilltop remains of **Stafford Castle** (01785-257698; Newport Rd; admission free; visitor centre 11am-4pm Wed-Sun Apr-Oct, 11am-4pm Sat & Sun Nov-Mar), a classic Norman moat and bailey, sit romantically in a forest glade about 1 mile southwest of town, just off the A518.

Buses X1 and 101 run between Stafford and Hanley (Stoke-on-Trent; £6.90, 1¼ hours, hourly). Trains run to Birmingham (£8.70, 40 minutes, every 20 minutes), Manchester (£17.40, one hour, every 30 minutes) and London Euston (£48.90, 1½ hours, hourly).

Around Stafford

On the edge of Cannock Chase, the regal, neoclassical mansion of **Shugborough** (01889-881388; www.shugborough.org.uk; adult/child £12/7, parking £3; 11am-5pm Tue-Sun Mar-Oct) is the ancestral home of renowned royal photographer Lord Lichfield; accordingly, a good proportion of the wall space is devoted to his work. Unless you're an ardent monarchist, a more compelling reason to visit is the collection of exquisite Louis XV and XVI furniture in the state rooms. Kids may get more out of the grounds, where costumed actors demonstrate what life was like for landowners and the hoi polloi in the 19th century.

Shugborough is 6 miles east of Stafford on the A513; bus 825 from Stafford to Lichfield runs nearby (20 minutes, half-hourly Monday to Saturday).

Lichfield

POP 27,900

Even without its magnificent Gothic cathedral (one of the most spectacular in the country) this quaintly cobbled market town would be worth a visit to tread in the footsteps of lexicographer and wit Samuel Johnson, and natural philosopher Erasmus Darwin, grandfather of Charles. Johnson once described Lichfield folk as 'the most sober, decent people in England', which was rather generous considering that this was the last place in the country to stop burning people at the stake!

Sights & Activities

FREE **Lichfield Cathedral** CATHEDRAL
(01543-306100; donation requested; 7.30am-6.15pm, to 5pm Sun low season) Crowned by three dramatic towers, Lichfield Cathedral is a stunning Gothic fantasy, constructed in stages from 1200 to 1350. The enormous vaulted nave is set slightly off line from the choir, creating a bizarre perspective when viewed from the west door, and carvings inside the cathedral still bear signs of damage caused by soldiers sharpening their swords during the English Civil War.

In the octagonal Chapter House, you can view the illuminated *Chad Gospels*, created around 730AD, and an ornate Anglo-Saxon bas-relief known as the Lichfield Angel. The Lady Chapel features 16th-century Flemish stained glass, and along the north and south aisles are memorials to generations of Lichfield bishops.

Erasmus Darwin House MUSEUM
(01543-306260; www.erasmusdarwin.org; Beacon St; adult/child £3/1; noon-5pm Tue-Sun, last admission 4.15pm) After turning down the job of royal physician to King George III – perhaps a lucky escape, considering the monarch's descent into madness – Erasmus Darwin became a leading light in the Lunar Society, debating the origins of life with such luminaries as Wedgwood, Boulton and Watt, decades before his grandson Charles came up with the theory of evolution. His former house contains some intriguing personal effects, and at the back is a fragrant herb garden leading to Cathedral Close.

FREE Samuel Johnson Birthplace Museum MUSEUM
(☎01543-264972; www.samueljohnsonbirthplace.org.uk; Breadmarket St; ⊙10.30am-4.30pm Apr-Sep, 11am-3.30pm Oct-Mar) A short walk south of Erasmus Darwin House, this small but absorbing museum charts the life of the pioneering lexicographer Samuel Johnson, who moved to London from his native Lichfield and devoted nine years to producing the first dictionary of the English language.

Sleeping & Eating

No 8 The Close B&B ££
(☎01543-418483; www.ldb.co.uk/accommodation.htm; 8 The Close; s/d from £38/58) Right on Cathedral Close (so, in a prime location), this family-run B&B is set in a listed 19th-century town house. There are three comfortable rooms but be sure to book in advance.

George Hotel PUB/HOTEL ££
(☎01543-414822; www.thegeorgelichfield.co.uk; 12-14 Bird St; r from £80; P @ ☰) Now part of the Best Western chain, this old Georgian pub has been upgraded into a comfortable midrange hotel, but it scores points for location rather than atmosphere.

Eating & Drinking

Chandlers' Grande Brasserie MODERN EUROPEAN ££
(☎01543-416688; Bore St; mains £10-23; ⊙closed lunch Sun) Set in the old Corn Exchange and decked out with natural wood and polished brass, this is where locals go for a big night out, as much for the ambience as for the Mediterranean-inspired main courses.

Information

The **tourist office** (☎01543-412112; www.visitlichfield.com; Lichfield Garrick, Castle Dyke; ⊙9am-5pm Mon-Sat) doubles as the box office for the Lichfield Garrick theatre.

Getting There & Away

The bus station is opposite the main train station on Birmingham Rd. Bus 112 runs to Birmingham (1¼ hours, hourly), while the 825 serves Stafford (1¼ hours, hourly).

Lichfield has two stations. Trains to Birmingham (40 minutes, every 20 minutes) leave from Lichfield City station in the centre. To reach London Euston (£36.50, 2¼hours), travel from Lichfield Trent Valley station to Rugby and change.

Stoke-on-Trent

POP 240,636

At the heart of the Potteries – the famous pottery-producing region of Staffordshire – Stoke-on-Trent is famed for its ceramics, but don't expect cute little artisanal producers. This was where pottery shifted to mass production during the Industrial Revolution, and Stoke is a sprawl of industrial townships tied together by flyovers and bypasses. There are dozens of active potteries that you can visit, including the famous Wedgwood factory, but the town museum presents a good overview for less ceramic-obsessed visitors. Hanley is the official 'city centre' with the main bus station, surrounded by the suburbs of Tunstall, Burslem, Fenton, Longton and Stoke (with the train station).

Sights & Activities

Ceramics are the big money attraction in Stoke-on-Trent. The tourist office has leaflets on all the potteries that are open to the public.

Wedgwood Visitor Centre POTTERY
(☎0870 606 1759; www.wedgwoodvisitorcentre.com; Barlaston; adult/child £9.50/7; ⊙9am-5pm Mon-Fri, 10am-5pm Sat & Sun) Set in attractive parkland, the modern production centre for Josiah Wedgwood's porcelain empire displays an extensive collection of historic pieces, including plenty of Wedgwood's delicate, neoclassical blue-and-white jasperware. You can observe the fascinating industrial process and there's an interesting film on Josiah's life, and his work in the fields of pottery, canal building and the abolishment of slavery.

FREE Potteries Museum & Art Gallery MUSEUM
(☎01782-232323; Bethesda St, Hanley; ⊙10am-5pm Mon-Sat, 1-2pm Sun Nov-Feb) This museum houses an impressively extensive ceramics display, from Toby jugs and jasperware to outrageous ornamental pieces like the Minton Peacock.

Sleeping & Eating

Verdon Guest House B&B £
(☎01782-264244; www.verdonguesthouse.co.uk; 44 Charles St, Hanley; s/d from £26/40; P @ ☰) Set in an unlovely area but central and lovingly kept, this B&B offers comfy rooms a few short steps from the bus station.

Victoria on the Square PUB £
(www.victoriaonthesquare.co.uk; Victoria Sq, Hanley; mains £6-13) Part pub, part cabaret, this reliable local serves decent steaks and other pub staples. It's a popular venue for speed-dating so watch whose eye you catch!

Information

Tourist office (☎01782-236000; www.visitstoke.co.uk; Victoria Hall, Bagnall St, Hanley; ⌚9am-5pm Mon-Fri, 10am-2pm Sat) Ask for a map with the locations of the various potteries.

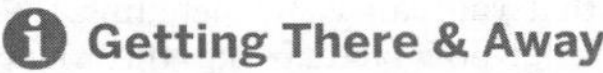

Getting There & Away

From Stoke-on-Trent station in Stoke, trains run to Stafford (20 minutes, half-hourly) and London (£53.50, 1½ hours, two hourly). The Hanley bus station is on Lichfield St:

Alton Towers Bus 32A, one hour, every two hours

London National Express, £23.80, four hours, seven daily

Manchester National Express, £6.50, 1½ hours, eight daily

Stafford First Bus 101, 1¼ hours, hourly

WORCESTERSHIRE

Probably best known for its famous condiment, invented by two Worcester chemists in 1837, Worcestershire marks the transition from the industrial heart of the Midlands to the peaceful countryside of the Welsh Marches. The southern and western fringes of the county burst with lush countryside and sleepy market towns, while the capital is a classic English county town, whose magnificent cathedral inspired the composer Elgar to write some of his greatest works.

THEME PARK SHENANIGANS

Staffordshire is rightly famous for its theme parks, which resound with the screams of adrenalin junkies lured here by fast and furious thrill rides like Thirteen, the world's first vertical drop roller coaster. Buckle up, it's going to be a bumpy ride...

Alton Towers

The phenomenally popular **Alton Towers** (☎0870 444 4455; www.altontowers.com; adult/under 12yr £38/29; ⌚main hours 10am-5.30pm, open later for school holidays, weekends & high season) offers maximum G-forces for your buck. Roller-coaster fans are well catered for – as well as Thirteen, you can ride lying down, sitting down or suspended from the rails on the Nemesis, Oblivion, Air and Rita. Gentler thrills include log flumes, carousels, stage shows, a pirate-themed aquarium and a splashtastic water-park (adult/child £14/10). For discounted entry fees, book online.

The **Dimmingsdale YHA** (☎0845 371 9513; www.yha.org.uk; Oakamoor; dm from £14) is a miniature hostel 2 miles northwest of the park, set in pleasant walking country.

Alton Towers is east of Cheadle off the B5032. Most large towns in the area offer package coach tours (enquire at tourist offices), or you can ride the Alton Towers bus from Stoke-on-Trent, Nottingham and Derby (see the Alton Towers website for details).

Drayton Manor

Alton Towers' closest rival, **Drayton Manor** (☎0844 472 1950; www.draytonmanor.co.uk; adult/child £23/19; ⌚10.30am-5pm Easter-Oct, longer hours May-Sep) has been serving up screams since 1949. Crowd-pleasers include the Apocalypse free-fall tower, voted Britain's scariest ride, and Shockwave, Europe's only stand-up roller coaster. Younger kids will be just as thrilled by Thomas Land, dedicated to the animated steam-train character.

The park currently has no on-site accommodation, but Tamworth is just 2 miles away, with plenty of B&Bs and hotels – contact **Tamworth Tourist Information** (☎01827-709581; Market St) for recommendations. Drayton Manor is on the A4091, between junctions 9 and 10 of the M42. Package coach tours run from Birmingham, or you can take bus 110 from Birmingham Bull St to Fazeley (one hour, every 20 minutes) and walk the last 15 minutes.

Activities

The longest riverside walk in the UK, the 210-mile **Severn Way** (www.severnway.com) winds its way through Worcestershire en route from Plynlimon in Wales to the sea at Bristol. A shorter challenge is the 100-mile **Three Choirs Way**, linking Worcester to Hereford and Gloucester. The Malvern Hills are also prime country for walking, cycling and paragliding, though are no official cycling routes.

Information

Visit Worcestershire (www.visitworcestershire.org)

Getting Around

Worcester is a convenient rail hub, and Kidderminster is the southern railhead of the quaint Severn Valley Railway. Buses connect larger towns, but services to rural areas can be frustratingly infrequent – search the transport pages at www.worcestershire.gov.uk for bus companies and timetables.

Worcester

POP 94,029

Worcester – pronounced *woos*-ter, as in 'Jeeves and...' – has enough historic treasures to forgive the architectural eyesores thrown up during the postwar love affair with all things concrete. The home of Lea & Perrins and that famous sauce (an unlikely combination of fermented tamarinds and anchovies), this ancient cathedral city was the site of the last battle of the Civil War. The defeated Charles II only narrowly escaped the pursuing Roundheads by hiding in an oak tree, an event still celebrated in Worcester every 29 May, when government buildings are decked out with oak sprigs.

Sights

Worcester Cathedral CATHEDRAL
(☎01905-732900; www.worcestercathedral.org.uk; suggested donation £5; ⊙7.30am-6pm) Rising above the River Severn, Worcester's majestic cathedral is best known as the final resting place of Magna Carta signatory King John, damned by history for attempting to seize the throne while his brother Richard the Lionheart was away fighting in the Crusades.

The strong-legged can tackle the 249 steps to the top of the **tower** (adult/child £4/2; ⊙11am-5pm Sat & school holidays Easter-Sep), where Charles II surveyed his troops during the disastrous Battle of Worcester. Hour-long **cathedral tours** (adult/child £3/free; ⊙11am & 2.30pm Mon-Sat Apr-Sep, Sat Oct-Mar) run from the gift shop.

Commandery MUSEUM
(☎01905-361821; www.worcestercitymuseums.org.uk; College St; adult/child £5.40/2.30; ⊙10am-5pm Mon-Sat, 1.30-5pm Sun) The town's history museum is housed in a splendid Tudor building that served as King Charles II's headquarters during the battle of Worcester. Engaging audio guides and interactive exhibits tell the story of Worcester during key periods in its history.

Royal Worcester Porcelain Works MUSEUM
(☎01905-21247; www.worcesterporcelainmuseum.org.uk; Severn St; adult/concession £6/5; ⊙10am-5pm Mon-Sat Easter-Oct, 10.30am-4pm Tue-Sat low season) Up there with Crown Derby and Wedgwood, the Royal Worcester porcelain factory gained an edge over its rivals by picking up the contract to provide fine crockery to the English monarchy. An entertaining audio tour reveals some quirkier sides to the Royal Worcester story, including its brief foray into porcelain dentures and 'portable fonts' designed for cholera outbreaks.

Tours

Worcester Walks (☎01905-726331; www.worcesterwalks.co.uk; adult £4; ⊙11am Mon-Fri) Offers popular half-hour walking tours.

Worcester River Cruises (☎01905-611060; www.worcesterrivercruises.co.uk; adult/child £5/3; ⊙hourly 11am-5pm) Runs 45-minute cruises on the Severn.

Discover History Walking Tours (☎07949 222137; www.discover-history.co.uk; adult £5) Offers a variety of themed historic tours.

Sleeping

Diglis House Hotel HOTEL ££
(☎01905-353518; www.diglishousehotel.co.uk; Severn St; s/d from £75/95; P) This rambling Georgian house has an idyllic setting right by the water, a short stroll from the cathedral. The best rooms have four posters, luxe bathrooms and river views.

Barrington House B&B ££
(☎01905-422965; www.barringtonhouse.eu; 204 Henwick Rd; r £80-90; P@☜) A lovely Georgian house by the river with wonderful views, a pretty walled garden, three plush bedrooms full of brocade and trim and hearty breakfasts served with eggs from the owners' hens.

Eating

Phat Nancy's CAFE £
(☎01905-612658; www.phatnancys.co.uk; 16 New St; sandwiches from £3; ⌚9am-4pm Mon-Sat) A sandwich shop for the Facebook generation, Nancy's has a punk diner vibe and quirky sandwich fillings chalked up on the walls. It's takeaway only, and busy, busy at lunchtime.

Little Ginger Pig CAFE £
(☎01905-338913; www.littlegingerpig.co.uk; 9-11 Copenhagen St; dishes from £6; ⌚8am-3pm Mon-Wed, to 11pm Thu-Sat) The focus is on local produce and independent labels at this airy cafe. Locally sourced meats crop up in everything from the steak dinners to the lunchtime BLTs.

Glasshouse MODERN BRITISH ££
(☎01905-611120; www.theglasshouse.co.uk; Danesbury House, College St; mains £13-19, 2-/3-course set lunch £10-14; ⌚closed dinner Sun) Designer details abound at this magenta-hued restaurant near the Commandery. The Mediterranean-inspired food is as flawless as the decor, but staff are friendly and the mood is unpretentious.

Drinking & Entertainment

Cardinal's Hat PUB
(31 Friar St) Despite looking as English as Tudor ruffs, this atmospheric Worcester institution sells Austrian beers in traditional steins and serves authentic Austrian delicacies at lunchtime.

Marr's Bar LIVE MUSIC
(www.marrsbar.co.uk; 12 Pierpoint St; ⌚from 8pm) The best live-music venue for miles around, Marr's still has its original sprung dance floors from its days as a dance studio. You can bounce on them to your heart's content most nights, thanks to a lively schedule of gigs and shows.

Information

The **tourist office** (☎01905-726311; www.visitworcester.com; Guildhall, High St; ⌚9.30am-5pm Mon-Sat) has stacks of brochures.

Getting There & Around

Worcester Foregate is the main rail hub, but services also run from Worcester Shrub Hill. Regular trains run to London Paddington (£31, 2½ hours, twice hourly) and Hereford (£9.80, 50 minutes, hourly).

The bus station is inside the Crowngate Centre on Friary Walk. Services:

Birmingham Bus 144, 1¾ hours, every 20 minutes (hourly Sunday)

Great Malvern Bus 44, 30 minutes, twice hourly

Ledbury Bus 417, 50 minutes, five daily Monday to Saturday

London National Express, £21.10, four hours, two daily

Great Malvern

POP 35,558

Tumbling down the side of a forested ridge about 7 miles southwest of Worcester, the picturesque spa town of Great Malvern is the gateway to the Malverns, a soaring range of volcanic hills that rise unexpectedly from the surrounding meadows. In Victorian times, the medicinal waters were prescribed as a panacea for everything from gout to 'sore eyes' – should you wish to test the theory, you can sample Malvern water straight from the ground at a series of public wells dotted around the town. In June, classical musicians flock to town for the biannual **Elgar Festival** (www.elgar-festival.com). This festival celebrates the life and works of great English composer Edward Elgar, who lived nearby at Malvern Link.

Sights & Activities

Great Malvern Priory PRIORY
(☎01684-561020; www.greatmalvernpriory.org.uk; Church St; suggested donation £3; ⌚9am-5pm Apr-Oct, reduced hours low season) The 11th-century Great Malvern Priory is packed with remarkable features, from original Norman pillars to surreal modernist stained glass. The choir is enclosed by a screen of 15th-century tiles and the monks' stalls are decorated with delightfully irreverent 14th-century misericords, depicting everything from three rats hanging a cat to the mythological basilisk.

Malvern Museum of Local History MUSEUM
(☎01684-567811; Priory Gatehouse, Abbey Rd; adult/child £2/50p; ⌚10.30am-5pm Mar-Oct, except Wed during school terms) Straddling Abbey Rd in the grand Priory Gatehouse (from 1470), the town museum offers a thorough exploration of the things for which Great Malvern is renowned, including spring waters, medieval monasteries, the Malvern Hills and Morgan motors.

WORTH A TRIP

ELGAR BIRTHPLACE MUSEUM

England's most popular classical composer is celebrated with appropriate pomp and circumstance at **Elgar Birthplace Museum** (☎01905-333224; www.elgarmuseum.org; Lower Broadheath; adult/child £7/3; ⊙11am-5pm, closed late-Dec–Jan), housed in the humble cottage where Edward Elgar was born in 1857. Admission includes an audio tour with musical interludes so that you can appreciate what all the fuss is about.

FREE **Morgan Motor Company** MUSEUM
(☎01684-584580; www.morgan-motor.co.uk; Pickersleigh Rd, Malvern Link; museum admission free, tours £10; ⊙8.30am-5pm Mon-Thu) The Morgan Motor Company has been hand-crafting elegant and beautiful sports cars since 1909, and you can still see the mechanics at work on guided tours of the factory (prebooking essential). The museum has a fine fleet of vintage classics. Bus 44 from Church St runs past the factory.

Tours

Walking tours (adult/child £3/1.50) leave from the tourist office at 10.30am Saturday and 2.30pm Sunday, exploring the town's medieval and Victorian history.

Sleeping

Bredon House HOTEL ££
(☎01684-566990; www.bredonhouse.co.uk; 34 Worcester Rd; s/d from £50/80; P @) A short saunter from the centre, this genteel family- and pet-friendly Victorian hotel backs onto a stunning vista. Rooms are decorated in a quirky but tasteful mix of new and old, and the books, magazines and family photographs dotted around the place make it feel like staying with family.

Como House B&B ££
(☎01684-561486; www.comohouse.co.uk; Como Rd; s/d £40/62; P @ ᯤ) This handsome Malvern-stone house benefits from a quiet location away from the central bustle. Rooms are snug, the garden is a delight and the mood is restoratively calm. The owners will pick you up from the station and drop you off by the walking trails.

Abbey Hotel HOTEL £££
(☎01684-892332; www.savora.co.uk; Abbey Rd; s/d from £130/140; P @) Cloaked by a crazy tangle of vines, like a Brother's Grimm fairy-tale castle, this stately property offers Great Malvern's grandest bedrooms, in a prime location by the museum and priory.

Eating

Pepper and Oz MODERN EUROPEAN ££
(☎01684-562676; www.pepperandoz.co.uk; 23 Abbey Rd; mains £8-18.50; ⊙closed Sun & Mon) Wedged in beside the museum, this bijou brasserie has a lovely alfresco terrace and a superior wine list. The menu is full of locally sourced classics like smoked duck and Herefordshire steaks, with special promos for pre-theatre diners.

Anupam INDIAN ££
(☎01684-573814; www.anupam.co.uk; 85 Church St; mains £9-14) Hidden in an arcade just off the main road, this stylish place has a menu that roams the subcontinent, from hearty Mughlai curries to Keralan treats like tandoori kingfish.

Entertainment

Malvern Theatres THEATRE
(www.malvern-theatres.co.uk; Grange Rd) One of the country's best provincial theatres, this long-established cultural hub packs in a lively program of classical music, dance, comedy, drama and cinema. Several nearby restaurants offer good value pre-theatre menus.

Theatre of Small Convenience THEATRE
(www.wctheatre.co.uk; Edith Walk) This curious place is set in a converted Victorian public lavatory decked out with theatrical Italianate flourishes. With just 12 seats, and a program that runs from puppet shows to opera, it feels like something cooked up by Monty Python's Terry Gilliam.

Information

The **tourist office** (☎01684-892289; www.malvernhills.gov.uk; 21 Church St; ⊙10am-5pm) is a mine of walking and cycling information. The post office on the square has a bureau de change.

Getting There & Around

The train station is east of the centre, off Ave Rd. Trains run to Hereford (£6.90, 35 minutes, hourly), Worcester (15 to 20 minutes, two or three hourly) and Ledbury (13 minutes, hourly).

WALKING IN THE MALVERN HILLS

The jack-in-the-box Malvern Hills, which dramatically pop up out of the Severn plains on the boundary between Worcestershire and Herefordshire, rise to the lofty peak of the Worcester Beacon (419m), reached by a steep 3-mile climb above Great Malvern. More than 100 miles of trails traipse over the various summits, which are mostly capped by exposed grassland, offering the kind of views that inspire orchestral movements. The tourist office has racks of pamphlets covering popular hikes, including a map of the mineral water springs, wells and fountains dotted around the town and the surrounding hills. The enthusiast-run website www.malverntrail.co.uk is also a goldmine of useful walking information.

National Express runs one bus daily to London (£21.70, 3½ hours). For Worcester (30 minutes, twice hourly), take bus 44 or 362/363 (the Malvern Link).

HEREFORDSHIRE

Slumbering quietly in the English countryside, Herefordshire is a patchwork of fields, hills and cute little black-and-white villages, many dating back to the Tudor era and beyond. Getting around is complicated by infrequent bus services and meandering country lanes, but taking the scenic route is part of the appeal of this laid-back rural idyll.

Activities

As well as the famous Offa's Dyke Path – see boxed text, p718 – walkers can follow the **Herefordshire Trail** (www.herefordshiretrail.com) on a 150-mile circular loop through Leominster, Ledbury, Ross-on-Wye and Kington. Only slightly less ambitious is the 107-mile **Wye Valley Walk** (www.wyevalleywalk.org), which runs from Chepstow in Wales through Herefordshire and back out again to Rhayader. Then there's the **Three Choirs Way**, a 100-mile route connecting the cathedrals of Hereford, Worcester and Gloucester. Cyclists can trace the **Six Castles Cycleway** (NCN Route 44) from Hereford to Leominster and Shrewsbury, or NCN Route 68 to Great Malvern and Worcester. Climbers and canoeists make a beeline for the gorge of the River Wye at Symonds Yat.

Information

Visit Herefordshire (www.visitherefordshire.co.uk)

Getting Around

Trains run frequently to Hereford, Leominster and Ledbury, with regular bus connections on to the rest of the county. For bus timetables, search for 'bus' at www.herefordshire.gov.uk. Alternatively, pick up the chunky *Bus and Train Timetable* from any tourist office (50p).

Hereford

POP 56,353

Best known for prime steaks, cider and the Pretenders (three of the original band members were local boys), Hereford dozes in the midst of apple orchards and rolling pastures at the heart of the Marches. Straddling the River Wye, the town seems more preoccupied with agriculture than tourism, but there are some interesting things to see, including a vast Norman cathedral whose organist, George Sinclair, was a mentor to the young Edward Elgar.

Sights

Hereford Cathedral CATHEDRAL

(☎01432-374200; www.herefordcathedral.org; 5 College Cloisters; suggested donation £4; ⏰9.15am Evensong) After Welsh marauders torched the original Saxon cathedral, the Norman rulers of Hereford erected a larger, grander cathedral on the same site, which was subsequently remodelled in a succession of medieval architectural styles. Memorials to past bishops – some worn smooth with age – are dotted around the nave and transept.

However, all fades into insignificance compared to the magnificent **Mappa Mundi** (adult/child £4.50/3.50; ⏰10am-5pm Mon-Sat May-Sep, to 4pm Mon-Sat Oct-Apr), a piece of calfskin vellum intricately painted with some rather fantastical assumptions about the layout of the globe in around 1290 – see boxed text, p421. The same wing contains the world's largest surviving chained library, with rare manuscripts manacled to the shelves.

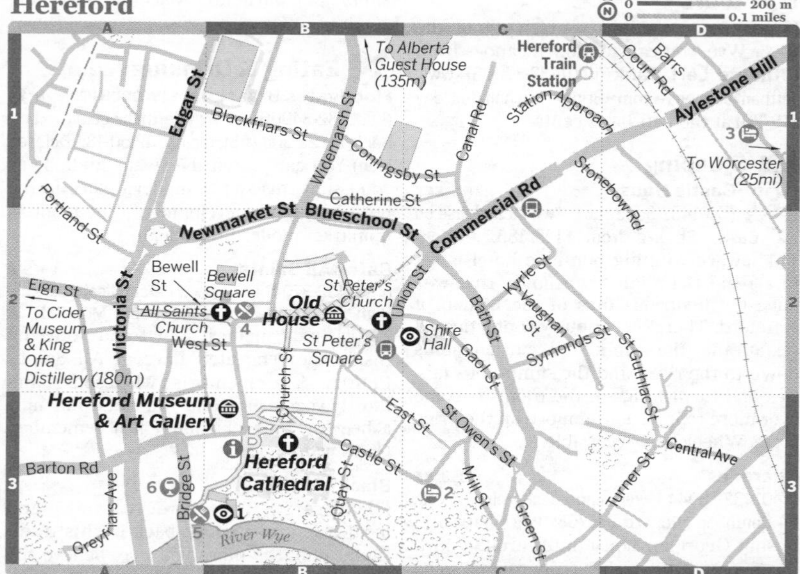

The cathedral comes alive with Evensong at 5.30pm Monday to Saturday and at 3.30pm on Sunday, and every three years in August it holds the famous **Three Choirs Festival** (www.3choirs.org), shared with Gloucester and Worcester Cathedrals.

FREE **Old House** MUSEUM
(☎01432-260694; ⏲10am-5pm Tue-Sat year-round, plus to 4pm Sun Apr-Sep) Marooned in a sea of shops, this wonderfully creaky black-and-white, three-storey wooden house was built in 1621. Inside you can see a series of medieval rooms full of period furniture and carved wood panelling.

FREE **Hereford Museum & Art Gallery** MUSEUM
(☎01432-260692; Broad St; ⏲10am-5pm Tue-Sat year-round, plus to 4pm Sun Apr-Sep) The quirky collection at the town museum has displays on just about everything from 19th-century witches' curses to Roman antiquities. There's also some dressing-up gear to keep kids entertained.

Cider Museum & King Offa Distillery BREWERY
(☎01432-354207; www.cidermuseum.co.uk; 21 Ryelands St; adult/child £4/2.50; ⏲10am-5pm Tue-Sat Apr-Oct, 11am-3pm Tue-Sat Nov-Mar) The name is the giveaway at this brewery and museum. Displays cover cider-making history, and you can sample the delicious modern brews. Look for the fine *costrels* (minibarrels) used by agricultural workers to carry their wages, which were partially paid in cider. To reach the brewery, follow Eign St west from the centre and turn south along Ryelands St.

Hereford

Top Sights
Hereford Cathedral B3
Hereford Museum & Art Gallery B3
Old House B2

Activities, Courses & Tours
1 Ultimate Left Bank B3

Sleeping
2 Castle House C3
3 Charades D1

Eating
4 Cafe@All Saints B2
5 Floodgates Brasserie A3

Drinking
6 Black Lion A3

Tours

If you fancy guiding yourself along the River Wye, you can rent open canoes from **Ultimate Left Bank** (01432-360057; www.leftbankcanoehire.com; Bridge St; half/full day £15/20) at the Left Bank centre.

Sleeping

TOP CHOICE Castle House HOTEL £££
(01432-356321; www.castlehse.co.uk; Castle St; s/d from £125/185; P @) This award-winning boutique hotel is set in a regal Georgian town house that was once the luxurious digs of the Bishop of Hereford. There's a seriously sophisticated restaurant, the sun-kissed garden spills down to the river, and the sumptuous fabrics and furnishings in the rooms become ever more refined as you move up the price scale. Wheelchair accessible.

Charades B&B ££
(01432-269444; www.charadeshereford.co.uk; 34 Southbank Rd; s/d £45/65; P @) This imposing Georgian house built around 1870 has five inviting, rather frilly rooms, some with soothing countryside views. The house itself has character in spades – look for old service bells in the hall. It's handy for the bus station, but a 1km walk from the cathedral.

Other possibilities:

Alberta Guest House B&B £
(01432-270313; www.thealbertaguesthouse.co.uk; 5-13 Newtown Rd; s/d £30/45; P) Simple but warm and welcoming; in the north of town.

BLACK-AND-WHITE VILLAGES

A triangle of Tudor England survives almost untouched in northwest Herefordshire, where higgledy-piggledy black-and-white houses cluster round idyllic village greens, seemingly oblivious to the modern world. A delightful 40-mile circular drive follows the **Black-and-White-Village Trail**, meandering past the most handsome timber-framed buildings, starting at Leominster and looping round through Eardisland and Kington (the southern terminus of the Mortimer Trail from Ludlow). You can pick up guides to exploring the villages by car, bus or bicycle from any tourist office.

Eating & Drinking

Floodgates Brasserie MODERN EUROPEAN ££
(01432-349000; www.leftbank.co.uk; Left Bank, 20-22 Bridge St; mains £12.50-18; closed Mon) You can watch the swans glide by as you eat at this swish, modern place in the posh Left Bank development. The menu is upmarket modern European.

Cafe@All Saints CAFE £
(01432-370414; www.cafeatallsaints.co.uk; High St; mains £6-9; 8am-5pm Mon-Sat) A surprisingly modern and trendy offering inside the renovated nave of All Saint's Church. The menu is wholesome and mostly vegetarian, and you can even enjoy a beer or glass of wine – just remember, God's watching.

Black Lion PUB
(31 Bridge St) The more real ales and local ciders you knock back in this traditional pub, the more you may believe the tales that there are resident ghosts from the site's history as a monastery, an orphanage, a brothel and even a Chinese restaurant.

Information

Tourist office (01432-268430; www.visitherefordshire.co.uk; 1 King St; 10am-5pm Mon-Sat) Opposite the cathedral.

Getting There & Around

The bus station is on Commercial Rd, northeast of the town centre. National Express goes to London (£21.70, 4½ hours, three daily) and Gloucester (£6.20, 1¼ hours, five daily). Local services:

Hay-on-Wye Bus 39/39A, one hour, twice hourly (three Sunday services)

Ledbury Bus 476, 30 minutes, hourly (five Sunday services)

Ludlow Bus 492, 1¼ hours, twice hourly (three Sunday services)

Ross-on-Wye Bus 38, 45 minutes, hourly (six Sunday services)

Worcester Bus 420, one hour, twice hourly (four services Sunday)

The train station is northeast of the centre, with hourly trains to Birmingham (£13.20, 1½ hours) and London Paddington (£56.70, three hours), either direct or with a change in Newport, South Wales.

THE WORLD AS VIEWED FROM HEREFORD

There are many medieval *mappa mundi* (maps of the world) in existence, but the vellum map held by Hereford Cathedral is perhaps the most intricate. Created by a Lincolnshire monk named Richard de Bello in the 13th century, the map is a pictorial representation of the total world knowledge of the most informed men in England at the time it was created – which was based largely on hearsay, rumours and the exaggerations of drunken seafarers. Consequently, the oceans are populated by mermaids and sea serpents, and landmasses play host to dragons, half-plant–half-human mandrakes and sciapods, mythical inhabitants of India, with one giant foot used to shelter their heads from the sun. Author CS Lewis drew inspiration from this map for some of the more outlandish creatures in his Narnia books.

Ross-On-Wye

POP 10,085

Laid-back Ross-on-Wye, which sits prettily on a red sandstone bluff over a kink in the River Wye, is an easy paddle from Symonds Yat, but there are enough sights to warrant a trip by road. The town was propelled to fame in the 18th century by Alexander Pope and Samuel Taylor Coleridge, who penned tributes to philanthropist John Kyrle, Man of Ross, who dedicated his life and fortune to the poor of the parish.

Sights & Activities

The 17th-century **Market House** (☎01989-260675; ⏲10am-5pm Mon-Sat & 10.30am-4pm Sun Apr-Oct, 10.30am-4pm Tue-Sun Nov-Mar) sits atop weathered sandstone columns in the Market Pl; inside the salmon-pink building is an agreeably hand-crafted heritage centre with local-history displays.

Crowning the hilltop, pin-straight **St Mary's Church** (Church St; ⏲9am-5pm) is a 13th-century construction with a fine east window and grand alabaster memorials, including the grave of John Kyrle and the outrageously ostentatious tombs of the noble Rudhall family. Behind the church, Royal Parade runs to the edge of the bluff, lined with realistic-looking but ersatz **castle ruins**, constructed in 1833.

Sleeping & Eating

White House Guest House GUESTHOUSE ££
(☎01989-763572; www.whitehouseross.com; Wye St; s/d £45/65; P @) This 18th-century stone house has a great location across the road from the River Wye. Vivid window boxes give it a splash of colour, and the rooms, decorated in shades of burgundy and crisp white, are quiet and comfortable.

Bridge at Wilton RESTAURANT, GUESTHOUSE ££
(☎01989-562655; www.bridge-house-hotel.com; Wilton; s/d from £80/98; P) A distinguished Georgian country house restaurant a mile west of Ross, with smart rooms and a highly praised menu of modern British food.

Drinking

Hope & Anchor PUB
(Wye St; mains £6-17) At the foot of the bluff on the riverside, this friendly pub is a great place to while away the time; tables spread right down to the water's' edge, attracting lots of visiting canoeists in summer.

Information

Tourist office (☎01989-562768; tic-ross@herefordshire.gov.uk; Edde Cross St; ⏲9am-5pm Mon-Sat, to 4pm low season) Has

WORTH A TRIP

GOLDEN VALLEY

Nudging the foot of the Black Mountains, this lush valley was made famous by children's author CS Lewis, of Narnia acclaim. Following the meandering River Dore, the valley is peppered with historic relics, including **Arthur's Stone**, a 5000-year-old Neolithic chamber-tomb near the village of Dorestone, and the handsome 12th-century **Dore Abbey** (www.doreabbey.org.uk) in the appropriately named village of Abbey Dore. Bus 39 between Hereford and Hay-on-Wye (five daily, Monday to Saturday) follows the valley, stopping at Dorestone and Peterchurch. For accommodation and dining ideas, visit www.herefordholidays.co.uk.

nformation on sights and walks – ask for the *Ross-on-Wye Heritage Trail* booklet (50p).

Getting There & Around

The bus stand is on Cantilupe Rd. From Monday to Saturday, bus 38 runs hourly to Hereford (45 minutes), and bus 33 runs hourly to Gloucester (40 minutes). For Monmouth, take bus 34 (45 minutes, every two hours Monday to Saturday).

For local exploring, you can hire bikes from **Revolutions** (01989-562639; www.revolutionsatross.co.uk; 48 Broad St; per day from £10).

Forest of Dean

The Forest of Dean spills over the Gloucestershire border near the village of Goodrich, just off the A40 between Ross-on-Wye and Monmouth. The River Wye skirts the edge of the forest, offering glorious views to canoeists who paddle out from the delightful village of Symonds Yat.

GOODRICH

Seemingly part of its craggy bedrock, **Goodrich Castle** (EH; 01600-890538; adult/child £5.50/2.80; 10am-5pm Apr-Oct, to 6pm Jul & Aug, 10am-4pm Wed-Sun Nov-Mar) is an exceptionally complete medieval castle, topped by a superb 12th-century keep that affords spectacular views. A small exhibition tells the story of the castle from its 11th-century origins to its demise in the 1600s.

Welsh Bicknor YHA (0845 371 9666; www.yha.org.uk; dm from £10; Apr-Oct; P) is an austere-looking former Victorian rectory surveying a grand sweep of countryside from its lovely riverside grounds. It's on the Wye Valley Walk, 1½ miles from Goodrich; follow the signed road near Goodrich Castle and take the right fork where the road splits.

Bus 34 stops here every two hours on its way between Ross (20 minutes) and Monmouth (20 minutes), except on Sundays.

SYMONDS YAT

Right on the edge of the forest, squeezed between the River Wye and the towering limestone outcrop known as **Symonds Yat Rock**, Symonds Yat East is an endearing tangle of pubs and guest houses, with great walks and an excellent canoeing centre and campsite right in the middle of the village.

An ancient hand-hauled ferry (adult/child/bicycle £1/50p/50p) crosses the Wye to Symonds Yat West on the other side of the valley, where you'll find a riverside caravan park and some family-friendly amusements for campers.

Activities

This area is renowned for canoeing and rock climbing and there's also good hiking and cycling in the nearby Forest of Dean – the scenic **Peregrine Path** follows the riverbanks from Symonds Yat East to Monmouth.

The most popular walk from Symonds Yat East picks its way up the side of the 504m **Symonds Yat Rock**, affording fabulous views of river and valley. In July and August, you may be lucky enough to spot peregrine falcons soaring by the drop-off.

Rock climbers follow a series of mainly trad routes directly up the face of the cliff, but routes in the easier grades tend to be very polished, and rock falls are common – bring a varied rack and wear your helmet. *Symonds Yat* by John Willson is the definitive guidebook.

The **Wyedean Canoe Centre** (01594-833238; www.wyedean.co.uk; half-day hire from £28; 8.30am-8.30pm) hires out canoes and kayaks, and also organises multiday kayaking trips, white-water trips, and caving and climbing.

Fair-weather water-babies can enjoy the Wye without the hard work on a sedate, 40-minute gorge cruise run by **Kingfisher Cruises** (01600-891063; adult/child £5.50/3), leaving from beside the ferry crossing.

Sleeping & Eating

Garth Cottage B&B **££**
(01600-890364; www.garthcottage-symondsyat.com; Symonds Yat East; B&B per person £37.50; Apr-Oct; P) The pick of accommodation on the east side, this friendly, family-run B&B sits by the riverside near the ferry crossing, and has spotlessly maintained, bright rooms with river views.

Wyedean Canoe Centre Campsite CAMPSITE **£**
(01594-833238; www.wyedean.co.uk; sites per adult/child £9.50/6) This popular canoe centre has a lovely campsite with a clean bathroom block, set right by the river – perfect for a weekend of splashing around in the Wye. Rates drop by 30% from Monday to Thursday.

Royal Lodge HOTEL ££
(☎01600-890238; www.royallodgesymondsyat.co.uk; Symonds Yat East; mains £5-17, s/d from £35/80) With a pretty tree-sheltered garden, neat modern rooms and a fine restaurant, the Royal Lodge is great value. It's worth swinging by for a drink in the pretty gardens, even if you don't stay here.

Getting There & Away

There is no direct public transport, but bus 34 between Ross-on-Wye and Monmouth can drop you off on the main road 1.5 miles from the village (services run every two hours). Bikes are available for hire from the Royal Hotel (Symonds Yat East) for £15 per day.

Ledbury

POP 8491

An atmospheric little town creaking with history and dotted with antique shops, Ledbury is a favourite destination for day trippers. The best way to pass the time is to wander the crooked black-and-white streets, which zero in on a delightfully leggy medieval market house. The timber-framed structure is precariously balanced atop a series of wooden posts supposedly taken from the wrecked ships of the Spanish Armada.

Almost impossibly cute Church Lane runs its cobbled way from the High St to the town church, crowded with tilting timber-framed buildings, like JK Rowling's Diagon Alley.

At the top of the lane lies the 12th-century church of **St Michael and All Angels** (www.ledburyparishchurch.org.uk; ⏲8.30am-6pm, to 4pm low season) with a splendid 18th-century spire and tower divided from its medieval nave.

Sleeping & Eating

The town pubs offer reasonably priced meals, but budget travellers will struggle to find cheap accommodation.

Feathers Hotel PUB/HOTEL £££
(☎01531-635266; www.feathers-ledbury.co.uk; High St; mains £10-17, s/d from £89.50/135; P) This charming black-and-white Tudor hotel looms over the main road. Rooms in the oldest part of the building come with slanting floorboards, painted beams and much more character than the modern rooms. There's an atmospheric wood-panelled restaurant and a swimming pool.

Cameron & Swan DELI-CAFE £
(☎01531-636791; www.cameronandswan.co.uk; 15 The Homend; mains £6-7; ⏲breakfast & lunch Mon-Sat) A bustling cafe serving tasty deli sandwiches, giant meringues and other tasty homemade treats in a bright, airy dining room.

Information

Tourist office (☎01531-636147; www.visitledbury.co.uk; 3 The Homend; ⏲10am-5pm Mon-Sat Apr-Oct, to 4pm Nov-Mar) Just off the High St, behind St Katherine's Chapel, this helpful office has information on tours of the town.

Getting There & Away

Trains run to Great Malvern (15 minutes, hourly), Hereford (£5, 20 minutes, hourly), Worcester (£5.40, 30 minutes, hourly) and further afield. Bus 476 runs to Hereford hourly (40 minutes, every two hours on Sunday); bus 132 runs to Gloucester (one hour, hourly Monday to Saturday).

Eastnor Castle

Built more for fancy than fortification, the extravagant medieval-revival folly of **Eastnor Castle** (☎01531-633160; www.eastnorcastle.com; adult/child £8.50/5.50, grounds only £5.50/3.50; ⏲11am-4.30pm Sun-Thu Jul & Aug, Sun only Jun & Sep) is still the family home of the grandchildren of the first Earl Somers, who constructed this elaborate confection in 1810. The grounds are delightful and the opulent interior continues the romantic theme, with Gothic and Italianate flourishes and the kinds of antiques that make collectors weak at the knees.

The castle is just over 2 miles east of Ledbury on the A438; a taxi from Ledbury station will cost around £10.

SHROPSHIRE

Travellers in search of England as it was before the arrival of the chain stores and out-of-town shopping centres will find their dreams fulfilled in peaceful Shropshire, a glorious scattering of hills, castles and timber-framed villages tucked against the Welsh border.

Highlights include food-obsessed Ludlow, industrial Ironbridge and the beautiful Shropshire hills, which offer the best walking and cycling in the Marches.

SIPPING YOUR WAY AROUND CIDER COUNTRY

Crisp, dry ciders have been produced in Herefordshire since medieval times. The **Herefordshire Cider Route** (www.ciderroute.co.uk) drops in on numerous local cider producers, where you can try before you buy, and then totter off to the next cidery. Putting road safety first, tourist offices have maps and guide booklets to help you explore by bus or bicycle.

If you only have time to visit one cider-maker, make it **Westons Cider Mills** (☎01531-660233; www.westons-cider.co.uk; The Bounds; ⊙9am-4.30pm Mon-Fri, 10am-4pm Sat & Sun), whose house brew is even served in the Houses of Parliament! Informative tours (adult/child £6/3.25, 1¼ hours) start at 11am, 12.30pm and 2.30pm, with free tastings for the grown-ups. Westons is just under a mile west of Much Marcle.

Activities

WALKING

Between Shrewsbury and Ludlow, the landscape rucks up into dramatic folds, with spectacular trails climbing the flanks of Wenlock Edge and the Long Mynd near Church Stretton – see those sections for details. The county is also crossed by long-distance trails, including the famous **Offa's Dyke Path** and the popular **Shropshire Way**, which meanders around Ludlow, Craven Arms and Church Stretton. For general information on walking in the county, visit www.shropshirewalking.co.uk.

CYCLING

Mountain bikers head for the muddy tracks that scramble over the Long Mynd near Church Stretton, or the rugged forest trails of **Hopton Wood**, near Craven Arms, while road riders aim for the **Six Castles Cycleway** (NCN 44), which runs for 58 miles from Shrewsbury to Leominster.

Tourists offices sell copies of *Cycling for Pleasure in the Marches,* a pack of five maps and guides covering the entire county. Alternatively, you can download cycling pamphlets free from www.shropshirecycling.co.uk.

Information

Shropshire Tourism (www.shropshiretourism.co.uk)

Getting Around

Shrewsbury is the local transport hub, and handy rail services go to Church Stretton, Craven Arms and Ludlow. The invaluable *Shropshire Bus & Train Map,* available free from tourist offices, shows useful routes. **Shropshire Hills Shuttles** (www.shropshirehillsshuttles.co.uk) runs useful bus services along popular hiking routes on weekends and bank holidays.

Shrewsbury

POP 67,126

A delightful jumble of winding medieval streets and timbered Tudor houses leaning at precarious angles, Shrewsbury (*shroos-*

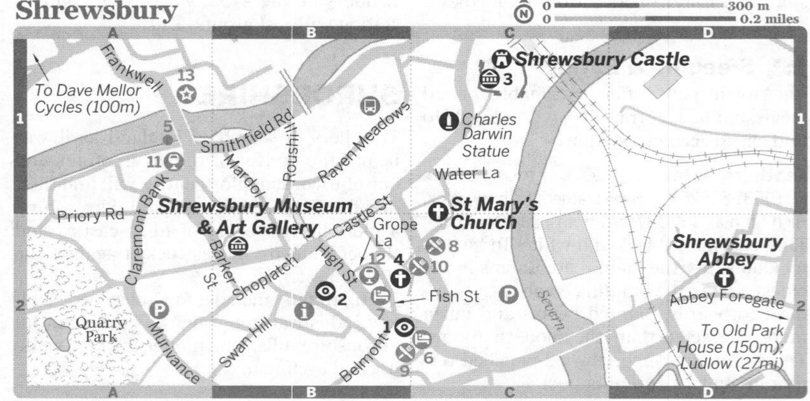

bree) was a crucial front in the conflict between English and Welsh in medieval times. The town was once an important centre for the wool trade, but its biggest claim to fame is being the birthplace of Charles Darwin (1809–82), who went on to rock the world with his theory of evolution.

Sights

Shrewsbury Abbey ABBEY

(☎01743-232723; www.shrewsburyabbey.com; Abbey Foregate; suggested donation adult/child £2/1; ⌚10.30am-3pm Mon-Sat, 11.30am-2.30pm Sun) Famous as the setting for Ellis Peters' *Chronicles of Brother Cadfael,* the lovely red-sandstone Shrewsbury Abbey is all that remains of a vast, cruciform Benedictine monastery founded in 1083. Nevertheless, you can still see some impressive Norman, Early English and Victorian features, including an exceptional 14th-century west window.

FREE **Shrewsbury Museum & Art Gallery** MUSEUM

(☎01743-281205; www.shrewsburymuseums.com; Barker St; ⌚10am-5pm Mon-Sat, to 4pm Sun May-Sep) The town museum is currently housed in the timbered, Tudor-era Rowley's House, with an eclectic selection of exhibits, from Roman treasures to Darwin memorabilia. In 2012 the museum and tourist office will move to the Music Hall on the Square – visit the website for the latest news.

Shrewsbury Castle CASTLE

(☎01743-358516; adult/child £2.50/1.50; ⌚10.30am-5pm Fri-Wed Jun-Sep, 10.30am-4pm Mon-Wed & Fri-Sat Feb-May & Sep-Dec) Hewn from sunset-red Shropshire sandstone, the town castle contains the **Shropshire Regimental Museum**, plus fine views from its battlements.

St Mary's Church CHURCH

(St Mary's St; ⌚10am-4pm Mon-Sat) The magnificent spire of this roughly hewn medieval church is one of the highest in England, and the interior is graced with an impressive collection of stained glass, including a 14th-century window depicting the Tree of Jesse, a Biblical representation of the lineage of Jesus.

Other Sights

The most handsome buildings can be found on the narrow lanes surrounding **St Alkmond's Church**, particularly along **Fish St** and amorously named **Grope Lane**. At the bottom of the High St on Wyle Cop, the seriously overhanging **Henry Tudor House** was where Henry VII stayed before the Battle of Bosworth.

At the other end of the High St in a cute cobbled square is Shrewsbury's 16th-century **Old Market Hall** (www.oldmarkethall.co.uk), whose upper levels contain the town's pocket-sized cinema.

Tours

Guided **walking tours** (adult/child £4/2.50) leave the tourist office at 2.30pm from Monday to Saturday, and at 11am on Sunday. Tours only run on Saturday from November to April.

Alternatively, enjoy Shrewsbury from the water on board the **Sabrina** (☎01743-369741;

Shrewsbury

Top Sights
Shrewsbury Abbey ... D2
Shrewsbury Castle ... C1
Shrewsbury Museum & Art Gallery ... B2
St Mary's Church ... C1

Sights
1 Henry Tudor House ... B2
2 Old Market Hall ... B2
3 Shropshire Regimental Museum ... C1
4 St Alkmond's Church ... B2

Activities, Courses & Tours
5 Sabrina Boat Trips ... A1

Sleeping
6 Lion Hotel ... C2
7 Tudor House ... B2

Eating
8 Drapers Hall ... C2
9 Good Life Wholefood Restaurant ... B2
10 Mad Jack's ... C2

Drinking
11 Armoury ... A1
12 Three Fishes ... B2

Entertainment
Old Market Hall Film & Digital Media Centre ... (see 2)
13 Theatre Severn ... A1

www.sabrinaboat.co.uk; from £5), which cruises the River Severn. Trips leave roughly hourly between 10am and 4pm (March to October).

Sleeping

As well as the following choices, pretty Abbey Foregate is lined with B&Bs.

Lion Hotel HOTEL ££
(☎01753-353107; www.thelionhotelshrewsbury.co.uk; Wyle Cop; s/d from £80/98; P) A gilded wooden lion crowns the doorway of this famous coaching inn, decked out inside with portraits of lords and ladies in powdered wigs. The guest lounge is warmed by a grand stone fireplace and the rooms are note-perfect, down to the period-pattern fabrics and ceramic water jugs.

Old Park House HOTEL ££
(☎01743-289750; 37 Abbey Foregate; s/d £60/75; P@) Despite the age of this fine old building you won't find any faux Tudor interiors here. Fifteenth-century timbered rooms have received a tasteful modern makeover, with bright contemporary fabrics and quirky artwork.

Tudor House B&B ££
(☎01743-351735; www.tudorhouseshrewsbury.com; 2 Fish St; s/d from £69/79; @) A bowing frontage festooned with hanging baskets and window boxes sets the scene at this Tudor cottage on a delightful Tudor lane. It's handy for everything in the centre, and rooms are adorned with shimmery fabrics and flowery trim. Not all rooms have an en suite.

Eating

Drapers Hall FRENCH £££
(☎01743-344679; St Mary's Pl; mains £14-25, s/d from £100/120) The sense of history is palpable in this beautifully preserved 16th-century hall, fronted by an elegant Elizabethan facade. Award-wining Anglo-French haute cuisine is served in rooms adorned with wood panelling and artwork, and upstairs are some spectacular, heirloom-filled rooms.

Mad Jack's MODERN EUROPEAN ££
(☎01743-358870; www.madjacksuk.com; 15 St Mary's St; mains £11-16, s/d from £70/80) A classy place that straddles the boundary between cafe, restaurant and bar, with an elegant dining room and a plant-filled courtyard. The menu features inventive modern European cuisine prepared with ingredients from local farms and suppliers. There are swish contemporary bedrooms upstairs.

Good Life Wholefood Restaurant VEGETARIAN £
(☎01743-350455; Barracks Passage; mains £3.50-7; ⊙lunch Mon-Sat) Healthy, freshly prepared vegetarian food is the name of the game in this cute little refuge off Wyle Cop. Favourites include quiches, nut loaf, salads, soups and veggie lasagne.

Drinking

Armoury PUB
(www.armoury-shrewsbury.co.uk; Victoria Ave) Despite being a modern invention, the Armoury still manages to feel like it has been here for generations. Inside this inviting pub are long wooden tables, dotted around among floor-to-ceiling bookshelves and assorted collectibles.

Three Fishes PUB
(4 Fish St) The quintessential creaky Tudor alehouse, it has a jolly publican, mellow regulars and hops hanging from the 15th-century beamed ceiling.

Entertainment

To view mainstream and art-house movies in a charming Elizabethan setting, visit the **Old Market Hall Film & Digital Media Centre** (www.oldmarkethall.co.uk; The Square).

Theatre Severn THEATRE
(www.theatresevern.co.uk; Frankwell Quay) This expansive riverside theatre and music venue opened in 2009 to great acclaim, hosting everything from pop gigs and comedy nights to plays and classical concerts.

Information

Royal Shrewsbury Hospital (☎01743-261000; Mytton Oak Rd)

Tourist office (☎01743-281200; www.visitshrewsbury.com; Shrewsbury Museum & Art Gallery, Barker St; ⊙9.30am-5.30pm Mon-Sat, 10am-4pm Sun May-Sep, 10am-5pm Mon-Sat Oct-Apr) Come for walking tours and stacks of brochures.

Getting There & Away

Bus

The bus station is beside the river on Smithfield Rd. Bus 435 runs to Ludlow (1½ hours, hourly Monday to Saturday), via Church Stretton. Other useful services:

Birmingham National Express, £6.80, 1½ hours, twice daily

Ironbridge Bus 96, 35 minutes, every two hours Monday to Saturday

London National Express, £21.30, 4½ hours, twice daily

Train

From the train station at the bottom of Castle Foregate, trains run half-hourly to Ludlow (£9.60, 30 minutes, hourly at weekends). Trains also go direct to London Marylebone (£52, 2¾ hours, four daily Monday to Saturday, two Sunday services). Alternatively, take one of the regular trains to Birmingham or Crewe and change.

If you're bound for Wales, **Arriva Trains Wales** (☎0845 606 1660; www.arrivatrainswales.co.uk) runs to Swansea (£33.80, 3¾ hours, hourly) and Holyhead (£34.80, three hours, hourly).

Getting Around

You can hire bikes at **Dave Mellor Cycles** (www.davemellorcycles.com; 9 New St).

Attingham Park

The most impressive of Shropshire's stately homes, **Attingham Park** (NT; ☎01743-708123; house & grounds adult/child £8.50/5.15, grounds only £3.80/2; ⊙house 11am-5.30pm Thu-Tue mid-Mar–early Nov, grounds 9am-6am daily) was built in imposing neoclassical style in 1785. With its grand columned facade and manicured lawns, and a stagecoach turning-circle in the courtyard, the house could have been plucked straight from a bodice-ripping period drama. Inside you can see an elegant picture gallery by John Nash, plus two wings, decorated in very different Regency styles – highlights include the cherub-filled ladies' boudoir and the grand dining room, laid out as if the banquet guests could arrive any minute. Home to some 300 fallow deer, the landscaped grounds swirl around an ornamental lake.

Attingham Park is 4 miles southeast of Shrewsbury at Atcham – take bus 81 or 96 (18 minutes, six daily Monday to Friday, less frequently at weekends).

Ironbridge Gorge

Strolling or cycling through the woods, hills and villages of this peaceful river gorge, it's hard to believe such a sleepy enclave could really have been the birthplace of the Industrial Revolution. Nevertheless, it was here that Abraham Darby perfected the art of smelting iron ore with coke in 1709, making it possible to mass-produce cast iron for the first time.

Abraham Darby's son, Abraham Darby II, invented a new forging process for producing single beams of iron, allowing Abraham Darby III to astound the world with the first-ever iron bridge, constructed in 1779. The bridge remains the focal point of this World Heritage Site, and 10 very different museums tell the story of the Industrial Revolution in the very buildings where it took place.

Sights & Activities

The Ironbridge museums are administered by the **Ironbridge Gorge Museum Trust** (☎01952-884391; www.ironbridge.org.uk), and all are open from 10am to 5pm from late March to early November, unless stated otherwise. You can buy tickets as you go, but the good-value **passport ticket** (adult/child £21.95/14.25) allows year-round entry to all of the sites.

Museum of the Gorge MUSEUM
(The Wharfage; adult/child £3.60/2.35) Kick off your visit at the Museum of the Gorge, which offers an overview of the World Heritage Site using film, photos and 3D models. Housed in a Gothic warehouse by the river, it's filled with entertaining, hands-on exhibits.

Coalbrookdale Museum of Iron MUSEUM
(Wellington Rd; adult/child; £7.40/4.95) Set in the brooding buildings of Abraham Darby's original iron foundry, the Museum of Iron contains some excellent interactive exhibits. Combined tickets with Darby Houses also available.

Darby Houses MUSEUMS
(☎01952-433522; adult/child £4.60/3; ⊙Apr-Oct) Just uphill from the Museum of Iron are these beautifully restored 18th-century homes, which housed generations of the Darby family in gracious but modest Quaker comfort.

Iron Bridge & Tollhouse BRIDGE
The flamboyant, arching **Iron Bridge** that gives the area its name was constructed to flaunt the new technology invented by the inventive Darby family. At the time of its construction in 1779, nobody could believe that anything so large could be built from cast iron without collapsing under its own weight. There's a small exhibition on the bridge's history at the former **tollhouse** (admission free).

Ironbridge Gorge

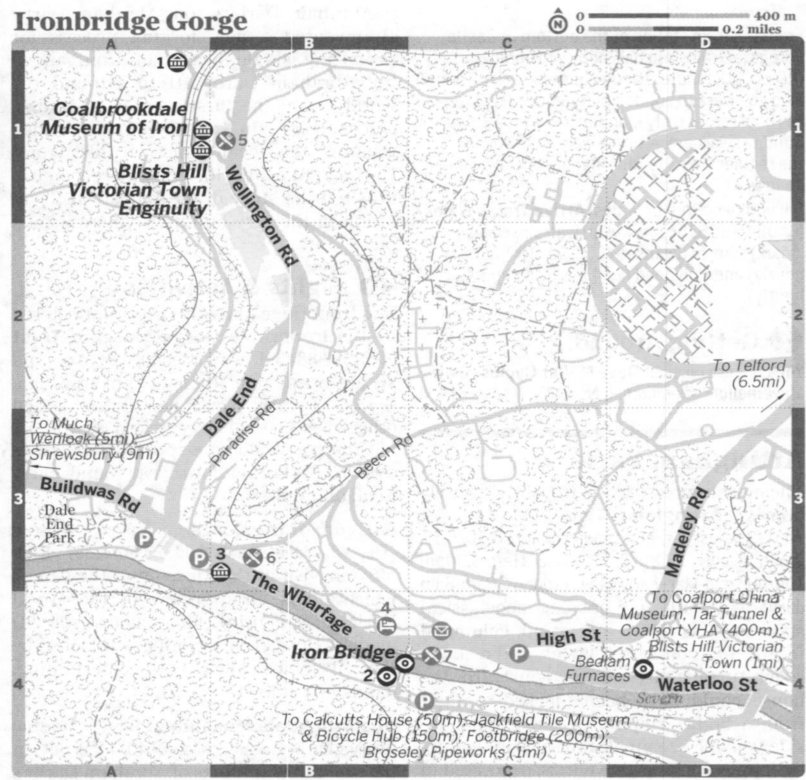

Blists Hill Victorian Town MUSEUM
(☎01952-433522; Legges Way, Madeley; adult/child £14.60/9.35) Set at the top of the Hay Inclined Plane (a cable lift that once transported coal barges uphill from the Shropshire Canal), Blists Hill is a lovingly restored Victorian village that has been repopulated with townsfolk in period costume, carrying out day-to-day activities like washing clothes, mending hobnail boots and working the village iron foundry. There's even a bank, where you can exchange your modern pounds for shillings to use at the village shops.

Coalport China Museum & Tar Tunnel MUSEUM
Dominated by a pair of towering bottle kilns, the atmospheric old china works now contains an absorbing **museum** (adult/child £7.40/4.95) tracing the history of the industry, with demonstrations of traditional pottery techniques.

A short stroll along the canal brings you to the 200-year-old **Tar Tunnel** (adult/child £2.50/1.95; ⏲Apr-Sep), an artificial watercourse that was abandoned when natural bitumen started trickling from its walls. You can don a hard hat and stoop in deep enough to see the black stuff ooze.

Jackfield Tile Museum MUSEUM
(Jackfield; adult/child £7.40/4.95) Gas-lit galleries re-create ornately tiled rooms from past centuries, from Victorian public conveniences to fairy-tale friezes from children's hospital wards. The museum is on the south bank of the Severn, near the footbridge to the Coalport China Museum.

Broseley Pipeworks MUSEUM
(adult/child £4.55/3; ⏲1-5pm mid-May–Sep) This was once the biggest clay tobacco pipemaker in the country, but the industry took a nose-dive after the introduction of prerolled cigarettes in the 1880s, and the fac-

Ironbridge Gorge

Top Sights

Blists Hill Victorian Town
Enginuity A1
Coalbrookdale Museum of Iron.......... A1
Iron Bridge B4

Sights

1 Darby Houses A1
2 Iron Bridge Tollhouse........................B4
3 Museum of the Gorge........................B3

Sleeping

4 Library House B4

Eating

5 Fat Frog B1
6 Malthouse B3
7 Restaurant Severn C4

tory was preserved much as the last worker left it when the doors finally closed in 1957. The pipeworks is a 1-mile walk south of the river, on a winding lane that passes the old workers' cottages (ask the tourist office for the *Jitties* leaflet).

Enginuity MUSEUM
(Wellington Rd; adult/child £7.65/6.55) If the kids are tired of fusty historical displays, recharge their batteries at this levers-and-pulleys science centre beside the Museum of Iron, where you can control robots, move a steam locomotive with your bare hands (and a little engineering know-how) and power up a vacuum cleaner with self-generated electricity.

Sleeping

There are two YHA hostels at Ironbridge, but the Coalbrookdale hostel is reserved for groups.

TOP CHOICE **Library House** B&B ££
(☎01952-432299; www.libraryhouse.com; 11 Severn Bank; s/d from £60/70; P@) Up an alley off the main street, this lovingly restored Georgian library building is hugged by vines, backed by a beautiful garden and decked out with stacks of v intage books, curios, prints and lithographs. There are three charming, individually decorated rooms, each named after a famous writer.

Coalport YHA HOSTEL £
(☎0845 371 9325; www.yha.org.uk; High St, Coalport; dm/f from £16/50; P) This superior hostel is set in a converted china factory next to the China Museum and canal. Rooms are modern and functional; the big drawcards are the facilities, including a laundry, kitchen and licensed cafe, and its location in the quietest, prettiest corner of Ironbridge.

Calcutts House B&B ££
(☎01952-882631; www.calcuttshouse.co.uk; Calcutts Rd; s/d/tr from £45/53/90; P) This former ironmaster's pad, built in the 18th century, is tucked away on the south bank, a few paces from the Jackfield Tile Museum. Its traditionally decorated rooms have heaps of character, and each is named after a famous former resident or guest at the house.

Eating & Drinking

Most places to eat are along the High St, but there are old-fashioned pubs scattered along both banks of the River Severn.

Restaurant Severn FRENCH £££
(☎01952-432233; www.restaurantseven.co.uk; 33 High St; 2-/3-course dinner from £23/25; dinner Wed-Sat, lunch Sun) The highly praised food is a hybrid of English and French at this elegant fine-dining waterfront restaurant. The simple decor and laid-back service attests to the fact that the real star here is the food – and the delectable, locally sourced menu changes weekly.

Fat Frog FRENCH ££
(☎01952-432240; www.fat-frog.co.uk; Wellington Rd; mains £10-17; closed dinner Sun) The quirky French bar-bistro at the Grove Hotel is cluttered with toy frogs and showbiz memorabilia, amassed by its Gallic proprietor. The food is excellent, and, as you'd expect, there's a great wine list with plenty of half-bottles.

Malthouse PUB ££
(☎01952-433712; www.themalthouseironbridge.com; The Wharfage; mains £10-15, s/d £60/70) Facing the river, this former malting house is the best of several similar pubs strung out along the Wharfage. Food comes in generous portions and there's live music nightly from Thursday to Saturday. Tasteful contemporary rooms are also available.

Information

Tourist office (☎01952-884391; www.visitironbridge.co.uk; The Wharfage; 10am-5pm) Located at the Museum of the Gorge.

Getting There & Away

The nearest train station is 6 miles away at Telford, but you can continue on to Ironbridge on bus 96 (20 minutes, every two hours Monday to Saturday). The same bus continues from the Visitor Centre to Shrewsbury (40 minutes). Bus 9 runs from Bridgnorth (30 minutes, four daily, no Sunday service) and bus 39 runs to Much Wenlock (30 minutes, four daily, no Sunday service).

Getting Around

At weekends and on bank holidays from Easter to October, the Gorge Connect bus (free to Museum Passport holders) runs from Telford bus station to all of the museums on the north bank of the Severn. A Day Rover pass costs £2.50/1.50 per adult/child. To reach the Jackfield Tile Museum, cross the footbridge at the bottom of the Hay Inclined Plane; to reach the Broseley Pipeworks, cross the Ironbridge and follow the signs.

Bikes can be rented from **Bicycle Hub** (☎01952-883249; Jackfield; rental per day from £15; ⌚10am-5pm Mon-Sat) in the Fusion centre, behind the Jackfield Tile Museum.

Much Wenlock

POP 1959

With one of those quirky names that abound in the English countryside, Much Wenlock is as charming as it sounds. Surrounding the time-worn ruins of Wenlock Priory, the streets are studded with Tudor, Jacobean and Georgian houses, and locals say hello to everyone. As well as being a perfect English village, Much Wenlock also claims to have jump-started the modern Olympics (see boxed text, p431).

The **tourist office** (☎01952-727679; www.muchwenlockguide.info; The Square; ⌚10.30am-1pm & 1.30-5pm Apr-Oct, 10.30am-1pm & 1.30-5pm Tue, Fri & Sat morning Nov-Mar) has stacks of brochures on local sights and walks, and a modest **museum** (admission free) of local history.

Sights & Activities

Wenlock Priory RUINS

(EH; ☎01952-727466; adult/child incl audio tour £3.80/1.90; ⌚10am-5pm May-Aug, 10am-5pm Wed-Sun Mar, Apr, Sep & Oct, 10am-4pm Thu-Sun Nov-Feb) The atmospheric ruins of Wenlock Priory rise up from vivid green lawns, sprinkled with animal-shaped topiaries. Raised by Norman monks over the ruins of a Saxon monastery from 680AD, the hallowed ruins include a finely decorated chapterhouse and an unusual carved lavabo, where monks came to ceremonially wash before eating.

Across from the tourist office, the wonky **Guildhall** (☎01952-727509; admission £1; ⌚10.30am-1pm & 2-4.30pm Mon-Sat, 2-4.30pm Sun Apr-Oct), built in classic Tudor style in 1540, features some splendidly ornate woodcarving. A short walk north, the ancient, eroded **Holy Trinity Church** (www.muchwenlockchurch.co.uk; ⌚9am-5pm) was built in 1150 over Saxon foundations.

Sleeping & Eating

Raven Hotel HOTEL £££

(☎01952-727251; www.ravenhotel.com; Barrow St; mains £10-20; s/d £85/130; P) Much Wenlock's finest, this 17th-century coaching inn and converted stables has oodles of historical charm and rich country-chic styling throughout. The excellent restaurant overlooks a flowery courtyard and serves up classic British and Mediterranean fare.

Fox PUB ££

(☎01952-727292; www.the-fox-inn.co.uk; 46 High St; mains £8-17, s/d from £65/85; @ 📶) Warm

WORTH A TRIP

COSFORD ROYAL AIR FORCE MUSEUM

About 13 miles east of Ironbridge, this famous aerospace **museum** (☎01902-376200; www.rafmuseum.org; Shifnal; ⌚10am-6pm, closed 2nd week Jan) is run by the Royal Air Force, whose pilots once steered many of these winged wonders across the skies. Aircraft on display range from fearsome war machines like the Vulcan bomber (which once carried Britain's nuclear deterrent) to strange experimental aircraft like the FA330 Bachstelze, a tiny helicopterlike glider towed behind German U-boats to warn them of approaching enemy ships. The museum is a half-mile walk from Cosford train station, on the Birmingham–Shrewsbury line. Visit in June for the annual **Cosford Air Show** (www.cosfordairshow.co.uk), when the Red Arrows stunt team paint the sky with coloured smoke.

GRANDADDY OF THE MODERN OLYMPICS

All eyes will be on London when the Olympic Games arrive in 2012, but tiny Much Wenlock will be holding its own Olympic Games in July the same year, as it has every year since 1850. The idea of holding a sporting tournament based on the games of ancient Greece was the brainchild of local doctor William Penny Brookes, who was looking for a healthy diversion for bored local youths. Accordingly, he created a tournament for 'every kind of man', with running races, high and long jumps, tilting, hammer throwing and wheelbarrow races – plus glee singing, knitting and sewing so every kind of woman didn't feel left out!

The games soon piqued the interest of Baron Pierre Coubertin, who visited Much Wenlock in 1890 and consulted Brookes extensively before launching the modern Olympic Games in Athens in 1896. Unfortunately, Brookes was effectively airbrushed out of the Olympic story until 1994, when International Olympic Committee President Juan Antonio Samaranch visited Much Wenlock to pay his respects to 'the founder of the Modern Olympic Games'.

The Much Wenlock Olympics are still held every July, with events that range from the triathlon to volleyball. You can find details at www.wenlock-olympian-society.org.uk.

yourself by the massive fireplace, then settle down in the dining room to enjoy locally sourced venison, pheasant and beef, swished down with a pint of Shropshire ale. It also has some surprisingly contemporary rooms.

The closest hostel is Wilderhope Manor YHA on Wenlock Edge.

ℹ Getting There & Away

Buses 436 and 437 run from Shrewsbury to Much Wenlock (35 minutes, hourly, every two hours Sunday) and on to Bridgnorth (20 minutes). Bus 39 runs to Ironbridge (30 minutes, four daily, no Sunday service).

Around Much Wenlock

The spectacular limestone escarpment of **Wenlock Edge** swells up like an immense petrified wave, breaking over the Shropshire countryside. Formed from limestone that once lined the bottom of Silurian seas, the ridge sprawls for 15 miles from Much Wenlock to Craven Arms along the route of the B4371, providing a fantastic hiking back-route from Ludlow and Ironbridge.

For a bite, a beer or a bed, point your hiking boots towards the 17th-century **Wenlock Edge Inn** (☎01746-785678; Hilltop, Easthope; s/d £50/75; Ⓟ), perched atop the Edge about 4.5 miles southwest of Much Wenlock. It's a down-to-earth place with above-average pub grub (mains £9 to £15) and five chintzy but cosy rooms.

Alternatively, ramble out to the remote **Wilderhope Manor YHA** (☎0845 371 9149; www.yha.org.uk; Longville-in-the-Dale; dm/f £14/45; ⏲Fri, Sat & school holidays; Ⓟ), a gloriously atmospheric gabled greystone Elizabethan manor, with spiral staircases, wood-panelled walls, an impressive stone-floored dining hall and spacious, oak-beamed rooms. This is hostelling for royalty!

Bus 155 from Ludlow and buses 153/154 from Bridgnorth run infrequently to Shipton, a half-mile walk from Wilderhope – call the hostel for the latest timetable.

Bridgnorth

POP 11,891

Cleaved in two by a dramatic sandstone bluff that tumbles down to the River Severn, Bridgnorth is worth a trip for a nostalgic ride on the **Bridgnorth Cliff Railway** (☎01746-762052; www.bridgnorthcliffrailway.co.uk; return £1; ⏲8am-8pm Mon-Sat & noon-8pm Sun May-Sep, to 6.30pm Oct-Apr), the steepest inland railway in Britain. Looking like a Victorian omnibus jacked up on girders, the train has been trundling its way up the cliff since 1892.

Bridgnorth is also the northern terminus of the **Severn Valley Railway** (☎01299-403816; www.svr.co.uk; adult one way/return £15.50/11, children half-price; ⏲daily May-Sep, weekends winter), whose trains chug down the valley to Kidderminster (one hour), starting from the station on Hollybush Rd.

Several narrow lanes drop down from the High Town to the Low Town, including the pedestrian Cartway, where the **Cinnamon Cafe** (☎01746-762944; Waterloo House, Cartway; mains £5-8; ⏰9am-6pm Mon-Wed & Fri, 10am-4pm Sat & Sun) serves up savoury bakes (many vegetarian and vegan) plus quiches and homemade cakes, which you can munch indoors or in front of the views from the terrace.

Based at the town library, the **tourist office** (☎01746-763257; www.visitbridgnorth.co.uk; ⏰9.30am-5pm Mon-Sat Apr-Oct, closed Thu Nov-Mar) can advise on local B&Bs.

Getting There & Away

Buses 436 and 437 run hourly from Shrewsbury to Bridgnorth (one hour, five Sunday services), via Much Wenlock (25 minutes). Bus 9 runs to Ironbridge (30 minutes, four daily, no Sunday service).

Church Stretton & Around

POP 3841

Set in a deep valley formed by the Long Mynd and the Caradoc Hills, Church Stretton is an ideal base for walks or cycle tours through the Shropshire Hills. Although black-and-white timbers are heavily in evidence, most of the buildings in town are 19th-century fakes, built by the Victorians who flocked here to take the country air. The Norman-era **St Laurence's Church** features an exhibitionist sheila-na-gig over its north door.

The **tourist office** (☎01694-723133; www.churchstretton.co.uk; Church St, Church Stretton; ⏰9.30am-5pm Mon-Sat, closed 12.30-1.30pm winter), adjoining the library, has abundant walking information as well as free internet access.

Activities

Walking

Church Stretton clings to the steeply sloping sides of the **Long Mynd**, Shropshire's most famous hill, which rises to 517m. Dubbed 'Little Switzerland' by the Victorians, this desolate but dramatic bluff is girdled by walking trails that offer soaring views over the surrounding countryside. Most people start walking from the National Trust car park at the end of the **Carding Mill Valley** (www.cardingmillvalley.org.uk), half a mile west of Shrewsbury Rd – a small **tearoom** (⏰11am-5pm) provides refreshments.

A maze of single-track roads climbs over the Long Mynd to the adjacent ridge of **Stiperstones**, which is crowned by a line of spooky-looking crags where Satan is said to hold court. You can continue right over the ridge to the village of Snailbeach, with its intriguing mining relics, passing the **Bog** (www.bogcentre.co.uk; Snailbeach; ⏰10am-5pm Wed-Sun Easter-Oct), a cosy cafe and information centre next to the ruins of an abandoned mining village.

Other Activities

The tourist office has maps of local mountain-biking circuits and details of local riding stables. To soar above the Long Mynd like a bird of prey, contact **Beyond Extreme** (☎01691-682640; www.beyondextreme.co.uk; 2 Burway Rd, Church Stretton) for hill-launch paragliding lessons and tandem flights.

Sleeping

Bridges Long Mynd YHA HOSTEL £
(☎01588-650656; www.yha.org.uk; Bridges; dm from £13; P) On the far side of the Long Mynd, this superior YHA property is housed in a former school in the tiny hamlet of Bridges near Ratlinghope. Popular with hikers, the hostel is wonderfully isolated, but meals and liquid refreshment are available at the nearby Horseshoe Inn pub. To get here, cross the Mynd to Ratlinghope, or take the Long Mynd shuttle bus.

Jinlye Guest House B&B ££
(☎01694-723243; www.jinlye.co.uk; Castle Hill, All Stretton; s/d £60/80; P) High above the village of All Stretton on the top of the Mynd, Jinlye is a beautifully restored crofter's cottage. In contrast to the rugged terrain on all sides, the interior is warm and cosy, with old beams, log fires and bright bedrooms full of historic odds and ends. Wheelchair accessible.

Mynd House B&B ££
(☎01694-722212; www.myndhouse.com; Ludlow Rd, Little Stretton; s/d from £40/75; P @ ᯤ). South of Church Stretton in Little Stretton, this inviting, family-friendly guest house has splendid views across the valley, and it backs directly onto the Mynd. The tastefully furnished rooms are bright and airy, there's a small bar and lounge stocked with local books, and the owners are full of hiking advice.

Eating & Drinking

As well as the following places, there are several cosy pubs along the High St.

Berry's Coffee House CAFE £
(☎01694-724452; www.berryscoffeehouse.co.uk; 17 High St, Church Stretton; meals £6-8; ⏲10am-5pm) A sociable cafe in an 18th-century house with a pretty conservatory, just off the main street. Berry's is proud of its organic, free-range, fair-trade, wholesome menu, but makes up for all that goodness with wicked desserts.

Studio MODERN EUROPEAN £££
(☎01694-722672; www.thestudiorestaurant.net; 59 High St, Church Stretton; 2/3 courses £24/26.50; ⏲dinner Wed-Sat) A former artist's studio (still littered with interesting works) sets the scene for the town's most intimate restaurant, which features an award-winning menu of modern English and traditional French food.

Van Doesburg's DELI £
(www.vandoesburgs.co.uk; 3 High St, Church Stretton; sandwiches from £3; ⏲9am-5pm Mon-Sat) You'll find everything you need for a posh picnic at this excellent patisserie-delicatessen, which sources its ingredients from local farms and small producers.

Getting There & Around

Trains between Ludlow and Shrewsbury stop here every hour, taking 20 minutes from either end. Alternatively, take bus 435 from Shrewsbury or Ludlow (40 minutes, hourly Monday to Saturday).

From April to September, the **Long Mynd & Stiperstones Shuttle** (www.shropshirehillsshuttles.co.uk; all-day adult/child £7/2.50, seven daily Sat, Sun & bank holiday Mon) runs from the Carding Mill Valley in Church Stretton to the villages atop the Long Mynd, passing the YHA at Bridges, the Stiperstones and the Snailbeach mine.

You can hire good-quality road and mountain bikes from **Shropshire Hills Bike Hire** (☎01694-723302; 6 Castle Hill, All Stretton; per day from £12.50).

Bishop's Castle

POP 1630

Set amid blissfully peaceful Shropshire countryside, Bishop's Castle is a higgledy-piggledy tangle of timbered town houses and Old Mother Hubbard cottages. Lined with surprisingly posh boutiques, the High St climbs from the town church to the adorable Georgian **town hall** abutting the crooked 16th-century **House on Crutches** (☎01588 630007; admission free; ⏲2-5pm Sat & Sun Apr-Sep), which also houses the town **museum**.

The pleasingly potty **Old Time** (☎01588-638467; www.oldtime.co.uk; 29 High St; ⏲10am-6pm Mon-Sat, to 2pm Sun) is part furniture workshop and part tourist information office.

Activities

Walkers can hike from north Bishops Castle along the **Shropshire Way**, which joins up with the long-distance **Offa's Dyke Path** and **Kerry Ridgeway** to the west. The northern sections of the Shropshire Way climb to the high country of the Stiperstones and the Long Mynd near Church Stretton. Bishops Castle also lies on the popular **Six Castles Cycleway** (NCN Route 44) between Shrewsbury and Leominster.

Sleeping & Eating

Poppy House B&B ££
(☎01588-638443; www.poppyhouse.co.uk; 20 Market Sq; s/d from £30/60, dishes from £6; ⏲10am-5pm Wed-Sun, to 10pm Sat) An artistic air pervades this sweet guest house, attached to a friendly cafe that upgrades to fine dining on Saturday nights. Rooms are bright and welcoming and the Saturday menu runs to braised lamb shanks and cod mornay.

Castle Hotel HOTEL ££
(☎01588-638403; www.thecastlehotelbishopscastle.co.uk; The Square; s/d £45/90; P) Boasting a delightful pergola and water-feature-filled garden, this solid-looking 18th-century coaching inn was allegedly built from the ruins of the vanished Bishop's Castle. The wood-panelled rooms are great value and the pub kitchen serves up hearty English meals.

Other possibilities:

Porch House B&B ££
(☎01588-638854; www.theporchhouse.com; High St; s/d from £45/70; P @ wi-fi) Part of a terrace of timbered 16th-century buildings, this stylish place has imaginatively modernised rooms full of family ornaments and tasteful little details.

Yarborough House CAFE £
(www.yarboroughhouse.com; The Square; ⏲10am-5pm Tue-Sun) Excellent coffee and cakes in a quirky classical music shop and secondhand bookshop.

Drinking

Three Tuns PUB

(www.thethreetunsinn.co.uk; Salop St) Bishop's Castle's finest watering hole is attached to the tiny **Three Tuns Brewery** (www.threetunsbrewery.co.uk), which has been rolling barrels of nut-brown ale across the courtyard since 1642.

Six Bells Inn PUB

(Church St; mains £8-13; ⏱lunch Tue-Sun, dinner Wed-Sat) This historic 17th-century coaching inn is alive with loyal locals and ramblers who come to sample ales from its adjoining brewery.

Getting There & Away

Bus 553 runs to and from Shrewsbury (one hour, six daily). On Saturdays and bank holiday weekends, you can jump on the Secret Hills Shuttle from Craven Arms (40 minutes, four per day).

Ludlow

POP 9548

Fanning out from the rambling ruins of a fine Norman castle, beautiful Ludlow's muddle of narrow streets are a mecca for foodies from across the country. Quite why this genteel market town became a national gastronomic phenomenon is not entirely clear, but the centre is crammed with independent butchers, bakers, grocers, cheesemongers and exceptional restaurants.

Sights & Activities

Ludlow Castle CASTLE

(☎01584-873355; www.ludlowcastle.com; Castle Sq; adult/child £4.50/2.50; ⏱10am-7pm Aug, to 5pm Apr-Jul & Sep, to 4pm Oct-Mar, Sat & Sun only Dec & Jan). Perched in an ideal defensive location atop a cliff above a crook in the river, the town castle was built to ward off the marauding Welsh – or to enforce the English expansion into Wales, according to those west of the border. Founded after the Norman conquest, the castle was dramatically expanded in the 14th century by the notorious Roger Mortimer, the first Earl of March, who conspired to cause the grisly death of Edward II and was the de facto ruler of England for three years (before getting his comeuppance at the hands of Edward III).

Despite the passing centuries, the ruins are in impressive shape, with a tangle of secret passageways, ruined rooms and time-worn stairways. The Norman chapel in the inner bailey is one of the few surviving round chapels in England, and the sturdy keep (built around 1090) offers wonderful views over the hills.

Church of St Laurence CHURCH

(www.stlaurences.org.uk; King St; requested donation £2; ⏱10am-5.30pm Apr-Sep, 11am-4pm Oct-Mar) One of the largest parish churches in Britain, the church of St Laurence contains grand Elizabethan alabaster tombs and some delightfully cheeky medieval misericords carved into its medieval choir stalls, including a beer-swilling chap raiding his barrel. Climb the tower (£3) for stunning views of town and countryside.

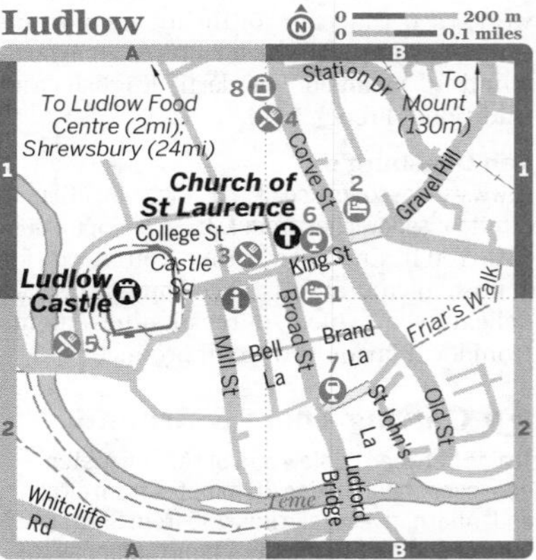

Ludlow

Top Sights

Church of St Laurence ... B1
Ludlow Castle ... A1

Sleeping

1 De Grey's ... B1
2 Feathers Hotel ... B1

Eating

3 Courtyard ... A1
De Grey's ... (see 1)
4 La Bécasse ... B1
5 Mr Underhill's ... A2

Drinking

6 Church Inn ... B1
7 Wheatsheaf Inn ... B2

Shopping

8 Myriad Organics ... A1

Cycling & Walking

Ludlow is ringed by wonderful landscapes that call out to cyclists and walkers. Starting just outside the castle entrance, the waymarked **Mortimer Trail** runs for 30 miles through idyllic English countryside to Kington in Herefordshire. The tourist office has various leaflets describing the route, or visit www.mortimercountry.co.uk.

Another fine walking or cycling route is the **Shropshire Way**, which runs northwest to Craven Arms, or northeast to Wenlock Edge over the dramatic summit of **Clee Hill** (540m), the highest point in the county. The hill affords awe-inspiring views south to Worcestershire's Malvern Hills.

Tours

Popular **town tours** (www.ludlowhistory.co.uk; per person £2.50) run at weekends from April to October, leaving the Cannon in Castle Sq at 2.30pm on Saturday and Sunday. Alternatively, search for spooks on the **ghost walk** (www.shropshireghostwalks.co.uk; adult/child £4/3; 8pm Fri) from outside the Church Inn on the Buttercross.

Festivals & Events

The town's busy calendar peaks with the **Ludlow Festival** (www.ludlowfestival.co.uk), a fortnight of theatre and music in June and July that uses the castle as its dramatic backdrop. The **Ludlow Food & Drink Festival** (www.foodfestival.co.uk) is one of Britain's best foodie celebrations, spanning a long weekend in September.

Sleeping

TOP CHOICE **Feathers Hotel** HOTEL ££
(01584-875261; www.feathersatludlow.co.uk; Bull Ring; s/d from £75/95, 2/3 courses £32/39.50; P) Stepping through the almost impossibly ornate timbered Jacobean facade of the Feathers, you can almost hear the Cavaliers toasting the health of King Charles. The best rooms are in the old building – rooms in the newer wing lack the character and romance. The restaurant is also highly recommended.

De Grey's B&B ££
(01584-872764; www.degreys.co.uk; 73 Broad St; s/d from £60/80) Above the tearooms of the same name, this classy B&B has nine luxurious rooms with low ceilings, beams, leaded windows and reassuringly solid oak beds. The balance of period features and modern luxury is spot on.

Mount B&B ££
(01584-874084; www.themountludlow.co.uk; 61 Gravel Hill; s/d from £30/55; P) On the hill northeast of the centre, this agreeable Victorian house offers lovely valley views and a warm welcome for walkers and cyclists. Rooms have crisp white linen and the hostess offers lifts from the railway station.

Eating

La Bécasse MODERN FRENCH £££
(01584-872325; www.labecasse.co.uk; 17 Corve St; 2/3 courses £49/55; lunch Wed-Sun, dinner Tue-Sat) Artistically presented Modern French cuisine bursting with inventive flavours is served in an oak-panelled, brick-walled dining room in a 17th-century coach house. Michelin-starred chef Will Holland has created some remarkable dishes – try the pigeon ballotine with wasabi and mango salsa.

Mr Underhill's MODERN BRITISH £££
(01584-874431; www.mr-underhills.co.uk; Dinham Weir; 9-course set menu from £49.50, s/d from £120/130; dinner Wed-Sun) This dignified and award-winning restaurant is set in a converted corn mill that dips its toes in the river, and the modern British food is exquisitely prepared, using market-fresh ingredients. Should you be too full to walk home, it has some extremely elegant rooms decked out with designer fabrics and all mod cons.

De Grey's TEAROOM £
(www.degreys.co.uk; 73 Broad St; light meals from £4; breakfast & lunch) A swooningly nostalgic tearoom that easily could be plucked from an Agatha Christie mystery, it serves excellent breakfasts, lunches and afternoon teas, and superior cakes and patisserie throughout the day.

Courtyard CAFE £
(www.thecourtyard.uk.com; 2 Quality Sq; mains £5.50-10; lunch Mon-Sat, dinner Fri & Sat) Offering light relief from too much gastronomic extravagance, this simple cafe, tucked away in a tranquil courtyard near the market square, has a faithful local following for its lightning service and tasty seasonal food.

Drinking

Of the many pubs, the hop-strewn **Church Inn** (Buttercross) is a cosy little escape, tucked away on the narrow lane beside the old butter market. The quiet little **Wheatsheaf Inn** (Lower Broad St), under the medieval Broadgate, has a good choice of local ales.

Shopping

Markets fill Castle Sq on Monday, Wednesday, Friday and Saturday.

If you can't wait till market day, try **Myriad Organics** (☎01584-872665; 22 Corve St; ⏰8.30am-6pm Mon-Sat) or the **Ludlow Food Centre** (☎01584-856000; Bromfield; ⏰9.30am-5.30pm Mon-Sat, 10.30am-4.30pm Sun), a handy one-stop-shop for wholefoods and gourmet ingredients, about 2 miles northwest of Ludlow on the A49.

Information

Tourist office (☎01584-875053; www.ludlow.org.uk; Castle Sq; ⏰10am-5pm Mon-Sat, 10.30am-5pm Sun) This office contains an inside-out **museum** (☎01584-813666, admission free, ⏰10am to 5pm Monday to Saturday, plus Sunday from June to August) featuring the town and surrounding area.

Getting There & Around

Trains run frequently from the station on the north edge of town to Hereford (£7.40, 25 minutes, every half-hour) and Shrewsbury (£9.60, 30 minutes, every half-hour) via Church Stretton (16 minutes). You can also reach Shrewsbury on bus 435 (1½ hours, hourly Monday to Saturday), which runs via Craven Arms (20 minutes) and Church Stretton (40 minutes).

You can hire bikes from **Wheely Wonderful** (☎01568-770755; www.wheelywonderfulcycling.co.uk; Petchfield Farm, Elton; bike per day from £24), 5 miles west of Ludlow.

NOTTINGHAMSHIRE

Say Nottinghamshire and people think of one thing – Robin Hood. Whether the hero woodsman ever really existed is hotly debated, but the county makes much of its connections to the outlaw from Locksley. The city of Nottingham is the bustling hub, but venture into the surrounding countryside and you'll find a wealth of historic towns and stately homes surrounding the green bower of Sherwood Forest.

Information

Visit Nottinghamshire (www.visitnottingham.co.uk)

Getting There & Around

Trains run frequently to most large towns, and many smaller villages in the Peak District. **National Express** (☎0871 781 8178; www.nationalexpress.com) and **Trent Barton Buses** (☎01773-712265; www.trentbarton.co.uk) provide the bulk of the bus services. See www.nottinghamshire.gov.uk/buses for timetables, or use the handy journey planner at www.itsnottingham.info.

Nottingham

POP 266,988

Forever associated with men in tights and a sheriff with anger-management issues, Nottingham is a county capital with big-city aspirations. Predictably, the Robin Hood connection is Nottingham's biggest drawcard, but look beyond the arrows and outlaws and you'll find a vibrant and historic metropolis with loads of cultural offerings and a buzzing music and club scene.

Sights & Activities

Nottingham Castle Museum & Art Gallery MUSEUM

(adult/child £3.50/2; ⏰10am-5pm Tue-Sun) Set atop a sandstone outcrop worm-holed with caves and tunnels, the original Nottingham castle was founded by William the Conqueror and held by a succession of English kings before falling in the English Civil War. Its 17th-century replacement contains a diverting museum of local history, with an extensive collection of costumes, jewellery, Wedgwood jasperware and paintings, including works by Dante Gabriel Rossetti. Your ticket also gains you entry to the Museum of Nottinghamshire Life at Brewhouse Yard.

Museum of Nottingham Life at Brewhouse Yard

At the foot of the cliffs, housed in five 17th-century cottages and accessed on the same ticket as Nottingham Castle, this charming little museum will take you back through 300 years of Nottingham life using reconstructions of traditional shops and living quarters.

Mortimer's Hole

(45min tours adult/child £2.50/1.50; ⏰tours 11am, 2pm & 3pm Mon-Sat, noon, 1pm, 2pm & 3pm Sun) Burrowing through the bedrock beneath the castle, this atmospheric underground passageway emerges at Brewhouse Yard. In 1330, supporters of Edward III used this tunnel to breach the castle security and capture Roger Mortimer, the machiavellian Earl of March, who briefly appointed himself ruler of England after deposing Edward II.

City of Caves CAVERN

(☎0115-988 1955; www.cityofcaves.com; adult/child £5.75/4.25; ⏰10.30am-4pm) Over the centuries, the sandstone underneath the city of Nottingham has been carved into a veritable Swiss cheese of caverns and passageways. From the top level of the Broadmarsh shopping centre, atmospheric audio tours (or guided tours at weekends) plunge into the wormholes, visiting a WWII air-raid shelter, a medieval underground tannery, several pub cellars and a mock-up of a Victorian slum dwelling.

FREE **Nottingham Contemporary** GALLERY (www.nottinghamcontemporary.org; Weekday Cross; ⏲10am-7pm Tue-Fri, 10am-6pm Sat, 11am-5pm Sun) Housed in an eye-catching building fronted with lace-patterned concrete, this sleek gallery lives up to its name, with lots of edgy, design-oriented exhibitions of paintings, prints, photography and sculpture.

Galleries of Justice MUSEUM (☎0115-952 0555; www.galleriesofjustice.org.uk; High Pavement; adult/child audio tour £5.75/4.25, performance tour £8.75/6.75; ⏲10.30am-5pm) Set in the grand Georgian precincts of the Shire Hall building, the Galleries of Justice offers an entertaining stroll through centuries of British justice, from medieval trials by fire and water to the controversial policing of the Miners Strike. Audio tours run on Monday and Tuesday; live-action tours with 'gaolers' run Wednesday to Sunday.

Tours

Original Nottingham Ghost Walk GHOST WALK (☎01623-721660; www.ghost-walks.co.uk; adult/child £5/3; ⏲7pm Sat Jan-Nov) Departs from Ye Olde Salutation Inn, Maid Marian Way – descend into the medieval caves if you dare…

Shaw's Heritage Services WALKING TOUR (☎0115-925 9388; www.nottinghamtours.com) Runs various tours of the city, including popular walking tours, coach trips to Sherwood Forest and boat trips on the Trent.

Festivals & Events

Nottingham hosts an interesting selection of festivals – for details, use the search form at www.nottinghamcity.gov.uk.

Held in October in the Forest Recreation Ground, a mile north of the city centre, the medieval **Goose Fair** has evolved from a travelling market to a boisterous modern funfair. Robin Hood gets his moment in the sun during the family-friendly **Robin Hood Pageant**, held every October in Nottingham Castle.

DON'T MISS

WOLLATON HALL

Built in 1588 for land owner and coal mogul, Sir Francis Willoughby, **Wollaton Hall** (Wollaton Park, Derby Rd; admission free, tours adult/child £2.50/2; ⏲11am-5pm) has more frills and ruffs than an Elizabethan banquet hall. This fabulous manor was created by architect Robert Smythson, who designed the equally avant-garde Longleat in Wessex (p266) and Doddington Hall (p446) near Lincoln. As well as extravagant rooms from the Tudor, Regency and Victorian periods, the hall boasts a natural history museum, an industrial museum and peaceful hectares of landscaped grounds and gardens.

Wollaton Hall is on the western edge of the city, 2.5 miles from the centre; get here on bus 30, 35 or 2 from Victoria bus station (15 minutes).

Sleeping

Hart's HOTEL ££ (☎0115-988 1900; www.hartsnottingham.co.uk; Standard Hill, Park Row; s & d from £120; P @) In the compound of the old Nottingham General Hospital, this swish boutique hotel is a cut above the competition. The ultra-modern rooms are in a striking modernist building, while the restaurant is housed in a historic old hospital wing. Check the website for discount rates.

Lace Market Hotel HOTEL ££ (☎0115-852 3232; www.lacemarkethotel.co.uk; 29-31 High Pavement; s/d £90/115; P) In the heart of the trendy Lace Market area, this rather lovely boutique hotel is set in an elegant Georgian town house, but rooms are sleek and contemporary. Check the website for weekend promotions.

Greenwood Lodge City Guest House B&B ££ (☎0115-962 1206; www.greenwoodlodgecityguesthouse.co.uk; Third Ave, Sherwood Rise; s/d £47.50/80; P) A fantastic B&B set in a large Victorian house north of the centre. The location is quiet, the house is full of period character, there's a pretty courtyard garden and rooms are frilly but comfortable.

Nottingham

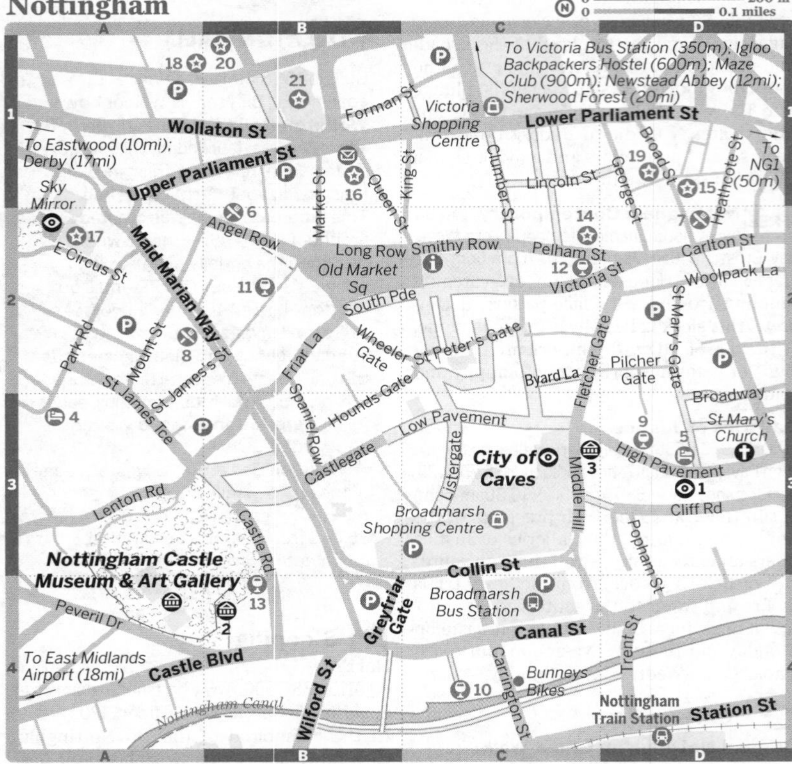

Igloo Backpackers Hostel HOSTEL £
(☎0115-947 5250; www.igloohostel.co.uk; 110 Mansfield Rd; dm £15) A favourite with international backpackers, this independent hostel is a short walk north of Victoria bus station, opposite the Golden Fleece pub. Always full at weekends so book ahead. Breakfast is extra.

Eating

TOP CHOICE **Restaurant Sat Bains** MODERN EUROPEAN £££
(www.restaurantsatbains.com; Lenton Lane; tasting menus £55-85; ⏰dinner Tue-Sat) Tucked away on the outskirts, two miles southwest of the centre, Nottingham's only Michelin-starred restaurant delivers outstanding, inventive modern European cooking. Like the outfits worn by the clientele, the food and surroundings are exquisite, but book well in advance. To get here, follow the A52 to Wilford and turn off near the Nottingham Trent University campus.

Alley Cafe VEGETARIAN £
(www.alleycafe.co.uk; Cannon Court; mains £5-6; ⏰lunch & dinner Mon & Tue, till late Wed-Sat) Tucked away down a hidden alleyway, this place sets out to prove that vegetarian food can be cool. The globe-trotting menu ranges from tofu and tempeh to hemp-seed burgers, which you can munch to a DJ soundtrack.

Memsaab INDIAN ££
(☎0115-957 0009; www.mem-saab.co.uk; 12-14 Maid Marian Way; mains £10-18; ⏰dinner) The best of the glamorous modern Indian eateries on Maid Marion Way, serving fabulous regional specialties in stylish, dinner-date friendly surroundings. Bookings are recommended.

Kayal INDIAN £
(www.kayalrestaurant.com; 8 Broad St; mains £5-13) The Nottingham branch of this small Midlands chain trades the chicken

Nottingham

Top Sights
City of Caves C3
Nottingham Castle Museum & Art Gallery A4

Sights
1 Galleries of Justice D3
2 Museum of Nottingham Life at Brewhouse Yard B4
3 Nottingham Contemporary C3

Sleeping
4 Hart's A3
5 Lace Market Hotel D3

Eating
6 Alley Cafe B2
7 Kayal D2
8 Memsaab A2

Drinking
9 Brass Monkey D3
10 Canal Hose C4
11 Malt Cross B2
12 Pit & Pendulum C2
13 Ye Olde Trip to Jerusalem B4

Entertainment
14 Bodega Social Club C2
15 Broadway Cinema D1
16 Gatecrasher B1
17 Nottingham Playhouse A2
18 Rock City A1
Royal Concert Hall ..... (see 21)
19 Screen Room D1
20 Stealth B1
21 Theatre Royal B1

tikka masala clichés for the spicy flavours of Kerala. Highlights of the menu include delicious dosas (lentil-flour pancakes) and zingy crab and kingfish curries.

Drinking

Weekends in Nottingham are boisterous affairs, and the streets throng with lads on stag nights, girls on hen parties, student revellers and intoxicated grown-ups who should really know better. If you fancy something more low-key, try the bars at the Broadway Cinema or Nottingham Playhouse – see p440.

TOP CHOICE **Ye Olde Trip to Jerusalem** PUB
(www.triptojerusalem.com; Brewhouse Yard, Castle Rd) Tucked into the cliff below the castle, this fantastically atmospheric alehouse claims to be England's oldest pub. Founded in 1189, it supposedly slaked the thirst of departing crusaders and its low-ceiling rooms and cobbled courtyards still hum with atmosphere.

Malt Cross PUB
(www.maltcross.com; 16 St James's St) A genuinely convivial drinking hole in a stately old Victorian music hall that looks like the last variety act just can-canned out the door. A fine place for a pint or a pub meal.

Pit & Pendulum PUB
(17 Victoria St) Local goths, emos and indie kids flock to this dimly lit pub for the vampire vibe and theatrical decor. For our money, it's more *Rocky Horror Picture Show* than *Hammer House of Horrors,* but it's an enjoyable spot to shake off the coffin dust.

Brass Monkey BAR
(www.brassmonkeybar.co.uk; High Pavement; 4pm-1am, till midnight Sun) Small and sultry, Brass Monkey rocks the Lace Market with sets by trendy DJs and quirky takes on cocktail favourites – rum and raisin daiquiri anyone? The roof terrace gets packed out on summer evenings.

Canal House PUB
(0115-955 5060; 48-52 Canal St; till midnight Thu, till 1am Fri & Sat, till 10.30pm Sun) The best of the giant waterside public houses crowding the canal, run by the independent Castle Rock Brewery and split in two by a watery inlet.

Entertainment

Nightclubs

Nightclub fads come and go at breakneck speed in Nottingham. Check the local press to see which venues are catching the popular imagination this week.

Stealth NIGHTCLUB
(www.stealthattack.co.uk; Masonic Pl, Goldsmith St; till 6am Fri & Sat) Around the back of Rock City, reached from Goldsmith St, this underground club caters to dancey types who like their bass heavy and their drums supercharged. The attached **Rescue**

Rooms (www.rescuerooms.com) has a varied line-up of live bands and DJs.

Gatecrasher NIGHTCLUB
(www.gatecrasher.com; Elite Bldg, Queen St; ⏲10pm-4am Fri & Sat, to 3am Thu) It's mainstream all the way at this spin-off from the famous Sheffield original. Spread over numerous rooms, it throbs to the sound of house, R&B, hip hop and club classics, and there are regular slots from international guest DJs.

Live Music

TOP CHOICE **Bodega Social Club** LIVE MUSIC
(www.thebodegasocialclub.co.uk; 23 Pelham St) Agreeably grungy, the Bodega boasts a popular beer garden and a stage that attracts bands of the calibre of the Strokes, Arctic Monkeys and Coldplay.

Maze Club LIVE MUSIC
(www.themazerocks.com; 257 Mansfield Rd; ⏲6pm-midnight Sun-Thu, 6pm-2am Fri & Sat) Behind the Forest Tavern pub, this revamped venue hosts singer-songwriters and kooky stage performers.

Rock City LIVE MUSIC
(www.rock-city.co.uk; 8 Talbot St) This monster venue has hosted everything from goth rock and Midlands metal to northern soul. It shares a compound with Stealth and the Rescue Rooms.

Theatre & Classical Music

For singalong musicals, touring theatre shows and veteran music acts, try the Royal Concert Hall or the Theatre Royal, which share a **booking office** (☎0115-989 5555; www.royalcentre-nottingham.co.uk; Theatre Sq) and an imposing building close to the centre. Ask at the tourist office for information on smaller theatres.

Nottingham Playhouse THEATRE
(☎0115-941 9419; www.nottinghamplayhouse.co.uk; Wellington Circus) Beside the shining bowl of Anish Kapoor's enormous *Sky Mirror,* the Playhouse hosts serious theatre, from stage classics to the avant-garde. The attached restaurant and bar attracts plenty of arty types.

Cinema

Broadway Cinema CINEMA
(www.broadway.org.uk; 14-18 Broad St) Fans of the arty and strange head to this funky independent cinema and gallery in the cultural part of town. The Broadway bar is one of the few drinking spots in the city centre where you can actually hear yourself talk.

Screen Room CINEMA
(www.screenroom.co.uk; 25 Broad St) Small but perfectly formed, this tiny cinema has just 21 seats, and an interesting program of arty movies.

 Information

There are numerous banks in the streets around Old Market Sq.

Post office (Queen St; ⏲9am-5.30pm Mon-Fri, 9am-4.30pm Sat) With bureau de change.

Tourist office (www.visitnottingham.com; The Exchange, 1-4 Smithy Row; ⏲9am-5.30pm Mon-Fri, to 5pm Sat, 10am-4pm Sun) Has internet terminals (£3 per hour), brochures and racks of Robin Hood merchandise.

 Getting There & Away

Air

East Midlands Airport (☎0871 919 9000; www.eastmidlandsairport.com) is about 18 miles south of Nottingham; Indigo buses pass the airport (one hour, hourly) en route to Derby.

Bus

Local services run from the Victoria bus station, behind the Victoria Shopping Centre on Milton St. Bus 100 runs to Southwell (50 minutes, every 20 to 30 minutes Monday to Saturday).

Long-distance buses operate from the dingy confines of Broadmarsh bus station, south of Bridlesmith Gate. For the Peak, the hourly Transpeak service runs to Derby (40 minutes), Matlock Bath (1¼ hours), Bakewell (two hours) and Buxton (2½ hours). Useful National Express services:

Birmingham £10, two hours, seven daily

Leicester 45 minutes, 10 daily

London £20.60, 3½ hours, 10 daily

Sheffield £8.20, 80 minutes, hourly

Train

The train station is just south of the town centre. Train services include the following:

Derby £5.50, 25 minutes, three hourly

Lincoln £9.20, one hour, hourly

London £49, two hours, every two hours

Manchester £18.40, two hours, hourly

Sheffield £10.70, one hour, every half hour

 Getting Around

For information on buses within Nottingham, call **Nottingham City Transport** (☎0115-950 6070; www.nctx.co.uk). The Kangaroo ticket gives you unlimited travel on buses and trams within the city for £3.40.

The single tram line operated by **Nottingham Express Transit** (www.thetram.net; single/day ticket from £1.50/2.70) runs from Nottingham train station to Hucknall, passing close to Broadmarsh bus station, the tourist office and Theatre Royal.

Bunneys Bikes (www.bunneysbikes.com; 97 Carrington St; bike hire per day £12.99) is near the train station.

Around Nottingham

NEWSTEAD ABBEY

The evocative lakeside ruins of **Newstead Abbey** (www.newsteadabbey.org.uk; adult/child £8/3.50, gardens only £4/2.50; ⌚house noon-5pm Fri-Mon Apr-Sep, garden 9am-dusk year-round) are forever associated with the original tortured romantic, Lord Byron (1788–1824), who owned the house until 1817. Founded as an Augustinian priory in around 1170, the building was converted into a residence after the dissolution of the monasteries in 1539, and Byron's old living quarters are full of suitably eccentric memorabilia.

The house is 12 miles north of Nottingham, off the A60. Pronto buses run from Victoria bus station, stopping at Newstead Abbey gates (30 minutes, every 20 minutes Monday to Saturday, half-hourly on Sunday), a mile from the house and gardens. Trains run to Newstead station, about 2.5 miles from the abbey.

SHERWOOD FOREST NATIONAL NATURE RESERVE

If Robin Hood wanted to hide out in Sherwood Forest today, he'd have to disguise himself and the Merry Men as day trippers on mountain bikes. Covering 182 hectares of old-growth forest, the park is a major destination for Nottingham city dwellers looking to fill their lungs with fresh air and chlorophyll, but there are still some peaceful corners.

On the outskirts of the forest on the B6034, the **Sherwood Forest tourist office** (www.sherwoodforest.org.uk; Swinecote Rd; parking £3; ⌚10am-5pm) has visitor information, copious quantities of Robin Hood merchandise and the lame 'Robyn Hode's Sherwode', with wooden cut-outs, murals and mannequins telling the tale of the famous woodsman.

Numerous walking trails lead through the forest, passing such Sherwood Forest landmarks as the **Major Oak**, a broad-boughed oak tree that is certainly old enough to have sheltered Robin of Locksley, if he did indeed exist. The **Robin Hood Festival** is a massive medieval re-enactment that takes place here every August.

Sherwood Forest YHA (☎0845 371 9139; www.yha.org.uk; Forest Corner, Edwinstowe; dm from £10) is a modern hostel with comfortable dorms just an arrow's flight from the tourist office.

MAD, BAD & DANGEROUS TO KNOW

The Romantic poet George Gordon Byron (1788–1824) was born of eccentric stock. His father was John 'Mad Jack' Byron, a playboy army captain who married a succession of women for their money, and his great-uncle, William Byron – aka the 'Wicked Lord' – allowed the family manor of Newstead Abbey to fall into ruin to spite his son and heir. With relatives like these, it was little wonder that the sixth Lord Byron fell into a life of debauchery and scandal.

Although Byron married only once, to Anne Isabella Milbanke, he had a string of affairs with married women, including Lady Caroline Lamb, who came up with that famous 'mad, bad' description. He was also alleged to have had liaisons with numerous male lovers and with his half-sister Augusta Leigh. After the breakdown of his marriage, Byron fled to Switzerland, where he befriended the ill-fated Romantic poet Percy Bysshe Shelly and his wife-to-be Mary Godwin, who would go on to write *Frankenstein*.

In between his many affairs, Byron was an active member of the House of Lords, campaigning on behalf of Luddites who were sentenced to death for destroying the industrial machinery that was robbing them of their livelihoods. Befitting a great Romantic, Byron died pursuing another idealistic dream, succumbing to a fever while fighting against the Ottomans in the Greek War of Independence. His legacy lives on in such epic works as *Don Juan* and the revealingly autobiographical *Childe Harold's Pilgrimage*.

The Sherwood Forester (bus 150) runs to the park from Sheffield on Sunday and bank holiday Mondays (May to September). From Nottingham, catch the Sherwood Arrow (bus 33, 30 minutes, four daily Monday to Saturday, two Sunday services).

Southwell

POP 6285

A graceful scattering of grand, wisteria-draped country houses, Southwell is straight out of the pages of an English Romantic novel. In the centre, **Southwell Minster** (www.southwellminster.org; suggested donation £3, photo pass £5; ⌚8am-7pm) is a fascinating blend of 12th- and 13th-century features, built over Saxon and Roman foundations.

On the outskirts of town on the road to Newark, **Southwell Workhouse** (NT; Upton Rd; adult/child £5.80/3; ⌚noon-5pm Wed-Sun) is a sobering reminder of the tough life faced by paupers in the 19th century. Visitors can explore the factory floors and workers' chambers in the company of an audio guide, narrated by 'inmates' and 'officials'.

For a comfortable bed for the night, head to the **Saracen's Head Hotel** (☎01636-812701; www.saracensheadhotel.net; s/d from £75/110, meals £8-10), a rambling, wood-timbered coaching inn by the main junction.

Bus 100 runs from Nottingham (50 minutes, every 20 minutes, four services Sunday).

LINCOLNSHIRE

One of the most sparsely populated corners of England, Lincolnshire is a blanket of farmland laid over a gently undulating landscape of low hills and pancake-flat fens. Surrounding beguiling Lincoln are seaside resorts, scenic waterways, serene nature reserves and stone-built towns that seem tailor-made for English period dramas.

Activities

Although it lacks the drama of the Lakes or Peaks, Lincolnshire is wonderfully quiet and unpopulated, perfect for cyclists and walkers. The 140-mile **Viking Way** snakes across the gentle hills of the Lincolnshire Wolds from the banks of the River Humber to Oakham in Leicestershire.

Cyclists can find information on routes across the county in any of the local tourist offices; the **Water Rail Way** is a flat but sculpture-lined on-road cycling route that follows the River Witham through classic fens countryside between Lincoln and Boston.

Information

Visit Lincolnshire (www.visitlincolnshire.com)

Getting There & Around

East Midlands trains connect Lincoln and Nottingham. Local buses connect the towns of Lincolnshire, but services are slow and infrequent. For local transport information, check the transport pages at www.lincolnshire.gov.uk. The same site offers some excellent digital pamphlets on cycle routes around the county – search for 'Cycling' and follow the links.

Lincoln

POP 85,595

A bustling metropolis by Lincolnshire standards, but a sleepy backwater compared with almost anywhere else, delightful Lincoln is a tangle of cobbled medieval streets surrounding a vast 12th-century cathedral. This is one of the Midlands' most beautiful cities – the lanes that topple over the edge of Lincoln Cliff are lined with Tudor town houses, ancient pubs and quirky independent shops. Flanking the River Witham at the base of the hill, the new town is less interesting, but the revitalised Brayford Waterfront development by the university is a pleasant place to watch the boats go by.

Sights

As well as the following sights, set aside some time to explore the achingly atmospheric medieval lanes around **Steep Hill**, which are crammed with historic buildings, including the Romanesque **Jew's**

LINCOLN'S LITTLE GREEN BUS

Despite the abundance of lovely architecture, walking between the two parts of Lincoln can feel like an Everest expedition. Fortunately, the handy **Walk & Ride** (all-day pass adult/child £2.50/1.50) bus service runs every 20 minutes from the Stonebow at the corner of High St and Saltergate to the cathedral and Newport Arch, then back via Brayford Waterfront and the train station.

DON'T MISS

LINCOLN CITY GATES

Lincoln seems to have more historic city gates than there are possible directions on the compass. Starting at the north end of the city, the **Newport Arch** on Bailgate is a relic from the original Roman settlement; traffic has been passing beneath this arch for at least 1500 years. A short walk south, the 13th-century **Exchequergate** leads from Castle Hill to the courtyard of Lincoln Cathedral, marking the spot where tenant farmers gathered to pay rent to the land-owning Bishops of Lincoln.

Behind the cathedral, Pottergate is bookended by the free-standing **Priory Gate**, built in Victorian times, and the ancient **Pottergate**, part of the fortifications that once protected the Bishops' Palace. At the bottom of the hill, by the junction of High St and Saltergate, the glorious **Stonebow** marks the southern entrance to the medieval city. Constructed in 1520, this Gothic gatehouse contains the **Lincoln Guildhall**, which is periodically open to the public for guided tours.

House, constructed in around 1160 (it now houses an upmarket restaurant).

The tourist office sells the Lincoln Time Travel Pass, which gives access to several heritage sites including the castle, cathedral and Bishops' Palace (single/family £10/20) and lasts three days.

Lincoln Cathedral CATHEDRAL
(www.lincolncathedral.com; Minister Yard; adult/child £6/1, audio guide £1; ⌚7.15am-8pm Mon-Fri, to 6pm Sat & Sun) Towering over Lincoln like a medieval skyscraper, Lincoln's magnificent cathedral is a breathtaking representation of divine power on earth. The great tower rising above the crossing is the third-highest in England at 83m, but in medieval times a lead-encased wooden spire added a further 79m to this height, topping even the great pyramids of Giza.

The first Lincoln cathedral was constructed between 1072 and 1092, but it fell in a devastating fire in 1141, and the second cathedral was destroyed by an earthquake in 1185. Putting trust in the motto 'third time lucky', Bishop Hugh of Avalon (St Hugh) rebuilt and massively expanded the cathedral, creating one of the largest Gothic buildings in Europe.

The glory of Lincoln cathedral is in the detail. The choir stalls are accessed through a magnificent stone screen carved with a riot of demons and grotesque faces. Look north to see the stunning rose window known as the **Dean's Eye** (from 1192), mirrored to the south by the floral flourishes of the **Bishop's Eye**, created by master glaziers in 1330.

Other interesting details include the curious Gilbert candlesticks, the dragon-carved font, the grand mausoleums of the Bishops of Lincoln, and the 10-sided **chapterhouse** – where Edward I held his parliament, and where the climax of *The Da Vinci Code* was filmed in 2005. Also look out for the tiny carving of the Lincoln Imp – a cheeky horned pixie, allegedly turned to stone by the angels after being sent by the devil to vandalise the church.

There are one-hour tours at least twice a day plus less-frequent tours of the roof and the tower. You can hear the organ resounding through the cathedral during Evensong (daily at 5.30pm; 3.45pm on Sunday) and the Sunday Eucharist at 9.30am.

Lincoln Castle CASTLE
(www.lincolnshire.gov.uk/lincolncastle; adult/child £5/3.30; ⌚10am-6pm) One of the first castles thrown up by the victorious William the Conqueror to keep his new kingdom in line, Lincoln Castle offers awesome views over the city and its miles of surrounding countryside. Highlights include the chance to view one of the four surviving copies of the **Magna Carta** (dated 1215), and the grim **Victorian prison chapel**, dating back to the days when this was the county jailhouse and execution ground.

Free tours of the castle run at 11am and 2pm daily from April to September and on weekends in winter.

Bishops' Palace HISTORIC RUIN
(EH; ☎01522-527468; adult/child £4.20/2.10; ⌚10am-5pm) Beside the cathedral are the time-ravaged but still imposing ruins of the 12th-century Bishops' Palace, gutted by parliamentary forces during the Civil War. From here, the local bishops once controlled a diocese stretching from the Humber to the Thames. You can roam around the ruins and undercroft in the company of an entertaining audio guide.

Lincoln

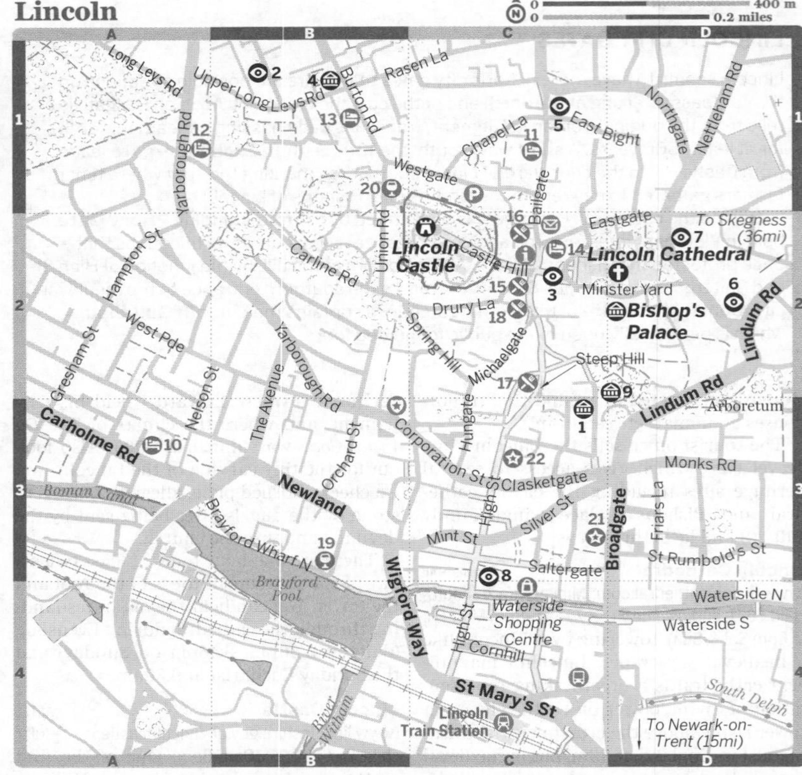

FREE Collection MUSEUM

(www.thecollection.lincoln.museum; Danes Tce; ⏲10am-5pm) An angular, modernist museum where archaeology bursts into life, with loads of hands-on displays where kids can handle artefacts and dress up in period costume. Check out the crushed skull of a 4000-year-old 'yellowbelly' (the local term for, well, the locals), pulled from a Neolithic burial site near Sleaford.

FREE Usher Gallery GALLERY

(Lindum Rd; ⏲10am-5pm Tue-Sat, 1-5pm Sun) Set in a handsome Edwardian building decorated with carvings of cow skulls, the town gallery has an impressive collection of works by such greats as Turner, Lowry and English watercolourist Peter de Wint (1784–1849). The gallery is set to reopen after renovations in 2010.

FREE Museum of Lincolnshire Life MUSEUM

(Old Barracks, Burton Rd; ⏲10am-4pm Mon-Sat) A short trek north of the centre and set in an old Victorian barracks, this community museum displays everything from Victorian farm implements to the tin-can tank built in Lincoln for WWI. Round the corner from the museum is the cute little **Ellis Mill** (Mill Rd; admission free; ⏲2-5pm Sat & Sun), the windmill that used to grind the town's flour in the 18th century.

Tours

History-focused 1½-hour guided **walking tours** (adult/child £4/free) run from outside the tourist office in Castle Hill at 11am daily in July and August, and at weekends only from October to June. Genuinely spooky 1¼-hour **ghost walks** (adult/child £4/2) depart from outside the tourist office at 7pm Wednesday to Saturday.

Boat trips along the River Witham and Fossdyke Navigation, a canal system dating back to Roman times, start from Brayford Waterfront. The **Brayford Belle** (☎01522-881200; www.lincolnboattrips.com; adult/child

Lincoln

Top Sights
Bishop's Palace ... D2
Lincoln Castle ... C2
Lincoln Cathedral ... D2

Sights
1 Collection ... C3
2 Ellis Mill ... B1
3 Exchequergate ... C2
Lincoln Guildhall ... (see 8)
4 Museum of Lincolnshire Life ... B1
5 Newport Arch ... C1
6 Pottergate ... D2
7 Priory Gate ... D2
8 Stonebow ... C3
9 Usher Gallery ... D2

Sleeping
10 Admiral Guest House ... A3
11 Bail House ... C1
12 Carline Guest House ... A1
13 Old Bakery ... B1
14 White Hart Hotel ... C2

Eating
15 Brown's Pie Shop ... C2
16 Gino's ... C2
17 Jew's House ... C2
Old Bakery ... (see 13)
18 Wig & Mitre ... C2

Drinking
19 Royal William IV ... B3
20 Victoria ... B1

Entertainment
21 Lincoln Drill Hall ... C3
22 Sakura ... C3

£6/4) runs five times daily from Easter to September, and just at weekends in October.

Sleeping

Bail House B&B ££
(☎01522-541000; www.bailhouse.co.uk; 34 Bailgate; r from £99; P@) Stone walls, worn flagstones, secluded gardens and one room with an extraordinary timber-vaulted ceiling are just some of the charms of this lovingly restored Georgian town house in central Lincoln. There's even a heated outdoor swimming pool.

White Hart Hotel HOTEL ££
(☎01522-526222; www.whitehart-lincoln.co.uk; Bailgate; s/d from £85/99; P@) You can't get more venerable than this grand dame of Lincoln hotels, sandwiched between castle and cathedral. With a history dating back 600 years, it offers vast rooms with appealing country-style fabrics and tasteful trim.

Old Bakery B&B ££
(☎01522-576057; www.theold-bakery.co.uk; 26-28 Burton Rd; r from £53; P@) This charming guest house, set above the excellent restaurant of the same name, has four quaint, sunlit rooms and delicious breakfasts, as you might expect from such foodie owners. Free parking is available out front.

Carline Guest House B&B ££
(☎01522-530422; www.carlineguesthouse.co.uk; 1-3 Carline Rd; s/d from £38/58; P) An elegant brick house, in an elegant residential part of town, with big, flowery rooms.

Admiral Guest House B&B £
(☎01522-544467; www.admiralguesthouse.co.uk; 16-18 Nelson St; s/tw/d £30/45/50; P) A hike from the old town in the industrial terraces northwest of Brayford Wharf, the Admiral mainly scores points for its prices.

Eating

As well as the following restaurants, there are numerous tearooms dotted along Steep Hill. Unless otherwise stated, reservations are recommended in the evenings at the following eateries.

TOP CHOICE **Brown's Pie Shop** PIE SHOP ££
(☎01522-527330; www.brownspieshop.co.uk; 33 Steep Hill; pies £9-17) Forget Mrs Miggins and Sweeny Todd; this long-established pie shop is one of Lincoln's top r estaurants, spread over a smart upstairs dining room and a cosy brick-lined basement. Come for hearty pies stuffed with locally sourced beef, rabbit and game.

Gino's ITALIAN £££
(☎01522-513770; www.ginoslincoln.co.uk; 7 Gordon Rd, Bailgate; mains £13-26) Run by Italian-born chef Vito Cataffo, who became famous for serving British food to Italians in Bologna, this superior restaurant serves fine dishes from northern and southern Italy.

Wig & Mitre PUB ££
(www.wigandmitre.com; 30 Steep Hill; mains £11-20; breakfast, lunch & dinner) Civilised pub-restaurant the Wig & Mitre has an excellent, upmarket menu but manages to retain the mellow mood of a friendly local. Food is served throughout the day, from morning fry-ups to lunchtime sandwiches and filling evening roasts. Bookings are not necessary.

Old Bakery MODERN BRITISH £££
(01522-576057; www.theold-bakery.co.uk; 26-28 Burton Rd; mains £17-22; Tue-Sun) This eccentric restaurant is where visiting actors and celebs come to eat when performing in the city. The menu is built around impeccably-presented local produce, and – appropriately – freshly baked bread.

Drinking

Bland chain pubs crowd the High St, but there are a few worthy independent public houses.

Victoria PUB
(6 Union Rd) A serious beer-drinker's pub with a pleasant patio looking up at the castle's western walls, the Victoria has a huge selection of guest brews, cask ales, thick stouts and superb ciders. Meals start at £7.

Royal William IV PUB
(Brayford Wharf N) Part of the regenerated Brayford Waterfront development, this student-friendly stone pub offers a more intimate drinking environment than the brash chain restaurants on all sides.

Entertainment

Ask at the tourist office about theatre venues.

Lincoln Drill Hall ARTS VENUE
(www.lincolndrillhall.com; Freeschool Lane) Downhill near the station, this stern-looking building hosts bands, orchestras, stage shows, comedy and daytime book and beer festivals.

Sakura NIGHTCLUB
(www.sakuralincoln.com; 280-281 High St; from 10pm Mon & Wed-Sat) There's a Tokyo Underground feel at this Japanese-themed basement club, which shakes to a different beat each night.

Information

The High St has numerous banks and ATMs. Check www.lincoln.gov.uk for events listings.

County hospital (01522-512512; off Greetwell Rd)

Post office (90 Bailgate; 9am-5.30pm Mon-Fri, 9am-5pm Sat) With bureau de change.

Tourist office (www.visitlincolnshire.com; 9 Castle Hill; 10.30am-4pm Mon-Sat) In a handsome 16th-century building by the castle.

Getting There & Away

Bus

National Express runs direct bus services from Lincoln to London (£25.20, 4¾ hours, daily) and Birmingham (£15.30, three hours, daily). Local buses mainly run Monday to Saturday; useful services include the following:

Boston Bus 5, 1½ hours, hourly (also five Sunday services)

Louth Bus 10, one hour, six daily

Skegness Bus 6, 1½ hours, hourly

Train

Getting to and from Lincoln by rail usually involves changing trains.

Boston £11, 1¼ hours, hourly, change at Sleaford

Cambridge £24, 2½ hours, hourly, change at Peterborough and Ely

Sheffield £12.40, one hour 40 minutes, hourly

Stamford

POP 19,525

One of England's prettiest towns, Stamford seems frozen in time, with elegant streets lined with honey-coloured limestone buildings and hidden alleyways dotted

WORTH A TRIP

DODDINGTON HALL

About 5 miles west of Lincoln on the B1190, peaceful **Doddington Hall** (www.doddingtonhall.com; adult/child £8.50/4.25, garden only £5/2.75; 11am-5pm Wed, Sun & bank holidays Apr-Sep, house open from 1pm) was another creation of the talented Robert Smythson, who also designed Longleat (p266) and Hardwick Hall (p462). Completed in 1600, this handsome Elizabethan pile boasts hectares of gorgeous ornamental gardens and all the tapestries, oil paintings and heirlooms you could ask for. The easiest way to get here is by taxi from Lincoln.

DON'T MISS

BURGHLEY HOUSE

Lying just a mile south of Stamford, flamboyant **Burghley House** (www.burghley.co.uk; adult/child incl sculpture garden £11.80/5.80; ⏱11am-5pm Sat-Thu) – pronounced bur-lee – was built by Queen Elizabeth's chief adviser William Cecil, whose descendants have lived here ever since. Needless to say, the family only uses a handful of the 115 rooms, and the remainder of the house is open to the public.

Set in more than 810 hectares of grounds, landscaped by the famous Lancelot 'Capability' Brown, the house bristles with cupolas, pavilions, belvederes and chimneys, and the staterooms are a treasure-trove of ormolu clocks, priceless oil paintings, Louis XIV furniture and magnificent murals of Greco-Roman deities and Rubenesque ladies in various states of undress, painted by the 17th-century Italian master Antonio Verrio. In the aptly titled Heaven Room, a writhing mass of deities and demons spills off the ceiling and down the walls; death is depicted in classic form as a scythe-wielding skeleton and the damned enter the Inferno through the gaping mouth of a diabolical cat.

Make time for a stroll around the lovely gardens and deer park, where an atmospheric Sculpture Garden erupts with disembodied faces and skeletal forms. To reach Burghley, followed the marked path for 15 minutes through the park by Stamford train station.

with hearty alehouses, interesting eateries and small independent boutiques. A forest of historic church spires rises overhead and the gently gurgling River Welland meanders through the town centre. Unsurprisingly, the town is a top choice for filmmakers looking for the postcard vision of England, appearing in everything from *Pride and Prejudice* to *The Da Vinci Code.*

Sights

The town's top attraction is nearby **Burghley House**, but just walking around the streets is a delight. Drop in on **St Mary's Church** (St Mary's St), with its charmingly wonky broach spire, or explore the 15th-century chapel and chambers of the **William Browne Hospital** (Broad St; adult/child £2.50/1; ⏱11am-4pm Sat & Sun).

The **Stamford Museum** (Broad St; admission free; ⏱10am-4pm Mon-Sat) has a muddle of displays on the town's history, including an exhibit on man-mountain Daniel Lambert (see boxed text, p451) who died here in 1809.

Close to pint-sized St George's Church at the Stamford Arts Centre, the **tourist office** (☎01780-755611; stamfordtic@southkesteven.gov.uk; 27 St Mary's St; ⏱9.30am-5pm Mon-Sat, 10.30am-3.30pm Sun) can arrange guided walks and boat trips.

Sleeping

TOP CHOICE George Hotel HOTEL £££
(☎01780-750750; www.georgehotelofstamford.com; 71 St Martin's; s/d from £93/132.50, 4-poster d £210.50; P @ wi-fi) Marked by a gallows sign across the road, this magnificent inn opened its doors in 1597, on the site of a former hostelry for the crusading Knights of St John of Jerusalem, but its rooms perfectly blend period charm and modern elegance. This level of luxury comes with a hefty price tag, as does the superior modern British food at the attached restaurant.

Rock Lodge B&B ££
(☎01780-481758; www.rock-lodge.co.uk; 1 Empingham Rd; s/d £72/90; P) Just a short stroll northwest of the centre, this imposing Edwardian town house sits haughtily above clipped green lawns, but the welcome is warm. The cosy country-style rooms are lovingly maintained and the breakfasts will definitely set you up for the day.

Dolphin Guest House B&B £
(☎01780-757515; mik@mikdolphin.demon.co.uk; 12 East St; s/d £45/60; P) A rare cheap option in Stamford, with modest rooms in a modern house north of the centre.

Eating

The best meals in town are served at the George Hotel.

Tobie Norris PUB ££
(www.tobbienorris.com; 12 St Pauls St; mains £10-13; ⏱lunch daily, dinner Mon-Thu) A fine, stone-walled pub in a delightful, flagstone-floored town house serving hearty pub grub and wholesome ales from the Ufford microbrewery.

Voujon INDIAN ££
(☎01780-757030; www.voujonrestaurant.co.uk; 26 Broad St; mains £7-11) Well-prepared Indian favourites are served up in stylish surroundings near the museum. Bookings recommended.

☆ Entertainment

Stamford Arts Centre VENUE
(☎01780-763203; www.stamfordartscentre.com; 27 St Mary's St) This cultured establishment hosts everything from live jazz and art-house cinema to stand-up comedy.

Getting There & Away

Cross-country trains run to Birmingham (£31.50, 1½ hours, hourly) and Stansted Airport (£31, 1¾ hours) via Cambridge (£17.40, 1¼ hours) and Peterborough (£6.20, 15 minutes). Bus services:

London National Express, £14.30, three hours, one daily

Peterborough Delaine Buses 201, one hour, hourly Monday to Saturday

Boston

POP 35,124

It's hard to believe that sleepy Boston was the inspiration for its larger and more famous American cousin. Although no Boston citizens sailed on the *Mayflower,* the town became a conduit for persecuted Puritans fleeing Nottinghamshire for religious freedom in the Netherlands and America. In the 1630s, the fiery sermons of Boston vicar John Cotton inspired many locals to follow their lead, among them the ancestors of John Quincy-Adams, the sixth American president. These pioneers founded a namesake town in the new colony of Massachusetts, and the rest, as they say, is history.

Sights

Built in the early 14th-century, **St Botolph's Church** (church free, tower adult/child £3/1; ⊙10am-4pm Mon-Sat, btwn services Sun) is known locally as the Stump – a comment on the truncated appearance of its 88m-high tower. Puff your way up the 365 steps on a clear day and you'll see Lincoln, 32 miles away. Linguists may be interested to note that the name Boston is actually a corruption of 'St Botolph's Stone'.

Before escaping to the New World, the Pilgrim Fathers were briefly imprisoned in the 14th-century **Guildhall** (South St; adult/child £3.30/1.60; ⊙10am-4.30pm Wed-Sat), one of Lincolnshire's oldest brick buildings. Inside are fun, interactive exhibits, as well as a restored 16th-century courtroom and a mock up of a Georgian kitchen.

About 800m northeast of Market Pl, the **Maud Foster Windmill** (www.maudfoster.co.uk; adult/child £2.50/1.50; ⊙10am-5pm Wed & Sat) is the tallest working windmill in the country, with seven floors that creak and tremble with every turn of the sails.

Sleeping & Eating

Palethorpe House B&B ££
(☎01205-359000; 138 Spilsby Rd; r £60; P @) This pretty vine-covered Victorian villa has just two beautifully refurbished en suite rooms complete with living room, and it's just a 10-minute walk from Boston's centre.

White Hart PUB ££
(☎01205-311900; www.whitehartboston.com; 1-5 High St; s/d £75/95, dishes from £10; P @) Right in the middle of town, this handsome pub-hotel has tastefully modernised rooms and a decent menu of meaty mains in the modern British mould.

Information

Tourist office (South St; ticboston@boston.gov.uk; ⊙10.30am-3.30pm Wed-Fri, 10.30am-3pm Sat) Inside the Guildhall, close to the River Witham.

Getting There & Away

InterConnect bus 5 runs between Lincoln and Boston (1½ hours, hourly, five Sunday services) and bus 7 runs to Skegness (one hour, hourly, reduced service Sunday). For Lincoln, you can also take the train (£11, 1¼ hours), changing at Sleaford.

Skegness

POP 16,806

Spread out along the better-than-average yellow sand beach at Skegness ('Skeggy' to the locals) you'll find the ABC of the English seaside – amusements, bingo and candy floss, accompanied by a constant soundtrack of tweets, klaxons and bells from the abundant slot machines and fairground rides. Culture vultures will probably run a mile, but it's all good family fun if you immerse yourself in the whole tacky spectacle.

There are plenty of faded seaside hotels, and cheap and cheerful B&Bs start at just £18 per person – the **tourist office** (Grand Pde; ⌚9.30am-5pm) has listings and leaflets on local walks.

Trains run between Skegness and Boston (40 minutes, at least hourly Monday to Saturday, nine on Sunday). Bus services include the Interconnect 7 to Boston (one hour, hourly, reduced service Sunday) and the Interconnect 6 to Lincoln (1½ hours, hourly).

NORTHAMPTONSHIRE

While it's hard to pin down a 'must-see' attraction, peaceful Northamptonshire has more than its fair share of stately homes, including the ancestral homes of George Washington and Lady Diana. The county capital is worth a visit for its museums and churches, and the countryside is dotted with villages full of pincushion cottages with thatched roofs and Tudor timbers.

Information

Explore Northamptonshire (www.explorenorthamptonshire.co.uk)

Getting Around

Northampton is the hub for bus services around the county, but some run only a few times daily and there are fewer buses on Sundays. See the 'Transport & Streets' pages at www.northamptonshire.gov.uk for routes and timetables. Trains run by London Midlands are useful for getting to and from Northampton; Corby and Kettering are on the East Midlands line.

Northampton

POP 194,458

Rebuilt after a devastating fire in 1675, Northampton was once one of the prettiest towns in the Midlands, but WWII bombers and postwar town planners wreaked their usual havoc. Nevertheless, the heart of the town, around Market Sq and George Row, is actually rather grand, and there are some ancient monuments dotted among the pedestrian shopping arcades and concrete flyovers. Historically the town played a significant role in the Wars of the Roses and the English Civil War, before shifting its attention to manufacturing shoes.

Sights & Activities

Constructed after the 1675 fire, **All Saints' Church** (www.allsaintsnorthampton.com; George Row; ⌚8am-6pm) owes an obvious debt to the churches built by Sir Christopher Wren after the Great Fire of London, with an ornate barrel-vaulted ceiling and dark-wood organ and reredos.

Even those without a shoe fetish can get a kick out of the impressive displays at **Northampton Museum & Art Gallery** (www.northampton.gov.uk/museums; Guildhall Rd; admission free; ⌚10am-5pm Mon-Sat, 2-5pm Sun), where you can learn about the history of shoemaking and footwear fashions and faux pas.

Northampton's oldest buildings are dotted around the inner ring road. West of Market Sq, **St Peter's Church** (Marefair; ⌚10am-4pm Wed-Sat) is a marvellous Norman edifice built in 1150 and adorned with ancient carvings. North of the centre, on the far side of the eyesore bus station, **Church of the Holy Sepulchre** (⌚2-4pm Wed & Sat) is one of the few surviving round churches in the country, founded when the first Earl of Northampton returned from the Crusades in 1100.

Sleeping & Eating

The tourist office can advise on B&Bs in the area.

Ibis Hotel HOTEL £

(☎1604-608900; www.ibishotel.com; Sol Central, Marefair; r from £45) The Ibis offers chain-hotel rooms in a chain-hotel setting, but you can't fault the location, just a few hundred yards from Market Sq in the Sol Central entertainment complex.

Church Bar & Restaurant MODERN EUROPEAN ££

(☎01604-603800; www.thechurchrestaurant.com; 67-83 Bridge St; mains £12-18; ⌚Mon-Sat) A deeply funky redevelopment of an old church, where you can feast on modern European cooking on the terrace, or sip a cocktail under the stained-glass windows in the bar.

Information

Tourist office (www.explorenorthamptonshire.co.uk; Sessions House, George Row; ⌚8.30am-5.30pm Mon-Fri, 10am-2pm Sat Apr-Sep)

Getting There & Away

Northampton has good rail links with Birmingham (£12.60, one hour, hourly) and London Euston (£26, one hour, three hourly). The train station is about half a mile west of town along Gold St.

Famously ugly Greyfriars bus station is on Lady's Lane, just north of the Grosvenor shopping centre. National Express coaches run services to the following places:

Birmingham £7.50, one hour 40 minutes, three daily

London £13.40, 2¼ hours, five daily

Nottingham £13.40, 2½ hours, once daily

Around Northampton

ALTHORP

The ancestral home of the Spencer family, **Althorp House** (bookings 01604-770107; www.althorp.com; adult/child £12.50/6, access to upper floors extra £2.50; 11am-5pm Jul & Aug, last entry 4pm) – pronounced altrup – is the final resting place of Diana, Princess of Wales, who is commemorated by a memorial and museum. You don't have to be a follower of the cult of Diana to enjoy the outstanding art collection, with works by Rubens, Gainsborough and Van Dyck. Profits from ticket sales go to the charities supported by the Princess Diana Memorial Fund. The limited number of tickets available must be booked by phone or on the web.

Althorp is off the A428, 5.5 miles northwest of Northampton. Stagecoach bus 96 (hourly, not Sundays) runs from Northampton to Rugby, passing the gates to the Althorp estate, where you can call to arrange a pick up from the estate minibus.

STOKE BRUERNE

POP 395

About 8 miles south of Northampton, this charming little village nestles against the Grand Union Canal, the main drag of England's canal network. From here, you can follow the waterways all the way to Leicester, Birmingham or London. Set in a converted corn mill, the entertaining **National Waterways Museum** (www.nwm.org.uk/stoke; adult/child £4.75/2.75; 10am-5pm) charts the history of the canal network and the bargemen, lock keepers and pit workers whose livelihoods depended on it.

The Grand Union Canal is still frequented by brightly painted barges. In summer, you can cruise on the **Indian Chief** (01604-862428; Sun & bank holiday weekends only), run by the Boat Inn.

For overnight stays, try **Waterways Cottage** (01604-863865; www.waterwayscottage.co.uk; Bridge Rd; s/d incl breakfast £48/60), an adorable thatched cottage right off the front of a biscuit box.

Meals and brews are served up at the cosy **Boat Inn** (01604-862428; www.boatinn.co.uk; mains £5-12) alongside the canal.

Buses 86 and 87 both run between Stoke Bruerne and Northampton (30 minutes, six daily Monday to Saturday).

SULGRAVE MANOR

While **Sulgrave Manor** (www.sulgravemanor.org.uk; adult/child £6.55/3.15; noon-5.30pm Sat & Sun Apr-Oct, also 2-5.30pm Tue-Thu May-Oct, last entry 4pm) is certainly an impressively preserved Tudor mansion, the main draw for most visitors is the connection between Lawrence Washington, who built the house in 1539, and a certain George Washington of Virginia. The Washington family lived here for almost 120 years before Colonel John Washington, the great-grandfather of America's first president, sailed to Virginia in 1656.

Sulgrave Manor is southwest of Northampton, just off the B4525 near Banbury. The easiest way to get here is to take a train to Banbury, and then a taxi from there.

KIRBY HALL

Known as the 'Jewel of the English Renaissance', **Kirby Hall** (EH; adult/child £5.30/2.70; 10am-5pm) was constructed for Christopher Hatton, Lord Chancellor to Elizabeth I, in around 1570. The house is all the more atmospheric for being partly ruined; ravens perch on the carved stone lintels and empty window frames look out over brilliantly restored parterre gardens. The Great Hall and state rooms were renovated to something of their original glory in 2004.

Kirby Hall is 4 miles northeast of Corby, which is 24 miles northeast of Northampton along the A43. Come by car or take a taxi from Corby train station.

LEICESTERSHIRE

Leicestershire was a vital creative hub during the Industrial Revolution, but its factories were a major target for German air raids in WWII and most towns in the county still bear the scars of wartime bombing. Nevertheless, there's some impressive history among the urban chaos, from Elizabethan castles to Roman ruins, and the busy capital, Leicester, offers a taste of India with its rainbow temples and pure-veg curry houses.

Information

Discover Rutland (www.discover-rutland.co.uk)
Leicestershire Tourism (www.goleicestershire.com)

Getting There & Around

Leicester is well served by buses and trains. For bus routes and timetables, visit the 'Roads & Transport' pages at www.leics.gov.uk. Regular buses connect Rutland to Leicester, Stamford and other surrounding towns.

Leicester

POP 279,923

Built over the buried ruins of two millennia of history, Leicester (*les*-ter) is another Midlands town that suffered at the hands of the Luftwaffe and postwar planners. However, a massive influx of textile workers from India and Pakistan since the 1960s has transformed the city from drab industrial workhouse to bustling global melting pot. Modern Leicester is alive with the sights, sounds and flavours of the subcontinent, creating a strange juxtaposition with the Victorian factories and eyesore concrete architecture. The city also has some surprising historical treasures, including perhaps the finest medieval guildhall in the country.

Sights

Apart from the National Space Centre, all of Leicester's **museums** (www.leicester.gov.uk/museums) are free.

FREE **New Walk Museum & Art Gallery** MUSEUM
(New Walk; 10am-5pm Mon-Sat, from 11am Sun) Southeast of the centre on pedestrian New Walk, this grand Victorian museum is full of eye-catching, thought-provoking displays that show off the collection to its best advantage. Highlights include the revamped dinosaur galleries, the painting collection (with works by Francis Bacon, TS Lowry and Stanley Spencer) and the Egyptian gallery, where real mummies rub shoulders with displays on Boris Karloff's *The Mummy*.

A MAN OF MAMMOTH PROPORTIONS

An unlikely folk hero, Daniel Lambert was born a healthy baby in 1770, but he soon began to tip the scales at ever more alarming totals. Despite being an enthusiastic swimmer and eating just one meal per day, Lambert ballooned to an astounding 336kg. When he became too large to continue in his job as a prison guard, he took to the road as a professional curiosity, granting public audiences to paying onlookers who marvelled at the size of the 'Human Mammoth'. When he died in 1809, the wall of the pub where he was staying had to be dismantled to remove the coffin. Despite his fame, Lambert was a relative lightweight compared to modern levels of obesity – the world's current heaviest man, Manuel Uribe, weighs in at a ground-shaking 597kg!

FREE **Guildhall** HISTORIC BUILDING
(Guildhall Lane; 11am-4.30pm Mon-Wed & Sat, 1-4.30pm Sun) Leicester's perfectly preserved 14th-century guildhall is reputed to be the most haunted building in Leicester. You can search for spooks in the magnificent Great Hall, the wood-panelled 'Mayor's Parlour' and the old police cells, which contain a reconstruction of a 19th-century gibbet.

National Space Centre MUSEUM
(www.spacecentre.co.uk; adult/child £12/10; 10am-5pm Tue-Sun, last entry 3.30pm) Before you get too excited, British space missions usually launch from French Guyana or Kazakhstan, but Leicester's space museum is still a fascinating introduction to the mysteries of the spheres. The ill-fated Beagle 2 mission to Mars was controlled from here and fun, kiddie-friendly displays cover everything from astronomy to the status of current space missions.

The centre is off the A6 about 1.5 miles north of the city centre. Take bus 54 from Charles St in the centre.

FREE **Newarke Houses Museum** MUSEUM
(The Newarke; 10am-5pm Mon-Sat, from 11am Sun) Sprawling over two 16th-century mansions, this entertaining museum has exhibits detailing the lifestyles of local people through the centuries. Don't

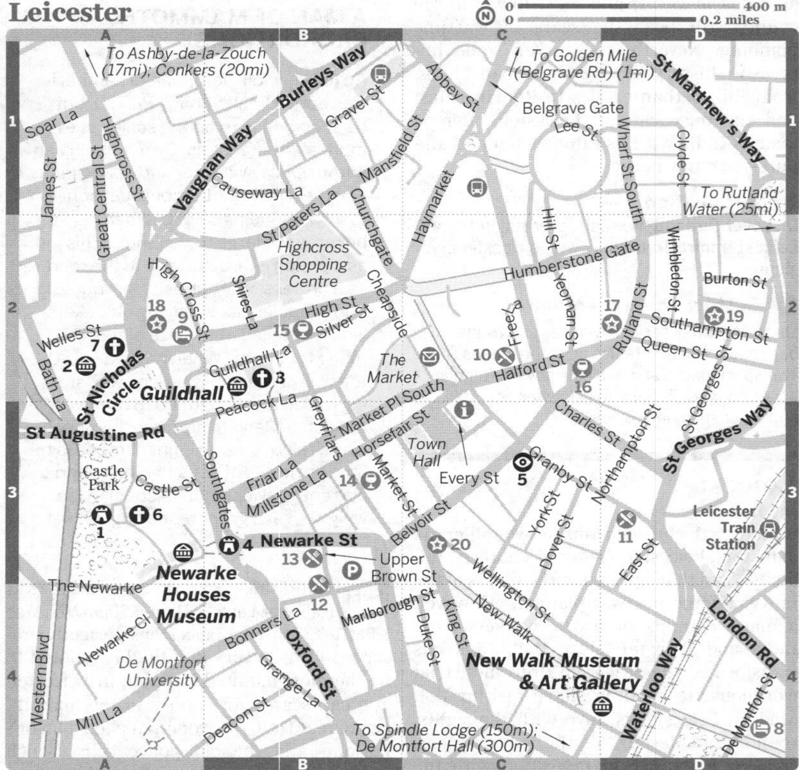

miss the displays on Daniel Lambert (see boxed text, p451), the walk-through recreation of a WWI trench and the trophies of the Royal Leicestershire Regiment, including an outrageous snuff box made from a tiger's head.

FREE **Leicester Castle** CASTLE

Dotted around the Newarke Houses Museum are the scattered ruins of Leicester's medieval castle, where Richard III spent his final days before the Battle of Bosworth. The most impressive chunk of masonry is the monumental gateway known as the **Magazine** (Newarke St), once a storehouse for cannonballs and gunpowder. Clad in Georgian brickwork, the 12th-century **Great Hall** (Castle Yard), stands behind a 15th-century gate near the church of **St Mary de Castro** (Castle St), where Geoffrey Chaucer was married in 1336. The hall is open for tours on the first Saturday of the month – contact the tourist office for details.

Jewry Wall Museum MUSEUM

(St Nicholas Circle; ⌚11am-4.30pm) You can see fine Roman mosaics and frescoes in this museum exploring the history of Leicester from Roman times to the modern day. In front of the museum is the **Jewry Wall**, part of Leicester's Roman baths. Tiles and masonry from the baths were incorporated in the walls of neighbouring **St Nicholas' Church**.

FREE **Leicester Cathedral** CATHEDRAL

(www.cathedral.leicester.anglican.org; 21 St Martin's; ⌚8am-6pm Mon-Sat, 7am-5pm Sun) In the midst of the shopping district on Guildhall Lane, this substantial medieval church features some striking carvings on its roof supports. Inside, you can see a memorial to Richard III, who rode out from Leicester to fatal defeat at the Battle of Bosworth.

Leicester

Top Sights
Guildhall ... B2
New Walk Museum & Art Gallery ... D4
Newarke Houses Museum ... A3

Sights
1 Great Hall ... A3
2 Jewry Wall Museum ... A2
3 Leicester Cathedral ... B2
4 Magazine ... B3
5 Ramada Hotel ... C3
6 St Mary de Castro ... A3
7 St Nicholas Church ... A2

Sleeping
8 Belmont House Hotel ... D4
9 Hotel Maiyango ... A2

Eating
10 Good Earth ... C2
11 Kayai ... D3
12 Tinseltown Diner ... B4
13 Watson's ... B3

Drinking
14 Firebug ... B3
15 Globe ... B2
Maiyango ... (see 9)
16 Quarter ... C2

Entertainment
17 Curve Theatre ... D2
18 Mosh ... A2
19 Phoenix Square ... D2
20 Superfly ... C3

Tours

In summer, **Discover Leicester** (☎0844 888 5151; adult/child £7/5; ⊙10am-4pm) runs jump-on jump-off open-topped bus tours around the city and up to Belgrave Rd, the Great Central Railway and the National Space Centre, departing from the Thomas Cook statue outside Leicester train station.

Festivals & Events

Leicester Comedy Festival COMEDY
(☎0116-261 6812; www.comedy-festival.co.uk) Held in February, this is the country's longest-running comedy festival, drawing big names as well as fresh talent.

Leicester Caribbean Carnival CULTURE
(www.leicestercarnival.com) In August the city hosts the biggest Caribbean celebration in the country after London's Notting Hill Carnival, with lots of colourful costumes.

Diwali RELIGION
Held in October or November, depending on the lunar calendar, the Festival of Lights is the biggest annual festival for Leicester's Hindu community, with fireworks, parades and ornate street lights on Belgrave Rd.

Sleeping

TOP CHOICE **Hotel Maiyango** HOTEL £££
(☎0116-251 8898; www.maiyango.com; 13-21 St Nicholas Pl; d from £148; @) A surprisingly sophisticated place to stay in a surprising setting at the end of the pedestrian High St. Attached to Leicester's funkiest bar, the hotel boasts spacious, sexy rooms, decorated with handmade Asian furniture, contemporary art and massive plasma TVs.

Belmont House Hotel HOTEL ££
(☎0116-254 4773; www.belmonthotel.co.uk; De Montfort St; s/d £115/120; P @) In a quiet location near De Montfort Hall, the Belmont has benefited from a hotel-wide refurbishment that has added plenty of modern style and colour to the rooms. There are great deals to be had if you book ahead.

Spindle Lodge B&B ££
(☎0116-233 8801; www.spindlelodge.com; 2 West Walk; s/d from £35/55; P @) Set in a grand Victorian house in the university quarter, this friendly place is cheaper than most, but you get what you pay for – rooms are plain and rather dated.

Ramada Hotel HOTEL ££
(☎0844 815 9012; www.ramadajarvis.co.uk; Granby St; r from £59; P @) Despite being set in a listed Victorian building, the Ramada spills out onto a noisy street that gets even noisier on weekend evenings. Rates vary day to day so check the web for the latest prices.

Eating

Watson's MODERN EUROPEAN ££
(☎0116-255 1928; 5-9 Upper Brown St; mains £12-17; ⊙Tue-Sat) Set in a converted cotton mill south of the shopping district, this upmarket eatery is a swirl of white linen

and fluted glasses. Artfully prepared and exquisitely presented modern European food is served to a jazz soundtrack. Bookings recommended.

Tinseltown Diner FAST FOOD £
(www.tinseltown.co.uk; 5-9 Upper Brown St; mains £5-11; ⏰noon-4am) Fancy a triple-decker chilli burger or an Oreo cookie and peanut butter milkshake at three in the morning? Then come on down to Tinseltown. With this being Leicester, the effect is more Bollywood than Hollywood, but kids will love the menu and razzmatazz.

Kayal INDIAN ££
(☎0116-255 4667; www.kayalrestaurant.com; 153 Granby St; dishes £5-13) This inviting restaurant offers an upmarket take on the steamy South Indian cuisine served up by the curry houses on Belgrave Rd. Try the *kappayum meenum* – the tasty fish curry served up by Keralan toddy shops. Bookings recommended.

Good Earth VEGETARIAN £
(☎0116-262 6260; 19 Free Lane; mains £3.25-6.25; ⏰noon-3pm Mon-Fri, 10am-4pm Sat) Tucked away on a side street, this wholesome vegetarian restaurant is justifiably popular for its veggie bakes, huge, fresh salads and homemade cakes.

Drinking

Maiyango BAR
(www.maiyango.com; 13-21 St Nicholas Pl) Moroccan lamps, silky scatter cushions and smooth beats create a chilled-out atmosphere in this moody cocktail bar and restaurant attached to the Maiyango hotel.

Quarter BAR
(41 Halford St; ⏰noon-midnight) Leading the way in the city's new cultural quarter, this place has an airy bar and restaurant full of two-tone designer furniture that spills outside in summer. The funky basement lounge is all mood lighting, plush sofas and world beats.

Firebug BAR
(www.firebug.co.uk; 1 Millstone Lane; ⏰noon-2am, till 4am Fri & Sat, till 1am Sun) A lava lounge for the student crowd, with theme nights, stage shows, gigs and a decent selection of beers on tap.

Globe PUB
(43 Silver St; ⏰to midnight Fri & Sat) In the atmospheric Lanes – a tangle of alleys south of the High St – this old-fashioned boozer offers fine draught ales and a crowd who rate their drinks by quality rather than quantity.

Entertainment

Nightclubs & Live Music

As well as the following venues, there are numerous mainstream clubs clustered around Churchgate and Gravel St.

De Montfort Hall LIVE MUSIC
(www.demontforthall.co.uk; Granville Rd) Big-name stars, big orchestras, and big song-and-dance acts are on the bill at this huge venue near Leicester University.

Mosh NIGHTCLUB
(www.moshleicester.com; 37 St Nicholas Place) Unleash your inner indie kid at this loud and lively rock joint near the end of the High St.

DON'T MISS

THE GOLDEN MILE

Lined with sari stores, jewellery emporiums and pure-veg curry houses, Belgrave Rd – aka the Golden Mile – is *the* place to come for blisteringly authentic Indian vegetarian food. Menus are built around the spicy flavours of the south, with delicious staples such as dosas (lentil-flour pancakes), *idli* (steamed rice cakes) and huge thalis (plate meals), with a mix of vegetable curries, flatbreads, rice and condiments. Belgrave Rd is about 1 mile northeast of the centre – follow Belgrave Gate and cross Burleys Flyover.

There are more top-notch eateries on the Golden Mile than you can shake a chapatti at. Our top pick is **Bobby's** (www.eatatbobbys.com; 154-6 Belgrave Rd; mains £5-12; ⏰Tue-Sun), which has been serving pure-veg classics since 1976. As well as spicy thalis and scrumptious samosas (curry-stuffed pastries), Bobby's is famous for its *namkeen* – tongue-tingling lentil-flour snacks that come in myriad shapes and sizes.

Superfly NIGHTCLUB
(www.superfly-city.com; 2 King St) Behind a towering mock-Tudor facade, this place serves up four floors of diverse beats, with guest DJs and gigs appealing to Leicester party people.

Theatre & Cinema

Curve Theatre THEATRE
(www.curveonline.co.uk; Rutland St) A sleek artistic space with big-name shows and some innovative modern theatre. The bar is a sophisticated place for lunch or a sun-downer.

Phoenix Square CINEMA
(www.phoenix.org.uk; Midland St) Part of the new Cultural Quarter, this is Leicester's premier venue for art-house films and digital media.

 Information

Post office (39 Gallowtree Gate; ⏲9am-5.30pm Mon-Sat) With a bureau de change.

Tourist office (www.goleicestershire.com; 7-9 Every St; ⏲10am-5.30pm Mon-Fri, 10am-5pm Sat) Brochures and information on local tours.

 Getting There & Away

East Midlands trains run to London's St Pancras Station (£46.80, 1¾ hours, two to four hourly) and Birmingham (£15, one hour, twice hourly).

Buses operate from St Margaret's bus station on Gravel St, north of the centre. The useful Skylink bus runs to East Midlands airport (£6, 50 minutes, every 30 minutes, 24 hours). Bus 440 runs to Derby (£7.90, one hour, 10 daily); one bus a day continues to Buxton (£14.30, two hours). National Express services:

Coventry £6.60, 45 minutes, four daily

London £18.30, 2¾ hours, one or two hourly

Nottingham 45 minutes, two hourly

 Getting Around

The centre is cut off from the suburbs by a tangle of underpasses and flyovers, but the centre of Leicester is easy to get around on foot. For unlimited transport on local buses, buy a £2.70 CityDay ticket.

> DON'T MISS
>
> **STEAMING AROUND LEICESTER**
>
> A fun jaunt rather than a serious way to get from A to B, the classic **Great Central Railway** (www.gcrailway.co.uk; return adult/child £14/9) operates steam locomotives from Leicester North station on Redhill Circle to Loughborough Central, following the 8-mile route along which Thomas Cook ran the original package tour in 1841. The locos chug several days a week from June to August and most weekends for the rest of the year – see the website for the latest timetable. To reach Leicester North station, take bus 70 from the Haymarket.

Around Leicester

BOSWORTH BATTLEFIELD

Given a few hundred years, every battlefield ends up just being a field, but the site of the Battle of Bosworth – where Richard III met his maker in 1485 – is enlivened by an entertaining **Heritage Centre** (☎01455-290429; www.bosworthbattlefield.com; admission £6; ⏲11am-5pm) full of skeletons and musket balls. The best time to visit is in August, when the battle is re-enacted by a legion of enthusiasts in period costume.

The battlefield is 16 miles southwest of Leicester at Sutton Cheny, off the A447. Arriva bus 153 runs hourly from Leicester to Market Bosworth, a 3-mile walk from the battlefield. Alternatively, book a taxi from **Bosworth Gold Cars** (☎01455-291999).

CONKERS & THE NATIONAL FOREST

The **National Forest** (www.nationalforest.org) is an ambitious project to generate new areas of sustainable woodland by planting 30 million trees in Leicestershire, Derbyshire and Staffordshire. More than seven million saplings have already taken root, and all sorts of visitor attractions are springing up in the forest, including the fun-filled **Conkers** (www.visitconkers.com; Rawdon Rd, Moira; adult/child £7.23/5.41; ⏲10am-6pm), a family-oriented nature centre, with interactive displays, indoor and outdoor playgrounds and lots of hands-on activities. Conkers is 20 miles northwest of Leicester off the A444. To get here, take bus 29/9 from Leicester to Ashby-de-la-Zouch (1½ hours, two hourly), then bus 23 to Moira (15 minutes, hourly). **National Forest YHA hostel** (☎0845 371 9672; www.yha.org.uk; beds from £14; P @), about 300m west of Conkers' entrance along Bath Lane, is packed with ecofriendly features and has a great restaurant serving local produce and organic wines.

DERBYSHIRE

Derbyshire is a country painted in two distinct tones – the lush green of rolling valleys, criss-crossed by a delicate tracery of dry stone walls, and the mottled brown of barren hilltops covered with the scrubby vegetation of the high moorlands. The big attraction here is the Peak District National Park, which preserves some of England's most evocative scenery, attracting legions of hikers, climbers, cyclists and fans of cramped dark places underground.

Activities

The Peak District National Park is the hub for outdoor enthusiasts – see the Activities heading in that section (p466).

Information

Peak District & Derbyshire (www.visitpeakdistrict.com)

Getting There & Around

East Midlands Airport (0871 919 9000; www.eastmidlandsairport.com) is the nearest air hub, and Derby is well served by trains, but there are few connecting services to smaller towns. In the Peak District, the Derwent Valley Line runs from Derby to Matlock. Edale and Hope lie on the Hope Valley Line from Sheffield to Manchester. For a comprehensive list of Derbyshire bus routes, visit the 'Transport' pages at www.derbyshire.gov.uk.

Derby

POP 229,407

Forever linked to football manager Brian Clough, who took Derby County to the top of the first division before his ill-fated tenure at Leeds United (a story powerfully told in the movie *The Damned United*), Derby was one of the crucibles of the Industrial Revolution. Almost overnight, a sleepy market town was transformed into a major manufacturing centre, producing everything from silk to bone china, and later locomotives and Rolls-Royce aircraft engines.

Derby suffered the ravages of industrial decline in the 1980s, but the city has bounced back with some impressive cultural developments, including the Silk Mill and Quad, a futuristic artistic space partly run by the British Film Institute.

Sights

FREE **Derby Cathedral** CATHEDRAL
(www.derbycathedral.org; 18 Irongate; 9.30am-4.30pm Mon-Sat & during services Sun) Founded in 943 AD, but extensively reconstructed in the 18th century, the vaulted ceiling of Derby Cathedral towers over a fine collection of medieval tombs, including the opulent grave of the oft-married Bess of Hardwick, who at various times held court at Hardwick Hall (p462) and Chatsworth House (p473).

WORTH A TRIP

SPLASHING ABOUT ON RUTLAND WATER

Aside from the modest claim to fame of being England's smallest county, tiny Rutland is noteworthy for the outdoorsy activities that are possible on **Rutland Water**, a vast artificial reservoir created by the damming of the Gwash Valley in 1976.

At Skyes Lane near Empingham, the **Rutland Water tourist office** (01780-686800; www.anglianwater.co.uk; 10am-4pm) has a snack kiosk, walking and cycling trails and information on the area.

A mile down the road, the **Whitwell Centre** (01780-460705; www.rutlandactivities.co.uk) has a vertigo-inducing high-ropes course, an outdoor climbing wall and bikes for hire (adult/child per day £21/10) for a gentle pedal around the lakeshore. In the same compound, **Rutland Watersports** (01780-460154; www.anglianwater.co.uk/leisure) offers a full range of watery activities, including sailing, windsurfing and kayaking.

From April to October, the **Rutland Belle** (01572-787630; www.rutlandwatercruises.com; adult/child £7/4.50) offers afternoon cruises from Whitwell to Normanton on the southern shore of the reservoir, where a stone causeway leads out across the water to **Normanton Church** (adult/child £2/1; 11am-4pm Mon-Fri, 11am-5pm Sat & Sun), saved from inundation by a limestone barrier wall.

The nearest places to stay are in Oakham and Stamford in Lincolnshire. Bus 19 runs from Nottingham (1¼ hours, hourly) and bus 9 runs from Stamford (20 minutes, hourly), passing along the north shore of Rutland Water.

FREE **Derby Museum of Industry & History** MUSEUM
(Silk Mill Lane; ⌚11am-5pm Mon, 10am-5pm Tue-Sat, 1-4pm Sun & bank holidays) Below the cathedral, overlooking the River Derwent, this well laid-out museum is housed in a former silk mill that was one of Britain's first modern factories. Displays inside tell the story of manufacturing in Derby, from water-powered spinning wheels to the development of the Rolls-Royce aero-engine.

FREE **Derby Museum & Art Gallery** MUSEUM
(The Strand; ⌚11am-5pm Mon, 10am-6pm Tue-Sun, 1-4pm Sun) Attached to the town library, this nicely presented museum has more displays on local history and industry, with a focus on the fine ceramics produced by Royal Crown Derby.

FREE **Quad** GALLERY
(☎01332-290606; www.derbyquad.co.uk; Market Pl; ⌚gallery 11am-6pm, from noon Sun, Mediatheque 11am-8pm, from noon Sun) A striking modernist cube on Market Pl, Quad contains a futuristic art gallery, a cinema and the Mediatheque, an archive of films and TV covering decades of broadcasting, run by the British Film Institute.

Royal Crown Derby Factory POTTERY
(www.royalcrownderby.co.uk; Osmaston Rd; tour & museum adult/child £5/4.75; ⌚10am-5pm Mon-Sat, tours 11am & 1.30pm Tue-Fri) Ceramic fans will enjoy a tour around this historic pottery works, which still turns out some of the finest bone china in England, from edgy Asian-inspired designs to the kind of stuff your grandma used to collect. Only children over 10 years can join the tours.

Sleeping

Chuckles B&B £
(☎01332-367193; www.chucklesguesthouse.co.uk; 48 Crompton St; s/d incl breakfast £30/50) The friendliest of several homey B&Bs just south of the centre, Chuckles is run by a cheerful couple with arty leanings. Rooms are simple but snug and there's a good breakfast. To get here, take Green Lanes and turn onto Crompton St by the church.

Cathedral Quarter Hotel HOTEL ££
(☎01332-546080; www.thefinessecollection.com/cathedralquarter; 16 St Mary's Gate; s/d from £80/100; @📶) Just a bell's peal from the cathedral in a grand Georgian edifice, this is the top choice for travellers with money to spend. The service is as polished as the grand marble staircase and there's an on-site spa and a lavish fine-dining restaurant.

Eating

Weekend bookings are recommended at the following eateries.

European Restaurant MODERN EUROPEAN ££
(☎01332-368732; 22 Irongate; mains £10-18; ⌚lunch Tue-Sat, dinner Mon-Sat) Opposite the cathedral, this trendy spot serves up good food in stylish surroundings, though 'European' generally translates to Italian when it comes to the menu.

Anoki INDIAN ££
(☎01332-292888; www.anoki.co.uk; 129 London Rd; mains £10-20; ⌚Mon-Sat) The best of a long line of Indian eateries on London Rd, Anoki offers an upmarket take on Midlands balti cooking. The vaulted dining room drips with baroque flourishes.

Drinking & Entertainment

Chain pubs and dance bars abound on Wardwick, Friargate and the pedestrian lanes around Market Pl, but weekend nights can be almost Bacchanalian in their excesses.

Old Bell Inn LIVE MUSIC
(☎01332-343701; www.myspace.com/theoldbellinnderby; Sadlergate) On a pedestrian lane just north of Market Pl, this old-school, spit-and-sawdust pub is the setting for gigs by rebel rockers and ageing punk veterans.

Quad CINEMA
(www.derbyquad.co.uk; Market Pl) Links to the British Film Institute in London ensure that there are some interesting art-house and old-classic movies shown here among the family films and blockbusters.

Brunswick Inn PUB
(www.brunswickinn.co.uk; 1 Railway Tce) Set at the end of a working-class terrace near the station, this award-winning inn is a warren of cosy rooms where you can enjoy the nut-brown ales fermented by the house brewery.

Information

Bureau de change (Victoria St; ⌚closed Sun) At the post office.

Tourist office (www.visitderby.co.uk; Market Pl; ⌚9.30am-5pm Mon-Sat, 10.30am-2.30pm Sun) This helpful office is under the Assembly Rooms in the main square.

BUS PASSES

There are several handy bus passes covering travel in the Peak District. The Zigzag Plus ticket offers all-day travel on Trent Barton buses, including the Transpeak between Derby and Buxton, for £7.80 (one child travels free with each adult). The Derbyshire Wayfarer (adult/child £8.60/£4.30) covers buses and trains throughout the county and as far afield as Manchester and Sheffield.

Getting There & Away

Air

About 8 miles northwest of Derby, **East Midlands Airport** (www.eastmidlandsairport.com) is served by regular Skylink buses (30 minutes, half-hourly, hourly 8.20pm to 6.20am).

Bus

Local and long-distance buses run from the shiny new Derby bus station, immediately east of Westfield. From Monday to Saturday, Transpeak has hourly buses between Derby and Buxton (1½ hours), via Matlock (45 minutes) and Bakewell (one hour). Five buses continue to Manchester (three hours).

Other services:

Leicester Skylink, 1½ hours, half-hourly (hourly 8.20pm to 6.20am)

Nottingham Transpeak/Indigo, 30 minutes, half-hourly

Train

The train station is about half a mile southeast of the centre on Railway Tce.

Birmingham £13.80, 45 minutes, four hourly

Leeds £33.50, 1½ hours, every 15 minutes.

London £53.30, 1¾ hours, two hourly

Sheffield £17, 35 minutes, hourly

Around Derby

KEDLESTON HALL

Sitting pretty in vast landscaped grounds, the superb neoclassical mansion of **Kedleston Hall** (NT; house adult/child £8.58/4.27; ⌚noon-5pm Sat-Wed Feb-Nov, grounds open daily) is a must for fans of stately homes. The Curzon family has lived here since the 12th century, but the current wonder was built by Sir Nathaniel Curzon in 1758. Meanwhile, the poor old peasants in Kedleston village had their humble dwellings moved a mile down the road, as they interfered with the view. Ah, the good old days...

Entering the house through a grand portico, you'll reach the breathtaking Marble Hall with its massive alabaster columns and statues of Greek deities. Other highlights include richly decorated bedrooms, a museum of Indian treasures amassed by Viceroy George Curzon, and a circular saloon with a domed roof, modelled on the Pantheon in Rome. Before you leave, take a walk around the 18th-century-style pleasure gardens, and pop into All Saints' Church to see the Curzon memorials.

Kedleston Hall is 5 miles northwest of Derby, off the A52. Arriva bus 109 between Derby and Ashbourne passes the Smithy, about 1 mile from Kedleston (25 minutes, every two hours Monday to Saturday). On summer Saturdays, the bus goes right to the hall.

CALKE ABBEY

Like an enormous, long-neglected cabinet of wonders, **Calke Abbey** (NT; ☎01332-863822; Ticknall; adult/child £9/4; ⌚12.30-5pm Sat-Wed) is not your average stately home. Built around 1703, the house was occupied by a dynasty of eccentric and reclusive baronets, who filled it with wonderful clutter, much of which can still be found in its rooms and corridors today.

The result is a ramshackle maze of rooms crammed with ancient furniture, mounted animal heads, dusty books, stuffed birds and endless piles of bric-a-brac spanning three centuries.

A stroll round the grounds is a similar time-warp experience – nature buffs should explore the ancient oak forests of **Calke Park**, preserved as a National Nature Reserve. You can visit the gardens at any time, but admission to the house is by timed ticket at busy times – advance bookings are recommended.

Calke is 10 miles south of Derby off the A514, close to the village of Ticknall. Arriva bus 61 from Derby to Swadlincote stops at Ticknall, a half-mile walk from the abbey.

ASHBOURNE

POP 7600

Perched at the southern edge of the Peak District National Park, Ashbourne is a pretty spread of steeply slanting stone streets, lined with cafes, pubs and antique shops.

On summer weekends, the town is a magnet for walkers, cyclists and bikers bound for Matlock Bath. Try to visit on Shrove Tuesday when Ashbourne goes football crazy.

At other times of year, the main attraction is the chance to walk or cycle along the **Tissington Trail**, part of NCN Route 68, which runs north for 13 miles to Parsley Hay, connecting with the **Pennine Cycleway** (NCN Route 68) and the **High Peak Trail** towards Buxton or Matlock. The track climbs gently along the tunnels, viaducts and cuttings of the disused railway line which once transported local milk to London, and a well-stocked cycle-hire centre rents out bikes for day trippers.

The **tourist office** (Market Pl; ⏲10am-5pm) can provide leaflets or advice on B&Bs in the area.

Sleeping & Eating

As well as the following places, you can embrace the glory of the English sausage roll at **Spencers the Bakers** (35-39 Market Pl; ⏲till 4.30pm) on the main square.

Just B B&B ££

(☎01335-346158; www.just-b.me.uk; 6 Buxton Rd; r from £65) A modern update on a lovely old house just uphill from the main market square. Rooms range from the comfortable to the stylish, and there's a piano bar and a ritzy restaurant serving modern British cuisine.

Patrick & Brooksbank CAFE £

(☎01335-342631; 22 Market Pl; sandwiches from £3; ⏲9.30am-3pm Mon, to 4pm Tue & Wed, to 5pm Thu-Sat) A great little deli and cafe with posh light meals and sandwiches and excellent homemade pastries, cheeses, breads and cold meats.

Getting There & Away

Without your own transport, buses are the only way to get to/from Ashbourne. Useful services:

Buxton Bowers 42/442, 35 minutes, every one to two hours

Derby Arriva 109/Trent Barton One, 40 minutes, hourly Monday to Saturday

Getting Around

About a mile above town along Mapleton Lane, the **Cycle Hire Centre** (☎01335-343156; half/full day from £12/15; ⏲9am-5.30pm Mar-Oct, reduced low-season hours) is right on the Tissington Trail, at the end of a huge and atmospheric old railway tunnel leading under Ashbourne. You can also rent children's bikes, bikes with baby seats, trailers for buggies and tandems. Ask for a map of pubs and teashops along the way.

DOVEDALE

About 3 miles northwest of Ashbourne, the River Dove winds through the steep-sided valley of Dovedale, where a famous set of stepping stones provides the perfect photo opportunity. Attracting hordes of visitors on summer weekends, the valley is every inch the green and pleasant land, and the final scenes of Ridley Scott's 2010 blockbuster *Robin Hood* were filmed along the riverbanks. Ashbourne's tourist office has various guides and walking pamphlets.

Matlock Bath

POP 2202

Unashamedly tacky, Matlock Bath looks like a seaside resort that somehow lost its way and ended up at the foot of the Peak District National Park. Following the River Derwent through a sheer-walled gorge, the main promenade is a continuous string of amusement arcades, tacky fairground attractions, tearooms, fish and

ROYAL SHROVETIDE FOOTBALL

Some people celebrate Shrove Tuesday (the last day before Lent) by eating pancakes or dressing up in carnival finery, but Ashbourne marks the occasion with riotous game of football where the ball is wrestled as much as kicked from one end of town to the other by vast crowds of revellers. Following rules first cooked up in the 12th century, villagers are split into two teams – those from north of the river and those living to the south – and the 'goals' are two millstones, set 3 miles apart. Participants are free to kick, carry or throw the ball, though it is usually squeezed through the crowds like a rugby ball in a scrum. Sooner or later, both players and ball end up in the river. Local shops board up their windows and the whole town comes out to watch or play – fearless visitors are welcome to participate in the melee but under a quirk of the rules, only locals are allowed to score goals.

MATLOCK ILLUMINATIONS

From the beginning of September to October, don't miss the **Matlock Illuminations** (Derwent Gardens; adult/child £4/free; from dusk Sat & Sun), with long chains of pretty lights, firework displays and a flotilla of outrageously decorated Venetian boats on the river.

chip shops, pubs and motorcycle accessory shops, catering to the vast hordes of bikers who gather here on summer weekends. On warm, sunny days, the smell of leather and petrol can be almost overpowering.

Sights & Activities

To enter into the spirit of Matlock Bath, buy yourself a punnet of chips and take a turn along the promenade, then work it off by following one of the steep paths that climb the eastern side of the gorge (several pedestrian bridges run across from the A6). The tourist office has free pamphlets describing some longer, more challenging walks in the hills.

Gulliver's Kingdom THEME PARK
(www.gulliversfun.co.uk; admission £12.50; 10.30am-4.30pm) A step up from the amusements on the promenade, this old-fashioned amusement park offers plenty of splashing, churning, looping attractions for anyone as tall as the signs at the start of the rides.

Heights of Abraham THEME PARK
(adult/child £11/8; 10am-5pm) Further north, this long-established hilltop leisure park has profited immeasurably from the addition of a spectacular cable-car ride from the bottom of the gorge. Once you reach the top, atmospheric cave and mine tours and fossil exhibitions add extra kiddie-appeal.

Peak District Mining Museum MUSEUM
(www.peakmines.co.uk; The Pavilion; adult/child £3.50/2.50; 10am-5pm) A more educational introduction to the mining history of Matlock is provided by this enthusiast-run museum, set in an old Victorian dance-hall. The museum is a maze of tunnels and shafts that little ones can wriggle through, while adults browse displays on mining history. For £2.50/1.50 extra per adult/child, you can go into the workings of the **Temple Mine** by Gulliver's Kingdom and pan for 'gold' (well, shiny minerals).

Masson Mills Working Textile Museum MUSEUM
(adult/child £2.50/1.50; 10am-4pm Mon-Fri, 11am-5pm Sat, to 4pm Sun) A mile south of Matlock Bath, housed in the vast brick buildings of an 18th-century mill, this museum tells the story of the textile mills that once dominated the Derwent Valley (see p461). The attached 'shopping village' is full of outlet stores for big clothing brands.

Sleeping

Hodgkinson's Hotel & Restaurant HOTEL ££
(01629-582170; www.hodgkinsons-hotel.co.uk; 150 South Pde; s/d from £40/75; P) Right in the thick of things on the parade, this eccentric hotel has an agreeably Victorian outlook. Rooms conjure up Matlock's golden age with antique furnishings, flowery wallpaper and cast-iron fireplaces.

Ashdale Guest House B&B ££
(01629-57826; www.ashdaleguesthouse.co.uk; 92 North Pde; s/d from £35/60) A tall stone house just beyond the tacky part of the promenade, with smart, tasteful rooms and organic breakfasts.

Temple Hotel HOTEL ££
(01629-583911; www.templehotel.co.uk; Temple Walk; s/d from £55/80; P) The views from this hillside inn are so lovely that Lord Byron once felt inspired to etch a poem on the restaurant window. Inside, everything is a little dated, but the rooms are comfy and the pub turns out filling meals and plenty of real ales.

Eating & Drinking

The official breakfast, lunch and dinner of Matlock is fish and chips, served at dozens of artery-clogging cafes along the strip. For a superior meal, head to the dining rooms at the Temple Hotel and Hodgkinson's Hotel.

Victorian Tea Shop TEAROOM £
(118 North Pde; snacks from £3; 10am-5.30pm Sat-Mon, Wed & Thu Jun-Sep, reduced hours at other times) The pick of the tearooms, this place is a cavern of chintz, with all the prerequisite frilly curtains, trays of iced buns and lace doilies.

DERWENT VALLEY MILLS

Unlikely as it may sound, the industrial mills that line the Derwent Valley are ranked up there with the Pyramids and the Taj Mahal on the Unesco World Heritage list. Founded in the 1770s by Richard Arkwright, the Cromford Mill near Matlock Bath was the first modern factory, producing cotton on automated machines, powered by a series of waterwheels along the River Derwent. This prototype inspired a succession of copycat mills at Derby, Matlock, Belper, Milford and Darley Abbey, ushering in the industrial age.

For an atmospheric introduction to Derbyshire's industrial history, take a tour of the original **Cromford Mill** (www.arkwrightsociety.org.uk; tour adult/child £3/2.50; 9am-5pm), run by the Arkwright Society. Buses 140 and 141 run here hourly from Matlock Bath (15 minutes, no Sunday service). Another fascinating industrial relic is **Strutt's North Mill** (www.belpernorthmill; adult/child £3/2; 1-5pm Wed-Sun) at Belper, accessible on the Transpeak bus between Derby and Matlock. Alternatively, you can drop into the museums housed in Derby's Silk Mill (p457) and Masson Mills near Matlock (p460).

Fishpond PUB

(204 South Pde) This pub gets a lively, spirited crowd, including legions of bikers. It has a mixed bag of live music and a decent selection of ales.

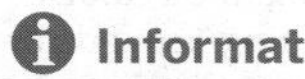

Information

Tourist office (www.derbyshire.gov.uk; The Pavilion; 10am-5pm Mar-Oct, to 4pm Nov-Feb) Run by the helpful staff at the Mining Museum.

Getting There & Away

Trains run hourly between Matlock and Derby (30 minutes). Matlock is also a hub for buses around the Peak District.

Bakewell Bus 172, one hour, hourly (not Sunday)

Chesterfield Bus 17, 35 minutes, hourly

Derby Transpeak, 1¼ hours, hourly

Sheffield Bus 214, 1¼ hours, hourly

Around Matlock Bath

From a tiny platform just north of the Sainsbury's on the outskirts of Matlock village, the nostalgic steam trains run by **Peak Rail** (www.peakrail.co.uk; adult/6-15yr/under 5yr £6.50/3.50/1.50) trundle along a 4-mile length of track to the nearby village of Rowsley.

Services run five times a day Saturday and Sunday (and some weekdays) from May to October, and some Sundays at other times of the year (see the website for details).

Chesterfield

POP 100,879

The eastern gateway to the Peak, Chesterfield is noteworthy for the bizarre crooked spire that rises atop **St Mary & All Saints Church** (01246-206506; www.chesterfieldparishchurch.org.uk; admission free, spire tours adult/child £3.50/1.50; 9am-5pm). Dating from 1360, the 68m-high spire is twisted in a right-handed corkscrew and it leans several metres southwest – a result of warping of the green timbers used in its construction. Locals prefer the legend that the spire twisted itself to witness the unlikely event of a virgin getting married in the church. Staff run regular tours of the spire; call to confirm a time.

The Chesterfield **tourist office** (Rykneld Sq; 9am-5.30pm Mon-Sat) is right opposite the crooked spire.

Chesterfield lies on the main rail line between Nottingham/Derby (20 minutes) and Sheffield (10 minutes), with hourly services in both directions. The station is just east of the centre. The Chesterfield Coach Station is on Beetwell St – useful local services include bus 170 to Bakewell (45 minutes, hourly) and bus 66 to Buxton (1½ hours, twice daily, one Sunday bus). National Express buses run to Coventry (£15.90, two hours, eight daily), Leicester (£8, 1¾ hours, five daily), Nottingham (£5.20, one hour, seven daily) and Sheffield (30 minutes, every 35 minutes).

Hardwick Hall

Perhaps the most stately of the East Midlands' stately homes, **Hardwick Hall** (NT; adult/child £9.50/4.75; ⊙11am-4.30pm Wed-Sun) is one of the most complete Elizabethan mansions in the country. It was home to the 16th century's second-most powerful woman, Elizabeth, Countess of Shrewsbury – known to all as Bess of Hardwick – who amassed a staggering fortune by marrying wealthy noblemen with one foot in the grave. Hardwick Hall was constructed using the money left behind when hubby number four shuffled off his mortal coil in 1590.

Designed by eminent architect Robert Smythson, the hall featured all the latest mod-cons of the time, including fully glazed windows – a massive luxury in the 16th century, inspiring the contemporary ditty 'Hardwick Hall, more glass than wall'. The atmospheric interiors are decked out with magnificent tapestries and time-darkened oil paintings of forgotten dignitaries. Set aside some time to explore the formal gardens, or take longer walks on the peaceful trails of **Hardwick Park**. Ask at the ticket office for details of routes.

Next door to the manor is Bess' first house, **Hardwick Old Hall** (EH; adult/child £4.20/2.10, joint ticket £11/5; ⊙10am-5pm Wed-Sun), now a romantic ruin administered by English Heritage.

Hardwick Hall is 10 miles southeast of Chesterfield, just off the M1. The Stagecoach Chesterfield-to-Nottingham bus stops at Glapwell, from where it's a 2-mile walk to Hardwick Hall.

PEAK DISTRICT

Rolling across the southernmost hills of the Pennines, the Peak District is one of the most beautiful parts of the country. Ancient stone villages are folded into creases in the landscape and the hillsides are littered with famous stately homes and rocky outcrops that attract hordes of walkers, climbers and cavers. No one knows for certain how the Peak District got its name – certainly not from the landscape, which has hills and valleys, gorges and lakes, wild moorland and gritstone escarpments, but no peaks. The most popular theory is that the region was named for the Pecsaetan, the Anglo-Saxon tribe that once populated this part of England.

As well as being England's first national park (it was founded in 1951), the Peak District National Park is the busiest national park in Europe, but don't be put off by its popularity – there are 555 sq miles of open English countryside to play with, and escaping the crowds is easy if you avoid summer weekends.

Locals divide the Peak District into the Dark Peak – dominated by exposed moorland and gritstone 'edges' – and the White Peak, made up of the limestone dales to the south.

Activities

CAVING & CLIMBING

The limestone sections of the Peak District are riddled with caves and caverns, including a series of 'showcaves' in Castleton, Buxton and Matlock Bath (described in each of those sections). For serious caving (or potholing) trips, the first port of call should be the website www.peakdistrictcaving.info, run by the caving shop **Hitch n Hike** (www.hitchnhike.co.uk; Mytham Bridge, Bamford), near Castleton.

If you're keen on climbing, the Peak District has long been a training ground for England's top mountaineers. Climbing in the Peak is predominantly on old-school trad routes, requiring a decent rack of friends, nuts and hexes. Top gritstone crags include Froggatt Edge, Curbar Edge, Stanage and the Roaches, while High Tor is the pick of the limestone outcrops. Numerous climbing guidebooks cover the area, including the comprehensive *Eastern Grit* and *Western Grit* published by Rockfax.

CYCLING

The plunging dales and soaring scarps are a perfect testing ground for cyclists, and local tourist offices are piled high with cycling maps and pamphlets. For easy traffic-free riding, head for the 17.5-mile **High Peak Trail**, which follows the old railway line from Cromford, near Matlock Bath, to Dowlow near Buxton. The trail winds through beautiful hills and farmland to Parsley Hay, where the **Tissington Trail**, part of NCN Route 68, heads south for 13 miles to Ashbourne.

Mirroring the Pennine Way, the **Pennine Bridleway** is another top spot to put your calves through their paces. You could also follow the **Pennine Cycleway** (NCN Route 68) from Derby to Buxton and beyond. Other popular routes include the **Limestone Way**, running south from Castleton to Staffordshire, and the **Monsal Trail** between Bakewall and Buxton.

Peak District National Park

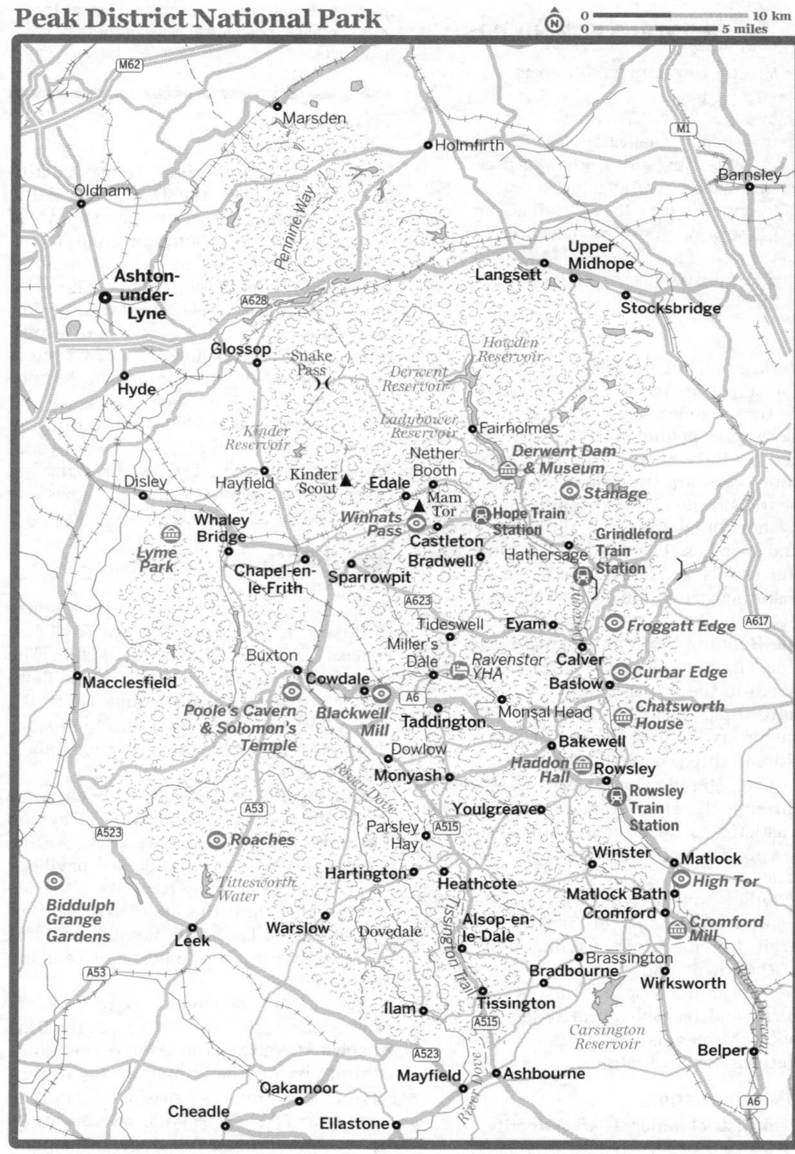

Peak Tours (www.peak-tours.com; mountain bike per day £18) will deliver its rental bikes to anywhere in the Peak District, and it also offers guided cycling tours. Derbyshire council operates several cycle-hire centres in the Peak District charging standard rates of £12/15 for a half/full day (£8/10 for a child's bike).

WALKING

The Peak District is one of the most popular walking areas in England, attracting legions of hikers in the summer months. The White

HOSTELS FOR HIKERS

Hikers, outdoors types and shoestring travellers can take advantage of some useful YHA hostels, including the phenomenally popular properties at Edale, Castleton, Tideswell and Eyam, plus a series of rudimentary 'camping barns' (beds from £6 per person) in remote locations around the peak. Contact the **YHA** (☎01629-592700; www.yha.org.uk) for details and locations.

Peak is perfect for leisurely strolls, which can start from pretty much anywhere – just be sure to follow the Countryside Code and close gates behind you. To explore the rugged territory of the Dark Peak, make sure your boots are waterproof and prepare to be transformed into a dripping, muddy blob by horizontal rain and slips into rivulets and marshes. The reward will come when the clouds suddenly part to reveal awe-inspiring vistas of hills, dales and sky.

The Peak's most famous walking trail is the **Pennine Way**, which runs north from Edale for more than 250 miles, finishing far north in the Scottish Borders. If you don't have three weeks to spare, you can reach the pretty town of Hebden Bridge in Yorkshire in three comfortable days.

The 46-mile **Limestone Way** winds through the Derbyshire countryside from Castleton to Rocester in Staffordshire, following a mix of footpaths, tracks and quiet lanes.

Other popular routes include the **High Peak Trail**, **Tissington Trail** and **Monsal Trail**, described under Cycling (p462). Most of the towns and villages in the Peak are well set up for visiting walkers with pubs, B&Bs and tearooms that welcome muddy boots. Numerous short walks are described in the following sections.

Information

Peak District National Park Authority (☎01629-816200; www.peakdistrict.org)

Getting There & Away

Trains run to Matlock Bath, Buxton, Edale and several other towns and villages, and buses run from regional centres like Sheffield and Derby to destinations across the Peak District. Be aware that buses are much more frequent at weekends, and many services close down completely in winter. Timetables are available from all the tourist offices, or online at www.derbyshire.gov.uk/buses.

Buxton

POP 24,112

Imagine Bath or Brighton transported to the rolling hills of the Derbyshire dales. That's Buxton, a picturesque sprawl of Georgian terraces, Victorian amusements and pretty parks, set in the very heart of the Peak District National Park. The town built its fortunes on its natural warm-water springs, which attracted hordes of health tourists in Buxton's heyday. Today visitors are drawn here by the flamboyant Regency architecture, the cute shops and cafes and the abundant natural wonders waiting in the surrounding countryside. Tuesday and Saturday are market days, bringing an extra dash of colour to the grey limestone market place.

Sights

Victoriana

At the foot of the Slopes, the historic centre of Buxton is a riot of Victorian pavilions, concert halls and glasshouse domes. The most famous building in town is the flamboyant, turreted **Opera House** (Water St), which hosts an impressive variety of stage shows, with a notable preference for Gilbert & Sullivan.

The Opera House shares an entrance with the equally flamboyant **Pavilion Gardens** (www.paviliongardens.co.uk; ⊙10am-4.30pm), where a series of domed pavilions sprawls across a pretty park like a seaside pier dropped into the middle of the Derbyshire Dales. The main building contains a tropical greenhouse, a nostalgic cafe and the tourist office.

Uphill from the Pavilion Gardens is another glorious piece of Victoriana, the **Devonshire Hospital**, whose enormous dome contains part of the campus for the University of Derby and – surprisingly – an opulent **spa** (☎01332-594408; www.devonshire-spa.co.uk) offering a full range of pampering treatments.

Buxton Spa ARCHITECTURE

In Victorian times, spa activities were centred on the extravagant Buxton Baths complex, built in grand Regency style in 1854. The various bath buildings are fronted by a grand, curving facade, known as **the**

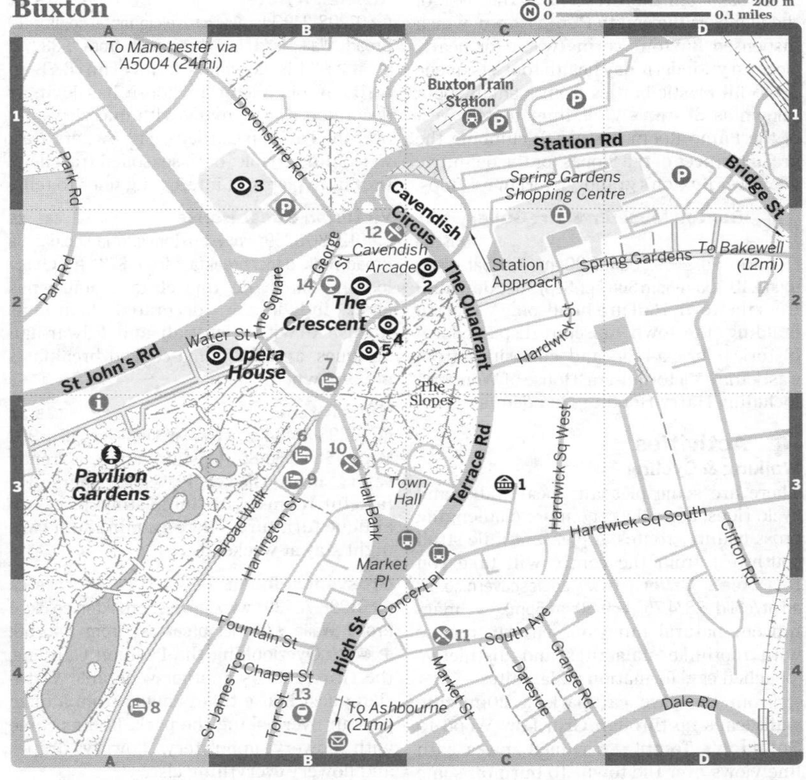

Buxton

Top Sights

Opera House B2
Pavilion Gardens A3
The Crescent B2

Sights

1 Buxton Museum & Art Gallery C3
2 Cavendish Arcade C2
3 Devonshire Hospital B1
4 Pump Room B2
Spa .... (see 3)
5 St Ann's Well B2

Sleeping

6 Grosvenor House B3
Nat's Kitchen .... (see 11)
7 Old Hall Hotel B2
8 Roseleigh Hotel A4
9 Victorian Guest House B3

Eating

10 Columbine Restaurant B3
11 Nat's Kitchen C4
12 Simply Thai B2

Drinking

13 Old Sun Inn B4
14 Project X B2

Crescent, inspired by the Royal Crescent in Bath. Today it sits empty, awaiting a developer with enough money to restore the town spa. For a taste of what the baths looked like in their heyday, pop around the corner to **Cavendish Arcade**, where the walls retain their original eggshell-blue art-deco tiles.

Across from the Crescent at the base of the Slopes is the empty **Pump Room**, which dispensed Buxton's spring water for nearly a century. Modern-day health tourists queue up to fill plastic bottles from a small spout known as **St Ann's Well**, immediately west of the Pump Room. It's worth climbing the green terraces of the Slopes for the definitive view over Buxton's grand Victorian rooftops.

FREE **Buxton Museum & Art Gallery** MUSEUM
(Terrace Rd; 9.30am-5.30pm Tue-Sat year-round, 10.30am-5pm Sun Apr-Sep) Just downhill from the Town Hall in a handsome Victorian building, the town museum displays local historical bric-a-brac and curiosities from Castleton's Victorian-era 'House of Wonders', including Harry Houdini's handcuffs.

Activities

Walking & Cycling

There are some pleasant local walks and cycle rides, as well as the more challenging cross-country routes. A pleasant mile stroll southwest from the centre will take you to **Poole's Cavern** (www.poolescavern.co.uk; adult/child £8/4.75; 9.30am-5pm), a magnificent natural limestone cavern, replete with toothlike stalactites and distinctive 'poached egg' formation stalagmites.

From the cave car park, a 20-minute walk leads up through Grin Low Wood to **Solomon's Temple**, a ruined tower with fine views over the town. To burn off some serious calories, set your sights on the **Monsal Trail**, beginning 3 miles east of the town and running all the way to Bakewell.

Good-quality bikes (both road and mountain bikes) can be rented from **Parsley Hay Cycle Hire** (01298-84493), about 8 miles south of Buxton at the junction of the High Peak and Tissington Trails (half/full day £11/14).

Sleeping

The nearest hostel is the Ravenstor YHA near Tideswell (p467).

TOP CHOICE **Old Hall Hotel** HOTEL ££
(01298-22841; www.oldhallhotelbuxton.co.uk; The Square; s/d incl breakfast from £65/100; @ wi-fi) There is a tale to go with every creak of the floorboards at this history-soaked establishment, supposedly the oldest hotel in England. Among other esteemed residents, Mary, Queen of Scots, stayed here from 1576 to 1578, albeit against her will. The rooms are still the grandest in town.

Roseleigh Hotel B&B ££
(01298-24904; www.roseleighhotel.co.uk; 19 Broad Walk; s/d incl breakfast from £38/72; P @ wi-fi) This gorgeous family-run B&B in a roomy old Victorian house has lovingly decorated rooms, many with fine views out over the Pavilion Gardens. The owners are a welcoming couple, both seasoned travellers; they have plenty of interesting tales to tell.

Victorian Guest House B&B ££
(01298-78759; www.buxtonvictorian.co.uk; 3a Broad Walk; d incl breakfast from £78; P) Overlooking the park, this elegant house has eight individually decorated bedrooms furnished with Victorian and Edwardian antiques, and the home-cooked breakfasts are renowned.

Nat's Kitchen B&B ££
(01298-214642; www.natskitchen.co.uk; 9-11 Market St; r £60-85) Upstairs above a trendy eatery near Market Pl, Nat's offers five tasteful rooms with interesting pieces of antique furniture. There's a minimum two-night stay at weekends.

Grosvenor House B&B ££
(01298-72439; www.grosvenorbuxton.co.uk; 1 Broad Walk; s/d incl breakfast from £45/60; P @ wi-fi) Overlooking the Pavilion Gardens, the Grosvenor is another venerable Victorian guest house that benefits from a huge parlour overlooking the park. Rooms come with flowery upholstery, flowery drapes and flowery everything else.

Eating

Columbine Restaurant MODERN BRITISH ££
(01298-78752; 7 Hall Bank; mains £11-17; dinner Mon-Sat, closed Tue Nov-Apr) On the lane leading down beside the Town Hall, this understated restaurant is top choice among Buxtonites in the know. The chef conjures up some imaginative dishes using mainly local produce and there's a sinful list of fattening puddings. Bookings recommended.

Pavilion Cafe CAFE £
(snacks £3-7; 9.30am-5pm Apr-Sep) Set in a renovated wing of the Pavilion, these peaceful tearooms conjure up images of jazz-fuelled tea-dances sometime between the wars.

Nat's Kitchen MODERN BRITISH ££
(01298-214642; www.natskitchen.co.uk; 9-11 Market St; mains £9.50-17) A relaxing dining room full of natural wood tones provides the

backdrop to some inventive modern British cooking at this cosmopolitan option near Market Pl. Ingredients are sourced from local suppliers and there are some smart B&B rooms upstairs. Bookings recommended.

Simply Thai THAI £
(2-3 Cavendish Circus; mains £7.50-13.50) This uptown Thai – all polished wood floors, Siamese sculptures and silk-attired staff – is a great place to enjoy a bit of Asian spice.

Drinking & Entertainment

Project X BAR
(www.project-x-cafe.com; The Old Court House, George St; 8am-midnight) Young folk in Buxton thank their lucky stars for this sultry cafe and bar at the back of the baths complex. Moroccan tables, hanging lanterns and deep violet walls create a casbah vibe. By day, people sip lattes and munch on paninis (snacks £5 to £10); after dark, drinkers move on to beers and cocktails.

Old Sun Inn PUB
(33 High St) The cosiest of the High St pubs, with a warren of rooms full of original features and a lively crowd that spans the generations. The pub grub (mains £6 to £9.50), while predictable, is inexpensive and tasty.

Opera House OPERA
(www.buxtonoperahouse.org.uk; Water St) Buxton's gorgeously restored Victorian Opera House hosts a full program of drama, dance, concerts and comedy, as well as some renowned festivals and events.

Information

There are several banks with ATMs along Spring Gardens and opposite Cavendish Arcade.

Grove Movie Centre (2 Eagle Pde; per 30min £2; 11am-9pm Mon-Fri, 10am-9pm Sat, noon-9pm Sun; @) Video shop with several internet terminals.

Post office (High St) With a bureau de change.

Tourist office (www.visitpeakdistrict.com; Pavilion Gardens; 9.30am-5pm Oct-Mar, 10am-4pm Apr-Sep)

Getting There & Away

Northern Rail has trains to and from Manchester (£9.20, one hour, hourly). Buses stop on both sides of the road at Market Pl. The hourly Transpeak runs to Derby (1¾ hours) and Nottingham (2½ hours), via Bakewell (one hour) and Matlock Bath (1½ hours). There are also six daily Transpeak buses to Manchester (one hour).

Other services:

Chesterfield Bus 66, 1¼ hours, two daily.

Sheffield Bus 65, one hour, five daily (three services Sunday)

Tideswell

POP 2000

About 8 miles east of Buxton, deep in the Derbyshire countryside, the former lead-mining village of Tideswell makes a good base for walking and cycling around the White Peak. As well as the popular **Limestone Way** and **Monsal Trail**, there are numerous short local circuits, including the 6-mile round trip to Litton Mill, which became notorious during the Industrial Revolution for exploiting the children of impoverished families as cheap labour.

Tideswell's centrepiece is the massive parish church of St John the Baptist – known as the **Cathedral of the Peak** (daylight hours) – which has stood here virtually unchanged for 600 years. Look out for the wooden panels inscribed with the Ten Commandments and the grand 14th-century tomb of local landowner Thurston de Bower, depicted in full medieval armour.

For accommodation, **Poppies** (01298-871083; www.poppiesbandb.co.uk; Bank Sq; s/d from £23/46) is frequently recommended by walkers for its cosy welcome and hearty evening meals.

About 2 miles from Tideswell at Miller's Dale, the **Ravenstor YHA** (0845 371 9655; www.yha.org.uk; dm from £16) is a great base for walkers, set in a huge, rambling country house with a cafe and bar.

Bus 65 from Buxton to Sheffield and bus 66 from Buxton to Chesterfield both pass through Tideswell and Miller's Dale.

Castleton

POP 1200

Guarding the entrance to the forbidding gorge known as Winnats Pass, Castleton is blessed with more than its fair share of visitor attractions. The streets are lined with leaning stone houses, walking trails criss-cross the surrounding hills, a wonderfully atmospheric castle crowns the ridge above town, and the bedrock under Castleton is riddled with caves that were once mined for Blue John Stone, a vivid violet form of flourspar. On summer weekends, it can seem like the entire population of the East Midlands has descended on the town, so come in the week to enjoy the sights in relative peace and quiet.

Sights

Peveril Castle CASTLE
(EH; adult/child £4.20/2.10; 10am-5pm Apr-Oct, 10am-4pm Nov-Mar) Topping the ridge to the south of Castleton, this evocative castle has been so ravaged by the centuries that it almost looks like a crag itself. Constructed by William Peveril, son of William the Conqueror, the castle was used as a hunting lodge by Henry II, King John and Henry III, and the crumbling ruins offer swoon-inducing views over the Hope Valley.

Castleton Caves CAVES
The limestone caves around town have been mined for lead, silver and the semiprecious John Blue Stone for centuries; four are open to the public on guided tours.

Peak Cavern
(01433-620285; www.devilsarse.com; adult/child £7.75/5.75; 10am-5pm, tours hourly till 4pm) A short walk from the castle tourist office is the largest natural cave entrance in England, known locally as the Devil's Arse. Should you choose to enter Beelzebub's rocky crevasse, you'll see some dramatic limestone formations, lit with fibre-optic cables.

Speedwell Cavern
(01433-621888; www.speedwellcavern.co.uk; adult/child £8.25/6.25; 10am-5pm, tours hourly till 4pm) About half a mile west of Castleton at the mouth of Winnats Pass, this cave is reached via an eerie boat ride through flooded tunnels, emerging by a huge subterranean lake called the Bottomless Pit. New chambers are being discovered here all the time by potholing expeditions.

Treak Cliff Cavern
(01433-620571; www.bluejohnstone.com; adult/child £7.95/4; 10am-5pm, last tour 4.20pm) A short walk across the fields from Speedwell Cavern, Treak Cliff is notable for its forest of stalactites and exposed seams of colourful Blue John Stone, which is still mined to supply the jewellery trade. Tours focus on the history of mining, and kids can polish their own piece of Blue John Stone on school holidays.

Blue John Cavern
(01433-620638; www.bluejohn-cavern.co.uk; adult/child £9/4.50; 10am-5.30pm) Up the side of Mam Tor, Blue John is a maze of natural caverns with rich seams of Blue John Stone that are still mined every winter. You can get here on foot up the closed section of the Mam Tor road.

FREE **Castleton Museum** MUSEUM
(01433-620679; Castleton tourist office, Buxton Rd; 9.30am-5.30pm) Attached to the tourist office, the cute town museum has displays on everything from mining and geology to rock climbing, hang-gliding and the curious Garland Festival (see Flowery Kings & Queens).

Activities

Set at the base of 517m Mam Tor, Castleton is the northern terminus of the **Limestone Way**, which follows narrow, rocky Cave Dale, far below the east wall of the castle.

For a scenic 6-mile circuit (three to four hours), follow the Limestone Way up Cave Dale and then loop round on paths and tracks to the west of Rowter Farm to meet the Buxton Rd. Go straight (north) across fields and cross another road to reach Mam

FLOWERY KINGS & QUEENS

Every 29 May – or on the 28th if the 29th is a Sunday – Castleton celebrates **Oak Apple Day** with a flamboyant village festival that can trace its origins back to at least the 17th century, and possibly all the way back to Celtic times. Every year, two residents of the village are chosen to be Garland King and Queen and paraded through the village on horseback, with the Garland King buried under an enormous headdress woven with flowers. It's all very *Wicker Man*, and the strange behaviour of the Nettle Man, who whips anyone not wearing a sprig of oak leaves with a bunch of stinging nettles, only adds to the surreal mood. In fact, the tradition of wearing oak leaves dates back to the English Civil War, when it served as a badge of identification for supporters of Charles II, who escaped capture at the Battle of Worcester by hiding in an oak tree. However, scholars believe the festival may have its ultimate roots in the worship of the pagan fertility goddess Brigantia. Needless to say, if anyone asks for help looking for a mysterious child, be very afraid...

Nick, where the Edale road passes through a gap in the ridge. From here, steps climb to the summit of Mam Tor, offering spectacular views along the Hope Valley.

The path then strikes northwest along the ridge to another gap called Hollins Cross, where several tracks lead back down to Castleton. From Hollins Cross, you can extend any walk by dropping down to Edale. Maps and leaflets on these and other walking trails are available at the Castleton tourist office.

Sleeping

Castleton YHA HOSTEL £
(☎0845 371 9628; www.yha.org.uk; Castle St; dm members/non-members from £14/17; P @) The inviting town hostel scores extra points for being in the middle of Castleton, rather than out in the sticks. Set in a rambling stone house, the hostel has tidy rooms, knowledgeable staff and – good news for thirsty walkers – a licensed bar.

Causeway House B&B ££
(☎01433-623921; www.causewayhouse.co.uk; Back St; s/d £33/65) The floors within this ancient character-soaked stone cottage are worn and warped with age, but the quaint bedrooms are bright and welcoming.

Ye Olde Nag's Head Hotel HOTEL ££
(☎01433-620248; www.yeoldenagshead.co.uk; Cross St; r from £50) The cosiest of a long line of 'residential' pubs along the main road, it offers comfortable, well-appointed rooms, some with luxuries such as four-poster beds and Jacuzzis. There's also a quality restaurant.

Rowter Farm CAMPSITE£
(☎01433-620271; sites per person £5; ⏲Easter-Sep) A simple campsite about 1 mile west of Castleton in a stunning location up in the hills. Drivers should approach via Winnats Pass; on foot, follow the Cave Dale path.

Eating & Drinking

Castle Inn PUB £
(Castle St; mains £5-10) On the road up to the castle, unsurprisingly, with a cosy flagstone lounge bar, an open fire and a decent selection of hearty meals including good Sunday roasts.

Ye Olde Cheshire Cheese Inn PUB ££
(☎01433-620330; www.cheshirecheeseinn.co.uk; How Lane; mains £5-14) Tradition is everything at this well-known alehouse, set in a fine old timbered building on the main road. The pub menu is more exotic than most (try the rabbit hot pot) and there are also comfy rooms for rent (singles/doubles £35/65).

Teashops abound in Castleton – probably the most popular purveyor of cream teas and light meals is **Three Roofs Cafe** (The Island; light meals £5-9; ⏲10am-5pm), opposite the turn-off to the tourist office.

Information

Tourist office (Buxton Rd; ⏲9.30am-5.30pm Mar-Oct, 10am-5pm Nov-Feb) Has a snack kiosk, museum and lots of leaflets on local walks.

Getting There & Away

The nearest train station is at Hope, about 3 miles east of Castleton on the line between Sheffield and Manchester. On summer weekends, a bus runs between Hope station and Castleton to meet the trains, but it's an easy walk.

Bus 272 runs to Sheffield (1¼ hours, hourly) and bus 173 to Bakewell (50 minutes, three daily) via Hope (10 minutes) and Tideswell (25 minutes). From Monday to Saturday, bus 68 goes from Castleton to Buxton (one hour) in the morning, returning in the afternoon. On Sundays only, bus 260 runs between Castleton and Edale (25 minutes, six services).

Derwent Reservoirs

North of the Hope Valley, the upper reaches of the Derwent Valley were flooded between 1916 and 1935 to create three huge reservoirs to supply Sheffield, Leicester, Nottingham and Derby with water. These artificial lakes soon proved their worth – the Dambusters squadron carried out practice runs over Derwent Reservoir before unleashing their 'bouncing bombs' on the Ruhr Valley in Germany in WWII. One of the towers atop the Derwent Dam contains a small **museum** (admission free; ⏲10am-4pm Sun) detailing their exploits.

These days, the Ladybower, Derwent and Howden Reservoirs are popular destinations for walkers, cyclists and mountain-bikers – and ducks, lots of ducks, so drive slowly! The focal point for visitors is **Fairholmes**, near the Derwent Dam, which has a **tourist office** (⏲9.30am-5.30pm), a car park, a snack bar and a good **cycle hire centre** (☎01433-651261; ⏲9.30am-5.30pm), charging the standard Peak rates.

Off-road routes for mountain-biking climb high into the hills – the tourist office stocks maps and guidebooks.

Fairholmes is 2 miles north of the A57, the main road between Sheffield and Manchester. Bus 273 from Sheffield Interchange runs out to Fairholmes in the morning, returning in the afternoon.

Edale

POP 316

Surrounded by majestic Peak District countryside, this tiny cluster of stone houses set around a pretty parish church is an enchanting place to pass the time. Edale lies between the White and Dark Peak areas, and is the southern terminus of the Pennine Way – despite the remote location, the Manchester–Sheffield line passes through the village, bringing legions of outdoorsy types on summer weekends.

Activities

Predictably, walking is the number one drawcard, and the **Pennine Way** – running north for 268 miles to the Scottish Borders – is the number-one choice for hardcore hikers. However, there are plenty of diverting strolls for less committed hill walkers.

As well as trips to Hollins Cross and Mam Tor, on the ridge dividing Edale from Castleton, you can walk north onto the **Kinder Plateau**, dark and brooding in the mist, but gloriously high and open when the sun's out. This was the setting for a famous act of civil disobedience by ramblers in 1932 that paved the way for the legal 'right to roam' and the creation of England's national parks.

Weather permitting, a fine circular walk starts by following the Pennine Way through fields to **Upper Booth**, then up a path called Jacobs Ladder and along the southern edge of Kinder, before dropping down to Edale via the steep rocky valley of Grindsbrook Clough, or the ridge of Ringing Roger.

About 1.5 miles east of Edale, **Ladybrook Equestrian Centre** (☎01433-670205; www.ladybooth.co.uk; Nether Booth) offers horse-riding trips around the Peak, lasting anything from one hour to a full day.

Sleeping

Upper Booth Farm CAMPSITE £

(☎01433-670250; www.upperboothcamping.co.uk; sites per person/car £5/2; ⊙Feb-Nov; P) Located along the Pennine Way about a mile from Edale, this peaceful campsite is set on a working farm and is surrounded by spectacular scenery. For hikers, there's a camping barn and small shop.

Edale YHA HOSTEL £

(☎0845 371 9514; www.yha.org.uk; Nether Booth; dm from £16; P @) This substantial hostel is set in a slightly austere-looking country house 1.5 miles east of Edale, with spectacular views across to Back Tor. To get here, follow the signed road past a rather fragrant farm from the Hope road.

Stonecroft B&B ££

(☎01433-670262; www.stonecroftguesthouse.co.uk; Grindsbrook; r from £75; P) This handsomely fitted-out stone house, built in the 1900s, has two comfortable bedrooms. Vegetarians and vegans are well catered for – the organic breakfast is excellent. The owner also runs landscape-photography courses.

Cooper's Camp CAMPSITE £

(☎01433-670372; sites per person/car £4.50/2; P) Simple site at the far end of the village on a farm. Caravans are also welcome and there is a shop, post office and cafe by the entrance.

Fieldhead Campsite CAMPSITE £

(☎01433-670386; www.fieldhead-campsite.co.uk; sites per person/car £5/2; P) Right next to the Moorland Centre, this pretty and well-equipped campsite spreads over six fields, with some pitches right by the river.

Eating

To stock up on carbs for hiking, head to **Cooper's Cafe** (☎01433-670401; Cooper's Camp; sandwiches & burgers £2-5; ⊙8am-4pm; @ wi-fi), a cheerful greasy spoon with wi-fi internet, close to the village school.

Walker-friendly pubs:

Old Nag's Head PUB ££

(Grindsbrook; meals £8-15) Refurbished, warm and welcoming.

Rambler Inn PUB ££

(☎01433-670268; www.thetramblerinn.com; Grindsbrook; mains £8-16) Ales, B&B rooms (from £38 per person) and a petting zoo for the kids.

Information

Moorland tourist office (☎01433-670207; www.edale-valley.co.uk; Grindsbrook; ⊙9.30am-5pm Mon-Fri, to 5.30pm Sat & Sun, shorter hours in low season) Has brochures, maps, displays on the moors, a kiosk and a campsite.

Getting There & Away

Trains run from Edale to Manchester (£8.90, every two hours, 45 minutes) and Sheffield (£5.50, every two hours, 30 minutes) via Hope. From Monday to Friday, bus 200 runs between Edale and Castleton (20 minutes, three daily) via Hope. On Sunday and on bank holidays, take bus 260 (six services) via Winnats Pass.

Eyam

POP 926

Quaint little Eyam (ee-em), a former lead-mining village, has a tragic and touching history. In 1665 the town was infected by the dreaded Black Death plague, carried here by fleas on a consignment of cloth from London, and the village rector, William Mompesson, convinced villagers to quarantine themselves rather than transmit the disease further. Some 270 of the village's 800 inhabitants succumbed, while surrounding villages remained relatively unscathed. Even independently of this poignant story, Eyam is a delightful place to wander around, with its sloping streets of old cottages backed by rows of green hills.

Sights

Eyam Parish Church CHURCH

(⊙9am-6pm Mon-Sat) Inside this church, where many of the plague victims were buried, you can view stained-glass panels and moving displays telling the story of the outbreak, and a plague register, recording those who died, name by name, day by day.

Eyam Hall HISTORIC HOUSE

(www.eyamhall.co.uk; adult/child £6.25/4; ⊙noon-4pm Sun-Fri) This solid-looking 17th-century manor house with stone windows and door-frames is home to a **craft centre** (admission free; ⊙10.30am-5pm, closed Mon) and several eateries, surrounding a traditional English walled garden.

Eyam Museum MUSEUM

(www.eyammuseum.demon.co.uk; Hawkhill Rd; adult/child £2/1.50; ⊙10am-4.30pm Tue-Sun) The town's museum has some vivid displays on the Eyam plague, plus exhibits on the village's history of lead-mining and silk-weaving.

Sleeping & Eating

Eyam YHA HOSTEL £

(☎0845 371 9738; www.yha.org.uk; Hawkhill Rd; dm £18) A simple place in a dignified old Victorian house with a folly tower, perched up a hill overlooking the village.

Miner's Arms HOTEL ££

(☎01433-630853; Water Lane; s/d £45/70) Although its age isn't immediately obvious, this traditional village inn was built shortly before the plague hit Eyam. Inside you'll find beamed ceilings, affable staff, a cosy stone fireplace, comfy en suite rooms and decent pub food (meals £8 to £12).

Crown Cottage B&B ££

(☎01433-630858; www.crown-cottage.co.uk; Main Rd; s/d from £45/64) Very walker- and cyclist-friendly, this stone house full of pottery ornaments is crammed to the rafters most weekends. Book ahead to be sure of a spot.

Eyam Tea Rooms TEAROOM £

(The Square; snacks from £2; ⊙till 4pm, closed Tue) All chintz and doilies, this tearoom serves delicious homemade cakes and pastries as well as hearty lunches.

Getting There & Away

Bus services from Eyam:

Bakewell Bus 175, 25 minutes, five daily Monday to Saturday

Buxton Bus 65/66, 40 minutes, seven daily (four Sunday)

Chesterfield Bus 66/66A, 40 minutes, 10 daily (four Sunday)

Sheffield Bus 65, 40 minutes, seven daily (three Sunday)

Bakewell

POP 3979

The second-largest town in the Peak District, Bakewell lacks the spa-town grandeur of Buxton, but it's still a pretty place to see and a great base for exploring the White Peak. The town is ring-fenced by famous walking trails and stately homes, but it's probably best known for its famous pudding (of which the Bakewell Tart is just a poor imitation). Like other Peak towns, Bakewell is mobbed during the summer months – expect traffic jams and cut-throat competition for hotel rooms at weekends.

Sights

Up on the hill above Rutland Sq, **All Saints Church** (9am-4.30pm) is packed with ancient features, including a 14th-century font, a pair of Norman arches, some fine heraldic tombs and a collection of crude stone gravestones and crosses dating back to the 12th century.

Set in a time-worn stone house near the church, the **Old House Museum** (Cunningham Pl; adult/child £3/1.50; 11am-4pm) explores local history. Check out the Tudor loo and the displays on wattle and daub, a traditional technique for building walls using woven twigs and cow dung.

Activities

Unsurprisingly, walking and cycling are the main attractions, and the popular and scenic **Monsal Trail** follows the path of a disused railway line from Combs Viaduct on the outskirts of Bakewell to Topley Pike in Wye Dale, about 3 miles east of Buxton. A number of old railway tunnels are set to be opened to visitors in 2011, extending the route all the way from Bakewell to Buxton.

For a rewarding shorter walk, follow the Monsal Trail for 3 miles to the dramatic viewpoint at Monsal Head, where you can pause for refreshment at the **Monsal Head Hotel** (www.monsalhead.com; mains from £8). The tourist offices at Bakewell and Buxton have a *Monsal Trail* leaflet with all the details.

Other walking routes go to the stately homes of Haddon Hall (p473) and Chatsworth House (p473).

Sleeping

Melbourne House B&B ££
(01629-815357; Buxton Rd; r from £55; P) Located in a picturesque, creeper-covered building dating back more than three centuries, this is an inviting B&B situated on the main road leading to Buxton.

Rutland Arms Hotel HOTEL ££
(01629-812812; www.rutlandarmsbakewell.co.uk; The Square; s/d £50/125; P) Aristocratic but slightly careworn, this hotel is the most refined offering in Bakewell. It's a substantial stone coaching inn, and the more expensive rooms have lots of flowery Victorian flourishes.

Eating & Drinking

Bakewell's streets are lined with cute tearooms and bakeries, most with 'pudding' in the name.

Piedaniels FRENCH ££
(01629-812687; www.piedaniels-restaurant.co.uk; Bath St; mains £12; Tue-Sat) The toast of the local restaurant scene, Piedaniels serves exquisitely presented modern-French cuisine in stunning surroundings. Weekday lunch menus (three courses for £12) are fantastic value.

Castle Inn PUB ££
(Bridge St; mains from £8) The ivy-draped Castle Inn is one of the better pubs in Bakewell, with four centuries' practice in warming the cockles of hamstrung hikers.

Information

Tourist office (01629-813227; Bridge St; 9.30am-5pm, from 10am Nov-Mar) In the old Market Hall, this helpful place has racks of leaflets and books and can help book accommodation.

Getting There & Away

Bakewell lies on the popular Transpeak bus route. Buses run hourly to Nottingham (1¾ hours), Derby (1¼ hours), Matlock Bath (30 minutes) and Buxton (50 minutes). Five services a day continue to Manchester (1¾ hours).

PUDDING OF CHAMPIONS

The Peak District's most famous dessert is – as any Bakewell resident will tell you – a pudding, not a tart. Invented following an accidental misreading of a recipe in around 1820, the Bakewell Pudding is a pastry shell spread with jam and topped with frangipane, a mixture of egg and ground almonds. If you've only ever seen the glazed version produced by commercial bakeries, the Bakewell original can look crude and misshapen, but we can confirm from experience that it's delicious. Numerous shops in Bakewell, all claiming to be the 'original' progenitor of the Bakewell Pudding, serve this tasty Derbyshire treat.

Around Bakewell

HADDON HALL

Glorious **Haddon Hall** (www.haddonhall.co.uk; adult/child £8.95/4.95; ⏲noon-5pm, last admission 4pm) looks exactly like a medieval manor house should look – all stone turrets, time-worn timbers and walled gardens. The house was founded in the 12th century, and then expanded and remodelled throughout the medieval period. The 'modernisation' stopped when the house was abandoned in the 18th century, saving Haddon Hall from the more florid excesses of the Victorian period. If the house looks familiar, it was used as a location for the period blockbusters *Jane Eyre* (1996), *Elizabeth* (1998) and *Pride and Prejudice* (2005).

The house is 2 miles south of Bakewell on the A6. You can get here on the Transpeak bus from Bakewell to Matlock and Derby (hourly) or walk along the footpath through the fields, mostly on the east side of the river.

CHATSWORTH HOUSE

It's easy to get stately home fatigue with all the grand manors dotted around the Midlands, but sumptuous **Chatsworth House** (www.chatsworth.org; adult/child house & garden £10.50/6.25, garden only £7.50/4.50; ⏲11am-5.30pm) is really something else. Known as the 'Palace of the Peak', this vast edifice has been occupied by the earls and dukes of Devonshire for centuries. The manor was founded in 1552 by the formidable Bess of Hardwick and her second husband, William Cavendish, who earned grace and favour by helping Henry VIII dissolve the English monasteries. Bess was onto her fourth husband, George Talbot, Earl of Shrewsbury, by the time Mary, Queen of Scots was imprisoned at Chatsworth on the orders of Elizabeth I in 1569.

While the core of the house dates from the 16th century, Chatsworth was altered and enlarged repeatedly over the centuries, and the current building has a Georgian feel, dating back to the last overhaul in 1820. Inside, the lavish apartments and mural-painted staterooms are packed with paintings and priceless items of period furniture. Among the historic treasures, look out for the portraits of the current generation of Devonshires by Lucian Freud.

The house sits in 25 sq miles of grounds and ornamental gardens, some landscaped by Lancelot 'Capability' Brown. When the kids tire of playing hide-and-seek around the fountains, take them to the **farmyard adventure playground** (admission £5.25) with loads of ropes, swings and slides, and farmyard critters.

Chatsworth is 3 miles northeast of Bakewell. Bus 214 from Sheffield Interchange to Matlock goes right to Chatsworth (hourly, 50 minutes) and bus 215 runs from Bakewell (20 minutes, hourly) on Sunday. On other days, take the Transpeak bus towards Derby and change to the 214 at Darley Dale.

Coming from Bakewell, walkers can take footpaths through Chatsworth park via the mock-Venetian village of Edensor (en-sor), while cyclists can pedal via Pilsley.

Yorkshire

Includes »

SOUTH YORKSHIRE........478
WEST YORKSHIRE ..480
Leeds............. 480
YORKSHIRE DALES NATIONAL PARK....490
EAST RIDING OF YORKSHIRE........497
NORTH YORKSHIRE........500
York 501
Scarborough 517
NORTH YORK MOORS NATIONAL PARK.... 521

Best Places to Eat

- » J Baker's Bistro Moderne (p509)
- » Stone Trough Inn (p513)
- » Star Inn (p523)

Best Places to Stay

- » Millgate House (p496)
- » Beiderbecke's Hotel (p519)
- » Holme House (p488)

Why Go?

With a population as big as Scotland's and an area half the size of Belgium, Yorkshire is almost a country in itself. It has its own flag, its own dialect and its own Yorkshire Day celebration (1 August). While local folk are proud to be English, they're even prouder to be natives of 'God's Own Country'.

What makes Yorkshire so special? First there's the landscape – from the brooding moors and green dales that roll their way to the dramatic coastline, Yorkshire has some of Britain's finest scenery. Second, there's the sheer breadth of history – every facet of the British experience is represented here, from Roman times to the 20th century.

But Yorkshire's greatest appeal is its people. Industrious and opinionated, they have a wry wit and a shrewd friendliness. Stay here for a while and you'll come away believing, like the locals, that God is indeed a Yorkshirewoman.

When to Go

In February the week-long Jorvik Festival sees York taken over by a Viking invasion.

In July, the Great Yorkshire Show happens in Harrogate, and Yorkshire's coastal sea-cliffs become a frenzy of nesting seabirds.

The ideal time for hiking in the Yorkshire Dales is September; the Walking Festival in Richmond also takes place in September.

History

As you drive through Yorkshire on the main A1 road, you're following in the footsteps of the Roman legions who conquered northern Britain in the 1st century AD. In fact, many Yorkshire towns – including York, Catterick and Malton – were founded by the Romans, and many modern roads (including the A1, A59, A166 and A1079) follow the lines of Roman roads.

When the Romans departed in the 5th century, native Britons battled for supremacy with invading Angles and, for a while, Yorkshire was part of the Kingdom of Northumbria. In the 9th century the Vikings arrived and conquered most of northern Britain. They divided the territory that is now Yorkshire into *thridings* (thirds), which all met at Jorvik (York), their thriving commercial capital.

In 1066 Yorkshire was the scene of a pivotal showdown in the struggle for the English crown, when the Anglo-Saxon king Harold II rode north to defeat the forces of the Norwegian king Harold Hardrada at the Battle of Stamford Bridge, before returning south to meet his appointment with William the Conqueror – and a fatal arrow – at the Battle of Hastings.

The inhabitants of northern England did not take the subsequent Norman invasion lying down. The Norman nobles built a chain of formidable castles throughout Yorkshire, including those at York, Richmond, Scarborough, Pickering and Helmsley. They also oversaw the establishment of the great abbeys of Rievaulx, Fountains and Whitby.

The Norman land grab formed the basis of the great estates that supported England's medieval aristocrats. By the 15th century, the duchies of York and Lancaster had become so wealthy and powerful that they ended up battling for the English throne – known as the Wars of the Roses (1455–87), it was a recurring conflict between the supporters of King Henry VI of the House of Lancaster (the red rose) and Richard, Duke of York (the white rose). They ended with the defeat of the Yorkist king Richard III by the earl of Richmond, Henry Tudor, at the Battle of Bosworth Field.

Yorkshire prospered quietly, with fertile farms in the north and the cutlery business of Sheffield in the south, until the big bang of the Industrial Revolution transformed the landscape: south Yorkshire became a centre of coal mining and steel works, while west Yorkshire was home to a massive textile industry, and the cities of Leeds, Bradford, Sheffield and Rotherham flourished. By the late 20th century another revolution was taking place. The heavy industries had died out, and the cities of Yorkshire were reinventing themselves as shiny, high-tech centres of finance, higher education and tourism.

Activities

Yorkshire's varied landscape of wild hills, tranquil valleys, high moors and spectacular coastline offers plenty of opportunities for outdoor activities. See www.outdoor yorkshire.com for more details.

CYCLING

Yorkshire has a vast network of country lanes, although the most scenic areas also attract lots of motorists so even minor roads can be busy at weekends. Options include the following:

North York Moors
(www.mtb-routes.co.uk/northyorkmoors) Off-road bikers can avail themselves of the networks of bridleways, former railways and disused mining tracks now converted to two-wheel use.

Moor to Sea Cycle Route
(www.moortoseacycle.net) A network of routes between Pickering, Danby and the coast, including a 20-mile traffic-free route that follows a disused railway line between Whitby and Scarborough.

White Rose Cycle Route
(NCN route 65; www.sustrans.org.uk) A 120-mile cruise from Hull to York and on to Middlesbrough, via the rolling Yorkshire Wolds and the dramatic western scarp of the North York Moors, with a traffic-free section on the old railway between Selby and York.

Yorkshire Dales Cycleway
(www.cyclethedales.org.uk) An exhilarating 130-mile loop, taking in the best of the national park. There's also lots of scope for off-road riding, with around 500 miles of bridleways and trails – check out www.mtbthedales.org.uk for inspiration.

WALKING

For shorter walks and rambles the best area is the **Yorkshire Dales**, with a great selection of walks through scenic valleys or over wild hilltops, with a few higher summits thrown in for good measure. The East

Yorkshire Highlights

1. Exploring the medieval streets of **York** (p501) and its awe-inspiring cathedral
2. Pulling on your hiking boots and striding out across the moors of the **Yorkshire Dales** (p490)
3. Chilling out in **Leeds** (p480): shopping, eating, drinking, dancing
4. Being beside the seaside at **Scarborough** (p517) with its traditional bucket-and-spade atmosphere
5. Riding on the **North Yorkshire Moors Railway** (p524), one of England's most scenic railway lines
6. Discovering mining's dark side at the **National Coal Mining Museum for England** (p487)

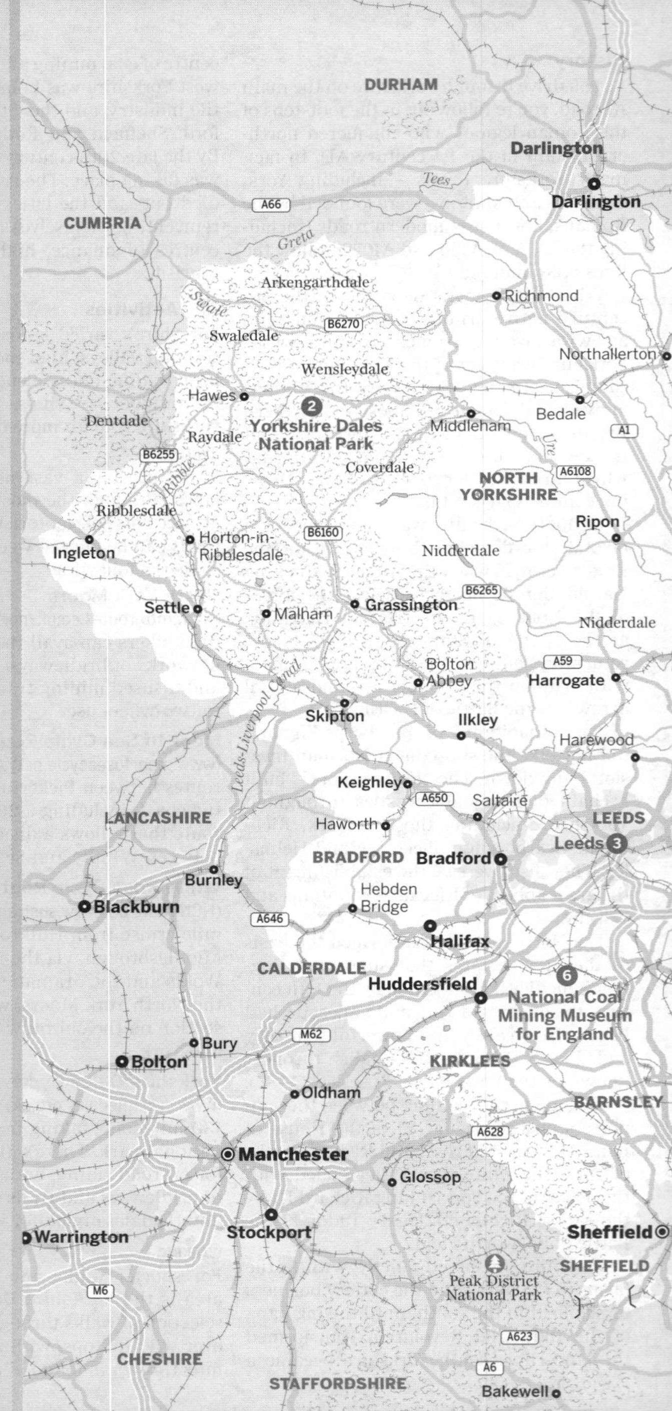

0 20 km
0 10 miles
North Sea
Billingham
Middlesbrough
Stockton-on-Tees
Egglescliffe
Stokesley
Danby
Whitby
Grosmont
Robin Hood's Bay
North York Moors National Park
North Yorkshire Moors Railway
Hambleton Hills
Hutton-le-Hole
Scarborough
Pickering
Helmsley
Thirsk
Bempton Cliffs Nature Reserve
Flamborough Head
Malton
Cleveland Hills
Bridlington
Bridlington
Boroughbridge
Great Driffield
York
YORK
EAST RIDING OF YORKSHIRE
Beverley
Hull
Hull Ferry Terminal
Patrington
Easington
Kilnsea
Spurn Head
WAKEFIELD
NORTH LINCOLNSHIRE
Grimsby
Cleethorpes
Scunthorpe
DONCASTER
Doncaster
To Rotterdam & Zeebrugge
NORTHEAST LINCOLNSHIRE
Rotherham
ROTHERHAM
Gainsborough
Market Rasen
Louth
LINCOLNSHIRE
Worksop
NOTTINGHAMSHIRE
Chesterfield
Lincoln
DERBYSHIRE
Sherwood Forest
Horncastle
A174
A171
A171
A19
A19
B1363
A64
A59
A166
A1079
A1
A19
A164
A15
A15
A18
A46
A158
A57
Ouse
Trent
Humber
Hull
Derwent
Rye
Seven
Hertford
Leven
Seph

Riding's **Yorkshire Wolds** hold hidden delights, while the quiet valleys and dramatic coast of the **North York Moors** also have many good opportunities.

Long-distance trails include the following:

Cleveland Way

(www.nationaltrail.co.uk/clevelandway) A venerable moor-and-coast classic that circles the North York Moors National Park on its 109-mile, nine-day route from Helmsley to Filey.

Coast to Coast Walk

(www.wainwright.org.uk/coasttocoast.html) England's number-one walk, 190 miles across northern England from the Lake District across the Yorkshire Dales and North York Moors. The Yorkshire section takes a week to 10 days and offers some of the finest walking of its kind in England.

Dales Way

(www.dalesway.org.uk) A charming and not-too-strenuous amble from the Yorkshire Dales to the Lake District, following the River Wharfe through the heart of the Dales, and finishing at Bowness-on-Windermere.

Pennine Way

(www.nationaltrail.co.uk/pennineway) The Yorkshire section of England's most famous walk runs for over 100 miles via Hebden Bridge, Malham, Horton-in-Ribblesdale and Hawes, passing near Haworth and Skipton.

Wolds Way

(www.nationaltrail.co.uk/yorkshirewoldsway) A beautiful but oft-overlooked walk that winds through the most scenic part of the East Riding of Yorkshire.

Information

Yorkshire Tourist Board (www.yorkshire.com; 312 Tadcaster Rd, York, YO24 1GS) Has plenty of general leaflets and brochures (postal and email enquiries only). For more detailed information contact the local tourist offices listed throughout this chapter.

Getting There & Around

The major north–south transport routes – the M1 and A1 motorways and the main London-to-Edinburgh railway line – run through the middle of Yorkshire, serving the key cities of Sheffield, Leeds and York.

If you're arriving by sea from northern Europe, Hull (in the East Riding) is the region's main port. More specific details for each area are given under Getting There & Away sections throughout this chapter. **Traveline Yorkshire** (☎0871 200 22 33; www.yorkshiretravel.net) provides public transport information for the whole of Yorkshire.

BUS Long-distances coaches run by **National Express** (☎08717 81 81 78; www.nationalexpress.com) serve most cities and large towns in Yorkshire from London, the south of England, the Midlands and Scotland. More details are given under Getting There & Away in the individual town and city sections.

Bus transport around Yorkshire is frequent and efficient, especially between major towns. Services are more sporadic in the national parks but still adequate for reaching most places, particularly in the summer months (June to September).

TRAIN The main line between London and Edinburgh runs through Yorkshire, with at least 10 trains per day calling at York and Doncaster, where you can change trains for other Yorkshire destinations. There are also direct services between the major towns and cities of Yorkshire and other northern cities such as Manchester and Newcastle. For timetable information contact **National Rail Enquiries** (☎08457 48 49 50; www.nationalrail.co.uk).

SOUTH YORKSHIRE

As in the valleys of South Wales, it was a confluence of natural resources – coal, iron ore and ample water – that made South Yorkshire a crucible of the British iron, steel and mining industries. From the 18th century to the 20th, the region was the industrial powerhouse of northern England.

The blast furnaces of Sheffield and Rotherham and the coal pits of Barnsley and Doncaster may have closed long ago, but the hulking reminders of that irrepressible Victorian dynamism remain, not only in the old steel works and pit-heads – some of which have been converted into enthralling museums and exhibition spaces – but also in the grand civic buildings that grace Sheffield's city centre, fitting testaments to the untrammelled ambitions of their 19th-century patrons.

Sheffield

POP 525,800

Steel is everywhere in Sheffield. Today, however, it's not the steel of the foundries, mills and forges that made the city's fortune, nor the canteens of cutlery that made 'Sheffield steel' a household name, but the steel of scaffolding and cranes, of modern sculptures and supertrams, and of new steel-framed buildings rising against the skyline.

The steel industry that made the city famous is long since gone, but after many years of decline Sheffield is on the up again – like many of northern England's cities it has grabbed the opportunities presented by urban renewal with both hands and is working hard to reinvent itself. The new economy is based on services, shopping and the 'knowledge industry' that flows from the city's universities.

Sights

Since 2000 the city centre has been in the throes of a massive redevelopment that will continue into 2020 and beyond, so expect building sites and road works for several years to come.

Of the parts that are already complete, pride of place goes to the **Winter Gardens** (admission free; ⌚8am-6pm), a wonderfully ambitious public space with a soaring glass roof supported by graceful arches of laminated timber. The 21st-century architecture contrasts sharply with the Victorian **town hall** nearby, and is further enhanced by the **Peace Gardens** – complete with fountains, sculptures and lawns full of lunching office workers whenever there's a bit of sun.

Sheffield's cultural revival is spearheaded by the **Millennium Gallery** (www.museums-sheffield.org.uk; Arundel Gate; admission free; ⌚10am-5pm Mon-Sat, 11am-5pm Sun), a collection of four galleries under one roof. Inside, the **Ruskin Gallery** houses an eclectic collection of paintings, drawings and manuscripts established and inspired by Victorian artist, writer, critic and philosopher John Ruskin, while the **Metalwork Gallery** charts the transformation of Sheffield's steel industry into craft and design – the 'Sheffield Steel' stamp on locally made cutlery and tableware now has the cachet of designer chic.

The nearby **Graves Gallery** (Surrey St; admission free; ⌚10am-5pm Mon-Sat) has a neat and accessible display of British and European modern art; the big names represented include Cézanne, Gauguin, Miró, Klee and Picasso.

In the days before steel mills, metalworking was a cottage industry (just like wool and cotton). For a glimpse of that earlier, more innocent era, explore the restored 18th-century forges, workshops and machines at the **Abbeydale Industrial Hamlet** (www.simt.co.uk; admission free; ⌚10am-4pm Mon-Thu, 11am-4.45pm Sun, closed early Oct-early Apr), 4 miles southwest of the centre on the A621 (towards the Peak District).

Sleeping & Eating

Leopold Hotel BOUTIQUE HOTEL ££
(☎0845 078 0067; www.leopoldhotel.co.uk; 2 Leopold St; r £70-90; wi-fi) Housed in a former grammar school building, Sheffield's first boutique hotel brings some much-needed style and sophistication to the city's accommodation scene (but without a London-sized price tag). Can suffer late-night noise from the bars on Leopold Square – ask for a quiet room at the back.

Houseboat Hotels HOUSEBOAT ££
(☎01909-569393; www.houseboathotels.com; Victoria Quays, Wharfe St; s/d/q from £59/69/95; P) Here's something a bit different: kick off your shoes and relax on board your very own permanently moored houseboat, complete with self-catering kitchen and patio area. Guests are entitled to use the gym and pool facilities at the Hilton across the road.

TOP CHOICE **Gusto Italiano** ITALIAN £
(18 Church St; lunch mains £6-10; ⌚breakfast & lunch Mon-Sat) A *real* Italian cafe, from the Italian owners serving homemade Italian food to the genuine Italian coffee being enjoyed by Italian customers reading the Italian newspapers... You get the idea. Daily lunch specials include dishes such as fennel sausage casserole, and vegetable lasagne with mushrooms and rosemary.

22a CAFE £
(22a Norfolk Row; mains £4-8; ⌚breakfast & lunch Mon-Sat) Nice music, nice people, nice place – this homely cafe serves hearty breakfasts and offers a mean wrap at lunchtime (hummus and roasted veggie is our favourite) and serves it with a decent cup of java.

Blue Moon Cafe VEGETARIAN £
(2 St James St; mains £5-7; ⌚breakfast, lunch & dinner Mon-Sat) Tasty veggie and vegan creations, soups and other healthy dishes, all served with the ubiquitous salad, in a very pleasant atmosphere – perfect for a spot of Saturday afternoon lounging.

Information

Post office (Norfolk Row; ⌚8.30am-5.30pm Mon-Fri, to 3pm Sat)

Tourist office (☎0114-221 1900; www.sheffieldcitycentre.com; 14 Norfolk Row; ⌚10am-5pm Mon-Fri, 10am-4pm Sat)

Getting There & Away

For all travel-related info in Sheffield and South Yorkshire, call ☎01709-51 51 51 or consult www.travelsouthyorkshire.com.

BUS The bus station – called the Interchange – is just east of the centre, about 250m north of the train station. National Express services link Sheffield with most major centres in the north; there are frequent buses linking Sheffield with Leeds (£5.20, one hour, hourly), Manchester (£8, 1½ hours, four daily) and London (£18, 4½ hours, eight daily).

TRAIN Sheffield is served by trains from all directions: Leeds (£8.70, one hour, twice hourly); London St Pancras (£70, 2½ hours, hourly) via Derby or Nottingham; Manchester Piccadilly (£16, one hour, twice hourly); and York (£15, 1¼ hours, twice hourly).

WEST YORKSHIRE

What steel was to South Yorkshire, wool was to West Yorkshire. It was the tough and unforgiving textile industry that drove the county's economy from the 18th century on. The wool mills, factories and canals that were built to transport raw materials and finished products defined much of this landscape. But that's all in the past, and recent years have seen the transformation of this once hard-bitten area into quite the picture postcard.

Leeds and Bradford, two adjoining cities so big that they've virtually become one, are the perfect case in point. Though both were founded amid the dark, satanic mills of the Industrial Revolution, both are undergoing radical redevelopment and reinvention, prettifying their town centres and trying to tempt the more adventurous tourist with a slew of new museums, galleries, restaurants and bars.

Beyond the cities, West Yorkshire is a landscape of bleak moorland dissected by deep valleys dotted with old mill towns and villages. The relics of the wool and cloth industries are still visible in the rows of weavers' cottages and workers' houses built along ridges overlooking the towering chimneys of the mills in the valleys – landscapes that were so vividly described by the Brontë sisters, West Yorkshire's most renowned literary export and biggest tourist draw.

Getting Around

The Metro is West Yorkshire's highly efficient train and bus network, centred on Leeds and Bradford – which are also the main gateways to the county. For transport information call **Metroline** (☎0113-245 7676; www.wymetro.com).

Day Rover (£6.20) tickets are good for travel on buses and trains after 9.30am on weekdays and all day at weekends. There's a range of additional Rover tickets covering buses and/or trains, plus heaps of useful Metro maps and timetables, available from bus and train stations and most tourist offices in West Yorkshire.

Leeds

POP 750,200

One of the fastest growing cities in the UK, Leeds is the glitzy, glamorous embodiment of newly rediscovered northern self-confidence. More than a decade of redevelopment has seen the city centre transform from near-derelict mill town into a vision of 21st-century urban chic, with skyscraping office blocks, glass and steel waterfront apartment complexes and renovated Victorian shopping arcades. However, the financial crisis of 2008–10 saw many flagship development projects grind to a halt.

Known as the 'Knightsbridge of the North', Leeds has made itself into a shopping mecca, its streets lined with bustling malls sporting the top names in fashion. And when you've shopped till you've dropped there's a plethora of pubs, clubs and excellent restaurants to relax in. From cutting-edge couture to contemporary cuisine, Leeds will serve it to you on a plate (or more likely in a stylishly designed bag). Amid all this cutting-edge style, it seems fitting that the network of city bus routes includes peach, mauve and magenta lines as well as the more humdrum red, orange and blue.

Sights

FREE **Royal Armouries** MUSEUM
(www.royalarmouries.org; Armouries Dr; ⏲10am-5pm) Leeds' most interesting museum is undoubtedly the Royal Armouries, beside the snazzy Clarence Dock residential development. It was originally built to house the armour and weapons from the Tower of London but was subsequently expanded to cover 3000 years' worth of fighting and self-defence. It all sounds a bit macho, but the exhibits are as varied as they are fascinating: films, live-action demonstrations and hands-on technology can awaken interests you never thought you had, from jousting to Indian elephant

armour – we dare you not to learn something! To get here, walk east along the river from Centenary Footbridge (10 minutes), or take bus 28 from Albion St.

Leeds Industrial Museum MUSEUM
(www.leeds.gov.uk/armleymills; Canal Rd; adult/child £3.10/1.10; ⏱10am-5pm Tue-Sat, 1-5pm Sun) One of the world's largest textile mills has been transformed into the Leeds Industrial Museum, telling the story of Leeds' industrial past, both glorious and ignominious. The city became rich off the sheep's back, but at some cost in human terms – working conditions were, well, Dickensian. As well as a selection of working machinery, there's a particularly informative display on how cloth is made. Take bus 5 from the train station to get here.

FREE **Leeds Art Gallery** ART GALLERY
(www.leeds.gov.uk/artgallery; The Headrow; ⏱10am-5pm Mon, Tue & Thu-Sat, noon-5pm Wed, 1-5pm Sun) The municipal gallery is packed with 19th- and 20th-century British heavyweights – Turner, Constable, Stanley Spencer, Wyndham Lewis et al – along with contemporary pieces by more recent arrivals such as Antony Gormley, sculptor of the *Angel of the North*.

FREE **Henry Moore Institute** ART GALLERY
(www.henry-moore-fdn.co.uk; The Headrow; ⏱10am-5.30pm Thu-Mon, 10am-9pm Wed) Housed in a converted Victorian warehouse in the city centre, this gallery showcases the work of 20th-century sculptors, but not, despite the name, anything by Henry Moore (1898–1986), who graduated from the Leeds School of Art. To see works by Moore, head to the Yorkshire Sculpture Park.

Festivals

The August Bank Holiday (the weekend preceding the last Monday in August) sees 50,000-plus music fans converge on Bramham Park, 10 miles outside the city centre, for the **Leeds Festival** (www.leedsfestival.com), one of England's biggest rock music extravaganzas, spread across four stages.

Sleeping

There are no budget options in the city centre, and the midrange choices here are either chain hotels or places we wouldn't recommend. If you want somewhere cheapish you'll be forced to head for the 'burbs, where there are plenty of decent B&Bs and smallish hotels.

TOP CHOICE **Quebecs** BOUTIQUE HOTEL £££
(☎0113-244 8989; www.theetoncollection.com; 9 Quebec St; s/d/ste from £170/190/325; @📶) Victorian grace at its opulent best is the theme of our favourite hotel in town, a conversion of the former Leeds & County Liberal Club. The elaborate wood panelling and heraldic stained-glass windows in the public areas are matched by the contemporary design of the bedrooms. Pre-booking online can get you a room for as little as half the rack rate.

42 The Calls BOUTIQUE HOTEL £££
(☎0113-244 0099; www.42thecalls.co.uk; 42 The Calls; r/ste from £150/280; @📶) This snazzy boutique hotel in what was once a 19th-century grain mill overlooking the river is a big hit with the trendy business crowd, who love its sharp, polished lines and designer aesthetic. The smaller 'study' rooms are pretty compact, and breakfast is not included; it'll cost you an extra £15 for the full English.

Bewleys Hotel HOTEL ££
(☎0113-234 2340; www.bewleyshotels.com/leeds; City Walk, Sweet St; r from £69; P@📶) Bewleys is super-convenient for motorists, just off Junction 3 on the M621 but also just 10 minutes' walk from the city centre, and with secure basement parking. Rooms are stylish and well appointed, with soundproofed walls and windows. The flat rate accommodates up to two adults plus two kids under 12.

Roomzzz Central APARTMENTS ££
(☎0113-233 0400; www.roomzzz.co.uk; 2-person apt from £89; P@📶) This outfit offers bright and modern luxury apartments complete with fitted kitchen, with the added advantage of a 24-hour hotel reception. Roomzzz City (10 Swinegate S) is right in the city centre; Roomzzz Central (2 Burley Rd) is half a mile west.

Malmaison BOUTIQUE HOTEL £££
(☎0113-398 1000; www.malmaison.com; 1 Swinegate; s/d/ste from £160/190/369; 📶) Self-consciously stylish, this typical Malmaison property is set in a former bus and tram company HQ. It has a fabulous waterfront location and all of the trademark touches: huge, comfy beds, sexy lighting and all the latest designer gear.

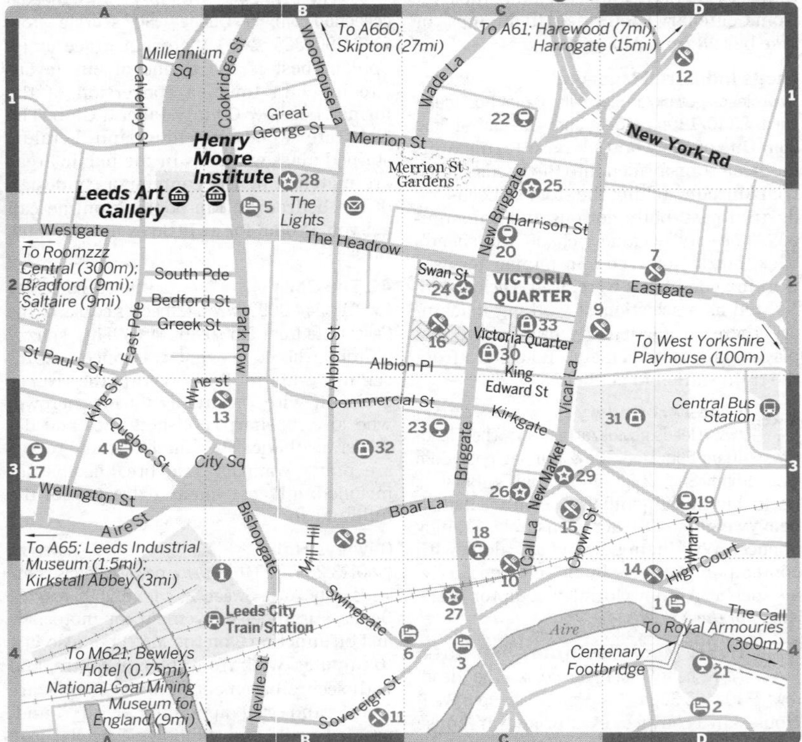

Jury's Inn HOTEL ££

(☎0113-283 8800; www.jurysinns.com; Kendell St, Brewery Pl; r £69-115; P@) The successful Irish hotel chain has another hit with its Leeds hotel: large, functional rooms, plenty of personal charm and few complaints. If you're walking, it's just across the Centenary footbridge from the city centre, in the heart of the fashionable Brewery Wharf district.

Radisson Blu HOTEL ££

(☎0113-236 6000; www.radissonblu.co.uk/hotel-leeds; 1 The Light, Cookridge St; r £90-130; P@) An extraordinary conversion of the former HQ of the Leeds Permanent Building Society, the Radisson inhabits a listed building dating from 1930, with 'standard' rooms that are anything but. You have a choice of three styles: high-tech, art deco and Italian, while the business-class rooms are truly luxurious.

Eating

The Leeds restaurant scene is constantly evolving, with new places springing up in the wake of new shopping and residential developments. The newly refurbished **Corn Exchange** (www.cornx.net), a beautiful Victorian building with a spectacular domed roof, now houses a new branch of Anthony's, while celebrity chef Jamie Oliver's new restaurant – **Jamie's Italian** (www.jamieoliver.com/italian/leeds; 35 Park Row; ⊙lunch & dinner) – opened in 2010, just too late to be reviewed here.

Brasserie Blanc FRENCH ££

(☎0113-220 6060; www.brasserieblanc.com; Victoria Mill, Sovereign St; mains £11-20; ⊙lunch & dinner;) Raymond Blanc manages to create a surprisingly intimate and romantic space amid the cast-iron pillars and red brick of an old Victorian warehouse, with a scatter of outdoor tables for sunny lunchtimes beside the river. The menu is unerr-

Leeds

Top Sights
Henry Moore Institute ... B2
Leeds Art Gallery ... A2

Sleeping
1 42 The Calls ... D4
2 Jury's Inn ... D4
3 Malmaison ... C4
4 Quebecs ... A3
5 Radisson Blu ... B2
6 Roomzzz City ... C4

Eating
7 Akbar's ... D2
8 Anthony's ... B3
9 Anthony's at Flannel's ... C2
10 Art's Cafe Bar & Restaurant ... C4
11 Brasserie Blanc ... B4
12 Hansa's Gujarati ... D1
13 Jamie's Italian ... B3
14 Livebait ... D4
15 Piazza by Anthony ... C3
16 Pickles & Potter ... C2

Drinking
17 Baby Jupiter ... A3
18 Bar Fibre ... C3
19 Duck & Drake ... D3
20 Northbar ... C2
21 Oracle ... D4
22 Sandinista ... C1
23 Whitelocks ... C3

Entertainment
24 City Varieties ... C2
Cockpit ... (see 6)
25 Grand Theatre & Opera House ... C1
26 HiFi Club ... C3
27 Mission ... C4
28 Vue Cinema ... B1
29 Wire ... C3

Shopping
30 Harvey Nichols ... C2
31 Leeds City Market ... D3
32 Trinity Leeds ... B3
33 Victoria Quarter ... C2

ingly French, from escargots (edible snails) to Toulouse sausage. The pre-7pm menu (6.30pm Saturday) offers three courses plus a glass of wine for £15.

Livebait SEAFOOD ££
(www.livebaitrestaurants.co.uk; 11-15 Wharf St, High Court; mains £12-20; ⏲breakfast Mon-Thu, lunch & dinner Mon-Sat) Quality seafood – from Whitby crab and Canadian lobster to fresh oysters and langoustines – is the order of the day in this friendly and welcoming restaurant. Classic fish and chips is done with a light and crispy batter and served with homemade tartare sauce and deliciously minty mushy peas.

Hansa's Gujarati INDIAN £
(www.hansasrestaurant.com; 72-74 North St; mains £6-8; ⏲lunch Sun, dinner Mon-Sat) A Leeds institution, Hansa's has been dishing up wholesome Gujarati vegetarian cuisine for 20 years. The restaurant is plain and unassuming (save for a Hindu shrine), but the food is exquisite – specialities of the house include *samosa chaat,* a mix of spiced potato and chickpea samosas with a yogurt and tamarind sauce.

Piazza by Anthony INTERNATIONAL ££
(www.anthonysrestaurant.co.uk; Corn Exchange, Call Lane; mains £7-12; ⏲lunch & dinner;) Leeds' landmark new development is the refurbished Corn Exchange, with this cool and contemporary restaurant taking pride of place. The all-day menu ranges from gourmet salads and sandwiches to pasta, meat and fish dishes such as bouillabaisse (Mediterranean fish stew) with confit potatoes and rouille (sauce of olive oil, breadcrumbs, garlic, saffron and chilli).

Pickles & Potter DELI, CAFE £
(18-20 Queens Arcade; mains £3-5; ⏲breakfast & lunch) This rustic cafe is famous for its superb sandwiches, especially the sumptuous roast-beef version compete with mustard, onion marmalade and fresh salad. There's also homemade soup, delicious cakes, and a meat or vegetarian main course of the day.

Akbar's INDIAN £
(www.akbars.co.uk; 15 Eastgate; mains £7-9; ⏲dinner) Bit of an Egyptian theme going on at this exceptionally popular Indian restaurant – sarcophagi and cat gods watch over the cutting-edge decor beneath a 'night in the desert' ceiling. The traditional curry dishes come in pyramid-size portions, and they don't take bookings – expect to wait 30 minutes for a table on weekend nights.

Art's Cafe Bar & Restaurant INTERNATIONAL ££
(www.artscafebar.co.uk; 42 Call Lane; mains lunch £5-7, dinner £10-15; ⏲lunch & dinner) Local art on the walls and a Bohemian vibe throughout make this a popular place for quiet reflection, a chat and a really good cup of coffee. The dinner menu offers a half-dozen classic dishes, including tarragon-crusted chicken, and roast butternut squash risotto.

Anthony's MODERN BRITISH £££
(☎0113-245 5922; www.anthonysrestaurant.co.uk; 19 Boar Lane; 2-/3-course dinner £36/45; ⏲lunch & dinner Tue-Sat) Probably the most talked-about restaurant in town, Anthony's serves top-notch modern British cuisine (try sea bream with smoked potatoes, peas and mint jelly) to a clientele so eager that they'll think nothing of booking a month in advance. If you go at any other time except Saturday evening, you'll get away with making your reservations a day or so earlier.

Anthony's at Flannel's FRENCH ££
(www.anthonysatflannels.co.uk; 3rd fl, Flannel's Fashion Centre, 68-78 Vicar Lane; mains £8-12, 2-/3-course lunch £18/22; ⏲breakfast Tue-Sat, lunch Tue-Sun, dinner Fri & Sat) The brasserie-style brother of the award-winning Anthony's, this bright and cheerful modern restaurant set amid white walls and timber beams features much of Anthony's style stuffed into its excellent sandwiches, salads, lunches and luxurious afternoon teas (£13). If you want to see and be seen, there's also **Anthony's Patisserie** in the classy setting of the Victoria Quarter arcade across the street.

Drinking

Leeds is justifiably renowned for its selection of pubs and bars. Glammed-up hordes of party animals crawl the cluster of venues around Boar Lane and Call Lane, where bars are opening (and closing) all the time. Most bars open till 2am; many turn into clubs after 11pm or midnight, with an admission charge.

Northbar BAR
(www.northbar.com; 24 New Briggate) There's a continental feel to this long, narrow, minimalist bar that's enhanced by the unfamiliar beer labels, from Dortmunder and Duvel to Schneider and Snake Dog. In fact, Northbar is dedicated to introducing Leeds to the best of world beers, with more than a dozen ales on tap and dozens more in bottles.

Duck & Drake PUB
(www.duckndrake.co.uk; 43 Kirkgate) A down-to-earth, traditional boozer with a well-worn atmosphere, a cast of regular pub characters and no fewer than 16 hand-pulled real ales to choose from. The Duck also provides a stage for local rock and blues bands from Wednesday to Sunday nights.

Whitelocks PUB
(www.whitelocks.co.uk; 6-8 Turk's Head Yard) There's lots of polished wood, gleaming brass and colourful stained glass in this popular, traditional pub dating from 1715. Theakstons, Deuchars IPA and several other real ales are on tap, and in summer the crowds spill out into the courtyard.

Baby Jupiter BAR
(11 York Pl) A retro gem with lots of purple velvet, hanging fishbowls and images from old sci-fi films, this basement bar sports a cool soundtrack that ranges from indie, funk and soul to punk, new wave and electro.

Sandinista COCKTAIL BAR
(www.sandinistaleeds.co.uk; 5/5a Cross Belgrave St) This laid-back bar has a Latin look but a unifying theme, attracting an eclectic clientele with its mixed bag of music and unpretentious atmosphere. If you enjoy a well-mixed cocktail but aren't too fussed about looking glam, this is the spot for you.

Bar Fibre BAR
(www.barfibre.com; 168 Lower Briggate) Leeds' most popular gay bar, which spills out onto the cleverly named Queen's Court, is where the beautiful set congregates. There's another cluster of gay bars downhill at the junction of Lower Briggate and The Calls.

Oracle COCKTAIL BAR
(www.oraclebar.com; 3 Brewery Pl) *The* place to be seen on a summer afternoon, Oracle has a huge outdoor terrace overlooking the River Aire. It serves gourmet burgers, cocktails and a great selection of international beers, from Guinness to Grolsch to Tsingtao.

Entertainment

In order to make sense of the ever-evolving scene, get your hands on the fortnightly *Leeds Guide* (www.leedsguide.co.uk; £1.50).

Clubs

The tremendous Leeds club scene attracts people from miles around. In true northern tradition, people brave the cold wearing next to nothing, even in winter, which is a spectacle in itself. Clubs charge a variety of admission prices, ranging from as little as £1 on a slow weeknight to £10 or more on Saturday.

HiFi Club CLUB
(www.thehificlub.co.uk; 2 Central Rd) This intimate club is a good break from the hardcore sound of four-to-the-floor: if it's Tamla Motown or the percussive beats of dance-floor jazz that shake your booty, this is the spot for you.

Cockpit LIVE MUSIC
(www.thecockpit.co.uk; Swinegate) Snugly ensconced in a series of railway arches, the legendary Cockpit is the antidote to dance clubs. A live music venue of note (Coldplay, the White Stripes, the Flaming Lips and Amy Winehouse have all cut their teeth here), it also hosts the Session on Friday nights, a superb indie/electro/guitar club night.

Mission CLUB
(www.clubmission.com; 8-13 Heaton's Ct) A massive club that redefines the term 'up for it'. Thursday sees the 'Full Moon Thai Beach Party' student night, while Saturdays offer a range of house, dance and classic-anthem club nights.

Wire CLUB
(www.wireclub.co.uk; 2-8 Call Lane) This small, atmospheric basement club, set in a forest of Victorian cast-iron pillars, throbs to a different beat every night, from rock and roll to drum and bass. Popular with local students.

Theatre & Opera

Grand Theatre & Opera House MUSICALS, THEATRE
(www.leedsgrandtheatre.com; 46 New Briggate) Hosts musicals, plays and opera, including performances by the acclaimed **Opera North** (www.operanorth.co.uk).

West Yorkshire Playhouse THEATRE
(www.wyp.org.uk; Quarry Hill Mount) The Playhouse has a reputation for excellent live drama, from the classics to cutting-edge new writing.

City Varieties MUSIC HALL
(www.cityvarieties.co.uk; Swan St) This old-fashioned music hall features anything from clairvoyants to comedy acts to country music. Closed for major refurbishment at time of research.

Cinema

Hyde Park Picture House ART HOUSE
(www.hydeparkpicturehouse.co.uk; Brudenell Rd) This Edwardian cinema shows a meaty range of art-house and mainstream choices. Take bus 56 from the city centre to get here.

Vue Cinema MULTIPLEX
(www.myvue.com; 22 The Light, The Headrow) For mainstream, first-run films, head for the Vue on the second floor of The Light entertainment complex.

Sport

Leeds United Football Club SOCCER
(www.leedsunited.com; Elland Rd) Leeds supporters know all about pain: the team was relegated from the Premiership in 2004, and then from the Championship to League One in 2007. Loyal fans were rewarded with promotion back to the Championship in 2010, and continue to pack the Elland Rd stadium in their masses. Take bus 93 or 96 from City Sq.

Yorkshire County Cricket Club CRICKET
(www.yorkshireccc.com; Headingley Carnegie Cricket Ground, St Michael's Lane) Headingley, the spiritual home of Yorkshire cricket, has been hosting cricket matches since 1890 and is still used for test matches. To get to the ground, take bus 18 or 56 from the city centre.

Shopping

Leeds' city centre has so many shopping arcades that they all seem to blend into one giant mall. The latest development – **Trinity Leeds** (www.trinityleeds.com) between Commercial St and Boar Lane, still under construction at the time of research – will be the city's biggest.

The mosaic-paved, stained-glass-roofed Victorian arcades of **Victoria Quarter** (www.v-q.co.uk), between Briggate and Vicar Lane, are well worth visiting for aesthetic reasons alone. Dedicated shoppers can join the footballers' wives browsing boutiques by Louis Vuitton, Vivienne Westwood and Swarovski. The flagship store here, of course, is **Harvey Nichols** (www.harveynichols.com; 107-111 Briggate).

Just across the street to the east you'll find the opposite end of the retail spectrum in **Leeds City Market** (www.leedsmarket.com; Kirkgate; 9am-5pm Mon-Sat, to 1pm Wed, open-air market Thu-Tue). Once the home of Michael Marks, who later joined Spencer, this is Britain's largest covered market, selling fresh meat, fish, fruit and vegetables, as well as household goods.

Information

Gateway Yorkshire/Leeds tourist office (☎0113-242 5242; www.visitleeds.co.uk; The Arcade, Leeds City Train Station; ⌚9am-5.30pm Mon-Sat, 10am-4pm Sun)

Post office (St John's Centre, 116 Albion St; ⌚9am-5.30pm Mon-Sat)

Getting There & Away

AIR Eleven miles northwest of the city via the A65, **Leeds Bradford International Airport** (www.lbia.co.uk) offers flights to a range of domestic and international destinations. The Metroconnect 757 bus (£2.50, 40 minutes, every 30 minutes, hourly on Sunday) runs between Leeds bus station and the airport. A taxi costs about £20.

BUS **National Express** (www.nationalexpress.com) serves most major cities, including services from London (£22, 4½ hours, hourly) and Manchester (£9.20, 1¼ hours, every 30 minutes).

Yorkshire Coastliner (www.coastliner.co.uk) has useful services from Leeds to York, Castle Howard, Goathland and Whitby (840 and 842); to York and Scarborough (843); and to Filey and Bridlington (845 and X45). A Freedom Ticket (£13) gives unlimited bus travel for a day.

TRAIN Leeds City Station has hourly services from London King's Cross (£85, 2½ hours), Sheffield (£12, one hour), Manchester (£16, one hour) and York (£11, 30 minutes).

Leeds is also the starting point for services on the famous Settle-Carlisle Line; for details see p495.

Getting Around

Metro's **FreeCityBus** (www.wymetro.com) service runs every few minutes from 6.30am to 7.30pm Monday to Saturday, linking the bus and train stations to all the main shopping areas in the city centre.

The various Day Rover passes (see p486) covering trains and/or buses are good for reaching Bradford, Haworth and Hebden Bridge.

Around Leeds

SALTAIRE

A Victorian-era landmark, Saltaire was a model industrial village built in 1851 by philanthropic woolbaron and teetotaller Titus Salt. The rows of neat, honey-coloured cottages – now a Unesco World Heritage site – overlook what was once the largest factory in the world.

The factory is now **Salt's Mill** (www.saltsmill.org.uk; admission free; ⌚10am-5.30pm Mon-Fri, 10am-6pm Sat & Sun), a splendidly bright and airy building where the main draw is a permanent exhibition of art by local boy David Hockney (1937–). In a fitting metaphor for the shift in the British economy from making things to selling them, this former engine of industry is now a shrine to retail therapy, housing shops selling books, crafts and outdoor equipment, and a cafe and restaurant.

Saltaire's **tourist office** (www.saltairevillage.info; 2 Victoria Rd; ⌚10am-5pm) has maps of the village and runs hour-long guided walks (adult/child £3.50/2.50) through the town throughout the year.

Saltaire is 9 miles west of Leeds centre, and 3 miles north of Bradford centre. It's easily reached by Metro rail from either.

HAREWOOD

The great park, sumptuous gardens and mighty edifice of **Harewood House** (www.harewood.org; adult/child £14.30/7.25; ⌚grounds 10am-6pm, house noon-4.30pm Apr-Oct; 👪) could easily fill an entire day trip from Leeds, and also makes a good port of call on the way to Harrogate.

A classic example of a stately English pile, the house was built between 1759 and 1772 by the era's superstar designers: John Carr designed the exterior, Lancelot 'Capability' Brown laid out the grounds, Thomas Chippendale supplied the furniture (the largest commission he ever received, costing the unheard of amount of £10,000), Robert Adams designed the interior, and Italy was raided to create an appropriate art collection. The superb terrace was added 100 years later by yet another top name, Sir Charles Barry – he of the Houses of Parliament.

Many locals come to Harewood just to relax or saunter through the **grounds** (grounds-only ticket £10/6.10), without even thinking of going inside the house. Hours of entertainment can be had in the **Bird Garden**, with many exotic species including penguins (feeding time at 2pm is a highlight), and there's also a boating lake, cafe and adventure playground. For more activity, there's a network of walking trails around the lake or through the parkland.

Harewood is about 7 miles north of Leeds on the A61. Take bus 36 (20 minutes, at least half-hourly Monday to Saturday, hourly on Sunday), which continues to Harrogate. Visitors coming by bus get half-price admission, so hang on to your ticket. From the main gate, it's a 2-mile walk through the grounds to the house and gardens, or you can use the free shuttle service.

NATIONAL COAL MINING MUSEUM FOR ENGLAND

For close to three centuries, West and South Yorkshire were synonymous with coal production; the collieries shaped and scarred the landscape, while entire villages grew up around the pits, each male inhabitant and their descendants destined to spend their working lives underground. The industry came to a shuddering halt in the 1980s, but the imprint of coal is still very much in evidence, even if there's only a handful of collieries left. One of these, at Claphouse, is now the **National Coal Mining Museum for England** (www.ncm.org.uk; Overton, near Wakefield; admission free; ⌚10am-5pm, last tour 3.15pm), a superb testament to the inner workings of a coal mine.

The highlight of a visit is the underground tour (departing every 10 minutes): equipped with helmet and head-torch you descend almost 150m in the 'cage' then follow subterranean passages to the coal seam where massive drilling machines now stand idle. Former miners work as guides, and explain the details – sometimes with a suitably authentic and almost impenetrable mix of local dialect (known in Yorkshire as Tyke) and technical terminology.

Up on top, there are audiovisual displays, some fascinating memorabilia (including sketches by Henry Moore) and exhibits about trade unions, strikes and the wider mining communities – only a bit over-romanticised in parts. You can also stroll round the pit-pony stables (their equine inhabitants also now retired) or the slightly eerie bathhouse, unchanged since the miners scrubbed off the coal dust for the last time and emptied their lockers.

The museum is about 10 miles south of Leeds on the A642 between Wakefield and Huddersfield, which drivers can reach via Junction 40 on the M1. By public transport, take a train from Leeds to Wakefield (15 minutes, at least hourly), and then bus 232 towards Huddersfield (25 minutes, hourly).

YORKSHIRE SCULPTURE PARK

One of England's most impressive collections of sculpture is scattered across the formidable 18th-century estate of Bretton Park, 200-odd hectares of lawns, fields and trees. A bit like the art world's equivalent of a safari park, the **Yorkshire Sculpture Park** (www.ysp.co.uk; Bretton, near Wakefield; admission free, parking £4; ⌚10am-6pm Apr-Sep, to 5pm Oct-Mar) showcases the work of dozens of sculptors both national and international. But the main focus of this outdoor gallery is the work of local kids Barbara Hepworth (1903–75), who was born in nearby Wakefield, and Henry Moore (1898–1986).

The rural setting is especially fitting for Moore's work, as the artist was hugely influenced by the outdoors and preferred his art to be sited in the landscape rather than indoors. Other highlights include pieces by Andy Goldsworthy and Eduardo Paolozzi. There's also a program of temporary exhibitions and installations by visiting artists, plus a bookshop and cafe.

The park is 12 miles south of Leeds and 18 miles north of Sheffield, just off Junction 38 on the M1 motorway. If you're on public transport, take a train from Leeds to Wakefield (15 minutes, at least hourly), or from Sheffield to Barnsley (20 minutes, at least hourly); then take bus 444 that runs between Wakefield and Barnsley via Bretton Park (30 minutes, hourly Monday to Saturday).

Hebden Bridge

POP 4086

Tucked tightly into the fold of a steep-sided valley, Yorkshire's funkiest little town is a former mill town that refused to go gently into that good night with the dying of industry's light. Instead it raged a bit and then morphed into an attractive little tourist trap with a distinctly bohemian atmosphere. Besides the honest-to-God Yorkshire folk who have lived here for years, the town is home to university academics, artists, die-hard hippies and a substantial gay community (it allegedly boasts the highest proportion of lesbians per head of population in the UK) – all of which explains the abundance of craft shops, organic cafes and secondhand bookshops.

From the town centre, a short stroll along the attractive waterfront of the Rochdale Canal leads to the **Alternative Technology Centre** (www.alternativetechnology.org.uk; Hebble End Mill; admission free; ⌚10am-5pm Mon-Fri, noon-4pm Sat, 1-4pm Sun), which promotes renewable energy, recycling and sustainable lifestyles through a series of intriguing exhibits and workshops.

Above the town is the much older village of **Heptonstall**, its narrow cobbled street lined with 500-year-old cottages and the ruins of a beautiful 13th-century church. But it is the churchyard of the newer St Thomas' Church that draws literary pilgrims, for here is buried the poet Sylvia Plath (1932–63), wife of another famous poet, Ted Hughes (1930–98), who was born in nearby Mytholmroyd.

The **Hebden Bridge tourist office & Canal Centre** (☎01422-843831; Butlers Wharf, New Rd; ⏲9.30am-5.30pm Mon-Fri, 10.30am-5pm Sat & Sun mid-Mar–mid-Oct, shorter hours rest of year) has a good stock of maps and leaflets on local walks, including a saunter to **Hardcastle Crags**, the local beauty spot, and nearby **Gibson Mill** (NT; adult/child £3.60/1.80; ⏲11am-4pm Tue-Thu, Sat & Sun Mar-Oct, 11am-3pm Sat & Sun Nov-Feb), a renovated 19th-century cotton mill. The mill houses a visitor centre with exhibitions covering the industrial and social history of the mill and its former workers.

Sleeping & Eating

Holme House B&B ££
(☎01422-847588; www.holmehousehebdenbridge.co.uk; New Rd; s/d from £60/75; 📶) Holme House is an elegant Victorian villa right in the heart of town, with stylish and spacious bedrooms and fluffy robes and towels in the bathrooms. At breakfast you can choose from smoked haddock with poached egg, fresh fruit and yoghurt, or a fry-up prepared using local produce.

Mankinholes YHA HOSTEL £
(☎0845 371 9751; www.yha.org.uk; Todmorden; dm £16; P) A converted 17th-century manor house 4 miles southwest of Hebden Bridge, this hostel has limited facilities (no TV room) but is very popular with walkers (the Pennine Way passes only half a mile away). There are buses from New Rd in Hebden to Todmorden every 10 minutes; from there, bus T6/T8 goes to the hostel.

Mooch CAFE-BAR £
(www.moochcafe.co.uk; 24 Market St; mains £5-7; ⏲9am-8pm Mon & Tue-Sat, 10am-7pm Sun) This chilled-out little cafe-bar exemplifies Hebden's alternative atmosphere, with a menu that includes a full-vegan breakfast, brie-and-grape ciabatta, and Mediterranean lunch platters of olives, hummus, stuffed vine leaves, tabouleh and more. There's also Krombacher beer on draught, and excellent espresso.

Relish VEGETARIAN ££
(☎01422-843587; www.relishhebden.co.uk; Old Oxford House, Albert St; mains £10-11; ⏲dinner Thu-Sat) Voted one of the UK's Top Five vegetarian restaurants in 2008, Relish adopts a gourmet attitude towards veggie and vegan cuisine, serving dishes such as leek, sage and walnut risotto with parmesan shavings, and Sri Lankan red curry with plantain, lemongrass and black bean cakes. Best book a table to avoid disappointment.

Organic House CAFE £
(www.organic-house.co.uk; 2 Market St; mains £6-11; ⏲breakfast & lunch; 🚸) Practically everything on the menu at this busy local caff is organic, locally produced or fair-trade, from the veggie breakfast to the pâté *du jour* (served with toast and chutney). There are outdoor tables in the garden, and a shiatsu and reflexology studio upstairs.

Getting There & Away

Hebden Bridge is on the Leeds–Manchester train line (£4.05, 50 minutes, every 20 minutes Monday to Saturday, hourly on Sunday). Get off at Todmorden for the Mankinholes YHA.

Haworth

POP 6100

It seems that only Shakespeare himself is held in higher esteem than the beloved Brontë sisters – Emily, Anne and Charlotte – at least, judging by the 8 million visitors a year who trudge up the hill from the train station to pay their respects at the handsome parsonage where the literary classics *Jane Eyre* and *Wuthering Heights* were born.

Not surprisingly, the whole village is given over to Brontë-linked tourism, but even without the literary associations Haworth is still worth a visit, though you'll be hard pushed not to be overwhelmed by the cottage industry that has grown up around the Brontës and their wonderful creations.

Sights

FREE **Haworth Parish Church** CHURCH
(Church St; ⏲9am-5.30pm) Your first stop should be Haworth Parish Church, a lovely old place of worship built in the late 19th century on the site of the older church that the Brontë sisters knew, which was demolished in 1879. In the surrounding churchyard, gravestones are covered in moss

BAD-LUCK BRONTËS

The Rev Patrick Brontë, his wife Maria and six children moved to Haworth Parsonage in 1820. Within four years Maria and the two eldest daughters had died from cancer and tuberculosis. The treble tragedy led the good reverend to keep his remaining family close to him, and for the next few years the children were home-schooled in a highly creative environment.

The children conjured up mythical heroes and fantasy lands, and produced miniature homemade books. It was an auspicious start, at least for the three girls, Charlotte, Emily and Anne; the lone boy, Branwell, was more of a painter but lacked his sisters' drive and discipline. After a short stint as a professional artist, he ended up spending most of his days in the Black Bull pub, drunk and stoned on laudanum obtained across the street at Rose & Co Apothecary.

While the three sisters were setting the London literary world alight with the publication of three superb novels – *Jane Eyre*, *Wuthering Heights* and *Agnes Grey* – in one extraordinary year (1847), Branwell was fading quickly and died of tuberculosis in 1848. The family was devastated, but things quickly got worse. Emily fell ill with tuberculosis soon after her brother's funeral; she never left the house again and died on 19 December. Anne, who had also been sick, was next; Charlotte took her to Scarborough to seek a sea cure but she died on 28 May 1849.

The remaining family never recovered. Despite her growing fame, Charlotte struggled with depression and never quite adapted to her high position in literary society. Despite her misgivings she eventually married, but she too died, in the early stages of pregnancy, on 31 March 1855. All things considered, it's hardly surprising that poor old Patrick Brontë spent the remaining years of his life going increasingly insane.

or thrust to one side by gnarled tree roots, giving the place a tremendous feeling of age.

Brontë Parsonage Museum MUSEUM
(www.bronte.info; Church St; adult/child £6.50/3.50; ⏲10am-5.30pm Apr-Sep, 11am-5pm Oct-Mar) Set in a pretty garden overlooking the church and graveyard, the house where the Brontë family lived from 1820 till 1861 is now a museum. The rooms are meticulously furnished and decorated exactly as they were in the Brontë era, with many personal possessions on display. There's also a neat and informative exhibition, which includes the fascinating miniature books the Brontës wrote as children.

Activities

Above Haworth stretch the bleak moors of the South Pennines – immediately familiar to Brontë fans – and the tourist office has leaflets on local walks to endless Brontë-related places. A 6.5-mile favourite leads to **Top Withins**, a ruined farm thought to have inspired *Wuthering Heights*, even though a plaque clearly states that the farmhouse bore no resemblance to the one Emily wrote about.

Other walks can be worked around the **Brontë Way**, a longer route linking Bradford and Colne via Haworth. Alternatively, you can walk or cycle the 8 miles south to Hebden Bridge via the scenic valley of Hardcastle Crags.

Sleeping & Eating

Virtually every second house on Main St offers B&B; they're mostly indistinguishable from each other but some are just that little bit cuter. There are a couple of good restaurants in town, and many of the B&Bs also have small cafes that are good for a spot of lunch.

Old Registry B&B ££
(☎01535-646503; www.theoldregistryhaworth.co.uk; 2-4 Main St; r £75-120; wi-fi) This place is a bit special. It's an elegantly rustic guest house where each of the carefully themed rooms has a four-poster bed, whirlpool bath or valley view. The Blue Heaven room is just that – at least for fans of Laura Ashley's delphinium blue.

Ye Sleeping House B&B ££
(☎01535-546992; www.yesleepinghouse.co.uk; 8 Main St; s/d from £29/58) There's a cosy, country cottage atmosphere at this welcoming B&B, with just three small rooms and two friendly resident cats. Try to get the one en-suite room, which can sleep a family of four and has great views over the valley.

Aitches B&B ££
(☎01535-642501; www.aitches.co.uk; 11 West Lane; s/d from £40/58) A very classy, stone-built Victorian house with four en suite rooms, each differently decorated with a pleasantly olde-worlde atmosphere. There's a residents' dining room (three-course meal costs £16 (prebooked, minimum four persons).

Cobbles and Clay CAFE £
(www.cobblesandclay.co.uk; 60 Main St; mains £4-8;) This attractive, child-friendly cafe not only offers fair-trade coffee and healthy salads and snacks – Tuscan bean stew, or hummus with pita bread and raw veggie sticks – but also the opportunity to indulge in a bit of pottery painting.

Weaver's Restaurant with Rooms RESTAURANT, B&B ££
(☎01535-643822; www.weaversmallhotel.co.uk; 15 West Lane; s/d £65/110, mains £13-19; ⏲lunch Wed-Fri, dinner Tue-Sat) A stylish and atmospheric restaurant, it offers a menu featuring local produce (such as slow-cooked shoulder of Pennine lamb with fennel seed and coriander stuffing) or simple lunches like an Ellison's pork pie with mushy peas and mint sauce. Upstairs are three comfy bedrooms, two of which have views towards the moors.

Other options:

Apothecary Guest House B&B ££
(☎01535-643642; www.theapothecaryguesthouse.co.uk; 86 Main St; s/d £35/55;) Oak beams and narrow, slanted passageways lead to smallish rooms with cheerful decor.

Old White Lion Hotel HOTEL ££
(☎01535-642313; www.oldwhitelionhotel.com; West Lane; s/d from £63/88;) Pub-style accommodation – comfortable if not spectacular – sits above an oak-panelled bar and highly rated restaurant (mains £8 to £13).

Haworth YHA HOSTEL £
(☎0845 371 9520; www.yha.org.uk; Longlands Dr; dm £16; P @) A big old house with a games room, lounge, cycle store and laundry. It's on the northeastern edge of town, off Lees Lane.

Haworth Old Hall PUB ££
(☎01535-642709; www.hawortholdhall.co.uk; Sun St; mains £9-15) A 16th-century pub serving real ale and decent food. If you want to linger longer, two comfortable doubles cost £65 each.

Information

Post Office (98 Main St; ⏲9am-5.30pm Mon-Fri, to 12.30pm Sat)

Tourist Office (☎01535-642329; www.haworth-village.org.uk; 2-4 West Lane; ⏲9am-5.30pm Apr-Sep, to 5pm Oct-Mar)

Venables & Bainbridge (111 Main St; ⏲11am-5pm daily) Secondhand books including many vintage Brontë volumes.

Getting There & Away

From Leeds, the easiest approach is via Keighley, which is on the Metro rail network. Bus 500 runs from Keighley bus station to Haworth (15 minutes, hourly) and continues to Todmorden and Hebden Bridge. However, the most interesting way to get from Keighley to Haworth is via the Keighley & Worth Valley Railway (see boxed text, p490).

STEAM ENGINES & RAILWAY CHILDREN

Haworth is on the **Keighley & Worth Valley Railway** (www.kwvr.co.uk; adult/child return £9.40/4.70, adult/child Day Rover £14/7), which runs steam and classic diesel engines between Keighley and Oxenhope. It was here, in 1969, that the classic movie *The Railway Children* was shot: Mr Perks was stationmaster at Oakworth, where the Edwardian look has been meticulously maintained. Trains operate about hourly at weekends all year; in holiday periods they run hourly every day.

YORKSHIRE DALES NATIONAL PARK

The Yorkshire Dales – named from the old Norse word *dalr,* meaning 'valleys' – is the central jewel in the necklace of three national parks strung across of northern England, with the dramatic fells of the Lake District to the west and the brooding heaths of the North York Moors to the east.

From well-known names such as Wensleydale and Ribblesdale to obscure and evocative Langstrothdale and Arkengarthdale, these glacial valleys are characterised by a distinctive landscape of high heather moorland, stepped skylines and flat-topped hills. Down in the green valleys, patchworked with drystone dykes, are picture-postcard towns and hamlets, where sheep

Yorkshire Dales National Park

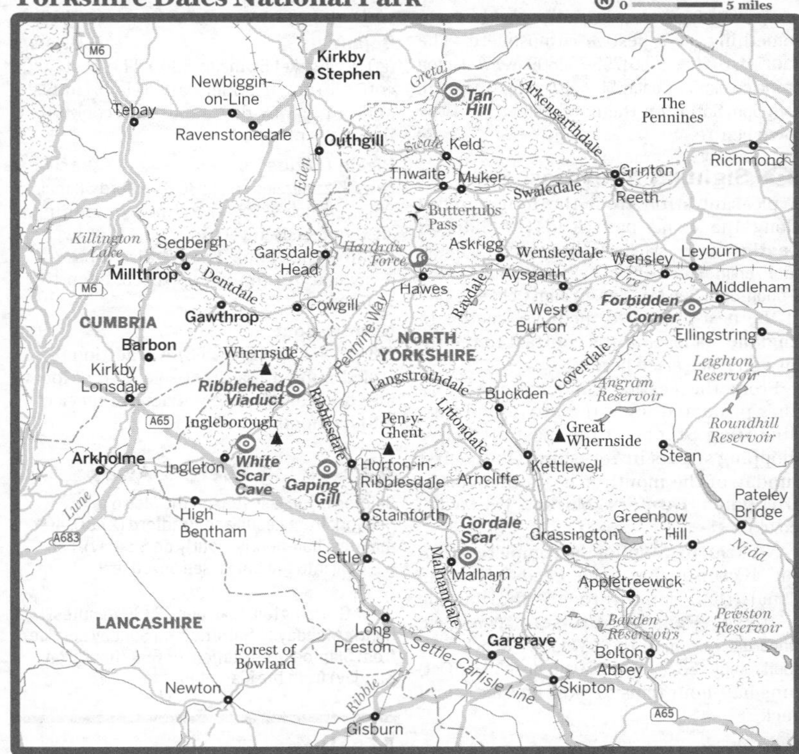

and cattle still graze on village greens. And in the limestone country in the southern Dales you'll find England's best examples of karst scenery.

The Dales have been protected as a national park since the 1950s, assuring their status as a walker's and cyclist's paradise. But there's plenty for nonwalkers as well, from exploring the legacy of literary vet James Herriot of *All Creatures Great And Small* fame to sampling Wallace and Gromit's favourite teatime snack at the Wensleydale Creamery.

The *Visitor* newspaper, available from tourist offices, lists local events and walks guided by park rangers, as well as many places to stay and eat. The official park website (www.yorkshiredales.org.uk) is also useful.

Getting There & Around

Around 90% of visitors to the park arrive by car, and the narrow roads can be extremely crowded in summer; parking can also be a serious problem. If you can, try to use public transport as much as possible.

Pick up a *Dales Bus Timetable* from tourist offices, or consult the **Traveldales** (www.traveldales.org.uk) and **Dalesbus** (www.dalesbus.org) websites.

By train, the best and most interesting access to the Dales is via the famous **Settle-Carlisle Line** (p495). Trains run between Leeds and Carlisle, stopping at Skipton, Settle and numerous small villages, offering unrivalled access to the hills straight from the station platform.

Skipton

POP 14,300

This busy market town on the southern edge of the Dales takes its name from the Anglo-Saxon *sceape ton* (sheep town) – no prizes for guessing how it made its money. Monday, Wednesday, Friday and

Saturday are market days on High St, bringing crowds from all over and giving the town something of a festive atmosphere. The **tourist office** (☎01756-792809; www.skiptononline.co.uk; 35 Coach St; ⊙10am-5pm Mon-Fri, 9am-5pm Sat) is on the northern edge of the town centre.

Sights & Activities

A pleasant stroll from the tourist office along the canal path leads to **Skipton Castle** (www.skiptoncastle.co.uk; High St; adult/child £6.20/3.70; ⊙10am-6pm Mon-Sat & noon-6pm Sun Mar-Sep, to 4pm Oct-Feb), one of the best-preserved medieval castles in England – a fascinating contrast to the ruins you'll see elsewhere.

From the castle, wander along Skipton's pride and joy – the broad and bustling **High St**, one of the most attractive shopping streets in Yorkshire. On the first Sunday of the month it hosts the **Northern Dales Farmers Market** (www.ndfm.co.uk).

No trip to Skipton is complete without a cruise along the Leeds-Liverpool Canal that runs through the middle of town. **Pennine Cruisers** (www.penninecruisers.com; The Wharf, Coach St; adult/child £3/2; ⊙10.30am-dusk Mar-Oct) runs half-hour trips to Skipton Castle and back.

Sleeping & Eating

There's a strip of B&Bs just outside the centre on Keighley Rd. All those between Nos 46 and 57 are worth trying.

Carlton House B&B ££
(☎01756-700921; www.carltonhouse.rapidial.co.uk; 46 Keighley Rd; s/d from £30/60) A handsome house with five pretty, comfortable rooms – no frills but lots of floral prints. The house is deservedly popular on account of the friendly welcome.

Le Caveau FRENCH ££
(☎01756-794274; www.lecaveau.co.uk; 86 High St; mains £13-18; ⊙lunch Tue-Fri, dinner Tue-Sat) Set in a stylishly decorated 16th-century cellar with barrel-vaulted ceilings, this friendly bistro offers a seasonal menu built lovingly around fresh local produce. Daily specials include dishes such as a light and flavourful quiche made with black pudding, bacon and mushrooms, and a succulent fish pie topped with mashed potato. On weekdays you can get a two-course lunch for £10.

Bojangles CAFE, BAR £
(20 Newmarket St; mains £3-6) The best coffee in town. American-style breakfasts and burgers by day; tapas and cocktails in the evening.

Bizzie Lizzies FISH & CHIPS £
(www.bizzielizzies.co.uk; 36 Swadford St; mains £6-8; ⊙lunch & dinner) An award-winning, sit-down fish-and-chip restaurant overlooking the canal. There's also a takeaway counter (mains £3 to £5, open till 11.15pm).

Narrow Boat PUB £
(38 Victoria St; mains £5-8) A traditionally styled pub with a great selection of local ales and foreign beers, friendly service and bar food.

Getting There & Away

Skipton is the last stop on the Metro rail network from Leeds and Bradford (£7.50, 40 minutes, half-hourly, hourly on Sunday). For heading into the Dales, see boxed text p495.

For Grassington, take bus 72 (30 minutes, hourly Monday to Saturday, no Sunday service) from Skipton train station, or 66A (hourly on Sunday) from the Market Pl.

Malham

POP 120

Stretching west from Grassington to Ingleton is the largest area of limestone country in England, which has created a distinctive landscape dotted with dry valleys, potholes, limestone pavements and gorges. Two of the most spectacular features – Malham Cove and Gordale Scar – lie near the pretty village of Malham.

The **national park centre** (☎01969-652380; www.yorkshiredales.org.uk; ⊙10am-5pm daily Apr-Oct, 10am-4pm Sat & Sun Nov-Mar) at the southern edge of the village has the usual wealth of information. Note that Malham can only be reached via narrow roads that can be very congested in summer; leave your car at the national park centre and walk into the village.

Sights & Activities

A half-mile walk north from Malham village leads to **Malham Cove**, a huge rock amphitheatre lined with 80m-high vertical cliffs. You can hike steeply up the left-hand end of the cove (on the Pennine Way footpath) to see the extensive limestone pavement above the cliffs. Another 1.5 miles further north is **Malham Tarn**, a glacial lake and nature reserve.

A mile east of Malham along a narrow road (very limited parking) is spectacular **Gordale Scar**, a deep limestone canyon with scenic cascades and the remains of an Iron-Age settlement. The national park centre has a leaflet describing the **Malham Landscape Trail**, a 5-mile circular walk that takes in Malham Cove, Gordale Scar and the Janet's Foss waterfall.

The **Pennine Way** passes through Malham; Horton-in-Ribblesdale lies a day's hike away to the northwest.

Sleeping & Eating

Beck Hall HOTEL ££
(☎01729-830332; www.beckhallmalham.com; s/d from £36/54; P Wi-Fi) This rambling 17th-century country house on the edge of the village has 15 individually decorated rooms – we recommend the Green Room, with its old-style furnishings and four-poster bed. There's a rustling stream flowing through the garden and a nice tearoom (mains £3 to £5, open for lunch Tuesday to Sunday).

Malham YHA HOSTEL £
(☎0845 371 9529; www.yha.org.uk; dm £18; P) In the village centre you will find this purpose-built hostel; the facilities are top-notch and young children are well catered for.

Ribblesdale & The Three Peaks

Scenic Ribblesdale cuts through the southwestern corner of the Yorkshire Dales National Park, where the skyline is dominated by a trio of distinctive hills known as the **Three Peaks** – Whernside (735m), Ingleborough (724m) and Pen-y-ghent (694m). Easily accessible via the Settle-Carlisle railway line, this is one of England's most popular areas for outdoor activities, attracting thousands of hikers, cyclists and cavers each weekend.

SETTLE

POP 3621

The busy market town of Settle, dominated by its grand neo-Gothic town hall, is the gateway to Ribblesdale and marks the beginning of the scenic part of the famous Settle-Carlisle railway line. Narrow cobbled streets lined with shops and pubs lead out from the central market square (Tuesday is market day), and the town offers plenty of accommodation options.

Around the main square there are several good cafes, including **Ye Olde Naked Man** (Market Pl; mains £4-7), formerly an undertakers (look for the 'naked man' on the outside wall, dated 1663); and the excellent **Shambles** (Market Pl; fish & chips £5-7).

The **tourist office** (☎01729-825192; Town Hall, Cheapside; ⏲9.30am-4.30pm Apr-Oct, to 4pm Nov-Mar) has maps and guidebooks.

Trains from Leeds or Skipton heading to Carlisle stop at the station near the town centre; those heading for Morecambe (on the west coast) stop at Giggleswick, about 1.5 miles outside town.

THREE PEAKS CHALLENGES

Since 1968 more than 200,000 hikers have taken up the challenge of climbing Yorkshire's Three Peaks in less than 12 hours. The circular 25-mile route begins and ends at the Pen-y-ghent Cafe in Horton-in-Ribblesdale – where you clock-in and clock-out to verify your time – and takes in the summits of Pen-y-ghent, Whernside and Ingleborough. Succeed, and you're a member of the cafe's Three Peaks of Yorkshire Club. You can find details of the route at www.merseyventure.com/yorks and download a guide (£4) at www.walkingworld.com (walk ID 4228 and 4229).

Fancy a more gruelling test of your endurance? Then join the fell-runners in the annual **Three Peaks Race** (www.threepeaksrace.org.uk) on the last Saturday in April, and run the route instead of walking it. First held in 1954 when six people competed, it now attracts around 900 entries; the course record is two hours, 43 minutes and three seconds.

In the last week of September, cyclists get their chance in the **Three Peaks Cyclo-Cross** (www.3peakscyclocross.org.uk), which covers 38 miles of rough country and 1524m of ascent.

HORTON-IN-RIBBLESDALE

POP 560

A favourite with outdoor enthusiasts, the little village of Horton and its railway station is 5 miles north of Settle. Everything centres on the Pen-y-ghent Cafe, which acts as the village tourist office, wet-weather retreat and hikers' information centre.

Horton is the starting point for climbing Pen-y-ghent and for doing the **Three Peaks Walk** (see boxed text, p493); it's also a stop on the Pennine Way. At the head of the valley, 5 miles north of Horton, is the spectacular **Ribblehead Viaduct**, built in 1874 and the longest on the Settle-Carlisle line – more than 30m high and 400m long. You can hike there along the Pennine Way and travel back by train from Ribblehead station.

Sleeping & Eating

Horton is popular, so it's wise to book accommodation in advance.

Golden Lion B&B, BUNKHOUSE £
(☎01729-860206; www.goldenlionhotel.co.uk; s/d from £40/60, bunkhouse per person £12) The Golden Lion is a lively pub that offers comfortable B&B bedrooms, a brand-new 40-bed bunkhouse, and three public bars where you can tuck into a bit of grub washed down with a pint of hand-pulled ale.

Holme Farm Campsite CAMPSITE £
(☎01729-860281; per person/tent £2/1) Basic, no-frills campsite right next door to the Golden Lion pub, much used by Pennine Way hikers.

Pen-y-ghent Cafe CAFE £
(mains £2-6; ⏲breakfast & lunch) A traditional cafe run by the same family since 1965, the Pen-y-ghent fills walkers' fuel tanks with fried egg and chips, homemade scones and pint-sized mugs of tea. It also sells maps, guidebooks and walking gear.

INGLETON

POP 2000

The village of Ingleton, perched precariously above a river gorge, is the caving capital of England. It sits at the foot of one of the country's most extensive areas of limestone upland, crowned by the dominating peak of Ingleborough and riddled with countless potholes and cave systems.

The **tourist office** (☎01524-241049; www.visitingleton.co.uk; ⏲10am-4pm Apr-Sep) is beside the main car park, while **Bernie's Cafe** (4 Main St; ⏲9am-4pm Mon, Wed & Thu, 9am-6pm Fri-Sun) is the centre of the local caving scene.

Ingleton is the starting point for two famous Dales hikes. The shorter and easier of the two is the circular, 4.5-mile **Waterfalls Walk** (www.ingletonwaterfallswalk.co.uk), which passes through native oak woodland on its way past a series of spectacular waterfalls on the River Twiss and River Doe. The more strenuous option is **Ingleborough** (724m). Around 120,000 people climb this hill every year, but that doesn't make the 6-mile round trip any less of an effort; this is a proper hill walk, so pack waterproofs, food, water, a map and a compass.

Although most of the local caves are accessible only to experienced potholers, some are open to the general public. **White Scar Cave** (www.whitescarcave.co.uk; 80min guided tour adult/child £7.95/4.95; ⏲10am-4.30pm Feb-Oct, Sat & Sun only Nov-Jan) is the longest show cave in England, with a series of underground waterfalls and impressive dripstone formations leading to the 100m-long Battlefield Cavern, one of the largest cave chambers in the country. The cave is 1.5 miles northeast of the village on the B6255 road.

Gaping Gill, on the southeastern flank of Ingleborough, is one of the most famous caves in England. A huge vertical pothole 105m deep, it was the largest known cave shaft in the UK until the discovery of Titan in Derbyshire in 1999. Gaping Gill is normally off-limits to non-cavers but, twice a year on the May and August bank holiday weekends, local caving clubs set up a winch so that members of the public can descend into the depths in a special chair (£10 per person). For details see www.bpc-cave.org.uk and www.cravenpotholeclub.org, and click on the Gaping Gill link.

Ingleton is 10 miles northwest of Settle; take bus 581 from Settle train station (25 minutes, two daily).

Hawes

POP 700

The beating heart of Wensleydale is Hawes, a thriving and picturesque market town (market day is Tuesday) that has the added attraction of its own waterfall in the village centre. On busy summer weekends, however, Hawes' narrow arteries can get seriously clogged with traffic – leave the car in the parking area beside the **national park centre** (☎01969-666210; Station Yard; ⏰10am-5pm year round) at the eastern entrance to the village.

Sights & Activities

Sharing a building with the park centre is the **Dales Countryside Museum** (☎01969-666210; Station Yard; adult/child £3/free), a beautifully presented social history of the area that explains the forces that shaped the landscape, from geology to lead mining to land enclosure.

At the other end of the village lies the **Wensleydale Creamery** (www.wensleydale.co.uk; ⏰9.30am-5pm Mon-Sat, 10am-4.30pm Sun), devoted to the production of Wallace and Gromit's favourite crumbly, white cheese. You can visit the cheese museum and then 'try before you buy' in the shop, which is free to enter. There are one-hour tours of the creamery (adult/child £2.50/1.50) between 10am and 3pm.

About 1.5 miles north of Hawes is 30m-high **Hardraw Force**, the highest unbroken waterfall in England. By international standards it's not that impressive (except after heavy rain); access is through the Green Dragon pub, which levies a £2 admission fee.

Sleeping & Eating

Herriot's Guest House B&B ££
(☎01969-667536; www.herriotsinhawes.co.uk; Main St; r per person from £38; 📶) A delightful guest house set in an old stone building close to the bridge by the waterfall, Herriot's has seven comfy, en-suite bedrooms set above an art gallery and coffee shop.

Green Dragon Inn B&B ££
(☎01969-667392; www.greendragonhardraw.co.uk; Hardraw; s/d from £26/50) A fine old pub with flagstone floors, low timber beams, ancient oak furniture and Theakstons on draught, the Dragon serves up a tasty steak-and-ale pie and offers B&B accommodation in plain but adequate rooms.

Bainbridge Ings Caravan & Camp Site CAMPSITE £
(☎01969-667354; www.bainbridge-ings.co.uk; tent, car & 2 adults £13, hikers & cyclists per person £5) An attractive site set in stone-walled fields around a spacious farmhouse about half a mile east of town. Gas, milk and eggs are sold on site.

Hawes YHA HOSTEL £
(☎0845 371 9120; www.yha.org.uk; Lancaster Tce; dm £16; P 👪) A modern place on the western edge of town, at the main A684 (Aysgarth Rd) and B6255 junction, this is a family-friendly hostel with great views of Wensleydale.

THE SETTLE-CARLISLE LINE

The 72-mile Settle-Carlisle Line (SCL), built between 1869 and 1875, offers one of England's most scenic railway journeys. The line's construction was one of the great engineering achievements of the Victorian era: 5000 navvies armed with picks and shovels built 325 bridges, 21 viaducts and blasted 14 tunnels in horrific conditions – nearly 200 of them died in the process.

Trains run between Leeds and Carlisle via Settle about eight times per day. The first section of the journey from Leeds is along the Aire Valley, stopping at **Keighley**, where the Keighley & Worth Valley Railway branches off to **Haworth**, **Skipton** (gateway to the southern Dales) and **Settle**. The train then labours up the valley beside the River Ribble, through **Horton-in-Ribblesdale**, across the spectacular **Ribblehead Viaduct** and then through Blea Moor Tunnel to reach remote **Dent station**, at 350m the highest main-line station in the country.

The line reaches its highest point (356m) at Ais Gill where it leaves the Dales behind before easing down to **Kirkby Stephen**. The last halts are **Appleby** and **Langwathby**, just northwest of Penrith (a jumping-off point for the Lake District), before the train finally pulls into **Carlisle**.

The entire journey from Leeds to Carlisle takes two hours and 40 minutes and costs £23.10/27.80 for a single/day return. Various hop-on/hop-off passes for one or three days are also available. You can pick up a free SCL timetable – which includes a colour map of the line and brief details about places of interest – from most Yorkshire stations. For more information contact **National Rail Enquiries** (☎08457 48 49 50) or see www.settle-carlisle.co.uk.

Chaste BISTRO ££
(www.chaste-food.co.uk; Market Pl; mains lunch £4-8, dinner £13-15;) It's an unusual name for a bistro, but this place is far from coy when it comes to promoting Yorkshire produce – almost everything on the menu, from the all-day breakfast to the vegetable burger to the lamb chops with peppercorn-and-strawberry gravy, is either homemade or locally sourced.

Cart House TEAROOM £
(01969-667691; www.hardrawforce.co.uk; Hardraw; mains £6; Mar-Nov) Across the bridge from the Green Dragon, this craft shop and tearoom offers a healthier diet of homemade soup, organic bread and a 'Fellman's Lunch' of Wensleydale cheese, pickle and salad. There's a basic campsite at the back (£11 for two adults, tent and car).

Getting There & Away

Dales & District buses 156 and 157 run from Bedale to Hawes (1¼ hours, eight daily Monday to Saturday, four on Sunday) via Leyburn, where you can connect with transport to/from Richmond. To get to Bedale from Northallerton train station on the main York-Newcastle line, take bus 73 (25 minutes, half-hourly Monday to Saturday, every two hours Sunday).

From Garsdale station on the Settle-Carlisle line, bus 113 runs to Hawes (20 minutes, three daily Monday to Saturday); on Sundays and bank holidays bus 808 goes to Hawes from Ribblehead station (50 minutes, two daily). Check the bus times at www.yorkshiretravel.net or a tourist office before using these routes.

Richmond

POP 8200

The handsome market town of Richmond is one of England's best-kept secrets, perched on a rocky outcrop overlooking the River Swale and guarded by the ruins of a massive castle. A maze of cobbled streets radiates from the broad, sloping market square (market day is Saturday) lined with elegant Georgian buildings and photogenic stone cottages, with glimpses of the surrounding hills and dales peeking through the gaps.

Sights

Top of the pile is the impressive heap that is **Richmond Castle** (EH; www.english-heritage.org.uk; Market Pl; adult/child £4.50/2.30; 10am-6pm Apr-Sep, to 4pm Oct-Mar), founded in 1070 and one of the first castles in England since Roman times to be built of stone. It's had many uses through the years, including a stint as a prison for conscientious objectors during WWI (there's a small and sobering exhibition about their part in the castle's history). The best part is the view from the top of the remarkably well-preserved 30m-high keep that towers over the River Swale.

Military buffs will enjoy the **Green Howards Museum** (www.greenhowards.org.uk; Trinity Church Sq; adult/child £3.50/free; 10am-4.30pm Mon-Sat, closed 24 Dec-31 Jan), which pays tribute to the famous Yorkshire regiment. In a different vein, the **Richmondshire Museum** (www.richmondshiremuseum.org.uk; Ryder's Wynd; adult/child £2.50/2; 10.30am-4.30pm Apr-Oct) is a delight, with local history exhibits including an early Yorkshire cave-dweller and displays on lead mining, which forever altered the Swaledale landscape a century ago. You can also see the original set that served as James Herriot's surgery in the TV series *All Creatures Great and Small*.

Built in 1788, the **Georgian Theatre Royal** (www.georgiantheatreroyal.co.uk; Victoria Rd; tours per person £3.50; tours hourly 10am-4pm Mon-Sat mid-Feb–mid-Dec) is the most complete Georgian playhouse in Britain. Tours include a look at the country's oldest surviving stage scenery, painted between 1818 and 1836.

Activities

Walkers can follow paths along the River Swale, both upstream and downstream from the town. A longer option is to follow part of the famous long-distance **Coast to Coast Walk** all the way to Reeth (11 miles) and take the bus back (see www.dalesbus.info/richmond).

In September/October the town hosts the **Richmond Walking & Book Festival** (www.booksandboots.org), 10 days of guided walks, talks, films and other events.

Cyclists can also follow Swaledale – as far as Reeth may be enough, while a trip along Arkengarthdale and then over the high wild moors to Kirkby Stephen via the Tan Hill Inn is a more serious (but very rewarding) 40-mile undertaking.

Sleeping

TOP CHOICE **Millgate House** B&B £££
(01748-823571; www.millgatehouse.com; Market Pl; r £110-145; P @) Behind an unassuming green door lies the unexpected pleasure of one of the most attractive guest houses in England. While the house itself is a Georgian

gem crammed with period details, it is overshadowed by the multi-award-winning garden at the back, which has superb views over the River Swale and the Cleveland Hills – if possible, book the Garden Suite.

Frenchgate Hotel HOTEL ££
(01748-822087; www.thefrenchgate.co.uk; 59-61 Frenchgate; s/d from £88/118; P) Nine elegant bedrooms occupy the upper floors of this converted Georgian town house, now a boutique hotel decorated with local art. The rooms have cool designer fittings that set off a period fireplace here, a Victorian roll-top bath there; downstairs there's an excellent restaurant (three-course dinner £34) and a hospitable lounge with oak beams and an open fire.

Willance House B&B ££
(01748-824467; www.willancehouse.com; 24 Frenchgate; s/d £50/70;) This is an oak-beamed house, built in 1600, with three immaculate rooms (one with a four-poster bed) that combine old-fashioned charm and all mod cons.

There's also a batch of pleasant places to stay along Frenchgate, and a couple more on Pottergate (the road into town from the east). These include the following:

66 Frenchgate B&B ££
(01748-823421; www.66frenchgate.co.uk; 66 Frenchgate; s/d from £40/60;) One of the three rooms has a superb river view.

Pottergate Guesthouse B&B ££
(01748-823826; 4 Pottergate; d from £50) Compact and chintzy, with a friendly and helpful landlady.

Eating & Drinking

Rustique FRENCH ££
(01748-821565; Chantry Wynd, Finkle St; mains £10-16; lunch & dinner Mon-Sat) Newly opened and hard to find (tucked away in an arcade), this cosy bistro has consistently impressed with its mastery of French country cooking, from *confit de canard* (duck slow roasted in its own fat) to *paupiette de poulet* (chicken breast stuffed with brie and sun-dried tomatoes). Booking recommended.

Cross View Tearoom CAFE £
(38 Market Pl; mains £4-9; 9am-5.50pm Mon-Sat) So popular with locals that you might have to queue for a table at lunchtime, the Cross View is the place to go for a hearty breakfast, homemade cakes, a hot lunch or just a nice cup of tea.

Seasons Restaurant & Cafe INTERNATIONAL ££
(www.restaurant-seasons.co.uk; Richmond Station, Station Rd; mains £8-11; breakfast, lunch & dinner) Housed in the restored Victorian station building, this attractive, open-plan eatery shares space with a boutique brewery, artisan bakery, ice-cream factory and cheesemonger – and yes, all this local produce is on the menu.

Barkers FISH & CHIPS £
(Trinity Church Sq; mains £6-10; lunch & dinner) Barkers has the best fish and chips in town, for sit down or takeaway.

Black Lion Hotel PUB
(Finkle St) This hotel has cosy bars, low beams and good beer and food.

Unicorn Inn PUB
(2 Newbiggin) The Unicorn is a determinedly old-fashioned free house serving Theakstons and Old Speckled Hen.

Information

The **tourist office** (01748-828742; www.richmond.org; Friary Gardens, Victoria Rd; 9.30am-5.30pm Apr-Oct, to 4.30pm Nov-Mar) has the usual maps and guides, plus several leaflets showing walks in town and the surrounding countryside.

Getting There & Away

From Darlington (on the railway between London and Edinburgh) it's easy to reach Richmond on bus X26 or X27 (35 minutes, every 15 minutes, every 30 minutes on Sunday). All buses stop in Market Pl.

On Sundays and bank holiday Mondays only, from late May to late October, the Eastern Dalesman bus 820 runs from Leeds to Richmond (3½ hours, one daily) via Fountains Abbey, Ripon, Masham and Middleham.

EAST RIDING OF YORKSHIRE

In command of the East Riding of Yorkshire is the tough old sea dog known as Hull, a no-nonsense port that looks to the North Sea and the broad horizons of the Humber estuary for its livelihood. Just to its north, and in complete contrast to Hull's salt and grit, is East Riding's most attractive town, Beverley, with lots of Georgian character and one of England's finest churches.

Hull

POP 256,200

Tough and uncompromising, Hull is a curmudgeonly English seaport with a proud seafaring tradition. It has long been the principal cargo port of England's east coast, with an economy that grew up around carrying wool out and bringing wine in. It was also a major whaling and fishing port until the trawling industry died out, but it remains a busy cargo terminal and departure point for ferries to the Continent.

Sights

The Deep AQUARIUM

(www.thedeep.co.uk; Tower St; adult/child £9.50/7.50; 10am-6pm, last entry 5pm;) Hull's biggest tourist attraction is The Deep, a vast aquarium housed in a colossal, angular building that appears to lunge above the muddy waters of the Humber like a giant shark's head. Inside it's just as dramatic, with echoing commentaries and computer-generated interactive displays that guide you through the formation of the oceans and the evolution of sea life. The largest aquarium is 10m deep, filled with sharks, stingrays and colourful coral fish, with moray eels draped over rocks like scarves of iridescent slime. A glass elevator plies up and down inside the tank, though you'll get a better view by taking the stairs. Don't miss the cafe on the very top floor, which has a great view of the Humber estuary.

FREE **Museum Quarter** MUSEUMS

Hull has several city-run **museums** (www.hullcc.gov.uk/museums; 36 High St; 10am-5pm Mon-Sat, 1.30-4.30pm Sun) concentrated in an area promoted as the Museum Quarter. All share the same contact details and opening hours, and all are free.

The fascinating **Streetlife Museum** contains re-created street scenes from Georgian and Victorian times and from the 1930s, with all sorts of historic vehicles to explore, from stagecoaches to bicycles to buses and trams. Behind the museum, marooned in the mud of the River Hull, is the **Arctic Corsair** (tours 10am-4.30pm Wed & Sat, 1.30-4.30pm Sun). Tours of this Atlantic trawler, a veteran of the 1970s 'Cod Wars', demonstrate the hardships of fishing north of the Arctic Circle.

Nearby you'll find the **Hull & East Riding Museum** (local history and archaeology), and **Wilberforce House** (the birthplace of William Wilberforce, now a museum about the slave trade and its abolition).

Festivals

Hull Literature Festival LITERATURE

(www.humbermouth.org.uk) Besides the Larkin connection, poets Andrew Marvell and Stevie Smith and playwrights Alan Plater and John Godber all hail from Hull. Held in the last two weeks of June.

Hull Jazz Festival JAZZ

(www.hulljazz.org.uk) This week-long July festival brings an impressive line-up of great jazz musicians to the city.

Sleeping & Eating

Good accommodation in the city centre is pretty thin on the ground – mostly business-oriented chain hotels and a few mediocre guest houses. The tourist office will help book accommodation for free.

The best concentration of eating places is to be found along Princes Ave, from Welbeck St to Blenheim St, a mile northwest of the centre.

Kingston Theatre Hotel HOTEL ££

(01482-225828; www.kingstontheatrehotel.com; 1-2 Kingston Sq; s/d/ste from £50/65/90;) Overlooking leafy Kingston Sq, close to the New Theatre, this recently refurbished hotel is one of the best options in the city centre, with elegant bedrooms, friendly service and an excellent breakfast.

Fudge CAFE/BRASSERIE ££

(www.fudgecafe-restaurant.com; 93 Princes Ave; mains £9-15; breakfast & lunch Tue-Sun, dinner Tue-Sat;) This funky cafe serves hearty breakfasts, cakes and coffee all day, but also offers a tempting brasserie menu at lunch and dinner times, with dishes that include juicy burgers (beef or veggie), seafood gumbo and chickpea casserole with chilli and coriander.

Boar's Nest MODERN BRITSH ££

(01482-445577; www.theboarsnesthull.com; 22-24 Princes Ave; mains £14-19; lunch & dinner) Set in a former butcher's shop with quirky Edwardian decor, the Boar's Nest has built its reputation on sourcing quality British produce and serving it in a straightforward fashion: from Bridlington crab (on granary toast with a quail's egg on top) to roast rib of beef (with mashed potato and cauliflower cheese). Bookings recommended at weekends.

Hitchcock's Vegetarian Restaurant VEGETARIAN ££

(☎01482-320233; www.hitchcocksrestaurant.co.uk; 1 Bishop Lane, High St; per person £15; ⏲dinner Tue-Sat) The word 'quirky' could have been invented to describe this place. It's an atmospheric maze of small rooms, and has an all-you-can-eat vegetarian buffet whose theme – Thai, Indian, Spanish, whatever – is chosen by the first person to book that evening. But hey, the food is excellent and the welcome is warm. Bookings necessary.

Drinking & Entertainment

Come nightfall – especially at weekends – Hull can be raucous and often rowdy, especially in the streets around Trinity Sq in the Old Town, and on the strip of pubs along Beverley Rd to the north of the city centre.

Hull Truck Theatre THEATRE

(www.hulltruck.co.uk; Spring St) Home to acclaimed playwright John Godber, who made his name with gritty comedies *Bouncers* and *Up'n'Under* (he is one of the most-performed playwrights in the English-speaking world), Hull Truck presents a lively program of drama, comedy and Sunday jazz. It's just northwest of the Old Town.

Welly Club CLUB

(www.giveitsomewelly.com; 105-107 Beverley Rd; admission £5-12; ⏲10pm-3am Thu-Sat) The East Riding's top nightclub offers two venues – the mainstream Welly:One (which hosts Shuffle, the regular Saturday night dance club) and the more alternative Welly:Two (more house, techno, drum and bass). First Friday of the month is the famed Déjà vu house night, while Thursday is devoted to indie rock.

Minerva PUB

(Nelson St) If you're more into pubbing than clubbing, try a pint of Black Sheep at this lovely, 200-year-old pub down by the waterfront; on a sunny day you can sit outdoors and watch the ships go by.

Hull New Theatre THEATRE

(www.hullcc.gov.uk; Kingston Sq) A traditional regional theatre hosting popular drama, concerts and musicals.

Information

Post office (63 Market Pl; ⏲9am-5.30pm Mon-Sat)

Tourist office (☎0844 811 2070; www.realyorkshire.co.uk; 1 Paragon St; ⏲10am-5pm Mon-Sat, 11am-3pm Sun)

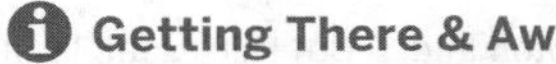

Getting There & Away

BOAT The ferry port is 3 miles east of the centre at King George Dock; a bus connects the train station with the ferries.

BUS There are buses direct from London (£26, 6½ hours, one daily), Leeds (£7, 1¾ hours, six daily Monday to Friday, eight Saturday, two Sunday) and York (£7.60, 1¾ hours, one daily).

TRAIN Hull has good rail links north and south to Newcastle (£30, 2½ hours, hourly, change at York or Doncaster) and London King's Cross (£50, 2¾ hours, every two hours), and west to York (£18, 1¼ hours, every two hours) and Leeds (£16, one hour, hourly).

Beverley

POP 29,110

Handsome, unspoilt Beverley is one of the most attractive towns in Yorkshire, largely on account of its magnificent minster – a rival to any cathedral in England – and the tangle of streets that lie beneath it, each brimming with exquisite Georgian and Victorian buildings.

All the sights are a short walk from either train or bus station. There's a large market in the main square on Saturday, and a smaller one on Wednesday on the square called...Wednesday Market.

Sights

Beverley Minster CHURCH

(www.beverleyminster.org; admission by donation; ⏲9am-4pm Mon-Sat & noon-4pm Sun, till 5pm Mon-Sat May-Aug) One of the great glories of English religious architecture, Beverley Minster is the most impressive church in the country that is not a cathedral. Construction began in 1220 – it was the third church to be built on this site, the first dating from the 7th century – and continued for two centuries, spanning the Early English, Decorated and Perpendicular periods of the Gothic style.

The soaring lines of the exterior are imposing, but it is inside that the charm and beauty lie. The 14th-century **north aisle** is lined with original stone carvings, mostly of musicians. Indeed, much of our knowledge of early musical instruments comes from these images. You'll also see goblins, devils and grotesque figures. Look out for the bagpipe player.

Close to the altar, the elaborate and intricate **Percy Canopy** (1340), a decorative frill above the tomb of local aristocrat Lady Eleanor Percy, is a testament to the skill of the sculptor and the finest example of Gothic stone carving in England. In complete contrast, in the nearby chancel is the 10th-century Saxon **frith stool,** a plain and polished stone chair that once gave sanctuary to anyone escaping the law.

In the roof of the tower is a restored **treadwheel crane** (guided tours £5; 11.15am, 2.15pm & 3.30pm Mon-Sat), where workers ground around like hapless hamsters to lift the huge loads necessary to build a medieval church. Access is by guided tour only.

FREE St Mary's Church CHURCH

(9.30am-4.30pm Mon-Fri, 10am-4pm Sat, 2-4pm Sun Apr-Sep, reduced hours Oct-Mar) Doomed to play second fiddle to Beverley Minster, St Mary's Church at the other end of town was built between 1120 and 1530. The west front (early 15th century) is considered one of the finest of any parish church in England. In the north choir aisle there is a **carving** (c 1330) of a rabbit dressed as a pilgrim that is said to have inspired Lewis Carroll's White Rabbit.

Sleeping & Eating

Friary YHA HOSTEL £

(0845 371 9004; www.yha.org.uk; Friar's Lane; dm from £14; P) Beverley's cheapest accommodation also has the best setting and location. This hostel is housed in a beautifully restored 14th-century Dominican friary mentioned in Chaucer's *The Canterbury Tales*, and is only 100m from the minster and a short walk from the train station.

Kings Head B&B ££

(01482-868103; www.kingsheadpubbeverley.co.uk; 38 Saturday Market; r from £73; @) A Georgian coaching inn that has been given a modern makeover, the Kings Head is a lively, family-friendly pub with 12 bright and cheerful rooms above the bar. The pub opens late on weekend nights, but earplugs are supplied for those who don't want to join the revelry!

Dine on the Rowe BRASSERIE ££

(01482-502269; www.dineontherowe.com; 12-14 Butcher Row; mains £16-18; lunch daily, dinner Wed-Sat) This new kid on the block rivals Grant's Bistro in its dedication to local produce, but offers a rather less formal atmosphere. Try the roast duck from Leven farm (just northeast of Beverley) with a sweet-and-sour Yorkshire rhubarb jus. Lunch dishes such as sausage and mash are available noon to 7.30pm, and a sharing platter for two, including two glasses of wine, costs £25.

Grant's Bistro MODERN BRITISH ££

(01482-887624; www.grantsbistro.co.uk; 22 North Bar Within; mains £15-21; lunch Fri & Sat, dinner Mon-Sat) Grant's is a great place for a romantic dinner *à deux,* with darkwood tables, fresh flowers and candlelight. The menu makes the most of fresh local beef, game and especially seafood, with dishes such as pan-fried scallops with black pudding. From Monday to Thursday you can get a two-course dinner including a glass of wine for £15.

Eastgate Guest House B&B ££

(01482-868464; www.eastgateguesthouse.com; 7 Eastgate; s/d £50/80) A red-brick Victorian town house with comfortable rooms in a central location.

Boutique du Café Lempicka CAFE £

(13 Wednesday Market; mains £5-7) Stylish and sepia-toned little cafe with a 1930s art-deco atmosphere. Serves fair-trade coffee and tea, wicked hot chocolate, homemade cakes and daily lunch specials.

Information

Post office (Register Sq; 9am-5.30pm Mon-Fri, to 12.30pm Sat)

Tourist office (01482-391672; www.beverley.gov.uk; 34 Butcher Row; 9.30am-5.15pm Mon-Fri & 10am-4.45pm Sat year-round, 11am-3pm Sun Jul & Aug)

Getting There & Away

BUS There are frequent bus services from Hull, including numbers 121, 122, 246 and X46/X47 (30 minutes, every 20 minutes). Bus X46/X47 links Beverley with York (1¼ hours, hourly).

TRAIN There are regular trains to Scarborough via Filey (£11.40, 1½ hours, every two hours) and Hull (£5.50, 15 minutes, twice hourly).

NORTH YORKSHIRE

The largest of Yorkshire's four counties – and the largest county in England – is also the most beautiful. Unlike the rest of northern England, it has survived almost unscarred by the Industrial Revolution. On the contrary, North Yorkshire has always, since the Middle Ages, been about sheep and the woolly wealth that they produce.

Instead of closed-down factories, mills and mines, the artificial monuments that dot the landscape round these parts are of the magnificent variety – the great houses and wealthy abbeys that sit ruined or restored, a reminder that there was plenty of money to be made off the sheep's back.

All the same, North Yorkshire's biggest attraction is an urban one. Sure, the genteel spa town of Harrogate and the bright and breezy seaside resorts of Scarborough and Whitby have many fans, but nothing compares to the unparalleled splendour of York, England's most-visited city outside London.

York

POP 181,100

Nowhere in northern England says 'medieval' quite like York, a city of extraordinary cultural and historical wealth that has lost little of its pre-industrial lustre. Its medieval spider's web of narrow streets is enclosed by a magnificent circuit of 13th-century walls. At the heart of the city lies the immense, awe-inspiring minster, one of the most beautiful Gothic cathedrals in the world. The city's long history and rich heritage is woven into virtually every brick and beam, and modern, tourist-oriented York – with its myriad museums, restaurants, cafes and traditional pubs – is a carefully maintained heir to that heritage.

Just to avoid the inevitable confusion, remember that round these parts *gate* means street and *bar* means gate.

Sights

York Minster CATHEDRAL

(www.yorkminster.org; adult/child £8/free; 9am-5.30pm Mon-Sat, noon-3.45pm Sun) Not content with being Yorkshire's most important historic building, the awe-inspiring York Minster is also the largest medieval cathedral in all of Northern Europe. Seat of the archbishop of York, primate of England, it is second in importance only to Canterbury, home of the primate of *all* England – the separate titles were created to settle a debate over whether York or Canterbury was the true centre of the English church. But that's where Canterbury's superiority ends, for this is without doubt one of the world's most beautiful Gothic buildings. If this is the only cathedral you visit in England, you'll still walk away satisfied – as long as you have the patience to deal with the constant flow of school groups and organised tours that will invariably clog up your camera's viewfinder.

> **WANT MORE?**
>
> Head to **Lonely Planet** (www.lonelyplanet.com/england/yorkshire/york) for planning advice, author recommendations, traveller reviews and insider tips.

The first church on this spot was a wooden chapel built for the baptism of King Edwin of Northumbria on Easter Day 627; its location is marked in the crypt. It was replaced with a stone church that was built on the site of a Roman basilica, parts of which can be seen in the foundations. The first Norman minster was built in the 11th century; again, you can see surviving fragments in the foundations and crypt.

The present minster, built mainly between 1220 and 1480, manages to encompass all the major stages of Gothic architectural development. The transepts (1220–55) were built in Early English style; the octagonal chapter house (1260–90) and the nave (1291–1340) in the Decorated style; and the west towers, west front and central (or lantern) tower (1470–72) in Perpendicular style.

Choir, Chapter House & Nave

You enter via the south transept, which was badly damaged by fire in 1984 but has now been fully restored. To your right is the 15th-century **choir screen** depicting the 15 kings from William I to Henry VI. Facing you is the magnificent **Five Sisters Window**, with five lancets over 15m high. This is the minster's oldest complete window; most of its tangle of coloured glass dates from around 1250. Just beyond it to the right is the 13th-century **chapter house**, a fine example of the Decorated style. Sinuous and intricately carved stonework – there are more than 200 expressive carved heads and figures – surrounds an airy, uninterrupted space.

Back in the main church, take note of the unusually tall and wide **nave**, the aisles of which (to the sides) are roofed in stone, in contrast to the central roof, which is wood painted to look like stone. On both sides of the nave are painted stone shields of the nobles who met with Edward II at a parliament in York. Also note the **dragon's head** projecting from the gallery – it's a crane believed to have been used to lift a font cover.

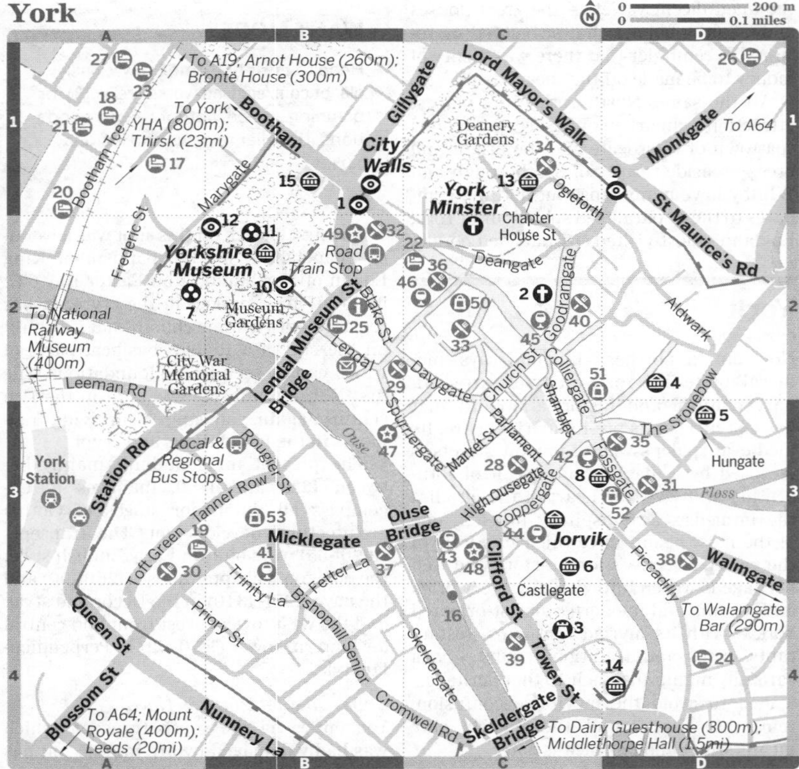

There are several fine windows dating from the early 14th century, but the most impressive is the **Great West Window** (1338), with its beautiful stone tracery.

Beyond the screen and the choir is the **lady chapel** and, behind it, the **high altar**, which is dominated by the huge **Great East Window** (1405). At 23.7m by 9.4m – roughly the size of a tennis court – it is the world's largest medieval stained-glass window and the cathedral's single most important treasure. Needless to say, its epic size matches the epic theme depicted within: the beginning and end of the world as described in Genesis and the Book of Revelations.

Undercroft, Treasury & Crypt

A set of stairs in the south transept leads down to the undercroft, where you'll also find the treasury and crypt – these should on no account be missed. In 1967 the foundations were shored up when the central tower threatened to collapse; while engineers worked frantically to save the building, archaeologists uncovered Roman and Norman remains that attest to the site's ancient history – one of the most extraordinary finds is a **Roman culvert**, still carrying water to the Ouse. The **treasury** houses 11th-century artefacts including relics from the graves of medieval archbishops.

The **crypt** contains fragments from the Norman cathedral, including the font showing King Edwin's baptism that also marks the site of the original wooden chapel. Look out for the **Doomstone**, a 12th-century carving showing a scene from the Last Judgement with demons casting doomed souls into Hell.

Tower

At the heart of the minster is the massive **tower** (extra admission adult/child £5/3), which is well worth climbing for the unparalleled **views of York**. You'll have to tackle a fairly claustrophobic climb of 275 steps and, most

York

Top Sights

	City Walls	B1
	Jorvik	C3
	York Minster	C2
	Yorkshire Museum	B2

Sights

1	Bootham Bar	B1
2	Church of the Holy Trinity	C2
	City Wall Access Steps	(see 1)
	City Wall Access Steps	(see 9)
3	Clifford's Tower	C4
4	Dig	D2
5	Dig Hungate	D3
6	Fairfax House	C3
7	Gatehall	A2
	Hospitium	(see 7)
8	Merchant Adventurers' Hall	C3
9	Monk Bar	D1
10	Multangular Tower	B2
	Richard III Museum	(see 9)
11	St Mary's Abbey	B2
12	St Mary's Lodge	B2
13	Treasurer's House	C1
14	York Castle Museum	D4
15	York City Art Gallery	B1

Activities, Courses & Tours

16	YorkBoat	C4

Sleeping

17	23 St Mary's	A1
18	Abbeyfields	A1
19	Ace Hotel	A3
20	Briar Lea Guest House	A1
21	Elliotts B&B	A1
22	Guy Fawkes Inn	C2
23	Hedley House Hotel	A1
24	Hotel 53	D4
25	Judges Lodging Hotel	B2
26	Monkgate Guesthouse	D1
27	St Raphael	A1

Eating

28	Ate O'Clock	C3
29	Betty's	B2
30	Blake Head Vegetarian Cafe	A3
31	Blue Bicycle	D3
32	Café Concerto	B2
33	El Piano	C2
34	Gray's Court	C1
35	J Baker's Bistro Moderne	D3
36	Little Betty's	C2
37	Living Room	B3
38	Melton's Too	D3
39	Olive Tree	C4
40	Siam House	C2

Drinking

41	Ackhorne	B3
42	Blue Bell	C3
43	King's Arms	C3
44	Little John	C3
45	Old White Swan	C2
46	Ye Olde Starre	C2

Entertainment

47	City Screen	B3
48	Grand Opera House	C3
49	York Theatre Royal	B2

Shopping

50	Antiques Centre	C2
51	Azendi	C2
52	Barbican Books	D3
53	Ken Spellman Booksellers	B3

probably, a queue of people with cameras in hand. Access to the tower is near the entrance in the south transept, dominated by the exquisite **Rose Window**, commemorating the union of the royal houses of Lancaster and York through the marriage of Henry VII and Elizabeth of York, which ended the Wars of the Roses and began the Tudor dynasty.

FREE **National Railway Museum** MUSEUM (www.nrm.org.uk; Leeman Rd; ⏲10am-6pm, closed 24-26 Dec) Many railway museums are the sole preserve of lone men in anoraks comparing dog-eared notebooks and getting high on the smell of machine oil, coal smoke and nostalgia. But this place is different. York's National Railway Museum – the biggest in the world, with more than 100 locomotives – is so well presented and full of fascinating stuff that it's interesting even to folk whose eyes don't mist over at the thought of a 4-6-2 A1 Pacific class chuffing into a tunnel.

Highlights for the trainspotters among us include a replica of George Stephenson's *Rocket* (1829), the world's first 'modern' steam locomotive; the sleek and streamlined *Mallard,* which set the world speed record for a steam locomotive in 1938

(126mph); a 1960s Japanese *Shinkansen* bullet train; and the world-famous *Flying Scotsman,* the first steam engine to break the 100mph barrier (currently undergoing restoration; should be in full working order by 2011). There's also a massive 4-6-2 loco from 1949 that's been cut in half so you can see how it works.

But even if you're not a rail nerd you'll enjoy looking around the gleaming, silk-lined carriages of the royal trains used by Queen Victoria and Edward VII, or having a *Brief*

YORK: FROM THE BEGINNING

York – or the marshy area that preceded the first settlement – has been coveted by pretty much everyone that has ever set foot on this island. In the beginning there were the Brigantes, a local tribe that minded their own business. In AD 71 the Romans – who were spectacularly successful at minding everyone else's business – built their first garrison here for the troops fighting the poor old Brigantes. They called it Eboracum, and in time a civilian settlement prospered around what became a large fort. Hadrian used it as the base for his northern campaign, while Constantine the Great was proclaimed emperor here in AD 306 after the death of his father. When the Roman Empire collapsed, the town was taken by the Anglo-Saxons who renamed it Eoforwic and made it the capital of the independent kingdom of Northumbria.

Enter the Christians. In 625 a Roman priest, Paulinus, arrived and managed to convert King Edwin and all his nobles. Two years later, they built the first wooden church; for most of the next century the city was a major centre of learning, attracting students from all over Europe.

The student party lasted until 866, when the next wave of invaders arrived. This time it was those marauding Vikings, who chucked everybody out and gave the town a more tongue-friendly name, Jorvik. It was to be their capital for the next 100 years, and during that time they reined in their pillaging ways and turned the city into an important trading port. The next arrival was King Eadred of Wessex, who drove out the last Viking ruler in 954 and reunited Danelaw with the south, but trouble quickly followed. In 1066 King Harold II managed to fend off a Norwegian invasion/rebellion at Stamford Bridge, east of York, but his turn came at the hands of William the Conqueror a few months later at the Battle of Hastings.

Willie exercised his own brand of tough love in York. After his two wooden castles were captured by an Anglo-Scandinavian army, he torched the whole city (and Durham) and the surrounding countryside so that the rebels knew who was boss – the 'harrying of the north'. The Normans then set about rebuilding the city, including a new minster. From that moment, everything in York was rosy – except for a blip in 1137 when the whole city caught fire – and over the next 300 years it prospered through royal patronage, textiles, trade and the church.

No sooner did the church finally get built, though, than the city went into full recession. In the 15th century Hull took over as the region's main port and the textile industry moved elsewhere. Henry VIII's inability to keep a wife and the ensuing brouhaha with the church that resulted in the Reformation also hit York pretty hard. Henry did establish a branch of the King's Council here to help govern the north, and this contributed to the city's recovery under Elizabeth I and James I.

The council was abolished during Charles I's reign, but the king established his court here during the Civil War, which drew the devastating attentions of the Parliamentarians. They besieged the rabidly promonarchist York for three months in 1644, but by a fortunate accident of history their leader was a local chap called Sir Thomas Fairfax, who prevented his troops from setting York alight, thereby preserving the city and the minster.

Not much happened after that. Throughout the 18th century the city was a fashionable social centre dominated by the aristocracy, who were drawn by its culture and new racecourse. When the railway was built in 1839 thousands of people were employed in the new industries that sprung up around it, such as confectionery. These industries went into decline in the latter half of the 20th century, but by then a new invader was asking for directions at the city gates, armed only with a guidebook.

LOCAL KNOWLEDGE

ANDY DEXTROUS: GHOST TOUR GUIDE, YORK

Things I love about York include its outstanding architecture, the maze of 'snickleways' (narrow alleys), the array of small independent shops, the street entertainment and festivals, and central, green spaces like **Museum Gardens** (p506). All year round the streets are full of appreciative visitors from all over the world enjoying the city, relaxing and adding to the atmosphere.

York's Spookiest Spots

Haunted pubs like the **Old White Swan** (p511). Plus the **Antiques Centre** (p511) on Stonegate, which is also haunted. In the streets around the Minster you're always within a breath of a ghost tale.

Best of York

For beer and atmosphere, the **Blue Bell** (p511). For veggie and vegan food and a place that welcomes children, **El Piano** (p510). And for sheer ambience, **Gray's Court** (p510).

Best of Yorkshire

Take the **North Yorkshire Moors Railway** (p524) to Goathland, then walk to Mallyan Spout waterfall. Include a drink at the Birch Hall Inn at Beck Hole.

For a special meal there's the **Star Inn** (p523) at Harome or the **Stone Trough** (p513) at Kirkham; stroll down to the abbey ruins before or after your meal.

Encounter moment over tea and scones at the museum's station platform cafe called, erm, Brief Encounter. Allow at least two hours to do the museum justice.

The museum is about 400m west of the train station; if you don't fancy walking you can ride the road train (adult/child £2/1) that runs every 30 minutes from 11am to 4pm between the minster and the museum.

Jorvik MUSEUM
(www.vikingjorvik.com; Coppergate; adult/child £8.95/6, Jorvik & Dig combined £13/9.75; ⏲10am-5pm Apr-Oct, to 4pm Nov-Mar) Interactive multimedia exhibits aimed at 'bringing history to life' often achieve just the opposite, but the much-hyped Jorvik – the most visited attraction in town after the minster – manages to pull it off with admirable aplomb. It's a smells-and-all reconstruction of the Viking settlement that was unearthed here during excavations in the late 1970s, brought to you courtesy of a 'time-car' monorail that transports you through 9th-century Jorvik (the Viking name for York). While some of the 'you will now travel back in time' malarkey is a bit naff, it's all done with a sense of humour tied to a historical authenticity that will leave you with a pretty good idea of what life must have been like in Viking-era York. In the exhibition at the end of the monorail, look out for the **Lloyds Bank Turd** – a fossilised human stool that measures an eye-watering nine inches long and half a pound in weight, and must be the only jobbie in the world to have its own Wikipedia entry.

You can cut time spent waiting in the queue by booking your tickets online and choosing the time you want to visit – it only costs £1 extra.

FREE **City Walls** CITY WALLS
(⏲8am-dusk) If the weather's good, don't miss the chance to walk the City Walls, which follow the line of the original Roman walls – it gives a whole new perspective on the city. The full circuit is 4.5 miles (allow 1½ to two hours); if you're pushed for time, the short stretch from Bootham Bar to Monk Bar is worth doing for the views of the minster.

Start and finish in the Museum Gardens or at **Bootham Bar** (on the site of a Roman gate), where a multimedia exhibit provides some historical context, and go clockwise. Highlights include **Monk Bar**, the best-preserved medieval gate, which still has a working portcullis, and **Walmgate Bar**, England's only city gate with an intact barbican (an extended gateway to ward off uninvited guests).

At Monk Bar you'll find the **Richard III Museum** (www.richardiiimuseum.co.uk; adult/child £2.50/free; ⏲9am-5pm Mar-Oct, 9.30am-

4pm Nov-Feb). The museum sets out the case of the murdered 'Princes in the Tower' and invites visitors to judge whether their uncle, Richard III, killed them.

You can download a free guide to the wall walk at www.visityork.org/explore/walls.html.

Yorkshire Museum MUSEUM

(www.yorkshiremuseum.org.uk; Museum St; adult/child £7/free; ⏲10am-5pm) Most of York's Roman archaeology is hidden beneath the medieval city, so the displays in the Yorkshire Museum are invaluable if you want to get an idea of what Eboracum was like. There are excellent exhibits on Viking and medieval York too, including priceless artefacts such as the 8th-century Coppergate helmet; a 9th-century Anglian sword decorated with silver; and the 15th-century Middleham Jewel, an engraved gold pendant adorned with a giant sapphire.

In the peaceful **Museum Gardens** (⏲dawn-dusk) you can see the **Multangular Tower**, a part of the city walls that was once the western tower of the Roman garrison's defensive ramparts. The Roman stonework at the base has been built over with 13th-century additions.

On the other side of the Museum Gardens are the ruins of **St Mary's Abbey** (founded 1089), dating from 1270–1294. The ruined **Gatehall** was its main entrance, providing access from the abbey to the river. The adjacent **Hospitium** dates from the 14th century, although the timber-framed upper storey is a much-restored survivor from the 15th century; it was used as the abbey guest house. **St Mary's Lodge** was built around 1470 to provide VIP accommodation.

Shambles MEDIEVAL STREET

(www.yorkshambles.com) The narrow, cobbled lane known as the Shambles, lined with 15th-century Tudor buildings that overhang so much they seem to meet above your head, is the most visited street in Europe. Quaint and picturesque it most certainly is, and it hints at what a medieval street may have looked like – if it is overrun with people told they have to buy a tacky souvenir and be back on the tour bus in 15 minutes. It takes its name from the Saxon word *shamel*, meaning 'slaughterhouse' – in 1862 there were 26 butcher shops on this one street.

York Castle Museum MUSEUM

(www.yorkcastlemuseum.org.uk; Tower St; adult/child £8/free; ⏲9.30am-5pm) This excellent museum contains displays of everyday life through the centuries, with reconstructed domestic interiors, a Victorian street and a less-than-homely prison cell where you can try out a condemned man's bed – in this case the highwayman Dick Turpin's (he was imprisoned here before being hanged in 1739). There's a bewildering array of evocative objects from the past 400 years, gathered together by a certain Dr Kirk from the 1920s onwards for fear that the items would become obsolete and disappear completely. He wasn't far wrong, which makes this place all the more interesting.

Treasurer's House HISTORIC BUILDING

(NT; www.nationaltrust.org.uk; Minster Yard; adult/child £6/3; ⏲11am-4.30pm Sat-Thu Apr-Oct, 11am-3pm Sat-Thu Nov) The Treasurer's House was home to the York Minster's medieval treasurers. Substantially rebuilt in the 17th and 18th centuries, the 13 rooms here house a fine collection of furniture and provide a good insight into 18th-century life. The house is also the setting for one of the city's most enduring ghost stories: during the 1950s a plumber working in the basement swore he saw a band of Roman soldiers walking *through* the walls. His story remains popular if unproven – but you can explore the cellar to find out.

Dig MUSEUM

(www.digyork.co.uk; St Saviour's Church, St Saviourgate; adult/child £5.50/5, Dig & Jorvik £13/9.75; ⏲10am-5pm, closed 24-26 Dec; 👪) Under the same management as Jorvik, Dig cashes in on the popularity of archaeology programs on TV by giving you the chance to be an 'archaeological detective', unearthing the secrets of York's distant past as well as learning something of the archaeologist's world – what they do, how they do it and so on. Aimed mainly at kids, it's much more hands-on than Jorvik, and a lot depends on how good – and entertaining – your guide is.

Up to the end of 2011 you can also visit a real live archaeological dig at **Dig Hungate** (www.dighungate.com; tours per person £1); ask at Dig or check the website for times and details.

Clifford's Tower CASTLE

(EH; www.english-heritage.org.uk; Tower St; adult/child £3.50/1.80; ⏲10am-6pm Apr-Sep, to 5pm Oct, to 4pm Nov-Mar) There's precious little left of York Castle except for this evocative stone tower, a highly unusual figure-of-eight design built into the castle's keep after the original one was destroyed in 1190 during anti-Jewish riots. An angry mob forced 150 Jews to be locked inside the tower and the hapless victims took their own lives rather than be killed. There's not much to see inside, but the views over the city are excellent.

FREE **Church of the Holy Trinity** CHURCH
(Goodramgate; ⏲10am-5pm Tue-Sat May-Sep, 10am-4pm Oct-Apr) Tucked away behind an inconspicuous gate and seemingly cut off from the rest of the town, the Church of the Holy Trinity is a fantastically atmospheric old building, having survived almost unchanged for the last 200 years. Inside are rare 17th- to 18th-century box pews, 15th-century stained glass, and wonky walls that seem to have been built without plumb line or spirit level.

Other sights worth exploring:

FREE **York City Art Gallery** ART GALLERY
(www.yorkartgallery.org.uk; Exhibition Sq; ⏲10am-5pm) Includes works by Reynolds, Nash, Boudin, LS Lowry and controversial York artist William Etty, who, back in the 1820s, was the first major British artist to specialise in nude painting.

Merchant Adventurers' Hall HISTORIC BUILDING
(www.theyorkcompany.co.uk; Fossgate; adult/child £5/free; ⏲9am-5pm Mon-Thu, 9am-3.30pm Fri & Sat, noon-4pm Sun Apr-Sep, 9am-3.30pm Mon-Sat Oct-Mar) One of the most handsome timber-framed buildings in Europe, built between 1357 and 1361. Displays include oil paintings and antique silver, but the building itself is the star.

Fairfax House HISTORIC BUILDING
(www.fairfaxhouse.co.uk; Castlegate; adult/child £6/free; ⏲11am-4.30pm Mon-Thu & Sat, 1.30-5pm Sun, guided tours 11am & 2pm Fri) Built in 1762 by John Carr (of Harewood House fame), Fairfax House contains a superb collection of Georgian furniture.

Tours

There's a bewildering range of tours on offer, from historic walking tours to a host of ever more competitive night-time ghost tours (York is reputed to be England's most haunted city). For starters, check the tourist office's own suggestions for walking itineraries at www.visityork.org/explore.

Ghost Hunt of York WALKING TOURS
(www.ghosthunt.co.uk; adult/child £5/3; ⏲tours 7.30pm) Award-winning and highly entertaining 75-minute tour laced with authentic ghost stories; the kids will just love this one. Begins at the Shambles, whatever the weather (they never cancel). No need to book, just turn up.

Yorkwalk WALKING TOURS
(www.yorkwalk.co.uk; adult/child £5.50/3.50; ⏲tours 10.30am & 2.15pm) Offers a series of two-hour themed walks on an ever-growing list of themes, from the classics – Roman York, the snickelways (alleys) and City Walls – to specialised walks on chocolates and sweets, women in York, secret York and the inevitable graveyard, coffin and plague tour. Walks depart from Museum Gardens Gate on Museum St; no need to book.

YorkBoat BOAT TOURS
(www.yorkboat.co.uk; King's Staith; adult/child £7.50/3.50; ⏲tours 10.30am, noon, 1.30pm & 3pm Feb-Nov) Runs one-hour cruises on the River Ouse departing from King's Staith (and Lendal Bridge 10 minutes later). Also special lunch, dinner and evening cruises.

Original Ghost Walk of York WALKING TOURS
(www.theoriginalghostwalkofyork.co.uk; adult/child £4.50/3; ⏲tours 8pm) An evening of ghouls, ghosts, mystery and history courtesy of a well-established group departing from the King's Arms pub by Ouse Bridge.

York CitySightseeing BUS TOURS
(www.city-sightseeing.com; day tickets adult/child £10/4; ⏲9am-5pm) Hop-on/hop-off route with 16 stops, calling at all the main sights. Buses leave every 10 minutes from Exhibition Sq near York Minster.

FREE **Association of Voluntary Guides** WALKING TOURS
(www.visityork.org; ⏲tours 10.15am, also 2.15pm Apr-Sep & 6.45pm Jun-Aug) Two-hour walking tours of the city starting from Exhibition Sq in front of York City Art Gallery.

Festivals & Events

Check out a full calendar of events at www.yorkfestivals.com.

Jorvik Viking Festival HISTORY
(www.vikingjorvik.com) For a week in mid-February, York is invaded by Vikings once again as part of this festival, which features battle re-enactments, themed walks, markets and other bits of Viking-related fun.

THE YORKSHIRE PASS

If you plan on visiting a lot of sights, you can save yourself some money by using a **Yorkshire Pass** (www.yorkshirepass.com; 1/2/3/6 days adult £28/38/44/68, child £18/22/26/44). It grants you free access to more than 70 pay-to-visit sights in Yorkshire, including all the major attractions in York. It's available at York tourist office, or you can buy online.

York Food Festival FOOD & DRINK
(www.yorkfoodfestival.com) Ten-day celebration of all that's good to eat and drink in Yorkshire – food stalls, markets, tastings, beer tent, cookery demonstrations etc.

York Christmas SHOPPING
(www.visityork.org/christmas) Kicking off with St Nicholas Fayre market in late November, the run-up to Christmas is an extravaganza of street decorations, market stalls, carol singers and mulled wine.

Sleeping

Beds are tough to find midsummer, even with the inflated prices of the high season. The tourist office's accommodation booking service charges £4, which might be the best four quid you spend if you arrive without a booking.

Needless to say, prices get higher the closer to the city centre you are. However, there are plenty of decent B&Bs on the streets north and south of Bootham. Southwest of the town centre, there are B&Bs clustered around Scarcroft Rd, Southlands Rd and Bishopthorpe Rd.

It's also worth looking at serviced apartments if you're planning to stay two or three nights. **City Lets** (01904-652729; www.citylets york.co.uk) offers a good selection of places from around £90 a night for a two-person apartment – we particularly like the stylish, modern flats in the peaceful courtyard at Talbot Court on Low Petergate.

Abbeyfields B&B ££
(01904-636471; www.abbeyfields.co.uk; 19 Bootham Tce; s/d from £49/78; wi-fi) Expect a warm welcome and thoughtfully arranged bedrooms here, with chairs and bedside lamps for comfortable reading. Breakfasts are among the best in town, with sausage and bacon from the local butcher, freshly laid eggs from a nearby farm, and the smell of newly baked bread.

Elliotts B&B B&B ££
(01904-623333; www.elliottshotel.co.uk; 2 Sycamore Pl; s/d from £55/80; P @ wi-fi) A beautifully converted 'gentleman's residence', Elliotts leans towards the boutique end of the guest-house market with stylish and elegant rooms, and high-tech touches such as flatscreen TVs and free wi-fi. Excellent location, both quiet and central.

Hedley House Hotel B&B ££
(01904-637404; www.hedleyhouse.com; 3 Bootham Tce; s/d/f from £50/80/90; P wi-fi family) Run by a couple with young children, this smart red-brick terrace-house hotel could hardly be more family-friendly – plus it has private parking at the back, and is barely five minutes' walk from the city centre through the Museum Gardens.

Arnot House B&B ££
(01904-641966; www.arnothouseyork.co.uk; 17 Grosvenor Tce; r £70-85; P) With three beautifully decorated rooms (provided you're a fan of Victorian floral patterns), including two with impressive four-poster beds, Arnot House sports an authentically old-fashioned look that appeals to a more mature clientele. No children allowed.

Brontë House B&B ££
(01904-621066; www.bronte-guesthouse.com; 22 Grosvenor Tce; s/d from £40/76; wi-fi) The Brontë offers five homely en suite rooms, each decorated differently; our favourite is the double with a carved, 19th-century canopied bed, William Morris wallpaper and assorted bits and pieces from another era.

23 St Mary's B&B ££
(01904-622738; www.23stmarys.co.uk; 23 St Mary's; s/d £55/90; P @) A smart and stately town house with nine chintzy, country house-style rooms, some with hand-painted furniture for that rustic look, while others are decorated with antiques, lace and polished mahogany.

Dairy Guesthouse B&B ££
(01904-639367; www.dairyguesthouse.co.uk; 3 Scarcroft Rd; s/d from £55/75; wi-fi) A lovely Victorian home that has retained many of its original features, including pine doors, stained glass and cast-iron fireplaces. But the real treat is the flower- and plant-filled courtyard that leads to the cottage-style rooms. Minimum two-night stay at weekends.

Guy Fawkes Inn HOTEL ££
(☎0845 460 2020; www.guy-fawkes-hotel.co.uk; 25 High Petergate; s/d/ste from £65/90/200; 📶) Directly opposite the minster is this comfortable and atmospheric hotel complete with gas lamps and log fires. The premises include a cottage that is reputed to be the birthplace of Guy Fawkes himself. We're not convinced, but the cottage is still the handsomest room in the building, complete with a four-poster and lots of red velvet.

York YHA HOSTEL £
(☎0845 371 9051; www.yha.org.uk; 42 Water End, Clifton; dm £18-20; P@📶👪) Originally the Rowntree (Quaker confectioners) mansion, this handsome Victorian house makes a spacious and child-friendly youth hostel, with most of the rooms being four-bed dorms. It's about a mile northwest of the city centre; there's a riverside footpath from Lendal Bridge (poorly lit so avoid after dark). Alternatively, take bus 2 from Station Ave or Museum St.

Judges Lodgings Hotel HOTEL £££
(☎01904-638733; www.judgeslodgings.com; 9 Lendal; s/d from £120/185; P) Despite being housed in an elegant Georgian mansion that was built for a wealthy physician, this is really a place for the party crowd to crash – it's within easy reach of city centre pubs, and the hotel's own lively courtyard bar rocks late into the night.

Mount Royale HOTEL £££
(☎01904-628856; www.mountroyale.co.uk; The Mount; r £100-210; P📶) A grand, early 19th-century listed building that has been converted into a superb luxury hotel, complete with a solarium, beauty spa and outdoor heated tub and swimming pool. The rooms in the main house are gorgeous, but the best of the lot are the open-plan garden suites, reached via a corridor of tropical fruit trees and bougainvillea.

Middlethorpe Hall HOTEL £££
(☎01904-641241; www.middlethorpe.com; Bishopsthorpe Rd; s/d from £130/200; P📶) York's top spot is this breathtaking 17th-century country house set in 20 acres of parkland that was once the home of diarist Lady Mary Wortley Montagu. The rooms are spread between the main house, the restored courtyard buildings and three cottage suites. Although we preferred the grandeur of the rooms in the main house, every room is beautifully decorated with original antiques and oil paintings carefully collected so as to best reflect the period.

WORTH A TRIP

YORK YURTS

Only a 15-minute drive from York, but half a world away in ambience, **York Yurts** (☎01759-380901; www.yorkyurts.com; Tadpole Cottage, Sutton Lane, Barmby Moor; d £65-75; P) offers the chance to sleep under canvas without having to rough it. There are four yurts (circular, wood-framed tents originating from Mongolia) in a three-acre field, complete with double beds, candles (no electricity), wood-burning stoves, cooking tents and barbecues (though you can order breakfast brought to you in bed if you want). There's also a communal bathroom tent with a rolltop bath and hot tub.

Ace Hotel HOSTEL £
(☎01904-627720; www.acehotelyork.co.uk; 88-90 Micklegate; dm/tw from £20/60; @) Housed in a Grade I Georgian building (once home to the High Sheriff of Yorkshire), this is a large, well-equipped hostel that's popular with school groups and stag and hen parties – don't expect peace and quiet!

Briar Lea Guest House B&B ££
(☎01904-635061; www.briarlea.co.uk; 8 Longfield Tce; s/d from £37/62; 📶) Clean, simple rooms and a friendly welcome in a central location.

St Raphael B&B ££
(☎01904-645028; www.straphaelguesthouse.co.uk; 44 Queen Annes Rd; s/d from £65/76; 📶) Historic house with that half-timbered look, great central location and home-baked bread for breakfast.

Monkgate Guesthouse B&B ££
(☎01904-655947; www.monkgateguesthouse.com; 65 Monkgate; s/d from £42/70; P👪) Attractive guest house with special family suite with separate bedroom for two kids.

Hotel 53 HOTEL ££
(☎01904-559000; www.hotel53.com; 53 Piccadilly; r from £86; P📶) Modern and minimalist, but very central with secure parking just across the street.

Eating

TOP CHOICE **J Baker's Bistro Moderne** MODERN BRITISH ££
(☎01904-622688; www.jbakers.co.uk; 7 Fossgate; lunch mains £10, 2-/3-course dinner £25/29.50;

lunch & dinner Tue-Sat) Superstar chef Jeff Baker left a Michelin star in Leeds to pursue his own vision of modern British cuisine here. The ironic '70s-style decor (think chocolate/oatmeal/tango) with moo-cow paintings is echoed in the unusual menu, which offers witty, gourmet interpretations of retro classics – try Tongue'n'Cheek (a crisp pie containing ox tongue, beef cheeks and beef jelly) or Whitby crab cocktail with apple and avocado. And don't miss his signature dessert, lemon tops.

Gray's Court CAFE ££
(www.grayscourtyork.com; Chapter House St; mains £6-7; breakfast & lunch) An unexpected find right in the very heart of York, this 16th-century house has more of a country atmosphere. Enjoy gourmet coffee and cake in the sunny garden, or indulge in a light lunch in the historic setting of the oak-panelled Jacobean gallery (extra points if you grab the alcove table above the main door). The menu runs from smoked salmon and scrambled eggs to roast butternut squash, red pepper and goat's cheese tart, and from lavender shortbread to lemon drizzle cake.

Blake Head Vegetarian Cafe VEGETARIAN £
(104 Micklegate; mains £5-7; breakfast & lunch) A bright and airy space at the back of a bookshop, filled with modern oak furniture and funky art, the Blake Head offers a tempting menu of daily lunch specials such as spicy bean burger with salsa, or hummus and roast red pepper open sandwich. Great ginger and lemon cake, too. Veggie breakfasts served till 11.30am.

Ate O'Clock BISTRO ££
(01904-644080; www.ateoclock.co.uk; 13a High Ousegate; mains £14-17; lunch & dinner Tue-Sat) A tempting menu of classic bistro dishes (fillet of beef with mushrooms, pork-and-chive sausage with mash and onion gravy) made with fresh Yorkshire produce has made this place hugely popular with locals – best book a table to avoid disappointment. Three-course dinner is £16.75 from 6pm to 7.55pm Tuesday to Thursday.

Olive Tree MEDITERRANEAN ££
(01904-624433; www.theolivetreeyork.co.uk; 10 Tower St; mains £9-18; lunch & dinner) Local produce gets a Mediterranean makeover at this bright and breezy bistro with a view across the street to Clifford's Tower. Classic pizza and pasta dishes are complemented by more ambitious recipes such as seared scallops with chorizo, and sea bass with asparagus, cherry tomatoes and saffron cream sauce. The lunchtime and early evening menu offers two courses for £13.

Café Concerto CAFE/BISTRO ££
(01904-610478; www.cafeconcerto.biz; 21 High Petergate; snacks £3-8, mains £10-17; 8.30am-10pm) Walls papered with sheet music, chilled jazz on the stereo and battered, mismatched tables and chairs set the bohemian tone in this comforting coffee shop. During the day expect breakfasts, bagels and cappuccinos big enough to float a boat in, and a sophisticated bistro menu in the evening.

Betty's TEAROOM ££
(www.bettys.co.uk; St Helen's Sq; mains £6-11, afternoon tea £16; breakfast, lunch & dinner) Afternoon tea, old-school style, with white-aproned waitresses, linen tablecloths and a teapot collection ranged along the walls. The house speciality is the Yorkshire Fat Rascal – a huge fruit scone smothered in melted butter – but the smoked haddock with poached egg and hollandaise sauce is our favourite lunch dish.

El Piano VEGAN £
(www.elpiano.com; 15 Grape Lane; mains £4-7; lunch daily, dinner Mon-Sat;) With a menu that is 100% vegan, nut-free and gluten-free, this colourful, Hispanic-style spot is a vegetarian haven. There's a lovely cafe downstairs and three themed rooms upstairs. The menu offers dishes such as falafel, onion bhaji, corn fritters and mushroom-and-basil salad, either in tapas-size portions or as mixed platters. There's also a takeaway counter.

Melton's Too BAR/BISTRO ££
(www.meltonstoo.co.uk; 25 Walmgate; mains £9-12; breakfast, lunch & dinner) A comfortable, chilled-out cafe-bar and bistro, Melton's Too serves everything from cake and cappuccino (or Bombay Sapphire gin and tonic) to tapas-style snacks or a three-course dinner of smoked mackerel and watercress salad, duck confit with apple salad, and Yorkshire rhubarb crumble.

Blue Bicycle FRENCH/FUSION ££
(01904-673990; www.thebluebicycle.com; 34 Fossgate; mains £15-24; lunch Thu-Sun, dinner daily) Once upon a time, this building was a well-frequented brothel; these days it's a romantic, candlelit restaurant that makes for a top-notch dining experience.

Little Betty's TEAROOM ££
(www.bettys.co.uk; 46 Stonegate; mains £8-10; ⏲10am-5.30pm) Betty's younger sister is more demure and less frequented, but just as good.

Living Room INTERNATIONAL ££
(www.thelivingroom.co.uk; 1 Bridge St; mains £10-17; ⏲breakfast, lunch & dinner) Balcony tables overlooking the river and a menu focused on quality versions of classic dishes from around the world. Sunday brunch served noon to 6pm.

Siam House THAI ££
(63a Goodramgate; mains £9-15; ⏲dinner Mon-Sat) Delicious Thai food in about as authentic an atmosphere as you could muster up 6000km from Bangkok.

Drinking

With only a couple of exceptions, the best drinking holes in town are the older, traditional pubs. In recent years, the area around Ousegate and Micklegate has gone from moribund to mental, especially at weekends.

TOP CHOICE **Blue Bell** PUB
(53 Fossgate) This is what a real English pub looks like – a tiny, wood-panelled room with a smouldering fireplace, decor (and beer and smoke stains) dating from c 1798, a pile of ancient board games in the corner, friendly and efficient bar staff, and Timothy Taylor and Black Sheep ales on tap. Bliss, with froth on top.

Ye Olde Starre PUB
(40 Stonegate) Licensed since 1644, this is York's oldest pub – a warren of small rooms and a small beer garden, with a half-dozen real ales on tap. It was used as a morgue by the Roundheads during the Civil War, but the atmosphere's improved a lot since then.

Ackhorne PUB
(9 St Martin's Lane) Tucked away off beery, sloppy Micklegate, this locals' inn is as comfortable as old slippers – some of the old guys here look like they've merged with the furniture. There's a pleasant beer garden at the back, and an open-mic night for local musicians on the first Tuesday of the month.

Little John PUB
(5 Castlegate) This historic pub – the third oldest in York – is the city's top gay venue, with regular club nights and other events. In 1739 the corpse of executed highwayman Dick Turpin was laid out in the cellar here for the public to view at a penny a head; the pub is said to be haunted by his ghost. Not sure what's scarier though – the ghost story or the Thursday night karaoke session...

Old White Swan PUB
(80 Goodramgate) Popular and atmospheric old pub with small beer garden and a good range of guest real ales. And it's haunted...

King's Arms PUB
(King's Staith) York's best-known pub in fabulous riverside location, with tables spilling out onto the quayside – a perfect spot for a summer's evening, but be prepared to share it with a few hundred other people.

Entertainment

There are a couple of good theatres in York, and an interesting art-house cinema, but as far as clubs are concerned, forget it: historic York is best enjoyed without them anyway.

York Theatre Royal THEATRE
(www.yorktheatreroyal.co.uk; St Leonard's Pl) Stages well-regarded productions of theatre, opera and dance.

Grand Opera House MUSIC/COMEDY
(www.grandoperahouseyork.org.uk; Clifford St) Despite the name there's no opera here but a wide range of productions from live bands and popular musicals to stand-up comics and pantomime.

City Screen CINEMA
(www.picturehouses.co.uk; 13-17 Coney St) Appealing modern building in a converted printing works, screening both mainstream and art-house films. There's also a nice cafe-bar on the terrace overlooking the river.

Shopping

Coney St, Davygate and the adjoining streets are the hub of York's high-street shopping scene, but the real treat for visitors are the antique, bric-a-brac and secondhand bookshops, which are concentrated in Colliergate, Micklegate and Fossgate.

Ken Spelman Booksellers BOOKS
(www.kenspelman.com; 70 Micklegate) This fascinating shop has been selling rare, antiquarian and secondhand books since 1910. With an open fire crackling in the grate in winter, it's a browser's paradise.

Antiques Centre ANTIQUES
(www.antiquescentreyorkeshop.co.uk; 41 Stonegate) A Georgian town house with a veritable maze of rooms and corridors, showcasing the wares of around 120 dealers: everything from lapel pins and snuff boxes to oil paintings and longcase clocks. And the house is haunted, too...

Barbican Books BOOKS
(www.barbicanbookshop.co.uk; 24 Fossgate) Wide range of secondhand titles, with special subjects that include railways, aviation, walking and mountaineering.

Azendi JEWELLERY
(www.azendi.com; 20 Colliergate) This jewellery boutique sells a range of beautiful contemporary designs in silver, white gold and platinum.

Information

American Express (6 Stonegate; 9am-5.30pm Mon-Fri, 9am-5pm Sat) With foreign exchange service.

Post office (22 Lendal; 8.30am-5.30pm Mon & Tue, 9am-5.30pm Wed-Sat)

York District Hospital (01904-631313; Wiggington Rd) A mile north of the centre.

York tourist office (01904-550099; www.visityork.org; 1 Museum St; 9am-6pm Mon-Sat, 10am-5pm Sun Apr-Sep, shorter hours Oct-Mar; @) Brand-new tourist office with visitor and transport info for all of Yorkshire, accommodation booking, ticket sales and internet access.

Getting There & Away

Bus

For timetable information call **Traveline Yorkshire** (0871 200 2233; www.yorkshiretravel.net) or check the computerised 24-hour information points at the train station and Rougier St. All local and regional buses stop on Rougier St, about 200m northeast of the train station.

There are National Express coaches to London (£26, 5½ hours, four daily), Birmingham (£26, 3¼ hours, one daily) and Newcastle (£15, 2¾ hours, four daily).

Car

A car is more of a hindrance than a help in the city centre; use one of the Park & Ride car parks on the edge of the city. If you want to explore the surrounding area, rental options include **Europcar** (01904-654040; www.europcar.co.uk) by platform 1 in the train station (which also rents bicycles and stores luggage for £4 per bag); and **Hertz** (01904-612586; www.hertz.co.uk) near platform 3 in the train station.

Train

York is a major railway hub with frequent direct services to Birmingham (£45, 2¼ hours), Newcastle (£15, one hour), Leeds (£11, 30 minutes), London's King's Cross (£80, two hours), Manchester (£15, 1½ hours) and Scarborough (£10, 50 minutes).

There are also trains to Cambridge (£70, 2¾ hours), changing at Peterborough.

Getting Around

York is easy to get around on foot – you're never really more than 20 minutes from any of the major sights.

Bicycle

The tourist office has a useful free map showing York's cycle routes. If you're energetic you could pedal out to Castle Howard (15 miles), Helmsley and Rievaulx Abbey (12 miles) and Thirsk (a further 12 miles), and then catch a train back to York. There's also a section of the Trans-Pennine Trail cycle path from Bishopthorpe in York to Selby (15 miles) along the old railway line.

You can rent bikes from **Bob Trotter** (13 Lord Mayor's Walk; 9am-5.30pm Mon-Sat, 10am-4pm Sun), outside Monk Bar; and **Europcar** (8am-8.30pm Mon-Sat, 9am-8.30pm Sun), by platform 1 in the train station; both charge around £15 per day.

Bus

Local bus services are operated by **First York** (www.firstgroup.com); single fares range from £1 to £2.70, and a day pass valid on all local buses is £3.70 (available at Park & Ride car parks).

Taxi

Station Taxis (01904-623332) has a kiosk outside the train station.

Around York

CASTLE HOWARD

Stately homes may be two a penny in England, but you'll have to try pretty damn hard to find one as breathtakingly stately as **Castle Howard** (www.castlehoward.co.uk; house & grounds adult/child £12.50/7.50, grounds only £8.50/6; house 11am-4.30pm, grounds 10am-6.30pm Mar-Oct & 1st 3 weeks of Dec), a work of theatrical grandeur and audacity set in the rolling Howardian Hills. This is one of the world's most beautiful buildings, instantly recognisable from its starring role in the 1980s TV series *Brideshead Revisited* and more recently in the 2008 film of the same name (both based on Evelyn Waugh's 1945 novel of nostalgia for the English aristocracy).

WORTH A TRIP

KIRKHAM PRIORY & STONE TROUGH INN

While the crowds queue up to get into Castle Howard, you could turn off on the other side of the A64 along the minor road to the hamlet of Kirkham. Here, the picturesque ruins of **Kirkham Priory** (EH; www.english-heritage.org.uk; adult/child £3.20/1.60; ⏲10am-5pm Thu-Mon Apr-Sep, daily Aug) rise gracefully above the banks of the River Derwent, sporting an impressive 13th-century gatehouse encrusted with heraldic symbols.

After a stroll by the river, head up the hill on the far side to the **Stone Trough Inn** (www.stonetroughinn.co.uk; mains £8-16; ⏲lunch & dinner Tue-Sun; 📶) for a spot of lunch. This traditional country inn serves gourmet-style pub grub (try the roast cod with creamed leek sauce) and has an outdoor terrace with a great view over the valley.

When the earl of Carlisle hired his pal Sir John Vanbrugh to design his new home in 1699, he was hiring a bloke who had no formal training and was best known as a playwright. Luckily Vanbrugh hired Nicholas Hawksmoor who had worked for Christopher Wren as his clerk of works – not only would Hawksmoor have a big part to play in the house's design but the two would later work wonders with Blenheim Palace. Today the house is still home to the Hon Simon Howard and his family; he can often be seen around the place.

If you can, try to visit on a weekday, when it's easier to find the space to appreciate this hedonistic marriage of art, architecture, landscaping and natural beauty. As you wander about the peacock-haunted grounds, views open up over the hills, Vanbrugh's playful Temple of the Four Winds and Hawksmoor's stately mausoleum, but the great baroque house with its magnificent central cupola is an irresistible visual magnet. Inside, it is full of treasures – the breathtaking Great Hall with its soaring Corinthian pilasters, pre-Raphaelite stained glass in the chapel, and corridors lined with classical antiquities.

Castle Howard is 15 miles northeast of York, off the A64. There are several organised tours from York – check with the tourist office for up-to-date schedules. Yorkshire Coastliner bus 840 (40 minutes from York, one daily) links Leeds, York, Castle Howard, Pickering and Whitby.

Harrogate

POP 85,128

The quintessential Victorian spa town, prim, pretty Harrogate has long been associated with a certain kind of old-fashioned Englishness, the kind that seems to be the preserve of retired army chaps and formidable dowagers who always vote Tory. They come to Harrogate to enjoy the flower shows and gardens that fill the town with a magnificent display of colour, especially in spring and autumn. It is fitting that the town's most famous visitor was Agatha Christie, who fled here incognito in 1926 to escape her broken marriage.

Yet this picture of Victoriana redux is not quite complete. While it's undoubtedly true that Harrogate remains a firm favourite of visitors in their golden years, the New Britain makeover has left its mark in the shape of smart new hotels and trendy eateries catering to the boom in Harrogate's newest trade – conferences. All those dynamic young sales-and-marketing guns have to eat and sleep somewhere...

Sights & Activities

Royal Pump Room Museum MUSEUM
(www.harrogate.gov.uk/harrogate-987; Crown Pl; adult/child £3.30/1.90; ⏲10am-5pm Mon-Sat & 2-5pm Sun Apr-Oct, to 4pm Nov-Mar) The ritual of visiting a spa town to 'take the waters' as a health cure became fashionable in the 19th century and peaked during the Edwardian era in the years before WWI. Charles Dickens visited Harrogate in 1858 and described it as 'the queerest place, with the strangest people in it, leading the oddest lives of dancing, newspaper-reading and dining': sounds quite pleasant, really.

You can learn all about the history of Harrogate as a spa town in the ornate Royal Pump Room, built in 1842 over the most famous of the sulphur springs. It gives an insight into how the phenomenon shaped the town and records the illustrious visitors that it attracted; at the end you get the chance to sample the spa water, if you dare.

BLACK SHEEP OF THE BREWING FAMILY

The village of Masham is a place of pilgrimage for connoisseurs of real ale – it's the frothing fountainhead of Theakston's beers, which have been brewed here since 1827. The company's most famous brew, Old Peculier, takes its name from the Peculier of Masham, a parish court established in medieval times to deal with religious offences, including drunkenness, brawling and 'taking a skull from the churchyard and placing it under a person's head to charm them to sleep'. The court seal is used as the emblem of Theakston Ales.

To the horror of real-ale fans, and after much falling out among members of the Theakston family, the Theakston Brewery was taken over by much-hated megabrewer Scottish & Newcastle in 1987. Five years later, Paul Theakston – who had refused to go and work for S&N, and was determined to keep small-scale, artisan brewing alive – bought an old maltings building in Masham and set up his own brewery, which he called Black Sheep. He managed to salvage all kinds of traditional brewing equipment, including six Yorkshire 'stone square' brewing vessels, and was soon running a successful enterprise.

History came full circle in 2004 when Paul's four brothers took the Theakston brewery back into family ownership. Both breweries now have tourist offices – the **Black Sheep Brewery** (www.blacksheepbrewery.com; ⏲10.30am-4.30pm Sun-Thu, 10.30am-11pm Fri & Sat) and the **Theakston's Brewery** (www.theakstons.co.uk; ⏲10.30am-5.30pm Jul & Aug, to 4.30pm May, Jun, Sep & Oct); both offer guided tours (best booked in advance).

Masham (pronounced 'Massam') is 9 miles northwest of Ripon on the A6108 to Leyburn. Bus 159 from Ripon (25 minutes, every two hours Monday to Saturday) and the Eastern Dalesman bus 820 from Leeds (2¾ hours, one daily, Sunday and bank holidays only, late May to late September) stop at Masham.

Montpellier Quarter DISTRICT
(www.montpellierharrogate.com) The most attractive part of town is the Montpellier Quarter, overlooking Prospect Gardens between Crescent Rd and Montpellier Hill. It's an area of pedestrianised streets lined with restored 19th-century buildings that are now home to art galleries, antique shops, fashion boutiques, cafes and restaurants – an upmarket annex to the main shopping area around Oxford St and Cambridge St.

Turkish Baths HISTORIC BUILDING
(☎01423 556746; www.harrogate.gov.uk/harrogate-1100; Parliament St; admission £13-19; ⏲9.30am-9pm Mon-Fri, 9am-8.30pm Sat & Sun) If drinking the water isn't enough, you can immerse yourself in it at Harrogate's fabulously tiled Turkish Baths. This mock-Moorish facility is gloriously Victorian and offers a range of watery delights – hot rooms, steam rooms, plunge pools and so on; a visit should last around 1½ hours. There's a complicated schedule of opening hours that are by turns single-sex and mixed – call or check online for details.

Festivals & Events

All three of Harrogate's major events are held at the Great Yorkshire Showground, just off the A661 on the southeastern edge of town.

Spring Flower Show HORTICULTURE
(www.flowershow.org.uk; admission £12-13) The year's main event, held in late April. A colourful three-day extravaganza of blooms and blossoms, flower competitions, gardening demonstrations, market stalls, crafts and gardening shops.

Great Yorkshire Show AGRICULTURE
(www.greatyorkshireshow.co.uk; adult/child £21/10) Staged over three days in mid-July by the Yorkshire Agricultural Society. Expect all manner of primped and prettified farm animals competing for prizes, and entertainment ranging from show-jumping and falconry to cookery demonstrations and hot-air balloon rides.

Autumn Flower Show HORTICULTURE
(www.flowershow.org.uk; admission £12-13) Held in late September. Fruit- and vegetable-growing championships, heaviest-onion competition, cookery demonstrations, children's events...

Harrogate

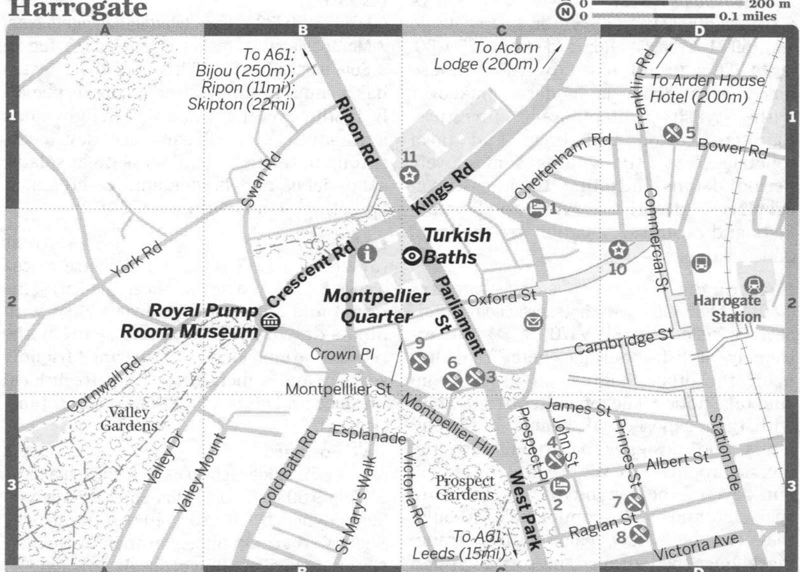

Harrogate

Top Sights
Montpellier Quarter B2
Royal Pump Room Museum B2
Turkish Baths C2

Sleeping
1 Harrogate Brasserie & Hotel C1
2 Hotel du Vin C3

Eating
3 Betty's C2
4 Fodder C3
5 Le D2 .... D1
6 Le Jardin C2
7 Sasso D3
8 Tannin Level D3
9 Van Zeller C2

Entertainment
10 Harrogate Theatre D2
11 Royal Hall C1

Sleeping

There are lots of excellent B&Bs and guest houses just north of Harrogate town centre on and around Franklin Rd and Ripon Rd.

Bijou B&B ££
(01423-567974; www.thebijou.co.uk; 17 Ripon Rd; s/d from £65/85; P @ wi-fi) Bijou by name and bijou by nature, this Victorian villa sits firmly at the boutique end of the B&B spectrum – you can tell that a lot of thought and care has gone into the design of the place. The husband-and-wife team who own the place make fantastic hosts: warm and helpful but unobtrusive.

Acorn Lodge B&B ££
(01423-525630; www.acornlodgeharrogate.co.uk; 1 Studley Rd; s/d from £47/80; P wi-fi) Attention to detail makes the difference between an average and an excellent B&B, and the details at Acorn Lodge are spot on – stylish decor, crisp cotton sheets, powerful showers and perfect poached eggs for breakfast. Location is good too, just 10 minutes' walk from the town centre.

Harrogate Brasserie & Hotel BOUTIQUE HOTEL ££
(01423-505041; www.harrogatebrasserie.co.uk; 26-30 Cheltenham Pde; s/d from £60/80; P wi-fi) Stripped pine, leather armchairs and subtle colour combinations make this one of Harrogate's most appealing places to stay. The cheerful and cosy accommodation is complemented by an excellent restaurant and bar, with live jazz every evening except Monday.

Arden House Hotel B&B ££
(01423-509224; www.ardenhousehotel.co.uk; 69-71 Franklin Rd; s/d from £50/80; P) This grand old Edwardian house has been given a modern makeover with stylish contemporary furniture, Egyptian cotton bed linen and posh toiletries, but still retains some lovely period details including tiled, cast-iron fireplaces. Attentive service, good breakfasts and a central location are the icing on the cake.

Hotel du Vin BOUTIQUE HOTEL £££
(01423-856800; www.hotelduvin.com; Prospect Pl; r/ste from £110/170; P@) An extremely stylish boutique hotel that has made the other lodgings in town sit up and take notice. The loft suites (from £280) with their exposed oak beams, hardwood floors and designer bathrooms are the nicest rooms we've seen in town, but even the standard rooms are spacious and very comfortable (though they can be noisy), each with a trademark huge bed draped in soft Egyptian cotton.

Eating

Tannin Level BISTRO ££
(01423-560595; 5 Raglan St; mains £10-15; lunch & dinner Tue-Sat) Old terracotta floor tiles, polished mahogany tables and gilt-framed mirrors and paintings create a relaxed yet elegant atmosphere at this hugely popular neighbourhood bistro. A competitively priced menu based on seasonal local produce – think a shank of lamb with honey-roasted carrots, or fish pie with mustard mash and smoked-cheese crust – means that you'd best book a table or face being turned away.

Betty's TEAROOM ££
(www.bettys.co.uk; 1 Parliament St; mains £8-11, afternoon tea £16; breakfast, lunch & dinner) A classic tearoom in a classic location with views across the park, Betty's is a local institution. It was established in 1919 by a Swiss immigrant confectioner who took the wrong train, ended up in Yorkshire and decided to stay. It has exquisite home-baked breads, scones and cakes, quality tea and coffee, and a downstairs gallery lined with art nouveau marquetry designs of Yorkshire scenes commissioned by the founder in the 1930s.

Le Jardin BISTRO £
(01423-507323; www.lejardin-harrogate.com; 7 Montpellier Pde; mains £5-8; lunch Tue-Fri & Sun, dinner Tue-Sat) This cool little bistro has a snug, intimate atmosphere, especially in the evening when candlelight adds a romantic glow. During the day locals throng to the tables, enjoying great salads, sandwiches and homemade ice cream. A two-/three-course dinner is £9/13.

Le D2 BISTRO ££
(www.led2.co.uk; 7 Bower Rd; 2-course lunch/dinner £10/15; lunch & dinner Tue-Sat) This bright and airy bistro is always busy, with diners drawn back again and again by the relaxed atmosphere, warm and friendly service, and a menu that takes fresh local produce and adds a twist of French sophistication.

Fodder CAFE £
(www.fodderweb.co.uk; 4 John St; mains £3-5; 9.30am-5.30pm Mon-Sat, 10am-4pm Sun) Owned by the Yorkshire Agricultural Society (there's a bigger branch at the Great Yorkshire Showground), this cafe serves fresh, healthy salads, sandwiches and lunch specials such as mung beans, chorizo and roast veg.

Van Zeller FRENCH £££
(01423-508762; www.vanzellerrestaurants.co.uk; 8 Montpellier St; mains £18-29; lunch Tue-Sun, dinner Tue-Sat) New fine-dining restaurant from Michelin-trained Yorkshire chef Tom van Zeller. Lunch and pre-theatre menu: four courses for £20.

Sasso ITALIAN ££
(01423-508838; 8-10 Princes Sq; mains £14-22; lunch & dinner Mon-Sat) A top-class basement trattoria where homemade pasta is served in a variety of traditional and authentic ways, along with a host of other Italian specialties.

Entertainment

Harrogate Theatre VARIETY
(www.harrogatetheatre.co.uk; Oxford St) An historic Victorian building that dates from 1900, staging variety, comedy, musicals and dancing.

Royal Hall MUSIC
(www.royalhall.co.uk; Ripon Rd) A gorgeous Edwardian theatre that is now a part of the Harrogate International conference centre. The musical program covers orchestral and choral performances, piano recitals, jazz etc.

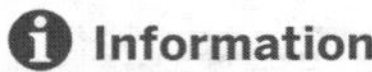

Information

Post office (11 Cambridge Rd; 9.30am-5.30pm Mon-Sat)

Tourist office (0845 389 3223; www.harrogate.gov.uk/tourism; Crescent Rd; 9am-6pm Mon-Sat & 10am-1pm Sun Apr-Sep, 9am-5pm Mon-Fri & 9am-4pm Sat Oct-Mar)

Getting There & Away

BUS National Express coaches run from Leeds (£3.60, 40 minutes, five daily). Bus 36 comes from Ripon (30 minutes, every 20 minutes), continuing to Leeds.

TRAIN Trains run to Harrogate from Leeds (£6.60, 40 minutes, about half-hourly) and York (£6.60, 45 minutes, hourly).

Scarborough

POP 57,649

Scarborough is where the whole tradition of English seaside holidays began. And it began earlier than you might think – it was in the 1660s that a book promoting the medicinal properties of a local spring (now the site of Scarborough Spa) pulled in the first flood of visitors. A belief in the health-giving effects of sea bathing saw wheeled bathing carriages appear on the beach in the 1730s, and with the arrival of the railway in 1845 Scarborough's fate was sealed. By the time the 20th century rolled in, it was all donkey rides, fish and chips, seaside rock and boat trips round the bay, with saucy postcards, kiss-me-quick hats and blokes from Leeds with knotted hankies on their heads just a decade or two away.

Like all British seaside towns, Scarborough suffered a downturn in recent decades as people jetted off to the Costa Blanca on newly affordable foreign holidays, but things are looking up again. The town retains all the trappings of the classic seaside resort, but is in the process of reinventing itself as a centre for the creative arts and digital industries – the Victorian spa is being redeveloped as a conference and entertainment centre, a former museum has been converted into studio space for artists, and there's free, open-access wi-fi along the promenade beside the harbour – an area being developed as the town's bar, cafe and restaurant quarter.

FOUNTAINS ABBEY

Nestled in the secluded valley of the River Skell lie two of Yorkshire's most beautiful attractions – absolute musts on any northern itinerary. The beautiful and strangely obsessive water gardens of the **Studley Royal** estate were built in the 19th century to enhance the picturesque ruins of 12th-century **Fountains Abbey** (NT; www.fountainsabbey.org.uk; adult/child £8.50/4.55; 10am-5pm Apr-Sep, to 4pm Oct-Mar). Together they present a breathtaking picture of pastoral elegance and tranquillity that have made them a UNESCO World Heritage Site, and the most visited of all the National Trust's pay-to-enter properties.

After falling out with the Benedictines of York in 1132, a band of rebel monks came here to what was then a desolate and unyielding patch of land to establish their own monastery. Struggling to make it on their own, they were formally adopted by the Cistercians in 1135; by the middle of the 13th century the new abbey had become the most successful Cistercian venture in the country. It was during this time that most of the abbey was built, including the church's nave, transepts and eastern end, and the outlying buildings (the church tower was added in the late 15th century).

After the Dissolution, the abbey's estate was sold into private hands, and between 1598 and 1611 Fountains Hall was built using stone from the abbey ruins. The hall and ruins were united with the Studley Royal estate in 1768.

Studley Royal was owned by John Aislabie (once Chancellor of the Exchequer), who dedicated his life to creating the park after a financial scandal saw him expelled from parliament. The main house of Studley Royal burnt down in 1946, but the superb landscaping, with its serene artificial lakes, survives almost unchanged from the 18th century.

Fountains Abbey is 4 miles west of Ripon off the B6265. Public transport is limited to shuttle bus 139 from Ripon on Sunday and bank holidays only (10 to 20 minutes, eight daily) from April to October.

Scarborough

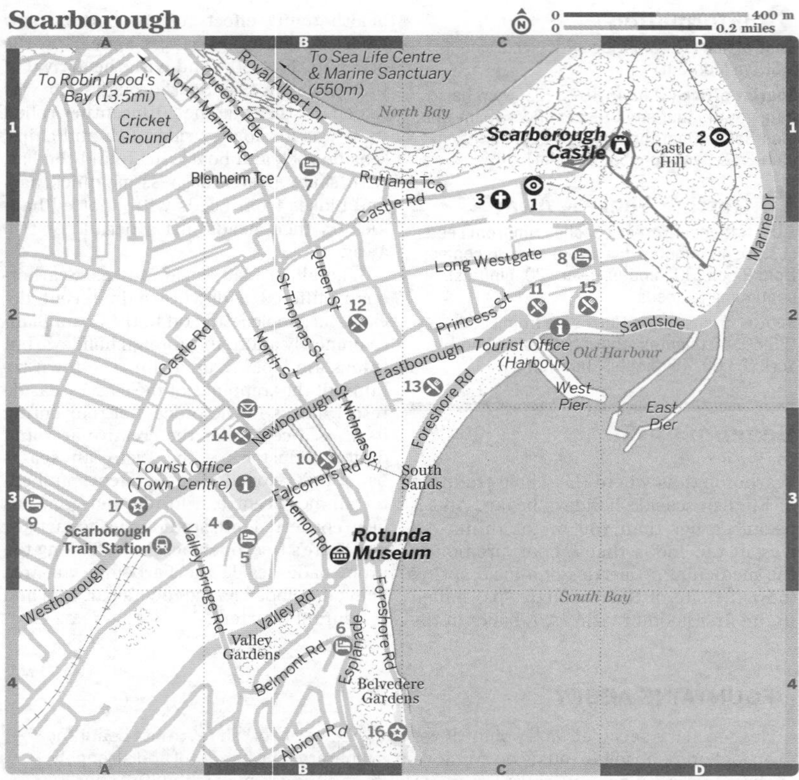

As well as the usual seaside attractions, Scarborough offers excellent coastal walking, a new geology museum, one of Yorkshire's most impressively sited castles, and a renowned theatre that is the home base of popular playwright Alan Ayckbourn, whose plays always premiere here.

Sights

Scarborough Castle CASTLE

(EH; www.english-heritage.org.uk; adult/child £4.70/2.40; 10am-6pm Apr-Sep, 10am-4pm Thu-Mon Oct-Mar) Scarborough is not exclusively about sandcastles, seaside rock and walks along the prom. The massive medieval keep of Scarborough Castle occupies a commanding position atop its headland – legend has it that Richard I loved the views so much his ghost just keeps coming back. Take a walk out to the edge of the cliffs where you can see the 2000-year-old remains of a **Roman signal station** – the Romans appreciated this viewpoint too.

Rotunda Museum MUSEUM

(www.rotundamuseum.co.uk; Vernon Rd; adult/child £4.50/free; 10am-5pm Tue-Sun;) The newly restored Rotunda Museum is dedicated to seaside rock of a different kind – the coastal geology of northeast Yorkshire, which has yielded many of Britain's most important dinosaur fossils. The strata in the local cliffs here were also important in deciphering the geological history of England. Founded by William Smith, the 'father of English geology', who lived in Scarborough in the 1820s, the museum displays original Victorian exhibits, as well as having a hands-on gallery for kids.

Sea Life Centre & Marine Sanctuary AQUARIUM

(www.sealife.co.uk; Scalby Mills; adult/child £14.50/10.95; 10am-6pm) Of all the family-oriented attractions on the waterfront, the best of the lot is the Sea Life Centre overlooking North Bay. You can see coral reefs,

Scarborough

Top Sights
Rotunda Museum ... B3
Scarborough Castle ... D1

Sights
1 Grave of Anne Brontë ... C1
2 Roman Signal Station ... D1
3 St Mary's Church ... C1

Activities, Courses & Tours
4 Secretspot Surf Shop ... B3

Sleeping
5 Beiderbecke's Hotel ... B3
6 Crown Spa Hotel ... B4
7 Hotel Helaina ... B1
8 Interludes ... C2
9 Windmill ... A3

Eating
10 Bonnet's ... B3
11 Golden Grid ... C2
12 Lanterna ... B2
Marmalade's ... (see 5)
13 Roasters ... C2
14 Roasters ... B3
15 Tunny Club ... C2

Entertainment
16 Scarborough Spa ... B4
17 Stephen Joseph Theatre ... A3

turtles, octopuses, seahorses, otters and many other fascinating creatures, though the biggest draw is the **Seal Rescue Centre** (feeding times 11.30am and 2.30pm). It's at the far north end of North Beach; the miniature **North Bay Railway** (www.nbr.org.uk; return adult/child £3/2.40; ⌚10.30am-4.45pm Apr-Sep) runs the 0.75-mile route.

FREE **St Mary's Church** CHURCH
(Castle Rd; ⌚10am-4pm Mon-Fri, 1-4pm Sun May-Sep) This church dates from 1180. In the little cemetery across the lane from the church is the **grave of Anne Brontë**.

Activities

There are some decent waves on England's northeast coast, which support a growing surfing scene. A top spot is **Cayton Bay**, 4 miles south of town, where you'll find **Scarborough Surf School** (www.scarboroughsurfschool.co.uk) offering full-day lessons for £45 per person, and equipment hire.

Back in town, you can get information and advice from the **Secretspot Surf Shop** (www.secretspot.co.uk; 4 Pavilion Tce) near the train station.

Sleeping

In Scarborough, if a house has four walls and a roof it'll offer B&B. Competition is intense, and in such a tough market multinight-stay special offers are two a penny, which means that single-night rates are the highest of all.

TOP CHOICE **Hotel Helaina** B&B ££
(☎01723-375191; www.hotelhelaina.co.uk; 14 Blenheim Tce; r £54-92; Wi-Fi) Location, location, location – you'd be hard pushed to find a place with a better sea view than this elegant guest house perched on the clifftop overlooking North Beach. And the view inside the rooms is pretty good too, with sharply styled contemporary furniture and cool colours. The standard rooms are a touch on the small side – it's well worth splashing out on the deluxe sea-view room with the bay window.

Beiderbecke's Hotel HOTEL ££
(☎01723-365766; www.beiderbeckes.com; 1-3 The Crescent; s/d from £85/115; P Wi-Fi) Set in an elegant Georgian terrace in the middle of town, on a quiet street overlooking gardens, this hotel combines stylish and spacious rooms with attentive but friendly and informal service. It's not quite boutique, but with its intriguing modern art on the walls and snazzily coloured toilet seats it's heading in that direction.

Windmill B&B ££
(☎01723-372735; www.windmill-hotel.co.uk; Mill St; tw/d from £75/85; P) Quirky doesn't begin to describe this place – a beautifully converted 18th-century windmill in the middle of town. There are tight-fitting but comfortable doubles around a cobbled courtyard, but try to get the balcony suite (£120 a night) in the upper floors of the windmill itself, with great views from the wrap-around balcony.

Interludes B&B ££
(☎01723-360513; www.interludeshotel.co.uk; 32 Princess St; s/d £36/66; Wi-Fi) Owners Ian and Bob have a flair for the theatrical and have brought it to bear with visible success on this lovely, gay-friendly Georgian

home plastered with old theatre posters, prints and other thespian mementos. The individually decorated rooms are given to colourful flights of fancy that can't but put a smile on your face. Children, alas, are not welcome.

Wrea Head Country House Hotel HOTEL £££
(☎01723-378211; www.englishrosehotels.co.uk; Barmoor Lane, Scalby; s/d from £110/180; P) This fabulous country house about 2 miles north of the centre is straight out of *Remains of the Day*. The 20 individually styled bedrooms have canopied four-poster beds, plush fabrics and delicate furnishings, while the leather couches in the bookcased, wood-heavy lounges are tailor-made for important discussions over cigars and expensive brandy. Check website for special rates that can be as low as half the rack rate.

Scarborough YHA HOSTEL £
(☎0845 371 9657; www.yha.org.uk; Burniston Rd; dm £18; P) An idyllic hostel set in a converted 17th-century water mill. It's 2 miles north of town along the A166 to Whitby; take bus 3, 12 or 21.

Crown Spa Hotel HOTEL ££
(☎0800 072 6134; www.crownspahotel.com; Esplanade; s/d from £58/99; P) This grand old hotel opened its doors in 1845 and has been going strong ever since, offering superb sea views and a luxurious spa.

Eating

Marmalade's BRASSERIE ££
(☎01723-365766; 1-3 The Crescent; mains £11-17; lunch & dinner) The stylish brasserie in Beiderbecke's Hotel – cream and chocolate colours, art with a musical theme, and cool jazz in the background – has a menu that adds a gourmet twist to traditional dishes such as cider-braised belly pork with mustard mash and onion gravy, lavender-crusted rack of lamb, and smoked fish pie with sautéed greens.

Glass House CAFE/BISTRO £
(☎01723-368791; www.glasshousebistro.co.uk; Burniston Rd; mains £4-8; cafe breakfast & lunch daily, bistro dinner Fri & Sat) Homemade lasagne, steak-and-ale pie and filled baked potatoes pull in the crowds at this appealing (and always busy) cafe beside the start of the North Bay Railway. The bistro menu (mains £11 to £16) ranges from sesame-crusted tuna steak with soy and lime dressing to pan-fried venison with red-wine gravy. Reservations recommended for dinner.

Roasters CAFE £
(www.roasterscoffee.co.uk; 8 Aberdeen Walk; mains £5-6; breakfast & lunch) A funky coffee shop with chunky pine tables, brown leather chairs and an excellent range of freshly ground coffees. There's a juice and smoothie bar too, and the lunch menu includes ciabatta sandwiches, salads and jacket potatoes.

Lanterna ITALIAN £££
(☎01723-363616; www.lanterna-ristorante.co.uk; 33 Queen St; mains £15-21; dinner Mon-Sat) A snug, old-fashioned Italian trattoria that specialises in fresh local seafood (including lobster, from £32), and classic dishes from the old country such as *stufato de ceci* (old-style chickpea stew with oxtail) and white-truffle dishes in season (October to December). As well as sourcing Yorkshire produce, the chef

THE TUNNY CLUB

Strange but true: in the 1930s Atlantic bluefin tuna (also known as tunny) started to follow the herring shoals into the North Sea, and Yorkshire became the hub of a US-style big-game fishery. Professional hunter Lorenzo Mitchell-Henry set the record for a rod-caught fish in British waters when he landed a 386kg monster in 1933, and Scarborough was soon home to the Tunny Club of Great Britain. Visiting millionaires and movie stars chartered local boats and vied with each other to smash the record.

Overfishing led to the disappearance of the herring shoals in the 1950s, and with them the tunny. However, in recent years the ocean giants have returned, attracted by warmer waters (a result of climate change) and recovering herring stocks. Meanwhile, all that remains in Scarborough is the former premises of the Tunny Club at 1 Sandgate, now a fish-and-chip shop; the upstairs dining room is filled with big-game fishing memorabilia.

imports delicacies direct from Italy, including truffles, olive oil, prosciutto and a range of cheeses.

Golden Grid SEAFOOD ££
(www.goldengrid.co.uk; 4 Sandside; mains £7-18; ⏲lunch & dinner) Whoever said fish and chips can't be eaten with dignity hasn't tried the Golden Grid, a sit-down fish restaurant that has been serving the best cod in Scarborough since 1883. It's staunchly traditional, with starched white tablecloths and starched white aprons, as is the menu – as well as fish and chips there's freshly landed crab, lobster, prawns and oysters, plus sausage and mash, liver and bacon, and steak and chips.

Bonnet's TEAROOM £
(38-40 Huntriss Row; mains £5-10; ⏲breakfast Mon-Sat, lunch daily) One of the oldest cafes in town (open since 1880), Bonnet's serves delicious cakes and light meals in a quiet courtyard.

Roasters CAFE £
(www.roasterscoffee.co.uk; 24 Foreshore Rd; ⏲breakfast & lunch) Seaside branch of the excellent coffee shop, with outdoor tables.

Tunny Club FISH & CHIPS £
(1 Sandgate; mains £3-5; ⏲lunch & dinner) Decent chippie whose upstairs dining room is a shrine to Scarborough's history of big-game fishing.

☆ Entertainment

Stephen Joseph Theatre THEATRE
(www.sjt.uk.com; Westborough) Stages a good range of drama – renowned chronicler of middle-class mores Alan Ayckbourn premieres his plays here.

Scarborough Spa VARIETY
(www.scarboroughspa.co.uk; South Bay) The revitalised spa complex stages a wide range of entertainment, especially in the summer months – orchestral performances, variety shows, popular musicals and old-fashioned afternoon-tea dances.

ℹ Information

FreeBay Wifi Free wi-fi internet access along harbourfront from West Pier to East Pier.

Post office (11-15 Aberdeen Walk; ⏲9am-5.30pm Mon-Fri, to 12.30pm Sat)

Tourist office (☎01723-383637; www.discoveryorkshirecoast.com) Town Centre (Brunswick Shopping Centre, Westborough; ⏲9.30am-5.30pm daily Apr-Oct, 10am-4.30pm Mon-Sat Nov-Mar) Harbour (Sandside; ⏲10am-5.30pm Apr-Oct, to 9pm Jul & Aug)

ℹ Getting There & Away

BUS Bus 128 goes along the A170 from Helmsley to Scarborough (1½ hours, hourly) via Pickering, while buses 93 and X93 come from Whitby (one hour, every 30 minutes) via Robin Hood's Bay (hourly). Bus 843 arrives from Leeds (£12, 2¾ hours, hourly) via York.

TRAIN There are regular trains from Hull (£12.50, 1½ hours, hourly), Leeds (£22, one hour 20 minutes, hourly) and York (£16, 50 minutes, hourly).

ℹ Getting Around

Tiny, Victorian-era funicular railways rattle up and down Scarborough's steep cliffs between town and beach daily from February till the end of October (70p). Local buses leave from the western end of Westborough and outside the train station.

For a taxi call ☎01723-361009; £5 should get you to most places in town.

NORTH YORK MOORS NATIONAL PARK

Inland from the north Yorkshire coast, the wild and windswept North York Moors rise in desolate splendour. Three-quarters of all the world's heather moorland is to be found in Britain, and this is the largest expanse in all of England. Ridge-top roads climb up from lush green valleys to the bleak open moors where weather-beaten stone crosses mark the line of ancient drove roads. In summer the heather blooms in billowing drifts of purple haze.

This is classic walking country, and the moors are criss-crossed with footpaths old and new, and dotted with pretty, flower-bedecked villages. The national park is also home to one of England's most picturesque steam railways.

The park produces the very useful *Moors & Coast* visitor guide, available at tourist offices, hotels etc, with information on things to see and do. See also www.northyorkmoors.org.uk.

ℹ Getting Around

The **Moorsbus** (www.northyorkmoors.org.uk/moorsbus) operates on Sundays and bank holiday Mondays from May to October, plus Wednesdays in July and September, and daily from late

North York Moors National Park

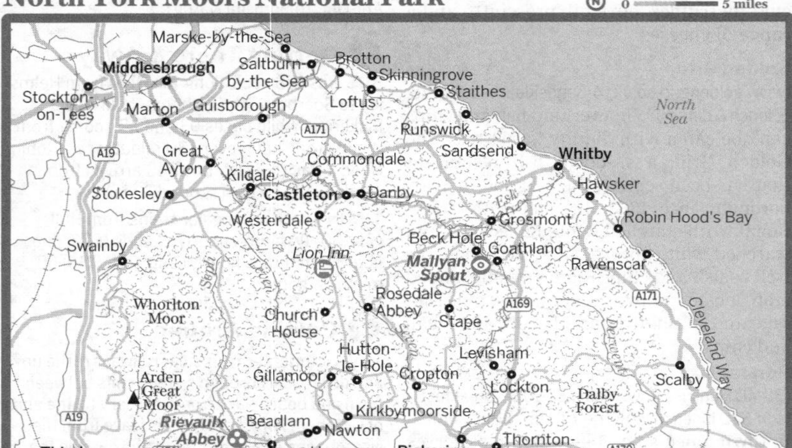

July to early September. Pick up a timetable and route map from tourist offices or download one from the website. A standard day pass costs £5. Family tickets and one-off fares for short journeys are also available.

There's also a free public transport map, the *Moors Explorer Travel Guide*, available from tourist offices.

If you're planning to drive on the minor roads over the moors, beware of wandering sheep and lambs – hundreds are killed by careless drivers every year.

Helmsley

POP 1620

Helmsley is a classic North Yorkshire market town, a handsome place full of old houses, historic coaching inns and – inevitably – a cobbled market square (market day Friday), all basking under the watchful gaze of a sturdy Norman castle. Nearby are the romantic ruins of Rievaulx Abbey and a fistful of country walks.

Sights & Activities

The impressive ruins of 12th-century **Helmsley Castle** (EH; www.english-heritage.org.uk; adult/child £4.70/2.40; ⏲10am-6pm Apr-Sep, 10am-5pm Mar & Oct, 10am-4pm Thu-Mon Nov-Feb) are defended by a striking series of deep ditches and banks to which later rulers added the thick stone walls and defensive towers – only one tooth-shaped tower survives today following the dismantling of the fortress by Sir Thomas Fairfax after the Civil War. The castle's tumultuous history is well explained in the tourist office.

Just outside the castle, **Helmsley Walled Garden** (www.helmsleywalledgarden.org.uk; adult/child £4/free; ⏲10.30am-5pm daily Apr-Oct, Mon-Fri Nov-Mar) would be just another plant-and-produce centre were it not for its dramatic position and fabulous selection of flowers, fruits and vegetables – some of which are rare – not to mention the herbs, including 40 varieties of mint. If you're into horticulture with a historical twist, this is Eden.

South of the castle stretches the superb landscape of Duncombe Park estate with the stately home of **Duncombe Park House** (www.duncombepark.com; adult/child house & gardens £8.25/3.75, gardens only £5/3; ⏲11am-5.30pm Sun-Thu Apr-Oct) at its heart. From the house (guided tours depart hourly 12.30pm to 3.30pm) and formal gardens, wide grassy walkways and terraces lead through woodland to mock-classical temples, while longer walking trails are set out in the parkland, now protected as a nature reserve. The house is 1.5 miles south of town, an easy walk through the park.

You could easily spend a day here, especially if you take in one of the many walks. Cream of the crop is the 3.5-mile route to **Rievaulx Abbey** – the tourist office can provide route leaflets and advise on buses if you don't want to walk both ways. This route is also the opening section of the **Cleveland Way**.

Sleeping

Feathers Hotel B&B ££
(☎01439-770275; www.feathershotelhelmsley.co.uk; Market Pl; s/d from £50/90) One of a number of old coaching inns on Market Pl that offer B&B, half-decent grub and a pint of hand-pumped real ale. There are four-poster beds in some rooms and historical trimmings throughout.

Feversham Arms B&B £££
(☎01439-770766; www.fevershamarms.com; r from £155; P Wi-Fi) For something plusher try the Feversham, where country charm meets boutique chic.

Helmsley YHA HOSTEL £
(☎0845 371 9638; www.yha.org.uk; Carlton Lane; dm £18; P family) Looks a bit like an ordinary suburban home; its location (400m east of the market square) at the start of the Cleveland Way means that it's often busy, so book in advance.

Wrens of Rydale CAMPSITE £
(☎01439-771260; www.wrensofryedale.co.uk; Gale Lane, Nawton; tent & 2 adults £9, with car £15; ⊙Apr-Oct) Sheltered campsite with three acres of pristine parkland 3 miles east of Helmsley, just south of Beadlam.

Eating

Helmsley is a bit of a foodie town, sporting a couple of quality delicatessens on the main square. There's **Perns** (18 Market Pl; ⊙7.30am-5.30pm Mon-Sat, 10am-4pm Sun), a butcher, deli and wine merchant under the same ownership as the Star Inn at Harome; and flower-bedecked **Hunters of Helmsley** (www.huntersofhelmsley.com; 13 Market Pl; ⊙8am-5.30pm), a cornucopia of locally made chutneys, jams, beers, cheeses, bacon, humbugs and ice cream – a great place to stock up for a gourmet picnic.

TOP CHOICE **Star Inn** GASTROPUB £££
(☎01439-770397; www.thestaratharome.co.uk; Harome; mains £15-24; ⊙lunch Tue-Sun, dinner Mon-Sat; V) This thatch-roofed country pub is home to one of Yorkshire's best restaurants, with a Michelin-starred menu that revels in top-quality produce from the surrounding farms – slow-roasted pork belly with black pudding, apple salad and a fried duck egg, or roast roe deer venison with mushrooms and tarragon jus. It's the sort of place you won't want to leave, and the good news is you don't have to: the adjacent lodge has eight magnificent bedrooms (£150 to £240), each decorated in classic but luxurious country style. It's about 2 miles south of Helmsley just off the A170.

Information

The **tourist office** (☎01439-770173; ⊙9.30am-5.30pm Mar-Oct, 10am-4pm Fri-Sun Nov-Feb) at the castle entrance sells maps and books, and helps with accommodation.

Getting There & Away

All buses stop in the main square. Bus 31X runs from York to Helmsley (£7, 1¼ hours, two daily Monday to Saturday). From Scarborough take bus 128 (£7.40, 1½ hours, hourly Monday to Saturday, four on Sunday) via Pickering.

Around Helmsley

RIEVAULX

In the secluded valley of the River Rye, amid fields and woods loud with birdsong, stand the magnificent ruins of **Rievaulx Abbey** (EH; www.english-heritage.org.uk; adult/child £5.30/2.70; ⊙10am-6pm Apr-Sep, to 5pm Thu-Mon Oct, to 4pm Thu-Mon Nov-Mar). This idyllic spot was chosen by Cistercian monks in 1132 as a base for missionary activity in northern Britain. St Aelred, the third abbot, famously described the abbey's setting as, 'everywhere peace, everywhere serenity, and a marvellous freedom from the tumult of the world'. But the monks of Rievaulx (pronounced 'ree-voh') were far from unworldly, and soon created a network of commercial interests ranging from sheep farms to lead mines that formed the backbone of the local economy. The extensive ruins give a wonderful feel for the size and complexity of the community that once lived here – their story is fleshed out in a series of fascinating exhibits in the neighbouring tourist office.

In the 1750s landscape-gardening fashion favoured a Gothic look, and many aristocrats had mock ruins built in their parks. The Duncombe family went one better, as their lands contained a real medieval ruin – Rievaulx Abbey. They built **Rievaulx Terrace & Temples** (NT; www.nationaltrust.org.uk; adult/child £5.25/2.90; ⌚11am-5pm Mar-Oct) so that lords and ladies could stroll effortlessly in the 'wilderness' and admire the abbey in the valley below. Today, we can do the same, with views over Ryedale and the Hambleton Hills forming a perfect backdrop.

Rievaulx is about 3 miles west of Helmsley. Note that there's no direct access between the abbey and the terrace. Their entrance gates are about a mile apart, though easily reached along a lane – steeply uphill if you're going from the abbey to the terrace.

Hutton-le-Hole

POP 210

With a scatter of gorgeous stone cottages, a gurgling brook and a flock of sheep grazing contentedly on the village green, Hutton-le-Hole must be a contender for the best-looking village in Yorkshire. The dips and hollows on the green may have given the place its name – it was once called simply Hutton Hole but wannabe posh Victorians added the Frenchified 'le', which the locals defiantly pronounce 'lee'.

The **tourist office** (☎01751-417367; ⌚10am-5.30pm mid-Mar–early Nov) has leaflets on walks in the area, including a 5-mile circuit to the nearby village of Lastingham.

Attached to the tourist office is the largely open-air **Ryedale Folk Museum** (☎01751-417367; www.ryedalefolkmuseum.co.uk; adult/child £5.50/4; ⌚10am-5.30pm mid-Mar–Oct, 10am-dusk Nov–mid-Mar, closed mid-Dec–mid-Jan), a constantly expanding collection of North York Moors buildings from different eras, including a medieval manor house, simple farmers' houses, a blacksmith's forge and a row of 1930s village shops. Demonstrations and displays throughout the season give a fascinating insight into local life as it was in the past.

The **Daffodil Walk** is a 2½-mile circular walk following the banks of the River Dove. As the name suggests, the main draws are the daffs, usually at their best in the last couple of weeks in April.

Sleeping & Eating

Lion Inn PUB, B&B ££
(☎01751-417320; www.lionblakey.co.uk; Blakey Ridge; s/d from £42/64; mains £10-18; Ⓟ) From Hutton, the Blakey Ridge road climbs over the moors to Danby and, after 6 miles, passes one of the highest and most remote pubs in England (altitude 404m). With its low-beamed ceilings and cosy fireplaces, hearty grub and range of real ales, the Lion is a firm favourite with hikers and bikers.

Burnley House B&B ££
(☎01751-417548; www.burnleyhouse.co.uk; d £75-90; Ⓟ) This elegant Georgian home offers comfortable bedrooms and a hearty breakfast, but the best features are the lovely sitting room and garden where you can relax with a cup of tea and a book.

Getting There & Away

Hutton-le-Hole is 2½ miles north of the main A170 road, about halfway between Helmsley and Pickering. Moorsbus services (p521) through Hutton-le-Hole include the M3 between Helmsley and Danby (seven per day) and the M1 and M2 between Pickering and Danby (eight per day) via the Lion Inn. Outside times when the Moorsbus runs, you'll need your own transport to get here.

Pickering

POP 6600

Pickering is a lively market town with an imposing Norman castle that advertises itself as the 'Gateway to the North York Moors'. That gateway is the terminus of the wonderful North Yorkshire Moors Railway, a picturesque survivor from the great days of steam.

The **tourist office** (☎01751-473791; www.yorkshiremoorsandcoast.com; The Ropery; ⌚9.30am-5.30pm Mon-Sat, 9.30am-4pm Sun Mar-Oct, 10am-4pm Mon-Sat Nov-Feb) has the usual details as well as plenty of NYMR-related info.

Sights

The privately owned **North Yorkshire Moors Railway** (NYMR; www.nymr.co.uk; Pickering-Whitby Day Rover ticket adult/child £21/10.50) runs for 18 miles through beautiful countryside to the village of Grosmont, with connections to Whitby. Lovingly restored steam locos pull period carriages, resplendent with polished brass and bright paintwork. For visitors without wheels, it's ideal for reaching out-of-the-way villages in the middle of the moors. Grosmont is also on the main railway line between Middlesbrough and Whitby, opening up yet more possibilities for walking and sightseeing. Check the website for the latest on hours of operation.

Dating mostly from the 13th and 14th centuries, **Pickering Castle** (EH; www.english-heritage.org.uk; adult/child £3.70/1.90; ⏲10am-6pm Apr-Sep, 10am-4pm Thu-Mon Oct) is a lot like the castles we drew as kids: thick stone walls around a central keep, perched atop a high motte (mound) with great views of the surrounding countryside.

Sleeping & Eating

White Swan Hotel PUB/HOTEL £££
(☎01751-472288; www.white-swan.co.uk; Market Pl; s/d from £115/150, mains £11-20; P 🛜) The top spot in town successfully combines a smart pub, a superb restaurant serving local dishes with a Continental twist, and a luxurious boutique hotel. Nine modern rooms in the converted coach house up the ante with flatscreen TVs and other stylish paraphernalia that add to the luxury found throughout the hotel.

There's a strip of B&Bs on tree-lined Eastgate (the A170 to Scarborough) and a few more on Westgate (heading towards Helmsley). Decent options include **Eleven Westgate** (☎01751-475111; www.elevenwestgate.co.uk; 11 Westgate; s/d £50/70; P 🛜), a pretty house with patio and garden; and the elegant Georgian town house at **17 Burgate** (☎01751-473463; www.17burgate.co.uk; 17 Burgate; s/d from £79/89; P @ 🛜).

There are several cafes and teashops on Market Pl, but don't overlook the **tearoom** (Pickering Station; mains £2-6) at Pickering station, which serves excellent home-baked goodies and does a tasty roast-pork roll with apple sauce, crackling and stuffing.

Getting There & Away

In addition to the NYMR trains, bus 128 between Helmsley (40 minutes) and Scarborough (50 minutes) runs hourly via Pickering. Yorkshire Coastliner service 840 between Leeds and Whitby links Pickering with York (£12, 70 minutes, hourly).

Danby

POP 290

The Blakey Ridge road from Hutton-le-Hole swoops steeply down to Danby, a compact, stone-built village set deep amid the moors at the head of Eskdale. It's home to the **Moors Centre** (www.visitthemoors.co.uk; ⏲10am-5pm Apr-Oct, 10.30am-3.30pm Nov, Dec & Mar, 10.30am-3.30pm Sat & Sun Jan-Feb), the national park's HQ, which has interesting exhibits on the natural history of the moors as well as a cafe, an accommodation booking service and a huge range of local guidebooks, maps and leaflets.

You can reach Danby on the delightful **Esk Valley Railway** (www.eskvalleyrailway.co.uk) – Whitby is 20 minutes east, Middlesbrough 45 minutes west. There are four departures daily Monday to Saturday, and two on Sunday.

WORTH A TRIP

GOATHLAND

This picture-postcard halt on the North Yorkshire Moors Railway stars as Hogsmeade train station in the Harry Potter films, and the village appears as Aidensfield in the British TV series *Heartbeat*. It's also the starting point for lots of easy and enjoyable walks, often with the chuff-chuff-chuff of passing steam engines in the background.

One of the most popular hikes is to head northwest from the station (via a gate on the platform on the far side from the village) to the hamlet of Beck Hole, where you can stop for a pork pie and a pint of Black Sheep at the wonderfully atmospheric **Birch Hall Inn** (www.beckhole.info) – it's like stepping into the past. Return to Goathland via the waterfall at **Mallyan Spout**.

Whitby

POP 13,600

Whitby is a town of two halves, split down the middle by the mouth of the River Esk. It's also a town with two personalities – on the one hand a busy commercial and fishing port with a bustling quayside fishmarket; on the other a traditional seaside resort, complete with sandy beach, amusement arcades and promenading holidaymakers slurping ice-cream cones in the sun.

It's the combination of these two facets that makes Whitby more interesting than your average resort. The town has managed to retain much of its 18th-century character, recalling the time when James Cook – Whitby's most famous adopted son – was making his first forays at sea on his way towards becoming one of the best-known explorers in history. The narrow streets and alleys of the old town hug the riverside,

Whitby

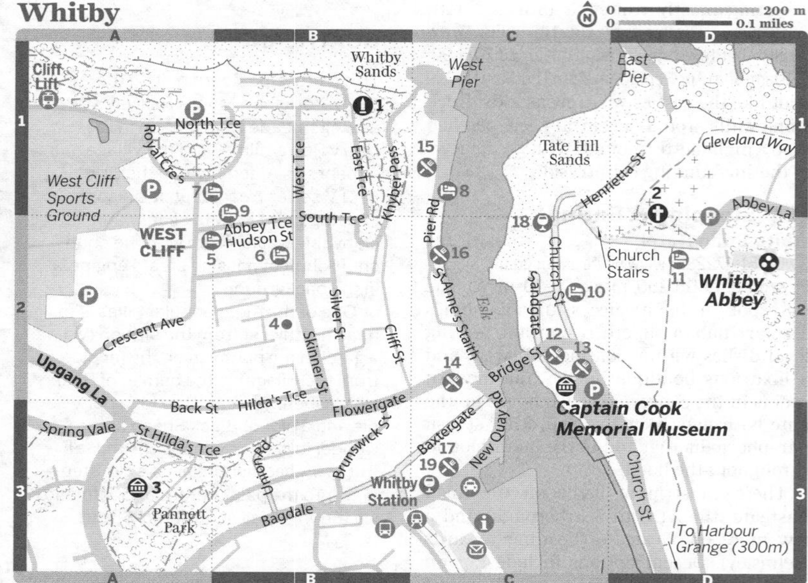

now lined with restaurants, pubs and cute little shops, all with views across the handsome harbour where colourful fishing boats ply to and fro. Keeping a watchful eye over the whole scene is the atmospheric ruined abbey atop the East Cliff.

But Whitby also has a darker side. Most famously, it was the inspiration and setting for part of Bram Stoker's Gothic horror story *Dracula*. Less well known is the fact that Whitby is famous for the jet (fossilised wood) that has been mined from the local sea cliffs for centuries; this smooth, black substance was popularised in the 19th century when Queen Victoria took to wearing mourning jewellery made from Whitby jet. In recent years these morbid associations have seen the rise of a series of hugely popular goth festivals.

Sights

Whitby Abbey ABBEY RUINS

(EH; www.english-heritage.org.uk; adult/child £5.80/2.90; 10am-6pm Apr-Sep, 10am-4pm Thu-Mon Oct-Mar) There are ruined abbeys and there are picturesque ruined abbeys, and then there's Whitby Abbey, dominating the skyline above the East Cliff like a great Gothic tombstone silhouetted against the sky. Looking more like it was built as an atmospheric film set than as a monastic establishment, it is hardly surprising that this medieval hulk inspired the Victorian novelist Bram Stoker – who holidayed in Whitby – to make it the setting for Count Dracula's dramatic landfall.

From the end of **Church St**, which has many shops selling jet jewellery, the 199 steps of **Church Stairs** lead steeply up to Whitby Abbey passing the equally atmospheric **St Mary's Church** (admission free; 10am-5pm Apr-Oct, to 4pm Nov-Mar) and its spooky graveyard, a favourite haunt of courting Goth couples.

Captain Cook Memorial Museum MUSEUM

(www.cookmuseumwhitby.co.uk; Grape Lane; adult/child £4.50/3; 9.45am-5pm Apr-Oct, 11am-3pm Mar) This fascinating museum occupies the house of the ship owner with whom Cook began his seafaring career. Highlights include the attic where Cook lodged as a young apprentice, Cook's own maps and letters, etchings from the South Seas and a wonderful model of the *Endeavour*, with all the crew and stores laid out for inspection.

Whitby Sands BEACH

Whitby's days as a seaside resort continue with donkey rides, ice-cream and bucket-and-spade escapades on Whitby Sands, stretching west from the harbour mouth. Atop the cliff on the harbour's west side, the **Captain Cook**

Whitby

Top Sights

	Captain Cook Memorial Museum	C2
	Whitby Abbey	D2

Sights

1	Captain Cook Monument	B1
2	St Mary's Church	D1
	Whalebone Arch	(see 1)
3	Whitby Museum	A3

Activities, Courses & Tours

4	Dr Crank's Bike Shack	B2

Sleeping

5	Argyle House	A2
6	Bramblewick	B2
7	Langley Hotel	A1
8	Marine Hotel	C1
9	Rosslyn House	B1
10	Shepherd's Purse	C2
11	Whitby YHA	D2

Eating

12	Green's	C2
13	Humble Pie'n'Mash	C2
14	Java Cafe-Bar	C2
15	Magpie Café	C1
16	Moon & Sixpence	C2
17	Trenchers	C3

Drinking

18	Duke of York	C2
19	Station Inn	C3

Monument shows the great man looking out to sea, often with a seagull perched on his head. Nearby is the **Whalebone Arch**, which recalls Whitby's days as a whaling port. Whitby Sands can be reached from West Cliff via the **cliff lift** (rides 70p; May-Sep only), an elevator that has been running since 1931.

Whitby Museum MUSEUM
(www.whitbymuseum.org.uk; Pannett Park; adult/child £3/1; 9.30am-4.30pm Tue-Sun) Set in a park to the west of the town centre is the wonderfully eclectic Whitby Museum with displays of fossil plesiosaurs and dinosaur footprints, Cook memorabilia, ships in bottles, jet jewellery and the 'Hand of Glory' – a preserved human hand reputedly cut from the corpse of an executed criminal.

Activities

For a cracking day out, take a bus to Robin Hood's Bay, explore the village, have lunch, then hike the 6-mile **clifftop footpath** back to Whitby (allow three hours).

First choice for a bike ride is the excellent 20-mile Whitby-to-Scarborough **Coastal Cycle Trail**, which starts a mile south of the town centre and follows the route of an old railway line via Robin Hood's Bay. Bikes can be hired from **Dr Crank's Bike Shack** (20 Skinner St; 10am-5pm Mon, Tue & Thu-Sat) in Whitby, or **Trailways** (www.trailways.info) at Hawsker for £12 to £20 a day.

Festivals & Events

Whitby Gothic Weekends COUNTER CULTURE
(www.wgw.topmum.co.uk; tickets £40) Goth heaven, with gigs, events and the Bizarre Bazaar – dozens of traders selling goth gear, jewellery, art and music. Twice yearly on the last weekends of April and October.

Whitby Spring Session MUSIC & ARTS
(www.moorandcoast.co.uk; tickets from £35) Beards, sandals and real ale galore at this traditional festival of folk music, dance and dubious Celtic art. May Bank Holiday weekend.

Sleeping

B&Bs are concentrated in West Cliff in the streets to the south and east of Royal Cres; if a house here ain't offering B&B, the chances are it's derelict. Accommodation can be tough to find at festival times; it's wise to book ahead.

TOP CHOICE **Marine Hotel** HOTEL £££
(01947-605022; www.the-marine-hotel.co.uk; 13 Marine Pde; r £150) Feeling more like mini-suites than ordinary hotel accommodation, the four bedrooms at the Marine are quirky, stylish and comfortable – the sort of place that makes you want to stay in rather than go out. Ask for one of the two rooms that have a balcony – they have great views across the harbour.

Langley Hotel B&B ££
(01947-604250; www.langleyhotel.com; 16 Royal Cres; s/d from £70/100; P) With a cream-and-crimson colour scheme, and a gilt four-poster bed in one room, this grand old guest house exudes a whiff of Victorian splendour. Go for room 1 or 2, if possible, to make the most of the panoramic views from West Cliff.

WHITBY'S DARK SIDE

The famous story of *Dracula*, inspiration for a thousand lurid movies, was written by Bram Stoker while staying at a B&B in Whitby in 1897. Although most Hollywood versions of the tale concentrate on deepest, darkest Transylvania, much of the original book was set in Whitby, and many sites can still be seen today. The tourist office sells an excellent *Dracula Trail* leaflet.

Shepherd's Purse B&B ££
(☎01947-820228; www.theshepherdspurse.com; 95 Church St; r £55-70) This place combines a beads-and-baubles boutique with a wholefood shop and guest-house accommodation in the courtyard at the back. The plainer rooms share a bathroom and are perfectly adequate, but we recommend the rustic en suite bedrooms situated around the courtyard; the four-poster beds feel a bit like they've been shoehorned in, but the atmosphere is cute rather than cramped. (Breakfast is not provided.)

Whitby YHA HOSTEL £
(☎0845 371 9049; www.yha.org.uk; Church Lane; dm £18-22; P @ wi-fi) With an unbeatable position next to the abbey, this hostel doesn't have to try too hard, and it doesn't. You'll have to book well in advance to get your body into one of the basic bunks. Hike up from the station or take bus 97 (hourly Monday to Saturday).

Harbour Grange HOSTEL £
(☎01947-600817; www.whitbybackpackers.co.uk; Spital Bridge; dm £17) Overlooking the harbour and less than 10 minutes' walk from the train station, this tidy hostel is conveniently located but has an 11.30pm curfew – good thing we're all teetotalling early-to-bedders, right?

Trailways HOTEL ££
(☎01947-820207; www.trailways.info; from £290 for 3 nights; P) If travelling on the North Yorkshire Moors Railway has given you a taste for trains, how about sleeping in one? Trailways has a beautifully converted InterCity125 coach parked at the old Hawsker train station on the Whitby–Scarborough cycle route, offering luxurious self-catering accommodation with all mod cons for two to seven people.

Rosslyn House B&B ££
(☎01947-604086; www.guesthousewhitby.co.uk; 11 Abbey Tce; s/d £35/55) Bright and cheerful with a friendly welcome.

Bramblewick B&B ££
(☎01947-604504; www.bramblewickwhitby.com; 3 Havelock Pl; s/d £32/66; P wi-fi) Friendly owners, hearty breakfasts and abbey views from the top-floor room.

Argyle House B&B ££
(☎01947-602733; www.argyle-house.co.uk; 18 Hudson St; s/d £40/66; wi-fi) Comfortable as old slippers, with kippers for breakfast.

Eating & Drinking

Green's SEAFOOD, BRITISH ££
(☎01947-600284; www.greensofwhitby.com; 13 Bridge St; bistro mains £10-19, restaurant 2-/3-course dinner £34/41; ⊙lunch & dinner Mon-Fri) The classiest eatery in town is ideally situated to take its pick of the fish and shellfish freshly landed at the harbour. Grab a hearty lunch in the ground floor bistro (*moules-frites,* sausage and mash, fish and chips) or head to the upstairs restaurant for a sophisticated dinner date.

Moon & Sixpence BRASSERIE ££
(☎01947-604416; 5 Marine Pde; mains £10-18; ⊙breakfast, lunch & dinner) This brand-new brasserie and cocktail bar has a prime position, with views across the harbour to the abbey ruins. The seafood-dominated menu ranges from hearty winter warmers, such as chunky vegetable soup and fish pie, to more sophisticated dishes like a half-dozen oysters *au naturel* and seared scallops with black pudding.

Magpie Café SEAFOOD ££
(www.magpiecafe.co.uk; 14 Pier Rd; mains £9-18; ⊙lunch & dinner) The Magpie flaunts its reputation for serving the 'World's Best Fish and Chips'. Damn fine they are too, but the world and his dog knows about it, and summertime queues can stretch along the street. Fish and chips from the takeaway counter cost £5; the sit-down restaurant is dearer, but offers a wide range of seafood dishes, from grilled sea bass to paella.

Java Cafe-Bar CAFE £
(2 Flowergate; mains £4-6; ⊙8am-6pm; wi-fi) A cool little diner with stainless-steel counters and retro decor, with internet access, music vids on the flatscreen and a menu of healthy salads, sandwiches and wraps washed down with excellent coffee.

CAPTAIN COOK – WHITBY'S ADOPTED SON

Although he was born in Marton (now a suburb of Middlesbrough), Whitby has adopted the famous explorer Captain James Cook, and ever since the first tourists got off the train in Victorian times local entrepreneurs have mercilessly cashed in on his memory, as endless 'Endeavour Cafes' and 'Captain Cook Chip Shops' testify.

Still, Whitby played a key role in Cook's eventual success as a world-famous explorer. It was here that he first went to sea, serving his apprenticeship with local ship owners, and the design of the ships used for his voyages of discovery – including the famous *Endeavour* – were based on the design of Whitby 'cats', flat-bottomed ships that carried coal from Newcastle to London.

Humble Pie'n'Mash PIES £
(www.humblepienmash.com; 163 Church St; mains £5; ⏰lunch daily, dinner Mon-Sat) Superb homemade pies with fillings ranging from lamb, leek and rosemary to roast veg and goat's cheese, served in a cosy, timber-framed cottage.

Trenchers FISH & CHIPS ££
(www.trenchersrestaurant.co.uk; New Quay Rd; mains £10-15; ⏰lunch & dinner) Top-notch fish and chips minus the 'World's Best' tagline – this place is your best bet if you want to avoid the queues at the Magpie (don't be put off by the modern look).

Station Inn PUB
(New Quay Rd) Best place in town for atmosphere and real ale with an impressive range of cask-conditioned beers including Theakston's Black Bull and Black Dog Abbey Ale.

Duke of York PUB
(Church St) Popular watering hole at the bottom of the Church Stairs, with great views over the harbour. Serves Timothy Taylor ales.

ℹ Information

Post office (⏰8.30am-5.30pm Mon-Sat) Inside the Co-op supermarket.

Tourist office (☎01947-602674; www.visitwhitby.com; Langborne Rd; ⏰10am-6pm May-Sep, 10am-4.30pm Oct-Apr)

ℹ Getting There & Away

BUS Buses 93 and X93 run south to Scarborough (one hour, every 30 minutes) via Robin Hood's Bay (15 minutes, hourly), and north to Middlesbrough (hourly), with fewer services on Sunday. See p486 for details of the Yorkshire Coastliner service from Leeds to Whitby.

TRAIN Coming from the north, you can get to Whitby by train along the Esk Valley Railway from Middlesbrough (£4.70, 1½ hours, four per day), with connections from Durham and Newcastle. From the south, it's easier to get a train from York to Scarborough, then a bus from Scarborough to Whitby.

Around Whitby

ROBIN HOOD'S BAY

Picturesque Robin Hood's Bay (www.robin-hoods-bay.co.uk) has nothing to do with the hero of Sherwood Forest – the origin of the name is a mystery, and the locals call it Bay Town, or just Bay. But there's no denying that this fishing village is one of the prettiest spots on the Yorkshire coast.

Leave your car at the parking area in the upper village, where 19th-century ship's captains built comfortable Victorian villas, and walk downhill to **Old Bay**, the oldest part of the village (don't even think about driving down). This maze of narrow lanes and passages is dotted with tearooms, pubs, craft shops and artists' studios – there's even a tiny cinema – and at low tide you can go down onto the beach and fossick around in the rock pools. There are several pubs and cafes – best pub for ambience and real ale is **Ye Dolphin** (King St), while the **Swell Cafe** (www.swell.org.uk; Chapel St; mains £4-7; ⏰breakfast & lunch) does great coffee and has a terrace with a view over the beach.

Robin Hood's Bay is 6 miles south of Whitby; you can walk here along the coastal path in two or three hours, or bike it along the cycle trail in 40 minutes. Also, bus 93 runs hourly between Whitby and Scarborough via Robin Hood's Bay – the bus stop is at the top of the hill, in the new part of town.

Manchester, Liverpool & Northwest England

Includes »

MANCHESTER 531
CHESHIRE 547
Chester 548
LIVERPOOL 552
Speke............. 562
LANCASHIRE....... 562
Blackpool 562
Lancaster 564
Ribble Valley 565
ISLE OF MAN 566
Douglas........... 568

Best Places to Eat

- » Lime Tree (p542)
- » Italian Club (p558)
- » Mark Addy (p542)
- » Upstairs at the Grill (p551)
- » Tanroagan (p568)

Best Places to Stay

- » Green Bough (p550)
- » Hard Days Night Hotel (p558)
- » Hope St Hotel (p557)
- » Velvet Hotel (p540)
- » Number One (p563)

Why Go?

Music, history and hedonism: three great reasons to venture into England's once-mighty industrial heartland, the cradle of capitalism and the Industrial Revolution. Among the hulking relics of the region's industrial past are two of the most exciting cities in the country, a picture-postcard town dripping with Tudor charm and the most stomach-turning roller coaster we've ever been on. If you fancy a bit of respite from the concrete paw print of humankind, there's some of the most beautiful countryside in England. Oh, and a rich musical tradition that defines your MP3 playlists as much as anywhere else in the world.

The northwest helped define the progress of the last two centuries, but these days it's all about making an imprint on the 21st. A tall order, but the region knows a thing or two about mighty achievements, urban redesign and bloody good music: look and listen for yourself.

When to Go?

Steeplechase lovers should head to the world-famous Aintree Grand National, run just outside Liverpool, on the first weekend of April, while petrol heads should make a beeline to the Isle of Man's TT Festival, held for two weeks in May/June. For fans of the region's most important sport, football (soccer), August/September is a good time to visit as it's the start of the season.

Those with an appreciation of culture shouldn't miss the Manchester International Arts Festival, a biennial showstopper held in July. To appreciate the area's rich musical past visit Liverpool in the last week of August for madness at Creamfields (dance) and Matthew St Festival, an ode to all things Beatles.

Activities

Although predominantly an urban area, the northwest does have some decent walking and cycling options, most notably in the Ribble Valley in northern Lancashire, home to plenty of good walks including the 70-mile **Ribble Way**. The historic village of Whalley, in the heart of the Ribble Valley, is the meeting point of the two circular routes that make up the 260-mile **Lancashire Cycle Way**.

The Isle of Man has top-notch walking and cycling opportunities. Regional tourism websites contain walking and cycling information, and tourist offices stock free leaflets as well as maps and guides (usually £1 to £5) that cover walking, cycling and other activities.

Information

Discover England's Northwest (www.visitnorthwest.com) is the centralised tourist authority; for the Isle of Man, check out the main **Isle of Man Government** (www.gov.im) site.

Getting Around

The towns and cities covered in this chapter are all within easy reach of each other, and are well linked by public transport. The two main cities, Manchester and Liverpool, are only 34 miles apart and are linked by hourly bus and train services. Chester is 18 miles south of Liverpool, but is also easily accessible from Manchester by train or via the M56. Blackpool is 50 miles to the north of both cities, and is also well connected. Try the following for transport information:

Greater Manchester Passenger Transport Authority (www.gmpte.com) Extensive info on Manchester and its environs.

Merseytravel (www.merseytravel.gov.uk) Taking care of all travel in Merseyside.

National Express (www.nationalexpress.com) Extensive coach services in the northwest; Manchester and Liverpool are major hubs.

MANCHESTER

POP 394,270

'Manchester has everything but a beach.' Former Stone Roses' frontman Ian Brown's description of his native city has become Manchester's unofficial motto – and even accounting for a bit of northern bluster Brown isn't far wrong. The uncrowned capital of the north was the world's first modern city and the birthplace of capitalism; it is where the Industrial Revolution blossomed; where communism and feminism were given theoretical legs; and where the first computer beeped into life.

Manchester was raised on lofty ambition, so it stands to reason that it likes to plan on an impressive scale. Its world-class museums and heavyweight art galleries – spread across the city centre and west in Salford Quays – are noteworthy, but what makes this city truly special are its distractions of pure pleasure: you can dine, drink and dance yourself into happy oblivion in the swirl of nightlife that once made the city a key stop on the global party tour, from the boho Northern Quarter to the elegant eateries of the southern suburb of Didsbury.

History

Canals and steam-powered cotton mills were what transformed Manchester from a small disease-infested provincial town into a big disease-infested industrial city. It all happened in the 1760s, with the opening of the Bridgewater Canal between Manchester and the coal mines at Worsley in 1763, and with Richard Arkwright patenting his super cotton mill in 1769. Thereafter Manchester and the world would never be the same again. When the canal was extended to Liverpool and the open sea in 1776, Manchester – dubbed 'Cottonopolis' – kicked into high gear and took off on the coal-fuelled, steam-powered gravy train.

There was plenty of gravy to go around, but the good burghers of 19th-century Manchester made sure that the vast majority of the city's swollen citizenry (with a population of 90,000 in 1801, and 100 years later, two million) who produced most of it never got their hands on any of it. Their reward was life in a new kind of urban settlement: the industrial slum. Working conditions were dire, with impossibly long hours, child labour, work-related accidents and fatalities commonplace. Mark Twain commented

WANT MORE?

For in-depth information, reviews and recommendations at your fingertips, head to the Apple App Store to purchase Lonely Planet's *Manchester City Guide* iPhone app.

Alternatively, head to **Lonely Planet** (www.lonelyplanet.com/england/northwest-england/manchester) for planning advice, author recommendations, traveller reviews and insider tips.

Manchester, Liverpool & Northwest England Highlights

1. Learning a valuable history lesson at the outstanding **International Slavery Museum** (p556) in Liverpool
2. Having your insides churned and twisted at Blackpool's **Pleasure Beach** (p563)
3. Learning exactly what kind of hell war is in the **Imperial War Museum North** (p535) in Manchester
4. Sampling's Manchester culinary delights at one (or more!) of the city's superb **restaurants** (p541)

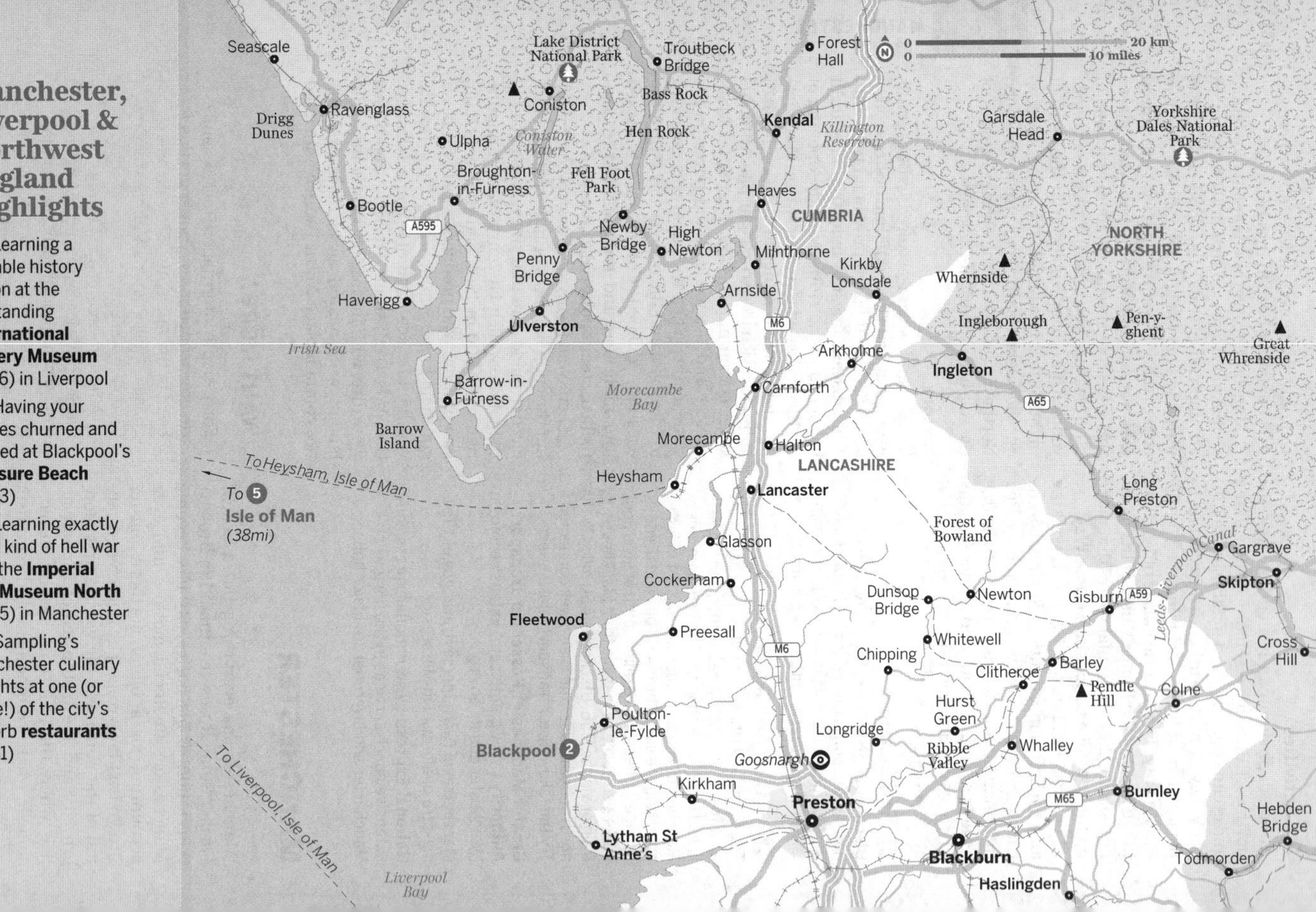

5 Getting to grips with the **Isle of Man** (p566) – about as exotic as England gets

6 Tramping Chester's **city walls** (p548), like the Romans did 2000 years ago.

that he would like to live here because the 'transition between Manchester and Death would be unnoticeable'. So much for Victorian values.

The wheels started to come off towards the end of the 19th century. The USA had begun to flex its own industrial muscles and was taking over a sizeable chunk of the textile trade; production in Manchester's mills began to slow, and then it stopped altogether. By WWII there was hardly enough cotton produced in the city to make a tablecloth. The postwar years weren't much better: 150,000 manufacturing jobs were lost between 1961 and 1983, and the port – still the UK's third largest in 1963 – finally closed in 1982 due to declining traffic. The nadir came on 15 June 1996, when an IRA bomb wrecked a chunk of the city centre, but the subsequent reconstruction proved to be the beginning of the glass-and-chrome revolution so much in evidence today.

Sights & Activities

CITY CENTRE

FREE Museum of Science & Industry MUSEUM
(MOSI; www.msim.org.uk; Liverpool Rd; admission free, charge for special exhibitions; 10am-5pm) The city's largest museum comprises 2.8 hectares in the heart of 19th-century industrial Manchester. It's in the landscape of enormous, weather-stained brick buildings and rusting cast-iron relics of canals, viaducts, bridges, warehouses and market buildings that makes up Castlefield, now deemed an 'urban heritage park'.

If there's anything you want to know about the Industrial (and post-Industrial) Revolution and Manchester's key role in it, you'll find the answers among the collection of steam engines and locomotives, factory machinery from the mills, and the excellent exhibition telling the story of Manchester from the sewers up.

FREE People's History Museum MUSEUM
(www.phm.org.uk; Left Bank, Bridge St; 10am-5pm) A major refurb of an Edwardian pumping station – including the construction of a striking new annexe – has resulted in the expansion of one of the city's best museums, which is devoted to British social history and the labour movement. It's compelling stuff, and a marvellous example of a museum's relevance to our everyday lives.

National Football Museum MUSEUM
(www.nationalfootballmuseum.com; Urbis, Cathedral Gardens, Corporation St) It's the world's most popular game and Manchester is home to the world's most popular team, so when this museum went looking for a new home (from its previous location in the stand of Preston North End Football Club, winners of the first professional league championship in 1889), it made sense that it would find its way to the stunning glass triangle that is Urbis. Slated to open in 2011, the museum will be a major stop in the football fan's Manchester pilgrimage and promises a major revamp of the displays exhibited in Preston.

FREE Manchester Art Gallery GALLERY
(www.manchestergalleries.org; Mosley St; 10am-5pm Tue-Sun) A superb collection of British art and a hefty number of European masters are on display at the city's top gallery. The older wing, designed by Charles Barry (of Houses of Parliament fame) in 1834, has an impressive collection that includes 37 Turner watercolours, as well as the country's best collection of Pre-Raphaelite art. The newer gallery features a permanent collection of 20th-century British art starring Lucien Freud, Francis Bacon, Stanley Spencer, Henry Moore and David Hockney.

FREE John Rylands Library LIBRARY
(www.library.manchester.ac.uk; 35 Deansgate; 10am-5pm Mon & Wed-Sat, noon-5pm Tue & Sun) Less a library and more a cathedral to books, Basil Champneys' stunning building is arguably the most beautiful library in Britain – although there's not much argument when you're standing in the simply exquisite Gothic 'Reading Room', complete with high-vaulted ceilings and stained-glass windows.

Town Hall SIGNIFICANT BUILDING
(0161-234 5000; www.manchester.gov.uk; Albert Sq; tours adult/child £5/4; tours 2pm Sat Mar-Sep) The city's main administrative centre is this superb Victorian Gothic building. The interior is rich in sculpture and ornate decoration, while the exterior is crowned by an impressive 85m-high tower.

FREE Central Library LIBRARY
(0161-234 1900; St Peter's Sq; 10am-8pm Mon-Thu, 10am-6pm Fri & Sat) Just behind the town hall, the elegant Roman Pantheon lookalike was built in 1934. It is the country's largest municipal library, with more than 20 miles of shelves.

MANCHESTER IN...

Two Days

After exploring the **Museum of Science & Industry**, explore the newly renovated **People's History Museum** and come to grips with the beautiful game at the **National Football Museum**. Pick a restaurant such as **Yang Sing** to kick off the evening, then try **A Place Called Common** and round off the night in **Bluu**.

The next day, hop on the Metrolink for the Salford Quays and its trio of top attractions: the **Imperial War Museum North**, the **Lowry** and the **Manchester United Museum** at Old Trafford. Back in the city, indulge your retail chi in either the **Millennium Quarter** or the boutiques and offbeat shops of the **Northern Quarter**. Finish your day with a jaunt to the suburb of **West Didsbury** and its selection of fantastic restaurants.

Four Days

Follow the two-day itinerary and also tackle some of the city's lesser-known museums – the **John Rylands Library** and **Whitworth Art Gallery**. Examine the riches of the **Manchester Art Gallery**. End the evening with a dance at the new **Fac 251: The Factory** club. The next day, take a walking tour – the tourist office has details of a whole host of themed ones – and if you're serious about clubbing, be sure to make the pilgrimage to Ancoats for the absolutely fabulous **Sankey's**.

SALFORD QUAYS

It's a cinch to get here from the city centre via Metrolink (£2); for the Imperial War Museum North and the Lowry, look for the Harbour City stop; get off at Old Trafford for the eponymous stadium.

FREE **Imperial War Museum North** MUSEUM
(www.iwm.org.uk/north; Trafford Wharf Rd; ⏲10am-6pm) War museums generally appeal to those with a fascination for military hardware and battle strategy (toy soldiers optional), but Daniel Libeskind's visually stunning Imperial War Museum North takes a radically different approach. War is hell, it tells us, but it's a hell we revisit with tragic regularity.

Although the audiovisuals and displays are quite compelling, the extraordinary aluminium-clad building itself is a huge part of the attraction, and the exhibition spaces are genuinely breathtaking. Libeskind designed three distinct structures (or shards) that represent the three main theatres of war: air, land and sea.

FREE **Lowry** ARTS CENTRE
(www.thelowry.com; Pier 8, Salford Quays; ⏲11am-8pm Tue-Fri, 10am-8pm Sat, 11am-6pm Sun & Mon) Looking more like a shiny steel ship than an arts centre, the Lowry is the quays' most notable success. It attracts more than one million visitors a year to its myriad functions, which include everything from art exhibits and performances to bars, restaurants and, inevitably, shops. You can even get married in the place.

The complex is home to more than 300 paintings and drawings by northern England's favourite artist, LS Lowry (1887–1976), who was born in nearby Stretford. He became famous for his humanistic depictions of industrial landscapes and northern towns, and gave his name to the complex.

Old Trafford (Manchester United Museum & Tour) STADIUM
(☎0870 442 1994; www.manutd.com; Sir Matt Busby Way; ⏲9.30am-5pm) Home of the world's most famous club, the Old Trafford stadium is both a theatre and a temple for its millions of fans worldwide, many of whom come in pilgrimage to the ground to pay tribute to the minor deities disguised as highly paid footballers that play there. Ironically, Manchester United is not as popular in Manchester as its cross-town rival Manchester City, whose fans have traditionally regarded United's enormous wealth and success in strictly Faustian terms.

Still, a visit to the stadium is one of the more memorable things you'll do here. We strongly recommend that you take the **tour** (adult/child £12.50/8.50; ⏲every 10min except match days 9.40am-4.30pm), which includes a seat in the stands, a stop in the changing rooms, a peek at the players' lounge (from which the manager is banned unless invited by the players) and a walk down the tunnel to the pitchside dugout, which is as close to

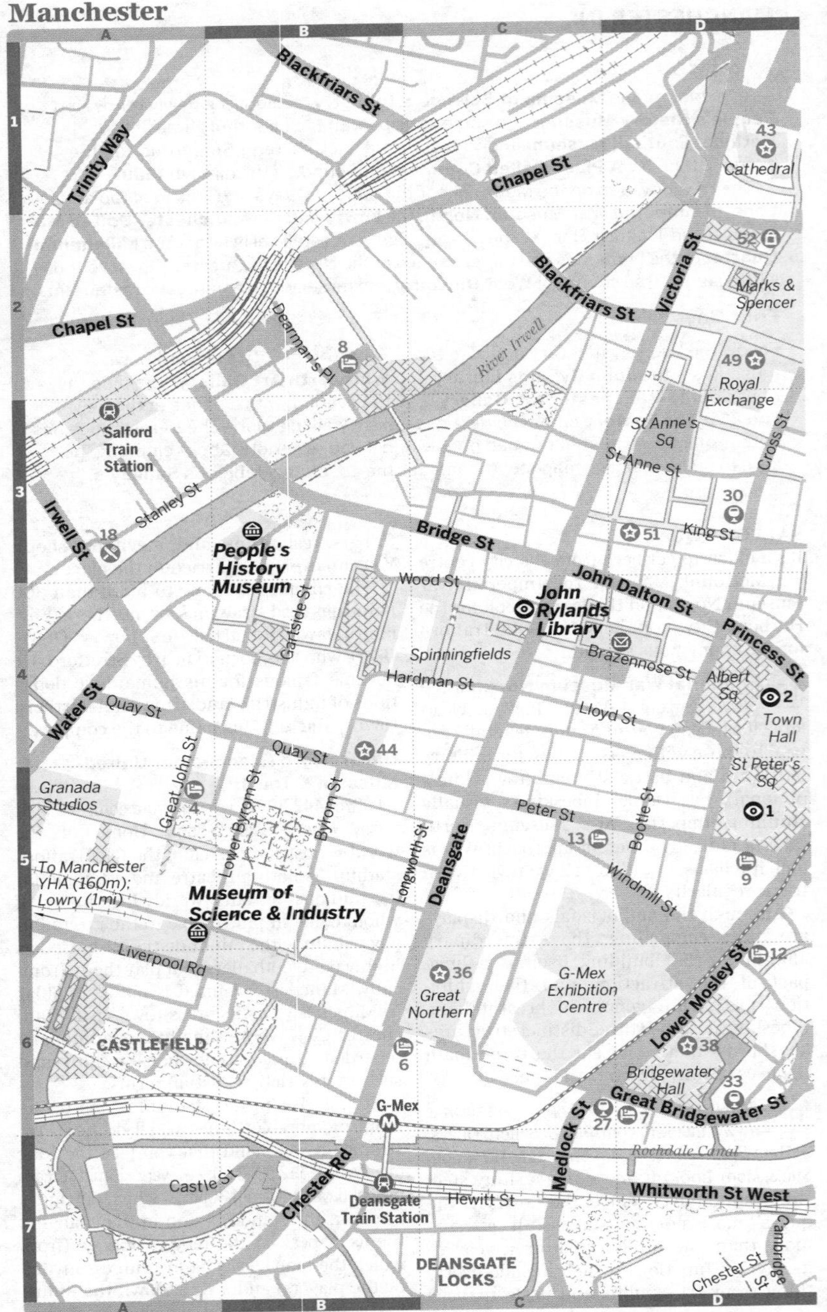

A
B
C
D
1
2
3
4
5
6
7
Blackfriars St
Trinity Way
Chapel St
43
Cathedral
52
Victoria St
Blackfriars St
Marks & Spencer
Chapel St
Dearman's Pl
8
River Irwell
49
Royal Exchange
Salford Train Station
St Anne's Sq
Cross St
St Anne St
Irwell St
Stanley St
30
18
People's History Museum
Bridge St
51
King St
Wood St
John Dalton St
John Rylands Library
Gartside St
Spinningfields
Brazennose St
Princess St
Hardman St
Albert Sq
2
Town Hall
Water St
Quay St
Lloyd St
Quay St
44
St Peter's Sq
Granada Studios
Great John St
4
Lower Byrom St
Byrom St
Peter St
1
Bootle St
13
Longworth St
Deansgate
9
To Manchester YHA (160m); Lowry (1mi)
Windmill St
Museum of Science & Industry
12
Liverpool Rd
36
Great Northern
G-Mex Exhibition Centre
Lower Mosley St
CASTLEFIELD
6
38
Bridgewater Hall
33
G-Mex
Great Bridgewater St
Medlock St
27
7
Rochdale Canal
Castle St
Chester Rd
Deansgate Train Station
Hewitt St
Whitworth St West
DEANSGATE LOCKS
Chester St
Cambridge St

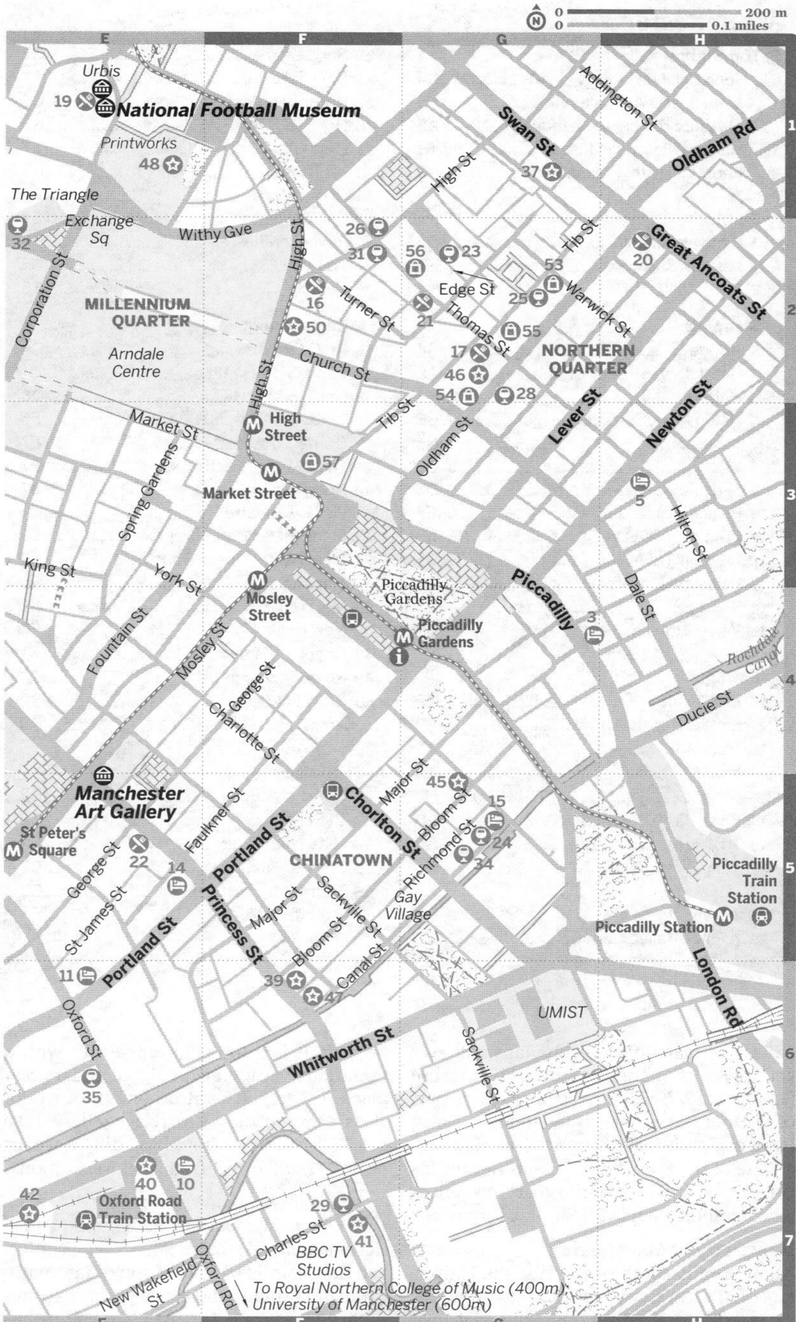

200 m
0.1 miles
E
F
G
H
1
2
3
4
5
6
7
Urbis
19
National Football Museum
Printworks
48
The Triangle
32
Exchange Sq
Withy Gve
Corporation St
MILLENNIUM QUARTER
Arndale Centre
High St
26
31
56
23
Edge St
16
Turner St
21
Thomas St
50
Church St
Swan St
Addington St
High St
37
Oldham Rd
Tib St
53
25
Warwick St
55
20
Great Ancoats St
17
46
54
28
NORTHERN QUARTER
Lever St
Newton St
Tib St
Oldham St
High Street
Market St
57
Market Street
Spring Gardens
5
Hilton St
King St
York St
Mosley Street
Piccadilly Gardens
Piccadilly Gardens
Piccadilly
3
Dale St
Rochdale Canal
Fountain St
Mosley St
George St
Charlotte St
Ducie St
Manchester Art Gallery
St Peter's Square
Faulkner St
Portland St
Chorlton St
Major St
45
Bloom St
15
Richmond St
24
34
CHINATOWN
George St
22
14
St James St
Princess St
Major St
Sackville St
Gay Village
Bloom St
Canal St
Piccadilly Train Station
Piccadilly Station
Portland St
11
39
47
London Rd
Oxford St
UMIST
Whitworth St
Sackville St
35
40
10
42
Oxford Road Train Station
29
41
Charles St
BBC TV Studios
New Wakefield St
Oxford Rd
To Royal Northern College of Music (400m); University of Manchester (600m)
MANCHESTER

Manchester

Top Sights
- John Rylands Library C4
- Manchester Art Gallery E5
- Museum of Science & Industry A5
- National Football Museum E1
- People's History Museum B3

Sights
- 1 Central Library D5
- Lesbian & Gay Foundation .... (see 39)
- 2 Town Hall D4

Sleeping
- 3 ABode G4
- 4 Great John Street Hotel A5
- 5 Hatters H3
- 6 Hilton Manchester Deansgate B6
- 7 Jury's Inn D6
- 8 Lowry B2
- 9 Midland D5
- 10 Palace Hotel E7
- 11 Premier Travel Inn E6
- 12 Premier Travel Inn D6
- 13 Radisson Edwardian C5
- 14 Roomzzz E5
- 15 Velvet Hotel G5

Eating
- 16 Earth Cafe F2
- 17 Love Saves the Day G2
- 18 Mark Addy A3
- 19 Modern E1
- 20 Ning H2
- River Bar & Restaurant .... (see 8)
- 21 Trof G2
- 22 Yang Sing E5

Drinking
- 23 A Place Called Common G2
- 24 AXM G5
- 25 Bar Centro G2
- 26 Bluu F2
- 27 Britons Protection C6
- 28 Dry Bar G2
- 29 Lass O'Gowrie F7
- 30 Mr Thomas' Chop House D3
- 31 Odd F2
- 32 Old Wellington Inn E2
- 33 Peveril of the Peak D6
- 34 Taurus G5
- 35 Temple E6

Entertainment
- 36 AMC Cinemas C6
- 37 Band on the Wall G1
- 38 Bridgewater Hall D6
- 39 Club Alter Ego F6
- 40 Cornerhouse E7
- 41 Fac 251: The Factory F7
- 42 Green Room E7
- Library Theatre .... (see 1)
- 43 Manchester Cathedral D1
- 44 Manchester Opera House B4
- 45 Mancunia G5
- 46 Moho Live G2
- 47 New Union Hotel F6
- 48 Odeon Cinema E1
- 49 Royal Exchange D2
- 50 Ruby Lounge F2
- 51 South D3

Shopping
- 52 Harvey Nichols D2
- 53 Oi Polloi G2
- 54 Oxfam Originals G2
- 55 Rags to Bitches G2
- 56 Thomas St Post Office G2
- 57 Tib Street Market F3

ecstasy as many of the club's fans will ever get. It's pretty impressive stuff. The **museum** (adult/child £9/7; ⌚9.30am-5pm), which is part of the tour but can be visited independently, has a comprehensive history of the club, and a state-of-the-art call-up system that means you can view your favourite goals – as well as a holographic 'chat' with Sir Alex Ferguson.

University of Manchester UNIVERSITY

About a mile south of the city, the University of Manchester is one of England's most extraordinary institutions, and not just because it is a top-class university with a remarkable academic pedigree and a great place to party. It is also home to a world-class museum and a superb art gallery. Take bus 11, 16, 41 or 42 from Piccadilly Gardens or bus 47, 190 or 191 from Victoria station.

FREE *Manchester Museum*
(www.museum.manchester.ac.uk; University of Manchester, Oxford Rd; ⌚10am-5pm Tue-Sat, 11am-4pm Sun & Mon) If you're into natural history and social science, this extraordinary museum is the place for you. It has

galleries devoted to archaeology, archery, botany, ethnology, geology, numismatics and zoology. The real treat here, though, is the Egyptology section and its collection of mummies. One particularly interesting part is devoted to the work of Dr Richard Neave, who has rebuilt faces of people who have been dead for more than 3000 years; his pioneering techniques are now used in criminal forensics.

FREE *Whitworth Art Gallery* (www.whitworth.manchester.ac.uk; University of Manchester, Oxford Rd; ⏲10am-5pm Mon-Sat, noon-4pm Sun) Manchester's second most important art gallery has a wonderful collection of British watercolours. It also houses the best selection of historic textiles outside London, and has a number of galleries devoted to the work of artists from Dürer and Rembrandt to Lucien Freud and David Hockney.

All this high art aside, you may find that the most interesting part of the gallery is the group of rooms dedicated to wallpaper – proof that bland pastels and horrible flowery patterns are not the final word in home decoration.

Tours

The tourist office sells tickets for guided walks on all aspects of the city, from architecture to radical history, which operate almost daily year-round and cost £6/5 per adult/child.

Festivals & Events

Queer Up North LGBT
(www.queerupnorth.com) This biennial festival is the country's biggest gay and lesbian arts festival – the next will be in spring 2011.

FutureEverything CONTEMPORARY ARTS
(www.futureeverything.org) A superb music and media arts festival that takes place in various venues over a week in mid-May.

Manchester Day PARADE
(www.themanchesterdayparade.co.uk) Inaugurated in 2010, a parade to celebrate all things Manchester, with music, performances and fireworks; in June.

Manchester International Festival ARTS
(www.manchesterinternationalfestival.com) With its exciting showcasing of only new, commissioned work, this largely musical biennial festival (held in July) is already the city's most popular.

Manchester Jazz Festival MUSIC
(www.manchesterjazz.com) Takes place in 50 venues throughout the city over the last week in July.

Manchester Pride LGBT
(www.manchesterpride.com) One of England's biggest celebrations of gay, bisexual and transgender life, held in August.

GAY & LESBIAN MANCHESTER

The city's gay scene is unrivalled outside London, and caters to every taste. Its healthy heart beats loudest in the Gay Village, centred on handsome Canal St. Here you'll find bars, clubs, restaurants and – crucially – karaoke joints that cater almost exclusively to the pink pound.

The country's biggest gay and lesbian arts festival, **Queer Up North** (☎0161-833 2288; www.queerupnorth.com), takes place every two years – the next in spring 2011. **Manchester Pride** (www.manchesterpride.com) is a 10-day festival from the middle of August each year and attracts more than 500,000 people.

There are bars to suit every taste, but you won't go far wrong in **AXM** (www.axm-bar.co.uk; 10 Canal St), which is more of a cocktail lounge for the city's flash crowd; or **Taurus** (www.taurus-bar.co.uk; 1 Canal St), which is a little shabbier but equally good fun.

For your clubbing needs, look no further than **Club Alter Ego** (www.clubalterego.co.uk; 105-107 Princess St; ⏲11pm-5am Thu-Sat) and **Mancunia** (www.mancuniaclub.co.uk; 8 Minshull St; ⏲11pm-5am Thu-Sat), which is just as popular.

And then there's karaoke, the ultimate choice for midweek fun. The best of the lot is at the **New Union Hotel** (www.newunionhotel.com; 111 Princess St; ⏲9pm-2am), where you can find your inner Madonna and Cyndi Lauper every Tuesday and Thursday – for a top prize of £50.

For more information, check with the **Lesbian & Gay Foundation** (☎0161-235 8035; www.lgf.org.uk; 105-107 Princess St; ⏲4-10pm). The city's best pink website is www.visitgaymanchester.co.uk.

Manchester International Film Festival FILM

(www.kinofilm.org.uk) A biennial film festival held in late-October. The festival was launched in 2007.

Sleeping

Manchester's hotels recognise that the business traveller is their best bet, but in keeping with their capital of cool status, they like to throw in more than a bit of style, so you'll find plenty of designer digs around town. Remember that during the football season (August to May), rooms can be almost impossible to find if either of the city's football clubs are playing at home (especially United). If you are having difficulty finding a bed, the tourist office's free accommodation service can help.

CITY CENTRE

TOP CHOICE **Velvet Hotel** BOUTIQUE HOTEL ££

(0161-236 9003; www.velvetmanchester.com; 2 Canal St; r from £99;) Nineteen beautiful bespoke rooms, each decorated with exquisite taste and style, make this a real contender for best in the city. We ooh'd and aah'd over every element of this gorgeous new hotel – the sleigh bed in Room 24, the double bath of Room 34, the saucy framed photographs of a stripped-down David Beckham (this is Gay Village, after all!). Despite the tantalising decor and location, this is not an exclusive hotel and is as popular with straight visitors as it is with the same-sex crowd.

Great John Street Hotel HOTEL £££

(0161-831 3211; www.greatjohnstreet.co.uk; Great John St; r £85-345; @) Elegant, designer luxury? Present. Fabulous rooms with all the usual delights (Egyptian cotton sheets, fabulous toiletries, free-standing baths and lots of high-tech electronics)? Present. A butler to run your bath in the Opus Grand Suite? Present. This former schoolhouse (ah, now you get it) is small and sumptuous – and just across the street from Granada TV studios.

Roomzzz SERVICED ACCOMMODATION ££

(0161-236 2121; www.roomzzz.co.uk; 36 Princess St; r £89-199; @) The short-lived Yang Sing Oriental Hotel was just a little bit too luxurious for the changing times; enter the Roomzzz group who converted this superb hotel in a Grade II building into equally elegant serviced apartments – at a fraction of the price. Highly recommended if you're planning a longer stay.

Hatters HOSTEL £

(0161-236 9500; www.hattersgroup.com; 50 Newton St; dm/s/d/tr from £14.50/27.50/50/67.50; P@) The old-style lift and porcelain sinks are the only leftovers of this former milliner's factory, now one of the best hostels in town – smack in the heart of the Northern Quarter, you won't have to go far to get the best of alternative Manchester.

ABode HOTEL ££

(0161-247 7744; www.abodehotels.co.uk; 107 Piccadilly St; r from £60; @) Modern British style is the catchphrase at this converted textile factory. The original fittings have been combined successfully with 61 bedrooms divided into four categories of ever-increasing luxury: Comfortable, Desirable, Enviable and Fabulous, the latter being five seriously swanky top-floor suites. Vi-Spring beds, Monsoon showers, LCD-screen TVs and stacks of Aqua Sulis toiletries are standard throughout. In the basement, star chef Michael Caines has a champagne and cocktail bar adjacent to his very own restaurant.

Radisson Edwardian HOTEL ££

(0161-835 9929; www.radissonedwardian.com/manchester; Peter St; r from £90; P@) The Free Trade Hall saw it all, from Emmeline Pankhurst's suffragette campaign to the Sex Pistols' legendary 1976 gig. Today, those rabble-rousing noisemakers wouldn't be allowed to set foot in the door of what is now a sumptuous five-star hotel, all minimalist Zen and luxury.

Manchester YHA HOSTEL £

(0845 371 9647; www.yha.org.uk; Potato Wharf; dm incl breakfast from £16; P@) This purpose-built canalside hostel in the Castlefield area is one of the best in the country. It's a top-class option with four- and six-bed dorms, all with bathroom, as well as three doubles and a host of good facilities. Potato Wharf is just left off Liverpool Rd.

Palace Hotel BOUTIQUE HOTEL ££

(0161-288 1111; www.principal-hotels.com; Oxford St; s/d from £85/105;) An elegant refurbishment of one of Manchester's most magnificent Victorian palaces has resulted in a special boutique hotel, combining the grandeur of the public areas with the modern look of the bedrooms.

Hilton Manchester Deansgate HOTEL ££
(☎0161-870 1600; www.hilton.co.uk; Beetham Tower, 303 Deansgate; r from £99; 📶) A no-surprises Hilton occupying the lower 23 floors of the city's tallest landmark, the Beetham Tower. The tower is growing on even the most reluctant Mancunians; the hotel has been a hit with the business crowd since the day it opened.

Other options worth considering:

Jury's Inn HOTEL ££
(☎0161-953 8888; www.jurysdoyle.com; 56 Great Bridgewater St; r from £55) Comfortable Irish chain hotel a few doors down from the Bridgewater Hall.

Park Inn Hotel HOTEL ££
(☎0161-832 6565; www.sasparkinn.com; 4 Cheetham Hill Rd; r from £99; 📶) Spacious, modern rooms (with floor-to-ceiling windows) in a massive hotel overlooking the MEN Arena; perfect if you're going to a gig. The hotel is about 300m north of Victoria Station along Cheetham Hill Rd.

Premier Travel Inn HOTEL ££
(☎0870 990 6444; www.premiertravelinn.com; r from £60) G-Max (Bishopsgate, 11 Lower Mosley St); Portland St (The Circus, 112 Portland St) Two convenient city-centre locations for this tidy chain.

Midland HOTEL ££
(☎0161-236 3333; www.themidland.co.uk; Peter St; r from £104; @) Mr Rolls and Mr Royce sealed the deal in the elegant lobby of this fancy business hotel.

SALFORD QUAYS

Lowry HOTEL £££
(☎0161-827 4000; www.roccofortecollection.com; 50 Dearman's Pl, Chapel Wharf; r £120-950; P 📶 @) Simply dripping with designer luxury and five-star comfort, Manchester's top hotel (not to be confused with the arts centre in the Salford Quays) has fabulous rooms with enormous beds, ergonomically designed furniture, walk-in wardrobes and bathrooms finished with Italian porcelain tiles and glass mosaics. You can soothe yourself with a skin-brightening treatment or an aromatherapy head-massage at the health spa.

Eating

The choice of restaurants in Manchester is unrivalled outside of London, with something for every palate and every budget. There are good restaurants throughout the city, including a superb selection in Chinatown and the organic havens of the Northern Quarter, where you'll also find some excellent veggie spots. If you want to dine like an in-the-know Mancunian, you'll have to go to suburbs such as Didsbury (divided into East and West), about 5 miles south of the city centre. The best way to get there is by buses 43 or 143 from Oxford Rd.

CITY CENTRE

Yang Sing CHINESE ££
(☎0161-236 2200; 34 Princess St; mains £9-17) A serious contender for best Chinese restaurant in England, Yang Sing attracts diners from all over with its exceptional Cantonese cuisine. From a dim-sum lunch to a full evening banquet, the food is superb, and the waiters will patiently explain the intricacies of each item to punters who can barely pronounce the dishes' names. Bookings suggested for evening meals.

Earth Cafe VEGETARIAN £
(www.earthcafe.co.uk; 16-20 Turner St; chef's special £3.20; ⏲10am-5pm Tue-Sat) Below the Manchester Buddhist Centre, this gourmet vegetarian cafe's motto is 'right food, right place, right time', which is reflected in its overriding commitment to ensuring that it serves as much local seasonable produce as possible. The result is wonderful: here you'll eat well in the knowledge that you're eating right. The chef's special (a main dish, side and two salad portions) is generally excellent and always filling.

Modern MODERN BRITISH ££
(☎0161-605 8282; Urbis, Cathedral Gardens, Corporation St; 2-/3-course lunch £12/15, dinner mains £11-21) Top fare on top of the world, or an excellent meal atop Manchester's most distinctive landmark, Urbis (soon to be home to the National Football Museum) is one of the city's most enjoyable dining experiences. The food – mostly modern British cuisine – will not disappoint, but being able to sit at a table close to the floor-to-ceiling windows make this place worthwhile; book a table in advance.

Ning MALAYSIAN ££
(www.ningcatering.com; 92-94 Oldham St; mains £9.50-11.50; ⏲dinner Tue-Sun) Head chef Norman Musa has become one of the Northern Quarter's biggest draws, thanks to his exquisite presentations of Malaysian dishes such as *ikan goreng masam manis* (pan-fried sea bass fillets with sweet and sour chilli gravy) and *sambal udang* (prawns

with onions and vegetables, coated with spicy chilli gravy) and a handful of Thai selections, all served in a beautiful room that has the informal feeling of a canteen.

Love Saves the Day CAFE £
(☎0161-832 0777; Tib St; lunch £6-8; ⊙8am-7pm Mon-Wed, to 9pm Thu, to 8pm Fri, 10am-6pm Sat, 10am-4pm Sun) The Northern Quarter's most popular cafe is a New York–style deli, small supermarket and sit-down eatery in one large, airy room. Everybody comes here – from crusties to corporate types – to sit around over a spot of (locally sourced) lunch and discuss the day's goings-on. A wonderful spot. The house salad is £5.50.

Trof CAFE £
(☎0161-832 1870; 5-8 Thomas St; sandwiches £4, mains £8; ⊙breakfast, lunch & dinner) Great music, top staff and a fab selection of sandwiches, roasts and other dishes (the huge breakfast is a proper hangover cure), as well as a broad selection of beers and tunes (Tuesday night is acoustic night), have made this hang-out a firm favourite with students.

SALFORD QUAYS

Mark Addy MODERN BRITISH ££
(☎0161-832 4080; www.markaddy.co.uk; Stanley St; mains £8.90-12.50; ⊙lunch & dinner Wed-Fri, dinner Sat) A contender for best pub grub in town, the Mark Addy owes its culinary success to Robert Owen Brown, whose loving interpretations of standard British classics – pork hop with honey-roasted bramley, pan-friend Dab with cockles and spring onion et al (all locally sourced) – has them queuing at the door for a taste.

River Bar & Restaurant MODERN BRITISH £££
(☎0161-832 1000; www.theriverrestaurant.com; Lowry Hotel, 50 Dearman's Pl, Chapel Wharf; mains £18-39; ⊙Mon-Sat) Head chef Oliver Thomas won the 'Taste of Manchester' award in 2010 for his outstanding British cuisine, which emphasises the use of local produce and traditional cooking methods. The result is terrific: how about grilled native lobster with garlic butter and chips, or Welsh Salt Marsh lamb with sweet potato, apricots and sugar-snap peas?

DIDSBURY & SOUTHERN SUBURBS

TOP CHOICE **Lime Tree** MODERN BRITISH £££
(☎0161-445 1217; www.thelimetreerestaurant.co.uk; 8 Lapwing Lane, West Didsbury; mains £15-23; ⊙lunch & dinner Tue-Fri & Sun, dinner Mon & Sat) The ambience is refined without being stuffy, the service is relaxed but spot on. and the food is divine – this is as good a restaurant as you'll find anywhere in the northwest. The fillet steak in peppercorn sauce (£21.50) is to die for; the second time we visited we opted for the pan-fried Goosnargh duck with a cranberry and ginger compote (£15.95). We'll be back. And back again.

Cachumba Cafe INTERNATIONAL £
(☎0161-445 2479; www.cachumba.co.uk; 220 Burton Rd; mains £4-9; ⊙dinner Tue-Sat) Cachumba does for food what the 'global beats' section in a record shop does for music: it brings together flavours from all over the world (Southeast Asia, India and a selection from Africa) and serves them up in small, tapas-style portions. Friendly, relaxed, informal and exactly the kind of cafe we like to linger in. Recommended.

Fat Loaf MODERN BRITISH ££
(☎0161-438 0319; www.thefatloaf.co.uk; 846 Wilmslow Rd; mains £10.95-15.95; ⊙lunch & dinner Mon-Sat, noon-7pm Sun) This increasingly popular restaurant is in a Grade II–listed building on Didsbury Green. Dishes are sourced locally (slow-braised English lamb shank, roast Gressingham duck) and are done to perfection.

Drinking

There's every kind of drinking hole in Manchester, from the really grungy ones that smell but have plenty of character to the ones that were designed by a team of architects but have the atmosphere of a freezer. Every neighbourhood in town has its favourites; here's a few to get you going.

Temple BAR
(Great Bridgewater St; ⊙noon-midnight Mon-Thu, to 1am Fri & Sat, noon-11pm Sun) This tiny basement bar with a capacity of about 30 has a great jukebox and a fine selection of spirits, all crammed into a converted public toilet. If you want to get up close and personal, this is the perfect spot to do it in. Hardly your bog-standard pub.

Britons Protection PUB
(50 Great Bridgewater St) Whisky – 200 different kinds of it – is the beverage of choice at this liver-threatening, proper English pub that also does Tudor-style meals (boar, venison and the like; mains £8). An old-fashioned boozer with open fires in the back rooms and a cosy atmosphere...perfect on a cold evening.

LOCAL KNOWLEDGE

OLIVER THOMAS: CHEF, THE RIVER RESTAURANT

The food scene in Manchester

It's been pretty well-established since Marco Pierre White first started this restaurant about 10 years ago.

Secrets to its success?

Manchester's best restaurants are committed to discovering their own locality, and using produce from local farms, especially from the Goosnargh area north of Preston, which is fabulous for all kinds of produce, from cheese to geese.

Where would you go for a good meal?

I'm a big fan of Robert Owen Brown's food at the **Mark Addy** (p542); really good renditions of classic British dishes. I also rate the food in **Harvey Nichols** (p546) and the **Fat Loaf** (p542) in Didsbury.

Bluu BAR
(www.bluu.co.uk; Unit 1, Smithfield Market, Thomas St; ⏲noon-midnight Sun-Mon, to 1am Tue-Thu, to 2am Fri & Sat) Our favourite of the Northern Quarter's collection of great bars. Bluu is cool, comfortable and comes with a great terrace on which to enjoy a pint and listen to music selected by folks with really good taste.

Lass O'Gowrie PUB
(36 Charles St) A Victorian classic off Princess St that brews its own beer in the basement. It's a favourite with students, old-timers and a clique of BBC employees who work just across the street in the Beeb's Manchester HQ. It also does good-value bar meals (£6).

A Place Called Common BAR
(www.aplacecalledcommon.co.uk; 39-41 Edge St; ⏲noon-midnight Mon-Wed, to 1am Thu, to 2am Fri & Sat, 2pm-midnight Sun) Common by name but great by nature, this is a terrific boozer favoured by an unpretentious crowd who like the changing artwork on the walls and the DJs who play nightly.

Odd BAR
(www.oddbar.co.uk; 30-32 Thomas St; ⏲11am-11pm Mon-Sat, to 10.30pm Sun) This eclectic little bar – with its oddball furnishings, wacky tunes and anti-establishment crew of customers – is the perfect antidote to the increasingly similar look of so many modern bars. A slice of Mancuniana to be treasured.

Bar Centro BAR
(72-74 Tib St; ⏲noon-midnight Mon-Wed, to 1am Thu, to 2am Fri & Sat, 2pm-midnight Sun) A Northern Quarter stalwart, it's very popular with the bohemian crowd precisely because it doesn't try to be. Great beer, nice staff and a better-than-average bar menu (mains £6 to £9) make this one of the choice spots in the area.

Dry Bar BAR
(28-30 Oldham Rd; ⏲noon-midnight Mon-Wed, noon-2am Thu-Sat, 6pm-midnight Sun) The former HQ of Madchester's maddest protagonists (legend has it Shaun Ryder once pulled a gun on Tony Wilson here), Dry has remained cool long after the scene froze over, and it's still one of the best bars in the Northern Quarter.

Other decent boozers:

Mr Thomas' Chop House PUB
(52 Cross St) An old-style boozer that is very popular for a pint as well as for food (mains £10).

Old Wellington Inn PUB
(4 Cathedral Gates) One of the oldest buildings in the city and a lovely spot for a pint of genuine ale.

Peveril of the Peak PUB
(127 Great Bridgewater St) An unpretentious pub with wonderful Victorian glazed tilework outside.

☆ Entertainment

Nightclubs

A handy tip: if you want to thrive in Manchester's excellent nightlife, drop all mention of Madchester and keep talk of being 'up for it' to strict irony. Otherwise, you'll risk being labelled a saddo nostalgic or, worse, someone who should have gone

THE MADCHESTER SOUND

It is often claimed that Manchester is the engine room of British pop. If this is indeed the case, then the chief engineer was TV presenter and music impresario Tony Wilson (1950–2007), founder of Factory Records. This is the label that in 1983 released New Order's ground-breaking 'Blue Monday', to this day the best-selling 12in in British history, which successfully fused the guitar-driven sound of punk with a pulsating dance beat.

When the money started pouring in, Wilson took the next, all-important step: he opened his own nightclub that would provide a platform for local bands to perform. The Haçienda opened its doors with plenty of fanfare but just wouldn't take off. Things started to turn around when the club embraced a brand new sound coming out of Chicago and Detroit: house. DJs Mike Pickering, Graeme Park and Jon Da Silva were the music's most important apostles, and when ecstasy hit the scene late in the decade, it seemed that every kid in town was 'mad for it'.

Heavily influenced by these new arrivals, the city's guitar bands took notice and began shaping their sounds to suit the clubbers' needs. The most successful was the Stone Roses, who in 1989 released 'Fools Gold', a pulsating hit with the rapid shuffle of James Brown's 'Funky Drummer' and a druggie guitar sound that drove dancers wild. Around the same time, Happy Mondays, fronted by the laddish Shaun Ryder and the whacked-out Bez (whose only job was to lead the dancing from the stage), hit the scene with the infectious 'Hallelujah'. The other big anthems of the day were 'The One I Love' by the Charlatans, 'Voodoo Ray' by A Guy Called Gerald, and 'Pacific' by 808 State – all local bands and producers. The party known as Madchester was officially opened.

The party ended in 1992. Overdanced and overdrugged, the city woke up with a terrible hangover. The Haçienda went bust, Shaun Ryder's legendary drug intake stymied his musical creativity and the Stone Roses withdrew in a haze of postparty depression. The latter were not to be heard of again until 1994 when they released *Second Coming*, which just couldn't match their eponymous debut album. They lasted another two years before breaking up. The fertile crossover scene, which had seen clubbers go mad at rock gigs, and rock bands play the kind of dance sounds that kept the floor thumping until the early hours, virtually disappeared and the two genres withdrew into a more familiar isolation.

Madchester is legendary precisely because it is no more, but it was exciting. If you missed the party, you can get a terrific sense of what it was like by watching Michael Winterbottom's *24-Hour Party People* (2002), which captures the hedonism, extravagance and genius of Madchester's cast of characters; and the superb *Control* (2007) by Anton Corbijn, which tells the story of Ian Curtis, Joy Division's tragic lead singer.

home and grown up a decade ago. But fear not: there is still a terrific club scene and Manchester remains at the vanguard of dance-floor culture. There's a constantly changing mixture of club nights, so check the *Manchester Evening News* for details of what's on. Following are our favourite places.

TOP CHOICE Sankey's NIGHTCLUB
(www.sankeys.info; Radium St, Ancoats; ⏲10pm-3am Thu & Fri, 10pm-4am Sat) Sankey's has earned itself legendary status for being at the vanguard of dance music (Chemical Brothers, Daft Punk and others got their start here) and its commitment to top-class DJs is unwavering: these days, you'll hear the likes of Timo Maas, Seb Leger and Thomas Schumacher mix it up with the absolutely superb residents. Choon! The best way to get here is to board the free Disco Bus that picks up at locations throughout the city from 10.30pm to 2am Friday and Saturday, and between 10.10pm and 1am the rest of the week. See the website for details.

FAC 251: The Factory NIGHTCLUB
(www.factorymanchester.com; 112-118 Princess St; ⏲9.30pm-3am Mon-Sat) Tony Wilson's legendary Factory Records label HQ has been converted into a brand-new club and live-music venue part-owned by Peter Hook, ex-bass player of Joy Division and New Order.

Ex-Stone Roses bass player Mani is on the decks for Wednesday's Fuel.

South NIGHTCLUB
(4a South King St; ⌚10pm-3am Fri & Sat) An excellent basement club to kick off the weekend: Friday night is CWord with Strangerways, featuring everything from Ibrahim Ferrer to northern soul, and Saturday is the always excellent Disco Rescue with Clint Boon (once of the Inspiral Carpets), which is more of the same eclectic mix of alternative and dance.

Cinemas

Cornerhouse ART HOUSE
(www.cornerhouse.org; 70 Oxford St) Your only destination for good art-house releases; also has a gallery, bookshop and cafe.

Odeon Cinema MULTIPLE
(www.odeon.co.uk; The Printworks, Exchange Sq) An ultramodern 20-screen complex in the middle of the Printworks centre.

AMC Cinemas MULTIPLEX
(www.amccinemas.co.uk; The Great Northern, 235 Deansgate) A 16-screen multiplex in a retail centre that was formerly a goods warehouse for the Northern Railway Company.

Theatre

Green Room THEATRE
(☎0161-236 1677; 54 Whitworth St W) The premier fringe venue in town.

Manchester Opera House MUSIC VENUE
(☎0161-242 2509; www.manchestertheatres.co.uk; Quay St) West End shows and lavish musicals make up the bulk of the program.

Library Theatre THEATRE
(☎0161-236 7110; Central Library, St Peter's Sq) Old plays and new work in a small theatre beneath the Central Library.

Royal Exchange THEATR
(☎0161-833 9833; St Anne's Sq) Interesting contemporary plays are standard at this magnificent, modern theatre-in-the-round.

Live Music

ROCK MUSIC

Band on the Wall BAR
(www.bandonthewall.org; 25 Swan St) A top-notch venue that hosts everything from rock to world music, with splashes of jazz, blues and folk thrown in for good measure.

FAC 251: The Factory NIGHTCLUB
(www.factorymanchester.com; 112-118 Princess St; ⌚9.30pm-3am Mon-Sat) Indie rock is the mainstay of the live-music gigs at the former HQ of the legendary Factory Records. Gigs usually go from 9pm to 10.30pm.

MEN Arena VENUE
(Great Ducie St) A giant arena north of the centre that hosts large-scale rock concerts (as well as being the home of the city's ice-hockey and basketball teams). It's about 300m north of Victoria Station.

Moho Live VENUE
(www.moholive.com; 21-31 Oldham St) A new 500-capacity live-music venue that has already proven incredibly popular with its line-up of live music and club nights.

Ruby Lounge BAR
(☎0161-834 1392; 26-28 High St) Terrific live-music venue in the Northern Quarter that features mostly rock bands.

CLASSICAL MUSIC

Bridgewater Hall CONCERT HALL
(☎0161-907 9000; www.bridgewater-hall.co.uk; Lower Mosley St) The world-renowned Hallé Orchestra has its home at this enormous and impressive concert hall, which hosts up to 250 concerts and events a year. It has a widespread program that includes opera, folk music, children's shows, comedy and contemporary music.

Lowry THEATRE
(☎0161-876 2000; www.thelowry.com; Pier 8, Salford Quays) The Lowry has two theatres – the 1750-capacity Lyric and 460-capacity Quays – hosting a diverse range of performances, from dance to comedy.

Manchester Cathedral CATHEDRAL
(☎0161-833 2220; www.manchestercathedral.org; Victoria St) Hosts a summer season of concerts by the Cantata Choir and ensemble groups.

Royal Northern College of Music COLLEGE
(☎0161-907 5555; www.rncm.ac.uk; 124 Oxford Rd) Presents a full program of extremely high-quality classical music and other contemporary offerings.

Sport

For most people, Manchester plus sport equals football, and football means Manchester United. This is why United is covered in the Sights & Activities section. Manchester United's reign may be about to end as the scrappy underdog with the big heart that is Manchester City is poised to establish itself as a major presence in world football thanks to the arrival of a consortium of oil-rich sheiks.

Manchester City FOOTBALL
Manchester's best-loved team is the perennial underachiever, Manchester City. In 2008 the club was taken over by the Abu Dhabi United Group, who proceeded to invest £210 million (and counting) in new players and a new manager, all with the stated intent of becoming the most successful club in Britain. In the meantime, you can enjoy the **Manchester City Experience** (☎0870 062 1894; www.mcfc.co.uk; tours adult/child £7.50/6; ⊙tours 11am, 1.30pm & 3.30pm Mon-Sat, 11.45am, 1.45pm & 3.30pm Sun except match days) – a tour of the ground, dressing rooms and museum before the inevitable steer into the kit shop. Tours must be booked in advance. Take bus 53, 54, 185, 186, 216, 217, 230, 231, 232, 233, 234, 235, 236, 237, X36 or X37 from Piccadilly Gardens.

Lancashire County Cricket Club CRICKET
Cricket is a big deal here, and **Lancashire** (☎0161-282 4000; www.lccc.co.uk; Warwick Rd), founded in 1816 as the Aurora before changing its name in 1864, is one of the most beloved of England's county teams. This is despite the fact that it hasn't won the county championship since 1934. Matches are played at Old Trafford (same name, but different ground adjacent to the football stadium) and the key fixture in Lancashire's calendar is the Roses match against Yorkshire. If you're not around for that, the other games in the county season (admission £11 to £17) are a great day out. The season runs throughout the summer. International test matches are also played here occasionally. Take the Metrolink to Old Trafford.

Shopping

The huge selection of shops here will send a shopper's pulse into orbit; every taste and budget is catered for. The huge Millennium Quarter in the heart of the city centre encompasses the newly refurbed Arndale Centre and a host of high-street shops as well the upmarket boutiques of New Cathedral St. Otherwise, King St is full of lovely boutiques, while for all things boho just head to the Northern Quarter.

Oi Polloi BOUTIQUE
(www.oipolloi.com; 70 Tib St) Besides the impressive range of casual footwear, this trendy boutique also stocks a range of designers including APC, Lyle & Scott, Nudie Jeans and Fjallraven.

Thomas St Post Office BOUTIQUE
(www.thomasstpostoffice.com; 61 Thomas St) Carhartt, Edwin, Pointer and Undefeated are just some of the trendy labels represented on the racks of this lovely boutique housed in a converted post office.

Harvey Nichols DEPARTMENT STORE
(21 New Cathedral St) The king of British department stores has an elegant presence on fashionista row. The 2nd-floor **restaurant** (mains £8-16; ⊙lunch daily, dinner Tue-Sat) is excellent and even has a list of more than 400 different wines.

Tib Street Market MARKET
(Tib St; ⊙10am-5pm Sat) Up-and-coming local designers get a chance to display their wares at this relatively new weekly market where you can pick up everything from purses to lingerie and hats to jewellery.

Oxfam Originals VINTAGE
(Unit 8, Smithfield Bldg, Oldham St) If you're into retro, this terrific store has high-quality gear from the 1960s and '70s. Shop in the knowledge that it's for a good cause.

Rags to Bitches VINTAGE
(www.rags-to-bitches.co.uk; 60 Tib St) An award-winning vintage boutique with fashions from the 1930s to the '80s, this is the place to go to pick up unusual, individual pieces or that outfit for the fancy-dress ball.

Information

Bookshops

Cornerhouse (www.cornerhouse.org; 70 Oxford St) Art and film books, specialist magazines and kitschy cards.

Waterstone's Biggest bookshop in town, with branches on Deansgate and St Anne's Sq.

Emergency

Ambulance (☎0161-436 3999)

Police station (☎0161-872 5050; Bootle St)

Rape Crisis Centre (☎0161-273 4500)

Samaritans (☎0161-236 8000)

Internet Access

L2K Internet Gaming Cafe (32 Princess St; per 30min £2; ⊙9am-10pm Mon-Fri, 9am-9pm Sat & Sun)

Loops Computer (83 Princess St; per 30min £2; ⏲9am-10pm Mon-Fri, 9am-9pm Sat & Sun)

Internet Resources

Manchester After Dark (www.manchesterad.com) Reviews and descriptions of the best places to be when the sun goes down.

Manchester City Council (www.manchester.gov.uk) The council's official website, which includes a visitors' section.

Manchester Evening News (www.menmedia.co.uk) The city's evening paper in electronic form.

Manchester Online (www.manchesteronline.co.uk) Local online newspaper.

Real Manchester (www.realmanchester.com) Online guide to nightlife.

Restaurants of Manchester (www.restaurantsofmanchester.com) Thorough, reliable and up-to-date reviews of restaurants in the city and suburbs.

Virtual Manchester (www.manchester.com) Restaurants, pubs, clubs and where to sleep.

Visit Manchester (www.visitmanchester.com) The official website for Greater Manchester.

Medical Services

Cameolord Chemist (St Peter's Sq; ⏲10am-10pm)

Manchester Royal Infirmary (Oxford Rd)

Post

Post office (Brazennose St; ⏲9am-5.30pm Mon-Fri)

Tourist Information

Tourist office (www.visitmanchester.com; Piccadilly Plaza, Portland St; ⏲10am-5.15pm Mon-Sat, 10am-4.30pm Sun)

 Getting There & Away

Air

Manchester Airport (☎0161-489 3000; www.manchesterairport.co.uk), south of the city, is the largest airport outside London and is served by 13 locations throughout Britain as well as more than 50 international destinations.

Bus

National Express (www.nationalexpress.com) serves most major cities almost hourly from Chorlton St coach station in the city centre. Sample destinations:

Leeds £8.40, one hour, hourly

Liverpool £6.30, 1¼ hours, hourly

London £24.40, 3¾ hours, hourly

Train

Manchester Piccadilly (east of the Gay Village) is the main station for trains to and from the rest of the country, although Victoria station (north of the National Football Museum) serves Halifax and Bradford. The two stations are linked by Metrolink. Off-peak fares are considerably cheaper.

Blackpool £13.50, 1¼ hours, half-hourly

Liverpool Lime St £9.80, 45 minutes, half-hourly

London Euston £131, three hours, seven daily

Newcastle £51.20, three hours, six daily

 Getting Around

To/From the Airport

The airport is 12 miles south of the city. A train to or from Victoria station costs £2, and a coach is £3. A taxi is nearly four times as much in light traffic.

Public Transport

The excellent public transport system can be used with a variety of **Day Saver tickets** (bus £3.70, train £4, Metrolink £6, bus, train & Metrolink £10). For enquiries about local transport, including night buses, contact **Travelshop** (☎0161-228 7811; www.gmpte.com; 9 Portland St, Piccadilly Gardens; ⏲8am-8pm).

BUS Centreline bus 4 provides a free service around the heart of Manchester every 10 minutes. Pick up a route map from the tourist office. Most local buses start from Piccadilly Gardens.

METROLINK There are frequent **Metrolink** (www.metrolink.co.uk) trams between Victoria and Piccadilly train stations and G-Mex (for Castlefield), as well as further afield to Salford Quays. Buy your tickets from the platform machine.

TRAIN Castlefield is served by Deansgate station with rail links to Piccadilly, Oxford Rd and Salford stations.

CHESHIRE

Generally overshadowed by the loud, busy conurbations of Liverpool and Manchester, Cheshire gets on with life in a quiet, usually pastoral kind of way, happy enough with its reputation as a contemporary version of ye olde Englande. Fields full of Friesian cows are interspersed with clusters of half-timbered Tudor houses and working farmyards, an idyll that in recent decades has attracted the soccerati millionaires from the nearby cities, whose blinged up mansions remain largely unseen behind tall security walls. For the rest of us mere mortals, however, Cheshire is really just about Chester.

Chester

POP 80,130

Marvellous Chester is one of English history's greatest gifts to the contemporary visitor. Its red-sandstone wall, which today gift-wraps a tidy collection of Tudor and Victorian buildings, was built during Roman times. The town was then called Castra Devana, and was the largest Roman fortress in Britain.

It's hard to believe today, but throughout the Middle Ages Chester made its money as the most important port in the northwest. However, the River Dee silted up over time and Chester fell behind Liverpool in importance.

Sights & Activities

City Walls ARCHITECTURE

A good way to get a sense of Chester's unique character is to walk the 2-mile circuit along the walls that surround the historic centre. Originally built by the Romans around AD 70, the walls were altered substantially over the following centuries but have retained their current position since around 1200.

Of the many features along the walls, the most eye-catching is the prominent **East-**

Chester

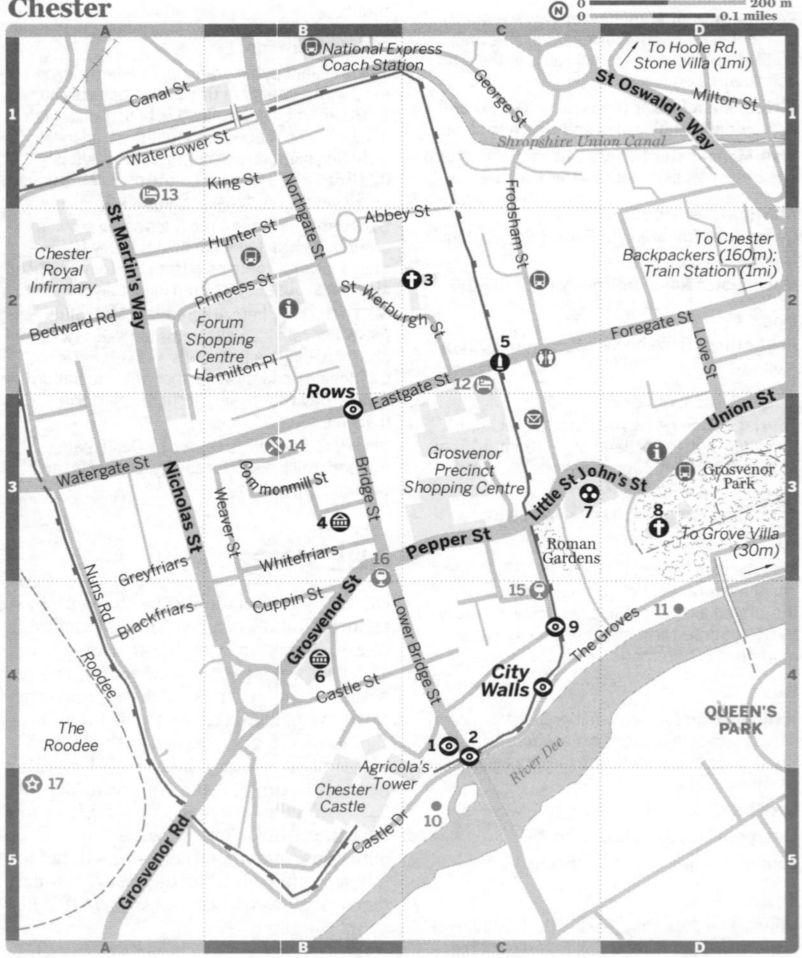

gate, where you can see the most famous **clock** in England after London's Big Ben, built for Queen Victoria's Diamond Jubilee in 1897.

At the southeastern corner of the walls are the **wishing steps**, added in 1785; local legend claims that if you can run up and down these uneven steps while holding your breath your wish will come true. We question the veracity of this claim because our wish was not to twist an ankle.

Just inside Southgate, known here as **Bridgegate** (as it's at the northern end of the Old Dee Bridge), is the 1664 **Bear & Billet** pub, Chester's oldest timber-framed building and once a tollgate into the city.

Rows ARCHITECTURE

Chester's other great draw is the **Rows**, a series of two-level galleried arcades along the four streets that fan out in each direction from the **Central Cross**. The architecture is a handsome mix of Victorian and Tudor (original and mock) buildings that house a fantastic collection of individually owned shops. The origin of the Rows is a little unclear, but it is believed that as the Roman walls slowly crumbled, medieval traders built their shops against the resulting rubble banks, while later arrivals built theirs on top.

Chester

Top Sights

City Walls ... C4
Rows ... B3

Sights

1 Bear & Billet ... C4
2 Bridgegate ... C4
3 Chester Cathedral ... C2
4 Dewa Roman Experience ... B3
5 Eastgate Clock ... C2
6 Grosvenor Museum ... B4
7 Roman Amphitheatre ... C3
8 St John the Baptist Church ... D3
9 Wishing Steps ... C4

Activities, Courses & Tours

10 Bithell Boats ... C5
11 Boat Hire ... D4

Sleeping

12 Chester Grosvenor Hotel & Spa ... C2
13 Chester Townhouse ... A1

Eating

Simon Radley at the Chester Grosvenor ... (see 12)
14 Upstairs at the Grill ... B3

Drinking

15 Albion ... C4
16 Falcon ... B3

Entertainment

17 Roodee ... A5

Chester Cathedral CATHEDRAL

(www.chestercathedral.com; Northgate St; adult/child £5/2.50; 9am-5pm Mon-Sat, 1-4pm Sun) Originally a Benedictine abbey built on the remains of an earlier Saxon church dedicated to St Werburgh (the city's patron saint), it was shut down in 1540 as part of Henry VIII's dissolution frenzy but reconsecrated as a cathedral the following year. Although the cathedral itself was given a substantial Victorian facelift, the 12th-century cloister and its surrounding buildings are essentially unaltered and retain much of the structure from the early monastic years. There are 1¼-hour **guided tours** (free; 9.30am-4pm Mon-Sat) to really get to grips with the building and its history.

FREE **Grosvenor Museum** MUSEUM

(www.grosvenormuseum.co.uk; Grosvenor St; 10.30am-5pm Mon-Sat, 2-5pm Sun) Excellent museum with the country's most comprehensive collection of Roman tombstones. At the back of the museum is a preserved Georgian house, complete with kitchen, drawing room, bedroom and bathroom.

Dewa Roman Experience MUSEUM

(www.dewaromanexperience.co.uk; Pierpoint Lane; adult/child £4.95/3.25; 9am-5pm Mon-Sat, 10am-5pm Sun) Walk through a reconstructed Roman street to reveal what Roman life was like. It's just off Bridge St.

FREE **Roman Amphitheatre** RUINS

Just outside the city walls is what was once an arena that seated 7000 spectators (making it the country's largest); now it's little more than steps buried in grass.

St John the Baptist Church CHURCH

(Vicar's Lane; 9.15am-6pm) Built on the site of an older Saxon church in 1075, it's been a peaceful ruin since 1581. It includes the remains of a Norman choir and medieval chapels.

Tours

The tourist office and Chester Visitors' Centre offer a broad range of walking tours departing from both centres. Each tour lasts between 1½ and two hours.

City Sightseeing Chester BUS TOURS
(01244-347452; www.city-sightseeing.com; adult/child £8.50/3; every 15-20min) Offers open-top bus tours of the city, picking up from the tourist office and Chester Visitors' Centre.

Bithell Boats BOAT TOURS
(01244-325394; www.chesterboats.co.uk) Runs 30-minute and hour-long cruises up and down the Dee, including a foray into the gorgeous Eaton Estate, home of the duke and duchess of Westminster. All departures are from the riverside along the promenade known as the Groves and cost from £6.50 to £14.

Chester Rows: The Inside Story WALKING TOURS
(adult/child £5/4; 2pm) The fascinating history of Chester's most outstanding architectural feature.

Ghosthunter Trail WALKING TOURS
(adult/child £5/4; 7.30pm Thu-Sat Jul-Oct) The ubiquitous ghost tour, looking for things that go bump in the night.

History Hunter WALKING TOURS
(adult/child £5/4; 10.30am) Two thousand years of Chester history.

Roman Soldier Patrol WALKING TOURS
(adult/child £5/4; 2pm Thu, Fri & Sat, Jul & Aug) Patrol Fortress Deva in the company of Caius Julius Quartus.

Taste of Chester WALKING TOURS
(adult/child £5/4; 2pm Thu & Sat May-Oct) Two thousand years of Chester history and samples of local produce.

Secret Chester WALKING TOURS
(adult/child £5/4; 2pm Tue, Thu, Sat & Sun May-Oct) Exactly what it says on the tin.

Sleeping

If you're visiting between Easter and September, you'd better book early if you want to avoid going over budget or settling for far less than you bargained for. Except for a handful of options most of the accommodation is outside the city walls but within easy walking distance of the centre.

TOP CHOICE **Green Bough** BOUTIQUE HOTEL £££
(01244-326241; www.chestergreenboughhotel.co.uk; 60 Hoole Rd; r from £150; P @) The epitome of the boutique hotel, this exclusive, award-winning Victorian town house has individually styled rooms dressed in the best Italian fabrics. The rooms come adorned with wall coverings, superb antique furniture and period cast-iron and wooden beds, including a handful of elegant four-posters.

Stone Villa B&B ££
(01244-345014; www.stonevillachester.co.uk; 3 Stone Pl, Hoole Rd; s/d from £45/75) Twice winner of Chester's B&B of the Year in the last 10 years, this beautiful villa has everything you need for a memorable stay. Elegant bedrooms (from standard to executive, which have flatscreen TVs), a fabulous breakfast and welcoming, friendly owners all add up to one of the best lodgings in town.

Chester Grosvenor Hotel & Spa HOTEL £££
(01244-324024; www.chestergrosvenor.com; 58 Eastgate St; r from £180; P @) This hotel is perfectly located and has huge, sprawling rooms with exquisite period furnishings and all mod cons. The spa (which is open to nonguests) offers a range of body treatments, including reiki, LaStone therapy, Indian head massage and four-handed massage. There's also a Michelin-starred restaurant downstairs.

Chester Backpackers HOSTEL £
(01244-400185; www.chesterbackpackers.co.uk; 67 Boughton; dm from £13.50;) Comfortable dorm rooms with nice pine beds in a typically Tudor white-and-black building. It's just a short walk from the city walls and there's also a pleasant garden.

Other good options:

Bawn Lodge B&B ££
(01244-324971; www.bawnlodge.co.uk; 10 Hoole Rd; r from £75; P) Spotless rooms with plenty of colour make this charming guest house a very pleasant option. Rates go up during the Chester Races.

Chester Townhouse B&B ££
(01244-350021; www.chestertownhouse.co.uk; 23 King St; s/d £45/75; P) Five beautifully decorated rooms in a handsome 17th-century house within the city walls make Chester Townhouse a terrific option – you're close to the action and you'll sleep in relative luxury.

Grove Villa B&B ££
(01244-349713; www.grovevillachester.com; 18 The Groves; r from £65; P) A wonderfully positioned Victorian home overlooking

the Dee. The rooms have antique beds and great river views.

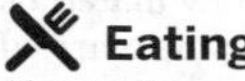

Eating

Chester has great food – it's just not in any of the tourist-oriented restaurants that line the Rows. Besides the better restaurants, you'll find the best grub in some of the pubs (see p551).

Upstairs at the Grill STEAKHOUSE £££
(☎01244-344883; www.upstairsatthegrill.co.uk; 70 Watergate St; mains £15-25; ⏲dinner Mon-Sat, lunch & dinner Sun) A superb Manhattan-style steakhouse almost hidden on the 2nd floor, this is the place to devour every cut of meat from American-style porterhouse to a sauce-sodden chateaubriand.

Simon Radley at the Chester Grosvenor FRENCH £££
(☎01244-895618; www.chestergrosvenor.com; Chester Grosvenor Hotel & Spa, 58 Eastgate St; 3-course à la carte £89; ⏲dinner Tue-Sat) Formerly the Arkle, the hotel opted to rename the Michelin-starred restaurant in recognition of their brilliant head chef, whose French-influenced cuisine continues to earn rave reviews. Bookings are most definitely required.

Old Harker's Arms PUB ££
(www.harkers arms-chester.co.uk; 1 Russell St; mains £9-14; ⏲11am-late) An old-style boozer with a gourmet kitchen, this is the perfect place to tuck into Cumberland sausages or a Creole rice salad with sweet potatoes, and then rinse your palate with a pint of local ale such as Cheshire Cat or a 'guest beer' from around the country. To get here, follow Eastgate St east for 100m and take a left onto Russell St.

Drinking

Albion PUB
(4 Albion St) No children, no music, and no machines or big screens (but plenty of Union Jacks). This 'family hostile' Edwardian classic pub is a throwback to a time when ale-drinking still had its own *rituals*. Still, this is one of the finest pubs in northwest England precisely because it doggedly refuses to modernise.

Falcon PUB
(Lower Bridge St) This is an old-fashioned boozer with a lovely atmosphere; the surprisingly adventurous menu offers up dishes such as Jamaican peppered beef or spicy Italian sausage casserole. Great for both a pint and a bite (mains from £5.50).

Entertainment

Roodee HORSE RACING
(www.chester-races.co.uk; ⏲May-Sep) Chester's ancient and very beautiful racetrack is on the western side of the walls, which has been hosting races since the 16th century. Highlights of the summer flat season include the two-day July Festival and the August equivalent.

Information

Cheshire Constabulary (☎01244-350000; Town Hall, Northgate St)

Chester Visitors' Centre (www.visitchester.com; Vicar's Lane; ⏲9.30am-5.30pm Mon-Sat, 10am-4pm Sun)

Countess of Chester Hospital (☎01244-365000; Health Park, Liverpool Rd)

Post office (2 St John St; ⏲9am-5.30pm Mon-Sat)

Tourist office (www.chester.gov.uk; Town Hall, Northgate St; ⏲9am-5.30pm Mon-Sat, 10am-4pm Sun)

Getting There & Away

Bus

National Express (www.nationalexpress.com) coaches stop on Vicar's Lane, just opposite the tourist office by the Roman amphitheatre. Destinations include the following:

Birmingham £12.40, 2¼ hours, four daily

Liverpool £7.20, one hour, four daily

London £24.60, 5½ hours, three daily

Manchester £6.80, 1¼ hours, three daily

For information on local bus services, ring the **Cheshire Bus Line** (☎01244-602666). Local buses leave from the Town Hall Bus Exchange on Princess St.

Train

The train station is about a mile from the city centre via Foregate St and City Rd, or Brook St. City-Rail Link buses are free for people with rail tickets, and operate between the station and Bus Stop A on Frodsham St. Destinations:

Liverpool £4.35, 45 minutes, hourly

London Euston £65.20, 2½ hours, hourly

Manchester £12.60, one hour, hourly

Getting Around

Much of the city centre is closed to traffic from 10.30am to 4.30pm, so a car is likely to be a hindrance. Anyway, the city is easy to walk around and most places of interest are close to the wall.

City buses depart from the Town Hall Bus Exchange.

Chester Zoo

The largest of its kind in the country, **Chester Zoo** (www.chesterzoo.org; adult/child £16.90/12.45; ⏲10am-dusk, last admission 4pm Mon-Fri, till 5pm Sat & Sun) is about as pleasant a place as caged animals in artificial renditions of their natural habitats could ever expect to live. It's so big that there's even a **monorail** (adult/child £2/1.50) and a **waterbus** (adult/child £2/1.50) on which to get around. The zoo is on the A41, 3 miles north of Chester's city centre. Buses 11C and 12C (every 15 minutes Monday to Saturday, half-hourly Sunday) run between Chester's Town Hall Bus Exchange and the zoo.

LIVERPOOL

POP 469,020

Beleaguered by a history of hard times and chronic misfortune, Liverpool's luck has changed dramatically in recent years. The city centre, which for decades was an unattractive mix of ugly retail outlets and depressing dereliction, is in the process of being transformed, largely on the back of a substantial program of urban regeneration.

Besides giving us a host of new buildings such as the impressive, ultraswish Liverpool ONE shopping district, the city's rebirth has breathed new life into its magnificent cultural heritage, established more than 200 years ago when the city was a thriving trading port and one of the empire's most important cities. This legacy of power is best exemplified by the magnificent waterfront around Albert Dock, which has more listed buildings than any city in England except London and is now a Unesco World Heritage Site. Now home to some of the best museums and galleries north of the Watford Gap, Albert Dock is proof that Liverpool doesn't want to celebrate its glorious past as much as create an exciting, contemporary equivalent of it.

The main attractions are Albert Dock (west of the city centre), and the trendy Ropewalks area (south of Hanover St and west of the two cathedrals). Lime St station, the Paradise St bus station, the 08 Place tourist office and the Cavern Quarter – a mecca for Beatles fans – lie just to the north.

History

Liverpool grew wealthy on the back of the triangular trading of slaves, raw materials and finished goods. From 1700 ships carried cotton goods and hardware from Liverpool to West Africa, where they were exchanged for slaves, who in turn were carried to the West Indies and Virginia, where they were exchanged for sugar, rum, tobacco and raw cotton.

As a great port, the city drew thousands of Irish and Scottish immigrants, and its Celtic influences are still apparent. However, between 1830 and 1930 nine million emigrants – mainly English, Scots and Irish, but also Swedes, Norwegians and Russian Jews – sailed from here for the New World.

The start of WWII led to a resurgence of Liverpool's importance. More than one million American GIs disembarked here before D-Day and the port was, once again, hugely important as the western gateway for transatlantic supplies. The GIs brought with them the latest American records, and Liverpool was thus the first European port of call for the new rhythm and blues that would eventually become rock and roll. Within 20 years, the Mersey Beat was *the* sound of British pop, and four mop-topped Scousers had formed a skiffle band...

Sights

The wonderful Albert Dock is the city's biggest tourist attraction and the key to understanding the city's history, but the city centre is where you'll find most of Liverpool's real day-to-day life.

CITY CENTRE

FREE **World Museum Liverpool** MUSEUM (www.liverpoolmuseums.org.uk/wml; William Brown St; ⏲10am-5pm) Natural history, science and technology are the themes of this sprawling museum, whose exhibits range from birds of prey to space exploration. It also includes the country's only free planetarium. This vastly entertaining and educational museum is divided into four major sections: the **Human World**, one of the top anthropological collections in the country; the **Natural World**, which includes a new aquarium as well as live insect colonies; **Earth**, a geological treasure trove; and **Space & Time**, which includes the planetarium. Highly recommended.

LIVERPOOL IN…

Two Days

Head to the waterfront and explore the Albert Dock museums – the **Tate Liverpool**, the **Merseyside Maritime Museum** and the unmissable **International Slavery Museum** – before paying tribute to the Fab Four at the **Beatles Story**. Keep to the Beatles theme and head north towards the Cavern Quarter around Mathew St before surrendering to the retail giant that is **Liverpool ONE**, with its hundreds of shops. Round off your evening with dinner at **London Carriage Works** and a pint at the marvellous **Philharmonic**, and wrap yourself in the crisp linen sheets of the **Hope Street Hotel**. Night hawks can tear it up in the bars and clubs of the hip **Ropewalks** area. The next day, explore the city's two **cathedrals** and check out the twin delights of the **World Museum Liverpool** and the **Walker Art Gallery**.

Four Days

Follow the two-day itinerary but add in a **Yellow Duckmarine Tour** to experience the docks from the water.On day three, make a pilgrimage to **Mendips** and **20 Forthlin Rd**, the childhood homes of John Lennon and Paul McCartney respectively. That evening, get some good Italian food at the **Italian Club**. The next day, walk on holy ground at Anfield, home of **Liverpool Football Club**. Race junkies can head out to the visitor centre at **Aintree racecourse**, which hosts England's most beloved race, the Grand National.

FREE **Walker Art Gallery** GALLERY
(www.liverpoolmuseums.org.uk/walker; William Brown St; ⏲10am-5pm) Touted as the 'National Gallery of the North', the city's foremost gallery is the national gallery for northern England, housing an outstanding collection of art from the 14th to the 21st centuries. Its strong suits are Pre-Raphaelite art, modern British art and sculpture – not to mention the rotating exhibits of contemporary expression. It's a family-friendly place, too: the ground-floor **Big Art for Little People** gallery is designed especially for under-eights and features interactive exhibits and games that will (hopefully) result in a life-long love affair with art.

Liverpool Cathedral CATHEDRAL
(www.liverpoolcathedral.org.uk; Hope St; ⏲8am-6pm) Liverpool's Anglican cathedral is a building of superlatives. Not only is it Britain's largest church, it's also the world's largest Anglican cathedral, and it's all thanks to Sir Giles Gilbert Scott, who made its construction his life's work. Sir Scott also gave us the red telephone box and the Southwark Power Station in London, now the Tate Modern. The central bell is the world's third-largest (with the world's highest and heaviest peal), while the organ, with its 9765 pipes, is likely the world's largest operational model.

The visitor centre features the **Great Space** (adult/child £5/3.50; ⏲9am-4pm Mon-Sat, noon-2.30pm Sun), a 10-minute, panoramic high-definition movie about the history of the cathedral. It's followed by your own audiovisual tour, courtesy of a snazzy headset.

Your ticket also gives you access to the cathedral's 101m tower, from which there are terrific views of the city and beyond – on a clear day you can see Blackpool Tower.

FREE **St George's Hall** CULTURAL CENTRE
(www.stgeorgesliverpool.co.uk; William Brown St; ⏲10am-5pm Tue-Sat, 1-5pm Sun) Arguably Liverpool's most impressive building is the Grade I–listed St George's Hall, a magnificent example of neoclassical architecture that is as imposing today as it was when it was completed in 1854. Curiously, it was built as law courts *and* a concert hall – presumably a judge could pass sentence and then relax to a string quartet. Today it serves as an all-purpose cultural and civic centre, hosting concerts, corporate gigs and a host of other civic get-togethers; it is also the focal point of any city-wide celebration. **Tours** (☎0151-225 6909; £3.50; ⏲2pm Wed, 11am & 2pm Sat & Sun) of the hall are run in conjunction with the tourist office; the tour route can vary depending on what's going on in the building.

Liverpool

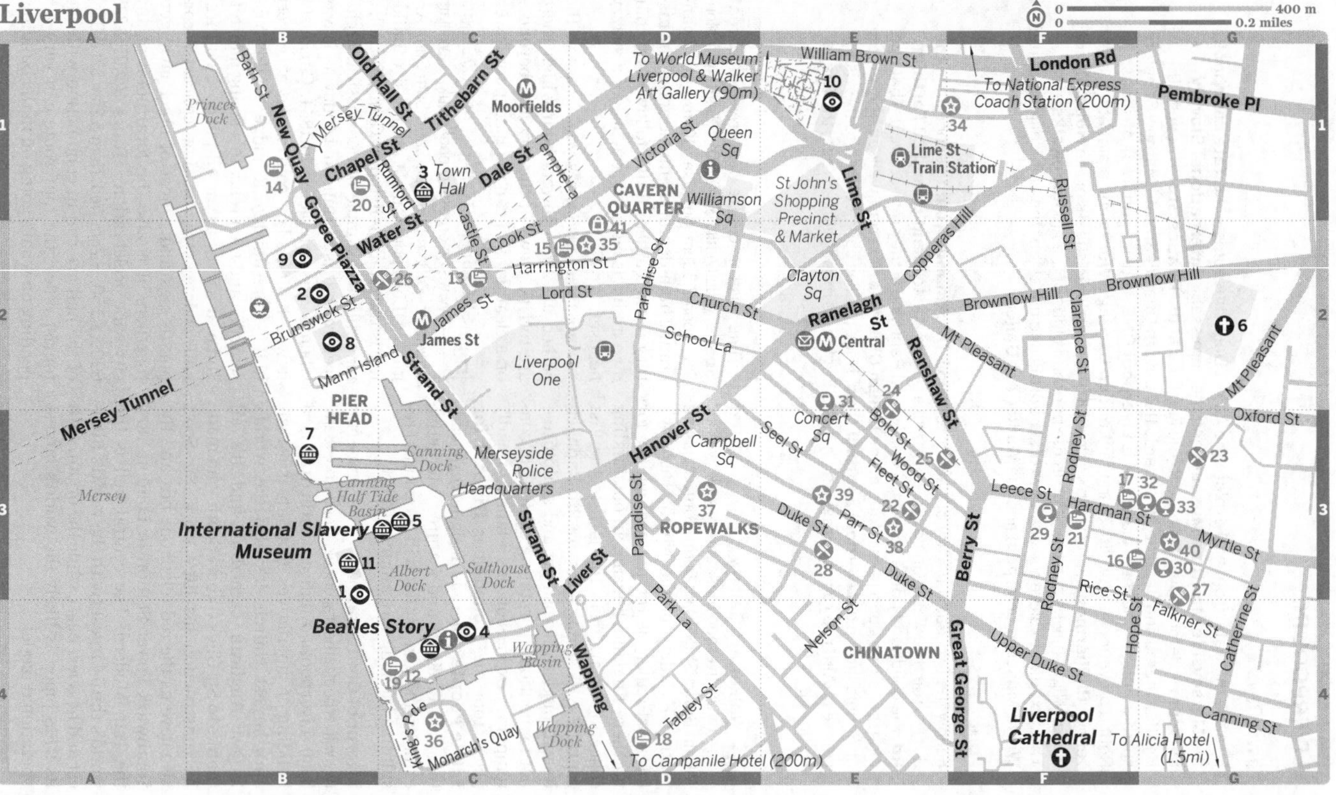
0 400 m
0 0.2 miles
A
B
C
D
E
F
G
1
2
3
4
Bath St
Princes Dock
New Quay
Mersey Tunnel
Old Hall St
Tithebarn St
Moorfields
Chapel St
Rumford St
3 Town Hall
Dale St
Temple La
Water St
Goree Piazza
Castle St
Cook St
Victoria St
To World Museum Liverpool & Walker Art Gallery (90m)
William Brown St
10
London Rd
To National Express Coach Station (200m)
Pembroke Pl
34
Lime St Train Station
Queen Sq
CAVERN QUARTER
Williamson Sq
St John's Shopping Precinct & Market
Lime St
Copperas Hill
Russell St
14
20
41
15
35
Harrington St
13
26
9
2
8
Brunswick St
James St
Lord St
Paradise St
Church St
Clayton Sq
Ranelagh St
Central
Brownlow Hill
Clarence St
6
Mt Pleasant
School La
Liverpool One
Mann Island
Strand St
PIER HEAD
Mersey Tunnel
7
Canning Dock
Merseyside Police Headquarters
Hanover St
Campbell Sq
Seel St
Concert Sq
31
24
Bold St
Renshaw St
Oxford St
23
Wood St
25
Fleet St
Leece St
Rodney St
17 32
33
Hardman St
Mersey
Canning Half Tide Basin
5
International Slavery Museum
11
Albert Dock
Salthouse Dock
1
Beatles Story
4
37
ROPEWALKS
39
Duke St
22
Parr St
38
28
Berry St
29
21
40
Myrtle St
16
30
Rice St
27
Falkner St
Hope St
Catherine St
Liver St
Park La
Nelson St
CHINATOWN
Upper Duke St
Wapping Basin
Wapping
19
12
King's Pde
36
Monarch's Quay
Wapping Dock
Tabley St
18
To Campanile Hotel (200m)
Great George St
Liverpool Cathedral
To Alicia Hotel (1.5mi)
Canning St

Liverpool

Top Sights
- Beatles Story C4
- International Slavery Museum C3
- Liverpool Cathedral F4

Sights
- 1 Bugworld Experience B3
- 2 Cunard Building B2
- 3 Liverpool War Museum C1
- 4 Magical Mystery Tour Bus Stop C4
- 5 Merseyside Maritime Museum C3
- 6 Metropolitan Cathedral of Christ the King G2
- 7 Museum of Liverpool B3
- 8 Port of Liverpool Building B2
- 9 Royal Liver Building B2
- 10 St George's Hall E1
- 11 Tate Liverpool B3

Activities, Courses & Tours
- 12 Yellow Duckmarine Tour Bus Stop C4

Sleeping
- 13 62 Castle St C2
- 14 Crowne Plaza Liverpool B1
- 15 Hard Days Night Hotel C2
- 16 Hope Street Hotel F3
- 17 International Inn F3
- 18 Liverpool YHA D4
- 19 Premier Inn C4
- 20 Racquet Club B1
- 21 Roscoe House F3

Eating
- 22 Alma de Cuba E3
- 23 Everyman Bistro G3
- 24 Italian Club E2
- 25 Italian Club Fish E3
- London Carriage Works .... (see 16)
- 26 Meet Argentinean C2
- 27 Quarter G3
- 28 Sapporo Teppanyaki E3

Drinking
- 29 Hannah's F3
- 30 Korova G3
- 31 Lime Kiln (Loyd's Bar) E2
- 32 Magnet G3
- 33 Philharmonic G3

Entertainment
- 34 Academy F1
- 35 Cavern Club D2
- 36 ECHO Arena C4
- Everyman Theatre .... (see 23)
- 37 Le Bateau D3
- 38 Masque E3
- 39 Nation E3
- 40 Philharmonic Hall G3

Shopping
- 41 Beatles Shop D2

Metropolitan Cathedral of Christ the King CATHEDRAL
(www.liverpoolmetrocathedral.org.uk; Mt Pleasant; ⏲8am-6pm Mon-Sat, 8am-5pm Sun Oct-Mar) Known colloquially as Paddy's Wigwam, Liverpool's Catholic cathedral is a mightily impressive modern building that looks like a soaring concrete teepee, hence its nickname. It was completed in 1967 according to the design of Sir Frederick Gibberd, and after the original plans by Sir Edwin Lutyens, whose crypt is inside. The central tower frames the world's largest stained-glass window, created by John Piper and Patrick Reyntiens.

Liverpool War Museum MUSEUM
(www.liverpoolwarmuseum.co.uk; 1 Rumford St; adult/child £5.50/3.75; ⏲10.30am-4.30pm Mon-Thu & Sat) The secret command centre for the Battle of the Atlantic in the Western Approaches, it was abandoned at the end of the war with virtually everything left intact. You can get a good glimpse of the labyrinthine nerve centre of Allied operations, including the all-important map room, where you can imagine playing a real-life, full-scale version of Risk.

ALBERT DOCK

Liverpool's biggest tourist attraction is **Albert Dock** (admission free), 2.75 hectares of water ringed by enormous cast-iron columns and impressive five-storey warehouses; these make up the country's largest collection of protected buildings and are a World Heritage Site. A fabulous development program has really brought the dock to life; here you'll find several outstanding museums and an extension of London's Tate Gallery, as well as a couple of top-class restaurants and bars.

TOP CHOICE **International Slavery Museum** MUSEUM
(www.liverpoolmuseums.org.uk/ism; Albert Dock; admission free; ⏲10am-5pm) Museums are, by their very nature, like a still of the past, but the extraordinary International Slavery Museum resonates very much in the present. It reveals slavery's unimaginable horrors – including Liverpool's own role in the triangular slave trade – in a clear and uncompromising manner. It does this through a remarkable series of multimedia and other displays, and it doesn't baulk at confronting racism, slavery's shadowy ideological justification for this inhumane practice.

It's heady, disturbing stuff, but as well as providing an insightful history lesson, we are reminded of our own obligations to humanity and justice throughout the museum, not least in the Legacies of Slavery exhibit, which explores the continuing fight for freedom and equality. A visit to this magnificent museum is unmissable.

Beatles Story MUSEUM
(www.beatlesstory.com; Albert Dock; adult/child £12.95/6.50; ⏲9am-7pm, last admission 5pm) Liverpool's most popular museum won't illuminate any dark, juicy corners in the turbulent history of the world's most famous foursome – there's ne'er a mention of internal discord, drugs or Yoko Ono – but there's plenty of genuine memorabilia to keep a Beatles fan happy. The museum is also the departure point for the Yellow Duckmarine Tour (see p557).

FREE **Merseyside Maritime Museum** MUSEUM
(www.liverpoolmuseums.org.uk/maritime; Albert Dock; ⏲10am-5pm) The story of one of the world's great ports is the theme of this excellent museum and, believe us, it's a graphic and compelling page-turner. One of the many great exhibits is Emigration to a New World, which tells the story of nine million emigrants and their efforts to get to North America and Australia; the walk-through model of a typical ship shows just how tough conditions on board really were.

FREE **Tate Liverpool** GALLERY
(www.tate.org.uk/liverpool; Albert Dock; special exhibitions adult/child from £5/4; ⏲10am-5.50pm) Touted as the home of modern art in the north, this gallery features a substantial checklist of 20th-century artists across its four floors, as well as touring exhibitions from the mother ship on London's Bankside. But it's all a little sparse, with none of the energy we'd expect from the world-famous Tate.

FREE **Bugworld Experience** MUSEUM
(www.bugworldexperience.co.uk; Grand Hall, Colonnades, Albert Dock; ⏲10am-5pm) Get up close and personal with 36 different species of bug and insect by clambering around six distinctive habitats; see the world from their eyes; and, for an extra-special treat, sample some oven-baked tarantula, chilli locusts or a meal worm pancake. This is just part of the fun at this brand-new interactive museum, which will surely have the kids pestering you to buy a book on insects and their funny habits when you're done.

NORTH OF ALBERT DOCK

The area to the north of Albert Dock is known as **Pier Head**, after a stone pier built in the 1760s. This is still the departure point for ferries across the River Mersey, and was, for millions of migrants, their final contact with European soil.

Their story – and that of the city in general both past and present – will be told in the eye-catching, giant-X-shaped **Museum of Liverpool** (Mann Island) currently being built on an area known as Mann Island and not slated to open until sometime in 2011. Until then, this part of the dock will continue to be dominated by a trio of Edwardian buildings known as the 'Three Graces', dating from the days when Liverpool's star was still ascending. The southernmost, with the dome mimicking St Paul's Cathedral, is the **Port of Liverpool Building**, completed in 1907. Next to it is the **Cunard Building**, in the style of an Italian palazzo, once HQ to the Cunard Steamship Line. Finally, the **Royal Liver Building** (pronounced *lie*-ver) was opened in 1911 as the head office of the Royal Liver Friendly Society. It's crowned by Liverpool's symbol, the famous 5.5m copper Liver Bird.

Tours

Beatles Fab Four Taxi Tour MUSIC TOURS
(☎0151-601 2111; www.thebeatlesfabfourtaxitour.co.uk; per tour £50) Get your own personalised 2½-hour tour of the city's mop-top landmarks. Pick-ups arranged when booking. Up to five people per tour.

Magical Mystery Tour MUSIC TOURS
(☎0151-709 3285; www.beatlestour.org; per person £14.95; ⏲2.30pm year-round, plus noon Sat Jul &

LIVERPOOL FOR CHILDREN

The museums on Albert Dock are extremely popular with kids, especially the brand-new **Bugworld Experience** (p556) and the **Merseyside Maritime Museum** (p556) – which has a couple of boats for kids to mess about on. The **Yellow Duckmarine Tour** (p557) is a sure-fire winner. The Big Art for Little People gallery at the **Walker Art Gallery** (p552) is perfect for kids who want to find out that art is more than just something adults stare at.

Need a break from the tots? Drop them off at **Zoe's Childminding Service** (☎0151-228 2685; 15 Woodbourne Rd), about 2 miles east of the city centre.

Aug) Two-hour tour that takes in all Beatles-related landmarks – their birthplaces, childhood homes, schools and places such as Penny Lane and Strawberry Field – before finishing up in the Cavern Club (which isn't the original). Departs from outside the tourist office at the 08 Place.

Yellow Duckmarine Tour BOAT TOURS
(☎0151-708 7799; www.theyellowduckmarine.co.uk; adult/child £11.95/9.95; ⏲from 11am) Take to the dock waters in a WWII amphibious vehicle after a quickie tour of the city centre's main points of interest. It's not especially educational, but it is a bit of fun. Departs from Albert Dock, near the Beatles Story.

Festivals & Events

Aintree Festival HORSE RACING
(www.aintree.co.uk) A three-day race meeting culminating in the world-famous Grand National steeplechase, held on the first Saturday in April.

Merseyside International Street Festival CULTURE
(www.brouhaha.uk.com) A three-week extravaganza of world culture beginning in mid-July and featuring indoor and outdoor performances by artists and musicians from pretty much everywhere.

Creamfields MUSIC
(www.cream.co.uk) An alfresco dance-fest that brings together some of the world's best DJs and dance acts during the last weekend in August. It takes place at the Daresbury Estate near Halton, Cheshire.

Mathew St Festival MUSIC
(☎0151-239 9091; www.mathewstreetfestival.org) The world's biggest tribute to the Beatles features six days of music, a convention and a memorabilia auction during the last week of August.

Sleeping

There are some pretty fancy pillows upon which to lay your head, from sexy boutique hotels to stylish upmarket properties. For the rest, it's all about standard business hotels and midrange chains. Beds are rarer than hen's teeth when Liverpool FC are playing at home (it's less of an issue with Everton) and during the mobbed out Beatles convention in the last week of August. If you fancy self-catering options, the tourist office has all the information you need.

CITY CENTRE

Hope Street Hotel BOUTIQUE HOTEL £££
(☎0151-709 3000; www.hopestreethotel.co.uk; 40 Hope St; r/ste from £120/180; @) Luxurious Liverpool's pre-eminent flag-waver is this stunning boutique hotel, on the city's most elegant street. King-sized beds draped in Egyptian cotton, oak floors with underfloor heating; LCD wide-screen TVs and sleek modern bathrooms (with REN bath and beauty products) are but the most obvious touches of class at this supremely cool address. Breakfast, taken in the marvellous London Carriage Works, is not included.

Racquet Club BOUTIQUE HOTEL ££
(☎0151-236 6676; www.racquetclub.org.uk; Hargreaves Bldg, 5 Chapel St; r £110;) Eight individually styled rooms with influences that range from French country house to Japanese minimalist chic (often in the same room) make this boutique hotel one of the most elegant choices in town. Antique beds, sumptuous Frette linen, free-standing baths and exclusive toiletries are all teasers to a pretty classy stay.

International Inn HOSTEL £
(☎0151-709 8135; www.internationalinn.co.uk; 4 South Hunter St; dm/d from £15/36;) A superb converted warehouse in the middle of uni-land: heated rooms with tidy wooden beds and bunks accommodate from two to 10 people. Facilities include a lounge, baggage storage, laundry and 24-hour front desk. The staff is terrific and CafeLatte.net internet cafe is next door.

62 Castle St BOUTIQUE HOTEL ££
(0151-702 7898; www.62castlest.com; 62 Castle St; r from £79; P @) This elegant property – voted one of Britain's top 100 lodgings in 2010 by the *Sunday Times* – successfully blends the traditional Victorian features of the building with a sleek, contemporary style. The 20 fabulously different suites come with HD plasma screen TVs, drench showers and Elemis toiletries as standard.

Hard Days Night Hotel HOTEL £££
(0151-236 1964; www.harddaysnighthotel.com; Central Bldgs, North John St; r £110-160, ste £750; @) You don't have to be a fan to stay here, but it helps: unquestionably luxurious, the 110 ultramodern, fully equipped rooms are decorated with specially commissioned drawings of the Beatles. And if you opt for one of the suites, named after Lennon and McCartney, you'll get a white baby grand piano in the style of 'Imagine' and a bottle of fancy bubbly on arrival.

Roscoe House BOUTIQUE HOTEL ££
(0151-709 0286; www.hotelliverpool.net; 27 Rodney St; r from £50;) A handsome Georgian home once owned by Liverpool-born writer and historian William Roscoe (1753–1831) has been given the once-over and is now a chic boutique hotel. The elegant rooms combine period touches (original coving, fireplaces and furnishings) with contemporary comforts such as flatscreen TVs and fancy Egyptian cotton linen.

Alicia Hotel HOTEL ££
(0151-727 4411; www.feathers.uk.com; 3 Aigburth Dr, Sefton Park; r from £84; P) Once a wealthy cotton merchant's home, this is a handsome place. Most of the rooms have extra luxuries, such as CD players and PlayStations. There's also a nice park on the grounds. The hotel is southeast of the city centre.

AROUND ALBERT DOCK

Crowne Plaza Liverpool HOTEL ££
(0151-243 8000; www.cpliverpool.com; St Nicholas Pl, Princes Dock, Pier Head; r from £79; P @) The paragon of the modern and luxurious business hotel, the Crowne Plaza has a marvellous waterfront location and plenty of facilities including a health club and swimming pool.

Liverpool YHA HOSTEL £
(0845 371 9527; www.yha.org.uk; 25 Tabley St; dm incl breakfast from £16; P) It may have the look of an Eastern European apartment complex, but this award-winning hostel, adorned with plenty of Beatles memorabilia, is one of the most comfortable you'll find anywhere in the country. The dorms with attached bathroom even have heated towel rails.

Other dockside options:

Campanile Hotel HOTEL ££
(0151-709 8104; www.campanile-liverpool-queens-dock.co.uk; Chaloner St, Queen's Dock; r from £50; P) Functional, motel-style rooms in a purpose-built hotel. Great location and perfect for families – children under 12 stay for free.

Premier Inn HOTEL ££
(0870 990 6432; www.premierinn.co.uk; Albert Dock; r from £49; P) Decent chain hotel about two steps away from the Beatles Story museum on Albert Dock.

Eating

Top grade international cuisine, the best of British and the greasy spoon...you'll find plenty of choices to satisfy every taste. Best spots include Ropewalks, along Hardman St and Hope St, or along Nelson St in the heart of Chinatown.

Italian Club ITALIAN £
(85 Bold St; mains £6-10; 10am-7pm Mon-Sat) The Crolla family must have been homesick for southern Italy, so they opened this fabulous spot, adorned it with family pictures and began serving the kind of food relatives visiting from the home country would be glad to tuck into. They've been so successful that they recently opened **Italian Club Fish** (0151-707 2110; 128 Bold St; mains £8-14; Tue-Sun) just down the street, specialising in, erm, fish.

London Carriage Works MODERN BRITISH £££
(0151-705 2222; www.thelondoncarriageworks.co.uk; 40 Hope St; 2-/3-course meals £15/20, mains £14-33) Liverpool's dining revolution is being led by Paul Askew's award-winning restaurant, which successfully blends ethnic influences from around the globe with staunch British favourites and serves up the result in a beautiful dining room – actually more of a bright glass box divided only by a series of sculpted glass shards. Reservations are recommended.

Everyman Bistro CAFE £
(0151-708 9545; www.everyman.co.uk; 13 Hope St; mains £5-8; noon-2am Mon-Fri, 11am-2am

Sat, 7-10.30pm Sun) Out-of-work actors and other creative types on a budget make this great cafe-restaurant (beneath the Everyman Theatre) their second home – with good reason. Great tucker and a terrific atmosphere.

Alma de Cuba CUBAN £££
(www.alma-de-cuba.com; St Peter's Church, Seel St; mains £16-24) This extraordinary venture has seen the transformation of a Polish church into a Miami-style Cuban extravaganza: a bar and restaurant where you can feast on a suckling pig (the menu heavily favours meat) or clink a perfectly made mojito at the long bar. *¡Salud!*

Meet Argentinean STEAKHOUSE ££
(☎0151-258 1816; www.meetrestaurant.co.uk; 2 Brunswick St; mains £11-26) Liverpool's first Argentine restaurant is really an elegant tribute to grilled beef served the size of a small wheel – just as any self-respecting gaucho would demand. Thankfully there are some cuts that are smaller but just as good; the 450g grilled fillet steak was plenty for us.

Other dining options:

Sapporo Teppanyaki JAPANESE £££
(☎0151-705 3005; www.sapporo.co.uk; 134 Duke St; teppanyaki sets £25-40, mains £15-25) As good a teppan-yaki (food that is grilled on a hot plate in front of you) experience as you'll have outside of Japan. Also decent sushi and sashimi.

Quarter BISTRO ££
(☎0151-707 1965; 7-11 Falkner St; mains £9-13) A gorgeous little wine bar and bistro with outdoor seating for that elusive summer's day.

Drinking

Unless specified, all the bars included here open 11am until 2am Monday to Saturday, although most have a nominal entry charge after 11pm.

Magnet DJ BAR
(39 Hardman St; ⌚11am-2am Mon-Sat) Red leather booths, plenty of velvet and a suitably seedy New York–dive atmosphere where Iggy Pop or Tom Waits would feel right at home. The upstairs bar is very cool but totally chilled out, while downstairs the dance floor shakes to the best music in town, spun by up-and-comers and supported with guest slots by some of England's most established DJs.

Philharmonic PUB
(36 Hope St; ⌚11am-11.30pm) This extraordinary bar, designed by the shipwrights who built the *Lusitania,* is one of the most beautiful bars in all of England. The interior is resplendent with etched and stained glass, wrought iron, mosaics and ceramic tiling – and if you think that's good, just wait until you see inside the marble men's toilets, the only heritage-listed lav in the country.

Korova MUSIC BAR
(32 Hope St; ⌚11am-2am Mon-Sat) A new, supercool bar that takes its name from the Russian for 'cow' (fans of *A Clockwork Orange* take note), it is a great place to drink, hang out and hear some decent live music from a range of up-and-coming bands. Very trendy, but not at all stuck up.

Hannah's BAR
(2 Leece St; ⌚11am-2am Mon-Sat) One of the top student bars in town. Try to land yourself a table on the outdoor patio, which is covered in the event of rain. Staying open late, a friendly, easygoing crowd and some pretty decent music make this one of the better places in which to have a drink.

Lime Kiln (Lloyd's Bar) BAR
(26 Fleet St; ⌚11am-2am Mon-Sat) It's a chain bar, but it's immensely popular with revellers in Ropewalks, who come for the cheap drinks, charty music and the surprisingly pleasant covered outdoor area where you can smoke and observe the carnage on Concert Sq.

☆ Entertainment

Nightclubs

Most of the city's clubs are concentrated in Ropewalks, where they compete for customers with a ton of late-night bars; considering the number of punters in the area on a Friday or Saturday night, we're guessing there's plenty of business for everyone.

Masque NIGHTCLUB
(90 Seel St; ⌚11pm-3am Mon-Sat) This converted theatre is home to our favourite club in town. The fortnightly Saturday **Chibuku** (www.chibuku.com) is one of the best club nights in all of England, led by a mix of superb DJs including Yousef (formerly of Cream nightclub) and superstars such as Dmitri from Paris and Gilles Peterson. The music ranges from hip hop to deep house – if you're in town, get in line.

Nation NIGHTCLUB
(40 Slater St, Wolstenholme Sq; ⏱11pm-3am) It looks like an air-raid shelter, but it's the big-name DJs dropping the bombs at the city's premier dance club, formerly the home of Cream. These days, it also hosts live bands as well as pumping techno nights.

Le Bateau NIGHTCLUB
(62 Duke St; ⏱11pm-3am Thu-Sat) This oddly named club – there's nothing boatlike about this building – is home to a superb indie club, where 500 punters cram the dance floor and shake it to sounds that have nothing to do with the charts – you'll hear everything from techno to hard rock. Friday night is the excellent Indiecation.

Music

Philharmonic Hall CLASSICAL MUSIC
(☎0151-709 3789; Hope St) One of Liverpool's most beautiful buildings, the art-deco Phil is home to the city's main classical orchestra, but it also stages the work of avant-garde musicians such as John Cage and Nick Cave.

Academy LIVE MUSIC
(Liverpool University, 11-13 Hotham St) Good spot to see midsize bands on tour.

Cavern Club LIVE MUSIC
(8-10 Mathew St) Reconstruction of 'world's most famous club'; good selection of local bands.

ECHO Arena LIVE MUSIC
(☎0844 800 0400; Monarch's Quay) Brand-new megavenue that hosts the city's pop shows, from top artists to Broadway extravaganzas.

Sport

LIVERPOOL FC

Doff o' the cap to Evertonians and Beatlemaniacs, but no single institution represents the Mersey spirit and strong sense of identity more powerfully than **Liverpool FC** (☎0151-263 9199, ticket office 220 2345; www.liverpoolfc.tv; Anfield Rd), England's most successful football club. Virtually unbeatable for much of the 1970s and '80s, they haven't won the league championship since 1990 but they did bag the European Champions' League in 2005 for the fifth time under the tenure of Spanish manager Rafael Benitez, who left the club in 2010 after yet another disappointing season.

But the fans' love of their club remains undiminished, as does their affection for the utterly marvellous **Anfield Road** (☎0151-260 6677; www.liverpoolfc.tv; Anfield Rd; tour & museum adult/child £14/8, museum only adult/child £6/4; ⏱ hourly 10am-3pm except match days), where the experience of a live match is one of the sporting highlights of an English visit, especially the sound of 40,000 fans singing the club's anthem, 'You'll Never Walk Alone', before cheering

DOING THE BEATLES TO DEATH

It doesn't matter that two of them are dead, that the much-visited Cavern Club is a reconstruction of the original club that was the scene of their earliest gigs, or that, if he were alive, John Lennon would have devoted much of his cynical energy to mocking the 'Cavern Quarter' that has grown up around Mathew St. No, it doesn't matter at all, because the phenomenon lives on and a huge chunk of the city's visitors come to visit, see and touch anything – and we mean anything – even vaguely associated with the Beatles.

Which isn't to say that a wander around Mathew St isn't fun: from shucking oysters in the Rubber Soul Oyster Bar to buying a Ringo pillowcase in the From Me to You shop, virtually all of your Beatles needs can be taken care of. For decent memorabilia, check out the **Beatles Shop** (www.thebeatleshop.co.uk; 31 Mathew St).

True fans will undoubtedly want to visit the National Trust–owned **Mendips**, the home where John lived with his Aunt Mimi from 1945 to 1963 (which is also the time period covered by Sam Taylor-Wood's superb 2009 biopic of the young Lennon, *Nowhere Boy*) and **20 Forthlin Road**, the plain terraced home where Paul grew up; you can only do so by prebooked **tour** (☎0151-427 7231; adult/child £16.80/3.15; ⏱10.30am & 11.20am Wed-Sun Easter-Oct) from outside the **National Conservation Centre** (www.liverpoolmuseums.org.uk/conservation; Whitechapel; ⏱10am-5pm). Visitors to Speke Hall (see p562) can also visit both from there.

If you'd rather do it yourself, the tourist offices stock the *Discover Lennon's Liverpool* guide and map, and *Robin Jones' Beatles Liverpool*.

their heroes, which include local lad and Liverpool legend Steven Gerrard. Take bus 26 or 27 from Paradise St Interchange or 17 or 217 from the Queen St Bus Station.

EVERTON FOOTBALL CLUB

Liverpool's 'other' team are the blues of **Everton Football Club** (☎0151-330 2400, ticket office 330 2300; www.evertonfc.com; Goodison Park), who may not have their rivals' winning pedigree but are just as popular locally.

Tours (☎0151-330 2277; adult/child £8.50/5; ⏰11am & 2pm Sun-Wed & Fri) of Goodison Park run throughout the year, except on the Friday before home matches. Take bus 19, 20 or 21 from Paradise St Interchange or Queen St Bus Station.

 Shopping

In 2008, Liverpool's city centre was transformed by the opening of the simply enormous **Liverpool ONE** (www.liverpool-one.com) shopping district ('centre' just feels too small), 17 hectares of retail and restaurant pleasure between Hanover St to the south, Paradise St to the east, James and Lord Sts to the north and Albert Dock to the west.

 Information

Bookshops

Waterstone's (14-16 Bold St)

Emergency

Merseyside police headquarters (☎0151-709 6010; Canning Pl) Opposite Albert Dock.

Internet Access

CafeLatte.net (4 South Hunter St; per 30min £2; ⏰9am-6pm)

Planet Electra (36 London Rd; per 30min £2; ⏰9am-5pm)

Internet Resources

Clubbing Liverpool (www.clubbingliverpool.co.uk) Everything you need to know about what goes on when the sun goes down.

Itchy Liverpool (www.itchyliverpool.co.uk) Irreverent guide to the city.

Liverpool Magazine (www.liverpool.com) Insiders' guide to the city, including lots of great recommendations for food and nights out.

Mersey Guide (www.merseyguide.co.uk) Guide to the Greater Mersey area.

Tourist office (www.visitliverpool.com)

Medical Services

Mars Pharmacy (68 London Rd) Open until 10pm every night.

THE GRAND NATIONAL

The world's most famous steeplechase – and one of England's most cherished events – takes place on the first Saturday in April across 4.5 miles and over the most difficult fences in world racing. Its protagonists are 40-odd veteran stalwarts of the jumps, ageing bruisers full of the oh-so-English qualities of grit and derring-do.

You can book **tickets** (☎0151-522 2929; www.aintree.co.uk) for the Grand National, or visit the **Grand National Experience** (☎0151-523 2600; www.aintree.co.uk; adult/child with tour £10/6, without tour £5/4), a visitor centre that includes a race simulator – those jumps are very steep indeed. Redevelopment work on the centre means you have to book the tour in advance – call to make sure.

Royal Liverpool University Hospital (☎0151-706 2000; Prescot St)

Post

Post office (Ranelagh St; ⏰9am-5.30pm Mon-Sat)

Tourist Information

Liverpool's tourist office has three branches in the city. It also offers an **accommodation hotline** (☎0845 601 1125; ⏰9am-5.30pm Mon-Fri, 10am-4pm Sat).

08 Place tourist office (☎0151-233 2008; Whitechapel; ⏰9am-8pm Mon-Sat, 11am-4pm Sun) The main branch of the tourist office.

Albert Dock tourist office (☎0151-478 4599; ⏰10am-6pm) Two branches: Anchor Courtyard and Merseyside Maritime Museum.

 Getting There & Away

Air

Liverpool John Lennon Airport (☎0870 750 8484; www.liverpoolairport.com) serves a variety of international destinations as well as destinations in the UK (Belfast, London and the Isle of Man).

Bus

The **National Express Coach Station** (Norton St) is 300m north of Lime St station. There are services to/from most major towns:

Birmingham £12.40, 2¾ hours, five daily

London £25.60, five to six hours, six daily

Manchester £6.30, 1¼ hours, hourly

Newcastle £21.60, 6½ hours, three daily

Train

Liverpool's main station is Lime St. It has hourly services to almost everywhere, including the following:

Chester £4.35, 45 minutes

London Euston £65.20, 3¼ hours

Manchester £9.80, 45 minutes

Wigan £5.40, 50 minutes

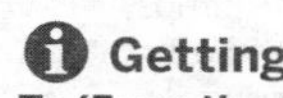

Getting Around

To/From the Airport

The airport is 8 miles south of the centre. **Arriva Airlink** (per person £1.90; ⏲6am-11pm) buses 80A and 180 depart from Paradise St bus station, and **Airportxpress 500** (per person £2.90; ⏲5.15am-12.15am) buses leave from outside Lime St station. Buses from both stations take half an hour and run every 20 minutes. A taxi to the city centre should cost no more than £18.

Boat

The famous cross-Mersey **ferry** (adult/child £1.55/1.25) for Woodside and Seacombe departs from Pier Head Ferry Terminal, next to the Royal Liver Building (to the north of Albert Dock).

Car & Motorcycle

You won't really have much use for a car in Liverpool, and it'll no doubt end up costing you plenty in parking fees. If you have to drive, there are parking meters around the city and a number of open and sheltered car parks. Car break-ins are a significant problem, so leave absolutely nothing of value in the car.

Public Transport

Local public transport is coordinated by **Merseytravel** (www.merseytravel.gov.uk). Highly recommended is the **Saveaway ticket** (adult/child £4.50/2.30), which allows for one day's off-peak (after 9.30am) travel on all bus, train and ferry services throughout Merseyside. Tickets are available at shops and post offices throughout the city. Paradise St bus station is in the city centre.

Merseyrail (www.merseyrail.org) is an extensive suburban rail service linking Liverpool with the Greater Merseyside area. There are four stops in the city centre: Lime St, Central (handy for Ropewalks), James St (close to Albert Dock) and Moorfields (for the Liverpool War Museum).

Taxi

Mersey Cabs (☎0151-298 2222) operates tourist taxi services and also has some wheelchair-accessible cabs.

AROUND LIVERPOOL

Speke

A marvellous example of a black-and-white half-timbered hall can be visited at **Speke Hall** (NT; www.nationaltrust.org.uk; house & gardens adult/child £8.40/4.20, gardens only adult/child £5/2.60; ⏲11am-5.30pm Wed-Sun), 6 miles south of Liverpool in the plain suburb of Speke. It contains several priests' holes where 16th-century Roman Catholic priests could hide when they were forbidden to hold Masses. Any airport bus from Paradise St will drop you within a half-mile of the entrance. Speke Hall can also be combined with a National Trust 1½-hour **tour** (☎0151-486 4006; with Speke Hall adult/child £16.80/3.15) to the childhood homes of both Lennon and McCartney (see boxed text, p560) – you can book at Speke Hall or at the tourist offices in Liverpool.

LANCASHIRE

As isolated as it is industrious, not all of Lancashire is an endless stretch of urban jungle. Its southern half has its fair share of concrete (no part of England is so heavily urbanised) and it includes both Liverpool and Manchester, which are so big that they've been administered separately since 1974. But as you travel north, beyond Blackpool – the belle of the beach holiday – you'll arrive at the undulating folds of the Ribble Valley, a gentle warm-up for the Lake District that lies just beyond Lancashire's northern border. North of the Ribble Valley is the county's handsome Georgian capital, Lancaster.

Blackpool

POP 142,290

The queen bee of England's fun-by-the-sea-type resorts is unquestionably Blackpool. It's bold and brazen in its efforts to cement its position as the country's second-most-visited town after London. Tacky, trashy and, in recent years, just a little bit tawdry, Blackpool doesn't care because 16 million annual visitors don't either.

The town is famous for its tower, its three piers, its Pleasure Beach and its Illuminations, the latter being a successful ploy to extend the brief summer holiday season. From early September to early November, 5 miles of the Promenade are illuminated with thousands of electric and neon lights.

Sights

Pleasure Beach AMUSEMENT PARK
(www.blackpoolpleasurebeach.com; Central Promenade; Pleasure Beach Pass £5; ⏲from 10am Feb-Oct, Sat & Sun only Nov) The main reason for Blackpool's immense popularity is the Pleasure Beach, a 16-hectare collection of more than 145 rides that attracts some seven million visitors annually, and, as amusement parks go, is easily the best in Britain.

The high-tech, modern rides draw the biggest queues, but spare a moment to check out the marvellous collection of old-style wooden roller coasters, known as 'woodies'. You can see the world's first **Big Dipper** (1923), but be sure to have a go on the **Grand National** (1935), whose carriages trundle along a 1½-mile track in an experience that is typically Blackpool – complete with riders waving their hands (despite the sombre-toned announcement not to).

Rides are divided into categories, and once you've gained entry to the park with your Freedom Ticket you can buy tickets for individual categories or for a mixture of them all. Alternatively, an Unlimited Ride **wristband** (1-day adult/child £30/25, 2-day £40/32) includes the £5 entrance fee; there are great discounts if you book your tickets online in advance.

There are no set times for closing; it depends how busy it is.

Blackpool Tower ENTERTAINMENT COMPLEX
(www.theblackpooltower.co.uk; adult/child £17/14; ⏲10am-6pm) Blackpool's most recognisable landmark is the 150m-high tower built in 1894. Inside is a vast entertainment complex including a dinosaur ride, Europe's largest indoor jungle gym and a Moorish circus.

The highlight is the magnificent rococo **ballroom** (⏲10am-6pm Mon-Fri & Sun, to 11pm Sat), with extraordinary sculptured and gilded plasterwork, murals, chandeliers and couples gliding across the beautifully polished wooden floor to the melodramatic tones of a huge Wurlitzer organ.

Sandcastle Waterpark WATERPARK
(www.sandcastle-waterpark.co.uk; adult/child £15/13; ⏲from 10am May-Oct, from 10am Sat & Sun Nov-Feb) Across from the Pleasure Beach is this indoor water complex with 15 different slides and rides, including the Master Blaster, the world's largest indoor waterslide.

Sealife Centre AQUARIUM
(www.sealifeeurope.com; New Bonny St; adult/child £13.95/10.95; ⏲10am-8pm) State-of-the-art sealife centre that features 2.5m-long sharks and a giant octopus.

FREE **North Pier** ARCHITECTURAL LANDMARK
(Promenade) Built in 1862 and opening a year later, the most famous of the three Victorian piers once charged a penny for admission; its plethora of unexciting rides are now free.

Sleeping

If you want to stay close to the waterfront, prepare for a noisy, boisterous night; accommodation along Albert and Hornby Rds, 300m back from the sea, is that little bit quieter. The tourist office will assist you in finding a bed.

Number One BOUTIQUE HOTEL ££
(☎01253-343901; www.numberoneblackpool.com; 1 St Lukes Rd; s/d from £70/120; P 📶) Far fancier than anything else around, this stunning boutique guest house is all luxury and contemporary style. Everything exudes a kind of discreet elegance, from the dark-wood furniture and high-end mod cons to the top-notch breakfast. It's on a quiet road just set back from the South Promenade near the Pleasure Beach.

Big Blue Hotel HOTEL ££
(☎0845 367 3333; www.bigbluehotel.com; Blackpool Pleasure Beach; s/d/ste from £69/89/119; P @ 📶) A handsome family hotel with smartly kitted-out rooms. Kids' needs are met with DVD players and computer games, while its location at the southern entrance to the Pleasure Beach should ensure that everyone has something to do.

Eating

Forget gourmet meals – the Blackpool experience is all about stuffing your face with burgers, doughnuts, and fish and chips. Most people eat at their hotels, where roast and three vegetables often costs just £5 per head.

There are a few restaurants around Talbot Sq (near the tourist office) on Queen St, Talbot Rd and Clifton St. Our favourite meal in town is at the Mediterranean **Kwizeen** (www.kwizeenrestaurant.co.uk; 49 King St; mains £13), which serves a delicious suckling pig in a Sardinian style, topped with a bacon roulade.

Information

Tourist office (☎01253-478222; www.visitblackpool.com; 1 Clifton St; ⏲9am-5pm Mon-Sat)

Getting There & Away

Bus

The central coach station is on Talbot Rd, near the town centre.

London £29, 6½ hours, four daily

Manchester £7.30, 1¾ hours, four daily

Train

The main train station is Blackpool North, about five blocks east of the North Pier on Talbot Rd. There is a direct service from Manchester (£13.50, 1¼ hours, half-hourly) and Liverpool (£14.60, 1½ hours, seven daily), but most other arrivals change in Preston (£6.70, 30 minutes, half-hourly).

Getting Around

A host of travel-card options for trams and buses ranging from one day to a week are available at the tourist office and most newsagents. With more than 14,000 car-parking spaces in Blackpool, you'll have no problem parking. The **land train service** (one way/return £2/3; ⏲from 10.30am Apr-Oct) shuttles funsters between the central corridor car parks and the main entrance to the Pleasure Beach every five minutes or so throughout the day. Otherwise, the town has recently introduced a **bike hire scheme** (www.hourbike.com/blackpool; per 3hr £6) with bikes available for hire from stations along the Promenade and in Stanley Park.

Lancaster

POP 45,960

Lancashire's county seat is genteel, austere and much, much quieter than it was in its 18th-century heyday, when it served as an important trading port for all manner of goods, including people. The city's handsome Georgian architecture was one of the slave trade's ancillary benefits.

Sights

Lancaster Castle & Priory CASTLE

(☎01524-64998; www.lancastercastle.com; Castle Park; adult/child £5/4; ⏲10am-5pm) Lancaster's imposing castle was originally built in 1150. Later additions include the **Well Tower**, more commonly known as the Witches' Tower because it was used to incarcerate the accused of the famous Pendle Witches Trial of 1612, and the impressive twin-towered **gatehouse**, both of which were added in the 14th century. However, most of what you see today dates from the 18th and 19th centuries, when the castle was substantially altered to suit its new, and still current, role as a prison. Consequently, you can only visit the castle as part of a 45-minute **guided tour** (⏲every 30min 10.30am-4pm), but you do get a chance to experience what it was like to be locked up in the dungeon.

Immediately next to the castle is the equally fine **priory church** (Priory Cl; admission free; ⏲9.30am-5pm), founded in 1094 but extensively remodelled in the Middle Ages.

Judges' Lodgings MUSEUM

(Church St; adult/child £3/2; ⏲10am-4pm Mon-Fri, noon-4pm Sat & Sun) Once the home of witch-hunter Thomas Covell (he who 'caught' the poor Pendle women), Lancaster's oldest town house, a Grade I–listed Georgian building, is now home to a Museum of Furnishings by master builders Gillows of Lancaster, whose work graces the Houses of Parliament. It also houses a Museum of Childhood, which has memorabilia from the turn of the 20th century.

Williamson Park & Tropical Butterfly House GARDENS

(www.williamsonpark.com; ⏲10am-5pm) Lancaster's highest point is the 22-hectare spread of this elegant park, from which there are great views of the town, Morecambe Bay and the Cumbrian fells to the north. In the middle is the **Ashton Memorial**, a 67m-high baroque folly built by Lord Ashton (the son of the park's founder, James Williamson) for his wife.

More beautiful, however, is the Edwardian Palm House, now the **Tropical Butterfly House** (adult/child £4.50/3.50), full of exotic and stunning species. Take bus 25 or 25A from the station, or else it's a steep short walk up Moor Lane.

Sleeping & Eating

Sun Hotel & Bar HOTEL ££

(☎01524-66006; www.thesunhotelandbar.co.uk; 63 Church St; s/d from £72/82; P 📶) An excellent hotel in a 300-year-old building with a rustic, old-world look that stops at the bedroom door; a recent renovation has resulted in 16 pretty snazzy rooms. The pub downstairs is one of the best in town and a top spot for a bit of grub; the two-course roast of the day (£9.95) is excellent.

Royal King's Arms Hotel HOTEL ££
(☎01524-32451; www.oxfordhotelsandinns.com; Market St; s/d from £59/79; P 📶) Lancaster's swankiest hotel is a period house with modern, comfortable rooms and an all-round businesslike interior. The hotel restaurant is an excellent dining choice, with mains around £11.

Whale Tail Cafe VEGETARIAN £
(www.whaletailcafe.co.uk; 78a Penny St; mains £6-8; ⊙10am-4pm Mon-Fri, to 5pm Sat, to 3pm Sun) This gorgeous 1st-floor veggie restaurant has an elegant dining room and a more informal plant-filled yard for lunch on a sunny day. The spicy bean burger (£6) is particularly good. Food here is locally produced and, when possible, organic.

Information

Post office (85 Market St; ⊙9am-5.30pm Mon-Fri, 9am-12.30pm Sat)

Tourist office (☎01524-841656; www.citycoastcountryside.co.uk; 29 Castle Hill; ⊙9am-5pm Mon-Sat)

Getting There & Away

Lancaster is on the main west-coast railway line and on the Cumbrian coast line. Destinations include Carlisle (£17.40, one hour, hourly), Manchester (£13.90, one hour, hourly) and Morecambe (£2.10, 15 minutes, half-hourly).

Ribble Valley

Lancashire's most attractive landscapes lie east of the brash tackiness of Blackpool and north of the sprawling conurbations of Preston and Blackburn.

The northern half of the valley is dominated by the sparsely populated moorland of the Forest of Bowland, which is a fantastic place for walks, while the southern half features rolling hills, attractive market towns and ruins, with the River Ribble flowing between them.

Activities

WALKING & CYCLING

The **Ribble Way**, a 70-mile footpath that follows the River Ribble from its source at Ribblehead (in the Yorkshire Dales) to the estuary at Preston, is one of the more popular walks in the area and passes through Clitheroe. For online information check out www.visitlancashire.com.

The valley is also well covered by the northern loop of the **Lancashire Cycle Way**; for more information about routes, safety and so on contact **Blazing Saddles** (☎01442-844435; www.blazingsaddles.co.uk), a Yorkshire-based bike shop.

The tourist office in Clitheroe has three useful publications: *Bowlands by Bike* (£1), *Mountain Bike Ribble Valley Circular Routes* (£2.50) and *Mountain Bike Rides in Gisburn Forest* (£2).

CLITHEROE

POP 14,700

Located northeast of Preston, the Ribble Valley's largest market town is best known for its impressive **Norman keep** (admission free; ⊙dawn-dusk), built in the 12th century and now, sadly, standing empty; from it there are great views of the river valley below.

The extensive grounds are home to the newly refurbished **castle museum** (Castle Hill; adult/child £3.50/free; ⊙11am-5pm Apr-Oct, noon-4pm Nov-Mar), which explores 350 *million* years of local history.

Sleeping & Eating

Old Post House Hotel HOTEL ££
(☎01200-422025; www.posthousehotel.co.uk; 44-48 King St; s/d from £40/65; P 📶) A former post office is now Clitheroe's most handsome hotel, with 11 superbly decorated rooms.

Eaves Hall Hotel HOTEL ££
(☎01200-425271; www.eaveshall.co.uk; Eaves Hall Lane, West Bradford; s/d from £50/90; 📶) Just north of the village, this is the archetypal country house hotel with 34 well-appointed rooms in a beautiful building surrounded by 5 hectares of lush, landscaped gardens.

Halpenny's of Clitheroe TEAROOM £
(Old Toll House, 1-5 Parson Lane; mains £6) A traditional teashop that serves sandwiches, and dishes such as Lancashire hotpot.

Information

Tourist office (☎01200-425566; www.visitribblevalley.co.uk; Church Walk; ⊙9am-5pm Mon-Sat) Information on the town and surrounding area.

PENDLE HILL

The valley's top attraction is Pendle Hill (558m), made famous in 1612 as the stomping ground of the Pendle Witches. These were 10 women who, allegedly, practised all kinds of malefic doings until they were convicted on the sole testimony of a child, and hanged. The tourist authority makes a big deal of the mythology surrounding the unfortunate women, and every Halloween a pseudomystical ceremony is performed here to commemorate their 'activities'.

If that isn't enough, the hill is also renowned as the spot where George Fox had a vision in 1652 that led him to found the Quakers. Whatever your thoughts on witchcraft and religious visions, the hill, a couple of miles east of Clitheroe, is a great spot for a walk.

FOREST OF BOWLAND

This vast, grouse-ridden moorland is somewhat of a misnomer. The use of 'forest' is a throwback to an earlier definition, when it served as a royal hunting ground. Today it is an Area of Outstanding Natural Beauty (AONB), which makes for good walking and cycling. The **Pendle Witch Way**, a 45-mile walk from Pendle Hill to northeast of Lancaster, cuts right through the area, and the **Lancashire Cycle Way** runs along the eastern border. The forest's main town is **Slaidburn**, about 9 miles north of Clitheroe on the B6478.

Other villages worth exploring are **Newton**, **Whitewell** and **Dunsop Bridge**.

Sleeping & Eating

Inn at Whitewell INN ££
(☎01200-448222; www.innatwhitewell.com; Whitewell Village; s/d from £70/96) Once the home of Bowland's forest keeper, this is now a superb guest house with antique furniture, peat fires and Victorian claw-foot baths. The restaurant (mains £10 to £16) specialises in traditional English game dishes.

Hark to Bounty Inn INN ££
(☎01200-446246; www.harktobounty.co.uk; Slaidburn; s/d £42/85) Marvellous 13th-century inn with atmospheric rooms with exposed oak beams. An excellent restaurant (mains £8 to £13) downstairs specialises in homemade herb breads.

Slaidburn YHA HOSTEL £
(☎0845 371 9343; www.yha.org.uk; King's House, Slaidburn; dm £16; ⊙Apr-Oct) A converted 17th-century village inn that is especially popular with walkers and cyclists.

Getting There & Away

Clitheroe is served by regular buses from Preston and Blackburn as well as by hourly trains from Manchester (£8.70, 75 minutes) and Preston (£5.90, 50 minutes). Once here, you're better off having your own transport, as there is only a Sunday bus service between Clitheroe and the rest of the valley villages.

ISLE OF MAN

It pays to be different. Best known as a tax haven, petrol-head heaven and the home of the tailless cat, the Isle of Man (Ellan Vannin in Manx, the local lingo) doggedly refuses to relinquish its quasi-independent status, which gives rise to the oft-quoted mainland prejudice that the islanders' rejection of England's warm embrace must mean there's something odd about them.

We've noticed nothing of the kind, but the island undoubtedly has a different feel about it, as though it has deliberately avoided efforts to hurry up and modernise. Crass commercialism and mass tourism have no place here, except of course for the world-famous summer season of Tourist Trophy (TT) motorbike racing, which attracts around 50,000 punters and bike freaks every May and June, bringing noise and mayhem to the otherwise lush valleys, barren hills and rugged coastlines of this beautiful island. Needless to say, if you want a slice of silence, be sure to avoid the high-rev bike fest.

Home to the world's oldest continuous parliament, the Isle of Man enjoys special status in Britain, and its annual parliamentary ceremony honours the thousand-year history of the Tynwald (a Scandinavian word meaning 'meeting field'). Douglas, the capital, is a run-down relic of Victorian tourism with fading B&Bs.

Activities

WALKING & CYCLING

With plenty of great marked trails, the Isle of Man is a firm favourite with walkers and is regularly voted one of the best walking destinations in Britain. Ordnance Survey (OS) Landranger Map 95 (£6.99) covers the whole island, while the free *Walks on the Isle of Man* is available from the tourist office in Douglas. The **Millennium Way** is a walking path that runs the length of the island amid some spectacular scenery. The most demanding of all the island's walks is the 95-mile **Raad ny Foillan** (Road of the Gull), a well-marked path that makes a complete circuit of the island and normally takes about five days to complete. The **Isle of Man**

Isle of Man

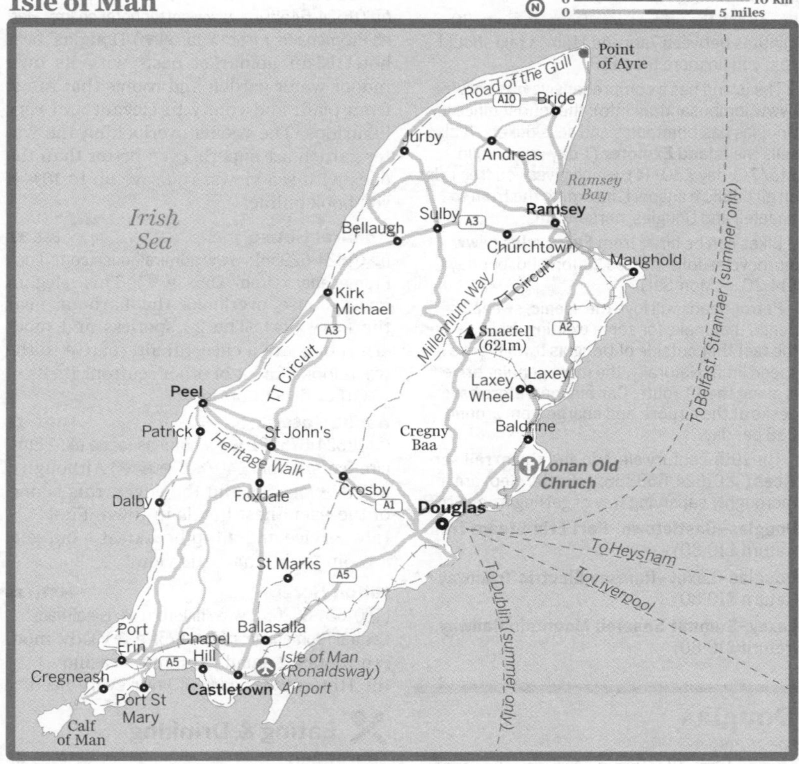

Walking Festival (www.isleofmanwalking.com) takes place over five days in June.

There are six designated off-road mountain-biking trails on the island, each with varying ranges of difficulty. See www.gov.im/tourism/activities/events/mountainbiking.xml for details.

Information

Most of the island's historic sites are operated by Manx Heritage, which offers free admission for National Trust or English Heritage members. Unless otherwise indicated, **Manx Heritage** (MH; www.gov.im/mnh) sites are open 10am to 5pm daily, from Easter to October. The Manx Heritage **5 Site Pass** (adult/child £16/8) grants you entry into five of the island's heritage attractions; pick it up at any of the tourist offices or online.

Getting There & Away

AIR **Ronaldsway Airport** (www.iom-airport.com; Ballasalla) is 10 miles south of Douglas near Castletown.

Airline contacts:

Aer Arann (www.aerarann.com; from £10) From Dublin and London City.

Blue Islands (www.blueislands.com; from £157) From Guernsey and Jersey.

easyJet (www.easyjet; from £19) From Liverpool.

Flybe (www.flybe.com; from £21) From Birmingham, Bristol, London Gatwick, Luton, Liverpool, Manchester, Glasgow and Edinburgh.

Manx2 (www.manx2.com; from £20) From Belfast, Blackpool, Leeds-Bradford, Gloucester M5, Newcastle and East Midlands.

BOAT **Isle of Man Steam Packet** (www.steam-packet.com; foot passenger single/return £19/30.50, car & 2 passengers £154/145) is a car ferry and high-speed catamaran service from Liverpool and Heysham to Douglas. There is also a summer service (mid-April to mid-September) to Dublin (three hours) and Belfast (three hours). It's usually cheaper to buy a return ticket than to pay the single fare.

Getting Around

Buses link the airport with Douglas every 30 minutes between 7am and 11pm; a taxi should cost you no more than £18.

The island has a comprehensive **bus service** (www.iombusandrail.info); the tourist office in Douglas has timetables and sells tickets. It also sells the **Island Explorer** (1-day adult/child £15/7, 3-day £30/14), which gives you free rides on all public transport, including the tram to Snaefell and Douglas' horse-trams.

Bikes can be hired from **Eurocycles** (www.eurocycles.iofm.net; 8a Victoria Rd; per day £14-20; Mon-Sat).

Petrol-heads will love the scenic, sweeping bends that make for some exciting driving – and the fact that outside of Douglas town there's no speed limit. Naturally, the most popular drive is along the TT route. Car-hire operators have desks at the airport, and charge from around £38 per day.

The 19th-century electric and steam **rail services** (01624-663366; Easter-Sep) are a thoroughly satisfying way of getting from A to B:

Douglas–Castletown–Port Erin Steam Train (return £10.80)

Douglas–Laxey–Ramsey Electric Tramway (return £10.80)

Laxey–Summit Snaefell Mountain Railway (return £10.80)

Douglas

POP 26,218

Much like Blackpool across the water, Douglas' heyday was in the middle of the 19th century, when it was a favourite destination for Victorian mass tourism. It's not nearly as popular – or as pretty – today, but it still has the best of the island's hotels and restaurants – as well as the bulk of the finance houses that are frequented so regularly by tax-allergic Brits.

The **Manx Museum** (MH; www.gov.im/mnh; Kingswood Grove; admission free; 10am-5pm Mon-Sat) gives an introduction to everything from the island's prehistoric past to the latest TT race winners.

Sleeping

The seafront promenade is crammed with B&Bs. Unless you booked back at the beginning of the millennium, however, there's little chance of finding accommodation during TT week and the weeks either side of it. The tourist office's camping information sheet lists sites all around the island.

Sefton Hotel HOTEL ££
(01624-645500; www.seftonhotel.co.im; Harris Promenade; r from £95; P) Douglas' best hotel is an upmarket oasis with its own indoor water garden and rooms that range from plain and comfy to elegant and very luxurious. The rooms overlooking the water garden are superb, even better than the ones with sea views. You save up to 10% if you book online.

Admiral House B&B ££
(01624-629551; www.admiralhouse.com; Loch Promenade; r from £55; P) This elegant guest house overlooks the harbour near the ferry port. The 23 spotless and modern rooms are a cheerful alternative to the worn look of a lot of other seafront B&Bs.

Other decent options:

Ascot Hotel HOTEL ££
(01624-675081; www.hotel-ascot.co.uk; 7 Empire Tce; s/d from £40/80; P@) Although a little worn around the edges, this is one of the friendliest hotels in town. First-rate service and a top breakfast – but get a room with a harbour view.

Hilton Hotel HOTEL ££
(01624-662662; www.hilton.co.uk/isleofman; Central Promenade; r from £75; P@) Tidy, modern rooms, a small gym and a casino – the Hilton takes care of your every need.

Eating & Drinking

Tanroagan SEAFOOD ££
(01624-472411; www.tanroagan.co.uk; 9 Ridgeway St; mains £9-18; lunch & dinner Tue-Fri, dinner Sat) The place for all things from the sea, this elegant eatery is the trendiest in Douglas. It serves fresh fish straight off the boats, giving them the merest of Continental twists or just a spell on the hot grill. Reservations are recommended.

Cacio e Pepe ITALIAN ££
(6 Victoria St; mains £8-13; Mon-Sat) Authentic Italian cuisine served in warm, friendly surroundings. The pasta with parma ham is divine, the side salads fresh and crisp.

There are a few good pubs around, including the trendy **Bar George** (St George's Chambers, 3 Hill St) and **Rover's Return** (11 Church St), which specialises in the local brew, Bushy Ales.

Information

Tourist office (01624-686766; www.visitisleofman.com; Sea Terminal Bldg; 9.15am-7pm) Makes free accommodation bookings.

Around Douglas

You can follow the TT circuit up and over the mountain or wind around the coast. The mountain route goes close to the summit of **Snaefell** (621m), the island's highest point. It's an easy walk up to the summit, or take the electric tram from Laxey, near the coast.

On the edge of Ramsey, on the north of the island, is the **Grove Rural Life Museum** (MH; Andreas Rd; admission £3.50; ⏲10am-5pm Apr-Oct). The church in the small village of **Maughold** is on the site of an ancient monastery; a small shelter houses quite a good selection of stone crosses and ancient inscriptions.

It's no exaggeration to describe the **Lady Isabella Laxey Wheel** (MH; Mines Rd, Laxey; admission £3.50; ⏲10am-5pm Apr-Oct), built in 1854 to pump water from a mine, as a 'great' wheel; it measures 22m across and can draw 1140L of water per minute from a depth of 550m. It is named after the wife of the then lieutenant-governor and is the largest wheel of its kind in the world.

The wheel-headed cross at **Lonan Old Church**, just north of Douglas, is the island's most impressive early Christian cross.

Castletown & Around

At the southern end of the island is Castletown, a quiet harbour town that was originally the capital of the Isle of Man. The town is dominated by the impressive 13th-century **Castle Rushen** (MH; Castletown Sq; admission £5; ⏲10am-5pm Apr-Oct). The flag tower affords fine views of the town and coast. There's also a small **Nautical Museum** (MH; Bridge St; admission £4; ⏲10am-5pm Easter-Oct) displaying, among other things, its pride and joy, *Peggy*, a boat built in 1791 and still housed in its original boathouse. There is a school dating back to 1570 in **St Mary's church** (MH; admission free), behind the castle.

Between Castletown and Cregneash, the Iron Age hillfort at **Chapel Hill** encloses a Viking ship burial site.

On the southern tip of the island, the **Cregneash Village Folk Museum** (MH; admission £4; ⏲10am-5pm Apr-Oct) recalls traditional Manx rural life. The **Calf of Man**, the small island just off Cregneash, is a bird sanctuary. **Calf Island Cruises** (☎01624-832339; adult/child £12/6; ⏲10.15am, 11.30am & 1.30pm Apr-Oct, weather permitting) run between Port Erin and the island.

The **Garrison Tapas Bar** (5 Castle St; tapas £5-8; ⏲lunch & dinner Mon-Sat, lunch Sun) brings Iberian flavour to a handsome 17th-century building in the town centre. The paella (£26.50) is fantastic, but it feeds four.

PORT ERIN & PORT ST MARY

Port Erin, another Victorian seaside resort, plays host to the small **Railway Museum** (Station Rd; adult/child £1/50p; ⏲10am-5pm Apr-Oct), which reveals the history of steam railway on the island.

Port Erin has a good range of accommodation, as does Port St Mary, across the headland and linked by steam train.

Our Port Erin accommodation choice would be the Victorian **Falcon's Nest Hotel** (☎01624-834077; falconsnest@enterprise.net; Station Rd; r from £42; 📶), once supremely elegant, now just handsome in a nostalgic sort of way. The rooms are nothing special, but the views over the water are superb.

The slightly more splendid Victorian-style **Aaron House** (☎01624-835702; www.aaronhouse.co.uk; The Promenade, Port St Mary; s/d from £35/70) is a B&B that has fussed over every detail, from the gorgeous brass beds and claw-foot baths to the old-fashioned photographs on the walls. The sea views are also sensational.

Peel & Around

The west coast's most appealing town, Peel has a fine sandy beach, but its real attraction is the 11th-century **Peel Castle** (MH; admission £3.80; ⏲10am-5pm Apr-Oct), stunningly positioned atop St Patrick's Island and joined to Peel by a causeway.

The **House of Manannan** (MH; admission £6; ⏲10am-5pm Apr-Oct) museum uses interactive displays to explain Manx history and its seafaring traditions. A combined ticket for both the castle and museum costs £7.70.

Three miles east of Peel is **Tynwald Hill** at St John's, where the annual parliamentary ceremony takes place on 5 July.

Peel has several B&Bs, including the **Fernleigh Hotel** (☎01624-842435; www.isleofman.com/Business/f/fernleigh; Marine Pde; r per person incl breakfast from £26; ⏲Feb-Nov), which has 12 decent bedrooms. For a better-than-average bite, head for the **Creek Inn** (☎01624-842216; East Quay; mains around £8), opposite the House of Manannan, which serves Manx queenies (scallops served with white cheese sauce) and has self-catering rooms from £35.

The Lake District & Cumbria

Includes »

THE LAKE DISTRICT . . 574
Windermere & Bowness 577
Grasmere 585
Hawkshead 586
Coniston 588
Wasdale. 591
Ullswater & Around . . 597
CUMBRIAN COAST . . 598
Furness Abbey 599
NORTHERN & EASTERN CUMBRIA . . 600
Carlisle 600

Why Go?

If it's grandstand views you're looking for, nowhere in England can match Cumbria. It's a place where the superlatives simply run dry – home to the nation's longest and deepest lakes, as well as its smallest church, steepest road, highest town and loftiest peak. The glaciers that carved out this landscape during the last ice age have long since melted, leaving behind a string of crags, fells and sparkling tarns that form the core of one of England's oldest national parks – the stunning Lake District, founded in 1951 and still considered by many to be the spiritual heartland of English hiking.

But there's much more to this region than just fine views. With a wealth of literary and artistic connections, a history stretching back over 5000 years and some of the halest and heartiest cooking anywhere in England, it's packed with more natural appeal than almost anywhere else in Britain.

When to Go?

Cumbria's largest mountain festival is held in Keswick in mid-May, while the Beer Festival in June welcomes ale aficionados from across the globe. Ambleside's traditional sports day on the last Saturday in July features events such as houndtrailing and Cumbrian wrestling; Grasmere's annual sports day takes place on the August Bank Holiday. In November, the world's greatest liars congregate on Santon Bridge for their annual fibbing contest.

Best Places to Eat

- Punch Bowl Inn (p582)
- Jumble Room (p586)
- Drunken Duck (p587)
- Yanwath Gate Inn (p604)

Best Places to Stay

- Moss Grove Organic (p585)
- Waterhead Hotel (p582)
- Yewfield (p587)
- Howe Keld (p594)
- Summer Hill Country House (p590)

History

The earliest settlers arrived in the Lake District 5000 years ago, building stone circles like Castlerigg and quarrying flint and stone around Stonethwaite and Seatoller. The region was subsequently occupied by Celts, Angles, Vikings and Romans, and during the Dark Ages marked the centre of the kingdom of Rheged, which extended across much of modern Cumbria, Dumfries and Galloway in Scotland, and was annexed by neighbouring Northumbria sometime in the 8th century.

During the Middle Ages Cumbria marked the start of 'The Debatable Lands', the wild frontier between England and Scotland. Bands of Scottish raiders known as Border Reivers regularly plundered the area, prompting the construction of distinctive *pele* towers, built to protect the inhabitants from border raiders, and the stout fortresses at Carlisle, Penrith and Kendal.

The area was a centre for the Romantic movement during the 19th century, and writers including Coleridge, de Quincey and William Wordsworth were among the first to champion the area's natural beauty above its potential for industrial resources (a cause later taken up by other literary luminaries, including John Ruskin and Beatrix Potter). The Lake District became one of the nation's first national parks in 1951, and the modern county of Cumbria was formed from the old districts of Cumberland and Westmorland in 1974.

Activities

CYCLING

Cycling is popular in Cumbria, especially mountain biking on the fells, but you'll need nerves (and legs) of steel on the more challenging routes. Cycle-hire shops are widespread, and tourist offices stock a cycling map showing traffic-free routes. Bike hire starts at around £15 per day.

Long-distance bikers can follow the 72-mile **Cumbria Way** (www.cumbriawaycycleroute.co.uk) between Ulverston, Keswick and Carlisle, and the Cumbrian section of the 140-mile **Sea to Sea Cycle Route** (C2C; www.c2c-guide.co.uk) from Whitehaven via the northern Lake District en route to the North Pennines and Newcastle.

WALKING

For many people, hiking on the fells is the main reason for a Lake District visit. Trails range from low-level rambles to full-blown mountain ascents; most tourist offices sell maps and guidebooks, including Collins' *Lakeland Fellranger*, Ordnance Survey's *Pathfinder Guides*, and Alfred Wainwright's classic hand-drawn, seven-volume set, *A Pictorial Guide to the Lakeland Fells* (recently updated by experienced hiker and Wainwright devotee Chris Jesty).

If you're planning on anything more than a low-level stroll in the Lakes, a decent-quality map is essential. Walkers have a choice of two map publishers: traditionalists generally opt for the Ordnance Survey 1:25,000 *Landranger* series maps, although many hikers prefer Harvey *Superwalker* 1:25,000 maps, which are specifically made for walkers and clearly mark major trail routes (as well as all 214 fells detailed by Alfred Wainwright in his classic walking guides).

There are endless fell trails to choose from, but if you're up for something more challenging, how about Alfred Wainwright's **Coast to Coast Walk** (http://www.thecoasttocoastwalk.info/), which cuts west to east from St Bees to Robin Hood's Bay in North Yorkshire, a distance of 191 miles. The Cumbrian section passes through Honister Pass, Grasmere, Patterdale, Kirkby Stephen and Shap en route to the Yorkshire Dales, a five- to seven-day hike of 82 miles.

Door-to-door baggage services can be useful; contact **Coast to Coast Packhorse** (☎017683-71777; www.c2cpackhorse.co.uk) or **Sherpa Van** (☎0871 520 0124; www.sherpavan.com).

OTHER ACTIVITIES

Cumbria is a haven for adrenalin-fuelled activities, ranging from rock climbing and orienteering to quad biking, fell running and *ghyll* scrambling (a cross between coasteering and river canyoning along a steep ravine). Sailing, kayaking and windsurfing are popular too, especially around Windermere, Derwent Water and Coniston.

Check out www.lakedistrictoutdoors.co.uk for the low-down.

Getting There & Away

BUS National Express coaches run direct from London and Glasgow to Windermere, Carlisle and Kendal. Count on seven hours between London Victoria and Windermere.

TRAIN Carlisle is on the main Virgin West Coast line from London Euston to Manchester to Glasgow, with trains running roughly hourly from both north and south. To get to the Lake District, you need to change at Oxenholme, where regular trains travel west into Kendal and Windermere. There are at least three direct trains from

The Lake District & Cumbria Highlights

1. Slogging to the top of England's highest mountain, **Scafell Pike** (p591)
2. Cruising across the silvery waters of **Derwentwater** (p593) and **Coniston Water** (p589)
3. Visiting the former homes of William Wordsworth at **Dove Cottage** (p585) and **Rydal Mount** (p584)
4. Drinking in the dramatic fell views from **Wasdale** (p591)
5. Spotting England's only resident ospreys on **Bassenthwaite Lake** (p596)
6. Exploring the outdoor art and wooded trails of **Grizedale Forest** (p587)
7. Staring out from the redbrick battlements of **Carlisle Castle** (p600)
8. Hopping aboard the miniature steam trains of **La'al Ratty** (p599), aka the Ravenglass & Eskdale Railway

Canonbie
Catlowdy
Bewcastle
Northumberland National Park
Sewingshields
Esk
Gretna Green
Longtown
Kirkcambeck
Once Brewed
Acomb
Birdoswald Roman Fort
Gilsland
Bardon Mill
Greenhead
Haydon Bridge
Hexham
A6071
Haltwhistle
Blackford
Brampton
Burgh by Sands
Houghton
Kingstown
Gelt Woods
Lambley
NORTHUMBERLAND
Allendale Town
Moorhouse
7
Warwick Bridge
Castle Carrock
Carlisle
A686
Slaggyford
Carleton
Orton Grange
Blanchland
Micklethwaite
Cotehill
Kirkhaugh
Alston
Bolt's Law
Allenheads
Armathwaite
Low Hesket
Nenthead
Leadgate
Rookhope
Eden
Garrigill
A686
South Tyne
Lazonby
Hesket Newmarket
Ireshopeburn
Plumpton
Long Meg & Her Daughters
Little Salkeld
Plumpton Head
Langwathby
Langdon Beck
Mungrisdale
Greystoke
Penrith
Jacksons Fold
Newbiggin
Saddleback
Penruddock
Threlkeld
Troutbeck
CUMBRIA
Middleton-in-Teesdale
Castlerigg Stone Circle
Pooley Bridge
Askham
A66
Dockray
M6
Coupland
Thirlspot
Shap
A591
Brough
Helvellyn
Haweswater Reservoir
A66
Fairfield
Soulby
Kirkby Stephen
Grasmere
Dove Cottage
Newbiggin-on-Line
3
Rydal Mount
Nateby
3
Elterwater
Ambleside
Kentmere
A6
Tebay
Ravenstonedale
Lake District National Park
Troutbeck Bridge
Keld
Forest hall
Outhgill
Swale
Staveley
A683
Buttertubs Pass
Thwaite
Red Nab
Hawkshead
Bowness-on-Windermere
A593
Windermere
Kendal
NORTH YORKSHIRE
2
6
Winster
Sedbergh
Garsdale Head
Coniston Water
Grizedale Forest
Crosthwaite
Killington Reservoir
Skinner Pastures
Bowland Bridge
Sizergh Castle
Hawes
Newby Bridge
Dent
Cowgill
Yorkshire Dales National Park
Gawthwaite
CUMBRIA
Heaves
Witherslack
Penny Bridge
High Newton
Milnthorne
Whernside
Kirkby Lonsdale
Ribblehead
A590
Cark
Arnside
Ulverston
Grange-over-Sands
A65
Ingleborough
Pen-y-Ghent
Bardsea
A6
Arkholme
Arncliffe
Ingleton
Horton-in-Ribblesdale
Carnforth
Newbiggin
Morecambe Bay
LANCASHIRE
High Bentham

CUMBRIAN BUS PASSES

Cumbria has a really good bus network, and several useful bus passes are available, all of which can be purchased from the driver or any Stagecoach office.

North West Explorer (one-/four-day pass adult £9.75/22, child £6.50/15.50) The best-value ticket, allowing unlimited travel on services in Cumbria and Lancashire.

Borrowdale Day Rider (adult/child £5.60/4.20) Valid on Bus 79 between Keswick and Seatoller.

Carlisle Day Rider (£3.30) Unlimited travel in Carlisle.

Central Lakes Dayrider (adult/child £6.30/4.70) Covers Bowness, Ambleside, Grasmere, Langdale and Coniston; includes the 599, 505 and 516.

Honister Dayrider (adult/child £6.50/4.75) Valid on Bus 77 between Keswick and Borrowdale.

Windermere and Kendal south to Lancaster, Manchester and Manchester Airport. Call ☎08457-484950 for information on Day Ranger passes covering the Cumbrian rail network.

For something more soulful, Carlisle sits along some of the UK's most scenic railways:

Cumbrian Coast Line via Ulverston and Ravenglass (see p603)

Settle-Carlisle Railway across the Yorkshire Dales (see p495)

Lakeside & Haverthwaite Steam Railway from Bowness/Ambleside to Windermere (p579)

Ravenglass & Eskdale Railway (p599), often known as La'al Ratty

Getting Around

Traveline (☎0871-200 22 33; www.travelinenortheast.info) provides travel information. Tourist offices stock the free *Getting Around Cumbria* booklet, with timetables for buses, trains and ferries.

BOAT Windermere, Coniston Water, Ullswater and Derwent Water all offer ferry services, providing time-saving links for walkers. Boats on Coniston and Windermere also tie in with the Cross-Lakes Experience (p576).

BUS The main bus operator is **Stagecoach** (www.stagecoachbus.com). Bus suggestions in this chapter are based on summer timetables; most routes run a reduced winter service. You can download timetables from the Stagecoach website or the **Cumbria County Council** (www.cumbria.gov.uk) site.

Useful bus routes:

555 (Lakeslink) between Lancaster and Carlisle, stopping at all the main towns.

505 (Coniston Rambler) linking Kendal, Windermere, Ambleside and Coniston.

X4/X5 Penrith to Workington via Troutbeck, Keswick and Cockermouth.

CAR Driving in the Lake District can be a headache, especially on holiday weekends; you might find it easier to leave the car wherever you're staying and get around using local buses.

Many Cumbrian towns use a timed parking permit for on-street parking, which you can pick up for free from local shops and tourist offices.

THE LAKE DISTRICT

If you're a lover of the great outdoors, the Lake District is one corner of England where you'll want to linger. This sweeping panorama of slate-capped fells, craggy hilltops, misty mountain tarns and glittering lakes has been pulling in the crowds ever since the Romantics pitched up in the early 19th century, and it remains one of the country's most popular beauty spots. Literary landmarks abound, from Wordsworth's boyhood school to the lavish country estate of John Ruskin at Brantwood, and there are enough hilltop trails, hidden pubs and historic country hotels to fill a lifetime of visits.

Information

The Lake District's tourist offices are among the best in England, crammed with information on local hikes, activities and accommodation, and stocked with trail books, maps and hiking supplies. The main offices are in Windermere, Ambleside, Keswick and Carlisle, and there's a fantastic visitor centre at Brockhole (p581).

Kendal

POP 28,398

Technically Kendal isn't in the Lake District, but it's a major gateway town. Often known as the 'Auld Grey Town' thanks to the sombre grey stone used for many of its buildings, Kendal is a bustling shopping centre with some good restaurants, a funky arts centre and intriguing museums. But it'll forever be synonymous in many people's minds with its famous mint cake, a staple item in the nation's hiking packs ever since Edmund Hillary and Tensing Norgay munched it during their ascent of Everest in 1953.

The Lake District

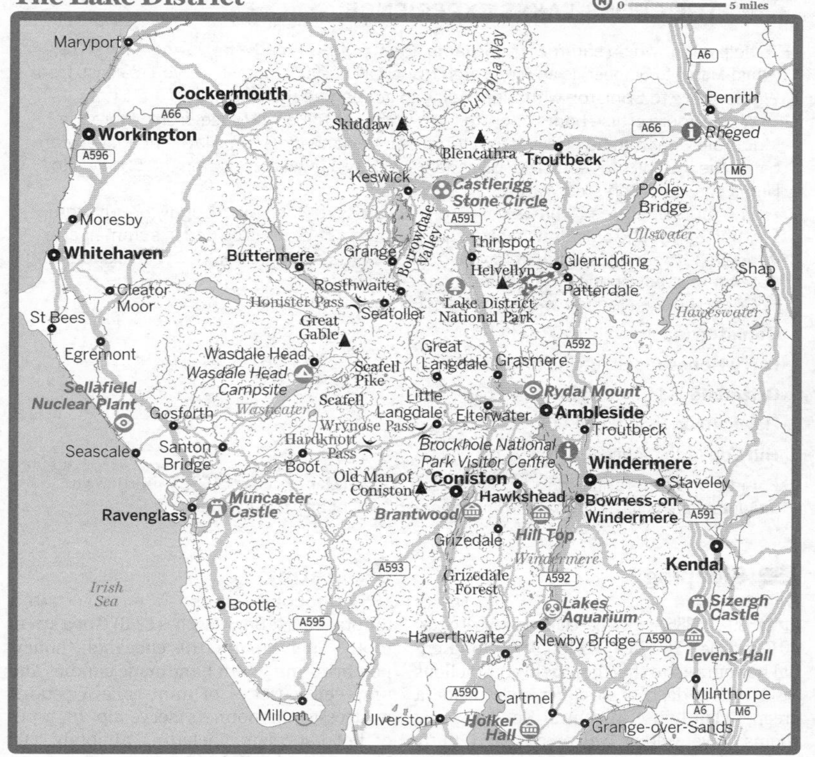

Sights

Kendal Museum MUSEUM
(☎01539-721374; www.kendalmuseum.org.uk; Station Rd; adult/child £2.80/free; ⏰noon-5pm Thu-Sat) Founded in 1796 by the inveterate Victorian collector William Todhunter, this mixed-bag museum features everything from stuffed beasts to medieval coin hoards (look out for the Alethiometer, from Philip Pullman's *His Dark Materials* trilogy). There's also a reconstruction of the office of Alfred Wainwright, the famous hill-walker and author of the classic *Pictorial Guides*, who served as honorary curator at the museum from 1945 to 1974.

Abbot Hall Art Gallery GALLERY
(☎01539-722464; www.abbothall.org.uk; adult/child £5.75/free; ⏰10.30am-5pm Mon-Sat Apr-Oct, to 4pm Nov-Mar) Kendal's gallery houses one of the northwest's best collections of 18th- and 19th-century art; it's especially strong on portraiture and Lakeland landscapes. Look out for works by Constable, Varley and Turner, as well as portraits by John Ruskin and local boy George Romney, born in Dalton-in-Furness in 1734, and a key figure in the 'Kendal School'.

Museum of Lakeland Life & Industry MUSEUM
(☎01539-722464; www.lakelandmuseum.org.uk; adult/child £4.75/3.40; ⏰10.30am-5pm Mon-Sat Apr-Oct, to 4pm Nov-Mar) This museum recreates various scenes from Lakeland life during the 18th and 19th centuries, including a farmhouse parlour, a Lakeland kitchen, an apothecary and the study of Arthur Ransome, author of *Swallows and Amazons*.

Festivals & Events

Kendal Mountain Festival OUTDOOR ACTIVITIES
(www.mountainfest.co.uk) Annual mountain-themed celebration encompassing books, film and live talks in November.

THE CROSS-LAKES EXPERIENCE

To help cut down on summer traffic jams, the **Cross-Lakes Experience** (Map p578; mid-March to October) is an integrated transport service that allows you to cross from Windermere to Coniston without needing to get behind the wheel.

Windermere cruise boats operate from Bowness to Ferry House, from where the Mountain Goat minibus travels to Hill Top and Hawkshead. From Hawkshead, you can catch the X30 bus to Moor Top, Grizedale and Haverthwaite, or catch the 505 bus to High Cross and Coniston Water.

The route operates 10 times daily from Bowness to Coniston (roughly hourly from 10am to 5pm). The only drawback is that the buses get very crowded in summer, and if they're full you'll have to wait for the next one (you can't prebook). Cyclists should note there's only space for five bikes on the minibuses.

Current prices for one-way fares from Bowness:

Coniston (adult/child £10.60/5.65)

Ferry House (adult/child £2.45/1.40)

Grizedale (adult/child £7.65/4.25)

Hawkshead (adult/child £6/3.25)

Hill Top (adult/child £5.10/2.80)

For info and timetables, contact **Mountain Goat** (Map p578; 015394-45161; www.mountain-goat.com; Victoria Rd, Windermere) or ask at any tourist office.

Sleeping

Beech House B&B ££

(01539-720385; www.beechhouse-kendal.co.uk; 40 Greenside; s £60-75, d £80-100; P wi-fi) Top Kendal honours go to this thoroughly marvellous B&B with a dash of designer style inside a creeper-clad house in central Kendal. Some rooms have velour bedspreads and fluffy cushions, others roll-top tubs and mini-fridges; Sebergh Soap Company goodies are standard throughout. The 'Penthouse' and 'Serpentine' rooms are particularly swish.

Hillside B&B ££

(01539-722836; www.hillside-kendal.co.uk; 4 Beast Banks; s £33-41, d £66-82; wi-fi) Another decent guest-house option in Kendal, in a Victorian town house dating from the late 19th century. Rooms are small and quite traditional but comfy nonetheless; parking permits are available for the street outside.

Kendal YHA HOSTEL ££

(0845-371 9641; kendal@yha.org.uk; 118 Highgate; dm from £16; reception 7.30-10am & 1-11.30pm; @) It's definitely not on the level of some of the Lakeland hostels, but this Georgian house next door to the Brewery Arts Centre is decent enough, in a functional YHA way. Dorms are mostly small five- or six-bed rooms, and there's a kitchen, lounge and pool room on the ground floor. No kitchen.

Eating

1657 Chocolate House CAFE £

(54 Branthwaite Brow; lunches £2-8) Got a sweet tooth? Then dip into this chocaholic honeypot, brimming with handmade candies and umpteen varieties of mint cake. Upstairs, waitresses in bonnets serve up 18 types of hot chocolate, including almondy 'Old Noll's Potion' and the bitter-choc 'Dungeon'. Take that, Willy Wonka…

New Moon RESTAURANT ££

(01539-729254; 129 Highgate; 2-course lunch £9, mains £10-17; Tue-Sat) Kendal's best food is served at the fresh and funky New Moon, which takes the best of Lakeland produce and gives it a zippy Mediterranean spin – roast duck breast in a five-spice-and-honey marinade, pork with Parma ham, hake with a pesto crust. The two-course Early Supper menu, served before 7pm, is great value at £9.95.

Waterside Wholefoods CAFE £

(Kent View, Waterside; light meals £4-10; 8.30am-4.30pm Mon-Sat) Kendal's veggies make a beeline for this lovely riverside cafe, a long-standing staple for chunky doorstep sandwiches, soups and naughty-but-nice cakes.

Grain Store BISTRO £

(pizzas £6.50-9, mains £9-16.50; 10am-11pm Mon-Sat) The buzzy bistro at the Brewery Arts centre is great for stone-baked pizzas and swish fish after dark, but it's just as good for a lunchtime wrap or a pre-show coffee.

☆ Entertainment

Brewery Arts Centre THEATRE, CINEMA
(☎01539-725133; www.breweryarts.co.uk; Highgate) Excellent arts complex with two cinemas, gallery space, cafe and a theatre hosting dance, performance and live music.

ℹ Information

Library (75 Stricklandgate; per hr £2; ⏰9.30am-5.30pm Mon & Tue, 9.30am-7pm Wed & Fri, 9.30am-1pm Thu, 9am-4pm Sat, noon-4pm Sun) Internet access.

Tourist office (☎01539-725758; kendaltic@southlakeland.gov.uk; Highgate; ⏰10am-5pm Mon-Sat)

ℹ Getting There & Around

BUS Useful buses from Kendal:

555/556 Lakeslink (hourly Monday to Saturday, 10 on Sunday) Hits Kendal en route to Windermere (30 minutes), Ambleside (40 minutes) and Grasmere (1¼ hours), or Lancaster (one hour) in the opposite direction.

505 Coniston (one hour, 10 daily Monday to Saturday, six on Sunday) via Windermere, Ambleside and Hawkshead.

X35 Travels south to Grange (30 minutes) before returning via Haverthwaite Station, Ulverston and Barrow (hourly Monday to Saturday, four on Sunday).

TRAIN The train line from Windermere runs to Kendal (£3.80, 15 minutes, hourly) en route to Oxenholme.

Around Kendal

Sizergh Castle CASTLE
(NT; ☎015395-60070; adult/child £7.15/3.60, gardens only £4.65/2.40; ⏰gardens 11am-5pm, castle noon-5pm Sun-Thu mid-Mar–Nov) Three and half miles south of Kendal along the A591, this impressive castle is the feudal seat of the Strickland family. The castle is renowned for its *pele* tower and for the lavish wood panelling on display in the Great Hall.

Levens Hall HISTORIC HOME
(☎015395-60321; www.levenshall.co.uk; adult/child £11/4.50, gardens only £8/3.50; ⏰gardens 10am-5pm, house noon-5pm Sun-Thu mid-Mar–mid-Oct) Two miles further south along the A6 is another Elizabethan manor built around a mid 13th-century *pele* tower. Fine Jacobean furniture is on display throughout the house, but the real draw is the 17th- century topiary garden: a surreal riot of pyramids, swirls, curls, pom-poms and peacocks straight out of *Alice in Wonderland*. Rather peculiarly, it holds a chilli festival in August.

The *555/556* bus (hourly Monday to Saturday, 10 on Sunday) from Grasmere, Ambleside, Windermere and Kendal runs past the castle gates.

LOW SIZERGH BARN

Food shop (☎015395-60426; www.lowsizerghbarn.co.uk; ⏰shop 9am-5.30pm, tearoom 9.30am-5.30pm) is a fantastic farm shop spot near Sizergh Castle and it's the place to go when you want to be sure your goodies are 100% food-mile free. Nearly everything in the shop is sourced from the Lakeland area, from homemade chutneys to farm-reared hams and traditional Cumbrian puddings (look out for the award-winning flapjacks from Kendal Jacksmiths and organic wines from Mansergh Hall).

The shop is off the A590 from Kendal. Follow the brown signs to Sizergh Castle and look out for signs to Low Sizergh Barn. Bus 555/6 also stops nearby.

Windermere & Bowness

POP 8432

Of all England's lakes, none carries quite the cachet of regal Windermere. Stretching for 10.5 silvery miles from Ambleside to Newby Bridge, it's one of the classic Lake District vistas, and has been a centre for Lakeland tourism since the first steam trains chugged into town in 1847 (much to the chagrin of the local gentry, including William Wordsworth). The town itself is split between Windermere, 1.5 miles uphill from the lake, and bustling Bowness – officially 'Bowness-on-Windermere' – where a bevy of boat trips, ice cream booths and frilly teashops jostle for space around the shoreline. It's busy, brash and a touch tatty in places, but the lake itself is still a stunner, especially when viewed from one of Windermere's historic cruise boats.

Windermere

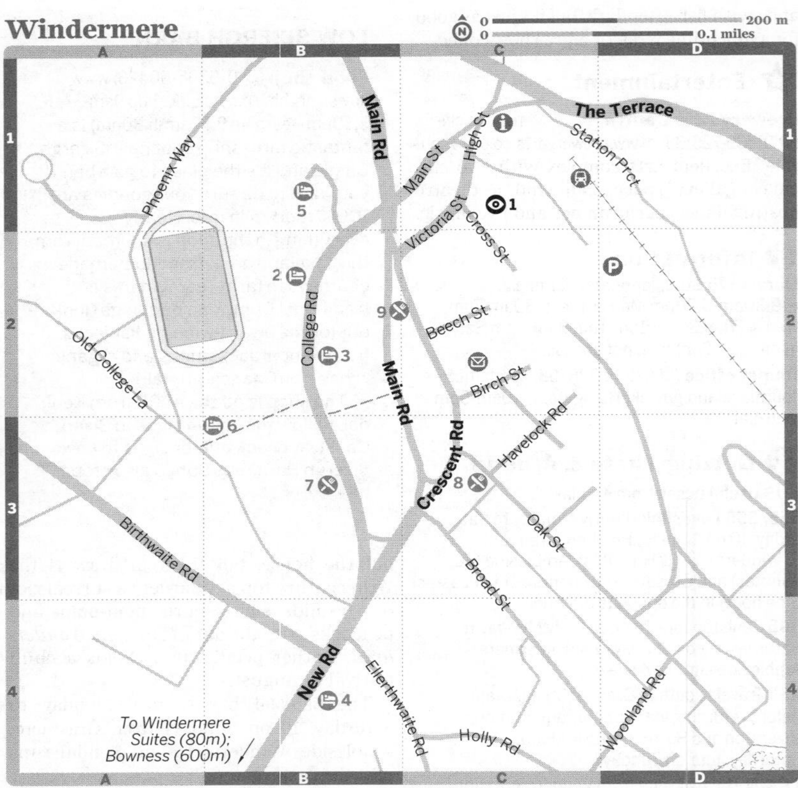

The A592 travels into Bowness from southern Cumbria, tracking the lakeshore before joining the A591 northwest of town. The train and bus stations are in Windermere town. Most of the hotels and B&Bs are dotted around Lake Rd, which leads downhill to Bowness and the lakeshore.

Sights

Lakes Aquarium AQUARIUM
(015395-30153; www.lakesaquarium.co.uk; Lakeside, Newby Bridge; adult/child £8.95/5.95; 9am-6pm Apr-Oct;) At the southern end of the lake near Newby Bridge, this small aquarium explores underwater habitats from tropical Africa through to Morecambe Bay. You could arrive by ferry from Bowness or Ambleside, aboard the Lakeside & Haverthwaite Railway, or via bus 618 from Windermere. Last admission is at 5pm. Discounts are available for buying tickets in advance online.

World of Beatrix Potter CHILDREN'S MUSEUM
(www.hop-skip-jump.com; adult/child £6.75/3.50; 10am-5.30pm Apr-Sep, 10am-4.30pm Oct-Mar;) This decidedly odd theme attraction brings to life scenes from Beatrix Potter's books (including Peter Rabbit's garden and Mr McGregor's greenhouse) using a combination of life-size models and themed rooms.

Be prepared for queues: for some reason, Japanese visitors are obsessed with all things Beatrix Potter, and this place is number one on their list after Hill Top.

Activities

Boat Trips

Windermere Lake Cruises CRUISES
(015395-31188; www.windermere-lakecruises.co.uk) Top on the list of things to do in Windermere is to take a lake cruise. The first passenger ferry was launched back in 1845, and cruising on the lake is still

Windermere

Sights

1 Mountain Goat / Cross-Lakes Experience C1

Sleeping

2 Applegarth Hotel B2
3 Archway B2
4 Howbeck B4
5 Lake District Backpackers Lodge B1
6 Wheatlands Lodge B3

Eating

7 Jericho's B3
8 Lazy Daisy's Lakeland Kitchen C3
9 Lighthouse B2

a hugely popular pastime: some of the vessels are modern, but there are a couple of period beauties dating back to the 1930s. Cruises allow you to jump off at one of the ferry landings (Waterhead/Ambleside, Wray Castle, Brockhole, Bowness, Ferry Landing, Fell Foot Ferry and Lakeside) and catch a later boat back.

Blue Cruise (adult/child/family £6.75/3.40/18.50) 45-minute cruise around Windermere's islands and bays.

Green Cruise (adult/child/family £6.20/3.10/17) 45-minute cruise from Waterhead/Ambleside via Wray Castle and Brockhole Visitor Centre.

Red Cruise (adult/child/family £9.15/5.30/26) North lake cruise from Bowness to Ambleside.

Yellow Cruise (adult/child/family £9.45/5.50/27) South cruise from Bowness to Lakeside and the Lakes Aquarium.

Bowness to Ferry House (single adult/child/family £2.45/1.50/7) Ferry service that links up with the Cross-Lakes shuttle to Hill Top and Hawkshead.

If you'd rather explore under your own steam, from April to October rowing boats can be hired along the waterfront for £5/2.50 per adult/child. Open-top motorboats cost £15 per hour, or there's a closed-cabin version for £18. There's a 10mph speed limit on Windermere, much to the dismay of local power-boaters and water-skiers.

Train Rides

Lakeside & Haverthwaite Railway STEAM RAILWAY

Classic standard-gauge steam trains puff their way along this vintage **railway** (☎015395-31594; www.lakesiderailway.co.uk; Haverthwaite Station; ⊙mid-Mar–Oct) from Haverthwaite, near Ulverston, to Newby Bridge and Lakeside. There are five to seven daily trains in season, timed to correspond with the Windermere cruise boats. There are various combo tickets available for local attractions – see boxed text (p580) or ask at the ticket office. Standard fares from Haverthwaite:

Lakeside (adult/child £5.90/2.95)

Bowness (adult/child £14.00/7.50)

Ambleside (adult/child £19.40/9.70)

Sleeping

Windermere's popularity means accommodation tends to be pricier than elsewhere around the Lakes.

TOP CHOICE **Wheatlands Lodge** B&B ££

(☎015394-43789; www.wheatlandslodge-windermere.co.uk; Old College Lane; d £70-150; P 📶) Set back from the hustle of Windermere town, this elegant detached residence looks venerably Victorian, but inside it reveals some contemporary surprises: lovely, large rooms each with their own keynote colour (maroon, coffee, pistachio), big bathrooms with a choice of walk-in shower or jacuzzi hot tub, and an extremely upmarket dining room serving one of the best breakfasts we had in Windermere.

Cranleigh HOTEL ££

(☎015394-43293; www.thecranleigh.com; Kendal Rd; d £85-148, ste £240-325; P 📶) They certainly haven't spared any expense at this pimped-up pamper-palace. The rooms simply ooze invention: for an out-and-out spoil, the newly opened Sanctuary bungalow is the one to go for, with a remote-controlled fire, huge headboard and a glass bath that's straight out of *Blade Runner*. The rest of the rooms are less starry, but still a distinct cut above most places in town.

Windermere Suites B&B £££

(☎01539-444739; www.windermeresuites.co.uk; New Rd; d £140-280; P 📶) Newly renovated by the owners of the Howbeck, the rooms here are simply enormous: all are named after different Lakeland locations but share a similar taste for soothing whites, gloss-wood

LAKE CRUISE TICKETS

Various combination tickets are available covering lake cruises and admission to local attractions.

Freedom of the Lake ticket (adult/child/family £15/7.50/40) A day's unlimited travel on the lake boats.

Boat & Train (return from Bowness; adult/child/family £14/8.50/39.50) Cruise and travel on the Lakeside & Haverthwaite Steam Railway.

Boat & Aquarium (return from Bowness; adult/child/family £15.90/8.95/46.80). Cruise and entry to the Lakes Aquarium.

floors, enormous flatscreen TVs and the odd touch of boutique wallpaper or funky artwork. In fact, it might all be a bit much for some, and it is a little on the pricey side.

Aphrodite's Themed Lodge HOTEL ££
(015394-45052; www.aphroditesthemedlodge.co.uk; Longtail Hill; d £90-160; P) Something must have got into the water around Windermere – this is another wildly over-the-top design project, where every suite takes on a different theatrical theme: a Tarzan and Jane room with bamboo walls and jungle plants, an Austin Powers pop art room, or a Flintstones suite – complete with faux furs and mock-rock plaster walls. It's completely insane, but you've got to give them an A for effort. The lodge is about 0.8 miles south of Bowness.

Applegarth Hotel HOTEL £££
(015394-43206; www.lakesapplegarth.co.uk; College Rd; s £57-62, d £100-196; P) Traditional in style, undoubtedly, but then this is one of the loveliest Arts & Crafts houses in Windermere, built in the 19th century by industrial bigwig John Riggs. Polished panels, burnished furniture and the odd bit of stained glass conjure up the restrained Victorian vibe, although cheaper rooms are a tad bland.

Howbeck B&B ££
(015394-44739; www.howbeck.co.uk; New Rd; d £100-160; P) Not quite as spangly as Windermere Suites, its sister business up the road, the Howbeck, is still a top B&B choice, with 10 rooms, crisply finished in up-to-date fabrics and a minimum of clutter. A bit more cash buys plusher furnishings, but you won't completely dodge the road noise.

Archway B&B ££
(015394-45613; www.the-archway.com; 13 College Rd; d £50-55) There's nothing particularly fancy about this stone-fronted B&B (although there are spanking fell views from the front rooms), but it's worth a mention for its breakfast: Manx kippers, smoked haddock and American-style pancakes are all on offer.

Number 80 Bed Then Breakfast B&B ££
(015394-43584; www.number80bed.co.uk; 80 Craig Walk; d £80-90;) This Bowness refuge is still off the radar, so keep it under your hats. Just four rooms, but each one has its own decorative tics: room 1 feels traditional with a pine four-poster, but the other three are more modern.

Lake District Backpackers Lodge HOSTEL £
(015394-46374; www.lakedistrictbackpackers.co.uk; High St; dm £15-17; @) The only hostel in Windermere proper, and it's a little underwhelming, with cramped bunk-bed dorms squeezed into a slate-roofed house down a cul-de-sac near the station. Still, the beds are cheap, there's a cosy lounge (with Sky TV) and the managers organise biking and hiking trips.

Eating & Drinking

Lazy Daisy's Lakeland Kitchen CAFE £
(015394-43877; 31-33 Crescent Rd; lunch £4-10, dinner £10-16; 10am-9pm Mon-Sat) Cute as they come, and chock-full of Lakeland goodness, this little Windermere cafe has something to suit regardless of the hour of the day: morning coffee, lunchtime sandwiches, afternoon tea and cakes, and rich dinner dishes along the lines of buttered trout and steak-and-merlot pie.

Jericho's RESTAURANT £££
(015394-42522; www.jerichos.co.uk; Waverly Hotel, College Rd; dinner mains £15-24; dinner Tue-Sun) Now installed at the Waverley Hotel, the town's most upmarket restaurant is a favourite with the foodie guides, and head chef Chris Blaydes has acquired a deserved name as one of the Lake District's most talented chefs. The town house setting is

an ideal counterpoint for the modern Brit bistro food.

Lucy 4 at the Porthole BISTRO ££
(3 Ash St; tapas £5-10; ⏲lunch Sat & Sun, dinner daily) The homely old Porthole has been overhauled courtesy of Lucy Nicholson, of Lucy's of Ambleside fame (see p583). It boasts the same laid-back atmosphere, pick-and-mix tapas menu and wine-bar feel as the original Lucy 4, only this time steps from the Windermere shoreline.

Angel Inn GASTROPUB ££
(☎015394-44080; www.the-angelinn.com; Helm Rd; mains £11-16) The Lake District isn't just about cosy country inns – it has its fair share of gastropubs too, like this one on a grassy hump beside the Bowness shoreline. Stripped wood, banquette seats and leather sofas conjure an urban-chic ambiance, and the menu's stocked with solid gastropub stuff – mussels, beer-battered haddock and seared sea bass.

Lighthouse CAFE £
(Main Rd; mains £8-15; ⏲breakfast, lunch & dinner) This triple-floored cafe at the top of Windermere offers a continental-style menu, quality cappuccino and fresh-baked pastries.

ℹ Information

Brockhole National Park Visitor Centre (☎015394-46601; www.lake-district.gov.uk; ⏲10am-5pm Easter-Oct) The Lake District's flagship visitor centre is 3 miles north of Windermere on the A591, with a teashop, adventure playground and gardens.

Library (☎015394-62400; Broad St; per 30min £1; ⏲9am-7pm Mon, to 5pm Tue, Thu & Fri, to 1pm Sat, closed Wed & Sun) Internet access.

Tourist office Bowness (☎015394-42895; bownesstic@lake-district.gov.uk; Glebe Rd; ⏲9.30am-5.30pm Easter-Oct, 10am-4pm Fri-Sun Nov-Easter); Windermere (☎015394-46499; windermeretic@southlakeland.gov.uk; Victoria St; ⏲9am-5.30pm Mon-Sat, 9.30am-5.30pm Sun Apr-Oct, shorter hours in winter) The latter branch is opposite NatWest Bank.

ℹ Getting There & Away

BOAT The **Windermere Ferry** (car/bike/foot passenger £4/1/50p; ⏲6.50am-9.50pm Mon-Fri, 9.10am-9.50pm Sat & Sun Mar-Oct, last ferry one hr earlier in winter) carries vehicles and foot passengers roughly every 20 minutes from Ferry Nab, just south of Bowness, across the lake to Ferry House on the lake's west side. Ferries can be cancelled at short notice due to bad weather, and summer queues can be long.

BUS There's one daily National Express coach from London (£37, eight hours) via Lancaster and Kendal. Local buses:

555/556 Lakeslink Tracks the lake to Brockhole Visitor Centre (seven minutes, at least hourly), Ambleside (15 minutes) and Grasmere (30 minutes), or Kendal in the opposite direction.

505 Coniston Rambler To Coniston (50 minutes, 10 daily Monday to Saturday, six on Sunday) via Brockhole, Ambleside and Hawkshead.

599 Lakes Rider (three times hourly Monday to Saturday, hourly on Sunday, reduced service in winter) To Bowness, Windermere, Troutbeck, Brockhole, Rydal Church (for Rydal Mount, p584), Dove Cottage and Grasmere.

TRAIN Windermere is the only town inside the national park accessible by train. It's on the branch line to Kendal and Oxenholme, from where there are frequent connections north and south.

Train services:

DESTINATION	FARE (ONE WAY)	DURATION (HR)
Oxenholme	£4.30	20min
Kendal	£3.80	15min
Manchester	£28.40	1½-2
Lancaster	£11	45min
London	£82	3¼
Glasgow	£42	2¾
Edinburgh	£46.50	2½

Around Bowness

Blackwell Arts & Crafts House HISTORIC HOME
(www.blackwell.org.uk; adult/child £6.50/4.20; ⏲10.30am-5pm Apr-Oct, to 4pm Feb-Mar & Nov-Dec) Two miles south of Bowness on the B5360, Blackwell House is one of the finest examples of the 19th-century Arts and Crafts Movement. Inspired by the aesthetic principles of John Ruskin and William Morris, Arts and Crafts was a reaction against the machine-driven mentality of the Industrial Revolution, placing emphasis on simple architecture, high-quality craftsmanship and natural light. Designed by Mackay Hugh Baillie Scott, the house has all the hallmarks of classic Arts and Crafts: light, airy rooms, serene decor, and bespoke craftwork ranging from Delft tiles to handmade doorknobs and wood panelling. There's a tearoom

and gift shop for when you've finished moseying round the house.

Townend HISTORIC HOME
(NT; ☎01539-432628; adult/child £4.20/2.10; ⊙1-5pm Wed-Sun Mar-Oct, earlier guided tours by arrangement) Hidden on a hilltop in the tiny hamlet of Troutbeck, a mile from Windermere, this Lakeland farmhouse was built for a wealthy yeoman farmer in the 17th century. Topped by cylindrical chimneys and grey slate tiles, the house contains rustic artefacts, books and vintage farming tools, plus original wooden furniture carved by the Browne family, who owned the house until 1943.

Getting There & Away

Bus 517, the Kirkstone Rambler, travels through Troutbeck en route to Ullswater (one hour, three daily mid-July to August, weekends only other times of year).

Ambleside

POP 3382

Tucked at the northern head of Windermere and backed by a cluster of dramatic fells, Ambleside feels a lot less commercialised than its sister towns further to the south, but that doesn't stop it getting jam-packed throughout the summer months. It's a favourite base for hikers, with plenty of quality outdoors shops dotted round town, and it marks the start of several classic fell hikes.

Sights & Activities

The town's best-known landmark is **Bridge House**, a tiny cottage that spans the clattering brook of Stock Ghyll; now occupied by a National Trust shop, it's thought to have originally been built as an apple store.

Armitt Museum MUSEUM
(www.armitt.com; Rydal Rd; adult £2.50; ⊙10am-5pm) Artefacts at Ambleside's modest town museum include a lock of John Ruskin's hair, a collection of botanical watercolours by Beatrix Potter, and prints by the pharmacist-turned-photographer Herbert Bell.

Fell Hikes WALKING
Ambleside marks the start of several well-known walks, including the wooded trail up to the 60ft waterfall of **Stock Ghyll Force**, or the three-hour round trip via **Wansfell** and **Jenkins Crag**, with views across to Coniston and the Langdale Pikes. Serious hikers can tackle the 10-mile **Fairfield Horseshoe** via Nab Scar, Heron Pike, Fairfield and Dove Crag.

Low Wood Watersports BOAT HIRE
(☎015394-39441; watersports@elhmail.co.uk) If you feel like getting out on the lake, this watersports centre rents row boats (one/four hours £12/34), kayaks (two/four hours £16/21), canoes (two/four hours £20/30) and motor boats (one/four hours £20/45).

Sleeping

Waterhead Hotel HOTEL £££
(☎08458-504503; www.elh.co.uk/hotels/waterhead; r £106-256; P ᯤ) Outside, it's quintessential Lakeland: stone, slate, watery views. Inside, it's bespoke and boutique: cream-and-beige rooms, leather chairs, LCD TVs, flashy fabrics. The lakeside patio-bar's a beauty, too and the upmarket Bay Restaurant serves some of Ambleside's best bistro food (mains £12.95 to £19.95).

Cote How Organic Guest House B&B £££
(☎015394-32765; www.bedbreakfastlakedistrict.com; Rydal, near Ambleside; s £98-£108, d £120-160; P ᯤ) If it's an eco-conscious sleep you're after, Cote How's the place – it's one of only three UK B&Bs licensed by the Soil Association. Food is 100% local and organ-

WORTH A TRIP

PUNCH BOWL INN

Having scooped oodles of awards over the last couple of years, this cracking **country pub** (☎015395-68237; www.the-punchbowl.co.uk; Crosthwaite; mains £14-28; r £160-310; P) is unfortunately no longer the secret tip it used to be. Even so, it's still an essential stop for gastropub connoisseurs, and serves up some of the finest food in Lakeland.

We're a long world away from scampi-and-chips here – you might feel like tucking into roast veal blanquette, skate wing with shrimp butter or home-smoked duck, washed down perhaps with a choice ale from the in-house Barngates Brewery. Indulged too much? No problem: upstairs rooms dazzle, with reclaimed beams, Roberts Revival radios and underfloor heating.

The pub's in the hamlet of Crosthwaite, about 6 miles southeast of Windermere along the A5074.

ic, power's sourced from a green supplier, and they'll even lend you wind-up torches and candles (5% discount if you arrive by bus, too). The three rooms are elegantly Edwardian, with cast-iron beds, roll-top baths and fireplaces. The house is in Rydal, 1.5 miles north of Ambleside.

Lakes Lodge B&B ££
(015394-33240; www.lakeslodge.co.uk; Lake Rd; r £89-129;) Trendy cross between a minihotel and a modern guest house: the rooms are all clean lines, stark walls and zero clutter, and there are several extra-big rooms that are ideal for families.

Compston House Hotel B&B ££
(015394-32305; www.compstonhouse.co.uk; Compston Rd; d from £76) Quirky Stateside-style B&B, run by expat New Yorkers. Every room is themed after a different state: sunny Hawaii, airy Florida, maritime Maine – you get the idea. Needless to say, there are muffins and maple pancakes for breakfast.

The Gables B&B ££
(015394-33272; www.thegables-ambleside.co.uk; Church Walk; s £40-50, d £60-80; P) Gabled by name, gabled by nature, this double-fronted house is in a quiet spot overlooking the recreation ground. The 14 rooms vary in size – ask for the largest that's available. The owners run Sheila's Cottage restaurant, and guests receive a discount when they dine.

Low Wray CAMPSITE £
(lowwraycampsite@nationaltrust.org.uk; tent sites for 1 adult, car and small tent £8-11, per extra adult £5, extra child £2.50, lake view supplement £7.50-10; campsite arrivals 3-7pm Sat-Thu, 3-9pm Fri) Lovely lakeside campsite run by the National Trust, recently supplemented by the addition of yurts, ecopods and tepees. The site is 3 miles from town along the B5286; bus 505 stops nearby. For ecopod and tent bookings, contact the National Trust, but for yurt and tepee hire, try **4Winds Lakeland Tipis** (01539-821227; www.4windslakelandtipis.co.uk; tipi per week £270-440), **Long Valley** (01539-731089; www.long-valley-yurts.co.uk; yurts per week £385-460), or **Wild in Style** (07909-446381; www.wildinstyle.co.uk; yurts per week £350-450), which has more-luxurious yurts.

Ambleside YHA HOSTEL £
(0845-371 9620; ambleside@yha.org.uk; Windermere Rd; dm from £14; P) Fresh from a refit, this flagship YHA is open for business again with fresh rooms (including plenty of doubles), lake views and a host of organised activities (from kayaking to *ghyll*-scrambling). Great facilities (kitchen, bike rental, boat jetty and bar) mean it's heavily subscribed in high season.

NATIONAL TRUST CAMPSITE BOOKINGS

The NT's three Lake District campsites at Low Wray, Wasdale and Great Langdale have recently started to accept **bookings**, much to the delight of regular Lakeland campers. Pitches can be reserved up to 24 hours before your stay for periods of two nights or longer. There's an online booking fee of £5, or £7.50 for telephone and email bookings. Discounts are also available if you arrive by 'green transport' (eg by showing a train or bus ticket).

Contact the **Bookings Coordinator** (015394-63862; campsite.bookings@nationaltrust.org.uk; 1-5pm Mon-Fri), or search for the relevant campsite with the **National Trust** (www.nationaltrust.org.uk) online.

Ambleside Backpackers HOSTEL ££
(015394-32340; www.englishlakesbackpackers.co.uk; Old Lake Rd; dm £16; P @) Cottage hostel a short walk south from Ambleside's centre.

Full Circle CAMPSITE £££
(07975-671928; www.lake-district-yurts.co.uk; yurts £295-440; P) Yurt camping in the grounds of Rydal Hall, near Rydal Mount.

Eating

It's wise to book the following places.

TOP CHOICE **Lucy's on a Plate** RESTAURANT ££
(015394-31191; www.lucysofambleside.co.uk; Church St; mains lunch £6-15, dinner £15-25; 10am-9pm) Lucy's started life in 1989 as a specialist grocery, but over the last decade it's mushroomed into a full-blown gastronomic empire, with premises dotted all over Ambleside, as well as a Windermere outpost and even a cookery school in Staveley. The original bistro is still the best of the bunch, though: a light and inviting space with pine tables and a sweet conservatory, serving Lucy's trademark quirkily named food, such as 'fruity porker', 'fell-walker filler' or 'pruned piggy-wig'. It gets very busy,

so bookings are essential at busy times and weekends.

Glass House RESTAURANT ££
(☎015394-32137; Rydal Rd; mains lunch £8-14, dinner £13-19) Ritzy restaurant in a converted watermill (with the original mill wheel and machinery still on site), serving some of the most accomplished Med and French food in the Lakes, underpinned by top-quality local ingredients – Herdwick lamb, Lakeland chicken, and fish from the north coast ports.

Fellini's VEGETARIAN ££
(☎015394-32487; Church St; mains £10.95; ⊙dinner only, closed Mon in winter) Fear not, vegetarians: you might be in the land of the Cumberland sausage and the tattie hotpot, but thanks to this new veggie venture you won't have to go without a good meal. It's a long way from tired old nut roasts: think grilled courgette towers, potato filo baskets and walnut and pear cannelloni. It's run by the owners of Ambleside's cinema and Zeffirelli's restaurant (as well as the lovely Yewfield B&B, see p587). The movie-meal combo costs £19.95.

Zeffirelli's BISTRO £
(☎015394-33845; Compston Rd; pizzas & mains £8-10; ⊙until 10pm) Affectionately known as Zeff's by the locals, this buzzy pizza and pasta joint doubles as Ambleside's jazz club after dark. Artful lighting and big curvy seats conjure a cool vibe. The movie-meal combo costs £17.95, including a two-course meal and a ticket to the flicks.

Tarantella RESTAURANT ££
(10 Lake Rd; mains £10-16) Snazzy Italian served in elegant surroundings, with wood-fired pizzas and authentic pastas partnered by unusual regional fare such as duck-and-chilli sausage and roast tuna.

Lucy 4 TAPAS £
(2 St Mary's Lane; tapas £4-10; ⊙5-11pm Mon-Sat, to 10.30pm Sun) Tapas and wine-bar offshoot of Lucy's eating empire.

Apple Pie CAFE £
(Rydal Rd; lunch £4-10; ⊙breakfast & lunch) Sunny cafe popular for its cakes, sandwiches, Bath buns and hearty pies.

Lucy's Specialist Grocery DELI £
(Compston Rd) The deli that started it all, relocated to Compston Rd. Shelves stocked with chutneys, chocs, plus chiller cabinets full of Lakeland produce.

Drinking & Entertainment

Ambleside has plenty of pubs: locals favour the **Golden Rule** (Smithy Brow) for its ale selection, while the **Royal Oak** (Market Pl) packs in the posthike punters.

Ambleside's two-screen **Zeffirelli's Cinema** (☎015394-33100; Compston Rd) is next to Zeff's, with extra screens in a converted church down the road.

Shopping

Compston Rd has enough equipment shops to launch an assault on Everest, with branches of **Rohan** and **Gaymer Sports** on Market Cross. Also on Compston Rd, **Black's** is a favourite with hikers, and the **Climber's Shop** specialises in rock-climbing gear.

Information

Library (Kelsick Rd; per hr £3; ⊙10am-5pm Mon & Wed, to 7pm Tue & Fri, to 1pm Sat) Internet access.

Tourist office (☎015394-32582; tic@thehubofambleside.com; Central Buildings, Market Cross; ⊙9am-5pm)

Getting There & Around

BICYCLE For mountain-bike hire, including maps, pump, helmet and lock:

Biketreks (☎015394-31505; www.biketreks.net; Compston Rd; per day £20)

Ghyllside Cycles (☎015394-33592; www.ghyllside.co.uk; The Slack; per day £18)

BUS Lots of buses run through Ambleside.

555 to Grasmere and Windermere (hourly, 10 buses on Sunday)

505 to Hawkshead and Coniston (10 a day Monday to Saturday, six on Sunday, mid-March to October)

516 (six daily, five on Sunday) to Elterwater and Langdale.

Around Ambleside

TOP CHOICE **Rydal Mount** HISTORIC HOME
(www.rydalmount.co.uk; adult/child £6/2.50, gardens only adults £4; ⊙9.30am-5pm daily Mar-Oct, 11am-4pm Wed-Mon Nov & Feb) While most people flock to Dove Cottage in search of William Wordsworth, those in the know head for Rydal Mount, the Wordsworth family home from 1813 until his death in 1850.

Still owned by the poet's distant descendants, the house is a treasure trove of Wordsworth memorabilia. On the top floor is Wordsworth's attic study, containing his encyclopedia and a sword belonging to his younger brother John, who was killed in a shipwreck in 1805.

Below the house is **Dora's Field**, which Wordsworth planted with daffodils in memory of his eldest daughter, who succumbed to tuberculosis in 1847.

The house is 1.5 miles northwest of Ambleside, off the A591. Bus 555 (and bus 599 from April to October), between Grasmere, Ambleside, Windermere and Kendal, stops at the end of the drive.

Grasmere

POP 1458

Even without its Romantic connections, gorgeous Grasmere would still be one of the Lakes' biggest draws. It's one of the prettiest of the Lakeland hamlets, huddled at the base of a sweeping valley dotted with woods, pastures and slate-coloured hills, but most of the thousands of trippers come in search of its famous former residents: opium-eating Thomas de Quincey, unruly Coleridge and grand old man William Wordsworth. With such a rich literary heritage, Grasmere unsurprisingly gets crammed; avoid high summer if you can.

Sights

Dove Cottage HISTORIC HOME

(015394-35544; www.wordsworth.org.uk; adult/child £7.50/4.50; 9.30am-5.30pm, last admission 4pm winter) Originally an inn called The Dove and Olive, this tiny cottage just outside Grasmere is the most famous former home of William Wordsworth.

Covered with climbing roses, honeysuckle and tiny latticed windows, the cottage contains some fascinating artefacts – keep your eyes peeled for some fine portraits of Wordsworth, a cabinet containing his spectacles, shaving case and razor, and a set of scales used by de Quincey to weigh out his opium. Entry is by timed ticket to prevent overcrowding, and includes a half-hour tour.

Next door is the **Wordsworth Museum & Art Gallery**, which houses a collection of letters, portraits and manuscripts relating to the Romantic movement, and regularly hosts events and poetry readings.

St Oswald's Church CHURCH

Parts of Grasmere's delightful village church date back to the 13th century. The Wordsworth family regularly came here to worship: inside you'll see a memorial to the poet alongside his own prayer book, and in the churchyard you'll find the graves of William, Mary and Dorothy; the Wordsworth children Dora, Catherine and Thomas; and Samuel Taylor Coleridge's son Hartley.

Activities

Popular **fell hikes** starting from Grasmere include Helm Crag (1328ft), often known as the 'Lion and the Lamb', thanks to its distinctive shape, Silver Howe (1292ft), Loughrigg Fell (1099ft) and the multi-peak circuit known as the Easedale Round (five to six hours, 8.5 to 9 miles).

Sleeping

TOP CHOICE **Moss Grove Organic** HOTEL £££

(015394-35251; www.mossgrove.com; r £225-325; P) This Victorian villa has been lavishly redeveloped as Lakeland's loveliest eco-chic hotel, second to none in terms of green credentials: sheep-fleece insulation, natural-ink wallpapers, organic paints, reclaimed-timber beds. It's expensive, but definitely one to remember.

How Foot Lodge B&B ££

(015394-35366; www.howfoot.co.uk; Town End; d £70-78; P) Wordsworth groupies will adore this stone cottage just a stroll from William's digs at Dove Cottage. The six rooms are light and contemporary, finished in fawns and beiges; ask for the one with the private sun lounge for that indulgent edge. The rates are fantastic, too, especially considering the heritage and location.

Harwood Hotel B&B ££

(015394-35248; www.harwoodhotel.co.uk; Red Lion Square; d £95-135;) Despite the 'hotel' in the name, this is a really a B&B – but a very classy one. Nestled right in the middle of Grasmere above Heidi's cafe, the six rooms are chocolate-box cute, if a tad feminine – expect plenty of Cath Kidston–style patterns and frilly heart-shape cushions.

Raise View House B&B ££

(015394-35215; www.raiseviewhouse.co.uk; White Bridge; s/d £90/110; P) For that all-essential fell view, you can't really top this excellent B&B. All the rooms have a different outlook (the ones from Helm Crag, Easedale and Stone Arthur are particularly impressive), and the rest of the house is beautifully appointed: Farrow & Ball paints, Gilchrist & Soames bathstuffs, and Wedgwood china on the breakfast table.

Grasmere Hostel HOSTEL £
(☎015394-35055; www.grasmerehostel.co.uk; Broadrayne Farm; dm £18.50; P @) When was the last time you stayed at a hostel with a Nordic sauna? It might be pricier than Grasmere's two YHAs, but you'll be treating yourself to a superior sleep: bathrooms en suite for every room, a mountain-view lounge and two kitchens. The hostel's just off the A591 near the Traveller's Rest pub. Bus 555 stops nearby.

Butharlyp How YHA HOSTEL £
(☎0845-371 9319; www.yha.org.uk; Easedale Rd; dm £15.50; ⊙reception 7am-10pm Feb-Nov, weekends only Dec & Jan; P @) The biggest of Grasmere's two YHA hostels is in a fine Victorian house plonked amidst grassy grounds. The dorms are starting to show their age, but the idyllic setting and decent bar-restaurant make this another superior YHA. The hostel also handles bookings for Thorney How.

Thorney How YHA HOSTEL £
(☎0845-371 9319; grasmere@yha.org.uk; Easedale Rd; dm from £14; ⊙reception 7.30-10am & 5-11pm Apr-Oct) For rustic character, try this old farmhouse tucked away on a back lane 15 minutes from Grasmere. The rooms are spartan and the facilities basic, but you'll be staying in a historic spot – Thorney How was the first property purchased by the YHA back in 1931.

Eating & Drinking

TOP CHOICE **Jumble Room** RESTAURANT £££
(☎015394-35188; Langdale Rd; mains £13-24; ⊙lunch weekends, dinner Wed-Mon) Husband-and-wife team Andy and Crissy Hill have turned this tiny boho bistro into a real gastronomic heavy-hitter. Mixing quality Lakeland produce with Mediterranean influences (particularly from Spain and Italy), it attracts diners from far and wide, and the decor oozes oddball appeal, from the jumble-shop-chic furniture and polka dot plates to the colourful cow pictures on the downstairs walls. Reserve ahead.

Sara's Bistro BISTRO ££
(Broadgate; mains £10-16) Hearty homespun cooking is Sarah's raison d'être – big portions of roast chicken, lamb shanks and apple crumble, served without the faintest hint of fuss.

Heidi's of Grasmere CAFE £
(Red Lion Sq; lunch mains £4-8; ⊙9am-5.30pm) Yummy little sandwich shop and cafe beneath the Harwood Hotel. Pull up a pine table for some piping-hot soup, a toasted sandwich or the house special, 'cheese smokey'.

Sarah Nelson's Gingerbread Shop CONFECTIONERY SHOP
(www.grasmeregingerbread.co.uk; Church Stile; 12 pieces of gingerbread £3.50; ⊙9.15am-5.30pm Mon-Sat, 12.30-5pm Sun) Don't think about leaving Grasmere without sampling Sarah Nelson's legendary gingerbread, produced to the same secret recipe for the last 150 years and still served by ladies in frilly pinnies and starched bonnets.

Other options:

Rowan Tree CAFE £
(Stocks Lane; mains £3-10, pizzas £6-9) Riverside cafe good for lunchtime ciabattas, fish dishes and veggie plates.

Miller Howe Cafe CAFE ££
(Red Lion Sq; mains £5-14) Chic cafe on the main village square.

Getting There & Away

The hourly 555 runs from Windermere to Grasmere (15 minutes), via Ambleside, Rydal Church and Dove Cottage. The open-top 599 (two or three per hour March to August) runs from Grasmere south via Ambleside, Troutbeck Bridge, Windermere and Bowness.

Hawkshead

POP 1640

Lakeland villages don't come much more postcard-perfect than Hawkshead, a muddle of whitewashed cottages, cobbled lanes and old pubs lost among bottle-green countryside between Ambleside and Coniston. Chuck in connections to both Wordsworth and Beatrix Potter, and you won't be surprised to find Hawkshead awash with visitors in the high summer – although the fact that cars are banned in the village centre keeps things a bit more tranquil.

Sights

Hawkshead Grammar School HISTORIC BUILDING
(www.hawksheadgrammar.org.uk; admission £2; ⊙10am-1pm & 2-5pm Mon-Sat, 1-5pm Sun Apr-Sep, 10am-1pm & 2-3.30pm Mon-Sat, 1-3.30pm Sun Oct) In centuries past, promising young Lakeland gentleman were sent to Hawkshead's village school for their educational foundations, including a young William Wordsworth, who attended the school from 1779 to 1787. The curriculum was punishing:

ten hours' study a day, covering weighty subjects such as Latin, Greek, geometry, science and rhetoric. Hardly surprising young Willie (among others) felt the urge to carve his name into one of the desks.

Upstairs is a small exhibition exploring the history of the school.

Beatrix Potter Gallery GALLERY
(NT; Red Lion Sq; adult/child £4.40/2.10; 10.30am-4.30pm Sat-Thu mid-Mar–Oct) Beatrix Potter's husband, the solicitor William Heelis, was based in Hawkshead. His former office is now owned by the National Trust and contains a selection of delicate wildife watercolours by Beatrix Potter, illustrating her considerable skills as a botanical painter and amateur naturalist.

Discounted admission is available if you keep hold of your ticket from Hill Top.

Sleeping & Eating

TOP CHOICE **Yewfield** B&B ££
(015394-36765; www.yewfield.co.uk; Hawkshead Hill; d £96-120; P) Run by the owners of Zeff's in Ambleside, the rooms at this all-veggie house combine oriental fabrics, slinky finishes and Edwardian features (although the Tower Room has a more classic feel). Breakfast is organic, vegetarian and sourced from the kitchen garden, and the gardens are gorgeous: there are also self-catering apartments in the Swallows Nest (£280 to £550 per week). The house is 2 miles west of Hawkshead on the B5285.

Hawkshead YHA HOSTEL £
(0845-371 9321; hawkshead@yha.org.uk; dm from £14; P @) Hawkshead's hostel occupies a Regency house a mile along the Newby Bridge road. Like many Lakeland YHAs, the period architecture is impressive – cornicing, panelled doors, a veranda – and the big dorms boast big views. There's bike rental and a kitchen, and buses stop outside the door.

Queen's Head Hotel PUB, B&B ££
(015394-36271; Main St; mains £14-22, d £40-90) Hawkshead has several decent pubs, but our pick is the old Queen's Head, which fairly brims with oak-panelled appeal. Hale and hearty country food (Esthwaite trout, Winster pork, Gressingham duck) in the low-ceilinged bar, partnered by small, prim rooms upstairs and a less appealing lodge out back.

Hawkshead Relish Company DELI £
(015394-36614; www.hawksheadrelish.com; The Square; 9.30am-5pm Mon-Fri, from 10am Sun) Award-winning chutneys, relishes and mustards, from classic piccalilli to damson jam.

DON'T MISS

THE DRUNKEN DUCK

TOP CHOICE **Drunken Duck** (015394-36347; www.drunkenduckinn.co.uk; Barngates; mains £13-25, r £95-275; P wi-fi) This designer place is much, much more than a bog-standard gastropub – it's a brewery, boutique B&B, historic boozer and lip-smacking bistro rolled into one indulgent bundle. Inside the 400-year-old inn, vintage architecture marries up with modern touches. Slate fireplaces and old signs sit alongside leather chairs and neutral shades, and while the rooms are small, they're all fresh and inviting, with Roberts radios, enamel baths and rolling rural views (some even overlook a private tarn). The real treat, though, is the pub itself, where home-brewed ales from the Barngates Brewery accompany a menu oozing with sophisticated flavours – crab-claw salad, venison loin, pan-fried turbot. Simply super.

Getting There & Away

Hawkshead is linked with Windermere, Ambleside and Coniston by bus 505 (10 Monday to Saturday, six on Sunday mid-March to October), and to Hill Top and Coniston by the Cross-Lakes Shuttle.

Around Hawkshead

TARN HOWS

About 2 miles off the B5285 from Hawkshead, a windy country lane wends its way to **Tarn Hows**, a famously photogenic artificial lake built on land donated to the National Trust by Beatrix Potter in 1930. Trails wind their way around the lakeshore – keep you eyes peeled for rare red squirrels frolicking in the treetops.

Parking can be difficult in summer and on weekends, so you might prefer to catch the bus. Several services, including the 505, the X31/32 and the Cross-Lakes Experience, stop nearby.

GRIZEDALE FOREST

Stretching across the hills between Coniston Water and Esthwaite Water is Grizedale (from the Old Norse for 'wild boar'), a dense woodland of oak, larch and pine that has been almost entirely replanted over the last hundred years after extensive logging during the 19th century.

The forest is now a hugely popular spot with mountain bikers and walkers; eight marked walking paths and five mountain bike routes wind their way through the trees. On your way around, look out for some of the 90-odd outdoor sculptures that have been created in the forest by local and international artists over the course of the last 30 years.

Budding 'Gorillas' (adults) and 'Baboons' (children) can also test their skills at **Go Ape** (www.goape.co.uk; adult/child £30/25; ⌚9-5pm Mar-Oct, plus winter weekends), a gravity-defying assault course along rope ladders, bridges, platforms and hair-raising zip-slides.

For general information on the forest, the new **Grizedale Visitors Centre** (☎01229-860010; www.forestry.gov.uk/grizedaleforestpark; ⌚10am-5pm, 11am-4pm winter) provides trail leaflets and forest maps. It's also home to the small **Café in the Forest** (⌚10am-5pm) and **Grizedale Mountain Bike Hire** (www.grizedalemountainbikes.co.uk; per day adult/child from £25/10; ⌚9am-5.30pm Mar-Oct, last hire 2pm).

HILL TOP

(NT; ☎015394-36269; hilltop@nationaltrust.org.uk; adult/child £6.50/3.10; ⌚10am-4.30pm mid-May–Aug, 10.30am-4.30pm mid-Mar–mid-May & Sep-Oct, 11.30am-3.30pm mid-Feb–mid-Mar) In the tiny village of Near Sawrey, 2 miles south of Hawkshead, this farmhouse is a must for Beatrix Potter buffs: it was the first house she lived in after moving to the Lake District, and it's also where she wrote and illustrated many of her famous tales.

Purchased in 1905 (largely on the proceeds of her first bestseller, *The Tale of Peter Rabbit*), Hill Top is crammed with decorative details that fans will recognise from the author's illustrations.

Thanks to its worldwide fame (helped along by the 2006 biopic *Miss Potter*), Hill Top is one of the Lakes' most popular spots. Entry is by timed ticket, and the queues can be seriously daunting during the summer holidays.

Getting There & Away

For details on the Cross-Lakes Experience, see p576.

X30 Grizedale Wanderer (four daily March to November) Runs from Haverthwaite to Grizedale via Hawkshead and Moor Top.

505 Stops at Hawkshead en route between Coniston and Windermere.

Coniston

POP 1948

Hunkered beneath the pockmarked peak of the Old Man (803m), the lakeside village of Coniston was originally established as a centre for the copper-mining industry, but the only remnants of the industry left are the many abandoned quarries and mine shafts that now litter the surrounding hilltops.

Coniston's main claim to fame is as the location for a string of world-record speed attempts made here by Sir Malcolm Campbell and his son, Donald, between the 1930s and 1960s. Tragically, after beating the record several times, Donald was killed during an attempt in 1967, when his futuristic jet-boat *Bluebird* flipped at around 320mph. The boat and its pilot were recovered in 2001, and Campbell was buried in the cemetery near St Andrew's church.

Coniston is a fairly quiet village these days, mainly worth a visit for its lovely lake cruises and a trip to the former house of John Ruskin at Brantwood.

Sights

Brantwood HISTORIC HOME

(☎015394-41396; www.brantwood.org.uk; adult/child £6.30/1.35, gardens only £4.50/1.35; ⌚11am-5.30pm mid-Mar–mid-Nov, to 4.30pm Wed-Sun mid-Nov–mid-Mar) John Ruskin (1819–1900), the Victorian polymath, philosopher and critic, was one of the great thinkers of 19th-century society, expounding views on everything from Venetian architecture to the finer points of traditional lace-making. In 1871 he purchased Brantwood and spent the next 20 years expanding the house and grounds, championing the value of traditional 'Arts and Crafts' over soulless factory-made materials.

Upstairs you can view a collection of his watercolours before stopping for lunch at the excellent **Jumping Jenny** (lunches £4-8) cafe and catching a leisurely boat back to Coniston. The boat trip from Brantwood back to Coniston takes about half an hour.

Alternatively you can drive to the house – take the B5285 towards Hawkshead and follow the brown signs to Brantwood.

Ruskin Museum MUSEUM
(www.ruskinmuseum.com; adult/child £5.25/2.50; ⏲10am-5.30pm Easter–mid-Nov, 10.30am-3.30pm Wed-Sun mid-Nov–Easter) Coniston's museum explores the village's history, touching on copper mining, Arthur Ransome and the Campbell story. There's also an extensive section on John Ruskin, with displays of his writings, watercolours and sketchbooks. An extension is currently being built to house Campbell's K7 boat: if it's not finished by the time you get here, you can see the boat's tail fin, air intake and engine. The museum also arranges **guided walks** (adult/child £7/3.50) exploring the Campbell story and the area's John Ruskin connections.

Activities

Boating

Lake Coniston famously inspired Arthur Ransome's classic children's tale *Swallows & Amazons*. Peel Island, towards the southern end of **Coniston Water**, doubles in the book as 'Wild Cat Island', while the Gondola steam yacht allegedly gave Ransome the idea for Captain Flint's houseboat. **Coniston Boating Centre** (☎015394-41366; Coniston Jetty) hires out rowing boats, Canadian canoes and motorboats, or you can take one of the two cruise services which glide out across the glassy waters.

Steam Yacht Gondola LAKE CRUISE
(☎015394-63850; adult/child £8.50/4.50) Built in 1859 and restored in the 1980s by the National Trust, this wonderful steam yacht looks like a cross between a Venetian *vaporetto* and an English houseboat, complete with cushioned saloons and polished wood seats. There are five trips daily from mid-March to October, plus less frequent commentated Explorer cruises covering Ransome, the Campbells and Ruskin.

And don't fret about carbon emissions; since 2008 the Gondola's been running on ecofriendly waste-wood logs, cutting her carbon footprint by 90%.

Coniston Launch LAKE CRUISE
(☎015394-36216; www.conistonlaunch.co.uk) A more contemporary way to get around the lake is aboard Coniston's two modern launches, which have run on solar panels since 2005. There are two routes: the **Northern service** (adult/child return £8.90/4.95) calls at the Waterhead Hotel, Torver and Brantwood, while the **Southern service** (adult/child return £12.50/6.25) sails to the jetties at Torver, Water Park, Lake Bank, Sunny Bank and Brantwood via Peel Island. You can break your journey and walk to the next jetty. There are between five and nine daily trips depending on the time of year.

As with the Gondola, cruises (commentated) on the Campbells (adult/child £11.70/5.75) and *Swallows & Amazons* (£12/6) are available throughout the year. Ask at the ticket office for details.

Walking

If you're in Coniston to hike, chances are you've come to conquer the **Old Man** (7.5 miles, four to five hours). It's a steep but rewarding climb past Coniston's abandoned copper mines to the summit, from where the views stretch to the Cumbrian Coast on a clear day.

The tourist office has leaflets on possible routes up the Old Man and other walks, as well as the annual **Coniston Walking Festival** (www.conistonwalkingfestival.org), held in September.

Sleeping

TOP CHOICE **Yew Tree Farm** B&B ££
(☎015394-41433; www.yewtree-farm.com; d £100-124; P) Farmhouses don't come finer than this whitewashed, slate-roofed beauty, which doubled for Hill Top in *Miss Potter* (fittingly, since Beatrix Potter owned Yew Tree in the 1930s). It's still a working farm, but these days it offers luxurious lodgings alongside the cowsheds. If it's fully booked, console yourself with a nutty flapjack or a Hot Herdwick sandwich at the delightful Yew Tree Tea Room next door.

Bank Ground Farm B&B ££
(☎015394-41264; www.bankground.com; East of the Lake; d £70-80; P) This lakeside farmhouse has literary clout: Arthur Ransome used it as the model for Holly Howe Farm in *Swallows & Amazons*. Parts of the house date back to the 15th century, so the rooms are obviously snug, but they're all smartly done, some with sleigh beds, others with exposed beams. The tearoom (⏲noon-5pm Fri-Sun Easter-Oct) is a beauty, too, and there are several pretty cottages if you can't bear to tear yourself away.

Summer Hill Country House HOTEL ££
(☎015394-36180; www.summerhillcountryhouse.com; Hawkshead Hill; d £70-104; P@🛜) You'll need a car to get to this elegant house-hotel, as it's halfway between Coniston and Hawkshead, but it's really worth the drive. There are only five rooms, but each has its own feel: we particularly recommend the monochrome No 4 and crimson No 5.

Holly How YHA HOSTEL £
(☎0845-371 9511; conistonhh@yha.org.uk; Far End; dm £16) Coniston's main hostel occupies a slate-fronted period house along the road towards Ambleside, and offers the usual YHA facilities: kitchens, evening meals and bike hire, with a choice of four-, eight- or 10-bed dorms. It's a school-trip favourite, so book ahead.

Coppermines YHA HOSTEL £
(☎0845-371 9630; coppermines@yha.org.uk; dm £16; ⊙Easter-Oct) Mountain hostel popular with hikers setting out for the Old Man. It's 1.5 miles from Coniston; no car access.

Coniston Hall Campsite CAMPSITE £
(☎015394-41223; sites from £12; ⊙Easter-Oct) Busy lakeside campsite a mile from town.

Eating & Drinking

Black Bull PUB ££
(www.conistonbrewery.com; Yewdale Rd; mains £6-14) Quality pub grub right in the middle of Coniston village: the Cumberland Sausage is particularly noteworthy, as are the house-brewed ales, including Bluebird Bitter, Old Man Ale and Winter Warmer Blacksmiths.

Sun Hotel PUB ££
(www.thesunconiston.com; mains £12-20) Dine under hefty beams or in a fell-view conservatory at the Sun, perched on a little hill just behind the village and famously used as a HQ by Donald Campbell during his final fateful campaign.

Harry's CAFE £
(4 Yewdale Rd; mains £6-12) Part wine bar, part cafe, part bistro, serving solid (if rather unstarry) steaks, pizzas, pastas and club sandwiches, along with the prodigious Harry's Big Breakfast.

Bluebird Cafe CAFE £
(Lake Rd; lunch mains £4-8; ⊙breakfast & lunch) Perfectly placed by the Coniston jetty, the Bluebird is a fine spot for tea and cakes or a quick ice cream before hopping aboard the cross-lake launch.

Information

Coniston Tourist Office (☎015394-41533; www.conistontic.org; Ruskin Ave; ⊙9.30am-5.30pm Easter-Oct, till 4pm Nov-Easter) The Coniston Loyalty Card (£2) offers local discounts. The Ruskin Explorer ticket (adult/child £14.95/6.50) includes Windermere bus fare, a Coniston launch ticket and entrance to Brantwood; pick it up here or from the bus driver.

Hollands Cafe (☎015394-41303; Tilberthwaite Ave; per hr £5; ⊙9am-4pm or 5pm Mon-Sat) Internet access.

Getting There & Away

Bus 505 runs from Windermere (10 Monday to Saturday, six on Sunday mid-March to October), via Ambleside, with a couple of daily connections to Kendal (1¼ hours).

Langdale

Travelling north from Coniston, the road passes into increasingly wild, empty countryside. Barren hilltops loom as you travel north past the old Viking settlement of Elterwater en route to Great Langdale, where the main road comes to an end and many of the Lakes' greatest trails begin – including the stomp up the Langdale Pikes past Harrison Stickle (736m) and Pike o' Stickle (709m), and the spectacular ascent of Crinkle Crags (819m).

The classic place to stay in Great Langdale is the **Old Dungeon Ghyll** (☎015394-37272; www.odg.co.uk; d £102-112; P). It's been the getaway of choice for many well-known walkers and it's still endearingly old-fashioned: country chintz and venerable furniture in the rooms; oak beams, wood tables and a crackling fire in the walkers' bar; and more history per square inch than practically anywhere in the Lakes.

The **Stickle Barn** (☎015394-37356; mains £4-12) is a popular choice for a posthike dinner, with curries, casseroles and stews to warm those weary bones. There's basic dorm accommodation in the bunkhouse out back.

Many hikers choose to kip at the **Great Langdale Campsite** (langdalecamp@nationaltrust.org.uk; tent sites 1 adult with car £8-11, extra adult/child £5/2.50; ⊙arrivals 3-7pm Sat-Thu, 3-9pm Fri), a typically well-run NT campground a mile up the valley, with glorious mountain views and the recent addition of eco-pods (£20 to £40 per night) and Long Valley yurts (£285 to £460 per week).

Getting There & Away

Bus 516 (the Langdale Rambler; six daily, five on Sunday) is the only scheduled bus service to the valley, with stops at Ambleside, Skelwith Bridge, Elterwater, and the Old Dungeon Ghyll Hotel in Great Langdale.

Wasdale

Hunkered down amidst a dramatic amphitheatre of brooding peaks, Wasdale feels considerably wilder and more remote than many of the Lake District's gentler valleys. Overlooked by the snow-flecked summits of Scaféll Pike and Great Gable, it's a famously scenic corner of the Lakes – in fact, it topped a recent TV poll to find the nation's favourite view.

Sleeping & Eating

TOP CHOICE **Wasdale Head Inn** B&B, PUB ££
(019467-26229; www.wasdale.com; d £118, mains £4-12, menus £28; P) This historic inn can stake a claim as the spiritual home of English mountain climbing: one of the inn's early owners, Will Ritson, was among the adventurous gaggle of Victorian gents who pioneered the techniques of early mountaineering in the late 19th century. Dog-eared photos and climbing memorabilia are dotted around the inn, and upstairs you'll find simple, snug rooms crammed with character – and a refreshing absence of TVs.

TOP CHOICE **Wasdale Head Campsite** CAMPSITE £
(www.wasdalecampsite.org.uk; sites for 1 adult with car £8-11, extra adult/child £5/2.50; arrivals 8-11am & 5-8pm) This NT campsite is in a fantastically wild spot, nestled beneath the Scaféll range a mile from Wastwater. Facilities are basic (laundry room, showers and not much else), but the views are simply out of this world. A new barrier system has been installed; if you've prebooked you'll have an access card, otherwise you need to arrive between 8am and 11am or 5pm and 8pm.

Wastwater YHA HOSTEL £
(0845-371 9350; wasdale@yha.org.uk; Wasdale Hall, Nether Wasdale; dm £14) Nestled beside the green-grey waters of Wastwater, this is yet another stunningly situated hostel in a half-timbered 19th-century mansion in Nether Wasdale, at the lake's western end. There's a restaurant serving Cumbrian nosh and real ales, and many dorms have outlooks across the water.

Rainors Farm B&B ££
(019467-25934; www.rainorsfarm.co.uk; Gosforth; s/d £45/65) Three sweet rooms in a whitewashed farmhouse cottage, prettied up with checks, crimson spreads and country views. There's a choice of traditional or veggie breakfasts, and campers can bunk down in a couple of backgarden yurts (£340 to £595 per week). Gosforth is about 5 miles west of Nether Wasdale.

THE ROOF OF ENGLAND

In Scotland it's Ben Nevis (1344m, 4409ft), in Wales it's Snowdon (1085m, 3560ft), and in England the highest peak is **Scaféll Pike** (978m, 3210ft). While they might not be on quite the same scale as the French Alps or the Canadian Rockies, many a hiker has set out to conquer this sky-topping trio, the ultimate goal for British peak-baggers (especially for hardy souls attempting the Three Peaks Challenge, in which all three mountains are conquered in 24 hours).

The classic ascent up Scaféll Pike is from Wasdale Head; there's also a more scenic route that starts near Seathwaite in Borrowdale. Either way, you're looking at around six hours out on the mountain; don't even think about tackling it without proper supplies (rucksack, OS map, compass, food and water, and decent hiking boots) and a favourable weather forecast.

Getting There & Away

The **Wasdale Taxibus** (019467-25308) runs between Gosforth and Wasdale twice daily on Thursday, Saturday and Sunday, but only if there are enough people to make it worthwhile – you need to ring and book a seat.

Cockermouth

POP 8225

Plonked in flat fields beyond the northerly fells, the Georgian town of Cockermouth was hitherto best known as the birthplace of William Wordsworth and the home base of one of Cumbria's largest beer makers, Jenning's Brewery. But in November 2009 the town hit the national headlines after flash floods inundated the town centre, causing millions of pounds of damage and forcing the emergency evacuation of many residents by RAF helicopter.

Sights

Wordsworth House HISTORIC HOME
(NT; ☎01900-824805; Main St; adult/child £5.60/2.80; ⏰11am-4.30pm Mon-Sat mid-Mar–Oct) At the eastern end of Main St, this elegant Georgian mansion is the celebrated birthplace of all five Wordsworth children (William was the second to arrive, born on 7 April 1770, followed a year later by Dorothy). Built around 1745, the house had been painstakingly restored using authentic materials based on family accounts from the Wordsworth archive.

Since the floods, the house has been thoroughly dried out, dehumidified and given a fresh lick of paint, and it's now (almost) back to its former self – don't miss the flagstoned kitchen, the grand 1st-floor drawing room and the bedroom thought to have belonged to wee Willie himself.

Jenning's Brewery BREWERY
(☎01900-821011; www.jenningsbrewery.co.uk; adult/child 12-18yrs £6/3) The town's historic brewer, in business since 1874, fared rather less well. The floods left the brewery's main site under around five feet of water, and production at the plant was halted until January 2010. Once again, however, Cockermouth's fighting spirit kicked in, and the brewery is now back up and running. **Guided tours** (⏰11am & 2pm Mon-Sat Mar-Oct, plus Sun Jul & Aug) include a tasting session in the Cooperage Bar. Admirably, since November 2009 Jenning's has donated 10p from every pint of its beer sold in British pubs to the Cumbria Flood Recovery Fund.

Sleeping

TOP CHOICE **Old Homestead** B&B ££
(☎01900-822223; www.byresteads.co.uk; Byresteads Farm; d £76-96; P) This spankingly good farm conversion is 2 miles west of Cockermouth. The farmhouse clutter has been cleared to leave light, airy rooms with just a few rustic touches for character (a wood rafter here, a stone tile or hardwood mirror there).

Six Castlegate B&B ££
(☎01900-826749; www.sixcastlegate.co.uk; 6 Castlegate; s/d £48/65; wi-fi) Saved from the floods by its fortunate position on a slight rise at the far end of Main St, this Grade II-listed town house offers Georgian heritage with a modern twist. Feathery pillows, lofty ceilings and shiny showers make this one of Cockermouth's top sleeps.

Cockermouth YHA HOSTEL £
(☎0845-371 9313; www.yha.org.uk; Double Mills; dm £14; ⏰reception 7.30-10am & 5-10.30pm Apr-Oct) A simple hostel in a converted 17th-century watermill, about half a mile's walk from town. Camping space and cycle storage are available.

Eating & Drinking

Quince & Medlar RESTAURANT ££
(13 Castlegate; www.quinceandmedlar.co.uk; mains £12-16; ⏰dinner Tue-Sat) This renowned veggie establishment was another fortunate flood escapee, and it's a good thing too: it serves some of the fanciest meat-free food you could ever hope to taste. Burnished panels, candles and squeaky leather chairs give it the atmosphere of a private drawing room.

Merienda CAFE £
(7a Station St; mains £4-8; ⏰breakfast & lunch, to 10pm Fri) Savour light bites, authentic tapas and open-face sandwiches at this sunny Med-style diner with an admirable penchant for fair-trade goods, local produce and specialist coffees.

Bitter End PUB ££
(Kirkgate) Much-loved pub/microbrewery, which produces its own beers – Cockermouth Pride, Lakeland Honey Beer and the fantastically named Cuddy Lugs.

Information

Cockermouth (www.cockermouth.org.uk) Useful town guide.

Tourist office (☎01900-822634; cockermouthtic@co-net.com; ⏰9.30am-5pm Mon-Sat, 10am-2pm Sun Jul-Aug, 9.30am-4.30pm Mon-Sat Apr-Jun & Sep-Oct, 9.30am-4pm Mon-Fri, 10am-2pm Sat Jan-Mar & Nov-Dec) Inside the town hall.

Getting There & Away

The X4/X5 (13 to 15 Monday to Saturday, six on Sunday) travels from Workington via Cockermouth on to Keswick (35 minutes) and Penrith (1¼ hours).

Keswick

POP 5257

The sturdy slate town of Keswick is nestled alongside one of the region's most idyllic lakes, Derwent Water, a silvery curve studded by wooded islands and criss-crossed by puttering cruise boats.

Sights

The heart of Keswick is the old Market Pl, in the shadow of the town's former prison and meeting rooms at the **Moot Hall** (now occupied by the tourist office).

FREE **Keswick Museum & Art Gallery** MUSEUM

(☎017687-73263; Station Rd; ⏰10am-4pm Tue-Sat Feb-Oct) Hardly anything has changed since Keswick's municipal museum opened its doors in 1898. Dusty cases fill the halls: the most famous exhibits are a centuries-old mummified cat and the celebrated Musical Stones of Skiddaw, a truly weird instrument made from hornsfel rock that was once played for Queen Victoria.

FREE **Castlerigg Stone Circle** MONUMENT

Set on a fabulously wild hilltop a mile east of town, the famous stone circle of Castlerigg consists of 48 stones between 3000 and 4000 years old, surrounded by a dramatic circle of mountain peaks.

Cars of the Stars Motor Museum MUSEUM

(☎017687-73757; www.carsofthestars.com; Standish St; adult/child £5/3; ⏰10am-5pm) houses a fleet of celebrity vehicles: Chitty Chitty Bang Bang, Mr Bean's Mini, a Batmobile, KITT from *Knight Rider,* the A-Team van and the Delorean from *Back to the Future,* as well as lots of Bond cars.

Pencil Museum MUSEUM

(☎017687-73626; www.pencilmuseum.co.uk; Southy Works; adult/child £3.25/1.75; ⏰9.30am-5pm) For over 350 years, Keswick was a centre for graphite mining and pencil manufacture (Derwent colouring pencils are still a favourite among discerning artists). At the southern end of Main St, the former Cumberland Pencil Factory now houses various exhibits exploring the industry, including a reconstruction of the old Borrowdale slate mine and the world's longest pencil (measuring 8m end to end).

Activities

Boating

Studded with wooded islands and ringed by high fells, **Derwentwater** is unquestionably one of the most beautiful of all the Lakeland lakes (it's also supposed to have been Beatrix Potter's favourite).

From the jetty near Crow Park, a short walk south of the town centre, **Keswick Launch Company**(☎017687-72263; www.keswick-launch.co.uk) runs cruise boats to seven landing stages around the lake shore: Ashness Gate, Lodore Falls, High Brandlehow, Low Brandlehow, Hawse End, Nichol End and back to Keswick.

A ticket all the way around the lake costs £9.00/4.50 for adult/child. Single and return fares are available to each of the seven jetties.

Walking

Keswick has enough hikes to fill a lifetime of tramping. The most popular walk is the ascent of **Lattrigg Fell**, along an old railway path that's now part of the C2C cycle trail. Other possible routes climb **Walla Crag** (379m), **Skiddaw** (931m) and **Blencathra** (868m), or you can catch the boat to Hawse End for the scenic family-friendly hike up **Catbells** (451m).

WHINLATTER FOREST PARK

Encompassing 1200 hectares of pine, larch and spruce, **Whinlatter** is England's only true area of mountain forest, rising sharply to 790m around the Whinlatter Pass, about 5 miles from Keswick.

The forest is a designated red squirrel reserve; you can check out live video feeds from squirrel cams at the **Whinlatter visitor centre** (☎017687-78469; Braithwaite; ⏰10am-5pm).

Thrill-junkies can monkey about in the trees at **Go Ape** (☎017687-78469; adult/10-17yr £30/25; ⏰9am-5pm mid-Mar–Oct, closed Mon in term time) or mountain bike along the **Altura** and **Quercus** trails.

You can hire bikes at **Cyclewise** (☎017687-78711; www.cyclewisetraining.co.uk), next to the visitor centre.

Bus 77 (four daily) goes to Whinlatter from Keswick.

Keswick

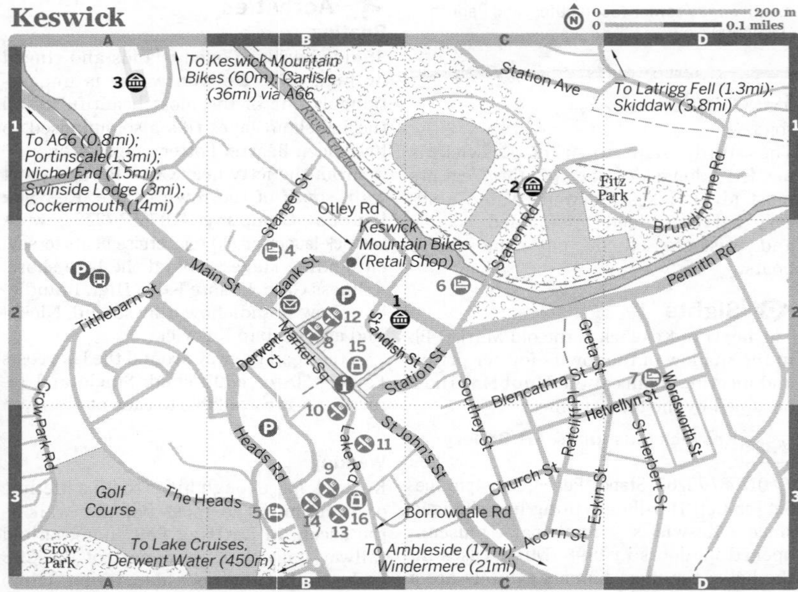

Festivals & Events

Keswick Mountain Festival OUTDOOR ACTIVITIES

(www.keswickmountainfestival.co.uk) This May festival celebrates all things mountainous.

Keswick Beer Festival BEER

(www.keswickbeerfestival.co.uk) Lots and lots of beer is drunk during Keswick's June real ale fest.

Keswick Agricultural Show FARMING

(www.keswickshow.co.uk) Held every year since 1860 on August Bank Holiday.

Sleeping

Keswick is crammed with B&Bs, especially around Stanger St and Helvellyn Rd.

TOP CHOICE **Howe Keld** B&B ££

(☎017687-72417; www.howekeld.co.uk; 5-7 The Heads; s £50, d £90-100; wi-fi) This revamped Crow Park B&B pulls out all the stops. The kitsch clutter has been jettisoned for goose-down duvets, slate-floored bathrooms and handmade furniture courtesy of a local joiner; TVs are flatscreen, the decor's sleek, and the key-fobs are fashioned from local slate.

TOP CHOICE **Swinside Lodge** HOTEL ££

(☎017687-72948; www.swinsidelodge-hotel.co.uk; Newlands; d £92-136 incl dinner; P) Tucked below Catbells, this fancy number has scooped awards for its gourmet food and Georgian finery. It's classy without being chichi: rooms are furnished in country style, and the house is a reassuring mix of creaky floorboards, cosy lounges and book-stocked shelves. Supper at the bistro is included in rates. Take the A66 from Keswick towards Cockermouth and look our for signs to Newlands Valley, Portinscale and Grange; the hotel is about 2 miles from the turning.

Powe House B&B ££

(☎017687-73611; www.powehouse.com; Portinscale, Keswick; s £40-50, d £60-80; wi-fi) Pleasantly removed from the Keswick crush about a mile from town in Portinscale, this detached house has six great-value bedrooms, all with integrated DVD/TVs and bags of understated style. You might even spot Skiddaw from some.

Oakthwaite House B&B ££

(☎017687-72398; www.oakthwaite-keswick.co.uk; 35 Helvellyn St; d £60-76) In the B&B-heavy neighbourhood round Helvellyn Rd, this is one of our choicest finds: just four rooms (so not too crowded), with power showers, white linen and cool shades throughout. Ask for the king-size rooms for fell views.

Keswick

Sights
1 Cars of the Stars Motor Museum B2
2 Keswick Museum & Art Gallery C1
3 Pencil Museum A1

Sleeping
4 Ellergill B2
5 Howe Keld B3
6 Keswick YHA C2
7 Oakthwaite House D2

Eating
8 Bryson's B2
9 Cafe-Bar 26 .... B3
10 Dog & Gun B3
11 Good Taste B3
12 Lakeland Pedlar Wholefood Cafe B2
13 Mayson's B3
14 Morrel's B3

Shopping
15 Cotswold Outdoor B2
16 George Fisher B3

Ellergill B&B ££
(☎017687-73347; www.ellergill.co.uk; 22 Stanger St; d £64-72) Velour bedspreads, plumped-up cushions and either regal purples or fiery reds give this B&B an opulent edge, marrying well with the house's Victorian features (including tiled hearths and a lovely hallway floor).

Keswick YHA HOSTEL £
(☎0845-371 9746; www.yha.org.uk; Station Rd; dm from £14; @) In a converted wool mill beside the clattering river, this efficient hostel offers roomy dorms, doubles and triples, some with balconies overlooking Fitz Park.

Eating

Morrel's RESTAURANT ££
(☎017687-72666; Lake Rd; 2/3-course menu £13.50/16; ⊙dinner Tue-Sun) Keswick's top table is this glossy restaurant, smoothly done in shades of cappuccino, cream and chocolate and enlivened by pop art movie prints. Expect quality bistro food spiced by the occasional Spanish, Catalan or Italian influence.

Good Taste CAFE £
(www.simplygoodtaste.co.uk; 19 Lake Rd; lunches £3-6; ⊙8.30am-4.30pm Mon-Sat) Peter Sidwell's snazzy cafe is one of the town's most popular places for lunch, and it's not really surprising. Tuck into gourmet sandwiches, fresh-made smoothies and mo[...] filling mains shot through with Italian [...] French flavours. Best coffee in Keswick, too.

Mayson's DINER £
(33 Lake Rd; mains £6-10) Buffet dining in a cosy space sprinkled with potted plants and bench seating. Select your daily special from one of the woks on the counter, choose a drink and wait for your grub to arrive in double-quick time.

Lakeland Pedlar Wholefood Cafe CAFE £
(www.lakelandpedlar.co.uk; Hendersons Yard; mains £3-10; ⊙9am-5pm) You'll be hard-pressed to find a heartier lunch in the Lakes than the ones served up at this long-standing establishment, noted for its chunky sandwiches, homemade soups, veggie chillis and inch-thick cakes. There's a bike shop upstairs.

Dog & Gun PUB £
(2 Lake Rd; mains from £8) Plenty of pubs in Keswick, but this is the pick: deep booths, flickering hearths, a well-worn wooden bar and proper pub grub and ale, including 'Thirst rescue', which helps fund the Keswick Mountain Rescue Team.

Bryson's CAFE £
(42 Main St; cakes £2-5) Much-loved bakery known for its fruit cakes, Battenburgs and florentines.

Cafe-Bar 26 CAFE £
(26 Lake Rd; mains £3-10) Smart cafe and wine bar that also turns out snacky tapas, burgers and bruschetta.

Shopping

Keswick has plenty of outdoor shops. There's a huge branch of **Cotswold Outdoor** (16 Main St), but the traditionalists' choice is **George Fisher** (2 Borrowdale Rd).

Information

Keswick & the North Lakes (www.keswick.org) Comprehensive guide to all things Keswick.

Tourist office (☎017687-72645; keswicktic@lake-district.gov.uk; Moot Hall, Market Pl; ⊙9.30am-5.30pm Apr-Oct, to 4.30pm Nov-Mar) Sells discounted launch tickets.

U-Compute (48 Main St; ⊙9am-5.30pm; per hr £3) Net access above the post office.

Getting There & Away

Buses from Keswick:

555/556 Lakeslink Hourly to Ambleside (40 minutes), Windermere (50 minutes) and Kendal (1½ hours)

THE BASSENTHWAITE OSPREYS

In 2001 the first wild ospreys to breed in England for 150 years set up home at Bassenthwaite Lake, near Keswick. These magnificent birds of prey were once widespread, but were driven to extinction by hunting, environmental degradation and egg collectors. The last wild breeding pair was destroyed in Scotland in 1916, but following years of careful conservation, the ospreys have slowly recolonised several areas of the British Isles.

Over the last few years, the birds have usually arrived at Bassenthwaite in April, spending the summer at the lake before heading for Africa in late August or early September. There are two official viewpoints, both in **Dodd Wood**, about 3 miles north of Keswick on the A591 (follow signs for Dodd Wood and Cattle Inn). The **lower hide** (10am-5pm) is about 15 minutes' walk from the car park at Mirehouse, and the new **upper hide** (10.30am-4.30pm) is half an hour further. There's an informative osprey display and live video feed at the **Whinlatter Forest Park visitor centre** (p593).

From Keswick, the 73/73A bus stops at nearby Mirehouse, or there's a special 47/74A Osprey Bus (six on weekends April to mid-July, daily July and August).

Find out more at www.ospreywatch.co.uk.

X4/X5 Penrith to Workington via Keswick (hourly Monday to Friday, six on Sunday).

77/77A Honister Rambler (four daily) The main Buttermere bus, including stops at Seathwaite, Lorton and Whinlatter. The bus then crosses Honister Pass and travels through Borrowdale back to Keswick.

78 Borrowdale Rambler Regular bus to the Borrowdale valley (hourly Monday to Saturday, seven on Sunday).

Getting Around

Hire full-suspension bikes, hard tails and hybrids at **Keswick Mountain Bikes** (017687-75202; 1 Daleston Ct) from £20 per day. They have a second branch on Otley Rd.

Borrowdale

The B5289 tracks Derwent Water into the heart of Borrowdale Valley, overlooked by the impressive peaks of Scaféll and Scaféll Pike. Past the small village of **Grange-in-Borrowdale**, the valley winds into the jagged ravine of the **Jaws of Borrowdale**, a well-known hiking spot with wonderful views, notably from the summit of **Castle Crag** (290m) at the southern end of Derwent Water.

A mile or so further south from Grange, a turn-off leads up to a National Trust car park and the geological curiosity of the **Bowder Stone**, a 1870-ton lump of rock thought to have been left behind by a retreating glacier. A small stepladder leads up to the top of the rock.

Sleeping & Eating

TOP CHOICE **Langstrath Inn** B&B ££
(017687-77239; www.thelangstrath.com; Stonethwaite; d £99-108; P) Borrowdale digs are on the pricey side, which makes this whitewashed inn in Stonethwaite a doubly welcome discovery. The slate-topped building surrounded by valley views is attractive enough: throw in elegant rooms finished in crimsons and cool whites, and a rustic pub-restaurant downstairs serving classic Cumbrian dishes, and you have a very tempting Borrowdale option indeed. The house even once featured in a novel by Ian McEwan – and you can't say that every day, now can you?

Seatoller House B&B ££
(017687-77218; www.seatollerhouse.co.uk; s/d £55/122; P) Another tiny hideaway with an air of a Beatrix Potter burrow, tucked beneath the climb up to Honister Pass. All the rooms are named after animals – attic Osprey has sky views through a Velux window, Rabbit is pleasantly pine-filled and Badger has views over the garden.

Yew Tree Farm B&B ££
(017687-77675; www.borrowdaleherdwick.co.uk; Rosthwaite; d from £75; P) Cottage style rules the roost at this button-cute farmhouse, with three rooms snuggled in under low ceilings, and the lovely Flock In tea-

room across the way serving sticky toffee pud, giant flapjacks and piping-hot tea.

Derwentwater YHA HOSTEL £
(☎0845-371 9314; derwentwater@yha.org.uk; Barrow House; dm £16; ⏲Feb-Nov, weekends Nov-Jan; Ⓟ@) The first of Borrowdale's two hostels is in an impressive mansion built for the 19th-century notable Joseph Pocklington, who built an artificial waterfall in the back garden that now runs the hostel's hydro-electric turbine. The rooms are fairly old-time YHA, but there's a billiard room and a big lounge for post-trek chilling.

Borrowdale YHA HOSTEL £
(☎0845-371 9624; borrowdale@yha.org.uk; Longthwaite; dm from £16; ⏲Feb-Dec) Purpose-built chalet-style hostel further up the valley, specialising in walking and activity trips. The facilities are great, but it's often booked out throughout the summer.

ℹ Getting There & Away

Bus 78 runs from Keswick through Borrowdale as far as Seatoller. Bus 77/77A goes from Keswick through the Buttermere Valley, across the Honister Pass and through Borrowdale back to Keswick.

Honister Pass

From Borrowdale, a narrow, winding and perilously steep road snakes up the fellside to Honister Pass and the Buttermere valley beyond.

Overlooking the top of the pass is the **Honister Slate Mine** (☎017687-77230; www.honister-slate-mine.co.uk; adult/child £9.75/4.75; ⏲tours 10.30am, 12.30pm & 3.30pm Mar-Oct), where underground tours venture deep into the bowels of the old 'Edge' and 'Kimberley' mines (a tour into the 'Cathedral' mine runs on Friday by request, but you'll need eight people and it costs £19.75).

Honister's latest attraction is the UK's first **Via Ferrata** (Iron Way; adult/10-15yr £25/20). Modelled on the century-old routes across the Italian Dolomites, this vertiginous clamber follows the cliff trail once used by the Honister slate miners, using a system of fixed ropes and iron ladders. It's exhilarating and great fun, but unsurprisingly you'll need a head for heights.

Buttermere

From the high point of Honister, the road drops sharply into the deep bowl of Buttermere, skirting the lakeshore to Buttermere village, 4 miles from Honister and 9 miles from Keswick. From here, the B5289 cuts past Crummock Water (once joined with its neighbour) before exiting the valley's northern edge.

Buttermere marks the start of Alfred Wainwright's all-time favourite circuit: up **Red Pike** (755m), and along **High Stile**, **High Crag** and **Haystacks** (597m). In fact, the great man liked it so much he decided to stay here for good: after his death in 1991, his ashes were scattered across the top of Haystacks as was requested in his will.

Buttermere has limited accommodation. Walkers bunk down at the **Buttermere YHA** (☎0845-371 9508; buttermere@yha.org.uk; dm £16), a slate-stone house above Buttermere Lake, while those looking for more luxury try one of the valley's two hotels, the upmarket **Bridge Hotel** (☎017687-70252; www.bridge-hotel.com; r £130-150, incl dinner £185-210; Ⓟ) or the **Fish Hotel** (☎017687-70253; 2-night minimum stay d £200; Ⓟ).

Better still, if you're up for a night under canvas there's one of the Lake District's best rural campsites, **Syke Farm** (☎01768-770222; sites adult/child £7/3.50; ⏲Feb-Nov) Facilities are limited to basic loos and his-and-hers showers, but pick your spot and you'll wake up to views of Red Pike, High Stile and Haystacks. There's a river to chill your booze in, and the farmer makes ice cream with milk straight from his dairy herd (the marzipan and vanilla are to die for).

ℹ Getting There & Away

Bus 77/77A serves Buttermere and Honister Pass.

Ullswater & Around

After Windermere, the second-largest lake in the Lake District is Ullswater, a silvery slash that stretches for 7.5 miles between Pooley Bridge, and Glenridding and Patterdale in the south. Carved out by a long-extinct glacier, the deep valley in which the lake sits is flanked by an impressive string of fells, most notably the razor ridge of **Helvellyn**, Cumbria's third-highest mountain.

From Pooley Bridge **Ullswater 'Steamers'** (☎017684-82229; www.ullswater-steamers.co.uk) putter south along the lake, making stops at Howtown and Glenridding before looping back to Pooley Bridge. Round trips are adult/child £9.00/4.50 to Howtown, or £12.30/6.15 for an all-day pass.

Sleeping & Eating

Old Water View B&B ££

(☎017684-82175; www.oldwaterview.co.uk; Patterdale; d £84) Frilly B&B with something to cover all bases: split-level 'Bothy' is ideal for families with attic beds for the kids, while 'Little Gem' overlooks the tinkling stream and 'Place Fell' is reputed to be have been a favourite of Alfred Wainwright.

Cherry Holme B&B ££

(☎017684-82512; www.cherryholme.co.uk; Glenridding; s £60, d £80-120;) There are plenty of luxury extras at this roomy house on the edge of Glenridding, including a Nordic-style sauna that makes a perfect place to soothe those bones post-Helvellyn – although the fairly standard rooms are underwhelming considering the price.

Patterdale YHA HOSTEL £

(☎0845-371 9337; patterdale@yha.org.uk; Patterdale; dm £14; reception 7.30-10am & 5-10.30am Easter-Oct) This modern hostel makes a nice change from the heritage settings enjoyed by some of the other Lakeland YHAs. It's got a whiff of the '70s around it – a patch of timber cladding here, some pop-art colours there – but the facilities are good (cafe-bar, bike hire, spacious kitchen).

Helvellyn YHA HOSTEL £

(☎0845-371 9742; www.yha.org.uk; Greenside; dm £12; Easter-Oct, rest of year by reservation) Formerly occupied by high-mountain miners, this basic hostel-in-the-wilds sits 274m above Glenridding along a rocky mountain track. It's miles from anything, but if you're after a solitude hit and don't mind the ¾-mile trek, you'll be in for a treat. The hostel's mainly used by hikers looking for an early start on Helvellyn; guided walks can be arranged through the hostel staff.

Traveller's Rest PUB ££

(Glenridding; mains £5.50-15) Typically friendly Cumbrian pub known for its 'Traveller's Mixed Grill' (£14.70) of steak, lamb chop, gammon, black pudding and Cumberland sausage, all crowned with a fried egg.

Fellbites CAFE ££

(Glenridding; lunch mains £6-12; evening menus £17.50-21.50; lunch daily, dinner Thu-Sat) Attractive village cafe good for soups and sarnies (sandwiches) at lunch, plus more sophisticated stuff after dark.

Information

Ullswater Information Centre (☎017684-82414; ullswatertic@lake-district.gov.uk; Beckside car park; 9am-5.30pm Apr-Oct)

Getting There & Away

The Ullswater Bus-and-Boat Combo ticket (£13.60) includes a day's travel on the 108 with a return trip on an Ullswater Steamer; buy the ticket on the bus. Useful buses:

108 Penrith to Patterdale via Pooley Bridge and Glenridding (six Monday to Friday, five on Saturday, four on Sunday).

517 (Kirkstone Rambler; three daily July and August, otherwise weekends only) over the Kirkstone Pass from Bowness and Troutbeck, stopping at Glenridding and Patterdale.

CUMBRIAN COAST

While the central lakes and fells pull in a never-ending stream of visitors, surprisingly few ever make the trek west to explore Cumbria's coastline. And that's a shame: while it might not compare to the wild grandeur of Northumberland or the rugged splendour of Scotland's shores, Cumbria's coast is well worth exploring. Less attrac-

THE MORECAMBE BAY CROSSING

Before the coming of the railway, the sandy expanse of **Morecambe Bay** provided the quickest route into the Lake District from the south of England. The traditional crossing is made from Arnside on the eastern side of the bay over to Kents Bank, near Grange-over-Sands. Morecambe Bay is notorious for its fast-rising tide and treacherous sands, but it's possible to walk across the flats at low tide, in the company of the official **Queen's Guide**, a role established in 1536. You'll need to register a fortnight in advance; ask at the Grange tourist office for details of the next crossing. The 8-mile crossing takes around 3½ hours.

Find out more about this unique waterway at www.morecambebay.org.uk.

tive is the nuclear plant of Sellafield, still stirring up controversy some 50 years after its construction.

Getting Around

The railway line loops 120 miles from Lancaster to Carlisle, stopping at the coastal resorts of Grange, Ulverston, Ravenglass, Whitehaven and Workington.

Holker Hall

Holker Hall (☎015395-58328; www.holker-hall.co.uk; adult/child £10/5.50, grounds only £6.50/3.50; ⊙house 10.30am-4.30pm Sun-Fri, grounds 10am-6pm Mar-Oct) has been the family seat of the Cavendish family for nigh on 400 years. Though parts of the house date from the 16th century, the house was almost entirely rebuilt following a devastating fire in 1871. It's a typically ostentatious Victorian affair, covered with mullioned windows, gables and copper-topped turrets. Among its wealth of grand rooms are the drawing room (packed with antique furniture, including a choice few Chippendales), the library (stocked with over 3500 tomes) and the lavish Long Gallery (renowned for its elaborate plasterwork).

Outside, Holker's grounds sprawl for over 10 hectares, encompassing a rose garden, woodland, ornamental fountains and a 22m-high lime tree. There's also a fantastic **food hall** (☎015395-59084; www.holderfoodhall.co.uk) stocking produce from the estate.

Furness Abbey

Eight and a half miles southwest of Ulverston, the rosy runs of **Furness Abbey** (EH; www.english-heritage.org.uk/daysout/properties/furness-abbey; adult/child £3.70/1.90; ⊙10am-6pm Apr-Sep, to 5pm Oct, to 4pm Wed-Sun Nov-Mar) are all that remains of one of northern England's most powerful monasteries. Founded in the 12th century, the abbey's lands and properties once stretched across southern Cumbria and the Lakes, but like many of England's monasteries, it met an ignominious end in 1537 during the dissolution. An informative audio guide is included in the admission price.

Several buses, including the hourly X35 from Ulverston, stop nearby.

Ravenglass & Eskdale Railway

Built in 1875 to ferry iron ore from the Eskdale mines to the coast, and affectionately known as **La'al Ratty**, the pocket-size choo-choos chug of the **Ravenglass & Eskdale Railway** (☎01229-717171; www.ravenglass-railway.co.uk; single fares adult/child £6.60/3.30, day tickets £11.20/5.60) chug for 7 miles from the coastal town of Ravenglass into Eskdale and the Lake District foothills, terminating at Dalegarth Station, near Boot. There are up to 17 trips daily in summer, dropping to two in winter.

While you wait for your train, there's an interesting **museum** exploring the railway's history, and good grub and ales at the **Ratty Arms** (mains £8-15), which is covered with memorabilia from the railway's heyday.

Ravenglass has frequent rail links north to Whitehaven (£4.20, 30 minutes) and, in the other direction, Ulverston (£7.40, 1¼ hours), Grange-over-Sands (£10.70, 1½ hours) and beyond.

WORTH A TRIP

LAUREL & HARDY MUSEUM

Founded by avid Laurel & Hardy collector Bill Cubin back in 1983, this eclectic cinematic **museum** (www.laurel-and-hardy.co.uk; Brogden St, Ulverston; adult/child £4/2; ⊙10am-4.30pm Feb-Dec) has new premises in Ulverston's old Roxy cinema. The museum still houses all the old floor-to-ceiling memorabilia relating to the duo, but presented in a rather less chaotic fashion than at the former site; happily, the much-loved little 15-seat cinema has been retained, and still shows back-to-back Laurel & Hardy classics.

The hourly X35 bus travels from Ulverston via Haverthwaite, Newby Bridge, Grange and Kendal from Monday to Saturday (three times on Sunday). Regular trains from Carlisle (£33.50, two hours) and Lancaster (£8, 40 minutes) stop at Ulverston station, five minutes' walk south of the centre.

Muncaster Castle

Like many Cumbrian castles, **Muncaster** (www.muncaster.co.uk; adult/child £11/7.50, gardens only £8.50/6; ⏲gardens 10.30am-dusk, castle noon-4.30pm Sun-Fri Feb-Nov) was originally built around a 14th-century *pele* tower, constructed to resist Reiver raids from across the Scottish border. Home to the Pennington family for the last seven centuries, the castle's celebrated features include its majestic great hall and octagonal library, and on its grounds you'll find an ornamental maze and an owl centre.

NORTHERN & EASTERN CUMBRIA

Many visitors speed through the northern and eastern reaches of Cumbria in a headlong dash for the Lake District, but this is an area that's worth exploring – a bleakly beautiful landscape of isolated farms, barren heaths and solid hilltop towns, cut through by the Roman barrier of Hadrian's Wall.

Carlisle

POP 69,527

Precariously perched on the tempestuous border between England and Scotland, in the area once ominously dubbed the 'Debatable Lands', Carlisle is a city with a notoriously stormy past. Sacked by the Vikings, pillaged by the Scots, and plundered by the Border Reivers, Carlisle has stood on the frontline of England's defences for the last 1000 years. The battlements and keeps of the stout medieval castle still stand watch, built from the same rosy red sandstone as the city's cathedral and terraced houses. But Cumbria's only city is a more peaceful place these days, with a buzzy student population that keeps this old city young at heart.

Sights & Activities

Carlisle Castle CASTLE

(☎01228-591922; www.english-heritage.org.uk/daysout/properties/carlisle-castle/; adult/child £4.50/2.30; ⏲9.30am-5pm Apr-Sep, 10am-4pm Oct-Mar) Carlisle's brooding, rust-red castle lurks dramatically on the north side of the city.

The castle has witnessed some dramatic events over the centuries: Mary, Queen of Scots was imprisoned here in 1568, and the castle was the site of a notorious eight-month siege during the English Civil War, when the Royalist garrison survived by eating rats, mice and the castle dogs before finally surrendering in 1645. Look out for the 'licking stones' in the dungeon, which Jacobite prisoners supposedly lapped for moisture.

Admission includes entry to the **Kings Own Royal Border Regiment Museum**, which explores the history of Cumbria's Infantry Regiment. There are guided tours from April to September.

Carlisle Cathedral CHURCH

(www.carlislecathedral.org.uk; 7 The Abbey; donation £2; ⏲7.30am-6.15pm Mon-Sat, to 5pm Sun) Built from the same rosy stone as many of the city's buildings, Carlisle's cathedral began life as a priory church in 1122, before later being raised to cathedral status when its first abbot, Athelwold, became the first Bishop of Carlisle. Among its notable features are the 15th-century choir stalls, the impressive barrel-vaulted roof and the wonderful 14th-century East Window, one of the largest Gothic windows in England. Surrounding the cathedral are other priory relics, including the 16th-century **Fratry** (see Prior's Kitchen Restaurant) and the **Prior's Tower**.

Tullie House Museum MUSEUM

(www.tulliehouse.co.uk; Castle St; adult/child £5.20/free; ⏲10am-5pm Mon-Sat, 11am-5pm Sun Jul & Aug, 10am-5pm Mon-Sat, noon-5pm Sun Apr-Jun & Sep-Oct, earlier closing at other times) The city museum ranges through Carlisle's turbulent history, starting from its Celtic foundation through to the development of modern Carlisle. The museum has a strong archaeology collection, including a Bronze Age spear-mould, Roman tablets collected from Hadrian's Wall, and artefacts recovered from Viking burial sites in nearby Ormside and Hesket.

Guildhall Museum MUSEUM

(Greenmarket; admission free; ⏲noon-4.30pm Tue-Sun Apr-Oct) This tiny museum is housed in a wonky 15th-century town house built for Carlisle's trade guilds. Among the modest exhibits are a ceremonial mace, the city's stocks and a section of exposed wall

Carlisle

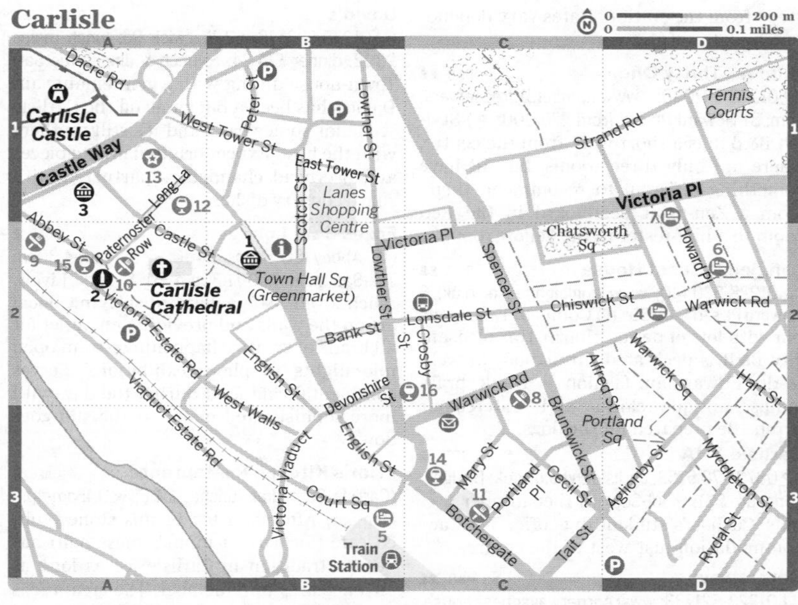

Carlisle

Top Sights
- Carlisle Castle A1
- Carlisle Cathedral A2

Sights
- Fratry ..... (see 10)
- 1 Guildhall Museum B2
- 2 Prior's Tower A2
- 3 Tullie House Museum A1

Sleeping
- 4 Cornerways D2
- 5 Hallmark Hotel B3
- 6 Langleigh Guest House D2
- 7 Number Thirty One D1

Eating
- 8 David's C2
- 9 Foxes Cafe Lounge A2
- 10 Prior's Kitchen Restaurant A2
- 11 Teza Indian Canteen C3

Drinking
- 12 Alcoves Cafe Bar A1
- 13 Brickyard A1
- 14 Cafe Solo C3
- 15 Fats A2
- 16 Gilded Lily C2

showing the building's wattle-and-daub construction.

Tours

Open Book Visitor Guiding SIGHTSEEING TOURS

(01228-670578; www.greatguidedtours.co.uk) Tours of Carlisle and the surrounding area, including visits to Carlisle Castle and Hadrian's Wall. Tours leave from the tourist office.

Sleeping

Hallmark Hotel HOTEL ££

(01228-531951; carlisle.reception@hallmarkhotels.co.uk; Court Sq; d from £75; P wi-fi)Chain it may be, but the reborn Lakes Court Hotel is now a superior Carlisle sleep. It's certainly not "boutique" (despite what the brochure says), but it's perfectly comfortable: rooms in golds and yellows (all with big beds, wi-fi and flatscreen tellies), posh function rooms, and a handy location steps from the station. Rates vary depending on dates of stay.

Number Thirty One B&B ££
(☎01228-597080; www.number31.freeservers.com; 31 Howard Pl; s/d from £70/100; P) Stylish B&B digs a short walk from the centre. There are only three rooms, but all have something different to recommend them, from a Zen-print headboard in the Red room to a half-tester in the Yellow room.

Langleigh Guest House B&B ££
(☎01228-530440; www.langleighhouse.co.uk; 6 Howard Pl; s/d £45/80; P) Completely chaotic, but with lots of period charm, this pleasant city B&B is decorated throughout in well-to-do Edwardian fashion – think brass lamps, antique clocks and watercolour prints. Be prepared for the dogs.

Carlisle YHA HOSTEL £
(☎0870-770 5752; carlisle@yha.org.uk; Bridge Lane; dm £21; ⏲Jul-Sep) In the summer hols, Carlisle's student digs offer YHA accommodation just west of the centre.

Cornerways B&B ££
(☎01228-521733; www.cornerwaysguest house.co.uk; 107 Warwick Rd; s £30-35, d £55-65; P @) This rambling redbrick is basic as they come, but offers some of the cheapest B&B rooms in the city.

Eating

Teza Indian Canteen INDIAN ££
(4a English Gate Plaza; mains £8-14; ⏲lunch & dinner Mon-Sat) After a disappointing dip in form, Teza's groundbreaking Indian is back in vogue, especially since the return of head chef Dinesh Rawat (who helped launch the restaurant back in 2005). This award-winning Indian does the usual *bhunas* (medium-hot dry curries) and bhajis, but it's the regionally influenced cuisine that fires things up: flavours from Kerala, Goa and Kashmir all make it into the mix.

Holme Bistro RESTAURANT ££
(56-58 Denton St; mains £11-15; ⏲lunch & dinner Mon-Sat) A little stroll southwards from the train station brings you to this little-known local gem, where the British bistro food is streets ahead of the competition. There's nary a whiff of pretension here, either in the simply done dining room or the simply done food. Tuck into confit duck or pan-fried pork chop, or pitch up on Friday for steak night.

David's BISTRO ££
(☎01228-523578; 62 Warwick Rd; lunch mains £8-12, dinner £14-24; ⏲lunch & dinner Tue-Sat) Town-house dining with a gentlemanly air. David's has been a big name on the Carlisle scene for some years, and it's still up there with the best. Expect original mantelpieces and overhead chandeliers partnered with suave country dishes.

Foxes Cafe Lounge CAFE £
(18 Abbey St; mains £4-10; ⏲9.30am-4.30pm Tue-Sat, plus 7.30-11.30pm Fri & Sat) Lively, much-loved cafe-gallery displaying local art on the walls and providing an outlet for all kinds of creative happenings, from open mic nights to photo exhibitions. Serves continental cafe food during the day, with more sophisticated mains as the sun goes down.

Prior's Kitchen Restaurant CAFE £
(Carlisle Cathedral; lunches £4-6; ⏲9.45am-4pm Mon-Sat) Afternoon tea in this stone-vaulted cafe (formerly a monk's mess hall) has been a tradition in Carlisle for as long as anyone cares to remember. The cream teas are cracking, or there are quiches, cakes and rounds of sandwiches for something more filling.

Drinking

Botchergate's the place for late-night action, but it gets notoriously rowdy so watch your step.

Gilded Lily PUB
(6 Lowther St; ⏲9am-midnight Mon-Thu, 9am-2am Fri & Sat, noon-midnight Sun) Former bank turned sprawling city pub. Indulge in continental beers and bespoke cocktails beneath the original skylight, and be prepared for plenty of dolled-up drinkers come the weekend.

Fats PUB
(48 Abbey St; ⏲11am-11pm) Slate, steel and an open fireplace attract a classy clientele to Fats. The world beers behind the bar, while open-mic nights, scratch sessions and hot-tip DJs pull in the crowds.

Alcoves Cafe Bar BAR
(Up Long Lane, 18 Fisher Street; ⏲6pm-late Tue-Sat) Easy to miss, but this alleyway hang-out near the cathedral is a popular spot for late-night drinks and DJs when you're wanting to evade the Botchergate hullabaloo. Look out for the lane off Fisher St.

Cafe Solo BAR
(1 Botchergate) Spanish-themed cocktails, late-night tapas and Sol beers at a tiny corner-bar on the edge of Botchergate.

Brickyard CONCERT HALL
(www.thebrickyardonline.com; 14 Fisher St) Carlisle's main (read: only) regular gig venue, housed in the former Memorial Hall.

Information

@Cybercafe (www.atcybercafe.co.uk; 8-10 Devonshire St; per hr £3; ⏲10am-10pm Mon-Sat, 1-10pm Sun)

Cumberland Infirmary (☎01228-523444; Newtown Rd) Half a mile west of the city centre.

Police station (☎0845-330 0247; English St; ⏲8am-midnight)

Tourist office (☎01228-625600; www.historic-carlisle.org.uk; Greenmarket; ⏲9.30am-5pm Mon-Sat, 10.30am-4pm Sun)

Getting There & Away

BUS Carlisle is Cumbria's main transport hub. National Express coaches depart from the bus station on Lonsdale St. Popular routes:

London £35, 7½ hours, three direct daily (with extra buses via Birmingham

Glasgow £20.70, two hours, 14 daily

Manchester £28, 3¼ hours, eight daily

Useful links to the Lakes:

104 (40 minutes, hourly Monday to Saturday, nine on Sunday) Penrith.

554 (70 minutes, three daily) Keswick.

555/556 (at least hourly) Windermere and Ambleside.

600 (one hour, seven daily Monday to Saturday) Cockermouth and towns in between.

AD 122 (Hadrian's Wall bus; six daily late May to late September) Connects Hexham and Carlisle.

TRAIN Carlisle is on the London Euston (£91, 3¼ to 4¼ hours) to Glasgow (£22, 1¼ to 1½ hours) line. It's also the terminus for several regional railways:

Cumbrian Coast Line Loops round the coastline all the way to Lancaster (£26, three to four hours via the coast, 45 minutes direct).

Settle-Carlisle Line (www.settle-carlisle.co.uk) Cuts southeast across the Yorkshire Dales (£23 return, 1½ hours); see also p495.

Tyne Valley Line Follows Hadrian's Wall to Newcastle-upon-Tyne (£13, 1½ hours).

Getting Around

To book a taxi, call **Radio Taxis** (☎01228-527575), **Citadel Station Taxis** (☎01228-523971) or **County Cabs** (☎01228-596789).

DON'T MISS

BIRDOSWALD ROMAN FORT

Though most of the forts along Hadrian's Wall have long since been plundered for building materials, you can still visit **Birdoswald Roman Fort** (EH; ☎01697-747602; adult/child £4.80/2.40; ⏲10am-5.30pm mid-Mar–Sep, 10am-4pm Oct–mid-Mar). Built to replace an earlier timber-and-turf fort, Birdoswald would have been the operating base for around 1000 Roman soldiers; excavations have revealed three of the four gateways, as well as granary stores, workshops, exterior walls and a military drill hall. A visitors centre explores the fort's history and the background behind the wall's construction. The AD 122 bus connecting Carlisle with Hexham passes by the fort.

Alston

POP 2227

Surrounded by the bleak hilltops of the Pennines, isolated Alston's main claim to fame is its elevation: at 305m above sea level, it's thought to be the highest market town in England (despite no longer having a market). It's also famous among steam enthusiasts thanks to the **South Tynedale Railway** (☎01434-381696, timetable 01434-382828; www.strps.org.uk; adult/child return £6/3; ⏲Apr-Oct), which puffs and clatters through the hilly country between Alston and Kirkhaugh, along a route that originally operated from 1852 to 1976. The return trip takes about an hour; there are up to five daily trains in midsummer.

Penrith

POP 14,882

Traditional butchers, greengrocers and quaint little teashops line the streets of Penrith, a stout, red-brick town that feels closer to the no-nonsense villages of the Yorkshire Dales than to the chocolate-box villages of the Central Lakes.

Cunningly disguised as a Lakeland hill 2 miles west of Penrith, the **Rheged** (www.rheged.com; ⏲10am-6pm) visitor centre houses a large-screen Imax cinema and an exhibition on the history and geology of Cumbria, as well as a retail hall selling Cumbrian goods from handmade paper to chocolate and chutneys. The frequent X4/X5 bus stops at the centre.

Sleeping

Brooklands B&B ££
(☎01768-863395; www.brooklandsguesthouse.com; 2 Portland Pl; s £38, d £75-85; wi-fi) The town's most elegant B&B is this Victorian redbrick on Portland Place. Rich furnishings and posh extras (such as White Company toiletries, fridges and chocs on the teatray) keep it a cut above the crowd.

Brandelhow B&B ££
(☎01768-864470; www.brandelhowguesthouse.co.uk; 1 Portland Pl; s/d £35/70; wi-fi) Bang next door to Brooklands, things are more staid at this friendly, family-run guest house. Nothing remarkable about the rooms, but the little treats make it worth considering – such as the sit-down welcome tea accompanied by Bootle Gingerbread or Lanie's Expedition Flapjack.

George Hotel HOTEL ££
(☎01768-862696; www.lakedistricthotels.net/georgehotel; d £108-180; P wi-fi) You won't find a better location in Penrith than the one belonging to this scarlet-bricked stalwart right on the market square. Once the town's main coaching inn, it's now mainly frequented by business travellers – expect efficient service and corporate rooms in creams, taupes and beiges, plus a rather quaint bar and country restaurant.

Eating

TOP CHOICE **Yanwath Gate Inn** GASTROPUB ££
(☎01768-862886; Yanwath; mains £16-19) Gastropub gorgeousness is at the order of the day at the Yat, 2 miles south of town. It's been named Cumbria's Top Dining Pub three times by the *Good Pub Guide*, and the grub puts many of the county's gastronomic restaurants to shame: wild venison, saltmarsh lamb, Brougham Hall chicken and crispy pork belly, chased down by Cumbrian cheeses and beers from three local breweries.

No 15 CAFE ££
(15 Victoria Rd; lunches £6-10; ⏲9am-5pm Mon-Sat)
Our tip for the town's top lunch is this groovy cafe-gallery, proffering tempting pies, salads and wraps accompanied by first-rate coffee and freshly-mixed smoothies. Look out for art and photography exhibitions in the annexe, and late-night music sessions.

Information

Tourist office (☎01768-867466; pen.tic@eden.gov.uk; Middlegate; ⏲9.30am-5pm Mon-Sat, 1-4.45pm Sun) Also houses Penrith's local museum.

Getting There & Away

BUS The bus station is northeast of the centre, off Sandgate. There are regular services to eastern Cumbria and the Eden Valley.

104 Penrith to Carlisle (45 minutes, hourly Monday to Saturday, nine on Sunday).

X4/X5 Travels via Rheged, Keswick and Cockermouth en route to the Cumbrian coast (hourly Monday to Saturday, six on Sunday).

TRAIN Penrith has frequent connections to Carlisle (£5.70, 15 minutes, hourly) and Lancaster (£13.70, one hour, hourly).

Newcastle & Northeast England

Includes »

NEWCASTLE-UPON-TYNE 609
Angel of the North... 616
Segedunum 617
COUNTY DURHAM .. 617
Durham 617
North Pennines 622
HADRIAN'S WALL ... 622
NORTHUMBERLAND NATIONAL PARK 628
NORTHUMBERLAND 630
Farne Islands 632
Bamburgh 632
Holy Island (Lindisfarne) 633

Best Places to Eat

» Oldfields (p613)

» Jesmond Dene House (p614)

» Bouchon Bistrot (p625)

Best Places to Stay

» Ashcroft (p627)

» No 1 Sallyport (p634)

» Fallen Angel (p619)

Why Go?

Ask a Kentish farmer or Cornish fisherman about northeast England and they may describe a forbidding industrial wasteland inhabited by soccer-mad folk with impenetrable accents. What they won't mention are the untamed landscapes, Newcastle's cultural renaissance, the wealth of Roman sites and the no-nonsense likeability of the locals. Some post-industrial gloom remains, but there's so much more to this frontier country than slag heaps and silenced steelworks.

In fact, if it's silence you are looking for, the northeast is ideal for flits into unpeopled backcountry – from the rounded Cheviot Hills, to the brooding Northumberland National Park to the harsh remoteness of the North Pennines, you're spoilt for choice when it comes to fleeing the urban hullabaloo. Spectacular Hadrian's Wall cuts a lonely path through this wild landscape dotted with dramatic castle ruins, haunting reminders of a long and bloody struggle with the Scots to the north.

When to Go?

The best time to discover Northumberland's miles of wide sandy beaches is during the June to August season. In May you can join the toga party at the Hadrian's Wall spring festival, while September through October is great for losing yourself in the autumnal landscapes of the North Pennines. September is also the month to grab a Newkie Brown ale, or your running shoes, and join the party along the route of Tyneside's Great North Run, the world's biggest half marathon.

Newcastle & Northeast England Highlights

1. Viewing cutting-edge contemporary art and the River Tyne at the **BALTIC Centre for Contemporary Art** (p612)
2. Enjoying a thumping **night out** on the tiles in Newcastle's raucous city centre (p614)
3. Hugging the XXL ankles of the **Angel of the North** (p616)
4. Gazing in awe at **Durham Cathedral** (p617), a spectacular Unesco World Heritage Site
5. Getting all hands-on with the northeast's industrial past at **Beamish Open-Air Museum** (p621)

6 Walking like a Roman – by taking a hike along **Hadrian's Wall** (p622)

7 Clambering to the top of the **Cheviot** (p629) the highest peak in the Northumberland National Park.

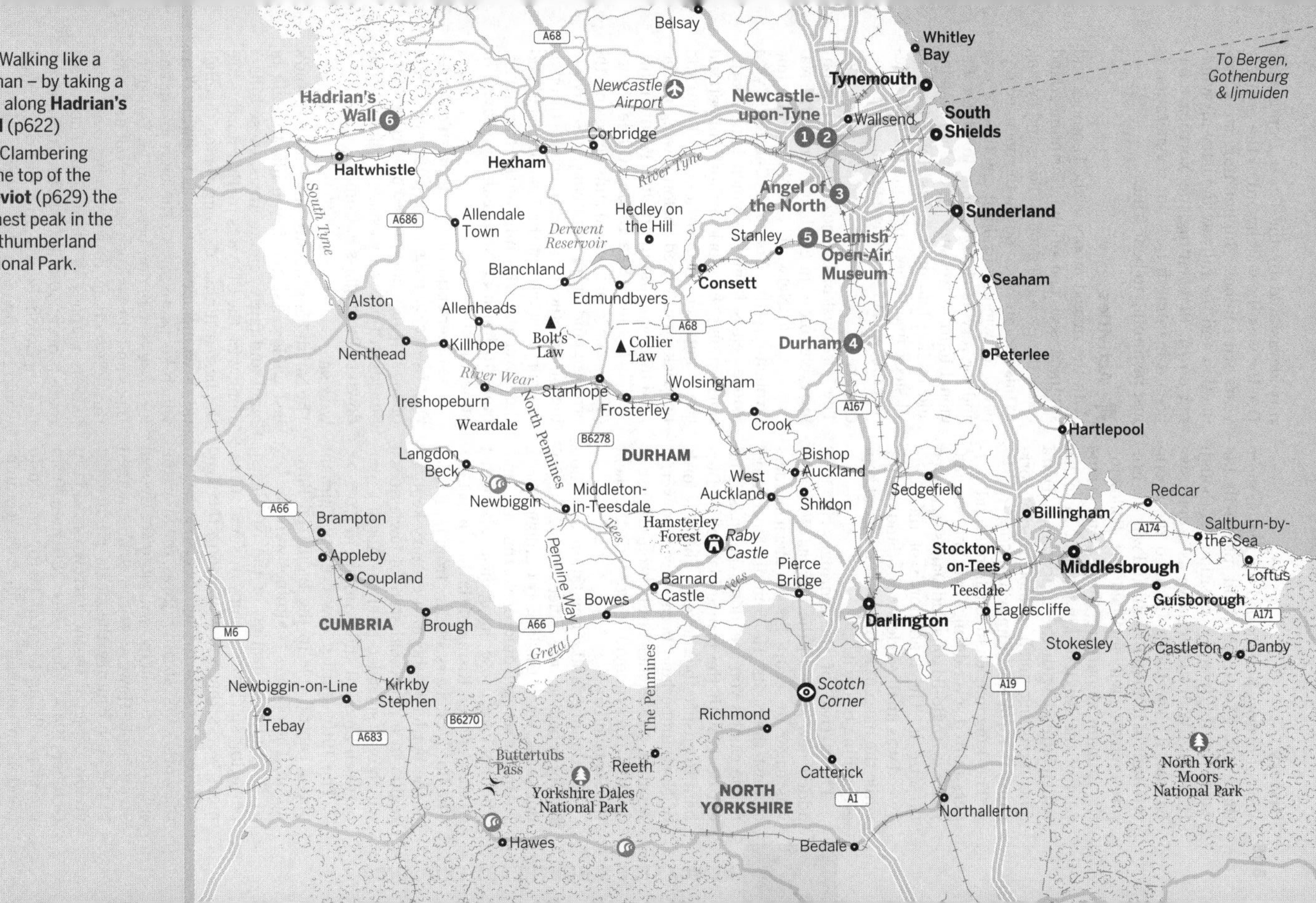

History

Violent history has shaped the region more than any other in England, primarily because of its frontier position. Although Hadrian's Wall didn't serve as a defensive barrier, it nevertheless marked the northern limit of Roman Britain and was the Empire's most heavily fortified line. Following the Romans' departure, the region became part of the Anglian kingdom of Bernicia, which united with the kingdom of Deira (encompassing much of modern-day Yorkshire) to form Northumbria in 604.

The kingdom changed hands and borders shifted several times over the next 500 years as Anglo-Saxons and Danes struggled to seize it. The land north of the River Tweed was finally ceded to Scotland in 1018, while the nascent kingdom of England kept everything below it.

The arrival of the Normans in 1066 added new spice to the mix, as William I was eager to secure his northern borders against the Scots. He commissioned most of the castles you see along the coast, and cut deals with the prince bishops of Durham to ensure their loyalty. The new lords of Northumberland became very powerful because, as Marcher Lords (from the use of 'march' as a synonym of 'border'), they kept the Scots at bay.

Northumberland's reputation as a hotbed of rebellion intensified during the Tudor years, when the largely Catholic north, led by the seventh duke of Northumberland, Thomas Percy, rose up against Elizabeth I in the defeated Rising of the North in 1569. The Border Reivers, raiders from both sides of the border in the 16th century kept the region in a perpetual state of lawlessness, which only subsided after the Act of Union between England and Scotland in 1707.

The 19th century saw County Durham play a central role in the Industrial Revolution. The region's coalmines were the key to the industrialization of the Northeast, powering steelworks, shipyards and armament works that grew up along the Tyne and Tees. In 1825 the mines also spawned the world's first steam railway, the Stockton & Darlington built by local engineer George Stephenson. However social strife emerged in the 20th century, the locals' plight most vividly depicted by the Jarrow Crusade in October 1936, which saw 200 men from the shipbuilding town of Jarrow march to London to demand aid for their community devastated by the Great Depression. Decline was the watchword of the postwar years with mines, shipbuilding, steel production and the railway industry all winding down. Reinventing the Northeast has been a mammoth task but regeneration is just beginning to bear fruit.

Activities

With the rugged moors of the Pennines and stunning seascape of the Northumberland coast, there's some good walking and cycling in this region. When out in the open, be prepared for wind and rain at any time of year and for very harsh conditions in winter. Regional tourism websites all contain walking and cycling information, and tourist offices all stock free leaflets plus maps and guides covering walking, cycling and other activities.

CYCLING

The northeast has some of the most inspiring cycle routes in England. Part of the National Cycle Network (NCN), a long-time favourite is the **Coast & Castles Cycle Route** (NCN Route 1), which runs south–north along the glorious Northumberland coast between Newcastle-upon-Tyne and Berwick-upon-Tweed, before swinging inland into Scotland to finish at Edinburgh.

The 140-mile **Sea to Sea Cycle Route** (C2C; www.c2c-guide.co.uk) runs across northern England from Whitehaven or Workington on the Cumbrian coast, through the northern part of the Lake District, and then over the wild hills of the North Pennines to finish at Newcastle-upon-Tyne or Sunderland.

The other option is the **Hadrian's Cycleway** (www.cycle-routes.org), a 191-mile route opened in July 2006 that runs from South Shields in Tyneside, west along the wall and down to Ravenglass in Cumbria.

WALKING

The North Pennines are billed as 'England's last wilderness', and if you like to walk in quiet and fairly remote areas, these hills – along with the Cheviots further north – are the best in England. Long routes through this area include the famous **Pennine Way**, which keeps mainly to the high ground as it crosses the region between the Yorkshire Dales and the Scottish border, but also goes through sections of river valley and some tedious patches of plantation. The whole route is over 250 miles, but the 70-mile section between Bowes and Hadrian's Wall would be a fine four-day taster.

Elsewhere in the area, the great Roman ruin of **Hadrian's Wall** is an ideal focus for walking. There's a huge range of easy loops taking in forts and other historical highlights.

The Northumberland coast has endless miles of open beaches, and little in the way of resort towns, so walkers can often enjoy this wild, windswept shore in virtual solitude. One of the finest walks is between the villages of Craster and Bamburgh via Dunstanburgh, which includes two of the county's most spectacular castles.

Getting There & Around

Bus

Bus transport around the region can be difficult, particularly around the more remote reaches of western Northumberland. Contact **Traveline** (☎0871-2002233; www.travelinenortheast.info) for information on connections, timetables and prices.

Several one-day Explorer tickets are available; always ask if one might be appropriate. The Explorer North East (adult/child £8/7), available on buses, covers from Berwick down to Scarborough, and allows unlimited travel for one day, as well as numerous admission discounts.

Train

The main lines run north to Edinburgh via Durham, Newcastle and Berwick, and west to Carlisle roughly following Hadrian's Wall.

There are numerous Rover tickets for single-day travel and longer periods, so ask if one might be worthwhile. For example, the North Country Rover (adult/child £72/36) allows unlimited travel throughout the north (not including Northumberland) any four days out of eight.

NEWCASTLE-UPON-TYNE

POP 189,863

Of all northern England's cities, Newcastle is perhaps the most surprising to the first-time visitor, especially if they come armed with the preconceived notions that have dogged the city's reputation since, well, always. A sooty, industrial wasteland for salt-of-the-earth toughies whose favourite hobby is drinking and braving the elements bare-chested. Coal slags and cold slags? You may be in for a pleasant surprise.

Welcome to the hipster capital of the northeast, a cool urban centre that knows how to take care of itself and anyone else who comes to visit with an unexpected mix of culture, heritage and sophistication, best exemplified not just by its excellent new art galleries and magnificent concert hall, but by its growing number of fine restaurants, choice hotels and interesting bars. It's not just about the Tyne bridges – although the eclectic, cluttered array of Newcastle's most recognisable feature is pretty impressive.

Sights

QUAYSIDE

Newcastle's most recognisable attractions are the seven bridges that span the Tyne and some of the striking buildings that line it. Along the Quayside, on the river's northern side, is a handsome boardwalk that makes for a pleasant stroll during the day but really comes to life at night, when the bars, clubs and restaurants that line it are full to bursting.

FREE **Bessie Surtee's House**
MERCHANT'S HOUSE

(EH; 41-44 Sandhill; ⌚10am-4pm Mon-Fri) The Tyne's northern bank was the hub of commercial Newcastle in the 16th century and on Sandhill a row of leaning merchant houses has survived from that era. One of them is the Bessie Surtee's House where three rooms are open to the public. The daughter of a wealthy banker, feisty Bessie annoyed Daddy by falling in love with John Scott (1751–1838), a pauper. It all ended in smiles as John went on to become Lord Chancellor.

BRIDGING THE TYNE

The most famous view in Newcastle is the cluster of Tyne bridges, the most famous of these being the **Tyne Bridge** (1925–28). Its resemblance to Australia's Sydney Harbour Bridge is no coincidence as both were built by the same company (Dorman Long of Middlesbrough) around the same time. The quaint little **Swing Bridge** pivots in the middle to let ships through. Nearby, **High Level Bridge**, designed by Robert Stephenson, was the world's first combined road and railway bridge (1849). The most recent addition is the multiple-award-winning **Millennium Bridge** (aka Blinking Bridge; 2002), which opens like an eyelid to let ships pass.

Newcastle-upon-Tyne

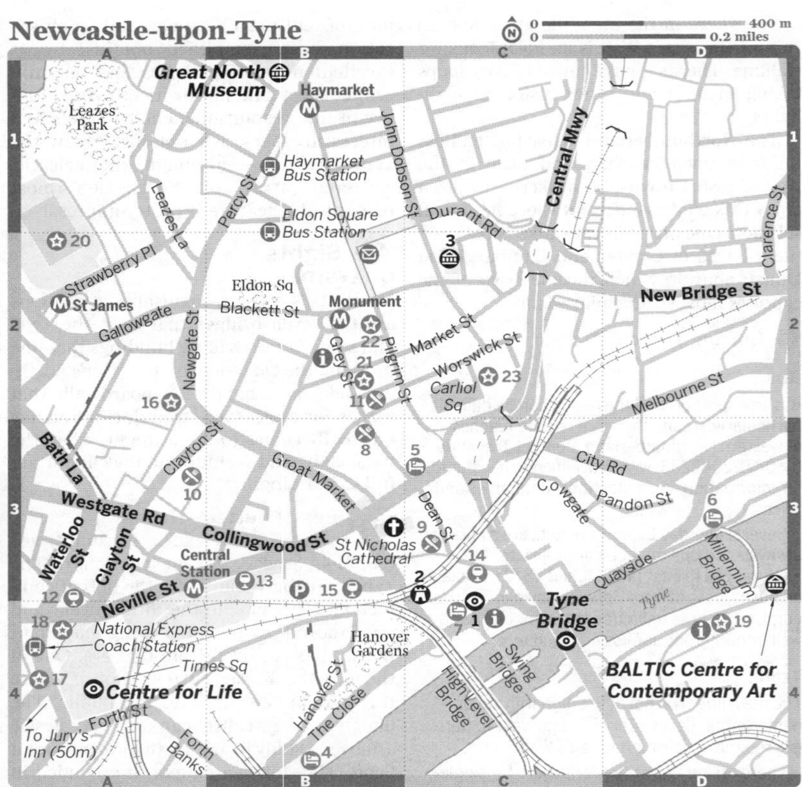

CITY CENTRE

Newcastle's Victorian centre, a compact area bordered roughly by Grainger St to the west and Pilgrim St to the east, is supremely elegant and one of the most compelling examples of urban rejuvenation in England. At its heart is the extraordinarily handsome Grey St, lined with fine classical buildings – undoubtedly one of the country's finest thoroughfares: it was even voted the UK's 3rd prettiest street in the Google Street View Awards 2010.

FREE **Great North Museum** MUSEUM
(www.greatnorthmuseum.org; Barras Bridge; ⏲10am-5pm Mon-Sat, 2-5pm Sun) This outstanding new museum has been created by bringing together the contents of Newcastle University's museums and adding them to the natural history exhibits of the prestigious Hancock Museum in the latter's renovated neoclassical building. The result is a fascinating jumble of dinosaurs, Roman altar stones, Egyptian mummies, Samurai warriors and some impressive taxidermy, all presented in an engaging and easily digestible way. The indisputable highlights are a life-size model of a *Tyrannosaurus rex* and an interactive model of Hadrian's Wall showing every milecastle and fortress. There's also lots of hands-on stuff for the kids, a planetarium with screenings throughout the day and a decent snack bar.

Centre for Life SCIENCE VILLAGE
(www.life.org.uk; Times Sq; adult/child £9.95/6.95; ⏲10am-6pm Mon-Sat, 11am-6pm Sun, last admission 4pm) This excellent science village, part of the sober-minded complex of institutes devoted to the study of genetic science, is one of the more interesting attractions in town. Through a series of hands-on exhibits and the latest technology you (or your kids) can discover the incredible secrets of life. The highlight is the Motion Ride, a motion simulator that lets you

Newcastle-upon-Tyne

Top Sights
- BALTIC Centre for Contemporary Art D3
- Centre for Life A4
- Great North Museum B1
- Tyne Bridge C4

Sights
1. Bessie Surtee's House C4
2. Castle Garth Keep C3
3. Laing Art Gallery C2

Sleeping
4. Copthorne B4
5. Greystreethotel C3
6. Malmaison D3
7. Waterside Hotel C4

Eating
8. Blake's Coffee House B3
9. Oldfields C3
10. Scrumpy Willow & Singing Kettle A3
11. Starters & Puds B2

Drinking
12. Camp David A3
13. Centurion Bar B3
14. Crown Posada C3
15. Tokyo B3

Entertainment
16. Beyond Bar & Grill A2
17. Loft A4
18. Powerhouse Nightclub A4
19. Sage Gateshead D4
20. St James' Park A2
21. Theatre Royal B2
22. Tyneside Cinema B2
23. World Headquarters C2

'feel' what it's like to experience things like bungee jumping and other extreme sports (the 3D film changes every year).

FREE **Discovery Museum** MUSEUM
(www.twmuseums.org.uk; Blandford Sq; 10am-5pm Mon-Sat, 2-5pm Sun) Tyneside's rich history is uncovered through a fascinating series of exhibits at this unmissable museum. The exhibitions, spread across three floors of the former Co-operative Wholesale Society building, surround the mightily impressive 30m-long *Turbinia*, the fastest ship in the world in 1897. There's an absorbing section dedicated to shipbuilding on the Tyne including a scale model of the river as it was in 1929, a buzzers-and-bells science maze for the kids and a 'Story of Newcastle' section giving the low-down on the city's history from Pons Aelius (Newcastle's Roman name) to Cheryl Cole.

The museum is about a ten minute walk west of Central Station along Neville St and Westmorland Rd.

Castle Garth Keep CASTLE
(adult/child £4/free; 10am-5pm Mon-Sat, from noon Sun) The stronghold that put both the 'new' and 'castle' into Newcastle has been largely swallowed up by the railway station, leaving only the square Norman keep as one of the few remaining fragments. Inside you'll discover a fine chevron-covered chapel and an exhibition of architectural models ranging from Hadrian's Wall to 20th-century eyesores. The 360-degree city views from the rooftop are much better than from the BALTIC's 'Viewing Box' across the water.

FREE **Laing Art Gallery** GALLERY
(www.twmuseums.org.uk; New Bridge St; 10am-5pm Mon-Sat, 2-5pm Sun) The exceptional collection at the Laing includes works by Gainsborough, Gauguin and Henry Moore, and an important collection of paintings by Northumberland-born artist John Martin (1789–1854). Free guided tours run Saturdays at 11am.

OUSEBURN VALLEY

About a mile east of the city centre is the much-touted Ouseburn Valley, the 19th-century industrial heartland of Newcastle and now an up-and-coming, semi-regenerated district, dotted with potteries, glass-blowing studios and other skilled craftspeople, as well as a handful of great bars, clubs and a superb cinema (though much of the area is still an unsightly industrial estate). For more info, check out www.ouseburntrust.org.uk.

Biscuit Factory COMMERCIAL GALLERY
(www.thebiscuitfactory.com; 16 Stoddart St; 11am-5pm Sun & Mon, 10am-6pm Tue-Sat, to 8pm Thu) No prizes for guessing what this commercial art gallery used to be. What it

THE GREAT NORTH RUN

First held in 1981, the world's biggest **half-marathon** sees over 50,000 runners grunt and sweat a gruelling 13.1 miles from just north of the city centre, along the central motorway, across the Tyne Bridge and east along the Tyne to slump on the seafront at South Shields. Held in early autumn, it's one of the largest annual occasions in the city's sporting calendar and brings out the Geordie crowds, who line the route egging on the athletes with applause and, less appropriately, plastic cups of Newkie Brown beer. Bands pump out Geordie anthems at strategic points, adding to the festival atmosphere.

is now, though, is the country's biggest art shop, where you can peruse and buy work by artists from near and far in a variety of mediums, including painting, sculpture, glassware and furniture, much of which has a northeast theme.

Seven Stories – the Centre for Children's Books LITERATURE MUSEUM
(www.sevenstories.org.uk; 30 Lime St; adult/child £6/5; ⌚10am-5pm Mon-Sat, to 4pm Sun) A marvellous conversion of a handsome Victorian mill has resulted in Seven Stories, a very hands-on museum dedicated to the wondrous world of children's literature. Across the seven floors you'll find original manuscripts, a growing collection of artwork from the 1930s onwards, and a constantly changing program of exhibitions, activities and events designed to encourage the AA Milnes of the new millennium.

36 Lime Street ARTISTS COOPERATIVE
(www.36limestreet.co.uk; Ouseburn Warehouse, 36 Lime St) The artistic, independent spirit of Ouseburn is particularly well represented in this artists cooperative, the largest of its kind in the northeast, featuring an interesting mix of artists, performers, designers and musicians. They all share a historic building designed by Newcastle's most important architect, John Dobson (1787–1865), who also designed Grey St and Central Station in the neoclassical style. As it's a working studio you can't just wander in, but there are regular exhibitions and open days.

GATESHEAD

You probably didn't realise that that bit of Newcastle south of the Tyne is the 'town' of Gateshead, but local authorities are going to great lengths to put it right, even promoting the whole kit-and-caboodle-on-Tyne as 'NewcastleGateshead', a clumsy piece of marketing indeed.

FREE **BALTIC Centre for Contemporary Art** GALLERY
(www.balticmill.com; Gateshead Quays; ⌚10am-6pm Wed-Mon, from 10.30am Tue) Once a huge, dirty, yellow grain store overlooking the Tyne, BALTIC is now a huge, dirty, yellow art gallery to rival London's Tate Modern. Unlike the Tate, there are no permanent exhibitions here, but the constantly rotating shows feature the work and installations of some of contemporary art's biggest show stoppers. The complex has artists in residence, a performance space, a cinema, a bar, a spectacular rooftop restaurant (you'll need to book) and a ground-floor restaurant with riverside tables. There's also a viewing box for a fine Tyne vista.

Sleeping

Although the number of city-centre options is on the increase, they are still generally restricted to the chain variety – either budget or business – that caters conveniently to the party people and business folk that make up the majority of Newcastle's overnight guests. Most of the other accommodations are in the handsome northern suburb of Jesmond, where the forces of gentrification and student power fight it out for territory; Jesmond's main drag, Osborne Rd, is lined with all kinds of bed types as well as bars and restaurants – making it a strong rival with the city centre for the late-night party scene. As the city is a major business destination, weekend arrivals will find that most places drop their prices for Friday and Saturday nights.

CITY CENTRE

As you'd expect, bedrooms in the city centre are pricier than almost anywhere else, but there are some good budget and midrange options that don't involve too much of a hike.

Malmaison HOTEL £££
(☎0191-245 5000; www.malmaison-newcastle.com; Quayside; r from £125, ste from £195; P @ ☎) The affectedly stylish Malmaison touch has been applied to this former

warehouse with considerable success, even down to the French-speaking lifts. Big beds, sleek lighting and designer furniture embellish the bouncy boudoirs and slick chambers.

Backpackers Newcastle HOSTEL £
(0191-340 7334; www.backpackersnewcastle.com; 262 Westgate Rd; dm from £17.95;) This clean, well-run budget flophouse has just 26 beds lending it a bit more of a backpacker vibe than its competitors in the city. Bike storage, kitchen, a big games room, power-showers and a mildly design feel make this a great kip on the Tyne.

Waterside Hotel HOTEL ££
(0191-230 0111; www.watersidehotel.com; 48-52 Sandhill, Quayside; s/d £75/85;) The rooms are a tad small, but they're among the most elegant in town: lavish furnishings and heavy velvet drapes in a heritage-listed building. The location is excellent.

Greystreethotel HOTEL ££
(0191-230 6777; www.greystreethotel.com; 2-12 Grey St; d from £109; P) A bit of designer class along the classiest street in the city centre has been long overdue: the rooms are gorgeous if a tad poky, all cluttered up with flatscreen TVs, big beds and handsome modern furnishings.

Copthorne HOTEL ££
(0191-222 0333; www.millenniumhotels.com; The Close, Quayside; s/d from £93/112; P) A superb waterside location makes this modern hotel a perfect choice – especially if you pick a room overlooking the water (the Connoisseur rooms, for instance). You may even bump into the odd celebrity performing at the nearby Newcastle Arena. Book online for the best rates.

JESMOND

The shabby chic suburb of Jesmond is the place to head for budget and mid-range accommodation. Catch the Metro to Jesmond or West Jesmond. Bus 80A from near Central Station, or the 38 from Westgate Rd.

Jesmond Dene House HOTEL £££
(0191-212 3000; www.jesmonddenehouse.co.uk; Jesmond Dene Rd; s £165, d £175-250, ste £295-375; P@) As elegant a hotel as you'll find anywhere, this exquisite property is the perfect marriage between traditional styles and modern luxury. The large, gorgeous bedrooms are furnished in a modern interpretation of the Arts and Crafts style and are bedecked with all manner of technological goodies (flatscreen digital TVs, digital radios) and wonderful bathrooms complete with underfloor heating. The restaurant is not bad either.

Avenue B&B ££
(0191-281 1396; 2 Manor House Rd; s/d £39.50/60) Buried in a sleepy residential area but just a couple of blocks' walk from the action on Osborne Rd, this well-run, family-friendly B&B goes big on busy floral flounce and faux country style.

Newcastle YHA YOUTH HOSTEL £
(0845 371 9335; www.yha.org.uk; 107 Jesmond Rd; dm from £18) This nice, rambling place has small dorms that are generally full, so book in advance. It's close to the Jesmond Metro stop.

Eating

The Geordie palate is pretty refined these days and there are a host of fine dining options in all price categories that make their mark. Of course for many locals, Geordies plus food equals the legendary **Greggs** (8am-5pm), Newcastle's very own fast-food chain (15 locations throughout the city centre) serving cheap and filling cakes, sandwiches, pastries and drinks since 1951.

CITY CENTRE

TOP CHOICE **Oldfields** BRITIS ££
(www.oldfieldsrealfood.co.uk; Milburn House, Dean St; mains £12-19; Mon-Sat, lunch Sun) Top-notch, no-nonsense British gourmet fare, using locally sourced ingredients wherever possible, is Oldfields' tasty trade. Tuck into rich and satisfying dishes such as Durham rabbit and crayfish pie, mutton hotpot and Eccles cake with custard in the circular, wood-panelled dining room, before finishing off with a shot of Wylam gin or locally microbrewed ale.

Blake's Coffee House CAFE £
(0191-261 5463; 53 Grey St; breakfast £1.95-8.95, sandwiches £3-4; 9am-6pm) There is nowhere better than this high-ceilinged cafe for a Sunday-morning cure on any day of the week. It's friendly, relaxed and serves up the biggest selection of coffees in town.

Starters & Puds RESTAURANT ££
(www.startersandpuds.com; 2-6 Shakespeare St; starters £3.50-7, puddings £4.70; Mon-Sat) Situated in a low-lit cellar next to the

Theatre Royal, the idea here is to come for a pre-theatre starter, cross the road for a thespian main course then head back for a post-performance dessert (and drink). However word has got round about the award-winning fare served up here so now there's a lunch menu (£10).

Scrumpy Willow & Singing Kettle ORGANIC RESTAURAN ££
(☎0191-221 2323; 89 Clayton St; mains £5-10; ⊙Mon-Sat, lunch Sun) Voted one of the UK's top organic eateries by Guardian readers, this incredibly popular place bursts at the seams at mealtimes, and one mouthful is enough to understand why. Vegans, veggies and gluten-freers are all catered for with an eclectic menu featuring everything from peanut butter sarnies to Irish stew. Booking recommended.

JESMOND

TOP CHOICE **Jesmond Dene House** REGIONAL CUISINE £££
(☎0191-212 5555; www.jesmonddenehouse.co.uk; Jesmond Dene Rd; mains £13-40) Head chef Pierre Rigothier is the architect of an exquisite menu heavily influenced by the northeast – venison from County Durham, oysters from Lindisfarne and the freshest herbs plucked straight from the garden – all infused with a touch of French sophistication. The result is a gourmet delight and one of the best dining experiences in the city.

Pizzeria Francesca PIZZERIA ££
(134 Manor House Rd, Jesmond; pizzas & pastas £5, other mains £7-15; ⊙Mon-Sat) One of the northeast's best pizza and pasta joints, this chaotic, friendly place is how all Italian restaurants should be. Excitable, happy waiters and huge portions of pizza and pasta keep them queuing at the door – get in line and wait because you can't book in advance.

Drinking

It's no secret that Geordies like a good night on the razzle but you may be surprised to know that not only is there nightlife beyond the coloured cocktails of the Bigg Market, but that it is infinitely more interesting and satisfying than the sloppy boozefest that defines the stereotype. The Ouseburn attracts a mellower crowd, and the western end of Neville St has a decent mix of great bars and is also home to the best of the gay scene.

CITY CENTRE

Centurion Bar BAR
(Central Station) Voted Newcastle's best bar in 2008, the former first-class waiting room at Central Station is ideal for a pre-club drink in style or a pre-train brew on the hop. The exquisitely ornate Victorian tile decoration reaching from floor to ceiling is said to be worth four million pounds. There's an adjoining cafe and deli platform-side.

Crown Posada PUB
(31 The Side) An unspoilt, real-ale pub that is a favourite with more seasoned drinkers, be they the after-work or instead-of-work crowd.

Tokyo COCKTAIL BAR
(17 Westgate Rd) Tokyo has a suitably darkened atmosphere for what the cognoscenti consider the best cocktail bar in town, but we loved the upstairs garden bar where you can drink, smoke and chat with a view.

OUSEBURN VALLEY

Cumberland Arms PUB
(off Byker Bank, Ouseburn) Sitting on a hill at the top of the Ouseburn, this 19th-century bar has a sensational selection of ales and ciders as well as a range of Northumberland meads. There's a terrace outside, where you can read a book from the Bring One, Borrow One library inside.

☆ Entertainment

Are you up for it? You'd better be, because Newcastle's nightlife doesn't mess about. There is action beyond the club scene – you'll just have to wade through a sea of staggering, glassy-eyed clubbers to get to it.

The Crack (www.thecrackmagazine.com) is a free monthly magazine available from clubs, tourist offices and some hotels containing comprehensive club, theatre, music and cinema listings for the northeast's nightlife hotspots.

Cinema

Tyneside Cinema CINEMA
(www.tynesidecinema.co.uk; Pilgrim St) Opened in 1937 as Newcastle's first newsreel cinema, this period picture house, all plush red-velvet seats and swish art deco design, screens a blend of mainstream and offbeat movies as well as archive Newsreel films (11.30am; free). Free guided tours of the building (one hour) run on Tuesday, Wednesday, Friday and Saturday at 11.15am.

Live Music

Sage Gateshead MUSIC VENUE
(☎0191-443 4666; www.thesagegateshead.org; Gateshead Quays) Few contemporary pieces of architecture will stand the test of time, but Norman Foster's magnificent chrome-and-glass horizontal bottle might just be one that does. Most come to gape and wander, some to hear live music, from folk to classical orchestras, or engage in educational or research activities. It is the home of the Northern Sinfonia and Folkworks.

Head of Steam@The Cluny MUSIC VENUE
(☎0191-230 4474; www.headofsteam.co.uk; 36 Lime St, Ouseburn Valley) This is one of the best-known spots in town to hear live music, attracting all kinds of performers, from experimental prog-rock heads to up-and-coming pop goddesses. Touring acts and local talent fill the bill every night of the week.

Nightclubs

World Headquarters NIGHTCLUB
(www.welovewhq.com; Curtis Mayfield House, Carliol Sq) Dedicated to the genius of black music in all its guises – funk, rare groove, dance-floor jazz, northern soul, genuine R&B, lush disco, proper house and reggae – this fabulous club is strictly for true believers, and judging from the numbers, there are thousands of them.

Beyond Bar & Grill NIGHTCLUB
(www.beyondbar.co.uk; The Gate, Newgate St) Cheapo student nights, sexy urban R&B events, and Saturday mash-ups – with slabs of vinyl from the '60s to Brit pop going under the needle – fill this popular venue at the Gate.

Theatre

Theatre Royal THEATRE
(☎08448-112121; www.theatreroyal.co.uk; 100 Grey St) The winter home of the Royal Shakespeare Company is full of Victorian splendour and has an excellent program of drama.

Sport

Newcastle United Football Club FOOTBALL CLUB
(www.nufc.co.uk) NUFC is more than just a football team: it is the collective expression of Geordie hope and pride as well as the release for decades of economic, social and sporting frustration. The club's fabulous ground, **St James' Park** (Strawberry Pl), is always packed, but you can get a **stadium tour** (☎0844-372 1892; adult/child £10/7; ⏰11am, 1.30pm daily & 4hr before kick-off on match days) of the place, including the dugout and changing rooms. Match tickets go on public sale about two weeks before a game or you can try the stadium on the day.

GAY & LESBIAN NEWCASTLE

Newcastle's gay scene is pretty dynamic, with its hub at the 'Pink Triangle' formed by Waterloo, Neville and Collingwood Sts, but stretching as far south as Scotswood Rd. There are plenty of gay bars in the area and a few great clubs.

Camp David (www.campdavidnewcastle.com; 8-10 Westmorland Rd) Mixed bar as trendy with straights as it is with the gay community.

Loft (10A Scotswood Rd) Loud, proud and completely cheesy, this 1st-floor club is open seven nights a week from 11pm.

Powerhouse Nightclub (www.clubph.co.uk; 9-19 Westmorland Rd) Newcastle's brashest queer nightclub, with flashing lights, video screens and lots of suggestive posing.

Information

City Library (33 New Bridge St W; ⏰8.30am-8pm Mon-Thu, to 5.30 Fri & Sat) Free internet access at Newcastle's stomping new library building. Bring ID.

Police station (☎03456-043043; cnr Pilgrim & Market Sts)

Post office (36 Northumberland St; ⏰9am-5.30pm Mon-Sat) On the second floor of WH Smith. Has a bureau de change.

Newcastle General Hospital (☎0191-233 6161; Westgate Rd) Has an Accident and Emergency unit.

Tourist offices (www.visitnewcastlegateshead.com) Main branch (☎0191-277 8000; Central Arcade, Market St; ⏰9.30am-5.30pm Mon-Fri, from 9.30 Sat); Gateshead Library (☎0191-433 8420; Prince Consort Rd; ⏰9am-7pm Mon, Tue, Thu & Fri, to 5pm Wed, to 1pm Sat); Guildhall (☎0191-277 8000; Newcastle Quayside; ⏰10am-5pm Mon-Fri, 9am-5pm Sat, 9am-4pm Sun); Sage Gateshead (☎0191-478 4222; Gateshead Quays; ⏰10am-5pm) All offices listed here provide a booking service as well as other assorted tourist sundries.

Getting There & Away

Air

Newcastle International Airport (0871-882 1121; www.newcastleairport.com) Seven miles north of the city off the A696. It has direct services to many UK and European cities as well as long-haul flights to Dubai. Tour operators fly charters to the Americas and Africa.

Bus

Local and regional buses leave from Haymarket or Eldon Sq bus stations. National Express buses arrive and depart from the coach station on St James Blvd. For local buses around the northeast, the excellent-value Explorer North East ticket (£8) is valid on most services.

Berwick-upon-Tweed Bus 501/505, two hours, five daily

Edinburgh National Express, £17.50, three hours, three daily

London National Express/Megabus £10-27, seven hours, nine daily

Manchester National Express, £19.50, five hours, five daily

Train

Newcastle is on the main rail line between London and Edinburgh and is the starting point of the scenic Tyne Valley Line west to Carlisle.

Alnmouth (for bus connections to Alnwick) £7.70, 25 minutes, hourly

Berwick £21.50, 45 minutes, hourly

Carlisle £14.50, 1½ hours, hourly

Edinburgh £32, 1½ hours, half-hourly

London King's Cross £105, three hours, half-hourly

York £23.50, one hour, every 20 minutes

Getting Around

To/From the Airport

The airport is linked to town by the Metro (£2.90, 20 minutes, every 15 minutes).

Public Transport

There's a large bus network, but the best means of getting around is the excellent Metro, with fares from £1.40. Several saver passes are also available. The tourist office can supply you with route plans for the bus and Metro networks.

The DaySaver (£4.80, £3.90 after 9am) gives unlimited Metro travel for one day, and the DayRover (adult/child £6.50/3.50) gives unlimited travel on all modes of transport in Tyne and Wear for one day.

Taxi

On weekend nights taxis can be as rare as covered flesh; try **Noda Taxis** (0191-222 1888), which has a kiosk outside the entrance to Central Station.

AROUND NEWCASTLE

If you're in town for a longer stretch there's plenty to keep you entertained even beyond the city limits. All of the following are easily reached on the city's superb public transport system.

Angel of the North

Nicknamed the Gateshead Flasher, this extraordinary 200-tonne, rust-coloured human frame with wings, more soberly known as the *Angel of the North,* has been looming over the A1 (M) about 5 miles south of Newcastle for almost a decade and a half. At 20m high and with a wingspan wider than a Boeing 767, Antony Gormley's most successful work is the UK's largest sculpture and the most viewed piece of public art in the country, though Mark Wallinger's *White Horse* in Kent may pinch both titles over the next decade. Buses 21 and 22 from Eldon Sq will take you there.

Tynemouth

One of the most popular Geordie days out is to this handsome seaside resort 6 miles east of the city centre. Besides being the mouth of the Tyne, this is one of the best surf spots in all England, with great all-year breaks off the immense, crescent-shaped Blue Flag beach. The town even occasionally hosts the **National Surfing Championships** (www.britsurf.co.uk).

For all your surfing needs, including lessons, call into the **Tynemouth Surf Company** (0191-258 2496; www.tynemouthsurf.co.uk; Grand Parade), which provides two-hour group lessons for £25 or one-hour individual lesson for the same price.

If riding nippy surf is not your thing, the town's other main draw is the 11th-century ruins of **Tynemouth Priory** (EH; adult/child £4.20/2.10; 10am-5pm Apr-Sep), built by Benedictine monks on a strategic bluff above the mouth of the Tyne, but ransacked during the Dissolution in 1539. The military took over for four centuries, only leaving in 1960, and today the skeletal remains of the priory church sit alongside old military installations, their guns aimed out to sea at an enemy that never came.

From Newcastle city centre take the Metro to Tynemouth or bus 306 from the Haymarket.

Segedunum

The last strong post of Hadrian's Wall was the fort of **Segedunum** (www.twmuseums.org.uk; adult/child £4.35/free; ⏲10am-5pm Apr-Oct), 6 miles east of Newcastle at Wallsend. Beneath the 35m-high tower, which you can climb for some terrific views, is an absorbing site that includes a reconstructed Roman bathhouse (with steaming pools and frescoes) and a fascinating museum that gives visitors a well-rounded picture of life during Roman times.

Take the Metro to Wallsend.

COUNTY DURHAM

Best known for its strikingly beautiful capital that is one of England's star attractions, County Durham spreads itself across the lonely, rabbit-inhabited North Pennines and the gentle ochre hills of Teesdale, each dotted with picturesque, peaceful villages and traditional market towns.

Ironically, this pastoral image, so resonant of its rich medieval history, has only been reclaimed in recent years; it took the final demise of the coal industry, all-pervasive for the guts of 300 years, to render the county back to some kind of pre-industrial look. A brutal and dangerous business, coal mining was the lifeblood of entire communities and its sudden end in 1984 by the stroke of a Conservative pen has left some purposeless towns and an evocatively scarred landscape.

Durham

POP 42,940

The sheer magnificence of Durham is best appreciated if arriving by train on a clear morning: emerging from the train station, the view across the River Wear to the hilltop peninsula will confirm your reason for coming. England's most beautiful Romanesque cathedral, a masterpiece of Norman architecture and a resplendent monument to the country's ecclesiastical history, rates pretty highly in any Best of Britain list.

Durham is unquestionably beautiful, but once you've visited the cathedral and walked the old town looking for the best views there isn't much else to do; a day trip from Newcastle or an overnight stop on your way to explore the rest of the county is the best way to see the city of the Prince Bishops.

Sights

Durham Cathedral CATHEDRAL

(www.durhamcathedral.co.uk; donation requested; ⏲7.30am-6pm, to 5.30pm Sun) Durham's most famous building – and the main reason for visiting unless someone you know is at university here – has earned superlative praise for so long that to add more would be redundant; how can you do better than the 19th-century novelist Nathaniel Hawthorne, who wrote fawningly: 'I never saw so lovely and magnificent a scene, nor (being content with this) do I care to see better.' This may be overstating things a bit but no one can deny that as the definitive structure of the Anglo-Norman Romanesque style, Durham Cathedral is one of the world's greatest places of worship.

The cathedral is enormous and has a pretty fortified look; this is due to the fact that although it may have been built to pay tribute to God and to house the holy bones of St Cuthbert, it also needed to withstand any potential attack by the pesky Scots and Northumberland tribes who weren't too thrilled by the arrival of the Normans a few years before.

First up is the main door and the famous (and much-reproduced) **Sanctuary Knocker,** which medieval felons would strike to gain 37 days asylum within the cathedral before standing trial or leaving the country.

Once inside, things get genuinely spectacular. The superb nave is dominated by massive, powerful piers – every second one round, with an equal height and circumference of 6.6m, and carved with geometric designs. Durham was the first European cathedral to be roofed with stone-ribbed vaulting, which upheld the heavy stone roof and made it possible to build pointed transverse arches – the first in England, and a great architectural achievement. The central tower dates from 1262, but was damaged in a fire caused by lightning in 1429, and was unsatisfactorily patched up until it was entirely rebuilt in 1470. The western towers were added in 1217–26.

Built in 1175 and renovated 300 years later, the **Galilee Chapel** is one of the most beautiful parts. The northern side's **paintings** are rare surviving examples of 12th-century wall painting and are thought to feature Sts Cuthbert and Oswald. The chapel also contains the **Venerable Bede's tomb**. Bede was an 8th-century Northumbrian monk, a great historian and polymath

Durham

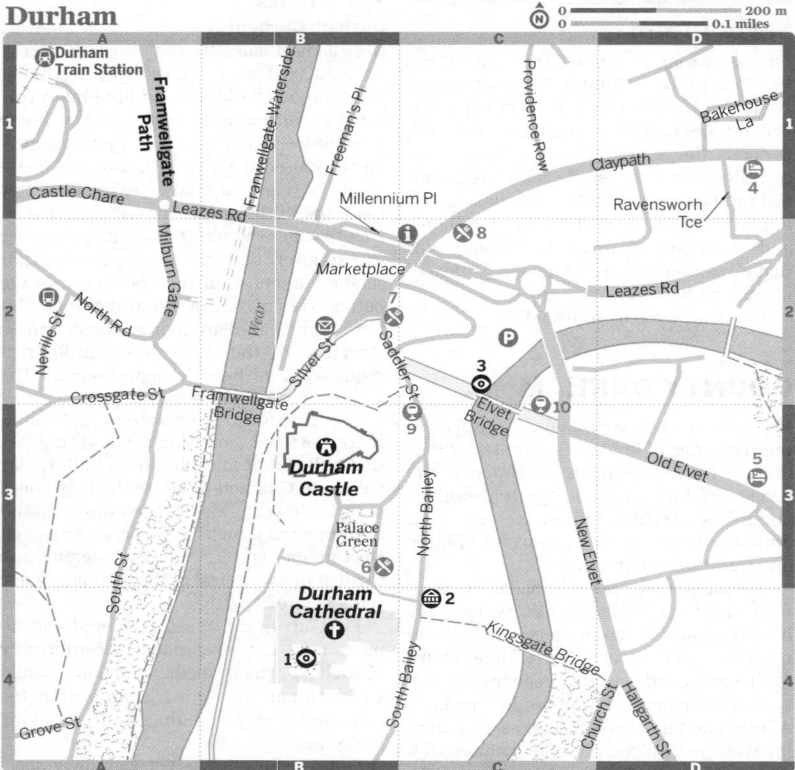

whose work *The Ecclesiastical History of the English People* is still the prime source of information on the development of early Christian Britain. Among other things, he introduced the numbering of years from the birth of Jesus. He was first buried at Jarrow, but in 1022 a miscreant monk stole his remains and brought them here.

The **Bishop's Throne**, built over the tomb of Bishop Thomas Hatfield, dates from the mid-14th century. Hatfield's effigy is the only one to have survived another turbulent time: the Reformation. The **high altar** is separated from **St Cuthbert's tomb** by the beautiful stone **Neville Screen**, made around 1372–80. Until the Reformation, the screen included 107 statues of saints.

The cathedral has worthwhile **guided tours** (adult/child £4/free; ⏲10.30am, 11am & 2pm Mon & Sat). Evensong is at 5.15pm from Monday to Saturday and at 3.30pm on Sunday.

The **tower** (adult/child £5/2.50; ⏲10am-4pm Mon-Sat Apr-Sep, to 3pm Oct-Mar) provides show-stopping vistas, but you've got to climb 325 steps (and part with a hefty £5) to enjoy them.

Other attractions include the mostly 19th-century **Cloisters** where you'll find the **Monk's Domitory** (adult/child £1/30p; ⏲10am-4pm Mon-Sat, 12.30-4pm Sun Apr-Sep), now a library of 30,000 books and displaying Anglo-Saxon carved stones. There are also **audiovisual displays** (adult/child £1/30p; ⏲10am-3pm Mon-Sat) on the building of the cathedral and the life of St Cuthbert.

The **Treasures** (adult/child £2.50/70p; ⏲10am-4.30pm Mon-Sat, 2-4.30pm Sun) refer to the relics of St Cuthbert, but besides his cross and coffin, there's very little here related to the saint, the collection consisting mostly of religious paraphernalia from later centuries. This exhibition may be moving to another site in coming years.

Durham

Top Sights

Durham Castle ... B3
Durham Cathedral ... B4

Sights

1 Cloisters & Treasures ... B4
2 Durham Heritage Centre ... C4

Activities, Courses & Tours

Browns Boathouse ... (see 3)
3 Prince Bishop River Cruiser ... C2

Sleeping

4 Cathedral View ... D1
5 Fallen Angel ... D3

Eating

6 Almshouse ... B3
7 Greggs ... B2
8 Oldfields ... C2

Drinking

9 Shakespeare ... C3
10 Swan & Three Cygnets ... C3

Durham Castle CASTLE
(www.dur.ac.uk; adult/concession £5/3.50; tours 2pm, 3pm, 4pm term time, 10am, 11am & noon during university vacations) Built as a standard motte-and-bailey fort in 1072, Durham Castle was the prince bishops' home until 1837, when it became the first college of the new university. It remains a university hall, and you can stay here.

The castle has been much altered over the centuries, as each successive prince bishop sought to put his particular imprint on the place, but heavy restoration and reconstruction were necessary anyway as the castle is built of soft stone on soft ground. Highlights of the 45-minute tour include the groaning 17th-century **Black Staircase**, the 16th-century **chapel** and the beautifully preserved **Norman chapel** (1080).

Other sights:

Durham Heritage Centre MUSEUM
(www.durhamheritagecentre.org.uk; North Bailey; admission £2; 2-4.30pm Easter-Oct) Near the cathedral, in what was the St Mary-le-Bow Church, this museum has a pretty crowded collection of displays on Durham's history from the Middle Ages to mining. It's all suitably grim, especially the reconstructed Victorian prison cell.

Crook Hall GARDENS
(www.crookhallgardens.co.uk; Frankland La, Sidegate; adult/child £6/5; 11am-5pm Sun-Thu Apr-Sep) This medieval hall with 1.6 hectares of charming small gardens is about 200m north of the city centre. From the tourist office, cross the main road bridge across the Wear then follow the river north.

Activities

Prince Bishop River Cruiser RIVER TRIPS
(0191-386 9525; www.princebishoprc.co.uk; Elvet Bridge; adult/child £6/3; cruises 2pm & 3pm Jun-Sep) One-hour cruises on the Wear.

Browns Boathouse BOAT HIRE
(per hr per person £5) Rowing boats can be hired from below Elvet Bridge.

Sleeping

There's only one view that counts – a cathedral view. But when you consider that it's visible from pretty much everywhere, it's quality, not quantity, that counts. The tourist office makes local bookings free of charge, which is a good thing considering that Durham is always busy with visitors.

TOP CHOICE **Fallen Angel** BOUTIQUE HOTEL £££
(0191-384 1037; www.fallenangelhotel.com; 34 Old Elvet; d from £150) Possibly the northeast's most bizarre digs, the ten rooms at this fun place leave few indifferent. Each room has a theme with the 'Le Jardin' featuring a shed and garden furniture, the 'Sci-fi' room containing a *Doctor Who* Tardis and the 'Premiere' boasting a huge projection screen and popcorn machine, while the 'Edwardian Express' recreates a night in a yesteryear sleeper compartment. The most 'normal' room is the Library though even here military uniforms hang from the bookcases as if their owners could return any moment. The restaurant is superb and some rooms have cathedral views. Pricey, but worth every penny.

Cathedral View B&B ££
(0191-386 9566; www.cathedralview.com; 212 Gilesgate; s/d from £60/80) This anonymous Georgian house has no sign, but inside it does exactly what it says on the tin. Six large rooms decorated with lots of cushions and coordinated bed linen and window dressings make up the numbers, but it's the two at the back that are worth the fuss: the views of the cathedral are fantastic. Breakfast is cooked to order and served out on the vista-rich terrace or in the dining room lined with Beryl Cook prints.

Eating

Cheap eats aren't a problem in Durham thanks to the students, but quality is a little thin on the ground. Some pubs do good bar food and if you're really desperate, there's always bakers **Greggs** (14 Saddler St) to fall back on for some good old northern stodge.

Oldfields BRITISH **££**
(18 Claypath; mains £12-19) With its strictly seasonal menus that use only local or organic ingredients sourced within a 60-mile radius of Durham, this award-winning restaurant is one of the county's finest, though it's not quite as good as its Newcastle sister. With dishes such as smoked haddock pan haggerty and wild boar pie on the menu, all served in the old boardroom of the former HQ of the Durham Gas Company (1881), it's still the best meal in town.

Almshouse CAFE **££**
(Palace Green; dishes £5-9; 9am-5pm, to 8pm Jul & Aug) Fancy imaginative and satisfying snacks served in a genuine 17th-century house right on Palace Green? It's a shame about the interior, which has been restored to look like any old museum canteen. All the artwork on the walls is for sale.

Drinking

Durham may be a big student town, but most scholars seem to take the whole study thing really seriously, and the nightlife here isn't as boisterous as you might expect from a university town.

Shakespeare PUB
(63 Saddler St) As authentic a traditional bar as you're likely to find in these parts, this is the perfect locals' boozer, complete with dartboard, cosy snugs and a small corner TV to show the racing. Needless to say, the selection of beers and spirits is terrific.

Swan & Three Cygnets PUB
(Elvet Bridge) This high-ceilinged riverside pub with courtyard tables overlooks the river. It also serves some pretty good food (mains around £8) – usually fancy versions of standard bar fare such as bangers and mash.

Information

Post office (Silver St)

Public Library (Millennium Pl; 9.30am-7pm Mon-Fri, 9am-5pm Sat, 10.30am-4pm Sun) Bring ID to surf the web.

Tourist office (0191-384 3720; www.thisisdurham.com; 2 Millennium Pl; 9.30am-5.30pm Mon-Sat, 10am-4pm Sun) In the Gala complex, which includes a theatre and cinema.

Getting There & Away

Bus

Darlington Buses 5 and 7; one hour, four hourly.

London National Express; £29.80, 6½ hours, four daily.

Newcastle Buses 21, 44, X41, X2; one hour to 1¾ hours, several per hour.

Train

The East Coast mainline arches over Durham meaning speedy connections to many destinations across the country:

Edinburgh £50.30, two hours, hourly.

London £103.60, three hours, hourly.

Newcastle £5.20, 15 minutes, five hourly.

York £21.90, one hour, four hourly.

Getting Around

Cycle Force (29 Claypath) Charges £10/16 per half-/full day for mountain-bike hire.

Pratt's (0191-386 0700) A trustworthy taxi company.

Darlington

POP 97,838

The old Quaker market town of Darlington may be best known these days as a shopping mecca, but its main claim to fame came in 1825, when it found itself at one end of the world's first passenger railway, the Stockton & Darlington. The first train was pulled by George Stephenson's aptly named *Locomotion No 1,* which rumbled along the new cast-iron rail link to docks on the Tees at the breakneck speed of 10mph to 13mph, carrying 350 people – mostly in coal trucks.

The event – and the subsequent effect on transport history – is the subject of the town's top attraction, the excellent **Head of Steam** (www.head-of-steam.co.uk; North Rd; adult/child £4.95/3; 10am-4pm Tue-Sun Apr-Sep), aka Darlington Railway Museum, which is actually situated on the original 1825 route, in 19th-century Stockton & Darlington railway buildings attached to North Rd Station, one of the oldest in the world. Pride of place goes to the surprisingly small and fragile-looking *Locomotion,* but railway buffs will also enjoy a close look at other engines, such as the *Derwent,* the earliest surviving Darlington-built locomo-

WORTH A TRIP

BEAMISH OPEN-AIR MUSEUM

County Durham's greatest attraction is **Beamish** (www.beamish.org.uk; adult/child £16/10; ⏲10am-5pm Apr-Oct), a living, breathing, working museum that offers a fabulous, warts-and-all portrait of industrial life in the northeast during the 19th and 20th centuries. Instructive and lots of fun to boot, this huge museum spread over 121 hectares will appeal to all ages.

You can go underground, explore mine heads, a working farm, a school, a dentist and a pub, and marvel at how every cramped pit cottage seemed to find room for a piano. Don't miss a ride behind an 1815 Steam Elephant locomotive or a replica of Stephenson's *Locomotion No 1*.

Allow at least three hours to do the place justice. Many elements (such as the railway) aren't open in the winter (when the admission price is lower); check the web for details.

Beamish is about 8 miles northwest of Durham. Buses 28 from Newcastle (one hour, half hourly) and 720 from Durham (30 minutes, hourly) operate to the museum.

tive. Railway memorabilia is complemented by an impressive range of audiovisuals that tell the story of the railway, Darlington's locomotive building industry (and its demise in the 1960s) and the impacts of these events on the town. There's also a 19th-century ticket office that seems to have been dunked in formaldehyde and an original Victorian Gents toilets. The museum is about a mile north of the centre.

There aren't many other reasons to linger, but you should definitely pop your head into Our Lady of the North, better known as **St Cuthbert's Church** (www.stcuthbertsdarlington.net; Market Pl; ⏲11am-1pm Mon-Sat Easter-Sep plus during services), founded in 1183 and one of the finest examples of the Early English Perpendicular style, topped with a 14th-century tower. Guided tours of the church can be arranged through the tourist office.

Information

Tourist office (☎01325-388666; www.visitdarlington.com; Dolphin Centre, Horsemarket; ⏲9am-5pm Mon-Fri, to 3pm Sat)

Getting There & Away

Most buses arrive and depart opposite the Town Hall on Feethams, just off Market Place. There are no direct bus services to Newcastle.

Darlington Bus 7/7A; 50 minutes, hourly.

Richmond (North Yorkshire) X26 and X27; 40 minutes, twice hourly.

Darlington is on the east coast main line with connections to York (£16.10, 30 minutes, three hourly), Newcastle (£8.90, 30 minutes, three hourly) and London (£99.40, two hours 40 minutes, hourly).

Barnard Castle

POP 6720

Barnard Castle, or just plain Barney, is anything but: this thoroughly charming market town is a traditionalist's dream, full of antiquarian shops and atmospheric old pubs that serve as a wonderful setting for the town's twin-starred attractions, a daunting ruined castle at its edge and an extraordinary French chateau on its outskirts. If you can drag yourself away, it is also a terrific base for exploring Teesdale and the North Pennines.

Sights

Barnard Castle CASTLE RUINS

(EH; adult/child £4.20/2.10; ⏲10am-6pm Easter-Sep) Partly dismantled during the 16th century, one of northern England's largest castles built on a cliff above the Tees still manages to cover more than two very impressive hectares. Founded by Guy de Bailleul and rebuilt around 1150, its occupants spent their time suppressing the locals and fighting off the Scots – on their days off they sat around enjoying the wonderful river views.

Bowes Museum MUSEUM

(www.thebowesmuseum.org.uk; adult/child £8/free; ⏲10am-5pm) About half a mile east of town stands a Louvre-inspired French chateau containing an extraordinary and wholly unexpected museum. Funded by 19th-century industrialist John Bowes, but largely the brainchild of his Parisienne actress wife Josephine, the museum was built by French architect Jules Pellechet to display a collection the Bowes had travelled the world to assemble. Opened in 1892, this spectacular museum has lavish furniture and paintings by Canaletto, El Greco and Goya as well as 15,000 other objets d'art including 55 paintings by Josephine herself. A new section examines textiles through the ages, with some incredible dresses from the 17th century to the 1970s, while the precious metals exhibition displays clocks, watches and tableware in gold and silver. The museum's star attraction, however, is the marvellous mechanical silver swan, which performs every day at 2pm. If you miss it or arrive too early, there's now a film showing it in action.

Sleeping & Eating

Marwood House B&B ££
(01833-637493; www.marwoodhouse.co.uk; 98 Galgate; s/d from £29/58) A handsome Victorian property with tastefully appointed rooms (the owner's tapestries feature in the decor and her homemade biscuits sit on a tray), Marwood House's standout feature is the small fitness room in the basement, complete with a sauna that fits up to four people.

Jersey Farm Country Hotel HOTEL ££
(01833-638223; www.jerseyfarm.co.uk; Darlington Rd; s/d from £72/99; P) Another genteel farmhouse conversion, right? Wrong. From the moment you step into the funky reception you know you're not in for the usual frills-and-flowers B&B experience. Although the owners haven't gone the whole design-boutique hog, rooms sport cool retro colour schemes, ultra sleek bathrooms in several shades of black and gadgets galore. The restaurant is a clean-cut affair. It's a mile east of the town just off the A67.

Old Well Inn HOTEL ££
(01833-690130; www.theoldwellinn.co.uk; 21 The Bank; r from £69;) You won't find larger bedrooms in town than at this old coaching inn, built over a huge well (not visible). Of the 10 rooms, No 9 is the most impressive with its own private entrance, flagstone floors and a bath. The pub has a reputation for excellent, filling pub grub and real ales from Darlington and Yorkshire.

Information

Tourist office (01833- 696356; www.teesdalediscovery.com; Woodleigh, Flatts Rd; 9.30am-5pm Mon-Sat, 10am-4pm Sun Easter-Oct) Has information on all the sights, a small cafe and internet access for £1.50 per half hour.

Getting There & Away

Darlington Buses 75 and 76; 40 minutes, twice hourly.

Egglestone Abbey

The ransacked, spectral ruins of **Egglestone Abbey** (EH; dawn-dusk), dating from the 1190s, overlook a lovely bend of the Tees. You can envisage the abbey's one-time grandeur despite the gaunt remains. They're a pleasant 1.5-mile-long walk southeast of Barnard Castle.

North Pennines

The North Pennines stretch from western Durham to just short of Hadrian's Wall in the north. In the south is Teesdale, the gently undulating valley of the River Tees; to the north is the much wilder Weardale, carved through by the River Wear. Both dales are marked by ancient quarries and mines – industries that date back to Roman times. The wilds of the North Pennines are also home to the picturesque Derwent and Allen Valleys, north of Weardale.

For online information, check out www.northpennines.org.uk and www.exploreteesdale.co.uk.

HADRIAN'S WALL

What exactly have the Romans ever done for us? The aqueducts. Law and order. And this enormous wall, built between AD 122 and 128 to keep 'us' (Romans, subdued Brits) in and 'them' (hairy Pictish barbarians from Scotland) out. Or so the story goes. Hadrian's Wall, named in honour of the emperor who ordered it built, was one of Rome's greatest engineering projects, a spectacular 73-mile testament to ambition and the practical Roman mind. Even today, almost 2000 years after the first stone was laid, the sections that are still standing remain an awe-inspiring sight, proof that when the Romans wanted something done, they just knuckled down and did it.

It wasn't easy. When completed, the mammoth structure ran across the narrow neck of the island, from the Solway Firth in the west almost to the mouth of the Tyne in the east. Every Roman mile (0.95 miles) there was a gateway guarded by a small fort (milecastle) and between each milecastle

WORTH A TRIP

RABY CASTLE

About 7 miles northeast of Barnard Castle is the sprawling, romantic **Raby Castle** (www.rabycastle.com; adult/child £9.50/4; ⏲1-5pm Sun-Wed May, Jun & Sep, Sun-Fri Jul & Aug), a stronghold of the Catholic Neville family until it engaged in some ill-judged plotting (the 'Rising of the North') against the oh-so Protestant Queen Elizabeth in 1569. Most of the interior dates from the 18th and 19th centuries, but the exterior remains true to the original design, built around a courtyard and surrounded by a moat. There are beautiful formal gardens and a deer park. Bus 8 zips between Barnard Castle and Raby (15 minutes, eight daily).

were two observation turrets. Milecastles are numbered right across the country, starting with Milecastle 0 at Wallsend and ending with Milecastle 80 at Bowness-on-Solway.

A series of forts was developed as bases some distance south (and may predate the wall), and 16 lie astride it. The prime remaining forts on the wall are Cilurnum (Chesters), Vercovicium (Housesteads) and Banna (Birdoswald). The best forts behind the wall are Corstopitum at Corbridge, and Vindolanda, north of Bardon Mill.

Carlisle, in the west, and Newcastle, in the east, are obviously good starting points, but Brampton, Haltwhistle, Hexham and Corbridge all make good bases. The B6318 follows the course of the wall from the outskirts of Newcastle to Birdoswald; from Birdoswald to Carlisle it pays to have a detailed map. The main A69 road and the railway line follow 3 or 4 miles to the south.

History

Emperor Hadrian didn't order the wall built from fear of a northern invasion. Truth is no part of the wall was impenetrable – a concentrated attack at any single point would have surely breached it – but it was meant to mark the border as though to say that the Roman Empire would extend no further. By drawing a physical boundary, the Romans were also tightening their grip on the population to the south – for the first time in history, passports were issued to citizens of the empire, marking them out not just as citizens but, more importantly, as taxpayers.

But all good things come to an end. It's likely that around 409, as the Roman administration collapsed, the frontier garrisons ceased receiving Roman pay. The wall communities had to then rely on their own resources and were gradually reabsorbed into the local population. Most of the foreign soldiers posted to Hadrians Wall at the zenith of the Roman Empire had long since returned home.

Activities

The **Hadrian's Wall Path** (www.nationaltrail.co.uk/hadrianswall) is an 84-mile National Trail that runs the length of the wall from Wallsend in the east to Bowness-on-Solway in the west. The entire route should take about seven days on foot, giving plenty of time to explore the rich archaeological heritage along the way. Anthony Burton's *Hadrian's Wall Path – National Trail Guide* (Aurum Press, £12.99) available at most bookshops and tourist offices in the region, is good for history, archaeology and the like, while the *Essential Guide to Hadrian's Wall Path National Trail* (Hadrian's Wall Heritage Ltd, £3.95) by David McGlade is a guide to everyday facilities and services along the walk.

Information

Carlisle and Newcastle tourist offices are good places to start gathering information, but there are also tourist offices in Hexham, Haltwhistle, Corbridge and Brampton.

Hadrian's Wall (www.hadrians-wall.org) The official portal for the whole of Hadrian's Wall Country. An excellent, easily navigable site.

Hadrian's Wall information line (☎01434-322002)

Northumberland National Park Visitor Centre (☎01434-344396; Once Brewed; ⏲9.30am-5pm Apr-Oct) Off the B6318.

May sees a **spring festival**, with lots of re-creations of Roman life along the wall (contact tourist offices for details).

Getting There & Around

Bus

The AD 122 Hadrian's Wall bus (eight daily, April to October) is a hail-and-ride service that runs between Hexham and Carlisle, with one bus a day starting and ending at Newcastle's Central

Hadrian's Wall & Northumberland National Park

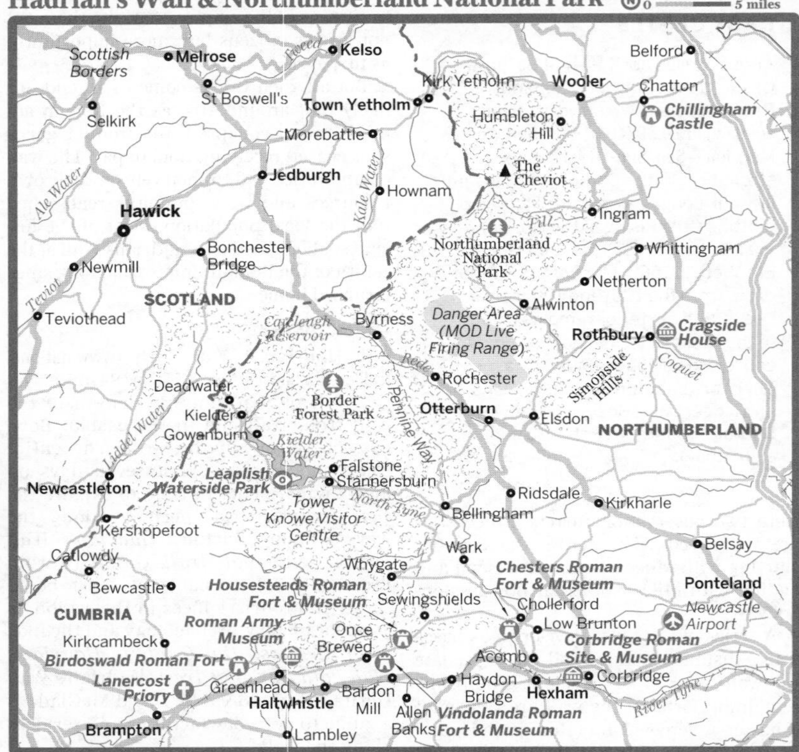

Station and not all services cover the entire route. Bus 185 zips along the wall the rest of the year (Monday to Saturday only).

West of Hexham the wall runs parallel to the A69, which connects Carlisle and Newcastle. Bus 685 runs along the A69 hourly, passing near the YHA hostels and 2 miles to 3 miles south of the main sites throughout the year.

The **Hadrian's Wall Rover ticket** (adult/child one-day £8/5, three-day £16/10) is available from bus drivers and tourist offices, where you can also get timetables.

Car & Motorcycle

This is obviously the most convenient method of transport with one fort or garrison usually just a short hop from the next. Parking costs £3 and the ticket is valid at all other sites along the wall.

Train

The railway line between Newcastle and Carlisle (Tyne Valley Line) has stations at Corbridge, Hexham, Haydon Bridge, Bardon Mill, Haltwhistle and Brampton. Trains run hourly but not all services stop at all stations.

Corbridge

POP 2800

The mellow commuter town of Corbridge is a handsome spot above a green-banked curve in the Tyne, its shady, cobbled streets lined with old-fashioned shops. Folks have lived here since Saxon times when there was a substantial monastery, while many of the buildings feature stones nicked from nearby Corstopitum.

Corbridge Roman Site & Museum

ROMAN GARRISON

(EH; adult/child £4.80/2.40; ⏲10am-5.30pm Apr-Sep) What's left of the Roman garrison town of Corstopitum lies about a half a mile west of Market Pl on Dere St, once the main road from York to Scotland. It is the oldest fortified site in the area, predating the wall itself by some 40 years, when it was used by troops launching retaliation raids into Scotland. Most of what you see here, though, dates from around AD 200, when the fort had developed into a civilian settlement and was the main base along the wall.

You get a sense of the domestic heart of the town from the visible remains, and the Corbridge Museum displays Roman sculpture and carvings, including the amazing 3rd-century **Corbridge Lion**.

Sleeping & Eating

2 The Crofts B&B ££

(☎01434-633046; www.2thecrofts.co.uk; B6530; s/d from £38/62; P) By far the best place in town to drop your pack, this secluded B&B occupies a beautiful period home around half a mile's walk east of the town centre. The three high-ceilinged, spacious rooms are all en suite and one has impressive carved wardrobes said to be from the *Olympic,* sister ship to the *Titanic*. The energetic owners cook a mean breakfast.

The Black Bull BRITISH ££

(Middle St; mains £7-16) A menu of British comfort food, such as beef burgers, fish in beer batter and slow-cooked New Zealand lamb, and a series of low-ceilinged, atmospheric dining rooms, make this restaurant/tavern a fine spot to fill the hole.

Valley Restaurant INDIAN ££

(Station Rd; mains £8-12; dinner Mon-Sat) Taking up the entire train station building, this temple to spice was declared 'best Indian in the north' by the Curry Club, and they're a bunch who know good subcontinental grub when they taste it. A group of 10 or more diners from Newcastle can catch the 'Passage to India' train to Corbridge accompanied by a waiter, who will supply snacks and phone ahead to have the meal ready when the train arrives!

Information

Tourist office (☎01434-632815; www.thisiscorbridge.co.uk; Hill St; 10am-5pm Mon-Sat, 1-5pm Sun Easter-Oct) Occupies a corner of the library.

Getting There & Away

Bus 685 between Newcastle and Carlisle comes through Corbridge, as does the half-hourly bus 602 from Newcastle to Hexham, where you can connect with the Hadrian's Wall bus AD 122. Corbridge is also on the Newcastle-Carlisle railway line.

Hexham

POP 10,690

Bustling Hexham is a handsome if somewhat scuffed little market town long famed for its grand Augustinian abbey. Its cobbled alleyways boast more shops and amenities than any other wall town between Carlisle and Newcastle, making it a good place to take on provisions if you're heading out into the windswept wilds beyond.

Sights

Hexham Abbey ABBEY

(www.hexhamabbey.org.uk; 9.30am-5pm) Dominating tiny Market Pl, Hexham's stately abbey is a marvellous example of early English architecture. It cleverly escaped the Dissolution of 1537 by rebranding as Hexham's parish church, a role it still has today. The highlight is the 7th-century **Saxon crypt** (11am & 3.30pm), the only surviving element of St Wilfrid's Church, built with inscribed stones from Corstopitum in 674.

Old Gaol HISTORICAL JAIL

(adult/child £4/2.10; 11am-4.30pm Tue-Sat) This strapping stone structure was completed in 1333 as England's first purpose-built prison; today its four floors tell the history of the jail in all its gruesome glory. The history of the Border Reivers – a group of clans who fought, kidnapped, blackmailed and killed each other in an effort to exercise control over a lawless tract of land along the Anglo-Scottish border throughout the 16th century – is also retold, along with tales of the punishments handed out in the prison.

Sleeping & Eating

TOP CHOICE **Bouchon Bistrot** FRENCH ££

(www.bouchonbistrot.co.uk; 4-6 Gilesgate; mains £12-19; Tue-Sat) Hexham may be an unlikely setting for some true fine dining, but this Gallic affair has such an enviable reputation and was voted the UK's best local French restaurant in 2010 by Channel 4 viewers. Country-style menus are reassuringly brief, ingredients as fresh as nature can provide and the wine list an elite selection of champagnes, reds and whites. The owners have also created a cosy, understated interior in which to enjoy all of the above.

Hallbank Guest House B&B ££

(☎01434-605567; www.hallbankguesthouse.com; Hallgate; s/d from £60/80; P📶) Behind the Old Gaol is this fine Edwardian house with eight stylishly furnished rooms, which combine period elegance with flatscreen TVs and huge beds. Very popular so book ahead.

Dipton Mill PUB £

(Dipton Mill Rd; mains around £6-10) This superb country pub 2 miles out on the road to Blanchland, among woodland and by a river, offers real ploughman's lunches and real ale by real fires – really.

Information

Tourist office (☎01434-652220; Wentworth Car Park; ⊙9am-6pm Mon-Sat, 10am-5pm Sun) Northeast of the town centre.

Getting There & Away

Bus 685 between Newcastle and Carlisle comes through Hexham hourly. The AD 122 and the winter-service bus 185 connect with other towns along the wall, and the town is on the scenic railway line between Newcastle (twice hourly) and Carlisle (hourly).

Chesters Roman Fort & Museum

The best-preserved remains of a Roman cavalry fort in England are at **Chesters** (EH; ☎01434-681379; Chollerford; adult/child £4.80/2.40; ⊙10am-6pm Apr-Sep), set among idyllic green woods and meadows near the village of Chollerford and originally constructed to house a unit of troops from Asturias in northern Spain. They include part of a bridge (beautifully constructed and best appreciated from the eastern bank) across the River North Tyne, four well-preserved gatehouses, an extraordinary bathhouse and an underfloor heating system. The museum has a large collection of Roman sculpture. Take bus 880 or 882 from Hexham (5.5 miles away); it is also on the route of Hadrian's Wall bus AD 122.

Haltwhistle & Around

POP 3810

It's one of the more important debates in contemporary Britain: where exactly is the centre of the country? The residents of Haltwhistle, basically one long street just north of the A69, claim that they're the ones. But then so do the folks in Dunsop Bridge, 71 miles to the south. Will we ever know the truth? In the meantime, Haltwhistle is the spot to get some cash and load up on gear and groceries. Thursday is market day.

Sights

Vindolanda Roman Fort & Museum ROMAN FORT

(www.vindolanda.com; adult/child £5.90/3.50, with Roman Army Museum £9/5; ⊙10am-6pm Apr-Sep, to 5pm Feb-Mar & Oct) The extensive site of Vindolanda offers a fascinating glimpse into the daily life of a Roman garrison town. The time-capsule museum displays leather sandals, signature Roman toothbrush-flourish helmet decorations, and a new exhibition featuring numerous writing tablets recently returned from the British Library. These include a student's marked work ('sloppy'), and a parent's note with a present of socks and underpants (things haven't changed – in this climate you can never have too many).

The museum is just one part of this large, extensively excavated site, which includes impressive parts of the fort and town (excavations continue) and reconstructed turrets and temple.

It's 1.5 miles north of Bardon Mill between the A69 and B6318 and a mile from Once Brewed.

Housesteads Roman Fort & Museum ROMAN FORT

(EH; adult/child £4.80/2.40; ⊙10am-6pm Apr-Sep) The wall's most dramatic site – and the best-preserved Roman fort in the whole country – is at Housesteads. From here, high on a ridge and covering 2 hectares, you can survey the moors of Northumberland National Park, and the snaking wall, with a sense of awe at the landscape and the aura of the Roman lookouts.

The substantial foundations bring fort life alive. The remains include an impressive hospital, granaries with a carefully worked-out ventilation system and barrack blocks. Most memorable are the spectacularly situated communal flushable latrines, which summon up Romans at their most mundane. Information boards show what the individual buildings would have looked like in their heyday and there's a scale model of the entire fort in the small museum at the ticket office.

Housesteads is 2.5 miles north of Bardon Mill on the B6318, and about 6 miles from Haltwhistle.

Roman Army Museum MUSEUM
(www.vindolanda.com; adult/child £4.50/2.50, with Vindolanda £9/5; ⏲10am-6pm) A mile northwest of Greenhead, near Walltown Crags, this kid-pleasing museum provides lots of colourful background detail to wall life, such as how the soldiers spent their R&R time in this lonely outpost of the empire.

Birdoswald Roman Fort ROMAN FORT
(EH; adult/child £4.80/2.40; ⏲10am-5.30pm Mar-Oct) *Technically* in Cumbria (we won't tell if you don't), the remains of this once-formidable fort on an escarpment overlooking the beautiful Irthing Gorge are on a minor road off the B6318, about 3 miles west of Greenhead; a fine stretch of wall extends from here to Harrow Scar Milecastle.

Lanercost Priory PRIORY
(EH; adult/child £3.20/1.60; ⏲10am-5pm Apr-Sep, to 4pm Thu-Mon Oct) About 3 miles further west along the A69 from Birdoswald, these peaceful raspberry-coloured ruins are all that remain of a priory founded in 1166 by Augustinian canons. Post-dissolution it became a private house and a priory church was created from the Early English nave. The AD 122 bus drops off at the gate.

Sleeping

TOP CHOICE **Ashcroft** B&B ££
(☎01434-320213; www.ashcroftguesthouse.co.uk; Lanty's Lonnen, Haltwhistle; s/d from £48/78; 📶) In the world of British B&Bs, things don't get better than this. Picture a large, elegant Edwardian vicarage surrounded by two acres of beautifully manicured, layered lawns and gardens from which there are stunning views. Inside, the nine rooms, some with private balconies and terraces, hoist preposterously high ceilings and are fitted out in an understated style but also contain every gadget 21st-century people need for survival. The dining room is grander than some snooty hotels and the welcome certainly more genuine. Ashcroft is highly recommended.

Centre of Britain HOTEL ££
(☎01434-322422; www.centre-of-britain.org.uk; Haltwhistle; s/d from £59/70) Just across from where locals claim the 'Centre of Britain' to be, this Norwegian-owned hotel (hence the slightly Scandinavian feel) incorporates a sturdy 15th-century *pele* (fortified) tower, one of the oldest chunks of architecture in town. The most spacious rooms (two have their own full-blown sauna!) are located in the historical main building, there are smaller, quite oddly designed two-level rooms in the courtyard and a separate annex almost next door takes the spill-over.

Holmhead Guest House B&B ££
(☎01697-747402; www.bandbhadrianswall.com; Greenhead; dm/s/d from £12.50/42.50/65) Built using recycled bits of the wall on whose foundations it stands, this superb farmhouse B&B offers everything from comfy rooms to a basic bunk barn to camping pitches. Both the Pennine Way and the Hadrian's Wall Path pass through the grounds and the jagged ruins of Thirwall Castle loom above the scene. The owners will gladly show you their piece of 3rd-century Roman graffiti. Half a mile north of Greenhead.

There are three hostels in the area:

Once Brewed YHA YOUTH HOSTEL £
(☎0845 371 9753; www.yha.org.uk; Military Rd, Bardon Mill; dm £12; ⏲Feb-Nov) This modern and well-equipped hostel is central for visiting both Housesteads Fort, 3 miles away, and Vindolanda, 1 mile away. The Hadrian's Wall bus drops at the door.

Greenhead YOUTH HOSTEL £
(☎016977-47411; Greenhead; dm £15) No longer affiliated to the YHA, this hostel occupies a converted Methodist chapel by a trickling stream and a pleasant garden, 3 miles west of Haltwhistle. Served by bus AD 122 or 685.

Birdoswald YHA YOUTH HOSTEL £
(☎0845 371 9551; www.yha.org.uk; dm £14; ⏲Jul-Sep, call to check other times) Within the grounds of the Birdoswald complex this hostel has basic facilities, including a self-service kitchen and laundry. The price includes a visit to the fort.

Information

Tourist office (☎01434-322002; ⏲9.30am-1pm & 2-5.30pm Mon-Sat, 1-5pm Sun) Haltwhistle's tourist office is in the train station, but may soon be moving to the library in Main St.

NORTHUMBERLAND NATIONAL PARK

England's last great wilderness is the 405 sq miles of natural wonderland that make up Northumberland National Park, spread about the soft swells of the Cheviot Hills, the spiky moors of autumn-coloured heather and gorse, and the endless acres of forest. Even the negligible human influence (this is England's least populated national park with only 2000 inhabitants) has been benevolent: the finest sections of Hadrian's Wall run along the park's southern edge and the landscape is dotted with prehistoric remains and fortified houses – the thick-walled *peles* were the only solid buildings built here until the mid-18th century.

Activities

The most spectacular stretch of the **Hadrian's Wall Path** is between Sewingshields and Greenhead in the south of the park.

There are many fine walks through the Cheviots, frequently passing by prehistoric remnants; the towns of Ingram, Wooler and Rothbury make good bases, and their tourist offices can provide maps, guides and route information.

Though at times strenuous, cycling in the park is a pleasure; the roads are good and the traffic is light here. There's off-road cycling in Border Forest Park.

Information

For information, contact **Northumberland National Park** (01434-605555; www.northumberland-national-park.org.uk; Eastburn, South Park, Hexham). Besides the tourist offices listed in each town, there are national park offices in **Once Brewed** (01434-344396; 9.30am-5pm Apr-Oct) and **Ingram** (01665-578890; 10am-5pm Apr-Oct). All the tourist offices handle accommodation bookings.

Getting There & Around

Public transport options are limited, aside from buses on the A69. See the Hadrian's Wall section for access to the south. Bus 808 (55 minutes, two daily Monday to Saturday) runs between Otterburn and Newcastle. Bus 880 (50 minutes, twice daily Tuesday, Friday & Saturday) runs between Hexham and Bellingham. A National Express service calls at Otterburn (£5.70, 50 minutes, daily) on its way from Newcastle to Edinburgh.

Rothbury

POP 1740

The one-time prosperous Victorian resort of Rothbury is an attractive, restful market town on the River Coquet that makes a convenient base for the Cheviots.

Visitors flock to Rothbury to see **Cragside House, Garden and Estate** (NT; 01669-620333; admission £13.90, gardens & estate only £9; house 1-5pm or 11am-5pm Tue-Sun depending on the month, gardens 10.30am-5pm Tue-Sun mid-Mar–Oct), the quite incredible country retreat of the first Lord Armstrong. In the 1880s the house had hot and cold running water, a telephone and alarm system, and was the first in the world to be lit by electricity, generated through hydropower – the original system has been restored and can be observed in the Power House. The Victorian gardens are also well worth exploring: huge and remarkably varied, they feature lakes, moors and one of Europe's largest rock gardens. Visit late-May to mid-June to see Cragside's famous rhododendrons in bloom.

The estate is 1 mile northeast of town just off the B6341; there's no public transport to the front gates from Rothbury; try **Rothbury Motors** (01669-620516) if you need a taxi.

Beamed ceilings, stone fireplaces and canopied four-poster beds make **Katerina's Guest House** (01669-620691; www.katerinasguesthouse.co.uk' Sun Buildings, High St; r £74;) one of the town's better choices, though the three rooms are a little small for the price. Alternatively, the **Haven** (01669-620577; www.thehavenrothbury.co.uk; Back Crofts; s/d/ste £40/80/130; P) is a beautiful Edwardian home up on a hill with six comfy bedrooms and one elegant suite.

There's plenty of pub grub available along High St or you could try **Sun Kitchen** (High St; snacks & meals £3.60-6.50): it's been serving sandwiches, jacket potatoes and other snacks for four decades. **Rothbury Bakery** (High St) do great takeaway pies and sandwiches.

The **tourist office** (01669-620887; Church St; 10am-5pm Apr-Oct) has a free exhibition on the Northumberland National Park.

Bus 144 runs hourly to and from Morpeth (30 minutes) Monday to Saturday.

Bellingham

The small, remote village of Bellingham (bellin-*jum*) is a pleasant-enough spot on the banks of the North Tyne, surrounded by beautiful, deserted countryside on all sides. It's an excellent launch pad for trips into the national park and a welcome refuelling halt on the Pennine Way.

The **Bellingham Heritage Centre** (☎01434-220050; Station Yard, Woodburn Rd; admission £3; ⏲9.30am-4.30pm Mon-Sat Apr-Sep) houses a new **museum** with heaps of railway paraphernalia, an interesting section on the Border Reivers and mock-ups of old village shops. The heritage centre shares its premises with the tourist office.

The only other sights of note are the 12th-century **St Cuthbert's Church**, unique as it retains its original stone roof, and **St Cuthbert's Well**, outside the churchyard wall, which is alleged to have healing powers on account of its blessing by the saint.

The **Hareshaw Linn Walk** passes through a wooded valley and over six bridges, leading to a 9m-high waterfall 2.5 miles north of Bellingham (*linn* is an Old English name for waterfall).

Bellingham is popular with hikers so book ahead for accommodation in summer. Most of the B&Bs cluster around the village green.

Demesne Farm (☎01434-220107; www.demesnefarmcampsite.co.uk; Woodburn Rd; dm/site £16/12) is a working smallholding in the middle of the village but with a very comfortable 15-bed bunkhouse and lots of soft green grass for tents. There's also cycle storage, a drying room and kitchen. It's affiliated with the YHA.

The **Lyndale Guest House** (☎01434-220361; www.lyndaleguesthouse.co.uk; s/d from £35/65; P 📶) provides a cosy, homely experience and knowledgeable hosts Joy and Ken make you feel like a distant relative come to kip in the spare room.

Bellingham's pub grub is nothing to write home about so try the **Happy Valley** Chinese takeaway in Main St or the **Riverside Hall Hotel**, just outside the village heading towards Kielder, for superior fare.

The **tourist office** (☎01434-220616; Station Yard, Woodburn Rd; ⏲9.30am-4.30pm Mon-Sat Apr-Sep) handles visitor enquiries (and is the same building as the heritage centre).

Wooler

POP 1860

A harmonious, stone-terraced town, Wooler owes its sense of unified design to a devastating fire in 1863, which resulted in an almost complete rebuild. It is an excellent spot in which to catch your breath, especially as it is surrounded by some excellent forays into the nearby Cheviots (including a clamber to the top of the Cheviot, the highest peak in the range). It's also the midway point for the 65-mile St Cuthbert's Way, which runs from Melrose in Scotland to Holy Island on the coast.

Activities

A popular walk from Wooler takes in **Humbleton Hill**, the site of an Iron Age hill fort and the location of yet another battle (1402) between the Scots and the English. It's immortalised in 'The Ballad of Chevy Chase' and Shakespeare's *Henry IV*. There are great views of the wild Cheviot Hills to the south and plains to the north, merging into the horizon. The well-posted 4-mile trail starts and ends at the bus station (follow the signs to Wooler Common). It takes approximately two hours. Alternatively, the yearly **Chevy Chase** (www.woolerrunningclub.co.uk) is a classic 20-mile fell run with over 4000ft of accumulated climb, run at the beginning of July.

A more arduous hike leads to the top of the **Cheviot** (815m), 6 miles southeast. The top is barren and wild, but on a clear day you can see the castle at Bamburgh and as far out as Holy Island. It takes around four hours to reach the top from Wooler. Check with the tourist office for information before setting out.

Sleeping & Eating

Tilldale House B&B ££
(☎01668-281450; www.tilldalehouse.co.uk; 34-40 High St; s/d from £40/60) One of the houses to survive the fire of 1863 now contains comfortable, spacious rooms that radiate a welcoming golden hue. The five-star breakfast includes veggie and gluten free options.

Wooler YHA YOUTH HOSTEL £
(☎01668-281365; www.yha.org.uk; 30 Cheviot St; dm £14) In a low, red-brick building above the town, the northernmost YHA hostel (at least until the new Berwick hostel opens) contains 46 beds in a variety of rooms, a modern lounge and a small cafe.

Spice Village INDIAN RESTAURANT **£**
(3 Peth Head; mains from £5; ⏲dinner) There's bog-standard pub grub galore in Wooler, but for a bit more flavour, head for this small takeaway/restaurant that does spicy Indian and Bangladeshi dishes.

Information

Tourist office (☎01668-282123; www.wooler.org.uk; Cheviot Centre, 12 Padgepool Pl; ⏲10am-4.30pm Easter-Oct) A mine of information on walks in the hills.

Getting There & Around

Wooler has good bus connections to the major towns in Northumberland. To reach Wooler from Newcastle change at Alnwick.

Alnwick Buses 470 and 473; nine daily Monday to Saturday.

Berwick Buses 464 and 267; 50 minutes, nine daily Monday to Saturday.

Cycle hire is available at **Haugh Head Garage** (☎01668-281316; per day from £15) in Haugh Head, 1 mile south of Wooler on the A697.

Around Wooler

Recently voted best castle in Europe by readers of the *Independent*, **Chillingham** (☎01668-215359; www.chillingham-castle.com; adult/child £7/3.50; ⏲noon-5pm Sun-Fri Easter-Sep) is steeped in history, warfare, torture and ghosts: it is said to be one of the country's most haunted places, with ghostly clientele ranging from a phantom funeral to Lady Mary Berkeley in search of her errant husband.

The current owner, Sir Humphrey Wakefield, has gone to great lengths to restore the castle to its eccentric, noble best. This followed a 50-year fallow period when the Grey family (into which Sir Humphrey married) abandoned it, despite having owned it since 1245, because they couldn't afford the upkeep.

Today's visitor is in for a real treat, from the extravagant medieval staterooms that have hosted a handful of kings in their day to the stone-flagged banquet halls. Below ground, Sir Humphrey has gleefully restored the grisly torture chambers, which have a polished rack and the none-too-happy face of an Iron Maiden. There's also a museum with a fantastically jumbled collection of objects.

It's possible to stay at the medieval fortress in the seven apartments designed for guests, where the likes of Henry III and Edward I once snoozed. Prices vary depending on the luxury of the apartment; the **Grey Apartment** (£170) is the most expensive – it has a dining table to seat 12 – or there's the **Tower Apartment** (£130), in the Northwest Tower. All of the apartments are self-catering.

Chillingham is 6 miles southeast of Wooler. Bus 470 running between Alnwick and Wooler (three daily Monday to Saturday) stops at Chillingham.

NORTHUMBERLAND

The utterly wild and stunningly beautiful landscapes of Northumberland don't stop with the national park. Hard to imagine an undiscovered wilderness in a country so modern and populated, but as you cast your eye across the rugged interior you will see ne'er a trace of Man save the fortified houses and lonely villages that dot the horizon.

While the west is covered by the national park, the magnificent and pale sweeping coast to the east is the scene of long, stunning beaches, bookmarked by dramatic wind-worn castles and tiny islands offshore that really do have an air of magic about them. Hadrian's Wall emerges from the national park and slices through the south.

Alnwick

POP 7770

Northumberland's historic ducal town, Alnwick (no tongue gymnastics: just say 'annick') is an elegant maze of narrow cobbled streets spread out beneath the watchful gaze of a colossal medieval castle. England's most perfect bookshop, the northeast's most visited attraction at Alnwick Garden and some olde-worlde emporiums attract secondhand book worms, antique fans, castle junkies and the green-fingered in equal measure, and there's even a little something for Harry Potter nerds.

Most of the action takes place around Bondgate Within, Bondgate Without and Clayport St with the castle to the north overlooking the River Aln.

Sights

Alnwick Castle CASTLE

(www.alnwickcastle.com; adult/child £12.50/5.50, with Alnwick Garden £20.80/5.50; ⏲10am-6pm Apr-Oct) The outwardly imposing ancestral home of the Duke of Northumberland and a favourite set for film-makers (it was Hogwarts for the first couple of Harry Potter films) has changed little since the 14th century. The interior is sumptuous and extravagant; the six rooms open to the public – staterooms, dining room, guard chamber and library – have an incredible display of Italian paintings, including Titian's *Ecce Homo* and many Canalettos.

A free Harry Potter tour runs every day at 2.30pm and includes details of other productions – period drama *Elizabeth* and the British comedy series *Blackadder* to name but two – to have used the castle as a backdrop.

The castle is set in parklands designed by Lancelot 'Capability' Brown. The woodland walk offers some great aspects of the castle, or for a view looking up the River Aln, take the B1340 towards the coast.

Alnwick Garden GARDENS

(www.alnwickgarden.com; adult/child £9.50/free; ⏲10am-6pm Apr-Oct) As spectacular a bit of green-thumb artistry as you'll see in England, this is one of the northeast's great success stories. Since the project began in 2000, the 4.8-hectare walled garden has been transformed from a derelict site into a spectacle that easily exceeds the grandeur of the castle's 19th-century gardens, a series of magnificent green spaces surrounding the breathtaking Grand Cascade – 120 separate jets spurting over 30,000L of water down 21 weirs for everyone to marvel at and kids to splash around in.

There are a half-dozen other gardens, including the Franco-Italian-influenced **Ornamental Garden** (with more than 15,000 plants), the **Rose Garden** and the particularly fascinating **Poison Garden**, home to some of the deadliest – and most illegal – plants in the world, including cannabis, magic mushrooms, belladonna and even tobacco.

Sleeping

Alnwick packs them in at weekends from Easter onwards so book ahead. B&Bs cluster near the castle.

TOP CHOICE **Alnwick Lodge** B&B ££

(☎01665-604363; www.alnwicklodge.com; West Cawledge Park; s/d from £45/100; P wi-fi) Is it a B&B, is it a lonely Victorian farmstead, is it an antiques gallery? The answer is, it's all of these and more. The never-ending jumble of rooms, each one different and all containing restored antiques; the quirky touches such as free-standing baths with lids; the roaring fire in the Victorian guest lounge; the friendly, flexible owners and the cooked breakfasts around a huge circular banqueting table – all its features make this a truly unique place to stay. The catch – you'll need a car or taxi to get there (West Cawledge Park is 2 miles S off the A1).

White Swan Hotel HOTEL ££

(☎01665-602109; www.classiclodges.co.uk; Bondgate Within; s/d from £80/105; P wi-fi) Alnwick's top address is this 300-year-old coaching inn right in the heart of town. Its rooms are all of a pretty good standard (LCD screen TVs, DVD players and free wi-fi), but this spot stands out for its dining room, filched in its entirety from the *Olympic,* sister ship to the *Titanic,* elaborate panelling, ceiling and stained-glass windows included.

Blackmore's BOUTIQUE HOTEL ££

(☎01665-602395; www.blackmoresofalnwick.com; Bondgate Without; s/d £90/115; P wi-fi) Trendy Blackmore's motto of 'Eat well, sleep well and party hard' may be a touch incongruous in slow-paced Alnwick, but this takes nothing away from the 14 very comfortable rooms with boutique elements and up-to-the-minute bathrooms. The timber and leather bar-restaurant downstairs is where Alnwick's suited and booted come to booze and get hitched.

Eating & Drinking

Art House INTERNATIONAL ££

(www.arthouserestaurant.com; 14 Bondgate Within; mains £9-16 ⏲Thu-Mon) Located partially within the 15th-century Hotspur Tower (known locally as the Bondgate Tower), this bright, sharp-edged restaurant/art gallery offers simple but flavoursome combos such as salmon in white wine and pesto sauce, and chicken breast with wild mushrooms and tarragon. Ingredients are locally picked, caught and reared wherever possible. All the art on the walls is for sale.

Market Tavern PUB

(7 Fenkle St; stottie £6) Near Market Sq, this is the place to go for a traditional giant beef stottie (round loaf) sluiced down with a yard of real ale. B&B available (£30).

Ye Old Cross PUB

(Narrowgate) Known as 'Bottles', after the dusty bottles in the window, this is another atmospheric stottie-and-pint halt. Legend has it that 150 years ago the owner collapsed and died while trying to move the bottles and no one's dared attempt it since; the irony is that the old window is now behind plexiglass to stop revellers stealing them!

Shopping

Barter Books SECONDHAND BOOKSHOP

(☎01665-604888; www.barterbooks.co.uk; Alnwick Station; ⏲9am-7pm) One of the country's largest secondhand bookshops is the magnificent, sprawling Barter Books, housed in a Victorian railway station with coal fires, velvet ottomans and reading (once waiting) rooms. You could spend days in here.

Information

Tourist office (☎01665-511333; www.visitalnwick.org.uk; 2 The Shambles; ⏲9am-5pm Mon-Sat, 10am-4pm Sun) Located by the marketplace; staff can help find accommodation.

Getting There & Away

Alnwick's nearest train station is at Alnmouth, connected to Alnwick by bus every 15 minutes.

Berwick-upon-Tweed Buses 501 & 505; 50 minutes, 10 daily.

Newcastle Buses 501, 505, 518; one hour, two to three hourly.

Farne Islands

One of England's most incredible seabird conventions is found on a rocky archipelago of islands about 3 miles offshore from the undistinguished fishing village of **Seahouses**.

The best time to visit the **Farne Islands** (NT; admission £6, ⏲depending on island & time of year) is during breeding season (roughly May to July), when you can see feeding chicks of 20 species of seabird, including puffin, kittiwake, Arctic tern, eider duck, cormorant and gull. This is a quite extraordinary experience, for there are few places in the world where you can get so close to nesting seabirds. The islands are also home to a colony of grey seals.

To protect the islands from environmental damage, only two are accessible to the public: Inner Farne and Staple Island. Inner Farne is the more interesting of the two, as it is also the site of a tiny **chapel** (1370, restored 1848) to the memory of St Cuthbert, who lived here for a spell and died here in 687.

Information

The **tourist office** (☎01665-720884; Seafield car park; ⏲10am-5pm Apr-Oct) near the harbour in Seahouses and a **National Trust Shop** (16 Main St; ⏲10am-5pm Apr-Oct) are on hand to provide island-specific information.

Getting There & Away

There are various tours, from 1½-hour cruises to all-day specials, and they get going from 10am April to October. Crossings can be rough, and may be impossible in bad weather. Some of the boats have no proper cabin, so make sure you've got warm, waterproof clothing if there's a chance of rain. Also recommended is an old hat – those birds sure can ruin a head of hair!

Of the four operators that sail from the dock in Seahouses, **Billy Shiel** (☎01665-720308; www.farne-islands.com; 3hr tour adult/child £13/9, all-day tour with landing £25/15) is probably the best known – he even got an MBE for his troubles.

Bamburgh

POP 450

Cute little Bamburgh is dominated by its castle, a massive, imposing structure roosting high up on a basalt crag and a solid contender for England's best. The village itself – a tidy fist of houses around a pleasant green – will be forever associated with the valiant achievements of local lass, Grace Darling.

Bamburgh Castle CASTLE

(www.bamburghcastle.com; adult/child £8/4, audio guide £2.50; ⏲10am-5pm Mar-Oct) Northumberland's most dramatic castle was built around a powerful 11th-century Norman keep by Henry II, although its name is a derivative of Bebbanburgh, after the wife of Anglo-Saxon ruler Aedelfrip, whose fortified home occupied this basalt outcrop 500 years earlier. The castle played a key role in the border wars of the 13th and 14th centuries, and in 1464 was the first English castle to fall as the result of a sustained artillery attack, by Richard Neville, Earl of Warwick, during the Wars of the Roses. It was restored in the 19th century by the great industrialist Lord Armstrong, who died before work was completed. The castle is still home to the Armstrong family.

Once through the gates, head for the **museum** to view scraps of WWII German bombers washed up on Northumberland's beaches, plus exhibits illustrating just how the Armstrongs raked in their millions (ships, weapons, locomotives), before entering the castle proper. The 12 rooms and chambers inside are crammed with antique furniture, suits of armour, priceless ceramics and works of art, but top billing must go to the **King's Hall**, a stunning piece of 19th-century neo-Gothic fakery, all wood panelling, leaded windows and hefty beams supporting the roof.

RNLI Grace Darling Museum MUSEUM

(1 Radcliffe Rd; adult/child £2.75/1.75; ⌚10am-5pm) Born in Bamburgh, Grace Darling was the lighthouse keeper's daughter on Outer Farne who rowed out to the grounded, flailing SS *Forfarshire* in 1838 and saved its crew in the middle of a dreadful storm. This recently refurbished museum is dedicated to the plucky Victorian heroine and even has the actual coble (rowboat) in which she braved the churning North Sea, as well as a film on the events of that stormy night. Grace was born just three houses down from the museum and is buried in the churchyard opposite, her ornate wrought-iron and sandstone tomb built tall so as to be visible to passing ships.

Getting There & Away

Alnwick Bus 401 or 501; one hour, four to six daily.

Newcastle Bus 501; 2½ hours, three daily Monday to Saturday, two Sunday. Stops at Alnwick and Seahouses.

Holy Island (Lindisfarne)

Holy Island is often referred to as an unearthly place, and while a lot of this talk is just that (and a little bit of bring-'em-in tourist bluster), there *is* something almost other-worldly about this small island (it's only 2 sq miles). It's slightly tricky to reach, as it's connected to the mainland by a narrow causeway that only appears at low tide. It's also fiercely desolate and isolated, barely any different from when St Aidan arrived to found a monastery in 635. As you cross the empty flats to get here, it's not difficult to imagine the marauding Vikings who repeatedly sacked the settlement between 793 and 875, when the monks finally took the hint and left. They carried with them the illuminated *Lindisfarne Gospels* (now in the British Library in London) and the miraculously preserved body of St Cuthbert, who lived here for a couple of years but preferred the hermit's life on Inner Farne. A priory was re-established in the 11th century but didn't survive the Dissolution in 1537.

Pay attention to the crossing-time information, posted at tourist offices and on notice boards throughout the area. Every year a handful of go-it-alone fools are caught midway by the incoming tide and have to abandon their cars.

Sights

Lindisfarne Priory PRIORY

(EH; adult/child £4.50/2.30; ⌚9.30am-5pm Apr-Sep) The skeletal, red and grey ruins of the priory are an eerie sight and give a fleeting impression of the isolated life lead by the Lindisfarne monks. The later 13th-century St Mary the Virgin Church is built on the site of the first church between the Tees and the Firth of Forth and the adjacent museum displays the remains of the first monastery and tells the story of the monastic community before and after the Dissolution.

Lindisfarne Heritage Centre HERITAGE CENTRE

(www.lindisfarne.org.uk; Marygate; adult/child £3/1; ⌚10am-5pm Apr-Oct, according to tides Nov-Mar) Twenty pages of the luminescent *Lindisfarne Gospels* can be flicked through on touch-screens here, though there's normally a queue for the two terminals. While you wait your turn there are fascinating exhibitions on the Vikings and the sacking of Lindisfarne in 793.

Lindisfarne Castle CASTLE

(NT; adult/child £6/3; ⌚10.30am-3pm or noon-4.30pm Tue-Sun Mar-Oct) Half a mile from the village stands this tiny, storybook castle, moulded onto a hunk of rock in 1550, and extended and converted by Sir Edwin Lutyens from 1902 to 1910 for Mr Hudson, the owner of *Country Life* magazine. You can imagine some decadent parties have graced its alluring rooms – Jay Gatsby would have been proud.

Sleeping & Eating

It's possible to stay on the island, but you'll need to book well in advance.

Open Gate HOTEL ££
(☎01289-389222; www.aidanandhilda.org; Marygate; s/d £40/65) This spacious Elizabethan stone farmhouse with comfortable rooms caters primarily to those looking for a contemplative experience – you're not as much charged a room rate as 'encouraged' to give the listed price as a donation. There's a small chapel in the basement and a room full of books on Celtic spirituality.

Manor House Hotel HOTEL ££
(☎01289-389207; www.manorhouselindisfarne.com; s/d £55/95) Check in at the bar before heading up the tartan-carpeted stairway to one of the ten smart rooms, the six at the front enjoying spectacular castle views. The restaurant downstairs (mains £7 to £11) is a very popular tourist refuelling stop.

Ship Inn PUB, B&B ££
(☎01289-389311; www.theshipinn-holyisland.co.uk; Marygate; s/d from £82/104) Four exceptionally comfortable rooms – one with a four-poster – sit above an 18th-century public house known here as the Tavern. There's good local seafood in the bar.

Getting There & Away

Holy Island can be reached by bus 477 from Berwick (Wednesday and Saturday only, Monday to Saturday July and August). People taking cars across are requested to park in one of the signposted car parks (£4.40 per day). The sea covers the causeway and cuts the island off from the mainland for about five hours each day.

If arriving by car, a **shuttle bus** (£2; every 20min) runs from the car park to the castle.

Berwick-upon-Tweed

POP 11,665

The northernmost city in England is a salt-encrusted fortress town and the stubborn holder of two unique honours: it is the most fought-over settlement in European history (between 1174 and 1482 it changed hands 14 times between the Scots and the English); and its football team, Berwick Rangers, are the only English team to play in the Scottish League – albeit in lowly Division Three. Although firmly English since the 15th century, Berwick retains its own peculiar identity, an odd blend of Scottish and English with locals born south of the border very often speaking with a noticeable Scottish whirr.

Sights & Activities

FREE **Berwick's Walls** DEFENSIVE WALLS
(EH) Berwick's hefty Elizabethan walls were begun in 1558 to reinforce an earlier set built during the reign of Edward II. They represented state-of-the-art military technology of the day and were designed both to house artillery (in arrowhead-shaped bastions) and to withstand it (the walls are low and massively thick, but it's still a long way to fall).

You can walk almost the entire length of the walls, a circuit of about a mile. It's a must, with wonderful, wide-open views. Only a small fragment remains of the once mighty **border castle**, most of the building having been replaced by the train station.

Berwick Barracks MUSEUMS/GALLERIES
(EH; The Parade; adult/child £3.70/1.90; 10am-5pm Apr-Sep) Designed by Nicholas Hawksmoor, the oldest purpose-built barracks (1717) in Britain now house an assortment of museums and art galleries.

The **By Beat of Drum** exhibition charges through the history of British soldiery from 1660 to 1900, while the **Regimental Museum** is only really for those with a burning interest in the King's Own Scottish Borderers. The **Berwick Museum and Art Gallery** romps through the town's history and holds 400 works of art from the Burrell collection (the other 9,000 make up Glasgow's famous museum). The **Gymnasium Gallery** (noon-4pm Wed-Sun) hosts big-name contemporary art exhibitions.

Cell Block Museum MUSEUM
(Marygate; adult/child £2/50p; tours 10.30am & 2pm Mon-Fri Apr-Sep) The original jail cells in the upper floor of the town hall (1750–61) have been preserved as a museum devoted to crime and punishment. Tours take in the public rooms, museum, jail and belfry.

Sleeping

There's a cluster of fairly basic B&Bs in Church St. The new Granary development by the river will contain a brand-new YHA hostel expected to open in 2011.

TOP CHOICE **No 1 Sallyport** BOUTIQUE B&B £££

(☎01289-308827; www.sallyport.co.uk; 1 Sallyport, off Bridge St; r £110-150) Not just the best in town, but one of the best B&Bs in England, No 1 Sallyport has only six suites – each carefully appointed to fit a theme. The Manhattan Loft, crammed into the attic, makes the minimalist most of the confined space; the Lowry Room is a country-style Georgian classic; the Smuggler's Suite has a separate sitting room complete with widescreen TV, DVD players and plenty of space to lounge around in. The Tiffany Suite has a grand fireplace and the attic Mulberry Suite has a sexy freestanding bath. The downstairs **restaurant** (mains £8.95-14.95) is Berwick's finest serving Cheviot lamb, North Sea fish and homemade cakes and pastries. The ambitious owners are hoping to gain Northumberland's first Michelin star in 2011.

Berwick Backpackers HOSTEL ££

(☎01289-331481; www.berwickbackpackers.co.uk; 56-58 Bridge St; dm/s/d from £16.95/29.95/70; P@) This well-appointed hostel, basically a series of rooms in the outhouses of a Georgian home positioned around a central courtyard, has a variety of spick-and-span rooms including two mixed dorms. Highly recommended.

Eating & Drinking

Foxton's CONTINENTAL ££

(26 Hide Hill; mains £9-14.50; Mon-Sat) This decent brasserie-style restaurant has Continental dishes to complement the local fare, which means there's something for everyone.

Barrels Alehouse PUB

(56 Bridge St) Berwick's best watering hole attracts a mixed, laid-back crowd who can be found supping real ales and micro-distilled gins and whiskies at all hours. There's regular live music in the atmospherically dingy basement bar.

Information

Berwick Library (Walkergate; closed Thu & Sun) Bring ID to access the internet.

Tourist office (☎01289-330733; www.visitnorthumberland.com; 106 Marygate; 10am-5pm Mon-Sat, 11am-3pm Sun Easter-Oct) Can help find accommodation and runs one-hour guided walks at 10am, 11.45am & 2pm on weekdays (£4).

Getting There & Away

Bus

Buses stop on Golden Sq (where Marygate becomes Castlegate).

Edinburgh National Express; £13.70, one hour 20 minutes, twice daily.

Holy Island Bus 477; 35 minutes, two services on Wednesday and Saturday, Monday to Saturday in August.

London National Express; £35.30, eight hours, twice daily.

Newcastle Buses 505, 501 (via Alnwick); 2½ hours, nine daily.

Train

Berwick is almost exactly halfway between Edinburgh (£13.60, 50 minutes, half hourly) and Newcastle (£19.70, 50 minutes, half hourly) on the main east-coast London-Edinburgh line.

Wales

CHERYL FORBES

Wales Highlights

1. Exploring **Cardiff** (p638), the Welsh capital, with its fantasy castle, Victorian shopping arcades and lively nightlife
2. Catching some breaks or just enjoying the views along the **Gower Peninsula** (p668)
3. Hitting the long-distance coast path in **Pembrokeshire** (p673) for stunning scenery
4. Enjoying tiny **St Davids** (p679) with its beautiful cathedral and idyllic setting
5. Climbing Wales's highest peak, **Snowdon** (p745), or enjoying more gentle exercise in **Snowdonia** (p744)
6. Buying some fish and chips and strolling along the pier in **Llandudno** (p726)
7. Seeing **Caernarfon Castle** (p737), arguably the most impressive of all of Wales's many fortresses
8. Wandering through **Hay-on-Wye** (p704), a bookworm's heaven
9. Walking in the mountains then eating in the gastropubs of the **Brecon Beacons** (p693)

Cardiff (Caerdydd)

TELEPHONE CODE: 029 / POP: 324,800 / AREA: 54 SQ MILES

Includes »

Sights 640
Tours............... 645
Festivals & Events.... 646
Sleeping 647
Eating 648
Drinking 649
Entertainment....... 650
Shopping 651
AROUND CARDIFF ..653

Best Places to Eat

» Woods Bar & Brasserie (p649)

» Le Gallois (p649)

» Brava (p649)

» Cameo Club & Bistro (p649)

» Garçon! (p649)

Best Places to Stay

» Tŷ Rosa (p648)

» NosDa Budget Hotel (p647)

» Jolyon's Boutique Hotel (p647)

» Park Plaza (p647)

» Parc Hotel (p647)

Why Go?

The capital of Wales since only 1955, Cardiff has embraced its new role with vigour, emerging as one of Britain's leading urban centres in the 21st century. Caught between an ancient fort and an ultramodern waterfront, compact Cardiff seems to have surprised even itself with how interesting it's become. If its mid-20th-century decline at one stage seemed terminal, the city has entered the new millennium pumped up on steroids, flexing its new architectural muscles as if it's still astonished to have them. This newfound confidence is infectious; people now actually travel *to* Cardiff for a good night out, bringing with them a buzz that reverberates through the streets. The city makes a great base for day trips in the surrounding countryside, where you'll find castles, Roman ruins, Neolithic stone monuments and beachside amusements.

When to Go?

January and February are the coldest months, although Wales' home matches in the Six Nations Rugby Championship warm spirits in February and March. June is the driest month and in July the summer-long Cardiff Festival kicks off, incorporating theatre, comedy, music and a food festival. In August, the warmest month, knights storm the castle, classic cars converge and gay pride takes over the streets. By November, the wettest month, the average daily high temperature is 10°C – it doesn't scrape into two digits again until March.

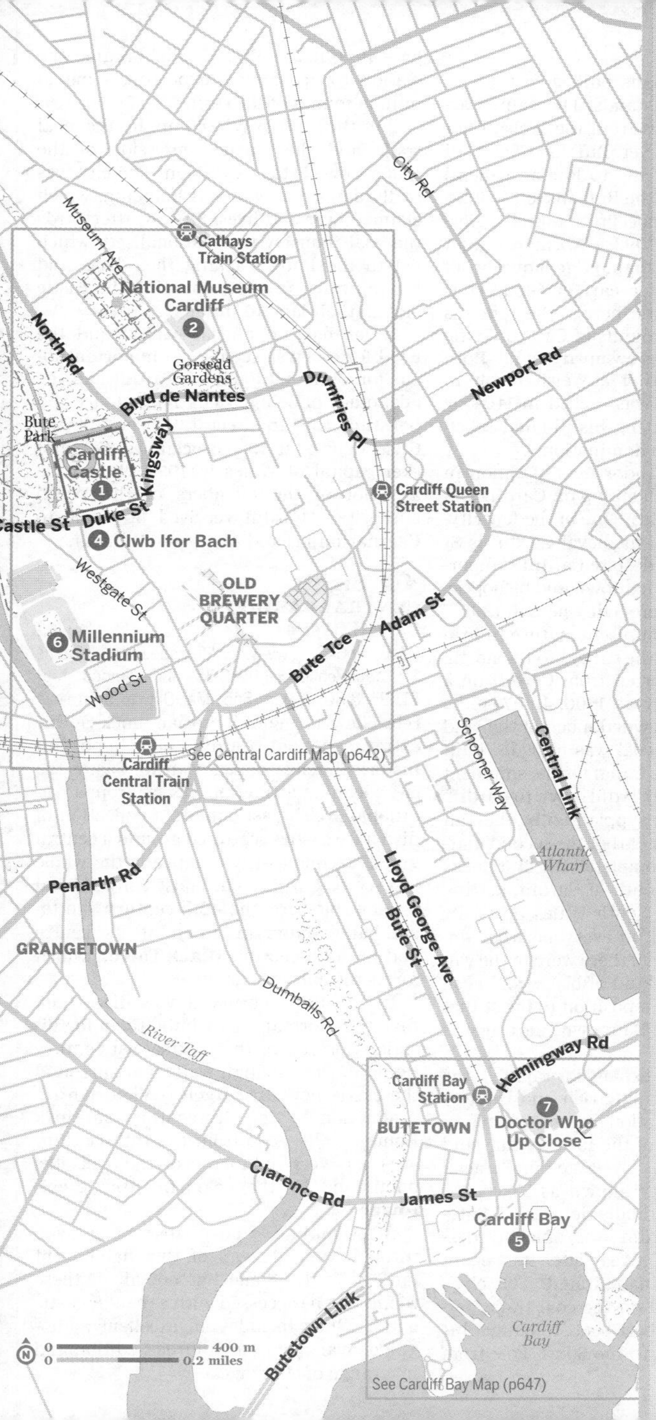

Cardiff Highlights

1. Marvelling at the over-the-top Victorian interiors that add bling to **Cardiff Castle** (p640), the city's ancient citadel
2. Taking an engrossing journey via the big bang, archaeological artefacts and art at the **National Museum Cardiff** (p641)
3. Joining the nighttime revellers hopping between the central city's **bars** (p649) as the city's streets thrum with live music after dark
4. Catching the next big thing on the Welsh music scene at **Clwb Ifor Bach** (p650)
5. Admiring the architectural showpieces that make up the glitzy entertainment precinct at **Cardiff Bay** (p643)
6. Getting swept away by the exhilaration of a fired-up rugby test at **Millennium Stadium** (p641)
7. Coming face to face with a Dalek, without even a couch to hide behind, in **Doctor Who Up Close** (p645)

History

In AD 75 the Romans built a fort where Cardiff Castle now stands. The name Cardiff probably derives from the Welsh Caer Tâf (Fort on the River Taff) or Caer Didi (Didius' Fort), referring to Roman general Aulus Didius. After the Romans left Britain the site remained unoccupied until the Norman Conquest. In 1093 a Norman knight named Robert Fitzhamon (conqueror of Glamorgan and later earl of Gloucester) built himself a castle here – the remains stand within the grounds of Cardiff Castle – and a small town grew up around it. Both were damaged during a Welsh revolt in 1183 and the town was sacked in 1404 by Owain Glyndŵr during his ill-fated rebellion against English domination.

The first of the Tudor Acts of Union in 1536 put the English stamp on Cardiff and brought some stability. One of the few city-centre reminders of medieval Cardiff is St John's Church. But despite Cardiff's importance as a port, market town and bishopric, only 1000 people were living here in 1801.

The city owes its present stature to iron and coal mining in the valleys to the north. Coal was first exported from Cardiff on a small scale as early as 1600. In 1794 the Bute family – who owned much of the land from which Welsh coal was mined – built the Glamorganshire Canal for the shipment of iron from Merthyr Tydfil down to Cardiff.

In 1840 this was supplanted by the Taff Vale Railway. A year earlier the second marquess of Bute had completed the first docks at Butetown, just south of Cardiff, getting the jump on other South Wales ports. By the time it dawned on everyone what immense reserves of coal there were in the valleys – setting off a kind of black gold rush – the Butes were in a position to insist that it be shipped from Butetown. Cardiff was off and running.

The docklands expanded rapidly, the Butes grew staggeringly rich and the city boomed, its population mushrooming to 170,000 by the end of the 19th century and to 227,000 by 1931. A large, multiracial workers' community known as Tiger Bay grew up in the harbourside area of Butetown. In 1905 Cardiff was officially designated a city, and a year later its elegant Civic Centre was inaugurated. The city's wealth and its hold on the coal trade persuaded Captain Robert Scott to launch his ill-fated expedition to the South Pole from here in 1910. In 1913 Cardiff became the world's top coal port, exporting some 13 million tonnes of the stuff.

But the post-WWI slump in the coal trade and the Great Depression of the 1930s slowed this expansion. The city was badly damaged by WWII bombing, which claimed over 350 lives. Shortly afterwards the coal industry was nationalised, which led to the Butes packing their bags and leaving town in 1947, donating the castle and all their land to the city.

Wales had no official capital and the need for one was seen as an important focus for Welsh nationhood. Cardiff had the advantage of being Wales' biggest city and boasting the architectural riches of the Civic Centre. It was proclaimed the first ever capital of Wales in 1955, chosen via a ballot of the members of the Welsh authorities. Cardiff received 36 votes to Caernarfon's 11 and Aberystwyth's four.

Sights

CENTRAL CARDIFF

Cardiff Castle CASTLE

(Map p642; www.cardiffcastle.com; Castle St; adult/child £8.95/6.35, incl guided tour £11.95/8.50; ⏲9am-6pm Mar-Oct, to 5pm Nov-Feb) The grafting of Victorian mock-Gothic extravagance onto Cardiff's most important historical relics makes Cardiff Castle the city's leading attraction. It's far from a traditional Welsh castle, more a collection of disparate castles scattered around a central green, encompassing practically the whole history of Cardiff. The most conventional castle-y bits are the 12th-century motte-and-bailey **Norman keep** at its centre and the 13th-century **Black Tower**, which forms the entrance gate.

In the 19th century it was discovered that the Normans had built their fortifications on top of the original 1st-century Roman fort. The high walls that surround the castle now are largely a Victorian reproduction of the 3rd-century 3m-thick Roman walls. Also from the 19th century are the towers and turrets on the west side, dominated by the colourful 40m **clock tower**.

A 50-minute guided tour takes you through the interiors of this flamboyant fantasy world. Some but not all of these rooms can be accessed with a regular castle entry, which includes an excellent audioguide (available in a children's edition and in a range of languages).

CARDIFF IN...

Two Days

Begin with our walking tour to orient yourself in the central city. If you stop along the way to explore **Cardiff Castle** and the **National Museum Cardiff** you'll quickly find that the day has disappeared. Lunch could be a picnic in **Bute Park** with treats acquired at **Cardiff Central Market** or, if the weather's not cooperating, a meal at any of the reasonably priced eateries in central Cardiff. Finish the day with a slap-up meal in the genteel area around **Cathedral Rd**. Spend your second day heading back to the future at **Cardiff Bay**: immerse yourself in forward-thinking architecture and get acquainted with **Doctor Who Up Close**.

Four Days

Spend your third morning steeped in history at **St Fagans National History Museum** then check out Barry Island. On your last day, head north to explore **Llandaff Cathedral**, then continue on to **Castell Coch** and **Caerphilly Castle**. For your last night in the capital, blast out the cobwebs in one of the city's live-music venues.

One Week

Stretch things out to a leisurely pace, allowing plenty of time for shopping and wandering the streets. Head to **Penarth** on the Waterbus, tour the Millennium Stadium and take a **Creepy Cardiff Ghost Tour**.

Housed below the **Interpretation Centre** to the right of the entrance is the **Welch Regiment Museum** (⌚Wed-Mon), which records the military achievements of South Wales' infantry regiment.

FREE National Museum Cardiff MUSEUM
(Map p642; www.museumwales.ac.uk; Gorsedd Gardens Rd; ⌚10am-5pm Tue-Sun) Set around the green lawns and colourful flowerbeds of **Alexandra Gardens** is the Civic Centre, an early-20th-century complex of neo-Baroque buildings in gleaming white Portland stone. They include the **City Hall**, police headquarters, law courts, crown offices, Cardiff University and this excellent museum, one of Britain's best, covering natural history, archaeology and art.

The Evolution of Wales exhibit takes you through 4600 million years of geological history, with a rollicking multimedia display that places Wales into a global context. Films of volcanic eruptions and aerial footage of the Welsh landscape explain how its scenery was formed, while model dinosaurs and woolly mammoths keep the kids interested.

The natural-history displays range from brightly coloured insects to the 9m-long skeleton of a humpback whale that washed up near Aberthaw in 1982. The world's largest turtle (2.88m by 2.74m), which was found on Harlech beach, is also here, suspended on wires from the ceiling.

The art gallery houses an excellent collection, including many impressionist and postimpressionist pieces. Treasures include works by Monet, Renoir, Matisse and Van Gogh, along with modern luminaries Francis Bacon and David Hockney. Welsh artists such as Richard Wilson, Thomas Jones, David Jones, Gwen John and Augustus John are well represented.

Millennium Stadium STADIUM
(Map p642; ☎029-2082 2228; www.millenniumstadium.com; Westgate St; tours adult/child £6.50/4; ⌚10am-5pm Mon-Sat, to 4pm Sun) The spectacular Millennium Stadium squats like a stranded spaceship on the River Taff's east bank. Attendance at international rugby and football matches has increased dramatically since this 72,500-seat, three-tiered stadium with sliding roof was completed in time to host the 1999 Rugby World Cup. The famous **Cardiff Arms Park** (Map p642), its predecessor, lies literally in its shadow.

Not everyone is happy with it: one critic called it 'an absurdly overexcited structure...that rears over the surrounding streets like a sumo wrestler'. The stadium cost £110 million to build and big matches paralyse the city centre, but when the crowd

Central Cardiff

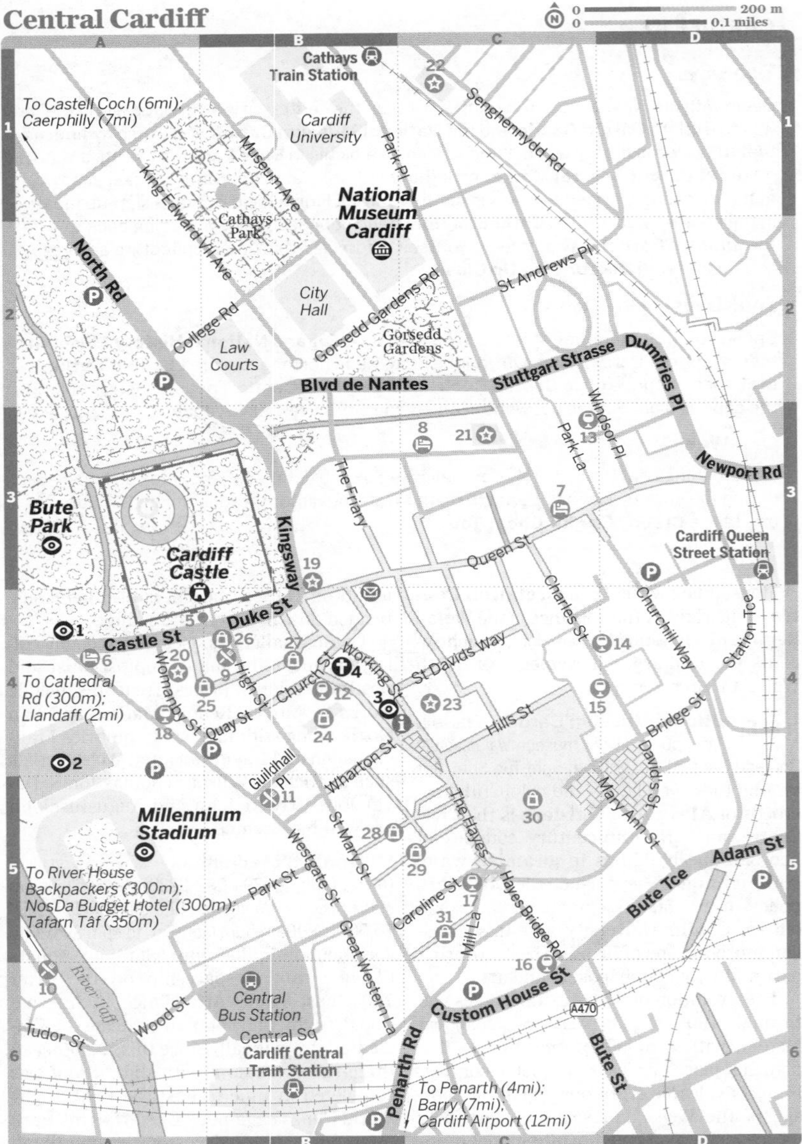

begins to sing, the whole city resonates and all is forgiven.

It's well worth taking a tour – you get to walk through the players' tunnel and sit in the VIP box. The entrance for guided tours is at Gate 3 on Westgate St.

Cardiff Story MUSEUM

(Map p642; ☎029-2078 8334; www.cardiffstory.com; the Old Library, the Hayes; ⏰10am-5pm Mon-Sat, to 4pm Sun) We can't say too much about this museum, as it hadn't quite opened when we were researching this

Central Cardiff

Top Sights
Bute Park A3
Cardiff Castle A4
Millennium Stadium A5
National Museum Cardiff B2

Sights
1 Animal Wall A4
2 Cardiff Arms Park A4
3 Cardiff Story B4
4 St John the Baptist Church B4

Activities, Courses & Tours
5 City Sightseeing Bus Stop A4

Sleeping
6 Barceló Cardiff Angel Hotel A4
7 Parc Hotel C3
8 Park Plaza C3

Eating
Cafe Minuet ..... (see 25)
9 Goat Major B4
Madame Fromage ..... (see 25)
Plan ..... (see 28)
10 Riverside Real Food Market A6
11 Zerodegrees B5

Drinking
12 10 Feet Tall B4
13 Buffalo Bar C3
14 Club X D4
15 Exit Club C4
16 Golden Cross C6
17 King's Cross C5
18 Pica Pica A4

Entertainment
19 Barfly B3
20 Clwb Ifor Bach A4
21 New Theatre C3
22 Sherman Theatre C1
23 St David's Hall C4

Shopping
24 Cardiff Central Market B4
25 Castle Arcade B4
26 Castle Welsh Crafts B4
27 High Street Arcade B4
28 Morgan Arcade B5
29 Royal Arcade C5
Spiller's Records ..... (see 28)
30 St David's C5
31 Wyndham Arcade C5

book. It aims to tell the story of Cardiff's transformation from a small market town into the world's biggest coal port and then into the capital city you see today.

St John the Baptist Church CHURCH
(Map p642; Working St) A graceful Gothic lantern tower rises from this 15th-century church, its delicate stonework almost like filigree. A church has stood on this site since at least 1180. Inside are simple, elegant arches. Regular lunchtime organ concerts are held here.

Bute Park PARK
(Map p642) With Sophia Gardens, Pontcanna Fields and Llandaff Fields, Bute Park forms a green corridor that stretches northwest alongside the River Taff for 1.5 miles to Llandaff. All were once part of the Bute's vast holdings. Forming the park's southern edge, the **Animal Wall** is topped with stone figures of lions, seals, bears and other creatures. In the 1930s they were the subject of a newspaper cartoon strip and many Cardiff kids grew up thinking the animals came alive at night.

CARDIFF BAY

Cardiff Bay Waterfront NEIGHBOURHOOD
(Map p646) Lined with important national institutions, Cardiff Bay is where the modern Welsh nation is put on display in an architect's playground of interesting buildings, large open spaces and public art. It wasn't always this way. By 1913 more than 13 million tonnes of coal was being shipped from Cardiff's docks. Following the post-WWI slump the docklands deteriorated into a wasteland of empty basins, cut off from the city by the railway embankment. The bay outside the docks – which has one of the highest tidal ranges in the world (more than 12m between high and low water) – was ringed for up to 14 hours a day by smelly, sewage-contaminated mudflats.

Since 1987 the area has been completely redeveloped. The turning point came with the erection of a state-of-the-art tidal barrage, completed in 1999, which transformed the mudflats into a freshwater lake by containing the waters at the mouth of the Rivers Taff and Ely. It was a controversial project, as its construction flooded 490 acres of intertidal mudflats which, despite their unpleasant aspects, were an important habitat for waterfowl. The barrage includes sluice gates to control the water flow, three lock gates to allow passage for boats, and a fish pass that lets migrating salmon and sea trout pass between the river and the sea.

Cardiff Bay's main commercial centre is **Mermaid Quay** (Map p646), packed with bars, restaurants and shops. To its east is **Roald Dahl Plass** (Map p646), a large public space (it used to be a dock basin), named after the Cardiff-born writer, that serves as an open-air performance area, overseen by a soaring, stainless-steel **water sculpture**.

FREE **Wales Millennium Centre** ARTS CENTRE
(Map p646; ☎029-2063 6464; www.wmc.org.uk; Bute Pl) The centrepiece and symbol of Cardiff Bay's regeneration, the Millennium Centre is an architectural masterpiece of stacked Welsh slate in shades of purple, green and grey topped with an overarching bronzed steel shell. Designed by Welsh architect Jonathan Adams, it opened in 2004 as Wales' premier arts complex, housing the Welsh National Opera, National Dance Company, National Orchestra, Academi (Welsh National Literature Promotion Agency), HiJinx Theatre and Ty Cerdd (Music Centre of Wales).

The roof above the main entrance is pierced by 2m-high, letter-shaped windows, spectacularly backlit at night, that spell out phrases from poet Gwyneth Lewis: *'Creu Gwir fel Gwydr o Ffwrnais Awen'* (Creating truth like glass from inspiration's furnace) and 'In these stones horizons sing'.

You can wander through the public areas at will, or take an official **guided tour** (adult/child £5.50/4.50; ⌚9am-5pm) that leads behind the giant letters, onto the main stage and into the dressing rooms, depending on what shows are on.

FREE **Senedd (National Assembly Building)** GOVERNMENT BUILDING
(Map p646; ☎0845 010 5500; www.assemblywales.org/sen-home; ⌚10.30am-4.30pm, extended during plenary sessions) Designed by Lord Richard Rogers (the architect behind London's Lloyd's Building and Paris' Pompidou Centre), the Senedd is a striking structure of concrete, slate, glass and steel with an undulating canopy roof lined with red cedar. It's won awards for an environmentally friendly design, which includes a huge rotating cowl on the roof for power-free ventilation and a gutter system that collects rainwater for flushing the toilets. The lobby and surrounding area are littered with public artworks.

The Welsh National Assembly usually meets in a plenary session from 1.30pm on Tuesday and Wednesday, and seats in the public gallery may be pre-booked, although you can always take your chances on the day.

THE BEAUT BUTES

The Butes, an aristocratic Scottish family related to the Stuart monarchy, arrived in Cardiff in 1766 in the shape of John, Lord Mountstuart, who had served briefly as prime minister under King George I. He married a local heiress, Charlotte Jane Windsor, acquiring vast estates and mineral rights in South Wales in the process.

Their grandson, the second marquess of Bute, grew fabulously wealthy from coal mining and then in 1839 gambled his fortune to create the first docks at Cardiff. The gamble paid off. The coal-export business boomed, and his son, John Patrick Crichton-Stuart, the third marquess of Bute, became one of the richest people on the planet. He was not your conventional Victorian aristocrat; an intense, scholarly man with a passion for history, architecture, ritual and religion (Catholic), he neither hunted nor fished but instead supported the antivivisection movement and campaigned for a woman's right to a university education.

The Butes had interests all over Britain and never spent more than about six weeks at a time in Cardiff. By the end of WWII they had sold or given away all their Cardiff assets, the fifth marquess gifting Cardiff Castle and Bute Park to the city in 1947. The present marquess, the seventh, lives in the family seat at Mount Stuart House on the Isle of Bute in Scotland's Firth of Clyde; another maverick, he's better known as Johnny Dumfries, the former Formula One racing driver.

WORTH A TRIP

LLANDAFF CATHEDRAL

Set in a hollow on the west bank of the River Taff, on the site of a 6th-century monastery, is beautiful **Llandaff Cathedral** (www.llandaffcathedral.org.uk; Cathedral Rd; ⏲10am-4pm). The present cathedral was begun in 1120 – it crumbled throughout the Middle Ages, and during the Reformation and Civil War it was used as an alehouse and then an animal shelter. Derelict by the 18th century, it was largely rebuilt in the 19th century and extensively restored after being damaged by a German bomb in 1941. The towers at the western end epitomise the cathedral's fragmented history – one was built in the 15th century, the other in the 19th. Inside, a giant arch supports Sir Jacob Epstein's huge, aluminium sculpture *Majestas*, its modern style a bold contrast in this gracious, vaulted space.

Buses 24, 25, 33, 33A and 62 (15 minutes, every 10 to 15 minutes) run along Cathedral Rd to Llandaff.

FREE **Pierhead** MUSEUM
(Map p646; ☎029-0845 010 5500; www.pierhead.org; ⏲10.30am-4.30pm Mon-Fri & most weekends) One of the area's few Victorian remnants, Pierhead is a red-brick French-Gothic Renaissance confection – nicknamed Wales' Big Ben – built with Bute family money. It's now part of the National Assembly complex and at the time of research was about to open as an interactive museum 'highlighting issues that matter in Wales'.

Doctor Who Up Close EXHIBITION
(Map p646; www.doctorwhoexhibitions.com; Red Dragon Centre; adult/child £6.50/5; ⏲10am-6.30pm) The huge success of the reinvented classic TV series *Doctor Who*, produced by BBC Wales, has brought Cardiff to the attention of sci-fi fans worldwide. City locations have featured in many episodes and the spin-off series *Torchwood* is set in Cardiff Bay (the hidden lift to their headquarters emerges beneath the water sculpture in Roald Dahl Plass). Capitalising on Timelord tourism, this permanent exhibition has opened in the Red Dragon Centre, with props and costumes from both shows displayed alongside video clips from the episodes they feature in. It's great fun – especially when you come face to face with full-size Daleks in full 'ex-ter-min-ate' mode. Fans can pick up a locations guide (30p) from the nerdalicious shop.

The Red Dragon Centre also has an IMAX cinema, a casino and restaurants.

Butetown NEIGHBOURHOOD
Victorian Butetown, spanning out from Mount Stuart Sq, just northwest of the waterfront, was the heart of Cardiff's coal trade – a multiethnic community that propelled the city to world fame. The old **Coal Exchange** (Map p646; www.coalexchange.co.uk; Mount Stuart Sq) was the place where international coal prices were set. It was here in March 1908 that a coal merchant wrote the world's first-ever £1 million cheque. It now houses an arts and performance venue.

FREE **Butetown History & Arts Centre** ARTS CENTRE
(Map p646; www.bhac.org; 4-5 Dock Chambers, Bute St; ⏲10am-5pm Tue-Fri, 11am-4.30pm Sat & Sun) This centre is devoted to preserving oral histories, documents and images of the docklands. Its exhibits put the area into both a historical and present-day context.

Tours

City Sightseeing BUS
(Map p642; ☎029-2047 3432; www.city-sightseeing.com; adult/child £9/4; ⏲daily Feb-Oct, Sat & Sun only Nov-Jan) Open-top, hop-on/hop-off bus tours of the city, departing every 30 to 60 minutes from outside Cardiff Castle; tickets are valid for 24 hours.

CARDIFF FOR CHILDREN

Compact and easy to navigate, Cardiff is welcoming to families. Interactive **Techniquest** (Map p646; www.techniquest.org; Stuart St; adult/child £7/5; ⏲10am-4.30pm) is the primary attraction to challenge little brains, while the National Museum Cardiff is full of weird and wonderful animals and fascinating exhibits. For a day trip, try the living history of Caerphilly Castle or Castell Coch.

Creepy Cardiff Ghost Tour WALKING
(07980 975135; www.creepycardiff.com; adult/child £5/4, minimum £40 if fewer than 10 bookings) A one-hour walking tour promising frights and laughs in equal doses.

Festivals & Events

Cardiff Festival SUMMER FESTIVAL
(www.cardiff-festival.com) Runs throughout summer, from July to early September. Includes: Welsh Proms (two weeks of classical concerts at St David's Hall); Big Weekend (funfair, bands and the Lord Mayor's parade); Cardiff Comedy Festival; Cardiff International Food & Drink Festival; Grand Medieval Melee; lesbian and gay Mardi Gras; National Classic Car & Motor Boat Rally; Everyman Summer Theatre Festival; and lots of crazy one-offs.

Great British Cheese Festival FOOD
(www.greatbritishcheesefestival.co.uk) Brush shoulders with the big cheeses in Cardiff Castle, late September.

Cardiff Winter Wonderland WINTER FESTIVAL
(www.cardiffswinterwonderland.com; Civic Centre) An outdoor ice-skating rink, Christmas lights, Santa's grotto and family-friendly activities.

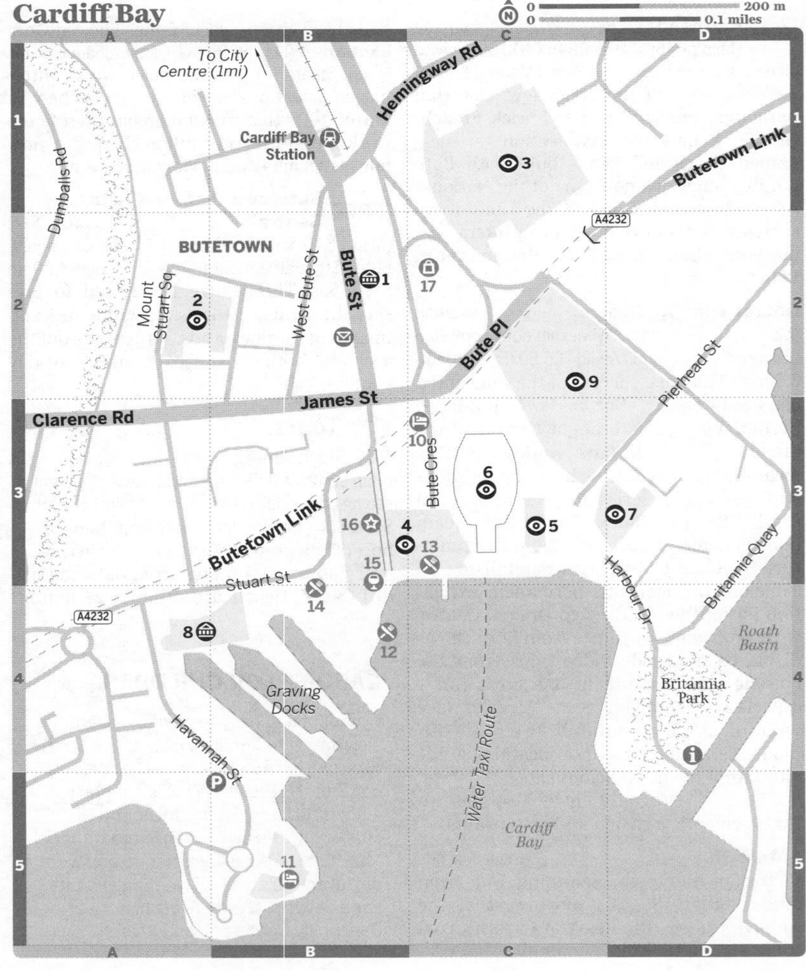

Sleeping

CENTRAL CARDIFF

TOP CHOICE **NosDa Budget Hotel** HOSTEL £
(029-2037 8866; www.nosda.co.uk; 53-59 Despenser St; dm/tw from £19/43; P@) You won't find a better budget bed any closer to the city centre than this stylishly refurbished hostel right across the river from the Millennium Stadium. It's family-friendly, and there's an in-house bar, restaurant and gym.

Park Plaza HOTEL ££
(Map p642; 029-2011 1111; www.parkplazacardiff.com; Greyfriars Rd; r from £109; @) Luxurious without being remotely stuffy, the Plaza has all the five-star facilities you'd expect from a business-orientated hotel. For something more offbeat, it offers *Doctor Who* breaks complete with remote-controlled Daleks.

Parc Hotel HOTEL ££
(Map p642; 0871-376 9011; www.thistle.com/theparchotel; Park Pl; r from £99; @) A smart contemporary hotel located right at the heart of the main shopping area, with tasteful rooms, good facilities and helpful staff.

River House Backpackers HOSTEL £
(029-2039 9810; www.riverhousebackpackers.com; 59 Fitzhamon Embankment; dm/r from £18/35; @) Professionally run by a young brother-and-sister team, the River House has a well-equipped kitchen, a small garden and a TV lounge. Free breakfast (cereal and toast) and pizza nights are a nice touch, but the private rooms are very dorm-like.

Barceló Cardiff Angel Hotel HOTEL ££
(Map p642; 029-2064 9200; www.barcelo-hotels.co.uk; Castle St; r from £71; @) Across the street from the castle, this lavish Victorian hotel was founded in 1883 by the third marquess of Bute. The rooms don't quite live up to the promise of the sparkling chandeliers and painted ceilings of the atrium, but cheap advance-purchase rates compensate for any scuffed edges.

CARDIFF BAY

TOP CHOICE **Jolyon's Boutique Hotel** HOTEL ££
(Map p646; 029-2048 8775; www.jolyons.co.uk; 5 Bute Cres; r £65-140;) A touch of Georgian elegance in the heart of Cardiff Bay, Jolyon's has six individually designed rooms combining antique furniture with contemporary colours and crisp cotton sheets.

St David's Hotel & Spa HOTEL ££
(Map p646; 029-2045 4045; www.thestdavidshotel.com; Havannah St; r from £99; @) A glittering, glassy tower topped with a sail-like flourish, St David's epitomises Cardiff Bay's transformation from wasteland to stylish place-to-be. Every room has a private balcony with a harbour view.

CATHEDRAL ROAD AREA

Lincoln House B&B ££
(029-2039 5558; www.lincolnhotel.co.uk; 118 Cathedral Rd; s/d from £65/85; P) At the top end of the guest-house scale, Lincoln House is a large Victorian property with a guest lounge and bar. For added romance, book the four-poster room.

Town House B&B ££
(029-2023 9399; www.thetownhousecardiff.co.uk; 70 Cathedral Rd; s/d from £50/70; P) Succinctly named, this is yet another elegant Victorian town house with a welcoming owner. It retains lots of period features, including tiled hallway, original fireplaces and stained glass.

Cardiff Bay

Sights

1	Butetown History & Arts Centre	B2
2	Coal Exchange	A2
3	Doctor Who Up Close	C1
4	Mermaid Quay	B3
5	Pierhead	C3
6	Roald Dahl Plass	C3
7	Senedd	D3
8	Techniquest	A4
9	Wales Millennium Centre	C2

Sleeping

10	Jolyon's Boutique Hotel	C3
11	St David's Hotel & Spa	B5

Eating

12	Bosphorus	B4
13	Garçon!	C3
14	Woods Bar & Brasserie	B4

Drinking

	Cwtch	(see 10)
15	Salt	B3

Entertainment

16	Glee Club	B3

Shopping

17	Craft in the Bay	C2

Beaufort Guest House B&B ££
(☎029-2023 7003; www.beauforthousecardiff.co.uk; 65 Cathedral Rd; s/d from £55/79; 📶) Despite having had a thorough refurbishment, the Beaufort retains a Victorian atmosphere, with period-style furniture, gilt mirrors, heavy drapes and even a portrait of the old queen herself.

Saco House APARTMENTS ££
(☎0845 122 0405; www.sacoapartments.co.uk; 74-76 Cathedral Rd; apt from £82; P) This Victorian town house has been given a contemporary makeover and converted into serviced apartments, complete with comfortable lounges and fitted kitchens. The two-bedroom apartments are good value for families with kids and there's an extra sofa bed in the lounge. It's set up for longer visits, but a two-day stay is the minimum.

GRANGETOWN

TOP CHOICE **Tŷ Rosa** B&B £
(☎0845 643 9962; www.tyrosa.com; 118 Clive St; s/d from £42/49; 📶) Half an hour's walk from either Central Cardiff or the bay (follow the river south from the city centre, turn right onto Penarth Rd and then left after 650m), this wonderful gay-friendly B&B is noted for its sumptuous breakfasts and affable hosts. The thoughtfully equipped rooms are split between the main house and a less impressive annexe across the road. Some rooms share bathrooms.

Eating

As Cardiff has become more glossy, cosmopolitan and multicultural, so has its food scene. A diverse array of restaurants is scattered around the city, with a particularly ritzy batch lining Cardiff Bay. Burger joints, curry houses and kebab shops cater to the central city's throngs of young drinkers, well into the small hours. While there are cafes everywhere, the UK has been slow to wake up to the joys of a well-made coffee – but Cardiff, unlike the rest of Wales, does now have a few exemplars of the art. A good cuppa tea is much easier to find.

CENTRAL CARDIFF

TOP CHOICE **Riverside Real Food Market** MARKET £
(Map p642; Fitzhamon Embankment; ⏲10am-2pm Sun) What it lacks in size it makes up for in sheer yumminess. This riverside market has stalls heaving with cooked meals, cakes, cheese, organic meat, charcuterie, apple juice and real ale. There are lots of options for vegetarians and the Welsh cakes hot off the griddle are exceptional.

Plan CAFE £
(Map p642; 28 Morgan Arcade; mains £5-8; ⏲9am-5pm) Serving quite possibly Wales' best coffee, this satisfying cafe specialises in healthy, organic, locally sourced food, including vegan options. Grab a window seat and a copy of the *Guardian* newspaper and caffeinate to your (racing) heart's content.

Zerodegrees MICROBREWERY, ITALIAN £
(Map p642; 27 Westgate St; mains £7-13) Within a big factory-like space this microbrewery and restaurant combines all-day food with lip-smacking artisan-crafted beers – try the Black Lager, with hints of caramel and coffee. The excellent dining options include a UN of pizza toppings (Thai, Mexican, Indian, Portuguese), pasta, risotto and kilo pots of mussels, the house specialty.

Cafe Minuet ITALIAN £
(Map p642; 42 Castle Arcade, High St; mains £6-10; ⏲10am-5pm Mon-Sat) It may look a bit greasy spoon from the outside, but this unassuming eatery produces excellent cheap and cheerful Italian food. The menu includes good vegetarian dishes, including lots of pasta options. Get in early at lunchtime or expect to wait for a table.

Goat Major PUB £
(Map p642; 33 High St; mains £7-8; ⏲food noon-6pm Mon-Sat, to 4pm Sun) A solidly traditional pub with armchairs, a fireplace and lip-smacking Brains Dark real ale on tap, the Goat Major's gastronomic contribution comes in the form of its selection of homemade pies. Its Wye Valley pie (a mixture of buttered chicken, leek, asparagus and Tintern Abbey cheese) was named Britain's best in 2010.

Madame Fromage DELICATESSAN CAFE £
(Map p642; www.madamefromage.co.uk; 18 Castle Arcade, High St; mains £3-6; ⏲10am-5.30pm Mon-Sat, noon-5pm Sun) One of Cardiff's finest delicatessens, with a wide range of charcuterie and French and Welsh cheeses. The Madame also has a cafe with tables spilling into the arcade, where you can read French newspapers and eat a mixture of Breton dishes and Welsh caffi food: rarebit, lamb cawl and bara brith.

CARDIFF BAY

TOP CHOICE **Woods Bar & Brasserie** MODERN EUROPEAN ££

(Map p646; ☎029-2049 2400; Stuart St; mains £11-18; ⏰ closed dinner Sun) The historic Pilotage Building has been given a modern makeover – zany wallpaper, exposed stone walls and a floor-to-ceiling glass extension – to accommodate Cardiff Bay's best restaurant. The cuisine is modern European, light and flavoursome, with an emphasis on local ingredients.

Garçon! FRENCH ££

(Map p646; ☎029-2049 0990; Mermaid Quay; mains £11-18; ⏰closed Mon Oct-Feb) The name may conjure up the worst Brits-do-French stereotypes, but this place is the real deal. Seemingly beamed in directly from Normandy, the ambience and menu are perfectly authentic, even down to offering reasonable prix-fixe deals (two/three courses £13/16, served before 6pm).

Bosphorus TURKISH ££

(Map p646; ☎029-2048 7477; 31 Mermaid Quay; mains £10-14) While the food is good, it's the setting that really distinguishes this upmarket Turkish restaurant. Jutting out over the water on its own private pier, Bosphorus enjoys wonderful views all round; the best of all are from the outdoor tables at the end. Early eaters can take advantage of the pre-7pm offer: two courses plus a drink for £13.

CATHEDRAL ROAD AREA

Le Gallois FRENCH £££

(☎029-2034 1264; 6-10 Romilly Cres; lunch 2/3 courses £20/25, dinner £25/30; ⏰Tue-Sat) One of Cardiff's finest, Le Gallois (the Welshman) majors in an inspirational blend of Welsh produce and French cuisine. The decorous dining room of grey walls, walnut-veneer tables and starched-linen napkins makes sure the focus is on the seasonal menu of half-a-dozen starters and half-a-dozen main courses.

Brava CAFE ££

(71 Pontcanna St; brunch £3-7, dinner £9-15) With local art on the walls and an informal vibe, this cool cafe is our favourite brunch spot on the strength of its eggs Benedict, silky white coffee and attentive service. Tables spill out onto the pavement in summer and in the evening it morphs into a licensed bistro. Brava indeed.

Cameo Club & Bistro BISTRO ££

(☎029-2037 1929; 3 Pontcanna St; mains £13-21; ⏰breakfast & lunch daily, dinner Mon-Sat; ) Once a notorious after-hours drinking den, this private members' club is much more respectable these days, but it's still the hub for Cardiff's arts and media scene. Anyone can now partake in the delicious food offered in its effortlessly hip bistro, but the bar is members-only after 5pm.

Drinking

Cardiff is a prodigious boozing town – Friday and Saturday nights see the city centre invaded by hordes of generally good-humoured, beered-up lads and ladettes tottering from bar to club to kebab shop, whatever the weather (someone fetch that young woman a coat). It's not all as tacky as it sounds – a lively alternative scene, some swish bars and a swath of old-fashioned pubs keep things interesting. Try the local Brains SA (meaning Special Ale, Same Again or Skull Attack depending on how many you've had), brewed by the same family concern since 1882.

CENTRAL CARDIFF

TOP CHOICE **10 Feet Tall** BAR, LIVE MUSIC

(Map p642; www.thisis10feettall.co.uk; 11-12 Church St) The newer sister property to Buffalo Bar, this hip venue over three floors merges a cafe, cocktail and tapas bar, and a live music venue. Chic bar-keeps swish together two-for-one cocktails between 5pm and 8pm, weekdays and all day Sunday.

Buffalo Bar BAR, LIVE MUSIC

(Map p642; www.myspace.com/wearebuffalobar; 11 Windsor Pl) A haven for cool kids about town, the laid-back Buffalo features retro furniture, tasty daytime food, life-affirming cocktails and cool tunes with DJ sets. Upstairs a roster of cutting-edge indie bands take to the stage.

Tafarn Tâf HOSTEL BAR

(53-9 Despenser St) A cool little bar attached to an upmarket backpacker hostel, Tafarn has outdoor tables on a riverside terrace, a big screen for watching all the rugby action and an all-day menu of tasty Welsh snacks.

Pica Pica TAPAS BAR

(Map p642; 15-23 Westgate St) Housed in a series of low-ceiling brick vaults, this cool bar serves tapas, *mezze* and two-for-one cocktails before 8pm.

GAY & LESBIAN CARDIFF

Cardiff has a relaxed and thriving gay and lesbian scene, with a cluster of venues on Charles St (for listings and general information check www.gaycardiff.co.uk). The big event is the annual **Mardi Gras** (www.cardiffmardigras.co.uk), held as part of the Cardiff Festival in late August or early September.

Club X (Map p642; www.clubxcardiff.net; 35 Charles St; admission £4-10; ⌚8pm-6am Fri-Sun) Cardiff's biggest gay club has two dance floors, with a chill-out bar and covered beer garden upstairs.

Exit Club (Map p642; www.exitclubcardiff.com; 48 Charles St) A long-standing, attitude-free bar, with disco and pop filling the two dance floors until the early hours.

Golden Cross (Map p642; 283 Hayes Bridge Rd) One of the oldest pubs in the city and a long-standing gay venue, this Victorian bar retains its handsome stained glass, polished wood and ceramic tiles.

Kings Cross (Map p642; 25 Caroline St) Prominently positioned in the shopping district, KX (as its known) is a stalwart of the gay scene, with DJs, cabaret, karaoke and quiz nights.

CARDIFF BAY

Cwtch BAR

(Map p646; 5 Bute Cres) A cwtch is either a warm, safe place or a cuddle and this little bar, below Jolyon's hotel, is certainly the former and imparts a cosy feeling that's almost as good as the latter. Lethal two-for-one cocktail deals add to the merriment, as do occasional open-mic nights. Sink into a sofa and slip into Cwtch's warm embrace.

Salt BAR

(Map p646; Mermaid Quay) A large, modern, nautical-themed bar with plenty of sofas and armchairs for lounging around and a 1st-floor open-air terrace with a view of the yachts out in the bay.

☆ Entertainment

Pick up a copy of *Buzz,* a free monthly magazine with up-to-date entertainment listings in the city, available from the tourist office and entertainment venues.

Live Music

Most classical companies are now based at the Wales Millennium Centre, but **St David's Hall** (Map p642; ☎029-2087 8444; www.stdavidshallcardiff.co.uk; The Hayes), the national concert hall, hosts the Welsh Proms in July and a full program of performances.

See the Drinking section for bars hosting live bands.

TOP CHOICE **Clwb Ifor Bach** CLUB

(Map p642; ☎029-2023 2199; www.clwb.net; 11 Womanby St) Truly an independent music great, *Y Clwb* has broken many a Welsh band since the early 1980s. It started as a venue for Welsh-language music in Anglophone Cardiff and has survived the Cool Cymru backlash with its reputation as Cardiff's most eclectic and important venue. It now hosts bands performing in many tongues and it's the best place to catch gigs by up-and-coming new acts as well as more established artists.

Barfly CLUB

(Map p642; ☎0844 847 2424; www.barflyclub.com; Kingsway) Part of a UK-wide chain of music clubs, the Cardiff Barfly is a major live-music venue with gigs six nights a week, providing a stage for local talent as well as major bands on tour, and alternative and electronica club nights.

Cinema, Theatre & Comedy

Other companies are based at the Wales Millennium Centre.

Chapter THEATRE, CINEMA

(☎029-2030 4400; www.chapter.org; Market Rd, Canton; @) The city's edgiest arts venue, the Chapter has a varied program of contemporary drama, as well as art exhibitions, arthouse cinema, workshops, alternative theatre and dance performances. To get here from Castle St, cross the river and head west along Cowbridge Rd East. Market Rd is on the right after 0.8 miles.

Sherman Theatre THEATRE

(Map p642; ☎029-2064 6900; www.shermancymru.co.uk; Senghennydd Rd, Cathays) South Wales' leading theatre company, staging a wide range of material from classics and children's theatre to works by new playwrights.

Glee Club COMEDY
(Map p646; ☎0871 472 0400; www.glee.co.uk; Mermaid Quay) A busy comedy club with a well-regarded program of comedy nights.

New Theatre THEATRE
(Map p642; ☎029-2087 8889; www.newtheatrecardiff.co.uk; Park Pl) This restored Edwardian playhouse hosts touring productions, musicals and pantomime.

Sport

Cardiff is the home of Welsh sport. All international rugby and football matches take place at the giant Millennium Stadium.

Cardiff City Stadium FOOTBALL STADIUM
(☎0845 345 1400; www.cardiffcitystadium.co.uk; Leckwith Rd, Canton) Greedy Cardiff couldn't stop at one new stadium – this 26,800-seater opened in 2009. It's home to both the Cardiff Blues (www.cardiffblues.com), Wales' most star-studded professional rugby union club, and Cardiff City Football Club (www.cardiffcityfc.co.uk). Local football fans still hark back to 1927 when the Bluebirds took the English FA Cup out of England for the first (and only) time – Welsh football's equivalent of Owain Glyndŵr's rebellion. They now play in the Championship League. From Castle St head west along Cowbridge Rd East and Wellington St, turn left onto Leckwith Rd and look for the stadium on your left.

SWALEC Stadium CRICKET GROUND
(☎029-2041 9311; www.swalecstadium.co.uk; Sophia Gardens) This is the home of the Glamorgan Cricket Club (www.glamorgancricket.com), the only Welsh club belonging to the England and Wales Cricket Board. Not to be outdone, it also has a fancy, redeveloped stadium. The stadium is on the east bank of the river, opposite Bute Park.

Shopping

If you thought Cardiff's 21st-century makeover was all about political edifices, arts centres and sports stadia, think again. One of the most dramatic developments in the central city is the transformation of the Hayes shopping strip, with the giant, glitzy extension of the St David's shopping centre now eating up its entire eastern flank. Costing £675 million, it's one of the UK's largest. Balancing this ultramodern mall is a historic network of Victorian and Edwardian arcades spreading their dainty tentacles either side of St Mary St.

Craft in the Bay ART, CRAFT
(Map p646; Lloyd George Ave; ⏲10.30am-5.30pm daily) This retail gallery showcases work by contemporary Welsh artists and craftspeople, with a wide range of ceramics, textiles, woodwork, jewellery, glassware, canvases and ironwork.

St David's MALL
(Map p642; www.stdavidscardiff.com; The Hayes; ⏲9.30am-8pm Mon-Fri, 9.30am-6pm Sat, 10.30am-5pm Sun) Immense is the best way to describe this shiny new shopping centre. All of the high-street chains you could name have a home here, along with a smorgasbord of eateries, a cinema multiplex and a large branch of the John Lewis department store, which dominates its south end.

Spillers Records MUSIC
(Map p642; www.spillersrecords.com; Morgan Arcade) The world's oldest record shop, founded in 1894 (when it sold wax phonograph cylinders), Spillers stocks a large range of CDs and vinyl, prides itself on catering to the nonmainstream end of the market (it's especially good on punk), and promotes local talent through in-store gigs.

Royal Arcade & Morgan Arcade ARCADES
(Map p642; www.royalandmorganarcades.co.uk; btwn St Mary St & The Hayes) Cardiff's oldest arcade (1858), the Royal Arcade is home to the excellent, large Wally's Delicatessen and Melin Tregwynt (Welsh woven fabric designs – cushions, blankets, lampshades, scarves, coats, hats). It connects to Morgan Arcade, where you can stop for a coffee break at Plan and visit Spillers Records.

Cardiff Central Market MARKET HALL
(Map p642; www.cardiff-market.co.uk; btwn St Mary St & Trinity St; ⏲8am-5.30pm Mon-Sat) For an age-old shopping experience, head to this Victorian covered market, which is packed with stalls selling everything from fresh fish to mobile phones. Stock up here for a picnic in Bute Park with goodies such as fresh bread, cheese, cold meats, barbecued chicken, cakes and pastries.

Castle Welsh Crafts SOUVENIRS
(Map p642; www.castlewelshcrafts.co.uk; 1 Castle St) If you're after stuffed dragons, lovespoons, Cardiff T-shirts or a suit of armour (£1600 and wearable, if you're interested), this is the city's biggest souvenir shop, conveniently located across the street from the castle.

High St Arcade ARCADE
(Map p642; btwn High & St John Sts) Divergent points of the music spectrum come together in this arcade: traditional music specialist Telynau Vining Harps (sheet music and instruments) and dance-music gurus Catapult 100% Vinyl (DJ equipment and records). Pussy Galore stocks funky women's fashion and sparkly accessories, while Hobo's is great for secondhand 1960s and '70s clothing.

Castle Arcade ARCADE
(Map p642; btwn Castle & High Sts) The most decorative of the city's arcades, it houses Troutmark Books (secondhand and Welsh-language books), Madame Fromage and Cafe Minuet.

Wyndham Arcade ARCADE
(Map p642; btwn St Mary St & Mill Lane) Yet another historic arcade, this one has the gloriously old-fashioned Bear Shop – a specialist tobacconist from a bygone era.

Information

Cardiff Bay tourist office (Map p646; 029-2087 7927; Harbour Dr; 10am-6pm) Known as 'The Tube' and shaped like a squashed aeroplane fuselage, this distinctive construction is more attraction than tourist office per se. It hosts exhibitions, screens information videos and is home to a scale model of the bay area.

Cardiff tourist office (Map p642; 029-2087 3573; www.visitcardiff.com; Old Library, The Hayes; 9.30am-5.30pm Mon-Sat, 10am-4pm Sun; @) Piles of information, an accommodation-booking service and a good stock of OS maps, plus Welsh literature and internet access.

Police (029-2022 2111; King Edward VII Ave)

University Hospital of Wales (029-2074 7747; Heath Park) Located 2 miles north of the Civic Centre, with an accident and emergency department.

Getting There & Away

Air

Cardiff Airport (01446-711111; www.tbicardiffairport.com) is mainly used by budget operators. Aside from summer charters, these are the airlines flying into Cardiff and the destinations they serve:

Aer Lingus (www.aerlingus.com) Cork and Dublin.

bmibaby (www.bmibaby.com) Edinburgh, Jersey, Munich, Murcia and Geneva.

Eastern Airways (www.easternairways.com) Newcastle.

flybe (www.flybe.com) Newcastle, Glasgow, Edinburgh, Jersey, Belfast and Paris.

KLM (www.klm.com) Amsterdam.

Manx2 (www.manx2.com) Anglesey.

Bus

Intercity buses depart from the central bus station on Wood St (Map p642). The **First** (www.firstgroup.com) Shuttle100 service heads regularly between Cardiff and Swansea (peak/off-peak £6.50/5 return, one hour). Other buses head to many Welsh towns, including Caerphilly, Abergavenny and Aberystwyth. **National Express** (www.nationalexpress.com) coach destinations include Swansea (£7.30, one hour), Brecon (£4.10, 1¼ hours), Monmouth (£9.70, 1¼ hours), Chepstow (£5.20, one hour) and London (£22, 3¼ hours).

Car

Depending on where you're coming from, Cardiff is reached from any of exits 29 to 33 from the M4 (which runs from London to northwest of Swansea); it's very well signposted. Cardiff has branches of all the major rental car companies.

Train

Trains from major UK cities arrive at Cardiff Central station (Map p642), on the southern edge of the city centre. **Arriva Trains Wales** (www.arrivatrainswales.co.uk) operates all train services in Wales. Direct services from Cardiff include London Paddington (£43, 2¾ hours), Swansea (£7.80, one hour), Fishguard Harbour (£20, 2¼ hours), Abergavenny (£11, 40 minutes) and Bangor (£40, 4¼ hours).

Getting Around

To/From the Airport

Cardiff airport is 12 miles southwest of Cardiff, past Barry. A shuttle bus (free with train ticket) links the airport terminal to nearby Rhoose Cardiff Airport train station, which has trains into the city (£3.30, 35 minutes); they run hourly Monday to Saturday and every two hours on Sunday. The X91 bus (£3.40, 35 minutes, every two hours) runs from the airport to the central bus station (stand F1). A taxi from the airport to the city centre takes 20 to 30 minutes, depending on traffic, and costs about £26.

Public Transport

Local buses are operated by **Cardiff Bus** (www.cardiffbus.com; single trip/day pass £1.50/3); buy your ticket from the driver (no change given). Free route maps and timetables are available from its Wood St office. **Free B** (www.cardiff.gov.uk/freeb; 8am-8pm Mon-Fri, 8am-6pm Sat, 9am-6pm Sun) buses loop around the inner city, departing every 10 minutes; rides are free.

Frequent trains run from Cardiff Queen St station (Map p642) to Cardiff Bay station (Map p646; £1, four minutes), which is 500m from the harbour. From Cathays or Central stations you have to change at Queen St.

The most appealing way to reach Cardiff Bay is on the **Cardiff Aquabus** (www.cardiffaquabus.com), which stops at jetties from Bute Park to Mermaid Quay along the River Taff (£3 one way, 25 minutes, hourly 10.30am to 4.30pm).

Taxi

Reliable companies include **Capital Cabs** (☎029-2077 7777) and **Dragon Taxis** (☎029-2033 3333).

AROUND CARDIFF

If you're basing yourself in Cardiff there's a diverting selection of day trips to choose between.

Penarth

POP 24,300

Penarth is an old-fashioned seaside resort – stuck somewhere between the 19th and 21st centuries – with a tatty, turquoise Victorian pier staggering out to sea, a trim seafront lined with Victorian terraces, and a mature population wielding Thermos flasks. It's connected to Cardiff Bay by the freshwater lake formed by the erection of the barrage and it now sports a busy marina on the lakefront.

FREE **Turner House Gallery** (☎029-2070 8870; www.ffotogallery.org; Plymouth Rd; ⊙11am-5pm Tue-Sat), a red-brick building a block east of the train station, has changing photographic exhibitions, and runs summer workshops where kids can do stuff like print-making and pinhole photography. From the town centre, it's a five-minute walk through pretty, topiary-filled **Alexandra Gardens** down to the esplanade.

From June to September, **Waverley Excursions** (☎0845 130 4647; www.waverleyexcursions.co.uk) runs cruises on either the *Waverley,* the world's last seagoing paddle steamer, or its sister ship the *Balmoral,* departing from Penarth pier for a trip across the Bristol Channel to Holm Island, Clevedon, Minehead or Ilfracombe.

Cardiff buses 89, 92, 93 and 94 (20 minutes, half-hourly Monday to Saturday, hourly Sunday) run to Penarth, and there are frequent trains from Cardiff Central (£2.10, 20 minutes). There's also a **Waterbus** (☎07940 142409; www.cardiffcats.com), with departures from Penarth (near the barrage) every 45 minutes from 10am to 4pm daily, and Cardiff Bay (Pierhead Pontoons) half an hour later (single/return £2/4, 20 minutes).

Barry

POP 47,900

The massive popularity of the BBC Wales comedy *Gavin and Stacey* has put Barry Island back on the map. Like nearby Penarth, it's a faded seaside resort but with a better beach and a waterfront lined with amusement arcades and fun parks. Fans of the BAFTA (British Academy of Film and TV Arts) award-winning show won't have trou-

FREEWHEELING THROUGH WALES

Two of Wales' most coveted long-distance rides come under the auspices of the NCN, a charity that coordinates over 12,000 miles of cycling and walking paths throughout the UK. **Lôn Las Cymru** (Greenways of Wales/Welsh National Route; NCN routes 8 and 42) is the more demanding of the two. The 254-mile route runs from Holyhead through to Hay-on-Wye, then on to Cardiff via Brecon or Chepstow via Abergavenny. Encompassing three mountain ranges, Snowdonia, the Brecon Beacons and the Cambrian Mountains, there's a fair amount of uphill, low-gear huffing and puffing to endure along the way. That said, each peak promises fantastic views and plenty of downhill, freewheeling delights.

Lôn Geltaidd (Celtic Trail; NCN routes 4 and 47) is a 337-mile route, snaking from Fishguard through the West Wales hills, the Pembrokeshire Coast, the former coalfields of South Wales and ending at Chepstow Castle. The glorious, ever-changing landscape provides a transient backdrop.

Tackle the routes in their entirety, or pick and mix parts in tandem with your pedalling power and scenery wish list. End points are linked with the rail network, so you can make your way back to the start by train.

Around Cardiff

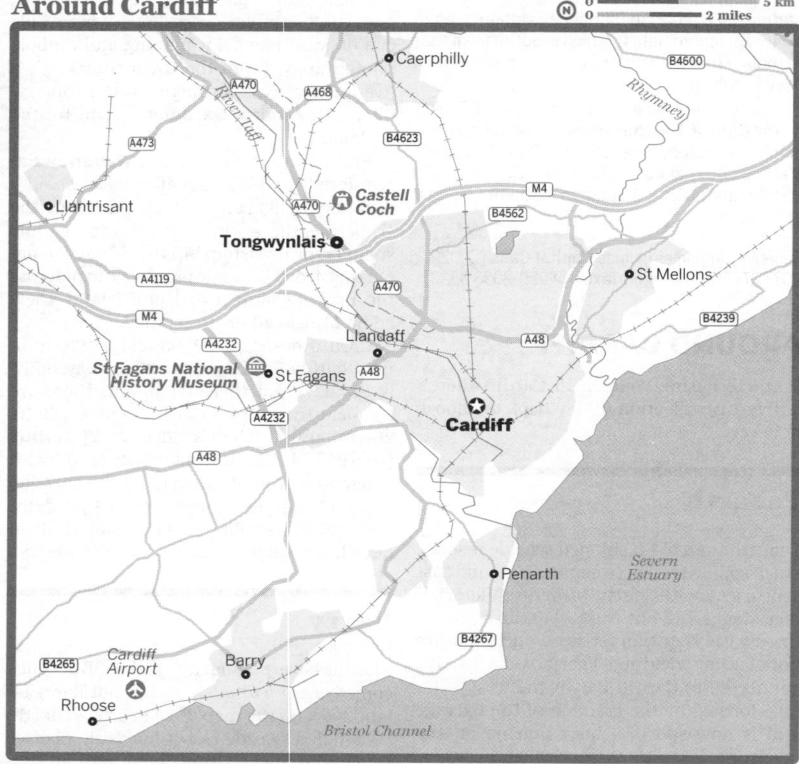

ble picking many of the locations used. The staff at Island Leisure (on the Promenade) are used to pilgrims stopping to pay homage at the booth where Nessa (played in the show by co-writer Ruth Jones) worked. Other sites include Trinity St, where Stacey's mum and Uncle Bryn live, and the Colcot Arms pub (Colcot Rd).

Barry is 8 miles southwest of Cardiff, and Barry Island is well signposted at the south end of the town. It stopped being a real island in the 1880s when it was joined to the mainland with a causeway. There are frequent Cardiff Bus services (route 95, £2.10, one hour) and trains (£2.60, 30 minutes) from the city centre.

St Fagans National History Museum

Historic buildings from all over the country have been dismantled and re-erected in a beautiful rural setting at **St Fagans National History Museum** (☎029-2057 3500; www.museumwales.ac.uk/en/stfagans; admission free, carpark £3; ⏲10am-5pm). More than 40 buildings are on show, including farmhouses of timber and stone, barns, a watermill, a school and an 18th-century Unitarian chapel, with native breeds of livestock grazing in the surrounding fields.

St Fagans Castle is no Johnny-come-lately construction; this medieval fortress with a 16th-century manor house at its heart was donated by the Earl of Plymouth in 1948, along with its extensive formal gardens, forming the basis of the museum. You'll need at least half a day to do the whole complex justice and you could easily spend longer, picnicking in the grounds.

Highlights include a farmhouse dating from 1508, redolent with the smells of old timber, beeswax and wood smoke, and a row of six miners' cottages from Merthyr

Tydfil, each one restored and furnished to represent different periods in the town's history, from the austere minimalism of 1805 to all the mod cons of 1985. It took 20 years to move St Teilo's church here (built 1100 to 1520), stone by stone. It's been restored to its original look, before Protestant whitewash covered the vividly painted interior.

Not original but equally fascinating is the reproduction of three circular Celtic houses based on the archaeological remains of actual buildings.

You can see craftspeople at work in many of the buildings, showing how blankets, clogs, barrels, tools and cider were once made, and the woollen mill sells its own handmade blankets. It's a great place for kids, with special events in the summer.

The indoor galleries hold plenty of interest also, exploring the nature of Welshness through traditional costume, farming implements and the accounts of immigrants. Look for the 'Welsh Not', wooden signs that children were forced to wear as punishment if they had the temerity to speak their native tongue at school.

St Fagans is 5 miles west of central Cardiff; take bus 32 or 320 (25 minutes, hourly) from the bus station.

Castell Coch

Perched atop a thickly wooded crag on the northern fringes of the city is Cardiff Castle's little brother. Fanciful **Castell Coch** (Cadw; ☎029-2081 0101; Tongwynlais; adult/child £3.60/3.20; ⏰9am-5pm Apr-Oct, 9.30am-4pm Mon-Sat & 11am-4pm Sun Nov-Mar) was the summer retreat of the third marquess of Bute and, like Cardiff Castle, was designed by William Burges in gaudy Victorian Gothic style.

Raised on the ruins of Gilbert de Clare's 13th-century Castell Coch (Red Castle), the Butes' Disneyesque holiday home is a monument to high camp. Lady Bute's huge, circular bedroom is pure fantasy – her bed, with crystal globes on the bedposts, sits in the middle beneath an extravagantly decorated and mirrored cupola, with 28 painted panels around the walls depicting monkeys (fashionable at the time, apparently; just plain weird now). The corbels are carved with images of birds nesting or feeding their young, and the washbasin is framed between two castle towers.

Lord Bute's bedroom is small and plain in comparison, but the octagonal drawing room is another hallucinogenic tour de force, the walls painted with scenes from Aesop's fables, the domed ceiling a flurry of birds and stars, and the fireplace topped with figures depicting the three ages of men and women. The tower to the right of the entrance houses exhibits explaining the castle's history.

Stagecoach buses 26 and 132 (30 minutes) stop at Tongwynlais, a 10-minute walk to the castle. Bus 26 continues to Caerphilly Castle, and the two can be combined in a day trip. Bus 26A (four daily Monday to Friday) stops right at the castle gates.

Caerphilly (Caerffili)

POP 31,000

The town of Caerphilly – now almost a suburb of Cardiff – guards the entrance to the Rhymney valley to the north of the capital. Its name is synonymous with a popular variety of hard, slightly crumbly white cheese

THE BIG CHEESE

Any festival that includes a Cheese Olympics and a Tommy Cooper Tent has got to be worth a look. Each year, at the end of July, Caerphilly welcomes more than 70,000 people to the **Big Cheese** (www.caerphilly.gov.uk/bigcheese; admission free), three days of family-oriented fun and games that offers everything from fireworks to falconry, comedy acts to cheese-tasting, along with medieval battle re-enactments, food and craft stalls, archery demonstrations, live music and a traditional funfair.

The Cheese Olympics are held Friday evening, and include cheese-throwing, -rolling and -stacking events. The Tommy Cooper Tent – named after the much-loved British comedian, who was born in Caerphilly and died in 1984 – stages comedy acts, including a Tommy Cooper tribute act. A statue to Cooper, in his trademark fez and with a rabbit at his feet, overlooks the castle near the tourist office.

(similar to cheddar, but saltier) that originated in the surrounding area.

You could be forgiven for thinking that **Caerphilly Castle** (Cadw; ☎029-2088 3143; adult/child £3.60/3.20; ⌚9am-5pm Apr-Oct, 9.30am-4pm Mon-Sat & 11am-4pm Sun Nov-Mar) – with its profusion of towers and crenellations reflected in a duck-filled lake – was a film set rather than an ancient monument. Indeed, it often *is* used as a film set, but it is also one of Britain's finest examples of a 13th-century fortress with water defences.

Unusually, Caerphilly was never a royal castle. Most of the construction was completed between 1268 and 1271 by the powerful English baron Gilbert de Clare (1243–95), Lord Marcher of Glamorgan, in response to the threat of Prince Llywelyn ap Gruffydd, prince of Gwynedd (and the last Welsh Prince of Wales). In the 13th century Caerphilly was state-of-the-art, being one of the earliest castles to use lakes, bridges and a series of concentric fortifications for defence; to reach the inner court you had to overcome no fewer than three drawbridges, six portcullises and five sets of double gates.

Edward I's subsequent campaign against the Welsh princes put an end to Llywelyn's ambitions and Caerphilly's short-lived spell on the front line came to an end without ever tasting battle; the famous leaning tower at the southeast corner is a result of subsidence rather than sabotage. In the early 14th century it was remodelled as a grand residence and the magnificent Great Hall was adapted for entertaining, but from the mid-14th century onward the castle began to fall into ruin.

Much of what you see results from restoration from 1928 to 1939 by the fourth marquess of Bute; work continued after the state bought the castle in 1950. The Great Hall was given a splendid wooden ceiling in the 19th century and the Gothic windows were restored in the 1960s; it is now used to host special events. On the south dam platform you can see reconstructions of medieval siege weapons; they are working models and lob stone projectiles into the lake during battle re-enactments.

You can buy Caerphilly cheese from the **tourist office** (www.visitcaerphilly.com; Twyn Sq; ⌚10am-5.30pm), just east of the castle, itself clearly visible 500m north of Caerphilly train station (along Cardiff Rd). The easiest way to reach Caerphilly from Cardiff is by train (£3.30, 19 minutes), or you can catch Stagecoach buses 26A and B (45 minutes).

Pembrokeshire & South Wales

Includes »

SOUTHEAST WALES . 659
Lower Wye Valley . . . 660
SWANSEA & THE GOWER 663
Mumbles (Y Mwmbwls) 667
Gower Peninsula (Y Gŵyr). 668
CARMARTHENSHIRE (SIR GAERFYRDDIN). 670
PEMBROKESHIRE (SIR BENFRO) 673
Pembroke (Penfro) . .677
St Davids (Tyddewi). .679
Preseli Hills 686

Best Places to Eat

» Crown at Whitebrook (p660)

» Llys Meddyg (p685)

» Angel Vaults (p672)

Best Places to Stay

» Llys Meddyg (p685)

» Morgans (p665)

» Tides Reach Guest House (p667)

Why Go?

Stretching from historic border town Chepstow in the east, via the industrial heritage of the valleys, through to the jagged Pembrokeshire coast in the west, South Wales really packs it in. Hugging the border, the Wye Valley is the birthplace of British tourism. For more than 200 years people have come to explore this tranquil waterway and its winding, wooded vale, where the majestic ruins of Tintern Abbey have inspired generations of poets and artists. In contrast, Blaenavon provides a stark reminder of Wales' contribution to the Industrial Revolution. Reborn Swansea offers something approaching big city sophistication; the Gower Peninsula revels in its coastal beauty; while the fecund heartland of rural Carmarthenshire offers country comfort in abundance. The biggest draw in the south, however, remains Pembrokeshire, where almost 200 miles of magical shoreline has been declared a national park, delineated by craggy cliffs, golden sands, chocolate-box villages and seaside resorts.

When to Go?

Average daily temperatures scrape above 10°C in March – spend St David's Day in the saint's city and look out for early daffodils. In May, Fishguard serenades summer with folk music, while Swansea Bay kicks off its Summer Festival, which continues until September. Chepstow and Fishguard both have festivals in June, which is the driest month. July and August are the only months with average highs over 20°C, making them the best for a beach holiday.

South Wales Highlights

1 Strolling among romantic ruins on the banks of the Wye at **Tintern Abbey** (p660)

2 Experiencing World Heritage industrial sites and world-class cheese at **Blaenavon** (p661)

3 Using whiz-bang interactive displays to trace Wales' industrial heritage at Swansea's **National Waterfront Museum** (p663)

4 Watching the surf break against the great dragon at **Rhossili Bay** (p668)

5 Gazing up at **Carreg Cennen Castle** (p670), Wales' most dramatically positioned fortress

6 Viewing Norman Foster's intriguing dome, signalling a monumental garden in the making at **National Botanic Garden of Wales** (p671)

7 Exploring **St Davids** (p679), Wales' most beguiling little city

8 Entering a Celtic village brought back to life on its original foundations at **Castell Henllys Iron Age Fort** (p686)

SOUTHEAST WALES

You need only ponder the preponderance of castles to realise that the pleasantly rural county of Monmouthshire was once a wild frontier. The Norman Marcher lords kept stonemasons extremely busy, erecting mighty fortifications to keep the unruly Welsh at bay. The River Wye forms the Wales–England border before emptying into the River Severn below Chepstow. Much of it is designated an Area of Outstanding Natural Beauty (AONB; www.wyevalleyaonb.org.uk), famous for its limestone gorges and dense broadleaved woodland.

To the west, the serried South Wales Valleys were once the heart of industrial Wales. Although the coal, iron and steel industries have withered, the valleys still evoke a world of tight-knit working-class communities, male voice choirs and rows of neat terraced houses set amid a scarred, coal-blackened landscape. Today, the region is fighting back against decline by creating a tourist industry based on industrial heritage.

Chepstow (Cas Gwent)

POP 14,200

Chepstow is an attractive market town nestled in a great S-bend in the River Wye, with a splendid Norman castle perched dramatically on a cliff above the water. The town is also home to one of Britain's best-known racecourses.

The town was first developed as a base for the Norman conquest of southeast Wales, later prospering as a port for the timber and wine trades. As river-borne commerce gave way to the railways, Chepstow's importance diminished to reflect its name, which means 'marketplace' in Old English.

Sights

Chepstow Castle CASTLE

(Bridge St; adult/child £3.60/3.20; 9am-5pm Apr-Oct, 9.30am-4pm Mon-Sat, 11am-4pm Sun Nov-Mar) Magnificent Chepstow Castle perches atop a limestone cliff overhanging the river, guarding the main river crossing from England into South Wales. It is one of the oldest castles in Britain (building began in 1067) and the impressive Great Tower retains its original Norman architecture.

Chepstow Museum MUSEUM

(Bridge St; admission free; 11am-5pm Mon-Sat, 2-5pm Sun;) Housed in an 18th-century town house across the road from the castle, this small, child-friendly museum covers Chepstow's industrial and social history.

Sleeping & Eating

Castle View Hotel HOTEL, GASTROPUB ££

(01291-620349; www.hotelchepstow.co.uk; 16 Bridge St; s/d from £55/77, mains £9-17) This 300-year-old, castle-gazing hotel serves up solid, meaty, country fare – much of it sozzled in vodka or wine-based sauces. Nor is it short on atmosphere, heightened in the evening when candles flicker in moody corners and the young owner is in host-with-the-most mode. Most rooms are small and the floors are creaky, but there's plenty of character.

TOP CHOICE **Mythos!** GREEK ££

(01291-627222; Welsh St; mains £11-16; noon-2am Mon-Sat, 5pm-midnight Sun) Exposed beams, stone walls and dramatic lighting make this lively Greek bar and restaurant memorable, but it's the authentic, delicious food that justifies that pretentious exclamation mark in the name: tzatziki, grilled haloumi, spanakopita (spinach-filled pastries), lamb and chicken souvlaki, moussaka – served as meze or main-sized portions.

Boat Inn PUB £

(The Back; mains £3-6) A great riverside pub strewn with nautical knick-knacks and a particularly snug 'snug', the Boat dishes up better-than-average pub grub and a good menu of daily specials.

Information

Tourist office (01291-623772; Castle car park, Bridge St; 9.30am-5.30pm Apr-Oct, 9.30am-3.30pm Nov-Mar) Ask about local walking trails, such as the Tintern & Return path.

Getting There & Away

BUS Route 69 links Chepstow with Monmouth (40 minutes) via Tintern (15 minutes). **National Express** (www.nationalexpress.com) coach destinations include London (£22, three hours), Cardiff (£5.20, one hour), Swansea (£12, two hours), Carmarthen (£19, 2¼ hours), Tenby (£24, three hours) and Pembroke (£22, 3¼ hours).

TRAIN There are direct **Arriva Trains Wales** (www.arrivatrainswales.co.uk) services from Cardiff (£7.30, 40 minutes) and Gloucester (£7.40, one hour).

Lower Wye Valley

The A466 road follows the snaking, steep-sided valley of the River Wye from Chepstow to Monmouth, passing through the straggling village of Tintern. It's a beautiful drive, rendered particularly mysterious when a twilight mist rises from the river and shrouds the illuminated ruins of **Tintern Abbey** (www.cadw.wales.gov.uk; adult/child £3.60/3.20; ⌚9am-5pm Apr-Oct, 9.30am-4pm Mon-Sat, 11am-4pm Sun Nov-Mar; P). Founded in 1131 by the Cistercian order, this sprawling monastic complex and its riverside setting have inspired poets and artists through the centuries. The huge abbey church was built between 1269 and 1301, the stone shell of which remains surprisingly intact; the finest feature is tracery that once contained the magnificent west windows.

There are plenty of possibilities for riverside walks around Tintern. One of the best begins at the old railway bridge just upstream from the abbey, and leads up to the **Devil's Pulpit**, a limestone crag on the east side of the river with a spectacular view over the abbey (2.5 miles round trip).

If you take the narrow country lane along the west bank of the Wye, a mile north of the turn-off where the A466 crosses the river into England, and 5 miles north of the abbey, you'll find the Michelin-starred **Crown at Whitebrook** (☎01600-860254; www.crownatwhitebrook.co.uk; Whitebrook; 2-/3-course lunch £25/28, 3-/6-/9-course dinner £48/55/70; ⌚closed Sun dinner). Its elegant dining room and riverside setting may conspire to ignite romance in the hardest of hearts, while the fine cuisine (combining fusion flavours with game meats) may melt them completely. If you don't fancy driving afterwards, or the romantic ambience has worked its magic, get a room (doubles £125 to £150).

Monmouth (Trefynwy)

POP 9500

The compact market town of Monmouth sits at the confluence of the Rivers Wye and Monnow, and has hopped in and out of Wales over the centuries as the border shifted back and forth. It's famous as the birthplace of Henry V and the home of Charles Stewart Rolls, co-founder of Rolls-Royce. In modern times Monmouth's main claim to fame is the nearby Rockfield recording studio, which has produced a string of hit albums for the likes of Oasis, Coldplay and Super Furry Animals.

Monmouth's main drag, Monnow St, starts at car-free **Monnow Bridge**, the UK's only complete example of a medieval fortified bridge. It was built in 1270, although much of what you see now was restored in 1705. Before you cross into town, it's worth poking your head into **St Thomas the Martyr's Church**. Parts of it date from around 1180 – there's an im-

COOL CYMRU

With such a small population and a culture that's been overshadowed by England for centuries, it's something of a surprise that Wales has produced plenty of musical maestros who have hit the big time. Everyone knows perma-tanned warbler Tom Jones, who, together with the likes of Shirley Bassey, has kept Welsh pop on the map since the 1960s.

Along with Lou Reed, Valleys-born John Cale was responsible for the experimental edge that made the Velvet Underground one of the most influential bands of all time. He's gone on to become a respected solo performer and producer.

In the 1980s the Alarm emerged as Wales' leading act, with a string of U2-inspired rock ballads to its name. Since then major names have included Manic Street Preachers, Catatonia, Stereophonics, Gorky's Zygotic Mynci, Charlotte Church, Jem, Christopher Rees, Bullet For My Valentine, Kate Le Bon, Duffy and Lostprophets. The genre-defying Super Furry Animals produced the biggest-selling Welsh-language album of all time, the dreamy *Mwng*.

At the time of writing Marina & the Diamonds were storming the charts with their brand of New Wave–influenced pop, while indie group Kids In Glass Houses were splashing around in the lower reaches. The Welsh Wave shows no signs of breaking anytime soon.

pressive Norman Romanesque arch, and pews and a gallery fashioned out of dark wood.

The meagre remains of **Monmouth Castle** (Castle Hill; no admission), where in 1397 Henry V was born, are set back from Monnow St. Except for the great tower, it was dismantled in the 17th century and the stone used to build **Great Castle House** next door, now headquarters of the Royal Monmouthshire Regiment.

Just across the Monnow Bridge from Monmouth town centre, **Monnow Bridge Camping** (☎01600-714004; Drybridge St; sites £11) has a quiet riverside location.

ℹ Information

Tourist office (☎01600-713899; www.visitwyevalley.com; Priory St; ⏰9.30am-3.30pm Mon-Sat)

ℹ Getting There & Away

Bus route 69 runs along the Wye Valley from Monmouth to Chepstow (40 minutes) via Tintern (35 minutes) and route 83 heads to Abergavenny (45 minutes) via Raglan (20 minutes). National Express coaches head to Monmouth from Birmingham (£20, 1½ hours) and Cardiff (£9.70, 1¼ hours).

Skenfrith

A chocolate-box village of stone buildings set around a hefty castle and ancient church and skirted by the River Monnow, Skenfrith encapsulates the essence of the Monmouthshire countryside. **Skenfrith Castle** was built around 1228 by Hubert de Burgh on the site of earlier Norman fortifications. Its keep and walls remain reasonably intact and there are no barriers to prevent you entering and picnicking on the central lawn. Nearby, a squat tower announces 750-year-old **St Bridget's Church**, accessed by a low wooden door with a foot-high step.

The riverside village pub, **The Bell at Skenfrith** (☎01600-750235; www.skenfrith.co.uk; r £110-220; P 📶), has had a gastronomic makeover and is now an esteemed restaurant serving upmarket country fare (mains £15 to £19). Upstairs there are elegant rooms that marry an antique feel with contemporary comfort. The Bell produces its own walk pamphlets (50p) – one route leads over the English border to **Garway Church**, which is adorned with swastikas and mason's marks from its Knights Templar past.

Skenfrith is 8 miles northwest of Monmouth via the B4233, B4347 and B4521. There's no public transport.

Blaenavon (Blaenafon)

POP 6000

Of all the valley towns that were decimated by the demise of heavy industry, the one-time coal and iron town of Blaenavon shows the greenest shoots of regrowth, helped in large part by the awarding of Unesco World Heritage site status in 2000 to its conglomeration of industrial sites. Its proximity to Brecon Beacons National Park and Abergavenny doesn't do it any harm either.

Blaenavon is an interesting town to visit, but not necessarily to stay in; the nearest recommended accommodation is in Abergavenny.

Sights & Activities

FREE **Blaenavon World Heritage Centre** INFORMATION CENTRE
(☎01495-742333; www.world-heritage-blaenavon.org.uk; Church Rd; ⏰9am-4pm Tue-Sun) Housed in an artfully converted old school, this centre houses a cafe, tourist office, gallery, gift shop and, more importantly, excellent interactive, audiovisual displays which explore the industrial heritage of the region.

RAGLAN CASTLE

Magnificent **Raglan Castle** (www.cadw.wales.gov.uk; adult/child £3/2.60; ⏰9am-5pm Apr-Oct, 9.30am-4pm Mon-Sat, 11am-4pm Sun Nov-Mar) was the last great medieval castle to be built in Wales and was designed more as a swaggering declaration of wealth and power than a defensive fortress. A sprawling complex built of dusky pink sandstone, its centrepiece is the lavish Great Tower, a hexagonal keep ringed by a moat, which was badly damaged during the Civil Wars of the 1640s.

Bus 83 from Monmouth (20 minutes) and Abergavenny (25 minutes) stops in Raglan; it's a five-minute walk to the castle.

Big Pit: National Coal Museum MINE, MUSEUM
(☎01495-790311; www.museumwales.ac.uk; admission free; ⌚9.30am-5pm, guided tours 10am-3.30pm) Big Pit provides an opportunity to descend 90m into a real coal mine in the company of an ex-miner guide and get a taste of what life was like for those who worked here. It's cold underground, so take extra layers, and wear sturdy shoes. Children must be at least 1m tall.

Blaenavon Ironworks IRONWORKS, MUSEUM
(www.cadw.wales.gov.uk; North St; admission free; ⌚10am-5pm Apr-Oct, 9.30am-4pm Fri & Sat, 11am-4pm Sun Nov-Mar) When it was completed in 1788, Blaenavon Ironworks was one of the most advanced in the world. Today the site is one of the best-preserved of all the Industrial Revolution ironworks. You can follow the whole process of production, from the charging of the furnaces to the casting of molten iron. Also on display are the ironworkers' tiny terraced cottages.

Blaenavon Cheddar Co CHEESE, TOURS
(www.chunkofcheese.co.uk; 80 Broad St; ⌚10am-5pm Mon-Sat) The award-winning cheese company is both a champion for the town and evidence of its gradual resurgence. The shop stocks their range of handmade cheese, some of which are matured down in the Big Pit mineshaft. The Pwll Mawr is particularly good, having won a bronze in the British cheese awards, but for extra kick try the chilli- and ale-laced Dragon's Breath. It also stocks a range of Welsh speciality ales, wines and whisky. The same crew arranges guided **walking and mountain-biking tours** (walks per person from £2.50) for all ability levels and offers **bike hire** (half-/full day £8/15).

Pontypool & Blaenavon Railway STEAM TRAIN
(☎01495-792263; www.pontypool-and-blaenavon.co.uk; adult/child £4.50/2.25; ⌚check online for hours) Built to haul coal and passengers, this railway has been restored by local volunteers, allowing you to catch a steam train from the town centre to Big Pit and on to Whistle Halt, the highest train station in England and Wales (396m).

Getting There & Away

Buses X24 and 30 head here from Newport (50 minutes). See also Beacons Bus B15 (boxed text, p696).

Caerleon

POP 8700

After the Romans invaded Britain in AD 43, they controlled their new territory through a network of forts and military garrisons. The top tier of military organisation was the legionary fort, of which there were only three in Britain – at Eboracum (York), Deva (Chester) and Isca (Caerleon).

Caerleon ('fort of the legion') was the headquarters of the elite 2nd Augustan Legion for more than 200 years, from AD 75 until the end of the 3rd century. It wasn't just a military camp but a purpose-built township some 9 miles in circumference, complete with a 6000-seat amphitheatre and a state-of-the-art Roman baths complex. Today it is one of the largest and most important Roman settlements in Britain. The Cadw guidebook *Caerleon Roman Fortress* (£3.50) is worth buying for its maps, sketches and aerial views, which help to visualise the settlement among the distractions of the modern town.

Begin with a visit to the excellent **National Roman Legion Museum** (www.museumwales.ac.uk/en/roman; High St; admission free; ⌚10am-5pm Mon-Sat, 2-5pm Sun), which displays a host of intriguing Roman artefacts, from jewellery to armour and teeth to tombstones, and shows what life was like for Roman soldiers in one of the remotest corners of Empire.

Head next for the **Roman Baths** (www.cadw.wales.gov.uk; High St; admission free; ⌚9.30am-5pm Apr-Oct, 9.30am-5pm Mon-Sat, 11am-4pm Sun Nov-Mar; P), a block to the southeast. Parts of the outdoor swimming pool, apodyterium (changing room) and frigidarium (cold room) are on show under a protective roof, and give some idea of the scale of the place.

Broadway, the side street opposite the museum, leads to a park on the left where you'll find the turf-covered terraces of the **Roman Amphitheatre** (admission free; ⌚9.30am-5pm). The oval structure is the only fully excavated Roman amphitheatre in Britain; it lay just outside the old Roman city walls. Follow the signs on the other side of the road to see the foundations of the **Barracks**.

Two miles to the southeast of Caerleon, in the village of Christchurch, the **Old Rectory** (☎01633-430700; www.the-oldrectory.co

.uk; s/d £50/75; P) offers a warm welcome and three luxurious rooms with views over the estuary to England.

Caerleon is 4 miles northeast of Newport. Buses 27D, 28A-E, 28X, 29 and 29B (15 minutes, four per hour) run from Newport bus station to Caerleon High St.

SWANSEA & THE GOWER

Wales' second-largest city sprawls along the 5-mile sweep of Swansea Bay, ending to the southwest in the smart seaside suburb of Mumbles at the head of the beautiful Gower Peninsula.

Swansea (Abertawe)

POP 229,100

Dylan Thomas called Swansea an 'ugly, lovely town', and that remains a fair description today. It's currently in the grip of a Cardiff-esque bout of regeneration that's slowly transforming the drab, postwar city centre into something worthy of its natural assets. A new marina, national museum, waterpark, architecturally tricksy footbridge and transport centre have already opened and plans are afoot to bulldoze and rebuild the central shopping precinct and create a fitting seaside boulevard out of shabby Oystermouth Rd.

Swansea makes up for its visual shortcomings with a visceral charm. A hefty student population takes to the city's bars with enthusiasm and a newly minted restaurant scene has emerged from among all the Chinese and Indian takeaways.

Swansea's Welsh name, Abertawe, describes its location at the mouth of the Tawe, where the river empties into Swansea Bay. The Vikings named the area Sveins Ey (Swein's Island), probably referring to the sandbank in the river mouth.

The Normans built a castle here, but Swansea didn't really get into its stride until the Industrial Revolution, when it developed into an important copper-smelting centre. Ore was first shipped in from Cornwall, across the Bristol Channel, but by the 19th century it was arriving from Chile, Cuba and the USA, in return for Welsh coal.

By the 20th century the city's industrial base had declined, although Swansea's oil refinery and smaller factories were still judged a worthy target by the Luftwaffe, which devastated the city centre in 1941. It was rebuilt as a rather soulless retail development in the 1960s, '70s and '80s, and now has another date with destruction, courtesy of a wrecking ball.

Sights & Activities

A small pocket of the central city around Wind St and Castle Sq escaped the wartime bombing and retains a remnant of Georgian and Victorian Swansea as well as the ruins of 14th-century **Swansea Castle** (closed to the public). The castle was mostly destroyed by Cromwell in 1647, but had a brief lease of life as a prison in the 19th century.

TOP CHOICE **National Waterfront Museum** MUSEUM

(www.waterfrontmuseum.co.uk; South Dock Marina; admission free; ⌚10am-5pm) Housed in a 1901 dockside warehouse with a striking glass and slate extension, the museum's 15 hands-on galleries explore Wales' industrial history and the impact of industrialisation on its people, from 1750 to the present day, making much use of interactive computer screens and audiovisual presentations. The effect can be a bit overwhelming, but there is a lot of interesting stuff here, enough to occupy several hours.

Swansea Museum MUSEUM

(www.swanseaheritage.net; Victoria Rd; admission free; ⌚10am-5pm Tue-Sun) It would be hard to find a more complete contrast to the Waterfront Museum – Dylan Thomas referred to it as 'the museum which should have *been* in a museum'. Founded in 1834, it remains charmingly low-tech, from the eccentric Cabinet of Curiosities to the glass cases of archaeological finds from Gower caves. Pride of place goes to the Mummy of Hor.

FREE **Dylan Thomas Centre** MUSEUM

(www.swansea.gov.uk/dtc; Somerset Pl; ⌚10am-4.30pm) Housed in the former Guildhall, this centre contains an absorbing exhibition on the Swansea-born poet's life and work. Aside from the collection of memorabilia, what really brings his work to life is a series of recordings, including the booming baritone of Richard Burton performing *Under Milk Wood* and Thomas himself reading *Do Not Go Gentle Into That Good Night,* the celebrated paean to his dying father.

Swansea

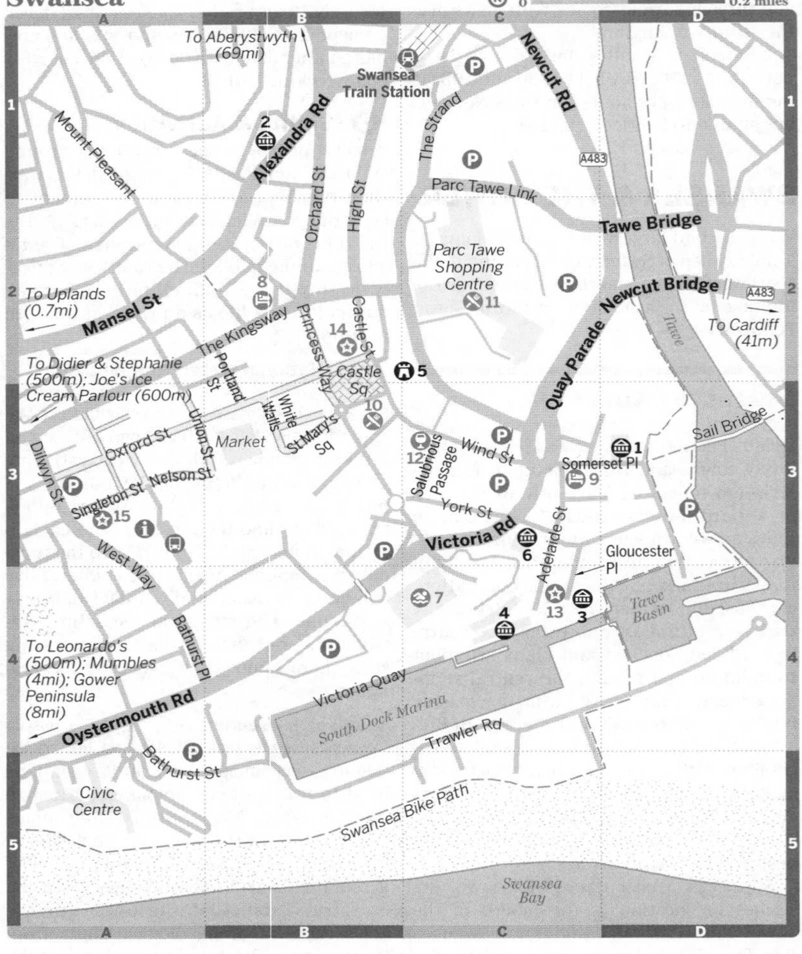

Glynn Vivian Art Gallery GALLERY

(www.swansea.gov.uk/glynnvivian; Alexandra Rd; admission free; ⌚10am-5pm Tue-Sun) Housed in an elegant Italianate building, the city's main gallery displays a wide range of Welsh art (Richard Wilson, Gwen John, Ceri Richards, Shani Rhys James) alongside works by Claude Monet and Lucien Freud and a large ceramics collection.

FREE **Egypt Centre** MUSEUM

(www.swan.ac.uk/egypt; Taliesin Arts Centre, Singleton Park, Mumbles Rd; ⌚10am-4pm Tue-Sat) Swansea University is in the suburb of Sketty, halfway between the city centre and the Mumbles, and possesses the UK's biggest collection of Egyptian antiquities outside the British Museum. It displays a fascinating collection of everyday ancient Egyptian artefacts, ranging from a 4000-year-old razor and cosmetics trays to a mummified crocodile.

LC2 AQUATIC CENTRE

(www.thelcswansea.com; Oystermouth Rd; waterpark adult/child £7/3; ⌚6.30am-10pm Mon-Fri, 8am-9pm Sat & Sun, waterpark 4-9pm Mon-Fri, 9am-8pm Sat & Sun) The Marine Quarter's new £32-million leisure centre includes a gym and a 9m indoor climbing wall, but

Swansea

Sights

1 Dylan Thomas Centre D3
2 Glynn Vivian Art Gallery B1
3 Mission Gallery C4
4 National Waterfront Museum C4
5 Swansea Castle C2
6 Swansea Museum C3

Activities, Courses & Tours

7 LC2 .... C4

Sleeping

8 Dragon Hotel B2
9 Morgans C3

Eating

10 Chelsea Restaurant B3
11 Joe's Ice Cream Parlour C2

Drinking

12 No Sign Bar C3

Entertainment

13 Dylan Thomas Theatre C4
14 Monkey B2
15 Swansea Grand Theatre A3

best of all is the waterpark, complete with a wave pool, water slides and the world's first indoor surfing ride.

Mission Gallery GALLERY
(www.missiongallery.co.uk; Gloucester Pl; admission free; 11am-5pm) Set in a converted 19th-century seamen's chapel, it stages Swansea's most striking exhibitions of contemporary art, as well as selling glassware, ceramics, jewellery and art magazines.

Festivals & Events

Swansea Bay Summer Festival SUMMER FESTIVAL
(www.swanseabayfestival.net) From May to September, the waterfront is taken over by shows, fun fairs, carnivals, music and exhibitions.

Swansea Bay Film Festival FILM FESTIVAL
(www.swanseafilmfestival.com) Held over a week in May, includes workshops and screenings.

Escape into the Park DANCE MUSIC
(www.escapefestival.com) Wales' biggest outdoor dance music festival, a one-day mid-June event featuring big-name DJs in Singleton Park.

Swansea Festival of Music and the Arts ARTS FESTIVAL
(www.swanseafestival.org) Concerts, drama, lectures and exhibitions, staged during the first three weeks of October.

Dylan Thomas Festival POETRY, PERFORMANCES
(www.dylanthomas.com) Poetry readings, talks, films and performances; held from 27 October (Thomas' birthday) to 9 November (the date he died).

Sleeping

TOP CHOICE **Morgans** HOTEL ££
(01792-484848; www.morganshotel.co.uk; Somerset Pl; r £65-250; P @) The city's first boutique hotel, set in the gorgeous red-brick and Portland stone former Ports Authority building, Morgans combines historic elegance with contemporary design, and a high pamper factor – Egyptian cotton bed linen, suede curtains, big bathrobes, flatscreen TVs. An annexe across the road has lower ceilings but similar standards.

Crescent Guest House B&B ££
(01792-465782; www.crescentguesthouse.co.uk; 132 Eaton Cres, Uplands; r £65-70; wi-fi) The Crescent has a great location, perched on a slope with great views across the rooftops to Swansea Bay. The bedrooms are immaculate, with an antique feel (without being chintzy), in keeping with the house.

Mirador Town House B&B ££
(01792-466976; www.themirador.co.uk; 14 Mirador Cres, Uplands; s/d from £59/69) Kooky in the extreme, all seven B&B rooms are elaborately themed – Roman, Mediterranean, African, Spanish, Egyptian, Oriental, French – with murals on the walls and sometimes the ceilings as well.

Christmas Pie B&B B&B ££
(01792-480266; www.christmaspie.co.uk; 2 Mirador Cres, Uplands; s/d from £48/75; P @ wi-fi) The name suggests something warm and comforting, and this suburban villa does not disappoint – three tastefully decorated en suite bedrooms, fresh fruit and an out-of-the-ordinary, vegetarian-friendly breakfast selection.

Dragon Hotel HOTEL ££
(01792-657141; www.dragon-hotel.co.uk; Kingsway Circle; r £69-129; P pool) This 1960s city-centre hotel has been given an expensive upgrade, with dragon-red carpets, orange backlighting and well-turned-out bedrooms. There's also a good-sized gym and pool.

Leonardo's B&B £
(☎01792-470163; www.leonardosguesthouse.co.uk; 380 Oystermouth Rd; s/d from £23/40;) Leonardo's is the best in the long strip of budget seafront guest houses on Oystermouth Rd, with small rooms in bright, sunny colours. Five of the nine bedrooms enjoy views over Swansea Bay and some have en suites.

Eating

The main eat streets are Wind St and St Helen St, with a range of pubs, cafes and restaurants to cater to all budgets and appetites.

TOP CHOICE **Joe's Ice Cream Parlour** ICE CREAM £
(85 St Helen's Rd; noon-7.30pm) For an ice-cream sundae or a cone, locals love Joe's – a Swansea institution founded in 1922 by Joe Cascarini, son of immigrants from Italy's Abruzzi mountains. There are also branches at **Parc Tawe Shopping Centre** (Park Tawe Link; 10.30am-6pm) and **Mumbles** (524 Mumbles Rd; 11am-5.30pm).

Chelsea Restaurant SEAFOOD ££
(☎01792-464068; 17 St Mary's St; mains £12-19, 2-/3-course lunch £13/17; Mon-Sat) Perfect for a romantic liaison, this elegant little dining room is discreetly tucked away behind the frenzy of Wind St. Seafood's the focus and blackboard specials are chalked up daily. While the name sounds flash, the prices aren't too bad: a £20 three-course set dinner is offered from Monday to Thursday.

Didier & Stephanie FRENCH ££
(☎01792-655603; 56 St Helen's Rd, Uplands; mains £16-19; Tue-Sat) Swansea's top restaurant is an intimate and relaxed place, run by the Gallic duo with their names on the door. It's well regarded for its French cooking, refined setting and attentive service, and it offers good-value set menus at lunch (two/three courses £14/17).

Drinking & Entertainment

In a city synonymous with Dylan Thomas you'd expect some hard drinking to take place…and you'd be right. Swansea's main boozing strip is Wind St (pronounced to rhyme with 'blind', as in drunk) and on weekends it can be a bit of a zoo, full of generally good-natured alcopop-fuelled teens teetering around on high heels.

Buzz magazine (free from the tourist office and bars around town) has its finger on the pulse of the local scene.

TOP CHOICE **No Sign Bar** PUB, MUSIC
(56 Wind St) Once frequented by Dylan Thomas (it appears as the Wine Vaults in his story *The Followers*), the No Sign stands out as the only vaguely traditional bar left on Wind St. On weekends there's live music downstairs in the Vault. The window seats, looking out over the acres of goose-bumped flesh on the street outside, offer a frisson of schadenfreude.

Uplands Tavern PUB, MUSIC
(www.myspace.com/uplandstavern; 42 Uplands Cres) Yet another Thomas hang-out, Uplands still serves a quiet daytime pint in the Dylan Thomas snug. Come nightfall and it turns into a different beast altogether as the hub of the city's live music scene.

Monkey CAFE-BAR, MUSIC
(www.monkeycafe.co.uk; 13 Castle St) An organic, veg-friendly cafe-bar by day, with chunky tables, big sofas, modern art and cool tunes, this funky little venue transforms after dark into Swansea's best alternative club, hosting DJs, live musicians, burlesque and salsa upstairs.

Swansea Grand Theatre THEATRE
(☎01792-475715; www.swanseagrand.co.uk; Singleton St) The city's largest theatre stages a mixed line-up of ballet, opera, musicals, theatre, pantomimes and a regular comedy club.

Taliesin Arts Centre ARTS CENTRE
(☎01792-602060; www.taliesinartscentre.co.uk; Singleton Park) Part of the University of Wales, Swansea, this vibrant arts centre features live music, theatre, dance and film.

Dylan Thomas Theatre THEATRE
(☎01792-473238; www.dylanthomastheatre.org.uk; Gloucester Pl) Home to Swansea Little Theatre, an amateur dramatic group of which DT was once a member, the company stages a wide repertoire of plays, including regular performances of your man's *Under Milk Wood*.

Information

Morriston Hospital (☎01792-702222; Heol Maes Eglwys, Morriston) Accident and emergency department, 5 miles north of centre.

Police (☎01792-456999; Grove Pl)

Swansea Tourist Office (☎01792-468321; www.visitswanseabay.com; Plymouth St; 9.30am-5.30pm Mon-Sat year-round, 10am-4pm Sun Jun-Sep)

THE DYLAN THOMAS TRAIL

The legacy of Dylan Thomas is inescapable in this part of Wales. Whether you're a fan or whether you're just interested to know what all the fuss is about, you'll find plenty of sites in Swansea to stalk the shade of the maverick poet and writer. When you've exhausted them all, you can always head on to Laugharne (p672).

Start at the Dylan Thomas Centre (p663) and then check out his statue gazing across the marina outside the Dylan Thomas Theatre (p666). In Uplands, a plaque marks Thomas' **birthplace** (5 Cwmdonkin Dr), an unassuming terraced house where he wrote two-thirds of his poetry.

Perhaps the places where you're most likely to feel Thomas' presence are his beloved drinking haunts, which include No Sign Bar (p666), Uplands Tavern (p666) and Mermaid (p668).

Getting There & Away

BICYCLE Part of the Celtic Trail (Sustrans National Route 4) hugs the bay from downtown Swansea to Mumbles. **Action Bikes** (☎01792-464640; 5 St David's Sq) rents bicycles.

BOAT **Fastnet Line** (☎0844 576 8831; www.fastnetline.com; King's Dock) sails to Cork (Ireland) three to four times per week; the 10-hour trip costs £85 to £149 for a standard car plus one passenger, one way. The ferry terminal is a mile east of the centre, on the east side of the river mouth. At the time of writing **Severn Link** (www.severnlink.com), a new ferry service from Swansea to Ilfracombe in Devon, was awaiting official approval.

BUS Bus X63 links Swansea with Brecon (two hours); X40 with Carmarthen (45 minutes) and Aberystwyth (3¼ hours); and X13 with Llandeilo (1½ hours). See also the Cardiff–Swansea Shuttle100 (p652) and Beacons Bus B15 (boxed text, p696). National Express coach destinations include London (£26, five hours), Chepstow (£12, two hours), Cardiff (£7.30, one hour), Carmarthen (£6, 45 minutes), Tenby (£8, 1½ hours) and Pembroke (£8, 1¾ hours).

TRAIN Direct trains from Swansea head to London Paddington (£28, three hours), Cardiff (£7.80, one hour), Carmarthen (£7, 45 minutes), Tenby (£12, 1½ hours), Llandeilo (£5.60, 57 minutes) and Llandrindod Wells (£9.70, 2¼ hours).

Getting Around

First Cymru (www.firstgroup.com) runs local services. A Swansea Bay Day Ticket offers all-day bus travel in the Swansea and Mumbles area for £4.25; buy tickets from the driver.

Mumbles (Y Mwmbwls)

Strung out along the shoreline at the southern end of Swansea Bay, Mumbles has been Swansea's seaside retreat since 1807, when the Oystermouth Railway was opened. Built for transporting coal, the horse-drawn carriages were soon converted for paying customers, and the now defunct Mumbles train became the first passenger railway service in the world.

Once again fashionable, with restaurants vying for trade along the promenade, Mumbles' reputation received a boost when its most famous daughter, Hollywood actress Catherine Zeta-Jones, built a £2 million luxury mansion at Limeslade, on the south side of the peninsula. Singer Bonnie Tyler also has a home here.

The origin of Mumbles' unusual name is uncertain, although one theory is that it's a legacy of French seamen who nicknamed the twin rounded rocks at the tip of the headland Les Mamelles ('the breasts').

Sights

Oystermouth Castle CASTLE
(http://oystermouthcastle.wordpress.com; Castle Ave; adult/child £1/80p; 11am-5pm Apr-Sep) It wouldn't be Wales without a castle, hence the trendy shops and bars of Newton Rd are guarded by a majestic ruin. Once the stronghold of the Norman lords of Gower it's now the focus of summer Shakespeare performances. There's a fine view over Swansea Bay from the battlements.

Mumbles Pier PIER
(www.mumbles-pier.co.uk; Mumbles Rd) At the end of its mile-long strip of pastel-painted houses, pubs and restaurants is a rocky headland abutted by a Victorian pier with a sandy beach below. Built in 1898, it houses the usual amusement arcade and a once-grand cafe, festooned with chandeliers.

Sleeping

TOP CHOICE **Tides Reach Guest House** B&B ££
(☎01792-404877; www.tidesreachguesthouse.com; 388 Mumbles Rd; s/d from £50/75; @) Delicious eco-conscious breakfasts and stacks of local information are served

with a smile at this smart waterfront guest house. Some rooms have sea views; our favourite is suitelike room nine, where the dormer windows open out to create a virtual deck from within the sloping roof.

Patricks with Rooms BOUTIQUE HOTEL ££
(☎01792-360199; www.patrickswithrooms.com; 638 Mumbles Rd; d £115-170; P) Patricks has 16 individually styled designer bedrooms in bold contemporary colours, with art on the walls, fluffy robes and, in some of the rooms, roll-top baths and sea views.

Eating & Drinking

The famous Mumbles Mile – a pub crawl along Mumbles Rd – is not what it once was; many of the old faithful inns have succumbed to the gastropub bug. Newton Rd does have some rather nice wine bars though, which aren't too bad for a drop of celebrity spotting.

Mermaid RESTAURANT, BAR ££
(☎01792-367744; 686 Mumbles Rd; 2-course lunch £13, 3-course dinner £25; ⏲Tue-Sun) Fresh-from-the-bay mains and local organic produce are the cornerstones of this sleek, sea-facing eatery, divided between a lounge area for tapas and the main restaurant. In a former incarnation it was a favourite haunt of Dylan Thomas and a quote from a poem referencing the Mermaid is painted on a wall.

Jones WINE BAR
(www.jonesbar.co.uk; 61 Newton Rd, Mumbles) Jones buzzes with 40-somethings giving the chandeliers a run for their money in the bling stakes. There's no chance Dylan Thomas ever did, or would, hang out here, but there's a good wine list and a friendly vibe.

Information

Mumbles tourist office (☎01792-361302; www.mumblestic.co.uk; Methodist Church, Mumbles Rd; ⏲10am-5pm Mon-Sat, noon-5pm Sun Jul & Aug, 10am-4pm Mon-Sat Sep-Jun)

Getting There & Away

Buses 2, 3 and 37 head to Newton Rd in Mumbles (20 minutes), departing from Oxford St, Swansea. On weekends from May to August the **Swansea Bay Rider** (adult/child £2.20/1.60), a toy-town road-train, runs along the promenade between Swansea and the Mumbles.

Gower Peninsula (Y Gŵyr)

With its broad butterscotch beaches, pounding surf, precipitous clifftop walks and rugged, untamed uplands, the Gower Peninsula feels a million miles away from Swansea's urban bustle – yet it's just on the doorstep. This 15-mile-long thumb of land stretching west from Mumbles was designated the UK's first official Area of Outstanding Natural Beauty (AONB) in 1956. The National Trust (NT) owns about three-quarters of the coast and although there is no continuously waymarked path, you can hike almost the entire length of the coastline. The peninsula also has the best surfing in Wales outside Pembrokeshire.

The main family beaches, patrolled by lifeguards during the summer, are Langland Bay, Caswell Bay and Port Eynon.

Sights

Heading west along the south coast from the family-magnet beach of **Port Eynon**, the village of **Rhossili** looks north along the 3-mile sweep of **Rhossili Bay** at the western tip of the peninsula. The village of **Llangennith**, at the north of Rhossili Bay, is the infrastructure hub for surfers, with **PJ's Surfshop** (www.pjsurfshop.co.uk), run by former surf champion Peter Jones, the centre of activity.

From Rhossili village follow the 1-mile tidal causeway to rocky, wave-blasted **Worm's Head** (from Old English *wurm*, meaning dragon) but *only* for a two-hour period either side of low tide. The **seabird colony** at the Outer Head includes razorbills, guillemots and oystercatchers, while seals often bob in the swell.

At the heart of peninsula is Cefn Bryn, a ruggedly beautiful expanse of moorland that rises to a height of 186m. On a suitably desolate ridge above the village of **Reynoldston** stands a mysterious neolithic burial chamber capped by the 25-tonne quartz boulder known as **Arthur's Stone** (Coeten Arthur).

Activities

Parc-Le-Breos Pony Trekking HORSE RIDING
(☎01792-371636; www.parc-le-breos.co.uk; Parkmill; half-/full day £30/43) The rural byways and bridleways of Gower are ideal territory for exploring on horseback.

Welsh Surfing Federation Surf School SURFING
(☎01792-386426; www.wsfsurfschool.co.uk; Llangennith) The governing body for surfing in Wales offers initial two-hour surfing lessons for £25 and subsequent lessons for £20.

Sam's Surf Shack SURFING
(☎01792-390519; www.samssurfshack.com; Rhossili; per hr $20) Learn to surf at the Gower's most beautiful beach.

Euphoria Sailing SAILING, WATER-SKIING
(☎01792-234502; www.euphoriasailing.co.uk; Oxwich Bay) Try your hand water-skiing, wake-boarding (both £45 per 30 minutes) or dinghy sailing (one-day intro course £90).

Gower Coast Adventures SPEEDBOAT TRIPS
(☎07866-250440; www.gowercoastadventures.co.uk) Speedboat trips to Worms Head from Port Eynon (adult/child £30/20) or Mumbles (adult/child £38/24), or from Mumbles to Three Cliffs and Oxwich Bay (adult/child £24/16).

Sleeping & Eating

King's Head B&B ££
(☎01792-386212; www.kingsheadgower.co.uk; Llangennith; r from £85; P 📶) The centre of Llangennith's social life is the King's Head, which serves real ales and home-cooked bar meals (mains £6 to £12). Behind it are two stone blocks, stylishly fitted out with modern bathrooms and pale tiles.

Culver House APARTMENTS ££
(☎01792-390755; www.culverhousehotel.co.uk; Port Eynon; apt from £90; @ 📶) This 19th-century house offers eight modern self-contained apartments with dishwashers, TVs that double as computers, laundry facilities and continental breakfasts delivered daily to your fridge.

Maes-Yr-Haf RESTAURANT-WITH-ROOMS ££
(☎01792-371000; www.maes-yr-haf.com; Parkmill; s/d £95/125, mains £12-18; ⊙lunch Tue-Sun, dinner Tue-Sat; P 📶) The restaurant part of this restaurant-with-rooms has a focus on game, seafood and locally farmed meat, with just a hint of a Greek influence courtesy of head chef Christos Georgakis. The small but stylish rooms are a treat for gadget fans, with iPod docking stations and PlayStations that double as DVD players.

Fairyhill RESTAURANT-WITH-ROOMS £££
(☎01792-390139; www.fairyhill.net; s/d from £155/175; 2-/3-course lunch £16/20, 2-/3-course dinner £35/45; P 📶) Hidden (as any proper fairy place should be) down a narrow lane north of Reynoldston, Fairyhill's restaurant draws on local produce, including organic homegrown goodies from their kitchen garden. The Georgian country house setting is suitably magical, and the menu is pleasantly Welshy.

King Arthur Hotel PUB, B&B ££
(☎01792-390775; www.kingarthurhotel.co.uk; Higher Green, Reynoldston; s/d from £55/65; P) As traditional as swords in stone and ladies of the lake, this King Arthur serves real ales in a cosy wood-panelled bar and a lengthy menu in the neighbouring dining room (mains £6 to £17). The bedrooms above are less atmospheric but clean and comfortable. For true romance, enquire about the stone-walled 18th-century Guinevere's Cottage.

Parc-le-Breos House B&B ££
(☎01792-371636; www.parc-le-breos.co.uk; Parkmill; s/d £45/70; P 📶) Set in its own private estate north of the main road, Parc-le-Breos offers en suite B&B accommodation in a Victorian hunting lodge. The majestic lounge and dining room downstairs have log fires in winter.

Port Eynon YHA HOSTEL £
(☎0845 371 9135; www.yha.org.uk; dm from £18) Worth special mention for its spectacular location, this former lifeboat station is as close as you could come to the sea without sleeping on the beach itself. It's cosier than your average youth hostel, with an attractive lounge with sea views, and well stocked with board games.

Hillend CAMPSITE £
(☎01792-386204; Llangennith; sites around £20; ⊙Easter-Oct) This large campsite is as close to Rhossili Bay as you can get. The on-site **Eddy's Restaurant** (mains £6-8) has brilliant views, and rustles up breakfast for under a fiver.

Nicholaston Farm CAMPSITE £
(☎01792-371209; www.nicholastonfarm.co.uk; Penmaen; sites £11-13; ⊙Apr-Oct) A working farm that's a short walk from Tor Bay and Three Cliffs Bay.

Information

Rhossili Visitor Centre (www.nationaltrust.org.uk; Coastguard Cottages, Rhossili;

⌚10.30am-5pm Apr-Oct, 11am-4pm Fri-Sun Nov-Mar) The National Trust's centre has information on local walks and wildlife, and an audiovisual display upstairs.

Getting There & Around

Swansea's First Cymru buses head to Langland Bay, Caswell Bay, Parkmill, Oxwich Bay, Port Eynon and Rhossili in summer. The **Gower Explorer** (day ticket adult/child £4/2.20) has year-round services looping the peninsula: 115 Llangennith–Reynoldston–Port Eynon; 117 Port Eynon–Oxwich–Parkmill; 118 Rhossili–Port Eynon–Reynoldston–Swansea.

CARMARTHENSHIRE (SIR GAERFYRDDIN)

Castle-dotted Carmarthenshire has gentle valleys, deep-green woods and a small, partly sandy coast. Caught between dramatic neighbours – Pembrokeshire to the west and the Brecon Beacons to the east – it remains much quieter and less explored. Yet the appeal of its tranquil countryside hasn't gone entirely unnoticed and charming places like Llandeilo are sprouting upmarket eateries, galleries and shops. If your interests stretch to gardens, stately homes and all things green, add this quiet county to your itinerary.

Llandeilo & Around

POP 3000

Set on a hill encircled by the greenest of fields, Llandeilo is little more than a handful of narrow streets lined with grand Georgian and Victorian buildings and centred on a picturesque church and graveyard. The surrounding region was once dominated by large country estates and, though they have long gone, the deer, parkland trees and agricultural character of the landscape are their legacy. The genteel appeal of such a place can't be denied, so it's small wonder that Llandeilo's little high street is studded with fashionable shops and eateries.

Sights

TOP CHOICE **Carreg Cennen Castle** CASTLE
(www.carregcennencastle.com; adult/child £3.60/3.25; ⌚9.30am-6.30pm Apr-Oct, 9.30am-4pm Nov-Mar) Perched atop a steep limestone crag high above the River Cennen is Wales' ultimate romantic ruined castle, visible for miles in every direction. The current structure was built at the end of the 13th century in the course of Edward I's conquest of Wales. It was partially dismantled in 1462 during the Wars of the Roses. The most unusual feature is a stone-vaulted passage running along the top of the sheer southern cliff, which leads down to a long, narrow, natural cave; bring a torch or hire one from the ticket office (£1.50).

Carreg Cennen is signposted from the A483, heading south from Llandeilo.

Dinefwr Park & Castle MANOR, CASTLE
(www.nationaltrust.org.uk; adult/child £6.09/3.04; ⌚11am-5pm mid-Feb–Oct, 11am-4pm Fri-Sun Nov–mid-Dec) At the heart of this large estate, immediately west of Llandeilo, is **Newton House**, a wonderful 17th-century manor made over with a Victorian facade. It's presented as it was in Edwardian times, focusing particularly on the experience of servants in their downstairs domain. Striking 13th-century **Dinefwr Castle** is set on a hilltop in the southern corner of the estate. In the 17th century it suffered the indignity of being converted into a picturesque garden feature. There are several marked walking routes around the grounds.

Bus 280 (Carmarthen–Llandeilo) stops here.

WORTH A TRIP

NATIONAL WETLAND CENTRE

Covering 97 hectares on the northern shore of the Burry Inlet, across from the Gower Peninsula, the **National Wetland Centre** (☎01554-741087; www.wwt.org.uk/llanelli; Llanelli; adult/child £7.05/3.86; ⌚9.30am-4.30pm; P) is one of Wales' most important habitats for waders and waterfowl. Winter is the most spectacular season, when up to 60,000 birds converge on the salt marsh and mudflats. Flashiest of all are the resident flock of nearly fluorescent pink Caribbean flamingos.

There's always plenty on for the littl'uns during the school holidays. Late spring's Duckling Days are filled with downy cuteness, while in the summer months there are canoes and bikes to borrow.

Aberglasney Gardens GARDENS

(www.aberglasney.org; Llangathen; adult/child £6.36/3.63; ⏲10am-6pm Apr-Sep, 10.30am-4pm Oct-Mar) Wandering through these formal walled gardens feels a bit like walking into a Jane Austen novel. They date back to the 17th century and contain a unique cloister built solely as a garden decoration. There's also a pool garden, a 250-year-old yew tunnel and a 'wild' garden in the bluebell woods to the west. Several derelict rooms in the central courtyard of Aberglasney House have been converted into a glass-roofed atrium garden full of subtropical plants such as orchids, palms and cycads.

Aberglasney is in the village of Llangathen, just off the A40, 4 miles west of Llandeilo. Bus 280 between Carmarthen and Llandeilo stops on the A40, 500m north of the gardens.

National Botanic Garden of Wales BOTANIC GARDENS

(www.gardenofwales.org.uk; Llanarthne; adult/child £8.50/4; ⏲10am-6pm Apr-Oct, 10am-4.30pm Nov-Mar) Concealed in the rolling Tywi valley countryside, this lavish complex is twice the size of London's Kew Gardens. Opened in 2000, it's still a work in progress, with new features being added every year.

Formerly an aristocratic estate, the garden has a wide range of plant habitats, from lakes and bogs to woodland and heath, with lots of decorative areas and educational exhibits on plant medicine and organic farming. The centrepiece is the Norman Foster–designed **Great Glasshouse**, an arresting glass dome sunken into the earth.

The garden is 8 miles southwest of Llandeilo, signposted from the road to Carmarthen (A40).

Sleeping

TOP CHOICE **Fronlas** B&B ££

(☎01558-824733; www.fronlas.com; 7 Thomas St; s/d from £80/95; P Wi-Fi) A Victorian town house given a chic makeover, Fronlas has three rooms dressed in fresh tones, designer wallpaper and travertine marble tiles. A similarly well-attired guest lounge has an honesty bar and DVD library.

Plough Inn HOTEL ££

(☎01558-823431; www.ploughrhosmaen.com; s/d from £60/80; P Wi-Fi) On the A40, just north of Llandeilo, this baby-blue inn offers hip, contemporary rooms, some with countryside views. The standard rooms are spacious enough but the corner-hogging executives have cat-swinging space and then some.

Eating

TOP CHOICE **Heavenly** BAKERY, CHOCOLATES £

(60 Rhosmaen St; ⏲9.30am-5pm Mon-Sat) Believe the name and enter an Aladdin's cave stacked with handcrafted chocolates, artisanal ice cream and enticing pastries and cakes. Grab something yummy and head to the benches by the churchyard for a taste of sweet paradise.

Y Capel Bach Bistro at The Angel GASTROPUB ££

(62 Rhosmaen St; lunch £5-10; ⏲closed Sun) A lively blackboard menu, hung between an unusual display of historical wedding photos, announces fresh daily specials at this popular gastropub. Thursday nights are devoted to ethnically themed buffets (£10), while a set-price menu is offered otherwise (two/three courses £10/12, add £2 on Saturdays).

Getting There & Away

BUS Buses 280 and 281 from Carmarthen (40 minutes) and X13 from Swansea (1½ hours) stop here. See also Beacons Bus B10 (boxed text, p696).

TRAIN Llandeilo is on the Heart of Wales railway line, with direct services to Swansea (£5.60, 57 minutes), Llanwrtyd Wells (£3.90, 45 minutes), Llandrindod Wells (£6.10, 1¼ hours), Knighton (£8.60, two hours) and Shrewsbury (£11, three hours).

Carmarthen (Caerfyrddin)

POP 14,600

Carmarthenshire's county town is a place of legend and ancient provenance. Though not the kind of place you'll feel inclined to linger in, it's a handy transport and shopping hub. The Romans built a town here, complete with a fort and amphitheatre. A couple of solid walls and a few crumbling towers are all that remain of Carmarthen's Norman Castle, which was largely destroyed in the Civil War.

Most intriguingly, Carmarthen is reputed to be the birthplace of the most famous wizard of them all (no, not Harry Potter) – Myrddin of the Arthurian legends, better known in English as Merlin. An oak tree planted in 1660 for Charles II's coronation came to be called 'Merlin's Tree' and was linked to a prophecy that its death would mean curtains for the town. The tree died in the 1970s, but the town, while a little down at heel, is still standing.

Sights

Carmarthen Market MARKET
(www.carmarthenmarket.co.uk; Market Way; ⏲9am-5pm Mon-Sat) There's been a market here since Roman times and in 1180 it was given a royal charter. The main indoor market has an edgy modern home and sells a bit of everything, from produce to antiques. On Wednesday and Saturday the general market spills out onto Red St, while on Friday there's a farmers market.

Oriel Myrddin GALLERY
(Merlin Gallery; www.orielmyrddingallery.co.uk; Church Lane; admission free; ⏲10am-5pm Mon-Sat) Stages changing exhibitions of contemporary art.

King Street Gallery GALLERY
(www.kingstreetgallery.co.uk; King St; ⏲10am-4pm Mon-Sat) Sells interesting work by a cooperative of 29 local painters, sculptors, ceramicists and printmakers.

Eating

Carmarthen's contribution to Welsh gastronomy is a salt-cured, air-dried ham. Local legend has it that the Romans liked the recipe so much they took it back to Italy with them. Look for it at the market.

TOP CHOICE **Angel Vaults** MODERN WELSH ££
(☎01267-238305; 3 Nott Sq; mains £14-22; ⏲lunch Mon-Sat, dinner Tue-Sat) For a swanky night out, locals head to Angel Vaults for heavenly food and then finish off across the square at Diablo's for devilish cocktails. A locally focused menu features Pembrokeshire salmon and scallops, Gower salt-marsh lamb, and Welsh black beef and cheeses.

Cafe at No 4 Queen St CAFE £
(4 Queen St; mains £4-8; ⏲9am-5pm Mon-Sat) This chic little corner cafe, right in the middle of Carmarthen, brews the best coffee in town and serves fantastic homemade cakes and scones as well as soups, salads, sandwiches and daily specials.

Information

Tourist Office (☎01267-231557; www.discovercarmarthenshire.com; 113 Lammas St; ⏲10am-5pm Apr-Sep, 10am-4pm Mon-Sat Oct-Mar)

Getting There & Away

BUS Bus X40 links Carmarthen with Cardiff (two hours), Swansea (45 minutes) and Aberystwyth (2¼ hours); 280 and 281 head to Llandeilo (40 minutes); 322 to Haverfordwest (one hour); and 460 to Cardigan (1½ hours). See also Beacons Bus B10 (boxed text, p696).

National Express destinations include London (£26, 5¾ hours), Chepstow (£19, 2¼ hours), Swansea (£6, 45 minutes), Tenby (£5.10, 40 minutes), Pembroke (£5.10, one hour) and Haverfordwest (£6.70, 1½ hours).

TRAIN The station is 300m south of town across the river. There are direct trains to Cardiff (£15, 1¾ hours), Swansea (£7, 45 minutes), Fishguard Harbour (£7.10, 49 minutes), Tenby (£7.20, 41 minutes) and Pembroke (£7.20, 1¼ hours).

Laugharne (Talacharn)

POP 2900

Sleepy little Laugharne (pronounced 'larn') sits above the tide-washed shores of the Taf Estuary, overlooked by a Norman castle. Dylan Thomas, one of Wales'

MYTHS & LEGENDS

Wales is awash with sagas inspired by medieval ancestry, bloody conflict and untamed landscapes. From generation to generation, elaborate tales of enchantment and wizardry have been bequeathed like rich family legacies. As early as the 9th century tales of mystery and heroism were compiled in the *Historia Britonum*. But the finest impressions come from the *Mabinogion*, a 14th-century tome containing occasionally terrifying tales of Celtic magic.

King Arthur is a recurrent character, especially in the *Mabinogion*. One of British legend's most romanticised heroes, he was believed to have been a 5th- or 6th-century cavalry leader who rallied British fighters against the marauding Saxon invaders. Time transformed Arthur into a king of magic deeds, with wise magician Myrddin (Merlin) by his side and a loyal band of followers in support. Arthur went on to slay Rita Gawr, a giant who butchered kings, in an epic battle on Snowdon. Finally, Myrddin delivered the dying hero to Avalon, which may well have been saintly Bardsey Island off the Llŷn Peninsula.

The world of Welsh myths is richly imaginative. For more see Robin Gwyndaf's detailed bilingual *Chwedlau Gwerin Cymru: Welsh Folk Tales*.

greatest writers, spent the last four years of his life here, during which he produced some of his most inspired work, including *Under Milk Wood;* the town is one of the inspirations for the play's fictional village of Llareggub (spell it backwards and you'll get the gist).

On Thomas' first visit he described it as the 'strangest town in Wales', but returned repeatedly throughout his restless life. Many Dylan fans make a pilgrimage here to see the Boathouse where he lived, the shed where he wrote, Brown's Hotel where he drank (he used to give the pub telephone number as his contact number; sadly it's now closed) and the churchyard where he's buried.

Sights

Dylan Thomas Boathouse MUSEUM
(www.dylanthomasboathouse.com; Dylan's Walk; adult/child £3.50/1.75; 10am-5.30pm May-Oct, 10.30am-3.30pm Nov-Apr) Dylan Thomas lived here from 1949 to 1953 with his wife Caitlin and their three children. It's a beautiful setting, looking out over the estuary with its 'heron-priested shore'. The parlour has been restored to its 1950s appearance, with the desk that once belonged to Thomas' schoolmaster father and recordings of the poet reading his own works. Upstairs are photographs, manuscripts, a short video about his life, and his death mask, which once belonged to Richard Burton, while downstairs is a cafe.

Along the lane from the Boathouse is the old shed where Thomas did most of his writing. It looks as if he has just popped out, with screwed-up pieces of paper littered around.

Dylan and Caitlin Thomas are buried in a grave marked by a simple white, wooden cross in the grounds of **St Martin's Church**, on the northern edge of the town. **Dylan's Walk** is a scenic 2-mile loop that continues north along the shore beyond the Boathouse, then turns inland past a 17th-century farm and back via St Martin's Church. It's clearly signposted.

Laugharne Castle CASTLE
(www.cadw.wales.gov.uk; adult/child £3/2.60; 10am-5pm Apr-Oct) Built in the 13th century, Laugharne Castle was converted into a mansion in the 16th century for John Perrot, thought to be the illegitimate son of Henry VIII. It was landscaped with lawns and gardens in Victorian times.

Sleeping & Eating

Boat House B&B ££
(01994-427263; www.theboathousebnb.co.uk; 1 Gosport St; s/d from £40/70; @) Friendly, homely and tastefully decorated, this is the smartest B&B in town. The building was formerly the Corporation Arms pub, where Dylan Thomas told stories in exchange for free drinks. The home-cooked breakfasts would assuage even Thomas' legendary hangovers.

Hurst House HOTEL £££
(01994-427417; www.hurst-house.co.uk; East Marsh; r from £175; P) Having had a £5 million makeover, you would expect this converted Georgian farm on the salt-marsh flats south of Laugharne to be luxurious. And it is. Rooms have big beds, bold colours and roll-top baths, there's massage therapy on tap, and a convivial, clubbish lounge bar and restaurant.

Keepers Cottage B&B ££
(01994-427404; www.keepers-cottage.com; s/d £50/70; P) Sitting on the top of the hill by the main approach to town, this pretty cottage has simply decorated but very comfortable rooms. Complimentary bottled water and glasses of wine are a nice touch.

Green Room CAFE, BISTRO ££
(01994-427870; www.thegreenroomcafe.co.uk; 6 The Grist; lunch £7-10, dinner £13-17; Thu-Mon) Laugharne doesn't exactly abound with gastronomic options, making this cafe a welcome find. It serves lighter dishes by day (salads, quiches, pasta) and hearty home-cooked bistro meals after dark. Delicious desserts, views of the castle and comfy sofas add to a cosy, welcoming ambience.

Getting There & Away

Bus 222 runs from Carmarthen to Laugharne (30 minutes).

PEMBROKESHIRE (SIR BENFRO)

The rugged Pembrokeshire coast is what you would imagine the world would look like if God was a geology teacher. There are knobbly hills of volcanic rock, long thin inlets scoured by glacial meltwater, and stratified limestone pushed up vertically and eroded into natural arches, blowholes and sea stacks. Stretches of towering red

WORTH A TRIP

NATIONAL WOOL MUSEUM

The Cambrian Mills factory, world famous for its high-quality woollen products, closed in 1984 and this interesting **museum** (☎01559-370929; www.museumwales.ac.uk; Dre-fach Felindre; admission free; ⊙10am-5pm Tue-Sat Oct-Mar, daily Apr-Sep) has taken its place. Former mill workers are often on hand to get the machines clickety-clacking, but there's also a working commercial mill next door where you can watch the operations from a viewing platform. There's a cafe onsite and a gift shop selling snug woollen blankets.

The museum is positioned in verdant countryside, 14 miles north of Carmarthen and 14 miles southeast of Cardigan, signposted from the A484.

and grey cliff give way to perfect sandy beaches, only to resume around the headland painted black.

It's a landscape of Norman castles, Iron Age hill forts, holy wells and Celtic saints – including the nation's patron, Dewi Sant (St David). Predating even the ancient Celts are the remnants of an older people, who left behind them dolmens and stone circles – the same people who may have transported their sacred bluestones all the way from the Preseli Hills to form the giant edifice at Stonehenge.

Tenby (Dinbych Y Pysgod)

POP 4900

Perched on a headland with sandy beaches either side, Tenby is postcard-maker's dream. Houses are painted from the pastel palette of a classic fishing village, interspersed with the white elegance of Georgian mansions. The main part of town is still constrained by its Norman-built walls, funnelling holidaymakers through medieval streets lined with pubs, ice-creameries and gift shops. Without the tackiness of the promenade-and-pier beach towns, in the off season it tastefully returns to being a sleepy little place. In the summer months it has a boisterous, boozy, holiday-resort feel.

Tenby flourished in the 15th century as a centre for the textile trade, exporting cloth in exchange for salt and wine. Clothmaking declined in the 18th century, but the town soon reinvented itself as a fashionable watering place, assisted by the coming of the railway in the 19th century.

Sights & Activities

St Mary's Church CHURCH
(High St) The graceful arched roof of this 13th-century church is studded with fascinating wooden bosses, mainly dating from the 15th century and carved into flowers, cheeky faces, mythical beasts, fish and even a mermaid holding a comb and mirror. There's a memorial here to Robert Recorde, the 16th-century writer and mathematician who invented the 'equals' sign, along with a confronting cadaver-topped tomb, intended to remind the viewer of their own mortality.

The young Henry Tudor – later to become Henry VII – was hidden here before fleeing to Brittany. It's thought that he left by means of a tunnel into the cellars under Mayor Thomas White's house across the road (where Boots is now).

Caldey Island ISLAND, MONASTERY
(☎01834-844453; www.caldey-island.co.uk; adult/child £11/6; ⊙Mon-Sat Apr-Oct) Boat trips run from Tenby harbour to Caldey Island, home to lots of grey seals and seabirds, and a red-topped, whitewashed monastery that houses a community of around 15 Cistercian monks. There are guided tours of the monastery and great walks around the island, with good views from the lighthouse.

Tudor Merchant's House HISTORIC BUILDING
(Quay Hill; adult/child £3/1.50; ⊙11am-5pm Sun-Fri Easter-Oct) Tenby's handsomely restored, 15th-century Tudor house has period furnishings and the remains of early frescos on the interior walls.

Tenby Museum & Art Gallery MUSEUM
(www.tenbymuseum.org.uk; Castle Hill; adult/child £4/2; ⊙10am-5pm Mon-Fri Nov-Easter, daily Easter-Oct) Housed within the ruins of a Norman castle, this museum covers local history and includes paintings by Augustus and Gwen John.

Sleeping

St Brides Spa Hotel HOTEL £££
(☎01834-812304; www.stbridesspahotel.com; St Brides Hill, Saundersfoot; s/d from £135/150; P ≋) Pembrokeshire's premier spa hotel offers the chance to relax after a massage

Pembrokeshire

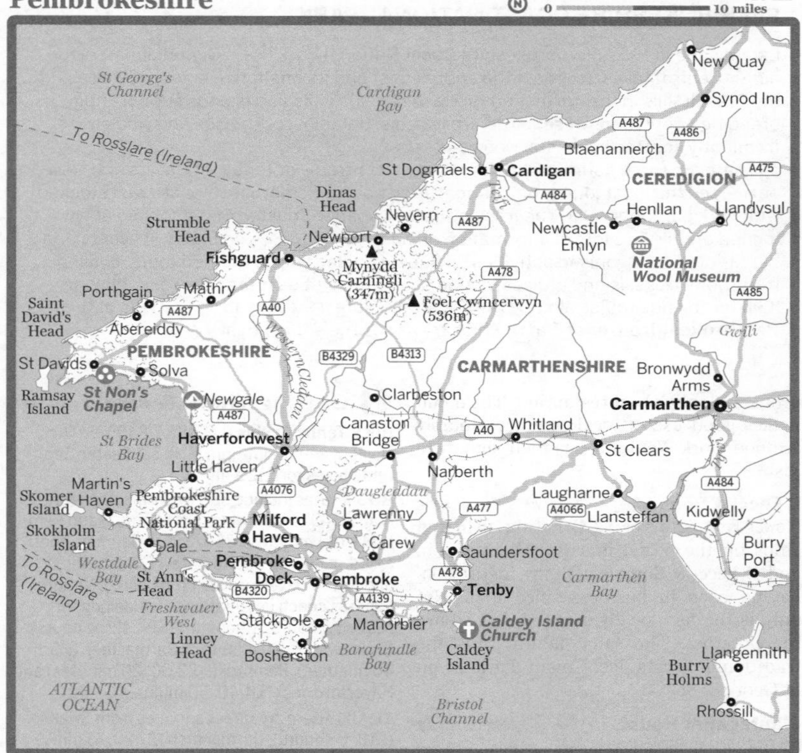

in the infinity-edge pool overlooking the beach, before dining in the candle-lit **Cliff restaurant** (mains £17-22). The bedrooms are stylish and modern, in colours that evoke the seaside. It's in Saundersfoot, 3 miles north of Tenby.

Bay House B&B ££
(☎01834-849015; www.bayhousetenby.co.uk; 5 Picton Rd; r from £70) A stylish, modern take on the seaside B&B, Bay House offers a relaxed, friendly atmosphere, airy rooms with flatscreen TVs and DVDs, and an emphasis on local, organic produce.

Myrtle House B&B ££
(☎01834-842508; St Mary's St; s/d £40/64) A handy location a few metres from the steps down to Castle Beach; tastefully decorated spacious rooms, great breakfasts and a friendly, helpful owner make this late-Georgian house an attractive place to stay.

Lindholme House B&B ££
(☎01834-843368; www.lindholmehouse.co.uk; 27 Victoria St; s/d from £30/60) A traditional B&B with friendly owners and fry-up breakfasts, salmon-hued Lindholme is a little chintzy but clean, comfy and central.

Trevayne Farm CAMPSITE £
(☎01834-813402; www.camping-pembrokeshire.co.uk; Monkstone, Saundersfoot; sites £8-12) Large clifftop field site on the Pembrokeshire Coast Path.

Eating & Drinking

There are around two dozen pubs crammed into the area around Tudor Sq.

Blue Ball Restaurant RESTAURANT ££
(☎01834-843038; www.theblueballrestaurant.co.uk; Upper Frog St; mains £9-22; ⌚dinner Thu-Sun low season, daily summer) Polished wood, old timber beams and exposed brickwork create a cosy, rustic atmosphere in what is

PEMBROKESHIRE COAST NATIONAL PARK

Established in 1952, Pembrokeshire Coast National Park (Parc Cenedlaethol Arfordir Sir Benfro) takes in almost the entire coast and its offshore islands, as well as the Preseli Hills in the north. Pembrokeshire's sea cliffs and islands support huge breeding populations of seabirds, while seals, dolphins, porpoises and whales are frequently spotted in coastal waters.

There are three national park information centres – in Tenby, St Davids and Newport – and the local tourist offices scattered across Pembrokeshire are well stocked with park paraphernalia. The free annual newspaper *Coast to Coast* (online at www.pcnpa.org.uk) has lots of information on park attractions, a calendar of events and details of park-organised activities, including guided walks, themed tours, cycling trips, pony treks, island cruises, canoe trips and minibus tours. It's worth picking it up for the tide tables alone – they're an absolute necessity for many legs of the **Pembrokeshire Coast Path**, which traverses the entire coast.

probably Tenby's best restaurant. The menu makes good use of local produce, notably seafood. Pork Wellington is their signature dish.

D Fecci & Sons TAKEAWAYS, ICE CREAM **£**
(Lower Frog St; mains £2-4) Eating fish and chips on the beach is a British tradition, and D Fecci & Sons is a Tenby institution, having been in business since 1935. Not only is the fish locally sourced, but so are the potatoes. The same family runs the traditional Fecci's Ice Cream Parlour on St George's St.

Plantagenet House RESTAURANT **££**
(☎01834-842350; Quay Hill; mains £14-22; ⏲lunch Sat & Sun, dinner Fri & Sat low season, daily summer) Atmosphere-wise, this place instantly impresses; perfect for a romantic, candle-lit dinner. Tucked down an alley in Tenby's oldest house, it's dominated by an immense 12th-century Flemish hearth. The menu ranges from acclaimed seafood to organic beef.

Tenby House PUB
(www.tenbyhousehotel.com; Tudor Sq) A hotel bar with cool tunes on Friday and Saturday nights, and a sunny, flower-bedecked courtyard for summer afternoon sessions.

ℹ Information

National Park Centre (☎01834-845040; South Pde; ⏲9.30am-5pm Apr-Sep, 10am-4.30pm Mon-Sat Oct-Mar)

Police station (☎0845 330 2000; Warren St)

Tourist office (☎01834-842402; Upper Park Rd; ⏲10am-4pm daily Easter-Oct, Mon-Sat Nov-Easter)

ℹ Getting There & Away

BIKE Tenby Cycles (☎01834-845573; The Norton; ⏲9.30am-5pm Mon-Sat Easter-Sep) rents bikes for £12 a day.

BUS Routes include 333 to Carmarthen (one hour); 349 to Manorbier (18 minutes) and Pembroke (43 minutes); 350/351 to Saundersfoot (eight minutes); 360 to Carew (17 minutes); and 381 to Haverfordwest (one hour). National Express coach destinations include London (£30, 6½ hours), Chepstow (£24, three hours), Swansea (£8, 90 minutes), Carmarthen (£5.10, 40 minutes), Pembroke (£2.60, 20 minutes) and Haverfordwest (£4.40, 50 minutes).

TRAIN There are direct services from Swansea (£12, 1½ hours), Carmarthen (£7.20, 41 minutes), Manorbier (£2.50, 10 minutes) and Pembroke (£4.20, 34 minutes).

West of Tenby

Craggy, lichen-spotted **Manorbier Castle** (www.manorbiercastle.co.uk; adult/child £3.50/1.50; ⏲10am-6pm Easter-Sep) guards over a little village of leafy, twisting lanes nestled above a lovely sandy beach, 5.5 miles southwest of Tenby. **Manorbier YHA** (☎0845 371 9031; www.yha.org.uk; dm/d from £16/31; Ⓟ) occupies a futuristic ex–Ministry of Defence building, 1.5 miles east of the village centre, on a remote clifftop.

Further west, the National Trust's **Stackpole Estate** takes in 8 miles of coast, including two fine beaches (**Barafundle Bay** and **Broad Haven**), a wooded valley and the **Bosherston Lily Ponds**, a system of artificial ponds famous for their spectacular display of water lilies.

From the car park at the end of the St Govan's Head road, steps hacked into the rock lead down to tiny **St Govan's Chapel**, wedged into a slot in the cliffs just out of reach of the sea. The chapel dates from the 5th or 6th century, and is named for an itinerant 6th-century Irish preacher. The car park at **Stack Rocks**, 3 miles to the west, gives access to even more spectacular cliff scenery, including the **Green Bridge of Wales**, the biggest natural arch in the country.

Wild and windblown **Freshwater West**, a 2-mile strand of golden sand and silver shingle backed by acres of dunes, is Wales' best surf beach, sitting wide open to the Atlantic rollers. But beware – although it's great for surfing, big waves, powerful rips and quicksand make it dangerous for swimming; several people have drowned here and the beach has year-round red-flag status. In 2009 scenes from *Harry Potter and the Deathly Hallows* and Ridley Scott's *Robin Hood* were filmed here.

At the southern head of the Milford Haven waterway, the village of **Angle** feels a long way off the beaten track. The main attraction is the tiny beach in **West Angle Bay**, which has great views across the mouth of Milford Haven to St Ann's Head, and offers good coastal walks with lots of rock pools to explore.

If you're walking the coast path, it's a good idea to catch the **Havenlink** (☎01646-600288; www.ruddersboatyard.co.uk; about £5; ⏰Fri-Sun Jun-Sep) ferry from Angle to Dale and skip two grim days passing the giant oil refineries lining Milford Haven. Another option is the **Coastal Cruiser bus** (⏰daily May-Sep, Mon, Thu & Sat Oct-Apr), which loops in both directions between Pembroke, Angle, Freshwater West, Bosherston and Stackpole, terminating at Pembroke Dock.

Pembroke (Penfro)

POP 7200

Pembroke is not much more than a single street of neat Georgian and Victorian houses sitting beneath a whopping great castle – the oldest in west Wales and birthplace of Henry VII, the first Tudor king. Spectacular and forbidding **Pembroke Castle** (www.pembrokecastle.co.uk; Main St; adult/child £4.50/3.50; ⏰10am-4pm) was the home of the earls of Pembroke for over 300 years. A fort was established here in 1093, but most of the present buildings date from the 12th and 13th centuries. It's a great place for kids to explore – wall walks and passages run from tower to tower, and there are vivid exhibitions detailing the castle's history. Guided tours are available from May to August (£1; phone for times). Falconry displays and costumed re-enactments are held in summer.

Sleeping & Eating

TOP CHOICE **Tregenna** B&B ££
(☎01646-621525; www.tregennapembroke.co.uk; 7 Upper Lamphey Rd; s/d £40/60; P 🛜) Treats in the rooms include a sewing kit, shaving kit, mini toothbrush and toothpaste, bottled water and Welsh cakes. It's a newly built house, so everything's modern and shiny.

High Noon Guest House B&B ££
(☎01646-683736; www.highnoon.co.uk; Lower Lamphey Rd; s/d £25/50; P 🛜) Handy for Pembroke train station, and offering good value rather than atmosphere, this modern house has decent, though smallish, rooms with a pleasant garden terrace out back. The single rooms share bathrooms.

Beech House B&B £
(☎01646-683740; www.beechhousepembroke.com; 78 Main St; s/d £19/37) Wearing a garland of ivy, this simple place at the western end of the main street has spick-and-span rooms with period Georgian features. It's handy for the train station and family friendly.

Old King's Arms Hotel PUB £££
(Main St; mains £15-22) Dark timber beams, ochre walls and polished copperware lend a country kitchen atmosphere to the restaurant here. The locally sourced protein (black beef, Carmarthen ham, daily seafood specials) comes accompanied with enough potatoes and vegetables to fill even a Tudor king.

Information

Tourist office (☎01437-776499; Commons Rd; ⏰10am-4pm Mon-Fri, 10am-1pm Sat Apr-Oct, 10am-1pm Tue-Sat Nov-Mar; @)

Getting There & Away

BOAT **Irish Ferries** (☎+353 818 300 400; www.irishferries.co.uk) has two sailings a day on the four-hour route between Pembroke Dock and Rosslare in the southeast of Ireland (car and driver from £89, additional adult/child £23/13, foot passenger from £26).

BUS The 349 heads to Tenby (43 minutes), Manorbier (25 minutes), Pembroke Dock (10 minutes) and Haverfordwest (45 minutes). National Express destinations include London (£30, seven hours), Chepstow (£22, 3¼ hours), Swansea (£8, 1¾ hours), Carmarthen (£5.10, one hour), Tenby (£2.60, 20 minutes) and Haverfordwest (£4.40, 30 minutes).

TRAIN There are direct trains to Swansea (£12, 2¼ hours), Carmarthen (£7.20, 1¼ hours), Manorbier (£3.30, 19 minutes) and Tenby (£4.20, 34 minutes).

Carew

Looming romantically over the River Carew, its gaping windows reflected in the glassy water, craggy **Carew Castle** (www.carewcastle.com; adult/child £4.50/3; ⏲10am-5pm Apr-Oct) is an impressive sight. These rambling limestone ruins range from functional 12th-century fortification to Elizabethan country house. Abandoned in 1690, the castle is now inhabited by a large number of bats. A summer program of events includes battle re-enactments and open-air theatre. The castle ticket also gives you admission to **Carew Tidal Mill**, the only intact tidal mill in Wales.

Near the castle entrance is the 11th-century **Carew Cross**, one of the grandest of its kind – around 4m tall and covered in psychedelic Celtic squiggles. Directly across the road, **Carew Inn** (mains £8-18) serves lunch and dinner (with veg options), and has a beer garden overlooking the castle.

Carew is 4 miles northeast of Pembroke and 6 miles northwest of Tenby. Bus 360 heads here from Tenby (17 minutes).

Haverfordwest (Hwlffordd)

POP 13,400

A workaday town rather than a tourist hot spot, Haverfordwest is Pembrokeshire's main transport and shopping hub. Though it retains some fine Georgian buildings, it lacks the prettiness and historic atmosphere of many of its neighbours. Founded as a fortified Flemish settlement by the Norman Lord Gilbert de Clare in about 1110, its castle became the nucleus for a thriving market and its port remained important until the railway arrived in the mid-19th century.

Today the Riverside Shopping Centre is the main focus of activity and home to an excellent farmers market with organic and local produce stalls every other Friday.

PUFFIN SHUTTLE

Between May and September walkers can make use of the Puffin Shuttle (route 315/400, fares less than £4), which crawls around the coast three times daily in each direction from Haverfordwest to St Davids. Stops include Milford Haven, Dale, Marloes Village, Martin's Haven, Little Haven, Broad Haven, Newgale Sands and Solva. For the rest of the year the route is split, with 315 heading from Haverfordwest to Marloes (no Sunday service) and 400 heading from St Davids to Marloes (Monday, Thursday and Saturday only).

Sleeping & Eating

College Guest House B&B ££
(☎01437-763710; www.collegeguesthouse.com; 93 Hill St; s/d from £50/70; @📶) Set in a spacious Georgian town house in the town centre, the College offers eight homely rooms with high ceilings and remodelled bathrooms. There's a free car park directly across the road.

Georges CAFE ££
(☎01437-766683; 24 Market St; mains £10-18; ⏲10am-5.30pm Tue-Thu, 10am-11pm Fri & Sat; ✎) Gargoyles on leashes guard the door of this trippy, hippy gift shop that doubles as an offbeat cafe. The Georges has cosy nooks of stained glass and candlelight, lanterns and fairy lights, along with a simple menu of home-cooked food ranging from steak to pasta to curry.

Information

Police station (☎0845 330 2000; Merlin's Hill)

Tourist office (☎01437-763110; 19 Old Bridge St; ⏲10am-4pm Mon-Sat)

Withybush General Hospital (☎01437-764545; Fishguard Rd)

Getting There & Away

BUS Routes include 322 to Carmarthen (one hour); 349 to Pembroke (45 minutes), Manorbier (1¼ hours) and Tenby (1½ hours); 411 to Lower Solva (29 minutes) and St Davids (40 minutes); 412 to Fishguard (37 minutes), Newport (52 minutes), Castell Henllys (one hour) and Cardigan (1¼ hours); and the Puffin Shuttle.

National Express destinations include Chepstow (£24, four hours), Swansea (£8.50, 2½ hours), Carmarthen (£6.70, 1½ hours), Tenby (£4.40, 50 minutes) and Pembroke (£4.40, 30 minutes).

TRAIN There are direct trains to Newport (£23, 2¾ hours), Cardiff (£20, 2½ hours), Swansea (£12, 1½ hours) and Carmarthen (£7.10, 35 minutes).

Dale & Around

The fishing village of **Dale** sits on a rugged and remote peninsula, forming the northern head of the Milford Haven waterway. As you round beautiful **St Ann's Head**, all vestiges of the harbour's heavy industry and, indeed, human habitation disappear from view. Little **Westdale Bay** follows and then the impressive sweep of **Marloes Sands**, with views over **Gateholm Island** – a major Iron Age Celtic settlement where the remains of 130 hut circles have been found. Housed in a group of National Trust–owned farm buildings near the Pembrokeshire Coast Path, **Marloes Sands YHA** (☎0845 371 9333; www.yha.org.uk; Runwayskiln; dm/d from £16/32; ⊙Easter-Oct; P) offers a mixture of dorms and private rooms.

Around Wooltack Point is **Martin's Haven**, the tiny harbour that is the jumping-off point for boat trips to Skomer and Skokholm Islands. An unstaffed **information room** here has displays on the marine environment, including touchscreen displays of wildlife activity around Skomer. Look for a 7th-century **Celtic cross** set into the wall outside.

Further around the headland the cliffs change from red to black and **Musselwick Sands** comes in to view: a large, sandy beach with plenty of craggy inlets to explore.

The Puffin Shuttle stops at Dale, Marloes Village and Martin's Haven.

Skomer, Skokholm & Grassholm Islands

The rocky islands at the south end of St Brides Bay are home to more than half a million seabirds, including guillemots, puffins and Manx shearwaters, as well as grey seals. Skomer and Skokholm Islands are nature reserves run by the **Wildlife Trust of South and West Wales** (www.welshwildlife.org), which offers bunkhouse accommodation on Skomer (dorm/single from £25/38). **Dale Sailing Company** (☎01646-603123; www.pembrokeshire-islands.co.uk; adult/child £10/7; ⊙10am, 11am & noon Tue-Sun Apr-Oct) runs boats to Skomer on a first-come, first-served basis, departing from Martin's Haven. If you go ashore, there's an additional landing fee (£7).

Eleven miles offshore, Grassholm Island has one of the largest gannet colonies in the northern hemisphere. Grassholm is owned by the **Royal Society for the Protection of Birds** (RSPB; www.rspb.org.uk) and landing is not permitted, but Dale Sailing Company runs three-hour, round-the-island trips (£30); book ahead.

Lower Solva

Lower Solva sits at the head of a peculiar L-shaped harbour, where the water drains away completely at low tide leaving its flotilla of yachts tilted onto the sand. Its single street is lined with brightly painted, flower-laden cottages housing little galleries, pubs and tearooms.

If sailing takes your fancy, you can enjoy a cruise aboard a 24ft yacht (up to three passengers) with **Solva Sailboats** (☎01437-720972; www.solva.net/solvasailboats; 1 Maes-y-Forwen; per 3hr/day £70/120). It also rents sailing dinghies (per hour £22) and runs official Royal Yachting Association sailing courses.

The **Old Pharmacy** (☎01437-720005; 5 Main St; mains £13-19; ⊙dinner) is the village's gastronomic highlight, with a cosy cottage atmosphere, outdoor tables in a riverside garden, and a bistro-style menu that includes Solva lobster (£25 for half) and crab, Pembrokeshire rabbit and Welsh black beef.

Both the Puffin Shuttle and bus 411 between Haverfordwest and St Davids stop here.

St Davids (Tyddewi)

POP 1800

Charismatic St Davids (yes, it has dropped the apostrophe from its name) is Britain's smallest city, its status ensured by the magnificent 12th-century cathedral that marks Wales' holiest site. The birth and burial site of the nation's patron saint, St Davids has

St Davids

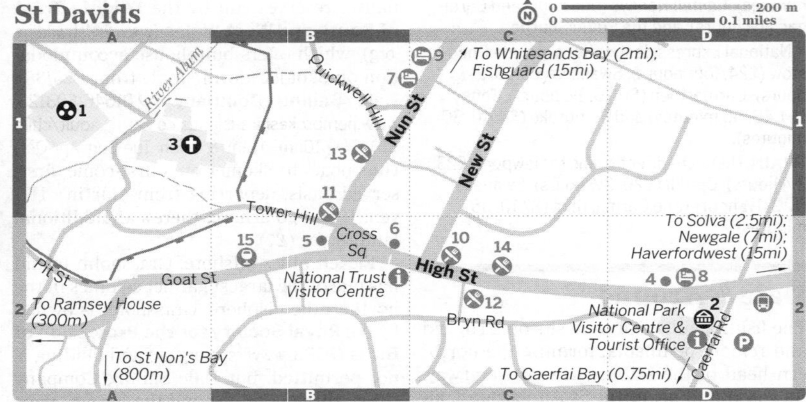

been a place of pilgrimage for more than 1500 years.

The setting itself has a numinous presence. With the sea just beyond the horizon on three sides, you're constantly surprised by glimpses of it at the ends of streets. Then there are those strangely shaped hills in the distance, sprouting from a seemingly ancient landscape.

Dewi Sant (St David) founded a monastic community here in the 6th century, only a short walk from where he was born at St Non's Bay. In 1124 Pope Calixtus II declared that two pilgrimages to St Davids were the equivalent of one to Rome, and three were equal to one to Jerusalem. The cathedral has seen a constant stream of visitors ever since.

Today St Davids attracts hordes of non-religious pilgrims too, drawn by the town's laid-back vibe and the excellent hiking, surfing and wildlife-watching in the surrounding area.

Sights & Activities

St David's Cathedral CATHEDRAL
(www.stdavidscathedral.org.uk; £4 suggested donation; ⌚8.30am-5.30pm Mon-Sat, 12.45-5.30pm Sun) Hidden in a hollow and behind high walls, St David's Cathedral is intentionally unassuming. The valley site was chosen in the vain hope that the church would be overlooked by Viking raiders, but it was ransacked at least seven times. Yet once you pass through the gatehouse that separates it from the town and its stone walls come into view, it's as imposing as any of its contemporaries.

Built on the site of a 6th-century chapel, the building dates mainly from the 12th to the 14th centuries. Extensive works were carried out in the 19th century by Sir George Gilbert Scott (architect of the Albert Memorial and St Pancras in London) to stabilise the building. The distinctive **west front**, with its four pointed towers of purple stone, dates from this period.

The atmosphere inside is one of great antiquity. As you enter the **nave**, the oldest surviving part of the cathedral, the first things you notice are the sloping floor and the outward lean of the massive, purplish-grey pillars linked by semicircular Norman Romanesque arches, a result of subsidence. Above is a richly carved 16th-century oak ceiling, adorned with pendants and bosses.

At the far end of the nave is a delicately carved 14th-century Gothic **pulpitum** (screen), separating it from the magnificent **choir**. Check out the mischievous carved figures on the 16th-century misericords (under the seats), one of which depicts pilgrims being seasick over the side of a boat. Don't forget to look up at the colourfully painted lantern tower above (those steel tie rods around the walls were installed in the 19th century to hold the structure together).

In a recess in the **Holy Trinity Chapel** at the east end of the cathedral is the object of all those religious pilgrimages – a simple oak casket that contains the bones of St David and St Justinian. The chapel ceiling is

St Davids

Sights

1 Bishop's Palace....A1
2 Oriel y Parc....D2
3 St David's Cathedral....A1

Activities, Courses & Tours

4 Aquaphobia....D2
5 Thousand Islands Expeditions....B2
6 TYF Adventure....B2
Voyages of Discovery....(see 6)

Sleeping

7 Alandale....B1
8 Grove....D2
9 Y Glennydd....C1

Eating

10 Bench....C2
11 Chapel Chocolates....B1
12 Cwtch....C2
13 Sampler....B1
14 St Davids Food & Wine....C2

Drinking

15 Farmer's Arms....B2

distinguished by superb fan vaulting dating from the early 16th century.

Accessed from the north wall of the nave the **Treasury** (admission free) displays vestments and religious paraphernalia crafted from precious metals and stones. Just as valuable are the treasures in the neighbouring **Library** (admission £1; ⏲2-4pm Mon), the oldest of which dates to 1505.

The **St David's Cathedral Festival** is 10 days of classical music performances, starting on the Spring Bank Holiday weekend at the end of May. Many other concerts are performed at the cathedral throughout the year.

Bishop's Palace RUINED PALACE

(www.cadw.wales.gov.uk; adult/child £3/2.60; ⏲9am-5pm Apr-Oct, 9.30am-4pm Mon-Sat, 11am-4pm Sun Nov-Mar) Across the river from the cathedral, this atmospheric ruined palace was begun at the same time as the cathedral, but its final, imposing form owes most to Henry de Gower, bishop from 1327 to 1347.

Its most distinctive feature is the arcaded parapet that runs around the courtyard, decorated with a chequerboard pattern of purple and yellow stone blocks. The corbels that support the arches are richly adorned with a menagerie of carved figures – lions, monkeys, dogs and birds, as well as grotesque mythical creatures and human heads.

The palace courtyard provides a spectacular setting for open-air plays in summer.

TOP CHOICE **St Non's Bay** CHURCH, RUINS

Immediately south of St Davids is this ruggedly beautiful spot, named after St David's mother and traditionally accepted as his birthplace. A path leads down to the 13th-century **ruins of St Non's Chapel**. Only the base of the walls remains, along with a stone marked with a cross within a circle, believed to date from the 7th century. Standing stones in the surrounding field suggest that the chapel may have been built within an ancient pagan stone circle.

On the approach to the ruins is a pretty little **holy well**. The spring is said to have emerged at the moment of the saint's birth and the water is believed to have curative powers.

Nearby, the Catholic **Chapel of Our Lady and St Non** was built in 1935 out of the stones of ruined religious buildings. Its dimensions echo those of the original chapel.

Oriel y Parc GALLERY, INFORMATION

(☎01437-720392; www.orielyparc.co.uk; High St; admission free; ⏲10am-4.30pm) Occupying a bold, semicircular, environmentally friendly building on the edge of town, Oriel y Parc (Landscape Gallery) is a winning collaboration between the Pembrokeshire Coast National Park Authority and the National Museum Wales. Not only does it function as a tourist office and national park visitor centre, but it houses changing exhibitions from the museum's art collection.

Ramsey Island NATURE RESERVE

Ramsey Island lies off the headland to the west of St Davids, ringed by dramatic sea cliffs and an offshore armada of rocky islets and reefs. The island is an RSPB reserve famous for its large breeding population of choughs – members of the crow family with glossy black feathers and distinctive red bills and legs – and for its grey seals.

You can reach the island by boat from the tiny harbour at St Justinian's, 2 miles west of St Davids. Longer boat trips run up to 20 miles offshore, to the edge of the

Celtic Deep, to spot whales, porpoises and dolphins. What you'll see depends on the weather and the time of year: July to September are the best months. Porpoises are seen on most trips, dolphins on four out of five, and there's a 40% chance of seeing whales. The most common species is the minke, but pilot whales, fin whales and orcas have also been spotted.

Thousand Islands Expeditions (☎01437-721721; www.ramseyisland.com; Cross Sq) is the only operator permitted to land day trippers on the island (adult/child £15/7.50). They have a range of other boat trips, including 2½-hour whale- and dolphin-spotting cruises (£55/30) and one-hour jet-boat trips (£24/12).

Voyages of Discovery (☎01437-721911; www.ramseyisland.co.uk; 1 High St) and **Aquaphobia** (☎01437-720471; www.aquaphobia-ramseyisland.co.uk; Grove Hotel, High St) offer a similar selection of cruises.

Sleeping

TOP CHOICE **Ramsey House** B&B ££
(☎01437-720321; www.ramseyhouse.co.uk; Lower Moor; r £100; P 📶) The young owners have fashioned a fresh-looking B&B from their new house on the outskirts of town, which is still only a short stroll west from the centre. The six rooms are all different, but it's the kind of place where the chandeliers match the wallpaper.

Alandale B&B ££
(☎01437-720404; www.stdavids.co.uk/guesthouse/alandale.htm; 43 Nun St; s/d £36/80; @ 📶) A neat terraced house built in the 1880s for coastguard officers, Alandale has a bright, cheerful atmosphere – ask for one of the rooms at the back, which are quieter and have sweeping countryside views.

Y Glennydd B&B ££
(☎01437-720576; www.yglennydd.co.uk; 51 Nun St; s/d £40/65; 📶) Mixing maritime memorabilia and antique oak furniture, this 10-room guest house has a traditional bordering on old-fashioned feel, with smallish, unfussy bedrooms and a cosy lounge bar.

Grove PUB ££
(☎01437-720341; www.grovestdavids.com; High St; r/ste £95/110; P 📶) Offering upmarket pub accommodation, the Grove's rooms have been given a fresh, up-to-the-moment look in a recent refurbishment. Expect a bit of noise from the drinkers downstairs – pack earplugs or join in.

St Davids YHA HOSTEL £
(☎0845 371 9141; www.yha.org.uk; Llaethdy, Whitesands Bay) A former farmhouse tucked beneath Carn Llidi, 2 miles northwest of town, with snug dorms in the cow sheds.

Caerfai Bay CAMPSITE £
(☎01437-720274; www.caerfaibay.co.uk; sites £12) A 15-minute walk south of St Davids, this large site has good facilities and great coastal views across St Brides Bay.

Eating & Drinking

TOP CHOICE **Cwtch** MODERN WELSH £££
(☎01437-720491; www.cwtchrestaurant.co.uk; 22 High St; 3-course dinner £29; ⏲dinner Wed-Sun, daily summer) Stone walls and wooden beams mark this out as a sense-of-occasion place, as indeed does the price, yet there's a snugness that lives up to its name

COASTEERING

If you fancy a spot of rock climbing, gully scrambling, cave exploration, wave riding and cliff jumping, all rolled together, then try coasteering. More or less conceived on the Pembrokeshire coast, this demanding activity is the mainstay of the local adventure sports scene. It's also risky, so take guidance from an instructor and don't be tempted to take flight from the nearest precipice.

Preseli Venture ADVENTURE ACTIVITIES
(☎01348-837709; www.preseliventure.com; Parcynole Fach) Has its own lodge near Abermawr, on the coast between St Davids and Fishguard. Activities include coasteering, sea kayaking, mountain biking, surfing and coastal hiking.

TYF Adventure ADVENTURE ACTIVITIES
(☎01437-721611; www.tyf.com; 1 High St, St Davids) Organises coasteering, surfing, sea-kayaking and rock-climbing trips from its St Davids base.

(*cwtch* means a cosy place or a cuddle). There's an emphasis on local produce, so expect plenty of fresh seafood on the menu.

Sampler TEAROOM £
(17 Nun St; mains $5-6; ⏲10am-5.30pm Mon-Thu, extended hours in summer) Named after the embroidery samples blanketing the walls, this may be the perfect exemplar of the traditional Welsh tearoom. Pembrokeshire clotted cream tea comes served with freshly baked scones and *bara brith* (a rich, fruit tea-loaf), and there are Welsh cheese platters, jacket potatoes, soups and sandwiches.

Farmer's Arms PUB
(14 Goat St) Even though St Davids is a bit of a tourist trap, you'd be hard-pressed finding a more authentic country pub. There's real ale and Guinness on tap and it's the place to be when the rugby's playing. The beer garden out back is a pleasant place to watch the sun go down on a summer's evening.

Bench BAR, BISTRO £
(www.bench-bar.co.uk; 11 High St; mains £5-17; ⏲9am-late; @📶) A bustling rabbit warren of a bar-bistro with a strong Mediterranean motif, the Bench serves up all-day snacks and lip-smacking ice creams.

Chapel Chocolates CONFECTIONERY
(www.chapelchocolates.com; The Pebbles) Dieters beware – the shelves in this shop are stacked floor to ceiling with more than 100 varieties of handmade Welsh chocolates, truffles and other confectionery.

St Davids Food & Wine DELICATESSEN
(High St; ⏲8.30am-5pm Mon-Sat) Stock up on picnic supplies at this delicatessen, which specialises in local organic produce.

Information

National Park Information Centre & Tourist Office See Oriel y Parc, p681.

National Trust Visitor Centre (☎01437-720385; High St; ⏲10am-5.30pm Mon-Sat, 10am-4pm Sun mid-Mar–Dec, 10am-4pm Mon-Sat Jan–mid-Mar) Sells local-interest books and guides to NT properties in Pembrokeshire.

Getting There & Around

Buses include the Puffin Shuttle; 411 to Lower Solva (nine minutes) and Haverfordwest (40 minutes); and 413 to Fishguard (50 minutes). The Strumble Shuttle (404; Tuesday, Thursday and Saturday October to April, daily May to September) follows the coast between St Davids and Fishguard, calling at Porthgain.

Porthgain

For centuries the tiny harbour of Porthgain consisted of little more than a few sturdy cottages wedged into a rocky cove. In the mid-19th century it began to prosper as the port for shipping out slate quarried just down the coast at Abereiddy, and by the 1870s its own deposits of granite and fine clay had put it on the map as a source of building stone. The post-WWI slump burst the bubble, and the sturdy stone quays and overgrown brick storage 'bins' are all that remain.

Despite having been an industrial harbour, Porthgain is surprisingly picturesque and today it is home to a couple of art galleries and restaurants. The Strumble Shuttle coastal bus service stops here.

Eating

Shed SEAFOOD £££
(☎01348-831518; www.theshedporthgain.co.uk; lunch £9-17, dinner £19-26; ⏲lunch Fri-Sun, dinner Mon, Fri & Sat low season, daily high season) Housed in a beautifully converted machine shop right by the little harbour, the Shed has grown into one of Pembrokeshire's finest seafood restaurants; the menu lists Porthgain crab and lobster, and locally caught sea bass, gurnard, mullet and squid.

Sloop Inn PUB ££
(☎01348-831449; www.sloop.co.uk; mains £10-17) With wooden tables worn smooth by many a bended elbow, old photos of Porthgain in its industrial heyday and interesting nautical clutter all over the place, the Sloop is a cosy and deservedly popular pub. It dishes up breakfast (to 11am) and hearty, home-cooked meals to hungry walkers.

Fishguard (Abergwaun)

POP 3200

Perched on a headland between its modern ferry port and former fishing harbour, Fishguard is often overlooked by travellers, most of them passing through on their way to or from Ireland. It doesn't have any sights as such, but it's an appealing little town and was the improbable setting for the last foreign invasion of Britain.

THE LAST INVASION OF BRITAIN

While Hastings in 1066 may get all the press, the last invasion of Britain was actually at Carregwastad Point, northwest of Fishguard, on 22 February 1797. The ragtag collection of 1400 French mercenaries and bailed convicts had intended to land at Bristol and march to Liverpool, keeping English troops occupied while France mounted an invasion of Ireland. But bad weather blew them ashore at Carregwastad, where, after scrambling up a steep cliff, they set about looting the Pencaer peninsula for food and drink.

The invaders had hoped that the Welsh peasants would rise up to join them in revolutionary fervour but, not surprisingly, their drunken pillaging didn't endear them to the locals. The French were quickly seen off by volunteer 'yeoman' soldiers, with help from the people of Fishguard including, most famously, one Jemima Nicholas who, armed with a pitchfork, single-handedly captured 12 mercenaries.

Fishguard is split into three distinct areas. The main town is centred on Market Sq, where the buses stop. To the east is the picturesque harbour of the Lower Town (Y Cwm), which was used as a setting for the 1971 film version of *Under Milk Wood*. The train station and ferry terminal lie a mile to the northwest of the town centre in Goodwick.

Much that goes on in Fishguard happens in the Town Hall on Market Sq. The tourist office is here, as is the library (handy for free internet access) and the market hall. It hosts a country market on Tuesdays, a town market on Thursdays and a farmers market on Saturdays. Upstairs is the **Last Invasion Gallery** (admission free; ⌚9.30am-5pm Mon-Sat Apr-Sep, until 1pm Sat Oct-Mar), which displays the Fishguard Tapestry. Inspired by the Bayeux Tapestry, which recorded the 1066 Norman invasion at Hastings, it was commissioned in 1997 to commemorate the bicentenary of the failed Fishguard invasion. It uses a similar cartoonish style as Bayeux's (albeit with less rude bits) and tells the story in the course of 37 frames and 30m of cloth. A film about its making demonstrates what a huge undertaking it was.

Activities

Celtic Diving DIVING
(☎01348-871938; www.celticdiving.co.uk; The Parrog, Goodwick) Runs half-day scuba-diving taster sessions in its own practice pool (£65), as well as PADI-certificated diving courses. Dive sites include several wrecks.

Mike Mayberry Kayaking KAYAKING
(☎01348-874699; www.mikemayberrykayaking.co.uk) Offers instruction courses (one/two days £87/147) and guided kayaking tours for more experienced paddlers.

Sleeping

Pentower B&B ££
(☎01348-874462; www.pentower.co.uk; Tower Hill; s/d £45/75; Ⓟ) Built by Sir Evan Jones, the architect who designed the harbour, this rambling home is perched on a hill at the edge of town, overlooking his creation. Rooms are spacious and romantic.

Manor Town House B&B ££
(☎01348-873260; www.manortownhouse.com; Main St; s/d £45/70; wi-fi) This graceful Georgian house has a lovely garden terrace where you can sit and gaze over the harbour. The young owners are charm personified and there's a generally upmarket ambience, although the decor doesn't always quite hit the spot.

Eating & Drinking

Royal Oak Inn PUB £
(Market Sq; mains £5-15) Suffused with character, this old inn was the site of the French surrender in 1797 and the table on which it was signed takes pride of place at the back of the dining room. The pub has turned into something of an invasion museum, filled with memorabilia. It also serves the best pub food in town and hosts a popular live folk night on Tuesdays where musicians are welcome to join in.

Bar Five BAR, BISTRO ££
(☎01348-875050; www.barfive.com; 5 Main St; mains £13-16; ⌚lunch Fri & Sun, dinner Thu-Sun, extended hours in summer) For a completely different ambience, try this hip, upmarket bar and restaurant in a cleverly renovated Georgian town house with a terrace overlooking the harbour. The bistro menu focuses on fresh local produce, especially crab and lobster hauled in from the restaurant's own boat.

Ship Inn PUB
(Old Newport Rd, Lower Town) This is a lovely little pub with an open fire in winter and lots of memorabilia on the walls, including photos of Richard Burton filming *Under Milk Wood* outside (the street and nearby quay haven't changed a bit).

Information

Fishguard Tourist office (☎01437-776636; Town Hall, Market Sq; ⏰10am-4pm Mon-Sat; @)

Goodwick Tourist office (☎01348-874737; Ocean Lab, Goodwick; ⏰10am-4pm; @) Houses an exhibition on marine life and the environment aimed mainly at kids.

Getting There & Away

BOAT **Stena Line** (☎08447-707070; www.stenaline.co.uk) has two regular ferries a day, year-round (car and driver from £69, additional adult/child £23/13, foot passenger £25, bike £5), and a 'Fastcraft' most days in July and August (car and driver from £94, other details the same), between Rosslare in the southeast of Ireland and Fishguard Harbour.

BUS Buses include 412 to Haverfordwest (37 minutes), Newport (19 minutes), Castell Henllys (28 minutes) and Cardigan (41 minutes); and 413 to St Davids (50 minutes). Walkers' services include the Strumble Shuttle, Poppit Rocket and the Green Dragon Bus.

TRAIN There's a daily direct train to Fishguard Harbour from Cardiff (£20, 2¼ hours) via Carmarthen (£7.10, 49 minutes). On Sunday there's a slower service via Swansea (£11.60, two hours).

Newport (Trefdraeth)

POP 1200

In stark contrast to the industrial city of Newport in Gwent, the Pembrokeshire Newport is a pretty cluster of flower-bedecked cottages huddled beneath a small, privately owned, Norman **castle**. It sits at the foot of **Mynydd Carningli** (347m), a large bump on the seaward side of the Preseli Hills, and in recent years has gained a reputation for the quality of its restaurants and guest houses.

Newport makes a pleasant base for walks along the coastal path or south into the Preseli Hills, but it does get crowded in summer. At the northwest corner of the town is little **Parrog Beach**, dwarfed by **Newport Sands** (Traeth Mawr) across the river.

There's a little dolmen right in town, well signposted from the main road just past the Golden Lion. At first glance it looks like **Carreg Coetan**'s capstone is securely supported by four standing stones. A closer inspection suggests that some old magic has held it together all these thousands of years, as it's balanced on only two of them.

POPPIT ROCKET

Between May and September, the Poppit Rocket (405) heads three times daily in each direction from Fishguard to Cardigan. Stops include Pwllgwaelod, Newport, Moylgrove, Poppit Sands and St Dogmaels. For the rest of the year it only covers the stops between Newport and Cardigan (Monday, Thursday and Saturday only).

Sleeping & Eating

TOP CHOICE **Llys Meddyg** RESTAURANT-WITH-ROOMS ££
(☎01239-820008; www.llysmeddyg.com; East St; r £100-150; @☎) This converted doctor's residence takes contemporary big-city cool and plonks it firmly by the seaside. Bedrooms are large and bright, the lounge boasts leather sofas and a period fireplace, and there's a secluded garden at the back. The restaurant (mains £17 to £34) is superb, with the menu changing with the seasons and reflecting the best of local produce, combined with an international palate of flavours.

Cnapan B&B, RESTAURANT ££
(☎01239-820575; www.cnapan.co.uk; East St; s/d £54/84; ☎) Light-filled rooms and a flower-filled garden are offered at this listed Georgian town house above a popular restaurant (two-/three-course dinner £24/30, open Wednesday to Monday). If you're man enough for the floral wallpaper, ask for room four: it's bigger. The somewhat formal dining rooms offer candlelight and crisp white linen tablecloths, but the service is friendly and relaxed. Local seafood (Penclawdd mussels and the fresh catch of the day) features on the set menu, alongside Welsh beef and a tempting array of desserts.

Golden Lion Hotel PUB ££
(☎01239-820321; www.goldenlionpembrokeshire.co.uk; East St; s/d £60/85; P☎) Sunny decor, golden pine furniture and

DON'T MISS

CASTELL HENLLYS IRON AGE FORT

From about 600 BC and right through the Roman occupation there was a thriving Celtic fortified village at what's now **Castell Henllys** (www.castellhenllys.com; Felindre Farchog; adult/child £4/3; ⏲10am-5pm Easter-Oct, 11am-3pm Nov-Easter). A visit is like travelling back in time. There are reconstructions of the settlement's buildings – four thatched roundhouses, animal pens, a smithy and a grain store – that you can enter and touch. Costumed staff, craft demonstrations, Celtic festivals and other events bring it to life.

Castell Henllys is 4 miles east of Newport. Bus 412 from Cardigan (15 minutes) to Haverfordwest (1¼ hours), via Newport (nine minutes) and Fishguard (25 minutes), stops at Castell Henllys junction hourly.

colourful flower arrangements make for a warm atmosphere in this appealing country inn. There's also a snug traditional bar with log fire, serving real ales, and a good restaurant (mains £10 to £20).

Canteen CAFE **££**
(☎01239-820131; www.thecanteen.org; Market St; lunch £4-9, dinner £10-14; ⏲lunch Mon-Sat, dinner Fri & Sat) The name, reasonable prices and stark decor suggest a no-nonsense approach, echoed by a menu focusing on crowd-pleasers like fish and chips, chicken Caesar salad and mushrooms on toast. Yet there's no skimping on quality. A good selection of wine is offered by the glass and meals are kicked off with complimentary bread and olive oil.

ℹ Information

National Park Information Centre & Tourist Office (☎01239-820912; Long St; ⏲10am-6pm Mon-Sat Easter-Oct, 10.30am-3pm Mon & Fri, 10.30am-1pm Tue-Thu & Sat Nov-Easter)

ℹ Getting There & Away

BICYCLE The back roads around the Preseli Hills and Cwm Gwaun offer some of the best on-road cycling in southwest Wales. You can rent a bike from **Newport Bike Hire** (☎01239-820773; www.newportbikehire.com; East St; per half-/full day £10/15), based in Wholefoods of Newport. It also stocks cycling guides and outdoor pursuits books.

BUS Buses include 412 to Haverfordwest (52 minutes), Fishguard (19 minutes), Castell Henllys (nine minutes) and Cardigan (26 minutes); plus the Poppit Rocket.

Preseli Hills

The only upland area in the Pembrokeshire Coast National Park is the Preseli Hills (Mynydd Preseli), rising to 536m at Foel Cwmcerwyn. These hills are at the centre of a fascinating prehistoric landscape, scattered with hill forts, standing stones and burial chambers, and are famous as the source of the mysterious bluestones of Stonehenge. An ancient track called the **Golden Road**, once part of a 5000-year-old trade route between Wessex and Ireland, runs along the crest of the hills, passing prehistoric cairns and the stone circle of **Bedd Arthur**.

The largest dolmen in Wales, **Pentre Ifan** is a 4500-year-old neolithic burial chamber set on a remote hillside 3 miles southeast of Newport, signposted from the A487. The huge, 5m-long capstone, weighing more than 16 tonnes, is delicately poised on three tall, pointed, upright bluestones.

The 430 from Cardigan heads to Crymych (30 minutes, no service Sunday), at the eastern end of the hills. From here you can hike along the Golden Road to the car park at Bwlch Gwynt on the B4329 (7.5 miles). You can return to Crymych (34 minutes) or continue through the Gwaun Valley to Fishguard (50 minutes) on the 15-seater **Green Dragon Bus** (☎0845 686 0242; www.greendragonbus.co.uk; membership £5; ⏲Tue, Thu & Sat Jul-Sep). It's a members-only service; pay £5 on top of your fare to the driver the first time you use it.

Hay-on-Wye & Mid-Wales

Includes »

CEREDIGION 689
Devil's Bridge & Rheidol Falls....... 693
BRECON BEACONS NATIONAL PARK....693
Black Mountain & Fforest Fawr 695
Black Mountains (Y Mynyddoedd Duon)............. 703
Hay-on-Wye (Y Gelli Gandryll).......... 704
POWYS 713
Llanwrtyd Wells (Llanwrtyd).........714
Llandrindod Wells (Llandrindod).......715
Machynlleth........719

Best Places to Eat

» Ynyshir Hall (p693)
» Hardwick (p702)
» Ultracomida (p692)

Best Places to Stay

» Ynyshir Hall, Eglwysfach (p693)
» Bodalwyn (p691)
» Gwyn Deri (p701)

Why Go?

The big draw here is the magnificent upland scenery of Brecon Beacons National Park, with book-loving Hay-on-Wye within its confines and food-loving Abergavenny on its doorstep. By contrast the Ceredigion and Powys countryside is something of a well-kept secret and certainly worthy of a closer look. This is Wales at its most rural – a landscape of lustrous green fields, wooded river valleys and small market towns; it's the part that the Industrial Revolution missed. It's also thoroughly Welsh, with around 40% of people speaking the mother tongue (over 50% in Ceredigion). Apart from exuberant, student-populated Aberystwyth, you won't find a lot of excitement in the urban areas. It's the places in between that are much more interesting, criss-crossed as they are with cycling and walking routes, and plenty of country lanes to tootle about in.

When to Go?

In the midst of spring, in May, the world's intelligentsia gets Hay fever. In August, cap off the Green Man and Brecon Jazz music festivals with a spot of bog snorkelling. As the weather starts to cool down, in September, fill up at the Abergavenny Food Festival.

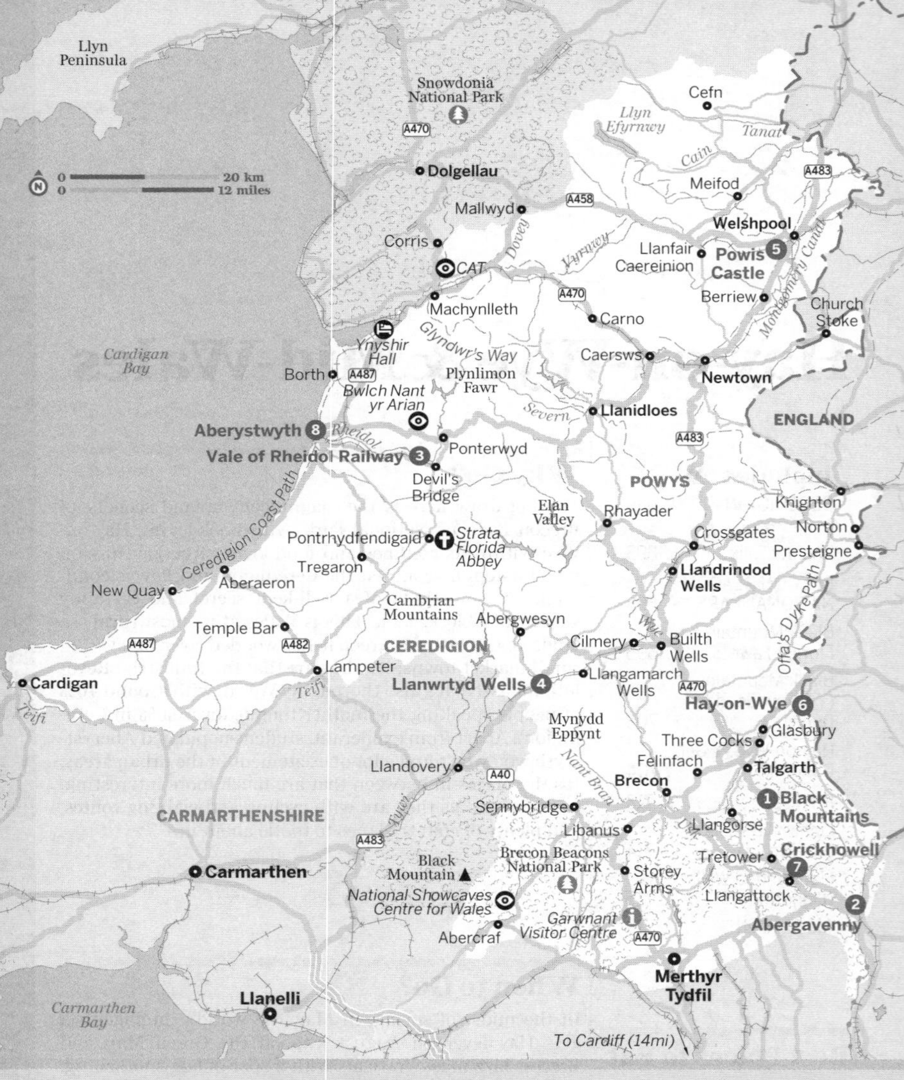

Hay-on-Wye & Mid-Wales Highlights

1. Soaking up the tranquillity of the remote Vale of Ewyas in the **Black Mountains** (p703)

2. Exploring a countryside seasoned with Wales' best restaurants in the fields around **Abergavenny** (p701)

3. Reliving the age of steam with a scenic ride to Devil's Bridge on the **Vale of Rheidol Railway** (p690)

4. Trying your hand bog snorkelling or real ale wobbling at **Llanwrtyd Wells** (p714)

5. Letting the sculptured yew paths of **Powis Castle** (p721) lead you through Welsh history

6. Experiencing charming **Hay-on-Wye** (p704), a town surrounded by nature but infatuated with books

7. Settling into village life in the heart of Brecon Beacons National Park in peaceful **Crickhowell** (p700)

8. Revelling in the high culture and student-inspired high jinks that come together by the seaside at **Aberystwyth** (p690)

CEREDIGION COAST PATH

Not to be outdone by its showy neighbour across the Teifi in Pembrokeshire, Ceredigion has opened up its own shoreline to the relentless march of coastal walkers. You can now walk 63 miles along a waymarked path between the mouths of the Rivers Teifi and Dovey. The truly hardcore could tack this on to the end of the 13- to 15-day Pembrokeshire Coast Path – a total of 249 continuous coastal miles.

For more information, visit www.walkcardiganbay.co.uk. The **Cardi Bach bus** (600; ⏲Thu-Tue Jul-Sep) covers the coast between Cardigan and New Quay in summer, making it easy to split this stretch into day-long walks.

CEREDIGION

The Welsh language is stronger in Ceredigion than most other parts of Wales, kept alive in rural communities that escaped the massive population influxes of the coal-mining valleys of the south and the slate mining towns of the north. That lack of heavy industry has left Ceredigion with some of Britain's cleanest beaches. And with no rail access south of Aberystwyth, they tend to be less crowded. Adding to the isolation is the natural barrier known as the Desert of Wales, consisting of the barren uplands of the Cambrian Mountains, which separate Ceredigion from Powys. If any area could be described as off-the-beaten-track in Wales, this is it.

Cardigan (Aberteifi)

POP 4100

Refusing to be typecast by the town's name, the folk of Cardigan are much more likely to be found ambling along the main street in hoodies and trainers than in any grandfatherly knitwear. Yet this is the sort of town where taking up knitting might just help the time pass faster – there's not a lot to do or see here. In fact, all of the most interesting places to visit are just across the river in Pembrokeshire. It is, however, the closest town to the end of the Pembrokeshire Coast Path and the first town at the beginning of the new Ceredigion Coast Path, so it sees plenty of hikers coming and going.

The shored-up and overgrown walls of **Cardigan Castle** (www.cardigancastle.com; Bridge St) make for a sorry sight – a contrasting vision of ragged stone, rampant ivy, plastic tarpaulin and metal stanchions. Long neglected by its private owner, the crumbling castle was purchased by Ceredigion Council in 2003. Plans are under way to restore it and it's occasionally used for special events. It holds an important place in Welsh culture, having been the venue for the first competitive National Eisteddfod, held in 1176.

The neo-Gothic **Guildhall** (High St) dates from 1860, and is now home to **Cardigan Market**. A country market is held here every Friday.

Sleeping & Eating

Llety Teifi B&B ££
(☎01239-615566; www.llety.co.uk; Pendre; s/d from £45/70; P 📶) New and stylish, this is Cardigan's first boutique B&B and easily its best. Breakfast is served at the much less hip place next door belonging to the owner's mother-in-law.

Fforest CAMPSITE £
(☎01239-615286; www.coldatnight.co.uk; d per week from £335) Perched on the edge of Teifi Marshes Nature Reserve, Fforest's large tents, tepees and geodesic domes challenge the notion that camping means roughing it.

Poppit Sands YHA HOSTEL £
(☎0845 371 9037; www.yha.org.uk; dm £14) Rural and secluded, this simple hostel is 4 miles northwest of town, tucked into a hillside overlooking the beach, and near the trailhead of the Pembrokeshire Coast Path.

Abdul's Tandoori Spice INDIAN £
(☎01239-621416; 2 Royal Oak, Quay St; mains £4-16; ⏲dinner) A cut above your usual curry house, gaining a loyal local following with its consistently tasty tandoori dishes and excellent service. Serves are substantial, so resist the urge to over-order. No alcohol is available.

Information

Cardigan Hospital (☎01239-612214; Pont-y-Cleifion)

Tourist Office (☎01239-613230; www.tourism.ceredigion.gov.uk; Bath House Rd; ⏰10am-5pm Mon-Sat) In the lobby of the Theatr Mwldan.

Getting There & Around

BICYCLE You can hire bikes from **New Image Bicycles** (☎01239-621275; www.newimagebicycles.co.uk; 29-30 Pendre; per half-day/day £12/18).

BUS Routes include X50 to Aberystwyth (1½ hours); 407 to Poppit Sands (15 minutes); 412 to Castell Henllys (15 minutes), Newport (24 minutes), Fishguard (40 minutes) and Haverfordwest (1¼ hours); 460 to Carmarthen (90 minutes); and the Poppit Rocket (see boxed text, p685).

Aberystwyth

POP 16,000

Thanks to its status as one of the liveliest university towns in Wales, with an admirable range of options for eating out, drinking and partaking in Welsh culture, Aberystwyth is an essential stop along the Ceredigion coast. Welsh is widely spoken here and locals are proud of their heritage. It's a particularly buzzy town during term time and retains a cosmopolitan feel year-round.

When pub culture and student life get too much for you, the quintessential Aberystwyth experience remains soaking up the sunset over Cardigan Bay. Here the trappings of a stately Georgian seaside resort remain, with an impressive promenade skirted by a sweep of pastel-coloured buildings.

Sights & Activities

National Library of Wales LIBRARY, GALLERIES
(☎01970-623800; www.llgc.org.uk; admission free; ⏰9.30am-5pm Mon-Sat) Sitting proudly on a hilltop half a mile east of town, the National Library is a cultural powerhouse, holding millions of books in many languages. The **Hengwrt Room** is where it displays all of the really important stuff, such as the 12th-century *Black Book of Carmarthen* (the oldest existing Welsh text) and the 13th-century Tintern Abbey Bible. Other galleries display an ever-stimulating set of changing exhibitions.

Ceredigion Museum MUSEUM
(☎01970-633088; http://museum.ceredigion.gov.uk; Terrace Rd; admission free; ⏰10am-5pm Mon-Sat Apr-Sep, noon-4.30pm Oct-Mar) Houses entertaining exhibitions on Aberystwyth's history – everything from old chemist furnishings to hand-knitted woollen knickers and a wall devoted to the *Little Britain* TV series.

Vale of Rheidol Railway STEAM RAILWAY
(☎01970-625819; www.rheidolrailway.co.uk; Park Ave; adult/child return £14/3.50; ⏰Apr-Oct, check online timetable) Old steam locomotives (built between 1923 and 1938) have been lovingly restored by volunteers and chug for almost 12 miles up the valley of the River Rheidol to Devil's Bridge (an hour each way). The line opened in 1902 to bring lead and timber out of the valley.

Cliff Railway FUNICULAR
(www.aberystwythcliffrailway.co.uk; adult/child £3.50/2.50; ⏰10am-5pm daily Apr-Oct, Wed-Sun mid-Feb–Mar) If your constitution's not up to the climb of Constitution Hill (135m), at the northern end of North Beach, you can catch a lift on the trundling little **Cliff Railway**, the UK's longest electric funicular (1896) and possibly the slowest, too, at a G-force-busting 4mph.

From the wind-blown balding hilltop there are tremendous coastal views. One relic of the Victorian era is a **camera obscura** (admission £1) that allows you to see practically into the windows of the houses below.

WORTH A TRIP

STRATA FLORIDA ABBEY

On an isolated, peaceful site southeast of Aberystwyth lies this ruined Cistercian **abbey** (www.cadw.wales.gov.uk; adult/child £3/2.60; ⏰10am-5pm Apr-Sep, unattended & free in other months). The best-preserved remnant is a simple, complete arched doorway, with lines like thick rope. At the rear of the site a roof has been added to protect two chapels which still have some of their 14th-century tiling, including one depicting a man admiring himself in a mirror.

The site is a mile down a rural road from the village of Pontrhydfendigaid on the B4343; the village is 15 miles from Aberystwyth or 9 miles south of Devil's Bridge.

Aberystwyth

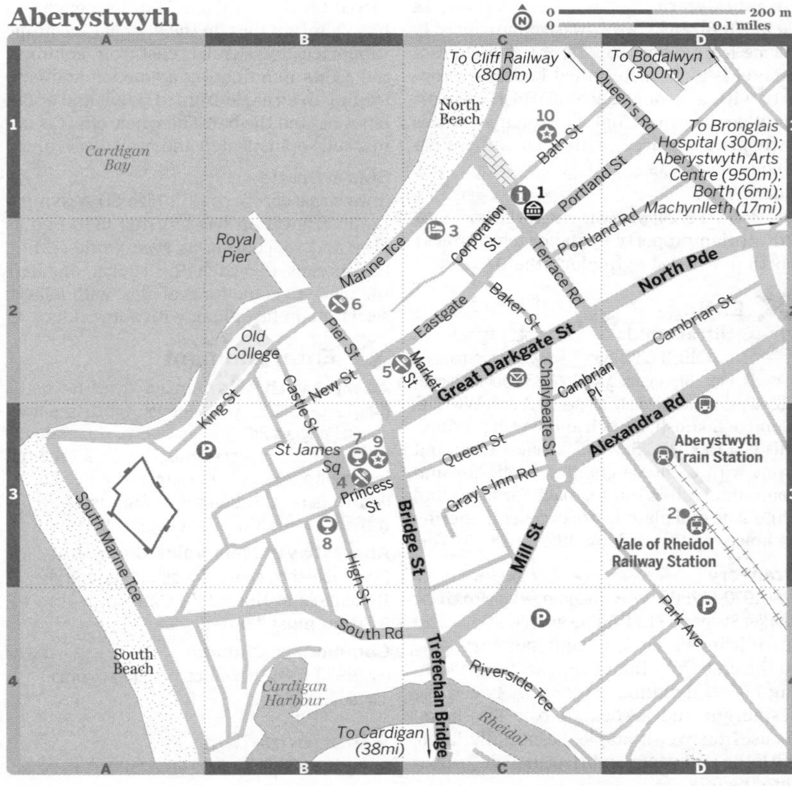

Ystwyth Trail CYCLING, WALKING

Suitable for cyclists and walkers, this 20-mile waymarked route mainly follows an old rail line from Aberystwyth southeast to Tregaron, at the foot of the Cambrian Mountains. For the first 12 miles it shadows the River Ystwyth, while at the end it enters the Teifi Valley. At the Aberystwyth end you can pick up the trail from the footbridge on Riverside Tce; although you'll get more downhills if you start from Tregaron.

Sleeping

TOP CHOICE **Bodalwyn** B&B ££

(☎01970-612578; www.bodalwyn.co.uk; Queen's Ave; s/d/f from £45/65/80;) Simultaneously upmarket and homely, this handsome Edwardian B&B goes the extra mile, offering tasteful rooms and a hearty cooked breakfast (with vegetarian options). Ask for room 3, with the bay window.

Aberystwyth

Sights

1 Ceredigion Museum C1

Activities, Courses & Tours

2 Vale of Rheidol Railway Station D3

Sleeping

3 Gwesty Cymru C2

Eating

4 Blue Creek Cafe B3
5 Orangery B2
6 Ultracomida B2

Drinking

7 Academy B3
8 Ship & Castle B3

Entertainment

9 Aberystwyth Male Voice Choir B3
10 Commodore Cinema C1

Gwesty Cymru BOUTIQUE HOTEL ££
(☎01970-612252; www.gwestycymru.com; 19 Marine Tce; s/d from £65/85; 📶) This gem of a hotel is a character-filled boutique property with a strong sense of Welsh identity, right on the waterfront. Local slate features throughout, paired with rich aubergine-coloured carpets.

Borth YHA HOSTEL £
(☎0845 371 9724; www.yha.org.uk; dm from £10) Edwardian property by the beach, 7 miles north of Aberystwyth along the B4572.

Eating

TOP CHOICE **Ultracomida** TAPAS, DELICATESSEN ££
(☎01970-630686; www.ultracomida.co.uk; 31 Pier St; tapas £4, 1-/2-/3-course dinner £12/16/19; ⊙lunch daily, dinner Fri & Sat) With its blend of Spanish, French and Welsh produce, this is a foodie's Nirvana: a delicatessen out front with a cheese counter to die for and communal tables out the back for tapas and wine. The deli platters are excellent, offering a choice of meat, fish or cheese (£8.95).

Orangery MODERN WELSH ££
(☎01970-617606; www.theorangerybistro.co.uk; Market St; mains £13-15) The smartest place in town brings a sense of contemporary style to the erstwhile Talbot Inn, an 1830 coaching house, dividing the space between the restaurant and a cocktail bar. The menu focuses on Welsh staples, especially lamb, with the odd pasta and risotto dish thrown into the mix.

Blue Creek Cafe CAFE £
(11 Princess St; ⊙10am-6pm Mon-Sat; 📶) The best coffee we've found outside of Cardiff. Plus it stocks a good selection of homemade cakes and snacks, and offers free wireless internet and newspapers to read.

Drinking

Thanks to its large student population, during term time Aberystwyth has a livelier nightlife than anywhere else in the northern half of the country, so if you're going to go out bar-hopping anywhere, make it here. Wednesday nights can be a surreal experience when the various university clubs hit the town in costume: one minute you might be sitting in an empty pub and the next minute the whole place may fill up with Kiss impersonators, or cross-dressers, or school girls.

TOP CHOICE **Academy** BAR
(New Darkgate St) An incongruous setting for a booze palace, perhaps, but an incredibly beautiful one. This former chapel has Victorian tiles on the floor, a mezzanine supported by slender cast-iron columns, red lights illuminating a wooden staircase leading to an eagle-fronted pulpit and organ pipes behind the bar. The whole effect is upmarket, sophisticated and, well, heavenly.

Ship & Castle PUB
(www.shipandcastle.co.uk; 1 High St) A sympathetic renovation has left this 1830 pub as cosy and welcoming as ever, while adding big screens to watch the rugger on. It is the place to come for real ales, with a large selection on tap, along with a few ciders.

Entertainment

Aberystwyth Arts Centre THEATRE, CINEMA
(☎01970-623232; www.aberystwythartscentre.co.uk; Penglais Rd) Stages opera, drama, dance and concerts, plus there's a cinema, bookshop, art gallery, bar and cafe. The centre is on the Penglais campus of the university, half a mile east of the town.

Aberystwyth Male Voice Choir MALE CHOIR
(www.aberchoir.co.uk; Bridge St; free entry) Rehearses at the RAFA Club from 7pm to 8.30pm most Thursdays.

Commodore Cinema CINEMA
(☎01970-612421; www.commodorecinema.co.uk; Bath St)

Information

Bronglais Hospital (☎01970-623131; Caradoc Rd)

Tourist office (☎01970-612125; www.tourism.ceredigion.gov.uk; cnr Terrace Rd & Bath St; ⊙10am-5pm Mon-Sat Sep-May, daily Jun-Aug) Located below the Ceredigion Museum.

Getting There & Away

BUS Routes include X18 to Rhayader (1¼ hours), Llandrindod Wells (1½ hours) and Builth Wells (1¾ hours); 28 to Machynlleth (45 minutes) and Fairbourne (two hours); X32 to Corris (one hour), Dolgellau (1¼ hours), Porthmadog (2¼ hours), Caernarfon (three hours) and Bangor (3½ hours); X40 to Carmarthen (2¼ hours), Swansea (3¼ hours) and Cardiff (4¼ hours); and X50 to Cardigan (1½ hours). A daily National Express coach heads to/from Newtown (£9.40, 80 minutes), Welshpool (£11, 1¾ hours), Shrewsbury (£14, 2¼ hours), Birmingham (£27, four hours) and London (£33, seven hours).

TRAIN Aberystwyth is the terminus of the Cambrian line, which crosses Mid-Wales every two hours en route to Birmingham (£17, three hours) via Machynlleth (£4.90, 33 minutes), Newtown (£9.80, 1¼ hours), Welshpool (£11, 1½ hours) and Shrewsbury (£15, two hours).

DON'T MISS

YNYSHIR HALL

Tucked away to the south of the River Dovey estuary, just off the main Aberystwyth-Machynlleth road (A487), this grand manor house with a 15th-century core was once kept as a hunting lodge by Queen Victoria. It's now a wonderful boutique **hotel** (☎01654-781209; www.ynyshirhall.co.uk; r £160-395; P 📶) which has hosted Hollywood royalty (Richard Gere stayed in the Vermeer room) and its **restaurant** (3-course lunch/dinner £22/70) is one of Wales' finest; part of a very small club of Welsh Michelin star holders. The house's Victorian purpose is reflected in a menu that includes game birds such as quail, partridge and pheasant, all faultlessly prepared. The friendly (rather than fawning) staff are never less than professional.

Bwlch Nant yr Arian

Part of a forestry commission block, **Bwlch Nant yr Arian** (www.forestry.gov.uk/bwlchnantyrarian; ⏲10am-5pm summer, 11am-dusk winter) is a picturesque piece of woodland set around a lake, ringed with mountain biking and walking tracks. The main drawcard, however, is the red kite feeding which takes place at 2pm daily (3pm daylight saving time). Even outside of mealtime you'll quite often see the majestic birds of prey circling around. You can watch all the action from the terrace of the attractive turf-roofed visitor centre and cafe.

It's 9 miles east of Aberystwyth on the A44.

Devil's Bridge & Rheidol Falls

Dramatic **Devil's Bridge** (www.devilsbridgefalls.co.uk; adult/child £3.50/1.50; ⏲9.45am-5pm Apr-Oct, other times access via turnstile £2) spans the Rheidol Valley on the lush western slopes of Plynlimon (Pumlumon Fawr; 752m), source of the Rivers Wye and Severn. Here the Rivers Mynach and Rheidol tumble together in a narrow gorge.

The Mynach is spanned by three famous stone bridges, stacked on top of each other. The lowest and oldest is believed to have been built by the monks of Strata Florida Abbey before 1188. It's one of many bridges associated with an arcane legend which involves the devil building the bridge on the condition that he gets the first thing to cross it. An old lady outwits the devil by throwing some food over, which her dog chases and everybody's happy – except the devil and, presumably, the dog.

However it's not the bridges that are the real attraction here. Just above the confluence, the Rheidol drops 90m in a series of spectacular waterfalls. There are two possible walks: one, just to view the three bridges, takes only 10 minutes (£1); the other, a half-hour walk, descends 100 steps (Jacob's Ladder), crosses the Mynach and ascends the other side.

The Vale of Rheidol Railway heads to Devil's Bridge from Aberystwyth, as does the 18-mile Rheidol Cycle Trail.

BRECON BEACONS NATIONAL PARK

Rippling dramatically for 45 miles from Llandeilo in the west, all the way to the English border, Brecon Beacons National Park (Parc Cenedlaethol Bannau Brycheiniog) encompasses some of the finest scenery in Mid-Wales. High mountain plateaux of grass and heather, their northern rims scalloped with glacier-scoured hollows, rise above wooded, waterfall-splashed valleys and green, rural landscapes. It couldn't be more different than rock-strewn Snowdonia to the north, but it offers comparable thrills.

There are four distinct regions within the park, neatly bounded by main roads: the wild, lonely Black Mountain in the west, with its high moors and glacial lakes; Fforest Fawr, which lies between the A4067 and A470, whose rushing streams and spectacular waterfalls form the headwaters of the Rivers Tawe and Neath; the Brecon Beacons proper, a group of very distinctive, flat-topped hills that includes **Pen-y-Fan** (886m), the park's highest peak; and, from the A40 northeast to the English border, the rolling heathland ridges of the Black Mountains – don't confuse them with the Black Mountain (singular) in the west.

Brecon Beacons National Park

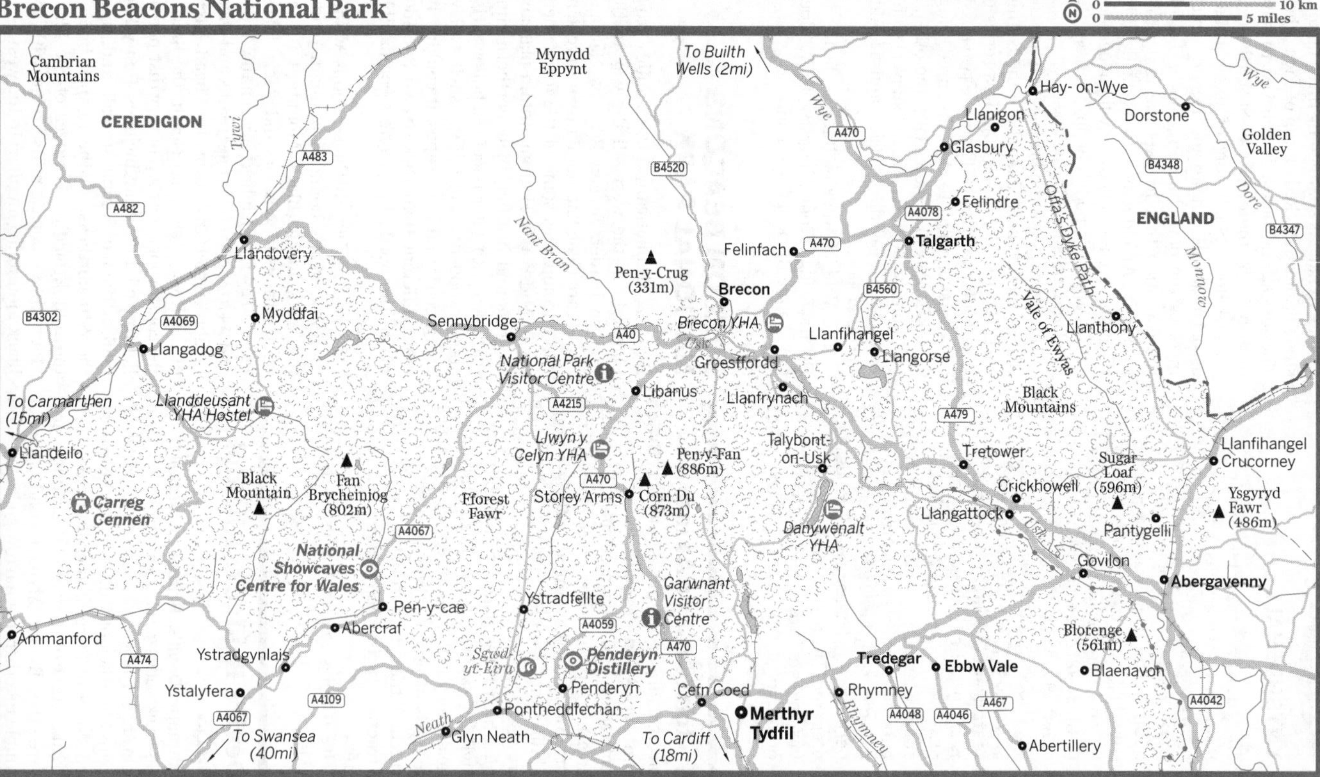

There are hundreds of walking routes in the park, ranging from gentle strolls to strenuous climbs. The park's staff organise guided walks and other active events throughout the summer. A set of six *Walk Cards* (£1 each) is available from the tourist offices of all the towns in and around the park, as well as the main park visitor centre near Libanus.

Likewise, there are many excellent off-road mountain-biking routes, including a series of 14 graded and waymarked trails detailed in a map and guidebook pack (£7.50); see also www.mtbbreconbeacons.co.uk for more information.

Ordnance Survey (OS) Landranger maps 160 and 161 cover most of the park, and they have walking and cycling trails marked.

Black Mountain & Fforest Fawr

West of the A470, this entire half of the national park is sparsely inhabited, without any towns of note. **Black Mountain** (Mynydd Du) contains the wildest, loneliest and least visited walking country. Its finest feature is the sweeping escarpment of **Fan Brycheiniog** (802m), which rises steeply above the scenic glacial lakes of Llyn y Fan Fach and Llyn y Fan Fawr. It can be climbed from Llanddeusant; the round trip is 12 miles.

Fforest Fawr (Great Forest; www.fforestfawrgeopark.org.uk), once a Norman hunting ground, is now a Unesco geopark famous for its varied landscapes, ranging from bleak moorland to flower-flecked limestone pavement and lush, wooded ravines choked with moss and greenery.

Sights & Activities

National Showcaves Centre for Wales CAVES

(☎01639-730284; www.showcaves.co.uk; adult/child £13/7; ⏰10am-4pm Apr-Oct) The limestone plateau of the southern Fforest Fawr, around the upper reaches of the River Tawe, is riddled with some of the largest and most complex cave systems in Britain. Most can only be visited by experienced cavers, but this set of three caves is well lit, spacious and easily accessible, even to children.

The highlight of the 1.5-mile self-guided tour is the **Cathedral Cave**, a high-domed chamber with a lake fed by two waterfalls that pour from openings in the rock. Nearby is the **Bone Cave**, where 42 Bronze Age skeletons were discovered. **Dan-yr-Ogof Cave**, part of a 10-mile complex, has interesting limestone formations.

The admission fee also gives entry to various other attractions on-site, including a museum, a reconstructed Iron Age farm, a prehistoric theme park filled with life-sized fibreglass dinosaurs, a shire-horse centre and a children's playground. The complex is just off the A4067 north of Abercraf.

Sgwd-yr-Eira WATERFALLS

Between the villages of Pontneddfechan and Ystradfellte is a series of dramatic waterfalls, where the Rivers Mellte, Hepste and Pyrddin pass through steep forested gorges. The finest is **Sgwd-yr-Eira** (Waterfall of the Snow), where you can actually walk behind the torrent. At one point the River Mellte disappears into **Porth-yr-Ogof** (Door to the Cave), the biggest cave entrance in Britain (3m high and 20m wide), only to reappear 100m further south.

Walks in the area are outlined on the national park's *Wood of the Waterfalls* walk card (£1), available from visitor centres.

Penderyn Distillery WHISKY DISTILLERY

(☎01685-813300; www.welsh-whisky.co.uk; adult/child £5/2; ⏰9.30am-5pm) Before the ascendency of the chapels in the 19th century, the Welsh were as fond of whisky as their Celtic cousins in Scotland and Ireland. This boutique, independently owned distillery released its first malt whiskey in 2004, marking the resurgence of Welsh whisky-making after a more than 100-year absence. It's distilled with fresh spring water drawn from directly beneath the distillery, then matured in bourbon casks and finished in rich Madeira wine casks to create a golden-hued drop of liquid fire. It also produces Brecon Gin, Brecon Five Vodka and Merlyn Cream Liqueur.

From the imposing black visitors centre you can watch the spirits being made, and adult tickets include tastings of two products. If the weather's a bit cold and wet, it's a great way to warm up. Enthusiasts can take a 2½-hour Master Class, which includes a guided tour and tastings (per person £45, bookings essential).

BEACONS BUSES

The **Beacons Buses** (☎01873-853254; www.travelbreconbeacons.info; day ticket £8) only run on Sundays and bank holidays from April to September. With a day ticket (buy it on the first bus you board) and a careful analysis of the online timetable you can plan a full day of sightseeing and activities. On the B16 and B17 circular routes you can get on and off at any point (adult/child £5/3.50). Some services allow bikes to be transported.

Useful routes include:

» B1 – Cardiff, Storey Arms, Libanus, Brecon

» B2 – Storey Arms, Libanus, Brecon

» B3 – Penderyn, Storey Arms, Libanus, Brecon

» B4 – Abergavenny, Crickhowell, Tretower, Brecon

» B5 – Cardiff, Caerphilly, Libanus, Brecon

» B6 – Swansea, National Showcaves Centre, Brecon

» B10 – Carmarthen, National Botanic Garden, Llandeilo, Brecon

» B11 – Brecon, National Park Visitor Centre

» B12 – Brecon, Llangorse Lake, Hay-on-Wye

» B13 (Geopark Circular) – Brecon, National Park Visitor Centre, Storey Arms, National Showcaves Centre, Penderyn

» B15 – Brecon, Tretower, Crickhowell, Big Pit, Blaenavon

» B16 (Taff Trail Roundabout) – Brecon, National Park Visitor Centre, Storey Arms, Brecon Mountain Railway, Llanfrynach

» B17 (Offa's Dyke Flyer) – Hay-on-Wye, Llanthony Priory, Llanfihangel Crucorney, Pandy

Sleeping

Llanddeusant YHA HOSTEL £
(☎0845 371 9750; www.yha.org.uk; Old Red Lion; dm from £12) This hostel is a former inn, nestled in the western fringes of Black Mountain.

Llwyn y Celyn YHA HOSTEL £
(☎0845 371 9029; www.yha.org.uk; dm from £18) An 18th-century farmhouse in 6 hectares of woodland 6 miles south of Brecon on the A470.

Information

Garwnant Visitor Centre (☎01685-723060; www.forestry.gov.uk) At the head of Llwyn Onn Reservoir, 5 miles north of Merthyr Tydfil on the A470. It's the starting point for a couple of easy forest walks and a cycle trail. It also has a cafe, an adventure play area and a rope-swing 'assault course' for kids.

Waterfalls Centre (☎01639-721795; Pontneathvaughan Rd, Pontneddfechan; ⏲9.30am-5pm Apr-Oct, 9.30am-3pm Sat & Sun Nov-Mar)

Getting There & Away

Bus 63 between Swansea and Brecon stops at the National Showcaves Centre.

Brecon (Aberhonddu) & Around

POP 7900

The handsome stone market town of Brecon stands at the meeting of the River Usk and the River Honddu. For centuries the town thrived as a centre of wool production and weaving; today it's the main hub of the national park and a natural base for exploring the surrounding countryside. The conical hill of **Pen-y-Crug** (331m), capped by an Iron Age hill fort, rises to the northwest of the town, and makes a good objective for a short hike (2.5 miles round trip).

Sights

Brecon Cathedral CHURCH
(www.breconcathedral.org.uk; Cathedral Close) Perched on a hill above the River Honddu, Brecon Cathedral was founded as part of a Benedictine monastery in 1093, though little remains of the Norman structure except the carved font and parts of the nave. It's a lovely church and very visitor-friendly; seven information points provide information about key features.

In the cathedral grounds is a **Heritage Centre** (admission free; ⏲10am-4.30pm Mon-

Sat), cafe and gift shop housed in a restored 15th-century tithe barn.

Brecknock Museum & Art Gallery MUSEUM (www.powys.gov.uk; Captain's Walk; adult/child £1/50p; ⏲10am-5pm Mon-Sat) Behind the stolid neoclassical exterior of the former Shire Hall, the town's museum focuses on the archaeology, history and natural history of the Brecon area.

Activities

Monmouthshire & Brecon Canal CANAL
Brecon is the northern terminus of this canal, built between 1799 and 1812 for the movement of coal, iron ore, limestone and agricultural goods. The 33 miles from Brecon to Pontypool is back in business, transporting a generally less grimy cargo of holidaymakers and river-dwellers. The busiest section is around Brecon, with craft departing from the canal basin, 400m south of the town centre. **Dragonfly Cruises** (☎01874-685222; www.dragonfly-cruises.co.uk; adult/child £7/4.50; ⏲Mar-Oct) runs 2½-hour narrowboat trips.

You can also take to the water with **Beacon Park Boats** (☎01873-858277; www.beaconparkboats.com; ⏲10am-5pm Mar-Oct), which rents out electric-powered boats (per hour/half-day/day from £16/35/50; up to six people) and three-seater Canadian canoes (per hour/half-day/day from £10/20/30). It also has a fleet of luxury narrowboats for longer live-in voyages, as does **Cambrian Cruisers** (☎01874-665315; www.cambriancruisers.co.uk; Ty Newydd, Pencelli). **Backwaters Adventure Equipment Ltd** (☎01873-831825; www.backwatershire.co.uk; per day kayak/canoe £28/40) rents kayaks and canoes, including buoyancy aids and waterproof barrels.

A peaceful 8.5-mile walk along the towpath leads to the picturesque village of Talybont-on-Usk. You can return on the X43 bus or, on summer Sundays, the Beacons Bus B4 or B16.

Cantref Adventure Farm & Riding Centre HORSE RIDING
(☎01874-665223; www.cantref.com; Upper Cantref Farm, Llanfrynach; adult/child £7.50/6.50; ⏲10.30am-5.30pm Easter-Nov, weekends & school holidays only Dec-Easter) In the countryside south of Brecon, Cantref operates a child-focused fun farm, complete with pig races, lamb feeding and unfortunates dressed as horses, dancing for the little troops. More interesting for adults are the pony trekking and hacking – ie more advanced terrain – expeditions (per hour/half-/full day £18/27/50), heading out into the Brecon Beacons.

It's reached by a set of narrow country lanes; follow the horseshoe signs from the A40, southeast of town. Bunkhouse

CLIMBING PEN-Y-FAN

One of the most popular hikes in the national park is the ascent of Pen-y-Fan (886m), the highest peak in the Brecon Beacons (around 120,000 people make the climb each year, giving it the nickname 'the motorway'). The shortest route to the summit begins at the Pont ar Daf car park on the A470, 10 miles southwest of Brecon. It's a steep but straightforward slog up a deeply eroded path (now paved with natural stone) to the summit of Corn Du (873m), followed by a short dip and final ascent to Pen-y-Fan (4.5 miles round trip; allow three hours). A slightly longer (5.5 miles round trip) but just as crowded path starts at the Storey Arms outdoor centre, a mile to the north. The X43 and various Beacons Buses stop at the Storey Arms. (Note: the Storey Arms is not a pub!)

You can avoid the crowds by choosing one of the longer routes on the north side of the mountain, which also have the advantage of more interesting views on the way up. The best starting point is the Cwm Gwdi car park, at the end of a minor road 3.5 miles southwest of Brecon. From here, you follow a path along the crest of the Cefn Cwm Llwch ridge, with great views of the neighbouring peaks, with a final steep scramble up to the summit. The round trip from the car park is 7 miles; allow three to four hours. Starting and finishing in Brecon, the total distance is 14 miles.

Remember that Pen-y-Fan is a serious mountain – the weather can change rapidly, and people have to be rescued here every year. Wear hiking boots and take warm clothes, waterproofs, and a map and compass. You can get advice and weather forecasts at the National Park Visitor Centre or from the **Met Office** (☎0870 900 0100; www.metoffice.gov.uk).

Brecon

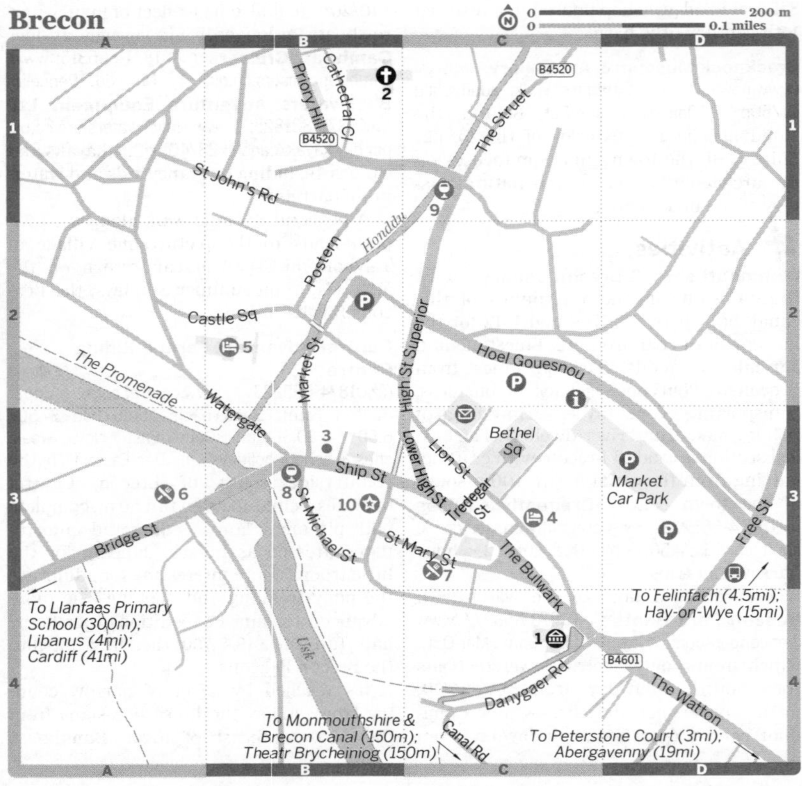

accommodation (from £14) and basic camping is available.

Llangorse Lake WATER SPORTS

Reed-fringed Llangorse Lake (Llyn Syfaddan), to the east of Brecon, may be Wales' second-largest natural lake (after Llyn Tegid), but it's barely more than a mile long and half a mile wide. Close to the northern shore is a **crannog**, a lake dwelling built on an artificial island. Such dwellings or refuges were used from the late Bronze Age until early medieval times. Tree-ring dating shows that this one (of which only the base remains) was built around AD 900, probably by the royal house of Brycheiniog. Among the artefacts found here was a dugout canoe, now on display in Brecon's Brecknock Museum; other finds can be seen at the National Museum Cardiff. There's a reconstruction of a crannog house on the shore.

The lake is the national park's main water sports location, used for sailing, windsurfing, canoeing and water-skiing. **Lakeside Caravan Park** (☎01874-658226; www.llangorselake.co.uk), on the north shore, rents rowing boats (per hour/day £12/30), Canadian canoes (per hour/day £12/36) and Wayfarer sailing dinghies (per hour £25; you'll need to know how to rig it yourself).

Festivals & Events

Brecon Jazz Festival JAZZ

(www.breconjazz.co.uk; concerts free-£32) Organised by the team behind the Hay Festival, in the second weekend in August Brecon hosts one of Europe's leading jazz events.

Brecon Beast MOUNTAIN BIKING

(www.breconbeast.co.uk; entry £28) A gruelling mountain bike challenge over 44 or 68 miles, held in mid-September. The fee covers camping, refreshments on the route, a 'pasta party' and a brag-worthy T-shirt.

Brecon

Sights

1 Brecknock Museum & Art Gallery C4
2 Brecon Cathedral B1

Activities, Courses & Tours

3 Biped Cycles B3

Sleeping

4 Cantre Selyf C3
5 Castle of Brecon Hotel B2

Eating

6 Bridge Cafe A3
7 Roberto's C3

Drinking

8 Boar's Head B3
9 Bull's Head C1

Entertainment

10 Coliseum Cinema B3

Sleeping & Eating

BRECON

TOP CHOICE Cantre Selyf B&B ££

(☎01874-622904; www.cantreselyf.co.uk; 5 Lion St; s/d from £56/72; P wi-fi) This elegant 17th-century town house, right in the middle of Brecon, has atmospheric period decor and furnishings, including plaster mouldings, original fireplaces and cast-iron bedsteads.

Castle of Brecon Hotel HOTEL ££

(☎01874-624611; www.breconcastle.co.uk; Castle Sq; s/d from £65/75; P) Built into the ruined walls of Brecknock Castle, this grand old hotel had been getting a bit creaky but an ongoing renovation has been leaving a trail of comfortable, refurbished rooms. The welcome remains as warm as ever.

Bridge Cafe B&B, CAFE ££

(☎01874-622024; www.bridgecafe.co.uk; 7 Bridge St; s/d from £30/50; wi-fi) With a particular focus on refuelling weary walkers and mountain bikers, Bridge Cafe offers home-cooked meals (mains £8), such as hearty casseroles, in cosy surrounds. Local, organic ingredients are used wherever possible. Upstairs are three plain but comfortable bedrooms with down-filled duvets and crisp, cotton sheets.

Roberto's ITALIAN ££

(☎01874-611880; St Mary St; mains £9-20; ⊙dinner daily, closed Sun winter; vegetarian) They may be plastic vines hanging from the trellis on the ceiling, but everything else about Roberto's is authentically Italian, from the relaxed atmosphere to the free olives and crostini, to the *puttanesca* (tomatoes, garlic, olive and anchovies) sauce. Though, of course, that's Welsh beef lurking underneath the gorgonzola.

AROUND BRECON

TOP CHOICE Felin Fach Griffin RESTAURANT-WITH-ROOMS ££

(☎01874-620111; www.felinfachgriffin.co.uk; Felinfach; mains £17-19, 1-/2-/3-course set supper £15/22/26; ⊙closed Mon lunch) With a string of awards as long as its extensive wine list, the Griffin offers gourmet dining in a relaxed and unpretentious setting. Open fires, leather sofas and timber beams create a comfortable atmosphere, while the kitchen follows a 'simple things done well' mantra, making the most of local fish, meat and game. Upstairs are a set of chintz-free rooms (singles/doubles from £85/120), with just a splash of colour to set off antique four-poster beds equipped with goose-down pillows and duvets. The Griffin is 5 miles northeast of Brecon on the A470.

Peterstone Court HOTEL, RESTAURANT ££

(☎01874-665387; www.peterstone-court.com; A40, Llanhamlach; r £120-220; P wi-fi swimming pool) An elegant Georgian manor house overlooking the River Usk, Peterstone enjoys views across the valley to the peaks of Cribyn and Pen-y-Fan. The large bedrooms combine antiques with modern designer furniture and crisp linen. Its restaurant (mains £13 to £19) has the added advantage of serving produce straight from the manor's farm, turned out by a Ritz-trained chef who won the Welsh International Culinary Championships in 2010. Llanhamlach is 3 miles southeast of Brecon, just off the A40.

White Swan PUB ££

(☎01874-665276; www.the-white-swan.com; Llanfrynach; mains £14-16; ⊙Tue-Sun) A traditional village inn that offers a candle-lit dining room with old wooden floors, a bar with comfortably worn leather sofas and armchairs, and a beautiful garden terrace. The White Swan is a great place to relax after a walk along the canal or a hike in the Brecon Beacons. The menu emphasises Welsh lamb, beef and venison, with daily fish and vegetarian specials. Llanfrynach is 3.5 miles southeast of Brecon off the B4558.

Danywenallt YHA HOSTEL £
(☎0845 371 9548; Talybont-on-Usk; dm from £18) Converted farmhouse nestling beneath the dam of Talybont Reservoir, halfway between Brecon and Crickhowell.

Brecon YHA HOSTEL £
(☎0845 371 9506; www.yha.org.uk; Groesffordd; dm from £14) Victorian farmhouse hostel, 2 miles east of Brecon.

Drinking

Bull's Head PUB
(86 The Struet) Arguably the best real-ale pub in town, with Evan Evans beer from Llandeilo and a range of guest ales, the riverside Bull's Head is cosy, quiet and friendly. It also serves good pub grub and occasionally hosts live music.

Boar's Head PUB
(Ship St) A lively local pub, with sofas in the back room and the full range of Breconshire Brewery real ales on tap. There's a sunny beer garden overlooking the river, and regular live music.

Entertainment

Brecon & District Male Choir CHOIR
(www.breconchoir.co.uk; Llanfaes Primary School, Orchard St; ⏲7.30-9.30pm Fri) For booming harmonies, head to the practice sessions of the local men's choir; visitors are welcome.

Theatr Brycheiniog THEATRE
(☎01874-611622; www.theatrbrycheiniog.co.uk; Canal Rd) This attractive canalside theatre complex is the town's main venue for drama, dance, comedy and music. It sometimes hosts surprisingly big-name touring acts.

Coliseum Cinema CINEMA
(☎01874-622501; www.coliseumbrecon.co.uk; Wheat St; tickets £6) As well as mainstream films, the local film society shows art-house films on Monday evenings.

Information

Brecon War Memorial Hospital (☎01874-622443; Cerrigcochion Rd)

National Park Visitor Centre (☎01874-623366; www.breconbeacons.org; Libanus; ⏲9.30am-5pm) The park's main visitor centre, with full details of walks, hiking and biking trails, outdoor activities, wildlife and geology. The centre is off the A470 road 5 miles south-west of Brecon.

Tourist Office (☎01874-622485; Market car park; ⏲9.30am-5.30pm Mon-Sat, 10am-4pm Sun)

Getting There & Away

BICYCLE Biped Cycles (☎01874-622296; www.bipedcycles.co.uk; 10 Ship St; per half-/full day £16/20) rents bikes and can arrange guided rides. The Taff Trail heads south from here to Cardiff. This forms part of the Lôn Las Cymru national cycling route which also heads north to Builth Wells.

BUS Bus X43 heads to Crickhowell (26 minutes), Abergavenny (50 minutes) and Cardiff (1½ hours); X63 to Swansea (two hours); 39 to Hay-on-Wye (41 minutes); and 704 to Newtown (two hours) via Builth Wells (40 minutes) and Llandrindod Wells (55 minutes). National Express coaches head to Birmingham (£27, 4¼ hours) and Cardiff (£4.10, 1¼ hours).

TAXI Ride and Hike (☎07971-527660; www.rideandhike.com) offers regular taxi services as well as a walkers' shuttle. Indicative fares: National Park Visitor Centre (£12), Cardiff (£60).

Crickhowell (Crughywel) & Llangattock (Llangatwg)

These prosperous, picturesque, flower-bedecked villages face each across the River Usk, linked by an elegant 17th-century stone bridge famous for having 12 arches on one side, and 13 on the other. Crickhowell is named after the distinctive flat-topped Crug Hywel (Hywel's Rock; 451m), better known as Table Mountain, which rises to the north. You can hike to the remains of an Iron Age fort at the top (3 miles round trip). The village grew up around a Norman motte (mound) and bailey castle, of which all that remains are a few tumbledown towers. There's not a lot to see in either village, but they're pleasant places for an overnight stop.

Sights & Activities

Tretower Court & Castle CASTLE, MANOR
(www.cadw.wales.gov.uk; Tretower; admission £3; ⏲10am-5pm Apr-Oct, 9.30am-4pm Fri & Sat, 11am-4pm Sun Nov-Mar) Originally the home of the Vaughan family, Tretower gives you two historic buildings for the price of one – the sturdy circular tower of a Norman motte-and-bailey castle, and a 15th-century manor house with a fine medieval garden. Together they illustrate the transition from military stronghold to country house that took place in late medieval times.

Tretower is 3 miles northwest of Crickhowell on the A479.

Arts and Craft Market MARKET
(Old Market Hall, High St, Crickhowell: ⏲Fri & Sat)

Golden Castle Riding Stables HORSE RIDING
(☎01873-812649; www.golden-castle.co.uk; Llangattock; per 90min/day from £35/55) Offers pony trekking, hacking and trail riding in the surrounding countryside.

Festivals & Events

Green Man Festival ALTERNATIVE MUSIC
(www.greenman.net; Glanusk Park; adult/child £120/50) Staged in late August, 2 miles west of Crickhowell via the B4558, Green Man is a summer music festival with a strong green ethos that caters well for children and people with disabilities. Yet that would all count for naught if the line-up wasn't any good, and here's where Green Man excels. Despite its relatively small size (around 10,000 people), it consistently attracts the current 'it' bands of the alternative music firmament – acts like Animal Collective, Joanna Newsom, Flaming Lips and Wilco, and dead-set legends such as Jarvis Cocker and Robert Plant. Unsurprisingly, it sells out early. Tickets include the weekend's camping.

Sleeping & Eating

Gwyn Deri B&B ££
(☎01873-812494; www.gwynderibedandbreakfast.co.uk; Mill St, Crickhowell; s/d £40/60; P 📶) The friendly couple who run this homely B&B keep the modern rooms immaculately clean. Bonuses include iPod docks, fresh fruit in the rooms and an excellent breakfast selection.

Gliffaes Hotel HOTEL ££
(☎01874-730371; www.gliffaeshotel.com; s/d from £89/99; P 📶) This Victorian mansion makes quite an impression with its Romanesque towers rising through its thickly wooded grounds on the banks of the Usk. Standard doubles start from £160, but the considerably cheaper 'small doubles' have the same facilities. It's about 4 miles northwest of Crickhowell, off the A40.

Tŷ Gwyn B&B ££
(☎01873-811625; www.tygwyn.com; Brecon Rd, Crickhowell; s/d from £40/64; P @) Once the home of Regency architect John Nash, Tŷ Gwyn is a lovely old Georgian house with four spacious en suite rooms.

Old Rectory HOTEL ££
(☎01873-810373; www.rectoryhotel.co.uk; s/d from £45/75; P 📶) Surprisingly grand for the price, this partly 16th-century stone mansion was once the home of poet Henry Vaughan. Now it has its own golf course and a clubby atmosphere pervades in the downstairs bar and restaurant. Rooms are chic and comfortable.

Riverside CAMPSITE £
(☎01873-810397; www.riversidecaravanscrickhowell.co.uk; New Rd; sites £10; ⏲Mar-Oct) Well kept and very central, next to the Crickhowell bridge, but it can get crowded in high summer; no under 18s.

Bear Hotel HOTEL, RESTAURANT ££
(☎01873-810408; www.bearhotel.co.uk; Beaufort St; s/d from £73/90; P 📶) The Bear is a fine old coaching inn with low-ceilinged rooms, stone fireplaces, blackened timber beams and antique furniture. Some rooms have four-poster beds and Jacuzzis. The menu (mains £7 to £16) ranges from hearty country fare (roast venison, slow-roasted pork belly) to more exotic dishes (Moroccan lemon chicken, salmon marinated in chilli, lime and coriander).

Nantyffin Cider Mill RESTAURANT ££
(☎01873-810775; mains £13-19; ⏲closed dinner Sun Oct-Mar & Mon) One of Mid-Wales' gastronomic pioneers, this 16th-century drovers' inn takes great pride in using local produce to create simple, unfussy dishes that allow the quality of the ingredients to shine through. The dining room is a stylish blend of bare stone, exposed roof beams, designer chairs and white table linen, set around the original 19th-century cider press. Nantyffin is a mile northwest of Crickhowell on the A40.

Information

Tourist Office (☎01873-812105; www.crickhowellinfo.org.uk; Beaufort St, Crickhowell) Has leaflets for local walks.

Getting There & Away

Bus X43 connects Crickhowell with Abergavenny (17 minutes), Brecon (26 minutes) and Cardiff (2¼ hours).

Abergavenny (Y Fenni)

POP 14,000

Bustling, workaday Abergavenny is set amid shapely, tree-fringed hills on the eastern edge of Brecon Beacons National Park. While not the most immediately attractive town, it's well worth trying to get under the skin of this place.

Abergavenny was traditionally best known as a place for outdoor pursuits – it makes a fine base for walks, cycling and paragliding in the surrounding hills – but it is as the capital of a burgeoning food scene that the town has really come into its own. Its position at the heart of Wales' new cuisine, which celebrates the best in fresh, local and organic produce, is generating international interest in both its food festival and its acclaimed eateries, the best of which are just out of town in the surrounding countryside.

Abergavenny sits between three impressive protrusions: Blorenge (561m) to the southwest; Ysgyryd Fawr (486m) to the northeast; and Sugar Loaf (596m) to the northwest. Each has rewarding walks and fine views of the Usk Valley and the Black Mountains, of which the last two form the southernmost summits. For more leisurely walks, you can follow easy paths along the banks of the River Usk or explore the towpath of the Monmouthshire and Brecon Canal, which passes a mile southwest of the town.

Sights

St Mary's Priory Church & Tithe Barn

CHURCH

(www.stmarys-priory.org; Monk St; ⏲10am-4pm) Relatively modest-looking, St Mary's contains a remarkable treasury of aristocratic tombs within. It was founded at the same time as the castle (1087) as part of a Benedictine priory, but the present building dates mainly from the 14th century, with 15th- and 19th-century additions and alterations. In the northern transept is one of the most important medieval carvings in Europe – a monumental 15th-century wooden representation of the biblical figure of Jesse.

The priory's 13th century **tithe barn** (⏲9am-5pm) has recently been restored and converted into an excellent heritage centre and a food hall focusing on locally sourced Welsh products.

Abergavenny Castle & Museum

CASTLE, MUSEUM

(www.abergavennymuseum.co.uk; Castle St; admission free; ⏲11am-5pm Mon-Sat, 2-5pm Sun Mar-Oct, 11am-4pm Mon-Sat Nov-Feb) Not much remains of Abergavenny Castle except for an impressive stretch of curtain wall on either side of the gatehouse on the northwest side. The castle keep, converted into a hunting lodge by the Victorians, now houses a small museum devoted to the history of the castle and the town.

Festivals & Events

South Wales Three Peaks Trial

WALKING

(www.threepeakstrial.co.uk) Annual walking challenge held in March.

DON'T MISS

GOOD FOOD COUNTRY

Many of the eateries that cemented Abergavenny's reputation as Wales' culinary capital are secluded within the surrounding fields.

Hardwick

MODERN WELSH ££

(☎01873-854220; www.thehardwick.co.uk; Old Raglan Rd, Abergavenny; mains £14-20, 2-/3-course lunch £19/24; ⏲Tue-Sat) The Hardwick is a traditional pub-style restaurant with an old stone fireplace, low ceiling beams and terracotta floor tiles. Ex-Walnut Tree alumnus Stephen Terry has created a gloriously unpretentious menu that celebrates the best of country cooking; save room for the homemade ice cream. The Hardwick is 2 miles south of Abergavenny on the B4598.

Walnut Tree

MODERN WELSH ££

(☎01873-852797; www.thewalnuttreeinn.com; Llandewi Skirrid; mains £12-20, 2-/3-course lunch £18/23; ⏲Tue-Sat) Established in 1963, the legendary Walnut Tree remains one of Wales' finest restaurants despite a change of ownership, with a Michelin star to prove it. Fresh, local produce dominates, and with wood pigeon and hare on the menu last time we visited, we wouldn't be all that surprised if some of it was once scurrying around the backyard. The Walnut Tree is 3 miles northeast of Abergavenny on the B4521.

Abergavenny Festival of Cycling CYCLING
(www.abergavennyfestivalofcycling.co.uk) Mid-July lycra-enthusiasts' meet incorporating the Iron Mountain Sportif, a participatory event with 25-mile, 50-mile and 100-mile courses.

Abergavenny Food Festival FOOD
(www.abergavennyfoodfestival.co.uk) The most important gastronomic event in Wales, held on the third weekend in September.

Sleeping & Eating

TOP CHOICE **Highfield House** B&B ££
(☎01873-852371; www.highfieldabergavenny.co.uk; 6 Belmont Rd; s/d £45/68; P) A handsome Victorian villa set in attractive gardens, not far from the town centre. Peaceful Highfield has three comfortable guest bedrooms, and front-facing rooms have views over Sugar Loaf Mountain.

Angel Hotel HOTEL ££
(☎01873-857121; www.angelhotelabergavenny.com; 15 Cross St; s/d from £69/89; P 📶) Abergavenny's top hotel is a fine Georgian building that was once a famous coaching inn. Seemingly in the middle of a never-ending refurbishment, the completed communal areas downstairs feel sleek and sophisticated. Those rooms that have been finished have designer Villeroy and Boch bathrooms, and there's one with a four-poster bed. The menu makes the most of local produce (mains £7 to £21) and there's an excellent wine list.

Guest House B&B ££
(☎01873-854823; www.theguesthouseabergavenny.co.uk; 2 Oxford St; s/d from £35/65; 📶) This family-friendly B&B with cheerful, flouncy rooms (not all en suite) has a mini-menagerie of pigs, rabbits, chickens and a parrot that can match the gregarious owners in colourful language. It's certainly not lacking in character.

Mulberry House HOSTEL £
(☎01873-855959; www.mulberrycentre.com.co.uk; Pen-y-Pound Rd; dm/d £27/54; P @ 📶) Housed in an old convent (and reputedly haunted by a nun), Mulberry House is a joint venture between an educational facility and the YHA. It's popular with school groups but the family room will give you all the privacy you need.

King's Arms PUB ££
(☎01873-855074; 29 Nevill St; mains £10-17) Cosy and atmospheric, the King's Arms is a great old tavern (at least 14th-century) where you can down a pint in the bar accompanied with a quality steak-and-ale pie or bangers-and-mash. The restaurant menu (Brecon venison, Swansea Bay sea bass) takes dining to the next level of sophistication, while still keeping a rustic edge.

Information

Nevill Hall Hospital (☎01873-732732; Brecon Rd) Twenty-four-hour emergency department.

Tourist Office (☎01873-853254; www.visitabergavenny.co.uk; Swan Meadow, Cross St; ⊙10am-4pm) Merged with the Brecon Beacons National Park visitor centre.

Getting There & Away

BUS Bus routes include 83 to Monmouth (45 minutes) via Raglan (20 minutes); X3 to Cardiff (1½ hours); and X43 to Brecon (50 minutes) via Crickhowell (15 minutes). National Express coaches head to Birmingham (£12, three hours).

TRAIN There are direct trains from Cardiff (£11, 40 minutes), Shrewsbury (£22, 1¼ hours), Bangor (£35, 3½ hours) and Holyhead (£37, 4¼ hours).

Black Mountains (Y Mynyddoedd Duon)

The hills that stretch northward from Abergavenny to Hay-on-Wye, bordered by the A479 road to the west and the English border to the east, are bleak, wild and largely uninhabited, making this a popular walking area. The scenic and secluded Vale of Ewyas runs through the heart of them, from Llanfihangel Crucorney to the 542m-high Gospel Pass, which leads down to Hay-on-Wye. It's a magical place, with only a very narrow, single-track road running along it, best explored on foot, bike or horseback.

Sights & Activities

Llanthony Priory RUINS
Halfway along the Vale of Ewyas lie these atmospheric 13th-century ruins, set among grasslands and wooded hills by the River Honddu. Though not as grand as Tintern Abbey, the setting is even more romantic; JMW Turner painted the scene in 1794.

Llanthony Riding & Trekking HORSE RIDING
(☎01873-890359; www.llanthony.co.uk; Court Farm; half-/full day beginners £28/50, experienced £35/60) Next to Llanthony Priory and the Abbey Hotel. Apart from pony trekking and hacking, it also offers basic campsites (per person £3) and rents self-catering cottages.

Sleeping & Eating

Skirrid Inn PUB, B&B ££
(☎01873-890258; www.skirridmountaininn.co.uk; Llanfihangel Crucorney; r £90) Those with a taste for the macabre and ghostly will love this place. Wales' oldest inn (dating prior to 1110) once doubled as a court and over 180 people were hung here. Just so you don't forget, a noose dangles from the well-worn hanging beam, directly outside the doors to the bedrooms – which, incidentally, are very nice. The Skirrid serves decent pub grub and it makes a good base camp or finishing point for an ascent of Ysgyryd Fawr; it's a 4-mile round trip from pub to summit.

Llanthony Priory Hotel PUB, B&B ££
(☎01873-890487; www.llanthonyprioryhotel.co.uk; r £80) Seemingly growing out of the priory ruins, and incorporating some of the original medieval buildings, the Abbey Hotel is wonderfully atmospheric, with four-poster beds, stone spiral staircases and rooms squeezed into turrets; there are only five rooms and no en suites. It's also a great spot for a beer and snack.

Hay-on-Wye (Y Gelli Gandryll)

POP 1500

Hay-on-Wye, a pretty little town on the banks of the River Wye just inside the Welsh border, has developed a reputation disproportionate to its size. First came the explosion in secondhand bookshops, a charge led by the charismatic and forthright local maverick Richard Booth. Booth opened his eponymous bookshop in the 1960s and went on to proclaim himself the King of Hay, among other elaborate publicity stunts, while campaigning for an international network of book towns to support failing rural economies. With Hay becoming the world's secondhand book capital, a festival of literature and culture was established in 1988, growing in stature each year to become a major international fixture.

But Hay is not all about book browsing and celebrity spotting – it also makes an excellent base for active pursuits, with the Black Mountains, River Wye and Offa's Dyke Path all within easy access of the superb facilities of the town. The small town centre is made up of narrow sloping lanes, peppered by interesting shops, and peopled by the differing types that such individuality and so many books tend to attract. Even outside of festival time, it has a vaguely alternative ambience.

Activities

Drover Holidays CYCLING, WALKING
(☎01497-821134; www.droverholidays.co.uk; St Johns Pl) Rents mountain and touring bikes (per half-day/day/week £18/25/70) and arranges logistics for long-distance cycling or walking expeditions anywhere in Wales.

Paddles & Pedals CANOEING
(☎01497-820604; www.canoehire.co.uk; 15 Castle St) Take to the Wye waters at Hay and get collected further downstream.

Festivals

Hay Festival LITERATURE, ARTS
(☎01497-822629; www.hayfestival.com) The 10-day Hay Festival in late May has become Britain's leading festival of literature and the arts – a kind of bookworm's Glastonbury or, according to Bill Clinton, 'the Woodstock of the mind'. Like those legendary music festivals, it pulls more than its fair share of internationally famous guest stars. As well as readings, workshops, book signings, concerts and club nights, there's also a very successful children's festival called Hay Fever.

Sleeping & Eating

TOP CHOICE **Start** B&B ££
(☎01497-821391; www.the-start.net; Bridge St; s/d £45/70; P) Peacefully set on the fringes of town, this little place boasts an unbeatable riverside setting, homely rooms in a renovated 18th-century house and a flagstone-floored breakfast room. The owner can advise on local activities and walks.

(Continued on page 713)

Big Ben (p65)
The Palace of Westminster's most famous features are its 13-ton clock and its tower

DAVID TOMLINSON

SEAN CAFFREY

1. Lindisfarne Castle (p633)
This tiny, storybook castle was moulded onto a hunk of rock in 1550

2. Oxford (p182)
One of the world's most famous university towns, it's soaked in history and dripping with august buildings

3. The Lake District (p574)
A sweeping panorama of craggy hilltops, misty mountain tarns and glittering lakes

4. Wales Millennium Centre (p644)

Cardiff's premier arts complex has stacked Welsh slate, topped with a bronzed steel shell.

5. South West Coast Path (p224)

Pick it up at many points along the coast for a short (and spectacular) day's stroll, or tackle longer stretches

DAVID TOMLINSON

3

4

MANFRED GOTTSCHALK

EOIN CLARKE

NEIL SETCHFIELD

1. Hadrian's Wall (p622)

This enormous wall was to keep the 'hairy Pictish barbarians from Scotland' out of Roman England

2. Caernarfon Castle (p737)

Majestic (and intact) Caernarfon has served as a military stronghold, a seat of government and a royal palace

2

NEIL SETCHFIELD

3. Llandudno (p726)
Developed as an upmarket Victorian seaside holiday town, it still retains much of its 19th-century grandeur

4. St Paul's Cathedral (p74)
Designed by Christopher Wrenn, its dome is second in size only to St Peter's in Rome

5. Snowdonia National Park (p744)
Wales' best known and most heavily used slice of nature, including Mt Snowdon (1085m).

3

1

1. Urquhart Castle (p896)
With outstanding views, the castle is a Nessie-watching hot spot

2. Edinburgh Castle (p764)
The castle, built on brooding, black crags, is the reason for Edinburgh's existence

3. Balmoral Castle (p883)
Built in 1855, the Queen's Highland holiday home revived the Scottish Baronial architecture style

4. Three Sisters, Glen Coe (p902)
Looming over Glen Coe are massive spurs known as the Three Sisters

JONATHAN SMITH

Callanish Standing Stones (p938)

They make up one of the most complete stone circles in Britain and are one the most atmospheric prehistoric sites

(Continued from page 704)

Bear B&B ££
(01497-821302; www.thebearhay.co.uk; Bear St; s/d £33/72; P) A homely and rustic atmosphere, exposed stone walls and original beams, plus a liberal sprinkling of books, make this former coaching inn (1590) an excellent choice. It only has four rooms, of which two are en suite.

Old Black Lion GASTROPUB, B&B ££
(01497-820841; www.oldblacklion.co.uk; Lion St; s/d £53/90; P) As traditional and atmospheric as they come, this inn looks 17th-century but parts of it date from the 13th – expect low ceilings and uneven floors. The accumulated weight of centuries of hospitality is cheerfully carried by the current staff. The food is many leagues beyond pub grub: think stuffed Guinea fowl, or pork loin with black pudding (mains £12 to £18).

Three Tuns GASTROPUB ££
(01497-821855; Broad St; mains £12-19; Wed-Sun) Rebuilt and expanded after a fire partially destroyed the 16th-century building, this smart gastropub has a large garden area for alfresco food and a fancier restaurant upstairs. The international menu follows that increasingly common mantra: local, organic and sustainable.

Shepherds Ice Cream Parlour ICE CREAM £
(9 High Town; single scoop £1.50; 9.30am-6pm) Nobody should leave Hay without trying the homemade ice cream from Shepherds. It's made from sheep's milk for a lighter, smoother taste.

Drinking & Entertainment

Globe at Hay CLUB, CAFE
(01497-821762; www.globeathay.co.uk; Newport St) Converted from a Methodist chapel and filled with mismatched chairs and sofas, this very cool venue is part cafe, part bar, part club, part theatre and all-round community hub – hosting DJs, live music, comedy, theatre, film, kid's events, chess clubs and political talks.

Blue Boar PUB
(Castle St) This cosy, traditional pub is ideal for whiling away a wet afternoon with a pint of Timothy Taylor's ale, a home-cooked lunch of Glamorgan sausage and a good book.

Shopping

There are 26 secondhand and antiquarian bookshops in Hay, with hundreds of thousands of tomes stacked floor to ceiling across town. Each store is profiled on a free map, available from the tourist office and from venues around town. There are also excellent stores selling antiques, craft, art and historic maps.

Booth Books BOOKS
(www.boothbooks.co.uk; 44 Lion St) The most famous, and still the best.

Mostly Maps ANTIQUARIAN MAPS
(www.mostlymaps.com; 2 Castle St)

Hay Castle Books BOOKS
(Hay Castle, Oxford Rd) Richard Booth's primary domain these days.

Murder & Mayhem BOOKS
(5 Lion St) Detective fiction, true crime and horror.

Rose's Books BOOKS
(www.rosesbooks.com; 14 Broad St) Rare children's and illustrated books.

Information

Tourist office (01497-820144; www.hay-on-wye.co.uk; Oxford Rd; 11am-4pm; @)

Getting There & Away

Bus 39 stops in Hay-on-Wye, en route between Brecon (41 minutes) and Hereford (one hour).

POWYS

By far Wales' biggest county, Powys took the name of an ancient Welsh kingdom when it was formed in 1974 from the historic counties of Montgomeryshire, Radnorshire and Brecknockshire. Overwhelmingly rural, the majority of its 132,000 population live in villages and small towns. Newtown is easily the largest, yet even it only just scrapes above the 10,000-person mark. This county isn't just green in a literal sense – Machynlleth has become a focal point for the nation's environmentally friendly aspirations, and all over the county efforts to restore the threatened red kite have been met with outstanding success. The bird is now the very symbol of Powys, the county at Wales' green heart.

LLANWRTYD'S TWISTED EVENTS

While mulling over how to encourage tourism in Llanwrtyd in the dark winter months, some citizens started an inspired roll call of unconventionality. There's something on each month (see www.green-events.co.uk for more details) but these are the wackiest.

» **Saturnalia Beer Festival & Mountain Bike Chariot Racing** (mid-Jan) Roman-themed festival including a 'best dressed Roman' competition, the devouring of stuffed bulls' testicles and the chariot race.

» **Man vs Horse Marathon** (mid-Jun) The event that kicked all the craziness off, it's been held every year since 1980 and has resulted in some tense finishes. Two-legged runners have won only twice, the first in 2004.

» **World Bog Snorkelling Championships** (Aug bank holiday) The most famous event of all. Competitors are allowed wetsuits, snorkels and flippers to traverse a trench cut out of a peat bog, using no recognisable swimming stroke and surfacing only to navigate. Spin-off events include Mountain Bike Bogsnorkelling ('like trying to ride through treacle') and the Bogsnorkelling Triathlon, both held in July.

» **Real Ale Wobble & Ramble** (Nov) In conjunction with the Mid-Wales Beer Festival, cyclists and walkers follow waymarked routes (10, 15 or 25 miles, or 35 miles for the wobblers), supping real ales at the 'pintstops' along the way.

» **Mari Llwyd** (New Year's Eve) A revival of the ancient practice of parading a horse's skull from house to house while reciting Welsh poetry.

Llanwrtyd Wells (Llanwrtyd)

POP 600

Llanwrtyd (khlan-*oor*-tid) Wells is an odd little town: mostly deserted except during one of its oddball festivals when it's packed to the rafters with an influx of crazy contestants and their merrymaking supporters. According to the *Guinness Book of Records* it is the UK's smallest town – some local residents even claim that in order to cling onto this status there's a periodic cull.

Apart from its newfound position as the capital of wacky Wales, Llanwrtyd Wells is surrounded by beautiful walking, cycling and riding country, with the Cambrian Mountains to the northwest and the Mynydd Eppynt to the southeast.

Sleeping

TOP CHOICE **Ardwyn House** B&B ££
(☎01591-610768; www.ardwynhouse.co.uk; Station Rd; s/d £49/70; P 📶) The young owners have been busy, restoring the art-nouveau grandeur of this once derelict house. Some rooms have claw-foot baths and rural views, and there is oak parquet flooring, period wallpaper and a guest lounge with a pool table and bar.

Carlton Riverside RESTAURANT-WITH-ROOMS ££
(☎01591-610248; www.carltonriverside.com; Irfon Cres; s £50-60, d £75-100) This upmarket restaurant-with-rooms has a boutique feel and a mantelpiece that positively groans under the strain of awards for its foodie achievements. The rooms are modern, simple and tasteful, and well catered to bon vivants with late breakfasts and checkouts. Ask about all-inclusive foodie breaks.

Eating & Drinking

TOP CHOICE **Neuadd Arms Hotel** PUB £
(☎01591-610236; www.neuaddarmshotel.co.uk; Y Sgwar; mains £7) Like any good village pub should be, the Neuadd Arms is a focal point for the community. It was here that former landlord Gordon Green and his punters cooked up many of the kooky events that have put Llanwrtyd Wells on the tourist trail. If you want to find out anything about mountain biking, pony trekking or hiking in the area, it's the place to come. During the winter you might join one of the farmers' dogs on the couch in front of the fire. There's also a surprisingly interesting menu (mains around £7), which when we visited included an excellent goat's cheese, pear and walnut tart; rabbit and beef pie; and some

hefty-looking desserts. And they even brew their own beer!

Drovers Rest RESTAURANT-WITH-ROOMS ££
(☎01591-610264; www.food-food-food.co.uk; Y Sgwar; lunch £6-11, dinner £14-18) A well-regarded restaurant-with-rooms, the Drovers has a snug little restaurant serving up the best of local produce and lots of fresh fish mains. The Sunday roasts are excellent (£13). The owners also run regular cooking classes, including a Welsh Cooking Day (£185).

Information

In the Pink (☎01591-610666; Irfon Tce; ⏲hours vary) As kooky as you'd hope for in such a place, the tourist office operates out of this little cafe/gift shop, where you can stock up on hiking and camping accessories and check your email (per 20 minutes £1).

Getting There & Away

BUS Bus 48 heads to Builth Wells (23 minutes).

TRAIN Llanwrtyd is on the **Heart of Wales** (www.heart-of-wales.co.uk) railway line, with direct services to Swansea (£8.40, two hours), Llandeilo (£3.90, 45 minutes), Llandrindod Wells (£3.20, 30 minutes) and Shrewsbury (£11, two hours).

Builth Wells (Llanfair-Ym-Muallt)

POP 2350

Builth (pronounced bilth) Wells is by far the liveliest of the former spa towns, with a bustling, workaday feel. Once the playground of the Welsh working classes, it has a pretty location on the River Wye. It's a handy base for walkers or cyclists tackling any of the long-distance paths that pass through.

Festivals & Events

Royal Welsh Agricultural Show AGRICULTURAL SHOW
(www.rwas.co.uk) Builth Wells fills to bursting at the beginning of July, when 230,000 people descend for the show (founded 1904), which involves everything from livestock judging to lumberjack competitions.

Sleeping & Eating

TOP CHOICE **Greyhound Hotel** PUB ££
(☎01982-553255; www.thegreyhoundhotel.co.uk; 3 Garth Rd; s/d £55/80; P📶) Currently being spruced up from the top down, this friendly local pub will soon have a complete set of up-to-the-minute rooms. It's at the northwest end of town by the Wesley Methodist Church.

Woodlands B&B ££
(☎01982-552354; woodlandsbandb@hotmail.co.uk; Hay Rd; s/d £35/55; P) A traditional Edwardian house, this place is set up a driveway off the A470, east of the township. The four rooms, all en suite, offer simple home comforts at a budget price.

Cosy Corner TEAROOM £
(☎01982-551700; 55 High St; mains £3-7; ⏲10am-4pm Mon-Sat) An atmospheric and, yes, cosy tearoom, offering homemade cakes, sandwiches and jacket potatoes in an 18th-century building.

Entertainment

Wyeside Arts Centre THEATRE, CINEMA
(☎01982-552555; www.wyeside.co.uk; Castle St) A great little venue with a bar, exhibition space, cinema and live shows.

Builth Male Voice Choir MALE CHOIR
(www.builthmalechoir.org.uk) You can catch a rehearsal from 8pm on Monday nights in the upper room of the Greyhound Hotel.

Information

Curio & Welsh Craft (☎01982-552253; www.visitbuilthwells.co.uk; 24 High St; ⏲9am-6pm Mon-Sat) There's no tourist office any more, but maps and brochures are available here.

Getting There & Away

Buses include X18 from Llandrindod Wells (17 minutes), Rhayader (45 minutes) and Aberystwyth (1¾ hours); 48 from Llanwrtyd Wells (23 minutes); and 704 from Brecon (40 minutes) and Newtown (1½ hours).

Llandrindod Wells (Llandrindod)

POP 5100

This spa town struck gold in Victorian times by touting its waters to the well-to-do gentry who rolled in for rest and recuperation. The grand architecture of the era remains, but now it's the town that's sleepy – you'd need to prod it with a sharp stick to rouse it on a Wednesday afternoon, when most of the shops close.

Roman remains at nearby Castell Collen show that it wasn't the Victorians who first discovered the healthy effects of the local spring waters, but it was the arrival of the Central Wales railway (now the Heart of Wales line) in 1865 that brought visitors en masse.

Sights

National Cycle Collection MUSEUM
(www.cyclemuseum.org.uk; Temple St; adult/child £3.50/1.50; ⏲10am-4pm daily Mar-Oct, Tue, Thu & Sun Nov-Feb) The art-nouveau Automobile Palace houses over 250 bikes, tracing the progression from clunky boneshakers to slick modern-day examples. Curios include circus-reminiscent penny farthings, bamboo bikes from the 1890s and the vertiginous 'Eiffel Tower' of 1899 (used to display billboards).

Rock Park PARK, SPRING
In 1670 the local spring was given the name the 'Well of the Blacksmith's Dingle', but it was not till the mid-18th century that its therapeutic qualities were discovered. However, the allure of stinky water gradually diminished and it closed in 1972. You can still sup from the rusty-looking and -tasting Chalybeate Spring beside Arlais Brook as it tinkles through the forested park – apparently the water is good for treating gout, rheumatism, anaemia and more (chalybeate refers to its iron salts).

Llandrindod Lake LAKE
Just southeast of the centre is a sedately pretty, tree-encircled lake, built at the end of the 19th century to allow Victorians to take their exercise without appearing to do so. The lake's centrepiece is a sculpture of a Welsh dragon.

Radnorshire Museum MUSEUM
(www.powys.gov.uk/radnorshiremuseum; Temple St; adult/child £1/50p; ⏲10am-4pm Tue-Fri, 10am-1pm Sat) Small and low-key, rather like the town itself, this museum offers a taste of local history.

Festivals & Events

Victorian Festival VICTORIANA
(www.victorianfestival.co.uk) In the middle of August Llandrindod Wells indulges in nine days of 19th-century costumes and shenanigans.

Sleeping

TOP CHOICE **Cottage** B&B ££
(☎01597-825435; www.thecottagebandb.co.uk; Spa Rd; s/d £38/58) This large, appealing Edwardian house, set in a flower-adorned garden, has comfortable rooms with heavy wooden furniture and lots of original features. Not all rooms are en suite and the only TV is in the guest lounge.

Metropole Hotel HOTEL ££
(☎01597-823700; www.metropole.co.uk; Temple St; s/d from £94/120; P 📶) Dating from the town's Victorian heyday, this grand turreted hostelry has spacious, updated rooms and an excellent leisure complex with a swimming pool, sauna and gym.

Eating

TOP CHOICE **Spencer's Bar & Brasserie** BRASSERIE ££
(☎01597-823700; Temple St; mains £11-18) Echoes of Victorian grandeur linger in the Metropole Hotel, not least in Spencers with its elegant verandah and bowtie-bedecked waiters. The formal dining area is tucked in the back and here too there's a touch of the classic (Welsh beef and lamb, and a perfect coq au vin) alongside Thai and Italian dishes.

Herb Garden Café CAFE £
(☎01597-823082; www.herbgardencafe.co.uk; 5 Spa Centre; mains £3-7; ⏲9.30am-5pm Mon-Sat; @📶🌿) Tucked down an alley by the Co-op supermarket, this eatery serves tasty light meals made from organic and wholefood produce. While not strictly vegetarian they make an effort to cater for various dietary requirements. It gets busy at lunchtime, so book ahead.

Van's Good Food Shop DELICATESSAN £
(Middleton St; ⏲9am-5.30pm Mon-Sat; 🌿) This excellent vegetarian deli features the best of local produce, including organic fruit, cheese and wine, plus ecofriendly cleaning products and other ethically selected goods.

Information

Llandrindod Wells Memorial Hospital
(☎01597-822951; Temple St)

Tourist Office (☎01597-822600; Temple St; ⏲10am-1pm Mon-Sat Oct-Mar, to 4pm Apr-Sep)

Getting There & Around

BUS Bus routes include X18 to Builth Wells (17 minutes), Rhayader (17 minutes) and Aberystwyth (1½ hours); and 704 to Newtown (one hour) and Brecon (55 minutes).

TRAIN Llandrindod is on the Heart of Wales railway line, with direct services to Swansea (£9.70, 2¼ hours), Llandeilo (£6.10, 80 minutes), Llanwrtyd Wells (£3.20, 30 minutes), Knighton (£3.50, 34 minutes) and Shrewsbury (£11, 1½ hours).

Rhayader (Rhaeadr Gwy)

POP 2100

Rhayader is a small livestock-market town revolving around a central crossroads marked by a war-memorial clock. It's a place that appeals to walkers visiting the nearby Elan Valley and tackling the 136-mile Wye Valley Walk. Rhayader is deserted on Thursdays when businesses trade for only half a day, but market day on Wednesdays attracts a crowd.

Sights & Activities

Gigrin Farm Red Kite Feeding Station WILDLIFE

(www.gigrin.co.uk; adult/child £4/1.50; 2pm Nov-Mar, 3pm Apr-Oct) Once the most common bird of prey throughout Britain, by the 19th century the red kite was flirting with extinction. Concerted conservation efforts over the last century have meant that red kites are once again a familiar sight in Welsh skies.

Anywhere from 12 to 500 red kites at a time may partake in the daily feeding frenzy at this working farm on the A470, half a mile south of the town centre. Once the meat scraps from a local abattoir are spread on the field the crows descend, then the acrobatically swooping kites – often mugging the crows to get the meat – and later ravens and buzzards. There's an interpretive centre, live camera feeds and marked nature trails.

Elan Valley CONSERVATION AREA

In the early 19th century, dams were built on the River Elan (pronounced ellen), west of Rhayader, with a fourth large dam following in 1952 on the tributary River Claerwen. Together they provide over 264 million litres of water daily for Birmingham and parts of South and Mid-Wales and 4.2 megawatts of hydroelectric power. The need to protect the 70-sq-mile watershed has turned it into an important wildlife conservation area.

Located just downstream of the lowest dam is Welsh Water's **Elan Valley Visitor Centre** (www.elanvalley.org.uk; 10am-5.30pm Mar-Oct), with interesting exhibits on the scheme and leaflets on the estate's 80 miles of nature trails and footpaths. Check the website for details of the frequent guided walks and birdwatching trips, which are mostly free.

The **Elan Valley Trail** is an 8-mile traffic-free walking, horse-riding and cycling path that mostly follows the line of the long-gone Birmingham Corporation Railway alongside the River Elan and its reservoirs. It starts just west of Rhayader at Cwmdauddwr.

Clive Powell Mountain Bike Centre MOUNTAIN BIKING

(01597-811343; www.clivepowellmountainbikes.co.uk; West St) Run by a former cycling champion who offers a program of 'Dirty Weekends', all-inclusive mountain-biking weekends hit trails around the Elan Valley (£176 to £299). You also can hire a mountain/off-road bike (£20/15 per day), including helmet and puncture kit.

Sleeping & Eating

Brynafon Workhouse HOTEL ££

(01597-810735; www.brynafon.co.uk; South St; s/d from £46/72; P) Rest assured, you won't be enduring any Dickensian treatment at this former workhouse. There's an attractive range of rooms, some with four-poster beds, some with exposed beams, but all with leafy outlooks over the River Wye and Elan Valley.

Triangle Inn PUB £

(www.thetriangleinn.co.uk; mains £7-13) Located just over the bridge from the town centre, this tiny 16th-century inn is the pick of the local places to eat and drink for its unique sense of character and history. It's so small that the toilets are located across the road and the ceiling is so low that there's a trapdoor in the floor so darts players can stand in a hole to throw their arrows.

Getting There & Away

Bus X18 from Builth Wells (45 minutes) to Aberystwyth (1¼ hours) via Llandrindod Wells (17 minutes) passes through Rhayader.

OFFA'S DYKE PATH *BECKY OHLSEN*

They say that good fences make good neighbours, but King Offa may have taken the idea a bit far. The 8th-century Mercian king built Offa's Dyke, Britain's longest archaeological monument, to mark the boundary between his kingdom and that of the Welsh princes and even today, though only 80 miles of the dyke remains, the modern Wales-England border roughly follows the line it defined.

The Offa's Dyke Path national trail criss-crosses that border around 30 times in its journey from the Severn Estuary near Chepstow, through the beautiful Wye Valley and Shropshire Hills, to the coast at Prestatyn in North Wales. The dyke itself usually takes the form of a bank next to a ditch, although it's overgrown in some places and built over in others. The trail often strays from the dyke, covering an astonishing range of scenery and vegetation, including river valleys, hill country, oak forests, heathland and bracken, conifer forest, green fields, high moors and the mountainous terrain of the Clwydian range in the north.

While it can be walked in either direction, it's best done south to north, with the wind and sun mainly on your back. Most people take 12 days to complete the 178-mile walk, though it's wise to allow at least two rest days, bringing your adventure to an even two weeks.

The Offa's Dyke Centre in Knighton is the best source of information about the route, stocking maps, guidebooks and pamphlets.

Presteigne (Llanandras)

At the far east of the vanished country of Radnorshire, pressed right up against the English border, is Presteigne (www.presteigne.org.uk), its former county town. It's a quaint little place, lined with attractive old buildings and surrounded by beautiful countryside.

The **Judge's Lodging** (www.judgesloding.org.uk; adult/child £5.95/3.95; ⏲10am-5pm Tue-Sun Mar-Oct, 10am-4pm Sat & Sun Nov-Dec) offers an intriguing glimpse into Victorian times via an audioguided wander through the town's 19th-century courthouse, lock-up and judge's apartments. The commentary does tend to ramble on but the displays are interesting. The local tourist office is based here.

In the neighbouring village of Norton, the **Old Vicarage** (☎01544-260038; www.oldvicarage-nortonrads.co.uk; s/d from £78/104; 🅿) is a three-room, gay-friendly, boutique B&B featuring opulent Victorian fittings.

Bus 41 heads to Knighton (20 minutes).

Knighton (Tref-Y-Clawdd)

POP 2800

Hilly Knighton (www.visitknighton.co.uk) is so close to the border that its train station is actually in England. It sits midway along the Offa's Dyke Path national trail and at one end of the Glyndŵr's Way national trail. The two-in-one **Tourist Office & Offa's Dyke Centre** (☎01547-528753; www.offasdyke.demon.co.uk; West St; ⏲10am-5pm Apr-Oct, 10am-4pm Mon-Sat Nov-Mar) is full of information for walkers and interactive displays about the dyke, a section of which runs behind the centre.

The town's best refuelling option is the **Horse & Jockey** (☎01547-520062; www.thehorseandjockeyinn.co.uk; Station Rd; mains bar £4-7, restaurant £6-14; s/d £45/70), a 14th-century coaching inn. You can eat in the bar or sit down to a more substantial meal in the restaurant; it does an excellent Sunday lunch. The five upmarket en-suite rooms have flatscreen TVs, modern fittings, ancient exposed stone walls and flash bathrooms.

Knighton is one of the stops on the Heart of Wales line; destinations include Swansea (£25, 3¼ hours), Llandeilo (£8.60, two hours), Llanwrtyd Wells (£3.20, 30 minutes), Llandrindod Wells (£3.50, 34 minutes) and Shrewsbury (£7.50, 52 minutes). Bus 41 heads to Presteigne (20 minutes).

Newtown (Y Drenewydd)

POP 10,400

Newtown's a former mill town with lots of history but, as a destination, it's also a sleepy place these days – absolutely soporific on a Sunday, but waking up for the Tuesday and Saturday markets. Its big claim to fame is that Robert Owen (1771–1858), the factory reformer, founder of the cooperative movement and 'father of Socialism', was born and died here. Monuments to his esteemed memory abound in the town centre.

Newtown was also once the home of Welsh flannel, and a major UK textile centre. When competition began driving wages down, Wales' first Chartist meeting was held here in October 1838. Pryce Jones, the world's first-ever mail-order firm, got its start here, on the back of the textile trade. By the end of the 19th century Newtown's boom days were over – and they've never been back. There are several small museums devoted to those long-gone salad days.

Newtown is almost the home of Laura Ashley, who opened her first shop in Carno, 10 miles west of the centre.

Sights

Robert Owen Museum MUSEUM
(www.robert-owen-museum.org.uk; The Cross; admission free; 9.30am-noon & 2-3.30pm Mon-Fri, 9.30-11.30am Sat; @) If you're not aware of Robert Owen's legacy, you're best to start here. The displays on Owen's life are broken up with mementos and pictures; it's quite text-heavy but it makes fascinating reading. It also serves at the de facto tourist office. Owen's well-tended grave is in the grounds of **St Mary's Old Parish Church** (Old Church St).

Oriel Davies ART GALLERY
(www.orieldavies.org; The Park; admission free; 10am-5pm Mon-Sat) One of Wales' leading contemporary spaces hosting often edgy exhibitions. Its sunny, glassed-in **cafe** (mains £5 to £7) is the best place for a light meal, such as homemade soup, quiche or baked potatoes.

FREE **Textile Museum** MUSEUM
(www.powys.gov.uk; 5-7 Commercial St; 2-5pm Mon, Tue & Thu-Sat May-Sep) Located in former weavers' cottages and workshops, just north of the river, impressively recreated rooms show what workers' conditions were like in the 1820s.

Sleeping

Highgate B&B ££
(01686-623763; www.highgatebandb.co.uk; Bettws Cedewain; s/d £45/75; P) Fields still surround this heritage-listed half-timbered farmhouse (1651), making it a particularly bucolic retreat. The decor is understated, keeping the focus on the original oak beams and other period features. From Newtown, cross the bridge at the end of the main street, turn right, veer left at All Saints Church and continue for 2.5 miles.

Getting There & Away

BUS Bus routes include X75 to Welshpool (25 minutes) and Shrewsbury (1¼ hours); X85 to Machynlleth (54 minutes); and 704 to Llandrindod Wells (one hour), Builth Wells (1½ hours) and Brecon (two hours). The daily National Express coach from Aberystwyth (£9.40, 80 minutes) to London (£30, 5½ hours), via Welshpool (£4.30, 25 minutes), Shrewsbury (£7.50, 55 minutes) and Birmingham (£10, 2½ hours), stops here.

TRAIN Newtown is on the Cambrian line, which crosses from Aberystwyth (£9.80, 1¼ hours) to Birmingham (£13, 1¾ hours) every two hours, via Machynlleth (£7.40, 42 minutes), Welshpool (£3.90, 15 minutes) and Shrewsbury (£5.60, 39 minutes).

Machynlleth

POP 2200

Little Machynlleth (ma-*hun*-khleth) punches well above its weight. It was here that nationalist hero Owain Glyndŵr established the country's first Parliament in 1404. But even that legacy is close to being trumped by the town's reinvention as the green capital of Wales – thanks primarily to the Centre for Alternative Technology (CAT).

Sights

CAT TECHNOLOGY CENTRE
(01654-705950; www.cat.org.uk; adult/child £8.50/4; 10am-5.30pm) Founded in 1974, CAT is a virtually self-sufficient workers' cooperative which acts as an ecologically driven laboratory and information source for alternative technologies. There are more than 3 hectares of displays dealing with topics such as composting, organic gardening, environmentally friendly construction, renewable energy sources, sewage treatment and recycling. It has about 130 on-site workers and 15 full-time residents. To explore the whole site takes about two hours – take rainwear as it's primarily outdoors. Kids love the interactive displays and adventure playground.

There are workshops and games for children during the main school holidays and an extensive program of residential courses for adults throughout the year (day courses start from around £45). Volunteer helpers willing to commit to a six-month stint are welcome, but you'll need to apply.

To get to the CAT from Machynlleth you can take the 32, X32 or 34 bus (six minutes). Arriving by bus or bicycle gets you a discount of £1.

MOMA Wales ART GALLERY
(www.momawales.org.uk; Penrallt St; admission free; ⏲10am-4pm Mon-Sat) Housed partly in a neoclassical chapel (1880), the Museum of Modern Art exhibits work by contemporary Welsh artists as well as an annual international competition (mid-July to early September).

Owain Glyndŵr Centre MEDIEVAL HOUSE
(www.canolfanglyndwr.org; adult/child £2/free; ⏲10am-4pm Tue-Sat Easter-Sep) Housed in a rare example of a late-medieval Welsh town house, the Owain Glyndŵr Centre has somewhat dry displays but nevertheless tells a rip-roaring story of the Welsh hero's fight for independence. Although it's called the Old Parliament Building, it was probably built around 1460, some 50 years after Glyndŵr instituted his parliament on this site, but it's believed to closely resemble the former venue.

Activities

Dyfi Mountain Biking BIKE TRAILS
(www.dyfimountainbiking.org.uk) Dyfi maintains three waymarked mountain-bike routes from Machynlleth, the Mach 1 (10 miles), 2 (14 miles) and 3 (19 miles), each more challenging than the last. The Mach 3's not for beginners. In the Dyfi Forest, near Corris, is the custom-built, 9-mile, Climachx loop trail. In May the same crew run the **Dyfi Enduro**, a noncompetitive, long-distance, mountain-bike challenge, limited to 650 riders.

Holey Trail BIKE HIRE
(☎01654-700411; 31 Maengwyn St; ⏲10am-6pm Mon-Sat) Hires mountain bikes (per day £25), performs repairs, offers bunkhouse accommodation and is a mine of information on the local trails.

Sleeping & Eating

TOP CHOICE **Wynnstay Hotel** HOTEL, RESTAURANT ££
(☎01654-702941; www.wynnstay-hotel.com; Maengwyn St; s/d from £59/90; P 🛜) This erstwhile Georgian coaching inn (1780) has charming older-style rooms, one with a four-poster bed, and creaky, uneven floors. Downstairs is given over to a rustic bar-eatery. Flying in the face of Machynlleth's veg-warrior image, the Wynnstay's menu (mains £11 to £17) revels in game meats.

Plas Llwyngwern B&B £
(☎01654-703970; www.plas-llwyngwern.com; Pantperthog; s/d from £35/55; P) A welcoming place located 300m north of the CAT, this grand house (1750) has substantial grounds for children to run wild in. Most of the spacious and eccentrically decorated bedrooms share bathrooms.

Quarry Cafe CAFE £
(Maengwyn St; mains £3-7; ⏲breakfast & lunch Mon-Sat; 🛜 ✎) Run by the same people as the CAT, this popular place dishes up delicious, wholesome, vegetarian lunch specials, using mostly organic ingredients. It's also very baby friendly with organic baby food on the menu, and changing facilities.

GLYNDŴR'S WAY NATIONAL TRAIL

Named after the renowned Welsh leader, Glyndŵr's Way cuts an arc through Powys from Knighton to Welshpool, taking in many sites connected with him, including Machynlleth. Most people take nine days to complete the 132-mile walk. Accommodation is scarce along the route, so book ahead. On some of the more remote sections you'll need to pack a lunch and carry enough water for the day.

The hilly terrain and difficulty of route-finding can make for pretty slow going, so it's wise to allow more time than you would for more established trails. It's essential to carry a compass and a good set of maps. Your best bet is to pick up the *Glyndŵr's Way* official National Trail Guide by David Perrott, which includes extracts from the relevant Ordnance Survey 1:25,000 Explorer maps.

DON'T MISS

POWIS CASTLE & GARDEN

Surrounded by magnificent gardens, **Powis Castle** (www.nationaltrust.org.uk; adult/child castle & gardens £10.40/5.10, garden only £7.70/3.85; castle & garden 1-5pm Thu-Mon Mar-Oct, garden 11am-3.30pm Sat & Sun Nov) rises from its terraces as if floating on a fantastical cloud of manicured yew trees. It was originally constructed in the 13th century by Gruffydd ap Gwenwynwyn, prince of Powys, and subsequently enriched by generations of the Herbert and Clive families. The extravagant mural-covered, wood-panelled interior contains one of Wales' finest collections of furniture and paintings along with curios such as Mary, Queen of Scot's rosary beads and an exquisite cache of jade, ivory, armour, textiles and other treasures brought back from India by Baron Clive.

The castle is just over a mile south of Welshpool.

Delicatessen Blasau DELICATESSAN £
(Penrallt St; 10am-5pm Mon-Sat) A superb little deli selling takeaway sandwiches, organic produce and fair-trade supplies. Specialising in local produce, it has a good selection of fruit wines, mead, liqueurs and chocolate – all of which would make excellent gifts for the cat-sitter back home.

Farmers Market MARKET
(Maengwyn St; Wed) Has been held for over seven centuries and remains a lively affair.

Information

Dyfi Craft & Clothing (01654-703369; Owain Glyndŵr Centre, Maengwyn St; 10am-4pm Mon-Sat) Following the demise of the official tourist office, this little store stocks brochures, maps and accommodation information.

Getting There & Away

BUS Routes include 28 to Aberystwyth (45 minutes) and Fairbourne (1¼ hours); X32 to Corris (13 minutes), Dolgellau (35 minutes), Porthmadog (1½ hours), Caernarfon (2¼ hours) and Bangor (2¾ hours); and X85 to Newtown (54 minutes).

TRAIN Machynlleth is on both the Cambrian and Cambrian Coast lines. Destinations include Aberystwyth (£4.90, 33 minutes), Porthmadog (£11, 1¾ hours), Pwllheli (£13, 2¼ hours), Newtown (£7.40, 42 minutes) and Birmingham (£15, 2¼ hours).

Snowdonia & North Wales

Includes »

NORTH COAST & BORDERS 724
Llangollen 724
Llandudno 726
Conwy 730
ISLE OF ANGLESEY 733
WEST OF SNOWDONIA 736
Caernarfon 736
Llŷn Peninsula 739
SNOWDONIA NATIONAL PARK 744
Snowdon & Around 745
Betws-y-Coed 749
Bala (Y Bala) & Around 750

Why Go?

From rugged mountain trails and historic train lines to World Heritage castles and rejuvenated seaside towns, Wales' north holds its own against the arguably more famous attractions down south. The region's dominated by Snowdonia National Park, where the mightiest peaks south of Scotland scrape moody skies. With such a formidable mountain shield, it's little wonder that the less-visited Llŷn Peninsula and the ancient island enclave of Anglesey have held tightly to their language and culture. In fact, the whole region feels properly Welsh: you'll hear the language on the street, see the Celtic legacy in the landscape and soak up the cultural pride in galleries, museums and attractions, from the beaches of the North Coast to the burgeoning heartland of northeast Wales. I n many ways, North Wales distils the very essence of Welshiness – just don't mention that to the folks in Cardiff.

Best Places to Eat

» Castle Restaurant & Armoury Bar (p755)

» Fish Tram Chips (p728)

» Gales of Llangollen (p725)

» Ann's Pantry (p734)

Best Places to Stay

» Ffynnon (p753)

» Escape B&B (p727)

» manorhaus (p727)

» Venetia (p741)

When to Go?

May is the driest month and Llandudno celebrates the warming weather with much Victorian merriment. In June, as summer kicks in, the Snowdon train can once again make it to the summit and Llangollen gets the giggles with its annual comedy festival. In July you can shuttle between the beaches and Llangollen's International Musical Eisteddfod and Fringe Festival. July and August offer the warmest weather. The north is at its wettest between October and December. Average temperatures rarely scrape into two digits anytime between December and March.

Snowdonia & North Wales Highlights

1. Exploring the island hub of **Beaumaris** (p733), then eating and sleeping in style
2. Making a weekend of it at the reborn seaside resort of **Llandudno** (p726)
3. Taking a ride across **Pontcysyllte Aqueduct** (p724), Wales' latest World Heritage Site, near Llangollen
4. Seeing Wales rise to a crescendo at the (accessible) peak of **Snowdon** (p745)
5. Walking through a postcard of stone cottages and cascading rivers at **Betws-y-Coed** (p749)
6. Witnessing the Byzantine beauty and strength of **Caernarfon Castle** (p737)
7. Taking a (nearly) coast-to-coast alpine train journey you'll never forget with the **Welsh Highland Railway** (p742)
8. Gazing toward the holy island of Bardsey from this magical land's end of **Braich-y-Pwll** (p740)

NORTH COAST & BORDERS

The North Wales coast has both perennial charms and cultural black spots in equal measure. Stick with the former and you'll not be disappointed – they include a glorious, Unesco-listed castle at Conwy and the Victorian resort of Llandudno, now reinventing itself as a stylish, family-holiday hub.

Moving southeast towards the English border, Llangollen has a burgeoning reputation for its adventure sports and cultural festivals. Most of all, it is known as the home of the annual International Musical Eisteddfod.

More details on this region are available from www.borderlands.co.uk, www.visitllandudno.com and www.visitconwy.org.uk.

Llangollen

POP 3500

Llangollen (lan-goch-len), huddled in the fertile Vale of Llangollen around the banks of the tumbling River Dee, has long been a scenic gem of North Wales. It was traditionally seen as more of a day-trip destination, but its appeal has evolved rapidly in recent years with a slew of smart new places to eat, a developing walking and outdoors scene, and a growing reputation for its arts festivals.

Sights & Activities

Horse Drawn Boat Centre BOAT TRIP

(www.horsedrawnboats.co.uk; adult/child £5/2.50; ⏲11am-4.30pm Apr-Oct) The 45-minute, horse-drawn boat excursion along the towpath from Llangollen Wharf leads to Wales' latest addition to the Unesco World Heritage list, the **Pontcysyllte Aqueduct**. Standing 126ft above the water, it is the tallest navigable aqueduct in the world and an engineering marvel.

Plas Newydd HISTORIC HOUSE

(☎01978-861314; Hill St, adult/child £3.50/2.50; ⏲10am-5pm Apr-Oct) Ornate Plas Newydd was home to the Ladies of Llangollen. Highlights of the visit include exploring the tranquil grounds, an audio tour (included in the admission) and arts events staged in the gardens. Don't confuse it with the National Trust (NT) stately home of the same name on Anglesey (p737).

Llangollen Railway HERITAGE RAIL

(www.llangollen-railway.co.uk; adult/child return £11/5.50; ⏲daily high season, special services low season) The 7.5-mile jaunt through the Dee

Llangollen

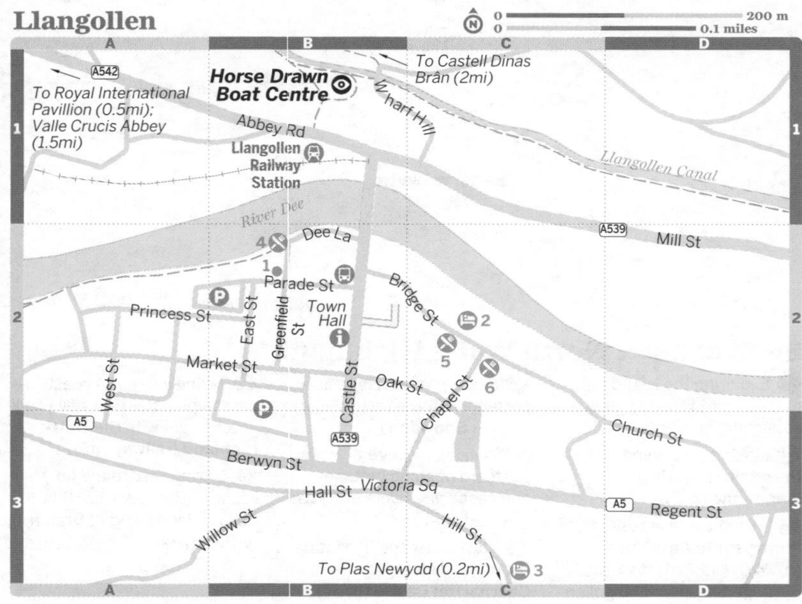

THE LADIES OF LLANGOLLEN

Lady Eleanor Butler and Miss Sarah Ponsonby, the 'Ladies of Llangollen', lived in Plas Newydd from 1780 to 1829 with their maid Mary Carryl. Their love affair blossomed in Ireland and, after their Anglo-Irish families discouraged the relationship, they eloped to Wales disguised as men in an attempt to start a new life. They settled in Llangollen, devoting themselves to 'friendship, celibacy and the knitting of stockings'.

Their relationship became well known, so much so that national and literary figures of the day, including the Duke of Wellington and William Wordsworth, paid them visits. Wordsworth penned the charming words 'Sisters in love, a love allowed to climb, even on this earth above the reach of time'.

Lady Eleanor died in 1829, Sarah Ponsonby two years later. They are buried at St Collen's Parish Church in the centre of Llangollen.

Valley via Berwyn (near Horseshoe Falls) and Carrog on the former Ruabon to Barmouth line is a superb day out for families and heritage rail lovers alike.

Castell Dinas Brân CASTLE & WALKING TRAIL
One of North Wales' best-known ancient sites, Dinas Brân marks the stark remnants of an Iron Age fort and the tumbledown ruins of a castle whose past is shrouded in mystery. There's a walking trail to the site north of Llangollen.

Valle Crucis Abbey ABBEY & WALKING TRAIL
(Cadw; adult/child £2.60/2.25; ⏲10am-5pm Apr-Oct) Also within walking distance of Llangollen, the dignified ruins of the abbey – another of the region's ancient treasures – evoke the lives of Wales' Cistercian monks through interpretation material.

ProAdventure Activity Centre CLIMBING WALL
(www.llangollenclimbing.co.uk; Parade St; ⏲6-10pm Mon-Fri, 10am-9pm Sat, 10am-5pm Sun) Home to the Llangollen Climbing Centre with its dedicated indoor climbing wall.

Llangollen

Top Sights
Horse Drawn Boat Centre B1

Activities, Courses & Tours
1 ProAdventure Activity Centre B2

Sleeping
2 Cornerstones Guesthouse C2
3 Hillcrest Guesthouse C3

Eating
4 Corn Mill B2
5 Gales of Llangollen C2
6 Hand Hotel C2

Festivals & Events

Llangollen Comedy Festival COMEDY
(www.llancomedy.com) Recently launched; comes to the Royal International Pavilion every June.

International Musical Eisteddfod MUSIC
Staged at the Royal International Pavilion in early July; see boxed text, p726.

Llangollen Fringe Festival ENTERTAINMENT
(www.llangollenfringe.co.uk) A smaller version of the famous Edinburgh Fringe Festival; staged at the Town Hall each July.

Sleeping

TOP CHOICE **Cornerstones Guesthouse** B&B ££
(☎01978-861569; www.cornerstones-guesthouse.co.uk; 15 Bridge St; r £80-100; P @) This converted 16th-century house, all sloping floorboards and oak beams, has charm and history. The River Room is the cosiest of the five rooms, with the gentle lapping of the River Dee to send you off to sleep.

Hillcrest Guesthouse B&B £
(☎01978-860208; www.hillcrest-guesthouse.com; Hill St; r from £50) Pet friendly and charmingly traditional, it's a simple but homely place that attracts consistently good reports from visitors.

Eating & Drinking

TOP CHOICE **Gales of Llangollen** WINE BAR ££
(☎01978-860089; www.galesofllangollen.co.uk; 18 Bridge St; mains £7.95-15.95; ⏲noon-2pm & 6-9.30pm Mon-Sat) Gales, a Llangollen institution, is consistently the best place in town to eat. With a 100-strong wine list that spans the globe, this wood-lined eatery boasts a daily-changing menu best enjoyed with a good glass of wine. The owners also

ESSENTIAL EISTEDDFOD

The **National Eisteddfod** (www.eisteddfod.org.uk), pronounced *ey-steth-vot*, a celebration of Welsh culture, is Europe's largest festival of competitive music-making and poetry. Descended from ancient Bardic tournaments, it is conducted in Welsh, but the festival welcomes all entrants and visitors. Many people come in search of Welsh ancestry, while musical fringe events featuring local bands lend a slight Glastonbury-style atmosphere. It's generally held in early August, and the venue swings annually between north and south Wales.

Urdd Eisteddfod (www.urdd.org) is a separate young people's festival – *urdd* (pronounced *irth*) is Welsh for 'youth' – held every May at changing venues. The format resembles its bigger brother, although any self-respecting teenager prefers to hang out on the fringe at the main event.

Most famous of all is the **International Musical Eisteddfod** (www.llangollen2010.co.uk), established after WWII to promote international harmony. Held in early July, it attracts participants from more than 40 countries, transforming the town into a global village. In addition to daily folk music and dancing competitions, gala concerts feature international stars. It was nominated for the Nobel Peace Prize in 2004.

run the **Wine Shop** (⌚10am-5.30pm Mon-Sat, to 4pm Sun) next door.

Corn Mill GASTROPUB ££
(Dee Lane; mains £8.75-16.50; ⌚noon-9pm) The water mill still turns at the heart of this converted mill – now an all-day bar and eatery – while the deck is the best spot in town for an alfresco lunch.

Hand Hotel BAR MEALS £
(www.hand-hotel-llangollen.com; Bridge St; Sunday lunch £7.95) Don't miss the excellent, pile-it-high Sunday lunches. The hotel also hosts the Llangollen Male Voice Choir each Friday evening for a pint and an impromptu sing-along in the bar.

Information

Llangollen tourist office (☎01978-860828; The Chapel, Castle St; ⌚9.30am-5.30pm high season, to 5pm low season) Helpful tourist office, well stocked with Ordnance Survey (OS) maps, books and gifts. It shares the Chapel Building with the library and stages regular art exhibitions.

Getting There & Away

BUS Arriva (www.arrivabus.co.uk) Runs bus service 5A to Wrexham (30 minutes, half-hourly Monday to Saturday, hourly Sunday) and X94 to Barmouth (one hour, bi-hourly Monday to Saturday, five daily on Sunday). Buses stop on Market St.

CAR Short-stay car park (Market St; per hr £1)

TRAIN The nearest mainline station is at Ruabon, 6 miles east on Arriva Trains' Holyhead–Cardiff line.

Around Llangollen

The Yorke family home for over two centuries (until 1973), **Erddig** (NT; adult/child £9.35/4.68, grounds only £6.10/3.05; ⌚house noon-5pm Sat-Thu high season, to 4pm Sat & Sun low season, grounds 11am-6pm Sat-Thu high season, to 4pm Sat & Sun low season) offers an illuminating glimpse into 19th-century life for the British upper class. Much of the family's original furniture is on display in the fine staterooms, while a formal, walled garden has been restored in Victorian style.

Erddig lies 12 miles northeast of Llangollen on the A483 in the village of Rhostyllen.

Llandudno

POP 15,000

Llandudno is a master of reinvention. Developed as an upmarket Victorian holiday town, it still retains much of its 19th-century grandeur, yet continues to find new fans with its booming boutique accommodation, upmarket dining, big-name retail outlets and Welsh art and performance. No wonder the American travel writer Bill Bryson was moved to describe Llandudno as his 'favourite seaside resort'.

The dominating feature is the **Great Orme** (207m), a spectacular 2-mile-long limestone headland jutting into the Irish Sea. Old-school tramway and cable-car rides go to the summit, providing breathtaking views of the Snowdonia range. On the seafront, traditional delights include strolling along the pier and catching Professor Codman's historic Punch and Judy show.

The opening of arts hub Venue Cymru has boosted the town's cultural life, and a major new retail park, Parc Llandudno, located at the east end of town, has brought big-name shops to the resort.

Llandudno's biggest annual event is its **Victorian Extravaganza** (www.victorian-extravaganza.co.uk), held over the early-May Bank Holiday weekend – book ahead for accommodation.

The town straddles its own peninsula, with Llandudno Bay and North Shore Beach to the northeast and Conwy Bay and West Shore Beach to the southwest.

Sights & Activities

Great Orme Country Park NATURE RESERVE
From sea level it's difficult to gauge the sheer scale of the Great Orme, designated a Site of Special Scientific Interest (SSSI). The peak is home to several Neolithic sites, a cornucopia of flowers, butterflies and sea birds, three waymarked summit trails (of which the Haulfre Gardens Trail is the easiest stroll to negotiate) and its own **visitor centre** (www.conwy.gov.uk/countryside; ⌚9.30am-5pm) with picnic tables, a cafe and a gift shop.

You can walk to the summit; take the **Great Orme Tramway** (www.greatormetramway.co.uk; adult/child return £5.60/3.80; ⌚10am-6pm high season, to 5pm Mar & Oct), which leaves every 20 minutes from Church Walks; or ride Britain's longest **cable car** (☎01492-877205; adult/child return £6.50/4.50; ⌚10am-5pm) from the Happy Valley Gardens above the pier – departures are weather dependent.

FREE **Mostyn Gallery** GALLERY
(www.mostyn.org; 12 Vaughan St; ⌚10am-5pm Mon-Sat) Finally re-opened after a three-year renovation program, the gallery is now North Wales' premier arts space. Call in to explore the shop or grab a coffee upstairs at Café Lux even if you're not a fan of modern art.

Llandudno Pier SEASIDE
(⌚9am-6pm) The 1878-built Victorian pier is, at 670m, the longest pier in Wales and extends into the sea with amusements, candyfloss and slot machines. High art it isn't, but the kids will love it.

City Sightseeing BUS TOUR
(www.city-sightseeing.com; adult/child £7.50/3; ⌚May-Sep) Departs the pier half-hourly for a hop-on/hop-off bus tour of Llandudno and Conwy; tickets are valid for 24 hours.

Llandudno Land Train BUS TOUR
(⌚Apr-Oct) Runs a regular loop shuttle from the pier to the quieter West Shore and back (£1.50 each way).

Sleeping

TOP CHOICE **Escape B&B** HOTEL ££
(☎01492-877776; www.escapebandb.co.uk; 48 Church Walks; r £85-135; P 📶) Escape, Llandudno's first boutique B&B, recently upped the ante again, giving the rooms a major, design-led makeover to include a host of energy-saving and trend-setting features. Don't miss the honesty-bar

WORTH A TRIP

RUTHIN

Ruthin feels very on the up. Offa's Dyke Path national trail passes through the nearby Clwydian Range Area of Outstanding Natural Beauty (AONB) and the town is packed with history: the 15th-century **Nantclwyd y Dre** (adult/child £3.60/2.50; ⌚10am-5pm Fri-Sun Apr-Sep) is the oldest timber-framed building in Wales.

Ruthin Craft Centre (www.ruthincraftcentre.org.uk; Park Rd; admission free; ⌚10am-5.30pm) is the town's new arts hub, with galleries, events and a decent cafe. And local independent shops, such as the mouth-watering deli **Leonardo's** (www.leonardosdeli.co.uk; 4 Well St; ⌚9.30am-5.30pm Mon-Sat) are showcasing local produce and enterprise.

The place to stay is the town's art-themed boutique hotel, **manorhaus** (☎01824-704830; www.manorhaus.com; Well St; d £85-150, per person half board £135-200; 📶), with eight artistically styled rooms, each one showcasing the works of different local and national artists.

More from **Visit Ruthin** (www.visitruthin.com).

Llandudno

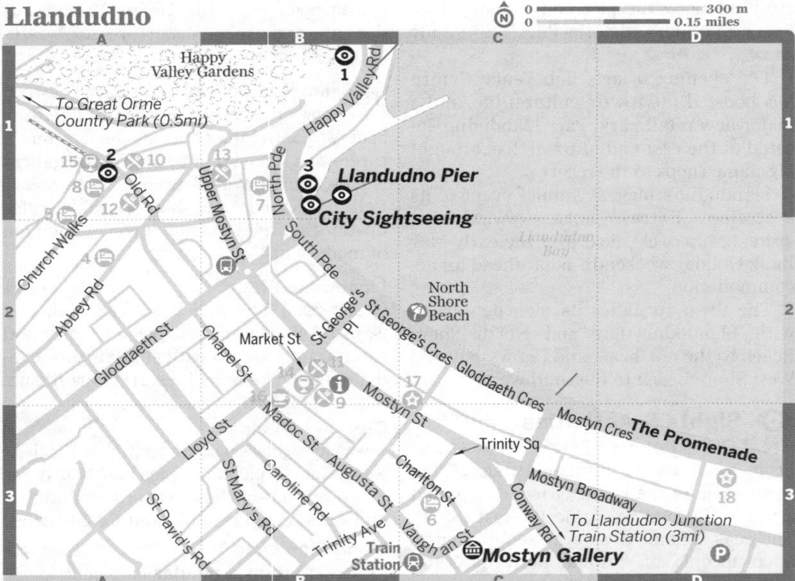

lounge, DVD library, tasty breakfasts and atmosphere of indulgence.

Osborne House HOTEL £££
(☎01492-860330; www.osbornehouse.com; 17 North Pde; ste £150-190; P@) All marble, antique furniture and fancy drapes, the lavish Osbourne House takes a more classical approach to aesthetics, but the results are no less impressive. The best suites are on the 1st floor with Victorian-style sitting rooms and sea views. Guests have use of spa facilities at nearby sister property the Empire Hotel.

Abbey Lodge B&B ££
(☎01492-878042; 14 Abbey Rd; s/d £45/75; P@) The owners of Abbey Lodge keep this four-room property fresh and provide some homely touches, such as a small collection of local-interest books in each room. Hang out in the garden on a sunny day or read in the cosy lounge.

Plas Madoc B&B ££
(☎01492-876514; www.plasmadocguesthouse.co.uk; 60 Church Walks; s/d from £40/60; P) Formerly a fully vegetarian and vegan guesthouse, the new owners have widened the remit to non-vegetarian guests, but maintained the soya milk and free-range eggs tradition for those who request it. The five cosy rooms are light and airy with lots of homely touches.

Quay Hotel & Spa HOTEL £££
(☎01492-564100; www.quayhotel.co.uk; Deganwy Quay; r from £175-285; P) High-end suites, a popular day spa and fine dining, the latter with superb views of Conwy Castle illuminated by night, are the big draws at this stylish, quayside property.

Llandudno Hostel HOSTEL £
(☎01492-877430; www.llandudnohostel.co.uk; 14 Charlton St; dm £18, tw £44-48, f £72-100) This is a family-run, Victorian-pile independent hostel with friendly, knowledgeable owners and a location close to the train station. Rooms are clean and a continental breakfast is included, but there are no self-catering facilities.

Eating & Drinking

TOP CHOICE **Fish Tram Chips** CAFE £
(Old Rd; set menu £6.95; ⊙noon-2pm, 5-7.30pm Tue-Sat, noon-2.15pm Sun winter, noon-3pm & 4.30-7.30pm daily summer) One of the tastiest and best-value fish suppers in North Wales, Fish Tram Chips is a pretty low-frills place but big on tasty, fresh fish and homemade side dishes with views across to the Great Orme Tram-

Llandudno

Top Sights
- City Sightseeing ... B1
- Llandudno Pier ... B1
- Mostyn Gallery ... C3

Sights
1 Cable Car Terminus ... B1
2 Great Orme Tramway ... A1
3 Llandudno Land Train ... B1

Sleeping
4 Abbey Lodge ... A2
5 Escape B&B ... A1
6 Llandudno Hostel ... C3
7 Osborne House ... B1
8 Plas Madoc ... A1

Eating
9 Badgers Tearooms ... B2
10 Fish Tram Chips ... A1
11 Hambone Food Hall ... B2
12 Number 1 Bistro ... A1
13 Seahorse ... B1

Drinking
14 Cottage Loaf ... B2
15 King's Head ... A1
16 Nineteen ... B2

Entertainment
17 St John's Methodist Church ... C2
18 Venue Cymru ... D3

way station. Probably the best bargain in town.

Hambone Food Hall DELICATESSEN CAFE £
(Lloyd St; 9.30am-5.30pm Mon-Sat) The best deli in Llandudno, the Hambone has a huge range of freshly made sandwiches to eat in or take away. Perfect for an alfresco picnic on the nearby promenade.

Number 1 Bistro FRENCH ££
(01492-875424; Old Rd; set menu 2/3 courses £12/18; 5.30-9.30pm Mon-Sat) French bistro with some interesting twists on the standard fare with venison and ostrich, plus lots of fresh fish. The early-evening set menu is cracking value but only available until 6.30pm each evening.

Seahorse SEAFOOD ££
(01492-875315; www.the-seahorse.co.uk; 7 Church Walks; set menu £21; 5pm-late Tue-Sat) The menu at the Seahorse (formerly Richard's Bistro) appropriately features lots of fresh fish. It's a split-level affair with the more intimate cellar room better suited to informal dining and the street-level restaurant the domain of a good-value set menu (except weekends).

Cottage Loaf PUB ££
(www.the-cottageloaf.co.uk; 1 Market St; mains £9-12) A cosy pub with real ales and satisfyingly hearty pub food.

King's Head PUB ££
(Old Rd; mains £7-12) For a quiet pint and pub grub at a Victorian pub overlooking the tramway station.

Nineteen CAFE £
(19 Lloyd St; 9am-5pm Mon-Sat;) This place is a chilled-out little coffee bar for smoothies and snacks, as well as coffee. Read the papers or use your laptop with the free wi-fi.

Badgers Tearooms CAFE £
(Victoria Shopping Centre, Mostyn St; 10am-4.30pm Mon-Fri, 9.30am-5pm Sat, 10.30am-4pm Sun) A traditional tearoom, best known for its creamy afternoon teas and gooey cakes. The Victorian attire of the staff adds a frisson of genteel nostalgia.

Entertainment

Venue Cymru THEATRE
(01472-872000; www.venuecymru.co.uk; The Promenade; box office 9.30am-8.30pm Mon-Sat, noon-4pm Sun, plus before performances) The town's leading arts venue for shows and events from rock gigs to highbrow classical performances.

FREE **St John's Methodist Church** CHOIR
(Mostyn St; 8pm Tue & Thu Jul-Oct) Male-voice-choir performances.

Information

Llandudno Hospital (01492-860066) One mile south of the centre of town.

Llandudno tourist office (www.visitllandudno.org.uk; Mostyn St; 9am-5.30pm Mon-Sat, 9.30am-4.30pm Sun Apr-Oct, 9am-5pm Mon-Sat Nov-Mar) Housed in the library building.

Getting There & Away

BUS Buses stop on the corner of Upper Mostyn St and Gloddaeth St.

Arriva (www.arrivabus.co.uk) Runs bus 5 to Caernarfon (1¾ hours, half-hourly Monday to Saturday, hourly Sunday) and bus 19/19A to Llanrwst (30 minutes, half-hourly Monday to Saturday, hourly Sunday).

LOCAL KNOWLEDGE

JACQUELINE MILLBAND CODMAN: PUNCH & JUDY PUPPETEER

The family celebrates 150 years of Mr Punch in Llandudno this year. My great grandfather, Richard Codman, started a Punch and Judy Show outside the Empire Hotel in 1860. He moved to the Promenade in 1864 and went on to perform for Queen Victoria. We're part of the town's history now. Llandudno is moving with the times, but it retains its genteel Victorian ambience. Llandudno always did cater for top-end clientele with private jazz clubs and cafes in its postwar heyday.

Top Tables

The Seahorse is still superb for fresh fish and Fish Tram Chips remains perennially popular for a simple but good-value supper. Personally, I rather like Fortes, a cafe on Mostyn St, for a snack lunch.

Best for Families

Take a picnic to Happy Valley, or head to West Shore to feed the swans on the boating pool. Taking the Great Orme Tramway is also perfect for nostalgia.

Favourite Escape

My tip for visitors is, after a couple of days exploring the resort itself, take the train down to Betws-y-Coed. From Llandudno, you're just 20 minutes from the seaside into the heart of the Snowdonia National Park.

National Express (www.nationalexpress.com) Runs to London (£32, 8½ hours).

CAR Parking on the promenade is at a premium. For easiest parking, head for the large number of spaces within the Parc Llandudno complex and its accompanying Asda supermarket.

TRAIN Llandudno's train station, the subject of a long-awaited and much-needed regeneration plan, is located three blocks south of Mostyn St; taxis wait by the station.

Arriva Trains (www.arrivatrainswales.co.uk) Runs services to Holyhead (£11, 1½ hours) and nearby Llandudno Junction station (£2.10, 10 minutes) on the North Coast line. Also runs services from Llandudno Junction station to Blaenau Ffestiniog (£6.40, one hour) via Betws-y-Coed (£4.70, 30 minutes) on the Conwy Valley line.

Virgin Trains (www.virgintrains.co.uk) Runs direct services to London Euston (£70, three hours) from Llandudno Junction station on the West Coast main line.

Conwy

POP 4000

Conwy Castle, the Unesco-designated cultural treasure, dominates the walled town of Conwy. Even today, it invests the approach to town with a sense of pomp and ceremony, while the three bridges spanning the river – namely Thomas Telford's 1826 (now-pedestrianised) suspension bridge, Robert Stephenson's 1848 steel railway bridge and the newer road-crossing bridge – add a sense of theatrical flourish.

The lengthy project to regenerate the rundown Conwy Quay has finally been completed, but more comprehensive eating and sleeping options remain in nearby Llandudno.

A highlight of the year is the increasingly well-regarded **Gwledd Conwy Feast** (www.gwleddconwyfeast.co.uk), held annually in October – book accommodation well in advance.

Sights

Conwy Castle & Town Wall CASTLE
(Cadw; adult/child £4.60/4.10; ⏲9am-5pm high season, 9.30am-4pm Mon-Sat, 11am-4pm Sun low season) Probably the most stunning of all Edward I's Welsh fortresses, built between 1277 and 1307, Conwy Castle rises from a rocky outcrop with commanding views across the estuary and Snowdonia National Park. Exploring the castle's nooks and crannies makes for a superb, living-history visit but, best of all, head to the battlements for panoramic views and an overview of Conwy's majestic complexity.

The 1200m-long Conwy **town wall** was built simultaneously with the castle, guarding Conwy's residents at night. You can walk part-way round the wall; the best views are to be had from Upper Gate.

Conwy

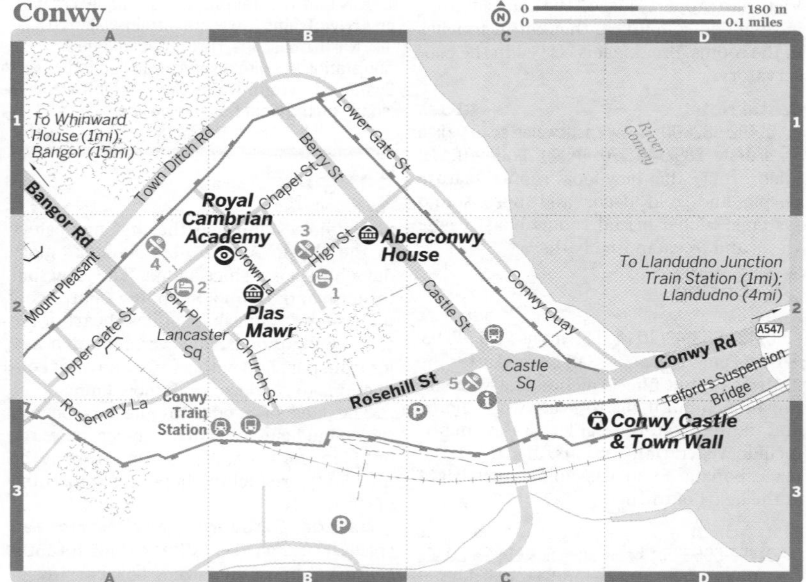

Plas Mawr HISTORIC HOUSE
(Cadw; High St; adult/child £4.90/4.50; 9.30am-5pm Tue-Sun high season, to 4pm Oct) Plas Mawr, one of Britain's finest surviving Elizabethan town houses, was built in 1585. The tall, whitewashed exterior is an indication of the owner's status, but gives no clue of the vivid friezes of the interior. The admission price includes a helpful audio tour; a combined ticket including entrance to the castle costs £6.85/5.85 per adult/child.

Aberconwy House HISTORIC HOUSE
(NT; Castle St; adult/child £3/1.50; 11am-5pm daily high season, Wed-Mon low season) Near to Plas Mawr, this timber-and-plaster building is the town's oldest medieval merchant's house, dating from around 1300. It has a gift shop downstairs for souvenirs.

FREE **Royal Cambrian Academy** GALLERY
(www.rcaconwy.org; Crown Lane; 11am-5pm Tue-Sat, 1-4.30pm Sun) The twin white-walled galleries host a full program of exhibitions by members, plus visiting shows from the National Museum Wales and elsewhere. The academy also hosts the excellent Annual Summer Exhibition from July to September, featuring the cream of fine art in Wales under one roof.

Conwy

Top Sights
Aberconwy House ... B2
Conwy Castle & Town Wall ... C3
Plas Mawr ... B2
Royal Cambrian Academy ... B2

Sleeping
1 Castle Hotel ... B2
2 Gwynfryn ... A2

Eating
3 Amelie's ... B2
4 Bistro Bach ... A2
5 Press Room Café ... C2

Sleeping

Whinward House B&B ££
(01492-573275; www.whinwardhouse.thefoxgroup.co.uk; s/d £60/70; P) This three-room B&B, located just outside Conwy's city walls, is a cosy, homely affair. A conservatory and outside decking area for summer nights, the latter with a maritime theme, add to the overall appeal. Book ahead.

Gwynfryn B&B ££
(01492-576733; www.gwynfrynbandb.co.uk; 4 York Pl; r £60-80;) The owners of this family B&B – set in a refurbished, five-bedroom

Victorian property just off the main square – have added some nice, thoughtful touches to the rooms. Breakfast is served in the conservatory.

Castle Hotel HOTEL £££
(☎01492-582800; www.castlewales.co.uk; High St; s/d/ste £89/140/170; P @) Following a major refit, the new-look rooms feature purple and gold decor and Bose sound systems; higher-priced rooms boast castle views and freestanding baths.

Eating

Amelie's FRENCH ££
(☎01492-583142; 10 High St; mains £9.95-16.95; ⏲11am-2pm & 6-9pm Tue-Sat) Named after the Audrey Tautou film, Amelie's is a welcoming French-motif bistro with wood floors and flowers on the tables. Tasty mains include vegetarian options. It's a relaxed place, popular for an easygoing lunch, right at the heart of town.

Bistro Bach WELSH ££
(☎01492-596326; Chapel St; mains £14.95-20.95; ⏲6.30-9pm Mon-Sat) For modern Welsh food in an intimate bistro setting, the recently renamed Bistro Bach remains the smartest option for dinner in town. The menu takes in the traditional Welsh mains of lamb and beef, but gives them a more contemporary spin.

Press Room Café CAFE £
(☎01492-592242; 3 Rosehill St; mains £4.50-8.50; ⏲10.30am-4.30pm Tue-Sun) Located by the entrance to the castle and with an outdoor courtyard, this arty cafe is a useful spot for lunches and coffee, followed by a visit to the gift shop next door.

Information

Conwy tourist office (☎01492-592248; Castle Sq; ⏲9.30am-6pm daily high season, 9.30am-4pm Mon-Sat, 11am-4pm Sun low season) A cramped box of an office within the castle complex, it can be heaving during the high season.

Getting There & Away

BUS Most buses stop by the train station.

Arriva (www.arrivabus.co.uk) Runs bus 5 to Caernarfon (40 minutes, half-hourly Monday to Saturday, hourly Sunday) and bus 19 to Llandudno (30 minutes, half-hourly Monday to Saturday, hourly Sunday) via Llandudno Junction (five minutes) for train connections. But Arriva bus 19 stops on Castle St for Llanrwst (1¾ hours, hourly Monday to Saturday).

TRAIN Conwy's train station is a request stop on **Arriva Trains** (www.arrivatrainswales.co.uk) North Coast line. Nearby Llandudno Junction station has direct services to London Euston with **Virgin Trains** (www.virgintrains.co.uk) on the West Coast main line.

Bangor

POP 12,000

St Deiniol established the first monastery in the city in AD 525, but Bangor's glory days have long since faded. The new, but rather bland, Deiniol Shopping Centre now makes for a somewhat soulless heart of the town. Bangor does, however, remain a major transport hub with a raft of onward connections to Anglesey and Snowdonia.

The lack of a cultural life has been a major bugbear for Bangor in recent years, but plans for a new £35m arts centre at the university are fuelling hopes for something of a renaissance.

Bangor Cathedral (www.churchinwales.org.uk; admission free) is known for its 15th-century, almost life-sized, oak carving of Christ. The **Gwynedd Museum & Art Gallery** (Ffordd Gwynedd; admission free; ⏲12.30-4.30pm Tue-Fri, 10.30am-4.30pm Sat) has a section devoted to tracing the evolution of the Welsh identity.

Sleeping & Eating

Eryl Mor Hotel HOTEL ££
(☎01248-353789; www.erylmorhotel.com; 2 Upper Garth Rd; s/d/f £48/75/80; P @) Bangor isn't exactly blessed with accommodation options, but this place, while a bit stuck in the past, is the best of the bunch, notably for the superb views across the Menai Strait.

TOP CHOICE **Kyffin** CAFE £
(☎01248-355161; 129 High St; lunch mains £5, evening menu £13; ⏲10am-5pm Mon-Thu, to 9pm Fri & Sat) Hidden-gem, fair-trade, vegetarian and vegan cafe with jazz music, a cosy lounge and antique-shop fittings, plus a deli counter for lots of organic goodies. Kyffin now offers evening meals at weekends and world cinema nights with an accompanying menu.

1815 DELICATESSEN CAFE £
(☎01248-355969; 2 Waterloo Pl; mains £7, tapas £8; ⏲8.30am-6pm Mon-Thu & Sun, to 10pm Fri & Sat) Fresh local produce and a strong Mediterranean influence are the key themes of this lively, friendly cafe-bar. By day it's a

buzzy place for coffees and snack lunches, by night it takes on more of a wine-bar vibe.

Shopping

Cob Records MUSIC

(www.cobrecordsbangor.com; 320 High St) An old-school independent record shop, it has everything for vinyl junkies and serious collectors, plus a section dedicated to Welsh music.

Information

Gwynedd Hospital (01248-384384; Penrhos Rd) Located 2 miles southwest of the centre, this is the regional hub for medical emergencies.

Bangor tourist office (01248-352786; Deiniol Rd; 9.30am-1.30pm & 2-4pm Mon-Fri Apr-Sep) Bangor's hit-and-miss tourist office can at least advise on the dearth of local accommodation.

Getting There & Away

BUS The station is located behind the Deiniol Shopping Centre; some buses also stop just outside the station.

Arriva (www.arrivabus.co.uk) Bus 4/X4/44 runs to Holyhead (one hour 10 minutes, half-hourly Monday to Saturday, twice-hourly Sunday); bus 5/X5 runs to Caernarfon (30 minutes, every 15 minutes Monday to Saturday, hourly Sunday); and bus 53/57/58 runs to Beaumaris (30 minutes, every 35 minutes Monday to Saturday, twice-hourly Sunday).

National Express (www.nationalexpress.com) Runs daily to London (£33, nine hours).

TRAIN Bangor's train station has direct services with the following.

Virgin Trains (www.virgintrains.co.uk) To London Euston (£40, 3½ hours).

Arriva (www.arrivatrainswales.co.uk) To Holyhead (£7.20, 35 minutes).

ISLE OF ANGLESEY

At 276 sq miles, the Isle of Anglesey is the largest island in England and Wales. It's a popular destination for visitors, with miles of inspiring coastline, hidden beaches, chocolate-box villages and Wales' greatest concentration of ancient and prehistoric sites. The new A55 expressway also means that getting round the island by car is now much easier.

Fertile farming land attracted early settlers, while the island was holy to the Celts and the last part of Wales to fall to the Romans around AD 60. Given its outpost status and singular character, Anglesey stakes a fair claim to being the Welsh heartland. Gerald of Wales quoted the ancient name for the island 'Môn mam Cymru' (Mother of Wales) at the end of the 12th century.

The industrial age arrived in 1826 when Thomas Telford established the first permanent link to the mainland. His iconic 174m Menai Suspension Bridge across the Menai Strait has a 30m-high central span, allowing the passage of tall ships. It was joined in 1850 by Robert Stephenson's Britannia Bridge to carry the newly laid railway.

Beaumaris makes for the most convenient base on the island, with the best range of infrastructure. Off-the-beaten-track highlights include Cemaes Bay rock pools for crabbing and Church Bay for its idyllic beach.

The two official tourist offices are at Llanfair PG (p730) and Holyhead. Menai Bridge is the island's bus hub, with regular local connections across the region.

For more information about the island, see www.visitanglesey.co.uk.

Beaumaris (Biwmares)

POP 2000

The attractive visitor hub of the island, Beaumaris boasts a winning combination of an attractive waterfront location, a romantic castle lording it over a pretty collection of Georgian buildings, and a growing number of boutiques, deli-cafes and galleries. Sailing and walking lure a new generation of Anglesey converts to its smart hotels and chic eateries, while a major new project to extend the pier and introduce fast-track water-taxi services across the Menai Strait keeps the town moving with the times.

Sights & Activities

Beaumaris Castle CASTLE

(Cadw; adult/child £3.60/3.20; 9.30am-6pm high season, 9.30am-4pm Mon-Sat, 11am-4pm Sun low season) The last of Edward I's great castles of North Wales, and the largest, Beaumaris is deservedly a World Heritage Site. The four successive lines of fortifications and concentric 'walls within walls' make it the most technically perfect castle in Great Britain – the castle with the wow factor.

TOP FIVE HIDDEN GEMS FOR FOOD LOVERS

Ann's Pantry (01248-410386; www.annspantry.co.uk; Moelfre; snacks £2.50-7.50; 9am-5pm, dinner Thu-Sat) With a delightful garden setting and a funky, beach hut-chic interior, plus great homemade food and fair-trade drinks, it's little wonder that Ann's Pantry was voted Bistro of the Year at the Anglesey Tourism Awards 2010.

White Eagle (01407-860267; Rhoscolyn; mains £7.95-19.95; lunch & dinner Mon-Fri, all day weekends & holidays) High-end and busy gastropub with a huge, sun-trap decking area and gardens for kids to explore.

Wavecrest Café (01407-730650; Church Bay; snacks £4.95-7.95; 10.30am-5pm Thu-Mon) Cosy, relaxed cafe with great snack lunches (try the homemade fish pie) and creamy afternoon teas.

Lobster Pot (01407-730241; www.lobster-pot.net; Church Bay; mains £12.95-26.95; noon-1.30pm & 6-8.30pm) Local institution for fresh seafood in a delightful location; call ahead for bookings.

Ship Inn (01248-852568; Red Wharf Bay; mains £9.95-16.45; lunch & dinner) Hearty pub grub and local ales served with appetite-whetting bay views.

Puffin Island Cruises BOAT TRIP
(01248-810746; www.beaumarismarine.com; adult/child £7/5; Apr-Oct) Puffin Island is a hotbed of bird and marine life, designated a Special Protection Area. The (weather-dependent) boat trips take in spectacular views across the Menai Strait to the Snowdonia range and promise encounters with 12 species of sea birds in their natural habitat. Book at the kiosks at the entrance to the pier, or by phone.

Beaumaris Courthouse & Gaol HISTORIC BUILDING
(combined ticket adult/child £6/4.50; 10.30am-5pm Easter-Sep) Atmospheric and eerie, the courthouse is nearly 400 years old and the Victorian jail contains the last-surviving treadwheel in Britain (for hard-labour prisoners). The jail and courthouse are separate buildings, but the combined ticket gets you admission to both.

Sleeping

TOP CHOICE **Townhouse** HOTEL £££
(01248-810329; www.bullsheadinn.co.uk; Castle St; s/d/ste £80/120/155;) From the team that brought you Beaumaris' stately Ye Olde Bulls Head, this funky, new little-sister property, located just across the road, provides quite a contrast. While the Bulls Head is historic and elegant, Townhouse is contemporary, high-tech and design driven. Breakfast and drinks are back across the road at its big sister.

Cleifiog B&B ££
(01248-811507; www.cleifiogbandb.co.uk; Townsend; s/d from £60/90) A charmingly dotty little gem, this artistic town house oozes character ands history, and boasts superb views of the Menai Strait. Of the three rooms, all stylishly designed, Tapestry is the largest and features the original 18th-century panelling. The owner displays her artworks around the house.

Eating

TOP CHOICE **Loft at the Ye Olde Bulls Head Inn** MODERN WELSH £££
(01248-810329; www.bullsheadinn.co.uk; Castle St; 3 courses £39.50; lunch & dinner Tue-Sat) Compared to the hotel's more pedestrian Brasserie restaurant, the Loft is more of a fine-dining experience. Peruse the menu over aperitifs in the lounge before climbing the stairs for elegant decor, a refined ambience and lovingly crafted food, centring on seasonal Anglesey produce.

Court's BRASSERIE ££
(01248-810565; www.courtyardcuisine.com; Regent House, Church St; mains £8.95-21; 11am-3pm & 6-9pm Wed-Mon) Chi-chi Courts serves quality brasserie fare in stylish, contemporary surroundings. The menu plays to both local strengths and European influences with lots of fresh fish and locally reared meat.

Red Boat Ice Cream Parlour ICE CREAM £
(www.redboatgelato.com; 34 Castle St; 10am-6pm) Red Boat is a stylish little gelato parlour, using authentic Italian recipes to prepare the tastiest frozen ice cream this

side of Florence. Try the exotic strawberry, mascarpone and balsamic vinegar flavour.

Sarah's Delicatessen & the Coffee Shop
DELICATESSEN CAFE £
(11 Church St; ⏲9am-5.30pm Mon-Sat) This excellent deli champions local produce, such as cheese and ales, with a well-stocked selection of treats. The owners also run a small cafe round the corner with daily specials (try the Anglesey dressed crab), good coffee and heavenly desserts.

ℹ Information

Tourist office (☎01248-810040; Castle St; ⏲10.30am-4.30pm Mon-Thu Apr-Sep) This unofficial tourist office is in the Town Hall. It's a useful resource but, as it is volunteer run, it can keep irregular hours.

ℹ Getting There & Away

Buses stop on Church St. **Arriva** (www.arrivabus.co.uk) runs bus services 53, 57 and 58 to Bangor (30 minutes, half-hourly Monday to Saturday) for onward connections.

Holyhead (Caergybi)

POP 12,000

Holyhead remains a major travel hub for ferries to Ireland, but the town has fallen on hard times. The first shoots of regeneration are now brightening the formerly moribund town centre. The Celtic Gateway bridge, linking the train station to the main thoroughfare, Market St, invites visitors to 'Pass this way with a pure heart', while major plans to overhaul the harbour were at the planning stage at the time of writing.

Holyhead is divided from the west coast of Anglesey by a narrow channel on Holy Island (Ynys Gybi), a 7-mile stretch of land. It's 'Holy' because this was the domain of St Cybi, a well-travelled monk thought to have lived in the 6th century.

Holyhead is the starting point for the Lôn Las Cymru cycle route (see boxed text, p653) and St Cybi's Church marks the official starting point for the Isle of Anglesey Coastal Path.

The **Holyhead Maritime Museum** (www.holyheadmaritimemuseum.co.uk; Newry Beach; adult/child £3.50/2; ⏲10am-4pm Apr-Sep) is housed in what is believed to be the oldest lifeboat house in Wales (c 1858). It's a family-friendly visit with model ships, photographs and exhibits on Holyhead's maritime history from Roman times onwards.

For an ends-of-the-earth escape, **South Stack Lighthouse** (www.trinityhouse.co.uk; tours adult/child £4.25/2.25; ⏲10.30am-5pm Apr-Sep), and the accompanying **nature reserve** (www.rspb.org.uk/wales; Plas Nico;

WALKING THE ISLE OF ANGLESEY COASTAL PATH

Anglesey is a big draw for walkers thanks to the **Isle of Anglesey Coastal Path** (www.angleseycoastalpath.co.uk), a 125-mile coastal walking path with clear, yellow waymarking and spectacular views. The full trail, a 12-day walk appealing to all ability ranges and reaching a maximum altitude of just 219m, passes through a changing landscape of coastal heath, saltmarsh, beaches and even a National Nature Reserve.

The official trailhead is at St Cybi's Church in Holyhead, but the 12 stages can easily be tackled as individual day hikes, ranging from seven to 13 miles per day. Some of the stages, particularly the far-northern legs from Cemaes Bay to Church Bay, make for bracing strolls against a dramatic backdrop of wild, wind-swept scenery.

A great, introductory day walk from Beaumaris takes in the ancient monastic site of Penmon Priory, Penmon Point with views across to Puffin Island, and Llanddona, a Blue Flag beach for a refreshing dip.

Alternatively, Moelfre is one of the prettiest harbour villages on the east coast. It's home to both Ann's Pantry and the **Seawatch Centre** (☎01248-410277; admission free; ⏲11am-5pm Tue-Sat, 1-5pm Sun Apr-Sep), where a statue of local coxwain Richard Evans, who won the first Royal National Lifeboat Institute (RNLI) gold medal in 1959, overlooks the sea.

Walkers should equip themselves with a copy of the *OS Explorer Maps 262 (west coast)* and *263 (east coast)* before setting out.

Anglesey Walking Holidays (www.angleseywalkingholidays.com; per person from £395) offers self-guided walking packages, including accommodation, luggage transfers and transport between trailheads.

admission free; ⏲11am-5pm Apr-Sep) – run by the Royal Society for the Protection of Birds (RSPB); visitor centre at Ellins Tower – is gloriously remote.

Sleeping & Eating

Yr Hendre B&B ££
(☎01407-762929; www.yr-hendre.net; Porth-y-Felin Rd; s/d £45/60; P @) Yr Hendre remains the best place to stay in Holyhead and a welcome change from the town's recent proliferation of budget chain hotels. Professionally managed and homely, the rooms are elegant; some have sea views. No credit cards.

Ucheldre Kitchen CAFE £
(www.ucheldre.org; Millbank; ⏲10am-4.30pm Mon-Sat, 2-4.30pm Sun) Attached to Holyhead's excellent arts hub, the Ucheldre Arts Centre, is this relaxed, friendly cafe for lunches and coffees. Time your lunch well and you could catch one of the community arts events in the studio next door.

Harbourfront Bistro BISTRO ££
(Newry Beach; mains £8.95-14.95; ⏲noon-2.15pm daily, 6-9pm Thu-Sat) For good food and marina views, this cosy little bistro adjoining the Holyhead Maritime Museum is hard to beat.

Information

Holyhead tourist office (⏲9.30am-5.30pm daily high season, Mon-Wed, Fri & Sat low season) Located in ferry terminal 1.

Getting There & Away

BUS The station is on Summer Hill.

Arriva (www.arrivabus.co.uk) Bus 4/X4 runs to Bangor (1½ hours, half-hourly Monday to Saturday); bus 44 (twice hourly, five daily) runs on Sunday.

National Express (www.nationalexpress.com) Coach destinations include Birmingham (£27, four hours), Cardiff (£52, 11 hours) and London (£28, 7½ hours).

FERRY Terminal 1 is connected to the train station for foot passengers; terminal 2 is for car passengers; terminal 3 is reserved for Irish Ferries. A free shuttle-bus service runs between terminals for foot passengers.

Irish Ferries (www.irishferries.com) Two daily slow ferries (3¼ hours) and two fast services (one hour 50 minutes).

Stena Line (www.stenaline.co.uk) Four daily services to Dublin for car passengers (3¼ hours); two daily services to Dun Laoghaire for foot passengers (one hour 10 minutes).

TRAIN Holyhead's station has the following direct services.

Virgin Trains (www.virgintrains.co.uk) To London Euston (£45, four hours) on the West Coast main line.

Arriva Trains Wales (www.arrivatrainswales.co.uk) To Chester (£20, 1¾ hours) via Bangor (£7, 30 minutes).

WEST OF SNOWDONIA

The region between the western fringe of the Snowdonia National Park and the Isle of Anglesey is a staunchly Welsh-speaking area. Indeed, the county of Gwynedd is the traditional heartland of Welsh nationalism; around 70% of people here still use Welsh as their first language.

Caernarfon

POP 9600

Wedged between the gleaming Menai Strait and the deep-purple mountains of Snowdonia, Caernarfon is home to a fantastical castle, its main claim to fame. Given the town's crucial historical importance, its proximity to the national park and its reputation as a centre of Welsh culture (it has the highest percentage of Welsh speakers of anywhere), parts of the town centre are surprisingly down-at-heel. Still, there's a lot of charm and a tangible sense of history in the streets around the castle. Within the cobbled lanes of the old walled town are some fine Georgian buildings, while the waterfront area has started on the inevitable march towards gentrification.

The castle was built by Edward I as the last link in his 'iron ring' and it's now part of the Castles and Town Walls of King Edward in Gwynedd Unesco World Heritage Site. In an attempt by then-Prime Minister David Lloyd George (himself a Welshman) to bring the royals closer to their Welsh constituency, the castle was designated as the venue for the 1911 investiture of the Prince of Wales. In retrospect, linking the modern royals to such a powerful symbol of Welsh subjugation may not have been the best idea. It incensed the largely nationalist local population, and at the next crowning, that of Prince Charles in 1969, the sentiment climaxed in an attempt to blow up his train.

EXPLORING MORE OF ANGLESEY

» **Llanfair PG**, the small town with the absurdly famous multi-syllable moniker (Llanfairpwllgwyngyllgogerychwyrndrobwllllantysiliogogogoch), is an unlikely hotspot for visitors. Coach parties are all jostling for a photo opportunity on the train station platform by the sign, but more practical is the **Llanfair PG tourist office** (☎01248-713177; ⏲9.30am-5.30pm Mon-Sat, 10am-4pm Sun), for information, maps and souvenirs.

» Anglesey is synonymous with the twin iconic bridges that connect the island to the Welsh mainland. The **Menai Heritage Experience** (www.menaibridges.co.uk; Menai Bridge; adult/child £3/free; ⏲10am-4pm Sun-Thu Apr-Oct) explains the feat of Victoria engineering and explores the ecology of the Menai Strait.

» Anglesey's leading arts centre, **Oriel Ynys Môn** (www.kyffinwilliams.info; Llangefni; ⏲10.30am-5pm) is the lynchpin of Anglesey's visual arts centre. The History Gallery explores Anglesey's past, but the main draw is the Oriel Kyffin Williams, featuring 400-odd works by Wales' most celebrated artist.

» If you only visit one NT property in North Wales, make it **Plas Newydd** (NT; Llanfair PG; adult/child £7.80/3.90; ⏲house & garden noon-5pm Sat-Wed), home to the first Marquess of Anglesey, who commanded the cavalry during the 1815 battle of Waterloo. Don't confuse this stately property with Llangollen's Plas Newydd (p726).

Sights & Activities

Caernarfon Castle CASTLE, MUSEUM

(Cadw; adult/child/family £4.95/4.60/15; ⏲9am-5pm Apr-Oct, 9.30am-4pm Mon-Sat & 11am-4pm Sun Nov-Mar) Majestic Caernarfon Castle was built between 1283 and 1330 as a military stronghold, a seat of government and a royal palace. Inspired by the dream of Macsen Wledig recounted in the *Mabinogion,* Caernarfon echoes the 5th-century walls of Constantinople, with colour-banded masonry and polygonal towers, instead of the traditional round towers and turrets.

Despite its fairytale aspect it is thoroughly fortified. It repelled Owain Glyndŵr's army in 1404 with a garrison of only 28 men, and resisted three sieges during the Civil War before surrendering to Cromwell's army in 1646.

A year after the construction of the building was begun, Edward I's second son was born here, becoming heir to the throne four months later when his elder brother died. To consolidate Edward's power he was made Prince of Wales in 1301, and his much-eroded statue is over the **King's Gate**. He came to a very nasty end via a red-hot poker, but that did not destroy the title.

Caernarfon Castle is a large, relatively intact structure. You can walk on and through the interconnected walls and towers gathered around the central green, most of which are well preserved but empty. Start at the **Eagle Tower**, the one with the flagpoles to the right of the entrance. On the turrets you can spot the weathered eagle from which it gets its name, alongside stone helmeted figures intended to swell the garrison's numbers (they're easier to spot from the quay). Inside there are displays on Edward I and the construction of the castle as well as a short film, *The Eagle & The Dragon,* which screens on the half-hour.

There is an exhibition plus a cinematic glimpse of the investiture of today's Prince of Wales, HRH Prince Charles, in the **North East Tower**. In the **Queen's Tower** (named after Edward I's wife Eleanor) is the **Regimental Museum of the Royal Welsh Fusiliers**.

FREE **Segontium Roman Fort** RUINS, MUSEUM

(www.segontium.org.uk; Ffordd Cwstenin; ⏲12.30-4.30pm Tue-Sun) Just east of the centre, these excavated foundations represent the westernmost Roman legionary fort of the Roman Empire. Overlooking the Menai Strait, the fort dates back to AD 77, when the conquest of Wales was completed by capturing the Isle of Anglesey. It was designed to accommodate a force of up to 1000 infantrymen, and coins recovered from the site indicate that it was an active garrison until AD 394 – a reflection of its crucial strategic position.

The on-site museum explains the background to the stark remains, although it's not always open as it's staffed by volunteers. The site is located about half a mile along the A4085 (to Beddgelert), which crosses through the middle of it

Plas Menai WATERSPORTS CENTRE
(☎01248-670964; www.plasmenai.co.uk) The excellent National Watersports Centre, 3 miles out along the A487 towards Bangor, offers a year-round range of water-based courses for all interests and ability levels (sailing, power-boating, kayaking, windsurfing) plus multi-activity courses suitable for families and youth groups. Advance reservations are necessary. The centre also offers B&B accommodation (singles/doubles £45/70) and a bunkhouse (dorms £25). Bus 1A (Caernarfon to Bangor) stops here.

Beics Menai CYCLING
(☎01286-676804; www.beicsmenai.co.uk; 1 Slate Quay; per 2/4/6/8hr £13/15/17/20; ⏰9.30am-4pm Tue-Sat) Hires bikes (including tandems, children's bikes and child seats) and can advise on local cycle routes. Recreational cycle routes include the 12.5-mile Lôn Eifion (starting near the Welsh Highland Railway station and running south to Bryncir) and the 4.5-mile Lôn Las Menai (following the Menai Strait to the village of Y Felinheli).

GreenWood Forest Park AMUSEMENT PARK
(www.greenwoodforestpark.co.uk; Y Felinheli; adult/child £11/9.90; ⏰11am-5pm Mar-Oct) This 7-hectare adventure park with a slew of rides and activities is underpinned by a strong green ethos. Grab a ride on the Green Dragon, the world's first people-powered roller coaster. It's signposted from the A487 near Y Felinheli, 4 miles north-east of Caernarfon.

Sleeping & Eating

TOP CHOICE **Totters** HOSTEL £
(☎01286-672963; www.totters.co.uk; 2 High St; dm/d/tr incl breakfast £15/45/60) Modern, clean and very welcoming, this excellent independent hostel is the best-value place to stay in town. In addition to traveller-friendly facilities, the 14th-century arched basement gives a sense of history to guests' breakfasts. As well as dorms, there's a two-bed attic apartment.

Victoria House B&B ££
(☎01286-678263; www.thevictoriahouse.co.uk; 15 Church St; d £50-70; 📶) Victoria House is an exceptional four-bedroom guesthouse with a homely feel, spacious modern rooms and some nice touches, such as an impressive selection of free toiletries and a DVD on the town's history in each room.

Black Boy Inn PUB, B&B ££
(☎01286-673604; www.black-boy-inn.com; Northgate St; s/d £65/95; P📶) Dating from 1522, the creaky but atmospheric rooms at this traditional inn have original wooden beams and panelling but a modern sensibility. The public areas are divided into a series of snug rooms and, although the wine might come out of a box, the place serves real ale and excellent hearty meals (mains £7 to £16) such as cassoulet and game pie.

Caer Menai B&B ££
(☎01286-672612; www.caermenai.co.uk; 15 Church St; s/d from £40/60; @📶) A former county school (1894), this elegant building is the biggest and brightest on the street. New owners are in the process of updating the seven en-suite rooms; number seven has sunset sea views.

Castell BAR £
(33 Castle Sq; mains £8-9) Caernarfon's chicest bar looks on to Castle Sq from behind its grand facade. Inside it's all black furniture and pink trim – which isn't anywhere near as much of a 1980s nightmare as it sounds. Drop in for soup or a sandwich at lunchtime (about £4) or a more substantial evening meal.

Stones Bistro FRENCH ££
(☎01286-671152; 4 Hole in the Wall St; mains £11-16; ⏰dinner Tue-Sat, lunch Sun) Housed in what was a 17th-century temperance house, this dark but cosy French-style bistro is open for dinner and Sunday lunch, with specialty roast lamb and some decent options for vegetarians.

Entertainment

Galeri Caernarfon THEATRE, CINEMA
(☎01286-685222; www.galericaernarfon.com; Victoria Dock) This excellent multipurpose arts centre hosts exhibitions, theatre, film and events; check the program online for details. The stylish in-house DOC Cafe Bar serves all-day snacks and pre-event suppers.

Information

Tourist office (☎01286-672232; Castle Ditch; ⏰9.30am-4.30pm Apr-Oct, 10am-3.30pm Mon-Sat Nov-Mar) Opposite the castle's main entrance; incorporates the Pendeitsh Gallery.

Getting There & Away

BUS Buses stop at stands along Penllyn, two blocks north of Pool St. Buses include 1/1A to

Bangor (25 minutes), Plas Menai (five minutes), Criccieth (35 minutes), Tremadog (37 minutes) and Porthmadog (45 minutes); X5 to Conwy (1¼ hours) and Llandudno (1½ hours); 12 to Pwllheli (45 minutes); and 87/88 to Llanberis (30 minutes).

Snowdon Sherpa (www.snowdoniagreenkey.co.uk) bus S4 heads to Beddgelert (30 minutes) via the Snowdon Ranger (20 minutes) and Rhyd Ddu (24 minutes) trailheads. A National Express coach stops here daily, en route between Pwllheli (£6.80, one hour) and London (£31, 10½ hours), via Bangor (£6, 25 minutes), Llandudno (£7.30, one hour) and Birmingham (£24, six hours).

TRAIN Caernarfon is the northern terminus of the Welsh Highland Railway tourist train, which currently runs to just past Beddgelert (£22 return, 1½ hours) and will connect to Porthmadog in 2011. The station is near the river on St Helen's Rd.

Llŷn Peninsula

Jutting out into the Irish Sea from the mountains of Snowdonia, the Llŷn Peninsula is a green finger of land, some 25 miles long and averaging 8 miles in width. It's a peaceful and largely undeveloped region with isolated walking and cycling routes, some good beaches, a scattering of small fishing villages and 70 miles of wildlife-rich coastline (much of it in the hands of the NT, and almost 80% of it designated an AONB). Over the centuries the heaviest footfalls have been those of pilgrims on their way to Bardsey Island.

Welsh is the language of everyday life here. Indeed, as places go, this is about as Welsh as it gets. The Llŷn (pronounced khlee'en) and the Isle of Anglesey were the last places on the Roman and Norman itineraries, and both have maintained a separate identity, the Llŷn especially so. Isolated physically and culturally, it's been an incubator of Welsh activism. It was the birthplace of David Lloyd George, the first Welsh prime minister of the UK, and of Plaid Cymru (the Welsh Party), which was founded in Pwllheli in 1925 and is now the main opposition party in the Welsh Assembly.

With a population of 3900, Pwllheli (poolth-*heh*-lee; meaning 'salt-water pool') is the largest town on the Llŷn. While it's staunchly Welsh and has a long sandy beach, it's not a particularly interesting or attractive town to linger in. It is, however, the peninsula's public transport hub.

Sights & Activities

FREE **Welsh Language & Heritage Centre** LANGUAGE CENTRE

(☎01758-750334; www.nantgwrtheyrn.org; ⏲call ahead for times) The village of Nant Gwrtheyrn was built for workers in the 19th century, but the granite quarries closed after WWII and it was gradually abandoned. In 1978 it was given a new lease of life when it was bought and restored as the home of this residential training centre. Even if you don't take a course, it's a magical place – eerily quiet and ideal for a tranquil walk along world's-end cliffs.

The heritage centre has a small but compelling exhibition on the history of the Welsh language, but its main focus is offering Welsh language and literature courses to suit all levels of ability (from £280 for three days including full board). It's reached from the village of Llithfaen (on the B4417) by following a path down a steep valley. If you're driving take it very slowly.

THE BARDSEY PILGRIMAGE

At a time when journeys from Britain to Italy were long, perilous and beyond the means of most people, the Pope decreed that three pilgrimages to the holy island of Bardsey would have the same spiritual value as one to Rome. Tens of thousands of penitents took advantage of this get-out-of-purgatory-free (or at least quickly) card and many came here to die. In the 16th century, Henry VIII's ban on pilgrimages put paid to the practice – although a steady trickle of modern-day pilgrims still walk the route.

The traditional path stops at ancient churches and holy wells along the way. It's broken into nine legs on the **Edge of Wales Walk** (www.edgeofwaleswalk.co.uk) website, run by a cooperative of local residents. They can help to arrange a 47-mile, self-guided walking tour, including five nights' accommodation and baggage transfers (around £56 per night). A similar service is also offered for the 84-mile **Llŷn Coastal Path**, which circumnavigates the peninsula.

Porth Dinllaen BEACH, PUB

It's hard to believe that this was once a busy cargo, shipbuilding and herring port, the only safe haven on the peninsula's north coast. Today, it's owned in its entirety by the NT, which maintains a small information kiosk in its car park (parking £3 in summer, free to NT members).

At the western end of the beach are an isolated cluster of buildings, which include the legendary **Tŷ Coch Inn** (www.tycoch.co.uk; ⌚noon-4pm Sat & Sun, daily summer). It was famous for its views and toes-in-the-water pints even before Demi Moore shot key scenes from the 2006 movie *Half Light* here.

Braich-y-Pwll HEADLAND

While the boats for Bardsey now leave from Porth Meudwy, this rugged NT property on the very tip of the Llŷn Peninsula is where the medieval pilgrims set off from – and one glimpse of the surf-pounded rocks will reinforce what a terrifying final voyage that would have been. It's an incredibly dramatic, ancient-looking landscape, with Bardsey rising out of the slate-grey sea like the mystical Avalon. A path leads down past the earthworks that are all that remains of **St Mary's Abbey** to a Neolithic standing stone known as **Maen Melyn**, bent like a finger towards the island and suggesting this was a holy place long before the Celts or their saints arrived.

Aberdaron BEACH, CHURCH

Aberdaron (population 1000) is an ends-of-the-earth kind of place with whitewashed, windswept houses contemplating Aberdaron Bay. It was traditionally the last resting spot before pilgrims made the treacherous crossing to Bardsey.

Lingering from this time is **St Hywyn's Church** (⌚10am-4pm), stoically positioned above the pebbly beach. The left half of the church dates from 1100, while the right half was added 400 years later, to cope with the volume of pilgrims. With their spiritual needs sorted, the Bardsey-bound saints could then claim a meal at **Y Gegin Fawr** (The Big Kitchen; ⌚9am-6pm). Dating from 1300, it still dishes up meals.

Bardsey Island (Ynys Enlli) ISLAND

This rugged island, 2 miles long and 2 miles off the tip of the Llŷn, is a magical place. In the 6th or 7th century the obscure St Cadfan founded a monastery here, giving shelter to Celts fleeing the Saxon invaders, and medieval pilgrims followed in their wake. A Celtic cross amidst the abbey ruins commemorates the pilgrims who came here to die and gave the island its poetic epithet: the Isle of 20,000 Saints. Their bones still periodically emerge from unmarked graves; it's said that in the 1850s they were used as fencing, there were so many of them. To add to its mythical status, it's one of many candidates for the Isle of Avalon from the Arthurian legends. It's said that the wizard Merlin is asleep in a glass castle somewhere on the island.

Its Welsh name means 'Isle of the Currents', a reference to the treacherous tidal surges in Bardsey Sound, which doubtless convinced medieval visitors that their lives were indeed in God's hands. Most modern pilgrims to Bardsey are sea-bird-watchers (the island is home to an important colony of Manx shearwaters).

The **Bardsey Island Trust** (☎08458 11 22 33; www.bardsey.org) is Bardsey's custodian and can arrange holiday lets in cottages on the island. In the summer months both **Bardsey Boat Trips** (☎07971-769895; www.bardseyboattrips.com) and **Enlli Charters** (☎0845 811 3655; www.enllicharter.co.uk) take boats to Bardsey from Porth Meudwy (adult/child £30/15). Enlli Charters also departs from Pwllheli (adult/child £35/20).

Abersoch BEACH TOWN

Abersoch (population 1000) comes alive in summer with a 30,000-person influx of boaties, surfers and beachbums. Edged by gentle blue-green hills, the town's main attraction is its beaches. Surfers head for the Atlantic swell at Porth Neigwl (Hell's Mouth) and Porth Ceiriad, while sailors, windsurfers and boaters prefer the gentle waters of Abersoch Bay.

West Coast Surf Shop (www.westcoastsurf.co.uk; Lôn Pen Cei; ⌚9.30am-5pm) hires out boards and wetsuits all year around. Its website features a live surfcam and daily surf reports. **Offaxis** (☎01758-713407; www.offaxis.co.uk; Lôn Engan; lessons incl equipment from £30) is another outdoors and surf shop, which specialises in wakeboarding, windsurfing and surfing lessons.

Abersoch Sailing School (☎01758-712963; www.abersochsailingschool.co.uk) offers sailing lessons (from £45) and joy rides (per person £25), and hires laser fun boats (one/two/three hours £30/45/60), catamarans (one/two/three hours £40/60/80), sea kayaks (per hour single/double £10/20) and skippered day racers and keelboats (per hour £75, minimum two hours).

FREE **Oriel Plas Glyn-y-Weddw** GALLERY, MANOR

(www.oriel.org.uk; Llanbedrog; ⊙10am-5pm Wed-Mon, daily summer) Only part of the attraction of this excellent gallery is the lively collection of work by contemporary Welsh artists, all of which is available for purchase. The gallery is worth visiting just to gape at the flamboyant Victorian Gothic mansion it's housed in, with its flashy exposed beams and stained glass. There's also a nice little cafe and paths through the wooded grounds, which roll down to NT-owned Llandbedrog beach.

It's 3 miles from Abersoch and 4 miles west of Pwllheli.

Llanystumdwy VILLAGE, MUSEUM

The village of Llanystumdwy is the boyhood home and final resting place of David Lloyd George, one of Wales' finest ever political statesmen, and the British prime minister from 1916 to 1922. There's a small **Lloyd George Museum** (adult/child £4/3; ⊙10.30am-5pm Mon-Fri), which gives an impression of the man and to some extent illustrates the tension between his nationality and position, through photos, posters and personal effects. Highgate, the house he grew up in, is 50m away, and his grave is about 150m away on the other side of the car park.

The turn-off to the village is to be found 1.5 miles west of Criccieth on the A497.

Criccieth CASTLE, BEACH

This genteel slow-moving seaside town (population 1800) sits above a sweep of sand-and-stone beach about 5 miles west of Porthmadog. It's main claim to fame is ruined **Criccieth Castle** (Cadw; adult/child £3/2.60; ⊙10am-5pm Apr-Oct, 11am-4pm Fri-Sun Nov-Mar) perched up on the clifftop and offering views stretching along the southern coast and across Tremadog Bay to Harlech. Constructed by Welsh prince Llywelyn the Great in 1239, it was overrun in 1283 by Edward I's forces and recaptured for the Welsh in 1404 by Owain Glyndŵr, who promptly burnt it. Today there is a small but informative exhibition centre at the ticket office.

Sleeping & Eating

TOP CHOICE **Venetia** RESTAURANT-WITH-ROOMS ££

(☎01758-713354; www.venetiawales.com; Lôn Sarn Bach, Abersoch; r £108-148; P) No sinking old Venetian palazzo, just five beautifully styled rooms above an excellent Italian **restaurant** (mains £9-20; ⊙Thu-Sun winter, daily summer), decked out with designer lighting and modern art. Cinque has a TV above its bathtub.

Plas Bodegroes RESTAURANT-WITH-ROOMS ££

(☎01758-612363; www.bodegroes.co.uk; s £50, d £55-88; P wi-fi) Set in a stately 1780 manor house with immaculately coiffured gardens, this restaurant-with-rooms is a romantic option. The emphasis is on the eating, which perhaps explains why the comfortable rooms are so reasonably priced. The slick **restaurant** (3-course dinner £43; ⊙lunch Sun, dinner Tue-Sat) has an elegant dining room but ups the Welshiness by serving its dishes on slabs of slate. It's a mile inland from Pwllheli along the A497.

Tŷ Newydd HOTEL ££

(☎01758-760207; www.gwesty-tynewydd.co.uk; Aberdaron; s/d from £60/95) Right on the beach, this friendly hotel has fully refurbished, light-drenched, spacious rooms and some truly wonderful sea views. The terrace off the pub restaurant seems designed with afternoon gin and tonics in mind.

Poachers Restaurant RESTAURANT ££

(☎01766-522512; www.poachersrestaurant.co.uk; 66 High St, Criccieth; mains £11-19; ⊙lunch Sun, dinner Wed-Sat) Look past the paper serviettes and limited wine choice and you'll find tasty Welsh dishes married with some flavours of Asia. Try the good-value three-course set menu (£17).

Information

Abersoch Tourist Office (www.abersochandllyn.co.uk; High St, Abersoch; ⊙10.30am-4.30pm Apr-Aug; @)

Pwllheli Tourist Office (☎01758-613000; Station Sq; ⊙10.30am-3pm Mon-Wed, Fri & Sat Nov-Mar, 9am-5pm Apr-Oct)

Getting There & Away

BUS Bus 1 (Porthmadog–Caernarfon–Bangor) stops in Criccieth. All of the peninsula's other bus services originate or terminate at Pwllheli, including 3 to Llanystumdwy (20 minutes), Criccieth (24 minutes), Tremadog (37 minutes) and Porthmadog (41 minutes); 12 to Caernarfon (45 minutes); 17/17B to Llanbedrog (10 minutes) and Aberdaron (45 minutes); and 18 to Llanbedrog (12 minutes) and Abersoch (25 minutes). A National Express coach heads between Pwllheli and London (£31, 10½ hours) daily, via Criccieth (£5.20, 17 minutes), Caernarfon (£6.80, one hour), Bangor (£7.30, 1½ hours) and Birmingham (£24, seven hours).

TRAIN Pwllheli is the terminus of the Cambrian Coast line, with direct trains to Criccieth (£2.70, 13 minutes), Porthmadog (£3.90, 22 minutes), Harlech (£6.30, 45 minutes), Barmouth (£8.70, 1¼ hours), Fairbourne (£8.70, 1¼ hours) and Machynlleth (£13, 2¼ hours).

Porthmadog & Around

POP 4200

Given its abundance of transport connections and its position straddling both the Llŷn Peninsula and Snowdonia National Park, busy little Porthmadog (port-*mad*-uk) makes an excellent place to base yourself for a few days. While the town centre is nothing to look at, its estuarine setting offers nice views and walks. Despite a few rough edges, Porthmadog has a considerable amount of charm and a conspicuously friendly populace.

The town was founded by an 1821 Act of Parliament granting permission to slate magnate William Alexander Madocks – after whom the town is named – to reclaim estuary land and create a new harbour. Madocks begun by laying a mile-long causeway called the Cob across Traeth Mawr, the estuary at the mouth of the River Glaslyn. Some 400 hectares of wetland habitat behind the Cob was drained and turned into farmland. The resulting causeway provided the route Madocks needed to transport slate on the new Ffestiniog Railway down to the new port. In the 1870s it was estimated that over a thousand vessels per year departed from the harbour and, at its 1873 peak, over 116,000 tons of slate.

Today Porthmadog is the southern terminus for two of Wales' finest narrow-gauge train journeys, the Ffestiniog and Welsh Highland Railways. On its doorstep is the village of Portmeirion, a fantasy-style pocket of *la dolce vita* Italy in North Wales.

Sights & Activities

Ffestiniog & Welsh Highland Railways
HERITAGE RAILWAYS

(☎01766-516024; www.festrail.co.uk) There are 'little trains' all over Wales, a legacy of Victorian industry, but Porthmadog is doubly blessed. These two lines top and tail the town, with a station at each end of the High St. They're run by the oldest independent railway company in the world, established by an Act of Parliament in 1832.

Departing from the south end, near the Cob, the **Ffestiniog Railway** (adult/child return £18/17) is a fantastic, twisting and precipitous narrow-gauge railway that was built between 1832 and 1836 to haul slate down to Porthmadog from the mines at Blaenau Ffestiniog. Horse-drawn wagons were replaced in the 1860s by steam locomotives and the line became a passenger service. Saved after years of neglect, it is one of Wales' most spectacular and beautiful narrow-gauge journeys. Because it links the Cambrian Coast and Conwy Valley main lines, it also serves as a serious public transport link. Nearly all services are steam-hauled.

Exciting things are afoot at its sibling, the **Welsh Highland Railway** (Caernarfon-Pont Croesor; adult/child return £28/26). An amalgamation of several late-19th-century slate railways, the line opened for passenger traffic in 1923 but closed just 14 years later. It reopened as a tourist attraction in 1997 and until recently was offering only short trips from Porthmadog and rather longer ones from Caernarfon as far as the trailheads of the Snowdon Ranger and Rhyd Ddu tracks on the slopes of Snowdon.

STEAM RIDES AGAIN

Wales' narrow-gauge railways are testament to an industrial heyday of mining and quarrying. Using steam and diesel engines, these railways often crossed terrain that defied standard-gauge trains. By the 20th century, industrial decline and road-building had left many lines defunct and the infamous Beeching report of 1963 closed dozens of rural branch lines. Five years later, British Rail fired up its last steam engine.

Passionate steam enthusiasts formed a preservation group, buying and restoring old locomotives, rolling stock, disused lines and stations – a labour of love financed by offering rides to the public, often with former railway workers helping out.

Ten restored lines around Wales form a group called **Great Little Trains of Wales** (www.greatlittletrainsofwales.co.uk). A discount card (£10) entitles the holder to a 20% discount for a return trip on each of the 10 railways.

In 2010 the line was extended to Beddgelert and through the outrageously beautiful Aberglaslyn Pass to Pont Croesor, 2 miles from Porthmadog. By the time you're reading this, the last small gap should have been plugged, connecting Caernarfon with Porthmadog, with a final leg along the main street to a new terminus near the Ffestiniog Railway.

Portmeirion TOURIST VILLAGE
(www.portmeirion-village.com; adult/child £8/4; 9.30am-5.30pm) Set on its own tranquil peninsula reaching into the estuary, Portmeirion is an oddball, gingerbread collection of buildings with a heavy Italian influence, masterminded by the Welsh architect Sir Clough Williams-Ellis. Starting in 1926, Clough collected bits and pieces from disintegrating stately mansions to create this weird and wonderful seaside utopia over the course of 50 years. When it was deemed to be finished in 1976, Clough had reached the ripe old age of 90 and had designed and built many of the structures himself. Today the buildings are all listed and the site is a conservation area.

It's really much more like an amusement park or a stage set than an actual village and, indeed, it formed the ideally surreal set for cult TV series *The Prisoner*, which was filmed here from 1966 to 1967; it still draws fans of the show in droves, with *Prisoner* conventions held annually in April.

Most of the kooky cottages or scaled-down mansions scattered about the site are available for holiday lets, while other buildings contain cafes, restaurants and gift shops. Portmeirion pottery (the famously florid pottery designed by Susan, Sir Clough's daughter) is available, even though these days it's made in Stoke-on-Trent (England).

Portmeirion is 2 miles east of Porthmadog. It's an easy enough walk, but bus 99B has services at 9.55am and 1.05pm Monday to Saturday (10 minutes).

Borth-y-Gest SEASIDE VILLAGE
The best views over the estuary are from Terrace Rd, which becomes Garth Rd above the harbour. At its end a path heads down to Borth-y-Gest, a pretty horseshoe of candy-coloured houses overlooking a sandy bay. At the other end of the crescent the path continues around the cliffs; if you look carefully you should be able to spot Harlech Castle in the distance.

Purple Moose Brewery MICROBREWERY
(www.purplemoose.co.uk; Madoc St; 9am-5pm Mon-Fri) One of approximately 30 microbreweries across Wales, Purple Moose has grown from humble beginnings to employ four people and supply pubs across North Wales. Its award-winning tipples include Snowdonia Ale, Madog's Ale, Glaslyn Ale and Dark Side of the Moose. You can buy these and associated memorabilia from the brewery shop. Tours are given on request, if it's not too busy.

Sleeping & Eating

Yr Hen Fecws ROOMS, CAFE ££
(01766-514625; www.henfecws.com; 16 Lombard St; s/d £43/55; P) Stylishly restored, this stone cottage has seven simply decorated en-suite rooms with exposed-slate walls and fireplaces. Add £6 per person for breakfast at the excellent cafe below.

Golden Fleece Inn PUB £
(01766-512421; www.goldenfleeceinn.com; Market Sq, Tremadog; s/d £25/40;) An inviting and friendly old inn with hop flowers hanging from the ceilings, real ales, decent pub grub (mains £4 to £12), an open fire for cold nights and a sunny courtyard for balmy days. The budget rooms upstairs are much more comfortable and atmospheric than you'd expect for the price. Be prepared for noise until closing, or just join the party. A roster of live music and jam sessions entertains the troops, although the punters can be pretty entertaining themselves.

Hotel Portmeirion & Castell Deudraeth HOTELS, COTTAGES £££
(01766-70000; www.portmeirion-village.com; r £170-300) You can live the fantasy and stay within the famous fairytale village itself. The original Hotel Portmeirion (1926) has classic, elegant rooms and a dining room designed by Sir Terence Conran. Up the drive, storybook Castell Deudraeth is, perversely, a more modern alternative. Better still, there are 17 whimsical self-catering cottages on site, hired out according to a complex series of rates for weekly, weekend or midweek stays.

Information

Tourist office (01766-512981; High St; 9.30am-5pm Easter-Oct, 10am-3.30pm Mon-Sat Nov-Easter)

Getting There & Away

BUS Bus route 1B heads to Blaenau Ffestiniog (31 minutes); 3 to Tremadog (four minutes), Criccieth (13 minutes), Llanystumdwy (23 minutes), and Pwllheli (41 minutes); and X32 to Aberystwyth (2¼ hours), Machynlleth (1½ hours), Dolgellau (1½ hours), Caernarfon (43 minutes) and Bangor (1¼ hours). Snowdon Sherpa bus S97 goes to Beddgelert (25 minutes) and Pen-y-Pass (45 minutes). A National Express coach heads between Pwllheli (£7, 30 minutes) and London (£31, 10 hours) daily, via Caernarfon (£6.80, 35 minutes), Llandudno (£7.30, 1½ hour) and Birmingham (£24, 6½ hours).

TRAIN Porthmadog is on the Cambrian Coast line, with direct trains to Machynlleth (£11, 1¾ hours), Fairbourne (£6.20, 58 minutes), Barmouth (£5.40, 48 minutes), Harlech (£3, 22 minutes) and Pwllheli (£3.90, 22 minutes). See also the Ffestiniog & Welsh Highland Railways (p742) for steamy services to Blaenau Ffestiniog, the Snowdon trailheads and Caernarfon.

SNOWDONIA NATIONAL PARK

Snowdonia National Park (Parc Cenedlaethol Eryri) was founded in 1951 (making it Wales' first national park), primarily to keep the area from being loved to death. This is, after all, Wales' best known and most heavily used slice of nature, with the busiest part around Snowdon (1085m) itself. Around 750,000 people climb, walk or take the train to the summit each year, and all those sturdy shoes make trail maintenance a never-ending task for park staff. Yet the park is so much more than just Snowdon, stretching some 35 miles east to west and over 50 miles north to south and incorporating coastal areas, rivers and Wales' biggest natural lake.

The Welsh name for Snowdonia, is Eryri (eh-*ruh*-ree) meaning highlands. The Welsh call Snowdon itself Yr Wyddfa (uhr-*with*-vuh), meaning Great Tomb – according to legend a giant called Rita Gawr was slain here by King Arthur and is buried at the summit.

Like Wales' other national parks, this one is very lived-in, with sizeable towns at Dolgellau, Bala, Harlech and Betws-y-Coed. Two-thirds of the park is privately owned, with over three-quarters used for raising sheep and cattle. While the most popular reason for visiting the park is to walk, you can also go climbing, white-water rafting, kayaking, pony trekking and even windsurfing.

The park authority publishes a free annual visitor newspaper, which includes information on getting around, park-organised walks and other activities. The Met Office keeps the weather conditions constantly updated on its website (www.metoffice.gov.uk/loutdoor/mountainsafety/).

In the alpine reaches you'll need to be prepared to deal with hostile conditions at any time of the year; the sudden appearance of low cloud and mist is common, even on days that start out clear and sunny. Never head into isolated reaches without food, drink, warm clothing and waterproofs, whatever the weather. Carry *and* know how to read the appropriate large-scale Ordnance Survey (OS) map for the area, and carry a compass. Also be aware that even some walks described as easy may follow paths that go near very steep slopes and over loose scree.

Beddgelert

POP 500

Charming little Beddgelert is a conservation village of rough grey stone buildings, overlooking the trickling River Glaslyn with its ivy-covered bridge. Flowers festoon the village in spring and the surrounding hills are covered in a purple blaze of heather in summer, reminiscent of a Scottish glen.

The name, meaning 'Gelert's Grave', is said to refer to a folk tale concerning 13th-century Welsh prince Llywelyn. Believing that his dog Gelert had savaged his baby son, Llywelyn slaughtered the dog, only to discover that Gelert had fought off the wolf that had attacked the baby. More likely, the name Beddgelert is derived from a 5th-century Irish preacher, Celert, who is believed to have founded a church here. Regardless, the 'grave' of Gelert the dog is a popular attraction, reached by a pretty riverside trail. It was probably constructed by an unscrupulous 19th-century hotelier in an attempt to boost business.

Sights & Activities

Sygun Copper Mine MINE

(www.syguncoppermine.co.uk; adult/child £8.75/6.75; ⌚9.30am-5pm Mar-Oct) A mile east of Beddgelert, this mine dates from Roman times, although extraction was stepped up in the 19th century. Abandoned in 1903, it has since been converted into a museum, with an audiovisual underground tour that evokes the life of Victorian miners. You can also try your hand at archery (£3) or panning for gold (£2).

Beddgelert Forest MOUNTAIN BIKING

Within this forestry commission block, 2 miles north of Beddgelert along the A4805, is a popular campsite and two mountain bike trails: the 9½km Hir Trail and the easier 4km Byr Trail. **Beics Beddgelert** (01766-890434; www.beddgelertbikes.co.uk; per 2/4/8hr £12/18/25) rents out mountain bikes, tandems and child seats.

Sleeping & Eating

Plas Tan Y Graig B&B ££

(01766-890310; www.plastanygraig.co.uk; s/d £49/78;) This bright, friendly place is the best B&B in the heart of the village. It has seven uncluttered rooms, five with bathrooms, and a lounge full of maps and books.

Glaslyn Ices & Cafe Glandwr ICE CREAM, PIZZA £

(www.glaslynices.co.uk; mains £4-14) In summer, this excellent ice-cream parlour is the busiest place in the village. It serves a huge array of homemade flavours and is attached to a family restaurant offering simple meals, especially pizza.

Lyn's Cafe CAFE £

(meals £3-12; 10am-5.30pm winter, plus dinner summer) A family-friendly all-rounder (with a separate children's menu), split between a restaurant serving big breakfasts and Sunday roasts, and a tearoom around the back with seats by the river for simple snacks.

Information

Tourist Office & National Park Information Centre (01766-890615; Canolfan Hebog; 9.30am-5.30pm daily Easter-Oct, to 4.30pm Fri-Sun Nov-Mar; @)

Getting There & Away

Beddgelert is a stop on the historic Welsh Highland Railway, which currently runs from Caernarfon (£22 return, 1½ hours) and will connect to Porthmadog in 2011. Snowdon Sherpa bus S4 heads from here to Caernarfon (30 minutes) and Pen-y-Pass (15 minutes), while S97 heads to Porthmadog (25 minutes).

Snowdon & Around

No Snowdonia experience is complete without coming face-to-face with Snowdon (1085m), one of Britain's most awe-inspiring mountains and the highest summit in Wales (it's actually the 61st highest in Britain, with the other 60 all in Scotland). On a clear day the views stretch to Ireland and the Isle of Man over Snowdon's fine jagged ridges, which drop away in great swoops to sheltered *cwms* (valleys) and deep lakes. Even on a gloomy day you could find yourself above the clouds. Thanks to the Snowdon Mountain Railway it's extremely accessible – however, the summit and some of the tracks can get frustratingly crowded.

Sights & Activities

Climbing Snowdon WALKING TRACKS

Six paths of varying length and difficulty lead to the summit. Simplest (and dullest) is the **Llanberis Path** (10 miles, six hours return) running beside the railway line. The **Snowdon Ranger Path** (7 miles, five hours) starts at the Snowdon Ranger YHA; this is the shortest and also the safest in winter.

The two options which start from Pen-y-Pass require the least amount of ascent: the **Miner's Track** (7 miles, six hours) starts out gently but ends steeply; the **Pyg Track** (7 miles, six hours) is more interesting and meets the Miner's Track where it steepens. The classic **Snowdon Horseshoe** route (7.5 miles, six to seven hours) combines the Pyg Track to the summit (or via the precipitous ridge of Crib Goch if you're very experienced) with a descent over the peak of Llewedd and a final section down the Miner's Track.

The straightforward **Rhyd Ddu Path** (8 miles, six hours) is the least-used route; the trailhead is on the Caernarfon–Beddgelert road (A4085). Most challenging is the **Watkin Path** (8 miles, six hours), involving an ascent of more than 1000m on its southerly approach from Nantgwynant.

Make sure you're well prepared with warm, waterproof clothing and sturdy footwear. Check the weather forecast before setting out.

Snowdon Mountain Railway RAILWAY

(0844 493 8120; www.snowdonrailway.co.uk; return adult/child £25/18; 9am-5pm Mar-Oct) If you're not physically able to climb a mountain, short on time or just plain lazy, those industrious, railway-obsessed Victorians have gifted you an alternative. Opened in 1896, this is the UK's highest and only public rack-and-pinion railway. Vintage steam and modern diesel

Snowdonia & Llŷn Peninsula

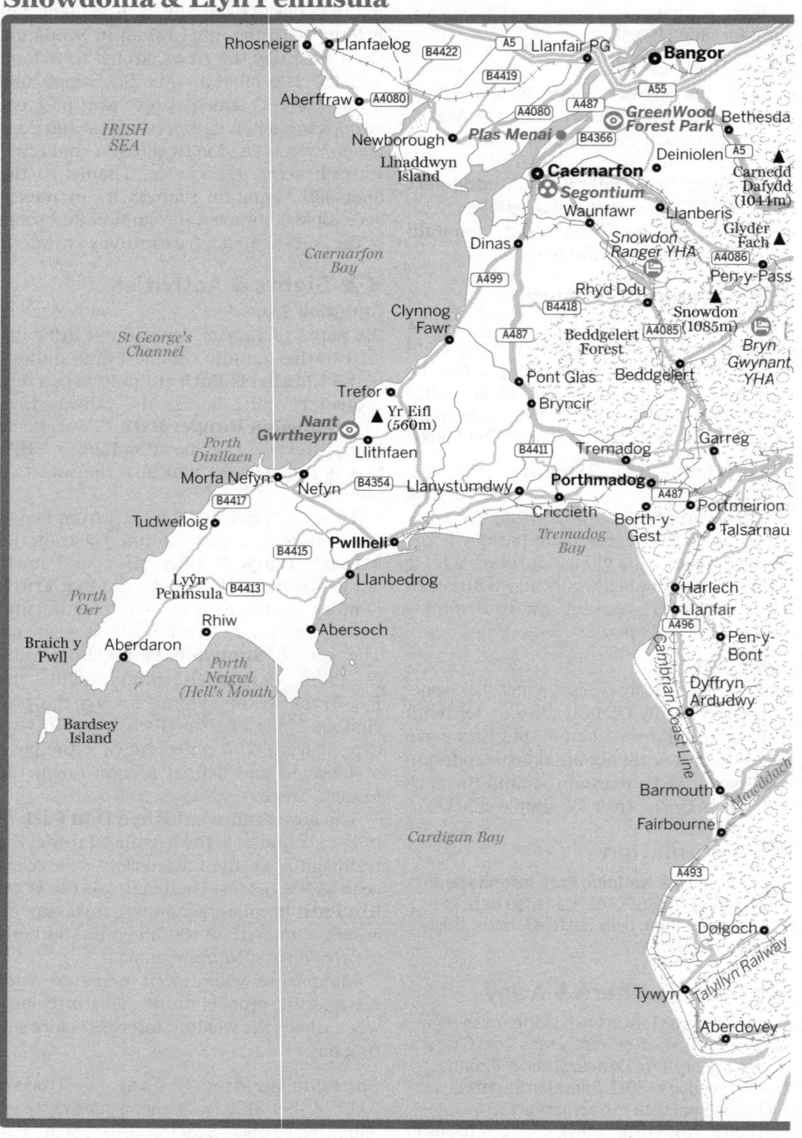

locomotives haul carriages from Llanberis up to Snowdon's very summit in an hour. Return trips involve a scant half-hour at the top before heading back down again. Single tickets can only be booked for the journey up (adult/child £18/15).

In the first season after the opening of Hafod Eryri, the trains carried 159,000 people to the summit, so make sure you book well in advance or you may miss out. Departures are weather dependent and from March to May the trains can only head as

far as Clogwyn Station (adult/child £18/14) – an altitude of 762m.

Hafod Eryri VISITOR CENTRE

Just below the cairn that marks Snowdon's summit, this striking piece of architecture opened in 2009 to replace the dilapidated 1930s visitor centre which Prince Charles famously labelled 'the highest slum in Europe'. Clad in granite and curved to blend into the mountain, it's a wonderful building, housing a cafe, toilets and ambient interpretative elements built into the structure itself. A wall of picture windows gazes down towards the west, while a small row faces the cairn. The centre (including the toilets) closes in the winter or if the weather's terrible; it's open whenever the train is running.

Sleeping

Pen-y-Gwyrd HOTEL £

(01286-870211; www.pyg.co.uk; Nant Gwynant; r with/without bathroom 48/40) Eccentric but full of atmosphere, Pen-y-Gwryd was used as a training base by the 1953 Everest team, and memorabilia from their stay includes their signatures on the dining-room ceiling. At the time of research the hotel was closed for renovations; it's usually open January to October. You'll find it below Pen-y-Pass, at the junction of the A498 and A4086.

Snowdon Ranger YHA HOSTEL £

(0845 371 9659; www.yha.org.uk; dm from £12) On the A4085, 5 miles north of Beddgelert, at the trailhead for the Snowdon Ranger Path, this former inn is full of character and has its own adjoining lakeside beach.

Pen-y-Pass YHA HOSTEL £

(0845 371 9534; www.yha.org.uk; dm from £16) Superbly situated on the slopes of Snowdon, 5.5 miles up the A4086 from Llanberis.

Bryn Gwynant YHA HOSTEL £

(0845 371 9108; www.yha.org.uk; Nantgwynant; dm from £10) Victorian mansion overlooking the lake, 4 miles east of Beddgelert.

Getting There & Away

The Welsh Highland Railway stops at the trailheads of the Snowdon Ranger and Rhyd Ddu paths, while Snowdon Sherpa buses stop at all of them. Even if you've got your own car, it's worth considering this as the Pen-y-Pass car park, in particular, can fill up quickly. Another option is to take the Snowdon Mountain Railway to the top and walk back down. It's more difficult to do this the other way around as the train will only take on new passengers at the top if there are gaps.

Llanberis

POP 1900

While not the most instantly attractive town in the area, Llanberis is a mecca for walkers and climbers, hosting a steady flow of rugged polar fleece wearers year-round, but especially in July and August when accommodation is at a premium. It's actually positioned just outside the national park but functions as a hub, partly because the Snowdon Mountain Railway leaves from here.

Llanberis straddles the A4086 with nearly all points of interest spread out along the High St, which runs parallel to it. Across the A4086 are the village's two lakes, Llyn Padarn and Llyn Peris.

The town was originally built to house workers in the Dinorwig slate quarry; the massive waste tips are hard to miss as you approach from the east. While tourism is the cornerstone of Llanberis life these days, the town wears its industrial heritage on its sleeve. Indeed, Dinorwig, which once boasted the largest artificial cavern in the world, has now become part of Europe's biggest pumped-storage power station. Some of the old quarry workshops have been reincarnated as a museum of the slate industry, and the narrow-gauge railway that once hauled slate to the coast now tootles along Llyn Padarn.

Sights & Activities

FREE National Slate Museum MUSEUM

(www.museumwales.ac.uk/en/slate; 10am-5pm Apr-Oct, to 4pm Sun-Fri Nov-Mar) Even if you're not all that fussed by industrial museums, this one's well worth checking out. At Llanberis, much of the slate was carved out of the open mountainside – leaving behind a jagged, sculptural cliff face that's fascinating if not quite beautiful. The museum occupies the Victorian workshops beside Llyn Padarn, featuring video clips, a huge working water wheel, reconstructed workers' cottages and demonstrations.

Electric Mountain POWER STATION

(01286-870636; www.electricmountain.co.uk; 10am-4.30pm) The Dinorwig Power Station's visitor centre has free interactive exhibits on the history of hydropower and runs interesting **guided tours** (adult/child £7.50/3.75; bookings required) into the station's guts under the mountain. It's located by the lakeside on the A4086, near the south end of High St.

Dolbadarn Castle CASTLE

Wales is so spoilt for castles that this one gets little attention. Built before 1230 by the Princes of Gwyneth, the keep rises like a perfect chessboard rook from a green hilltop between the two lakes. It's a brief stroll from town, rewarded by wonderful views of the lakes, quarries and Snowdon itself.

Llanberis Lake Railway STEAM TRAIN

(01286-870549; www.lake-railway.co.uk; adult/child £7.20/6.70; see online timetable) This little steam train departs on a tame but scenic one-hour return trip beside Llyn Padarn.

Sleeping

Glyn Afon B&B ££

(01286-872528; www.glyn-afon.co.uk; 72 High St; s/d £38/60; P) The recently refurbished rooms have no frills but are warm and homely at this midrange guesthouse. A hearty breakfast is assured and all dietary needs catered for.

Dolafon B&B, TEAROOMS ££

(01286-870993; www.dolafon.com; High St; s/d from £30/60; P) Set back from the road, this imposing 19th-century house offers a series of traditional rooms, most of them with en suites. The hearty breakfast includes vegetarian options, served in the oriental-wallpapered specialty tearoom downstairs.

Llanberis YHA HOSTEL £

(0845 371 9645; dm from £18) Former quarry manager's house on the slopes above the town.

Eating

Peak Restaurant WELSH ££

(01286-872777; www.peakrestaurant.co.uk; 86 High St; mains £12-15; dinner Wed-Sun) Charming owners and adventurer-sized portions underpin this restaurant's popularity and longevity. It continues to serve the best hearty, Welsh-style dinners in town.

Snowdon Honey Farm & Winery CAFE, STORE £

(www.snowdonhoneyfarmandwinery.co.uk; High St; snacks £4-5) All manner of honey-related goodies are sold here, including a range of mead. It also functions as a cafe, serving ice cream, cream tea, cakes and sandwiches.

Pete's Eats CAFE £

(01286-870117; www.petes-eats.co.uk; 40 High St; meals £4-6; @) A busy, bright cafe where hikers and climbers swap tips over monster portions in a hostel-like environment. There's bunkhouse accommodation upstairs, a huge noticeboard full of travellers' information, a book exchange, a map and guidebook room, and computers for internet access.

Information

Tourist office (☎01286-870765; 41 High St; ⏲9.30am-4.30pm Apr-Oct, to 3pm Fri-Mon Nov-Mar)

Getting There & Away

Snowdon Sherpa bus S1 heads to Pen-y-Pass (15 minutes) while S2 continues on to Capel Curig (23 minutes), Swallow Falls (28 minutes) and Betws-y-Coed (33 minutes). Buses 85 and 86 head directly to Bangor (44 minutes) while 87 and 88 head first to Caernarfon (30 minutes).

Capel Curig

POP 190

Tiny Capel Curig, 5 miles west of Betws-y-Coed, is one of Snowdonia's oldest hill stations, and has long been a magnet for walkers, climbers and other outdoor junkies. The village spreads out along the A5, but the main clump of activity is at the intersection of the A4086. It's a heady setting, ringed by looming mountains.

The **Plas y Brenin National Mountain Centre** (☎01690-720214; www.pyb.co.uk), at the western edge of the village, is a multiactivity centre offering an array of residential courses including rock climbing, mountaineering, kayaking and canoeing. Taster days run throughout the school holidays with an introduction to three activities for £35.

The basic **Capel Curig YHA** (☎0845 371 9110; dm from £16) offers great views across to the Snowdon Horseshoe.

Snowdon Sherpa buses S2 and S6 stop here.

Betws-y-Coed

POP 950

If you're looking for a base with an Alpine feel from which to explore Snowdonia National Park, the bustling little stone village of Betws-y-Coed *(bet-us-ee-koyd)* stands out as a natural option. It boasts a postcard-perfect setting above an inky river, engulfed in the verdant leafiness of the Gwydyr Forest and near the junction of three river valleys: the Llugwy, the Conwy and the Lledr.

The town has been Wales' most popular inland resort since Victorian days when a group of countryside painters founded an artistic community to record the diversity of the landscape. The arrival of the railway in 1868 cemented its popularity and today Betws-y-Coed is as busy with families and coach parties as it is with walkers.

Sights & Activities

Swallow Falls WATERFALLS

Betws-y-Coed's main natural tourist trap is located 2 miles west of town alongside the A5. It's a beautiful spot, with the torrent weaving through the rocks into a green pool below. Bring a £1 coin for the turnstile.

Gwydyr Forest WALKING, CYCLING

The 28-sq-mile Gwydyr Forest, planted since the 1920s with oak, beech and larch, encircles Betws-y-Coed. It's an ideal setting for a day's walking close to town, though it gets very muddy in wet weather. There are two challenging mountain biking loops and over a dozen marked tracks, many of which are outlined in *The Gwydyr Forest Guide* (£2) and *Walks Around Betws-y-Coyd* (£5), both available from the National Park Information Centre.

Beics Betws (☎01690-710766; www.bikewales.co.uk; Vicarage Rd; ⏲9am-5pm) can advise on cycling trails, performs repairs and hires mountain bikes from £25 per day.

Gwydir Stables HORSE RIDING

(☎01690-760248; www.horse-riding-wales.co.uk; Penmachno; per hr/half-day/day £19/34/53) Arranges rides through the forest for novice and regular riders alike. It also offers a pub ride for £40, lasting around four hours and stopping off for a pint at a couple of local pubs along the way.

Sleeping & Eating

TOP CHOICE **Tŷ Gwyn Hotel** HOTEL, RESTAURANT **££**

(☎01690-710383; www.tygwynhotel.co.uk; r £52-120; P 📶) This ex-coaching inn has been welcoming guests since 1636, its venerable age borne out by misshapen rooms, low ceilings and exposed beams. Predictably, not all rooms have en suites. The menu focuses on hearty, meaty mains (£13 to £18), but vegetarian choices and lighter bar-style meals are also available. It's located on the A5, just across Waterloo Bridge.

Afon Gwyn BOUTIQUE B&B ££
(☎01690-710442; www.guest-house-betws-y-coed.com; Coed-y-Celyn, A470; r £80-109; P) Down in the valley, this old stone house has been skilfully converted into a grand boutique guesthouse. The decor is faultlessly tasteful, with white-painted wooden panelling, hushed tones, glittering chandeliers and bathrooms bedecked in Italian tiles and marble. While all the rooms are spacious, the Alice Suite is massive.

Maes-y-Garth B&B ££
(☎01690-710441; www.maes-y-garth.co.uk; Lon Muriau, off A470; r £66-70; P) Just across the river and a field from the township, this completely ordinary-looking newly built home has earned itself many fans. Inside you'll find a warm welcome and three quietly stylish guest rooms.

Bistro Betws-y-Coed RESTAURANT ££
(☎01690-710328; www.bistrobetws-y-coed.com; Holyhead Rd; lunch £6-9, dinner £12-17; ⊙Wed-Sun, daily summer) This cottage-style eatery's statement of intent is 'modern and traditional Welsh'. Expect the likes of locally made sausages, rarebit and haddock-and-chips – battered with Llandudno Orme real ale, naturally.

Betws-y-Coed YHA HOSTEL £
(☎01690-710796; www.yha.org.uk; Swallow Falls; dm from £16) A functional hostel that's part of a bustling traveller hub with camping and a pub.

Information

National Park Information Centre (www.betws-y-coed.co.uk; Royal Oak Stables; ⊙9.30am-4.30pm) Sells books and maps. The adjoining free exhibition includes a virtual-reality helicopter ride over Snowdon.

Ultimate Outdoors (www.ultimateoutdoors.co.uk; Holyhead Rd) An adventure shop with equipment and specialist references for walkers, climbers and cyclists.

Getting There & Away

BUS Snowdon Sherpa buses S2 and S6 stop outside the train station, with services to Swallow Falls (five minutes), Capel Curig (10 minutes), Pen-y-Pass (25 minutes) and Llanberis (33 minutes).

TRAIN Betws-y-Coed is on the **Conwy Valley Line** (www.conwyvalleyrailway.co.uk), with six daily services (three on Sunday) to Llandudno (£4.70, 52 minutes) and Blaenau Ffestiniog (£3.80, 32 minutes).

Bala (Y Bala) & Around

POP 2000

The town of Bala is synonymous with beautiful **Llyn Tegid** (Bala Lake), Wales' largest freshwater lake – 4 miles long, three-quarters of a mile wide and, in places, over 43m deep. In recent years it has built a reputation as a centre for water sports, making it a very lively little place in summer. It's also a predominantly Welsh-speaking town – about 80% speak Welsh as a first language.

Sights & Activities

Bala Lake Railway RAILWAY
(☎01678-540666; www.bala-lake-railway.co.uk; adult/child return £9/3; ⊙Apr-Oct) Vintage locomotives depart from a little station at Penybont, half a mile from Bala town centre, for a scenic 90-minute return journey skirting the lake.

Canolfan Tryweryn National Whitewater Centre RAFTING
(☎01678-521083; www.ukrafting.co.uk; Frongoch; 1/2hr trip £32/60) Runs rafting trips on a 1.5-mile stretch of the Tryweryn that is almost continuous class-III white water with class IV sections. The **Adventure Breaks** program marries rafting with another activity, such as rock climbing, mountain biking, pony trekking, high ropes, bushcraft, 4x4 off-road driving, canyoning, clay pigeon shooting or quad biking; from £135 including accommodation. The centre is 3.5 miles northwest of Bala on the A4212.

Bala Adventure & Watersports Centre ACTIVITIES, HIRE
(☎01678-521059; www.balawatersports.com; Pensarn Rd) Bala offers windsurfing, sailing, canoeing, kayaking, white-water rafting, mountain biking, rock-climbing and abseiling courses (prices start from £35/60 per half-/full day). Rental gear includes kayaks (£10), canoes (£20), rowing boats (£24), pedalos (£15), windsurfers (£16) and wayfarers (£30); all prices are per hour.

Sleeping

TOP CHOICE **Abercelyn Country House** B&B ££
(☎01678-521109; www.abercelyn.co.uk; Llanycil; s/d £60/90; P) Located on the A494, 1 mile from the centre of Bala, this former rectory (1729) has stylish rooms, a homely atmosphere, excellent breakfasts and a lovely setting in gardens with a gurgling brook.

WORTH A TRIP

BLAENAU FFESTINIOG

Most of the slate used to roof 19th-century Britain came from Wales, and much of that came from the mines of Blaenau (*blay*-nye) Ffestiniog. However, only about 10% of mined slate is usable, so for every ton that goes to the factory, nine tons are left as rubble. Despite being in the very centre of Snowdonia National Park, the grey mountains of waste that surround Blaenau prevented it from being officially included in the park – a slap in the face for this close-knit but impoverished town in the days before Wales' industrial sites were recognised as part of its heritage.

Blaenau's main attraction, the **Llechwedd Slate Caverns** (01766-830306; www.llechwedd-slate-caverns.co.uk; either tour adult/child £9.45/7.15, both tours £15.20/11.60; from 10am daily, last tour 5.15pm Apr-Sep, 4.15pm Oct-Mar) offer a chance to descend into a real slate mine. Of the two tours offered, the more evocative **Deep Mine Tour** includes a descent on the UK's steepest passenger railway and recreates the harsh working conditions of the 19th-century miners – be prepared to duck and scramble around dark tunnels. If you can't manage a lot of steps, go for the **Miner's Tramway Tour**, a ride through the huge 1846 network of tunnels and caverns.

Today, although slate mining continues on a small scale, Blaenau has a mournful feel to it, not helped by famously miserable weather. It's an interesting place to stop, but you're unlikely to be tempted to stay. It makes a great day trip from Porthmadog via the historic Ffestiniog Railway and it's also connected to Betws-y-Coed by the Conwy Valley line.

Bala Backpackers HOSTEL £
(01678-521700; www.bala-backpackers.co.uk; 32 Tegid St; dm/tw from £15/45) A leap up in comfort from most of Wales' hostels, the main building has brightly painted dorms with a maximum of four single beds (it's a bunk-free zone) and a newly renovated kitchen and bathrooms. Across the road in a separate building are four smartly decorated twins, some with en suites.

Eating

TOP CHOICE **Siop y Gornel** BAKERY, CAFE £
(www.siop-y-gornel.co.uk; 21 Tegid St; breakfast & lunch Mon-Sat) It takes 24 hours to make sourdough this good and that's just one of the homemade, organic delights on sale at this wonderful little delicatessen-bakery-cafe. It also concocts delicious baguettes, croissants, cakes, slices and pies. Stop in to fill up your picnic hamper or settle in with a newspaper and coffee.

Eagles Inn (Tafarn Yr Eryod) PUB £
(www.theeagleinn-bala.co.uk; Llanuwchllyn; mains £7-15; lunch Fri-Sun, dinner daily) Right down the other end of the lake, this is your consummate North Welsh village pub – a friendly community boozer with a popular dartboard. The food, however, is a step above. Most of the vegetables and some of the meat comes from its own garden, and for dessert there's a delicious array of homemade pies and puddings.

Plas-yn-Dre WELSH ££
(01678-521256; 23 High St (Stryd Fawr); lunch £5-11, dinner £12-16) The decor in this smart eatery is a tasteful take on country-kitchen chic, finished with soft-leather chairs. The hearty dinner menu has lots of interesting Welsh dishes, including fresh Menai mussels.

Information

Tourist office (01678-521021; Pensarn Rd; 10am-5pm Apr-Oct, 9.30am-3pm Fri-Mon Nov-Mar) Southwest of the centre, by the lake.

Getting There & Away

BICYCLE **Roberts Cycles** (01678-520252; www.rhroberts-cycles.co.uk; High St; per day £13) Rents out mountain bikes. The tourist office stocks a *Bike Routes Around Bala* pamphlet.

BUS X94 from Dolgellau (35 minutes), Barmouth (1½ hours) and Llangollen (one hour) stops on the High St.

Dolgellau

POP 2400

Dolgellau is a little place steeped in history with a palpable old-world feel. More than 200 of its stern stone buildings are listed for preservation – the highest concentration in Wales. It was a regional centre for Wales' prosperous wool industry in the 18th century and early 19th century. Many of the town's finest buildings, sturdy and unornamented, were built at that time, and the town centre hasn't changed all that much since.

Today, however, this grey-slate, charmingly gruff little market town relies on tourism. One of Snowdonia's premier peaks, bulky Cader Idris, rises to the south, the lovely Mawddach Estuary lies to the west and, to the north, the Coed y Brenin Forest offers glorious mountain biking. In recent years some plush boutique accommodation options have sprung up, making it an appealing base from which to explore the national park.

Sights & Activities

Tŷ Siamas FOLK MUSIC

(☎01341-421800; www.tysiamas.com; Eldon Sq; adult/child £4/2; ⊙10am-5pm Mar-Oct, to 4pm Tue-Sat Nov-Feb) Dolgellau has been an important folk-music hub ever since it held the first Welsh folk festival in 1952. In recognition of that, the town's former market hall has been transformed into the National Centre for Welsh Folk Music. The permanent exhibition includes audiovisual clips, musical instruments and interesting displays about folk traditions. Yet it's not just a museum – it has a recording studio, stages workshops and performances, and offers lessons on traditional instruments.

**Coed y Brenin Forest Park** MOUNTAIN BIKING

Covering 3600 hectares, this woodland park is the premier location for mountain biking in Wales. It's laced with 70 miles of purpose-built cycle trails, divided into seven graded routes to suit beginners or guns, and impressively presented by way of old-fashioned waterproof trail cards or downloadable geocaches and MP3 audio files. The park's impressive environmentally friendly **visitor centre** (☎01341-440747; www.forestry.gov.uk/wales; ⊙9.30am-4.30pm), 8 miles north of Dolgellau off the A470, has a cafe, toilets and a children's play area, while downstairs you can hire bikes from **Beics Brenin** (☎01341-440728; www.beicsbrenin.co.uk; per day £25-50). At the time of research a new highwires course called **Go Ape** (☎0845 643 9215; www.goape.co.uk; adult/child from £30/20; ⊙Easter-Oct) was about to open.

Cader Idris MOUNTAIN

Cader Idris (893m), or the 'Seat of Idris' (a legendary giant), is a hulking, menacing-looking mountain with an appropriate mythology attached. It's said that hounds of the underworld fly around its peaks, and strange light effects are often sighted in the area. It's also said that anyone who spends the night on the summit will awake either mad or a poet – although perhaps you'd have to be a little mad or romantic to attempt it in the first place. Regardless of its repute, it's popular with walkers and it's the park's favourite locale for rock climbers.

When tackling Cader Idris, the standard route is up the 'Dolgellau' or Ty Nant Path (6 miles, five hours), heading southeast from Ty Nant Farm on the A493. The longest but easiest is the Tywyn or Llanfihangel y Pennant Path (10 miles, six hours), northeast from the Talyllyn Railway terminus at Abergynolwyn. The shortest and steepest trail is the Minffordd Path (6 miles, five hours), northwest from the Dol Idris car park, a few hundred metres down the B4405 from Minffordd on the A487 road to Machynlleth. Whichever route you choose, always carry appropriate clothing and check weather conditions before departure.

TYDDYN LLAN

The glowing reputation of this country **restaurant-with-rooms** (☎01490-440264; www.tyddynllan.co.uk; Llandrillo; r £70-140, dinner B&B £115-185; ⊙lunch Fri-Sun, dinner daily; P), located 7½ miles east of Bala on the B4401, was given a boost in 2010 by some Michelin starlight. An elegant property set among gardens in the tranquil Vale of Edeyrnion, it's a cosy bolthole for a rural retreat. The 12 rooms each boast their own individual style, some frou-frou romantic, some shabby-chic modern.

On our last visit to the **restaurant** (2-/3-course lunch £24/30, dinner £39/48; ⊙lunch Fri-Sun, dinner daily) some dishes were extraordinary and some merely good, but overall it was a memorable experience. Proceedings kick off with complementary canapés served in the sitting room before you progress into the elegant dining area.

Sleeping

TOP CHOICE Ffynnon BOUTIQUE B&B ££
(☎01341-421774; www.ffynnontownhouse.com; Love Lane; s/d from £85/125; P 📶) With a keen eye for contemporary design and a super-friendly welcome, this first-rate boutique guesthouse feels both homely and stylish. French antiques are mixed in with modern chandeliers, claw-foot tubs and electronic gadgets, and there's a children's play area.

Bryn Mair House B&B ££
(☎01341-422640; www.brynmairbedandbreakfast.co.uk; Love Lane; r £85-90; P 📶) Right next to Ffynnon on wistfully monikered Love Lane, this is another impressive stone house with three comfortable B&B rooms. They're all kitted out with DVDs and iPod docks and some have sublime mountain views.

Penmaenuchaf Hall HOTEL £££
(☎01341-422129; www.penhall.co.uk; s/d from £95/150; P) With imposing furnishings and elaborate gardens, this stately country-house hotel is the former pile of Bolton cotton magnate James Leigh. The 14 rooms have a lavish old-world air but also CD players and satellite TV. It's located 2.5 miles southwest of Dolgellau on the A493.

Kings YHA HOSTEL £
(☎0845 371 9327; www.yha.org.uk; dm from £14) Remote country-house hostel set in woods, southwest of Dolgellau. The nearest shop is 5 miles away; don't expect a mobile-phone signal.

Eating

TOP CHOICE Y Sospan CAFE, BISTRO ££
(☎01341-423174; Queen's Sq; breakfast & lunch £3-7, dinner £10-17; ⊙breakfast & lunch daily, dinner Wed-Sun) In a book-lined and woody 1606 building that once served as a prison, this relaxed eatery serves fry-up breakfasts, sandwiches, jacket potatoes and light cooked meals during the day. At night, it switches to a heavier bistro menu, where lamb plays a starring role and most of the desserts have been on the booze, including an excellent bread-and-butter pudding.

Parliament House CAFE £
(Glyndŵr St; mains £4-6; ⊙9.30am-5.30pm Mon-Sat; 📶) With a fantastic period setting in a Grade II–listed former ironmonger's shop, still with its original fittings, this atmospheric coffee shop has light meals (soup, Welsh rarebit, sandwiches, ciabatta, baguettes), newspapers to browse and a huge range of speciality teas.

Mawddach Restaurant & Bar MODERN WELSH ££
(☎01341-424020; www.mawddach.com; Llanelltyd; mains £10-17; ⊙lunch Wed-Sun, dinner Wed-Sat) Located 2 miles west of Dolgellau on the A496, Mawddach brings a touch of urban style to what was once a barn. Slate floors, leather seats and panoramic views across to Cader Idris set the scene. The food is equally impressive: meat straight from nearby farms, fresh local fish specials and traditional Sunday roasts (two/three courses £13/17).

Dylanwad Da TAPAS, WELSH ££
(☎01341-422870; www.dylanwad.co.uk; 2 Smithfield St; mains £13-19; ⊙Thu-Sat Apr-Sep) Informal cafe, wine and tapas bar by day, contemporary restaurant by night, this well-run, low-lit eatery has been serving up high-quality food for over 20 years. A long-standing favourite on the Snowdonia scene, it has a healthy wine list and an imaginative menu.

Drinking

For a straightforward pint with the locals, try the following:

Unicorn PUB
(Smithfield Sq)

Royal Ship Hotel PUB
(www.royalshiphotel.co.uk; Queen's Sq)

Information

Tourist office & National Park Information Centre (☎01341-422888; Eldon Sq; ⊙9.30am-4.30pm) Sells maps, local-history books and trail leaflets for climbing Cader Idris. Upstairs there's a permanent exhibition on the region's Quaker heritage in a suitably dour wood-panelled room.

Getting There & Away

BICYCLE Dolgellau Cycles (☎01341-423332; Smithfield St) Rents bikes, performs repairs and offers advice on local cycle routes. Lôn Las Cymru, the Welsh National Cycle Route (NCN route 8), passes through Dolgellau, heading north to Porthmadog and south to Machynlleth.

BUS Buses stop on Eldon Sq in the heart of town. Routes include X32 to Aberystwyth (1¼ hours), Machynlleth (35 minutes), Porthmadog

(50 minutes), Caernarfon (1½ hours) and Bangor (two hours); 35 to Coed y Brenin (15 minutes) and Blaenau Ffestiniog (54 minutes); and X94 to Barmouth (24 minutes), Bala (35 minutes) and Llangollen (1½ hours).

Mawddach Estuary

An important bird habitat, the glorious Mawddach Estuary is a striking sight – flanked by woodlands, wetlands and the romantic mountains of southern Snowdonia. Following its southern edge, the 9½-mile **Mawddach Trail** (www.mawddachtrail.co.uk) is a flat walking and cycling path that follows an old railway line from the bridge in Dolgellau, through woods and past wetlands, before crossing over the rail viaduct to Barmouth (where you can grab the bus back).

The **Mawddach Way** (www.mawddachway.co.uk) is a 30-mile, two- to three-day track looping through the hills on either side. Although the highest point is 346m, by the end of the undulating path you'll have climbed 2226m. An A5 booklet can be ordered or downloaded online (booklet/download £10/5); GPS route data can be downloaded for free.

WORTH A TRIP

TALYLLYN RAILWAY

Famous as the inspiration behind Rev W Awdry's *Thomas the Tank Engine* stories, the narrow-gauge **Talyllyn Railway** (☎01654-710472; www.talyllyn.co.uk; Wharf Station, Tywyn; adult/child £13/6.25; ⏲check online timetable) was saved from closure in 1950 by the world's first railway-preservation society. It's one of Wales' most enchanting little railways and puffs for 7.3 scenic, steam-powered miles up the Fathew Valley to Abergynolwyn. There are five stations along the way, each with waymarked walking trails (and waterfalls at Dolgoch and Nant Gwernol). Your ticket entitles you to all-day travel.

At Tywyn's Wharf Station, the **Narrow Gauge Railway Museum** (www.ngrm.org.uk; admission free; ⏲10am-4.30pm May-Sep, to 2pm Oct) is one for the history buffs, with shiny narrow-gauge steam locomotives and the story of the volunteers who preserved the railway.

Fairbourne

Fairbourne has a lovely, long beach but little else to offer except the steam-hauled **Fairbourne Railway** (☎01341-250362; www.fairbournerailway.com; Beach Rd; adult/child £7.80/4.20; ⏲check online timetable), Wales' only seaside narrow-gauge railway. The line heads north along the coast for 2.5 miles to Penrhyn Point, where there are ferries across the mouth of the Mawddach to Barmouth, timed to meet the trains.

Fairbourne is on the Cambrian Coast line and bus 28 from Aberystwyth (two hours) to Dolgellau (20 minutes) stops here.

Barmouth (Abermaw)

POP 2300

Despite a Blue Flag beach, the seaside resort of Barmouth has a faded feel to it. In the summer months it becomes a typical kiss-me-quick seaside resort – all chip shops and dodgem cars – catering to the trainloads arriving in their thousands from England's West Midlands. Outside of the brash neon of high summer it's considerably mellower but still has its rough edges.

Wales' only surviving wooden rail viaduct spans the estuary and has a handy pedestrian walkway across it. Behind the town rises rocky Dinas Oleu, the first property ever bequeathed to the NT (in 1895) and an irresistible temptation for walkers.

Sleeping & Eating

Richmond House B&B ££

(☎01341-281366; www.barmouthbedandbreakfast.co.uk; High St; s/d £55/70; P@☜) This handsome town house has big, contemporary rooms and an attractive garden area for summer lounging on chunky, wooden furniture. Thoughtful touches include in-room DVD players and free biscuits.

Last Inn PUB ££

(www.lastinn-barmouth.co.uk; Church St; mains £9-13) Dating from the 15th century, this is easily the best place to eat, drink and hang out in. Most unusually, the mountain forms the rear wall, with a spring emerging right inside the pub. Kids are welcome and the menu's full of crowd-pleasers, including a traditional Sunday roast. There's also live music from time to time.

Information

Tourist office (☎01341-280787; train station, Station Rd; ⏲10am-5pm Apr-Oct, 9.30am-3pm Mon-Fri Nov-Mar)

Getting There & Away

BUS Routes include 38 to Harlech (34 minutes) and X94 to Dolgellau (24 minutes), Bala (1½ hours) and Llangollen (2½ hours).

TRAIN Barmouth is on the Cambrian Coast line, with direct trains to Machynlleth (£7, 57 minutes), Fairbourne (£2, 7 minutes), Harlech (£3.70, 24 minutes), Porthmadog (£5.40, 48 minutes) and Pwllheli (£8.70, 1¼ hours).

Harlech

POP 2000

Hilly Harlech is best known for the mighty, grey-stone towers of its castle, framed by gleaming Tremadog Bay. Some sort of fortified structure has probably surmounted the rock since Iron Age times, but Edward I removed all traces when he commissioned the construction of his castle. Finished in 1289, Harlech Castle is the southernmost of four fortifications included in the Castles and Town Walls of King Edward in Gwynedd Unesco World Heritage Site.

Harlech is such a thoroughly pleasant place that it has become one of the more gentrified destinations in Snowdonia – every other shop seems to sell antiques or tea and there are some sophisticated places to eat and sleep in. While it's bustling in summer, it can be deliciously sleepy otherwise. It makes a great base for a beach holiday or for day trips into the national park – and those views never get boring.

Sights

Harlech Castle CASTLE

(Cadw; adult/child £3.60/3.20; ⏲9am-5pm Apr-Oct, 9.30am-4pm Mon-Sat, 11am-4pm Sun Nov-Mar) Edward I finished this intimidating building in 1289, the southernmost of his 'iron ring' of fortresses designed to keep the Welsh firmly beneath his boot. Despite its might, the storybook fortress has been called the 'Castle of Lost Causes' because it has been lucklessly defended so many times. Owain Glyndŵr captured it after a long siege in 1404. He was in turn besieged here by the future Henry V.

During the Wars of the Roses the castle is said to have held out against a siege for seven years and was the last Lancastrian stronghold to fall. The siege inspired the popular Welsh hymn *Men of Harlech,* which is still played today in regimental marches and sung with patriotic gusto at rugby matches. The castle was also the last to fall in the Civil War, finally giving in to Cromwell's forces in 1647.

The grey sandstone castle's massive, twin-towered gatehouse and outer walls are still intact and give the illusion of impregnability even now. Enter through the ticket office–gift shop and cross the drawbridge through the gatehouse into the compact inner ward. Four gloomy round towers guard the corners and you can climb onto the ramparts for views in all directions. Some are closed off and partly ruined, but you still get a good feel for what it was once like. The fortress's great natural defence is the seaward cliff face. When it was built, ships could sail supplies right to the base.

Sleeping & Eating

TOP CHOICE **Maelgwyn House** B&B ££

(☎01766-780087; www.maelgwynharlech.co.uk; Ffordd Isaf; r £70-95; P 📶) A model B&B, Maelgwyn has interesting hosts, delicious breakfasts and a small set of elegant rooms stocked with DVD players, tea-making facilities and Ferrero Rocher chocolates. Full marks.

Castle Cottage RESTAURANT-WITH-ROOMS ££

(☎01766-780479; www.castlecottageharlech.co.uk; Ffordd Pen Llech; s/d from £80/120; P 📶) Within arrow's reach of the castle, Castle Cottage has spacious bedrooms in a contemporary style with exposed beams, in-room DVD players and a bowl of fresh fruit for each guest. The fine-dining restaurant (three-course dinner £37) serves a deliciously patriotic menu, revelling in local produce (Welsh lamb, beef and cod, Ruthin chicken, Menai mussels, wild duck, woodcock, cheeses) and traditional dishes (bara brith, rarebit). Yet the execution is in the classical French style.

TOP CHOICE **Castle Restaurant & Armoury Bar** CARIBBEAN ££

(☎01766-780416; Castle Sq; mains £12-15; ⏲lunch & dinner Tue-Sun) If this place were transported to London it would have queues out the door, so one has to admire the gumption of opening such a wonderful

Caribbean restaurant in Wales, let alone in sleepy Harlech. Upstairs is the coolest cocktail bar in North Wales – red curtains, bauble chandeliers and a smooth soundtrack of Trojan reggae. Downstairs, the locals are switching on to the spicy delights of goat curry, jerk chicken and blackened salmon.

Cemlyn Tea Shop TEAROOMS **£**
(www.cemlyntea.co.uk; High St; snacks around £5; ⌚10.30am-5pm Wed-Sun) The Coles (Jan and Geoff) may be merry old souls, but it's tea that's king here. There are over 30 varieties on offer, along with a simple range of snacks to accompany them and a slew of Tea Guild Awards of Excellence on the walls. Best of all are the views from the terrace.

Information

Tourist office (☎01766-780658; High St; ⌚9.30am-5.30pm Apr-Oct)

Getting There & Away

Harlech is on the Cambrian Coast line, with direct trains to Machynlleth (£9.20, 1½ hours), Fairbourne (£4.50, 46 minutes), Barmouth (£3.70, 24 minutes), Porthmadog (£3, 22 minutes) and Pwllheli (£6.30, 45 minutes). Bus 38 heads to Barmouth (34 minutes).

Scotland

WILL SALTER

Scotland Highlights

❶ Exploring Scotland's capital, **Edinburgh** (p759), one of the world's most fascinating cities

❷ Seeing glorious Victorian architecture, great nightlife and friendly locals in **Glasgow** (p789)

❸ Getting permanent jaw-drop along the **northwest Highlands coast** (p913)

❹ Experiencing the romantic ruins of the **Border Abbeys** (p810)

❺ Uncovering beauty and tragic history at **Glen Coe** (p902)

❻ Capturing the brooding beauty of Skye's **Cuillin Hills** (p923)

❼ Climbing **Ben Nevis** (p906), the highest point in Britain

❽ Enjoying magnificent forests and lochs in **Perthshire** (p864)

❾ Finding 5000-year-old neolithic sites on **Orkney** (p948)

Edinburgh

POP: 430,000 / AREA: 116 SQ KM

Includes »

Sights 762
Activities............ 774
Tours................. 774
Festivals & Events..... 776
Sleeping.............. 778
Eating............... 780
Drinking.............. 782
Entertainment......... 783
Shopping.............. 785
AROUND EDINBURGH........ 787

Best Places to Eat

» Ondine (p780)
» Oloroso (p781)
» Café Marlayne (p781)
» Fishers Bistro (p782)

Best Places to Stay

» Hotel Missoni (p778)
» Six Mary's Place (p778)
» Southside Guest House (p779)

Why Go?

Edinburgh is a city that begs to be explored. From the vaults and wynds that riddle the Old Town to the urban villages of Stockbridge and Cramond, it's filled with quirky, come-hither nooks that tempt you to walk just a little bit further. And every corner turned reveals sudden views and unexpected vistas – green sunlit hills, a glimpse of rust-red crags, a blue flash of distant sea.

But there's more to Edinburgh than sightseeing – there are top shops, world-class restaurants and a bacchanalia of bars to enjoy. This is a city of pub crawls and impromptu music sessions, mad-for-it clubbing and all-night parties, overindulgence, late nights and wandering home through cobbled streets at dawn.

All these superlatives come together in August at festival time, when it seems as if half the world descends on Edinburgh for one enormous party. If you can possibly manage it, join them.

When to Go

In May there's good weather (usually), flowers and cherry blossoms everywhere, and (gasp!) no crowds. August is festival time! Crowded and mad but unmissable. In December there are Christmas decorations, cosy pubs with open fires and ice skating in Princes St Gardens.

Edinburgh Highlights

1 Taking in the views from the battlements of **Edinburgh Castle** (p764)

2 Feasting on fresh seafood at **Ondine** (p780)

3 Nosing around the Queen's private quarters on the former **Royal Yacht Britannia** (p774) at Leith

4 Listening to live folk music at **Sandy Bell's** (p784)

5 Trying to decipher the Da Vinci Code at mysterious **Rosslyn Chapel** (p788)

EDINBURGH IN...

Two Days

A two-day trip to Edinburgh should start at **Edinburgh Castle**, followed by a stroll down the **Royal Mile** to the **Scottish parliament building** and the **Palace of Holyroodhouse**. You can work up an appetite by climbing **Arthur's Seat**, then satisfy your hunger with dinner at **Oloroso** while you watch the sun set over the **Firth of Forth**. On day two spend the morning in the **Museum of Scotland** then catch the bus to **Leith** for a visit to the **Royal Yacht Britannia**. In the evening have dinner at one of Leith's many excellent restaurants, or scare yourself silly on a guided **ghost tour**.

Four Days

Two more days will give you time for a morning stroll around the **Royal Botanic Garden**, followed by a trip to the enigmatic and beautiful **Rosslyn Chapel**. Relax with a visit to the seaside village of **Cramond** – bring along binoculars (for birdwatching and yacht-spotting) and a book (to read in the sun). Dinner at the **Cafe Royal Oyster Bar** could be before or after your sunset walk to the summit of **Calton Hill**. On day four head out to the pretty harbour village of **Queensferry**, nestled beneath the **Forth Bridges**, and take a cruise to **Inchcolm Island**.

History

Back in the 7th century the Castle Rock was called Dun Eiden (meaning 'Fort on the Hill Slope'). When it was captured by invaders from the kingdom of Northumbria in northeast England in 638, they took the existing Gaelic name 'Eiden' and tacked it onto their own Old English word for fort, 'burh', to create the name Edinburgh.

Originally a purely defensive site, Edinburgh began to expand in the 12th century when King David I held court at the castle and founded the abbey at Holyrood. The city's first effective town wall was constructed around 1450, enclosing the Old Town; this overcrowded area became a medieval Manhattan, forcing its inhabitants to build tenements five and six storeys high.

The capital played an important role in the Reformation (1560–1690), led by the firebrand John Knox. Mary, Queen of Scots held court in the Palace of Holyroodhouse for six brief years, but when her son James VI succeeded to the English throne in 1603 he moved his court to London. The Act of Union in 1707 further reduced Edinburgh's importance.

Nevertheless, cultural and intellectual life flourished during the Scottish Enlightenment (roughly 1740–1830), and Edinburgh became known as 'a hotbed of genius'. In the second half of the 18th century the New Town was built, and in the 19th century the population quadrupled to 400,000 as suburbs of Victorian tenements spread to the north and south.

In the 1920s the city's borders expanded again to encompass Leith in the north, Cramond in the west and the Pentland Hills in the south. Following WWII, the city's cultural life blossomed, stimulated by the Edinburgh International Festival and its fellow traveller the Fringe, both held for the first time in 1947 and now recognised as world-class arts festivals.

Edinburgh entered a new era following the 1997 referendum vote in favour of a devolved Scottish parliament, which first convened in July 1999. The parliament is housed in a controversial new building in Holyrood at the foot of the Royal Mile,

DON'T MISS

CASTLE HIT LIST

Pushed for time? Here's a list of the top things to see at Edinburgh Castle:

» Views from Argyle Battery

» One O'Clock Gun

» Great Hall

» Honours of Scotland

» Prisons of War

Old Town

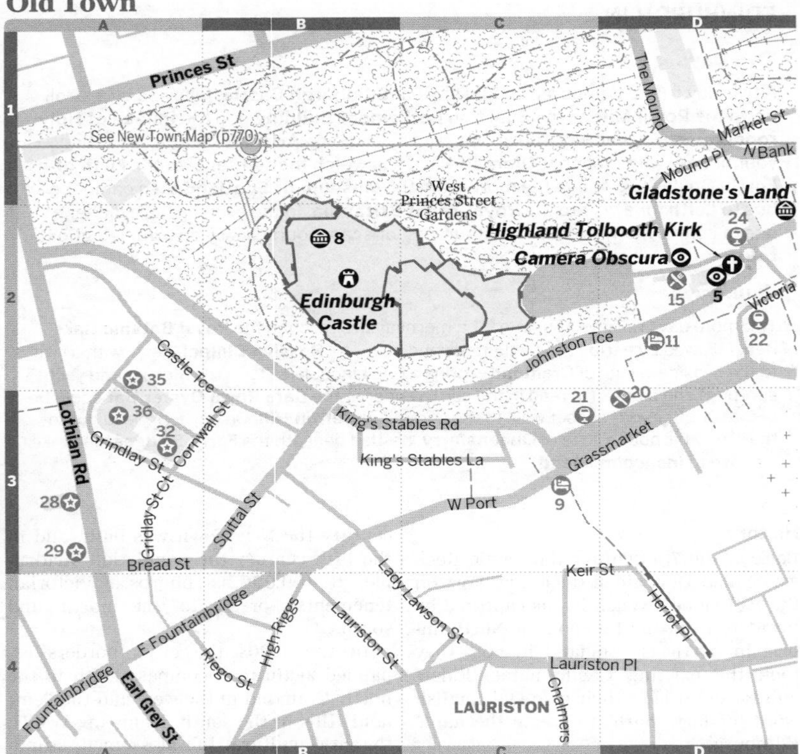

where the 2007 elections saw the Scottish National Party – whose long-term aim is independence for Scotland – take power for the first time.

Sights

Edinburgh's main attractions are concentrated in the city centre – on and around the Old Town's Royal Mile between the castle and Holyrood, and in New Town. A major exception is the Royal Yacht *Britannia,* which is in the redeveloped docklands district of Leith, 2 miles northeast of the centre.

OLD TOWN

Edinburgh's Old Town stretches along a ridge to the east of the castle, and tumbles down Victoria St to the broad expanse of the Grassmarket. It's a jagged and jumbled maze of masonry riddled with closes (alleys) and wynds (narrow lanes), stairs and vaults, and cleft along its spine by the cobbled ravine of the Royal Mile.

Until the founding of New Town in the 18th century, old Edinburgh was an overcrowded and insanitary hive of humanity squeezed between the boggy ground of the Nor' Loch (North Loch, now drained and occupied by Princes Street Gardens) to the north and the city walls to the south and east. The only way for the town to expand was upwards, and the five- and six-storey tenements that were raised along the Royal Mile in the 16th and 17th centuries were the skyscrapers of their day, remarked upon with wonder by visiting writers such as Daniel Defoe. All classes of society, from beggars to magistrates, lived cheek by jowl in these urban ants' nests, the wealthy occupying the middle floors – high enough to be above the noise and stink of the streets, but not so high that climbing the

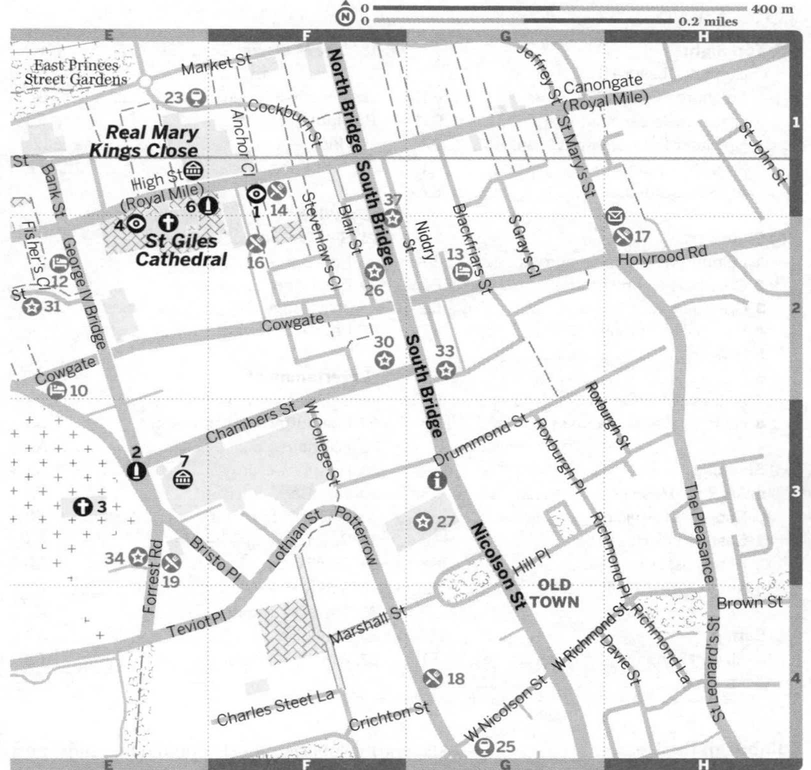

stairs would be too tiring – while the poor squeezed into attics, basements, cellars and vaults amid the rats, rubbish and raw sewage.

THE ROYAL MILE

This mile-long street earned its regal nickname in the 16th century when it was used by the king to travel between the castle and the Palace of Holyroodhouse. There are five sections – the Castle Esplanade, Castlehill, Lawnmarket, High St and Canongate – whose names reflect their historical origins:

Castlehill: the short slope connecting the Castle Esplanade to the Lawnmarket.

Lawnmarket: a corruption of 'Landmarket', a market selling goods from the land outside the city. Takes its name from the large cloth market that flourished here until the 18th century. This was the poshest part of the Old Town, where many of its most distinguished citizens made their homes.

High St: stretches from George IV Bridge down to the Netherbow at St Mary's St, and is the heart and soul of the Old Town, home to the city's main church, the Law Courts, the city council and – until 1707 – the Scottish parliament.

Canongate: the stretch of the Royal Mile from Netherbow to Holyrood takes its name from the Augustinian canons (monks) of Holyrood Abbey. From the 16th century it was home to aristocrats attracted to the Palace of Holyroodhouse. Originally governed by the monks, Canongate was an independent burgh separate from Edinburgh until 1856.

Old Town

Top Sights
Camera Obscura ... D2
Edinburgh Castle ... B2
Gladstone's Land ... D2
Highland Tolbooth Kirk ... D2
Real Mary King's Close ... E1
St Giles Cathedral ... E2

Sights
1 Edinburgh Festival Fringe Office ... F1
2 Greyfriars Bobby Statue ... E3
3 Greyfriars Kirk ... E3
4 Heart of Midlothian ... E2
5 Hub ... D2
6 Mercat Cross ... E1
7 National Museum of Scotland ... E3
8 National War Museum of Scotland ... B2

Sleeping
9 Art Roch Hostel ... C3
10 Budget Backpackers ... E2
11 Castle Rock Hostel ... D2
12 Hotel Missoni ... E2
13 Smart City Hostel ... G2

Eating
14 Always Sunday ... F1
15 Amber ... D2
16 Café Marlayne ... F2
17 David Bann ... H2
18 Mosque Kitchen ... G4
19 Mums ... E3
Ondine ... (see 12)
20 Petit Paris ... D3

Drinking
21 Beehive Inn ... C3
22 Bow Bar ... D2
23 Ecco Vino ... E1
24 Jolly Judge ... D2
25 Pear Tree House ... G4

Entertainment
26 Cabaret Voltaire ... F2
27 Edinburgh Festival Theatre ... G3
28 Filmhouse ... A3
29 Henry's Cellar ... A3
30 Jazz Bar ... F2
31 Liquid Room ... E2
32 Royal Lyceum Theatre ... A3
33 Royal Oak ... G2
34 Sandy Bell's ... E3
35 Traverse Theatre ... A2
36 Usher Hall ... A3
37 Whistle Binkie's ... F2

Edinburgh Castle CASTLE
(Map p762; www.edinburghcastle.gov.uk; Castlehill; adult/child incl audioguide £14/7.50; ⌚9.30am-6pm Apr-Sep, 9.30am-5pm Oct-Mar, last admission 45min before closing, closed 25 & 26 Dec) The brooding, black crags of Castle Rock rising above the western end of Princes St are the very reason for Edinburgh's existence. This rocky hill was the most easily defended hilltop on the invasion route between England and central Scotland, a route followed by countless armies from the Roman legions of the 1st and 2nd centuries AD to the Jacobite troops of Bonnie Prince Charlie in 1745.

Edinburgh Castle has played a pivotal role in Scottish history, both as a royal residence – King Malcolm Canmore (r 1058–93) and Queen Margaret first made their home here in the 11th century – and as a military stronghold. The castle last saw military action in 1745; from then until the 1920s it served as the British army's main base in Scotland. Today it is one of Scotland's most atmospheric, most popular – and most expensive – tourist attractions.

The **Entrance Gateway**, flanked by statues of Robert the Bruce and William Wallace, opens to a cobbled lane that leads up beneath the 16th-century **Portcullis Gate** to the cannon ranged along the Argyle and Mills Mount batteries. The battlements here have **great views** over New Town to the Firth of Forth.

At the far end of Mills Mount Battery is the famous **One O'Clock Gun**, where crowds gather to watch a gleaming WWII 25-pounder fire an ear-splitting time signal at exactly 1pm (every day except Sundays, Christmas Day and Good Friday).

South of Mills Mount, the road curls up leftwards through **Fog's Gate** to the highest part of Castle Rock, crowned by the tiny, Romanesque **St Margaret's Chapel**, the oldest surviving building in Edinburgh. It was probably built by David I or Alexander I in memory of their mother, Queen Margaret, sometime around 1130 (she was canonised in 1250). Beside the chapel stands **Mons Meg**, a giant 15th-century siege gun built at Mons (in what is now Belgium) in 1449.

The main group of buildings on the summit of Castle Rock are ranged around Crown Sq, dominated by the shrine of the **Scottish National War Memorial**. Opposite is the **Great Hall**, built for James IV (r 1488–1513) as a ceremonial hall and used as a meeting place for the Scottish parliament until 1639. Its most remarkable feature is the original, 16th-century hammer-beam roof.

The **Castle Vaults** beneath the Great Hall (entered from Crown Sq via the Prisons of War exhibit) were used variously as storerooms, bakeries and a prison. The vaults have been renovated to resemble 18th- and early-19th-century prisons, where graffiti carved by French and American prisoners can be seen on the ancient wooden doors.

On the eastern side of the square is the **Royal Palace**, built during the 15th and 16th centuries, where a series of historical tableaux leads to the highlight of the castle – a strongroom housing the **Honours of Scotland** (the Scottish crown jewels), the oldest surviving crown jewels in Europe. Locked away in a chest following the Act of Union in 1707, the crown (made in 1540 from the gold of Robert the Bruce's 14th-century coronet), sword and sceptre lay forgotten until they were unearthed at the instigation of the novelist Sir Walter Scott in 1818. Also on display here is the **Stone of Destiny**.

Among the neighbouring **Royal Apartments** is the bedchamber where Mary, Queen of Scots gave birth to her son James VI, who was to unite the crowns of Scotland and England in 1603.

National War Museum of Scotland

(www.nms.ac.uk; admission incl in Edinburgh Castle ticket; ⌚9.45am-5.45pm Apr-Oct, 9.45am-4.45pm Nov-Mar) At the western end of the castle, down a road to the left of the castle restaurant, is the National War Museum of Scotland, which brings Scotland's military history vividly to life. The

THE STONE OF DESTINY

On St Andrew's Day 1996 a block of sandstone – 26.5 inches by 16.5 inches by 11 inches in size, with rusted iron hoops at either end – was installed with much pomp and ceremony in Edinburgh Castle. For the previous 700 years it had lain in London, beneath the Coronation Chair in Westminster Abbey. Almost all English, and later British, monarchs from Edward II in 1307 to Elizabeth II in 1953 have parked their backsides firmly over this stone during their coronation ceremony.

The legendary Stone of Destiny – said to have originated in the Holy Land, and on which Scottish kings placed their feet during their coronation (not their bums; the English got that bit wrong) – was stolen from Scone Abbey near Perth by King Edward I of England in 1296. It was taken to London and there it remained for seven centuries – except for a brief removal to Gloucester during WWII air raids, and a three-month sojourn in Scotland after it was stolen by Scottish Nationalist students at Christmas in 1950 – an enduring symbol of Scotland's subjugation by England.

The Stone of Destiny returned to the political limelight in 1996, when the then Scottish Secretary and Conservative Party MP, Michael Forsyth, arranged for the return of the sandstone block to Scotland. A blatant attempt to boost the flagging popularity of the Conservative Party in Scotland prior to a general election, Forsyth's publicity stunt failed miserably. The Scots said thanks very much for the stone and then, in May 1997, voted every Conservative MP in Scotland into oblivion.

Many people, however, believe that Edward I was fobbed off with a shoddy imitation in 1296 and that the true Stone of Destiny remains safely hidden somewhere in Scotland. This is not impossible – some descriptions of the original state that it was made of black marble and decorated with elaborate carvings. Interested parties should read *Scotland's Stone of Destiny* by Nick Aitchison, which details the history and cultural significance of Scotland's most famous lump of rock.

exhibits have been personalised by telling the stories of the original owners of the objects on display, making it easier to empathise with the experiences of war than any dry display of dusty weaponry ever could.

Highland Tolbooth Kirk CHURCH

(Map p762; Castlehill; admission free; ⌚9.30am-7pm) Edinburgh's tallest spire (71.7m) is at the foot of Castlehill and is a prominent feature of the Old Town's skyline. The interior has been refurbished and it now houses the **Hub** (www.thehub-edinburgh.com), the ticket office and information centre for the Edinburgh Festival. There's also a good cafe here.

Camera Obscura CAMERA OBSCURA

(Map p762; www.camera-obscura.co.uk; Castlehill; adult/child £9.25/6.25; ⌚9.30am-7.30pm Jul & Aug, 9.30am-6pm Apr-Jun, Sep & Oct, 10am-5pm Nov-Mar) Edinburgh's 'camera obscura' is a curious 19th-century device – in constant use since 1853 – that uses lenses and mirrors to throw a live image of the city onto a large horizontal screen. The accompanying commentary is entertaining and the whole experience has a quirky charm, complemented by an intriguing exhibition dedicated to illusions of all kinds. Stairs lead up through various displays to the **Outlook Tower**, which offers great views over the city.

Gladstone's Land HISTORIC HOUSE

(Map p762; NTS; www.nts.org.uk; 477 Lawnmarket; adult/child £5.50/4.50; ⌚10am-6.30pm Jul & Aug, 10am-5pm Apr-Jun, Sep & Oct) One of Edinburgh's most prominent 17th-century merchants was Thomas Gledstanes, who in 1617 purchased the tenement later known as Gladstone's Land. It contains fine painted ceilings, walls and beams, and some splendid furniture from the 17th and 18th centuries. The volunteer guides provide a wealth of anecdotes and a detailed history.

St Giles Cathedral CHURCH

(Map p762; www.stgilescathedral.org.uk; High St; £3 donation suggested; ⌚9am-7pm Mon-Fri, 9am-5pm Sat, 1-5pm Sun May-Sep, 9am-5pm Mon-Sat, 1-5pm Sun Oct-Apr) Dominating High St is the great grey bulk of St Giles Cathedral. Properly called the High Kirk of Edinburgh (it was only a true cathedral – the seat of a bishop – from 1633 to 1638 and from 1661 to 1689), St Giles Cathedral was named after the patron saint of cripples and beggars. A Norman-style church was built here in 1126 but was destroyed by English invaders in 1385; the only substantial remains are the central piers that support the tower.

The present church dates largely from the 15th century – the beautiful **crown spire** was completed in 1495 – but much of it was restored in the 19th century. The interior lacks grandeur but is rich in history: St Giles was at the heart of the Scottish Reformation, and John Knox served as minister here from 1559 to 1572. One of the most interesting corners of the kirk is the **Thistle Chapel**, built in 1911 for the Knights of the Most Ancient & Most Noble Order of the Thistle. The elaborately carved Gothic-style stalls have canopies topped with the helms and arms of the 16 knights – look out for the bagpipe-playing angel amid the vaulting.

By the side of the street, outside the western door of St Giles, is a cobblestone **Heart of Midlothian** set into the paving. This marks the site of the Tolbooth. Built in the 15th century and demolished in the early 19th century, the Tolbooth served variously as a meeting place for parliament, the town council and the General Assembly of the Reformed Kirk, before becoming law courts and, finally, a notorious prison and place of execution. Passers-by traditionally spit on the heart for luck (don't stand downwind!).

At the other end of St Giles is the **Mercat Cross**, a 19th-century copy of the 1365 original, where merchants and traders met to transact business and royal proclamations were read.

Real Mary King's Close HISTORIC BUILDING

(Map p762; ☎0845 070 6255; www.realmarykingsclose.com; 2 Warriston's Close, Writers Ct, High St; adult/child £11/6; ⌚10am-9pm Apr-Oct, to 11pm Aug, 10am-5pm Sun-Thu & 10am-9pm Fri & Sat Nov-Mar) Part of the Royal Exchange was built over the sealed-off remains of Mary King's Close, and the lower levels of this medieval Old Town alley have survived almost unchanged in the foundations of the City Chambers for 250 years. Now open to the public as the Real Mary King's Close, this spooky, subterranean labyrinth gives a fascinating insight into the daily life of 16th- and 17th-century Edinburgh. Costumed characters give tours through

SCOTTISH PARLIAMENT BUILDING

The **Scottish parliament building** (☎0131-348 5200; www.scottish.parliament.uk; admission free; ⌚9am-6.30pm Tue-Thu, 10am-5.30pm Mon & Fri in session, 10am-6pm Mon-Fri in recess Apr-Oct, 10am-4pm in recess Nov-Mar; 📶), built on the site of a former brewery close to the Palace of Holyroodhouse, was officially opened by HM the Queen in October 2005.

The public areas of the parliament building – the Main Hall, where there is an exhibition, a shop and cafe, and the **public gallery** in the Debating Chamber – are open to visitors (tickets needed for public gallery – see website for details). You can also take a free, one-hour **guided tour** (advance booking recommended) that includes a visit to the Debating Chamber, a committee room, the Garden Lobby and, when possible, the office of an MSP (Member of the Scottish Parliament). If you want to see the **parliament in session**, check the website to see when it will be sitting – business days are normally Tuesday to Thursday year-round.

Enric Miralles (1955–2000), the architect who conceived the Scottish parliament building, believed that a building could be a work of art. However, the weird concrete confection that has sprouted at the foot of Salisbury Crags has left the good people of Edinburgh staring and scratching their heads in confusion. What does it all mean? The strange forms of the exterior are all symbolic in some way, from the oddly shaped windows on the west wall (inspired by the silhouette of the *Reverend Robert Walker Skating on Duddingston Loch,* one of Scotland's most famous paintings), to the ground plan of the whole complex, which represents a 'flower of democracy rooted in Scottish soil' (best seen looking down from Salisbury Crags).

The **Main Hall**, inside the public entrance, has a low, triple-arched ceiling of polished concrete, like a cave, or cellar, or castle vault. It is a dimly lit space, the starting point for a metaphorical journey from this relative darkness up to the **Debating Chamber** (sitting directly above the Main Hall), which is, in contrast, a palace of light – the light of democracy. This magnificent chamber is the centrepiece of the parliament, designed not to glorify but to humble the politicians who sit within it. The windows face Calton Hill, allowing MSPs to look up to its monuments (reminders of the Scottish Enlightenment), while the massive, pointed oak beams of the roof are suspended by steel threads above the MSPs' heads like so many Damoclean swords.

a 16th-century town house and the plague-stricken home of a 17th-century gravedigger. Advance booking recommended.

FREE **Museum of Edinburgh** MUSEUM
(142 Canongate; ⌚10am-5pm Mon-Sat year-round, 2-5pm Sun Aug) Across the street from a museum called the People's Story is Huntly House. Built in 1570, it now houses a museum covering the history of Edinburgh from prehistory to the present. Exhibits of national importance include an original copy of the National Covenant of 1638, but the big crowd-pleaser is the dog collar and feeding bowl that once belonged to **Greyfriars Bobby**, the city's most famous canine citizen.

HOLYROOD

Palace of Holyroodhouse ROYAL PALACE
(www.royalcollection.org.uk; Canongate; adult/child £10.25/6.20; ⌚9.30am-6pm Apr-Oct, 9.30am-4.30pm Nov-Mar) This palace is the royal family's official residence in Scotland, but is most famous as the 16th-century home of the ill-fated **Mary, Queen of Scots**. The palace developed from a guest house attached to Holyrood Abbey, which was extended by King James IV in 1501. The oldest surviving part of the building, the northwestern tower, was built in 1529 as a royal apartment for James V and his wife, Mary of Guise. Mary, Queen of Scots spent six turbulent years here, during which time she debated with John Knox, married both her first and second husbands, and witnessed the murder of her secretary. The palace is closed to the public when the royal family is visiting

and during state functions (usually in mid-May, and mid-June to early July; check the website for exact dates).

The guided tour leads you through a series of impressive royal apartments, ending in the **Great Gallery**. The 89 portraits of Scottish kings were commissioned by Charles II and supposedly record his unbroken lineage from Scota, the Egyptian pharaoh's daughter who discovered the infant Moses in a reed basket on the banks of the Nile.

But the highlight of the tour is **Mary, Queen of Scots' Bed Chamber**, home to the unfortunate Mary from 1561 to 1567, and connected by a secret stairway to her husband's bedchamber. It was in this room that her jealous first husband, Lord Darnley, restrained the pregnant queen while his henchmen murdered her secretary – and favourite – David Rizzio. A plaque in the neighbouring room marks the spot where he bled to death.

Our Dynamic Earth MULTIMEDIA EXHIBITION

(www.dynamicearth.co.uk; Holyrood Rd; adult/child £10.50/7; 10am-6pm Jul & Aug, 10am-5.30pm Apr-Jun, Sep & Oct, 10am-5pm Wed-Sun Nov-Mar, last admission 90min before closing;) The modernistic white marquee pitched beneath Salisbury Crags marks Our Dynamic Earth, billed as an interactive, multimedia journey of discovery through Earth's history from the big bang to the present day. Hugely popular with kids of all ages, it's a slick extravaganza of whiz-bang special effects and 3D movies cleverly designed to fire up young minds with curiosity about all things geological and environmental. Its true purpose, of course, is to disgorge you into a gift shop where you can buy model dinosaurs and souvenir T-shirts.

Holyrood Park PARK

In Holyrood Park Edinburgh is blessed with a little bit of wilderness in the heart of the city. The former hunting ground of Scottish monarchs, the park covers 263 hectares of varied landscape, including crags, moorland and loch. The highest point is the 251m summit of **Arthur's Seat**, the deeply eroded remnant of a long-extinct volcano. Holyrood park can be circumnavigated by car or bike along Queen's Dr (it is closed to motorised traffic on Sunday), and you can hike from Holyrood to the summit in around 45 minutes.

SOUTH OF THE ROYAL MILE

FREE **National Museum of Scotland** MUSEUM

(Map p762; www.nms.ac.uk; Chambers St; fee for special exhibitions; 10am-5pm) Broad, elegant Chambers St is dominated by the long facade of the National Museum of Scotland. Its extensive collections are spread between two buildings, one modern, one Victorian.

The golden stone and striking modern architecture of the museum building, opened in 1998, is one of the city's most distinctive landmarks. The five floors of the museum trace the history of Scotland from geological beginnings to the 1990s, with many imaginative and stimulating exhibits – audioguides are available in several languages. Highlights include the **Monymusk Reliquary**, a tiny silver casket dating from AD 750, which is said to have been carried into battle with Robert the Bruce at Bannockburn in 1314, and some of the **Lewis chessmen**, a set of charming 12th-century chess pieces made from walrus ivory. Don't forget to take the lift to the **roof terrace** for a fantastic view of the castle.

The Museum of Scotland connects with the Victorian **Royal Museum** building, dating from 1861, whose stolid, grey exterior gives way to a bright and airy, glass-roofed entrance hall. The museum houses an eclectic collection covering natural history, archaeology, scientific and industrial technology, and the decorative arts of ancient Egypt, Islam, China, Japan, Korea and the West. (The Royal Museum was undergoing a major rebuild at the time of research; it is due to reopen in mid-2011.)

Greyfriars Kirk CHURCH

(Map p762; www.greyfriarskirk.com; Candlemaker Row; 10.30am-4.40pm Mon-Fri & 10.30am-2pm Sat, 1.30-3.30pm Thu only Nov-Mar) Candlemaker Row leads from the eastern end of the Grassmarket towards one of Edinburgh's most famous churches. **Greyfriars Kirk** was built on the site of a Franciscan friary and opened for worship on Christmas Day 1620. In 1638 the **National Covenant** was signed here, rejecting Charles I's attempts to impose episcopacy and a new English prayer book, and affirming the independence of the Scottish Church. Many who signed were later executed at the Grass-

UNDERGROUND EDINBURGH

As Edinburgh expanded in the late 18th and early 19th centuries, many old tenements were demolished and new bridges were built to link the Old Town to the newly built areas to its north and south. South Bridge (built between 1785 and 1788) and George IV Bridge (built between 1829 and 1834) lead southwards from the Royal Mile over the deep valley of Cowgate, but so many buildings have been built closely around them that you can hardly tell they are bridges – George IV Bridge has a total of nine arches but only two are visible; South Bridge has no less than 18 hidden arches.

These **subterranean vaults** were originally used as storerooms, workshops and drinking dens. But as early-19th-century Edinburgh's population was swelled by an influx of penniless Highlanders cleared from their lands, and Irish refugees from the potato famine, the dark, dripping chambers were given over to slum accommodation and abandoned to poverty, filth and crime.

The vaults were eventually cleared in the late 19th century, then lay forgotten until 1994 when the **South Bridge vaults** were opened to guided tours (see Mercat Tours, p776). Certain chambers are said to be haunted and one particular vault was investigated by paranormal researchers in 2001.

Nevertheless, the most ghoulish aspect of Edinburgh's hidden history dates from much earlier – from the plague that struck the city in 1645. Legend has it that the disease-ridden inhabitants of **Mary King's Close** (a lane on the northern side of the Royal Mile on the site of the City Chambers – you can still see its blocked-off northern end from Cockburn St) were walled up in their houses and left to perish. When the lifeless bodies were eventually cleared from the houses, they were so stiff that workmen had to hack off limbs to get them through the small doorways and narrow, twisting stairs.

From that day on, the close was said to be haunted by the spirits of the plague victims. The few people who were prepared to live there reported seeing apparitions of severed heads and limbs, and the largely abandoned close fell into ruin. When the Royal Exchange (now the City Chambers) was constructed between 1753 and 1761, it was built over the lower levels of Mary King's Close, which were left intact and sealed off beneath the building.

Interest in the close revived in the 20th century when Edinburgh's city council began to allow occasional guided tours to enter. Visitors have reported many supernatural experiences – the most famous ghost is 'Sarah', a little girl whose sad tale has prompted people to leave gifts of dolls in a corner of one of the rooms. In 2003 the close was opened to the public as the Real Mary King's Close.

market and, in 1679, 1200 Covenanters were held prisoner in terrible conditions in the southwestern corner of the kirkyard. There's a small exhibition inside the church.

Surrounding the church, hemmed in by high walls and overlooked by the brooding presence of the castle, **Greyfriars Kirkyard** is one of Edinburgh's most evocative cemeteries, a peaceful green oasis dotted with elaborate monuments. Many famous Edinburgh names are buried here, including the poet Allan Ramsay (1686–1758), architect William Adam (1689–1748) and William Smellie (1740–95), the editor of the first edition of the *Encyclopedia Britannica*.

In July and August you can join a **guided tour** (free; donation suggested) of the kirkyard; check the website for times and dates. If you want to experience the graveyard at its scariest – inside a burial vault, in the dark, at night – go on one of Black Hart Storytellers' guided tours.

Greyfriars Bobby Statue MONUMENT

The memorials inside Greyfriars Kirkyard are interesting, but the one that draws the biggest crowds is outside, in front of the pub beside the kirkyard gate. It's the tiny

New Town

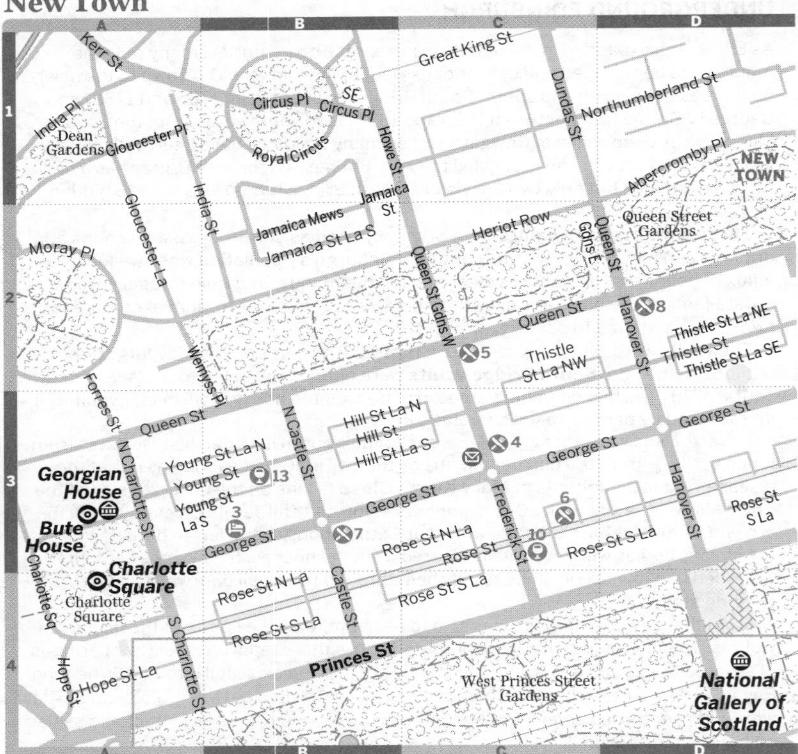

statue of Greyfriars Bobby, a Skye terrier who, from 1858 to 1872, maintained a vigil over the grave of his master, an Edinburgh police officer. The story was immortalised (and romanticised) in a novel by Eleanor Atkinson in 1912, and in 1963 was made into a movie by – who else? – Walt Disney. Bobby's own grave, marked by a small, pink granite stone, is just inside the entrance to the kirkyard. You can see his original collar and bowl in the Museum of Edinburgh.

NEW TOWN

Edinburgh's New Town lies north of the Old Town, on a ridge running parallel to the Royal Mile and separated from it by the valley of Princes Street Gardens. Its regular grid of elegant, neoclassical terraces is the world's most complete and unspoilt example of Georgian architecture and town planning. Along with the Old Town, it was declared a Unesco World Heritage site in 1995.

PRINCES STREET

Princes St is one of the world's most spectacular shopping streets. Built up on the north side only, it catches the sun in summer and allows expansive views across Princes Street Gardens to the castle and the crowded skyline of the Old Town.

Princes Street Gardens lie in a valley that was once occupied by the Nor' Loch, a boggy depression that was drained in the early 19th century. The gardens are split in the middle by **The Mound**, which was created by around two million cart-loads of earth excavated from the foundations of New Town being dumped here to provide a road link across the valley to the Old Town. It was completed in 1830.

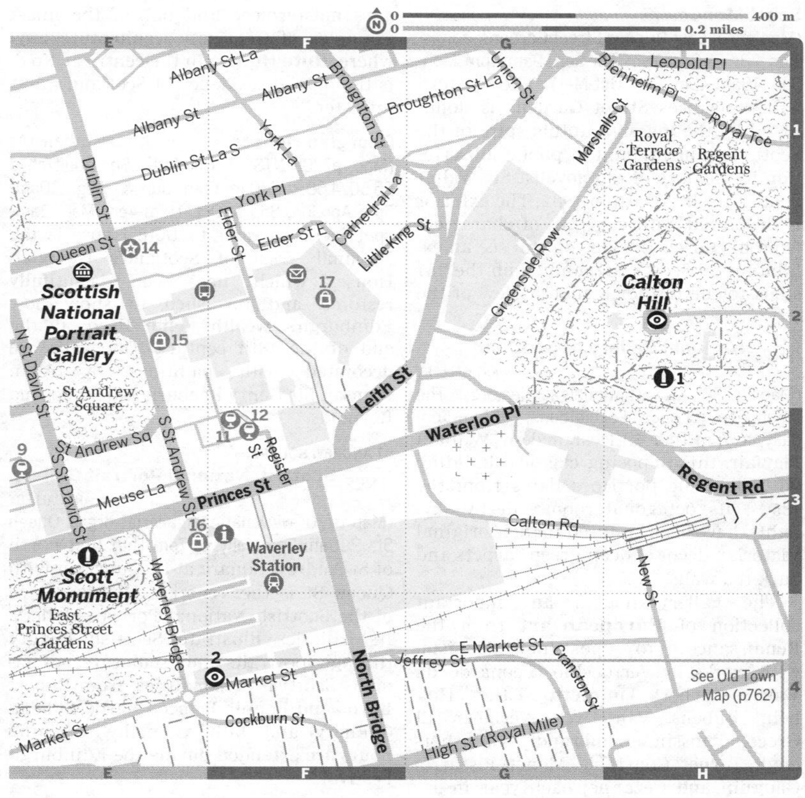

New Town

Top Sights

- Bute House A3
- Calton Hill H2
- Charlotte Square A4
- Georgian House A3
- National Gallery of Scotland D4
- Scott Monument E3
- Scottish National Portrait Gallery E2

Sights

1 Nelson Monument H2
2 Tattoo Office F4

Sleeping

3 Tigerlily B3

Eating

4 Eteaket C3
5 La P'tite Folie C2
6 Mussel Inn C3
7 Oloroso B3
8 Urban Angel D2

Drinking

9 Abbotsford E3
10 Amicus Apple C3
11 Café Royal Circle Bar F3
12 Guildford Arms F3
13 Oxford Bar B3

Entertainment

14 Stand Comedy Club E2

Shopping

15 Harvey Nichols E2
16 Princes Mall E3
17 St James Shopping Centre F2

Scott Monument MONUMENT

(Map p770; East Princes Street Gardens; admission £3; ⏲10am-7pm Apr-Sep, 9am-4pm Mon-Sat, 10am-4pm Sun Oct-Mar) The eastern half of Princes Street Gardens is dominated by the massive Gothic spire of the Scott Monument, built by public subscription in memory of the novelist Sir Walter Scott after his death in 1832. The exterior is decorated with carvings of characters from his novels; inside you can see an exhibition on Scott's life, and climb the 287 steps to the top for a superb view of the city.

FREE **National Gallery of Scotland** ART GALLERY

(Map p770; www.nationalgalleries.org; The Mound; fee for special exhibitions; ⏲10am-5pm daily, to 7pm Thu; 📶) Designed by William Playfair, this imposing classical building with its Ionic porticoes dates from the 1850s. Its octagonal rooms, lit by skylights, have been restored to their original Victorian decor of deep-green carpets and dark-red walls.

The gallery houses an important collection of **European art** from the Renaissance to post-Impressionism, with works by Verrocchio (Leonardo da Vinci's teacher), Tintoretto, Titian, Holbein, Rubens, Van Dyck, Vermeer, El Greco, Poussin, Rembrandt, Gainsborough, Turner, Constable, Monet, Pissarro, Gauguin and Cézanne; each year in Janary the gallery exhibits its collection of **Turner watercolours**, bequeathed by Henry Vaughan in 1900. Room X is graced by Antonio Canova's white marble sculpture, **The Three Graces**; it is owned jointly with London's Victoria & Albert Museum.

GEORGE STREET & CHARLOTTE SQUARE

Until the 1990s George St – the major axis of New Town – was the centre of Edinburgh's financial industry and Scotland's equivalent of Wall St. Today the big financial firms have moved to premises in the Exchange office district west of Lothian Rd, and George St's former banks and offices house upmarket shops, pubs and restaurants.

At the western end of George St is **Charlotte Square**, the architectural jewel of New Town, designed by Robert Adam shortly before his death in 1791. The northern side of the square is Adam's masterpiece and one of the finest examples of Georgian architecture anywhere. **Bute House**, in the centre at No 6, is the official residence of Scotland's first minister.

Georgian House HISTORIC HOUSE

(Map p770; NTS; 7 Charlotte Sq; adult/child £5.50/4.50; ⏲10am-6pm Jul & Aug, 10am-5pm Apr-Jun, Sep & Oct, 11am-4pm Mar, 11am-3pm Nov) Next door to Bute House is the National Trust of Scotland's Georgian House, which has been beautifully restored and furnished to show how Edinburgh's wealthy elite lived at the end of the 18th century. The walls are decorated with paintings by Allan Ramsay, Sir Henry Raeburn and Sir Joshua Reynolds.

ST ANDREW SQUARE

FREE **Scottish National Portrait Gallery** ART GALLERY

(Map p770; www.nationalgalleries.org; 1 Queen St; ⏲10am-5pm daily, to 7pm Thu) Just north of St Andrew Square at the junction with Queen St is the Venetian Gothic palace of the Scottish National Portrait Gallery. Its galleries illustrate Scottish history through portraits and sculptures of famous Scottish personalities, from Robert Burns and Bonnie Prince Charlie to Sean Connery and Billy Connolly. Opening hours are extended during the Edinburgh Festival.

CALTON HILL

Calton Hill (100m), rising dramatically above the eastern end of Princes St, is Edinburgh's acropolis, its summit scattered with grandiose memorials mostly dating from the first half of the 19th century. It is also one of the best viewpoints in Edinburgh, with a panorama that takes in the castle, Holyrood, Arthur's Seat, the Firth of Forth, New Town and the full length of Princes St.

Looking a bit like an upturned telescope – the similarity is intentional – and offering even better views, the **Nelson Monument** (Calton Hill; admission £3; ⏲1-6pm Mon, 10am-6pm Tue-Sat Apr-Sep, 10am-3pm Mon-Sat Oct-Mar) was built to commemorate Admiral Lord Nelson's victory at Trafalgar in 1805.

DEAN VILLAGE

If you follow Queensferry St northwards from the western end of Princes St,

Leith

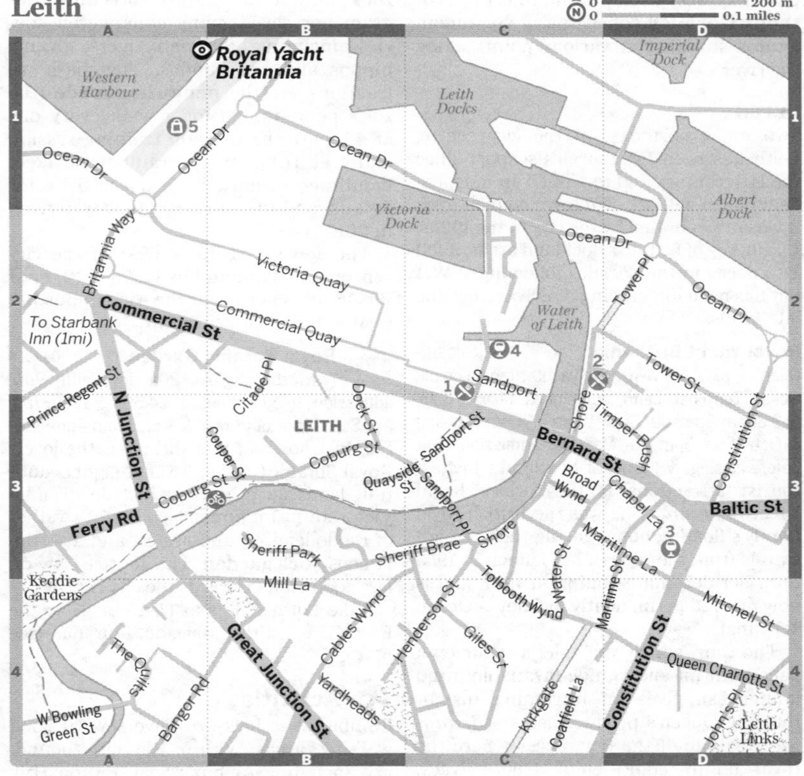

Leith

Top Sights

Royal Yacht Britannia A1

Eating

1 Chop Chop C2
2 Fishers Bistro C2

Drinking

3 Port O'Leith D3
4 Teuchter's Landing C2

Shopping

5 Ocean Terminal A1

you come to **Dean Bridge**, designed by Thomas Telford and built between 1829 and 1832. Down in the valley just west of the bridge is **Dean Village** (from 'dene', a Scots word for valley). It was founded as a milling community by the canons of Holyrood Abbey in the 12th century and by 1700 there were 11 watermills here operated by the Incorporation of Baxters (the bakers' trade guild).

FREE **Scottish National Gallery of Modern Art** ART GALLERY

(www.nationalgalleries.org; 75 Belford Rd; fee for special exhibitions; ⏲10am-5pm) This collection concentrates on **20th-century art**, with various European movements represented by the likes of Matisse, Picasso, Kirchner, Magritte, Miró, Mondrian and Giacometti. There's an excellent **cafe** downstairs, and the surrounding **park** features sculptures by Henry Moore, Rachel Whiteread and Barbara Hepworth among others, as well as a 'landform artwork' by Charles Jencks.

A footpath and stairs at the rear of the gallery lead down to the **Water of Leith Walkway**, which you can follow along the river for 4 miles to Leith. This takes you past **6 Times**, a sculptural project by **Anthony Gormley** consisting of six human figures standing at various points along the river.

LEITH

Two miles northeast of the city centre, Leith has been Edinburgh's seaport since the 14th century and remained an independent burgh with its own town council until it was incorporated by the city in the 1920s. Like many of Britain's dockland areas, it fell into decay in the decades following WWII but has been undergoing a revival since the late 1980s.

Royal Yacht Britannia HISTORIC SHIP

(Map p773; www.royalyachtbritannia.co.uk; Ocean Terminal, Leith; adult/child £10.50/6.75; ⌚9.30am-6pm Jul-Sep, 10am-5.30pm Apr-Jun & Oct, 10am-5pm Nov-Mar, last admission 1½hr before closing; 📶) One of Scotland's biggest tourist attractions is the former Royal Yacht *Britannia*. She was the British royal family's floating home during their foreign travels from the time of her launch in 1953 until her decommissioning in 1997, and is now moored permanently in front of Ocean Terminal.

The tour, which you take at your own pace with an audioguide (available in 20 languages), gives an intriguing insight into the Queen's private tastes – *Britannia* was one of the few places where the royal family could enjoy true privacy. The entire ship is a monument to 1950's decor and technology, and the accommodation reveals Her Majesty's preference for simple, unfussy surroundings – the Queen's own bed is surprisingly tiny and plain.

Britannia was joined in 2010 by the 1930s racing yacht **Bloodhound**, which was owned by the Queen in the 1960s.

The Majestic Tour bus (see p776) runs from Waverley Bridge to *Britannia* during opening times. Alternatively, take Lothian Bus 11, 22, or 35 to Ocean Terminal.

GREATER EDINBURGH

Edinburgh Zoo ZOO

(www.edinburghzoo.org.uk; 134 Corstorphine Rd; adult/child £15.50/11; ⌚9am-6pm Apr-Sep, 9am-5pm Oct & Mar, 9am-4.30pm Nov-Feb) Opened in 1913, Edinburgh Zoo is one of the world's leading conservation zoos. Edinburgh's captive breeding program has saved many endangered species, including Siberian tigers, pygmy hippos and red pandas. The main attractions are the **penguin parade** (the zoo's penguins go for a walk every day at 2.15pm), the sea lion training session (daily at 11.15am), the rainbow lorikeet handling session (check the website for details) and the sun bears (newly arrived in 2010).

The zoo is 2.5 miles west of the city centre; take Lothian Bus 12, 26 or 31, First Bus 16, 18, 80 or 86, or the Airlink Bus 100 westbound from Princes St.

FREE **Royal Botanic Garden** GARDEN

(www.rbge.org.uk; 20a Inverleith Row; admission to glasshouses £4.50; ⌚10am-7pm Apr-Sep, 10am-6pm Mar & Oct, 10am-4pm Nov-Feb) Just north of Stockbridge is the lovely Royal Botanic Garden. Twenty-eight beautifully landscaped hectares include splendid Victorian **palm houses**, colourful swathes of rhododendron and azalea, and a world-famous **rock garden**. The Terrace Cafe offers good views towards the city centre.

Take Lothian Bus 8, 17, 23 or 27 to the East Gate, or the Majestic Tour bus (see p776).

Activities

Edinburgh is lucky to have several good walking areas within the city boundary, including Arthur's Seat, Calton Hill, Blackford Hill, Hermitage of Braid, Corstorphine Hill, and the coast and river at Cramond.

You can follow the **Water of Leith Walkway** from the city centre to Balerno (8 miles), and continue across the Pentlands to Silverburn (6.5 miles) or Carlops (8 miles), and return to Edinburgh by bus. Another good walk is along the towpath of the **Union Canal**, which begins in Fountainbridge and runs all the way to Falkirk (31 miles).

Tours

Bus Tours

Open-topped buses leave from Waverley Bridge outside the main train station and offer hop-on/hop-off tours of the main sights, taking in New Town, the Grassmarket and the Royal Mile. They're a good way to get your bearings, although with a bus map and a Day Saver bus ticket (£3) you could do much the same thing

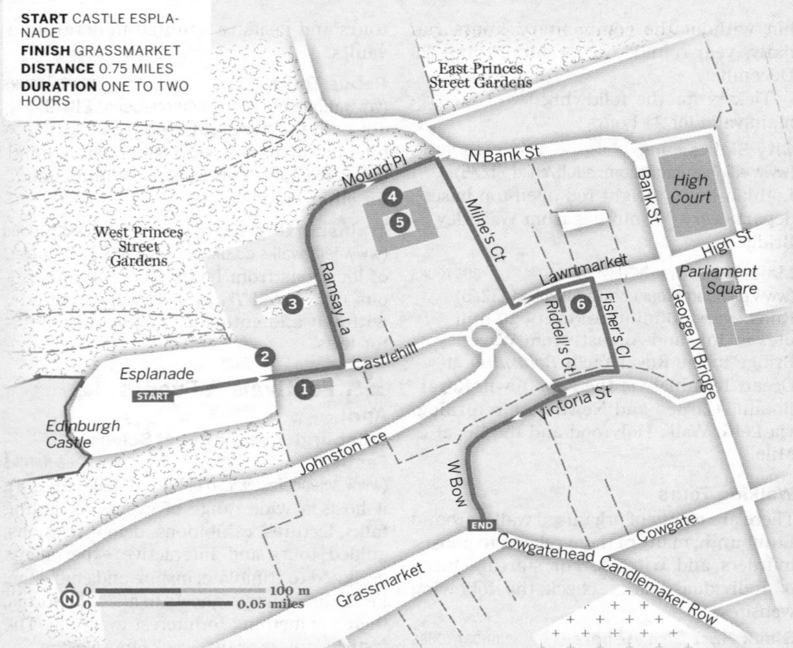

Walking Tour
Old Town Alleys

This walk explores the alleys and closes around the upper part of the Royal Mile, and involves a bit of climbing up and down steep stairs.

From the Esplanade head down Castlehill. The 17th-century house on the right is known as **Cannonball House** because of the iron ball lodged in the wall (look between, and slightly below, the two largest windows). It was not fired in anger, but marks the gravitation height to which water would flow naturally from the city's first piped water supply.

The building across the street was originally the reservoir for the Old Town's water supply. On its west wall is the **Witches Well**, where a bronze fountain commemorates around 4000 people (mostly women) who were executed between 1479 and 1722 on suspicion of witchcraft.

Turn left down Ramsay Lane and take a look at **Ramsay Garden** where late-19th-century apartments were built around the octagonal Ramsay Lodge, once home to poet Allan Ramsay. The cobbled street continues around to **New College**, home to Edinburgh University's Faculty of Divinity. Nip into the courtyard to see the **statue of John Knox**.

Just past New College turn right and climb up the stairs into Milne's Court, a student residence. Exit into Lawnmarket, cross the street (bearing slightly left) and duck into **Riddell's Court** at No 322-328, a typical Old Town close. You'll find yourself in a small courtyard, but the house in front of you (built in 1590) was originally the edge of the street (the building you just walked under was added in 1726). The arch with the inscription *Vivendo discimus* ('we live and learn') leads into the original 16th-century courtyard.

Go back into the street, turn right and right again down Fisher's Close, which leads to delightful Victoria Terrace, poised above Victoria St. Go right, then down the stairs at the foot of Upper Bow and continue downhill to the Grassmarket where you can take your pick of cafes and bars.

but without the commentary. Tours run daily, year-round, except for 24 and 25 December.

Tickets for the following two tours remain valid for 24 hours.

City Sightseeing BUS TOURS
(www.edinburghtour.com; adult/child £12/5) Lothian Buses' bright red open-top buses depart every 20 minutes from Waverley Bridge.

Majestic Tour BUS TOURS
(www.edinburghtour.com; adult/child £12/5) Runs every 30 minutes (every 20 minutes in July and August) from Waverley Bridge to the Royal Yacht *Britannia* at Ocean Terminal via the New Town, Royal Botanic Garden and Newhaven, returning via Leith Walk, Holyrood and the Royal Mile.

Walking Tours

There are plenty of organised walks around Edinburgh, many of them related to ghosts, murders and witches. For starting times of individual walks, check the following websites:

Black Hart Storytellers GHOST TOURS
(www.blackhart.uk.com; adult/concession £9.50/7.50) Not suitable for young children. The 'City of the Dead' tour of Greyfriars Kirkyard is probably the scariest of Edinburgh's 'ghost' tours. Many people have reported encounters with the 'McKenzie Poltergeist'.

Cadies & Witchery Tours GHOST TOURS
(www.witcherytours.com; adult/child £7.50/5) The becloaked and pasty-faced Adam Lyal (deceased) leads a 'Murder & Mystery' tour of the Old Town's darker corners. These tours are famous for their 'jumper-ooters' – costumed actors who 'jump oot' when you least expect it.

Edinburgh Literary Pub Tour LITERARY TOURS
(www.edinburghliterarypubtour.co.uk; adult/student £10/8) An enlightening two-hour trawl through Edinburgh's literary history – and its associated howffs – in the entertaining company of Messrs Clart and McBrain. One of the best of Edinburgh's walking tours.

Mercat Tours HISTORY TOURS
(www.mercattours.com; adult/child £9/5) Mercat offers a wide range of fascinating tours including history walks in the Old Town and Leith, 'Ghosts & Ghouls' tours and visits to haunted underground vaults.

Rebus Tours LITERARY TOURS
(www.rebustours.com; adult/student £10/9) Tours of the 'hidden Edinburgh' frequented by novelist Ian Rankin's fictional detective John Rebus. Not recommended for children under 10.

Trainspotting Tours LITERARY TOURS
(www.leithwalks.co.uk; per person £8) A tour of locations from Irvine Welsh's notorious 1993 novel *Trainspotting,* delivered with wit and enthusiasm. Not suitable for kids.

Festivals & Events

April

Edinburgh International Science Festival SCIENCE & NATURE
(www.sciencefestival.co.uk) First held in 1987, it hosts a wide range of events, including talks, lectures, exhibitions, demonstrations, guided tours and interactive experiments designed to stimulate, inspire and challenge. From dinosaurs to ghosts to alien life forms, there's something to interest everyone. The festival runs over two weeks in April.

May

Imaginate Festival CHILDREN'S THEATRE
(www.imaginate.org.uk) This is Britain's biggest festival of performing arts for children, with events suitable for kids from three to 12. Groups from around the world perform classic tales like *Hansel and Gretel* as well as new material written specially for children. The festival takes place annually in the last week of May.

June

Scottish Real Ale Festival BEER
(www.scottishbeerfestival.org.uk; Assembly Rooms, 54 George St) A celebration of all things fermented and yeasty, Scotland's biggest beer-fest gives you the opportunity to sample a wide range of traditionally brewed beers from Scotland and around the world. Froth-topped bliss. The festival is held over a weekend in June.

Royal Highland Show AGRICULTURAL
(www.royalhighlandshow.org; Royal Highland Centre, Ingliston) Scotland's hugely popular national agricultural show is a four-day feast of all things rural, with everything from show-jumping and tractor-driving

FESTIVAL CITY

August in Edinburgh sees a frenzy of festivals, with half a dozen world-class events running at the same time.

Edinburgh Festival Fringe

When the first Edinburgh Festival was held in 1947, there were eight theatre companies who didn't make it onto the main program. Undeterred, they grouped together and held their own mini-festival, on the fringe, and an Edinburgh institution was born. Today the **Edinburgh Festival Fringe** (Map p762; ☎0131-226 0026; www.edfringe.com; Edinburgh Festival Fringe Office, 180 High St) is *the* biggest festival of the performing arts anywhere in the world.

The Fringe take place over 3½ weeks in August, the last two weeks overlapping with the first two of the Edinburgh International Festival.

Edinburgh International Festival

First held in 1947 to mark a return to peace after the ordeal of WWII, the **Edinburgh International Festival** (☎0131-473 2099; www.eif.co.uk) is festooned with superlatives – the oldest, the biggest, the most famous, the best in the world. The original was a modest affair, but today hundreds of the world's top musicians and performers congregate in Edinburgh for three weeks of diverse and inspirational music, opera, theatre and dance.

The festival takes place over the three weeks ending on the first Saturday in September; the program is usually available from April. Tickets for popular events – especially music and opera – sell out quickly, so it's best to book as far in advance as possible. You can buy tickets in person at the **Hub** (Map p762), or by phone or internet.

Edinburgh Military Tattoo

The month kicks off with the **Edinburgh Military Tattoo** (Map p770; ☎0131-225 1188; www.edintattoo.co.uk; Tattoo Office, 32 Market St), a spectacular display of military marching bands, massed pipes and drums, acrobats, cheerleaders and motorcycle display teams, all played out in front of the magnificent backdrop of the floodlit castle. The Tattoo takes place over the first three weeks of August (from a Friday to a Saturday); there's one show at 9pm Monday to Friday and two (at 7.30pm and 10.30pm) on Saturday, but no performance on Sunday.

Edinburgh International Book Festival

Held in a little village of marquees in the middle of Charlotte Sq, the **Edinburgh International Book Festival** (☎0845 373 5888; www.edbookfest.co.uk) is a fun fortnight of talks, readings, debates, lectures, book signings and meet-the-author events, with a cafe and tented bookshop thrown in. The festival lasts for two weeks in August (usually the first two weeks of the Edinburgh International Festival).

to sheep-shearing and falconry. Countless pens are filled with coiffed show-cattle and pedicured prize ewes. The show is held over a long weekend (Thursday to Sunday) in late June.

Edinburgh International Film Festival FILM

(www.edfilmfest.org.uk) One of the original Edinburgh Festival trinity, having first been staged in 1947 along with the International Festival and the Fringe, the two-week film festival is a major international event, serving as a showcase for new British and European films, and staging the European premieres of one or two Hollywood blockbusters.

July

Edinburgh International Jazz & Blues Festival JAZZ & BLUES

(www.edinburghjazzfestival.com) Held annually since 1978, the Jazz & Blues

Festival pulls in top talent from all over the world. The festival runs for nine days, beginning on the last Friday in July (the week before the Fringe and Tattoo begin). The first weekend sees a Mardi Gras street parade on Saturday from the City Chambers, up the Royal Mile and down Victoria St into the Grassmarket, for an afternoon of free, open-air music. On the Sunday there's a series of free concerts at the Ross Bandstand in Princes Street Gardens.

August

See boxed text, p777, for details of August's festivals.

December

Edinburgh's Christmas CHRISTMAS
(www.edinburghschristmas.com) The youngest of the Scottish capital's festivals, first held in 2000, the Christmas bash includes a big street parade, a fairground and Ferris wheel, and an open-air ice rink in Princes Street Gardens. The celebrations are held over the three weeks before Christmas Day.

Edinburgh's Hogmanay NEW YEAR'S
(www.edinburghshogmanay.com) The biggestwinter festival in Europe. Events run from 29 December to 1 January and include a torchlight procession, huge street party and a New Year's Day triathlon. To get into the main party area in the city centre after 8pm on 31 December you'll need a ticket – book well in advance.

Sleeping

Edinburgh is not short of accommodation, but you can guarantee that the city will be packed to the gills during the festival period (August) and over Hogmanay (New Year). If you want a room during these periods, book as far in advance as possible. In general, it's best to book ahead for accommodation at Easter and from mid-May to mid-September.

OLD TOWN

TOP CHOICE **Hotel Missoni** BOUTIQUE HOTEL £££
(Map p762; ☎0131-220 6666; www.hotelmissoni.com; 1 George IV Bridge; r £180; 📶) The Italian fashion house has established a style icon in the heart of the medieval Old Town with this bold statement of a hotel – modernistic architecture, black and white decor with well-judged splashes of colour, impeccably mannered staff and – most importantly – very comfortable bedrooms and bathrooms with lots of nice little touches, from fresh milk in the minibar to plush bathrobes.

Smart City Hostel HOSTEL £
(Map p762; ☎0870 892 3000; www.smartcityhostels.com; 50 Blackfriars St; dm £9-22, tw £80; @📶) A big (620 beds), bright, modern hostel that feels more like a hotel, with a convivial cafe where you can buy breakfast, and mod cons such as keycard access and secure charging stations for mobile phones, MP3 players and laptops. Lockers in every room, bike parking and a central location just off the Royal Mile make this the city's new favourite place to stay.

Art Roch Hostel HOSTEL £
(Map p762; ☎0131-228 9981; www.artrochhostel.com; 2 West Port, Grassmarket; dm from £10; @📶) The new Art Roch Hostel tries to be all things to all people, and pretty much succeeds. There are mixed and female-only dorms, family rooms, an executive floor for business travellers, and a specially equipped room for wheelchair users. There's a very cool common room with loads of sofas, a hammock and pool table, 24-hour reception, and great location close to the castle.

Castle Rock Hostel HOSTEL £
(Map p762; ☎0131-225 9666; www.scotlands-top-hostels.com; 15 Johnston Tce; dm from £13.50, d £40-55; @) Bright, spacious, single-sex dorms, superb views and a great location – the only way to get closer to the castle would be to pitch a tent on the esplanade.

Budget Backpackers HOSTEL £
(Map p762; ☎0131-226 6351; www.budgetbackpackers.com; 39 Cowgate, The Grassmarket; dm from £12.50-16, tw £48; @) This fun spot piles on the extras, with bike storage, pool tables, laundry and a colourful chill-out lounge. Only downside is that prices increase at weekends.

NEW TOWN & AROUND

TOP CHOICE **Six Mary's Place** B&B ££
(☎0131-332 8965; www.sixmarysplace.co.uk; 6 Mary's Pl, Raeburn Pl; s/d/f from £50/94/150; @📶) Six Mary's Place is an attractive Georgian town house with a

designer mix of period features, contemporary furniture and modern colours. Breakfasts are vegetarian-only, served in an attractive conservatory with a view of the garden, while the lounge, with its big, comfy sofas, offers free coffee and newspapers.

Tigerlily BOUTIQUE HOTEL £££
(Map p770; ☎0131-225 5005; www.tigerlilyedinburgh.co.uk; 125 George St; r from £195; 📶) Georgian meets gorgeous at this glamorous, glittering boutique hotel (complete with its own nightclub) decked out in mirror mosaics, beaded curtains, swirling Timorous Beasties textiles and wall coverings, and atmospheric pink uplighting. Book the Georgian Suite (£375) for a truly special romantic getaway.

Dene Guest House B&B ££
(☎0131-556 2700; www.deneguesthouse.com; 7 Eyre Pl; per person £25-50; 👪) The Dene is a friendly and informal place, set in a charming Georgian town house, with a welcoming owner and spacious bedrooms. The inexpensive single rooms make it ideal for solo travellers; children under 10 staying in their parents' room pay half price.

Belford Hostel HOSTEL £
(☎0131-220 2200; www.hoppo.com; 6/8 Douglas Gardens; dm £13-20, d £45-65; @) An unusual hostel housed in a converted church. Although some people complain about noise – there are only thin partitions between dorms, and no ceilings – it's cheerful and well run with good facilities. This hostel is about 20 minutes' walk west of Waverley train station. If you're arriving by train from Glasgow or the north, get off at Haymarket station, which is much closer.

SOUTH EDINBURGH

TOP CHOICE **Southside Guest House** B&B ££
(☎0131-668 4422; www.southsideguesthouse.co.uk; 8 Newington Rd; s/d £70/90; 📶) Though set in a typical Victorian terrace, the Southside transcends the traditional guest-house category and feels more like a modern boutique hotel. Its eight stylish rooms just ooze interior design, standing out from other Newington B&Bs through the clever use of bold colours and modern furniture.

45 Gilmour Rd B&B ££
(☎0131-667 3536; www.edinburghbedbreakfast.com; 45 Gilmour Rd; s/d £60/110) A peaceful setting, large garden and friendly owners contribute to the appeal of this Victorian terraced house, which overlooks the local bowling green. The decor is a blend of 19th- and 20th-century influences, with bold Victorian reds, pine floors and period fireplace in the lounge, a rocking horse and art nouveau lamp in the hallway, and a 1930s vibe in the three spacious bedrooms. Located 1 mile southeast of the city centre.

Aonach Mor Guest House B&B ££
(☎0131-667 8694; www.aonachmor.com; 14 Kilmaurs Tce; r per person £30-70; @📶) This elegant Victorian terraced house is located on a quiet back street and has seven bedrooms, beautifully decorated, with many original period features. Our favourite is the four-poster bedroom with polished mahogany furniture and period fireplace. Located 1 mile southeast of the city centre.

Town House B&B ££
(☎0131-229 1985; www.thetownhouse.com; 65 Gilmore Pl; per person £40-58; P📶) The five-room Town House is a plush little place, offering the sort of quality and comfort you might expect from a much larger and more expensive hotel. It's an elegant Victorian terraced house with big bay windows, spacious bedrooms (all en suite) and a breakfast menu that includes salmon fishcakes and kippers alongside the more usual offerings.

Argyle Backpackers HOSTEL £
(☎0131-667 9991; www.argyle-backpackers.co.uk; 14 Argyle Pl; dm £14-20, d & tw £50-60; 📶) The Argyle, spread across three adjacent terraced houses, is a quiet and relaxed hostel offering double and twin rooms as well as four- to eight-bed dorms (mixed sex). There is a comfortable TV lounge, an attractive little conservatory, and a pleasant walled garden at the back where you can sit outside in summer.

Sherwood Guest House B&B ££
(☎0131-667 1200; www.sherwood-edinburgh.com; 42 Minto St; s £30-60, d £40-75; P📶) One of the most attractive guest houses on Minto St's B&B strip, the Sherwood is a refurbished Georgian terrace house with six en suite rooms.

Menzies Guest House B&B £
(☎0131-229 4629; www.menzies-guesthouse.co.uk; 33 Leamington Tce; s £50, d £45-65) Clean, friendly and well-run place with seven high-ceilinged Victorian rooms spread over three floors.

Robertson Guest House B&B ££
(☎0131-229 2652; www.robertson-guesthouse.com; 5 Hartington Gardens; s/d £65/75;) Homely Victorian house in a quiet back street, range of healthy breakfasts including yogurt, fruit and vegetarian fry-up.

NORTHEAST EDINBURGH

Edinburgh Central Youth Hostel HOSTEL £
(SYHA; ☎0131-524 2090; www.edinburghcentral.org; 9 Haddington Pl, Leith Walk; dm £16-26, s/tw from £34/51; @) This modern, purpose-built hostel, about a half-mile north of Waverley train station, is a big (300 beds), flashy, five-star establishment with its own cafe-bistro as well as self-catering kitchen, smart and comfortable eight-bed dorms and private rooms, and mod cons including keycard entry and plasma-screen TVs.

Millers 64 B&B ££
(☎0131-454 3666; www.millers64.com; 64 Pilrig St; s from £80, d £90-140; P) Luxury textiles, colourful cushions, stylish bathrooms and fresh flowers added to a warm Edinburgh welcome make this Victorian town house a highly desirable address. There are just two bedrooms (and a minimum three-night stay during festival periods) so book well in advance.

Ardmor House B&B ££
(☎0131-554 4944; www.ardmorhouse.com; 74 Pilrig St; s £50-75, d £75-145;) The 'gay-owned, straight-friendly' Ardmor is a stylishly renovated Victorian house with five en-suite bedrooms, and all those little touches that make a place special – an open fire, thick towels, crisp white bed linen and free newspapers at breakfast.

Eating

In the last decade there has been a boom in the number of restaurants in Edinburgh – the city now has more restaurants per head of population than London.

For good-value eats, head for the student-populated areas south of the city centre: Bruntsfield, Marchmont and Newington. Fine dining is concentrated in the New Town, Stockbridge and Leith.

OLD TOWN

TOP CHOICE **Ondine** SEAFOOD £££
(Map p762; ☎0131-226 1888; www.ondinerestaurant.co.uk; 2 George IV Bridge; mains £14-24; ⏲noon-10pm) New on the scene in 2009 (part of the Hotel Missoni), Ondine has rapidly become one of Edinburgh's finest seafood restaurants, with a menu based on sustainably sourced fish. Take an octopus-inspired seat at the curved Crustacean Bar and tuck into lobster thermidor or roast shellfish platter. The two-course lunch (noon to 2.30pm) and pre-theatre (5pm to 6.30pm) menu costs £15.

Mums CAFE £
(Map p762; www.monstermashcafe.co.uk; 4a Forrest Rd; mains £6-8; ⏲8am-10pm Mon-Fri,

TOP THREE LUNCH SPOTS

Many restaurants in Edinburgh offer good-value lunches. Here are a few suggestions from various parts of the city.

» **Urban Angel** (Map p770; ☎0131-225 6215; www.urban-angel.co.uk; 121 Hanover St; mains £8-12; ⏲9am-10pm Mon-Sat, 10am-5pm Sun) A wholesome deli that puts the emphasis on fair-trade, organic and locally sourced produce, Urban Angel also has a delightfully informal cafe-bistro that serves all-day brunch (porridge with honey, French toast, eggs Benedict), tapas, and a wide range of light, snacky meals.

» **La P'tite Folie** (Map p770; ☎0131-225 7983; 61 Frederick St; mains £16-18; ⏲noon-3pm & 6-11pm Mon-Sat, 6-11pm Sun) This is a delightful little restaurant with a Breton owner whose menu includes French classics – onion soup, *moules marinières* – alongside steaks, seafood and a range of *plats du jour*. The two-course lunch is a bargain at £9.

» **Petit Paris** (Map p762; ☎0131-226 2442; www.petitparis-restaurant.co.uk; 38-40 Grassmarket; mains £14-18; ⏲noon-3pm & 5.30-11pm, closed Mon Oct-Mar) Like the name says, this is a little piece of Paris, complete with checked tablecloths, friendly waiters and good-value grub – the *moules-frîtes* (mussels and chips) are excellent. There's a lunch deal offering the *plat du jour* and a coffee for £8; add a starter and it's £11.

9am-10pm Sat, 10am-10pm Sun) After a change of name due to management fall-outs, the original founder of Monster Mash has reopened with a new name. This nostalgia-fuelled cafe continues to serve up classic British comfort food of the 1950s – bangers and mash, shepherd's pie, fish and chips. But there's a twist – the food is all top-quality nosh freshly prepared from local produce, including Crombie's gourmet sausages. And there's even a wine list!

Always Sunday CAFE £
(Map p762; www.alwayssunday.co.uk; 170 High St, Royal Mile; mains £4-8; ⏲8am-6pm Mon-Fri, 9am-6pm Sat & Sun) If the thought of a greasy fry-up is enough to put you off your breakfast, head instead for this bright and breezy cafe that dishes up hearty but healthy grub such as fresh fruit smoothies, crisp salads, homemade soups and speciality sandwiches, washed down with fair-trade coffee or herbal tea.

Café Marlayne FRENCH ££
(Map p762; www.cafemarlayne.com; 7 Old Fishmarket Close, High St; 2-course dinner £15; ⏲lunch & dinner Tue-Sat) This little bistro is a hidden gem, down a steep cobbled alley off the Royal Mile, with a changed-daily menu of market-fresh produce and a lovely little lunchtime sun-trap of an outdoor terrace.

Mosque Kitchen INDIAN £
(Map p762; 50 Potterrow; mains £2-5; ⏲noon-7pm Sat-Thu, noon-1pm & 1.45-7pm Fri) Sophisticated it ain't – expect shared tables and disposable plates – but this is the place to go for cheap, authentic and delicious homemade curries, kebabs, pakora and naan bread washed down with lassi or mango juice. Caters to Edinburgh's Central Mosque, but welcomes all – local students have taken to it big time. No alcohol.

David Bann VEGETARIAN ££
(Map p762; ☎0131-556 5888; www.davidbann.com; 56-58 St Mary's St; mains £9-13; ⏲noon-10pm Mon-Fri, 11am-10pm Sat & Sun) If you want to convince a carnivorous friend that cuisine à la veg can be as tasty and inventive as a meat-muncher's menu, take them to David Bann's stylish restaurant – dishes such as beetroot, apple and Dunsyre blue cheese pudding, and crepe of Thai-spiced broccoli and smoked tofu are guaranteed to win converts.

Amber SCOTTISH ££
(Map p762; ☎0131-477 8477; www.amber-restaurant.co.uk; 354 Castlehill; mains £12-18; ⏲noon-3.45pm daily, 7-9pm Tue-Sat) You've got to love a place where the waiter greets you with the words, 'My name is Craig, and I'll be your whisky adviser for this evening'. Located in the Scotch Whisky Experience, this whisky-themed restaurant manages to avoid the tourist clichés and create genuinely interesting and flavoursome dishes such as fillet of pork with black pudding and whisky and apple compote, or vegetarian haggis with a whisky cream sauce.

NEW TOWN

TOP CHOICE **Oloroso** SCOTTISH £££
(Map p770; ☎0131-226 7614; www.oloroso.co.uk; 33 Castle St; mains £16-25; ⏲restaurant noon-2.30pm & 7-10.30pm, bar 11am-1am) Oloroso is one of Edinburgh's most stylish restaurants, perched on a glass-encased New Town rooftop with views across a Mary Poppins' chimney-scape to the Firth of Forth and Fife hills. Swathed in sophisticated cream linen and charcoal upholstery enlivened with splashes of deep yellow, the dining room serves top-notch Scottish produce with Asian and Mediterranean touches. Two-course lunch £18.50.

Mussel Inn SEAFOOD ££
(Map p770; www.mussel-inn.com; 61-65 Rose St; mains £10-22; ⏲noon-3pm & 5.30-10pm Mon-Thu, noon-10pm Fri-Sun) Owned by west-coast shellfish farmers, the Mussel Inn provides a direct outlet for fresh Scottish seafood. The busy restaurant, decorated with bright beechwood indoors, spills out onto the pavement in summer. A kilogram pot of mussels with a choice of sauces – try leek, Dijon mustard and cream – costs £11.50.

Eteaket CAFE £
(Map p770; www.eteaket.co.uk; 41 Frederick St; mains £4-6; ⏲8am-7pm Mon-Sat, 10am-7pm Sun) A 'tea boutique' serving more than 40 varieties of leaf tea, this cosy cafe also offers a tempting range of breakfasts (bagels, toasted croissants, scrambled eggs) and fresh, wholesome sandwiches (ciabatta with hummus, feta cheese and sunblush tomatoes) and afternoon tea (scones with jam and clotted cream).

Blue Moon Cafe CAFE £
(www.bluemooncafe.co.uk; 1 Barony St; mains £7-8; ⏲10am-10pm) The Blue Moon is the

focus of Broughton St's gay social life, always busy, always friendly, and serving up delicious nachos, salads, sandwiches and baked potatoes. It's famous for its home-made burgers (beef, chicken or falafel), which come with a range of toppings, and delicious daily specials.

LEITH

TOP CHOICE Fishers Bistro SEAFOOD ££
(Map p773; ☎0131-554 5666; www.fishersbistros.co.uk; 1 The Shore; mains £10-35; ⏰noon-10.30pm) This cosy little restaurant, tucked beneath a 17th-century signal tower, is one of the city's best seafood places. The menu ranges widely in price, from cheaper dishes such as mackerel with beetroot, chilli and orange dressing, to more expensive delights such as North Berwick lobster served with garlic and herb butter.

Chop Chop CHINESE £
(Map p773; ☎0131-553 1818; 76 Commercial St; mains £7-10; ⏰noon-2pm & 5.30-10pm Mon & Wed-Sat, noon-10pm Sun) Chop Chop is a Chinese restaurant with a difference, in that is serves dishes popular in China rather than Britain; as their slogan says, 'Can a billion people be wrong?' No sweet and sour pork here, but a range of delicious dumplings filled with pork and coriander, beef and chilli, or lamb and leek, and unusual vegetarian dishes such as aubergine fried with garlic and Chinese spices.

Drinking

Edinburgh has more than 700 bars, which are as varied as the population – everything from Victorian palaces to rough-and-ready drinking dens, and from bearded, real-ale howffs (pubs) to trendy cocktail bars.

OLD TOWN

Bow Bar PUB
(Map p762; 80 West Bow) One of the city's best traditional-style pubs (it's not as old as it looks) serving a range of excellent real ales and a vast selection of malt whiskies, the Bow Bar often has standing room only on Friday and Saturday evenings.

Jolly Judge PUB
(Map p762; www.jollyjudge.co.uk; 7a James Crt; 📶) A snug little howff tucked away down a close, the Judge exudes a cosy 17th-century atmosphere (low, timber-beamed painted ceilings) and has the added attraction of a cheering open fire in cold weather. No music or gaming machines, just the buzz of conversation.

Ecco Vino WINE BAR
(Map p762; www.eccovinoedinburgh.com; 19 Cockburn St) With outdoor tables on sunny afternoons, and cosy candle-lit intimacy in the evenings, this comfortably cramped Tuscan-style wine bar offers a tempting range of Italian wines, though not all are available by the glass – best to share a bottle.

Beehive Inn PUB
(Map p762; 18-20 Grassmarket) The historic Beehive – a former coaching inn – is a big, buzzing party-pub, with a range of real ales, but the main attraction is sitting out the back in the Grassmarket's only beer garden, with views up to the castle.

Pear Tree House PUB
(Map p762; 38 West Nicolson St) The Pear Tree is another student favourite, with comfy sofas and board games inside, plus the city's biggest and most popular beer garden in summer.

NEW TOWN

Oxford Bar PUB
(Map p770; www.oxfordbar.com; 8 Young St) The Oxford is that rarest of things these days, a real pub for real people, with no 'theme', no music, no frills and no pretensions. 'The Ox' has been immortalised by Ian Rankin, author of the Inspector Rebus novels, who is a regular here, as is his fictional detective.

Cumberland Bar PUB
(www.cumberlandbar.co.uk; 1-3 Cumberland St) Immortalised as the stereotypical New Town pub in Alexander McCall-Smith's serialised novel *44 Scotland Street,* the Cumberland has an authentic, traditional wood-brass-and-mirrors look (despite being relatively new), and serves well-looked-after, cask-conditioned ales and a wide range of malt whiskies. There's also a pleasant little beer garden outside.

Guildford Arms PUB
(Map p770; www.guildfordarms.com; 1 West Register St) Located next door to the Cafe Royal Circle Bar, the Guildford is another classic Victorian pub full of polished mahogany, brass and ornate cornices. The bar lunches are good – try to get a table in the unusual upstairs gallery, with a view over the sea of drinkers down below.

TOP FIVE TRADITIONAL PUBS

Edinburgh is blessed with a large number of traditional 19th- and early-20th-century pubs, which have preserved much of their original Victorian or Edwardian decoration and serve cask- conditioned real ales and a staggering range of malt whiskies.

» **Athletic Arms** (Diggers; 1-3 Angle Park Tce) Named after the cemetery across the street – the grave-diggers used to nip in and slake their thirst after a hard day's interring – the Diggers dates from the 1890s. It's still staunchly traditional – the decor has barely changed in 100 years – and has recently revived its reputation as a real-ale drinker's mecca by serving locally brewed Diggers' 80-shilling ale. Packed to the gills with football and rugby fans on match days.

» **Abbotsford** (Map p770; www.theabbotsford.com; 3 Rose St) One of the few pubs in Rose St that has retained its Edwardian splendour, the Abbotsford has long been a hang-out for writers, actors, journalists and media people, and has many loyal regulars. Dating from 1902, and named after Sir Walter Scott's country house, the pub's centrepiece is a splendid, mahogany island bar. Good selection of Scottish and English real ales.

» **Bennet's Bar** (8 Leven St) Situated beside the King's Theatre, Bennet's has managed to hang on to almost all of its beautiful Victorian fittings, from the leaded, stained-glass windows and ornate mirrors to the wooden gantry and the brass water taps on the bar (for your whisky – there are over 100 malts to choose from).

» **Cafe Royal Circle Bar** (Map p770; www.caferoyal.org.uk; 17 West Register St) Perhaps the classic Edinburgh bar, the Cafe Royal's main claims to fame are its magnificent oval bar and the series of Doulton tile portraits of famous Victorian inventors. Check out the bottles on the gantry – staff line them up to look like there's a mirror there, and many a drink-befuddled customer has been seen squinting and wondering why he can't see his reflection.

» **Sheep Heid** (www.sheepheid.co.uk; 43-45 The Causeway, Duddingston) Possibly the oldest inn in Edinburgh – with a licence dating back to 1360 – the Sheep Heid feels more like a country pub than an Edinburgh bar. Set in the semi-rural shadow of Arthur's Seat, it's famous for its 19th-century skittles alley and the lovely little beer garden.

Amicus Apple COCKTAIL BAR
(Map p770; www.amicusapple.com; 15 Frederick St) This laid-back cocktail lounge is the hippest hang-out in the New Town. The drinks menu ranges from retro classics such as Bloody Mary and mojito, to original and unusual concoctions such as the Cuillin Martini (Tanqueray No 10 gin, Talisker malt whisky and smoked rosemary).

LEITH

Teuchter's Landing PUB
(Map p773; 1 Dock Pl) A cosy warren of timber-lined nooks and crannies housed in a single-storey red-brick building (once a waiting room for ferries across the Firth of Forth), this real ale and malt whisky bar also has outdoor tables on a floating terrace in the dock.

Port O'Leith PUB
(Map p773; 58 Constitution St) This is a good, old-fashioned, friendly local boozer, swathed with flags and cap bands left behind by visiting sailors – the harbour is just down the road. Pop in for a pint and you'll probably stay until closing time.

☆ Entertainment

The comprehensive source for what's-on info is *The List* (www.list.co.uk), an excellent listings magazine covering both Edinburgh and Glasgow. It's available from most newsagents, and is published fortnightly on a Thursday.

Live Music

Henry's Cellar ROCK/INDIE
(www.theraft.org.uk; 8a Morrison St) One of Edinburgh's most eclectic live-music venues, Henry's has something going on every

night of the week, from rock and indie to 'Balkan-inspired folk', funk to hip-hop to hardcore, staging both local bands and acts from around the world. Open till 3am at weekends.

Whistle Binkie's ROCK/BLUES
(Map p762; www.whistlebinkies.com; 4-6 South Bridge) This crowded cellar-bar just off the Royal Mile has live music every night till 3am, from rock and blues to folk and jazz. Open mic night on Monday and breaking bands on Tuesday are showcases for new talent.

Jazz Bar JAZZ
(Map p762; www.thejazzbar.co.uk; 1a Chambers St; 🛜) This atmospheric cellar bar, with its polished parquet floors, bare stone walls, candle-lit tables and stylish steel-framed chairs is owned and operated by jazz musicians. There's live music every night from 9pm to 3am, and on Saturday from 3pm.

Sandy Bell's FOLK
(Map p762; 25 Forrest Rd) This unassuming bar has been a stalwart of the traditional-music scene since the Corrs were in nappies. There's music almost every evening at 9pm, and also from 3pm Saturday and Sunday.

Royal Oak FOLK
(Map p762; www.royal-oak-folk.com; 1 Infirmary St) This popular folk pub is tiny, so get there early (9pm start weekdays, 2.30pm Saturday) if you want to be sure of a place. Sundays from 4pm to 7pm is open-session – bring your own instruments (or a good singing voice).

Nightclubs

Bongo Club MULTI-ARTS VENUE
(www.thebongoclub.co.uk; Moray House, Paterson's Land, 37 Holyrood Rd) The weird and wonderful Bongo Club is home to Big N Bashy, a Saturday night club dedicated to reggae, grime, dubstep and jungle. Also worth checking out is the booming bass of roots and dub reggae night Messenger Sound System (boasting 'a sound system that could knock you out'). The club is open as a cafe and exhibition space during the day.

Cabaret Voltaire CLUB/LIVE MUSIC
(Map p762; www.thecabaretvoltaire.com; 36 Blair St) An atmospheric warren of stone-lined vaults houses Edinburgh's most 'alternative' club, which eschews huge dance floors and egotistical DJ-worship in favour of a 'creative crucible' hosting an eclectic mix of DJs, live acts, comedy, theatre, visual arts and the spoken word. Well worth a look.

Liquid Room CLUB/LIVE MUSIC
(Map p762; www.liquidroom.com; 9c Victoria St) Set in a subterranean vault deep beneath Victoria St, the Liquid Room is a superb club venue with a thundering sound system. There are regular club nights Wednesday to Saturday as well as live bands. The long-running and recently relaunched Evol (Friday from 10.30pm) is an Edinburgh institution catering to the indie-kid crowd, and is regularly voted as Scotland's top club night out.

Studio 24 CLUB
(24 Calton Rd) Studio 24 is the dark heart of Edinburgh's underground music scene, with a program that covers all bases, from house to nu metal via punk, ska, reggae, crossover, tribal, electro, techno and dance. Mission (Saturday from 11pm) is the city's classic hard rock, metal and alt night.

Cinemas

Cameo CINEMA
(www.picturehouses.co.uk; 38 Home St) An imaginative mix of mainstream and art-house movies.

Filmhouse CINEMA
(Map p762; www.filmhousecinema.com; 88 Lothian Rd; 🛜) Main venue for the annual Edinburgh International Film Festival; screens a full program of art-house, classic, foreign and second-run films.

Classical Music, Opera & Ballet

Edinburgh Festival Theatre BALLET/OPERA
(Map p762; www.eft.co.uk; 13-29 Nicolson St; ⏲box office 10am-6pm Mon-Sat, to 8pm show nights, 4pm-showtime Sun) The city's main venue for opera, dance and ballet; also stages musicals, concerts, drama and children's shows.

Usher Hall CLASSICAL MUSIC
(Map p762; www.usherhall.co.uk; Lothian Rd; ⏲box office 10.30am-5.30pm, to 8pm show nights) Hosts concerts by the Royal Scottish National Orchestra (RSNO) and performances of popular music.

Sport

Edinburgh is home to two rival **football** teams playing in the Scottish Premier League. **Heart of Midlothian** (aka Hearts) has its home ground at **Tynecastle Stadium** (www.heartsfc.co.uk; Gorgie Rd), while the **Hibernian** (aka Hibs) home ground is at **Easter Road Stadium** (www.hibs.co.uk; 12 Albion Pl).

Each year, from January to March, Scotland's national **rugby** team takes part in the Six Nations Rugby Union Championship. **Murrayfield Stadium** (www.scottishrugby.org; 112 Roseburn St), about 1.5 miles west of the city centre, is the venue for international matches.

Theatre, Musicals & Comedy

Royal Lyceum Theatre DRAMA/MUSICALS
(Map p762; www.lyceum.org.uk; 30b Grindlay St; box office 10am-6pm Mon-Sat, to 8pm show nights) Stages drama, concerts, musicals and ballet.

Traverse Theatre DRAMA/DANCE
(Map p762; www.traverse.co.uk; 10 Cambridge St; box office 10am-6pm Mon-Sat, till 8pm on show nights) Main focus is new Scottish writing; stages an adventurous program of contemporary drama and dance.

King's Theatre DRAMA/MUSICALS
(www.eft.co.uk; 2 Leven St, Bruntsfield; box office open 1hr before show) A traditional theatre with a program of musicals, drama, comedy and its famous Christmas pantomime.

Stand Comedy Club COMEDY
(Map p770; www.thestand.co.uk; 5 York Pl) Edinburgh's main comedy venue, with performances every night and a free Sunday lunchtime show.

Shopping

Princes St is Edinburgh's principal shopping street, lined with all the big high-street stores, with many smaller shops along pedestrianised Rose St, and more expensive designer boutiques on George St. There are also two big shopping centres in the New Town – **Princes Mall**, at the eastern end of Princes St, and the nearby **St James Shopping Centre** at the top of Leith St, plus a designer shopping complex with a flagship **Harvey Nichols** store on the eastern side of St Andrew Sq. The huge **Ocean Terminal** in Leith is the biggest shopping centre in the city.

For more off-beat shopping – including fashion, music, crafts, gifts and jewellery – head for the cobbled lanes of Cockburn, Victoria and St Mary's Sts, all near the Royal Mile in the Old Town; William St in the western part of New Town; and the Stockbridge district, immediately north of the New Town.

Information

Emergency

In an emergency, dial 999 or 112 (free from public phones) and ask for police, ambulance, fire brigade or coastguard.

Edinburgh Rape Crisis Centre (08088 01 03 02; www.rapecrisisscotland.org.uk)

Lothian & Borders Police HQ (0131-311 3131; www.lbp.police.uk; Fettes Ave)

Lothian & Borders Police Information Centre (0131-226 6966; 188 High St; 10am-7.30pm Mar-Oct, 10am-6pm Nov-Feb) Report a crime or make lost property enquiries here.

Internet Access

There are several internet-enabled telephone boxes (10p a minute, 50p minimum) scattered around the city centre, and countless wi-fi hot spots – search on www.jiwire.com. Internet cafes are spread around the city. Some convenient ones:

easyInternetcafe (www.easy-everything.com; 58 Rose St; 7.30am-10.30pm)

e-corner (www.e-corner.co.uk; 54 Blackfriars St; per 20min £1; 7.30am-9pm Mon-Fri, 8am-9pm Sat & Sun)

G-Tec (www.grassmarket-technologies.com; 67 Grassmarket; per 20min £1; 10am-6pm Mon-Fri, 10am-5.30pm Sat)

Internet Resources

Edinburgh Architecture (www.edinburgh architecture.co.uk) Informative site dedicated to the city's modern architecture.

Edinburgh & Lothians Tourist Board (www.edinburgh.org) Official tourist-board site, with listings of accommodation, sights, activities and events.

Edinburgh Festival Guide (www.edinburgh festivals.co.uk) Everything you need to know about Edinburgh's many festivals.

Events Edinburgh (www.eventsedinburgh.org.uk) The city council's official events guide.

The List (www.list.co.uk) Listings of restaurants, pubs, clubs and nightlife.

Left Luggage

Edinburgh airport left-luggage office (per

item per 24hr £5; ⊙5.15am-10.45pm) On the ground floor in the UK arrivals area.

Edinburgh bus station (Map p770; small/medium/large locker per 24hr £3/4/5; ⊙6am-midnight)

Waverley train station left-luggage office (Map p770; per item per 24hr £6; ⊙7am-11pm) Beside platform 1.

Medical Services

For urgent medical advice you can call the **NHS 24 Helpline** (☎08454 24 24 24; www.nhs24.com). Chemists (pharmacists) can advise you on minor ailments. At least one local chemist remains open round the clock – its location will be displayed in the windows of other chemists.

For urgent dental treatment you can visit the walk-in **Chalmers Dental Centre** (3 Chalmers St; ⊙9am-4.45pm Mon-Thu, 9am-4.15pm Fri). In the case of a dental emergency in the evenings or at weekends, call **Lothian Dental Advice Line** (☎0131-536 4800).

Royal Infirmary of Edinburgh (☎0131-536 1000; www.nhslothian.scot.nhs.uk; 51 Little France Cres, Old Dalkeith Rd) Edinburgh's main general hospital; has 24-hour accident and emergency department.

Post

Main post office (Map p770; St James Centre, Leith St; ⊙8.30am-5.30pm Mon-Fri, to 6pm Sat) Hidden away inside shopping centre.

Tourist Information

Edinburgh & Scotland Information Centre (ESIC; Map p770; ☎0845 225 5121; www.edinburgh.org; Princes Mall, 3 Princes St; ⊙9am-9pm Mon-Sat, 10am-8pm Sun Jul & Aug, 9am-7pm Mon-Sat, 10am-7pm Sun May, Jun & Sep, 9am-5pm Mon-Wed, 9am-6pm Thu-Sun Oct-Apr) Includes an accommodation booking service, currency exchange, gift and bookshop, internet access, and counters selling tickets for Edinburgh city tours and Scottish Citylink bus services.

Old Craighall tourist office (☎0131-653 6172; Old Craighall Junction, A1) In a service area on the main A1 road, about 5 miles east of the city centre.

Tourist & Airport Information Desk (☎0845 225 5121) At Edinburgh airport.

 Getting There & Away

Air

Edinburgh Airport (☎0131-333 1000; www.edinburghairport.com), 8 miles west of the city, has numerous flights to other parts of Scotland and the UK, Ireland and mainland Europe. **Fly-Be/Loganair** (☎0871 700 2000; www.loganair.co.uk) operates daily flights to Inverness, Wick, Orkney, Shetland and Stornoway.

Bus

Edinburgh Bus Station (Map p770) is at the northeast corner of St Andrew Sq, with pedestrian entrances from the square and from Elder St. For timetable information, call **Traveline** (☎0871 200 22 33; www.travelinescotland.com).

Scottish Citylink (☎0871 266 3333; www.citylink.co.uk) buses connect Edinburgh with all of Scotland's cities and major towns. The following are sample one-way fares departing from Edinburgh.

DESTINATION	FARE (£)	DURATION (HR)	FREQUENCY
Aberdeen	26	3¼	3 daily
Dundee	14	2	hourly
Fort William	30	4-5	8 daily
Glasgow	6	1¼	every 15min
Inverness	26	4	hourly
Portree	46	7	1 daily
Stirling	7	1	hourly

It's also worth checking with **Megabus** (☎0900 160 0900; www.megabus.com) for cheap intercity bus fares (from as little as £3) from Edinburgh to Aberdeen, Dundee, Glasgow, Inverness and Perth.

Train

The main terminus in Edinburgh is Waverley train station (Map p770), located in the heart of the city. Trains arriving from, and departing for, the west also stop at Haymarket station, which is more convenient for the West End.

You can buy tickets, make reservations and get travel information at the **Edinburgh Rail Travel Centre** (⊙4.45am-12.30am Mon-Sat, 7am-12.30am Sun) in Waverley station. For fare and timetable information, phone the **National Rail Enquiry Service** (☎08457 48 49 50; www.nationalrail.co.uk) or use the Journey Planner on the website.

First ScotRail operates a regular shuttle service between Edinburgh and Glasgow (£11, 50 minutes, every 15 minutes), and frequent daily services to all Scottish cities including Aberdeen (£40, 2½ hours), Dundee (£20, 1¼ hours) and Inverness (£55, 3¼ hours).

 Getting Around

To/From the Airport

The Lothian Buses **Airlink** (www.flybybus.com) service 100 runs from Waverley Bridge, outside the train station, to the airport (£3/6 one way/

return, 30 minutes, every 10 to 15 minutes) via the West End and Haymarket.

An airport taxi to the city centre costs around £16 and takes about 20 minutes. Both buses and taxis depart from outside the arrivals hall; go out through the main doors and turn left.

Car & Motorcycle

Though useful for day trips beyond the city, a car in central Edinburgh is more of a liability than a convenience. There is restricted access on Princes St, George St and Charlotte Sq, many streets are one way and finding a parking place in the city centre is like striking gold. Queen's Dr around Holyrood Park is closed to motorised traffic on Sunday.

CAR RENTAL

All the big, international car-rental agencies have offices in Edinburgh.

There are many smaller, local agencies that offer better rates. One of the best is **Arnold Clark** (☎0131-657 9120; www.arnoldclarkrental.co.uk; 20 Seafield Rd East) near Portbello, which charges from £26 a day, or £128 a week for a small car, including VAT and insurance.

Public Transport

For the moment, Edinburgh's public transport system consists entirely of buses (a tram network is under construction, due to come into operation in 2012). The main operators are **Lothian Buses** (www.lothianbuses.co.uk) and **First** (www.firstedinburgh.co.uk); for timetable information contact **Traveline** (☎0871 200 22 33; www.travelinescotland.com).

Adult **fares** are £1.20 from the driver or £1.10 from automatic ticket machines at bus stops; children aged under five travel free and those aged five to 15 pay a flat fare of 70p. On Lothian Buses you must pay the driver the exact fare, but First buses will give change. Lothian Bus drivers also sell a Daysaver ticket (£3) that gives unlimited travel (on Lothian Buses only, excluding night buses) for a day. **Night-service buses** (www.nightbuses.com), which run hourly between midnight and 5am, charge a flat fare of £3.

Taxi

Central Taxis (☎0131-229 2468)

City Cabs (☎0131-228 1211)

ComCab (☎0131-272 8000)

AROUND EDINBURGH

Queensferry

Queensferry is at the narrowest part of the Firth of Forth, where ferries have sailed to Fife from the earliest times. The village takes its name from Queen Margaret (1046–93), who gave pilgrims free passage across the firth on their way to St Andrews. Ferries continued to operate until 1964 when the graceful **Forth Road Bridge** – now Europe's fifth longest – was opened.

Predating the road bridge by 74 years, the magnificent **Forth Bridge** – only outsiders ever call it the Forth Rail Bridge – is one of the finest engineering achievements of the 19th century. Completed in 1890 after seven years' work, its three huge cantilevers span 1447m and took 59,000 tonnes of steel, eight million rivets and the lives of 58 men to build.

Queensferry Museum — MUSEUM

(53 High St; admission free; ⏲10am-1pm & 2.15-5pm Mon & Thu-Sat, noon-5pm Sun) In the pretty, terraced High St in Queensferry is this small museum, which contains some interesting background information on the bridges, and a fascinating exhibit on the 'Burry Man', part of the village's summer gala festivities.

Inchcolm — ISLAND

Known as the 'Iona of the East', the island of Inchcolm (meaning 'St Columba's Island') lies east of the Forth bridges, less than a mile off the coast of Fife. Only 800m long, it is home to the ruins of **Inchcolm Abbey** (HS; Inchcolm, Fife; adult/child £4.70/2.80; ⏲9.30am-5.30pm Apr-Sep, 9.30am-4.30pm Oct), one of Scotland's best-preserved medieval abbeys, founded by Augustinian priors in 1123.

The ferry boat **Maid of the Forth** (www.maidoftheforth.co.uk) sails to Inchcolm from Hawes Pier in Queensferry. There are one to four sailings most days from May to October. The return fare is £14.70/5.85 per adult/child, including admission to Inchcolm Abbey. It's a half-hour sail to Inchcolm and you get 1½ hours ashore. As well as the abbey, the trip gives you the chance to see the island's grey seals, puffins and other seabirds.

Hopetoun House — STATELY HOME

(www.hopetoun.co.uk; adult/child £8/4.25; ⏲10.30am-5pm Easter-Sep, last admission 4pm) Hopetoun is one of Scotland's finest stately homes, with a superb location in lovely grounds beside the Firth of Forth. There are two parts – the older built to Sir William Bruce's plans between 1699 and 1702 and dominated by a splendid stairwell with (modern) trompe l'oeil paintings; and the newer designed between 1720 and 1750 by three members of the Adam family, William and sons Robert and John. The highlights are the red and yellow **Adam drawing rooms**, lined in silk damask, and the view from the roof terrace.

Hopetoun House is 2 miles west of Queensferry along the coast road.

Getting There & Away

Queensferry lies on the southern bank of the Firth of Forth, 8 miles west of Edinburgh city centre. To get there, take **First bus** 43 (£3, 30 minutes, three hourly) westbound from St Andrew Sq. It's a 10-minute walk from the bus stop to the Hawes Inn and the Inchcolm ferry.

Trains go from Edinburgh's Waverley and Haymarket stations to Dalmeny station (£3.60, 15 minutes, two to four hourly). From the station exit, the Hawes Inn is five minutes' walk along a footpath (across the road, behind the bus stop) that leads north beside the railway and then downhill under the bridge.

Rosslyn Chapel

The success of Dan Brown's novel *The Da Vinci Code* and the subsequent Hollywood film has seen a flood of visitors descend on Scotland's most beautiful and enigmatic church – **Rosslyn Chapel** (Collegiate Church of St Matthew; www.rosslynchapel.com; Roslin; adult/child £7.50/free; 9.30am-6pm Mon-Sat, noon-4.45pm Sun Apr-Sep, 9.30am-5pm Mon-Sat, noon-4.45pm Sun Oct-Mar). The chapel was built in the mid-15th century for William St Clair, third earl of Orkney, and the ornately carved interior – at odds with the architectural fashion of its time – is a monument to the mason's art, rich in symbolic imagery. As well as flowers, vines, angels and biblical figures, the carved stones include many examples of the pagan 'Green Man'; other figures are associated with Freemasonry and the Knights Templar. Intriguingly, there are also carvings of plants from the Americas that predate Columbus' voyage of discovery. The symbolism of these images has led some researchers to conclude that Rosslyn is some kind of secret Templar repository, and it has been claimed that hidden vaults beneath the chapel could conceal anything from the Holy Grail or the head of John the Baptist to the body of Christ himself. The chapel is owned by the Episcopal Church of Scotland and services are still held here on Sunday mornings.

The chapel is on the eastern edge of the village of Roslin, 7 miles south of Edinburgh's centre. Lothian Bus 15 (not 15A) runs from the west end of Princes St in Edinburgh to Roslin (£1.20, 30 minutes, every 30 minutes).

A refreshing alternative to the mainstream tours is offered by **Celtic Trails** (www.celtictrails.co.uk) whose knowledgeable owner Jackie Queally leads guided tours of Rosslyn Chapel and other ancient and sacred sites covering subjects such as Celtic mythology, geomancy, sacred geometry and the Knights Templar. Half-/whole-day tours of the chapel and surrounding area are £33/60 per person, not including admission fees.

Glasgow & Southern Scotland

Includes »

GLASGOW 792
Sights 793
Activities. 798
Tours 799
Festivals & Events. . . . 799
Sleeping 799
Eating 803
Drinking 805
Entertainment. 806
Shopping 807
Lanark & New Lanark. 809
BORDERS REGION . . 810
AYRSHIRE & ARRAN. 816
Isle of Arran 817
South Ayrshire. 820
DUMFRIES & GALLOWAY 822

Best Places to Eat

» Café Gandolfi (p803)

» Left Bank (p804)

» Ubiquitous Chip (p804)

» Stravaigin (p804)

» Cobbles Inn (p811)

Best Places to Stay

» Brunswick Hotel (p801)

» Malmaison (p801)

» Corsewall Lighthouse Hotel (p827)

» Kildonan Hotel (p819)

» Lochranza SYHA (p819)

Why Go?

For many southern Scotland is what you drive through on the way to big cities Glasgow or Edinburgh, or even points further north. Big mistake – but it means plenty of peaceful corners here. The South's proximity to England brought strife, but the ruins of Borders castles and the abbeys they protected make wonderfully atmospheric historic sites. The hillier west enjoys extensive forest cover; hills cascade down to sandy coasts blessed with Scotland's sunniest weather. Visible offshore, Arran is an island jewel offering top cycling and walking.

The region's premier attraction, however, is urban. Glasgow is a fascinatingly vital place. Victorian buildings house top-notch restaurants to tickle your taste buds, as well as a hedonistic club culture – Glasgow's pounding live-music scene is one of the best in Britain. Yet nightlife is only the beginning: top-drawer museums and galleries abound; Charles Rennie Mackintosh's sublime works dot the town; and the River Clyde, traditionally associated with Glasgow's earthier side, is now a symbol of the city's renaissance.

When to Go?

June sees music festivals in Glasgow, and spectacular gardens in bloom at the region's numerous castles and stately homes. Glasgow is super-friendly at any time, but in the August sunshine there's no happier city in Britain. In autumn, hit Galloway's forests to see red deer, high on stag testosterone, battle it out in the rutting season.

Glasgow & Southern Scotland Highlights

1 Gazing at the Glasgow Boys' paintings in the **Burrell Collection** (p798), the **Kelvingrove Art Gallery & Museum** (p797) and the **Hunterian Art Gallery** (p797)

2 Catching a match in one of Celtic or Rangers' massive cauldrons of **football** (p807)

3 Showing your latest dance moves among Glasgow's plethora of **nightclubs** (p806)

4 Deciding just which one of the West End's excellent **restaurants** (p804) you are going to dine at next

5 Discovering the work of **Charles Rennie Mackintosh** (p798) – genius is an overused

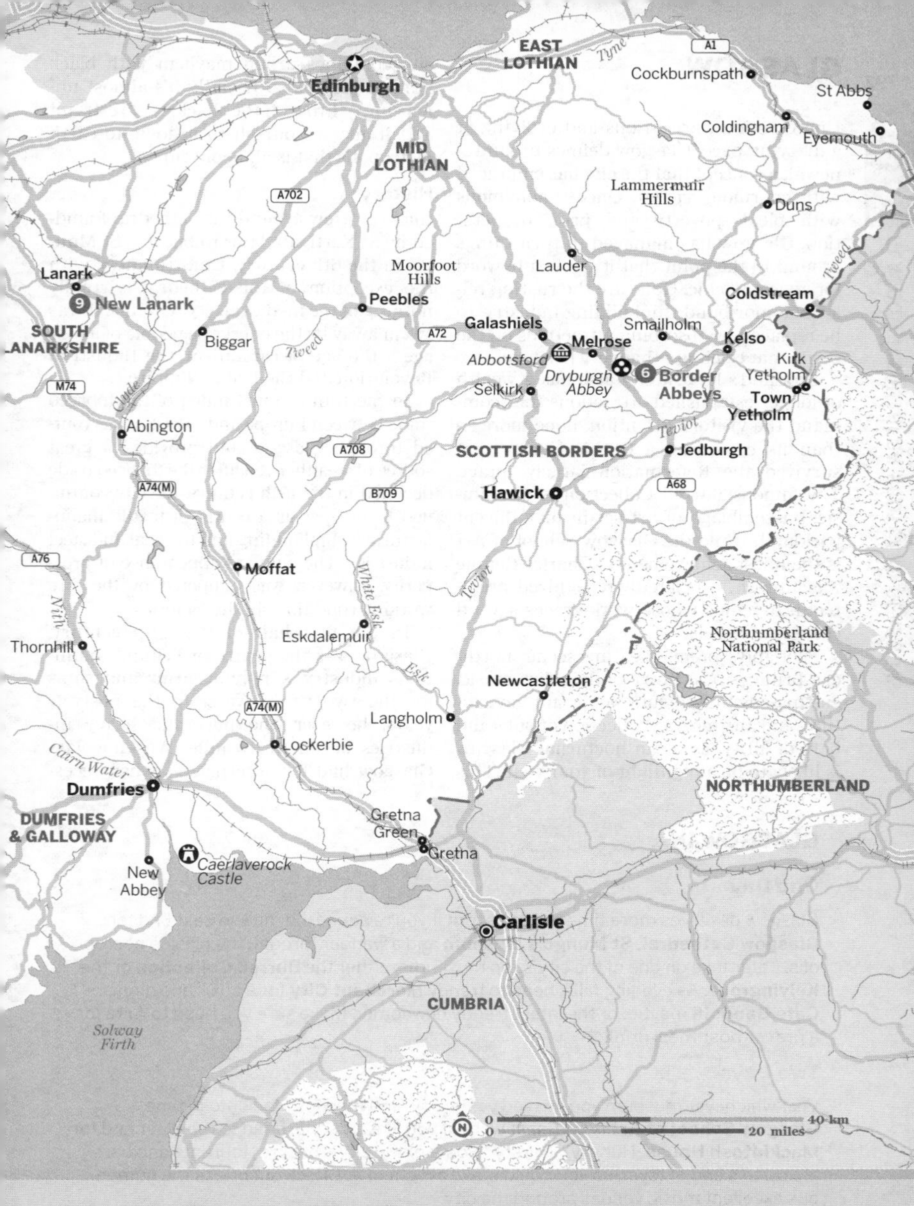

word, but few would argue here

6 Hiking or cycling between the noble ruins of the **Border Abbeys** (p810)

7 Learning some Lallans words from the Scottish Bard's verses at the new **Robert Burns Birthplace Museum** (p821)

8 Whooshing down forest trails at the **7stanes mountain-biking hubs** (p826)

9 Marvelling at the radical social reform instituted in the mill community of **New Lanark** (p809)

10 Blowing away the cobwebs on scenic, activity-packed **Isle of Arran** (p817)

GLASGOW

POP 634,680

Unpretentious, gregarious and evolving at a dizzying pace, Glasgow defines urban renewal, a concept that the city has embraced with enormous vigour. Once synonymous with bleak poverty and grim desperation, Glasgow has managed to turn things around to the point that it's now a byword for style and chic. Gone are the rusting relics of a moribund shipbuilding industry, to be replaced by absorbing attractions on the Clyde that celebrate that very heritage.

Scotland's largest city also has a wealth of longer-established attractions that command the visitor's attention, none more so than its cathedral, a Gothic beauty that survived the Reformation largely intact. The famous Burrell Collection is a whimsical assemblage of art set in magnificent parkland, while the Glasgow School of Art is the finest achievement of Charles Rennie Mackintosh, a belatedly-recognized architectural genius whose work graces several corners of the city.

Scotland's premier eating scene, northern Britain's best range of daily live music, cutting-edge nightclubs, a vibrant gay culture, and an amazing collection of pubs and bars of all types mean nocturnal Glasgow is likely to be a highlight of your visit. This city combines urban mayhem with black humour, and is so friendly it's almost unnerving – throw off the shackles of restraint and immerse yourself in a down-to-earth metropolis that is all about fun.

History

Glasgow grew around the cathedral founded by St Kertigan, later to become St Mungo, in the 6th century. Unfortunately, with the exception of the cathedral, virtually nothing of the medieval city remains. It was swept away by the energetic people of a new age – the age of capitalism, the Industrial Revolution and the British Empire.

In the 18th century, much of the tobacco trade between Europe and the USA was routed through Glasgow and provided a great source of wealth. Even after the tobacco trade declined in the 19th century, the city continued to prosper as a centre of textile manufacturing, shipbuilding and the coal and steel industries. The outward appearance of prosperity, however, was tempered by the dire working conditions in the factories.

In the first half of the 20th century, Glasgow was the centre of Britain's munitions industry, supplying arms and ships for the two world wars. In the postwar years, however, the port and heavy industries began to dwindle. Working-class Glasgow had few alternatives when reces-

GLASGOW IN...

One Day

Glasgow deserves more time than this, but if you're squeezed, hit the East End for **Glasgow Cathedral**, **St Mungo's Museum** and a wander through the hillside necropolis. Later take on one of the city's top museums: either the **Burrell Collection** or the **Kelvingrove**. As evening falls, head to trendy **Merchant City** for a stroll and dinner – **Café Gandolfi** maybe, or the latest trendy newcomer. Make sure you head to **Artá** for a pre- or post-meal drink.

Two Days

Visit whichever museum you missed yesterday, and then it's Mackintosh time. **Glasgow School of Art** is his finest work: if you like his style, head to the West End for **Mackintosh House**. Hungry? Thirsty? Some of the city's best restaurants and bars are up this end of town, so you could make a night of it. Check out one of the numerous excellent music venues around the city.

Five Days

Better. Much better. Spend a day along the Clyde – explore the new **Riverside Museum** and the **Science Centre**. Plan your weekend around a night out at **Arches** or the legendary **Sub Club**, a day at the boutiques of the **Italian Centre**, earthier shopping at the **Barras flea market** and a football game. Don't miss trying at least one of the city's curry classics.

sion hit and the city became synonymous with unemployment, economic depression and urban violence. More recently, urban development and a booming cultural sector have injected style and confidence into the city; though the standard of living remains low for Britain and life continues to be tough for many, the ongoing regeneration process gives grounds for optimism.

Sights

CITY CENTRE

Glasgow School of Art MACKINTOSH BUILDING
(Map p794; ☎0141-353 4526; www.gsa.ac.uk/tours; 167 Renfrew St; adult/child £8.75/7; ⏲9.30am-6.30pm Apr-Sep, 10am-5pm Oct-Mar) Mackintosh's greatest building, the Glasgow School of Art, still fulfils its original function, so just follow the steady stream of eclectically dressed students up the hill to find it. It's hard not to be impressed by the thoroughness of the design; the architect's pencil seems to have shaped everything inside and outside the building. The visitor entrance is at the side of the building on Dalhousie St; here you'll find a shop with a small but useful interpretative display. Excellent hour-long guided tours (roughly hourly summer, 11am and 3pm winter) run by architecture students leave from here; this is the only way (apart from enrolling) you can visit the building's interior. They're worth booking by phone at busy times.

FREE **Gallery of Modern Art** GALLERY
(Map p794; www.glasgowmuseums.com; Royal Exchange Sq; ⏲10am-5pm Mon-Wed & Sat, to 8pm Thu, 11am-5pm Fri & Sun; wi-fi) Scotland's most popular contemporary art gallery features modern works from artists worldwide in a graceful neoclassical building. The original interior is used to make a daring, inventive art display. Social issues are a focal point of the museum but it's not all heavy going: there's a big effort made to keep the kids entertained.

FREE **Willow Tearooms** MACKINTOSH BUILDING
(Map p794; www.willowtearooms.co.uk; 217 Sauchiehall St; ⏲9am-5pm Mon-Sat, 11am-5pm Sun) Admirers of the great Mackintosh will love the this authentic reconstruction of tearooms Mackintosh designed and furnished in the early 20th century for restaurateur Kate Cranston. Relive the original splendour of this unique tearoom and admire the architect's stroke in just about everything. He had a free rein and even the teaspoons were given his distinctive touch.

EAST END

The oldest part of the city, given a facelift in the 1990s, is concentrated around Glasgow Cathedral, to the east of the modern centre. It takes 15 to 20 minutes to walk from George Sq, but numerous buses pass nearby, including buses 11, 12, 36, 37, 38 and 42.

FREE **Glasgow Cathedral** CHURCH
(HS; Map p794; www.historic-scotland.gov.uk; Cathedral Sq; ⏲9.30am-5.30pm Mon-Sat, 1-5pm Sun Apr-Sep, 9.30am-4.30pm Mon-Sat, 1-4.30pm Sun Oct-Mar) An attraction that shouldn't be missed, Glasgow Cathedral has a rare timelessness. The dark, imposing interior conjures up medieval might and can send a shiver down the spine. It's a shining example of Gothic architecture, and the only mainland Scottish cathedral to have survived the Reformation. Most of the current building dates from the 15th century, and only the western towers were destroyed in the turmoil.

The most interesting part of the cathedral, the **lower church**, is reached by a stairway. Its forest of pillars creates a powerful atmosphere around St Mungo's tomb (St Mungo founded a monastic community here in the 5th century), the focus of a famous medieval pilgrimage that was believed to be as meritorious as a visit to Rome.

Behind the cathedral, the **necropolis** stretches picturesquely up and over a green hill. Its elaborate Victorian tombs of the city's wealthy industrialists make for an intriguing stroll, great views and a vague Gothic thrill.

TOP CHOICE **St Mungo's Museum of Religious Life & Art** MUSEUM
(Map p794; www.glasgowmuseums.com; 2 Castle St; admission free; ⏲10am-5pm Mon-Thu & Sat, 11am-5pm Fri & Sun) A startling achievement, this museum, set in a reconstruction of the bishop's palace that once stood here in the cathedral forecourt, is an audacious attempt to capture the world's major religions in an artistic nutshell, while presenting the similarities and differences in how they approach common themes such as birth, marriage and death. The result is commendable. The attraction is twofold: firstly, impressive art that blurs the lines between religion and culture; and secondly, the opportunity to delve into different faiths, an experience that can be as deep or shallow as you wish. There are three galleries, representing religion as art, religious life and, on the top floor, religion in Scotland. A Zen garden is outside.

Central Glasgow

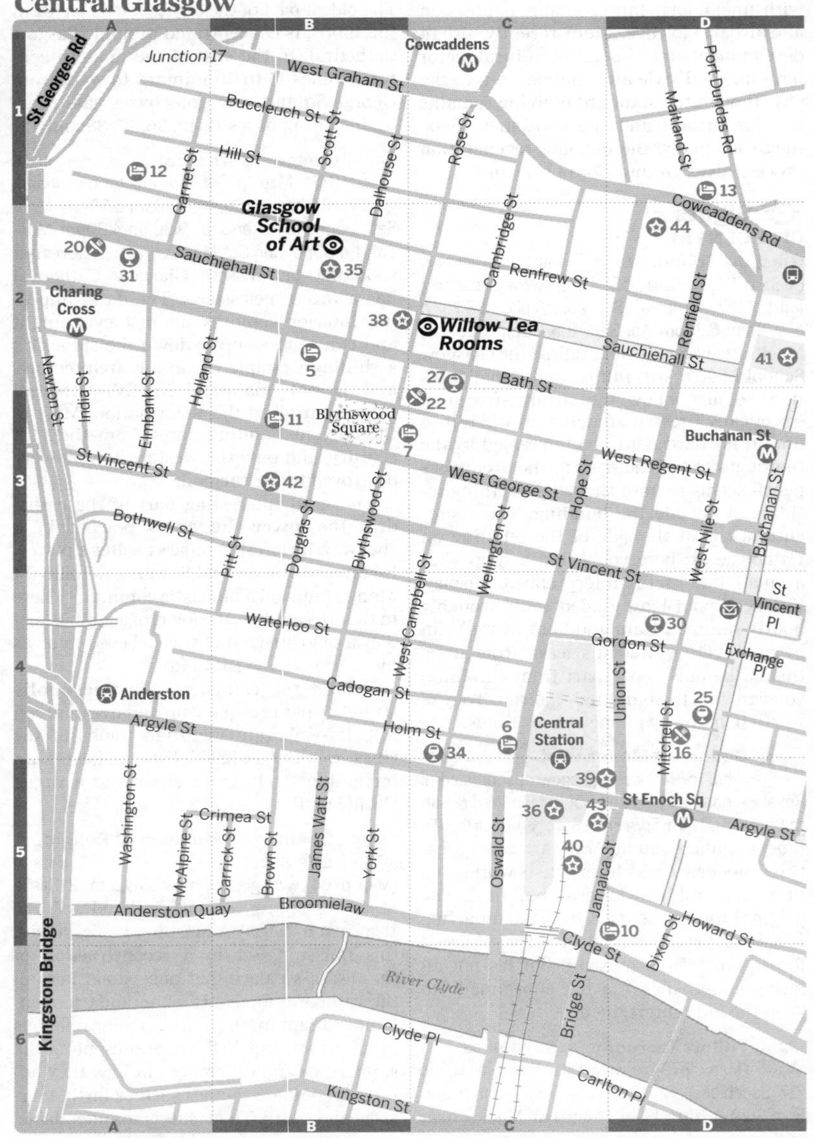

FREE **Provand's Lordship** HISTORIC HOUSE (Map p794; www.glasgowmuseums.com; 3 Castle St; ⏲10am-5pm Mon-Thu & Sat, 11am-5pm Fri & Sun) Across the road from St Mungo's Museum is Provand's Lordship, the oldest house in Glasgow. A rare example of 15th-century domestic Scottish architecture, it was built in 1471 as a manse for the chaplain of St Nicholas Hospital. The ceilings and doorways are low, and the rooms are sparsely furnished with period artefacts, except for an upstairs

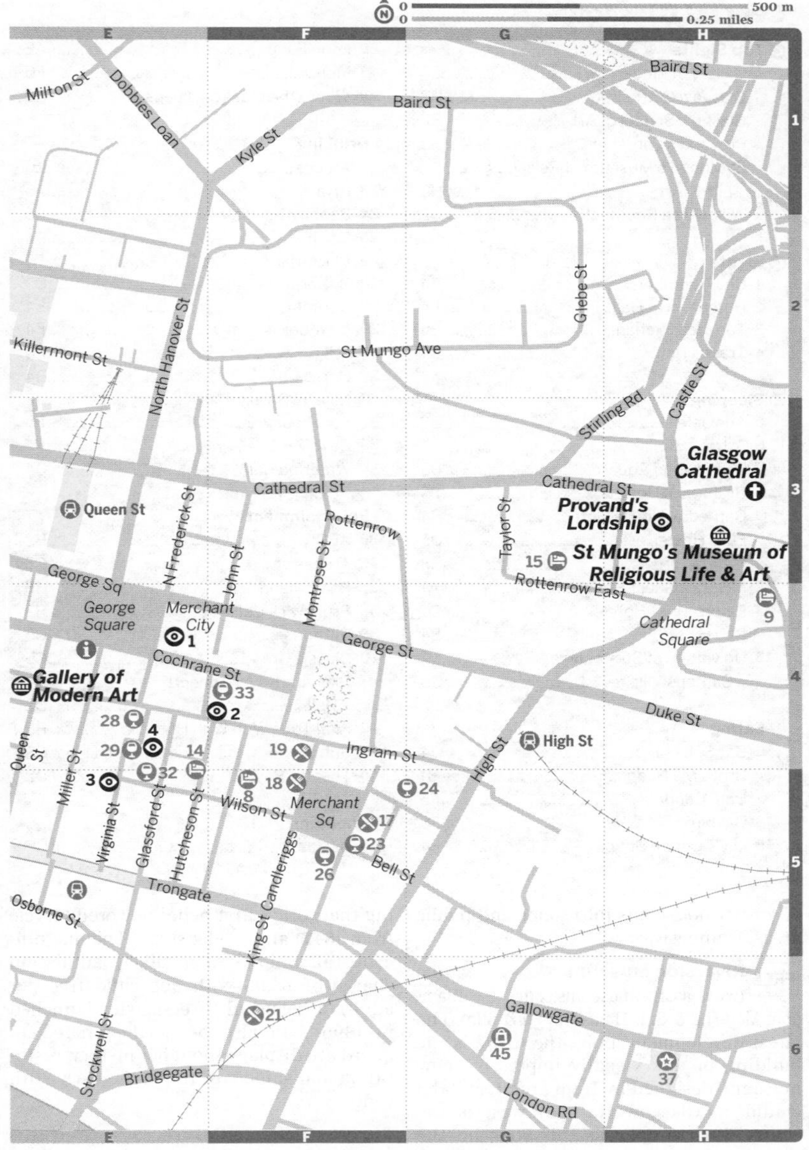

room, which has been furnished to reflect the living space of an early-16th-century chaplain. The building's best feature is its authentic feel – if you ignore the tacky imitation-stone linoleum covering the ground floor.

THE CLYDE

Once a thriving shipbuilding area, the Clyde sank into dereliction but is being rejuvenated. A major campaign to redevelop Glasgow Harbour, involving the conversion

Central Glasgow

Top Sights
Gallery of Modern Art E4
Glasgow Cathedral H3
Glasgow School of Art B2
Provand's Lordship H3
St Mungo's Museum of Religious Life & Art H3
Willow Tea Rooms C2

Sights
1 City Chambers E4
2 Hutcheson's Hall F4
3 Tobacco Exchange E5
4 Trades Hall E4

Sleeping
5 Adelaide's B2
6 Artto C4
7 Blythswood Square B3
8 Brunswick Hotel F5
9 Cathedral House Hotel H4
10 Euro Hostel D5
11 Malmaison B3
12 McLay's Guest House A1
13 Pipers Tryst Hotel D1
14 Rab Ha's E4
15 University of Strathclyde Campus Village G3

Eating
16 Bar Soba D4
Brutti Ma Buoni ..... (see 8)
17 Café Gandolfi F5
18 Dakhin F5
19 Lily's Coffee Shop F4
20 Loon Fung A2
21 Mono F6
22 Where the Monkey Sleeps C3

Drinking
Arches ..... (see 36)
23 Artà F5
24 Babbity Bowster G5
25 Bar 10 ..... D4
26 Blackfriars F5
27 Butterfly & Pig C2
28 Corinthian E4
29 Delmonica's E4
FHQ ..... (see 33)
30 Horse Shoe D4
31 Nice 'n' Sleazy A2
32 Polo Lounge E5
33 Revolver F4
34 Waterloo Bar C4

Entertainment
35 ABC B2
36 Arches C5
37 Barrowland H6
38 Brunswick Cellars B2
39 Cathouse C5
40 Classic Grand C5
41 Glasgow Royal Concert Hall D2
42 King Tut's Wah Wah Hut B3
43 Sub Club C5
44 Theatre Royal D2

Shopping
45 Barras G6

of former docklands into shops and public areas, is underway.

FREE **Riverside Museum** MUSEUM
(www.glasgowmuseums.com; ⏲10am-5pm Mon-Thu & Sat, 11am-5pm Fri & Sun) The latest development along the Clyde is the building of this visually impressive new museum, designed by Iraqi architect Zaha Hadid, at Glasgow Harbour west of the centre. Due to open as this book hit the shelves, it was to house a varied collection, including three recreated Glasgow streets from various points in history, a display of maritime heritage and much of what was formerly in the Museum of Transport: a display of cars made in Scotland, plus assorted railway locos, trams, bikes (including the world's first pedal-powered bicycle from 1847) and model ships. The magnificent Tall Ship *Glenlee* (likely admission charge of £5.95 with one child free per adult), a beautiful three-master launched in 1896, will also be berthed here. On board are displays about her history, restoration and shipboard life in the early 20th century.

Glasgow Science Centre MUSEUM
(www.glasgowsciencecentre.org; 50 Pacific Quay; Science Mall adult/child £9.95/7.95, extras for IMAX, tower or planetarium £2.50; ⏲10am-5pm) Scotland's flagship millennium project, the superb, ultramodern Glasgow Science Centre will keep the kids entertained for hours (that's middle-aged kids, too!). It brings

science and technology alive through hundreds of interactive exhibits on four floors. Look out for the illusions (like rearranging your features through a 3D head-scan) and the cloud chamber, showing tracks of natural radiation. It consists of an egg-shaped titanium-covered **IMAX** theatre (phone for current screenings) and an interactive **Science Mall** with floor-to-ceiling windows – a bounty of discovery for young, inquisitive minds. There's also a rotating **observation tower**, 127m high. And check out the planetarium, where the **Scottish Power Space Theatre** brings the night sky to life and a **Virtual Science Theatre** treats visitors to a 3D molecular journey. To get here take Arriva bus 24 from Renfield St or First Glasgow bus 89 or 90 from Union St.

WEST END

With its expectant buzz, trendy bars and cafes and nonchalant swagger, the West End is great for people-watching, and is as close as Glasgow gets to bohemian. From the centre, buses 9, 16 and 23 run towards Kelvingrove, 8, 11, and 16 to the university, and 20, 44 and 66 to Byres Rd (among others).

FREE Kelvingrove Art Gallery & Museum — MUSEUM/GALLERY

(www.glasgowmuseums.com; Argyle St; ⌚10am-5pm Mon-Thu & Sat, 11am-5pm Fri & Sun) In a magnificent stone building, this grand Victorian cathedral of culture has been revamped into a fascinating and unusual museum, with a bewildering variety of exhibits, but not too tightly packed to overwhelm. Here you'll find fine art alongside stuffed animals, and Micronesian shark tooth swords alongside a Spitfire plane, but it's not mix 'n' match: rooms are carefully and thoughtfully themed, and the collection is a manageable size. There's an excellent room of Scottish art, and a room of fine French Impressionist works, alongside quality Renaissance paintings from Italy and Flanders. Salvador Dalí's superb *Christ of St John of the Cross* is also here. Best of all, everything – including every painting – has an easy-reading paragraph of interpretation next to it: what a great idea. You can learn a lot about art and more here, and it's excellent for the children with plenty for them to do, and displays aimed at a variety of ages. Bus 17, among many others, runs here from Renfield St.

FREE Hunterian Museum — MUSEUM

(www.hunterian.gla.ac.uk; University Ave; ⌚9.30am-5pm Mon-Sat) Housed in the glorious sandstone main building of the university, which is in itself reason enough to pay a visit, this quirky museum contains the collection of renowned one-time student of the university, William Hunter (1718–83). Hunter was primarily an anatomist and physician, but as one of those gloriously well-rounded Enlightenment figures, he interested himself in everything the world had to offer. Pickled organs in glass jars take their place alongside geological phenomena, potsherds gleaned from ancient brochs, dinosaur skeletons and a creepy case of deformed animals. The main halls of the exhibition, with their high vaulted roofs, are magnificent in themselves. A highlight is the 1674 'Map of the Whole World' in the World Culture section.

FREE Hunterian Art Gallery — GALLERY

(www.hunterian.gla.ac.uk; 82 Hillhead St; ⌚9.30am-5pm Mon-Sat) Across the road from the Hunterian Museum, the bold tones of the Scottish Colourists (Samuel Peploe, Francis Cadell, JD Fergusson) are well represented in this gallery, which also forms part of Hunter's bequest to the university. There are also Sir William MacTaggart's impressionistic Scottish landscapes and a gem by Thomas Millie Dow. There's a special collection of James McNeill Whistler's limpid prints, drawings and paintings. Upstairs, in a section devoted to late-19th-century Scottish art, you can see works by several of the Glasgow Boys.

TOP CHOICE Mackintosh House — MACKINTOSH BUILDING

(www.hunterian.gla.ac.uk; 82 Hillhead St; admission £3, after 2pm Wed free; ⌚9.30am-5pm Mon-Sat) Attached to the Hunterian Art Gallery, this is a reconstruction of the first home that Charles Rennie Mackintosh bought with his wife, noted artist Mary Macdonald. It's fair to say that interior decoration was one of their strong points; the Mackintosh House is startling even today. The quiet elegance of the hall and dining room on the ground floor give way to a stunning drawing room. There's something otherworldly about the very mannered style of the beaten silver panels, the long-backed chairs and the surface decorations echoing Celtic manuscript illuminations. You wouldn't have wanted to be a guest that spilled a glass of red on this carpet.

THE GENIUS OF CHARLES RENNIE MACKINTOSH

Great cities have great artists, designers and architects contributing to the cultural and historical roots of their urban environment while expressing its soul and individuality. Charles Rennie Mackintosh was all of these. His quirky, linear and geometric designs have had almost as much influence on the city as have Gaudí's on Barcelona. Many of the buildings Mackintosh designed in Glasgow are open to the public, and you'll see his tall, thin, art nouveau typeface repeatedly reproduced.

Born in 1868, Mackintosh studied at the Glasgow School of Art. In 1896, when he was aged only 27, he won a competition for his design of the School of Art's new building. The first section was opened in 1899 and is considered to be the earliest example of art nouveau in Britain, as well as Mackintosh's supreme architectural achievement. This building demonstrates his skill in combining function and style.

Although Mackintosh's genius was quickly recognised on the Continent, he did not receive the same encouragement in Scotland. His architectural career here lasted only until 1914, when he moved to England to concentrate on furniture design. He died in 1928, and it is only since the last decades of the 20th century that Mackintosh's genius has been widely recognised. For more about the man and his work, contact the **Charles Rennie Mackintosh Society** (☎0141-946 6600; www.crmsociety.com; Mackintosh Church, 870 Garscube Rd). Check its website for special events.

If you're planning to go CRM crazy, the Mackintosh Trail ticket, available at the tourist office or any Mackintosh building, gives you a day's free admission to all his creations as well as unlimited bus and subway travel. It costs £16.

SOUTH SIDE

The south side is a tangled web of busy roads with a few oases giving relief from the urban congestion. It does contain some excellent attractions, though.

FREE **Burrell Collection** GALLERY

(www.glasgowmuseums.com; Pollok Country Park; ⏲10am-5pm Mon-Thu & Sat, 11am-5pm Fri & Sun) One of Glasgow's top attractions is the Burrell Collection. Amassed by wealthy industrialist Sir William Burrell before being donated to the city, it is housed in an outstanding museum, 3 miles south of the city centre. This idiosyncratic collection of treasure includes everything from Chinese porcelain and medieval furniture to paintings by Renoir and Cézanne. It's not so big as to be overwhelming, and the stamp of the collector lends an intriguing coherence.

Within the spectacular interior, carved-stone Romanesque doorways are incorporated into the structure so you actually walk through them. Floor-to-ceiling windows admit a flood of light, and enable the surrounding landscape outside to enhance the effect of the exhibits. It feels like you're wandering in a huge tranquil greenhouse.

In springtime, it's worth making a full day of your trip here and spending some time wandering in the beautiful park, studded with flowers. Once part of the estates of Pollok House, which can be visited, the grounds have numerous enticing picnic spots; if you're not heading further north, here's the place to see shaggy Highland cattle, as well as heavy horses.

Many buses pass the park gates (including buses 45, 47, 48 and 57 from the city centre), and there's a twice-hourly bus service between the gallery and the gates (a pleasant 10-minute walk). Alternatively catch a train to Pollokshaws West from Central station (four per hour; you want the second station on the line for East Kilbride or Kilmarnock).

Activities

Walking & Cycling

The **Clyde Walkway** extends from Glasgow upriver to the Falls of Clyde near New Lanark (p809), some 40 miles away. The tourist office has a good leaflet pack detailing different sections of this walk. The 10-mile section through Glasgow has interesting parts, though modern buildings have replaced most of the old shipbuilding works.

The well-trodden, long-distance footpath called the **West Highland Way** begins in Milngavie, 8 miles north of Glasgow (you can walk to Milngavie from Glasgow along the River Kelvin), and runs for 95 spectacular miles to Fort William.

There are several long-distance pedestrian/cycle routes that begin in Glasgow and follow off-road routes for most of the way. Check www.sustrans.org.uk for more details.

Tours

City Sightseeing BUS TOUR
(0141-204 0444; www.citysightseeingglasgow.co.uk; adult/child £11/5) These double-decker tourist buses run a circuit along the main sightseeing routes, starting outside the tourist office on George Square. You get on and off as you wish. A ticket, bought from the driver or in the tourist office, is valid for two consecutive days. All buses have wheelchair access and multilingual commentary.

Seaforce BOAT TRIPS
(0141-221 1070; www.seaforce.co.uk; Riverside Museum) Departing from the new Riverside Museum, Seaforce offers speedy all-weather powerboat jaunts along the Clyde. There's a variety of trips, including a half-hour ride around central Glasgow (adult/child £10/6), an hour trip to the Erskine Bridge (£15/10) or four-hour rides to local wildlife hot spots (£50/35).

Festivals & Events

Not to be outdone by Edinburgh, Glasgow has some kicking festivals of its own.

Celtic Connections MUSIC
(0141-353 8000; www.celticconnections.com) Two-week music festival held in January.

Glasgow Jazz Festival JAZZ
(0141-552 3552; www.jazzfest.co.uk) Excellent festival held in June; George Sq is a good place for free jazz at this time.

International Festival of Visual Art VISUAL ART
(0141-276 8384; www.glasgowinternational.org) Held in late April in even years, this festival features a range of innovative installations, performances and exhibitions around town.

West End Festival MUSIC/ARTS
(0141-341 0844; www.westendfestival.co.uk) This music and arts event is Glasgow's biggest festival, running for two weeks in June.

Sleeping

The city centre gets very rowdy at weekends, and accommodation options fill up fast, mostly with groups who will probably roll in boisterously some time after 3am. If

GAY & LESBIAN GLASGOW

Glasgow has a vibrant gay scene, with the gay quarter found in and around the Merchant City (particularly Virginia, Wilson and Glassford Sts). The city's gay community has a reputation for being very friendly.

To tap into the scene, check out *The List*, the free *Scots Gay* (www.scotsgay.co.uk) magazine and the **GayScotland website** (www.gayscotland.com/glasgow/glasgow_index.htm). If you're in Glasgow in autumn check out **Glasgay** (0141-552 7575; www.glasgay.co.uk), a gay performing arts festival, held around October/November each year. The following are just a few of the gay and lesbian pubs and clubs in Glasgow:

» **Delmonica's** (Map p794; 68 Virginia St; noon-midnight) Attached to the Polo Lounge, Delmonica's is a world away, with its predatory feeling of people on the pull. It's packed on weekday evenings. Friday night is glam night with chart tunes and Sunday is a karaoke free-for-all.

» **FHQ** (Map p794; 10 John St) In-fashion women-only location in the heart of the Pink Triangle.

» **Polo Lounge** (Map p794; 84 Wilson St) Staff claim 'the city's best talent' is found here; a quick glance at the many glamour pusses – male and female – proves their claim. The downstairs club is packed on weekends; just the main bars open on other nights.

» **Revolver** (Map p794; www.revolverglasgow.com; 6a John St) Hip little Revolver, downstairs on cosmopolitan John St, sports a relaxed crowd and, crucially, a free jukebox. You'll be listening to indie rather than Abba here.

» **Waterloo Bar** (Map p794; 306 Argyle St) This is a traditional pub that's Scotland's oldest gay bar. It attracts punters of all ages. It's very friendly and, with a large group of regulars, a good place to meet people away from the scene.

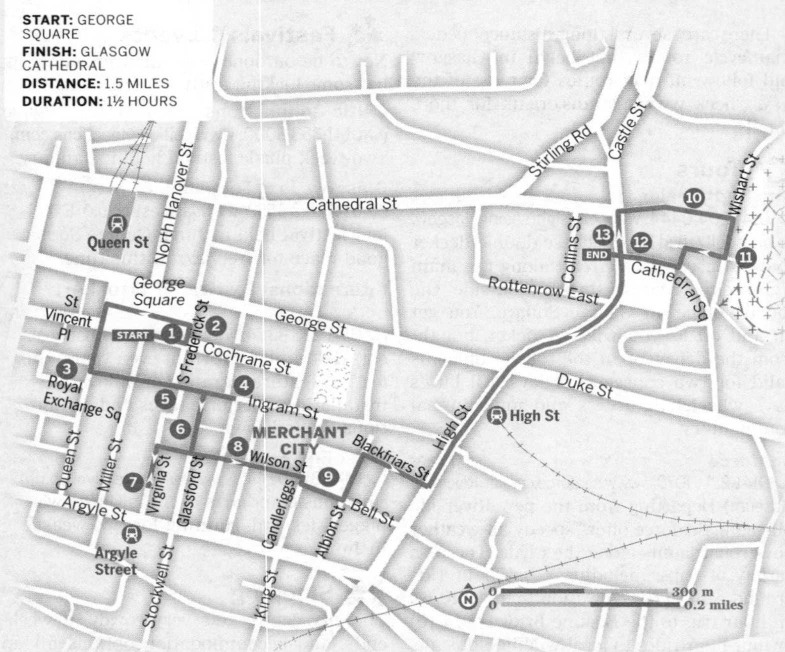

Walking Tour
Glasgow

This stroll takes you to Glasgow Cathedral through trendy Merchant City, once headquarters for Glasgow industrialists.

The tourist office on 1 **George Square** is a good starting point. The square is surrounded by imposing Victorian architecture: the old post office, the Bank of Scotland and the grandiose 2 **City Chambers**. Statues include Robert Burns, James Watt, and, atop a Doric column, Sir Walter Scott.

Walk one block south down Queen St to the 3 **Gallery of Modern Art**. This striking colonnaded building was once the Royal Exchange and now hosts some of the country's best contemporary art displays.

The gallery faces Ingram St, which you should cross and then follow east four blocks to 4 **Hutcheson's Hall**. Built in 1805, this elegant building is now maintained by the National Trust for Scotland (NTS). On your way, duck into the former Court House cells now housing the 5 **Corinthian** pub/club for a glimpse of the extravagant interior. Retrace your steps one block and continue south down Glassford St past 6 **Trades Hall**, designed by Robert Adam in 1791 to house the trades guild. The exterior is best viewed from Garth St. Turn right into Wilson St and left along Virginia St, lined with the old warehouses of the Tobacco Lords; many of these have been converted into posh flats. The 7 **Tobacco Exchange** became the Sugar Exchange in 1820.

Back on Wilson St, the 8 **Sheriff Court** fills a whole block and was originally Glasgow's town hall. Continue east on Wilson St past Ingram Square to 9 **Merchant Square**, a covered courtyard that was once the city's fruit market but now bustles with cafes and bars.

Head up Albion St, then right into Blackfriars St. Emerging onto High St, turn left and follow it up to the 10 **cathedral**. Behind the cathedral wind your way up through the 11 **Necropolis**, which offers great city views. On your way back check out the fabulous 12 **St Mungo's Museum of Religious Life & Art** and 13 **Provand's Lordship**.

you prefer an earlier appointment with your bed, you'll be better off in a smaller, quieter lodging or in the West End. Booking ahead is essential anywhere at weekends and in July and August.

CITY CENTRE

TOP CHOICE Brunswick Hotel HOTEL ££
(Map p794; ☎0141-552 0001; www.brunswickhotel.co.uk; 106 Brunswick St; compact d/standard d/d/king d £50/65/85/95;) Some places have dour owners threatening lockouts if you break curfew. Then there's the Brunswick, which every-now-and-then converts the whole hotel into a party venue, with DJs in the lifts and art installations in the rooms. You couldn't ask for a more relaxed and friendly Merchant City base. The rooms are all stylish with a mixture of minimalism and rich, sexy colours. Compact and standard doubles will do if you're here for a night out, but king-size rooms are well worth the £10 upgrade. There's an excellent restaurant downstairs and occasional nightclub in the basement.

Malmaison HOTEL £££
(Map p794; ☎0141-572 1000; www.malmaison.com; 278 West George St; standard r Fri-Sun £135, standard r Mon-Thu £155;) Heavenly Malmaison is the ultimate in seductive urban accommodation. Cutting-edge but decadently stylish living at its best, this sassy sister of hospitality is super slinky and a cornerstone of faith in Glaswegian accommodation. Stylish rooms with their moody lighting have a dark, brooding tone, plush furnishings and a designer touch. It's best to book online, as it's cheaper, and various suite offers can be mighty tempting.

Blythswood Square HOTEL £££
(Map p794; ☎0141-248 8888; www.blythswoodsquare.com; 11 Blythswood Sq; r £195-285;) Recently opened in a gorgeous Georgian terrace, this elegant five-star offers plenty of inner-city luxury, with grey and cerise tweeds offering casual soft-toned style throughout. Grades of rooms range from standard to penthouse with corresponding increases in comforts; it's hard to resist the traditional 'classic' ones with windows onto the delightful square, but at weekends you'll have a quieter sleep in the new wing at the back. There's an excellent bar and superb restaurant, as well as a very handsome floorboarded and colonnaded salon space on the first floor that functions as an evening spot for cocktails. Other facilities include valet parking and, ready by the time you read this, a spa complex.

Artto HOTEL ££
(Map p794; ☎0141-248 2480; www.arttohotel.com; 37 Hope St; s/d £70/90;) Right by the train station, this modish but affordable hotel offers soft white, fawn, and burgundy tones in its compact but attractive rooms above a popular bar and eatery. Large windows make staying at the front appealing but, though the double glazing does a good job of subduing the street noise, light sleepers will be happier at the rear. Rates vary widely by the day; the above is a worst-case scenario.

Rab Ha's INN ££
(Map p794; ☎0141-572 0400; www.rabhas.com; 83 Hutcheson St; r £79-89;) This Merchant City favourite is an atmospheric pub/restaurant with four stylish upstairs rooms. Each is a good size with a dark polished wood theme and a spotless en suite. It's the personal touches, such as fresh flowers in the rooms, and designer photographic prints on the walls, that make you feel special. Breakfast can be delivered to your room and you can come and go as you please, long after the bar downstairs has closed.

Pipers Tryst Hotel HOTEL ££
(Map p794; ☎0141-353 5551; www.thepipingcentre.co.uk; 30-34 McPhater St; s/d £50/65;) The name is no strategy to lure tartan tourists; this intimate, cosy hotel is in a noble building actually run by the adjacent bagpiping centre. Cheery staff, great value and a prime city centre location make this a cut above other places. Of the eight well-appointed rooms, Nos 6 and 7 are our faves; you won't have far to migrate after a night of Celtic music and fine single malts in the snug bar-restaurant downstairs.

Euro Hostel HOSTEL £
(Map p794; ☎0141-222 2828; www.euro-hostels.co.uk; 318 Clyde St; dm £15-25, s £35-50, d £40-70;) With hundreds of beds, this mammoth hostel is handily close to the station and centre. While it feels a bit institutional, it has excellent facilities, though the kitchen is very compact. Dorms range in size, and price varies on a daily basis, so book ahead for the best rates. Private rooms aren't great value. It's very popular with groups and has a rockin' bar on-site.

Adelaide's B&B ££
(Map p794; ☎0141-248 4970; www.adelaides.co.uk; 209 Bath St; standard £35, s/d/f £50/60/82; @) Quiet and cordial, this is ideal for folk who want location at a reasonable price. It's an unusual place – a simple, friendly guest house on prestigious Bath St set in an historic church conversion and still Baptist-run, though there's not a hint of preachiness in the air. Tariffs are room only – various breakfast options are available – and families are very welcome. Aim for the back to minimize weekend noise.

McLay's Guest House B&B £
(Map p794; ☎0141-332 4796; www.mclays.com; 260 Renfrew St; s/d £36/56, without bathroom £28/48; @) The string of cheapish guest houses along the western end of Renfrew St are a mixed bag but offer a tempting location right by the Sauchiehall nightlife and a block or so from the College of Art. This is among the best of them; a solid choice with decent warm rooms and fair prices. It's sometimes a little cheaper via online booking agencies.

EAST END

Cathedral House Hotel HOTEL ££
(Map p794; ☎0141-552 3519; http://cathedralhousehotel.org; 28-32 Cathedral Sq; s/d £55/85; P) Who said you had to get out of town for those Scottish Baronial mansions, turrets and all? Right opposite the cathedral, this convivial spot has eight individual rooms above an attractive bar and restaurant. The corner rooms – seven is the best – offer sumptuous beds and great views of St Mungo's and the Necropolis. It's a great spot; the only catch is that the less mobile might struggle with the steep spiral stairs.

University of Strathclyde Campus Village UNIVERSITY ACCOMMODATION £
(Map p794; ☎0141-553 4148; www.rescat.strath.ac.uk; Rottenrow East; s £36, without bathroom £30; mid-Jun–mid-Sep;) The uni opens its halls of residence to tourists over summer. The Campus Village, opposite Glasgow Cathedral, offers B&B accommodation in single rooms (couples can relive the thrill of having to sneak into each others' room at midnight) at good prices. Cheaper, self-catering prices may also be available.

WEST END

Glasgow SYHA HOSTEL £
(☎0141-332 3004; www.syha.org.uk; 8 Park Tce; dm/tw £23/62; @) Perched on a hill overlooking Kelvingrove Park in a charming town house, this place is simply fabulous and one of Scotland's best official hostels. Dorms are mostly four to six beds with padlock lockers and all have their own en suite – very posh. The common rooms are spacious, plush and good for lounging about. There's no curfew, a good kitchen, and breakfast is available. The prices above reflect maximums and are usually cheaper.

Hotel Du Vin HOTEL £££
(☎0141-339 2001; www.hotelduvin.com; 1 Devonshire Gardens; r from £150, ste from £410; P @) This is the favoured hotel for the rich and famous, and the patriarch of sophistication and comfort. A study in elegance, it's sumptuously decorated and occupies three classical terrace houses. There are 35 rooms, all individually furnished, and two fine restaurants are on-site with a wine selection exceeding 600 varieties.

Embassy Apartments APARTMENTS ££
(☎0141-946 6698; www.mcquadehotels.com; 8 Kelvin Dr; 2/4 person flat per night £77/95;) If you're after a self-catering option, it's hard to go past this elegant place both for facilities and location. Situated in the leafy West End on a quiet, exclusive street right on the edge of the Botanical Gardens, it sleeps one to seven in studio-style apartments that have fully equipped kitchens and are sparkling clean. Particularly good option for couples and families with older kids. They are available by the day, but prices drop for three- and seven-day rentals. Prices vary extensively according to demand; the above are guides only.

Alamo Guest House B&B ££
(☎0141-339 2395; www.alamoguesthouse.com; 46 Gray St; s/d/tw £42/64/68, d with bathroom £84;) The Alamo may not sound like a quiet, peaceful spot, but that's exactly what this great little place is. Opposite Kelvingrove Park, it feels miles from the hustle of the city, but the city centre and West End are within walking distance, and several of the best museums and restaurants in town are close by. The decor is an enchanting mixture of antique furnishings and modern design, and the breezy owners will make you very welcome. All rooms have DVD players and there's an extensive collection to borrow from.

Kirklee Hotel HOTEL ££
(☎0141-334 5555; www.kirkleehotel.co.uk; 11 Kensington Gate; s/d £59/75;) Want to spoil someone special? In a leafy neighbourhood, Kirklee is a quiet little gem that combines the luxury of a classy hotel with the warmth

of staying in someone's home. The rooms are simply gorgeous, beautifully furnished and mostly looking onto lush gardens. For families there is an excellent downstairs room with enormous en suite. This could be Glasgow's most beautiful street.

Bunkum Backpackers HOSTEL £
(0141-581 4481; www.bunkumglasgow.co.uk; 26 Hillhead St; dm/tw £14/36;) A tempting budget headquarters for assaults on the eateries and pubs of the West End, Bunkum Backpackers occupies a noble old Victorian terrace on a quiet street. The dorms are spacious – one exaggeratedly so – and the common room and kitchen are also large. There's no curfew but it's not a party hostel. Watch the street numbers; the place isn't well signposted.

Eating

Glasgow is the best place to eat in Scotland, with an excellent range of eateries. The West End is the culinary centre of the city, with Merchant City also boasting an incredible concentration of quality restaurants and cafes.

CITY CENTRE

Café Gandolfi CAFE/BISTRO ££
(Map p794; 0141-552 6813; 64 Albion St; mains £8-14; 9am-11.30pm Mon-Sat, noon-11.30pm Sun) In the fashionable Merchant City, this cafe was once part of the old cheese market. It's been pulling in the punters for years and packs an interesting clientele: die-hard Gandolfers, the upwardly mobile and tourists. It's an excellent, friendly bistro and upmarket coffee shop – very much the place to be seen. Book a Tim Stead-designed, medieval-looking table in advance for well-prepared Scottish and Continental food. There's an expansion, specialising in fish, next door.

Loon Fung CHINESE ££
(Map p794; 0141-332 1240; www.loonfungglasgow.co.uk; 417 Sauchiehall St; mains £10-13; noon-4am) It's rare to get such an authentically Chinese experience in Scotland and it's quite a surprise after a spot of late-night dining to emerge to Sauchiehall rather than Hong Kong. There are various set meal options but be adventurous and pick dishes off the pages of Chinese specials rather than the Westernised plates; there are some real gems here.

Brutti Ma Buoni BISTRO ££
(Map p794; 0141-552 0001; www.brunswickhotel.co.uk; 106 Brunswick St; mains £8-13; 11am-10pm;) If you like dining in a place that has a sense of fun, Brutti delivers – it's the antithesis of some of the pretentious places around the Merchant City. With dishes such as 'ugly but good' pizza and 'angry or peaceful' prawns, Brutti's menu draws a smile for its quirkiness and its prices. The Italian and Spanish influences give rise to tapas-like servings or full-blown meals, which are imaginative, fresh and frankly delicious.

Lily's Coffee Shop CAFE £
(Map p794; 103 Ingram St; mains £4-6; 9.30am-5pm Mon-Sat) Don't be put off by the slightly sterile feel, Lily's is a top lunch spot fusing a creative blend of East and West. It's a unique cross between a Chinese bistro and chic cafe with made-to-order Chinese food (such as dumpling buns and mandarin duck wraps) and standards like burgers and baked potatoes that are tarted up almost beyond recognition. The Chinese food is outstanding – fresh, lively and served with fruits and salad.

Dakhin INDIAN ££
(Map p794; 0141-553 2585; www.dakhin.com; 89 Candleriggs; mains £6-16) This south Indian restaurant breathes some fresh air into the city's curry scene. Dishes are from all over the south, and include *dosas* – thin rice-based crêpes – and a yummy variety of fragrant coconut-based curries. If you're really hungry, try a thali: an assortment of Indian 'tapas'.

Bar Soba ASIAN FUSION £
(Map p794; 0141-204 2404; www.barsoba.co.uk; 11 Mitchell Lane; mains £8-10) With seating around the edges of the room and candles flickering in windows there's a certain sense of intimacy in stylish and very friendly Bar Soba. You can eat in the plush downstairs restaurant, or in the bar. The food is Asian fusion and the laksas go down a treat – followed up of course with an irresistible chocolate brownie. Background beats are perfect for chilling and it can be a good spot to escape Friday evening crowds.

Where the Monkey Sleeps CAFE £
(Map p794; www.monkeysleeps.com; 182 West Regent St; dishes £5-7; 7am-5pm Mon-Fri, 10am-5pm Sat) This funky little number in the middle of the business district is just what you need to get away from the ubiquitous coffee chains. Laid-back and a little hippy, the bagels and paninis, with names like maverick or renegade, are highlights as are some very inventive dishes, such as the 'nuclear' beans, dripping with cayenne and Tabasco.

Mono VEGETARIAN £

(Map p794; www.myspace.com/monoglasgow; 12 Kings Ct, King St; mains £3-8) Combining vegetarian food with music, Mono is one of Glasgow's best vegan eateries. Monorail is in the same premises, which means you can browse through an indie record shop while waiting for your food to be prepared. The all-day bar-menu provides classics such as the breakfast fry-up while the main menu has a touch of flair demonstrating a Mediterranean influence. The lasagne is well worth ploughing through. Mono also makes a relaxing place for a coffee or a beer.

WEST END

There are numerous excellent restaurants in the West End. They cluster along Byres Rd, and, just off it, on Ashton Lane and Ruthven Lane. Gibson St and Great Western Rd also have plenty to offer.

Left Bank BISTRO ££

(☎0141-339 5969; www.theleftbank.co.uk; 33 Gibson St; mains £8-14; ⏰9am-10pm) Huge windows fronting the street greet you at this outstanding eatery specialising in gastronomic delights and lazy afternoons. There are lots of little spaces filled with couches and chunky tables reflecting a sense of intimacy. The large starter-menu can be treated like tapas making it good for sharing plates. There are lots of delightful creations that use seasonal and local produce.

Ubiquitous Chip SCOTTISH £££

(☎0141-334 5007; www.ubiquitouschip.co.uk; 12 Ashton Lane; 2-/3-course dinner £35/40) The original champion of Scottish produce, The Ubiquitous Chip has won lots of awards for its unparalleled Scottish cuisine, and for its lengthy wine list. Named to poke fun at Scotland's perceived lack of finer cuisine, it offers a French touch but resolutely Scottish ingredients, carefully selected and following sustainable principles. Above, **Upstairs at the Chip** (mains £12 to £20) provides cheaper, bistro-style food with a similarly advanced set of principles. There are also bar meals at the atmospheric upstairs pub, while the cute 'Wee Pub' down the side alley offers plenty of drinking pleasure.

Stravaigin SCOTTISH ££

(☎0141-334 2665; www.stravaigin.com; 28 Gibson St; mains £10-19; ⏰dinner Mon-Fri, lunch & dinner Sat & Sun) Stravaigin is a serious foodie's delight, with a menu constantly pushing the boundaries of originality and offering creative culinary excellence. The cool contemporary dining space in the basement has booth seating, and helpful, laid-back waiting-staff to assist in deciphering the audacious menu. Entry-level has a buzzing two-level bar that's open 11am to midnight daily; you can also eat here. There are always plenty of menu deals and special culinary nights.

Mother India INDIAN ££

(☎0141-221 1663; www.motherindiaglasgow.co.uk; 28 Westminster Tce, Sauchiehall St; mains £9-14; ⏰lunch Fri-Sun, dinner daily; 👪) Glasgow curry buffs are forever debating the merits of the city's numerous excellent south Asian restaurants, and Mother India features in every discussion. It may lack the trendiness of some of the up-and-comers but it's been a stalwart for years and the quality and innovation on show is superb. It also makes a real effort for kids, with a separate menu.

Heart Buchanan CAFE £

(www.heartbuchanan.co.uk; 380 Byres Rd; light meals £4-7; ⏰9am-6.30pm) The famous West End deli – give your nose a treat and drop in – has a small cafe space next door. Break any or all of the 10 commandments to bag a table, then enjoy some of Glasgow's best breakfasts, all with an exquisite quality of produce, a refreshing juice or milkshake, or regularly changing light-lunch options. If you failed in the table quest, the deli also does some of these meals to take away.

Stravaigin II SCOTTISH ££

(☎0141-334 7165; www.stravaigin.com; 8 Ruthven Lane; mains £9-17) Top service makes all feel welcome at this relaxed eatery just off Byres Rd. The menu changes regularly but always features a few surprises from around the globe. Slow cooking features prominently in preparation of both meat and vegetables, so expect those flavours to burst out at you. But it's also got a legendary reputation for its burgers, fish 'n' chips, and haggis, so there's something here for any appetite.

Konaki GREEK ££

(☎0141-342 4010; www.konakitaverna.co.uk; 920 Sauchiehall St; mains £9-13; ⏰lunch Mon-Sat, dinner daily) Not far from the Kelvingrove museum, Konaki is a friendly and unpretentious Greek restaurant that makes a great morning or evening pita stop. The starters are a particular highlight of the authentic menu – in fact, ordering a whole lot of them to share is the most enjoyable way to eat here. There are several Greek wines

LOCAL KNOWLEDGE

CINDY-LOU RAMSAY: TV CAMERA OPERATOR & PHOTOGRAPHER

Top photography spot? Pollok Park. The park itself is gorgeous and full of lots of good walks for walkers and cyclists to explore. It also takes you to the famous Burrell Collection, which may not look like much from the outside, but it's a really calming, beautiful building on the inside and jam-packed with exhibits from all over the world.

Favourite spots for live music? Barrowland and King Tut's Wah Wah Hut. Barrowland is an old, tired looking ballroom badly in need of a bit of a wee facelift, but you're guaranteed to get an unforgettable atmosphere; this is the reason that the biggest bands in the world continue to grace its stage. King Tut's is a much smaller venue for getting 'up close and personal' with some great bands.

Pub for a pint and read of the paper? Blackfriars in the Merchant City.

Typical local words? Blethering (chatting)! Glaswegians tend to do a lot of it, especially if you decide to ask them about their city!

to accompany your meal; knock back a traditional thick coffee afterwards.

Drinking

Some of Scotland's best nightlife is found in the din and sometimes roar of Glasgow's pubs and bars. There are as many different styles of bar as there are punters to guzzle in them; a month of solid drinking wouldn't get you past the halfway mark.

CITY CENTRE

TOP CHOICE Artà BAR

(Map p794; www.arta.co.uk; 13-19 Walls St; ⌚until 3am) This extraordinary place is so baroque that when you hear a Mozart concerto over the sound system, it wouldn't surprise you to see the man himself at the other end of the bar. Set in a former cheese market, it really does have to be seen to be believed. As its door slides open, Artà's opulent, cavernous candle-lit interior is exposed. There's floor-to-ceiling velvet, with red curtains revealing a staircase to the tapas bar and restaurant above in a show of decadence that the Romans would have appreciated. Despite the luxury, it's got a relaxed, chilled vibe and a mixed crowd. The big cocktails are great.

Horse Shoe PUB

(Map p794; www.horseshoebar.co.uk; 17 Drury St) This legendary city pub and popular meeting place dates from the late 19th century and is largely unchanged. It's a picturesque spot, with the longest continuous bar in the UK, but its main attraction is what's served over it – real ale and good food. Upstairs in the lounge is some of the best value pub food (dishes £3 to £6) in town.

Blackfriars PUB

(Map p794; www.blackfriarsglasgow.com; 36 Bell St) Merchant City's most relaxed and atmospheric pub, Blackfriars' friendly staff and chilled-out house make it special. Cask ales are taken seriously here, and there's a seating area with large windows that are great for people-watching.

Butterfly & Pig PUB

(Map p794; www.thebutterflyandthepig.com; 153 Bath St) A breath of fresh air along trendy Bath St, the piggery is a little offbeat, a little zany and makes you feel comfortable as soon as you plunge into its basement depths. The decor is an eclectic bunch with a retro feel and this adds to its familiarity.

Babbity Bowster PUB

(Map p794; 16-18 Blackfriars St) In a quiet corner of Merchant City, this handsome spot is perfect for a tranquil daytime drink, particularly in the adjoining beer garden. Service is attentive, and the smell of sausages may tempt you to lunch. This is one of the centre's most charming pubs, in one of its noblest buildings.

Arches BAR

(Map p794; www.thearches.co.uk; 253 Argyle St) A one-stop culture/entertainment fix, Arches doubles as a theatre showing contemporary, avant-garde productions and there's also a club (p806). The hotel-like entrance belies the deep interior, which make you feel as though you've discovered Hades' bohemian underworld. The crowd is mixed – hiking boots are as welcome as Versace.

Corinthian BAR
(Map p794; www.thecorinthianclub.co.uk; 191 Ingram St) A breathtaking, domed ceiling and majestic chandeliers make Corinthian an awesome venue. Originally a bank and later Glasgow's High Court, this regal building also houses a plush club, downstairs in old court cells, and a piano bar. Closed at time of research for renovation, it'll be open again by the time you read this.

Bar 10 BAR
(Map p794; 10 Mitchell Lane) A tiny city treasure that will cause the canny Glasgow drinker to give you a knowing glance if you mention its name. As laid-back as you could ask for in a hip city bar, the friendly, tuned-in staff complete the happy picture. It transforms from a quiet daytime bar to a happening weekend pub on Friday and Saturday nights. It also does decent, cheap paninis, salads, and the like during the day.

Nice 'n' Sleazy BAR, CLUB
(Map p794; www.nicensleazy.com; 421 Sauchiehall St) Students from the nearby School of Art make the buzz here reliably friendly on the rowdy Sauchiehall strip. If you're over 35 you'll feel like a professor not a punter, but retro decor, a big selection of tap and bottled beers, 3am closing, and nightly alternative live music downstairs followed by a club at weekends make this a winner.

WEST END

Uisge Beatha PUB
(www.uisgebeathabar.co.uk; 232 Woodlands Rd) If you enjoy a drink among dead things, you'll love Uisge Beatha (Gaelic for whisky, literally 'water of life'). This mishmash of church pews, stuffed animal heads and portraits of depressed nobility (the Maggie mannequin is our favourite) is patrolled by Andy Capp-like characters during the day and students at night. With 100 whiskies and four quirky rooms to choose from, this unique pub is one of Glasgow's best – an antidote to style bars.

Oran Mor BAR
(www.oran-mor.co.uk; 731 Great Western Rd) Now some may be a little uncomfortable with the thought of drinking in a church. But we say – the lord giveth. Praise be and let's give thanks – a converted church and an almighty one at that is now a bar, brasserie and club venue. The bar feels like it's been here for years – all wood and thick, exposed stone giving it warmth and a celestial air. There's an excellent array of whiskies. The only thing missing is holy water on your way in.

Brel BAR
(www.brelbarrestaurant.com; 39 Ashton Lane) Perhaps the best on Ashton Lane, this bar can seem tightly packed, but there's a conservatory out the back so you can pretend you're sitting outside when it's raining, and when the sun does peek through there's a beer garden. It has a huge range of Belgian beers, and also does mussels and other Lowlands favourites.

☆ Entertainment

Glasgow is Scotland's entertainment city, from classical music, fine theatres and ballet, to cracking nightclubs pumping out state-of-the-art hip-hop, electro, or techno to cheesy chart tunes, and contemporary Scottish bands at the cutting edge of modern music.

For theatre tickets book directly with the venue. For concerts, a useful booking centre is **Tickets Scotland** (☎0141-204 5151, 0870 220 1116; www.tickets-scotland.com; 239 Argyle St).

Nightclubs

Sub Club NIGHTCLUB
(Map p794; www.subclub.co.uk; 22 Jamaica St) Saturdays at the Sub Club are one of Glasgow's legendary nights, offering serious clubbing with a sound system that aficionados usually rate the city's best. The claustrophobic, last-one-in vibe, is not for those faint of heart.

Arches NIGHTCLUB
(Map p794; www.thearches.co.uk; 253 Argyle St) R-e-s-p-e-c-t is the mantra with the Arches. The Godfather of Glaswegian clubs, it has a design based around hundreds of arches slammed together, and is a must for funk and hip-hop freaks. It is one of the city's biggest clubs pulling top DJs, and you'll also hear some of the UK's up-and-coming turntable spinners. It's off Jamaica St.

Cathouse NIGHTCLUB
(Map p794; www.cathouseglasgow.co.uk; 15 Union St; ⏲Thu-Sun) Mostly rock, emo and metal at this long-standing indie, goth and alternative venue. There are two dance floors: upstairs is pretty intense with lots of metal and hard rock, downstairs is a little less scary if you're not keen on moshing.

Live Music

Glasgow is the king of Scotland's live-music scene. Pick up a copy of the *Gig Guide* (www.gigguide.co.uk), published monthly and available free in most pubs and venues for the latest on music gigs.

One of the city's premier live-music pub venues, the excellent **King Tut's Wah Wah Hut** (Map p794; www.kingtuts.co.uk; 272a St Vincent St) hosts bands every night of the week. Oasis were signed after playing here.

Two bars to see the best, and worst, of Glasgow's newest bands are **Brunswick Cellars** (Map p794; 239 Sauchiehall St) and **Classic Grand** (Map p794; 18 Jamaica St). Several of the bars mentioned under Drinking above are great for live music, including **Nice 'n' Sleazy** (p806).

Other recommendations:

ABC CONCERT VENUE
(O2 ABC; Map p794; www.abcglasgow.com; 300 Sauchiehall St) Former cinema; medium- to large-size acts.

Barrowland CONCERT VENUE
(Map p794; www.glasgow-barrowland.com; 244 Gallowgate) An exceptional old dancehall catering for some of the larger acts that visit the city.

Captain's Rest PUB
(www.captainsrest.co.uk; 185 Great Western Rd) Variety of indie bands

Clyde Auditorium AUDITORIUM
(☎0870 040 4000; www.secc.co.uk; Finnieston Quay) Also known as the Armadillo because of its bizarre shape, adjoins SECC, and caters for big national and international acts.

SECC AUDITORIUM
(☎0870 040 4000; www.secc.co.uk; Finnieston Quay) Adjoins Clyde Auditorium and hosts major national and international acts. A new venue, Glasgow Arena, is being built alongside.

Theatres & Concert Halls

Theatre Royal OPERA/BALLET/THEATRE
(Map p794; ☎0141-332 3321; www.ambassadortickets.com; 282 Hope St) This is the home of Scottish Opera, and the Scottish Ballet often has performances here. Ask about standby tickets if you'll be in town for a few days.

Glasgow Royal Concert Hall CONCERT HALL
(Map p794; ☎0141-353 8080; www.grch.com; 2 Sauchiehall St) A feast of classical music is showcased at this concert hall, the modern home of the Royal Scottish National Orchestra.

Citizens' Theatre THEATRE
(☎0141-429 0022; www.citz.co.uk; 119 Gorbals St) This is one of the top theatres in Scotland and it's well worth trying to catch a performance here.

Sport

Two football clubs dominate the sporting scene in Scotland, having vastly more resources than other clubs and a long history (and rivalry). This rivalry is also along partisan lines, with Rangers representing Protestant supporters, and Celtic, Catholic. It's worth going to a game; both play in magnificent arenas with great atmosphere. Games between the two (four a year) are fiercely contested, but tickets aren't sold to the general public; you'll need to know a season ticket holder.

Celtic Football Club FOOTBALL CLUB
(☎0871 226 1888; www.celticfc.co.uk; Celtic Park, Parkhead) There are daily stadium tours (adult/child £8.50/5.50). Get bus 61 or 62 from outside St Enoch centre.

Rangers Football Club FOOTBALL CLUB
(☎0871 702 1972; www.rangers.co.uk; Ibrox Stadium, 150 Edmiston Dr) Tours of the stadium and trophy room run daily (£8/5.50 per adult/child). Get the subway to Ibrox station.

Shopping

Boasting the UK's largest retail phalanx outside London, Glasgow is a shopaholic's paradise. The 'Style Mile' around Buchanan St, Argyle St and Merchant City is a fashion hub, while the West End has quirkier, more bohemian shopping options.

Barras FLEA MARKET
(Map p794; btwn Gallowgate & London Rd; ⌚9am-4pm Sat & Sun) Glasgow's flea market, the Barras on Gallowgate, is the living, breathing heart of this city in many respects. It has almost a thousand stalls and people come here just for a wander as much as for shopping, which gives the place a holiday air. The Barras is notorious for designer frauds, so be cautious. Watch your wallet, too.

Information

The List (£2.20; www.list.co.uk), available from newsagents, is Glasgow and Edinburgh's invaluable fortnightly guide to films, theatre, cabaret, music, clubs – the works. The excellent *Eating & Drinking Guide* (£5.95), published by *The List* every April, covers Glasgow and Edinburgh.

Internet Access

Gallery of Modern Art (☎0141-229 1996; Royal Exchange Sq; ⌚10am-5pm Mon-Wed

& Sat, 10am-8pm Thu, 11am-5pm Fri & Sun) Basement library; free internet access. Bookings recommended.

ICafe (cnr Great Western Rd & Dunearn St; per hr £2; ⌚10am-11pm) Sip a coffee and munch on a pastry while you check your emails on super-fast connections. Wi-fi too.

Mitchell Library (☎0141-287 2999; North St; ⌚9am-8pm Mon-Thu, to 5pm Fri & Sat) Free internet access; bookings recommended.

Yeeh@ (48 West George St; per hr £2; ⌚9.30am-7pm Mon-Fri, 10am-6pm Sat, 11am-6pm Sun)

Medical Services

Glasgow Royal Infirmary (☎0141-211 4000; 84 Castle St)

Money

There are numerous ATMs around the centre. The post office and the tourist office have bureaux de change.

American Express (Amex; 66 Gordon St)

Post

Main post office (Map p794; 47 St Vincent St; ⌚Mon-Sat)

Tourist Information

Tourist Office (Map p794; ☎0141-204 4400; www.seeglasgow.com; 11 George Sq; ⌚9am-5pm Mon-Sat) Excellent tourist office; makes local and national accommodation bookings (£4). Closes later and opens Sundays in summer.

Getting There & Away

Air

Ten miles west of the city, **Glasgow International Airport** (www.glasgowairport.com) handles domestic traffic and international flights. **Glasgow Prestwick Airport** (www.gpia.co.uk), 30 miles southwest of Glasgow, is used by **Ryanair** (www.ryanair.com) and some other budget airlines, with many connections to the rest of Britain and Europe.

Bus

All long-distance buses arrive and depart from **Buchanan bus station** (Map p794; ☎0141-333 3708; www.spt.co.uk/bus/bbs; Killermont St), which has pricey lockers, ATMs, and a cafe with wi-fi.

Buses from London are very competitive. **Megabus** (www.megabus.com) should be your first port of call if you're looking for the cheapest fare. It has one-way fares for around £11; check the website for your date of departure.

National Express (☎08717 81 81 81; www.nationalexpress.com) and **First** (☎0141-423 6600; www.firstgroup.com) also run to London (£25 to £35, eight hours). Most of these services are overnight. The 10.30pm National Express service stops at Heathrow. It's often cheaper to buy in advance online.

National Express also runs daily to several English cities. Check Megabus and the National Express website for heavily discounted fares on these routes.

Scottish Citylink (☎0870 550 5050; www.citylink.co.uk) has buses to most major towns in Scotland, including: Edinburgh (£6.30, 1¼ hours, every 15 minutes), Inverness (£25.50, 3½ hours, eight daily), Aberdeen (£26.50, 2¾ to four hours, hourly), Oban (£16.40, three hours, four direct daily) and Fort William (£20.50, three hours, seven daily).

Car & Motorcyle

There are numerous car-rental companies; the big names have offices at Glasgow and Prestwick airports. Companies include the following:

Arnold Clark (☎0141-423 9559; www.arnoldclarkrental.com; 43 Allison St)

Avis (☎0141-544 6064; www.avis.co.uk; 70 Lancefield St)

Europcar (☎0141-249 4106; www.europcar.com; 76 Lancefield Quay)

Train

As a general rule, Glasgow Central station serves southern Scotland, England and Wales, and Queen St station serves the north and east. There are buses every 10 minutes between them. There are direct trains from London's King's Cross and Euston stations; they're much quicker (advance purchase single £60, full fare £144, 4½ hours, more than hourly) and more comfortable than the bus.

First ScotRail (☎08457 55 00 33; www.scotrail.co.uk) runs Scottish trains. Destinations include: Edinburgh (£11.50, 50 minutes, every 15 minutes), Oban (£19.30, three hours, three to four daily), Fort William (£23.40, 3¾ hours, four to five daily), Dundee (£22.60, 1½ hours, hourly), Aberdeen (£40.30, 2½ hours, hourly) and Inverness (£70.40, 3½ hours, 10 daily, four on Sunday).

Getting Around

To/From the Airport

There are buses every 10 or 15 minutes from Glasgow International Airport to Buchanan bus station (single/return £4.50/7). A taxi costs £20 to £25.

Bike

There are several places to hire a bike; the tourist office has a full list. Prices start at around £10/15/60 for a half-day/day/week. A couple of options:

West End Cycles
(☎0141-357 1344; 16 Chancellor St) Good quality mountain bikes.

Gear Bikes
(☎0141-339 1179; www.gearbikes.com; 19 Gibson St) Decent hybrids.

Public Transport

BUS City bus services, mostly run by **First Glasgow** (☎0141-423 6600; www.firstglasgow.com), are frequent. You can buy tickets when you board buses but on most you must have the exact change. Short journeys in town cost £1.25 or £1.70; a day ticket (£3.75) is good value and is valid until 1am, when a night network starts. The tourist office hands out the highly complicated SPT Bus Map, detailing all routes in and around the city.

TRAIN & UNDERGROUND There's an extensive suburban network of trains in and around Glasgow; tickets should be bought before travel if the station is staffed or from the conductor if it isn't. There's also an underground line that serves 15 stations in the centre, west and south of the city (single £1.20). The train network connects with the subway at Buchanan St station. The Discovery Ticket (£3.50) gives unlimited travel on the subway for a day, while the Roundabout ticket gives a day's unlimited train and subway travel for £5.25.

AROUND GLASGOW

Other appealing destinations within easy reach of Glasgow are covered elsewhere, such as Loch Lomond (p840).

Blantyre

POP 17,300

The birthplace of David Livingstone is an outlying suburb of Glasgow these days. It was founded as a cotton mill in the late 18th century and that zealous and pious doctor, missionary and explorer was raised in a one-room tenement and worked in the mill by day from the age of 10, going to the local school at night.

The **David Livingstone Centre** (NTS; www.nts.org.uk; adult/child £5.50/4.50; ⏲10am-5pm Mon-Sat, 12.30-5pm Sun Apr-Dec) tells the story of his life from his early days in Blantyre to the 30 years he spent in Africa, where he named the Victoria Falls on one of his numerous journeys. It's a good display and brings to life the incredible hardships of his missionary existence, his battles against slavery, and his famous meeting with Stanley. There's a child-friendly African wildlife feature and the grassy park the museum is set in makes a perfect picnic spot.

It's a 30-minute walk along the river to **Bothwell Castle** (HS; www.historic-scotland.gov.uk; adult/child £3.70/2.20; ⏲9.30am-5.30pm Apr-Sep, 9.30am-4.30pm Sat-Wed Oct-Mar), regarded as the finest 13th-century castle in Scotland. The stark, roofless, red-sandstone ruins are substantial and, largely due to their beautiful green setting, romantic.

Trains run from Glasgow Central station to Blantyre (20 minutes, three hourly). Head straight down the hill from the station to reach the museum.

Lanark & New Lanark

POP 8253

Below the market town of Lanark, in an attractive gorge by the River Clyde, is the World Heritage site of **New Lanark** – an intriguing collection of restored mill buildings and warehouses.

Once the largest cotton-spinning complex in Britain, it was better known for the pioneering social experiments of Robert Owen, who managed the mill from 1800. New Lanark is really a memorial to this enlightened capitalist. You'll need at least half a day to explore this site, as there's plenty to see, and appealing walking along the riverside.

Sights & Activities

New Lanark Visitor Centre MUSEUM
(www.newlanark.org; adult/child/family £7/6/22; ⏲10am-5pm Apr-Sep, 11am-5pm Oct-Mar) You will need to buy a ticket to enter the main attractions. These include a huge working spinning mule, producing woollen yarn, the **Historic Schoolhouse**, which contains an innovative, high-tech journey to New

Lanark's past via a 3D hologram of the spirit of Annie McLeod, a 10-year-old mill girl who describes life here in 1820. The kids will love it as it's very realistic, although the 'do good for all mankind' theme is a little overbearing.

Also included in your admission is a **millworker's house**, Robert Owen's **home** and exhibitions on 'saving New Lanark'. There's also a 1920s-style **village store**.

Falls of Clyde EXHIBITION, WALK

The **Falls of Clyde Wildlife Centre** (www.swt.org.uk; adult/child £2/1; ⏲11am-5pm Mar-Dec, noon-4pm Jan & Feb) is also by the river in New Lanark. This place has child-friendly displays focused on badgers, bats, peregrine falcons and other prominent species. In season, there's a live video feed of peregrines nesting nearby. Outside is a bee tree, where you can see honey being made.

From the centre, you can walk up to Corra Linn (30 minutes) and Bonnington Linn (one hour), two of the **Falls of Clyde** that inspired Turner and Wordsworth, through the beautiful nature reserve managed by the Scottish Wildlife Trust.

Sleeping

New Lanark makes a very relaxing, attractive place to stay.

New Lanark Mill Hotel HOTEL ££

(☎01555-667200; www.newlanark.org; New Lanark; s/d £80/120; P @ ᯤ ♿) Cleverly converted from an 18th-century mill, this hotel is full of character and is a stone's throw from the major attractions. It has luxury rooms (only £25 extra for a spacious suite and added decadence) or self-catering accommodation in charming **cottages** (from £285/525 per week in winter/summer). The hotel also serves good **meals** (bar meals £6 to £9, 2-course dinner £23).

New Lanark SYHA HOSTEL £

(SYHA; ☎01555-666710; www.syha.org.uk; New Lanark; dm/tw £17/38; ⏲mid-Mar–mid-Oct; P @) This hostel has a great location in an old mill building by the River Clyde. It's been recently renovated and has a really good downstairs common area, and spruce en suite dormitories.

Information

Tourist office (☎01555-661661; lanark@visitscotland.com; Ladyacre Rd, Lanark; ⏲10am-5pm) Close to the bus and train stations. Closed Sundays October to March.

Getting There & Around

Lanark is 25 miles southeast of Glasgow. Express buses from Glasgow, run by Irvine's Coaches, make the hourly run from Monday to Saturday (one hour).

Trains also run daily between Glasgow Central station and Lanark (£5.45, 55 minutes, every 30 minutes).

It's a pleasant walk to New Lanark, but there's also a half-hourly bus service from the train station (daily).

BORDERS REGION

Domestic tourists grease the wheel of the Borders' economy – they flock here from north and south of the border, eager to explore links to the country's medieval past. It's a distinctive region – centuries of war and plunder have left a battle-scarred landscape, encapsulated by the remnants of the great Border abbeys. They were an irresistible magnet during the Border wars, and were destroyed and rebuilt numerous times. The monasteries met their scorched end in the 16th century and were never rebuilt. Today these massive stone shells are the region's finest attractions.

Kelso

POP 5116

Kelso, a prosperous market town with a broad, cobbled square flanked by Georgian buildings, has a French feel to it and an historic appeal. During the day it's a busy little place, but after 8pm you'll have the streets to yourself. The town has a lovely site at the junction of the Rivers Tweed and Teviot, and is one of the most enjoyable places in the Borders.

Sights

FREE **Kelso Abbey** ABBEY

(HS; www.historic-scotland.gov.uk; Bridge St; ⏲9.30am-6.30pm Apr-Sep, 9.30am-4.30pm Sat-Wed Oct-Mar) Once one of the richest abbeys in southern Scotland, Kelso Abbey was built by the Tironensians, an order founded at Tiron in Picardy and brought to the Borders around 1113 by David I. English raids in the 16th century reduced it to ruins, though what remains today is some of the finest surviving Romanesque architecture in Scotland.

Nearby, the rare, octagonal **Kelso Old Parish Chuch** (The Butts; ⏲10am-4pm Mon-Fri May-Sep), built in 1773, is intriguing.

BORDERS WALKING & CYCLING

The region's most famous walk is the challenging 212-mile **Southern Upland Way** (www.southernuplandway.gov.uk). If you want a sample, one of the best bits is the three- to four-day section from St John's Town of Dalry to Beattock. Another long-distance walk is the 62-mile **St Cuthbert's Way** (www.stcuthbertsway.fsnet.co.uk), inspired by the travels of St Cuthbert (a 7th-century saint who worked in Melrose Abbey), which crosses some superb scenery between Melrose and Lindisfarne (in England).

The **Borders Abbeys Way** (www.bordersabbeysway.com) links all the great Border abbeys in a 65-mile circuit. For shorter walks and especially circular loops in the hills, the towns of Melrose, Jedburgh and Kelso all make ideal bases.

The **Tweed Cycle Way** is a waymarked route running 62 miles along the beautiful Tweed Valley, following minor roads from Biggar to Peebles (13 miles), Melrose (16 miles), Coldstream (19 miles) and Berwick-upon-Tweed (14 miles). Jedburgh tourist office (p814) has details.

Floors Castle CASTLE
(www.floorscastle.com; adult/child £7.50/3.50; 11am-5pm May-Oct) Grandiose Floors Castle is Scotland's largest inhabited mansion and overlooks the Tweed about a mile west of Kelso. Built by William Adam in the 1720s, the original Georgian simplicity was 'improved' in the 1840s with the addition of rather ridiculous battlements and turrets. Inside are vividly coloured 17th-century Brussels tapestries in the drawing room and intricate oak carvings in the ornate ballroom. Palatial windows reveal a ribbon of green countryside extending well beyond the estate.

Sleeping

TOP CHOICE **Old Priory** B&B ££
(01573-223030; www.theoldpriorykelso.com; 33 Woodmarket St; s/d £50/75; P Wi-Fi) The doubles in this atmospheric place are fantastic and the family room has to be seen to be believed; rooms are both sumptuous and debonair with gorgeous dark polished wood pieces. The good news extends to the garden – perfect for a coffee in the morning – and a most comfortable sitting room. The huge windows are another feature, flooding the rooms with natural light.

TOP CHOICE **Ednam House Hotel** HOTEL ££
(01573-224168; www.ednamhouse.com; Bridge St; s/d from £78/115; P Wi-Fi family) The genteel, Georgian Ednam House, touched with a quiet dignity, contains many of its original features and is the top place in town, with fine gardens overlooking the river and the excellent **Ednam House Restaurant**. It's very popular with fisher folk and during salmon season, from the end of August until November, the hotel is very busy. Rooms with a river view cost more.

Central Guest House B&B £
(01890-883664; www.thecentralguesthousekelso.co.uk; s/d £30/45) A bargain in sometimes pricey Kelso and just on the central square. The owners live off-site so call ahead first. The rooms are fine: spacious, with firm beds, new carpets and good bathrooms. Rates are room-only, but you get a fridge, toaster, and microwave so you can create your own breakfast.

Eating & Drinking

Cobbles Inn PUB ££
(01573-223548; www.thecobblesinn.co.uk; 7 Bowmont St; mains £10-16; lunch & dinner Tue-Sun) We've included the phone number for a reason: this pub off the main square is so popular you should book for a meal at weekends. Why does it pack out? Because it's cheery, very welcoming, warm, and serves excellent upmarket pub food in generous portions. There's a decent wine selection and proper coffee, but the wise leave room for dessert too. The bar always has an interesting guest ale or two as well. A cracking place.

Oscar's BISTRO ££
(01573-224008; www.oscars-kelso.com; 33 Horsemarket; mains £10-16; lunch Mon & Wed-Sat, dinner Wed-Mon) Posh comfort food and the work of local artists sit side by side in this likeable bar/restaurant/gallery in the centre of town. The menu changes, but when you see avocados, serrano ham, sea bass, sizzling lamb, hummus, and haggis on the same menu, it means one thing: you might have to come back again to try everything. A wide selection of wines accompanies the food, and you can browse the exhibition space downstairs while you wait for your plate.

Information

Kelso Library (Bowmont St; ⌚Mon-Sat) Free internet access.

Tourist office (☎01573-223464; www.visitscottishborders.com; The Square; ⌚daily Apr-Nov, Mon-Sat Dec-Mar)

Getting There & Away

There are six buses daily (three on Sunday) to **Berwick-upon-Tweed** (one hour). Buses run to/from **Jedburgh** (25 minutes, up to 11 daily Monday to Saturday, five Sunday) and **Hawick** (one hour, seven daily Monday to Saturday, four Sunday). There are also frequent services to Edinburgh.

Around Kelso

SMAILHOLM TOWER

Perched on a rocky knoll above a small lake, the narrow, stone **Smailholm Tower** (HS; www.historic-scotland.gov.uk; Smailholm; adult/child £3.70/2.20; ⌚9.30am-5.30pm Apr-Sep, 9.30am-4.30pm Sat & Sun Oct-Mar) provides one of the most evocative sights in the Borders and keeps the bloody uncertainties of its history alive. Although the displays inside are sparse, the panoramic view from the top is worth the climb.

The nearby farm, **Sandyknowe**, was owned by Sir Walter Scott's grandfather. As Scott himself recognised, his imagination was fired by the ballads and stories he heard as a child at Sandyknowe, and by the ruined tower a stone's throw away.

The tower is 6 miles west of Kelso, a mile south of Smailholm village on the B6397. You pass through the farmyard to get to the tower. Munro's bus 65 between Melrose and Kelso stops in Smailholm village.

Melrose

POP 1656

Tiny, charming Melrose is a polished village running on the well-greased wheels of tourism. This little enclave is a complete contrast with overbearing Galashiels, whose urban sprawl laps at its western edges. Sitting at the feet of the three heather-covered Eildon Hills, Melrose has a classic market square and one of the great abbey ruins.

Sights

Melrose Abbey ABBEY

(HS; www.historic-scotland.gov.uk; adult/child £5.20/3.10; ⌚9.30am-5.30pm Apr-Sep, 9.30am-4.30pm Oct-Mar) Perhaps the most interesting of all the great Border abbeys, the red-sandstone Melrose Abbey was repeatedly destroyed by the English in the 14th century. The remaining broken shell is pure Gothic and the ruins are famous for their decorative stonework – see if you can glimpse the pig gargoyle playing the bagpipes on the roof. You can climb to the top for tremendous views. The abbey was founded by David I in 1136 for Cistercian monks from Rievaulx in Yorkshire. It was rebuilt by Robert the Bruce, whose heart is buried here. The ruins date from the 14th and 15th centuries, and were repaired by Sir Walter Scott in the 19th century.

The adjoining **museum** (free for abbey ticket holders) has many fine examples of 12th- to 15th-century stonework and pottery found in the area. Note the impressive remains of the 'great drain' outside – a medieval sewerage system.

Festivals & Events

In mid-April rugby followers fill the town to see the week-long **Melrose Rugby Sevens** (www.melrose7s.com) competition. The **Borders Book Festival** (www.bordersbookfestival.org) stretches over four days in late June.

Sleeping

Townhouse HOTEL ££

(☎01896-822645; www.thetownhousemelrose.co.uk; Market Sq; s/d £90/120; P Wi-Fi) The classy Townhouse, exuding warmth and professionalism, has some of the best rooms in town – tastefully furnished with attention to detail. There are two superior rooms (£132) that are enormous in size with lavish furnishings; the one on the ground floor in particular has an excellent en suite, which includes a Jacuzzi. It's well worth the price.

Old Bank House B&B ££

(☎01896-823712; www.oldbankhousemelrose.co.uk; 27 Buccleuch St; s/d £40/60) Right in the middle of town, this noble building offers B&B that stands out for its friendly welcome and helpful attitude. Spacious rooms and inviting beds make this a top Borders base.

Melrose SYHA HOSTEL £

(☎01896-822521; www.syha.org.uk; Priorwood; dm/tw £17/36; ⌚late Mar–late Oct; P @) A short walk from the abbey, this stately Georgian house is in a quiet location with a big grassy garden to relax in. The dorms vary substantially in number of beds and have no lockers, but it's all spotless and the common areas are good.

Eating

Townhouse RESTAURANT ££
(☎01896-822645; www.thetownhousemelrose.co.uk; Market Sq; mains £11-13; ⊙lunch & dinner) The brasserie and restaurant here turn out just about the best gourmet cuisine in town – the sister hotel Burt's, opposite, comes a close second – and offers decent value. There's some rich, elaborate, beautifully presented fare here, but you can always opt for the range of creative lunchtime sandwiches for a lighter feed.

Marmion's Brasserie RESTAURANT ££
(☎01896-822245; www.marmionsbrasserie.co.uk; 5 Buccleuch St; mains £10-16; ⊙lunch & dinner Mon-Sat) This atmospheric, oak-panelled niche serves snacks all day, but the lunch and dinner menus include gastronomic delights, featuring things like local lamb, venison steaks, or pan-seared cod. For lunch the focaccias with creative fillings are a good choice.

Information

Melrose Library (18 Market Sq; ⊙Mon-Fri) Free internet access.

Tourist office (☎01896-822283; melrose@visitscotland.com; Abbey St; ⊙10am-4.30pm Mon-Sat, noon-4pm Sun Apr-Oct, 10am-4pm Fri & Sat Nov-Mar) By the abbey.

Getting There & Away

First buses run to/from **Edinburgh** (£6, 2¼ hours, hourly) via Peebles. Change in **Galashiels** (20 minutes, frequent) for more frequent Edinburgh services and for other Borders destinations.

Around Melrose

DRYBURGH ABBEY

The most beautiful, complete Border abbey is **Dryburgh Abbey** (HS; www.historic-scotland.gov.uk; adult/child £4.70/2.80; ⊙9.30am-5.30pm Apr-Sep, 9.30am-4.30pm Oct-Mar), partly because the neighbouring town of Dryburgh no longer exists (another victim of the wars) and partly because it has a lovely site in a sheltered valley by the River Tweed, accompanied only by a symphony of birdsong. The abbey conjures up images of 12th-century monastic life more successfully than its counterparts in nearby towns. Dating from about 1150, it belonged to the Premonstratensians, a religious order founded in France. The pink-hued stone ruins were chosen as the burial place for Sir Walter Scott.

The abbey is 5 miles southeast of Melrose on the B6404, which passes famous **Scott's View** overlooking the valley. You can hike there along the southern bank of the River Tweed, or take a bus to the nearby village of Newtown St Boswells.

ABBOTSFORD

Fans of Sir Walter Scott should visit his former residence, **Abbotsford** (www.scottsabbotsford.co.uk; adult/child £7/3.50; ⊙9.30am-5pm Mon-Sat, 11am-4pm Sun Mar-May & Oct, 9.30am-5pm Sun Jun-Sep). The inspiration he drew from the surrounding 'wild' countryside influenced many of his most famous works. A collection of Scott memorabilia is on display, including many personal possessions.

The mansion is about 2 miles west of Melrose between the River Tweed and the B6360. Frequent buses run between Galashiels and Melrose; alight at the Tweed bank roundabout and follow the signposts (it's a 15-minute walk). You can also walk from Melrose to Abbotsford in an hour along the southern bank of the Tweed.

Jedburgh

POP 4090

Attractive Jedburgh is a lush, compact oasis, where many old buildings and wynds (narrow alleys) have been intelligently restored, inviting exploration by foot. It's constantly busy with domestic tourists, but wander into some of the pretty side streets and you won't hear a pin drop.

Sights

Jedburgh Abbey ABBEY
(HS; www.historic-scotland.gov.uk; Abbey Rd; adult/child £5.20/3.10; ⊙9.30am-5.30pm Apr-Sep, 9.30am-4.30pm Oct-Mar) Dominating the town skyline, Jedburgh Abbey was the first great Border abbey to be passed into state care, and it shows – audio and visual presentations telling the abbey's story are scattered throughout the carefully preserved ruins (good for the kids or if it's raining). The red-sandstone ruins are roofless but relatively intact, and the ingenuity of the master mason can be seen in some of the rich (if somewhat faded) stone carvings in the nave (be careful of the staircase in the

nave – it's slippery when wet). The abbey was founded in 1138 by David I as a priory for Augustinian canons.

FREE **Mary Queen of Scots House** HISTORIC HOUSE
(Queen St; ⏲10am-4.30pm Mon-Sat, 11am-4.30pm Sun Mar-Nov) Mary stayed at this beautiful 16th-century tower house in 1566 after her famous ride to visit the injured earl of Bothwell, her future husband, at Hermitage Castle. The interesting displays evoke the sad saga of Mary's life.

Sleeping

Maplebank B&B £
(☎01835-862051; maplebank3@btinternet.com; 3 Smiths Wynd; s/d £25/40; P) It's very pleasing to come across places like this, where it really feels like you're staying in someone's home. That someone in this case is like your favourite aunt: friendly and chaotic and generous. There's lots of clutter and it's very informal. The rooms are comfortable and large, and share a good bathroom. Breakfast (particularly if you like fruit, homemade yogurts and a selection of everything) is better than you'll get at a posh guest house.

Willow Court B&B ££
(☎01835-863702; www.willowcourtjedburgh.co.uk; The Friars; d £65-70; P wi-fi) With superb views over Jedburgh from the conservatory, where you are served a three-meals-in-one breakfast, Willow Court is a traditional B&B with homespun décor, smiling hosts and a large garden. Ask about the self-catering cottage just out of town.

Jedburgh Camping & Caravanning Club CAMPING £
(☎01835-863393; www.campingandcaravanningclub.co.uk/jedburgh; Elliot Park, A68; tent sites with/without car £15/7.50; ⏲Apr-Oct; P wi-fi) About a mile north of the town centre, opposite Jedburgh Woollen Mill, this site is set on the banks of Jed Water and is quiet and convenient, particularly if you're interested in fishing.

Eating

Nightjar RESTAURANT ££
(☎01835-862552; www.thenightjar.co.uk; 1 Abbey Close; mains £10-15; ⏲dinner Thu-Sat) Casual but classy, this is a highly commended restaurant dishing out a mix of creative meals, including seafood and Thai cuisine. The real highlight is if you're lucky enough to be here on the last Saturday of the month when a special Thai menu is revealed; locals rave about this night.

Carters Rest PUB ££
(Abbey Pl; mains £9-12; ⏲lunch & dinner; wi-fi) Right opposite the abbey, this place offers upmarket pub grub in an attractive lounge bar. The standard fare is fleshed out with an evening dinner menu featuring local lamb and other goodies. Portions are generous and served with a smile.

Information

There's a free wi-fi zone around the centre.

Library (Castlegate; ⏲Mon-Fri) Free internet.

Tourist office (☎01835-863170; jedburgh@visitscotland.com; Murray's Green; ⏲9.30am-5pm Mon-Sat, 10am-4pm Sun) Head tourist office for the Borders region. Extended hours in summer. Closed Sunday in winter.

Getting There & Away

Jedburgh has good bus connections to **Hawick** (25 minutes, roughly hourly), **Melrose** (30 minutes, at least hourly Monday to Saturday) and **Kelso** (25 minutes, at least hourly Monday to Saturday, four Sunday). Munro's runs from Jedburgh to **Edinburgh** (£6, two hours, at least hourly Monday to Saturday, five Sunday).

Hermitage Castle

The 'guardhouse of the bloodiest valley in Britain', **Hermitage Castle** (HS; www.historic-scotland.gov.uk; adult/child £3.70/2.20; ⏲9.30am-5.30pm Apr-Sep) embodies the brutal history of the Scottish Borders. Desolate but proud with its massive squared stone walls, it looks more like a lair for orc raiding parties than a home for Scottish nobility, and is one of the bleakest and most stirring of Scottish ruins.

Strategically crucial, the castle was the scene of many a dark deed and dirty deal with the English invaders, all of which rebounded heavily on the perfidious Scottish lord in question. Here, in 1338, Sir William Douglas imprisoned his enemy Sir Alexander Ramsay and deliberately starved him to death. Ramsay survived for 17 days by eating grain that trickled into his pit (which can still be seen) from the granary above. In 1566, Mary Queen of Scots famously visited the wounded tenant of the castle, Lord Bothwell, here. Fortified, he recovered to (probably) murder her husband, marry her himself, then abandon her months later and flee into exile.

The castle is about 12 miles south of Hawick on the B6357.

Peebles

POP 8065

With a picturesque main street set on a ridge between the River Tweed and the Eddleston Water stream, Peebles is one of the most handsome of the Border towns. Though it lacks a major sight as a focus to things, the agreeable atmosphere and good walking options in the rolling, wooded hills hereabouts will entice you to linger for a couple of days.

Two miles east of town off the A72, in **Glentress forest**, is one of the **7stanes** (www.7stanes.gov.uk) mountain-biking hubs (see boxed text, p826). It also has osprey viewing and marked walking trails.

Sleeping & Eating

Cringletie House HOTEL £££
(☎01721-725750; www.cringletie.com; s/d from £210/230; P@) Luxury without snobbery is this enchanting hotel's hallmark, and more power to them. To call it a house is being coy; it's an elegant baronial mansion, 2 miles north of Peebles on the A703 and set in lush, wooded grounds. Rooms are plush and feature genteel elegance and linen so soft you could wrap a newborn in it. There's an excellent **restaurant** (mains £23) and an excellent atmosphere.

Rowanbrae B&B ££
(☎01721-721630; www.aboutscotland/rowanbrae; 103 Northgate; s/d £35/60;) A marvellously hospitable couple run this great B&B in a quiet cul-de-sac not far from the main street; you'll soon feel like you're staying with friends. There are three upstairs bedrooms, two with en suite, and an excellent guest lounge for relaxation.

Sunflower Restaurant RESTAURANT ££
(☎01721-722420; www.thesunflower.net; 4 Bridgegate; mains £10-15; lunch Mon-Sat, dinner Thu-Sat;) The Sunflower, with its warm yellow dining room, is in a quiet spot off the main drag and has a reputation that brings lunchers from all over southern Scotland. It serves good salads for lunch and has an admirable menu in the evenings, with creative and elegant dishes that always include some standout vegetarian fare.

Tontine Hotel RESTAURANT ££
(☎01721-720892; www.tontinehotel.com; High St; mains £7-14; lunch & dinner; P) Glorious is the only word to describe the Georgian dining room here, complete with musicians' gallery, fireplace, and windows the like of which we'll never see again. It'd be worth it even if they served catfood on mouldy bread, but luckily the meals – ranging from pub classics like steak-and-ale pie to more ambitious fare – are tasty and backed up by very welcoming service. **Rooms** (single/double £75/110) are decent too: there's a small supplement for river views.

Information

Tourist office (☎01721-723159; bordersinfo@visitscotland.com; High St; 9am-5pm Apr-Dec, 10am-4pm Mon-Sat Jan-Mar) To 6pm in summer.

Getting There & Away

The bus stop is beside the post office on Eastgate. First bus 62 runs half hourly to **Edinburgh** (1¼ hours), **Galashiels** (45 minutes) and **Melrose** (one hour).

Around Peebles

TRAQUAIR HOUSE

One of Scotland's great country houses, **Traquair House** (www.traquair.co.uk; Innerleithen; adult/child/family £7.50/4/21; 10.30am-5pm Jun-Aug, noon-5pm Apr-May & Sep, 11am-4pm Oct, 11am-3pm Sat & Sun Nov) has a powerful ethereal beauty, and an exploration here is like time travel. Since the 15th century, the house has belonged to various branches of the Stuart family, and the family's unwavering Catholicism and loyalty to the Stuart cause are largely why development ceased when it did.

One of its most interesting places is the concealed room where priests secretly lived and performed Mass – up until 1829 when the Catholic Emancipation Act was finally passed.

In addition to the house, there's a **garden maze**, an **art gallery**, a small **brewery** producing the tasty Bear Ale, and an active craft community. The **Traquair Fair** takes place here in early August.

Traquair is 1.5 miles south of Innerleithen, about 6 miles southeast of Peebles. Bus 62 runs from Edinburgh via Peebles to Innerleithen and on to Galashiels and Melrose.

AYRSHIRE & ARRAN

Ayrshire is synonymous with golf and with Robert Burns – and there's plenty on offer here to satisfy both of these pursuits. Troon has six golf courses for starters, and plenty of yachties, and there's enough Burns memorabilia in the region to satisfy his most fanatic admirers.

This region's main drawcard though is the irresistible Isle of Arran. With the most varied and scenic countryside of the southern Hebridean islands, this easily accessible island shouldn't be missed.

North Ayrshire

LARGS

POP 11,241

On a sunny day, there are few more beautiful places in southern Scotland than Largs, where green grass meets the sparkling water of the Firth of Clyde. It's a resort-style waterfront town that harks back to seaside days in times of gentler pleasures.

The main attraction in Largs is **Vikingar!** (www.kaleisure.com; Greenock Rd; adult/child £4.50/3.50; 10.30am-4.30pm Apr-Sep, 10.30am-3.30pm Oct & Mar, 10.30am-3.30pm Sat & Sun Nov & Feb). This multimedia exhibition describes Viking influence in Scotland until its demise at the Battle of Largs in 1263. Tours with staff in Viking outfits run every hour.

Sleeping & Eating

Brisbane House Hotel HOTEL ££
(01475-687200; www.brisbanehousehotel.com; 14 Greenock Rd, Esplanade; s/d £80/85, d/ste with sea view £95/120;) We're not sure about the modern facade on this genteel old building, but the rooms are quite luxurious, and some – it's aimed at wedding parties – have Jacuzzis and huge beds. It's on the waterfront road, so paying the extra for a sea view will reward in fine weather, as the sun sets over the island opposite. There's a decent bar and restaurant downstairs and a comfortable contemporary feel.

Nardini CAFE, BISTRO ££
(www.nardinis.co.uk; Esplanade; mains £11-18; 9am-10pm;) Nothing typifies the old-time feel of Largs more than this giant art deco gelateria, well into its second century. The ice creams are decadently delicious, with rich flavours that'll have parents licking more than their fair share from the kids. There's also a cafe with outdoor seating, and a restaurant which does pizzas, pastas, and some surprisingly decent dishes like duck breast and delicious sardines on toast.

Haven House B&B £
(01475-676389; m.l.mcqueen@btinternet.com; 18 Charles St; r per person £25) One of several good options on a street close to the water, this has comfortable rooms with good shared bathrooms. It's an easy-going place typical of the friendliness of this town. Room-only rates are a fiver less per person.

Information

Tourist office (01475-689962; www.ayrshire-arran.com; 10.30am-3pm Mon-Sat Easter-Oct) At the train station, a block back from the waterfront on the main street.

Getting There & Away

Largs is 32 miles west of Glasgow by road. There are very regular buses to Glasgow (45 minutes) and roughly one or two hourly to **Ardrossan** (30 minutes) and **Ayr** (1¼ hours). There are trains to Largs from **Glasgow Central station** (£6.35, one hour, hourly).

ISLE OF GREAT CUMBRAE

POP 1200

Walking or cycling is the best way to explore this accessible, hilly island (it's only 4 miles long), ideal for a day trip from Largs. **Millport** is the only town, strung out a long way around the bay overlooking neighbouring Little Cumbrae.

The town boasts Britain's smallest cathedral, the lovely **Cathedral of the Isles** (01475-530353; College St; daylight hours), which was completed in 1851. Inside it's quite ornate with a lattice woodwork ceiling and fragments of early Christian carved stones.

The island's minor roads have well-marked **walking** and **cycling** routes. Take the Inner Circle route up to the island's highest point, **Glaid Stone**, where you get good views of Arran and Largs, and even as far as the Paps of Jura on a clear day. You can walk between the ferry and the town via here in about an hour. There are several bike-hire places in Millport.

If you're staying overnight on the island there are several choices. Try the unusual **College of the Holy Spirit** (01475-530353; www.island-retreats.org; College St; s/d £35/60, with en suite £50/70;), next to the cathedral; there's a refectory-style dining room and a library.

A very frequent 15-minute CalMac ferry ride links Largs with Great Cumbrae (passenger/car £4.70/20.35) daily. Buses meet the ferries for the 3.5-mile journey to Millport (£1.80/2.80 single/return).

ARDROSSAN

POP 10,952

The main reason – OK the *only* reason – for coming here is to catch a CalMac ferry to Arran. Trains leave Glasgow Central station (£5.85, one hour, half-hourly) to connect with ferries.

Isle of Arran

POP 4800

Enchanting Arran is a jewel in Scotland's tourism crown. Strangely undiscovered by foreign tourists, the island is a visual feast, and boasts culinary delights, cosy pubs (including its own brewery) and stacks of accommodation. The variations in Scotland's dramatic landscape can all be experienced on this one small island, best explored by pulling on the hiking boots or jumping on a bicycle. Arran offers some challenging walks in the mountainous north, often compared to the Highlands, while the island's circular road is very popular with cyclists.

BRODICK & AROUND

Most visitors arrive in Brodick, the heartbeat of the island.

Sights

Brodick Castle & Park CASTLE

(NTS; www.nts.org.uk; adult/child castle & park £10.50/7.50, park only £5.50/4.50; castle 11am-4pm Sat-Wed Apr-Oct, open daily late Jun-early Sep, park 9.30am-sunset) The first impression of this estate 2.5 miles north of Brodick is that of an animal morgue – you enter via the hunting gallery, wallpapered with prized deer heads. On your way to the formal dining room (with its peculiar table furnishings), note the intricacy of the fireplace in the library. The castle has more of a lived-in feel than some NTS properties. Only a small portion is open to visitors. The extensive grounds, now a country park with various trails among the rhododendrons, justify the steep entry fee.

On the main road not far from the castle entrance are a number of attractions. In Duchess Court, **Arran Aromatics** (01770-302595; www.arranaromatics.com; 9.30am-5pm) has a popular visitor centre where you can purchase any number of scented items and watch the production line at work. Free factory tours run on Thursdays in summer at 6pm. It also runs **Soapworks** (soapmaking from £7.50; 10am-4pm), a fun little place where kids (and adults, of course) can experiment by making their own soaps, combining colours and moulds to make weird and wonderful creations.

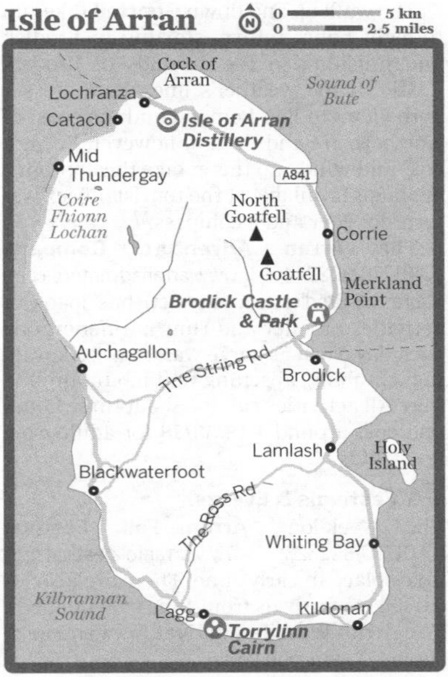

Nearby, the Cladach centre has an excellent self-guided tour of the **Isle of Arran Brewery** (01770-302353; www.arranbrewery.com; Cladach; tour £2.50; 10am-5pm Mon-Sat, 12.30-5pm Sun Apr-Sep, 10am-3.30pm Mon & Wed-Sat Oct-Mar), which includes tastings in the shop. Arran beers are pure quality.

Activities

Drop into the tourist office for plenty of walking and cycling suggestions around the island. The 50-mile circuit on the coastal road is popular with cyclists and has few serious hills – more in the south than the north. There are plenty of walking booklets and maps available. There are many walking trails clearly signposted around the island. Several leave from Lochranza, including the spectacular walk to the island's northeast tip, **Cock of Arran**, and finishing in the village of Sannox (8 miles one-way).

The walk up and down **Goatfell** takes up to eight hours return, starting in Brodick and finishing in the grounds of Brodick Castle. If the weather's fine, there are superb views to Ben Lomond and the coast of Northern Ireland. It can, however, be very cold and windy up there; take the appropriate maps (available at the tourist office), waterproof gear and a compass.

The **Arran Adventure Company** (01770-302244; www.arranadventure.com; Shore Rd, Brodick; Easter-Oct) has loads of activities on offer and runs a different one each day (such as gorge walking, sea kayaking, climbing, abseiling and mountain biking). All activities run for about three hours and cost around £48/38/28 for adults/solo teens/kids.

Festivals & Events

The week-long **Arran Folk Festival** (01770-302623; www.arranfolkfestival.org) takes place in early June. There are also local village festivals from June to September. The **Arran Wildlife Festival** (www.arranwildlife.co.uk) is in mid-May.

Sleeping

TOP CHOICE Kilmichael Country House Hotel HOTEL £££
(01770-302219; www.kilmichael.com; Glen Cloy; s £95, d £160-199; P) The island's best hotel, the Kilmichael is also the oldest building – it has a glass window dating from 1650. The hotel is a luxurious, tastefully decorated spot, a mile outside Brodick, with eight rooms and an excellent **restaurant** (3-course dinner £42). It's an ideal, utterly relaxing hideaway, and feels very classy without being overly formal.

Glenartney B&B ££
(01770-302220; www.glenartney-arran.co.uk; Mayish Rd; s/d £56/78; late Mar–Sep; P) Uplifting bay views and genuine, helpful hosts make this a cracking option. Airy, stylish rooms make the most of the natural light available here at the top of the town. Cyclists will appreciate the bike wash and storage facilities, while hikers can benefit from the drying rooms and expert trail advice. The owners make big efforts to be sustainable, too.

Fellview B&B ££
(01770-302153; fellviewarran@yahoo.co.uk; 6 Strathwhillan Rd; r per person £30) This lovely house near the ferry is an excellent place to stay. The two rooms – which share a good bathroom – are full of thoughtful personal touches like bathrobes, and breakfast is in a pretty garden conservatory. The owner is warm, friendly and encapsulates Scottish hospitality; she doesn't charge a supplement for singles (because, in her words, 'it's not their fault'). To get here, head south out of Brodick and take the left-hand turn to Strathwhillan. Fellview is just up on the right.

Glen Rosa Farm CAMPING £
(01770-302380; sites per person £4; P) In a lush glen by a river, 2 miles from Brodick, this large place has plenty of nooks and crannies to pitch a tent. It's remote camping with cold water and toilets only. To get there from Brodick head north, take String Rd, then turn right almost immediately on the road signed to Glen Rosa. After 400m, on the left is a white house where you book in; the campground is further down the road.

Eating & Drinking

Eilean Mòr CAFE £
(www.eileanmorarran.com; Shore Rd; mains £8-10; food 10am-9pm, bar 11am-midnight;) Upbeat and modern, this likeable little cafe/bar does tasty meals through the day, with pizzas and pastas featuring. But it's not afraid to give them a Scottish twist; try the haggis ravioli.

Ormidale Hotel PUB £
(01770-302293; www.ormidalehotel.co.uk; Glen Cloy; mains £8-10; lunch & dinner;) This hotel has decent bar food. Dishes change regularly, but there are always some good vegetarian options, and daily specials. Quantities and value-for-money are high, and Arran beers are on tap.

LOCHRANZA

The village of Lochranza is in a stunning location in a small bay at the north of the island. On a promontory stand the ruins of the 13th-century **Lochranza Castle** (HS; www.historic-scotland.gov.uk; 24hr), said to be the inspiration for the castle in *The Black Island,* Hergé's Tintin adventure. It's basically a draughty shell inside, with interpretative signs to help you decipher the layout.

Also in Lochranza is the **Isle of Arran Distillery** (01770-830264; www.arranwhisky.com; tours adult/child £5/free; 10am-6pm Mon-Sat, 11am-6pm Sun mid-Mar–Oct), which produces a light, aromatic single malt. The tour is a good one; it's a small distillery, and the whisky-making process is thoroughly explained.

Sleeping & Eating

Lochranza SYHA HOSTEL £
(01770-830631; www.syha.org.uk; Lochranza; dm/f £17.50/72; mid-Feb–Oct; P @) A recent refurbishment has made a really excellent hostel of what was always a charming place, with lovely views. The rooms are great, with chunky wooden furniture, keycards, and lockers. Rainwater toilets, a heat exchange system, and excellent disabled room shows the thought that's gone into the redesign, while plush lounging areas, a kitchen you could run a restaurant out of, laundry, drying room, red deer in the garden, and welcoming management make this a top option.

Apple Lodge B&B ££
(01770-830229; Lochranza; s/d/ste £54/78/90; P) Once the village manse, this rewarding choice is most dignified and hospitable. Rooms are individually furnished, and very commodious. One has a four-poster bed, while another is a self-contained suite in the garden. The guest lounge is perfect for curling up with a good book, and courteous hosts mean you should book this one well ahead in summer.

Catacol Bay Hotel PUB ££
(01770-830231; www.catacol.co.uk; Catacol; r per person £30; P @) Genially run, and with a memorable position overlooking the water, this no-frills pub 2 miles south of Lochranza offers comfortable-enough rooms with shared bathroom and views to lift the heaviest heart. No-frills bar food comes out in generous portions, there's a Sunday lunch buffet (£10.50), and the beer garden is worth a contemplative pint or two as you gaze off across the water into the west.

SOUTH COAST

The landscape in the southern part of the island is much gentler; the road drops into little wooded valleys, and it's particularly lovely around **Lagg**. There's a 10-minute walk from Lagg Hotel to **Torrylinn Cairn**, a chambered tomb over 4000 years old where at least eight bodies were found. **Kildonan** has pleasant sandy beaches, a gorgeous water outlook, a hotel, a campground and an ivy-clad ruined castle.

Sleeping & Eating

TOP CHOICE **Kildonan Hotel** HOTEL ££
(01770-820207; www.kildonanhotel.com; Kildonan; s/d/ste £70/95/125; P) Luxurious rooms and a grounded attitude – dogs and kids are made very welcome – combine to make this one of Arran's best options. Oh, and it's right by the water, with fabulous views and seals basking on the rocks. The standard rooms are beautifully furnished and spotless, but the suites – with private terrace or small balcony – are superb. Other amenities include great staff, a bar serving good bar meals, a restaurant doing succulent seafood, an ATM, book exchange, and laptops lent to guests if you didn't bring one. Applause.

Royal Arran Hotel B&B ££
(01770-700286; www.royalarran.co.uk; Whiting Bay; s £50, d £90-105; P) This personalised, intimate spot has just four rooms. The double upstairs is our idea of accommodation heaven – four-poster bed, big heavy linen, a huge room and gorgeous water views. Room No 1 downstairs is a great size and has a private patio. The hosts couldn't be more welcoming (except to kids under 12, who aren't allowed).

Sealshore Campsite CAMPING £
(01770-820320; www.campingarran.com; Kildonan; sites per person £6, per tent £1-3; P) Living up to its name, this small campsite is right by the sea (and, happily, the Kildonan Hotel) with one of Arran's finest views from its grassy camping area. There's a good washroom area with heaps of showers, and the breeze keeps the midges away.

LAMLASH

An upmarket town (even the streets feel wider here), Lamlash is in a dazzling setting, strung along the beachfront. The bay was used as a safe anchorage by the navy during WWI and WWII.

Just off the coast is **Holy Island**, owned by the Samye Ling Tibetan Centre and used as a retreat, but day visits are allowed. Depending on tides, the **ferry** (01770-600998) makes around seven trips a day (adult/child return £10/5, 15 minutes) from Lamlash and runs between May and September. The same folk also run fun mackerel-fishing expeditions (£20 per person).

Built in the 17th century, the **Lilybank Guest House** (01770-600230; www.lilybank-arran.co.uk; Shore Rd, Lamlash; s/d £50/70; P) retains its heritage but has been refurbished for 21st-century needs. Rooms are clean and comfortable, with one adapted for disabled use. The front ones have great views over Holy Island. Breakfast includes oak-smoked kippers and Arran goodies.

Information

In Brodick there are banks with ATMs.

Arran Library (☎01770-302835; Brodick Hall; ⌚10am-5pm Tue, 10am-7.30pm Thu & Fri, 10am-1pm Sat) Free internet access.

Hospital (☎01770-600777; Lamlash)

Tourist office (☎01770-303774; www.ayrshire-arran.com; ⌚9am-5pm Mon-Sat) Efficient; by Brodick pier.

Getting There & Away

CalMac runs a car ferry between **Ardrossan** and **Brodick** (passenger/car return £9.70/59, 55 minutes, four to eight daily), and from April to late October runs services between **Claonaig** and **Lochranza** (passenger/car return £8.75/39.10, 30 minutes, seven to nine daily).

Getting Around

BICYCLE Several places hire out bicycles in Brodick, including **Arran Adventure Company** (☎01770-302244; www.arranadventure.com; Shore Rd, Brodick; day/week £15/55) and the **Boathouse** (☎01770-302868; Brodick Beach; day/week £12.50/45).

CAR At the service station near the ferry pier, **Arran Transport** (☎01770-700345; Brodick) hires cars from £25/32 per half/full day.

PUBLIC TRANSPORT Four to seven buses daily go from Brodick pier to Lochranza (45 minutes), and many daily go from Brodick to Lamlash and Whiting Bay (30 minutes), then on to Kildonan and Blackwaterfoot. Pick up a timetable from the tourist office. An **Arran Rural Rover ticket** costs £4.75 and permits travel anywhere on the island for a day (buy it from the driver). For a **taxi**, call ☎01770-302274 in Brodick or ☎01770-600903 in Lamlash.

South Ayrshire

AYR

POP 46,431

Reliant on tourism, Ayr, whose long sandy beach has made it a popular family seaside resort since Victorian times, has struggled in the recent economic climate. Parts of the centre have a neglected air, though there are many fine Georgian and Victorian buildings, and it makes a convenient base for exploring this section of coast.

Sights

Most things to see in Ayr are Robert Burns-related. The bard was baptised in the **Auld Kirk** (Old Church) off High St. Several of his poems are set here in Ayr; in *Twa Brigs*, Ayr's old and new bridges argue with one another. The **Auld Brig** (Old Bridge) was built in 1491 and spans the river just north of the church. **St John's Tower** (Eglinton Tce) is the only remnant of a church where a parliament was held in 1315, the year after the celebrated victory at Bannockburn.

Festivals & Events

The **Burns an' a' That** (www.burnsfestival.com) festival, held in Ayr in late May, has a bit of everything, from wine-tasting to horseracing to concerts, some of it Burns-related.

Sleeping

Crescent B&B ££

(☎01292-287329; www.26crescent.co.uk; 26 Bellevue Cres; s £50, d £70-80; 📶) When the blossoms are out, Bellevue Cres is Ayr's prettiest street, and this is an excellent place to stay on it. The rooms are impeccable – a tenner to upgrade to the spacious four-poster room is a sound investment – but it's the warm welcome given by the hosts that makes this special. Numerous little extras, like Arran toiletries, bottled water in the rooms, and silver cutlery at breakfast add appeal.

Eglinton Guest House B&B ££

(☎01292-264623; www.eglinton-guesthouse-ayr.com; 23 Eglinton Tce; r per person £26; 📶) A short walk west of the bus station, this friendly family-run Georgian property is in a quiet cul-de-sac and has a range of traditional, tidy rooms. The location is brilliant – between the beach and the town, and it offers plenty of value, with comfortable beds and compact en suite bathrooms.

Eating & Drinking

Fouter's RESTAURANT £££

(☎01292-261391; www.fouters.co.uk; 2a Academy St; mains £16-20; ⌚dinner Tue-Sat) The best place to eat in town, Fouter's is a class act set in a former bank vault opposite the town hall. It's an ideal place to splash out on a top-class dinner without breaking the budget. It specialises in Ayrshire produce (such as new season local lamb with pine nut, garlic and herb crust) and Mediterranean-style seafood. There's an early-dining menu (£15 for two courses) from 5pm to 7pm.

Beresford BISTRO ££

(☎01292-280820; www.theberesfordayr.co.uk; 22 Beresford Tce; mains £10-16; ⌚food 9am-9pm) Style and fun go hand in hand at this upbeat establishment serving afternoon martinis in teapots and luring churchgoing ladies with artisanal chocolates. The food is a creative fusion of influences based on solid local produce, with Ayrshire pork, west coast oysters, and Scottish lamb often featuring. Some dishes hit real heights, and are solidly backed by a wide choice of wines, with 10 available by the glass. It stays open as a bar after the kitchen close. Top service seals the deal.

Tam o'Shanter PUB

(230 High St; mains £7) Opened in the mid-18th century and featured in the Burns poem whose name it now bears, this is an atmospheric old pub with traditional pub grub (served noon to 9pm).

Information

Carnegie Library (12 Main St; Mon-Sat) Offers fast, free internet access.

Tourist office (01292-290300; www.ayrshire-arran.com; 22 Sandgate; 9am-5pm Mon-Sat, 10am-5pm Sun Apr-Sep, 9am-5pm Mon-Sat Oct-Mar)

Getting There & Around

The main bus operator in the area is **Stagecoach Western** (01292-613500; www.stagecoachbus.com), which runs very frequent express services to **Glasgow** (one hour) and also serves **Stranraer** (£6.90, two hours, four to eight a day), other Ayrshire destinations, and **Dumfries** (£5.70, 2¼ hours, five to seven a day).

There are at least two trains an hour that run to Ayr from **Glasgow Central station** (£6.70, 50 minutes), and some trains continue south from Ayr to **Stranraer** (£13, 1½ hours).

ALLOWAY

The pretty, lush town of Alloway (3 miles south of Ayr) should be on the itinerary of every Robert Burns fan – he was born here on 25 January 1759.

The brand new **Robert Burns Birthplace Museum** (NTS; www.nts.org.uk; adult/child £8/5; 10am-5pm Oct-Mar, 10am-5.30pm Apr-Sep) displays a solid collection of Burnsiana, including manuscripts and possessions of the poet like the pistols he packed in order to carry out his daily work – as a taxman. A Burns jukebox allows you to select readings of your favourite Burns verses, and there are other entertaining audio and visual performances.

The admission ticket (valid for three days) also covers the atmospheric **Burns Cottage**, by the main road from Ayr, and connected by a sculpture-lined walkway from the Birthplace Museum. Born in the little box bed in this cramped thatched dwelling, the poet spent the first seven years of his life here. It's an attractive display which gives you a context for reading plenty of his verse. Much-needed translation of some of the more obscure Scots farming terms he loved to use decorate the walls.

Near the Birthplace Museum are the ruins of **Alloway Auld Kirk**, the setting for part of *Tam o'Shanter*. Burns' father, William Burnes (his son dropped the 'e' from his name), is buried in the kirkyard; read the poem on the back of the gravestone.

The **Burns Monument & Gardens** are nearby. The monument was built in 1823 and affords a view of the 13th-century **Brig o'Doon House**.

Getting There & Away

Stagecoach Western bus 57 operates hourly between Alloway and Ayr from 8.45am to 3.45pm Monday to Saturday (10 minutes). Otherwise, rent a bike and cycle here.

TROON

POP 14,766

Troon, a major sailing centre on the coast 7 miles north of Ayr, has excellent sandy beaches and six golf courses. The demanding championship course **Royal Troon** (01292-311555; www.royaltroon.co.uk; Craigend Rd) has offers on its website; the standard green fee is £165 (caddie hire is £40 extra).

Getting There & Away

There are half-hourly trains to **Ayr** (10 minutes) and **Glasgow** (£6.15, 45 minutes).

P&O (0871 66 44 777; www.poirishsea.com) sails twice daily to **Larne** (£24 for passengers, £79 for a car and driver, two hours) in Northern Ireland.

CULZEAN CASTLE & COUNTRY PARK

The Scottish National Trust's flagship property, magnificent **Culzean** (NTS; 01655-884400; www.culzeanexperience.org; adult/child/family £13/9/32, park only adult/child £8.50/5.50; castle 10.30am-5pm Apr-Oct, park 9.30am-sunset year round) is one of the most impressive of Scotland's great stately homes. The entrance to Culzean (kull-*ane*) is a converted viaduct, and on approach the castle appears like a mirage, floating into view. Designed by Robert Adam, who was encouraged to exercise his romantic genius in its design, this 18th-century mansion is perched dramatically on the edge of the cliffs. Robert Adam was the most influential architect of his time,

THE SCOTTISH BARD

Best remembered for penning the words of *Auld Lang Syne*, Robert Burns (1759–96) is Scotland's most famous poet and a popular hero whose birthday (25 January) is celebrated as Burns Night by Scots around the world.

Burns was born in 1759 in Alloway to a poor family, who scraped a living gardening and farming. At school he soon showed an aptitude for literature and a fondness for the folk song. He later began to write his own songs and satires. When the problems of his arduous farming life were compounded by the threat of prosecution from the father of Jean Armour, with whom he'd had an affair, he decided to emigrate to Jamaica. He gave up his share of the family farm and published his poems to raise money for the journey.

The poems were so well reviewed in Edinburgh that Burns decided to remain in Scotland and devote himself to writing. He went to Edinburgh in 1787 to publish a second edition, but the financial rewards were not enough to live on and he had to take a job as an excise man in Dumfriesshire. Though he worked well, he wasn't a taxman by nature, and described his job as 'the execrable office of whip-person to the blood-hounds of justice'. He contributed many songs to collections published by Johnson and Thomson in Edinburgh, and a 3rd edition of his poems was published in 1793. To give an idea of the prodigious writings of the man, Robert Burns composed more than 28,000 lines of verse over 22 years. Burns died of rheumatic fever in Dumfries in 1796, aged 37.

Burns wrote in Lallans, the Scottish Lowland dialect of English that is not very accessible to the Sassenach (Englishman), or foreigner; perhaps this is part of his appeal. He was also very much a man of the people, satirising the upper classes and the church for their hypocrisy.

The Burns connection in southern Scotland is milked for all it's worth and tourist offices have a *Burns Heritage Trail* leaflet leading you to every place that can claim some link with the bard. Burns fans should have a look at www.robertburns.org.

renowned for his meticulous attention to detail and the elegant classical embellishments with which he decorated his ceilings and fireplaces.

Getting There & Away

Culzean is 12 miles south of Ayr; Maybole is the nearest train station, but since it's 4 miles away it's best to come by bus from Ayr (30 minutes, 11 daily Monday to Saturday). Buses pass the park gates, from where it's a 20-minute walk through the grounds to the castle.

DUMFRIES & GALLOWAY

Some of the region's finest attractions lie in the gentle hills and lush valleys of Dumfries & Galloway. Ideal for families, there's plenty on offer for the kids and, happily, restaurants, B&Bs and guest houses that are very used to children. Galloway Forest is a highlight, with its sublime views, mountain-biking and walking trails, red deer, kites and other wildlife, as are the dream-like ruins of Caerlaverock Castle.

Dumfries

POP 31,146

Lovely, red-hued sandstone bridges crisscross pleasant Dumfries, which is bisected by the wide River Nith, and there are pleasant grassed areas along the river bank. Historically, Dumfries held a strategic position in the path of vengeful English armies. Consequently, although it has existed since Roman times, the oldest standing building dates from the 17th century.

Sights

The red-sandstone bridges arching over the River Nith are the most attractive features of the town: **Devorgilla Bridge** (1431) is one of the oldest bridges in Scotland. You can download a multilingual MP3 audio tour of the town at www.dumgal.gov.uk/audiotour.

FREE **Burns House** MUSEUM
(www.dumgal.gov.uk/museums; Burns St; ⏲10am-5pm Mon-Sat & 2-5pm Sun Apr-Sep, 10am-1pm & 2-5pm Tue-Sat Oct-Mar) This is a place of pilgrimage for Burns enthusiasts. It's here that the poet spent the last years

of his life, and there are various items of his possessions in glass cases, as well as manuscripts and, entertainingly, letters: make sure you have a read.

FREE **Robert Burns Centre** MUSEUM
(www.dumgal.gov.uk/museums; Mill Rd; audiovisual presentation £2; 10am-5pm Mon-Sat & 2-5pm Sun Apr-Sep, 10am-1pm & 2-5pm Tue-Sat Oct-Mar) A worthwhile Burns exhibition in an old mill on the banks of the River Nith. It tells the story of the poet and Dumfries in the 1790s. The optional audiovisual presentations give more background on Dumfries, and explain the exhibition's contents.

You'll find Robert Burns' **mausoleum** in the graveyard at **St Michael's Kirk**; there's a grisly account of his reburial on the information panel. At the top of High St is a **statue** of the bard; take a close look at the sheepdog at his feet.

Sleeping

Merlin B&B ££
(01387-261002; 2 Kenmure Tce; r per person £30;) Beautifully located on the riverbank across a pedestrian bridge from the centre, this is a top place to hole up in Dumfries. So much work goes on behind the scenes here that it seems effortless: numerous small details and a friendly welcome make this a very impressive set-up. Rooms share a bathroom, and have super-comfy beds; the breakfast table is also quite a sight.

Ferintosh Guest House B&B ££
(01387-252262; www.ferintosh.net; 30 Lovers Walk; s £35, d £54-60;) A Victorian villa, opposite the train station, Ferintosh has sumptuous rooms done in individual themes. The whisky room is our fave – no matter which you choose, there'll probably be a free dram awaiting you on arrival. These people have the right attitude towards hospitality. The owner's original artwork complements the decor and mountain bikers are welcomed with a shed out the back for bikes.

Eating & Drinking

Cavens Arms PUB £
(20 Buccleuch St; mains £7-12; lunch & dinner Tue-Sun) Engaging staff, nine real ales on tap, and a warm contented buzz make this a legendary Dumfries pub. Generous portions of typical pub nosh backed up by a long list of more adventurous daily specials make it one of the town's most enjoyable places to eat too. If you were going to move to Dumfries, you'd make sure you were within a block or two of here.

Globe Inn PUB
(www.globeinndumfries.co.uk; 56 High St) A traditional, rickety old nook-and-cranny pub down a narrow wynd off the main pedestrian drag, this was reputedly Burns' favourite watering hole, and scene of one of his numerous seductions. It's got a great atmosphere created by its welcoming locals and staff as much as the numerous pictures of the 'ploughman poet' himself.

Information

Ewart library (01387-253820; Catherine St; 9.15am-7.30pm Mon-Wed & Fri, 9.15am-5pm Thu & Sat) Free internet access.

Tourist office (01387-245550; www.visitdumfriesandgalloway.co.uk; 64 Whitesands; 9.30am-5pm Mon-Sat, plus Sun Jul–mid-Oct)

Getting There & Away

Bus

Local buses run regularly to **Kirkcudbright** (one hour, roughly hourly Monday to Saturday, six on Sunday) and towns along the A75 to **Stranraer** (£7.40, 2¼ hours, eight daily Monday to Saturday, three on Sunday).

Bus 100/101 runs to/from **Edinburgh** (£7, 2¾ hours, four to seven daily), via Moffat and Biggar.

Train

There are trains between **Carlisle** and Dumfries (£8.60, 35 minutes, every hour or two Monday to Saturday), and direct trains between Dumfries and **Glasgow** (£12.90, 1¾ hours, eight daily Monday to Saturday); there's a reduced service on Sunday.

South Of Dumfries

CAERLAVEROCK

The ruins of **Caerlaverock Castle** (HS; www.historic-scotland.gov.uk; adult/child £5.20/3.10; 9.30am-5.30pm Apr-Sep, 9.30am-4.30pm Oct-Mar), by Glencaple on a beautiful stretch of the Solway coast, are among the loveliest in Britain. Surrounded by a moat, lawns and stands of trees, the unusual pink-stoned triangular castle looks impregnable. In fact, it fell several times, most famously when it was attacked in 1300 by Edward I: the siege became the subject of an epic poem, *The Siege of Caerlaverock*. The current castle dates from the late 13th century but, once defensive purposes were no longer a design necessity, it was refitted as a luxurious Scottish Renaissance mansion house in 1634. Ironically, the rampaging Covenanter militia sacked it a few years later. With nooks and crannies to explore, passageways and remnants of fireplaces, this castle is great for the whole family.

From Dumfries, bus D6A runs several times a day (just twice on Sunday) to Caerlaverock Castle. By car take the B725 south.

NEW ABBEY

The small, picturesque village of New Abbey lies 7 miles south of Dumfries and contains the remains of the 13th-century Cistercian **Sweetheart Abbey** (HS; www.historic-scotland.gov.uk; adult/child £3/1.80; ⌚9.30am-5.30pm Apr-Sep, to 4.30pm Oct, 9.30am-4.30pm Sat-Wed Nov-Mar). The shattered, red-sandstone remnants of the abbey are impressive and stand in stark contrast to the manicured lawns surrounding them. The abbey, the last of the major monasteries to be established in Scotland, was founded by Devorgilla of Galloway in 1273 in honour of her dead husband John Balliol (with whom she had founded Balliol College, Oxford). On his death, she had his heart embalmed and carried it with her until she died 22 years later. She and the heart were buried by the altar – hence the name.

Bus 372 from Dumfries travels to New Abbey.

Castle Douglas & Around

POP 3671

Castle Douglas attracts a lot of day trippers but hasn't been 'spruced up' for tourism. It's an open, attractive, well-cared-for town. There are some remarkably beautiful areas close to the centre, such as the small Carlingwark Loch. The town was laid out in the 18th century by Sir William Douglas, who had made a fortune in the Americas.

Two miles further west of Castle Douglas, **Threave Castle** (HS; www.historic-scotland.gov.uk; adult/child incl ferry £4.20/2.50; ⌚9.30am-5pm Apr-Sep) is an impressive tower on a small island in the River Dee. Built in the late 14th century, it became a principal stronghold of the Black Douglases. It's now basically a shell, having been badly damaged by the Covenanters in the 1640s, but it's a romantic ruin nonetheless. It's a 15-minute walk from the car park to the ferry landing, where you ring a bell for the custodian to take you across to the island in a small boat.

Sleeping & Eating

Douglas House B&B ££

(☎01556-503262; www.douglas-house.com; 63 Queen St; s/d £38/78; 📶) A keen designer's eye is obviously present at this luxurious, attractively renovated place. Big beautiful bathrooms complement the light, stylish chambers, which include flatscreen digital TVs with inbuilt DVD player. The two upstairs doubles are the best, although the downstairs double is huge and has a king-size bed – you could sleep four in it…if you're into that kinda thing.

Douglas Arms Hotel HOTEL ££

(☎01556-502231; www.douglasarmshotel.com; 206 King St; s/d dinner, bed & breakfast £55/80; 📶) Smack bang in the middle of town, Douglas Arms was originally a coaching inn, but these days all the mod cons comfort the weary traveller. If you want to splash out, go for the honeymoon suite, which has a four-poster bed, Jacuzzi and views over the main drag from a collage of windows. The lively bar serves scrumptious food (bar meals £8 to £12), although the atmosphere is a bit staid. The steak-and-ale pie made with Galloway beef is recommended.

Information

Library (☎01556-502643; King St; ⌚10am-7.30pm Mon-Wed & Fri, 10am-5pm Thu & Sat) Free internet access.

Tourist office (☎01556-502611; King St; ⌚10am-5pm Mon-Sat Apr-Oct) In a small park on King St. Also open Sundays in July and August.

Getting There & Away

Buses 501 and 502 pass through Castle Douglas roughly hourly en route to **Dumfries** (45 minutes) and **Kirkcudbright** (20 minutes). Bus 520 along the A713 connects Castle Douglas with **New Galloway** (30 minutes, six daily Monday to Saturday, one Sunday) and **Ayr** (£6.80, 2¼ hours, two or three daily Monday to Saturday, one Sunday).

Kirkcudbright

POP 3447

Kirkcudbright (kirk-*coo*-bree), with its dignified streets of 17th- and 18th-century merchants' houses and its appealing harbour, is the ideal base from which to explore the south coast. With its architecture and setting, it's easy to see why Kirkcudbright has been an artists' colony since the late 19th century.

Sights & Activities

Kirkcudbright is a charming town for a wander, dropping into galleries as you go; it won't be long before you stumble across its main sights.

MacLellan's Castle CASTLE
(HS; www.historic-scotland.gov.uk; Castle St; adult/child £3.70/2.20; ⌚9.30am-5.30pm Apr-Sep) Near the harbour, this is a large, atmospheric ruin built in 1577 by Thomas MacLellan, then provost of Kirkcudbright, as his town residence. Inside look for the 'lairds' lug', a 16th-century hidey hole designed for the laird to eavesdrop on his guests.

FREE **Tolbooth Art Centre** EXHIBITION SPACE
(High St; ⌚11am-4pm Mon-Sat, 2-5pm Sun) As well as catering for today's local artists, this centre has an exhibition on the history of the town's artistic development. The place is as interesting for the building itself as for the artistic works on display. It's one of the oldest and best-preserved tolbooths in Scotland and interpretative signboards reveal its past. Extended hours in summer.

Broughton House GALLERY
(NTS; www.nts.org.uk; 12 High St; adult/child £5.50/4.50; ⌚noon-5pm Apr-Oct) The 18th-century Broughton House displays paintings by EA Hornel (he lived and worked here), one of the Glasgow Boys group of painters. Behind the house is a lovely Japanese-style garden (also open in February and March). The library with its wood panelling and stone carvings is probably the most impressive room.

Sleeping & Eating

Kirkcudbright has a swathe of good B&Bs.

TOP CHOICE **Selkirk Arms Hotel** HOTEL ££
(☎01557-330402; www.selkirkarmshotel.co.uk; High St; s/d/superior d £82/116/136; P@📶👪) What a haven of good hospitality this is. Superior rooms are excellent – wood furnishings and views over the back garden give them a rustic appeal. Try No 20. The **bistro** (mains £10 to £18) serves top pub nosh – the fish and chips come wrapped in the hotel newsletter – and the restaurant, **Artistas** (2-course dinner £23), serves more refined but equally tasty fare. Staff are happy to be there, and you will be too.

Castle Restaurant RESTAURANT ££
(☎01557-330569; www.thecastlerestaurant.net; 5 Castle St; mains £12-14; ⌚lunch Thu-Sun, dinner Mon-Sat; 👪) The Castle Restaurant is the best place to eat in town and uses organic produce where possible. It covers a few bases with chicken, beef and seafood dishes on offer as well as tempting morsels for vegetarians. Lunch mains are lighter and cheaper, and there's a good-value evening 2-course offer for £16.

Greengate B&B ££
(☎01557-331895; www.thegreengate.co.uk; 46 High St; s/d £50/70; 📶) The artistically inclined should snap up the one double room in this lovely place, with both historic and current painterly connections.

Anchorlee B&B ££
(☎01557-330197; www.anchorlee.co.uk; 95 St Mary St; s/d £55/75; P📶) Top-floor rooms are a bit frilly but very spacious and neat as a pin. Very friendly.

Information

Check out **www.kirkcudbright.co.uk** and **www.artiststown.org.uk** for heaps of information on the town.

Tourist office (☎01557-330494; kirkcudbrighttic@visitscotland.com; Harbour Sq; ⌚daily mid-Feb–Nov) Handy office with useful brochures detailing walks and road tours in the surrounding district.

Getting There & Away

Kirkcudbright is 28 miles southwest of Dumfries. Buses 501 and 505 run hourly to **Dumfries** (one hour) via Castle Douglas and Dalbeattie respectively. Change at Gatehouse of Fleet for Stranraer.

Galloway Forest Park

South and northwest of the small town of New Galloway is 300-sq-mile Galloway Forest Park, with numerous lochs and great whale-backed, heather- and pine-covered mountains. The highest point is **Merrick** (843m). The park is criss-crossed by some superb signposted walking trails, from gentle strolls to long-distance paths, including the **Southern Upland Way** (see boxed text, p811). The park is very family focused; look out for the booklet of annual events, and the park newspaper, *The Galloway Ranger*, in tourist offices.

The park is also great for stargazing; it's been named a Dark Sky Park by the International Dark-Sky Association.

On the shore of Clatteringshaws Loch, 6 miles west of New Galloway, is **Clatteringshaws Visitor Centre** (☎information 01671-402420; www.forestry.gov.uk/scotland; car-park fee £2; ⏲10.30am-4.30pm mid-Mar–Oct, to 5.30pm Jul & Aug), with an exhibition on the area's flora and fauna. Pick up a copy of the *Galloway Red Kite Trail* leaflet here, which details a circular route through impressive scenery that offers a good chance to spot one of these majestic reintroduced birds.

About a mile west of Clatteringshaws, **Raiders Rd** is a 10-mile drive through the forest with various picnic spots, child-friendly activities, and short walks marked along the way. It costs £2 per vehicle; drive slowly as there's plenty of wildlife about.

Farther west is the **Galloway Red Deer Range** where you can observe Britain's largest land-based beast. During rutting season in autumn it's a bit like watching a bullfight as snorting, charging stags compete for the harem. During summer there are guided **ranger-led walks** (adult/child £3.50/2.50).

Walkers and cyclists head for **Glentrool** in the park's west, accessed by the forest road east from Bargrennan off the A714, north of Newton Stewart. Located just over a mile from Bargrennan is the **Glentrool Visitor Centre** (⏲10.30am-4.30pm mid-Mar–Oct, to 5.30pm Jul & Aug), which stocks information on activities, including mountain biking, in the area. There is a coffee shop with snacks and an opportunity to rest those weary legs. The road then winds and climbs up to Loch Trool, where there are magnificent views.

The Machars

The Galloway Hills give way to the softly rolling pastures of the triangular peninsula known as the Machars. The south has many early Christian sites and the loping 25-mile **Pilgrims Way**.

Buses running between Stranraer and Dumfries stop in Newtown Stewart, from where you can get a bus to Wigtown and Whithorn.

MOUNTAIN-BIKING HEAVEN

A brilliant way to experience southern Scotland's forests is by pedal power. The **7stanes** (stones) are seven mountain-biking centres around the region with trails through some of the finest forest scenery you'll find in the country. **Glentrool** is one of these centres and the Blue Route here is 5.6 miles in length and a lovely ride climbing up to Green Torr Ridge overlooking Loch Trool. If you've more serious intentions, the Big Country Route is 36 miles of challenging ascents and descents that afford magnificent views of the Galloway Forest. It takes a full day and is not for wimps.

Another of the trailheads is at **Kirroughtree Visitor Centre**, 3 miles southeast of Newton Stewart. This offers plenty of singletrack at four different skill levels. You can hire bikes at both of these places (www.thebreakpad.com). For more information on routes see www.7stanes.gov.uk.

WIGTOWN

POP 987

Wigtown is a huge success story. Economically run down for many years, the town's revival began in 1998 when it became Scotland's National Book Town. Today 24 bookshops offer the widest selection of books in Scotland and give book enthusiasts the opportunity to get lost here for days. A major **book festival** (www.wigtownbookfestival.com) is held here in late September.

The **Bookshop** (www.the-bookshop.com; 17 North Main St; ⏲9am-5pm Mon-Sat) claims to be Scotland's largest secondhand bookshop, and has a great collection of Scottish and regional titles. **ReadingLasses Bookshop Café** (www.reading-lasses.com; 17 South Main St; ⏲10am-5pm Mon-Sat, also noon-5pm Sun May-Oct) sells caffeine to prolong your reading time and does a cracking smoked salmon salad sourced locally. It specialises in books on the social sciences and women's studies.

Wow! That's what we said when we saw the rooms in **Hillcrest House** (☎01988-402018; www.hillcrest-wigtown.co.uk; Station Rd; s £40, d £65-75; P 👪 📶). A noble stone building in a quiet part of town, the house features high ceilings and huge windows; spend the extra and get a superior room, which have stupendous views overlooking rolling green hills and the sea beyond. This is all complemented by a ripper breakfast involving fresh local produce.

Pop into the bright dining room at **Café Rendezvous** (2 Agnew Cres; dishes £4-7; ⏲10am-4.30pm) for fresh, home-cooked paninis and filled crepes. There's also decent coffee, gooey treats and outdoor seating.

WHITHORN

POP 867

Whithorn has a broad, attractive High St which is virtually closed at both ends (it was designed to enclose a medieval market). There are few facilities in town, but it's worth visiting because of its fascinating history.

In 397, while the Romans were still in Britain, St Ninian established the first Christian mission beyond Hadrian's Wall in Whithorn (predating St Columba on Iona by 166 years). After his death, Whithorn Priory, the earliest recorded church in Scotland, was built to house his remains, and Whithorn became the focus of an important medieval pilgrimage.

Today the ruined priory is part of the excellent **Whithorn Trust Discovery Centre** (www.whithorn.com; 45 George St; adult/child £4.50/2.25; ⏲10.30am-5pm Apr-Oct), which introduces you to the history of the place with a good audiovisual and very informative exhibition. There's ongoing archaeological investigation here, and you can see the site of earlier churches. There's also a museum with some fascinating early Christian stone sculptures, including the Latinus Stone (c 450), reputedly Scotland's oldest Christian artefact. Learn about the influences their carvers drew from around the British Isles and beyond.

Stranraer

POP 10,851

The friendly but somewhat ramshackle ferry port of Stranraer is gradually seeing its boat services to Northern Ireland move up the road to Cairnryan. Though locals fear it'll turn their town into a ghostly shadow of what it was, it'll probably become a more pleasant place if the scheduled waterfront redevelopment takes place.

Sleeping & Eating

TOP CHOICE **Corsewall Lighthouse Hotel** HOTEL £££

(☎01776-853220; www.lighthousehotel.co.uk; Kirkcolm; d incl 5-course dinner £150-250; P) It's just you and the cruel sea out here at this fabulously romantic 200 year-old lighthouse, right at the northwest tip of the peninsula, 13 miles northwest of Stranraer. On a sunny day, the water shimmers with light, and you can see Ireland, Kintyre, Arran, and Ailsa Craig. But when the wind and rain beat in, it's just great to be cosily holed up in the snug bar/restaurant or snuggling under the covers in your room. Rooms in the lighthouse building itself are attractive if necessarily compact; there are also chalets available.

Balyett Farm Hostel & B&B B&B, HOSTEL ££

(☎01776-703395; www.balyettbb.co.uk; Cairnryan Rd; dm/s/d £20/45/65; P 📶) A mile north of town on the A77, Balyett provides tranquil accommodation in its tidy hostel section, which accommodates five people and has a kitchen/living area. The relaxed B&B at the nearby ivy-covered farmhouse could be the best deal in town. The rooms are light, bright and clean as a whistle. Room No 2 is our fave but all are beautifully furnished and come with lovely aspects over the surrounding country.

Ivy House B&B ££

(☎01776-704176; www.ivyplace.worldonline.co.uk; 3 Ivy Pl; s/d £30/56) This is a great guest house and does Scottish hospitality proud, with excellent facilities, tidy en suite rooms and a smashing breakfast. Nothing is too much trouble for the hosts, who always have a smile for their guests. The room at the back overlooking the churchyard is particularly light and quiet.

L'Aperitif BISTRO ££

(☎01776-702991; London Rd; mains £11-14; ⏲lunch & dinner Mon-Sat) Purgatory at dinnertime can look uncannily like Stranraer at times, so thank the powers that be for this cheerful local. It's definitely the town's best restaurant and is close to being its best pub too. Despite the name, dishes are more Italian than French, with great pastas alongside roasts, saltimbocca, and delicious appetizers featuring things like smoked salmon or greenlip mussels. Early dining (£13.50 for two courses) is lighter on the wallet.

Information

Library (North Strand St; 9.15am-7.30pm Mon-Wed & Fri, to 5pm Thu & Sat) Free internet access.

Tourist office (01776-702595; www.visit-dumfriesandgalloway.com; 28 Harbour St; 10am-4pm Mon-Sat) Efficient and friendly.

Getting There & Away

Boat

Cairnryan is 6 miles north of Stranraer on the eastern side of Loch Ryan. Bus 358 runs frequently to Cairnryan (terminating at the post office).

P&O (0871 66 44 777; www.poirishsea.com) Runs six to seven ferries a day from Cairnryan to **Larne** (Northern Ireland).

Stena Line (08447 70 70 70; www.stenaline.co.uk; passenger/car £27/100) Runs five to seven HSS and Superferries from Stranraer to **Belfast**. This service is set to move to Cairnryan in late 2011.

Bus

Scottish Citylink buses run to **Glasgow** (£16.20, 2½ hours, twice daily) and **Edinburgh** (£18.80, 3¾ hours, twice daily).

There are also several daily local buses to **Kirkcudbright** and the towns along the A75, such as **Newton Stewart** (45 minutes, at least hourly) and **Dumfries** (£7.40, 2¼ hours, nine daily Monday to Saturday, three on Sunday).

Train

First Scotrail runs to/from **Glasgow** (£19.30, 2¼ hours, two to seven trains daily); it may be necessary to change at Ayr.

Around Stranraer

Magnificent **Castle Kennedy Gardens** (www.castlekennedygardens.co.uk; Rephad; adult/child £4/1; 10am-5pm daily Apr-Sep, 10am-5pm Sat & Sun Feb-Mar & Oct), 3 miles east of Stranraer, are among the most famous in Scotland. They cover 30 hectares and are set on an isthmus between two lochs and two castles (Castle Kennedy, burnt in 1716, and Lochinch Castle, built in 1864). The landscaping was undertaken in 1730 by the earl of Stair, who used unoccupied soldiers to do the work. Buses 430 (hourly) and 500 from Stranraer stop here.

Portpatrick

POP 585

Portpatrick is a charming port on the rugged west coast of the Rhinns of Galloway peninsula. Until the mid-19th century it was the main port for Northern Ireland but it's now a quiet holiday resort.

It is also a good base from which to explore the south of the peninsula, and it's the starting point for the **Southern Upland Way** (p811). You can follow part of the Way to Stranraer (9 miles). It's a clifftop walk, followed by sections of farmland and heather moor. Start at the Way's information shelter at the northern end of the harbour. The walk is waymarked until 800m south of Stranraer, where you get the first good views of the village.

Harbour House Hotel (01776-810456; www.theharbourhousehotel.co.uk; 53 Main St; s/d £40/80) was formerly the customs house but is now a popular, solid old pub. Some of the tastefully furnished rooms have brilliant views over the harbour. The hotel is also a warm nook for a traditional bar meal (£8 to £10).

For a real dose of luxury, head 3 miles southeast to **Knockinaam Lodge** (01776-810471; www.knockinaamlodge.com; dinner, bed & breakfast for two £320-420; P), a former hunting lodge on a little sandy bay. It's where Churchill plotted the endgame of the Second World War – you can stay in his suite – and it's a very romantic place to get away from it all. The excellent French-influenced cuisine (lunch/dinner £38/50) is backed up by a great range of wines and single malts.

See also the Corsewall Lighthouse Hotel (p827) for accommodation not too far away.

Buses 358 and 367 run to **Stranraer** (20 minutes, eight Monday to Saturday, three Sunday).

Stirling & Central Scotland

Includes »

STIRLING REGION. . .832
Stirling 833
ARGYLL 840
Isle of Islay 844
Isle of Iona. 854
FIFE 855
St Andrews 856
East Neuk 861
PERTHSHIRE 864
West Perthshire 870
DUNDEE & ANGUS . . 871
ABERDEENSHIRE & MORAY. 876
Aberdeen 876
Deeside 882

Best Places to Eat & Drink

» Café Fish (p853)
» Breizh (p865)
» Moulin Hotel (p869)
» Café 52 (p880)

Best Places to Stay

» Monachyle Mhor (p840)
» Achnadrish House (p853)
» Luigino's (p862)
» Globe Inn (p879)

Why Go?

Covering everything from the green pastures of the northeast to the mountain landscapes of Glen Lyon, from urban Dundee to the far Mull of Kintyre, central Scotland is less a geographical region than a catch-all term for everything between the Lowlands and the northern Highlands. Anything you ever dreamed about Scotland can be found here: lochs aplenty, from romantic Lomond to the picturesque Trossachs; castles, ranging from royal Balmoral to noble Stirling; whiskies, from the honeyed lotharios of Speyside to the peaty clan chiefs of Islay; and islands, from brooding, deer-studded Jura to emerald Iona, birthplace of Scottish Christianity.

The active are well catered for, with a welter of hills to climb and some of Britain's best long-distance trails to hike. Cyclists and walkers are spoiled for choice, with scenery ranging from mighty Perthshire forests to the rugged Argyll hills; from the fishing hamlets of Fife to the epic landscapes of Mull.

When to Go?

If the weather is kind, May is a magical time for exploring before summer crowds arrive. August is the best month of the year for whale-watching off the west coast. In September there are the Braemar Gathering (Highland games) and Spirit of Speyside whisky and music festival in Dufftown.

Stirling & Central Scotland Highlights

1. Opening your jaw in amazement at the epic splendour of **Glen Lyon** (p870), gateway to a faerie land
2. Admiring the views from magnificent **Stirling Castle** (p833), overlooking ancient independence battlefields
3. Scoffing at critics of British cuisine as you sample the super seafood in **Tobermory** (p853), **Oban** (p849) or **Loch Fyne** (p842)
4. Strolling the verdant **Speyside Way** (p832) and sauntering into distilleries for a sly dram along the way
5. Unwinding totally on delightful tiny **Iona** (p854), holy island and tomb of Scottish kings
6. Experiencing the astonishing hospitality of **Islay** (p844), whisky and bird paradise and Scotland's friendliest island
7. Exploring the castles, villages, forests and hills of **Royal Deeside** (p882), home to the Queen's Balmoral Castle

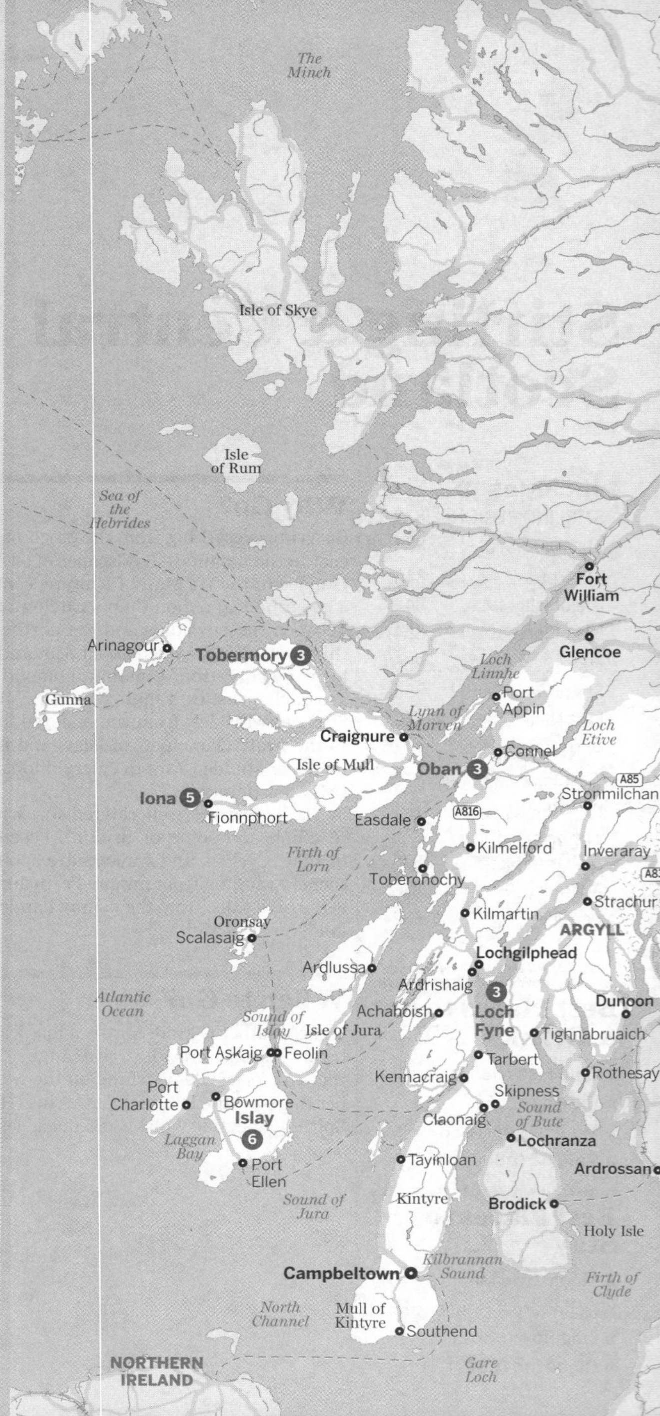

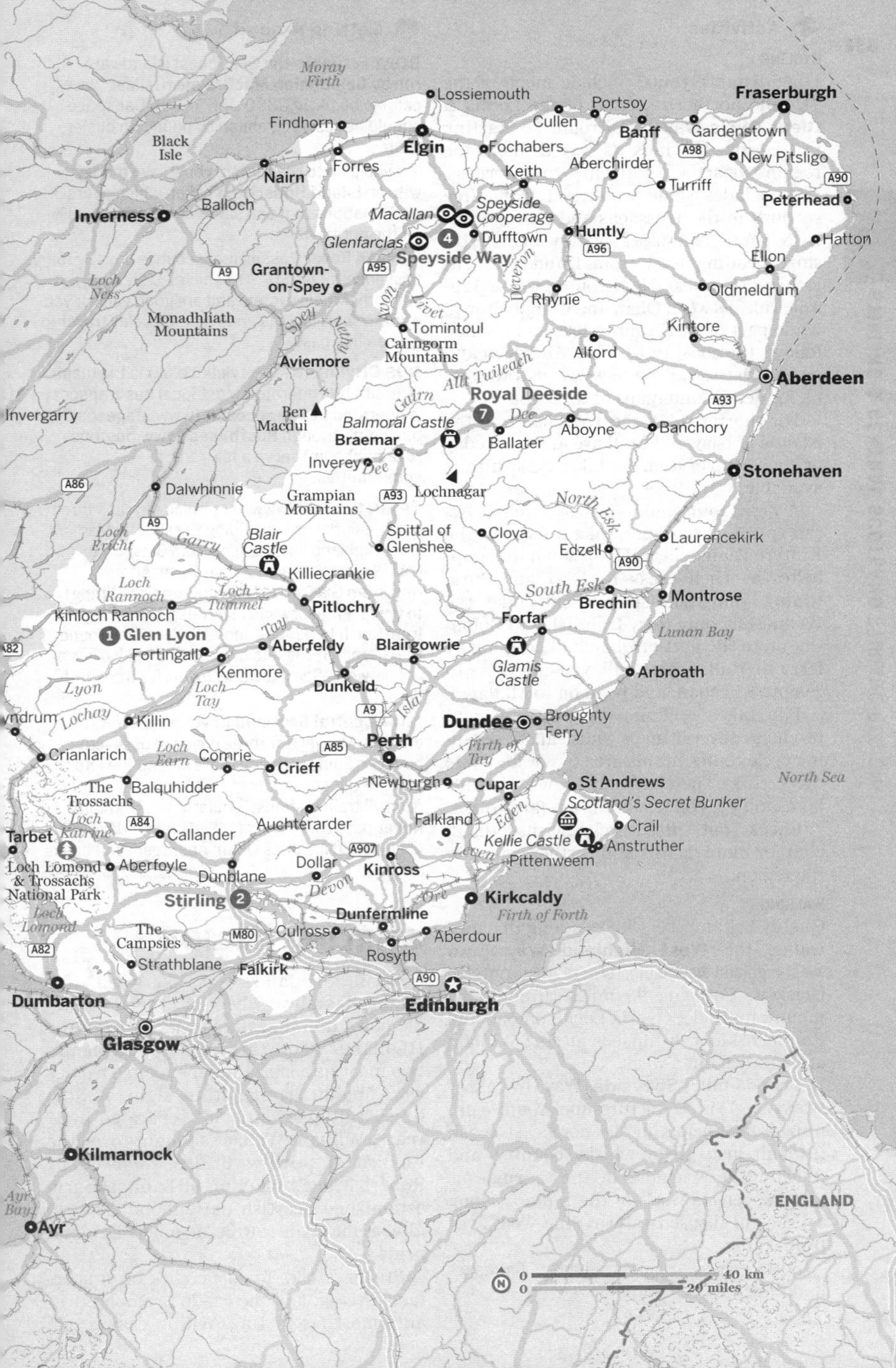

Moray Firth
Lossiemouth
Portsoy
Fraserburgh
Cullen
Findhorn
Banff
Gardenstown
Black Isle
Elgin
Fochabers
A98
New Pitsligo
Forres
Aberchirder
Nairn
Keith
Turriff
A90
Balloch
Speyside Cooperage
Peterhead
Inverness
Macallan
Glenfarclas
4
Dufftown
Huntly
Hatton
A96
Speyside Way
Ellon
A9
Grantown-on-Spey
A95
Deveron
Loch Ness
Avon
Livet
Rhynie
Oldmeldrum
Monadhliath Mountains
Spey
Nethy
Tomintoul
Kintore
Cairngorm Mountains
Alford
Aviemore
Allt Tuileach
Aberdeen
Gairn
Royal Deeside
A93
Ben Macdui
7
Dee
Invergarry
Balmoral Castle
Aboyne
Banchory
Braemar
Ballater
Inverey
Dee
Stonehaven
A86
Lochnagar
Dalwhinnie
Grampian Mountains
A93
North Esk
A9
Spittal of Glenshee
Clova
Loch Ericht
Blair Castle
Laurencekirk
Garry
Edzell
A90
Killiecrankie
Loch Rannoch
Loch Tummel
South Esk
Montrose
Brechin
Kinloch Rannoch
Pitlochry
Forfar
Tay
Lunan Bay
1 Glen Lyon
A82
Aberfeldy
Blairgowrie
Fortingall
Kenmore
Glamis Castle
Arbroath
Lyon
Loch Tay
Dunkeld
A9
Isla
Broughty Ferry
Tyndrum
Lochay
Killin
Dundee
A85
Perth
Firth of Tay
Crianlarich
Loch Earn
Comrie
Crieff
North Sea
The Trossachs
Balquhidder
Newburgh
Cupar
St Andrews
Scotland's Secret Bunker
Loch Katrine
A84
Auchterarder
Falkland
Eden
Crail
Tarbet
Callander
Kellie Castle
Anstruther
Loch Lomond & Trossachs National Park
Aberfoyle
A907
Leven
Pittenweem
Dollar
Kinross
Dunblane
Devon
Ore
Kirkcaldy
Stirling
2
Firth of Forth
Loch Lomond
The Campsies
M80
Culross
Dunfermline
Aberdour
A82
Rosyth
Strathblane
Falkirk
A90
Edinburgh
Dumbarton
Glasgow
Kilmarnock
ENGLAND
Ayr Bay
Ayr
0
40 km
0
20 miles
N

Activities

CYCLING

Long-distance routes include much of the 217-mile northern section of the **Lochs & Glens Cycle Way** (NCN route 7). Starting in Glasgow, it winds its way through the region's heart via Pitlochry to Inverness, and includes some wonderful traffic-free sections in the Trossachs and Cairngorms. NCN route 77 crosses picturesque Perthshire heading west from Dundee to Pitlochry (54 miles). NCN route 78 is a 120-mile ride between Oban and Campbeltown, while part of NCN route 1 bisects Fife then follows the coast to Dundee, Aberdeen and on to Inverness. Browse www.sustrans.org.uk for details and maps of these routes.

For shorter rides, the Trossachs and the islands of Islay and Mull are ideal for a day or more exploration by bike; cycle hire is available.

A great tour could start by circling Arran (p817). From here, take a ferry to the Kintyre Peninsula and loop down to Campbeltown. Then cross to Islay and Jura, timing your trip so you can take the Wednesday-only ferry from Islay to Colonsay, on to the port of Oban and crossing by ferry to Mull. From Mull, you can cross to remote Kilchoan, and head on to Mallaig.

Fife takes cycling very seriously, and produces several maps and leaflets detailing cycle routes in this area (www.fife-cycleways.co.uk). There are only a few steep hills here, and the country roads are fairly quiet.

Check out http://cycling.visitscotland.com for more details and further routes in the region.

WALKING

One of Britain's best-known long-distance walks, the **West Highland Way** (www.west-highland-way.co.uk), starts just outside Glasgow. Covering 95 miles through the mountains and glens via Loch Lomond and Rannoch Moor, it finishes at Fort William and takes about a week.

The 65-mile **Speyside Way** (www.speysideway.org) is a picturesque route running from Buckie on the northeast coast, through lush green whisky country, and finishing at Aviemore in the Cairngorms (or vice versa). Much of the route is along a peaceful disused railway line well away from traffic.

Both these routes have baggage-handling services available.

Getting Around

BOAT Ferries to the west-coast islands are run by **Caledonian MacBrayne** (CalMac; www.calmac.co.uk; ☎0800 066 5000). Car space should be reserved ahead by phone on busier routes.

If you plan to island-hop, you'll save money with an **Island Hopscotch** ticket, which offers 30 combinations that can save you more than 20% off the normal fares.

Island Rover Passes (consecutive days 8/15, passengers £48.50/70, vehicles £232/348) cover the whole system and are good value if you want to see a lot of islands fast. Bicycles travel free on this pass.

BUS Citylink (www.citylink.co.uk) is the major intercity bus operator. Most local bus transport is operated by **Stagecoach** (www.stagecoachbus.com), though **Postbuses** (www.postbus.royalmail.com) serve a few remote communities.

TRAIN Scotrail (www.scotrail.co.uk) runs three north–south lines, including the spectacular West Highland line, running from Glasgow to Fort William with a branch to Oban. Another runs from Glasgow and Edinburgh (via Stirling) to Perth, Pitlochry and Inverness; the third goes from Perth to Dundee and Aberdeen, and round the Grampian coast to Inverness. Fife also has a rail network. See individual towns for transport details.

The **Central Scotland Rover** pass allows unlimited travel (for three days out of seven) between Edinburgh and Glasgow and the Fife and Stirling areas. It costs £33 and is available from all train stations. Similarly, the **Highland Rover** pass (£74) allows travel on four days out of eight and includes Oban, Aberdeen, and buses on Mull.

STIRLING REGION

Covering Scotland's wasplike waist, this region has always been a crucial strategic point dividing the Lowlands from the Highlands. For this reason, Scotland's two most important independence battles were fought here, within sight of Stirling's hilltop stronghold. Separated by 17 years, William Wallace's victory over the English at Stirling Bridge, followed by Robert Bruce's triumph at Bannockburn, established Scottish nationhood. The region remains a source of much national pride.

Stirling's Old Town perches on a spectacular crag, and the castle is among Britain's most fascinating. Within easy reach, the dreamy Trossachs, home to Rob Roy and inspiration to Walter Scott, offer great walking and cycling in the eastern half of Scotland's first national park.

Getting Around

Trains service Stirling but not the rest of the region, so you'll be relying on buses if you don't have your own transport. **First** (01324-602200; www.firstgroup.com) is the main operator.

Stirling

POP 32,673

With an utterly impregnable position atop a mighty wooded crag (the plug of an extinct volcano), Stirling's beautifully preserved Old Town is a treasure-trove of noble buildings and cobbled streets winding up to the ramparts of its dominant castle, which offer views for miles around. Clearly visible is the brooding Wallace Monument, a strange Victorian Gothic creation honouring the legendary freedom fighter of *Braveheart* fame. Nearby is Bannockburn, scene of Robert the Bruce's major triumph over the English.

The castle makes a fascinating visit, but make sure you spend time exploring the Old Town and the picturesque path that encircles it. Near the castle are a couple of snug pubs in which to toast Scotland's hoary heroes. Below the Old Town, retail-minded modern Stirling doesn't offer the same appeal; stick to the high ground as much as possible and you'll love the place.

Sights

Stirling Castle CASTLE

(HS; www.historic-scotland.gov.uk; 9.30am-6pm Apr-Sep, to 5pm Oct-Mar) Hold Stirling and you control Scotland. This maxim has ensured that a fortress of some kind has existed here since prehistoric times. Commanding superb views, you cannot help drawing parallels with Edinburgh castle – but many find Stirling's fortress more atmospheric; the location, architecture and historical significance combine to make it a grand and memorable visit. This means it draws plenty of visitors, so it's advisable to visit in the afternoon; many tourists come on day trips from Edinburgh or Glasgow, so you may have the castle to yourself by about 4pm.

The current castle dates from the late 14th to the 16th century, when it was a residence of the Stuart monarchs. The **Great Hall** and **Gatehouse** were built by James IV; observe the hammer-beam roof and huge fireplaces in the largest medieval hall in Scotland – the result of 35 years of restoration. In another part of the castle, the **Great Kitchens** are especially interesting, bringing to life the bustle and scale of the enterprise of cooking for the King. Near the entrance, the **Castle Exhibition** gives good background information on the Stuart kings and updates on current archaeological investigations.

After a long restoration project, the **Royal Palace** is scheduled to re-open as this book hits the shelves. It'll be a sumptuous recreation of how this luxurious Renaissance palace would have looked when it was constructed by French masons under the orders of James V (in the early 16th century) to impress his (also French) bride and other crowned heads of Europe.

Admission costs for the castle will rise once the Royal Palace opens. The mooted price at time of research was £14 for adults, which would include an audio guide.

By the castle car park, the **Stirling tourist office** (admission free; 9.30am-6pm Apr-Sep, to 5pm Oct-Mar) has an audiovisual presentation and exhibition about Stirling, including the history and architecture of the castle.

Old Town DISTRICT

Below the castle, the steep Old Town has a remarkably different feel to modern Stirling, its cobblestone streets packed with 15th- to 17th-century architectural gems. Stirling has the best surviving **town wall** in Scotland. It can be explored on the **Back Walk**, which follows the line of the wall from Dumbarton Rd (near the tourist office) to the castle. You pass the town cemeteries (check out the Star Pyramid, an outsized affirmation of Reformation values dating from 1863), then the path continues around the back of the castle to Gowan Hill where you can see the **Beheading Stone**, now encased in iron bars to prevent contemporary use.

The **Church of the Holy Rude** (www.holyrude.org; St John St; admission free; 11am-4pm May-Sep) has been the town's parish church for 600 years; James VI was crowned here in 1567. The nave and tower date from 1456, and the church has one of the few surviving medieval open-timber roofs. Stunning stained-glass windows and huge stone pillars create a powerful effect.

Stirling

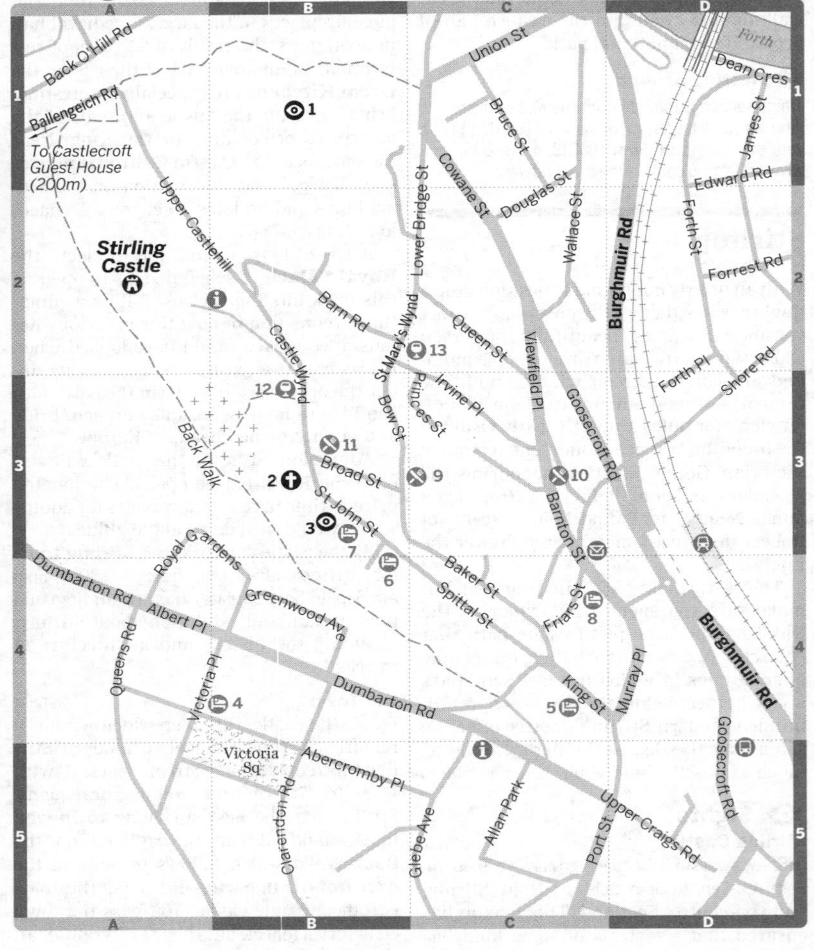

The **Old Town Jail** (www.oldtownjail.com; St John St; adult/child/family £6.50/4/17; ⏲10am-5pm Apr-Oct, 10.30am-4pm Nov-Mar) is a great one for kids, as actors take you through the complex, portraying a cast of characters that illustrate the hardships of Victorian prison life in innovative, entertaining style.

National Wallace Monument MONUMENT
(www.nationalwallacemonument.com; adult/child £7.50/4.50; ⏲10am-5pm Apr-Oct, to 6pm Jul & Aug, 10.30am-4pm Nov-Mar) Towering over Scotland's narrow waist, this nationalist memorial is so Victorian Gothic it deserves circling bats and ravens. It commemorates the bid for Scottish independence depicted in the film Braveheart. From the tourist office, walk or shuttle-bus up the hill to the building itself. Once there, break the climb up the narrow staircase inside to admire Wallace's 66 inches of broadsword and see the man himself recreated in a 3D audiovisual display. More staid is the marble pantheon of lugubrious Scottish heroes, but the view from the top over the flat, green gorgeousness of the Forth Valley, including the site of Wallace's 1297 victory over the English at Stirling Bridge, justifies the steep entry fee.

Stirling

Top Sights

Stirling Castle A2

Sights

1 Beheading Stone B1
2 Church of the Holy Rude B3
3 Old Town Jail B3

Sleeping

4 Garfield Guesthouse B4
5 Sruighlea C4
6 Stirling Highland Hotel B4
7 Stirling SYHA B3
8 Willy Wallace Backpackers Hostel C4

Eating

9 Darnley Coffee House C3
10 East India Company C3
11 Hermann's B3

Drinking

12 Portcullis B3
13 Settle Inn C2

Buses 62 and 63 run from Murray Place in Stirling to the visitor centre, otherwise it's a half-hour walk from central Stirling. There's a cafe here, too.

Bannockburn BATTLEFIELD

Though Wallace's heroics were significant, it was Robert the Bruce's defeat of the English on 24 June 1314 at Bannockburn, just outside Stirling, that eventually established lasting Scottish nationhood. Exploiting the marshy ground, Bruce won a great tactical victory against a much larger and better-equipped force, and sent Edward II 'homeward, tae think again', as Flower of Scotland commemorates. At **Bannockburn Heritage Centre** (NTS; www.nts.org.uk; adult/child £5.50/4.50; 10am-5pm Mar-Oct, to 5.30pm Apr-Sep) the history pre- and post-battle is lucidly explained. The audiovisual could do with a remake, but there's lots to do for kids, and an intriguing recreation of Bruce's face which suggests that he may have suffered from leprosy in later life.

The battlefield itself (which never closes) is harder to appreciate; apart from a statue of the victor astride his horse and a misbegotten flag memorial, there's nothing to see. Bannockburn is 2 miles south of Stirling; you can reach it on bus 51 from Murray Pl in the centre.

Sleeping

Castlecroft Guest House B&B ££

(01786-474933; www.castlecroft-uk.com; Ballengeich Rd; s/d £45/60; P @ wi-fi) Nestling into the hillside under the back of the castle, this great hideaway feels like a rural retreat but is a short, spectacular walk from the heart of historic Stirling. The lounge boasts 180-degree views over green fields to the hills that gird the town, and the compact rooms are appealing and well-maintained.

Willy Wallace Backpackers Hostel HOSTEL £

(01786-446773; www.willywallacehostel.com; 77 Murray Pl; dm/tw £17/36; @ wi-fi) This highly convenient central hostel is friendly, spacious and sociable. The colourful, spacious dormitories are clean and light, there's free tea and coffee, a good kitchen, and a laissez-faire atmosphere. Other amenities include a laundry service and free internet and wi-fi.

Sruighlea B&B ££

(01786-471082; www.sruighlea.com; 27 King St; s/d £40/60; wi-fi) This place feels like a secret hideaway – there's no sign – but it's conveniently located smack-bang in the centre of town. You'll feel like a local staying here, and there are eating and drinking places practically on the doorstep. It's a B&B that welcomes guests with the kind of warmth that keeps them returning.

Stirling SYHA HOSTEL £

(01786-473442; www.syha.org.uk; St John St; dm/tw £17.25/45; P @ wi-fi) Right in the Old Town, this hostel has an unbeatable location and great facilities. Though its facade is that of a former church, the interior is modern and efficient. The dorms are compact but comfortable with lockers and ensuite bathrooms; other highlights include a pool table, bike shed and, at busy times, cheap meals on offer. Lack of atmosphere can be the only problem.

Garfield Guesthouse B&B ££

(01786-473730; www.garfieldgh.com; 12 Victoria Sq; small/large d £60/65) Though close to the centre of town, Victoria Sq is a quiet oasis, with noble Victorian buildings surrounding a verdant swath of lawn. The Garfield's huge rooms, bay windows, ceiling roses and other period features make it a winner. There's a great family room, and some rooms have views to the castle towering above.

Linden Guest House B&B ££
(☎01786-448850; www.lindenguesthouse.co.uk; 22 Linden Ave; s/d £50/72; P@) Handy if arriving by car from the south, this guest house's warm welcome and easy parking offer understandable appeal. The rooms, of which two are suitable for families, have fridges, and the gleaming bathrooms could feature in ads for cleaning products. Breakfast features fresh fruit and kippers, among other choices.

Stirling Highland Hotel HOTEL £££
(☎01786-272727; www.barcelo-hotels.co.uk; Spittal St; s/d £105/134; P@) The smartest hotel in town, Stirling Highland Hotel is a sympathetic refurbishment of the old high school. This curious place still feels institutional in parts, but has great facilities that include pool, spa, gym, sauna and squash courts. It's very convenient for the castle and Old Town, and the rooms have been recently refitted, though they vary widely in size. Prices are flexible: those listed above are a guide.

Neidpath B&B ££
(☎01786-469017; www.neidpath-stirling.co.uk; 24 Linden Ave; d £58; P) Spotless rooms and a filling breakfast.

Eating & Drinking

Portcullis PUB £
(☎01786-472290; www.theportcullishotel.com; Castle Wynd; bar meals £8-12; ⊙lunch & dinner) Built in stone as solid as the castle that it stands below, this former school is just the spot for a pint and a pub lunch after your visit. With bar meals that would have had even William Wallace loosening his belt a couple of notches, a little beer garden, and a cosy buzz indoors, it's well worth a visit; there are also rooms here (single/double £67/87).

East India Company INDIAN £
(7 Viewfield Pl; mains £6-11; ⊙dinner) This basement Indian restaurant is one of the best spots in Central Scotland for a curry. Sumptuously decorated to resemble a ship's stateroom, with portraits of tea barons on the wall to conjure images of the days of the clippers, it offers exquisite dishes from all parts of India. There's a buffet dinner available Monday to Thursday (£8.95), but go à la carte and savour the toothsome flavours.

Hermann's RESTAURANT £££
(☎01786-450632; www.hermanns.co.uk; 58 Broad St; 2-course lunch/3-course dinner £13/20, mains £16-20; ⊙lunch & dinner) Solidly set on a corner above the Mercat Cross and below the castle, this elegant Scottish-Austrian restaurant is a reliable and popular choice. The solid, conservative decor is weirdly offset by magazine-style skiing photos, but the food doesn't miss a beat and ranges from Scottish favourites to gourmet schnitzel and spätzle noodles. Vegetarian options are good, and quality Austrian wines provide an out-of-the-ordinary accompaniment.

Darnley Coffee House CAFE £
(www.darnley.connectfree.co.uk; 18 Bow St; snacks £3.50-5; ⊙breakfast & lunch) Just down the hill from the castle, beyond the end of Broad St, Darnley Coffee House is a good pitstop for home baking and speciality coffees during a walk around the Old Town. The building is an historic 16th-century house where Darnley, lover then husband of Mary Queen of Scots, once stayed while visiting her.

Settle Inn PUB
(91 St Mary's Wynd) A warm welcome is guaranteed at Stirling's oldest pub (1733), a spot redolent with atmosphere, what with its log fire, vaulted back room, and low-slung ceilings. Guest ales, atmospheric nooks for settling in for the night, and a blend of local characters make it a classic of its kind.

Information

Stirling Royal Infirmary (☎01786-434000; Livilands Rd) Hospital; south of the town centre.

Stirling Visitor Centre (☎01786-450000; ⊙9.30am-6pm Apr-Sep, to 5pm Oct-Mar) Near the castle entrance.

Tourist office (☎01786-475019; www.visitscottishheartlands.com; 41 Dumbarton Rd; ⊙10am-5pm Mon-Sat year-round, plus Sun Jun–mid-Sep; @)

Getting There & Away

BUS The **bus station** (☎01786-446474) is on Goosecroft Rd. **Citylink** (www.citylink.co.uk) offers a number of services to/from Stirling:

Dundee £12.50, 1½ hours, hourly
Edinburgh £6.70, one hour, hourly
Glasgow £6.60, 45 minutes, hourly
Perth £7.70, 50 minutes, at least hourly
Some buses continue to Aberdeen, Inverness, and Fort William; more frequently a change will be required.

TRAIN First ScotRail (www.scotrail.co.uk) has services to/from a number of destinations, including:
Aberdeen £38.60, 2¼ hours, regular services
Dundee £15.80, one hour, regular services
Edinburgh £6.90, 55 minutes, twice hourly Monday to Saturday, hourly Sunday
Glasgow £7.10, 40 minutes, twice hourly Monday to Saturday, hourly Sunday
Perth £10.40, 35 minutes, regular services

TROSSACHS TRANSPORT

In a bid to cut public transport costs, 'Demand Responsive Transport', or DRT, was being brought to the Trossachs when we researched this guide. Sounds complex, but basically it means you get a taxi to where you want to go, for the price of a bus (eg 10 miles for £3.30). Taxis run Monday to Saturday and need to be booked in advance; call or text ☎0844 567-5670 between 7am and 7pm Monday to Saturday, or book online at www.aberfoylecoaches.com.

The Trossachs

The Trossachs region has long been a favourite weekend getaway, offering outstanding natural beauty and excellent walking and cycling routes within easy reach of the southern population centres. With thickly forested hills, romantic lochs and an increasingly interesting selection of places to stay and eat, its popularity is sure to continue, protected by its National Park status.

The Trossachs first gained popularity as a tourist destination in the early 19th century, when curious visitors came from all over Britain drawn by the romantic language of Walter Scott's poem *Lady of the Lake*, inspired by Loch Katrine, and *Rob Roy*, about the derring-do of the region's most famous son.

In summer the Trossachs can be overburdened with coach tours, but many of these are day trippers – peaceful, long evenings gazing at the reflections in the nearest loch are still possible. It's worth timing your visit not to coincide with a weekend.

ABERFOYLE & AROUND

POP 576

Crawling with visitors on most weekends and dominated by a huge car park, little **Aberfoyle** is a fairly uninteresting place, easily overwhelmed by day trippers. Instead of staying here, we recommend Callander or other Trossachs towns.

Half a mile north of Aberfoyle on the A821 is the **David Marshall Lodge tourist office** (www.forestry.gov.uk/qefp; admission free, car park £2; ⏲10am-4pm Nov-Mar, 10am-5pm Apr-Oct, to 6pm Jul & Aug) in the **Queen Elizabeth Forest Park**, which has info about the many walks and cycle routes in and around the park (many departing from the tourist office). The Royal Society for the Protection of Birds (RSPB) has a display here on local bird life, the highlight being a live video link to the resident osprey family. The centre is worth visiting solely for the views.

Three miles east is the **Lake of Menteith** (called lake not loch due to a mistranslation from Gaelic). A ferry takes visitors to the substantial ruins of **Inchmahome Priory** (HS; www.historic-scotland.gov.uk; adult/child incl ferry £4.70/2.80; ⏲9.30am-5.30pm Apr-Sep, last return ferry 4.30pm). Mary, Queen of Scots was kept safe here as a child during Henry VIII's 'Rough Wooing'. Henry attacked Stirling trying to force Mary to marry his son in order to unite the kingdoms.

Activities

Several picturesque but busy waymarked **trails** start from the David Marshall Lodge tourist office centre in the forest park. These range from a light 20-minute stroll to a nearby waterfall to a hilly 4-mile circuit. Also here, **Go Ape!** (www.goape.co.uk; adult/child £30/20; ⏲daily Apr-Oct, Sat & Sun Mar & Nov) will bring out the monkey in you on its exhilarating adventure course of long ziplines, swings and rope bridges through the forest.

An excellent 20-mile circular **cycle route** links with the boat at Loch Katrine. From Aberfoyle, join the Lochs & Glens Cycle Way on the forest trail, or take the A821 over Duke's Pass. Following the southern shore of Loch Achray, you reach the pier on Loch Katrine. The ferry can take you to Stronachlachar (one-way with bike £14) on the western shore, from where you can follow the beautiful B829 via Loch Ard back to Aberfoyle.

Sleeping & Eating

Forth Inn PUB £
(01877-382372; www.forthinn.com; Main St; mains £6-9; breakfast, lunch & dinner;) In the middle of the village, the solid Forth Inn seems to be the lifeblood of the town, with locals and visitors alike queuing up for good, honest pub fare. The tasty bar meals are the best in town. It also provides accommodation and beer, with drinkers spilling outside into the sunny courtyard. Single/double rooms are available for £50/80, but they can be noisy at weekends.

Information

The **tourist office** (01877-382352; aberfoyle@visitscotland.com; Main St; 10am-5pm Apr-Oct, 10am-4pm Sat & Sun Nov-Mar; @) details a history of the Trossachs and provides currency exchange and a soft play area.

Getting There & Away

First (www.firstgroup.com) has up to four daily buses from Stirling (40 minutes); you'll have to connect at Balfron on Sundays. See boxed text, p837, for transport around the region.

CALLANDER

POP 2754

Callander has been pulling in the tourists for over 150 years, and has a laid-back ambience along its main thoroughfare. It's a far better place than Aberfoyle to spend time in, quickly lulling visitors into lazy pottering. There's also an excellent array of accommodation options here.

The Trossachs is a lovely area to cycle around. On a cycle route and based at Trossachs Tryst hostel, the excellent **Wheels Cycling Centre** (01877-331100; www.wheelscyclingcentre.com) has a wide range of hire bikes starting from £10/15 per half-/full day.

Sleeping

TOP CHOICE **Roman Camp Hotel** HOTEL £££
(01877-330003; www.roman-camp-hotel.co.uk; s/d/superior d £95/145/185; P) Callander's best hotel. It's centrally located but feels rural, set by the river in its own beautiful grounds with birdsong the only sound. Its endearing features include a lounge with blazing fire, and a library with a tiny, secret chapel. There are three grades of room; the standards are certainly luxurious, but the superior ones are even more appealing, with period furniture, armchairs and a fireplace. The upmarket restaurant is open to the public. Reassuringly, the name refers not to toga parties but to a ruin in the adjacent fields.

Trossachs Tryst HOSTEL £
(01877-331200; www.scottish-hostel.co.uk; Invertrossachs Rd; dm/tw £17.50/45; P@) Set up to be the perfect hostel for outdoorsy people, this cracking spot is in fresh-aired surroundings a mile from Callander. Facilities and accommodation are excellent, with dorms offering acres of space and their own bathrooms, and cycle hire with plenty of route advice. Help yourself to a continental breakfast in the morning, and enjoy the great feel that pervades this helpful place. To get there, take Bridge St off Main St, then turn right onto Invertrossachs Rd and continue for a mile.

Abbotsford Lodge B&B ££
(01877-330066; www.abbotsfordlodge.com; Stirling Rd; s/d £50/75; P@) This friendly Victorian house offers something different to the norm, with tartan and florals consigned to the bonfire, replaced by stylish comfortable contemporary design that enhances the building's original features. Ruffled fabrics and ceramic vases with flower arrangements characterise the renovated rooms.

Arden House B&B ££
(01877-330235; www.ardenhouse.org.uk; Bracklinn Rd; s/d £35/70; Apr-Oct; P) A redoubt of peaceful good taste, this elegant home features faultlessly welcoming hospitality and a woodsy, hillside location close to the centre but far from the crowds. The commodious rooms have flatscreen TV and plenty of little extras, including a suite (£80) with great views. Homebaked banana bread and a rotating dish-of-the-day keep breakfast well ahead of the competition.

White Shutters B&B £
(01877-330442; 6 South Church St; s/d £22/39) A cute little house just off the main street, White Shutters offers pleasing rooms with shared bathroom and a friendly welcome. The mattresses aren't exactly new, but it's comfortable and offers great value for this part of the world.

Linley Guest House B&B ££
(01877-330087; www.linleyguesthouse.co.uk; 139 Main St; s/d incl breakfast £36/52) A spick-and-span B&B with bright rooms and helpful owners. The double en suite is worth the extra: it's beautifully appointed with a large window drawing in lots of natural light. Room-only rate available.

Eating & Drinking

TOP CHOICE **Mhor Fish** BISTRO, TAKEAWAY ££
(☎01877-330213; www.mhor.net; 75 Main St; fish supper £5.50, mains £8-12; ⊙lunch & dinner Tue-Sun) Both chip shop and fish restaurant, but wholly different, this endearing black-and-white-tiled cafe displays the day's fresh catch. You can choose how you want it cooked, whether pan-seared and accompanied with one of many good wines, or fried and wrapped in paper with chips to take away. The fish and seafood comes from sustainable stock, and includes oysters and other goodies. If it runs out of fresh fish, it shuts, so opening hours can be a bit variable.

Callander Meadows RESTAURANT ££
(☎01877-330181; www.callandermeadows.co.uk; 24 Main St; lunch £7.95, mains £11-17; ⊙lunch & dinner Thu-Sun) Informal but smart, this well-loved restaurant in the centre of Callander occupies the two front rooms of a house on the main street. There's a contemporary flair for presentation and unusual flavour combinations, but a solidly British base underpins the cuisine, with things like mackerel, red cabbage, salmon and duck making regular and welcome appearances. It also opens on Mondays from April to September, and Wednesdays too in high season.

Lade Inn PUB £
(www.theladeinn.com; Kilmahog; bar meals £8-11; ⊙lunch & dinner;) Callander's best pub isn't in Callander – it's a mile north of town. It does decent, large and popular bar meals, don't mind kids, and pull a good pint (the real ales here are brewed to a house recipe). Next door, the owners run a shop with a dazzling selection of Scottish beers. There's low-key live music here at weekends too, but it shuts early if it's quiet midweek.

Information

Loch Lomond & the Trossachs National Park tourist office (☎01389-722600; ww.lochlomond-trossachs.org; 52 Main St; ⊙9.30am-4.30pm Mon-Fri, 9.30am-12.30pm Sat) This place is a useful centre for specific information on the park.

Rob Roy & Trossachs tourist office (☎01877-330342; callander@visitscotland.com; Ancaster Sq; ⊙10am-5pm daily Apr-Oct, 10am-4pm Mon-Sat Nov-Mar; @) This centre has heaps of info on the area.

Getting There & Away

First (www.firstgroup.com) operates buses from Stirling (45 minutes, hourly Monday to Saturday), while **Kingshouse** (www.kingshousetravel.co.uk) buses run from Killin (45 minutes, three to six daily Monday to Saturday). There are also **Citylink** (www.citylink.co.uk) buses from Edinburgh to Oban or Fort William via Callander (£15.10, 1¾ hours, daily).

Aberfoyle Coaches (www.aberfoylecoaches.com) runs between Callander and Aberfoyle (half-hour, four times daily Monday to Saturday).

See boxed text on p837 for other transport around the region.

LOCH KATRINE

This rugged area, 6 miles north of Aberfoyle and 10 miles west of Callander, is the heart of the Trossachs. From April to October two **boats** (☎01877-332000; www.lochkatrine.com; 1hr cruise adult/child £10/7) run cruises from Trossachs Pier at the eastern tip of Loch Katrine. At 10.30am there's a departure to Stronachlachar at the other end of the loch before returning (single/return adult £12/14, child £8/9). From Stronachlachar (also accessible by car via Aberfoyle), you can reach the eastern shore of Loch Lomond at isolated Inversnaid. A tarmac path links Trossachs Pier with Stronachlachar, so you can also take the boat out and walk/cycle back (12 miles). At Trossachs Pier, you can hire good bikes from **Katrinewheelz** (www.wheelscyclingcentre.com; hire per half-/full day from £10/15; ⊙daily Apr-Oct). It even has electric buggies for the less mobile or inclined (£40 for two hours).

KILLIN

POP 666

A fine base for the Trossachs or Perthshire, this lovely village sits at the western end of Loch Tay and has a spread-out, relaxed sort of a feel, particularly around the scenic **Falls of Dochart** which tumble through the centre. On a sunny day people sprawl over the rocks by the bridge, pint or picnic in hands. Killin offers some fine walking around the town, and mighty mountains and glens close at hand.

The helpful, informative **tourist office** (☎01567-820254; killin@visitscotland.com) is in the **Breadalbane Folklore Centre** (www.breadalbanefolklorecentre.com; adult/child £2.95/1.95; ⊙10am-4pm Wed-Mon Apr-Oct), in an old water mill overlooking the falls.

Activities

Five miles northeast of Killin, **Ben Lawers** (see boxed text, p871) rises above Loch Tay. Other routes abound; one rewarding **circular walk** heads up into the Acharn forest south of town, emerging above the tree-line

WORTH A TRIP

MONACHYLE MHOR

Four miles from Balquihidder is a luxury **hideaway** (01877-384622; www.mhor.net; dinner, bed & breakfast s/d from £166/220; P 📶 @) with a fantastically peaceful location overlooking two lochs. It's a great fusion of country Scotland and contemporary attitudes to design and food. The rooms and suites are superb and feature quirkily original decor. The restaurant offers set lunch (£20 for two courses) and dinner (£46) menus which are high in quality, sustainably sourced, and deliciously innovative. Enchantment lies in its successful combination of top-class hospitality with a relaxed rural atmosphere; dogs and kids happily romp on the lawns, and no-one looks askance if you come in flushed and muddy after a day's fishing or walking.

to great views of Loch Tay and Ben Lawers. The tourist office has stacks of walking leaflets and maps covering the area.

Killin is on the Lochs & Glens cycle route from Glasgow to Inverness. Hire bikes at **Killin Outdoor Centre** (01567-820652; www.killinoutdoor.co.uk; Main St; daily). It also rents out canoes and kayaks.

Sleeping & Eating

There are numerous good guest houses strung along the road through town, and a couple of supermarkets for trail supplies.

Falls of Dochart Inn PUB ££
(01567-820270; www.falls-of-dochart-inn.co.uk; s/d from £60/80; P 📶) In a prime position overlooking the falls, this is an excellent place to stay and eat. Handsome renovated rooms are comfortable, with slate bathrooms; it's worth the investment for one overlooking the falls themselves (double £95), but readers warn they can be chilly in winter. Downstairs is a very snug, atmospheric space with a roaring fire, personable service and really satisfying pub food, ranging from light meals to tasty, tender steaks and a couple of more advanced creations.

Braveheart Backpackers HOSTEL £
(07796-886899; info@cyclescotland.co.uk; dm/s/d £17.50/20/40) Tucked away alongside the Killin Hotel (on the main road through town), these two adjoining cottages offer several types of room, all wood-clad with comfortable beds and bunks including sheets. The comfy kitchen and lounge area won't appeal to hygiene nuts, but make the place feel like a home rather than a hostel. There's a rather negotiable attitude to prices and bookings: in short, it's not for everyone, but we like it.

Getting There & Away

Two daily **Citylink** (www.citylink.co.uk) buses between Edinburgh and Oban/Fort William stop here. There's also a **postbus** (www.royalmail.com) to Crianlarich and Tyndrum twice on weekdays and once on Saturday. **Kingshouse Travel** (www.kingshousetravel.co.uk) runs buses to Callander, where you can change to a Stirling service.

ARGYLL

An ancient and disparate area, Argyll comprises a series of peninsulas and islands along Scotland's ragged southwestern coast, pierced by long sea lochs knifing their way into the hilly, moody landscape. Because of its dramatic geography, places such as the Mull of Kintyre – not so far from Glasgow as the crow flies – can seem impossibly remote.

The islands offer great diversity. Romantic Mull is the gateway to holy Iona, whereas cheery Islay reverberates with the names of the heavyweights of the whisky world and Jura's wild hillscapes show nature's ultimate mastery and majesty. Meanwhile, the banks of Loch Lomond, the oysters of Loch Fyne and the prehistoric sites of Kilmartin Glen – all within easy striking distance of Glasgow – mean the mainland has nothing to envy.

Loch Lomond & Around

The 'bonnie banks' and 'bonnie braes' of Loch Lomond have long been Glasgow's rural retreat – a scenic region of hills, lochs and healthy fresh air within easy reach of Scotland's largest city. Since the 1930s Glaswegians have made a regular weekend exodus to the hills – by car, by bike and on foot – and today the loch's popularity shows no sign of decreasing (Loch Lomond is within an hour's drive of 70% of Scotland's population).

The main tourist focus is along the A82 on the loch's western shore, and at the southern end, around Balloch, which can occasionally be a nightmare of jet skies and motorboats. The eastern shore, which is followed by the West Highland Way long-distance footpath, is a little quieter.

The region's importance was recognised when it became the heart of **Loch Lomond & the Trossachs National Park** (www.lochlomond-trossachs.org) – Scotland's first national park, created in 2002.

Activities

Walking

The big walk around here is the **West Highland Way** (www.west-highland-way.co.uk), which runs along the eastern shore of the loch. There are shorter lochside walks at Firkin Point on the western shore and at several other places around the loch.

Rowardennan is the starting point for an ascent of **Ben Lomond** (974m), a popular and relatively easy five- to six-hour round trip. The route starts at the car park just past the Rowardennan Hotel.

Boat Trips

The main centre for boat trips is Balloch, where **Sweeney's Cruises** (www.sweeney.uk.com; Balloch Rd) offers a range of trips including a one-hour cruise to Inchmurrin and back (adult/child £7/4, departs hourly).

Cruise Loch Lomond (www.cruiselochlomondltd.com) is based in Tarbet and offers trips to Inversnaid and Rob Roy MacGregor's Cave. You can also be dropped off at Rowardennan and picked up at Inversnaid after a 9-mile hike along the West Highland Way.

Lomond Adventure (☎01360-870218), in Balmaha, rents out Canadian **canoes** (£30 per day) and **sea kayaks** (£25).

Sleeping & Eating

TOP CHOICE **Drover's Inn** PUB £
(☎01301-704234; www.thedroversinn.co.uk; Inverarnan; bar meals £8-10, steaks £15-17; lunch & dinner; P) This is one howff (drinking den) you shouldn't miss – a low-ceilinged place with smoke-blackened stone, barmen in kilts and walls festooned with moth-eaten stag's heads. We recommend this inn more as a place to eat and drink than to stay – accommodation (single/double from £40/78) varies from eccentric, old-fashioned and rather run-down rooms in the old building (including a ghost in room 6), to more comfortable rooms (with en-suite bathrooms) in the modern annexe across the road (ask to see your room before taking it, though).

Loch Lomond Youth Hostel HOSTEL £
(SYHA; ☎01389-850226; www.syha.org.uk; Arden; dm £18; Mar-Oct; P@) Forget about roughing it, this is one of the most impressive hostels in the country – an imposing 19th-century country house set in beautiful grounds overlooking the loch. It's 2 miles north of Balloch and very popular, so book in advance in summer. And yes, it *is* haunted.

Oak Tree Inn INN ££
(☎01360-870357; www.oak-tree-inn.co.uk; Balmaha; dm/s/d £30/60/75; P) An attractive traditional inn built in slate and timber, the child-friendly Oak Tree offers luxurious guest bedrooms for pampered hikers, and two four-bed bunkrooms for hardier souls. The rustic **restaurant** dishes up hearty meals (£8 to £15; open noon to 9pm).

ROB ROY

Nicknamed 'Red' ('ruadh' in Gaelic, anglicised to 'roy') for his ginger locks, Robert MacGregor (1671–1734) was the wild leader of the wildest of Scotland's clans. Although they had rights to the lands the clan occupied, these estates stood between powerful neighbours who had the MacGregors outlawed, hence their sobriquet 'Children of the Mist'. Incognito, Rob became a prosperous livestock trader, before a dodgy deal led to a warrant for his arrest.

A legendary swordsman, the fugitive from justice then became notorious for his daring raids into the Lowlands to carry off cattle and sheep. He was forever hiding from potential captors; he was twice imprisoned, but escaped dramatically on both occasions. He finally turned himself in, and received his liberty and a pardon from the King. He lies buried in the churchyard at Balquhidder; his uncompromising epitaph reads 'MacGregor despite them'. His life has been glorified over the years due to Walter Scott's novel and the 1995 film. Many Scots see his life as a symbol of the struggle of the common folk against the unequable ownership of vast tracts of the country by landed aristocrats.

Rowardennan Youth Hostel HOSTEL £
(☎01360-870259; Rowardennan; dm £17; ⏲Mar-Oct) Housed in an attractive Victorian lodge, this hostel has a superb setting right on the loch shore, beside the West Highland Way.

Cashel Campsite CAMPSITE £
(☎01360-870234; www.forestholidays.co.uk; Rowardennan; dm £6.50, tent sites per 2 people incl car £15-17; ⏲Mar-Oct;) This is the most attractive campsite in the area. It's 3 miles north of Balmaha, by the loch.

Information

Balloch tourist office (☎0870 720 0607; Balloch Rd; ⏲9.30am-6pm Jun-Sep, 10am-6pm Apr-May & Oct)

Balmaha National Park Centre (☎01389-722100; Balmaha; ⏲9.30am-4.15pm Apr-Sep)

National Park Gateway Centre (☎01389-751035; www.lochlomondshores.com; Loch Lomond Shores, Balloch; ⏲10am-6pm Apr-Sep, 10am-5pm Oct-Mar; @)

Tarbet tourist office (☎0870-720 0623; ⏲10am-6pm Jul & Aug, 10am-5pm Easter-Jun, Sep & Oct) At the junction of the A82 and the A83.

Getting There & Away

BUS First (www.firstgroup.com) Glasgow buses 204 and 215 run from Argyle St in central Glasgow to Balloch and Loch Lomond Shores (1½ hours, at least two per hour).

Citylink (www.citylink.co.uk) coaches from Glasgow to Oban and Fort William stop at Luss (£8, 55 minutes, six daily), Tarbet (£8, 65 minutes) and Ardlui (£14, 1¼ hours).

TRAIN There are frequent trains from Glasgow to Balloch (£4.15, 45 minutes, every 30 minutes) and a less-frequent service on the West Highland line from Glasgow to Arrochar & Tarbet station (£10, 1¼ hours, three or four daily), halfway between the two villages, and Ardlui (£13, 1½ hours), continuing to Oban and Fort William.

Inveraray

POP 700

You can spot Inveraray long before you get here – its neat, whitewashed buildings stand out from a distance on the shores of Loch Fyne. It's a planned town, built by the Duke of Argyll in Georgian style when he revamped his nearby castle in the 18th century. The **tourist office** (☎0845 225 5121; Front St; ⏲9am-6pm Jul & Aug, 10am-5pm Mon-Sat Apr-Jun, Sep & Oct, 10am-3pm Mon-Sat Nov-Mar; @) is on the seafront.

Sights

Inveraray Castle CASTLE
(www.inveraray-castle.com; adult/child £9/6.10; ⏲10am-5.45pm Apr-Oct) Inveraray Castle has been the seat of the dukes of Argyll – chiefs of Clan Campbell – since the 15th century. The 18th-century building, with its fairy-tale turrets and fake battlements, houses an impressive armoury hall, its walls patterned with a collection of more than 1000 pole arms, dirks, muskets and Lochaber axes. The castle is 500m north of town, entered from the A819 Dalmally road.

Inveraray Jail MUSEUM
(www.inverarayjail.co.uk; Church Sq; adult/child £8.25/5.50; ⏲9.30am-6pm Apr-Oct, 10am-5pm Nov-Mar) Inveraray Jail is an award-winning, interactive tourist attraction where you can sit in on a trial, try out a cell, and discover the harsh torture meted out to unfortunate prisoners. The attention to detail – including a life-sized model of an inmate squatting on a 19th-century toilet – more than makes up for the sometimes tedious commentary.

Sleeping & Eating

TOP CHOICE **George Hotel** HOTEL ££
(☎01499-302111; www.thegeorgehotel.co.uk; Main St E; s/d from £35/70; P) The George Hotel boasts a magnificent choice of opulent rooms, complete with four-poster beds, period furniture, Victorian roll-top baths and private Jacuzzis (superior rooms cost £130 to £165 per double). The cosy wood-panelled bar, with its rough stone walls, flagstone floor and peat fires, is a delightful place for a bar meal (mains £7 to £10, open for lunch and dinner).

Inveraray Youth Hostel HOSTEL £
(SYHA; ☎01499-302454; www.syha.org.uk; Dalmally Rd; dm £16; ⏲Apr-Oct; @) To get to this hostel, housed in a comfortable, modern bungalow, go through the arched entrance on the seafront – it's set back on the left of the road about 100m further on.

Loch Fyne Oyster Bar RESTAURANT ££
(www.lochfyne.com; Clachan, Cairndow; mains £10-22; ⏲breakfast, lunch & dinner) Six miles northeast of Inveraray in Cairndow, this rustic-themed restaurant serves excellent seafood, though the service can be a bit hit-and-miss. It's housed in a converted byre, and the menu includes locally farmed oysters, mussels and salmon. The neighbouring shop sells packaged seafood

and other deli goods to take away, as well as bottled beer from the nearby Fyne Ales microbrewery.

Getting There & Away

Citylink (www.citylink.co.uk) buses run from Glasgow to Inveraray (£10, 1¾ hours, six daily Monday to Saturday, two Sunday). Three of these buses continue to Lochgilphead and Campbeltown (£11, 2½ hours); the others continue to Oban (£9, 1¼ hours).

Kilmartin Glen

In the 6th century, Irish settlers arrived in this part of Argyll and founded the kingdom of Dalriada, which eventually united with the Picts in 843 to create the first Scottish kingdom. Their capital was the hill fort of Dunadd, on the plain to the south of Kilmartin Glen.

This magical glen is the focus of one of the biggest concentrations of prehistoric sites in Scotland. Burial cairns, standing stones, stone circles, hill forts and cup-and-ring-marked rocks litter the countryside. Within a 6-mile radius of Kilmartin village there are 25 sites with standing stones and over 100 rock carvings.

Sights

Your first stop should be **Kilmartin House Museum** (www.kilmartin.org; Kilmartin; adult/child £5/2; 10am-5.30pm Mar-Oct, 11am-4pm Nov-23 Dec), in Kilmartin village, a fascinating interpretive centre that provides a context for the ancient monuments you can go on to explore, alongside displays of artefacts recovered from various sites. The project was partly funded by midges – the curator exposed his body in Temple Wood on a warm summer's evening and was sponsored per midge bite!

The oldest monuments at Kilmartin date from 5000 years ago and comprise a linear cemetery of **burial cairns** that runs south from Kilmartin village for 1.5 miles. There are also ritual monuments (two stone circles) at **Temple Wood**, three-quarters of a mile southwest of Kilmartin. The museum bookshop sells maps and guides.

Kilmartin Churchyard contains some 10th-century Celtic crosses and medieval grave slabs with carved effigies of knights. Some researchers have surmised that these were the tombs of Knights Templar who fled persecution in France in the 14th century.

The hill fort of **Dunadd**, 3.5 miles south of Kilmartin village, was the seat of power of the first kings of Dalriada, and may have been where the **Stone of Destiny** (p765) was originally located. The faint rock carvings of a wild boar and two footprints with an Ogham inscription may have been used in some kind of inauguration ceremony. A slippery path leads to the summit where you can gaze out on much the same view that the kings of Dalriada enjoyed 1300 years ago.

Sleeping & Eating

Burndale B&B B&B ££
(01546-510235; www.burndale.net; s/d from £35/54; P) Set in a lovely Victorian manse (minister's house), this homely and hospitable B&B is just a short walk north from the Kilmartin House Museum. Expect a warm welcome and Loch Fyne kippers for breakfast. Credit cards not accepted.

Kilmartin Hotel INN ££
(01546-510250; www.kilmartin-hotel.com; s/d £40/65; P) Though the rooms here are a bit on the small side, this attractively old-fashioned hotel is full of atmosphere. There's a **restaurant** here too, and a whisky bar with real ale on tap where you can enjoy live folk music at weekends.

TOP CHOICE **Glebe Cairn Café** CAFE £
(Kilmartin House Museum; mains £5-8; breakfast & lunch, dinner Thu-Sat Jun-Aug) The cafe in the Kilmartin House Museum has a lovely conservatory with a view across fields to a prehistoric cairn. Dishes include homemade Cullen Skink and a Celtic cheese platter.

Getting There & Away

Bus 423 between Oban and Ardrishaig (four daily Monday to Friday, two on Saturday) stops at Kilmartin (£4.50, one hour 20 minutes).

You can **walk or cycle** along the Crinan Canal from Ardrishaig, then turn north at Bellanoch on the minor B8025 road to reach Kilmartin (12 miles one way).

Kintyre

Almost an island, the 40-mile-long Kintyre Peninsula has only a narrow isthmus at Tarbert connecting it to the rest of Scotland. Magnus Barefoot the Viking, who could claim any island he circumnavigated, made his people drag their longship across this strand to validate his claim to Kintyre.

TARBERT

POP 1500

The attractive fishing village and yachting centre of Tarbert is the gateway to Kintyre, and well worth a stopover for lunch or dinner. There's a **tourist office** (☎01880-820429; Harbour St; ⏰9am-5pm Mon-Sat Apr-Oct) here.

The picturesque harbour is overlooked by the crumbling, ivy-covered ruins of **Tarbert Castle**, built by Robert the Bruce in the 14th century. You can hike up to it via a signposted footpath beside the **Loch Fyne Gallery** (www.lochfynegallery.com; Harbour St; ⏰10am-5pm), which showcases the work of local artists.

There are plenty of B&Bs and hotels here, but be sure to book ahead during festivals and major events. The **Springside B&B** (☎01880-820413; www.scotland-info.co.uk/springside; Pier Rd; s/d £35/60; P) is an attractive fisherman's cottage that overlooks the entrance to the harbour, where you can sit out front and watch the yachts and fishing boats come and go. There are four comfy rooms, three with en suite, and the house is just five minutes' walk from the village centre in one direction, and a short stroll from the Portavadie ferry in the other.

TOP CHOICE **Corner House Bistro** (☎01880-820263; Harbour St; mains £14-26; ⏰lunch & dinner) is worth a trip to Tarbert even just for dinner. This relaxed and romantic restaurant, with log fires and candlelight, has an award-winning French chef who knows exactly what to do with top-quality local seafood. The entrance is on the side street around the corner from the Corner House pub – look for the green awning. Best to book a table.

CAMPBELTOWN

POP 6000

Campbeltown, with its ranks of gloomy, grey council houses, feels a bit like an Ayrshire mining town that's been placed incongruously on the shores of a beautiful Argyllshire harbour. It was once a thriving fishing port and whisky-making centre, but industrial decline and the closure of the former air force base at nearby Machrihanish saw Campbeltown's fortunes decline.

But renewal is in the air – the spruced-up seafront, with its flower beds, smart Victorian buildings and restored art-deco cinema, lends the town a distinctly optimistic air.

There were once no fewer than 32 distilleries in the Campbeltown area, but most closed down in the 1920s. Today, **Springbank Distillery** (www.springbankwhisky.com; tours £4; ⏰by arrangement 10am & 2pm Mon-Fri, 2pm only Oct-Apr) is one of only three that now operate in town. It is also one of the very few distilleries in Scotland that distils, matures and bottles all its whisky on the one site.

Mull of Kintyre Seatours (☎0870 720 0609; www.mull-of-kintyre.co.uk) operates two-hour, high-speed boat trips (adult/child from £30/20) out of Campbeltown harbour to look for wildlife: seals, porpoises, minke whales, golden eagles and peregrine falcons live in the turbulent tidal waters and on the spectacular sea cliffs of the Mull of Kintyre. Book in advance by phone or at the tourist office.

The **tourist office** (☎01586-552056; the Pier, Campbelltown; ⏰9am-5.30pm Mon-Sat) is beside the harbour.

Loganair/FlyBe (www.loganair.co.uk) operates two flights daily, Monday to Friday, from Glasgow to Campbeltown (£50, 35 minutes). **Citylink** (www.citylink.co.uk) buses run from Campbeltown to Glasgow (£17, four hours, three daily) via Tarbert, Inveraray, Arrochar and Loch Lomond.

MULL OF KINTYRE

A narrow winding road, about 18 miles long, leads south from Campbeltown to the **Mull of Kintyre**, passing some good **sandy beaches** near Southend. The name of this remote headland was immortalised in Paul McCartney's famous song – the former Beatle owns a farmhouse in the area. A **lighthouse** marks the spot closest to Northern Ireland, whose coastline, only 12 miles away, is visible across the North Channel.

Isle of Islay

POP 3400

The home of the world's greatest and peatiest whiskies, whose names reverberate on the tongue like a pantheon of Celtic deities, Islay (*eye*-lah) is a wonderfully friendly place whose warmly welcoming inhabitants offset its lack of majestic scenery. Even if you're not into your drams, the birdlife, fine seafood, turquoise bays and basking seals are ample reason to visit this island. There are currently eight working distilleries; perhaps this is why the locals are so genial. A wave or cheerio to passers-by is mandatory, and you'll soon find yourself slowing down to Islay's relaxing pace.

Fèis Ìle (Islay Festival; www.theislayfestival.co.uk) is a week-long celebration of traditional Scottish music and whisky at the end of May. Events include *ceilidhs* (informal entertainment and dance), pipe-band performances, distillery tours, barbecues and whisky tastings.

Information

Islay Service Point (Jamieson St, Bowmore; 9am-12.30pm & 1.30-5pm Mon-Fri; @) Free internet access.

Islay tourist office (0870-720 0617; The Square, Bowmore; 10am-5pm Mon-Sat & 2-5pm Sun Apr-Aug, shorter hr Sep-Mar)

MacTaggart Community CyberCafé (www.islaycybercafe.co.uk; 30 Mansfield Pl, Port Ellen; 9am-10pm Mon & Wed-Sat, 9am-5pm Tue & Sun; @) Internet access.

MacTaggart Leisure Centre (School St, Bowmore; wash £4, dry £2; noon-9pm Mon-Fri, 10.30am-5.30pm Sat & Sun) Coin-operated laundrette.

Getting There & Away

There are two ferry terminals on the island, both served by ferries from Kennacraig in West Loch Tarbert – Port Askaig on the east coast, and Port Ellen in the south. Islay airport lies midway between Port Ellen and Bowmore.

AIR **Loganair/FlyBe** (www.loganair.co.uk) flies from Glasgow to Islay (£70 one way, 45 minutes, two or three flights daily Monday to Friday, one or two Saturday and Sunday).

Hebridean Air Services (0845 805 7465; www.hebrideanair.co.uk) operates flights (£65 one way, twice daily Tuesday and Thursday) from Connel Airfield (near Oban) to Colonsay (30 minutes) and Islay (40 minutes).

BOAT **CalMac** (www.calmac.co.uk) runs ferries from Kennacraig in West Loch Tarbert to Port Ellen (passenger/car £9.20/49, 2¼ hours, one to three daily) and Port Askaig (£9.20/49, two hours, one to three daily). On Wednesday only in summer the ferry continues from Port Askaig to Colonsay (£4.85/24.70, 1¼ hours).

Getting Around

BIKE HIRE You can hire bikes from **Bowmore Post Office** (per day £10), and from the house opposite the Port Charlotte Hotel.

BUS A bus service links Ardbeg, Port Ellen, Bowmore, Port Charlotte, Portnahaven and Port Askaig (limited service on Sunday). Pick up a copy of the *Islay & Jura Public Transport Guide* from the tourist office.

CAR HIRE **D & N MacKenzie** (01496-302300; Port Ellen; from £30 a day).

TAXI Bowmore (01496-810449); Port Ellen (01496-302155).

PORT ELLEN & AROUND

Port Ellen is the main point of entry for Islay. While there's nothing to see in the town itself, the coast stretching northeast from Port Ellen is one of the loveliest parts of the island.

There are three **whisky distilleries** in close succession (check websites for tour times):

Laphroaig DISTILLERY
(www.laphroaig.com; tours £3; 9.30am-5.30pm Mon-Fri, also 10am-4pm Sat & Sun Mar-Dec)

Lagavulin DISTILLERY
(www.discovering-distilleries.com; tours £6; 9am-5pm Mon-Fri Apr-Oct, to 12.30pm Nov-Mar, plus 9am-5pm Sat & 12.30-4pm Sun Jul & Aug)

Ardbeg DISTILLERY
(www.ardbeg.com; tours £5; 10am-5pm Jun-Aug, 10am-4pm Mon-Fri Sep-May).

A pleasant bike ride leads past the distilleries to the atmospheric, age-haunted **Kildalton Chapel**, 8 miles northeast of Port Ellen. In the kirkyard is the exceptional late-8th-century **Kildalton Cross**, the only remaining Celtic high cross in Scotland (most surviving high crosses are in Ireland). There are carvings of biblical scenes on one side and animals on the other. There are also several extraordinary grave slabs around the chapel, some carved with swords and Celtic interlace patterns.

Sleeping & Eating

TOP CHOICE **Kintra Farm** CAMPSITE, B&B ££
(01496-302051; www.kintrafarm.co.uk; Kintra; tent sites £4-10, plus per person £3, r per person £30-38; Apr-Sep) At the southern end of Laggan Bay, 3.5 miles northwest of Port Ellen, Kintra offers three bedrooms in a homely farmhouse B&B. There's also a basic but beautiful campsite on buttercup-sprinkled turf amid the dunes, with a sunset view across the beach.

Oystercatcher B&B B&B ££
(01496-300409; www.islay-bedandbreakfast.com; 63 Frederick Cres, Port Ellen; r per person £32; @) If you like your breakfasts fishy, then this welcoming waterfront house is the place for you – there's smoked haddock, smoked salmon and kippers on the menu, as well as the usual stuff. Bedrooms are small but comfortable and nicely decorated.

Islay, Jura & Colonsay

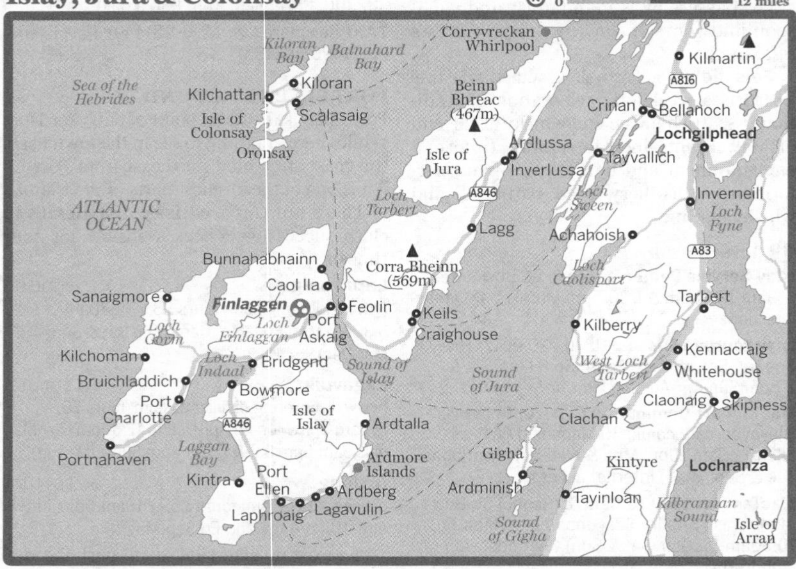

TOP CHOICE **Old Kiln Café** CAFE **£**
(Ardbeg; mains £4-10; ⏲breakfast & lunch daily Jun-Aug, Mon-Fri only Sep-May) Housed in the former malting kiln at Ardbeg Distillery, this well-run cafe serves hearty homemade soups such as sweet-potato and chilli, tasty light meals and a range of home-baked desserts.

BOWMORE

The attractive Georgian village of Bowmore was built in 1768 to replace the village of Kilarrow, which just had to go – it was spoiling the view from the laird's house. Its centrepiece is the distinctive **Round Church** at the top of Main St, built in circular form to ensure that the devil had no corners to hide in.

Bowmore Distillery (www.bowmore.co.uk; School St; tours adult/child £4/2; ⏲9am-5pm Mon-Fri & 9am-noon Sat, also 9am-5pm Sat Easter–mid-Sep & noon-4pm Sun Jul–mid-Sep) is the only distillery on the island that still malts its own barley. The tour (check website for times), which begins with an overblown 10-minute marketing video, is redeemed by a look at (and taste of) the germinating grain laid out in golden billows on the floor of the malting shed, and a free dram at the end.

Sleeping & Eating

Harbour Inn RESTAURANT WITH ROOMS **£££**
(☎01496-810330; www.harbour-inn.com; The Square; s/d from £95/130; @ wi-fi) The plush seven-room Harbour Inn, smartly decorated with a nautical theme, is the poshest place in town. The **restaurant** (mains £16-24; ⏲lunch & dinner) has harbour views and serves fresh local oysters, lobster and scallops, Islay lamb and Jura venison.

Lambeth House B&B **££**
(☎01496-810597; lambethguesthouse@tiscali.co.uk; Jamieson St; s/d £60/90; @ family) A short stroll from the harbour, the Lambeth is a simple, good-value guest house with comfy en suite bedrooms. Breakfasts are excellent, and it also offers a two-course evening meal for £12.

PORT CHARLOTTE

Eleven miles from Bowmore, on the opposite shore of Loch Indaal, is the attractive village of Port Charlotte. It has a **general store** (⏲9am-12.30pm & 1.30-5.30pm Mon-Sat, 11.30am-1.30pm Sun) and post office.

Islay's long history is lovingly recorded in the **Museum of Islay Life** (www.islaymuseum.org; adult/child £3/1; ⏲10am-5pm Mon-Sat, 2-5pm Sun Easter-Oct), housed in the former Free Church. Prize exhibits include an illicit still, 19th-century crofters' furniture, and a set of leather boots once worn by the horse that pulled the lawnmower at Islay House (so it wouldn't leave hoof-prints on the lawn!). There are also touch-screen computers displaying archive photos of Islay in the 19th and early 20th centuries.

The **Bruichladdich Distillery** (☎01496-850190; www.bruichladdich.com; tours £5; ⏲9am-5pm Mon-Fri & 10am-4pm Sat), at the northern edge of the village, re-opened in 2001 with all its original Victorian equipment restored to working condition. Independently owned and independently minded, Bruichladdich (brook-*lah*-day) produces an intriguing range of distinctive, very peaty whiskies. Call ahead to book a tour.

Sleeping & Eating

Port Charlotte Hotel HOTEL £££
(☎01496-850360; www.portcharlottehotel.co.uk; Port Charlotte; s/d £95/160; P 🛜 👪) This lovely old Victorian hotel has stylish, individually decorated bedrooms with sea views, and a candle-lit **restaurant** (mains £15-22; ⏲dinner) serving local seafood (seared scallops with braised leeks and truffle cream sauce), Islay beef, venison and duck. The bar (bar meals £7 to £10, open for lunch and dinner) is well stocked with Islay malts and real ales, and has a nook at the back with a view over the loch towards the Paps of Jura.

Debbie's Minimarket CAFE £
(Bruichladdich; ⏲9am-5.30pm Mon-Sat) The village shop and post office at Bruichladdich doubles as a deli that stocks good wine and posh picnic grub, and also serves the best coffee on Islay – sit at one of the outdoor tables and enjoy an espresso with a sea view.

Port Mor Campsite CAMPSITE £
(☎01496-850441; www.islandofislay.co.uk; Port Charlotte; tent sites per person £8; @ 🛜) The sports field to the south of the village doubles as a campsite – there are toilets, showers, laundry and a children's play area in the main building. Open all year.

Islay Youth Hostel HOSTEL £
(SYHA; ☎01496-850385; www.syha.org.uk; Port Charlotte; dm £15; ⏲Apr-Oct; @ 🛜) This modern and comfortable hostel is housed in a former distillery building with views over the loch.

FINLAGGAN

Lush meadows swathed in buttercups and daisies slope down to reed-fringed Loch Finlaggan, the medieval capital of the Lords of the Isles. This bucolic setting, 3 miles southwest of Port Askaig, was once the most important settlement in the Hebrides, the central seat of power of the Lords of the Isles from the 12th to the 16th centuries. From the little island at the northern end of the loch the descendants of Somerled administered their island territories and entertained visiting chieftains in their great hall. Little remains now except the tumbled ruins of houses and a chapel, but the setting is beautiful and the history fascinating. A wooden walkway leads over the reeds and water lilies to the island, where information boards describe the remains.

The **Finlaggan tourist office** (www.finlaggan.com; adult/child £3/1; ⏲10.30am-4.30pm Mon-Sat & 1.30-4.30pm Sun Apr-Sep), in a nearby cottage (plus modern extension), explains the site's history and archaeology. The island itself is open at all times.

Buses from Port Askaig stop at the road-end, from where it's a 15-minute walk to the loch.

Isle of Jura

POP 170

Jura lies off the coast of Argyll – long, dark and low like a vast Viking longship, its billowing sail the distinctive triple peaks of the Paps of Jura. A magnificently wild and lonely island, Jura is the perfect place for getting away from it all – as George Orwell did in 1948. Orwell wrote his masterpiece *1984* while living at the remote farmhouse of Barnhill in the north of the island. Jura takes its name from the Old Norse *dyr-a* (deer island) – an apt appellation, as the island supports a population of around 6000 red deer, who outnumber their human cohabitants by about 35-to-one.

Apart from the superb wilderness walking and wildlife-watching, there's not a whole lot to do on the island apart from visit the **Isle of Jura Distillery** (www.isleofjura.com; admission free; ⏲by appointment Mon-Fri) or wander around the beautiful walled gardens of **Jura House** (www.jurahouseandgardens.co.uk; adult/child £2.50/free; ⏲9am-5pm) at the southern end of the island.

You can hire bikes from **Jura Bike Hire** (☎07092-180747; www.jurabikehire.com; per day

£12.50) at Bramble Cottage in Keils, a mile northeast of Craighouse.

Sleeping & Eating

Places to stay on the island are very limited, so book ahead. Most of Jura's accommodation is in self-catering cottages that are let by the week (see www.juradevelopment.co.uk). You can **camp** for free in the field below the Jura Hotel.

Jura Hotel HOTEL, PUB **££**
(01496-820243; www.jurahotel.co.uk; Craighouse; s/d from £50/84; P) The 18-room Jura is the most comfortable place to stay on the island; ask for a room at the front with a view of the bay. The hotel also serves decent bar meals (£7 to £12).

Antlers BISTRO **££**
(01496-820123; www.theantlers.co.uk; Craighouse; mains £5-9, 2-/3-course dinner £25/29; 10.30am-4.30pm daily, 6.30-9.30pm Tue-Sun;) This brand-new bistro makes the most of locally sourced produce, offering soup, sandwiches and burgers during the day, and an unexpectedly classy menu at dinner time.

Getting There & Away

A **car ferry** (passenger/car/bicycle £1.25/7.60/free, five minutes, hourly Monday to Saturday, every two hours Sunday) shuttles between Port Askaig on Islay and Feolin on Jura.

From April to September **Jura Passenger Ferry** (07768-450000; www.jurapassengerferry.com) runs from Tayvallich on the mainland to Craighouse on Jura (£17.50, one hour, one or two daily except Wednesday). Booking is recommended.

Oban

POP 8120

Oban is a peaceful waterfront town on a delightful bay, with sweeping views to Kerrera and Mull. OK, that first bit about peaceful is true only in winter; in summer the town centre is a heaving mass of humanity, its streets jammed with traffic and crowded with holidaymakers, day trippers and travellers headed for the islands. But the setting is still lovely.

There's not a huge amount to see in the town itself, but it's an appealingly busy place with some excellent restaurants and lively pubs, and it's the main gateway to the islands of Mull, Iona, Colonsay, Barra, Coll and Tiree.

Sights

McCaig's Tower HISTORIC BUILDING
(admission free; 24hr) Crowning the hill above the town centre is the Victorian folly known as McCaig's Tower. Its construction was commissioned in 1890 by local worthy John Stuart McCaig, an art critic, philosophical essayist and banker, with the philanthropic intention of providing work for unemployed stonemasons. To reach it on foot, make the steep climb up **Jacob's Ladder** (a flight of stairs) from Argyll St and then follow the signs. The views over the bay are worth the effort.

Oban Distillery DISTILLERY
(www.discovering-distilleries.com; Stafford St; tour £7; 9.30am-5pm Mon-Sat Easter-Oct, plus noon-5pm Sun Jul-Sep, closed Sat & Sun Nov-Dec & Feb-Easter, closed Jan) This distillery has been producing Oban single-malt whisky since 1794. There are guided tours available (last tour begins one hour before closing time), but even without a tour, it's still worth a look at the small exhibition in the foyer.

FREE **War & Peace Museum** MUSEUM
(www.obanmuseum.org.uk; Corran Esplanade; 10am-6pm Mon-Sat & 10am-4pm Sun May-Sep, 10am-4pm daily Mar, Apr, Oct & Nov) Military buffs will enjoy the little War & Peace Museum, which chronicles Oban's role in WWII as a base for Catalina seaplanes and as a marshalling area for Atlantic convoys.

Activities

A tourist-office leaflet lists local **bike rides**, which include a 7-mile Gallanach circular tour, a 16-mile route to the Isle of Seil and routes to Connel, Glenlonan and Kilmore. You can hire mountain bikes from **Evo Bikes** (www.evobikes.co.uk; 29 Lochside St; 9am-5.30pm Mon-Sat), opposite Tesco supermarket, from £15 to £30 per day.

Various operators offer **boat trips** to spot seals and other marine wildlife, departing from the North Pier slipway (adult/child £8/5.50); ask for details at the tourist office.

Sleeping

Despite having lots of B&B accommodation, Oban's beds can still fill up quickly in July and August so try to book ahead. If you can't find a bed in Oban, consider staying at Connel, 4 miles to the north.

Barriemore Hotel B&B ££
(☎01631-566356; www.barriemore-hotel.co.uk; Corran Esplanade; s/d from £65/92; P) The Barriemore enjoys a grand location, overlooking the entrance to Oban Bay. There are 13 spacious rooms here (ask for one with a sea view), plus a guest lounge with magazines and newspapers, and plump Loch Fyne kippers on the breakfast menu.

Heatherfield House B&B ££
(☎01631-562681; www.heatherfieldhouse.co.uk; Albert Rd; s/d from £35/70; P@) The welcoming Heatherfield House occupies a converted 1870s rectory set in extensive grounds and has six spacious rooms. If possible, ask for room 1, complete with fireplace, sofa and a view over the garden to the harbour.

Old Manse Guest House B&B ££
(☎01631-564886; www.obanguesthouse.co.uk; Dalriach Rd; s/d from £62/74; P) Set on a hillside above the town, the Old Manse commands great views over to Kerrera and Mull. The sunny, brightly decorated bedrooms have some nice touches (a couple of wine glasses and a corkscrew), and kids are made welcome with Balamory books, toys and DVDs.

Manor House HOTEL £££
(☎01631-562087; www.manorhouseoban.com; Gallanach Rd; r £154-199; P) Built in 1780 for the Duke of Argyll as part of his Oban estates, the Manor House is now one of Oban's finest hotels. It has small but elegant rooms in Georgian style, a posh bar frequented by local and visiting yachties, and a fine **restaurant** serving Scottish and French cuisine. Children under 12 are not welcome.

Oban Backpackers Lodge HOSTEL £
(☎01631-562107; www.obanbackpackers.com; Breadalbane St; dm £12.50-13.50; @) This is a friendly place with a good vibe and a large and attractive communal lounge with lots of sofas and armchairs. Breakfast is included in the price, there's free tea and coffee, a laundry service (£2.50) and powerful showers.

Oban Caravan & Camping Park CAMPSITE £
(www.obancaravanpark.com; Gallanachmore Farm; tent & campervan sites £17; Apr-Oct) This spacious campsite has a superb location overlooking the Sound of Kerrera, 2.5 miles south of Oban (bus twice a day). The quoted rate includes up to two people and a car; extra people are £2 each. A one-person tent with no car is £8. No pre-booking – it's first-come, first-served.

Jeremy Inglis Hostel HOSTEL £
(☎01631-565065; 21 Airds Cres; dm/s £15/22;) This bargain place is more of an eccentric B&B than a hostel – most 'dorms' have only two or three beds, and are decorated with original artwork, books, flowers and cuddly toys. The kitchen is a little cramped, but the owner is friendly and knowledgeable (and makes delicious homemade jam). The price includes a continental breakfast.

Sand Villa Guest House B&B ££
(☎01631-562803; www.holidayoban.co.uk; Breadalbane St; r per person £28-33; P) Ground floor room with wheelchair access. No credit cards.

Roseneath Guest House B&B ££
(☎01631-562929; www.roseneathoban.com; Dalriach Rd; s/d from £40/60; P) Peaceful location with sea views.

Eating

TOP CHOICE **Waterfront Restaurant** SEAFOOD ££
(☎01631-563110; www.waterfrontoban.co.uk; Waterfront Centre, Railway Pier; mains £10-18; lunch & dinner) Housed on the top floor of a converted seamen's mission, the Waterfront's stylish, unfussy decor – dusky pink and carmine with pine tables and local art on the walls – does little to distract from the superb seafood freshly landed at the quay just a few metres away. Best to book for dinner.

TOP CHOICE **Shellfish Bar** SEAFOOD £
(Railway Pier; mains £2-7; breakfast & lunch) If you want to savour superb Scottish seafood without the expense of an upmarket restaurant, head for Oban's famous seafood stall – it's the green shack on the quayside near the ferry terminal. Here you can buy fresh and cooked seafood to take away – excellent prawn sandwiches (£2.75), dressed crab (£4.75), and fresh oysters for only 65p each.

Seafood Temple SEAFOOD £££
(☎01631-566000; Gallanach Rd; mains £15-25; dinner Thu-Sun) Locally sourced seafood is the god that's worshipped at this tiny temple – a former park pavilion with glorious views over the bay. Owned by a former fisherman who smokes his own salmon, what must be Oban's smallest restaurant serves up whole lobster cooked to order, scallops in garlic butter, plump langoustines,

and the 'platter magnifique' (£60 for two persons), which offers a taste of everything. Booking essential.

Cuan Mor BISTRO ££
(www.cuanmor.co.uk; 60 George St; mains £8-16; ⏲lunch & dinner) This always-busy bar and bistro sports a no-nonsense menu of old favourites – from haddock and chips to sausage and mash with onion gravy – spiced with a few more sophisticated dishes such as scallops with black pudding, and a decent range of vegetarian dishes. And the sticky toffee pudding is not to be missed!

Ee'usk SEAFOOD ££
(☎01631-565666; www.eeusk.com; North Pier; mains £12-20; ⏲lunch & dinner) Bright and modern Ee'usk (it's how you pronounce *iasg,* the Gaelic word for fish) occupies Oban's prime location on the North Pier. Floor-to-ceiling windows allow diners on two levels to enjoy views over the harbour to Kerrera and Mull, whilst sampling a seafood menu ranging from fragrant Thai fish cakes to langoustines with chilli and ginger. A little pricey, perhaps, but both food and location are first class.

Kitchen Garden CAFE £
(www.kitchengardenoban.co.uk; 14 George St; mains £3-8; ⏲9am-5pm Mon-Sat, 10.30am-5pm Sun, 6-9pm Thu-Sat) Deli packed with delicious picnic food. Also has a great little cafe above the shop – good coffee, scones, cakes, homemade soups and sandwiches.

Information

Fancy That (112 George St; per hr £3; ⏲10am-5pm; @) Internet access.

Lorn & Islands District General Hospital (☎01631-567500; Glengallan Rd) Southern end of town.

Main post office (Lochside St; ⏲8am-6pm Mon-Sat, 10am-1pm Sun) Inside Tesco supermarket.

Tourist office (☎01631-563122; www.oban.org.uk; Argyll Sq; ⏲9am-7pm daily Jul & Aug, 9am-5.30pm Mon-Sat & 10am-5pm Sun May, Jun & Sep, 9am-5.30pm Mon-Sat Oct-Apr; @) Internet access available (£1 per 20 minutes).

Getting There & Away

The bus, train and ferry terminals are all grouped conveniently together next to the harbour on the southern edge of the bay.

BOAT **CalMac** (www.calmac.co.uk) ferries link Oban with the islands of Kerrera, Mull, Coll, Tiree, Lismore, Colonsay, Barra and Lochboisdale. See the relevant island entries for details of ferry services. Information and reservations for all CalMac ferry services are available at the ferry terminal on Oban's West Pier. Ferries to the Isle of Kerrera depart from a separate jetty, about 2 miles southwest of Oban town centre.

BUS Scottish **Citylink** (www.citylink.co.uk) buses run to Oban from Glasgow (£17, three hours, four daily) via Inveraray; and from Perth (£12, three hours, twice daily Friday to Monday) via Tyndrum and Killin.

West Coast Motors (www.westcoastmotors.co.uk) bus 423 runs from Oban to Lochgilphead (£5, 1¾ hours, four daily Monday to Friday, two on Saturday) via Kilmartin. Bus 918 goes to Fort William via Appin and Ballachulish (£9, 1½ hours, three daily Monday to Saturday).

TRAIN Oban is at the terminus of a scenic route that branches off the West Highland line at Crianlarich. There are up to three trains daily from Glasgow to Oban (£19, three hours).

The train isn't much use for travelling north from Oban – to reach Fort William requires a detour via Crianlarich (3¾ hours). Take the bus instead.

Isle of Mull

POP 2600

From the rugged ridges of Ben More and the black basalt crags of Burg to the blinding white sand, rose-pink granite and emerald waters that fringe the Ross, Mull can lay claim to some of the finest and most varied scenery in the Inner Hebrides. Add in two impressive castles, a narrow-gauge railway, the sacred island of Iona and easy access from Oban and you can see why it's sometimes impossible to find a spare bed on the island.

The waters to the west of Mull provide some of the best whale-spotting opportunities in Scotland, with several operators offering **whale-watching cruises**.

Tours

Bowman's Tours
(☎01631-563221/566809; www.bowmanstours.co.uk; 3 Stafford St & 1 Queens Park Pl) From April to October, Bowman's offers a **Three Isles day trip** (adult/child £49/24.50, 10 hours, daily) from Oban that visits Mull, Iona and Staffa; the crossing to Staffa is weather dependent.

Information

MEDICAL **Dunaros Hospital** (☎01680-300392; Salen) Has a minor injuries unit; the nearest casualty department is in Oban.

Mull, Coll & Tiree

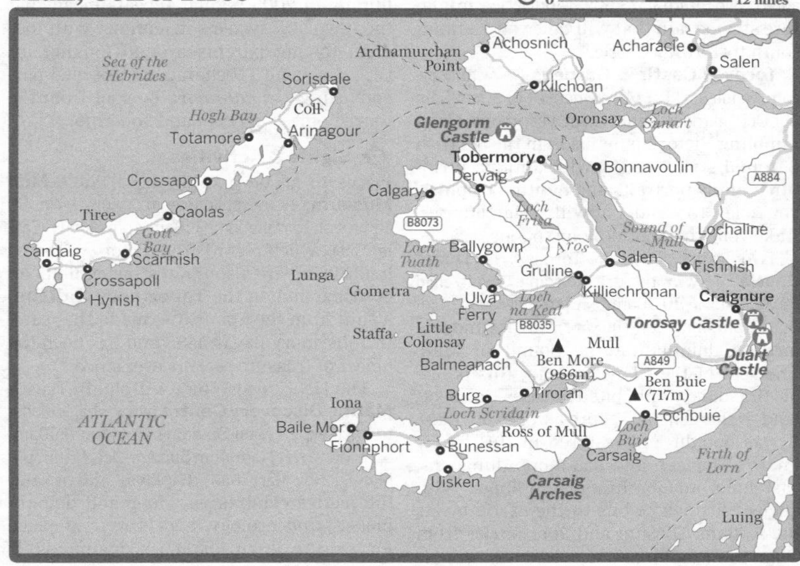

MONEY Clydesdale Bank (Main St, Tobermory; ⌚9.15am-4.45pm Mon-Fri) The island's only bank and 24-hour ATM. You can get cash using a debit card from the post offices in Salen and Craignure, or get cash back with a purchase from Co-op food stores.

POST Post office (Main St, Tobermory; ⌚9am-1pm & 2-5.30pm Mon, Tue, Thu & Fri, 9am-1pm Wed & Sat) There are also post-office counters in Salen, Craignure and Fionnphort.

TOURIST INFORMATION Craignure tourist office (☎01680-812377; Craignure; ⌚8.30am-5pm Mon-Sat, 10.30am-5pm Sun)

Tobermory tourist office (☎01688-302182; The Pier, Tobermory; ⌚9am-6pm Mon-Sat & 10am-5pm Sun Jul & Aug, 9am-5pm Mon-Sat & 11am-5pm Sun May & Jun, shorter hours rest of year)

ℹ Getting There & Away

There are frequent **CalMac** (www.calmac.co.uk) car ferries from Oban to Craignure (passenger/car £4.65/41.50, 40 minutes, every two hours). There's another car-ferry link from Lochaline to Fishnish, on the east coast of Mull (£2.80/12.55, 15 minutes, at least hourly).

A third CalMac car ferry links Tobermory to Kilchoan on the Ardnamurchan peninsula (£4.45/23, 35 minutes, seven daily Monday to Saturday). From June to August there are also five sailings on Sunday.

ℹ Getting Around

BICYCLE You can hire bikes for around £10 to £15 per day from the following places.

Brown's Hardware Shop (☎01688-302020; www.brownstobermory.co.uk; Main St, Tobermory)

On Yer Bike (☎01680-300501; Inverinate, Salen) Easter to October only. Also has an outlet by the ferry terminal at Craignure.

BUS Public transport on Mull is fairly limited. **Bowman's Tours** (☎01680-812313; www.bowmanstours.co.uk) is the main operator, connecting the ferry ports and the island's main villages. Bus 495 goes from Craignure to Tobermory (£7 return, one hour, six daily Monday to Friday, four or five Saturday and Sunday), and bus 496 links Craignure to Fionnphort (£11 return, 1¼ hours, three or four daily Monday to Saturday, one Sunday). Bus 494 goes from Tobermory to Dervaig and Calgary (three daily Monday to Friday, two on Saturday).

CAR Almost all of Mull's road network consists of single-track roads. There are petrol stations at Craignure, Fionnphort, Salen and Tobermory.

TAXI Mull Taxi (☎07760 426351; www.mulltaxi.co.uk) is based in Tobermory, and has a vehicle that is wheelchair accessible.

CRAIGNURE & AROUND

There's not much to see at Craignure other than the ferry terminal and the hotel, so turn left, walk 200m and hop onto the **Mull**

Railway (www.mullrail.co.uk; Old Pier Station; adult/child return £5/3.50; ⏲Apr-Oct), a miniature steam train that will take you 1.5 miles south to Torosay Castle.

Torosay Castle & Gardens (www.torosay.com; adult/child £7/4; ⏲house 10.30am-5pm Apr-Oct, gardens 9am-sunset year-round) is a rambling Victorian mansion in the Scottish Baronial style, stuffed with antique furniture, family portraits and hunting trophies. You're left to wander at will: a sign advises, 'Take your time but not our spoons.'

Two miles beyond Torosay is **Duart Castle** (www.duartcastle.com; adult/child £5.30/2.65; ⏲10.30am-5.30pm daily May–mid-Oct, 11am-4pm Sun-Thu Apr), a formidable fortress dominating the Sound of Mull. The seat of the Clan Maclean, this is one of the oldest inhabited castles in Scotland – the central keep was built in 1360. It was bought and restored in 1911 by Sir Fitzroy Maclean and has damp dungeons, vast halls and bathrooms equipped with ancient fittings. A bus to the castle meets the 9.50am, 11.55am and 2pm ferries from Oban to Craignure.

TOBERMORY

POP 750

Tobermory, the island's main town, is a picturesque little fishing port and yachting centre with brightly painted houses arranged around a sheltered harbour, with a grid-patterned 'upper town'. The village was the setting for the children's TV program *Balamory*, and while the series stopped filming in 2005 regular repeats mean that the town still swarms in summer with toddlers towing parents around looking for their favourite TV characters (frazzled parents can get a *Balamory* booklet from the tourist offices in Oban and Tobermory).

Sights & Activities

Places to go on a rainy day include **Mull Museum** (www.mullmuseum.org.uk; Main St; admission by donation; ⏲10am-4pm Mon-Fri Easter-Oct), which records the history of the island. There are also interesting exhibits on crofting, and on the **Tobermory Galleon**, a ship from the Spanish Armada that sank in Tobermory Bay in 1588 and has been the object of treasure seekers ever since.

The Hebridean Whale & Dolphin Trust's **Marine Discovery Centre** (www.whaledolphintrust.co.uk; 28 Main St; admission free; ⏲10am-5pm Mon-Fri & 11am-4pm Sun Apr-Oct, 11am-5pm Mon-Fri Nov-Mar) has displays, videos and interactive exhibits on whale and dolphin biology and ecology, and is a great place for kids to learn about sea mammals. It also provides information about volunteering and reporting sightings of whales and dolphins.

Sea Life Surveys (☎01688-302916; www.sealifesurveys.com), based in the new harbour building beside the main car park, runs whale-watching boat trips out of Tobermory harbour.

THAR SHE BLOWS!

The North Atlantic Drift – a swirling tendril of the Gulf Stream – carries warm water into the cold, nutrient-rich seas off the Scottish coast, resulting in huge blooms of plankton. Small fish feed on the plankton, and bigger fish feed on the smaller fish... This huge seafood smorgasbord attracts large numbers of marine mammals, from harbour porpoises and dolphins to minke whales and even – though sightings are rare – humpback and sperm whales.

In contrast to Iceland and Norway, Scotland has cashed in on the abundance of minke whales off its coast by embracing whale watching rather than whaling. There are now dozens of operators around the coast offering whale-watching boat trips lasting from a couple of hours to all day; some have whale-sighting success rates of 95% in summer.

While seals, porpoises and dolphins can be seen year-round, minke whales are migratory. The best time to see them is from June to August, with August being the peak month for sightings. The website of the **Hebridean Whale & Dolphin Trust** (www.whaledolphintrust.co.uk) has lots of information on the species you are likely to see, and how to identify them.

A booklet titled *Is It a Whale?* is available from tourist offices and bookshops, and provides tips on identifying the various species of marine mammal that you're likely to see.

Sleeping

Tobermory has dozens of B&Bs, but the place can still be booked solid in July and August, especially at weekends.

Sonas House B&B ££
(01688-302304; www.sonashouse.co.uk; The Fairways, Erray Rd; s/d £80/125; P) Here's a first – a B&B with a heated, indoor 10m swimming pool! Sonas is a large, modern house that offers luxury B&B in a beautiful setting with superb views over Tobermory Bay; ask for the 'Blue Poppy' bedroom, which has its own balcony.

Cuidhe Leathain B&B ££
(01688-302504; www.cuidhe-leathain.co.uk; Salen Rd; r per person £35;) A handsome 19th-century house in the upper town, Cuidhe Leathain (coo-*lane*), which means Maclean's Corner, exudes a cosily cluttered Victorian atmosphere. The breakfasts will set you up for the rest of the day, and the owners are a fount of knowledge about Mull and its wildlife.

2 Victoria St B&B £
(01688-302263; 2 Victoria St; s/d £25/40; Easter-Oct) Traditional, old-school B&B with simple, homely bedrooms (with shared bathroom) and a friendly and hospitable landlady.

Tobermory Campsite CAMPSITE £
(01688-302624; www.tobermorycampsite.co.uk; Newdale, Dervaig Rd; tent sites per adult/child £6/3; Mar-Oct;) Quiet, family-friendly campsite a mile west of town on the road to Dervaig.

Tobermory Youth Hostel HOSTEL £
(SYHA; 01688-302481; www.syha.org.uk; Main St; dm £15; Mar-Oct; @) Great location in a Victorian house right on the waterfront. Bookings recommended.

Eating & Drinking

TOP CHOICE **Café Fish** SEAFOOD ££
(01688-301253; www.thecafefish.com; The Pier; mains £10-16; lunch & dinner) Seafood doesn't come much fresher than the stuff served at this warm and welcoming little restaurant overlooking Tobermory harbour – as their motto says, 'The only thing frozen here is the fisherman'! Langoustines and squat lobsters go straight from boat to kitchen to join rich shellfish bisque, fat scallops, seafood pie and catch-of-the-day on the daily-changing menu. Freshly-baked bread, homemade desserts and a range of Scottish cheeses also available.

Fish & Chip Van SEAFOOD £
(Main St; mains £4-7; 12.30-9pm Mon-Sat Apr-Dec) If it's a takeaway you're after, you can tuck into some of Scotland's best gourmet fish and chips down on the waterfront. And where else will you find a chip van selling freshly cooked prawns and scallops?

MacGochan's PUB ££
(Ledaig; mains £9-15; lunch & dinner) A lively pub beside the car park at the southern end of the waterfront, MacGochan's does good bar meals (haddock and chips, steak pie, vegetable lasagne), and often has outdoor barbecues on summer evenings. There's a more formal **restaurant** upstairs, and live music in the bar on weekends.

Mishnish Hotel PUB ££
(www.mishnish.co.uk; Main St; mains £11-20; lunch & dinner;) 'The Mish' is a favourite hang-out for visiting yachties and a good place for a bar meal, or dinner at the more formal **restaurant** upstairs. Wood-panelled and flag-draped, this is a good old traditional pub where you can listen to live folk music, toast your toes by the open fire, or challenge the locals to a game of pool.

NORTH MULL

The road from Tobermory west to Calgary cuts inland, leaving most of the north coast of Mull wild and inaccessible. Just outside Tobermory a long, single-track road leads north for 4 miles to majestic **Glengorm Castle** (www.glengorm.com; Glengorm; admission free; 10am-5pm daily Easter–mid-Oct) with views across the sea to Ardnamurchan, Rum and the Outer Hebrides. The castle outbuildings house an art gallery featuring the work of local artists, a farm shop selling local produce, and an excellent coffee shop. The castle itself is not open to the public, but you're free to explore the beautiful castle grounds.

Mull's best (and busiest) silver-sand **beach**, flanked by cliffs and with views out to Coll and Tiree, is at **Calgary**, about 12 miles west of Tobermory. And yes – this is the place from which the more famous Calgary in Alberta, Canada, takes its name.

Sleeping & Eating

TOP CHOICE **Achnadrish House** B&B ££
(01688-400388; www.achnadrish.co.uk; Dervaig Rd; d from £85; P@) There aren't too many B&Bs where *pad Thai* noodles appear on the breakfast menu, but Achnadrish is one. The dish is a legacy of

the owner's extensive Asian travels, as are many of the decorative touches in this wonderfully welcoming guest house.

Calgary Farmhouse SELF-CATERING ££
(☎01688-400256; www.calgary.co.uk; Calgary; two-person apt per 2 nights from £120; P 📶) This farmhouse complex offers eight fantastic self-catering properties (sleeping from two to eight people), beautifully designed and fitted out with timber furniture and wood-burning stoves.

Glengorm Coffee Shop CAFE £
(www.glengorm.com; Glengorm Castle; mains £5-8; ⊙lunch) Set in a cottage courtyard in the grounds of Glengorm Castle, this cafe serves superb lunches (noon-4.30pm). The menu changes daily, but includes sandwiches and salads (much of the salad veg is grown on the Glengorm estate), soups and specials such as curry-flavoured salmon fishcakes with mint and cucumber salad.

Calgary Farmhouse Tearoom CAFE £
(www.calgary.co.uk; Calgary; mains £5-8; ⊙lunch; P 📶) Just a few minutes' walk from the sandy beach at Calgary Bay, this tearoom serves soups, sandwiches, coffee and cake using fresh local produce as much as possible.

Dervaig Hall Bunkhouse HOSTEL £
(☎01688-400491; www.dervaigbunkroomsmull.co.uk; Dervaig; dm/q £14/50; P) Basic but very comfortable bunkhouse accommodation in Dervaig's village hall, with self-catering kitchen and sitting room.

Calgary Bay CAMPSITE £
You can camp for free at the southern end of the beach at Calgary Bay – keep to the area south of the stream.

SOUTH MULL

The road from Craignure to Fionnphort climbs through some wild and desolate scenery before reaching the southwestern part of the island, which consists of a long peninsula called the **Ross of Mull**. The Ross has a spectacular south coast lined with black basalt cliffs that give way further west to white-sand beaches and pink granite crags.

At the western end of the Ross, 38 miles from Craignure, is **Fionnphort** (*finn*-a-fort) and the ferry to **Iona**. The coast here is a beautiful blend of pink granite rocks, white sandy beaches and vivid turquoise sea.

Isle of Iona

POP 130

There are few more uplifting sights on Scotland's west coast than the view of Iona from Mull on a sunny day – an emerald island set in a sparkling turquoise sea. From the moment you step off the ferry you begin to appreciate the hushed, spiritual atmosphere that pervades this sacred island.

St Columba sailed from Ireland and landed on Iona in 563 before setting out to spread Christianity throughout Scotland. He established a monastery on the island and it was here that the *Book of Kells* – the prize attraction of Dublin's Trinity College – is believed to have been transcribed. It was taken to Kells in Ireland when Viking raids drove the monks from Iona.

The monks returned and the monastery prospered until its destruction during the Reformation. The ruins were given to the Church of Scotland in 1899, and by 1910 a group of enthusiasts called the **Iona Community** (www.iona.org.uk) had reconstructed the abbey. It's still a flourishing spiritual community that holds regular courses and retreats.

Sights & Activities

Head uphill from the ferry pier and turn right through the grounds of a ruined 13th-century **nunnery** with fine cloistered gardens, and exit at the far end. Across the road is the **Iona Heritage Centre** (adult/child £2/free; ⊙10.30am-4.30pm Mon-Fri Apr-Oct), which covers the history of Iona, crofting and lighthouses; the centre's **coffee shop** serves delicious home baking.

Turn right here and continue along the road to **Reilig Oran**, an ancient cemetery that holds the graves of 48 of Scotland's early kings, including Macbeth, and a tiny Romanesque chapel. Beyond rises the spiritual heart of the island – **Iona Abbey** (HS; www.iona.org.uk; adult/child £4.70/2.80; ⊙9.30am-5.30pm Apr-Sep, 9.30am-4.30pm Oct-Mar). The spectacular nave, dominated by Romanesque and early Gothic vaults and columns, contains the elaborate, white marble tombs of the 8th duke of Argyll and his wife. A door on the left leads to the beautiful Gothic cloister, where medieval grave slabs sit alongside modern religious sculptures. A replica of the intricately carved **St John's Cross** stands just outside the abbey – the massive 8th-century original is in the **Infirmary Museum** (around the far side of the abbey) along with many other fine examples of early Christian and medieval **carved stones**.

Continue past the abbey and look for a footpath on the left signposted **Dun I** (dun-*ee*). An easy walk of about 15 to 20 minutes leads to the highest point on Iona, with fantastic views in all directions.

Sleeping & Eating

TOP CHOICE **Argyll Hotel** HOTEL ££
(☎01681-700334; www.argyllhoteliona.co.uk; Baile Mor; s/d from £61/97; ⊙Mar-Oct) The terrace of cottages above the ferry slip houses this cute little hotel – it has 16 snug rooms (a sea view costs rather more – £131 for a double) and a country house **restaurant** (mains £8-15; ⊙lunch & dinner) with wooden fireplace and antique tables and chairs. The kitchen is supplied by a huge organic garden around the back, and the menu includes Cullen Skink, home-grown salads, and venison-and-rabbit hotpot.

TOP CHOICE **Iona Hostel** HOSTEL £
(☎01681-700781; www.ionahostel.co.uk; Lagandorain; dm £18.50; ⊙check-in 4-7pm) This hostel is set in an attractive, modern timber building on a working croft, with stunning views out to Staffa and the Treshnish Isles. Rooms are clean and functional, and the well-equipped lounge/kitchen area has an open fire. It's at the northern end of the island – to get here, continue along the road past the abbey for 1.5 miles (a 20- to 30-minute walk).

Cnocoran Campsite CAMPSITE £
(☎01681-700112; cnocoran@yahoo.co.uk; Cnocoran; tent sites per person £5) Basic campsite about a mile west of the ferry. Open year-round.

Getting There & Away

The **passenger ferry** from Fionnphort to Iona (£4.30 return, five minutes, hourly) runs daily. There are also various day trips available from Oban to Iona (see Tours, p851).

FIFE

Protruding like a serpent's head from Scotland's east coast, Fife (www.visitfife.com) is a spit of land between the Firths of Forth and Tay. A royal history and atmosphere distinct from the rest of Scotland leads it to style itself as 'The Kingdom of Fife'.

Though overdeveloped southern Fife is commuter-belt territory, the eastern region's rolling green farmland and quaint fishing villages is prime turf for exploration and crab-crunching, and the fresh sea air feels like it's doing a power of good. Elsewhere in the county, little Falkland makes a great stop, and dignified Culross is a superbly preserved 17th-century burgh.

Fife's biggest attraction, St Andrews, has Scotland's most venerable university and a wealth of historic buildings. It's also, of course, the headquarters of golf and draws professionals and keen slashers alike to take on the Old Course – the classic links experience.

Activities

The **Fife Coastal Path** (www.fifecoastalpath.co.uk) runs more than 80 miles following the entire Fife coastline from the Forth Road Bridge to the Tay Bridge and beyond.

WORTH A TRIP

ISLE OF STAFFA

Felix Mendelssohn, who visited the uninhabited island of Staffa in 1829, was inspired to compose his *Hebrides Overture* after hearing waves echoing in the impressive and cathedral-like **Fingal's Cave**. The cave walls and surrounding cliffs are composed of vertical, hexagonal basalt columns that look like pillars (Staffa is Norse for 'Pillar Island'). You can land on the island and walk into the cave via a causeway. Nearby **Boat Cave** can be seen from the causeway, but you can't reach it on foot. Staffa also has a sizable puffin colony, north of the landing place.

Northwest of Staffa lies a chain of uninhabited islands called the **Treshnish Isles**. The two main islands are the curiously shaped **Dutchman's Cap** and **Lunga**. You can land on Lunga, walk to the top of the hill and visit the shag, puffin and guillemot colonies on the west coast at **Harp Rock**.

Unless you have your own boat, the only way to reach Staffa and the Treshnish Isles is on an organised boat trip – see the Tours section, p851, for details.

It's well waymarked, picturesque and not too rigorous, though winds can buffet. It's easily accessed for shorter sections or day walks, and long stretches of it can be tackled on a mountain bike too.

Getting Around

The main bus operator here is **Stagecoach Fife** (0871-2002233; www.stagecoachbus.com). For £6.80 you can buy a Fife Dayrider ticket, which gives unlimited travel around Fife on Stagecoach buses.

If you are driving from the Forth Road Bridge to St Andrews, a slower but much more scenic route than the M90/A91 is along the signposted **Fife Coastal Tourist Route**.

St Andrews

POP 14,209

For a small place, St Andrews made a big name for itself, firstly as religious centre, then as Scotland's oldest university town. But its status as the home of golf has propelled it to even greater fame, and today's pilgrims arrive with a set of clubs. But it's a lovely place to visit even if you've no interest in the game, with impressive medieval ruins, stately university buildings, idyllic white sands and excellent accommodation and eating options.

The Old Course, the world's most famous, has a striking seaside location at the western end of town. Although it's difficult to get a game (see boxed text, p857), it's still a thrilling experience to stroll the hallowed turf. Between the students and golfers, St Andrews can feel like the least Scottish of places as, although technically a city, it's not very large.

History

St Andrews is said to have been founded by St Regulus, who arrived from Greece in the 4th century bringing the bones of St Andrew, Scotland's patron saint. The town soon grew into a major pilgrimage centre and St Andrews developed into the ecclesiastical capital of the country. The university was founded in 1410, the first in Scotland.

Golf has been played here for more than 600 years; the Royal & Ancient Golf Club, the game's governing body, was founded in 1754 and the imposing clubhouse was built a hundred years later. The British Open Championship takes place here every few years in July.

Sights

St Andrews Cathedral CATHEDRAL RUINS

(HS; www.historic-scotland.gov.uk; The Pends; adult/child £4.20/2.50, incl castle £7.20/4.30; 9.30am-5.30pm Apr-Sep, to 4.30pm Oct-Mar) The ruins of this cathedral are all that's left of one of Britain's most magnificent medieval buildings. You can appreciate the scale and majesty of the edifice from the small sections that remain standing. Although founded in 1160, it was not consecrated until 1318, but stood as the focus of this important pilgrimage centre until 1559 when it was pillaged during the Reformation.

St Andrew's supposed bones lie under the altar; until the cathedral was built, they had been enshrined in the nearby Church of St Regulus (Rule). All that remains of this church is **St Rule's Tower**, worth the climb for the view across St Andrews. The tourist office includes a **museum** with a collection of Celtic crosses and gravestones found on the site. The entrance fee only applies for the tower and museum; you can wander freely around the atmospheric ruins.

St Andrews Castle CASTLE

(HS; www.historic-scotland.gov.uk; The Scores; adult/child £5.20/3.10, with cathedral £7.20/4.30; 9.30am-5.30pm Apr-Sep, to 4.30pm Oct-Mar) Not far from the cathedral and with dramatic coastline views, the castle is mainly in ruins, but the site itself is evocative. It was founded around 1200 as the bishop's fortified home. After the execution of Protestant reformers in 1545, other reformers retaliated by murdering Cardinal Beaton and taking over the castle. They spent almost a year holed up, during which they and their attackers dug a complex of **siege tunnels**, said to be the best surviving example of castle-siege engineering in Europe; you can walk (or stoop) along their damp mossy lengths. A tourist office gives a good audiovisual introduction and has a small collection of Pictish stones.

The Scores STREET

From the castle, the Scores follows the coast west down to the first tee at the Old Course. Family-friendly **St Andrews Aquarium** (www.standrewsaquarium.co.uk; adult/child £6.50/4.60; 10am-6pm Mar-Oct, 10am-4.30pm Nov-Feb, last entry 1hr before closing) has a seal pool, rays and sharks from Scottish waters and exotic tropical favourites. Once introduced to our finny friends, you can snack on them with chips in the cafe.

PLAYING THE OLD COURSE

Golf has been played at St Andrews since the 15th century. By 1457 it was so popular that James II placed a ban on it because it interfered with his troops' archery practice. Although it lies beside the exclusive, all-male (female bartenders, unsurprisingly, allowed) Royal & Ancient Golf Club, the Old Course is public.

Book in advance to play via **St Andrews Links Trust** (☎01334-466666; www.standrews.org.uk). You must reserve on or after the first Wednesday in September the year before you wish to play. No bookings are taken for Saturdays or the month of September.

Unless you've booked months in advance, getting a tee-off time is literally a lottery; enter the ballot at the **caddie office** (☎01334-466666) before 2pm on the day before you wish to play (there's no Sunday play). Be warned that applications by ballot are normally heavily oversubscribed, and green fees are £130 in summer. Singles are not accepted in the ballot and should start queuing as early as possible – 5.30am is good – in the hope of joining a group. You'll need a handicap certificate (24/36 for men/women). If your number doesn't come up, there are six other public courses in the area, including the prestigious, recently-opened Castle Course (£120). Other summer green fees: New £65, Jubilee £65, Eden £40, Strathtyrum £25 and Balgove (nine-holer for beginners and kids) £12. There are various multiple-day tickets available. If you play on a windy day expect those scores to balloon: Nick Faldo famously stated, 'When it blows here, even the seagulls walk.'

Guided walks (£2.50; 50 min) of the Old Course run at weekends in June and daily in July and August; these will take you to famous landmarks such as the Swilcan Bridge and the Road Hole bunker. They run from outside the shop roughly hourly from 11am to 4pm. On Sundays, a three-hour walk (£5) takes you around the whole course.

Nearby, the **British Golf Museum** (www.britishgolfmuseum.co.uk; Bruce Embankment; adult/child £6/3; ⊙9.30am-5pm Mon-Sat & 10am-5pm Sun Apr-Oct, 10am-4pm daily Nov-Mar) has an extraordinarily comprehensive overview of the history and development of the game and the role of St Andrews in it. Favourite fact: bad players were formerly known as 'foozlers'. Interactive panels allow you to relive former British Opens (watch Paul Azinger snapping his putter in frustration), and there's a large collection of memorabilia from Open winners both male and female.

Opposite the museum is the **Royal & Ancient Golf Club**, which stands proudly at the head of the **Old Course**, which you can stroll on once play is finished for the day, and all day on Sundays. Beside it stretches magnificent **West Sands** beach, made famous by the film *Chariots of Fire*.

Sleeping

St Andrews accommodation is often heavily booked (especially in summer), so you're well advised to book in advance. Almost every house on Murray Park and Murray Pl is a guest house: this area couldn't be more convenient, but prices are on the high side.

TOP CHOICE **Abbey Cottage** B&B ££
(☎01334-473727; www.abbeycottage.co.uk; Abbey Walk; s £40, d £59-64; P) You know you've strayed from B&B mainstream when your charming host's hobby is photographing tigers in the wild – don't leave without browsing her albums. This engaging spot sits below the town, surrounded by stone walls which enclose a rambling garden; it feels like you are staying in the country. There are three excellent rooms, all different, with patchwork quilts, sheepskins, and antique furniture.

Hazelbank Hotel HOTEL £££
(☎01334-472466; www.hazelbank.com; 28 The Scores; s/d £90/151; @ 🛜) Offering a genuine welcome, the family-run Hazelbank is the most likeable of the hotels along the Scores. The front rooms have marvellous views along the beach and out to sea; those at the back are somewhat cheaper and more spacious. Prices drop significantly outside the height of summer. There are good portents if you are playing a round – Bobby Locke won the Open in 1957 while staying here.

Five Pilmour Place B&B ££
(☎01334-478665; www.5pilmourplace.com; 5 Pilmour Pl; s £75, d £105-130; @ 🛜) Just around

St Andrews

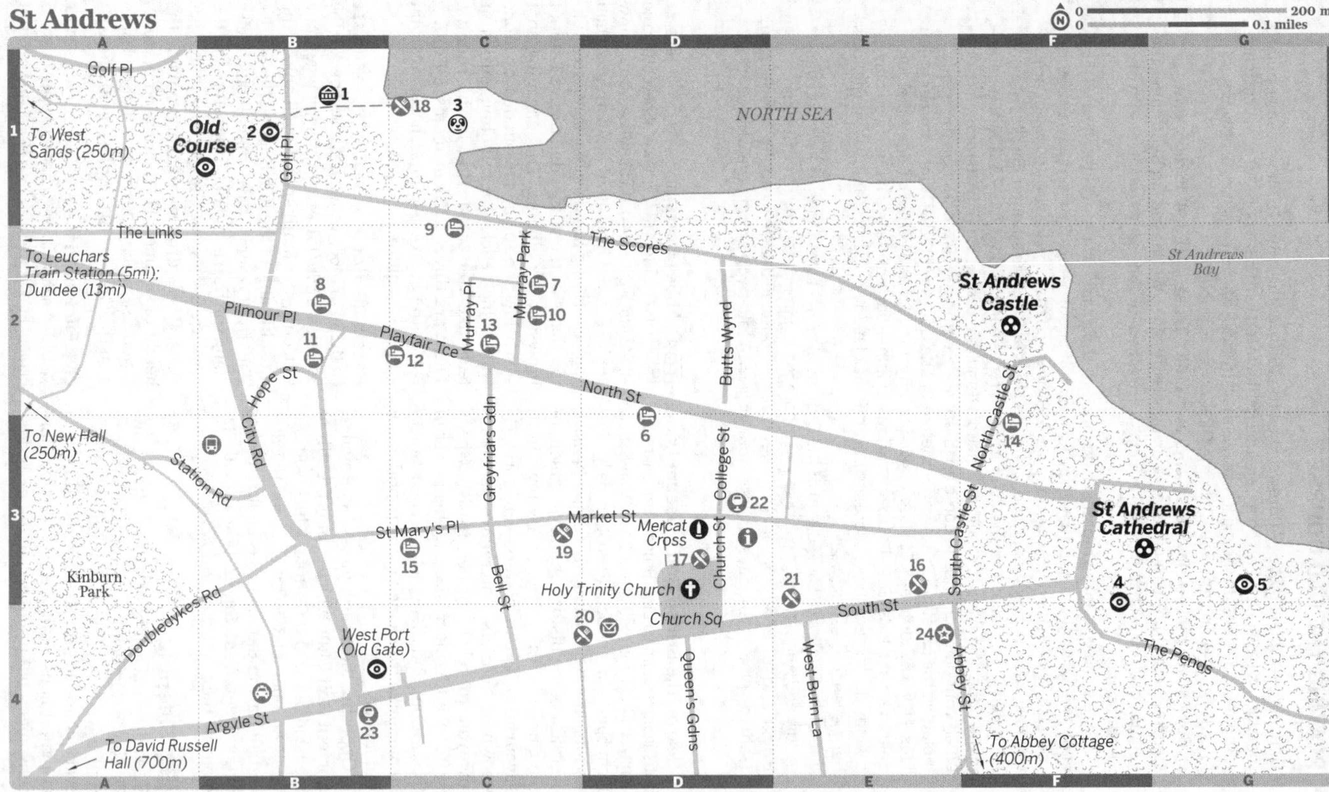
0 200 m
0 0.1 miles
NORTH SEA
St Andrews Bay
Golf Pl
To West Sands (250m)
Old Course
The Links
To Leuchars Train Station (5mi); Dundee (13mi)
Pilmour Pl
Hope St
City Rd
To New Hall (250m)
Station Rd
Kinburn Park
Doubledykes Rd
Argyle St
To David Russell Hall (700m)
West Port (Old Gate)
The Scores
Murray Pl
Murray Park
Playfair Tce
Greyfriars Gdn
Bell St
St Mary's Pl
Market St
North St
Butts Wynd
College St
Church St
Mercat Cross
Holy Trinity Church
Church Sq
Queen's Gdns
West Burn La
South St
South Castle St
North Castle St
Abbey St
To Abbey Cottage (400m)
St Andrews Castle
St Andrews Cathedral
The Pends
1
2
3
4
5
6
7
8
9
10
11
12
13
14
15
16
17
18
19
20
21
22
23
24
A
B
C
D
E
F
G

St Andrews

Top Sights

	Old Course	B1
	St Andrews Castle	F2
	St Andrews Cathedral	F3

Sights

1	British Golf Museum	B1
2	Royal & Ancient Golf Club	B1
3	St Andrews Aquarium	C1
4	St Andrews Cathedral Tourist Office & Museum	F3
5	St Rule's Tower	G3

Sleeping

6	Aslar House	D3
7	Cameron House	C2
8	Five Pilmour Place	B2
9	Hazelbank Hotel	C2
10	Lorimer House	C2
11	McIntosh Hall	B2
12	Meade B&B	C2
13	Ogstons on North Street	C2
14	Old Fishergate House	F3
15	St Andrews Tourist Hostel	C3

Eating

16	B Jannetta	E3
17	Doll's House	D3
	Grill House	(see 15)
18	Seafood Restaurant	C1
19	Tailend	C3
20	Vine Leaf	D4
21	Zizzi	E3

Drinking

22	Central Bar	D3
23	West Port	B4

Entertainment

24	Byre Theatre	E4

the corner from the Old Course, this luxurious and intimate spot offers stylish, compact rooms with an eclectic range of decor as well as modern conveniences such as flatscreen TV and DVD player. The king-size beds are especially comfortable, and the lounge area is a treat.

Meade B&B B&B ££
(01334-477350; annmeade10@hotmail.com; 5 Albany Pl; s with/without bathroom £55/30, d £60/40;) It's always sweet relief to find a B&B unconcerned with VisitScotland's fussy regulations. This economical gem is run by a friendly family and their pets, including a portly marmalade cat and affectionate black lab. The two comfortable rooms are colour-coded and have readable novels, photo albums and films on DVD. They might have moved to a new location by the time you read this, but the phone number will be the same.

Old Fishergate House B&B ££
(01334-470874; www.oldfishergatehouse.co.uk; North Castle St; s/d £75/100;) This historic 17th-century town house, furnished with period pieces, is in a great location – the oldest part of town, close to the cathedral and castle. The two twin rooms are very spacious and even have their own sitting room and cushioned ledges on their window sills. On a scale of one to 10 for quaintness, we'd rate it about a 9½. Cracking breakfasts feature fresh fish and pancakes.

St Andrews Tourist Hostel HOSTEL £
(01334-479911; www.standrewshostel.com; St Marys Pl; dm £13-14;) Laid-back and central, this hostel down the side of the Grill House restaurant is a little bit hard to spot. Occupying a stately old building, it has high corniced ceilings, especially in the huge lounge, and a laissez-faire approach. The dorms could use new mattresses, but are clean and bright. There's a supermarket close by.

University of St Andrews HOTEL, B&B, SELF-CATERING ££
(www.discoverstandrews.com; mid-Jun–mid-Sep;) When the university is out of session, three student residences open up as visitor accommodation. There's the hotel-style **New Hall** (01334-467000; North Haugh; s/d £56/83); self-catering rooms at **David Russell Hall** (01334-467100; Buchanan Gdns; apt for 3/7 days £290/560); and budget single rooms in the central **McIntosh Hall** (01334-467035; Abbotsford Cres; s/d £34/60). These prices are all good value for the standard of accommodation on offer.

Cameron House B&B ££
(01334-472306; www.cameronhouse-sta.co.uk; 11 Murray Park; s/d £45/90;) Beautifully decorated rooms and warm, cheerful hosts make this a real home-away-from-home on this guest-house-filled street.

Ogstons on North Street HOTEL £££
(01334-473387; www.ogstonsonnorthst.com; 127 North St; s £100-120, d £120-160;) If

you want to eat, drink and sleep in the same stylish place then this classy inn could be for you.

Aslar House B&B ££
(01334-473460; www.aslar.com; 120 North St; s/d £48/96;) Mod-cons in the rooms at this upmarket pad include iPod docks, DVD players and silent fridges, but they don't detract from the house's historical features, including a whimsical turret room.

Cairnsmill Caravan Park CAMPSITE £
(01334-473604; cairnsmill@aol.com; Largo Rd; tent sites per 2 people £15-16; Apr-Oct;) About a mile west of St Andrews on the A915, this camping ground has brilliant views over the town. There's not much space between sites – they pack 'em in.

Lorimer House B&B ££
(01334-476599; www.lorimerhouse.com; 19 Murray Park; d £90-110;) Smallish, sparklingly clean rooms with extra-comfy beds and a fab deluxe double on the top floor.

Eating

Vine Leaf RESTAURANT ££
(01334-477497; www.vineleafstandrews.co.uk; 131 South St; 2-course dinner £23.50; dinner Tue-Sat) Classy, comfortable, and well-established, the friendly Vine Leaf offers a changing menu of sumptuous Scottish seafood, game and vegetarian dishes. It's down a close off South St.

Seafood Restaurant RESTAURANT £££
(01334-479475; www.theseafoodrestaurant.com; The Scores; lunch/dinner £22/45; lunch & dinner) The Seafood Restaurant occupies a stylish glass-walled room, built out over the sea, with plush navy carpet, crisp white linen, an open kitchen and panoramic views of St Andrews Bay. It offers top seafood and an excellent wine list, and has won a clutch of awards. Look out for its special winter deal – three-course lunch for £15, or dinner for £20.

Doll's House RESTAURANT ££
(01334-477422; www.dolls-house.co.uk; 3 Church Sq; mains £10-15; lunch & dinner) With its high-backed chairs, bright colours and creaky wooden floor, the Doll's House blends a Victorian child's bedroom with modern stylings. The result is a surprising warmth and no pretensions. The menu makes the most of local fish and other Scottish produce, and the two-course lunch for £6.95 is unbeatable value. The early-evening two-course deal for £12.95 isn't bad either.

Grill House BISTRO £
(www.grillhouserestaurant.co.uk; St Mary's Pl; mains £6-15; lunch & dinner) This cheerful, sometimes boisterous restaurant offers something for every taste and bank balance, with a big selection ranging from Mexican, pizza and pasta to char-grilled salmon and quality steaks. The upbeat atmosphere and service are pluses, as is the £5 lunchtime deal.

Zizzi BISTRO £
(www.zizzi.co.uk; 87 South St; pasta £7-10; lunch & dinner) Beloved of local students, this Italian eatery has atmosphere without the tack. Rather than Mona Lisas, moribund love songs and phallic pepper grinders, it's got contemporary decor, an open kitchen, a chatty buzz and fast service. The food won't wow but it will satisfy.

Tailend BISTRO £
(130 Market St; mains £6-10; breakfast, lunch & dinner) Delicious fresh fish sourced from Arbroath just up the coast put this new St Andrews arrival a class above most chippies.

B Jannetta ICE CREAM £
(www.jannettas.co.uk; 31 South St; 2-dip cone £2.40; breakfast & lunch Mon-Sat) B Jannetta is a St Andrews institution, offering 52 varieties of ice-cream from the weird (Irn-Bru sorbet) to the decadent (strawberries-and-champagne).

Drinking

Central Bar PUB
(77 Market St) Rather staid compared to some of the wilder student-driven drinking options, this likeable pub keeps it real with traditional features, an island bar, lots of Scottish beers and filling (if uninspiring) pub grub.

West Port PUB
(www.maclay.com; 170 South St;) Just by the gateway of the same name, this sleek, modernised pub has several levels, as well as a great beer garden out the back.

Entertainment

Byre Theatre THEATRE
(01334-475000; www.byretheatre.com; Abbey St) This theatre company started life in a converted cow byre in the 1930s, and now occupies a flashy premises making clever use of light and space.

Information

J&G Innes (107 South St) Plenty of local-interest books, such as Fife's history of burning witches.

Library (Church Sq; 9.30am-5pm Mon, Fri & Sat, to 7pm Tue-Thu; @) Free internet access – drop-in only; no bookings.

St Andrews Memorial Hospital (01334-472327; Abbey Walk) Located south of Abbey St.

Tourist office (01334-472021; www.visit-standrews.co.uk; 70 Market St; 9.15am-6.30pm Mon-Sat & 9.30am-5pm Sun Jul-Sep, 9.15am-5pm Mon-Sat mid-Oct–Jun, plus 11am-4pm Sun Apr-Jun; @) Helpful staff with good knowledge of St Andrews and Fife.

Getting There & Away

BUS All buses leave from the bus station on Station Rd. There are frequent services to:

Anstruther 40 minutes, regularly

Crail 30 minutes, regularly

Dundee 30 minutes, half-hourly

Edinburgh via Kirkcaldy £9.40, two hours, hourly

Glasgow £9.40, 2½ hours, hourly

Stirling £7.30, two hours, six to seven Monday to Saturday

TRAIN There is no train station in St Andrews itself, but you can take a train from Edinburgh (grab a seat on the right-hand side of the carriage for great firth views) to Leuchars, 5 miles to the northwest (£11.20, one hour, hourly). From here, buses leave regularly for St Andrews.

Getting Around

To order a cab, call **Golf City Taxis** (01334-477788). A taxi between Leuchars train station and the town centre costs around £10.

Spokes (01334-477835; www.spokescycles.com; 37 South St; hire per half-/full day £8.50/13; 9am-5.30pm Mon-Sat) hires out mountain bikes.

East Neuk

This charming stretch of coast runs south from St Andrews to the point at Fife Ness, then west to Leven. Neuk is an old Scots word for corner, and it's certainly an appealing nook of the country to investigate, with picturesque fishing villages, some great restaurants and pretty coastal walks; the Fife Coastal Path's most scenic stretches are in this area. It's easily visited from St Andrews, but also makes a very pleasant place to stay.

CRAIL

POP 1695

Pretty and peaceful, little Crail has a much-photographed stone-sheltered harbour surrounded by wee cottages with red-tiled roofs. You can buy lobster and crab from a **kiosk** (lunch Sat & Sun) there. The benches in the nearby grassed area are perfectly placed for munching your alfresco crustaceans while admiring the view across to the Isle of May.

The village's history and involvement with the fishing industry is outlined in the **Crail Museum** (www.crailmuseum.org.uk; 62 Marketgate; admission free; 10am-1pm & 2-5pm Mon-Sat, 2-5pm Sun Jun-Sep, 2-5pm Sat & Sun Apr & May), which also offers tourist information.

Hazelton Guest House (01333-450250; www.thehazelton.co.uk; 29 Marketgate North; d/superior £70/80; Mar-Oct; wi-fi) is a welcoming, walker-friendly guest house across the road from the museum, while **Caiplie House** (01333-450564; www.caipliehouse.co.uk; 53 High St N; s/d £39/64; Apr-Nov; wi-fi) has large rooms with lots of light, and big soft beds perfect for flopping on at the end of the day. The top room here has views across to East Lothian. It also does reader-recommended evening meals.

Crail is 10 miles southeast of St Andrews. **Stagecoach** (www.stagecoachbus.com) bus 95 between Leven, Anstruther, Crail and St Andrews passes through Crail hourly every day (30 minutes to St Andrews).

ANSTRUTHER

POP 3442

Once among Scotland's busiest ports, cheery Anstruther has ridden the tribulations of the fishing industry better than some, and now has a very pleasant mixture of bobbing boats, historic streets, and visitors ambling around the harbour grazing on fish-and-chips or contemplating a trip to the Isle of May.

Sights

The displays at the excellent **Scottish Fisheries Museum** (www.scotfishmuseum.org; adult/child £6/free; 10am-5.30pm Mon-Sat & 11am-5pm Sun Apr-Sep, 10am-4.30pm Mon-Sat & noon-4.30pm Sun Oct-Mar) include the **Zulu Gallery**, which houses the huge, partly restored hull of a traditional Zulu-class fishing boat, redolent with the scent of tar and timber. Afloat in the harbour outside the museum lies the *Reaper*, a fully restored Fifie-class fishing boat built in 1902.

The mile-long **Isle of May**, 6 miles southeast of Anstruther, is a stunning nature reserve. Between April and July the intimidating cliffs are packed with breeding kittiwakes, razorbills, guillemots, shags and around 40,000 puffins.

The five-hour trip to the island on the **May Princess** (☎01333-310054; www.isleofmayferry.com; adult/child £19/9.50), including two to three hours ashore, sails almost daily from May to September. There's also a faster boat, the 12-seater rigid-hull inflatable *Osprey*, which makes non-landing circuits of the island (adult/child £20/12.50) and longer visits (£25/15).

Sleeping & Eating

TOP CHOICE **Spindrift** B&B ££
(☎01333-310573; www.thespindrift.co.uk; Pittenweem Rd; s/d £55/80; P 📶) Arriving from the west, there's no need to go farther than Anstruther's first house on the left, a redoubt of Scottish cheer and warm hospitality. The rooms are elegant, classy and extremely comfortable – some have views across to Edinburgh and one is like a ship's cabin, courtesy of the sea-captain who once owned the house. There are DVD players and teddies for company, an honesty-bar with characterful ales and malts and fine company from your hosts. Breakfast includes porridge once voted the best in the Kingdom. Dinner (from £22) is also available.

Dreel Tavern PUB £
(16 High St W; mains £8-12; ⊙lunch & dinner; 👪) This charming old pub on the banks of the Dreel Burn has bucket-loads of character and serves reliably tasty bar meals, with excellent handwritten daily specials. Chow down in the outdoor beer garden in summer. There are also some top-quality cask ales here.

Wee Chippie TAKEAWAY £
(4 Shore St; fish supper £5; ⊙lunch & dinner) The Anstruther Fish Bar is one of Britain's best chippies, but we – and plenty of locals – reckon this one is even better. The fish is of a very high quality, portions are larger and there's less of a queue too. Eat your catch by the water.

Cellar Restaurant RESTAURANT £££
(☎01333-310378; www.cellaranstruther.co.uk; 24 East Green; 2/3-course set dinner £35/40; ⊙lunch Fri & Sat, dinner Tue-Sat) Tucked away in an alley behind the museum, the Cellar is famous for its seafood and fine wines. Try the local crab, lobster or whatever delicacies they've brought in that day. Inside it's elegant and upmarket. Advance bookings are essential.

Information

Tourist office (☎01333-311073; anstruther@visitscotland.com; Harbourhead; ⊙10am-5pm Mon-Sat, 11am-4pm Sun Apr-Oct) The best tourist office in the East Neuk.

Getting There & Away

Stagecoach (www.stagecoachbus.com) bus 95 runs daily from Leven (more departures from St Monans) to Anstruther and on to St Andrews (40 minutes, hourly) via Crail.

Falkland

POP 1183

Below the soft ridges of the Lomond Hills in the centre of Fife is the charming village of Falkland. Rising majestically out of the town centre and dominating the skyline is the outstanding 16th-century **Falkland Palace** (NTS; www.nts.org.uk; adult/child £10.20/7.10; ⊙11am-5pm Mon-Sat, 1-5pm Sun Mar-Oct), a country residence of the Stuart monarchs. Mary, Queen of Scots is said to have spent the happiest days of her life 'playing the country girl in the woods and parks' at Falkland. The palace was built between 1501 and 1541 to replace a castle dating from the 12th century; French and Scottish craftspeople were employed to create a masterpiece of Scottish Gothic architecture. The **King's bedchamber** and the **chapel**, with its beautiful painted ceiling, have both been restored. Don't miss the prodigious 17th-century Flemish hunting **tapestries** in the hall. One feature of the royal leisure centre still exists: the oldest **royal tennis court** in Britain, built in 1539 for James V. It's in the grounds and still in use.

Opposite the church, the excellent **Luigino's** (Covenanter Hotel; ☎01337-857224; www.luiginos.co.uk; s/d/f £56/80/89; 📶) is an old coaching inn that's a joyful marriage of wonderful traditional architecture and exuberant Italian gastronomy. Rooms have been made over with smart black slate and wallpaper, and the quality restaurant, Luigino's (mains £9 to £13, open for lunch and dinner) serves authentic and tasty *saltimbocca* (Italian veal-and-ham dish), pasta that you can watch being made fresh, and wood-fired pizza. The enthusiasm and cheeriness of the owners and staff is a high point.

Falkland is 11 miles north of Kirkcaldy. Bus 36 travels between Glenrothes and Auchtermuchty via Falkland. From either of those two places, there are regular connections to St Andrews and other Fife destinations. Buses continue on to Perth (one hour) more or less hourly.

Southwestern Fife

Southwestern Fife is an odd mixture of urban sprawl – Fife's proximity to expensive Edinburgh has made it part of the commuter belt – and quiet country lanes. There are several worthwhile attractions here, within easy day trip range from St Andrews or Edinburgh.

DUNFERMLINE

POP 39,229

Historic, monastic Dunfermline is Fife's largest population centre, sprawling eastwards through once-distinct villages. Its noble history is centred on evocative **Dunfermline Abbey** (HS; www.historic-scotland.gov.uk; St Margaret St; adult/child £3.70/2.20; ⌚9.30am-5.30pm daily Apr-Sep, 9.30am-4.30pm Mon-Wed & Sat, 9.30am-12.30pm Thu & 2-4.30pm Sun Oct-Mar), founded by David I in the 12th century as a Benedictine monastery. Dunfermline was already favoured by religious royals; Malcolm III married the exiled Saxon princess Margaret here in the 11th century, and both chose to be interred here. There were many more royal burials, none more notable than Robert the Bruce, whose remains were discovered here in 1818.

What's left of the abbey are the **ruins** of the impressive three-tiered refectory building, and the atmosphere-laden nave of the church, endowed with geometrically patterned columns and fine Romanesque and Gothic windows. It adjoins the 19th-century **church** (closed October to April) where Robert the Bruce now lies under the ornate pulpit.

Next to the refectory (and included in your abbey admission price) is **Dunfermline Palace**. Once the abbey guest house, it was converted for James VI, whose son, the ill-fated Charles I, was born here in 1600. Below stretches the bosky, strollable **Pittencrieff Park**.

Dunfermline is a culinary desert, but the good folk at **Fresh** (2 Kirkgate; light meals £4-7; ⌚breakfast & lunch daily, dinner Sat & Sun), just up from the abbey, do decent sandwiches and coffee, as well as tasty daily specials based on deli produce. There's also wine, internet access, a gallery and book exchange.

There are frequent buses between Dunfermline and Edinburgh (40 minutes), Stirling (1¼ hours) and St Andrews (1¼ hours), and trains to/from Edinburgh (30 minutes).

CULROSS

POP 500

An enchanting little town, Culross (koo-*ross*) is Scotland's best-preserved example of a 17th-century Scottish burgh. Small, red-tiled, whitewashed buildings line the cobbled streets, and the winding Back Causeway to the abbey is embellished with whimsical stone cottages.

As birthplace of St Mungo, Glasgow's patron saint, Culross was an important religious centre from the 6th century. The burgh developed, under laird George Bruce, by mining coal through extraordinary underwater tunnels. Vigorous trade resulted, enabling Bruce to build and complete the palace by 1611. When mining was ended by flooding of the tunnels, the town switched to making linen and shoes.

Culross Palace (NTS; www.nts.org.uk; adult/child £8/5; ⌚noon-5pm Thu-Mon Apr-May & Sep, noon-5pm daily Jun-Aug, noon-4pm Thu-Mon Oct) is more a large house than a palace, and features extraordinary decorative painted woodwork, barrel-vaulted ceilings and an interior largely unchanged since the early 17th century. The **Town House** (tourist office downstairs) and the **Study**, also completed in the early 17th century, are open to the public (via guided tour included in palace admission).

Ruined **Culross Abbey** (HS; www.historic-scotland.gov.uk; admission free; ⌚9.30am-7pm Mon-Sat & 2-7pm Sun Apr-Sep, 9.30am-4pm Mon-Sat & 2-4pm Sun Oct-Mar), founded by the Cistercians in 1217, is on the hill in a lovely peaceful spot with vistas of the firth. The choir of the abbey church is now the parish church.

Above a pottery workshop near the palace, **Biscuit Café** (www.culrosspottery.com; light meals £4-7; ⌚breakfast & lunch) has a tranquil little garden and sells coffee, tempting organic cakes and scones, and tasty light meals.

Culross is 12 miles west of the Forth Road Bridge. **Stagecoach** (www.stagecoachbus.com) bus 78 runs to Culross from Dunfermline (25 minutes, hourly).

PERTHSHIRE

For sheer scenic variety, Perthshire is the pick of Scotland's regions and a place where everyone will find a special, personal spot – whether it's a bleak moor, snaking loch, postcard-perfect village or magnificent forest. Highlights are many: the enchanting valley of Glen Lyon strikes visitors dumb with its wild and remote beauty; stunning Loch Tay is nearby (the base for ascending Ben Lawers); and the River Tay runs east from here towards Dunkeld, whose cathedral is among the most beautifully situated in the country.

Things begin sedately in the southeast corner with Perth itself, a fine country town with a fabulous attraction in lavish Scone Palace, and get gradually wilder as you move northwards and westwards, moving through wooded slopes and river-blessed valleys and culminating in the bleak expanse of Rannoch Moor.

Getting Around

The A9 cuts across the region through Perth and Pitlochry. It's the fast route into the Highlands and to Inverness, and very busy.

The council produces a useful public transport map available at tourist offices. **Stagecoach** (☎01382-227201; www.stagecoachbus.com) runs local services.

Trains run alongside the A9, destined for Inverness. Another line connects Perth with Stirling (in the south) and Dundee (in the east).

Perth

POP 43,450

Sedately arranged along the banks of the Tay, this former capital of Scotland is a most liveable place with large tracts of enticing parkland surrounding an easily-managed centre. On its outskirts lies Scone Palace, a country house of staggering luxury built alongside the mound that was the crowning place of Scotland's kings. It's really a must-see, but the town itself, ennobled by stately architecture, fine galleries and a few excellent restaurants, merits exploration, and is within easy striking distance of both Edinburgh and Glasgow.

Sights

Scone Palace PALACE

(www.scone-palace.co.uk; adult/child/family £9/6/26; ⏲9.30am-5pm Apr-Oct) 'So thanks to all at once and to each one, whom we invite to see us crowned at Scone.' This line from *Macbeth* indicates the importance of this place (pronounced 'skoon'), 2 miles north of Perth. The palace itself was built in 1580 on a site intrinsic to Scottish history. Here in 838, Kenneth MacAlpin became the first king of a united Scotland and brought the **Stone of Destiny** (see p765), on which Scottish kings were ceremonially invested, to Moot Hill. In 1296 Edward I of England carted the talisman off to Westminster Abbey, where it remained for 700 years before being returned to Scotland.

These days, Scone doesn't really conjure up hoary days of bearded warrior-kings swearing oaths in the mist, however, as the palace, rebuilt in the early 19th century, is a Georgian mansion of extreme elegance and luxury.

The visit takes you through a succession of sumptuous **rooms** filled with fine French furniture and noble artworks. There's an astonishing collection of porcelain and fine portraits here, as well as a series of exquisite Vernis Martin papier-mâché. Scone has belonged for centuries to the Murray family, Earls of Mansfield, and many of the objects have fascinating history attached to them (friendly guides are on hand). Each room has comprehensive multilingual information; there are also panels relating histories of some of the Scottish kings crowned at Scone over the centuries.

Outside, peacocks – all named after a monarch – strut around the magnificent **grounds**, which incorporate woods, a butterfly garden, and a maze.

Ancient kings were crowned atop **Moot Hill**, topped by a chapel, next to the palace. It's said that the hill was created by bootfuls of earth, brought by nobles attending the coronations as an acknowledgement of the king's rights over their lands, although it's likelier the site of an ancient motte-and-bailey castle.

From Perth's centre, cross the bridge, turn left, and keep bearing left until you reach the gates of the estate (15 to 20 minutes). From here, it's a half-mile to the palace. Various buses from town stop here roughly hourly; the tourist office has a printout. There's a good cafe at the palace, too.

FREE **St John's Kirk** CHURCH
(www.st-johns-kirk.co.uk; St John St; 10am-4pm Mon-Sat, 10am-1pm Sun May-Sep) Daunting St John's Kirk, founded in 1126, is surrounded by cobbled streets and is still the centrepiece of the town. In 1559 John Knox preached a powerful sermon here that helped begin the Reformation, inciting a frenzied destruction of Scone abbey and other religious sites. Perth used to be known as St John's Town after this church; the football team here is still called St Johnstone.

FREE **JD Fergusson Gallery** GALLERY
(www.pkc.gov.uk; cnr Marshall Pl & Tay St; 10am-5pm Mon-Sat) Beautifully set in the round waterworks building, this gallery exhibits much of the work of the Scottish Colourist JD Fergusson in a most impressive display. Fergusson spent time in Paris, and the influence of artists like Matisse on his work is evident; his voluptuous female portraits against a tropical-looking Riviera background are memorable, as is the story of his lifelong relationship with noted Scottish dancer Margaret Morris.

FREE **Perth Museum** MUSEUM
(www.pkc.gov.uk; cnr George & Charlotte Sts; 10am-5pm Mon-Sat) The city's main museum is worth wandering through for the elegant neoclassical interior alone. There's a varied shower of exhibits, ranging from portraits of dour lairds to interesting local social history. A geological room provides more entertainment for the young, while there are often excellent temporary exhibitions.

Black Watch Museum MUSEUM
(www.theblackwatch.co.uk; Hay St; adult/child £4/2; 9.30am-5pm Mon-Sat, also 10am-4pm Sun Apr-Oct) Housed in a mansion on the edge of North Inch, this museum honours what was once Scotland's foremost regiment. Formed in 1725 to combat rural banditry, the Black Watch fought in numerous campaigns, re-created here with paintings, memorabilia and anecdotes. Little attempt at perspective is evident: there's justifiable pride in the regiment's role in the gruelling trench warfare of WWI, where it suffered nearly 30,000 casualties, but no sheepishness about less glorious colonial engagements, such as against the 'Fuzzy Wuzzies' of Sudan. In 2006 the Black Watch was subsumed into the new Royal Regiment of Scotland.

Sleeping

Someone should open a hostel in Perth.

Parklands HOTEL ££
(01738-622451; www.theparklandshotel.com; 2 St Leonard's Bank; s/d £89/129; P @) Tucked away near the train station, this relaxing hotel sits amidst a lush hillside garden overlooking the parklands of South Inch. While the rooms – which vary in size and shape – conserve the character of this beautiful building, formerly the residence of the town's mayors, they also offer modern conveniences such as flatscreen TVs and CD/DVD players. The restaurant has a fine reputation and a terrace to lap up the Perthshire sun.

Comely Bank Cottage B&B ££
(01738-631118; www.comelybankcottage.co.uk; 19 Pitcullen Cres; s/d £48/55; P) Pitcullen Cres is bristling with upmarket, flowery B&Bs. This is one of our favourites, a perfectly maintained family home offering large and commodious rooms with spacious bathrooms, and a solicitous owner who doesn't disappoint come breakfast time.

Pitcullen Guest House B&B ££
(01738-626506; www.pitcullen.co.uk; 17 Pitcullen Cres; d £68; P @) Readers rave about this place, and rightly so. Good B&B depends on the host, and this one gets it spot-on, with helpful tips to guide your stay in Perth and numerous small, thoughtful extras that make this more than the sum of its parts.

Kinnaird Guest House B&B ££
(01738-628021; www.kinnaird-guesthouse.co.uk; 5 Marshall Pl; s/d £45/75; P) The best of the handful of guest houses enjoying a privileged position across the road from the lovely South Inch parkland, this elegant old house has noble original features and boasts appealing, bright rooms with big beds. The owners of Kinnaird are engaging and extremely helpful; they are justifiably proud of what Perth has to offer. The back rooms do receive occasional train noise.

Eating & Drinking

TOP CHOICE **Breizh** BISTRO ££
(01738-444427; www.cafebreizh.co.uk; 28 High St; mains £7-14; breakfast Mon-Sat, lunch & dinner daily) This warmly decorated bistro – the place could define the word – is a treat. Dishes are served with

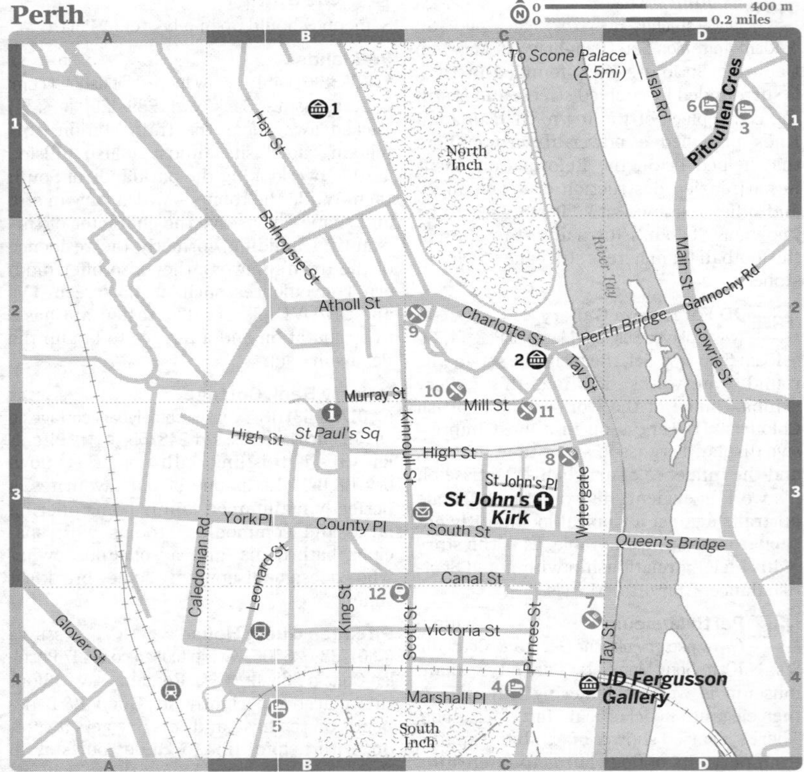

real panache, and the salads, featuring all sorts of delicious ingredients, are a feast of colour, texture, and subtle flavours. The blackboard meat and fish specials offer great value and a real taste of northwest France. Breakfasts, *galettes* (Breton buckwheat crêpes), tasty wines...If you like quality food served in an unpretentious way, you'll love it here.

63 Tay Street RESTAURANT ££
(☎01738-441451; www.63taystreet.com; 63 Tay St; mains £13-18; ⊙lunch & dinner Tue-Sat) Classy and warmly welcoming, this understated restaurant is Perth's best, featuring a lightly decorated dining area, excellent service and quality food. In a culinary Auld Alliance, French influence is applied to the best of Scottish produce to produce memorable game, seafood, beef and vegetarian plates.

Deans@Let's Eat RESTAURANT ££
(☎01738-643377; www.letseatperth.co.uk; 77 Kinnoull St; mains £14-19; ⊙lunch & dinner Tue-Sat) Noted for its excellent service, this award-winning bistro is the best place in town for splashing out on a special meal. Outstanding cuisine comes in the form of creative dishes on a short menu listed by main ingredient: halibut, lamb and beef reliably feature, but the manner of their cooking will change. Enjoy an aperitif on the comfy couches before indulging your palate.

Glassrooms CAFE £
(www.horsecross.co.uk; Mill St; light meals £5-8; ⊙breakfast & lunch Mon-Sat) Occupying part of the foyer of the ambitious, inspiring Perth Concert Hall, this open-plan cafe offers an eclectic range of daytime dishes. Expect several healthy and vegetarian choices as well as sandwiches and breakfasts.

Perth

Top Sights
JD Fergusson Gallery C4
St John's Kirk C3

Sights
1 Black Watch Museum B1
2 Perth Museum C2

Sleeping
3 Comely Bank Cottage D1
4 Kinnaird Guest House C4
5 Parklands B4
6 Pitcullen Guest House D1

Eating
7 63 Tay St C4
8 Breizh C3
9 Dean@Let's Eat C2
10 Glassrooms C2
11 Paco's C3

Drinking
12 Twa Tams B4

Paco's BISTRO ££
(www.pacos.co.uk; 3 Mill St; mains £7-13; lunch Sat, dinner daily;) Something of an institution, Paco's keeps Perthers coming back over and over, perhaps because it would take dozens of visits to even try half of the menu. There's something for everyone: steaks, seafood, pizza, pasta and Mexican, all served in generous portions. The fountain-tinkled terrace is the place for a sunny day.

Twa Tams PUB
(www.myspace.com/thetwatams; 79 Scott St) Perth's best pub has a strange outdoor space with windows peering out onto the street, an ornate entrance gate and large, cosy interior. There are regular events, including live music every Friday and Saturday night; it has a sound reputation for attracting talented young bands.

Information

AK Bell Library (York Pl; 9.30am-5pm Mon, Wed & Fri, to 8pm Tue & Thu, to 4pm Sat; @) Free internet; lots of terminals.

Perth Royal Infirmary (01738-623311; Taymount Tce) Hospital; west of the town centre.

Tourist office (01738-450600; www.perthshire.co.uk; West Mill St; 9.30am-5pm Mon-Sat & 10.30am-3.30pm Sun Apr-Oct, 10am-4pm Mon-Sat Nov-Mar) Efficiently run tourist office. Closes an hour later in summer.

Getting There & Away

Bus

From the bus station, **Citylink** (www.citylink.co.uk) operates buses to/from:

Dundee (£6.70, 40 minutes, hourly)
Edinburgh (£10.30, 1½ hours, hourly)
Glasgow (£10.70, 1½ hours, hourly)
Inverness (£18.80, 2½ hours, at least five daily)

Further buses run from the Broxden Park & Ride on Glasgow Rd; this is connected regularly with the bus station by shuttle bus. These include **Megabus** (www.megabus.com) discount services to Aberdeen, Edinburgh, Glasgow, Dundee, and Inverness.

Stagecoach (www.stagecoachbus.com) buses serve Perthshire destinations regularly, with reduced Sunday service.

Train

Trains run between Perth and destinations including:

Edinburgh (£12.90, 1¼ hours, at least hourly Monday to Saturday)
Glasgow (£12.90, one hour, at least hourly Monday to Saturday, every two hours Sunday) From Queen St.
Pitlochry (£11, 30 minutes, two hourly, fewer on Sunday)
Stirling (£10.40, 30 minutes, one or two per hour)

Perth to Blair Castle

There are a number of major sights strung along the busy but scenic A9, the main route north to the Cairngorms (p897) and Inverness (p890).

DUNKELD & BIRNAM

POP 1005

Ever been to a feel-good town? Well, Dunkeld and Birnam, with their enviable location nestled in the heart of Perthshire's big-tree country, await. The River Tay runs like a storybook river between the two. As well as Dunkeld's lovely cathedral, there's much walking to be done in this area of magnificent forested hills. These same walks inspired Beatrix Potter to create her children's tales.

Sights & Activities

Situated between open grassland between the River Tay on one side and rolling hills on the other, **Dunkeld Cathedral** (HS; www.historic-scotland.gov.uk; High St; admission free; ⏲9.30am-6.30pm Mon-Sat & 2-6.30pm Sun Apr-Sep, 9.30am-4pm Mon-Sat & 2-4pm Sun Oct-Mar) is one of the most beautifully sited cathedrals in Scotland. Don't miss it on a sunny day, as there are few more lovely places to be. Half the cathedral is still in use as a church; the rest is in ruins, and you can explore it all. It partly dates from the 14th century; the cathedral was damaged during the Reformation and burnt in the battle of Dunkeld (Jacobites vs Government) in 1689.

Across the bridge is Birnam, made famous by *Macbeth*. There's not much left of Birnam Wood, but there is a small, leafy **Beatrix Potter Park** (the children's author, who wrote the evergreen story of *Peter Rabbit*, spent childhood holidays in the area). Next to the park, in the Birnam Arts Centre, is a small **exhibition** (Station Rd, Birnam; admission £1; ⏲10am-4.30pm) on Potter and her characters.

Sleeping & Eating

Birnam Hotel HOTEL ££
(☎01350-728030; www.birnamhotel.com; Perth Rd, Birnam; s/d/f £79/98/135; P 📶) This grand-looking place with crow-stepped gables has tastefully fitted rooms opposite the Beatrix Potter park. Superior rooms (d £130) are substantially larger than the standards. Service is very welcoming, and there's a fairly formal restaurant as well as a livelier pub alongside serving creative bar meals.

TOP CHOICE **Taybank** PUB £
(www.thetaybank.com; Tay Tce, Dunkeld; bar mains £5-8) Top choice for a sun-kissed pub lunch by the river is the Taybank, a regular meeting place and performance space for musicians of all creeds and a wonderfully open and welcoming bar. The menu includes a tasty selection of traditional and offbeat stovies.

Information

Dunkeld's **tourist office** (☎01350-727688; dunkeld@visitscotland.com; The Cross; ⏲daily Apr-Oct, Fri-Sun Nov-Mar) has information on local trails and paths.

Getting There & Away

Dunkeld is 15 miles north of Perth. **Citylink** (www.citylink.co.uk) buses between Glasgow/Edinburgh and Inverness stop at Birnam House Hotel. Birnam to Perth (£7.90) or Pitlochry (£7.60) takes 20 minutes.

Stagecoach (www.stagecoachbus.com) has a bus between Blairgowrie (30 minutes) and Aberfeldy (40 minutes), via Dunkeld, twice daily Monday to Friday only.

Trains run to Edinburgh (£12.90, 1½ hours, approximately hourly Monday to Saturday, four on Sunday), Glasgow (£12.90, 1½ hours, roughly hourly Monday to Saturday, four on Sunday) and to Inverness (£21.50, two hours, eight daily Monday to Saturday, five on Sunday).

PITLOCHRY

POP 2564

Pitlochry, with its air already smelling of the Highlands, is a popular stop on the way north and convenient base for exploring northern Central Scotland. On a quiet spring evening it's a pretty place with salmon jumping in the Tummel and good things brewing at the Moulin Hotel. In summer the main street can be a conga-line of tour groups, but get away from that and it'll still charm you.

Sights

One of Pitlochry's attractions is its beautiful **riverside**; the River Tummel is dammed here, and you can watch salmon swimming (not jumping) up a **fish ladder** to the loch above.

FREE **Edradour Distillery** DISTILLERY
(☎01796-472095; www.edradour.co.uk; ⏲daily) This is proudly Scotland's smallest distillery and a great one to visit: you can see the whole process easily-explained in one room. It's 2.5 miles east of Pitlochry along the Moulin road, and it's a pleasant walk to get there.

Explorers Garden GARDEN
(www.explorersgarden.com; adult/child £3/1; Foss Rd; ⏲10am-5pm Apr-Oct) At the Pitlochry Festival Theatre, this excellent garden commemorates 300 years of plant collecting and those who hunted down 'new' species. The whole collection is based on plants brought back to Scotland by Scottish explorers.

Sleeping

Craigatin House B&B ££
(☎01796-472478; www.craigatinhouse.co.uk; 165 Atholl Rd; d standard/deluxe £78/88; P 📶) Several times more tasteful than the average Pitlochry lodging, this noble house and garden is set back from the main road at the western end of town. Chic contemporary fabrics covering expansive beds offer a standard of comfort above and beyond

the reasonable price; the rooms in the converted stable block are particularly inviting. Breakfast choices include whisky-laced porridge, smoked-fish omelettes, and apple pancakes.

Pitlochry Backpackers Hotel HOSTEL £
(☎01796-470044; www.scotlands-top-hostels.com; 134 Atholl Rd; dm/tw/d £15/38/40; P@📶) Friendly, laid-back and very comfortable, this is a cracking hostel smack-bang in the middle of town, with three- to eight-bed dorms that are in mint condition. There are also good-value en-suite twins and doubles, with beds, not bunks. Cheap breakfast and a pool table add to the convivial party atmosphere. No extra charge for linen.

Ashleigh B&B £
(☎01796-470316; nancy.gray@btinternet.com; 120 Atholl Rd; s/d £25/50; P) Genuine welcomes don't come much better than Nancy's, and her place on the main street makes a top Pitlochry pitstop. Three comfortable rooms share an excellent bathroom, and there's an open kitchen stocked with goodies where you make your own breakfast in the morning. A home-away-from-home and standout budget choice.

Tir Aluinn B&B ££
(☎01796-473811; www.tiraluinn.co.uk; 10 Higher Oakfield Rd; s/d £32/64; P) Tucked away above the main street, this is a little gem of a place with bright rooms with easy-on-the-eye furniture, and an excellent personal welcome.

Pitlochry SYHA HOSTEL £
(☎01796-472308; www.syha.org.uk; Knockard Rd; dm £17.25; ⏲Feb-Oct; P@📶) Great location overlooking the town centre. Popular with families and walkers.

Eating & Drinking

TOP CHOICE **Moulin Hotel** PUB/HOTEL £
(☎01796-472196; www.moulinhotel.co.uk; Moulin; bar mains £7-11; ⏲lunch & dinner) A mile away but a world apart, this atmospheric hotel was trading centuries before the tartan tack came to Pitlochry. With its romantic low ceilings, ageing wood and booth seating, the inn is a wonderfully atmospheric spot for a house-brewed ale or a portion of Highland comfort food: try the filling haggis or venison stew. A more formal restaurant (mains £13 to £16) serves equally delicious fare, and the hotel has a variety of rooms (single/double £60/75) as well as a self-catering annexe. The best way to get here from Pitlochry is walking: it's a pretty uphill stroll through green fields, and an easy roll down the slope afterwards.

Port-na-Craig Inn RESTAURANT/PUB ££
(☎01796-472777; www.portnacraig.com; Port Na Craig; mains £13-17; ⏲lunch & dinner) Right on the river, this top little spot sits in what was once a separate hamlet. Delicious main meals are prepared with confidence and panache – scrumptious scallops or lamb steak bursting with flavour might appeal, but simpler sandwiches, kids' meals and light lunches also tempt. Or you could just sit out by the river with a pint and watch the anglers whisking away.

Entertainment

Pitlochry Festival Theatre THEATRE
(☎01796-484626; www.pitlochry.org.uk; Foss Rd; tickets £14-25) This well-known theatre stages a different mainstream play for six nights out of seven during its season from May to mid-October.

Information

Computer Services Centre (☎473711; 67 Atholl Rd; per hr £3; ⏲9.30am-5.30pm Mon-Fri, to 12.30pm Sat; @) Internet access.

Tourist office (☎01796-472215; pitlochry@visitscotland.com; 22 Atholl Rd; ⏲8.30am-7pm Mon-Sat & 9.30am-5.30pm Sun Easter-Oct, 10am-4pm Mon-Sat Nov-Mar; @) Good information on local walks.

Getting There & Away

Citylink (www.citylink.co.uk) buses run roughly hourly to Inverness (£15.10, two hours), Perth (£9.40, 40 minutes), Edinburgh (£14.40, two hours) and Glasgow (£14.40, 2¼ hours). **Megabus** (www.megabus.com) discount services also run these routes.

Stagecoach (www.stagecoachbus.com) runs to Aberfeldy (30 minutes, hourly Monday to Saturday, three Sunday), Dunkeld (25 minutes, up to 10 daily Monday to Saturday) and Perth (one hour, up to 10 daily Monday to Saturday).

Pitlochry is on the main railway from Perth (£11, 30 minutes, nine daily Monday to Saturday, five on Sunday) to Inverness.

BLAIR CASTLE

One of the most popular tourist attractions in Scotland, magnificent **Blair Castle** (www.blair-castle.co.uk; Blair Atholl; adult/child/family £8.75/5.25/24; ⏲9.30am-5.30pm Apr-Oct) and the 108 square miles it sits on, is the seat of the Duke of Atholl, head of the Murray clan. It's an impressive white building set beneath forested slopes above the River Garry.

The original tower was built in 1269, but the castle has undergone significant remodelling since. Thirty rooms are open to the public and they present a wonderful picture of upper-class Highland life from the 16th century on. The **dining room** is sumptuous – check out the 9-pint wine glasses – and the **ballroom** is a vaulted chamber that's a virtual stag cemetery.

The current duke visits the castle every May to review the Atholl Highlanders, Britain's only private army.

Blair Atholl is 6 miles northwest of Pitlochry, and the castle a further mile beyond it. Local buses run a service between Pitlochry and Blair Atholl (25 minutes, three to seven daily). Four buses a day (Monday to Saturday) go directly to the castle. There's a train station in the village, but not all trains stop here.

West Perthshire

The jewel in central Scotland's crown, West Perthshire achieves a Scottish ideal with rugged, noble hills reflected in some of the nation's most beautiful lochs. Bring your hiking boots and camera and prepare to stay a few days.

LOCH TAY

Serpentine and picturesque, long Loch Tay reflects the powerful forests and mountains around it. The bulk of mighty **Ben Lawers** (1214m) looms above and is part of a National Nature Reserve that includes the nearby **Tarmachan Range**.

The main access point for the ascent of Ben Lawers (see the boxed text, p871) is the now-defunct tourist office, a mile off the A827 five miles east of Killin. There's also an easier nature trail leaving from here.

There's good accommodation in Kenmore and Killin, as well as **Culdees Bunkhouse** (☎01887-830519; www.culdeesbunkhouse.co.uk; dm/tw/f £17/44/66; P @), a wonderfully offbeat hostel with utterly majestic vistas: the whole of the loch stretches out before and below you. It's half a mile above the village of Fearnan, four miles west from Kenmore.

KENMORE

Pretty Kenmore lies at Loch Tay's eastern end, 6 miles west of Aberfeldy, and is dominated by church, clock tower, and the striking archway of privately owned **Taymouth Castle**. Just outside town on the loch is the fascinating **Scottish Crannog Centre** (www.crannog.co.uk; tours adult/child £6.50/4.50; ⏲10am-5.30pm mid-Mar–Oct, 10am-4pm Sat & Sun Nov). A crannog, perched on stilts in the water, was a favoured form of defence-minded dwelling in Scotland from the 3rd millennium BC onwards. This one has been superbly reconstructed, and the guided tour includes an impressive demonstration of firemaking. It's an excellent visit.

The heart of the village, **Kenmore Hotel** (☎01887-830205, www.kenmorehotel.com; s/d £85/140; P @) has a bar with a roaring fire and some verses scribbled on the chimneypiece by Robert Burns in 1787, when the inn was already a couple of centuries old. There's also a riverbank beer garden and a wide variety of rooms, some across the road. They sport modern conveniences; the nicest have bay windows and river views. Prices plummet off-season and midweek.

Regular buses link Aberfeldy with Kenmore, some continuing to Killin via the turnoff to the trailhead for Ben Lawers.

FORTINGALL

Fortingall is one of the prettiest villages in Scotland, with 19th-century thatched cottages in a very tranquil setting. The **church** has impressive wooden beams and a 7th-century **monk's bell**. In the churchyard, there's a 2000-year-old **yew**, probably the oldest tree in Europe. This tree was around when the Romans camped in the meadows by the River Lyon: popular if unlikely tradition says that Pontius Pilate was born here. Today the tree is a shell of its former self – at its zenith it had a girth of over 17m! But souvenir hunters have reduced it to two much smaller trunks.

Alongside, **Fortingall Hotel** (☎01887-830367; www.fortingallhotel.com; s/d £110/160; P) is a peaceful, old-fashioned country hotel with polite service and furnished with quiet good taste.

GLEN LYON

This remote and stunningly beautiful glen runs for some 34 unforgettable miles of rickety stone bridges, Caledonian pine for-

BAG A MUNRO: BEN LAWERS

The trip to the top of Ben Lawers and back can take up to five hours: pack wet-weather gear, water and food. From the now-closed tourist office, take the nature trail that heads northeast. After the boardwalk protecting a bog, cross a stile then fork left and ascend along the Edramucky burn (to the right). At the next rise, fork right and cross the burn. A few minutes later ignore the nature trail's right turn and continue ascending parallel to the burn's left bank for just over half a mile. Leave the protected zone by another stile and steeply ascend Beinn Ghlas's shoulder. Reaching a couple of large rocks, ignore a northbound footpath and continue zigzagging uphill. The rest of the ascent is a straightforward succession of three false summits. The last and steepest section alternates between erosion-sculpted rock and a meticulously crafted cobbled trail. Long views of majestic hillscapes, and even the North Sea and Atlantic, are your reward on a clear day.

est and sheer heather-splashed peaks poking through swirling clouds. It becomes wilder and more uninhabited as it snakes its way west, and is proof that hidden treasures still exist in Scotland. The ancients believed it to be a gateway to Faerieland, and even the most sceptical of people will be entranced by the valley's magic.

From Fortingall, a narrow road winds up the glen – another road from Loch Tay crosses the hills and reaches the glen halfway in, at **Bridge of Balgie**. The glen continues up to a dam (past a memorial to explorer Robert Campbell); bearing left here you can actually continue over a wild and remote road (unmarked on maps) to remote **Glen Lochay** and down to Killin. **Cycling** through Glen Lyon is a wonderful way to experience this special place.

There's little in the way of attractions in the valley – the majestic and lonely scenery is the reason to be here – but at **Glenlyon Gallery** (www.glenlyongallery.co.uk; Bridge of Balgie; admission free; ⌚10am-5pm Thu-Tue), next to the Bridge of Balgie post office (which does more-than-decent lunches), a selection of fine handmade pieces are for sale.

For utter tranquillity in a glorious natural setting, **Milton Eonan** (☎01887-866318; www.miltoneonan.com; Bridge of Balgie; d £70; P 📶) is a must. On an effervescent stream where an historic watermill once stood, it's a working croft that offers a romantic one-bedroom cottage (breakfast available for a little extra) at the bottom of the garden. It can sleep three at a pinch. The lively owners do packed lunches and evening meals (£18.50) using local and homegrown produce. After crossing the bridge at Bridge of Balgie, you'll see Milton Eonan signposted to the right.

There is no public transport in the glen.

LOCHS TUMMEL & RANNOCH

The route along Lochs Tummel and Rannoch is worth doing any way you can – by foot, bicycle or car – just don't miss it! Hills of ancient birch and forests of spruce, pine and larch make up the **Tay Forest Park** – the king of Scotland's forests. It's the product of a brilliant bit of forward thinking: the replanting of Tay Forest 300 years ago. These wooded hills roll into the glittering waters of the lochs; a visit in autumn is recommended, when the birch trees are at their finest.

Far beyond, the road ends at romantic, isolated **Rannoch train station**, which is on the Glasgow-Fort William line. Beyond is desolate, intriguing **Rannoch Moor**, a windy, vaguely threatening peat bog stretching as far as the A82 and Glen Coe. There's a tearoom on the platform, and a welcoming small hotel alongside the station.

DUNDEE & ANGUS

Angus is a region of fertile farmland stretching north from Dundee – Scotland's fourth-largest city – to the Highland border. It's an attractive area of broad straths (valleys) and low, green hills contrasting with the rich, red-brown soil of freshly ploughed fields. Romantic glens finger their way into the foothills of the Grampian Mountains, while the scenic coastline ranges from the red-sandstone cliffs of Arbroath to the long, sandy beaches around

Dundee

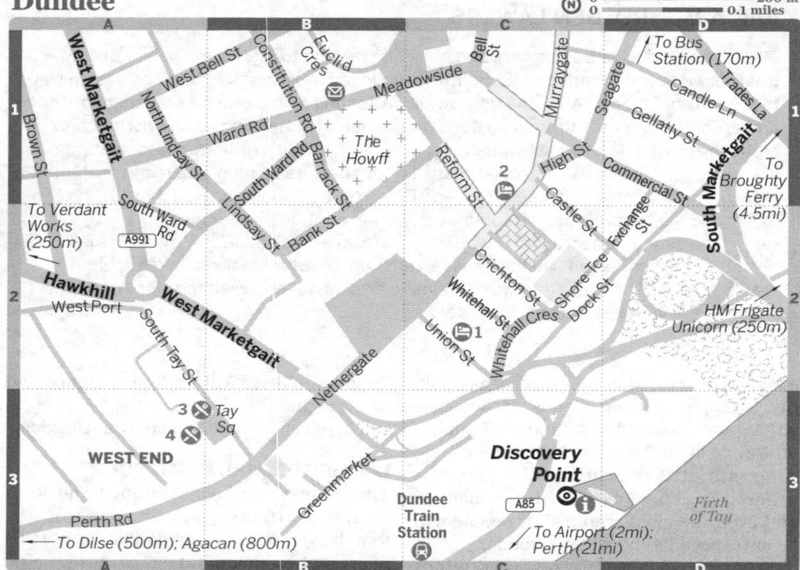

Montrose. This was the Pictish heartland of the 7th and 8th centuries, and many interesting Pictish symbol stones survive here.

Apart from the crowds visiting Discovery Point in newly confident Dundee and the coach parties shuffling through Glamis Castle, Angus is a bit of a tourism backwater and a good place to escape the hordes.

Dundee

POP 144,000

London's Trafalgar Sq has Nelson on his column, Edinburgh's Princes St has its monument to Sir Walter Scott and Belfast has a statue of Queen Victoria outside City Hall. Dundee's City Sq, on the other hand, is graced – rather endearingly – by the bronze figure of Desperate Dan. Familiar to generations of British school children, Dan is one of the best-loved cartoon characters from the children's comic *The Dandy,* published by Dundee firm DC Thomson since 1937.

Dundee is often called the city of the 'Three Js' – jute, jam and journalism. According to legend, it was a Dundee woman named Janet Keillor who invented marmalade in the late 18th century; her son founded the city's famous Keillor jam factory. Jute is no longer produced, and when the Keillor factory was taken over in 1988 production was transferred to England. Journalism still thrives, however, led by the family firm of DC Thomson. Best known for children's comics, such as *The Beano,* Thomson is now the city's largest employer.

Dundee enjoys perhaps the finest location of any Scottish city, spreading along the northern shore of the Firth of Tay, and can boast tourist attractions of national importance in Discovery Point and the Verdant Works museum. Add in the attractive seaside suburb of Broughty Ferry, some lively nightlife and the Dundonians themselves – among the friendliest, most welcoming and most entertaining people you'll meet – and Dundee is definitely worth a stopover.

Sights

Discovery Point MUSEUM

(www.rrsdiscovery.com; Discovery Quay; adult/child £7.75/4.75; ⌚10am-6pm Mon-Sat, 11am-6pm Sun Apr-Oct, 10am-5pm Mon-Sat, 11am-5pm Sun Nov-Mar) The three masts of Captain Robert Falcon Scott's famous polar expedition vessel the **RRS Discovery** dominate the riverside to the south of the city cen-

Dundee

Top Sights

Discovery Point....C3

Sleeping

1 Aabalree....C2
2 Dundee Backpackers....C1

Eating

3 Playwright....A3
4 Rep Theatre Cafe....A3

tre. The ship was built in Dundee in 1900, with a wooden hull at least half a metre thick to survive the pack ice, and sailed for the Antarctic in 1901 where it spent two winters trapped in the ice. From 1931 on it was laid up in London where its condition steadily deteriorated, until it was rescued by the efforts of Peter Scott (son of Robert) and the Maritime Trust, and restored to its 1925 condition. In 1986 the ship was given a berth in its home port of Dundee, where it became a symbol of the city's regeneration.

A joint ticket that gives entry to both Discovery Point and the Verdant Works costs £11.50/7 per adult/child.

HM Frigate Unicorn MUSEUM

(www.frigateunicorn.org; Victoria Dock; adult/child £5/3; 10am-5pm Apr-Oct, noon-4pm Wed-Fri, 10am-4pm Sat & Sun Nov-Mar) Unlike the polished and much-restored *Discovery*, Dundee's other floating tourist attraction retains the authentic atmosphere of a salty old sailing ship. Built in 1824, the 46-gun *Unicorn* is the oldest British-built ship still afloat – she was mothballed soon after launching and never saw action. Wandering around the four decks gives you an excellent impression of what it must have been like for the crew forced to live in such cramped conditions.

The *Unicorn* is berthed in Victoria Dock, just northeast of the Tay Road Bridge. The entry price includes a self-guided tour (also available in French and German).

Verdant Works MUSEUM

(www.verdantworks.com; West Henderson's Wynd; adult/child £7/4; 10am-6pm Mon-Sat, 11am-6pm Sun Apr-Oct, 10.30am-4.30pm Wed-Sat, 11am-4.30pm Sun Nov-Mar) One of the finest industrial museums in Europe, the Verdant Works explores the history of Dundee's jute industry. Housed in a restored jute mill, complete with original machinery still in working condition, the museum's interactive exhibits and computer displays follow the raw material from its origins in India through to the manufacture of a wide range of finished products, from sacking to rope to wagon covers for the pioneers of the American West. The mill is 250m west of the city centre.

Sleeping

Balgowan House B&B ££

(01382-200262; www.balgowanhouse.co.uk; 510 Perth Rd; s/d £63/84; P) Built in 1900 and perched in a prime location with stunning views over the Firth of Tay, Balgowan is a wealthy merchant's mansion converted into a luxurious guest house with two sumptuous en suite bedrooms. It's 2 miles west of the city centre, overlooking the university botanic gardens.

Apex City Quay Hotel HOTEL ££

(01382-202404; www.apexhotels.co.uk; 1 West Victoria Dock Rd; r from £98; P) Though it looks plain from the outside, the Apex overlooks the city's redeveloping waterfront and sports the sort of stylish, spacious, sofa-equipped rooms that make you want to lounge around all evening munching chocolate in front of the TV. If you can drag yourself away from your room, there are spa treatments, saunas and Japanese hot tubs to enjoy. The hotel is just east of the city centre, close to the Frigate Unicorn.

Errolbank Guest House B&B ££

(01382-462118; www.errolbank-guesthouse.com; 9 Dalgleish Rd; s/d £35/58; P) A mile east of the city centre, just north of the road to Broughty Ferry, Errolbank is a lovely Victorian family home with small but beautifully decorated en-suite rooms set on a quiet street.

Dundee Backpackers HOSTEL £

(01382-224646; www.hoppo.com; 71 High St; dm £13-15, s/tw from £25/40; @) New hostel in a beautifully converted historic building, with clean, modern kitchen, pool room, and an ideal location right in the city centre. Can get a bit noisy at night, but that's because it's close to pubs and nightlife.

Aabalree B&B £

(01382-223867; www.aabalree.com; 20 Union St; s/d £24/40) This is a pretty basic B&B – there are no en suites – but the owners are welcoming (don't be put off by the dark entrance) and it couldn't be more central, close to both train and bus stations. This makes it popular, so book ahead.

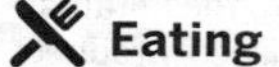

Eating

TOP CHOICE **Metro** BRASSERIE ££
(☎0845 365 0002; www.apexhotels.co.uk/eat; Apex City Quay Hotel, 1 West Victoria Dock Rd; mains £10-16) Sleek, slate-blue banquettes, white linen napkins, black-clad staff and a view of Victoria Dock lend an air of city sophistication to this stylish hotel brasserie, with a menu that ranges from steaks and burgers to Caribbean jerk chicken with coconut curry. There's a three-course dinner menu for £21.50. Located just east of the city centre, close to the Frigate Unicorn.

Playwright BISTRO ££
(☎01382-223113; www.theplaywright.co.uk; 11 Tay Sq; mains £23-25; ⊙10am-midnight) Next door to the theatre, and decorated with photos of Scottish actors, this innovative cafe-bar and bistro serves a 'grazing menu' of light meals (£5 to £8) from noon to 5pm, a lunch and pre-theatre menu £17/20 for two/three courses and a gourmet à la carte menu that concentrates on fine Scottish produce with dishes such as saddle of lamb with wild mushrooms and roast halibut with shellfish sauce.

Dil'se INDIAN ££
(www.dilse-restaurant.co.uk; 99 Perth Rd; mains £8-15; ⊙noon-2.30pm & 4.30-11pm Sun-Thu, noon-2am Fri & Sat) Dundee loves a curry, and nobody does it better than this sleek modern Bangladeshi restaurant most of the way up Perth Rd. The bold, contemporary approach extends beyond the delicious old favourites to new dishes, such as *Mas Bangla*, which brings the subcontinent to Scots salmon.

Rep Theatre Cafe CAFE-BAR ££
(www.dundeereptheatre.co.uk; Tay Sq; mains £9-15; ⊙cafe 10am-late, restaurant noon-3pm & 5-10pm Mon-Sat) The city's arty types hang out in this Continental-style cafe-bar and restaurant in the foyer at the Dundee Rep Theatre. Great sandwiches and pizza, as well as tasty steaks, fishcakes and veggie dishes.

Information

Ninewells Hospital (☎01382-660111; ⊙casualty 24hr) At Menzieshill, west of the city centre.

Tourist office (☎01382-527527; www.angusanddundee.co.uk; Discovery Point; ⊙10am-5pm Mon-Sat, noon-4pm Sun Jun-Sep, 10am-4pm Mon-Sat Oct-May)

Getting There & Away

AIR Two and a half miles west of the city centre, **Dundee Airport** (www.hial.co.uk/dundee-airport) has daily scheduled services to London City airport (CityJet), Birmingham and Belfast (FlyBe). Bus 8X runs between the airport and the city centre (five minutes, half-hourly Monday to Saturday). A taxi to the airport takes five minutes and costs £3.50.

BUS **National Express** (www.nationalexpress.com) operates one direct service a day from London to Dundee (£40, 11 hours).

Scottish Citylink (www.citylink.co.uk) has hourly buses from Dundee to Glasgow (£15, 2½ hours), Perth (£8, 35 minutes), Aberdeen (£15, 1½ hours) and Edinburgh (£14, two hours, change at Perth); book via www.megabus.com for fares as low as £5.

TRAIN Trains run to Dundee from Edinburgh (£20, 1¼ hours) and Glasgow (£23, 1½ hours) at least once an hour Monday to Saturday, hourly on Sunday from Edinburgh, and every two hours on Sunday from Glasgow.

Trains from Dundee to Aberdeen (£24, 1¼ hours) travel via Arbroath and Stonehaven. There are around two trains an hour, fewer on Sunday.

Broughty Ferry

Dundee's attractive seaside suburb, known locally as 'The Ferry', lies 4 miles east of the city centre. It has a castle, a long, sandy beach and a number of good places to eat and drink. It's also handy for the golf courses at nearby Carnoustie.

FREE **Broughty Castle Museum** MUSEUM
(Castle Green; ⊙10am-4pm Mon-Sat, 12.30-4pm Sun, closed Mon Oct-Mar) A 16th-century tower house that looms imposingly over the harbour, guarding the entrance to the Firth of Tay. There's a fascinating exhibit on Dundee's whaling industry, and the view from the top offers the chance of spotting seals and dolphins offshore.

Sleeping & Eating

Invermark House B&B ££
(☎01382-739430; www.invermark.co.uk; 23 Monifieth Rd; s/d from £30/50; P 📶) Invermark is a grand Victorian villa set in its own grounds, built for a jute baron in the mid-19th century. There are five large en-

suite bedrooms and an elegant lounge and dining room with a view of the gardens.

Fisherman's Tavern B&B ££
(☎01382-775941; www.fishermanstavern.co.uk; 10-16 Fort St; s/d £39/64) A delightful 17th-century terraced cottage just a few paces from the seafront, the Fisherman's was converted into a pub in 1827. It now has 11 stylishly modern rooms, most with en suite, and an atmospheric pub.

Ship Inn PUB/RESTAURANT ££
(www.theshipinn-broughtyferry.co.uk; 121 Fisher St; mains £10-18; ⏲food served noon-2pm & 5-10.30pm Mon-Fri, noon-10.30pm Sat & Sun) On the seafront around the corner from the Fisherman's is the snug, wood-panelled, 19th-century Ship Inn, which serves top-notch dishes ranging from gourmet haddock and chips to venison steaks; you can eat in the upstairs restaurant, or down in the bar (bar meals £7 to £9). It's always busy, so get there early to grab a seat.

Getting There & Away

City bus 5 and Stagecoach bus 73 run from Dundee High St to Broughty Ferry (20 minutes) several times an hour from Monday to Saturday, and hourly on Sunday.

WORTH A TRIP

GLAMIS CASTLE

Looking every inch the archetypal Scottish Baronial castle, with its roofline sprouting a forest of pointed turrets and battlements, **Glamis Castle** (www.glamis-castle.co.uk; adult/child £8.75/6; ⏲10am-6pm mid-Mar–Oct, 10.30am-4.30pm Nov & Dec, closed Jan–mid-Mar) claims to be the legendary setting for Shakespeare's *Macbeth* (his character is the Thane of Glamis at the start of the play). A royal residence since 1372, it is the family home of the earls of Strathmore and Kinghorne: the Queen Mother (born Elizabeth Bowes-Lyon; 1900–2002) spent her childhood at Glamis (pronounced 'glams') and Princess Margaret (the Queen's sister; 1930–2002) was born here. The one-hour guided tours depart every 15 minutes (last tour at 4.30pm, or 3.30pm in low season).

Glamis Castle is located 12 miles north of Dundee. There are two to four buses a day from Dundee (35 minutes) to Glamis; some continue to Kirriemuir.

Arbroath

POP 22,800

Arbroath is an old-fashioned seaside resort and fishing harbour, home of the famous **Arbroath smokie** (a form of smoked haddock). The humble smokie achieved European Union 'Protected Geographical Indication' status in 2004 – the term 'Arbroath smokie' can be only be used legally to describe haddock smoked in the traditional manner within an 8km radius of Arbroath. No visit is complete without buying a pair of smokies from one of the many fish shops and eating them with your fingers while sitting beside the harbour. Yum.

Sights

Arbroath Abbey ABBEY
(HS; Abbey St; adult/child £4.70/2.80; ⏲9.30am-5.30pm Apr-Sep, 9.30am-4.30pm Oct-Mar) The magnificent, red-sandstone ruins of Arbroath Abbey, founded in 1178 by King William the Lion, dominate the town centre. It is thought that Bernard of Linton, the abbot here in the early 14th century, wrote the famous Declaration of Arbroath in 1320, asserting Scotland's right to independence from England. You can climb to the top of one of the towers for a grand view over the town.

St Vigeans Museum MUSEUM
(HS; St Vigeans Lane; adult/child £3.70/2.20; ⏲10am-5pm Tue-Thu, Sat & Sun Apr-Oct, 11am-1pm Tue-Thu, Sat & Sun Nov-Mar) About a mile north of the town centre, this cottage museum houses a superb collection of Pictish and medieval sculptured stones. The museum's masterpiece is the **Drosten Stone**, beautifully carved with animal figures and hunting scenes on one side, and an interlaced Celtic cross on the other (look for the devil perched in the top left corner).

Sleeping & Eating

Harbour Nights Guest House B&B ££
(☎01241-434343; www.harbournights-scotland.com; 4 The Shore; s/d from £45/60) With a

superb location overlooking the harbour, five stylishly decorated bedrooms and a gourmet breakfast menu, Harbour Nights is our favourite place to stay in Arbroath. Rooms 2 and 3, with harbour views, are a bit more expensive (doubles £70 to £80), but well worth asking for when booking.

Smithie's CAFE £

(16 Keptie St; mains £3-6; ⌚9.30am-4.30pm Mon-Fri, 9.30am-4pm Sat) Housed in a former butcher's shop, with hand-painted tiles and meat hooks on the ceiling, Smithie's is a great little neighbourhood deli and cafe serving Fairtrade coffee, pancakes, wraps and freshly made pasta – butternut squash and sage tortellini make a tasty change from macaroni and cheese for a vegetarian lunch.

Getting There & Away

BUS Bus 140 runs from Arbroath to Auchmithie (15 minutes, six daily Monday to Friday, three daily on Saturday and Sunday).

TRAIN Trains from Dundee to Arbroath (£4.50, 20 minutes, two per hour) continue to Aberdeen (£19, 55 minutes) via Montrose and Stonehaven.

ABERDEENSHIRE & MORAY

Since medieval times Aberdeenshire and its northwestern neighbour Moray have been the richest and most fertile regions of the Highlands. Aberdeenshire is famed for its Aberdeen Angus beef cattle, its many fine castles and the prosperous 'granite city' of Aberdeen. Moray's main attractions are the Speyside whisky distilleries that line the valley of the River Spey and its tributaries.

Aberdeen

POP 197,300

Aberdeen is the powerhouse of the northeast, fuelled by the North Sea petroleum industry. Oil money has made the city as expensive as London and Edinburgh, and there are hotels, restaurants and clubs with prices to match the depth of oil-wealthy pockets. Fortunately, most of the cultural attractions, such as the excellent Maritime Museum and the Aberdeen Art Gallery, are free.

The name Aberdeen is a combination of two Pictish-Gaelic words, *aber* and *devana,* meaning 'the meeting of two waters'. Known throughout Scotland as the granite city, much of the town was built using silvery grey granite hewn from the now abandoned Rubislaw Quarry, at one time the biggest artificial hole in the ground in Europe. On a sunny day the granite lends an attractive glitter to the city, but when low, grey rain clouds scud in off the North Sea it can be hard to tell where the buildings stop and the sky begins.

Royal Deeside is easily accessible to the west, Dunnottar Castle to the south, sandy beaches to the north and whisky country to the northwest.

Sights

CITY CENTRE

FREE **Provost Skene's House** HISTORIC BUILDING

(www.aagm.co.uk; Guestrow; ⌚10am-5pm Mon-Sat) Surrounded by concrete and glass office blocks in what was once the worst slum in Aberdeen is Provost Skene's House, a late-medieval, turreted town house occupied in the 17th century by the provost (the Scottish equivalent of a mayor) Sir George Skene. It was also occupied for six weeks by the duke of Cumberland on his way to Culloden in 1746. The tempera-painted ceiling with its religious symbolism, dating from 1622, is unusual for having survived the depredations of the Reformation. It's a period gem featuring earnest-looking angels, soldiers and St Peter with crowing cockerels.

FREE **Marischal College & Museum** MUSEUM

(www.abdn.ac.uk/marischal_museum; Marischal College, Broad St; ⌚10am-5pm Mon-Fri, 2-5pm Sun) Across Broad St from Provost Skene's House is **Marischal College**, founded in 1593 by the 5th Earl Marischal, and merged with King's College (founded 1495) in 1860 to create the modern University of Aberdeen. The huge and impressive facade in Perpendicular Gothic style – unusual in having such elaborate masonry hewn from notoriously hard-to-work granite – dates from 1906 and is the world's second-largest granite structure (after L'Escorial near Madrid). At the time of research the building was being converted into Aberdeen City Council's new headquarters.

Founded in 1786, the **Marischal Museum** houses a fascinating collection of material donated by graduates and friends of the university over the centuries. In one room, the history of northeastern Scotland is depicted through its myths, customs, famous people, architecture and trade. The other gallery gives an anthropological overview of the world, incorporating objects from vastly different cultures, arranged thematically (Polynesian wooden masks alongside gas masks and so on). There are the usual Victorian curios, an Inuit kayak found in the local river estuary in the 18th century and Inuit objects collected by whalers. At the time of research, the museum was closed to the public during building work, but will reopen sometime in 2011.

FREE **Aberdeen Art Gallery** ART GALLERY
(www.aagm.co.uk; Schoolhill; ⌚10am-5pm Tue-Sat, 2-5pm Sun) Behind the grand facade of Aberdeen Art Gallery is a cool, marble-lined space exhibiting the work of contemporary Scottish and English painters, such as Gwen Hardie, Stephen Conroy, Trevor Sutton and Tim Ollivier. There are also several landscapes by Joan Eardley, who lived in a cottage on the cliffs near Stonehaven in the 1950s and '60s and painted tempestuous oils of the North Sea and poignant portraits of slum children. Among the Pre-Raphaelite works upstairs, look out for the paintings of Aberdeen artist William Dyce (1806–64), ranging from religious works to rural scenes.

ABERDEEN HARBOUR

Aberdeen has a busy, working harbour crowded with survey vessels and supply ships servicing the offshore oil installations, and car ferries bound for Orkney and Shetland. From dawn until about 8am the colourful **fish market** on Albert Basin operates as it has done for centuries.

FREE **Aberdeen Maritime Museum** MUSEUM
(www.aagm.co.uk; Shiprow; ⌚10am-5pm Mon-Sat, noon-3pm Sun) Overlooking the nautical bustle of the harbour is the Maritime Museum. Centred on a three-storey replica of a North Sea oil production platform, its exhibits explain all you ever wanted to know about the petroleum industry. Other galleries, some situated in **Provost Ross's House**, the oldest building in the city and part of the museum, cover the shipbuilding, whaling and fishing industries. Sleek and speedy Aberdeen clippers were a 19th-century shipyard speciality, used by British merchants for the importation of tea, wool and exotic goods (opium, for instance) to Britain, and, on the return journey, the transportation of emigrants to Australia.

ABERDEEN BEACH

Just 800m east of Castlegate is a spectacular 2-mile sweep of clean, **golden sand** stretching between the mouths of the Rivers Dee and Don. At one time Aberdeen Beach was a good, old-fashioned British seaside resort, but the availability of cheap package holidays has lured Scottish holidaymakers away from its somewhat chilly delights. On a warm summer's day, though, it's still an excellent beach. When the waves are right, a small group of dedicated **surfers** ride the breaks at the southern end.

OLD ABERDEEN

Just over a mile north of the city centre is the district called Old Aberdeen. The name is misleading – although Old Aberdeen is certainly old, the area around Castlegate is older still. This part of the city was originally called Aulton, from the Gaelic for 'village by the pool', and this was anglicised in the 17th century to Old Town.

FREE **St Machar's Cathedral** CATHEDRAL
(www.stmachar.com; The Chanonry; ⌚9am-5pm Mon-Sat Apr-Oct, 10am-4pm Mon-Sat Nov-Mar) The 15th-century St Machar's Cathedral, with its massive twin towers, is a rare example of a fortified cathedral. According to legend, St Machar was ordered to establish a church where the river takes the shape of a bishop's crook, which it does just here. The cathedral is best known for its impressive **heraldic ceiling**, dating from 1520, which has 48 shields of kings, nobles, archbishops and bishops. Sunday services are held at 11am and 6pm.

Sleeping

There are clusters of B&Bs on Bon Accord St and Springbank Tce (both 400m southwest of the train station) and along Great Western Rd (the A93, a 25-minute walk southwest of the city centre. Prices tend to be lower on weekends.

Aberdeen

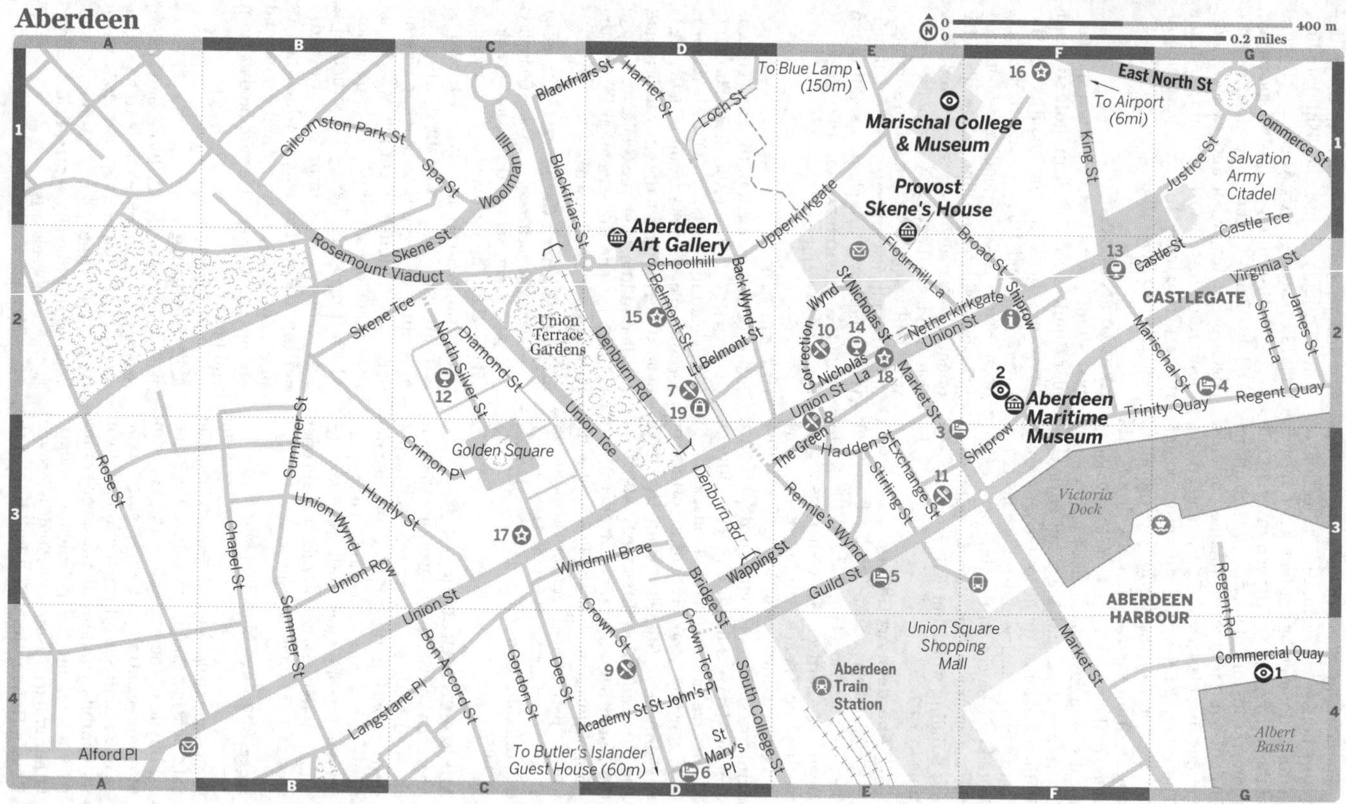
0 400 m
0 0.2 miles
East North St
To Airport (6mi)
Commerce St
Justice St
Salvation Army Citadel
Castle Tce
King St
Castle St
13
CASTLEGATE
Virginia St
James St
Shore La
Marischal St
4
Regent Quay
Trinity Quay
16
Marischal College & Museum
To Blue Lamp (150m)
Loch St
Provost Skene's House
Broad St
Shiprow
Flourmill La
Netherkirkgate
Union St
2
Aberdeen Maritime Museum
Upperkirkgate
Harriet St
Blackfriars St
Aberdeen Art Gallery
Schoolhill
Back Wynd
Belmont St
Lt Belmont St
15
7
19
St Nicholas St
Wynd
Correction
10
14
Nicholas La
18
Market St
3
Shiprow
Union St
8
The Green
Hadden St
Exchange St
Stirling St
11
Victoria Dock
ABERDEEN HARBOUR
Regent Rd
Commercial Quay
1
Albert Basin
Gilcomston Park St
Spa St
Woolman Hill
Skene St
Rosemount Viaduct
Skene Tce
North Silver St
Diamond St
12
Union Terrace Gardens
Denburn Rd
Union Tce
Golden Square
Crimon Pl
Rose St
Summer St
Union Wynd
Huntly St
17
Chapel St
Union Row
Windmill Brae
Denburn Rd
Rennie's Wynd
Wapping St
Guild St
5
Union Square Shopping Mall
Aberdeen Train Station
Market St
Union St
Bridge St
Crown St
Crown Tce
South College St
Summer St
Bon Accord St
Langstane Pl
Gordon St
Dee St
9
Academy St
St John's Pl
St Mary's Pl
To Butler's Islander Guest House (60m)
6
Alford Pl
A
B
C
D
E
F
G
1
2
3
4

Aberdeen

Top Sights

Aberdeen Art Gallery D2
Aberdeen Maritime Museum F2
Marischal College & Museum E1
Provost Skene's House E1

Sights

1 Fish Market G4
2 Provost Ross's House F2

Sleeping

3 Aberdeen Douglas Hotel E3
4 City Wharf Apartments G2
Globe Inn .... (see 12)
5 Jurys Inn E3
6 Royal Crown Guest House D4

Eating

7 Beautiful Mountain D2
8 Café 52 .... E2
9 Foyer D4
10 Moonfish Café E2
11 Musa Art Cafe E3

Drinking

12 Globe Inn C2
13 Old Blackfriars F2
14 Prince of Wales E2

Entertainment

Aberdeen Box Office .... (see 17)
15 Belmont Cinema D2
16 Lemon Tree Theatre F1
17 Music Hall C3
18 Tunnels E2

Shopping

19 One Up Records D2

TOP CHOICE City Wharf Apartments SERVICED APARTMENTS ££
(☎0845 094 2424; www.citywharfapartments.co.uk; 19-20 Regent Quay; d from £95;) You can watch the bustle of Aberdeen's commercial harbour as you eat breakfast in one of these luxury serviced apartments, complete with stylish, fully-equipped kitchen, champagne-stocked minibar and daily cleaning service. Available by the night or the week, with discounts for longer stays.

TOP CHOICE Globe Inn B&B ££
(☎01224-624258; www.the-globe-inn.co.uk; 13-15 North Silver St; s/d £65/70) This popular pub (see p880) has seven appealing and comfortable guest bedrooms upstairs, done out in dark wood with burgundy bedspreads. There's live music in the pub on weekends so it's not a place for early-to-bed types, but the price vs location factor can't be beat. No dining room, so breakfast is continental, served on a tray in your room.

Butler's Islander Guest House B&B ££
(☎01224-212411; www.butlersguesthouse.com; 122 Crown St; s £40-65, d £60-80; @) Butler's is a cosy place with a big breakfast menu that includes fresh fruit salad, kippers and kedgeree as alternatives to the traditional fry-up. It's often busy on weekdays; weekend (Friday to Sunday) rates are cheaper.

Aberdeen Douglas Hotel HOTEL £££
(☎01224-582255; www.aberdeendouglas.com; 43-45 Market St; r from £125;) You can't miss the grand Victorian façade of this historic landmark, which first opened its doors as a hotel in 1853. Now renovated, it offers classy modern rooms with polished woodwork and crisp white bed linen, and is barely a minute's walk from the train station.

Royal Crown Guest House B&B ££
(☎01224-586461; www.royalcrown.co.uk; 111 Crown St; s £35-70, d £60-80; P) The Royal Crown has eight small but nicely furnished bedrooms, and has a top location only five minutes' walk from the train station (though up a steep flight of stairs).

Aberdeen Youth Hostel HOSTEL £
(SYHA; ☎01224-646988; 8 Queen's Rd; dm £18-20; @) This hostel, set in a granite Victorian villa, is a mile west of the train station. Walk west along Union St and take the right fork along Alford (then Albyn) Pl until you reach a roundabout; Queen's Rd continues on the western side of the roundabout.

Jurys Inn HOTEL ££
(☎01224-381200; www.jurysinns.com; Union Sq, Guild St; s/d £88/96;) Stylish and comfortable new hotel right next to the train station.

Adelphi Guest House B&B ££

(☎01224-583078; www.adelphiguesthouse.com; 8 Whinhill Rd; s/d from £40/50;) 400m south from the western end of Union St.

Eating

TOP CHOICE Café 52 BISTRO ££

(☎01224-590094; www.cafe52.net; 52 The Green; mains £12-16; ⏲noon-9.30pm Mon-Sat, noon-6pm Sun;) This little haven of laid-back industrial chic – a high, narrow space lined with bare stonework, rough plaster and exposed ventilation ducts – serves some of the finest and most inventive cuisine in the northeast. Try starters such as wild game and garlic meatloaf with spiced swede chutney, or mains like roast cumin and honey pork loin with baked black pudding.

Silver Darling SEAFOOD £££

(☎01224-576229; www.silverdarlingrestaurant.co.uk; Pocra Quay, North Pier; lunch mains £10-15, dinner mains £18-27; ⏲noon-1.45pm Mon-Fri & 7-9.30pm Mon-Sat) The Silver Darling (an old Scottish nickname for herring) is housed in a former Customs office, with picture windows overlooking the sea at the entrance to Aberdeen harbour. Here you can enjoy fresh Scottish seafood prepared by a top French chef while you watch the porpoises playing in the harbour mouth. The lunch menu offers good-value gourmet delights, such as pan-fried turbot with chorizo and herb croquette; bookings are recommended.

Moonfish Café FRENCH ££

(☎01224-644166; www.moonfishcafe.co.uk; 9 Correction Wynd; 2-/3-course dinner £16/22; ⏲noon-11pm) A funky little eatery tucked away on a back street, the Moonfish menu concentrates on good value French bistro fare (two-course lunch £10) such as classic French onion soup, *moules-frites* (mussels with fries) with saffron and Pernod cream sauce, and crisp sea bass fillet with chorizo, *boudin noir* (blood sausage) and salsa verde.

Foyer FUSION ££

(☎01224-582277; www.foyerrestaurant.com; 82a Crown St; mains £10-19; ⏲11am-9.30pm Tue-Sat;) A light, airy space filled with blonde wood and bold colours, Foyer is an art gallery as well as a restaurant and is run by a charity that works against youth homelessness and unemployment. The seasonal menu is a fusion of Scottish, Mediterranean and Asian influences, with lots of good vegetarian (and gluten- or dairy-free) options. A light lunch menu is available from 11am to 4pm.

Musa Art Cafe MODERN SCOTTISH ££

(☎01224-571771; www.musaaberdeen.com; 33 Exchange St; lunch mains £6-12, mains £16-19; ⏲noon-11pm) The bright paintings on the walls match the vibrant furnishings and smart gastronomic creations at this great cafe-restaurant, set in a former church that was later used to store bananas. As well as a menu that focuses on quality local produce cooked in a quirky way – think haggis and coriander spring rolls with apricot chutney – there are Brewdog beers from Fraserburgh, and interesting music, sometimes live.

Beautiful Mountain CAFE £

(www.thebeautifulmountain.com; 11-13 Belmont St; mains £6-9; ⏲8am-4.30pm Mon-Fri, 8am-5pm Sat, 5.30-11pm Thu-Sat) This cosy cafe is squeezed into a couple of tiny rooms (seating upstairs), but serves all-day breakfasts and tasty sandwiches (smoked salmon, Thai chicken, pastrami) on sourdough, bagels, ciabatta and lots of other breads, along with exquisite espresso and consummate cappuccino.

Sand Dollar Café CAFE/BISTRO £

(www.sanddollarcafe.com; 2 Beach Esplanade; mains £4-7; ⏲9am-5pm) A cut above your usual seaside cafe – on sunny days you can sit at the wooden tables outside and share a bottle of chilled white wine, and there's a tempting menu that includes pancakes with maple syrup, homemade burgers and chocolate brownie with Orkney ice cream. An evening bistro menu (mains £11 to £20, served from 6pm Thursday to Saturday) offers steak and seafood dishes. The cafe is on the esplanade, 800m northeast of the city centre.

Drinking

Globe Inn PUB

(www.the-globe-inn.co.uk; 13-15 North Silver St) This lovely Edwardian-style pub with wood panelling, marble-topped tables and walls decorated with old musical instruments is a great place for a quiet lunchtime or afternoon drink. It serves good coffee as well as real ales and malt whiskies, and has live music (rock, blues, soul) in the evenings Friday and Saturday. And probably the poshest pub toilets in the country.

Prince of Wales PUB
(7 St Nicholas Lane) Tucked down an alley off Union St, Aberdeen's best-known pub boasts the longest bar in the city, and a great range of real ales and good-value pub grub. Quiet in the afternoons, but standing-room only in the evenings.

Old Blackfriars PUB
(www.old-blackfriars.co.uk; 52 Castlegate) One of the most attractive traditional pubs in the city, with a lovely stone and timber interior, stained-glass windows and a relaxed atmosphere – a great place for an afternoon pint.

☆ Entertainment

Cinemas

Belmont Cinema CINEMA
(www.picturehouses.co.uk; 49 Belmont St) The Belmont is a great little art-house cinema, with a lively program of cult classics, director's seasons, foreign films and mainstream movies.

Clubs & Live Music

Check out what's happening in the club and live-music scene at local record shops – try **One Up Records** (www.oneupmusic.co.uk; 17 Belmont St).

Snafu CLUB/LIVE MUSIC
(www.clubsnafu.com; 1 Union St) Aberdeen's coolest club – though admittedly there isn't much competition – cosy Snafu offers a wide range of rotating club nights and guest DJs, as well as a Tuesday night comedy club and live music gigs.

Tunnels CLUB/LIVE MUSIC
(www.thetunnels.co.uk; Carnegie's Brae) This cavernous, subterranean club – the entrance is in a road tunnel beneath Union St – is a great live music venue, with a packed program of up-and-coming Scottish bands. It also hosts regular DJ nights – check the website for the latest program.

Theatre & Concerts

You can book tickets for most concerts and other events at the **Box Office** (www.boxofficeaberdeen.com; ⏲9.30am-6pm Mon-Sat) next to the **Music Hall** (Union St), the main venue for classical music concerts.

Lemon Tree Theatre DRAMA, MUSIC
(www.boxofficeaberdeen.com; 5 West North St) An interesting program of dance, music and drama, and often has live rock, jazz and folk bands playing. There are also children's shows, ranging from comedy to drama to puppetry.

ℹ Information

Books & Beans (www.booksandbeans.co.uk; 22 Belmont St; per 15min £1; ⏲8am-6pm Mon-Sat) Internet access; also Fairtrade coffee and secondhand books.

Aberdeen Royal Infirmary (☎01224-681818; Foresterhill) Medical services. About a mile northwest of the western end of Union St.

Main post office (St Nicholas Shopping Centre, Upperkirkgate; ⏲9am-5.30pm Mon-Sat)

Union St post office (489 Union St)

Tourist office (☎01224-288828; www.aberdeen-grampian.com; 23 Union St; ⏲9am-6.30pm Mon-Sat, 10am-4pm Sun Jul & Aug, 9.30am-5pm Mon-Sat Sep-Jun). Internet access too.

ℹ Getting There & Away

AIR **Aberdeen Airport** (www.aberdeenairport.com) is at Dyce, 6 miles northwest of the city centre. There are regular flights to numerous Scottish and UK destinations, including Orkney and Shetland, and international flights to the Netherlands, Norway, Denmark and France.

Stagecoach Jet bus 727 runs regularly from Aberdeen bus station to the airport (single £1.70, 35 minutes). A taxi from the airport to the city centre takes 25 minutes and costs £15.

BOAT Car ferries from Aberdeen to Orkney (single passenger £17 to £26, single car £69 to £94, 6 hours, three or four weekly) and Shetland (single passenger £22 to £35, single car £92 to £124, 12 to 14 hours, daily) are run by **Northlink Ferries** (www.northlinkferries.co.uk). The **ferry terminal** is a short walk east of the train and bus stations.

BUS The **bus station** is next to Jurys Inn, close to the train station. National Express runs direct buses from London (£45, 12 hours) twice daily, one of them overnight. Scottish Citylink runs services to Dundee (£15, 1½ hours), Perth (£21, two hours), Edinburgh (£26, 3¼ hours) and Glasgow (£26, 4¼ hours).

TRAIN The **train station** is south of the city centre, next to the massive Union Square shopping mall. There are several trains a day from London's King's Cross to Aberdeen (£122, 7½ hours); some are direct, but most services involve a change of train at Edinburgh.

Other destinations served from Aberdeen by rail include Edinburgh (£40, 2½ hours), Glasgow

(£40, 2¾ hours), Dundee (£24, 1¼ hours) and Inverness (£25, 2¼ hours).

Getting Around

BUS The main city bus operator is **First Aberdeen** (www.firstaberdeen.com). Local fares cost from 70p to £2; pay the driver as you board the bus.

CAR For rental cars try **Arnold Clark** (01224-249159; www.arnoldclarkrental.com; Girdleness Rd) or **Enterprise Car Hire** (01224-642642; www.enterprise.co.uk; 80 Skene Sq).

Around Aberdeen

STONEHAVEN

POP 9600

Originally a small fishing village, Stonehaven has been the county town of Kincardineshire since 1600 and is now a thriving, family-friendly seaside resort. There's a **tourist office** (01569-762806; 66 Allardice St; 10am-7pm Mon-Sat, 1-5.30pm Sun Jul & Aug, 10am-1pm & 2-5.30pm Mon-Sat Jun & Sep, 10am-1pm & 2-5pm Mon-Sat Apr, May & Oct) near Market Sq in the town centre.

From the lane beside the tourist office, a boardwalk leads south along the shoreline to the picturesque cliff-bound **harbour**, where you'll find a couple of appealing pubs and the town's oldest building, the **Tolbooth**, built about 1600 by the Earl Marischal. It now houses a small **museum** (admission free; 10am-noon & 2-5pm Mon & Thu-Sat, 2-5pm Wed & Sun) and a restaurant.

A pleasant, 15-minute walk along the cliff tops south of the harbour leads to the spectacular ruins of **Dunnottar Castle** (www.dunnottarcastle.co.uk; adult/child £5/1; 9am-6pm daily Easter-Oct, 10.30am-dusk Fri-Mon Nov-Easter), spread out across a grassy promontory rising 50m above the sea. As dramatic a film set as any director could wish for, it provided the backdrop for Franco Zeffirelli's *Hamlet,* starring Mel Gibson. The original fortress was built in the 9th century; the keep is the most substantial remnant, but the drawing room (restored in 1926) is more interesting.

A recent makeover with bare timber, slate and dove-grey paintwork has given the popular harbour-side pub **Marine Hotel** (www.marinehotelstonehaven.co.uk; 9-10 The Shore; mains £8-13; food served noon-2.30pm & 5.30-9pm Mon-Fri, noon-9pm Sat & Sun) a boutique look; the bar has half a dozen real ales on tap, including Deuchars IPA and Timothy Taylor, and a bar meals menu that includes fresh seafood specials.

Stonehaven is 15 miles south of the city of Aberdeen and is served by a number of frequent **buses** travelling between Aberdeen (45 minutes, hourly) and Dundee (1½ hours). **Trains** to Dundee are faster (£12, 55 minutes, hourly) and offer a more scenic journey.

Deeside

The valley of the **River Dee** – often called **Royal Deeside** because of the royal family's long association with the area – stretches west from Aberdeen to Braemar, closely paralleled by the A93 road. From Deeside north to Strathdon is serious castle country – there are more examples of fanciful Scottish Baronial architecture here than anywhere else in the country.

BALLATER

POP 1450

The attractive little village of Ballater owes its 18th-century origins to the curative waters of nearby Pannanich Springs (now bottled commercially as Deeside Natural Mineral Water) and its prosperity to nearby Balmoral Castle.

When Queen Victoria travelled to Balmoral Castle she would alight from the royal train at Ballater's **Old Royal Station** (Station Sq; admission £2; 9am-6pm Jul & Aug, 10am-5pm Sep-Jun). The station has been beautifully restored and now houses the tourist office, a cafe and a museum with a replica of Victoria's royal coach. Note the crests on the shop fronts along the main street proclaiming 'By Royal Appointment' – the village is a major supplier of provisions to Balmoral.

You can hire bikes from **CycleHighlands** (www.cyclehighlands.com; The Pavilion, Victoria Rd; per day £16; 9am-6pm), who also offer guided bike rides and advice on local trails, and **Cabin Fever** (Station Sq; per 2hr £8; 9am-6pm), who can also arrange pony-trekking, quad-biking, clay-pigeon shooting or canoeing.

The **tourist office** (01339-755306; Station Sq; 9am-6pm Jul & Aug, 10am-5pm Sep-Jun) is in the Old Royal Station.

Bus 201 runs from Aberdeen to Ballater (£9, 1¾ hours, hourly Monday to Saturday, six on Sunday) via Crathes Castle, and continues to Braemar (30 minutes) every two hours.

BALMORAL CASTLE

Eight miles west of Ballater lies **Balmoral Castle** (www.balmoralcastle.com; adult/child £8.70/4.60; ⏲10am-5pm Apr-Jul, last admission 4pm), the Queen's Highland holiday home, screened from the road by a thick curtain of trees. Built for Queen Victoria in 1855 as a private residence for the royal family, it kicked off the revival of the Scottish Baronial style of architecture that characterises so many of Scotland's 19th-century country houses.

The admission fee includes an interesting and well thought out audioguide, but the tour is very much an outdoor one through garden and grounds; as for the castle itself, only the ballroom, which displays a collection of Landseer paintings and royal silver, is open to the public. Don't expect to see the Queen's private quarters! The main attraction is learning about Highland estate management, rather than royal revelations. Guided tours are available on Saturdays from October to December – check the website for details.

The massive, pointy-topped mountain that looms to the south of Balmoral is **Lochnagar** (1155m), immortalised in verse by Lord Byron, who spent his childhood years in Aberdeenshire:

> England, thy beauties are tame and domestic
> To one who has roamed o'er the mountains afar.
> O! for the crags that are wild and majestic:
> The steep frowning glories of dark Lochnagar.

Balmoral is beside the A93 at Crathie and can be reached on the Aberdeen to Braemar bus.

BRAEMAR

POP 400

Braemar is a pretty little village with a grand location on a broad plain ringed by mountains where the Dee valley and Glen Clunie meet. In winter this is one of the coldest places in the country – temperatures as low as minus 29°C have been recorded – and during spells of severe cold hungry deer wander the streets looking for a bite to eat. Braemar is an excellent base for hill walking, and there's skiing at nearby Glenshee.

Just north of the village, turreted **Braemar Castle** (www.braemarcastle.co.uk; adult/child £5/3; ⏲11am-6pm Sat & Sun, also Wed Jul & Aug) dates from 1628 and served as a government garrison after the 1745 Jacobite rebellion. It was taken over by the local community in 2007, and now offers guided tours of the historic castle apartments.

Five miles west of Braemar is the tiny settlement of Inverey. Numerous mountain walks start from here, including the adventurous walk through the **Lairig Ghru** pass to Aviemore (for experienced and well-equipped hikers only).

A good short walk (3 miles, 1½ hours) begins at the **Linn of Quoich** – a waterfall that thunders through a narrow slot in the rocks. Head uphill on a footpath on the east bank of the stream, past the impressive rock scenery of the **Punch Bowl** (a giant pothole), to a modern bridge that spans the narrow gorge and return via an unsurfaced road on the far bank.

BRAEMAR GATHERING

There are Highland games in many towns and villages throughout the summer, but the best known is the **Braemar Gathering** (www.braemargathering.org), which takes place on the first Saturday in September. It's a major occasion, organised every year since 1817 by the Braemar Royal Highland Society. Events include highland dancing, pipers, tug-of-war, a hill race up Morrone, tossing the caber, hammer- and stone-throwing and the long jump. International athletes are among those who take part.

Sleeping

TOP CHOICE **Rucksacks Bunkhouse** BUNKHOUSE £ (☎01339-741517; 15 Mar Rd; bothy £7, dm £12-15, tw £36; P @) An appealing cottage bunkhouse, with comfy dorm and cheaper beds in an alpine-style bothy (shared sleeping platform for 10 people, bring your own sleeping bag). Extras including a drying room (for wet weather gear), laundry and even a sauna (£10 an hour). Nonguests are welcome to use the internet (£3 per hour, open 10.30am to 4.30pm), laundry and even the showers (£2), and the friendly owner is a fount of knowledge about the local area.

Craiglea B&B ££
(☎01339-741641; www.craigleabraemar.com; Hillside Dr; r £70; P) Craiglea is a homely B&B set in a pretty stone-built cottage with three en-suite bedrooms. Vegetarian breakfasts are available and the owners can give advice on local walks.

Braemar Youth Hostel HOSTEL £
(SYHA; ☎01339-741659; 21 Glenshee Rd; dm £16-17; ⏲Jan-Oct; @) This hostel is housed in a grand former shooting lodge just south of the village centre on the A93 to Perth; it has a comfy lounge with pool table, and a barbecue in the garden.

St Margarets B&B ££
(☎01339-741697; 13 School Rd; s/tw £32/54; wifi) Grab this place if you can, but there's only one room – a twin with a serious sunflower theme. The genuine warmth of the welcome is heart-warming.

Invercauld Caravan Club Site CAMPSITE £
(☎01339-741373; tent sites £10-15; ⏲late Dec-Oct) Good camping here, or you can **camp wild** (no facilities) along the minor road on the east bank of the Clunie Water, 3 miles south of Braemar.

Eating

TOP CHOICE **Gathering Place** BISTRO ££
(☎01339-741234; www.the-gathering-place.co.uk; 9 Invercauld Rd; mains £15-18; ⏲dinner Tue-Sun) This bright and breezy bistro is an unexpected corner of culinary excellence, with a welcoming dining room and sunny conservatory, tucked below the main road junction at the entrance to the village.

Taste CAFE £
(www.taste-braemar.co.uk; Airlie House, Mar Rd; mains £3-5; ⏲10am-5pm Thu-Mon; family) Taste is a relaxed little cafe with armchairs in the window, serving soups, snacks, coffee and cakes.

BLAZE YOUR OWN WHISKY TRAIL

Visiting a distillery can be memorable, but only hardcore malthounds will want to go to more than two or three. Some are great to visit; others are depressingly corporate. The following are some recommendations.

» **Aberlour** (www.aberlour.com; tours £10; ⏲10.30am & 2pm daily Easter-Oct, Mon-Fri by appointment Nov-Mar) has an excellent, detailed tour with a proper tasting session. It's on the main street in Aberlour.

» **Glenfarclas** (www.glenfarclas.co.uk; admission £3.50; ⏲10am-4pm Mon-Fri Oct-Mar, 10am-5pm Mon-Fri Apr-Sep, plus 10am-4pm Sat Jul-Sep) Small, friendly and independent, Glenfarclas is 5 miles south of Aberlour on the Grantown road. The last tour leaves 90 minutes before closing. The in-depth Ambassador's Tour (Fridays only) is £15.

» **Glenfiddich** (www.glenfiddich.com; admission free; ⏲9.30am-4.30pm Mon-Fri year-round, 9.30am-4.30pm Sat & noon-4.30pm Sun Easter-mid-Oct) is big and busy, but handiest for Dufftown and foreign languages are available. The standard tour starts with an overblown video, but it's fun, informative and free. An in-depth Connoisseur's Tour (£20) must be prebooked. Glenfiddich kept single malt alive during the dark years.

» **Macallan** (www.themacallan.com; standard tours £5; ⏲9.30am-4.30pm Mon-Sat Apr-Oct, ring for winter hours) Excellent sherry-casked malt. Several small-group tours are available (last tour at 3.30pm), including an expert one (£15); all should be prebooked. Lovely location 2 miles northwest of Craigellachie.

» **Speyside Cooperage** (www.speysidecooperage.co.uk; admission £3.30; ⏲9am-4pm Mon-Fri) is a spot where you can see the fascinating art of barrel-making in action. It's a mile from Craigellachie on the Dufftown road.

» **Spirit of Speyside** (www.spiritofspeyside.com) is a bi-annual whisky festival in Dufftown with a number of great events. It takes place in early May and late September; both accommodation and events should be booked well ahead.

Getting There & Away

Bus 201 runs from Aberdeen to Braemar (£9, 2¼ hours, eight daily Monday to Saturday, five on Sunday). The 50-mile drive from Perth to Braemar is beautiful, but there's no public transport on this route.

Moray

The old county of Moray (*murr*-ree), centred on the county town of Elgin, lies at the heart of an ancient Celtic earldom and is famed for its mild climate and rich farmland – the barley fields of the 19th century once provided the raw material for the Speyside whisky distilleries, one of the region's main attractions for present-day visitors.

ELGIN

POP 21,000

Elgin's been the provincial capital of Moray for over eight centuries and was an important town in medieval times. Dominated by a hilltop monument to the 5th duke of Gordon, Elgin's main attraction is its impressive ruined cathedral, where the tombs of the duke's ancestors lie.

Sights

Elgin Cathedral CATHEDRAL

(HS; King St; adult/child £4.70/2.80, joint ticket with Spynie Palace £6.20/3.70; ⌚9.30am-5.30pm Apr-Sep, 9.30am-4.30pm Sat-Wed Oct-Mar) Many people think that the ruins of Elgin Cathedral, known as the 'lantern of the north', are the most beautiful and evocative in Scotland. Consecrated in 1224, the cathedral was burned down in 1390 by the infamous Wolf of Badenoch, the illegitimate son of Robert II, following his excommunication by the Bishop of Moray. The octagonal chapter house is the finest in the country.

Elgin Museum MUSEUM

(www.elginmuseum.org.uk; 1 High St; adult/child £4/1.50; ⌚10am-5pm Mon-Fri, 11am-4pm Sat Apr-Oct) Palaeontologists and Pict lovers will enjoy Elgin Museum, where the highlights are its collections of fossil fish and Pictish carved stones.

Sleeping & Eating

Croft Guesthouse B&B ££

(☎01343-546004; www.thecroftelgin.co.uk; 10 Institution Rd; s/d from £55/70; P) The Croft offers a taste of Victorian high society, set in a spacious mansion built for a local lawyer back in 1848. The house is filled with period features – check out the cast-iron and tile fireplaces – and the three large bedrooms are equipped with easy chairs and crisp bed linen.

Southbank Guest House B&B ££

(☎01343-547132; www.southbank-guesthouse.co.uk; 36 Academy St; s/d from £50/75; P) The family-run, 12-room Southbank is set in a large Georgian town house in a quiet street south of Elgin's centre, just five minutes' walk from the cathedral and other sights.

Mezzo BISTRO ££

(cnr Hay & South Sts; mains £8-15; ⌚lunch & dinner Mon-Sat, dinner Sun) This lively bar and restaurant is part of the Mansefield Hotel complex, and serves tasty bistro fare, including pasta, pizza, burgers and various vegetarian dishes.

Getting There & Away

BUS Elgin is a stop on the hourly Stagecoach bus 10 service between Inverness (£8, one hour) and Aberdeen (£10, two hours).

TRAIN There are frequent trains from Elgin to Aberdeen (£15, 1½ hours) and Inverness (£10, 45 minutes).

DUFFTOWN

POP 1450

Rome may be built on seven hills, but Dufftown's built on seven stills, say the locals. Founded in 1817 by James Duff, 4th earl of Fife, Dufftown is 17 miles south of Elgin and lies at the heart of the Speyside whisky-distilling region.

With seven working distilleries nearby, Dufftown has been dubbed Scotland's malt whisky capital. Ask at the tourist office for a **Malt Whisky Trail** (www.maltwhiskytrail.com) booklet, a self-guided tour around the seven stills plus the Speyside Cooperage.

Sleeping & Eating

Davaar B&B B&B ££

(☎01340-820464; www.davaardufftown.co.uk; 17 Church St; s/d from £40/60) Just along the street opposite the tourist office, Davaar is a sturdy Victorian villa with three smallish but comfy rooms; the breakfast menu is superb, offering the option of Portsoy kippers instead of the traditional fry-up (which uses eggs from the owners' own chickens).

WORTH A TRIP

DUFF HOUSE

Duff House (www.duffhouse.org.uk; adult/child £6.55/5.45; ⏲11am-5pm Apr-Oct, 11am-4pm Thu-Sun Nov-Mar) is an impressive baroque mansion on the southern edge of Banff (upstream from the bridge, and across from the tourist office), 35 miles east of Elgin. Built between 1735 and 1740 as the seat of the earls of Fife, it was designed by William Adam and bears similarities to that Adam masterpiece, Hopetoun House. Since being gifted to the town in 1906 it has served as a hotel, a hospital and a POW camp, but is now an art gallery. One of Scotland's hidden gems, it houses a superb collection of Scottish and European art, including important works by Raeburn and Gainsborough.

La Faisanderie FRENCH/SCOTTISH **£££**
(☎01340-821273; The Square; mains £18-21; ⏲noon-1.30pm & 5.30-8.30pm) This is a great place to eat, run by a local chef who shoots much of his own game, guaranteeing freshness. The interior is decorated in French auberge style with a cheerful mural and pheasants hiding in every corner. The set menus (three-course lunch £18.50, four-course dinner £32) won't disappoint, but you can order à la carte as well.

Information

The **tourist office** (☎01340-820501; ⏲10am-1pm & 2-5.30pm Mon-Sat, 11am-3pm Sun Easter-Oct) is in the clock tower in the main square; the adjoining museum contains some interesting local items.

Getting There & Away

Buses link Dufftown to Elgin (50 minutes, hourly), Huntly, Aberdeen and Inverness.

On summer weekends, you can take a train from Aberdeen or Inverness to Keith, and then ride the **Keith and Dufftown Railway** (www.keith-dufftown-railway.co.uk) to Dufftown.

Inverness, the Highlands & the Northern Islands

Includes »

INVERNESS & THE GREAT GLEN 890
Inverness.......... 890
Loch Ness......... 895
THE CAIRNGORMS..897
CENTRAL WESTERN HIGHLANDS........902
Glen Coe.......... 902
Fort William........ 903
CAITHNESS........910
NORTH & NORTHWEST COAST.............913
ISLE OF SKYE......920
OUTER HEBRIDES..927
ORKNEY ISLANDS..942
SHETLAND ISLANDS...........956

Best Places to Eat

» Lime Tree (p904)

» Cross (p901)

» Albannach (p916)

» Three Chimneys (p926)

Best Places to Stay

» West Manse (p955)

» Shetland Lighthouse Cottages (p961)

» Rocpool Reserve (p890)

» Mackays Hotel (p911)

Why Go?

Scotland's vast melancholy soul is here, an epic land whose stark beauty indelibly imprints upon the hearts of those who see it. Mist, peat, whisky, heather...and long, sun-blessed summer evenings that repay the many days of horizontal drizzle.

The region's capital, Inverness, is backed by the craggy Cairngorms, which draw skiers and walkers to its slopes. Further north, ancient stones are testament left by prehistoric builders in Caithness, and across the water on the magical Orkney and remote Shetland Islands – where wind keeps the vegetation at a minimum – isolation makes it a haven for sea birds and more.

The most epic scenery – you really need an orchestra to do it justice – is in the far northwest, and it continues onto Skye, where the mighty Cuillin Ridge towers jaggedly in the setting sun. Beyond here, the Outer Hebrides offer the nation's best beaches and a glimpse of traditional life.

When to Go

In January hit the Cairngorms for skiing or the Shetland Islands for Up Helly Aa, a fiery Viking festival. The long, long evenings in June up here bathe heartachingly sublime landscapes in a dreamlike light. September is the ideal time for hiking and hill walking – midges are dying off, but the weather is still reasonably good.

Inverness, the Highlands & Northern Islands Highlights

1. Hiking among the hills, lochs and forests of beautiful **Glen Affric** (p894)
2. Dipping your toes in the water at some of the world's most beautiful beaches on **Harris** (p939)
3. Shouldering the challenge of the **Cuillin Hills** (p923), whose rugged silhouettes brood over the skyscape of Skye.
4. Picking your jaw up off the floor as you marvel at the epic scenery between **Durness** and **Ullapool** (p915)
5. Relaxing in postcard-pretty **Plockton** (p919), where the Highlands meet the Caribbean
6. Launching into a **sea-kayak** to explore the otter-rich waters of the Outer Hebrides (p927)
7. Shaking your head in astonishment at extraordinary **Skara Brae** (p949) and **Maes Howe** (p948), prehistoric perfection that predates the pyramids
8. Island-hopping Orkney's **Northern Islands** (p953), where crystal azure waters lap against glittering white-sand beaches
9. Capering with puffins, spotting offshore orcas, or dodging dive-bombing skuas in the Shetland Islands' **nature reserves** (p964)

0 40 km
0 20 miles
Westray
Papa Westray
North Ronaldsay
Pierowall
Beltane
Northwall
Rapness
Sanday
Kettletoft
Northern Islands 8
Eday
Rousay
Papa Stronsay
Orkney Islands
Birsay
Backaland
Whitehall
Evie
Stronsay
Skara Brae 7
Auskerry
To Shetland Islands
Maes Howe 7
Stromness
Kirkwall
Mainland
North Sea
Moaness
Deerness
Copinsay
Hoy
Lyness
St Margaret's Hope
South Ronaldsay
Burwick
Pentland Firth
Dunnet Head
Scrabster
Duncansby Head
Durness
Sandwood Bay
4
Melvich
Castle of Mey
John O'Groats
Thurso
Coldbackie
Bettyhill
Sinclair's Bay
Kinlochbervie
Tongue
Watten
Wick
Tarbet
Laxford Bridge
Handa
Naver
Strathy
Halladale
Scourie
Thurso
Achavanich
Eddrachillis Bay
Lybster
Point of Stoer
Kylesku
Kinbrace
Dunbeath
North Sea
Clachtoll
Achmelvich
Lochinver
Helmsdale
Loch Shin
Brora
Helmsdale
Knockan
Tirry
Oykel
Achiltibuie
Ruhie
Lairg
Dunrobin Castle
Golspie
Gruinard Bay
Invercassley
Dornoch Firth
4 Ullapool
Bonar Bridge
Drumchork
Ardgay
Dornoch
Dundonnell
Midtown
Portmahomack
Tain
Gairloch
Moray Firth
Invergordon
Loch Maree
Cromarty Firth
Cromarty
Kinlochewe
Garve
Elgin
Dingwall
Fort George
Nairn
Torridon
Achnasheen
Brodie Castle
Fortrose
Shieldaig
Carron
Orrin
Cawdor Castle
Inverness
Culloden
Kishorn
Struy
Glass
Lochcarron
Findhorn
Grantown-on-Spey
5 Plockton
Cannich
Drumnadrochit
1
Affric
Urquhart Castle
Carrbridge
Glen Affric
Monadhliath Mountains
Glenelg
Invermoriston
Foyers
Cairngorm Mountains
Aviemore
Arnisdale
Fort Augustus
Killin
Kincraig
Tarff
Cairngorms National Park
Loch Quoich
Inverie
Invergarry
Kingussie
Newtonmore
Loch Lochy
Spey
Strathan
Loch Arkaig
Achnacarry
Pattack
Glenfinnan
Grampian Mountains
Roy Bridge
Dalwhinnie
Loch Eil
Fort William
Ben Nevis
Garry
Strontian
Kinlochleven
Pitlochry
Loch Linnhe
Glencoe

INVERNESS & THE GREAT GLEN

Inverness, one of the fastest growing towns in Britain, is the capital of the Highlands. It's a transport hub and jumping-off point for the central, western and northern Highlands, the Moray Firth coast and the Great Glen.

The Great Glen is a geological fault running in an arrow-straight line across Scotland from Fort William to Inverness. The glaciers of the last ice age eroded a deep trough along the fault line that is now filled by a series of lochs – Linnhe, Lochy, Oich and Ness. The glen has always been an important communication route – General George Wade built a military road along the southern side of Loch Ness in the early 18th century, and in 1822 the various lochs were linked by the Caledonian Canal to create a cross-country waterway.

Inverness

POP 55,000

Inverness, the primary city and shopping centre of the Highlands, has a great location astride the River Ness at the northern end of the Great Glen. In summer it overflows with visitors intent on monster hunting at nearby Loch Ness, but it's worth a visit in its own right for a stroll along the picturesque River Ness and a cruise on the Moray Firth in search of its famous bottlenose dolphins.

Sights & Activities

Ness Islands PARK

Save the indoor sights for a rainy day – the main attraction in Inverness is a leisurely stroll along the river to the Ness Islands. Planted with mature Scots pine, fir, beech and sycamore, and linked to the river banks and each other by elegant Victorian footbridges, the islands make an appealing picnic spot. They're a 20-minute walk south of the castle – head upstream on either side of the river (the start of the Great Glen Way), and return on the opposite bank. On the way you'll pass the red-sandstone towers of **St Andrew's Cathedral** (11 Ardross St), dating from 1869, and the modern Eden Court Theatre, which hosts regular art exhibits, both on the west bank.

Tours

Moray Firth Cruises BOAT

(01463-717900; www.inverness-dolphin-cruises.co.uk; Shore St Quay, Shore St; 10.30am-4.30pm Mar-Oct) Offers 1½-hour wildlife cruises (adult/child £14/10) to look for dolphins, seals and bird life. Follow the signs to Shore St Quay from the far end of Chapel St or catch the free shuttle bus that leaves from the tourist office 15 minutes before sailings (which depart every 1½ hours). In July and August there are also departures at 6pm.

Jacobite Cruises BOAT

(01463-233999; www.jacobite.co.uk; Glenurquhart Rd) Cruise boats depart at 10.35am and 1.35pm from Tomnahurich Bridge for a 3½-hour trip along Loch Ness, including visits to Urquhart Castle and Loch Ness 2000 Monster Exhibition (adult/child £26/20 including admission fees). You can buy tickets at the tourist office and catch a free minibus to the boat.

John O'Groats Ferries BUS, FERRY

(01955-611353; www.jogferry.co.uk; departs 7.30am) Daily tours (lasting 13½ hours; adult/child £57/28.50) are on offer from May to September, by bus and passenger ferry from Inverness bus station to Orkney.

Sleeping

Inverness has a good range of backpacker accommodation, and there are lots of guest houses and B&Bs along Old Edinburgh Rd and Ardconnel St on the east side of the river, and on Kenneth St and Fairfield Rd on the west bank.

TOP CHOICE **Trafford Bank** B&B ££

(01463-241414; www.traffordbankguesthouse.co.uk; 96 Fairfield Rd; s/d from £85/110; P) Lots of word-of-mouth rave reviews for Trafford Bank, an elegant Victorian villa that was once home to a bishop, just a mitre-toss from the Caledonian Canal and only 10 minutes' walk west from the city centre. The luxurious rooms include fresh flowers and fruit, bathrobes and fluffy towels – ask for the Tartan Room, with its wrought-iron king-size bed and Victorian roll-top bath.

TOP CHOICE **Rocpool Reserve** BOUTIQUE HOTEL £££

(01463-240089; www.rocpool.com; Culduthel Rd; s/d from £160/195; P) Boutique chic meets the Highlands in this slick and sophisticated little hotel, where an elegant Georgian exterior conceals an oasis of contemporary cool. A gleaming white entrance hall lined with contemporary art leads to designer rooms in shades of chocolate, cream and coffee; expect lots of high-tech gadgetry in the more expensive rooms, ranging from iPod docks to balcony hot tubs with aquavision TV. A new restaurant by Albert Roux completes the package.

Ardconnel House B&B ££
(01463-240455; www.ardconnel-inverness.co.uk; 21 Ardconnel St; per person from £35;) The six-room Ardconnel is another of our favourites – a terraced Victorian house with comfortable en-suite rooms, a dining room with crisp white table linen, and a breakfast menu that includes Vegemite for homesick Antipodeans. Kids under 10 not allowed.

Ach Aluinn B&B ££
(01463-230127; www.achaluinn.com; 27 Fairfield Rd; per person £25-35; P) This large, detached Victorian house is bright and homely, and offers all you might want from a guest house – private bathroom, TV, reading lights, comfy beds with two pillows each, and an excellent breakfast. Five minutes' walk west from city centre.

MacRae Guest House B&B ££
(01463-243658; joycemacrae@hotmail.com; 24 Ness Bank; s/d from £45/64; P[]) This pretty, flower-bedecked Victorian house on the eastern bank of the river has smart, tastefully decorated bedrooms – one is wheelchair accessible – and vegetarian breakfasts are available. Minimum two-night bookings in July and August.

Bazpackers Backpackers Hotel HOSTEL £
(01463-717663; 4 Culduthel Rd; dm/tw £14/38; @) This may be Inverness's smallest hostel (30 beds), but it's hugely popular – it's a friendly, quiet place with a convivial lounge centred on a wood-burning stove, a small garden and great views. Though the dorms can be a bit cramped, the showers are great.

Inverness Millburn Youth Hostel HOSTEL £
(SYHA; 01463-231771; Victoria Dr; dm £18.50; Apr-Dec; P@) Inverness' modern 166-bed hostel is 10 minutes' walk northeast of the city centre. With its comfy beds and flashy stainless-steel kitchen, some reckon it's the best hostel in the country. Booking is essential, especially at Easter, and in July and August.

Bluebell House B&B ££
(01463-238201; www.bluebell-house.com; 31 Kenneth St; r per person £30-45; P) Warm and welcoming hosts, top breakfasts, close to city centre.

Eating

TOP CHOICE **Contrast Brasserie** BRASSERIE ££
(01463-227889; www.glenmoristontownhouse.com/contrast; 22 Ness Bank; mains £10-19; noon-2.30pm & 5-10pm) Book early for what we think is the best restaurant in Inverness – a dining room that drips designer style, smiling professional staff, a jug of water brought to your table without asking, and truly delicious food. Try mussels with Thai red curry, wild mushroom risotto, or pork belly with glazed walnuts and watercress; 10 out of 10. And at £10 for a two-course lunch, the value is incredible.

TOP CHOICE **Café 1** BISTRO ££
(01463-226200; www.cafe1.net; 75 Castle St; mains £10-20; noon-2pm & 5.30-9.30pm Mon-Sat) Café 1 is a friendly and appealing little bistro with candle-lit tables amid elegant blonde-wood and wrought-iron decor. There is an international menu based on quality Scottish produce, from succulent Aberdeen Angus steaks to crisp sea bass with chilli, lime and soy sauce. Lunch and early bird menu (two course for £9.50) is served noon to 6.45pm weekdays, and noon to 3pm Saturday.

Rocpool MEDITERRANEAN ££
(01463-717274; www.rocpoolrestaurant.com; 1 Ness Walk; mains £13-18; noon-2.30pm & 5.45-10pm) Lots of polished wood, navy-blue leather and crisp white linen lend a nautical air to this relaxing bistro, which offers a Mediterranean-influenced menu that makes the most of quality Scottish produce, especially seafood. The two-course lunch (noon to 2.30pm Monday to Saturday) is £12.

Mustard Seed MODERN SCOTTISH ££
(01463-220220; www.mustardseedrestaurant.co.uk; 16 Fraser St; mains £12-16; noon-10pm) This bright and bustling bistro brings a dash of big-city style to Inverness. The menu changes weekly, but focuses on Scottish and French cuisine with a modern twist. Grab a table on the upstairs balcony if you can – it's the best outdoor lunch spot in Inverness, with a great view across the river. And a two-course lunch for £6 – yes, that's right – is hard to beat.

Inverness

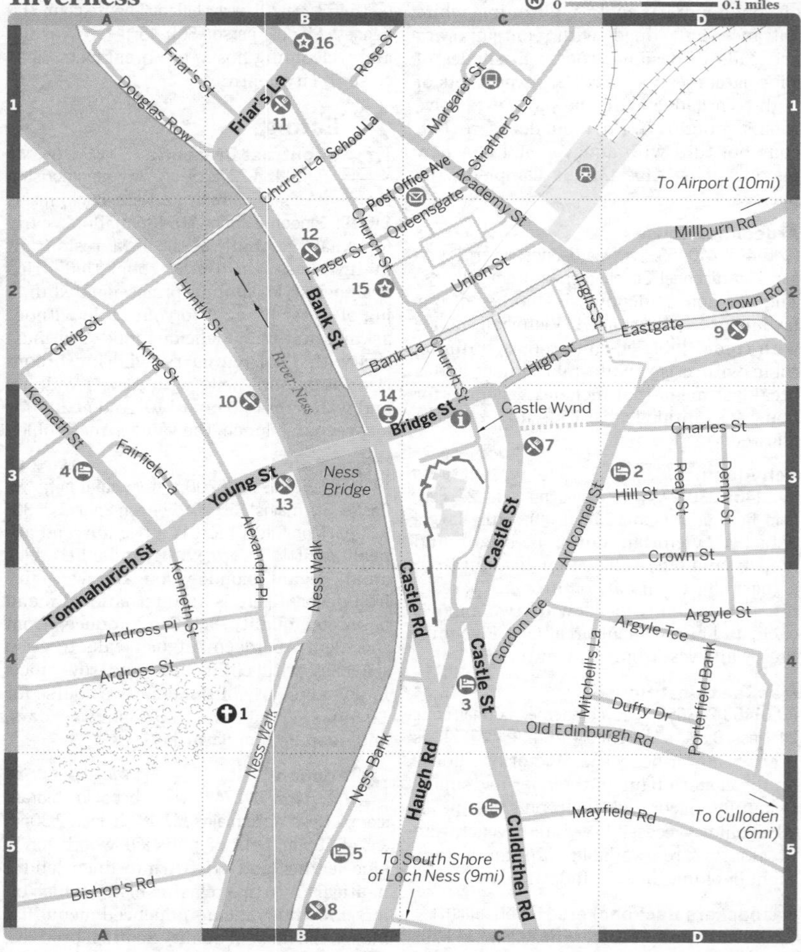

Délices de Bretagne FRENCH £
(6 Stephen's Brae; mains £3-7; ⏲9am-5pm Mon-Sat, 10am-5pm Sun) This cafe brings a little taste of France to the Highlands, with its art nouveau decor and a menu of tasty *galettes* (savoury pancakes), crepes, Breton cider and excellent coffee.

Kitchen MODERN SCOTTISH ££
(☎01436-259119; www.kitchenrestaurant.co.uk; 15 Huntly St; mains £12-16; ⏲noon-3pm & 5.30-10pm) This spectacular glass-fronted restaurant is under the same management as the Mustard Seed, and offers a similar menu with a view of the river.

Leakey's CAFE £
(Greyfriars Hall, Church St; mains £3-5; ⏲10am-5.30pm Mon-Sat) Cafe in secondhand bookshop.

Drinking

TOP CHOICE **Clachnaharry Inn** PUB
(www.clachnaharryinn.co.uk; 17-19 High St, Clachnaharry) Just over a mile northwest of the city centre, on the bank of the Caledonian Canal just off the A862, this is a delightful old coaching inn (with beer garden out back) serving an excellent range of real ales and good pub grub.

Inverness

Sights

1 St Andrew's Cathedral B4

Sleeping

2 Ardconnel House D3
3 Bazpackers Backpackers Hotel C4
4 Bluebell House A3
5 MacRae House B5
6 Rocpool Reserve C5

Eating

7 Café 1 .... C3
8 Contrast Brasserie B5
9 Délices de Bretagne D2
10 Kitchen B3
11 Leakey's B1
12 Mustard Seed B2
13 Rocpool B3

Drinking

14 Johnny Foxes B3

Entertainment

15 Hootananny B2
16 Ironworks B1

Johnny Foxes BAR
(www.johnnyfoxes.co.uk; 26 Bank St) Stuck beneath the ugliest building on the riverfront, Johnny Foxes is a big and boisterous Irish bar, with a wide range of food served all day and live music nightly. Part of the premises, The Den, is now a smart cocktail bar.

✩ Entertainment

Hootananny LIVE MUSIC
(www.hootananny.com; 67 Church St) Hootananny is the city's best live-music venue, with traditional folk and/or rock music sessions nightly, including big-name bands from all over Scotland (and, indeed, the world). The bar is well stocked with a range of beers from the local Black Isle Brewery.

Ironworks LIVE MUSIC, COMEDY
(www.ironworksvenue.com; 122 Academy St) With live bands (rock, pop, tribute) and comedy shows two or three times a week, the Ironworks is the town's main venue for big-name acts.

Information

ClanLAN (22 Baron Taylor St; 10am-8pm Mon-Fri, 11am-8pm Sat, noon-5pm Sun) Internet access £1 per 20 minutes.

New City Laundrette (17 Young St; 8am-8pm Mon-Fri, to 6pm Sat, 10am-4pm Sun) Charges £3 per load, £1.40 to dry. Internet access £1 per 20 minutes.

Tourist office (01436-234353; www.visithighlands.com; Castle Wynd; 9am-6pm Mon-Sat & 9.30am-5pm Sun Jul & Aug, 9am-5pm Mon-Sat & 10am-4pm Sun Jun, Sep & Oct, 9am-5pm Mon-Sat Apr & May) Bureau de change and accommodation booking service; also sells tickets for tours and cruises. Internet access £1 per 20 minutes. Openings hours limited November to March.

Getting There & Away

Air

Inverness airport (www.hial.co.uk/inverness-airport) At Dalcross, 10 miles east of the city. There are scheduled flights to London, Belfast, Stornoway, Benbecula, Orkney, Shetland and several other British airports. For more information, see p1066.

Stagecoach Jet (www.stagecoachbus.com) Buses run from the airport to Inverness bus station (£3, 20 minutes, every 30 minutes). A taxi costs around £15.

Bus

National Express (www.nationalexpress.com) operates a direct overnight bus from London to Inverness (£45, 13 hours, one daily), with more frequent services requiring a change at Glasgow.

Citylink (www.citylink.co.uk) has connections to Glasgow (£26, 3½ to 4½ hours, hourly), Edinburgh (£26, 3½ to 4½ hours, hourly), Fort William (£11, two hours, five daily), Ullapool (£9, 1½ hours, two daily except Sunday), Portree (£17, 3½ hours, five daily) on the Isle of Skye and Thurso (£18, 3½ hours, two daily).

If you book far enough in advance, **Megabus** (www.megabus.com) offers fares from as little as £5 for buses from Inverness to Glasgow and Edinburgh, and £15 to London.

Buses to Aberdeen (3¾ hours, hourly) and Aviemore (1¾ hours, three daily Monday to Friday) are operated by Stagecoach.

Train

There is one direct train daily from London to Inverness (£99, eight hours); others require a change at Edinburgh. There are several direct trains a day from Glasgow (£55, 3½ hours), Edinburgh (£55, 3¼ hours) and Aberdeen (£25, 2¼ hours), and three daily Monday to Saturday (one or two on Sunday) to Thurso and Wick (£16, four hours).

The line from Inverness to Kyle of Lochalsh (£18, 2½ hours, four daily Monday to Saturday, two Sunday) provides one of Britain's great scenic train journeys.

Getting Around

Bicycle

Great Glen Cycle Hire (☎07752 102700; www.greatglencyclehire.com; 18 Harbour Rd) Rent mountain bikes for £20 a day.

Bus

City services and buses to places around Inverness, including the Culloden battlefield, are operated by Stagecoach. An Inverness City Dayrider ticket costs £3.20 and gives unlimited travel for a day on buses throughout the city.

Car

Sharp's Vehicle Rental (☎01436-236694; www.sharpsreliablewrecks.co.uk; Inverness train station) Has rates starting at £30 per day.

Around Inverness

CULLODEN BATTLEFIELD

The Battle of Culloden in 1746, the last pitched battle ever fought on British soil, saw the defeat of Bonnie Prince Charlie and the end of the Jacobite dream when 1200 Highlanders were slaughtered by government forces in a 68-minute rout. The duke of Cumberland, son of the reigning king George II and leader of the Hanoverian army, earned the nickname 'Butcher' for his brutal treatment of the defeated Scottish forces. The battle sounded the death knell for the old clan system, and the horrors of the Clearances soon followed. The sombre moor where the conflict took place has scarcely changed in the ensuing 260-plus years.

The impressive new **visitor centre** (NTS; www.nts.org.uk/culloden; adult/child £10/7.50 ⌚9am-6pm Apr-Oct, 10am-4pm Nov-Mar) presents detailed information about the battle, including the lead-up and the aftermath, with perspectives from both sides. An innovative film puts you on the battlefield in the middle of the mayhem, and a wealth of other audio presentations must have kept Inverness' entire acting community in business for weeks. The admission fee includes an audio guide for a self-guided tour of the battlefield itself.

Culloden is 6 miles east of Inverness. Bus No 1 runs from Queensgate in Inverness to Culloden battlefield (30 minutes, hourly).

FORT GEORGE

The headland guarding the narrows in the Moray Firth opposite Fortrose is occupied by the magnificent and virtually unaltered 18th-century artillery fortification of **Fort George** (HS; adult/child £6.70/4; ⌚9.30am-5.30pm Apr-Sep, 9.30am-4.30pm Oct-Mar). One of the finest examples of its kind in Europe, it was established in 1748 as a base for George II's army of occupation in the Highlands – by the time of its completion in 1769 it had cost the equivalent of around £1 billion in today's money. The mile-plus walk around the ramparts offers fine views out to sea and back to the Great Glen. Given its size, you'll need at least two hours to do the place justice. The fort is off the A96 about 11 miles northeast of Inverness.

CAWDOR CASTLE

Built in the 14th century, **Cawdor Castle** (www.cawdorcastle.com; adult/child £8.30/5.20; ⌚10am-5.30pm May–mid-Oct) was the home of the Thanes of Cawdor, one of the titles prophesied by the three witches for the eponymous character of Shakespeare's *Macbeth*. Macbeth couldn't have moved in, though, since the central tower dates from the 14th century (the wings were 17th-century additions) and he died in 1057.

BRODIE CASTLE

Set in 70 hectares of parkland, **Brodie Castle** (NTS; adult/child £8/5; ⌚10.30am-5pm daily Jul & Aug, 10.30am-4.30pm Sun-Wed Apr-Jun, Sep & Oct) has several highlights, including a library with more than 6000 peeling, dusty volumes. There are wonderful clocks, a huge Victorian kitchen and a 17th-century dining room with wildly extravagant moulded plaster ceilings depicting mythological scenes. The Brodies have been living here since 1160, but the present structure dates mostly from 1567, with many additions over the years.

Stagecoach bus 10A or 11 from Inverness to Elgin stops at Brodie (35 minutes, hourly Monday to Saturday).

GLEN AFFRIC

The broad valley of **Strathglass** extends about 18 miles inland from the town of Beauly, followed by the A831 road to **Cannich**, the only village in the area, where there's a grocery store and a post office.

Glen Affric (www.glenaffric.org), one of the most beautiful glens in Scotland, extends deep into the hills beyond Cannich. The upper reaches of the glen, now designated as **Glen Affric National Nature Reserve**, is a scenic wonderland of shimmering lochs, rugged mountains and native Scots pine, home to pine marten, wildcat, otter, red squirrel and golden eagle.

It's possible to walk all the way from Cannich to **Glen Shiel** on the west coast (35 miles) in two days, spending the night at the remote Glen Affric Youth Hostel.

Sleeping & Eating

Kerrow House B&B ££
(☎01456-415243; www.kerrow-house.co.uk; Cannich; per person £35-40; P) This wonderful Georgian hunting lodge has bags of old-fashioned character – it was once the home of Highland author Neil M Gunn, and has spacious grounds with 3.5 miles of private trout fishing. It's a mile south of Cannich on the minor road along the east side of the River Glass.

Glen Affric Youth Hostel HOSTEL £
(SYHA; ☎bookings 0845 293 7373; Allt Beithe, Glen Affric; dm £18.50; ⊙Apr–mid-Sep) This remote and rustic hostel is set amid magnificent scenery at the halfway point of the cross-country walk from Cannich to Glen Shiel, 8 miles from the nearest road. Facilities are basic and you'll need to take all supplies with you. Book in advance. There is no phone at the hostel.

Getting There & Away

Stagecoach bus 17 runs from Inverness to Cannich (one hour, three a day Monday to Saturday) via Drumnadrochit.

BLACK ISLE

The Black Isle – a peninsula rather than an island – is linked to Inverness by the Kessock Bridge.

At **Fortrose Cathedral** you'll find the vaulted crypt of a 13th-century chapter house and sacristy, and the ruinous 14th-century south aisle and chapel. In Rosemarkie, the **Groam House Museum** (www.groamhouse.org.uk; admission by donation; ⊙10am-5pm Mon-Sat, 2-4.30pm Sun May-Oct, 2-4pm Sat & Sun Apr & Nov) has a superb collection of Pictish stones engraved with designs similar to those on Celtic Irish stones.

The pretty village of **Cromarty** at the northeastern tip of the Black Isle has lots of 18th-century red sandstone houses. The 18th-century **Cromarty Courthouse** (www.cromarty-courthouse.org.uk; Church St; adult/child £2/free; ⊙11am-4pm Apr-Sep) details the town's history using contemporary references. Kids will love the talking mannequins.

From Cromarty harbour, **Ecoventures** (☎01381-600323; www.ecoventures.co.uk) runs 2½-hour boat trips (adult/child £22/16) into the Moray Firth to see bottlenose dolphins and other wildlife.

Stagecoach buses 26 and 26A run from Inverness to Fortrose and Rosemarkie (30 to 40 minutes, twice hourly Monday to Saturday); half of them continue to Cromarty (one hour).

Loch Ness

Deep, dark and narrow, Loch Ness stretches for 23 miles between Inverness and Fort Augustus. Its bitterly cold waters have been extensively explored in search of Nessie, the elusive Loch Ness monster, but most visitors see her only in cardboard-cutout form at the monster exhibitions. The busy A82 road runs along the northwestern shore, while the more tranquil and picturesque B862 follows the southeastern shore. A complete circuit of the loch is about 70 miles – travel anticlockwise for the best views.

Activities

The 73-mile **Great Glen Way** (www.greatglenway.com) long-distance footpath stretches from Inverness to Fort William, where walkers can connect with the **West Highland Way**. The Great Glen Way footpath shares some sections with the 80-mile **Great Glen Mountain Bike Trail**, a waymarked mountain-bike route that follows canal towpaths and gravel tracks through forests, avoiding roads where possible.

DRUMNADROCHIT

POP 800

Seized by monster madness, its gift shops bulging with Nessie cuddly toys, Drumnadrochit is a hotbed of beastie fever, with two monster exhibitions battling it out for the tourist dollar.

The **Loch Ness Exhibition Centre** (www.loch-ness-scotland.com; adult/child £6.50/4.50; ⊙9am-6.30pm Jul & Aug, to 6pm Jun & Sep, 9.30am-5pm Feb-May & Oct, 10am-3.30pm Nov-Jan) is the better of the two Nessie-themed attractions, with a scientific approach that allows you to weigh the evidence for yourself.

One-hour monster-hunting cruises (adult/child £10/8), complete with sonar and underwater cameras, are available aboard the **Nessie Hunter** (☎01456-450395;

www.lochness-cruises.com). Cruises depart hourly from Drumnadrochit, 9am to 6pm daily from Easter to December.

URQUHART CASTLE

Commanding a brilliant location with outstanding views (on a clear day), **Urquhart Castle** (HS; adult/child £7/4.20; ⏲9.30am-6pm Apr-Sep, to 5pm Oct, to 4.30pm Nov-Mar) is a popular Nessie-watching hot spot. A huge visitor centre (most of which is beneath ground level) includes a video theatre (with a dramatic 'unveiling' of the castle at the end of the film), displays of medieval items discovered in the castle, a huge gift shop and a restaurant. The site is often very crowded in summer.

Sleeping & Eating

Loch Ness Inn INN ££
(☎01456-450991; www.staylochness.co.uk; Lewiston; s/d/f £69/99/140; P, wi-fi) Conveniently located in the quiet hamlet of Lewiston, between Drumnadrochit and Urquhart Castle, the Loch Ness Inn ticks all the weary traveller's boxes with comfortable bedrooms (the family suite sleeps two adults and two children), a cosy bar pouring real ales from the Cairngorm and Isle of Skye breweries, and a rustic **restaurant** (mains £8-16) serving hearty, wholesome fare such as smoked haddock chowder, and venison sausages with mash and onion gravy.

Drumbuie Farm B&B ££
(☎01456-450634; www.loch-ness-farm.co.uk; Drumnadrochit; per person from £30; ⏲Mar-Oct; P) A B&B in a modern house on a working farm – the surrounding fields are full of sheep and highland cattle – with views over Urquhart Castle and Loch Ness. Walkers and cyclists are welcome.

Loch Ness Backpackers Lodge HOSTEL £
(☎01456-450807; www.lochness-backpackers.com; Coiltie Farmhouse, East Lewiston; dm/d/f £12.50/30/45; P) This snug, friendly hostel housed in a cottage and barn has six-bed dorms, one double and a large barbecue area. It's about 0.75 miles from Drumnadrochit, along the A82 towards Fort William; turn left where you see the sign for Loch Ness Inn, just before the bridge.

Getting There & Away

Scottish Citylink and Stagecoach buses from Inverness to Fort William run along the shores of Loch Ness (six to eight daily, five on Sunday); those headed for Skye turn off at Invermoriston. There are bus stops at Drumnadrochit (£6.20, 30 minutes), Urquhart Castle car park (£6.60, 35 minutes) and Loch Ness Youth Hostel (£10, 45 minutes).

Fort Augustus

POP 510

Fort Augustus, at the junction of four old military roads, was originally a government garrison and the headquarters of General George Wade's road-building operations in the early 18th century. Today it's a neat and picturesque little place, often overrun by tourists in summer.

Sights & Activities

Caledonian Canal CANAL
At Fort Augustus, boats using the Caledonian Canal are raised and lowered 13m by a 'ladder' of five consecutive locks. It's fun to watch, and the neatly landscaped canal banks are a great place to soak up the sun or compare accents with fellow tourists. The **Caledonian Canal Heritage Centre** (admission free; ⏲10am-5pm Apr-Oct), beside the lowest lock, showcases the history of the canal.

The **Royal Scot** (www.cruiselochness.com; ⏲10am-4pm Mar-Oct, 2pm Sat & Sun only Nov & Dec) offers one-hour cruises (adult/child £11/6.50) on Loch Ness, accompanied by the latest high-tech sonar equipment so you can keep an underwater eye open for Nessie.

Sleeping & Eating

TOP CHOICE **Lovat Arms Hotel** HOTEL ££
(☎01456-459250; www.thelovat.com; Main Rd; d from £110; P, wi-fi, family-friendly) Recently given a luxurious but eco-conscious boutique-style makeover in shades of pink and grey, this former huntin'n'shootin' hotel is set apart from the tourist crush around the canal. The bedrooms are spacious and stylishly furnished, while the lounge is equipped with a log fire, comfy armchairs and grand piano. The **restaurant** (mains £10-17, separate kids' menu) serves top quality cuisine, from posh fish and chips to roast venison, seared sea bass, and wild mushroom risotto.

Morag's Lodge HOSTEL £
(☎01320-366289; www.moragslodge.com; Bunnoich Brae; dm/tw/f from £18/46/59; P, @, wi-fi) This large and well-run hostel is based in a big Victorian house with great views of Fort Augustus' hilly surrounds,

STRANGE SPECTACLE ON LOCH NESS

Highland folklore is filled with tales of strange creatures living in lochs and rivers, notably the kelpie (water horse) that lures unwary travellers to their doom. The use of the term 'monster', however, is a relatively recent phenomenon whose origins lie in an article published in the *Inverness Courier* on 2 May 1933, entitled 'Strange Spectacle on Loch Ness'.

The article recounted the sighting of a disturbance in the loch by Mrs Aldie Mackay and her husband: 'There the creature disported itself, rolling and plunging for fully a minute, its body resembling that of a whale, and the water cascading and churning like a simmering cauldron.'

The London newspapers couldn't resist. In December 1933 the *Daily Mail* sent Marmaduke Wetherall, a film director and big-game hunter, to Loch Ness to track down the beast. Within days he found 'reptilian' footprints in the shoreline mud (soon revealed to have been made with a stuffed hippopotamus foot, possibly an umbrella stand). Then in April 1934 came the famous 'long-necked monster' photograph taken by the seemingly reputable Harley St surgeon Colonel Kenneth Wilson. The press went mad and the rest, as they say, is history.

In 1994, however, Christian Spurling – Wetherall's stepson, by then 90 years old – revealed that the most famous photo of Nessie ever taken was in fact a hoax, perpetrated by his stepfather with Wilson's help. Today, of course, there are those who claim that Spurling's confession is itself a hoax. And, ironically, the researcher who exposed the surgeon's photo as a fake still believes wholeheartedly in the monster's existence.

Hoax or not, there's no denying that the bizarre mini-industry that has grown up around Loch Ness, and its mysterious monster since that eventful summer 75 years ago, is the strangest spectacle of all.

and has a convivial bar with open fire. It's hidden away in the trees up the steep side road just north of the tourist office car park.

Lock Inn PUB **££**
(Canal Side; mains £9-14) A superb little pub right on the canal bank, the Lock Inn has a vast range of malt whiskies and a tempting menu of bar meals (served noon-8pm) that includes Orkney salmon, Highland venison and daily seafood specials; the house speciality is beer-battered haddock and chips.

Information

There's an ATM and bureau de change (in the post office) beside the canal.

Tourist office (☎01320-366367; ⌚9am-6pm Mon-Sat, to 5pm Sun Easter-Oct) In the central car park.

Getting There & Away

Scottish Citylink and Stagecoach buses from Inverness to Fort William stop at Fort Augustus (£10, one hour, six to eight daily Monday to Saturday, five on Sunday).

THE CAIRNGORMS

The **Cairngorms National Park** (www.cairngorms.co.uk) encompasses the highest landmass in Britain – a broad mountain plateau, riven only by the deep valleys of the Lairig Ghru and Loch Avon, with an average altitude of over 1000m and including five of the six highest summits in the UK. This wild mountain landscape of granite and heather has a sub-Arctic climate and supports rare alpine tundra vegetation and high-altitude bird species, such as snow bunting, ptarmigan and dotterel.

The harsh mountain environment gives way lower down to scenic glens softened by beautiful open forests of native Caledonian pine, home to rare animals and birds such as pine marten, wildcat, red squirrel, osprey, capercaillie and crossbill.

This is prime hill-walking territory, but even couch potatoes can enjoy a taste of the high life by taking the Cairngorm Mountain Railway up to the edge of the Cairngorm plateau.

The Cairngorms

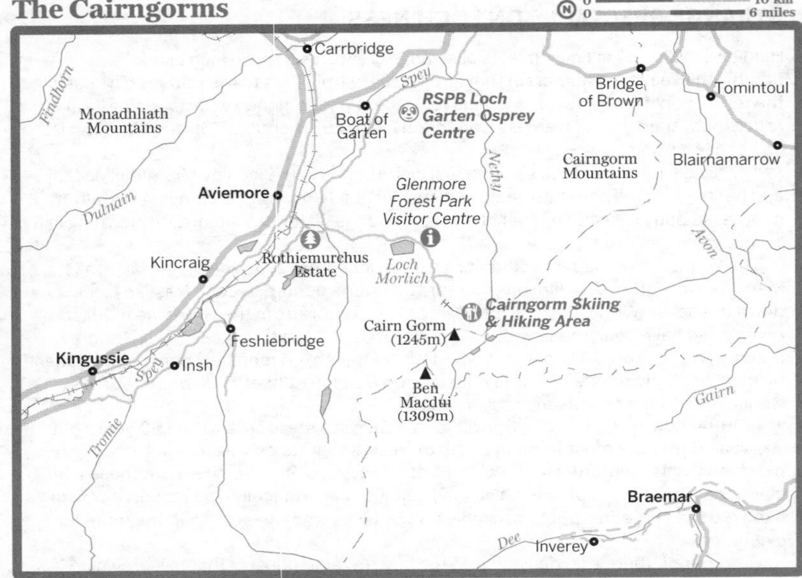

Aviemore

POP 2400

Aviemore is the gateway to the Cairngorms, the region's main centre for transport, accommodation, restaurants and shopping. It's not the prettiest town in Scotland by a long stretch, as the main attractions are in the surrounding area.

The Cairngorm skiing area and mountain railway lie 9 miles east of Aviemore along the B970 (Ski Rd) and its continuation through Coylumbridge and Glenmore.

Sights & Activities

Strathspey Steam Railway HERITAGE RAILWAY
(www.strathspeyrailway.co.uk; Station Sq) Aviemore's mainline train station is also home to the Strathspey Steam Railway, which runs steam trains on a section of restored line between Aviemore and Broomhill, 10 miles to the northeast, via Boat of Garten. There are four or five trains daily from June to September, and a more limited service in April, May, October and December; a return ticket from Aviemore to Broomhill is £10.50/5.25 per adult/child.

Rothiemurchus Estate WALKING, CYCLING
(www.rothiemurchus.net) The Rothiemurchus Estate, which extends from the River Spey at Aviemore to the Cairngorm summit plateau, is famous for having Scotland's largest remnant of **Caledonian forest**, the ancient forest of Scots pine that once covered most of the country. The forest is home to a large population of red squirrel, and is one of the last bastions of the Scottish wildcat.

The estate **visitor centre** (Inverdruie; admission free; ⌚9am-5.30pm), a mile southeast of Aviemore along the B970, sells an *Explorer Map* detailing more than 50 miles of footpaths and cycling trails, including the wheelchair-accessible 4-mile trail around **Loch an Eilein**, with its ruined castle and peaceful pine woods.

Visitors can also opt for ranger-guided walks, Land Rover tours, and trout-fishing at the estate's fish farm or in the River Spey.

Cairngorm Mountain WINTER SPORTS
(www.cairngormmountain.co.uk) Aspen or Val d'Isere it ain't, but with 19 runs and 23 miles of piste Cairngorm is Scotland's biggest ski area. When the snow is at its best and the sun is shining you can close your eyes and imagine you're in the Alps; sadly, low cloud, high winds and horizontal sleet are more common. The season usually runs from December until the snow melts, which may be as late as the end of April, but snowfall here is unpredictable.

A ski pass for one day is £30/18 for adults/under 16s. Ski or snowboard rental is around £20/14.50 per adult/child for a day; there are lots of rental outlets at Coire Cas, Glenmore and Aviemore.

Cairngorm Sled-Dog Centre DOG SLED
(☎07767 270526; www.sled-dogs.co.uk; Ski Rd) If you prefer the smell of wet dog to the whiff of petrol, you can be taken on a two- to three-hour sled tour of local forest trails in the wake of a team of huskies (adult/child £60/40). The sleds have wheels, so snow's not necessary, but it needs to be under 11°C, so the season generally lasts from September to April. There are also one-hour guided tours of the kennels (adult/child £8/4).

Alvie & Dalraddy Estate QUAD BIKE
(☎01479-810330; www.alvie-estate.co.uk; Dalraddy Holiday Park; per person £39) Join a cross-country quad-bike trek, 3 miles south of Aviemore on the B9152 (call first).

Sleeping

Old Minister's House B&B ££
(☎01479-812181; www.theoldministershouse.co.uk; Rothiemurchus; s/d £65/96; P 📶) This former manse dates from 1906 and has four rooms with a homely, country farmhouse feel. It's in a lovely setting amid Scots pines on the banks of the River Druie, just 0.75 miles southeast of Aviemore.

Aviemore Bunkhouse HOSTEL £
(☎01479-811181; www.aviemore-bunkhouse.com; Dalfaber Rd; dm/tw/f £15/50/60; P @ 📶) This independent hostel, next door to the Old Bridge Inn, provides accommodation in bright, modern six- or eight-bed dorms, each with private bathroom, and one twin/family room. There's a drying room, secure bike storage and wheelchair-accessible dorms. From the train station, cross the pedestrian bridge over the tracks, turn right and walk south on Dalfaber Rd.

Ravenscraig Guest House B&B ££
(☎01479-810278; www.aviemoreonline.com; Grampian Rd; r per person £30-40; P 📶) Ravenscraig is a large, flower-bedecked Victorian villa with six spacious en-suite rooms, plus another six in a modern annexe at the back (one wheelchair accessible). It serves traditional and veggie breakfasts in an attractive conservatory dining room.

Kinapol Guest House B&B ££
(☎01479-810513; www.kinapol.co.uk; Dalfaber Rd; s/d from £30/40; P 📶) The Kinapol is a modern bungalow offering basic but comfortable B&B accommodation, across the tracks from the train station. All three rooms have shared bathrooms.

Aviemore Youth Hostel HOSTEL £
(SYHA; ☎01479-810345; 25 Grampian Rd; dm £17; P @ 📶) Upmarket hostelling in a spacious, well-equipped building, five minutes' walk from the village centre. There are four- and six-bed rooms, and the doors stay open until 2am.

Rothiemurchus Camp & Caravan Park CAMPSITE £
(☎01479-812800; www.rothiemurchus.net; Coylumbridge; sites per person £7.50-8.50) The nearest camping ground is this year-round park set among Scots pines at Coylumbridge, 1.5 miles along the B970.

Eating & Drinking

Old Bridge Inn PUB ££
(www.oldbridgeinn.co.uk; 23 Dalfaber Rd; mains £10-16; 📶) The Old Bridge has a snug bar, complete with roaring log fire in winter, and a cheerful, chalet-style **restaurant** (food served noon to 3pm and 6pm to 9pm Sunday to Thursday, and to 10pm on Friday and Saturday) at the back serving quality Scottish cuisine.

Mountain Cafe CAFE £
(www.mountaincafe-aviemore.co.uk; 111 Grampian Rd; mains £4-9; ⏲8.30am-5pm Tue-Thu, to 5.30pm Fri-Mon; 👪) Fresh, healthy breakfasts of muesli, porridge and fresh fruit (till 11.30am), hearty lunches of seafood chowder, salads or burgers, and homebaked breads, cakes and biscuits. Vegan, coeliac and nut-allergic diets catered for.

Café Mambo CAFE-BAR £
(The Mall, Grampian Rd; mains £5-10; ⏲food noon-8.30pm Mon-Thu, noon-7.30pm Fri & Sat, 12.30-8.30pm Sun; 📶) The Mambo is a popular chill-out cafe in the afternoon, serving burgers, steaks and Tex-Mex grub, and turns into a clubbing and live-band venue in the evenings.

Information

Old Bridge Inn (23 Dalfaber Rd; per 30min £1; ⏲11am-11pm Sun-Thu, to midnight Fri & Sat) Internet access.

Tourist office (☎01479-810363; www.visitaviemore.com; The Mall, Grampian Rd; ⏲9am-6pm Mon-Sat, 9.30am-5pm Sun Jul & Aug, 9am-5pm Mon-Sat, 10am-4pm Sun Easter-Jun, Sep & Oct) Hours are limited October to Easter.

Getting There & Away

BUS Buses stop on Grampian Rd opposite the train station; buy tickets at the tourist office. Scottish Citylink connects Aviemore with Inverness (£9, 45 minutes), Perth (£18, 2¼ hours), Glasgow (£23, 3¾ hours) and Edinburgh (£23, 3¾ hours).

TRAIN There are direct train services to Glasgow/Edinburgh (£40, three hours, three daily) and Inverness (£10, 40 minutes, nine daily).

Getting Around

BIKE Several places in Aviemore, Rothiemurchus Estate and Glenmore have mountain bikes for hire.

Bothy Bikes (www.bothybikes.co.uk; Ski Rd, Rothiemurchus) Charges £20 a day for a quality bike with front suspension and disc brakes.

BUS Bus 34 links Aviemore to Cairngorm car park (20 to 30 minutes, hourly, no Sunday service late October to late December) via Coylumbridge and Glenmore. A Strathspey Dayrider/Megarider ticket (£6/20) gives one/seven days unlimited bus travel from Aviemore as far as Cairngorm, Carrbridge and Kingussie (buy from the bus driver).

Around Aviemore

CAIRNGORM MOUNTAIN RAILWAY

Aviemore's most popular attraction is the **Cairngorm Mountain Railway** (☎01479-861261; www.cairngormmountain.co.uk; adult/child return £9.75/6.15; ⌚10am-5pm May-Nov, 9am-4.30pm Dec-Apr), a funicular train that will whisk you to the edge of Cairngorm plateau (1085m) in just eight minutes. The bottom station is at the Coire Cas car park at the end of Ski Rd; at the top is an exhibition, a shop (of course) and a restaurant. Unfortunately, for environmental and safety reasons, you're not allowed out of the top station in summer, not even to walk down – you must return to the car park on the funicular. However, a trial project launched in 2010 offers 90-minute guided walks to the summit (adult/child £13/10) four times a day from mid-July to October. Check the website for details.

LOCH MORLICH

Six miles east of Aviemore, Loch Morlich is surrounded by some 8 sq miles of pine and spruce forest that make up the **Glenmore Forest Park**. Its attractions include a sandy beach (at the east end) and a visitor centre with a small exhibition on the Caledonian forest.

Sights & Activities

Loch Morlich Watersports Centre WATERSPORTS
(www.lochmorlich.com; Glenmore; ⌚9am-5pm May-Oct) Popular outfit which rents out Canadian canoes (£18 an hour), kayaks (£8.50), windsurfers (£16.50), sailing dinghies (£20) and rowing boats (£18).

Cairngorm Reindeer Centre WILDLIFE PARK
(www.cairngormreindeer.co.uk; Glenmore; adult/child £9.50/5) The warden here will take you on a tour to see and feed Britain's only herd of reindeer. Walks take place at 11am, plus another at 2.30pm from May to September, and 3.30pm Monday to Friday in July and August.

Glenmore Lodge ADVENTURE SPORTS
(www.glenmorelodge.org.uk; Glenmore; P) One of Britain's leading adventure sports training centres, offers courses in hill walking, rock climbing, ice climbing, canoeing,

MOUNTAIN WALKS IN THE CAIRNGORMS

The climb from the car park at the Coire Cas ski area to the summit of **Cairn Gorm** (1245m) takes about two hours (one way). From there, you can continue south across the high-level plateau to Ben Macdui (1309m), Britain's second-highest peak. This takes eight to 10 hours return from the car park and is a serious undertaking; for experienced and well-equipped walkers only.

The **Lairig Ghru trail**, which can take eight to 10 hours, is a demanding 24-mile walk from Aviemore through the Lairig Ghru pass (840m) to Braemar. An alternative to doing the full route is to make the six-hour return hike up to the summit of the pass and back to Aviemore. The path starts from Ski Rd, a mile east of Coylumbridge, and involves some very rough going.

Warning – the Cairngorm plateau is a sub-Arctic environment where navigation is difficult and weather conditions can be severe, even in midsummer. Hikers must have proper hill-walking equipment, and know how to use a map and compass. In winter it is a place for experienced mountaineers only.

mountain biking and mountaineering. The centre's comfortable **B&B accommodation** (per person £25-33) is available to all, even if you're not taking a course, as is the indoor-climbing wall, gym and sauna.

Sleeping

Cairngorm Lodge Youth Hostel HOSTEL £ (SYHA; ☎01479-861238; Glenmore; dm £17; ⏲closed Nov & Dec; @) Set in a former shooting lodge that enjoys a great location at the east end of Loch Morlich; prebooking is essential.

Glenmore Caravan & Camping Site CAMPSITE £ (☎01479-861271; www.forestholidays.co.uk; Glenmore; tents & campervans £19-20; ⏲year round) Campers can set up base at this attractive loch-side site with pitches amid the Scots pines; rates include up to four people per tent/campervan.

BOAT OF GARTEN

Boat of Garten is known as the Osprey Village because these rare and beautiful birds of prey nest nearby at the **RSPB Loch Garten Osprey Centre** (www.rspb.org.uk; Tulloch, Nethybridge; adult/child £3/50p; ⏲10am-6pm Apr-Aug) The ospreys migrate here each spring from Africa and nest in a tall pine tree – you can watch from a hide as the birds feed their young. The centre is signposted about 2 miles east of the village.

Boat of Garten is 6 miles northeast of Aviemore. The most interesting way to get here is on the Strathspey Steam Railway.

Kingussie & Newtonmore

The gracious old Speyside towns of Kingussie (kin-*yew*-see) and Newtonmore sit at the foot of the great heather-clad humps known as the Monadhliath Mountains. The towns are best known as the home of the excellent Highland Folk Museum.

Sights & Activities

FREE **Highland Folk Museum** OPEN-AIR MUSEUM (www.highlandfolk.museum; Kingussie Rd, Newtonmore; ⏲10.30am-5.30pm Apr-Aug, 11am-4.30pm Sep & Oct) The open-air Highland Folk Museum comprises a collection of historical buildings and relics revealing many aspects of Highland culture and lifestyle. The museum is laid out like a farming township and has a community of traditional thatch-roofed cottages, a sawmill, a schoolhouse, a shepherd's bothy and a rural post office. Actors in period costume give demonstrations of woodcarving, spinning and peat-fire baking. You'll need two to three hours to make the most of a visit here.

Sleeping & Eating

TOP CHOICE **Eagleview Guest House** B&B ££ (☎01540-673675; www.eagleviewguesthouse.co.uk; Perth Rd, Newtonmore; r per person £25-35; P 🛜 👪) The family-friendly Eagleview is one of the nicest places to stay in the area, with beautifully decorated bedrooms, super-kingsize beds, spacious bathrooms with power showers, and nice little touches like wall-mounted flatscreen TVs, cafetieres with real coffee on your hospitality tray and real milk rather than that yucky UHT stuff.

Homewood Lodge B&B ££ (☎01540-661507; www.homewood-lodge-kingussie.co.uk; Newtonmore Rd, Kingussie; r per person £25-30; P) This elegant Victorian lodge on the western outskirts of town offers double rooms with exquisite views of the Cairngorms – a nice way to wake up in the mornings! The owners are committed to recycling and energy efficiency, and have created a mini-nature reserve in the garden.

TOP CHOICE **Cross** RESTAURANT £££ (☎01540-661166; www.thecross.co.uk; Tweed Mill Brae, Ardbroilach Rd, Kingussie; 3-course dinner £50; ⏲7-9pm Tue-Sat, closed Jan; P) Housed in a converted water mill beside the Allt Mor burn, the Cross is one of the finest restaurants in the Highlands. The intimate, low-raftered dining room has an open fire and a patio overlooking the stream, and serves a daily-changing menu of fresh Scottish produce accompanied by a superb wine list. If you want to stay the night, there are eight stylish **rooms** (d or tw £100-140) to choose from.

Getting There & Away

BUS There are Scottish Citylink buses from Kingussie to Perth (£14, 1¾ hours, five daily), Aviemore (£7, 25 minutes, five to seven daily) and Inverness (£11, one hour, six to eight Monday to Saturday, three Sunday).

TRAIN From the train station at the southern end of town there are trains to Edinburgh (£32, 2½ hours, seven a day Monday to Saturday, two Sunday) and Inverness (£10, one hour, eight a day Monday to Saturday, four Sunday).

CENTRAL WESTERN HIGHLANDS

This area extends from the bleak blanket-bog of the Moor of Rannoch to the west coast beyond the valley Glen Coe and Fort William, and includes the southern reaches of the Great Glen. The scenery is grand throughout, with high and wild mountains dominating the glens. Great expanses of moor alternate with lochs and patches of commercial forest. Fort William, at the inner end of Loch Linnhe, is the only sizable town in the area.

Glen Coe

Scotland's most famous glen is also one of the grandest and, in bad weather, the grimmest. The southern side is dominated by three massive, brooding spurs, known as the **Three Sisters**, while the northern side is enclosed by the continuous steep wall of the knife-edged Aonach Eagach ridge. The main road threads its lonely way through the middle of all this mountain grandeur.

Glencoe village was written into the history books in 1692 when the resident MacDonalds were murdered by Campbell soldiers in what became known as the Glencoe Massacre.

Activities

There are several short, pleasant walks around **Glencoe Lochan**, near the village. A more strenuous hike, but well worth the effort on a fine day, is the climb to the **Lost Valley**, a magical mountain sanctuary still haunted by the ghosts of the murdered MacDonalds (only 2.5 miles round trip, but allow three hours). A rough path from the car park at Allt na Reigh (on the A82, 6 miles east of Glencoe village) climbs up the wooded valley between Beinn Fhada and Gearr Aonach (the first and second of the Three Sisters) before emerging – quite unexpectedly – into a broad, open valley with an 800m-long meadow as flat as a football pitch.

A few miles east of Glencoe proper, on the south side of the A82, is the car park and base station for the **Glencoe Mountain Resort** (www.glencoemountain.com). The **chairlift** (adult/child £10/5; 9.30am-4.30pm Thu-Mon May-Sep) continues to operate in summer – there's a grand view over the Moor of Rannoch from the top station – and provides access to a downhill mountain-biking track. In winter a lift pass costs £30 a day and equipment hire is £25 a day.

GLENCOE VILLAGE

POP 360

The little village of Glencoe stands on the south shore of Loch Leven at the western end of the glen.

Sights

Glencoe Folk Museum MUSEUM
(Glencoe; adult/child £2/free; 10am-5.30pm Mon-Sat Apr-Oct) This small, thatched museum houses a varied collection of military memorabilia, farm equipment, and tools of the woodworking, blacksmithing and slate-quarrying trades.

Glencoe Visitor Centre VISITOR CENTRE
(NTS; 01855-811307; www.glencoe-nts.org.uk; Inverigan; adult/child £5.50/4.50; 9.30am-5.30pm Apr-Aug, 10am-5pm Sep & Oct, 10am-4pm Thu-Sun Nov-Mar) About 1.5 miles east of the village, towards the glen, is this modern facility with an ecotourism angle. The centre provides comprehensive information on the geological, environmental and cultural history of Glencoe via hi-tech interactive and audiovisual displays, and tells the story of the Glencoe Massacre in all its gory detail.

Sleeping & Eating

TOP CHOICE **Clachaig Inn** HOTEL ££
(01855-811252; www.clachaig.com; Clachaig, Glencoe; s/d £70/88; P) The Clachaig has long been a favourite haunt of hill walkers and climbers. As well as comfortable en-suite accommodation, there's a smart, wood-panelled lounge bar, with lots of sofas and armchairs, mountaineering photos and climbing magazines to leaf through. Climbers usually head for the lively Boots Bar on the other side of the hotel – it has log fires, serves real ale and good pub grub (mains £8 to £12), and has live Scottish, Irish and blues music every Saturday night.

Glencoe Independent Hostel HOSTEL £
(01855-811906; www.glencoehostel.co.uk; Glencoe; dm £12-15, bunkhouse £11-12; P) This handily located hostel, just 10 minutes' walk from the Clachaig Inn, is set in an old farmhouse with six- and eight-bed dorms, and a bunkhouse with another 16 bed spaces in communal, Alpine-style bunks. There's also a cute little wooden cabin that sleeps up to three (£48 to £54 per night).

Getting There & Away

Scottish Citylink buses run between Fort William and Glencoe (£7, 30 minutes, eight daily) and from Glencoe to Glasgow (£19, 2½ hours, eight daily). Buses stop at Glencoe village, Glencoe Visitor Centre, and Glencoe Mountain Resort.

Stagecoach bus 44 links Glencoe village with Fort William (35 minutes, hourly Monday to Saturday, three on Sunday) and Kinlochleven (25 minutes).

Kinlochleven

POP 900

Kinlochleven is hemmed in by high mountains at the head of the beautiful fjord-like Loch Leven, about 7 miles east of Glencoe village.

Activities

The final section of the **West Highland Way** stretches for 14 miles from Kinlochleven to Fort William. The village is also the starting point for easier walks up the glen of the River Leven, through pleasant woods to the Grey Mare's Tail waterfall, and harder mountain hikes into the Mamores.

If you fancy trying your hand at ice-climbing, even in the middle of summer, head for **Ice Factor** (www.ice-factor.co.uk; Leven Rd; ⏲9am-10pm Tue & Thu, 9am-7pm Mon, Wed & Fri), the world's biggest indoor ice-climbing wall; a one-hour beginner's 'taster' session costs £30.

Sleeping & Eating

TOP CHOICE **Lochleven Seafood Cafe** SEAFOOD ££

(☎01855-821048; www.lochlevenseafoodcafe.co.uk; Loch Leven; mains £8-18; ⏲noon-9pm Wed-Sun) An outstanding and welcome addition to the region's restaurants, this place serves superb shellfish freshly plucked live from tanks – oysters on the half shell, razor clams, scallops, lobster and crab – plus a daily fish special, and a couple of nonseafood dishes. For warm summer days, there's an outdoor terrace with a view across the loch to the Pap of Glencoe, a distinctive conical-shaped mountain.

Blackwater Hostel HOSTEL £

(☎01855-831253; www.blackwaterhostel.co.uk; Lab Rd; dm/tw £14/32, tent sites per person £6) This 40-bed hostel has spotless, pine-panelled dorms with en-suite bathrooms and TV, and a level, well-sheltered camping ground.

Getting There & Away

Stagecoach bus 44 runs from Fort William to Kinlochleven (50 minutes, hourly Monday to Saturday, three on Sunday) via Ballachulish and Glencoe village.

Fort William

POP 9910

Basking on the shores of Loch Linnhe amid magnificent mountain scenery, Fort William has one of the most enviable settings in the whole of Scotland. If it wasn't for the busy dual carriageway crammed between the town centre and the loch, and one of the highest rainfall records in the country, it would be almost idyllic. Even so, the Fort has carved out a reputation as 'Outdoor Capital of the UK' (www.outdoorcapital.co.uk), and its easy access by rail and bus makes it a good place to base yourself for exploring the surrounding mountains and glens.

Sights

West Highland Museum MUSEUM

(www.westhighlandmuseum.org.uk; Cameron Sq; adult/child £4/1; ⏲10am-5pm Mon-Sat Jun-Sep, plus 2-5pm Sun Jul & Aug, 10am-4pm Mon-Sat Oct-May) The small but fascinating West Highland Museum is packed with all manner of Highland memorabilia. Look out for the secret portrait of Bonnie Prince Charlie – after the Jacobite rebellions all things Highland were banned, including pictures of the exiled leader, and this tiny painting looks like nothing more than a smear of paint until viewed in a cylindrical mirror, which reflects a credible likeness of the prince.

Events

UCI Mountain Bike World Cup MOUNTAIN BIKING

(www.fortwilliamworldcup.co.uk) In June, Fort William pulls in crowds of more than 18,000 spectators for this World Cup downhill mountain biking event. The gruelling downhill course is at nearby Nevis Range ski area.

Tours

Crannog Cruises BOAT

(☎01397-700714; www.crannog.net/cruises; Town Pier) Operates 1½-hour wildlife cruises (adult/child £10/5, four daily) on Loch Linnhe, visiting a seal colony and a salmon farm.

Fort William

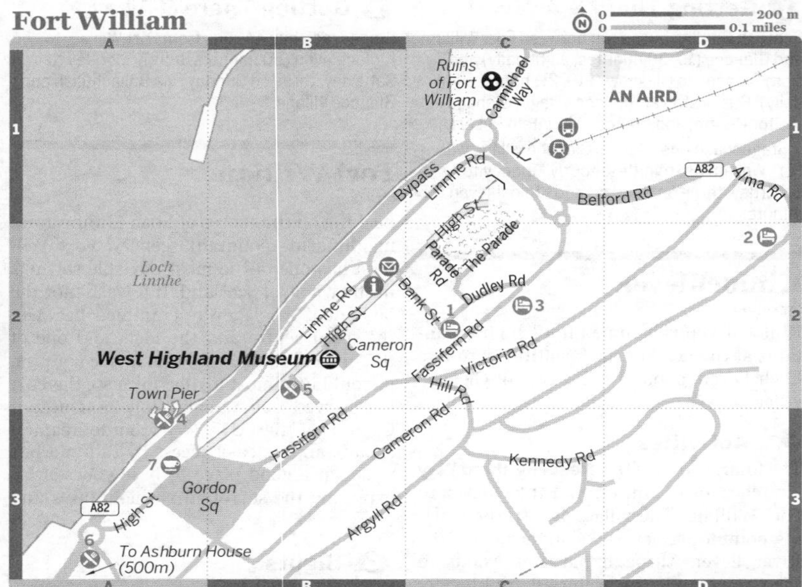

Sleeping

It's best to book well ahead in summer, especially for hostels. See also the Glen Nevis Sleeping & Eating section.

TOP CHOICE Lime Tree HOTEL ££
(01397-701806; www.limetreefortwilliam.co.uk; Achintore Rd; s/d from £70/100; P) Much more interesting than your average guest house, this former Victorian manse overlooking Loch Linnhe is an 'art gallery with rooms', decorated throughout with the artist-owner's atmospheric Highland landscapes. Foodies rave about the **restaurant** and the gallery space – a triumph of sensitive design – stages everything from serious exhibitions to folk concerts.

Grange B&B ££
(01397-705516; www.grangefortwilliam.com; Grange Rd; r per person £56-59; P) An exceptional 19th-century villa set in its own landscaped grounds, the Grange is crammed with antiques and fitted with log fires, chaise longues and Victorian roll-top baths. The Turret Room, with its window seat in the turret overlooking Loch Linnhe, is our favourite.

St Andrew's Guest House B&B ££
(01397-703038; www.standrewsguesthouse.co.uk; Fassifern Rd; r per person £22-28; P) Set in a lovely 19th-century building that was once a rectory and choir school, St Andrew's retains period features, such as carved masonry, wood panelling and stained-glass windows. It has six spacious bedrooms, some with stunning views – good value for the price.

Fort William Backpackers HOSTEL £
(01397-700711; www.scotlands-top-hostels.com; Alma Rd; dm/tw from £14/38; @) A 10-minute walk from the bus and train stations, this lively and welcoming hostel is set in a grand Victorian villa, perched on a hill side with great views over Loch Linnhe.

Bank Street Lodge HOSTEL £
(01397-700070; www.bankstreetlodge.co.uk; Bank St; dm/tw £14.50/48) Part of a modern hotel and restaurant complex, the Bank Street Lodge offers the most central budget beds in town, only 250m from the train station. It has kitchen facilities and a drying room.

Eating & Drinking

TOP CHOICE Lime Tree MODERN SCOTTISH £££
(01397-701806; www.limetreefortwilliam.co.uk; Achintore Rd; mains £19-25; dinner daily, noon-3pm Sun) Fort William is not over-endowed with great places to eat, but the restaurant at this small hotel-cum-art

Fort William

Top Sights
West Highland Museum B2

Sleeping
1 Bank Street Lodge C2
2 Fort William Backpackers D2
Lime Tree ..... (see 6)
3 St Andrew's Guest House C2

Eating
4 Crannog Seafood Restaurant A3
5 Grog & Gruel B2
6 Lime Tree A3

Drinking
7 Fired Art Cafe A3

gallery has certainly put the UK's Outdoor Capital on the gastronomic map. The chef won a Michelin star in his previous restaurant, and turns out technically accomplished dishes such as beer-braised beef with shallot mousse, and slow-roast pork belly with truffled honey.

Crannog Seafood Restaurant SEAFOOD ££
(01397-705589; www.crannog.net; Town Pier; mains £14-20; lunch & dinner) The Crannog easily wins the prize for the best location in town – it's perched on the Town Pier, giving window-table diners an uninterrupted view down Loch Linnhe. Informal and unfussy, it specialises in fresh local seafood – there are three or four daily fish specials plus the main menu – though there are beef, poultry and vegetarian dishes too. Two-course lunch £10.

Grog & Gruel PUB ££
(www.grogandgruel.co.uk; 66 High St; mains £9-12; bar meals noon-9pm) The Grog & Gruel is a traditional-style, wood-panelled pub with an excellent range of cask ales from regional Scottish and English microbreweries. Upstairs is a lively Tex-Mex **restaurant** (5-9pm), with a crowd-pleasing menu of tasty enchiladas, burritos, fajitas, burgers, steaks and pizza.

Fired Art Cafe CAFE £
(www.fired-art.co.uk; mains £3-4; 10am-5pm Mon-Sat;) Enjoy what is probably the best coffee in town at this colourful cafe, or go for a hot chocolate, milk shake or smoothie; the kids can be kept busy painting their own coffee mugs in the pottery studio at the back.

Information

Tourist office (01397-703781; www.visithighlands.com; 15 High St; 9am-6pm Mon-Sat, 10am-5pm Sun Apr-Sep, limited hr Oct-Mar) Internet access (£1 per 20 minutes).

Getting There & Away

Bus

Scottish Citylink buses link Fort William with Glasgow (£21, three hours, eight daily) and Edinburgh (£30, 4½ hours, one daily direct, seven with a change at Glasgow) via Glencoe and Crianlarich, as well as Oban (£9, 1½ hours, three daily), Inverness (£11, two hours, five daily) and Portree (£28, three hours, four daily), on the Isle of Skye.

Train

The spectacular West Highland line runs from Glasgow to Mallaig via Fort William. There are three trains daily (two on Sunday) from Glasgow to Fort William (£24, 3¾ hours), and four daily (three on Sunday) between Fort William and Mallaig (£10, 1½ hours). Travelling from Edinburgh (£40, five hours), you have to change at Glasgow's Queen St station.

The overnight Caledonian Sleeper service connects Fort William and London Euston (£103 sharing a twin-berth cabin, 13 hours).

Getting Around

Bike

Off-Beat Bikes (01436-704008; www.offbeatbikes.co.uk; 117 High St; 9am-5.30pm) Rents mountain bikes for £17/12 a day/half-day.

Bus

The Fort Dayrider ticket (£2.60) gives unlimited travel for one day on Stagecoach bus services in the Fort William area. Buy from the bus driver.

Around Fort William

GLEN NEVIS

You can walk the 3 miles from Fort William to scenic Glen Nevis in about an hour or so. The **Glen Nevis Visitor Centre** (01397-705922; www.bennevisweather.co.uk; 9am-5pm Apr-Oct) is situated 1.5 miles up the glen, and provides information on walking as well as specific advice on climbing Ben Nevis.

From the car park at the far end of the road along Glen Nevis, there is an excellent 1.5-mile walk through the spectacular Nevis Gorge to **Steall Meadows**, a verdant valley dominated by a 100m-high bridal-veil waterfall. You can reach the foot of the falls

CLIMBING BEN NEVIS

As the highest peak in the British Isles, Ben Nevis (1344m) attracts many would-be ascensionists who would not normally think of climbing a Scottish mountain – a staggering (often literally) 100,000 people reach the summit each year.

Although anyone who is reasonably fit should have no problem climbing Ben Nevis on a fine summer's day, an ascent should not be undertaken lightly. Every year people have to be rescued from the mountain. You will need proper walking boots (the path is rough and stony, and there may be soft, wet snowfields on the summit), warm clothing, waterproofs, a map and compass, and plenty of food and water. And don't forget to check the weather forecast (see www.bennevisweather.co.uk).

In thick cloud, visibility at the summit can be 10m or less; and in such conditions the only safe way off the mountain requires careful use of a map and compass to avoid walking over 700m cliffs.

There are three possible starting points for the tourist track (the easiest route to the top) ascent – Achintee Farm; the footbridge at Glen Nevis Youth Hostel; and the car park at Glen Nevis Visitor Centre. The path climbs gradually to the shoulder at Lochan Meall an t-Suidhe (known as the Halfway Lochan), then zigzags steeply up beside the Red Burn to the summit plateau.

The total distance to the summit and back is 8 miles; allow at least four or five hours to reach the top, and another 2½ to three hours for the descent. Afterwards, as you celebrate in the pub with a pint, consider the fact that the record time for the annual Ben Nevis Hill Race is just under 1½ hours – up *and* down. Then have another pint.

by crossing the river on a wobbly, three-cable wire bridge – one cable for your feet and one for each hand – a real test of balance!

Sleeping & Eating

TOP CHOICE **Ben Nevis Inn** HOSTEL £
(☎01397-701227; www.ben-nevis-inn.co.uk; Achintee; dm £14; P @) A good alternative to the youth hostel is this great barn of a pub (real ale and tasty bar meals available; mains £9 to £12), with a comfy 24-bed hostel downstairs. It's at the Achintee start of the path up Ben Nevis, and only a mile from the end of the West Highland Way. Food is served noon to 9pm; closed Monday to Wednesday in winter.

Achintee Farm HOSTEL, B&B £
(☎01397-702240; www.achinteefarm.com; Achintee; dm £15, tw £34) This attractive farmhouse offers excellent B&B accommodation and also has a small bunkhouse attached. It's just 100m from the Ben Nevis Inn, and ideally positioned for climbing Ben Nevis.

Glen Nevis Caravan & Camping Park CAMPSITE £
(☎01397-702191; www.glen-nevis.co.uk; tent £6.50, tent & car £11, campervan £11, per person £3; ⊙mid-Mar–Oct) This big, well-equipped site is a popular base camp for Ben Nevis and the surrounding mountains.

Getting There & Away

Bus 41 runs from Fort William bus station up **Glen Nevis** (10 minutes, five daily Monday to Saturday, three on Sunday, limited service October to April).

NEVIS RANGE

The **Nevis Range ski area** (☎01397-705825; www.nevisrange.co.uk), 6 miles north of Fort William, spreads across the northern slopes of Aonach Mor (1221m). The gondola that gives access to the bottom of the ski area at 655m operates year-round from 10am to 5pm; a return trip costs £10.50/6 for an adult/child (15 minutes each way. During the ski season a one-day lift pass costs £28/16.50 per adult/child; a one-day package, including equipment hire, lift pass and two hours' instruction, costs £62.

A world championship **downhill mountain-bike trail** (⊙11am-3pm mid-May–mid-Sep) – for experienced riders only – runs from the Snowgoose restaurant to the base station; bikes are carried on a rack on the gondola cabin. A single trip with your own bike costs £12; full-suspension bike hire costs from £40/70 per half-/full day depending on the bike. There are also 25 miles of waymarked mountain-bike trails in the nearby forest.

Bus 41 runs from Fort William bus station to Nevis Range (15 minutes, five daily Monday to Saturday, three on Sunday, limited service October to April).

Road To The Isles

The 46-mile A830 from Fort William to Mallaig is traditionally known as the Road to the Isles, as it leads to the jumping-off point for ferries to the Small Isles and Skye, itself a stepping stone to the Outer Hebrides.

GLENFINNAN

POP 100

Glenfinnan is hallowed ground for fans of Bonnie Prince Charlie, and its central shrine is the **Glenfinnan Monument**. This tall column, topped by a statue of a kilted Highlander, was erected in 1815 on the spot where the Young Pretender first raised his standard and rallied the clans on 19 August 1745, marking the start of the ill-fated campaign that would end in disaster 14 months later. The setting, at the north end of Loch Shiel, is hauntingly beautiful.

The nearby **Glenfinnan Visitor Centre** (NTS; adult/child £3/2; ⏲9.30am-5.30pm Jul & Aug, 10am-5pm Easter-Jun, Sep & Oct) recounts the story of the '45, as the Jacobite rebellion of 1745 is known – when the prince's loyal clansmen marched and fought from Glenfinnan south to Derby, then back north to final defeat at Culloden.

ARISAIG & MORAR

The 5 miles of coast between Arisaig and Morar is a fretwork of rocky islets, inlets and gorgeous silver-sand beaches backed by dunes and machair, with stunning sunset views across the sea to the silhouetted peaks of Eigg and Rum. The **Silver Sands of Morar**, as they are known, draw crowds of bucket-and-spade holidaymakers in July and August, when the many camping grounds scattered along the coast are filled to overflowing.

WORTH A TRIP

GLENUIG INN

Set on a peaceful bay on the Arisaig coast, halfway between Lochailort and Acharacle on the A830 road, the recently renovated **Glenuig Inn** (☎01687-470219; www.glenuig.com; Glenuig; B&B s/d/q £60/90/120, bunkhouse per person £25; Ⓟ📶) is a great place to get away from it all. As well as offering comfortable accommodation, good food (mains £9 to £19), and real ale on tap, it's a great base for exploring Arisaig, Morar and the Loch Shiel area.

MALLAIG

POP 800

If you're travelling between Fort William and Skye, you may find yourself overnighting in the bustling fishing and ferry port of Mallaig. The village's rainy-day attractions are limited to the **Mallaig Heritage Centre** (www.mallaigheritage.org.uk; Station Rd; adult/child £2/free; ⏲9.30am-4.30pm Mon-Sat, noon-4pm Sun) which covers the archaeology and history of the region, including the heart-rending tale of the Highland Clearances in Knoydart.

Sleeping & Eating

Seaview Guest House B&B ££

(☎01687-462059; www.seaviewguesthousemallaig.com; Main St; r per person £28-35; ⏲Mar-Nov; Ⓟ) Just beyond the tourist office, this comfortable three-bedroom B&B has grand views over the harbour, not only from the upstairs bedrooms but also from the breakfast room. There's also a cute little cottage next door that offers self-catering accommodation (www.selfcateringmallaig.com; one double and one twin room) for £350 to £450 a week.

Mallaig Backpacker's Lodge HOSTEL £

(☎01687-462764; www.mallaigbackpackers.co.uk; Harbour View; dm £14.50) Sheena's is a friendly, 12-bed hostel in a lovely old house overlooking the harbour. On a sunny day the hostel's Tea Garden **terrace cafe** (mains £5-10), with its flowers, greenery and cosmopolitan backpacker staff, feels more like the Med than Mallaig.

TOP CHOICE **Fish Market** SEAFOOD ££

(☎01687-462299; Station Rd; mains £9-20; ⏲lunch & dinner) There are at least half-a-dozen signs in Mallaig advertising 'seafood restaurant', but this bright, modern, bistro-style place next to the harbour is our favourite

Information

There's a **tourist office** (☎01687-462170; ⏲10am-5.30pm Mon-Fri, 10.15am-3.45pm Sat, noon-3.30pm Sun), a post office, a bank with ATM and a **Co-op supermarket** (⏲8am-10pm Mon-Sat, 9am-9pm Sun).

Getting There & Away

BOAT Ferries run from Mallaig to the Isle of Skye; see the transport information for Skye (p924) for more details.

BUS Shiel Buses bus 500 runs from Fort William to Mallaig (1½ hours, three daily Monday to Friday only) via Glenfinnan (30 minutes) and Arisaig (one hour).

TRAIN The West Highland line runs between Fort William and Mallaig (£10, 1½ hours) four times a day (three on Sunday).

NORTHEAST COAST

In both landscape and character, the east coast is where the real barrenness of the Highlands begins to unfold. While the interior is dominated by the vast and mournful Sutherland mountain range, along the coast great heather-covered hills heave themselves out of the wild North Sea. Rolling farmland drops suddenly into the icy waters, and small, historic towns are moored precariously on the coast's edge.

Tain

POP 3511

Scotland's oldest royal burgh, Tain is a proud sandstone town that rose to prominence as pilgrims descended to venerate the relics of St Duthac, who is commemorated by the 12th-century ruins of **St Duthac's Chapel**, and St Duthus Church. In the church grounds is entertaining **Tain Through Time** (www.tainmuseum.org.uk; Tower St; adult/child £3.50/2.50; ⏲10am-5pm Mon-Sat Apr-Oct), a heritage centre with a colourful and educational display on Duthac, King James IV and key moments in Scottish history. Another building focuses on the town's fine silversmithing tradition. Admission includes an audio-guided walk around town.

On Tain's northern outskirts, friendly **Glenmorangie Distillery** (www.glenmorangie.com; tours £2.50; ⏲9am-5pm Mon-Fri, plus 10am-4pm Sat & Sun Jun-Aug), with emphasis on the second syllable, produces a fine light malt, which is subjected to a number of different cask finishes for variation. The tour is less in-depth than some but finishes with a dram.

So much the heart of town that the main street has to detour around it, the **Royal Hotel** (☎01862-892013; www.royalhoteltain.co.uk; High St; s/d £50/85; 📶) is undergoing much-needed refurbishment that's leaving its good-sized rooms looking very spruce. For only a tenner more, you get a four-poster room in the old part of the hotel; these are great, with a choice of colour schemes, and well worth the upgrade. The restaurant is the best in town and bar meals are also decent.

Scottish Citylink and Stagecoach buses from Inverness to Thurso pass through Tain several times daily (£8.50, 50 minutes to 1¼ hours, five daily).

There are up to three trains daily to Inverness (£11.20, one hour) and Thurso (£13.70, 2½ hours).

Bonar Bridge & Around

The A9 crosses the Dornoch Firth, on a bridge and causeway, near Tain. An alternative route goes around the firth via the tiny settlements of **Ardgay** and **Bonar Bridge**, where the A836 to Lairg branches west.

From Ardgay, a single-track road leads 10 miles up Strathcarron to **Croick**, the scene of notorious evictions during the 1845 Clearances. You can still see the evocative messages scratched by refugee crofters from Glencalvie on the eastern windows of Croick Church.

Opulent **Carbisdale Castle SYHA** (☎01549-421232; www.hostellingscotland.com; Culrain; dm/s/d £20/25/50; ⏲mid-Mar–Oct; P @ 📶 👪) makes its home in Carbisdale Castle, which was built in 1914 for the dowager duchess of Sutherland. It's now Scotland's biggest and most luxurious hostel, its halls studded with statues and dripping with opulence. Kick back in the super-elegant library room or cook up a feast in the kitchen; catered meals (£11.50 for a three-course dinner) are also available. It's 10 minutes' walk north of Culrain train station. Advance bookings are highly recommended. Mountain bikers coming off the trails can shower here for a small fee.

Trains from Inverness to Thurso stop at Culrain (£13.50, 1½ hours, two to three daily), half a mile from Carbisdale Castle.

Dornoch

POP 1206

It's difficult to believe that Scotland's last executed witch perished in a vat of boiling tar in Dornoch in 1722, because today this graceful village is all happy families. On the coast, 2 miles off the A9, this symphony in sandstone bewitches visitors with flowers, greenery and affable locals at every turn.

Sights

Consecrated in the 13th century, **Dornoch Cathedral** (10am-7pm or later) is an elegant Gothic edifice with an interior softly illuminated through modern stained-glass windows. By the western door is the sarcophagus of Sir Richard de Moravia, who died fighting the Danes at the battle of Embo in the 1260s. Until he met his maker, the battle had been going rather well for him; he'd managed to slay the Danish commander with the unattached leg of a horse that was to hand.

If you've struck Dornoch on a sunny day make sure you have a walk along its golden sand **beach**, which stretches for miles.

Sleeping & Eating

TOP CHOICE **Dornoch Castle Hotel** HOTEL ££
(01862-810216; www.dornochcastlehotel.com; Castle St; garden s/d £71/118, superior/deluxe d £175/223;) This 16th-century former bishop's palace makes a wonderful place to stay, particularly if you upgrade to one of the superior rooms, which have views, space, malt whisky and chocolates on the welcome tray, and, in some cases, four-poster beds; the deluxe rooms are unforgettable. Cheaper rooms (s/d £51/66) are also available in adjoining buildings. In the evening toast your toes in the cosy bar before dining in style at the first-rate restaurant (dinner mains £16 to £20) tucking into dishes featuring plenty of game and seasonal produce. The restaurant's open for lunch and dinner; bar meals are also available during the day.

Trevose Guest House B&B ££
(01862-810269; jamackenzie@tiscali.co.uk; Cathedral Sq; s/d £35/60; Mar-Sep;) First impressions deceive at Trevose Guest House, a lovely stone cottage right by the cathedral. It looks compact but actually boasts very spacious rooms with significant comfort and well-loved old wooden furnishings. Character oozes from every pore of the place and a benevolent welcome is a given.

Information

The **tourist office** (01862-255121; Castle St; 9am-12.30pm, 1.30-5pm Mon-Fri, also Sat & Sun Jun-Aug) is in the Highland Council Building next to Dornoch Castle Hotel.

Getting There & Away

Scottish Citylink has four to five daily services to/from Inverness (£9, one hour) and Thurso (£14, 2¼ hours), stopping in the square at Dornoch.

Dunrobin Castle

Mighty **Dunrobin Castle** (www.dunrobincastle.co.uk; adult/child £8.50/5; 10.30am-4.30pm Mon-Sat, noon-4.30pm Sun Apr, May & Sep–mid-Oct, 10.30am-5.30pm Jun-Aug) is the largest house in the Highlands (187 rooms). Although it dates back to around 1275, most of what you see today was built in French style between 1845 and 1850. One of the homes of the earls and dukes of Sutherland, it's richly furnished and offers an intriguing insight into their opulent lifestyle. The pitiless first Duke of Sutherland cleared 15,000 people from the north of Scotland while residing here.

Only 22 rooms are on display, with hunting trophies much to the fore. The **museum** offers an eclectic mix of archaeological finds, natural-history exhibits, more non-PC animal remains and an excellent collection of Pictish stones found in Sutherland. The formal gardens host impressive **falconry** displays two to three times a day.

Buses between Inverness and Thurso stop in Golspie, one mile to the south of the castle. There are also trains from Inverness (£15, two hours, two or three daily) to Golspie and to Dunrobin Castle.

Helmsdale

POP 900

Surrounded by hills whose gorse explodes mad yellow in springtime, this sheltered fishing town, like many spots on this coast, was a major emigration point during the Clearances and also a booming herring port. It's surrounded by stunning, undulating coastline and the River Helmsdale is one of the best salmon rivers in the Highlands.

In the centre of town, **Timespan** (www.timespan.org.uk; 10am-5pm Mon-Sat, noon-5pm Sun Apr-Oct, 11am-4pm Sat & Sun, 2-5pm Tue Nov-Mar) has an impressive display covering local history (including the 1869 gold rush), and Barbara Cartland, late queen of romance novels, who was a Helmsdale regular. There are also local art exhibitions, a geology garden and a cafe.

Sleeping & Eating

Bridge Hotel HOTEL ££
(☎01431-821100; www.bridgehotel.net; Dunrobin St; s/d £65/105; 📶) Ideally located, this early 19th-century lodging is the smartest place to stay and the best place to eat in town. Proud rather than furtive about its Highland heritage, it displays a phalanx of antlers, even on the key fobs. But the rooms don't have the expected patina of age; they have wonderfully plush fabrics and a smart contemporary feel. The downstairs bar and restaurant hum with good cheer and relaxed hospitality; check out the replica of Britain's biggest landed salmon.

Helmsdale Hostel HOSTEL £
(☎01431-821636; www.helmsdalehostel.co.uk; Stafford St; dm/tw/f £15/40/60; ⊙Apr-Sep; 📶) This caringly run hostel is in very good nick and makes a cheerful, comfortable budget base for exploring Caithness. The dorm berths are mostly cosy single beds rather than bunks, and the en suite rooms are great for families. The lofty kitchen-lounge space has a wood stove and good kitchen.

La Mirage BISTRO £
(www.lamirage.org; 7 Dunrobin St; mains £8-10; ⊙noon-8.30pm) Created in homage to Barbara Cartland by the larger-than-life late owner, this minor legend is a medley of pink flamboyance, faded celebrity photos and show tunes. The meals aren't gourmet – think chicken Kiev – but the fish and chips (also available to take away: eat 'em down on the pretty harbour) are really tasty.

Getting There & Away

Buses from Inverness and Thurso stop in Helmsdale, as do trains (from Thurso £13.50, 1¼ hours, four daily).

CAITHNESS

Once you pass Helmsdale, you are entering Caithness, a place of jagged gorse-and-grass-topped cliffs hiding tiny fishing harbours. This top corner of Scotland was Viking territory, historically more connected to Orkney and Shetland than to the rest of the mainland. It's a magical and mystical land with an ancient aura, peopled by wise folk with long memories who are fiercely proud of their corner of Scotland.

Helmsdale to Wick

Lybster is a purpose-built fishing village dating from 1810, with a stunning harbour area surrounded by grassy cliffs. In its heyday, it was Scotland's third busiest port.

There are several interesting prehistoric sites near Lybster. Five miles to the northwest, on the minor road to Achavanich, just south of Loch Stemster, are the unsigned 30 **Achavanich Standing Stones**. In a desolate setting, these crumbling monuments of the distant past still capture the imagination with their evocative location.

A mile east of Lybster on the A99, a turn-off leads 4 miles north to the **Grey Cairns of Camster**. Dating from between 4000 BC and 2500 BC, these burial chambers are hidden in long, low mounds rising from an evocatively desolate stretch of moor.

Back on the A99, the **Hill o'Many Stanes**, 2 miles beyond the Camster turn-off, is a curious, fan-shaped arrangement of 22 rows of small stones that probably date from around 2000 BC.

Stagecoach buses between Thurso and Inverness run via Lybster (one hour, up to four daily). There's also a coastal service from Wick to Helmsdale stopping here.

Wick

POP 7333

More gritty than pretty, Wick has been down on its luck since the collapse of the herring industry. It was once the world's largest fish port for the 'silver darlings' but when the market dropped off after WWII, job losses were huge and the town hasn't totally recovered.

The **Wick Heritage Centre** (www.wickheritage.org; 20 Bank Row; adult/child £3/50p; ⊙10am-5pm Mon-Sat Apr-Oct, last entry 3.45pm) is a great town museum displaying everything from fishing equipment to complete herring fishing boats. Displays show the rise and fall of the herring industry, but the Johnston photographic collection is the museum's star exhibit. From 1863 to 1977, three generations of Johnstons photographed everything that happened around Wick, and the 70,000 photographs are an amazing portrait of the town's life.

Sleeping & Eating

Quayside B&B ££
(☎01955-603229; www.quaysidewick.co.uk; 25 Harbour Quay; s/d/f without breakfast £30/50/75; P) Quayside should be your first port of call for accommodation – it has been in the business for many years and knows what it's doing. Spruce rooms – including a great family room with kitchenette – can be taken at B&B or bed-only rates and there are self-catering flats available too. The owners couldn't be more helpful.

Mackays Hotel HOTEL ££
(☎01955-602323; www.mackayshotel.co.uk; Union St; s/d £89/119; @) The renovated MacKay's is Wick's best hotel. Rooms vary in layout and size so ask to see a few; prices drop if you're staying more than one night, and walk-up prices are usually quite a bit lower than the rack rates we list here. The 2.75m-long Ebenezer Pl, the shortest street in Britain, runs past one end of the hotel. The bistro is a fine-dining option for lunch or dinner (mains £10 to £13). Service is friendly and the ingredients are sourced locally.

Bord de L'Eau RESTAURANT ££
(☎01955-604400; 2 Market St; mains £14-21; ⊙lunch Tue-Sat, dinner Tue-Sun) This serene, upmarket French restaurant is the best place to eat in Wick. It overlooks the river and serves a changing menu of mostly meat French classics. The conservatory dining room overlooking the river is lovely on a sunny evening. It also opens for 'morning coffee' before lunch, when you can down tasty pastries with your cafe au lait.

Information

Tourist office (McAllans; 66 High St; ⊙9am-5.30pm Mon-Sat) Good selection of information upstairs in McAllans Clothing Store.

Wick Carnegie Library (Sinclair Tce; ⊙Mon-Sat) Free internet access.

Getting There & Away

Flybe/Loganair (☎0871 700 2000; www.flybe.com) flies between Edinburgh and Wick airport once daily except Saturday. **Eastern Airways** (☎01652-680600; www.easternairways.com) flies to Aberdeen (three daily Monday to Friday).

Stagecoach/Citylink operates buses to/from Inverness (£17.50, three hours, five daily) and Thurso (30 minutes, five daily) and also to John O'Groats (45 minutes, up to five daily).

Rapsons/Highland Country runs the connecting service to John O'Groats (40 minutes, four to seven Monday to Saturday) for the passenger ferry to Burwick, Orkney. It also runs by the Gills Bay ferry to St Margaret's Hope, Orkney.

Trains service Wick from Inverness (£16.10, four hours, four daily).

John O'Groats

POP 500

A car park surrounded by tourist shops, John O'Groats offers little to the visitor beyond a means to get across to Orkney; even the pub has been shut for a while now (there are a couple of cafes). Though it's not the northernmost point of the British mainland (that's Dunnet Head), it still serves as the endpoint of the 874-mile trek from Land's End in Cornwall, a popular if arduous route for cyclists and walkers, many of whom raise money for charitable causes.

Two miles east, **Duncansby Head** provides a more solemn end-of-Britain moment with a small lighthouse and 60m cliffs sheltering nesting fulmars. From here a 15-minute walk through a sheep paddock yields spectacular views of the sea-surrounded monoliths known as **Duncansby Stacks**.

The **tourist office** (☎01955-611373; ⊙10am-5pm Apr-Oct) is the best thing about the place, with its fine selection of local novels and books about Caithness and the Highland Clearances.

Getting There & Away

Stagecoach runs buses between John O'Groats and Wick (40 minutes, four to seven Monday to Saturday). There are also three to eight services Monday to Saturday to/from Thurso.

From May to September, a passenger ferry shuttles across to Burwick in Orkney (see p956). Ninety-minute wildlife cruises to the island of Stroma or Duncansby Head cost £15 (late June to August).

Castle of Mey

This **castle** (www.castleofmey.org.uk; adult/child £9.50/4; ⊙10.30am-4pm May–mid-Oct), a big crowd-puller for its Queen Mother connections, is about 6 miles from John O'Groats, off the A836 to Thurso. The exterior may seem grand but inside it feels domestic and everything is imbued with the character of the late Queen Mum. All the in-jokes are explained by staff who worked for the lady. The castle closes for a couple of weeks at the end of July.

Dunnet Head

Turn off 8 miles east of Thurso to reach the most northerly point on the British mainland, dramatic Dunnet Head, which banishes tacky pretenders with its majestic cliffs dropping into Pentland Firth. There are inspiring views of the Orkney Islands, flopping seals and nesting seabirds below, and a lighthouse built by Robert Louis Stevenson's granddad.

Just west, Dunnet Bay offers you one of Scotland's finest beaches, backed by high dunes.

Thurso & Scrabster

POP 7737

Britain's most northerly mainland town, Thurso makes a handy overnight stop if you're heading west or across to Orkney. There's a pretty town beach, riverbank strolls and a good new museum. Ferries cross from Scrabster, 2.5 miles west of Thurso, to Orkney.

Sights

FREE **Caithness Horizons** MUSEUM
(www.caithnesshorizons.co.uk; High St; 10am-6pm Mon-Sat, 11am-4pm Sun) All shiny and new, this museum brings much of the lore, history and sentiment of Caithness to life through its excellent displays. A couple of fine Pictish cross-slabs greet the visitor downstairs; the main exhibition is a wide-ranging look at local history that includes plenty of audiovisuals – check out the wistful one on the now-abandoned island of Stroma for an emotional slice of social history.

Sleeping

Forss House Hotel HOTEL £££
(01847-861201; www.forsshousehotel.co.uk; Forss by Thurso; s/d £95/125, superior s/d/ste £110/160/230; P) Tucked into a thicket of trees 4 miles west of Thurso is elegant accommodation in an old Georgian mansion that has both character and style. Sumptuous upstairs rooms are much better than basement rooms as they have lovely views of the garden. There are also separate, beautifully appointed suites in the garden itself, which provide both privacy and a sense of tranquillity.

Sandra's Hostel HOSTEL £
(01847-894575; www.sandras-backpackers.ukf.net; 24 Princes St; dm/d/f £14/34/50; P@) A byword for backpacker excellence, Sandra's was awash with free facilities when some hostels still had you scrubbing floors before checkout. Sporting an excellent kitchen, it offers free internet and wi-fi, a help-yourself continental breakfast, laundry and downstairs chip shop. Dorms, mostly four-berthers, are en suite and spotless.

Murray House B&B ££
(01847-895759; www.murrayhousebb.com; 1 Campbell St; s/d £35/70;) A solid 19th-century town house on a central corner, Murray House gives a good first impression with a genuine welcome. It continues with new carpets, smart rooms with solid wooden furniture, an appealing lounge space and the option of an evening meal, all at very punter-friendly prices. No cards.

Waterside House B&B £
(01847-894751; www.watersidehouse.org; 3 Janet St; s £25, d £35-50) This straight-up guest house is easy to find (turn left just after the bridge coming into town), has parking outside and comfortable beds in well-priced rooms. There's a range of them, from double en suites to cheaper attic rooms that share a spotless bathroom. Breakfast choices include egg-and-bacon rolls or takeaway if you've got an early ferry. No cards.

Eating

Captain's Galley RESTAURANT £££
(01847-894999; www.captainsgalley.co.uk; Scrabster; 3-course dinner £46; dinner Tue-Sat) Right by the ferry terminal in Scrabster, Captain's Gallery is a classy but friendly place offering a short, seafood-based menu that features local and sustainable-sourced produce prepared in relatively simple ways to let the natural flavours shine through. Most rate it the best eatery in Caithness.

Holborn BAR, RESTAURANT ££
(01847-892771; www.holbornhotel.co.uk; 16 Princes St; mains £13-18) A trendy, comfortable place decked out in light wood, the Holborn is quite a contrast to more traditional Thurso watering holes. Its bar, Bar 16, is a modern space with couches and comfy chairs. Bar meals here (£7 to £10) are uncomplicated but decent. The Red Pepper

restaurant takes things to a higher level, with very tasty seafood – delicious home-smoked salmon – the mainstay of a short but solid menu. Desserts are delicious too.

Information

Library (☎01847-893237; Davidson's Lane; ⊙10am-6pm Mon & Wed, to 8pm Tue & Fri, to 1pm Thu & Sat) Free internet.

Tourist office (☎01847-893155; thurso@visitscotland.com; Riverside Rd; ⊙Mon-Sat Apr-May & Sep-Oct, daily Jun-Aug)

Getting There & Around

From Inverness, Stagecoach/Citylink run via Wick to Thurso/Scrabster (£17.50, 3½ hours, five daily) and also head to John O'Groats (one hour, three to eight Monday to Saturday).

There are two or three daily train services from Inverness in summer (£16.10, 3¾ hours) but space for bicycles is limited so book ahead.

It's a 2-mile walk from Thurso train station to the ferry port at Scrabster or there are buses from Olrig St.

NORTH & NORTHWEST COAST

Quintessential Highland country such as this, marked by single-track roads, breathtaking emptiness and a wild, fragile beauty, is a rarity on the modern, crowded, highly urbanised island of Britain. You could get lost up here for weeks – and that still wouldn't be enough time.

The north and northwest coastline is a feast of deep inlets, forgotten beaches and surging peninsulas. Within the rugged confines, the deep interior is home to vast, empty spaces, enormous lochs and some of Scotland's highest peaks.

Thurso to Durness

It's 80 winding, and often spectacular, coastal miles from Thurso to Durness.

BETTYHILL

POP 550

The panorama of a sweeping, sandy beach backed by velvety green hills with bulbous, rocky outcrops makes a sharp contrast to the sad history of this area. Bettyhill is a crofting community of resettled tenant farmers kicked off their land during the Clearances.

Strathnaver Museum (www.strathnavermuseum.org.uk; adult/child £2/50p; ⊙10am-5pm Mon-Sat Apr-Oct), in an old church, tells the sad story of the Strathnaver Clearances. Outside the back door of the church is the Farr Stone, a fine carved Pictish cross-slab.

Just west of town, an enormous stretch of white sand flanks the River Naver as it meets the sea.

COLDBACKIE & TONGUE

POP 450

Coldbackie has outstanding views over sandy beaches, turquoise waters and offshore islands. Only 2 miles further on is Tongue, with the evocative 14th-century ruins of **Castle Varrich**, once a Mackay stronghold. To get to the castle, take the trail next to the Royal Bank of Scotland, near Ben Loyal Hotel – it's an easy stroll. Tongue has a shop, post office, bank and petrol station.

Sleeping & Eating

Cloisters B&B £
(☎01847-601286; www.cloistertal.demon.co.uk; Talmine; s/d £32.50/55; P) Vying for the position of best-located B&B in Scotland, Cloisters has three en-suite twin rooms with brilliant views over the Kyle of Tongue and offshore islands. Breakfast is in the artistically converted church alongside. To get here from Tongue, cross the causeway and take the turn-off to Melness, almost immediately on your right; Cloisters is a couple of miles down this road.

Tongue SYHA HOSTEL £
(☎01847-611789; www.syha.org.uk; dm/tw £16.25/39; ⊙Apr-Oct; P) In a wonderful spot right by the causeway across the Kyle of Tongue, a mile west of town, Tongue SYHA is the top budget option in the area with clean, comfortably refitted dorms, some with views, a decent kitchen and cosy lounge. The helpful warden has plenty of local advice and turns her hand to delicious home baking.

Tongue Hotel HOTEL, PUB ££
(☎01847-611206; www.tonguehotel.co.uk; s/d £65/100, superior £75/120; P) Tongue Hotel is a welcoming spot that offers cosy, recently renovated rooms in a former hunting lodge. It serves upmarket Highland restaurant fare (mains £16 to £18) in the evenings and great-value bar meals (£6,

CROFTING & THE CLEARANCES

The wild and empty spaces up in these parts of the Highlands are among Europe's least populated zones, but this wasn't always so. Ruins of cottages in the most desolate areas are mute witnesses to one of the most heartless episodes of Scottish history: the Highland Clearances.

Up until the 19th century the most common form of farming settlement here was the *baile*, a group of a dozen or so families who farmed the land granted to them by the local chieftain in return for military service and a portion of the harvest.

After Culloden, however, the king banned private armies and new laws made the clan chiefs actual owners of their traditional lands, often vast tracts of territory. With the prospect of unimagined riches allied to a depressing failure of imagination, the lairds decided that sheep were more profitable than agriculture and proceeded to evict tens of thousands of farmers from their lands. The Clearances forced these desperate folk to head for the cities in the hope of finding work or to emigrate to the Americas or Southern Hemisphere. Those who chose not to emigrate or move to the cities to find work were forced to eke a living from narrow plots of marginal agricultural land, often close to the coast. This was a form of smallholding that became known as crofting. The small patch of land barely provided a living and had to be supplemented by other work such as fishing and kelp-gathering. It was always precarious, as rights were granted on a year-by-year basis, so at any moment a crofter could lose not only the farm but also the house they'd built on it.

The economic depression of the late 19th century meant many couldn't pay their rent. This time, however, they resisted expulsion, instead forming the Highland Land Reform Association and their own political party. Their resistance led to several of their demands being acceded to by the government, including security of tenure, fair rents and eventually the supply of land for new crofts. Crofters now have the right to purchase their farmland and recent laws have abolished the feudal system, which created so much misery.

lunch and dinner) in the snug Brass Tap bar in the basement, a good spot to chat with locals or shelter from the weather.

Craggan Hotel RESTAURANT ££
(01847-601278; www.thecraggan.co.uk; mains £8-16; breakfast, lunch & dinner) On the same road as Cloisters, 2 miles from the other side of the Kyle, Craggan Hotel doesn't look much from outside but go in and you'll find smart, formal service and a menu ranging from exquisite burgers (£6.50) to classy game and seafood dishes, presented beautifully. The wine list's not bad for a pub either.

Durness

POP 350

The scattered village of Durness (www.durness.org) is strung out along cliffs, which rise from a series of pristine beaches. It has one of the finest locations in Scotland. When the sun shines the effects of blinding white sand, the cry of sea birds and the lime-coloured seas combine in a magical way.

There are shops, an ATM, petrol and plenty of accommodation options in Durness.

Sights & Activities

Walking around the sensational sandy coastline is a highlight here, as is a visit to Cape Wrath. Durness's beautiful **beaches**, include Rispond to the east, Sargo Sands below town and Balnakeil to the west; the sea offers **scuba-diving** sites complete with wrecks, caves, seals and whales. At **Balnakeil**, less than a mile beyond Durness, a craft village occupies what was once an early warning radar station.

A mile east of the village centre is a path down to **Smoo Cave**. From the vast main chamber, you can head through to a smaller flooded cavern where a waterfall sometimes cascades from the roof. From here you can take a **boat trip** (adult/child £3/2; Apr-Sep) across to explore a little further into the interior.

Sleeping & Eating

TOP CHOICE **Mackays** HOTEL ££

(☎01971-511202; www.visitmackays.com; Durness; d/deluxe d £110/125; ⊙Apr-Nov; 📶) You literally feel you're at the top corner of Scotland here; this is where the road turns 90 degrees. But no matter whether you're heading east or south, you'll go far before you find a better place to stay than this family-run haven of Highland hospitality. With big beds and soft fabrics, it's a romantic spot, but what impresses more than anything is the warm-hearted personal service. The restaurant (mains £11 to £17) presents local seafood and robust meat dishes.

Lazy Crofter Bunkhouse HOSTEL £

(☎01971-511202; www.durnesshostel.com; dm £15) Run out of Mackays, Lazy Crofter Bunkhouse is Durness's best budget accommodation. A bothy vibe gives it a Highland feel and it offers inviting dorms with plenty of room and lockers, a sociable shared table for meals and board games, and a great wooden deck with sea views, perfect for midge-free evenings.

Loch Croispol Bookshop CAFE £

(www.scottish-books.net; Balnakeil Craft Village; light meals £4-8; ⊙10.30am-5pm) At this place you can feed your body and your mind. Set among books featuring all things Scottish are a few tables where you can enjoy an all-day breakfast, sandwiches and other scrumptious fare at lunch, such as fresh Achiltibuie salmon.

Sango Sands Oasis CAMPING £

(☎01971-511222; www.sangosands.com; Durness; sites per adult/child £5.75/3.50; P) You couldn't imagine a better location for a campsite: great grassy areas on the edge of cliffs descend to two lovely sand beaches. Facilities are good and very clean and there's a pub next door.

Information

Durness Community Building (1 Bard Tce; per 30min £1) Coin-op internet access, opposite Mackays.

Tourist office (☎01971-511368; durness@visitscotland.com; ⊙10am-5pm Mon-Sat Apr-Oct, plus Sun Apr-Aug) Organises guided walks in summer. Closes an hour for lunch.

Durness to Ullapool

Perhaps Scotland's most spectacular road trip, the 69 miles connecting Durness to Ullapool is a scenic feast, almost too much to take in. A wide heathered valley gives way to rockier country studded with small lochs; gorse-covered hills preface the magnificent rugged ridge of Assynt, punctuated by its glacier-scoured mountains, including ziggurat-like Quinag, the distinctive saddle of Suilven and much-climbed Stac Pollaidh. It's no wonder the area has been dubbed a geopark (www.northwest-highlands-geopark.co.uk).

KYLESKU & LOCH GLENCOUL

Cruises on Loch Glencoul pass treacherous-looking mountains, seal colonies and the 213m-drop of **Eas a'Chual Aulin**, Britain's highest waterfall. In summer, the **MV Statesman** (☎01971-502345; ⊙daily Apr-Sep) runs two-hour trips twice daily from Kylesku pier for £15/5 per adult/child to see waterfalls and baby seals.

WORTH A TRIP

CAPE WRATH

Though its name actually comes from the Norse word for 'turning point', there is something daunting and primal about Cape Wrath, the northwesternmost point of the British mainland. It is crowned by a **lighthouse** (built by Robert Stevenson in 1828) and stands close to the seabird colonies of **Clo Mor**, Britain's highest coastal cliffs. Getting to Cape Wrath involves a **boat** (☎01971-511287) ride – passengers and bikes only – across the Kyle of Durness (return £5.50, 10 minutes) connecting with an optional **minibus** (☎01971-511343) running 12 miles to the cape (return £10, 40 minutes). This is a friendly but eccentric, sometimes shambolic service with limited capacity, so plan on waiting in high season, and ring before setting out to make sure the ferry is running. The ferry leaves from Keoldale pier, a couple of miles southwest of Durness, and runs two or more times daily from Easter to September. It's a spectacular ride or hike to Cape Wrath over bleak scenery occasionally used by the Ministry of Defence as a firing range. There's a cafe at the lighthouse serving soup and sandwiches.

While you wait for the boat you can toast your toes by a log fire, enjoy a pint (decent ales on tap) and tuck into a superb all-day bar meal at the **Kylesku Hotel** (☎01971-502231; www.kyleskuhotel.co.uk; Kylesku; small s/d £55/80, s/d 65/97, bar mains £9-13; ⊙noon-9pm; 📶) overlooking the pier. Seafood is the speciality including local mussels and smoked haddock and salmon fish cakes. There's also a restaurant open for even tastier fishy delights at dinner time (mains £13 to £17). If you fancy bunkering down for the night, a variety of rooms are available – the separate, motel-style ones with views are the best.

ACHMELVICH & AROUND

Not far south of Kylesku, a 30-mile detour on the narrow B869 rewards with spectacular views and fine beaches. From the lighthouse at **Point of Stoer**, a one-hour cliff walk leads to the **Old Man of Stoer**, a spectacular sea stack. On this stretch is the **Clachtoll Beach Campsite** (☎01571-855377; www.clachtollbeachcampsite.co.uk; tent £8-10 plus per person £2; ⊙Apr-Sep), a great coastal spot, and the **Achmelvich Beach SYHA** (☎01571-844480; www.syha.org.uk; Achmelvich; dm £15; ⊙Apr-Sep) a whitewashed cottage set beside a great beach at the end of a side road. There's a summer chip shop nearby, otherwise bring your own supplies; it's a 4-mile walk from Lochinver. Ullapool–Lochinver buses take you to the hostel on request. The hostel closes between 10am and 5pm.

LOCHINVER & ASSYNT

The distinctive region of Assynt comprises a landscape of spectacular peaks rising from the moorland. Lochinver is the main settlement; a busy little fishing port that's a popular port of call for tourists, with its laid-back attitude, good facilities, striking scenery and range of accommodation.

The stunningly shaped hills of Assynt are popular with walkers and include peaks such as Suilven (731m), Quinag (808m), Ben More Assynt (998m) and Canisp (846m). The tourist office has plenty of walking information: leaflets and more detailed booklets.

Sleeping & Eating

There are several B&Bs; for magnificent vistas head a mile around the bay to Baddidarrach, which looks back at Lochinver and the magnificent bulk of Suilven behind.

TOP CHOICE **Albannach** HOTEL, RESTAURANT £££
(☎01571-844407; www.thealbannach.co.uk; Baddidarrach; s/d/ste with dinner from £200/260/340; ⊙Mar-Dec; P📶) The Albannach is sheer indulgence, on a grand scale. You'll discover roaring fireplaces, furniture found only in antique shops and a demure, sophisticated atmosphere. Roomy lodgings decorated with elegant flair, spacious grounds studded with fruit trees, inspiring panoramas and wonderful dinners using organic ingredients and well-selected local produce (£55 for non-guests) combine to make it a special spot.

Veyatie B&B ££
(☎01571-844424; www.veyatie-scotland.co.uk; 66 Baddidarrach; s/d £48/76; ⊙Jan-Nov; P📶) Overseen by a personable Belgian shepherd (dog), this choice at the end of the road across the bay has perhaps the best views of all, as well as sweet rooms, a little conservatory and a grassy garden.

Lochinver Larder & Riverside Bistro CAFE, RESTAURANT ££
(www.lochinverlarder.co.uk; 3 Main St; pies £5.95, mains £10-16; ⊙10am-8.30pm) With an outstanding ensemble of inventive food made with local produce, Lochinver pies are a particular standout here and are famous in this part of the world: try the smoked haddock, or wild boar and apricot – very tasty. The bistro also churns out delicious seafood dishes in the evening. A top place.

Information

There's a supermarket in town, as well as a post office, bank (with an ATM) and petrol station.

Tourist office (☎01571-844373; lochinver@visitscotland.com; Main St; ⊙10am-5pm Mon-Sat Easter-Oct, also 10am-4pm Sun Jun-Aug) Has leaflets on hill walks in the area and a display on the story of Assynt, from flora and fauna to clans, conflict and controversy.

Ullapool

POP 1308

The pretty port of Ullapool is one of the most alluring Highlands spots, a wonderful destination in itself as well as a gateway for the Western Isles. Offering a row of whitewashed cottages arrayed along the harbour and special views of Loch Broom and its flanking hills, the town has a very distinctive appeal.

Sights & Activities

In summer, the ferry company **CalMac** (www.calmac.co.uk) runs day trips to Lewis and Harris.

Ullapool Museum MUSEUM
(www.ullapoolmuseum.co.uk; 7 West Argyle St; adult/child £3/50p; ⏲10am-5pm Mon-Sat Apr-Oct) In a converted Telford Parliamentary church, this museum relates the pre-, natural and social history of the town and Loch-Broom area with a particular focus on the emigration to Nova Scotia and other places; there's a genealogy section if you want to trace roots.

Seascape BOAT TRIPS
(☎01854-633708; www.sea-scape.co.uk)
These guys run you out to the Summer Isles in an orange RIB (rigid inflatable boat). Their two-hour trip costs £28.50 for adults, £20 for kids.

Summer Queen BOAT TRIPS
(☎07713-257219; www.summerqueen.co.uk)
The stately *Summer Queen* takes you out around Isle Martin (£17/8.50 per adult/child, two hours) or to the Summer Isles (£26/13, four hours), with a stop on Tanera Mor.

Sleeping

Note that during summer Ullapool is very busy and finding accommodation can be tricky – the answer: book ahead.

TOP CHOICE **Ceilidh Place** HOTEL ££
(☎01854-612103; www.theceilidhplace.com; 14 West Argyle St; d £100-146; P) Ceilidh Place is a celebration of Scottish culture and one of the more unusual and delightful places to stay in the Highlands. That's culture with a capital C: we're talking literature and traditional music, not tartan and Nessies. Rooms go for character rather than modern bathrooms or conveniences, and come with a selection of books personally chosen by Scottish literati, eclectic artwork and nice little touches like hot-water bottles. Best is the sumptuous guest lounge, with sofas, chaises longues and an honesty bar.

West House B&B ££
(☎01854-613126; www.accommodationullapool.net; West Argyle St; d £70;) Slap bang in the centre of Ullapool, this welcoming place, a solid white house that was once a manse, offers excellent rooms with a contemporary style and great bathrooms. Breakfast is continental: rooms come with a fridge stocked with fresh fruit salad and juice so you eat at your leisure in your own chamber. It also hires bikes so you can explore the surrounding area.

Ullapool SYHA HOSTEL £
(☎01854-612254; www.syha.org.uk; Shore St; dm/tw £17.25/38; ⏲Mar-Oct) You've got to hand it to the SYHA; it has chosen some very sweet locations for its hostels. This is as close to the water as it is to the town's best pub; about four seconds' walk. The front rooms have harbour views but the busy dining area and little lounge are also good spots for contemplating the water.

Point Cottage B&B ££
(☎01854-612494; www.pointcottage.co.uk; 22 West Shore St; d £70; ⏲Mar-Oct; P) A haven of good taste, the courteous and welcoming Point Cottage has a great headland location – even the back rooms have water views. It's one of those shorefront cottages you've already admired if you arrived by ferry, and it'll feel comfy for both hedonists – smoked fish for breakfast – and walkers, with plenty of maps and advice.

Ceilidh Clubhouse HOSTEL £
(☎01854-612103; West Lane; r per person £18-20; P) Opposite the Ceilidh Place, this place is run by them as no-frills accommodation for walkers, journeypeople and staff. A big building, it has hostel-style rooms with sturdy bunks and basin. Though showers and toilets are a little institutional, the big bonus is that rooms are private: if you're woken by snores, at least they'll be familiar ones.

Broomfield Holiday Park CAMPING £
(☎01854-612664; www.broomfieldhp.com; West Lane; 1/2 person tent £8/12, plus car £4; ⏲May-Oct) Great grassy headland location very close to centre. Midge-busting machines in action.

Eating & Drinking

Ferry Boat Inn PUB ££
(☎01854-612366; www.ferryboat-inn.com; Shore St; mains £9-12) Known as the FBI, this inn is to Ullapool what the castle is to Edinburgh. The pub's a little less traditional-looking these days with its bleached wood and non-stained carpet but it's still the place where locals and visitors mingle. The food offering is interesting; some of the dishes are a little bland, but a well-run dining room, quality ingredients and great presentation compensate.

Frigate Café CAFE £
(www.ullapoolcatering.co.uk; Shore St; mains £7-9; ⏲noon-9pm) Frigate Café, on the waterfront, is a popular venue for coffee, teas and ice cream; it also sells a very tasty local smoked cheese. But you can also sit down and graze the Italian-influenced menu of salads, pizzas and pastas, or just drop by for a glass of wine or a beer.

Information

Library (Mill St; ⏲9am-5pm Mon, Wed & Fri, 9am-5pm & 6-8pm Tue & Thu, closed Mon & Wed during holidays) Free internet access.

Tourist office (☎01854-612486; ullapool@visitscotland.com; Argyle St; ⏲daily Jun-Sep, Mon-Sat Apr-May & Oct, Mon-Fri Nov-Mar)

Getting There & Away

Citylink has three daily buses, Monday to Saturday and one on Sunday, from Inverness to Ullapool (£12, 1½ hours), connecting with the Lewis ferry. See p928 for details of this service.

Ullapool to Kyle of Lochalsh

Although it's less than 50 miles as the crow flies from Ullapool to Kyle of Lochalsh, it's more like 150 miles along the circuitous coastal road – but don't let that put you off. It's a deliciously remote region and there are fine views of beaches and bays backed by mountains all the way along.

The A832 doubles back to the coast from the A835, 12 miles from Ullapool. Just after the junction, the **Falls of Measach** ('ugly' in Gaelic) spill 45m into the spectacularly deep and narrow Corrieshalloch Gorge. You can cross from side to side on a wobbly suspension bridge, built by Sir John Fowler of Braemore. The thundering falls and misty vapours rising from the gorge are very impressive.

If you're in a hurry to get to Skye, head inland on the A835 (towards Inverness) and catch up with the A832 further down, near Garve.

GAIRLOCH

POP 1100

Gairloch is a group of villages (comprising Achtercairn, Strath and Charlestown) around the inner end of a loch of the same name. The surrounding area has beautiful sandy beaches, good trout-fishing and birdwatching. Hill walkers also use Gairloch as a base for the Torridon hills and An Teallach.

The **Old Inn** (☎01445-712006; www.theoldinn.net; Charlestown; s/d £57/99; P 📶) is a rustic classic with a range of excellent snug rooms, some (such as No 4) with four-poster beds. Downstairs, the bar is an atmospheric nook-and-cranny affair, with the best pint of ale in town, and serves recommended bar meals (£7 to £14) of the delectable seafood variety. The inn is just opposite Gairloch Pier.

Information

Tourist office (☎01445-712071; ⏲daily May-Sep) At the car park in Achtercairn where a road branches off to the main centre at Strath.

TORRIDON

Southwest from Kinlochewe, the A896 follows **Glen Torridon**, overlooked by multiple peaks, including Beinn Eighe (1010m) and Liathach (1055m). The drive along Glen Torridon is one of the most breathtaking in Scotland. Mighty, brooding mountains, often partly obscured by clumps of passing clouds, seemingly drawn to their peaks like magnets, loom over the tiny, winding, single-track road.

The road reaches the sea at Torridon, where there is a **Countryside Centre** (NTS; donation £3; ⏲10am-5pm Sun-Fri Easter-Sep) offering information on flora, fauna and walks in the rugged area.

The **camping ground** (☎01381-621252; Torridon; sites free) here has good showers and you get a grassy patch to pitch your tent, along with stunning views and wide-open, exhilarating space.

The modern, squat **Torridon SYHA** (☎01445-791284; www.syha.org.uk; dm/tw £16.25/40; ⏲Mar-Oct; P @) is in a magnificent location surrounded by spectacular mountains. It's a very popular walking base so book ahead in summer.

To stay in the lap of luxury try the **Torridon** (☎01445-791242; www.thetorridon.com; s/d/superior d/master d £180/295/345/505; P @ 📶), a lavish Victorian shooting lodge that has a romantic lochside position overlooking the peaks, with Liathach looming impossibly large opposite. Rooms are gradually being converted from a classic look to a more contemporary (but most tasteful) one. The dinners are sumptuous affairs and open to non-residents (£45). Friendly staff can organise any number of activities on land or water. Part of the same set-up, the adjacent Torridon Inn offers motel-style rooms (double £87) and a welcoming bar serving meals.

APPLECROSS

POP 200

A long side trip abandons the A896 to follow the coast road to the delightfully remote seaside village of Applecross. Or you can continue a bit further down the A896 to one of the best drives in the country (best in terms of the remote and incredibly rugged and spectacular scenery, not the actual road, which winds and twists and balances on sheer precipices). The road climbs steeply to the **Bealach na Ba pass** (626m), then drops dramatically to the village. This drive is pure magic and a must if you're in the area.

The remote settlement of Applecross feels like an island retreat, partly because of its isolation, and partly because of the magnificent views of Raasay and the hills of Skye that set the pulse racing, particularly at sunset. On a clear day it's an unforgettable place, but the tranquil atmosphere isn't quite the same when the campsite and pub fill to the brim in school holidays.

You can pitch your tent at the **Applecross Camp Site** (☎01520-744268; www.applecross.uk.com; sites per person £7, hut for 2 £30; P), which offers green grassy plots, cute little wooden cabins and a good cafe.

The hub of the spread-out community is the **Applecross Inn** (☎01520-744262; www.applecross.uk.com; Shore St; s/d £70/100; mains £7-13; food noon-9pm; P), which has a perfect shoreside location for a sunset pint, a wide variety of food (mostly daily blackboard specials) and rooms with a view.

PLOCKTON

POP 450

There's something distinctly tropical about idyllic little Plockton, a filmset-like village with palm trees, whitewashed houses and a small bay dotted with islets and hemmed in by green-fuzzed mountains.

Calum's Seal Trips (☎01599-544306; www.calums-sealtrips.com; cruises adult/child £8/5) runs seal-watching cruises. There are swarms of the slippery fellas just outside the harbour and the trip comes with an excellent commentary. Trips leave daily at 10am, noon, 2pm and 4pm.

Airily set in the one-time train station (it's now opposite), **Plockton Station Bunkhouse** (☎01599-544235; gillcoe@btinternet.com; dm £13; P wi-fi) has cosy four-bed dorms, a garden and kitchen-lounge with plenty of light and good perspectives over the frenetic comings and goings (OK, that last bit's a lie) of the platforms below.

Slap-bang by the sea, characterful **Shieling** (☎01599-544282; www.lochalsh.net/shieling; d £60; Easter-Oct) is surrounded by an expertly trimmed garden and has two carpeted rooms with views and big beds. Next door is a historic thatched blackhouse (a low-walled stone cottage with a turf roof and earthen floor).

The black-painted **Plockton Hotel** (☎01599-544274; www.plocktonhotel.co.uk; 41 Harbour St; s/d £85/120, cottage s/d £55/80; mains £8-13; lunch & dinner; wi-fi) is one of those classic Highland spots that manages to make everyone happy, whether it's thirst, hunger, or fatigue that brings you knocking. The assiduously tended rooms are a delight, with excellent facilities and thoughtful touches like bathrobes. The cosy bar (or wonderful beer garden on a sunny day) are memorable places for a pint, and food ranges from sound-value bar meals to seafood platters and local langoustines brought in on the afternoon boat.

KYLE OF LOCHALSH

POP 739

Before the controversial bridge, Kyle of Lochalsh was Skye's main ferry-port. Visitors now tend to buzz through town, but Kyle has an intriguing attraction if you're interested in marine life.

The tourist office is where to book for the **Seaprobe Atlantis** (☎0800 980 4846; www.seaprobeatlantis.com; Easter-Oct), a glass-hulled boat that takes a spin around the kyle to spot seabirds, seals and maybe an otter or two. The basic trip (£9.50/4.75 adult/child) includes an entertaining guided tour and plenty of beautiful jellyfish; longer trips take in a WWII shipwreck.

The **tourist office** (☎01599-534276; daily Easter-Oct), beside the main seafront car park, stocks information on Skye. Next to it is one of Scotland's most lavishly decorated public toilets.

Citylink run to Kyle a few times daily from Inverness (£18.60, 2¼ hours), and Glasgow (£34, 5¾ hours).

The train ride between Inverness and Kyle of Lochalsh (£18.20, 2½ hours, up to four daily) is one of Scotland's most scenic train routes.

MADDENING MIDGES

Forget Nessie; the Highlands have a real monster – a voracious, bloodsucking female, fully 3mm long, known as *Culicoides impunctatus*, or the Highland midge. The bane of campers and as much a symbol of Scotland as the kilt or dram, they drive sane folk to distraction as they descend in biting clouds.

Though normally vegetarian, the female midge needs a dose of blood in order to lay her eggs. And like it or not, if you're in the Highlands between June and August, you've just volunteered as a donor. Midges especially congregate near water, and are most active in the early morning, though squadrons also patrol in the late evening, around 10pm.

Repellents and creams are reasonably effective protection, though some walkers favour midge veils. Wearing light-coloured clothing also helps. Pubs and campsites increasingly have midge-zapping machines. Check www.midgeforecast.co.uk for activity levels by area.

EILEAN DONAN CASTLE

Photogenically sited at the entrance to Loch Duich, near Dornie village, **Eilean Donan Castle** (www.eileandonancastle.com; Dornie; adult/child £5.50/4.50; ⌚9.30am-6pm mid-Mar–mid-Nov) is one of Scotland's most evocative castles, and must be represented in millions of photo albums. It's on an offshore islet, magically linked to the mainland by an elegant, stone-arched bridge. It's very much a re-creation inside with an excellent introductory exhibition. Keep an eye out for the photos of castle scenes from the movie *Highlander*. There's also a sword used at the battle of Culloden in 1746. The castle was ruined in 1719 after Spanish Jacobite forces were defeated at the Battle of Glenshiel, and it was rebuilt between 1912 and 1932.

Citylink buses from Fort William and Inverness to Portree stop opposite the castle.

ISLE OF SKYE

POP 9900

The Isle of Skye (an t-Eilean Sgiathanach in Gaelic) takes its name from the old Norse *sky-a,* meaning 'cloud island', a Viking reference to the often mist-enshrouded Cuillin Hills. It's the biggest of Scotland's islands, a 50-mile-long smorgasbord of velvet moors, jagged mountains, sparkling lochs and towering sea cliffs. The stunning scenery is the main attraction, but when the mist closes in there are plenty of castles, crofting museums and cosy pubs and restaurants to retire to.

Activities

WALKING

Skye offers some of the finest – and in places the roughest and most difficult – walking in Scotland. There are many detailed guidebooks available. You'll need Ordnance Survey (OS) 1:50,000 maps 23 and 32. Don't attempt the longer walks in bad weather or in winter.

Skye Walking Holidays (☎01470-552213; www.skyewalks.co.uk; Duntulm Castle Hotel, Trotternish) organises three-day guided walking holidays for £400 per person, including four nights of hotel accommodation.

CLIMBING

The Cuillin Hills is a playground for rock climbers, and the two-day traverse of the Cuillin Ridge is the finest mountaineering expedition in the British Isles. There are several mountain guides who can provide instruction and safely introduce inexperienced climbers to the harder routes.

Skye Guides (☎01471-822116; www.skyeguides.co.uk) A five-day basic rock-climbing course costs around £800 and a private mountain guide can be hired for around £190 a day (both rates apply for up to two clients).

SEA KAYAKING

The sheltered coves and sea lochs around the coast of Skye provide magnificent sea-kayaking opportunities. The following centres provide kayaking instruction, guiding and equipment hire for beginners and experts. It costs around £35 for a half-day kayak hire with instruction.

Whitewave Outdoor Centre (☎01470-542414; www.white-wave.co.uk; 19 Linicro, Kilmuir; ⌚Mar-Oct)

Skyak Adventures (☎01471-820002; www.skyakadventures.com; 29 Lower Breakish, Breakish)

Skye & Outer Hebrides

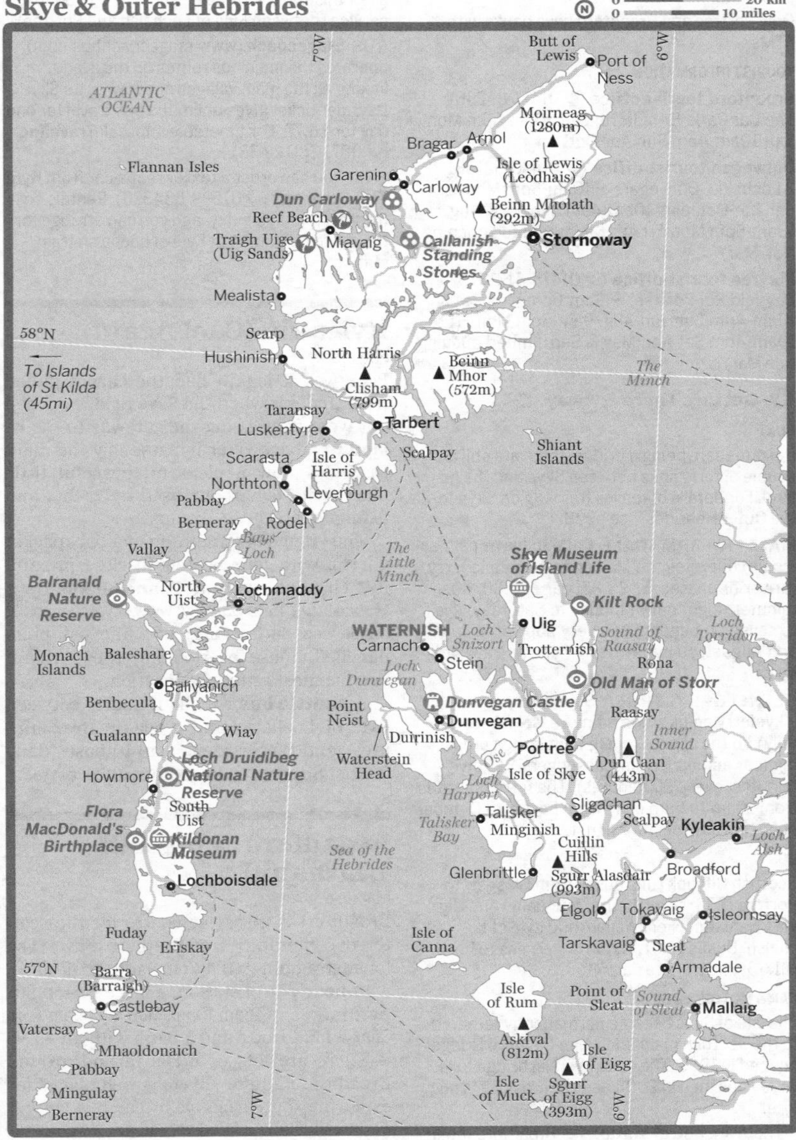

Information

INTERNET ACCESS

Portree tourist office (Bayfield Rd, Portree; per 20min £1; ⌚9am-6pm Mon-Sat & 10am-4pm Sun Jun-Aug, 9am-5pm Mon-Fri & 10am-4pm Sat Apr, May & Sep, limited opening Oct-Mar)

Seamus Bar (Sligachan Hotel, Sligachan; per 15min £1; ⌚11am-11pm; 📶)

South Skye Computers (Old Corrie Industrial Estate, Broadford; per 15min £1.25; ⌚10am-5pm Mon-Fri, 10am-1pm Sat)

MONEY

Only Portree and Broadford have banks with ATMs.

TOURIST INFORMATION

Broadford tourist office (☎01471-822361; The Car Park, Broadford; ⏲9.30am-5pm Mon-Sat, 10am-4pm Sun Apr-Oct)

Dunvegan tourist office (☎01470-521581; 2 Lochside, Dunvegan; ⏲10am-5pm Mon-Sat Jun-Oct, plus 10am-4pm Sun Jul & Aug, 10am-5pm Mon-Fri Apr & May, limited opening Nov-Mar)

Portree tourist office (☎01478-612137; Bayfield Rd, Portree; ⏲9am-6pm Mon-Sat & 10am-4pm Sun Jun-Aug, 9am-5pm Mon-Fri & 10am-4pm Sat Apr, May & Sep, limited opening Oct-Mar)

Getting There & Away

BOAT

Despite there being a bridge, there are still a couple of ferry links between Skye and the mainland. For details of ferries from Uig on Skye to the Outer Hebrides, see p928.

MALLAIG–ARMADALE **CalMac** (www.calmac.co.uk) operates the Mallaig to Armadale ferry (driver or passenger £3.85, car £20.30, 30 minutes, eight daily Monday to Saturday, five to seven on Sunday). It's very popular in July and August, so book ahead if you're travelling by car.

GLENELG–KYLERHEA **Skye Ferry** (www.skyeferry.co.uk) runs a tiny vessel (six cars only) on the short Glenelg to Kylerhea crossing (car and up to four passengers £12, five minutes, every 20 minutes). The ferry operates from 10am to 6pm daily from Easter to October only, till 7pm June to August.

BUS

Scottish Citylink runs buses from Glasgow to Portree (£38, seven hours, four daily) and Uig via Crianlarich, Fort William and Kyle of Lochalsh. Buses also run from Inverness to Portree (£17, 3½ hours, five daily).

CAR & MOTORCYCLE

The Isle of Skye became permanently tethered to the Scottish mainland when the Skye Bridge opened in 1995. The controversial bridge tolls were abolished in 2004 and the crossing is now free.

There are **petrol stations** at Broadford (open 24 hours), Armadale, Portree, Dunvegan and Uig.

Getting Around

Getting around the island by public transport can be a pain, especially if you want to explore away from the main Kyleakin–Portree–Uig road. Here, as in much of the Highlands, there are only a few buses on Saturdays, and only one Sunday service (between Kyle of Lochalsh and Portree).

BUS **Stagecoach** (www.stagecoachbus.com) operates the main bus routes on the island, linking all the main villages and towns. Its Skye Dayrider ticket gives unlimited bus travel for one day for £6.70. For timetable info, call **Traveline** (☎0871 200 22 33).

TAXI You can order a taxi or rent a car from **Kyle Taxi Company** (☎01599-534323). Rentals cost from around £38 a day, and you can arrange for the car to be waiting at Kyle of Lochalsh train station.

Kyleakin (Caol Acain)

POP 100

Poor wee Kyleakin had the carpet pulled from under it when the Skye Bridge opened – it went from being the gateway to the island to a backwater bypassed by the main road. It's now a pleasant, peaceful little place, with a harbour used by yachts and fishing boats.

The village is something of a backpacker ghetto, with four hostels in close proximity. The homely **Dun Caan Independent Hostel** (☎01599-534087; www.skyerover.co.uk; Castle View; dm from £15), in a fine, old, pine-panelled house overlooking the harbour, has the most attractive location.

A **shuttle bus** runs half-hourly between Kyle of Lochalsh and Kyleakin (five minutes), and there are eight to 10 buses daily (except Sunday) to Broadford and Portree.

Broadford (An T-Ath Leathann)

POP 1050

Broadford is a service centre for the scattered communities of southern Skye. The long, straggling village has a tourist office, a 24-hour petrol station, a large **Co-op supermarket** (⏲8am-10pm Mon-Sat, 9am-6pm Sun), a laundrette and a bank with an ATM.

There are lots of B&Bs in and around Broadford and the village is well placed for exploring southern Skye by car.

Sleeping & Eating

Broadford Hotel HOTEL **££**
(☎01471-822204; www.broadfordhotel.co.uk; Torrin Rd; s/d from £115/128; P wifi) The folks who own the Bosville in Portree have converted the old Broadford Hotel into a glamourous and stylish retreat with luxury fabrics and designer colour schemes.

There's a formal restaurant and the more democratic **Gabbro Bar** where you can enjoy a bar meal (mains £7 to £9, served noon to 9pm) of smoked haddock chowder or steak pie washed down with Isle of Skye Brewery ale.

Creelers SEAFOOD ££
(☎01471-822281; www.skye-seafood-restaurant.co.uk; Lower Harrapool; mains £12-18; ⏲noon-9.30pm Mon-Sat) Broadford has several places to eat but one really stands out. Creelers is a small, bustling, no-frills restaurant that serves some of the best seafood on Skye; the house speciality is a rich, spicy seafood gumbo. Book ahead, and if you can't get a table then nip around to the back door, where you'll find Ma Doyle's Takeaway, for fish and chips (£5) to go.

Berabhaigh B&B £
(☎01471-822372; www.isleofskye.net/berabhaigh; 3 Lime Park; r per person £34; ⏲Mar-Oct; P) A lovely, old croft house with views over the bay. Just off the main road, near Creelers restaurant.

Sleat

If you cross over the sea to Skye on the ferry from Mallaig you arrive in Armadale, at the southern end of the long, low-lying peninsula known as Sleat (pronounced 'slate').

Armadale, where the ferry from Mallaig arrives, is little more than a store, a post office and a couple of houses. There are six or seven buses a day (Monday to Saturday) from Armadale to Broadford and Portree.

Sights & Activities

Museum of the Isles MUSEUM, CASTLE
(www.clandonald.com; adult/child £6.95/4.95; ⏲9.30am-5.30pm Easter-Oct) Just along the road from the ferry is the part-ruined Armadale Castle, former seat of Lord Macdonald of Sleat. The neighbouring museum will tell you all you ever wanted to know about Clan Donald, as well as providing an easily digested history of the Lordship of the Isles. The ticket also gives admission to the lovely castle gardens.

Sleeping & Eating

TOP CHOICE **Toravaig House Hotel** HOTEL £££
(☎01471-820200; www.skyehotel.co.uk; Sleat; r from £169; P 📶) This hotel, 5 miles north of Armadale, is one of those places where the owners know a thing or two about hospitality – as soon as you arrive you'll feel right at home – whether relaxing on the plump sofas by the log fire in the lounge or admiring the view across the Sound of Sleat from the lawn chairs in the garden. The spacious bedrooms – ask for room No 1 (Eriskay), with its enormous sleigh bed – are luxuriously equipped, from the rich and heavy bed linen to the huge, high-pressure shower heads. The elegant restaurant **Iona** (4-course dinner £43) serves the best of local fish, game and lamb.

Cuillin Hills

The Cuillin Hills are Britain's most spectacular mountain range. Though small in stature (**Sgurr Alasdair**, the highest summit, is only 993m), the peaks are near-alpine in character, with knife-edge ridges, jagged pinnacles, scree-filled gullies and acres of naked rock. While they are a paradise for experienced mountaineers, the higher reaches of the Cuillin are off limits to the majority of walkers.

The good news is that there are also plenty of good, low-level hikes within the ability of most walkers. One of the best (on a fine day) is the steep climb from Glenbrittle camping ground to **Coire Lagan** (6 miles round trip; allow at least three hours).

There are two main bases for exploring the Cuillin – **Sligachan** to the north, and **Glenbrittle** to the south.

Sleeping & Eating

Sligachan Hotel HOTEL ££
(☎01478-650204; www.sligachan.co.uk; Sligachan; per person from £59; P @ 📶) The Slig, as it has been known to generations of climbers, is a near village in itself, encompassing a luxurious hotel, a microbrewery, self-catering cottages, a bunkhouse, a campsite, a big barn of a bar (see below) and an adventure playground.

Seamus's Bar PUB £
(Sligachan Hotel, Sligachan; mains £8-10; ⏲food served 11am-11pm; @ 📶 👪) This place dishes up decent bar meals, including haggis, neeps and tatties, steak and ale pie, and fish pie, and serves real ales from its own microbrewery plus a range of 200 malt whiskies in serried ranks above the bar. As well as the adventure playground outside, there are games, toys and a play area indoors.

Getting There & Away

Sligachan, on the main Kyle–Portree road, is easily accessible by bus; Glenbrittle is harder to reach. Bus 53 runs five times a day Monday to Friday (once on Saturday) from Portree to Carbost via Sligachan (50 minutes); from there, you'll have to hitch or walk the remaining 8 miles to Glenbrittle (this can be slow, especially late in the day).

Minginish

Loch Harport, to the north of the Cuillin, divides the Minginish Peninsula from the rest of Skye. On its southern shore lies the village of Carbost, home to the smooth, sweet and smoky Talisker malt whisky, produced at **Talisker Distillery** (www.discovering-distilleries.com; Carbost; guided tour £5; ⏲9.30am-5pm Mon-Sat Easter-Oct, noon-5pm Sun Jul & Aug, 10-5pm Mon-Fri Nov-Easter). This is the only distillery on Skye; the guided tour includes a free dram. Magnificent **Talisker Bay**, 5 miles west of Carbost, has a sandy beach, sea stack and waterfall.

The **Old Inn** (☎01478-640205; www.carbost.f9.co.uk; Carbost; s/d £42/74; P) is an atmospheric wee pub, offering accommodation in bright B&B bedrooms and an appealing chalet-style **bunkhouse** (from £14 per person). The bar is a favourite with walkers and climbers from Glenbrittle – there's an outdoor patio at the back with great views over Loch Harport – and between noon and 10pm, it serves excellent **pub grub** (£8 to £12), from fresh oysters to haddock and chips.

There are five buses a day on weekdays (one on Saturday) from Portree to Carbost via Sligachan.

Portree (Port Righ)

POP 1920

Portree is Skye's largest and liveliest town. It has a pretty harbour lined with brightly painted houses, and there are great views of the surrounding hills. Its name (from the Gaelic for King's Harbour) commemorates James V, who came here in 1540 to pacify the local clans.

Sleeping

Portree is well supplied with B&Bs but many of them are in bland, modern bungalows that, though comfortable, often lack character. Accommodation fills up fast in July and August so be sure to book ahead.

TOP CHOICE **Ben Tianavaig B&B** B&B ££
(☎01478-612152; www.ben-tianavaig.co.uk; 5 Bosville Tce; r £65-75; P wi-fi) A warm welcome awaits from the Aussie/Brit couple who run this appealing B&B bang in the centre of town. All four bedrooms have a view across the harbour to the hill that gives the house its name, and breakfasts include free range eggs and vegetables grown in the garden.

Bosville Hotel HOTEL ££
(☎01478-612846; www.bosvillehotel.co.uk; 9-11 Bosville Tce; s/d from £120/128; wi-fi) The Bosville brings a little bit of metropolitan style to Portree with its designer fabrics and furniture, flatscreen TVs, fluffy bathrobes and bright, spacious bathrooms. It's worth splashing out a bit for the 'premier' rooms, with leather recliner chairs from which you can lap up the view over the town and harbour.

Peinmore House B&B ££
(☎01478-612574; www.peinmorehouse.co.uk; r per person £55; P) Located around 2 miles south of Portree, this former manse has recently been cleverly converted into a stylish and comfortable guest house with a spectacular, oak-floored lounge, enormous bedrooms, excellent breakfasts and panoramic views.

Bayfield Backpackers HOSTEL £
(☎01478-612231; www.skyehostel.co.uk; Bayfield; dm from £13; @ wi-fi) Clean, central and modern, this hostel provides the best backpacker accommodation in town. The owner really makes you feel welcome and is a font of advice on what to do and where to go in Skye.

Bayview House B&B £
(☎01478-613340; www.bayviewhouse.co.uk; Bayfield; r per person from £23; P wi-fi) Bayview House is modern with spartan but sparklingly clean rooms and bathrooms with power showers. At this price and location, it's a bargain.

Eating & Drinking

TOP CHOICE **Café Arriba** CAFE £
(www.cafearriba.co.uk; Quay Brae; light meals £5-8, dinner mains £10-13; ⏲7am-10pm May-Sep, 8am-5.30pm Oct-Apr) Arriba is a funky little cafe, brightly decked out in primary colours and offering the best

choice of vegetarian grub on the island, ranging from a veggie breakfast fry-up to Indian-spiced bean cakes with mint yoghurt, as well as carnivorous treats such as slow-cooked haunch of venison with red wine and beetroot gravy. Also serves excellent coffee.

Bistro at the Bosville BISTRO ££
(☎01478-612846; www.bosvillehotel.co.uk; 7 Bosville Tce; mains £9-20; ⏲noon-2.30pm & 5.30-10pm) This hotel bistro sports a relaxed atmosphere, an award-winning chef and a menu that makes the most of Skye-sourced produce including lamb, game, seafood, cheese, organic vegetables and berries, and adds an original twist to traditional dishes.

Sea Breezes SEAFOOD ££
(☎01478-612016; 2 Marine Buildings, Quay St; mains £10-20; ⏲noon-2.30pm & 5.30-10pm Tue-Sun, closed Nov, Jan & Feb) A good choice for seafood, Sea Breezes is an informal, no-frills restaurant specialising in local fish and shellfish fresh from the boat – try the impressive seafood platter, a small mountain of langoustines, crab, oysters and lobster. Book early, as it's often hard to get a table.

Granary Bakery CAFE £
(Somerled Sq; light mains £5-8; ⏲8am-5pm Mon-Sat) Most of Portree seems to congregate at the Granary Bakery's cosy coffee shop to snack on tasty sandwiches, filled rolls, pies, cakes and pastries.

ℹ Getting There & Around

BUS The main bus stop is in Somerled Sq. There are seven Scottish Citylink buses a day, including Sundays, from Kyle of Lochalsh to Portree (£13, one hour) and on to Uig.

Stagecoach services (Monday to Saturday only) run from Portree to Broadford (40 minutes, at least hourly) via Sligachan (15 minutes); to Armadale (1¼ hours, connecting with the ferries to Mallaig); to Carbost (40 minutes, four daily); to Uig (30 minutes, six daily) and to Dunvegan Castle (40 minutes, five daily Monday to Friday, three on Saturday). There are also five or six buses a day on a circular route around Trotternish (in both directions) taking in Flodigarry (20 minutes), Kilmuir (1¼ hours) and Uig (30 minutes). See p944 for details of buses from the mainland.

BIKE You can hire bikes at **Island Cycles** (☎01478-613121; The Green; ⏲9am-5pm Mon-Sat) for £10/15 per half-/full day.

Dunvegan (Dun Bheagain) & Around

Skye's most famous historic building, and one of its most popular tourist attractions, is **Dunvegan Castle** (www.dunvegancastle.com; Dunvegan; adult/child £8/4; ⏲10am-5pm Easter-Oct, 11am-4pm Nov-Easter), seat of the chief of Clan MacLeod. It has played host to Samuel Johnson, Sir Walter Scott and, most famously, Flora MacDonald. The oldest parts are the 14th-century keep and dungeon but most of it dates from the 17th to 19th centuries.

There are some interesting artefacts, most famous being the **Fairy Flag**, a diaphanous silk banner that dates

FLORA MACDONALD

Flora MacDonald, who became famous for helping Bonnie Prince Charlie escape after his defeat at the Battle of Culloden, was born in 1722 at Milton in South Uist, where a memorial cairn marks the site of one of her early childhood homes.

In 1746, she helped Bonnie Prince Charlie make his way from Benbecula to Skye disguised as her Irish maidservant. With a price on the prince's head their little boat was fired on, but they managed to land safely and Flora escorted the prince to Portree where he gave her a gold locket containing his portrait before setting sail for Raasay.

Waylaid on the way home, the boatmen admitted everything. Flora was arrested and imprisoned in the Tower of London. She never saw or heard from the prince again.

In 1747, she returned to Skye, marrying Allan MacDonald and having nine children. Dr Samuel Johnson stayed with her in 1773 during his trip to the Western Isles, but later poverty forced her family to emigrate to North Carolina. There her husband was captured by rebels. Flora returned to Kingsburgh on Skye where she died in 1790. She was buried in Kilmuir churchyard, wrapped in the sheet on which both Bonnie Prince Charlie and Dr Johnson had slept.

from some time between the 4th and 7th centuries.

Sleeping & Eating

TOP CHOICE **Three Chimneys** RESTAURANT-WITH-ROOMS £££

(☎01470-511258; www.threechimneys.co.uk; Colbost, Dunvegan; 3-course lunch/dinner £35/55; ⏰12.30-2pm Mon-Sat Mar-Oct, 6.30-9pm daily year-round; P) In Colbost, halfway between Dunvegan and Waterstein, Three Chimneys is a superb romantic retreat combining a gourmet restaurant in a candle-lit crofter's cottage with sumptuous five-star rooms (double £285, dinner B&B per couple £405) in the modern house next door. Book well in advance, and note that children are not welcome in the restaurant in the evenings.

Trotternish

The Trotternish Peninsula to the north of Portree has some of Skye's most beautiful – and bizarre – scenery.

EAST COAST

First up is the 50m-high, potbellied pinnacle of crumbling basalt known as the **Old Man of Storr**, prominent above the road 6 miles north of Portree. North again, near Staffin (Stamhain), is spectacular **Kilt Rock**, a stupendous cliff of columnar basalt whose vertical ribbing is fancifully compared to the pleats of a kilt.

Sleeping & Eating

Flodigarry Country House Hotel HOTEL ££

(☎01470-552203; www.flodigarry.co.uk; Flodigarry; s/d from £90/120; P) Flora MacDonald lived in a farmhouse cottage at Flodigarry in northeast Trotternish from 1751 to 1759. The cottage and its pretty garden are now part of this delightful hotel – you can stay in the cottage itself (there are seven bedrooms), or in the more spacious rooms in the hotel. The bright, modern bistro (mains £10 to £25) has great views over the Inner Sound, and serves lunch and dinner featuring local produce such as langoustines, lobster, lamb and venison.

Dun Flodigarry Hostel HOSTEL £

(☎01470-552212; www.hostelflodigarry.co.uk; Flodigarry; dm/tw £13/30; @) If the local hotel is too expensive for you, this nearby hostel shares the same superb views, and you can still visit the hotel bar for afternoon tea – it's only a 100m walk away. You can camp nearby and use the hostel facilities (£6.50 per person).

WEST COAST

The peat-reek of crofting life in the 18th and 19th centuries is preserved in thatched cottages at **Skye Museum of Island Life** (www.skyemuseum.co.uk; Kilmuir; adult/child £2.50/50p; ⏰9.30am-5pm Mon-Sat Easter-Oct). Behind the museum is Kilmuir Cemetery, where a tall Celtic cross marks the **grave of Flora MacDonald**; the cross was erected in 1955 to replace the original, of which 'every fragment was removed by tourists'.

Whichever way you arrive at **Uig** (*oo*-ig), the picture-perfect bay, ringed by steep hills, rarely fails to impress. If you've time to kill while waiting for a ferry to the Outer Hebrides, visit the **Isle of Skye Brewery** (www.skyebrewery.co.uk; The Pier, Uig; ⏰9am-5pm Mon-Fri), which sells locally brewed cask ales and bottled beers.

There's a cluster of B&Bs in Uig, as well as the **Uig Youth Hostel** (SYHA; ☎01470-542746; Uig; dm £15; ⏰late Apr-Sep; wi-fi).

Isle Of Raasay

POP 160

Raasay is the rugged, 10-mile-long island that lies off Skye's east coast. There are several good walks here, including one to the flat-topped conical hill of **Dun Caan** (443m). Forest Enterprise publishes a free leaflet (available from the tourist offices in Portree or Kyle of Lochalsh) with suggested walks and forest trails.

The extraordinary ruin of **Brochel Castle**, perched on a pinnacle at the northern end of Raasay, was home to Calum Garbh MacLeod, an early 16th-century pirate.

Set in a rustic cottage high on the hill overlooking Skye, **Raasay Youth Hostel** (SYHA; ☎01478-660240; Creachan Cottage; dm £16; ⏰May-Sep) is a fair walk from the ferry pier (2.5 miles) but is a good base for exploring the island.

See www.raasay.com for a full listing of accommodation.

A CalMac **ferry** (passenger/car £3.10/11.90) runs from Sconser, on the road from Portree to Broadford, to the southern end of Raasay (15 minutes, hourly Monday to Saturday, twice daily Sunday). There are no petrol stations on the island.

OUTER HEBRIDES

POP 26,500

The Outer Hebrides – also known as the Western Isles, or Na h-Eileanan an Iar in Gaelic – are a 130-mile-long string of islands lying off the northwest coast of Scotland. There are 119 islands in total, of which the five main inhabited islands are: Lewis and Harris (two parts of a single island, although often described as if they are separate islands), North Uist, Benbecula, South Uist and Barra. The middle three (often referred to simply as 'the Uists') are connected by road-bearing causeways.

The ferry crossing from Ullapool or Uig to the Western Isles marks an important cultural divide – more than a third of Scotland's registered crofts are in the Outer Hebrides, and no less than 60% of the population are Gaelic speakers. The rigours of life in the old island blackhouses are still within living memory.

The name Hebrides is not Gaelic, and is probably a corruption of Ebudae, the Roman name for the islands. But the alternative derivation from the Norse *havbredey* – 'isles at the edge of the sea' – has a much more poetic ring, alluding to the broad vistas of sky and sea that characterise the islands' often bleak and treeless landscapes. But there is beauty here too, in the machair (grassy, wildflower-speckled dunes) and dazzling white-sand beaches, majesty in the rugged hills and sprawling lochs, and mystery in the islands' fascinating past. It's a past signalled by Neolithic standing stones, Viking place names, deserted crofts and folk memories of the Clearances.

Information

INTERNET ACCESS

Community Library (Community School, Castlebay, Barra; ⏲9am-4.30pm Mon & Wed, 9am-4.30pm & 6-8pm Tue & Thu, 9am-3.30pm Fri, 10am-12.30pm Sat) Free access.

Stornoway Public Library (19 Cromwell St, Stornoway, Lewis; ⏲10am-5pm Mon-Wed & Sat, 10am-6pm Thu & Fri) Free access.

Taigh Chearsabhagh (Lochmaddy, North Uist; per 20min 50p; ⏲10am-5pm Mon-Sat Feb-Jun & Sep-Dec, 10am-5pm Mon-Thu & Sat, to 8pm Fri Jul & Aug)

TOURIST INFORMATION

Castlebay tourist office (☎01871-810336; Main St, Castlebay, Barra; ⏲9am-1pm & 2-5pm Mon-Sat, noon-4pm Sun Apr-Oct)

Lochboisdale tourist office (☎01878-700286; Pier Rd, Lochboisdale, South Uist; ⏲9am-1pm & 2-5pm Mon-Fri, 9.30am-5pm Sat, 9-9.30pm Tue & Thu Apr-Oct)

Lochmaddy tourist office (☎01876-500321; Pier Rd, Lochmaddy, North Uist; ⏲9am-1pm & 2-5pm Mon-Fri, 9.30am-1pm & 2-5.30pm Sat, 8-9pm Mon, Wed & Fri Apr-Oct)

Stornoway tourist office (☎01851-703088; 26 Cromwell St, Stornoway, Lewis; ⏲9am-6pm & 8-9pm Mon, Tue & Thu, 9am-8pm Wed & Fri, 9am-5.30pm & 8-9pm Sat year-round)

Tarbert tourist office (☎01859-502011; Pier Rd, Tarbert, Harris; ⏲9am-5pm Mon-Sat, plus 8-9pm Tue, Thu & Sat Apr-Oct)

Getting There & Away

AIR There are flights to Stornoway from Edinburgh, Inverness, Glasgow and Aberdeen. There are daily flights from Glasgow to Barra and Benbecula. At Barra, the planes land on the hard-sand beach at low tide, so the timetable depends on the tides.

KEEPING THE SABBATH

The Protestants of the Outer Hebrides have succeeded in maintaining a distinctive fundamentalist approach to their religion, with Sunday being devoted largely to religious services, prayer and Bible reading. On Lewis and Harris, the last bastion of Sabbath observance in the UK, almost everything closes down on a Sunday. In fact, Stornoway must be the only place in the UK to suffer a Sunday rush hour as people drive to church around 10.30am; it's then a ghost town for an hour and a half until the services are over. But a few cracks have begun to appear.

There was outrage when British Airways/Loganair introduced Sunday flights from Edinburgh and Inverness to Stornoway in 2002, with members of the Lord's Day Observance Society spluttering that this was the thin end of the wedge. They were probably right – in 2003 a Stornoway petrol station began to open on a Sunday, and now does a roaring trade in Sunday papers and takeaway booze. Then in 2006 the CalMac ferry from Berneray to Leverburgh in Harris started a Sunday service, despite strong opposition from the residents of Harris (ironically, they were unable to protest at the ferry's arrival, as that would have meant breaking the Sabbath).

Airlines serving the Western Isles:

FlyBe/Loganair (☎0871 700 2000; www.loganair.com)

Eastern Airways (☎0870 366 9100; www.easternairways.com)

Highland Airways (☎0845 450 2245; www.highlandairways.co.uk)

BOAT **CalMac** runs car ferries from Ullapool to Stornoway (Lewis); from Uig (Isle of Skye) to Lochmaddy (North Uist) and Tarbert (Harris); and from Oban to Castlebay (Barra) and Lochboisdale (South Uist). One-way fares:

CROSSING	CAR	DRIVER/ PASSENGER	DURATION
Ullapool–Stornoway	£38	£7.55	2¾hr
Uig–Lochmaddy	£24	£5.15	1¾hr
Uig–Tarbert	£24	£5.15	1½hr
Oban–Castlebay	£51	£11.40	4¾hr
Oban–Lochboisdale	£51	£11.40	6¾hr

Advance booking for cars is essential in July and August; foot and bicycle passengers should have no problems. Bicycles are carried for free.

CalMac has 12 different Island Hopscotch tickets for set routes in the Outer Hebrides, offering a saving of around 10% (tickets are valid for one month). See the website for details.

Getting Around

Despite their separate names, Lewis and Harris are actually one island. Berneray, North Uist, Benbecula, South Uist and Eriskay are all linked by road bridges and causeways. There are car ferries between Leverburgh (Harris) and Berneray, Tarbert (Harris) and Lochmaddy (North Uist), Eriskay and Castlebay (Barra), and Lochboisdale (South Uist) and Castlebay (Barra).

The local council publishes two booklets of timetables (one covering Lewis and Harris, the other the Uists and Barra) that list all bus, ferry and air services in the Outer Hebrides. Timetables can also be found online at www.cne-siar.gov.uk/travel.

BICYCLE Many visiting cyclists plan to cycle the length of the archipelago, but if you're one of them, remember that the wind is often strong, so south to north is usually the easier direction. Bikes can be hired for around £10 a day or £45 a week in Stornoway (Lewis), Leverburgh (Harris), Howmore (South Uist) and Castlebay (Barra).

BUS The bus network covers almost every village in the islands, with around four to six buses a day on all the main routes; however, there are no buses at all on Sundays.

CAR & MOTORCYCLE Cars can be hired from around £30 per day from:

Arnol Motors (☎018510-710548; www.arnolmotors.com; Arnol, Lewis; ⏲closed Sun)

Lewis Car Rentals (☎01851-703760; www.lewis-car-rental.com; 14 Bayhead St, Stornoway; ⏲closed Sun)

Lewis (Leodhais)

POP 18,600

The northern part of Lewis is dominated by the desolate expanse of the Black Moor, a vast, undulating peat bog dimpled with glittering lochans, seen clearly from the Stornoway–Barvas road. But Lewis' finest scenery is on the west coast. The Outer Hebrides' most evocative historic sites – Callanish Standing Stones, Dun Carloway, and Arnol Blackhouse Museum – are also to be found here.

STORNOWAY (STEORNABHAGH)

POP 6000

Stornoway is the bustling 'capital' of the Outer Hebrides and the only real town in the whole archipelago. It's a surprisingly busy little place, with cars and people swamping the centre on weekdays. Though set on a beautiful natural harbour, the town isn't going to win any prizes for beauty or atmosphere, but it's a pleasant enough introduction to this remote corner of the country.

Sights

FREE **An Lanntair Art Centre** ARTS CENTRE (www.lanntair.com; Kenneth St; ⏲10am-9pm Mon-Wed, 10am-10pm Thu, 10am-midnight Fri & Sat; wi-fi) The modern, purpose-built An Lanntair Art Centre, complete with art gallery, theatre, cinema and restaurant, is the centre of the town's cultural life; it hosts changing exhibitions of contemporary art and is a good source of information on cultural events.

FREE **Museum nan Eilean** MUSEUM (Francis St; ⏲10am-5.30pm Mon-Sat, shorter winter hr) This museum strings together a loose history of the Outer Hebrides from the earliest human settlements some 9000 years ago to the 20th century, exploring traditional island life and the changes inflicted by progress and technology.

Festivals

Hebridean Celtic Festival (www.hebceltfest.com) A four-day extravaganza of folk/rock/Celtic music held in the second half of July.

(Continued on page 937)

Iconic Scotland

Royal Mile »
Rosslyn Chapel »
Stirling Castle »

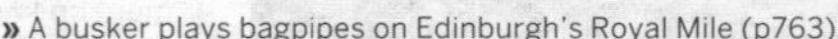

» A busker plays bagpipes on Edinburgh's Royal Mile (p763).

Royal Mile

A GRAND DAY OUT

Planning your own procession along the Royal Mile involves some tough decisions – it would be impossible to see everything in a single day, so it's wise to decide in advance what you don't want to miss and shape your visit around that. Remember to leave time for lunch, for exploring some of the Mile's countless side alleys and, during festival time, for enjoying the street theatre that is bound to be happening in High St.

The most pleasant way to reach the Castle Esplanade at the start of the Royal Mile is to hike up the zigzag path from the footbridge behind the Ross Bandstand in Princes Street Gardens (in springtime you'll be knee-deep in daffodils). Starting at Edinburgh Castle 1 means that the rest of your walk is downhill. For a superb view up and down the length of the Mile, climb the Camera Obscura's Outlook Tower 2 before visiting Gladstone's Land 3 and St Giles Cathedral 4.

JONATHAN SMITH

Edinburgh Castle

If you're pushed for time, visit the Great Hall, the Crown Jewels and the Prisons of War exhibit. Head for the Half-Moon Battery for a photo looking down the length of the Royal Mile.

Royal Visits to the Royal Mile

1561: Mary, Queen of Scots arrives from France and holds an audience with John Knox.
1745: Bonnie Prince Charlie fails to capture Edinburgh Castle, and instead sets up court in Holyroodhouse.
2004: Queen Elizabeth II officially opens the Scottish Parliament building.

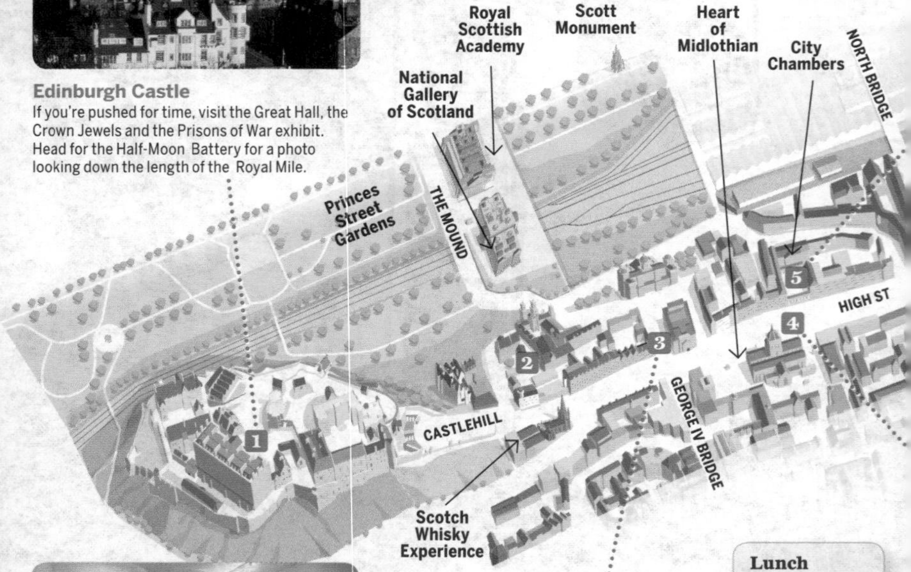

Royal Scottish Academy
Scott Monument
Heart of Midlothian
City Chambers
NORTH BRIDGE
National Gallery of Scotland
Princes Street Gardens
THE MOUND
HIGH ST
GEORGE IV BRIDGE
CASTLEHILL
Scotch Whisky Experience
1
2
3
4
5

KARL BLACKWELL

Gladstone's Land

The 1st floor houses a faithful recreation of how a wealthy Edinburgh merchant lived in the 17th century. Check out the beautiful Painted Bedchamber, with its ornately decorated walls and wooden ceilings.

Lunch Break

Pie and a pint at **Royal Mile Tavern**; soup and a sandwich at **Always Sunday**; bistro nosh at **Café Marlayne**.

If history's your thing, you'll want to add Real Mary King's Close 5, John Knox House 6 and the Museum of Edinburgh 7 to your must-see list.

At the foot of the mile, choose between modern and ancient seats of power – the Scottish Parliament 8 or the Palace of Holyroodhouse 9. Round off the day with an evening ascent of Arthur's Seat or, slightly less strenuously, Calton Hill. Both make great sunset viewpoints.

TAKING YOUR TIME

Minimum time needed for each attraction:

» **Edinburgh Castle:** two hours
» **Gladstone's Land:** 45 minutes
» **St Giles Cathedral:** 30 minutes
» **Real Mary King's Close:** one hour (tour)
» **Scottish Parliament:** one hour (tour)
» **Palace of Holyroodhouse:** one hour

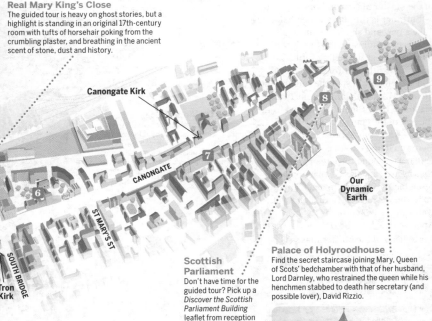

Real Mary King's Close

The guided tour is heavy on ghost stories, but a highlight is standing in an original 17th-century room with tufts of horsehair poking from the crumbling plaster, and breathing in the ancient scent of stone, dust and history.

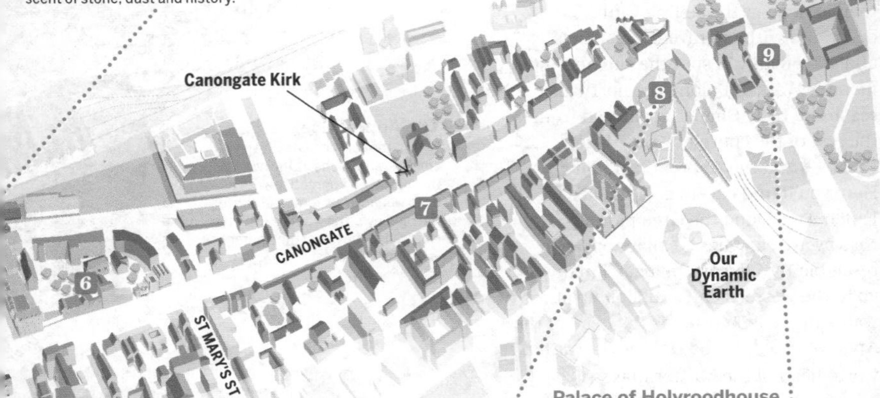

Scottish Parliament

Don't have time for the guided tour? Pick up a *Discover the Scottish Parliament Building* leaflet from reception and take a self-guided tour of the exterior, then hike up to Salisbury Crags for a great view of the complex.

COLIN PALMER PHOTOGRAPHY/ALAMY

Palace of Holyroodhouse

Find the secret staircase joining Mary, Queen of Scots' bedchamber with that of her husband, Lord Darnley, who restrained the queen while his henchmen stabbed to death her secretary (and possible lover), David Rizzio.

JEAN-CHRISTOPHE GODET/ALAMY

St Giles Cathedral

Look out for the Burne-Jones stained glass window (1873) at the west end, showing the crossing of the River Jordan, and the bronze memorial to Robert Louis Stevenson in the Moray Aisle.

EUROPHOTOS/ALAMY

Rosslyn Chapel

DECIPHERING ROSSLYN

Rosslyn Chapel is a small building, but the density of decoration inside can be overwhelming. It's well worth buying the official guidebook by the Earl of Rosslyn first; find a bench in the gardens and have a skim through before going into the chapel – the background information will make your visit all the more interesting. The book also offers a useful self-guided tour of the chapel, and explains the legend of the Master Mason and the Apprentice.

Entrance is through the north door **1**. Take a pew and sit for a while to allow your eyes to adjust to the dim interior; then look up at the ceiling vault, decorated with engraved roses, lilies and stars (can you spot the sun and the moon?). Walk left along the north aisle to reach the Lady Chapel, separated from the rest of the church by the Mason's Pillar **2** and the Apprentice Pillar **3**. Here you'll find carvings of Lucifer **4**, the Fallen Angel, and the Green Man **5**. Nearby are carvings **6** that appear to resemble Indian corn (maize). Finally, go to the western end and look up at the wall – in the left corner is the head of the Apprentice **7**; to the right is the (rather worn) head of the Master Mason **8**.

ROSSLYN CHAPEL & THE DA VINCI CODE

» Dan Brown was referencing Rosslyn Chapel's alleged links to the Knights Templar and the Freemasons – unusual symbols found among the carvings, and the fact that a descendant of its founder, William St Clair, was a Grand Master Mason – when he chose it as the setting for his novel's denouement. Rosslyn is indeed a coded work, written in stone, but its meaning depends on your point of view. See The Rosslyn Hoax? by Robert LD Cooper (www.rosslynhoax.com) for an alternative interpretation of the chapel's symbolism.

SANDRO VANNINI/CORBIS

Lucifer, the Fallen Angel
At head height, to the left of the second window from left is an upside-down angel bound with rope, a symbol often associated with Freemasonry. The arch above is decorated with the Dance of Death.

Explore Some More

After visiting the chapel, head downhill to see the spectacularly sited ruins of Roslin Castle, then take a walk along leafy Roslin Glen.

The Apprentice
High in the corner, beneath an empty statue niche, is the head of the murdered Apprentice, with a deep wound in his forehead above the right eye. The worn head on the side wall to the left of the Apprentice is that of his mother.

North Door

The Master Mason

8

Baptistery

Practical Tips

Buy your tickets in advance through the chapel's website (except in August, when no bookings are taken). No photography is allowed inside the chapel.

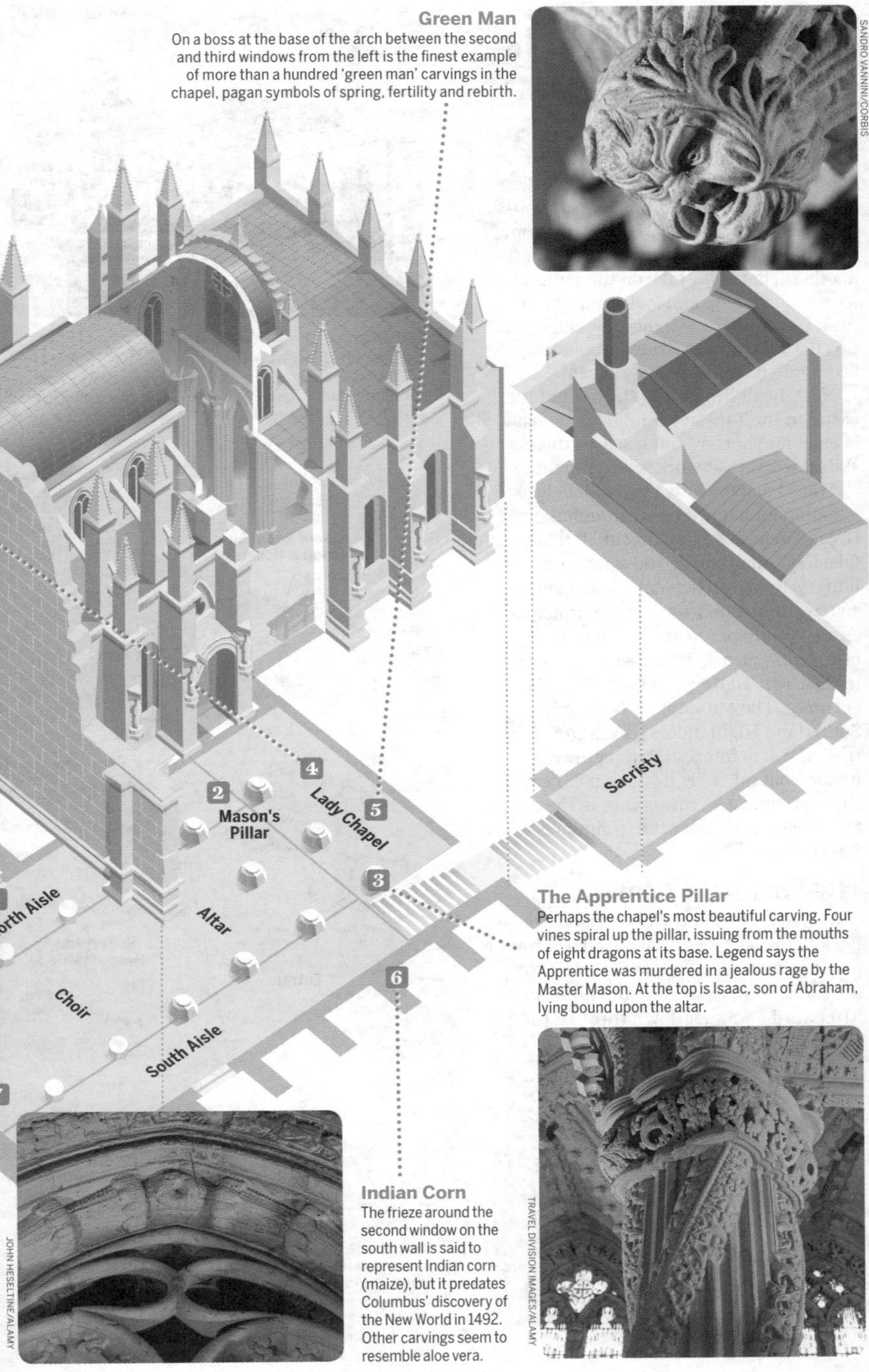

Green Man

On a boss at the base of the arch between the second and third windows from the left is the finest example of more than a hundred 'green man' carvings in the chapel, pagan symbols of spring, fertility and rebirth.

SANDRO VANNINI/CORBIS

The Apprentice Pillar

Perhaps the chapel's most beautiful carving. Four vines spiral up the pillar, issuing from the mouths of eight dragons at its base. Legend says the Apprentice was murdered in a jealous rage by the Master Mason. At the top is Isaac, son of Abraham, lying bound upon the altar.

TRAVEL DIVISION IMAGES/ALAMY

Indian Corn

The frieze around the second window on the south wall is said to represent Indian corn (maize), but it predates Columbus' discovery of the New World in 1492. Other carvings seem to resemble aloe vera.

JOHN HESELTINE/ALAMY

Stirling Castle

PLANNING YOUR ATTACK

Stirling's a sizeable fortress, but not so huge that you'll have to decide what to leave out – there's time to see it all. Unless you've got a working knowledge of Scottish monarchs, head to the Castle Exhibition 1 first: it'll help you sort one James from another. That done, take on the sights at leisure. First, stop and look around you from the ramparts 2; the views high over this flat valley, a key strategic point in Scotland's history, are magnificent.

Next, head through to the back of the castle to the Tapestry Studio 3, which is open for shorter hours; seeing these skilful weavers at work is a highlight.

Track back towards the citadel's heart, stopping for a quick tour through the Great Kitchens 4; looking at all that fake food might make you seriously hungry, though. Then enter the main courtyard. Around you are the principal castle buildings. During summer there are events (such as Renaissance dancing) in the Great Hall 5 – get details at the entrance. The Museum of the Argyll & Sutherland Highlanders 6 is a treasure trove if you're interested in regimental history, but missable if you're not. Leave the best for last – crowds thin in the afternoon – and enter the sumptuous Royal Palace 7.

THE WAY UP & DOWN

If you have time, take the atmospheric Back Walk, a peaceful, shady stroll around the Old Town's fortifications and up to the castle's imposing crag-top position. Afterwards, wander down through the Old Town to admire its facades.

TOP TIPS

» **Admission** Entrance is free for Historic Scotland members. If you'll be visiting several Scottish castles and ruins, a membership will save you plenty.

» **Vital Statistics** First constructed: before 1110; Number of sieges: at least 9; Last besieger: Bonnie Prince Charlie (unsuccessful); Money spent refurbishing the Royal Palace: £12 million.

DAVID ROBERTSON/ALAMY

Museum of the Argyll & Sutherland Highlanders
The history of one of Scotland's legendary regiments – now subsumed into the Royal Regiment of Scotland – is on display here, featuring memorabilia, weapons and uniforms.

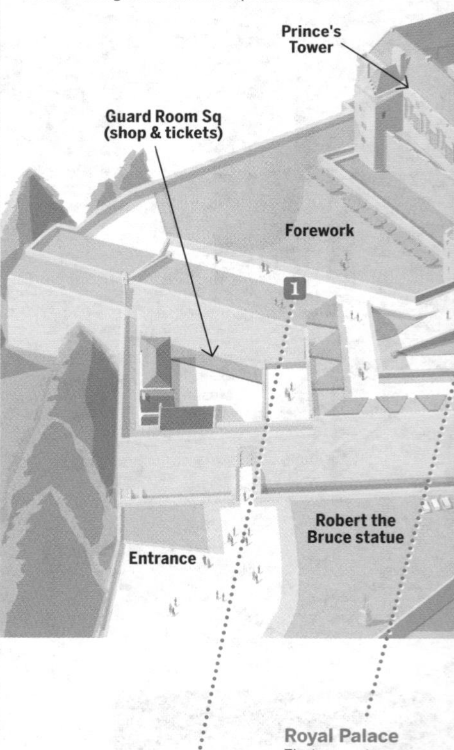

Castle Exhibition
A great overview of the Stewart dynasty here will get your facts straight, and also offers the latest archaeological titbits from the ongoing excavations under the citadel. Analysis of skeletons has revealed surprising amounts of biographical data.

Royal Palace
The impressive new highlight of a visit to the castle is this recreation of the royal lodgings originally built by James V. The finely worked ceiling, ornate furniture and sumptuous unicorn tapestries dazzle.

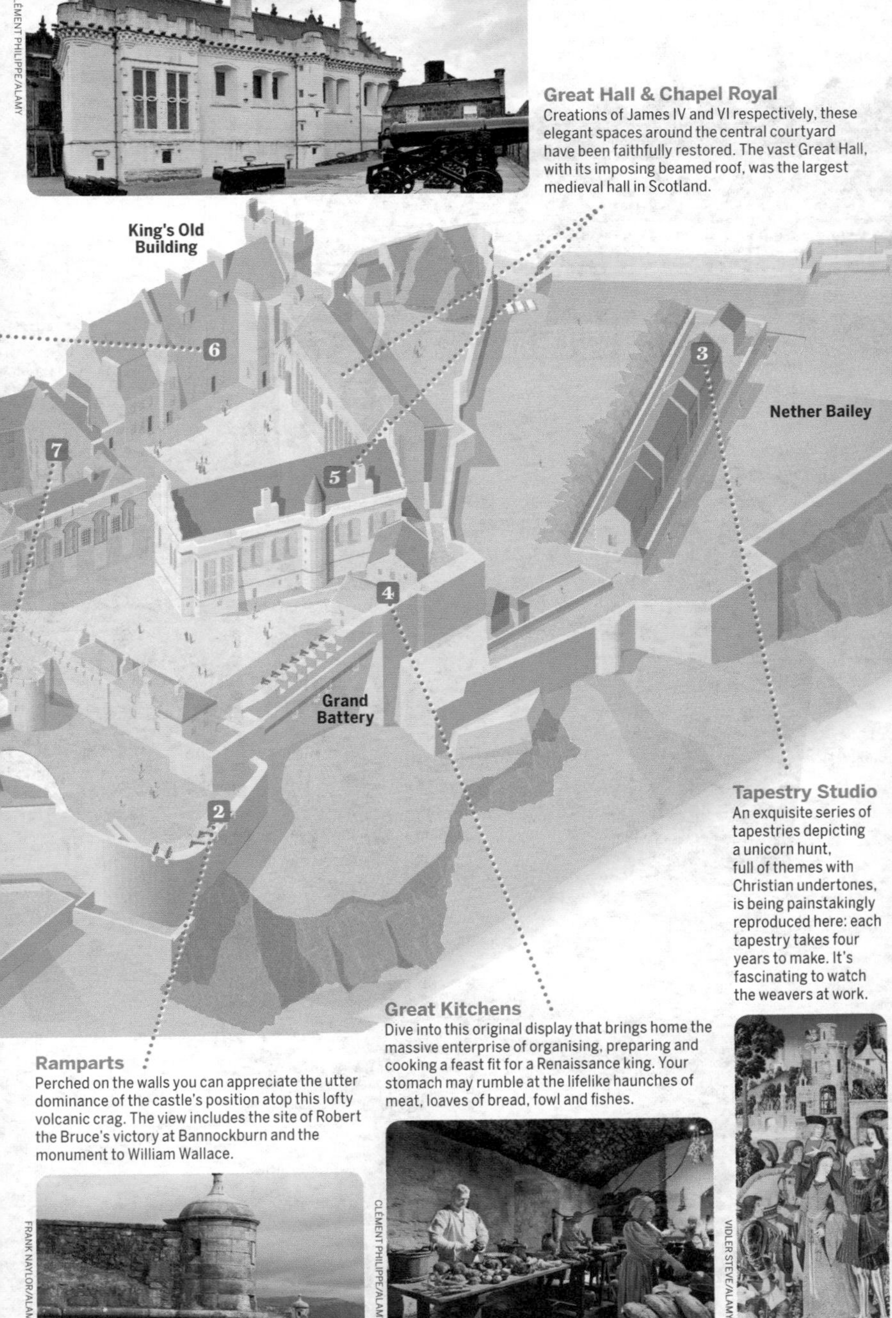

Great Hall & Chapel Royal

Creations of James IV and VI respectively, these elegant spaces around the central courtyard have been faithfully restored. The vast Great Hall, with its imposing beamed roof, was the largest medieval hall in Scotland.

Tapestry Studio

An exquisite series of tapestries depicting a unicorn hunt, full of themes with Christian undertones, is being painstakingly reproduced here: each tapestry takes four years to make. It's fascinating to watch the weavers at work.

Great Kitchens

Dive into this original display that brings home the massive enterprise of organising, preparing and cooking a feast fit for a Renaissance king. Your stomach may rumble at the lifelike haunches of meat, loaves of bread, fowl and fishes.

Ramparts

Perched on the walls you can appreciate the utter dominance of the castle's position atop this lofty volcanic crag. The view includes the site of Robert the Bruce's victory at Bannockburn and the monument to William Wallace.

» Scotland's most beautiful and enigmatic church, Rosslyn Chapel (p788), is filled with symbolic carvings with both Christian and pagan themes.

(Continued from page 928)

Sleeping

Braighe House B&B ££
(☎01851-705287; www.braighehouse.co.uk; 20 Braighe Rd; per person from £45; P) This spacious and comfortable guest house, 3 miles east of the town centre on the A866, has stylish, modern bedrooms and a great seafront location. Good bathrooms with powerful showers, hearty breakfasts and genuinely hospitable owners round off the perfect package.

Park Guest House B&B ££
(☎01851-702485; www.theparkguesthouse.co.uk; 30 James St; s/d from £58/86; P) A charming Victorian villa with a conservatory and eight luxurious rooms (mostly en suite), the Park Guest House is comfortable and central and has the advantage of an excellent restaurant. Rooms overlooking the main road can be noisy on weekday mornings.

Royal Hotel HOTEL ££
(☎01851-702109; www.royalstornoway.co.uk; Cromwell St; s/d £79/109; P) The 19th-century Royal is the most appealing of Stornoway's hotels – the rooms at the front retain period features such as wood panelling, and enjoy a view across the harbour to Lews Castle. Ask to see your room first, though, as some are a bit cramped.

Heb Hostel HOSTEL £
(☎01851-709889; www.hebhostel.co.uk; 25 Kenneth St; dm £15; @) The Heb is a friendly, easy-going hostel close to the ferry, with comfy wooden bunks, a convivial living room with peat fire and a welcoming owner who can provide all kinds of advice on what to do and where to go.

Eating

TOP CHOICE **Digby Chick** BISTRO £££
(☎01851-700026; 5 Bank St; mains £18-23; noon-10pm Mon-Sat) A modern restaurant that dishes up bistro cuisine such as haddock and chips, sesame-glazed pork belly or garlic-roasted mushroom with duck egg salad at lunchtime, the Digby Chick metamorphoses into a candle-lit gourmet restaurant in the evening, serving dishes such as grilled langoustines, seared scallops, roast lamb and steak. You can get a two-course lunch for £10 (11.30am to 2pm), and a three-course dinner for £20 (5.30pm to 6.30pm only).

SUNDAY EATS

Most restaurants in Stornoway are closed on Sundays. The few options for a sit-down meal include:

HS-1 Cafe-Bar (Royal Hotel, Cromwell St; mains £8-11; noon-4pm & 5-9pm)

Stornoway Balti House (24 South Beach; mains £8-13; noon-2.30pm & 6-11pm)

Thai Café THAI £
(☎01851-701811; 27 Church St; mains £5-7; noon-2.30pm & 5.30-11pm Mon-Sat) Here's a surprise – authentic, inexpensive Thai food in the heart of Stornoway. This spick-and-span little restaurant has a genuine Thai chef, and serves some of the most delicious, best-value Asian food in the Hebrides. If you can't get a table, it does takeaway, too.

Information

Sandwick Rd Petrol Station (Sandwick Rd) The only shop in town that's open on a Sunday (from 10am to 4pm); the Sunday papers arrive around 2pm.

Getting There & Around

BUS The bus station is on the waterfront, next to the ferry terminal. Bus W10 runs from Stornoway to Tarbert (one hour, four or five daily Monday to Saturday) and Leverburgh (two hours).

The Westside Circular bus W2 runs a circular route from Stornoway through Callanish, Carloway, Garenin and Arnol; the timetable means you can visit one or two of the sites in a day.

BIKE You can hire bikes from **Alex Dan's Cycle Centre** (☎01851-704025; www.hebrideancycles.co.uk; 67 Kenneth St; 9am-6pm Mon-Sat).

ARNOL

One of Scotland's most evocative historic buildings, the **Arnol Blackhouse** (HS; ☎01851-710395; adult/child £2.50/1.50; 9.30am-5.30pm Mon-Sat Apr-Sep, to 4.30pm Mon-Sat Oct-Mar, last admission 30min before closing) is not so much a museum as a perfectly preserved fragment of a lost world. Built in 1885, this traditional blackhouse – a combined byre, barn and home – was inhabited until 1964 and has not been changed since the last inhabitant moved out. The staff faithfully rekindle the central peat fire every morning so you can experience the distinctive peat-reek; there's no chimney, and the smoke finds its own way

FOR PEAT'S SAKE

In the Outer Hebrides, where trees are few and far between and coal is absent, peat has been the main source of domestic fuel for many centuries. Although oil-fired central heating is now the norm, many houses have held on to their peat fires for nostalgia's sake.

Peat in its raw state is extremely wet and can take a couple of months to dry out. It is cut from roadside bogs, where the cuttings are at least a metre deep. Rectangular blocks of peat are cut using a long-handled tool called a *tairsgeir* (peat-iron) and carefully assembled into a *cruach-mhonach* (peat stack), each balanced on top of the other in a grid pattern thus creating maximum air space. Once the peat has dried out it is stored in a shed.

Peat burns much more slowly than wood or coal and produces a not unpleasant smell, but in the old blackhouses (which had no chimney) it permeated every corner of the dwelling, not to mention the inhabitants' clothes and hair, hence the expression 'peat-reek' – the ever-present smell of peat smoke that was long associated with island life.

out through the turf roof, windows and door – spend too long inside and you might feel like you've been kippered! The museum is just off the A858, about 3 miles west of Barvas.

GARENIN (NA GEARRANNAN)

The picturesque and fascinating **Gearrannan Blackhouse Village** is a cluster of nine restored thatch-roofed blackhouses perched above the exposed Atlantic coast. One of the cottages is home to the **Blackhouse Museum** (www.gearrannan.com; adult/child £2.20/1; ⏲9.30am-5.30pm Mon-Sat Apr-Sep), a traditional 1955 blackhouse with displays on the village's history, while another houses the **Taigh an Chocair Cafe** (mains £3-6; ⏲9.30am-5.30pm Mon-Sat).

Garenin Crofters' Hostel (www.gatliff.org.uk; dm adult/child £10/6) occupies one of the village blackhouses, and is one of the most atmospheric hostels in Scotland (or anywhere else for that matter).

The other houses in the village are let out as self-catering **holiday cottages** (☎01851-643416; www.gearrannan.com; per 2 nights for 2 people £144-191) offering the chance to stay in a unique and luxurious, modernised blackhouse with attached kitchen and lounge. There's a minimum five-night let from June to August.

CARLOWAY (CARLABAGH)

Dun Carloway (Dun Charlabhaigh) is a 2000-year-old, dry-stone broch, perched defiantly above a beautiful loch with views to the mountains of North Harris. The site is clearly signposted along a minor road off the A858, a mile southwest of Carloway village. One of the best-preserved brochs in Scotland, its double walls (with internal staircase) still stand to a height of 9m and testify to the engineering skills of its Iron Age architects.

The tiny, turf-roofed **Doune Broch Centre** (admission free; ⏲10am-5pm Mon-Sat Apr-Sep) nearby has interpretative displays and exhibitions about the history of the broch and the life of the people who lived there.

CALLANISH (CALANAIS)

The **Callanish Standing Stones**, 15 miles west of Stornoway on the A858 road, form one of the most complete stone circles in Britain and are one of the most atmospheric prehistoric sites anywhere. Its ageless mystery, impressive scale and undeniable beauty leave a lasting impression. Sited on a wild and secluded promontory overlooking Loch Roag, 13 large stones of beautifully banded gneiss are arranged, as if in worship, around a 4.5m-tall central monolith. Some 40 smaller stones radiate from the circle in the shape of a cross, with the remains of a chambered tomb at the centre. Dating from 3800 to 5000 years ago, the stones are roughly contemporary with the pyramids of Egypt.

The nearby **Calanais Visitor Centre** (www.callanishvisitorcentre.co.uk; admission free, exhibition £2; ⏲10am-9pm Mon-Sat Apr-Sep, 10am-4pm Wed-Sat Oct-Mar) is a tour de force of discreet design. Inside is a small **exhibition** that speculates on the origins and purpose of the stones, and an excellent cafe (snacks £2 to £5).

Harris (Na Hearadh)

POP 2000

Harris, to the south of Lewis, is the scenic jewel in the necklace of islands that comprise the Outer Hebrides, a spectacular blend of rugged mountains, pristine beaches, flower-speckled machair and barren rocky landscapes. The isthmus at Tarbert splits Harris neatly in two – North Harris is dominated by mountains that rise forbiddingly above the peat moors to the south of Stornoway – Clisham (799m) is the highest point; South Harris is lower-lying, fringed by beautiful white-sand beaches on the west, and a convoluted rocky coastline to the east.

Harris is famous for Harris Tweed, a high-quality woollen cloth still hand-woven in islanders' homes. The industry employs around 400 weavers; staff at Tarbert tourist office can tell you about weavers and workshops that you can visit.

TARBERT (AN TAIRBEART)

POP 480

Tarbert is a harbour village with a spectacular location, tucked into the narrow neck of land that links North and South Harris. It has ferry connections to Uig on Skye.

Village facilities include a petrol station, bank, ATM and two general stores. The **Harris Tweed Shop** (www.isleofharristweedshop.co.uk; Main St; ⌚9.15am-5.30pm May-Sep) stocks a wide range of books on the Hebrides and sells gifts, crafts and the famous cloth itself.

Sleeping & Eating

Harris Hotel HOTEL ££
(☎01859-502154; www.harrishotel.com; s/d from £55/90; P 📶) Run since 1903 by four generations of the Cameron family, Harris Hotel is a 19th-century sporting hotel, originally built for deer-stalkers visiting the North Harris Estates. It has spacious, comfy rooms and a good restaurant; look out for JM Barrie's initials scratched on the dining-room window (the author of *Peter Pan* visited in the 1920s). The hotel is on the way out of the village, on the road north towards Stornoway.

Rockview Bunkhouse HOSTEL £
(☎01859-502081, 01859-502211; imacaskill@tiscali.co.uk; Main St; dm £10) This hostel on the street above the harbour is a bit cell-like with its cramped dorms and air of neglect, but it's close to the ferry. Not permanently staffed – if there's no answer, ask at the post office.

SOUTH HARRIS

The west coast of South Harris has some of the most beautiful beaches in Scotland. The blinding white sands and turquoise waters of **Luskentyre** and **Scarasta** would be major holiday resorts if they were transported to somewhere with a warm climate; as it is, they're usually deserted.

The culture and landscape of the Hebrides are celebrated in the fascinating exhibition at **Seallam! Visitor Centre** (www.seallam.com; Northton; adult/child £2.50/2; ⌚10am-5pm Mon-Sat). The centre, which is in Northton, just south of Scarasta, also has a genealogical research centre for people who want to trace their Hebridean ancestry.

The **east coast** is a complete contrast to the west – a strange, rocky moonscape of naked gneiss pocked with tiny lochans, the bleakness lightened by the occasional splash of green around the few crofting communities.

The village of **Leverburgh** (An t-Ob; www.leverburgh.co.uk) has a post office with an ATM, a general store and a petrol station.

Sleeping & Eating

Carminish Guest House B&B ££
(☎01859-520400; www.carminish.com; 1a Strond, Leverburgh; s/d £50/68; P 📶) One of the few B&Bs in Harris that is open all year, the welcoming Carminish is a modern house with three comfy guest bedrooms. There's a view of the ferry from the dining room, and lots of nice little touches such as handmade soaps, a tin of chocolate biscuits in the bedroom and the latest weather forecast posted on the breakfast table.

Sorrel Cottage B&B £
(☎01859-520319; www.sorrelcottage.co.uk; 2 Glen, Leverburgh; r per person from £30) Sorrel Cottage is a pretty crofter's house, about 1.5 miles west of the ferry at Leverburgh. Evening meals can be provided (£16 a head), and vegetarians and vegans are happily catered for. Bike hire available.

Getting There & Around

A CalMac **car ferry** zigzags through the reefs of the Sound of Harris from Leverburgh to Berneray (pedestrian/car £6.25/28.50, 1¼ hours, three or four daily Monday to Saturday). You can hire **bicycles** from Sorrel Cottage for £10 a day.

Berneray (Bearnaraigh)

POP 140

Berneray (www.isleofberneray.com) was linked to North Uist by a causeway in October 1998, but that hasn't altered the peace and beauty of the island. The beaches on its west coast are some of the most beautiful and unspoilt in Britain, and seals and otters can be seen in Bays Loch on the east coast.

The basic but atmospheric **Gatliff Hostel** (www.gatliff.org.uk; Baile; dm adult/child £10/6, camping per person £5), housed in a pair of restored blackhouses right by the sea, is the place to stay. You can camp outside, or on the grass above the gorgeous white-sand beach just to the north.

Bus W19 runs from Berneray (Gatliff Hostel and Harris ferry) to Lochmaddy (30 minutes, six daily Monday to Saturday). For details of ferries to Leverburgh (Harris), see p939.

North Uist (Uibhist A Tuath)

POP 1550

North Uist, an island half-drowned by lochs, is famed for its fishing but also has some magnificent beaches on its north and west coasts. For birdwatchers this is an earthly paradise, with regular sightings of waders and wildfowl ranging from redshank to red-throated diver to red-necked phalarope. The landscape is less wild and mountainous than Harris but it has a sleepy, subtle appeal.

LOCHMADDY (LOCH NAM MADADH)

Little Lochmaddy is the first village you hit after arriving on the ferry from Skye. There's a **tourist office** (☎01876-500321; Pier Rd; ⊙9am-1pm & 2-5pm Mon-Fri, 9.30am-1pm & 2-5.30pm Sat, 8-9pm Mon, Wed & Fri Apr-Oct), a couple of stores, a bank with an ATM, a petrol station, a post office and a pub.

Taigh Chearsabhagh (admission free, museum £1; ⊙10am-5pm Mon-Sat Feb-Jun & Sep-Dec, 10am-5pm Mon-Thu & Sat, to 8pm Fri Jul & Aug; @) is a museum and arts centre that preserves and displays the history and culture of the Uists, and is also a thriving community centre, post office and meeting place. The centre's lively cafe (mains £3 to £6) dishes up lovely homemade soups, sandwiches and cakes.

Buses from Lochmaddy to Berneray, Langass, Clachan na Luib, Benbecula and Lochboisdale run five or six times a day Monday to Saturday.

Sleeping & Eating

Tigh Dearg Hotel HOTEL ££
(☎01876-500700; www.tighdearghotel.co.uk; Lochmaddy; s/d £99/139; P 📶) It looks a little like a hostel from the outside but the 'Red House' (as the name means) is actually Lochmaddy's most luxurious accommodation, with nine designer bedrooms, a lounge with leather sofas around an open fire, a gym and even a sauna. There's a good restaurant too, with sea views from the terrace.

Old Courthouse B&B £
(☎01876-500358; oldcourthouse@tiscali.co.uk; Lochmaddy; r per person from £30; P) This charming, Georgian-style villa has four guest rooms and is within walking distance of the ferry, on the road that leads to Uist Outdoor Centre. Excellent porridge for breakfast and kippers are on the menu too.

Uist Outdoor Centre HOSTEL £
(☎01876-500480; www.uistoutdoorcentre.co.uk; Cearn Dusgaidh; dm £15; ⊙Mar–mid-Dec; P @ 📶) This shore-side activity centre has a smart bunkhouse with four-bed dorms and offers a range of activities including sea kayaking, rock climbing and diving.

BALRANALD NATURE RESERVE

Birdwatchers flock to this Royal Society for the Protection of Birds (RSPB) nature reserve, 18 miles west of Lochmaddy, in the hope of spotting the rare red-necked phalarope or hearing the distinctive call of the corncrake. There's a **visitors centre** (☎01876-510372; admission free; ⊙Apr-Sep) with a resident warden who offers 1½-hour guided walks (£5, depart visitor centre 10am on Tuesdays, May to August).

Benbecula (Beinn Na Faoghla)

POP 1200

Benbecula is a low-lying island whose flat, lochan-studded landscape is best appreciated from the summit of **Rueval** (124m), the island's highest point. There's a path around the south side of the hill (signposted from the main road; park beside the landfill site) that is said to be the route taken to the coast by Bonnie Prince Charlie and Flora MacDonald during the prince's escape in 1746.

The control centre for the British army's Hebrides Missile Range (located on the northwestern tip of South Uist) is the island's main source of employment, and **Balivanich** (Baile a'Mhanaich) – looking like a corner of a Glasgow housing estate planted incongruously on the machair – is the commercial centre serving the troops and their families. The village has a bank with an ATM, a post office, a large **Co-op supermarket** (8am-8pm Mon-Sat, 11am-6pm Sun) and a petrol station (open on Sundays).

South Uist (Uibhist A Deas)

POP 1900

South Uist is the second-largest island in the Outer Hebrides and saves its choicest corners for those who explore away from the main north–south road. The low-lying west coast is an almost unbroken stretch of white-sand beach and flower-flecked machair – a new waymarked hiking trail, the **Machair Way**, follows the coast – while the multitude of inland lochs provide excellent trout fishing. The east coast, riven by four large sea lochs, is hilly and remote, with spectacular **Beinn Mhor** (620m) the highest point.

THE NORTH

The northern part of the island is mostly occupied by the watery expanses of Loch Bee and Loch Druidibeg. **Loch Druidibeg National Nature Reserve** is an important breeding ground for birds such as dunlin, redshank, ringed plover, greylag goose and corncrake; you can take a 5-mile self-guided walk through the reserve (pick up a leaflet from the Scottish Natural Heritage office on the main road beside the loch).

Two miles south of Loch Druidibeg is the attractive hamlet of **Howmore** (Tobha Mor), with several restored, thatched blackhouses, one of which houses the **Tobha Mor Crofters' Hostel** (www.gatliff.org.uk; dm adult/child £10/6).

You can rent bikes from **Rothan Cycles** (01870-620283; www.rothan.com; 9 Howmore; per day/week from £10/43) where the road to the hostel leaves the main road.

THE SOUTH

Six miles south of Howmore, **Kildonan Museum** (01878-710343; Kildonan; adult/child £1.50/free; 10am-5pm Mon-Fri, 2-5pm Sun Easter-Oct) explores the lives of local crofters through its collection of artefacts.

Amid the ruined blackhouses of Milton, half a mile south of the museum, a cairn marks the site of **Flora MacDonald's birthplace**.

LOCHBOISDALE (LOCH BAGHASDAIL)

The ferry port of Lochboisdale is the island's largest settlement, with a tourist office, a bank with an ATM, a grocery store and a petrol station. There's a **Co-op supermarket** (8am-8pm Mon-Sat, 12.30-6pm Sun) at Daliburgh, 3 miles west of the village.

For details of ferries from Lochboisdale to Oban, see p928.

Sleeping & Eating

TOP CHOICE **Polochar Inn** INN ££
(01878-700215; www.polocharinn.com; Polochar; s/d from £60/90; P) Run by local sisters Morag McKinnon and Margaret Campbell, this 18th-century inn has been transformed into a stylish and welcoming hotel with a stunning location looking out across the sea to Barra. There's an excellent restaurant and bar menu (mains £9 to £19). Polochar is 7 miles southwest of Lochboisdale, on the way to Eriskay.

Lochside Cottage B&B £
(01878-700472; www.lochside-cottage.co.uk; r per person from £25; P) This friendly B&B, 1.5 miles west of the ferry, has rooms with views and a sun lounge barely a fishing-rod's length from its own trout loch.

Eriskay (Eiriosgaigh)

POP 170

In 1745, Bonnie Prince Charlie first set foot in Scotland on the west coast of Eriskay, on the sandy beach (immediately north of the ferry terminal) still known as **Prince's Strand** (Coilleag a'Phrionnsa).

More recently, the SS *Politician* sank just off the island in 1941. The islanders salvaged much of its cargo of around 250,000 bottles of whisky and, after a binge of dramatic proportions, the police intervened and a number of the islanders landed in jail. The story was immortalised by Sir Compton Mackenzie in his comic novel *Whisky Galore*, later made into a famous film.

A CalMac **car ferry** links Eriskay with Ardmhor at the northern end of Barra (pedestrian/car £6.70/19.55, 40 minutes, four or five daily).

Barra (Barraigh)

POP 1150

With its beautiful beaches, wildflower-clad dunes, rugged little hills and strong sense of community, diminutive Barra – just 14 miles in circumference – is the Outer Hebrides in miniature.

Castlebay (Bagh a'Chaisteil), in the south, is the largest village. There's a tourist office, a bank with an ATM, a post office and two grocery stores.

Sights & Activities

Kisimul Castle CASTLE

(HS; Castlebay; adult/child incl ferry £4.70/2.80; 9.30am-5.30pm Apr-Sep) Castlebay takes its name from Kisimul Castle, first built by the MacNeil clan in the 11th century. It was sold in the 19th century and restored in the 20th by American architect Robert MacNeil, who became the 45th clan chief; he gifted the castle to Historic Scotland in 2000 for an annual rent of £1 and a bottle of whisky. A short boat trip (weather permitting) takes you out to the island castle.

Sleeping & Eating

Wild camping (on foot or by bike) is allowed almost anywhere.

Castlebay Hotel HOTEL ££

(01871-810223; www.castlebayhotel.com; Castlebay; s/d from £60/95; P) The recently refurbished Castlebay Hotel offers spacious bedrooms decorated with a subtle tartan motif – it's worth paying a bit extra for a sea view – and a comfy lounge and conservatory with grand views across the harbour to the islands south of Barra. The hotel bar is the hub of island social life, with regular sessions of traditional music, and the restaurant specialises in local seafood and game (rabbit is often on the menu).

Dunard Hostel HOSTEL £

(01871-810443; www.dunardhostel.co.uk; Castlebay; dm/d from £15/38; P) Dunard is a friendly, family-run hostel just five minutes' walk from the ferry terminal. The owners can organise **sea-kayaking** tours for £30/55 a half-/full day.

Getting There & Around

See p928 for details of CalMac ferries from Castlebay to Oban and Lochboisdale (South Uist) and flights to the Scottish mainland; see p941 for the ferry from Ardmhor, at the northern end of Barra, to Eriskay.

Bus W32 makes a regular circuit of the island and also connects with flights at the airport.

You can hire bikes from **Island Adventures** (01871-810284; 29 St Brendan's Rd, Castlebay).

ORKNEY ISLANDS

There's a magic to the Orkney Islands that you'll begin to feel as soon as the Scottish mainland slips away astern. Consisting of 70 flat, green-topped islands stripped bare of trees by the wind, it's a place of ancient standing stones and prehistoric villages, an archipelago of old-style hospitality and Viking heritage narrated in the *Orkneyinga Saga* and still strong today, a region whose ports tell of lives led with the blessings and rough moods of the sea, and a destination where seekers can find melancholy wrecks of warships and the salty clamour of remote seabird colonies.

The principal island, confusingly called Mainland, has the two major settlements – bustling market-town Kirkwall, and Stromness with its grey-flagged streets – and the standout ancient sites. Ferries and flights give access to the other 15 inhabited islands.

Tours

Wildabout Orkney WILDLIFE, HISTORICAL

(01856-851011; www.wildaboutorkney.com) Operates tours covering Orkney's history, ecology, folklore and wildlife. Day trips operate year-round and cost £49, with pick-ups in Stromness and Kirkwall.

John O'Groats Ferries BOAT TRIPS

(01955-611353; www.jogferry.co.uk; John O'Groats) If you're in a hurry, these guys run a one-day tour of the main sites for £46, including the ferry from John O'Groats. You can do the whole thing as a long day trip from Inverness.

Getting There & Away

AIR

Flybe/Loganair (0871 700 0535; www.flybe.com) flies daily from Kirkwall to Aberdeen, Edinburgh, Glasgow, Inverness and Sumburgh (Shetland).

BOAT

During summer, book ahead for car spaces.

FROM SCRABSTER, SHETLANDS & ABERDEEN **Northlink Ferries** (0845 600 0449; www.northlinkferries.co.uk) operates ferries

Orkney Islands

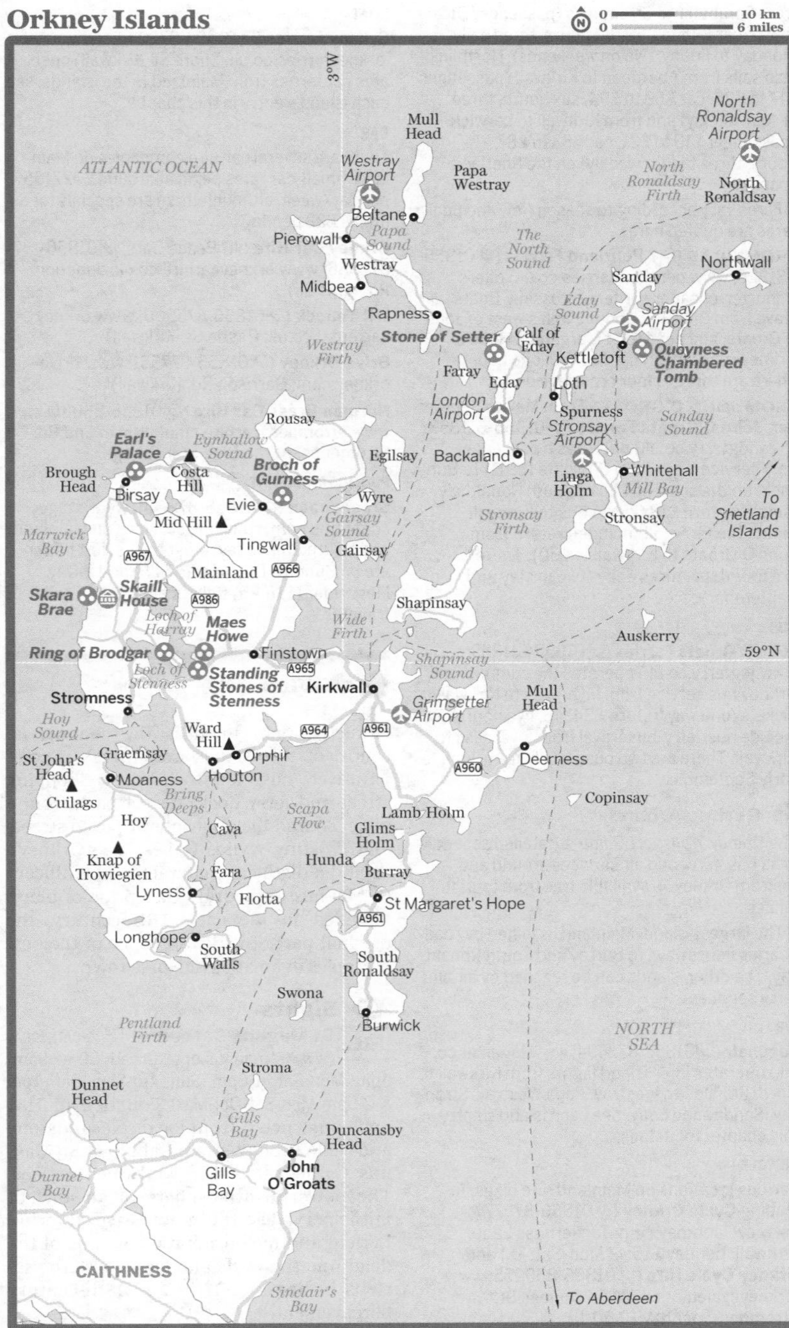

from Scrabster to Stromness (passenger £14 to £17, car £45 to £50, 1½ hours, three daily Monday to Friday, two on weekends). Northlink also sails from Aberdeen to Kirkwall (passenger £17 to £26, car £69 to £94, sux hours, three or four weekly) and from Kirkwall to Lerwick (passenger £15 to £21, car £53 to £87, 7½ hours, three to four weekly) on the Shetland Islands.

Fares vary according to season (low and peak fares are quoted here).

FROM GILLS BAY **Pentland Ferries** (☎01856-831226; www.pentlandferries.co.uk) offers a shorter, cheaper car-ferry crossing. Boats leave from Gills Bay, about 3 miles west of John O'Groats, and head to St Margaret's Hope in Orkney (passenger/car £13/30, one hour). There are three to four crossings daily.

FROM JOHN O'GROATS From May to September, **John O'Groats Ferries** (☎01955-611353; www.jogferry.co.uk) operates a passenger-only service from John O'Groats (p911) to Burwick, on the southern tip of South Ronaldsay (single/return £18/28). A bus to Kirkwall meets the ferry (all-included return from John O'Groats to Kirkwall is £30). There are four departures daily (two in May and September).

BUS

John O'Groats Ferries (☎01955-611353; www.jogferry.co.uk) operates the summer-only Orkney bus service from Inverness to Kirkwall. Tickets (one way/return £34/46, five hours) include bus-ferry-bus travel from Inverness to Kirkwall. There are two buses daily from June to early September.

Getting Around

The *Orkney Transport Guide*, a detailed schedule of all bus, ferry and air services around and to/from Orkney, is available free from tourist offices.

The largest island, Mainland, is joined by road-bearing causeways to Burray and South Ronaldsay. The other islands can be reached by air and ferry services.

AIR

Loganair (☎01856-872494; www.loganair.co.uk) operates inter-island flights from Kirkwall to North Ronaldsay, Westray, Papa Westray, Stronsay, Sanday and Eday. See each island's entry in this chapter for details.

BICYCLE

Various locations on Mainland hire bikes, including **Cycle Orkney** (☎01856-875777; www.cycleorkney.com; Tankerness Lane, Kirkwall; per day £15; ⏰Mon-Sat; 👪) and **Orkney Cycle Hire** (☎01856-850255; www.orkneycyclehire.co.uk; 54 Dundas St, Stromness; per day £7.50-10).

BOAT

Orkney Ferries (☎01856-872044; www.orkneyferries.co.uk; Shore St, Kirkwall) operates car ferries from Mainland to the islands; see each island's entry in this chapter.

CAR

There are several car-hire companies on Mainland. Small-car rates begin at around £32/165 per day/week, although there are specials for as low as £28 per day.

Orkney Car Hire (JD Peace Cars; ☎01856-872866; www.orkneycarhire.co.uk; Junction Rd, Kirkwall)

WR Tullock (☎01856-875500; www.orkneycarrental.co.uk; Castle St, Kirkwall)

Drive Orkney (☎01856-877551; www.driveorkney.com; Garrison Rd, Kirkwall)

Norman Brass Car Hire (☎01856-850850; www.stromnesscarhire.co.uk; North End Rd, Stromness) At the Blue Star Garage.

PUBLIC TRANSPORT

Stagecoach (☎01856-878014; www.stagecoachbus.com) runs bus services on Mainland and South Ronaldsay. Most buses don't operate on Sunday. Dayrider (£7.25) and 7-Day Megarider (£16.25) tickets allow unlimited travel.

Kirkwall

POP 6206

Orkney's main town is the commercial centre of the islands and there's a comparatively busy feel to its main shopping street and ferry dock. It's set back from a wide bay and the atmospheric paved streets and twisting wynds (lanes) give Orkney's capital a distinctive character. Magnificent St Magnus Cathedral takes pride of place. Founded in the early 11th century, the original part of Kirkwall is one of the best examples of an ancient Norse town.

Sights

FREE **St Magnus Cathedral** CATHEDRAL
(www.stmagnus.org; Broad St; ⏰9am-6pm Mon-Sat, 1-6pm Sun Apr-Sep, 9am-1pm & 2-5pm Mon-Sat Oct-Mar) Founded in 1137 and constructed from local red sandstone and yellow Eday stone, fabulous St Magnus Cathedral is Kirkwall's centrepiece. The powerful atmosphere of an ancient faith pervades the impressive interior. Lyrical and melodramatic epitaphs of the dead line the walls and emphasise the serious business of 17th- and 18th-century bereavement.

Kirkwall

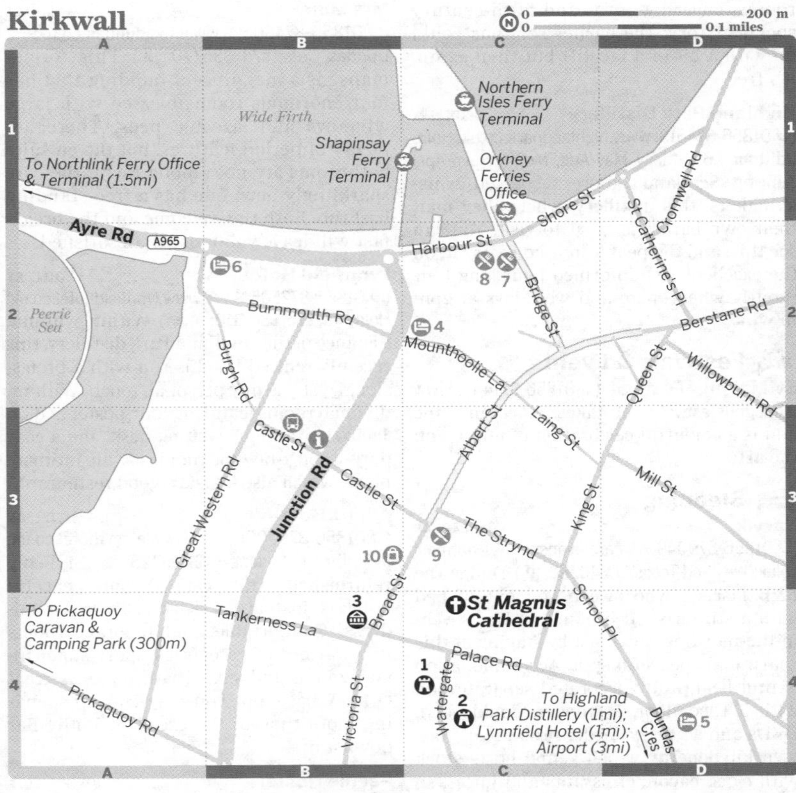

Earl's Palace & Bishop's Palace PALACES
(HS; www.historic-scotland.gov.uk; Watergate; adult/child £3.70/2.20; ⌚9.30am-5.30pm Apr-Sep) Near the cathedral, these two ruined palaces are worth poking around. The better of the two, Earl's Palace, was once known as the finest example of French Renaissance architecture in Scotland. One room features an interesting history of its builder, Earl Patrick Stewart, who was executed in Edinburgh for treason. He started construction in about 1600, but he ran out of money and it was never completed.

FREE **Orkney Museum** MUSEUM
(www.orkney.gov.uk; Broad St; ⌚10.30am-5pm Mon-Sat) Opposite the cathedral, this is a labyrinthine display in a former merchant's house. It has an overview of Orkney history and prehistory, including Pictish carvings and a display on the Ba'. Most engaging are the last

Kirkwall

Top Sights
St Magnus Cathedral C4

Sights
1 Bishop's Palace C4
2 Earl's Palace C4
3 Orkney Museum B4

Sleeping
4 Albert Hotel C2
5 Mrs Muir D4
6 Peedie Hostel B2

Eating
Bothy Bar ......(see 4)
7 Dil Se C2
8 Kirkwall Hotel C2
9 Reel C3

Shopping
10 Longship B3

rooms, covering 19th- and 20th-century social history; the earlier sections could do with a bit of a facelift but then again, it's free.

Highland Park Distillery DISTILLERY
(☎01856-874619; www.highlandpark.co.uk; Holm Rd; tour £6; ⊙daily May-Aug, Mon-Fri Sep-Apr) Among Scotland's more respected whiskymakers, this distillery, where they malt their own barley, is great to visit. You can see this, and the peat kiln used to dry it, on the excellent well-informed hour-long tour (hourly when open, and weekdays at 2pm in winter).

Festivals & Events

St Magnus Festival (☎01856-871445; www.stmagnusfestival.com) takes place in June and is a colourful celebration of music and the arts.

Sleeping

Narvik B&B ££
(☎01856-879049; carolevansnarvik@hotmail.co.uk; Weyland Tce; s/d £40/60; P) Dodge the B&B fascists who sweep you out of bed with a stiff-bristled broom for your seven-in-the-morning breakfast by staying at this charmingly peaceful spot. Accommodation is in a beautifully decorated separate flat, with a tiled floor, a wooden double bed, DVDs and a grassy garden. You've got your own kitchenette, which genial hosts stock with eggs, bacon, croissants and juices, so your morning meal is wholly at your own pace.

Orcades Hostel HOSTEL £
(☎01856-873745; www.orcadeshostel.com; Muddisdale Rd; dm/d £17/50; P Wi-Fi) Book ahead to get a bed in this cracking new hostel near the campsite on the western edge of town. It's a guest-house conversion so there's a very smart kitchen and lounge area, and great-value doubles. Comfortable dorms with just four bunks make for sound sleeping, and young enthusiastic owners give the place plenty of spark.

Mrs Muir B&B ££
(☎01856-874805; www.twodundas.co.uk; 2 Dundas Cres; s/d £35/70; P) This former manse is a magnificent building that has four enormous rooms blessed with large windows and sizeable beds. There are plenty of period features, but the en suite bathrooms are not among them; they are sparklingly new; one has a free-standing bathtub. Both the welcome and the breakfast will leave you more than satisfied.

Lynnfield Hotel HOTEL ££
(☎01856-872505; www.lynnfieldhotel.co.uk; Holm Rd; s/d £80/110; P Wi-Fi) Within whiffing distance of the Highland Park distillery, this recently refitted hotel is run with a professional, yet warmly personal, touch. With individual rooms featuring four-poster beds, a Jacuzzi or antique writing desk, and a cosy dark-wood drawing room, it's an intimate place, which also boasts a good restaurant.

Albert Hotel HOTEL ££
(☎01856-876000; www.alberthotel.co.uk; Mounthoolie Lane; s/d £110/128; Wi-Fi) Stylishly refurbished, this central but peaceful hotel is just about Kirkwall's finest address. Comfortable contemporary rooms in a variety of categories sport super-inviting beds and smart bathrooms. A great Orkney base, but you may end up spending more time in the excellent Bothy Bar downstairs.

Peedie Hostel HOSTEL £
(☎01856-875477; kirkwallpeediehostel@talk21.com; Ayre Rd; dm £15) Nestling into a corner at the end of the Kirkwall waterfront, this cute hostel squeezes in all the necessary features for a comfortable stay in a small space. The dorms actually have plenty of room – it's only in the tiny kitchen that territorial squabbles might break out.

Pickaquoy Caravan & Camping Park CAMPING £
(☎01856-879900; www.pickaquoy.co.uk; Pickaquoy Rd; sites for one/two to three £6.50/10.50; ⊙Apr-Sep; P) Plenty of grass and excellent

THE BA'

Every Christmas Day and New Year's Day, Kirkwall holds a staggering spectacle: a crazy ball game known as The Ba'. Two enormous teams, the Uppies and the Doonies, fight their way, no holds barred, through the streets, trying to get a leather ball to the other end of town. Violence, skulduggery and other stunts are common and the event, fuelled by plenty of strong drink, can last hours.

modern facilities. Check-in in the sports centre alongside.

Eating & Drinking

Reel CAFE £

(Albert St; sandwiches £3, 9am-6pm) Part music shop and part cafe, Kirkwall's best coffee-stop sits alongside the cathedral, and bravely puts tables outside at the slightest threat of sunshine. It's a relaxed spot that's good for morning-after debriefing, as well as lunchtime panini and musically named sandwiches (along with their cheese one...Skara Brie). It's a centre for local folk musicians, with regular evening sessions.

Kirkwall Hotel RESTAURANT ££

(01856-872232; www.kirkwallhotel.com; Harbour St; mains £9-15; lunch & dinner) This grand old Orcadian hotel on the waterfront is one of the capital's best places to dine. The elegant bar and eating area packs out; it's one of Kirkwall's favourite spots for an evening out with the clan. There's a fairly standard pub-food list that's complemented by a seasonal menu homing in on local seafood and meat – the lamb is delicious – that's well presented and very tasty.

Dil Se SOUTH ASIAN £

(01856-875242; 7 Bridge St; mains £8-11; 4-11pm) Upbeat and inventive, this main-street subcontinental choice tries to steer Orcadians away from the clichéd curry classics in favour of baltis – the spinach one is fabulous – and other creations. The late opening means you can enjoy those long summer evenings outdoors and not go hungry at the end of them.

Bothy Bar PUB £

(www.alberthotel.co.uk; Mounthoolie Lane; mains £7-10; lunch & dinner) In the Albert Hotel, the Bothy looks very smart these days with its modish floor and black-and-white photos of old-time Orcadian farming, but its low tables provide the customary cheer and sustaining food: think sausages, think haddock, think stews: good pub grub.

Shopping

Kirkwall has some gorgeous jewellery and crafts along Albert St. Try **The Longship** (www.olagoriejewellery.com; 7 Broad St) for Orkney-made crafts and gifts, and exquisite designer jewellery.

Information

Orkney Library (01856-873166; 44 Junction Rd; Mon-Sat) Fast free internet access (one-hour maximum).

Tourist office (01856-872856; www.visitorkney.com; 6 Broad St; 9am-6pm summer, 9am-5pm Mon-Fri, 10am-4pm Sat winter) Has a good range of publications on Orkney.

Getting There & Away

The **airport** (www.hial.co.uk) is 2.5 miles east of town. See p956 for flight information. For flights and ferries from Kirkwall to the islands, see the island sections.

Bus 1 runs direct from Kirkwall to Stromness (40 minutes, hourly, four to six Sunday); bus 2 runs to Orphir and Houton (20 minutes, four or five Monday to Saturday); bus 6 runs from Kirkwall to Evie (30 minutes, three to five daily Monday to Saturday) and the ferry at Tingwall to Rousay.

Mainland To South Ronaldsay

When a German U-boat sneaked into Scapa Flow and sank the battleship *Royal Oak* right under the Royal Navy's nose in 1939, Churchill decided it was time to better protect this crucial naval harbour. Using concrete blocks and discarded ships, the channels between Lamb Holm, Glimps Holm, Burray, South Ronaldsay and Mainland were blocked; the **Churchill Barriers** still link the islands, and carry the main road from Kirkwall to Burwick. There are good sandy beaches by barriers No 3 and 4.

Getting There & Away

There are buses from Kirkwall to South Ronaldsay's St Margaret's Hope (30 minutes, almost hourly Monday to Saturday).

LAMB HOLM

On the tiny island of Lamb Holm, the **Italian Chapel** (admission free; 9am-dusk) is all that remains of a POW camp that housed the Italian soldiers who worked on the Churchill Barriers. They built the chapel in their spare time, using two Nissen huts, scrap metal and their considerable artistic and decorative skills. One of the artists returned in 1960 to restore the paintwork. It's quite extraordinary inside and definitely worth seeing.

BURRAY

Sleepy Burray village is on the southern side of this island. The **Sands Hotel** (☎01856-731298; www.thesandshotel.co.uk; Burray; s/d/ste £80/100/155; P wi-fi) is a spiffy, refurbished 19th-century herring station, right on the pier. Very modern rooms have stylish furnishings, and all have great water views. Families and groups should consider a suite – these are two-level self-contained flats that sleep four and have a kitchen. The **restaurant** (mains £15, bar meals £8; ⊙lunch & dinner), with its genteel, nautical feel, dishes out decent nosh, and tables in the sunlit conservatory migrate outside in sunny weather.

SOUTH RONALDSAY

The main village on South Ronaldsay is **St Margaret's Hope**, named after Margaret, the Maid of Norway, who died here in 1290 on the way from her homeland to marry the future Edward II of England. This is where the Gills Bay ferry docks.

Sights

Tomb of the Eagles ARCHAEOLOGICAL SITE
(www.tomboftheeagles.co.uk; adult/child £6.50/3; ⊙9.30am-5.30pm Apr-Oct, 10am-noon Mar, by arrangement Nov-Feb) At the island's southern tip, this is the result of a local farmer finding two significant archaeological sites on his land. The first is a Bronze Age stone building with a firepit, indoor well and plenty of seating; orthodox theory suggests it was a communal cooking site, but we reckon it's the original Orkney pub. Beyond here, in a spectacular clifftop position, the Neolithic tomb (wheel yourself in prone on a trolley) is an elaborate stone construction that held the remains of up to 340 people who died some five millennia ago. Before you head out to the sites, an excellent personal explanation is given to you at the visitor centre; you meet a few spooky skulls and can handle some of the artefacts found. It's about a mile's airy walk to the tomb from the centre.

Sleeping & Eating

Bankburn House B&B ££
(☎08444 142310; www.bankburnhouse.co.uk; St Margaret's Hope; s/d £38/55, with en suite £48/65; P @ wi-fi) On the A961, just outside town, this place has four smashing upstairs rooms in a large rustic house. Two rooms have en suite, all are a brilliant size, and a lot of thought has been put into guests' comfort. There's also a huge stretch of lawn out the front, which overlooks the town and bay – perfect for sunbathing on those shimmering, summery Orkney days. There's a substantial discount if you stay more than one night.

St Margaret's Hope Backpackers HOSTEL £
(☎01856-831225; www.orkneybackpackers.com; St Margaret's Hope; dm £13; P) The backpackers, next to the Murray Arms, and a short walk from the ferry, is a lovely stone cottage and has small, simple rooms with up to four berths – good for families. There's a great lounge, a kitchen, a laundry and good hot showers. It's an excellent setup, particularly as the pub is right outside the front door and you can use the wi-fi in the adjacent cafe. Enquiries at the Trading Post shop next door.

Creel RESTAURANT £££
(☎01856-831311; www.thecreel.co.uk; Front Rd, St Margaret's Hope; 2/3 courses £32/38; ⊙dinner Tue-Sun) On the waterfront in an unassuming house, on unpretentious wooden tables, some of Scotland's best seafood has been served up for well over 20 years. Upstairs and next door, the three rooms (singles/doubles £75/110) face the spectacular sunset over the water, and are most spacious and comfortable. It was up for sale at the time of research, so fingers crossed.

West & North Mainland

This part of the island is sprinkled with outstanding prehistoric monuments: the journey up to Orkney is worth it for these alone.

MAES HOWE

Egypt has the pyramids, Scotland has **Maes Howe** (HS; ☎01856-761606; www.historic-scotland.gov.uk; adult/child £5.20/3.10; ⊙tours hourly 10am-3pm Oct-Mar, also 4pm Apr-Sep). Constructed about 5000 years ago, it's an extraordinary place, a Stone Age tomb built from enormous sandstone blocks, some of which weighed many tons and were brought from several miles away. Creeping down the long stone passageway to the central chamber, you feel the indescribable gulf of years that separate us from the architects of this mysterious place. Though nothing is known about who and what was interred here, the scope of the project suggests it was a structure of great significance.

In the 12th century, the tomb was broken into by Vikings searching for treasure. A couple of years later, another group sought shelter in the chamber from a blizzard that lasted three days. While they waited out the storm, they carved runic graffiti on the walls. As well as the some-things-never-change 'Olaf was 'ere' and 'Thorni bedded Helga', there are also more intricate carvings, including a particularly fine dragon and a knotted serpent.

Buy tickets in Tormiston Mill, on the other side of the road. Entry is by 45-minute guided tours that leave on the hour. Be sure to reserve your tour-slot ahead by phone. Due to the oversized groups, guides tend to only show a couple of the Viking inscriptions, but they'll happily show more if asked.

STANDING STONES OF STENNESS

Within sight of Maes Howe, four mighty **stones** (www.historic-scotland.gov.uk; ⏲24hr) remain of what was once a circle of 12. Recent research suggests they were perhaps erected as long ago as 3300 BC, and they impose by their sheer size; the tallest measures 5.7m in height. This narrow strip of land, the Ness of Brodgar, separates the Harray and Stenness lochs and was the site of a large settlement, inhabited throughout the Neolithic period (3500–1800 BC).

A short walk to the east are the excavated remains of **Barnhouse Neolithic Village**, thought to have been inhabited by the builders of Maes Howe. Don't skip this: it brings the area to life.

RING OF BRODGAR

Situated about a mile north of Stenness, along the road towards Skara Brae, is this wide circle of **standing stones** (www.historic-scotland.gov.uk; ⏲24hr), some over 5m tall. Last of the three Stenness monuments to be built (2500–2000 BC), it remains a most atmospheric location. Twenty-one of the original 60 stones still stand among the heather. These mysterious giants, their curious shapes mutilated by years of climatic onslaught, fire the imagination – what were they for?

SKARA BRAE & SKAILL HOUSE

A visit to extraordinary **Skara Brae** (HS; www.historic-scotland.gov.uk; Bay of Skaill; adult/child £6.70/4; ⏲9.30am-5.30pm Apr-Sep, 9.30am-4.30pm Oct-Mar), one of the world's most evocative prehistoric sites, offers the best opportunity in Scotland for a glimpse of Stone Age life. Idyllically situated by a sandy bay 8 miles north of Stromness, and predating Stonehenge and the pyramids of Giza, Skara Brae is northern Europe's best-preserved prehistoric village.

Even the stone furniture – beds, boxes and dressers – has survived the 5000 years since a community lived and breathed here. It was hidden until 1850, when waves whipped up by a severe storm eroded the sand and grass above the beach, exposing the houses underneath. There's an excellent interactive exhibit and short video, arming visitors with facts and theory, which will enhance the impact of the site. You then enter a reconstructed house, which gives the excavation that follows more meaning.

The joint ticket will also get you into **Skaill House** (⏲Apr-Sep), which is an early-17th-century mansion built for the local bishop in 1620. It's a bit anticlimactic, catapulting straight from the Neolithic to the 1950s decor.

Buses run to Skara Brae from Kirkwall and Stromness (Monday, Thursday and Saturday May to September only). It's possible to walk along the coast from Stromness to Skara Brae.

BIRSAY

The small village of Birsay is 6 miles north of Skara Brae. The ruins of the **Earl's Palace** (⏲24hr), built in the 16th century by the despotic Robert Stewart, earl of Orkney, dominate the village centre. Today it's a mass of half walls and crumbling columns, the latter climbing like dilapidated chimney stacks.

At low tide (check tide times at the shop in Earl's Palace) you can walk out to the **Brough of Birsay** (HS; www.historic-scotland.gov.uk; adult/child £3.20/1.90; ⏲9.30am-5.30pm mid-Jun–Sep), you'll find the extensive ruins of a Norse settlement and the 12th-century St Peter's Church.

Birsay makes a lovely, peaceful place to stay amid the Orkney countryside. **Birsay Hostel** (☎01856-873535; www.hostelsorkney.co.uk; dm £13, small/medium tent £5/8; ⏲May-Oct; P) is a former activity centre and school that now has dorms that vary substantially in spaciousness – go for one of the four-bedded ones. There's a big kitchen and grassy camping area. One of Orkney's most charming B&Bs is **Links House** (☎01856-721221; www.ewaf.co.uk; s/d £49/78; P), a most welcoming stone house near the sea. The beautiful rooms – one with comforting sloping ceiling, one with a toilet that has wonderful vistas – are complemented by a great little gazebo space. Breakfast is a treat – pancakes with blueberries and crème fraiche anyone?

EVIE

On an exposed headland at Aikerness, a 1.5-mile walk northeast from the straggling village of Evie, you'll find the **Broch of Gurness** (HS; www.historic-scotland.gov.uk; adult/child £4.70/2.80; ⏲9.30am-5.30pm Apr-Sep), a fine example of these drystone fortified towers that were both status symbol for powerful farmers and useful protection from raiders some 2200 years ago. The imposing entranceway and sturdy stone walls – originally 10m high – impress; inside you can see the hearth and where a mezzanine floor would have fitted. Around the broch are the remains of the settlement centred on it.

Eviedale Campsite (☎01856-751270; eviedale@orkney.com; Evie; sites £5-9; ⏲Apr-Sep; P 📶), at the northern end of the village, has a good grassed area for tent camping, with picnic tables. This would suit people looking to avoid the larger municipal sites. Next door is self-catering accommodation in excellent, renovated farm cottages.

Stromness

POP 1609

An elongated little port, Stromness lacks Kirkwall's size and punch but makes up for that with bucketloads of character. The rambling, winding streets flanking the town have changed little since the 18th century and the flagstone-paved main street curves along the waterfront, amid attractive stone cottages. Guest houses, pubs and eateries interrupt traditional trade along the main street, where cars and pedestrians move at the same pace as each other.

Sights

Pier Arts Centre GALLERY

(www.pierartscentre.com; 30 Victoria St; ⏲10.30am-5pm Mon-Sat) Resplendently redesigned, this has really rejuvenated the Orkney modern art scene with its sleek lines and upbeat attitude. It's worth a look as much for the architecture as its high-quality collection of 20th-century British art and changing exhibitions.

Stromness Museum MUSEUM

(www.orkneyheritage.com; 52 Alfred St; adult/child £3.50/1; ⏲10am-5pm Apr-Sep, 11am-3.30pm Mon-Sat Oct-Mar) A superb museum full of knick-knacks from maritime and natural-history exhibitions covering whaling, the Hudson's Bay Company and the sunken German fleet. You can happily nose around the place for a couple of hours. Across the street from the museum is the house where local poet and novelist George Mackay Brown lived.

Festivals & Events

The **Orkney Folk Festival** (www.orkneyfolkfestival.com) is a four-day event based in Stromness in the third week of May.

Sleeping

Orca Hotel HOTEL ££

(☎01856-850447; www.orcahotel.moonfruit.com; 76 Victoria St; s/d £40/54) Warm and homelike, this small hotel right in the heart of things is likeably out of the ordinary, and features cosy rooms with narrow, comfortable beds. Rates vary slightly depending on the room you choose; in winter you can use the hotel's kitchen.

Miller's House B&B ££

(☎01856-851969; www.millershouseorkney.com; 7 John St; s/d £50/70; ⏲Easter-Oct) Reached from up a side alley, Miller's House is a historic Stromness residence – check out the wonderful 1716 stone doorway – but most of the rooms are actually in a different building (Harbourside Guest House) around the corner. Here you can smell the cleanliness, and there's plenty of light and an optimistic feel. Showers hit the spot, and you can use the laundry. Exceptional breakfasts include vegetarian options and daily baked bread.

Hamnavoe Hostel HOSTEL £

(☎01856-851202; www.hamnavoehostel.co.uk; 10a North End Rd; dm £16-18; 📶) This well-equipped hostel lacks a bit of character but makes up for that with excellent facilities, including a fine kitchen and a lounge room with great perspectives over the water. The dorms are very commodious, with duvets and reading lamps, and the showers are good.

DIVING SCAPA FLOW'S WRECKS

One of the world's largest natural harbours, Scapa Flow has been in near-constant use by various fleets from the Vikings onwards. After WWI, 74 German ships were interned in Scapa; when the terms of the armistice were agreed on 6 May 1919, with the announcement of a severely reduced German navy, Admiral von Reuter, who was in charge of the fleet, decided to take matters into his own hands. On 21 June, a secret signal was passed from ship to ship and the British watched incredulously as every German ship began to sink. Fifty-two of them went to the bottom, with the rest left aground in shallow water.

Most of the ships were salvaged, but seven vessels remain to attract divers. There are three battleships – the *König*, the *Kronprinz Wilhelm* and the *Markgraf* – all of which weigh over 25,000 tonnes. The first two were subjected to blasting for scrap metal, but the Markgraf is undamaged and considered one of the best dives in the area.

As well as the German wrecks, numerous other ships rest on the sea bed in Scapa Flow. HMS *Royal Oak*, which was sunk by a German U-boat in October 1939, with the loss of 833 crew, is an official war grave.

Recommended diving contacts:

Diving Cellar (☎01856-850055; www.divescapaflow.co.uk; 4 Victoria St, Stromness)

Scapa Scuba (☎/fax 01856-851218; www.scapascuba.co.uk; Dundas St, Stromness)

Brown's Hostel HOSTEL £
(☎01856-850661; www.brownshostel.co.uk; 45 Victoria St; dm £14-15; @📶) On the main street, this handy, sociable place has cramped but cosy and homelike dorms (the upstairs ones are a pound more but have more space) as well as small private rooms. Life centres on its inviting common area where you can browse the free internet or swap pasta recipes in the open kitchen. There are overflow rooms in a house up the street.

Stromness Hotel HOTEL ££
(☎01856-850298; www.stromnesshotel.com; Victoria St; s/d £55/98; 📶) Proudly surveying the main street and harbour, this lofty Victorian hotel is a reminder of the way things used to be, with its posh revolving door and imposing facade. The pink-hued rooms are spacious, but the yielding beds have seen better days and the claustrophobic lift means your suitcase'll have to find its own way.

Ness Caravan & Camping Park CAMPING £
(☎01856-873535; 1-person/2-person/family tents £5.80/9/11; ⏲Apr-Sep; 🅿) This breezy, fenced-in camping ground overlooks the bay at the southern end of town and is as neat as a pin.

Eating & Drinking

Hamnavoe Restaurant RESTAURANT £££
(☎01856-850606; 35 Graham Pl; mains £13-19; ⏲dinner Tue-Sun Apr-Oct) Tucked away off the main street, this longstanding Stromness classic specialises in excellent local seafood backed up by professional service. There's always something good off the boats, and the chef prides himself on his lobster. Booking is a must. From November to March, it's only open Saturday and Sunday for dinner, while in summer it also opens for lobster lunches on Saturday.

Julia's Café & Bistro CAFE £
(20 Ferry Rd; mains £5-8; ⏲9am-5pm Sep-May, plus dinner Wed-Sun Jun-Aug; @📶) This cafe with a conservatory, opposite the port, keeps all-comers happy, with massive fry-ups offset on the cardiac karma scale by wraps, salads and tempting vegetarian dishes such as nut roast or couscous. In summer it opens for dinner with elaborated fare (£10 to £13) on offer.

Ferry Inn PUB £
(www.ferryinn.com; 10 John St; mains £7-11; ⏲breakfast, lunch & dinner) Every port has its pub, and in Stromness it's the Ferry. Convivial and central, it warms the cockles with folk music, local beers and characters, and pub food that's unsophisticated but generously proportioned and good value.

Information

Library (Alfred St; ⏲2-7pm Mon-Thu, 2-5pm Fri, 10am-5pm Sat) Free internet.

Tourist office (☎01856-850716; ⏲10am-4pm Mon-Sat Apr-Oct) In the ferry terminal. Also open on Sunday in summer.

Getting There & Away

For information on ferries to Scrabster, Lerwick and Aberdeen, see p956.

Bus 1 runs regularly to Kirkwall (40 minutes) and on to St Margaret's Hope.

Hoy

Orkney's second-largest island, Hoy (meaning 'High Island'), got the lion's share of this archipelago's scenic beauty. Shallow turquoise bays lace the perimeter, while peat and moorland cover Orkney's highest hills. Much of the northern part of the island is a Royal Society for the Protection of Birds (RSPB) reserve, with breeding guillemots, kittiwakes, fulmars, puffins and great skuas. Note that the ferry service from Mainland gets very busy over summer – book ahead.

Sights

The northern part of the island boasts spectacular coastal scenery, including some of Britain's highest vertical cliffs – St John's Head on the northwest coast rises 346m.

Lyness, on the eastern side of Hoy, was an important naval base during both world wars, when the British Grand Fleet was based in Scapa Flow. With the dilapidated remains of buildings and an uninspiring outlook towards the oil terminal on Flotta island, this isn't a pretty place. However, the **Scapa Flow Visitor Centre** (admission by donation; 9am-4.30pm Mon-Fri Mar-Oct, plus Sat & Sun May-Sep) is a fascinating naval museum and photographic display, located in an old pumphouse that once fed fuel to the ships.

Activities

First scaled in 1966, the **Old Man of Hoy** is a rock-climber's delight. The easiest approach to the Old Man is from Rackwick Bay, a two- to three-hour walk by road from Moaness Pier (in Hoy village on the east coast, where the ferries dock) through the beautiful **Rackwick Glen**. You'll pass the 5000-year-old **Dwarfie Stane**, the only example of a rock-cut tomb in Scotland and, according to Sir Walter Scott, the favourite residence of Trolld, a dwarf from Norse legend. On your return you can take the path via the **Glens of Kinnaird** and **Berriedale Wood**, Scotland's most northerly tuft of native forest.

The most popular walk climbs steeply westwards from Rackwick Bay, then curves northwards, descending gradually to the edge of the cliffs opposite the Old Man of Hoy. Allow seven hours for the return trip from Moaness Pier, or three hours from Rackwick, a village on the west coast – there's a hostel here from where the walk begins.

Sleeping & Eating

Hoy Centre HOSTEL £
(office hours only 01856-873535 ext 2415; www.hostelsorkney.co.uk; Moaness; dm/f £14/34; P) This is a pretty schmick place with an enviable location, around 15 minutes' walk from Moaness Pier, at the base of the rugged Cuilags. Rooms come with twin beds and a bunk bed, or there are family rooms, all with en suite.

Quoydale B&B £
(01856-791315; www.orkneyaccommodation.co.uk; s/d £25/42) There are several B&Bs on the island, including the welcoming Quoydale, nestled at the base of Ward Hill on a working farm one mile from the ferry terminal. It has spectacular views over Scapa Flow and offers tours and a taxi service.

Stromabank Hotel HOTEL, PUB ££
(01856-701494; www.stromabank.co.uk; Longhope; s/d £42/64; bar meals £6-10; lunch Sun, dinner Fri-Wed) Perched on the hill above Longhope, the small, atmospheric Stromabank has very acceptable refurbished en suite rooms and an attractive bar whose small menu offers tasty home-cooked meals using lots of local produce. Opens less in winter.

Getting There & Away

Orkney Ferries (01856-850624; www.orkneyferries.co.uk) runs passenger ferries between Stromness and Moaness Pier (£3.60, 30 minutes, two to five daily).

There's also a frequent **car ferry** (01856-811397) to Lyness (Hoy) from Houton on Mainland (passenger/car £3.60/11.50, 40 minutes, up to seven daily Monday to Friday, two or three Saturday and Sunday). The Sunday service only runs from May to September.

Getting Around

Transport on Hoy is very limited. Your best bet to explore is the **Hoy Hopper**, which runs Wednesday to Friday, mid-May to mid-September.

Departing from Kirkwall, it crosses to Hoy then does circuits around the island, allowing you to hop on and off at will, before returning to Kirkwall in the evening. Total cost is £17/8.50 per adult/child.

Northern Islands

The group of windswept islands north of Mainland provides a refuge for migrating birds and a nesting ground for seabirds; there are several RSPB reserves. Some of the islands are also rich in archaeological sites, but it's the beautiful scenery, with wonderful white-sand beaches and lime-green to azure seas, that is the main attraction.

The tourist offices in Kirkwall and Stromness have the useful *Islands of Orkney* brochure with maps and details of these islands. Note that the 'ay' at the end of each island name (from the Old Norse for 'island') is pronounced 'ee'.

Orkney Ferries (01856-872044; www.orkneyferries.co.uk) and **Loganair** (01856-872494; www.loganair.co.uk) enable you to make day trips to many of the islands from Kirkwall on most days of the week (Friday only to North Ronaldsay), but it's worth staying over.

ROUSAY

Just off the north coast of Mainland, hilly Rousay merits exploration for its fine assembly of prehistoric sites, great views and relaxing away-from-it-all ambience. Connected by regular ferry from Tingwall, it makes a great little day trip, but you may well feel a pull to stay longer.

Sights & Activities

FREE **Prehistoric Sites** ARCHAEOLOGICAL SITES
(HS; www.historic-scotland.gov.uk; 24hr)
The major archaeological sites are clearly labelled from the 14-mile road that rings the island. Heading west (left) from the ferry, you soon come to **Taversoe Tuick**, an intriguing burial cairn constructed on two levels, with separate entrances – perhaps a joint tomb for different families; a semi-detached solution in posthumous housing. You can squeeze into the cairn to explore both levels, but there's not much space. Not far beyond here, are two other significant cairns; **Blackhammer**, then **Knowe of Yarso**, the latter a fair walk up the hill but with majestic views.

Six miles from the ferry, the mighty **Midhowe Cairn** has been dubbed the 'Great Ship of Death'. Built around 3500 BC and enormous in size, it's divided into compartments, in which the remains of 25 people were found. Covered by a protective stone building, it's nevertheless a memorable sight. Next to it, **Midhowe Broch**, whose sturdy stone lines echo the striations of the rocky shoreline, is a muscular Iron Age fortified compound with a mezzanine floor. The sites are by the water, a ten-minute walk downhill from the main road.

Sleeping & Eating

Trumland Farm Hostel HOSTEL £
(01856-821252; trumland@btopenworld.com; sites £5, dm £10, bedding £2; P) An easy stroll from the ferry, this organic farm has a wee hostel, with rather cramped six-bed dorms and a pretty little kitchen and common area. You can pitch tents outside and use the facilities; there's also a well-equipped self-catering cottage.

Taversoe Hotel HOTEL ££
(01856-821325; www.taversoehotel.co.uk; s/d £45/75; P) About two miles west from the pier, the island's only hotel is a low-key place with neat, simple doubles with water vistas that share a bathroom and a twin with en suite but no view. The best views, however, are from the dining room, which serves good-value meals. The friendly owners will pick you up from the ferry.

Getting There & Around

A small **car ferry** (01856-751360; www.orkneyferries.co.uk) connects Tingwall on Mainland with Rousay (passenger/car £3.60/11.50, 30 minutes, up to six daily) and the nearby islands of Egilsay and Wyre.

Rousay Transport (01856-821234; www.visitrousay.co.uk) offers island tours, which include guided visits to the historic sites on Tuesday and Thursday (adult/child £16.50/3).

Bikes can be rented for £7 per day from Trumland Farm.

STRONSAY

Shaped like a bent crucifix, Stronsay attracts walkers and cyclists for its lack of serious inclines, and beautiful landscapes over its four curving bays. You can spot wildlife, with chubby seals basking on the rocks, puffins and other seabirds.

Sights & Activities

In the 19th century, Whitehall harbour became one of Scotland's major herring ports, but the fisheries collapsed in the 1930s. The old **Stronsay Fish Mart** (Whitehall; admission free; daily May-Sep) now houses a herring industry interpretation centre. There's also a hostel and cafe here.

At the southern end of the island, you can visit the **seal-watch hide** on the beach. There's also a chance to see otters at nearby **Loch Lea-shun**.

Sleeping & Eating

Stronsay Hotel HOTEL, PUB ££
(01857-616213; www.stronsayhotelorkney.co.uk; Whitehall; s/d £38/76; lunch & dinner;) The island's watering hole has immaculate refurbished rooms. There's also recommended pub grub (meals from £7) in the bar, with excellent seafood (including paella and lobster) in particular. There are good deals for multinight stays.

Stronsay Fish Mart HOSTEL £
(01857-616386; Whitehall; dm £14) Part of the island's former herring station has been converted into a 10-bed hostel with shower and kitchen. It's clean and well run, and the neighbouring cafe serves takeaways, snacks and meals all day.

Getting There & Away

Loganair (01856-872494; www.loganair.co.uk) flies from Kirkwall to Stronsay (£35 one-way, 20 minutes, two daily Monday to Saturday). A **car ferry** (01856-872 044) links Kirkwall with Stronsay (passenger/car £7.05/16.75, 1½ hours, two to three daily) and Eday.

EDAY

Eday has a hilly centre, with cultivated fields situated around the coast. There is the impressive standing **Stone of Setter** and, close by, the chambered cairns of **Braeside**, **Huntersquoy** and **Vinquoy**. Huntersquoy is a two-storey cairn, like Taversoe Tuick (p953) on Rousay.

Eday Heritage and Visitor Centre (www.edayheritagecentre.org.uk; 10am-6pm summer, Sun winter) has a range of local history exhibits, as well as an audiovisual about tidal energy initiatives. The early-17th-century **Carrick House** (01857-622260; adult/child £3/1; by appointment), with its floor bloodstained from a pirate skirmish, is worth a visit; tours of the house run in summer with advance notice.

Eday Minibus Tour (01857-622206) offers 2¼-hour guided tours (adult/child £12/8) from the ferry pier on Monday, Wednesday and Friday from May to August. It also operates as a taxi service.

Sleeping & Eating

Eday Hostel HOSTEL £
(07973-716278; www.syha.org.uk; dm £15; P @) Four miles north of the ferry pier, this recently renovated hostel is community-run and an excellent place to stay.

Getting There & Around

There are two flights from Kirkwall (one way £35, 30 minutes) to London airport – that's London, Eday – on Wednesday only. Ferries sail from Kirkwall, usually via Stronsay (passenger/car £7.05/16.75, two hours, two to three daily). There's also a link between Sanday and Eday (20 minutes).

SANDAY

Aptly named, blissfully quiet Sanday is ringed by Orkney's best beaches – with dazzling white sand of the sort you'd expect in the Caribbean. The island is almost entirely flat apart from a colossal sand dune and the cliffs at Spurness; the dunes are 12 miles long and growing, due to sand build-up.

There are several archaeological sites here, the most impressive being the **Quoyness chambered tomb** (admission free; 24hr), similar to Maes Howe (see p948) and dating from the 3rd millennium BC. It has triple walls, a main chamber and six smaller cells. At the northeastern tip of Sanday, there's **Tafts Ness**, with around 500 prehistoric burial mounds.

Sleeping & Eating

Kettletoft Hotel HOTEL, PUB ££
(01857-600217; www.kettletofthotel.co.uk; Kettletoft; s/d £35/70; P) The welcoming and family-friendly Kettletoft is a refurbished elderly statesman near the centre of the island. The pub here serves tasty bar meals for around £9, leaning towards the seaward side of things, with lobster even scuttling onto some dishes.

Ayre's Rock Hostel HOSTEL, CAMPSITE £
(01857-600410; www.ayres-rock-sanday-orkney.co.uk; dm/s £13.50/18, 1-/2-person tents £5/7; P) Cosy hostel sleeping eight in the outbuildings of a farm. There's a craft shop and chippie on site, breakfasts and dinners are available, and you can also pitch a tent.

Getting There & Around

There are flights from Kirkwall to Sanday (one way £35, 20 minutes, twice daily Monday to Saturday) and ferries (passenger/car £7.05/16.75, 1½ hours), with a link to Eday.

WESTRAY

If you've only time to visit one of Orkney's northern islands, make delightful Westray the one. With an ecological bent, rolling farmland, handsome sandy beaches, coastal walks and appealing places to stay, it's a green emerald in the archipelago's jewel box.

The main settlement, Pierowall, is 7 miles from the Rapness ferry dock. Arrayed around a picturesque natural harbour, Pierowall was once a strategic Viking base.

Sights & Activities

In Pierowall, the **Westray Heritage Centre** (adult/child £2/50p; daily May-Sep) has interesting displays including finds from archaeological digs – the famous Neolithic 'Westray Wife' among them. A half-mile west of Pierowall stand the muscular ruins of **Noltland Castle** (admission free), a tower house with a formidable array of shot holes from the defence of its deceitful owner Gilbert Balfour, who plotted to murder Cardinal Beaton and, after being exiled, the King of Sweden.

Westraak (01857-677777; www.westraak.co.uk) is a recommended operator that will take you on informative, engaged trips around the island, covering everything from Viking history to puffin mating habits.

The RSPB reserve at **Noup Head** coastal cliffs, in the northwest of the island, attracts vast numbers of breeding seabirds from April to July. There are big puffin posses here and at **Castle O'Burrian**, a mile north of Rapness.

Sleeping & Eating

West Manse B&B, SELF-CATERING ££
(01857-677482; www.millwestray.com; Westside; r £30-35 per person; P) Take the Westside road to its end to reach this imposing, noble house with arcing coastal vistas. Here no timetables reign; make your own breakfast when you feel like it. Your warmly welcoming hosts have introduced a raft of practical green solutions for heating, fuel and more.

The Barn HOSTEL, CAMPING £
(01857-677214; www.thebarnwestray.co.uk; Chalmersquoy, Pierowall; dm £16, sites £5 plus per person £1.50; P) This excellent, intimate, modern, 13-bed hostel is an Orcadian gem. It's heated throughout and has an inviting lounge, complete with DVD collection for when the weather turns foul. The price includes bed linen, shower and pristine kitchen facilities. Local advice comes free.

Pierowall Hotel PUB ££
(www.pierowallhotel.co.uk; Pierowall; mains £8-10; lunch & dinner) The heart of this island community, the local pub is famous throughout Orkney for its popular fish and chips – the fish is caught fresh by the hotel's boats and whatever has turned up in the day's catch is displayed on the blackboard. There are also some curries available, but the sea is the way to go here.

Getting There & Away

There are flights from Kirkwall to Westray (one way £35, 20 minutes, one or two daily Monday to Saturday). A ferry links Kirkwall with Rapness (passenger/car £7.05/16.75, 1½ hours, daily).

PAPA WESTRAY

Known locally as Papay (*pa*-pee), this exquisitely peaceful, tiny island (4 miles long by a mile wide) attracts superlatives. It is home to Europe's oldest domestic building, the **Knap of Howar** (built about 5500 years ago), and to Europe's largest colony of arctic terns (about 6000 birds) at North Hill. Even the two-minute hop from Westray airfield is featured in *Guinness World Records* as the world's shortest scheduled air service.

Beltane Guest House & Hostel (01857-644224; www.papawestray.co.uk; dm/s/d £12/20/30; P), owned by the local community co-op, comprises a 20-bed hostel and a guest house with four simple and immaculate rooms with en suite.

B&B and tasty evening meals (dinner £17) are available at warm, welcoming **School Place** (01857-644268; sonofhewitj@aol.com; r per person £20). The conservatory is good for quiet reflection and the owners are *the* people to speak to about life in their beloved island community.

Getting There & Away

There are daily flights to Papa Westray (£17, 15 minutes) from Kirkwall, Monday to Saturday; there's an excellent £20 return offer.

There's also a passenger-only ferry from Pierowall to Papa Westray (£3.55, 25 minutes, three to six daily in summer).

NORTH RONALDSAY

Three miles long and almost completely flat, North Ronaldsay is a real outpost surrounded by rolling seas and big skies. The delicious peace and quiet and excellent birdwatching – fulmars, oystercatchers and terns are particularly numerous – lures visitors here; the island is home to cormorant and seal colonies and is an important stopover for migratory birds. There are enough old-style sheep here to seize power, but a 13-mile **drystone wall** right around the flat island keeps them off the grass; they make do with seaweed, which gives their meat a unique flavour.

Powered by wind and solar energy, **Observatory Guest House** (01857-633200; www.nrbo.co.uk; dm/s/d £14/33/66; P @) is a great spot next to the ferry pier, and offers first-rate accommodation and ornithological activities. There's a cafe-bar with lovely coastal views and convivial communal dinners (£12.50) in a sun-kissed (sometimes) conservatory: if you're lucky, local mutton might be on the menu. You can also camp here.

There are two or three daily flights to North Ronaldsay (£17, 20 minutes) from Kirkwall. There's a £20 return offer available that's great value. There's a weekly ferry from Kirkwall on Friday (passenger/car £7.05/16.75, 2½ hours).

SHETLAND ISLANDS

Adrift in the North Sea, and close enough to Norway geographically and historically to make nationality an ambiguous concept here, the Shetland Islands are Britain's northernmost outpost. There's a distinct Scandinavian lilt to the local accent, and walking down streets named King Haakon or St Olaf recalls the fact that the Shetland Islands were under Norse rule until 1469 when they were gifted to Scotland in lieu of the dowry of a Danish princess.

Despite the famous ponies and woollens, it's no agricultural backwater: the oil industry and military bases have ensured a certain prosperity, and a growing tourism industry takes advantage of its rich prehistoric heritage. Away from the semi-bustle of the capital, Lerwick, though the isolation sweeps you off your feet – frequent thundering gales thrash across the raw landscape and mother nature whips up the wild Atlantic into white-cap frenzies that smash into imposing coastal cliffs.

One of the great attractions of the Shetland Islands is the birdlife (see boxed text, p964); it's worth packing binoculars even if you're not fanatical about it.

Getting There & Around

AIR

The oil industry ensures that air connections are good. The main **airport** (www.hial.co.uk) is at Sumburgh, 25 miles south of Lerwick. **Flybe** (0871 700 0535; www.flybe.com) have daily services to Aberdeen, Kirkwall, Inverness, Edinburgh, and Glasgow; they also fly to Bergen (Norway) in summer. See individual islands for inter-island flights.

BICYCLE

Hire bikes from **Grantfield Garage** (01595-692709; www.grantfieldgarage.co.uk; North Rd, Lerwick; per day/week £7.50/40), among several other places, including Sumburgh Hotel, near the airport.

BOAT

Northlink Ferries (0845 600 0449; www.northlinkferries.co.uk) runs car ferries between Lerwick and Kirkwall in Orkney (see p956).

Northlink also runs overnight car ferries from Aberdeen to Lerwick (passenger £23 to £35, car £92 to £124, 12 to 14 hours, daily) leaving Aberdeen at 5pm or 7pm.

See individual islands for inter-island ferries.

CAR & MOTORCYCLE

There are three car-hire outfits who process rentals with a minimum of fuss.

Bolts Car Hire (01595-693636; www.boltscarhire.co.uk; 26 North Rd, Lerwick) Small cars start from £39/177 per day/week. Office at airport.

Grantfield Garage (01595-692709; www.grantfieldgarage.co.uk; North Rd, Lerwick) The cheapest: from £23/118 per day/week.

Star Rent-a-Car (01595-692075; www.starrentacar.co.uk; 22 Commercial Rd, Lerwick) Opposite the bus station; from £36/164 per day/week. Office at airport.

Lerwick

POP 6830

Built on the herring trade, Lerwick is Shetland's only real town, home to about a third of the islands' population and dug into the hills of Bressay Sound. It has a solid maritime feel, with aquiline oil-boats competing for harbour space with the dwindling fishing fleet. The water's clear blue tones makes wandering along atmospheric Commercial

Shetland Islands

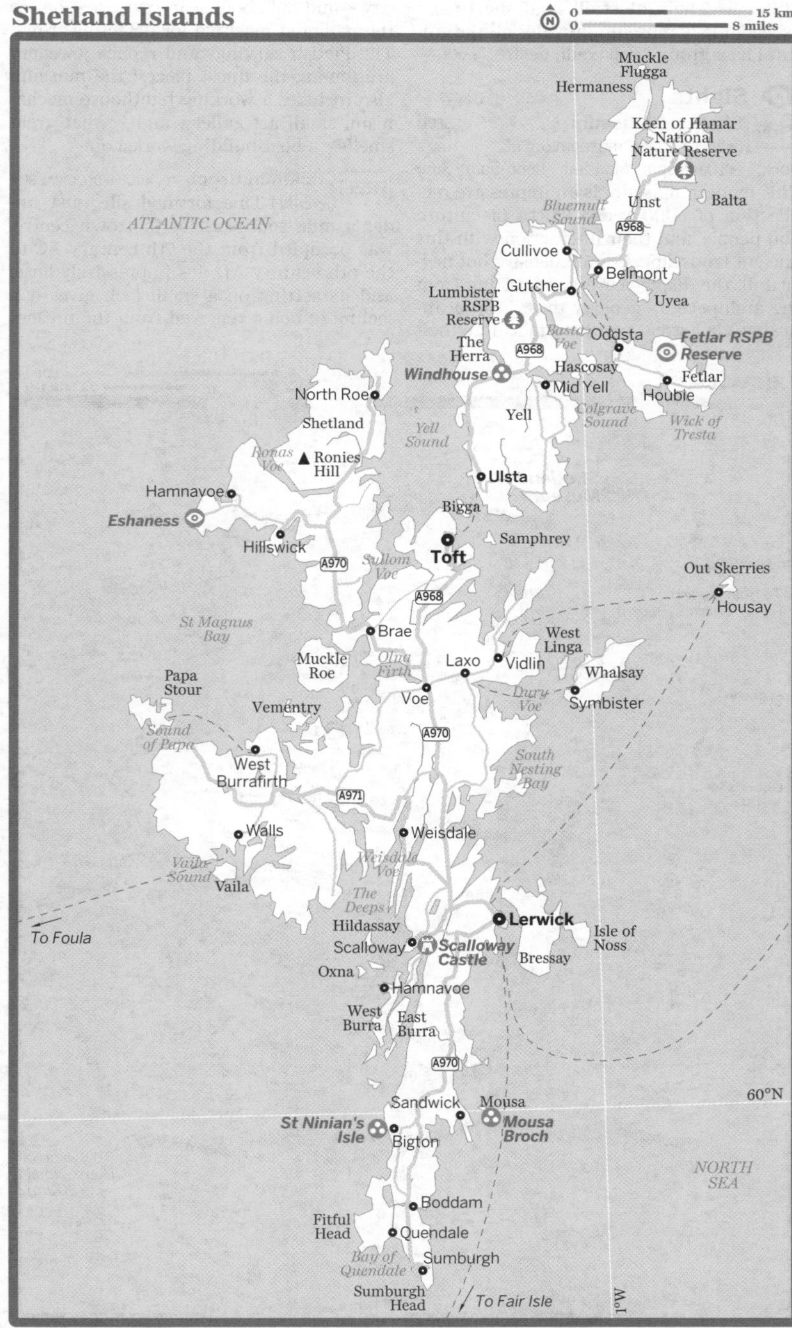

Street a delightful stroll, and the town's excellent new museum provides all the cultural background you could desire.

Sights

FREE Shetland Museum MUSEUM
(www.shetland-museum.org.uk; Hay's Dock; ⏲10am-5pm Mon-Sat, noon-5pm Sun) This modern museum is an impressive recollection of 5000 years' worth of culture and people, and their interaction with this ancient landscape. Comprehensive but never dull, the display covers everything from the archipelago's geology to its fishing industry, via a great section on local mythology – find out about scary nyuggles, or use the patented machine for detecting trows. The Pictish carvings and replica jewellery are among the finest pieces; the museum also includes a working lighthouse mechanism, small art gallery, and – what great smells – a boat-building workshop.

FREE Clickimin Broch ARCHAEOLOGICAL SITE
(⏲24hr) This fortified site, just under a mile southwest of the town centre, was occupied from the 7th century BC to the 6th century AD. It's impressively large and its setting on a small loch gives it a feeling of being removed from the present

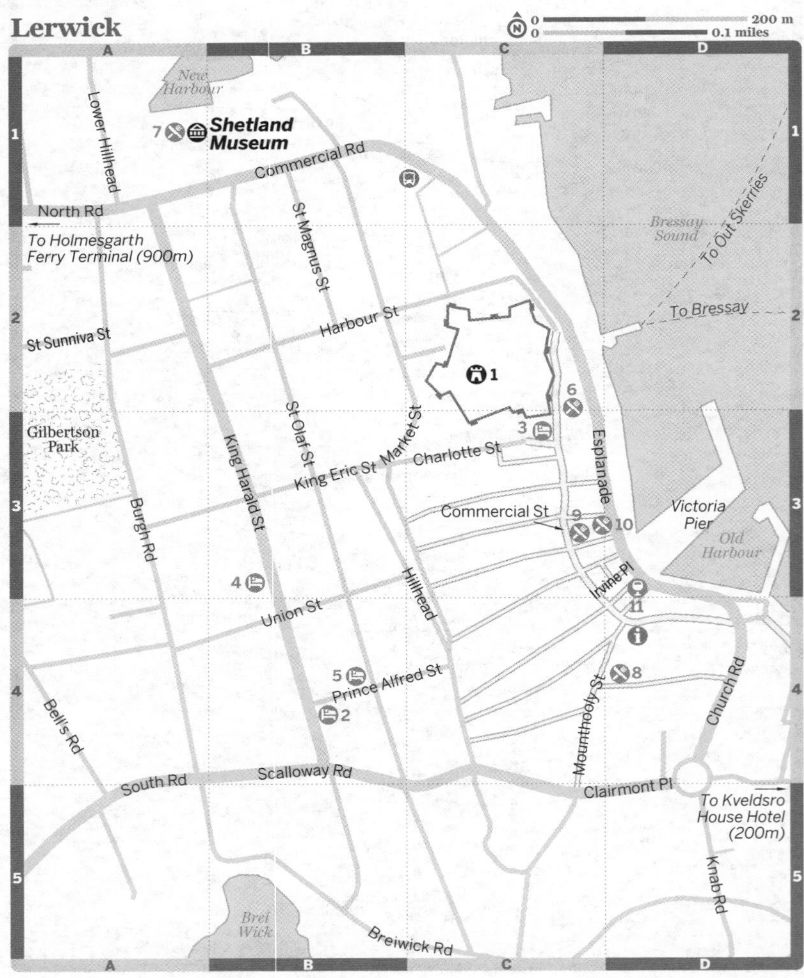

day – unusual given the surrounding urban encroachment.

FREE **Böd of Gremista** HISTORIC BUILDING
(Gremista; ⌚10am-1pm & 2-5pm Tue-Sat May–mid-Sep) Across the harbour from the centre, this is well worth a visit. Once the headquarters of a fish-curing station, it was also the birthplace of Arthur Anderson, who went on to found P&O and who ploughed much of his wealth back into the local community. The personable custodian is a delight.

FREE **Fort Charlotte** FORTIFICATION
(Charlotte St; ⌚9.30am-sunset) Above the town, there are excellent views from the battlements of Fort Charlotte, built in 1665 to protect the harbour from the Dutch navy.

Festivals & Events

See also boxed text, p960.

Folk Festival (www.shetlandfolkfestival.com) Last week of April.

Fiddle & Accordion Festival (www.shetlandaccordionandfiddle.com) Mid-October.

Sleeping

Fort Charlotte Guesthouse B&B ££
(☎01595-692140; www.fortcharlotte.co.uk; 1 Charlotte St; s £25-30, d £60;) Sheltering under the walls of the fortress, this great place offers very summery en suite rooms, including great singles. Views down the pedestrian street are on offer in some; sloping ceilings and oriental touches add charm to others. There's a bike shed and local salmon for breakfast. Very friendly; you'll need to book ahead.

Woosung B&B £
(☎01595-693687; sandraconroy43@btinternet.com; 43 St Olaf St; s/d £25/44) A budget gem in the heart of Lerwick B&B-land, this has a wise and welcoming host and comfortable, clean, good-value rooms that share a bathroom. The solid stone house dates from the 19th century, built by a clipper captain who traded tea out of the port it's named after.

Isleburgh House Hostel HOSTEL £
(☎01595-745100; www.isleburgh.org.uk; King Harald St; dm/f £16.50/50; ⌚Apr-Sep; P @) This typically grand Lerwick mansion houses an excellent Scottish Youth Hostels Association (SYHA)–affiliated hostel, with comfortable dorms, a shop, a laundry, a cafe and an industrial kitchen. Electronic keys that know too much mean there's excellent security and no curfew. It's wise to book ahead, and it's worth asking about winter availability as it sometimes opens for groups.

Kveldsro House Hotel HOTEL ££
(☎01595-692195; www.shetlandhotels.com; Greenfield Pl; s/d £98/120; P) Shetland's most luxurious hotel overlooks the harbour. It's a dignified small hotel that will appeal to older visitors or couples looking for a treat. Rooms 415 and 417 are doubles with striking views over the harbour, or, if after a twin, try room 413, which has two walls of windows and Shetland views.

Clickimin Caravan & Camp Site CAMPING £
(☎01595-741000; www.srt.org.uk; Lochside; sites per small/large tent £8/11; P) By the loch on the western edge of town, Clickimin is a small and tidy park with good grassy sites. There's a laundry and shower block, and you've got a leisure centre with pool and more as part of the complex.

Carradale Guest House B&B ££
(☎01595-692251; carradale@btinternet.com; 36 King Harald St; s/d £35/60;) It's very amicable at Carradale and perpetually busy. The rooms, although a mix of old and new, are large and well furnished and provide a concoction of comforts for visitors. Couples should ask for the huge family room, which is traditionally decked out and has a private bathroom.

Lerwick

Top Sights
Shetland Museum ... A1

Sights
1 Fort Charlotte ... C2

Sleeping
2 Carradale Guest House ... B4
3 Fort Charlotte Guesthouse ... C3
4 Isleburgh House Hotel ... B3
5 Woosung ... B4

Eating
6 Fort Café ... C2
7 Hay's Dock ... A1
8 Monty's Bistro ... D4
9 Osla's Café ... C3
10 Peerie Shop Cafe ... C3

Drinking
11 Captain Flint's ... D3

UP HELLY AA!!!

The long Viking history of the Shetland Islands has rubbed off in more ways than just street names and square-shouldered locals. Most villages have their own fire festival, a continuation of the old Viking midwinter celebrations of the rebirth of the sun. The most spectacular is in Lerwick.

Up Helly Aa (www.uphellyaa.org) takes place on the last Tuesday in January. Squads of 'guizers' dress in Viking costume and march through the streets with blazing torches, dragging a replica longship, which they then surround and burn, bellowing out Viking songs from behind bushy beards.

Eating

TOP CHOICE Peerie Shop Cafe CAFE £

(www.peerieshopcafe.com; Esplanade; snacks £2-5; ⏲9am-6pm Mon-Sat) If you've been craving proper espresso since leaving the mainland, head to this gem of a spot, with art exhibitions, wire-mounted halogens and industrial gantry chic. Newspapers, scrumptious cakes and sandwiches, hot chocolate that you deserve after that blasting wind outside, and, more rarely, outdoor seating, give everyone a reason to be here.

Monty's Bistro RESTAURANT ££

(☎01595-696555; 5 Mounthooly St; mains lunch £8-9, dinner £13-20; ⏲lunch Tue-Sat, dinner Mon-Sat) Though well tucked away behind the tourist office, this is far from a secret, and Shetlanders descend on its wee wooden tables with alacrity. The happy orange upstairs dining-room is fragrant with aromas of Gressingham duck and local mussels from the short, quality menu, and the wine list has some welcome old friends.

Hay's Dock CAFE, RESTAURANT ££

(☎01595-741569; www.haysdock.co.uk; light lunches £3-6, dinner mains £13-18; ⏲lunch daily, dinner Thu-Sat) Upstairs in the Shetland Museum you'll find this place, whose glass front and optimistic balcony looks right over the water. Its clean lines and light wood recall Scandinavia, but the smart food relies on carefully selected local and Scottish produce on a short, quality menu.

Osla's Café BISTRO £

(www.oslas.co.uk; 88 Commercial St; mains £7-13; ⏲lunch & dinner Mon-Sat, lunch Sun) Osla's is a sparky little joint that flips a mean pancake downstairs, but upstairs La Piazza is where you'll discover the joys of Italian cooking. Authentic, thin-crust pizzas are just like Papa used to make…well, almost.

Fort Café CAFE, TAKEAWAY £

(2 Commercial St; fish & chips £5-6; ⏲10am-8pm) Sometimes all that sea-salt air can make a body cry out for a haddock supper, and this well-loved local institution is the place to get it. Eat in, or munch down on the pier if you don't mind the seagulls' envious stares.

Drinking & Entertainment

Look out for Mareel, a new arts venue due to open on the waterfront near the museum in 2011.

Captain Flint's PUB

(2 Commercial St; ⏲to 1am) This lively bar throbs with happy conversation and has a distinctly nautical, creaky-wooden feel. There's a cross-section of young 'uns, tourists, boat folk and older locals. There's live music some nights and a pool table upstairs. By some distance Lerwick's best pub.

Information

Shetland Library (Lower Hillhead; ⏲10am-7pm Mon, Wed & Fri, 10am-5pm Tue, Thu & Sat; @) Free internet.

Tourist office (☎01595-693434; www.visitshetland.com; Market Cross; ⏲9am-5pm summer, 10am-4pm Mon-Sat winter) Helpful; good range of books and maps, and a comprehensive brochure selection.

Getting There & Around

For details of services to Lerwick, see p942. Ferries dock at Holmsgarth terminal, a 15-minute walk from the town centre. From Sumburgh airport, Leask's runs regular buses that meet flights.

Bressay & Noss

POP 350

Two islands lie across Bressay Sound east of Lerwick. The 34-sq-km island of Bressay (*bress*-ah) has some interesting walks, especially along the cliffs and up Ward Hill (226m), which has good views of the island.

The **Bressay Heritage Centre** (donation £2; ⏲10am-4pm Tue-Wed, Fri & Sat, 11am-5pm Sun May-Sep) is by the ferry dock and has an exhibition on Bressay life and history, as well as information about the mysterious Bronze Age mound that has been relocated alongside.

For serious **birdwatching**, visit Noss, a National Nature Reserve east of Bressay, to see huge seabird colonies on the island's 183m cliffs. Noss can only be visited from May to August, when Scottish Natural Heritage (SNH) operates a small visitor centre at Gungstie.

You can pause for an ale or excellent shellfish meal at **Maryfield Hotel** (☎01595-820207; mains £7-15; P), which offers secluded accommodation (singles/doubles £40/65) near the ferry.

Getting There & Away

Daily ferries (passenger/car return £3.60/8.40, seven minutes, frequent) link Lerwick and Bressay. It's then 2.5 miles across the island (some people bring rented bikes from Lerwick) to take the inflatable dinghy to Noss (adult/child £3/1.50, 10am to 5pm Tuesday, Wednesday and Friday to Sunday late April to August), but check with the **SNH** (☎0800 107 7818) before leaving Lerwick, as the dinghy doesn't operate in bad weather.

Central & West Mainland

SCALLOWAY

POP 812

The former capital of Shetland, Scalloway (*scall*-o-wah), on the west coast 6 miles from Lerwick, is now a busy fishing village set around bare, rolling hills. The main landmark is **Scalloway Castle** (HS; www.historic-scotland.co.uk), with a well-preserved 15th-century keep.

Close to the waterfront, the **Scalloway Hotel** (☎01595-880444; scalloway.hotel@btconnect.com; Main St; s/d £65/90; P) has modern, spotless rooms with small en suites. Some rooms have good views over the harbour and there's some really tasty, creative bar food here, as well as more upmarket fare in the restaurant.

Buses run from Lerwick (25 minutes, roughly hourly Monday to Saturday) to Scalloway.

South Mainland

From Lerwick, the main road south winds 25 miles down the eastern side of this long, narrow, hilly tail of land to Sumburgh Head.

SANDWICK & AROUND

Opposite the scattered village of Sandwick, where you pass the 60-degree latitude line, is the small isle of Mousa, an RSPB reserve protecting some 7000 breeding pairs of nocturnal storm petrels. Mousa is also home to rock-basking seals as well as impressive **Mousa Broch**, the best preserved of these northern fortifications. Rising to 13m, it's an imposing structure, typically double-walled, and with a spiral staircase to access a second floor. It features in two Viking sagas as a hide-out for eloping couples; these days petrels favour it as a nesting spot.

From April to mid-September, **Tom Jamieson** (☎01950-431367; www.mousaboattrips.co.uk) runs daily boat trips (adult/child £13/6.50, 25 minutes) from Leebitton harbour in Sandwick, allowing two hours on Mousa. He also conducts night trips to view the petrels.

There are buses between Lerwick and Sandwick (25 minutes, three to seven daily).

A LIGHT IN THE NORTH

Shetland offers intriguing options for getting off the beaten accommodation track. There's a great network of *böds* – simple rustic hostels with peat fires, which might mean bringing sleeping bag, coins for the meter, or even a campstove. We've listed some of these in the text, but there are more. Contact and book via **Shetland Amenity Trust** (☎01595-694688; www.camping-bods.com).

The same organisation runs three **lighthouse cottages** (☎01595-694688; www.lighthouse-holidays.com), all commanding dramatic views of rugged coastline: one near the airport at Sumburgh, one on the island of Bressay near Lerwick, and one in Mainland's northwest at Eshaness. Sleeping six to seven, the cottages cost from £190 to £230 for a three-night booking in high season.

BIGTON & AROUND

Buses from Lerwick stop twice daily (Monday to Saturday) in Bigton on the west coast, but it's another couple of miles to the **tombolo**, a narrow isthmus connecting Mainland to beautiful emerald-capped **St Ninian's Isle**. Walk across the tombolo to find there the ruins of a 12th-century church, beneath which are traces of an earlier Pictish church. During excavations in 1958, Pictish treasure, probably dating from AD 800 and consisting of 27 silver objects, was found beneath a broken sandstone slab. They're now kept in the Museum of Scotland in Edinburgh, though there are replicas in Lerwick's Shetland Museum.

SUMBURGH

With its clear waters, sea cliffs, and grassy headlands jutting out into sparkling blue waters, Sumburgh is one of the most scenic places to stay on the island. There's a 7-day **tourist office** at Sumburgh airport, with internet access.

Sights

Jarlshof ARCHAEOLOGICAL SITE

(HS; www.historic-scotland.gov.uk; adult/child £4.70/2.80, 20% off with Old Scatness ticket; 9.30am-5.30pm Apr-Sep) Old and new collide at Mainland's southern tip, where Sumburgh airport is only a few metres from Jarlshof, a picturesque and instructive archaeological site covering various periods of occupation from 2500 BC to AD 1500. You can clearly see the complete change that happened when the Vikings arrived: their rectangular longhouses are in marked contrast to the brochs, roundhouses, and wheelhouses that preceded them. Atop the site is the Old House of Sumburgh, built in the 16th century and named 'Jarlshof' in a novel by Sir Walter Scott. There's an informative audio tour included with admission.

Old Scatness ARCHAEOLOGICAL SITE

(www.shetland-heritage.co.uk/amenitytrust; Dunrossness; adult/child £4/3, 20% discount with Jarlshof ticket; 10am-5pm Sun-Thu May-Oct) This site brings Shetland's prehistoric past vividly and entertainingly to life; it's a must-see for archaeology buffs but fun for kids, too. Clued-up guides in Iron Age clothes show you around the site, which is still being studied, and has provided important clues on the Viking takeover, and the dating of these northern Scottish sites in general. Discovered when building an airport access road, the site has revealed an impressive broch from around 300 BC, roundhouses and later wheelhouses. Best of all is the reconstruction of one of these, complete with smoky peat fire and working loom.

Sumburgh Head BIRDWATCHING

(www.rspb.org.uk) Near Jarlshof, and clearly visible from the site, the spectacular cliffs of **Sumburgh Head**, a mile from the main road offer a good chance to get up close and personal with puffins, and also have huge nesting colonies of fulmars, guillemots and razorbills.

Sleeping & Eating

Another option is atmospheric Sumburgh Lighthouse cottage (see p961).

Betty Mouat's Böd HOSTEL £

(Dunrossness; dm £8, P) Just behind Old Scatness, this is a simple and comfortable hostel with peat fire (£5 a bag), power and decent hot-water bathrooms. Book via the Trust (see boxed text, p961) or at Old Scatness.

Sumburgh Hotel HOTEL ££

(01950-460201; www.sumburghhotel.com; Sumburgh; s/d £65/80; P@) Next to Jarlshof is an upmarket, country-style hotel with a high standard of accommodation. There are fine views for birdwatchers, prehistorians, and planespotters, comfortable pinkish rooms, and excellent restaurant and bar meals. Larger sea-view rooms cost more (singles/doubles £80/100).

Getting There & Away

To get to Sumburgh from Lerwick, take the airport bus (45 minutes, four to six daily).

North Mainland

The north of Mainland is very photogenic. Around Hillswick, there's stunning scenery and several good places to stay; this makes one of the best bases in the Shetland Islands.

BRAE & AROUND

Just outside Brae and built in 1588, luxurious, genteel **Busta House Hotel** (01806-522506; www.bustahouse.com; s/d £90/110, 4-course dinner £35; P) is perhaps Shetland's most characterful hotel, with a long, sad history and inevitable rumours of a (friendly) ghost. Refurbished rooms are tastefully decked out, and retain a classy but homely charm. They're all individually designed and named after places in Shetland. Rooms with sea view and/or four-poster bed cost a little more. The restaurant is excellent.

Buses from Lerwick to Eshaness and North Roe stop in Brae (35 minutes, up to seven daily Monday to Saturday).

ESHANESS & HILLSWICK

Eleven miles northwest of Brae the road ends at the red basalt cliffs of Eshaness, which form some of the most impressive, wild, coastal scenery in Shetland. Howling Atlantic gales whip the ocean into a white-cap frenzy before it crashes into the base of the cliffs. When the wind subsides there is superb **walking** and panoramic views from the lighthouse (closed to the public) on the headland.

A mile east of Eshaness, a side road leads south to the **Tangwick Haa Museum** (⊙11am-5pm mid-Apr–Sep), located in a restored 17th-century house. The wonderful collection of ancient black-and-white photos capture the sense of community here.

At **Hamnavoe**, which you reach from another side road heading north, about 3.5 miles east of Eshaness, is **Johnny Notions Camping Böd** (☎01595-694688; www.camping-bods.co.uk; beds £8; ⊙Apr-Sep), offering four spacious berths in a cute wee stone cottage with a challengingly low door.

Decent campsites and tasty light meals served in a cafe with stunning views over St Magnus Bay, and its weird and wonderful rock formations, are on offer at **Braewick Café & Caravan Park** (☎01806-503345; www.eshaness.shetland.co.uk; Braewick; sites/wigwams £7/33; ⊙10am-5pm Mar-Oct). It also offers 'wigwams', wooden huts with fridge and kettle that sleep four, six at a pinch.

Follow the puffin signpost a mile short of Hillswick to **Almara B&B** (☎01806-503261; www.almara.shetland.co.uk; Urafirth; s/d £30/60; P 📶) and get the most wonderful welcome in the Shetland Islands. With sweeping views over the bay, this house has a great lounge, a few unusual features in the excellent rooms and bathrooms, and a good eye on the environment. You'll feel completely at home and appreciated; this is B&B at its best.

In Hillswick itself, **St Magnus Bay Hotel** (☎01806-503372; www.stmagnusbayhotel.co.uk; s/d £65/95; P 📶) occupies a wonderful wooden mansion built in 1896 and transferred here from the Glasgow Exhibition. Enthusiastic new owners have injected some much-needed TLC and are renovating it beautifully. The rooms vary in size, shape, and views – grab one of the corner ones for a stunning double vista over the bay – but all are very appealing.

Buses from Lerwick run (evenings only) to Hillswick (1¼ hours) and Eshaness (1½ hours).

The North Isles

Yell, Unst and Fetlar make up the North Isles, all connected to each other by ferry.

YELL

POP 1100

Yell if you like but nobody will hear; the desolate peat moors here are typical Shetland scenery. Though many folk fire on through to Unst, Yell offers several good hill walks, especially around the **Herra peninsula**, about halfway up the west coast.

Across Whale Firth from the peninsula is **Lumbister RSPB Reserve**, where red-throated divers (called rain geese in Shetland), merlins, skuas and other bird species breed. The area is home to a large otter population, too, best viewed around Whale Firth, where you may also spot common and grey seals.

South of Lumbister, on the hillside above the main road, stand the reputedly haunted ruins of **Windhouse**, dating from 1707.

From the southern ferry terminal, the road leads 4 miles east to Burravoe. The **Old Haa Museum** (⊙10am-4pm Tue-Thu & Sat, 2-5pm Sun Apr-Sep) has a medley of curious objects (pipes, a piano, a doll-in-cradle, tiny bibles, ships-in-bottles and a sperm-whale jaw) as well as an archive of local history and a tearoom.

Sleeping & Eating

After a couple of closures, sleeping options are limited, to say the least. But there are lots of excellent self-catering cottages dotted around the island: check www.visitshetland.com for options.

Windhouse Lodge HOSTEL £
(☎01957-702475; www.camping-bods.co.uk; Mid Yell; beds £9) Below the haunted ruins of Windhouse, and on the A968, you'll find this well-kept, clean, snug camping *böd*

NATURE-WATCHING IN SHETLAND

For birdwatchers, Shetland is paradise. As well as being a stopover for migrating Arctic species, there are vast seabird breeding colonies. Every bird seems to have its own name here: rain geese are red-throated divers, bonxies are great skuas, and alamooties are storm petrels.

Of the 24 sea-bird species that nest in the British Isles, 21 are found here; June is the height of the breeding season. The **Royal Society for the Protection of Birds** (RSPB; ☎01950-460800; www.rspb.org.uk) maintains several reserves on south Mainland and on the island of Fetlar. There are National Nature Reserves at **Hermaness** (where you can't fail to be entertained by the clownish antics of the almost tame puffins), **Keen of Hamar** and on the **Isle of Noss**. **Fair Isle** also supports large sea-bird populations.

But keep an eye on the sea itself: killer whales are regularly sighted, as are other cetaceans, as well as sea-otters. A useful website for all species is www.nature-shetland.co.uk, which details latest sightings.

Take care when birdwatching as the cliff-edge sites can be dangerous.

with a pot-belly stove to warm your toes. Book via phone or the website.

Wind Dog Café CAFE £
(www.winddogcafe.co.uk; Gutcher; snacks & light meals £3-5; ⏲9am-5pm Mon-Fri, 10am-5pm Sat & Sun, dinner Jun-Aug; @) While you're waiting for the ferry to Unst, you can snack at this warm, eclectic little cafe. It serves up paninis, burgers and hot drinks. There's also a small library, ideal if the rain is pelting outside.

Getting There & Away

Yell is connected with Mainland by **ferry** (☎01957-722259; www.shetland.gov.uk/ferries) between Toft and Ulsta (passenger return £3.60, car and driver return £8.40, 20 minutes, frequent). Although you don't need to book, it's wise to do so in the summer months.

There are two buses Monday to Saturday from Lerwick to Yell and Unst, and a further one to Toft ferry pier (one hour). Connecting buses at Ulsta serve other parts of the island.

UNST

POP 1100

You're fast running out of Scotland once you cross to Unst, a rugged island of ponies and seabirds. It's prettier than Yell with bare, velvety-smooth hills and clusters of settlements that cling to their waterside locations, fiercely resisting the buffeting winds. It also feels less isolated and has more of a community.

Its stellar attraction is the marvellous headland of **Hermaness**, where a 4.5-mile round walk from the reserve entrance at the end of the road takes you to cliffs where gannets, fulmars and guillemots nest and numerous puffins frolic. The path is guarded by a small army of great skuas, known hereabouts as bonxies. They nest in the nearby heather, and dive-bomb at will if they feel threatened. From the cliffs, you can see Britain's most northerly point, the rocks of **Out Stack**, and **Muckle Flugga**, with its lighthouse built by Robert Louis Stevenson's uncle. Stevenson wrote *Treasure Island* while living on Unst. For more tips on wildlife-watching duck into the **Hermaness Visitor Centre** (⏲9am-5pm Apr–mid-Sep), near the reserve's entrance.

Unst Heritage Centre (Haroldswick; adult/child £2/free, joint Unst Boat Haven ticket £3; ⏲11am-5pm May-Sep) houses a modern museum with a history of the Shetland pony, and a nostalgic look at the past.

Unst Boat Haven (Haroldswick; adult/child £2/free, joint Unst Heritage Centre ticket £3; ⏲11am-5pm May-Sep) is housed in a large shed and is every boaty's delight, with rowing and sailing boats, photographs of more boats, and maritime artefacts.

Viking Unst (www.vikingshetland.com) is a project to promote the island's various Viking sites. The centrepiece, a reconstructed longhouse and replica longship, was being built on the main road just south of Haroldswick last time we passed by.

At the turnoff from the main road to Littlehamar, just north of Baltasound, don't miss Britain's most impressive **bus stop** (www.unstbusshelter.shetland.co.uk). Enterprising locals, tired of waiting in discomfort, have installed an armchair, novels, flowers, a telly, an old Amstrad computer and a visitors' book to sign. All in orange when we visited, but the colour scheme changes yearly.

Sleeping & Eating

TOP CHOICE **Gardiesfauld Hostel** HOSTEL £
(☎01957-755279; www.gardiesfauld.shetland.co.uk; Uyeasound; dm £12, tent & 2 people £6; ⏲Apr-Sep; P) This 35-bed hostel is very clean, has most spacious dorms with lockers, family rooms, a garden, an elegant lounge and a wee conservatory dining area with great bay views. You can camp here too. Nonresidents are welcome to use common areas. The bus stops right outside. Bring 20p coins for the shower.

Saxa Vord HOSTEL £
(☎01957-711711; www.saxavord.com; Haroldswick; s/d £18.50/37; P 📶) This former Royal Air Force base is something of a white elephant these days, but various plans are afoot. It's not the most atmospheric lodging-place, but the barracks-style rooms offer great value for singles and couples, and there's something nice about watching the rain squalls through the window and skylight. The restaurant (open mid-May to September) dishes out reasonable local food, there's a bar – Britain's northernmost, by our reckoning – and a friendly, helpful atmosphere. Self-catering holiday houses here are good for families.

Prestegaard B&B ££
(☎01957-755234; s/d £28/50; P) This solid old manse near the water in Uyeasound makes a great base. Rooms are spacious and very comfy, with water views and exterior, but private, bathroom. We particularly like the upstairs one. The breakfast room with Up Helly Aa shields and axes on the wall will bring out the Viking in you, and the kindly owner will make your stay a delightful one.

Getting There & Away

Unst is connected with Yell by a small car **ferry** (☎01957-722259; www.shetland.gov.uk/ferries) between Gutcher and Belmont (free, 10 minutes, frequent).

There are two buses Monday to Saturday from Lerwick to Yell and Unst.

FETLAR

POP 90

Fetlar is the smallest but most fertile of the North Isles. There's great birdwatching here, and the 705 hectares of grassy moorland around Vord Hill (159m) in the north form the **Fetlar RSPB Reserve**. Common and grey seals can also be seen on the shores. Much of the reserve is off-limits in the summer breeding season but it's still the best time to see birds, including the red-necked phalarope.

Four to seven daily free **ferries** (☎01957-722259; www.shetland.gov.uk/ferries) connect Fetlar with Gutcher on Yell and Belmont on Unst.

Channel Islands

IONAS KALTENBACH

The Channel Islands

Includes »

Jersey 969
Guernsey........... 972
Herm 973
Sark 974
Alderney 975

Best Places to Eat

- » Pier 17 (p973)
- » Hathaways Brasserie (p975)
- » Sails Brasserie (p970)
- » Braye Chippy (p976)
- » Mermaid Tavern (p974)

Best Places to Stay

- » La Valette Campsite (p975)
- » Harbourview (p970)
- » Old Government House Hotel (p972)
- » White House Hotel (p974)
- » Farm Court (p976)

Why Go?

Hedge-lined lanes meandering between sea cliffs and beaches give the islands of Jersey, Guernsey, Herm, Sark and Alderney an old-world English charm. But although English is now the predominant language, and many place-names remain in French, the islands are proudly independent, self-governing British Crown dependencies with their own intricate history and character.

During WWII, the Channel Islands were the only British soil to be occupied by the Nazis, and poignant museums – some housed in old war tunnels and bunkers – provide an insight into the islanders' fortitude. Subtropical plants and colourful flowers bloom thanks to the warm Gulf of St Malo, which also guarantees sublime local seafood and attracts an incredible array of bird life.

The islands are havens for sandcastles, surfing, cobweb-banishing walks and exploring secret coves, just a short hop across the channel from mainland Blighty.

When to Go?

Most of the islands' festivals and events take place in the warmer months (May to September), when accommodation can be scarce – book ahead! Highlights include learning about Alderney's rare fauna, marine life and seabirds during Wildlife Week in mid May. In August, don't miss floral-adorned floats parading through Jersey for its iconic Battle of Flowers. RAF jets and WWII aircraft roar overhead in Guernsey's Battle of Britain Air Display in early September.

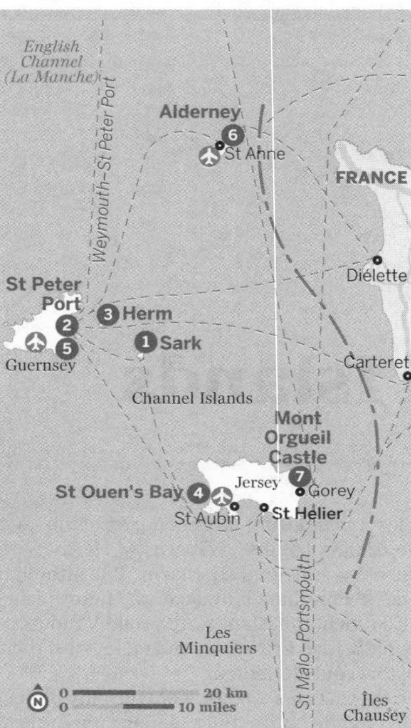

Channel Isands Highlights

1 Clip-clopping in a horse and cart along the car-free lanes of gorse-covered **Sark** (p974)

2 Crossing the breakwater to visit 13th-century **Castle Cornet** (p972) on a former islet in Guernsey's harbour

3 Touring tiny **Herm** (p974) with the island's gardener

4 Surfing off the wide beaches of Jersey's west coast at **St Ouen's Bay** (p970)

5 Marvelling at Victor Hugo's interior-design skills as well as his literary prowess at his home in exile, Guernsey's **Hauteville House** (p972)

6 Strolling along the headland to see gannets on **Alderney** (p975), or sailing around the island to spot puffins and seals

7 Learning about medieval life in the dark corners, twisting alleyways and spiralling staircases of Sir Walter Raleigh's former home, Jersey's **Mont Orgueil Castle** (p970)

History

The Channel Islands are rich in archaeological sites from the Stone Age onwards. Used by the Romans as trading posts, the islands were part of Normandy until William II of Normandy ('William the Conqueror') invaded England in 1066, and have been governed separately since 1204. For centuries the islands were used as sparring grounds, but in 1483 England and France agreed that the territory would remain neutral in the event of war.

During WWII, these happy-go-lucky resorts formed part of Hitler's Atlantic Wall, designed to protect German-controlled continental Europe from a British invasion, and were occupied by the Nazis from 1940 to 1945. Numerous islanders evacuated, while thousands were deported, and thousands more were brought in as slave labour to build fortifications. Alderney's defences alone included 27 military batteries and 30,000 landmines. Today, fortifications still dominate the islands' clifftops and beaches. Some serve as Occupation museums and others have been appropriated as snack kiosks and even accommodation.

Getting There & Away

Return flights from the UK to Jersey and Guernsey, the main points of entry, vary wildly from under £70 up to £250 – shop around.

JERSEY **Air Southwest** (www.airsouthwest.com) Bristol and Plymouth.

Aurigny Air Services (www.aurigny.com) Alderney, Bristol, East Midlands, France, Guernsey, London Gatwick, London Stansted and Manchester.

Condor Ferries (www.condorferries.com) Sails from Guernsey (from 55 minutes), Poole (four hours), Portsmouth (10 hours), St-Malo, France, (1¼ hours) and Weymouth (3½ hours). On most routes, there's at least one daily ferry between April and October, but services are severely reduced from November to March. Typical return fares from the UK are £90 for a foot passenger, and £255 for a car and driver.

Corsaire (www.compagniecorsaire.com; mid-Apr–late Sep) Runs passenger ferries from St-Malo, France.

Manche Îles Express (www.manche-iles-express.com; Apr-Sep) Has passenger ferries from Guernsey (single £37.50, one hour) and Carteret and Granville in France (£37.50, one hour).

POLITICS & PRACTICALITIES

The Channel Islands aren't part of the UK or the EU (although there's some cross-over). Rather, they're made up of two independent, self-governing bailiwicks: the **Bailiwick of Jersey** (www.gov.je) and the **Bailiwick of Guernsey** (www.gov.gg), which includes Guernsey itself as well as Alderney, Sark and Herm – though Alderney's and Sark's governments are also responsible for many of their own laws. It's a complex set of arrangements that even confuses islanders at times, but the main points affecting visitors are as follows:

Insurance The Channel Islands aren't covered by NHS or EHIC cards, so make sure your travel insurance includes medical treatment.

Duty-free shopping Visitors travelling to/from the EU (including the UK) and between the two bailiwicks can buy duty-free goods (subject to maximum allowance limits).

Money The bailiwicks have their own versions of Sterling, and both have their own £1 notes. UK-issued money is accepted on the islands, but Jersey- and Guernsey-issued money isn't legal tender in the UK. You can change unspent notes for equal value at banks. Some Channel Islands establishments also accept euros.

Opening hours Most shops shut on Sunday.

Post Stamps are issued by the bailiwicks; UK stamps aren't valid.

Visas The Channel Islands have their own immigration laws and policies. Tourist entry requirements are the same as for the UK. The UK Home Office can also issue visas for the islands where necessary.

Airlines serving Jersey:

Blue Islands (www.blueislands.com) Alderney, Guernsey, Isle of Man, Southampton and Switzerland.

bmibaby (www.bmibaby.com) Bournemouth, Cardiff, East Midlands and Manchester.

British Airways (www.ba.com) London Gatwick.

easyJet (www.easyjet.com) Liverpool.

Flybe (www.flybe.com) Over 20 airports in the UK, plus Guernsey, France and Switzerland.

Jet2 (www.jet2.com) Belfast, Blackpool and Leeds-Bradford.

GUERNSEY Condor Ferries sails from Jersey, Poole (2¾ hours), Portsmouth (10½ hours), St-Malo (2½ hours) and Weymouth (2¼ hours); Manche Îles Express sails from Jersey, Alderney and Carteret and Diélette in France.

Air Southwest, Aurigny Air Services, Blue Islands and Flybe fly from Alderney, Birmingham, Bristol, East Midlands, Exeter, France, Gatwick, Isle of Man, Jersey, London Stansted, Manchester, Norwich, Plymouth, Southampton and Switzerland.

HERM Ferries link Herm with Guernsey (see p974).

SARK Sark is served by ferries from Jersey and Guernsey (see p975).

ALDERNEY Manche Îles Express sails from Diélette and Guernsey. Aurigny Air Services and Blue Islands fly from Guernsey and Southampton.

Jersey

POP 91,626

Measuring 9 miles by 5 miles, Jersey is the biggest and, its rivals would say, the brashest of the Channel Islands. Shimmering steel and glass and pinstripe suits set the tone in the capital, St Helier, an offshore finance centre. Many visitors prefer the nautical charm of the harbour village of St Aubin, with a string of restaurants and cobbled streets climbing the hill from the boat masts. The coast is 48 miles long; exquisite sandy beaches fringe the south, east and west sides, while rugged cliffs frame the north. In between are tranquil lanes and museums that bring Jersey's rich history to life.

Sights & Activities

Durrell WILDLIFE PARK
(www.durrell.org; Les Augrès Manor, Trinity; adult/child £12.90/9.40; ⏲9.30am-6pm high season, to 5pm low season) Founded by writer and naturalist Gerald Durrell, this inspiring centre breeds and hand-rears endangered

species, releasing them into the wild. The layout allows remarkable freedom, with monkeys and lemurs roaming a natural, wooded environment. Enthusiastic keepers give free talks. Take bus 3A, 3B or 23 (Explorer bus green or yellow). See also p971.

Jersey War Tunnels MUSEUM
(www.jerseywartunnels.com; Les Charrières Malorey, St Lawrence; adult/child £10.50/6.50; 10am-6pm Mar-Nov, last admission 4.30pm) Flickering film footage and personal testimonies fill the chilling passages of this WWII underground military hospital, hacked out of solid rock by forced labour. Your ticket is an islander's identity card; find out what befell the individual in question at the end. History made human, the museum asks what you would have done in the situations faced by the 25,000 islanders who chose not to evacuate. Take bus 8 (Explorer bus red or yellow).

Mont Orgueil Castle MUSEUM
(www.jerseyheritage.org; Gorey; adult/child £10/6; 10am-6pm) Hugely entertaining for kids and kids-at-heart, this medieval concentric castle atmospherically houses catapults, artefacts and thought-provoking artwork. Storytellers, hawking demonstrations, sword fighting and more are scheduled during high season. Take bus 1, 1a or 1b (Explorer bus green).

Maritime Museum MUSEUM
(www.jerseyheritage.org; New North Quay, St Helier; adult/child £7.50/4.50; 9.30am-5pm Apr-Oct) Build boats, change the wind direction, make waves and generally play at being King Knut at this interactive, lever-pulling delight. There are conventional exhibits too, but it's largely excellent education by stealth.

St Ouen's Bay BEACH
On the wild west coast, the 5-mile-long sandy beach at St Ouen's Bay is backed by wind-sculpted dunes and interspersed with beach cafes and water-sports centres, including the **Jersey Surf School** (01534-484005; www.jerseysurfschool.co.uk; wetsuit & board hire per hr £8, 90-minute lesson £30; Apr-Oct).

Le Pinâcle QUARRY, SHRINE
North of St Ouen's Bay) is this Stone Age quarry and Roman shrine, where the pink granite outcrop is seen, somewhat inevitably, as a fertility symbol.

Sleeping

Jersey Tourism operates a free reservations service, **Jerseylink** (01534-448888; jerseylink@jersey.com).

Harbourview B&B ££
(01534-741585; www.harbourviewjersey.com; Le Boulevard, St Aubin; d £110, ste £120-140;) Rooms inside this creeper-covered early-18th-century inn have chic, contemporary nautical decor and bang-up-to-date bathrooms. Its excellent bistro overlooks St Aubin's waterfront.

Surrey Lodge B&B ££
(01534-734834; www.jersey.co.uk/hotels/surreylodge; 20 Belmont Rd, St Helier; d with/without en suite £70/64;) In a quiet street 10 minutes' stroll from the city centre and port, hosts Dave and Jean provide salt-of-the-earth Jersey hospitality at their flowerbox-adorned home. Dave's cooked breakfasts include veggie sausages on request, and spacious, spotless rooms come with chocolate biscuits.

Les Noyers HOSTEL £
(01534-860037; www.durrell.org; Trinity; dm/s/tw £25/35/64;) The islands' only hostel, this traditional farmhouse is on the grounds of the Durrell wildlife park. Dorms and rooms are available providing they're not occupied by training-course participants. Bonuses: free Durrell entry, ultra-cheap bike hire – and waking to the sounds of the park's adjacent Madagascan jungle.

Merton HOTEL £££
(01534-724231; www.mertonhotel.com; Belvedere Hill, St Saviour; d £150;) Indoor, outdoor and spa pools, a waterslide and cool Flowrider surfing wave, kids' activities and a babysitting service make Merton brilliant for families. Rooms are modern and comfortable and there's a slew of on-site eating options as well as live entertainment.

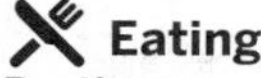

Eating

Boathouse REGIONAL CUISINE ££
(www.theboathousegroup.com/boat-house; 1 North Quay, St Aubin; mains £9-16) On St Aubin's waterfront, the downstairs **Quay Bar** (mains £9-15; lunch & dinner) serves quality bar food. Upstairs, the swish **Sails Brasserie** (3-course menu £25-35; dinner Mon-Sat, lunch Sun) excels at seafood dishes like scallop-and-mackerel fish cakes, and aromatic cheese platters.

LOCAL KNOWLEDGE

HARRIET WHITFORD: BIRD DEPARTMENT SUPERVISOR, DURRELL

Background?

I was born in Jersey and grew up wanting to work at Durrell. Jersey has some college courses but no universities, so I studied animal behaviour in Lincoln, England, with the idea of coming back.

Job?

Bird husbandry and research...it's very long hours in breeding season. I manage the European collections of the Meller's duck and Madagascan teal, keeping genes going and moving them around, and teach at Durrell's international training centre. I also do wild bird surveys. We're trying to reintroduce birds that were once in Jersey and are now gone, like the yellow hammer.

Insider island tips?

Everyone goes to the big, main beaches, but you don't have to look hard for quiet beaches and bays, like Belcroute and Portelet Bay – it only takes 1½ hours to cross from one side of Jersey to the other.

Favourite aspect of Jersey?

It's a stepping stone between the UK and Europe. It's a beautiful place.

Hungry Man KIOSK £

(Rozel; snacks £2.80-4; ⏲10am-5pm, weekends only winter; 🚼) One of Jersey's beloved seaside kiosks, this 60-plus-year-old institution serves Jersey cream teas, fresh-as-it-gets crab sandwiches and burgers such as the Double Decker Health Wrecker (double bacon, double cheese).

Cafe Jac CAFE £

(www.cafejac.co.uk; Phillips St, St Helier; mains £6-8; ⏲breakfast, lunch & dinner Mon-Sat; 📶) Thai green curry with organic brown rice, wok-fried tofu and falafel pittas are among the Arts Centre cafe's veggie creations, but it's also great for a full-monty fry-up breakfast or ham and eggs with hand-cut chips – plus events like summertime 'silent' movie nights (ie with headphones).

Corbiere Phare REGIONAL CUISINE ££

(www.corbierephare.com; St Brelade; mains £9-22; ⏲lunch & dinner) Overlooking its namesake lighthouse, floor-to-ceiling windows make this a prime sunset-watching spot. Jersey royal potatoes and local catches are on the menu, including a laden £70 seafood platter.

Central & Fish Markets MARKETS £

(Beresford St, St Helier; ⏲8.30am-5.30pm Mon-Sat, to 2pm Thu) Pack a beach picnic hamper at Jersey's Victorian central market and neighbouring fish market.

Drinking

Don't miss a pint at the 15th-century half-timbered **Old Court House Inn** (www.oldcourthousejersey.com; Le Blvd, St Aubin) at its schooner-shaped bar, made from old ship timbers.

Information

Curiosity Coffee Shop (14 Sand St, St Helier; 1st 30min free with purchase; ⏲7am-6pm Mon-Fri, 8am-6pm Sat; 📶) Internet access.

Jersey Tourism (www.jersey.com; Liberation Place, St Helier; ⏲8.30am-5.30pm Mon-Sat, 9am-1pm Sun high season, 8.30am-5.30pm Mon-Fri, 9am-1pm Sat low season) Beside the bus station, a short walk from the ferry terminal. The airport also has an information desk.

Murray's (La Neuve Rte, St Aubin; per min 5p; ⏲9am-10pm; 📶) Internet access.

Getting There & Around

For information on getting to Jersey, see p968.

TO/FROM THE AIRPORT A taxi from the **airport** (www.jerseyairport.com) to St Helier costs around £15. Bus 15 (airport–St Aubin–St Helier, 25 minutes) costs £1.60.

BUS Fares £1.10 to £1.60; routes originate at St Helier's bus station. Bus 12A travels to St Ouen's Bay via St Aubin. From approximately May to September, there are four Explorer bus routes – red, yellow, green and blue.

CAR Traffic and free parking are problematic. Major car-hire companies are located at the airport. **Zebra** (www.zebrahire.com; 9 Esplanade, St Helier) rents cars (from £34 per day) and bikes (from £12 per day).

Guernsey

POP 65,632

The most central of the Channel Islands, Guernsey makes a handy base for island hopping. On the eastern edge, narrow cobblestone streets winding downhill through its picturesque capital, St Peter Port ('town'), to the water's edge, where colourful yachts pack the harbour. With green lanes, crescent-shaped beaches and cliffs made for hiking, Guernsey measures around 7 miles long by 5 miles wide. The steep south coast has leg-testing cliff paths; land on the west and north coasts slopes more gently towards the sea.

Sights & Activities

A round-island coastal trip on bus 7 (clockwise) or 7A (anticlockwise) is ideal for mini hop-on/hop-off expeditions; a complete circuit takes one hour and twenty minutes.

Browse St Peter Port's quaint high-street shops for a **Guernsey jumper** (special pattern, special wool).

Hauteville House HISTORIC HOME
(www.victorhugo.gg; 38 Hauteville; adult/child £6/free; 1hr guided tours 10am-4pm Mon-Sat May-Sep, noon-4pm Mon-Sat Apr) Exiled from France in 1851 following Napoleon III's coup, Victor Hugo lived here for 14 years. Preserved in its full, eclectic glory, ornately decorated Hauteville has tapestry-covered ceilings, spiritual symbols, furniture such as the fireplace built using panels and legs from medieval chests, and a 'fire tree' light made from cotton bobbins. In the glass lookout tower, where Hugo wrote *Les Misérables* standing up, on a clear day you can see the French coast.

Castle Cornet MUSEUMS
(www.museums.gov.gg; adult/child £8/1.50; 10am-5pm Apr-Oct) Dominating St Peter Port's harbour, this ancient fortress was a royalist stronghold during the Civil War and a garrison in the Napoleonic Wars. Its four museums cover subjects including Guernsey's maritime heritage and the building's 800-year history.

Underground Military Museum MUSEUM
(01481-722300; La Vallette, St Peter Port; adult/child £4.50/2; 10am-5pm Mar–mid-Nov) One of 10 museums and sites in Guernsey addressing the Occupation; powerful relics in its dank tunnels recall the enforced labourers who died building the island's Nazi fortifications.

Fort Grey Shipwreck Museum MUSEUM
(www.museums.gov.gg; Rocquaine Coast Rd; adult/child £4/1.50; 10am-5pm late Mar-Oct) On the west coast, this 1804 Martello (defensive) tower dubbed the 'cup and saucer' crams in a wealth of detail about the hazardous local waters from the 14th century on. Take bus 5, 7 or 7A.

Guernsey Museum & Art Gallery MUSEUM & ART GALLERY
(www.museums.gov.gg; Candie Gardens, St Peter Port; adult/child £5/1.50; 10am-4pm or 5pm Feb-Dec) Evoking island life from the Iron Age onwards through thought-provoking exhibits, the museum can also give you the key to climb about 100 steps of the nearby crenellated **Victoria Tower** (1851).

Some other options:

Bathing pools SWIMMING
(St Peter Port) Join the locals at this rock-sculpted spot.

Guernsey Surf School SURFING
(01481-244855; www.guernseysurfschool.co.uk; 90min lesson £30) Based at west-coast surf spot **Vazon Bay**.

Pembroke Bay BEACH
Beach lovers are spoilt for choice; Pembroke, at Guernsey's northern tip, offers family fun.

Outdoor Guernsey OUTDOOR ACTIVITIES
(01481-267627; www.outdoorguernsey.co.uk) Runs activities from coasteering to kayaking.

Sleeping

Old Government House Hotel HOTEL £££
(01481-724921; www.theoghhotel.com; St Ann's Pl, St Peter Port; s/d/ste £125/160/215; P) Guernsey's top address, 'OGH' has gorgeous, French-accented guest rooms and cuisine, plus a spoil-yourself-silly spa with treatments, jacuzzis and a gym.

Fauxquets Valley Campsite CAMPSITE £
(01481-236951; www.fauxquets.co.uk; Candie Rd, Castel; sites adult/child £9.40/4.70, incl tent hire £44-48; P) Secluded in a lovely, lush spot with a stone-and-wood-beamed

THE CHANNEL ISLANDS

restaurant and bike hire. From bus 4 or 5, it's a 15-minute walk along Candie Rd.

Le Chêne HOTEL ££
(☎01481-235566; www.lechene.co.uk; Forest Rd, Forest; d £99; P 🛜 ≈) Free fishing rods, and (conditionally) free bikes, bus travel or car hire are among the incentives at this comfy, family-run country hotel, with wi-fi in some rooms. Catch bus 4, 7 or 7A.

Duke of Normandie Hotel HOTEL ££
(☎01481-721431; www.dukeofnormandie.com; Lefebvre St, St Peter Port; d £104-146; P 🛜) This central choice has a lively, wood-panelled bar and comfortable rooms (the modish 'Executive' rooms are definitely worth the extra cash), some up spiral stairs from the cobbled courtyard.

Le Friquet HOTEL ££
(☎01481-256509; www.lefriquethotel.com; Rue du Friquet, Castel; s £59.50-67.50, d £102-134; P 🛜 ≈ 👪) Rooms at this converted stone farmhouse are as flowery and perfumed as its award-winning garden. Take bus 2.

Eating

Summertime beach kiosks are a definitive slice of laidback island life, but Guernsey also has some stellar gastronomic restaurants. Look out for Gâche (pronounced 'gosh') fruit loaf served with Guernsey butter.

TOP CHOICE **Pier 17** MODERN BRITISH ££
(www.pier17restaurant.com; Albert Pier, St Peter Port; mains £12.50-18.50; ⏰lunch & dinner Mon-Sat) At the end of Albert Pier, this stylish restaurant has striped aqua-and-navy chairs, original wooden floors and a changing panorama of the busy harbour. Lime- and ginger-roasted sea bass, herb- and mustard-crusted rack of lamb, and Bailey's crème brûlée are among the highlights.

Swan GASTROPUB ££
(St Julian's Ave, St Peter Port; mains £13-17; ⏰lunch & dinner Mon-Sat) Tucked away from the action, you'll find one of Guernsey's oldest pubs by the tantalising aromas wafting from its kitchen. The formal dining room offers dishes like truffled Guernsey crab salad and brie-stuffed chicken breast; there's also a pub menu (mains £9 to £14).

Crabby Jack's SEAFOOD ££
(Vazon Bay; mains £8-15; ⏰noon-9.45pm) This island institution has all the vistas and scrumptious seafood you'd expect from a classic beach hang-out, including deliciously creamy crab soup.

Christies CAFE £
(The Pollet, St Peter Port; mains £5-16; ⏰8am-late) Bubble and squeak, smoked seafood chowder and tofu skewers feature on the diverse menu at this split-level spot opening onto a harbour-view balcony. Occasional live music.

Information

All Sorts (32 Mill St; per min 5p; ⏰10am-7pm Mon-Sat) Internet cafe.

Guernsey Information Centre (www.visitguernsey.com; North Plantation, St Peter Port; ⏰9am-5pm Mon-Sat, 9am-1pm Sun high season, 9am-5pm Mon-Fri, 10am-12.30pm Sat low season) On the waterfront, with free internet access. The airport also has an information desk.

Getting There & Around

For information on getting to Guernsey, see p969.

Guernsey has an excellent bus network. All services start at the harbourside station in town (any journey £1). Buses 4, 7 and 7A stop at the **airport** (www.guernsey-airport.gov.gg), which has car-rental desks. A taxi from the airport to St Peter Port takes about 15 minutes (£12).

Millard & Co (☎01481-720777; www.millards.org; Victoria Rd, St Peter Port) Hires bikes (£8.50) and scooters (per day £30).

Herm

POP 63

A tiny 1.5 miles long and half a mile wide, Herm is the smallest of the publicly accessible islands. Pretty white beaches and flower-strewn hills see its permanent population swell with summertime workers and bucket-and-spade-bearing visitors. Even then, it's possible to leave the crowds behind and luxuriate in the wheel-free atmosphere – not even bicycles are allowed.

Herm has been overseen by the same family since 1949. Previous occupants include Prince Blücher von Wahlstatt, a Prussian noble who tried to establish a wallaby population, and Sir Compton Mackenzie, who fictionalised the island in *Fairy Gold*.

Sights & Activities

A blustery walk to **Shell Beach**, a beautiful spot for a swim, takes in the common, dotted with the remains of **neolithic tombs** and a moss-covered **obelisk**, and **Alderney Point**, with views of the larger island and Normandy. At hilltop Le Manoir, Norman monks built the L-shaped **St Tugual's Chapel**.

The island gardener leads a 90-minute **tour** (per person £5.75; 11am Tue mid-Apr–mid-Sep) of his award-winning handiwork.

Sleeping & Eating

Book **self-catering accommodation** (cottages per week from £710; year-round;) and **camping** (sites per adult/child £6.60/3.80, equipped tents £59; May-Sep;) through the **administration office** (01481-750000; www.herm-island.com; 8.30am-5.30pm).

White House Hotel HOTEL ££
(01481-750075; www.herm-island.com; half-board per person from £105; Apr-early Oct;) Herm's upmarket hotel has a tranquil garden and rooms with stunning bay views. Its terraced **Ship Inn** (mains £8-14; lunch) restaurant serves decent pub grub, while the **Conservatory** (lunch mains £17-24, 4-course dinner menu £25; lunch & dinner) is a classy affair.

Mermaid Tavern PUB £
(mains £7.25-13; lunch & dinner;) Creaking with nauticalia and photos of Prince Blücher's wallabies, the cosy pub and laid-back courtyard are idyllic for fish and chips or a burger while waiting for the ferry.

Snack kiosks KIOSKS
(Apr-Oct) At Shell Beach and Belvoir Bay on the east coast.

Getting There & Away

Travel Trident (01481-721379; adult/child return £9.75/4.50) runs ferries from Guernsey (20 minutes). There are six to eight daily sailings from April to October. From November to March there's one sailing a day in each direction, with three return sailings on Wednesday and Saturday. Due to the high tidal ranges, departure docks vary.

Sark

POP 650

Measuring just 3 miles by 1.5 miles, this steep-sided island has a fretted coastline covering 40 miles of cliffs and beaches. On the plateau, seemingly lost flower-lined lanes, extraordinary views and a tangible sense of freedom make it reminiscent of childhood holidays you possibly never actually had. Tractors are the only motorised vehicles; horses and carts provide picturesque transportation, or you can walk or cycle.

In 2008 Sark dissolved feudal rule on the island after 450 years. While many people welcome democratisation, others say it takes power from the Seigneur (lord) only to hand it to the Barclay brothers, the *Daily Telegraph* owners who live on the neighbouring private island of Brecqhou. Regardless, anachronisms show no sign of disappearing from Sark, where signs measure distances in 'minutes to walk'.

Sights & Activities

La Seigneurie Gardens and Maze GARDENS & MAZE
(www.laseigneuriegardens.com; adult/child £3/1; 10am-5pm Mon-Sat Easter-Oct) In the shadow of the big man's 17th-century residence. A footpath leads to the **Window in the Rock**, with clifftop views.

Occupation and Heritage Museum MUSEUM
(admission by donation; hours vary) Housed in the old telephone exchange.

La Coupée ISTHMUS
Cross the 100m-high walkway linking Sark and Little Sark.

Venus Pool SWIMMING
This aquamarine pool appears at low tide on Little Sark; swimming is possible two hours either side.

Round-island trip BOAT TRIPS
(01481-832107; trips adult/child £22/11) For three hours of stories, join former fisherman George in his Sark-built boat.

Sleeping & Eating

Sark counts some six hotels, 11 B&Bs, two campsites and numerous self-catering cottages; the tourist office can help with bookings. Luggage is transferred between the ferry and your accommodation – be sure to label it.

La Sablonnerie HOTEL ££
(01481-832061; www.lasablonnerie.com; per person £75; late Apr–mid-Oct;) Across the isthmus on Little Sark, this deeply comfortable converted farmhouse has lush gardens and a gourmet **restaurant** (mains around £15). Its **tea garden** (mains around £8) serves mouth-watering seafood lunches and cream teas.

La Valette Campsite CAMPSITE £
(☎01481-832202; www.sercq.com; sites per adult/child £7/4) Spectacularly set on Sark's east coast, with fresh farm produce, solar-heated water, sea-view sites and equipped tents for hire.

Clos de Menage B&B ££
(☎01481-832091; david.curtis@cwgsy.net; per person £30-50;) Hiding behind its subtropical garden, this country-house B&B has quiet, colourful rooms, an open fire in the lounge and evening meals using homegrown produce by arrangement.

Hathaways Brasserie BRASSERIE ££
(www.hathawaysbrasserie.com; La Seigneurie Gardens; mains £9.50-13; breakfast, lunch & dinner;) Sophisticated cooking at this artistically decorated, low-lit spot spans homemade soups with fresh-baked bread to Moroccan lamb tajines, as well as late-night tapas and Illy coffee.

Information

There are no cash machines at Sark's NatWest and HSBC banks (both open 10am to 12.30pm and 2pm to 3pm Monday to Friday), but you can withdraw cash with purchases at Island Stores.

The Island Hall, adjoining the school, has free wi-fi.

Sark Tourism (www.sark.info; 9am-5pm Mon-Sat, to 1pm Sun high season, to 1pm Mon-Sat low season) The island's official (but not only) tourist office; at the far end of the Avenue next to Sark's two-cell prison (thought to be the world's smallest).

Getting There & Around

Isle of Sark Shipping (www.sarkshippingcompany.com) sails from St Peter Port, Guernsey (adult/child return £25.50/13, 45 minutes). Between late May and late September there are four or five return services a day (two on Sunday). For much of the winter, day trips are only possible on Monday, Wednesday and Friday.

Manche Îles Express (see p968) has a couple of ferries a week from Jersey (single £39, 50 minutes).

An open-sided, tractor-powered carriage, the '**toast rack**' (adult/child £1/50p) pulls you up the harbour hill (otherwise it's 15 minutes' walk) to the Avenue, which has the main concentration of shops, and is where **horse-drawn carriages** (1/2hr tour £7/10) congregate. Sark has three bicycle-rental outlets, charging from £6.50 per day.

Alderney

POP 2400

The third-largest island (3.5 miles by 1.5 miles) has a remote location and a singular atmosphere. Home to the world's only breeding population of blonde hedgehogs, it's also an avian hotspot: the 7000 birds that give Gannet Rocks their name are a breathtaking sight. The Nazis left a high concentration of fortifications and the crumbling remains are an eerie presence.

Alderney's village-sized, pastel-painted capital, St Anne, is 20 minutes' walk from both the airport and the port, Braye Harbour, and the island's isolation has preserved its sense of community. While the projectionist changes the reels at the cinema, the audience adjourns to the Georgian House Hotel bar during the interval to discuss the film so far – islanders enjoy the half-time ritual as much as the official entertainment.

Island-wide celebrations take place during **Alderney Week** in the first week of August.

Sights & Activities

Alderney Wildlife Trust WILDLIFE TRUST
(www.alderneywildlife.org; Victoria St; 10am-noon & 2-4pm Mon-Sat) Adjoining the tourist office, with displays on the island's diverse marine and bird life. Staff can point you in the direction of gannet colonies and the blonde hedgehog's habitat. From April to September, they also organise clear-bottom **kayaking** (adult/child per hr £12/6) and two-hour foot and bicycle **tours** (adult/child £6/3) investigating everything from Alderney's dawn chorus to its bat population, as well as island fortifications.

Museum MUSEUM
(www.alderneysociety.org; High St; adult/child £2/free; 10am-noon & 2.30-4.30pm Mon-Fri, 10am-noon Sat & Sun Apr-Oct) Displays include local history, geology exhibits, relics from the Victorian era and the Occupation, and an Elizabethan shipwreck.

McAllister's Fish Shop BOAT TRIPS
(☎01481-823666; Victoria St; adult/child £25/20; Apr-Sep) Buy tickets here for 2½-hour, round-island trips viewing gannet, puffin and grey Atlantic seal colonies.

Alderney Railway RAILWAY
(www.alderneyrailway.com; adult/child return £4.50/2.50) Check with the tourist office

for high-season weekend departure times for this 1840s-built, 870m-long railway, the Channel Islands' only one.

Sleeping & Eating

Farm Court B&B ££
(☎01481-822075; www.farmcourt-alderney.co.uk; St Anne; per person £49;) Huddled around a cobbled courtyard, these cosy stone farm buildings are filled with the owner's art (ask about dates for watercolour classes). Breakfast includes homemade jam.

Braye Beach Hotel HOTEL £££
(☎01481-824300; www.brayebeach.com; Braye Harbour; s £130-140, d £180-200;) Rooms at the island's best hotel ooze style, and its smart **restaurant** (mains £13.50-20) has glass tables and views down the beach.

Braye Chippy KIOSK/RESTAURANT £
(☎01481-823465; Braye Harbour; mains £8; ⊙dinner Tue-Sat;) Run by two chefs; sophisticated twists include Thai-style fishcakes, blue-cheese dressing and chilli burgers. Book a table or take away.

Old Barn TEA ROOM/RESTAURANT ££
(cwgsy.net/business/theoldbarn_alderney; Longis Rd; mains £8-12; ⊙10am-6.30pm daily plus dinner Thu-Sat high season, hours vary low season;) Opening onto a storybook garden home to resident rabbit Arthur, this hidden spot near Alderney's golf course serves dishes like pan-fried skate wing, plus a Sunday roast with all the trimmings.

Information

Alderney Tourism (www.visitalderney.com; Victoria St; ⊙10am-noon & 2-4pm Mon-Sat plus 10am-noon Sun high season) Has internet access (£1.50 per 15 minutes); there are two ATMs nearby.

Getting There & Around

See p969 for information on getting to Alderney. For car rental, contact **Europcar** (www.europcaralderney.com; per day from £37.50).

Bike-rental companies include **Cycle & Surf** (☎01481-822286; Les Rocquettes, St Anne; bike hire per day £6). Taxi operators including **ABC Taxis** (☎01481-823760) also run island tours. A taxi from the airport to St Anne/Braye Harbour costs £5.50/7.50.

› Understand Great Britain

GREAT BRITAIN TODAY 978

Around the globe, the 21st century's first decade was tumultuous, to say the least. How was it for Britain?

HISTORY 981

From ancient civilisations to contemporary characters, Britain's history is varied – and certainly never dull.

THE BRITISH TABLE 1008

Fish and chips, haggis or chicken tikka masala? Real ale, whisky or fine wine? This chapter will tickle your taste buds.

ARCHITECTURE IN BRITAIN 1020

In Britain you're never far from an ancient castle, soaring broch or graceful cathedral, while modern buildings continue to impress.

BRITISH LITERATURE 1025

Everyone knows Shakespeare. This chapter studies some other leading characters from the British canon of poetry and prose.

VISUAL & PERFORMING ARTS IN BRITAIN 1030

From proud traditions in painting to sculpture, theatre to film – they're all here. And everybody talks about pop music.

THE BRITISH LANDSCAPE 1041

A geographical variety pack, from sandy beaches to high mountains, with surprisingly diverse wildlife and stunning national parks.

SPORTING BRITAIN 1049

Where to see football, rugby, cricket, golf and more.

population per sq km

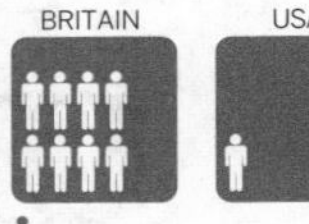

Great Britain Today

» Population: 58 million

» Size: 88,500 sq miles (230,000 sq km)

» Inflation: 2%

All Change Please

For Britain and the British, the first decade of the 21st century has been a time of significant change and national soul-searching. The year 2010 was especially pivotal, thanks to two events: a World Cup tournament where the England football squad floundered while Wales and Scotland didn't even make it through the qualifying rounds; and a general election that saw the end of 13 years of Labour government, and the arrival of a Conservative–Liberal-Democrat coalition for the first time.

Honeymoon Days

To understand the massive significance of the 2010 election result, we need to rewind a little. The 1980s had been dominated by the Conservatives under Margaret Thatcher, then the political pendulum swung the other way, culminating in the 1997 landslide for Labour and its leader Tony Blair. For the first few years, Blair and Labour remained popular and the Millennium celebrations across Britain to mark the start of the year 2000 were almost an extension of their victory parade. The next election, in 2001, was another walkover. And so it went on, with the Conservatives struggling and Labour winning a historic third term in 2005.

Labour Pains

But as the decade continued, the honeymoon period seemed a distant memory and the Labour government faced a seemingly unending string of controversies and crises. Most evident were the invasions of Iraq and Afghanistan and the threat of terrorism close at hand, brought shockingly to the surface in London on 7 July 2005, when bombers attacked underground trains and a bus, killing more than 50 people.

Manners

» **Queues** The British are notoriously polite, especially when it comes to queuing. Attempts to 'jump the queue' will result in outbursts of tutting.

» **Bargaining** Haggling over the price of goods (but not food) is OK in markets but very rare in shops. Politeness is still key, though.

Movies

» *Brief Encounter* (1945)

» *This Sporting Life* (1963)

» *Under Milk Wood* (1972)

» *Withnail and I* (1986)

» *Trainspotting* (1996)

» *The Full Monty* (1997)

» *Dead Man's Shoes* (2004)

belief systems
(% of population)

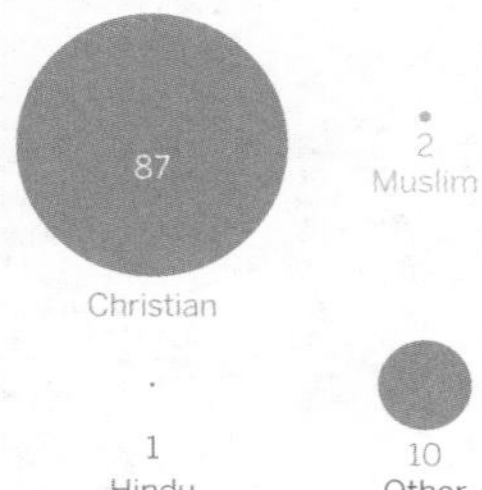

if Britain were 100 people

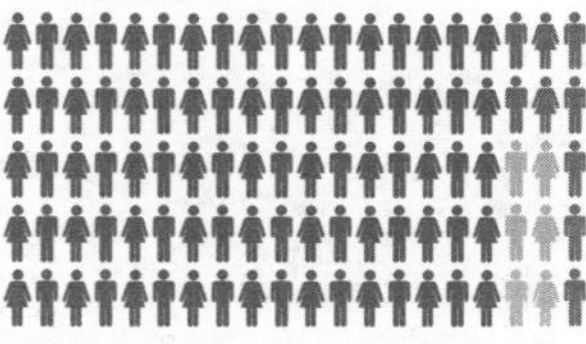

85 would be Caucasian
4 would be South Asian
2 would be African & Afro Caribbean
9 would be other

After 10 years at the helm, Tony Blair resigned as Labour leader in 2007, allowing Gordon Brown, the Chancellor of the Exchequer (the British term for Minister of Finance) and for so long the prime-minister-in-waiting, to finally get the top job. His first three months in office were promising, but then policies seemed to go awry and public support started to fall. The final nail in the Labour coffin was the coming of the global financial crisis. According to many commentators, the economic turbulence brought out the best in the fiscally astute Mr Brown, and Britain weathered the storm better than some other countries, but in the eyes of the public it was too late.

» Per capita GNP: £14,000 (US$26,000)

» Total number of mobile phones: 100 million

» Average number of cups of tea per person per day: 3

Unexpected Bedfellows

And that brings us back to the start of this story: Labour lost the 2010 election, and the new government was a seminal coalition between the centre-right Conservatives and the centre-left Liberal-Democrats – a result that very few political pundits would have ever predicted.

Unexpected or not, the new government got straight down to work and, despite coming from opposite sides of the centre ground, impressed most observers with displays of collaboration. Foundation policies were based around the tenets of 'fairness' and 'choice', most notably a major reform of National Health Service funding to give more flexibility to doctors and patients and new laws allowing parents to set up their own schools – both the cause of much debate in Britain, where health and education are always two of the biggest political hot potatoes.

Home & Away

On the international front, the new government remains committed to keeping Britain's forces in Iraq and Afghanistan, although public

Top Tunes

» 'God Save The Queen' by The Sex Pistols

» 'Take Me Out' by Franz Ferdinand

» 'Town Called Malice' by The Jam

» 'Sultans of Swing' by Dire Straits

» 'Waterloo Sunset' by The Kinks

» 'Country House' by Blur

» 'Ghost Town' by The Specials

» 'Rock n Roll Star' by Oasis

» 'This Charming Man' by The Smiths

» 'A Design for Life' by Manic Street Preachers

» 'I Predict a Riot' by Kaiser Chiefs

» 'Common People' by Pulp

» 'Our House' by Madness

» 'Shipbuilding' by Elvis Costello

sympathy for UK involvement is waning. It's likely, however, that the biggest single issue in British politics for the next few years will be dealing with the after-effects of the financial crisis. Speeches from newly installed ministers promised 'straight talking', but in reality they refrained from too much detail. Most commentators – from all sides of politics – agree that the government will reduce spending and raise taxes more than it has so far admitted. For the people of Britain, it remains to be seen exactly what gets cut and what gets spared.

» Average household weekly spend on fruit: £3

» Average household weekly spend on alcohol: £14

» Percentage of population overweight: 50%

Rule Britannia

Meanwhile, away from political battles there are deeper schisms at work. Where once the state of Great Britain was a single entity, the process of devolution has seen the constituent countries of Scotland and Wales get their own independent ruling bodies based in their own capital cities: the Welsh Assembly in Cardiff and the Scottish Parliament in Edinburgh. This has led to a reassessment by the people of England on what it actually means to be English rather than British (the difference has been hazy for centuries), while the broader cultural vagaries of Britishness have also become a subject of fierce debate, with the English, Welsh and Scots forced to reflect on the values and institutions that bind their countries together – and keep them apart.

But if there's one thing this plucky little nation has proven down the centuries, it's resilience. As long as there's a nice hot mug of tea to hand, of course. The wars are still raging, the economy is looking dicey and the national identity is under the glass, but there's still one thing for certain: Britain's days are far from over yet.

Books

» *Notes from a Small Island* by Bill Bryson. An American's fond, and spot-on, take on Britain.

» *Two Degrees West* by Nicholas Crane. A revealing walk (in a perfectly straight line) across Britain.

» *Slow Coast Home* by Josie Drew. The chatty tale of a 5000-mile cycle tour through England and Wales.

» *Great British Bus Journeys* by David McKie. Witty tales of 'unknown' towns off the beaten track, but on the bus route.

» *Pies and Prejudice* by Stuart Maconie. A search for the soul of Northern England.

» *On the Slow Train* by Michael Williams. A paean to the pleasure of British rail travel.

History

Britain may be a small country on the edge of Europe, but it has never been on the sidelines of history. For thousands of years, invaders and incomers have arrived, settled and made their mark. The result is Britain's fascinating mix of landscape, culture and language – a dynamic pattern that shaped the nation and continues to evolve today.

Among the earliest migrants were neolithic peoples; thanks to lower sea levels they could cross the land bridge between Britain and the continent of Europe. Much later the Celts took more or less the same route, and after them came Roman invaders; they established the province of Britannia and left a legacy of spectacular ruins that can still be visited.

After the Romans came a period once called the Dark Ages (because it was seen as a time of cultural decline), but the Anglo-Saxon migration that followed was a key turning point in English history. Thanks to kings like Alfred the Great, his battles against Viking invaders and the later consolidation of separate Saxon kingdoms, the foundations were laid for the modern state we now call England. At the same time, further west and north, the Celtic peoples established their own territories that would one day become the nations of Wales and Scotland.

Next came a pivotal date in British history, 1066, when the country was invaded by the French Norman army of William the Conqueror. This led to the great constructions of the medieval period – the sturdy castles and graceful cathedrals – that are such a feature on tourist itineraries today.

By the 18th century the aristocrats no longer needed castles, so instead they built great country mansions as even more potent symbols of their power and wealth. Today these 'stately homes' dot the British landscape, often containing vast hoards of art and priceless furniture, and set spectacularly at the heart of manicured parks.

For many visitors, this rich historic legacy – everything from Stonehenge to Glen Coe, via Hadrian's Wall, Canterbury Cathedral, Caernarfon Castle and the Tower of London – is Britain's main at-

The United Kingdom (UK) consists of Great Britain plus Northern Ireland. The British Isles is a *geographical* term for the whole group of islands that make up the UK and the Republic of Ireland, plus others such as the Channel Islands.

TIMELINE

4000 BC

Neolithic peoples migrate from continental Europe. They differ significantly from previous arrivals: instead of hunting and moving on, they settle in one place and start farming.

c 500 BC

The Celts, a group originally from Central Europe, arrive in Britain and by the middle of the 1st millennium BC have settled across much of the island, absorbing the indigenous people.

c 55 BC

Relatively small groups of Roman invaders under the command of Julius Caesar make forays into southern England from the northern coast of Gaul (today's France).

traction, so this chapter concentrates on high-profile events. We also mention historic locations you're likely to see on your travels. Even if you're no fan of dates and dynasties, we hope this overview will help you get the most from your trip.

First Arrivals

Stone tools discovered near the town of Lowestoft in Suffolk in East Anglia show that human habitation in Britain stretches back at least 700,000 years, although exact dates depend on your definition of 'human'. As the centuries rolled on, ice ages came and went, sea levels rose and fell, and the island now called Britain was frequently joined to the European mainland. Hunter-gatherers crossed the land bridge, moving north as the ice melted and retreating to warmer climes when the glaciers advanced once again.

Probably built around 3000 BC, Stonehenge has stood on Salisbury Plain for more than 5000 years and is older than the famous Great Pyramids of Egypt.

Around 4000 BC a group of migrants arrived from Europe that differed significantly from previous groups: instead of hunting and moving on, they settled in one place and started farming – most notably in open chalky hill areas such as the South Downs and Salisbury Plain in southern England.

Alongside the fields, Britain's Stone Age people used rocks and turf to build massive burial mounds, and the remains of many of these can still be seen, including West Kennet Long Barrow in Wiltshire, Pentre Ifan in Pembrokeshire and Maes Howe, Orkney.

But perhaps the most enduring, and certainly the most impressive, legacy left by these nascent Britons was the great stone circles such as Callanish on Lewis in Scotland, and – most famously – the elaborate and enigmatic great stone circles of Avebury and Stonehenge.

Iron & Celts

Move on a millennium or two, and it's the Iron Age. The population expanded and began to divide into specific groups or tribes. Across the whole island the forests were cleared with increasing efficiency as more land was turned to farming. This led to a patchwork pattern of fields,

THREE IN ONE

The countries of England, Wales and Scotland make up the state of Great Britain. Three countries in one might seem strange set-up, and visitors are sometimes confused about the difference between England and Britain – as are a lot of English people (although the Welsh and Scots are clear on the distinction). But getting a grip on this basic principle will aid your understanding of British history and culture, and make your travel more enjoyable, too.

AD 43

Emperor Claudius leads the first proper Roman invasion of England. His army wages a ruthless campaign, and the Romans control most of southern England by AD 50.

60

Warrior-queen Boudica leads an army against the Romans, destroys the Roman town of Colchester and gets as far as Londinium, the Roman port on the present site of London.

60

In Wales the Celts, led by their mystic faith-healers, the druids, fight a last stand on Anglesey against the Roman army; they are beaten but not totally conquered.

c 108

According to legend, Roman soldiers of the ninth legion sent to fight the Picts in Scotland mysteriously disappear. In reality the regiment is probably simply disbanded.

woods and small villages that still exists in many parts of rural lowland Britain. As the population grew, territorial defence became an issue, so the Iron Age people left another legacy – the great 'earthwork' castles of southern England, stone forts in northern England and brochs (defensive towers) in Wales and Scotland.

As landscapes altered, this was also a time of cultural change. The Celts, a people who originally migrated from Central Europe, had settled across much of the island of Britain by around 500 BC. (Historians are not clear if the new arrivals absorbed the indigenous people, or vice versa.) A Celtic-British population developed – sometimes known as the 'Ancient Britons' to distinguish them from contemporary natives – separated into about 20 tribes, including the Cantiaci (in today's county of Kent), the Iceni (Norfolk), the Brigantes (northwest England), the Picts and Caledonii (Scotland), the Ordivices (parts of Wales) and the Scotti (much of Ireland).

You noticed the Latin-sounding names? That's because the tribal tags were first handed out by the next arrivals on Britain's shores...

Enter the Romans

Think of the Romans, and you think of legions, centurions and aqueducts. They were all here, as Britain and much of Europe came under the power (or the yoke, for those on the receiving end) of the classical period's greatest military empire.

Julius Caesar, the ruler everyone remembers, made forays to the island of Britain from what is now France in 55 BC. But the real Roman invasion happened a century later when Emperor Claudius led a ruthless campaign resulting in the Romans controlling pretty much everywhere in southern England by AD 50.

Much of the occupation was straightforward: several Celtic-British tribal kings realised collaboration was more profitable than battle. For example, King Togidbnus of the Regnenses tribe changed his name to Tiberius Cogidumnus and built a Roman-style villa, which can still be seen today at Fishbourne near the town of Chichester; and a historian called Nennius suggests in his *Historia Britonum* (written around AD 800) that the people of Wales revered their Roman governors so much that one governor, Magnus Maximus, was transformed into a mythical hero called Maxen Wledig.

It wasn't all plain sailing, though: some locals fought back. The most famous freedom fighter was warrior-queen Boudica, who led an army as far as Londinium, the Roman port on the present site of London.

However, opposition was mostly sporadic and no real threat to the legions' military might. By around AD 80 the new province of Britannia (much of today's England and Wales) was firmly under Roman

BOUDICA

Boudica was queen of the Iceni, a Celtic-British tribe whose territory was invaded by the Romans around AD 60. A year later, she led an army of Britons against the Roman settlements of Camulodunum (now Colchester) and Londinium (London), but her army was eventually defeated at the Battle of Watling Street (in today's Shropshire).

122

Rather than conquer wild north British tribes, Emperor Hadrian settles for building a coast-to-coast barricade. For nearly 300 years, Hadrian's Wall marks the northernmost limit of the Roman Empire.

200

The Romans build a defensive wall around the city of London with four main entrance gates, still remembered today by the districts of Aldgate, Ludgate, Newgate and Bishopsgate..

VERONICA GARBUTT

» Housesteads Roman Fort (p150), Hadrian's Wall

HADRIAN DRAWS A LINE

The Romans may have found the occupation of their new province of Britannia relatively easy, but the lands to the north, which the Romans called Caledonia (one day to become Scotland), proved a harder place to find a fan club. So in AD 122 Emperor Hadrian decided that, rather than conquer the wild Caledonian tribes, he'd settle for keeping them at bay. So a great wall was built across northern England – between today's cities of Carlisle and Newcastle – and for nearly 300 years it marked the northernmost limit of the Roman Empire. In reality, it was as much a *symbol* of power as a defensive barricade, and a way to keep tabs on the locals as they passed through the wall's many gateways. Today, a remarkably well-preserved section of Hadrian's Wall in Northumberland is one of Britain's best-known historic sites.

rule. And although it's tempting to imagine noble natives battling courageously against occupying forces, in reality Roman control and stability was probably welcomed by a general population tired of feuding chiefs and insecure tribal territories.

Exit the Romans

Settlement by the Romans in Britain lasted almost four centuries, and intermarriage was common between locals and incomers (many from other parts of the empire, including today's Belgium, Spain and Syria, rather than Rome itself) so that a Romano-British population evolved, particularly in the towns, while indigenous Celtic-British culture remained in rural areas.

Along with stability and wealth, the Romans introduced another cultural facet – a new religion called Christianity, after it was recognised by Emperor Constantine in AD 313. But by this time, although Romano-British culture was thriving, back in its Mediterranean heartland the empire was already in decline.

It was an untidy finale. The Romans were not driven out by the Ancient Britons (by this time Romano-British culture was so established that there was nowhere for the 'invaders' to go 'home' to). In reality, Britannia was simply dumped by the rulers in Rome, and the colony slowly fizzled out of existence. But historians are neat folk, and the end of Roman power in Britain is generally dated at AD 410.

The Emergence of England

When Roman power faded, the province of Britannia went downhill. Coins were no longer minted, so the use of money dwindled and long-distance trade declined. Some Romano-British towns in England and

c 410

As the classical world's greatest empire finally declines after more than three centuries of relative peace and prosperity, Roman rule ends in Britain with more of a whimper than a bang.

5th century

Teutonic tribes – known today as the Anglo-Saxons – from the area now called Germany migrate to England, and quickly spread across much of the country.

Late 5th century

The Scotti people (from today's Ireland) invade the land of the Picts (today's Wales and Scotland). In today's Argyll they establish the kingdom of Dalriada.

Early 6th century

St Columba establishes a Christian mission on the Scottish island of Iona. By the late 8th century the mission is responsible for the conversion of most of Scotland.

Wales were abandoned (most of Scotland had escaped Roman control in the first place), and some rural areas became no-go zones as local warlords fought over fiefdoms.

Britain's post-Roman vacuum didn't go unnoticed and once again invaders crossed from the European mainland. Angles and Saxons – Teutonic tribes from the land we now call Germany – advanced across the former Roman turf.

Historians disagree on exactly what happened next. Either the Anglo-Saxons largely overcame, replaced or absorbed the Romano-British and Celts, or the indigenous tribes simply adopted the Anglo-Saxon language and culture. Either way, by the late 6th century much of the area we now call England was dominated by the Anglo-Saxons and divided into three separate kingdoms: Wessex (in today's southern England), Mercia (today's Midlands) and Northumbria (today's northern England).

In many areas the original inhabitants lived alongside the Anglo-Saxons and remained unaffected by the incomers (records show that the Celtic language was still being spoken in parts of southern England when the Normans invaded 500 years later), but the overall impact was immense: today the core of the English language is Anglo-Saxon, many place names have Anglo-Saxon roots, and the very term 'Anglo-Saxon' has become a (much-abused and factually incorrect) byword for 'pure English'.

Meanwhile, back in reality, Northumbria was initially the dominant Anglo-Saxon kingdom, covering much of today's northern England and extending its power into Scotland. In the 8th century, the kingdom of Mercia became stronger and its ruler, King Offa, marked a clear border between England and Wales – a defensive ditch called Offa's Dyke that

LEGACY OF THE LEGIONS

To control the territory they'd occupied, the Romans built castles and garrisons across Britain – especially in Wales and England. Many of these developed into towns, later called 'chesters' and today remembered by names such as Winchester, Manchester, Cirencester and Chester. The Romans are also well known for the roads they built – initially so the legions could march quickly from place to place, and later so that trade could develop. Wherever possible the roads were built in straight lines (because it was efficient, not – as the old joke goes – to stop the Ancient Britons hiding round corners) and included Ermine Street between London and York, Watling Street between London and Chester, and the Fosse Way between Exeter and Lincoln. As you travel around Britain today, you'll notice many ruler-straight Roman roads still followed by modern highways, and in a country better known for old lanes and turnpike routes winding through the landscape, they clearly stand out in the map.

6th century

St David is born, going on to establish a sacred place of worship in Pembrokeshire and becoming the patron saint of Wales.

597

Pope Gregory sends missionary St Augustine to southern England to revive interest in Christianity among the southern Anglo-Saxons. His colleague St Aidan similarly converts many people in northern England.

7th century

Anglo-Saxons from the expanding English kingdom of Northumbria attempt to colonise southeast Alba (today's southern Scotland) and are met by the Scotti.

685

The Pictish king Bridei defeats the Northumbrians at Nechtansmere in Angus, an against-the-odds victory that sets the foundations for Scotland as a separate entity.

can still be seen today. A century later, at the top of the league was the kingdom Wessex, covering today's southern England and ruled by King Egbert, grandfather of the future King Alfred.

The Waking of Wales

Away from the emerging kingdoms of England, the Celts on the outer fringes of the British Isles (particularly in Ireland) had kept alive their own distinct yet Roman-influenced culture, along with the ideals of Christianity. And while the Anglo-Saxons took advantage of the post-Roman void in eastern Britain, towards the end of the 5th century others played the same game on the west side of the island: the Scotti people (from today's Ireland) invaded the land of the Picts (today's Wales and Scotland).

In response to the invasion, people from the kingdom of Gododdin (in today's Scotland) came to northwest Wales. Their initial plan was to drive out the invaders, but they stayed and settled in the area, which became the kingdom of Gwynedd. (The modern county in northern Wales still proudly bears this name.)

The struggle between Welsh settlers and Irish raiders along the coast carried on for the rest of the Dark Ages. At the same time, more settlers came to Wales from today's Cornwall and western France, and Christian missionaries arrived from Ireland in the 6th and 7th centuries.

While these newcomers arrived from the west and south, the people of Wales were also under pressure to the east – harassed by the Anglo-Saxons of England pretty much constantly for hundreds of years. In response, by the 8th century the disparate tribes of Wales

BRITAIN'S MYTHICAL MONARCH

It was during the Dark Ages that a particularly powerful leader came to prominence, whose name just may have been Arthur. He may have been a Romano-Briton; he may have been a Celt. He may have come from southern England or he may have been born in Wales. Or maybe Scotland. He might have fought against the Anglo-Saxons or against pagan Celts. In truth, virtually nothing is known about this mythical figure from the mists of time, but King Arthur has nevertheless become the focus of many legends. Along with Merlin the magician and the Knights of the Round Table, Arthur inspired a huge body of literature, not least by the Welsh in the epic tale *Mabinogion*, and by Thomas Malory in his masterpiece *Morte d'Arthur.* Numerous sites in Britain, from Tintagel in Cornwall to Arthur's Seat in Edinburgh, via Snowdonia, Glastonbury and Pembrokeshire, claim Arthurian links that you'll undoubtedly come across as you travel around Britain today. For more tales see boxed text, p672.

8th century

King Offa of Mercia orders the construction of a clear border between his kingdom and Wales – a defensive ditch called Offa's Dyke still visible today.

8th century

The disparate tribes of Wales start to band together and sow the seeds of nationhood, calling themselves *cymry* (fellow countrymen).

850

Vikings come from today's Denmark and conquer east and northeast England. They establish their capital at Jorvik, today's city of York.

RICHARD PEEL

» Jorvik Viking Festival (p507)

MISSIONARY ENDEAVOURS

On the religious front, the Anglo-Saxons were pagans, and their invasion of Britain forced the Christian religion, along with other aspects of Celtic culture, to the western edge of the British Isles – to Wales, Scotland and Ireland. The pope of the time, Gregory, decided this was a poor show and in AD 597 sent missionaries to England to revive interest in the faith. One holy pioneer was St Augustine, who successfully converted Angles in Kent, and some good-looking specimens were sent to Rome as proof – giving rise to Pope Gregory's famous quip about Angles looking like angels. Meanwhile in northern England another missionary called St Aidan was even more successful. With admirable energy and fervour, he converted the entire populations of Mercia and Northumbria, and still had time to establish a monastery at Lindisfarne, a beautiful site on the coast which can still be visited today.

had started to band together and sow the seeds of nationhood. They called themselves *cymry* (fellow countrymen), and today Cymru is the Welsh word for Wales.

The Stirring of Scotland

While Wales was becoming established in the west of the island of Britain, similar events were taking place to the north, in the land the Romans had called Caledonia. The Picts were the region's dominant indigenous tribe and named their kingdom Alba, which still today is the Gaelic word for Scotland.

In the power vacuum that followed the fizzle-out of Roman rule in Britannia, Alba was invaded from two sides: first, towards the end of the 5th century, the Scotti crossed the sea from today's Ireland and established the kingdom of Dalriada (in today's Argyll), then in the 7th century Anglo-Saxons from the expanding English kingdom of Northumbria moved in to colonise southeast Alba. But by this time the Scotti were well dug in alongside the Picts, foreshadowing the time when yet another name - Scotland - would be applied to northern Britain.

The Viking Era

Just as the new territories of England, Wales and Scotland were becoming established, Britain was yet again invaded by a bunch of pesky continentals. This time, Vikings appeared on the scene.

It's another classic historical image: blonde Scandinavians, horned helmets, big swords, square-sailed longboats, raping and pillaging. Tradition has it that Vikings turned up, killed everyone, took everything, and left. There's *some* truth in that, but in reality many Vikings

872

The King of Norway creates an earldom in Orkney; Shetland is also governed from here. These island groups become a Viking base for raids and colonisation into Scotland and northern England.

9th century

King Rhodri Mawr of Wales defeats a Viking force and begins Welsh unification process. His grandson Hywel the Good draws up a set of laws.

9th century

Kenneth MacAilpin, the king of the Scotti, declares himself ruler of both the Scots *and* the Picts, thus uniting Scotland north of the Firth of Forth into a single kingdom.

927

Athelstan, grandson of Alfred the Great, son of Edward the Elder, is the first monarch to be specifically crowned King of England, building on his ancestors' success in regaining Viking territory.

The Year 1000 by Robert Lacey and Danny Danziger looks long and hard at English life a millennium ago. Apparently it was cold and damp then, too.

settled for good, and their legacy is still evident in parts of northern England – in the form of local dialect, geographical terms such as 'fell' and 'dale' (from the old Norse *fjell* and *dalr*), and even the traces of Nordic DNA in some of today's inhabitants.

The main wave of Vikings came from today's Denmark, conquering east and northeast England and establishing their capital at Jorvik (today's city of York, where many Viking remains can still be seen). By the middle of the 9th century, they spread southwards across central England. Standing in their way were the Anglo-Saxon armies, led by Alfred the Great – the king of Wessex and one of English history's best-known characters – and the battles that followed were seminal to the foundation of the nation-state of England.

But the fighting didn't all go Alfred's way. For a few months he was on the run, wading through swamps, hiding in peasant hovels and famously burning cakes. It was the stuff of legend, which is just what you need when the chips are down. By 886 Alfred had gathered his strength, garnered his forces and pushed the Vikings back to the north.

United England?

Thus England was divided in two: north and east was Viking 'Danelaw', while south and west was Anglo-Saxon territory. Alfred was hailed as king of the English – the first time the Anglo-Saxons regarded themselves as a truly united people.

Alfred's son and successor was Edward the Elder. After more battles, he gained control of the Danelaw, and thus became the first king to rule the whole of England. His son, Athelstan, took the process a stage further and was specifically crowned King of England in 927. But it was hardly cause for celebration: the Vikings were still around, and later in

WHOSE PATRON SAINT IS THIS?

Along the coast of Wales, the struggle between settlers and raiding Irish pirates was a major feature of life during the Dark Ages. Even St Patrick, the patron saint of Ireland, is reputed to have been a Welshman, captured by brigands and taken to Ireland as a slave.

At around the same time, other visitors from Ireland to Wales were Christian missionaries. Among them was a monk named Dewi, who became known as David, and later became patron saint of Wales.

So in a fair swap, the patron saint of Wales was an Irishman, while the patron saint of Ireland could well have been Welsh. It seems odd, but then the patron saint of England, St George, was a Turk, and the patron saint of Scotland, St Andrew, was a Palestinian, so maybe in the British Isles it's all par for the course.

1018

Scottish King Malcolm II defeats the Northumbrians at the battle of Carham and gains the Lothian region, thus expanding the size of Scotland.

1040

Macbeth takes the Scottish throne after defeating Duncan in battle. This, and the fact that he was later killed by Duncan's son Malcolm, are the only parallels with the Shakespeare version.

1066

Battle of Hastings – a crucial date in English history. Incumbent King Harold is defeated by an invading Norman army, and England has a new monarch: William the Conqueror.

1085–86

The new Norman rulers establish the Domesday Book census. Within three years they have a snapshot of England's current stock and future potential.

the 10th century more raids from Scandinavia threatened this fledgling English unity. Over the following decades, control swung from Saxon (King Edgar) to Dane (King Knut) and back to Saxon again (King Edward the Confessor). As England came to the end of the 1st millennium AD, the future was anything but certain.

Highs & Lows in Wales

Meanwhile, as England fought off the Viking threat, Wales was also dealing with the Nordic intruders. Building on the initial cooperation forced upon them by Anglo-Saxon oppression, in the 9th and 10th centuries the small kingdoms of Wales began cooperating, through necessity, to repel the Vikings.

King Rhodri Mawr (who died in 878) defeated a Viking force off the Isle of Anglesey and began the unification process. His grandson Hywel the Good is thought to have been responsible for drawing up a set of laws to bind the disparate Welsh tribes. Things were going well, but just as Wales was becoming a recognisable entity, the young country was faced with more destructive onslaughts than it could handle, and in 927 the Welsh kings recognised the Anglo-Saxon King Athelstan as their overlord in exchange for an anti-Viking alliance.

Myths and Legends of the British Isles by Richard Barber is an ideal read if you want a break from firm historical facts. Gen up on King Arthur and the Knights of the Round Table, plus much more from the mists of time.

Scotland Becomes a Kingdom

While the Welsh were forming their own nation, similar events were being played out in Alba. In the 9th century, the king of the Scotti of Dalriada was one Kenneth MacAilpin (usually anglicised to MacAlpin). His father was a Scotti, but his mother was a Pict princess, so MacAlpin took advantage of the Pictish custom of matrilineal succession to declare himself ruler of both the Scots *and* the Picts, and therefore king of all Alba.

In a surprisingly short time, the Scots gained cultural and political ascendancy. The Picts were absorbed, and Pictish culture simply – and quite suddenly – came to an end. As part of this process, Alba became known as Scotia.

In the 11th century, Scottish nation building was further consolidated by King Malcolm III (whose most famous act was the 1057 murder of Macbeth – as immortalised by William Shakespeare). With his English queen, Margaret, he founded the Canmore dynasty that would rule Scotland for the next two centuries.

1066 & All That

While Wales and Scotland laid the foundations of nationhood, back in England things were unsettled, as the royal pendulum was still swinging between Saxon and Danish-Viking monarchs. When King Edward

1095

The start of the First Crusade – a campaign of Christian European armies against the Muslim occupation of Jerusalem and the 'Holy Land'. A series of crusades continues until 1272.

1124–53

The rule of David I of Scotland. The Scottish aristocracy adopts the Norman feudal system, and the king grants land to great Norman families.

12th century

Oxford University is founded. There's evidence of teaching in the area since 1096, but King Henry II's 1167 ban on students attending the University of Paris solidified Oxford's importance.

1215

King John signs the Magna Carta, limiting the monarch's power for the first time in English history in an early step along the path towards constitutional rule.

the Confessor died, the crown passed to Harold, his brother-in-law. That should've settled things, but Edward had a cousin in Normandy (the northern part of today's France) called William, who thought *he* should have succeeded to the throne of England.

The result was the Battle of Hastings in 1066, the most memorable of dates for anyone who's studied English history – or for anyone who hasn't. William sailed from Normandy with an army of Norman soldiers, the Saxons were defeated and Harold was killed – according to tradition, by an arrow in the eye.

At the top of the feudal system came the monarch, followed by nobles (barons and baronesses, dukes and duchesses, plus the bishops), then earls, knights, lords and ladies. At the bottom were peasants or 'serfs'. This strict hierarchy became the basis of a class system in Britain that still exists today.

Norman Wisdom

William became king of England, earning himself the prestigious title William the Conqueror. It was no idle nickname. To control the Anglo-Saxons, the Norman invaders wisely built castles across their new-won territory, and by 1085–86 the Domesday Book provided a census of England's current stock and future potential.

William the Conqueror was followed by William II, but he was mysteriously assassinated during a hunting trip and succeeded by Henry I, another Norman ruler, and the first of a long line of kings called Henry.

In the years after the invasion, the French-speaking Normans and the English-speaking Anglo-Saxons kept pretty much to themselves. A strict hierarchy of class developed, known as the feudal system.

Intermarriage was not completely unknown, however. Henry himself married a Saxon princess. Nonetheless, such unifying moves stood for nothing after Henry's death: a bitter struggle for succession followed, finally won by Henry II, who took the throne as the first king of the House – or dynasty – of Plantagenet.

Post-Invasion Wales & Scotland

By the time the Normans invaded England, the Welsh no longer needed anti-Viking protection and had returned to their independent ways – but not if William the Conqueror had anything to do with it. To secure

LOOKING SOUTH

The arrival of William the Conqueror was a watershed event, as it marked the end of Britain's century-old ties to the Nordic countries (only in Orkney and Shetland did the Viking presence continue until the 15th century). The mainland's perspective turned to France, Western Europe and the Mediterranean, giving rise to massive cultural implications that were to last into our own time. In addition, the Norman landing capped an era of armed invasion. Since 1066, in the near-on thousand years to the present day, Britain has never again been seriously invaded by a foreign power.

13th century

Wales is invaded by English King Edward I, bringing to an end the rule of Welsh leader 'Llywelyn the Last'. Edward builds a ring of castles to suppress further Welsh uprisings.

1295

John Balliol of Scotland and Philip IV of France sign a mutual defence treaty that establishes the 'Auld Alliance' – this predominantly anti-English agreement remains in place for several centuries.

1296

King Edward I marches on Scotland with an army of 30,000 men, and in a brutal invasion captures the castles of Berwick, Edinburgh, Roxburgh and Stirling.

SEAN CAFFREY

» Main gate, Stirling Castle (p833)

DOMINATING THE LANDSCAPE

If you're travelling through Wales, it won't take you long to notice the country's most striking architectural asset: castles. There are around 600 in all, giving Wales the dubious honour of being Europe's most densely fortified country. Most were built in medieval times, first by William the Conqueror, then by other Anglo-Norman kings, to keep a lid on the Welsh. In the late 13th century, Edward I built the spectacular castles at Caernarfon, Harlech, Conwy and Beaumaris – now jointly listed as a Unesco World Heritage Site. Other castles to see include Rhuddlan, Denbigh, Cricceith, Raglan, Pembroke, Kidwelly, Chepstow and Caerphilly. Great for visitors, of course, but a sore point for patriotic Welsh; the writer Thomas Pennant called them 'the magnificent badge of our subjection'.

his new kingdom, and keep the Welsh in theirs, William built castles and appointed feudal barons along the border. The Lords Marcher, as they were known, became massively rich and powerful, and the parts of western England along the Welsh border are still called the Marches today.

In Scotland, King Malcolm III and Queen Margaret were more accommodating to Norman ways – or, at least, they liked the way the Normans ran a country. Malcolm's successor, David I (1124–53), was impressed too, and adopted the Norman feudal system as well as granting land to great Norman families. By 1212 a courtier called Walter of Coventry remarked that the Scottish court was 'French in race and manner of life, in speech and in culture'.

But while the French-Norman effect changed England and lowland Scotland over the following centuries, further north the Highland clans remained inaccessible in their glens – a law unto themselves for another 600 years.

Royal & Holy Squabbling

Meanwhile, back in England the rule of Henry I had come to an end, and the fight to take his place continued the enduring English habit of competition for the throne, and introduced an equally enduring tendency of bickering between royalty and the church. Things came to a head in 1170 when Henry II had 'turbulent priest' Thomas Becket murdered in Canterbury Cathedral. (The stunning cathedral is still an important shrine and a major destination for visitors to Britain today; see p138.)

Perhaps the next king, Richard I, wanted to make amends for his forebears' unholy sentiments by leading a crusade – a Christian 'holy war' – to liberate Jerusalem and the Holy Land (the area at the eastern end of the Mediterranean, today known as Israel and the Palestinian

1298–1305

William Wallace is proclaimed Guardian of Scotland in 1298. After Edward's army defeats the Scots at the Battle of Falkirk, Wallace goes into hiding but is betrayed and executed in 1305.

1314

An army under Robert the Bruce wins against the English at the Battle of Bannockburn – a victory that turns the tide in favour of the Scots for the next 400 years.

1328

Continuing raids by the Scots into northern England force Edward II to sue for peace; the Treaty of Northampton gives Scotland its independence, with Robert I, the Bruce, as king.

1337–1453

England battles against France in a long conflict known as the Hundred Years' War. It was actually a series of small conflicts. And it lasted for more than a century, too...

territories, plus parts of Syria, Jordan and Lebanon) from occupation by Muslim 'heathens' under their leader Saladin. The campaign became known as the Third Crusade, and although the Christian armies under Richard captured the cities of Acre and Jaffa, they did not take Jerusalem.

Unfortunately, Richard's overseas activities meant he was too busy crusading to bother about governing England – although his bravery and ruthlessness earned him the sobriquet Richard the Lionheart – and in his absence the country fell into disarray.

Richard was succeeded by his brother John, but under his harsh rule things got even worse for the general population. According to legend, during this time a nobleman called Robert of Loxley, better known as Robin Hood, hid in Sherwood Forest and engaged in a spot of wealth redistribution.

Expansionist Edward

The next king was Henry III, followed in 1272 by Edward I – a skilled ruler and ambitious general. During a busy 35-year reign, he expounded English nationalism and was unashamedly expansionist in his outlook, leading campaigns into Wales and Scotland.

Some decades earlier, the Welsh king Llywelyn the Great (who died in 1240) had attempted to set up a state in Wales along the lines of the new feudal system in England, and his grandson Llywelyn ('Llywelyn the Last') was recognised by Henry III as the first Prince (but not King) of Wales. But Edward I had no time for such niceties, and descended on Wales in a bloody invasion that lasted much of the 1270s. In the end, Wales became a dependent principality, owing allegiance to England. There were no more Welsh kings, and just to make it clear who was boss, Edward made his own son Prince of Wales. Ever since, the British sovereign's eldest son has been automatically given the title. (Most recently, Prince Charles was formally proclaimed Prince of Wales at Caernarfon Castle in 1969 – much to the displeasure of Welsh nationalists.)

KING JOHN CALLED TO BOOK

In 1215 the barons found King John's erratic rule increasingly hard to swallow and forced him to sign a document called Magna Carta (the Great Charter), limiting the monarch's power for the first time in British history. Although originally intended as a set of handy ground rules, Magna Carta was a fledgling bill of human rights that eventually led to the creation of parliament – a body to rule the country, independent of the throne. The signing took place at Runnymede, near Windsor, and you can still visit the site today.

1348

The bubonic plague – called the Black Death – arrives, ultimately killing more than a third of the population. For peasant labourers that survived, an upside was a rise in wages.

1371

The last of the Bruce dynasty dies, succeeded by the Stewards (Stewarts), who rule Scotland and then Britain for the next three centuries.

1381

Richard II is confronted by the Peasants' Revolt. This attempt by commoners to overthrow the feudal system is brutally suppressed, further injuring an already deeply divided country.

1399

Richard II, the last of the Plantagenet dynasty, is ousted by a powerful baron called Henry Bolingbroke, who becomes Henry IV – the first monarch of the House of Lancaster.

Edward I then looked north. For the past 200 years, Scotland had been ruled by the Canmores, but the dynasty effectively ended in 1286 with the death of Alexander III. He was succeeded by his four-year-old granddaughter Margaret ('the Maid of Norway'), who was engaged to the son of Edward I, but she died in 1290 before the wedding could take place.

There followed a dispute for the Scottish throne in which there were 13 *tanists* (contestants), but in the end it came down to two: John Balliol and Robert Bruce of Annandale. Arbitration was needed and Edward I was called in: he chose Balliol. But, having finished the job, Edward then sought to formalise his feudal overlordship and travelled through Scotland forcing clan leaders to swear allegiance. In a final blow to Scottish pride, Edward removed the Stone of Scone (also known as the Stone of Destiny or Fatal Stone), on which the kings of Scotland had been crowned for centuries, and sent it to London (see boxed text, p765).

That was just too much. In response, Balliol got in touch with Edward's old enemy, France, and arranged a treaty of cooperation – the start of an anti-English partnership, 'the Auld Alliance' – that was to last for many centuries (and to the present day when it comes to rugby or football).

Edward wasn't the sort of bloke to brook opposition, though. In 1296 the English army defeated Balliol, forcing the Scottish barons to accept Edward's rule, and his ruthless retaliation earned him the title 'Hammer of the Scots'. But still the Scottish people refused to lie down: in 1297, at the Battle of Stirling Bridge, the English were defeated by a Scots army under the leadership of William Wallace. Over 700 years later, Wallace is still remembered as the epitome of Scottish patriots (see p834).

Walks Through Britain's History (published by AA) guides you on foot to castles, battlefields and hundreds of other sites with a link to the past. Take the air. Breathe in history!

The story of William Wallace is told in the Mel Gibson epic *Braveheart*. In devolution debates of the 1990s, the patriotic pride engendered by this movie did more for Scottish nationalism than any politician's speech.

Hard Times

Back in England, Edward I was succeeded by Edward II, but the new model lacked the military success of his forebear, and his favouring of personal friends over barons didn't help. Edward failed in the marriage department too, and his rule came to a grisly end when his wife, Isabella, and her lover, Roger Mortimer, had him murdered. Fans of ghoulish ends can visit the very spot where it happened – Berkeley Castle.

By this time, Robert the Bruce (grandson of Robert Bruce of Annandale) had crowned himself king of Scotland (1290), been beaten in battle, gone on the run, and while hiding in a cave been famously inspired to renew his efforts by a spider persistently spinning its web. Bruce's army went on to defeat Edward II and the English at the Battle

1400

Welsh nationalist hero Owain Glyndŵr leads the Welsh in rebellion, declaring a parliament in Machynlleth, but his rebellion is short-lived and victory fleeting.

1459–71

The Wars of the Roses takes place – an ongoing conflict between two competing dynasties, the Houses of Lancaster and York. The Yorkists are eventually successful, enabling King Edward IV to gain the throne.

1468–69

Orkney and then Shetland are mortgaged to Scotland as part of a dowry from Danish King Christian I, whose daughter is to marry the future King James III of Scotland.

1485

Henry Tudor defeats Richard III at the Battle of Bosworth to become King Henry VII, establishing the Tudor dynasty and ending York-Lancaster rivalry for the throne.

Historic Websites

» www.royal.gov.uk

» www.bbc.co.uk/history

» www.englishmonarchs.co.uk

» www.victorianweb.org

of Bannockburn in 1314, another milestone in Scotland's long fight to remain independent.

Next in line was Edward III. Highlights of his reign – actually low-lights – include the start of the Hundred Years' War with France in 1337 and the arrival of a plague called the Black Death about a decade later, which eventually carried off 1.5 million people, more than a third of the country's population.

Another change of king didn't improve things either. Richard II had barely taken the throne when the Peasants' Revolt erupted in 1381. This attempt by commoners to overthrow the feudal system was brutally suppressed, further injuring an already deeply divided country.

Stewarts Enter the Scene

While the Hundred Years' War raged (or rather, rumbled) between England and France, things weren't much better in Scotland. After the death of Robert the Bruce in 1329, the country was ravaged by endless internal conflicts and plague epidemics.

Bruce's son became David II of Scotland, but he was soon caught up in battles against fellow Scots disaffected by his father and aided by England's Edward III. So when David died in 1371, the Scots quickly crowned Robert Stewart (Robert the Bruce's grandson) as king, marking the start of the House of Stewart, which was to crop up again in England a bit later down the line.

Houses of York & Lancaster

In 1399 the ineffectual Richard II was ousted by a powerful baron called Henry Bolingbroke, who became Henry IV – the first monarch of the House of Lancaster. Less than a year later, his rule was

HELL OF A JOB

The story of Britain's ruling dynasties clearly shows that life was never dull for the folk at the top. Despite immense power and privilege, the position of monarch (or, perhaps worse, *potential* monarch) probably ranks as one of history's least safe occupations. English kings have been killed in battle (Harold), beheaded (Charles I), assassinated (William II), murdered by a wicked uncle (Edward V) and knocked off by their queen and her lover (Edward II). Similarly, life was just as uncertain for the rulers of Wales and Scotland; threats came from rival warlords or ambitious clan chiefs – you only have to think of Shakespeare's *Macbeth* – and often from the English king next door. As you visit the castles and battlefields of Britain, you may feel a touch of sympathy – but only a touch – for those all-powerful figures continually looking over their shoulder.

1509–47

The reign of King Henry VIII. The Pope's disapproval of Henry's serial marriage and divorce results in the English Reformation – the founding of the Church of England.

1536 & 1543

English authority is exerted over Wales; the Laws in Wales Acts, also known as the Acts of Union, formally tie the two countries as a single political entity.

1560

The Scottish Parliament creates a Protestant Church that is independent of Rome and the monarchy, as a result of the Reformation. The Latin Mass is abolished and the pope's authority denied.

1588

The first complete translation of the Bible into Welsh helps the cause of Protestantism and also helps the survival of the neglected Welsh language.

disrupted by a final cry of resistance from the downtrodden Welsh, led by royal descendant Owain Glyndŵr (Owen Glendower to the English). It wasn't a good result for Wales: the rebellion was crushed, vast areas of farmland were destroyed, Glyndŵr died an outlaw and the Welsh elite were barred from public life for many years.

Henry IV was followed, neatly, by Henry V, who decided it was time to stir up the dormant Hundred Years' War. He defeated France at the Battle of Agincourt and the patriotic tear-jerker speech he was given by Shakespeare ('cry God for Harry, England and St George') has ensured his pole position among the most famous English kings of all time.

Still keeping things neat, Henry V was followed by Henry VI. Interspersed with great bouts of insanity, his main claim to fame was overseeing the building of great places of worship (King's College Chapel in Cambridge, and Eton Chapel near Windsor), architectural wonders that can still be explored and admired today.

When the Hundred Years' War finally ground to a halt in 1453, you'd have thought things would be calm for a while. But no. The English forces returning from France threw their energies into ano ther battle – a civil war dubbed the Wars of the Roses.

Briefly it went like this: Henry VI of the House of Lancaster (whose emblem was a red rose) was challenged by Richard, Duke of York (emblem, a white rose). Henry was weak and it was almost a walkover for Richard. But Henry's wife, Margaret of Anjou, was made of sterner mettle and her forces defeated the challenger. It didn't rest there: Richard's son Edward entered the scene with an army, turned the tables and finally drove out Henry. He became King Edward IV – the first monarch of the House of York.

HENRY V

Shakespeare's *Henry V* was filmed most recently in 1989 – a superb epic starring British cinema darling Kenneth Branagh as the eponymous king. Also worth catching is the earlier movie of the same name starring Laurence Olivier, made in 1944 as a patriotic rallying cry.

Dark Deeds in the Tower

Life was never easy for the guy at the top. Edward IV hardly had time to catch his breath before facing a challenger to his own throne. Enter scheming Richard Neville, Earl of Warwick, who liked to be billed as 'the kingmaker'. In 1470 he teamed up with the energetic Margaret of Anjou to shuttle Edward into exile and bring Henry VI to the throne. But a year later Edward IV came bouncing back, and this time there was no messing about: he killed Warwick, captured Margaret and had Henry snuffed out in the Tower of London.

Although Edward IV's position seemed secure, he ruled for only a decade before being succeeded by his 12-year-old son, now Edward V. But the boy-king's reign was even shorter than his dad's. In 1483 he

1558–1603

The reign of Queen Elizabeth I, a period of boundless English optimism. Enter stage right playwright William Shakespeare. Exit due west navigators Walter Raleigh and Francis Drake.

1603

James VI of Scotland inherits the English throne in the so-called Union of the Crowns, becoming James I of England and James VI of Scotland.

MARY EVANS PICTURE LIBRARY

» James VI of Scotland

1605

King James' attempts to smooth religious relations are set back by an anti-Catholic outcry following the infamous Gunpowder Plot, a terrorist attempt to blow up parliament led by Guy Fawkes.

was mysteriously murdered, along with his brother, and once again the Tower of London was the scene of the crime.

With the 'little princes' dispatched, this left the throne open for their dear old Uncle Richard. Whether he was the princes' killer is still the subject of debate, but his rule as Richard III was short-lived. Despite being given another famous Shakespearean sound bite ('A horse, a horse, my kingdom for a horse'), few tears were shed in 1485 when he was tumbled from the top job by a nobleman from Wales called Henry Tudor, who became King Henry VII.

Moves Towards Unity

There hadn't been a Henry on the throne for a while, and this new incumbent harked back to the days of his namesakes with a skilful reign. After the Wars of the Roses, his Tudor neutrality was important. He also diligently mended fences with his northern neighbours by marrying off his daughter to James IV of Scotland, thereby linking the Tudor and Stewart lines.

On top of his family links with Scotland, Henry was also half-Welsh. He withdrew many of the anti-Welsh restrictions imposed after the Glyndŵr uprising, and his countrymen were only too grateful to enjoy newfound preferential treatment at the English court and career opportunities in English public life.

Matrimony may have been more useful than warfare for Henry VII, but the multiple marriages of his successor, Henry VIII, were a very different story. Fathering a male heir was his problem – hence the famous six wives – but the pope's disapproval of divorce and remarriage led to a split with the Roman Catholic Church. Parliament made Henry the head of the Protestant Church of England – the beginning of a pivotal division between Catholics and Protestants that still exists in some areas of Britain.

In 1536 Henry followed this up by 'dissolving' many monasteries in Britain and Ireland, a blatant takeover of their land and wealth rather than a symptom of the struggle between church and state. Nonetheless, the general populace felt little sympathy for the wealthy and often corrupt abbeys, and in 1539–40 another monastic land grab swallowed the larger ones as well.

At the same time, Henry signed the Acts of Union (1536 and 1543), formally uniting England and Wales for the first time. This was welcomed by the aspiring Welsh gentry, as it meant English law and parliamentary representation for Wales, plus plenty of trade opportunities. The Welsh language, however, ceased to be recognised in the law courts.

Meanwhile, in Scotland, James IV had been succeeded by James V, who died in 1542, broken-hearted, it is said, after yet another defeat at

ELIZABETH

The 1998 movie *Elizabeth*, directed by Shekhar Kapur and starring Cate Blanchett, covers the early years of the Virgin Queen's rule, as she graduates from novice princess to commanding monarch – a time of forbidden love, unwanted suitors, intrigue and death.

1644–49

English Civil War between the king's Cavaliers and Oliver Cromwell's Roundheads, establishes the Commonwealth of England.

1688

William of Orange and his wife, Mary, daughter of King James II, jointly ascend the throne after William defeats his father-in-law in the Glorious Revolution.

1692

The Massacre of Glencoe causes further rifts between those clans loyal to the Scottish crown and those loyal to the old ways.

1707

The Act of Union brings England and Scotland under one parliament, one sovereign and one flag.

the hands of the English. His baby daughter Mary became queen and Scotland was ruled by regents.

The Elizabethan Age

Henry VIII died in 1547, succeeded by his son Edward VI, then by his daughter Mary I, but their reigns were short. So, unexpectedly, the third child, Elizabeth, came to the throne.

As Elizabeth I, she inherited a nasty mess of religious strife and divided loyalties, but after an uncertain start she gained confidence and turned the country round. Refusing marriage, she borrowed biblical imagery and became known as the Virgin Queen – perhaps the first British monarch to create a cult image.

It paid off. Her 45-year reign was a period of boundless optimism characterised by the naval defeat of the Spanish Armada, the expansion of trade due to the global explorations of seafarers such as Walter Raleigh and Francis Drake, not to mention a cultural flourishing thanks to writers such as William Shakespeare and Christopher Marlowe.

Mary, Queen of Scots

During Elizabeth's reign, her cousin Mary (daughter of Scottish King James V and a Catholic) had become known as Mary, Queen of Scots. She'd spent her childhood in France and had married the French *dauphin* (crown prince), thereby becoming queen of France as well. Why stop at two? After her husband's death, Mary returned to Scotland, from where she ambitiously claimed the English throne as well – on the grounds that Elizabeth I was illegitimate.

But Mary's plans failed; she was imprisoned and forced to abdicate in favour of her son (a Protestant, who became James VI of Scotland), but then she escaped to England and appealed to Elizabeth for help. This could have been a rookie error, or she might have been advised by courtiers with their own agenda. Either way, it was a bad move. Mary was seen – not surprisingly – as a security risk and imprisoned once again.

Mary, Queen of Scots, Slept Here

» Workington Hall, Cumbria

» Carlisle Castle, Cumbria

» Bolton Castle, North Yorkshire

» Tutbury Castle, Staffordshire

» Chatsworth House, Derbyshire

» Sheffield Castle & Manor, South Yorkshire

» Fotheringhay Castle, Northamptonshire

» St Mary's Guildhall, Coventry, Warwickshire

THE ROUGH WOOING

When the child Mary, daughter of James V, became queen of Scotland, the English King England Henry VIII sent a proposal that Mary should marry his son. But Mary's regents rejected his offer and – not forgetting the 'Auld Alliance' treaty with the French – Mary was sent to France instead. Henry was furious and sent his armies to ravage southern Scotland and sack Edinburgh in an (unsuccessful) attempt to force agreement to the wedding. With typical irony and understatement, the Scots dubbed it the Rough Wooing.

1721–42

Violent struggles for the throne seem a thing of the past and the Hanoverian kings increasingly rely on parliament to govern the country. Robert Walpole becomes Britain's first prime minister.

1745–46

The culmination of the Jacobite uprisings sees Bonnie Prince Charlie land in Scotland, gather an army and march southwards, to be eventually defeated at the Battle of Culloden.

1749

Author and magistrate Henry Fielding founds the Bow Street Runners, cited as London's first professional police force. A 1792 Act of Parliament allows the Bow Street model to spread across England.

CHARLOTTE HINDLE

» Police sign, London

In an uncharacteristic display of indecision, before finally ordering her execution, Elizabeth held Mary under arrest for 19 years, moving her frequently from house to house, so that today England has many stately homes (and even a few pubs) claiming 'Mary, Queen of Scots, slept here'.

United & Disunited Britain

When Elizabeth died in 1603, despite a bountiful reign, one thing the Virgin Queen failed to provide was an heir. She was succeeded by her closest relative, James, the safely Protestant son of the executed Mary. He became James I of England and James VI of Scotland, the first English monarch of the House of Stuart (Mary's time in France had Gallicised the Stewart name). Most importantly, James united England, Wales and Scotland into one kingdom for the first time in history – another step towards British unity, at least on paper – although the terms 'Britain' and 'British' were still not yet widely used in this context.

James' attempts to smooth religious relations were set back by the anti-Catholic outcry that followed the infamous Guy Fawkes Gunpowder Plot, a terrorist attempt to blow up parliament in 1605. The event is still celebrated every 5 November, with fireworks, bonfires and burning effigies of Guy himself.

Alongside the Catholic-Protestant rift, the divide between king and parliament continued to smoulder. The power struggle worsened during the reign of the next king, Charles I, and eventually degenerated into the Civil War of 1644–49. The antiroyalist (or 'parliamentarian') forces were led by Oliver Cromwell, a Puritan who preached against the excesses of the monarchy and established Church. His army (known as the Roundheads) was pitched against the king's forces (the Cavaliers) in a conflict that tore England apart – although it was the final civil war in English history. It ended with victory for the Roundheads, with the king executed and England declared a republic – and Cromwell hailed as 'Protector'.

The Civil War had been a bitter conflict, but it failed to exhaust Cromwell's appetite for mayhem; a devastating rampage to gain control of Ireland – the first British colony – followed quickly in its wake. Meanwhile, the Scots suffered their own parallel civil war between the royalists and radical 'Covenanters', who sought freedom from state interference in church government.

On the chilly day of his execution, the dethroned King Charles I reputedly wore two shirts to avoid shivering and being regarded as a coward.

CHARLES I

The Return of the King

By 1653 Cromwell was finding parliament too restricting and he assumed dictatorial powers, much to his supporters' dismay. On his death in 1658, he was followed half-heartedly by his son, but in 1660 parliament decided to re-establish the monarchy – as republican alternatives were proving far worse.

1776–83
The American War of Independence is the British Empire's first major reverse, forcing England to withdraw from the world stage, a fact not missed by French ruler Napoleon.

1799–1815
In the Napoleonic Wars, Napoleon threatens invasion on a weakened Britain, but his ambitions are curtailed by Nelson and Wellington at the famous battles of Trafalgar (1805) and Waterloo (1815).

1858 & 1860
The first modern national eisteddfods are held in Llangollen and Denbigh – although earlier ones had been organised from the end of the 18th century as part of a Welsh cultural revival.

1837–1901
The reign of Queen Victoria, during which the British Empire – 'the empire where the sun never sets' – expands from Canada through Africa and India to Australia and New Zealand.

Charles II (the exiled son of Charles I) came to the throne, and his rule – known as 'the Restoration' – saw scientific and cultural activity bursting forth after the straitlaced ethics of Cromwell's time. Exploration and expansion were also on the agenda. Backed by the army and navy (modernised, ironically, by Cromwell), English colonies stretched down the American coast, while the East India Company set up headquarters in Bombay (now Mumbai), laying foundations for what was to become the British Empire.

The next king, James II, had a harder time. Attempts to ease restrictive laws on Catholics ended with his defeat at the Battle of the Boyne by William III, the Protestant king of Holland, better known as William of Orange. Ironically, William was married to James' own daughter Mary, but it didn't stop him having a bash at his father-in-law.

William and Mary both had equal rights to the throne and their joint accession in 1688 was known as the Glorious Revolution. Lucky they were married or there might have been *another* civil war.

Killiecrankie & Glen Coe

In Scotland things weren't quite so glorious. Anti-English (essentially anti-William and anti-Protestant) feelings ran high, as did pro-James ('Jacobite') support. In 1689 Jacobite leader Graham of Claverhouse, better-known as 'Bonnie Dundee', raised a Highlander army and routed English troops at Killiecrankie.

Then in 1692 came the infamous Glen Coe Massacre. On English government orders members of the Campbell clan killed most of the MacDonald clan for failing to swear allegiance to William.

The atrocity further fuelled Catholic-Protestant divisions, and tightened English domination of Britain, although Jacobite sentiment surfaced in two rebellions (see p1000) before finally succumbing to history.

Full Final Unity

In 1694 Mary died, leaving just William as monarch. He died a few years later, and was succeeded by his sister-in-law Anne (the second daughter of James II). In 1707, during Anne's reign, the Act of Union was passed, bringing an end to the independent Scottish Parliament, and finally linking the countries of England, Wales and Scotland under one parliament (based in London) for the first time. The nation of Britain was now established as a single state, with a bigger, better and more powerful parliament, and a constitutional monarchy with clear limits on the power of the king or queen.

The new-look parliament didn't wait long to flex its muscles. The Act of Union also banned any Catholic, or anyone married to a Catholic, from ascending the throne – a rule still in force today. And although

HENRY VIII

Six Wives: The Queens of Henry VIII by historian David Starky is an accessible modern study of the multimarrying monarch.

1847

Publication of a government report, dubbed the 'Treason of the Blue Books', suggests the Welsh language is detrimental to education in Wales, and fuels the Welsh-language struggle.

1900

James Keir Hardie (usually known as just Keir Hardie) becomes the first Labour MP, winning a seat in the Welsh mining town of Merthyr Tydfyl.

1914

Archduke Franz Ferdinand of Austria is assassinated in the Balkan city of Sarajevo – the final spark in a decade-long crisis that starts the Great War, now called WWI.

1916

The Welsh Liberal MP David Lloyd George becomes the British prime minister in an alliance with the Conservative Party, having built a reputation for championing the poor and needy.

the Glorious Revolution was relatively painless in Britain, the impact on Ireland (where the Protestant ascendancy dates from William's victory) sowed the seeds for division that continue to the present day.

In 1714 Anne died without leaving an heir, marking the end of the Stuart line. The throne was then passed to distant (but still safely Protestant) German relatives – the House of Hanover.

Iconic Historical Sites

Don't miss invasion point **Battle**, near Hastings; **Bannockburn**, milestone of Scottish independence; **Caernarfon Castle**, focal point of Welsh-English conflict; **Runnymede**, where the Magna Carta was signed; ancient stone circle **Stonehenge**; **Westminster Abbey**, where monarchs have been crowned since 1066; or**Hadrian's Wall**, symbol of Roman rule.

The Jacobite Rebellions

Despite, or perhaps because of, the 1707 Act of Union, anti-English feeling in Scotland refused to disappear. The Jacobite rebellions, most notably those of 1715 and 1745, were attempts to overthrow the Hanoverian monarchy and bring back the Stuarts. Although these are iconic events in Scottish history, in reality there was never much support for the Jacobite cause outside the Highlands: the people of the lowlands were mainly Protestant, and feared a return to the Catholicism the Stuarts represented.

The 1715 rebellion was led by James Edward Stuart (the Old Pretender), the son of the exiled James II of England (James VII of Scotland). When the attempt failed, he fled to France, and to impose control on the Highlands, the English military (under the notorious General Wade) constructed roads into previously inaccessible glens.

In 1745 James' son Charles Edward Stuart (Bonnie Prince Charlie, the Young Pretender) landed in Scotland to claim the crown for his father. He was initially successful, moving south into England as far as Derby, but the prince and his Highland supporters suffered a catastrophic defeat at the Battle of Culloden in 1746, and his legendary escape to the western isles is eternally remembered in the *Skye Boat Song*. And in a different way, General Wade is remembered too – many of the roads his troops built are still in use today.

The Empire Strikes Out

By the mid-18th century, struggles for the British throne seemed a thing of the past, and the Hanoverian kings increasingly relied on parliament to govern the country. As part of the process, from 1721 to 1742 a senior parliamentarian called Sir Robert Walpole effectively became Britain's first prime minister.

Meanwhile, the British Empire – which, despite its official title, was predominantly an *English* entity – continued to grow in America, Canada and India. The first claims were made to Australia after Captain James Cook's epic voyage in 1768.

The empire's first major reverse came when the American colonies won the War of Independence (1776–83). This setback forced Britain to withdraw from the world stage for a while, a gap not missed by

1925

Plaid (Cenedlaethol) Cymru, the Welsh Nationalist Party, is formed, initiating the struggle for Welsh self-governance and laying the foundations for the modern-day party.

1926

Increasing mistrust of the government, fuelled by soaring unemployment, leads to the General Strike. Millions of workers – train drivers, miners, ship builders – down tools and bring the country to a halt.

1939–45

WWII rages across Europe, and much of Africa and Asia. Britain and Allies including America, Russia, Australia, India and New Zealand eventually defeat the armies of Germany, Japan and Italy.

DOUG MCKINLAY

» Imperial War Museum (p81)

French ruler Napoleon. He threatened to invade Britain and hinder the power of the British overseas, before his ambitions were curtailed by navy hero Viscount Horatio Nelson and military hero the Duke of Wellington at the famous battles of Trafalgar (1805) and Waterloo (1815).

Captain Cook's voyage to the southern hemisphere was primarily a scientific expedition. His objectives included monitoring the transect of Venus, an astronomical event that happens only twice every 180 years or so (most recently in 2004 and 2008). 'Discovering' Australia was just a sideline.

The Industrial Age

While the empire expanded abroad, at home Britain had become the crucible of the Industrial Revolution. Steam power (patented by James Watt in 1781) and steam trains (launched by George Stephenson in 1830) transformed methods of production and transport, and the towns of the English Midlands became the first industrial cities.

This population shift in England was mirrored in Scotland. From about 1750, much of the Highlands region had been emptied of people, as landowners casually expelled entire farms and villages to make way for more profitable sheep farming, a seminal event in Scotland's history known as the Clearances (see p914). Industrialisation just about finished off the job. Although many of the dispossessed left for the New World, others came from the glens to the burgeoning factories of the lowlands. The tobacco trade with America boomed, and then gave way to textile and engineering industries, as the cotton mills of Lanarkshire and the Clyde shipyards around Glasgow expanded rapidly.

The same happened in Wales. By the early 19th century, copper, iron and slate were being extracted in the Merthyr Tydfil and Monmouth areas. The 1860s saw the Rhondda valleys opened up for coal mining, and Wales soon became a major exporter of coal, as well as the world's leading producer of tin plate.

Across Britain, industrialisation meant people were on the move as never before. People left the land and villages their families had occupied for generations. Often they went to the nearest factory, but not always. People from rural Dorset migrated to the Midlands, for example, while farmers from Scotland and England settled in South Wales and became miners. The rapid change from rural to urban society caused great dislocation, and although knowledge of science and medicine also improved alongside industrial advances, for many people the adverse side effects of Britain's economic blossoming were poverty and deprivation.

A History of Britain by historian and TV star Simon Schama is a highly accessible set of three books, putting events from 3000 BC to AD 2000 in a modern context.

But despite the social turmoil of the early 19th century, by the time Queen Victoria took the throne in 1837, Britain's factories dominated world trade and Britain's fleets dominated the oceans. The rest of the 19th century was seen as Britain's Golden Age – a period of confidence not enjoyed since the days of the last great queen, Elizabeth I.

Victoria ruled a proud nation at home, and great swaths of territories

1945

WWII ends, and in the immediate postwar election the Labour Party under Clement Attlee defeats the Conservatives under Winston Churchill, despite the latter's pivotal rule in Britain's WWII victory.

1946–48

The Labour Party nationalises key industries such as shipyards, coal mines and steel foundries. Britain's 'big four' train companies are combined into British Railways.

1948

Aneurin Bevan, the health minister in the Labour government, launches the National Health Service – the core of Britain as a 'welfare state'.

1952

Princess Elizabeth becomes Queen Elizabeth II when her father, George VI, dies. Her coronation takes place in Westminster Abbey in June 1953.

abroad, from Canada through much of Africa and India to Australia and New Zealand – trumpeted as 'the empire where the sun never sets'. In a final move of PR genius, the queen's chief spin doctor and most effective prime minister, Benjamin Disraeli, had Victoria crowned Empress of India. She'd never even been to India, but the British people simply loved the idea.

The times were optimistic, but it wasn't all tub-thumping jingoism. Disraeli and his successor William Gladstone also introduced social reforms to address the worst excesses of the Industrial Revolution. Education became universal, trade unions were legalised and the right to vote was extended to commoners. Well, to male commoners. Women didn't get the vote for another few decades. Disraeli and Gladstone may have been enlightened gentlemen, but there *were* limits.

At its height, the British Empire covered 20% of the land area of the earth and contained a quarter of the entire world's population.

World War I

When Queen Victoria died in 1901, it seemed Britain's energy fizzled out too. The new king, Edward VII, ushered in the relaxed new Edwardian era – and a long period of decline.

Meanwhile, in continental Europe, other states were more active: four restless military powers (Russia, Austro-Hungary, Turkey and Germany) focused their sabre-rattling on the Balkan states, and the assassination of Archduke Ferdinand at Sarajevo in 1914 finally sparked a clash that became the great war we now call WWI. When German forces entered Belgium, on their way to invade France, soldiers from Britain and Allied countries were drawn into the war – a vicious conflict of stalemate and horrendous slaughter – most infamously on the killing fields of Flanders and the beaches of Gallipoli.

By the war's weary end in 1918 over a million Britons had died (not to mention millions more from many other countries) and there was hardly a street or village untouched by death, as the sobering lists of names on war memorials all over Britain still show. The conflict also added 'trench warfare' to the dictionary, and the divide that existed between aristocrat officers and their troops during the conflict further deepened the huge gulf between the ruling and working classes when the war was over.

Disillusion & Depression

For the soldiers who did return from WWI, disillusion led to questioning of the social order. Many supported the ideals of a new political force – the Labour Party, to represent the working class – upsetting the balance long enjoyed by the Liberal and Conservative Parties since the days of Walpole. The first Labour leader was Keir Hardie, a Scottish

1955 & 1959

Cardiff is declared the Welsh capital in 1955, and Wales gets its own official flag – the red dragon on a green and white field – in 1959.

1960s

It's the era of African and Caribbean independence, including Nigeria (1960), Tanzania (1961), Jamaica and Trinidad & Tobago (1962), Kenya (1963), Malawi (1964), The Gambia (1965) and Barbados (1966).

1960s

At home, it's the era of Beatlemania. Successful songs like 'Please, Please Me' ensure the Beatles become household names in Britain, then America – then the world.

1971

Britain adopts the 'decimal' currency (one pound equals 100 pence) and drops the ancient system of one pound equals 20 shillings or 240 pennies, the centuries-old bane of school maths lessons.

politician representing a Welsh constituency (the coal-mining town of Merthyr Tydfil) in the London-based parliament.

The right to vote was extended to all men over 21 and all women over 30, and the Labour Party won for the first time in the 1923 election, in coalition with the Liberals; James Ramsay MacDonald was the first Labour prime minister. A year later the Conservatives regained power, but by this time the world economy was in decline and a rankling 'them and us' mistrust in Britain, fertilised by soaring unemployment, led to the 1926 General Strike. When half a million workers marched through the streets, the government's response included sending in the army – setting the stage for a style of industrial conflict that was to plague Britain for the next 50 years.

One of the finest novels about WWI is *Birdsong* by Sebastian Faulks. Understated, perfectly paced and intensely moving, it tells of passion, fear, waste, incompetent generals and the poor bloody infantry.

Unrest at home was mirrored by unrest abroad – in Ireland, Britain's oldest colony. WWI was no sooner over than Britain was involved in the bitter Anglo-Irish War, which ended in mid-1921 with most of Ireland achieving full independence (although six counties in the north remained British). The new political entity may have been billed as the United Kingdom of Great Britain and Northern Ireland, but the decision to divide the island of Ireland in two was to have long-term repercussions that still dominate political agendas in both the UK and the Republic of Ireland today.

The unrest of the 1920s worsened in the '30s as the world economy slumped and the Great Depression took hold – a decade of misery and political upheaval. Even the royal family took a knock when Edward VIII abdicated in 1936 so he could marry a woman who was twice divorced and, horror of horrors, American. The ensuing scandal was good for newspaper sales and hinted at the prolonged 'trial by media' suffered by royals in more recent times.

The throne was taken by Edward's less-than-charismatic brother George VI and Britain dithered through the rest of the decade, with mediocre and visionless government failing to confront the country's deep-set social and economic problems.

World War II

Meanwhile, in mainland Europe, Germany saw the rise of Adolf Hitler, leader of the Nazi party. Many feared another Great War, but Prime Minister Neville Chamberlain met Hitler in 1938 and promised Britain 'peace for our time' (a phrase still remembered, though usually misquoted as 'peace in our time'). He was wrong. The following year Hitler invaded Poland. Two days later Britain was once again at war with Germany.

The German army moved with astonishing speed, sweeping west through France, and pushing back British forces to the beaches of

1970s

Much of the decade is characterised by inflation, inept governments (on the left and right), trade-union disputes, strikes, shortages and blackouts, culminating in the 1978–79 'Winter of Discontent'.

1970s

The discovery of oil and gas in the North Sea brings new prosperity to Aberdeen in Scotland and the surrounding area, and also to the Shetland Islands.

JONATHAN SMITH

» Aberdeen city centre and harbour (p876)

Dunkirk in June 1940. An extraordinary flotilla of rescue vessels turned total disaster into a brave defeat – and Dunkirk Day is still remembered with pride and sadness in Britain every year.

By mid-1940 most of Europe was controlled by Germany. In Russia, Stalin had negotiated a peace agreement. The USA was neutral, leaving Britain virtually isolated. Neville Chamberlain, reviled for his earlier 'appeasement', stood aside to let a new prime minister – Winston Churchill – lead a coalition government. (See p1005 for more Churchillian details.)

Normandy Landings Statistics

» Largest military armada in history

» More than 5000 ships

» Approximately 150,000 Allied troops landed

» Campaign time: four days

In 1941 the tide began to turn as the USA entered the war to support Britain, and Germany became bogged down on the eastern front fighting Russia. The following year, British forces were revitalised thanks to Churchill's focus on arms manufacturing, and the Germans were defeated in North Africa.

By 1944 Germany was in retreat. Britain and the USA controlled the skies, Russia's Red Army pushed back from the east, and the Allies were again on the beaches of France as the Normandy landings (D-Day, as it's better remembered) marked the start of the liberation of Europe from the west, and in Churchill's words, 'the beginning of the end of the war'. By 1945 Hitler was dead and his country a ruined shell. Two atomic bombs forced the surrender of Germany's ally Japan, and finally brought WWII to a dramatic and terrible close.

Swinging & Sliding

In Britain, despite the victory, there was an unexpected swing on the political front. An electorate tired of war and hungry for change tumbled Churchill's Conservatives, and voted in the Labour Party, led by Clement Attlee. This was the dawn of the 'welfare state': key industries (such as steel, coal and railways) were nationalised and the National Health Service was founded. But rebuilding Britain was a slow process, and the postwar 'baby boomers' experienced food rationing well into the 1950s.

The effects of depleted reserves were felt overseas too, as one by one the colonies became independent, including India and Pakistan in 1947, and Malaya in 1957, followed by much of Africa and the Caribbean. Through the next decade, people from these former colonies were drawn to the 'mother country'. In many cases they were specifically invited by the British government, as additional labour was needed to help rebuild postwar Britain.

But while the empire's sun may have been setting, Britain's royal family was still going strong. In 1952 George VI was succeeded by his daughter Elizabeth II and, following the trend set by earlier queens Elizabeth I and Victoria, she has remained on the throne for more

1972

In Uganda, East Africa, the dictator Idi Amin expels all people of Asian origin. Many have British passports and migrate to Britain, settling predominantly in London and the cities of the Midlands.

1979

A Conservative government led by Margaret Thatcher wins the national election, a major milestone of Britain's 20th-century history, ushering in a decade of dramatic political and social change.

» Margaret Thatcher

1982

Britain is victorious in a war against Argentina over the invasion of the Falkland Islands, leading to a rise in patriotic sentiment.

than five decades, overseeing a period of massive social and economic change.

By the late 1950s, recovery was strong enough for Prime Minister Harold Macmillan to famously remind the British people they had 'never had it so good'. Some saw this as a boast for a confident future, others as a warning about difficult times ahead, but most probably forgot all about it because by this time the 1960s had started and grey old Britain was suddenly more fun and lively than it had been for generations – especially if you were over 10 and under 30. There was the music of the Beatles, the Rolling Stones and Cliff Richard and the Shadows, while cinema audiences flocked to see Michael Caine, Peter Sellers and Glenda Jackson.

Alongside the glamour, 1960s business seemed swinging too. But by the 1970s economic decline had set in again. A deadly combination of

CHURCHILL: LIFE & LEGACY

Although he was from an aristocratic family, Churchill's early years were not auspicious; he was famously a 'dunce' at school – an image he actively cultivated in later life.

As a young man Churchill joined the British Army, and in 1901 he was elected to parliament as a Conservative MP. In 1904 he defected to the Liberals, the main opposition party at the time. A year later, after a Liberal election victory, he became a government minister.

Churchill rejoined the Conservatives in 1922, and held various ministerial positions through the rest of the 1920s. Notable statements during this period included calling Mussolini a 'genius' and Gandhi 'a half-naked fakir'.

The 1930s Churchill criticised Prime Minister Neville Chamberlain's 'appeasement' of Hitler and called for British rearmament to face a growing German threat, but his political life was generally quiet – so he concentrated on writing. His multi-volume *History of the English-Speaking Peoples* was drafted during this period; although biased and flawed by modern standards, it remains his best-known work.

In 1939 Britain entered WWII, and by 1940 Churchill was prime minister, taking additional responsibility as minister of defence. Hitler had expected an easy victory, but Churchill's extraordinary dedication (not to mention his radio speeches – most famously offering 'nothing but blood, toil, sweat and tears' and promising to 'fight on the beaches') inspired the British people to resist.

Between July and October 1940 the Royal Air Force withstood Germany's aerial raids to win what became known as the Battle of Britain – a major turning point in the war, and a chance for land forces to rebuild their strength. It was an audacious strategy, but it paid off and Churchill was lauded as a national hero – praise that continued to the end of the war, beyond his death in 1965, and up to today.

1990

Mrs Thatcher ousted as leader and the Conservative party enters a period of decline but remains in power thanks to inept Labour opposition.

1992

Labour remains divided between traditionalists and modernists. The Conservatives, under their new leader John Major, confound the pundits and unexpectedly win the general election.

1997

The general election sees Tony Blair lead 'New' Labour to victory in the polls, with a record-breaking parliamentary majority, ending more than 20 years of Tory rule.

1999

The first National Assembly is elected for Wales, with the members sitting in a new building in Cardiff; Rhodri Morgan becomes First Minister.

inflation, the oil crisis and international competition revealed the weakness of Britain's economy, and a lot that was rotten in British society too. The ongoing struggle between the ruling classes and the disgruntled working classes was brought to the boil once again; the rest of the decade was marked by strikes, disputes and all-round gloom – especially when the electricity was cut, as power stations went short of fuel or labour.

Even when 'local' reserves of oil and gas were discovered in the North Sea, off Britain's northeast coast, things improved only slightly. Prosperity came to the Aberdeen area and the Shetland Islands in Scotland, but most of the revenue was pipelined back to England. This, along with takeovers of many Scottish companies by English ones, fuelled increasing nationalist sentiment in Scotland.

Neither the Conservatives – also known as the Tories – under Edward Heath, nor Labour under Harold Wilson and Jim Callaghan proved capable of controlling the strife. The British public had had enough, and in the elections of 1979, the Conservatives won a landslide victory, led by a little-known politician named Margaret Thatcher.

THATCHER

One of Us: A Biography of Mrs Thatcher by respected journalist and commentator Hugo Young covers the early life of the 'iron lady' and her time in power – showing that her grip on events, and on her own party, wasn't as steely as it seemed.

The Thatcher Years

Soon everyone had heard of Mrs Thatcher. (As Britain's first female prime minister she was always known as *Mrs* Thatcher – at least by her supporters.) Love her or hate her, no one could argue that her methods weren't direct and dramatic. The industries nationalised in the late 1940s were now seen as inefficient and a drain on resources, so they were sold off with a sense of purpose that made Henry VIII's dissolution of the monasteries seem like a Sunday-school picnic.

Naturally, these moves were opposed by those working in the nationalised industries (and many other sections of society) via strikes, marches and demonstrations, but the Thatcher government waged a relentless assault on the power of trade unions, fronted by the closure of 'uneconomic' coal mines throughout Britain – most notably in the English Midlands, South Wales and parts of Scotland. In response, the nationwide strike by miners in the early 1980s was one of the most bitter labour disputes in British history, but Mrs Thatcher was victorious and the pit closures went ahead. (Since 1984 around 140 coal pits have closed, meaning a quarter of a million jobs lost, with major impacts on surrounding communities.)

And on top of all that, just in case there was any doubt about Mrs Thatcher's patriotism, in 1982 she led Britain into war against Argentina in a dispute over the Falkland Islands, leading to a bout of public flag-waving that hadn't been seen since WWII, or probably since Agincourt.

Looking back from a 21st-century vantage point, most commentators agree that by economic measures Mrs Thatcher's policies were largely

1999–2004

Scottish Parliament is convened for the first time on 12 May 1999. Five years later, after plenty of scandal and huge sums of money, a new parliament building is opened at Holyrood in Edinburgh.

JONATHAN SMITH

» Scottish parliament building (p767), Holyrood

2001

Tony Blair and Labour continue to enjoy a honeymoon period and another victory at the 2001 general election – although their majority is reduced.

successful, but by social measures they were a failure. The new competitive Britain created by the Thatcher government's monetarist policies was now a greatly polarised Britain. Once again a trench formed, but not between the classes; this time it was between the people who gained from the prosperous wave of Thatcherism and those left drowning in its wake – not only jobless, but jobless in a harsh environment. Even Thatcher fans were unhappy about the brutal and uncompromising methods favoured by the 'iron lady', but by 1988 she was the longest-serving British prime minister of the 20th century, although her repeated electoral victories were helped considerably by the Labour Party's total incompetence and destructive internal struggles.

Goodbye Margaret, Hello Tony

The pendulum started to swing in the early 1990s: Margaret Thatcher was finally dumped when her introduction of the hugely unpopular 'poll tax' breached even the Conservatives' limits of tolerance. The voters regarded Labour with even more suspicion, however, allowing new Conservative leader John Major to unexpectedly win the 1992 election.

Britain enjoyed another half-decade of political stalemate, as the Conservatives stagnated and Labour was rebuilt on the sidelines, but business continued to boom. In line with a global upswing, by the late 1990s the British economy was in better shape than it had been for years. In two decades the economic base had shifted massively from heavy industry and into the service industry. (Today the majority of Britons are employed in less labour-intensive light engineering, high-tech and electronic fields, including computers and telecommunications, and the finance and retail sectors.)

It all came to a head in the 1997 election, when 'New' Labour swept to power under fresh-faced leader Tony Blair. After nearly 18 years of Tory rule, to the majority of Brits it really seemed that Labour's rallying call ('things can only get better') was true – and some people literally danced in the street when the results were announced.

Things Can Only Get Better by John O'Farrell is a witty, self-deprecating tale of 1980s politics – the era of Conservative domination – from a struggling Labour viewpoint.

New Labour, New Millennium

Tony Blair and New Labour enjoyed an extended honeymoon period, and the next election (in 2001) was another walkover. The Conservative party continued to struggle, allowing Labour to win a historic third term in 2005, and a year later Mr Blair became the longest-serving Labour prime minister in British history. In 2010 a record 13 years of Labour rule came to an end, and a new coalition between the Conservative and Liberal-Democrat parties formed government.

2003

Britain joins America and other countries in the invasion of Iraq, initially with some support from parliament and public, despite large anti-war street demonstrations in London and other cities.

2005

Public support for the Iraq war wanes, and the Labour government faces several internal crises but still wins the general election for a historic third term.

2007

The Government of Wales Bill heralds the largest transfer of power from Westminster to Cardiff since the founding of the National Assembly.

2010

Labour is narrowly defeated in the general election as the minority Liberal-Democrats align with the Conservatives to form the first coalition government in Britain's postwar history.

The British Table

Once upon a time, British food was highly regarded. In the later medieval period and 17th century, many people – especially the wealthy – ate a varied diet. Then along came the Industrial Revolution, with mass migration from the country to the city, and food quality took a nosedive, a legacy that means there's still no English equivalent for the phrase *bon appétit*.

Today the tide has turned once again. A culinary landmark came in 2005, when food bible *Gourmet* magazine famously singled out London as having the best collection of restaurants in the world. In the years since then the choice for food lovers – whatever their budget – has continued to improve. London is now regarded as a global gastronomic capital, and it's increasingly easy to find decent food in other cities, towns and rural areas across Britain.

Having said that, a culinary heritage of ready-sliced white bread, fatty meats and vegetables boiled to death, all washed down by tea with four sugars, remains firmly in place in many parts of the country. But wherever you travel in Britain, for each greasy spoon or fast-food joint, there's a local pub or restaurant serving up enticing home-grown specialities. Epicures can splash out big bucks on fine dining, while the impecunious can also enjoy tasty eating that definitely won't break the bank.

According to leading organic-food campaign group the Soil Association (www.soilassociation.org), more than 85% of people in Britain want pesticide-free food. See www.whyorganic.org. for more information.

Eating in Britain

The infamous outbreaks of 'mad cow' disease in the 1990s are ancient history now, and British beef is once again exported to the world, but an upside of the bad press at the time was a massive surge in demand for good-quality food. Wherever you go in Britain, you'll find a plethora of organic, natural, unadulterated, chemical-free, free-range, hand-reared, nonintensive products available in shops, markets, cafes and restaurants.

Alongside this greater awareness of food quality and provenance, there have been other changes to British food thanks to outside influences. For decades most towns have boasted Chinese and Indian restaurants, so a vindaloo or a chow mein is no longer considered 'exotic'; in fact, curry is the most popular takeaway food, outstripping even fish and chips.

As well as the food available in Indian restaurants (which in many cases are actually owned, run and staffed by Pakistanis or Bangladesh-

EATING PRICE BANDS

In the restaurant reviews throughout this book, we've given an indication of their price-band.

- » £ means a budget place where a main dish is less than £9.
- » ££ means midrange; mains are £9 to £18
- » £££ means top end; mains are more than £18

is), dishes from Japan, Korea or Thailand and other Asian countries have become available in more recent times, too. From elsewhere in the world, there's been a growth in restaurants serving up South American, Middle Eastern, African and Caribbean cuisine. Closer to home, a wide range of Mediterranean dishes – from countries as diverse as Morocco and Greece – are commonplace, not only in smarter restaurants but also in everyday eateries.

The overall effect of these foreign influences has been the introduction to 'traditional' British cuisine of new techniques (eg steaming), new condiments (eg chilli or soy sauce), new implements (eg woks) and even revolutionary ingredients (eg crisp, fresh vegetables). So now we have 'modern British cuisine', where even humble bangers and mash rise to new heights when handmade pork, apple and thyme-flavoured sausages are paired with lightly chopped fennel and new potatoes, and 'fusion' dishes where native ingredients get new flavours from adding, for example, Oriental spices.

Perhaps the best example of fusion cuisine – although purist foodies will wince – is chicken tikka masala, the UK's favourite 'Indian' dish created specifically for the British palate and unheard of in India itself.

But beware the hype. While some restaurants in Britain experiment with new ideas and are undeniably excellent, others are not. Only a few months after *Gourmet* magazine called the capital 'the best place in the world to eat right now', one of the country's most respected food critics, the *Evening Standard*'s Fay Maschler, decried the domination of style over substance, and accused several top eateries of offering poor value for money, reiterating what any food fan will tell you: you're often better spending £5 on a top-notch curry in Birmingham or a homemade steak-and-ale pie in a country pub in Devon than forking out £30 in a restaurant for a 'modern European' concoction that tastes like it came from a can.

Of course, there's more to food than eating out. The lavishly illustrated food sections in weekend newspapers and the bookshop shelves groaning under the weight of countless new cookery books all indicate that food is now officially fashionable. Feeding on this are the so-called 'celebrity chefs', including Hugh Fernley-Whittingstall, who famously scored a £2 million deal with his publishers in the heady pre-recession days of 2006, and Gordon Ramsay, who featured in a list of Britain's richest self-made entrepreneurs a few months later. They are not alone; every night on a TV channel near you a star of the kitchen demonstrates imaginative and simple techniques for producing stylish, tasty and healthy food.

There's change afoot in the shops too. Supermarkets still dominate – four companies (Asda Wal-Mart, Morrisons, Sainsbury's, Tesco) account for around 80% of all grocery shopping – squeezing suppliers to sell at ever-lower prices, while forcing out old-fashioned butchers and bakers from high streets and neighbourhoods, but they're selling more organic food than ever before, and new labels show just how much fat, salt and sugar the foodstuffs contain.

In October 2009 Phaidon Press published a book called *Coco*, subtitled *10 World-Leading Masters Choose 100 Contemporary Chefs*. Of the up-and-coming culinary stars selected by the experts, 13 were based in London – presumably much to the scorn of food fans of New York (eight chefs selected) and Paris (just five).

Alongside these changes there's an increase in the number of independent shops selling high-quality food, while the relatively new phenomenon of farmers markets creates an opportunity for food producers to sell locally sourced meat, veg, fruit, eggs, honey and so on direct to the public. And they're not just in country towns where you might expect to see them, but in cities too: there are around 20 farmers markets in London alone.

But behind the scenes, and despite the growing availability of good food in shops, markets, pubs and restaurants, many British folk still have an odd attitude to eating at home. They love to sit on the sofa and *watch* TV food shows. Then, inspired, they rush out and buy all the TV-tie-in recipe books. Then on the way back, they pop into the supermarket and buy a stack of ready-made meals. Homemade food sounds great in theory, but in reality the recipe for dinner is more likely to be something like this: open freezer, take out package, throw in microwave, ping, eat.

Most farmers markets around England are certified as genuine by the Farmers' Retail & Markets Association (FARMA). The 2009 Market of the Year awards went to Brigg Farmers' Market in North Lincolnshire and Moseley Farmers' Market in Birmingham. For more information and a list of farmers markets around the country, see www.farmersmarkets.net.

In fact, more junk food and ready-made meals are consumed in the UK than in all the rest of the countries of Europe put together. So it's no surprise that the British are getting increasingly heavy, with around 50% of the adult population overweight and almost 25% obese. But despite the vast intakes, average nutrition rates are lower now than they were during 1950s postwar rationing.

So in summary: yes, as a local or a visitor you can definitely find great food in Britain. It's just that not all the British seem to like eating it.

The Full British

Although grazing on a steady supply of snacks is increasingly commonplace in Britain, as it is in many other industrialised nations, the British culinary day is still punctuated by the three traditional main meals of breakfast, lunch and dinner. And just to keep you on your toes, those very same meals are also called – depending on social class and geographical location – breakfast, dinner and tea.

Breakfast

Most working people make do with a bowl of cereal before dashing to the office or factory, but visitors staying in B&Bs will undoubtedly encounter a phenomenon called the 'Full English Breakfast' – or one of its regional equivalents. This usually consists of bacon, sausages, eggs, tomatoes, mushrooms, baked beans and fried bread, In Scotland the 'full Scottish breakfast' might include oatcakes instead of fried bread. In Wales you may be offered *lavabread* – not a bread at all but seaweed, a tasty speciality often served with oatmeal and bacon on toast. In northern England you may get black pudding (see Regional Specialties). And just in case you thought this insufficient, it's still preceded by cereal, and followed by toast and marmalade.

If you don't feel like eating half a farmyard first thing in the morning, it's OK to ask for just the egg and tomatoes, for example, while some B&Bs offer other alternatives such as kippers (smoked fish) or a 'continental breakfast' – which completely omits the cooked stuff and may even add something exotic such as croissants.

Lunch

For the midday meal, one of the many great inventions that Britain gave the world is the sandwich. Slapping a slice of cheese or ham between two bits of bread may seem a simple concept, but no one apparently thought of it until the 18th century when the Earl of Sandwich (his title comes from a town in southeast England – Sandwich – that originally gets its name from the Viking word for sandy beach) ordered his servants to bring cold meat between bread so he could keep working at his desk or, as some historians claim, keep playing cards late at night. Of course, the noble earl didn't really invent the idea – various cultures around the world had been doing it for millennia – but the name stuck and the sandwich became a fashionable food for the aristocracy. Its popularity grew among the lower classes in the early days of the Industrial Revolution – labourers heading for mines and mills needed a handy way to carry their midday meal – and today it's the staple of office and factory workers everywhere.

Like meat, but not battery pens? Go to the Royal Society for the Prevention of Cruelty to Animals (www.rspca.org.uk) and follow links to Freedom Food.

A favourite sandwich ingredient is Marmite, a dark and pungent yeast extract that generations of British kids have loved or hated. Ei-

THE PIG, THE WHOLE SHEEP & NOTHING BUT THE COW

One of the many trends enjoyed by modern British cuisine is the revival of 'nose to tail' cooking – that is, using the whole animal, not just the more obvious cuts such as chops and fillet steaks. This does not mean boiling or grilling a pig or sheep all in one go – although spit-roasts are popular. It means utilising the parts that may at first seem unappetising or, frankly, inedible. So as well as dishes involving liver, heart, chitterlings (intestines) and other offal, traditional delights such as bone marrow on toast or tripe (stomach) and onions once again grace the menus of fashionable restaurants. The movement is particularly spearheaded by chef Fergus Henderson at his St John restaurant in London (p115), and via his influential recipe book *Nose to Tail Eating: A Kind of British Cooking* and 2007's follow-up *Beyond Nose To Tail*.

ther way, it's a passion that continues through adulthood. In 2006, when the manufacturer of Marmite moved from selling the stuff in a near-spherical glass jar to a (more practical) plastic tube, much was the consternation across the land. Similar to the Australian icon, Vegemite (but not the same – oh no, sir!), it's also popular on toast at breakfast and especially great for late-night munchies.

Another British classic that perhaps epitomises British food more than any other – especially in pubs – is the ploughman's lunch. Basically it's bread and cheese, and although hearty yokels probably did carry such food to the fields (no doubt wrapped in a red spotted handkerchief) over many centuries, the meal is actually a modern phenomenon. It was invented in the 1960s by the marketing chief of the national cheese-makers' organisation as a way to boost consumption, neatly cashing in on public nostalgia and fondness for tradition.

You can still find a basic ploughman's lunch offered in some pubs – and it undeniably goes well with a pint or two of local ale at lunchtime – but these days the meal has usually been smartened up to include butter, salad, pickle, pickled onion and dressings. At some pubs you get a selection of cheeses. You'll also find other variations, such as a farmer's lunch (bread and chicken), stockman's lunch (bread and ham), Frenchman's lunch (brie and baguette) and fisherman's lunch (you guessed it, with fish).

For cheese and bread in a different combination, try Welsh rarebit – a sophisticated variation of cheese on toast, seasoned and flavoured with butter, milk and sometimes a little beer. Other traditional Welsh dishes include *cawl* (a thick broth) and for a takeaway lunch in Scotland, look out for *stovies* (tasty pies of meat, mashed onion and fried potato) and Scotch pies (hard-cased pies of minced meat, sometimes eaten cold). In restaurants and cafes, Scotch broth (a thick soup of barley, lentils and mutton stock) is sometimes offered as a starter, but it's filling enough as a meal in itself.

In the 16th century, Queen Elizabeth I decreed that mutton could only be served with bitter herbs – intended to stop people eating sheep in order to help the wool trade – but her subjects discovered mint sauce improved taste, and it's been roast lamb's favourite condiment ever since.

Dinner

For generations, a typical British dinner has been 'meat and two veg'. Dressed up as 'supper' or dressed down as 'cooked tea', there was little variation: the meat is pork, beef or lamb, one of the veg is potatoes and the other would inevitably be carrots, cabbage or cauliflower – and just as inevitably cooked long and hard. Although tastes and diets are changing, this classic combination still graces the tables of many British families several times a week.

Traditionally, the meat is roast beef (that's why the French call the British 'les rosbif'), and good-quality cuts from well-reared cattle grace menus everywhere from Cornwall to the Highlands. Perhaps the most famous beef comes from Scotland's Aberdeen Angus cattle, while the best-known food from Wales is lamb (although a lowly vegetable, the leek, is a national emblem). Venison – usually from red deer – is readily available in Scotland, as well as in parts of Wales and England, most notably in the New Forest.

And with the beef – especially at Sunday lunches – comes Yorkshire pudding. It's simply roast batter, but is very tasty when properly cooked. Another classic British dish brings Yorkshire pudding and sausages together, with the delightful name of 'toad-in-the-hole'.

Yorkshire pudding also turns up at dinner in another guise, especially in pubs and cafes in northern England, where menus may offer a big bowl-shaped Yorkshire pudding filled with meat stew, beans or vegetables. You can even find Yorkshire puddings filled with curry – a favourite multicultural crossover that says something about British society today.

In Yorkshire, the eponymous pudding is traditionally a starter, a reminder of days when food was scarce and the pudding was a pre-meal stomach-filler.

YORKSHIRE PUDDING

North of the border, you'll be introduced to haggis, Scotland's national dish, essentially a large sausage made from a sheep's stomach filled with minced meat and oatmeal. It's often available in restaurants, and also deep-fried at takeaways. If you're wary, search the menu for Highland chicken, a meal that stuffs portions of haggis mix into baked chicken – that way you can sample a small serving.

Scottish salmon is also well known, and available everywhere in Britain smoked or poached, but there's a big difference between bland fatty salmon from fish farms and the lean tasty wild version. The latter is more expensive, but as well as the taste, there are sound environmental reasons for preferring the nonfarmed variety. Other British seafood includes herring, trout and haddock; in Scotland the latter is best enjoyed with potato and cream in the old-style soup called *cullen skink*.

But perhaps the best-known fish dish is the British classic, fish and chips, often bought from the 'chippie' as a takeaway wrapped in paper to enjoy at home – especially popular with families on a Friday night. Later in the evening, epicures may order their fish and chips 'open' to eat immediately while walking back from the pub. It has to be said that quality varies outrageously; sometimes the chips can be limp and soggy, and fish can be greasy and tasteless, especially once you get away from the sea, but in towns with salt in the air this classic deep-fried delight is always worth trying.

Puddings

After the main course – usually at an evening meal, or if you're enjoying a hearty lunch – comes dessert or 'pudding'. A classic British pudding is rhubarb crumble, the juicy stem of a large-leafed garden plant, stewed and sweetened, then topped with a crunchy mix of flour, butter and more sugar – and served with custard or ice cream. For much of the 20th century, rhubarb was a very popular food, with overnight trains dubbed the 'rhubarb express' bringing huge cargoes of the stuff to London and the cities of the southern England from the farms of the north. The main growing area was between the Yorkshire towns of Leeds, Wakefield and Morely, known – inevitably – as the 'rhubarb triangle'. It

VEGETARIANS & VEGANS

It's official vegetarians are no longer unusual. Many restaurants and pubs in Britain have at least one token vegetarian dish (another meat-free lasagne, anyone?), but better places offer much more imaginative choices. Vegans will find the going trickier, except of course at dedicated veggie/vegan restaurants – and where possible we recommend good options throughout this book. For more ideas see www.happycow.com.

fell out of fashion around the 1980s but is currently enjoying a renaissance in gourmet restaurants as well as humble kitchens.

Moving onto another sweet option, Bakewell pudding blundered into the recipe books around 1860 when a cook at the Rutland Arms Hotel in the Derbyshire town of Bakewell was making a strawberry tart, but mistakenly (some stories say drunkenly) spread the egg mixture on top of the jam instead of stirring it into the pastry. Especially in northern England, the Bakewell pudding (pudding, mark you, not 'Bakewell tart' as it's sometimes erroneously called) features regularly on local dessert menus and is certainly worth sampling.

More of a cake than a pudding, Welsh speciality *bara brith* (spicy fruit loaf) is a delight, while Scottish bakeries usually offer milk scones and griddle scones as well as plain varieties. Other sweet temptations include *bannocks* (half-scone, half-pancake), shortbread (a sweet biscuit) and Dundee cake (a rich fruit mix topped with almonds).

Other favourite British puddings include treacle sponge, bread-and-butter pudding and plum pudding, a dome-shaped cake with fruit, nuts and brandy or rum, traditionally eaten at Christmas when it's called – surprise, surprise – Christmas pudding. This pudding is steamed (rather than baked), cut into slices and served with brandy butter. It's eaten after the traditional Christmas lunch of roast turkey, and shortly before the traditional sleep on the sofa when the annual Queen's speech airs on TV. Watch out for coins inserted in the pudding by superstitious cooks – if you bite one it means good luck for the next year, but it may play havoc with your fillings.

While key ingredients of most puddings are self-explanatory, they are perhaps not so obvious for another well-loved favourite: spotted dick. But fear not. The origin of 'dick' in this context is unclear (it may be a corruption of 'dough' or derived from the German *dicht* [thick] or even from 'spotted dog') but the ingredients are easy: it's just a white suet pudding dotted with black currants. Plus sugar, of course. Most British puddings have loads of butter or loads of sugar, preferably both. Light, subtle and healthy? Not on your life.

To polish off our tour de table, and staying with the sweet stuff, a reminder that the international favourite banoffee pie (a delightfully sticky dessert made from bananas and toffee) is also an British invention, first developed in a pub in Sussex in southern England in the early 1970s. A plaque on the wall of the pub proudly commemorates this landmark culinary event.

Sherry trifle was considered the height of sophistication at dinner parties of the 1970s, then fell out of fashion, but after a few decades this combination of custard, fruit, sponge cake, whipped cream, and – of course – sherry is now considered a classic, and is enjoying a renaissance in many English restaurants.

Regional Specialities

With Britain's large coastline, it's no surprise that seafood is a speciality in many parts of the country. If fish is your thing, head for Yorkshire's seaside resorts – particularly famous for huge servings of cod, despite it becoming an endangered species thanks to overfishing – while restaurants in Devon and Cornwall regularly conjure up prawns, lobster, oysters, mussels and scallops. Local seafood you may encounter elsewhere on your travels includes Norfolk crab, Northumberland kippers, and jellied eels in London, while restaurants in Scotland, west Wales and southwest England regularly conjure up prawns, lobsters, oysters, mussels and scallops.

Meat-based treats in northern and central England include Cumberland sausage – a tasty mix of minced pork and herbs, so large it has to be spiralled to fit on your plate – and Melton Mowbray pork pies (motto: 'gracious goodness for over 100 years'), which is cooked ham compressed in a casing of pastry and always eaten cold, ideally with pickle. A legal victory in 2005 ensured that only pies made in the eponymous

NAME THAT PASTY

A favourite speciality in southwest England is the Cornish pasty. Originally a mix of cooked vegetables wrapped in pastry, it's often available in meat varieties (much to the scorn of the Cornish people) and now sold everywhere in Britain. Invented long before Tupperware, the pasty was an all-in-one-lunch pack that tin miners carried underground and left on a ledge ready for mealtime. So pasties weren't mixed up, they were marked with their owners' initials – always at one end, so the miner could eat half and safely leave the rest to snack on later without it mistakenly disappearing into the mouth of a workmate. Before going back to the surface, the miners traditionally left the last few crumbs of the pasty as a gift for the spirits of the mine, known as 'knockers', to ensure a safe shift the next day.

Midlands town could carry the Melton Mowbray moniker – in the same way that fizzy wine from other regions can't be called Champagne.

Another British speciality that enjoys the same protection is Stilton – a strong white cheese, either plain or in a blue vein variety. Only five dairies all of Britain – four in the Vale of Belvoir, and one in Derbyshire – are allowed to produce cheese with this name. Bizarrely, the cheese cannot be made in the village of Stilton in Cambridgeshire, although this is where it was first sold – hence the name.

Eggs, Bacon, Chips & Beans by Russell Davies showcases 50 of the UK's finest traditional cafes, with tongue-in-cheek taster's notes on their various versions of the traditional fry-up.

Perhaps less appealing is black pudding, effectively a large sausage made from ground meat, offal, fat and blood, and traditionally served for breakfast. It's known in other countries as 'blood sausage', but the British version has a high content of oatmeal so that it doesn't fall apart in the pan when fried.

Eating Out

In Britain, 'eating out' means simply going to a restaurant or cafe – anywhere away from home. There's a huge choice across the country, and this section outlines just some of your options. For details on opening times, see p1057. The tricky issue of tipping is covered on p1061.

Picnics & Self-catering

When shopping for food, as well as the more obvious chain stores and corner shops, markets can be a great place for bargains – everything from dented tins of tomatoes to home-baked cakes and organic goat's cheese. Farmers markets are always worth a browse; they're a great way for producers to sell good food direct to consumers, with both sides avoiding the grip of the supermarkets.

Cafes & Teashops

Teashops are your best bet for sampling a 'cream tea' – a plate of scones, clotted cream and jam, served with a pot of tea.

The traditional British cafe is nothing like its continental European namesake. For a start, asking for a brandy with your coffee may cause confusion, as cafes in Britain rarely serve alcohol. Most are simple places serving simple meals such as a meat pie, beans on toast, baked potato or omelette with chips (costing around £3 to £4) and sandwiches, cakes and other snacks (£1 to £2). Quality varies enormously: some cafes definitely earn their 'greasy spoon' handle, while others are neat and clean.

In London and some other cities, a rearguard of classic cafes – with formica tables, seats in booths and decor unchanged from the their 1950s glory days – stand against the onslaught of the international chains. In rural areas, many market towns and villages have cafes catering for tourists, walkers, cyclists and other outdoor types, and in summer they're open every day. Whether you're in town or country, good British cafes are a wonderful institution and always worth a stop during your travels.

Smarter cafes are called teashops – also more often found in country areas – where you might pay a bit more for extras like quaint decor and table service. Teashops are your best bet for sampling a 'cream tea' – a plate of scones, clotted cream and jam, served with a pot of tea. This is known as a Devonshire tea in some other English-speaking countries, but not in Britain (except of course in the county of Devon, where it's a well-known – and much-hyped – local speciality).

As well as the traditional establishments, in most cities and towns you'll also find American-flavoured coffee shops – the inevitable Starbucks on every corner – and a growing number of Euro-style cafe-bars, serving decent lattes and espressos, and offering bagels or ciabattas rather than beans on toast (you'll probably be able to get that brandy, too). Some of these modern places even have outdoor chairs and tables – rather brave considering the narrow pavements and inclement weather much of Britain enjoys.

Restaurants

London has scores of excellent restaurants that could hold their own in major cities worldwide, while places in Bath, Cardiff, Manchester and Edinburgh can give the capital a fair run for its money (often for rather less money). We've taken great pleasure in seeking out some of the best and best-value restaurants in Britain, and have recommended a small selection throughout this book.

Prices vary considerably across the country, with a main course in a straightforward restaurant costing around £9 or less, and anywhere between £10 and £18 at midrange places. Utterly excellent food, service and surroundings can be enjoyed for £20 to £50 – although in London you can, if you want, pay double this.

Pubs & Gastropubs

Not so many years ago, a pub was the place to go for a drink. And that was it. If you felt peckish, your choice might be ham or cheese roll, with pickled onions if you were lucky. Today it's totally different. Many pubs sell a wide range of food, and some pubs sell more food than drink. And pub food is often a good-value option, whether you want a toasted sandwich between museum visits in London, or a three-course meal in the evening after touring the castles of Wales.

While the food in many pubs is good quality and good value, some raised the bar to such a degree that a whole new genre of eatery – the gastropub – was born. While some gastropubs are almost restaurants in style (with smart decor, neat menus and uniformed table service) others have gone for a more relaxed atmosphere where you'll find mismatched cutlery, no tablecloths, waiters in T-shirts and today's

RICK STEIN

Rick Stein is a TV chef, energetic restaurateur and good-food evangelist. His books *Food Heroes* and *Food Heroes: Another Helping* extol small-scale producers and top-notch local food, from organic veg to wild boar sausages.

WHERE THERE'S SMOKE...

All restaurants and cafes in Britain are nonsmoking throughout. Virtually all pubs have the same rule, which is why there's often a small crowd of smokers standing on the pavement outside. Some pubs provide specific outdoor smoking areas, ranging from a simple yard to elaborate gazebos with canvas walls and the full complement of lighting, heating, piped music and TV screens – where you'd never need to know you were 'outside' at all, apart from the pungent clouds of burning tobacco. It is permitted to smoke in pub gardens, such that nonsmokers sometimes need to go *inside* to escape the fumes.

choices chalked up on a blackboard. And in true pub style, you order and pay at the bar, just as you do for your drinks. The key for all, though, is top-notch no-frills food. For visitors relaxing after a hard day doing the sights, nothing beats the luxury of a wholesome shepherd's pie washed down with a decent ale without the worry of guessing which fork to use.

Drinking in Britain

Among alcoholic drinks, Britain is probably best known for its beer, and as you travel around the country, you should definitely try some local brew.

British beer typically ranges from dark brown to bright orange in colour, and is often served at room temperature. Technically it's called ale and is more commonly called 'bitter'. This is to distinguish it from lager – the drink that most of the rest of the word calls 'beer' – which is generally yellow and served cold.

The Campaign for Real Ale promotes the understanding of traditional British beer. Look for endorsement stickers on pub windows, and for more info see www.camra .org.uk.

Bitter that's traditionally brewed and served is called 'real ale' to distinguish it from mass-produced brands, and there the many different varieties around England. But be ready! If you're used to the 'amber nectar' or 'king of beers', a local English brew may come as a shock – a warm, flat and expensive shock. This is partly to do with England's climate, and partly to do with the beer being served by hand pump rather than gas pressure. Most important, though, is the integral flavour: traditional English beer doesn't need to be chilled or fizzed to make it palatable.

Another key feature is that real ale must be looked after, usually meaning a willingness on the part of the pub manager or landlord to put in extra effort – often translating into extra effort on food, atmosphere, cleanliness and so on, too. But the extra effort is why many pubs don't serve real ale, so beware of places where bar staff give the barrels as much care as they give the condom machine in the toilets. There's honestly nothing worse than a bad pint of real ale.

If beer doesn't tickle your palate, try cider – available in sweet and dry varieties. In western parts of England, notably Herefordshire and the southwestern counties such as Devon and Somerset, you could try 'scrumpy', a very strong dry cider traditionally made from local apples. Many pubs serve it straight from the barrel.

On hot summer days, you could go for shandy – beer and lemonade mixed in equal quantities. You'll usually need to specify 'lager shandy' or 'bitter shandy'. It may seem an astonishing combination for outsiders, but it's very refreshing and of course not very strong. Another hybrid is 'snakebite', an equal mix of cider and lager, favoured by students

THE OLDEST PUB IN BRITAIN?

Many drinkers are often surprised to learn that the word 'pub', short for 'public house', although apparently steeped in history, dates only from the 19th century. But places selling beer have been around for much longer, and the 'oldest pub in Britain' is a hotly contested title.

One of the country's oldest pubs, with the paperwork to prove it, is Ye Olde Trip to Jerusalem (Nottingham, p439), which was serving ale to departing crusaders in the 12th century.

Other contenders sniff that Ye Trip is a mere newcomer. A fine old inn called the Royalist Hotel in Stow-on-the-Wold (Gloucestershire, p202) claims to have been selling beer since around AD 947, while another pub called Ye Olde Fighting Cocks in St Albans (Hertfordshire, p215) apparently dates back to the 8th century – although the 13th is more likely.

But then back comes Ye Olde Trip with a counter-claim: one of its bars is a cave hollowed out of living rock, and that's more than a million years old.

TEA FOR TWO

In Britain, a drink means any ingestible liquid, so if you're from overseas and a local asks 'would you like a drink?', don't automatically expect a gin and tonic. They may well mean a 'cuppa' – a cup of tea – Britain's best-known beverage. Tea is sometimes billed as the national drink, although coffee is equally popular these days; the Brits consume 165 million cups a day and the British coffee market is worth almost £700 million a year – but with the prices some coffee shops charge, maybe that's not surprising. And a final word of warning: when you're ordering a coffee and the server says 'white or black', don't panic. It simply means 'do you want milk in it?'

as it's a cost-efficient way to get drunk, thanks to the lager's bubbles and the cider's strength – the very reason some pubs refuse to serve it.

Back to more sensible tipples, many visitors are surprised to learn that wine is produced in Britain, and has been since the time of the Romans. Today, more than 400 vineyards and wineries produce around two million bottles a year – many highly regarded and frequently winning major awards. English white sparkling wines have been a particular success story in recent years, with many produced in the southeast of the country where the chalky soil and climatic conditions are similar to those of the Champagne region in France.

Moving on to something stronger, the usual arrays of gin, vodka, rum and so on are served in pubs and bars, but the spirit most visitors associate with Britain – and especially Scotland – is whisky (note the spelling – it's *Irish* whiskey that has an 'e'). More than 2000 brands are produced, but the two main kinds are single malt, made from malted barley, and blended whisky, made from unmalted grain blended with malts. Single malts are rarer (there are only about 100 brands) and more expensive.

When ordering a dram in Scotland remember to ask for whisky – only the English and other foreigners say 'Scotch' (what else would you be served in Scotland?). And if you're bemused by the wide choice, ask to try a local whisky – although if your budget is low, you might want to check the price first. A measure of blended whisky costs around £2, a straightforward single malt around £3, while a rare classic could be £10 or more.

Bars & Pubs

In Britain the difference between a bar and a pub is sometimes vague, but generally bars are smarter, larger and louder than pubs, possibly with a younger crowd. Drinks are more expensive too, unless there's a gallon-of-vodka-and-Red-Bull-for-a-fiver promotion – which there often is.

As well as beer, cider, wine and the other drinks mentioned earlier in this chapter, pubs and bars offer the usual choice of spirits, often served with a 'mixer', producing English favourites such as gin and tonic, rum and coke or vodka and lime. These drinks are served in measures called 'singles' and 'doubles'. A single is 35ml – just over one US fluid ounce. A double is of course 70ml – still disappointingly small when compared with measures in other countries. To add further to your disappointment, the vast array of cocktail options, as found in America, is generally restricted to more upmarket city bars in Britain.

And while we're serving out warnings, here are two more: first, if you see a pub calling itself a 'free house', it's simply a place that doesn't belong to a brewery or pub company, and thus is 'free' to sell any brand of beer. Unfortunately, it doesn't mean the booze is free of charge. Second, remember that drinks in English pubs are ordered and paid for at the

Tipplers' tomes: *Good Beer Guide to Great Britain*, by the Campaign for Real Ale, *Good Pub Guide*, by Alisdair Aird and Fiona Stapley, and *300 Beers to Try Before you Die*, by Roger Protz.

EARLY DOORS, LATE NIGHTS

Pubs in towns and country areas usually open daily from 11am to 11pm Sunday to Thursday and sometimes to midnight or 1am Friday and Saturday. Most open all day, although some may shut from 3pm to 6pm. Throughout this book, we don't list pub opening and closing times unless they vary significantly from these hours.

In cities, some pubs open until midnight or later, but it's mostly bars and clubs that take advantage of new licensing laws ('the provision of late-night refreshment', as it's officially and charmingly called) to stay open to 1am, 2am or later. As every place is different, we list opening hours for all bars and clubs.

bar. You can always spot the freshly arrived tourists – they're the ones sitting forlornly at a empty table hoping to spot a waiter.

When it comes to gratuities, it's not usual to tip pub and bar staff. However, if you're ordering a large round, or the service has been good all evening, you can say to the person behind the bar '...and one for yourself'. They may not have a drink, but they'll add the monetary equivalent to the total you pay and keep it as a tip.

Apart from good service, what makes a good pub? It's often surprisingly hard to pin down, but in our opinion the best pubs follow a remarkably simple formula: they offer a welcoming atmosphere, pleasant surroundings, a good range of hand-pulled beer and a good menu of snacks and meals – cooked on the premises, not shipped in by the truck-full and defrosted in the microwave.

After months of painstaking research, this is the type of pub we recommend throughout this book. But, of course, there are many more pubs in Britain than even we could sample, and nothing beats the fun of doing your own research. So, armed with the advice in this chapter, we urge you to get out there and tipple your taste buds.

Food & Drink Glossary

aubergine	large purple-skinned vegetable; 'eggplant' in the USA and Australia
bangers	sausages (colloquial)
bap	a large, wide, flat, soft bread roll
bevvy	drink (originally from northern England)
bill	the total you need to pay after eating in a restaurant ('check' to Americans)
bitter	a type of ale
black pudding	type of sausage made from dried blood and other ingredients
bun	bread roll, usually sweet, eg currant bun, cream bun
BYO	bring your own (usually in the context of bringing your own drink to a restaurant)
caff	abbreviated form of cafe
candy floss	light sugar-based confectionary; called 'cotton candy' in the USA and 'fairy floss' in Australia
chips	sliced, deep-fried potatoes, eaten hot (what Americans call 'fries')
cider	alcoholic drink made from apples
clotted cream	cream so heavy or rich that it's become almost solid (but not sour)

corkage	a small charge levied by the restaurant when you *BYO*
courgette	green vegetable ('zucchini' to Americans and Australians)
cream cracker	white unsalted savoury biscuit
cream tea	pot of tea and a scone loaded with *jam* and *clotted cream*
crisps	thin slices of fried potato bought in a packet, eaten cold; called 'chips' or 'potato chips' in the USA and Australia
crumpet	circular piece of doughy bread, toasted before eating, usually covered with butter
double cream	heavy or thick cream
dram	whisky measure
fish fingers	strips of fish pieces covered in breadcrumbs, usually bought frozen, cooked by frying or grilling
greasy spoon	cheap cafe (colloquial)
ice lolly	flavoured ice on a stick; called 'popsicle' in the USA and 'icy pole' in Australia
icing	thick, sweet and solid covering on a cake
jam	fruit conserve often spread on bread; called 'jelly' in the USA
jelly	sweet dessert of flavoured gelatine; called 'jello' in the USA
joint	cut of meat used for roasting
kippers	salted and smoked fish, traditionally herring
pickle	a thick, vinegary vegetable-based condiment
Pimms	popular English spirit mixed with lemonade, mint and fresh fruit
pint	beer (as in 'let me buy you a pint')
salad cream	creamy vinegary salad dressing, much sharper than mayonnaise
scrumpy	a type of strong dry cider originally made in England's Westcountry; many pubs serve it straight from the barrel
shandy	beer and lemonade mixed together in equal quantities; when ordering, specify a bitter shandy or a lager shandy
shepherd's pie	two-layered oven dish with a ground beef and onion mixture on the bottom and mashed potato on the top on the top, cooked in the oven
shout	to buy a group of people drinks, usually reciprocated (colloquial)
single cream	light cream (to distinguish from *double cream* and *clotted cream*)
snakebite	equal mix of *cider* and lager; favoured by students as it reputedly gets you drunk quickly
snug	usually a small separate room in a pub
squash	fruit drink concentrate mixed with water
stout	dark, full-bodied beer made from malt; Guinness is the most famous variety
swede	large root vegetable; sometimes called 'yellow turnip' or 'rutabaga' in the USA
sweets	what Americans call 'candy' and Australians call 'lollies'
tipple	an old-fashioned word for drink, often used ironically, eg 'Do you fancy a tipple?'; a tippler is a drinker
treacle	molasses or dark syrup

Architecture in Britain

With an architectural heritage that stretches back three millennia or more, the many different buildings of Britain – from simple cottages to grand cathedrals – are an obvious highlight of any visit.

Early Foundations

The oldest buildings in the country are the grass-covered mounds of earth, called 'tumuli' or 'barrows', used as burial sites by Britain's prehistoric residents. These mounds – measuring anything from a rough semisphere just 2m high to much larger, elongated semi-ovoids 5m high and 10m long – are dotted across the countryside from Cornwall to Cumbria, and are especially common in chalk areas such as Salisbury Plain and the Wiltshire Downs in southern England.

Perhaps the most famous barrow – and certainly the largest and most mysterious – is Silbury Hill, near Marlborough. Historians are not sure exactly why this huge conical mound was built – there's no evidence of it actually being used for burial. Theories include the possibility of it being used at cultural ceremonies or as part of the worship of deities in the style of South American pyramids, but whatever the original purpose, it's still awe-inspiring today, many centuries after it was built.

Even more impressive than the giant tumuli are another legacy of the neolithic era: menhirs, or standing stones, especially well known when they're set out in rings. These include the iconic stone circle of Stonehenge and the even larger Avebury Stone Circle, both in Wiltshire

STANDING STONES

The Callanish Standing Stones on Scotland's Isle of Lewis, dating from 3800 to 5000 years ago, are even older than those at Stonehenge and Avebury.

Bronze Age & Iron Age

After the large stone circles of the neolithic era, the architecture of the Bronze Age that we can see today is on a more domestic scale. Hut circles from this period can still be seen in several parts of Britain, most notably on Dartmoor in Devon, while the Scottish islands also hold many of Europe's best surviving remains of Bronze Age and Iron Age times, such as the stone villages of Skara Brae in Orkney and Jarlshof in Shetland.

Also during the Iron Age, the early peoples of Britain were organising themselves into clans or tribes. Their legacy includes the forts they built to defend territory and protect themselves from rival tribes or other invaders. Most forts consisted of a large circular or oval ditch, with a steep mound of earth behind. A famous example is Maiden Castle in Dorset.

The Roman Era

Roman remains are found in many towns and cities, mostly in England and Wales as the Romans never colonised Scotland. There are impressive remains in Chester, Exeter and St Albans, as well as the lavish Roman spa and bathing complex in Bath, but Britain's largest and most impressive Roman relic is the 73-mile sweep of Hadrian's Wall, built in the 2nd century AD as a defensive line stretching coast to coast across the country. Originally built to separate marauding Pictish warriors to the north of the wall (in modern Scotland) from the Empire's territories to the south, it later became as much a symbol of Roman power as a necessary defence mechanism.

Castles & Cathedrals

In the centuries following the Norman Conquest of 1066, Britain saw an explosion of architecture inspired by the two most pressing concerns of the day: worship and defence. Churches, abbeys, monasteries and minsters sprang up during the early Middle Ages, as did many landmark cathedrals, such as Salisbury and Canterbury, and York Minster.

As for castles in Britain, you're spoilt for choice. Castles range from the atmospheric ruins of Tintagel and Dunstanburgh and the sturdy ramparts of Conwy and Beaumaris to the stunning crag-top fortresses of Sterling and Edinburgh. And then there's the most impressive of them all – the Tower of London, guardian of the capital for more than 900 years.

As well as many grand cathedrals, Britain has thousands of parish churches, many of historical or architectural significance, especially in rural areas.

Stately Homes

The medieval period was tumultuous, but by around 1600 life became more settled, and the nobility started to have less need for their castles. While they were excellent for keeping out rivals or the common riff-raff, they were often too cold and draughty to be comfortable. So many castles saw the home improvements of the day – the installation of larger windows, wider staircases and better drainage. Others were simply abandoned for a brand-new dwelling next door; an example of this is Hardwick Hall in Derbyshire.

Following the Civil War, the trend away from castles gathered pace; throughout the 17th century the landed gentry developed a taste for fine 'country houses' designed by the most famous architects of the day. Many became the 'stately homes' that are a major feature of the British landscape, and a major attraction for visitors. Among the most extravagant are Chatsworth House and Blenheim Palace in England, Powis Castle in Wales and Hopetoun House in Scotland.

The great stately homes all display the proportion, symmetry and architectural harmony so in vogue during the 17th and 18th centuries, styles later reflected in the fashionable town houses of the Georgian era – most notably in the city of Bath.

CHALK FIGURES

As you travel around Britain, look out for the chalk figures gracing many of the country's hilltops. They're made by cutting through the turf to reveal the white chalk soil below, so are most notably in Southwest England, especially the counties of Dorset and Wiltshire. Some figures, such as the Uffington White Horse, date from the Bronze Age, but most are more recent; the formidably endowed Cerne Abbas Giant is often thought to be an ancient pagan figure, although recent research suggests it was etched sometime in the 17th century.

The Victorian Era

The Victorian era was a time of great building. A style called Victorian-Gothic developed, echoing the towers and spires that were such a feature of the original Gothic cathedrals. The most famous example of this style is the Palace of Westminster, better known as the Houses of Parliament and the Tower of Big Ben, in London. Other highlights in England's capital include the Natural History Museum and St Pancras train station. The style was copied around the country, especially for civic buildings, the finest examples including Manchester Town Hall and Glasgow City Chambers.

Industrialisation

Through the late 19th and early 20th century, as Britain's cities grew in size and stature, the newly moneyed middle classes built streets and squares of smart town houses. In other suburbs, the first town planners oversaw the construction of endless terraces of 'back-to-back' and 'two-up-two-down' houses to accommodate the massive influx of workers required to fuel the country's factories. In South Wales, similar houses – though often single storey – were built for the burgeoning numbers of coal miners, while the industrial areas of Scotland saw the rise of 'tenements', usually three or four storeys with a central communal staircase and two dwelling on each floor. In many cases the terraced houses and basic tenements are not especially scenic, but are perhaps the most enduring mark of all on the British architectural landscape.

GEORGIAN ERA

The stunning Royal Crescent in Bath, with its magnificent curved facade of about 30 houses, with a perfect harmonious design, is the epitome of Georgian-era architecture.

Postwar Era

During WWII many of Britain's cities were damaged by bombing, and the rebuilding that followed showed scant regard for the overall aesthetic of the cities, or for the lives of the people who lived in them. The rows of terraces were swept away in favour of high-rise tower blocks, while the 'brutalist' architects of the 1950s and '60s employed the modern and efficient materials of steel and concrete.

Perhaps this is why, on the whole, the British are conservative in their architectural tastes, and often resent ambitious or experimental designs, especially when they're applied to public buildings, or when form appears more important than function. But a familiar pattern often unfolds: after a few years of resentment, first comes a nickname, then grudging acceptance, and finally comes pride and affection for the new building. The British just don't like to be rushed, that's all.

With this attitude in mind, over the last few decades British architecture has started to redeem itself, and many big cities now have contemporary buildings their residents can enjoy and be proud of. Highlights in London's financial district include the bulging cone of the SwissRE building (inevitably dubbed 'the gherkin') and the former Millennium

HOUSE & HOME

It's not all about big houses. Alongside the stately homes, ordinary domestic architecture can also still be seen in Britain's rural areas: black-and-white 'half-timbered' houses characterise counties such as Worcestershire, while brick-and-flint buildings pepper Suffolk and Sussex, and hardy centuries-old cottages and farms built with slate and local stone are a feature of North Wales. In northern Scotland, a classic basic dwelling is the blackhouse – with walls of dry stone (no mortar) packed with earth and a roof of straw and turf.

Dome (now rebranded as simply the O2), which has been transformed from a source of national embarrassment into one of the capital's leading live-music venues.

The 21st Century

Beyond London, many areas of Britain place a new importance on progressive, popular architecture as a part of wider regeneration. Top examples include Manchester's Imperial War Museum North, Birmingham's chic new Bullring shopping centre, the Welsh National Assembly building and the Wales Millennium Centre (both on the Cardiff waterfront), the interlocking arches of Glasgow's Scottish Exhibition & Conference Centre (already affectionately called 'the armadillo') and the Sage concert hall in Gateshead, Northeast England.

Skyscrapers are back in fashion again in many of Britain's cities: in the past few years Leeds, Manchester, Brighton and Birmingham all announced plans for new buildings over 200m high. Top of the heap, however, is the London Bridge Tower (because of its shape it was quickly nicknamed 'the Shard'), which, at 306m, is set to become one of Europe's tallest buildings when it's completed in around 2012.

But wait, there may be more. Although construction has yet to start, two more giant skyscrapers are planned, and yes, they already have nicknames. Ladies and gentlemen, I give you 'the Walkie-Talkie' and 'the Cheese-grater'. We look forward to seeing these new marvels for real some time in the next decade.

So British architecture continues to push new boundaries of style and technology. The buildings may look a little different, but it's great to see the spirit of Stonehenge alive and well after all these years.

Perhaps the best-known example of brutalist architecture is London's Southbank Centre. Very much a building of its time, it was applauded when finished, then reviled for its ugliness, and is now regarded by Londoners with something close to affection.

Glossary of British Architecture

aisle	passageway or open space along either side of a church's *nave*
apse	area for clergy, traditionally at the east end of the church
bailey	outermost wall of a castle
bar	gate (York, and some other northern cities)
barrel vault	semicircular arched roof
boss	covering for the meeting point of the ribs in a *vaulted* roof
brass	memorial consisting of a brass plate set into the floor or a tomb
buttress	vertical support for a wall; see also *flying buttress*
campanile	free-standing belfry or bell tower
chancel	eastern end of the church, usually reserved for choir and clergy
chantry	*chapel* established by a donor for use in their name after death
chapel	small church; shrine or area of worship off the main body of a cathedral
chapel of ease	*chapel* built for those who lived far away from the parish church
choir	area in the church where the choir is seated
cloister	covered walkway linking the church with adjacent monastic buildings
close	buildings grouped around a cathedral
cob	mixture of mud and straw for building
corbel	stone or wooden projection from a wall supporting a beam or arch
crossing	intersection of the *nave* and *transepts* in a church

EH	English Heritage
flying buttress	supporting *buttress* in the form of one side of an open arch
font	basin used for baptisms, often in a separate baptistry
frater	common or dining room in a medieval monastery
lady chapel	*chapel* dedicated to the Virgin Mary
lancet	pointed window in Early English style
lierne vault	*vault* containing many tertiary ribs
Martello tower	small, circular tower used for coastal defence
minster	church connected to a monastery
misericord	hinged choir seat with a bracket (often elaborately carved)
nave	main body of the church at the western end, where the congregation gathers
NT	National Trust
oast house	building containing a kiln for drying hops
pargeting	decorative stucco plasterwork
pele	fortified house
precincts	see *close*
presbytery	eastern area of *chancel* beyond the choir, where the clergy operates
priory	religious house governed by a prior
pulpit	raised box where the priest gives sermons
quire	medieval term for *choir*
refectory	monastic dining room
reredos	literally 'behind the back'; backdrop to an altar
rood	archaic word for cross (in churches)
rood screen	screen carrying a *rood* or crucifix, separating *nave* from *chancel*
squint	angled opening in a wall or pillar to allow a view of a church's altar
transepts	north–south projections from a church's *nave,* giving church a cruciform (cross-shaped plan)
undercroft	vaulted underground room or cellar
vault	roof with arched ribs, usually in a decorative pattern
vestry	priest's robing room

British Literature

The roots of Britain's literary heritage stretch back to Norse sagas and Early English epics such as *Beowulf*. As the English language spread around the world, especially in the colonial era, so too did English literature, so that the poetry and prose of this small region is surprisingly well known far from its original homeland.

As you travel around Britain today you'll see numerous towns and cities with literary links, as well as humble villages and grand stately homes, not to mention forests, beaches and mountain ranges that feature in novels, poems and other works. Wherever possible in this chapter we've mentioned real places where you can experience something of the life of your favourite poets and novelists or even walk in the footsteps of their characters.

For extra insight while travelling, the *Oxford Literary Guide to Great Britain & Ireland* edited by Daniel Hahn and Nicholas Robins gives details of towns, villages and countryside immortalised by writers, from Chaucer's Canterbury and Austen's Bath to Philip Pullman's Oxford.

First Stars

Modern British literature starts around 1387 (yes, that is 'modern' in history-soaked Britain) when England's first literary giant, Geoffrey Chaucer, produced *The Canterbury Tales*. Still a classic today, this mammoth poem is a collection of fables, stories and morality tales using travelling pilgrims – the Knight, the Wife of Bath, the Nun's Priest and so on – as a narrative hook.

The next big name came two centuries later, when William Shakespeare entered the scene. Still Britain's best-known playwright (see boxed text, p1039), he also wrote about 150 poems. Perhaps his most famous poetic line is 'Shall I compare thee to a summer's day?' from Sonnet No 18.

The 17th & 18th Centuries

The early 17th century saw the rise of the metaphysical poets, including John Donne and Andrew Marvell. Their vivid imagery and far-fetched 'conceits' or comparisons daringly pushed the boundaries. In *A Valediction: Forbidding Mourning,* for instance, Donne compares the points of a compass with a pair of conjoined lovers. Racy stuff in its day.

Another key landmark came in 1667 with the publication of John Milton's *Paradise Lost,* an epic poem inspired by the biblical tale of Adam and Eve's expulsion from the Garden of Eden, swiftly followed in 1678 by the equally seminal *Pilgrim's Progress* by John Bunyan, an allegorical tale of the everyday Christian struggle. For mere mortals, reading these books in their entirety can be hard going, but they're worth dipping into for a taste of the rich language. On a rather more prosaic level, everyday London life of the time is richly captured in the wonderful *Diaries* of Samuel Pepys.

Perhaps you're more familiar with *Auld Lang Syne,* traditionally sung at New Year throughout Britain. It was penned by prolific 18th-century poet and lyricist Robert Burns. His more unusual *Address to a Haggis* plays an important part of 'Burn's Night', a Scottish celebration held on 25 January (see also boxed text, p822).

Elsewhere during the 18th century, English literature took on a new political edge, with works such as Alexander Pope's *The Rape of the Lock* attacking the mores of contemporary society. Daniel Defoe wrote *Robinson Crusoe,* seen by many scholars as the first English novel, as well as being a discussion on civilisation, colonialism and faith, and a travel-lit blockbuster since its publication in 1719. It was later parodied by the Anglo-Irish writer Jonathan Swift in his satirical study of human nature, *Gulliver's Travels*.

The Romantic & Gothic Era

As the Industrial Revolution began to take hold in the late 18th and early 19th century, the response from a new generation of writers was to draw inspiration from the natural world and the human imagination (in many cases helped along by a healthy dose of laudanum). Leading lights of the movement were William Blake, John Keats, Percy Bysshe Shelley, Lord Byron and Samuel Taylor Coleridge, and perhaps the best known of all, William Wordsworth, a resident of the English Lake District, where his famous lines from *Daffodils,* 'I wandered lonely as a cloud', were inspired by a hike in the hills.

Gothic literature took the power of the human imagination a step further – to create horror rather than joy. A classic Gothic text is Mary Shelley's *Frankenstein,* a cautionary tale about the dangers of human ambition and perverted technology, a meditation on a post-Enlightenment society facing up to a godless world, and often quoted as the world's first work of science fiction.

Victoriana

Next came the reign of Queen Victoria and the era of industrial expansion, and key novels of the time explored social and political themes. Charles Dickens especially tackled many prevailing issues of his day: in *Oliver Twist,* he captures the lives of young thieves in the London slums; *Bleak House* is a critique of the English legal system and *Hard Times* criticises the excesses of capitalism.

At around the same time, but choosing a rural setting, George Eliot (the pen name of Mary Anne Evans) wrote *The Mill on the Floss* – where the central character, Maggie Tulliver, looks for true love and struggles against society's expectations.

Meanwhile, Thomas Hardy's classic *Tess of the D'Urbervilles* deals with the peasantry's decline, and *The Trumpet Major* paints a picture of idyllic English country life interrupted by war and encroaching modernity. Many of Hardy's works are in the fictionalised county of Wessex, largely based on today's Dorset and surrounding counties, where towns such as Dorchester are popular stops on tourist itineraries.

North of the border, Sir Walter Scott produced the classic Scottish novel *Waverley,* set in the time of the 1745 Jacobite rebellion.

BRITISH ENGLISH

The language of most English literature is of course English – the main 'indigenous' language of Britain, and known as British English, to distinguish it from American English, Australian English and so on. British English is spoken in England (of course) and most parts of Wales and Scotland. Other languages of Britain include Welsh (spoken in Wales), Lowland Scots and Scottish Gaelic (two distinct languages of southern and northern Scotland) and Cornish (Cornwall). The Isle of Man and Channel Islands also have their own languages, although English is predominant there, too.

AUSTEN & THE BRONTËS

As the 19th century dawned, a new generation of writers used the trials and tribulations of middle-class society as the basis for their novels. Best known and best loved are Jane Austen and the Brontë sisters.

Two centuries after her death, Jane Austen is still one of Britain's best-known novelists, thanks to her exquisite observations of class, society, love, friendship, intrigues and passions boiling under the stilted social convention of the provincial middle-class – and in no small part to an endless stream of movies and TV costume dramas based on her works such as *Pride and Prejudice* and *Sense and Sensibility*. For visitors today, the location most associated with Jane Austen is the city of Bath – a beautiful place even without the literary link. As one of her heroines said, 'who can ever be tired of Bath?'

Other major figures from this era are the Brontë sisters. Of the family's prodigious output, Emily Brontë's *Wuthering Heights* is the best known – an epic tale of obsession and revenge, where the dark and moody landscape plays a role as great as any human character. Charlotte Brontë's *Jane Eyre* and Anne Brontë's *The Tenant of Wildfell Hall* are classics of passion, mystery and love. Fans still flock to their former home in the Yorkshire town of Haworth, perched on the edge of the wild Pennine moors that inspired so many of their books.

While Dickens and Hardy tackled issues at home, other writers explored Britain's rapidly expanding frontiers abroad, notably Rudyard Kipling, perhaps the classic chronicler of empire, in works such as *Gunga Din* and *The Jungle Book*.

Also popular during this period were Robert Louis Stevenson, best known for his children's books *Treasure Island* and *Kidnapped,* and Sir Arthur Conan Doyle, inventor of detective Sherlock Holmes who, with sidekick Watson, starred in a string of murder mysteries.

The 20th Century

In the 20th century, the pace of writing increased. A landmark was the 1908 success of Welsh poet WH Davies, whose *The Autobiography of a Super-Tramp* contained the immortal words 'What is this life if, full of care/We have no time to stand and stare?'

But life – and British literature – changed forever following the devastating carnage of WWI. Patriotic poems such as Rupert Brooke's *The Soldier* ('If I should die, think only this of me...') gave way to excoriating dissections of the false glory of war in the work of Siegfried Sassoon and Wilfred Owen. Even Kipling recanted his unquestioning devotion to the cause following the death of his only son in the war; his devastating refrain 'If any question why we died/Tell them, because our fathers lied' has since become a mantra for the antiwar movement.

Brighton Graham Greene's novel *Brighton Rock* (1938) is a classic account of wayward English youth. For an even more shocking take, try Anthony Burgess' *A Clockwork Orange*, later infamously filmed by Stanley Kubrick in 1971 and withdrawn in the UK following a spate of violent copycat acts.

The ideological chaos and social disruption of the postwar period fed into the fractured narratives of modernism. Perhaps the greatest British novelist of the interwar period is DH Lawrence, best known for *Sons and Lovers,* following the lives and loves of generations in the English Midlands as the country changes from rural idyll to an increasingly industrial landscape, and his controversial exploration of sexuality, *Lady Chatterley's Lover,* originally banned as 'obscene'.

Other highlights of the interwar years included EM Forster's *A Passage to India,* about the hopelessness of British colonial rule, and Daphne du Maurier's romantic suspense novel *Rebecca,* set on the Cornish coast. Another major figure was Virginia Woolf; her best-known novel, *To the Lighthouse,* also set in Cornwall, examines the impact of war on English society, the emotional clash between men and women, and the need for artists to balance their creativity with the demands of real life.

Evelyn Waugh tackled the themes of moral and social disintegration in *Vile Bodies* and *Brideshead Revisited,* and Richard Llewellyn wrote the Welsh classic *How Green Was My Valley.* In a different world entirely, JRR Tolkien published *The Hobbit,* trumping it some 20 years later with his awesome trilogy *The Lord of the Rings.*

After WWII, Compton Mackenzie lifted postwar spirits with *Whisky Galore,* a comic novel about a cargo of booze washed up from a sinking ship onto a Scottish island. Elsewhere, a less whimsical breed of writer emerged, along with a new wave of self-examination and paranoia. George Orwell wrote his closely observed studies of totalitarian rule *Animal Farm* and *1984,* the novel that gave Big Brother to the wider world, while the Cold War inspired Graham Greene's *Our Man in Havana,* in which a secret agent studies the workings of a vacuum cleaner to inspire fictitious spying reports.

As the Pennine moors haunt Brontë novels, so the marshy Cambridgeshire Fens dominate *Waterland* by Graham Swift – a tale of personal and national history, betrayal and compassion, and rated a landmark work of the 1980s.

Another spook of that period was Ian Fleming's full-blooded British hero James Bond – today better known as a movie franchise. He first appeared in 1953 in the book *Casino Royale,* then swashbuckled through numerous thrillers for another decade.

Alongside the novelists, the first half of the 20th century was a great time for poets. Major works include WH Auden's *Funeral Blues* and TS Eliot's epic *The Wasteland,* although the latter is better known for *Old Possum's Book of Practical Cats* – turned into the musical *Cats* by Andrew Lloyd Webber.

Different again was the gritty verse of Ted Hughes, sometimes renowned as much for the stormy relationship with his wife (American poet Sylvia Plath) as for his works, although in 1984 he became Poet Laureate. Meanwhile, Dylan Thomas, also known for his energetic social diary, came to the fore with *Portrait of The Artist As A Young Dog,* although his most celebrated work is a radio play *Under Milk Wood* (1954), exposing the tensions of small-town Wales.

Then came the swinging '60s and '70s. The Liverpool poet Roger McGough and friends determined to make art relevant to daily life and produced *The Mersey Sound* – landmark pop poetry for the streets. Other new writers included Muriel Spark, who introduced the world to a highly unusual Edinburgh school mistress in *The Prime of Miss Jean Brodie,* and Martin Amis, who was just 24 in 1973 when he wrote *The Rachel Papers,* a witty, minutely observed story of sexual obsession in puberty. Since then Amis has published many books, including *London Fields* and *The Information,* all greeted with critical acclaim and high sales. Similarly, Ian McEwan was one of Britain's angriest young novelists, earning the nickname Ian Macabre for his early works like *The Cement Garden* and *The Comfort of Strangers.* In 1998 he cracked the establishment and became a Booker Prize winner with *Amsterdam,* followed by other finely observed studies of the British character such as *Atonement* and *On Chesil Beach.*

For a taste of surreal humour, try two of Britain's funniest (and most successful) writers: Douglas Adams *(The Hitchhiker's Guide to the Galaxy)* and Terry Pratchett (the *Discworld* series). Pratchett was the best-selling author in the UK for much of the 1990s.

Contemporary novels in a different vein include 1993's *Trainspotting* by Irvine Welsh, a deep, dark look at Edinburgh's drug culture, and the start of a new genre coined 'Tartan Noir'. Other successful modern Scottish novelists include Iain Banks (who also writes sci-fi under the cunning pseudonym of Iain M Banks) and Ian Rankin, whose Detective Inspector Rebus novels are always eagerly awaited.

The New Millennium

As the 20th century came to a close, the nature of multicultural Britain proved a rich inspiration for contemporary novelists. Hanif Kureishi sowed the seeds with his ground-breaking 1990 novel *The Buddha of Suburbia,* examining the hopes and fears of a group of suburban Anglo-Asians in London. Other star novelists covering (loosely defined) 'multicultural Britain' themes include Zadie Smith, who published her acclaimed debut *White Teeth* in 2000 followed by a string of literary best sellers including *The Autograph Man;* Monica Ali, whose *Brick Lane* was shortlisted for the 2003 Man Booker Prize; Hari Kunzru, who received one of the largest advances in publishing history in 2002 for his debut *The Impressionist;* and Andrea Levy, winner of the 2004 Orange Prize for her novel *Small Island* about a Jamaican couple settled in postwar London.

Other contemporary writers worth seeking out include Will Self, known for his surreal, satirical novels, including his most recent book, *Liver,* a typically imaginative tale that explores the livers of four London characters in various stages of disease, decay and disintegration; David Mitchell, whose multilayered, time-bending *Cloud Atlas* marked him out as a writer to watch; and Sarah Waters, a gifted novelist who often places lesbian issues at the core of her work, in books such as *Tipping the Velvet* and *Night Watch.* Also recommended is Irvine Welsh's *Bedroom Secrets of the Master Chefs,* a study of modern-day fixations – food, drugs, sex and celebrity – with a nod to Dorian Gray thrown in for good measure.

Helen Fielding's *Bridget Jones's Diary,* a fond look at the heartache of a modern single girl's blundering search for love, epitomised the late-1990s 'chick-lit' genre.

At the more popular end of the shelf is the best-selling author Nick Hornby, chronicling the fragilities and insecurities of the British middle-class male in novels like *Fever Pitch* and *High Fidelity,* while Sebastian Faulks established himself with his wartime novels *Birdsong* and *Charlotte Gray,* and was recently chosen to write the first new James Bond novel in over 50 years to mark the centenary of Ian Fleming's birth; the resulting *Devil May Care* has since become one of the fastest-selling hardbacks ever published, shifting over 44,000 copies in its first four days.

But even James Bond can't hold a candle to the literary phenomenon that is JK Rowling's *Harry Potter* series, the magical adventures that have entertained millions of children (and a fair few grown-ups too) over the last decade. The series is the latest in a long line of British children's classics enjoyed by adults, stretching back to the works of Lewis Carroll *(Alice's Adventures in Wonderland),* E Nesbit *(The Railway Children),* AA Milne *(Winnie-the-Pooh)* and CS Lewis *(The Chronicles of Narnia).* More recently, Philip Pullman's controversial *His Dark Materials* trilogy has been a big hit.

Alongside the work of British poets and novelists, it's impossible to overlook the recent trend for scurrilous celebrity autobiographies – penned by everyone from footballers to reality TV also-rans – a reminder of the increasing importance of hype over merit in the modern book market. But whatever you make of the literary qualities of these memoirs, it's hard to argue with the figures – the British public buys them by the bucket load.

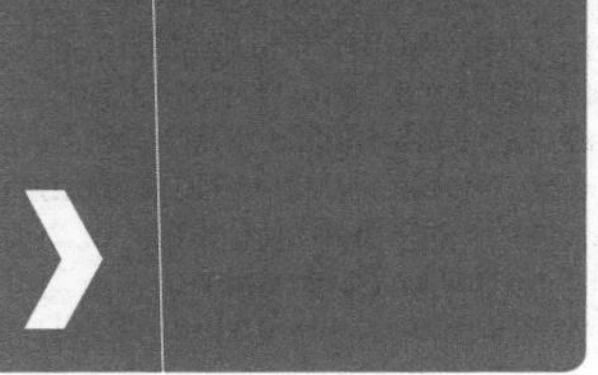

Visual & Performing Arts in Britain

Cinema

Early Days

Britain had a number of successful directors in the early days of cinema. Many cut their teeth in the silent-film industry, including Alfred Hitchcock, who directed *Blackmail,* one of the first British 'talkies' in 1929, and went on to direct a string of films during the 1930s before migrating to Hollywood in the early 1940s.

During WWII, British films were dominated by patriotic stories designed to keep up morale on the Home Front: films like *Went the Day Well?* (1942), *In Which We Serve* (1942) and *We Dive at Dawn* (1943) are classics of the genre. During this period the precocious young director David Lean directed a series of striking Dickens adaptations and the classic tale of buttoned-up passion, *Brief Encounter* (1945), before graduating to Hollywood epics including *Lawrence of Arabia* and *Doctor Zhivago.*

The UK's biggest film magazine is *Empire* (www.empireonline.co.uk). For less mainstream opinion check out *Little White Lies* (www.littlewhitelies.co.uk).

Another great film of the 1940s is *How Green Was My Valley,* a tale of everyday life in the coal-mining villages of Wales. Still perhaps the best-known Welsh film of all time, it also annoys more Welsh people than any other, as it features stereotypical characters, no Welsh actors, and was shot in a Hollywood studio. It is worth a watch, though, for a taste of the period.

The era also saw the start of one of the great partnerships of British cinema, between the British writer-director Michael Powell and the Hungarian-born scriptwriter Emeric Pressburger. During and after the war, they produced some of the most enduring films of British cinema, including *The Life and Death of Colonel Blimp* (1941), *A Matter of Life and Death* (1946) and *The Red Shoes* (1948).

Passport to Pimlico is an Ealing Studios film classic, the story of a London suburb declaring independence from the rest of the country.

After the War

Following the hardships of the war, British audiences were in the mood for escape and entertainment. During the late 1940s and early '50s, the domestic film industry specialised in eccentric British comedies epitomised by the work of Ealing Studios: notable titles include *Passport to Pimlico* (1949), *Kind Hearts and Coronets* (1949) and *The Titfield Thunderbolt* (1953).

More serious box-office hits of the time included *Hamlet,* starring Laurence Olivier (the first British film to win an Oscar in the Best Picture category) and Carol Reed's *The Third Man.* And in a Britain still struggling with rationing and food shortages, tales of heroic derring-do such as *The Dam Busters* (1955) and *Reach for the Sky* (1956) helped lighten the national mood.

Swinging Sixties

In the late 1950s 'British New Wave' and 'Free Cinema' explored the gritty realities of life in an intimate, semidocumentary style, borrowing techniques from the 'kitchen-sink' theatre of the '50s and the vérité style of the French New Wave. Lindsay Anderson and Tony Richardson crystallised the movement in films such as *This Sporting Life* (1961) and *A Taste of Honey* (1961). At the other end of the spectrum were the *Carry On* films, the cinematic equivalent of the smutty seaside postcard, packed with bawdy gags and a revolving troupe of actors including Barbara Windsor, Sid James and Kenneth Williams.

The 1960s also saw the birth of another classic British hero: James Bond, adapted from the Ian Fleming novels, and played by the Scottish actor Sean Connery. Since then about 20 Bond movies have been made, and Bond has been played by other British actors including Roger Moore, Timothy Dalton and Daniel Craig. More recent producers have brought the originally somewhat misogynist Bond into the modern age, and included the enlightened casting of Dame Judi Dench as Bond's boss 'M'.

The Ladykillers (1955) is a classic Ealing comedy about a band of hapless bank robbers holed up in a London guesthouse, and features Alec Guinness sporting quite possibly the most outrageous set of false teeth ever committed to celluloid.

Hard Times, Good Times

After the boom of the swinging '60s, British cinema entered troubled waters in the '70s. Dwindling production funds and increasing international competition meant that by the mid-1970s the only films being made in Britain were financed with foreign cash. Despite the hardships, new directors including Ken Russell, Nic Roeg, Ken Loach and Mike Hodges emerged, and the American director Stanley Kubrick produced some of his films in Britain, including *A Clockwork Orange* (1971).

In the 1980s the British film industry rediscovered its sense of self thanks partly to David Puttnam's Oscar success with *Chariots of Fire* in 1981. The newly established Channel Four invested in edgy films such as *My Beautiful Laundrette* (1985), and exciting new talents including Neil Jordan, Mike Newell and American-born, and member of the Monty Python team, Terry Gilliam.

Click on www.screenonline.org.uk – the website of the British Film Institute – for complete coverage of Britain's film and TV industry.

HAMMER HORROR

The low-budget flicks produced by Hammer Film Productions are revered among horror fans across the globe. Founded in 1934, the company was best known for its string of horror flicks produced in the 1950s and '60s, starting with *The Quatermass Xperiment* (1955) and *The Curse of Frankenstein* (1957). The two stars of the latter – Peter Cushing as Dr Frankenstein and Christopher Lee as the Monster – would feature in many of Hammer's best films over the next 20 years.

Hammer produced some absolute classics of the horror genre, including a string of nine *Dracula* films (most of which star Lee as Dracula and Cushing as Van Helsing or his descendants) and six *Frankenstein* sequels.

The studio also launched the careers of several other notable actors (including Oliver Reed, who made his film debut in *The Curse of the Werewolf*, 1961) and inspired a legion of low-budget horror directors: Wes Craven, John Carpenter and Sam Raimi have all acknowledged Hammer films as an early influence. The studio even spawned its very own spoof, *Carry On Screaming* – the ultimate British seal of approval.

The classic British youth movie is *Quadrophenia*, a visceral tale of mods, rockers, and pimped-up mopeds, with a top-notch soundtrack courtesy of The Who.

A film about love, betrayal, brass bands, coal-mine closures and the breakdown of society in 1980s England, *Brassed Off* makes you laugh, then cry, then laugh again – and shouldn't be missed.

Chariots of Fire is an inspiring dramatisation of a true story: the progress of two athletes from university to the 1924 Olympics. When receiving his Oscars, the director famously boasted: 'the British are coming.'

Meanwhile, the British producing duo of Ismail Merchant and James Ivory played Hollywood at its own game with epic tales including *Heat and Dust* (1983) and *A Room With A View* (1986), riding on the success of Richard Attenborough's big-budget *Gandhi* (1982), which bagged eight Academy Awards.

Brit-Flicks

The 1990s saw another renaissance in British films, ushered in by the massively successful *Four Weddings and a Funeral* (1994), introducing Hugh Grant in his trademark role as a likable and self-deprecating Englishman, a character type he reprised in subsequent hits including *Notting Hill, About a Boy* and *Love Actually*. All these films were co-financed by Working Title, a London-based production company that has become one of the big players of British cinema (and also unleashed Rowan Atkinson's hapless Mr Bean onto the global stage).

Four Weddings spearheaded a genre of 'Brit-flicks', including *Secrets and Lies* (1996), a Palme d'Or winner at Cannes, in which an adopted black woman traces her white mother; *Bhaji on the Beach,* a quirky East-meets-West-meets-Blackpool road movie; *Brassed Off* (1996) relating the trials of a struggling colliery band; *The Full Monty,* about a troupe of laid-off steel workers turned male strippers, which in 1997 became Britain's most successful film ever; *The Englishman Who Went Up a Hill and Came Down a Mountain,* an affectionate story about a peak in North Wales that was too short; and *Trainspotting,* a hard-hitting film about Edinburgh's drugged-out underbelly that launched the careers of Scottish actors Ewan McGregor and Robert Carlyle. They joined other British stars more frequently seen in Hollywood these days, including Welsh thespians Anthony Hopkins and Catherine Zeta-Jones.

More great films of the 1990s include *Lock, Stock and Two Smoking Barrels,* which spawned a host of gangster copycats, and the Oscar-winning series of *Wallace & Gromit* animations (see boxed text, p1034). *Breaking the Waves* is a perfect study of culture clash in 1970s Scotland, and *Human Traffic* is an edgy romp through Cardiff's clubland. Also released was *Sense and Sensibility,* with English doyennes Emma Thompson and Kate Winslet as the Dashwood sisters, and Hugh Grant as, you guessed it, a likable and self-deprecating Englishman.

Award-winning Welsh-language films of the 1990s include *Hedd Wynn,* a heartbreaking story of a poet killed in WWI, and *Solomon and Gaenor,* a passionate tale of forbidden love at the turn of the 20th century, staring Ioan Gruffudd and filmed twice – once with Welsh dialogue and once with English.

The decade ended with films such as *East Is East* (1999), a beautifully understated study of the clash between first- and second-generation immigrant Pakistanis in Britain, and *Billy Elliott* (2000) about a boy's quest to learn ballet and escape the slag-heaps of post-industrial northern England.

21st-Century Box

In the first decade of the 21st century, literary adaptations have continued to provide the richest seam of success in the British film industry. Hits of this genre include blockbuster adaptations of the *Bridget Jones* and *Harry Potter* books, as well as 2005's *The Constant Gardener* (based on a John Le Carré novel), 2007's *The Last King of Scotland* (featuring Forest Whittaker as Ugandan dictator Idi Amin) and *Atonement* (2008), a big-budget adaptation of Ian McEwan's novel.

Biopics are also a perennial favourite: recent big-screen subjects include Ian Curtis from Joy Division (in *Control,* 2007), Elizabeth I (in *Elizabeth: The Golden Age,* 2007), and even the Queen (in, er, *The Queen,* 2006).

But life remains tough for the British filmmaker, especially those at the low-budget end, and especially as the industry's support body, the UK Film Council, is one of many similar public sector organisations threatened with abolition in the harsh post-financial-crisis Britain of 2010. Nevertheless, names to look out for include Paul Greengrass, Andrea Arnold, Stephen Daldry, Stephen Frears, Danny Boyle and Andrew Macdonald. Sam Taylor-Wood is another name to watch, thanks to her sensitive film *Nowhere Boy* (2009), about the early life of John Lennon. Many talented names often take better-paid work abroad in order to finance home ventures, and genuinely British films about genuinely British subjects tend to struggle in an oversaturated marketplace: it's telling that two of Britain's best directors, Shane Meadows (*Dead Man's Shoes, This is England*) and Michael Winterbottom (*9 Songs, 24 Hour Party People*) have both yet to score a big splash at the box office.

Withnail and I is one of the great cult British comedies. Directed by Bruce Robinson, it stars Paul McGann and Richard E Grant as a pair of hapless out-of-work actors on a disastrous holiday to Wales.

More success has come to the comedy trio of Simon Pegg, Edgar Wright and Nick Frost with their zombie homage *Shaun of The Dead* (2004) and its cop-flick follow-up *Hot Fuzz* (2007), while music video director Garth Jennings followed his adaptation of *The Hitchhiker's Guide to the Galaxy* (2005) with a low-budget tale of youthful friendship and shoestring moviemaking in *Son of Rambow* (2007).

Veteran directors like Mike Leigh and Ken Loach are still going strong: Leigh's *Vera Drake* (2004), about a housewife turned backstreet abortionist in 1950s Britain, won the Golden Lion at the Venice Film Festival, while Loach's *The Wind that Shakes the Barley* (2006), a hard-hitting account of the Irish struggle for independence, scooped the Palme d'Or at Cannes.

Meanwhile the oldest of British film franchises trundles on: a tough, toned 21st-century James Bond appeared in 2006 courtesy of Daniel Craig and the blockbuster *Casino Royale.* His next film *Quantum of Solace* (2008) was due to be followed by another Bond movie (taking the total to 23) in 2010, but the project was delayed, keeping Bond fans on the edge of their seats for a little while longer than expected.

Bride & Prejudice is another Austen-inspired movie, given a brand-new slant by director Gurinder Chadha, this time with singing, dancing and outrageous Bollywood panache. Many of the locations are in Britain.

Television

If there's one thing the British excel at, it's the telly. Over the last 80-odd years of broadcasting, Britain has produced some of the world's finest programming, from classic comedy through to ground-breaking drama. Many of the world's most popular formats have their origins in British broadcasting (including the phenomenon known as reality TV), and while digital and satellite channels take ever-increasing shares of the market, the main British free-to-air channels (BBC1, BBC2, ITV1, Channel 4 and Five) remain major players.

The BBC is famous for its news and natural-history programming, epitomised by landmark series such as *Planet Earth* and *The Blue Planet* (reassuringly helmed by Sir David Attenborough, a similarly precious national institution since the 1970s).

The big-budget costume drama is another Sunday-night staple; BBC viewers have been treated to adaptations of practically every Dickens, Austen and Thackeray novel in the canon over the last decade. More recently ITV has been making inroads into costume-drama territory, notably with Jane Austen's *Persuasion, Mansfield Park* and *Northanger Abbey.*

THE PLASTICINE MAN

One of the great success stories of British television and cinema has been Bristol-based animator Nick Park and the production company Aardman Animations, best known for the award-winning animations starring the man-and-dog duo Wallace and Gromit. This lovable pair first appeared in Park's graduation film, *A Grand Day Out* (1989) and went on to star in *The Wrong Trousers* (1993), *A Close Shave* (1995) and their feature debut, *Wallace & Gromit in The Curse of the Were-Rabbit* (2005). Known for their intricate plots, film homages and amazingly realistic animation, the Wallace and Gromit films have scooped Nick Park four Oscars. Aardman Animations has also produced two successful animated features, *Chicken Run* (2000) and *Flushed Away* (2006), in partnership with Hollywood's DreamWorks studios.

The BBC is a public service broadcaster, financed by the licence fee – approximately £145, paid annually by every house in Britain with a TV set – rather than advertising. The other free-to-air stations are funded primarily by commercial breaks in the usual way.

BBC

Both channels are also known for their long-running 'soaps' – *Eastenders* (BBC), *Emmerdale* and *Coronation Street* (both ITV), which have collectively been running on British screens for well over a century.

Reality TV has dominated many channels in recent years, although the popularity of shows such as *Big Brother* and *I'm a Celebrity – Get Me Out of Here!* seems to be on the wane. On the flipside, talent and variety are making a big comeback, with programs like *Britain's Got Talent* and *Strictly Come Dancing* being syndicated all over the world (the latter under the brand of *Dancing with the Stars*). Game shows are another big success story, with *Who Wants to be a Millionaire?* and *The Weakest Link* spawning countless foreign versions.

While the main channels of BBC1 and ITV1 concentrate on high-profile programming, BBC2 and Channel 4 tend to produce edgier and more experimental content. Both channels are known for their documentaries – Channel 4 has a particular penchant for shocking subject matter (one of the channel's most controversial recent programs was *Autopsy,* which did exactly what it said on the label). Comedy is another strong point – the satirical news quiz *Have I Got News For You* is still going strong after 15 years, while classic British comedies such as *Monty Python, Steptoe & Son* and *Only Fools & Horses* have more recently been joined in comedy's hall of fame by cult hits *The Mighty Boosh, The League of Gentlemen, I'm Alan Partridge, Ali G, Spaced* and Ricky Gervais' *The Office* and *Extras.*

Pop & Rock Music

Britain's been putting the world through its musical paces ever since a mop-haired four-piece from Liverpool tuned up their Rickenbackers and created The Beatles. And while some may claim that Elvis invented rock and roll, it was the Fab Four that transformed it into a global phenomenon, backed by the other bands of the 1960s 'British Invasion' – The Rolling Stones, The Who, Cream, The Kinks and Welsh soul man Tom Jones.

In the 1970s, glam rock swaggered onto the stage, led by Marc Bolan and David Bowie in their tight-fitting costumes and chameleonic guises, succeeded by early boy-band Bay City Rollers, art-rockers Roxy Music and anthemic popsters Queen and Elton John. Meanwhile Led Zeppelin laid down the blueprint for heavy metal and hard rock, while the psychedelia of the previous decade morphed into the spacey noodlings of prog rock, epitomised by Pink Floyd, Genesis and Yes.

Punk Changes Everything

By the late 1970s the prog bands were looking out of touch in a Britain wracked by rampant unemployment and industrial unrest, and punk exploded onto the scene, summing up the general air of doom and gloom with nihilistic lyrics and short, sharp, three-chord tunes. The Sex Pistols produced one landmark album – *Never Mind the Bollocks, Here's the Sex Pistols* – and a clutch of (mostly banned) singles, plus a storm of controversy, ably assisted by other punk pioneers including The Clash, The Damned, The Buzzcocks and The Stranglers.

While punk burned itself out in a blaze of squealing guitars and ear-splitting feedback, New Wave acts including The Jam, The Tourists and Elvis Costello took up the torch, blending spiky tunes and sharp lyrics into a poppier, more radio-friendly sound. A little later, along came bands like The Specials, The Selecter and baggy-trousered rude boys Madness, mixing punk, reggae and ska into Two Tone. Meanwhile, another punk-and-reggae-influenced band called The Police – fronted by bassist Sting – became one of the biggest names of the decade.

Britain's longest-running soap is ITV's *Coronation Street*, which has charted everyday life in the fictional northern town of Weatherfield since 1960.

Mode, Metal & Miserabilism

The big money and conspicuous consumption of Britain in the early 1980s were reflected in the decade's pop scene. Big hair, shiny suits and shoulder pads became the uniform of New Romantics such as Spandau Ballet, Duran Duran and Culture Club, while the advent of synthesisers led to the development of a new electronic sound in the music of Depeche Mode and The Human League. More hits and highlights were supplied by Texas, Eurythmics and Wham! – a boyish duo headed by a bright young fellow called George Michael.

But the glitz of '80s pop concealed a murky underbelly: bands like The Cure, Bauhaus and Siouxsie & the Banshees employed doom-laden lyrics and apocalyptic riffs, while Britain's rock heritage inspired the birth of heavy-metal acts such as Iron Maiden, Judas Priest and Black Sabbath. In a different tone entirely, the disaffection of mid-1980s Britain was summed up by the arch-priests of 'miserabilism', The Smiths – fronted by extravagantly quiffed wordsmith Morrissey.

Brit-Pop

The beats and bleeps of 1980s electronica fuelled the burgeoning dance-music scene of the early '90s. Pioneering artists such as New Order (risen from the ashes of Joy Division) and The Orb used synthesised sounds to inspire the soundtrack for the ecstasy-fuelled rave culture, centred on famous clubs like Manchester's Haçienda and London's Ministry of Sound. Subgenres such as trip-hop, drum and bass, jungle, house and big-beat cropped up in other UK cities, with key acts including Massive Attack, Portishead and The Chemical Brothers.

Manchester was also a focus for the burgeoning British 'indie' scene, driven by guitar-based bands such as The Charlatans, The Stone Roses, James, Happy Mondays and Oasis. In the late 1990s, the term 'Britpop' was coined, covering a very wide range of bands including Blur, Elastica, Suede, Supergrass, Ocean Colour Scene, Manic Street Preachers, The Verve, Pulp, Travis, Feeder, Super Furry Animals, Stereophonics,

The British Film Institute (BFI) is dedicated to promoting film and cinema in Britain, and publishes the monthly academic journal *Sight & Sound*. For more, see www.bfi.org.uk.

MUSIC AT THE MOVIES

Some movies worth checking out to understand Britain's modern music scene: *Backbeat* (1994), a look at the early days of The Beatles; *Sid and Nancy* (1986), following The Sex Pistols bassist and his American girlfriend; *Velvet Goldmine* (1998), a tawdry glimpse of the glam-rock scene; and *24 Hour Party People* (2002), a totally irreverent and suitably chaotic film about the 1990s Manchester music scene.

Catatonia, Radiohead and (again) Oasis, whose distinctively British music chimed with the country's new sense of optimism following the landslide election of New Labour in 1997. Noel Gallagher of Oasis famously drinking tea with Prime Minister Tony Blair at No 10 Downing St in 1997 was regarded by many as a defining moment of the 'Cool Britannia' era, but the phenomenon was short-lived – and well and truly over by the end of the '90s.

New Millennium

The new millennium saw no let-up in the British music scene's continual shifting and reinvention, becoming ever more diverse thanks to the arrival of MySpace, iTunes and file sharing. Jazz, soul, R&B and hip-hop beats fused into a new 'urban' sound epitomised by artists like Jamelia, The Streets and Dizzee Rascal, while British folk and roots music, thanks largely to the rise of world music, enjoyed its biggest revival since the 1960s.

On the pop side, singer-songwriters – such as Amy Winehouse, Damien Rice, Ed Harcourt, Katie Mellua, James Blunt and Duffy – made a comeback, while the spirit of shoe-gazing British indie stayed alive and well thanks to Keane, Foals, Editors and world-conquering Coldplay, while traces of punk and postpunk survived thanks to Franz Ferdinand, Razorlight, Babyshambles, Muse, Klaxons, Dirty Pretty Things and 2008's download phenomenon Arctic Monkeys.

Pop Today, Gone Tomorrow

Today's music scene is as fast-moving and varied as ever. Big names like Muse, Dizzee Rascal and Franz Ferdinand continue to headline summer festivals, backed up by current favourites like Mumford & Sons, Bombay Bicycle Club, Foals and The XX. Beyond the festivals, Britain's live music scene continues to thrive; a vital opportunity for bands to make money in a business squeezed by free file sharing. Meanwhile, commercial pop acts like Leona Lewis and Diana Vickers are produced by endless – and obsessively followed – reality TV talent shows such as *X-Factor*.

By the time you read this book, half of the 'great new bands' of last year will have sunk without trace, and a fresh batch of unknowns will have risen to dominate the airwaves and download sites. One thing's for sure, the British music scene has never stood still, and it doesn't look like settling down any time soon.

Burning Bright

The painter, writer, poet and visionary William Blake (1757–1827) mixed fantastical landscapes and mythological scenes with motifs drawn from classical art, religious iconography and legend. For more see www.blakearchive.org.

Painting & Sculpture

Early Days

For many centuries, continental Europe – especially Holland, Spain, France and Italy – set the artistic agenda. The first artist with a truly British style and sensibility was arguably William Hogarth, whose riotous canvases exposed the vice and corruption of 18th-century London. His most celebrated work is *A Rake's Progress,* displayed today at Sir John Soane's Museum in London, which kick-started a long tradition of British caricatures that can be traced right through to the work of modern-day cartoonists such as Gerald Scarfe and Steve Bell.

While Hogarth was busy satirising society, other artists were hard at work showing it in its best light. The leading figures of 18th-century British portraiture were Sir Joshua Reynolds, Thomas Gainsborough, George Romney and George Stubbs, best known for his intricate studies of animals (particularly horses). Most of these artists are represented at Tate Britain or the National Gallery in London.

The 19th Century

In the 19th century, leading painters favoured the landscape. John Constable's idyllic depictions of the Suffolk countryside are summed up in *The Haywain* (National Gallery), while JMW Turner was fascinated by the effects of light and colour, with his works becoming almost entirely abstract by the 1840s – vilified at the time but prefiguring the Impressionist movement that was to follow 50 years later.

While Turner was becoming more abstract, the Pre-Raphaelite movement of the mid- to late 19th century harked back to the figurative style of classical Italian and Flemish art, tying in with the prevailing Victorian taste for fables, myths and fairy tales. Key members of the movement included John Everett Millais and William Holman Hunt. Millais' *Ophelia,* showing the damsel picturesquely drowned in a pool, is an excellent example of their style, and can be seen the Tate Britain gallery. However, one of the best collections of Pre-Raphaelite art is in the Birmingham Museum and Art Gallery.

The works of Henry Moore and Barbara Hepworth can be seen at the Yorkshire Sculpture Park, between Sheffield and Leeds, in northern England. Hepworth is also forever associated with St Ives in Cornwall.

A good friend of the Pre-Raphaelites was William Morris; he saw late-19th-century furniture and interior design as increasingly vulgar, and with Dante Gabriel Rossetti and Edward Burne-Jones founded the Arts and Crafts movement to encourage the revival of a decorative approach to features such as wallpaper, tapestries and windows. Many of his designs are still used today.

North of the border, Charles Rennie Mackintosh, fresh from the Glasgow School of Art, fast became a renowned artist, designer and architect. He is still Scotland's greatest art-nouveau exponent, and much of his work remains in this city (see p798 for more details). Mackintosh influenced a group of artists from the 1890s called the Glasgow Boys, among them James Guthrie and EA Walton, who were also much taken with French Impressionism. Perhaps inevitably, another group of decorative artists and designers emerged called the Glasgow Girls.

The Early 20th Century

In the tumultuous 20th century, British art became increasingly experimental, and its place on the international stage was ensured by Henry Moore's and Barbara Hepworth's monumental sculptures with natural forms and all kinds of new materials, Francis Bacon's contorted paintings influenced by Freudian psychoanalysis, and the works of a group known as the Scottish Colourists – Francis Cadell, SJ Peploe, Leslie Hunter and JD Ferguson.

The best places to see the Colourist seascapes of artists such as Francis Cadell and SJ Peploe are at Scottish attractions and points of interest – their works have been turned into the type of prints and postcards eternally favoured by souvenir shops.

Between the wars, Welsh sister-and-brother artists Gwen and Augustus John flourished, while Gwen John painted gentle, introspective portraits of women friends, cats and nuns – and famously became the model and lover of French artist Rodin. Her brother Augustus became Britain's leading portrait painter, with famous sitters such as Thomas Hardy and George Bernard Shaw. One place to admire works by the Johns is at the Glynn Vivian Art Gallery in Swansea.

The Scottish Colourists were followed in the interwar years by a group known as the Edinburgh School. This group included William MacTaggart, who was much influenced by the French expressionists and became one of Scotland's best-known painters. His rich and colourful landscapes can be seen in London's National Gallery and in Hunterian Art Gallery in Glasgow.

After WWII, Howard Hodgkin and Patrick Heron developed a British version of American abstract expressionism. At the same time, but in great contrast, Manchester artist LS Lowry was painting his much-loved 'matchstick men' figures set in an urban landscape of narrow streets and smoky factories. A good place to see his work is in the Lowry centre, Manchester.

Postwar

The mid-1950s and early '60s saw an explosion of British artists plundering TV, music, advertising and popular culture for inspiration. Leaders of this new 'pop-art' movement included David Hockney, who used bold colours and simple lines to depict his dachshunds and swimming pools, and Peter Blake, who designed the cut-up collage cover for the Beatles' landmark *Sgt Peppers...* album. The '60s also saw the rise of sculptor Anthony Caro, who held his first ground-breaking exhibition at the Whitechapel Art Gallery in 1963. Creating large abstract works in steel and bronze, he remains one of Britain's most influential sculptors.

The next big explosion in British art came in the 1990s, thanks partly to the interest (and money) of advertising tycoon and patron Charles Saatchi. Figureheads of the movement – dubbed, inevitably, 'Britart' – include Damien Hirst, famous for his pickled sharks, embalmed cows and more recently a diamond-encrusted skull; Tracy Emin, whose work has ranged from confessional videos to a tent entitled *All The People I Have Ever Slept With;* and the Chapman Brothers, known for their deformed child mannequins (often featuring genitalia in inappropriate places).

Another key artist of the 1990s – and still going strong today – is the sculptor Antony Gormley, whose *Angel of the North* overlooks the city of Gateshead near Newcastle. A massive steel construction of a human figure with outstretched wings, more fitting on a 747 than a heavenly being, it was initially derided by the locals, but it is now an instantly recognised symbol of Northeast England.

Standing beside the busy A1 London to Edinburgh road, *Angel of the North* is one of the most viewed works of art in the world. Millions of drivers each year can't help but see it. Even greater numbers will probably see the *White Horse at Ebbsfleet*.

New Millennium

The early years of the 21st century have, inevitably, been dubbed the 'post-Britart' era. A body of less obviously shocking artists is emerging, although none have become a household name yet – not even Simon Starling, winner of the 2005 Turner Prize. Of the previous generation, apart from Damien Hirst, one of the few Britart figures to find mainstream success is Rachel Whiteread, known for her resin casts of everyday objects. In 2008 she was one of five artists short-listed for the 'Angel of the South', a £2 million project to create a huge outdoor sculpture in Kent to counterbalance the celebrated *Angel of the North.*

Whiteread's idea for the project was a plaster-cast of a house interior on an artificial hill, but the final selection went to Mark Wallinger, winner of the 2007 Turner Prize, for his *White Horse at Ebbsfleet.* As the name implies, this work is a white horse, true to life in everything except size. When finished (it's due for completion by 2012) it will be over 50m high – that's more than 30 times bigger than a real horse, so it should be clearly seen from the nearby A2 main road and the railway line between London and Paris. It's due for completion by 2012, although a petition raised by local residents in July 2010 called for the project to be stopped.

ANISH KAPOOR

The sculptor Anish Kapoor has been working in London since the 1970s, but his work appears around the world. He's best known for his large outdoor installations, which often feature curved shapes and reflective materials, such as highly polished steel. His recent works include a major new installation in London, called *Arcelor Mittal Orbit,* to celebrate the 2012 Olympic Games. Based on the five Olympic rings, at over 110m high it will be the largest piece of public art in Britain when completed.

Theatre

However you budget your time and money, make sure that you see some British theatre as part of your travels. It easily lives up to its reputation as the finest in the world, and London is the international centre for theatrical arts – whatever New Yorkers say.

But first, let's set the stage with some history. Centuries after his death in 1616, English theatre's best-known name is, of course, William Shakespeare. Originally from the Midlands, he made his name in London, where most of his plays were performed (at the Globe Theatre).

His brilliant plots and spectacular use of language, plus the sheer size of his canon of work (including classics such as *Hamlet, Romeo and Juliet, Henry V* and *A Midsummer Night's Dream*), have turned him into a national – and international – icon. Today, the Globe has now been rebuilt, so you can see Shakespeare's plays performed in Elizabethan style, and you can also catch his works at the theatre in his birthplace Stratford-upon-Avon, now forever linked with the Bard himself.

Later in the 17th century, following the English Civil War, the puritanical Oliver Cromwell closed the nation's theatres, but when the exiled king Charles II returned to the throne in 1660 he reopened the doors and encouraged many radical innovations, including actresses (female roles had previously been played by boys). Bawdy comedies of the era satirised the upper classes and indulged in fabulously lewd jokes (William Wycherley's *The Country Wife* is a prime example). One of the leading actresses of the day, Nell Gwyn, became Charles II's mistress, and Britain's first female playwright, Aphra Behn, also emerged during this period.

In the 18th century, theatres were built in the larger cities (the Bristol Old Vic and The Grand in Lancaster date from this time), but drama went into something of a decline, mainly due to the rise in operas and burlesque entertainment. It wasn't until the Victorian era that serious drama came back into fashion: during the mid-19th century classical plays competed with a broad mix of melodramas, comic operas, vaudeville and music hall.

Of the Victorian and Edwardian dramatists, the most famous names include George Bernard Shaw, Noel Coward and Oscar Wilde (everyone's heard of *The Importance of Being Earnest,* even if they haven't seen it).

During the early 20th century, the theatre soldiered on despite increasing competition from the cinema, but it wasn't until the 1950s

WILLIAM SHAKESPEARE

This British Literature chapter covers poetry and prose, but it would be remiss to omit mention at least of theatre and especially the nation's best-known theatrical name: William Shakespeare.

Britain's best-known playwright was born in 1564 in the Midlands town of Stratford-upon-Avon. He started writing plays around 1585, and his early theatrical works were histories and comedies, many of which are household names today – such as *All's Well that Ends Well, The Taming of the Shrew, Henry IV Pts 1 & 2* and *Henry V*. Later in his career Shakespeare moved into tragedies such as *Hamlet* and *King Lear,* most of them performed at the Globe Theatre in London.

For visitors to Britain today, ground zero for the national poet is Stratford-upon-Avon, where you can see various houses associated with the Bard, as well as plays put on by the Royal Shakespeare Company. You can also see his works performed at a remarkably faithful replica of the original Globe on London's South Bank.

WHAT A PANTOMIME

If any British tradition is guaranteed to bemuse outsiders, it's the pantomime. This over-the-top Christmas spectacle graces stages throughout the land throughout December and January, and traces its roots back to Celtic legends, medieval morality plays and the British music hall. The modern incarnation is usually based on a classic fairy tale and features a mix of saucy dialogue, comedy skits, song-and-dance routines and plenty of custard-pie humour, mixed in with topical gags for the grown-ups. Tradition dictates that the leading 'boy' is played by a woman, and the leading lady, or 'dame', is played by a chap. B-list celebrities, struggling actors and soap stars famously make a small fortune hamming it up for the Christmas panto, and there are always a few staple routines that everyone knows and joins in ('Where's that dragon/wizard/pirate/lion?' – 'He's behind you!'). It's cheesy, daft and frequently rather surreal, but guaranteed to be great fun for the family. Oh, no it isn't! Oh, yes it is! Oh, no it isn't!

that a new generation of playwrights brought theatre back to life. The 'Angry Young Men', including John Osborne, Joe Orton and Terence Rattigan, railed against the injustices of mid-1950s Britain with a searing and confrontational new style of theatre. A contemporary was Harold Pinter, who developed a new dramatic style and perfectly captured the stuttering illogical diction of real-life conversation.

Other ground-breaking playwrights experimented with language and form during the 1960s and '70s – including Tom Stoppard *(Rosencrantz and Guildenstern are Dead)*, Peter Shaffer *(Amadeus)*, Michael Frayn *(Noises Off)* and Alan Ayckbourn *(The Norman Conquests)* – while emerging directors like Peter Hall and Peter Brook took new risks with dramatic staging. It was also a golden period for acting: the staid, declamatory style of the past steadily gave way to a new, edgy realism in the performances of Laurence Olivier and Richard Burton, succeeded by actors such as Antony Sher, Judi Dench, Glenda Jackson and Ian McKellen.

Many of these actors remain household names, although they're perhaps better known for their appearances in big-budget films from America. Other notable actors – including Ralph Fiennes, Brenda Blethyn, Toby Stephens and Simon Callow – also juggle high-paying Hollywood roles with appearances on the stage.

The British Landscape

Britain may be small, but even a relatively short journey takes you through a surprising mix of landscapes. Seeing the change – subtle in some areas, dramatic in others – as you travel is one of this country's great drawcards.

Location, Location, Location

The island of Britain sits on the eastern edge of the North Atlantic and consists of three nations: England in the south and centre, Scotland to the north and Wales to the west – together making up the state of Great Britain. Further west lies the island of Ireland. The islands of Ireland and Britain, plus several smaller islands, together make up the archipelago of the British Isles. Looking southeast, France is just 20 miles away, while to the northeast lie the countries of Scandinavia.

Geologically at least, Britain is part of Europe. It's on the edge of the Eurasian landmass, separated from the mother continent by the shallow English Channel. (The French are not so proprietorial, and call it La Manche – 'the sleeve'.) About 10,000 years ago, Britain was physically part of Europe, but then sea levels rose and created the island we know today. Only in more recent times has there been a reconnection, in the form of the Channel Tunnel.

When it comes to topology, Britain is not a place of extremes. There are no Himalayas or Lake Baikals here. But there's plenty to keep you enthralled.

Southern England is covered in a mix of cities, towns and gently undulating countryside. East Anglia is almost entirely low and flat, while the Southwest Peninsula has wild moors, granite outcrops and rich

Landscape & Environment Online

» www.aonb.org.uk

» www.environmentagency.gov.uk

» www.nationalparks.gov.uk

» www.wildaboutbritain.co.uk

COMPARING COVERAGE

Statistics can be boring, but these essential measurements may be handy for planning or perspective as you travel around:

» Wales: 8000 sq miles

» Scotland: 30,500 sq miles

» England: 50,000 sq miles

» Great Britain: 88,500 sq miles

» UK: 95,000 sq miles

» British Isles: 123,000 sq miles

For comparison, France is about 210,000 sq miles, Texas 260,000 sq miles, Australia nearly three million sq miles and the USA over 3.5 million sq miles. When Britain is compared with these giants, it's amazing that such a small island can make so much noise.

pastures (Devon's cream is world famous), plus a rugged coast with sheltered beaches, making it a favourite holiday destination.

In the north of England, farmland remains interspersed with towns and cities, but the landscape is noticeably more bumpy. A line of large hills called the Pennines (fondly tagged 'the backbone of England') runs from Derbyshire to the Scottish border, and includes the peaty plateaus of the Peak District, the wild moors around Haworth (immortalised in Brontë novels), the delightful valleys of the Yorkshire Dales and the frequently windswept but ruggedly beautiful hills of Northumberland.

Perhaps England's best-known landscape is the Lake District, a small but spectacular cluster of mountains in the northwest, where Scafell Pike (a towering 978m) is England's highest peak.

The landscape of Wales is also defined by hills and mountains: notably the rounded Black Mountains and Brecon Beacons in the south, and the spiky peaks of Snowdonia in the north, with Snowdon (1085m) the highest peak in Wales. In between lie the wild Cambrian Mountains of central Wales, rolling to the west coast of spectacular cliffs and shimmering river estuaries.

For real mountains, though, head to Scotland, especially the wild, remote and thinly populated northwest Highlands – separated from the rest of the country by a diagonal gash in the earth's crust called the Boundary Fault. Ben Nevis (1343m) is Scotland's – and Britain's – highest mountain, but there are many more to choose from. The Highlands are further enhanced by the vast cluster of beautiful islands that lie off the loch-indented west coast.

South of the Scottish Highlands is the relatively flat Central Lowlands, home to the bulk of Scotland's population. Further south, down to the border with England, things get hillier again; this is the Southern Uplands, a fertile farming area.

Top Areas of Outstanding Natural Beauty in England & Wales

- Anglesey
- Chilterns
- Cornwall
- Cotswolds
- Gower Peninsula
- Isles of Scilly
- Llŷn Peninsula
- North Pennines
- Northumberland Coast
- Suffolk Coast
- Wye Valley

National Parks

Back in 1810, English poet and outdoor fan William Wordsworth suggested that the wild landscape of the Lake District in Cumbria, northwest England, should be 'a sort of national property, in which every man has a right'. More than a century later the Lake District did indeed become a national park, along with Brecon Beacons, Cairngorms, Dartmoor, Exmoor, Loch Lomond & the Trossachs, New Forest, Norfolk and Suffolk Broads, Northumberland, North York Moors, Peak District, Pembrokeshire Coast, Snowdonia, South Downs and Yorkshire Dales.

Combined, Britain's national parks now cover over 10% of the country, but the term 'national park' can cause confusion. First, they are not state owned: nearly all land in Britain is private, belonging to farmers, estates and conservation organisations. Second, they are not areas of

BEACHES

Britain has a great many beaches, from tiny hidden coves in Cornwall and Pembrokeshire to vast neon-lined strands such as Brighton or Blackpool. Other great beaches, each with their own distinct character, can be found in Devon, Somerset and along the south coast, Suffolk, Norfolk, Lancashire, Yorkshire and Northumberland in England, and pretty much all the way around the Welsh coast between the Gower Peninsula and Llandudno. Scotland offers even more choice, from the rocky bays on the west coast to the flat sands of the east. The best resort beaches earn the coveted international **Blue Flag** (www.blueflag.org) award, meaning sand and water are clean and unpolluted. Other parameters include the presence of lifeguards, litter bins and recycling facilities – meaning some wild beaches may not earn the award, but are still stunning nonetheless.

PROTECTED LANDSCAPES

As well as national parks, other parts of England and Wales are designated Areas of Outstanding Natural Beauty (AONBs), the second tier of protected landscape after national parks. In Scotland there are National Scenic Areas. There are also Conservation Areas, Sites of Special Scientific Interest and many others that you'll undoubtedly come across as you travel around.

wilderness as in many other countries. In Britain's national parks you'll see crop-fields in lower areas and grazing sheep on the uplands, as well as roads, railways and villages, and even towns, quarries and factories in some parks. It's a reminder of the balance that needs to be struck in this crowded country between protecting the natural environment and catering for the people who live in it.

Despite these apparent anomalies, Britain's national parks still contain mountains, hills, downs, moors, woods, river valleys and other areas of quiet countryside, all ideal for long walks, easy rambles, cycle rides, sightseeing or just lounging around. To help you get the best from the parks, they all have information centres, and all provide various recreational facilities (trails, car parks, campsites etc) for visitors.

Finally, it's worth noting also that there are many beautiful parts of Britain that are not national parks (such as central Wales, the North Pennines in England and many parts of Scotland). These can be just as good for outdoor activities or simply exploring by car or foot, and are often less crowded than the popular national parks.

Top National Scenic Areas in Scotland

- » Ben Nevis & Glencoe
- » Cuillin of Skye
- » Glen Affric
- » Isle of Mull
- » Knoydart
- » North Arran
- » River Tay
- » Shetland

Wildlife

For a small country, Britain has a diverse range of plants and animals. Many native species are hidden away, but there are some undoubted gems, from lowland woods carpeted in shimmering bluebells to stately herds of deer on the high moors. Taking the time to have a closer look will enhance your trip enormously, especially if you have the time and inclination to enjoy some walking or cycling through the British landscape – see the Britain's Great Outdoors chapter.

Animals

Farmland

In farmland areas, rabbits are everywhere, but if you're hiking through the countryside be on the lookout for brown hares, an increasingly rare species. They're related to rabbits but much larger. Males who battle for territory by boxing on their hind legs in early spring are, of course, as 'mad as a March hare'.

Although hare numbers are on the decline, down on the riverbank the once-rare otter is making a comeback. In southern Britain they inhabit the banks of rivers and lakes, and in Scotland they frequently live on the coast. Although their numbers are growing, they are mainly nocturnal and hard to see, but keep your eyes peeled and you might be lucky.

You're much more likely to see a red fox; this classic British mammal was once seen only in the countryside, but these wily beasts adapt well to any situation, so these days you're just as likely to see them scavenging in towns, and even in city suburbs. Elsewhere, another British classic, the black-and-white striped badger, is under threat from farmers who believe they transmit bovine tuberculosis to cattle, although conservationists say the case is far from proven.

Common birds of farmland and similar landscapes (and urban gardens) include the robin, with its instantly recognisable red breast and cheerful whistle; the wren, whose loud trilling song belies its tiny size; and the yellowhammer, with a song that sounds like (if you use your imagination) 'a-little-bit-of-bread-and-no-cheese'. In open fields, the warbling cry of a skylark is another classic, but now threatened, sound of the English outdoors. You're more likely to see a pheasant, a large bird originally introduced from Russia to the nobility's shooting estates, but now considered naturalised.

Between the fields, hedges provide cover for flocks of finches, but these seedeaters must watch out for sparrowhawks – birds of prey that come from nowhere at tremendous speed. Other predators include barn owls, a wonderful sight as they fly silently along hedgerows listening for the faint rustle of a vole or shrew. In rural Wales or Scotland you may see a buzzard, Britain's most common large raptor.

Wildlife & Walking Books

» *Wildlife Walks* published by the Wildlife Trusts

» *Walking In Britain* by Lonely Planet

» *Wildlife Walks in Britain* published by the AA

Woodland

In woodland areas, mammals include the small white-spotted fallow deer and the even smaller roe deer. Woodlands are full of birds too, but you'll hear them more than see them. Listen out for willow warblers (which have a warbling song with a descending cadence) and chiffchaffs (which, also not surprisingly, make a repetitive 'chiff chaff' noise).

If you hear rustling among the fallen leaves it might be a hedgehog – a cute-looking, spiny-backed insect eater – but it's an increasingly rare sound these days; conservationists say they'll be extinct in Britain by 2025, due to insecticides in farming, increased building in rural areas and hedgehogs' notoriously poor ability to safely cross roads.

In no such danger are grey squirrels, originally introduced from North America. They have proved very adaptable, to the extent that native red squirrels are severely endangered because the greys eat all the food. Pockets of red squirrels survive in the English Lake District and in various parts of Scotland, notably the Isle of Arran. Much larger than squirrels are pine martens, which are seen in some forested regions, especially in Scotland. With beautiful brown coats, they were once hunted for their fur, but are now fully protected.

Britain is home to herds of 'wild' ponies, notably in the New Forest, Exmoor and Dartmoor; these animals certainly roam free, but in reality they are privately owned and regularly managed.

Mountain & Moorland

On mountains and high moors – including Exmoor, Dartmoor, the Lake District and Northumberland, and much of Scotland – the most visible mammal is the red deer. Males of the species grow their famous large antlers between April and July, and shed them again in February. Also on the high ground, well-known and easily recognised birds include the red grouse, which often hides in the heather until almost stepped on then flies away with a loud warning call. On the high peaks of Scotland you may see the grouse's northern cousin, the ptarmigan, dappled brown in the summer but white in the winter.

'THE UNSPEAKABLE IN PURSUIT OF THE INEDIBLE'

Fox hunting has been a traditional English countryside activity (or a savage blood sport, depending on whom you talk to) for centuries, but it was banned in 2005 by a controversial law. As this activity killed only a small proportion of the total fox population, opinion is still divided on whether the ban has had any impact on overall numbers.

ACTING THE GOAT

Perhaps unexpectedly, Britain is home to herds of wild goats. They've gambolled on the moorland near Lynmouth in Devon for almost 1000 years, although they narrowly escaped a cull in 2005. Wild goats can also be seen on the Great Orme peninsula in North Wales, but these are new kids on the block, having been introduced only a century ago.

Look out, too, for the curlew, with its stately long legs and elegant curved bill. With luck you may see beautifully camouflaged golden plovers, while the spectacular aerial displays of lapwings are impossible to miss.

Other mountain birds include red kites (there have been various successful projects around the country to reintroduce these spectacular fork-tailed raptors – see p717). Also in the Scottish mountains, keep an eye peeled for golden eagles, Britain's largest birds of prey, as they glide and soar along ridges.

Wildlife of Britain by George McGavin et al is subtitled 'the definitive visual guide'. Although too heavy to carry around, this beautiful photographic book is great for pre-trip inspiration or post-trip memories.

Rivers & Coasts

If you're near inland water, you have a chance of spotting an osprey; the best places in Britain to see this magnificent bird include Rutland Water (see boxed text, p456) and the Cairngorms in Scotland. You could also look along the riverbanks for signs of water voles, endearing rodents that were once very common but have been all but wiped out by wild mink, another American immigrant (first introduced to stock fur farms).

On the coasts of Britain, particularly in Cornwall, Pembrokeshire and northwest Scotland, the dramatic cliffs are a marvellous sight in early summer (around May), when they are home to hundreds of thousands of breeding seabirds. Guillemots, razorbills and kittiwakes, among others, fight for space on impossibly crowded rock ledges. The cliffs become white with droppings and the air is filled with their shrill calls. Even if you're not into bird spotting, this is one of Britain's finest wildlife spectacles.

Another bird to look out for in coastal areas is the comical puffin (especially common in Shetland), with its distinctive rainbow beak and 'nests' burrowed in sandy soil. In total contrast, gannets are one of the largest seabirds and make dramatic dives for fish, often from a great height.

Britain's Best Wildlife by Chris Pacham and Mike Dilger is a 'Top 40' countdown of favourites compiled by experts and the public, with details on when and where to see the country's wildlife at its finest.

Estuaries and mudflats are feeding grounds for numerous migrant wading birds; easily spotted are black-and-white oystercatchers with their long red bills, while flocks of small ringed plovers skitter along the sand.

And finally, the sea mammals. There are two species of seal that frequent British waters; the larger grey seal is more often seen than the (misnamed) common seal. Boat trips to see their offshore colonies are available at various points around the coast, and are especially popular when the seal pups are born. Dolphins, porpoises and minke whales can all be seen off the west coast of Britain, particularly off Scotland, and especially from May to September when viewing conditions are better. Whale-watching trips (also good for seeing other marine wildlife such basking sharks) are available from several harbour towns, especially in Scotland; we give details throughout this book.

Plants

In any part of Britain, the best places to see wildflowers are areas that evade large-scale farming. In the chalky downs of southern England

and in limestone areas such as the Peak District and Yorkshire Dales, for example, many fields erupt with great profusions of cowslips and primroses in April and May.

Perhaps surprisingly, Britain's most wooded county is Surrey, despite its proximity to London. The soil is too poor for agriculture, and while woodland areas elsewhere in Britain were cleared, Surrey's trees received a stay of execution.

Some flowers prefer woodland, and again the best time to visit is April and May. This is because the leaf canopy of the woods is not yet fully developed, allowing sunlight to break through to encourage plants such as bluebells (a beautiful and internationally rare species). Another classic British plant is gorse – you can't miss the swathes of this spiky bush in heath areas, most notably in the New Forest in southern England.

In contrast, the blooming season for heather is quite short. On the Scottish mountains, the Pennine moors of northern England, and Dartmoor in the south, the landscape is covered in a riot of purple in August and September.

Britain's natural deciduous trees include oak, ash, hazel and rowan, with seeds and leaves supporting a vast range of insects and birds. The New Forest in southern England and the Forest of Dean on the Wales–England border are good examples of this type of habitat. In some parts of Scotland, most notably Glen Affric, stands of indigenous Caledonian pine can still be seen. As you travel through Britain you're also likely to see non-native pines, often in vast plantations empty of wildlife, although an increasing number of deciduous trees are also planted these days.

Environmental Issues

With Britain's long history of human occupation, it's not surprising that the country's appearance is almost totally the result of people's interaction with the environment. Since the earliest times, people have been chopping down trees and creating fields for crops or animals, but the most dramatic changes in rural areas came in the late 1940s, continuing into the '50s and '60s, when a postwar drive to be self-reliant in food meant new and intensive, large-scale farming methods. The visible result: lowland Britain's ancient patchwork of small meadows became a landscape of vast prairies, as walls were demolished, woodlands felled, ponds filled, wetlands drained and, most notably, hedgerows ripped out.

Legend says that it's the season for kissing when gorse blooms. Luckily, these vivid yellow flowers show year-round.

In most cases the hedgerows were lines of dense bushes, shrubs and trees forming a network that stretched across the countryside, protecting fields from erosion, supporting a varied range of flowers, and providing shelter for numerous insects, birds and small mammals. But in the rush to improve farm yields, thousands of miles of hedgerows were destroyed in the postwar decades, and between the mid-1980s and the early 2000s another 25% disappeared.

WILDLIFE IN YOUR POCKET

Is it a rabbit or a hare? A gull or a tern? Buttercup or cowslip? If you need to know a bit more about Britain's plant and animal kingdoms the following field guides are ideal for entry-level naturalists:

» *Complete Guide to British Wildlife* by Paul Sterry is portable and highly recommended, covering mammals, birds, fish, plants, snakes, insects and even fungi, with brief descriptions and excellent photos.

» If feathered friends are enough, the *Complete Guide to British Birds* by Paul Sterry combines clear photos and descriptions, plus when and where each species may be seen.

» *Wildlife of the North Atlantic* by world-famous film-maker Tony Soper beautifully covers the animals seen from beach, boat and clifftop in the British Isles and beyond.

» Collins Gem series includes handy little books on wildlife topics such as *Birds, Trees, Fish* and *Wild Flowers*.

BRITAIN'S NATIONAL PARKS

NATIONAL PARK	FEATURES	ACTIVITIES	BEST TIME TO VISIT	PAGE
Brecon Beacons	great green ridgelines, waterfalls; Welsh mountain ponies, red kites, buzzards, peregrine falcons, otters, kingfishers, dinosaurs	horse riding, cycling, caving, canoeing, hang-gliding	Mar-Apr (spring lambs shaking their tails)	p693
Cairngorms	snowy peaks, pine forests; ospreys, pine martens, wildcats, grouse, capercaillies	skiing, birdwatching, walking	Feb (for the snow)	p897
Dartmoor National Park	rolling hills, rocky outcrops and serene valleys; wild ponies, deer, peregrine falcons	walking, mountain biking, horse riding	May & Jun (wildflowers in bloom)	p312
Exmoor National Park	sweeping moors and craggy sea cliffs; red deer, wild ponies, horned sheep	horse riding, walking	Sep (heather in bloom)	p291
Lake District	majestic fells, rugged mountains and shimmering lakes; ospreys, red squirrels, golden eagles	water sports, walking, mountaineering, rock climbing	Sep-Oct (summer crowds have left and autumn colours abound)	p574
Loch Lomond & the Trossachs	sparkling lochs, brooding mountains: deer, squirrels, badgers, foxes, buzzards, otters	climbing, walking, cycling	Sep & Oct (after the summer rush)	p840 & p837
New Forest	woodlands and heath; wild ponies, otters, Dartford warblers southern damselflies	walking, cycling, horse riding	Apr-Sep (lush vegetation, wild ponies grazing)	p234
Norfolk & Suffolk Broads	expansive shallow lakes, rivers and marshlands; water lilies, wildfowl, otters	walking, cycling, boating	Apr & May (birds most active)	p381
North York Moors National Park	heather-clad hills, deep-green valleys, lonely farms and isolated villages; merlins, curlews and golden plovers	walking, mountain biking	Aug-Sep (heather flowering)	p521
Northumberland National Park	wild rolling moors, heather and gorse; black grouse, red squirrels; Hadrian's Wall	walking, cycling, climbing	Apr-May (lambs) & Sep (heather flowering)	p628
Peak District National Park	high moors, tranquil dales, limestone caves; kestrels, badgers, grouse	walking, cycling, mountain biking, hang-gliding, rock climbing	Apr-May (even more lambs)	p462
Pembrokeshire Coast	wave-ravaged shoreline of cliffs and beaches; puffins, fulmars, shearwaters, grey seals, dolphins, porpoises	walking, kayaking, coasteering, mountain biking, horse riding	Apr-May (lambs again)	p673
Snowdonia	major mountain ranges, lakes and estuaries; curlews, choughs, red kites, wild goats, Snowdon lilies, buzzards, polecats	walking, kayaking, coasteering, mountain biking, horse riding	May-Sep (summit temperatures mellow out)	p744
South Downs National Park	rolling chalky hills, tranquil farmland, woods, sheer white sea-cliffs: buzzards, red kites, peregrine falcons, Adonis blue butterflies, specialist chalk flowers such as Bastard Toadflax	walking, mountain biking, cycling, horse riding	any time of year (thanks to mild climate)	p166
Yorkshire Dales	rugged hills & lush valleys crossed by stone walls & dotted with monastic ruins	walking, cycling, climbing	Apr-May (you guessed it, when lambs outnumber visitors)	p490

WILDLIFE ON THE WEB

» National Trust (England & Wales) – www.nationaltrust.org.uk
» National Trust for Scotland – www.nts.org.uk
» Royal Society for the Protection of Birds – www.rspb.org.uk
» Wildlife Trusts – www.wildlifetrusts.org
» Woodland Trust – www.woodland-trust.org

Hedgerows have come to symbolise many other environmental issues in rural areas, and in recent years the destruction has abated, partly because farmers recognise their anti-erosion qualities, and partly because they're encouraged – with financial incentives from UK or European agencies – to 'set aside' such areas as wildlife havens.

Britain's new 'hedgerows' are the long strips of grass and bushes alongside motorways and major roads. Rarely trod by humans, they support rare flowers and thousands of insect species, plus mice, shrews and other small mammals – so kestrels are often seen hovering nearby.

In addition to hedgerow clearance, other farming techniques remain hot environmental issues. Studies have shown that the use of pesticides and intensive irrigation results in rivers running dry or being poisoned by run-off. Meanwhile, monocropping means vast fields with one type of grass and not another plant to be seen. These 'green deserts' support no insects, so in turn wild bird populations have plummeted. This is not a case of wizened old peasants recalling the idyllic days of their forebears; you only have to be over about 40 in Britain to remember a countryside where birds such as skylarks or lapwings were visibly much more numerous.

But all is not lost. In the face of apparently overwhelming odds, Britain still boasts great biodiversity, and some of the best wildlife habitats are protected (to a greater or lesser extent) by the creation of national parks and similar areas, or private reserves owned by conservation campaign groups such as the Wildlife Trusts, Woodland Trust and the Royal Society for the Protection of Birds. Many of these areas are open to the public – ideal spots for walking, birdwatching or simply enjoying the peace and beauty of the countryside – and well worth a visit as you travel around.

Sporting Britain

The British may have invented many of the world's favourite sports – or at least codified the modern rules – including cricket, tennis, rugby, golf and football, but, unfortunately, the national teams aren't always very good at playing them. It says something about the nation's footballing prowess, and something about the nation itself, when the most famous victory is still England winning the World Cup, way back in 1966.

But even when the British national teams aren't winning, a poor result doesn't dull the enthusiasm of the fans. Every weekend, thousands of people turn out to cheer their favourite football or rugby team, and sporting highlights such as the FA Cup, Wimbledon or the Derby keep the entire nation enthralled. The phenomenal success of the swimmers, cyclists and rowers at the Beijing Olympics engendered an outbreak of patriotic sporting pride – helped of course by London's hosting of the next Games in 2012.

This chapter gives a brief overview of spectator sports you might encounter as part of your travels around Britain; the regional chapters have more details on specific football stadia, cricket grounds and so on. For information on participatory sports, see the Britain's Great Outdoors chapter.

You can often buy tickets on the spot at the stadium for non-Premiership football games. Alternatively, go to the club websites or online agencies like www.ticketmaster.co.uk and www.myticketmarket.com.

Football (Soccer)

Despite what the fans may say in Madrid or Sao Paulo, the English Premier League has some of the finest teams in the world, dominated in recent years by the four top teams – Arsenal, Liverpool, Chelsea and Manchester United, all (with the notable exception of Arsenal) owned by multimillionaire foreigners whose limitless transfer budgets have allowed the clubs to attract many of the world's best – and now richest – players.

Down from the Premiership, 72 other teams play in the English divisions called the Championship, League One and League Two, while the Scottish Premier League is dominated by Glasgow Rangers and Glasgow Celtic. In Wales, football is less popular (rugby is the national sport), and the main Welsh teams such as Wrexham, Cardiff and Swansea play in lower English leagues.

SOCK IT TO ME

The word 'soccer' (the favoured term in countries where 'football' means another game) is reputedly derived from 'Association'. The sport is still officially called Association Football, to distinguish it from Rugby football, Gaelic football, American football, Aussie Rules football and so on. Another source is the word 'sock'; in medieval times this was a tough leather foot-cover worn by peasants – ideal for kicking around a pig's bladder in the park on a Saturday afternoon.

The football season is the same for all divisions (August to May), so seeing a match can easily be tied into most visitors' itineraries. However, tickets for the Premier League are like gold dust – your chances of bagging one are pretty much zilch unless you're a club member, or know someone who is. So you're better off buying a ticket for a lower-division game, which are cheaper and more easily available.

Rugby

A wit once said that football was a gentlemen's game played by hooligans, while rugby was the other way around. That may be true, but rugby is very popular, especially since England became world champions in 2004, and nearly did it again in 2008. It's worth catching a game for the display of skill (OK, and brawn), and the fun atmosphere in the grounds.

The international rugby union calendar is dominated by the annual Six Nations Championship between January and April, in which England does battle with neighbours Scotland, Wales, Ireland, France and Italy.

There are two versions of the game in Britain: Rugby Union (www.rfu.com) is played more in southern England, Wales and Scotland, and is traditionally the game of the middle and upper classes, while Rugby League (www.therfl.com) is played predominantly in northern England, traditionally by the working classes – although these days there's a lot of crossover.

Both 'codes' trace their roots to a football match in 1823 at Rugby School, in Warwickshire. A player called William Ellis, frustrated at the limitations of mere kicking, reputedly picked up the ball and ran with it towards the opponents' goal. True to the British tradition of fair play, rather than Ellis being dismissed from the game, a whole new sport was developed around his tactic, and the Rugby Football Union was formally inaugurated in 1871. Today, the Rugby World Cup is named the Webb Ellis trophy after this enterprising young tearaway.

Leading rugby union clubs include Leicester, Bath and Gloucester, while London has a host of good-quality teams (including Wasps and Saracens). In rugby league, teams to watch include the Wigan Warriors, Bradford Bulls and Leeds Rhinos. Tickets for games cost around £15 to £40 depending on the club's status and fortunes.

THE SWEET FA CUP

The Football Association held its first interclub knockout tournament in 1871. Fifteen clubs took part, playing for a nice piece of silverware called the FA Cup – then worth about £20.

Nowadays, around 600 clubs compete for this legendary and priceless trophy. It differs from many other competitions in that every team – from the lowest-ranking part-timers to the stars of the Premier League – is in with a chance. The preliminary rounds begin in August, and the world-famous Cup Final is held in May at the iconic Wembley Stadium in London.

The team with the most FA Cup victories is Manchester United, but public attention, and affection, is invariably focused on the 'giant-killers' – minor clubs that claw their way up through the rounds, unexpectedly beating higher-ranked competitors. The best-known giant-killing event occurred in 1992, when Wrexham, then ranked 24th in Division 3, famously beat league champions Arsenal. Other shocks include non-league Kidderminster Harriers' 1994 defeat of big boys Birmingham City, and Oldham Athletic beating premier leaguers Manchester City in 2005.

In recent years, the FA Cup has become one football competition among many. The Premier League and Champions League (against European teams) have a higher profile, bigger kudos and simply more money to play with. But, just as a country gets behind their national side, nothing raises community spirit more than a town team doing better than expected. Perhaps the FA Cup will one day be consigned to history – but what a sweet and glorious history it's been!

THE ASHES

The historic test cricket series between England and Australia known as the Ashes has been played every other year since 1882 (bar a few interruptions during the World Wars). It is played alternately in England and Australia with each of the five matches in the series held at a different cricket ground, always in the summer in the host location.

The contest's name dates back to the landmark test match of 1882, won (for the very first time) by the Australians. Defeat of the mother country by the colonial upstarts was a source of profound national shock: a mock obituary in the *Sporting Times* lamented the death of English cricket and referred to the sport's ashes being taken to Australia.

Later the name was given to a terracotta urn presented the following year to the English captain Ivo Bligh, purportedly containing the cremated ashes of a stump or bail used in this landmark match. Since 1953 this hallowed relic has resided at the Marylebone Cricket Club (MCC) Museum at the Lord's Cricket Ground. Despite the vast importance given to winning the series, the urn itself is a diminutive 6in high (152cm).

The recent history of the Ashes is not without drama. After eight straight defeats, England won the series in 2005, then handed the prize straight back to the Aussies after a humiliating thrashing in 2007, before 'regaining the Ashes' once again in 2009. In the 2010–11 series England thrashed Australia, winning in Australia for the first time since 1986–87.

Cricket

One of the most popular sports in Britain, cricket remains a predominantly English game at home, although it became an international game during Britain's colonial era, when it was exported to the countries of the Commonwealth, particularly in the Indian sub-continent, the West Indies and Australasia. A century on, the former colonies still delight in giving the old country a good spanking on the cricket pitch.

While many English people follow cricket like a religion, to the uninitiated it's an impenetrable spectacle. Spread over one-day games or five-day test matches, progress seems so *slow* (surely, say the unbelievers, this is the game for which TV highlights were invented), and dominated by arcane terminology like innings, overs, googlies, outswingers, leg-byes and silly mid-offs. Nonetheless, at least one cricket match should feature in your travels. If you're patient and learn the intricacies, you could find cricket as enriching and enticing as all the fans who remain glued to their radio or computer all summer, 'just to see how England's getting on'.

One-day games and international tests are played at grounds including Lord's in London, Edgbaston in Birmingham and Headingley in Leeds. Tickets cost from £30 to well over £200. The County Championship pits together the best teams from around the country; tickets cost £15 to £25, and only the most crucial games tend to sell out. Details are on the website of the English Cricket Board (www.ecb.co.uk).

The easiest option of all – and often the most enjoyable – is stumbling across a local game on a village green as you travel around. There's no charge for spectators, and no one will mind if you nip into the pub during a quiet period.

Causing ructions in the cricket world, the Twenty20 format emphasises fast big-batting scores, rather than slow and careful run-building. Traditionalists say it's changing the character of the game, but there's no doubting its popularity – many Twenty20 matches in Britain sell out.

Golf

Britain's main golfing tournament for spectators is the Open Championship, often referred to simply as The Open (or the British Open outside the UK). It's the oldest of professional golf's 'major' championships (dating back to 1860) and the only one held outside the USA. Usually played over the third weekend in July, the location changes each year,

SPORTING COVERAGE

Perhaps surprisingly, unlike many countries, Britain has no dedicated large circulation sports newspaper (apart from perhaps *The Sportsman*, concentrating mainly on the betting angle). But read the excellent coverage in the back pages of the *Daily Telegraph*, the *Times* and the *Guardian* and you'll see there's no need for one. The tabloid newspapers also cover sport, especially if a star has been caught with their pants down. Talking of which, the *Daily Sport* is not a sports paper, despite the name, unless photos of glamour models wearing only a pair of Arsenal socks counts as 'sport'.

using nine courses around the country: 2007 Carnoustie; 2008 Royal Birkdale; 2009 Turnberry; 2010 St Andrews ('the birthplace of golf'); 2011 Royal St George, Kent; 2012 Royal Lytham & St Annes, Lancashire; 2013 Muirfield.

Other important competitions include the British Amateur Championship and the Welsh Open at Celtic Manor Hotel near Newport, South Wales – the course for 2010's Ryder Cup. Spectator tickets start at about £10, going up to £75 for a good position at the major events.

Horse Racing

The tradition of horse racing in Britain stretches back centuries, and there's a 'meeting' somewhere pretty much every day. For all but the major events you should be able to get a ticket on the day, or buy in advance from the British Horse Racing Authority's website (www.gotoheraces.com), which also has lots of information about social events such as music festivals that coincide with the races.

The top event in the calendar is Royal Ascot (www.royalascot.co.uk) in mid-June, where the rich and famous come to see and be seen, and the fashion is almost as important as the nags –even the Queen turns up to put a fiver each way on Lucky Boy in the 3.15.

Other highlights include the Grand National steeplechase at Aintree in early April; and the Derby at Epsom on the first Saturday in June. The latter is especially popular with the masses so, unlike Ascot, you won't see morning suits and outrageous hats anywhere.

Tennis

Over 27 tonnes of strawberries and 7000L of cream are consumed every year during the two weeks of the Wimbledon Tennis Championships.

Tennis is widely played at club and regional level, but the best known tournament for spectators is the All England Championships – known to everyone as Wimbledon – when tennis fever sweeps through Britain in the last week of June and first week of July. There's something quintessentially English (yes, more English than British) about the combination of grass courts, polite applause and umpires in boaters, with strawberries and cream devoured by the truck-load.

Demand for seats at Wimbledon always outstrips supply, but to give everyone an equal chance tickets are sold through a public ballot. You can also take your chance on the spot; about 6000 tickets are sold each day (but not the last four days), but you'll need to be an early riser: dedicated fans start queuing before dawn. For more information see www.wimbledon.org.

Survival Guide

DIRECTORY A-Z . . .1054
Accommodation . . . 1054
Business Hours 1057
Climate Charts. 1058
Customs Regulations 1058
Electricity 1058
Embassies & Consulates 1058
Gay & Lesbian Travellers 1058
Health. 1059
Heritage Organisations 1059
Insurance 1060
Internet Access 1060
Legal Matters 1060
Money 1060
Public Holidays 1061
Safe Travel 1062
Telephone 1062
Tourist Information. 1062
Travellers with Disabilities. 1063
Visas. 1063
Work. 1063

TRANSPORT 1064
GETTING THERE & AWAY 1064
Air 1064
Land 1064
Sea 1065
GETTING AROUND . 1066
Air 1066
Bicycle 1066
Bus & Coach. 1066
Car & Motorcycle. . . . 1067
Hitching 1068
Local Transport 1068
Train 1068

GLOSSARY 1071

Directory A-Z

Accommodation

Accommodation in Britain is as varied as the sights you visit. From hip hotels to basic barns, the wide choice is all part of the attraction.

B&Bs & Guesthouses

The B&B ('bed and breakfast') is a great British institution. At smaller places it's pretty much a room in somebody's house, and you'll really feel part of the family. Larger B&Bs may have around 10 rooms and more facilities. Sometimes a larger B&B may call itself a 'guest house'. Facilities usually reflect price: for around £20 per person you get a simple bedroom and share the bathroom; for around £25 to £30 you get a private bathroom – either down the hall or en suite.

B&B prices are usually quoted per person, based on two people sharing a room. Single rooms for solo travellers are harder to find, and attract a 20% to 50% premium. Some B&Bs simply won't take single people (unless you pay the full double-room price), especially in summer.

» In country areas, B&Bs might be in the heart of a village or an isolated farm; in cities it's usually a suburban house.

» Advance reservations are always preferred at B&Bs, and are essential during popular tourist periods. Many require a minimum two nights at the weekends.

» If a B&B is full, owners may recommend another place nearby (possibly a private house taking occasional guests, not in tourist listings).

» In cities, some B&Bs are for long-term residents or people on welfare; they don't take passing tourists.

» In country areas, most B&Bs cater for walkers and cyclists, but some don't, so let them know if you'll be turning up with dirty boots or wheels.

» Some places reduce rates for longer stays (two or three nights).

» Most B&Bs serve enormous breakfasts; some offer packed lunches (around £5) and evening meals (around £12 to £15).

» If you're on a flexible itinerary and haven't booked in advance, most towns have a main drag of B&Bs; those with spare rooms hang up a 'Vacancies' sign.

» When booking, check where your B&B actually is. In country areas, postal addresses include the nearest town, which may be 20 miles away – important if you're walking! Some B&B owners will pick you up by car for a small charge.

Bunkhouses & Camping Barns

A bunkhouse is a simple place to stay, handy for walkers, cyclists or anyone on a budget in the countryside. They usually have a communal sleeping area and bathroom, heating and cooking stoves. You provide the sleeping bag and possibly cooking gear. Most charge around £10 per person per night.

Camping barns are even more basic: they're usually converted farm buildings, with sleeping platforms, a cooking area, and basic toilets outside. Take everything you'd need to camp except the tent. Charges are from around £5 per person.

CAMPING

If you're touring Britain with a tent or campervan (motorhome), it's worth joining the **Camping & Caravanning Club** (www.campingandcaravanningclub.co.uk). The club owns almost 100 campsites and lists thousands more in the invaluable *Big Sites Book* (free to members).

Camping

The opportunities for camping in Britain are numerous – ideal if you're on a tight budget or simply enjoy the great outdoors. In rural areas, campsites range from farmers' fields with a tap and a basic toilet, costing as little as £3 per person per night, to smarter affairs with hot showers and many other facilities, charging £10 or more.

Whatever your style, you'll usually need all your own kit. Britain doesn't have the huge sites of permanent tents, as found in France and some other European countries. Having said that, a few campsites in Britain also offer self-catering accommodation in chalets and caravans, or in more exotic options such as tepees and yurts. Some options are very smart and stylish – dubbed 'glamping' by the UK press.

Hostels

There are two types of hostel in Britain: those run by the **Youth Hostels Association** (YHA; www.yha.org.uk) and **Scottish Youth Hostels Association** (SYHA; www.syha.org.uk); plus independent hostels – most of which are listed in the Independent Hostels guidebook and website (www.independenthostelguide.co.uk). You'll find hostels in rural areas, towns and cities. They're aimed at all types of traveller and you don't have to be young.

Some hostels are purpose-built but many are converted cottages, country houses and even castles, often in wonderful locations. Facilities include showers, drying room, lounge and equipped self-catering kitchen. Sleeping is usually in dormitories. Many hostels also have twin or four-bed rooms, some with private bathroom.

YHA & SYHA HOSTELS

The simplest YHA and SYHA hostels cost around £10 per person per night.

NO SUCH THING AS A 'STANDARD' HOTEL RATE

You'll notice as you're travelling through Britain that there's often no such thing as a 'standard' hotel rate. Many hotels, especially larger places or chains, vary prices according to demand – or have different rates for online, phone or walk-in bookings – just like airlines and train operators. So if you book early for a night when the hotel is likely to be quiet, rates are cheap. If you book late, or aim for a public holiday weekend, you'll pay a lot.

However, if you're prepared to be flexible and leave booking to the very last minute you can sometimes get a bargain as drop rates again. The end result: you can pay anything from £19 to £190 for the very same hotel room. With that in mind, the hotel rates we quote throughout this book are often guide prices only (B&B prices tend to be much more consistent).

PRACTICALITIES

» Newspapers – Tabloids include the *Sun, Mail and Mirror,* and *Daily Record* (in Scotland); quality 'broadsheets' include (from right to left, politically) the *Telegraph, Times, Independent* and *Guardian*.

» TV – Leading free-to-air options include BBC 1 and BBC 2, closely followed by ITV and Channel 4. Satellite and cable TV is dominated by Sky.

» Weights & Measures – Britain uses a bizarre mix of metric and imperial measures; for example, petrol is sold by the litre but beer by the pint and mountain heights are in metres but road distances are in miles.

» Radio – Main BBC stations and wavelengths are Radio 1 (98-99.6MHz FM), Radio 2 (88-92MHz FM), Radio 3 (90–92.2 MHz FM), Radio 4 (92–94.4MHz FM) and Radio 5Live (909 or 693 AM). National commercial stations include Virgin Radio (1215Hz MW) and non-highbrow classical specialist Classic FM (100–102MHz FM). All are available on digital.

» Video & DVD – PAL format (incompatible with NTSC/Secam).

» Discount Card – There's no specific discount card for visitors to Britain, although travel cards are discounted for younger and older people – see p1066.

Larger hostels with more facilities are £15 to £20. London's YHA hostels cost from £25. Most hostel prices vary according to demand and season (just like train fares in Britain). Book early for a Tuesday night in May and you'll get the best rate. Book late for a weekend in August and you'll pay top price – if there's space at all. Throughout this book, we have generally quoted the cheaper rates (in line with those listed on the YHA's website); you may find yourself paying more.

All charge extra if you're not a member (£3 at YHA hostels; £1 at SYHA hostels). Reservations and advance payments with credit card are usually possible. You don't *have* to be a member of the YHA/SYHA (or another Hostelling International organisation) to stay at YHA/SYHA hostels, but it's usually worth joining. Annual YHA membership costs £16; annual SYHA membership costs £10; younger people and families get discounts. Throughout this book we have generally quoted the member rates for YHA/SYHA hostels.

YHA hostels tend to have complicated opening times and days, especially in remote locations or out of tourist season, so check before turning up.

INDEPENDENT HOSTELS

In rural areas some independent hostels are little more than simple bunkhouses (charging around £6), while others are almost up to B&B standard (£15 or more). In cities, independent backpacker hostels are usually aimed at young budget travellers and are open 24/7, with a lively atmosphere, good range of rooms (doubles or dorms), bar, cafe, internet computer, wi-fi and laundry, charging around £15 for a dorm bed, or £20 to £35 for a bed in a private room.

PRICE RANGES

Throughout this book, reviews of places to stay use the following price ranges, all based on double room with private bathroom in high season. Hotels in London are more expensive than the rest of the country, so have different price ranges in this book.

BUDGET	LONDON	ELSEWHERE
budget (£)	<£80	<£50
midrange (££)	£80-180	£50-130
top end (£££)	>£180	>£130

Hotels

A hotel in Britain might be a small and simple place, perhaps a former farmhouse now stylishly converted, where peace and quiet – along with luxury – are guaranteed. Or it might be a huge country house with fancy facilities, grand staircases, acres of grounds and lines of stag heads on the wall.

Charges vary as much as quality and atmosphere. At the bargain end, you can find singles/doubles costing £30/40. Move up the scale and you'll pay £100/150 or beyond. More money doesn't always mean a better hotel though – whatever your budget, some are excellent value, while others overcharge.

If all you want is a place to put your head down, budget chain hotels can be a good option. Most are totally lacking in style or ambience, but who cares? You'll only be there for eight hours, and six of them you'll be asleep. Most offer rooms at variable prices based on demand; on a quiet night in November twin-bed rooms with private bathroom start at around £20, and at the height of the tourist season you'll pay £45 or more.

Options include the following:

Etap Hotels (www.etaphotel.com)

Hotel Formule 1 (www.hotelformule1.com)

Premier Inn (www.premierinn.com)

Travelodge (www.travelodge.co.uk)

BOOK YOUR STAY ONLINE

For more accommodation reviews by Lonely Planet authors, check out hotels.lonelyplanet.com/GreatBritain. You'll find independent reviews, as well as recommendations on the best places to stay. Best of all, you can book online.

Pubs & Inns

As well as selling drinks, many pubs and inns offer lodging, particularly in country areas. Staying in a pub can be good fun – you're automatically at the centre of the community – although accommodation varies enormously.

Expect to pay around £20 per person at the cheap end, and around £30 to £35 for something better. An advantage for solo tourists is that pubs are more likely to have single rooms.

If a pub does B&B, it normally does evening meals,

served in the bar or an adjoining restaurant.

Rental Accommodation

If you want to slow down and get to know a place, renting for a week or two can be ideal. Choose from neat apartments in towns and cities, or quaint old houses and farms (always called cottages, whatever the size) in country areas. Cottages for four people cost between £200 and £600 in high season. Rates fall at quieter times, and you may be able to rent for a long weekend.

Handy websites include the following:

Bed & Breakfast Nationwide (www.bedandbreakfastnationwide.com)

Cottages & Castles (www.cottages-and-castles.co.uk)

Cottages4U (www.cottages4u.co.uk)

Hoseasons (www.hoseasons.co.uk)

National Trust (www.nationaltrust.org.uk/accommodation)

Stilwell's (www.stilwell.co.uk)

University Accommodation

Many universities offer student accommodation to visitors during holidays. You usually get a functional single bedroom with private bathroom, and self-catering flats are also available.

Prices range from £15 to £30 per person. A handy portal is www.universityrooms.co.uk.

> **OPENING HOURS**
>
> London and other cities have 24/7 convenience stores. In smaller towns and in country areas, shops often shut for lunch (normally 1pm to 2pm) and on Wednesday or Thursday afternoon, too.

Business Hours

Throughout this book we work on the basis that most restaurants and cafes are open for lunch or dinner or both, so precise opening times and days are given only if they differ markedly from the pattern outlined here.

Banks

» Monday to Friday, open 9.30am until 4pm or 5pm.

» Saturday, main branches open 9.30am to 1pm.

» Sunday closed.

Bars & Clubs

» In cities, bars (and some pubs) open until midnight or later, especially at weekends.

» Clubs often stay open to 2am or beyond.

Cafes

» In cities, many cafes open from 7am to 6pm, sometimes later.

» In country areas, teashops open for lunch, and stay open all afternoon until 5pm (often later in summer).

» In winter months, country cafe hours are reduced; some close completely October to April.

Museums & Sights

» Large museums and sights usually open virtually every day of the year.

» Some smaller places open Saturday and Sunday but are closed Monday and/or Tuesday.

» Smaller places open daily in high season; but on weekends only or are completely closed in low season.

Post Offices

» Monday to Friday, 9am to 5pm (5.30pm or 6pm in cities).

» Saturday 9am to 12.30pm. Main branches to 5pm.

» Sunday closed.

> **SOMETHING DIFFERENT FOR THE WEEKEND?**
>
> For some more unusual accommodation options, the Landmark Trust rents historic buildings; your options include ancient cottages, medieval castles, Napoleonic forts and 18th-century follies. Or try Distinctly Different, specialising in unusual and bizarre places to stay. See www.landmarktrust.org.uk and www.distinctlydifferent.co.uk.

Pubs

» Pubs open daily 11am to 11pm Sunday to Thursday, sometimes to midnight or 1am Friday and Saturday.

» Some pubs shut from 3pm to 6pm.

Restaurants

» Most restaurants open Monday to Sunday; some close Sunday evening or all day Monday.

» Most open for lunch (about noon to 3pm) *and* dinner (about 6pm to 11pm, to midnight or later in cities). Some restaurants open only for lunch *or* dinner.

» A few restaurants open at around 7am and serve breakfast, but mainly cafes do this.

Shops

» Monday to Friday, 9am to 5pm (5.30pm or 6pm in cities).

» Saturday, 9am to 5pm.

» Sunday, larger shops open 10am to 4pm.

Customs Regulations

Britain has a two-tier customs system: one for goods bought duty-free outside the EU; the other for goods bought in another European Union (EU) country where tax and duty is paid. Below is a summary of the rules; for more details go to www.hmce.gov.uk and search for 'Customs Allowances'.

Duty-Free

For duty-free goods from outside the EU, the limits include 200 cigarettes, 2L of still wine, plus 1L of spirits or another 2L of wine, 60cc of perfume, and other duty-free goods (including beer) to the value of £300.

Tax & Duty Paid

There is no limit to the goods you can bring from within the EU (if taxes have been paid), but customs officials use the following guidelines to distinguish personal use from commercial imports: 3200 cigarettes, 200 cigars, 10L of spirits, 20L of fortified wine, 90L of wine and 110L of beer. Still enough to have one hell of a party.

Electricity

Climate

London

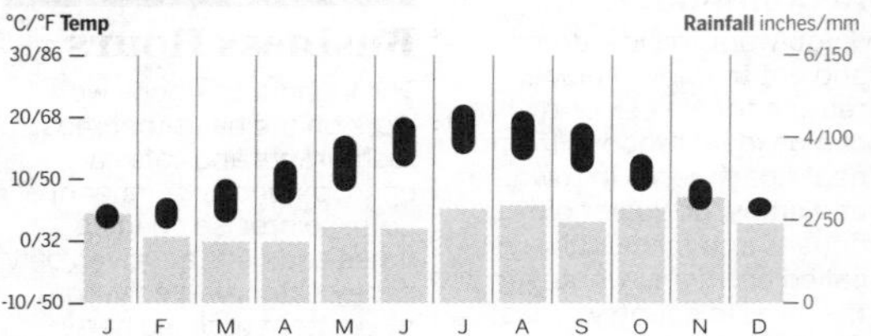

Newquay

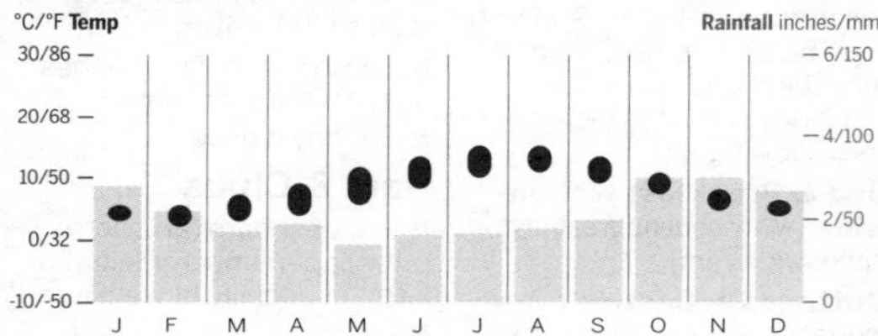

York

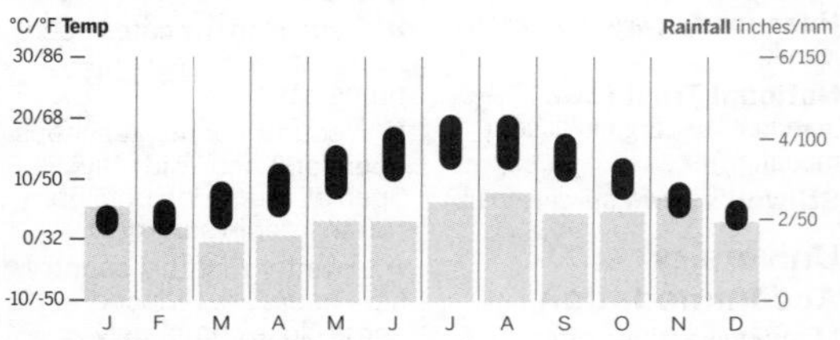

Embassies & Consulates

Opposite is a selection of embassies, consulates and high commissions in London. For a complete list of embassies in Britain, see the website of the **Foreign & Commonwealth Office** (www.fco.gov.uk), which also lists Britain's diplomatic missions overseas.

Gay & Lesbian Travellers

Britain is a generally tolerant place for gays and lesbians. London, Manchester and Brighton have flourishing gay scenes, and in other sizeable cities (even some small towns) you'll find communities not entirely in the closet. That said, you'll still find pockets of homophobic hostility in some areas. Resources include the following:

Diva (www.divamag.co.uk)

Gay Times (www.gaytimes.co.uk)

London Lesbian & Gay Switchboard (☎020-7837 7324; www.llgs.org.uk, www.queery.org.uk)

Pink Paper (www.pinkpaper.com)

Health

No immunisations are mandatory for visiting Britain.

Cardiff

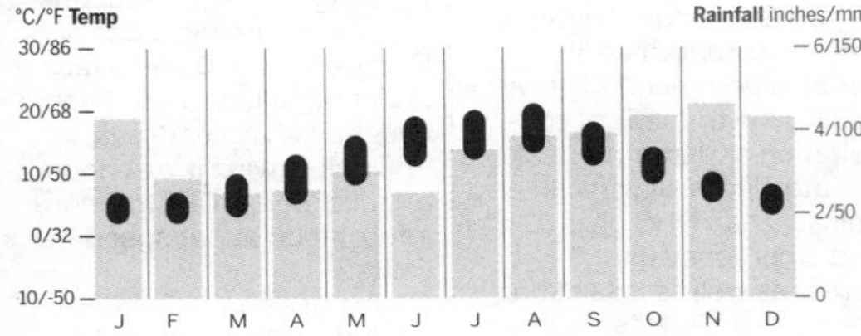

Inverness

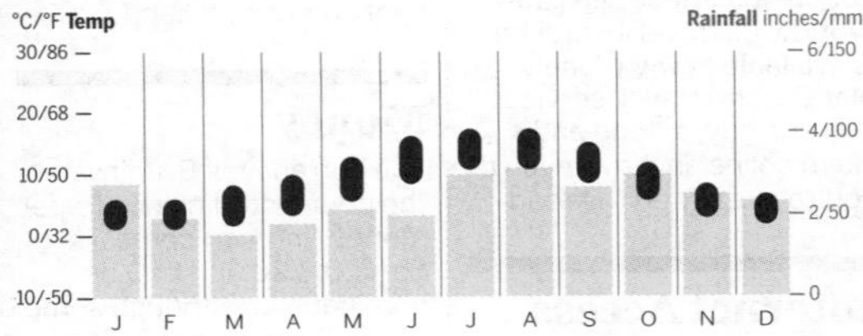

Edinburgh

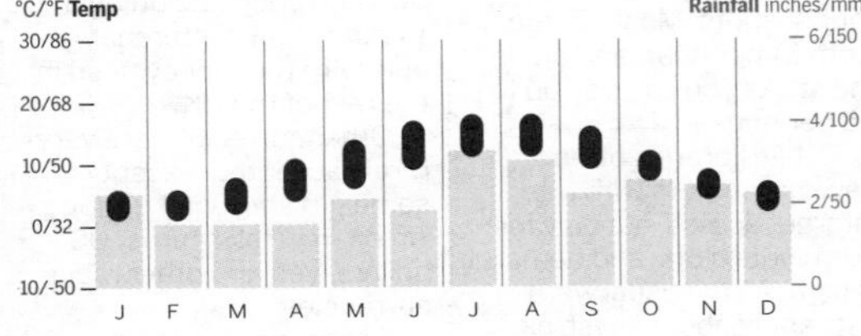

Regardless of nationality, everyone receives free emergency treatment at accident and emergency (A&E) departments of state-run NHS hospitals. European Economic Area (EEA) nationals get free nonemergency treatment (ie the same service British citizens receive) with a European Health Insurance Card (EHIC) validated in their home country. Reciprocal arrangements between Britain and some other countries (including Australia) allow free medical treatment at hospitals and surgeries, and subsidised dental care.

If you don't need full-on hospital treatment, chemists (pharmacies) can advise on minor ailments such as sore throats and earaches. In large cities, there's always at least one 24/7 chemist.

For more details see the **Department of Health** (www.doh.gov.uk) website and follow the links to 'Health Care', 'Entitlements' and 'Overseas Visitors'.

Heritage Organisations

A highlight of a journey through Britain is visiting the numerous castles and historic sites that pepper the country. Membership of a heritage organisation gets you free admission (usually

EMBASSIES & CONSULATES IN LONDON

COUNTRY	PHONE	WEBSITE	ADDRESS
Australia	020-7379 4334	www.australia.org.uk	The Strand, WC2B 4LA
Canada	020-7258 6600	www.canada.org.uk	1 Grosvenor Sq, W1X 0AB
China	020-7299 4049	www.chinese-embassy.org.uk	49-51 Portland Pl, W1B 4JL
France	020-7073 1000	www.ambafrance-uk.org	58 Knightsbridge, SW1 7JT
Germany	020-7824 1300	www.london.diplo.de	23 Belgrave Sq, SW1X 8PX
Ireland	020-7235 2171	www.embassyofireland.co.uk	17 Grosvenor Pl, SW1X 7HR
Japan	020-7465 6500	www.uk.emb -japan.go.jp	101 Piccadilly, W1J 7JT
Netherlands	020-7590 3200	www.netherlands-embassy.org.uk	38 Hyde Park Gate, SW7 5DP
New Zealand	020-7930 8422	www.nzembassy.com/uk	80 Haymarket, SW1Y 4TQ
Poland	0870 774 2700	www.polishembassy.org.uk	47 Portland Pl, W1B 1HQ
USA	020-7499 9000	www.usembassy.org.uk	24 Grosvenor Sq, W1A 1AE

CAN YOU DRINK THE WATER?

Tap water in Britain is safe unless there's a sign to the contrary (eg on trains). Don't drink from streams in the countryside – you never know if there's a dead sheep upstream.

a good saving) as well as information handbooks and so on. If you join an English heritage organisation, it covers you for Wales and Scotland, and vice versa.

The **National Trust** (NT; www.nationaltrust.org.uk) protects hundreds of historic buildings plus vast tracts of land with scenic importance across England and Wales. Annual membership costs £49 (with discounts for under-26s and families). A Touring Pass allows free entry to NT properties for one/two weeks (£21/26 per person); families and couples get cheaper rates. The **National Trust for Scotland** (NTS; www.nts.org.uk) is similar.

English Heritage (EH; www.english-heritage.org.uk) is a state-funded organisation responsible for numerous historic sites. Annual membership costs £44 (couples and seniors get discounts). An Overseas Visitors Pass allows free entry to most sites for seven/14 days for £20/25 (with cheaper rates for couples and families). In Wales and Scotland the equivalent organisations are **Cadw** (www.cadw.wales.gov.uk) and **Historic Scotland** (HS; www.historic-scotland.gov.uk).

We have included the relevant acronym (NT, NTS, EH etc) in the information brackets after properties listed throughout this book. You can join at the first NT/NTS/EH/HS/Cadw site you visit.

Insurance

Although everyone receives free emergency treatment, regardless of nationality, travel insurance is still highly recommended. It will usually cover medical consultation and treatment at private clinics, which can be quicker than NHS places, and emergency dental care – as well as loss of baggage or valuable items and, most importantly, the cost of any emergency flights home. For car insurance see p1067. Worldwide travel insurance is available at www.lonelyplanet.com/travel_services. You can buy, extend and claim online anytime, even if you're already on the road.

Internet Access

Internet cafes are surprisingly rare in Britain, especially away from big cities and tourist spots. Most charge from £1 per hour, and out in the sticks you can pay up to £5 per hour.

Public libraries often have computers with free internet access, but only for 30-minute slots, and demand is high. All the usual warnings apply about keystroke-capturing software and other security risks.

If you'll be using your laptop to get online, an increasing number of hotels, hostels, stations and coffee shops (even some trains) have wi-fi access, charging anything from nothing to £5 per hour. Wi-fi is often free, but some places (typically, upmarket hotels) charge.

Legal Matters

You must be over 18 to buy alcohol and cigarettes. You usually have to be 18 to enter a pub or bar, although rules are different for under-18s if eating (see p45). Some bars and clubs are over-21 only.

Illegal drugs are widely available, especially in clubs. Cannabis possession is a criminal offence; punishment for carrying a small amount may be a warning, a fine or imprisonment. Dealers face stiffer penalties, as do people caught with other drugs.

Drink-driving is a serious offence. See p1067 for more information about speed limits.

On buses and trains (including the London Underground), people without a valid ticket are fined on the spot – usually around £20.

Money

The currency of Britain is the pound sterling (£). Paper money ('notes') comes in £5, £10, £20 and £50 denominations, although some shops don't accept £50 notes because fakes circulate. Scotland issues its own currency (including a £1 note) that's interchangeable with the money used in the rest of the UK.

Other currencies are very rarely accepted, except some gift shops in London, which may take euros, US dollars, yen and other major currencies.

For a rundown of exchange rates and costs see p19.

SCOTTISH POUNDS

Although Scottish pounds are exactly the same value as (and freely interchangeable with) pounds in the rest of the UK, in reality you'll find shops more readily accept them in the north of England than in the south. Banks will always change them.

ATMs

ATMs (often called 'cash machines') are easy to find in cities and even small towns. Watch out for ATMs that might have been tampered with; a common ruse is to attach a card-reader to the slot.

Changing Money

Cities and larger towns have banks and bureaus for changing your money (cash or travellers cheques) into pounds. Check rates first; some bureaus offer poor rates or levy outrageous commissions. You can also change money at some post offices – very handy in country areas, and exchange rates are fair.

Credit & Debit Cards

Visa and MasterCard credit and debit cards are widely accepted in Britain; they're good for larger hotels, restaurants, shopping, flights, long-distance travel, car hire etc. Smaller businesses, such as pubs or B&Bs, prefer debit cards (or charge a fee for credit cards), and some take cash or cheque only.

Nearly all credit and debit cards use a 'Chip and PIN' system (instead of signing). If your card isn't Chip and PIN enabled, you should be able to sign in the usual way, but some places may not accept your card.

Tipping

In Britain you're not obliged to tip if the service or food was unsatisfactory (even if it's been automatically added to your bill as a 'service charge').

» Restaurants – around 10%. Also teashops and smarter cafes with full table service. At smarter restaurants waiters can get a bit sniffy if the tip isn't nearer 12% or even 15%.

» Taxis – 10%, or rounded up to the nearest pound, especially in London. It's less usual to tip minicab drivers.

» Toilet attendants – around 50p.

» Pubs – around 10% if you order food at the table and your meal is brought to you. If you order and pay at the bar (food or drinks), tips are not expected.

Travellers Cheques

Travellers cheques are safer than cash, but are rarely used in Britain, as credit/debit cards and ATMs have become the method of choice. They are rarely accepted for purchases (except at large hotels), so for cash you'll still need to go to a bank or change bureau.

PUBLIC HOLIDAYS

Roads get busy and hotel prices go up during school holidays. Exact dates vary from year to year and region to region, but are roughly as follows:

» **Easter Holiday** Week before and week after Easter

» **Summer Holiday** Third week of July to first week of September

» **Christmas Holiday** Mid-December to first week of January

There are also three week-long 'half-term' school holidays – usually late February (or early March), late May and late October. These vary between Scotland, England and Wales.

Public Holidays

Holidays for the whole of Britain:

New Year's Day 1 January

Easter March/April (Good Friday to Easter Monday inclusive)

May Day First Monday in May

Spring Bank Holiday Last Monday in May

Summer Bank Holiday Last Monday in August

Christmas Day 25 December

Boxing Day 26 December

If a public holiday falls on a weekend, the nearest Monday is usually taken instead. In England and Wales most businesses and banks close on official public holidays (hence the quaint term 'bank holiday'). In Scotland Bank Holidays are just for the banks, and many businesses stay open. Many Scottish towns normally have a spring and autumn holiday, but the dates vary.

On public holidays, some small museums and places of interest close, but larger attractions have their busiest times. If a place closes on Sunday, it'll probably be shut on bank holidays as well. Virtually

TRAVEL HEALTH WEBSITES

Before visiting Britain from overseas, consult your government's travel health website. These include:

» **Australia** (www.dfat.gov.au/travel)

» **Canada** (www.travelhealth.gc.ca)

» **USA** (www.cdc.gov/travel/)

GOVERNMENT ADVICE

The following government websites offer travel advisories and information on current hot spots:

Australian Department of Foreign Affairs (www.smarttraveller.gov.au)

British Foreign Office (www.fco.gov.uk/countryadvice)

Canadian Department of Foreign Affairs (www.dfait-maeci.gc.ca)

US State Department (http://travel.state.gov)

everything – attractions, shops, banks, offices – closes on Christmas Day, although pubs are open at lunchtime.

There's usually no public transport on Christmas Day, and a very minimal service on Boxing Day.

Safe Travel

Britain is a remarkably safe country, but crime is not unknown in London and other cities. When travelling by tube, tram or urban train services at night, choose a carriage containing other people.

Unlicensed minicabs – a bloke with a car earning money on the side – operate in large cities, and are worth avoiding unless you know what you're doing. Annoyances include driving round in circles, then charging an enormous fare. Dangers include driving to a remote location then robbery or rape. To avoid this, use a metered taxi or phone a reputable minicab company and get an up-front quote for the ride.

Telephone

In this book, area codes and individual numbers are listed together, separated by a hyphen.

Area codes in Britain do not have a standard format or length, eg ☎020 for London, ☎0161 for Manchester, ☎01225 for Bath, ☎029 for Cardiff, ☎0131 for Edinburgh, ☎015394 for Ambleside, followed as usual by the individual number.

Other codes:

» ☎0500 or ☎0800 – free calls

» ☎0845 – calls at local rate, wherever you're dialling from within the UK

» ☎087 – calls at national rate

» ☎089 or ☎09 – premium rate

» ☎07 – mobile phones, more expensive than calling a landline

To call outside the UK dial ☎00, then the country code (☎1 for USA, ☎61 for Australia etc), the area code (you usually drop the initial zero) and the number.

» operator ☎100

» international operator ☎155 – also for reverse-charge (collect) calls

For directory enquiries, a host of agencies compete for your business and charge from 10p to 40p; numbers include ☎118 192, ☎118 118, ☎118 500 and ☎118 811.

Tourist Information

All British cities and towns, and some villages, have a tourist information centre (TIC). Some TICs are run by national parks and often have small exhibits about the area. You'll also see 'visitor welcome centres' or 'visitor information centres' – for ease we've called all these places 'tourist offices' in this book.

Whatever the name, these places have helpful staff, books and maps for sale, leaflets to give away and loads of advice on things to see or do. They can also assist with booking accommodation. Most tourist offices keep regular business hours; in quiet areas they close from October to March, while in popular areas they open daily year-round.

For a list of all tourist offices around Britain see www.visitmap.info/tic.

Travellers with Disabilities

All new buildings have wheelchair access, and even hotels in grand old country houses often have lifts,

USEFUL ORGANISATIONS FOR TRAVELLERS WITH DISABILITIES

» **Good Access Guide** (www.goodaccessguide.co.uk)

» **Royal Association for Disability & Rehabilitation** (RADAR; www.radar.org.uk) Published titles include *Holidays in Britain and Ireland*. Through RADAR you can get a key for 7000 public disabled toilets across the UK.

» **RNIB** (www.rnib.org.uk)

» **RNID** (www.rnid.org.uk)

» **Tourism For All** (www.tourismforall.org.uk)

TOURISM SITES

Before leaving home, check the informative, comprehensive and wide-ranging website of Britain's official tourist board, **VisitBritain** (www.visitbritain.com), covering all the angles of national tourism, with links to numerous other sites.

ramps and other facilities. Smaller B&Bs are often harder to adapt, so you'll have less choice here. Many theatres, most banks and some public buildings have hearing loops, while the main public areas in cities and towns have some facilities for blind people, such as audible signals and special paving at road-crossings.

Cities

Getting around in cities, new buses have low floors for easy access, but few have conductors who can lend a hand when you're getting on or off. Many taxis take wheelchairs, or just have more room in the back.

Long-Distance Coach

Coaches may present problems if you can't walk, but the main operator, **National Express** (www.nationalexpress.com) has wheelchair-friendly coaches on many routes. For details, ring their dedicated Disabled Passenger Travel Helpline on ☎0121-423 8479 or go to the website and follow links to 'Our Service' then 'Disabled Facilities'.

Intercity Trains

On most intercity trains there's more room and better facilities, compared with travel by coach, and usually station staff around; just have a word and they'll be happy to help.

Visas

If you're a European Economic Area (EEA) national, you don't need a visa to visit (or work in) Britain. Citizens of Australia, Canada, New Zealand, South Africa and the USA are given leave to enter the UK at their point of arrival for up to six months (three months for some nationalities), but are prohibited from working. For more info see www.ukvisas.gov.uk or www.ukba.homeoffice.gov.uk.

Work

Nationals of most European countries don't need a permit to work in Britain, but everyone else does. Exceptions include most Commonwealth citizens with a UK-born parent: the 'Right of Abode' allows you to live and work in Britain and the rest of the UK. Most Commonwealth citizens under 31 are eligible for a Working Holidaymaker Visa – it's valid for two years, you can work for a total of 12 months, and it must be obtained in advance.

Useful websites are listed below. Also very handy is the 'Living & Working Abroad' thread on the Thorntree forum at lonelyplanet.com.

BUNAC (www.bunac.org)

Go Work Go Travel (www.goworkgotravel.com)

UK Border Agency (www.ukba.homeoffice.gov.uk)

UK Employment & Recruitment Agencies (www.employmentrecruitment.co.uk)

Working Holiday Guru (www.workingholidayguru.com)

Transport

GETTING THERE & AWAY

London is a global transport hub, so you can easily fly to Britain from just about anywhere. In recent years, the massive growth of budget ('no-frills') airlines has increased the number of routes – and reduced the fares – between Britain and other countries in Europe.

Your other main option for travel between Britain and mainland Europe is ferry, either port-to-port or combined with a long-distance bus trip, although journeys can be long and financial savings not huge compared with budget airfares. International trains are much more comfortable and a 'green' option; the Channel Tunnel allows direct rail services between Britain, France and Belgium, with onward connections to many other European destinations.

Flights, tours and rail tickets can be booked online at www.lonelyplanet.com/travel_services.

Air

Airports

London's main airports:

Heathrow (LHR; www.heathrowairport.com) The world's busiest airport, and the UK's main airport for international flights, it's often chaotic and crowded. About 15 miles west of central London.

Gatwick (LGW; www.gatwickairport.com) The UK's number-two airport, also mainly for international flights, 30 miles south of central London.

Stansted (STN; www.stanstedairport.com) About 35 miles northeast of central London, mainly handling charter and budget European flights.

Luton (LTN; www.london-luton.co.uk) Some 35 miles north of central London, especially well known as a holiday flight airport.

London City (LCY; www.londoncityairport.com) A few miles east of central London, specialising in flights to/from European and other UK airports.

For details on getting between these airports and central London, see p131.

Some planes on European and long-haul routes go direct to major regional airports including Manchester and Glasgow, while smaller regional airports such as Southampton, Cardiff and Birmingham are served by flights to and from continental Europe and Ireland.

Land

Bus & Coach

You can easily get between Britain and other European countries via long-distance bus or coach. The international network **Eurolines** (www.eurolines.com) connects a huge number of destinations; you can buy

CLIMATE CHANGE & TRAVEL

Every form of transport that relies on carbon-based fuel generates CO_2, the main cause of human-induced climate change. Modern travel is dependent on aeroplanes, which might use less fuel per kilometre per person than most cars, but travel much greater distances. The altitude at which aircraft emit gases (including CO_2) and particles also contributes to their climate change impact. Many websites offer 'carbon calculators' that allow people to estimate the carbon emissions generated by their journey and, for those who wish to do so, to offset the impact of the greenhouse gases emitted with contributions to portfolios of climate-friendly initiatives throughout the world. Lonely Planet offsets the carbon footprint of all staff and author travel.

tickets online via one of the national operators.

Services to/from Britain are operated by **National Express** (www.nationalexpress.com). Some sample journey times to/from London:

» Amsterdam, 12 hours

» Barcelona, 24 hours

» Dublin, 12 hours

» Paris, eight hours

If you book early, and can be flexible with timings (ie travel when few other people want to), you can get some very good deals – some branded as 'fun fares' and 'promo fares'. For example, London to Paris or Amsterdam one way starts at just £18, although paying nearer £25 is more usual.

Train

CHANNEL TUNNEL SERVICES

The Channel Tunnel makes direct train travel between Britain and continental Europe a fast and enjoyable option. High-speed **Eurostar** (www.eurostar.com) passenger services hurtle at least 10 times daily between London and Paris (journey time 2½ hours) or Brussels (two hours). You can buy tickets from travel agencies, major train stations or direct from the Eurostar website. The normal single fare between London and Paris/Brussels is around £150, but if you buy in advance and travel at a less busy period, deals drop to around £90 return or even less. You can also buy 'through fare' tickets from many cities in Britain – for example York to Paris, or Manchester to Brussels. You can also get very good train and hotel combination deals – bizarrely sometimes cheaper than train fare only.

Drivers use **Eurotunnel** (www.eurotunnel.com). At Folkestone in southern England or Calais in France, you drive onto a train, get carried through the tunnel and drive off at the other end. The trains run about four times an hour from 6am to 10pm, then hourly. Loading and unloading takes an hour; the journey takes 35 minutes. You can book in advance online or pay on the spot. The one-way cost for a car and passengers is around £90 to £150 depending on the time of day (less busy times are cheaper); promotional fares often bring it nearer to £50.

TRAIN & FERRY CONNECTIONS

As well as Eurostar, many 'normal' trains run between Britain and mainland Europe. You buy one ticket, but get off the train at the port, walk onto a ferry, then get another train on the other side. Routes include Amsterdam–London (via Hook of Holland and Harwich). Travelling between Ireland and Britain, the main train–ferry–train route is Dublin to London, via Dun Laoghaire and Holyhead. Ferries also run between Rosslare and Fishguard or Pembroke (Wales), with train connections on either side.

Sea

The main ferry routes between Britain and mainland Europe include Dover to Calais or Boulogne (France), Harwich to Hook of Holland (Netherlands), Hull to Zeebrugge (Belgium) or Rotterdam (Netherlands), Rosyth to Zeebrugge, Portsmouth to Santander or Bilbao (Spain), and Rosyth and Newcastle to Bergen (Norway) or Gothenburg (Sweden). Routes to/from Ireland include Holyhead to Dun Laoghaire.

Competition from Eurotunnel and budget airlines has forced ferry operators to discount heavily and offer flexible fares, meaning great bargains at quiet times of day or year. For example, the short cross-channel routes such as Dover to Calais or Boulogne can be as low as £20 for a car plus up to five passengers, although around £50 is more likely. If you're a foot passenger, or cycling, there's often less need to book ahead, and cheap fares on the short crossings start from about £10 each way.

Main operators include the following:

Brittany Ferries (www.brittany-ferries.com)

DFDS Seaways (www.dfds.co.uk)

Irish Ferries (www.irishferries.com)

Norfolkline (www.irishferries.com)

P&O Ferries (www.poferries.com)

Speedferries (www.speedferries.com)

Stena Line (www.stenaline.com)

Transmanche (www.transmancheferries.com)

Broker sites covering all routes and options include www.ferrybooker.com and www.directferries.co.uk.

INFORMATION SERVICE

Traveline (☎0871 200 2233; www.traveline.org.uk) is a very useful information service covering bus, coach, taxi and train services nationwide, with numerous links to help plan your journey. By phone, you get transferred automatically to an adviser in the region you're phoning *from;* for details on another part of the country, you need to key in a code number (81 for London, 874 for Cumbria etc) – for a full list of codes, go to the Traveline website.

GETTING AROUND

For getting around Britain your first main choice is going by car or public transport. While having your own car makes the best use of your time, and helps reach remote places, rental and fuel costs can be expensive for budget travellers (while the trials of traffic jams and parking in major cities hit everyone) so public transport is often the better way to go.

Your main public transport options are train and long-distance bus (called coach in Britain). Services between major towns and cities are generally good, although at 'peak' (busy) times you must book in advance to be sure of getting a ticket. Conversely if you book ahead early or travel at 'off-peak' periods, ideally both, train and coach tickets can be very cheap.

As long as you have time, using a mix of train, coach, local bus, the odd taxi, walking and occasionally hiring a bike, you can get almost anywhere in Britain without having to drive. You'll certainly see more of the countryside than you might slogging along grey motorways.

Air

Britain's domestic air companies include British Airways, BMI, BMIbaby, EasyJet and Ryanair. If you're really pushed for time, flights on longer routes across Britain (eg Exeter or Southampton to Newcastle, Edinburgh or Inverness) are handy, although you miss the glorious scenery in between. On some shorter routes (eg London to Newcastle, or Manchester to Newquay) trains can compare favourably with planes on time, once airport downtime is factored in. On costs, you might get a bargain airfare, but trains can be cheaper if you buy tickets in advance.

DO I NEED A PASSPORT?

Getting between Britain's three nations of England, Scotland and Wales is easy. The bus and train systems are fully integrated and in most cases you won't even know you've crossed the border. Passports are not required – although some Scots and Welsh may think they should be!

Bicycle

Britain is a compact country, and getting around by bicycle is perfectly feasible – and a great way to really see the country – if you've got time to spare. For more inspiration see p39.

Renting a bike is easy in London; the capital is dotted with automatic docking stations where bikes can be hired on the spot – and they're free for the first 30 minutes. For info go to the Transport for London site (www.tfl.gov.uk) and follow the links to Cycling. Other hire options are listed at www.lcc.org.uk.

Rental is also possible in tourist spots such as Oxford and Cambridge, and in country areas, especially at forestry sites and reservoirs now primarily used for leisure activities, eg Kielder Water in Northumberland, Grizedale Forest in the Lake District and the Elan Valley in Mid-Wales. In some areas, disused railway lines are now bike routes, notably the Peak District in Derbyshire. The Great Glen Way in Scotland is another great option. Rates start at about £10 per day, or £20 for something half decent.

Bus & Coach

If you're on a tight budget, long-distance buses (called coaches in Britain) are nearly always the cheapest way to get around, although they're also the slowest – sometimes by a considerable margin. Many towns have separate stations for local buses and long-distance coaches; make sure you go to the right one!

National Express (www.nationalexpress.com/coach) is the main coach operator, with a wide network and frequent services between main centres. North of the border, services tie in with those of **Scottish Citylink** (www.citylink.co.uk), Scotland's leading coach company. Fares vary: they're cheaper if you book in advance and travel at quieter times, and more expensive if you buy your ticket on the spot and it's Friday afternoon. As a guide, a 200-mile trip (eg London to York) will cost around £15 to £20 if you book a few days in advance.

Megabus (www.megabus.com) operates a budget-airline-style coach services between about 30 destinations around the country. Go at a quiet time, book early and your ticket will be very cheap. Book later, for a busy time and... You get the picture.

For information about short-distance and local bus services, see p1068.

Bus Passes & Discounts

National Express offers discount passes to full-time students and under-26s, called Young Persons Coachcards. They cost £10 and get you 30% off standard adult fares. Also available are coachcards for people over 60, families and disabled travellers.

For touring the country, National Express offers Brit Xplorer passes, allowing unlimited travel for seven days (£79), 14 days (£139) and 28 days (£219). You don't need to book journeys in advance: if the coach has a spare seat, you can take it.

Car & Motorcycle

Travelling by car or motorbike means you can be independent and flexible, and reach remote places. Downsides for drivers include traffic jams and high parking costs in cities.

Hire

Compared with many countries (especially the USA), hire rates are expensive in Britain; you should expect to pay around £250 per week for a small car (unlimited mileage), but rates rise at busy times and drop at quiet times. Some main players: **Avis** (www.avis.co.uk), **Budget** (www.budget.co.uk), **Europcar** (www.europcar.co.uk), **Sixt** (www.sixt.co.uk) and **Thrifty** (www.thrifty.co.uk).

Many international websites have separate web pages for customers in different countries, and the prices for a car in Britain on the UK webpages can differ from the same car's prices on the USA or Australia pages. You have to surf a lot of sites to find the best deals.

Another option is to look online for small local car-hire companies in Britain that can undercut the international franchises. Generally those in cities are cheaper than in rural areas. See under Getting Around in the main city sections for more details, or see a rental-broker site such as **UK Car Hire** (www.ukcarhire.net).

Yet another option is to hire a motorhome or campervan. It's more expensive than hiring a car, but saves on accommodation costs, and gives almost unlimited freedom. Sites to check:

Cool Campervans (www.coolcampervans.com)

Just Go (www.justgo.uk.com)

Wild Horizon (www.wildhorizon.co.uk)

Insurance

Nearly all rental vehicles in Britain have insurance included in the price, although you may be liable for an 'excess' (ie paying for damage up to the value of anywhere between £200 and £500). This can be reduced to about £100 by paying a small extra fee.

Parking

Many cities have short-stay and long-stay car parks; the latter are cheaper though may be less convenient. 'Park and Ride' systems allow you to park on the edge of the city then ride to the centre on regular buses for an all-in-one price.

Yellow lines (single or double) along the edge of the road indicate restrictions. Find the nearby sign that spells out when you can and can't park. In London and other big cities, traffic wardens operate with efficiency; if you park on the yellow lines at the wrong time, your car will be clamped or towed away, and it'll cost you £100 or more to get driving again. In some cities there are also red lines, which mean no stopping at all. Ever.

Roads & Rules

Motorways and main A-roads are dual carriageways and deliver you quickly from one end of the country to another. Lesser A-roads, B-roads and minor roads are much more scenic and fun, as you wind through the countryside from village to village – ideal for car or motorcycle touring. You can't travel fast, but you won't care.

A foreign driving licence is valid in Britain for up to 12 months. If you plan to bring a car from Europe, it's illegal to drive without (at least) third-party insurance.

Some other important rules:

» drive on the left (!)

» wear fitted seat belts in cars

» wear crash helmets on motorcycles

» give way to your right at junctions and roundabouts

» always use the left-side lane on motorways and dual-carriageways, unless overtaking (although so many people ignore this rule, you'd think it didn't exist)

» don't use a mobile phone while driving unless it's fully hands-free (another rule frequently flouted)

Speed limits are 30mph (48km/h) in built-up areas, 60mph (96km/h) on main roads and 70mph (112km/h) on motorways and most (but not all) dual carriageways. Drinking and driving is taken very seriously; you're allowed a maximum blood-alcohol level of 80mg/100mL (0.08%) – campaigners want it reduced to 50mg/100mL.

MOTORING ORGANISATIONS

Motoring organisations include the **Automobile Association** (www.theaa.com) and the **Royal Automobile Club** (www.rac.co.uk); annual membership starts at around £35, including 24-hour roadside breakdown assistance. A greener alternative is the **Environmental Transport Association** (www.eta.co.uk); it provides all the usual services (breakdown assistance, roadside rescue, vehicle inspections etc) but doesn't campaign for more roads.

Hitching

Hitching is not as common as it used to be in Britain: maybe because more people have cars and maybe because few drivers give lifts any more. It's perfectly possible, however, if you don't mind long waits, although travellers should understand that they're taking a small but potentially serious risk, and we don't recommend it. If you decide to go by thumb, note that it's illegal to hitch on motorways; you must use approach roads or service stations.

However, it's all different in remote rural areas such as Mid-Wales or northwest Scotland, where hitching is a part of getting around – especially if you're a walker. On some Scottish islands, local drivers may stop and offer a lift without you even asking.

Local Transport

British cities usually have good local public transport systems – a combination of bus, train and tram – often run by a confusing number of separate companies. Tourist offices can provide maps and information. More details are given in the city sections throughout this book.

POSTBUS SERVICES

These are vans on usual mail services that also carry passengers, operating in some rural areas (often the most scenic and remote parts of the country) and especially useful for walkers and backpackers: www.royalmail.com/postbus.

Bus

There are good local bus networks year-round in cities and towns. Buses also run in some rural areas year-round, although timetables are designed to serve schools and businesses, so there aren't many midday and weekend services (and they may stop running during school holidays), or buses may link local villages to a market town on only one day each week. In tourist spots (especially national parks) there are frequent services from Easter to September. It's always worth double-checking at a tourist office before planning your day's activities around a bus that may not actually be running.

In this book, along with the local bus route number, frequency and duration, we have provided indicative prices if the fare is over £5. If it's less than this, we have generally omitted the fare.

BUS PASSES

If you're taking a few local bus rides in a day of energetic sightseeing, day passes (with names like Day Rover, Wayfarer or Explorer) are cheaper than buying several single tickets. If you plan to linger longer in one area, three-day passes are also available; often they can be bought on your first bus, and may include local rail services. It's always worth asking ticket clerks or bus drivers about your options.

Ferry

Local ferries, for example from the mainland to the Isle of Wight or the Scottish islands, are covered in the relevant sections in the regional chapters.

Taxi

There are two sorts of taxi in Britain: the famous black cabs (some with advertising livery in other colours), which have meters and can be hailed in the street; and minicabs, which are cheaper but can only be called by phone. In London and other big cities, taxis cost £2 to £3 per mile. In rural areas it's about half that. The best place to find the local taxi's phone number is the local pub. Alternatively, call **National Cabline** (☎0800 123444) from a landline phone; the service pinpoints your location and transfers you to an approved local taxi company. Also useful is www.traintaxi.co.uk – designed to help you 'bridge the final gap' between the train station and your hotel or other final destination.

Train

For long-distance travel around Britain, trains are generally faster and more comfortable than coaches but can be more expensive, although with discount tickets they're competitive – and often take you through beautiful countryside. The British like to moan about their trains, but around 85% run on time. The other 15% that get delayed or cancelled mostly affect commuters rather than long-distance services.

About 20 different companies operate train services in Britain (eg First Great Western runs from London to Bristol, Cornwall and South Wales; National Express East Coast runs London to Leeds, York and Scotland; and Virgin Trains runs the 'west coast' route from London to Birmingham, Carlisle and Scotland), while Network Rail operates track and stations. For some passengers this system can be confusing at first, but information and ticket-buying services are mostly centralised. If you have to change trains, or use two or more train operators, you still buy one ticket – valid for the whole of your journey. The main

BIKES ON TRAINS

Bicycles can be taken free of charge on most local urban trains (although they may not be allowed at peak times when the trains are too crowded with commuters) and on shorter trips in rural areas, on a first-come, first-served basis – though there may be space limits. Bikes can be carried on long-distance train journeys free of charge as well, but advance booking is required for most conventional bikes. (Folding bikes can be carried on pretty much any train at any time.) In theory, this shouldn't be too much trouble as most long-distance rail trips are best bought in advance anyway, but you have to go a long way down the path of booking your seat before you start booking your bike – only to find space isn't available. A better course of action is to buy in advance at a major rail station, where the booking clerk can help you through the options, or phone the relevant operator's Customer Service department. Have a large cup of coffee and a stress-reliever handy. And a final warning: when railways are repaired, cancelled trains are replaced by buses – and they won't take bikes.

A very useful leaflet called *Cycling by Train* is available at major stations or downloadable from www.nationalrail.co.uk/passenger_services/cyclists.html.

railcards are also accepted by all operators.

Your first stop should be **National Rail Enquiries** (☎08457-484950; www.nationalrail.co.uk), the nationwide timetable and fare information service. This site also advertises special offers, and has real-time links to station departure boards. Once you've found the journey you need, links take you to the relevant train operator or to centralised ticketing services (eg www.thetrainline.com, www.qjump.co.uk, www.raileasy.co.uk) to buy the ticket. To use these websites you always have to state a preferred time and day of travel, even if you don't mind when you go, but with a little delving around they can offer some real bargains.

You can also buy train tickets on the spot at stations, which is fine for short journeys, but discount tickets for longer trips are usually not available and must be bought in advance by phone or online.

For planning your trip, some very handy maps of the UK's rail network can be downloaded from the National Rail Enquiries website.

Classes

There are two classes of rail travel: first and standard. First class costs around 50% more than standard and, except on very crowded trains, is not really worth it. At weekends some train operators offer 'upgrades' for an extra £10 to £15 on top of your standard class fare.

Costs & Reservations

For short journeys (under about 50 miles) it's usually best to buy tickets on the spot at rail stations. For longer journeys, on-the-spot fares are always available, but tickets are much cheaper if bought in advance. Essentially, the earlier you book, the cheaper it gets. You can also save if you travel 'off-peak' (ie the days and times that aren't busy). Advance purchase usually gets a reserved seat, too. The cheapest fares are nonrefundable, so if you miss your train you'll have to buy a new ticket.

If you buy online, you can have the ticket posted (UK addresses only), or collect it at the station on the day of travel from automatic machines.

Whichever operator you travel with and wherever you buy tickets, these are the three main fare types:

HOW MUCH TO...?

When travelling long-distance by train or bus/coach in Britain, it's important to realise that there's no such thing as a standard fare. Prices vary according to demand and when you buy your ticket. Book long in advance and travel on Tuesday mid-morning and it's cheap. Buy your ticket on the spot late Friday afternoon and it'll be a lot more expensive. Ferries use similar systems. Throughout this book, we have generally quoted sample fares somewhere in between the very cheapest and most expensive options. The price you pay will almost certainly be different.

Anytime Buy anytime, travel anytime – usually the most expensive option

Off-peak Buy ticket any time, travel off-peak

Advance Buy ticket in advance, travel only on specific trains – usually the cheapest option

For an idea of the price difference, an Anytime single ticket from London to York will cost around £100 or more, an Off-peak around £80, while an Advance is around £20, and even less if you book early enough or don't mind arriving at midnight.

If the train doesn't get you all the way to your destination, a **PlusBus** (www.plusbus.info) supplement (usually around £2) validates your train ticket for onward travel by bus – it's more convenient, and usually cheaper, than buying a separate bus ticket. For details, see the website.

Train Passes

DISCOUNT PASSES

Local train passes usually cover rail networks around a city (many include bus travel too), and are mentioned in the individual city sections throughout this book. If you're staying in Britain for a while, passes known as 'railcards' are available:

16-25 Railcard For those aged 16 to 25, or a full-time UK student

Senior Railcard For anyone over 60

Family & Friends Railcard Covers up to four adults and four children travelling together

These railcards cost around £26 (valid for one year, available from major stations or online) and get you a 33% discount on most train fares, except those already heavily discounted. With the Family card, adults get 33% and children get 60% discounts, so the fee is easily repaid in a couple of journeys.

A **Disabled Person's Railcard** costs £18. You can get an application from stations or from the railcard website.

For full details on all discount passes see www.railcard.co.uk.

REGIONAL PASSES

If you're concentrating your travels on southeast England (eg London to Dover, Weymouth, Cambridge or Oxford) a **Network Railcard** covers up to four adults and up to four children travelling together outside peak times.

NATIONAL PASSES

For country-wide travel, **BritRail** (www.britrail.com) passes are available for visitors from overseas. They must be bought in your country of origin (not in Britain) from a specialist travel agency. They're available in three different versions (England only; all Britain; UK and Ireland) and for periods from four to 30 days.

Glossary

almshouse – accommodation for the aged or needy
ap – prefi x in a Welsh name meaning 'son of'
bag – reach the top of (as in to 'bag a couple of peaks' or '*Munro* bagging')
bailey – outermost wall of a castle
bar – gate (York, and some other northern cities)
beck – stream (northern England)
bill – the total you need to pay after eating in a restaurant ('check' to Americans)
billion – the British billion is a million million (unlike the American billion – a thousand million)
birlinn – Hebridean galley
blackhouse – traditional low-walled stone cottage with thatch or turf roof and earth floors; shared by both humans and cattle and typical of the Outer Hebrides until the early 20th century (Scotland)
bloke – man (colloquial)
Blue Flag – an award given to beaches for their unpolluted sand and water
böd – once a simple trading booth used by fishing communities, today it refers to basic accommodation for walkers etc
bothy – hut or mountain
brae – hill (Scotland)
bridleway – path or track that can be used by walkers, horse riders and cyclists
broch – defensive tower
burgh – town
burn – stream
bus – local bus; see also *coach*
Cadw – the Welsh historic-monuments agency
cairn – pile of stones marking path or junction; also peak
CalMac – Caledonian MacBrayne, the main Scottish island ferry operator
camanachd – Gaelic for *shinty*
canny – good, great, wise (northern England)
castell – castle (Welsh)
ceilidh – (*kay*-lay) – a session of traditional music, song and dance (originally Scottish, now more widely used across Britain)
Celtic high cross – a large, elaborately carved stone cross decorated with biblical scenes and Celtic interlace designs dating from the 8th to 10th centuries
cheers – goodbye; thanks (colloquial); also a drinking toast
chemist – pharmacist
chine – valley-like fissure leading to the sea (southern England)
chippy – fish-and-chip shop
circus – junction of several city streets, usually circular, and usually with a green or other feature at the centre
Clearances – eviction of Highland farmers from their land by lairds wanting to use it for grazing sheep
Clootie dumpling – rich steamed pudding filled with currants and raisins
close – entrance to an alley
coach – long-distance bus
coasteering – adventurous activity that involves making your way around a rocky coastline by climbing, scrambling, jumping or swimming
cob – mixture of mud and straw for building
corrie – circular hollow on a hillside
cot – small bed for a baby ('crib' to Americans)
court – courtyard
craic – lively conversation
craig – exposed rock
crannog – an artificial island in a loch built for defensive purposes
crofting – smallholding in marginal agricultural areas following the Clearances
Cymraeg – Welsh language (Welsh); also Gymraeg
dene – valley
dirk – dagger
DIY – do-it-yourself, ie home improvements
dram – a measure of whisky
dodgy – suspect, bad, dangerous
dolmen – chambered tomb (Wales)
dough – money (colloquial)
downs – rolling upland, characterised by lack of trees
duvet – quilt replacing sheets and blankets ('doona' to Australians)

EH – English Heritage; state-funded organisation responsible for historic sites

en suite room – hotel room with private attached bathroom (ie shower, basin and toilet)

eisteddfod – literally a gathering or session; festival in which competitions are held in music, poetry, drama and the fine arts; plural eisteddfodau (Welsh)

Evensong – daily evening service (Church of England)

fell race – tough running race through hills or moors

fen – drained or marshy low-lying flat land

firth – estuary

fiver – £5 note

flat – apartment (colloquial)

flip-flops – plastic sandals with a single strap over toes ('thongs' to Australians)

footpath – path through countryside and between houses, not beside a road (that's called a 'pavement')

gate – street (York, and some other northern cities)

gloup – natural arch

graft – work (not corruption, as in American English; colloquial)

grand – 1000 (colloquial)

gutted – very disappointed (colloquial)

guv, guvner – from governor, a respectful term of address for owner or boss; can sometimes be used ironically

hart – deer

HI – Hostelling International (organisation)

hire – rent

Hogmanay – Scottish celebration of New Year's Eve

howff – pub or shelter (Scotland)

HS – Historic Scotland; organisation that manages historic sites in Scotland

inn – pub with accommodation

jumper – woollen item of clothing worn on torso ('sweater' to Americans)

ken – Scottish term for 'understand' or 'know', as in 'you know'

kirk – church (northern England and Scotland)

knowe – burial mound (Scotland)

kyle – strait or channel (Scotland)

laird – estate owner (Scotland)

lass – young woman (northern England and Scotland)

lift – machine for carrying people up and down in large buildings ('elevator' to Americans)

linn – waterfall (Scotland)

loch – lake (Scotland)

lochan – small *loch*

lock – part of a canal or river that can be closed off and the water levels changed to raise or lower boats

lolly – money (colloquial); candy on a stick (possibly frozen)

lorry (s), lorries (pl) – truck

Mabinogion – key source of Welsh folk legends

machair – grass- and wildflower-covered sand dunes

mad – insane (not angry, as in American English)

Marches – borderlands (ie between England and Wales or Scotland) after the Anglo-Saxon word *mearc*, meaning 'boundary'

Martello tower – small, circular tower used for coastal defence

menhir – standing stone

Mercat Cross – a symbol of the trading rights of a market town or village, usually found in the centre of town and usually a focal point for the community

mere – a body of water, usually shallow; technically a lake that has a large surface area relative to its depth

merthyr – burial place of a saint (Welsh)

midge – mosquito-like insect

motorway – major road linking cities (equivalent to 'interstate' or 'freeway')

motte – early Norman fortification consisting of a raised, flattened mound with a keep on top; when attached to a *bailey* it is known as a motte-and-bailey

Munro – hill or mountain 3000ft (914m) or higher, especially in Scotland. (Those over 2500ft are called Corbetts.)

Munro bagger – a hill walker who tries to climb all the *Munros* in Scotland

naff – inferior, in poor taste (colloquial)

NCN – National Cycle Network

newydd – new (Welsh)

NNR – National Nature Reserve, managed by the *SNH*

NT – National Trust; organisation that protects historic buildings and land with scenic importance in England and Wales

NTS – National Trust for Scotland; organisation dedicated to the preservation of historic sites and the environment in Scotland

nyvaig – Hebridean galley

oast house – building containing a kiln for drying hops

ogham – ancient Celtic script

oriel – gallery (Welsh)

OS – Ordnance Survey

p (pronounced pee) – pence (ie 2p is 'two p' not 'two pence' or 'tuppence')

pargeting – decorative stucco plasterwork

pele – fortified house

Picts – early inhabitants of north and east Scotland (from Latin pictus, or 'painted', after their body-paint decorations)

pile – large imposing building

pissed – slang for drunk (not angry)

pissed off – angry (slang)

pitch – playing field

postbus – minibus delivering the mail, also carrying passengers – found in remote areas

provost – mayor

punter – customer (colloquial)

quid – pound (colloquial)

ramble – short easy walk

reiver – warrior or raider (historic term; northern England)

return ticket – round-trip ticket

RIB – rigid inflatable boat

rood – an old Scots word for a cross

RSPB – Royal Society for the Protection of Birds

RSPCA – Royal Society for the Prevention of Cruelty to Animals

sarsen – boulder, a geological remnant usually found in chalky areas (sometimes used in neolithic constructions, eg Stonehenge and Avebury)

Sassenach – from Gaelic 'Sasannach': anyone who is not a Highlander (including Lowland Scots)

sheila-na-gig – Celtic fertility symbol of a woman with exaggerated genitalia, often carved in stone on churches and castles. Rare in England, found mainly in the Marches, along the border with Wales

shinty – fast and physical ball-and-stick sport similar to Ireland's hurling

single ticket – one-way ticket

SMC – Scottish Mountaineering Club

SNH – Scottish Natural Heritage, a government organisation directly responsible for safeguarding and improving Scotland's natural heritage

snickelway – narrow alley (York)

snug – usually a small separate room in a pub

sporran – purse worn around waist with the kilt (Scotland)

SSSI – Site of Special Scientific Interest

Sustrans – sustainable transport charity encouraging people to walk, cycle and use public transport

SYHA – Scottish Youth Hostel Association

tarn – a small take or pool, usually in mountain areas in England, often in a depression caused by glacial erosion

tenner – £10

TIC – Tourist Information Centre

ton – 100 (colloquial)

tor – pointed hill

torch – flashlight

Tory – Conservative (political party)

towpath – path running beside a river or canal, where horses once towed barges

twitcher – obsessive birdwatcher

Tube, the – London's underground railway system (colloquial)

Underground, the – London's underground railway system

verderer – officer upholding law and order in the royal forests

wolds – open, rolling countryside

wynd – lane or narrow street (northern England and Scotland)

YHA – Youth Hostels Association

behind the scenes

SEND US YOUR FEEDBACK

We love to hear from travellers – your comments keep us on our toes and help make our books better. Our well-travelled team reads every word on what you loved or loathed about this book. Although we cannot reply individually to postal submissions, we always guarantee that your feedback goes straight to the appropriate authors, in time for the next edition. Each person who sends us information is thanked in the next edition – and the most useful submissions are rewarded with a free book.

Visit **lonelyplanet.com/contact** to submit your updates and suggestions or to ask for help. Our award-winning website also features inspirational travel stories, news and discussions.

Note: We may edit, reproduce and incorporate your comments in Lonely Planet products such as guidebooks, websites and digital products, so let us know if you don't want your comments reproduced or your name acknowledged. For a copy of our privacy policy visit lonelyplanet.com/privacy.

OUR READERS

Many thanks to the travellers who used the last edition and wrote to us with helpful hints, useful advice and interesting anecdotes:

A Vimal Abraham **B** Dolores Baldasare **C** Gerard Chan **D** Theo De Bray **E** Kursat Engin **G** Oliver Gardner, Paul Gerrard **J** Amelie Jennequin **K** Andy Kent **L** Bob Llewelyn, Meredith Lloyd **M** Richard Morris **P** Trent Paton, Edward Pinnegar, Greg Pogson, Doug Powell, Natalie Pullen **S** Kate Saggers, Eloise Singh, Margaret Snowball **T** Mike Thomas, David Townsend **W** Alyssa Webb, Lorayne Woodend **Z** Tarryn Zank

AUTHOR THANKS

David Else

As always, massive appreciation goes to my wife Corinne, for joining me on many of my research trips around Britain, and for not minding when I locked myself away for 12 hours at a time to write this book – and for bringing coffee when it got nearer 18 hours. Thanks also to the co-authors of this book; my name goes down as coordinating author, but I couldn't have done it without this team. And finally, thanks to Cliff Wilkinson, my commissioning editor at Lonely Planet London, and to all the friendly faces in the production departments at Lonely Planet Melbourne who helped bring this book to final fruition.

David Atkinson

Diolch yn fawr to Visit Wales for its advice and assistance, especially Ceri Jones for acting as a North Wales sounding board. Thanks also to Melanie Salisbury for her valuable input and Pip Cockeram for Anglesey tips.

Oliver Berry

Big thanks as always to everyone for keeping the home fires burning, but biggest thanks as always to Susie Berry and Molly Berry. Huge thanks also to lots of helpful people along the way who helped me during the research of this book, including Simon Harvey, Mark Jenkin, Adam Laity, Dan Mallett, Lee Trewhela, Alice Marston, Rhona Gardiner, Zoey Cotton, Jo Woodcock, Gabby Rogers, Anna Murphy, Sally Williams, Laura Martin and Laura Bower. Lastly thanks to Cliff Wilkinson for the gig, David Else for steering the ship, and of course all my co-authors, along with the Hobo for keeping me company when all other lights went out.

Joe Bindloss

First up, thanks as always to my partner Linda and my little boy Tyler, for going without bedtime stories while I was researching this book. In Shropshire, thanks to Tony and Petra Bindloss and my kid brothers Peter and Eddie, for providing a home away from home. Across the Midlands, thanks to all the travellers who provided top tips and recommendations. Thanks also to David Else, for fielding questions on the road, and to Clifton Wilkinson at Lonely Planet for calmly managing this new edition.

Fionn Davenport

A big thanks to Trevor Evers and the staff of Marketing Manchester, who were as helpful and as gracious as always. Thanks to Oliver Thomas for taking time out of his busy day to answer my questions. Thanks to the staff at the tourist offices in Liverpool, Blackpool, Douglas and elsewhere – you may not know why I asked so many questions, but your help in answering them is much appreciated. Thanks to Cliff, David and everyone else at Lonely Planet. And finally thanks to Caroline, who makes coming home the best bit of all.

Marc Di Duca

Big thanks must go to fellow Darlingtonian Clifton for entrusting me with the Northeast and Southeast chapters of this guide, and to David Else for his guidance throughout. A huge 'ta' to my parents Jacqueline and Paul in Whitley Bay for all their Tyneside insights and for letting me kip in their back bedroom between flits into the wilds of Northumberland. Undying gratitude goes to all the staff at tourist offices around the land, especially those in Brighton, Canterbury, Newcastle, Rye, Haltwhistle, Barnard Castle and Berwick. Also thanks to Madeleine in Berwick, Colin in Sandwich, my sister Selene in Darlington, Geoff in Killhope and Mykola and Vira in Kyiv. Last but certainly not least, heartfelt thanks must go to my wife Tanya and son Taras for all the long days we spend apart.

Belinda Dixon

It's always a true collaboration, so sincere thanks to all who've supported and advised along the way. As ever, tourist office staff have been unfailingly helpful, but particular thanks go to those at Portsmouth (Southsea), Poole, Salisbury, Lyme, Lulworth Cove and at the Dartmoor National Park – they even managed to explain the baffling complexities of the bus 82 timetable. Finally smiles to the AD, for serenity, sanity and sea swims.

Peter Dragicevich

Thanks to my London crew for assisting in 'researching' London's bars and restaurants, particularly Vanessa Irvine, Tim Benzie, Ed Lee and Sue Ostler. Special thanks to Kerri Tyler for joining me for the Bala research.

Catherine Le Nevez

Thanks to all of the locals, tourism professionals and fellow travellers who provided insider tips and fascinating insights into Channel Islands life. In particular, thanks to Jackie on Jersey, Jason on Guernsey, Andrew on Herm, Penny on Sark and Jo on Alderney, as well as Cliff Wilkinson for signing me up, and everyone at Lonely Planet. As ever, *merci surtout* to my family.

Etain O'Carroll

Sincere thanks to Peter Berry in Oxford and Mark Wilkinson in Norwich for giving me their time and inside tips for use in this book. Thanks to Pedro Honwana for all his help with the Cheltenham section and to all the staff in tourist offices across the country who answered my endless questions. Thanks to Cliff and David for making the whole process so smooth and to the inhouse staff who helped with legions of queries on the new styling. Lastly, thanks to Maria Leon Ferreiro for her endless patience and goodwill and to Mark, Osgur and Neven for company on the road and keeping me sane on return.

Andy Symington

I owe special thanks to much-appreciated Edinburgh accommodation-option and on-the-road companion Jenny Neil, and to ever-hospitable Juliette and David Paton, as well as to all my friends in Scotland. Particular thanks for various reasons to Cindy-Lou Ramsay, John Bain, Len Bloom, Colin Bell and Amy Allanson, Andrew Burns, Riika Åkerlind, and Mark and Diane Hayward. Applause to helpful tourist-office staff, big thanks to Neil for the pints, and gracias to Cliff for a top organizing job. Gratitude too to my parents for first taking me to Scotland, and to Ruthy for solidarity and love despite the absences.

Neil Wilson

Thanks to the many Yorkshire folk who freely offered advice and recommendations; to the tourist office staff for answering dumb questions; and to eerie Andy Dextrous in York for his help – much appreciated. Thanks also to Lonely Planet's editors and cartographers, and to Carol for good company in many Yorkshire restaurants.

ACKNOWLEDGMENTS

Climate map data adapted from Peel MC, Finlayson BL & McMahon TA (2007) 'Updated World Map of the Köppen-Geiger Climate Classification', Hydrology and Earth System Sciences, 11, 163344.

Cover photograph: Stonehenge, Wiltshire, England, Great Britain. Holger Leue / Lonely Planet Images

Illustrations: p146-7, p148-9, p150-1 by Javier Zarracina and p930-1, p932-3 and p934-5 by Michael Ruff.

Many of the images in this guide are available for licensing from Lonely Planet Images: www.lonelyplanetimages.com.

THIS BOOK

This 9th edition of *Great Britain* was researched and written by David Else (coordinating author), David Atkinson, Oliver Berry, Joe Bindloss, Fionn Davenport, Marc Di Duca, Belinda Dixon, Peter Dragicevich, Catherine Le Nevez, Etain O'Carroll, Andy Symington and Neil Wilson. The previous edition was also researched by James Bainbridge and Nana Luckham. This guidebook was commissioned in Lonely Planet's London office and produced by the following:

Commissioning Editors Glenn van der Knijff, Clifton Wilkinson

Coordinating Editor Gina Tsarouhas

Coordinating Cartographer Amanda Sierp

Coordinating Layout Designer Adrian Blackburn

Managing Editors Imogen Bannister, Melanie Dankel, Annelies Mertens

Managing Cartographers Adrian Persoglia, Herman So

Managing Layout Designers Laura Jane, Indra Kilfoyle, Celia Wood

Assisting Editors Holly Alexander, Elisa Arduca, Sarah Bailey, Pete Cruttenden, Kate Daly, Kate Evans, Chris Girdler, Carly Hall, Victoria Harrison, Trent Holden, Evan Jones, Amy Karafin, Ali Lemer, Shawn Low, Anne Mulvaney, Alan Murphy, Joanne Newell, Katie O'Connell, Susan Paterson, Martine Power, Charles Rawlings-Way, Erin Richards, Alison Ridgway, Louisa Syme, Angela Tinson, Branislava Vladisavljevic, Jeanette Wall, Helen Yeates

Assisting Cartographers Ildiko Bogdanovits, Csanad Csutoros, Xavier Di Toro, Julie Dodkins, Alex Leung, Wayne Murphy, Anthony Phelan

Assisting Layout Designer Lauren Egan, Jacqui Saunders

Internal Image & Cover Research Aude Vauconsant

Thanks to Mark Adams, Sasha Baskett, Jessica Boland, David Connolly, Melanie Dankel, Stefanie Di Trocchio, Janine Eberle, Brigitte Ellemor, Ryan Evans, Joshua Geoghegan, Mark Germanchis, Michelle Glynn, Liz Heynes, Lauren Hunt, Carol Jackson, David Kemp, Yvonne Kirk, Lisa Knights, Nic Lehman, John Mazzocchi, Naomi Parker, Piers Pickard, Averil Robertson, Lachlan Ross, Michael Ruff, Jacqui Saunders, Julie Sheridan, Laura Stansfeld, John Taufa, Sam Trafford, Phil Watkinson, Juan Winata, Emily K Wolman, Nick Wood

index

A

A La Ronde 302
Aardman Animations 1034
Abbey Dore 421
Abbey Road Studios 89
Abbeydale Industrial Hamlet 479
abbeys 21
  Bath Abbey 279, **4**
  Buckland Abbey 312
  Dryburgh Abbey 813
  Egglestone Abbey 622
  Forde Abbey 257
  Fountains Abbey 517
  Furness Abbey 599
  Hartland Abbey 319
  Hexham Abbey 625, **150**
  Iona Abbey 854
  Jedburgh Abbey 813-14
  Kelso Abbey 810
  Malmesbury Abbey 266
  Rievaulx Abbey 523-4
  St Augustine's Abbey 139-40
  Strata Florida Abbey 690
  Sweetheart Abbey 824
  Tintern Abbey 660
  Westminster Abbey 62-5
  Woburn Abbey 215
Abbotsbury Swannery 254
Abbotsford 813
Aberdeen 876-82, **878**, **1003**
Aberdeenshire 876-86
Aberfoyle 837
Abergavenny 701-3
Abergwaun 683-5
Aberhonddu 696-700
Abermaw 754-5
Abertawe 663-7
Aberteifi 689-90
Aberystwyth 690-2, **691**
abseiling 750

Map Pages **p000**
Image Pages **p000**

accommodation 1054-7, *see also individual locations*
Achmelvich 916
activities 36-43, *see also individual activities*
Acts of Union 996, 999-1000
Adam, Robert 788
air show, Cosford 430
air travel
  to/from Great Britain 1064
  within Great Britain 1066
airports
  Gatwick 131, 1064
  Heathrow 131-2, 1064
  Liverpool John Lennon Airport 561
  London City 132, 1064
  Luton 132, 1064
  Stansted 132, 1064
Albert Dock 555-6
Albert Memorial 85
Aldeburgh 372
Alderney 975-6
Alfred the Great 988
Alfriston 166
Alloway 821
Alnwick 630-2
Alston 603
Althorp 450
Alton Towers 414
Alum Chine 243
Amis, Martin 1028
amusement parks
  Alton Towers 414
  Bewilderwood 381-2
  Blackgang Chine Fun Park 241
  Drayton Manor 414
  GreenWood Forest Park 738
  Gulliver's Kingdom 460
  Heights of Abraham 460
  Legendary Land's End 331
  Legoland Windsor 218-19
  Pleasure Beach 563
  Puzzle Wood 213
  Sandcastle Waterpark 563
  Zooropia 273
An Tairbeart 939
An T-Ath Leathann 922-3
Ancient Golf Club 857
Angel of the North 616, 1038
Angle 677
Anglo-Irish War 1003
Anglo-Saxon people 985-6
Angus 871-6
Animal Wall 643
animals 1043-5, *see also individual animals*, wildlife sanctuaries
Anstruther 861-2
Applecross 919
aquariums
  Blue Reef (Portsmouth) 231
  Blue Reef Aquarium (Bristol) 273
  Blue Reef Aquarium (Hastings) 164
  Deep, The 498
  Lakes Aquarium 578
  National Marine Aquarium 308
  National Sea Life Centre 394
  Sea Life 84, 253
  Sea Life Centre & Marine Sanctuary 518-19
  Sealife Centre 563
  St Andrews Aquarium 856
Arbroath 875-6
archaeological sites, *see also* burial cairns, chambers & tombs, burial mounds, Roman sites, standing stones
  Avebury Stone Circle 267
  Blackhammer 953
  Clickimin Broch 958
  Cursus 265
  Dwarfie Stane 952
  Grey Wethers 315
  Grimspound 315
  Hadrian's Wall 150-1, 622-7, **624**, **6**, **150-2**, **708**, **983**
  Jarlshof 962
  Kilmartin 843
  Knap of Howar 955
  Knowe of Yarso 953
  Lesser Cursus 265
  Midhowe Cairn 953
  Old Scatness 962
  Quoyness 954
  Ridgeway National Trail 269
  Sanctuary 269
  Silbury Hill 269
  Skara Brae 949
  Stonehenge 263-5, **264**, **7**
  Taversoe Tuick 953
  Tomb of the Eagles 948
  West Kennet Long Barrow 269
  Woodhenge 265
architecture 1020-4
Ardgay 908
Ardrossan 817
area codes 1062
Areas of Outstanding Natural Beauty 1043
Argyll 840-55
Arisaig 907

Arlington Row 204, **10**
Arran 816-22
art galleries, *see* galleries, museums
Arthur, King 986
arts 1030-40, *see also individual genres*
Arts & Crafts movement 1037
Arundel 174-5
Ashbourne 458-9
Assynt 916
ATMs 1061
Attingham Park 427
Austen, Jane 227, 228, 282, 1027
Avebury 267-70, **268**
Aviemore 898-900
Ayr 820-1
Ayrshire 816-22

B

B&Bs 1054
Ba, The 946
Babbacombe 302
Backs, the 357-8, **10**
Bakewell 471-2
Bakewell Pudding 472
Bala 750-1
Ballater 882-3
Balloch 841
balti 398
Bamburgh 632-3
Bangor 732-3
Banksy 276
Barafundle Bay 676
Bardsey Island 739, 740
bargaining 978
Barmouth 754-5
Barra 942
Barraigh 942
Barry Island 654
bars 1017-18
Bassenthwaite 596
Bath 278-85, **280**
bathrooms 130-1
Battle 162-3
battles
  Anglo-Irish War 1003
  Bannockburn 835, 994
  Battle 162-3
  Battle of Bosworth 455
  Battle of Culloden 894
  Battle of Hastings 162
  Carregwastad Point 684
  Culloden 1000
  Hastings 990
  Hundred Years' War 994-5
  Killiecrankie 999
  Wars of the Roses 99
BBC 1034
beaches 25, 1042
  Aberdeen Beach 877
  Arisaig 907
  Barafundle Bay 676
  Bournemouth 243
  Broad Haven 676
  Calgary 853
  Carbis Bay 327
  Chesil Beach 254-5
  Cornwall 324
  Durness 914
  Falmouth 337
  Freshwater West 677
  Godrevy Towans 327
  Gwithian 327
  Morar 907
  Newquay 324
  Padstow 322-3
  Porthgwidden 327
  Porthmeor 327
  Porthminster 327
  Sanday 954
  St Ouen's Bay 970
  Summerleaze 320
  Torquay 302
  Weymouth 252
  Whitesand Bay 331
Beachy Head 166
Bealach na Ba pass 919
Bearnaraigh 940
Beatles, The 89, 556, 560
Beaulieu 236-7
Beaumaris 733-5
Becket, Thomas 140
Bedd Arthur 686
Beddgelert 744-5
Bedfordshire 215-16,
Bedruthan Steps 324, **9**
Beinn Na Faoghla 940-1
Bellingham 629
Ben Lawers 870, 871
Ben Lomond 841
Ben Nevis 906, **13**
Benbecula 940-1
Berkshire 216-20
Berneray 940
Berry, Peter 189
Berwick-upon-Tweed 634-5
Bettyhill 913
Betws-y-Coed 749-50
Beverley 499-500
Bibury 204
bicycle travel, *see* cycling
Big Ben 65, **145**, **705**
Bigton 962
birdwatching
  Abbotsbury Swannery 254
  Bassenthwaite 596
  Beaumaris 734
  Bird Garden 486
  Gigrin Farm Red Kite Feeding Station 717
  Grassholm Island 679
  Isles of Scilly 346
  Knap of Howar 955
  Lumbister RSPB Reserve 963
  Noss 961
  RSPB Minsmere 373
  Sandwick 961
  Shetland Islands 964
  Skokholm Island 679
  Skomer Island 679
  Sumburgh Head 962
Birmingham 392-402, **394-5**
  accommodation 397
  activities 393-6
  drinking 399
  emergency services 401
  entertainment 399-400
  festivals 396-7
  food 398-9
  itineraries 393
  medical services 401
  safety 401
  shopping 401
  sights 393-6
  tourist information 401
  tours 396
  travel to/from 401-2
  travel within 402
Birnam 867-8
Birsay 949-50
Bishop's Castle 433-4
Biwmares 733-5
Black Book of Carmarthen 690
Black Death 994
Black Isle 895
Black Mountain 695-6
Black Mountains 703-4
Black-and-White-Village Trail 420
Blackhammer 953
Blackpool 562-4
Blaenafon 661-2
Blaenau Ffestiniog 751
Blaenavon 661-2
Blair, Tony 978, 1007
Blake, William 1036
Blakeney Point 385

Blantyre 809
blonde hedgehogs 975
boat travel, *see also* boat trips, canal cruises
to/from Great Britain 1065
boat trips, *see also* canal cruises
Bardsey Island 740
Bath 281
Beaumaris 734
Birmingham 396
Blakeney Point 385
Brecon 697
Bristol 274
Brownsea Island 245
Cambridge 359
Canterbury 141
Chester 550
Coniston Water 589
Dorset 243
Durham 619
Durness 914
East Neuk 862
Eastbourne 165
Falmouth 337
Fort William 903
Glasgow 799
Inverness 890
Isle of Man 569
Isle of Mull 850
Isles of Scilly 346
Lincoln 444-5
Liverpool 557
Llangollen 724
Llŷn Peninsula 740
Loch Katrine 839
Loch Lomond 841
London 77, 81, 96, 97, 98, 149
Looe Island 343
Lymington 237
Mull of Kintyre 844
Norfolk Broads 383
Norwich 377
Oban 848
Orkney Islands 942
Padstow 322
Plymouth 308
Portland Harbour 252
Portsmouth 231
Rutland Water 456
Sandwich 155
Stratford-upon-Avon 407
Unst 964
West Wight 242
whale watching 852
Windermere Lake 578-9
Windsor 219
Worcester 415
Bodmin Moor 345
Boleyn Cup 203
Bonar Bridge 908
Bond, James 1028, 1029, 1031, 1033
Bonnie Prince Charlie 941, 1000
books 980, *see also* literature
cycling 39
drinking 1017
food 1009, 1014, 1015
hiking 993
history 988, 993, 1006, 1007
legends 989
shopping 713
travel 1025
walking 39, 993, 1044
wildlife 1045
Borders region 810-15
Borrowdale 596-7
Borth-y-Gest 743
Boscastle 321-2
Boscombe Pier 244
Bosherston Lily Ponds 676
Boston 448
Boudica 982, 983
Bournemouth 243-5
Bournville Village 395
Bowness 577-81
Brae 962-3
Braemar 883-5
Braich-y-Pwll 740
Brantwood 588
Braunton 317-18
Brecon 696-700, **698**
Bressay Sound 960-1
breweries
Black Sheep Brewery 514
Cider Museum & King Offa Distillery 419
Greene King Brewery 371
Harveys Brewery 161
Isle of Skye Brewery 926
Jenning's Brewery 592
Purple Moose Brewery 743
Shepherd Neame Brewery 161
Theakston's Brewery 514
bridges
Bridge of Sighs 188, 357
Clifton Suspension Bridge 271
Devil's Bridge 693
Devorgilla Bridge 822
Forth Bridge 787
Forth Road Bridge 787
High Level Bridge 609
Iron Bridge 427
London Bridge 84
Mathematical Bridge 358
Menai Suspension Bridge 733
Millennium Bridge 609
Monnow Bridge 660
Swing Bridge 609
Tower Bridge 74-5
Tyne Bridge 609
Bridgnorth 431-2
bridleways & towpaths
Brecon 697
Cotswolds 197
Exmoor 292
Fen Rivers Way 365
Gower 668
Hindhead 178
Llangollen 724
Loch Ness 895
Monmouthshire & Brecon Canal 702
North York Moors 475
Pennine Bridleway 462
Stratford-upon-Avon Canal 407
Union Canal 774
Windsor Castle 217
Yorkshire Dales Cycleway 475
Brighton & Hove 166-73, **168**, **25**
Bristol 270-8, **272-3**
accommodation 274-5
entertainment 277
food 275-6
itineraries 270
safety 277
sights 270-3
tours 273-4
travel to/from 277
travel within 278
British Museum 90-1, **15**
Brixham 304-5
Broad Haven 676
Broadford 922-3
Broadstairs 153
Broadway 200-1
brochs, *see* archaeological sites, castles & fortifications
Brodick 817-18
Brontë family 489, 519, 1027
Broughty Ferry 874-5

Map Pages **p000**
Image Pages p000

Brown, Gordon 979
Brown, Lancelot 'Capability' 177, 195, 257, 263, 281, 386, 411, 442, 486, 631
Brown Willy 345
Brownsea Island 245
brutalist architecture 1023
Bryher 347-8
Buckingham Palace 66
Buckinghamshire 215-16
Buckler's Hard 237
Bude 320-1
budget 18, 19
Builth Wells 715
Burford 198-9
burial cairns, chambers & tombs
  Arthur's Stone 421
  Belas Knap 202
  Carreg Coetan 685
  Dwarfie Stane 952
  Grey Cairns of Camster 910
  Herm 974
  Kilmartin Glen 843
  London Tombs 84
  Maes Howe 948-9
  Midhowe Cairn 953
  Pentre Ifan 686
  Preseli Hills 686
  Quoyness 954
  Taversoe Tuick 953
burial mounds
  Knowe of Yarso 953
  New King Barrows 265
  Tafts Ness 954
  Sutton Hoo 367
  West Kennet Long Barrow 269
Burlington Arcade 73
Burne-Jones, Edward 1037
Burnham Deepdale 386
Burns, Robert 821, 822-3
Burray 948
Bury St Edmunds 369-72, **370**
bus travel
  to/from Great Britain 1064-5
  to/from London 131
  within Great Britain 1066-7
  within London 133
bushcrafting 246, 382
business hours 1057
Bute family 644
Buttermere 597
Buxton 464-7, **465**
Bwlch Nant yr Arian 693
Byron, George Gordon (Lord Byron) 441

C

Cadbury World 395
Cader Idris 752
Caerdydd, *see* Cardiff
Caerfyrddin 671-2
Caergybi 735-6
Caerleon 662-3
Caernarfon 736-9
Caerphilly 655-6
cafes 1014-15
Cairn Gorm 900
cairns, *see* burial cairns, chambers & tombs
Caithness 910-13
Caldey Island 674
Calgary 853
Callander 838-9
Cambridge 353-63, **354**, **10**
  accommodation 359-60
  activities 359
  drinking 361-2
  entertainment 362
  food 360-1
  sights 353-9
  tourist information 362
  tours 359
  travel to/from 362-3
  travel within 363
Cambridgeshire 352-65
Campbeltown 844
camping 1054-5
canal cruises
  Birmingham 396
  Brecon 697
  Fort Augustus 896
  Fossdyke Navigation 444
  Kennet & Avon Canal 259
  Leeds-Liverpool Canal 492
canals, *see also* canal cruises
  Birmingham 394-5
  Caledonian Canal 896
  Exeter Canal 299
  Fossdyke Navigation 444
  Kennet & Avon Canal 259
  Leeds-Liverpool Canal 492
  Monmouthshire & Brecon Canal 697, 702
  Union Canal 774
canoeing, *see also* kayaking
  Cairngorms 900
  Exeter 299
  Forest of Dean 422
  Hay-on-Wye 704
  Hereford 420
  Loch Lomond 841
  Norfolk Broads 382
  Snowdonia National Park 750
Canterbury 135-43, **138**
  accommodation 141-2
  drinking 142
  entertainment 142-3
  festivals 141
  food 142
  sights 138-40
  tourist information 143
  travel to/from 143
  travel within 143
Canterbury Tales, The 141
Caol Acain 922
Cape Wrath 915
Capel Curig 749
car travel 19
  to/from London 131
  within Great Britain 1067
  within London 132
Caradoc Hills 432
Carbis Bay 327
Cardiff 49, 638-56, **639**, **642**, **12**
  accommodation 638, 647-8
  Cardiff Bay 643-5, **646**
  children, travel with 645
  drinking 649-50
  emergency services 652
  entertainment 650-1
  festivals 646-7
  food 638, 648-9
  highlights 639
  itineraries 641
  planning 638
  shopping 651-2
  sights 640-5
  tourist information 652
  tours 645-6
  travel seasons 638
  travel to/from 652
  travel within 652-3
Cardigan 689-90
Carew 678
Carlabagh 938
Carlisle 600-3, **601**
Carloway 938
Carmarthen 671-2
Carmarthenshire 670-3
Carne 340
Caro, Anthony 1038
Carr, Colin 156
Carreg Coetan 685
Cas Gwent 659
Castle Douglas 824
Castle Howard 512-13

castles & fortifications 21
Arundel Castle 174
Balmoral Castle 883, **711**
Bamburgh Castle 632-3
Barnard Castle 621-2
Beaumaris Castle 733
Birdoswald Roman Fort 150, 603, 627, **150**
Blair Castle 869-70
Bodiam Castle 163
Broch of Gurness 950
Brodie Castle 894
Caerlaverock Castle 823-4
Caernarfon Castle 737, **709**
Caerphilly Castle 656
Cardiff Castle 640-1
Carisbrooke Castle 240
Carlisle Castle 600
Carreg Cennen Castle 670
Castell Coch 655
Castell Henllys 686
Castle of Mey 911-12
Castle Rising Castle 388
Cawdor Castle 894
Chesters Roman Fort & Museum 150, 626, **150**
Chillingham 630
Colchester Castle 365
Conwy Castle 730
Corfe Castle 248-9
Culzean Castle & Country Park 821-2
Duart Castle 852
Dun Carloway 938
Dunnottar Castle 882
Dunrobin Castle 909
Dunstanburgh Castle 609, **15**
Durham Cathedral 617-18
Eastnor Castle 423
Edinburgh Castle 764-6, 930, **711**, **930**
Eilean Donan Castle 920
Glamis Castle 875
Greyfriars Kirk 768
Harlech Castle 755
Hermitage Castle 814-15
Housesteads Roman Fort & Museum 150-1, 626-7, **150-1**
Inveraray Castle 842
Kenilworth Castle 405-6
Leeds Castle 159-60
Lincoln Castle 443
Lindisfarne Castle 633, **706**
Maiden Castle 251
Mousa Broch 961
Muncaster Castle 600
Needles Old Battery 242
Old Sarum 262-3
Old Wardour Castle 258
Pendennis Castle 336-7
Pevensey Castle 166
Powderham Castle 302
Powis Castle 721
Raby Castle 623
Raglan Castle 661
Scarborough Castle 518
Segontium Roman Fort 737
Sizergh Castle 577
St Andrews Castle 856
St Giles Cathedral 766, **931**
St Mawes 340
Stirling Castle 833, 934-5, **934-5**, **983**, **990**
Sudeley Castle 202
Threave Castle 824
Urquhart Castle 896, **710**
Vespasian's Camp 265
Vindolanda Roman Fort & Museum 626
Warwick Castle 403-4
Windsor Castle 216-17
Wolvesey Castle 227
Castleton 467-9
Castletown 569
CAT 719-20
cathedrals, *see* churches & cathedrals
Cave Dale 468
Cavern Club 560
caves & caving
Blue John Cavern 468
Boat Cave 855
Castleton 468
Cheddar Gorge 288
City of Caves 436-7
Clearwell Caves 213
Fingal's Cave 855
Gaping Gill 494
Llechwedd Slate Caverns 751
National Showcaves Centre for Wales 695
Peak Cavern 468
Peak District National Park 462
Poole's Cavern 466
Porth-yr-Ogof 695
Smoo Cave 914
Speedwell Cavern 468
Symonds Yat 422
Treak Cliff Cavern 468
Wookey Hole 287-8
cell phones 19
Celtic crosses
Arbroath 875
Kilmartin Glen 843
Llŷn Peninsula 740
St Andrews 856
Trotternish 926
Wooltack Point 679
Celtic people 983
cemeteries
Highgate Cemetery 97
pet cemetery 388
Reilig Oran 854
central Scotland 51, 829-86, **830-1**
accommodation 829
food 829
highlights 830
planning 829
travel seasons 829
Ceredigion 689-93
Cerne Abbas 251-2
Cerne Giant 251
Chagford 316-17
chalk figures 251-2, 1021
changing of the guard 66, 217
Channel Islands 51, 966-76, **968**
accommodation 967
food 967
highlights 968
planning 967, 969
travel seasons 967
Channel Tunnel 1065
Charlecote Park 411
Charles I 998
Charles II 999
Chaucer, Geoffrey 141, 1025
Chawton 228
Cheddar 288
Chelsea Flower Show 27, 99
Cheltenham 206-10, **206**
Cheshire 547-52
Chesil Beach 254-5
Chester 548-52, **548**
Chesterfield 461
Cheviot 629
Chevy Chase 629
Chichester 175-6
children, travel with 44-6
Cardiff 645
Liverpool 557
London 98
Chillingham 630
Chipping Campden 200

Map Pages **p000**
Image Pages **p000**

Chipping Norton 199
Christie, Agatha 20, 304, 305
Church Stretton 432-3
churches & cathedrals 21, *see also* abbeys
Arundel 174
Beverley Minster 499-500
Canterbury Cathedral 138-9, **11**
Cathedral of the Peak 467
Chapel Royal of St Peter ad Vincula 73, 146, **146**
Elgin Cathedral 885
Ely Cathedral 363-4
Exeter Cathedral 297-9
Glasgow Cathedral 793
Gloucester Cathedral 211
Great St Mary's Church 358
Highland Tolbooth Kirk 766
King's College Chapel 353-5
Lincoln Cathedral 443
Liverpool Cathedral 553
Llandaff Cathedral 645
Norwich Cathedral 375
Rosslyn Chapel 788, 932-3, **932-3**, **936**
Round Church 358
Salisbury Cathedral 259-60
Southwark Cathedral 83
St Albans Cathedral 214
St Andrews Cathedral 856
St David's Cathedral 680-1, **16**
St John's Chapel 147, **147**
St Martin's Church 140
St Paul's Cathedral 74
Westminster Cathedral 66-7
Winchester Cathedral 225-7
Worcester Cathedral 415
York Minster 501-3, **13**
Churchill Barriers 947
Churchill, Winston 1004, 1005
cider makers 424
cinema 978
festivals 274, 540, 665, 777
history 993, 996
internet resources 1030, 1031, 1035
London 126
Cinque Ports 155
Cirencester 203
City Hall 83
classical music 124-5
Clee Hill 435
Cley Marshes 385
Clickimin Broch 958
Clifford's Tower 506-7
Clifton 271
climate 18, 1058-9, *see also individual locations*
climate change 1064
climbing
Ben Nevis 906
Cairngorms 900
Capel Curig 749
Cuillin Hills 920
Isle of Arran 818
Llanberis Path 745
Miner's Track 745
Peak District National Park 462
Pen-y-Fan 697
Pyg Track 745
Rhyd Ddu Path 745
Snowdon 745
Snowdon Horseshoe 745
Snowdon Ranger Path 745
Via Ferrata 597
Watkin Path 745
Clitheroe 565
Clouds Hill 247
Clovelly 319
coach travel, *see* bus travel
coasteering 41, 682
Cockermouth 591-3
Colchester 365-6
Coldbackie 913-14
colleges, *see also* universities
All Souls College 188
Brasenose College 188
Christ Church College 186-7
Christ's College 357
Corpus Christi College 189, 356
Emmanuel College 357
Eton College 217
Exeter College 188
Gonville & Caius College 356-7
Jesus College 357
Magdalen College 187
Marischal College 876
Merton College 188
New College 188
Old Royal Naval College 96
Peterhouse 357
Queens' College 357
St Edmund Hall 188
St John's College 357
Trinity College 188, 355-6
Trinity Hall College 356
Winchester College 227
Colourist painters 1037
comedy 125-6
Compton Verney 411
Coniston 588-90
Conservation Areas 1043
Constable, John 1037
consulates 1058-9
Conwy 730-2
Cook, James 529
cooking courses 295
Corbridge 624-5
Cornish pasties 1014
Cornwall 319-44, **335**, **9**
Cosford Air Show 430
costs 18
Cotehele 344
Cotswolds, the 196-205, **197**, **14**
County Durham 617-22
courses
abseiling 750
bushcrafting 246, 382
canoeing 750, 900
climbing 900
cooking 295
diving 684
language 739
kayaking 309, 684, 749, 750
mountain biking 292
mountaineering 749, 750, 900
sailing 246, 379, 750
surfing 43
windsurfing 246, 309, 750
Covent Garden 72
Coventry 402-3
Craignure 851-2
Crail 861
credit cards 1061
Criccieth 741
cricket 126, 1051
Crickhowell 700-1
crofting 914
Croick 908
Cromer 385
Cromwell, Oliver 364, 998
Cross-Lakes Experience 576
Crown Jewels 73, **147**
Croyde 317-18
Crughywel 700-1
Crusades, the 991-2
Cuillin Hills 920, 923-4
Culross 863
culture 67, 978-9
Cumbria 598-604, **572-3**
accommodation 570
food 570
highlights 572
planning 570
travel seasons 570
currency 18, 1060
customs regulations 1057-8

cycling 39-41, 1066, 1069, *see also* cycling trails, mountain biking
access 40
books 39
internet resources 40, 42, 224
maps 43
road rules 41
sporting events 239, 493, 703
within London 132
cycling trails
Beddgelert Forest 745
Black-and-White-Village Trail 420
Borders, the 811
Borders Abbeys Way 811
Camel Trail 224, 322
Coast & Castles Cycle Route 608
Coast to Coast Cycle Route 224
Coastal Cycle Trail 527
Coed y Brenin Forest Park 752
Dartmoor National Park 313
Devon Coast to Coast Cycle Route 292
Downs & Weald Cycle Route 135
Elan Valley Trail 717
Garden of England Cycle Route 135
Glasgow 798
Glentrool 826
Granite Way 224
Great Glen Mountain Bike Trail 895
Hadrian's Cycleway 608
High Peak Trail 462
Hopton Wood 424
Lancashire Cycle Way 531, 565
Limestone Way 462, 467
Lochs & Glens Cycle Way 832
Lôn Geltaidd 653
Lôn Las Cymru 653
Mawddach Trail 754
Monsal Trail 462, 466, 467, 472
Moor to Sea Cycle Route 475
Mortimer Trail 435
New Forest 234
North York Moors 475
Oxfordshire Cycleway 182
Peak District National Park 462
Pennine Bridleway 462
Pennine Cycleway 392, 462
Peregrine Path 422
Rothiemurchus Estate 898
Sea to Sea Cycle Route 608
Shropshire Way 435
Six Castles Cycleway 418, 424, 433
Southern Upland Way 811
St Cuthbert's Way 811
Thames Valley Cycle Way 181
Tissington Trail 462
Trossachs, The 837-8
Tweed Cycle Way 811
Viking Way 442
Wales 653
Water Rail Way 442
West Country Way 224, 292
White Rose Cycle Route 475
Wiltshire Cycleway 224
Yorkshire Dales Cycleway 475
Ystwyth Trail 691

D

Dale 679
Danby 525
dance 125, 665
dangers, *see* safety
Darlington 620-1
Dartmouth 305-6
Darwin Centre 20, 85
Darwin, Charles 160
David Livingstone Centre 809
Davies, WH 1027
debit cards 1061
Defoe, Daniel 1026
Derbyshire 456-62
Derwent Reservoirs 469-70
Derwent Valley 461
Devon 296-319
Dextrous, Andy 505
Diana, Princess of Wales 85, 88
Dickens, Charles 91-6, 153, 1026
Dig Hungate 506
Dinbych Y Pysgod 674-6
disabilities, travellers with 1062-3
distilleries
Aberlour 884
Ardbeg 845
Bruichladdich Distillery 847
Cider Museum & King Offa Distillery 419
English Whisky Company 20, 381
Glenfarclas 884
Glenfiddich 884
Glenmorangie Distillery 908
Highland Park Distillery 946
Isle of Arran Distillery 818
Isle of Jura Distillery 847
Lagavulin 845
Laphroaig 845
Macallan 884
Malt Whisky Trail 885
Oban Distillery 848
Penderyn Distillery 695
Plymouth Gin Distillery 308
Speyside Cooperage 884
Springbank Distillery 844
Talisker Distillery 924
diving
Durness 914
Fishguard 684
Isles of Scilly 348
Portland Harbour 252
Scapa Flow 951
divers, red-throated *963*
Doctor Who exhibition 645
dog sledding 899
Dolgellau 751-4
dolphins 852
Dorchester 250-1
Dorestone 421
Dornoch 908-9
Dorset 242-58
Douglas 568
Dovedale 459
Dover 156-9, **157**
Doyle, Arthur Conan 314, 1027
Dozmary Pool 345
Drake's Drum 312
Drayton Manor 414
drinking 1016-18, *see also* breweries, distilleries, *individual locations*, vineyards
Herefordshire Cider Route 424
driving, *see* car travel
Drosten Stone 875
drugs, illegal 1060
druids 982
Drumnadrochit 895-6
Drusillas 166
Dufftown 885-6
Dulverton 293-4
Dumfries 822-3
Dunadd 843
Duncansby Head 911
Dundee 871-6, **872**
Dunfermline 863
Dunkeld 867-8
Dunnet Head 912
Dunster 296
Dunvegan 925-6
Dunwich 372
Durdle Door 249
Durham 617-20, **618**
Durness 914-15
Durrell, Gerald 969

Map Pages **p000**
Image Pages **p000**

DVDs 1055
Dwarfie Stane 952

E

Eas a'Chual Aulin 915
East Anglia 48, 349-88, **350-1**
  accommodation 349
  food 349
  highlights 350
  planning 349
  travel seasons 349
East Neuk 861-2
East Riding of Yorkshire 497-500
East Sussex 160-73
Eastbourne 164-5
Eastbridge Hospital 140
economy 978, 979, 980
Edale 470-1
Eday 954
Eden Project 341
Edinburgh 50, 759-88, **760**, **762-3**, **770-1**, **773**, **5**, **711**
  accommodation 759, 778-80
  activities 774
  climate 759
  drinking 782-3
  emergency services 785, 786
  entertainment 783-5
  festivals & events 776-8
  food 759, 780-2
  highlights 760
  internet access 785
  itineraries 761
  medical services 786
  planning 761
  shopping 785
  sights & attractions 762-74
  tours 774-6
  travel seasons 759
  travel to/from 786
  travel within 786-7
Edinburgh Castle 764-6
Edward I 992-3
Edward II 993
Edward III 994
Edward IV 995
Edward V 995-6
Edward VII 1002-3
Edward the Confessor 989-90
Edward the Elder 988
Elan Valley 717
Electric Mountain 748
electricity 1058
Elgar, Edward 417
Elgin 885
Eliot, TS 1028
Elizabeth I 997
Elizabeth II 1004-5
Ely 363-5
email access 1060
embassies 1058-9
emergency services 19, 1059
  Birmingham 401
  Brighton 173
  Cardiff 652
  Edinburgh 785, 786
  Liverpool 561
  London 130
  Manchester 546
  Newcastle-upon-Tyne 615
Emin, Tracy 1038
England 55-635, **56-7**
  itineraries 34, 35
environmental issues 1041-8
  Alternative Technology Centre 487
  CAT 719-20
  climate change 1064
  Eden Project 341
  food 1010
  internet resources 679, 1008, 1041, 1048
  National Forest 455
  Tunny Club 520
Erddig 726
Eshaness 963
Essex 365-7
etiquette 67, 978
Eton 216-20, **218**
events, *see* festivals, sporting events
Evie 950
exchange rates 19
Exeter 297-302, **298**
Eyam 471

F

Fairbourne 754
Fairholmes 469
Falkland 862-3
Falkland Islands War 1006
Falls of Clyde 810
Falmouth 336-8
Fan Brycheiniog 695-6
Farne Islands 632
Farnham 177-8
Farr Stone 913
Faulks, Sebastian 1029
Fawkes, Guy 998
Fearnley-Whittingstall, Hugh 303
Fèis Ìle 845
fell hiking, *see* Munro bagging, walking, walking trails
festivals 24, *see also* film festivals, literature festivals, music festivals, sporting events
  Abergavenny Food Festival 29, 703
  Aintree Festival 557
  Aldeburgh Festival 372
  Artsfest 397
  Autumn Flower Show 514
  Bath Fringe Festival 283
  Beltane 27
  Big Cheese festival 655
  Birmingham Pride 396
  Bonfire Night 29
  Braemar Gathering 29
  Brighton Festival 27
  Burns an' a' That 820
  Cheese Olympics 655
  Chelsea Flower Show 27, 99
  Cheltenham 208
  Creamfields 557
  Crufts Dog Show 396
  Cycling Festival 239
  Edinburgh International Festival & Fringe 28, 777
  Edinburgh Military Tattoo 777
  Escape into the Park 665
  Fèis Ìle 845
  Fort William Mountain Festival 26
  Gay Pride 167
  Goose Fair 437
  Great British Cheese Festival 646
  Great Yorkshire Show 28, 514
  Guy Fawkes Night 29
  Hay Festival 27, 704
  Henley Festival 196
  Horse of the Year Show 397
  International Balloon Fiesta 274
  Isle of Wight Festival 238
  Jorvik Viking Festival 26, 507, **986**
  Kendal Mountain Festival 575
  Keswick Beer Festival 594
  Latitude Festival 28, 373
  Leicester Caribbean Carnival 453
  Llangollen Comedy Festival 725
  Llangollen Fringe Festival 725
  London Parade 26
  Ludlow Food & Drink Festival 435
  Manchester International Festival 539
  Mari Llwyd 714
  Matlock Illuminations 460
  Merseyside International Street Festival 557
  National Eisteddfod of Wales 28-9

festivals *continued*
Notting Hill Carnival 28, 99
Oak Apple Day 468
Orkney Folk Festival 950
Pride 28, 99
Richmond Walking & Book Festival 496
Robin Hood Festival 441
Robin Hood Pageant 437
Royal Academy Summer Exhibition 99
Royal Ascot 27
Royal Welsh Agricultural Show 715
Royal Welsh Show 28
Saturnalia Beer Festival & Mountain Bike Chariot Racing 714
Science Festival 208
Spirit of Speyside 27, 884
Spring Flower Show 514
St Albans Beer Festival 215
St Magnus Festival 946
Stonehaven Fireball Festival 29
Trooping the Colour 27, 99
Up Helly-Aa 26, 960
Victorian Festival 716
Walking Festival 239
Whitby Gothic Weekends 527
Wigtown book festival 826
Fetlar 965
Fife 855-63
film festivals
Edinburgh International Film Festival 777
Encounters 274
Manchester International Film Festival 540
Swansea Bay Film Festival 665
Finch Foundry 317
Finlaggan 847
Fionnphort 854
Fishguard 683-5
Fleet St 77
Fleming, Ian 1028
folk tales, *see* legends
food 1008-19, *see also individual locations*
Bakewell Puddng 472
balti 398
books 1009, 1014, 1015
cafes 1014-15
Cornish pasties 1014
costs 1008
environmental issues 1010
festivals 646, 655, 703
gastropubs 1015-16
pubs 1015-16
puddings 1012-13
regional cuisine 1013-14
restaurants 1015
sherry trifle 1013
smoking regulations 1015
teashops 1014-15
Yorkshire Pudding 1012
football 1049-50
Liverpool FC 560
Manchester United Museum 535
Old Trafford stadium 535, **16**
sporting events 459, 1050
Forest of Bowland 566
Forest of Dean 212-13, 422-3
forests, *see* national parks & forests, nature reserves
Forster, EM 1027
Fort Augustus 896-7
Fort George 894
Fort William 903-5, **904**
fortifications, *see* castles & fortifications
fossil hunting 255
Fowey 341-2
fox hunting 1044
Freshwater West 677

G

Gairloch 918
galleries 24, 164-5
Aberdeen Art Gallery 877
BALTIC Centre for Contemporary Art 612
Barber Institute of Fine Art 395
Beatrix Potter Gallery 587
Biscuit Factory 611-12
Gallery of Modern Art 793
Graves Gallery 479
Hayward Gallery 84
Henry Moore Institute 481
Hunterian Art Gallery 797
Institute of Contemporary Arts 67
Kelvingrove Art Gallery & Museum 797
Laing Art Gallery 611
Leeds Art Gallery 481
Manchester Art Gallery 534
Modern Art Oxford 190
MOMA Wales 720
National Gallery 71
National Gallery of Scotlan 772
National Portrait Gallery 71-2
Oriel Plas Glyn-y-Weddw 741
Pallant House Gallery 175
Penlee House Gallery & Museum 332
Royal Academy of Arts 72
Ruskin Gallery 479
Sainsbury Centre for Visual Arts 376-7
Scottish National Gallery of Modern Art 773-4
Scottish National Portrait Gallery 772
Serpentine Gallery 85
Somerset House 72, 148, **148**
Tate Britain 84
Tate Liverpool 556
Tate Modern 77, 149, **149**
Tate St Ives 327
Turner Contemporary 20, 144
Turner House Gallery 653
Walker Art Gallery 553
Wallace Collection 89
White Cube 95
Whitworth Art Gallery 539
gannets 679
Gaping Gill 494
Garenin 938
gastropubs 1015-16
gay travellers 1058
Birmingham 400
Birmingham Pride 396
Brighton 172
Cardiff 650
festivals 28, 99, 167, 539
Glasgow 799
London 120
Manchester 539
Newcastle-upon-Tyne 615
geese, rain 963
geography 25, 1041-2
geology 1041-2
Durdle Door 249
Jurassic Coast 248
George VI 1003
ghost tours
Arundel 174
Canterbury 141
Cardiff 646
Ludlow 435
Nottingham 437
Salisbury 261
Stratford-upon-Avon 407
Winchester 228
York 505, 507
Glasgow 792-809, **794-5**, **9**
accommodation 799-803
activities 798-9

Map Pages **p000**
Image Pages **p000**

drinking 805-6
entertainment 806-7
festivals 799
food 803-5
itineraries 792
medical services 808
shopping 807
sights 793-8
tours 799
travel to/from 808
travel within 809
walking tour 800, **800**

Glasgow School of Art 793
Glastonbury 288-91, **289**
Glen Affric 894-5
Glen Coe 902-3, **711**
Glen Nevis 905-6
Glencoe Lochan 902
Glencoe village 902-3
Glenfinnan 907
Glentrool 826
Glorious Revolution 999
Gloucester 211-12, **212**
Gloucestershire 205-13
Glyndebourne 27
Goathland 525
goats, wild 1045
Godrevy Towans 327
Golden Hind 304
Golden Road 686
golf 1051-2
golf courses
Broughty Ferry 874
St Andrews 857
Troon 821

Goodrich 422
Gordale Scar 493
Gormley, Antony 1038
government 978, 979, 980
Gower Peninsula 668-70, **14**
Grantchester 363
Grasmere 585-6
Grassholm Islands 679
Great Depression 1003
Great Glen, the 890
Great Malvern 416-18
Great Orme 726
Great Tew 199
Great Yarmouth 383-4
Green Bridge of Wales 677
Greenway 20, 305
Greenwich 95-6, 106
Greyfriars Bobby 769-70, **757**
Guernsey 972-3, **966**
guillemots 679
Gunpowder Plot 998
Gurnard's Head 330
Gwithian 327

H

hacking, *see* horse riding, pony trekking
Hadrian's Wall 150-1, 622-7, **624**, **6**, **150-2**, **708**, **983**
Segedunum 617

Haltwhistle 626-7
Hampshire 225-34
Hardraw Force 495
Hardy, Thomas 250, 1026
Harlech 755-6
Harold 990
Harris 939
Harrogate 513-17, **515**
Harworth 488-90
Hastings 163-4
Haverfordwest 678-9
Hawes 494-6
Hawkshead 586-7
Hay-on-Wye 704, 713
Haystacks 597
health 1058-9, 1061
Hebden Bridge 487-8
Hebridean Whale & Dolphin Trust 852
hedgehogs, blonde 975
Helm Crag 585
Helmsdale 909-10
Helmsley 522-3
Helvellyn 597
Henley-on-Thames 195-6
Henry I 990
Henry II 990-1
Henry III 992
Henry IV 994-5
Henry V 995
Henry VI 995
Henry VII 996
Henry VIII 996-7
Heptonstall 488
Hepworth, Barbara 327, 1037
Hereford 418-20, **419**
Herefordshire 418-23
Herefordshire Cider Route 424
heritage organisations 135, 1059-60
Herm 973-4
Hertfordshire 214-15
Hexham 625-6
High Crag 597
High Stile 597
Highland Clearances 914
Highland Games 29
Highlands, the 51, 887-965
accommodation 887
food 887
highlights 888
planning 887
travel seasons 887

hiking, *see* Munro bagging, walking, walking trails
Hill o'Many Stanes 910
Hill Top 588
hill walking, *see* Munro bagging, walking, walking trails
Hillswick 963
Hindhead 178
Hirst, Damien 1038
history 981-1007, *see also* battles
Acts of Union 996, 999-1000
Anglo-Saxon people 985-7
books 988, 993, 1006, 1007
Celts 983
Crusades, the 991-2
early settlers 982
Elizabethan era 997
Great Depression 1003
Highland Clearances 914
Industrial Revolution 1001-2
internet resources 994
Iron Age 982-3
missionaries 987
Restoration 999
Roman era 983-5
Stone Age 982
Thatcher era 1006-7
Viking era 987-8
WWI 1002
WWII 1003-4

hitching 1068
Hogarth, William 1036
Hogmanay 778
holidays 1061-2
Holkham 386
Hollins Cross 469
Holnicote Estate 295
Holst, Gustav 208
Holy Island (England) 633-4
Holy Island (Scotland) 819
Holyhead 735-6
Hornby, Nick 1029
horse racing 1052
Aintree Festival 557
Derby Week 27
Grand National steeplechase 27, 561
Royal Ascot 27

horse riding 41-2, *see also* pony trekking
  Betws-y-Coed 749
  Brecon 697
  Dartmoor National Park 313
  Elan Valley Trail 717
  Exmoor National Park 292
  Llangattock 701
  New Forest 235
  Peak District 470
Horsey Windpump 382
Horton-in-Ribblesdale 494
Hospital, Eastbridge 140
Hospital of St Cross 227-8
hostels 1055-6
hotels 1055-6
Houses of Parliament (London) 65, 148, 1022, **705**
Hoy 952-3
Hughes, Ted 1028
Hugo, Victor 972
Hull 498-9
Humbleton Hill 629
Hundred Years' War 994-5
Hutton-le-Hole 524
Hwlffordd 678-9
Hyde Park 85-8

I

Ilfracombe 318-19
Inchcolm 787
industrial heritage 23
industrial museums
  Abbeydale Industrial Hamlet 479
  Beamish open-air museum 621
  Blists Hill Victorian Town 428
  Broseley Pipeworks 428-9
  Building of Bath Museum 282
  Coalbrookdale Museum of Iron 427
  Coalport China Museum & Tar Tunnel 428
  Cromford Mill 461
  Design Museum 83
  Fox Talbot Museum of Photography 267
  Jackfield Tile Museum 428
  Leeds Industrial Museum 481
  Masson Mills Working Textile Museum 460
  Museum of Nottingham Life at Brewhouse Yard 436
  National Coal Mining Museum for England 487
  National Slate Museum 748
  National Waterfront Museum 663
  National Waterways Museum 211, 450
  Peak District Mining Museum 460
  Rotunda Museum 518
  Royal Pump Room Museum 513
  Strutt's North Mill 461
  Verdant Works 873
Industrial Revolution 1001-2
inflation 978
Ingleton 494
Inns of Court 77
insurance 1060, 1067
internet access 1060
  Birmingham 401
  London 130
internet resources 19, *see also individual locations*
  accommodation 102, 583, 1054, 1056-7
  camping 583
  children, travel with 45
  cinema 1030, 1031, 1035
  cycling 40, 42, 224
  disabilities, travellers with 1062
  environmental issues 679, 1008, 1041, 1048
  football tickets 1049
  health 1061
  history 994
  markets 1010
  travel advisories 1062
  walking 39
Inveraray 842-3
Inverness 890-4, **892**
Iron Age logboat 245
Ironbridge Gorge 427-30, **428**
Isle of Anglesey 733-6
Isle of Arran 817-20, **817**
Isle of Colonsay 848, **846**
Isle of Great Cumbrae 816-17
Isle of Iona 854-5
Isle of Islay 844-7, **846**
Isle of Jura 847-8, **846**
Isle of Man 566-9, **567**
Isle of May 862
Isle of Mull 850-4, **851**
Isle of Portland 253-4
Isle of Raasay 926
Isle of Skye 920-6, **921**
Isle of Staffa 855
Isle of Thanet 153
Isle of Tiree 848, **851**
Isle of Wight 238-42, **239**
Isles of Scilly 344-8, **344**
itineraries 30-5, *see also individual locations*

J

James I 998
James II 999
James VI 995, **995**
James, Henry 161
Jarlshof 962
Jedburgh 813-14
Jersey 969-72
John O'Groats 911
John, King 992
Johnson, Samuel 413
Jones, Inigo 67, 72, 96, 263
Jurassic Coast 248

K

Kapoor, Anish 1038
kayaking, *see also* canoeing
  Alderney 975
  Capel Cureg 749
  Dartmoor National Park 313
  Fishguard 684
  Isle of Arran 818
  Isle of Skye 920
  Lulworth Cove 249
  Pembrokeshire 682
  Plymouth 749
  Poole Harbour 246
  Snowdonia National Park 750
Kelso 810-12
Kendal 574-7
Kenilworth 405-6
Kenmore 870
Kensington Palace 85
Kent 135-60
Keswick 593-6, **594**
Kettle's Yard 358
Kildalton Cross 845
Killin 839-40
Kilmartin Glen 843
Kinder Plateau 470
King Arthur 672, 986
King's Lynn 387-8
Kingston Lacy 247
Kingussie 901
Kinlochleven 903
Kintyre 843-4
Kipling, Rudyard 1027
Kirkcudbright 824-5
Kirkwall 944-7, **945**
kite-boarding 42

Map Pages **p000**
Image Pages **p000**

kitebuggying 41, 324-5
kitesurfing 43, 246, 252
Knap of Howar 955
Knighton 718
Knowe of Yarso 953
König 951
Kronprinz Wilhelm 951
Kyle of Lochalsh 919, **14**
Kyleakin 922
Kylesku 915-16

L

La'al Ratty 599
Labour party 978, 979
Lacock 266-7
Ladies of Llangollen 724, 725
Lady Isabella Laxey Wheel 569
Lake District 49, 574-98, **572-3**, **575**, **707**
 accommodation 570
 food 570
 highlights 572
 planning 570
 travel seasons 570
Lake of Menteith 837
Lamb Holm 947
Lambert, Daniel 451
Lamlash 819-20
Lanark 809-10
Lancashire 562-6
Lancaster 564-5
land yachting 352
Land's End 331
Langdale 590-1
language 18, 1026
Lanhydrock 343-4
Largs 816
Laugharne 672-3
Lavenham 368-9, **22**
Lawrence, DH 1027
Lawrence, TE 247
Le Pinâcle 970
Ledbury 423
Leeds 480-6, **482**
legal matters 1060
legends
 Beddgelert 744
 books 989
 King Arthur 672, 986
 Loch Ness 897
 Merlin 672
 Robin Hood 992
Leicester 451-5, **452**
Leicestershire 450-5
Leodhais 928-38
Lerwick 956-60, **958**
lesbian travellers 1058
 Birmingham 400
 Birmingham Pride 396
 Brighton 172
 Cardiff 650
 festivals 28, 99, 167, 539
 Glasgow 799
 London 120
 Manchester 539
 Newcastle-upon-Tyne 615
Lewis 928-38
Lewis chessmen 768
Liberal-Democrat coalition 978, 979
libraries
 Bodleian Library 187
 British Library 91
 John Rylands Library 534
 Long Library 195
 National Library of Wales 690
 Radcliffe Camera 187-8
Lichfield 412-13
Lincoln 442-6, **444**
Lincolnshire 442-9
Lindisfarne 633-4
literature 1025-9, *see also* books, literature festivals
literature festivals
 Bath Literature Festival 282
 Bristol Shakespeare Festival 274
 Cheltenham Literature Festival 208
 Daphne du Maurier Literary Festival 341
 Dickens Festival 153
 Dylan Thomas Festival 29, 665
 Hull Literature Festival 498
 Edinburgh International Book Festival 777
 Hay Festival 27, 704
Liverpool 552-62, **554**
 accommodation 557-8
 children, travel with 557
 drinking 559
 emergency services 561
 entertainment 559-61
 festivals 557
 food 558-9
 internet access 561
 internet resources 561
 medical services 561
 shopping 561
 sights 552-6
 tourist information 561
 tours 556-7
 travel to/from 561-2
 travel within 562
Livingstone, David 809
Lizard Peninsula 334-6
Lizard Point 335
Llanandras 718
Llanberis 748-9
Llandeilo 670-1
Llandrindod Wells 715-17
Llandudno 726-30, **728**, **709**
Llanfair PG (Llanfairpwllgwyngyll-gogerychwyrndrobwllllantysili-ogogogoch) 737
Llanfair-Ym-Muallt 715
Llangattock 700-1
Llangatwg 700-1
Llangollen 724-6, **724**
Llangorse Lake 698
Llanwrtyd Wells 714-15
Llanystumdwy 741
Lloyds Bank Turd 505
Llŷn Peninsula 739-42, **746-7**
Llyn Tegid 750
Llywelyn the Great 992
Loch Glencoul 915-16
Loch Katrine 839
Loch Lomond 840-2
Loch Morlich 900
Loch nam Madadh 940
Loch Ness 895-6
Loch Rannoch 871
Loch Tay 870
Loch Tummel 871
Lochinver 916
Lochmaddy 940
Lochnagar 883
Lochranza 818-19
London 47, 58-133, **60-1**
 accommodation 58, 99-107
 airports 107
 Bayswater 103, 112, 119, 129, **104**
 Belgravia 101, 111
 Bloomsbury 89-93, 103-6, **92**
 Camden Town 93, 121, **114**
 Chelsea 84-8, 102, 111-12, 119, **86-7**
 children, travel with 98
 City, the 73-7, 101, 110, 118, **74-5**
 Clerkenwell 115, 121, 130, **108**
 discount tickets 76, 132
 Docklands 95
 drinking 117-22
 Earl's Court 102-3
 emergency services 130
 entertainment 122-6
 Farringdon 106, 115, 121, 130, **108**
 festivals 99

London *continued*
Fitzrovia 103, 113
food 58, 107-17
Fulham 102-3
Greenwich 95-6, 106
Hampstead 96-7, 106-7, 121-2
Highgate 96-7, 106-7, 121-2
highlights 60-1
Hoxton 93-5, 106, 115-17, 121, 130, **94**
internet access 130
internet resources 130
Islington 113-15, 129, **116**
itineraries 63
Kensington 84-8, 102, 111-12, 119, **86-7**
King's Cross 121
Knightsbridge 102, 111, 128, **86-7**
Marylebone 89, 113, 119-20, 129, **90**
medical services 130
Notting Hill 103, 112, 119, 129, **104**
Paddington 103, 112, 119, 129
Pimlico 84, 101
planning 58
safety 130, 133
Shepherd's Bush 130
shopping 127-33
Shoreditch 93-5, 106, 115-17, 121, 130, **94**
sights 62-98
South Bank 77-84, 101, 110, 119, **80**, **82**
Spitalfields 93-5, 106, 115-17, 121, 130, **94**
St James's 62-7, 100, **64**
St Pancras 89-93, 103-6, **92**
tourist information 131
tours 98
travel seasons 58
travel to/from 131
travel within 131-3
walking tours 78-9, 96, **78**
West End 67-73, 100-1, 107-10, 118, 127-8, **68-9**
Westminster 62-7, 100, **64**
London Dungeon 83
London Eye 81, 148, **55**, **148**
London Tombs 84
London Underground 133
Long Melford 368
Longleat 266

Map Pages **p000**
Image Pages **p000**

Looe 342-3
Looe Island 343
Lord's Cricket Ground 126
Lost Valley 902
Lower Solva 679
Lower Wye Valley 660
Lowry, LS 535, 1037
Ludlow 434-6, **434**
Lulworth Cove 249
Lulworth Crumple 249
Lunar Society 395, 397
Luskentyre 939
Lydford Gorge 317
Lyme Regis 255-6
Lymington 237-40
Lyndhurst 236
Lynmouth 294-5
Lynton 294-5

M

MacDonald, Flora 925, 926, 941
MacGregor, Robert 841
Machynlleth 719-21
Mackenzie, Compton 1028
Mackintosh, Charles Rennie 798, 1037
Madame Tussauds 89
Madchester sound 544
Maes Howe 948-9
Magna Carta 220, 259, 443
Major Oak 441
Malham 492-3
Mallaig 907-8
Malvern Hills 418
Mam Tor 468
Manchester 531-47, **536-7**
accommodation 540-1
activities 534-9
drinking 542-3
emergency services 546
entertainment 543-6
festivals 539-40
food 541-2
internet access 546-7
internet resources 547
itineraries 535
medical services 547
shopping 546
sights 534-9
tourist information 547
tours 539
travel to/from 547
travel within 547
Manx shearwaters 679
Mappa Mundi 418, 421
maps 43, 73
Marble Arch 88
Marches, the 48, 389-473, **390-1**
accommodation 389
food 389
highlights 390
planning 389
travel seasons 389
Margate 144-53
maritime museums, *see also* military museums, war museums
Aberdeen Maritime Museum 877
Buckler's Hard 237
Fort Grey Shipwreck Museum 972
Holyhead Maritime Museum 735
Maritime Heritage Centre 271
Mary Rose Museum 230
Merseyside Maritime Museum 556
National Maritime Museum (Falmouth) 336
National Maritime Museum (London) 96
Ramsgate Maritime Museum 154
Royal Naval Museum 230
markets
Cardiff 651
Carmarthen Market 672
internet resources 1010
London 128-9
Markgraf 951
Mary, Queen of Scots 767-8, 997-8
Matlock Bath 459-61
Maud Foster Windmill 448
Maurier, Daphne du 1027
Mawddach Estuary 754
Matthew 271
Max Gate 250
Mayfair 67
McEwan, Ian 1028
McGough, Roger 1028
measures 1055
medical services
Aberdeen 881
Birmingham 401
Edinburgh 786
Glasgow 808
Liverpool 561
London 130
Manchester 547
Oxford 194
Melrose 812-13
Merlin 672
Merrick 825
Midlands, the 48, 389-473, **390-1**
accommodation 389
food 389

highlights 390
planning 389
travel seasons 389
Mid-Wales 50, 687-721, **688**
accommodation 687
food 687
highlights 688
planning 687
travel seasons 687
military museums, *see also* maritime museums, war museums
Commandery 415
Cosford Royal Air Force Museum 430
D-Day Museum 231
Gurkha Museum 228
Horsepower 228
Rifles 261
Royal Armouries 480-1
Royal Green Jackets Museum 228
Royal Naval Museum 230
Royal Norfolk Regimental Museum 376
Underground Military Museum 972
Millais, John Everett 1037
Millband Codman, Jacqueline 730
Millennium Stadium 641-2
Minack 333
mines
Big Pit: National Coal Museum 662
Blue Hills Tin Streams 326
Cornwall & West Devon Mining Landscape 340
Geevor Tin Mine 330
Honister Slate Mine 597
Levant Mine & Beam Engine 331
Sygun Copper Mine 744-5
Minginish 924
minke whales 852
Minster Lovell 198
mobile phones 19
Moelfre 735
monarchies, *see also individual monarchs*
Elizabethan era 997
Lancaster, House of 994-5
Plantagenets, House of 990, 992
Victoria era 1022
York, House of 994-5
monasteries & priories
Caldey Island 674
Great Malvern Priory 416
Inchmahome Priory 837
Kirkham Priory 513
Lanercost Priory 627
Lindisfarne Priory 633
Llanthony Priory 703, **636**
Wenlock Priory 430
Whithorn 827
money 18, 19, 1060-1
discount cards 1055
Monmouth 660-1
Monument 76
Moore, Henry 481, 487, 1037
moors 22
Morar 907
Moray 885-6
Morecambe Bay 598
Moreton-in-Marsh 199
Mortimer's Hole 436
motorcycle travel 1067
mountain biking
Camel Trail 224
Caradoc Hills 432
Cardinham Woods 345
Chilterns 181
Cotswolds 181
Exmoor National Park 292
Forest of Dean 181
Granite Way 224
Isle of Arran 818
Long Mynd 432
Machynlleth 720
Nevis Range 906
Pembrokeshire 682
mountain boarding 42
mountaineering 42
Bala 750
Cairngorms 900
Capel Curig 749
mountains 22
Mousehole 331
Much Wenlock 430-1
Mull of Kintyre 844
Mumbles 667-8
Munro bagging 38, 871, 591
museums, *see also* galleries, industrial museums, maritime museums, military museums, railway museums, science museums, transport museums, war museums
Ashmolean Museum 20, 189
Bank of England Museum 76
Barbara Hepworth Museum & Sculpture Garden 327
Beatles Story 556
Blaenavon Ironworks 662
Bowes Museum 621-2
British Golf Museum 857
British Museum 90-1, **15**
Brontë Parsonage Museum 489
Cardiff Story 642-3
Charles Dickens Museum 91-3
Churchill Museum 67
Clockmakers' Museum 76
Corinium Museum 203
Cromwell's House 364
Dennis Severs' House 93
Dickens House Museum 153
Dig 506
Discovery Museum 611
dog collar museum 160
Dorset County Museum 250
Dover Castle 157-8
Dr Johnson's House 76-7
Dylan Thomas Boathouse 673
Dylan Thomas Centre 663
Elgar Birthplace Museum 417
Fitzwilliam Museum 358
Florence Nightingale Museum 84
Foundling Museum 91
Freud Museum 97
Geffrye Museum 93-5
Gordon Russell Museum 201
Great North Museum 610
Handel House Museum 73
Holst Birthplace Museum 208
Hunterian Museum 797
International Slavery Museum 556
Jane Austen Centre 282
Jane Austen house museum 228
Jorvik 505
Kelvingrove Art Gallery & Museum 797
Laurel & Hardy Museum 599
Madame Tussauds 89
Manchester United Museum 535
Museum of Edinburgh 767
Museum of London 75-6
Museum of London Docklands 95
Museum of Witchcraft 321
National Football Museum 534
National Museum Cardiff 641
National Museum of Scotland 768
National Roman Legion Museum 662
National Wool Museum 674
Natural History Museum 20, 85
Old Operating Theatre Museum 81
Pencil Museum 593
Pierhead 645
River & Rowing Museum 195
RNLI Grace Darling Museum 633
Robert Burns Birthplace Museum 821
Robert Burns Centre 823
Royal Cornwall Museum 339

museums *continued*
Royal Worcester Porcelain Works 415
Ruskin Museum 589
Russell-Cotes 243
Samuel Johnson Birthplace Museum 413
Scott Polar Research Institute 358
Scottish Fisheries Museum 861
Seven Stories – the Centre for Children's Books 612
Sir John Soane's Museum 72
St Fagans National History Museum 654-5
St Mungo's Museum of Religious Life & Art 793
Torquay Museum 304
University Museum 189-90
Victoria & Albert Museum 84
Wellcome Collection 91
World Museum Liverpool 552
World of Beatrix Potter 578
World Rugby Museum 126
music 544, 979, 1034-6, *see also* music festivals
music festivals 24
Bath International Music Festival 282-3
Bestival 29, 238
Brecon Jazz Festival 29, 698
Camden Crawl 27, 99
Celtic Connections 26
Cheltenham Folk Festival 208
Cheltenham Jazz Festival 208
Cheltenham Music Festival 208
Download Festival 27
Eden Sessions 341
Edinburgh International Festival 777
Edinburgh International Jazz & Blues Festival 777-8
Escape into the Park 665
Fiddle & Accordion Festival 959
Glastonbury Festival 28, 289
Glyndebourne 27
Green Man Festival 701
Hull Jazz Festival 498
International Musical Eisteddfod 28, 725, 726
Leeds Festival 28, 481
Lovebox 99
Manchester Jazz Festival 539
Mathew St Festival 557
Meltdown Festival 28, 99
National Eisteddfod 726
opera 27
Reading Festival 28
St David's Cathedral Festival 681
T in the Park 28
Truck 28
Urdd Eisteddfod 726
West End Festival 28
Womad 28
Musselwick Sands 679
Mynydd Preseli 686
myths, *see* legends

N

Na Gearrannan 938
national parks & forests 1042-3, 1047, *see also* nature reserves
Beddgelert Forest 745
Brecon Beacons National Park 693-704, 713, **694**
Cairngorms National Park 897-901, **898**
Caledonian forest 898
Coed y Brenin Forest Park 752
Dartmoor National Park 312-18, **312**,
Exmoor National Park 291-6, **291**
Galloway Forest Park 825-6
Glenmore Forest Park 900
Glentress forest 815
Grizedale Forest 587-8
Gwydyr Forest 749
Lake District National Park 574, **5**
Loch Lomond & the Trossachs 840-1
National Forest 455
Norfolk Broads 381-3
North York Moors National Park 521-9, **522**
Northumberland National Park 628-30, **624**
Peak District National Park 462-73, **463**
Pembrokeshire Coast National Park 676
Queen Elizabeth Forest Park 837
Snowdonia National Park 744-56, **8**, **708**
South Downs National Park 166
Trossachs, The 837-40
Whinlatter Forest Park 593
Yorkshire Dales National Park 490-7, **491**, **7**, **14**
National Scenic Areas 1043
National Trust 1060
National Wallace Monument 834-5
National Wetland Centre 670
nature reserves, *see also* national parks & forests, wildlife sanctuaries
Balranald Nature Reserve 940
Calke Park 458
Elan Valley 717
Fetlar RSPB Reserve 965
Galloway Red Deer Range 826
Glen Affric National Nature Reserve 894
Great Orme Country Park 727
Isle of May 862
Loch Druidibeg National Nature Reserve 941
Longleat 266
Lumbister RSPB Reserve 963
National Wetland Centre 670
Noss 961
Orford Ness 373
RSPB Minsmere 373
Sherwood Forest National Nature Reserve 441-2
Wildfowl & Wetlands Centre 174
Woburn Safari Park 215
Ness Islands 890
Nevis Range 906-7
New Forest 234-8, **235**
New Lanark 809-10
Newcastle-upon-Tyne 609-16, **610**
drinking 614
emergency services 615
entertainment 614-15
food 613-14
sights 609-12
sleeping 612-13
tourist information 615
travel to/from 616
travel within 616
Newlyn 331-4
Newport 685-6
Newquay 323-6, **324**
newspapers 1055
Newstead Abbey 441
Newtonmore 901
Newtown 718-19
Norfolk 374-88
Norfolk & Suffolk Broads 381-3
North Atlantic Drift 852
North Isles 963-5
North Pennines 622
North Ronaldsay 956
North Uist 940
north Wales 50, 722-56, **723**
accommodation 722
food 722

highlights 723
planning 722
travel seasons 722
Northampton 449-50
Northamptonshire 449-50
northeast England 49, 605-35, **606-7**
accommodation 605
food 605
highlights 606-7
planning 605
travel seasons 605
Northern Islands, the 51, 887-965
accommodation 887
food 887
highlights 888
planning 887
travel seasons 887
Northumberland 630-5, **12**
northwest England 49, 530-69, **532-3**
accommodation 530
food 530
highlights 532-3
planning 530
travel seasons 530
Norwich 375-80, **376**
Noss 961
Nottingham 436-41, **438**
accommodation 437-8
activities 436-7
drinking 439
entertainment 439-40
festivals 437
food 438-9
sights 436-7
tourist information 440
tours 437
travel to/from 440
travel within 440-1
Nottinghamshire 436-42

O

O2 96
Oban 848-50
Okehampton 317
Old Man 589
Old Man of Hoy 952
Old Sarum 262-3
Old Scatness 962
Old Trafford 535, **16**
Oliver, Jamie 115, 325, 482
open-air museums, *see* industrial museums
opening hours 1057
opera 125
Orford 373
Orford Ness 373
Orkney Islands 942-56, **943**
Orwell, George 1028
ospreys 596
Outer Hebrides 927-42, **921**
Oxford 182-94, **184-5**, **8**, **706**
accommodation 191-2
drinking 193
entertainment 193
food 192-4
internet resources 194
medical services 194
sights 183-90
tourist information 194
tours 190-1
travel to/from 194
travel within 194
Oxfordshire 182-96
Oyster card 132

P

Padstow 322-3
Paignton 302
Painswick 205
painting 1036-8
Palace of Westminster 65, **705**
palaces
Blenheim Palace 194-5, **8**
Buckingham Palace 66
Hampton Court Palace 97-8
Kensington Palace 85
Palace of Holyroodhouse 767-8 931, **705**, **931**
Scone Palace 864
St James's Palace 66
Pandora Inn 338
pantomime 1040
Papa Westray 955
Papay 955
parks & gardens
Aberglasney Gardens 671
Alnwick Garden 631
Alum Chine 243
Backs, the 357-8
Bird Garden 486
Calke Park 458
Cambridge University Botanic Garden 359
Castle Kennedy Gardens 828
Chalice Well & Gardens 290
Chelsea Physic Garden 88
Covent Garden 72
Cragside House, Garden & Estate 628
Green Park 66
Greenwich Park 96
Hampstead Heath 97
Hidcote Manor Garden 200
Holyrood Park 768
Hyde Park 85-8
Kensington Gardens 85
Kew Gardens 97
Lost Gardens of Heligan 341
National Botanic Garden of Wales 671
Ness Islands 890
Oxford Botanic Garden 187
Painswick Rococo Garden 205
Petworth Park 177
Prior Park 281-2
Regent's Park 89
Richmond Park 98
Royal Botanic Garden 774
St James's Park 66
Studley Royal 517
Trelissick Gardens 339
Williamson Park & Tropical Butterfly House 564
passports 1066
patron saints 988
peat 938
Peebles 815
Peel 569
Peggy 569
Pembroke 677-8
Pembrokeshire 673-86, **675**, **16**
Penarth 653
Pendle Hill 565-6
Pendower 340
Penfro 677-8
Penrith 603-4
Pen-y-Crug 696
Pen-y-Fan 697
Penzance 331-4, **332**
Perth 864-7, **866**
Perthshire 864-71, **15**
Peterhouse 357
petrels, storm 961
Piccadilly Circus 67
Pickering 524-5
Pictish stones
Black Isle 895
Drosten Stone 875
Dundee 872
Dunrobin Castle 909
Farr Stone 913
St Andrews 856
Thurso 912
Pinter, Harold 1040
Pitlochry 868-9

planning, *see also individual locations*
accommodation costs 1056
budgeting 18, 19
calendar of events 26-9
children, travel with 44-6
food costs 1008
Great Britain basics 18-19
Great Britain's regions 47-51
internet resources 19
itineraries 30-5
repeat visitors 20
travel seasons 18
weather 43
plants 1045-6
Plas Newydd 737
Plockton 919
Plymouth 307-12, **310**
politics 978, 979, 980
Polperro 342
Pontcysyllte Aqueduct 724
pony trekking 41-2
Black Mountains 704
Exmoor National Park 292
Llangattock 701
Poole 245-7
Pope, Alexander 1026
population 978, 979
Porlock 295-6
porpoises 852
Port Charlotte 846-7
Port Eliot 343
Port Ellen 845-6
Port Erin 569
Port Righ 924-5
Port St Mary 569
Porthgain 683
Porthgwidden 327
Porthmadog 742-4
Porthmeor 327
Porthminster 327
Porth-yr-Ogof 695
Portloe 340
Portmeirion 743
Portpatrick 828
Portree 924-5
Portsmouth 230-4, **232**
Postbridge 314-15
potholing, *see* caves & caving
Potter, Beatrix 578, 587, 588
Powys 713-21
Pre-Raphaelites 1037

Map Pages **p000**
Image Pages **p000**

Preseli Hills 686
Presteigne 718
Princess of Wales memorials, Diana 85, 88
Princetown 314
priories, *see* monasteries & priories
Provand's Lordship 794-5
public holidays 1061-2
pubs 1015-16, 1017-18
puddings 1012-13
puffins 679
Punch & Judy 730
punting 190, 359, **10**

Q

quad biking 899
Queensferry 787-8

R

Radcliffe Camera 187-8
radio 1055
rafting, *see* canoeing, kayaking
railway lines
Bodmin & Wenford Railway 345
Bridgnorth Cliff Railway 431
Bure Valley Steam Railway 382
Cairngorm Mountain Railway 900
Channel Tunnel 1065
Cliff Railway 294
East Cliff Lift Railway 243
East Hill Cliff Railway 164
Esk Valley Railway 525
Fairbourne Railway 754
Ffestiniog Railway 742
Great Central Railway 455
Great Little Trains of Wales 742
La'al Ratty 599
Lakeside & Haverthwaite Railway 579
Llanberis Lake Railway 748
narrow-gauge steam train 385
North Yorkshire Moors Railway 524
Paignton & Dartmouth Steam Railway 304
Peak Rail 461
Pontypool & Blaenavon Railway 662
Ravenglass & Eskdale Railway 599
Settle-Carlisle Line 495
Severn Valley Railway 431
Shakespeare Express steam train 401
Snowdon Mountain Railway 745-7
South Tynedale Railway 603
Strathspey Steam Railway 898
Swanage Steam Railway 248
Talyllyn Railway 754
Vale of Rheidol Railway 690
Welsh Highland Railway 742
railway museums
Head of Steam 620
Narrow Gauge Railway Museum 764
National Railway Museum 503-5
Port Erin 569
rain geese 963
Ramsay, Cindy-Lou 805
Ramsgate 154
Red Pike 597
red-throated divers 963
Reilig Oran 854
religion 979
restaurants 1015
Rhayader 717
Ribble Valley 565-8
Ribblehead Viaduct 494
Richard I 991-2
Richard II 994
Richard III 996
Richborough 156
Richmond 496-7
Ridgeway National Trail 269
Ring of Brodgar 949
Ripon 517
River Cottage Canteen 303
River Thames 148-9, **148-9**
Roald Dahl Plass 644
Rob Roy 841
Robert, Adam 486, 772, 788, 800, 821
Robert the Bruce 993
Robin Hood 992
Robin Hood's Bay 529
rock climbing 42
Cuillin Hills 920
Dartmoor National Park 313
Forest of Dean 422
Old Man of Hoy 952
Pembrokeshire 682
Symonds Yat Rock 422
Roman sites 23, 627
Birdoswald Roman Fort 150, 603, 627, **150**
Brading Roman Villa 241
Chester 549
Chesters Roman Fort & Museum 626, **150**
Corbridge Roman Site & Museum 624-5

Corinium Museum 203
Fishbourne Roman Palace & Museum 176-7
Hadrian's Wall 150-1, 622-7, **624**, **6**, **150-2**, **708**, **983**
Housesteads Roman Fort & Museum 150-1, 626-7, **150-1**
Jewry Wall 452
Le Pinâcle 970
Richborough Roman Fort 156
Roman Amphitheatre 662
Roman Baths 279, 662
Roman lighthouse 157
Roman Painted House 158
Roman signal station 518
Roman Town House 250
Segedunum 617
Segontium Roman Fort 737
Verulamium Museum & Roman Ruins 214
Verulamium Park 214
Vindolanda Roman Fort & Museum 626
Roseland, The 340
Ross of Mull 854
Rossetti, Dante Gabriel 1037
Rosslyn Chapel 788, 932-3, **932-3**, **936**
Ross-on-Wye 421-2
Rothbury 628
Rothiemurchus Estate 898
Rough Tor 345
Rousay 953
Rowling, JK 1029
Royal Albert Hall 124
Royal & Ancient Golf Club 857
Royal Crown Derby Factory 457
Royal Hospital Chelsea 88
Royal Mile 763-7, 929-30, **929-31**
Royal Observatory 96
Royal Opera House 125
royal pageants, *see* festivals
Royal Shakespeare Company 122
Royal Society for the Protection of Birds 679, 964
Royal Worcester porcelain 415
RSPB Minsmere 373
Rueval 940
rugby 1050
Runnymede 220
Ruthin 727
Rutland Water 456
Rydal Mount 584-5
Ryde 241
Rye 160-2

S

safaris
Exmoor National Park 292
Longleat 266
New Forest 235
Wildfowl & Wetlands Centre 174
Woburn Safari Park 215
safety 1062
Birmingham 401
Bristol 277
Dartmoor National Park 316
London 130, 133
midges 920
sailing 42-3
Bala 750
Cowes Week 240
Llŷn Peninsula 740
Lower Solva 679
Plymouth 309
Poole Harbour 246
Portland Harbour 252
sporting events 28
Salisbury 259-62, **260**
Saltaire 486
Samson 347-8
Sanday 954-5
Sandwich 154-6
Sandwick 961
Sandyknowe 812
Sark 974-5
Scafell Pike 591
Scalloway 961
Scapa Flow 951
Scarasta 939
Scarborough 517-22, **518**
science museums
At-Bristol 273
Bugworld Experience 556
Centre for Life 610-11
Dinosaurland 255
Enginuity 429
Glasgow Science Centre 796-7
Lyme Regis Museum 255
Museum of the History of Science 190
Museums of Science & Industry 534
National Space Centre 451
Science Museum 85
Scotland 757-975, **758**
itineraries 34
Scott Polar Research Institute 358
Scott, Walter 1026
Scottish Parliament 65, 931, **931**, **1006**
Scrabster 912-13
scrambling 43
sculpture 1036-8
Angel of the North 616, 1038
Tout Quarry 253-4
White Horse at Ebbsfleet 1038
seal spotting 155
seals 679, 852, 919
Selworthy 295
Senedd (National Assembly Building) 644
Sennen 331
Settle 493
Seven Sisters Cliffs 166
Sgurr Alasdair 923
Sgwd-yr-Eira 695
Shaftesbury 258
Shakespeare, William 1025, 1039
birthplace 406
sites 406-7
Shakespeare's Globe 80-1, 149, **149**
Shambles 506
Shanklin 241
shearwaters, Manx 679
Sheffield 478-80
Shelley, Mary 1026
Sherborne 256-8
sherry trifle 1013
Shetland Islands 956-65, **957**
ships
Golden Hind 304
HM Frigate *Unicorn* 873
HMS *Belfast* 83
HMS *Royal Oak* 947, 951
HMS *Victory* 230
HMS *Warrior* 230
Iron Age logboat 245
König 951
Kronprinz Wilhelm 951
Markgraf 951
Mary Rose 230
Matthew 271
Peggy 569
Royal Yacht Britannia 774
RRS *Discovery* 872-3
SS *Great Britain* 270-1
Sutton Hoo 367
Tobermory Galleon 852
Zulu-class fishing boat 861
shopping 24
Beatles memorabilia, The 560
markets 128-9, 651, 672
secondhand books 713
Shrewsbury 424-7 **424**
Shropshire 423-36
Shugborough 412

Silbury Hill 269
Sir Benfro 673-86
Sir Gaerfyrddin 670-3
Sites of Special Scientific Interest 1043
Skara Brae 949
Skegness 448-9
Skenfrith 661
skiing 42, 906
Skipton 491-2
Skokholm Island 679
Skomer Island 679
Sleat 923
Smailholm Tower 812
Smith, Zadie 1029
smoking regulations 1015
Snaefell 569
snorkelling, *see* diving
snowboarding 42
Snowdonia 745-7, **746-7**, **8**
soccer, *see* football
Somerset 285-91
South Ronaldsay 948
South Uist 941
south Wales 50, 657-86, **658**
  accommodation 657
  food 657
  highlights 658
  planning 657
  travel seasons 657
Southend-on-Sea 366-7
Southwell 442
southeast England 47, 134-78, **136-7**
  accommodation 134
  food 134
  highlights 136-7
  travel seasons 134
southern Scotland 51, 789-828, **790-1**, **794-5**, **9**
  accommodation 789
  food 789
  highlights 790-1
  planning 789
  travel seasons 789
southwest England 48, 221-348, **222-3**
  accommodation 221
  food 221
  highlights 222-3
  travel seasons 221
Southwold 373-4
Spark, Muriel 1028
spas, *see* thermal baths
Speaker's Corner 88
Spencer, Lady Diana, *see* Diana, Princess of Wales
sporting events
  Abergavenny Festival of Cycling 703
  Aintree Festival 557
  Ashes, the 1051
  Ba, The 946
  Big Cheese 655
  Brecon Beast 698
  Cheese Olympics 655
  Chevy Chase 629
  Coniston Walking Festival 589
  Cosford Air Show 430
  Cotswolds Olimpicks 27
  Cowes Week 28, 240
  Derby Week 27
  FA Cup 27, 1050
  Grand National steeplechase 27, 561
  Great North Run 29, 612
  Henley Royal Regatta 196
  Horse of the Year Show 29
  Isle of Man Walking Festival 566
  London Marathon 27, 99
  Man vs Horse Marathon 714
  Much Wenlock Olympics 431
  National Surfing Championships 616
  Real Ale Wobble & Ramble 714
  Royal Regatta 28
  Royal Shrovetide Football 459
  Saturnalia Beer Festival & Mountain Bike Chariot Racing 714
  Six Nations Rugby Championship 26
  Three Peaks Challenge 591
  Three Peaks Cyclo-Cross 493
  Three Peaks Race 493
  Twenty20 cricket series 1051
  UCI Mountain Bike World Cup 903
  University Boat Race 26, 99
  Wimbledon Lawn Tennis Championships 27, 99
  Wimbledon Tennis Championships 1052
  World Bog Snorkelling Championships 714
sports 1049-52, *see also* cricket, football, golf, horse racing, rugby, tennis
  London 126
St Agnes 326, 348
St Albans 214-15
St Andrews 856-61, **858**
St Davids 679-83, **680**, **16**
St Ives 326-30, **328**
St Just-in-Penwith 330-1
St Just-in-Roseland 340
St Katharine Docks 77
St Martin's 348
St Mary's 346-7
St Ninian's Isle 962
St Ouen's Bay 970
St Paul's Cathedral 74, **708-9**
St Scholastica's Day 183
Stafford 412
Staffordshire 411-14
Stamford 446-8
standing stones 1020
  Achavanich Standing Stones 910
  Avebury Stone Circle 267
  Bedd Arthur 686
  Callanish Standing Stones 938, 1020, **712**
  Carreg Coetan 685
  Castlerigg Stone Circle 593
  Grey Wethers 315
  Gugh 348
  Hill o'Many Stanes 910
  Kilmartin Glen 843
  Llŷn Peninsula 740
  Merrivale Stone Rows 315
  Newport 685
  Pentre Ifan 686
  Preseli Hills 686
  Ring of Brodgar 949
  Scorhill 315
  St Davids 681
  Stenness 949
  Stone of Setter 954
  Stonehenge 263-5, **264**, **6**
  Temple Wood 843
  West Kennet Avenue 269
stately homes & historic houses 22, 1021
  Abbotsford 813
  Althorp House 450
  Anne Hathaway's Cottage 407
  Arnol Blackhouse 937-8
  Attingham Park 427
  Babington House 285
  Beaulieu 236-7
  Blackwell Arts & Crafts House 581-2
  Blickling Hall 380
  Brantwood 588-9
  Broughton House 825
  Burghley House 447
  Calke Abbey 458

Map Pages **p000**
Image Pages **p000**

Castle Howard 512-13
Charlecote Park 411
Chatsworth House 473
Clarence House 66
Clouds Hill 247
Coleton Fishacre 305
Combe House 301
Compton Verney 411
Cotehele 344
Cragside House, Garden & Estate 628
Doddington Hall 446
Dove Cottage 585
Down House 160
Duff House 886
Duncombe Park House 522-4
Eastbridge Hospital 140
Erasmus Darwin House 412
Erddig 726
Georgian House 772
Gladstone's Land 766, 930, **930**
Greenway 305
Guildhall (London) 76
Haddon Hall 473
Hardwick Hall 462
Hardy's Cottage 250
Harewood House 486-7
Hill Top 588
Holker Hall 599
Hopetoun House 787-8
Kedleston Hall 458
Kenwood House 97
Kingston Lacy 247
Kirby Hall 450
Lanhydrock 343-4
Levens Hall 577
Longleat 266
Lulworth Castle 249
Mackintosh House 797
Mary Queen of Scots House 814
Max Gate 250
Mompesson House 260
Nash's House 406
Newstead Abbey 441
Osborne House 240
Petworth House 177
Plas Newydd 724, 737
Port Eliot 343
Provand's Lordship 794-5
Provost Skene's House 876
Ragley Hall 411
Royal Hospital Chelsea 88
Rydal Mount 584-5
Sandringham House 388
Shugborough 412
Skaill House 949
Speke Hall 562
Spencer House 67
Sulgrave Manor 450
Traquair House 815
Trerice 325
Tyntesfield 275
Waddesdon Manor 215-16
Willow Tearooms 793
Wilton House 263
Wollaton Hall 437
Wordsworth House 592
Steall Meadows 905
Steephill Cove 241
Stein, Rick 323, 336, 1015
Stenness 949
Steornabhagh 928-37
Stiperstones 432
Stirling 833-7, **834**
Stirling region 832-40
Stoke Bruerne 450
Stoke-on-Trent 413-14
Stoker, Bram 528
Stone of Destiny 765, 843, 864, 993
Stonehaven 882
Stonehenge 263-5, **264**, **6**
storm petrels 961
Stornoway 928-37
Stour Valley 367
Stourhead 265
Stow-on-the-Wold 202-3
Stranraer 827-8
Stratford-upon-Avon 406-11, **408**, **11**
Strathglass 894
Stromness 950-2
Stronsay 953-4
Stuart, Charles Edward 941, 1000
Studley Royal 517
Suffolk 367-74
Suffolk Broads, *see* Norfolk & Suffolk Broads
Sumburgh 962
surfing 43
artificial surf reef 244
Braunton 318
Cornwall 320, 323
Freshwater West 677
Ilfracombe 318
Llŷn Peninsula 740
National Surfing Championships 616
Pembrokeshire 682
southwest England 224
Surrey 177-8
Sutton Hoo 367
Swansea 663-7, **664**
Symonds Yat 422

T

Tafts Ness 954
Tain 908
Talacharn 672-3
Tar Tunnel 428
Tarbert 844, 939
Tarn Hows 587
Tate Britain 84
Taversoe Tuick 953
taxes 1058
taxi travel 1068
within London 133
tea 1017
teashops 1014-15
Techniquest 645
telephone services 19, 1062
Temple Wood 843
Tenby 674-6, **16**
tennis 1052
Terry, Stephen 702
Tetbury 204-5
Tewkesbury 210-11
Thatcher, Margaret 978, 1006, **1004**
theatre 1039-40
theatres
Almeida 122
Donmar Warehouse 122
Georgian Theatre Royal 496
London 122
Menier Chocolate Factory 122
Minack 333
National Theatre 122
Old Vic 122
Royal Court Theatre 122
Shakespeare's Globe 80-1, 149, **149**
Sheldonian Theatre 187
Young Vic 122
theft 133
theme parks, *see* amuseument parks
thermal baths
Bristol Lido 272
Thermae Bath Spa 282
Turkish Baths 514
Thomas, Dylan 663, 667, 673, 1028
Thomas, Oliver 543
Thorpeness 373
Three Peaks 493
Three Sisters 902, **711**
Thurso 912-13

Tideswell 467
Tinside Lido 309
Tintagel 322
tipping 1061
Tobermory 852-3
Tobermory Galleon 852
toilets 130-1
Tolkien, JRR 1028
Tomb of the Eagles 948
tombs, *see* burial cairns, chambers & tombs
Tongue 913-14
Top Withins 489
Torquay 302-4
Torre Abbey Sands 302
Torridon 918-19
Totnes 306-7
tourist information 1063
tours, see also boat trips, ghost tours, *individual locations*, safaris, walking tours, wildlife sanctuaries
  Beatles sites, The 98, 556, 557, 560
  Dover wartime tunnels 157
  subterranean 157, 299
Tower Bridge 74-5, 149, **149**
Tower Green scaffold site 146, **146**
Tower of London 73-4, 146-7, **146-7**
Trafalgar Square 70-1
train travel, *see also* railway lines
  to/from Great Britain 1065
  to/from London 131
  within Great Britain 1068-70
transport museums, *see also* railway museums
  Cars of the Stars Motor Museum 593
  Coventry Transport Museum 403
  London Transport Museum 72
  Morgan Motor Company 417
  National Cycle Collectio 716
  National Motor Museum 237
  National Waterways Museum 450
travel to/from Great Britain 1064-5
travel within Great Britain 1066-70
travellers cheques 1061
Trefdraeth 685-6
Tref-Y-Clawdd 718
Trefynwy 660-1
trekking, *see* Munro bagging, walking, walking trails
Trerice 325
Tresco 347

Map Pages **p000**
Image Pages **p000**

Treshnish Isles 855
Troon 821
Trooping the Colour 27, 99
Trossachs, The 837-40
Trotternish 926
Truro 338-40
Tube, the 133
tunnels
  Channel Islands 970
  Channel Tunnel 1065
  Dover wartime tunnels 157
  St Andrew's Castle 856
  Tar Tunnel 428
Tunnelsbeaches 318
Tunny Club 520
Turner, JMW 1037
TV 1033-4, 1055
Tyddewi 679-83
Tyddyn Llan 752
Tynemouth 616
Tyntesfield 275

U

Uffington White Horse 1021
Uibhist A Deas 941
Uibhist A Tuath 940
Uig 926
Ullapool 916-18
Ullswater 597-8
Unesco World Heritage sites, *see* World Heritage sites
universities, *see also* colleges
  Cambridge University 353-7
  University of Manchester 538-9
Unst 964-5
Up Helly-Aa 960
Upper Booth 470

V

vacations 1061-2
vegetarian travellers 1012
Ventnor 241-2
Verdant Works 873
Veryan 340
Via Ferrata 597
Victoria 1001-2
Victoria & Albert Museum 84
video 1055
Viking era 987-8
village idylls 22
vineyards
  Biddenden Vineyards 161
  Chapel Down Vinery 161
  Sharpham Vineyard 306-7
visas 19, 1063

W

wakeboarding 246
Wales 636-756, **654**
  itineraries 35
Wales Millennium Centre 644, **707**
walking 37-9, *see also* bridleways & towpaths, Munro bagging, walking tours, walking trails
  access 39
  accommodation 464
  baggage-carrying services 38, 374
  books 39, 993, 1044
  internet resources 39, 224
  maps 43
  'right of way' rules 39
  sporting events 239
walking tours
  Bath 282
  Birmingham 396
  Bristol 273
  Cambridge 359
  Canterbury 141
  Cheltenham 208
  Chester 550
  Edinburgh 775, 776
  Glasgow 800, **800**
  Great Malvern 417
  Isles of Scilly 346
  Lincoln 444
  London 78-9, 96, **78**
  Norwich 377
  Nottingham 437
  Oxford 189, 190-1
  Portsmouth 231
  Shrewsbury 425
  Winchester 228
  Worcester 415
  York 507
walking trails 38-9, *see also* bridleways & towpaths
  Ambleside 582
  Angles Way 374
  Around Norfolk Walk 374
  Assynt 916
  Borders, the 811
  Borders Abbeys Way 811
  Brontë Way 489
  Cairngorm National Park 900
  Capel Curig 749
  Cardinham Woods 345
  Ceredigion Coast Path 689
  Cleveland Way 478, 523
  Coast to Coast Walk 39, 478, 496
  Coleridge Way 224, 292
  Coniston 589

Cotswold Way 39, 181, 197
Cumbria Way 39
Daffodil Walk 524
Dales Way 478
Dartmoor National Park 313, 314
Dartmoor Way 314
Edge of Wales Walk 739
Elan Valley Trail 717
Fife Coastal Path 855-6
Glasgow 798
Glyndŵr's Way 720
Goatfell 818
Grasmere 585
Great Glen Way 39, 895
Hadrian's Wall Path 39, 609, 623, 628
Herefordshire Trail 418
High Peak Trail 464
Isle of Anglesey Coastal Path 735
Keats' Walk 228
Kerry Ridgeway 433
Lairig Ghru trail 900
Lake District, the 597
Limestone Way 392, 464, 467, 468-9
Llanberis Path 745
Llŷn Coastal Path 739
Long Mynd 432
Malham Landscape Trail 493
Mawddach Trail 754
Mawddach Way 754
Millennium Way 566
Miner's Track 745
Monsal Trail 464, 466, 467, 472
Mortimer Trail 435
New Forrest 235
North Downs Way 135
North York Moors 478
Offa's Dyke Path 39, 424, 433, 718
Oxfordshire Way 182, 718
Peddars Way & Norfolk Coast Path 352
Pembrokeshire Coast Path 39
Pennine Way 39, 392, 464, 470, 478, 493, 608
Peregrine Path 422
Pilgrims Way 826
Pyg Track 745
Raad ny Foillan 566
Rhyd Ddu Path 745
Ribble Way 531, 565
Ridgeway National Trail 181, 224
Rothiemurchus Estate 898
Severn Way 415
Shropshire Way 424, 433, 435
Snowdon Horseshoe 745
Snowdon Ranger Path 745
South Downs Way National Trail 135
South Wales Three Peaks Trial 702
South West Coast Path 39, 224, 292, **706**
Southern Upland Way 39, 811
Speyside Way 832
St Cuthbert's Way 39, 811
Suffolk Coast Path 352
Symonds Yat Rock 422
Tarka Trail 292
Templer Way 314
Thames Path 39, 181
Three Choirs Way 415, 418
Tissington Trail 464
Trossachs, The 837-8
Tweed Cycle Way 811
Two Moors Way 292, 294, 314
Viking Way 442
Watkin Path 745
Weavers Way 374
Wenlock Edge 431
West Devon Way 314
West Highland Way 39, 832, 841, 895, 903
Wherryman's Way 374
Wolds Way 478
Wychwood Way 182
Wye Valley Walk 418
Yorkshire Dales 475
Yorkshire Wolds 478
Ystwyth Trail 691
Wallace, William 993
Walter Scott, Sir 772
war museums
Britain at War Experience 83
Cabinet War Rooms 67
Imperial War Museum (Duxford) 363
Imperial War Museum (London) 81, 363, **1000**
Imperial War Museum North (Manchester) 535
Jersey War Tunnels 970
Liverpool War Museum 555
National War Museum of Scotland 765-6
Roman Army Museum 627
War & Peace Museum 848
Wareham 247-8
Wars of the Roses 995
Warwick 403-5, **404**
Warwickshire 402-11
Wasdale 591
water 1060
Waters, Sarah 1029
water-skiing 246
watersports, *see individual activities*
Waugh, Evelyn 1028
weather 18, 43, 1058-9, *see also individual locations*
websites, *see* internet resources
Wedgwood pottery 413
weights 1055
Wells 286-7
Wells-next-the-Sea 385-6
Welsh Assembly 980
Welsh, Irvine 1028
Wenlock Edge 431
West Kennet Long Barrow 269
West Sussex 174-7
West Wight 242
Westminster Abbey 62-5
Westons Cider Mills 424
Westray 955
Weymouth 252-3
whale watching 850, 852, 1045
Whalebone Arch 527
whales, minke 852
whisky, *see* distilleries
Whitby 525-9, **526**
White Horse at Ebbsfleet 1038
White Tower 146, **146**
Whitford, Harriet 971
Whithorn 827
Whitstable 143-4
Wick 910-11
Widecombe-in-the-Moor 315-16
wi-fi 1060
Wigtown 826-7
wild goats 1045
wildlife 1043-6, *see also individual species*, wildlife sanctuaries, safaris
books 1045
wildlife sanctuaries, *see also* safaris
Cairngorm Reindeer Centre 900
Durrell 969-70
Falls of Clyde Wildlife Centre 810
Gigrin Farm Red Kite Feeding Station 717
National Lobster Hatchery 322
National Seal Sanctuary 335
Norfolk Wildlife Conservation Centre 382
Sea Life Centre & Marine Sanctuary 518-19
Seal Rescue Centre 519
Wild Futures Monkey Sanctuary 343
Wilkinson, Mark 384

William III (of Orange) 999
William the Conqueror 990-1
Willow Tearooms 793
Wiltshire 258-70
Winchcombe 201-2
Winchester 225-30, **226**
Windermere 577-81, **578**
Windsor 216-20
windsurfing 42-3
  Bala 750
  Plymouth 309
  Poole 246
wineries, *see* vineyards
Winnats Pass 467
Woburn Safari Park 215
Woodstock 194-5
Wookey Hole 287-8
Wooler 629-30
Woolf, Virginia 1027
Worcester 415-16
Worcester Beacon 418
Worcestershire 414-18
Wordsworth, William 584-5, 592, 1026
work 1063
World Heritage sites
  Albert Dock 555-6
  Bath 278-85, **280**
  Beaumaris Castle 733
  Blaenavon 661-2
  Blenheim Palace 194-5, **8**
  Caernarfon Castle 737, **709**
  Canterbury Cathedral 138-9, **11**
  Conwy Castle 730
  Cornwall & West Devon Mining Landscape 340
  Durham Cathedral 617-18
  Edinburgh 770
  Fountains Abbey 517
  Greenwich 95-6, 106
  Harlech Castle 755
  Ironbridge Gorge 427-30
  Jurassic Coast 248
  New Lanark 809-10
  Pontcysyllte Aqueduct 724
  Saltaire 486
  Stonehenge 263-5, **264**
  Studley Royal 517
  Tower of London 73-4, 146-7, **146-7**
  Westminster Abbey 62-5
Wren, Christopher 59, 74, 76, 79, 88, 96, 97, 148, 186, 187, 188, 357, 449
WWI 1002
WWII 1003-4

Y

Y Bala 750-1
Y Drenewydd 718-19
Y Fenni 701-3
Y Gelli Gandryll 704, 713
Y Gŵyr 668-70
Y Mwmbwls 667-8
Y Mynyddoedd Duon 703-4
yachting, *see* sailing
Yell 963-4
Ynys Enlli 740
York 501-12, **502**, **13**
  accommodation 508-9
  drinking 511
  entertainment 511
  festivals 507-8
  food 509-11
  shopping 511-12
  sights 501-7
  tourist information 512
  travel to/from 512
  travel within 512
Yorkshire 48, 474-529, **476-7**
  accommodation 474
  food 474
  highlights 476
  planning 474
  travel seasons 474
Yorkshire Pudding 1012

Z

Zennor 330
zoos 272-3
  Chester Zoo 552
  Edinburgh Zoo 774
  Isle of Wight Zoo 241
  London Zoo 89
  Monkey World 247
  Paignton Zoo 302-3
Zulu-class fishing boat 861

Map Pages **p000**
Image Pages **p000**

how to use this book

These symbols will help you find the listings you want:

- Sights
- Activities
- Courses
- Tours
- Festivals & Events
- Sleeping
- Eating
- Drinking
- Entertainment
- Shopping
- Information/ Transport

These symbols give you the vital information for each listing:

- Telephone Numbers
- Opening Hours
- Parking
- Nonsmoking
- Air-Conditioning
- Internet Access
- Wi-Fi Access
- Swimming Pool
- Vegetarian Selection
- English-Language Menu
- Family-Friendly
- Pet-Friendly
- Bus
- Ferry
- Metro
- Subway
- London Tube
- Tram
- Train

Reviews are organised by author preference.

Look out for these icons:

- TOP CHOICE — Our author's recommendation
- FREE — No payment required
- A green or sustainable option

Our authors have nominated these places as demonstrating a strong commitment to sustainability – for example by supporting local communities and producers, operating in an environmentally friendly way, or supporting conservation projects.

Map Legend

Sights
- Beach
- Buddhist
- Castle
- Christian
- Hindu
- Islamic
- Jewish
- Monument
- Museum/Gallery
- Ruin
- Winery/Vineyard
- Zoo
- Other Sight

Activities, Courses & Tours
- Diving/Snorkelling
- Canoeing/Kayaking
- Skiing
- Surfing
- Swimming/Pool
- Walking
- Windsurfing
- Other Activity/ Course/Tour

Sleeping
- Sleeping
- Camping

Eating
- Eating

Drinking
- Drinking
- Cafe

Entertainment
- Entertainment

Shopping
- Shopping

Information
- Post Office
- Tourist Information

Transport
- Airport
- Border Crossing
- Bus
- Cable Car/ Funicular
- Cycling
- Ferry
- Metro
- Monorail
- Parking
- S-Bahn
- Taxi
- Train/Railway
- Tram
- Tube Station
- U-Bahn
- Other Transport

Routes
- Tollway
- Freeway
- Primary
- Secondary
- Tertiary
- Lane
- Unsealed Road
- Plaza/Mall
- Steps
- Tunnel
- Pedestrian Overpass
- Walking Tour
- Walking Tour Detour
- Path

Boundaries
- International
- State/Province
- Disputed
- Regional/Suburb
- Marine Park
- Cliff
- Wall

Population
- Capital (National)
- Capital (State/Province)
- City/Large Town
- Town/Village

Geographic
- Hut/Shelter
- Lighthouse
- Lookout
- Mountain/Volcano
- Oasis
- Park
- Pass
- Picnic Area
- Waterfall

Hydrography
- River/Creek
- Intermittent River
- Swamp/Mangrove
- Reef
- Canal
- Water
- Dry/Salt/ Intermittent Lake
- Glacier

Areas
- Beach/Desert
- Cemetery (Christian)
- Cemetery (Other)
- Park/Forest
- Sportsground
- Sight (Building)
- Top Sight (Building)

Etain O'Carroll

Oxford, Cotswolds & Around, Cambridge & East Anglia Travel writer and photographer Etain grew up in rural Ireland but now calls Oxford home. She has worked on more than 20 Lonely Planet books including numerous *England* and *Great Britain* guides as well as *Cycling Britain*. Her top tip? Oxford and the Cotswolds are expensive to live in but great places to visit on a budget. There are world-class museums, stunning architecture, gorgeous villages and ancient pubs – most of them free to visit.

Read more about Etain at:
lonelyplanet.com/members/EtainOCarroll

Andy Symington

Glasgow & Southern Scotland; Stirling & Central Scotland; Inverness, the Highlands & the Northern Islands Andy's Scottish forebears make their presence felt in a love of malt, a debatable ginger colour to his facial hair and a love of wild places. From childhood slogs up the M1 he graduated to making dubious road trips around the firths in a disintegrating Mini Metro and thence to peddling whisky in darkest Leith. Whilst living there, he travelled widely around the country in search of the perfect dram; now resident in Spain, he continues to visit very regularly.

Read more about Andy at:
lonelyplanet.com/members/andy_symington

Neil Wilson

Yorkshire; Edinburgh; Stirling & Central Scotland; Inverness, the Highlands & the Northern Islands Neil has made many cross-border forays into 'God's own country' from his home in Edinburgh, as well as regular expeditions around Scotland. Good weather on this research trip allowed for a memorable ascent of Ingleborough hill, a knee-trashing mountain-bike descent of the Pennine Way into Hawes, and a sunset panorama of the Applecross hills from a campsite on Skye's Trotternish Ridge. Neil has written more than 50 guidebooks for various publishers, including Lonely Planet's *Scotland* and *England* guides.

Read more about Neil at:
lonelyplanet.com/members/neilwilson

Joe Bindloss

Nottingham & the East Midlands; Birmingham, the West Midlands & the Marches Born of English stock, albeit in Cyprus, Joe spends a lot of time in the Marches, not least because his parents and brothers live in the sleepy village of Clun (hell, they even go Morris dancing). For this book, Joe juggled exploring rugged uplands and picturesque medieval villages with writing for newspapers and magazines and being a full-time dad in London. Joe has been writing guidebooks for Lonely Planet since 1999, covering everywhere from rural England to the high reaches of the Himalaya.

Read more about Joe at:
lonelyplanet.com/members/bindibhaji

Fionn Davenport

Manchester, Liverpool & the Northwest Dublin-born and bred, Fionn has been traipsing about his favourite bits of England (north of the Watford gap) for more than a decade, all the while falling in love with a country so near to his own yet so utterly unknown to most who assume that England is just one giant suburb dotted with roundabouts. His favourite place is his beloved Anfield in Liverpool, but he'd also settle for the streets of Manchester's Northern Quarter and the fine restaurants of West Didsbury.

Marc Di Duca

Canterbury & the Southeast, Newcastle & the Northeast From Farnham to the Farne Islands, Marc topped and tailed his native land for this edition of *England*. Born a mile from the Stockton & Darlington railway, Marc spent a decade in central Europe before becoming a full-time travel-guide author based in the southeast. Chilling extremities in the nippy River Tees, sinking ale in Cinque Ports, scrambling along Hadrian's Wall and stalking Dickens across six counties all formed part of his research for this guide.

Read more about Marc Di Duca at:
lonelyplanet.com/members/madidu

Belinda Dixon

Southwest England (Hampshire, New Forest, Isle of Wight, Dorset, Wiltshire, Devon) Belinda made a gleeful bolt for the southwest 17 years ago and has worked as a writer, journalist and local radio broadcaster there ever since. This is her sixth mission for Lonely Planet in the region, and it's seen her hugging sarsens in the stone circle at Avebury, rummaging for fossils at Lyme, and cresting tor tops on Dartmoor. All that and rigorously (very rigorously) testing all the food and drink she can manage.

Read more about Belinda at:
lonelyplanet.com/members/belindadixon

Peter Dragicevich

London, Cardiff, Pembrokeshire & South Wales, Hay-on-Wye & Mid-Wales, Snowdonia & North Wales (West of Snowdonia, Snowdonia National Park) After a dozen years reviewing music and restaurants for publications in New Zealand and Australia, London's bright lights and loud guitars could no longer be resisted. And maybe it's because he's got half a dragon in his surname, but Wales has held a fascination ever since Peter was sent there to write about castles for one of his first ever travel features. He has contributed to 20 Lonely Planet titles, including *Wales*, *England*, *Walking in Britain* and the last edition of this book.

Read more about Peter at:
lonelyplanet.com/members/peterdragicevich

Catherine Le Nevez

Channel Islands Catherine's hopped back-and-forth from France to the UK since age four, completing her Doctorate of Creative Arts in Writing, Masters in Professional Writing, and post-grad qualifications in Editing and Publishing along the way. But – six flights and four ferry rides later – this was her first chance to discover the islands in between. Catherine has authored or co-authored over two dozen guidebooks worldwide, including several editions of Lonely Planet's *France*, *Paris Encounter* and *Ireland* guidebooks, plus newspaper and magazine articles.

OUR STORY

A beat-up old car, a few dollars in the pocket and a sense of adventure. In 1972 that's all Tony and Maureen Wheeler needed for the trip of a lifetime – across Europe and Asia overland to Australia. It took several months, and at the end – broke but inspired – they sat at their kitchen table writing and stapling together their first travel guide, *Across Asia on the Cheap*. Within a week they'd sold 1500 copies. Lonely Planet was born.

Today, Lonely Planet has offices in Melbourne, London and Oakland, with more than 600 staff and writers. We share Tony's belief that 'a great guidebook should do three things: inform, educate and amuse'.

OUR WRITERS

David Else

Coordinating Author (Plan Your Trip, Understand, Survival Guide) As a professional writer, David has authored over 40 books, including several editions of Lonely Planet's *England*, *Great Britain* and *Walking in Britain*. His knowledge comes from a lifetime of travel around the country – often on foot – a passion dating from university years, when heading for the hills was always more attractive than visiting the library. Originally from London, David has lived in Yorkshire, Derbyshire and Wales, and is now a resident of the Cotswolds. For this current edition of *Great Britain*, David's research took him from Cornwall to Scotland – via two favourite spots: Porthcurno Beach and the northwest Highlands.

Read more about David at:
lonelyplanet.com/members/davidelse

David Atkinson

Snowdonia & North Wales (North Coast & Borders, Isle of Anglesey) Lapsed Welshman David Atkinson has been chasing the call of *hiraeth* for two editions of Lonely Planet's *Great Britain* guide, focusing this time exclusively on the green, green grass of north Wales. David writes widely for newspapers and magazines, and blogs at Hit the North (nowhitthenorth.wordpress.com) about travel around northwest England and Wales.

Oliver Berry

Southwest England (Cornwall, Bristol, Bath, Somerset), The Lake District & Cumbria Oliver is a writer and photographer based in Cornwall. Among many other projects for Lonely Planet, Oliver has written the first editions of *Devon, Cornwall & Southwest England* and *The Lake District*, and worked on several previous editions of the *England* and *Great Britain* guides. Research highlights for this edition were sampling some traditional 'scrumpy' on a Somerset cider farm and watching the sun rise over Glastonbury Tor. You can see some of his latest work at www.oliverberry.com.

Read more about Oliver at:
lonelyplanet.com/members/oliverberry

OVER PAGE MORE WRITERS

Published by Lonely Planet Publications Pty Ltd
ABN 36 005 607 983
9th edition – May 2011
ISBN 978 1 74179 566 0

10 9 8 7 6 5 4 3 2 1
Printed in Singapore